The Descendants of George Abbott of Andover and Hannah Chandler Through Six Generations

Including Male and Female Lines of Descent from Generation One to Generation Six

Compiled by:

Patricia A. Abbott

ISBN-13: 978-0-578-51595-3 (Patricia A. Abbott)
ISBN-10: 0-578-51595-4

Dedication: For Elizabeth, Bill, Martha, Bob, Stephen, Kathryn, Gerard and Mary – all my Abbotts

Introduction

This compilation is an attempt to provide as complete information as possible of the descendants of George Abbott and Hannah Chandler including complete families through five generations and all of the children that comprise the sixth generation. This includes coverage of more than 1,200 complete families. Both the male and female lines are included so there are many Chandlers, Holts, Ingalls, Fryes, Blanchards, Ballards, and many more names.

Within these pages you will find the full range of human behavior: individuals with great accomplishments, those with humble, ordinary lives, and those who faced incredible hardship and tragedy. There are personal struggles including poverty and reliance on almshouses for subsistence, out-of-wedlock children, and persons who wrestled with alcoholism, depression, and other mental illness. There are also Harvard graduates, attorneys, physicians, and clergymen. There are women pioneers persevering in the face of tremendous challenges. There are the first settlers of many communities in Massachusetts, Connecticut, New Hampshire, Maine, Vermont, Pennsylvania, and upstate New York. Moving into the fifth generation who will find more descendants who made their way to Canada and into Ohio and Michigan and the southern colonies.

Although this is a genealogical compilation, I hope that the presentation of the individual families will allow at least some sense of the humanity of these individuals and their contributions to the founding and development of the country.

Why this book?

This book is a continuation of *The Descendants of George Abbott of Andover and Hannah Chandler* which was published in 2018 and covered the first four generations of descendants. There have been previously published genealogies of the descendants of George Abbott of Andover, so why this book? There were several motivations for creating this new genealogy. First, earlier genealogies, for the most part, do not follow the female lines of descent. Not only does this result in an incomplete consideration of the descendants, it prevents a full appreciation of the degree of inter-connectedness of this kinship network. Next, although prior genealogies are very detailed, some information is omitted (e.g., not all the birth or death dates are provided, some names of spouses are not included). As far as possible, this work attempts to provide a more complete detailing of the individual descendants. Prior genealogies are, on a whole, remarkably accurate, but there are some errors. This work also likely has inaccuracies, but when there are areas of disagreement with other genealogies, I have attempted to lay out the reasoning for making one decision over another. One further consideration: an easier to read format. Hopefully, you will be able to read the information without a magnifying glass.

I have attempted to verify each piece of information with documents (birth, death, and marriage records; wills and probate records; and land transactions) to the degree that these could be accessed online. Admittedly this is a quite limited record access, but even within these limits, a large amount of information was able to be verified. Vital records present their own problems as what are mostly available are transcriptions of records, not original records. There are doubtless errors that crept into the transcriptions. I imagine I also made errors entering my data from the transcriptions. There are inconsistencies in records. For example, there are birth records for a single family in which one child is listed as born in April and a second child is recorded as being born in October of the same year. Often, birth records were recorded in more than one location, so it is not possible to *really* know where the person was born. But within the limits of available records, I have done my very best to be accurate.

Of course, there are not available records for all events (certainly not yet online), or even any records for some persons. For that, I have relied on previously published and unpublished genealogical material and town and county histories. Chief among these were the 1847 "Genealogical Register of the Descendants of George Abbot of Andover. . ." prepared by Abiel Abbot and Ephraim Abbot and the unpublished family notes documents prepared by Charlotte Helen Abbott. There were many other sources and you will find a complete list of these at the end of the book. Sources are also noted in footnotes. Even in those cases in which previously published work was used, I attempted to verify the information contained in those documents. In several cases, there was information that conflicted with available vital records or wills and I have noted those discrepancies and how they were resolved.

One "t" or two?

Some Abbott members use the double "t" and some use one. The patterns of use are often confusing. The original George Abbott of Andover used both; he signed his will with the double "t", so he is a double "t" in this book. Other individuals switched back and forth. Sometimes, members of the same family unit used one while others used two. So, what do we have in this book? When individuals consistently used a single "t", I have attempted to do that, but I am sure I did not always do that consistently. Please do not be offended if you are from the single "t" line. When "Abbott" or "Abbot" was used as a first name or a middle name, I did use the version contained in the records.

How the book is organized

The book is divided into chapters based on generations. When an individual is first introduced, if that person married and had children, you will see a number at the start of the entry that will allow you to know where to look for the next generation for that person. For example, you will see this type of entry when a person is first introduced:

2) i JOHN ABBOTT, b. 1648; d. 19 Mar 1720/1; m. at Andover, 17 Nov 1673 SARAH BARKER, b. at Andover, 23 Nov 1647 daughter of Richard and Joanna (-) Barker; Sarah d. 10 Feb 1728/9.

The "2)" indicates that you will find follow-up information later in the book. (The "i" indicates that this is the first child in that family.) Of course, there are complications. There are many instances in which descendants of the immigrant George Abbott married each other. In those cases, I have cross-referenced the information, so you hopefully will be able to find what you are looking for from either side of the couple.

The book is organized by generations. All the second generation, followed by all the third generation, then all the fourth, and then all the fifth. There are some complications with this, for example when a descendant from the second generation married a descendant from the third generation. In those cases, that couple and their children are included in the generation that appears first.

When moving down the generations, you will find in parentheses the track back to George Abbott the original. For example, Hannah Chandler, the daughter of Hannah Abbott and John Chandler, married Daniel Abbott, the son of George Abbott and Dorcas Graves. When the family of Hannah Chandler and Daniel Abbott is introduced, you will see this:

22) HANNAH CHANDLER (*Hannah Abbott Chandler^2, George^1*) and DANIEL ABBOTT (*George^2, George^1*)

From this, you can see that Hannah Chandler was the daughter of Hannah Abbott Chandler who was the daughter of George Abbott. You will also see that Daniel Abbott was the son of George Abbott who was the son of George Abbott. When just the first name is given, the last name is Abbott. A note about the descendancy path listed in parentheses after the names: For many of the individuals in this generation, there are two or more paths that might be taken back to George Abbott and Hannah Chandler. For some individuals there are as many as five paths. For simplicity, just one path is listed.

Table of Contents

Descendants of George Abbott and Hannah Chandler of Andover

Generation One

1) GEORGE ABBOTT baptized 22 May 1617 Bishops Stortford, Hertfordshire son of George and Elizabeth (-) Abbott;[1] d. at Andover, 24 Dec 1681; m. 12 Dec 1646 at Roxbury

HANNAH CHANDLER; baptized 22 May 1630 Bishops Stortford, Hertfordshire daughter of William and Annis (Bayford) Chandler. Hannah Chandler Abbott m. 2nd at Andover about 1690, Francis Dane. Hannah Chandler d. at Andover, 2 Jun 1711.

George Abbott and Hannah Chandler were both from Hertfordshire. Although the exact dates of emigration are not known, they likely both arrived sometime in the mid 1630's. Hannah traveled as a young child to New England with her parents William and Annis Chandler, and it is probable that George arrived as a single young man and may have been sponsored by the Chandler family or the family of John Dane. In any event, the Chandler family was first in Roxbury where William Chandler died in 1641. George Abbott and his wife Hannah Chandler settled in Andover as first proprietors in 1643.[2]

Although George Abbott was a first proprietor in Andover, he was not among the largest landholders. He received a 4-acre home lot in the first division of land and still had four acres just prior to 1662.[3] The four largest original land owners in Andover were Simon Bradstreet (who received 20 acres in the first division), John Osgood (20 acres), Nicholas Holt (15 acres), and Joseph Parker (10 acres).

But what the Abbott family lacked in terms of the size of the original property, they made up for in the sheer size of their families and the tendency of the Abbott family members to stay in Andover rather than move on to other locations. In 1730, there were 23 Abbott males on the tax rate lists out of a total of 199 males on the list. They accounted for 11.5% of the males paying taxes in the town. As comparison, the next highest number was the Holt family with 15 males on the tax rate lists in 1730.[4]

George Abbott and his family lived originally in what was North Parish in Andover. In 1663, George Abbott obtained property from Richard Sutton in the area of the current Central Street in Andover. It was here that George Abbott built his garrison house in the South Parish. This was one of twelve garrison houses in Andover at that time. It is believed that it is in this area that on 8 April 1676, Joseph, the 24-year old son of George and Hannah, was killed by Indians and another son, 13-year old Timothy, was taken captive for several months.[5]

George Abbott wrote his will on 12 December 1681 and signed his last name with the double-t (Georg Abbott). It begins "To all christen people to hom this presont righting may com." After making the customary statements related to giving his soul to god, he continues (in modernized version here) *And as for that portion of worldly goods that god has given me, considering the great love and affection I have unto my loving wife Hannah Abbott, and considering her tender love and respect she had to me, and also considering her care and diligence in helping to get and save what god has blessed us with. . . leave my whole estate to her.*[6]

The total value of the estate in the inventory was 587 pounds, 12 shillings, 5 pence. This inventory excludes portions of the property that had previously been given to the eldest son, John Abbott, as his portion of the estate. Hannah was left the responsibility of disposing of the property she and George Abbott had acquired. She did this 10 February 1706/7 when she conveyed property to her sons Timothy, Thomas, and Nathaniel.[7]

George Abbott and Hannah Chandler had thirteen children all born at Andover.[8]

---

[1] Moriarty, G. Andrews, "Ancestry of George Abbott of Andover," *The New England Historic and Genealogical Register,* 85 (1931): 79-86

[2] Marjorie W. Otten (2000), "The Two George Abbots of Andover, Massachusetts," *The Essex Genealogist*, 20 (2000): 19-23.

[3] Philip J. Greven, *Four Generations: Population, Land, and Family in Colonial Andover, Massachusetts*. (Ithaca, NY: Cornell University Press, 1970).

[4] Greven, *Four Generations*

[5] Claude Moore Fuess, 1959, *Andover, Symbol of New England: Evolution of a Town*, (Andover, MA: Andover Historical Society, 1959), p 70

[6] *Essex County, MA: Probate File Papers, 1638-1881.*Online database. *AmericanAncestors.org.* New England Historic Genealogical Society, 2014. (From records supplied by the Massachusetts Supreme Judicial Court Archives.) Probate of George Abbot, file #43

[7] Sarah Loring Bailey, *Historical Sketches of Andover*, (Boston: Houghton, 1880), 85-86

[8] All vital records from *Early Vital Records of Massachusetts from 1600 to 1850*, http://ma-vitalrecords.org/ unless otherwise noted.

2) i JOHN ABBOTT, b. 1648;[9] d. 19 Mar 1720/1; m. at Andover, 17 Nov 1673 SARAH BARKER, b. at Andover, 23 Nov 1647 daughter of Richard and Joanna (-) Barker; Sarah d. 10 Feb 1728/9.

ii JOSEPH ABBOTT, b. 11 Mar 1649; d. 24 Jun 1650.

3) iii HANNAH ABBOTT, b. 9 Jun 1650; d. 2 Mar 1740/1; m. at Andover, 20 Dec 1676 JOHN CHANDLER, b. at Andover, 14 Mar 1655 son of Thomas and Hannah (Brewer) Chandler; John d. 19 Sep 1721.

iv JOSEPH ABBOTT, b. 3 Mar 1652; d. 8 Apr 1676, a casualty of conflict with the Indians. Death record transcription reads Joseph, s. George and Hannah (Chandler), "killed by ye Indians," Apr. 8, 1676.

4) v GEORGE ABBOTT, b. 7 Jun 1655; d. 27 Feb 1736; m. 17 Apr 1678 DORCAS GRAVES, b. at Lynn, about 1655 daughter of Mark and Amy (-) Graves; Dorcas d. 19 Feb 1739/40.

5) vi WILLIAM ABBOTT, b. 18 Nov 1657; d. 24 Oct 1713; m. at Roxbury, 19 Jun 1682 ELIZABETH GEARY, b. at Roxbury, 10 Jul 1661 daughter of Nathaniel and Anne (Douglas) Geary; Elizabeth d. 26 Nov 1712.

6) vii SARAH ABBOTT, b. 14 Nov 1659; d. 28 Jun 1711; m. 11 Oct 1680, EPHRAIM STEVENS, b. about 1649 son of John and Elizabeth (Parker) Stevens; Ephraim d. 26 Jun 1718.

7) viii BENJAMIN ABBOTT, b. 20 Dec 1661; d. 30 Mar 1703; out-of-wedlock relationship with Naomi Hoyt in 1683; m. 22 Apr 1685 SARAH FARNUM, b. 14 Jan 1661 daughter of Ralph and Elizabeth (Holt) Farnum; Sarah d. before 1726.[10]

8) ix TIMOTHY ABBOTT, b. 17 Nov 1663; d. 9 Sep 1730; m. 27 Dec 1689 HANNAH GRAVES, b. at Lynn, 14 Dec 1657 daughter of Mark and Amy (-) Graves (sister of Dorcas who married George); Hannah d. 16 Nov 1726.

9) x THOMAS ABBOTT, b. 6 May 1666; d. 28 Apr 1728; m. 7 Dec 1697, HANNAH GRAY, b. at Salem 30 Jan 1674/5 daughter of Robert and Hannah (Holt) Gray; Hannah d. 25 Jan 1763.

xi EDWARD ABBOTT; b. abt. 1668; died young when drowned.[11]

10) xii NATHANIEL ABBOTT, b. 4 Jul 1671; d. 1 Dec 1749; m. 1 Nov 1695, DORCAS HIBBERT, b. about 1675 daughter of Joseph and Elizabeth (Graves) Hibbert of Salem and Beverly; Dorcas d. 17 Feb 1742/3.

11) xiii ELIZABETH ABBOTT, b. 9 Feb 1673; d. 4 May 1750; m. 24 Oct 1692, NATHAN STEVENS, b. 5 Apr 1665 son of John and Hannah (Barnard) Stevens; Nathan d. 25 Sep 1740.

Generation Two

2) JOHN ABBOTT (*George*[1]), b. 1648[12] son of George and Hannah (Chandler) Abbott; d. 19 Mar 1720/1; m. at Andover 17 Nov 1673, SARAH BARKER, b. at Andover 23 Nov 1647 daughter of Richard and Joanna (-) Barker; Sarah d. 10 Feb 1728/9.

John Abbott wrote his will 16 May 1716. The will includes bequests to "my well-beloved wife Sarah" who receives £10 and all the moveable estate, and after Sarah's death, the moveable estate will be divided between his two daughters Sarah Chandler and Priscilla Abbott. Well-beloved son John Abbott receives one part of the homestead, with the other part of the homestead going to well-beloved son Joseph Abbott. To his well-beloved son Stephen Abbott, he grants one-half of a property that he purchased, the other half going to well-beloved son Ebenezer. Well-beloved son Ephraim receives £40 (which he has already received) and a 3-acre plot near Ephraim's house and another 2.5 acres that are part of the common land. Beloved son Joshua is granted £45 (which he has already received). Well-beloved daughter Sarah Chandler receives two cows and six sheep as does well-beloved daughter Priscilla Abbott. Sons John Abbott and Joseph Abbott are named executors.[13]

John Abbott and Sarah Barker had nine children born at Andover.

12) i JOHN ABBOT, b. 2 Nov 1674; d. 1 Jan 1754; m. 6 Jan 1702/3 ELIZABETH HARNDEN, b. at Wilmington 25 Sep 1672 daughter of Richard and Mary (-) Harnden; Elizabeth m. 2nd Zebadiah Chandler 29 Mar 1756; Elizabeth d. 9 Aug 1756.

---

[9] Massachusetts: Legislators of the General Court, 1691-1780 (Online database: *AmericanAncestors.org*, New England Historic Genealogical Society, 2002), (Orig. Pub. by Northeastern University Press, Boston, MA. John A. Schutz, *Legislators of the Massachusetts General Court 1691–1780 A Biographical Dictionary*, 1997.)

[10] Charlotte Helen Abbott, "Early Notes and Records of the Farnum Family of Andover," undated manuscript. Retrieved from https://www.mhl.org/sites/default/files/files/Abbott/Farnum%20Family.pdf

[11] Abiel Abbot and Ephraim Abbot, *Genealogical Register of the Descendants of George Abbot of Andover, George Abbot of Rowley, Thomas Abbot of Andover, Arthur Abbot of Ipswich, Robert Abbot of Branford, CT, and George Abbot of Norwalk, CT*, (Boston: James Munroe and Company, 1847)

[12] Massachusetts: Legislators of the General Court, 1691-1780 (Online database: *AmericanAncestors.org*, New England Historic Genealogical Society, 2002).

[13] *Essex County, MA: Probate File Papers, 1638-1881.* Probate of John Abbot, 10 Apr 1721, Case number 66.

13) ii JOSEPH ABBOT, b. 29 Dec 1676; d. 9 Jan 1757; m. 4 Apr 1722, HANNAH ALLEN, b. 12 Sep 1690 daughter of John and Mercy (Peters) Allen; Hannah d. 4 Mar 1755.

14) iii STEPHEN ABBOT, b. 14 Feb 1678; d. 27 May 1766; m. 22 Jul 1708, SARAH STEVENS, b. 28 Oct 1681 daughter of Ephraim and Sarah (Abbott) Stevens; Sarah d. 28 Dec 1750.

15) iv SARAH ABBOTT, b. 26 Nov 1680; d. 6 Mar 1754; m. 9 Jan 1707, ZEBADIAH CHANDLER, b. 1 Apr 1683 son of John and Hannah (Abbott) Chandler. Zebadiah m. 2nd, Elizabeth Harnden Abbott (see above, Family #12); Zebadiah d. 20 Jun 1766.

16) v EPHRAIM ABBOT, b. 6 Aug 1682; d. 3 Jun 1748; m. 6 Jan 1714/5 Sarah Hunt (a widow most likely SARAH CROSBY the widow of Thomas Hunt, identity discussed with Family #16 below), b. 12 Jun 1694 daughter of Joseph and Sarah (French) Crosby. Sarah m. 3rd John Dane; Sarah d. about 1760.

17) vi JOSHUA ABBOTT, b. 17 Jun 1685; d. at Billerica 11 Feb 1769; m. 1st, 10 Jun 1710 REBEKAH SHED, b. at Billerica, 21 May 1685 daughter of John and Sarah (Chamberlain) Shed; Rebekah d. 7 Apr 1720. Joshua m. 2nd, 2 Mar 1720/1, DORCAS WHITING, b. at Billerica, 21 Mar 1692 daughter of Oliver and Anna (Danforth) Whiting; Dorcas d. 23 Dec 1765.

vii MARY ABBOTT, b. 9 Jan 1687; d. 22 Dec 1688.

18) viii EBENEZER ABBOT, b. 27 Sep 1689; d. 14 Jan 1761; m. 5 Apr 1720, HANNAH TURNER, widow of Francis Dane; Hannah was b. at Charlestown about 1694 daughter of James and Hannah (Lazell) Turner; Hannah d. 1788.

ix PRISCILLA ABBOT, b. 7 Jul 1691; d. 24 May 1791. Priscilla did not marry. According to the genealogy by Abiel Abbot and Ephraim Abbot, she often nursed the sick, was meek and cheerful. An anecdote is that her nephew Barachias, when he was aged, sent Priscilla a message via his son: "Tell my aged aunt Priscilia, that I am likely to shoot the gulf before her." Her answer was "Ah! I wish I was as fit to shoot the gulf as I think he is."[14]

3) HANNAH ABBOTT (*George¹*), b. 9 Jun 1650 daughter of George and Hannah (Chandler) Abbott; d. 2 Mar 1740/1; m. at Andover 20 Dec 1676 JOHN CHANDLER, b. at Andover, 14 Mar 1655 son of Thomas and Hannah (Brewer) Chandler; John d. 19 Sep 1721.

Hannah Abbott and John Chandler were first cousins, John being Hannah Chandler Abbott's nephew.

The will of John Chandler was written 16 July 1721 and proved 4 December 1721. He made the following bequests: dear and loving wife Hannah Chandler received eight bushels of Indian corn plus two bushels each of rye, wheat, and ground meal, plus some sheep's wool, 100 pounds of good pork, 50 pounds of good beef (and other provisions too numerous to mention here); son John receives all the living from the property he is already working including the housing, orchards, and pastures; son Zebadiah receives some additional land beyond what has already been given to him (this land lying near that of "son" Daniel Abbott who is the husband of Hannah Chandler); daughters Hannah Abbott and Sarah Wright receive some household goods beyond what they have already received; he gives his daughter-in-law Hephzibah Chandler two cows, some other provisions and household items, and the use of the back house as long as she is a widow; and his granddaughter Abial Chandler is the receive £50.[15] (Hephzibah is the widow of John's son Abiel.)

Hannah Abbott and John Chandler had six children whose births are recorded at Andover. Some sources list another son, Josiah, in this family. However, there are no records related to him and he is not in the will.

i JOHN CHANDLER, b. 23 Oct 1677; d. 10 Jul 1679.

19) ii JOHN CHANDLER, b. 14 Mar 1679/80; d. 3 May 1741; m. 4 Jun 1701, HANNAH FRYE, b. 12 Apr 1683 daughter of Samuel and Mary (Aslett) Frye; Hannah d. 1 Aug 1727.

15) iii ZEBADIAH CHANDLER, b. 1 Apr 1683; d. 20 Jun 1766; m. 9 Jan 1707, SARAH ABBOTT (Same as Family #15 above); Zebadiah and Sarah were first cousins.

---

[14] Abbot and Abbot, *Genealogical Register of Descendants*, p 2

[15] *Essex County, MA: Probate File Papers, 1638-1881.* Probate of John Chandler, 4 Dec 1721, Case number 4939.

20) iv ABIEL CHANDLER, b. 9 Jan 1686/7; d. 1 Sep 1711; m. 22 Mar 1711, HEPHZIBAH HARNDEN, b. at Reading 19 Sep 1688, daughter of Richard and Mary (-) Harnden. Hephzibah m. 2nd Timothy Chandler; Hephzibah d. 17 Mar 1783.

21) v HANNAH CHANDLER, b. 12 May 1690; d. at Woodstock, CT, 3 Mar 1755; m. 1st DANIEL ABBOTT, b. 10 Jan 1687/8 son of George and Dorcas (Graves) Abbott; Hannah and Daniel were first cousins; Daniel d. Aug 1731 at Woodstock. Hannah m. 2nd John Bartholomew.

22) vi SARAH CHANDLER, b. 8 Oct 1693; d. at Woodstock, CT 15 Mar 1737;[16] m. 12 Jan 1712/3 as his 1st wife, JOSEPH WRIGHT, b. 29 Oct 1693 son of Walter and Elizabeth (Peters) Wright. Joseph m. 2nd Elizabeth Chamberlain and m. 3rd Hannah Ashley.[17] Joseph d.? (a Joseph Wright of Norwich with a wife Hannah has a will probated in 1753; the will requests the division of his estate equally "among all my children" but they are not named).

4) GEORGE ABBOTT (*George[1]*), b. 7 Jun 1655 son of George and Hannah (Chandler) Abbott; d. 27 Feb 1736; m. 17 Apr 1678, DORCAS GRAVES, b. at Lynn, about 1655 daughter of Mark and Amy (-) Graves; Dorcas d. 19 Feb 1739/40.

The will of George Abbott was written 7 February 1735/6. His will includes a bequest to his dearly beloved wife Dorcas, beyond the customary widow's third, "the use of all my silver money, and the liberty to spend it so far as she shall have need of" for her support and comfort during her widowhood. He makes a bequest to the children of his son Daniel late of Woodstock who is deceased "besides the money and lands I have given to my said son in his lifetime to the value of many hundred pounds," an additional gift of 20 pounds in bills of credit to be paid when they come of age. Well-beloved "eldest surviving" son George receives an additional grant of land beyond what has been given him. There are also bequests for well-beloved son Henry, well-beloved daughter Hannah, grandchild Sarah who is the daughter of Elizabeth who is deceased, and to "youngest well-beloved son Isaac" who receives an additional money bequest beyond what he has already been given for his "learning."[18]

George Abbott and Dorcas Graves had ten children whose births are recorded at Andover.

i SARAH ABBOTT, b. 26 Aug 1679; d. 17 Nov 1679.

ii JOSEPH ABBOTT, b. 7 Oct 1680; probably died young.

iii NATHAN ABBOTT, b. 12 Feb 1682; probably died young.

iv MARTHA ABBOTT, b. 12 Feb 1682; d. 4 Dec 1683.

23) v HANNAH ABBOTT, b. 27 Feb 1684; d. 25 Dec 1774; m. 16 Sep 1708, JOHN OSGOOD, b. 28 Jun 1683 son of John and Hannah (Eires) Osgood; John d. 22 Nov 1765.

21) vi DANIEL ABBOTT, b. 10 Jan 1687/8; d. at Woodstock, CT, Aug 1731; m. 12 Sep 1711, HANNAH CHANDLER, b. 12 May 1690, daughter of John and Hannah (Abbott) Chandler (the same as Family #21 above).

24) vii ELIZABETH ABBOTT, b. 25 Jul 1690; d. 3 Sep 1718; m. 24 Dec 1716, BENJAMIN ABBOTT, b. 11 Jul 1686 son of Benjamin and Sarah (Farnum) Abbott; Elizabeth and Benjamin were first cousins. Benjamin m. 2nd Mary Carleton and 3rd Abigail Abbott (his second cousin and great granddaughter of the immigrant George Abbott of Rowley). Benjamin died before 5 Dec 1748 the date of probate of his estate.

25) viii GEORGE ABBOTT, b. 22 Dec 1692; d. 19 Mar 1768; m. 29 Nov 1721, MARY PHILLIPS, b. at Salem 5 Aug 1694, daughter of Samuel and Mary (Emerson) Phillips; Mary d. 4 Oct 1785.

26) ix HENRY ABBOTT, b. 12 Jun 1696; d. Feb 1776; m. 27 Oct 1721, MARY PLATTS, b. at Rowley 5 Sep 1700, daughter of James and Lydia (Hale) Platts; Mary d. Aug 1784.

27) x ISAAC ABBOTT, b. 4 Apr 1699; d. 9 Aug 1784; m. 1st, 29 Nov 1739, PHEBE LOVEJOY, b. 20 Jan 1715 daughter of William and Sarah (Frye) Lovejoy; Phebe d. 17 Dec 1751. Isaac m. 2nd, 3 Jan 1754, LYDIA STIMSON, b. at Charlestown, 10 Oct 1703 daughter of Andrew and Abigail (Sweetser) Stimson;[19] Lydia d. 28 Feb 1791. Lydia Stimson was the widow of Robert Calley.

---

[16] Vital Records of Woodstock 1686-1854 (accessed through archive.org)

[17] Vital Records of Woodstock 1686-1854 (accessed through archive.org)

[18] *Essex County, MA: Probate File Papers, 1638-1881.* Probate of George Abbott, 15 Mar 1736, Case number 46.

[19] The 1726 will of Abigail Sweetser Stimson includes a bequest to her daughter Lydia Calle. Lydia was the widow of Robert Calley when she married Isaac Abbott.

5) WILLIAM ABBOTT (*George¹*), b. 18 Nov 1657 son of George and Hannah (Chandler) Abbott; d. at Andover, 24 Oct 1713; m. at Roxbury, 19 Jun 1682 ELIZABETH GEARY, b. at Roxbury, 10 Jul 1661 daughter of Nathaniel and Anne (Douglas) Geary; Elizabeth d. 26 Nov 1712.

The estate of William Abbott entered probate 16 November 1713. His will includes bequests to the following persons: beloved wife Elizabeth, son William, son Ezra, sons James and Paul, son Philip, son Caleb, daughter Elizabeth, daughter Hannah, son Nathan, and son Zebadiah. The will was written 2 January 1711/12 and son Ezra died in 1712. The property division in 1716 includes "Joseph Phelps and his wife."[20]

William Abbott and Elizabeth Geary had twelve children born at Andover.

28) i ELIZABETH ABBOTT, b. 29 Apr 1683; d. 18 Jul 1762 at Pomfret, CT;[21] m. 13 Mar 1710/1, JOSEPH PHELPS, b. 8 Feb 1688/9 son of Samuel and Sarah (Chandler) Phelps; Joseph d. about 1773 at Pomfret when his will was probated.

28a ii WILLIAM ABBOTT, b. 16 Mar 1684/5; d. at Roxbury, 28 Oct 1713; m. at Roxbury, 25 Mar 1709, REBECCA BOYLSTON, b. at Roxbury, 15 Sep 1685 daughter of Thomas and Mary (Gardner) Boylston; Rebecca d. 7 Sep 1762.

iii GEORGE ABBOTT, b. 19 Mar 1686/7; d. 16 Nov 1690.

iv EZRA ABBOTT, b. 7 Jul 1689; d. 19 Nov 1712.

v GEORGE ABBOTT, b. 21 Dec 1691; d. 30 Dec 1691.

vi NATHAN ABBOTT b. 10 Dec 1691; d. 9 Jan 1712/3.

29) vii JAMES ABBOTT, b. 12 Feb 1694/5; d. 27 at Concord, NH, possibly in 1778;[22] m. 6 Jan 1713/4, ABIGAIL FARNUM, b. 3 May 1692, daughter of Ralph and Sarah (Sterling) Farnum; Abigail's date of death is not known.

30) viii PAUL ABBOTT, b. 28 Mar 1697; d. at Hampton, CT, 8 May 1752; m. 8 Feb 1719/20, ELIZABETH GRAY, b. 28 Mar 1700 daughter of Henry and Mary (Blunt) Gray; Elizabeth d. at Pomfret, CT 9 Jul 1765.[23]

31) ix PHILIP ABBOTT, b. 3 Apr 1699; d. 4 Nov 1748 at Hampton;[24] m. 8 Oct 1723 at Windham, ABIGAIL BIGFORD whose origins are not known; Abigail's date of death is not known although it is after 1748 as she was living at the time of the codicil to Philip's will that was written 1 Nov 1748.[25]

32) x HANNAH ABBOTT, b. 5 Apr 1701; d. 11 Feb 1751/2 at Windham; m. 21 Feb 1721 ABIEL HOLT, b. 28 Jun 1698 son of Nicholas and Mary (Russell) Holt. Abiel m. 2nd Sarah Downer; Abiel d. 11 Nov 1772 at Willington.

33) xi CALEB ABBOTT, b. 8 Oct 1704; died at Union, CT, 31 Jan 1778; m. at Pomfret 3 Dec 1730,[26] ELIZABETH PAINE, b. 9 Aug 1710 at Pomfret daughter of Samuel and Ruth (Perrin) Paine; Elizabeth d. 1 Apr 1772 at Union, CT.

xii ZEBADIAH ABBOTT, b. 1706; he was living at the time of his father's will in 1713. According to the Abbot genealogy he married a woman named Hannah and had one daughter named Hannah who died at age 12. There were no records located related to this family.

6) SARAH ABBOTT (*George¹*), b. 14 Nov 1659 daughter of George and Hannah (Chandler) Abbott; d. 28 Jun 1711; m. 11 Oct 1680, EPHRAIM STEVENS, b. about 1649 (based on age at time of death) son of John and Elizabeth (Parker) Stevens; Ephraim d. 26 Jun 1718.

Ensign Ephraim Stevens was a selectman of Andover and he was also charged with the security of the town's supply of weapons and ammunition. Town records for 20 February 1712/13 state "we have left the keas of the Town Stock of

[20] *Essex County, MA: Probate File Papers, 1638-1881.* Probate of William Abbott, 16 Nov 1713, Case number 148.

[21] Connecticut Town Death Records, pre-1870 (Barbour Collection). The vital records for Connecticut are from the Barbour Collections unless otherwise noted.

[22] The death date for James Abbott is not certain. Published genealogies, including the Abbott genealogy by Abiel Abbot and Ephraim Abbot list a date of 27 Dec 1787, but I cannot locate a record that supports this. There is a transcription of a death record for a James Abbott in Concord, NH for 1778 that lists the age at death as 83 which would be the right age for this James Abbott.

[23] Connecticut Town Death Records, pre-1870 (Barbour Collection).

[24] Connecticut, Hale Collection of Cemetery Inscriptions and Newspaper Notices, 1629-1934

[25] Connecticut, Wills and Probate Records, 1609-1999 (accessed through ancestry.com)

[26] New England Historical and Genealogical Register, 1913, volume LXVII, Marriages at Pomfret, Conn., p. 372

Ammunition with Ensign Ephraim Stevens, to be at ye selectmen's service, when they shall have ocation for them, and there is two dry casks of the Towns left standing on ye chest that the Amonition is locked up in."[27]

Ephraim Stevens wrote his will 11 June 1718 and his estate entered probate 7 July 1718.[28] To his son-in-law Robert Swan and daughter Hannah, he left his buildings and lands except one-half of the house being reserved for the use of his younger daughters while they are unmarried. He bequeaths to the other five daughters, Sarah, Elizabeth, Mary, Mehitabel, and Deborah, £20 each. The three younger daughters are to receive amounts equal to the amounts the three older daughters received at the time. His six daughters receive his stock of cattle and all the household goods. The daughters also receive £55 to be divided equally among them. Son-in-law Robert Swan was named executor.

On 7 April 1731, the children in this family, in consideration of payment of £20, quitclaimed their rights to the property in "Penne Cook" that was awarded by the General Court to their uncle Benjamin Stevens to Ebenezer Stevens. Those quitclaiming their rights were Stephen Abbott and Sarah his wife, Joseph Robinson and Elizabeth his wife, Robert Swan and Hannah his wife, James Ingalls and Mary his wife, Mehitabel Stevens, and Samuel Carlton and Deborah his wife. On 26 March 1733, the six daughters and their respective spouse, with Mehitabel single, and all children of Ephraim Stevens, in consideration of £83, quitclaimed to Job Marble property in Andover that was part of the estate of Capt. Benjamin Stevens. On 24 December 1742, Mehitable Stevens, spinster of Andover, and Samuel Carlton, mariner of Salem and his wife Deborah, in consideration of £7.10, conveyed to James Ingalls a tract of land in Andover. On 20 March 1754, Joseph and Elizabeth Robinson, Robert and Hannah Swan, and Mehitable Stevens daughter of Ephraim Stevens deceased joined other of their cousins in a quitclaim of property to Job Marble.[29][30]

Sarah Abbott and Ephraim Stevens had eight children all born at Andover.

14) i SARAH STEVENS, b. 28 Oct 1681; d. 28 Dec 1750; m. 22 Jul 1708, STEPHEN ABBOTT son of John and Sarah (Barker) Abbott; the same as Family #14 above.

34) ii ELIZABETH STEVENS, b. 7 Aug 1683; d. 28 Apr 1763; m. 20 Mar 1706/7, JOSEPH ROBINSON, b. about 1678 son of Joseph and Phebe (Dane) Robinson; Joseph d. at Andover, 9 Apr 1761.

35) iii HANNAH STEVENS, b. 18 Nov 1685; d. before 28 Sep 1773 when her will was probated; m. 17 Mar 1708/9, ROBERT SWAN, b. at Haverhill 28 May 1686 son of Robert and Elizabeth (Storie) Swan; Robert died before 4 Sep 1770 when his estate was probated.

iv MEHITABLE STEVENS, b. 29 Sep 1691; died young.

36) v MARY STEVENS, b. 10 Feb 1693/4; d. at Pomfret, 9 Mar 1773; m. 5 Nov 1719, JAMES INGALLS, b. 9 Aug 1695 son of James and Hannah (Abbott) Ingalls; Hannah Abbott Ingalls is from the Rowley Abbott line; James d. at Pomfret 6 Mar 1767.

vi EPHRAIM STEVENS, b. 13 Jul 1698; d. 9 Nov 1702.

vii MEHITABLE STEVENS, b. 31 Aug 1700; Mehitable was living in Andover and unmarried in 1754.

38) viii DEBORAH STEVENS, b. 4 Oct 1704; d. 17 Jun 1748 at Salem; m. 20 Jun 1726, SAMUEL CARLETON, b. 3 Jun 1696 son of John and Hannah (Osgood) Carleton; Samuel d. at Salem 9 Mar 1767.

7) BENJAMIN ABBOT (*George*[1]), b. 20 Dec 1661 son of George and Hannah (Chandler) Abbott; d. 30 Mar 1703; out-of-wedlock relationship with NAOMI HOYT 1683; m. 22 Apr 1685 SARAH FARNUM, b. 14 Jan 1661 daughter of Ralph and Elizabeth (Holt) Farnum; Sarah d. before 1726.[31]

Although Benjamin made important contributions to his community, he is also known as being the accuser of Martha Carrier for witchcraft. There was a property dispute that may also have been a factor in the accusations of witchery. Martha Carrier and her husband Thomas owned a property adjacent to Benjamin Abbot. There was dispute about the property line and, during an argument between Martha and Benjamin, she cursed him for seven years. At some point following this, Benjamin developed a series of maladies including a swollen foot and a pustule on his side. He attributed this to Martha's witchery. Martha was arrested and jailed, the first accused witch from Andover. She was also accused of witchcraft by the infamous Salem girls who fell in hysterics during her trial. Martha was tried, convicted, and hanged in Salem on August 19, 1692.[32]

---

[27] Bailey, "Andover in the Indian Wars," *Historical Sketches of Andover*, 185.

[28] *Essex County, MA: Probate File Papers, 1638-1881,* Probate of Ephraim Stevens, 7 Jul 1718, Case number 26333.

[29] The others involved in this quitclaim were John and Joanna Farnum, Abiel and Deborah Stevens, John 3rd and Deborah Foster, Nathan Barker, and Nathan Stevens. These cousins are descended from Benjamin Stevens's sister Mary Stevens wife of John Barker.

[30] Massachusetts Land Records, Essex County, 89:68, 116:229, 88:46, 116:234

[31] Charlotte Helen, "Early Notes and Records of the Farnum Family of Andover," undated manuscript. Retried from https://www.mhl.org/sites/default/files/files/Abbott/Farnum%20Family.pdf

[32] Information summarized from Bill Dalton, 2010, Witches and Switches: The Benjamin Abbot House, The Andover Townsman Online, Retrieved from http://www.andovertownsman.com/community/dalton-column-witches-and-switches-the-benjamin-abbot-house/article_6954f4c3-c022-5274-814e-a15d94ac99d5.html

Benjamin Abbot was the builder of what is now one of the two oldest houses in Andover located at 9 Andover Street. The house was placed on the National Register in 1976.[33]

Benjamin Abbot's estate entered probate 26 April 1703.[34] He did not leave a will. Sarah Abbott was administrator of the estate. Sarah Abbott was named guardian for the minor children Benjamin, David, Jonathan, and Samuel Abbott. (Although records for the father Benjamin Abbot are most often the one "t", the records for Sarah and the children are most often two "t's".)

Benjamin Abbot had a relationship with Naomi Hoyt Lovejoy when he was about age 22 and she was a young widow about age 28. There was a daughter born of this relationship recorded in the Andover vital records: "Abbot, Ben Naomie, d. illegitimate, Benjamin and Naomie Lovejoy, 1684." It is not known what became of this child.

Benjamin Abbot and Sarah Farnum had four children whose births are recorded at Andover.

24) 39) i BENJAMIN ABBOTT, b. 11 Jul 1686; d. before 5 Dec 1748; m. 1st, 24 Dec 1716 ELIZABETH ABBOTT, b. 25 Jul 1690 daughter of George and Dorcas (Graves) Abbott. BENJAMIN m. 2nd, 23 Oct 1722 MARY CARLETON, b. 7 Apr 1700 daughter of John and Hannah (Osgood) Carleton; Mary died 19 Jan 1725/6. BENJAMIN m. 3rd 1729, ABIGAIL ABBOTT, b. 7 Oct 1699 daughter of Nehemiah and Abigail (Lovejoy) Abbott. Abigail Abbott is from the George Abbott of Rowley line; Abigail d. 8 Dec 1753. Benjamin Abbott and his families with his three wives are covered in Families #24 and #39.

40) ii JONATHAN ABBOTT, b. Sep 1687; death reported as 21 Mar 1770 although record was not located;[35] m. 6 May 1713, ZERVIAH HOLT, b. 24 Mar 1688/9 daughter of Henry and Sarah (Ballard) Holt; Zerviah d. 26 Mar 1768.

41) iii DAVID ABBOTT, b. 18 Jan 1688/9; d. 14 Nov 1753; m. 20 Mar 1717/8, HANNAH DANFORTH, b. at Billerica, 20 Aug 1698 daughter of Samuel and Hannah (Crosby) Danforth; Hannah d. 8 Jan 1788.

iv SAMUEL ABBOTT, b. 19 May 1694; d. 29 Oct 1762; m. 8 Aug 1735, MARY PRESTON, widow of Christopher Lovejoy; Mary b. 31 Mar 1699 daughter of Samuel and Sarah (Bridges) Preston; Mary d. 15 Apr 1754. Samuel and Mary had no children. In his will, Samuel makes bequests to his three "sons-in-law" (stepsons) who were the sons of his deceased wife Mary (the sons of Mary with first husband Christopher Lovejoy): Christopher, Nathan, and Isaac Lovejoy, and a bequest to Nathan's wife Apphia. He also makes bequests to the six daughters of his deceased brother Benjamin (Sarah, Mary, Abigail, Elizabeth, Anna, and Dorcas), three sons of his brother Benjamin (Benjamin, Daniel, and Abiel), the sons of his brother Jonathan (Jonathan, David, Nathaniel, and Samuel), three sons of his deceased brother David (David, Solomon, and Jonathan), Zuriah daughter of brother Jonathan, Hannah and Sarah daughters of brother David, and the children of deceased Job Abbott (Job being a son of Samuel's brother Jonathan).

8) TIMOTHY ABBOTT (*George*[1]), b. 17 Nov 1663 son of George and Hannah (Chandler) Abbott; d. 9 Sep 1730; m. 27 Dec 1689 HANNAH GRAVES, b. at Lynn, 14 Dec 1657 daughter of Mark and Amy (-) Graves (sister of Dorcas who married Timothy's brother George); Hannah d. 16 Nov 1726.

Timothy was taken captive by the Indians on 8 April 1676, an attack in which his older brother was killed. Timothy was returned the following August in nearly starved condition. According to Fuess in his *Andover: Symbol of New England*, there is story tradition that as an adult Timothy never allowed his three children to complain of hunger as they did not know what true hunger was.[36]

Timothy Abbott wrote his will 3 March 1730 and his estate entered probate 21 September 1730. Timothy bequeaths to his only and well-beloved son Timothy, husbandman of Andover, several parcels of land including a parcel that was formerly owned by the elder Timothy's brother William who is now deceased. Eldest and well-beloved daughter Hannah receives £43 and youngest and well-beloved daughter Dorcas receives £21. These money amounts are in addition to payments previously made to them and constitute their whole portion. The two daughters also receive all the household items. In addition, after any debts are paid from the estate, any other money or bills of credit are to be equally divided among the three children. Son Timothy Abbott is named sole executor of the estate.[37]

Timothy Abbott and Hannah Graves had three children all born at Andover.

---

[33] Andover Historic Preservation, 9 Andover Street, Retrieved from https://preservation.mhl.org/9-andover-st

[34] *Essex County, MA: Probate File Papers, 1638-1881*, Probate of Benjamin Abbot, 26 Apr 1703, Case number 21.

[35] Holt Association of America, *First Three Generations of Holts in America*, (Newburgh, NY: Moore, 1930), 316

[36] Fuess, *Andover: Symbol of New England*, 71.

[37] *Essex County, MA: Probate File Papers, 1638-1881*, Probate of Timothy Abbott, 21 Sep 1730, Case number 143.

42) i TIMOTHY ABBOTT, b. 20 Jun 1693; d. 10 Jul 1766; m. Dec 1717, MARY FOSTER, b. at Boxford, 2 Aug 1698 daughter of William and Sarah (Kimball) Foster; Mary d. 31 Aug 1784.

43) ii HANNAH ABBOTT, b. 8 Oct 1695; d. 22 Apr 1769; m. 16 Mar 1732 as his 2nd wife, JOHN LANE, b. 20 Oct 1691 son of John and Susannah (Whipple) Lane; John d. 23 Sep 1763.

44) iii DORCAS ABBOTT, b. 25 Apr 1698; d. 25 Oct 1758; m. 12 Apr 1717 as his 2nd wife, NICHOLAS HOLT, b. 21 Dec 1683 son of Nicholas and Mary (Russell) Holt; Nicholas d. 1 Dec 1756.

9) THOMAS ABBOTT (*George¹*), b. 6 May 1666 son of George and Hannah (Chandler) Abbott; d. 28 Apr 1728; m. 7 Dec 1697 HANNAH GRAY, b. at Salem 30 Jan 1674/5 daughter of Robert and Hannah (Holt) Gray; Hannah d. 25 Jan 1763.

A probate record for Thomas Abbott was not located. Thomas Abbott and Hannah Gray had ten children all born at Andover.

45) i THOMAS ABBOTT, b. 3 Jan 1698/9; d. 11 Jul 1774; m. 28 Jan 1724/5, ELIZABETH BALLARD, b. 14 Jan 1700/1 daughter of Joseph and Rebecca (Johnson) Ballard; Elizabeth d. 31 Jul 1782.

ii HANNAH ABBOTT, b. 11 Sep 1700; d. at Rumford, NH, 22 Jul 1746; Hannah did not marry but accompanied some of her siblings to New Hampshire.

46) iii EDWARD ABBOTT, b. 9 Jun 1702; died at Concord, NH, 14 Apr 1759; m. 15 Jul 1728, DORCAS CHANDLER, b. about 1705 daughter of Thomas and Mary (Peters) Chandler; Dorcas d. 16 May 1748. Edward married 2nd, 23 Jan 1748/9, MEHITABLE EASTMAN, b. at Haverhill 17 Nov 1707 daughter of Jonathan and Hannah (Green) Eastman.

47) iv DEBORAH ABBOTT, b. 1 Dec 1704; d. at Concord, NH, 25 Oct 1801; m. at Andover 5 Jul 1736, JOSEPH HALL, b. 15 Dec 1707 son of Joseph and Sarah (Kimball) Hall; Joseph d. 8 Apr 1784 at Concord.[38]

48) v GEORGE ABBOTT, b. 7 Nov 1706; d. at Concord, NH, 6 Oct 1785; m. 1 Feb 1737, SARAH ABBOTT (who was his first cousin, once removed), b. Oct 1711 daughter of Samuel and Sarah (Stevens) Abbott and granddaughter of John and Sarah (Barker) Abbott; Sarah d. at Concord 14 Jun 1769.

vi ZEBADIAH ABBOTT, b. 25 Jan 1708/9; d. 17 May 1745 in the siege of Louisbourg.

49) vii BENJAMIN ABBOTT, b. 31 Mar 1710; d. at Concord, NH, 8 Mar 1794; m. 23 Jun 1742, HANNAH ABBOTT (who was his first cousin once removed), b. 30 Jul 1716 daughter of Samuel and Sarah (Stevens) Abbott and granddaughter of John and Sarah (Barker) Abbott; Hannah d. at Concord 27 Jul 1786.

viii CATHERINE ABBOTT, b. 31 Mar 1710; d. at Andover, 14 Sep 1744; Catherine did not marry.

ix AARON ABBOTT, b. 8 Aug 1714; d. 9 Apr 1730.

x ISAACK ABBOTT, b. 13 Feb 1715/6; d. 3 Nov 1745 in the siege of Louisbourg from illness; Isaac, s. Thomas and Hannah, "sickness in ye Kings Service at Lewisburg," Nov. 3, 1745, a. 28 y. 8m. 21 d.[39]

10) NATHANIEL ABBOTT (*George¹*), b. 4 Jul 1671 son of George and Hannah (Chandler) Abbott; d. 1 Dec 1749; m. 1 Nov 1695 DORCAS HIBBERT, b. about 1675 daughter of Joseph and Elizabeth (Graves) Hibbert of Salem and Beverly; Dorcas d. 17 Feb 1742/3.

Nathaniel Abbott and Dorcas Hibbert had ten children all born at Andover. There are two daughters, Sarah and Hannah, for whom there are no birth records, but these daughters are included in published genealogies including the Abbot genealogy.[40] For the daughter Hannah, there is no further record. The is a marriage reported for Sarah and that information is included here.

50) i MARY ABBOTT, b. 28 Jan 1697/8; d. unknown; m. 29 Dec 1718, BENJAMIN BLANCHARD, b. 14 Feb 1693 son of Jonathan and Anne (Lovejoy) Blanchard; Benjamin d. perhaps at NH.

51) ii NATHANIEL ABBOTT, b. 9 Jun 1700; d. at Concord, NH 1770;[41] m. 23 Nov 1726, PENELOPE BALLARD, b. 1705 daughter of Joseph and Rebecca (Johnson) Ballard; Penelope d. at Concord, date unknown (there is a death record transcription that gives the place of death, but not the date).

---

[38] New Hampshire Death and Disinterment Records, 1754-1947, accessed through ancestry.com

[39] Massachusetts: Vital Records, 1620-1850

[40] Abbot and Abbot, *Genealogical Register of Descendants*, p 144

[41] New Hampshire Death and Disinterment Records, 1754-1947

52) iii SARAH ABBOTT, b. about 1702 (based on age of 56th year at time of death); d. 11 Nov 1757; m. 4 Apr 1722, JOSEPH BLANCHARD, b. 19 Feb 1701 son of Thomas and Rose (Holmes) Blanchard. Joseph m. 2nd the widow Mary Frost.

53) iv JOSEPH ABBOTT, b. 22 Jan 1704/5; d. 23 Aug 1787 at Wilton, NH; m. 12 Aug 1731, DEBORAH BLANCHARD, b. 18 Apr 1712 daughter of Thomas and Rose (Holmes) Blanchard; Deborah d. at Andover 21 Jul 1773.

54) v TABITHA ABBOTT, b. about 1707; d. at Concord, NH date unknown, but before her husband; m. 5 Jan 1726/7, her first cousin once removed and George Abbott descendant, JOHN CHANDLER, b. May 1702 son of John and Hannah (Frye) Chandler; John d. at Concord 26 Jul 1775.

55) vi JEREMIAH ABBOTT, b. 4 Nov 1709; d. at Billerica 28 Aug 1748; m. 2 Jan 1734/5, HANNAH BALLARD, b. 27 Jun 1714 daughter of Hezekiah and Rebecca (Davis) Ballard. Hannah m. 2nd William Stickney; Hannah d. 11 Feb 1789 at Billerica.

vii JOSHUA ABBOTT, b. 3 Feb 1712. The Abbot genealogy[42] lists Joshua the son of Nathaniel and Dorcas (Hibbert) Abbott as marrying Lydia in Ashford, CT. However, there is another Joshua Abbott born 22 Feb 1711/2 in Ashford who is the son of Nathaniel and Mary (Hutchinson) Abbott. It would seem the Joshua born in Ashford is the more likely choice to marry Lydia in Ashford. Nathaniel Abbott who married Mary Hutchinson is from the George Abbott of Rowley line (through the "son" Thomas, Jr.). *Descendants of George Abbott of Rowley* lists Joshua of the Rowley line marrying Lydia and that is supported with land records and seems a sound case.[43] There is no further record that I could locate for this Joshua the son of Nathaniel and Dorcas.

56) viii ELIZABETH ABBOTT, b. 1 Feb 1713; d. 25 Jul 1799; m. 26 May 1741, TIMOTHY MOOAR, b. 16 Jun 1713 son of Timothy and Anne (Blanchard) Mooar; Timothy d. 20 Jan 1787.

57) ix REBECCA ABBOTT, b. 24 Apr 1717; d. 13 Feb 1803 at Concord, NH; m. 18 Mar 1741/2, ABIEL CHANDLER, b. 14 Mar 1717 son of John and Hannah (Frye) Chandler; Abiel d. abt. 1752 at Concord. Rebecca m. 2nd by 1754, her first cousin, once removed, AMOS ABBOTT, b. 18 Feb 1725/6 son of James and Abigail (Farnum) Abbott.

x HANNAH ABBOTT; she is listed in the Abbot genealogy, but I cannot find any record.

11) ELIZABETH ABBOTT (*George¹*), b. 9 Feb 1673 daughter of George and Hannah (Chalder) Abbott; d. 4 May 1750; m. 24 Oct 1692 NATHAN STEVENS, b. 5 Apr 1665 son of John and Hannah (Barnard) Stevens; Nathan d. 25 Sep 1740.

Nathan Stevens wrote his will 13 May 1740.[44] Beloved wife Elizabeth is to receive one-third of the produce of his tillage lands, two cows to be at her disposal, plus other provisions needed for her care and support. His grandchildren, who are the children of his daughter Elizabeth who is deceased who was the wife of Timothy Pearl, receive six pounds to be divided among them. Daughter Hannah the wife of Samuel Eams receives five pounds by the end of three years after his decease. Daughter Pheby the wife of Nicholas Steel receives ten pounds. There is an interesting bequest to granddaughter "Eunos Ginnins" (or perhaps Germin, but it is not clear in the will) who is the oldest daughter of his daughter Pheby who is to receive ten pounds when she reaches the age of 21. This granddaughter is not from Phebe's marriage to Nicholas Steel and this will be addressed with Phebe's family (Family #61). Daughter Lydia Stevens receives 60 pounds, and if she remains single will receive the use of the portion of the house that her mother occupies after mother's decease, as well as some other considerations. Son Nathan, who is named executor, receives all the lands and the remainder of the estate not otherwise distributed.

On 27 September 1746, Elizabeth Abbott Stevens signed a quit claim releasing her dower portion in exchange for a settlement of a payment to her of 40 pounds per year. This allowed grandson Nathan Stevens to take full control of the real property. Elizabeth's son Nathan died just a few months after his father. In 1746, grandson Nathan Stevens was 22 years old and ready to assume his adult responsibilities.

The births of six children of Elizabeth Abbott and Nathan Stevens are recorded at Andover.

---

[42] Abbot and Abbot, *Genealogical Register of Descendants*, 143

[43] Lemuel Abbott, *Descendants of George Abbott of Rowley*, 912

[44] *Essex County, MA: Probate File Papers, 1638-1881*. Probate of Nathan Stevens, 6 Oct 1740, Case number 26408.

58) i NATHAN STEVENS, b. 22 Sep 1693; d. 20 Sep 1741; m. 3 Nov 1715, HANNAH ROBINSON, b. 29 Jan 1694/5 daughter of Dane and Mary (Chadwick) Robinson; Hannah d. possibly at Boxford in 1753 (see discussion in Family #58 in Generation Three).

59) ii ELIZABETH STEVENS, b. 14 Oct 1697; d. at Windham, CT, 28 Aug 1736; m. 24 Aug 1722, TIMOTHY PEARL, b. at Bradford 23 Feb 1695 son of John and Elizabeth (Holmes) Pearl. Timothy m. 2nd Mary Leach; Timothy d. at Windham 9 Oct 1773.

60) iii HANNAH STEVENS, b. 1701; d. after 1782; m. 13 Jan 1720/1 as his 2nd wife, SAMUEL AMES, b. 6 Feb 1695/6 son of Robert and Bethia (Gatchell) Ames; Samuel d. at Groton 1784.

61) iv PHEBE STEVENS, b. 1704; date of death is unknown, although she is perhaps the Phebe Steel who is the head of household in the 1790 U.S. Census for Andover;[45] m. 7 Nov 1734, NICHOLAS STEEL whose origins are unknown, but described as a laborer.[46] The births of six children are recorded at Andover, but there are no death records in Massachusetts for either Phebe or Nicholas.

v LYDIA STEVENS, b. 1 Aug 1706; d. before 6 Jul 1790 when her estate entered probate;[47] m. 9 Jan 1744 as his 2nd wife, FRANCIS INGALLS, b. 20 Dec 1694 son of Henry and Abigail (Emery) Ingalls; Francis d. 26 Jan 1759. Lydia and Francis did not have children. In her will, Lydia left her estate to her son (stepson) Francis Ingalls, his wife Eunice, and their children Eunice and Asa.

vi Unknown child STEVENS, b. and d. 30 May 1709.

---

[45] 1790 United States Federal Census; Year: 1790; Census Place: Andover, Essex, Massachusetts; Series: M637; Roll: 4; Page: 20; Image: 35; Family History Library Film: 0568144. Household headed by Phebe Steel and household consists of two females.

[46] Charlotte Helen Abbott, Notes on the Steele Family

[47] *Essex County, MA: Probate File Papers, 1638-1881.* Probate of Lydia Ingalls, 6 Jul 1790, Case number 14537.

Generation Three

Children of John Abbott and Sarah Barker

12) JOHN ABBOT (*John², George¹*), b. 2 Nov 1674 son of John and Sarah (Barker) Abbott; d. 1 Jan 1754; m. 6 Jan 1702/3 ELIZABETH HARNDEN, b. at Wilmington, 25 Sep 1672 daughter of Richard and Mary (-) Harnden. Elizabeth m. 2nd Zebadiah Chandler, 29 Mar 1756; Elizabeth d. 9 Aug 1756.

John Abbot remained in Andover his entire life. He served as deacon of the church at Andover for 34 years. He was active in other town affairs including serving as selectman.[48]

John and his wife Elizabeth had six children, one of whom died in infancy. Another son, Abiel, attended Harvard College graduating in 1737. However, he died just two years later cutting short a promising career as a minister. The Reverend J. Barnard delivered a sermon at the funeral of Abiel lamenting the loss of a young life.[49]

Elizabeth was widowed in 1754. That same year, her brother-in-law Zebadiah Chandler was widowed when his wife Sarah Abbot (sister to John Abbot) died. Elizabeth and Zebadiah married in 1756, but Elizabeth died about five months after the marriage.

John Abbot wrote his will 12 August 1747 and it was proved 21 January 1754.[50] His will included bequests to the following persons: "Elizabeth, my dear and well-beloved wife" who received a fairly typical widow's bequest of the use of the west end of the house and a detailed list of requirements for her son to meet for her continued maintenance; eldest and well-beloved son John received all the homestead lands and some other property and livestock including "one-quarter part of my stock of brute creatures"; second and well-beloved son Barachias received the full deed to the land on which he currently lived; "well-beloved and only daughter Elizabeth" received another quarter of the brute stock and a bequest of money which is to offset a bill of credit that she owes to her father; and youngest and well-beloved son Joseph gets the last quarter of the brute stock and the deed to land on which he has been living. John made additional dispositions of his silver money, paper money, and bills of credit among his wife and his four children.

The children of John and Elizabeth Abbot were all born at Andover.

i JOHN ABBOT, b. 1 Sep 1703; d. 10 Sep 1703.[51]

62) ii JOHN ABBOT, b. 3 Aug 1704; d. 10 Nov 1793; m. 28 Sep 1732, PHEBE FISKE, b. at Boxford 4 Aug 1712 daughter of John and Abigail (Poore) Fiske; Phebe d. 7 Dec 1802.

63) iii BARACHIAS ABBOT, b. 14 May 1707; d. 2 Oct 1784; m. 22 Mar 1733, HANNAH HOLT, b. 18 Dec 1709 daughter of Timothy and Rhoda (Chandler) Holt; Hannah d. 2 Aug 1775.

64) iv ELIZABETH ABBOT, b. 28 Oct 1711; d. 4 Jul 1758; m. 26 Oct 1732, ASA FOSTER, b. 16 Jun 1710 son of William and Sarah (Kimball) Foster; Asa d. 17 Jul 1787.

v ABIEL ABBOT, b. 7 Jan 1715/6; d. 18 May 1739. He graduated from Harvard in 1737.[52]

65) vi JOSEPH ABBOT, b. 24 Apr 1719; d. 30 Jan 1790 at Chester, MA; m. 12 Nov 1741 his first cousin, HANNAH ABBOTT, b. 29 Dec 1721 daughter of Ebenezer and Hannah (Turner) Abbott; Hannah d. 2 Jun 1805 at Chester.

13) JOSEPH ABBOT (*John², George¹*), b. 29 Dec 1676 son of John and Sarah (Barker) Abbott; d. 9 Jan 1757; m. 4 Apr 1722 HANNAH ALLEN, b. 12 Sep 1690 daughter of John and Mercy (Peters) Allen; Hannah d. 4 Mar 1755.

There is little known from the records for Joseph Abbot and Hannah Allen. Hannah Allen was orphaned by the time she was three months old as both her parents died in the 1690 smallpox epidemic. There are just two children recorded at Andover for this family, one of whom died in early infancy. A probate record could not be located for Joseph.

---

[48] Abbot and Abbot, *Genealogical Register of Descendants*
[49] William B. Sprague, *Annals of the American Pulpit, Volume 1.* (New York: Robert Carter, 1859).
[50] *Essex County, MA: Probate File Papers, 1638-1881.* Probate of John Abbot, 21 Jan 1754, Case number 67.
[51] *Early Vital Records of Massachusetts from 1600 to 1850*
[52] Harvard University, *Quinquennial Catalogue*, 119

66) i JOSEPH ABBOT, b. 31 May 1724; d. 10 Dec 1766; m. 9 Feb 1748/9 ANNA PEABODY, b. at Boxford 21 Jul 1723 daughter of Jonathan and Alice (Pearl) Peabody; Anna d. 20 May 1766. Joseph married 2nd, 1 Nov 1766, EDNA PLATTS, b. 15 Nov 1737 at Bradford. Joseph died just one month after his second marriage.

ii WILLIAM ABBOT; b. 3 Dec 1730; d. 17 Dec 1730.

14) STEPHEN ABBOT (*John², George¹*), b. 14 Feb 1678 son of John and Sarah (Barker) Abbott; d. 27 May 1766; m. 22 Jul 1708, SARAH STEVENS (*Sarah Abbott Stevens², George¹*), b. 28 Oct 1681 daughter of Ephraim and Sarah (Abbott) Stevens; Sarah d. 28 Dec 1750.

Stephen Abbot and Sarah Stevens were first cousins and both descendants of George Abbott. Stephen and Sarah had nine children whose births were recorded at Andover. One of these children died in infancy. Son Samuel Abbot died at Lake George, New York during the French and Indian War.

Stephen had considerably less land than his older brothers having an estate of 150 to 190 acres at the time of his death. He made provisions for each of his three sons to settle on this single estate. Two of his sons died before Stephen. As a result, nearly all his lands were bequeathed to his remaining son Stephen, Jr. Stephen, Sr. had retained legal control of all his land until his death at the age of 88.[53]

The will of Stephen Abbot was written 3 November 1759 and proved 8 July 1766.[54] In his will, Stephen made bequests to the following persons: well-beloved son Stephen receives lands and buildings; daughter Elizabeth receives half of whatever grain and corn is on hand at the time of his death; beloved son Ephraim the son of Ephraim who is deceased receives a portion of land; his grandson Ephraim is to make a money payment to each of his five sisters from his bequest, those granddaughters being Hannah, Mehitable, Sarah, Abiel, and Rhoda; beloved daughter Sarah receives one-fifth of the moveable estate as do beloved daughter Hannah and beloved daughter Priscilla and beloved daughter Elizabeth. The last fifth of the moveable estate is granted to his granddaughters Sarah and Mary who are the children of his daughter Mary who is deceased. On the other hand, his two granddaughters Elizabeth and Hannah who are the children of his deceased son Samuel receive a bequest of land.

67) i EPHRAIM ABBOTT, b. 1710; d. 14 Apr 1745; m. 14 Feb 1733/4 HANNAH PHELPS, b. 1709 (est. based on age at death) daughter of Samuel and Hannah (Dane) Phelps; Hannah m. 2nd John Chandler; Hannah d. 5 Aug 1781.

48) ii SARAH ABBOTT, b. Oct 1711; d. at Concord, NH 14 Jun 1769;[55] m. 1 Feb 1737, GEORGE ABBOTT her first cousin, once removed, b. 7 Nov 1706 son of Thomas and Hannah (Gray) Abbott; George d. at Concord 6 Oct 1785.[56] (This is Family #48 in Generation Two.)

68) iii MARY ABBOTT, b. 4 Aug 1713; d. at Lunenburg, 5 Aug 1748; m. 14 Aug 1742, JOSEPH HOLT, b. 28 Feb 1715/6 son of Thomas and Alice (Peabody) Holt. Joseph m. 2nd Dorcas Frost; Joseph d. at Lunenburg 1754 (based on date of probate 26 Sep 1754).

49) iv HANNAH ABBOTT, b. 30 Jul 1716; d. at Concord, NH 26 Jul 1786;[57] m. 23 Jun 1742, BENJAMIN ABBOTT her first cousin, once removed, b. 31 Mar 1710 son of Thomas and Hannah (Gray) Abbott; Benjamin d. at Concord 8 Mar 1794. (This is Family #49 in Generation Two.)

69) v STEPHEN ABBOT, b. 2 Mar 1717/8; d. 8 Nov 1768; m. 24 May 1743, MARY ABBOTT, his second cousin, b. 12 Mar 1722/3 daughter of George and Mary (Phillips) Abbott. Mary m. 2nd as his second wife, her second cousin Jonathan Abbott son of Jonathan and Zerviah (Holt) Abbott; Mary d. 8 Aug 1792.

vi PRISCILLA ABBOTT, b. 20 Feb 1719/20; d. 28 Dec 1796; m. 28 Mar 1771 as his 2nd wife, JACOB FOWLE of Lancaster; there were no children from this marriage; Jacob d. 6 Mar 1774 at Lancaster.

vii ELIZABETH ABBOTT, b. 29 Dec 1721; d. about 1786;[58] she does not seem to have married.

70) viii SAMUEL ABBOT, b. 23 Jun 1726; d. 1758 at Ft. George, NY during the French and Indian War; m. 14 Dec 1754, ELIZABETH WYMAN probably born about 1730, described as “of Pelham” but no further information has been located on her origins. Elizabeth m. 2nd Joseph Dane; Elizabeth d. 26 Sep 1778.

ix MEHITABLE ABBOTT, b. 17 Mar 1727/8; d. 16 Apr 1728.

---

[53] Greven, *Four Generations*

[54] *Essex County, MA: Probate File Papers, 1638-1881.* Probate of Stephen Abbot, 8 Jul 1766, Case number 132.

[55] Abbot and Abbot, *Genealogical Register of Descendants*

[56] Confirmed by probate date 16 November 1785

[57] New Hampshire Death and Disinterment Records, 1754-1947, accessed through ancestry.com

[58] Abbot and Abbot, *Genealogical Register of Descendants*

15) SARAH ABBOTT (*John*[2], *George*[1]), b. 26 Nov 1680 daughter of John and Sarah (Barker) Abbott; d. 6 Mar 1754; m. 9 Jan 1707 ZEBADIAH CHANDLER (*Hannah Abbott Chandler*[2], *George*[1]), b. 1 Apr 1683 son of John and Hannah (Abbott) Chandler. Zebadiah m. 2nd Elizabeth Harnden Abbott (widow of John Abbott); Zebadiah d. 20 Jun 1766.

Sarah and Zebadiah Chandler were members of the South Parish church in Andover. Zebadiah held some positions in the town including surveyor 1721-1726 and was chosen constable 3 Mar 1734/5.[59] Sarah and Zebadiah had five daughters. The estate of Zebadiah Chandler was probated 8 July 1766. He made bequests to the following persons: beloved daughter Sarah Chandler (who married Joshua Chandler), beloved daughter Joanna Shaddock, beloved daughter Priscilla Phelps, beloved daughter Mehitable Lovejoy, beloved daughter Elizabeth Lovejoy, and beloved grandson Joshua Chandler son of daughter Sarah. Grandson Joshua Chandler was the executor.

71) i SARAH CHANDLER, b. 1707 (based on age at time of death); d. 28 Mar 1768; m. 18 Feb 1728/9, JOSHUA CHANDLER, her 1st cousin (and a descendant of George Abbott), b. 1705 son of John and Hannah (Frye) Chandler; Joshua d. 24 Mar 1734; Sarah did not remarry.

72) ii JOANNA CHANDLER, b. 1710 (based on age at time of death); d. 12 Sep 1791; m. 3 Jun 1728, JOSEPH SHATTUCK, b. 1707 (based on age at time of death); Joseph d. 21 Mar 1772.

73) iii PRISCILLA CHANDLER, b. 26 Apr 1713; d. 4 Jan 1778; m. 29 Jan 1735/6, SAMUEL PHELPS, b. 5 Feb 1712/3 son of Samuel and Hannah (Dane) Phelps; Samuel d. 17 Apr 1795.

74) iv MEHITABLE CHANDLER, b. 1717; d. 26 Jan 1786 (reported, but no record found); m. 26 Jan 1738, CALEB LOVEJOY, b. 28 Dec 1716 son of Henry and Sarah (Farnum) Lovejoy. The family relocated to Suncook, NH and Caleb is reported to have died there 1781 (this is the date used by the Daughters of the American Revolution and Carter's *History of Pembroke*).

75) v ELIZABETH CHANDLER, b. 5 Feb 1721; d. probably in NH, date unknown; m. 26 Mar 1741, DAVID LOVEJOY, b. 10 Oct 1715 son of Henry and Sarah (Farnum) Lovejoy. The family relocated to Suncook, NH. The DAR gives the death date of David as 18 Feb 1819, although I believe this to be the death date of his son David Lovejoy.

16) EPHRAIM ABBOT (*John*[2], *George*[1]), b. 6 Aug 1682 son of John and Sarah (Barker) Abbott; d. 3 Jun 1748; m. 6 Jan 1714/5 Sarah Hunt (a widow most likely SARAH CROSBY the widow of Thomas Hunt; identity discussed below), b. 12 Jun 1694 daughter of Joseph and Sarah (French) Crosby. Sarah m. 3rd John Dane; Sarah d. about 1760.

On 6 January 1714/5, Ephraim Abbot married Sarah Hunt, widow of Billerica. The Billerica records show that Thomas Hunt, the husband of Sarah and son of Samuel, Sr., died 16 September 1709. Thomas Hunt is recorded as marrying Sarah Crosby, although the date of the marriage did not survive in the records; there is just a record that a marriage occurred. There is one child born to Thomas and Sarah Hunt, a daughter Sarah born 20 November 1709. In the Billerica records, there are two potential Sarah Crosbys who might be the wife of Thomas Hunt. First is Sarah Crosby born in 1684 the daughter of Simon and Rachel Crosby. The second is Sarah the daughter of Joseph and Sarah Crosby. These two Sarah's were aunt and niece, the older Sarah being the sister of Joseph. However, the elder Sarah Crosby was married to a man named Rawson established by the 1724 will of Simon Crosby which includes a bequest to his daughter Sarah Rawson. The only real concern about this identification of Sarah daughter of Joseph being the wife of Thomas Hunt is her very young age (either 15 or 16) at the time of her first marriage. However, Thomas Hunt was born in 1689 making him a quite young husband in 1709. No death record or guardian record could be located for the child Sarah Hunt born to Thomas and Sarah.

In his will, Ephraim Abbot has bequests to the following persons: dearly and well-beloved wife Sarah, eldest and well-beloved son Ephraim, second and well-beloved son Joshua, and his other well-beloved sons Daniel, Josiah, Ebenezer, and Peter, and well-beloved daughters Sarah, Mary, Elizabeth, and Martha. Daniel is the executor of the estate.[60]

Ephraim Abbot and Sarah Crosby had eleven children all born at Andover.

76) i SARAH ABBOTT, b. 25 Jan 1715/6; d. at NH; m. 8 Sep 1736, SAMUEL GRAY, b. Jul 1711 son of Henry and Mary (Blunt) Gray; Samuel d. probably in New Hampshire.

77) ii EPHRAIM ABBOT, b. 22 Jul 1718; d. about 1775 at Amherst, NH; m. 1st, 3 Nov 1740 his 2nd cousin (and George Abbott descendant) MARY ABBOTT, b. 7 Jan 1723/4 daughter of Timothy and Mary (Foster)

---

[59] George Chandler. *The Chandler family: The descendants of William and Annis Chandler who settled in Roxbury, Mass 1637.* (Worcester, MA: Charles Hamilton, 1883).

[60] *Essex County, MA: Probate File Papers, 1638-1881.* Probate of Ephraim Abbot, 4 Jul 1748, Case number 41.

Abbott; Mary d. 9 Mar 1744. Ephraim m. 2nd 1 Feb 1745/6, MARY KNEELAND,[61] b. about 1720 of Ipswich; death is not known but likely at Amherst, NH.

78) iii MARY ABBOTT, b. Jul 1720; date of death unknown but likely in Amherst, NH; m. 11 May 1743, ROBERT READ, b. 25 Dec 1720 at Chelmsford son of William and Hannah (Bates) Read; Robert d. at Amherst, NH 11 Sep 1803.[62]

79) iv JOSHUA ABBOTT, b. 25 Sep 1722; d. at Amherst, NH after 2 Mar 1772 (the date of his will); m. 7 Jul 1749, PHEBE INGALLS, b. 10 Aug 1730 daughter of Joseph and Phebe (Farnum) Ingalls; Phebe d. after 2 Mar 1772.

v DANIEL ABBOTT, b. 3 Sep 1724; d.10 Aug 1761; m. 21 May 1752, Lydia Henfield widow. Daniel and Lydia had no children. In his will probated 31 Aug 1761, Daniel Abbott has bequests to the following persons: beloved wife Lydia, beloved brother Ebenezer Abbott, beloved brother Peter Abbott, beloved cousin Daniel Abbott, and his brethren and sisters: Ephraim Abbott, Joshua Abbott, Josiah Abbott, Ebenezer Abbott, Peter Abbott, Sarah Gray, Mary Reed, Elizabeth Abbott, and Martha Towne.[63] The will addresses the reports in published genealogies that Archelaus Towne first married Mary Abbott and then her younger sister Martha. Archelaus Towne and Martha Abbott were married by at least 1761. Martha's sister Mary was at that same time married to Robert Reed.

80) vi ELIZABETH ABBOTT, b. 29 Jun 1726; d. 18 Dec 1819; m. 20 Sep 1744, her 2nd cousin ASA ABBOT, b. 17 Oct 1721 son of Timothy and Mary (Foster) Abbot; Asa d. 22 Dec 1796.

81) vii JOSIAH ABBOTT, b. 26 Sep 1728; d. at Lyndeborough, NH, Dec 1777 at Lyndeborough, NH; m. by 1755 HANNAH HOBBS, b. at Middleton, 28 Aug 1729 daughter of William and Amme (Towne) Hobbs.

82) viii EBENEZER ABBOTT, b. 20 Feb 1731; d. 19 Dec 1771; m. 1 Jan 1752, LYDIA FARRINGTON, b. 24 Oct 1735 daughter of John and Sarah (Houghton) Farrington. Lydia was deceased by 1786 when her father wrote his will.

ix MARTHA ABBOTT, b. 30 Mar 1733; d. 5 May 1733.

83) x PETER ABBOTT, b. 8 May 1734; d. 19 Apr 1774 at Kingston, NH; m. 22 Sep 1757, ELIZABETH HOLT (widow of Edmund Damon), b. at Reading, about 1733 daughter of Joseph and Abigail (Rich) Holt; Elizabeth d. after 1774.

84) xi MARTHA ABBOTT, b. 13 Jul 1737; d. 13 Aug 1773 at Amherst, NH; m. about 1757 ARCHELAUS TOWNE,[64] b. 1734 at Topsfield son of Israel and Grace (Gardner) Towne; Archelaus d. Nov 1779 at Fishkill, NY during the Revolution.

17) JOSHUA ABBOTT (*John*[2], *George*[1]), b. 17 Jun 1685 son of John and Sarah (Barker) Abbott; d. at Billerica 11 Feb 1769; m. 1st, 10 Jun 1710 REBEKAH SHED, b. at Billerica, 21 May 1685 daughter of John and Sarah (Chamberlain) Shed; Rebekah d. 7 Apr 1720. Joshua m. 2nd, 2 Mar 1720/1, DORCAS WHITING, b. at Billerica 21 Mar 1692 daughter of Oliver and Anna (Danforth) Whiting; Dorcas d. 23 Dec 1765.

In his will, Joshua Abbott makes bequests to the following persons: "Tis my will and pleasure and I do give to Dorcas my beloved wife" one third part of the personal estate and other bequests to son John Abbott, daughter Sarah Goodwin, daughter Mary Jefts, daughter Elizabeth Walker, daughter Dorcas Abbott, granddaughter Hannah Osgood got forty shillings in full for the remainder of her mother's portion, son Joshua Abbott, son Oliver Abbott, and son David Abbott.[65]

Six children of Joshua Abbott and Rebekah Shed were born at Billerica.

i REBEKAH ABBOTT, b. 27 Mar 1711; d. 9 May 1761; she did not marry.

85) ii JOHN ABBOTT, b. 5 May 1713; d. 22 Oct 1791 at Westford; m. 30 Dec 1735, HANNAH RICHARDSON, b. 2 Apr 1714 at Billerica daughter of Jonathan and Hannah (French) Richardson; Hannah d. 29 Nov 1795.

---

[61] The Abiel Abbot and Ephraim Abbot Genealogy gives her name as Hannah Kneeland, but the marriage record says Mary Kneeland and the birth records for each of her children with Ephraim Abbot give the mother's name as Mary. She is possibly Mary Neeland (Kneeland) baptized in Topsfield 21 May 1721 daughter of Philip. Philip died in 1742 and his son Philip relocated to Ipswich which would make it possible that Mary accompanied her brother to Ipswich.

[62] His grave site has been located at the Amherst Town Hall Burying Ground and bears this inscription: Erected to the Memory of Col. Robert Read who died Sept. 11, 1803 in the 83 Year of his age. (findagrave.com)

[63] *Essex County, MA: Probate File Papers, 1638-1881.* Probate of Daniel Abbot, 31 Aug 1761, Case number 27.

[64] Several marriages are reported for Archelaus Towne in various published sources, but he seems to have married only Martha and they were married by 1761 when her brother Daniel leaves a bequest to his sister Martha Town in his will.

[65] *Middlesex County, MA: Probate File Papers, 1648-1871.* Probate of Joshua Abbott, 1769, Case number 36.

86) iii SARAH ABBOTT, b. 24 Feb 1714/5; d. about 1798; m. 1 Jan 1736, CHRISTOPHER OSGOOD, b. 21 Jul 1712 at Billerica son of Christopher and Mary (Keyes) Osgood; Christopher d. 26 Aug 1748. Sarah m. 2nd, about 1750, JAMES GOODWIN, b. at Reading, 1 Nov 1714 son of John and Tabitha (Pearson) Goodwin; James d. at Worcester, 2 Jun 1776. James was first married to Mary Mansfield who died in 1749.

87) iv MARY ABBOTT, b. 28 Aug 1717; d. about 1800; m. 29 Nov 1743, HENRY JEFTS, b. at Billerica, 24 Apr 1717 son of Henry and Elizabeth (Hayward) Jefts; Henry d. at Billerica 19 Aug 1772.

88) v HANNAH ABBOTT, twin of MARY, b. 28 Aug 1717; d. 11 Jan 1753; m. 6 Feb 1739, PHINEAS OSGOOD, b. at Billerica 20 Jun 1714 son of Christopher and Mary (Keyes) Osgood; Phineas d. 3 Jun 1756.

89) vi ELIZABETH ABBOTT, b. 7 Dec 1719; d. about 1803; m. 7 Dec 1743, ROBERT WALKER whose origin is unknown to me; he is *perhaps* the son of John and Abigail (Wesson) Walker of Chelmsford; Robert d. 26 Jan 1757.

Five children of Joshua Abbott and Dorcas Whiting were born at Billerica.

90) i JOSHUA ABBOTT, b. 28 Oct 1722; 7 Aug 1807; m. 6 Mar 1746, SARAH STEARNS, b, at Billerica, 10 Dec 1726 daughter of Isaac and Alice (-) Stearns; Sarah d. 7 Sep 1803.

ii DORCAS ABBOT, b. 6 Nov 1724; d. 7 Jan 1810; Dorcas did not marry. Dorcas did leave a will which includes bequests to niece Dorcas Bowers, niece Abigail Kidder, niece Elizabeth Abbot, grandniece Abigail E. A. Kidder, nephew Blaney Abbot, and niece Joanna Winship. Blaney Abbot is named executor.[66]

91) iii OLIVER ABBOTT, b. 26 Mar 1727; d. 10 Apr 1796; m. 13 Feb 1752, JOANNA FRENCH, b. at Billerica 27 Nov 1729 daughter of William and Joanna (Hill) French; Joanna d. 20 Aug 1768. OLIVER m. 2nd at Westford, 1 Aug 1769, ABIGAIL HALL, b. 19 Jul 1734 daughter of Willard and Abigail (Cotton) Hall; Abigail d. 4 Aug 1804.

92) iv DAVID ABBOTT, b. 27 Apr 1729; d. 15 Nov 1801; m. 25 Aug 1752, HANNAH ELLIS, b. about 1727 but origin is unknown; Hannah d. 17 Dec 1767. DAVID m. 2nd 28 Jun 1768 HULDAH PAINE of Malden who d. 8 Sep 1797.

v LYDIA ABBOTT, b. 26 Jun 1732; d. 13 Oct 1748.

18) EBENEZER ABBOT (*John*[2], *George*[1]), b. 27 Sep 1689 son of John and Sarah (Barker) Abbott; d. 14 Jan 1761; m. 5 Apr 1720, HANNAH TURNER, widow of Francis Dane; Hannah was b. at Charlestown about 1694 daughter of James and Hannah (Lazell) Turner; Hannah d. 1788.

In his will, Ebenezer Abbot had bequests to the following persons: beloved wife Hannah, son Isaac, son James, daughter Hannah, daughter Mary, daughter Phebe, and grandson Joseph Chandler.[67]

The original gravestone of Ebenezer Abbot in the Old South Burying Ground bore the inscription HERE LIES BURIED THE BODY ON ENs EBENEZER ABBOT WHO DEPARTED THIS LIFE JANRY 14 1761 IN YE 72 YEAR OF HIS AGE.[68]

Ebenezer Abbot and Hannah Turner had eight children whose births are recorded at Andover.

i EBENEZER ABBOTT, b. 1 Jan 1720/1; d. 18 Jul 1721.

65) ii HANNAH ABBOTT, b. 29 Dec 1721; d. 2 Jun 1805 at Chester, MA; m. 12 Nov 1741, her first cousin JOSEPH ABBOTT, b. 24 Apr 1719 son of John and Elizabeth (Harnden) Abbott; Joseph d. 30 Jan 1790.

iii EBENEZER ABBOTT, b. 23 Nov 1723; d. 28 Apr 1725.

93) iv MARY ABBOTT, b. 2 Apr 1725; d. 20 Apr 1760; m. 1st 4 Oct 1742, JOSEPH CHANDLER, b. 20 Nov 1720 son of Thomas and Mary (Stevens) Chandler (confirmed by the will of Thomas Chandler); Joseph d. 31 Mar 1745. MARY m. 2nd 8 Apr 1746, ISAAC BLUNT, b. 5 Nov 1712 son of William and Sarah (Foster) Blunt; Isaac d. 6 Jan 1798.

[66] *Middlesex County, MA: Probate File Papers, 1648-1871. Probate of* Dorcas Abbot, *1810, Case number* 15.

[67] *Essex County, MA: Probate File Papers, 1638-1881.* Probate of Ebenezer Abbot, 2 Feb 1761, Case number, p 32

[68] The Essex Antiquarian, volume 2, number 8, Salem, Mass., August 1898, Andover Inscriptions Old South Burying Ground

v NEHEMIAH ABBOTT, b. 5 Feb 1726/7; d. 25 Mar 1727.

94) vi ISAAC ABBOTT, b. 30 Jun 1728; d. after 1790 at Fryeburg, ME; m. 29 May 1753, SUSANNA FARNUM, whose origins are not firmly known but most likely the daughter of Ebenezer and Priscilla (Ingalls) Farnum.

95) vii PHEBE ABBOTT, b. 3 Jan 1731/2; d. Feb 1805; m. 30 May 1751, JAMES GRIFFIN whose origins are unknown; James d. 9 Oct 1815.

96) viii JAMES ABBOTT, b. 14 Apr 1736; d. unknown; m. at Dracut, 25 Feb 1758, LYDIA COBURN whose origins are not known definitively, although she is probably the daughter of Joseph and Hannah (Jones) Coburn of Dracut. The family seems to have relocated to New Hampshire.

Children of Hannah Abbott and John Chandler

19) JOHN CHANDLER (*Hannah Abbott Chandler*[2], *George*[1]), b. 14 Mar 1679/80 son of John and Hannah (Abbott) Chandler; d. 3 May 1741; m. 4 Jun 1701, HANNAH FRYE, b. 12 Apr 1683 daughter of Samuel and Mary (Aslett) Frye; Hannah d. 1 Aug 1727.

In his will, John Chandler has bequests to the following persons: well-beloved sons John, Nathan, and Abiel; well-beloved daughters Hannah Ballard, Phebe Lovejoy, and Lydia Chandler; and well-beloved grandsons Zebadiah and Joshua Chandler who are the sons of Joshua deceased. Nathan is named executor of the estate.[69]

John Chandler and Hannah Frye had twelve children all born at Andover.

54) i JOHN CHANDLER, b. May 1702; d. 26 Jul 1775 at Concord, NH; m. 5 Jan 1726/7, his first cousin, once removed TABITHA ABBOTT, b. about 1707 daughter of Nathaniel and Dorcas (Hibbert) Abbott; Tabitha d. probably at Concord, NH, date unknown.

71) ii JOSHUA CHANDLER, b. 1705; d. 24 Mar 1734; m. 18 Feb 1728/8 his first cousin SARAH CHANDLER, b. 1707 daughter of Zebadiah and Sarah (Abbott) Chandler; Sarah d. 28 Mar 1768.

97) iii NATHAN CHANDLER, b. 31 Jan 1708; d. 31 Jul 1784; m. 14 May 1729, PRISCILLA HOLT, b. about 1709 daughter of Timothy and Rhoda (Chandler) Holt; Priscilla d. 25 Nov 1803.

98) iv HANNAH CHANDLER, b. 1710; d. 29 May 1784; m. 4 Jun 1729, TIMOTHY BALLARD, b. 1702 son of Joseph and Rebecca (Johnson) Ballard; Timothy d. 30 Oct 1773.

v MARY CHANDLER; b. 7 May 1712; d. 28 Dec 1728

99) vi PHEBE CHANDLER, b. 2 Jan 1714/5; d. Jan 1805? at Concord, NH; m. 1 Jan 1735, HENRY LOVEJOY, b. 14 Aug 1714 son of Henry and Sarah (Farnum) Lovejoy; Henry d. 15 Mar 1793 at Concord.[70]

57) vii ABIEL CHANDLER, b. 14 Nov 1717; d. about 1752 at Concord, NH; m. 18 Mar 1741/2, his first cousin, once removed REBECCA ABBOTT, b. 24 Apr 1717 daughter of Nathaniel and Dorcas (Hibbert) Abbott. REBECCA m. 2nd by 1754, her first cousin, once removed AMOS ABBOTT,[71] b. 18 Feb 1725/6 son of James and Abigail (Farnum) Abbott; Rebecca d. 13 Feb 1803 at Concord;[72] Amos d. 3 Dec 1821 at Concord.

viii SAMUEL CHANDLER, b. 14 Nov 1717; d. 9 Dec 1717.

100) ix LYDIA CHANDLER, b. 10 Aug 1720; d. 9 Nov 1803; m. 30 Nov 1741, HEZEKIAH BALLARD, b. Jun 1720 son of Hezekiah and Rebecca (Davis) Ballard; Hezekiah d. 31 Dec 1801.

x SAMUEL CHANDLER, b. 2 Aug 1723; d. 29 Sep 1723.

xi ISAAC CHANDLER, b. 22 Feb 1725; d. 10 Mar 1725.

xii DORCAS CHANDLER, b. 18 Jul 1727; d. 2 Aug 1727.

---

69 *Essex County, MA: Probate File Papers, 1638-1881.* Probate of John Chandler, 1 Jun 1741, Case number 4940.

70 New Hampshire, Death and Burial Records Index, 1654-1949, ancestry.com

71 Ezra R. Stearns, William F. Witcher, and Edward E. Parker. *Genealogical and Family History of the State of New Hampshire*. (Lewis Publishing Company, 1908).

72 New Hampshire Death and Disinterment Records, 1754-1947, ancestry.com

20) ABIEL CHANDLER (*Hannah Abbott Chandler*[2], *George*[1]), b. 9 Jan 1686/7 son of John and Hannah (Abbott) Chandler; d. 1 Sep 1711; m. 22 Mar 1711 HEPHZIBAH HARNDEN, b. at Reading 19 Sep 1688, daughter of Richard and Mary (-) Harnden. Hephzibah m. 2nd Timothy Chandler; Hephzibah d. 17 Mar 1783.

Abiel Chandler and Hephzibah Harnden had one child born at Andover. Hephzibah's second husband, Timothy Chandler, wrote his will December 1770 and in that will he includes a bequest to Abial Chandler his wife's daughter by her first husband.[73]

101) i ABIAL (f) CHANDLER, b. 11 Dec 1711; d. 29 Jun 1780; m. 13 May 1731, DAVID CHANDLER, b. 11 Jan 1697/8 son of Thomas and Mary (Peters) Chandler; David d. before 1774 probably at Pembroke, NH.[74]

21) HANNAH CHANDLER (*Hannah Abbott Chandler*[2], *George*[1]), b. 12 May 1690 daughter of John and Hannah (Abbott) Chandler; d. at Woodstock, CT 3 Mar 1755; m. 1st DANIEL ABBOTT (*George*[2], *George*[1]), b. 10 Jan 1687/8 son of George and Dorcas (Graves) Abbott; Hannah and Daniel were first cousins; Daniel d. about Jul 1731 at Woodstock. Hannah m. 2nd John Bartholomew.

Hannah Chandler and Daniel Abbott were married in Andover and the births of their first eight children were recorded there. The family then relocated to Woodstock, Connecticut which was an area to which several members of this kinship network migrated in the early to mid-18th century.

Daniel Abbott wrote his will 3 November 1729 and it was presented at court for probate 19 July 1731. "I Daniel Abbott of Woodstock in the County of Suffolk in his majesty's Province of the Massachusetts Bay in New England. . . give and bequeath to Hannah my dearly beloved wife all my household goods whatsoever."[75] Other bequests are to son Daniel Abbott, £30 when he reaches the age of 21 and a gun; son Joseph Abbott, £15 when he reaches the age of 21 and a gun; to his daughters Hannah, Dorcas, Elizabeth, Phebe, and Sarah who will divide the household goods after their mother's death or remarriage; and all the rest to be divided among his nine children: Daniel, Joseph, Nathan, John, Hannah, Dorcas, Elizabeth, Phebe, and Sarah. (The youngest son of Daniel and Hannah, George, was born 21 January 1730 after the will was written.)

The births of the first eight children are recorded at Andover and the youngest two children at Woodstock.[76]

i HANNAH ABBOTT, b. 12 Sep 1712; d. 3 Mar 1734.

102) ii DORCAS ABBOTT, b. 16 Dec 1713; d. 22 Aug 1798 at Woodstock; m. 11 17 1740, THOMAS CHAFFEE, b. at Swansea 18 Oct 1716 son of Joseph and Jemima (Chadwick) Chaffee; Thomas d. at Woodstock 3 May 1753.

iii DANIEL ABBOTT, b. 18 Feb 1715; d. Feb 1741; Daniel did not marry. His will includes a bequest to his honored mother Hannah Bartholomew.

103) iv JOSEPH ABBOTT, b. 19 Sep 1716; m. at Woodstock, 22 Apr 1738, ABIGAIL CUTLER, b. 28 Aug 1711 at Colchester, CT, daughter of Jonathan and Abigail (Bigelow) Cutler; published genealogies (Bigelow and Abbot genealogies) give the dates of death for both Joseph and Abigail as 22 Sep 1776, but I have located no records for the deaths of either of them.

104) v ELIZABETH ABBOTT, b. 9 Jul 1719; d. at Woodstock, 1 Jan 1785; m. at Woodstock, 27 May 1737, MATTHEW MURRAY, perhaps of Scotland; d. at Pomfret about 1788 when his estate was probated.

105) vi PHEBE ABBOTT, b. 7 Apr 1721; d. at Woodstock after 10 Jul 1756 (the birth of her last child);[77] m. at Woodstock 20 Aug 1742, EBENEZER HOLMES, b. at Woodstock 27 Feb 1720/1 son of Ebenezer and Joanna (Ainsworth) Holmes. Ebenezer m. 2nd Martha Howlet, 12 Apr 1759; Ebenezer d. at Woodstock, 28 Jun 1794.[78]

106) vii NATHAN ABBOTT, b. 16 Oct 1723; d. likely at Brimfield after 1790 (listed as head of household in 1790 Census); m. at Woodstock 2 Jun 1746, ANNA LEACH.

---

73 *Essex County, MA: Probate File Papers, 1638-1881. Probate of* Timothy Chandler, 2 Dec 1771, *Case number* 4978.

74 Chandler, *The Descendants of William and Annis Chandler*. The Chandler Genealogy notes that the widow Abial Chandler was received at the church in Andover September 1774 from the church in Pembroke. The family had been dismissed from the church at Andover to Pembroke 21 May 1738.

75 *Probate Records (Worcester County, Massachusetts); Index 1731-1881*, Case number 17, accessed through ancestry.com

76 Barbour and Newton, *Vital Records of Woodstock 1686-1854.*

77 Published sources give her death as 30 May 1756, but the birth date of her youngest child in the Woodstock records in 10 Jul 1756.

78 Barbour and Newton, *Vital Records of Woodstock 1686-1854.*

107) viii JOHN ABBOTT, b. 11 Jan 1726; d. at Woodstock 7 Mar 1806; m. at Ashford, 28 Nov 1750, MARY WRIGHT, b. at Ashford, 29 Sep 1730 daughter of John and Judith (Wyman) Wright; Mary d. 30 May 1811.

108) ix SARAH ABBOTT, b. 5 May 1728; d. 7 Oct 1802; m. 1st, 1758, JABEZ CORBIN, b. at Woodstock, 21 Mar 1724 son of Jabez and Hannah (Peake) Corbin; Jabez d. 1774 (probate 7 Jun 1774). Sarah m. 2nd 31 May 1780, as his second wife, William Chapman; William d. 1792.

109) x GEORGE ABBOTT, b. 21 Jan 1730; d. before 18 Dec 1772; m. 16 Jan 1754, MARY WHITNEY, b. at Uxbridge, 27 Oct 1732 daughter of Joshua and Hannah (Rockett) Whitney.

22) SARAH CHANDLER (*Hannah Abbott Chandler², George¹*), b. 8 Oct 1693 daughter of John and Hannah (Abbott) Chandler; d. at Woodstock, CT 15 Mar 1737;[79] m. 12 Jan 1712/3 as his 1st wife, JOSEPH WRIGHT, b. 29 Oct 1693 son of Walter and Elizabeth (Peters) Wright. Joseph m. 2nd Elizabeth Chamberlain and m. 3rd Hannah Ashley.[80] Joseph d.? (A Joseph Wright of Norwich with a wife Hannah has a will probated in 1753; the will requests the division of his estate equally "among all my children" but they are not named).

The family of Sarah Chandler and Joseph Wright was beset by tragedy when Sarah, 11-year old son Abiel, and a servant John Page died in a house fire. "Mrs. Sarah Wright the wife of Leut. Joseph Wright Aged about 44 years and Abial Wright Son of the Said Joseph wright by Sarah his wife having Jest Completed the Eleventh year of his age and John Page, a Servent to Said Wright aged about 30 years ware all burnt to Death the following night after the fifteenth Day of March 1736/7 in the Dissolation of his house by fire."[81]

Sarah Chandler and Joseph Wright had twelve children. The births of the oldest five children are recorded at Andover, the remainder at Woodstock.

110) i JOSEPH WRIGHT, b. Mar 1712/3; d. at Winchester, NH, 27 May 1785; m. 1st at Woodstock, ABIGAIL CHAFFEE, b. at Swansea, 5 Mar 1715 daughter of Joseph and Jemima (Chadwick) Chaffee;[82] it is not known when Abigail died. Joseph had a second wife named Mary about whom nothing else is known.

111) ii SARAH WRIGHT, b. 7 Aug 1715; d. not known; m. 17 Jan 1733/4, EDMUND CHAMBERLAIN, b. 6 Mar 1701/2 son of Edmund and Elizabeth (Bartholomew) Chamberlain; Edmund d. 9 Dec 1779; it is possible that Sarah remarried but that is not verified.

112) iii HANNAH WRIGHT, b. 20 Jun 1717; no death record found (the Peters genealogy reports her death as 1796); m. 6 Jan 1734/5, BEAMSLEY PETERS, b. at Andover 1710 son of Samuel and Phebe (Frye) Peters.

113) iv ELIZABETH WRIGHT, b. 13 Feb 1718/9; death unknown; m. 23 Nov 1738, JOHN CARPENTER, b. at Woodstock, 17 Jul 1713 son of Eliphalet and Rebecca (Gardner) Carpenter.

114) v HEPHZIBAH WRIGHT, b. 14 Oct 1720; d, at Woodstock, 1797; m. 16 Dec 1736, ENOS BARTHOLOMEW, b. about 1714 possibly the son of John and Mary (Harrington) Bartholomew. John Bartholomew and his family relocated from Branford to Woodstock 7 Feb 1732/3.[83]

vi MARY WRIGHT, b. 3 Aug 1722; no further record found.

vii JOHN WRIGHT, b. 20 Apr 1724; d. 13 Jan 1733/4.

viii ABIEL WRIGHT, 11 Mar 1725/6; d. 15 Mar 1737.

115) ix ABIGAIL WRIGHT, b. 15 Feb 1727/8; m. 22 Mar 1748/9, ABIJAH CORBIN, b. 8 Feb 1722 son of Jabez and Hannah (Peake) Corbin; d. at Woodstock, 16 Oct 1808.

116) x DOROTHY WRIGHT, b. 3 Apr 1730; death not known; m. 3 Aug 1747, PENUEL BACON, b. at Woodstock, 8 Jan 1725/6 son of Joseph and Rebekah (Carpenter) Bacon.

xi DORCAS WRIGHT, b. 12 Mar 1731/2; death not known; m. 26 Apr 1750, THOMAS JEWELL.; Thomas d. 1753 at Mansfield, estate inventoried 28 Nov 1753; widow Dorcas is administrator; no births for this couple were located. It is possible that she is the Dorcas Jewell who married Ezekiel Corbin in Woodstock, 27 Dec 1758. On that same date (27 Dec 1758), Ezekiel's brother Jabez married Dorcas's first cousin Sarah Abbott. In any event, no further records were located for Dorcas either as Dorcas Jewell or Dorcas Corbin. No birth records for children were located.

---

[79] Barbour and Newton, *Vital Records of Woodstock 1686-1854.*

[80] Barbour and Newton, *Vital Records of Woodstock* 1686-1854.

[81] Barbour and Newton, *Vital Records of Woodstock, 1686-1854.*

[82] William Henry Chaffee, *The Chaffee Genealogy*. (Grafton Press, 1909), 78

[83] Connecticut Church Record Abstracts 1630-1920, volume 010, Brandford

xii JOHN WRIGHT, b. 29 Jun 1734; d. 22 Oct 1734.

Children of George Abbott and Dorcas Graves

23) HANNAH ABBOTT (*George*[2], *George*[1]), b. 27 Feb 1684 daughter of George and Dorcas (Graves) Abbott; d. 25 Dec 1774; m. 16 Sep 1708 JOHN OSGOOD, b. 28 Jun 1683 son of John and Hannah (Eires) Osgood; John d. at Andover, 22 Nov 1765.

In the probate record for John Osgood (he did not leave a will), widow Hannah (Annah) requests that her son John be the administrator. In the division of the estate in April 1768, the first division is assigned to John Osgood, the second to John Osgood as eldest son, third division to Mary Allen, the fourth to the heirs of Elizabeth Frye who is deceased, the fifth to Joseph Osgood, and the sixth to the heirs of Hannah Chickering deceased. Co-signers are William Allen and Dudley Woodbridge.[84]

In another document, widow Hannah Osgood signs over her parts of the inheritance in the following manner: 2/7 to John Osgood, 1/7 to Joseph, 1/7 to the children of daughter Hannah Chickering who is deceased (was married to Samuel Chickering); nine children of daughter Hannah are named Samuel, John, Zachariah, Hannah, Sarah, Susanna, Dorcas, Mary, and Phebe, and each is given 1/10 of the seventh; the final 1/10 of the seventh goes to the children of her granddaughter Elizabeth [this is the 10th child of daughter Hannah] (wife of Moses Sargent) who are Elizabeth, Susanna, Christopher, Hannah, and Moses; to the children of her daughter Elizabeth (wife of James Frye) who is deceased namely James, Jonathan, Elizabeth, Sarah, Hannah, Dorcas, and Molly (each gets 1/8 of the seventh); and 1/8 of the seventh to the children of her granddaughter Joanna (wife of Thomas Farrington) who is deceased namely Elizabeth, Thomas, Mareh, Frederick, and Daniel; daughter Mary the wife of William Allen gets 1/7; granddaughter Dorcas the wife of Dudley Woodbridge 1/7.

Hannah Abbott and John Chandler had seven children born at Andover.

117) i HANNAH OSGOOD, b. 22 Aug 1710; d. 16 Mar 1761; m. 24 Jun 1728, SAMUEL CHICKERING, b. at Charlestown, 10 Jul 1704 son of John and Susanna (Symmes) Chickering. Samuel m. 2nd the widow Mehitable Stevens; Samuel died about 1787 the year his estate was probated.

118) ii JOHN OSGOOD, b. 22 Aug 1711; d. 10 Jul 1775; m. 1st 20 Feb 1746, MARTHA CARLETON, b. 12 Jun 1722 daughter of Christopher and Martha (Barker) Carleton; Martha d. about 1755. JOHN m. 2nd 1760, HULDAH FRYE, b. 13 May 1737 daughter of Isaac and Naamah (Haskell) Frye. Huldah Osgood was listed in the 1800 Census as a head of household in Andover, but no record of her after that time.

iii CHILD OSGOOD, unnamed; 17 Jul 1712.

119) iv ELIZABETH OSGOOD, b. 15 Aug 1714; d. 8 Dec 1756; m. 28 Nov 1734, JAMES FRYE, b. at Bradford 24 Jun 1710 son of James and Joanna (Sprague) Frye. James married 2nd Sarah Robey; James d. 8 Jan 1776.

120) v JOSEPH OSGOOD, b. 5 Sep 1718; d. 11 Jan 1797; m. at Boston 1 Dec 1743, MARGARET BINNEY, b. at Hull 12 Apr 1719 daughter of Thomas and Margaret (Miller) Binney; Margaret d. 16 Feb 1797.

121) vi DORCAS OSGOOD, b. Sep 1721; d. at Boston about 1749 (Thomas remarried in 1750); m. at Boston 5 Jan 1743/4, THOMAS MARCH whose origins are unknown to me; Thomas d. at Boston about 1752 (when his will was probated). Thomas married 2nd Mary Hill on 7 Aug 1750.

122) vii MARY OSGOOD, b. 10 Jun 1726; d. 1806 at New Gloucester, ME; m. 11 Apr 1745, WILLIAM ALLEN, b. at Gloucester Jun 1717 son of Joseph and Mary (Coit) Allen; a death record for William was not located.

24) ELIZABETH ABBOTT (*George*[2], *George*[1]), b. 25 Jul 1690 daughter of George and Dorcas (Graves) Abbott; d. 3 Sep 1718; m. 24 Dec 1716, BENJAMIN ABBOTT (*Benjamin*[2], *George*[1]), b. 11 Jul 1686 son of Benjamin and Sarah (Farnum) Abbott; Elizabeth and Benjamin were first cousins. Benjamin m. 2nd Mary Carleton and 3rd Abigail Abbott (his second cousin and great granddaughter of the immigrant George Abbott of Rowley); Benjamin died before 5 Dec 1748 the date of probate of his estate.

Elizabeth and Benjamin Abbott had one child born at Andover. Benjamin's families with his two other wives are covered in Family #39.

123) i SARAH ABBOTT, b. 2 Aug 1718; d. 5 Mar 1778; m. 10 Apr 1746, her second cousin and George Abbott descendant JAMES HOLT, b. 13 Jan 1722/3 son of Nicholas and Dorcas (Abbott) Holt. James m. 2nd Phebe

[84] *Essex County, MA: Probate File Papers, 1638-1881.* Probate of John Osgood, 7 Apr 1766, Case number 20218.

Ballard who was the widow of Abiel Abbott son of Benjamin and Abigail (Abbott) Abbott; James Holt d. 22 Aug 1812.

25) GEORGE ABBOTT (*George², George¹*), b. 22 Dec 1692 son of George and Dorcas (Graves) Abbott; d. 19 Mar 1768; m. 29 Nov 1721, MARY PHILLIPS, b. at Salem 5 Aug 1694, daughter of Samuel and Mary (Emerson) Phillips; Mary d. 4 Oct 1785.

In his will George Abbott made bequests to the following persons: beloved wife Mary, eldest and beloved son George Abbott, beloved son Samuel Abbott, beloved daughter Mary Abbott (who married an Abbott), beloved daughter Elizabeth Abbott (who married an Abbott), beloved daughter Sarah Holt, and beloved daughter Hannah Foster. Son George is named executor.[85]

George Abbott and Mary Phillips had seven children all born at Andover.

69) i MARY ABBOTT, b. 12 Mar 1722/3; d. 8 Aug 1792; m. 24 May 1743, her second cousin STEPHEN ABBOTT, b. 2 Mar 1717/8 son of Stephen and Sarah (Stevens) Abbott; Stephen d. 8 Nov 1768. Mary m. 2nd JONATHAN ABBOTT, also a second cousin, who was the widower of Martha Lovejoy.

124) ii GEORGE ABBOTT, b. 14 Dec 1724; d. 26 Dec 1775; m. 1 Jan 1746/7, HANNAH LOVEJOY, b. 27 Dec 1724 daughter of John and Hannah (Foster) Lovejoy; Hannah d. 8 Sep 1813.

iii ELIZABETH ABBOTT, b. 10 Sep 1726; d. 7 Jan 1727.

125) iv ELIZABETH ABBOTT, b. 5 Nov 1727; d. at Westford, about 1802 (date of will 10 Aug 1802); m. 2 Apr 1747, her second cousin BENJAMIN ABBOT, b. 21 Oct 1723 son of Benjamin and Mary (Carleton) Abbott; Benjamin d. at Hollis, 1770 (probate 13 Jul 1770).[86] Elizabeth m. 2nd, James Pollard and 3rd, Josiah Bowers.

126) v SARAH ABBOTT, b. 14 Jan 1729/30; d. 29 Dec 1797; m. 4 Aug 1757, her second cousin and George Abbott descendant NATHAN HOLT, b. 28 Feb 1725 son of Nicholas and Dorcas (Abbott) Holt; Nathan d. at Danvers, 2 Aug 1792.

vi SAMUEL ABBOTT, b. 25 Feb 1731/2; d. 12 Apr 1812; m. 21 Feb 1760, SARAH MULBERRY, b. 31 Dec 1727 daughter of Benjamin and Ann (Everton) Mulberry; Sarah was the widow of John Kneeland; Sarah d. about 1815. Samuel and Sarah did not have any children. He was a merchant in Boston but maintained a residence in Andover. Samuel reared Sarah's three children from her first marriage. In his will, Samuel makes generous allowance for his wife, but provides a bequest to the trustees of Phillips Academy in Andover.

127) vii HANNAH ABBOTT, b. 14 Dec 1733; d. 26 Mar 1820; m. 9 Jan 1755, WILLIAM FOSTER, b. 4 Mar 1729/30 son of John and Mary (Osgood) Foster; William d. 1 Sep 1803.

26) HENRY ABBOT (*George², George¹*), b. 12 Jun 1696 son of George and Dorcas (Graves) Abbott; d. Feb 1776; m. 27 Oct 1721, MARY PLATTS, b. at Rowley 5 Sep 1700, daughter of James and Lydia (Hale) Platts; Mary d. Aug 1784.

The will of Henry Abbot includes bequests to the following persons: dear and well-beloved wife Mary, beloved son Henry, eldest and beloved daughter Lydia, beloved daughter Dorcas, and beloved daughter Mary.[87]

Henry Abbot and Mary Platts had five children born at Andover.

128) i LYDEA ABBOTT, b. 10 Feb 1722/3; d. 11 Sep 1807; m. 24 Mar 1742/3, JOSHUA LOVEJOY, b. 2 Dec 1719 son of Henry and Sarah (Farnum) Lovejoy; Joshua d. 2 Feb 1812.

129) ii HENRY ABBOTT, b. 31 Jan 1724; d. 21 Feb 1805; m. 1st 2 Oct 1750, ELIZABETH SIBSON (I think the daughter of Joseph); Elizabeth d. about 1764. Henry m. 2nd his first cousin PHEBE ABBOTT, b. 14 Nov 1746 daughter of Isaac and Phebe (Lovejoy) Abbott; Phebe d. 29 Jun 1833.

iii MARY ABBOTT, b. 28 Mar 1727; d. 27 Jan 1734.

130) iv DORCAS ABBOTT, b. 11 May 1729; d. at Nottingham, NH 10 Apr 1789; m. 17 Apr 1754, BENJAMIN BUTLER, b. at Edgartown, 9 Apr 1729 son of Malachi and Jemima (Dagget) Butler; Benjamin d. at Nottingham 26 Oct 1804.

131) v MARY ABBOTT, b. 13 Aug 1737; d. 26 Nov 1813; m. 22 Mar 1759, THOMAS HOVEY, b. at Ipswich 1 Oct 1736 son of Thomas and Sarah (Rust) Hovey; Thomas d. 29 Jul 1826.

---

[85] *Essex County, MA: Probate File Papers, 1638-1881.* Probate of George Abbott, 5 Apr 1768, Case number 47.

[86] There is a 1771 probate record at Middlesex County, MA for Benjamin Abbot of Hollis with widow Elizabeth Abbot of Hollis.

[87] *Essex County, MA: Probate File Papers, 1638-1881.* Probate of Henry Abbot, 4 Mar 1776, Case number 56.

27) ISAAC ABBOT (*George²*, *George¹*), b. 4 Apr 1699 son of George and Dorcas (Graves) Abbott; d. 9 Aug 1784; m. 1st 29 Nov 1739, PHEBE LOVEJOY, b. 20 Jan 1715, daughter of William and Sarah (Frye) Lovejoy; Phebe d. 17 Dec 1751. Isaac m. 2nd Lydia Stimson.

Isaac Abbot attended Harvard graduating in 1723. He was deacon of South Church of Andover for 44 years.[88] Isaac Abbot and Phebe Lovejoy had six children all born at Andover.

In his will, Isaac Abbott made bequests to the following persons: Lydia my dearly beloved wife, beloved son Isaac, beloved daughter Phebe wife of Capt. Henry Abbot, and beloved daughter Sarah wife of Timothy Abbott. Isaac is the executor of the estate.[89]

i SON ABBOTT, b. 21 Jul 1741; d. 21 Jul 1741.

ii WILLIAM ABBOTT, b. 21 Jul 1741; d. 29 Dec 1768.

132) iii ISAAC ABBOTT, b. 3 Feb 1745; d. 21 May 1836; m. 22 Apr 1766, his second cousin, once removed and George Abbott descendant PHEBE CHANDLER, b. 2 Jun 1742 daughter of Nathan and Priscilla (Holt) Chandler; Phebe d. 1 Jul 1800.

129) iv PHEBE ABBOTT, b. 14 Nov 1746; d. 29 Jun 1833; m. 21 Mar 1765 her first cousin, HENRY ABBOTT, b. 31 Dec 1724 son of Henry and Mary (Platts) Abbott; Henry d. 21 Feb 1805.

v SON ABBOTT; b. 12 Nov 1747; d. 14 Nov 1747.

133) vi SARAH ABBOTT, b. 2 Jan 1749/50; d. 2 Apr 1835; m. 2 Jan 1770, her second cousin once removed, TIMOTHY ABBOTT, b. 2 Jun 1745 son of Asa and Elizabeth (Abbott) Abbott; Timothy d. 22 Mar 1826.

Children of William Abbott and Elizabeth Geary

28) ELIZABETH ABBOTT (*William²*, *George¹*), b. 29 Apr 1683 daughter of William and Elizabeth (Geary) Abbott; d. 18 Jul 1762 at Pomfret, CT;[90] m. 13 Mar 1710/1 JOSEPH PHELPS, b. 8 Feb 1688/9 son of Samuel and Sarah (Chandler) Phelps; Joseph d. about 1773 at Pomfret when his will was probated.

Elizabeth and Joseph married and had their children in Andover. They then relocated to Pomfret, Connecticut. In the first two decades of the 18th century, more than 20 Andover men and their families had relocated to Windham County in Connecticut. This included seven Abbott family units.[91]

Joseph Phelps wrote his will 29 July 1762. He added a codicil to the will 19 March 1770. The will was probated 5 March 1773. In his will, Joseph made bequests to the following persons: beloved daughter Elizabeth Barrett; grandson Joseph Lawrence son of daughter Hannah who is deceased; youngest and well-beloved daughter Sarah Phelps; and grandson Joseph Barrett. Grandson Joseph Barrett was named executor. The codicil seems to relate to a conflict with his grandson Joseph Lawrence. Joseph Phelps had bequeathed several household items to his grandson in the 1762 will. But as he lived longer than he thought he might, Joseph had gone ahead and delivered these items to his grandson. But Joseph Lawrence refused to sign a statement that he had received his inheritance, so Joseph Phelps added the codicil to make it clear that his grandson had already received his whole inheritance.[92]

Elizabeth Abbott and Joseph Phelps had three children born at Andover.

134) i ELIZABETH PHELPS, b. 29 Oct 1712; d. at Brooklyn, CT 19 Jul 1787; m. at Pomfret 14 May 1741, BENONI BARRETT, b. 17 Aug 1718 son of Moses and Sarah (-) Barrett; Benoni d. 20 Jun 1755 at Brooklyn, CT.

135) ii HANNAH PHELPS, b. 20 May 1715; d. at Pomfret 13 Jan 1746/7; m. at Pomfret 15 Nov 1744, SAMUEL LAWRENCE; no definite information about Samuel has been obtained. He may have been a member of a Lawrence family in Killingly, CT.

---

88 Chandler, *The Descendants of William and Annis Chandler*, p. 7

89 *Essex County, MA: Probate File Papers, 1638-1881.* Probate of Isaac Abbot, 5 Oct 1784, Case number 58.

90 Connecticut Town Death Records, pre-1870 (Barbour Collection). The vital records for Connecticut are from the Barbour Collections unless otherwise noted.

91 Greven, *Four Generations*

92 *Connecticut Wills and Probate, 1609-1999*, Probate of Joseph Phelps, Hartford, 1773, Case number 3237.

iii SARAH PHELPS, b. Jun 1717; she was living at the time of her father's will in 1762 and there is no adjustment in the 1770 codicil so likely still living then; she was unmarried at the time of her father's will.

28a) WILLIAM ABBOTT (*William², George¹*), b. at Andover, 16 Mar 1684/5 son of William and Elizabeth (Geary) Abbott; d. at Roxbury, 28 Oct 1713; m. at Roxbury, 25 Mar 1709, REBECCA BOYLSTON, b. at Roxbury, 15 Sep 1685 daughter of Thomas and Mary (Gardner) Boylston; Rebecca d. 7 Sep 1762.

William, the oldest son of William Abbott and Elizabeth Geary, was raised by his uncle William Geary in Roxbury.[93]

William's estate entered probate 27 January 1713/4 with widow Rebecca Abbot as administratrix and Peter Boylston providing surety. Real estate was valued at £600 and personal estate at £139.8.5.[94]

William and Rebecca were parents of three children born at Roxbury.

i MARY ABBOTT, b. 24 Feb 1708/9; d. 16 May 1714.

ii WILLIAM ABBOTT, b. 6 Nov 1710; d. 14 Dec 1723.

135a iii REBECCA ABBOTT, b. 3 Jul 1712; d. at Roxbury, 30 Apr 1790;[95] m. at Roxbury, 24 Apr 1735, Rev. NATHANIEL WALTER, b. at Roxbury, 15 Aug 1711 son of Nehemiah and Sarah (Mather) Walter; Nathaniel d. at Roxbury, 11 Mar 1776.

29) JAMES ABBOTT (*William², George¹*), b. 12 Feb 1694/5 son of William and Elizabeth (Geary) Abbott; d. 27 at Concord, NH possibly in 1778;[96] m. 6 Jan 1713/4, ABIGAIL FARNUM, b. 3 May 1692, daughter of Ralph and Sarah (Sterling) Farnum; Abigail's date of death is not known.

James was a farmer. He and Abigail married and had all their fifteen children in Andover. The family then relocated to New Hampshire about 1735. He lived for a time in one of the garrison houses of early Concord.[97]

136) i ABIGAIL ABBOTT, b. 1 Jan 1714/5; d. at Charlestown about 1737; m. 13 May 1734, JOHN KIDDER, b. at Charlestown 13 Feb 1709 son of Stephen and Mary (Johnson) Kidder. John married second Anna Walker and third Mary Snow.

137) ii JAMES ABBOTT, b. 12 Jan 1716/7; d. at Newbury, VT, 27 Dec 1803; m. about 1742, SARAH BANCROFT, b. 19 Feb 1722 daughter of Samuel and Sarah (Lampson) Bancroft; Sarah d. 1765.[98]

iii ELIZABETH ABBOTT, b. 24 Jun 1718.

iv WILLIAM ABBOTT, b. 8 Sep 1719; d. 29 Oct 1741.

v RACHEL ABBOTT, b. 17 Nov 1720; (little other information yet). The Abbot genealogy states she had husbands named Manning and Russell and a daughter named Phebe. She was also reported to have gone to Londonderry, but no information has been found for her.

vi EZRA ABBOTT, b. 11 Mar 1721/2; d. 5 Dec 1741.

138) vii REUBEN ABBOTT, b. 4 Apr 1723; d. at Concord, NH, 13 May 1822; m. 1st RHODA WHITTEMORE, b. at Malden, 18 Aug 1729 daughter of Elias and Rhoda (Holt) Whittemore; d. 29 Jan 1785. Reuben m. 2nd widow Diana Blanchard; Diana d. 11 Mar 1826.

viii SIMEON ABBOTT, b. 18 Sep 1724; d. 15 Nov 1741.

57) ix AMOS ABBOTT, b. 18 Feb 1725/6; d. at Concord 3 Dec 1821; m. by 1754, as her 2nd husband, REBECCA ABBOTT (widow of ABIEL CHANDLER), b. 24 Apr 1717 daughter of Nathaniel and Dorcas (Hibbert) Abbott; Rebecca d. 13 Feb 1803. These families are considered together in Family #57.

139) x PHEBE ABBOTT, b. 22 Nov 1727; d. at Conway NH, 29 Sep 1754; m. 5 Nov 1747, as his 1st wife, THOMAS MERRILL, b. 5 Feb 1723/4 at Haverhill son of John and Lydia (Haynes) Merrill. Thomas had a total of four marriages, his 2nd to Mehitable Harriman, 3rd to Abigail Goodhue, and 4th to Elizabeth Abbott daughter of Benjamin and Abigail (Abbott) Abbott. Thomas Merrill d. at Conway 21 Jun 1788.

---

93 Abbot Genealogies, Essex Antiquarian, volume 1, number 3, p 36

94 *Suffolk County, MA: Probate File Papers.*Online database. *AmericanAncestors.org.* New England Historic Genealogical Society, 2017-2019. Case 3540

95 Walter, Rebecca, Madam [wid. Rev. Mr. N. R. 3.], Apr. 30, 1790, a. 78 y. C. R. 2.

96 The death date for James Abbott is not certain. Published genealogies, including the Abbott genealogy by Abiel Abbot and Ephraim Abbot, list a date of 27 Dec 1787, but I cannot locate a record that supports this. There is a transcription of a death record for a James Abbott in Concord, NH for 1778 that lists the age at death as 83 which would be the right age for this James Abbott.

97 Bouton, *History of Concord*, p 627

98 A gravestone engraved with the names James Abbott and Sarah Bancroft is in Oxbow Cemetery in Newbury, VT.

xi SON ABBOTT, b. and d. 1729.

140) xii REBECCA ABBOTT, b. 13 Aug 1730; d. at NH date unknown; m. 1750, ENOCH EASTMAN, b. at Salisbury, 1 Jun 1725 son of Joseph and Abigail (Merrill) Eastman.

141) xiii SARAH ABBOTT, twin of Rebecca, b. 13 Aug 1730; m. about 1751, as her 1st husband, her second cousin, JOB ABBOTT, b. 3 Oct 724 son of Jonathan and Zerviah (Holt) Abbott. Sarah m. 2nd about 1765, RICHARD EASTMAN, b. at Haverhill, 9 Aug 1712 son of Jonathan and Hannah (Green) Eastman; Richard d. at Lovell, ME, 29 Dec 1807.

142) xiv MARY ABBOTT, b. 12 Oct 1732; d, about 1780; m. by 1760 ADONIJAH TYLER, b. 26 Nov 1738[99] son of Moses and Miriam (Bailey) Tyler; Adonijah d. 12 Oct 1812 at Hopkinton, NH.

xv HANNAH ABBOTT, b. 12 Jan 1734/5; d. 10 Sep 1736.

30) PAUL ABBOTT (*William²*, *George¹*), b. 28 Mar 1697 son of William and Elizabeth (Geary) Abbott; d. at Hampton, CT 8 May 1752; m. 8 Feb 1719/20, ELIZABETH GRAY, b. 28 Mar 1700 daughter of Henry and Mary (Blunt) Gray; Elizabeth d. at Pomfret, CT 9 Jul 1765.[100]

In his will dated 20 February 1752, Paul Abbott has bequests to the following persons: beloved wife Elizabeth who receives the whole of the house in which they live plus many provisions for grain, beef, etc. to be provided by the executor; dearly beloved sons William, Nathan, Benjamin, Isaac, Asa, and Darius; and dearly beloved daughters Mary Holt, Sarah Ingalls, Elizabeth Abbott, and Hannah Abbott.[101]

Paul and Elizabeth had twelve children. The birth of the oldest child was recorded at Andover and those of the other eleven were recorded at Pomfret, Connecticut.

143) i NATHAN ABBOTT, b. 10 Apr 1721; d. unknown but he might have gone to Pennsylvania; m. 1st at Pomfret, 24 Nov 1742, EUNICE MARSH, b. at Plainfield, CT 17 Feb 1724 daughter of Thomas and Eunice (Parkhouse) Marsh; Eunice d. at Ashford 27 Oct 1760. Nathan m. 2nd HEPHZIBAH BROWN, b. about 1727; Hepzibah d. 26 May 1790 at Hampton, CT.

144) ii WILLIAM ABBOTT, b. 18 Feb 1723; d. at Pomfret 1 Nov 1805; m. 1st 9 May 1745, JERUSHA STOWELL, b. 22 Sep 1721 at Newton, MA daughter of David and Mary (Dillaway) Stowell; Jerusha d. 29 Feb 1768. William m. 2nd 4 Jun 1778, HANNAH EDMUND; Hannah d. 5 Feb 1808; nothing else is known of her at this time.

145) iii BENJAMIN ABBOTT, b. 25 Jul 1724; d. at Brookfield, VT, 21 Jun 1807;[102] m. 1st at Ashford, 16 Jan 1745/6, MARY ANN ANDREWS, b. at Windham 25 Jul 1727 daughter of John and Hannah (-) Andrews; Mary Ann d. 8 Dec 1788. Benjamin m. 2nd 30 Jun 1793 the widow HANNAH BROWN about whom nothing else is known.

iv ELIZABETH ABBOTT, b. 5 Feb 1726; d. 10 Sep 1736.

146) v MARY ABBOTT, b. 3 Mar 1728/9; d. at Windham 10 Aug 1769; m. 28 Jun 1749, JOSHUA HOLT, b. 19 Mar 1728/9 son of Joshua and Keturah (Holt) Holt. Joshua m. 2nd Susanna Goodell; Joshua d. 5 Jul 1791.

147) vi SARAH ABBOTT, b. 15 Oct 1730; d. 17 Dec 1811; m. 24 May 1749, JOSEPH INGALLS, b. at Andover, 9 Aug 1723 son of Joseph and Phebe (Farnum) Ingalls; Joseph d. 26 Oct 1790.

148) vii ISAAC ABBOTT, b. 29 Aug 1732; d. at Milford, NH about 1800;[103] m. 29 Apr 1756, MARY BARKER about whom nothing else concrete is known.[104]

149) viii DARIUS ABBOTT, b. 16 Oct 1734; d. about 1817 at Hillsborough, NH;[105] m. at Andover 1 Nov 1757, MARY HOLT, b. 30 Apr 1739 daughter of Henry and Rebecca (Gray) Holt; Mary d. about 1787.

---

[99] New Hampshire: Births, Deaths and Marriages, 1654-1969 (accessed through americanancestors.org)

[100] Connecticut Town Death Records, pre-1870 (Barbour Collection).

[101] Probate Records, 1747-1918; Author: Connecticut. Probate Court (Plainfield District); Probate Place: Windham, Connecticut

[102] His grave site is in the Brookfield, VT cemetery. (findagrave.com)

[103] 1800 is the year of death used by the Daughters of the American Revolution.

[104] Abbot and Abbot, *Genealogical Register of Descendants* gives her name as Sarah Barker, but the marriage record and all the birth records for the children give her name as Mary.

[105] Abbot and Abbot, *Genealogical Register of Descendants*

150) ix ELIZABETH ABBOTT, b. 20 Jul 1737; d. possibly 1828;[106] m. 28 Sep 1761 as his 2nd wife, JOSEPH PHELPS, b. 27 Feb 1723/4 son of Samuel and Hannah (Dane) Phelps; Joseph d. at Andover 27 Jan 1802.

x HARRIET ABBOTT, b. 18 Sep 1740; d. 18 Sep 1740.

xi HANNAH ABBOTT, b. 24 Jun 1741; d. 18 Nov 1763.

xii ASA ABBOTT, b. 7 Jan 1743; d. 5 Sep 1754.

31) PHILIP ABBOTT (*William², George¹*), b. 3 Apr 1699 son of William and Elizabeth (Geary) Abbott; d. 4 Nov 1748 at Hampton;[107] m. 8 Oct 1723 at Windham ABIGAIL BIGFORD whose origins are not known; Abigail's date of death is not known although it is after 1748 as she was living at the time of the codicil to Philip's will that was written 1 Nov 1748.[108]

Philip Abbott was a farmer. He relocated to Windham with his family as a young man in 1722. He acquired property in Windham, Pomfret, and Willington.

Philip Abbott wrote his will 1 November 1748. One-third of the estate in both Windham and Pomfret is set off for the support of well-beloved wife Abigail. Son Abiel receives all the estate in Pomfret and Windham. Son Stephen receives all the land in Willington when he reaches age 21. Daughter Hannah Abbott is to receive the equivalent of 183 ounces of silver to be paid when she reaches age 21 or at marriage. Son Joseph Abbott is to receive 316 ounces of silver and there is also a second payment of 100 ounces after his mother's decease. Daughter Mary Abbott receives the same bequest as Hannah. Son John receives the same bequest as Joseph.

Phillip Abbott and Abigail Bigford had eight children all born at Windham.

i JOHN ABBOTT, b. 12 Jul 1724; d. 18 Jul 1740.

151) ii ABIEL ABBOTT, b. 3 Mar 1726; d. 21 May 1772; m. 5 Jun 1750, ABIGAIL FENTON, b. at Willington, 27 Aug 1730 daughter of Francis and Ann (Berry) Fenton. Abigail m. 2nd John Chamberlain; Abigail d. 14 Aug 1776.

152) iii STEPHEN ABBOT, b. 21 Apr 1728; d. at Ashford, 29 Sep 1801; m. 3 Jan 1750, FREELOVE BURGESS, b. at Windham 14 Jul 1731 daughter of Benjamin and Susannah (Sabin) Burgess. The date of death for Freelove is not known, but after 1801 as she was living at the time of the probate of Stephen's estate.

153) iv HANNAH ABBOTT, b. 16 Mar 1730; d. 18 Dec 1801; m. Aug 1748, SAMUEL UTLEY, b. at Windham 28 May 1723 son of James and Annah (-) Utley; Samuel d. 15 Nov 1782.

v ZEBADIAH ABBOTT; d. 2 Dec 1731.

154) vi MARY ABBOTT, b. 6 Jul 1732; d. at Sheshequin, PA, 5 May 1803; m. 17 Oct 1751, STEPHEN FULLER, b. at Windham 3 Nov 1730 son of Stephen and Hannah (Moulton) Fuller; Stephen d. at Sheshequin 24 May 1813.

155) vii JOSEPH ABBOTT, b. 14 Feb 1735; d. at Ellington, CT 5 Jan 1815; m. 1st 20 Apr 1758, ELIZABETH STEDMAN, b. at Windham 30 Apr 1739 daughter of Thomas and Anna (-) Stedman; Elizabeth d. 2 Mar 1766. Joseph m. 2nd OLIVE PEARCE, b. at Brooklyn, CT, Mar 1738 daughter of Benjamin and Naomi (Richards) Pearce; Olive d. at Vernon, CT 9 Sep 1822.

156) viii JOHN ABBOTT, b. 27 Sep 1741; d. at Jacobs Plains, PA, 18 Jul 1778; m. 4 Nov 1762, ALICE FULLER, b. 1741 daughter of Stephen and Hannah (Moulton) Fuller. Alice m. 2nd Stephen Gardner; Alice d. at Plains, PA 1 Jun 1816.[109]

32) HANNAH ABBOTT (*William², George¹*), b. 5 Apr 1701 daughter of William and Elizabeth (Geary) Abbott; d. 11 Feb 1751/2 at Windham; m. 21 Feb 1721 ABIEL HOLT, b. 28 Jun 1698 son of Nicholas and Mary (Russell) Holt. Abiel m. 2nd Sarah Downer; Abiel d. 11 Nov 1772 at Willington.

Hannah and Abiel were part of the migration of several Andover families to Windham. There are records for ten children, all born at Windham, Connecticut. Most of the children in this family relocated to Willington.

157) i HANNAH HOLT, b. 17 Apr 1723; d. 25 Jan 1750/1; m. 14 Jul 1742, her first cousin WILLIAM HOLT, b. at Andover 10 Dec 1720 son of Thomas and Alice (Peabody) Holt. William m. 2nd Sybel Durkee; William d. at Hampton 2 Aug 1793.

---

[106] Abbot and Abbot, *Genealogical Register of Descendants* gives a death date of June 1828, but I have not located a record.
[107] Connecticut, Hale Collection of Cemetery Inscriptions and Newspaper Notices, 1629-1934
[108] Connecticut, Wills and Probate Records, 1609-1999 (accessed through ancestry.com)
[109] William Blair, *The Michael Shoemaker Book (Schumacher).* (Scranton PA: International Textbook Press, 1924), 66

158) ii ELIZABETH HOLT, b. 16 Feb 1724/5; d. about 1753; m. 10 Jun 1746, FRANCIS FENTON, b. at Willington, b. 16 Mar 1718 son of Francis and Ann (Berry) Fenton.[110] Francis m. 2nd Ann Newcomb.

159) iii ABIEL HOLT, b. 1 Feb 1726/7; d. 2 Oct 1785; m. 1st 22 Apr 1755, MARY DOWNER whose origins are unknown; Mary d. 28 Jan 1766. Abiel m. 2nd 2 Apr 1767, EUNICE KINGSBURY (widow of John Marshall), b. about 1733; Eunice d. 2 Jun 1784.

160) iv CALEB HOLT, b. 6 Mar 1729; d. 18 Aug 1810; m. 29 Jan 1755, MARY MERRICK, b. 6 Dec 1726 daughter of John and Sarah (Parsons) Merrick; Mary d. 4 Jun 1790. Caleb m. 2nd Chloe Hatch.

161) v NATHAN HOLT, b. 18 Apr 1733; d. 31 May 1800; m. 1st 19 Jan 1758, ABIGAIL MERRICK, b. 17 Jun 1737 daughter of John and Sarah (Parsons) Merrick; Abigail d. 1 Dec 1765. Nathan m. 2nd 26 Nov 1766, BATHSHEBA WILLIAMS, b. at Lebanon, 22 Mar 1737 daughter of Samuel and Deborah (Throope) Williams; Bathsheba d. 1 Aug 1769. Nathan m. 3rd 6 Jun 1770, LYDIA KINGSBURY, b. at Bolton, 1737 daughter of John and Deborah (Spaulding) Kingsbury; Lydia d. 22 Mar 1776.

162) vi ANNA HOLT, b. 14 Jan 1735; d. 10 Oct 1806; m. 29 Jan 1755, JOSEPH MERRICK, b. 17 Oct 1733 son of John and Sarah (Parsons) Merrick; Joseph d. 9 Apr 1787.

163) vii ISAAC HOLT, b. 2 Mar 1737/8; d. 14 Oct 1822; m. 26 May 1762, SARAH ORCUTT, b. at Stafford, 7 Nov 1740 daughter of William and Sarah (Leonard) Orcutt; Sarah d. 30 Mar 1816.

164) viii TIMOTHY HOLT, b. 2 Dec 1739; d. 7 May 1807; m. 7 May 1761 as her 2nd husband, REBECCA CHAMBERLAIN (widow of Nathaniel Fenton);[111] Rebecca was b. about 1730 probably the daughter of Edmund and Sarah (Furbush) Chamberlain; Rebecca d. 11 Apr 1809.

165) ix MARY HOLT, b. 4 May 1742; d. 13 Jan 1823; m. 27 Nov 1760, JOSEPH PERSONS, birth record not found but son of Joseph and Hannah (-) Persons; Joseph d. at Willington, 4 Nov 1812.

166) x JAMES HOLT, b. 27 Aug 1746; d. 30 Sep 1818; m. 1st 20 Apr 1769, ESTHER OWENS, b. 20 Feb 1747 son of Eleazer and Jerusha (Russ) Owens; Esther d. 5 Dec 1774. JAMES m. 2nd LUCE SAWINS, b. 28 Sep 1740 daughter of George and Anne (Farrar) Sawins; Luce d. 25 Dec 1824.

33) CALEB ABBOTT (*William², George¹*), b. 8 Oct 1704 son of William and Elizabeth (Geary) Abbott; died at Union, CT 31 Jan 1778; m. at Pomfret 3 Dec 1730[112] ELIZABETH PAINE, b. 9 Aug 1710 at Pomfret daughter of Samuel and Ruth (Perrin) Paine; Elizabeth d. 1 Apr 1772 at Union, CT.

Caleb was one of the first Abbotts to leave the Andover area. He purchased a farm in Pomfret Connecticut in 1726.[113] He married Elizabeth Paine there in 1730. He relocated again from Pomfret to Union Connecticut in 1749. Caleb and Elizabeth had seven children all born at Pomfret. Their oldest child, Caleb, Jr., died in the Revolutionary War.

i CALEB ABBOTT, b. 9 Sep 1731; d. by Mar 1776 when his estate entered probate; m. at unknown date, MARGARET PAUL, b. about 1727; d. 11 Jan 1806 at Union, CT; there are no known children. Caleb died during the Revolutionary War.[114] The inventory of Caleb Abbott's estate had a value of about £39. His widow, Margaret Abbott, requested that Abner Sepians be named administrator of the estate.

ii ELIZABETH ABBOTT, b. 12 Mar 1733; d. 31 Aug 1742.

167) iii HANNAH ABBOTT, b. 27 Oct 1734; d. 19 Apr 1813 at Hartland, VT; m. at Union, CT, 24 Mar 1761, JOHN HENDRICK, b. at Norwich, 3 Oct 1722 son of Israel and Ann (Babson) Hendrick; John d. at Hartland 8 Nov 1810.[115]

---

110 William Weaver, *Genealogy of the Fenton Family*. (Willimantic, CT, 1867).

111 This information is confirmed by the 1809 probate record of Rebecca Holt which includes heirs from her first marriage to Nathaniel Fenton.

112 New England Historical and Genealogical Register, 1913, volume LXVII, Marriages at Pomfret, Conn., p. 372

113 Margaret T. Abbott, Ten Generations of Abbotts in America, 1952, unpublished, Retrieved from https://www.mhl.org/sites/default/files/files/Abbott/Abbott%20Family.pdf

114 The death date for Caleb, Jr. is often confused with the death date of his father Caleb who died 31 Jan 1778. Caleb, Jr.'s estate was probated in 1776 with his widow Margaret declining administration of the estate.

115 Vermont, Vital Records, 1720-1908. (ancestry.com)

168) iv SARAH ABBOTT, b. 6 Jul 1736; d. 12 Nov 1761 at Brimfield, MA; m. 11 Nov 1754, JONATHAN BURK, b. 26 Feb 1733 son of Jonathan and Thankful (Waite) Burk. Jonathan m. 2nd Sarah Gould; Jonathan d. 18 May 1775 at Hartland, VT.

v MARY ABBOTT, b. 21 Mar 1739; she m. JOHN CAPEN of Hartland, VT; they moved to Scipio, NY and they did not have children.[116]

169) vi SAMUEL ABBOTT, b. 4 Mar 1743; d. 25 Sep 1825 at Hartland, VT; m. 1st at Union, CT, RACHEL WARD, b. about 1748 (based on age at death); Rachel d. at Hartland, VT 15 Oct 1774. Samuel m. 2nd 3 Dec 1778 the widow LYDIA STONE; Lydia d. 25 Sep 1825.

170) vii WILLIAM ABBOTT, b. 17 Oct 1745; d. 25 Jul 1832 at Clinton, NY; m. 1st at Union, CT, 15 Nov 1770, MARY COY; Mary d. 10 Dec 1776. William m. 2nd 24 Sep 1778, ESTHER GREEN, b. at Thompson, CT, 31 Dec 1753 daughter of Amos and Lydia (Johnson) Green;[117] Esther d. at Clinton, NY 23 Dec 1839.

Children of Sarah Abbott and Ephraim Stevens

34) ELIZABETH STEVENS (*Sarah Abbott Stevens², George¹*), b. 7 Aug 1683 daughter of Ephraim and Sarah (Abbott) Stevens; d. 28 Apr 1763; m. 20 Mar 1706/7 JOSEPH ROBINSON, b. about 1678 son of Joseph and Phebe (Dane) Robinson; Joseph d. at Andover, 9 Apr 1761.

The will of Joseph Robinson was dated 1 May 1758 and has bequests to the following persons: well beloved wife Elizabeth, son Joseph Robinson, son Isaac Robinson, son Ephraim Robinson, daughter Sarah wife of Samuel Barker, and daughter Elizabeth wife of James Seaton. Isaac is named the executor.[118]

There are records for eight children, all born at Andover.

i ELIZABETH ROBINSON, b. 1707; d. 19 Jan 1723/4.

171) ii JOSEPH ROBINSON, b. 22 Dec 1710; d. at Boxford, 29 Nov 1777; m. 25 Jul 1733, MEHITABLE EAMS, of Boxford, b. 1713 (based on age at time of death); her parentage is not clear; Mehitable d. 11 Aug 1782.

iii Unnamed child, b. and d. 1 Jun 1713.

172) iv ISAAC ROBINSON, b. Sep 1715; d. at Boxford, 15 Apr 1804; m. 19 Jun 1740, DOROTHY POOR, b. at Andover 1716 daughter of Daniel and Dorothy (Kimball) Poor; Dorothy d. 13 Jul 1801.

173) v SARAH ROBINSON, b. about 1716;[119] d.?; m. 10 Apr 1746, as his second wife, SAMUEL BARKER, b. 13 Feb 1691/2 son of William and Mary (Dix) Barker; Samuel d. 13 May 1770.

vi PHEBE ROBINSON, b. 25 Nov 1717; d. 2 Sep 1738.

174) vii EPHRAIM ROBINSON, b. 11 Aug 1723; death date not located; m. 2 Aug 1750, HANNAH KIMBALL, b. at Bradford 19 Mar 1730/1 daughter of Joseph and Abial (Peabody) Kimball; no death record was located for Hannah.

viii ELIZABETH ROBINSON, b. 7 Aug 1727; d. likely at Amherst, NH, date unknown; m. 5 May 1748, JAMES SEATON of unknown birth or origin, but seems to have been the brother of Deacon John Seaton thought to have come from Ireland (of Scottish origin); no death record or probate record was found for James. There is one birth record for a child born in Andover, but no further record for that child, and there is no record of Elizabeth and James having children while they lived in Amherst, NH.[120]

35) HANNAH STEVENS (*Sarah Abbott Stevens², George¹*), b. 18 Nov 1685 daughter of Ephraim and Sarah (Abbott) Stevens; d. before 28 Sep 1773 when her will was probated; m. 17 Mar 1708/9 ROBERT SWAN, b. at Haverhill 28 May 1686 son of Robert and Elizabeth (Storie) Swan; Robert died before 4 Sep 1770 when his estate was probated.

Robert Swan was from Haverhill and Hannah joined him there where they lived and raised their four children. They did relocate to Andover, apparently, as their deaths are recorded there.

---

[116] Abbot and Abbot, *Genealogical Register of Descendants*

[117] Esther's birthdate and name of her father are engraved on her gravestone. (findagrave.com)

[118] *Essex County, MA: Probate File Papers, 1638-1881. Probate of* Joseph Robinson, 6 Jul 1761, *Case number* 23905.

[119] Sarah is mentioned in her father's will, but no birth record was located for her.

[120] Daniel F. Secomb, *History of the Town of Amherst, Hillsborough County, New Hampshire.* (Concord, NH: Evans, Sleeper, and Woodbury, 1883)

The will of Robert Swan has bequests to the following persons: well beloved wife Hannah, daughter Elizabeth wife of Nathan(iel) Lovejoy, daughter Hannah wife of Peter Parker, to six grandsons, sons of son Robert of Methuen who is deceased (Jonathan, Joseph, Benjamin, Richard, Robert, and Phineas), and son Ephraim. Son Ephraim is the executor.[121]

In her will (probate 28 September 1773), Hannah Stevens Swan made the following bequests: four granddaughters who are Sarah Swan the daughter of Ephraim, Mary Isley, Hannah Parker, and Lydia Parker who are the daughters of Hannah the wife of Peter Parker; son Ephraim Swan; grandsons Jonathan, Robert, Richard, and Phineas Swan sons of Robert who is deceased; Joseph Swan who is the son of grandson Benjamin Swan of Methuen who is deceased; grandson Nathaniel Lovejoy who is son of daughter Elizabeth who is deceased; and grandsons Nathan, Peter, Robert, Isaac, Simeon Parker who are the sons of daughter Hannah who is deceased. Her grandson Ephraim Swan is named executor. She also makes mention of property she received as inheritance from her father Ephraim Stevens.[122]

There are records for four children, all born at Haverhill.

175) i ELIZABETH SWAN, b. 14 Feb 1709/10; d. at Andover 21 Jun 1770; m. 4 Jul 1743, NATHANIEL LOVEJOY, b. 16 Feb 1698/9 son of Nathaniel and Dorothy (Hoyt) Lovejoy; Nathaniel d. 25 Aug 1768.

176) ii ROBERT SWAN, b. 2 Mar 1711/2; d. at Methuen, 31 Oct 1752; m. 1731, ELIZABETH FARNUM, b. at Andover, 9 Nov 1711. Elizabeth m. 2nd James Howe; Elizabeth d. 5 Dec 1780.

177) iii EPHRAIM SWAN, b. 3 Sep 1713; d. at Andover before Oct 1777 (when his will was probated); m. 23 May 1738, SARAH POOLE, b. at Lynn, 11 Sep 1713 daughter of John and Mary (Gooding) Poole; Sarah d. likely after 1790 (she seems to be listed as the head of household with her daughter living with her in the 1790 Census).

178) iv HANNAH SWAN, b. 28 Dec 1716; d. at Andover, 7 Jul 1761; m. 14 Aug 1734, PETER PARKER, b. Jul 1714 son of Joseph and Lydia (Frye) Parker; Peter d. 9 Jan 1795.

36) MARY STEVENS (*Sarah Abbott Stevens*[2]*, George*[1]), b. 10 Feb 1693/4 daughter of Ephraim and Sarah (Abbott) Stevens; d. at Pomfret, 9 Mar 1773; m. 5 Nov 1719, JAMES INGALLS, b. 9 Aug 1695 son of James and Hannah (Abbott) Ingalls. Hannah Abbott Ingalls is from the Rowley Abbott line; James d. at Pomfret 6 Mar 1767.

This family was part of the migration from Andover to Pomfret in the mid-1730's. James and Mary had eight children all born at Andover.

In his will, James Ingalls has bequests for the following persons: beloved wife Mary, beloved son James of Methuen, beloved son Ephraim, beloved son Zebadiah, and beloved daughter Abiah Rogers.[123]

179) i JAMES INGALLS, b. 20 Aug 1720; d. at Methuen 8 May 1804; m. 6 Dec 1744, MARY FRYE, b. at Andover, 16 Feb 1724/5 daughter of Joshua and Mary (-) Frye;[124] Mary d. 6 Apr 1797.

ii DEBORAH INGALLS, b. 22 Apr 1722; d. at Pomfret, 5 Dec 1752; m. 19 Dec 1751, BENJAMIN SHARPE, b. about 1714 with parents unproved at this point. Benjamin m. 2nd MARY CRAFT. Benjamin d. about 1782 when his will was proved. Deborah and Benjamin had an infant daughter, Deborah, b. 27 Nov 1752 and d. 17 Apr 1753; mother Deborah died one week after her daughter's birth.

iii EPHRAIM INGALLS, b. 26 Nov 1723; d. 19 Jan 1724/5.

180) iv EPHRAIM INGALLS, b. 6 Nov 1725; d. at Pomfret 16 May 1805; m. 19 Dec 1751, MARY SHARP, b. at Pomfret, b. 10 Jul 1733 daughter of John and Dorcas (Davis) Sharp; Mary d. 16 Feb 1809.

v MARY INGALLS, b. 7 Sep 1727; d. 13 Mar 1750/1. Mary did not marry.

181) vi ZEBADIAH INGALLS, b. 3 Nov 1729; 11 Jun 1800; m. 20 Feb 1755, ESTHER GOODELL, b. at Pomfret, 19 May 1735 daughter of Zachariah and Hannah (Cheney) Goodell; Esther d. 30 Sep 1778.

---

[121] *Essex County, MA: Probate File Papers, 1638-1881. Probate of* Robert Swan, 4 Sep 1770, *Case number* 26899.

[122] *Essex County, MA: Probate File Papers, 1638-1881. Probate of* Hannah Swan, 28 Sep 1773, *Case number* 26887.

[123] *Connecticut Wills and Probate, 1609-1999*, Probate of James Ingalls, Hartford, 1767, Case number 2276.

[124] The 1768 probate of Joshua Frye includes heirs James and Mary Ingalls; *Essex County, MA: Probate File Papers, 1638-1881.* Online database. *AmericanAncestors.org.* New England Historic Genealogical Society, 2014. Case 10314

182) vii ABIAH INGALLS, b. 19 Oct 1731; d. likely at Palmer or Monson, MA; m. 16 Mar 1753, NATHANIEL ROGERS, b. about 1730 of not yet proved origins; d. probably about 1786, but no records were located.[125]

viii SIMEON INGALLS, b. 12 Jan 1735/6; d. 4 Apr 1753.

38) DEBORAH STEVENS (*Sarah Abbott Stevens², George¹*), b. 4 Oct 1704 daughter of Ephraim and Sarah (Abbott) Stevens; d. 17 Jun 1748 at Salem; m. 20 Jun 1726, SAMUEL CARLETON, b. 3 Jun 1696 son of John and Hannah (Osgood) Carleton; Samuel d. at Salem 9 Mar 1767.

Several of the children of Deborah and Samuel were either mariners or married to mariners. One of their sons, William, died while on a return voyage from Barbados. Two sons-in-law, Jacob Crowninshield and John Bowditch, also died at sea: Jacob in 1774 on a voyage from Jamaica and John in 1793.

In his will, Samuel Carleton has bequests for the following persons: son Ephraim, son Samuel, son William, daughter Hannah Crowninshield, and daughter Mary Bowditch. He specifies that he has five children.[126]

There are eight children recorded for Deborah and Samuel. The oldest child was born at Andover and the others at Salem.

i DEBORAH CARLETON, b. 17 Mar 1728/9; a death record was not found, but she died prior to the time of her father's will in 1767.

187) ii SAMUEL CARLETON, b. 11 Aug 1731; d. 25 Mar 1804; m. 27 Oct 1754, EUNICE HUNT, b. 25 Oct 1730 daughter of William and Eunice (Bowditch)Hunt; Eunice d. 12 Aug 1827.

188) iii HANNAH CARLETON, b. 26 Jul 1734; d. 14 May 1824; m. 30 Mar 1756, JACOB CROWNINSHIELD, b. 9 Jan 1732/3 son of John and Anstus (Williams) Crowninshield; Jacob was a mariner who died on a passage from Jamaica in Nov 1774.

iv BENJAMIN CARLETON, b. 5 Apr 1736; no death record found but not living at the time of his father's will in 1767.

189) v MARY CARLETON, b. about 1738; d. 24 Dec 1805; m. 12 Jul 1759, JOHN BOWDITCH, b. 3 Apr 1732 son of Ebenezer and Mary (Turner) Bowditch; John was a mariner and died at sea around April 1793.

vi EPHRAIM CARLETON, b. 20 Jan 1739; no further record found although he was living at the time of his father's will in 1767.

vii JOHN CARLETON, b. 24 May 1741; no death record found but before the time of his father's will in 1767.

190) viii WILLIAM CARLETON, b. 8 Apr 1744 son of Samuel and Deborah (Stevens) Carleton; d. Jun 1791 while on a trip to Barbados; m. 1st, (-) Palfrey who died before 1777. William m. 2nd, at Boston, 1 May 1777, MARY FARMER whose origins are uncertain but perhaps the daughter of Paul and Thankful (Sprague) Farmer of Boston.

Children of Benjamin Abbott and Sarah Farnum

24) BENJAMIN ABBOTT (*Benjamin², George¹*) and ELIZABETH ABBOTT (*George², George¹*) (Please see the family of Benjamin Abbott with his first wife Elizabeth Abbott at Family #24.)

39) BENJAMIN ABBOTT, b. 11 Jul 1686 son of Benjamin and Sarah (Abbott) Farnum; d. before 5 Dec 1748; m. 1st 24 Dec 1716 ELIZABETH ABBOTT, b. 25 Jul 1690 daughter of George and Dorcas (Graves) Abbott. BENJAMIN m. 2nd 23 Oct 1722 MARY CARLETON, b. 7 Apr 1700 daughter of John and Hannah (Osgood) Carleton; Mary died 19 Jan 1725/6. BENJAMIN m. 3rd 1729, ABIGAIL ABBOTT, b. 7 Oct 1699 daughter of Nehemiah and Abigail (Lovejoy) Abbott. Abigail Abbott is from the George Abbott of Rowley line; Abigail d. 8 Dec 1753.

As the oldest son, Benjamin assumed ownership of his father's farm. His father died when Benjamin was about 17.

Benjamin did not leave a will. His estate entered probate 5 December 1748 and includes an 81-page probate document. The probate settlement dated 18 February 1754 includes the following heirs: eldest son Benjamin, second son Daniel, daughter Mary, daughter Sarah the wife of James Holt, daughter Abigail, son Abiel, son Jacob, daughter Elizabeth, daughter Anna, and daughter Dorcas. Jacob, Elizabeth, Anna, and Dorcas have guardians who represent their interests, so

---

125 This is the date used by the SAR and the DAR as his approximated death, although it is not clear why this date was chosen. There is a marriage record for Abijah Rogers marrying Gideon Graves in Palmer in October 1786, but I do not think this is the widow Abijah marrying. The Gideon Graves in question seems to be about 30 years younger than Abijah. Perhaps this record is for a daughter Abijah.

126 *Essex County, MA: Probate File Papers, 1638-1881. Probate of* Samuel Carleton, 7 Apr 1767, *Case number* 4689.

these youngest four children are under age. Sarah the wife of James Holt is the daughter of Benjamin with his first wife Elizabeth Abbott.[127]

Children of Benjamin Abbott and his second wife, Mary Carleton, born at Andover:

125) i BENJAMIN ABBOT, b. 21 Oct 1723; d. at Hollis, NH, 1770 (probate 13 Jul 1770);[128] m. 2 Apr 1747, his second cousin, ELIZABETH ABBOTT, b. 5 Nov 1727 daughter of George and Mary (Phillips) Abbott. Elizabeth m. 2nd, 22 Mar 1775, James Pollard.[129] Elizabeth m. 3rd, Josiah Bowers of Billerica who died in 1794. Elizabeth died about 1802 at Westford (date of will 10 Aug 1802). There is a 1790 deed from Josiah Bowers of Billerica to his son Benjamin and named in the deed record is Josiah's wife Elizabeth.[130] Benjamin Abbott and Elizabeth Abbott are Family #125.

191) ii DANIEL ABBOTT, b. 29 Dec 1725; d. Apr 1793;[131] m. 3 Apr 1756, LUCY PARKER, b. 5 Jun 1732 daughter of Thomas and Lydia (Richardson) Parker; the date of death of Lucy is not known.

Benjamin Abbott and third wife, Abigail Abbott, had nine children born at Andover.

i ABIGAIL ABBOTT, b. 28 Mar 1731; d. 21 Oct 1733.

192) ii MARY ABBOTT, b. 21 Jul 1732; d. at Milford, NH, 9 Aug 1798; m. 13 Nov 1759, NEHEMIAH BARKER, b. at Methuen, 11 Feb 1734 son of Ebenezer and Abigail (Morse) Barker; Nehemiah d. 20 Jan 1810.

193) iii ABIGAIL ABBOTT, b. 13 Jan 1733/4; d. 1 Feb 1807; m. 1 Jun 1758, her second cousin, once removed, JOHN ABBOTT, b. 12 Sep 1735 son of John and Phebe (Fiske) Abbott; John d. 24 Apr 1818.

194) iv ABIEL ABBOT, b. 24 Jul 1735; d. 24 Jun 1764; m. 5 Feb 1761, his third cousin PHEBE BALLARD, b. 25 Jul 1738 daughter of Josiah and Mary (Chandler) Ballard. Phebe m. 2nd as his second wife, her third cousin (and great grandson of George Abbott), JAMES HOLT son of Nicholas and Dorcas (Abbott) Holt; Phebe d. 9 Jun 1815.

v JACOB ABBOTT, b. 2 Feb 1736/7; d. at Albany while in the army "of cold and fatigue" Feb 1760.[132]

195) vi ELIZABETH ABBOTT, b. 27 Oct 1738; d. at Conway, NH, 12 Oct 1789;[133] m. 1st 1 Jun 1758, EBENEZER CUMMINGS, b. at Groton, 17 Apr 1735 son of William and Lucy (Colburn) Cummings; Ebenezer d. 1 Jun 1778. Elizabeth m. 2nd as his fourth wife, THOMAS MERRILL, b. at Haverhill, 5 Feb 1723/4 son of John and Lydia (Haynes) Merrill. Thomas had married as his first wife, Phebe Abbott (Family #139); Thomas Merrill d. at Conway, NH, 21 Jul 1788.

196) vii ANNA ABBOTT, b. 13 Oct 1740; d. at Hollis, NH, 15 Jan 1810; m. Jan 1762, EPHRAIM BURGE, b. at Westford, 1 May 1738 son of Josiah and Susannah (Jaquith) Burge; Ephraim d. 21 Jul 1784.

viii JOEL ABBOTT, b. 20 Oct 1742; d. 23 Mar 1742/3.

197) ix DORCAS ABBOT, b. 1 Aug 1744; d. at Wilton, NH, 23 Feb 1829;[134] m. 20 Nov 1764, her second cousin, once removed, ABIEL ABBOT, b. 19 Apr 1741 son of John and Phebe (Fiske) Abbott; Abiel d. 19 Aug 1809.

40) JONATHAN ABBOTT (*Benjamin*[2], *George*[1]), b. Sep 1687 son of Benjamin and Sarah (Abbott) Farnum; d. reported as 21 Mar 1770 although record was not located;[135] m. 6 May 1713, ZERVIAH HOLT, b. 24 Mar 1688/9 daughter of Henry and Sarah (Ballard) Holt; Zerviah d. 26 Mar 1768 (recorded at Andover).

---

[127] *Essex County, MA: Probate File Papers, 1638-1881. Probate of* Benjamin Abbott, 5 Dec 1748, *Case number* 23.

[128] There is a probate record in Middlesex County, MA in 1771 related to Benjamin's estate and includes information about Benjamin being a mortgagee of Samuel Abbott. Twenty-three acres were set off to widow Elizabeth Abbott. Perley's article in the Essex Antiquarian gives a date of 5 Jan 1770.

[129] This marriage may not be accurate. There is a record for a marriage in Hollis 22 Mar 1775 for "Captain Jonas Pollard" of Westford and Mrs. Elizabeth Abbott. There is a Captain James Pollard of Westford who died in 1781 with a widow Elizabeth named in the will. James Pollard was born about 1708 and he was widowed in 1774. I believe the marriage transcription in the Hollis records is an error and the spouse is James Pollard.

[130] Middlesex County Deeds, 1792-1827, volumes 110-112, Images 85-86, Familysearch.org.

[131] Abbot and Abbot, *Genealogical Register of Descendants*

[132] Abbot and Abbot, *Genealogical Register of Descendants*

[133] *New Hampshire, Death and Disinterment Records, 1754-1947*

[134] *New Hampshire: Births, Deaths and Marriages, 1654-1969.* (From microfilmed records. Online database: *AmericanAncestors.org*, New England Historic Genealogical Society, 2014.)

[135] Holt Association of America. *First Three Generations of Holts in America*, Newburgh, NY, p. 316

The births of seven children of Jonathan Abbott and Zerviah Holt are recorded at Andover. Published genealogies include a daughter Mary in this family, but I can find no record of her.

198) i JONATHAN ABBOTT, b. Dec 1714; d. 31 May 1794; m. 1st 8 Oct 1739, MARTHA LOVEJOY, b. 2 Nov 1720 daughter of Henry and Sarah (Farnum) Lovejoy; Martha d. about 1768. Jonathan m. 2nd as her second husband, his second cousin MARY ABBOTT daughter of George and Mary (Phillips) Abbott.

199) ii DAVID ABBOTT, b. Dec 1716; d. 1777 at Rockingham, NH (probate 31 Dec 1777); m. 10 Aug 1741, his second cousin, once removed, HANNAH CHANDLER, b. 1724 daughter of Joseph and Mehitable (Russell) Chandler; Hannah's death not known but she was living at the time of her husband's will.

iii NATHAN ABBOTT, b. Apr 1719; d. 28 Jun 1798; m. 12 Mar 1744/5, his second cousin and George Abbott descendant, ABIGAIL AMES, b. about 1722 daughter of Samuel and Hannah (Stevens) Ames; Abigail d. 27 Aug 1812. Nathan Abbott and Abigail Ames did not have any children. Nathan Abbott wrote his will 21 March 1776 and the estate entered probate 3 September 1798. Dearly beloved wife Abigail receives "all my household stuff proper for woman's use." She receives other provisions for her support and the use and improvements of one-third of the real property. He makes a bequest to his "cousin" Nathan Abbott who is the son of his brother Job who is deceased. The nephew Nathan is named executor and has the remainder of the estate bequeathed to him.

200) iv ZERVIAH ABBOTT, b. Aug 1722; d. likely at Pembroke, NH; m. 17 Sep 1745, EPHRAIM BLUNT, b. 5 Feb 1720/1 son of William and Sarah (Foster) Blunt.

141) v JOB ABBOTT, b. 3 Oct 1724; d. likely at Pembroke, NH; m. about 1751, his second cousin, SARAH ABBOTT, b. 13 Aug 1730 daughter of James and Abigail (Farnum) Abbott.

201) vi SAMUEL ABBOTT, b. 20 Sep 1727; m. 12 Jul 1749, MIRIAM STEVENS whose origins are undetermined but may be the Miriam baptized in 1730 at Newbury.

vii JEREMIAH ABBOTT, b. 30 Sep 1733; d. 1755 in the French and Indian War.

41) DAVID ABBOT (*Benjamin*[2], *George*[1]), b. 18 Jan 1688/9 son of Benjamin and Sarah (Abbott) Farnum; d. 14 Nov 1753; m. 20 Mar 1717/8, HANNAH DANFORTH, b. at Billerica 20 Aug 1698 daughter of Samuel and Hannah (Crosby) Danforth; Hannah d. 8 Jan 1788.

David had a farm at Merrimack Corner in Andover. He and his wife Hannah had nine children all born at Andover.

The will of David Abbot, written 7 November 1753, has the following bequests: beloved wife Hannah receives the widow's third; beloved son Solomon receives land and meadows above the brook, and "all the rest" of the children receive the rest of the estate. These children are David, Josiah, Jonathan, Benjamin, Hannah, and Sarah. The four boys share equally while the two daughters get half as much as each of the boys. The bequests to the younger children do include bequests of land. David calls on his "trusty friends" Ebenezer Abbot, Samuel Abbot, and Thomas Abbot to divide the land and the sons are to buy out the value of the portion of the daughters.[136]

Two of the sons, Josiah and Benjamin, died within a week after the death of their father. A third child, daughter Elizabeth, died two months before her father. The family might have been a victim of one of the several epidemics that came through the colonies. In 1753, some areas of Massachusetts had an outbreak of "putrid fever"[137] and there was also a smallpox outbreak. The causes of death are not given on the death records for these four family members.

i HANNAH ABBOT, b. 21 Oct 1721; d. 25 Feb 1721/2.

ii HANNAH ABBOT, b. 23 Dec 1723; d. 12 Mar 1813; Hannah did not marry.

202) iii SARAH ABBOT, b. 7 Apr 1726; d. at Bedford, 5 Mar 1814; m. 1st 30 Jan 1753, ROBERT HILDRETH, b. at Dracut, 18 May 1713 son of Ephraim and Mercy (Richardson) Hildreth; Robert d. 1760. Sarah m. 2nd 28 May 1761, JOHN LANE, b. at Bedford, 2 Oct 1720 son of Job and Martha (Ruggles) Lane; John d. 7 Dec 1789. Sarah m. 3rd 14 Jul 1791, Benjamin Parker.

203) iv DAVID ABBOT, b. 28 Mar 1728; d. at Billerica 1 Nov 1798; m. 28 Dec 1752, PRUDENCE SHELDON, b. at Billerica 31 Aug 1732 daughter of Samuel and Sarah[138] (Hutchinson) Richardson. A death record for Prudence was not located, although she was living at the time of her husband's death and she was on the tax rolls in Billerica for 1798.

[136] *Essex County, MA: Probate File Papers, 1638-1881. Probate of* David Abbot, 26 Nov 1753, *Case number* 28.

[137] Ernest Caulfield (1950, January). The Pursuit of a Pestilence. In *Proceedings of the American Antiquarian Society* (Vol. 60, No. 1, p. 21). American Antiquarian Society

[138] The marriage record lists her name as Mary Hutchinson, but all the births of the children, including a daughter Sarah born in 1719, list the mother's name as Sarah.

204) v SOLOMON ABBOT, b. 14 Feb 1730/1; d. probably at Dracut 17 Dec 1797;[139] m. 3 May 1756, HANNAH COLBE, b. 22 Oct 1735 daughter of Daniel and Hannah (Gray) Colbe; Hannah's date of death is not known.

vi ELIZABETH ABBOT, b. 2 Aug 1733; d. 31 Aug 1753.

vii JOSIAH ABBOT, b. 1735; d. 26 Nov 1753.

205) viii JONATHAN ABBOT, b. 24 Oct 1739; d. 10 Apr 1817; m. 13 Nov 1759, his second cousin, once removed and George Abbott descendant, MARY CHANDLER, b. 15 Jun 1740 daughter of Nathan and Priscilla (Holt) Chandler; Mary d. 1 Apr 1824.

ix BENJAMIN ABBOT, b. 16 Jan 1743; d. 20 Nov 1753.

Children of Timothy Abbott and Hannah Graves

42) TIMOTHY ABBOT (*Timothy², George¹*), b. 20 Jun 1693 son of Timothy and Hannah (Graves) Abbott; d. 10 Jul 1766; m. Dec 1717, MARY FOSTER, b. at Boxford 2 Aug 1698 daughter of William and Sarah (Kimball) Foster; Mary d. 31 Aug 1784.

As the only son of his father Timothy, Timothy the younger took over his father's homes and lands. He and his wife Mary had eleven children all born at Andover.

In his will, Timothy Abbot has bequests to the following persons: son Asa gets all his lands; well beloved wife Mary receives mourning apparel, but also receives all the money in hand and a regular supply of apples; other bequests go to son Nathan, daughter Hannah Parker, daughter Sarah Farmer, daughter Lydia Farnam, daughter Dorcas Abbot, daughter Phebe Abbot, and grandchildren who are the children of daughter Mary who is deceased namely Mary, Ephraim, and Hannah. Son Asa is the sole executor.[140]

i MARY ABBOT, b. 5 Oct 1718; d. 28 Oct 1718.

ii TIMOTHY ABBOT, b. 26 Oct 1719; 26 Mar 1745.

80) iii ASA ABBOT, b. 17 Oct 1721; d. 22 Dec 1796; m. 20 Sep 1744, his second cousin, ELIZABETH ABBOTT, b. 29 Jun 1726 daughter of Ephraim and Sarah (Crosby) Abbott; Elizabeth d. 18 Dec 1819.

77) iv MARY ABBOT, b. 7 Jan 1723/4; d. 9 Mar 1744; m. her second cousin, EPHRAIM ABBOTT, b. 22 Jul 1718 son of Ephraim and Sarah (Crosby) Abbott. Ephraim m. 2nd Mary Kneeland; Ephraim d. at Amherst, NH about 1775.

206) v HANNAH ABBOTT, b. 21 Jun 1726; d. likely at Pembroke, NH but unknown; m. 25 Apr 1754, JOSEPH PARKER, b. 15 Jul 1726 son of Joseph and Mary (Emery) Parker.

207) vi NATHAN ABBOTT, b. 7 Jan 1728/9; d. likely at Wilton, NH; m. 11 Jan 1759, JANE PAUL, described as "resident of Andover," but whose origins are unknown; Jane d. at Wilton, 28 May 1772.

208) vii SARAH ABBOTT, b. 5 May 1731; m. 1 Mar 1757, EDWARD FARMER.

209) viii LYDIA ABBOTT, b. 28 Mar 1733; d. at Andover, 13 Mar 1816; m. 13 Jan 1756, THOMAS FARNUM, b. 6 Sep 1734 son of Thomas and Phebe (Towns) Farnum; Thomas's death is not known but was perhaps in NH.

ix DORCAS ABBOTT, b. 2 Oct 1735; d. after 1798 (when she is on the Andover tax list); m. 3 Jan 1775 as his second wife, SAMUEL BAILEY, b. at Bradford, 20 Feb 1705 son of James and Hannah (Wood) Bailey; Samuel d. 5 Jan 1784. Dorcas married later in life and did not have any children with her husband Samuel Bailey.

210) x PHEBE ABBOTT, b. 16 Feb 1736/7; d. not certain but perhaps before 1799; m. 22 Jul 1766 as his second wife, WILLIAM DANE, b. 15 Mar 1727/8 son of John and Sarah (Chandler) Dane. William is likely the William Dane that died at Brookfield in 1825 at age 99.

xi CALEB ABBOT, b. 9 Aug 1738; d. 7 Sep 1738.

---

[139] Abbot and Abbot, *Genealogical Register of Descendants* gives this date of death; a death record or probate record was not located.

[140] *Essex County, MA: Probate File Papers, 1638-1881. Probate of* Timothy Abbot, 7 Oct 1766, *Case number* 144.

43) HANNAH ABBOTT (*Timothy^2, George^1*), b. 8 Oct 1695 daughter of Timothy and Hannah (Graves) Abbott; d. 22 Apr 1769; m. 16 Mar 1732 as his 2nd wife JOHN LANE, b. 20 Oct 1691 son of John and Susannah (Whipple) Lane; John d. at Bedford, 23 Sep 1763.

There are discrepancies in published genealogies as to which Hannah Abbott married Abiel Holt and went to Connecticut and which Hannah Abbott married John Lane. This issue seems to be settled by probate records for Timothy Abbott, father of Hannah. Timothy died in 1730. During the probate, Hannah files a document as Hannah Abbott, spinster of Andover, acknowledging the settlement from her brother Timothy related to the estate of their father Timothy. This would eliminate Hannah the daughter of Timothy as the wife of Abiel Holt as Abiel Holt and Hannah Abbott were married in 1721. It seems that Abiel Holt married Hannah the daughter of William Abbott, and Hannah the daughter of Timothy married John Lane.

Hannah married late at age 36 and had just two children with her husband John Lane. One of those children died in childhood. The will of John Lane, written 1 April 1761 and proved in 1763, includes bequests for his four children from his first marriage and his son Samuel, his son with Hannah.[141]

i HANNAH LANE, b. 16 May 1734; d. 22 Apr 1769.

211) ii SAMUEL LANE, b. 21 Oct 1737; d. 1822 (year of probate); m. 8 Dec 1763, ELIZABETH FITCH, b. 6 Jan 1738/9 daughter of Zachariah and Elizabeth (Grimes) Fitch; Elizabeth d. 19 Sep 1807.[142]

44) DORCAS ABBOTT (*Timothy^2, George^1*), b. 25 Apr 1698 daughter of Timothy and Hannah (Graves) Abbott; d. 25 Oct 1758; m. 12 Apr 1717 as his 2nd wife NICHOLAS HOLT, b. 21 Dec 1683 son of Nicholas and Mary (Russell) Holt; Nicholas d. 1 Dec 1756.

In his will, Nicholas Holt makes bequests to the following persons: dearly beloved wife Dorcas, eldest and well-beloved son Benjamin, well-beloved son Stephen, well-beloved son Nicholas, well-beloved son Timothy, well-beloved son James, well-beloved son Nathan, well-beloved son Joshua, well-beloved son Daniel, eldest and well-beloved daughter Mary, and well-beloved daughter Dorcas. Benjamin, Mary, Stephen, and Nicholas are Nicholas's children from his first marriage to Mary Manning.[143]

Nicholas and Dorcas had six children all born at Andover.

212) i TIMOTHY HOLT, b. 17 Jan 1720/1; d. at Wilton, NH, Nov 1801; m. 18 Sep 1744, his second cousin, ELIZABETH HOLT, b. Jun 1718 daughter of John and Mehitable (Wilson) Holt; Elizabeth d. at Wilton 21 Mar 1776.

123) ii JAMES HOLT, b. 13 Jan 1722/3; d. 22 Aug 1812; m. 1st, SARAH ABBOTT, b. 2 Aug 1718 daughter of Benjamin and Elizabeth (Abbott) Abbott; Sarah d. 5 Mar 1778. James m. 2nd, 22 Jun 1779, PHEBE BALLARD daughter of Josiah and Mary (Chandler) Ballard and widow of Abiel Abbot (Family #194); Phebe d. 9 Jun 1815.

126) iii NATHAN HOLT, b. 28 Feb 1725; d. at Danvers, 2 Aug 1792; m. 4 Aug 1757, SARAH ABBOTT, b. 14 Jan 1729/30 daughter of George and Mary (Phillips) Abbott; Sarah d. 29 Dec 1797.

213) iv DORCAS HOLT, b. 4 Sep 1727; death unknown but may have been at Wilton, NH; m. 26 Jan 1749, as his second wife, her first cousin, THOMAS HOLT, b. Mar 1711/2 son of Thomas and Alice (Peabody) Holt; Thomas d. at Andover, 21 Nov 1776.

214) v JOSHUA HOLT, b. 30 Jun 1730; d. 24 Jul 1810; m. 2 Dec 1755, PHEBE FARNUM, b. 10 Oct 1731 daughter of Timothy and Dinah (Ingalls) Farnum; Phebe d. 26 Jan 1806.

215) vi DANIEL HOLT, b. 10 Feb 1732/3; d. at Andover, 15 Feb 1796; m. 29 Nov 1759, his first cousin once removed, HANNAH HOLT, b. 11 Feb 1738/9 daughter of Thomas and Hannah (Kimball) Holt; Hannah d. at Andover, 2 Aug 1831.

---

141 *Middlesex County, MA: Probate File Papers, 1648-1871. Probate of* John Lane, *1766, Case number* 13578.

142 The death record states just __, w. Samuel, complicated complaint, Sept. 19, 1807, a. 69. C.R. There was another Samuel Lane in town with a wife also born in 1738. However, that woman, Frances Hutchins Blood Lane, died in 1811 in Carlisle and has the following death listing: Lane, Frances, wid. "first wid. Stephen Blood, jr.," Apr. 17, 1811, a. 73 y. G. R. 1.

143 *Essex County, MA: Probate File Papers, 1638-1881. Probate of* Nicholas Holt, 27 Dec 1756, *Case number* 13680.

Children of Thomas Abbott and Hannah Gray

45) THOMAS ABBOTT (*Thomas*[2], *George*[1]), b. 3 Jan 1698/9 son of Thomas and Hannah (Gray) Abbott; d. 11 Jul 1774; m. 28 Jan 1724/5, ELIZABETH BALLARD, b. 14 Jan 1700/1 daughter of Joseph and Rebecca (Johnson) Ballard; Elizabeth d. 31 Jul 1782.

Thomas Abbott and Elizabeth Ballard lived their lives in Andover where all their children were born. However, four sons of this family relocated to Concord, New Hampshire near the time of the first settlement of Concord. Of those four, Jabez, Aaron, and Nathan, seem to have stayed in New Hampshire. Jesse seems to have returned to Massachusetts prior to his death.

No probate record was located for Thomas Abbott. Thomas Abbott and Elizabeth Ballard had ten children whose births are recorded at Andover.

i SAMUEL ABBOTT, b. 1 Nov 1725; d. 19 Nov 1725.

216) ii ELIZABETH ABBOTT, b. 10 Jan 1726/7; d. at Andover 27 Sep 1792; m. 4 Jan 1753, as his 2nd wife, SAMUEL OSGOOD, b. 29 May 1714 son of Ezekiel and Rebecca (Wardwell) Osgood; Samuel d. 16 Mar 1774.

217) iii THOMAS ABBOTT, b. 4 Apr 1729; d. at Andover 29 Mar 1775; m. 12 Feb 1756, LYDIA BLUNT, b. 6 Apr 1731 daughter of David and Lydia (Foster) Blunt; Lydia d. 16 Nov 1798.

218) iv JABEZ ABBOTT, b. 18 Apr 1731; d. 7 Jan 1804 at Concord; m. 1st by 1756, his first cousin, PHEBE ABBOTT, b. 13 Feb 1732 daughter of Edward and Dorcas (Chandler) Abbott; Phebe d. 6 Jan 1770. Jabez m. 2nd 8 Aug 1772, HEPHZIBAH STEVENS, b. 28 Feb 1739/40 daughter of Samuel and Hephzibah (Ingalls) Stevens.

219) v AARON ABBOTT, b. 17 Feb 1732/3; d. at Concord 31 Dec 1812; m. his first cousin, LYDIA ABBOTT, b. 15 Jun 1737 daughter of Edward and Dorcas (Chandler) Abbott; Lydia d. 15 Dec 1811.

vi JOSEPH ABBOTT, b. 27 Dec 1734; d. at Quebec in prison Jun 1758; Joseph was taken captive by the Indians at Lake George 19 Sep 1756 and was carried to Canada and died in prison at Quebec sometime in Jan 1758. This information is recorded in the death records.[144]

220) vii NATHAN ABBOTT, b. 7 Feb 1736/7; d. at Concord, 18 Jan 1805; m. 1766, BETTY FARNUM, b. 1743 daughter of Joseph and Zerviah (Hoit) Farnum; Betty d. 11 Nov 1821.

viii JESSE ABBOTT, b. 3 May 1740; d. 15 Jul 1740.

ix JESSE ABBOTT, b. 4 Oct 1741; d. 12 May 1808 recorded at Haverhill; m. at Andover, 27 Sep 1765, SARAH SCALES, b. 11 Sep 1743 daughter of Moses and Rebecca (Barnard) Scales; Sarah's date of death is not known. Jesse and Sarah did not have any children.

x LYDIA ABBOTT, b. 5 Oct 1743; d. 2 Jun 1749.

46) EDWARD ABBOTT (*Thomas*[2], *George*[1]), b. 9 Jun 1702 son of Thomas and Hannah (Gray) Abbott; died at Concord, NH 14 Apr 1759; m. 15 Jul 1728, DORCAS CHANDLER, b. about 1705 daughter of Thomas and Mary (Peters) Chandler; Dorcas d. 16 May 1748. Edward married 2nd 23 Jan 1748/9, MEHITABLE EASTMAN, b. at Haverhill 17 Nov 1707.

Edward Abbott was a first proprietor at Concord.[145] The births of all ten children of Edward and Dorcas are recorded at Rumford or Concord, New Hampshire.[146] No probate record was located for Edward.

221) i DORCAS ABBOTT, b. at Rumford 15 Feb 1728/9; d. 28 Sep 1797; m. 17 Jun 1746, EBENEZER HALL, b. at Bradford, 19 Sep 1721 son of Joseph and Sarah (Kimball) Hall; Ebenezer d. 24 Apr 1801. Ebenezer was the brother of Joseph Hall who married Deborah Abbott [daughter of Thomas and Hannah (Gray) Abbott].

---

[144] Joseph, s. Thomas and Elizabeth, "taken Captive by the Indians at Lake George, Sept. 19, 1756, and carry'd to Canada and dyed in prison at Quebeck sometime in Jan. 1758," in his 24th y. Massachusetts: Vital Records, 1620-1850

[145] Bouton, *The History of Concord*

[146] *New Hampshire, Births and Christenings Index, 1714-1904 (accessed through ancentry.com)*

222) ii EDWARD ABBOTT, b. 27 Dec 1730; d. 15 Sep 1801; m. about 1760 DEBORAH STEVENS, origins not certain but likely the Deborah born 1738 in Rumford, NH daughter of Aaron and Deborah (Stevens) Stevens; Aaron Stevens was an early settler at Concord; Deborah d. Nov 1817.

218) iii PHEBE ABBOTT, b. 13 Feb 1732; d. 6 Jan 1770; m. by 1756, her first cousin, JABEZ ABBOTT, b. 18 Apr 1731 son of Thomas and Elizabeth (Ballard) Abbott. Jabez m. 2nd Hephzibah Stevens; Jabez d. 7 Jan 1804.

iv LYDIA ABBOTT, b. 7 May 1735; d. 18 Jun 1736.

219) v LYDIA ABBOTT, b. 15 Jun 1737; d. 15 Dec 1811; m. her first cousin, AARON ABBOTT, b. 17 Feb 1732/3 son of Thomas and Elizabeth (Ballard) Abbott; Aaron d. 31 Dec 1812.

vi TIMOTHY ABBOTT, b. 21 Jul 1739; d. at Concord, 1814; no marriages or children are known for him; his probate from 1814 specifies he left no widow or children.

vii RACHEL ABBOTT, b. 31 Mar 1742; d. 26 Jul 1742.

223) viii BETSEY ABBOTT, b. 25 Aug 1743; d. 2 Oct 1827 at Goffstown, NH; m. 1759, THOMAS SALTMARSH, b. at Watertown, 2 Mar 1736 son of Thomas and Mary (Hazen) Saltmarsh; Thomas d. at Goffstown, NH 8 May 1826.[147]

ix JEMIMA ABBOTT, b. 23 Jun 1746; d. 13 Jul 1746.

x JEMIMA ABBOTT, b. 29 Apr 1748; d. 31 Jul 1748.

47) DEBORAH ABBOTT (*Thomas², George¹*), b. 1 Dec 1704 daughter of Thomas and Hannah (Gray) Abbott; d. at Concord, NH 25 Oct 1801; m. 5 Jul 1736, JOSEPH HALL, b. at Bradford 15 Dec 1707 son of Joseph and Sarah (Kimball) Hall; Joseph d. 8 Apr 1784 at Concord.[148]

Deacon Joseph Hall was from Bradford. He was deacon of the church at Concord for 40 years. Deborah is reported to have died after she lost her way while walking to pick berries, and then fell causing injuries that led to her death at the age of 97.[149]

Deborah Abbott and Joseph Hall had five children born at Concord.

i JOSEPH HALL, b. 17 Jul 1737; d. 10 Jun 1807; Joseph was a deacon and does not seem to have married or had children. His will leaves several bequests to what seem to be nieces and nephews (Wilkins and Thorndike who may be his sister Mary's children or grandchildren), a bequest to a local doctor, and he left his plot of land to the town of Concord.

ii SARAH HALL, b. 20 Sep 1738; d. 21 Oct 1746.

iii HANNAH HALL, b. 24 Nov 1740; d. 21 Oct 1746.

224) iv MARY HALL, b. 17 Mar 1743; d. 12 Dec 1773; m. THOMAS WILSON who d. at Concord 23 May 1818. After Mary's death, Thomas married Mary Hopkins Bancroft.

v JEREMIAH HALL, b. 6 Jan 1746; d. 6 Oct 1770; m., 1769, ESTHER WHITTEMORE, b. 2 Aug 1752 daughter of Aaron and Abigail (Coffin) Whittemore; Esther d. 12 Jul 1803. Esther m. 2nd, Joseph Woodman.

48) GEORGE ABBOTT (*Thomas², George¹*), b. 7 Nov 1706 son of Thomas and Hannah (Gray) Abbott; d. at Concord, NH 6 Oct 1785; m. 1 Feb 1737, SARAH ABBOTT (*Samuel³, John², George¹*) (who was his first cousin, once removed), b. Oct 1711 daughter of Samuel and Sarah (Stevens) Abbott and granddaughter of John and Sarah (Barker) Abbott; Sarah d. at Concord 14 Jun 1769.

George Abbott settled in Concord around 1732. He served as deacon of the church for 41 years.

In his will dated 28 February 1774, George made the following bequests: beloved son Daniel has already received his inheritance; to beloved son George, he orders that the executor provide him with a comfortable maintenance as long as he is single; beloved son Stephen receives 20 acres of land; beloved son Ezra receives a land bequest; and beloved son Joseph is named executor and also receives a parcel of land. The wording of the will suggests that son George may have had some type of disability. The inventory of his estate included real estate in Concord and Warner.[150]

George and Sarah had nine children born at Concord.

---

147 The graves of Elizabeth Abbott and Thomas Saltmarsh are in the Westlawn Cemetery at Goffstown with a gravestone that lists their names as Thomas Saltmarsh and Elisabeth Abbott, his wife. (accessed through findagrave.com)

148 New Hampshire Death and Disinterment Records, 1754-1947, accessed through ancestry.com

149 Bouton, *The History of Concord*

150 *New Hampshire Wills and Probate Records 1643-1982,* Probate of George Abbott, Rockingham, 16 Oct 1785, Case number 5147.

225) i DANIEL ABBOTT, b. 7 Aug 1738; d. 11 Jun 1804; m. 1st by 1761, his second cousin RACHEL ABBOTT, b. 7 Apr 1743 daughter of Nathaniel and Penelope (Ballard) Abbott; Rachel d. 13 Jun 1788. Daniel m. 2nd 1 Jan 1789 at Boscawen, MERCY KILBURN whose origins are not fully verified; she was born about 1760 based on the birth of her last child in 1799; she was living in 1830 when she was listed as a head of household in the 1830 US Census of Concord (between age 60-70).

ii GEORGE ABBOTT, b. 9 Apr 1740; d. 17 Sep 1791; George did not marry.

226) iii JOSEPH ABBOTT, b. 23 Oct 1741; d. at Concord, NH, 19 Jan 1832; m. 25 Apr 1765, PHEBE LOVEJOY, b. 20 Sep 1735 daughter of Henry and Phebe (Chandler) Lovejoy; Phebe d. 4 Jan 1789.

iv SAMUEL ABBOTT, b. 30 Mar 1743; d. 5 Nov 1761 at Crown Point during the French and Indian War.

v STEPHEN ABBOTT, b. 10 Dec 1744; d. 10 Oct 1746.

227) vi STEPHEN ABBOTT, 28 Oct 1746; d. 12 May 1811; m. 11 Apr 1778, MARY GILE, b. about 1755 (parentage not verified at this point); Mary d. Jan 1822.

vii NATHAN ABBOTT, b. 16 Nov 1748; d. 7 Mar 1749

viii NATHAN ABBOTT; b. 3 Jul 1752; d. 15 Nov 1758.

228) ix EZRA ABBOTT, b. 22 Aug 1756; d. 21 Feb 1837; m. 1st 21 Nov 1782, BETTY ANDREWS, b. 12 May 1762 daughter of Thomas and Mary (Burnham) Andrews; Betty d. 25 Aug 1794. Ezra m. 2nd 10 May 1795, ANNER CHOATE, b. at Ipswich 12 Jan 1758 daughter of Thomas and Dorothy (Proctor) Choate; Anner d. 21 Mar 1798. Ezra m. 3rd 15 Nov 1798, JANE JACKMAN, b. at Boscawen, 20 Dec 1767 daughter of Benjamin and Jane (-) Jackman; Jane d. 2 May 1847.

49) BENJAMIN ABBOTT (*Thomas²*, *George¹*), b. 31 Mar 1710 son of Thomas and Hannah (Gray) Abbott; d. at Concord, NH 8 Mar 1794; m. 23 Jun 1742, HANNAH ABBOTT (*Samuel³*, *John²*, *George¹*) (who was his first cousin once removed), b. 30 Jul 1716 daughter of Samuel and Sarah (Stevens) Abbott and granddaughter of John and Sarah (Barker) Abbott; Hannah d. at Concord 27 Jul 1786.

Benjamin was also an early settler of Concord. He was renowned for his physical prowess, including a report that he hoed four acres of corn in one day when he was over the age of 80.[151]

The will of Benjamin Abbott has bequests for the following persons (although one whole page of the will appears to be missing): son Benjamin, son Isaac, and daughter Hannah. Son Isaac is named executor.[152]

Benjamin and Hannah had eight children, all born at Concord.

229) i HANNAH ABBOTT, b. 22 Jan 1743; d. 22 Oct 1820; m. at Hopkinton, 25 Sep 1783, JEREMIAH STORY, JR. (origins not fully verified, but perhaps the Jeremiah Story of Ipswich); d. about 1806 based on the date of probate of his estate May 1806 with widow Hannah Story as administrator.

ii ISAAC ABBOTT, b. 7 Feb 1745; d. 24 Nov 1746.

iii ISAAC ABBOTT, b. 30 Aug 1747; d. 4 Mar 1799; m. at Ipswich, 28 Feb 1771, LUCY BURNHAM of Ipswich, b. about 1738 (as reported on death record); d. 3 Sep 1826. Isaac and Lucy do not seem to have had any children. The estate of Isaac Abbott entered probate 12 March 1799 in Rockingham County, New Hampshire. Isaac did not leave a will. Lucy Abbott declined administration of the estate and requested that Isaac's brother Benjamin take on that duty. The estate had a value of $745.

230) iv BENJAMIN ABBOTT, b. 10 Feb 1750; d. 11 Dec 1815; m. 29 Jan 1778, SARAH BROWN, b. 1758 at Brunswick, ME; Sarah d. 27 Sep 1801. Benjamin m. 2nd, 17 Jun 1805, HANNAH GREENLEAF who was still living at the time of Benjamin's death.

v EPHRAIM ABBOTT, b. 15 Jun 1752; d. 30 Oct 1778; Ephraim did not marry. He was wounded at the Battle of Bennington.

vi THOMAS ABBOTT, b. 7 Oct 1754; d. 2 Sep 1773.

---

[151] Bouton, *The History of Concord*

[152] *New Hampshire Wills and Probate Records 1643-1982,* Probate of Benjamin Abbott, Rockingham, 1 Apr 1794, Case number 5986.

vii THEODORE ABBOTT; b. 7 Mar 1759; d. 22 Sep 1778.

viii SARAH ABBOTT; b. 20 Feb 1761; d. 4 Jul 1761.

Children of Nathaniel Abbott and Dorcas Hibbert

50) MARY ABBOTT (*Nathaniel², George¹*), b. 28 Jan 1697/8 daughter of Nathaniel and Dorcas (Hibbert) Abbott; d.?; m. 29 Dec 1718, BENJAMIN BLANCHARD, b. 14 Feb 1693 son of Jonathan and Anne (Lovejoy) Blanchard; Benjamin d. likely in NH.

Benjamin and Mary had twelve children whose births are recorded at Andover. Their family fell victim to an epidemic of throat distemper in 1739. The family relocated to Hollis, New Hampshire where Benjamin was elected "fence viewer" at the first town meeting in 1746.[153] The family lived in West Parish of the District of Dunstable.

231) i MARY BLANCHARD, b. 6 Dec 1719; m. at Andover, 11 Jan 1742/3, EDWARD TAYLOR. The family resided in Hollis, NH.

232) ii BENJAMIN BLANCHARD, b. 19 Mar 1720/1; d. 7 Mar 1791 at Canterbury, NH; m. at Hollis, 27 Dec 1744, KEZIAH HASTINGS, b. at Lexington, 7 Jul 1723 daughter of Thomas and Sarah (White) Hastings.

233) iii ANNE BLANCHARD, b. 22 Nov 1722; d. at Hollis, before 1758 (when her second husband remarried); m. 26 Feb 1743, JONATHAN DANFORTH, b. at Billerica, 1 Nov 1714 son of Jonathan and Elizabeth (Manning) Danforth; Jonathan d. 1747 at Hollis, NH. Anne m. 2nd, STEPHEN MARTIN. After Anne's death, Stephen m. 21 Mar 1759, Patience Pope.

234) iv JACOB BLANCHARD, b. 11 May 1724; d. at Groton, 26 Apr 1770; m 1745, REBECCA LAWRENCE, b. at Groton, 17 Apr 1724 daughter of Nathaniel and Anne (Scripture) Lawrence. Rebecca m. 2nd, 1772 John Sheple who died in 1785; it is not known what became of Rebecca after that. She was living in 1786 at the time of the settlement of John Sheple's estate.

235) v JOSHUA BLANCHARD, b. 29 Mar 1726; d. 10 Oct 1818 at Wilton, NH; m. 23 Dec 1747, SARAH BURGE, b. 30 May 1728 daughter of John and Sarah (Taylor) Burge.

vi JONATHAN BLANCHARD, b. 7 Feb 1727/8; d. 16 Oct 1739.

vii DORCAS BLANCHARD, b. 28 Mar 1730; d. 13 Oct 1739.

viii DAVID BLANCHARD. B. 14 Feb 1731/2; d. 19 Oct 1739.

ix ELIZABETH BLANCHARD, b. 17 May 1734; no further record.

x ABIEL BLANCHARD, b. 25 Sep 1737; d. 15 Oct 1739.

xi DAVID BLANCHARD, b. 19 Feb 1739/40; d. 10 Apr 1740.

xii ABIEL BLANCHARD, b. 20 Oct 1741; d. 28 Jan 1742/3.

51) NATHANIEL ABBOTT (*Nathaniel², George¹*), b. 9 Jun 1700 son of Nathaniel and Dorcas (Hibbert) Abbott; d. at Concord, NH 1770;[154] m. 23 Nov 1726, PENELOPE BALLARD, b. 1705 daughter of Joseph and Rebecca (Johnson) Ballard; Penelope d. at Concord, date unknown (there is a death record transcription that gives the place of death, but not the date).

Nathaniel and Penelope married in Andover and had their first two children there. The family then headed up to Concord, New Hampshire as first settlers in that new development. Nathaniel Abbott was prominent in the early history of Concord serving multiple official functions.[155]

In his will dated 25 August 1769 (proved 29 August 1770), Nathaniel Abbott gentleman of Concord directed that his beloved wife Mehitable be comfortably maintained from the estate while she is a widow. Beloved son Nathaniel is to receive half of all money in his possession or owed to him at the time of his decease and son Jeremiah is to receive the other half. His daughters received the following bequests: Dorcas Merrill, one Spanish milled dollar; Rebecca Doyen, four Spanish milled dollars; Elizabeth Hazeltine, four Spanish milled dollars; Mary Walker, four Spanish milled dollars; Hannah Moor, four Spanish milled dollars; Rebecca Abbott, two Spanish milled dollars; Ruth Walker, four Spanish milled dollars; Dorothy George, four Spanish milled dollars; and Sarah Farnham, four Spanish milled dollars. The household goods are to be divided equally among

153 Worcester, *History of the Town of Hollis*

154 New Hampshire Death and Disinterment Records, 1754-1947

155 Bouton's *History of Concord* is relied on heavily for information about this family. When records have been located, they coincide exactly with the information provided in the Bouton text.

his nine daughters after his wife's decease. Son Joshua receives all the lands and buildings, the husbandry tools, and the stock animals. Joshua is named executor and is responsible for the legacies, debts, and the support of Mehitable. Estate was valued at £509.0.11.[156]

The births of the oldest two children are recorded in Andover and the youngest ten children are recorded in Concord.

236) i NATHANIEL ABBOTT, b. 10 Mar 1726/7; d. at Concord 4 Feb 1806; m. by 1749, MIRIAM CHANDLER, b. at Amesbury 24 Nov 1728 daughter of Nathaniel and Susannah (Rowel) Chandler; Miriam d. at Concord Jan 1811.

237) ii DORCAS ABBOTT, b. 11 Nov 1728; d. probably at Concord date unknown; m. by 1749, MOSES MERRILL, b. at Haverhill 27 Sep 1727 son of John and Lydia (Haynes) Merrill; Moses d. 1767.

238) iii REBECCA ABBOTT, b. 27 May 1731; d. after 1799 at Thetford, VT date unknown; m. 1st by 1750 JOHN MERRILL, b. at Haverhill 25 Nov 1725 son of John and Lydia (Haynes) Merrill; John d. at Bow, NH 1760. Rebecca m. 2nd JACOB DOYEN, b. about 1729; d. 1799 at Pembroke where his will was probated May 1799 with his widow Rebecca as administrator.

239) iv ELIZABETH ABBOTT, b. 1 Jul 1733; d. at Concord 25 Jan 1834; m. by 1755, JOSEPH HAZELTINE, b. at Rumford 27 Dec 1731 son of Richard and Sarah (Barnes) Hazeltine; Joseph d. 30 May 1798.

240) v MARY ABBOTT, b. 7 Mar 1735; d. Mar 1795; m. JOSEPH WALKER,[157] b. at Concord, 24 Apr 1732 son of Isaac and Sarah (Breed) Walker; Joseph d. about 1800 at Fryeburg, ME.

241) vi HANNAH ABBOTT, b. 7 Mar 1736; d. after 1792 when dower rights were set off to her; m. EPHRAIM MOOR whose origin is not yet established. Ephraim d. at Bow, NH about 1791 when his estate was probated. This record includes documents related to the dower of Hannah Moor.

242) vii RUTH ABBOTT, b. 28 Jan 1738; d. 27 Feb 1817; m. by 1759, JAMES A. WALKER, b. at Concord 2 Sep 1739 son of Isaac and Sarah (Breed) Walker; James d. 9 Feb 1821.

243) viii JOSHUA ABBOTT, b. 24 Feb 1740; d. Mar 1815; m. at Bradford 23 Oct 1766, ELIZA CHANDLER, b. at Bradford 20 Jul 1739 daughter of Josiah and Sara (Parker widow) Chandler; Eliza d. 27 May 1812.

225) ix RACHEL ABBOTT, b. 7 Apr 1743; d. 13 Jun 1788; m. by 1761 as his 1st wife, her second cousin DANIEL ABBOTT, b. 7 Aug 1738 son of George and Sarah (Abbott) Abbott. Daniel m. 2nd MERCY KILBURN; Daniel d. 11 Jun 1804.

244) x JEREMIAH ABBOTT, b. 17 Mar 1744; d. at Conway, NH 8 Nov 1823; m. ELIZABETH STICKNEY, b. at Rumford 7 Dec 1753 daughter of Thomas and Anna (Osgood) Stickney; Elizabeth d. 1846 (probate 3 Mar 1846).

245) xi DOROTHY ABBOTT, b. 28 Dec 1746; d. 27 Sep 1776; m. 29 May 1766, DAVID GEORGE, b. at Haverhill, 27 Oct 1745 son of David and Anne (Cottle) George; David d. about 1816 (date of probate) at Littleton, NH. David m. 2nd, Hannah Colby.

246) xii SARAH ABBOTT, b. 3 Dec 1748 daughter of Nathaniel and Penelope (Ballard) Abbott; d. Jun 1842; m. 1 Dec 1764, SAMUEL FARNUM, b. at Concord, 10 Feb 1743 son of Zebadiah and Mary (Walker) Farnum.

52) SARAH ABBOTT (*Nathaniel[2], George[1]*), b. about 1702 daughter of Nathaniel and Dorcas (Hibbert) Abbott; d. 11 Nov 1757; m. 4 Apr 1722, JOSEPH BLANCHARD, b. 19 Feb 1701 son of Thomas and Rose (Holmes) Blanchard. Joseph m. 2nd, 17 May 1758, the widow Mary Frost.

Sarah Abbott and Joseph Blanchard had eight children whose births are recorded at Andover. After the death of Sarah, Joseph married the widow Mary Frost and left Andover. He was for a time in Tewksbury and in 1772 he was in Wilmington.[158]

i SARAH BLANCHARD, b. 25 Jul 1723; d. 15 Apr 1729.

---

[156] New Hampshire State Papers, 39:302-304

[157] E. W. Foster and Philip Walker, "The Walkers of Woburn," *Massachusetts, Historical Bulletin, volumes 6-9*, pp 64-65

[158] Charlotte Helen Abbott, Early Records of the Blanchard Family of Andover

ii ELIZABETH BLANCHARD, b. 17 Jul 1726; d. 29 Mar 1728.

247) iii HANNAH BLANCHARD, b. 8 Oct 1728; d. likely at Hillsborough, NH; m. 19 May 1748, her third cousin, STEPHEN BLANCHARD, b. 9 Aug 1726 son of Stephen and Deborah (Phelps) Blanchard. Stephen had a second marriage to Elizabeth whose identity is not known; Stephen d. at Hillsborough about 1802 (will written 4 Mar 1796 and probate 1802).

248) iv JOSEPH BLANCHARD, b. 9 Feb 1730/1; d. 22 Mar 1776; m. 27 Feb 1753, his third cousin, DINAH BLANCHARD, b. 28 Dec 1731 daughter of Stephen and Deborah (Phelps) Blanchard. Dinah m. 2nd, as his second wife, REUBEN ABBOTT son of James and Abigail (Farnum) Abbott; Dinah d. 11 Mar 1826.

249) v JEREMIAH BLANCHARD, b. Jun 1733; d. at Weston, VT, 29 Jan 1826; m. 1st, 17 May 1759, DOROTHY SMITH who d. about 1770. Jeremiah m. 2nd, Aug 1772, SUSANNA MARTIN, b. 6 Apr 1743 daughter of John and Hannah (-) Martin.

250) vi DANIEL BLANCHARD, b. 15 Jul 1735; d. 19 Mar 1776; m. 29 Sep 1757, JERUSHA EATON, b. 19 Sep 1737 daughter of Silas and Jerusha (Gould) Eaton.

251) vii JOHN BLANCHARD, b. 19 Jul 1737; d. at Concord, NH, 10 Feb 1823; m. 5 Feb 1761, ELEANOR STEVENS, b. 1739 daughter of Samuel and Ann (Huse) Stevens.

viii PHEBE BLANCHARD, b. 3 Nov 1741; d. 29 Sep 1749.

53) JOSEPH ABBOTT (*Nathaniel*[2], *George*[1]), b. 22 Jan 1704/5 son of Nathaniel and Dorcas (Hibbert) Abbott; d. 23 Aug 1787 at Wilton, NH[159]; m. 12 Aug 1731, DEBORAH BLANCHARD, b. 18 Apr 1712 daughter of Thomas and Rose (Holmes) Blanchard; Deborah d. at Andover 21 Jul 1773.

Joseph Abbott was a farmer and lived on his father's homestead.[160] Joseph and his wife Deborah Blanchard had fourteen children born in Andover. Of their fourteen children, eight of them died in early childhood. A few years after Deborah's death in 1773, Joseph relocated to Wilton, New Hampshire. He served as a deacon. A probate record was not located.

i DEBORAH ABBOTT, b. 17 Sep 1732; d. 9 Jul 1736.

ii JOSHUA ABBOTT, b. 21 Jan 1733/4; d. 31 Dec 1736.

252) iii BATHSHEBA ABBOTT, b. 16 Sep 1735; d. 8 Dec 1784; m. 2 Jul 1752, NATHAN BLANCHARD, b. 30 Mar 1730 son of Stephen and Deborah (Phelps) Blanchard; Nathan d. before 1784 probably at Wilton, NH (Bathsheba was listed as a widow on her death record.

iv NATHANIEL ABBOTT, b. 12 Aug 1737; d. 5 Apr 1740.

v JOSHUA ABBOTT, b. 27 Apr 1739; d. 15 Oct 1739.

vi DEBORAH ABBOTT, b. 15 Jul 1740; d. 22 Nov 1745.

vii JOSEPH ABBOTT, b. 16 Jul 1740; d. 14 Sep 1741.

253) viii HANNAH ABBOTT, b. 15 Jun 1742; d. about 1770 at Wilton, NH (about this time her husband remarried); m. 15 Jan 1761, TIMOTHY DALE, b. at Danvers, 9 May 1733 son of John and Abigail (Putnam) Dale. Timothy m. 2nd Rebekah (-); date of death of Timothy is not known.

254) ix JOSEPH ABBOTT, b. 2 Apr 1744; d. at Wilton, NH about 1792; m. about 1763 MARY BARKER whose parentage is uncertain.

255) x JACOB ABBOTT, b. 9 Feb 1745/6; d. 5 Mar 1820 at Brunswick, ME; m. 1 Dec 1767, LYDIA STEVENS, b. 3 May 1745 daughter of John and Lydia (Gray) Stevens; Lydia d. Jun 1821.

xi DORCAS ABBOTT, b. 19 Jan 1747/8; d. 17 Oct 1749.

xii ODEDIAH ABBOTT, b. 23 Nov 1749; d. 8 Feb 1750.

256) xiii NATHANIEL ABBOTT, b. 27 Oct 1751; d. Mar 1791 at Wilton, NH; m. 31 Aug 1773, SARAH STEVENS.

257) xiv REBECCA ABBOTT, b. 19 Jun 1754; d. 19 Apr 1795 at Wilton, NH; m. 6 Apr 1775, DANIEL BATCHELDER, b. 2 Oct 1751 son of Joseph and Judith (Rea) Batchelder. Daniel m. 2nd Mrs. Sarah Kidder; Daniel d. 17 May 1832.

---

[159] Grave is in the Vale End Cemetery, Wilton, NH and bears the following inscription: "Erected in memory of Deacon Joseph Abbot who Departed this life August ye 23erd 1787 in the 83rd year of his age." Findagrave.com

[160] Abbot Genealogy, p 128

54) TABITHA ABBOTT (*Nathaniel², George¹*), b. abt. 1707 daughter of Nathaniel and Dorcas (Hibbert) Abbott; d. at Concord, NH date unknown but before her husband's will in 1775; m. 5 Jan 1726/6, her first cousin once removed, JOHN CHANDLER (*John Chandler³, Hannah Abbott Chandler², George¹*), b. May 1702 son of John and Hannah (Frye) Chandler; John d. at Concord 26 Jul 1775.

The will of John Chandler has the following bequests: grandsons Timothy and Abiel who are the sons of his son Timothy, his two granddaughters Tabitha and Elizabeth who are the daughters of son Timothy, son Daniel Chandler, son Joshua Chandler, and son John Chandler.

There are six children recorded to this couple, the eldest two born in Andover and the youngest four in Rumford, New Hampshire.

i HANNAH CHANDLER, b. 10 Jul 1728; d. 4 Aug 1728.

258) ii JOHN CHANDLER, b. 15 Aug 1730; d. at Concord, 1 Mar 1807; m. Oct 1751, MARY CARTER, b. 1729 (based on age at time of death) whose parents are unknown; Mary d. 9 Jun 1793.

259) iii TIMOTHY CHANDLER, b. 15 Aug 1733; d. 24 Mar 1770; m. by 1760, ELIZABETH COPP, b. at Amesbury, 5 Apr 1740 daughter of Solomon and Elizabeth (Davis) Copp; Elizabeth d. at Concord, 20 Mar 1830. Elizabeth m. 2nd, Feb 1774, STEPHEN WARD.

260) iv DANIEL CHANDLER, b. 15 Feb 1735; d. at Concord, 25 Oct 1795; m. 1st, about 1755, SARAH EASTMAN, b. 14 Jul 1737 daughter of Ebenezer and Eleanor (-) Eastman; Sarah died by 1757 (after the birth of her only child). Daniel m. 2nd, by 1759, SARAH MERRILL, b. 24 Apr 1741 daughter of John and Lydia (Haynes) Merrill; Sarah d. at Chatham, NH, 1810.

261) v JOSHUA CHANDLER, b. 9 Jun 1740; d. 3 Dec 1816; m. 1768, IRENE COPP, b. at Amesbury, 17 May 1745 daughter of Solomon and Elizabeth (Davis) Copp; Irene d. 7 Dec 1810.

vi HANNAH CHANDLER, b. 3 Sep 1744; d. before 1775 (father's will); m. JACOB? WORTHEN and AUSTIN? There is no confirmed information on Hannah other than the birth record which lists John Chandler and Tabitha Abbott as her parents. Both the Chandler genealogy book and the Abbot genealogy book suggest these spouses (Worthen and Austin), but no record has been located. As Hannah is not mentioned in her father's will, and no heirs of hers are mentioned, it seems she died before 1775 and likely had no children that lived until 1775.

55) JEREMIAH ABBOTT (*Nathaniel², George¹*), b. 4 Nov 1709 son of Nathaniel and Dorcas (Hibbert) Abbott; d. at Billerica 28 Aug 1748; m. 2 Jan 1734/5, HANNAH BALLARD, b. 27 Jun 1714 daughter of Hezekiah and Rebecca (Davis) Ballard. Hannah m. 2nd WILLIAM STICKNEY; Hannah d. 11 Feb 1789 at Billerica.

William Stickney who married the widow Hannah Abbott is one of the persons assigned to take the inventory of Jeremiah Abbott's estate. Hannah is the administrator. Jeremiah did not leave a will. There is a guardianship case for the children in 1749 at the time of Hannah's remarriage. Daughter Hannah at age 15 selected Joshua Davis of Billerica as her guardian. Rebecca, William, and Jeremiah also have Joshua Davis as guardian.

Jeremiah and Hannah had six children, all born at Billerica.

262) i HANNAH ABBOTT, b. 10 Oct 1735; d. 13 Sep 1819; m. 3 Jul 1766, OLIVER FARMER, b. 31 Jul 1728 son of Oliver and Abigail (Johnson) Farmer; Oliver d. 24 Sep 1814.

ii JEREMIAH ABBOTT, b. 24 Aug 1738; d. 12 Apr 1740.

263) iii REBECCA ABBOTT, b. 13 Jul 1741, m. 29 Oct 1761, RICHARD BOYNTON, b. at Tewksbury, 22 Mar 1741 son of Richard and Jerusha (Hutchins) Boynton.

iv JEREMIAH ABBOTT, b. 20 Jul 1745; d. 7 Aug 1745.

264) v WILLIAM ABBOTT, b. 21 Jul 1746; d. after 1800 at Wheelock, VT; m. 28 Dec 1769, BRIDGET SPAULDING, b. 11 Mar 1748/9 daughter of David and Phebe (-) Spaulding; Bridget's death is not known but likely in Vermont about 1795. William married second, Mehitable Scott (according to the Abbot genealogy book).[161]

---

[161] Abbot and Abbot, *Genealogical Register of Descendants*

265) vi JEREMIAH ABBOTT, b. 11 Aug 1748; d. ; m. 19 Jan 1769, SUSANNAH BALDWIN, b. 1746 (probably the daughter of Josiah Baldwin of Tewksbury); Susanna d. 9 Apr 1825.

56) ELIZABETH ABBOTT (*Nathaniel*[2], *George*[1]), b. 1 Feb 1713 daughter of Nathaniel and Dorcas (Hibbert) Abbott; d. 25 Jul 1799; m. 26 May 1741, TIMOTHY MOOAR, b. 16 Jun 1713 son of Timothy and Anne (Blanchard) Mooar; Timothy d. 20 Jan 1787.

Timothy Mooar did not leave a will. His widow Elizabeth requested that Nehemiah Abbot be named administrator. The debts of the estate exceeded the value of the estate.[162]

There are birth records for five children, all born at Andover.

i TIMOTHY MOOAR, b. 14 Feb 1742; d. 9 Sep 1817; Timothy did not marry.

266) ii JOHN MOOAR, b. Jun 1745; d. 1777 at Saratoga, NY during the Revolution; m. 28 Jul 1774, MARY BALLARD, b. 1754 daughter of William and Hannah (Howe) Ballard. Mary m. 2nd 13 Dec 1781, JONATHAN BOYNTON; Mary d. by 1795 when probate petition filed related to John Mooar's estate requesting administration of her widow's portion which reverted to creditors as she is deceased.

267) iii ELIZABETH MOOAR, b. 8 Mar 1747/8; d. 16 Mar 1818; m. 29 Jul 1766, MOSES BAILEY, b. at Bradford, 16 Jan 1743/4 son of Nathan and Mary (Palmer) Bailey; Moses d. 14 Mar 1842. Moses Bailey was the proprietor of what is now known as the Moses Bailey Abbott homestead at 72 Brundrett Avenue in Andover.[163]

268) iv JOSHUA MOOAR, b. 3 Jun 1751; d. at Milford, NH, 10 Sep 1824; m. 17 Sep 1776, DEBORAH CHANDLER, b. 26 Apr 1757 daughter of Zebadiah and Deborah (Blanchard) Chandler; Deborah was still living in 1822 when Joshua wrote his will.

269) v MARY MOOAR, b. 26 May 1760; d. 2 Aug 1820; m. 30 Jul 1778, WILLIAM HARRIS whose origins are not pinned down; his death is unknown but was before Mary died in 1820.

57) REBECCA ABBOTT (*Nathaniel*[2], *George*[1]), b. 24 Apr 1717 daughter of Nathaniel and Dorcas (Hibbert) Abbott; d. 13 Feb 1803 at Concord, NH; m. 18 Mar 1741/2, ABIEL CHANDLER *(John Chandler*[3], *Hannah Abbott Chandler*[2], *George*[1]*)*, b. 14 Mar 1717 son of John and Hannah (Frye) Chandler; Abiel d. abt. 1752 at Concord. Rebecca m. 2nd by 1754, AMOS ABBOTT *(James*[3], *William*[2], *George*[1]*)*, b. 18 Feb 1725/6 son of James and Abigail (Farnum) Abbott; Amos d. at Concord 3 Dec 1821.

Abiel Chandler and Rebecca Abbott had four children, the first recorded at Andover and the youngest three in Rumford/Concord, New Hampshire.

i ABIEL CHANDLER, b. 27 Jun 1742; died young.

270) ii ABIEL CHANDLER, b. 11 May 1744; d. 27 Aug 1776 at Long Island, NY during the Revolutionary War; m. about 1766, JUDITH WALKER, b. at Rumford, 21 Dec 1744 daughter of Timothy and Sarah (Burbeen) Walker. Judith m. 2nd Nathaniel Rolfe; Judith d. at Concord 1806.

iii PETER CHANDLER, b. 9 Oct 1747; d. 25 Jun 1776 while serving in the Army.

iv SARAH CHANDLER, b. about 1749; Sarah is included as a child in published genealogies, but there seem to be no records related to her.

Rebecca Abbott and Amos Abbott had three children.

271) i AMOS ABBOTT, b. 15 Jul 1754; d. at Concord 11 Oct 1834; m. JUDITH MORSE, b. at Newbury, 1 Mar 1766 daughter of Moses and Sarah (Hale) Morse.

ii JOHN ABBOTT, b. 23 Jun 1756; d. 31 Aug 1779. John served in the Revolutionary War.

272) iii REBECCA ABBOTT, b. 26 Sep 1760; d. at Loudon, NH, 24 Dec 1846; m. 9 Oct 1781, MOSES CHAMBERLAIN, b. at Hopkinton, 5 Oct 1757 son of Samuel and Martha (Mellen) Chamberlain; Moses d. 21 Oct 1811.

---

[162] *Essex County, MA: Probate File Papers, 1638-1881. Probate of* Timothy Mooar, 8 May 1787, *Case number* 18696.

[163] Andover Historic Preservation, retrieved from https://preservation.mhl.org/72-brundrett-avenue

Children of Elizabeth Abbott and Nathan Stevens

58) NATHAN STEVENS (*Elizabeth Abbott Stevens*[2], *George*[1]), b. 22 Sep 1693 son of Nathan and Elizabeth (Abbott) Stevens; d. at Andover, 20 Sep 1741; m. 3 Nov 1715 HANNAH ROBINSON, b. 29 Jan 1694/5 daughter of Dane and Mary (Chadwick) Robinson; Hannah d.? (possible death is 1753 in Boxford).

The will of Nathan Stevens has bequests for the following persons: well-beloved wife Hannah, eldest son Nathan, he makes a provision for early payment of the portions of daughters Hannah and Elizabeth in case either of them marries before son Nathan is 21, eldest daughter Mary Stevens, son Benjamin, son Phineas, and youngest daughter Sarah Stevens.[164]

The births of ten children are recorded at Andover. There are no clear records for any of these children beyond their births. A marriage for one of the children has been reasonably established. There are also marriages for two other children suggested by Charlotte Helen Abbott and these are also noted. But all marriages for these children should be considered preliminary. It is likely that other children married, but that cannot be firmly established at this time.

Charlotte Helen Abbott thinks it is possible that Mary married Samuel Parker. She states that Elizabeth married Samuel Ames. I think it is reasonable that Hannah married Abner Tyler of Boxford. There are two reasons to propose this marriage for Hannah. There is a death record in Boxford for the widow Hannah Stevens in Boxford in 1753 at age 58 and this would be the right age for Hannah Robinson Stevens. If her daughter Hannah married a man in Boxford, that would explain the mother Hannah's presence there. Also, Abner Tyler is a signer of one of the receipts in the probate record of Nathan Stevens attesting that he has received the settlement from the estate. It is possible that Abner Tyler was simply a creditor of the estate, but I have concluded for the time being that he is the husband of Hannah Stevens. In addition, the oldest child of Hannah and Abner was named Nathan, the name of Hannah's father who died just the prior year. Some sources suggest that the Hannah who married Abner Tyler was the daughter of Benjamin Stevens and Hannah Farnum, but their daughter seems to have married Aaron Gage, as indicated by Hannah Stevens alias Gage receiving a disbursement from the estate of her father Benjamin Stevens.

273) i MARY STEVENS, b. Apr 1716; d.?; m. 3 May 1742, SAMUEL PARKER, b. at Bradford, 6 Oct 1716 son of Daniel and Anne (Morse) Parker; Samuel d. 4 Oct 1796.

ii RACHEL STEVENS, b. 6 Feb 1719/20; d. 1 May 1738.

274) iii HANNAH STEVENS, b. about 1721; d. at Brookfield, 17 Nov 1789; m. 11 Feb 1741/2, ABNER TYLER of Boxford, b. 15 Feb 1708/9 son of John and Anna (Messenger) Tyler; Abner d. 8 Dec 1777.

275) iv ELIZABETH STEVENS, b. 2 Jul 1722; d.?; m. 11 Jul 1744, SAMUEL AMES, b. 1719 son of Samuel and Abigail (Spofford) Ames.

275a v NATHAN STEVENS, b. 16 Mar 1723/4; d. at Wendell, MA, 14 Nov 1794; m. at Andover, 22 Apr 1746, MARY POOR, b. at Andover, about 1726 daughter of John and Mary (Faulkner) Poor.

vi ABIGAIL STEVENS, b. 18 May 1726; d. 27 Oct 1736.

vii BENJAMIN STEVENS, b. 1 Apr 1729.

viii PHINEAS STEVENS, b. 7 Mar 1730/1; there are no further records for Phineas beyond his mention in his father's will.

ix SARAH STEVENS, b. 17 Jan 1733/4; d. 5 May 1738.

x SARAH STEVENS, b. 1 Feb 1740/1.

59) ELIZABETH STEVENS (*Elizabeth Abbott Stevens*[2], *George*[1]), b. 14 Oct 1697 daughter of Nathan and Elizabeth (Abbott) Stevens; d. at Windham, CT 28 Aug 1736; m. 24 Aug 1722, TIMOTHY PEARL, b. at Bradford 23 Feb 1695 son of John and Elizabeth (Holmes) Pearl. Timothy m. 2nd Mary Leach; Timothy d. at Windham 9 Oct 1773.

---

[164] *Essex County, MA: Probate File Papers, 1638-1881. Probate of* Nathan Stevens, 26 Oct 1741, *Case number* 26409.

The will of Timothy Pearl has bequests to the following persons: "faithful well-beloved wife Mary," eldest son Timothy, son John, son Nathan, eldest daughter Elizabeth Hibbard, daughter Phebe Durkee, daughter Lydia Denison, son James Pearl, son Richard, daughter Mary Towbridge, son David, daughter Ruth Pearl, daughter Hannah Pearl, son Phineas, and son Philip.[165] Some of these heirs are Timothy's children from his second marriage to Mary Leach.

Elizabeth Stevens and Timothy Pearl had six children, all born at Windham.[166]

276) i TIMOTHY PEARL, b. 24 Oct 1723; d. at Willington, 19 Oct 1789; m. 6 Nov 1746, DINAH HOLT, b. at Windham, 17 Mar 1725/6 daughter of Joshua and Keturah (Holt) Holt; Dinah d. at Willington, 25 Sep 1806.

ii JOHN PEARL, b. 20 Jan 1725/6; d.?; m. 17 Jun 1750, KETURAH HOLT, b. 22 Nov 1729 daughter of John and Keturah (Holt) Holt; Keturah d. at Willington, 1805. There do not seem to be any children for this couple. There is a probate record for Keturah from 1805. The distributions of the estate of Keturah Holt Pearl are to the following persons: sister Dinah Pearl; sister Phebe Goodale; and heirs of brother Joshua Holt who is deceased.

277) iii NATHAN PEARL, b. 22 Nov 1727; d.?; m. 7 Mar 1748, ELIZABETH UTLEY, b. 22 Apr 1729 daughter of James and Annah (-) Utley.

278) iv ELIZABETH PEARL, b. Jan 1729/30; d. ?; m. 24 May 1749, JOHN HIBBARD, b. 9 Dec 1727 son of John and Martha (Durkee) Hibbard; John d. at Royalton, VT, 31 Dec 1804.

279) v PHEBE PEARL, b. 12 May 1732; d. at Yarmouth, Nova Scotia, date unknown; m. 29 Nov 1750, PHINEAS DURKEE, b. 16 Sep 1730 son of Stephen and Lois (Moulton) Durkee; Phineas d. at Yarmouth, Nova Scotia, 5 Nov 1801.[167]

280) vi LYDIA PEARL, b. 31 Jul 1734; d. Sep 1819; m. 27 Nov 1753, DANIEL DENISON, b. 5 Sep 1730 son of Daniel and Hannah (Crocker) Denison; Daniel d. at Hampton, 4 Aug 1823.

60) HANNAH STEVENS (*Elizabeth Abbott Stevens²*, *George¹*), b. 1701 daughter of Nathan and Elizabeth (Abbott) Stevens; d. after 1782; m. 13 Jan 1720/1 as his 2nd wife, SAMUEL AMES, b. 6 Feb 1695/6 son of Robert and Bethia (Gatchell) Ames; Samuel d. at Groton 1784.

Samuel and Hannah moved several times during their marriage. They lived first in Andover, spent some time in Natick where son Nathan was born in 1729, were then in Andover again for the birth of the rest of their children, and finally settled in Groton. Samuel had one child, a son Samuel, from his first marriage to Abigail Spofford.

Samuel wrote his will 13 February 1782 and the estate went to probate 29 March 1784. The will is in poor condition, but it is possible to make out the names of the heirs. His wife is mentioned. The children named in the will are oldest son Samuel; "youngest son" Robert who receives the husbandry tools; the remaining sons Benjamin, Nathan, and Amos; and daughter Abigail Abbott. Abigail Abbott is clearly the only daughter.[168]

Samuel Ames and Hannah Stevens had seven children, all of them born or baptized in Andover except Nathan whose baptism is recorded at Natick.

i ABIGAIL AMES, b. about 1722; d. 27 Aug 1812; m. 12 Mar 1744/5, NATHAN ABBOTT, b. Apr 1719 son of Jonathan and Zerviah (Holt) Abbott; Nathan d. 28 Jun 1798. Nathan Abbott and Abigail Ames did not have any children. Nathan Abbott wrote his will 21 March 1776 and the estate entered probate 3 September 1798. Dearly beloved wife Abigail receives "all my household stuff proper for woman's use." She receives other provisions for her support and the use and improvements of one-third of the real property. He makes a bequest to his "cousin" Nathan Abbott who is the son of his brother Job who is deceased. The nephew Nathan is named executor and has the remainder of the estate bequeathed to him.

ii HANNAH AMES, b. about 1722; death unknown but she is not in her father's will and there is not a marriage record.

281) iii BENJAMIN AMES, b. 6 Jun 1724; d. 10 Jan 1809; m. 1st 4 Dec 1746, his second cousin, HEPHZIBAH CHANDLER, b. 7 Apr 1726 daughter of Timothy and Hephzibah (Harnden) Chandler; Hephzibah d. 19 Jan 1768. Benjamin m. 2nd about 1770, his second cousin, once removed and George Abbott descendant, DORCAS LOVEJOY, b. 18 Aug 1749 daughter of Joshua and Lydea (Abbott) Lovejoy; Dorcas d. 25 Jun 1843.

---

165 *Connecticut Wills and Probate, 1609-1999*, Probate of Timothy Pearl, Hartford, 1773, Case number 2980.

166 Lorraine Cook White, ed., *The Barbour Collection of Connecticut Town Vital Records. Vol. 1-55.* Baltimore, MD, USA: Genealogical Publishing Co., 1994-2002. (accessed through ancestry.com)

167 *Yarmouth, Nova Scotia, Genealogies* [database on-line]. (ancestry.com)

168 *Middlesex County, MA: Probate File Papers, 1648-1871. Probate of* Samuel Ames, *1784, Case number* 400.

282) iv NATHAN AMES, b. Apr 1729; d. at Groton 7 Mar 1791; m. 19 Apr 1763, DEBORAH BOWERS, b. at Groton, 2 Sep 1746 daughter of Samuel and Deborah (Farnsworth) Bowers; Deborah d. 8 Apr 1782.

283) v AMOS AMES, baptized 20 Jan 1733/4; d. 4 Aug 1817; m. 27 Oct 1757, ABIGAIL BULKLEY, b. at Concord, 28 Oct 1733 daughter of John and Abigail (-) Bulkley; Abigail d. 20 Aug 1809.[169]

284) vi ROBERT AMES, baptized 1737; d. ?; m. 1st 2 Dec 1762, SARAH WOODS, b. 19 Aug 1742 daughter of Isaac and Abigail (Stevens) Woods; Sarah d. 23 Nov 1774. Robert m. 2nd 29 Apr 1777, SUSANNA GREEN (widow of Abijah Warren), b. 20 Mar 1746 daughter of Isaac and Martha (Boyden) Green.

vii SIMEON AMES, b. 23 Jun 1741; d. 10 Dec 1760 of smallpox.

61) PHEBE STEVENS (*Elizabeth Abbott Stevens*[2], *George*[1]), b. 1704 daughter of Nathan and Elizabeth (Abbott) Stevens; date of death is unknown, although she is perhaps the Phebe Steel who is the head of household in the 1790 US Census for Andover; m. 7 Nov 1734, NICHOLAS STEEL whose origins are unknown.

The births of six children are recorded at Andover, but there are no death records in Massachusetts for either Phebe or Nicholas. Phebe Steel is listed in the 1790 US Census for Andover as the head of household which consists of two females[170], so it is assumed that Nicholas died before that time.

In her father's will, there is a bequest to the oldest daughter of Phebe who is named as "Eunos Ginnins" (or perhaps Germin, but it is not clear) in the will. Phebe's daughter is to receive ten pounds when she reaches age 21. This child is not from Phebe's marriage to Nicholas Steel and Phebe does not have a marriage prior to her marriage to her marriage to Nicholas as the marriage transcription lists her name as Phebe Stevens. One possibility is the Eunice is a child born out-of-wedlock. Phebe was about 30 years old when she married Nicholas, so it is certainly possible she had a child prior to this marriage. No other records associated with this daughter have been located. Search based on the last name as written in the will is difficult as the spelling of the last name is so uncertain. For the time being, the child mentioned in the will remains an interesting puzzle. One possibility is that "Eunos Ginnins" is the Eunice Jennings who married Francis Ingalls, Jr. who was the step-son of Phebe's sister Lydia. In her will, Lydia Stevens Ingalls leaves her entire estate to the family of Eunice and Francis Ingalls and three of their children. This will includes a bequest to "daughter Eunes" all the estate that is not otherwise disposed of. Although Lydia Stevens Ingalls had other living step-grandchildren, the only bequests are to Eunice and Francis and their children. Published genealogies give the parents of Eunice Jennings who married Francis Ingalls, Jr. as Joseph Jennings and Elizabeth Rolfe, but there is no birth record for Eunice (although there are records for all the other children of Joseph and Elizabeth).

285) i PHEBE STEEL, b. 27 Sep 1735; d. unknown but still living in 1783; m. 22 Nov 1776, as his second wife, JOHN ABBOTT (of the George Abbott of Rowley line), b. 10 Mar 1724/5 son of Uriah and Sarah (Mitchell) Abbott; John d. of smallpox 3 Jan 1779.

286) ii ELIZABETH STEEL, b. 21 Feb 1737; date of death not known but she appears to be the Elizabeth Ingalls in Andover in the 1810 US Census; m. 9 Sep 1760, JOSHUA INGALLS, b. 13 Aug 1732 son of Joseph and Phebe (Farnum) Ingalls; Joshua d. 1785, his will probated 5 Jul 1785.

287) iii RACHEL STEEL, b. 1 Jul 1739; death unknown; m. 11 Dec 1767, DUDLEY FOSTER, b. at Boxford, 21 Feb 1737/8 son of Zebadiah and Margaret (Tyler) Foster.

288) iv BENJAMIN STEEL, b. 25 Jan 1741; d. at Wilton, NH 14 Nov 1817; m. 16 Jun 1768, HANNAH LOVEJOY, b. 1748 (parentage uncertain); Hannah d. at Wilton, 31 Aug 1812.

v HANNAH STEEL, b. 17 Sep 1743; d. at Andover 23 Mar 1827; Hannah did not marry.

vi LYDIA STEEL, b. 20 Nov 1745; d. 14 Feb 1747/8.

---

[169] Green, *Groton Historical Series*, volume 3, p 159. Abigail Ames the wife of Amos Ames departed this life August ye 20th day, age 77 years.

[170] Year: 1790; Census Place: Andover, Essex, Massachusetts; Series: M637; Roll: 4; Page: 20; Image: 35; Family History Library Film: 0568144. (ancestry.com)

Generation Four

Grandchildren of John Abbott and Sarah Barker

62) JOHN ABBOT *(John³, John², George¹)*, b. 3 Aug 1704 son of John and Elizabeth (Harnden) Abbot; d. 10 Nov 1793; m. 28 Sep 1732, PHEBE FISKE, b. at Boxford 4 Aug 1712 daughter of John and Abigail (Poore) Fiske; Phebe d. 7 Dec 1802.

In his will, Captain John Abbot has bequests to his loving wife Phebe who receives improvements of half the dwelling house and half the cellar plus other bequests of a money payment and other provisions needed for her maintenance (a lengthy and specific list), eldest and beloved son John receives all of the lands and buildings in Andover, beloved son Abiel receives a tract of land in Wilton, beloved son Jeremiah also receives land in Wilton, beloved son William receives land in Wilton, and beloved daughter Phebe receives one-half of the household goods and a token of £1 which supplements the £57 she received at the time of her marriage. The land bequests in Wilton total in the hundreds of acres.[171]

There are birth records for seven children, all born at Andover. Of the four children in this family that married, three of them married fellow George Abbott descendants.

289) i PHEBE ABBOTT, b. 14 Apr 1733; d. 26 Jul 1812; m. 18 Apr 1754, her third cousin and George Abbott descendant, NATHAN CHANDLER, b. 19 Feb 1729/30 son of Nathan and Phebe (Holt) Chandler; Nathan d. 30 Apr 1786.

193) ii JOHN ABBOTT, b. 12 Sep 1735; d. 24 Apr 1818; m. 1 Jun 1758, his second cousin once removed, ABIGAIL ABBOTT, b. 13 Jan 1733/4 daughter of Benjamin and Abigail (Abbott) Abbott; Abigail d. 1 Feb 1807.

iii EZRA ABBOTT, b. 27 Sep 1737; d. 15 Sep 1760.

197) iv ABIEL ABBOT, b. 19 Apr 1741; d. at Wilton, NH, 19 Aug 1809; m. 20 Nov 1764, his second cousin once removed, DORCAS ABBOT, b. 1 Aug 1744 daughter of Benjamin and Abigail (Abbott) Abbott; Dorcas d. 23 Feb 1829.

290) v JEREMIAH ABBOTT, b. 14 May 1743; d. 2 Nov 1825 at Wilton, NH; m. 16 Sep 1766, CLOE ABBOTT (from the George Abbott of Rowley line), b. 5 Nov 1737 daughter of Zebadiah and Anne (Lovejoy) Abbott; Cloe d. at Wilton 21 Aug 1809.

291) vi WILLIAM ABBOTT, b. 3 Jan 1747/8; d. at Wilton, NH 30 Nov 1793; m. 12 Nov 1772, his third cousin and George Abbott descendant, PHEBE BALLARD, b. 5 Nov 1752 daughter of Timothy and Hannah (Chandler) Ballard; Phebe d. at Wilton, Jan 1846.

vii BENJAMIN ABBOTT, b. 29 May 1751; d. 1 Aug 1751.

63) BARACHIAS ABBOT *(John³, John², George¹)*, b. 14 May 1707 son of John and Elizabeth (Harnden) Abbot; d. 2 Oct 1784; m. 22 Mar 1733, his second cousin once removed, HANNAH HOLT, b. 18 Dec 1709 daughter of Timothy and Rhoda (Chandler) Holt; Hannah d. 2 Aug 1775. Hannah was the great-granddaughter of William Chandler and Annis Bayford.

The death record for Barachias lists his cause of death as cancer. A probate record has not been located for Barachias. There are birth records for eleven children all born at Andover.

i BARACHIAS ABBOTT, b. 16 Jan 1733/4; d. 24 Jun 1738.

292) ii MOSES ABBOTT, b. 9 Aug 1735; d. 23 Feb 1826; m. 31 Dec 1761, his third cousin, ELIZABETH HOLT, b. 8 Jun 1743 daughter of Henry and Rebecca (Gray) Holt; Elizabeth d. 23 Sep 1838.

293) iii HANNAH ABBOTT, b. 18 May 1737; d. Nov 1812 at Wilton, NH; m. 21 Apr 1756, her third cousin, JEREMIAH HOLT, b. 31 Mar 1734 son of John and Mary (Lewis) Holt; Jeremiah's death record not located, but after the 1790 US Census.

294) iv BARACHIAS ABBOT, b. 22 May 1739; d. 29 Jan 1812; m. 6 Dec 1770, his third cousin and George Abbott descendant, SARAH HOLT, b. 7 Mar 1746/7 daughter of James and Sarah (Abbott) Holt; Sarah d. 11 Feb 1808.

295) v ELIZABETH ABBOTT, b. 2 Nov 1740; d. 9 Sep 1780; m. 30 Aug 1759, her second cousin and George Abbott descendant, ZEBADIAH SHATTUCK, b. 26 Oct 1736 son of Joseph and Joanna (Chandler) Shattuck.

[171] *Essex County, MA: Probate File Papers, 1638-1881. Probate of* John Abbot, 2 Jun 1794, *Case number* 73.

Zebadiah m. 2nd 25 Dec 1781, Sarah Chandler (widow of Ralph Holbrook) and George Abbott descendant, b. 8 May 1751 daughter of Zebadiah and Deborah (Blanchard) Chandler; Zebadiah d. 10 Mar 1826.

296) vi PRISCILLA ABBOTT, b. 13 Feb 1742/3; d. likely at Bethel, ME; m. 16 Nov 1762, ZELA HOLT, b. 29 Dec 1738 son of James and Mary (Chandler) Holt.

297) vii LYDIA ABBOTT, b. 7 Mar 1744/5; d. 11 Jul 1829; m. 15 Aug 1771, URIAH RUSSELL, b. 1743 son of Thomas and Abigail (Ballard) Russell; Uriah d. 9 Nov 1822.

viii RHODA ABBOTT, b. 23 Apr 1747; d. 11 Aug 1775; Rhoda did not marry.

ix TIMOTHY ABBOTT, b. 23 Apr 1747; d. 30 Mar 1772.

298) x PHEBE ABBOTT, b. 29 Aug 1749; d. 17 Apr 1809; m. 1 Feb 1774, JOHN RUSSELL, b. 1 Jul 1746 son of John and Hannah (Foster) Russell. John m. 2nd Mary Wilkins; John d. 12 Aug 1830.

299) xi ABIGAIL ABBOTT, b. 25 Jul 1751; d. at Greenfield, NH, 1841; m. 10 Oct 1786, as his second wife, JOHN JOHNSON, b. at Andover, 1748 *perhaps* the son of John and Lydia (Osgood) Johnson (gravestone gives his age as 85); d. at Greenfield, NH 3 Oct 1833. He was first married to Hannah Abbott daughter of John and Hannah (Farnum) Abbott who died in 1785 and then married Abigail.

64) ELIZABETH ABBOT (*John*[3], *John*[2], *George*[1]), b. 28 Oct 1711 daughter of John and Elizabeth (Harnden) Abbot; d. 4 Jul 1758; m. 26 Oct 1732, ASA FOSTER, b. 16 Jun 1710 son of William and Sarah (Kimball) Foster; Asa d. 17 Jul 1787. Asa m. 2nd, Lucy Wise the widow of Richard Rogers. Lucy Wise was born at Ipswich, Mar 1723.

There are records for nine children for Elizabeth and Asa, all born at Andover. Five sons and one daughter relocated to New Hampshire, and most remained in Canterbury. One son, Benjamin, could not be reliably traced; the only record for him is a baptism in Andover. One child died in early infancy. A second daughter, Elizabeth, married and stayed in Andover where she died at age 31.

Captain Asa Foster served in the Revolutionary War. Asa Foster did not leave a will. His estate entered probate 7 August 1787. His widow Lucy Foster declined administration of the estate due to her ill health. Abiel Foster was named administrator.[172]

300) i ASA FOSTER, b. 29 Aug 1733; d. at Canterbury, NH 23 Sep 1814; m. 1st HANNAH SYMONDS, b. at Boxford, 5 Nov 1733 daughter of Joseph and Mary (-) Symonds; Hannah d. 29 Jun 1775. Asa m. 2nd 1776, HANNAH PETERS, b. at Andover 11 Dec 1730 daughter of Samuel and Mary (Robinson) Peters; Hannah Peters d. 11 Jan 1815.

301) ii ABIEL FOSTER, b. 8 Aug 1735; d. at Canterbury, NH 6 Feb 1806; m. 1st 15 May 1761, HANNAH BADGER, b. at Haverhill, 16 Nov 1742 daughter of Joseph and Hannah (Pearson) Badger; Hannah d. 10 Jan 1768. Abiel m. 2nd 11 Oct 1769, MARY ROGERS, b. 11 Nov 1745 daughter of Samuel and Hannah (Wise) Rogers; Mary d. 12 Mar 1813.

302) iii DANIEL FOSTER, b. 25 Sep 1737; d. at Canterbury 25 Jan 1833; m. 16 Dec 1760, HANNAH KITTREDGE, b. Aug 1742 daughter of Jacob and Hannah (French) Kittredge.

iv DAVID FOSTER, b. 7 May 1740; died in infancy.

303) v DAVID FOSTER, b. 24 Sep 1741; d. at Canterbury, 9 Dec 1810; m. 24 Nov 1768, SARAH FOSTER, b. about 1750 who parents are not yet determined; Sarah d. about 1830.[173]

304) vi ELIZABETH FOSTER, b. 14 Apr 1744; d. at Andover 24 Apr 1775; m. 3 Nov 1768, her third cousin and George Abbott descendant, (General) NATHANIEL LOVEJOY, b. 29 Apr 1744 son of Nathaniel and Elizabeth (Swan) Lovejoy; Nathaniel d. 5 Jul 1812.

vii BENJAMIN FOSTER; baptized 1747; no further certain record.

305) viii JONATHAN FOSTER, b. 28 Jul 1747; d. about 1818 at Canterbury, NH (will dated 5 Sep 1818); m. Nov 1770, LUCY ROGERS, b. 19 Oct 1748 daughter of Samuel and Hannah (Wise) Rogers; Lucy d. about 1830.

---

[172] *Essex County, MA: Probate File Papers, 1638-1881. Probate of* Asa Foster, 7 Aug 1787, *Case number* 9812.

[173] Lyford, *History of Canterbury*, p. 135

306) ix SARAH FOSTER, b. 15 Feb 1749/50; d. at Concord, NH, 7 Feb 1825; m. at Andover, 23 Dec 1773, TIMOTHY BRADLEY b. at Rumford, 30 Oct 1743 son of Timothy and Abiah (Stevens) Bradley; Timothy d. 31 Jul 1811 at Concord (will 27 May 1811).

65) JOSEPH ABBOT *(John³, John², George¹)*, b. 24 Apr 1719 son of John and Elizabeth (Harnden) Abbot; d. 30 Jan 1790 at Chester, MA; m. 12 Nov 1741 his first cousin, HANNAH ABBOTT *(Ebenezer³, John², George¹)*, b. 29 Dec 1721 daughter of Ebenezer and Hannah (Turner) Abbott; Hannah d. 2 Jun 1805 at Chester.

After their marriage and the birth of their first child, Joseph and Hannah relocated to the western part of Massachusetts, first in Lancaster and finally in Chester. Their children all married spouses from that general area of the state, and most of the children settled in Chester.

Joseph and Hannah had nine children, the birth of the oldest child recorded at Andover and the remainder recorded at Lancaster.

307) i JOSEPH ABBOTT, b. 29 Mar 1742; d.?; m. at Lancaster, 22 Aug 1774,[174] HANNAH PITSON, b. at Boston, 28 Feb 1740 daughter of James and Rachel (Danforth) Pitson.

308) ii HANNAH ABBOTT, b. 23 Sep 1743; d. at Chester, 2 Mar 1802; m. 27 Sep 1774, as his second wife, JOHN NEWTON PARMENTER, b. at Boston, Sep 1742 son of Benjamin and Elizabeth (Bigelow) Parmenter; John d. 6 Dec 1828. John married Mrs. Dolly Blair 19 Feb 1806. John was first married to Lydia Baldwin.

309) iii ELIZABETH ABBOTT, b. 6 Jul 1746; d.?; m. 31 Jan 1779, JACOB FOWLE, b. at Lancaster, 14 Sep 1749 son of Jacob and Phebe (Osgood) Fowle. Elizabeth Abbott's first cousin once removed, Priscilla Abbott, was the second wife of Jacob Fowle the elder, father of Jacob.

310) iv ABIEL ABBOTT, b. about 1749; d. at Chester, 7 Dec 1831; m. 23 Jan 1783, SARAH MANN, b. 12 Nov 1764 daughter of Nathan and Jane (Fleming) Mann; Sarah d. 22 Mar 1841.

311) v JOHN ABBOTT, b. 8 Oct 1751; d. 1798; m. 4 Feb 1775, LOIS BENNET, b. at Lancaster, 2 Sep 1757 daughter of Elisha and Lois (Wilder) Bennet. Lois seems to have remarried Aaron Bell 31 Jan 1811.

312) vi EBENEZER ABBOTT, b. 14 Oct 1753; d. ; m. 13 Dec 1781, ANNA WRIGHT, b. at Spencer, 23 Feb 1758 daughter of Edward and Tryphena (Hinds) Wright.

vii PHEBE ABBOTT, b. about 1756; there is no further record.

313) viii RELIEF ABBOTT, b. 11 May 1759; d. at Chester, 9 Feb 1817; m. 29 May 1784, JOHN WILLIAMS, b. at Middleborough, 23 Jan 1761 son of Larkin and Anna (Warren) Williams; John d. 28 Mar 1813.

314) ix DOROTHY ABBOTT, b. Dec 1762; d. 8 Mar 1848; m. 28 Dec 1784, ROBERT MOOR, *possibly* the Robert b. at Palmer, 1 May 1760 son of James and Elizabeth (Little) Moor, although there is also a Robert Moor born in Bolton son of John and Rhosanna who has been suggested; the family seems to have relocated to New York; Robert perhaps d. 26 Oct 1810 at Ulster County, New York.[175] It is possible that this family moved on from New York to perhaps Kentucky but that is not yet fully verified.

66) JOSEPH ABBOT *(Joseph³, John², George¹)*, b. 31 May 1724 son of Joseph and Hannah (Allen) Abbot; d. 10 Dec 1766; m. 9 Feb 1748/9 ANNA PEABODY, b. at Boxford 21 Jul 1723 daughter of Jonathan and Alice (Pearl) Peabody; Anna d. 20 May 1766. Joseph married 2nd 1 Nov 1766, EDNA PLATTS, b. 15 Nov 1737 at Bradford; Joseph died just one month after his second marriage.

Joseph Abbott did not leave a will. The estate entered probate 3 February 1767. Edna Abbott, widow, requests that George Abbott be administrator. There are four minor children under the age of 14 and Henry Abbott, Jr. and John Abbott are suggested as guardians. Guardians are named for six children altogether including Anna and Sarah who are over 14. The guardianships are for daughter "Anner", Sarah, Dorcas, Lydia, Huldah, and Joseph.[176]

315) i ANNA ABBOTT, b. 15 Nov 1749; d. at NH perhaps in 1788 (when the estate of widow Anna Stevens was probated); m. 18 Aug 1774, her third cousin, THEODORE STEVENS, b. 20 May 1750 son of John and Mary (Phelps) Stevens.

---

[174] Nourse, *Register of Lancaster, Massachusetts*, p 135

[175] Some of the vital records information is that used by the DAR.

[176] *Essex County, MA: Probate File Papers, 1638-1881. Probate of* Joseph Abbot, 3 Feb 1767, *Case number* 87 and Case number 126 for the guardianships.

316) ii SARAH ABBOTT, b. 14 Sep 1751; d. at Salem 19 Apr 1820; m. 1st 23 Mar 1775, BENJAMIN HERRICK, b. 6 Dec 1752 son of Edward and Mary (Kimball) Herrick; Edward d. by 1782 when his estate was probated. Sarah m. 2nd WILLIAM WHITTIER in 1789.

317) iii LYDIA ABBOTT, b. 23 Oct 1753; d. at Wilton, NH 20 Sep 1826; m. by 1775, SAMUEL LOVEJOY, b. 1750 son of William and Hannah (Evans) Lovejoy; Samuel d. 6 Oct 1801.

318) iv DORCAS ABBOTT, b. 26 Oct 1755; d. at Salem 19 Aug 1821; m. 12 Nov 1780, her fourth cousin, JOSEPH CHANDLER, b. 30 Jan 1753 son of John and Hannah (Phelps) Chandler; Joseph d. 27 Nov 1827.

319) v JOSEPH ABBOTT, b. 16 Feb 1758; d. at Andover, VT 3 May 1835;[177] m. 30 Dec 1784, LUCY KING, b. 18 May 1760 daughter of Richard and Lucy (Butterfield) King; Lucy d. at Andover, VT 2 Nov 1842.

320) vi HULDAH ABBOTT, b. 21 Oct 1760; d. 6 Apr 1830 at Roxbury, NH; m. by 1785, her third cousin and George Abbott descendant, JOSHUA ABBOTT, b. at Wilton, NH, 5 Nov 1765 son of Joseph and Mary (Barker) Abbott; Joshua d. 30 Nov 1798. Huldah m. 2nd Gideon Phillips.

67) EPHRAIM ABBOTT *(Stephen³, John², George¹)*, b. 1710 son of Stephen and Sarah (Stevens) Abbott; d. 14 Apr 1745; m. 14 Feb 1733/4 HANNAH PHELPS, b. 1709 (est. based on age at death) daughter of Samuel and Hannah (Dane) Phelps. Hannah m. 2nd John Chandler; Hannah d. 5 Aug 1781.

Ephraim Abbott did not leave a will. His estate entered probate 10 June 1745. Hannah Abbott and Stephen Abbott, Jr. serve as administrators. The available probate records include an inventory and then multiple receipts for payments made to creditors of the estate.[178]

Ephraim Abbott and Hannah Phelps had seven children born at Andover.

i HANNAH ABBOTT, b. 26 Dec 1734; d. 17 Nov 1798; Hannah did not marry. Her grave has the following inscription: In memory of Miss HANNAH ABBOT, who died 17 Nov. 1798. Aged 64 years. *Death thou hast concord me, I by thy dart are slain, But Christ has concord thee, And I shall rise again.*[179]

321) ii MEHITABLE ABBOTT, b. 11 Aug 1736; d. 1 Jan 1777; m. about 1762, her third cousin and George Abbott descendant, JONATHAN ABBOTT, b. at Lunenburg, 29 Aug 1740 son of Jonathan and Martha (Lovejoy) Abbott. Jonathan m. 2nd, another cousin, DORCAS ABBOTT, b. 23 Sep 1758 daughter of Stephen and Mary (Abbott) Abbott; Jonathan d. 26 Dec 1821.

iii SARAH ABBOTT, b. Nov 1737, d. 20 Mar 1831; Sarah did not marry. As reported in the Abbott genealogy, she lived with Judge Phillips and after his death took care of his farm and orchards.[180] She did leave a will in which she has bequests for her numerous nieces and nephews.

iv EPHRAIM ABBOTT, b. 22 Jun 1739; d. 3 Nov 1739.

322) v RHODA ABBOTT, b. 22 Jun 1741; d. 12 Jan 1821 at Albany, ME; m. 22 Mar 1764, JACOB HOLT, b. 29 Mar 1739 son of Jacob and Mary (Osgood) Holt; Jacob d. 12 May 1816.

vi EPHRAIM ABBOTT, b. 8 May 1743; d. 23 Apr 1809; m. 1st 27 Aug 1774, LYDIA POOR, b. 18 Jul 1751 daughter of Timothy and Mary (Stevens) Poor; Lydia d. 3 Jul 1788. Ephraim m. 2nd 26 Aug 1789, SARAH who was the widow of Thomas Safford, and she was the widow Sarah Lasser when she married Thomas Safford. It is possible, but not yet determined, that her maiden name was Herrick and that her first husband was John Lacer. Ephraim does not seem to have had children. In his will, he left his entire estate to his wife Sarah.

323) vii ABIEL ABBOTT (f), b. 14 Apr 1745; d. May 1795; m. 1st, 4 Apr 1763, BENJAMIN WALKER, b. at Billerica 6 Aug 1741 son of Benjamin and Hannah (Frost) Walker. Benjamin was wounded at the Battle of Bunker Hill, taken prisoner, and died in prison at Boston Aug 1775. Abiel m. 2nd 23 Apr 1778, as his second wife, SAMUEL FITCH, b. 9 Nov 1736 son of Jeremiah and Elizabeth (-) Fitch; Samuel Fitch d. 21 Jul 1809.

---

[177] Vermont, Vital Records, 1720-1908 (ancestry.com)

[178] *Essex County, MA: Probate File Papers, 1638-1881. Probate of* Ephraim Abbott, 10 Jun 1745, *Case number* 40.

[179] The Essex Antiquarian, 1898, Andover Inscriptions, Old South Burying Ground.

[180] Abbot and Abbot, *Genealogical Register of Descendants.*

68) MARY ABBOTT *(Stephen³, John², George¹)*, b. 4 Aug 1713 daughter of Stephen and Sarah (Stevens) Abbott; d. at Lunenburg 5 Aug 1748; m. 14 Aug 1742, JOSEPH HOLT, b. 28 Feb 1715/6 son of Thomas and Alice (Peabody) Holt. Joseph m. 2nd Dorcas Boynton (widow of Thomas Frost); Joseph d. at Lunenburg 1754 (based on date of probate 26 Sep 1754).

Joseph Holt wrote his will 16 February 1754. Dearly beloved wife Dorcas receives the improvements on the farm, house, and barn. This full use of the family homestead is just until the youngest son, Joseph Holt, is 7 years 4 months old, and that is with the provision that she keeps the house, barn, and fence in good repair and keeps the brush cut down. After Joseph reaches seven years old, she will have improvements on one-third of the property. Dorcas does receive all the livestock, husbandry tools, smith tools, smith shop, and household items for her use forever except what is bequeathed to the daughters Mary Holt and Sarah Holt. Because of this bequest, Dorcas is obliged to pay all his debts. Dorcas is also to pay her daughter Dorcas Frost three pounds six shillings for services she has provided to the family and a small payment to Joseph's brother Daniel Holt. Dorcas also needs to care for the sons Abiel and Joseph until the age of seven years. Sons Abiel and Joseph receive two-thirds of the real estate after Joseph reaches the age of seven. His two daughters, Mary and Sarah, receive household items and some clothing items that belonged to their mother which are currently in the care of Stephen Abbott in Andover. His books are to be equally divided among his four children. Dorcas and Joseph's brother Thomas Holt are named executors.[181] Of the children mentioned in the will, Mary, Sarah, and Abiel are from the marriage of Joseph Holt and Mary Abbott. Joseph Holt is the son of Joseph Holt and Dorcas Boynton. Dorcas Frost is the daughter of Thomas Frost and Dorcas Boynton.

Mary Abbott and Joseph Holt had four children all born at Lunenburg.

i JOSEPH HOLT, b. 4 Apr 1744; d. in infancy.

324) ii MARY HOLT, b. 17 Aug 1745; m. 26 Jun 1766, BENJAMIN DARLING, b. 28 Apr 1728 son of John and Lois (Gowing) Darling; Benjamin d. at Lunenburg, about 1783 based on date of probate.

iii SARAH HOLT, baptized 14 Dec 1746; m. 1 Feb 1767, BARNABAS WOOD.

325) iv ABIEL HOLT, b. 14 Jul 1748; d. at Temple, NH, 7 Jan 1811; m. 25 Nov 1773, his third cousin once removed and George Abbott descendant, SARAH ABBOTT, b. at Suncook, 1751 daughter of Job and Sarah (Abbott) Abbott; Sarah d. 9 Oct 1854 (age at death inscribed as 103 years, 2 months, 25 days on her gravestone).[182]

69) STEPHEN ABBOT *(Stephen³, John², George¹)*, b. 2 Mar 1717/8 son of Stephen and Sarah (Stevens) Abbott; d. 8 Nov 1768; m. 24 May 1743, MARY ABBOTT *(George³, George², George¹)*, his second cousin, b. 12 Mar 1722/3 daughter of George and Mary (Phillips) Abbott. Mary m. 2nd as his second wife, her second cousin JONATHAN ABBOTT (*Jonathan³, Benjamin², George¹*) son of Jonathan and Zerviah (Holt) Abbott; Mary d. 8 Aug 1792.

Stephen lived on his father's homestead in Andover. He died at the young age of 51 leaving his wife with 10 children ranging in age from 2 years to 24 years. Stephen Abbott did not leave a will. His estate entered probate 6 February 1769. Widow Mary declined being administrator of the estate and asked that George Abbott, Esq. be appointed. One-third of the estate was set aside for support of the widow. As part of the settlement of the estate, £100 was received by Jonathan Fisk the husband of Deborah. In an agreement dated 3 March 1772, Jonathan Fisk is to disburse payments of £20 to each of the following heirs: Jonathan Fisk as the right of his wife Deborah, Sarah Abbot, George Abbot, Abner Abbot, and Elizabeth Abbot. On 3 March 1772, a similar agreement included Stephen Abbot as receiving a £100 settlement and he is to make payments of £20 payments to Mary Abbot, Hannah Abbot, and Dorcas Abbot.

In an undated document with the probate file, Mary Abbot, now the wife of Jonathan Abbot, petitions that her one-third dower portion be released for sale with the remainder of the estate so that debts can be paid and there can be a settlement for the children. More than one-third of Stephen Abbot's estate was needed to pay his debts. "The remainder of the real estate is thrown into such an unhappy situation, it will not sell for what it is judged to be worth except the said dower might be sold with the same, and as her said Mary's other children by her said deceased husband stand in need of their respective parts of the remainder of said estate above mentioned. . . you petitioners viz. the said Mary and her son Stephen pray your Honor would empower them to make sale of said thirds."[183] It is likely that this petition is just prior to the settlement payments to the children in 1772.

In 1770, Mary remarried to Jonathan Abbott who was also widowed in 1768. Stephen and Mary had eleven children all born at Andover. Two children died in early childhood.

i MARY ABBOTT, b. 8 Mar 1743/4; d. 15 Sep 1820. Mary did not marry. She was called "Aunt Molly" and cared for the sick in Andover.

---

[181] *Worcester County, MA: Probate File Papers, 1731-1881*, Probate of Joseph Holt, 26 Sep 1754, Case number 30653.

[182] Findagrave.com

[183] *Essex County, MA: Probate File Papers, 1638-1881. Probate of* Stephen Abbott, 6 Feb 1769, *Case number* 133.

326) ii DEBORAH ABBOTT, b. 13 Oct 1745; d. after 1804 (husband's probate); m. 19 Sep 1766, JONATHAN FISKE; Jonathan d. at Groton about 1804 (date of probate). Births of two children are recorded at Andover and one at Groton.

327) iii SARAH ABBOTT, b. 1 Aug 1747; d. 8 Jul 1824; m. 7 Jul 1772, JOSEPH STEVENS, baptized at Boston, Oct 1750 son of Joseph and Hephzibah (Baker) Stevens; Joseph d. 20 Feb 1803.

328) iv STEPHEN ABBOTT, b. 1 Aug 1749; d. at Salem, 9 Aug 1813; m. 1st SARAH CROWELL, b. at Salem, Dec 1750 daughter of William and Sarah (Stone) Crowell; Sarah d. 14 Apr 1805. Stephen m. 2nd 5 Nov 1805, MARY BADGER of Dunstable, NH; Mary still living at the time of Stephen's probate in 1813.

v ABNER ABBOTT, b. 26 Aug 1751; d. 11 Mar 1758.

vi HANNAH ABBOTT, b. 10 Aug 1753; was living in 1769 when guardian appointed (over 14 years of age) and is still mentioned in the probate records in 1772 as Hannah Abbot. She might have married, but there is not an obvious marriage for her and no death record as Hannah Abbot that would fit.

329) vii GEORGE ABBOTT, b. 13 Jun 1756; d. likely in NH; m. 1 Apr 1779, REBECCA BLANCHARD, b. at Billerica, 1754 daughter of Simon and Rebekah (Sheldon) Blanchard.

321) viii DORCAS ABBOTT, b. 23 Sep 1758; d. 3 Mar 1844; m. 17 Dec 1778 as his second wife, her third cousin, JONATHAN ABBOTT, b. 29 Aug 1740 son of Jonathan and Martha (Lovejoy) Abbott. Jonathan's first wife was another cousin, Mehitable Abbott. Jonathan d. 26 Dec 1821.

330) ix ABNER ABBOTT, b. 29 Jan 1761; d. at Albany, ME, Sep 1833; m. 29 Jan 1784, RUTH HOLT, b. 25 Feb 1765 daughter of Joseph and Ruth (Johnson) Holt; Ruth d. 17 Nov 1806. Abner m. 2nd, DORCAS NASON, b. 1773 and d. 19 Jul 1862.

x SAMUEL ABBOTT, b. Apr 1763; d. 10 Aug 1769. Samuel was killed by a cart. The following inscription is on his gravestone: *Tho' sudden was the stroke, Which stopt his vital breath, He must obey, twas God who spoke, and yield to cruel death.*[184]

331) xi ELIZABETH ABBOTT, b. 22 Oct 1766; d. at Salem 19 Sep 1833; m. 27 Sep 1788, ABRAHAM VALPEY, b. 1766 (based on age at time of death) son of Richard and Hannah (Ives) Valpey; Abraham d. at Ipswich 26 Feb 1848.

70) SAMUEL ABBOT *(Stephen³, John², George¹)*, b. 23 Jun 1726 son of Stephen and Sarah (Stevens) Abbott; d. 1758 at Ft. George, NY during the French and Indian War; m. 14 Dec 1754, ELIZABETH WYMAN probably born about 1730, described as "of Pelham" but no further information has been located on her origins. Elizabeth m. 2nd Joseph Dane; Elizabeth d. 26 Sep 1778.

Samuel Abbot died at age 31 in 1758 near Lake George during the French and Indian Wars. Elizabeth was left with two young children. Elizabeth married Joseph Dane as the second of his three wives. She and Joseph had three children. Elizabeth died at age 57.

Samuel Abbot did not leave a will and his estate entered probate 4 December 1758. Widow Elizabeth was administrator of the estate. There is an accounting as administrator 27 April 1767 which she signs as Elizabeth Dane along with Joseph Dane.[185]

Samuel Abbot and Elizabeth Wyman had two children whose births are recorded at Andover.

332) i ELIZABETH ABBOTT, b. 2 Nov 1755; d. 28 Oct 1815; m. 15 Feb 1780, EBENEZER JONES, b. 1757 son of Jacob and Mary (Winn) Jones; Ebenezer m. 2nd 2 Dec 1819, Dorcas Dane, b. 1769 daughter of Joseph and Elizabeth (Wyman) Dane; Ebenezer d. 24 Aug 1832. Ebenezer's two wives, Dorcas Dane and Elizabeth Abbott, were half-sisters.

333) ii HANNAH ABBOTT, b. 24 Apr 1757; d. 31 Dec 1837; m. 24 Apr 1777, BENJAMIN GOLDSMITH, b. at Ipswich, 1755 son of William and Hannah (Burnham) Goldsmith; Benjamin d. 5 Apr 1817.

---

[184] Essex Antiquarian, 1898, Andover Inscriptions, Old South Burying Yard

[185] *Essex County, MA: Probate File Papers, 1638-1881. Probate of* Samuel Abbot, 4 Dec 1758, *Case number* 122.

71) SARAH CHANDLER *(Sarah Abbott Chandler[3], John[2], George[1]* **and** *Zebadiah Chandler[3], Hannah Abbott Chandler[2], George[1])*, b. 1707 (based on age at time of death) daughter of Zebadiah and Sarah (Abbott) Chandler; d. 28 Mar 1768; m. 18 Feb 1728/9, JOSHUA CHANDLER *(John Chandler[3], Hannah Abbott Chandler[2], George[1])*, her first cousin, b. 1705 son of John and Hannah (Frye) Chandler; Joshua d. 24 Mar 1734; Sarah did not remarry.

Joshua did not leave a will. His estate entered probate 26 April 1734. The total value of the estate available for disbursement to the heirs was £85. One-third, £28 was paid to the widow, £38 as the double portion to the older son Zebadiah Chandler, and £19 to son Joshua Chandler.[186]

334) i ZEBADIAH CHANDLER, b. 23 May 1729; d. 30 Jun 1775; m. 19 Jun 1750, DEBORAH BLANCHARD, baptized Nov 1727 daughter of Stephen and Deborah (Phelps) Blanchard; Deborah d. May 1799.

335) ii JOSHUA CHANDLER, b. 23 Jul 1732; d. 15 Mar 1807; m. 31 Mar 1757, his first cousin and George Abbott descendant, HANNAH CHANDLER, b. 20 May 1735 daughter of Nathan and Priscilla (Holt) Chandler; Hannah d. 14 Feb 1791. Joshua m. 2nd 7 Jun 1792, his first cousin (and George Abbott descendant), HANNAH BALLARD (the widow of Obadiah Foster); Hannah Ballard b. 6 Dec 1748 daughter of Hezekiah and Lydia (Chandler) Ballard; Hannah Ballard d. 22 Dec 1838.

72) JOANNA CHANDLER *(Sarah Abbott Chandler[3], John[2], George[1]* **and** *Zebadiah Chandler[3], Hannah Abbott Chandler[2], George[1])*, b. 1710 (based on age at time of death) daughter of Zebadiah and Sarah (Abbott) Chandler; d. 12 Sep 1791; m. 3 Jun 1728, JOSEPH SHATTUCK, b. 1707 (based on age at time of death); Joseph d. 21 Mar 1772.

Joseph and Joanna Shattuck lived in West Parrish of Andover. Joseph had a farm, part of which he had purchased from his father-in-law Zebadiah Chandler.[187][188] There is some uncertainty about his parentage and a couple of different families have been suggested but without confirming information.

In his will written 6 Jun 1761, Joseph has bequests for the following persons: well beloved wife Joanna, son Joseph, son Isaac, son Zebadiah, daughter Hannah the wife of Samuel Stevens, daughter Sarah the wife of John Barnard, daughter Mary who is single and not yet 21, and grandson Joseph Shattuck. His estate was valued at £232.[189]

Joanna and Joseph had nine children born at Andover.

336) i HANNAH SHATTUCK, b. 14 Jul 1729; death record not found; m. 18 Oct 1753, SAMUEL STEVENS, b. at Methuen, 27 Aug 1730 son of Samuel and Phebe (Bodwell) Stevens; Samuel d. 10 Aug 1810.

337) ii JOSEPH SHATTUCK, b. 27 Nov 1731; d. 9 Apr 1778; m. 13 Apr 1765, ANNA JOHNSON, b. at Haverhill, 6 Apr 1737 daughter of Cornelius and Lydia (Clement) Johnson; Anna reported to have died at Hillsborough.[190]

338) iii ISAAC SHATTUCK, b. 24 Mar 1733/4; d. 27 Apr 1822; m. 24 Mar 1757, MARY BARNARD, b. 4 Dec 1739 daughter of Nathaniel and Ruth (Preston) Barnard; Mary d. 2 Jun 1804.

295) iv ZEBADIAH SHATTUCK, b. 26 Oct 1736; d. 10 Mar 1826; m. 1st 30 Aug 1759, his second cousin (and George Abbott descendant) ELIZABETH ABBOTT, b. 2 Nov 1740 daughter of Barachias and Hannah (Holt) Abbott; Elizabeth d. 9 Sep 1780. Zebadiah m. 2nd 25 Jul 1781, his first cousin once removed (and George Abbott descendant), SARAH CHANDLER, b. 8 May 1751 daughter of Zebadiah and Deborah (Blanchard) Chandler.

339) v SARAH SHATTUCK, b. 9 Apr 1739; d. 9 Jan 1832; m. 6 Jan 1757, JOHN BARNARD, b. 8 May 1728 son of John and Sarah (Osgood) Barnard; John d. 27 Feb 1802.

vi ABIEL SHATTUCK, b. 25 Nov 1741; d. 12 Nov 1742.

340) vii MARY SHATTUCK, b. 13 Jul 1743; d. at Andover about 1815 (probate Feb 1816); m. 17 Oct 1765, THOMAS PHELPS, b. 1 Jun 1739 son of Thomas and Prudence (Wyman) Phelps; Thomas d. 28 May 1795.

viii ELIZABETH SHATTUCK, birth not found; d. 16 Dec 1747.

ix ELIZABETH SHATTUCK, b. 9 Oct 1749; d. 11 Mar 1753.

---

[186] *Essex County, MA: Probate File Papers, 1638-1881. Probate of* Joshua Chandler, 26 Apr 1734, *Case number* 4953.

[187] Chandler, *Descendants of William and Annis Chandler*, p 159

[188] Shattuck, *Memorials of the Descendants of William Shattuck*, pp 104-105

[189] *Essex County, MA: Probate File Papers, 1638-1881. Probate of* Joseph Shattuck, 7 Apr 1772, *Case number* 25124.

[190] Chandler, *The Descendants of William and Annis Chandler*

73) PRISCILLA CHANDLER *(Sarah Abbott Chandler*^{3}*, John*^{2}*, George*^{1} ***and*** *Zebadiah Chandler*^{3}*, Hannah Abbott Chandler*^{2}*, George*^{1}*)*, b. 26 Apr 1713 daughter of Zebadiah and Sarah (Abbott) Chandler; d. 4 Jan 1778; m. 29 Jan 1735/6, SAMUEL PHELPS, b. 5 Feb 1712/3 son of Samuel and Hannah (Dane) Phelps; Samuel d. 17 Apr 1795.

Samuel wrote his will 9 August 1775, 20 years before his death. In his will, he made bequests to the following persons: Prisilla dearly beloved wife (who died in 1778), beloved son Joshua, beloved son Henry, beloved daughter Hannah Moar wife of Benjamin Moar, and beloved daughter Prisilla Dane wife of Philemon Dane. His books are to be divided among his four children.[191]

Samuel and Priscilla had five children all born at Andover.

i SAMUEL PHELPS, b. 21 Oct 1736; d. 18 Oct 1756 at Lake George during the French and Indian War.

341) ii JOSHUA PHELPS, b. 25 Jun 1738; d. 22 Dec 1798; m. 17 Feb 1767, his second cousin (and George Abbott descendant), LOIS BALLARD, b. 19 Jul 1746 daughter of Hezekiah and Lydia (Chandler) Ballard; Lois d. 21 Dec 1836.

342) iii HENRY PHELPS, b. 5 Sep 1740; d. 31 Oct 1807; m. 31 Oct 1780, MARY BALLARD (also a George Abbott descendant), b. 27 Feb 1750/1 daughter of Hezekiah and Lydia (Chandler) Ballard; Mary d. 11 Aug 1835.

343) iv HANNAH PHELPS, b. 5 May 1745; d. 1826 at Lewiston, ME; m. 29 Sep 1767, BENJAMIN MOOAR, b. 28 Oct 1743 son of Benjamin and Abijah (Hill) Mooar; Benjamin d. 15 Aug 1828 at Lewiston.

344) v PRISCILLA PHELPS, b. 10 May 1748; d. 9 Sep 1799; m. 11 Jul 1769, her second cousin, PHILEMON DANE, b. 2 Feb 1741/2 son of John and Elizabeth (Chandler) Dane. Philemon m. 2nd 29 Jan 1801, widow Sarah Foster of Tewksbury; Philemon d. 13 May 1816.

74) MEHITABLE CHANDLER *(Sarah Abbott Chandler*^{3}*, John*^{2}*, George*^{1} ***and*** *Zebadiah Chandler*^{3}*, Hannah Abbott Chandler*^{2}*, George*^{1}*)*, b. 1717 daughter of Zebadiah and Sarah (Abbott) Chandler; d. 26 Jan 1786 (reported, but no record found); m. 26 Jan 1738, CALEB LOVEJOY, b. 28 Dec 1716 son of Henry and Sarah (Farnum) Lovejoy; the family relocated to Suncook, NH. Caleb reported to have died there 1781 (this is the date used by the Daughters of the American Revolution).

Six children have been located for this family. The primary information comes from the History of Pembroke, New Hampshire.[192]

345) i ELIZABETH LOVEJOY, b. 1738; d. after 1810 at Bow, NH;[193] m. about 1766, JOHN ROBERTSON, b. at Londonderry, 9 Jun 1732 son of Samuel and Margaret (Woodend) Robertson; John d. at Bow, NH 11 Oct 1816.

346) ii MEHITABLE LOVEJOY, b. 1745; d. 2 Mar 1835 at Allenstown, NH; m. JONATHAN HUTCHINSON, b. 20 Mar 1747 son of Jonathan and Theodate (Morrill) Hutchinson; Jonathan d. at Pembroke, 3 May 1830.

347) iii CALEB LOVEJOY, b. 1749; d. 1821 (estate probate 7 Sep 1821);[194] m. MEHITABLE KIMBALL. Caleb m. 2nd JEMIMA JUDKINS; Jemima d. 15 Sep 1853.

348) iv JERUSHA LOVEJOY, b. 5 Oct 1753; d. at Pembroke, 11 Oct 1841; m. 6 Jun 1775, JOHN LADD, b. at Kingston, 6 Jan 1755 son of Trueworthy and Lydia (Harriman) Ladd; John d. 8 Jun 1835.

349) v MARTHA LOVEJOY, b. about 1760 at Pembroke, NH; death record not found; m. at Pembroke, 21 May 1781, her third cousin (and George Abbott descendant) JOHN PARKER, b. 15 Aug 1760 son of Joseph and Hannah (Abbott) Parker; John d. at Pembroke 27 May 1825.

350) vi OBADIAH LOVEJOY, b. 1756; he is reported to have been in the Battle of Bunker Hill and is believed to have died while serving in the Army.[195] But the Lovejoy book says he married Tryphena Waugh.[196] More research needs to be done.

---

[191] *Essex County, MA: Probate File Papers, 1638-1881. Probate of* Samuel Phelps, 23 Jul 1795, *Case number* 21658.

[192] Carter and Fowler, *History of Pembroke, NH*

[193] She appears to still be living at the 1810 Census as a woman in her age category is in the household headed by John Robertson.

[194] Caleb's brothers-in-law Jonathan Hutchinson and John Ladd participate in the administration of the estate in addition to widow Jemima.

[195] Carter and Fowler, *The History of Pembroke, NH*

[196] Lovejoy, *The Lovejoy Genealogy*, p 105

vii Daughter, name not known who married John Moor of Pembroke the son of James and Agnes (Colbreath) Moor. This is a daughter listed in the Lovejoy Genealogy (p 74) and the History of Pembroke but her name is not yet found. However, the children that the History of Pembroke assigned to John Moor and the unknown daughter Lovejoy have birth records that list a mother's name as Martha. As Martha Lovejoy from this family married John Parker, it is not clear how all this disparate information fits together. This is most likely just a misidentification of the wife of John Moor.

75) ELIZABETH CHANDLER *(Sarah Abbott Chandler³, John², George¹* ***and*** *Zebadiah Chandler³, Hannah Abbott Chandler², George¹)*, b. 5 Feb 1721 daughter of Zebadiah and Sarah (Abbott) Chandler; d. probably in NH, date unknown; m. 26 Mar 1741, DAVID LOVEJOY, b. 10 Oct 1715 son of Henry and Sarah (Farnum) Lovejoy; the family relocated to Suncook, NH; the DAR gives the death date of David as 18 Feb 1819, although I believe this to be the death date of a different David Lovejoy.

According to the History of Pembroke, NH, David Lovejoy came to Pembroke between 1738 and 1740.[197] The births of eleven children were reported at Pembroke.

351) i ELIZABETH LOVEJOY, b. 10 Jan 1742; d. at Pembroke, 11 Apr 1815; m. 12 Jan 1764, JEREMIAH MORGAN, b. at Pembroke, 18 Aug 1741 son of Luther and Abigail (-) Morgan; Jeremiah d. 21 Jul 1819.

ii CHANDLER LOVEJOY, b. 9 Apr 1744; d. 15 Jul 1810; m. 9 Mar 1809, ABIGAIL DAVIS, Abigail d. 23 Mar 1831; there are no known children.

iii PRISCILLA LOVEJOY; b. 12 Mar 1746; d. 14 Apr 1832; Priscilla does not seem to have married.

352) iv MOLLY LOVEJOY, b. 29 Apr 1748; d. at Salisbury, NH, 23 Feb 1813; m. 21 Nov 1769, JEREMIAH WARDWELL, b. at Andover 6 Dec 1748 son of Thomas and Abigail (Gray) Wardwell; Jeremiah d. 9 Jan 1817. Jeremiah remarried to Betsy after the death of Molly.

353) v ABIGAIL LOVEJOY, b. 12 Sep 1750; d. 18 Mar 1833; m. about 1770, her third cousin once removed, DANIEL HOLT, b. at Pembroke 14 Sep 1744 son of Benjamin and Sarah (Frye) Holt; Daniel d. 5 Dec 1813.

vi MARTHA LOVEJOY, b. 16 Aug 1752; no further record was found for Martha.

354) vii PHEBE LOVEJOY, b. 28 Sep 1754; d. at Pembroke, Jun 1804; m. Feb 1779, NATHANIEL AMBROSE,[198] b. about 1752 (based on age at time of death). Nathaniel m. 2nd Elizabeth (-); Nathaniel d. 24 Mar 1835 at Deerfield, NH.[199]

355) viii OLIVE LOVEJOY, b. 13 Nov 1756; d. Feb 1843; m. 6 Mar 1781, THOMAS KIMBALL, b. at Andover, 17 Jul 1753 son of Thomas and Penelope (Johnson) Kimball; Thomas d. 20 Oct 1825.

356) ix DORCAS LOVEJOY, b. 1 Oct 1758; d. 1828 in Ohio; m. 28 Jan 1783, BENJAMIN MILLS, b. at Plaistow, NH, 30 Dec 1755 son of Reuben and Mary (Howard) Mills; Benjamin d. at Scioto County, OH, 15 Jul 1829.

357) x ESTHER LOVEJOY, b. 8 Mar 1764; d. likely in Vermont; m. 25 Aug 1792, AMOS LAKEMAN, b. at Bradford, 7 Jan 1762 son of Samuel ad Margaret (Kimball) Lakeman; Amos d. at Woodbury, VT 20 Dec 1850.

xi DAVID LOVEJOY, b. 16 Sep 1767; d. perhaps 1819; m. 16 Sep 1790, JANE COCHRAN, b, 1766 daughter of William and Betsy (Gile) Cochran;[200] Jane d. 28 Oct 1844. David and Jane did not have children.

76) SARAH ABBOTT *(Ephraim³, John², George¹)*, b. 25 Jan 1715/6 daughter of Ephraim and Sarah (Crosby) Abbott; d. at NH; m. 8 Sep 1736, SAMUEL GRAY, b. Jul 1711 son of Henry and Mary (Blunt) Gray; Samuel d. 3 Oct 1769 at Amherst, NH.[201]

Sarah and Samuel married in Andover and their first child was born there. They then moved on to New Hampshire, and the births of three children are recorded at Rumford. Samuel had some property in Pembroke that he sold to Moses Foster in 1742.[202] They settled in Amherst, New Hampshire.

No probate record was located for Samuel. Of the four children for whom there are birth records, three died in early childhood.

---

[197] Carter and Fowler, *History of Pembroke*, p 243

[198] Goodhue, *History and Genealogy of the Goodhue Family*. The Goodhue Family genealogy suggests parents as Jonathan and Abigail (Goodhue) Ambrose. The Pembroke, NH history suggests parent is Robert Ambrose.

[199] Nathaniel Ambrose's will was written 17 Mar 1835 and entered probate April 1835.

[200] Carter and Fowler, *History of Pembroke*, p. 36

[201] Secomb, *History of the Town of Amherst*, p. 667.

[202] Carter and Fowler, *History of Pembroke*, p. 98.

i SAMUEL GRAY, b. 11 Jan 1736/7; d. 15 Dec 1737.

ii SARAH GRAY, b. 25 Jan 1739; d. 10 May 1740.

iii SARAH GRAY, b. 16 Mar 1741; d. 4 Sep 1746.

358) iv MARY GRAY, b. 29 Dec 1743; d. at Amherst, NH 19 Oct 1775; m. at Amherst, 3 Dec 1762, MOSES TOWNE, b. at Topsfield, May 1739 son of Israel and Grace (Gardner) Towne; Moses d. at Milford, NH 9 Feb 1824.

77) EPHRAIM ABBOT *(Ephraim³, John², George¹)*, b. 22 Jul 1718 son of Ephraim and Sarah (Crosby) Abbott; d. abt. 1775 at Amherst, NH; m. 1st, 3 Nov 1740 his second cousin MARY ABBOTT *(Timothy³, Timothy², George¹)*, b. 7 Jan 1723/4 daughter of Timothy and Mary (Foster) Abbott; Mary d. 9 Mar 1744. Ephraim m. 2nd at Ipswich, 1 Feb 1745/6, MARY KNEELAND,[203] *possibly* b. at Topsfield, May 1721 daughter of Philip and Martha (Graves) Kneeland; death is not known but likely at Amherst, NH.

Ephraim Abbot and Mary Abbott had three children all born at Andover.

359) i MARY ABBOTT, b. 11 Mar 1741; d.?; m. 9 Dec 1762, PETER GOSS, b. at Bradford, 17 Jun 1737 son of John and Mehitable (Bailey) Goss.

360) ii EPHRAIM ABBOTT, b. 5 Dec 1742; d. 1827 at Bedford, NH; m. by 1765, DOROTHY STILES, b. 2 Sep 1740 daughter of Caleb and Sarah (Walton) Stiles.

361) iii HANNAH ABBOTT, b. 1 Mar 1744; d. unknown; m. NATHANIEL SHATTUCK; the information I have so far is a guess. Nathaniel Shattuck and a wife Hannah had two children in Hollis. There is a Nathaniel Shattuck married to Catherine Andrews and they have children in Temple starting in 1774, but I think that is a different Nathaniel. There is another Nathaniel Shattuck born in Hollis and later in Groton who married Eunice Hazen. The Abbot genealogy gives the name of Hannah's husband as ______ Shattuck and I cannot locate a record.

The children of Ephraim Abbott and Mary Kneeland were all born at Amherst, NH.

362) i KNEELAND ABBOTT, b. 17 May 1748; m. BETSEY STANLEY; relocated to Vermont.

363) ii SARAH ABBOTT, b. 14 Jun 1751; d. at Hillsborough, 22 Jan 1811; m. by 1775, WILLIAM CODMAN, b. 1748 son of William and Sarah (Wilkins) Codman; William d. 9 Nov 1813.

364) iii DORCAS ABBOTT, b. 7 Aug 1752; she is perhaps the Dorcas Wiley who died at Landgrove, VT in 1823; m. JOHN WILLEY.

365) iv ESTHER ABBOTT, b. 6 Mar 1755; d. likely at Montpelier, VT; m. 13 Dec 1781, BENJAMIN PIKE.

366) v ABIGAIL ABBOTT, b. 30 Jul 1756; d. 1852 at New Boston, NH; m. 25 Apr 1781, SAMUEL TWISS, b. at Tewksbury, 31 Jan 1755 son of John and Sarah (Patten) Twiss; Samuel d. at New Boston, NH, Oct 1799.

367) vi DANIEL ABBOTT, b. 1 Apr 1762; d. likely at Cavendish, VT; m. 28 Jul 1786, SARAH STEVENS possibly the daughter of Samuel and Rebecca (Stiles) Stevens.

78) MARY ABBOTT *(Ephraim³, John², George¹)*, b. Jul 1720 daughter of Ephraim and Sarah (Crosby) Abbott; date of death unknown but likely in Amherst, NH before 1792;[204] m. 11 May 1743, ROBERT READ, b. 25 Dec 1720 at Chelmsford son of William and Hannah (Bates) Read; Robert. Robert m. 2nd 11 Jan 1792, Joanna Danforth;[205] Robert d. at Amherst, NH 11 Sep 1803.[206]

---

[203] The Abiel Abbot and Ephraim Abbot Genealogy gives her name as Hannah Kneeland, but the marriage record says Mary Kneeland and the birth records for each of her children with Ephraim Abbot give the mother's name as Mary. She is possibly Mary Neeland (Kneeland) baptized in Topsfield 21 May 1721 daughter of Philip. Philip died in 1742 and his son Philip relocated to Ipswich which would make it possible that Mary accompanied her brother to Ipswich. Ipswich was the location for the marriage of Ephraim Abbot and Mary Kneeland. This is the identity made in Kneeland's *Seven Centuries in the Kneeland Family*, p. 153

[204] Secomb, *The History of Amherst*, p. 741 reports that Robert Read had a second marriage 11 January 1792 and this is confirmed by record.

[205] "New Hampshire Marriages, 1720-1920," database, *FamilySearch* (https://familysearch.org/ark:/61903/1:1:FDK1-FPD: 31 December 2014), Col. Robert Read and Joana Danforth, 11 Jan 1792; citing reference; FHL microfilm 1,001,296.

[206] His grave site has been located at the Amherst Town Hall Burying Ground and bears this inscription: Erected to the Memory of Col. Robert Read who died Sept. 11, 1803 in the 83 Year of his age. (findagrave.com)

The information for this family has been pieced together in a sketchy fashion from published genealogies and the History of Amherst, New Hampshire. There is consistency among sources in that five children are proposed, and records were located for three of these children. Marriages were located for three of the children. I did not locate a probate record for Robert Read. He relocated his family at least twice, starting in Massachusetts, being for a time in Litchfield, New Hampshire before settling in Amherst, New Hampshire. The information for this family should be considered, for the most part, preliminary.

i LEMUEL READ, b. about 1746; no records found.

ii ROBERT READ, b. at Litchfield 31 May 1748; no record found beyond birth record.

368) iii MARY READ,[207] b. at Litchfield 31 May 1748; d. by 1792 (date of husband's second marriage); m. by about 1775, BENJAMIN BRADFORD of Hillsborough. Benjamin m. 2nd 21 Dec 1792, Mary "Molly" Mc Adams.

369) iv WILLIAM READ, b. 14 Aug 1754; d. at Amherst, NH, 10 Sep 1834;[208] m. 1st BRIDGET GREELEY, b. at Hudson, NH, 3 Feb 1764 daughter of Ezekiel and Eunice (Lovewell) Greeley;[209] Bridget d. at Amherst, 2 Feb 1789. William m. 2nd 26 Jun 1791, ABIGAIL HOWARD, b. 1771 and d. 15 Jun 1852.

370) v OLIVE READ, b. at Hudson, NH, 23 Jul 1757; d. at Wilton, NH, 23 Feb 1811; m. at Nottingham, 8 Nov 1779,[210] SAMUEL GREELEY, b. at Nottingham, 29 Sep 1752 son of Samuel of Abigail (Blodgett) Greeley; Samuel d. 29 Sep 1798.

79) JOSHUA ABBOTT *(Ephraim³, John², George¹)*, b. 25 Sep 1722 son of Ephraim and Sarah (Crosby) Abbott; d. at Amherst, NH after 2 Mar 1772 (the date of his will); m. 7 Jul 1749, PHEBE INGALLS, b. 10 Aug 1730 daughter of Joseph and Phebe (Farnum) Ingalls; Phebe d. after 2 Mar 1772.

In his will dated 2 March 1772, Joshua Abbott orders that all his property (except his household furniture) be sold following his death. One-third of the proceeds is to be set aside for his wife Phebe. His wife is to also have her choice of one of his cows. The remainder of the proceeds are to be divided among his children: oldest son Joshua and other sons Stephen and Peter, with the sons to have £4 more than any of the daughters; daughter Phebe the wife of John Everden; daughters Elizabeth and Sarah are to have equal portions; and the youngest son Joseph to be provided for by the executor from the estate proceeds until he arrives at an age to be bound out as an apprentice. At the age of 21, Joseph will receive a cash payment for his portion.[211]

The birth of oldest daughter, Phebe, is recorded at Andover and the births of ten children are recorded at Amherst, New Hampshire.[212]

371) i PHEBE ABBOTT, b. 31 Aug 1750; m. about 1770, JOHN EVERDEN; the birth of one child for this couple is recorded at Amherst. John Everden seems to have seen service during the Revolution in Colonel Moses Nichols Regiment that marched from New Hampshire to Rhode Island in August 1778.[213] There is a John Everden that died 21 Aug 1837 at Winchester, NH but that may not be him.

ii SARAH ABBOTT, b. 27 Jan 1752; d. 4 Jan 1754.

iii JOSHUA ABBOTT, b. 10 May 1754. The Amherst, NH book[214] has Joshua Abbott marrying a Deborah Chandler, but I cannot find that anywhere else and there is no record of the marriage and I could not locate any possible children.

iv ELIZABETH ABBOTT, b. 12 Nov 1756.

v STEPHEN ABBOTT, b. 29 Sep 1759; m. 8 Aug 1782, SARAH LOVEJOY, b. 7 Nov 1765 daughter of Hezekiah and Hannah (Phelps) Lovejoy.[215] No children have yet been located for this couple and it is not clear where they might have settled.

---

207 Browne, *The History of Hillsborough, 1735-1921*, Volume 2, p 82

208 Date of death is found in his Revolutionary War pension payment index

209 Bridget's parents are confirmed by the 1793 will of Ezekiel Greeley that includes a bequest to Robert Read, Jr. son of William and his late wife Bridget. Robert Read, Jr. received one-third part of Ezekiel's estate.

210 New Hampshire, Marriage Records Index, 1637-1947 (ancestry.com)

211 *New Hampshire Wills and Probate Records 1643-1982*, Will of Joshua Abbot, Hillsborough, 2 Mar 1772.

212 Ancestry.com, *New Hampshire, Births and Christenings Index, 1714-1904* (Provo, UT, USA: Ancestry.com Operations, Inc., 2011).

213 "New Hampshire Revolutionary War Records, 1675-1835," database with images, *FamilySearch* (https://familysearch.org/ark:/61903/1:1:Q242-NWWR: accessed 6 February 2018), John Everden, 05 Aug 1778; citing New Hampshire, United States, Archives and Records Management, Concord.

214 Secomb, *History of the Town of Amherst*, p 478

215 The will of Hezekiah Lovejoy includes a bequest to daughter Sarah wife of Stephen Abbott.

372) vi SARAH ABBOTT, b. 19 Feb 1761; d. about 1848, Crown Point, NY; m. 29 Jan 1782, AARON NICHOLS, born about 1757; d. 13 Oct 1821 at Crown Point, NY.[216]

373) vii PETER ABBOTT, b. 28 Jul 1762; d. unknown but perhaps in NY; m. 23 Oct 1788, ABIGAIL FARNUM, b. at Amherst, 27 Dec 1767 daughter of Joseph and Mary (Lyon) Farnum. The children for this family are recorded in Windham, VT.

viii INFANT ABBOTT, b. and d. 16 Apr 1764.

ix INFANT ABBOTT, b. 3 Apr 1765; infant death.

x INFANT ABBOTT, b. 16 Feb 1767; infant death.

xi JOSEPH ABBOTT, b. 23 Jan 1772.

80) ELIZABETH ABBOTT *(Ephraim^3, John^2, George^1)*, b. 29 Jun 1726 daughter of Ephraim and Sarah (Crosby) Abbott; d. 18 Dec 1819; m. 20 Sep 1744, her second cousin ASA ABBOT *(Timothy^3, Timothy^2, George^1)*, b. 17 Oct 1721 son of Timothy and Mary (Foster) Abbot; Asa d. 22 Dec 1796.

The death record for Asa Abbot relates that he was injured by a blow from an ox's horn in 1791. This injury caused the loss of Asa's eye which brought about "a languishment" from which he ultimately died in 1796. No probate record for Asa Abbot was located.

Elizabeth and Asa had six children whose births are recorded at Andover.

133) i TIMOTHY ABBOTT, b. 4 Jun 1745; d. 22 Mar 1826; m. 2 Jan 1770, his second cousin once removed, SARAH ABBOTT, b. 2 Jan 1749/50 daughter of Isaac and Phebe (Lovejoy) Abbott; Sarah d. 2 Apr 1835. This is family #133 which is more fully covered further down in Generation Four.

374) ii ELIZABETH ABBOTT, b. 21 May 1747; d. by 1802 (when husband married his third wife); m. 30 May 1779 as his 2nd wife, JESSE MANNING, b. at Billerica, 18 Aug 1745 son of Jacob and Martha (Beard) Manning. Jesse m. 3rd Abigail Baldwin; Jesse's first wife was Anne Carleton. Jesse d. at Billerica about 1825 (will probated 1825). There are no children recorded for Elizabeth and Jesse, and the only two children mentioned in his will are from Jesse's first marriage to Anne Carleton.

iii ASA ABBOTT, b. 14 Jun 1749; d. 5 Jun 1763.

375) iv CALEB ABBOTT, b. 28 Oct 1751; d. 12 Apr 1837; m. 21 Jan 1779, LUCY LOVEJOY, b. 3 Aug 1757 daughter of Isaac and Mary (Peavey) Lovejoy; Lucy d. 21 Feb 1802. Caleb m 2nd 18 Nov 1802, his third cousin (and George Abbott descendant), DEBORAH AMES, b. 6 Apr 1768 daughter of Nathan and Deborah (Bowers) Ames. Deborah died 7 Dec 1819. He married for a third time to Hannah Shattuck Clark.

v DANIEL ABBOTT, b. 15 Jun 1754; d. 1776 while serving in the Army. "Daniel, s. Asa, in the Army, __, 1776."

376) vi NATHAN ABBOTT, b. 18 Nov 1756; d. at Billerica 10 Jan 1840; m. at Danvers, 22 May 1785, MARGARET "Peggy" WILSON, b. at Danvers, 25 Sep 1760 daughter of Benjamin and Lydia (Bancroft) Wilson; Margaret d. 21 Dec 1841.

81) JOSIAH ABBOTT *(Ephraim^3, John^2, George^1)*, b. 26 Sep 1728 son of Ephraim and Sarah (Crosby) Abbott; d. Dec 1777 at Lyndeborough, NH; m. by 1755 HANNAH HOBBS, b. at Middleton, 28 Aug 1729 daughter of William and Amme (Towne) Hobbs.[217]

There are eight children in this family for whom there is some evidence.[218] The births of the first seven children are recorded at Amherst, NH; the youngest daughter was likely born at Lyndeborough.

[216] Ancestry.com. *New York Pensioners, 1835* [database on-line]. Provo, UT, USA: Ancestry.com Operations Inc, 1998. Aaron Nichols who served in the Revolution in New Hampshire received a pension beginning 30 Apr 1818 in New York. Aaron Nichols is also head of household in the 1820 Census at Crown Point, Essex, NY.

[217] This identification of the parents of Hannah Hobbs is not proved, but there is circumstantial evidence. There were brothers William and Humphrey Hobbs both living in Middleton. It is known that Humphrey Hobbs relocated to Amherst, NH. It is not known what became of William as there is no death or probate record for him, but it seems reasonable that there could be a relationship established between the Hobbs and Abbott families in Amherst. In addition, two of the children of Josiah and Hannah Abbott were named William and Amy.

[218] Birth records through Ancestry.com. *New Hampshire, Births and Christenings Index, 1714-1904* [database on-line]. Provo, UT, USA: Ancestry.com Operations, Inc., 2011. The birth information for Sarah was obtained through the DAR Ancestor page of Josiah Abbott as no birth record was located for her.

377) i HANNAH ABBOTT, b. 18 Sep 1755; d. at Lyndeborough, NH 25 Sep 1784;[219] m. by 1775, SAMUEL CHAMBERLAIN, b. at Chelmsford, 4 Apr 1745 son of Jonathan and Elizabeth (Cram) Chamberlain. Samuel m. 2nd 8 Nov 1785, Naomi Richardson; Samuel d. about 1812 at Lyndeborough.[220]

ii AMY ABBOTT, b. 5 Jun 1757; d. about 1777.

iii JOSIAH ABBOTT, b. 18 Dec 1759; no further record.

iv WILLIAM ABBOTT, b. 21 Dec 1761; d. 23 Dec 1764.

378) v LEMUEL ABBOTT, b. 13 May 1764; d. at Windham, VT 19 Jan 1840;[221] m. by 1799, DEBORAH BALCH, b. at Dublin, NH, 13 Nov 1780 daughter of Hart and Dorcas (Somers) Balch; Deborah d. 15 Sep 1862.

vi WILLIAM ABBOTT, b. 28 Apr 1766; d. 10 May 1766.

379) vii DANIEL ABBOTT, b. 31 Jul 1769; d. at Westford, MA, 27 Jan 1854; m. 5 Jul 1798, SARAH ALLISON, b. at Londonderry, 12 Dec 1770 daughter of Samuel and Janet (McFarland) Allison; Sarah d. in New York, 22 Nov 1837.[222]

380) viii SARAH ABBOTT, b. 24 Apr 1773; d. at Cameron, NY 12 Jun 1870;[223] m. 19 Feb 1794, ENOCH ORDWAY, b. at Lyndeborough, 4 Aug 1762 son of John and Frances (Chase) Ordway; Enoch d. at Greenwood, NY 8 Jan 1843.

82) EBENEZER ABBOTT *(Ephraim³, John², George¹)*, b. 20 Feb 1731 son of Ephraim and Sarah (Crosby) Abbott; d. 19 Dec 1771; m. 1 Jan 1752, LYDIA FARRINGTON, b. 24 Oct 1735 daughter of John and Sarah (Houghton) Farrington; Lydia deceased by 1786 when her father wrote his will naming his four grandchildren children of Lydia.

Ebenezer did not leave a will. His widow Lydia was administrator of the estate. There are records for seven children all born at Andover.

381) i HANNAH ABBOTT, b. 27 Jun 1752; d. 24 Jul 1816; m. 18 Sep 1777, ABIJAH CLARK, b. 1742 (based on age at time of death); Abijah d. 25 May 1818.

ii LYDIA ABBOTT, b. 18 Jun 1754; d. 10 Jan 1775; m. 26 Dec 1773, PETER TOWNE, b. 10 Aug 1749 son of Nathan and Eunice (-) Towne. Peter m. 2nd Rebecca Sheldon; Peter d. 20 May 1830. Lydia and Peter had one son, Peter, who lived about 10 days and died the day before his mother died.

382) iii EBENEZER ABBOTT, b. 15 Jan 1757; d. at Reading 1803; m. 21 Oct 1783, SARAH GRAVES, b. at Reading, Mar 1765 daughter of Daniel and Sarah (-) Graves; Sarah was living at the time of Ebenezer's will in 1803. Sarah remarried to Lieutenant William Flint in 1804 and died in 1809.

383) iv EPHRAIM ABBOTT, b. 18 Mar 1759; d. 1 Jan 1834 at Sherbrooke, Québec; m. 26 Oct 1781, ESTHER EASTMAN of Conway, ME, b. 6 May 1761 daughter of Richard and Mary (Lovejoy) Eastman; Esther d. at Sherbrooke, Québec 30 Dec 1846.[224]

v JETHRO ABBOTT, b. 18 Apr 1761; d. 2 May 1764.

vi THEODORE ABBOTT, b. 10 Sep 1763; d. 14 May 1764.

384) vii SARAH ABBOTT, b. 7 Dec 1765; d. after 1834 and likely in 1856 in Ohio;[225] m. 28 Dec 1784, her third cousin, DAVID STEVENS, b. 3 Feb 1761 son of Thomas and Sarah (Gray) Stevens; David d. 29 Jan 1834.

---

[219] *New Hampshire: Births, Deaths and Marriages, 1654-1969.* (From microfilmed records. Online database: *AmericanAncestors.org*, New England Historic Genealogical Society, 2014.)

[220] Donovan, *The History of the Town of Lyndeborough, NH*, p. 180

[221] Ancestry.com. Vermont, Vital Records, 1720-1908

[222] Morrison, *A History of the Alison Family*, p 63

[223] In the 1870 U.S. Census, 97-year-old Sarah Ordway was living with her son Daniel and his wife Hannah. Year: 1870; Census Place: Cameron, Steuben, New York; Roll: M593_1094; Page: 506A; Family History Library Film: 552593

[224] Quebec, Canada, Vital and Church Records (Drouin Collection), 1621-1968 (ancestry.com)

[225] Sarah was still living at the time of the probate of her husband's estate. She seems to have traveled to Ohio to live with her son Ebenezer and his wife Lucy Herrick. There is a Sarah Stevens age 85 living with Ebenezer and Lucy Stevens in Springfield, Ohio in the 1850 US. Census. If this is indeed our Sarah (and it seems to be), Sarah died in Ohio in 1856.

83) PETER ABBOTT *(Ephraim^3, John^2, George^1)*, b. 8 May 1734 son of Ephraim and Sarah (Crosby) Abbott; d. 19 Apr 1774 at Kingston, NH; m. 22 Sep 1757, ELIZABETH HOLT (widow of Edmund Damon), b. at Reading, about 1733 daughter of Joseph and Abigail (Rich) Holt; Elizabeth d. after 1774.[226]

This was a family beset by tragedy. Four children ranging in age from three years to seven years old died between 2 March and 6 March 1765.

Peter Abbott did not leave a will, but his estate entered probate 25 May 1774 at Kingston, New Hampshire. Widow Elizabeth declined administration of the estate. David Clifford assumed the bond for the probate. There was an inventory in 1774 and an additional inventory 29 March 1777. The debts against the estate were £150 and the value of the personal estate was £106. There is nothing in the probate papers to suggest there are heirs other than the mention of the widow. There is no settlement to heirs included; there is just a list of creditors against the estate.[227]

There are seven births recorded for this family. The two oldest, twins Peter and Edmund, were recorded at Andover. The third child is recorded at Concord, and the youngest four are recorded at Kingston, New Hampshire.

385) i PETER ABBOTT, b. 22 Jun 1758; d. at Chester, NH Nov 1828; m. 7 Mar 1782, PHEBE SPRATT[228] who was "of Deerfield" but parents not located; Phebe d. at Chester 16 Feb 1846.

ii EDMUND ABBOTT, b. 22 Jun 1758; d. 2 Mar 1765.

iii BENJAMIN ABBOTT, b. Sep 1760; d. 4 Mar 1765.

iv DANIEL ABBOTT, b. 7 Jun 1762; d. 6 Mar 1765.

v BETTY ABBOTT, b. 7 Jun 1762; d. 4 Mar 1765.

vi EPHRAIM ABBOTT, b. 16 Dec 1764; no further record located.

vii BETTY ABBOTT, b. 15 Dec 1766; no further record located.

84) MARTHA ABBOTT *(Ephraim^3, John^2, George^1)*, b. 13 Jul 1737 daughter of Ephraim and Sarah (Crosby) Abbott; d. 13 Aug 1773 at Amherst, NH; m. about 1757 ARCHELAUS TOWNE, b. 1734 at Topsfield son of Israel and Grace (Gardner) Towne; Archelaus d. Nov 1779 at Fishkill, NY during the Revolution.

Archelaus Towne was a tavern owner in Monson, New Hampshire. He was a militia Captain in the Revolutionary War and raised a company in the Amherst area and joined the continental army. He was reported to have seen service at Bunker Hill and Bennington. He remained in the service until his death. He was also a selectman in Monson.[229]

Six children are reported in published genealogies, although a record was located for just one child.[230] The children were likely born at Monson or Amherst, New Hampshire.

i SARAH TOWNE, b. 23 May 1758; no further record.

386) ii ARCHELAUS TOWNE, b. 13 Jul 1760; d. at Hillsborough 8 Jul 1818; m. 22 Sep 1787, ESTHER WESTON, b. at Amherst 7 Jul 1763 daughter of Ebenezer and Esther (Kendall) Weston; Esther d. 6 Apr 1850 at Amherst.

387) iii SUSANNAH TOWNE, b. 29 Dec 1762; d. at Norwich, VT 2 Dec 1840; m. 21 Oct 1779, TIMOTHY NICHOLS, b. at Reading, 16 Feb 1756 son of Timothy and Mehitable (Weston) Nichols; Timothy d. at Norwich, VT 22 Aug 1846.

388) iv ABIGAIL TOWNE, b. 18 Feb 1765; d. at Merrimack, NH 11 Apr 1832; m. 12 Jan 1790, Dr. PETER ALLEN, b. at Surry, NH, 13 Feb 1764 son of Abel and Elizabeth (Chapin) Allen; d. 18 Mar 1809.[231]

389) v MARTHA TOWNE, b. 12 Nov 1771; d. about 1845 at Wells River, VT; m. 1792, DANIEL HOLT, b. 5 Feb 1767 son of Isaac and Mary (Marble) Holt; Daniel d. at Wells River, VT 18 Jun 1854.

---

[226] The death record of one of the children gives the mother's maiden name as Elizabeth Kent. However, the 1774 will of Joseph Holt of Reading includes a bequest to his daughter Elizabeth wife of Peter Abbott and she is likely the widow of Edmund Damon and daughter of Joseph and Abigail (Rich) Holt.

[227] *New Hampshire Wills and Probate Records 1643-1982,* Probate of Peter Abbott, Rockingham, 25 May 1774, Case number 4103.

[228] Some sources give her name as Pratt, but the marriage record and the birth records for the children give her name as Phebe Spratt.

[229] Spaulding, An Account of Some Early Settlers of West Dunstable, p 108

[230] Information on births obtained from Spaulding's, *An Account of Some of the Early Settlers of West Dunstable, Monson and Hollis, N.H.*, p 108

[231] Littlefield and Pfister, *Genealogies of the Early Settlers of Weston, Vermont*

vi MARY TOWNE, b. 12 Nov 1771; m. AMOS DODGE, b. 18 Jun 1769 son of Bartholomew and Martha (Hartshorne) Dodge; Mary and Amos do not seem to have had any children.[232]

85) JOHN ABBOTT *(Joshua³, John², George¹)*, b. 5 May 1713 son of Joshua and Rebekah (Shed) Abbott; d. 22 Oct 1791 at Westford, MA; m. 30 Dec 1735, HANNAH RICHARDSON, b. 2 Apr 1714 at Billerica daughter of Jonathan and Hannah (French) Richardson; Hannah d. 29 Nov 1795.

John Abbott was born in Billerica but relocated with his family to Westford where he served as deacon from 1762 through at least 1777. He was active in town functions and served on various building and other civic committees.[233]

In his will written 3 November 1785, John Abbott made bequests to the following persons: well beloved wife Hannah, daughter Martha Prescott, son John, and five grandchildren, the children of daughter Rebekah Jewett who is deceased (Jonathan, John, Patty, Leonard, and Joshua).[234]

There are births of six children record for this family, all at Westford.

i HANNAH ABBOTT, b. 4 Jan 1736/7; d. 5 Oct 1738.

390) ii REBECCA ABBOTT, b. 17 Feb 1738/9; d. 19 Feb 1785; m. 3 Nov 1763, JOSEPH JEWETT, b. at Littleton, 15 Jun 1740 son of Ezra and Mary (Herrick) Jewett. Joseph m. 2nd 1786, Hannah Richardson; Joseph d. 25 Aug 1814.

iii HANNAH ABBOTT, b. 11 Mar 1740/1; d. 5 Dec 1783; Hannah did not marry.

391) iv JOHN ABBOTT, b. 2 Dec 1743; d. 8 May 1804; m. 1st Jul 1769, LUCY PROCTOR, b. at Chelmsford, 28 Nov 1746 daughter of Daniel and Susanna (Hill) Proctor; Lucy d. 27 Apr 1779. John m. 2nd 22 Jun 1780, MARY FARRAR, b. at Concord, 4 Jul 1747 daughter of Jacob and Mary (Merriam) Farrar; Mary d. 26 Feb 1815.

v JOSHUA ABBOTT, b. 25 Oct 1750; d. 8 Oct 1752.

392) vi MARTHA ABBOTT, b. 17 Sep 1755; d. at Reading, 20 Oct 1842; m. 16 Nov 1776, JOHN PRESCOTT, b. 25 Apr 1752 son of Jonas and Rebecca (Jones) Prescott; John d. 30 Oct 1842.

86) SARAH ABBOTT *(Joshua³, John², George¹)*, b. 24 Feb 1714/5 daughter of Joshua and Rebekah (Shed) Abbott; d. about 1798;[235] m. 1 Jan 1736, CHRISTOPHER OSGOOD, b. 21 Jul 1712 at Billerica son of Christopher and Mary (Keyes) Osgood; Christopher d. 26 Aug 1748. Sarah m. 2nd, about 1750, JAMES GOODWIN, b. at Reading, 1 Nov 1714 son of John and Tabitha (Pearson) Goodwin; James d. at Worcester, 2 Jun 1776. James was first married to Mary Mansfield who died in 1749.

Christopher Osgood wrote his will 25 August 1748 just one day before his death. He wills that his real estate be sold and after the payment of debts that the proceeds be divided among his children. He orders that the timber at the mill be sawed and applied toward his debts. All his personal estate is at the disposal of his well-beloved wife Sarah. William Stickney and Thomas Kidder are appointed executors.[236]

At the time of Christopher Osgood's death in 1748, guardians were appointed for five minor children: Sarah, Mary, Christopher, Rebecca, and John. Sarah remarried about 1750 to James Goodwin of Worcester and the family relocated there. It is known that Sarah Abbott Osgood marries a Goodwin as the will of Joshua Abbott includes a bequest to his daughter Sarah Goodwin. James Goodwin of Worcester is one of the signers on the 1757 guardianship request for Christopher Osgood when he selects David Bancroft of Worcester as his guardian.

Children of Sarah Abbott and Christopher Osgood, born at Billerica:

393) i SARAH OSGOOD, b. 28 May 1738; d. at Lancaster 24 May 1805; m. at Worcester, 10 May 1756, TIMOTHY WHITING, b. 13 Feb 1731/2 son of Samuel and Deborah (Hill) Whiting; Timothy d. 12 Jul 1799.

394) ii MARY OSGOOD, b. 31 Aug 1740; d. at Worcester, 5 Sep 1761; m. 14 May 1757, JOHN GREEN, b. at Leicester, 14 Aug 1736 son of Thomas and Martha (Lynde) Green. John m. 2nd MARY RUGGLES; John d. 29 Oct 1799.

395) iii CHRISTOPHER OSGOOD, b. 12 Apr 1743; death uncertain; m. by 1765, HANNAH BROWN, b. 21 Sep 1742 daughter of Luke and Elizabeth (-) Brown; Hannah d. at Newfane, VT 1779.

iv REBEKAH OSGOOD, b. 11 Jun 1746; d. 22 Oct 1749.

v JOHN OSGOOD, b. 24 Apr 1748; d. 17 Oct 1749.

---

[232] Dodge. *Genealogy of the Dodge Family of Essex County, Mass.*, p 106
[233] Hodgman, *History of the Town of Westford*
[234] *Middlesex County, MA: Probate File Papers, 1648-1871.* Probate of John Abbott, 1791, Case number 30.
[235] It is possible that she is the widow Sarah Goodwin who died in Wakefield 24 July 1798 at age 86.
[236] *Middlesex County, MA: Probate File Papers, 1648-1871. Probate of* Christopher Osgood, *1748, Case number* 16268.

Sarah Abbott and James Goodwin had three children born at Worcester.

396) i REBECCA GOODWIN, b. 21 Oct 1751; m. at Worcester, 1 May 1781, AMOS JOHNSON, *possibly* b. at Worcester, 13 Jan 1756 son of John and Susannah (-) Johnson.

397) ii JOHN GOODWIN, b. 6 Aug 1753; d. at Putney, VT, 2 Sep 1801; m. at Leicester, 11 Feb 1773, MARTHA MOORE, b. at Worcester, 14 Jul 1752 daughter of Asa and Sarah (Hayward) Moore.[237]

398) iii TABITHA GOODWIN, b. 4 May 1756; d. at Shoreham, VT, 31 Jul 1825; m. 12 Jul 1776, JOEL DOOLITTLE, b. at Worcester, 8 Dec 1752 son of Ephraim and Sarah (Morton) Doolittle; Joel d. 19 Dec 1829.

87) MARY ABBOTT *(Joshua³, John², George¹)*, b. 28 Aug 1717 daughter of Joshua and Rebekah (Shed) Abbott; d. about 1800; m. 29 Nov 1743, HENRY JEFTS b. at Billerica 24 Apr 1717 son of Henry and Elizabeth (Hayward) Jefts; Henry d. 19 Aug 1772.

Henry Jefts did not leave a will. An inventory of his estate was filed 5 November 1772. The probate record does not include a distribution of the estate.

The births of five children are recorded at Billerica.

i JOHN JEFTS, b. 9 Nov 1744; d. 20 Apr 1750.

ii ELIZABETH JEFTS, b. 3 Oct 1746; no further record.

399) iii HENRY JEFTS, b. 7 Oct 1748; d. unknown but he appears on the 1810 Census in Billerica; m. 24 Feb 1774, ELIZABETH STEARNS, b. 20 Jun 1751 daughter of Samuel and Hannah (Trask) Stearns; Elizabeth was still living when her father wrote his will 1 May 1801.

iv MARY JEFTS, b. 24 Aug 1750; d.?; m. 15 May 1771, SAMUEL HAZELTINE, b. at Tewksbury, 24 Mar 1745, son of Samuel and Sarah (Bixby) Hazeltine. It is not clear what happened to this family. There are no records for them in either Massachusetts or New Hampshire after their marriage.

v ALICE JEFTS, b. 8 Sep 1756; no further record.

88) HANNAH ABBOTT *(Joshua³, John², George¹)*, twin of MARY, b. 28 Aug 1717 daughter of Joshua and Rebekah (Shed) Abbott; d. 11 Jan 1753; m. 6 Feb 1739, PHINEAS OSGOOD, b. at Billerica 20 Jun 1714 son of Christopher and Mary (Keyes) Osgood; Phineas d. 3 Jun 1756.

There are just two children recorded for this family. Phineas Osgood did not leave a will. David Osgood was named administrator of the estate. As part of the probate, Oliver Abbot was appointed guardian of daughter Hannah Osgood under 14 years of age. There are no other children mentioned.[238]

i PHINEAS OSGOOD, b. at Holliston 3 Sep 1739; d. at Billerica 25 Nov 1752.

ii HANNAH OSGOOD, b. at Billerica 24 Sep 1743; in Billerica records, there is this marriage record for Hannah: Hannah [d. Phinehas and Hannah] and —— Williams, —— —, ——, in Boston.* There is a marriage for Hannah Osgood and John Williams at Boston 3 Jun 1809, but I have no idea if this is her.

89) ELIZABETH ABBOTT *(Joshua³, John², George¹)*, b. 7 Dec 1719 daughter of Joshua and Rebekah (Shed) Abbott; d. about 1803;[239] m. 7 Dec 1743, ROBERT WALKER whose origin is unknown to me; he is perhaps the son of John and Abigail (Wesson) Walker of Chelmsford; Robert d. 26 Jan 1757.

Very little in terms of records have been located for Robert Walker. Hazen's *History of Billerica, Massachusetts* (p. 180) lists his seat in the meeting house as a second seat in the side gallery very near the seat of Henry Jefts, Jr. who was

---

[237] The will of Asa Moore written in 1798 includes a bequest to his daughter Patty Goodwin.

[238] *Middlesex County, MA: Probate File Papers, 1648-1871. Probate* of Phineas Osgood, *1756, Case number* 16280.

[239] This is the death date given in published genealogies (for example, Hazen's *The History of Billerica*, p. 154) but no source for this information is given and I could locate no records associated with it.

married to Elizabeth Abbott's sister Mary. There is no probate record for Robert Walker. There is no record that Elizabeth remarried. The births of eight children are recorded at Billerica.

i ELIZABETH WALKER, b. 9 Apr 1745; no further record.

400) ii ABIGAIL WALKER, b. 6 Oct 1746; d. at Grafton, VT, 7 Apr 1818; m. 10 Mar 1768, WILLIAM STICKNEY, b. 3 Apr 1743 son of William and Anna (Whiting) Stickney.

iii SAMUEL WALKER, b. 12 Apr 1748; no further record.

iv JOEL WALKER, b. 17 Feb 1749/50; no further record.

401) v LYDIA WALKER, b. 22 Mar 1752; d.?; m. 20 Oct 1770, JOSIAH RICHARDSON, b. 19 Jun 1751 son of Josiah and Judith (Kendall) Richardson.

402) vi REBEKAH WALKER, b. 12 Jun 1754; d. 17 May 1782; m. 25 Apr 1776, EBENEZER RICHARDSON, b. 25 Feb 1754 son of Ebenezer and Elizabeth (Shed) Richardson.

vii SARAH WALKER, b. 6 Jun 1756; no further record.

403) viii HANNAH WALKER, b. 6 Jun 1756; m. 4 Sep 1775, JOHN WRIGHT,[240] b. at Wilmington, 29 Jun 1756 son of Josiah and Abigail (Graves) Wright. The births of the children in this family are recorded at Billerica, but then there is no more record of them.

90) JOSHUA ABBOTT *(Joshua³, John², George¹)*, b. 28 Oct 1722 son of Joshua and Dorcas (Whiting) Abbott; d. at Billerica, 7 Aug 1807; m. 6 Mar 1746, SARAH STEARNS, b, at Billerica 10 Dec 1726 daughter of Isaac and Alice (Wilson) Stearns; Sarah d. 7 Sep 1803.

Just one child was located for this family. In his will, Joshua Abbott made bequests to his siblings, nieces, and nephews. There are bequests for the following persons: sister Dorcas Abbott who receives one-half of the homestead, Joshua Kidder who receives the other half of the homestead, Blaney Abbot gets his pew in the Billerica meeting house, Joanna Winship (niece) of Lexington, the widow Dorcas Bowers (niece) of Billerica, Abigail Kidder (niece), and Elizabeth Abbot of Billerica each receive $150; and to Henry Jefts (nephew), Elizabeth Jefts (nephew), Alice Jefts (niece), Lydia Richardson, and Hannah Wright (niece) all of Billerica; to Sarah Spaulding, Alice Trull, and Abigail Shattuck daughters of Oliver Stearns (children of Oliver Stearns and Susanna Winch?) late of Billerica each to receive $25; and to Polly Wilson who lives with him he gives some household items and $40; Samuel Stearns and Abbot Stearns sons of Oliver Stearns, and to James Abbot of Billerica who is also named executor.[241]

Child of Joshua Abbott and Sarah Stearns:

i JOSHUA ABBOTT, b. 2 Nov 1747; d. 7 Jun 1752.

91) OLIVER ABBOTT *(Joshua³, John², George¹)*, b. 26 Mar 1727 son of Joshua and Dorcas (Whiting) Abbott; d. 10 Apr 1796; m. 13 Feb 1752, JOANNA FRENCH, b. at Billerica 27 Nov 1729 daughter of William and Joanna (Hill) French; Joanna d. 20 Aug 1768. OLIVER m. 2nd at Westford 1 Aug 1769, ABIGAIL HALL, b. 19 Jul 1734 daughter of Willard and Abigail (Cotton) Hall; Abigail d. 4 Aug 1804.

The following heirs to the estate of Oliver Abbott signed approving of Simon Winship of Lexington as administrator of the estate: Abigail Abbott, Joanna Winship, Dorcas Bowers, Abigail Abbott (jr.), and Elizabeth Abbott.

Oliver and Joanna had nine children, but six of those children died in early childhood. Children of Oliver Abbott and Joanna French all born at Billerica:

i JOANNA ABBOTT, b. 15 Apr 1753; d. 19 Apr 1753.

ii LYDIA ABBOTT, b. 11 Jul 1754; d. 22 Jul 1788. Lydia did not marry.

404) iii JOANNA ABBOTT, b. 24 Jul 1755; d. at Lexington, 2 Feb 1826; m. 21 May 1776, SIMON WINSHIP, b. at Lexington, Nov 1749 son of Samuel and Abigail (Crosby) Winship; Simon d. at Lexington 24 Jan 1813.

iv OLIVER ABBOTT, b. 1 Dec 1756; d. 9 Feb 1757.

v OLIVER WHITING ABBOTT, b. 5 Dec 1757; d. 1 May 1758.

---

[240] Hazen's *The History of Billerica* gives the wife of John Wright as Hannah the daughter of Joseph Walker. But Hannah the daughter of Joseph was born in 1744 making her seemingly too old for this John. In addition, the 1807 will of Joshua Abbott (the brother of Elizabeth Abbott Walker) includes a bequest for his niece Hannah Wright. Also, John and Hannah Wright's last child was born in 1796 which would rule out Hannah born in 1744 as the mother in this family.

[241] *Middlesex County, MA: Probate File Papers, 1648-1871. Probate* of Joshua Abbott, *1807, Case number* 37.

vi BERIAH ABBOTT, b. and d. 1 Apr 1759.

vii SILENCE ABBOTT, b. and d. 21 Jul 1760.

viii SILENT ABBOTT, b. likely 1761; d. 13 May 1761.

405) ix DORCAS ABBOTT, b. 19 Dec 1764; d. after 1850 likely in Williamsburg, NY;[242] m. 21 Apr 1783, JONATHAN BOWERS, b. at Chelmsford, 18 Feb 1761 son of William and Hannah (Kidder) Bowers; Jonathan d. 21 Feb 1804.

Oliver Abbott had three children with his second wife Abigail Hall. The children were all born at Billerica.

i JOSHUA ABBOTT, b. 29 Jul 1772; d. 7 Jun 1795 at the Island of Hispaniola.[243]

406) ii ABIGAIL ABBOTT, b. 14 Dec 1774; d. at Boston 12 Sep 1816; m. 25 Dec 1796, EPHRAIM KIDDER, b. 10 Apr 1766 son of Ephraim and Lucy (Pollard) Kidder; Ephraim d. 22 Dec 1807.

iii ELIZABETH ABBOTT, b. 4 Dec 1779; d. at Boston 23 Feb 1852. Elizabeth did not marry. At the time of the 1850 US Census, she was living with her niece, Abigail Kidder, in Chelmsford.[244]

92) DAVID ABBOTT *(Joshua³, John², George¹)*, b. 27 Apr 1729 son of Joshua and Dorcas (Whiting) Abbott; d. 15 Nov 1801; m. 25 Aug 1752, HANNAH ELLIS, b. about 1727 but origin is unknown; Hannah d. 17 Dec 1767. DAVID m. 2nd 28 Jun 1768 HULDAH PAINE of Malden, who d. 8 Sep 1797.

There is just one child recorded for David Abbott and Hannah Ellis.

i DAVID ABBOTT, b. 5 Jun 1760; d. 19 Dec 1761.

Births of two children are recorded for David Abbott and Huldah Paine.

i DAVID ABBOTT, b. 18 Dec 1770; d. 9 Apr 1804; David does not seem to have married.

ii BLANEY ABBOTT, b. 25 Oct 1772; d. 17 Jul 1855. Blaney did not marry; his death record lists him as single. He did leave a will in which he leaves his estate to two nieces, Lydia Wilson and Betsy Wilson of Marblehead. The parents of Lydia and Betsy seem to be George Wilson and Polly Hooper (uncertain of that), but I have not worked out how these young women are his nieces.

93) MARY ABBOTT *(Ebenezer³, John², George¹)*, b. 2 Apr 1725 daughter of Ebenezer and Hannah (Turner) Abbot; d. 20 Apr 1760; m. 1st 4 Oct 1742, her second cousin once removed, JOSEPH CHANDLER, b. 20 Nov 1720 son of Thomas and Mary (Stevens) Chandler (confirmed by the will of Thomas Chandler[245]); Joseph d. 31 Mar 1745. MARY m. 2nd 8 Apr 1746, ISAAC BLUNT, b. 5 Nov 1712 son of William and Sarah (Foster) Blunt. Isaac m. 2nd Mary Kimball; Isaac d. at Andover, 6 Jan 1798.

Mary Abbott and Joseph Chandler had one child before Joseph's early death. Mary then remarried Isaac Blunt and they had six children.

The will of Isaac Blunt has bequests to the following persons: beloved wife Mary (who is Mary Kimball that he married after Mary Abbott died); daughter Anna; daughter Elizabeth (from his marriage to Mary Abbott) who is single and is allowed to live with her brother Isaac who gets the house; daughters get household goods (Elizabeth, Abigail, Anna, Tabitha, and Mehitable, the latter four being daughters form his marriage to Mary Kimball); and then three other daughters (Mary, Hannah, and Sarah who are daughters from his marriage to Mary Abbott) get a small amount of money; son John Blunt (land in Amherst, New Hampshire); and son Isaac the remainder of the estate.[246]

There is one child recorded at Andover for Mary Abbott and Joseph Chandler.

---

[242] In the 1850 U.S. Census, Dorcas Bowers age 85 was in the household of Mary and Alfred Curtis in Williamsburg, NY. Mary Bowers Curtis was Dorcas's granddaughter. Also in the home was Dorcas's son (and Mary Curtis's father) Alexander Bowers. Year: 1850; Census Place: Williamsburg, Kings, New York; Roll: M432_522; Page: 400A; Image: 530

[243] Ancestry.com, U.S., Newspaper Extractions from the Northeast, 1704-1930. Joshua Abbot son of Oliver Abbot d. at Island of Hispaniola, 7th June, age 23.

[244] 1850 U.S. Census, Chelmsford, enumerated 17 Oct 1850. Household consists of E. Abbott female age 71 and A. Kidder female age 50.

[245] The will of Thomas Chandler in 1751 includes a bequest to his grandson Joseph Chandler the only son of his son Joseph who is deceased.

[246] *Essex County, MA: Probate File Papers, 1638-1881. Probate of* Isaac Blunt, 6 Mar 1798, *Case number* 2654.

407) i JOSEPH CHANDLER, b. 8 Jun 1743; d. 8 Jun 1834 at Atkinson, NH; m. at Newbury, 7 Jan 1768, ELIZABETH COOK, b. at Newbury, 22 May 1747 daughter of Samuel and Elizabeth (-) Cook.

Mary Abbott and Isaac Blunt had six children whose births are recorded at Andover.

408) i MARY BLUNT, b. 14 Feb 1746/7; d. before 1818[247] likely at Exeter, NH; m. 2 May 1771; JEREMIAH LEAVITT, b. about 1749 and likely the son of Jeremiah and Mary (-) Leavitt; Jeremiah d. at Exeter, NH, 3 Aug 1818.

409) ii HANNAH BLUNT, b. 25 Sep 1755; d. likely at Wilmington, MA; m. 10 Aug 1773, EZRA CARTER, b. at Wilmington, 26 Feb 1745/6 son of Ezra and Lydia (Jenkins) Carter; Ezra d. at Wilmington, 11 Feb 1827.

iii SARAH BLUNT, b. 12 Dec 1750; d. at Haverhill, 2 Aug 1841; m. 13 Aug 1774, DAVID WEBSTER, b. at Haverhill, 13 Jul 1749 son of Jonathan and Abigail (Duston) Webster; David d. 9 Oct 1828. David and Sarah do not seem to have had any children. In his will, David Webster had bequests to his wife Sarah and to several nephews.

iv ELIZABETH BLUNT, b. 27 Jul 1752; d. 24 Mar 1801; Elizabeth did not marry.

410) v JOHN BLUNT, b. 31 Jan 1756; d. at Amherst, NH, 27 Nov 1836;[248] m. at Wilmington, 26 Oct 1780, SARAH EAMES daughter of Caleb and Mary (Harvey) Eames; Sarah d. at Milford, 25 Jan 1858.

vi ISAAC BLUNT, b. 12 Sep and d. 13 Sep 1757.

94) ISAAC ABBOTT *(Ebenezer³, John², George¹)*, b. 30 Jun 1728 son of Ebenezer and Hannah (Turner) Abbot; d. after 1790 at Fryeburg, ME; m. 29 May 1753, SUSANNA FARNUM, b. at Andover, 31 Aug 1735 daughter of Ebenezer and Priscilla (Ingalls) Farnum.

The births of seven children are recorded at Andover. Three other children born in Maine can be reasonably placed in this family. Each of them has a record for a marriage in Fryeburg.

411) i SUSANNA ABBOTT, b. 29 Aug 1754;[249] d. at Oxford County, ME, 21 Sep 1827; m. SAMUEL CHARLES, b. 28 Aug 1754 son of John and Abigail (Bliss) Charles; Samuel d. 14 Dec 1843.

412) ii OLIVE ABBOTT, b. 17 Feb 1756; d. in Oxford County, ME, 27 Aug 1828; m. about 1782, as his second wife, JOHN CHARLES, b. 28 Feb 1744 son of John and Abigail (Bliss) Charles; John d. 6 Jun 1831. John was first married to Phebe Russell.

413) iii LUCY ABBOTT, b. 20 Mar 1759; d. at Maine about 1790; m. WILLIAM KIMBALL. William m. 2nd, BETHIAH GORDON; William d. about 1813 (date of probate).

iv EBENEZER ABBOTT, b. 7 Dec 1760.

414) v ISAAC ABBOTT, b. 16 Jun 1762; d. at Fryeburg, ME, 23 Jun 1861; m. SUSANNA NOYES KNIGHT, b. about 1770 daughter of Stephen and Susanna (Noyes) Knight; Susanna d. 3 Sep 1851. Isaac is likely also the father of Enoch Eaton Abbott, an out-of-wedlock child born to Sarah Eaton in 1785.

415) vi SIMEON ABBOTT, b. 20 May 1764; d. at Stow, ME, 7 May 1851; m. 3 Jul 1791, MARY DAY, b. Feb 1768 daughter of Moses and Hannah (-) Day; Mary d. 14 Sep 1840.

vii MICAH ABBOTT, b. 15 May 1766; d. 16 Aug 1767.

416) viii JAMES ABBOTT, b. 1770 (based on age 89 at death); d. at Stow, ME, Dec 1859; m. at Fryeburg, 16 Aug 1795, ELIZABETH DAY, b. 18 Jun 1773 daughter of Moses and Hannah (-) Day; Elizabeth d. 6 Nov 1857.

417) ix MICAH ABBOTT, b. at Fryeburg, 1 Nov 1774; d. at Stow, ME, 2 Jul 1825; m. about 1795, ALICE WILEY, b. at Stow, 20 May 1778 daughter of Benjamin and Alice (Kilgore) Wiley; Alice d. 14 Sep 1858. After Micah's death, Alice married Samuel Huntress.

418) x DOROTHY "DOLLY" ABBOTT, b. 16 Aug 1778; d. at Richland, MI, 11 Nov 1858; m. at Fryeburg, 26 Oct 1795, JOSEPH CHARLES, b. 7 Apr 1773 son of Abner and Sarah (Walker) Charles; Joseph d. at Wyoming County, NY, 26 Jan 1846.

---

[247] She was not living at the time of the probate of her husband's estate 14 September 1818.

[248] The gravestone for this family has the following inscription: JOHN BLUNT DIED Nov. 27, 1836, AEt. 80; SARAH EAMES his wife Died Jan. 25, 1858, AEt. 93; Isaac 14 m's, Alva L. 3d's; Twin sons 1 d., Alva L. 17 d's & Rebecca K. 4 1/2 y's. Children of John & Sarah Blunt rest here. Blessed are the dead that die in the Lord. (findagrave.com, ID 61561179)

[249] The transcription of this record indicates the record was torn and only the last letter "a" is present.

95) PHEBE ABBOTT *(Ebenezer³, John², George¹)*, b. 3 Jan 1731/2 daughter of Ebenezer and Hannah (Turner) Abbot; d. Feb 1805; m. 30 May 1751, JAMES GRIFFIN whose origins are unknown; James d. at Andover, 9 Oct 1815.

The births of eight children of Phebe Abbott and James Griffin are recorded at Andover.

i PHEBE GRIFFIN, b. 1 Oct 1751; d. likely at Nottingham, NH; m. 29 Sep 1791, as his second wife, BENJAMIN BUTLER, b. at Edgartown, 9 Apr 1729 son of Malachi and Jemima (Dagget) Butler; Benjamin d. at Nottingham 26 Dec 1804. Benjamin was first married to Dorcas Abbott (Family #130).

ii HANNAH GRIFFIN, b. 5 Mar 1754; no further clear record.

iii ELIZABETH GRIFFIN, b. 7 Jul 1758.

418a) iv LYDIA GRIFFIN, b. 26 Mar 1761; d. at Bridgton, ME, 1843; m. at Andover, 15 Apr 1778, her third cousin, NATHAN INGALLS (*Eunice Jennings Ingalls⁴, Phebe Stevens³, Elizabeth Abbott Stevens², George¹*), b. at Andover, 12 Jun 1755 son of Francis and Eunice (Jennings) Ingalls; Nathan d. at Bridgton, 8 Jan 1835.

v SARAH GRIFFIN, b. 7 Oct 1764.

419) vi ABIGAIL GRIFFIN, b. 7 Oct 1764; d. at Middleton, 26 Jan 1860;[250] m. 1st at Wilmington, 9 Jan 1790, SAMUEL FROST; Samuel d. by 1796. Abigail m. 2nd, 9 Oct 1796, ASA HOLT, b. 26 Mar 1768 son of Asa and Dinah (Holt) Holt.

420) vii MARY "POLLY" GRIFFIN, b. 7 Aug 1768; d. before 1847 (not living when husband wrote his will); m. 9 May 1796, BENJAMIN CLEMENT, b. at Haverhill, about 1760 son of Benjamin and Mary (Bartlett) Clement; Benjamin d. at Haverhill about 1853 (probate 6 Apr 1853).

421) viii EBENEZER GRIFFIN, b. 5 Jun 1771; d. 1848 at Litchfield, NH; m. at Leominster, 20 Sep 1792, BETSY CARTER, b. 23 Nov 1774 daughter of Josiah and Elizabeth (Graves) Carter; Betsy d. at Litchfield, 1 Oct 1854.

96) JAMES ABBOTT *(Ebenezer³, John², George¹)*, b. 14 Apr 1736 son of Ebenezer and Hannah (Turner) Abbot; d. unknown, but his duties as town physician were taken over by Dr. Amos Bradley in 1785; m. at Dracut 25 Feb 1758, LYDIA COBURN, b. at Dracut, 18 Jan 1739 daughter of Joseph and Hannah (Jones) Coburn.

Dr. James Abbott was a physician in Dracut. His father-in-law, Dr. Joseph Coburn was the first town physician in Dracut. Dr. Abbott served in the Revolutionary War as a surgeon's mate. He and his family lived on a farm at Collinsville.[251]

The births of twelve children are recorded at Dracut. Five of the children relocated to New Hampshire. It is possible that the parents accompanied the children to New Hampshire, but that is not known.

422) i NEHEMIAH ABBOTT, b. 22 Nov 1759; d. likely at Glover, VT; m. 16 Oct 1788, ANNA VARNUM, b. at Dracut, 23 Apr 1767 daughter of Jonathan and Anna (East) Varnum.

423) ii RACHEL ABBOTT, b. 22 Mar 1761; d. at Lowell, 15 Mar 1844; m. 13 Dec 1783, JONATHAN COLBURN, b. 19 Aug 1757 son of Jonathan and Marcy (Hildreth) Colburn; Jonathan d. at Dracut, 17 Jun 1813.

iii LYDIA ABBOTT, b. 20 May 1762; d. 29 Jun 1767.

iv MOLLY ABBOTT, b. 14 Jan 1764; d. 13 Oct 1765.

424) v NATHANIEL ABBOTT, b. 19 Jan 1766; d. 28 Feb 1815 in NH; m. 3 Jan 1788, PHEBE CUMMINGS, b. at Westford, 2 Jun 1770 daughter of Thomas and Lucy (Laurence) Cummings; Phebe d. 14 Mar 1843.

vi JOSEPH ABBOTT, b. 17 Oct 1767; d. 7 Sep 1778.

425) vii HANNAH ABBOTT, b. 14 Jul 1769; d. at Glover, VT, 15 Jan 1857; m. 17 Dec 1795, JAMES VANCE, b. at Londonderry, 15 Apr 1769; James d. 26 Nov 1864.

viii EBENEZER ABBOTT, b. 25 Jan 1771; no further record.

ix RONE ABBOTT, b. 13 Jan 1773; d. 3 Sep 1778.

---

250 New England Historic Genealogical Society; Boston, Massachusetts; Massachusetts Vital Records, 1840–1911 (accessed through ancestry.com)

251 Coburn, *History of Dracut*, p 155 and p 281

426) x SIBYL ABBOTT, b. 21 Dec 1774; d. after 1850 in NH; m. 21 Dec 1797, DAVID WILSON, b. about 1770; David d. after 1850.[252]

427) xi RELIEF ABBOTT, b. 8 Sep 1778; d. likely in NH;[253] m. 13 Aug 1796, EBENEZER BROWN, b. at Dunstable, 12 Sep 1773 son of Samuel and Bridget (Bryant) Brown; Ebenezer d. at Dracut 3 Aug 1860.

428) xii MERCY ABBOTT, b. 24 Aug 1780; d. 1 Nov 1863 at Hancock; m. Feb 1808, EBENEZER BARTLETT, b. 10 Aug 1779 son of Thomas and Sarah (Rider) Bartlett; Ebenezer d. at Hancock, NH, 8 Nov 1854.

Grandchildren of Hannah Abbott and John Chandler

97) NATHAN CHANDLER *(John Chandler³, Hannah Abbott Chandler², George¹)*, b. 31 Jan 1708 son of John and Hannah (Frye) Chandler; d. at Andover, 31 Jul 1784; m. 14 May 1729, PRISCILLA HOLT, b. about 1709 daughter of Timothy and Rhoda (Chandler) Holt; Priscilla d. 25 Nov 1803.

Nathan was the lieutenant of a company that marched August 15, 1757 for the relief of Fort William Henry which had come under siege from the French.[254]

In his will (probate 5 October 1784), Nathan Chandler makes bequests to the following persons: dearly beloved wife Priscilla receives use of the house from the bottom of the cellar to the top of the house and the kitchen also and the liberty of using the well; Priscilla also receives several specific provisions for her continued maintenance and the "time and improvement" of his Negro woman Flora. Other bequests are to beloved son Nathan Chandler, beloved son Isaac Chandler, daughter Hannah wife of Joshua Chandler, Mary wife of Jonathan Abbott, and Phebe wife of Isaac Abbott.[255]

There are five births recorded at Andover for Nathan Chandler and Priscilla Holt. Four of the five children married other George Abbott of Andover descendants. The fifth child married a second cousin who was not a George Abbott descendant.

289) i NATHAN CHANDLER, b. 19 Feb 1729/30; d. 30 Apr 1786; m. 18 Apr 1754, his third cousin, PHEBE ABBOTT, b. 14 Apr 1733 daughter of John and Phebe (Fiske) Abbott; Phebe d. 26 Jul 1812. (This is the same couple as Family #62, child i.)

429) ii ISAAC CHANDLER, b. 8 Apr 1732; d. 6 Mar 1817; m. 14 Apr 1757, his second cousin once removed, HANNAH BALLARD, b. 3 Jan 1732/3 daughter of Josiah and Mary (Chandler) Ballard;[256] Hannah d. 2 Oct 1824.[257]

335) iii HANNAH CHANDLER, b. 20 May 1735; d. 14 Feb 1791; m. 31 Mar 1757, as his 1st wife, her first cousin (and George Abbott descendant), JOSHUA CHANDLER, b. 23 Jul 1732 son of Joshua and Sarah (Chandler) Chandler. Joshua m. 2nd 7 Jun 1792, Hannah Ballard the daughter of Hezekiah and Lydia (Chandler) Ballard who was the widow of Obadiah Foster; Joshua Chandler d. 15 Mar 1807. (This couple is the same as Family #71, child ii.)

205) iv MARY CHANDLER, b. 15 Jun 1740; d. 1 Apr 1824; m. 13 Nov 1759, her second cousin once removed, JONATHAN ABBOTT, b. 24 Oct 1739 son of David and Hannah (Danforth) Abbott; Jonathan d. 10 Apr 1817.

132) v PHEBE CHANDLER, b. 2 Jun 1742; d. 1 Jul 1800; m. 22 Apr 1766, her second cousin once removed, ISAAC ABBOTT, b. 3 Feb 1745 son of Isaac and Phebe (Lovejoy) Abbott; Isaac d. 21 May 1836.

98) HANNAH CHANDLER *(John Chandler³, Hannah Abbott Chandler², George¹)*, b. 1710 daughter of John and Hannah (Frye) Chandler; d. 29 May 1784; m. 4 Jun 1729, her second cousin, TIMOTHY BALLARD, b. 1702 son of Joseph and Rebecca (Johnson) Ballard; Timothy d. at Andover, 30 Oct 1773.

Timothy was a yeoman and owned a share of the Ballardvale saw and grist mill.[258] The inventory of his estate includes a share in the grist mill and one-fourth part of the saw mill. He also had several land parcels and the total value of the estate was £1057.

---

[252] Both Sibyl and David were living at the 1850 US Census living in the home of John and Sophia Ellenwood. They are listed as Sibyl A. Wilson age 75 and David Wilson age 79. John Ellenwood married Sophia Wilson at Pelham in 1844. Unsure how they are related. It certainly is possible that these are a different David and Sibyl Wilson, but they are the right ages.

[253] The births of their children are recorded at Londonderry. The family did return to Dracut but unsure whether this was before or after the death of Relief.

[254] Chandler, *The Descendants of William and Annis Chandler*, p 139

[255] *Essex County, MA: Probate File Papers, 1638-1881. Probate of* Nathan Chandler, 5 Oct 1784, *Case number* 4962.

[256] The 1780 will of Josiah Chandler includes a bequest to his daughter Hannah the wife of Mr. Isaac Chandler.

[257] This is the date of death used in *The Descendants of William and Annis Chandler*, p. 330. The deaths of both Isaac and Hannah are reported by the Chandler book as occurring in Concord, NH, but the record of Isaac's death is in the Andover records with the same specific date as the Chandler book.

[258] Charlotte Helen Abbott, Ballard Family

In his will (written 14 May 1770; probate 6 Dec 1773), Timothy Ballard made bequests to the following persons: Hannah his well-beloved wife, the male heirs of his son Timothy who is deceased, well-beloved son Joseph, well-beloved son Nathan, eldest and beloved daughter Mary Chandler, beloved daughter Hannah Abbott, beloved daughter Elizabeth, beloved daughter Phebe, and beloved daughter Dorothy. Joseph is named executor.[259]

The births of eleven children are recorded at Andover. Of the seven children known to have married, five married fellow George Abbott descendants.

430) i TIMOTHY BALLARD, b. 1 Mar 1729/30; d. 12 Jul 1768; m. 21 Jan 1755, his third cousin, SARAH ABBOTT, b. 3 Aug 1733 daughter of Zebadiah and Anne (Lovejoy) Abbott. Sarah did not remarry after Timothy's death and she died 2 Aug 1809.

431) ii MARY BALLARD, b. 1 May 1732; d. at Reading 15 Dec 1803; m. 30 Aug 1750, her third cousin once removed, DAVID CHANDLER, b. 15 Dec 1724 son of Josiah and Sarah (Ingalls) Chandler; David d. at Cambridge 1 Feb 1776. Mary m. 2nd 10 Nov 1779, Daniel Parker.

iii JOHN BALLARD, b. 9 Jun 1734; d. 11 Dec 1736.

432) iv HANNAH BALLARD, b. 8 Jun 1736; d. 27 Sep 1778; m. 11 Mar 1756, as his first wife, her third cousin, NEHEMIAH ABBOTT, b. 24 Aug 1731 son of Zebadiah and Anne (Lovejoy) Abbott. Nehemiah m. 2nd, LYDIA CLARK; Nehemiah d. 13 Oct 1808.

v JOHN BALLARD, b. 9 Apr 1739; no further record and he is not mentioned in his father's will.

vi JOSEPH BALLARD, b. 19 Jul 1741; d. 17 Jan 1746/7.

433) vii NATHAN BALLARD, b. 1 Nov 1744; d. at Concord, NH 14 Jan 1835; m. 1763, his third cousin, HANNAH HOLT, b. 19 Dec 1745 daughter of Jonathan and Lydia (Blanchard) Holt; Hannah d. 1 Dec 1818.

viii ELIZABETH BALLARD, b. 29 Nov 1746; Elizabeth was living at the time of her father's will (1770); it is not known what became of her.

434) ix JOSEPH BALLARD, b. Oct 1749; d. 15 Feb 1819; m. 1st 10 Sep 1771, MOLLY SMITH of Shrewsbury; Molly d. by 1773 when Joseph m. 2nd, 16 Dec 1773, his third cousin, HANNAH ABBOTT, b. 10 Oct 1749 daughter of George and Hannah (Lovejoy) Abbott; Hannah d. 29 May 1784.

291) x PHEBE BALLARD, b. 5 Nov 1752; d. at Wilton, NH Jan 1846; m. 12 Nov 1772, her third cousin, WILLIAM ABBOTT, b. 3 Jan 1747/8 son of John and Phebe (Fiske) Abbott; William d. at Wilton 13 Nov 1793.

435) xi DOROTHY BALLARD, b. 12 Dec 1757; d. at likely Bow, NH after 1820 (alive at the time of her husband's probate January 1820); m. 17 Apr 1783, her first cousin once removed (and George Abbott descendant), JOHN CHANDLER, b. 21 Nov 1759 son of Isaac and Hannah (Ballard) Chandler; John d. at Bow, NH Sep 1819.

99) PHEBE CHANDLER *(John Chandler³, Hannah Abbott Chandler², George¹)*, b. 2 Jan 1714/5 daughter of John and Hannah (Frye) Chandler; d. Jan 1805? at Concord, NH; m. 1 Jan 1735, HENRY LOVEJOY, b. 14 Aug 1714 son of Henry and Sarah (Farnum) Lovejoy; Henry d. 15 Mar 1793 at Concord.[260]

Phebe and Henry married in Andover and most of their children were born there. They left for Rumford, NH by 1745. Henry Lovejoy was a selectman in Concord in 1749.[261] There are records for seven children in this family, the oldest five recorded at Andover and the two youngest at Rumford, NH.

Although published genealogies report seven children in this family and there are records for the births of these seven children, it is likely there was an eighth child, Sarah, in this family. According to Bouton's *History of Concord* (p 660), Theodore Farnum of Concord married a Sarah Lovejoy and that couple had four children. Theodore Farnum was born in 1749 son of Josiah and Mary (Frye) Farnum. It is not known that Sarah Lovejoy belongs in this family, but there is no other obvious family for her in Concord at the time. The estate of Theodore Farnum entered probate in 1789 with widow Sarah as administrator and with Chandler Lovejoy and Phineas Virgin assuming the obligation of the bond. Chandler Lovejoy is a son in this family and Phineas Virgin is likely a brother-in-law to Chandler Lovejoy.

---

259 *Essex County, MA: Probate File Papers, 1638-1881.* Probate of Timothy Ballard, 6 Dec 1773, *Case number* 1602.

260 New Hampshire, Death and Burial Records Index, 1654-1949, ancestry.com

261 Lyford, *History of Concord*, p 1339

226) i PHEBE LOVEJOY, b. 20 Sep 1735; d. at Concord, 4 Jan 1789; m. 25 Apr 1765, her third cousin, JOSEPH ABBOTT, b. at Concord 23 Oct 1741 son of George and Sarah (Abbott) Abbott. Joseph married 2nd Abigail Tyler; Joseph d. at Concord 19 Jan 1832.

436) ii ABIEL LOVEJOY, b. 25 Jul 1737; d. at Conway, NH 27 May 1817; m. 1764, ANNA STICKNEY, b. at Rumford, 3 Sep 1741 daughter of Jeremiah and Elizabeth (Carleton) Stickney, Anna d. 15 Jan 1815.

437) iii DORCAS LOVEJOY, b. 10 Sep 1739; d. likely at Rumford, ME; m. EBENEZER VIRGIN, b. at Rumford, NH 28 May 1735 son of Ebenezer and Hannah (Foster) Virgin. This family relocated to Rumford, ME where they were first settlers.[262]

438) iv CHANDLER LOVEJOY, b. 23 Jan 1741/2; d. at Concord 20 Nov 1827; m. MIRIAM VIRGIN, b. at Rumford 23 May 1744 daughter of Ebenezer and Hannah (Foster) Virgin. Chandler m. 2nd 28 Sep 1814, AZUBAH GRAHAM.

v HENRY LOVEJOY, b. 19 Oct 1744; died in infancy.

vi HENRY LOVEJOY, b. 27 Sep 1746; d. 18 Aug 1747.

439) vii HANNAH LOVEJOY, b. 26 Jan 1749; d. at Thetford, VT 29 May 1809; m. JONATHAN WEST, b. at Rumford, 20 Oct 1749 son of Nathaniel and Sarah (Burbank) West; Jonathan d. 30 Aug 1826.

440) viii SARAH LOVEJOY, b. 8 Jun 1752; d. at Concord, 1815; m. about 1772, her second cousin, THEODORE FARNUM, b. at Andover, 24 Jan 1749 son of Josiah and Mary (Frye) Farnum; Theodore d. about 1789 (probate of estate). After Theodore's death, Sarah married Jedediah Hoit.

100) LYDIA CHANDLER *(John Chandler3, Hannah Abbott Chandler2, George1)*, b. 10 Aug 1720 daughter of John and Hannah (Frye) Chandler; d. 9 Nov 1803; m. 30 Nov 1741, HEZEKIAH BALLARD, b. Jun 1720 son of Hezekiah and Rebecca (Davis) Ballard; Hezekiah d. at Andover, 31 Dec 1801.

Deacon Hezekiah Ballard wrote his will 12 April 1801. In the will, he bequeaths to Lydia "my beloved wife, all my household stuff and furniture, proper for woman's use, to be entirely at her own disposal." She also has use of the easterly half of the dwelling house. Beloved son Hezekiah Ballard receives the westerly half of the dwelling house. Hezekiah also receives the remainder of the personal estate. He makes a token bequest of one dollar to each of his daughters as they have already received their portions of the estate. The daughters are Lydia, Rebecca, Lowis, Hannah, Mary, Sarah, and Lucy. He also grants to his grandson, Joshua Ballard the son of Hezekiah, all his lands on the easterly side of Boston road. Beloved grandson Zebadiah Abbot is named executor of the estate.[263]

The births of ten children were recorded at Andover. Of the eight children who married, seven of them married fellow George Abbott of Andover descendants.

441) i LYDIA BALLARD, b. 30 Jul 1742; d. 28 Nov 1813; m. 13 Dec 1763, her third cousin once removed, DANE HOLT, b. 1 Apr 1740 son of Timothy and Hannah (Dane) Holt; Dane d. 15 Dec 1818.

442) ii REBECCA BALLARD, b. 15 May 1744; d. 15 Sep 1821; m. 1 Oct 1765, her third cousin, ZEBADIAH ABBOTT, b. 27 Sep 1739 son of Zebadiah and Anne (Lovejoy) Abbott; Zebadiah d. 24 Nov 1793.

341) iii LOIS BALLARD, b. 19 Jul 1746; d. 21 Dec 1836; m. 17 Feb 1767, her second cousin (and George Abbott descendant) JOSHUA PHELPS, b. 25 Jun 1738 son of Samuel and Priscilla (Chandler) Phelps; Joshua d. 22 Dec 1798. This is the same couple as Family #73, child ii.

335) iv HANNAH BALLARD, b. 6 Dec 1748; d. 22 Dec 1838; m. 1st 30 May 1769, OBADIAH FOSTER, b. 25 May 1741 son of John and Mary (Osgood) Foster; Obadiah d. at Andover, 25 Jul 1780. Hannah m. 2nd as his second wife JOSHUA CHANDLER, b. 23 Jul 1732 son of Joshua and Sarah (Chandler) Chandler. Joshua's first wife was HANNAH CHANDLER daughter of Nathan and Priscilla (Holt) Chandler. This is the same as Family #71, child ii.

342) v MARY BALLARD, b. 27 Feb 1750/1; d. 11 Aug 1835; m. 31 Oct 1780, her second cousin (and George Abbott descendant) HENRY PHELPS, b. 5 Sep 1740 son of Samuel and Priscilla (Chandler) Phelps; Henry d. 31 Oct 1807.

vi JOSHUA BALLARD, b. 28 Jun 1753; d. 31 Jan 1755

[262] Lapham, *History of Rumford, Oxford County, Maine*

[263] *Essex County, MA: Probate File Papers, 1638-1881. Probate of* Hezekiah *Ballard,* 1 Feb 1802*, Case number* 1587.

443) vii SARAH BALLARD, b. 28 Dec 1755; d. 20 Aug 1825; m. 8 May 1777, her third cousin, NATHAN ABBOTT, b. at Pembroke, 4 Sep 1753 son of Job and Sarah (Abbott) Abbott; Nathan d. 1801.

viii DORCAS BALLARD, b. 16 Oct 1757; d. 25 Aug 1775.

444) ix LUCY BALLARD, b. 4 Apr 1760; d. 29 Jun 1827; m. 27 Nov 1782, her first cousin once removed (and George Abbott descendant) NATHAN CHANDLER, b. 16 Jun 1756 son of Nathan and Phebe (Abbott) Chandler; Nathan d. 27 Jun 1837.

445) x HEZEKIAH BALLARD, b. 18 Jul 1762; d. 4 Oct 1848; m. 10 Dec 1783, his first cousin once removed (and George Abbott descendant), MARY "Molly" CHANDLER, b. 4 Apr 1764 daughter of Zebadiah and Deborah (Blanchard) Chandler; Molly d. 30 Mar 1834.

101) ABIAL (f) CHANDLER *(Abiel Chandler³, Hannah Abbott Chandler², George¹)*, b. 11 Dec 1711 daughter of Abiel and Hephzibah (Harnden) Chandler; d. 29 Jun 1780; m. 13 May 1731, her first cousin once removed, DAVID CHANDLER, b. 11 Jan 1697/8 son of Thomas and Mary (Peters) Chandler; David d. before 1774 probably at Pembroke, NH.[264]

Seven children for this couple were found in the birth records. The births of the two oldest and the two youngest children are recorded at Andover; the three middle children were born at Suncook/Rumford. Chandler's *The Descendants of William and Annis Chandler* (p. 75) lists a son Samuel born 4 November 1757 with this family, but Samuel with that birthdate is recorded as the child of David and Mary (Ballard) Chandler.[265]

i INFANT CHANDLER, b. and d. 1731/2.

446a ii MARY CHANDLER, b. 8 Aug 1734; likely d. at Blue Hill, ME, 21 Mar 1830. *Likely* the wife of ISAAC INGALLS b. at Andover, 13 Sep 1733 son of Henry and Hannah (Martin) Ingalls.[266]

446) iii TIMOTHY CHANDLER, b. 5 Apr 1738 at Suncook; m. at Townsend, 26 Aug 1762, MARY WALKER whose identity is not certain, but born about 1742 (based on age at time of death); Mary d. at Shelburne, NH, 5 Sep 1777.

447) iv HULDAH CHANDLER, b. at Suncook, 16 Aug 1740; d. likely at Hillsborough; m. 1st, 27 Dec 1763, NATHAN WARDWELL, b. 20 Jan 1740/1 son of William and Margery (Gray) Wardwell; Nathan d. 14 Aug 1769. Huldah m. 2nd at Andover, 9 Jan 1772, STEPHEN STILES, b. at Andover, 27 Mar 1741 son of Hezekiah and Hannah (Barnard) Stiles.

448) v HEPHZIBAH CHANDLER, b. 16 Oct 1743; d. 25 Oct 1810; m. 12 Apr 1762, WILLIAM FARNSWORTH, b. at Pepperell, 27 Dec 1737 son of William and Ruth (Hobart) Farnsworth. William m. 2nd, 20 May 1813, Sarah Green; William d. about 1837 in New York.

449) vi LYDIA CHANDLER, b. 28 May 1746; d. after 1816 at Langdon, NH (received a distribution from her husband's estate in 1816); m. 1st, as his second wife, JOSEPH PARKER, b. 15 Jul 1726 son of Joseph and Mary (Emery) Parker; Joseph d. 1777. Joseph's first wife was Hannah Abbott and that family is considered elsewhere (Family #206). Lydia m. 2nd, THOMAS KENNEY, b. unknown but does not seem to be the son of Thomas Kenney who died in New Hampshire in 1762 (as he is not mentioned in that will); Thomas d. about 1814 at Langdon, NH (probate of will).

vii HANNAH CHANDLER, b. 21 Jun 1755; m. at Pepperell, 5 Mar 1778, SAMUEL FARLEY, b. at Reading, 1 May 1741 son of Samuel and Mary (Adams) Farley; Samuel d. at Scipio, NY, after 1820. Samuel was first married to Elizabeth Johnson. Hannah and Samuel had five children, and a marriage is likely for two of the children, Hephzibah who married William Lovejoy and David Chandler Farley who married Sally Nichols.

---

264 Chandler, *The Descendants of William and Annis Chandler* notes that the widow Abial Chandler was received at the church in Andover September 1774 from the church in Pembroke. The family had been dismissed from the church at Andover to Pembroke 21 May 1738.

265 Massachusetts: Vital Records, 1621-1850 (Online Database: *AmericanAncestors.org*, New England Historic Genealogical Society, 2001-2016).

266 Porter, Bangor Historical Magazine, volume 4, p 156 gives Isaac's wife as Mary Chandler. The Ingalls genealogy, p56, suggests she may be Mary Osgood or Mary Chandler, but the birth date they give is the birth date of Mary Chandler.

102) DORCAS ABBOTT *(Hannah Chandler Abbott[3], Hannah Abbott Chandler[2], George[1]* **and** *Daniel[3], George[2], George[1])*, b. 16 Dec 1713 daughter of Daniel and Hannah (Chandler) Abbott; d. 22 Aug 1798 at Woodstock; m. 17 Nov 1740, THOMAS CHAFFEE, b. at Swansea 18 Oct 1716 son of Joseph and Jemima (Chadwick) Chaffee; Thomas d. at Woodstock 3 May 1753.[267]

The family of Dorcas Abbott and Thomas Chaffee was part of the secondary migration in which families from the Massachusetts colony relocated to Connecticut, primarily settlements within Windham County. The couple had four daughters, three of whom lived to adulthood. Thomas died at 36 years old, but Dorcas did not remarry. She remained in Woodstock where she died in 1798.

Thomas did not leave a will, but there is a 1753 probate record which includes disbursements for the widow Dorcas and her three daughters Jemima, Dorcas, and Rhoda.[268]

One interesting element for this family is that two of the daughters, Jemima and Rhoda, seem to have children out-of-wedlock. The Woodstock Vital Records book has the following entry: "Asenath Hodges Daughter of Jemime Chaffe Born July 22nd 1760." The Connecticut Church Record Abstracts contain the following entries that may be related to this. On 2 August 1761, Jemima Chaffee "confessed and was pardoned." She had her daughter "Asenah" baptized on 21 February 1762.[269] Woodstock Vital Records have the following entry for Rhoda: "Anice Corbin Daughter of Rhoda Chaffe born May 18 - 177[1]." Rhoda confessed 17 March 1771 and had her daughter "Anise" baptized 20 October 1771. There were not corresponding confessions for either Mr. Hodge or Mr. Corbin, so it is not determined who those fathers might be. Both Rhoda and Jemima went on to marry other men.

450) i JEMIMA CHAFFEE, b. 12 May 1741; d. at Woodstock, 28 Aug 1818; out-of-wedlock relationship with Mr. Hodges 1759-1760; m. 5 Jun 1766, as his second wife, AMOS PERRIN son of Peter and Abigail (Carpenter) Perrin; Amos d. 11 Jan 1811.

ii DORCAS CHAFFEE, b. 17 May 1744; d. 31 Aug 1746.

451) iii DORCAS CHAFFEE, b. 12 Jun 1747; d. unknown (living at time of husband's death); m. at Ashford 6 Oct 1767, FRANCIS GREEN CHAFFEE,[270] b. 6 Apr 1745 son of Benjamin and Priscilla (Green) Chaffee; Francis d. 3 Jul 1786.

452) iv RHODA CHAFFEE, b. 10 May 1751; d. 19 Nov 1834; out-of-wedlock relationship with Mr. Corbin 1770-1771; m. by 1772, DARIUS TRUESDELL, b. at Pomfret 16 Jan 1752 son of Joseph and Mary (Holt) Truesdell; Darius d. at Woodstock 6 May 1808.

103) JOSEPH ABBOTT *(Hannah Chandler Abbott[3], Hannah Abbott Chandler[2], George[1]* **and** *Daniel[3], George[2], George[1])*, b. 19 Sep 1716 son of Daniel and Hannah (Chandler) Abbott; m. at Woodstock, 22 Apr 1738, ABIGAIL CUTLER, b. 28 Aug 1711 at Colchester, CT, daughter of Jonathan and Abigail (Bigelow) Cutler; published genealogies (Bigelow[271] and Abbot genealogies) give the dates of death for both Joseph and Abigail as 22 Sep 1776, but I have located no records for the deaths of either of them.

The Abbot genealogy book[272] adds children Olive and Zebadiah to this family. However, the Woodstock Vital Records attributes those two children to Nathan and Ann Abbott. There are only four births recorded for Joseph and Abigail at Woodstock.

i HANNAH ABBOTT, b. 12 Jul 1739.

453) ii DANIEL ABBOTT, b. 18 Oct 1740; d. likely at Lebanon, NH; m. at Belchertown, MA, 29 Nov 1764, MARY KENTFIELD.

454) iii JOSEPH ABBOTT, b. 17 Feb 1742/3; d. at Pittstown, NY, 26 Jan 1813; m. 11 Dec 1764, PERSIS PERRIN, b. 4 Jun 1742 daughter of Nathaniel and Abigail (Jackson) Perrin; Persis d. 23 Jan 1817.

455) iv SARAH ABBOTT, b. 8 Jul 1748; m. at Union, CT, 24 Nov 1768, JONAS HOUGHTON son of Edward and Abigail (-) Houghton; Jonas d. at Woodstock 13 Nov 1791.

104) ELIZABETH ABBOTT *(Hannah Chandler Abbott [3], Hannah Abbott Chandler[2], George[1]* **and** *Daniel[3], George[2], George[1])*, b. 9 Jul 1719 daughter of Daniel and Hannah (Chandler) Abbott; d. at Woodstock, 1 Jan 1785; m. at Woodstock, 27 May 1737, MATTHEW MURRAY, perhaps of Scotland; d. at Pomfret about 1788 when his estate was probated.

---

[267] Vital statistics for Woodstock are from Barbour and Brainard's Woodstock Vital Records unless otherwise noted.
[268] *Connecticut Wills and Probate, 1609-1999*, Probate of Thomas Chaffee, Hartford, 1753, Case number 873.
[269] Ancestry.com, *Connecticut, Church Record Abstracts, 1630-1920.* Original data: Connecticut Church Records Index. Connecticut State Library, Hartford, Connecticut.
[270] Connecticut, Town Marriage Records, pre-1870 (Barbour Collection)
[271] Howe, *Genealogy of the Bigelow Family*
[272] Abbot and Abbot, *Genealogical Register of Descendants*

Matthew Murray relocated to Pomfret after the death of Elizabeth. At the time of the probate of his estate in 1788, there were three heirs living and they signed quit claim deeds related to a property in Pomfret to settle the estate. These heirs were James Murray, Asa and Elizabeth Childs, and Jeremiah and Phebe Jackson.[273]

There are six children recorded at Woodstock for Matthew and Elizabeth.

i JAMES MURRAY, b. 29 Aug 1737; d. 1739.

456) ii PHEBE MURRAY, b. 2 Aug 1739; m. 16 Mar 1758, JEREMIAH JACKSON, b. 22 Aug 1739[274] son of Joseph and Zipporah (-) Jackson; Jeremiah d. at Lafayette, NY, 10 Mar 1802.[275]

457) iii ELIZABETH MURRAY, b. 10 Sep 1741; d. 28 Apr 1790; m. 17 Nov 1763, ASA CHILDS, b. at Woodstock, 6 Apr 1743 son of Ephraim and Mary (-) Childs; Asa d. 20 Oct 1826.

458) iv JAMES MURRAY, b. 8 Dec 1743; m. 26 Jan 1769, SARAH REYNOLDS who is not yet identified.

v SARAH MURRAY, b. 24 Jan 1745/6; no further record.

vi JOHN MURRAY, b. 1 Apr 1753; no further record.

105) PHEBE ABBOTT *(Hannah Chandler Abbott³, Hannah Abbott Chandler², George¹* **and** *Daniel³, George², George¹)*, b. 7 Apr 1721 daughter of Daniel and Hannah (Chandler) Abbott; d. at Woodstock after 10 Jul 1756 (the birth of her last child);[276] m. at Woodstock 20 Aug 1742, EBENEZER HOLMES, b. at Woodstock 27 Feb 1720/1 son of Ebenezer and Joanna (Ainsworth) Holmes. Ebenezer m. 2nd Martha Howlet, 12 Apr 1759 and 3rd 16 Nov 1775 Elizabeth Barrett. Ebenezer d. at Woodstock, 28 Jun 1794.[277]

Ebenezer Holmes did not leave a will, but the probate record does contain the disbursements to the heirs, four of whom are from his marriage to Phebe Abbott: eldest son Ebenezer, Ralph Vinton on behalf of his wife Phebe, John Vinton on behalf of his wife Dorothy, and Zephaniah Tucker on behalf of his wife Huldah.[278]

Phebe Abbott and Ebenezer Holmes had five children whose births are recorded at Woodstock.

459) i PHEBE HOLMES, b. 22 Jun 1743; d. at Dudley, MA 6 Feb 1828; m. at Dudley, 15 Jun 1766, RALPH VINTON, b. 17 Oct 1740 son of Joseph and Hannah (Baldwin) Vinton; Ralph d. 14 Apr 1832.

460) ii DOROTHY HOLMES, b. 13 Apr 1745; d. likely after 1830 when she seems to be the Dorothy Vinton as head of household in the 1830 Census; m. at Dudley, 11 Jan 1770, JOHN VINTON, b. 14 Feb 1742 son of Joseph and Hannah (Baldwin) Vinton; John d. at Charlton, MA Jul 1814.[279]

461) iii EBENEZER HOLMES, b. 1 Nov 1748; d. at Boston 29 Jan 1810; m. 7 Apr 1778, MARCELLA COLBURN, b. at Stafford, 11 May 1760 daughter of Jonathan and Hannah (Royce) Colburn; Marcella d. at Boston 28 Apr 1815, age at death given as 55 years.

iv CHANDLER HOLMES, b. 27 Dec 1750; d. 4 May 1755.

462) v HULDAH HOLMES, b. 10 Jul 1756; d. at Woodstock, 2 Feb 1853; m. 4 Feb 1779, ZEPHANIAH TUCKER, b. at Leicester, 15 Nov 1756 son of Stephen and Mary (Pike) Tucker; Zephaniah d. 25 Apr 1817.

106) NATHAN ABBOTT *(Hannah Chandler Abbott³, Hannah Abbott Chandler², George¹* **and** *Daniel³, George², George¹)*, b. 16 Oct 1723 son of Daniel and Hannah (Chandler) Abbott; d. after 1790 perhaps at Brimfield; m. at Woodstock 2 Jun 1746, ANNA LEACH who origins are unknown to me; a death record has not been located for Anna. There was a Leach family in Woodstock, but it is uncertain how she might be related to this family.

Nathan and Anna married at Woodstock and had three children there. The family then seems to have gone to Brimfield where at least two more children were born. The two oldest children in this family, who were born at Woodstock, married at Brimfield.

---

[273] *Connecticut Wills and Probate, 1609-1999*, Probate of Matthew Murry, Hartford, 1788, Case number 2983.

[274] Ancestry.com, *Mayflower Births and Deaths, Vol. 1 and 2* (Provo, UT, USA: Ancestry.com Operations, Inc., 2013).

[275] The grave of Jeremiah Jackson is in Lafayette Cemetery and includes an inscription with date of birth as 13 Aug 1739 and death as 10 Mar 1802. Findagrave.com memorial I.D. 44074277

[276] Published sources give her death as 30 May 1756, but the birth date of her youngest child in the Woodstock records is 10 Jul 1756.

[277] Barbour and Newton, *Vital Records of Woodstock 1686-1854*

[278] *Connecticut Wills and Probate, 1609-1999*, Probate of Ebenezer Holmes, Hartford, 1794, Case number 2118.

[279] The date of death is that used by the DAR Ancestor listing.

Nathan Abbott is listed in the History of Brimfield including his pew assignment in the meeting house in 1757. His name is listed as a signer of a 1774 covenant in support of the colonies and suspension of commerce with Great Britain.[280] It is possible that he is the Nathan Abbott listed in the 1790 U.S. Census at Brimfield with a household of seven persons.

There is disagreement in published genealogies related to Nathan Abbott which I believe results from the confusion of two different Nathan Abbotts (who were second cousins once removed) who were both in Woodstock near the same time. The second Nathan married Judith Stoddard and had several children with her in Woodstock. That Nathan died at Woodstock 19 January 1794 and his probate record includes administration by his widow Judith. According to the Abbot genealogy, it is Nathan born in 1744 son of Nathan and Eunice (Marsh) Abbott who married Judith Stoddard and remained in Woodstock and died there 14 January 1794 (or some state 14 January 1793). The Chandler genealogy, on the other hand, states it is Nathan the son of Daniel and Hannah (Chandler) Abbott that died in Woodstock in 1793 or 1794. But the probate record for that Nathan establishes that was the husband of Judith. That is also supported by records from the Connecticut cemetery inscriptions and newspaper notices that give the age at death in 1794 of 49 for Nathan Abbott. This fits for the age of Nathan son of Nathan born in 1744, but not for Nathan the son of Daniel born in 1723.[281] I have concluded that Nathan the son of Daniel and Hannah (Chandler) Abbott married Anna Leach in Woodstock and then relocated to Brimfield. Nathan the son of Nathan and Eunice (Marsh) Abbott married Judith Stoddard and remained in Woodstock where he died January 1794.

There are records of births of three children for Nathan and Anna at Woodstock and two at Brimfield. It is possible there were two other daughters in this family, Hannah and Mary. There are marriage records in Brimfield for Hannah and Mary about the time for them to be the right ages to be in this family, but that has not been established.

463) i ELLINOR ABBOTT, b. at Woodstock, 5 May 1747; m. at Brimfield, 28 May 1772, EPHRAIM BOND, b. at Leicester, 3 Dec 1746 son of John and Lydia (Gray) Bond.

464) ii OLIVE ABBOTT, b. at Woodstock, 27 May 1749; d. at Lebanon, CT, 7 Oct 1784; m. at Brimfield, 25 Oct 1770, ELEAZER HUTCHINSON, b. at Windham, 12 Feb 1744/5 son of Joseph and Ruth (Read) Hutchinson; Eleazer d. Apr 1824.[282] Olive and Eleazer had one child who died in childhood. They were admitted to the church in Lebanon in 1772 and their deaths are entered in the church records, but there are no baptism records for children and no birth or death records in the Lebanon records other than the one child.

465) iii ZEBADIAH ABBOTT, b. at Woodstock, 1750; m. at Sturbridge, 25 Mar 1780, MOLLY CHUBB, b. at Needham, 14 Nov 1754 daughter of Samuel and Prudence (Fisher) Chubb.

465a iv MARY ABBOTT, b. at Brimfield, about 1752;[283] d. at Brimfield, 22 Aug 1791; m. at Brimfield, 17 Jun 1773, SOLOMON CHARLES, b. at Brimfield, 8 Dec 1750 son of Jonathan and Judith (Smith) Charles; Solomon d. at Wilbraham, 7 Apr 1843. After Mary's death, Solomon married Hannah Tomblin.

466) v HENRY ABBOTT, b. at Brimfield, 30 May 1754;[284] d. at Brimfield, 31 Jul 1797; m. TABITHA RUSSELL, b. at Brimfield, 22 Aug 1749 the daughter of Ruth Blodget and unknown father Russell (apparently a child born out of wedlock);[285] Tabitha d. at Brimfield, 9 Mar 1832.

vi NATHAN ABBOTT, b. at Brimfield, 2 Jan 1757; d. 15 Sep 1758.

107) JOHN ABBOTT *(Hannah Chandler Abbott[3], Hannah Abbott Chandler[2], George[1]* **and** *Daniel[3], George[2], George[1])*, b. 11 Jan 1726 son of Daniel and Hannah (Chandler) Abbott; d. at Woodstock 7 Mar 1806; m. at Ashford, 28 Nov 1750, MARY WRIGHT, b. at Ashford, 29 Sep 1730 daughter of John and Judith (Wyman) Wright; Mary d. 30 May 1811.

The births of eleven children of John Abbott and wife Mary were located. The births of ten of these children were recorded at Ashford and the birth of one child, Mary, is recorded at Woodstock. There may be a question whether daughter Mary goes in this family, but she fits in terms of birthdate. I did not locate another John Abbott married to a Mary in Windham County around that time, so I am leaving her in this family. There is not a probate record for either John Abbott or his wife Mary Wright Abbott.

i JOHN ABBOTT, b. 18 Oct 1751; d. 22 Nov 1782.

---

[280] Hyde, *Historical Celebration of the Town of Brimfield, Hampden, Massachusetts*, p 305, p 311

[281] *Connecticut, Hale Collection of Cemetery Inscriptions and Newspaper Notices, 1629-1934.* Newspaper notice gives age at death as 49, and states he was in the Revolutionary War.

[282] *Connecticut, Church Record Abstracts, 1630-1920.*

[283] Mary is a presumed child of Nathan and Anna Abbott. She married in Brimfield at the time Nathan was there and no other Abbott families seem to have been there at that time. In any event, she is an Abbott even if she is later found to have other parents.

[284] Henery, s. Nathan and Annah, May 30, 1754, Brimfield births

[285] Tabitha, d. Ruth Blodget, Aug. 22, 1749. [Tabitha Blogget, C.R.]

467) ii MARY ABBOTT, b. 31 Aug 1753; d. at Ashford, 16 Nov 1790; m. at Ashford, 21 Oct 1784, EBENEZER WRIGHT.

468) iii ABIEL ABBOTT, b. 22 Mar 1756; d. 5 Apr 1812; m. 8 Jun 1786, JANE BARTLETT, b. about 1766; Jane d. after 1850 at Northampton, NY (living with son Daniel at the 1850 U. S. Census).

469) iv DAVID ABBOTT, b. 19 Apr 1758; d. 27 Feb 1827; m. POLLY PAINE.

v JUDAH ABBOTT, b. 20 Nov 1760; d. 27 Feb 1845.

470) vi NATHAN ABBOTT, b. 31 Jul 1763; d. at Cardiff, NY, 21 Mar 1836; m. 1st, 31 Aug 1785, ELIZABETH BOWEN, b. at Ashford, 13 Feb 1765 daughter of Joseph and Thankful (Chandler) Bowen; Elizabeth d. before 1808. Nathan m. 2nd, 16 Oct 1808 HULDAH SKINNER, b. at Stafford, 2 Feb 1777 daughter of Joseph and Mehitable (-) Skinner; Huldah d. at Cardiff, 15 Apr 1848.[286]

vii ABIGAIL ABBOTT, b. 26 Mar 1766; d. 7 Sep 1823.

viii DANIEL ABBOTT, b. 3 Sep 1768; d. at Woodstock?, 29 Mar 1812; m. IRENA CHAMBERLAIN, b. at Woodstock, 15 Nov 1765 daughter of Samuel and Anna (Kingsley) Chamberlain. Daniel and Irena did not have children.

471) ix JOSEPH ABBOTT, b. 13 Feb 1771; d. 24 Jun 1829; m. 6 Mar 1794, ANNA SKINNER, b. at Stafford, daughter of Joseph and Mehitable (-) Skinner. There are two sisters, Anna and Huldah Skinner, born at Woodstock in 1770 and 1771, but this is about six years too old for Huldah Skinner who married Nathan Abbott (based on her age at time of death). I did not locate probate records that would confirm one way of the other, so I am leaving Anna and Huldah as the sisters from Stafford for the time being.

472) x AMOS ABBOTT, b. 15 Nov 1772; d. at Otisco, NY, 21 Sep 1852; m. 9 Apr 1800, SARAH GRIGGS, b. at Ashford, 17 Sep 1776 daughter of Joseph and Rebecca (Chaffee) Griggs.

xi HANNAH ABBOTT, b. 1 Aug 1776; d. 24 Nov 1844; m. at Ashford, 16 Aug 1814, NATHANIEL ROUND of Bristol, RI. Hannah does not seem to have had children.

108) SARAH ABBOTT *(Hannah Chandler Abbott³, Hannah Abbott Chandler², George¹* **and** *Daniel³, George², George¹)*, b. 5 May 1728 daughter of Daniel and Hannah (Chandler) Abbott; d. 7 Oct 1802; m. 1st, JABEZ CORBIN, b. at Woodstock, 21 Mar 1724 son of Jabez and Hannah (Peake) Corbin; Jabez d. 1774 (probate 7 Jun 1774). Sarah m. 2nd, 31 May 1780, as his second wife, WILLIAM CHAPMAN; William d. 1792.

The estate of Jabez Corbin entered probate on 7 June 1774. Widow Sarah is administrator of the estate. There is an inventory of the estate, but no documents related to heirs. The value of the estate was just over £62.[287]

William Chapman wrote his will 5 April 1783. He makes mention of a settlement agreement with Sarah prior to their marriage executed 31 May 1780. In addition to this, she receives a list of specific household items including an iron trammel and a pewter chamber pot. If Sarah relinquishes her title and interest in his dwelling house which was part of the marital agreement, she will receive, on January 1 of each year, one-bushel wheat, one-bushel rye, and two bushels Indian corn as long as she remains his widow. He also makes bequests to his children from his first marriage.[288]

There are just two births recorded for Sarah Abbott and Jabez Corbin.

473) i JONATHAN CORBIN, b. 22 Aug 1760; d. at Dudley, MA; m. at Oxford, 24 Dec 1781, ABIGAIL WIGHT, b. at Thompson, CT, 30 Jan 1757 daughter of Levi and Susannah (Barstow) Wight; Abigail d. at Dudley 31 Jul 1825.

474) ii SARAH CORBIN, b. 11 Jan 1764; d. at Centerville, NY 15 Apr 1852; m. at Oxford, 24 Oct 1782, LEVI WIGHT, b. at Thompson, CT, 3 Jul 1761 son of Levi and Susannah (Barstow) Wight;[289] Levi d. at Centerville 2 Jan 1831.[290]

---

[286] The graves of Nathan and Huldah Abbott are in Cardiff Cemetery with Nathan's age on gravestone as 72 and Huldah his wife, age 70. It is not a certainty that these are the graves of this same couple.

[287] *Connecticut Wills and Probate, 1609-1999*, Probate of Jabez Corbin, Hartford, 1774, Case number 1264

[288] *Connecticut Wills and Probate, 1609-1999*, Probate of William Chapman, Hartford, 1792, Case number 735.

[289] Wight, *The Wights*, p 71

[290] The graves of Levi Wight and his wife Sarah are located at Bates Cemetery in Centerville, NY. Findagrave.com

109) GEORGE ABBOTT *(Hannah Chandler Abbott³, Hannah Abbott Chandler², George¹* and *Daniel³, George², George¹)*, b. 21 Jan 1730 son of Daniel and Hannah (Chandler) Abbott; d. before 18 Dec 1772[291]; m. 16 Jan 1754, MARY WHITNEY, b. at Uxbridge, 27 Oct 1732 daughter of Joshua and Hannah (Rockwood or Rockett) Whitney.

George and Mary married at Woodstock and their first child was born there. The young family then relocated to Palmer, Massachusetts where the births of six other children were recorded. No marriage or death records were located for the children. It is not known what became of Mary Whitney Abbott after her husband's death.

i GEORGE ABBOTT, b. 1755; died young

ii HANNAH ABBOTT, b. 22 Jun 1758

iii NATHAN ABBOTT, b. 26 Jun 1760

iv MOLLY ABBOTT, b. 20 Sep 1762

v SARAH ABBOTT, b. 25 Oct 1765

vi BETHIAH ABBOTT, b. 13 May 1768

vii GEORGE ABBOTT, b. 4 Sep 1770

110) JOSEPH WRIGHT *(Sarah Chandler Wright³, Hannah Abbott Chandler², George¹)*, b. Mar 1712/3 son of Joseph and Sarah (Chandler) Wright; d. at Winchester, NH, 27 May 1785; m. 1st at Woodstock, ABIGAIL CHAFFEE, b. at Swansea, 5 Mar 1715 daughter of Joseph and Jemima (Chadwick) Chaffee.[292] It is not known when Abigail died but likely by 1746 as Joseph and second wife Mary started having children in 1747. Joseph had a second wife named MARY about whom nothing else is known.

The 1786 New Hampshire probate of the son Samuel Wright makes a reference to the inventory of the possessions of the widow Mary Wright who is his step-mother. "An inventory of the household furniture of the Widow Wright mother to Samuel Wright late of Winchester, deceased."[293]

Births of five children of Joseph Wright and Abigail Chaffee are recorded at Woodstock.

475) i SARAH WRIGHT, b. 24 Sep 1737; d. likely at Winchester, NH; m. 23 Apr 1761, JOSEPH NARRAMORE, b. at Thompson, CT, 11 May 1735 son of Samuel and Lydia (Davis) Narrimore; Joseph d. at Winchester, 20 Feb 1802.

ii ABIEL WRIGHT, b. 9 Oct 1739; no further record.

iii ABIGAIL WRIGHT, b. 8 Sep 1741; died young.

476) iv SAMUEL WRIGHT, b. 28 Jan 1744/5; d. Jul 1786 at Winchester, NH; m. 27 Oct 1768, MARY COBURN, b. at Woodstock, 25 Oct 1745 daughter of John and Deborah (Goddard) Coburn.

v INFANT WRIGHT, abt. 1746.

Joseph Wright and Mary had four children whose births are recorded at Woodstock.

477) i HANNAH WRIGHT, b. 11 Dec 1747; d. at Winchester, 31 Mar 1812; m. 5 Nov 1767, ASAHEL JEWELL, b. 2 Aug 1744 son of Archibald and Rebecca (Leonard) Jewell; Asahel d. at Winchester, 30 Apr 1790.[294]

ii ABIGAIL WRIGHT, b. 8 Apr 1750; no further record.

478) iii BENJAMIN WRIGHT, b. 25 Feb 1753; d. in Caledonia County, VT 1839; m. 24 Jul 1776, SYBIL BRETT (Burt), b. at Bridgewater, 16 May 1756 daughter of Seth and Patience (Curtis) Brett.

479) iv LEMUEL WRIGHT, b. 15 May 1757; d. at Quebec, Canada, 13 Feb 1846; m. 21 Dec 1779, DEBORAH ERSKINE, b. about 1755 daughter of John and Deborah (Studley) Erskine; Deborah buried at Shefford, Québec in 1843.[295]

---

[291] Ward, "The Footloose Joshua Whitney", *American Genealogist* (1999, volume 74, p 200) states Mary Whitney Abbott was a widow in a deed of 18 Dec 1772. The Footloose Joshua Whitney

[292] Chaffee, *The Chaffee Genealogy*, p. 78

[293] *New Hampshire Wills and Probate Records 1643-1982*, Probate of Samuel Wright, Cheshire, 1786, Case number 47

[294] New Hampshire, Death and Disinterment Records, 1754-1947

[295] Ancestry.com, database, The New England Historical & Genealogical Register, 1847-2011

111) SARAH WRIGHT *(Sarah Chandler Wright³, Hannah Abbott Chandler², George¹)*, b. 7 Aug 1715 daughter of Joseph and Sarah (Chandler) Wright; d. 22 Dec 1783;[296] m. 17 Jan 1733/4, EDMUND CHAMBERLAIN, b. 6 Mar 1701/2 son of Edmund and Elizabeth (Bartholomew) Chamberlain; Edmund d.at Woodstock, 9 Dec 1779.

Sarah and Edmund Chamberlain had six children whose births are recorded at Woodstock.

i WILLIAM CHAMBERLAIN, b. 23 Oct 1734; d. 30 Oct 1739.

ii ZERVIAH CHAMBERLAIN, b. 29 Aug 1736; d. 2 Mar 1737.

480) iii ABIEL CHAMBERLAIN, b. 20 Dec 1737; d. at Woodstock, 12 Jan 1818; m. 1760, GRACE AINSWORTH, b. at Woodstock, 1 Jun 1743 daughter of Nathan and Huldah (Peake) Ainsworth; Grace d. 10 Jan 1788.

iv WILLIAM CHAMBERLAIN, b. 14 Mar 1740/1; no further record.

481) v EDMUND CHAMBERLAIN, b. 7 Mar 1742/3; d. 24 Oct 1824; m. 20 Nov 1766, ELIZABETH KINGSLEY possibly the daughter of Jonathan and Experience (Sabin) Kingsley b. at Pomfret 23 Jun 1747. Elizabeth d. perhaps at Sturbridge, MA, 12 Jul 1835

vi DAUGHTER CHAMBERLAIN, b. 14 Sep and d. 15 Sep 1745.

112) HANNAH WRIGHT *(Sarah Chandler Wright³, Hannah Abbott Chandler², George¹)*, b. 20 Jun 1717 daughter of Joseph and Sarah (Chandler) Wright; no death record found (the Peters genealogy reports her death as 1796);[297] m. 6 Jan 1734/5, BEAMSLEY PETERS, b. at Andover 1710 son of Samuel and Phebe (Frye) Peters; Beamsley d. unknown but was between 1757 and 1762. Beamsley is listed in his mother's 1757 will but he is not listed in the final estate settlement.

The birth of one child of Hannah and Beamsley Peters is recorded at Woodstock.

i HANNAH PETERS, b. at Woodstock, 28 Feb 1734/5; nothing else is known.

113) ELIZABETH WRIGHT *(Sarah Chandler Wright³, Hannah Abbott Chandler², George¹)*, b. 13 Feb 1718/9 daughter of Joseph and Sarah (Chandler) Wright; death unknown; m. 23 Nov 1738, JOHN CARPENTER, b. at Woodstock, 17 Jul 1713 son of Eliphalet and Rebecca (Gardner) Carpenter

The births of only three children were recorded at Woodstock. No probate record was found in Connecticut, Massachusetts, New Hampshire or Vermont. It is possible that the son Beamsley Carpenter went to Vermont as there is a marriage record there for a Beamsley Carpenter in 1827 who could be a son of Beamsley. The son John relocated to New York.

482) i JOHN CARPENTER, b. 22 Feb 1739/40; d. at Whitestown, NY, 12 Jan 1809; m. 9 Feb 1757, MERCY MORGAN. John served in the Revolutionary War along with his sons William and Abiel.

483) ii BEAMSLEY CARPENTER, b. 3 Jul 1743; m. MARTHA.

iii JOSEPH CARPENTER, b. 10 Jul 1752

114) HEPHZIBAH WRIGHT *(Sarah Chandler Wright³, Hannah Abbott Chandler², George¹)*, b. 14 Oct 1720 daughter of Joseph and Sarah (Chandler) Wright; d. 1797 at Woodstock; m. 16 Dec 1736, ENOS BARTHOLOMEW, b. about 1714 and perhaps the son of John and Mary (Harrington) Bartholomew; d. before 1797 (Hephzibah was a widow at the time of her death).

There are the births of five children recorded at Woodstock. No probate record was located. Daughter Mercy did have a son out-of-wedlock (Lemuel Dunham 1769-1779). That son died at about 10 years old and there is a marriage record for Marcy Bartholomew after her son died.

i SARAH BARTHOLOMEW, b. 4 Apr 1737; d. 31 Mar 1797. Sarah does not seem to have married.

484) ii HANNAH BARTHOLOMEW, b. 7 Jun 1739; *possibly* m. 13 Jul 1758, ELKANAH STEPHENS, b. at Dighton, 18 Mar 1736 son of Nicholas and Rachel (Andrews) Stephens.

485) iii JOHN BARTHOLOMEW, b. 20 Feb 1741/2; d. at Woodstock 8 Jul 1798; m. CANDACE AINSWORTH, b. at Woodstock, 31 Aug 1748 daughter of Daniel and Sarah (Bugbee) Ainsworth.

---

296 This is according to Cutter's *New England Families and Genealogy*.

297 Peters, *Peters of New England*, p 111

iv MERCY BARTHOLOMEW, b. 10 Apr 1744; out-of-wedlock relationship with Mr. Dunham 1769; *possibly* m. 23 Dec 1783, GEORGE COTENEY perhaps the son of George and Sarah (-) Coteney. Mercy had one son, Lemuel Dunham, who died about 10 years old. There are no known children for Mercy and George Coteney.

486) v MARY BARTHOLOMEW, b. 28 Jun 1746; perhaps the widow Mary Leach who d. at Woodstock, 7 Mar 1811; likely m. 25 Jul 1765, ROBERT LEACH, perhaps from Bridgewater b. 4 May 1740 the son of Nehemiah and Mercy (Staples) Leach. Robert d. at Tolland about 1800 (probate of estate). The children in this family do include a son named Enos.

115) ABIGAIL WRIGHT *(Sarah Chandler Wright³, Hannah Abbott Chandler², George¹)*, b. 15 Feb 1727/8 daughter of Joseph and Sarah (Chandler) Wright; death unknown; m. 22 Mar 1748/9, ABIJAH CORBIN, b. 8 Feb 1722 son of Jabez and Hannah (Peake) Corbin; d. at Woodstock, 16 Oct 1808.[298]

There are births of six children recorded for this family that were located. Only one possible marriage was identified from the Woodstock records. No probate record was located for Abijah Corbin.

i HANNAH CORBIN, b. 26 Apr 1750

ii ESTHER CORBIN, b. 24 Oct 1755

iii ABIGAIL CORBIN, b. 17 Jun 1759

iv ALICE CORBIN, b. 22 Mar 1766; d. unknown; *possibly* m. 9 Jan 1803, as his second wife, WILLIAM PAUL.

v DANIEL CORBIN, b. 6 Oct 1768

vi DAUGHTER CORBIN, b. 24 Oct 1775

116) DOROTHY WRIGHT *(Sarah Chandler Wright³, Hannah Abbott Chandler², George¹)*, b. 3 Apr 1730 daughter of Joseph and Sarah (Chandler) Wright; death not known; m. 3 Aug 1747, PENUEL BACON, b. at Woodstock, 8 Jan 1725/6 son of Joseph and Rebekah (Carpenter) Bacon.

There is the birth of one son recorded for this family at Woodstock, and then no further records. There is a Penuel Bacon who served in the French and Indian War from Connecticut, and that is probably this Penuel as he seems to have been the only one in Connecticut at the time. There is a Penuel Bacon who shows up in upstate New York in 1776 tax rolls and that might be him. However, there are no birth, death, or probate records for this family that could be located.

i PINIAS BACON, b. 15 Nov 1747; no further record. There is a Deacon Phineas Bacon in Middleton, Connecticut of about the right age, but that seems to be a different Phineas Bacon.

Grandchildren of George Abbott and Dorcas Graves

117) HANNAH OSGOOD *(Hannah Abbott Osgood³, George², George¹)*, b. 22 Aug 1710 daughter of John and Hannah (Abbott) Osgood; d. 16 Mar 1761; m. 24 Jun 1728, SAMUEL CHICKERING, b. at Charlestown 10 Jul 1704 son of John and Susanna (Symmes) Chickering. Samuel m. 2nd the widow Mehitable Stevens; Samuel died about 1787 the year his estate was probated.

The estate of Samuel Chickering entered probate 5 November 1787. He did not leave a will. His widow Mehitable is administrator of the estate. Henry Ingalls and Stephen Holt assume responsibility for the bond. There is an inventory, but no disbursement to heirs in the available probate papers.

The births of ten children to Samuel and Hannah are recorded at Andover.

487) i HANNAH CHICKERING, b. 13 Jul 1730; d. at Wakefield, 10 Aug 1791; m. 22 Mar 1753, BENJAMIN PETERS, b. 25 Aug 1728 son of Samuel and Mary (Robinson) Peters; Benjamin d. at Wakefield, 17 Apr 1812.

[298] Lawson, *History and Genealogy of the Descendants of Clement Corbin of Muddy River*, p. 51

488) ii SAMUEL CHICKERING, b. 28 Sep 1732; d. 16 Mar 1814; m. 17 Apr 1755, his third cousin once removed, MARY DANE, b. 27 Sep 1733 daughter of John and Sarah (Chandler) Dane; Mary d. 24 Jun 1824.

489) iii SARAH CHICKERING, b. 5 Mar 1734/5; d.?; m. 13 Dec 1753, JAMES FRYE, b. 13 Sep 1731 son of Samuel and Sarah (Osgood) Frye; James d. 17 Dec 1804.

490) iv ELIZABETH CHICKERING, b. 25 Jan 1736/7; d. at Methuen, 20 Sep 1767; m. 24 May 1757, MOSES SARGENT, b. 23 May 1738 son of Christopher and Sara (Peaslee) Sargent. Moses m. 2nd 29 Nov 1767, Esther Runnells.

v SUSANNA CHICKERING, b. 25 Jan 1738/9; there is no further record and perhaps died young.

vi DORCAS CHICKERING, b. 14 Jul 1742; d. about 1807 when the estate of Dorcas Chickering, single woman of Andover, was probated.

491) vii JOHN CHICKERING, b. 15 Aug 1744; d.; m. 13 Nov 1770, SARAH WEBSTER, b. 3 Oct 1748 daughter of Ebenezer and Sarah (Gage) Webster.[299]

492) viii ZACHARIAH CHICKERING, b. 29 Mar 1747; d. at Hartford, ME; m. 20 Nov 1771, SARAH POOR, b. 22 May 1750 daughter of John and Rebecca (Stevens) Poor.

493) ix MARY CHICKERING, b. 17 Jan 1749/50; d. at Danville, VT, 20 Aug 1820;[300] m. 24 Oct 1770, JOHN SHORT, b. at Newbury, 16 Aug 1741 son of Joseph and Hannah (Prowse) Short.

494) x PHEBE CHICKERING, b. 9 Nov 1751; d. likely in NH; m. 28 Jul 1778, THOMAS HUTCHINSON whose identity is uncertain, although he could be Thomas Hutchinson born in Lynn in 1750. Cutter reports he is the son of Jonathan and Elizabeth (Ganson) Hutchinson.[301]

118) JOHN OSGOOD *(Hannah Abbott Osgood3, George2, George1)*, b. 22 Aug 1711 son of John and Hannah (Abbott) Osgood; d. 10 Jul 1775; m. 1st 20 Feb 1746, MARTHA CARLETON, b. 12 Jun 1722 daughter of Christopher and Martha (Barker) Carleton; Martha d. about 1755. JOHN m. 2nd 20 Feb 1756, HULDAH FRYE, b. 13 May 1737 daughter of Isaac and Naamah (Haskell) Frye; Huldah was listed in the 1800 Census as a head of household in Andover, but no record of her after that time.

John Osgood wrote a will 14 Jun 1775. He has a bequest to his wife Huldah and "each of my children," but he does not name them.

John Osgood and Martha Carleton had six children born at Andover.

495) i MARTHA OSGOOD, b. 3 May 1747; d. at Exeter, NH 15 Jun 1830;[302] m. ENOCH POOR, b. 21 Jun 1736 son of Thomas and Mary (Adams) Poor. Brigadier General Enoch Poor d. at Hackensack, NJ while serving in the military, 8 Sep 1780. The cause of death of Enoch Poor is a mystery.[303] The National Archives have on file a letter written by George Washington to Brigadier General Enoch Poor 22 Feb 1779.[304]

ii HANNAH OSGOOD, b. 27 Dec 1748; d. 16 Feb 1754.

iii JOHN OSGOOD, b. 12 Nov 1750; d. 5 Apr 1754.

496) iv DORCAS OSGOOD, b. 24 Mar 1752; d. at Roxbury 17 Oct 1810;[305] m. 1st ISAAC MARBLE, b. 9 Jun 1740 son of Noah and Mary (Ingalls) Marble; Isaac d. by 1780. Dorcas m. 2nd as his second wife, HENRY DEARBORN; Henry d. 1829. General Henry Dearborn was the Secretary of War under President Jefferson.

---

299 Sarah's parentage is confirmed by the probate settlement of the estate of Ebenezer Webster which includes a disbursement to Sarah Chickering.

300 Vermont, Vital Records, 1720-1908. Ancestry.com

301 Cutter, *New England Families*, volume 3, p 1441

302 Ancestry.com. *New Hampshire, Death and Burial Records Index, 1654-1949* [database on-line]. Provo, UT, USA: Ancestry.com Operations, Inc., 2011.

303 A biography of Enoch Poor can be found at the site of the New Hampshire Division of Historical Resources at this link: http://rkc.org/poor/poorofnh.html

304 National Archives, letter from George Washington to Brigadier General Enoch Poor, retrieved from https://founders.archives.gov/documents/Washington/03-19-02-0260

305 Ancestry.com, *U.S., Newspaper Extractions from the Northeast, 1704-1930* (Provo, UT, USA: Ancestry.com Operations, Inc., 2014).

497) v MARY OSGOOD, b. 30 Jun 1753; d. 22 May 1820;[306] m. by 1771, ISAAC FARNUM, b. 19 Dec 1742 son of John and Sarah (Frye) Farnum; Isaac d. 8 Sep 1823.[307]

vi HANNAH OSGOOD, b. 6 Nov 1754; d. at Manchester, MA, 6 Nov 1827; m. 1st about 1774, SIMON GREENLEAF, baptized at Newbury, 21 Jun 1747 son of Jonathan and Mary (Presbury) Greenleaf; Simon d. at Newburyport, 7 Dec 1776. Hannah m. 2nd at Newburyport, 5 May 1779, as his second wife, JOHN LEE, b. at Manchester, MA, 16 May 1738 son of John and Joanna (Raymond) Lee; John d. at Andover, 26 Mar 1812.

John Osgood and Huldah Frye had four children born at Andover.

i CHARLOTTE OSGOOD, b. 27 Nov 1767; d. 25 Apr 1783.

498) ii JOHN OSGOOD, b. 2 Jun 1770; d. at Haverhill, NH, 29 Jul 1840; m. SARAH PORTER, b. at Boxford, 22 Apr 1777 daughter of William and Mary (Adams) Porter; Sarah d. at Haverhill, NH 5 Feb 1858.[308]

499) iii ALFRED OSGOOD, b. 7 Mar 1773; d. at Newburyport 25 May 1847; m. 18 Jun 1800, MARY SMITH, b. 4 Apr 1778 daughter of John and Mary (-) Smith; Mary d. at Newburyport 23 Sep 1855 at age 77. Mary's parents' names are given as John and Mary Smith on her death record.

500) iv ENOCH OSGOOD, b. 7 Nov 1775; d. at Newburyport 20 May 1848; m. 15 Feb 1807 MARY BROWN of not yet known origins; Mary d. Dec 1863.[309] She was known to be living in 1859 when her daughter's estate was probated.

119) ELIZABETH OSGOOD *(Hannah Abbott Osgood[3], George[2], George[1])*, b. 15 Aug 1714 daughter of John and Hannah (Abbott) Osgood; d. 8 Dec 1756; m. 28 Nov 1734, JAMES FRYE, b. at Bradford 24 Jun 1710 son of James and Joanna (Sprague) Frye. James married 2nd Sarah Robey. Colonel James Frye died 8 Jan 1776 "while in the Continental Service." His death is recorded at Andover.

James Frye had much military experience and was a Lieutenant Colonel in the French and Indian War. In 1775, he was a Colonel in charge of a regiment of Minutemen that fought at the Battle of Bunker Hill. He was wounded during the battle, although he continued to fight on after being wounded. He died of his wounds about six months later.[310]

The will of James Frye has bequests to the following persons: well beloved wife Sarah, son Frederick, son James, son Jonathan, daughter Elizabeth wife of Samuel Frye, his grandchildren who are the children of his daughter Joanna Farrington (Thomas, March, Elizabeth), daughter Sarah the wife of John Boyden, grandsons John and James Boyden, daughter Hannah the wife of Daniel Poor, daughter Dorcas the wife of Ezekiel Carleton, daughter Molly Frye (who is unmarried), and daughter Pamela Frye (who is under 18).[311] [Frederick is a son and Pamela is a daughter from James's second marriage to Sarah Robey. The other children are from his marriage to Elizabeth Osgood.]

Elizabeth Osgood and James Frye had eight children whose births are recorded at Andover.

501) i ELIZABETH FRYE, b. 7 Dec 1735; d. 14 May 1807; m. 24 May 1753, her second cousin once removed, SAMUEL FRYE, b. 22 Dec 1729 son of Samuel and Sarah (Osgood) Frye; Samuel d. 1819.

502) ii JOHANNA FRYE, b. 19 Feb 1736/7; d. at Groton 24 Jun 1767; m. by 1758, THOMAS FARRINGTON, b. 8 Mar 1735/6 son of Daniel and Elizabeth (Putnam) Farrington. Thomas m. 2nd Betty Woods and he relocated to Kennebec, ME for a time. Thomas m. 3rd Jerusha Hammond. Thomas d. 9 Apr 1808 at Delhi, NY.

503) iii SARAH FRYE, b. 8 Mar 1738/9; d. at Conway, MA 29 Jul 1785; m. about 1764, JOHN BOYDEN, b. at Groton, 12 Jan 1736 son of Josiah and Eunice (Parker) Boyden. John m. 2nd Esther Gilmore; John d. 10 Oct 1819.

504) iv JAMES FRYE, b. 9 Jan 1740/1; d. 28 Jan 1826; m. 1st 21 Feb 1765, his third cousin (and George Abbott descendant), MEHITABLE ROBINSON, b. at Boxford, Oct 1742 daughter of Joseph and Mehitable (Eams) Robinson;[312] Mehitable d. 6 Jun 1787. James m. 2nd Phebe Campbell.

---

306 Massachusetts Vital Records Project: Mary, w. Isaac, May 22, 1820, a. 66 y.

307 Massachusetts Vital Records Project: Isaac [h. Mary (Osgood). PR61], Sept. 8, 1823, a. 80 y. 8 m.

308 Ancestry.com. New Hampshire, Death and Burial Records Index, 1654-1949

309 Osgood, *Genealogy of Descendants. . . Osgood*, p 69

310 National History Society, "Colonel James Frye," http://www.nahistoricalsocietyexhibits.org/veterans/revolutionary-war/

311 *Essex County, MA: Probate File Papers, 1638-1881. Probate of* James Frye, 5 Feb 1776, *Case number* 10297.

312 The 1777 will of Joseph Robinson includes a bequest to his daughter Mehitable wife of James Frye.

505) v JONATHAN FRYE, b. 4 Dec 1742; d. at Bucksport, ME 12 Jul 1793; m. by 1766 to unidentified wife;[313] no marriage record has been located.

506) vi HANNAH FRYE, b. 12 Sep 1744; d. 16 Jan 1824; m. 31 Mar 1763, DANIEL POOR, b. 21 Sep 1740 son of Thomas and Mary (Adams) Poor; Daniel d. 20 Jun 1814.

507) vii DORCAS FRYE, b. 3 Jun 1750; d. 1 Dec 1821; m. 10 Nov 1768, EZEKIEL CARLETON, b. 22 Nov 1742 son of Ezekiel and Marcy (Kimball) Carleton; Ezekiel d. 1 Jan 1831.

508) viii MOLLY FRYE, b. 9 Mar 1752; d. at East Andover, ME, 13 Jun 1796; m. 9 May 1776, INGALLS BRAGG, b. 24 Jun 1753 son of Thomas and Dorothy (Ingalls) Bragg; Thomas d. at East Andover, ME about 1808 the year of the probate of his estate.

120) JOSEPH OSGOOD *(Hannah Abbott Osgood³, George², George¹)*, b. 5 Sep 1718 son of John and Hannah (Abbott) Osgood; d. at Andover, 11 Jan 1797; m. at Boston 1 Dec 1743, MARGARET BINNEY, b. at Hull 12 Apr 1719 daughter of Thomas and Margaret (Miller) Binney; Margaret d. 16 Feb 1797.

Joseph Osgood graduated Harvard in 1737[314] and was a physician in Andover.

The will of Joseph Osgood has bequests for the following persons: beloved wife Margaret, son Joseph, son John, son George, and grandson John Cushing is to be boarded for two years by George who is the executor.[315] John Cushing was the son of his daughter Mehitable from her marriage to John Cushing.

Joseph and Margaret had eight children, the oldest three born at Boston and the younger five children at Andover.

509) i JOSEPH OSGOOD, b. 25 Nov 1746; d. at Salem, Jun 1812; m. 14 Jun 1770, LUCRETIA WARD, b. at Salem, Sep 1748 daughter of Miles and Hannah (Derby) Ward; Lucretia d. Sep 1809. Lucretia's name is given as Mehitable in the Osgood genealogy, but the birth, marriage, and death record say Lucretia.

ii JOHN OSGOOD, b. 22 Oct 1748; d. Jun 1749.

510) iii MEHITABLE OSGOOD,[316] b. at Boston, 11 Dec 1749; d. 6 Oct 1788 (according to the Cushing Genealogy, but no record found); m. by 1770, JOHN CUSHING, b. at Haverhill, 11 Dec 1749 son of James and Anna (Wainwright) Cushing. John m. 2nd Mary Marsh; John d. at Goffstown, NH 1833.

iv JOHN GEORGE OSGOOD, b. 20 Aug 1742; d. 17 May 1754.

511) v JOHN OSGOOD, b. 14 Nov 1754; d. at Newbury, 5 Apr 1820; m. at Newbury, 3 Dec 1778, LYDIA NEWELL, b. at Brookline, 20 Apr 1754 daughter of Moses and Sarah (Gerrish) Newell; Lydia d. at West Newbury, 1 Feb 1836.

vi THOMAS OSGOOD, b. 29 Oct 1756; d. 12 Sep 1771.

512) vii GEORGE OSGOOD, b. 1 Dec 1758; d. 24 Oct 1823; m. 7 Jan 1782, ELIZABETH OTIS, b. at Barnstable, 12 Jan 1760 daughter of Joseph and Rebecca (Sturgis) Otis; Elizabeth d. 22 May 1802. George m. 2nd 8 Mar 1803, SARAH VOSE, b. at Milton, 29 Jul 1762 daughter of Joseph and Sarah (How) Vose; Sarah d. 17 Mar 1812. After Sarah's death, George married Mary Messer, 2 Oct 1815.

viii MARGARET OSGOOD, b. 4 Nov 1760; d. 25 Oct 1762. "Margaret, d. Joseph and Margaret, Oct. 25, 1762, a. 1 y. 11 m. 21 d. GR1"

121) DORCAS OSGOOD *(Hannah Abbott Osgood³, George², George¹)*, b. Sep 1721 daughter of John and Hannah (Abbott) Osgood; d. at Boston about 1749 (Thomas remarried in 1750); m. at Boston 5 Jan 1743/4, THOMAS MARCH whose origins are unknown to me; Thomas d. at Boston about 1752 (when his will was probated). Thomas married 2nd Mary Hill on 7 Aug 1750.

---

313 The "internet", the DAR, and even Barker's Frye genealogy identify his wife as Sarah Peabody (who was born 1729) daughter of Moses, but that is not correct. The marriage of Sarah Peabody and a different Jonathan Frye (born 1717) occurred in 1753 when this Jonathan was 11 years old. There are baptismal records for three children of Jonathan at Methuen but those records list only the father's name. Those three children can be supported as being this Jonathan's as one of the grandsons (Phineas Barnes) later placed a monument in the Wardwell Cemetery for this Jonathan. There are several other possible children born at Methuen for whom there are not available records.

314 Harvard University, *Quinquennial Catalogue of the Officers and Graduates of Harvard University*

315 *Essex County, MA: Probate File Papers, 1638-1881. Probate of* Joseph Osgood, 6 Feb 1797, *Case number* 20231.

316 Cushing, *The Genealogy of the Cushing Family*, p. 61

The will of Thomas March includes a bequest to his daughter Dorcas of a dozen of the gilt pictured plates and all the linen that was given to "me or my late wife by my father-in-law Mr. Osgood." He makes a general bequest to "all my children" but does not specify them. The guardianship of Dorcas was assumed by Joseph Osgood and John Osgood.[317]

There are birth records for two children of Dorcas and Thomas both born at Boston. However, the son, Thomas, died as an infant suggested by the fact that Thomas March named his first child with his second wife, Thomas.

i THOMAS MARCH, b. 26 May 1745; died young.

513) ii DORCAS MARCH, b. 11 Jun 1746; d. at Salem, Mar 1820; m. at Andover, 19 Jan 1763, DUDLEY WOODBRIDGE, b. at Salem, 3 Mar 1732/3 son of Benjamin and Mary (Osgood) Woodbridge; Dudley d. 21 Oct 1799.

122) MARY OSGOOD *(Hannah Abbott Osgood³, George², George¹)*, b. 10 Jun 1726 daughter of John and Hannah (Abbott) Osgood; d. 1806 at New Gloucester, ME; m. 11 Apr 1745, WILLIAM ALLEN, b. at Gloucester Jun 1717 son of Joseph and Mary (Coit) Allen; a death record for William was not located.

Mary Osgood and William Allen were early settlers in New Gloucester, Maine which was incorporated in 1774. The first land grants in that area were in the mid-1730's. The settlement was first called New Gloucester in 1738, likely named after the settlement in Massachusetts where most of the settlers were born. William and Mary Allen made their move to New Gloucester after the births of all their children at Gloucester. In 1770, the lot for the town meeting house was purchased from William Allen. He also served on a committee in 1774 related to the proposed boycott of British goods in the period prior to the Revolutionary War.[318]

There are births for thirteen children in this family recorded at Gloucester and two other births at New Gloucester, Maine.

i MARY ALLEN, b. 29 Mar 1746; d. 5 Apr 1746.

514) ii JOSEPH ALLEN, b. 24 Feb 1746/7; m. 30 Dec 1782, MARY BAKER. Joseph m. 2nd, DORCAS EMERY.

514a iii MARY ALLEN, b. 3 Nov 1748; m. 8 Jul 1775, as his second wife, PETER GRAFFAM[319] son of Caleb and Lois (Bennett) Graffam.

iv WILLIAM ALLEN, b. 30 Jul 1750; d. at Gloucester, MA, Mar 1826. He married and had children, but those details are not yet worked out.

515) v ELIZABETH ALLEN, b. 27 Oct 1752; d. at Portland, ME, Apr 1850; m. 12 Oct 1773, SAMUEL STEVENS, b. at Gloucester, 12 Mar 1748 son of William and Elizabeth (Allen) Stevens; Samuel d. at Gloucester, 9 Dec 1795.

516) vi DORCAS ALLEN, b. 11 Aug 1754; d. at Cumberland County, ME, 27 Dec 1785; m. 24 Jun 1779, DAVID HAYS, b. 12 Oct 1755 son of John and Judith (Moulton) Hays; David d. in Cumberland County, ME, 30 Aug 1793.

517) vii JOHN ALLEN, b. 25 Mar 1756; d. at Minot, ME, 6 Mar 1834; m. 9 Apr 1791, RACHEL WORTHLEY, b. at Yarmouth, ME, 24 Mar 1764 daughter of John and Martha (Bailey) Worthley.

viii BENJAMIN ALLEN, b. 4 Jan 1758

ix NATHANIEL COIT ALLEN, b. 29 Aug 1759. Served as paymaster in the 10th Massachusetts Regiment. He may not have married.

x AARON ALLEN, b. 12 Jan 1761; d. 16 Feb 1766.

xi CHRISTOPHER ALLEN, b. 29 Aug 1763; d. 17 Nov 1763.

518) xii CHRISTOPHER ALLEN, b. 16 Apr 1765; d. at Hebron, ME, 20 Jul 1819; m. 25 Jun 1808, DOLLY POOR, b. at Andover, 12 Oct 1772 daughter of Ebenezer and Susanna (Varnum) Poor; Dolly d. 1826.

519) xiii AARON ALLEN, b. 17 Dec 1766; m. at New Gloucester, ME, 27 Aug 1797, MARTHA PRINCE, b. at New Gloucester, 7 Jul 1773 daughter of John and Mary (-) Prince.

xiv JEREMIAH ALLEN, b. 13 May 1769; he is perhaps the Jeremiah Allen who died at New Gloucester, June 1843 at age 75. There is no record of a marriage.

---

[317] *Suffolk County, MA: Probate File Papers,* Probate of Thomas March, 1752, Case number 9976.

[318] Haskell, *The New Gloucester Centennial*

[319] The codicil of her brother Samuel's will incudes a mention of his sister Graffam.

xv SAMUEL ALLEN, b. 14 Apr 1771; d. at Oxford, ME about 1846 (date of codicil of will). Samuel did not marry. In his will, he left his estate to the four children of his brother Chrsitopher.

123) SARAH ABBOTT *(Elizabeth³, George², George¹* **and** *Benjamin³, Benjamin², George¹)*, b. 2 Aug 1718 daughter of Benjamin and Elizabeth (Abbott) Abbott; d. 5 Mar 1778; m. 10 Apr 1746, her second cousin, JAMES HOLT *(Dorcas Abbott Holt³, Timothy², George¹)*, b. 13 Jan 1722/3 son of Nicholas and Dorcas (Abbott) Holt. James m. 2nd, Phebe Ballard who was the widow of Abiel Abbott son of Benjamin and Abigail (Abbott) Abbott; James Holt d. at Andover, 22 Aug 1812

In his will written 24 March 1804, James Holt has bequests to the following persons: well beloved wife Phebe (second wife), grandson James Abbot (who has lived with him for 10 years), beloved daughter Sarah wife of Barachias Abbott, beloved daughter Abigail wife of Isaac Chandler, and his two sons-in-law Barachias Abbott and Isaac Chandler. Grandson James Abbot is named executor.[320]

In the will, James Holt elaborates on his bequest to his grandson: "For special and weighty reasons in my mind, I give to my beloved grandson, James Abbot, who has lived with me about ten years, and to his heirs and assigns, all my estate, both real and personal, not herein disposed of." He goes on to list several household items that are to go to him stating these were mostly items that had belonged to James Abbot's uncle. We can only imagine the nature of these "special and weighty reasons."

Sarah and James had seven children, all born at Andover.

i JAMES HOLT, b. 16 Apr 1749; d. 26 Nov 1800; m. 5 Jun 1778, HANNAH FOSTER, b. 23 Jul 1754 daughter of Jacob and Abigail (Frost) Foster; Hannah died from consumption 24 Oct 1794. They do not seem to have had any children that lived to adulthood. There is a daughter Hannah baptized in 1777 who is perhaps their child, but there is no further record for her and since she is not mentioned in the wills of either of her grandfathers, she likely died young. James is not mentioned in his father's will. Likewise, Hannah Foster is not mentioned in the will of her father Jacob who died in 1806.

ii ELIZABETH HOLT, b. 10 Mar 1750/1; d. 12 Nov 1777; Elizabeth did not marry.

iii JOEL HOLT, b. 7 Aug 1753; d. 20 Mar 1755.

iv DORCAS HOLT, b. 6 May 1756; d. 16 May 1778; Dorcas did not marry.

520) v ABIGAIL HOLT, b. 18 Jun 1758; d. 2 Oct 1824; m. 7 Dec 1780, her fourth cousin, ISAAC CHANDLER, b. 4 Oct 1754 son of William and Rebecca (Lovejoy) Chandler; Isaac d. 12 Jan 1832. After Abigail's death, Isaac married Elizabeth Upton.

294) vi SARAH HOLT, b. 7 Mar 1746/7; d. 11 Feb 1808; m. 6 Dec 1770, her third cousin (by two paths), BARACHIAS ABBOTT, b. 22 May 1739 son of Barachias and Hannah (Holt) Abbott; Barachias d. 29 Jan 1812.

vii SUSANNA HOLT, b. 27 Oct 1760; d. 26 Nov 1760.

69) MARY ABBOTT *(George³, George², George¹)*, b. 12 Mar 1722/3 daughter of George and Mary (Phillips) Abbott; d. 8 Aug 1792; m. 24 May 1743, her second cousin STEPHEN ABBOTT *(Stephen³, John², George¹)*, b. 2 Mar 1717/8 son of Stephen and Sarah (Stevens) Abbott; Stephen d. 8 Nov 1768; Mary m. 2nd JONATHAN ABBOTT *(Jonathan³, Benjamin², George¹)*, also a second cousin, who was the widower of Martha Lovejoy. This is the same as Family #69 covered above.

124) GEORGE ABBOT *(George³, George², George¹)*, b. 14 Dec 1724 son of George and Mary (Phillips) Abbott; d. at Andover, 26 Dec 1775; m. 1 Jan 1746/7, HANNAH LOVEJOY, b. 27 Dec 1724 daughter of John and Hannah (Foster) Lovejoy; Hannah d. 8 Sep 1813.

George Abbot's estate entered probate November 1776. In his will he has bequests for the following persons: dearly beloved wife Hannah, son George Abbot, beloved son John Lovejoy, beloved son Samuel Abbot, beloved daughter Hannah Ballard wife of Joseph Ballard, beloved daughter Mary Poor wife of Joseph Poor, beloved daughter Elizabeth Lummus wife of Samuel Lummus, beloved daughter Sarah, beloved daughter Martha, beloved daughter Dorcas, and beloved daughter Tammerson (Tamison).[321]

George and Hannah had 12 children whose births are recorded at Andover.

---

[320] *Essex County, MA: Probate File Papers, 1638-1881. Probate of* James Holt, 5 Nov 1812, *Case number* 13653.

[321] *Essex County, MA: Probate File Papers, 1638-1881. Probate of* George Abbot, 5 Nov 1776, *Case number* 49.

i GEORGE ABBOTT, b. 9 Feb 1747/8; d. at Salem 5 Oct 1784; m. 12 Mar 1772, PRISCILLA MANNING, b. at Ipswich, 17 Oct 1733 daughter of Joseph and Elizabeth (Boardman) Manning;[322] Priscilla d. 17 Mar 1804.[323] George and Priscilla had one daughter Priscilla who died at age 15. George Abbott did not leave a will; his widow Priscilla requested that William Gray be named administrator. In her will, Priscilla Abbott made bequests to her nieces and nephew.

434) ii HANNAH ABBOTT, b. 15 Oct 1749; d. 29 May 1784; m. 16 Dec 1773, as his second wife, her third cousin (and George Abbott descendant), JOSEPH BALLARD, b. Oct 1749 son of Timothy and Hannah (Chandler) Ballard. Joseph m. 1st in 1771, Molly Smith; Joseph d. 15 Feb 1819. This is the same as Family #98, child ix.

iii MARY ABBOTT, b. 4 Sep 1751; d. 12 Sep 1752.

521) iv MARY ABBOTT, b. 29 Jun 1753; d. 17 Aug 1820; m. 26 Dec 1768, JOSEPH POOR, b. 7 Nov 1748 son of Thomas and Mary (Adams) Poor; Joseph d. at Danvers 2 Mar 1815.

522) v ELIZABETH ABBOTT, b. 10 Jul 1755; d. 18 Aug 1821; m. 26 Jan 1775, SAMUEL LUMMUS, b. 31 Jul 1751 son of John and Hannah (Porter) Lummus; Samuel d. 10 Apr 1810.

523) vi JOHN LOVEJOY ABBOTT, b. 12 Apr 1757; d. 1 Nov 1837; m. 29 Oct 1782, his third cousin once removed, PHEBE ABBOTT, b. Apr 1763 daughter of Nehemiah and Hannah (Ballard) Abbot; Phebe d. about 1826.

vii SAMUEL ABBOTT, b. 12 Jun 1759; d. before 1760.

524) viii SAMUEL ABBOTT, b. 19 Sep 1760; d. at Saco, ME, 8 May 1792; m. 24 Jun 1788, MARY CUTTS, b. at Saco, 19 Jul 1763 daughter of Thomas and Elizabeth (Scammon) Cutts; Mary d. 27 Mar 1796.[324]

ix SARAH ABBOT, b. 3 Oct 1762; d. 2 Mar 1848; m. 3 Mar 1785, her third cousin once removed, NEHEMIAH ABBOT, b. 10 Mar 1757 son of Nehemiah and Hannah (Ballard) Abbot; Nehemiah d. 13 Dec 1822. Sarah and Nehemiah did not have children. Sarah Abbot used her wealth to help fund the Abbot Academy of Andover, an academy for females. The Abbot Academy is named for Sarah.[325]

525) x MARTHA ABBOTT, b. 17 Oct 1764; d. at Salem, 15 Sep 1798; m. 31 Aug 1788 as his second wife, JOHN JENKS, b. at Medford, 6 Dec 1751 son of John and Rebecca (Newhall) Jenks. John married first Hannah Andrew and third Annis Pauling. John d. 14 Oct 1817.

526) xi DORCAS ABBOTT, b. Dec 1766; d. 15 Mar 1841; m. 6 Jan 1792, her third cousin (and George Abbott descendant), JOHN HOLT, b. 12 Jan 1765 son of Joshua and Phebe (Farnum) Holt; John d. 11 Feb 1835. This couple is the same as Family #214, child vi.

xii TAMISON ABBOTT (some records spelled Tammerson), b. 14 Jan 1769; d. at Salem, 27 Jun 1850; m. 23 Jul 1797, as his second wife, WILLIAM APPLETON, b. at Ipswich, 30 Jun 1765 son of William and Sarah (Kinsman) Appleton. William had first married Anna Bowditch. William d. 23 Sep 1822 of "intemperance." Tamison does not seem to have had children.

125) ELIZABETH ABBOTT *(George³, George², George¹)*, b. 5 Nov 1727 daughter of George and Mary (Phillips) Abbott; d. about 1802 at Westford, MA; m. 2 Apr 1747, her second cousin BENJAMIN ABBOT *(Benjamin³, Benjamin², George¹)*, b. 21 Oct 1723 son of Benjamin and Mary (Carleton) Abbott; Benjamin d. at Hollis 1770 (probate 13 Jul 1770).[326] Elizabeth married 2nd, James Pollard of Westford 22 Mar 1775 and third married Josiah Bowers of Billerica.

There are records for nine children in this family, the oldest two recorded at Andover and the remainder at Hollis, New Hampshire.

Benjamin Abbot was active in the community of Hollis serving as selectman six times between 1752 and 1761. He also served on several committees and as the moderator of the town meeting in 1759. In 1757, he served in a regiment that participated in the French and Indian War.[327]

Benjamin Abbot did not leave a will and his estate entered probate 13 July 1770 with widow Elizabeth as administratrix.[328]

Elizabeth Bowers wrote her will at Westford 10 August 1802. Her will has bequests to the following persons: daughter Elizabeth Powers; daughter-in-law Lydia Abbott; granddaughter Betty Wright; Susan daughter of son Samuel Abbott;

---

322 Parents are confirmed by the 1784 probate record of Joseph Manning in which Priscilla Abbot signs that she has received her portion of the estate from her brother who is the administrator.

323 Massachusetts Vital Records Project: Abbott, Priscilla, Mrs., Mar. 17, 1804, a. 71 y. NR9

324 Howard, *Genealogy of the Cutts Family in America*, p. 85

325 McKeen, *Annals of Fifty Years: A History of Abbot Academy*

326 There is a probate record from 1771 in Middlesex County, MA for Benjamin Abbot of Hollis with widow Elizabeth Abbot of Hollis.

327 Worcester, *History of the Town of Hollis*

328 New Hampshire State Papers, 39:414-415

Abigail Read; and the remainder of the estate divided among "all my children" Benjamin Abbott, George Abbott, Joel Abbott, Jacob Abbott, Elizabeth Powers, and the children of daughter Polly Boynton.[329]

i BENJAMIN ABBOTT, b. 13 Apr 1748; d. 11 Jun 1748

527) ii BENJAMIN ABBOTT, b. 11 Apr 1749; d. at Hollis about 1838; m. by 1778, SARAH "SALLY" WRIGHT, b. 16 May 1763[330] daughter of Joshua and Abigail (Richardson) Wright.

528) iii ELIZABETH ABBOTT, b. 22 Feb 1751; d. at Hollis, 19 Feb 1836; m. 1st about 1770, EBENEZER NUTTING; he died at Hollis, 1773 (probate 24 Nov 1773). Elizabeth m. 2nd 4 Aug 1774, SAMPSON POWERS, b. at Hollis, 2 Apr 1748 son of Peter and Anna (Keyes) Powers; Sampson d. 2 Jan 1822 at Hollis (will written 10 Oct 1821).

529) iv SAMUEL ABBOTT, b. 13 Apr 1753; d. Feb 1794; m. SUSAN HUBBARD.

v MARY ABBOTT, b. 31 Dec 1754; d. 23 Jan 1755.

530) vi GEORGE ABBOTT, b. 29 Dec 1755; d. 15 Sep 1818; m. 29 Dec 1784, NAOMI TUTTLE, b. at Littleton, 28 Sep 1764 daughter of Samuel and Mary (Russell) Tuttle; Naomi d. about 1833.

531) vii JOEL ABBOTT, b. 4 Dec 1757; d. at Westford, 12 Apr 1806; m. 4 Sep 1786, LYDIA CUMMINGS, b. at Westford, 26 Nov 1769 daughter of Isaac and Elizabeth (Trowbridge) Cummings; Lydia d. at Littleton, 5 Mar 1813.

532) viii JACOB ABBOTT, b. 12 Apr 1760; d. at Westford, 11 Apr 1815; m. 14 Sep 1787, POLLY CUMMINGS, b. 12 Jul 1767 daughter of Thomas and Lucy (Laurence) Cummings.

533) ix MARY ABBOTT, b. about 1762; d. at Westford, 7 Jul 1797; m. 28 Jul 1782, ABEL BOYNTON, b. at Westford, 9 Aug 1755 son of Nathaniel and Rebekah (Barrett) Boynton. Abel m. 2nd Polly Pierce.

126) SARAH ABBOTT *(George³, George², George¹)*, b. 14 Jan 1729/30 daughter of George and Mary (Phillips) Abbott; d. 29 Dec 1797; m. 4 Aug 1757, her second cousin, NATHAN HOLT *(Dorcas Abbott Holt³, Timothy², George¹)*, b. 28 Feb 1725 son of Nicholas and Dorcas (Abbott) Holt; Nathan d. at Danvers 2 Aug 1792.

Sarah and Nathan had four children. The births of the three daughters are recorded at Danvers. The son James is attributed to this family in Durrie's Holt genealogy.[331] Nathan did not leave a will. The administrator of the estate was his son-in-law William Frost.

534) i SARAH HOLT, b. 29 Oct 1758; d. 17 Sep 1841; m. at Danvers, 2 Dec 1777, WILLIAM FROST, b. at New Castle, NH, 15 Nov 1754 son of William and Elizabeth (Prescott) Frost; William d. at Andover 28 Sep 1836. Sarah and William are second great grandparents of Robert Frost.

535) ii MARY HOLT, b. 3 Oct 1761; d. at Beverly, 7 Jan 1850; m. 1 Nov 1781, ROBERT ENDICOTT, b. 29 Oct 1756 son of John and Elizabeth (Jacobs) Endicott; Robert d. at Beverly, 6 Mar 1819.

536) iii HANNAH HOLT, b. 11 May 1769; d. at Beverly 26 Jul 1857; m. 23 Jan 1793, her first cousin and George Abbott descendant, PETER HOLT, b. at Andover 12 Jun 1763 son of Joshua and Phebe (Farnum) Holt; Peter d. at Greenfield, NH 25 Apr 1851. Two of the daughters of Hannah and Peter married Samuel Endicott son of Mary Holt and Robert Endicott (Hannah's sister Mary just above).

537) iv JAMES HOLT, b. 1772; d. in India, Aug 1807;[332] m. 30 Aug 1796, LUCY WHIPPLE, b. 8 Mar 1778; Lucy d. at Danvers, 6 Mar 1839. Although James's death is reported as August 1807, the probate of his estate was April 1807.

---

[329] *Middlesex County, MA: Probate File Papers, 1648-1924.* Will of Elizabeth Bowers, 10 Aug 1802. Case number 2269.

[330] This identification involves a young marriage for Sarah at age 15. However, her last child was born in 1807 so she would have to be very young at the time of the birth of the first child in 1778.

[331] Durrie, *Genealogical History of the Holt Family*, p 44

[332] James, h. Lucy (Whipple), at India, Aug. —, 1807.

127) HANNAH ABBOTT *(George³, George², George¹)*, b. 14 Dec 1733 of George and Mary (Phillips) Abbott; d. 26 Mar 1820; m. 9 Jan 1755, WILLIAM FOSTER, b. 4 Mar 1729/30 son of John and Mary (Osgood) Foster; William d. at Andover, 1 Sep 1803.

The will of William Foster has bequests for the following persons: beloved wife Hannah and his four children, son William, daughter Hannah the wife of Timothy Rogers, daughter Mary the wife of Timothy Ballard, and daughter Sarah the wife of Joseph Brown.[333]

The births of four children are recorded at Andover.

538) i HANNAH FOSTER, b. 20 Jun 1756; d. at Tewksbury 7 Nov 1830; m. 27 Feb 1777, TIMOTHY ROGERS, b. at Tewksbury 16 Jun 1745 son of Timothy and Rebecca (French) Rogers; Timothy d. 27 Feb 1814.

539) ii WILLIAM FOSTER, b. 1 Jun 1758; d. 20 Aug 1843; m. late in life, 18 Nov 1826, SALLY WELCH KIMBALL, b. at Plaistow, NH, 20 Dec 1786 daughter of Joseph and Anna (Welch) Kimball. Despite their late marriage, William and Sally did have one son. Sally d. 29 Jan 1850.

iii MARY FOSTER, b. 21 Jul 1763; d. 30 Mar 1834; m. 30 Oct 1783, her third cousin once removed (and George Abbott descendant), TIMOTHY BALLARD, b. 28 Jul 1757 son of Timothy and Sarah (Abbott) Ballard; Timothy d. 29 Feb 1828 when he committed suicide by cutting his throat.[334] Mary and Timothy did not have any children. Mary Foster Ballard wrote her will 3 March 1831. The will includes bequests to her brother William Foster and to her nieces and nephews who are named as follows: nephew Thadeus Brown, nephew George Brown, niece Sarah B. Gray, nephew Rev. Timothy Rogers, and niece Hannah Kidder wife of Samuel Kidder. These nieces and nephews receive money bequests of $20 except Thadeus who receives $100. The remainder of the estate is given to her two nieces who are the daughters of her late sister Sarah Brown: Mary Ballard Gould wife of Abraham Gould and Hannah Brown.

540) iv SARAH "SALLY" FOSTER, b. 9 Sep 1765; d. at Tewksbury 30 Nov 1807; m. 8 Jun 1794, JOSEPH BROWN, b. at Tewksbury, 19 Jun 1762 son of William and Mary (Osgood) Brown; Joseph d. 21 Nov 1829.

128) LYDEA ABBOTT *(Henry³, George², George¹)*, b. 10 Feb 1722/3 daughter of Henry and Mary (Platts) Abbott; d. 11 Sep 1807; m. 24 Mar 1742/3, JOSHUA LOVEJOY, b. 2 Dec 1719 son of Henry and Sarah (Farnum) Lovejoy; Joshua d. 2 Feb 1812.

Joshua and Lydea had six children whose births are recorded at Andover.

541) i JOSHUA LOVEJOY, b. 8 Jan 1743/4; d. at Sanbornton, NH 28 Jan 1832; m. 30 Apr 1769, SARAH PERKINS, b. at Middleton, 10 Mar 1744 daughter of Timothy and Phebe (Peters) Perkins; Sarah d. 3 May 1828.

ii MARY LOVEJOY, b. 13 Aug 1745; d. 15 Apr 1826; m. 24 Sep 1765, JAMES PARKER whose parentage is not entirely clear;[335] James d. 23 Oct 1801. Mary m. 2nd Jonathan Cummings. There are not any records of children for Mary and James.

542) iii LYDIA LOVEJOY, b. 21 Jul 1747; d. at Haverhill, MA, 3 Jan 1838; m. 23 Jun 1767, third cousin once removed, ABIEL HOLT, b. 3 Apr 1746 son of Thomas and Hannah (Kimball) Holt; Abiel d. 17 Nov 1824.

281) iv DORCAS LOVEJOY, b. 18 Aug 1749; d. 25 Jun 1843; m. about 1770, as his second wife, her second cousin once removed (and George Abbott descendant), BENJAMIN AMES, b. 6 Jun 1724 son of Samuel and Hannah (Stevens) Ames; Benjamin d. 10 Jan 1809. This is the same as Family #281 which also includes Benjamin's first wife Hephzibah Chandler.

543) v CHLOE LOVEJOY, b. 26 Mar 1753; d. 21 Nov 1843; m. 26 Dec 1776, her fourth cousin, JOHN POOR, b. 16 Apr 1754 son of John and Rebecca (Stevens) Poor; John d. 7 Jul 1823. John Poor is a descendant of George Abbott of Rowley.

544) vi LUCY LOVEJOY, b. 4 Aug 1755; d. at Andover, 2 Apr 1844; m. 11 Apr 1776, THEOPHILUS FRYE, b. at Andover, 12 Oct 1753 son of Samuel and Elizabeth (Frye) Frye; Theophilus d. 2 Apr 1830.

129) HENRY ABBOT *(Henry³, George², George¹)*, b. 31 Jan 1724 son of Henry and Mary (Platts) Abbot; d. 21 Feb 1805; m. 1st 2 Oct 1750, ELIZABETH SIBSON (I think the daughter of Joseph); Elizabeth d. about 1764. Henry m. 2nd his first cousin PHEBE ABBOT *(Isaac³, George², George¹)*, b. 14 Nov 1746 daughter of Isaac and Phebe (Lovejoy) Abbot; Phebe d. 29 Jun 1833.

Henry and Betsy Sibson did not have any children. The births of seven children of Henry and Phebe Abbot are recorded at Andover.

---

[333] *Essex County, MA: Probate File Papers, 1638-1881. Probate of* William Foster, 4 Oct 1803, *Case number* 10013.

[334] Massachusetts Vital Records Project: Timothy, "who cut his own throat," Feb. 29, 1828, a. 70 y. 7 m.

[335] His death record from 1801 gives his age as 66 years which would mean he was born in 1735. That conflicts with most published genealogies which have him born in 1745 son of James. The death record may be wrong.

The will of Henry Abbot was written 2 February 1805 and includes the following bequests: well beloved wife Phebe Abbot receives one-third of the real estate in Andover for her use during her life; after she is "done with it," two sons Henry and Isaac will divide that property. Isaac is the son charged with taking care of his mother. Son Henry Abbot receives a tract of land known as the Lovejoy lot and Peavy meadow. There are other land bequests and Henry also receives the silver tankard marked H.A.P. Daughter Phebe Porter wife of Jonathan Porter receives $50. Daughter Elizabeth Kneeland Abbot receives $600 in cash and a State Note of the Commonwealth of Massachusetts valued at $186.84. Elizabeth also is to receive cords of wood delivered to her door as long as she remains unmarried. Henry's wife Phebe further is allowed use of his clock and she can place it anywhere in the house she wants. She also receives use of the silver tankard marker I.A.P. as long as she remains a widow. Phebe is also to have one-half of the dwelling house for her use. Son Isaac receives the remainder of the real estate and buildings not otherwise disposed of in the will. Henry then goes on the describe the disposition of the estate if either of the sons dies before returning from sea. He also notes that if Isaac should die before his return from sea and if he shall not have made provision for "his particular friend Miss Charlotte Houghton," then Charlotte will receive $200 from the estate. His sons Henry and Isaac are named executors of the estate.[336] Isaac did return from the sea and went on the marry Miss Charlotte Houghton.

545) i PHEBE ABBOT, b. 25 Jan 1766; d. at Medford 10 Oct 1852; m. 7 Nov 1790, as his second wife, JONATHAN PORTER, b. at Braintree, 12 Mar 1745 son of Jonathan and Hannah (Hayden) Porter; Jonathan d. 4 Nov 1817.

ii MARY ABBOT, b. 4 Apr 1768; d. 17 Aug 1769.

iii HENRY ABBOT, b. Jul 1770; d. 10 Aug 1770.

iv HENRY ABBOT, b. 6 Sep 1771; d. 19 May 1776.

546) v HENRY ABBOT, b. 8 Apr 1777; d. 13 Jan 1862; m. 20 May 1807, JUDITH FOLANSBEE, b. 15 Dec 1782 likely the daughter of Moody and Judith (-) Folansbee of Newbury; Judith d. at Andover, 10 Feb 1864.

vi ISAAC ABBOT, b. 9 Jun 1779; d. 1838;[337] m. 22 Feb 1808, CHARLOTTE HOUGHTON, b. about 1780; Charlotte d. 21 Aug 1821. Isaac and Charlotte did not have children.

vii ELIZABETH KNEELAND ABBOT; b. 10 Jan 1783; d. 20 Aug 1812. Elizabeth did not marry.

130) DORCAS ABBOTT *(Henry³, George², George¹)*, b. 11 May 1729 daughter of Henry and Mary (Platts) Abbott; d. at Nottingham, NH 10 Apr 1789; m. 17 Apr 1754, BENJAMIN BUTLER, b. at Edgartown 9 Apr 1729 son of Malachi and Jemima (Dagget) Butler. Benjamin m. 2nd, 29 Sep 1791, Phebe Griffin daughter of James and Phebe (Abbott) Griffin; Benjamin d. at Nottingham 26 Oct 1804.

Benjamin studied at Harvard, was an ordained minister, and was the minister in Nottingham, New Hampshire. Dorcas and Benjamin's oldest child was born at Andover. Following that, the family relocated to Nottingham where seven other children were born including a set of triplets. Five of the children died in early childhood.[338] Only three children, Henry, Mary, and Dorcas, are mentioned in the will of Benjamin Butler.[339] After the death of his first wife Dorcas, Benjamin married Phebe Griffin who was the second cousin, once removed of Dorcas.

In his will, Benjamin Butler bequeaths to his beloved wife Phebe the full use of the dwelling house and the garden as long as she remains a widow. She also receives all the household furnishings she brought to the marriage and any that were procured after their marriage. Phebe also receives ten Spanish milled dollars annually. His son Henry is to provide for the ongoing maintenance (firewood, etc.) of Phebe. Daughters Dorcas and Mary receive the remainder of the household goods. Son Henry receives all the remainder of the estate, both real and personal, not otherwise disposed of in the will. The value of the estate was $1,923 not counting a one-third part of the dwelling.

547) i HENRY BUTLER, b. 27 Nov 1754; d. 17 Jan 1808; m. 11 Apr 1776, ISABELLA FISKE, b. at Epping, 2 Aug 1757 (or 2 Aug 1759)[340] daughter of Ebenezer and Elizabeth (Cotton) Fiske; Isabella d. 17 Jan 1808. After Isabella's death, Henry married Ruth Parsons.

ii BENJAMIN BUTLER, b. 23 Feb 1757; d. 30 Apr 1757.

---

336 *Essex County, MA: Probate File Papers, 1638-1881. Probate of* Henry Abbot, 6 Nov 1805, *Case number* 57.

337 Abbot and Abbot, *Genealogical Register of Descendants* report a death year as 1838, but I could not locate a death or a probate record.

338 Most of the information on children in this family obtained from Cogswell's *History of Nottingham, Deerfield, and Northwood*, p. 172

339 *New Hampshire Wills and Probate Records 1643-1982,* Probate of Benjamin Butler, Rockingham, 10 Jan 1805, Case number 7333.

340 Ancestry.com. New Hampshire, Births and Christenings Index, 1714-1904

iii BENJAMIN BUTLER, b. 14 Jun 1758; d. 29 Aug 1759.

548) iv MARY BUTLER, b. 30 Mar 1760; d. 1846; m. 1776, ABRAHAM BROWN, b. at Epping, 8 May 1753 son of Abraham and Hannah (Osgood) Brown; Abraham d. at Northfield 8 Mar 1824.

v ELIZABETH BUTLER, b. 30 Aug 1762; d. 3 Oct 1762.

549) vi DORCAS BUTLER, b. 9 Oct 1766; d. at Colerain Township, OH, 9 Oct 1857;[341] m. 5 Jun 1786, JONATHAN CILLEY, b. 8 Mar 1762 son of Joseph and Sarah (Longfellow) Cilley; Jonathan d. 21 Mar 1807.

vii JEMIMA BUTLER, b. 9 Oct 1766; d. 14 Oct 1766.

viii JAMES PLATT BUTLER, b. 9 Oct 1766; d. 19 Oct 1766.

131) MARY ABBOTT *(Henry³, George², George¹)*, b. 13 Aug 1737 daughter of Henry and Mary (Platts) Abbott; d. 26 Nov 1813; m. 22 Mar 1759, THOMAS HOVEY, b. at Ipswich 1 Oct 1736 son of Thomas and Sarah (Rust) Hovey; Thomas d. at Dracut, 29 Jul 1826.

Thomas Hovey wrote his will 13 December 1815 and his estate entered probate in 1826. His will includes bequests for the following persons: son Henry Abbot Hovey receives a token amount of $10 as he has already receive the full portion of his inheritance; son Samuel Hovey receives $100 to supplement what he has already been given; son Benjamin Hovey also receives $100; son Joseph Hovey receives $100 and a feather bed; daughter Mary Whiting wife of Moses Whiting receives a feather bed, a bedstead, and some pillows, in addition to what she received at the time of her marriage; daughter Elizabeth Hovey receives her mother's wearing apparel, silver teaspoons, and other household items, use of one room in the house as long as she remains unmarried, some sheep, and $100; and son James Platts Hovey receives land and buildings, and farming tools and utensils. James Platts Hovey is named executor.[342]

Mary and Thomas had ten children whose births were recorded at Dracut.

i THOMAS HOVEY, b. 15 Jan 1762; d. at Dracut, 7 Sep 1812; Thomas does not seem to have married.

550) ii HENRY ABBOTT HOVEY, b. 15 Jan 1764; d. at Milford about 1830;[343] m. 29 May 1791, HANNAH BRADLEY, b. at Dracut, 1 May 1768 daughter of Amos and Elizabeth (Page) Bradley; Hannah d. at Boston 14 May 1851.[344]

iii JOHN HOVEY, b. 14 Mar 1765; no further record; he is not mentioned in his father's will.

551) iv JAMES PLATTS HOVEY, b. 21 Jul 1767; d. at Dracut, 30 Nov 1831; m. 20 Feb 1801, REBEKAH HOVEY, b. at Boxford, about 1777 daughter of Ivory and Lucy (Peabody) Hovey; Rebekah d. at Lowell, 1 Feb 1853.

v MARY HOVEY, b. 13 Feb 1769; d. at Pelham, NH, 1837;[345] m. 10 May 1794, MOSES WHITING perhaps the son of Oliver and Mercy (Worcester) Whiting; Moses d. at Pelham about 1823. The date of Moses's will is 27 Jan 1823. Mary and Moses do not seem to have had children. No records for children were located and Moses's will leaves his entire estate to his wife.

vi ELIZABETH HOVEY, b. 26 Jul 1771; d. at Dracut, 6 Dec 1845. Elizabeth did not marry. In 1838, there was a probate case to appoint a guardian for her as she was found *non compos mentis*.[346]

552) vii SAMUEL HOVEY, b. 26 Oct 1773; d. after 1850;[347] m. 12 Sep 1795, MARTHA "PATTY" BRADLEY, b. at Dracut, 31 Jan 1774 daughter of Amos and Elizabeth (Page) Bradley; Martha d. 5 Jul 1825 at Dracut.

553) viii BENJAMIN HOVEY, b. 9 May 1775; d. at Dracut, 30 Mar 1866; m. at Medford, 2 Aug 1797, LOIS (Louisa) JENKINS, b. at Malden, 2 Aug 1767 daughter of Ezekiel and Margaret (Floyd) Jenkins;[348] Lois d. at Dracut, 8 Aug 1846.

ix JOSHUA HOVEY, b. 23 Sep 1778; d. at Dracut, 26 Jul 1804; Joshua does not seem to have married.

---

[341] Year: 1850; Census Place: Colerain, Hamilton, Ohio; Roll: M432_686; Page: 367B; Image: 256. In the 1850 U.S. Census, 83-year-old Dorcas Cilley, born in NH, was living in the household of Samuel and Mary Hardin who is Dorcas's daughter.

[342] *Middlesex County, MA: Probate File Papers, 1648-1871. Probate of* Thomas Hovey, *1826, Case number* 11965.

[343] U.S., Newspaper Extractions from the Northeast, 1704-1930; Columbian Centinel; Henry A. Hovey died at Milford in edition 31 Jul 1830.

[344] *Massachusetts: Vital Records, 1841-1910.* (From original records held by the Massachusetts Archives. Online database: *AmericanAncestors.org*, New England Historic Genealogical Society, 2004.)

[345] Daniel Hovey Association, *The Hovey Book*, p 153

[346] *Middlesex County, MA: Probate File Papers, 1648-1871.* Probate (non compos mentis) of Elizabeth Hovey, *1838*, Case number 11954.

[347] Year: 1850; Census Place: Cambridge, Middlesex, Massachusetts; Roll: M432_325; Page: 46B; Image: 98. Samuel Hovey living in Cambridge at the 1850 U.S. Census, age 76.

[348] Floyd, "Descendants of Joel Jenkins," NEHGR, p 319

554) x JOSEPH HOVEY, b. 25 May 1784; d. 29 Aug 1860; m. 4 Jul 1812, MARY HOVEY, b. at Boxford, Nov 1781 daughter of Ivory and Lucy (Peabody) Hovey.[349]

132) ISAAC ABBOT *(Isaac³, George², George¹)*, b. 3 Feb 1745 son of Isaac and Phebe (Lovejoy) Abbott; d. at Andover, 21 May 1836; m. 22 Apr 1766, his second cousin once removed, PHEBE CHANDLER *(Nathan Chandler⁴, John Chandler³, Hannah Abbott Chandler², George¹)*, b. 2 Jun 1742 daughter of Nathan and Priscilla (Holt) Chandler; Phebe d. 1 Jul 1800.

Isaac Abbot served in the Revolutionary War and was wounded at Bunker Hill.[350] He served as a deacon and was also the first postmaster of Andover. He lost his eyesight several years prior to his death.

Isaac Abbot made the following bequests in his will which was written 14 September 1833. His granddaughter Mrs. Mary Shattuck of Andover received one silver tablespoon, six silver teaspoons and $10. Daughter-in-law Mrs. Mary Abbot widow of his son Isaac received a clock and $10. Grandchildren Josiah F., Samuel, and Isaac Abbot children of son Isaac received $10 each. His wearing apparel was divided among William, Issac, and Moses Abbot who are the children of his son William Abbot of Concord. Granddaughter Phebe Abbot daughter of son William received the dictionary, the bible, and the umbrella. Granddaughter Rebekah Abbot daughter of William received the looking glass. All the named grandchildren received $10 each. His dwelling house and all the remainder of the estate is bequeathed to son William Abbot of Concord.[351]

Isaac and Phebe had four children whose births are recorded at Andover.

i PHEBE ABBOT, b. 27 May 1767; d. 8 Nov 1772.

555) ii ISAAC ABBOT, b. 9 Dec 1768; d. 27 Dec 1806; m. 1st, 5 Jul 1798, HEPHZIBAH FISKE, b. 21 Apr 1773 daughter of John and Hephzibah (-) Fiske; Hephzibah d. 22 Mar 1800. Isaac m. 2nd, 7 Oct 1801, MARY MOULTON, b. at Danvers, 16 Mar 1775 daughter of Ebenezer and Elizabeth (Curtis) Moulton; Mary d. 19 Aug 1851.

iii PRISCILLA ABBOT, b. 1 Jun 1770; d. 10 Feb 1830; m. 6 Jun 1820, as his third wife, JOHN KNEELAND, b. at Boston, 14 Oct 1748 son of John and Sarah (Mulberry) Kneeland. John married a fourth time after Priscilla's death; John d. 4 Sep 1831. John Kneeland was the stepson of Samuel Abbot who was Priscilla's first cousin once removed. Priscilla married late in life and did not have children.

556) iv WILLIAM ABBOT, b. 30 Oct 1772; d. at Concord, NH about 1856 (probate date 24 Jun 1856); m. 14 May 1801, his third cousin once removed (and George Abbott descendant) REBECCA BAILEY, b. 10 Apr 1781 daughter of Moses and Elizabeth (Mooar) Bailey; Rebecca was still living in 1860 when she was living in Concord with her son Moses.[352] This is the same as Family #267, child viii.

133) SARAH ABBOTT *(Isaac³, George², George¹)*, b. 2 Jan 1749/50 daughter of Isaac and Phebe (Lovejoy) Abbott; d. at Andover, 2 Apr 1835; m. 2 Jan 1770, her second cousin, once removed TIMOTHY ABBOTT *(Elizabeth Abbott Abbott⁴, Timothy³, Timothy², George¹)*, b. 2 Jun 1745 son of Asa and Elizabeth (Abbott) Abbott; Timothy d. 22 Mar 1826.

No probate record was located for Timothy. Sarah and Timothy had four children whose births are recorded at Andover.

557) i ASA ABBOTT, b. 15 Nov 1770; d. at Andover, 6 Jul 1850; m. at Billerica, 29 May 1798, JUDITH JAQUITH, b. 2 Feb 1777 daughter of Joseph and Elizabeth (Needham) Jaquith; Judith d. 15 Jul 1843.

ii TIMOTHY ABBOTT, b. 28 Sep 1774; d. by drowning, 17 Aug 1777.

558) iii DANIEL ABBOTT, b. 25 Feb 1777; d. at Nashua, NH, 3 Dec 1853; m. at Salem, 11 Aug 1805, ELIZABETH PICKMAN, b. at Salem, 11 Feb 1782 daughter of William and Elizabeth (Leavitt) Pickman; Elizabeth d. 29 Mar 1850.

---

349 There are two Mary Hoveys born in Boxford in 1781, one the daughter of Joseph (1746-1820) and one the daughter of Ivory. There is little to distinguish which Mary married Benjamin Pearl and which married Joseph Hovey (1784-1860). The one relevant document is the 1821 probate of Joseph Hovey (1746-1820) in which there is no daughter Mary living at the time of probate. This would fit with Joseph's daughter marrying Benjamin Pearl as Benjamin's wife died in 1819. The Mary Hovey who married Joseph Hovey lived until 1857.

350 The Essex Antiquarian, volume 1, Abbot Genealogy, p 80

351 *Essex County, MA: Probate File Papers, 1638-1881. Probate of* Isaac Abbot, 7 Jun 1836, *Case number* 60.

352 Year: *1860;* Census Place: *Concord Ward 7, Merrimack, New Hampshire;* Roll: *M653_675;* Page: *945;* Family History Library Film: *803675*

559) iv SARAH ABBOTT, b. 22 May 1783; d. at Andover, 11 Sep 1858; m. 27 Nov 1803, NATHANIEL SWIFT, b. at Dorchester, 15 Jul 1778 son of Nathaniel and Mary (Baker) Swift; Nathaniel d. 7 Dec 1840.

Grandchildren of William Abbott and Elizabeth Geary

134) ELIZABETH PHELPS *(Elizabeth Abbott Phelps^3, William^2, George^1)*, b. 29 Oct 1712 daughter of Joseph and Elizabeth (Abbott) Phelps; d. at Brooklyn, CT 19 Jul 1787; m. at Pomfret 14 May 1741, BENONI BARRETT, b. 17 Aug 1718[353] son of Moses and Sarah (-) Barrett; Benoni d. 20 Jun 1755 at Brooklyn, CT.

The final distribution of the estate of Benoni Barret was in January 1773 at the time the children had all reached age 18 years. Heirs receiving distributions were widow Elizabeth Barret, eldest son Joseph Barret who receives two-fifths, the heirs of daughter Elizabeth Barret who is deceased who receive one-fifth, son William Barret, and son James Barret who each also receive one-fifth.[354]

Elizabeth and Benoni had four children, the births of the sons recorded at Pomfret[355] and the birth of Elizabeth recorded at Woodstock.

560) i JOSEPH BARRETT, b. 12 Jul 1742; date of death uncertain; m. at Pomfret, 20 Feb 1765, JEMIMA CARPENTER, b. 9 Jan 1742/3 daughter of Samuel and Keziah (Carpenter) Carpenter.

ii ELIZABETH BARRETT, b. 6 Mar 1743/4;[356] d. before Jan 1773; likely the Elizabeth Barrett who had an out-of-wedlock child born at Pomfret 1765. That child was named Elizabeth Lawrence. There is not a record of the father, but it is *possible* that the father was her first cousin Joseph Lawrence. The daughter seems to be still living at the time of the final distribution of Benoni Barrett's estate in 1773 as it includes the "heirs of Elizabeth Barret deceased daughter to said Benoni Barret deceased," but no record was found of Elizabeth Lawrence after that time.

561) iii WILLIAM BARRETT, b. 12 Apr 1751; d. at Brooklyn, CT, 7 Mar 1838; m. 26 Feb 1778, LUCY ADAMS, b. at Pomfret, 25 May 1753 daughter of Paul and Mary (Hubbard) Adams; Lucy d. 4 Apr 1834.

iv JAMES BARRETT, b. 28 Feb 1754; d. 25 Jun 1776.

135) HANNAH PHELPS *(Elizabeth Abbott Phelps^3, William^2, George^1)*, b. 20 May 1715 daughter of Joseph and Elizabeth (Abbott) Phelps; d. at Pomfret 13 Jan 1746/7; m. at Pomfret 15 Nov 1744, SAMUEL LAWRENCE; no definite information about Samuel has been obtained. He may have been a member of a Lawrence family in Killingly, CT, most likely the son of Daniel Lawrence.[357]

Hannah and Samuel had just one child born at Pomfret. Following the death of his first wife, Samuel Lawrence married Hannah Tatman and relocated to Worcester where he had several children. He then seems to have left Worcester. It is possible he is the Samuel Lawrence who died in 1773 in Montague, MA with wife Hannah.

562) i JOSEPH LAWRENCE, b. 9 Aug 1745; d. at Pomfret 14 Oct 1775. There are births of three children at Pomfret for Joseph and wife Betty. There is no information on the identity of Betty.

135a) REBECCA ABBOTT (*William^3, William^2, George^1*), b. at Roxbury, 3 Jul 1712 daughter of William and Rebecca (Boylston) Abbott; d. at Roxbury, 30 Apr 1790;[358] m. at Roxbury, 24 Apr 1735, Rev. NATHANIEL WALTER, b. at Roxbury, 15 Aug 1711 son of Nehemiah and Sarah (Mather) Walter; Nathaniel d. at Roxbury, 11 Mar 1776.

Rev. Nathaniel Walter was pastor of the Second Church of Christ in Roxbury. He received his Bachelor of Arts degree from Harvard in 1729 and later completed the A. M. degree.[359] His was ordained at West Roxbury on 10 July 1734 with the ordination sermon given by his father Rev. Nehemiah Walter. He served as French interpreter for Gen, Pepperell at the siege of Louisburg in 1745.[360]

---

353 Ancestry.com, *Connecticut, Church Record Abstracts, 1630-1920* (Provo, UT, USA: n.p., 2013).

354 *Connecticut Wills and Probate, 1609-1999*, Probate of Benoni, Hartford, 1755, Case number 307.

355 Barbour Collection, Pomfret

356 Barbour and Newton, *Vital Records of Woodstock*

357 Collections of the Worcester Society of Antiquity, Volume 13, pp 57-58

358 Walter, Rebecca, Madam [wid. Rev. Mr. N. R. 3.], Apr. 30, 1790, a. 78 y. C. R. 2.

359 Harvard University, Quinquennial Catalogue, p 130

360 Weis, *The Colonial Clergy and the Colonial Churches of New England*, p 214

Two versions of Nathaniel Walter's will are provided in his probate file (probate 10 July 1777). In a version written 9 May 1757, he leaves his entire estate to his wife Rebecca to be at her own use and disposal, and after her death, to be equally divided among his surviving children. In a version written 25 April 1758 (which is crossed out), he leaves his estate to his wife Rebecca, but at her decease son William is to have from the estate what would allow for his education at college, with remaining estate to be divided among his daughters Sarah Hesilrige, Rebecca Walter, and Maria Walter, so that it should appear equitable with an eye to what Sarah has already received from the estate.[361]

Rebecca Abbott and Nathaniel Walter were parents of five children born at Roxbury.

562a i SARAH WALTER, b. 29 Mar 1736; d. at Leicestershire, England, 10 May 1775; m. at Quincy, MA, 31 Dec 1754, Sir ROBERT HESILRIGE, baptized at Northamptonshire, 27 Aug 1727 son of Arthur and Hannah (Sturges) Hesilrige.

562b ii WILLIAM WALTER, b. 7 Oct 1737; d. at Boston, 5 Dec 1800; m. at Boston, 30 Sep 1766, LYDIA LYNDE, b. at Salem, 14 Nov 1741 daughter of Benjamin and Mary (Bowles) Lynde; Lydia d. 25 Sep 1798.

562c iii REBECCA WALTER, baptized 22 Apr 1739; d. at Boston, 23 Jul 1775; m. at Roxbury, 12 May 1761, MATHER BYLES, b. at Boston, 12 Jan 1734 son of Mather and Ann (Noyes) Byles; Mather d. at St. John, New Brunswick, 12 Mar 1814.

iv NEHEMIAH WALTER, b. 13 Jun 1741

562d v MARIA WALTER, b. 19 Mar 1742/3; d. 19 Sep 1826; m. at Roxbury, 22 Feb 1770, as his second wife, Gen. JOSEPH OTIS, b. at Barnstable, 22 Feb 1725 son of James and Mary (Allyn) Otis; Joseph d. at West Barnstable, 21 Sep 1810. Joseph was first married to Rebeckah Sturgis.

136) ABIGAIL ABBOTT *(James³, William², George¹)*, b. 1 Jan 1714/5 daughter of James and Abigail (Farnum) Abbott; d. at Charlestown about 1737; m. 13 May 1734, JOHN KIDDER, b. at Charlestown 13 Feb 1709 son of Stephen and Mary (Johnson) Kidder; John married second Anna Walker and third Mary Snow.

The Abbot genealogy[362] lists Abigail as marrying Jacob Waldron, having children Sarah, Ezra, and Elizabeth and then marrying (-) Hibbard of Charlestown. However, available records give Jacob Waldron (who was born 1743) as marrying Abigail's niece Sarah [daughter of James and Sarah (Bancroft) Abbott]. There are also three birth records for children of Jacob and Sarah named Sarah, Ezra, and Elizabeth. The only marriage of Abigail seems to be to John Kidder of Charlestown and she seems to have died soon after the birth of her only child.

There is just one child and he likely died young as John Kidder named another son John that he had with his third wife.

i JOHN KIDDER, b. 12 Sep 1735; likely died young

137) JAMES ABBOTT *(James³, William², George¹)*, b. 12 Jan 1716/7 son of James and Abigail (Farnum) Abbott; d. at Newbury, VT, 27 Dec 1803; m. about 1742, SARAH BANCROFT, b. 19 Feb 1722 daughter of Samuel and Sarah (Lampson) Bancroft; Sarah d. 1765.

James Abbott and Sarah Bancroft had ten children. The oldest child's birth is recorded at Andover, and there are records of the births of some of the other children in New Hampshire. Information on other children was obtained from the Abbot genealogy, pp 28-29.[363]

563) i SARAH ABBOTT, b. 1 Mar 1743; death unknown; m. by 1765, JACOB WALDRON, b. at Rumford, 2 Mar 1743 son of Isaac and Susannah (Chandler) Waldron; the date or place of death is not known.

564) ii ABIGAIL ABBOT, b. 22 Jan 1745/6; d. at Bath, NH, 11 Feb 1815; m. 15 Apr 1767, ASA BAILEY, b. at Salem, NH, 13 May 1745 son of Edward and Elizabeth (Burbank) Bailey. Abigail divorced Asa in 1793 following years of abuse, the last straw being the sexual abuse of one of their daughters. What happened to Asa is not clear. *The Memoirs of Mrs. Abigail Bailey* recounting the events of her marriage was published in 1815 just after her death.[364]

---

361 *Suffolk County, MA: Probate File Papers.*Online database. *AmericanAncestors.org.* New England Historic Genealogical Society, 2017-2019. Case 16323

362 Abbot and Abbot, *Genealogical Register of Descendants*, p 28

363 Abbot and Abbot, *Genealogical Register of Descendants*

364 Bailey, *Memoirs of Mrs. Abigail Bailey*

565) iii MARY ABBOTT, b. 6 Feb 1748; m. 1st, 22 Oct 1773, RICHARD MINCHEN; Richard d. 1776. Mary m. 2nd, at Haverhill, NH, 22 Mar 1777, URIAH CROSS.[365]

566) iv JAMES ABBOTT, b. 10 Oct 1750; d. in Ohio 1814; m. at Groton, VT, 29 Mar 1781, ZILPHA SMITH. James m. 2nd, at Groton, VT, 25 Jul 1785, MEHITABLE HIDDEN.[366][367]

567) v JUDITH ABBOTT, b. 19 Feb 1753; d. at Newbury, VT, 30 Dec 1806; m. 27 Oct 1772, THOMAS BROCK, b. about 1745; Thomas d. at Newbury, 10 Jun 1811. Thomas Brock's origins are not clear at this point; he was perhaps born in Scotland.

568) vi WILLIAM ABBOTT, b. 24 Apr 1755; d. at Bath, NH, 14 Jun 1807; m. 9 Dec 1777, MABEL WHITTLESEY, b. at Guilford, CT, 25 Jun 1757 daughter of Josiah and Elizabeth (Jackson) Whittlesey; Mabel d. at Haverhill, NH, 2 Nov 1836.

569) vii BANCROFT ABBOTT, b. 4 Jun 1757; d. at Newbury, VT, 29 Oct 1829;[368] m. 1787, LYDIA WHITE, b. at Plaistow, NH, 1 Jan 1763 daughter of Ebenezer and Hannah (Merrill) White; Lydia d. 25 Jun 1853.

viii EZRA ABBOTT, b. 8 Oct 1759; died young.

ix SUSANNAH ABBOTT, b. 3 Mar 1763; no further record.

570) x EZRA ABBOTT, b. 2 Jun 1765; d. in Vermont, 5 Jul 1842; m. at Newbury, VT, 8 Aug 1788, his first cousin, HANNAH ABBOTT, b. 29 Mar 1762 daughter of Reuben and Rhoda (Whittemore) Abbott; Hannah d. 2 Sep 1832.

138) REUBEN ABBOTT *(James[3], William[2], George[1])*, b. 4 Apr 1723 son of James and Abigail (Farnum) Abbott; d. at Concord, NH, 13 May 1822; m. 1st, by 1752, RHODA WHITTEMORE, b. at Malden, 18 Aug 1729 daughter of Elias and Rhoda (Holt) Whittemore; d. 29 Jan 1785. Reuben m. 2nd DINAH BLANCHARD the widow of Joseph Blanchard; Dinah was b. 28 Dec 1731 daughter of Stephen and Deborah (Phelps) Blanchard; Dinah d. 11 Mar 1826.

Reuben and Rhoda had ten children whose births are recorded at Concord, New Hampshire. Of the six children who married, three married other George Abbott descendants.

i REUBEN ABBOTT, b. 18 May 1752; d. 11 Dec 1752.

571) ii REUBEN ABBOTT, b. 5 Feb 1754; d. 12 Dec 1834; m. 24 Sep 1776, his second cousin once removed, ZERVIAH FARNUM, b. at Concord, about 1752 daughter of Joseph and Zerviah (Hoit) Farnum; Zerviah d. at Concord, Dec 1818.[369]

572) iii RHODA ABBOTT, b. 31 Dec 1755; d. at Boscawen, 31 Aug 1839; m. at Concord, 8 Jan 1778, JONATHAN JOHNSON, b. at Boscawen, 29 Dec 1753 son of John and Eleanor (Eastman) Johnson; Jonathan d. 16 Sep 1820.

573) iv ELIAS ABBOTT, b. 24 Oct 1757; d. at Northfield, NH, 19 Mar 1847; m. Sep 1782, ELIZABETH BUSWELL, b. at Kingston, 4 Sep 1761 daughter of James and Elizabeth (Clough) Buswell; Elizabeth d. 25 Jan 1832.[370]

v PHEBE ABBOTT, b. 14 Apr 1759; d. 4 Jul 1760.

vi PHEBE ABBOTT, b. 6 Dev 1760; d. Nov 1777.

570) vii HANNAH ABBOTT, b. 29 Mar 1762; d. at Vermont, 2 Sep 1832; m. at Newbury, VT, 8 Aug 1788, her first cousin, EZRA ABBOTT, b. at Haverhill, 2 Jun 1765 son of James and Sarah (Bancroft) Abbott; Ezra d. 5 Jul 1842. This is the same couple as Family #137, child x.

viii RUTH ABBOTT, b. 14 Feb 1764; d. 2 Sep 1764

574) ix EZRA ABBOTT, b. 8 Aug 1765; d. 24 Apr 1839; m. his third cousin, MARY WALKER, b, about 1763 daughter of Joseph and Mary (Abbott) Walker; Mary d. at Concord, 22 Sep 1852. This is the same as Family #240, child v.

---

365 New Hampshire Marriage Record Index 1637-1947 (ancestry.com)
366 Abbott Family, Groton Families in 1790, Groton Vermont Historical Society.
367 Vermont Vital Records 1720-1908 (ancestry.com)
368 *Vermont, Vital Records, 1720-1908* (Provo, UT, USA: Ancestry.com Operations, Inc., 2013).
369 New Hampshire, Death and Disinterment Records, 1754-1947
370 History of the Town of Canterbury, p 1

575) x NATHAN ABBOTT, b. 8 Aug 1765; d. at Concord, 13 May 1849; m. his third cousin, PHEBE ABBOTT, b. 8 Aug 1764 daughter of Nathaniel and Miriam (Chandler) Abbott; Phebe d. 11 Aug 1854. This is the same as Family #236, child vii.

57) AMOS ABBOTT *(James[3], William[2], George[1])* and REBECCA ABBOTT; REBECCA ABBOTT and ABIEL CHANDLER. This family group is Family #57 in Generation Three.

139) PHEBE ABBOTT *(James[3], William[2], George[1])*, b. 22 Nov 1727 daughter of James and Abigail (Farnum) Abbott; d. at Conway NH, 29 Sep 1754; m. 5 Nov 1747, as his 1st wife, THOMAS MERRILL, b. 5 Feb 1723/4 at Haverhill son of John and Lydia (Haynes) Merrill. Thomas had a total of four marriages, his 2nd to Mehitable Harriman, 3rd to Abigail Goodhue, and 4th to Elizabeth Abbott daughter of Benjamin and Abigail (Abbott) Abbott. Thomas Merrill d. at Conway 21 Jun 1788.

Phebe Abbott and Thomas Merrill had five children born at Conway, New Hampshire. Three of the sons, William, Thomas, and Amos, bought adjoining farms on the Saco River in Conway.[371] Two of the sons married two Ambrose sisters who were the daughters of Jonathan and Abigail (Goodhue) Ambrose. Abigail Goodhue Ambrose was one of the wives of Thomas Merrill making these couples, step-siblings.

576) i THOMAS MERRILL, b. 31 Aug 1748; d. May 1821;[372] m. 7 Dec 1775, HANNAH AMBROSE, b, about 1750 daughter of Jonathan and Abigail (Goodhue) Ambrose.

ii WILLIAM MERRILL, b. about 1749. William did not marry.

577) iii ENOCH MERRILL, b. 10 Nov 1750; d. 1838; m. about 1772, MARY AMBROSE, b. at Exeter, 11 Nov 1755 daughter of Jonathan and Abigail (Goodhue) Ambrose; Mary d. at Conway, 27 Mar 1815.

578) iv AMOS MERRILL, b. Jul 1752; d, at Conway, 13 Mar 1840; m. 30 Dec 1779, LOIS WILLEY, b. Jan 1760; Lois d. 28 Mar 1855.

579) v PHEBE MERRILL, b. Dec 1753; d. at North Conway, 9 Oct 1839; m. 3 Dec 1775, her second cousin, ABIATHAR EASTMAN, b. 29 Apr 1745 son of Richard and Mary (Lovejoy) Eastman; Abiathar d. 10 Jan 1815.

Thomas Merrill and Elizabeth Abbott had two children born at Conway. (See Family #195)

140) REBECCA ABBOTT *(James[3], William[2], George[1])*, b. 13 Aug 1730 daughter of James and Abigail (Farnum) Abbott; d. at NH date unknown; m. 13 Aug 1750, ENOCH EASTMAN, b. at Salisbury, 1 Jun 1725 son of Joseph and Abigail (Merrill) Eastman.[373]

Rebecca ad Enoch were early settlers in Hopkinton. Enoch held the position of town clerk and fulfilled other civic responsibilities.[374]

Rebecca and Enoch were the parents of 12 children all born in Rumford[375] and Hopkinton.[376]

i ENOCH EASTMAN, b. 22 Feb 1752; d. 14 Mar 1756 by drowning.

ii EZRA EASTMAN, b. 25 Mar 1754; died young.

580) iii SIMEON EASTMAN, b. 23 Oct 1755; m. about 1780, MEHITABLE PIPER.

iv ENOCH EASTMAN, b. 2 Mar 1757; no further record.

581) v ABIGAIL EASTMAN, b. 25 Feb 1759; d. at Hopkinton, 19 Dec 1836; m. 14 Sep 1780, MOSES COLBY, b. at Newton, NH, 7 Jun 1751 son of Moses and Mary (Sargent) Colby; Moses d. at Hopkinton, 16 Mar 1790.

582) vi SAMUEL EASTMAN, b. 13 Nov 1760; d. at Hopkinton, NH after 1840;[377] m. SARAH HARRIS.

---

[371] Merrill, *A Merrill Memorial*, p 294
[372] Merrill, *A Merrill Memorial*, p 294
[373] Rix, *History and Genealogy of the Eastman Family of America*
[374] Lord, *Life and Times in Hopkinton, N.H.*
[375] Ancestry.com. *New Hampshire, Births and Christenings Index, 1714-1904*
[376] Ancestry.com. *New Hampshire, Births and Christenings Index, 1714-1904*
[377] Ancestry.com, New Hampshire, Compiled Census and Census Substitutes Index, 1790-1890. Samuel Eastman, age 79, is recorded living at Hopkinton in 1840.

583) vii REBEKAH EASTMAN, b. 10 Apr 1762; m. JAMES PUTNEY, b. at Hopkinton, 8 Feb 1761 son of John and Mary (-) Putney.

584) viii LUCY EASTMAN, b. 1 Dec 1763; d. 5 Jan 1816 at Tunbridge, VT; m. at Dunbarton, 16 Jan 1794, BENJAMIN ORDWAY, b. 1763 (based on age at time of death) perhaps the son of Moses and Susannah (Bly) Ordway; Benjamin d. 1 Dec 1849. After Lucy's death, Benjamin married Betsey Gilman.

585) ix EZRA EASTMAN, b. 15 Aug 1764; d. 14 Jun 1816; m. 28 Jun 1787, MOLLY EATON, b. 10 Aug 1769 daughter of Thomas and Molly (-) Eaton; Molly d. 11 Jan 1825.

586) x TAMISON EASTMAN, b. 19 Oct 1766; d. after 1850; m. SAMUEL FRENCH, b. at South Hampton, 3 Apr 1762 son of Offen and Abigail (French) French;[378] d. at Bradford, 7 Feb 1799.[379]

587) xi JOSEPH EASTMAN, b. 18 Sep 1768; d. at Contoocook, NH, 16 Feb 1823; m. 26 Oct 1790, BETSEY CLOUGH, b. 30 Jun 1770 daughter of James and Ruth (Webster) Clough; Betsey d. at Contoocook, NH, 1 Sep 1861.

588) xii SARAH EASTMAN, b. 27 Aug 1771; m. 5 Oct 1790, THOMAS EATON, b. 21 Jul 1771 son of Thomas and Molly (-) Eaton.

141) SARAH ABBOTT *(James[3], William[2], George[1])*, twin of Rebecca, b. 13 Aug 1730 daughter of James and Abigail (Farnum) Abbott; m. about 1751, as her 1st husband, her second cousin, JOB ABBOTT *(Jonathan[3], Benjamin[2], George[1])*, b. 3 Oct 1724 son of Jonathan and Zerviah (Holt) Abbott; Job died before 1765. Sarah m. 2nd about 1765, as his second wife, RICHARD EASTMAN, b. 9 Aug 1712 son of Jonathan and Hannah (Green) Eastman; Richard d. at Lovell, ME, 29 Dec 1807.

Sarah Abbott and Job Abbott had four children. Three of these four children married fellow George Abbott descendants. In addition, three of the children of the second child, Nathan, married three of the children of the third child, Job.

325) i SARAH ABBOTT, b. 1751 at Suncook; d. at Temple, NH, 9 Oct 1854;[380] m. 25 Nov 1773, her third cousin (and George Abbott descendant), ABIEL HOLT, b. at Lunenburg, 14 Jul 1748 son of Joseph and Mary (Abbott) Holt; Abiel d. 7 Jan 1811.

443) ii NATHAN ABBOTT, b. at Pembroke 4 Sep 1753; d. at Andover 1801 (probate of will 31 Mar 1801); m. 8 May 1777, his third cousin (and George Abbott descendant), SARAH BALLARD, b. 28 Dec 1755 daughter of Hezekiah and Lydia (Chandler) Ballard; Sarah d. 20 Aug 1825.

589) iii JOB ABBOTT, b. about 1755 at Pembroke; d. at Wilton 12 Jul 1805; m. at Andover, 12 Dec 1780, his third cousin once removed (and George Abbott descendant), ANNA BALLARD, b. 15 Nov 1762 daughter of Timothy and Sarah (Abbott) Ballard; Anna d. at Wilton, 7 Apr 1805.[381]

590) iv ABIGAIL ABBOTT, b. about 1757; d. 1 May 1845 at Lovell, ME;[382] m. by 1778, STEPHEN DRESSER, b. at Andover, 25 Oct 1754 son of Jonathan and Sarah (Foster) Dresser; Stephen d. at Frye, ME, 28 Sep 1829.

Richard Eastman was first married to Molly Lovejoy and had 12 children from his first marriage. He settled in Pembroke but relocated to Conway about 1768. Very soon after, the family made one more move to Lovell, Maine. Richard established a ferry across the Saco River in Maine.[383]

Sarah Abbott and Richard Eastman had five children, the oldest two born at Pembroke, and the three youngest born at Fryeburg, Maine.

591) i DANIEL EASTMAN, b. 21 Apr 1766; d. at Lovell, ME, 16 Jan 1844; m. at Dracut, 1 Mar 1787, SARAH WHITING, b. about 1762 (based on age of 44 at time of death) of parents not yet determined; Sarah d. at Lovell, 19 Jan 1806.

592) ii CYRUS EASTMAN, b. 10 Jul 1767; m. BETSEY WEBSTER. Betsey's origins are unknown, but the births for the two sons of this marriage, according to Rix's Eastman genealogy, are 1821 and 1827, so she would be born not much earlier than 1785-1790. However, there is a marriage record for Cyrus "Easton" and Betsey

[378] South Hampton Congregational Church, 1743-1801, marriages and baptisms, p 22
[379] Gould & Beals, *Early Families of Bradford*, p 168
[380] Gravestone inscription: Aged 103 yrs. 2 ms. & 25 ds.
[381] Date of death obtained from her gravestone which has the following inscription: Erected to the memory of Mrs. Anne Abbott, consort of Mr. Job Abbott, who died April 7, 1805, in the 43 year of her age. Findagrave Memorial ID: 34218725
[382] Ancestry.com, *U.S., Find A Grave Index, 1600s-Current* (Provo, UT, USA: Ancestry.com Operations, Inc., 2012).
[383] Rix, *History and Genealogy of the Eastman Family of America ...*, Volumes 1-5, pp 82-83

Webster in 1799.[384] There are questions yet to be resolved about this family. It may be that the two sons attributed to this couple are from a Cyrus from the following generation. There are other Cyrus Eastmans in the New Suncook area about 20 years younger than this Cyrus.

iii SUSANNAH EASTMAN, b. 29 Apr 1769; d. 1770.

593) iv JEREMY EASTMAN, b. 25 Apr 1771; d. at Stow, ME, 8 Oct 1846; m. by 1794, BETSEY KILGORE, b. 2 Apr 1776 daughter of Joseph and Abigail (Page) Kilgore; Betsey d. 16 Feb 1873.

v JAMES EASTMAN, b. 30 Jan 1775; d. 1778.

142) MARY ABBOTT *(James[3], William[2], George[1])*, b. 12 Oct 1732 daughter of James and Abigail (Farnum) Abbott; d, about 1780; m. by 1760 ADONIJAH TYLER, b. 26 Nov 1738[385] son of Moses and Miriam (Bailey) Tyler; Adonijah d. 12 Oct 1812 at Hopkinton, NH.

Mary Abbott and Adonijah Tyler had eight children. The births of the first six children are recorded at Henniker, New Hampshire[386] and the youngest two at Chester, New Hampshire. A probate record was not located. The family settled in Hopkinton, New Hampshire where Adonijah was a signer of the declaration of fidelity in 1776.[387]

594) i JAMES TYLER, b. 2 Apr 1760; d. at Thetford, VT, 20 Aug 1855;[388] m. by 1779, SARAH GOULD, b. at Hampton, 24 Jul 1760 daughter of Christopher and Abigail (Shepherd) Gould; Sarah's death record was not located.

595) ii RACHEL TYLER, b. 2 Mar 1762; d. in New York, Feb 1843; m. about 1782, JACOB STANLEY, b. at Hopkinton, 9 Sep 1761 son of Matthew and Mary (Putney) Stanley.

596) iii MIRIAM TYLER, b. 22 Mar 1764; d. Jun 1840; m. 11 May 1790, MOSES HASTINGS son of James and Mary (Foster) Hastings; Moses d. 25 Jan 1815.

597) iv JEREMIAH TYLER, b. 6 Apr 1766; d. at Thetford, VT, 19 Jan 1844; m. 31 Oct 1802, IRENE HEATON, b. 17 Apr 1774 daughter of William and Irene (King) Heaton; Irene died at Thetford, VT, 4 May 1840.[389]

598) v SIMEON TYLER, b. 22 Mar 1768; d. at Hopkinton, 24 Dec 1855; m. 14 Mar 1799, HANNAH ROWELL, b. 1776, parents unknown; Hannah d. 28 Jun 1831. Simeon m. 2nd, SUSAN PAIGE who was born about 1786 and d. 21 Mar 1865.

599) vi MOSES TYLER, b. 9 Apr 1770; d. at Tyler's Bridge, NH, 21 Dec 1857; m. 21 Jun 1798, BETSY MCCONNELL, b. at Pembroke, 30 Jan 1774 daughter of Samuel and Ann (Cunningham) McConnell; Betsy d. 9 Sep 1866.

600) vii MARY TYLER, b. 4 Jun 1773; d. 1839 at Gap Grove, IL; m. 16 Nov 1797, JACOB MARTIN, b. about 1770; Jacob d. after 1835, likely at Gap Grove.

601) viii SARAH TYLER, b. Mar 1775; d. at Ogle County, IL, 7 Feb 1839; m. at Hopkinton, 14 Jun 1796, ROBERT CROWELL *possibly* the son of Aaron and Elizabeth(-) Crowell; Robert d. 22 Sep 1862.[390]

143) NATHAN ABBOTT *(Paul[3], William[2], George[1])*, b. 10 Apr 1721 son of Paul and Elizabeth (Gray) Abbott; d. unknown but he might have gone to Pennsylvania; m. 1st at Pomfret, 24 Nov 1742, EUNICE MARSH, b. at Plainfield, CT 17 Feb 1724 daughter of Thomas and Eunice (Parkhouse) Marsh; Eunice d. at Ashford 27 Oct 1760. Nathan m. 2nd at Pomfret, 24 Nov 1761, HEPHZIBAH BROWN, b. about 1727; Hepzibah d. 26 May 1790 at Hampton, CT.

Nathan Abbott and Eunice Marsh had nine children whose births are recorded in Windham County, the oldest two children at Ashford and the remining six children at Pomfret. Five of the children are known to have died in early childhood,

---

[384] "Maine Marriages, 1771-1907," database, *FamilySearch* (https://familysearch.org/ark:/61903/1:1:F4FZ-NXX: 4 December 2014), Cyrus Easton and Betsy Webster, 1799; citing Fryeburg, Oxford, Maine, reference; FHL microfilm 10,915.

[385] New Hampshire: Births, Deaths and Marriages, 1654-1969 (accessed through americanancestors.org)

[386] Ancestry.com, *New Hampshire, Births and Christenings Index, 1714-1904* (Provo, UT, USA: Ancestry.com Operations, Inc., 2011).

[387] Lord, *Life and Times in Hopkinton*, p 59

[388] Ancestry.com, *Vermont, Vital Records, 1720-1908* (Provo, UT, USA: Ancestry.com Operations, Inc., 2013).

[389] Her grave is in Post Mills Cemetery, Vermont. Findagrave Memorial ID 121161310

[390] Brigham, *The Tyler Genealogy* p 237

four of the children dying in a two-week period in 1754. In 1754, there were outbreaks of "throat distemper" and "malignant fever" in various locations in the New England colonies.[391]

602) i NATHAN ABBOTT, b. 18 May 1744; d. at Woodstock, 19 Jan 1794;[392] m. JUDITH STODDARD, b. 24 Sep 1749 daughter of Ebenezer and Anna (Stowell) Stoddard. There is a probate record for Nathan Abbott from 1794 that names wife Judith as administrator of the estate with Ebenezer Stoddard as co-signer on the surety bond.[393]

ii EUNICE ABBOTT, b. 20 Nov 1746; no further record. There is a Eunice Abbott as head of household in the 1790 US Census in Fairfield, but there is no reason to believe that is this Eunice.

iii GIDEON ABBOTT, b. 3 Jun 1748; d. 5 Sep 1754.

iv HANNAH ABBOTT, b. 25 Mar 1750; d. 27 Aug 1754.

v PAUL ABBOTT, b. 11 Feb 1753; d. 30 Aug 1754.

vi ELIZABETH ABBOTT, b. 12 Feb 1754; d. 11 Sep 1754.

vii EXPERIENCE ABBOTT, b. 21 Jan 1756; d. at Hampton, 20 Dec 1835; m. 12 Mar 1820, as his third wife, THOMAS GROW, b. at Pomfret, 4 Apr 1743 son of Thomas and Susanna (Eaton) Grow.

603) viii STEPHEN ABBOTT, b. 20 Oct 1757; d. at North Providence, RI, 24 Jul 1813;[394][395] m. 28 Jun 1781, ESTHER INGALLS, b. 26 Nov 1762 daughter of Zebadiah and Esther (Goodell) Ingalls; Esther d. 4 Feb 1851. This is the same as Family #181, child v.

ix RUFUS ABBOTT, b. 18 Sep 1759; d. 1 Mar 1760.

144) WILLIAM ABBOTT *(Paul³, William², George¹)*, b. 18 Feb 1723 son of Paul and Elizabeth (Gray) Abbott; d. at Pomfret 1 Nov 1805; m. 1st 9 May 1745, JERUSHA STOWELL, b. 22 Sep 1721 at Newton, MA daughter of David and Mary (Dillaway) Stowell; Jerusha d. 29 Feb 1768. William m. 2nd 4 Jun 1778, HANNAH EDMUND; Hannah d. 5 Feb 1808; nothing else is known of her at this time.

There are four births records at Pomfret for William Abbott and his first wife Jerusha Stowell.

i ANNA ABBOTT, b. 29 Jun 1748; d. at Pomfret, 5 Nov 1791. Anna does not seem to have married.

604) ii WILLIAM ABBOTT, b. 27 May 1752; d. at Lisle, NY, 1806 (probate 15 Jul 1806); m. 8 Jul 1776, HANNAH SNOW, b. at Ashford, 2 Jul 1754 daughter of Samuel and Hannah (Mason) Snow.

iii ELIZABETH ABBOTT, b. 3 Mar 1758; d. 31 Dec 1769.

iv RHODA ABBOTT, b. 27 Jul 1761; d. likely in New York. The Abbot genealogy states she married and went to New York with her brother, but a spouse was not suggested. There was a Rhoda Abbott who married DAVID HEACOCK the son of David and Sarah (DeWulf) Heacock. Some sources suggest it was a daughter Rhoda of Jesse and Johannah (Kellogg) Abbott of the Rowley Abbott line, and that family was in Putnam County, NY where David Heacock also shows up. Remains an area for further research.

145) BENJAMIN ABBOTT *(Paul³, William², George¹)*, b. 25 Jul 1724 son of Paul and Elizabeth (Gray) Abbott; d. at Brookfield, VT, 21 Jun 1807;[396] m. 1st at Ashford, 16 Jan 1745/6, MARY ANN ANDREWS, b. at Windham 25 Jul 1727 daughter of John and Hannah (-) Andrews; Mary Ann d. 8 Dec 1788. Benjamin m. 2nd 30 Jun 1793 the widow HANNAH BROWN about whom nothing else is known.

Benjamin Abbott and Mary Ann Andrews had ten children whose births are recorded at several towns in Windham County including Ashford, Pomfret, and Windham. The Abbot genealogy[397] lists a daughter named Isabel in this family but omits the daughter Louisa; there are records for Louisa but not for Isabel, so she is not included here. This may just be a matter of the name being confused.

---

391 Caulfield, Ernest. "The Pursuit of a Pestilence." In *Proceedings of the American Antiquarian Society*, vol. 60, no. 1, p. 21. American Antiquarian Society., 1950.

392 *Connecticut, Hale Collection of Cemetery Inscriptions and Newspaper Notices, 1629-1934*. Newspaper notice gives age at death as 49, and states he was in the Revolutionary War.

393 *Connecticut Wills and Probate, 1609-1999*, Probate of Nathan Abbott, Hartford, 1794, Case number 4.

394 Ancestry.com, Rhode Island, Vital Extracts, 1636-1899

395 There is a Rhode Island probate record for Col. Stephen Abbott from August 1813 that contains an inventory and provides for widow Esther to administer the estate. Probate Files, Early to 1885 (Pawtucket, R.I.); Author: Pawtucket (Rhode Island). Court of Probate; Probate Place: Providence, Rhode Island

396 His grave site is in the Brookfield, VT cemetery. (findagrave.com)

397 Abbot and Abbot, *Genealogical Register of Descendants*

i HENRY ABBOTT, b. 12 Nov 1746; d. 27 Jan 1749.

605) ii HENRY ABBOTT, b. 3 Jun 1749; d. at Vermont, 31 Mar 1807; m. at Hampton, 7 Apr 1772, a fourth cousin, SARAH BURNHAM, b. 21 Aug 1750 daughter of Isaac and Eunice (Holt) Burnham. Sarah had married first John Greenslit with whom she had two children.

iii STEPHEN ABBOTT, b. 23 May 1751; d. 21 Aug 1754.

iv BENJAMIN ABBOTT, b. 21 Jan 1753; d, 21 Aug 1754.

606) v MARY ABBOTT, b. 4 Aug 1754; d. at Brookfield, VT, 28 Feb 1811; m. 17 May 1781, THOMAS ADAMS, b. at Canterbury, CT, 24 Apr 1757 son of Eliphalet and Mary (Frost) Adams; Thomas d. at Brookfield, 1803 (distribution of estate 5 Aug 1803).

607) vi ASA ABBOTT, b. 25 May 1756; d. at Hampton, 1834 (will dated 10 Apr 1834); m. by 1783, SARAH BIDLACK, b. at Hampton, 30 Sep 1756 daughter of James and Mehitable (Durkee) Bidlack. Sarah was first married to STEPHEN FULLER son of Stephen and Mary (Abbott) Fuller. Stephen died at the Battle of Wyoming. These families are considered together.

608) vii HANNAH ABBOTT, b. 10 Feb 1759; m. at Hampton, 24 May 1775, JOSIAH COLLINS, b. about 1749 (based on age 63 at time of death); Josiah d. at Hampton, 24 Feb 1812. There is a Josiah Collins who was born at Wethersfield in 1750 and died in 1826 but that is not this Josiah.

609) viii TRYPHENA ABBOTT, b. 22 Sep 1760; d. at Stafford, 21 Nov 1835; m. May 1781, ABNER ASHLEY, b. at Hampton, 19 Jan 1754 son of Abner and Mary (Crossley) Ashley; Abner d. at Tolland 1837 (will proved 2 January 1838).

610) ix LOUISA ABBOTT, b. 24 Dec 1762; d. at New York, 16 Mar 1806; m. at Canterbury, 1 Sep 1785, SAMUEL PRESTON, b. 19 Feb 1763 son of Jacob and Mary (Butts) Preston.

611) x BENJAMIN ABBOTT, b. 2 Oct 1764; d. at Brookfield, VT, 12 Sep 1829;[398] m. about 1786, LUCY FLINT, b. 10 Jun 1767 daughter of Nathaniel and Lucy (Martin) Flint; Lucy d. 24 Sep 1839.

146) MARY ABBOTT *(Paul^3, William^2, George^1)*, b. 3 Mar 1728/9 daughter of Paul and Elizabeth (Gray) Abbott; d. at Windham 10 Aug 1769; m. 28 Jun 1749, JOSHUA HOLT, b. 19 Mar 1728/9 son of Joshua and Keturah (Holt) Holt. Joshua m. 2nd Susanna Goodell; Joshua d. 5 Jul 1791.

In his will written 13 April 1791,[399] Joshua Holt has bequests for the following persons: dear and loving wife Susannah, daughter Dinah Stoel, daughter Mary Fuller, son Uriah, son Lemuel, daughter Keturah Amidown, daughter Sarah Durkee (although there are other last names for Sarah crossed out, one of them Holt), daughter Hannah Carpenter, daughter Dorcas Fuller, daughter Zilphia, and sons Samuel and Oliver who divide equally everything not given to the other children. Zilphia, Samuel, and Oliver are children from his second marriage to Susannah Goodell.

Mary Abbott and Joshua Holt had eight children whose births are recorded at Windham.

612) i DINAH HOLT, b. 22 Mar 1750; d. 21 Feb 1826; m. 30 Jun 1778, SETH STOWELL, b. 29 May 1742 son of Nathaniel and Margaret (Trowbridge) Stowell; Seth d. about 1798 (when estate went to probate). Dinah m. 2nd, 27 Nov 1800, PAUL HOLT, b. 1743 and d. 1827. Dinah was Paul Holt's third wife. Paul Holt and his first wife Sarah Welch were the parents of Sarah Holt who married Stephen Utley who is considered below in Family #153, child viii.

613) ii MARY HOLT, b. 11 Jul 1752; d. at Hampton, 23 Oct 1824; m. 7 Nov 1771, JOSEPH FULLER, b. at Ipswich, 1738 son of John and Hannah (Lord) Fuller; Joseph d. 29 Jan 1805.

614) iii URIAH HOLT, b. 23 Mar 1754; d. at West Springfield, MA, 22 Sep 1828; m. at Ashford, 11 Nov 1779, MARGARET MASON, b. at Ashford, 13 Aug 1754 daughter of Ebenezer and Mehitable (Holmes) Mason; Margaret d. 1817.

[398] Benjamin's estate entered probate in Orange County, VT in 1830.

[399] *Connecticut Wills and Probate, 1609-1999*, Probate of Joshua Holt, Hartford, 1791, Case number 1945.

615) iv LEMUEL HOLT, b. 28 Feb 1756; d. at Lyme, NH, 1 Aug 1836; m. 1778, his first cousin, MARY ABBOTT, b. 20 Jan 1757 daughter of Isaac and Mary (Barker) Abbott; Mary d. 8 Sep 1849. This is the same as Family #148, child i.

616) v KETURAH HOLT, b. 21 Aug 1758; d. at Randolph, VT, 25 Jul 1839;[400] m. 29 Jan 1784, JONATHAN AMIDON, b. 7 Feb 1759 son of Henry and Sarah (Doubleday) Amidon; Jonathan d. at Randolph, 15 Apr 1838.

617) vi SARAH HOLT, b. 26 Oct 1761; d. at Stockbridge, VT, 19 Feb 1813; m. 1783, JOHN DURKEE, b. at Windham, 2 Jul 1762 son of Joseph and Elizabeth (Fiske) Durkee; John d. at Stockbridge, 2 May 1838.

618) vii HANNAH HOLT, b. 24 May 1764; d. in Vermont, 7 Aug 1855; m. at Clarendon, VT, 21 Jan 1788, AARON CARPENTER, b. at Rehoboth, 9 May 1763 son of Jabez and Abigail (Dyer) Carpenter; Aaron d. 26 Sep 1836.[401]

619) viii DORCAS HOLT, b. 30 Mar 1767; d. at Middlebury, VT, 1 Jul 1800; m. JOSIAH FULLER, b. 30 Oct 1764 son of David and Hannah (Fuller) Fuller; Josiah d. Potsdam, NY, 4 Dec 1835.

147) SARAH ABBOTT *(Paul³, William², George¹)*, b. 15 Oct 1730 daughter of Paul and Elizabeth (Gray) Abbott; d. at Pomfret, 17 Dec 1811; m. 24 May 1749, JOSEPH INGALLS, b. at Andover, 9 Aug 1723 son of Joseph and Phebe (Farnum) Ingalls; Joseph d. 26 Oct 1790.

There is a 1791 probate record for Joseph Ingalls. There is no will. Part of the probate includes Sarah being named as the guardian of the youngest child Harvey. The estate was deemed to be insolvent. The whole of the real and personal estate was ordered to be sold, with most of the benefit of the sale to go to the creditors.[402]

There are records for twelve children of Joseph and Sarah all born at Pomfret.

i PHEBE INGALLS, b. 22 Aug 1750; d. 22 Sep 1759.

620) ii PETER INGALLS, b. 12 Feb 1752; d. at Pomfret, 11 Jun 1808; m. 20 Apr 1775, SARAH ASHLEY, b. at Windham, 2 Nov 1752 daughter of Joseph and Sarah (Cressy) Ashley, Sarah d. at Pomfret, 18 Nov 1811.

iii DORCUS INGALLS, b. 27 Jun 1754; no further record was located for Dorcus.

621) iv DARIUS INGALLS, b. 27 Jun 1754; d. likely in Vermont, 1824; m. Mar 1796, LODEMA LEE, b. at Killingly, 3 Nov 1757 daughter of Seth and Molly (Conant) Lee.

v ASA INGALLS, b. 29 Feb 1756; d. 25 Dec 1775.

622) vi LUTHER INGALLS, b. 24 Aug 1758; d. at Hanover, NH, 4 Jul 1855; m. 23 Jun 1781, LUCY UTLEY, born about 1760; Lucy d. 7 Jan 1831.

623) vii CALVIN INGALLS, b. 22 Nov 1760; d. at Stafford, Oct 1830; m. 1st, 28 Nov 1782, CATHERINE TERRINGTON; Catherine d. 31 Dec 1783. Calvin m. 2nd, 28 May 1795, MARY HORTON, b. at Union, 1 Oct 1759 daughter of Ezra and Mary (Hempstead) Horton; Mary d. 12 May 1833.

624) viii CHESTER INGALLS, b. 7 Aug 1762; d. at Hanover, NH, 27 May 1842; m. 4 Apr 1784, SYLVIA STEVENS, b. 25 Mar 1763 daughter of Robert and Mary (Hathaway) Stevens.

ix JOSEPH ROYAL INGALLS, b. 24 Aug 1764; d. 5 Sep 1783.[403]

625) x SARAH INGALLS, b. 18 Dec 1766; d. at Jericho, VT, 24 Apr 1833;[404] m. 22 Jan 1788, ABRAHAM FORD, b. 15 May 1764 son of Abraham and Abigail (Woodward) Ford; Abraham d. 9 Apr 1813 while on a trip to Lebanon, CT. The family settled in Vermont in 1803.

626) xi HANNAH INGALLS, b. 22 Aug 1769; m. 25 Jan 1791, JOSIAH INGERSOLL, *possibly* the son of Richard and Zipporah (-) Ingersoll; this family relocated to Westford, VT.

627) xii HARVEY INGALLS, b. 7 Jul 1775; d. 20 Dec 1833[405] at Brookfield, VT; m. ELLA FORD, b. at Windham, 6 Apr 1775 daughter of Abraham and Abigail (Woodward) Ford; Ella d. at Brookfield, 1857.

---

[400] Ancestry.com, *Vermont, Vital Records, 1720-1908* (Provo, UT, USA: Ancestry.com Operations, Inc., 2013).
[401] Ancestry.com, Vermont, Vital Records, 1720-1908
[402] *Connecticut Wills and Probate, 1609-1999*, Probate of Joseph Ingalls, Hartford, 1791, Case number 2280.
[403] Connecticut, Church Record Abstracts, 1630-1920
[404] *Vermont, Vital Records, 1720-1908*.
[405] The inscription on the gravestone gives exact age of 58 yrs. 5 mo. & 12 dys; Find a Grave Memorial # 92380131

148) ISAAC ABBOTT *(Paul3, William2, George1)*, b. 29 Aug 1732 son of Paul and Elizabeth (Gray) Abbott; d. at Milford, NH about 1800;[406] m. 29 Apr 1756, MARY BARKER about whom nothing else concrete is known.[407]

Isaac Abbott was a farmer. He was born in Pomfret and there married Mary (although some sources say Sarah) Barker who was also from Pomfret, but her parentage is not known. The births of their first seven children are recorded at Pomfret, but there is also a recording of these births at Princeton, Massachusetts. The young family left Pomfret by 1769, were for a time in Princeton where they were early settlers recorded there in 1769,[408] and finally settled in Milford, New Hampshire where they were about 1778.[409] Isaac Abbott served as a private in the company of Colonel Stickney during the Revolutionary War.

Isaac Abbott and Mary Barker had twelve children, the oldest seven recorded at Pomfret, the births of four children recorded at Princeton, and the youngest child whose birthplace is unknown. This youngest child died in Milford.

615) i MARY ABBOTT, b. at Pomfret, 20 Jan 1757; d. at Lyme, NH, 8 Sep 1849; m. 9 Dec 1778, her first cousin, LEMUEL HOLT, b. at Windham, 28 Feb 1756 son of Joshua and Mary (Abbott) Holt; Lemuel d. 1 Aug 1836. This is the same as Family #146, child iv.

628) ii HANNAH ABBOTT, b. at Pomfret, 2 Aug 1758; d. at Stoddard, NH, 9 Mar 1847; m. at Amherst, NH, 25 May 1781, ISRAEL TOWNE, b. at Stoddard, NH, 17 Jun 1761 son of Israel and Lydia (Hopkins) Towne; Israel d. 2 May 1848.

iii CHLOE ABBOTT, b. at Pomfret, 7 Aug 1760; d. at Lyme, 1835. Chloe is reported to have married twice, but the name of her first husband has not been found. She m. 2nd, about 1801, WILLIAM PORTER, b. 1761 son of William and Esther (Carpenter) Porter. William was a widower with several children, his wife Phebe Kingsbury having died in 1800. William d. 3 Mar 1847. Chloe did not have children.

629) iv SARAH "SALLY" ABBOTT, b. at Pomfret, 14 Oct 1762; d. at Mason, NH, 1846; m. at Amherst, 25 Oct 1795, JAMES BROWN.

v METYLDA ABBOTT, b. at Pomfret, 29 Aug 1764.

630) vi ISAAC ABBOTT, b. at Pomfret, 17 Jul 1766; d. at Milford, NH, 1 Sep 1831; m. 15 Oct 1793, RUTH AMES, b. at Wilmington, MA, 31 Jul 1776 daughter of Caleb and Mary (Harvey) Ames/Eams; Ruth d. at Milford, 29 Jul 1844.

vii ESTHER ABBOTT, b. at Pomfret, 28 Jun 1768.

viii FIDELIA ABBOTT, b. at Princeton, 29 May 1770.

631) ix OLIVE ABBOTT, b. at Princeton, 28 Oct 1772. It is possible that she married Isaac Parker 6 Feb 1794 at Amherst. The Olive Abbott that married Isaac was of Milford and she died 2 Jan 1862 at age 89 which fits for this Olive. Isaac Parker was b. at Monson, NH, 2 Mar 1769 son of Josiah and Hannah (Parkis) Parker.

x DOROTHY ABBOTT, b. at Princeton, 10 Sep 1774; d. at Milford, 16 Aug 1802.

xi DEBORAH ABBOTT, b. at Princeton, 10 Sep 1774; d. at Milford, 22 May 1806.

xii STEPHEN ABBOTT, b. 1778; d. at Milford, 9 Jul 1792.

149) DARIUS ABBOTT *(Paul3, William2, George1)*, b. 16 Oct 1734 son of Paul and Elizabeth (Gray) Abbott; d. about 1817 at Hillsborough, NH;[410] m. at Andover 1 Nov 1757, MARY HOLT, b. 30 Apr 1739 daughter of Henry and Rebecca (Gray) Holt; Mary d. about 1787.

Darius Abbott was born at Pomfret and married Mary Holt of Andover. Darius was a housewright and likely the builder of the historic Andover home at 142 Hidden Road. The property on which this home was built was purchased from the Holt family in 1760 and 1763 by Darius Abbott and Samuel Holt. Darius Abbott sold the homestead land with the dwelling to Jacob Jones 16 April 1776 with the deed recorded 17 March 1778.[411]

---

406 1800 is the year of death used by the Daughters of the American Revolution and in Ramsdell's *History of Milford, volume 1*.

407 Abbot and Abbot, *Genealogical Register of Descendants* gives her name as Sarah Barker, but the marriage record and all the birth records for the children give her name as Mary.

408 Blake, *The History of Princeton*, p 81

409 Ramsdell, *The History of Milford, volume 1*, p 560

410 Abbot and Abbot, *Genealogical Register of Descendants*

411 Andover Preservation Commission, 142 Hidden Road, https://preservation.mhl.org/142-hidden-road

The births of the first nine children of this family are recorded at Andover. The four youngest children were likely born at either Amherst or Hillsborough. The family went first to Amherst before finally settling at Hillsborough.[412]

i ANNA ABBOTT, b. 31 Aug 1758; d. 14 Oct 1775.

ii HENRY ABBOTT, b. 1 Jun 1761; no further record.

iii ELIZABETH ABBOTT, b. 23 Mar 1763; according to the Holt genealogy, Elizabeth married but not known to whom; she lived in Holderness, NH.[413]

iv HANNAH ABBOTT, b. Mar 1765; d. 11 Sep 1775.

632) v PAUL ABBOTT, b. 18 Mar 1767; death date not known but in NH; m. about 1795, NAOMI CARR whose origins are unknown.

633) vi TRYPHENA ABBOTT, b. 23 Feb 1769; d. at Putney, VT, Jun 1836; m. 2 Jun 1790, JOHN WALLACE, b. at Bedford, NH, 12 May 1764 son of John and Sarah (Woodburn) Wallace; John d. 1834 (probate 25 Nov 1834).

634) vii CALVIN HOLT ABBOTT, b. 15 Apr 1771; d. at Barre, VT, 14 Aug 1841; m. 10 Apr 1800, LUCY DUTTON, b. 16 May 1781 daughter of John and Elizabeth (Spaulding) Dutton; Lucy d. 15 Apr 1851.

viii LUTHER ABBOTT, b. May 1773; d. 14 Sep 1773.

ix ASA ABBOTT, b. Sep 1774; d. 12 Sep 1775.

x LUTHER ABBOTT, twin of Hannah, b. about 1778; no further record.

xi MARY ABBOTT, b. about 1780; no further record.

635) xii NANCY ABBOTT, b. about 1780; m. 23 Apr 1804, JOEL JONES (see Hannah below).

635) xiii HANNAH ABBOTT, b. 1783 (baptized 4 May 1783);[414] d. about 1803; m. about 1800, JOEL JONES, *possibly* the son of Joel and Mary (Bishop) Jones b. at Hillsborough, 7 Aug 1783. Joel m. 2nd, Hannah's sister Nancy (see above).

150) ELIZABETH ABBOTT *(Paul³, William², George¹)*, b. 20 Jul 1737 daughter of Paul and Elizabeth (Gray) Abbott; d. possibly 1828;[415] m. 28 Sep 1761 as his 2nd wife, JOSEPH PHELPS, b. 27 Feb 1723/4 son of Samuel and Hannah (Dane) Phelps; Joseph d. at Andover 27 Jan 1802.

Elizabeth Abbott married Joseph Phelps after he was widowed and with two small children. His first wife was Lydia Osgood who died at Pomfret 20 July 1761. Just two months later, Elizabeth and Joseph married. Elizabeth and Joseph had six children, the oldest two born at Pomfret. The family then returned to Massachusetts settling in Princeton in Worcester County where their youngest four children were born. In later life, the couple returned to their roots in Andover.

The will of Joseph Phelps includes bequests to the following persons: beloved wife Elisabeth, beloved son Joseph gets some oxen and a yoke to make up the rest of his part, beloved son Elisha gets carpenter tools to make up the rest of his part, and beloved daughters Hannah, Elisabeth, Lydia, and Tryphenea get one dollar each (which is in addition to what he has already given them). Legacies at the final settlement are to Hannah Adams, Elizabeth Harrington, Lydia Whittemore, Tryphena Russell, Elisha Phelps, and Joseph Phelps. Elizabeth Phelps also receives a payment.[416] Joseph Phelps and Hannah Adams are Joseph's children from his marriage to Lydia Osgood.

636) i ELIZABETH PHELPS, b. 1 Mar 1765; d. at Lexington, 26 Jun 1835; m. about 1787, NATHAN HARRINGTON, b. at Lexington, 29 Apr 1762 son of Daniel and Anna (Munroe) Harrington; Nathan d. 30 Jun 1837.

637) ii LYDIA PHELPS, b. 5 Feb 1767; d. at Cambridge, 10 Nov 1834; m. PHILIP CARTERET WHITTEMORE, b. at Arlington, 1 Sep 1766 son of William and Abigail (De Carteret) Whittemore; Philip d. 30 Jun 1855.

638) iii TRYPHENA PHELPS, b. 28 Sep 1769; d. at Woburn, 8 Oct 1818; m. at Woburn, 19 Jun 1791, WILLIAM "BILL" RUSSELL, b. 4 May 1763 son of Jesse and Elizabeth (Whipple) Russell. After Tryphena's death, Bill Russell married Mrs. Phebe Dorman. Bill Russell d. at Billerica, 4 Jul 1842.

---

412 Stearns, *Genealogical and Family History of the State of New Hampshire, volume 1*, p 360
413 Durrie, *Genealogical History of the Holt Family*
414 Historical Society of Amherst, Transcriptions of Baptisms of Children from Volume I of the Congregational Church of Amherst, New Hampshire, http://www.hsanh.org/Baptisms%202.htm
415 Abbot and Abbot, *Genealogical Register of Descendants* gives a death date of June 1828, but I have not located a record.
416 *Essex County, MA: Probate File Papers, 1638-1881. Probate of* Joseph Phelps, 10 Mar 1802, *Case number* 21650.

iv ELISHA PHELPS, b. 10 Oct 1771; d. at Andover, 27 Jan 1823; m. at Woburn, 28 Oct 1795, RHODA TAY, b. at Wilmington, 19 Nov 1770 daughter of Benjamin and Sybil (Marion) Tay; Rhoda d. 16 Oct 1841. Elisha and Rhoda do not seem to have had any children. Elisha died at the almshouse in Andover.[417]

v SAMUEL PHELPS, b. 5 Aug 1773; d. 19 Aug 1778.

vi POLLY PHELPS, b. 8 Oct 1775; d. 11 Aug 1778.

151) ABIEL ABBOTT *(Philip³, William², George¹)*, b. at Windham, 3 Mar 1726 son of Philip and Abigail (Bigford) Abbott; d. at Windham, 21 May 1772; m. 5 Jun 1750, ABIGAIL FENTON, b. at Willington, 27 Aug 1730 daughter of Francis and Ann (Berry) Fenton. Abigail m. 2nd John Chamberlain of Amenia Precinct in New York;[418] Abigail d. 14 Aug 1776.

Abiel Abbott was a farmer in Windham, Connecticut. He and Abigail had five children whose births are recorded at Windham. Their children seem to have had the wanderlust as all the children relocated to other states including one son settling in Quebec.

Abiel Abbott's estate entered probate in 1772 and the distributions of the estate property were made 18 Apr 1777, after the decease of the widow Abigail, in the following manner: eldest son Philip Abbott allotted two-sixths of the estate; second son James Abbott; son Abiel Abbott; daughter Abigail; and daughter Anne. Each of the younger children received one-sixth part of the estate.[419]

639) i PHILIP ABBOTT, b. 23 Mar 1751; d. at Kingston, PA, Mar 1834;[420] m. 6 Jul 1775, ANNA HEWETT, b. at Canterbury, 1 Jul 1754 daughter of Henry and Joanna (Denison) Hewett; Anna d. at Windham 29 Dec 1796. Philip m. 2nd, 17 Mar 1815 at Wilkes-Barre, MABEL MERRITT.

640) ii JAMES ABBOTT, b. 9 Mar 1753; d. at Cornell, NY, 2 May 1830; m. 1st, 1 Jan 1778, his third cousin, HANNAH DENISON, b. 18 Mar 1757 daughter of Daniel and Lydia (Pearl) Denison; Hannah d. 17 Jan 1784. James m. 2nd, as her second husband, PHEBE HOWE (widow of John Coray), married at Kingston, PA 17 Jan 1798; James and Phebe may have divorced after 1813. Phebe died at Naples, IL, 9 Sep 1842. Phebe Howe was born at Luzerne 21 Feb 1763 daughter of John and Mary (Stephens) Howe. This is the same as Family #280, child ii.

641) iii ABIEL ABBOTT, b. 28 Nov 1754; d. at Hatley, Quebec, 1838; m. 13 Nov 1777, RUTH HOVEY, b. 28 Aug 1754 daughter of Nathaniel and Ruth (Parker) Hovey; Ruth d. at Hatley 1832.

642) iv ABIGAIL ABBOTT, b. 21 Feb 1763; d. about 1843 perhaps in Ohio where she went to stay with her children; m. about 1784, JOSEPH UTLEY who was "of Hartford" but whose parents have not been fully verified, although *perhaps* the son of Joseph and Jerusha (Martin) Utley.

643) v ANNA ABBOTT, b. 18 Sep 1765; d. at Armada, MI, 13 Sep 1846; m. 29 Aug 1787, SETH LATHROP, b. at Springfield, 11 Apr 1762 son of Joseph and Elizabeth (Dwight) Lathrop; Seth d. 26 Feb 1831.

152) STEPHEN ABBOTT *(Philip³, William², George¹)*, b. 21 Apr 1728 son of Philip and Abigail (Bigford) Abbott; d. at Ashford 29 Sep 1801; m. 3 Jan 1750, FREELOVE BURGESS, b. at Ashford, 14 Jul 1731 daughter of Benjamin and Susannah (Sabin) Burgess; the date of death for Freelove is not known, but she was living at the time of probate of her husband's estate.

The estate of Captain Stephen Abbott entered probate 1 December 1801. There was not a will. Widow Freelove Abbot was administrator. The estate was valued at $719.99. The personal estate was used to pay debts and the real property was divided for distribution among the heirs. Distribution was to the widow Freelove Abbott, daughter Susannah, and son Reuben.[421]

Stephen Abbott and Freelove Burgess had four children. The births of the two oldest children are recorded at Windham. The youngest son, Reuben, was born at Ashford. There is not a record for daughter Lucy; she is just in published genealogies and perhaps she is mis-assigned to this family. In any event, there are just two children as heirs to the estate,

[417] *Massachusetts, Town and Vital Records, 1620-1988.*

[418] Abbot and Abbot, *Genealogical Register of Descendants*, p 51

[419] *Connecticut Wills and Probate, 1609-1999*, Probate of Abial Abbott, Hartford, 1772, Case number 34.

[420] Philip Abbott, age 70-79, is head of household in the 1830 U.S. Census; 1830; Census Place: *Plymouth, Luzerne, Pennsylvania*; Series: *M19*; Roll: *145*; Page: *431*; Family History Library Film: *0020619*

[421] *Connecticut Wills and Probate, 1609-1999*, Probate of Stephen Abbott, Hartford, 1772, Case number 5.

Susannah and Reuben. The youngest child, Reuben, was born about 20 years after his next oldest sibling, but there is a son Reuben in this family as evidenced by the probate distribution; Reuben married in 1798 which fits with a birth year of 1774.

644) i SUSANNAH ABBOTT, b. 23 Cot 1752; d. at Fort Ann, NY, Oct 1815;[422] m. 15 Sep 1773, STEPHEN BURGESS, b. at Ashford, 12 Jan 1751 son of Benjamin.

ii PHILIP ABBOTT, b. 1753; d. 1776. Philip served in the Revolutionary War. He was taken prisoner and died aboard a prison ship in the harbor of New York.[423]

iii LUCY ABBOTT, b. about 1755; she may not go in this family; no further record.

645) iv REUBEN ABBOTT, b. 15 Apr 1774; d. at Mansfield, CT, 1 Jan 1863; m. 8 Nov 1798, MARY "POLLY" SNOW, b. about 1773 (based on age at time of death; Abbot genealogy gives birth as 12 May 1773) whose parents are not verified; Polly d. 15 Apr 1857.

153) HANNAH ABBOTT *(Philip[3], William[2], George[1])*, b. 16 Mar 1730 daughter of Philip and Abigail (Bigford) Abbott; d. 18 Dec 1801; m. Aug 1748, SAMUEL UTLEY, b. at Windham 28 May 1723 son of James and Annah (-) Utley; Samuel d. 15 Nov 1782.

Samuel Utley did not leave a will, but his probate record includes a list of heirs who are to receive distributions. Those listed are the heirs of Abigail Butts (who is deceased), Ann Hare, Elizabeth Utley, Samuel, Phillip, Stephen, Timothy, Cyrus, Antipas, Rufus, and Elijah.[424]

Son Philip Utley did not marry, and he did leave a will dated 24 January 1832. He made bequests to his siblings and their heirs. Those named in the will are as follows: heirs of his brother Samuel who is deceased; heirs of his brother Cyrus who is deceased; heirs of his sister Anna Hare who is deceased; Betsy Utley daughter of his brother Stephen; brother Timothy; Lewis Utley son of his brother Antipas; to Orren Utley who is the brother of Lewis (and thus also a son of Antipas); and to Philip Utley who is the son of Rufus who is deceased, and to the other remaining heirs of brother Rufus. Mr. Royal Copeland is named executor.[425] Stephen, Timothy, and Antipas are not described as deceased. Elizabeth is not mentioned, so she is assumed to be deceased and without heirs. Elijah also is not mentioned. His oldest sister Abigail Butts is not mentioned. Abigail died in 1774 and had one daughter living at the time of her death. It is possible that Abigail's daughter was deceased by 1832.

Hannah Abbott and Samuel Utley had 13 children whose births are recorded at Windham.

646) i ABIGAIL UTLEY, b. 19 Nov 1749; d. at Canterbury, 4 Jul 1774; m. 15 Feb 1770, JAMES BUTTS, b. 14 Jun 1748 son of Samuel and Mary (Cleveland) Butts. James m. 2nd, Elizabeth Hibbard.

ii PHILIP UTLEY, b. 26 Jul 1751; d. 18 May 1754.

iii HANNAH UTLEY, b. 5 Jan 1753; d. 25 Feb 1778.

647) iv ANNA UTLEY, b. 6 Jan 1755; m. about 1780, STEPHEN HARE, b. at Ellington, 12 Sep 1755.[426]

v ELIZABETH UTLEY, b. 18 Jan 1757; d. at Hampton, 14 Nov 1825. Elizabeth did not marry.

648) vi SAMUEL UTLEY, b. 2 Feb 1759; d. at Ashford, CT, 13 Sep 1801; m. at Hampton, 7 Jan 1790, SARAH EASTMAN, b. at Ashford, 7 Aug 1761 daughter of Ebenezer and Mary (Fletcher) Eastman; Sarah d. 4 Jan 1828.

vii PHILIP UTLEY, b. 26 Feb 1760; d. about 1832. Philip did not marry.

649) viii STEPHEN UTLEY, b. 21 Nov 1762; d. 1 Mar 1841; m. 1797, SARAH HOLT, b. 3 Mar 1775 daughter of Paul and Sarah (Welch) Holt; Sarah d. 10 Feb 1833.

ix TIMOTHY UTLEY, b. 22 Mar 1765; d. after 1832

650) x CYRUS UTLEY, b. 11 Mar 1767; d. at Homer, NY between 1820 and 1832;[427] m. at Hampton, 4 Apr 1797, POLLY BENNET, b. at New Milford, 6 Jun 1771 daughter of Edward and Rhoda (Canfield) Bennett.

---

[422] Abbot and Abbot, *Genealogical Register of Descendants*, p 54

[423] Abbot and Abbot, *Genealogical Register of Descendants*, p 54

[424] *Connecticut Wills and Probate, 1609-1999*, Probate of Samuel Utley, Hartford, 1782, Case number 3893.

[425] *Connecticut Wills and Probate, 1609-1999*, Will of Philip Utley, Windham, 24 Jun 1832.

[426] The birth record in the Barbour Collection lists his date of birth but not the names of parents.

[427] He is listed in the 1820 U.S. Census at Homer, New York, but he is listed as deceased in his brother Philip's 1832 will. *1820 United States Federal Census*, 1820 U S Census; Census Place: Homer, Cortland, New York; Page: 555; NARA Roll: M33_66; Image: 308.

651) xi ANTIPAS UTLEY, b. 16 Feb 1770; d. after 1830; m. at Hampton, 29 May 1795, POLLY LUCE daughter of Nathan and Elizabeth (Lasel) Luce.[428] Polly seems to have died between 1810 and 1820.[429]

652) xii RUFUS UTLEY, b. 25 May 1773; m. MARY "POLLY" SILL probably the daughter of Ezra and Charity (Pratt) Sill.

xiii ELIJAH UTLEY, b. 15 Feb 1778; d. at Hampton, 15 Feb 1825. Elijah did not marry.

154) MARY ABBOTT *(Philip³, William², George¹)*, b. 6 Jul 1732 daughter of Philip and Abigail (Bigford) Abbott; d. at Sheshequin, PA, 5 May 1803; m. 17 Oct 1751, STEPHEN FULLER, b. at Windham 3 Nov 1730 son of Stephen and Hannah (Moulton) Fuller; Stephen d. at Sheshequin 24 May 1813.[430]

Several members of the Fuller and Abbott families relocated from Connecticut to the Wyoming Valley of Pennsylvania and became casualties in the Battle of Wyoming also known as the Wyoming Valley massacre. As a back-drop to the massacre, which occurred as part of the Revolutionary War, was a longer standing land dispute between earlier settlers in the Wyoming Valley and the newer settlers from Connecticut. This land dispute dated to the mid-17th century originating with competing claims between Dutch and English settlers, that followed by overlapping land grants from King Charles II to both William Penn and to the province of Connecticut. Thrown into the mix was conflict/resentment with Native American peoples in the area. The conflicts between the earlier settlers (Pennamites) and the Connecticut settlers (Yankees) were carried out from 1768 through 1784 and were finally settled by the young United States Congress after the end of the Revolutionary War.[431]

The Battle of Wyoming was part of a campaign by the British to wage a guerilla war against colonial frontier settlers. The British recruited colonial Loyalists who were under the command of Colonel John Butler; this militia was known as Butler's Rangers. Other British commanders recruited native warriors such as Seneca. These bands conducted raids on frontier settlements. In the summer of 1778, they decided on raids of the Wyoming Valley in Pennsylvania. The Loyalist troops with Seneca warriors engaged the little trained Patriot militia men on 3 July 1778. The Loyalist forces numbered about 1,000 compared to 350 Patriots. It is reported that the Loyalist forces had three killed while all but 60 of the Patriots were killed. This included the taking of 227 scalps. Raiding in the area in the aftermath included burning 1,000 homes of the settlers. There were reported follow-up raids by Iroquois with more killing of settlers. The aftermath also included regrouped Patriot militias conducting raids on Indian villages in the area.[432]

Two of the children of Mary Abbott and Stephen Fuller, Thomas and Stephen, died at the Battle of Wyoming.

Mary Abbott and Stephen Fuller had seven children whose births are recorded in Windham County, Connecticut. There is some disagreement in published genealogies about the marriages of daughters Abigail and Mary, but what I have provided matches the available records.

653) i ABIGAIL FULLER, b. at Windham, 3 Jan 1752; d. at Athens, PA, 31 Jan 1834; m. about 1772, JAMES BIDLACK, b. 26 Nov 1750 son of James and Mehitable (Durkee) Bidlack; James d. at Wyoming, PA, 3 Jul 1778. Abigail married 2nd, as his second wife, JOHN FRANKLIN, b. at Canaan, CT, 12 Sep 1749 son of John and Keziah (Pierce) Franklin. John Franklin d. at Athens, PA, 1 Mar 1831.

607) ii STEPHEN FULLER, b. 22 Jan 1755; d. at the Battle of Wyoming, 3 Jul 1778; m. SARAH BIDLACK, b. at Hampton, 30 Sep 1756 daughter of James and Mehitable (Durkee) Bidlack. Sarah m. 2nd, about 1783, ASA ABBOTT, b. at Pomfret, 25 May 1756 son of Benjamin and Mary Ann (Andrews) Abbott; Asa d. at Hampton, 1834.

iii THOMAS FULLER, b. 7 May 1757; d. at the Battle of Wyoming, 3 Jul 1778.

654) iv MARY FULLER, b. 28 May 1759; d. in New York after 1810 (living at the time of husband's probate); m. at Wilkes-Barre, 2 Jan 1782, THOMAS BALDWIN, b. 23 Feb 1755 son of Isaac and Patience (Rathburn) Baldwin; Thomas d. in New York about 1810.

655) v JOHN FULLER, b. at Windham, 26 Jan 1762; d. at Carlton, NY, 11 Mar 1817; m. about 1788, AMY SHAW, b. 1766 (based on age at time of death) whose parents are unknown to me; Amy d. 13 Nov 1834.

---

[428] Her parents are verified by the 1816 will of Nathan Luce which includes a bequest to his daughter Polly wife of Antipas Utley. Ancestry.com. *New York, Wills and Probate Records, 1659-1999* [database on-line]. Provo, UT, USA: Ancestry.com Operations, Inc., 2015. Original data: New York County, District and Probate Courts.

[429] Antipas is a head of household in 1800, 1810, 1820, and 1830 Census in Windham County, CT and there is a female of the right age for Polly through 1810, but not in 1820 or 1830.

[430] Information on this family derived from Fuller, *Genealogy of Some Descendants of Thomas Fuller*, p 92 and Bradsby, *History of Luzerne County*, p 718

[431] Boyer, "A Dangerous Combination of Villains"

[432] Trussell, "The Battle of Wyoming and Hartley's Expedition"

656) vi REUBEN FULLER, b. 19 Feb 1769; d. at Carlton, NY, 7 Jul 1837; m. 23 May 1793, MARY P. CASH, b. 10 Dec 1775 daughter of Daniel and Mary "Polly" (Tracy) Cash; Mary d. Sep 1849.

657) vii HANNAH FULLER, b. 17 Aug 1772; d. 1 Sep 1817; m. 18 Oct 1792, WILKES DURKEE, b. at Windham, 25 Jul 1768 son of Andrew and Mary (Benjamin) Durkee; Wilkes d. in Michigan, 23 Dec 1844.[433] Wilkes remarried Mariah after the death of Hannah.

155) JOSEPH ABBOT *(Philip³, William², George¹)*, b. 14 Feb 1735 son of Philip and Abigail (Bigford) Abbott; d. at Ellington, CT 5 Jan 1814; m. 1st 20 Apr 1758, ELIZABETH STEDMAN, b. at Windham 30 Apr 1739 daughter of Thomas and Anna (Seaver) Stedman; Elizabeth d. 2 Mar 1766.[434] JOSEPH m. 2nd OLIVE PEARCE, b. at Brooklyn, CT, Mar 1738 daughter of Benjamin and Naomi (Richards) Pearce; Olive d. at Vernon, CT 9 Sep 1822.

Joseph served in the militia during the Revolutionary War and held the rank of Lieutenant Colonel. He was a wealthy farmer in Ellington.

There is a probate record which has a first inventory 9 March 1814 and a second inventory in February 1815. Joseph, Delano, and Lemuel Abbot agree to complete the second inventory. The value of the estate given at the first inventory was $30,790. The disbursement of the estate includes distributions to the following persons: sons Joseph, Lemuel, Delano, and John, daughters Mary Scarborough and Abigail Whitman. There is also a distribution to widow Olive Abbot.[435]

Births of four children of Joseph Abbott and Elizabeth Stedman are recorded at Pomfret and Ellington.

658) i MARY ABBOTT, b. 6 Apr 1759; d. at Windsor, 25 Dec 1835; m. 1st, about 1785, DANIEL ELLSWORTH, b. 3 Dec 1758 son of Daniel and Mary (-) Ellsworth; Daniel d. at Presque Isle, 3 Mar 1798.[436] Mary m. 2nd, EBENEZER SCARBOROUGH, b. 1 Mar 1743 and d. 2 Oct 1813.

ii ELIZABETH ABBOTT, b. 11 Apr 1761; d. 1 Nov 1784.

659) iii ABIGAIL ABBOTT, b. at Ellington, 17 Dec 1762; d. at West Hartford, 11 Sep 1844; m. about 1784, SAMUEL WHITMAN, b. 26 Jul 1753 son of John and Abigail (Pantry) Whitman; Samuel d. 7 Feb 1810 when he was kicked by a horse.

iv JOSEPH ABBOT, b. 31 Jan 1766; d. 5 Feb 1834; m. around 1800 (the marriage record lists only 12 Mar with no year), LAURA WEST, b. 30 Dec 1781 daughter of Jeremiah and Amelia (Ely) West; Laura d. 26 Aug 1853. Joseph and Lucy did not have any children. Joseph did leave an extensive will that disposes of his large amount of property to siblings and nieces and nephews.

The births of four children of Joseph Abbot and Olive Pearce are recorded at Pomfret.

660) i LEMUEL ABBOT, b. 9 Mar 1768; d. at Vernon, 9 Jun 1846; m. 8 May 1792, LUCRETIA BINGHAM, b. 22 Jul 1766 daughter of Ithamar and Sarah (Kellogg) Bingham; Lucretia d. 17 Mar 1835.

ii OLIVE ABBOTT, b. 1772; d. 18 Dec 1776.

661) iii DELANO ABBOT, b. 16 Apr 1774; d. at Ira, NY, 11 Mar 1852; m. 1 Jan 1801, MARY "POLLY" BINGHAM, b. 1778 daughter of Ithamar and Sarah (Kellogg) Bingham; Polly d. at Ira, 11 Mar 1852.

662) iv JOHN ABBOT, b. 6 Jul 1784; d. at Vernon, 13 Mar 1859; m. 31 Mar 1813, ACHSAH CONE, b. at East Haddam, 17 Jul 1789 daughter of Daniel and Keziah (Chapman) Cone; Achsah d. 4 Aug 1882.

156) JOHN ABBOTT *(Philip³, William², George¹)*, b. 27 Sep 1741 son of Philip and Abigail (Bigford) Abbott; d. at Jacobs Plains, PA, 4 Aug 1778; m. 4 Nov 1762, ALICE FULLER, b. 1741 daughter of Stephen and Hannah (Moulton) Fuller. Alice m. 2nd Stephen Gardner; Alice d. at Plains, PA 1 Jun 1816.[437]

John Abbott fought during the Battle of Wyoming 3 July 1778 and survived the initial battle. He was killed at his home in August 1778 as part of the ongoing raids and skirmishes related to the guerilla campaign conducted against the Wyoming Valley, Pennsylvania settlers by Butler's Rangers and Indian allies.[438]

---

433 Wilkes Durkee was in New York for a time but received a homestead patent 22 Apr 1824 in the Michigan-Toledo strip. United States, Bureau of Land Management. *Michigan Pre-1908 Homestead & Cash Entry Patent and Cadastral Survey Plat Index*. General Land Office Automated Records Project, 1994. (accessed through ancestry.com)

434 Ancestry.com. *Connecticut Town Death Records, pre-1870 (Barbour Collection)*

435 *Connecticut Wills and Probate, 1609-1999*, Probate of Joseph Abbot, Hartford, 1814, Case number 38.

436 Connecticut, Hale Collection of Cemetery Inscriptions and Newspaper Notices, 1629-1934

437 Blair and Shoemaker, *The Shoemaker Book (Schumacher)*, p 66

438 Blair and Shoemaker, *The Shoemaker Book*, p 65

John Abbott and Alice Fuller had eleven children. Published genealogies give two daughters named Abigail, the first Abigail born 12 Dec 1764 dying early and then a second daughter Abigail with unknown birth date. However, there is a death record for Abigail, daughter of John and Alice, born about 1765 with a death date of 5 February 1790.[439] John and Alice married in November 1762 and had daughter Alice in April 1763. This would make it very unlikely that there is a second daughter Abigail as the Abigail born about 1765 lived until 1790.

663) i ALICE ABBOTT, b. at Windham 17 Apr 1763; d. at Hampton, 16 Jan 1809; m. 27 Apr 1790, AMOS UTLEY, b. at Windham, 22 Aug 1764 son of Amos and Grace (Martin) Utley; Amos d. at Hampton, 24 Apr 1810.

ii ABIGAIL ABBOTT, b. 12 Dec 1764; d. at Hampton, 5 Feb 1790.

664) iii CELINDA "LINDA" ABBOTT, b. 20 May 1766; d. at Scott, PA, 8 Apr 1854; m. about 1786, REUBEN TAYLOR, b. 28 Nov 1759 son of Reuben and Rebecca (Weeks) Taylor; Reuben d. at Greenfield, PA, 1849.

iv STEPHEN ABBOTT, b. 6 Dec 1767; d. 19 Jun 1770.

665) v CHARLES ABBOTT, b. 3 Jun 1769; d. at Delaware County, OH, after 1853; m. URANIA (also named Lorena in some sources) MANVILLE, b. 24 Mar 1775 daughter of Nicholas Manville; Urania d. at Sunbury, OH, 21 Dec 1848.[440]

666) vi STEPHEN ABBOTT, b. 19 Apr 1771; d. at Plains, PA, 22 Jul 1853;[441] m. 14 Jul 1799, ABIGAIL SEARLE, b. 25 Jun 1779 daughter of William and Philena (Frink) Searle; Abigail d. 2 Jun 1842. Stephen m. 2nd, 1 Jun 1843, SARAH DENISON the widow of Thomas Ferrier and daughter of Nathan and Elizabeth (Sill) Denison.

vii REUBEN ABBOTT, b. about 1774. Reuben is a son in published genealogies, but without any other information. There seem to be no records related to him.

667) viii LYDIA ABBOTT, b. about 1775; d. at Know County, OH after 1853; m. ARTEMAS SWETLAND, b. in Connecticut about 1769 son of Luke and Hannah (Tiffany) Swetland; Artemas d. 1855.

668) ix MARY ABBOTT, b. about 1776; m. JOHN CORTWRIGHT, b. 7 Apr 1774 son of Benjamin and Catherine (Hoover) Cortwright; John d. 4 Dec 1822. [Cortwright is also spelled Courtright.]

x HANNAH ABBOTT, b. about 1776, twin of Mary; no further information known.

669) xi SARAH ABBOTT, b. 28 Feb 1778; d. Tunkhannock, PA; m. 16 Apr 1800, JAMES KENNEDY, b. at Deer Park, NY, 13 Jul 1775 son of John and Mary (Van Fleet) Kennedy; James d. 19 Oct 1864.

157) HANNAH HOLT *(Hannah Abbott Holt³, William², George¹)*, b. 17 Apr 1723 daughter of Abiel and Hannah (Abbott) Holt; d. 25 Jan 1750/1; m. 14 Jul 1742, her first cousin WILLIAM HOLT, b. at Andover 10 Dec 1720 son of Thomas and Alice (Peabody) Holt. William m. 2nd SYBEL DURKEE daughter of Stephen and Lois (Moulton) Durkee; William d. at Hampton 2 Aug 1793.

Hannah Holt and William Holt had four children whose births are recorded at Windham.

670) i WILLIAM HOLT, b. 15 Jul 1743; d. at Hampton, 6 Aug 1815;[442] m. 8 Sep 1763, his third cousin, MERCY HOLT, b. 14 Feb 1740/1 daughter of Zebadiah and Sarah (Flint) Holt; Mercy d. 15 Sep 1799.

ii HANNAH HOLT, b. 26 Jan 1744/5; d. 30 Aug 1754.

671) iii ALICE HOLT, b. 26 Apr 1747; d. at Stockbridge, VT, 28 Nov 1814;[443] m. 13 Nov 1764, ROBERT LYON, b. at Pomfret, 30 Sep 1743 son of Peletiah and Sarah (Holt) Lyon; Robert d. 12 Feb 1809.

672) iv SARAH HOLT, b. 21 Jun 1748; d. at Hampton, 7 Apr 1777; m. 16 Nov 1769, HENRY DURKEE, b. 29 Sep 1749 son of Henry and Relief (Adams) Durkee. Henry m. 2nd, Sarah Loomis; Henry d. 22 Apr 1820.

---

[439] Connecticut, Deaths and Burials Index, 1650-1934; Connecticut State Library; Hartford, Connecticut; The Charles R. Hale Collection of Connecticut Cemetery Inscriptions

[440] Ancestry.com, *Web: Delaware County, Ohio, Burial Index, 1784-2011* (Provo, UT, USA: Ancestry.com Operations, Inc., 2013).

[441] Ancestry.com, *Pennsylvania, Deaths, 1852-1854* (Provo, UT, USA: Ancestry.com Operations, Inc., 2011), Pennsylvania State Archives; Reel Number: 671.

[442] *Connecticut, Deaths and Burials Index, 1650-1934.*

[443] *Vermont, Vital Records, 1720-1908.*

158) ELIZABETH HOLT *(Hannah Abbott Holt³, William², George¹)*, b. 16 Feb 1724/5 daughter of Abiel and Hannah (Abbott) Holt; d. about 1753; m. 10 Jun 1746, FRANCIS FENTON, b. at Willington, b. 16 Mar 1718 son of Francis and Ann (Berry) Fenton.[444] Francis m. 2nd Ann Newcomb, 31 Oct 1754. Francis Fenton d. at Willington, 1781 (date of probate).

Elizabeth Holt and Francis Fenton had two children whose births are recorded at Willington.

673) i MARY FENTON, b. 13 Apr 1749; d. at Willington, 14 Apr 1822; m. 1st, 21 May 1770, ISAAC SAWIN, b. 23 Sep 1748 son of George and Anna (Farrar) Sawin; Isaac d. 29 Oct 1776. Mary m. 2nd, 2 Jul 1778, as his second wife, JAMES NILES, b. at Braintree, 2 Apr 1747 son of John and Dorothy (Reynolds) Niles; James d. 18 Jan 1822.

674) ii FRANCIS FENTON, b. 13 Feb 1750/1; m. 25 May 1775, CHLOE GOODALE, b. at Pomfret, 28 Dec 1755 daughter of Ebenezer and Phebe (Holt) Goodale; Chloe d. at New Haven, Oct 1833.[445]

159) ABIEL HOLT *(Hannah Abbott Holt³, William², George¹)*, b. 1 Feb 1726/7 son of Abiel and Hannah (Abbott) Holt; d. at Willington, 2 Oct 1785; m. 1st 22 Apr 1755, MARY DOWNER whose origins are unknown, although perhaps the daughter of Andrew Downer and Sarah Lazell; Mary d. 28 Jan 1766. Abiel m. 2nd 2 Apr 1767, EUNICE KINGSBURY (widow of John Marshall), b. about 1733; Eunice d. 2 Jun 1784.

The distributions from the estate of Abiel Holt were made 19 December 1785 to the following heirs: Hannah Pearl, eldest daughter; Sarah Crocker, second daughter; Mary Needham, third daughter; Abial Holt, eldest son; Bethiah Holt, fourth daughter; Andrew Holt, second son; Abel Holt, third son; and Eunice Holt, youngest daughter. The first five children are from Abiel's marriage to Mary Downer; Eunice Kingsbury is the mother of the three youngest children.[446]

Abiel Holt and Mary Downer had six children born at Willington.

675) i HANNAH HOLT, b. 14 Mar 1756; d. 20 Nov 1832; m. 24 Apr 1782, as his second wife, her second cousin (and George Abbott descendant), OLIVER PEARL, b. 9 Oct 1749 son of Timothy and Dinah (Holt) Pearl. Oliver was married first to Mercy Hinkley. This is the same of Family #276, child iii.

676) ii SARAH HOLT, b. 8 Dec 1757; d. at Willington, 1856;[447] m. 24 Oct 1782, ZEBULON CROCKER, b. at Willington, 5 Mar 1757 son of Ebenezer and Hannah (Hatch) Crocker; Zebulon d. at Willington, 17 Jan 1826.

iii MARY HOLT, b. 13 Jul 1759; d. 4 Feb 1760.

677) iv MARY HOLT, b. 8 Dec 1760; m. at Charlton, MA, 17 Feb 1783,[448] DANIEL NEEDHAM possibly the son of Daniel and Hannah (Allen) Needham; Daniel d. at Paxton, MA 1801 (date of probate 6 Oct 1801; will written 4 Mar 1801).

678) v ABIEL HOLT, b. 12 Jul 1762; d. at Fairfax, VT, 6 Jun 1829; m. by 1787, MARY MOSHER, b. 21 Jul 1762 daughter of Nathaniel and Elizabeth (Crandall) Mosher; Mary d. 6 Sep 1827.

vi BETHIAH HOLT, b. 26 Mar 1764; d. 1833. Bethiah did not marry.

Abiel Holt and Eunice Kingsbury had three children born at Willington.

i ANDREW HOLT, b. 3 May 1768; d. at Hadley, MA, 21 Sep 1853;[449] m. HANNAH SMITH, b. at Hadley, 28 Aug 1775, daughter of Joseph and Nancy (Day) Smith; Hannah d. 28 Jul 1855. Andrew and Hannah did not have children.

679) ii ABEL HOLT, b. 1770; m. 1st, 17 Nov 1793, ANNA ABEL, b. at Norwich, 8 Jul 1771 daughter of Thomas and Zerviah (Hyde) Abel; Anna d. at Sharon, VT 13 Apr 1798. Abel m. 2nd, by 1798, RUTH KING, b. at Wilbraham, MA, 13 Feb 1779 daughter of Oliver and Ruth (Cooley) King. This family had nine children born in Vermont and then seem to have relocated to Oneida, New York.

iii EUNICE HOLT, b. 5 Mar 1772. She was living at the time of her father's will, but no record found following that.

---

444 Weaver, *Genealogy of the Fenton Family*

445 Connecticut, Deaths and Burials Index, 1650-1934

446 *Connecticut Wills and Probate, 1609-1999*, Probate of Abial Holt, Hartford, 1785, Case number 1057.

447 In the 1850 U.S. Census, 92-year old widow Sarah Crocker was living at the home of her daughter Bethiah Hull. Probate of estate was 1856 with Joseph Hull as administrator.

448 *Massachusetts, Compiled Marriages, 1633-1850*. Daniel and Mary Holt of Willington, int. Feb. 17, 1783.

449 *Massachusetts, Death Records, 1841-1915*, New England Historic Genealogical Society; Boston, Massachusetts; Massachusetts Vital Records, 1840–1911. Parents are listed on the death record as Abiel and Eunice Holt.

160) CALEB HOLT *(Hannah Abbott Holt[3], William[2], George[1])*, b. 6 Mar 1729 son of Abiel and Hannah (Abbott) Holt; d. at Willington, 18 Aug 1810; m. 29 Jan 1755, MARY MERRICK, b. 6 Dec 1726 daughter of John and Sarah (Parsons) Merrick; Mary d. 4 Jun 1790. Caleb m. 2nd Chloe Hatch.

Caleb wrote a will 11 Apr 1793.[450] There are bequests for wife Chloe, sons Elijah and Caleb, and daughter Elizabeth Howe(?). He wrote a codicil 4 April 1798, it which he bequeathed to his wife Chloe the whole of a farm that he purchased from Samuel Dunham so long as she gives up rights to property she brought with her into the marriage. There are no other changes to heirs. The estate entered probate 29 August 1810. The distribution documents include the division set off to widow Chloe and an acknowledgment from Elijah and Caleb that they have received their portions. There is not a distribution document related to Elizabeth. The will is difficult to decipher in terms of Elizabeth's married name (it might be Howe or Hovey or something else altogether or maybe it is a poorly written Holt). In any event, no marriage record was located for her and no death record.

Caleb Holt and Mary Merrick had five children whose births are recorded at Willington.

i ELIZABETH HOLT, b. 29 Apr 1756. From her father's will, it seems that Elizabeth married, but the last name is unclear. It could be Howe or Hovey or some other name. No marriage record was located that would fit with the name in the will. Durrie's Holt genealogy gives her spouse as Abiel Stevens. But Abiel Stevens and Elizabeth Holt married at Andover so that does not seem right, and other sources suggest it was Elizabeth the daughter of Nathaniel Holt that married Abiel Stevens.

680) ii ELIJAH HOLT, b. 24 Oct 1757; d. 4 Jul 1817; m. 5 Nov 1783,[451] MOLLY SIMMONS, b. 1754 possibly the daughter of Paul and Mary (Isham) Simmons, but this is not confirmed; Molly d. 6 May 1814. Elijah m. 2nd, Lovina *Marcy* Dunton 17 Aug 1815. Lovina Marcy was first married to Samuel Dunton.

681) iii CALEB HOLT, b. 23 Apr 1759; d. at Willington, 8 Sep 1826; m. 8 Jan 1783, SALLY GOODALE likely the daughter of Ebenezer and Phebe (Holt) Goodale; Sally d. 4 Oct 1831.

iv JOSHUA HOLT, b. 31 Mar 1763; d. 12 Aug 1790.

v JAMES HOLT, 24 Oct 1764; d. 25 Jan 1766.

161) NATHAN HOLT *(Hannah Abbott Holt[3], William[2], George[1])*, b. 18 Apr 1733 son of Abiel and Hannah (Abbott) Holt; d. at Willington, 31 May 1800; m. 1st 19 Jan 1758, ABIGAIL MERRICK, b. 17 Jun 1737 daughter of John and Sarah (Parsons) Merrick; Abigail d. 1 Dec 1765. Nathan m. 2nd 26 Nov 1766, BATHSHEBA WILLIAMS, b. 22 May 1737 daughter of Samuel and Deborah (Throope) Williams; Bathsheba d. 1 Aug 1769. Nathan m. 3rd 6 Jun 1770, LYDIA KINGSBURY, b. 1737 daughter of John and Deborah (Spaulding) Kingsbury; Lydia d. 22 Mar 1776.

In his will written March 1790, Nathan leaves his estate to his two children, Nathan and Abigail. In the will, Nathan is allowed used of one-half of the homestead including use of half the well (as long as he maintains it), a chamber in the house, and privilege to use of part of the cellar. The remainder of the estate is left to his daughter Abigail, both real and personal, and she is to pay her brother Nathan 50 pounds over a three-year period. Nathan and Abigail are the sole executors of the estate.[452] The will is unusual in that the daughter is bequeathed the whole estate and the son receives just use of part of the house.

Nathan Holt and Abigail Merrick had one child.

682) i NATHAN HOLT, b. 29 Aug 1761; d. at Willington, 5 Sep 1820; m. his second cousin, LOIS GOODALE, b. at Pomfret, 31 Jul 1764 daughter of Ebenezer and Phebe (Holt) Goodale; Lois d. 20 May 1842.

Nathan Holt and Bathsheba Williams had one child born at Willington.

i ABIGAIL HOLT, b. 4 Sep 1767; she was living at the time of probate of her father's estate in 1800 as Abigail Holt.

Nathan Holt and Lydia Kingsbury had two children born at Willington.

i BATHSHEBA HOLT, b. 11 Jan 1772; d. 20 Jan 1790.

---

[450] *Connecticut Wills and Probate, 1609-1999*, Probate of Caleb Holt, Hartford, 1810, Case number 1059.

[451] "Connecticut Marriages, 1640-1939," database with images, *FamilySearch* (https://familysearch.org/ark:/61903/1:1:F7PB-68K: 11 February 2018), Elijah Holt and Molley Simons, Marriage 05 Nov 1783, Willington Tolland, Connecticut, United States; Connecticut State Library, Hartford; FHL microfilm 1,376,042.

[452] *Connecticut Wills and Probate, 1609-1999*, Probate of Nathan Holt, Hartford, 1800, Case number 1066.

ii JOHN HOLT, b. 11 Apr 1774; d. 11 Mar 1776.

162) ANNA HOLT *(Hannah Abbott Holt³, William², George¹)*, b. 14 Jan 1735 daughter of Abiel and Hannah (Abbott) Holt; d. at Willington, 10 Oct 1806; m. 29 Jan 1755, JOSEPH MERRICK, b. 17 Oct 1733 son of John and Sarah (Parsons) Merrick; Joseph d. 9 Apr 1787.

Captain Joseph Merrick commanded a militia company during the Revolutionary War.

Anna Merrick's estate entered probate in 1806.[453] She did not leave a will. The value of the personal property resulted in a value of personal items of $56.67 to each of the heirs. There are distributions to the following heirs: Timothy Merrick, Thomas Merrick, Joseph Merrick, Caleb Merrick, Constant Merrick, Anna Hinkley, Hannah Merrick, and Elizabeth Nye.

Anna Holt and Joseph Merrick had eight children whose births are recorded at Willington.

683) i ANNE MERRICK, b. 19 Sep 1756; d. 2 May 1809; m. 10 Jan 1782, DAVID HINCKLEY, b. 24 Feb 1754 son of John and Susannah (Harris) Hinckley; David d. 24 Jan 1835.

684) ii TIMOTHY MERRICK, b. 31 Aug 1760; d. 4 Jan 1810; m. 29 Nov 1787, MEHITABLE ATWOOD, b. 1765 daughter of Thomas and Sarah (Fenton) Atwood; Mehitable d. 14 May 1855.

685) iii THOMAS MERRICK, b. 6 Jan 1763; d. at Willington, 8 Sep 1840; m. 10 Jan 1790, JOANNA NOBLE, b. 8 Oct 1769 daughter of Gideon and Christian (Cadwell) Noble; Joanna d. 28 Apr 1860.

686) iv JOSEPH MERRICK, b. 22 Feb 1765; death uncertain but about 1814 possibly by drowning; m. 21 Oct 1796, IRENA ALDEN, b. at Bellingham, MA, 24 Feb 1772 daughter of Elisha and Irene (Markham) Alden. Irena m. 2nd, Samuel Churchill; Irena d. at Pleasantville, PA, 13 Nov 1858.

687) v CALEB MERRICK, b. 17 May 1767; d. at Vernon, CT, Jun 1822; m. 15 Sep 1791, CHARLOTTE NOBLE, b. at Willington, 19 Aug 1771 daughter of Gideon and Christian (Cadwell) Noble; Charlotte d. at Franklin, CT, 21 Nov 1805.

vi HANNAH MERRICK, b. 23 Jul 1769; d. 31 May 1842. Hannah did not marry.

688) vii CONSTANT MERRICK, b. 14 Jan 1772; d. at Lebanon, NY, 29 Jul 1828; m. at Longmeadow, MA, 22 Sep 1796, EXPERIENCE BURT, b. 8 Aug 1776 daughter of Nathaniel and Experience (Chapin) Burt; Experience d. 1833 at Lebanon, NY, 24 Jul 1833.

689) viii ELIZABETH MERRICK, b. 13 Jul 1774; d. at Tolland, 29 Jun 1824; m. 24 Apr 1800, as his second wife, SAMUEL NYE, b. 25 Dec 1773 son of Samuel and Abigail (Benton) Nye. Samuel m. 3rd, Anna Hatch; Samuel's first wife was Elizabeth Brewster; Samuel d. at Tolland 25 Nov 1837.

163) ISAAC HOLT *(Hannah Abbott Holt³, William², George¹)*, b. 2 Mar 1737/8 son of Abiel and Hannah (Abbott) Holt; d. at Willington, 14 Oct 1822; m. 26 May 1762, SARAH ORCUTT, b. at Stafford, 7 Nov 1740 daughter of William and Sarah (Leonard) Orcutt; Sarah d. 30 Mar 1816.

Isaac and Sarah Holt made their home in Willington where they were admitted to full communion of the Church of Willington 12 July 1767.[454]

Isaac Holt wrote his will 8 May 1798. In the will, he makes special provision for his son Moses "being sensible that he is unable to provide for himself." The will has bequests for well beloved wife Sarah Holt, son Isaac, daughter Sarah, daughter Hannah, daughter Mary, daughter Elizabeth, son Leonard, daughter Anne, son Oliver, and son Moses. The estate entered probate 18 November 1822. Son Oliver Holt served as administrator.[455]

Isaac Holt and Sarah Orcutt had nine children whose births are recorded at Willington.

690) i ISAAC HOLT, b. 3 Nov 1763; d. at Sharon, VT, 7 Aug 1813; m. at Sharon, 1 Jan 1789,[456] MEHITABLE ORCUTT, b. at Stafford, CT, 17 Jan 1769 daughter of Caleb and Chloe (Parker) Orcutt; Mehitable d. 12 Nov 1851.

ii MOSES HOLT, b. 28 Oct 1765; d. 7 Mar 1819.

iii SARAH HOLT, b. 22 Feb 1769; d. 13 May 1836. Sarah did not marry.

---

[453] *Connecticut Wills and Probate, 1609-1999*, Probate of Anna Merrick, Hartford, 1806, Case number 1476.

[454] Talcott, Mary, "Records of the Church at Willington, Conn.", *New England Historical and Genealogical Register*, volume 67, 1913, p 217

[455] *Connecticut Wills and Probate, 1609-1999*, Probate of Isaac Holt, Hartford, 1822, Case number 1063.

[456] *Vermont, Vital Records, 1720-1908.*

691) iv HANNAH HOLT, b. 19 May 1771; d. likely at Clarksfield, OH before 1850;[457] m. 9 Apr 1795, ELEAZER FELLOWS, b. at Tolland, 2 Apr 1772 son of Verney and Hannah (Lathrop) Fellows; Eleazer d. after 1850 in Ohio.

692) v MARY HOLT, b. 1 May 1773; d. at Willington, 6 Jun 1861; m. 27 Nov 1799, WILLIAM CURTIS, b. about 1774; William d. 3 Nov 1860.

693) vi OLIVER HOLT, b. 16 Jul 1775; d. 6 Mar 1869; m. 16 May 1799, MARTHA "PATTY" SIBLEY,[458] b. 9 Feb 1776 daughter of Jonathan and Patty (Brooks) Sibley; Martha "Patty" d. 16 Dec 1846.

694) vii ELIZABETH HOLT, b. 6 Aug 1777; m. 11 Apr 1799, DANIEL GLAZIER, b. 2 Jun 1776 son of Silas and Suze (Johnson) Glazier; Daniel d. 28 Dec 1852.

695) viii LEONARD HOLT, b. 15 Feb 1782; d. 12 Mar 1857; m. 1st, 29 Dec 1809, his first cousin once removed (and George Abbott descendant), ASENATH HOLT, b. 26 Jan 1786 daughter of Nathan and Lois (Goodell) Holt; Asenath d. 13 Feb 1813. Leonard m. 2nd, about 1813, JOANNA ALDEN, b. 14 Jul 1782 daughter of Elisha and Irene (Markham) Alden; Joanna d. 30 Sep 1849.

696) ix ANNE HOLT, b. 21 Oct 1784; d. 27 Jun 1855; m. SIMON CARPENTER, b. 13 Dec 1783 son of Elijah and Sarah (Younglove) Carpenter; Simon d. 24 Aug 1862.

164) TIMOTHY HOLT *(Hannah Abbott Holt³, William², George¹)*, b. 2 Dec 1739 son of Abiel and Hannah (Abbott) Holt; d. 7 May 1807; m. 7 May 1761 as her 2nd husband, REBECCA CHAMBERLAIN (widow of Nathaniel Fenton).[459] Rebecca was b. about 1730 probably the daughter of Edmund and Sarah (Furbush) Chamberlain; Rebecca d. 11 Apr 1809.

The settlement of the estate of Timothy Holt in 1807 included distributions to the following persons: widow Mrs. Rebekah Holt, son Timothy Holt, and daughter Anna Crocker. The probate of the estate of Rebekah Chamberlain Fenton Holt in 1809 included distributions to the following persons: Timothy Holt, Nathaniel Fenton, Anna Crocker, Eleazer Fenton, and Rebecca Knowlton.[460] Nathaniel Fenton, Eleazer Fenton, and Rebecca Knowlton were children of Rebecca and her first husband Nathaniel Fenton.

Timothy Holt and Rebecca Chamberlain had two children whose births are recorded at Willington.

697) i ANNA HOLT, b. 12 Feb 1762; m. 17 Nov 1785, STEPHEN CROCKER, b. 14 Dec 1760 son of Ebenezer and Hannah (Hatch) Crocker. It is not firmly established where this family located, but they perhaps went to Schoharie County, New York. On the other hand, they may have stayed in Willington as a Stephen Crocker is of appropriate age there in the 1820 census.

698) ii TIMOTHY HOLT, b. 19 May 1765; d. 17 Apr 1850; m. 10 Dec 1789, ESTHER SCRIPTURE, b. 26 Aug 1765 son of John and Esther (Lee) Scripture; Esther d. 1 Aug 1841.

165) MARY HOLT *(Hannah Abbott Holt³, William², George¹)*, b. 4 May 1742 daughter of Abiel and Hannah (Abbott) Holt; d. 13 Jan 1823; m. 27 Nov 1760, JOSEPH PERSONS, birth record not found but son of Joseph and Hannah (-) Persons of Willington; Joseph d. at Willington, 4 Nov 1812.

Joseph and Mary do not seem to have had children. Joseph's will included bequests to his wife Mary and to his siblings and their heirs. In her will, written 10 June 1819 and proved 1 Feb 1823, Mary Parsons left her entire estate to the children of Joseph and Betsy Holt. Joseph and Betsy Holt were deceased at that time; their children who were heirs were Hannah Whitaker, Esther Heath, Alva Holt, Lucy Holt, Joseph P. Holt, and Mary Holt.[461] This is the family of Joseph and Betsy (Parker) Holt. Joseph Holt was a nephew of Mary Holt Persons, the son of Mary's brother James.

This Joseph Persons is often confused (at least in "internet" trees) with Joseph Parsons of Springfield, Massachusetts who married Naomi Hitchcock and had several children in Springfield. Joseph Persons, Jr. and Mary Holt lived in Willington. They were members of the church in Willington, Joseph, Jr. and Mary admitted as members February 1777. They were also listed as members in 1806 and Joseph's death is noted in the church records in 1813.[462] It is during this same time frame that

[457] In the 1850 U.S. Census, Eleazer Fellows, age 78, was living in Clarksfield OH; also in the home are Betsey Haskins age 43 and five children named Haskins. Betsey is the daughter of Eleazer and Hannah. Eleazer and Hannah's son Leonard also relocated to Huron County, Ohio.

[458] Connecticut, Marriage Index, 1620-1926; the handwritten marriage record confirms that the marriage is to Patty and not to her younger sister Polly.

[459] This information is confirmed by the 1809 probate record of Rebecca Holt which includes heirs from her first marriage to Nathaniel Fenton.

[460] *Connecticut Wills and Probate, 1609-1999*, Probate of Rebekah Holt, Hartford, 1809, Case number 1069.

[461] *Connecticut Wills and Probate, 1609-1999*, Probate of Mary Parsons, Hartford, 1823, Case number 1617.

[462] Ancestry.com, Connecticut, Church Record Abstracts, 1630-1920

Joseph Parsons and Naomi Hitchcock were married and having children in Springfield. Adding to the confusion is that each of these Josephs had fathers named Joseph and mothers named Hannah, but they are two different people.

166) JAMES HOLT *(Hannah Abbott Holt³, William², George¹)*, b. 27 Aug 1746 son of Abiel and Hannah (Abbott) Holt; d. at Willington, 30 Sep 1818; m. 1st 20 Apr 1769, ESTHER OWENS, b. 20 Feb 1747 son of Eleazer and Jerusha (Russ) Owens; Esther d. 5 Dec 1774. JAMES m. 2nd LUCE SAWINS, b. 28 Sep 1740 daughter of George and Anne (Farrar) Sawins; Luce d. 25 Dec 1824.

James Holt wrote his will 7 February 1814 (proved 19 October 1818) and includes bequests to the following persons: well beloved wife Lucy Holt who receives one half of the personal estate which is to be at her disposal forever; sons James, Joseph, and Solomon each receive $25; daughter Esther Parker, $1; son Abiel Holt, $25; and daughter Lucy Walker, $1. These are token money bequests as the children have previously received their full portions from the estate. The entire remainder of the estate is bequeathed to son John Holt who is also named the executor.[463]

James Holt and Esther Owens had four children whose birth are recorded at Willington, Connecticut.

699) i JAMES HOLT, b. 12 Apr 1770; d. at Willington, 16 Jan 1856; m. 4 Dec 1794, MARY POOL, b. at Willington, 14 Aug 1770 daughter of Timothy and Deborah (Presson) Pool; Mary d. 18 Jan 1853.

700) ii JOSEPH HOLT (twin of James), b. 12 Apr 1770; d. at Willington, 29 Jan 1816; m. 6 Mar 1794, BETSY PARKER, b. at Willington, 23 Feb 1775 daughter of Jonathan and Betsy (Johnson) Parker; Betsy d. 7 May 1814.

701) iii SOLOMON HOLT, b. 14 Apr 1772; d. in Iowa, 4 Jun 1838; m. at Franklin, CT, 7 Apr 1799, ZERVIAH ABELL, b. at Norwich, 26 Aug 1780 daughter of Thomas and Zerviah (Hyde) Abell; Zerviah d. 1845.

702) iv ESTHER HOLT, b. 20 Nov 1774; m. 9 Jan 1800, DANIEL PARKER, b. at Willington, 5 Mar 1777 son of Jonathan and Betsy (Johnson) Parker.

James Holt and Luce Sawins had three children whose births are recorded at Willington.

703) i JOHN HOLT, b. 11 Apr 1776; d. at Willington, 22 Apr 1841; m. 6 Sep 1804, CLARISSA HOLT, b. 1775 (based on age at time of death); Clarissa d. 25 Feb 1840. I have no idea who Clarissa Holt is and suspect she may be the widow of a Holt but have not been able to track her down.

704) ii LUCE HOLT, b. 11 Jun 1778; d. 22 Feb 1847;[464] m. at Ashford, 26 Jan 1809, AARON WALKER, b. 21 Jan 1776 son of Samuel and Alice (Case) Walker; Aaron d. at Ashford, 1 Nov 1815.

705) iii ABIEL HOLT, b. 14 Jan 1780; d. at Mansfield, about 1826 (probate of estate in 1826); m. 30 Apr 1805, SALLY CONVERSE, b. at Stafford, 9 Mar 1781 daughter of Stephen and Zerviah (Sanger) Converse;[465] Sally's date of death is uncertain. She was alive in 1823 when her father wrote his will but there is no mention of her in the probate of Abiel's estate. The probate includes some provisions of the support of the two younger sons (Sanford and Arnold) who were underage at the time.

167) HANNAH ABBOTT *(Caleb³, William², George¹)*, b. 27 Oct 1734 daughter of Caleb and Elizabeth (Paine) Abbott; d. 19 Apr 1813 at Hartland, VT; m. at Union, CT, 24 Mar 1761, JOHN HENDRICK, b. at Norwich, 3 Oct 1722 son of Israel and Ann (Babson) Hendrick; John d. at Hartland, 8 Nov 1810.[466]

Hannah and John married in Connecticut and started their family there. They relocated to Vermont with several other members of this family network. John was a farmer. John and Hannah were members of the congregational church in Hartland.[467]

Hannah and John had seven children; the births of the three oldest children are recorded in Union, Connecticut. The other children may have been born in Vermont, but records have not yet been located. The birth dates for the younger children are from published genealogies.[468]

i EZRA HENDRICK, b. 21 Feb 1762; d. Jun 1770.

ii JOHN HENDRICK, b. 4 Apr 1764; d. about 1826 in Chautauqua County, NY. John does not seem to have married and did not have any children.

---

[463] *Connecticut Wills and Probate, 1609-1999*, Probate of James Holt, Hartford, 1818, Case number 1064.
[464] Durrie, *A Genealogy of the Holt Family*, p 50
[465] The 1823 will of Stephen Converse includes a bequest to his daughter Sally Holt.
[466] Vermont, Vital Records, 1720-1908. (ancestry.com)
[467] Darling, *History and Anniversary of Hartland, Vermont*
[468] Abbot and Abbot, *Genealogical Register of Descendants*

706) iii MARY HENDRICK, b. 5 Dec 1765; d. after 1845 at Putney, VT; m. 14 Sep 1786, JOHN STODDARD, b. 19 Nov 1761 son of Joshua and Sarah (Humphrey) Stoddard; John d. at Westminster, VT, 13 Aug 1831.[469]

707) iv CALEB HENDRICK, b. 17 Sep 1767; d. at Hartland, VT, 26 Aug 1837; m. by 1796, his first cousin, SARAH ABBOTT, b. 15 Apr 1773 daughter of Samuel and Rachel (Ward) Abbott; Sarah d. 11 Feb 1849.

708) v HANNAH HENDRICK, b. 22 Mar 1770; d. at Waterford, VT, 12 Apr 1843; m. about 1800, ZEDEKIAH GOODELL, b. at Pomfret, 31 Aug 1769 son of Jacob and Mehitable (Goodell) Goodell; Zedekiah d. 11 Sep 1863.

709) vi EZRA HENDRICK, b. 13 Mar 1772; d. 28 Dec 1799; m. about 1797, ESTHER GOODELL, b. at Pomfret, 1 Jul 1776 son of Jacob and Mehitable (Goodell) Goodell.

vii ELIZABETH HENDRICK, b. 11 Jun 1775; d. at Fowlerville, NY, 7 May 1857; m. 12 Mar 1818, as his second wife, LOT JENNE, b. at Dartmouth, MA, 5 Jun 1760 son of Samuel and Bethiah (Rider) Jenne. Elizabeth did not have any children.

168) SARAH ABBOTT *(Caleb³, William², George¹)*, b. 6 Jul 1736 daughter of Caleb and Elizabeth (Paine) Abbott; d. 12 Nov 1761 at Brimfield, MA; m. 11 Nov 1754, JONATHAN BURK, b. 26 Feb 1733 son of Jonathan and Thankful (Waite) Burk. Jonathan m. 2nd Sarah Gould; Jonathan d. 18 May 1775 at Hartland, VT.

The births of four children of Sarah Abbott and Jonathan Burk are recorded at Brimfield, Massachusetts. The Abbot genealogy also lists a daughter Betsy, but she is the child of Jonathan and his second wife.[470]

710) i SARAH BURK, b. 18 Jan 1755; d. at Windsor, VT about 1783; m. at Windsor, 17 May 1774, LAZARUS BANNISTER, b. at Brookfield, 7 Feb 1748 son of Thomas and Mary (Wheeler) Bannister. Lazarus m. 2nd, about 1784, Anne Worcester. Lazarus d. at Windsor about 1813 (probate of estate).

ii JONATHAN BURK, b. 7 Jun 1756; died in the Army.

711) iii JOSEPH BURK, b. 27 Apr 1758; d. at Warner, NH, 7 May 1829; m. at Hartland, VT, 25 Apr 1784, JUDITH BARRELL, b. at Bridgewater, 1 May 1763 daughter of John and Judith (Snow) Barrell.

712) iv ABIGAIL BURK, b. 12 Nov 1761; d. at Westminster, VT, 18 Oct 1801;[471] m. 26 Aug 1779, REUBEN ROBINSON, b. at Cumberland, RI, 4 Aug 1753 son of Nathaniel and Kezia (Robbins) Robinson; Reuben d. 16 Dec 1839.

169) SAMUEL ABBOTT *(Caleb³, William², George¹)*, b. 4 Mar 1743 son of Caleb and Elizabeth (Paine) Abbott; d. 25 Sep 1825 at Hartland, VT; m. 1st at Union, CT, RACHEL WARD, b. about 1748 (based on age at death); Rachel d. at Hartland, VT 15 Oct 1774. Samuel m. 2nd 3 Dec 1778 the widow LYDIA STONE; Lydia d. 25 Sep 1825.

Samuel saw service during the Revolutionary War in the militia guarding frontier regions in Vermont. He had two children with his first wife, Rachel Ward; one of those children died as an infant. Samuel did not have children in his second marriage.

i SARAH ABBOTT, b. 12 Apr 1771; d. 3 Jul 1772.

707) ii SARAH ABBOTT, b. 15 Apr 1773; d. at Hartland, 11 Feb 1849; m. by 1796, her first cousin (and George Abbott descendant), CALEB HENDRICK, b. 17 Sep 1767 son of John and Hannah (Abbott) Hendrick; Caleb d. 26 Aug 1837. This is the same as Family #167, child iv.

170) WILLIAM ABBOTT *(Caleb³, William², George¹)*, b. 17 Oct 1745 son of Caleb and Elizabeth (Paine) Abbott; d. 25 Jul 1832 at Clinton, NY; m. 1st at Union, CT, 15 Nov 1770, MARY COY; Mary d. 10 Dec 1776. William m. 2nd 24 Sep 1778, ESTHER GREEN, b. at Thompson, CT, 31 Dec 1753 daughter of Amos and Lydia (Johnson) Green;[472] Esther d. at Clinton, NY 23 Dec 1839.

---

469 *Vermont, Vital Records, 1720-1908.*

470 Abbot and Abbot, *Genealogical Register of Descendants*, p 59

471 Vermont Births, Marriages and Deaths to 2008. (From microfilmed records. Online database: AmericanAncestors.org, New England Historic Genealogical Society, 2013.)

472 Esther's birthdate and name of her father are engraved on her gravestone. (findagrave.com)

William Abbott and Mary Coy had two children born at Union County, Connecticut.

713) i CALEB ABBOTT, b. 2 Feb 1774; d. at Colden, NY, 25 Jan 1851; m. by 1794, HANNAH WHEAT, b. at Bernardston, MA, 6 Jan 1772 daughter of Samuel and Jerusha (Allen) Wheat; Hannah d. 4 Sep 1842.

ii NEHEMIAH ABBOTT, b. 2 May 1776; d. 25 Sep 1776.

William Abbott and Esther Green had seven children born at Union County, Connecticut.

i MARY ABBOTT, b. 3 Aug 1779; d. after 1860 at Kirkland, NY.[473] Mary did not marry.

714) ii NEHEMIAH ABBOTT, b. 4 Jun 1781; d. 11 Jan 1867, Kirkland, NY; m. 4 Oct 1803, ESTHER BARKER, b. at Watertown, CT, 29 Oct 1776 daughter of Eliasaph and Mabel (Sanford) Barker; Esther d. 2 Jan 1857, Oneida County, NY.

715) iii PAUL ABBOTT, b. 7 May 1783; d. at Lowville, NY, 18 Mar 1831; m. 1st, 6 Mar 1807, MARY GAYLORD; Mary d. 2 Sep 1809. Paul m. 2nd, 7 Mar 1811, PATTY EELS, b. 26 Oct 1787 daughter of Daniel and Martha (Hamlin) Eels.

716) iv ESTHER ABBOTT, b. 4 Oct 1784; d. after 1860 at Kirkland, NY (living with her daughter at 1860 Census); m. 30 Jan 1810, ELIHU WAKELEE, b. 27 Dec 1789 son of Platt and Mary (Minor) Wakelee; Elihu d. 1 Aug 1833.

717) v ORINDA ABBOTT, b. 1 May 1786; d. at Panama, NY, 11 May 1850; m. 17 Oct 1805, JOEL HUBBARD, b. 15 Mar 1784; Joel d. 1 Apr 1862.

vi SAMUEL ABBOTT, b. 18 Jul 1789. Samuel was a mechanic. He did not marry.

vii WILLIAM ABBOTT, b. 2 Dec 1792; d. at Clinton, NY, 21 Oct 1819. William was a tailor. He did not marry.

Grandchildren of Sarah Abbott and Ephraim Stevens

171) JOSEPH ROBINSON *(Elizabeth Stevens Robinson³, Sarah Abbott Stevens², George¹)*, b. 22 Dec 1710 son of Joseph and Elizabeth (Stevens) Robinson; d. at Boxford, 29 Nov 1777; m. 25 Jul 1733, MEHITABLE EAMS, of Boxford, b. 1713 (based on age at time of death); her parentage is not clear; Mehitable d. 11 Aug 1782.

Joseph and Mehitable resided in Boxford where their six children were born. He owned a farm of about 100 acres in Boxford that he listed for sale in 1770, although he perhaps did not sell the property as he continued to live there until his death.[474]

Joseph wrote his will 17 November 1777. His widow Mehitable receives the use of all the household goods, one-half of the cow currently being fattened, and as much pork and other provisions that she requires for her support. Mehitable also receives the improvements from one-third part of the real estate. Son Joseph receives £260 which will be paid to him from the estate by son John. Jeremy is also bequeathed Joseph's best gun. Daughter Mary wife of Henry Bodwell receives £12. Daughter Mehitable wife of James Frye receives £12. His two daughters will also receive the household goods after the decease of their mother. Son John receives all the remainder of the estate and is named sole executor.[475] [Son Jeremy is called Jeremiah in the available vital records.]

Birth records were located for six children, the oldest three at Andover and the births of the youngest three children recorded at Boxford.

i NATHAN ROBINSON, b. 1 Sep 1734; d. 13 Jul 1736.

718) ii MARY ROBINSON, b. 3 Aug 1737; d. at Methuen, 16 Nov 1811; m. 20 Sep 1759, HENRY BODWELL, b. at Methuen, 26 Jul 1729 son of Henry and Anne (Pottelle) Bodwell; Henry d. 9 Apr 1816.

719) iii JOHN ROBINSON, b. 2 Sep 1739; d. at Boxford, 22 Jan 1810; m. 30 Jun 1763, REBECCA "BECKY" WOOD, b. Feb 1743/4 (baptized 12 Feb) daughter of Daniel and Sarah (Peabody) Wood; Becky d. 30 Mar 1810.

---

[473] In the 1860 U.S. Census, she was living with her brother Nehemiah in Kirkland, NY. Year: 1860; Census Place: Kirkland, Oneida, New York; Roll: M653_824; Page: 104; Family History Library Film: 803824

[474] "The Dwellings of Boxford," *Essex Institute Historical Collections*, volumes 27-29, p 87

[475] *Essex County, MA: Probate File Papers, 1638-1881.* Probate of Joseph Robinson, 2 Feb 1778, Case number 23906.

504) iv MEHITABLE ROBINSON, b. Oct 1742 (baptized 17 Oct); d. at Methuen, 6 Jun 1787; m. 21 Feb 1765, her third cousin (and George Abbott descendant), JAMES FRYE, b. at Andover, 9 Jan 1740/1 son of James and Elizabeth (Osgood) Frye; James d. 28 Jan 1826.

v ELIZABETH ROBINSON, b. Sep 1746 (baptized 7 Sep); d. 22 Oct 1777. Elizabeth did not marry.

vi JEREMIAH ROBINSON, b. 1754; d. 27 May 1780. Jeremiah did not marry.

172) ISAAC ROBINSON *(Elizabeth Stevens Robinson[3], Sarah Abbott Stevens[2], George[1])*, b. Sep 1715 son of Joseph and Elizabeth (Stevens) Robinson; d. at Boxford, 15 Apr 1804; m. 19 Jun 1740, DOROTHY POOR, b. at Andover 1716 daughter of Daniel and Dorothy (Kimball) Poor; Dorothy d. 13 Jul 1801.

Isaac Robinson wrote his will 20 March 1788.[476] His well-beloved wife Dorothy is to receive the improvement on one-third of the real estate. She is to have other considerations if needed to maintain her comfort. Son Isaac receives £5. Son Jonathan receives £50. Daughter Phebe the wife of Nathan Eams receives £5 as does daughter Hannah the wife of Jonathan Parker. His two daughters receive the household goods after the decease of their mother. Son John receives all the real estate in Andover and elsewhere. The three sons Isaac, Jonathan, and John receive wearing apparel. Wife Dorothy is mentioned in this 1788 will, but she died in 1801 prior to the probate of the estate.

Isaac Robinson and Dorothy Poor had eight children whose births are recorded at Andover.

i ISAAC ROBINSON, b. 24 Apr 1741; he was living in 1788 when his father wrote his will; it is not clear what became of him.

ii PHEBE ROBINSON, b. 3 Aug 1742; m. 27 Feb 1765, NATHAN EAMS, b. at Boxford, 16 Sep 1738 son of Jeremiah and Sarah (Kimball) Eams. It is unknown what became of this couple. Charlotte Helen Abbott attributes several children to them, but those are children of Nathan Ames and Deborah Bowers (that Nathan being the son of Samuel Ames and Hannah Stevens). There is no record of children for Nathan and Phebe in Massachusetts or New Hampshire and no probate record.

720) iii HANNAH ROBINSON, b. 27 Sep 1744; m. 17 Feb 1767, JONATHAN PARKER, b. 26 Mar 1738 son of Jonathan and Hannah (Frye) Parker.

iv DOLLY ROBINSON, b. 6 Feb 1746/7; d. at Boxford, Jun 1767.

v DANIEL ROBINSON, b. 8 Aug 1750; d. at St. Croix, Jul 1771; *Daniel, s. Isaac, at St. Croix, July —, 1771, a. 21 y. GR1.*

721) vi JONATHAN ROBINSON, b. 25 Jun 1753; d. at Surry, NH, 17 Mar 1838;[477] m. at Boxford, 24 Apr 1783, BETTY CHADWICK, b. at Boxford, 22 Aug 1756 daughter of John and Susannah (Peabody) Chadwick; Betty d. 23 Oct 1818.

vii NATHAN ROBINSON, b. 20 Apr 1756; d. 19 Sep 1762.

722) viii JOHN ROBINSON, b. 11 Apr 1758; d. at Boxford, 17 May 1807; m. at Boxford, 3 Apr 1781, SARAH TYLER, b. at Boxford, 8 Feb 1758 daughter of Gideon and Mehitable (Kimball) Tyler;[478] Sarah d. 3 May 1840 (*Sarah, wid. John, d. Gideon Tyler, May 3, 1840, a. 82 y. GR1*).

173) SARAH ROBINSON *(Elizabeth Stevens Robinson[3], Sarah Abbott Stevens[2], George[1])*, b. about 1716[479] daughter of Joseph and Elizabeth (Stevens) Robinson; d.?; m. 10 Apr 1746, as his second wife, SAMUEL BARKER, b. 13 Feb 1691/2 son of William and Mary (Dix) Barker; Samuel d. at Andover, 13 May 1770.

Samuel Barker wrote his will 21 November 1767. Wife Sarah receives one-third of the personal and real estate for use and improvement. Son-in-law Jedediah Holt and his wife Phebe receive all the estate real and personal. Jedediah Holt was named sole executor.[480]

Samuel's two children with his first wife died in infancy. Sarah Robinson and Samuel Barker had two children born at Andover.

---

[476] *Essex County, MA: Probate File Papers, 1638-1881.* Probate of Isaac Robinson, 7 May 1804, Case number 23887.

[477] Kingsbury, *The History of Surry, NH*

[478] The 1800 will of Gideon Tyler includes a bequest to daughter Sarah the wife of John Robinson. *Essex County, MA: Probate File Papers, 1638-1881.*

[479] Sarah is mentioned in her father's will, but no birth record was located for her.

[480] *Essex County, MA: Probate File Papers, 1638-1881.* Probate of Samuel Barker, 4 Jun 1770, Case number 1712.

i SARAH BARKER, b. 4 Oct 1747; d. 29 Sep 1763.

723) ii PHEBE BARKER, b. 2 Jan 1749/50; m. 19 Jun 1766, her second cousin once removed, JEDEDIAH HOLT, b. at Suncook, 23 Feb 1743/4 son of Stephen and Mary (Farnum) Holt; Jedediah d. at Andover, 12 Feb 1790.

174) EPHRAIM ROBINSON *(Elizabeth Stevens Robinson³, Sarah Abbott Stevens², George¹)*, b. 11 Aug 1723 son of Joseph and Elizabeth (Stevens) Robinson; death date not located; m. 2 Aug 1750, HANNAH KIMBALL, b. at Bradford 19 Mar 1730/1 daughter of Joseph and Abial (Peabody) Kimball; no death record was located for Hannah.

Little information has yet been located for this family. Some marriages for the children are suggested here, but these are preliminary. There are records for eight children, the oldest six and Andover and the youngest two at Haverhill.

i JOSEPH ROBINSON, b. 23 Aug 1751; m. at Haverhill, 8 Jun 1788, SUSANNA NOYES. No information has been found for this couple following their marriage.

ii SARAH ROBINSON, b. 21 May 1753; died young.

iii HANNAH ROBINSON, b. 28 Jun 1755

iv NAOMY ROBINSON, b. 1758; d. 20 Oct 1762.

v ELIZABETH ROBINSON, b. 17 Oct 1760; d. 9 Oct 1762.

vi NAOMY ROBINSON, b. 18 Mar 1763; d. unknown but living in 1828; m. at Haverhill, 8 Jul 1798, as his second wife, REUBEN CURRIER, b. at Haverhill, 21 Jul 1738 son of Reuben and Elizabeth (Robinson) Currier; Reuben d. at Haverhill, 15 Apr 1827. Reuben did not leave a will; Naomy Currier was administrator of the estate. Reuben and Naomy did not have children. Reuben's first wife was Lydia Atwood with whom he had several children.

vii SARAH ROBINSON, b. 31 Jan 1766.

viii ELIZABETH ROBINSON, b. 24 Nov 1768.

175) ELIZABETH SWAN *(Hannah Stevens Swan³, Sarah Abbott Stevens², George¹)*, b. 14 Feb 1709/10 daughter of Robert and Hannah (Stevens) Swan; d. at Andover 21 Jun 1770; m. 4 Jul 1743, NATHANIEL LOVEJOY, b. 16 Feb 1698/9 son of Nathaniel and Dorothy (Hoyt) Lovejoy; Nathaniel d. 25 Aug 1769.[481]

There are only two births recorded at Andover for Elizabeth Swan and Nathaniel Lovejoy. One son died in infancy. The second son was General Nathaniel Lovejoy, educated at Harvard and served in the Revolutionary War.

304) i NATHANIEL LOVEJOY, b. 29 Apr 1744; d. 5 Jul 1812; m. 3 Nov 1768, his third cousin (and George Abbott descendant), ELIZABETH FOSTER, b. 14 Apr 1744 daughter of Asa and Elizabeth (Abbott) Foster (same as Family #64, child vi). Elizabeth d. 24 Apr 1775. Nathaniel m. 2nd, by 1776, ELIZABETH BRANDON, b. at Cambridge, 18 Nov 1750 daughter of Benjamin and Elizabeth (Foxcroft) Brandon; Elizabeth Brandon d. 19 Nov 1788. Nathaniel m. 3rd, 1 Dec 1803, his third cousin once removed (and George Abbott descendant), BENJAMINA WOODBRIDGE, b. at Salem, Mar 1772 daughter of Dudley and Dorcas (March) Woodbridge. Benjamina d. at Worcester, 6 May 1851. Prior to her death, a guardian was appointed for her due to "insanity."

ii JONATHAN LOVEJOY, b. 22 Apr 1748; d. 5 Jan 1749/50.

176) ROBERT SWAN *(Hannah Stevens Swan³, Sarah Abbott Stevens², George¹)*, b. 2 Mar 1711/2 son of Robert and Hannah (Stevens) Swan; d. at Methuen, 31 Oct 1752; m. 1731, ELIZABETH FARNUM, b. at Andover, 9 Nov 1711 daughter of Jonathan and Elizabeth (Barker) Farnum. Elizabeth m. 2nd James Howe; Elizabeth d. 5 Dec 1780.

Robert Swan did not leave a will. The probate record contains a 1762 document which refers to his widow as Elizabeth Swan now Howe.

The births of eight children are recorded for Robert and Elizabeth. The oldest four and youngest two children have births recorded at Andover and the births of the other two children are recorded at Methuen.

724) i JONATHAN SWAN, b. 1 Sep 1732; d. at Methuen, 15 Aug 1783; m. 13 Dec 1759, as the second of her three husbands, ABIGAIL GREEN, b. at Haverhill, 7 Nov 1728 daughter of Peter and Martha (Singletary) Green.

481 1769 is the date on the transcription of the death record. The gravestone has a date of 1768.

ii JOSEPH SWAN, b. 17 May 1734; d. 29 Sep 1760 at Crown Point during the French and Indian War. *Joseph, s. Robert and Elezebeth, at Crown Point, Sept. 29, 1760, in his 26th y.*

iii BENJAMIN SWAN, b. 5 Jan 1737/8; d. 28 Jan 1738/9.

iv ELIZABETH SWAN, b. 1 Dec 1739; d. 14 May 1742.

v BENJAMIN SWAN, b. 27 Apr 1743

vi RICHARD SWAN, b. 8 Mar 1745/6

725) vii ROBERT SWAN, b. 19 Jan 1748/9; d. at Andover, 25 Dec 1832; m. 1st, 29 Apr 1773, APHIA FARRINGTON, b. 8 Mar 1756 daughter of John and Sarah (Holton) Farrington; Affa d. 11 Feb 1788. Robert m. 2nd, 21 May 1789, SUSANNAH EMERY, b. about 1759; Susannah d. 6 Apr 1842. Susannah's first husband was Nehemiah Abbott a descendant of George Abbott of Rowley.

726) viii PHINEAS SWAN, b. 14 Jun 1752; d. at Haverhill, NH, 16 Jan 1829; m. 21 Oct 1773, TRYPHENA WEBSTER, b. at Haverhill, 11 Sep 1754 daughter of Stephen and Susannah (Ladd) Webster; Tryphena d. 23 Mar 1843.

177) EPHRAIM SWAN *(Hannah Stevens Swan³, Sarah Abbott Stevens², George¹)*, b. 3 Sep 1713 son of Robert and Hannah (Stevens) Swan; d. at Andover before Oct 1777 (when his will was probated); m. 23 May 1738, SARAH POOLE, b. at Lynn, 11 Sep 1713 daughter of John and Mary (Gooding) Poole; Sarah d. likely after 1790 (she seems to be listed as the head of household with her daughter living with her in the 1790 Census).

In his will, Ephraim has bequests to the following persons: well-beloved wife Sarah receives one-half of the household; daughter Sarah Swan receives the improvements on the other half of the house sharing equal with her mother; granddaughter Martha Swan; daughter-in-law Martha Swan widow of son Ephraim receives the use of a room in his house; and grandson Ephraim receives the real property at the age of 21. Wife Sarah is named executor.[482]

Ephraim Swan and Sarah Poole had two children whose births are recorded at Andover. Daughter Sarah did not marry. Ephraim's son Ephraim also died in 1777, the younger Ephraim dying a few months before his father.

727) i EPHRAIM SWAN, b. 12 Oct 1739; d. likely early 1777 (probate 3 Apr 1777); m. 24 Oct 1765, MARTHA FARRINGTON, b. 5 Oct 1741 daughter of John and Sarah (Holton) Farrington. Martha m. 2nd, 30 Dec 1777, Thomas Clark.

ii SARAH SWAN, b. 13 Jun 1742; d. 7 Jun 1812.

178) HANNAH SWAN *(Hannah Stevens Swan³, Sarah Abbott Stevens², George¹)*, b. 28 Dec 1716 daughter of Robert and Hannah (Stevens) Swan; d. at Andover, 7 Jul 1761; m. 14 Aug 1734, PETER PARKER, b. Jul 1714 son of Joseph and Lydia (Frye) Parker; Peter d. at Andover, 9 Jan 1795.

The will of Peter Parker has bequests to the following persons: son Nathan Parker, son Peter Parker, son Robart Parker, son Isaac Parker, son Simeon Parker, grandson Parker Elsly son of daughter Mary Elsly who is deceased (who gets 100 acres in the newly incorporated Bluehill), and grandson Parker Elwell son of daughter Hannah Elwell who is deceased (also 100 acres in Bluehill), daughter Lydia wife of Hezekiah Coburn, and grandson Joseph Parker son of Nathan gets the house and barn. Son Isaac is named executor. Bluehill refers to Blue Hill, Maine first settled in 1762 by people from Andover.[483]

Hannah Swan and Peter Parker had eleven children whose births are recorded at Andover.

728) i MARY PARKER, b. 28 Nov 1734; died before 1795; m. ENOCH ILSLEY, b. at Newbury, 16 Dec 1730 son of Isaac and Abigail Moody Ilsley; Enoch d. at Falmouth/Portland, ME, 10 Nov 1811.

ii HANNAH PARKER, b. 20 Dec 1736; d. 15 Mar 1741/2.

729) iii NATHAN PARKER, b. 3 Jun 1739; d. at Blue Hill, ME, about 1819; m. at Blue Hill, 20 Dec 1764, MARY WOOD, b. at Beverly, 15 Nov 1748 daughter of Joseph and Mary (Haskell) Wood.

730) iv PETER PARKER, b. 28 May 1741; d. at Blue Hill, 24 Oct 1822; m. 5 Jun 1766, PHEBE MARBLE, b. at Andover, 29 Jul 1744 daughter of Job and Phebe (Barker) Marble; Phebe d. 1 Oct 1805.

---

[482] *Essex County, MA: Probate File Papers, 1638-1881.* Probate of Ephraim Swan, 6 Oct 1777, Case number 26885.

[483] *Essex County, MA: Probate File Papers, 1638-1881.* Probate of Peter Parker, 8 Apr 1795, Case number 20543.

v HANNAH PARKER, b. 2 Apr 1743; d. 26 Jan 1745/6.

731) vi ROBERT PARKER, b. 2 Mar 1744/5; d. at Blue Hill, 12 Feb 1818; m. 29 Nov 1773, RUTH WOOD, b. at Beverly, 18 Dec 1753 daughter of Joseph and Mary (Haskell) Wood; Ruth d. 20 Jan 1825.

732) vii HANNAH PARKER, b. 4 Apr 1747; d. about 1782; m. at Pelham, NH, 23 May 1775,[484] HENRY BUTLER ELWELL, b. at Gloucester, 27 Mar 1746 son of William and Elizabeth (Butler) Elwell.

733) viii ISAAC PARKER, b. 29 Aug 1749; d. 9 Oct 1814; m. a cousin, MARY "POLLY" PARKER, b. about 1761 (based on age at time of death) whose parents have not been fully verified; Mary d. at Andover 19 Nov 1834. It is also possible that Polly's maiden name is not Parker.

734) ix LYDEA PARKER, b. 24 Apr 1752; d. at Lowell, MA, 29 Mar 1849; m. at Dracut, 29 Oct 1774, HEZEKIAH COBURN, b. 29 Mar 1748 son of Samuel and Mary (Bradstreet) Coburn; Hezekiah d. at Dracut, 13 Mar 1816.

x SIMEON PARKER, b. 3 May 1754; Simeon likely married, but there are several Simeon Parkers of similar age in Massachusetts at this time and it is not clear yet where he settled. He does not seem to have gone to Blue Hill with his brothers. There is a Simeon Parker that married Mary Pratt, but that does not seem to be this Simeon.

xi PHEBE PARKER, b. 14 Nov 1757; d. 11 Jan 1759.

179) JAMES INGALLS *(Mary Stevens Ingalls[3], Sarah Abbott Stevens[2], George[1])*, b. 20 Aug 1720 son of James and Mary (Stevens) Ingalls; d. at Methuen 8 May 1804; m. 6 Dec 1744, MARY FRYE, b. at Andover, 16 Feb 1724/5 daughter of Joshua and Mary (-) Frye;[485] Mary d. 6 Apr 1797.

James Ingalls's will, written 5 April 1797, is of some interest as it omits the standard "In the name of god, amen" and the associated commending of his soul to god to start the will. He begins his will ". . . being advanced in years, have no means to flatter myself with long life, therefore think it my duty to discharge my mind of all temporal concerns, as far as the domestic and social duties of life which I owe my family and which the public will admit. . . I may with as little interruption as possible spend the remainder of my days in preparation for that further state to which I am hastening." He makes bequests to the following persons: daughter Mary Swan wife of Lieutenant Joshua Swan; daughter Hannah Hall the wife of Lieutenant Benjamin Hall; daughter Dorcas Swan the wife of Captain Caleb Swan; daughter Sarah Foster the wife of John Foster; daughter Lydia Ingalls who receives use of one room in the house for as long as she remains unmarried; to the children and heirs of his daughter Deborah Hibbard who is deceased namely Daniel Hibbard, Jr., Joshua Ingalls Hibbard, and Deborah Hibbard; son Charles Ingalls; and son Alfred receives the bulk of the estate including all the lands in Andover. Alfred is also executor of the estate.[486]

James Ingalls and Mary Frye had twelve children. The first six children were born at Andover and the youngest six children were born at Methuen.

735) i MARY INGALLS, b. 1 Dec 1745; d. in NH, 3 Jul 1811; m. 10 Oct 1765, her third cousin once removed, JOSHUA SWAN, b. at Methuen, 6 Aug 1745 son of Timothy and Mary (Abbott) Swan. Joshua Swan's mother Mary Abbott is from the Rowley Abbott line.

ii JAMES INGALLS, b. Aug 1747; d. 28 May 1748.

736) iii HANNAH INGALLS, b. 27 Dec 1748; d. 10 Jul 1811; m. 18 Nov 1765, BENJAMIN HALL; Benjamin d. at Gloversville, NY, 24 Dec 1830.

737) iv DORCAS INGALLS, b. 18 Feb 1750/1; d. at Methuen, 16 Jul 1821; m. 30 Sep 1777, her third cousin once removed, CALEB SWAN, b. 4 Oct 1749 son of Timothy and Mary (Abbott) Swan.

738) v DEBORAH INGALLS, b. 28 May 1753; d. 20 Sep 1779; m. 24 Mar 1773, DANIEL HIBBARD, b. at Methuen, 15 Sep 1748 son of Ebenezer and Abigail (Whittier) Hibbard. Daniel m. 2nd, Sarah Lovejoy.

vi JAMES INGALLS, b. 19 Jun 1755; d. 8 Jul 1775. James was wounded at the Battle of Bunker Hill and died from his wounds.

vii JOSHUA INGALLS, b. 30 Jul 1757; d. 12 May 1759.

viii JOSHUA INGALLS, b. 10 Aug 1759; d. 5 Apr 1761.

---

[484] Ancestry.com, New Hampshire, Marriage Records Index, 1637-1947

[485] The 1768 probate of Joshua Frye includes heirs James and Mary Ingalls; *Essex County, MA: Probate File Papers, 1638-1881.* Online database. *AmericanAncestors.org.* New England Historic Genealogical Society, 2014. Case 10314

[486] *Essex County, MA: Probate File Papers, 1638-1881.* Probate of James Ingalls, 5 Jun 1804, Case number 14514.

739) ix SARAH INGALLS, b. 5 Oct 1761; d. at Boxford, 25 Jul 1849; m. 25 Nov 1788, JOHN FOSTER, b. at Andover, 10 Dec 1759 son of Stephen and Abigail (Smith) Foster; John d. 30 Nov 1837.

740) x CHARLES INGALLS, b. 12 Oct 1763; d. at Greenwich, NY, 2 Sep 1812; m. CYNTHIA RUSSELL, b. 14 Mar 1769 daughter of Thomas and Mary (Patterson) Russell; d. 17 Mar 1801.

741) xi ALFRED INGALLS, b. 16 Oct 1765; d. at Methuen, 15 Sep 1843; m. 1st, 9 Nov 1790, ABIGAIL "NABBY" PAGE, b. 1768 *possibly* daughter of Daniel Page; Nabby d. 29 Nov 1795. Alfred m. 2nd, 24 Jul 1797, MARY STICKNEY (widow of William Carleton).

742) xii LYDIA INGALLS, b. 7 Dec 1767; d. at Corinth, VT, 7 Nov 1810; m. at Corinth, 28 Jan 1806, as his second wife, DAVID MCKEEN, b. at Londonderry, NH, 12 Jun 1750 son of James and Elizabeth (Dinsmore) McKeen; David d. 2 Dec 1824. David's first marriage was to Margaret McPherson.

180) EPHRAIM INGALLS *(Mary Stevens Ingalls[3], Sarah Abbott Stevens[2], George[1])*, b. 6 Nov 1725 son of James and Mary (Stevens) Ingalls; d. at Pomfret 16 May 1805; m. 19 Dec 1751, MARY SHARP, b. at Pomfret, b. 10 Jul 1733 daughter of John and Dorcas (Davis) Sharp; Mary d. 16 Feb 1809.

Ephraim Ingalls owned a tavern on the common in Pomfret and kept a public house.[487]

Ephraim Ingalls wrote his will 13 January 1795 and it was presented to the probate court 10 June 1805. In his will, Ephraim provides his well-beloved wife Mary improvements on one-third of the real estate during her natural life and one-third of the personal estate to be at her disposal. There are also other provisions for her care and support. Son Simeon receives £5 which together with the part of the estate he has already received constitutes his full portion. Daughter Deborah Allyn receives £25 with what she has already received constitutes her full portion. Daughter Sarah Grosvenor receives £15 to complete her portion. Daughter Mary Osgood receives £5 to complete her portion. Son Edmund receives £70 which is his full portion of the estate. Son Ephraim receives the remaining two-thirds of the real estate and stock animals as well as the carpentry and farming tools. It is Ephraim's responsibility to make the payments to his brothers and sisters per the schedule set out in the will. His wearing apparel is divided among sons Simeon, Edmund, and Ephraim. Ephraim is named sole executor. The inventory of the estate had a total value of $2,641.19 with $2,400 of that being the value of 80 acres of property with buildings.[488]

Ephraim Ingalls and Mary Sharp had eleven children whose births are recorded at Pomfret. Five of the children died in childhood, three of them in a two-week period in October 1764.

i MARY INGALLS, b. 5 Dec 1752; d. 29 Oct 1764

743) ii SIMEON INGALLS, b. 28 May 1754; d. at Hartwick, NY, 23 May 1827; m. 1st, OLIVE GROSVENOR, b. 17 May 1760 daughter of Joshua and Esther (Payson) Grosvenor; Olive d. 17 Apr 1782. Simeon m. 2nd, EUNICE WHEELER, b. 1 Nov 1756 daughter of Benjamin and Prudence (Huet) Wheeler; Eunice d. 5 Oct 1807. Simeon m. 3rd, 8 Mar 1808, RACHEL HARRIS.

iii DORCAS INGALLS, b. 9 Nov 1755; d. 25 Oct 1764.

iv DEBORAH INGALLS, b. 28 Aug 1757; d. at Walpole, NH, 7 Nov 1811;[489] m. 14 Dec 1780, General AMASA ALLEN, b. at Pomfret, 7 Apr 1752[490] son of Peter and Elizabeth (Craft) Allen; Amasa d. at Walpole, NH, 12 Jul 1821. Deborah and Amasa did not have children.

v RHODA INGALLS, b. 28 Nov 1759; d. 15 Oct 1764.

744) vi SARAH INGALLS, b. 17 Feb 1762; d. 10 Mar 1807; m. 10 Feb 1784, JOSHUA GROSVENOR, b. 24 Apr 1758 son of Joshua and Esther (Payson) Grosvenor; Joshua d. 2 Apr 1838.

745) vii EPHRAIM INGALLS, b. 6 Sep 1764; d. at Pomfret, 12 Feb 1831; m. 26 Apr 1801, LUCY GOODELL, b. at Pomfret, 22 Apr 1779 daughter of Amasa and Lucy(-) Goodell;[491] Lucy d. 2 Apr 1829. Several sources give the name of Lucy's mother as Lydia Chandler, and that may be correct, but the birth transcription for Lucy gives her mother's name as Lucy.

---

487 Griggs, *Early Homesteads of Pomfret and Hampton*

488 *Connecticut Wills and Probate, 1609-1999*, Will of Ephraim Ingalls, Windham, 13 Jan 1795.

489 New Hampshire, Death and Disinterment Records, 1754-1947

490 The transcription in the Barbour Collection has a mistyping of the birth date as 7 Apr 1852.

491 The 1814 will of Amasa Goodell includes a bequest to his daughter Lucy Ingalls.

746) viii MOLLY INGALLS, b. 27 Jan 1766; d. at Dedham, MA, 14 Oct 1859; m. 1st, MOSES OSGOOD, b. 28 Nov 1766 son of Zachariah and Rachel (Kenne) Osgood; Moses d. about 1801. Molly m. 2nd, John Wilson.

ix CHARLES INGALLS, b. 16 Sep 1768; d. 21 Nov 1772

747) x EDMUND INGALLS, b. 7 Sep 1770; d. at Cavendish, VT, 23 Dec 1850; m. 16 Apr 1801,[492] DOROTHY WHITE, b. at Westford, MA, 26 Oct 1776 daughter of Samuel and Hephzibah (Barrett) White; Dorothy d. 21 Aug 1853 (will 10 Sep 1852).

xi DORCAS INGALLS, b. 3 Apr 1772; d. 6 Dec 1774.

181) ZEBADIAH INGALLS *(Mary Stevens Ingalls[3], Sarah Abbott Stevens[2], George[1])*, b. 3 Nov 1729 son of James and Mary (Stevens) Ingalls; d. at Pomfret, 11 Jun 1800; m. 20 Feb 1755, ESTHER GOODELL, b. at Pomfret, 19 May 1735 daughter of Zachariah and Hannah (Cheney) Goodell; Esther d. 30 Sep 1778.

Zebadiah Ingalls lived on his father's homestead and after 1750 he built the FitzHenry Paine House in Pomfret. The family lived in this home until after the Revolution. Zebadiah then sold this property to his son Lemuel and Zebadiah returned to the family homestead. Zebadiah also had a blacksmith shop.[493]

Captain Zebadiah Ingalls was the leader of a militia company and on 22 April 1775 led his company in the march to Lexington.

Zebadiah Ingalls wrote his will 11 May 1799. He includes bequests to his beloved wife (who is not named), son Lemuel receives all the real estate, son James has already received his portion, son Oliver receives $200, daughter Esther Abbott receives $17, daughter Aly Holbrook receives $17, daughter Mary Williams receives $35, and daughter Allethiah Ingalls receives $117.[494]

There are birth records for 13 children of Zebadiah and Esther at Pomfret.

748) i LEMUEL INGALLS, b. 6 Dec 1755; d. at Pomfret, 17 Nov 1839; m. 24 Aug 1780, DOROTHY SUMNER, b. 20 Aug 1759 daughter of Samuel and Dorothy (Williams) Sumner; Dorothy d. 10 Mar 1851.

ii ZEBADIAH INGALLS, b. 19 Apr 1757; d. 17 Sep 1779. Zebadiah served in the Revolutionary War.

iii SILVANIUS INGALLS, b. 27 Jan 1759; d. 25 Sep 1776.

749) iv JAMES INGALLS, b. 31 Dec 1760; d. at Middlefield, NY, 19 Mar 1813; m. at Brooklyn, CT, 2 Feb 1786, SARAH WILLIAMS, b. at Pomfret, 12 May 1760 daughter of Thomas and Meriam (Wolcott) Williams; Sarah d. 27 Jan 1831.

603) v ESTHER INGALLS, b. 26 Nov 1762; d. at Providence, RI, 4 Feb 1851; m. 28 Jun 1781, her third cousin, STEPHEN ABBOTT, b. at Pomfret, 20 Oct 1757 son of Nathan and Eunice (Marsh) Abbott; Stephen d. at North Providence, RI, 24 Jul 1813. This is the same as Family #143, child vii.

vi ALICE INGALLS, b. 28 Oct 1764; d. at Woodstock, 8 Dec 1838; m. 13 Feb 1783, CALVIN HOLBROOK, b. at Pomfret, 10 Aug 1758 son of Ebenezer and Mary (Osgood) Holbrook; Calvin d. 4 Aug 1845. Alice and Calvin did not have children, at least not children for whom there is a record or who lived to adulthood. Calvin's will makes bequests to his brothers and sisters and their heirs.

vii OLIVE INGALLS, b. 20 Oct 1766; d. 13 Feb (year not given).

750) viii MARY "MOLLY" INGALLS, b. 31 Jul 1768; d. at Danielson, CT, 21 Apr 1839; m. 2 Dec 1790, ELEAZER WILLIAMS, b. at Pomfret, 29 Nov 1764 son of Samuel and Susannah (Danielson) Williams; Eleazer d. 16 Sep 1841.

751) ix OLIVER INGALLS, b. 7 Apr 1770; d. at Pomfret, 10 Apr 1815; m. Dec 1803, his niece,[495] BETSEY ABBOTT, b. likely at Providence, 4 May 1786 daughter of Stephen and Esther (Ingalls) Abbott; Betsey d. 17 Feb 1839 (will written at Providence, RI, 7 Feb 1839).

x OLIVE INGALLS, b. 16 May 1772; no further record and she is not living at the time of her father's will. See the note for Chloe below.

xi ALLETHIAH INGALLS, b. 15 Mar 1774; unmarried at the time of her father's will in 1799.

---

[492] *Vermont, Vital Records, 1720-1908.*

[493] Griggs, *Early Homesteads of Pomfret and Hampton*

[494] *Connecticut Wills and Probate, 1609-1999*, Probate of Zebadiah Ingalls, Hartford, 1800, Case number 2295.

[495] Although the relationship between Betsey and her husband is unusual, it seems to be true. Betsey Abbott Ingalls's gravestone (buried in Swan Point Cemetery in Providence) includes an inscription that she is the wife of Oliver and the daughter of Colonel Stephen Abbott and this makes Betsey the niece of her husband Oliver Ingalls. Oliver Ingalls was the brother of Esther Ingalls who married Colonel Stephen Abbott.

xii JOHN INGALLS, b. 26 Aug 1776; d. 23 Jan 1777.

xiii CHLOE INGALLS; there is not a birth record, just a death record that has just 26 Apr 17__. The transcription for this record suggests that the name is also torn, and Chloe seems to be a best guess for the name. It is possible that this is the death record for the daughter Olive for whom there is no further record after her birth.

182) ABIAH INGALLS *(Mary Stevens Ingalls³, Sarah Abbott Stevens², George¹)*, b. 19 Oct 1731 daughter of James and Mary (Stevens) Ingalls; d. likely at Palmer or Monson, MA; m. 16 Mar 1753, NATHANIEL ROGERS, b. about 1730 of not yet established origins but *possibly* the son of Nathaniel and Mary (Haggit) Rogers and born at Billerica; d. probably about 1786, but no records were located.[496]

The children of this family should be considered preliminary at least the youngest four children. There are records for the oldest three children born at Pomfret and for the next three children born at Monson. There is some at least circumstantial evidence for placing the remaining four children in this family.

752) i NATHANIEL ROGERS, b. at Pomfret, 18 Nov 1755; d. at Salem, CT, 12 Feb 1799; m. 23 Sep 1782, SARAH TUBBS, b. at Colchester, 1755 daughter of Alpheus Tubbs; Sarah d. about 1842.[497]

ii MOLLY ROGERS, b. at Pomfret, 6 Oct 1757.

iii ELIAS ROGERS, b. at Pomfret, 11 Aug 1759.

753) iv ABISHAI ROGERS, b. at Monson, 1 Feb 1762; d. at Sheldon, NY, 18 Jul 1831; m. 1st, Feb 1786, SARAH HAWKS who d. at Hawley, 1790; m. 2nd, 15 Mar 1792, ELIZABETH RUDD, b. 28 Jun 1765 daughter of Nathaniel and Alice (Kingsley) Rudd; Elizabeth d. 18 Jun 1848.

754) v SIMEON ROGERS, b. at Monson, 1 Feb 1762; d. at Whitestown, NY, 18 Jun 1848; m. ANNA (-), b. 1765 and d. 1849.[498]

755) vi JAMES AUGUSTUS ROGERS, b. at Monson, 2 May 1765; d. at Rockport, OH, 5 Aug 1837; m. 17 Nov 1790, DOROTHY LEONARD, b. at Rutland, MA, 6 Apr 1759 daughter of Andrew and Hannah (Pierce) Leonard; Dorothy d. at Pownal, VT, 5 Jun 1796. James m. 2nd, JEMIMA ROOT.

vii ABIAH ROGERS who perhaps married GIDEON GRAVES 3 Oct 1786 at Palmer. Gideon was b. at Palmer, 25 Aug 1758 son of Daniel and Joanna (-) Graves. Abiah the wife of Gideon died about 1787 and no children are known from this marriage. Gideon then married Hannah Dake.

756) viii DEBORAH ROGERS; m. about 1790, her third cousin once removed (and George Abbott descendant), WILLIAM FARNSWORTH, b. 15 Nov 1766 son of William and Hephzibah (Chandler) Farnsworth. The children of this couple include Oren Rogers Farnsworth and James Ingalls Farnsworth.

757) ix OREN ROGERS, b. at Monson about 1770; d. at Charlemont, MA, 15 Oct 1853; m. 23 Mar 1797, ABY BIRGE, b. at Deerfield, 22 Aug 1774 daughter of John and Esther (Pierce) Birge.

758) x MOSES ROGERS is also a possibility of a child in this family; he died 1 Feb 1808 with a child named Abishai. His wife was Mehitable Sears who was born 21 Dec 1778 daughter of Rowland Sears. Moses Rogers was a mill keeper in Hawley, MA and died when he was crushed by the wheel when trying to remove ice from the wheel.

187) SAMUEL CARLETON *(Deborah Stevens Carleton³, Sarah Abbott Stevens², George¹)*, b. 11 Aug 1731 son of Samuel and Deborah (Stevens) Carleton; d. at Salem, 25 Mar 1804; m. 27 Oct 1754, EUNICE HUNT, b. 25 Oct 1730 daughter of William and Eunice (Bowditch) Hunt; Eunice d. at Salem, 12 Aug 1827.

Samuel Carleton was an officer in the continental army during the Revolutionary War including service at Valley Forge. He was also a member of the Massachusetts General Court. He was a master mariner and member of the Masons.[499]

---

[496] This is the date used by the SAR and the DAR as his approximated death, although it is not clear why this date was chosen.

[497] Rogers, *James Rogers of New London, Ct.*, p 120

[498] Information from SAR

[499] *Massachusetts: Grand Lodge of Masons Membership Cards, 1733-1990.* Online database. *AmericanAncestors.org.* New England Historic Genealogical Society, 2010. (From records held by the Grand Lodge of Ancient Free and Accepted Masons of Massachusetts.)

The 1827 probate record for Eunice Hunt Carleton includes the following heirs-at-law who sign approving James Barr (husband of daughter Eunice) as administrator of the estate: John Carleton, Deborah Helme, Hannah Carleton, Elizabeth Carleton, and Elisabeth Carleton, Jr. The value of the estate was $800 in real estate and $32.49 for her personal estate.[500] Elizabeth Carleton, Jr. in the probate documents in the daughter of Eunice's son Benjamin who died in 1820.

Samuel Carleton and Eunice Hunt had eight children whose births are recorded at Salem.

764) i EUNICE CARLETON, b. 22 Dec 1754; d. at Salem, Mar 1838; m. 23 Dec 1779, JAMES BARR, b. at Salem, 1755 son of James and Mary (Ropes) Barr; James d. 19 Jan 1848.

ii SAMUEL CARLETON, b. 6 May 1757; no further clear record. It is possible that he married, but if so he did not have children as none are listed as heirs in either the estate of his mother or the will of his brother John who left his estate to siblings, nieces, and nephews. It is possible that Samuel died before adulthood.

765) iii DEBORAH CARLETON, b. 17 Dec 1759; d. at Salem, Apr 1831; m. 5 Oct 1783, HUGH HELME whose origins are unknown; Hugh d. 1792 (probate of estate 14 July 1792).

iv HANNAH CARLETON, b. 5 Sep 1762; d. 7 Sep 1842. Hannah did not marry.

766) v BENJAMIN CARLETON, b. 5 Jun 1765; d. 8 Sep 1820; m. 25 Mar 1787, his first cousin, ELIZABETH HOLMAN, b. 1762 daughter of Samuel and Ruth (Hunt) Holman; Elizabeth d. 25 Dec 1801.

vi MARY CARLETON, b. 29 Aug 1767; d. 18 Dec 1814. Mary did not marry.

vii JOHN CARLETON, b. 6 Nov 1770; d. at Philadelphia, 12 Aug 1847. He was a U.S. naval officer and sailing master. His will has bequests to his sisters, nieces, and nephew.

viii ELIZABETH CARLETON, b. 6 May 1773; d. after 1855 (still living at the 1855 Massachusetts Census when her niece Elizabeth, the daughter of Benjamin, was living with her).

188) HANNAH CARLETON *(Deborah Stevens Carleton[3], Sarah Abbott Stevens[2], George[1])*, b. 26 Jul 1734 daughter of Samuel and Deborah (Stevens) Carleton; d. 14 May 1824; m. 30 Mar 1756, JACOB CROWNINSHIELD, b. 9 Jan 1732/3 son of John and Anstus (Williams) Crowninshield; Jacob was a mariner who died on a passage from Jamaica in Nov 1774.

Captain Jacob Crowninshield was a member of the renowned Crowninshield mariner family. Jacob was lost at sea. He did not leave a will and his estate entered probate 4 January 1775. Hannah Crowninshield was administrator of the estate. The estate was declared insolvent and it was ordered to be sold 17 February 1790. The widow's dower had been set out to Hannah but was returned to the estate for sale in 1790, although she retained her right to live in a portion of the house. The estate included two Negros who claimed and took their freedom.[501]

Hannah Carleton Crowninshield's will was written 12 June 1810 and it was recorded 6 July 1824. Hannah's daughter Hannah and son Benjamin were executors of the estate. "Whereas the providence of God has blessed with prosperity my beloved son Benjamin Crowninshield, and he has no need of my assistance, I do will and bequeath to my only daughter, Hanna Crowninshield, the companion and friend of my widowhood, in reward for her faithful duty, all the property of every name. . . " Hannah did add a codicil in which "being disposed to express my fondest regards to my son Benjamin, I do will and bequeath to my said son Benjamin, the family tankard, as the best testimony of my affection."[502]

Hannah Carleton and Jacob Crowninshield lived in half of what is now known as the Crowninshield-Bentley house in Salem. This house was built about 1727 most likely by Jacob's grandfather. After Jacob's death, Hannah and her daughter lived in the East half of the house and supported themselves by taking in boarders. The Reverend William Bentley was one of the boarders from 1791 to 1819, and he kept a diary of the daily goings on in Salem. Hannah's son Benjamin inherited the West half of the house. Benjamin was quite successful and made substantial improvements to his half. In 1795, Benjamin's half was valued at $1,350 while his mother's half had a value of $250.[503]

There is record evidence for three children of Hannah Carleton and Jacob Crowninshield.

767) i BENJAMIN CROWNINSHIELD, b. 15 Feb 1758; d. at Salem, 1836; m. 9 Nov 1780, MARY LAMBERT, b. at Salem, Nov 1760 daughter of Joseph and Mary (Foote) Lambert;[504] Mary d. at Charlestown, 21 Jun 1851.

ii JOHN CROWNINSHIELD, b. 1762; d. at Salem, 19 Feb 1786; m. SARAH HATHORNE, b. about 1761 daughter of Daniel and Rachel (Phelps) Hathorne; Sarah d. 18 Jan 1829. John and Sarah do not seem to have had children. In her 1829 will, Sarah left her estate to her sister Ruth Hathorne. *John, m., mate with*

---

500 *Essex County, MA: Probate File Papers, 1638-1881.* Probate of Eunice Carleton, 2 Oct 1827, Case number 4642.

501 *Essex County, MA: Probate File Papers, 1638-1881.* Probate of Jacob Crowninshield, 4 Jan 1775, Case number 6677.

502 *Essex County, MA: Probate File Papers, 1638-1881.* Probate of Hannah Crowninshield, 6 Jul 1824, Case number 6675.

503 Crowninshield-Bentley House, Peabody Essex Museum, 2006. http://teh.salemstate.edu/educatorsguide/pages/Federal/CBHouse.pdf

504 Belknap, *The Lambert Family of Salem, Massachusetts*, p 30

Capt. Lambert, s. wid. Hannah [s. Jacob and Hannah, h. Sarah (Hathorne)], dysentery, Feb. 19, 1786, a. 24 y. CR4.

iii HANNAH CROWNINSHIELD, b. 1764; d. at Salem, Apr 1832. Hannah did not marry.

189) MARY CARLETON *(Deborah Stevens Carleton³, Sarah Abbott Stevens², George¹)*, b. about 1738 daughter of Samuel and Deborah (Stevens) Carleton; d. 24 Dec 1805; m. 12 Jul 1759, JOHN BOWDITCH, b. 3 Apr 1732 son of Ebenezer and Mary (Turner) Bowditch; John was a mariner and died at sea before 1797 and perhaps in 1793.

A son in this family, John Bowditch, died in April 1793 and there is an associated probate record for the son. There is not a death record or probate record for the father. It is certainly possible that father and son died in the same marine disaster and the elder John is deceased before 1797 when his widow wrote her will.

Mary Carleton Bowditch wrote her will 22 November 1797. She divided her wearing apparel equally among her three daughters namely Mary Hunt, Hannah Ingersoll, and Deborah Moriarty. The remainder of her personal estate is to be sold. She also orders that as soon as convenient that the one-fourth part of her pew in the East Meeting House and one-fourth of a plot of land on Cromwell Street (that she owns with other heirs) be sold. She bequeaths to her daughter Deborah Moriarty the southern part of her real estate where her house now stands which is on the west side of Union Street in Salem. The northern half of her real estate where her own house stands is to be let out along with the house; the rents are to be accumulated and draw interest and the interest reinvested until her two grandchildren, Nancy Bowditch and Polly Bowditch, are at lawful age or the age of marriage. Nancy and Polly will each receive one-fifth part of the accumulation of the value of the estate. Her three daughters also each receive one-fifth of that amount. Her daughters Mary Hunt and Deborah Moriarty are named executors.[505] Granddaughter Nancy Bowditch is the daughter of son Samuel who died in 1791 and Polly Bowditch is the daughter of son John who died in 1793.

There are records for seven children born at Salem.

768) i MARY BOWDITCH, b. Jun 1760; d. at Salem, 18 Mar 1829; m. 7 Apr 1782, as his second wife, LEWIS HUNT, b. 23 Mar 1746 son of William and Eunice Bowditch Hunt; Lewis d. 22 Oct 1797.

769) ii HANNAH BOWDITCH, b. Dec 1761; d. at Salem, 14 Dec 1825; m. 21 Jul 1792, as his second wife, JOHN INGERSOLL, b. Jun 1756 son of Nathaniel and Bethiah (Gardner) Ingersoll; John d. 12 Feb 1840.

770) iii JOHN BOWDITCH, b. Mar 1764; d. at sea, Apr 1793; m. 11 Mar 1791, POLLY WELMAN (widow of Samuel Cook), b. about 1760 whose parents are uncertain; Polly d. at Salem 28 Apr 1844.

771) iv DEBORAH BOWDITCH, b. Oct 1767; d. at Salem, 4 Jul 1823; m. 31 Oct 1782, THOMAS MORIARTY, b. in Cork, Ireland about 1760 son of John and Margaret (Moriarty) Moriarty;[506] Thomas d. 1790 (date of probate 5 Aug 1790). Some sources give his death as 1787 off the coast of Guinea, but that does not seem accurate.

772) v SAMUEL BOWDITCH, b. May 1769; d. at sea, 21 Mar 1791; m. 15 Aug 1790; ANNA "NANCY" WELMAN, baptized 2 Sep 1770 daughter of Samuel and Mary (Kempton) Welman. Nancy m. 2nd, William Richardson (or Richardson Russell, both names are given on the transcription of the marriage record).

vi SARAH BOWDITCH, b. May 1770; no further record; not living at the time of her mother's will.

vii EBENEZER BOWDITCH, b. Oct 1771; no further record and not living at the time of his mother's will.

190) WILLIAM CARLETON *(Deborah Stevens Carleton³, Sarah Abbott Stevens², George¹)*, b. 8 Apr 1744 son of Samuel and Deborah (Stevens) Carleton; d. Jun 1791 while on a trip to Barbados; m. 1st, (-) Palfrey who died before 1777. m. 2nd, at Boston, 1 May 1777, MARY FARMER whose origins are uncertain but perhaps the daughter of Paul and Thankful (Sprague) Farmer of Boston.

There is little information available about this family. There is record evidence for one son of William, who seems to be from a first marriage to a woman with the last name of Palfrey. That son was the editor of the Salem Register and this information is given for the transcription of his death recorded at Salem: William [editor of the Salem Register. NR9], printer, s. William and ——— (Palfry), h. ——— (Cooke), fever, July 24, 1805, a. 34 y. CR4

---

[505] *Massachusetts Wills and Probate Records 1635-1991,* Essex, Probate Record, Mary Bowditch; will and probate (15 Jan 1806), Case 2889.

[506] O'Laughlin, *Families of Co. Kerry Ireland*, p. 106

773) i WILLIAM CARLETON, b. 1771 (based on age at time of death); d. at Salem, 24 Jul 1805; m. at Salem, 22 May 1796, ELIZABETH COOKE, b. about 1771 daughter of Charles and (Stone) Cooke; Elizabeth d. at Salem, 22 Aug 1805. Salem vital records: *Elizabeth, d. Charles and____ (Stone) Cooke [proprietress of the Salem Register, G. R. 9.], wid. William, consumption. Aug. 25, 1805, a. 34 y.* William was the publisher of the *Salem Register* and his wife continued as publisher after his death until her death a few months later.

Grandchildren of Benjamin Abbott and Sarah Farnum

125) BENJAMIN ABBOT *(Benjamin³, Benjamin², George¹)*, b. 21 Oct 1723 son of Benjamin and Mary (Carleton) Abbott; d. at Hollis, NH, 1770 (probate 13 Jul 1770)[507]; m. 2 Apr 1747, his second cousin, ELIZABETH ABBOTT *(George³, George², George¹)*, b. 5 Nov 1727 daughter of George and Mary (Phillips) Abbott; Elizabeth d. at Westford, about 1802. Same as Family #125 previously covered.

191) DANIEL ABBOTT *(Benjamin³, Benjamin², George¹)*, b. 29 Dec 1725 son of Benjamin and Mary (Carleton) Abbott; d. Apr 1793;[508] m. 3 Apr 1756, LUCY PARKER, b. 5 Jun 1732 daughter of Thomas and Lydia (Richardson) Parker; the date of death of Lucy is not known.

The births of four children of Daniel Abbott and Lucy Parker are recorded at Dracut.

i DANIEL ABBOTT, b. 8 Sep 1757; d. at Claremont, NH, 10 Aug 1827. Daniel did not marry.

774) ii WILLIAM ABBOTT, b. 22 Feb 1760; d. likely at Bedford, NH; m. at Dracut, 13 Nov 1784, MARTHA "PATTY" COBURN, b. at Dracut about 1765.[509]

775) iii SAMUEL ABBOTT, b. 16 Feb 1765; d. at Claremont, NH, 13 Apr 1840; m. by 1794, his first cousin, ELIZABETH COTTON, b. about 1768 daughter of Rev. Samuel and Elizabeth (Parker) Cotton of Claremont; Elizabeth d. at Claremont, NH, 7 Jun 1837.[510] The mothers of Samuel Abbott and Elizabeth Cotton were sisters.

776) iv JONATHAN ABBOTT, b. 20 Jan 1772; d. at Litchfield, NH, 4 Jul 1855; m. 1st, 21 Feb 1795, REBECCA MASSEY, b. 24 Mar 1772 daughter of Bartholomew and Mary (Fox) Massey; Rebecca d. 19 Dec 1795. Jonathan m. 2nd, 31 Dec 1800, DOLLY PARKER, b. 12 Sep 1779.[511] Dolly died at Litchfield, 19 Sep 1824.[512] After Dolly's death, Jonathan married a widow named Miranda who d. at Claremont 23 Feb 1854.

192) MARY ABBOTT *(Benjamin³, Benjamin², George¹)*, b. 21 Jul 1732 daughter of Benjamin and Abigail (Abbott) Abbott; d. at Milford, NH, 9 Aug 1798; m. 13 Nov 1759, NEHEMIAH BARKER, b. at Methuen, 11 Feb 1734 son of Ebenezer and Abigail (Morse) Barker; Nehemiah d. 20 Jan 1810.

Nehemiah Barker was an inn owner in Methuen from 1777 to 1785. He also owned one-half of an iron works. This family relocated to Milford, New Hampshire about 1785.[513] Nehemiah Barker was listed as a taxpayer in Milford in 1794.[514]

Mary Abbott and Nehemiah Barker had five children, the oldest daughter's birth recorded at Andover and the youngest four at Methuen.

i ABIGAIL BARKER, b. 24 Jan 1762; d. Jul 1793.[515]

777) ii JOEL BARKER, b. 11 Aug 1764; d. at Milford, 5 Dec 1832; m. at Milford, 24 Dec 1793, SARAH "SALLY" FOSTER, b. at Milford, 1774 daughter of Edward and Phebe (Pierce) Foster; Sarah d. 5 Sep 1820. Joel m. 2nd, 27 Nov 1821, CATHERINE LOVEJOY of Bow.[516]

---

507 New Hampshire, Death and Burials Record Index, 1654-1949, ancestry.com

508 Abbot and Abbot, *Genealogical Register of Descendants*

509 *The History of Dracut*, p 130, gives Patty's parents as Jacob and Lydia, but their daughter Patty died unmarried in 1802 (at least the death record gives her name as Patty Caburn).

510 Spofford, *Gravestone Records: From the Ancient Cemeteries in the Town of Claremont*, p 6, Elizabeth (Cotton) Abbott wife of Samuel, June 7, 1837, 69y; Samuel Abbott, April 13, 1840, 76y

511 Family Tree Samplers, 1759-1894. Online database. AmericanAncestors.org. New England Historic Genealogical Society, 2013. (From the collection of Dan and Marty Campanelli.) Vital records for this family are contained in a sampler stitched by Dolly Parker.

512 Findagrave.com memorial ID 167676976

513 Charlotte Helen Abbott, Early Records of the Barker Family of Andover. https://www.mhl.org/sites/default/files/files/Abbott/Barker%20Family.pdf

514 History of Hillsborough County, New Hampshire, published 1885

515 Abbot and Abbot, *Genealogical Register of Descendants*, p 68

516 Ramsdell, *History of Milford, Volume 1*, p 576

iii MARY BARKER, b. 19 Sep 1766; d. 23 Oct 1766.

778) iv MARY BARKER, b. 18 Dec 1767; d. at Hollis, 3 Sep 1824; m. at Hollis, 6 Jan 1791, JACOB SPAULDING, b. at Chelmsford, 13 Dec 1767 son of Benjamin and Mary (Spaulding) Spaulding. Jacob m. 2nd, Susanna Robertson. Jacob d. at Hollis, 14 May 1838.

779) v DORCAS BARKER, b. 4 Sep 1770; d. at Peterborough, NH, 25 Jul 1840; m. About 1792, MERRILL PIERCE, b. at Chelmsford, 29 Jan 1764 son of Benjamin and Elizabeth (Merrill) Pierce. Merrill Pierce was the brother of Phebe Pierce (born 1748) the mother of Sarah Foster who married Dorcas's older brother Joel.

193) ABIGAIL ABBOTT *(Benjamin^3, Benjamin^2, George^1)*, b. 13 Jan 1733/4 daughter of Benjamin and Abigail (Abbott) Abbott; d. 1 Feb 1807; m. 1 Jun 1758, her second cousin, once removed, JOHN ABBOT *(John^4, John^3, John^2, George^1)*, b. 12 Sep 1735 son of John and Phebe (Fiske) Abbot; John d. at Andover, 24 Apr 1818.

John Abbot lived on the farm that he inherited from his father. He was apparently successful as he was able to pay for the college educations of three of his sons.

The estate of John Abbot entered probate 20 October 1818. His will, written 8 March 1805, has bequests for the following persons: dear and beloved wife Abigail (her yearly maintenance includes 50 pounds of good pork and 100 pounds of good beef plus all the other things she needs), eldest and well beloved son John, second and well beloved son Ezra (gets all the land in the town of Wilton), third and well beloved son Benjamin, eldest and well beloved daughter Abigail, well beloved daughter Elizabeth, third and well beloved daughter Phebe, youngest, and well beloved son Abiel. He notes having paid for the educations of John, Benjamin, and Abiel and that is considered part of their portion. The books are divided among the seven children. Abigail is mentioned in the will; however, she died between the time of the will and her husband's death.[517]

The births of eight children of Abigail and John Abbott are recorded at Andover.

i JOHN ABBOT, b. 8 Apr 1759; d. at Andover, 2 Jul 1843. John Abbot attended Harvard and graduated in 1784. Ill health prevented his entering the ministry which was his original plan. He was a tutor at Harvard for five years and later was a cashier at a Portland bank. He then found a position at Bowdoin College. His tenure as a professor of classical languages was rather lackluster. He was described as awkward and absentminded and fell victim to practical jokes.[518] He was criticized for his lack of scholarship. He later assumed the position of librarian which better suited him. He continued in this position at Bowdoin until 1828. He resided in Waterford, Maine. He was living with his brother in Andover at the time of his death. John did not marry.

780) ii EZRA ABBOTT, b. 3 Dec 1760; d. at Andover, 22 Jan 1844; m. 24 Apr 1798, his third cousin once removed (and George Abbott descendant), HANNAH POOR, b. 15 Jan 1770 daughter of Daniel and Hannah (Frye) Poor; Hannah d. 11 Sep 1861.

781) iii BENJAMIN ABBOTT, b. 17 Sep 1762; d. at Exeter, NH, 25 Oct 1849; m. 1st, HANNAH TRACY EMERY, b. at Exeter, 7 Mar 1771 daughter of John and Margaret (Gookin) Emery; Hannah d. 6 Dec 1793. Benjamin m. 2nd, at Boston, 1 May 1798, MARY PERKINS, b. at Boston, 24 May 1769 daughter of James and Elizabeth (Peck) Perkins; Mary d. at Exeter, 13 Mar 1863. Hannah Tracy Emery was mentioned in the diary of John Quincy Adams having met her on a visit to a Mr. Carter. "Miss H. Emery was there, a young lady with a beautiful countenance, an elegant person, and (I am told) an amiable mind."[519]

782) iv ABIGAIL ABBOTT, b. 15 Sep 1764; d. at Portland, ME, 22 Apr 1841; m. at Andover, 21 Apr 1791, WILLIAM DOUGLAS, baptized at Rutland, MA, 29 Mar 1761 son of Robert and Elinor (Fales) Douglas; William d. at Portland, 4 Dec 1827.

783) v ELIZABETH ABBOTT, b. 2 Aug 1766; d. at Peterborough, NH, 6 Apr 1853; m. 19 May 1796, her first cousin, ABIEL ABBOT, b. at Wilton, 14 Dec 1765 son of Abiel and Dorcas (Abbott) Abbot; Abiel d. at Cambridge, MA, 31 Jan 1859. This is a quadruple Abbott marriage; all four of the parents of this couple are Abbotts. Dr. Abiel Abbot was a distinguished minister and scholar. This is the same as Family #197, child i.

---

[517] *Essex County, MA: Probate File Papers, 1638-1881*. Probate of John Abbot, 20 Oct 1818, Case number 74.

[518] Hatch, *History of Bowdoin College*, pp 16-17

[519] John Quincy Adams, Charles Francis Adams, 1903, Life in a New England Town 1787, 1788: Diary of John Quincy Adams While a Student in the Office of Theophilus Parsons at Newburyport, p 45

784) vi PHEBE ABBOTT, b. 18 Nov 1768; d. at Portland, ME, 30 Apr 1852; m. 9 Apr 1789, EDWARD CARLETON, b. at Bradford, 2 Jul 1762 son of Dudley and Abigail (Wilson) Carleton; Edward d. 12 Jun 1825.

785) vii ABIEL ABBOT, b. 17 Aug 1770; d. at New York in transit from Cuba, 7 Jun 1828; m. at Haverhill, 19 Jul 1796, EUNICE WALES, b. at Roxbury, 21 Sep 1772 daughter of Ebenezer and Eunice (Davis) Wales; Eunice d. at Dorchester, 29 Dec 1831.

viii JACOB ABBOTT, b. 25 Jul 1771; d. Jul 1772.

194) ABIEL ABBOT *(Benjamin*[3]*, Benjamin*[2]*, George*[1]*)*, b. 24 Jul 1735 son of Benjamin and Abigail (Abbott) Abbott; d. 24 Jun 1764; m. 5 Feb 1761, his third cousin PHEBE BALLARD, b. 25 Jul 1738 daughter of Josiah and Mary (Chandler) Ballard. Phebe m. 2nd as his second wife, her third cousin (and great grandson of George Abbott), JAMES HOLT son of Nicholas and Dorcas (Abbott) Holt; Phebe d. 9 Jun 1815.

Abiel Abbot, called Dr. Abiel Abbot, attended Harvard for a time. He did study medicine and served as a physician during the French and Indian War.

Abiel Abbot did not leave a will. Joshua Holt, Jr. was administrator of the estate. There were many creditors to the estate and it was declared insolvent.[520]

Abiel Abbot and Phebe Ballard had two children born at Andover.

i ABIEL ABBOTT, b. 6 Nov 1761; d. 18 Aug 1828. Abiel did not marry. He did not leave a will but had many creditors and his property was sold at auction to settle the estate.

786) ii BENJAMIN ABBOTT, b. 28 May 1763; d. at Newburyport, 18 Aug 1821; m. 21 Nov 1786, JOANNA HOLMES, b. at Newburyport, 1765 daughter of Francis and Mary (Smith) Holmes; Joanna d. 11 Aug 1828.

195) ELIZABETH ABBOTT *(Benjamin*[3]*, Benjamin*[2]*, George*[1]*)*, b. 27 Oct 1738 daughter of Benjamin and Abigail (Abbott) Abbott; d. at Conway, NH, 12 Oct 1789;[521] m. 1st, 1 Jun 1758, EBENEZER CUMMINGS, b. at Groton, 17 Apr 1735 son of William and Lucy (Colburn) Cummings; Ebenezer d. of smallpox, 1 Jun 1778. Elizabeth m. 2nd as his fourth wife, THOMAS MERRILL, b. at Haverhill, 5 Feb 1723/4 son of John and Lydia (Haynes) Merrill; Thomas had married as his first wife, Phebe Abbott (Family #139).

Ebenezer Cummings enlisted in the army for service in the Revolutionary War. After his death from smallpox in 1778, the town agreed to care for the widows of the Continental soldiers including Mrs. Cummings.[522]

Elizabeth Abbott and Ebenezer Cummings had eight children born at Hollis, New Hampshire.

787) i ELIZABETH CUMMINGS, b. 23 Nov 1759; d. 3 Oct 1812; m. 13 Jun 1780, her third cousin, HENRY LOVEJOY, b. at Andover, 23 Nov 1753 son of William and Hannah (Evans) Lovejoy.

788) ii EBENEZER CUMMINGS, b. 15 Sep 1761; d, about 1842;[523] m. at Surry, NH, 29 May 1787, HANNAH WASHER, b. at Amherst, about 1767 daughter of Stephen and Sarah (Wilkins) Washer; Hannah d. at Andover, VT, 6 Aug 1837.

789) iii ABIGAIL CUMMINGS, b. 1 Jul 1763; d. Nov 1801; m. at Conway, 8 Apr 1788, JOSEPH SEAVEY, b. 1762 son of Jonathan and Comfort (Cates) Seavey; Joseph d. about 1812.

iv BRIDGET CUMMINGS, b. 15 Jul 1765; d. 24 Jan 1786.

790) v LUCY CUMMINGS, b. 9 Jul 1767; d. 15 Oct 1854; m. 8 Apr 1788, PETER PEAVEY, b. at Andover, 14 Apr 1762 son of Thomas and Dorcas (Holt) Peavey; Peter d. at Greenfield, NH, 28 Jul 1836.

791) vi MARY CUMMINGS, b. 22 Oct 1770; d. at Francestown, NH, 6 Apr 1856; m. 8 Dec 1810, WILLIAM BIXBY, b. 4 Nov 1779 son of Edward and Lucy (Barnes) Bixby; William d. 30 Oct 1862. Mary and William had one adopted child.[524]

---

520 *Essex County, MA: Probate File Papers, 1638-1881. Probate of* Abiel Abbot, 12 Jul 1764, *Case number* 6.

521 *New Hampshire, Death and Disinterment Records, 1754-1947*

522 Moorar, *The Cummings Memorial*, p 100

523 His death is reported by several sources as occurring in Wisconsin. However, he seems to have still been in Vermont in 1839 when his son Stephen made an appeal related to his father not having received his military service pension which he first applied for in 1832. It is possible that he relocated to Wisconsin in his very last years, perhaps to be with one of his children, but that needs further investigation. There is a death record for Ebenezer's wife 6 Aug 1837 in Vermont, so Ebenezer was still in Vermont in 1837. Some of his children did relocate to Wisconsin.

524 Cochrane and Wood, *History of Francestown*, p 518

792) vii JACOB ABBOT CUMMINGS, b. 2 Nov 1772; d. at Boston, 24 Feb 1820; m. 9 Aug 1807, ELIZABETH MERRILL, b. at Haverhill, 10 Mar 1781 daughter of Gyles and Lucy (Cushing) Merrill; Elizabeth d. at Portland, ME, 24 Dec 1867.

viii SARAH CUMMINGS, b. 28 Jan 1775; d. after 1850 likely at Francestown. Sarah did not marry. At the 1850 U.S. Census, she was living with her sister Mary Bixby in Francestown.[525]

Elizabeth Abbott and her second husband Thomas Merrill had two children born at Conway, New Hampshire.

793) i JOHN MERRILL, b. 2 Mar 1782; d. at Portland, ME, 7 Jun 1855; m. at Portland, 26 Sep 1820, MARY SOUTHGATE BOYD, b. at Portland, 20 Jan 1797 daughter of Joseph Coffin and Isabella (Southgate) Boyd; Mary d. Apr 1861.[526]

ii BENJAMIN MERRILL, b. 15 Mar 1784; d. at Salem, MA, 30 Jul 1847.[527] Benjamin did not marry. He did graduate from Harvard in 1804 and was awarded an LLD in 1845. He worked as an attorney, practicing first in Lynn, but for most of his career practiced in Salem. In his will, he makes bequests to his siblings Jonathan A. Merrill, Sally Cummings, and John Merrill.[528] Jonathan and Sally are half-siblings.

196) ANNA ABBOTT *(Benjamin³, Benjamin², George¹)*, b. 13 Oct 1740 daughter of Benjamin and Abigail (Abbott) Abbott; d. at Hollis, NH, 15 Jan 1810; m. Jan 1762, EPHRAIM BURGE, b. at Westford, 1 May 1738 son of Josiah and Susannah (Jaquith) Burge; Ephraim d. 21 Jul 1784.

Ephraim Burge was active in the civic life of Hollis, New Hampshire. For example, during the Revolutionary War, he was part of a 1781 committee to "class the town" which was a method of sectioning the town to answer call-ups for more soldiers for the war. He was also part of a committee charged with caring for the families of soldiers.[529]

There are records for the births of ten children at Hollis, New Hampshire.

794) i ANNA BURGE, b. 20 Nov 1762; d. at Dunstable, 31 Oct 1794; m. 17 Nov 1783, PHINEAS FLETCHER, b. 28 Nov 1757 son of Joseph and Elizabeth (Underwood) Fletcher. Phineas m. 2nd, Alice Ames; Phineas d. 31 Jul 1833.

795) ii EPHRAIM BURGE, b. 7 Jun 1764; d. at Hollis, 2 Mar 1853; m. 28 Jan 1793, PATTY BALDWIN, b. at Amherst, NH, 2 Mar 1764 daughter of Nahum and Mary (Lowe) Baldwin; Patty d. 2 Aug 1822.

iii JOSIAH BURGE, b. 15 Apr 1766; d. 25 Mar 1790. Josiah graduated from Harvard in 1787[530] and was a preacher.

iv JACOB BURGE, b. 7 Jan 1768; d. at Hollis, 10 Jun 1809. Jacob does not seem to have married.

v SUSANNAH BURGE, b. 5 Dec 1769; died young

796) vi SUSANNAH "SUKEY" BURGE, b. 21 Jul 1773; d. at Hollis, 6 Sep 1816; m. 16 Apr 1799, THOMAS FARLEY, b. 28 Dec 1769 son of Caleb and Elizabeth (Farley) Farley; Thomas d. 17 Mar 1832.

vii ABIAL BURGE, b. 27 May and d. 30 May 1775.

viii SARAH "SALLY" BURGE, b. 2 May 1777; d. at Bedford, NH, Oct 1825; m. at Hollis, 14 Apr 1821, as his second wife, Deacon STEPHEN THURSTON, b. at Rowley, 2 Jan 1770 son of Daniel and Judith (Chute) Thurston. Stephen married a third time after Sally's death; Stephen died 13 Sep 1833. Sally did not have any children.

---

525 *1850 United States Federal Census*, Year: 1850; Census Place: Francestown, Hillsborough, New Hampshire; Roll: M432_434; Page: 37A; Image: 75.

526 Chapman, *Monograph of the Southgate Family*, p 27

527 Benja[min], b. Conway, N. H., councillor-at-law, s. Thomas [and ____ (Abbot), N. R. 9.], apoplexy, July 30, 1847, a. 73 y. Massachusetts: Vital Records, 1620-1850

528 *Essex County, MA: Probate File Papers, 1638-1881. Probate of* Benjamin Merrill, 3 Aug 1847, *Case number* 46886.

529 Worcester, *History of the Town of Hollis*

530 Harvard University, *Quinquennial Catalogue*, p 140

797) ix SAMUEL BURGE, b. 28 Mar 1779; d. at Francestown, NH, 5 Sep 1824; m. by 1805, ANNA MAY,[531] b. 1787 (age 30 at time of death); d. 30 Oct 1817. Samuel m. 2nd, 5 Feb 1822, DEBORAH STARETT, b. 26 Dec 1782 daughter of William and Abigail (Fisher) Starett.

x BENJAMIN BURGE, b. 5 Aug 1782; d. at Hollis, 15 Jun 1815. Benjamin attended Harvard graduating in 1805 earning a medical degree.[532] Benjamin does not seem to have married.

197) DORCAS ABBOT *(Benjamin3, Benjamin2, George1)*, b. 1 Aug 1744 daughter of Benjamin and Abigail (Abbott) Abbott; d. at Wilton, NH, 23 Feb 1829;[533] m. 20 Nov 1764, her second cousin once removed, ABIEL ABBOT *(John4, John3, John2, George1)*, b. 19 Apr 1741 son of John and Phebe (Fiske) Abbott; Abiel d. 19 Aug 1809.

Dorcas Abbot and Abiel Abbot were born in Andover but had their children and raised their family in Wilton, New Hampshire. Abiel served in the Revolutionary War as paymaster in Baldwin's Regiment. He was a deacon in the church at Wilton. Three of their sons attended Harvard. The total number of children in the family is not certain. There are records for the births of 12 children, and some sources report there were 16 children. In any event, ten children lived to adulthood.

Abiel Abbot wrote his will 4 August 1809. Beloved wife Dorcas Abbott receives the use of the dwelling house, $200, and a lengthy list of provisions to be provided for her support. She also receives one-third part of the pew on the lower floor of the Wilton meeting house for as long as she remains his widow. Beloved son Abiel Abbot receives a one-tenth portion of his books and clothing in addition to the expense of his education which he has already received. Beloved son Jacob receives $100 in addition to the expense of his education. Son Benjamin receives the largest bored gun in addition to the lands and utensils he has received. Son Samuel receives a portion of books plus the expense of education. Daughter Dorcas Putnam receives one-tenth of the books in addition to what she has received. Daughters Abigail Livermore, Persis Lovejoy, Rhoda Peabody receive the same bequest of one-tenth portion of the books in addition to what they have already received. Daughter Phebe Abbot receives her portion of the books and $333, one-half on interest when she reaches the age of 18 and one-half when she reaches age 21. Son Ezra receives all the lands in Wilton, Mason, and Greenfield that have not otherwise been conveyed. Ezra also receives the tools of all kinds including the husbandry and cooper tools. Ezra is named executor.[534]

There are records for the following children born at Wilton, New Hampshire. Of the nine children who married, four of them married cousins who were George Abbott descendants.

783) i ABIEL ABBOT, b. 14 Dec 1765; d. at Cambridge, 31 Jan 1859; m. 19 May 1796, his first cousin, ELIZABETH ABBOTT, b. 2 Aug 1766 daughter of John and Abigail (Abbott) Abbott.

798) ii JACOB ABBOTT, b. 7 Jan 1768; d. 2 Nov 1834; m. 11 Feb 1802, CATHERINE THAYER, b. at Hampton, 28 Sep 1779 daughter of Ebenezer and Martha (Cotton) Thayer; Catherine d. 27 Jan 1843.

799) iii BENJAMIN ABBOTT, b. 17 Mar 1770; d. at Temple, ME, 10 Sep 1823; m. at Andover, 17 Jan 1793, his third cousin, PHEBE ABBOTT, b. at Wilton, 25 Jun 1774 daughter of Jacob and Lydia (Stevens) Abbott; Phebe d. 18 Apr 1857.

800) iv EZRA ABBOT, b. 8 Feb 1772; d. at Wilton, 3 Apr 1847; m. at Coventry, CT, 6 Oct 1799, REBEKAH HALE, b. at Coventry, 9 Jan 1781 daughter of Joseph and Rebecca (Harris) Hale; Rebekah d. 5 May 1860.[535]

801) v DORCAS ABBOTT, b. 30 Jan 1774; died after 2 Oct 1846, the date of her will;[536] m. 3 Jan 1795, ELIPHALET PUTNAM, b. at Wilton, 23 Jan 1766 son of Nathaniel and Mary (Eastman) Putnam; Eliphalet d. 25 Feb 1826.

vi CHILD ABBOTT, b. and d. 20 Apr 1776.

vii SAMUEL ABBOTT, b. 11 Jun 1777; d. 10 Jan 1782.

802) viii ABIGAIL ABBOTT, b. 13 Jul 1779; d. 5 Jun 1812; m. 19 May 1808, JONATHAN LIVERMORE, b. at Wilton, 10 Jul 1770 son of Jonathan and Elizabeth (Kidder) Livermore; Jonathan d. 24 Dec 1845.

---

[531] Cochrane's *History of Francestown, NH* suggests her name might be Charlotte Morrill. However, her grave stone gives her name as Anna wife of Samuel. In addition, the son of Samuel and Anna, Benjamin, was a graduate of Dartmouth College. Benjamin's biographical sketch for the alumni of Dartmouth College gives his mother's name as Anna May. Chapman, *Sketches of the Alumni of Dartmouth College*, p 275

[532] Harvard University, *Quinquennial Catalogue*, p 151

[533] *New Hampshire: Births, Deaths and Marriages, 1654-1969.* (From microfilmed records. Online database: *AmericanAncestors.org*, New England Historic Genealogical Society, 2014.)

[534] *New Hampshire Wills and Probate Records 1643-1982*, will of Abiel Abbot, Hillsborough, 4 Aug 1809.

[535] Abbott, *Family Tree of Ezra Abbot*. See this source of additional information.

[536] *Probate Records, 1771-1921; Indexes to Probate Records, 1771-1859, 1885-1961*; Author: New Hampshire. Probate Court (Hillsborough County); *Probate Place: Hillsborough, New Hampshire*

803) ix PERSIS ABBOTT, b. 25 Dec 1781; d. at Milford, NH, 13 Nov 1859; m. 12 Jan 1804, her third cousin (and George Abbott descendant of the 6th generation), HENRY LOVEJOY, b. 16 Aug 1781 son of Samuel and Lydia (Abbott) Lovejoy; Henry d. 23 Sep 1863.

804) x RHODA ABBOTT, b. 17 Mar 1784; d. at Peterborough, 19 Mar 1853; m. 14 Nov 1805, EPHRAIM PEABODY, b. at Wilton, 17 Jun 1776 son of Ephraim and Sarah (Hutchinson) Peabody; Ephraim d. 5 Jul 1816.

xi SAMUEL ABBOTT, b. 30 Mar 1786; d. 2 Jan 1839. Samuel did not marry. He attended Harvard, was admitted to the bar, but later developed an interest in chemistry.

805) xii PHEBE ABBOTT, b. 25 Jun 1788; d. at Jackson, ME, 25 Nov 1825, m. 25 Jun 1818, her first cousin, EZRA ABBOTT, b. at Wilton, 3 Jul 1785 son of William and Phebe (Ballard) Abbott; Ezra d. 7 Jun 1871. Ezra is a 6th generation descendant of George Abbott.

198) JONATHAN ABBOT *(Jonathan3, Benjamin2, George1)*, b. Dec 1714 son of Jonathan and Zerviah (Holt) Abbott; d. at Andover, 31 May 1794; m. 1st 8 Oct 1739, his second cousin, MARTHA LOVEJOY, b. 2 Nov 1720 daughter of Henry and Sarah (Farnum) Lovejoy; Martha d. about 1768. Jonathan m. 2nd as her second husband, his second cousin MARY ABBOTT daughter of George and Mary (Phillips) Abbott.

In his will written 13 November 1787 (probate 9 July 1794), Jonathan Abbot has bequests to the following persons: well beloved wife Mary, son William Abbot, daughter Martha Whiting, and son Jonathan Abbot who is named executor.[537]

Jonathan Abbot and Martha Lovejoy had four children. The births of the three oldest children are recorded at Lunenburg. The birth of the youngest child was recorded at Andover.

321) i JONATHAN ABBOT, b. 20 Aug 1740; d. at Andover, 26 Dec 1821; m. 1st, about 1762, his third cousin, MEHITABLE ABBOTT, b. at Andover 11 Aug 1736 daughter of Ephraim and Hannah (Phelps) Abbott; Mehitable d. 1 Jan 1777. Jonathan m. 2nd, 17 Dec 1778, his third cousin, DORCAS ABBOTT, b. 23 Sep 1758 daughter of Stephen and Mary (Abbott) Abbott; Dorcas d. 3 Mar 1844.

ii NATHAN ABBOT, b. Jan 1743/4; died young.

806) iii WILLIAM ABBOT, b. 24 Nov 1745; d. likely at Temple, NH; m. 26 Aug 1766, his third cousin, SARA HOLT, b. 11 Aug 1746 daughter of Timothy and Hannah (Dane) Holt.

807) iv MARTHA ABBOT, b. 23 Jan 1749/50; d. at Temple, NH, 10 Jan 1842; m. 3 May 1774; OLIVER WHITING, b. at Pelham, NH, 6 Apr 1750 son of Eleazer and Dorothy (Crosby) Whiting; Oliver d. 28 Sep 1829.

199) DAVID ABBOT *(Jonathan3, Benjamin2, George1)*, b. Dec 1716 son of Jonathan and Zerviah (Holt) Abbot; d. 1777 at Rockingham, NH (probate 31 Dec 1777); m. 10 Aug 1741, his second cousin, once removed, HANNAH CHANDLER, b. 1724 daughter of Joseph and Mehitable (Russell) Chandler; Hannah's death not known but she was living at the time of her husband's will.

The will of David Abbot, written 11 June 1771, includes bequests to the following persons: son John Abbot receives a pair of three year old steers, one cow and all his wearing apparel; daughter Hannah Holt receives 5 shillings; daughter Bridget Abbot receives 15 pounds and a yearling heifer; daughter Mehitable also get 15 pounds and a heifer at marriage or the age of 21; son Job Abbot is to be the sole executor; beloved wife Hannah has use of all the household during her widowhood; son Job receives remainder of real and personal estate, although noting that certain tracts of land have been granted to son John by warrantee deed.[538]

The five children listed in the will are given here. The History of Pembroke and other sources list a son Benjamin with this family. However, I believe that Benjamin is the son of David Abbott and Hannah Danforth, and as he is not mentioned/living at the time of the will, he is not included here. Five children were born at Pembroke.

808) i JOB ABBOT, b. about 1742; d. at West Barnet, VT, 15 Dec 1815; m. PHEBE FARNUM whose parentage is unknown at this time.

809) ii HANNAH ABBOT, b. 7 Sep 1743; d. at Pembroke, 17 Mar 1813; m. her third cousin, BENJAMIN HOLT, b. 28 Feb 1741 son of Benjamin and Sarah (Frye) Holt.

---

[537] *Essex County, MA: Probate File Papers, 1638-1881. Probate of* Jonathan Abbot, 9 Jul 1794, *Case number* 81.

[538] *New Hampshire Wills and Probate Records 1643-1982,* Probate of David Abbott, Rockingham, 31 Dec 1777, Case number 4406.

iii JOHN ABBOT, b. about 1752 (although he may be the oldest child in this family born in the early 1740's); still living in 1771. There are no records located yet for him. As he was an adult at the time of his father's will having already received land through deed, it is possible that he married although clear evidence not found yet.

810) iv BRIDGET ABBOT, b. about 1761; m. 24 Dec 1787, her third cousin (and George Abbott descendant), PHINEAS AMES, b. 7 Sep 1764 son of Samuel and Elizabeth (Stevens) Ames; Phineas d. about 1792. Bridget m. 2nd, 17 Dec 1793, STEPHEN HARRIMAN. This is the same as Family #275, child viii.

v MEHITABLE ABBOT, b. about 1762; still living in 1771.

200) ZERVIAH ABBOTT *(Jonathan³, Benjamin², George¹)*, b. Aug 1722 daughter of Jonathan and Zerviah (Holt) Abbott; d. likely at Pembroke, NH; m. 17 Sep 1745, EPHRAIM BLUNT, b. 5 Feb 1720/1 son of William and Sarah (Foster) Blunt.

There is record evidence for three children of Zerviah Abbott and Ephraim Holt. This family seems to have moved several times and were at various times in Massachusetts, New Hampshire, and Vermont.

i EPHRAIM BLUNT, b. at Andover, 9 Aug 1747; died young.

811) ii EPHRAIM BLUNT, b. at Danville, VT, 20 Jun 1754; d. at Danville, 15 Feb 1829; m. 21 Nov 1776, MARTHA ORDWAY, b. at Amesbury, 28 Mar 1753 daughter of Moses and Anna (-) Ordway.

812) iii ZERVIAH BLUNT, b. at Suncook, NH, 1759;[539] d. at Calais, VT, 18 Jan 1860; m. at Canterbury, NH, 26 Feb 1778, AARON HARTSHORN, b. at Reading, 1754 son of Thomas and Abia (-) Hartshorn; Aaron d. at Danville, VT, 19 Jun 1799.

201) SAMUEL ABBOTT *(Jonathan³, Benjamin², George¹)*, b. 20 Sep 1727 son of Jonathan and Zerviah (Holt) Abbott; m. 12 Jul 1749, MIRIAM STEVENS whose origins are undetermined but may be the Miriam baptized in 1730 at Newbury.

Samuel Abbott and Miriam Stevens had eleven children whose births are recorded at Pembroke, New Hampshire.

813) i SAMUEL ABBOTT, b. 16 Apr 1750; d. at North Pembroke, 11 Mar 1836; m. 22 Mar 1781, LYDIA PERRIN, b. about 1752 (based on age at time of death) parents not yet certain; Lydia d. 1 Apr 1829.

ii EBENEZER ABBOTT, b. 18 Oct 1751; no further record.

814) iii ABIGAIL ABBOTT, b. 6 Sep 1753; d. likely at Salisbury, NH; m. 23 Nov 1773, BENJAMIN WHITTEMORE, b. 4 Dec 1750 son of Aaron and Abigail (Coffin) Whittemore.

iv JUDITH ABBOTT, b. 28 Jul 1755; m. 18 Apr 1791, perhaps as his third wife, HEZEKIAH YOUNG. Published genealogies report that Judith was Hezekiah's first wife, but the available records are that Judith married Hezekiah in 1791 as his second, or perhaps even his third, wife. He married Mary Kimball in 1783 and Judith Abbott in 1791 at Pembroke. There is another marriage for Hezekiah Young and Mary Young in 1777 at Canterbury, but that may be a different Hezekiah. There are no records for any children for Judith and Hezekiah.[540]

815) v JEREMIAH ABBOTT, b. 9 May 1757; d. at Montville, ME, 27 Jan 1816; m. 29 Nov 1787, ELIZABETH "BETSEY" FRYE, b. 18 Feb 1767 daughter of Ebenezer and Hannah (Baker) Frye; Betsey d. 27 Aug 1841.

816) vi SARAH ABBOTT, b. 21 Jul 1759; m. 4 Nov 1790, as his second wife, JEREMIAH WHEELER, b. at Concord, MA, Feb 1745 son of Jeremiah and Esther (Russell) Wheeler; Jeremiah d. at Concord, NH, 17 Oct 1827.

817) vii LYDIA ABBOTT, b. 14 Jul 1761; d. at Bethel, VT, 9 Dec 1840; m. 29 Mar 1787, NATHANIEL MORRILL, b. at South Hampton, NH, 10 Jun 1761 son of Paul and Martha (Worthen) Morrill; Nathaniel d. 17 Nov 1832.

818) viii EZRA ABBOTT, b. 4 Aug 1763; d. at Sanbornton, NH, 16 Nov 1824; m. 30 Nov 1794, MOLLY BROWN daughter of William and Ruth (McDuffee) Brown;[541] Molly d. at Cabot, VT, 1836.

819) ix WILLIAM ABBOTT, b. 10 Sep 1765; d. at Pembroke, 22 Jul 1838; m. his third cousin (and George Abbott descendant), DORCAS PARKER, b. at Andover, 17 Feb 1769 daughter of Joseph and Hannah (Abbott) Parker; Dorcas d. 9 Nov 1853. This is the same as Family #206, child v.

---

539 Zerviah Hartshorn's death record lists her parents as Zerviah Blunt and Ephraim "Hartshorn" although this seems just to be a confusion of the name of her spouse and the name of her father. Her age on the death record is 100 years, 11 months, 21 days. *Vermont Vital Records 1720-1908*

540 Ancestry.com, New Hampshire, Marriage Records Index, 1637-1947

541 Chase, *History of Old Chester*, p 478

820) x RACHEL ABBOTT, b. 15 Jun 1768; d. at Pembroke, 28 Dec 1854; m. 30 Dec 1789, JOHN KELLEY, b. 22 Jul 1764 son of Samuel and Sarah (Barker) Kelley.

821) xi MARIAM ABBOTT, b. 5 Sep 1771; d. at Randolph, VT, 21 Jun 1820; m. JOHN MORRILL, b. 17 Jan 1759 son of Paul and Martha (Worthen) Morrill; John d. 21 Sep 1849.

202) SARAH ABBOT *(David³, Benjamin², George¹)*, b. 7 Apr 1726 daughter of David and Hannah (Danforth) Abbott; d. at Bedford, 5 Mar 1814[542]; m. 1st 30 Jan 1753, ROBERT HILDRETH, b. at Dracut, 18 May 1713 son of Ephraim and Mercy (Richardson) Hildreth; Robert d. at Chelmsford, 1760. Sarah m. 2nd 28 May 1761, JOHN LANE, b. at Bedford, 2 Oct 1720 son of Job and Martha (Ruggles) Lane; John d. 7 Dec 1789. Sarah m. 3rd 14 Jul 1791, BENJAMIN PARKER; Benjamin d. Feb 1801.

Robert Hildreth died in 1760 at Chelmsford. His estate entered probate in October 1760; his widow Sarah requested that David Abbott of Andover be named administrator of the estate. Robert did not leave a will. Only one child was located for Sarah and Robert.

After the death of her first husband, Sarah married John Lane of Bedford. John's first wife, Ruth Bowman, had died in 1759. The births of three children were recorded for Sarah and John Lane at Bedford. A probate record was not located for John Lane. After John Lane's death in 1789, Sarah married Benjamin Parker in 1791.

Child of Sarah Abbott and Robert Hildreth:

i BENJAMIN HILDRETH, b. at Dracut, 23 Jan 1754; d. 13 Feb 1754

Children of Sarah Abbott and John Lane all born at Bedford:

i JOSIAH LANE, b. 25 Feb 1762; d. 15 Mar 1762.

822) ii JONATHAN LANE, b. 15 Oct 1763; d. at Bedford, 4 Mar 1808; m. 1 Feb 1787, his second cousin (and George Abbott descendant), HANNAH LANE, b. 26 Feb 1765 daughter of Samuel and Elizabeth (Fitch) Lane; Hannah d. at Lowell, 1848 (date of probate). This is the same as Family #211, child i.

823) iii SARAH LANE, b. 1 Oct 1765; d. at Billerica, 11 Jun 1849; m. 1 Nov 1787, TIMOTHY STEARNS, b. at Billerica, 25 Sep 1763 son of Isaac and Sarah (Abbott) Stearns; Timothy d. 8 Aug 1816. Sarah's mother and Timothy's mother were both named Sarah Abbott. Timothy's mother Sarah Abbott was from the Rowley Abbott lane.

203) DAVID ABBOT *(David³, Benjamin², George¹)*, b. 28 Mar 1728 son of David and Hannah (Danforth) Abbott; d. at Billerica 1 Nov 1798; m. 28 Dec 1752, PRUDENCE SHELDON, b. at Billerica 31 Aug 1732 daughter of Samuel and Sarah[543] (Hutchinson) Richardson; a death record for Prudence was not located, although she was living at the time of her husband's death and she was on the tax rolls in Billerica for 1798.

David and Prudence had eleven children, the first ten births recorded at Andover and the youngest son born at Billerica. David owned property in Andover, Billerica, and New Suncook (now Lovell), Maine. The children in this family scattered to the four winds ending up in New Hampshire, Vermont, Maine, Ohio, and Quebec.

David Abbot wrote his will 7 December 1797. Beloved wife Prudence receives the use and improvements on one-half of the dwelling house and a horse to convey her to meetings and other occasions. There are also provisions made for her support in terms of annual allotments of grains, beef, firewood, etc. Sons Josiah and Samuel receive token bequests of six shillings in addition to their portions they have already received. Son David receives all his land in New Suncook in the county of York. Son Benjamin receives all the lands in Billerica and Andover. Son Jeremiah receives $167 to make up his full portion. Daughter Elizabeth Dugles (sic) receives one pound, six shillings, and six dollars to make up the rest of her portion. Daughter Prudence Sawyer receives six shillings, daughter Parker (this is Hannah who married Aaron Parker) receives $5, daughter Olive McDole receives $30, and daughter Dorcas Abbot receives $100. Son Benjamin is named executor.[544]

824) i ELIZABETH ABBOTT, b. 26 Feb 1754; m. at Cavendish, VT, 19 Aug 1792, WILLIAM DOUGLASS.

---

542 Sarah's death record at Bedford is reported as Parker, Sarah, wid., "formerly the wife of Mr. John Lane," Mar. 5, 1814, a. 88. G.R.

543 The marriage record lists her name as Mary Hutchinson, but all the births of the children, including a daughter Sarah born in 1719, list the mother's name as Sarah.

544 *Middlesex County, MA: Probate File Papers, 1648-1871. Probate of* David Abbot, *1798, Case number* 13.

ii Son, b. 7 Feb 1756; d. 2 Mar 1756.

825) iii PRUDENCE ABBOTT, b. 3 Oct 1757; d. at Salina, NY, 15 Dec 1839; m. 13 Oct 1778, NATHANIEL SAWYER, b. at Methuen, 16 Jun 1750 son of Josiah and Hannah (Gowing) Sawyer; Nathaniel d. 15 Oct 1807.

826) iv JOSIAH ABBOTT, b. 29 Dec 1759; d. Feb 1837; m. 1st, 15 May 1784, RUTH BODWELL; Ruth d. by 1790. Josiah m. 2nd, 30 Mar 1790, ANNA FURBUSH, b. Oct 1768 daughter of Charles and Sarah (Corey) Furbush.

827) v HANNAH ABBOTT, b. 5 Jan 1762; d. at Compton, Quebec, 1856; m. at Billerica, 21 Jan 1787, AARON PARKER, b. at Methuen, 22 Feb 1759 son of Timothy and Priscilla (Carleton) Parker; Aaron d. 1857; living in Compton in 1851 listed as 93 years old.[545]

828) vi SAMUEL ABBOTT, b. 27 Mar 1764; d. at Bennington, NH, 29 Mar 1833; m. 1st, at Billerica, 26 Jan 1786, his second cousin once removed, RHODA BLANCHARD, b. 17 Nov 1762 daughter of Samuel and Mary (Brown) Blanchard; Rhoda d. about 1800. Samuel m. 2nd at Hancock, NH, 22 Dec 1801, ANNA WALLACE.

829) vii DAVID ABBOTT, b. 4 Mar 1766; d. at Barton, VT, 11 Mar 1847; m. at Fryeburg, ME, Sep 1786, SARAH "SALLY" KEZAR;[546] Sally d. May 1816.

830) viii BENJAMIN ABBOTT, b. 26 Jun 1768; d. at Ashtabula, OH, 22 May 1856; m. at Hancock, NH, 6 Oct 1793, BETSEY NOONING whose origins are unknown; Betsey d. 4 Sep 1854.

831) ix OLIVE ABBOTT, b. 24 Jul 1770; d. at Thurso, Quebec, 27 Jun 1834; m. 1st, ALEXANDER MCDOLE, b. 15 Jun 1760 son of William McDowell and Rosannah (McLaughlin) McDole; Alexander d. at Grand Isle, VT, 26 Jan 1814. Olive m. 2nd 31 Mar 1816, as his second wife, DAVID TOWN, b. 25 Jun 1762; David d. at Waterbury, VT, 4 Sep 1828.

832) x DORCAS ABBOTT, b. 5 Dec 1773; d. likely at Chelmsford after 1850 (still living at the 1850 U.S. Census); m. 4 Feb 1798, JOHN SNOW, b. 5 Jul 1774 son of Richard and Lydia (Wright) Snow.

833) xi JEREMIAH ABBOTT, b. 18 May 1776; d. in New York, 28 Mar 1835;[547] Jeremiah lived in Portland, Maine much of his adulthood. He did marry and had some children. One child has been identified, but the identity of his wife has not been found. The most likely candidate for a wife is Susanna Centre who married Jeremiah Abbott at Boston in 1797. There is a Maine death record for her for 1844 with age of 74 at time of death. There are gravestones in Portland for Jeremiah and his wife Susanna with the appropriate death years so perhaps that is this Jeremiah and Susannah.

204) SOLOMON ABBOT *(David³, Benjamin², George¹)*, b. 14 Feb 1730/1 son of David and Hannah (Danforth) Abbott; d. probably at Dracut 17 Dec 1797;[548] m. 3 May 1756, HANNAH COLBE, b. 22 Oct 1735 daughter of Daniel and Hannah (Gray) Colbe; Hannah's date of death is not known.

Solomon and Hannah settled in Dracut soon after the birth of their first child. In 1758, Solomon Abbott bought property and rights to a ferry in Dracut from John White. Solomon then sold half of this property to Daniel Colby in 1759 and the other half to Amos Bradley in 1761. Solomon received a deed for 100 acres from John White in 1768. Solomon Abbott is also listed on the Roll of Honor for Dracut as serving in the Revolutionary War.[549]

Seven births are recorded for Solomon Abbott and Hannah Colbe, the oldest at Andover and the remainder in Dracut.

834) i HANNAH ABBOTT, b. 1 May 1757; d. after 1827 (living at the probate of her second husband's estate); m. 1st, 27 Feb 1776, PARKER BODWELL, b. at Methuen, 29 Oct 1750 son of Daniel and Abigail (Ladd) Bodwell; Parker d. 7 Aug 1795. Hannah m. 2nd, as his third wife, DAVID JONES, b. 12 Feb 1740/1 son of David and Hannah (Fox) Jones.

835) ii SOLOMON ABBOTT, b. 7 May 1759; d. at Dracut, 5 Jan 1842; m. about 1785, RACHEL BOWERS, b. 16 Jul 1763 daughter of John and Rachel (Varnum) Bowers; Rachel d. 7 Jan 1845.

---

545 1851 Census of Canada East, Canada West, New Brunswick, and Nova Scotia; Year: 1851; Census Place: Compton, Sherbrooke County, Canada East (Quebec); Schedule: A; Roll: C_1142; Page: 89; Line: 41

546 Published genealogies give her name as Sarah Keyser, but every birth record for this couple lists her name as Sarah Parker and Parker is included as the middle name of one of their children. But the marriage of David and Sarah says Keezer.

547 Ancestry.com, *U.S., Newspaper Extractions from the Northeast, 1704-1930* (Provo, UT, USA: Ancestry.com Operations, Inc., 2014). This notice gives place of death as New York but notes that he was until recently in Portland, Maine.

548 The date of death is given in Abbot and Abbot, *Genealogical Register of Descendants*; a death record or probate record was not located.

549 Coburn, *History of Dracut*

836) iii SARAH ABBOTT, b. 22 Mar 1761; m. at Methuen, 16 Mar 1786, SAMUEL MORSE, b. at Methuen, 28 Mar 1759 son of Joseph and Lydia (Huse) Morse.

837) iv DANIEL COLBY ABBOTT, b. 26 Oct 1766; d. at Dracut, 18 Sep 1842; m. about 1792, PATIENCE COBURN, b. at Methuen, 1768 daughter of Aaron and Phebe (Harris) Coburn; Patience d. 15 Apr 1830.

838) v ELIZABETH DANFORTH ABBOTT, b. 11 Oct 1768; d. at Walpole, NH, 5 Jul 1856; m. 18 Sep 1793, EPHRAIM LANE, b. at Bedford, 11 Mar 1767 son of Samuel and Ruth (Davis) Lane; Ephraim d. 15 Aug 1837.

839) vi LYDIA ABBOTT, b. 22 May 1771; m. JOSHUA MARTIN.[550]

840) vii DAVID ABBOTT, b. 18 May 1775; d. at Windham, NH, 1855 (probate 8 Aug 1855); m. 1st, 13 May 1797, HANNAH CROSBY, b. 20 Sep 1773 daughter of Jonathan and Hannah (Goodhue) Crosby; Hannah d. before 1816. David m. 2nd, 21 Feb 1816, DOLLY ABBOTT, b. at Amherst, 1775 daughter of Ephraim and Dorothy (Stiles) Abbott; Dolly d. 1822. David m. 3rd, about 1827, SARAH MCKINLEY, b. 1789 daughter of Robert and Sarah (Harriman) McKinley; Sarah d. 30 Jan 1869.

205) JONATHAN ABBOT *(David[3], Benjamin[2], George[1])*, b. 24 Oct 1739 son of David and Hannah (Danforth) Abbott; d. at Andover, 10 Apr 1817; m. 13 Nov 1759, his second cousin once removed, MARY CHANDLER *(Nathan Chandler[4], John Chandler[3], Hannah Abbott Chandler[2], George[1])*, b. 15 Jun 1740 daughter of Nathan and Priscilla (Holt) Chandler; Mary d. 1 Apr 1824.

Captain Jonathan Abbot was part of Johnson's Regiment of Militia. This regiment was part of the first alarm that marched in response to the Lexington alarm. This regiment participated at Bunker Hill.[551]

Jonathan Abbot did not leave a will. Nathan Abbott was administrator of the estate. The widow's third is set out to widow Mary. The personal estate was sold at public auction to pay debts. Mary petitioned to the Court asking for allowances from the estate as Jonathan left ten children, two of whom are dependent on her for support. The value of the personal estate was $3,160 and the real estate value was $4,442. There was a deduction for the widow's dower of $1,480, and the debts were $7,500. The heirs-at-law signing that they agree to the administration of the estate by Nathan Abbott are as follows: Mary Abbott, Jonathan Abbott, Jr., David Abbott, Solomon Abbott, Joseph Shattuck, Benjamin Abbott, Hannah Abbott, Sarah Abbott, and Joshua Chandler signing on behalf of Abiel Chandler and Gilbert Barker.[552]

Jonathan Abbott and Mary Chandler had twelve children whose births are recorded at Andover. Two of the children died as infants. Two children did not marry. Of the eight children who married, six married George Abbott descendants; three of the marriages were to first cousins.

The oldest son, Jonathan Abbott, did not marry but he did leave a will that created dissension in the family. One of the heirs-at-law of the will, Benjamin Abbott, questioned its validity claiming that Jonathan was not of sound mind and memory at the time the will was made. There was a suit involving Benjamin and Jonathan Abbott, Jr. (Jonathan's nephew), and some other parties. The witnesses to the will attested that Jonathan was of sound mind. The will that Jonathan did make has bequests to the following persons: sister Mary Chandler wife of Abiel Chandler receives $100; brother Nathan, $15; brother Benjamin, $50; sister Phebe Shattuck the wife of Joseph Shattuck, $100; brother Solomon, $30; sister Hannah Barker wife of Richard Barker, $100; sister Sarah Abbott, $30; sister Priscilla Barker wife of Gilbert Barker, $30; Rebecca Shattuck, $50; nephew David Abbott receives his pasture land that adjoins his land; nephew Ezra Abbott, $200; nephew Herman Abbott, $50; niece Phebe Abbott, $20; niece Hannah Shattuck, $5; niece Phebe Abbott, $5; niece Priscilla Abbott, $20; niece Mary Abbott, $10; niece Lucinna/Susanna? Abbott, $10; nephew Nathan the son of brother David who is deceased and Joseph Shattuck receive the homestead farm in Andover; Nathan, Jr. son of Nathan, $15; nephew Gilbert Abbott, $15; nephew Jonathan Abbott receives all the residue of the estate and Jonathan is to quit-claim about three acres of property to nephew David. Nephew Jonathan is named executor.[553]

i JONATHAN ABBOT, b. 3 Mar 1760; d. 21 May 1830. Jonathan did not marry.

---

550 This is a marriage reported in Abbot and Abbot, *Genealogical Register of Descendants*. There are limited records related to this family who relocated to Hookset, New Hampshire.

551 Patrakis, Joan, "Andover in the Revolutionary War," Andover Historical Society, retrieved from http://andoverhistorical.org/explore-andover-stories-blog/andover-in-the-revolutionary-war

552 *Essex County, MA: Probate File Papers, 1638-1881.* Probate of Jonathan Abbot, 6 May 1817, Case number 82.

553 *Essex County, MA: Probate File Papers, 1638-1881.* Probate of Jonathan Abbot, 1 Jun 1830, Case number 84.

841) ii MARY ABBOTT, b. 10 Jan 1762; d. 1 May 1845; m. 17 Oct 1782, her first cousin (and 6th generation George Abbott descendant), ABIEL CHANDLER, b. 28 Aug 1760 son of Joshua and Hannah (Chandler) Chandler; Abiel d. at Boston, 2 Nov 1833.

842) iii DAVID ABBOT, b. 11 Mar 1764; d. 1 Jun 1823; m. 26 May 1789, his first cousin, PRISCILLA CHANDLER, b. 30 Jun 1768 daughter of Nathan and Phebe (Abbott) Chandler; Priscilla d. 19 Feb 1831. Priscilla is a 6th generation descendant of George Abbott.

843) iv PHEBE ABBOTT, b. 26 Feb 1766; d 1 Dec 1848; m. 30 Mar 1790, her third cousin once removed (and George Abbott descendent), JOSEPH SHATTUCK, b. 8 Nov 1757 son of Joseph and Anna (Johnson) Shattuck; Joseph d. 8 Jul 1847. Joseph had first married Hannah Chandler (a 6th generation descendant) who died in the first year of the marriage.

844) v NATHAN ABBOT, b. 17 May 1768; d. at Andover, 7 Apr 1850; m. 11 Dec 1792, his second cousin (and George Abbott descendent), HANNAH PHELPS, b. 10 Sep 1769 daughter of Joshua and Lois (Ballard) Phelps; Hannah d. 17 Dec 1853.

845) vi BENJAMIN ABBOTT, b. 7 Jun 1770; d. at Andover, 20 Oct 1835; m. 26 Nov 1793, his first cousin (and a 6th generation George Abbott descendant), RHODA CHANDLER, b. 2 Mar 1774/5 daughter of Nathan and Phebe (Abbott) Chandler; Rhoda d. 19 Mar 1853.

846) vii SOLOMON ABBOTT, b. 1 Nov 1772; d. 1 Sep 1840; m. 8 Jul 1794, his third cousin once removed (and George Abbott descendent), LUCY FRYE, b. 4 Jul 1778 daughter of Theophilus and Lucy (Lovejoy) Frye; Lucy d. at Boston, 16 Jun 1854.

viii JOSHUA ABBOTT, b. 14 Nov 1774; d. 26 Mar 1775.

ix HANNAH ABBOTT, b. 14 Oct 1776; d. at Andover, 11 Jul 1840; m. 22 Dec 1818, RICHARD BARKER, b. at Methuen, 10 Dec 1775 son of John and Hannah (Dow) Barker. Hannah and Richard did not have children.

x SARAH ABBOTT, b. 9 Jul 1778; d. at Andover, 1 Jul 1860. Sarah did not marry. Sarah Abbott, age 81, single, died at the almshouse of chronic rheumatism.[554]

xi PRISCILLA ABBOTT, b. 29 Jul 1780; d. at Saugus, 23 Mar 1862; m. 30 May 1816, GILBERT BARKER, b. at Methuen, 25 Jan 1774 son of John and Hannah (Dow) Barker; Gilbert d. at Saugus, 21 Sep 1853. Priscilla and Gilbert did not have children.

xii JOSHUA ABBOTT, b. 9 Jun 1784; d. 9 Jul 1784.

Grandchildren of Timothy Abbott and Hannah Graves

206) HANNAH ABBOTT *(Timothy[3], Timothy[2], George[1])*, b. 21 Jun 1726 daughter of Timothy and Mary (Foster) Abbott; d. likely at Pembroke, NH; m. 25 Apr 1754, JOSEPH PARKER, b. 15 Jul 1726 son of Joseph and Mary (Emery) Parker.

Joseph and Hannah relocated to Pembroke after the births of their children. Joseph signed the association test at Pembroke in 1776. He also belonged in a militia company that was part of Colonel Daniel Moor's regiment.[555]

The births of five children of Hannah Abbott and Joseph Parker are recorded at Andover.

i JOSEPH PARKER, b. 10 May 1756; d. 14 Aug 1762

ii HANNAH PARKER, b. 30 Apr 1758; d. 23 Aug 1762

349) iii JOHN PARKER, b. 15 Aug 1760; d. at Pembroke, NH, 27 May 1825; m. at Pembroke, 21 May 1781, his third cousin (and George Abbott descendant), MARTHA LOVEJOY, b. about 1755 daughter of Caleb and Mehitable (Chandler) Lovejoy. Same as Family #74, child vi.

iv MOLLY PARKER, b. 7 Sep 1766

---

[554] *Massachusetts: Vital Records, 1841-1910.* (From original records held by the Massachusetts Archives. Online database: *AmericanAncestors.org*, New England Historic Genealogical Society, 2004.)

[555] Cutter, *New England Families*, volume 3, p 1246

819) v DORCAS PARKER, b. 17 Feb 1769; d. at Pembroke, 9 Nov 1853; m. 24 May 1792, WILLIAM ABBOTT, b. at Pembroke, 10 Sep 1765 son of Samuel and Miriam (Stevens) Abbott; William d. at Pembroke, 22 Jul 1838. This is the same as Family #201, child ix.

207) NATHAN ABBOTT *(Timothy³, Timothy², George¹)*, b. 7 Jan 1728/9 son of Timothy and Mary (Foster) Abbott; d. likely at Wilton, NH; m. 11 Jan 1759, JANE PAUL, described as "resident of Andover," but whose origins are unknown; Jane d. at Wilton, 28 May 1772. He is perhaps the Nathan Abbott listed as head of household in Wilton, NH in the 1790 U.S. Census with a total household of eight.

Some published sources (including the Abbot genealogy and the Granite State Monthly, volume 9) place a son Caleb in this family who marries Lucy Lovejoy and Deborah Ames. However, Caleb was born, had both marriages, and died in Andover and Nathan and Jane lived in New Hampshire. Caleb died in 1837 at the age of 86 making his birth in 1751 eight years before Nathan Abbott and Jane Paul married. There is no room for Caleb in the family of Nathan and Jane until 1764. I have concluded that Caleb that married Lucy Lovejoy is Caleb born in 1751 the son of Asa and Elizabeth (Abbott) Abbott. Asa and Nathan were brothers.

There are records for seven children of Nathan and Jane, the oldest two at Methuen and the youngest five at Wilton. Marriages for these children are uncertain. Asa married Miriam Smith and settled in Bradford, New Hampshire[556] and it is likely that Timothy married Miriam's sister Sarah Smith. Miriam and Sarah Smith were the daughters of Ezekiel and Ruth (Child) Smith of Henniker.[557] Timothy and Sarah (Smith) Abbott had children named Nathan and Jane and that would fit with this family.

i PAUL ABBOTT, b. 2 Dec 1759

ii NATHAN ABBOTT, b. 9 Mar 1761; died young

847) iii TIMOTHY ABBOTT, b. 15 Oct 1762; d. at Thetford, 8 Sep 1831; m. by 1788, SARAH SMITH, b. 1765 daughter of Ezekiel and Ruth (Childs) Smith; Sarah d. at Waterbury, VT, 9 Nov 1848.

848) iv ASA ABBOTT, b. 24 Jan 1765; d. at Bradford, NH, 5 Nov 1852; m. MIRIAM SMITH, b. 1770 daughter of Ezekiel and Ruth (Childs) Smith; Miriam d. 12 Feb 1819.

v NATHAN ABBOTT, b. 13 Feb 1767. Cutter suggests that Nathan married Mary Wilson and settled in Billerica but records that support that were not located.[558]

vi MARY "POLLY" ABBOTT, b. 14 May 1769

vii MARTHA "PATTY" ABBOTT, b. 12 Apr 1771

208) SARAH ABBOTT *(Timothy³, Timothy², George¹)*, b. 5 May 1731 daughter of Timothy and Mary (Foster) Abbott; m. at Andover, 1 Mar 1757, as his second wife, EDWARD FARMER. Edward Farmer was first married to Mary Winn the daughter of Samuel and Sara (-) Winn.

Birth records for six children were located for this couple, but a marriage was identified for just one of the children. The family lived in Hillsborough County, New Hampshire and Edward signed the association test at Hudson in 1776.[559] All the births are recorded in New Hampshire.

i SARAH FARMER, b. 6 Sep 1758

ii MOLLY FARMER, b. 29 Mar 1760

849) iii PHEBE FARMER, b. 21 Sep 1761; d. at Pelham, 23 Apr 1839; m. ENOS HADLEY, b. at Amesbury, 24 Oct 1755 son of Eliphalet and Elizabeth (Davis) Hadley; Enos d. about 1838.

iv LYDIA FARMER, b. 21 Jul 1763

v TIMOTHY FARMER, b. 23 Apr 1765

---

556 Gould and Beals, *Early Families of Bradford, New Hampshire*

557 Cogswell, *History of Town of Henniker*, p 736

558 Cutter, *New England Families*, volume I, p 452

559 Webster and Browne, *History of Hudson, NH*, p 237

vi CALEB FARMER, b. 30 Jun 1767

209) LYDIA ABBOTT *(Timothy³, Timothy², George¹)*, b. 28 Mar 1733 daughter of Timothy and Mary (Foster) Abbott; d. at Andover, 13 Mar 1816; m. 13 Jan 1756, THOMAS FARNUM, b. 6 Sep 1734 son of Thomas and Phebe (Towns) Farnum; Thomas death is not known but was perhaps in NH living with his grandchildren.

Lydia Abbott and Thomas Farnum had seven children whose births are recorded at Andover.

849a) i LYDIA FARNUM, b. 10 Nov 1756; m. 27 Oct 1774, her second cousin (and George Abbott descendant), THOMAS HOLT, b. 15 Jun 1750 son of Thomas and Dorcas (Holt) Holt. This is the same as Family #213, child i.

850) ii ISRAEL FARNUM, b. 14 Jun 1758; d. at Mont Vernon, NH, 1842; m. 3 Aug 1786, PHEBE SHELDON; Phebe d. 2 Feb 1824. Israel m. 2nd, 17 May 1825, SUSANNAH FARNUM, b. 22 Mar 1772 daughter of Asa and Susannah (Town) Farnum.[560]

851) iii TIMOTHY FARNUM, b. 13 May 1759; m. 23 Sep 1786, SUSANNA BERRY, b. 27 Apr 1767 daughter of Nathaniel and Susanna (-) Berry; Susanna d. 16 Jul 1854.

852) iv PHEBE FARNUM, b. 25 Jul 1762; m. SAVAGE (according to Charlotte Helen Abbott). No records for this marriage were located, and it may be that this is the Phebe Farnum that married David Hovey.

853) v SARAH FARNUM, b. 21 Sep 1764; m. ENOS ABBOTT of Andover, ME, b. 7 Feb 1769 son of Jonathan and Ruth (Bragg) Abbott of The Rowley Abbott line.

854) vi DORCAS FARNUM, b. 27 Dec 1766; m. 25 Dec 1789, NATHAN JONES, b. 1767; Nathan d. at Andover, 14 Aug 1804.

vii MARY FARNUM, b. 1770; d. at Andover, 25 Jan 1809. Mary did not marry.

210) PHEBE ABBOTT *(Timothy³, Timothy², George¹)*, b. 16 Feb 1736/7 daughter of Timothy and Mary (Foster) Abbott; d. not certain but perhaps before 1799; m. 22 Jul 1766 as his second wife, WILLIAM DANE, b. 15 Mar 1727/8 son of John and Sarah (Chandler) Dane. William is likely the William Dane who died at Brookfield in 1825 at age 99. William's first wife was Mary Osgood.

There are births for six children of Phebe Abbott and William Dane recorded at Andover.

855) i PHEBE DANE, b. 18 Dec 1767; d. at Greenfield, NH, 12 Sep 1854; m. 10 Nov 1794, BENJAMIN HARDY, b. at Tewksbury, 10 Aug 1768 son of James and Jemima (Palmer) Hardy; Benjamin d. 16 Apr 1834.

ii LYDIA DANE, b. 13 Jul 1769

856) iii DORCAS DANE, b. 22 Apr 1771; m. 9 Oct 1794, her first cousin, EZRA HOLT, b. 20 Mar 1762 son of Timothy and Hannah (Dane) Holt.

857) iv TIMOTHY DANE, b. 9 May 1773; d. at Hillsborough, Aug 1856; m. 2 Apr 1806, ESTHER WHEELER, b. at Hillsborough, 24 Mar 1778 daughter of Oliver and Hephzibah (Munroe) Wheeler.

v HANNAH DANE, b. 14 Nov 1776

vi JOHN DANE, b. 16 Nov 1779

211) SAMUEL LANE *(Hannah Abbott Lane³, Timothy², George¹)*, b. 21 Oct 1737 son of John and Hannah (Abbott) Lane; d. at Bedford, 1822 (year of probate); m. 8 Dec 1763, ELIZABETH FITCH, b. 6 Jan 1738/9 daughter of Zachariah and Elizabeth (Grimes) Fitch; Elizabeth d. 19 Sep 1807.[561]

Samuel Lane wrote his will 10 April 1818 and it was presented to probate 3 September 1822. He directs that his entire estate, real and personal, be sold at auction. Daughter Phebe is to receive $500 from the estate. Following that, the estate is to be divided equally among his four daughters (or their heirs). Those daughters are Hannah Lane, Dorcas White, Phebe Lane, and the children of his daughter Polly Stearns who is deceased. John Stearns, the father of Polly's children, is to hold their portion in trust. Moses Fitch, yeoman of Bedford, and his son-in-law John Stearns are name executors of the estate. The sale of the estate yielded just over $3,600. Phebe received her separate $500 legacy, although she did marry between the

---

560 Smith, *History of Mont Vernon*, p 63

561 The death record states just __, w. Samuel, complicated complaint, Sept. 19, 1807, a. 69. C.R. There was another Samuel Lane in Bedford with a wife also born in 1738. However, that woman, Frances Hutchins Blood Lane, died in 1811 in Carlisle and has the following death listing: Lane, Frances, wid. "first wid. Stephen Blood, jr.," Apr. 17, 1811, a. 73 y. G. R. 1.

time of the will and the settlement of the estate. Phebe married in 1822, David Lane who was widowed in 1820. David Lane signs the final settlement agreement along with his wife Phebe. The signers on the final settlement are John Stearns signing as guardian for Polly's seven children (Franklin, Mary, John O., Eliza Ann, Onslow, Lorenzo, and Barnard), David Lane, Phebe Lane, Hannah Lane, and Dorcas White.[562]

Samuel Lane and Elizabeth Fitch had four children born at Bedford.

822) i HANNAH LANE, b. 26 Feb 1765; d. at Lowell, 1848 (date of probate); m. 1 Feb 1787, her second cousin (and George Abbott descendant), JONATHAN LANE, b. 15 Oct 1763 son of John and Sarah (Abbott) Lane; Jonathan d. 4 Mar 1808. This is the same as Family #202, child ii.

858) ii DORCAS LANE, b. 8 Feb 1771; d. 11 Feb 1849; m. 3 Jan 1788, NATHAN WHITE.

iii PHEBE LANE, b. 12 Feb 1773; d. 8 Aug 1838; m. 30 Apr 1822, as his second wife, DAVID LANE, b. 11 Mar 1759 son of James and Mary (Wellington) Lane; David d. 10 Sep 1842. Phebe did not have children.

859) iv MARY "POLLY" LANE, b. 15 Aug 1776; d. at Billerica, 30 Nov 1815; m. 10 Feb 1801, JOHN STEARNS, b. 18 Sep 1765 son of Isaac and Sarah (Abbott of the Rowley Abbott line) Stearns; John d. at Woburn, 4 Nov 1836. After Mary's death, John married Susanna Winn.

212) TIMOTHY HOLT *(Dorcas Abbott Holt³, Timothy², George¹)*, b. 17 Jan 1720/1 son of Nicholas and Dorcas (Abbott) Holt; d. at Wilton, NH, Nov 1801; m. 18 Sep 1744, his second cousin, ELIZABETH HOLT, b. Jun 1718 daughter of John and Mehitable (Wilson) Holt; Elizabeth d. at Wilton 21 Mar 1776.

Timothy Holt and Elizabeth Holt had four children whose births are recorded at Andover. The family relocated to Wilton.

i TIMOTHY HOLT, b. 19 May 1746

860) ii ELIZABETH HOLT, b. 25 Nov 1748; m. 1 Jun 1769, ISAAC FRYE, b. at Andover, 6 Feb 1748 son of Abiel and Abigail (Emery) Frye; Isaac d. at Wilton, NH, 3 Nov 1791.

861) iii HANNAH HOLT, b. 18 Jan 1754; m. about 1774, as his second wife, RICHARD WHITNEY, b. at Oxford, MA, 22 Apr 1743 son of Israel and Hannah (Blodgett) Whitney. Richard was first married to Sarah Butterfield who died in 1773. This family lived in Wilton until 1795 but may have relocated to Vermont after all the children were born.

iv SARAH HOLT, b. 31 May 1757; m. WILLIAM PIERCE, b. about 1757 likely the son of William and Hannah (-) Pierce of Wilton, NH.[563] No firm information has been located for this couple.

213) DORCAS HOLT *(Dorcas Abbott Holt³, Timothy², George¹)*, b. 4 Sep 1727 daughter of Nicholas and Dorcas (Abbott) Holt; death unknown but may have been at Wilton, NH; m. 26 Jan 1749, as his second wife, her first cousin, THOMAS HOLT, b. Mar 1711/2 son of Thomas and Alice (Peabody) Holt; Thomas d. at Andover, 21 Nov 1776.

Thomas's first marriage was to Hannah Kimball with whom he had six children. Following her death, Thomas married his cousin Dorcas and they had six children. The story is that Thomas Holt was the largest landholder in Andover at that time. Dorcas was also a horse lover and is supposed to have had the first horse gig in town.[564] After the death of her husband, Dorcas went with one, or perhaps more, of her children to Wilton and she is believed to have died there.

Thomas wrote his will 8 Oct 1774. Dorcas was named executor of the estate in Thomas's will, but she requested that this duty be assumed by her brother Joshua Holt. In his will, Thomas Holt has bequests for the following persons: dearly beloved wife Dorcas who receives use of the West end of the dwelling house as well as other provisions for her support and son William is charged with seeing to her support and care; well-beloved son Nathan receives a token bequest of six shillings to make up his total portion; well-beloved son Daniel receives £13; well-beloved son Asa, six shillings; well-beloved son Thomas, a tract of land that was purchased from Samuel Ames; well-beloved son William, real and personal estate not otherwise disposed of; well-beloved son Joseph, a tract of land lying south of the land of the widow Rebecca Gray; beloved daughters Hannah and Mehitable receive six shillings each; beloved daughter Dorcas receives a piece of pasture land; beloved daughter Mary, £53; beloved daughter Lois, £53; daughters Lois and Mary also allowed use of a bed and chest in the house where they might stay in

---

[562] *Middlesex County, MA: Probate File Papers, 1648-1871. Probate of* Samuel Lane, 1822, *Case number* 13590.

[563] Livermore, *History of Wilton*, p 470

[564] Livermore, *History of the Town of Wilton*, p 404

times of sickness as long as they are unmarried.[565] Hannah, Mehitable, Nathan, Daniel, and Asa are children from Thomas's first marriage.

There are birth records for six children of Dorcas Holt and Thomas Holt recorded at Andover.

849a) i THOMAS HOLT, b. 15 Jun 1750; m. 27 Oct 1774, his second cousin, LYDIA FARNUM, b. 10 Nov 1756 daughter of Thomas and Lydia (Abbott) Farnum This is the same as Family #209, child i.

862) ii DORCAS HOLT, b. 19 Mar 1753; m. 25 Nov 1773, her third cousin, MOSES LOVEJOY, b. 9 Sep 1751 son of Daniel and Mary (Holt) Lovejoy.

iii MARY HOLT, b. 11 Mar 1758. Durrie's Holt genealogy lists Mary as the Mary Holt that married John Adams in 1776 (his third marriage). However, John Adams's Mary died in 1829 at age 89, meaning she was born about 1740 so that is not this Mary. There are several marriages for Mary Holts about the time this Mary would have married, but all those other options are not yet explored.

863) iv LOIS HOLT, b. 29 Oct 1760; d. at Andover, 17 Apr 1852; m. 4 Jan 1785, MOSES PEARSON, b. at Wilmington, about 1752 son of Nathan and Mary (Wilson) Pearson; Moses d. at Andover 11 Aug 1835.

864) v WILLIAM HOLT, b. 7 Sep 1763; m. 29 Jul 1784, ELIZABETH JONES daughter of Jacob Jones; Elizabeth d. at Weld, ME, 1829.

865) vi JOSEPH HOLT, b. 29 Sep 1766; d. at Andover, 8 Jun 1791; m. 27 Nov 1788, his third cousin once removed, ABIGAIL HOLT, b. 19 May 1767 daughter of Samuel and Abigail (Blanchard) Holt; Abigail d. 13 May 1821.

214) JOSHUA HOLT *(Dorcas Abbott Holt³, Timothy², George¹)*, b. 30 Jun 1730 son of Nicholas and Dorcas (Abbott) Holt; d. 24 Jul 1810; m. 2 Dec 1755, his second cousin once removed, PHEBE FARNUM, b. 10 Oct 1731 daughter of Timothy and Dinah (Ingalls) Farnum; Phebe d. 26 Jan 1806.

Joshua Holt and Phebe Farnum had as their homestead what is now 111 Reservation Road in Andover, known as the Solomon Holt farm. Joshua is believed to have built this homestead in 1790. His son Solomon, as noted in the will, received the homestead from his father.[566]

Joshua was deacon of the South Parish church in Andover for 34 years. He also served in the Revolutionary War as a member of the 4th Essex County militia.[567]

Joshua Holt revised his will 24 May 1807 in response to "great alterations" that had taken place in his family. Perhaps these "great alterations" related to the death of his wife Phebe in 1806. Four sons, John, Joshua, Timothy, and Stephen, each receive $40. Son Peter receives $110. Each of his daughters receive $33.34. These daughters are Phebe the wife of Joseph Batchelder, Mary the wife of Isaac Foster, Abiah the wife of Deacon Daniel Kimbal, Hannah the wife of Ephraim Holt, and Chloe the wife of Francis Bowers. The daughters also receive all the household goods and furniture. Son Solomon receives all the lands and buildings that Joshua still holds at the time as his death as well as his pew in the meeting house. His six sons will divide his wearing apparel, although Solomon is free to select what items he wants. Solomon is named sole executor.[568]

Solomon was the only child in this family that remained in Andover. All the other children moved to New Hampshire and settled in towns in Hillsborough County.

Joshua Holt and Phebe Farnum had eleven children whose births are recorded at Andover. Some sources (e. g., Durrie's *A Genealogical History of the Holt Family*) also list a child Ruth in this family, but there was another Joshua Holt married to Ruth Burnap who was in Andover at the same time and rearing a family. There were records for two girls named Ruth in Andover, one baptized in January 1756 and the other born 11 May 1758; both these dates conflict with births of other children of Joshua and Phebe, so perhaps Ruth was the daughter of Joshua and Ruth.

866) i PHEBE HOLT, b. 28 Nov 1756; d. at Greenfield, 1849; m. 11 Dec 1778, JOSEPH BATCHELDER, b. 6 Mar 1748 son of Joseph and Judith (Rea) Batchelder; Joseph d. 1826.

867) ii JOSHUA HOLT, b. 17 Jan 1758; d at Greenfield, 14 Mar 1835; m. 1787, HANNAH INGALLS, b. 20 Feb 1759 daughter of David and Priscilla (Howe) Ingalls; Hannah d. 1 Dec 1838.

868) iii MARY HOLT, b. 5 Dec 1759; d. at Greenfield, 9 Jul 1819; m. 26 Aug 1784, ISAAC FOSTER, b. 23 Dec 1751 son of Jacob and Abigail (Frost) Foster.

---

565 *Essex County, MA: Probate File Papers, 1638-1881. Probate of* Thomas Holt, 3 Feb 1777, *Case number* 13699.

566 Andover Historic Preservation. https://preservation.mhl.org/111-reservation-road

567 Massachusetts Soldiers and Sailors, volume 8, p 193

568 *Essex County, MA: Probate File Papers, 1638-1881. Probate of* Joshua Holt, 9 Aug 1810, *Case number* 13666.

869) iv ABIAH HOLT, b. 16 Apr 1761; d. at Hancock, NH, 4 May 1841; m. 21 Jun 1791, as his second wife, DANIEL KIMBALL, b. at Ipswich, 20 Oct 1755 son of Daniel and Hephzibah (Howe) Kimball; d. 24 May 1843. Daniel's first wife was Elizabeth Osgood.

536) v PETER HOLT, b. 12 Jun 1763; d. at Greenfield, 25 Apr 1851; m. 23 Jan 1793, his first cousin (and George Abbott descendant), HANNAH HOLT, b. at Danvers, 11 May 1769 daughter of Nathan and Sarah (Abbott) Holt; Hannah d. at Beverly, 26 Jul 1857.

526) vi JOHN HOLT, b. 12 Jan 1765; d, at Greenfield, 11 Feb 1835; m. 6 Jan 1792, his third cousin, DORCAS ABBOTT, b. Dec 1766 daughter of George and Hannah (Lovejoy) Abbott; Dorcas d. 15 Mar 1841. This is the same as Family #124, child xi.

870) vii TIMOTHY HOLT, b. Apr 1767; d. at Peterborough, 1856; m. 7 Nov 1793, his second cousin once removed, LYDIA HOLT, b. 18 Apr 1767 daughter of Joseph and Ruth (Johnson) Holt; Lydia d. 22 Nov 1825.

871) viii SOLOMON HOLT, b. Dec 1768; d. 15 Apr 1830; m. 22 May 1798, MARY CUMMINGS, b. 1 Nov 1774 daughter of Jonathan and Mary (Eastman) Cummings; Mary d. 8 Oct 1852.

872) ix HANNAH HOLT, b. Jun 1771; d. at Greenfield, 21 Apr 1842; m. 27 Nov 1794, her third cousin once removed (and George Abbott descendant of the 6th generation), EPHRAIM HOLT, b. 19 Mar 1769 son of Jacob and Rhoda (Abbott) Holt; Ephraim d. 24 Oct 1836.

873) x STEPHEN HOLT, b. May 1773; d. at Greenfield, 26 Mar 1868; m. 1799, FANNY BOWERS, b. at Chelmsford, Jun 1773 daughter of Francis and Elizabeth (Holt) Bowers; Fanny d. 18 Apr 1828. Stephen married in 1831, MARGARET BATCHELDER, b. 1784 and d. 1867.

874) xi CHLOE HOLT, b. Jun 1775; d. at Peterborough, 6 Nov 1849; m. 23 Oct 1798, FRANCIS BOWERS, b. at Chelmsford, 20 May 1775 son of Francis and Elizabeth (Holt) Bowers; Francis d. 15 Oct 1835.

215) DANIEL HOLT *(Dorcas Abbott Holt³, Timothy², George¹)*, b. 10 Feb 1732/3 son of Nicholas and Dorcas (Abbott) Holt; d. at Andover, 15 Feb 1796; m. 29 Nov 1759, his first cousin once removed, HANNAH HOLT, b. 11 Feb 1738/9 daughter of Thomas and Hannah (Kimball) Holt; Hannah d. at Andover, 2 Aug 1831.

There are births for three children in this family that are recorded at Andover. A probate record was not located, and no other specific information about this couple.

875) i DANIEL HOLT, b. Dec 1761; d. at Fitchburg, 27 Nov 1830; m. 5 Jan 1790, MARY JONES, b. at Andover, about 1769 daughter of Jacob and Mary (Winn) Jones.[569]

876) ii ABIEL HOLT, b. 8 Jun 1765; d. at Rindge, NH, 18 Jun 1825; m. 26 Jul 1791, PHEBE PUTNAM, b. at Fitchburg, 20 Sep 1770 daughter of Daniel and Rachel (-) Putnam; Phebe d. at Fitchburg, 12 Nov 1827.

iii NATHAN HOLT, b. 13 Jul 1767; d. 1 Sep 1778.

Grandchildren of Thomas Abbott and Hannah Gray

216) ELIZABETH ABBOTT *(Thomas³, Thomas², George¹)*, b. 10 Jan 1726/7 daughter of Thomas and Elizabeth (Ballard) Abbott; d. at Andover 27 Sep 1792; m. 4 Jan 1753, as his 2nd wife, SAMUEL OSGOOD, b. 29 May 1714 son of Ezekiel and Rebecca (Wardwell) Osgood; Samuel d. 16 Mar 1774. Samuel was first married to Dorothy Wardwell.

Samuel Osgood did not leave a will. His widow Elizabeth was administrator of the estate. The value of the estate was £1,085. The probate records contain the details of the portion that Elizabeth received but does not have the other distributions.[570] Elizabeth Osgood also did not leave a will and her estate entered probate 6 Nov 1792. The value of her estate was £42. Thomas Osgood was the administrator of Elizabeth's estate.[571]

Elizabeth Abbott and Samuel Osgood had eight children whose births are recorded at Andover.

---

569 The will of Jacob Jones includes a bequest to his granddaughter Mary Holt the child of his daughter Mary who is deceased.

570 *Essex County, MA: Probate File Papers, 1638-1881. Probate of* Samuel Osgood, 5 Jul 1774, *Case number* 20268.

571 *Essex County, MA: Probate File Papers, 1638-1881. Probate of* Elizabeth Osgood, 6 Nov 1792, *Case number* 20192.

i LYDIA OSGOOD, b. 31 May 1754; d. at Andover, 2 Oct 1816; m. 20 Dec 1791, as the second of his three wives, ABIEL FAULKNER, b. at Andover, 4 Sep 1755 son of Abiel and Mary (Poor) Faulkner; Abiel d. 26 Nov 1818. His first marriage was to Hannah Abbott who was Lydia Osgood's first cousin. Abiel's third marriage was to Clarissa Dillaway. Lydia did not have children.

ii ELIZABETH OSGOOD, b. 17 Dec 1755; d. 16 Sep 1764.

iii SARAH OSGOOD, b. 14 Sep 1758; d. 21 Oct 1764.

877) iv JOSEPH OSGOOD, b. 5 Oct 1760; d. at Blue Hill, ME, 15 Mar 1854; m. 31 May 1785, HANNAH BAILEY, b. at Andover, 21 Dec 1765 daughter of Nathan and Deborah (Johnson) Bailey; Hannah d. 10 Jul 1829.

878) v DORCAS OSGOOD, b. Mar 1763; d. at Blue Hill, ME, 27 Apr 1832; m. at Andover, 4 Oct 1791, THEODORE STEVENS, b. 12 Jul 1763 son of Benjamin and Hannah (Varnum) Stevens; Theodore d. 15 May 1820.

vi JOHN OSGOOD, b. 7 Sep 1765; d. at Allenstown, NH, Dec 1829; m. Oct 1802, MARY SLATER daughter of Benjamin and Mary (Henley) Slater.[572] No children have been identified for this couple.

879) vii THOMAS OSGOOD, b. 11 Jun 1767; d. at Charlestown, MA, 21 Mar 1818; m. 15 Mar 1792, HANNAH STEVENS, b. at Andover, 23 May 1770 daughter of Benjamin and Hannah (Wilkins) Stevens; Hannah d. 1 Sep 1830.

880) viii CHRISTOPHER OSGOOD, b. 25 Apr 1769; d. at Suncook, 3 Oct 1841; m. 7 Nov 1793, his third cousin once removed, ANNA ABBOTT, b. Sep 1767 daughter of Zebadiah and Rebecca (Ballard) Abbott; Anna d. 26 Dec 1827. Anna Abbott is a descendant of both George Abbott of Andover and George Abbott of Rowley.

217) THOMAS ABBOT *(Thomas³, Thomas², George¹)*, b. 4 Apr 1729 son of Thomas and Elizabeth (Ballard) Abbott; d. at Andover 29 Mar 1775; m. 12 Feb 1756, LYDIA BLUNT, b. 6 Apr 1731 daughter of David and Lydia (Foster) Blunt; Lydia d. 16 Nov 1798.

Thomas was a farmer in Andover having inherited the homestead as the oldest son in his family of origin.

Thomas Abbot wrote his will 24 Mar 1775. The will includes a request that his honored mother be well provided for. Thomas's father died in 1774 and as executor of his father's estate, Thomas would have been charged with the care of his mother. In his will, Thomas bequeaths to eldest son Thomas £80 or that value in land when he reaches age 21. Son Joel receives £60. Daughters Lydia, Hannah, Betty, Ane, and Chloe each receive £40. Dearly beloved wife Lydia receives all the remainder of the estate trusting that she in the future will make a just distribution of the estate. Lydia is also named executor of the estate.[573]

Thomas and Lydia had seven children whose births are recorded at Andover. The Andover record transcriptions contain a baptism in November 1771 for a daughter "Eleanor" but this is the same month as the birth of daughter Chloe; as there is Chloe, but not Eleanor, in the will, this is either an error in the records or there was a twin who died very young.

881) i LYDIA ABBOTT, b. 10 Apr 1757; d. at Deering, NH, 12 Nov 1826; m. at Andover, 4 May 1779, THOMAS ELIPHALET MERRILL, b. at South Hampton, NH, 25 Oct 1751 son of Eliphalet and Mary (Clough) Merrill; Thomas d. at Weare, NH, 19 Oct 1830.

882) ii HANNAH ABBOTT, b. 5 May 1759; d. 14 Nov 1789; m. at Andover, 16 Feb 1777, ABIEL FAULKNER, b. at Andover, 4 Sep 1755 son of Abiel and Mary (Poor) Faulkner; Abiel d. 26 Nov 1818.

883) iii THOMAS ABBOTT, b. 25 May 1761; d. at Providence, 11 Jun 1826;[574] m. at Providence, 5 Jan 1800, RUTH OWEN, b. 21 Feb 1766 daughter of Joseph and Mary (Tripp) Owen; Ruth d. 26 Apr 1849.

884) iv BETTE ABBOTT, b. 25 Jun 1763; d. at Temple, ME, 12 Feb 1842; m. 17 Dec 1789, JONATHAN BALLARD, b. May 1761; Jonathan d. 28 Nov 1830.

v JOEL ABBOTT, b. 22 Nov 1765; d. at Andover, Dec 1826. He does seem to have married and had a son Joel. The identity of his wife has not yet been found. There is not any specific information about the son Joel.

vi ANNA ABBOTT, b. 28 Feb 1769; d. 31 May 1847; m. at Derry, NH, 17 Feb 1829, CHRISTOPHER OSGOOD, b. at Andover, 25 Apr 1769 son of Samuel and Elizabeth (Abbott) Osgood. Christopher was first married to another Anna Abbott (see Family #880 above).

---

572 Her father's name is given in a Massachusetts Supreme Court Case involving a property dispute, not directly involving Mary, but concerning a property of her father Benjamin (a seaman who was an alien and never naturalized). She is listed as a daughter of Benjamin, Mary the wife of John Osgood. Massachusetts Reports: Cases Argued and Determined in the Supreme Judicial Court of Massachusetts, Volume 32, p 346

573 *Essex County, MA: Probate File Papers, 1638-1881.* Probate of Thomas Abbot, 6 May 1776, Case number 141.

574 *Rhode Island, Vital Extracts, 1636-1899.*

885) vii CHLOE ABBOTT, b. 4 Nov 1771; d. at Melbourne, Québec; m. 19 Jan 1799, PETER FRYE, b. about 1771; Peter d. at Melbourne, Québec, 29 Jul 1843.[575]

218) JABEZ ABBOTT *(Thomas³, Thomas², George¹)*, b. 18 Apr 1731 son of Thomas and Elizabeth (Ballard) Abbott; d. 7 Jan 1804 at Concord; m. 1st by 1756, his first cousin, PHEBE ABBOTT *(Edward³, Thomas², George¹)*, b. 13 Feb 1732 daughter of Edward and Dorcas (Chandler) Abbott; Phebe d. 6 Jan 1770. Jabez m. 2nd 8 Aug 1772, HEPHZIBAH STEVENS, b. 28 Feb 1739/40 daughter of Samuel and Hephzibah (Ingalls) Stevens.

Jabez participated in some civic duties in Concord including serving as a highway surveyor. He also signed a 1776 resolution related to pledging loyalty to the revolutionary cause: *We, the Subscribers, do solemnly engage and promise, that we will, to the utmost of our Power, at the Risque of our Lives and Fortunes, with ARMS, oppose the Hostile Proceedings of the British Fleet and Armies against the United American Colonies.*[576]

Jabez Abbott and Phebe Abbott had four children whose births are recorded at Concord.

i JOSEPH ABBOTT, b. 22 Apr 1757; d. 21 Nov 1758.

886) ii JOSEPH ABBOTT, b. 5 Aug 1759; d. at Boscawen, NH, 7 Oct 1837; m. at Salisbury, 3 Apr 1794, MOLLY MELOON, b. at Salisbury, 25 Jan 1769 daughter of Nathaniel and Bathsheba (Tucker) Meloon; Molly d. 17 Dec 1847.

887) iii PHEBE ABBOTT, b. 29 Oct 1762; d. at Boscawen, 14 Sep 1819; m. 29 Dec 1791, PAUL CLARK, b. at Newbury, 23 May 1762 son of Daniel and Mehitable (Hale) Clark;[577] Paul d. 11 Jan 1808.

888) iv NATHAN ABBOTT, b. 29 Jun 1765; d. at Concord, 19 Mar 1844; m. 24 Feb 1801, RHODA BRICKETT, b. at Newbury, MA, 24 Jul 1769 daughter of Thomas and Mary (Noyes) Brickett.

Jabez Abbott and Hephzibah Stevens had four children whose births are recorded at Concord.

889) i LYDIA ABBOTT, b. 10 Jun 1773; d, 23 Mar 1841; m. at Concord, 27 Oct 1796, CHRISTOPHER ROWELL, b. at Hampstead, 22 Aug 1769 son of Christopher and Ruth (Moors) Rowell.

ii HEPHZIBAH ABBOTT, b. 1 Feb 1780; d. at Concord, 23 Jan 1817. Hephzibah did not marry.

890) iii DYER ABBOTT, b. 18 Jun 1778; d. at Henniker, 8 Mar 1832; m. at Boscawen, 1 Oct 1807, SARAH ATKINSON, b. at Boscawen, 19 Jul 1785 daughter of Benjamin and Jane (Varney) Atkinson.

891) iv ASENATH ABBOTT, b. 3 Oct 1781; d. at Pembroke, NH after 1850;[578] m. 24 Feb 1801, THOMAS BRICKETT, b. at Pembroke, 7 Aug 1778 son of Thomas and Mary (Noyes) Brickett; Thomas d. about 1855 (probate of estate 25 Sep 1855).

219) AARON ABBOTT *(Thomas³, Thomas², George¹)*, b. 17 Feb 1732/3 son of Thomas and Elizabeth (Ballard) Abbott; d. at Concord 31 Dec 1812; m. his first cousin, LYDIA ABBOTT *(Edward³, Thomas², George¹)*, b. 15 Jun 1737 daughter of Edward and Dorcas (Chandler) Abbott; Lydia d. 15 Dec 1811.

There are perhaps eight children (according to the Abbot genealogy) but only two survived childhood.[579] There were no records located for the six children who died in childhood, so they are just listed here: Betsey, Betsey2, Samuel, Samuel2, Joseph, and Thomas. The two children who lived to adult age are listed below. Both these children married other Abbotts.

i LYDIA ABBOTT, b. 4 Apr 1771; m. at Concord, 17 Apr 1811, as his second wife, her first cousin, TIMOTHY ABBOTT, b. 12 Mar 1769 son of Edward and Deborah (Stevens) Abbott; Timothy d. 23 Jan 1819. Lydia and Timothy did not have children. Timothy was first married to Sarah Bradley.

---

[575] Ancestry.com, *Quebec, Canada, Vital and Church Records (Drouin Collection), 1621-1968* (Provo, UT, USA: Ancestry.com Operations, Inc., 2008), Institut Généalogique Drouin; Montreal, Quebec, Canada; Author: Gabriel Drouin, comp..

[576] Bouton, *History of Concord*, p 270

[577] Hale, *Genealogy of the Descendants of Thomas Hale*, p 248

[578] She and her husband Thomas Brickett are both listed in the 1850 U.S. Census living at Pembroke.

[579] Abbot and Abbot, *Genealogical Register of Descendants*, p 88; Bouton, *History of Concord*, p 624

892) ii AARON ABBOTT, b. at Concord, 11 Apr 1778; d. at Bethel, ME, 8 Sep 1856; m. 1 Jan 1800, his second cousin, SARAH ABBOTT, b. at Concord, 26 Jun 1780 daughter of Stephen and Mary (Gile) Abbott; Sarah d. at Bethel, 1853.

220) NATHAN ABBOTT *(Thomas[3], Thomas[2], George[1])*, b. 7 Feb 1736/7 son of Thomas and Elizabeth (Ballard) Abbott; d. at Concord, 18 Jan 1805; m. 1766, BETTY FARNUM, b. 1743 daughter of Joseph and Zerviah (Hoit) Farnum; Betty d. 11 Nov 1821 Nathan Abbott and Betty Farnum had ten children whose births are recorded at Concord.

i BETTY ABBOTT, b. 2 Jul 1767; d. 1774.

893) ii JACOB ABBOTT, b. 16 Jan 1769; d. 13 Jan 1838; m. 1802, BETSEY KNAPP, b. 4 Mar 1782; Betsey d. at Rumford, ME, 18 Mar 1831.

iii ASA ABBOTT, b. 11 Nov 1770; d. 11 Feb 1843. Asa did not marry.

894) iv DAVID ABBOTT, b. 22 Sep 1772. The Abbot genealogy reports he went to New York in 1794 and left no trace after that. He was a house-joiner. The Rutherford County Tennessee Historical Society suggests that this David Abbott made his way to Tennessee and died in Gibson County, TN in 1856. The historical society has prepared a summary on David and reports he married Elizabeth Cummins 15 Oct 1811.[580] David Abbott owned a mill and received a pension for service in the War of 1812.[581] There is an 1850 U.S. Census Record for Fall Creek, Rutherford, TN which lists David Abbott born about 1772 in NH as head of the household.[582] He wrote a will in 1855 that was in probate in Gibson County, TN in 1857.[583]

895) v HENRY ABBOTT, b. 22 Sep 1774; d. at Rumford, ME, 1 Feb 1862; m. 1 Jun 1798, his second cousin once removed (and George Abbott descendant), SUSANNAH HALL, b. at Concord, 13 Nov 1781 daughter of Stephen and Patience (Flanders) Hall; Susannah d. 20 Mar 1867.

vi ANNA ABBOTT, b. 7 Jun 1776; died young.

vii BETTY ABBOTT, b. 19 Apr 1778; d. 24 May 1831; m. 3 Jun 1816, JEREMIAH EASTMAN. Betty and Jeremiah did not have children.

896) viii ANNA ABBOTT, b. 8 Jan 1781; m. Feb 1806, her third cousin once removed (and George Abbott descendant), EDMUND BLANCHARD, b. at Canterbury, NH, 27 Jan 1778 son of Jonathan and Hannah (Chadwick) Blanchard; Edmund d. in Vermont, 29 Nov 1836.[584]

897) ix CHLOE ABBOTT, b. 10 Jun 1783; d. at Hollis, ME, after 1850; m. 19 Dec 1809, ZEBADIAH FARNUM, b. at Concord, 4 Mar 1781 son of John and Sally (West) Farnum; Zebadiah d. at Hollis, after 1850.

x ESTHER ABBOTT, b. 19 May 1789; d. at Concord after 1850. At the 1850 U.S. Census she was living with her nephew Asa Blanchard in Concord.

221) DORCAS ABBOTT *(Edward[3], Thomas[2], George[1])*, b. at Rumford 15 Feb 1728/9 daughter of Edward and Dorcas (Chandler) Abbott; d. at Concord, 28 Sep 1797; m. 17 Jun 1746, EBENEZER HALL, b. at Bradford, 19 Sep 1721 son of Joseph and Sarah (Kimball) Hall; Ebenezer d. 24 Apr 1801; Ebenezer was the brother of Joseph Hall who married Deborah Abbott [daughter of Thomas and Hannah (Gray) Abbott]. Ebenezer Hall was first married to Hephzibah Farnum.

Ebenezer Hall was a farmer in Concord and served as selectman. Dorcas Abbott is believed to be the "first white girl born in Concord."[585]

Ebenezer Hall wrote his will 8 June 1791. Beloved wife Dorcas receives the income from one-half of his real estate and one-half of the cattle during her natural life and all the household items. Beloved son Ebenezer receives a 60-acre lot in Warner. Beloved daughter Hephzibah Hazeltine receives £3. Well beloved son Obadiah receives six shillings. Beloved daughter Dorcas Carter receives £3. Beloved daughter Sarah Hazeltine also receives £3. Beloved sons Daniel, Timothy, and Abiel each receive six shillings. Daughter Lydia Cavis receives $8 as does daughter Deborah Barker. Beloved son Stephen receives the whole of the real estate in Concord. Son Stephen is also the sole executor of the estate. The 7 July 1801 inventory of the estate of Ebenezer Hall included real estate valued at $3,475.[586] The son Ebenezer Hall mentioned in the will is Ebenezer's son from his first marriage to Hephzibah Farnum.

---

[580] Rutherford County Tennessee Historical Society, "Some of the Earliest People in Rutherford County by Their Date of Birth Prior to 1800," retrieved from http://rutherfordtnhistory.org/wp-content/uploads/2017/10/Pioneers-before-1800.pdf

[581] National Archives, War of 1812 Pension and Bounty Land Warrant Application Files, www.fold3.com/image/270301070?xid=1945

[582] Year: 1850; Census Place: Fall Creek, Rutherford, Tennessee; Roll: M432_894; Page: 164B; Image: 321

[583] Tennessee Wills and Probate Records, 1779-2008, Gibson County, TN, Will Books Vol D-F, 1846-1862, Will of David Abbott.

[584] *Vermont, Vital Records, 1720-1908.*

[585] Hurd, *History of Merrimack and Belknap Counties*, Part 2, p 540

[586] *New Hampshire Wills and Probate Records 1643-1982,* Probate of Ebenezer Hall, Rockingham, 5 May 1801, Case number 6818.

Dorcas Abbott and Ebenezer Hall were parents to twelve children.

898) i HEPHZIBAH HALL, b. at Rumford, 29 Mar 1747; d. at Concord, 23 Nov 1817; m. about 1765, RICHARD HAZELTINE, b. 5 Apr 1742 son of Richard and Sarah (Barnes) Hazeltine; Richard d. 21 Apr 1817.

899) ii OBADIAH HALL, b. at Rumford, 13 Oct 1748; d. 24 Mar 1831; m. 3 Nov 1770, MARY PERHAM, b. 3 May 1749; Mary d. 27 Feb 1822. After Mary's death, Obadiah married Abigail Morrison.

900) iii DORCAS HALL; b. 13 Jan 1751; d. 5 Sep 1813 (or 1823); m. EPHRAIM CARTER, b. at Concord, 21 Oct 1746 son of Ezra and Ruth (Eastman) Carter.

901) iv SARAH HALL, b. at Rumford, 4 Feb 1753; d. May 1845; m. by 1774, WILLIAM HAZELTINE, b. at Rumford, 16 Jun 1744 son of Richard and Sarah (Barnes) Hazeltine; William d. at Canterbury, Jan 1826.

902) v DANIEL HALL, b. at Rumford, 13 Jan 1755; d. at Concord, 18 Feb 1835; m. 26 Sep 1775, DEBORAH DAVIS, b. at Concord, 15 Jul 1757 daughter of Robert and Sarah (Walker) Davis; Deborah d. 31 Oct 1822.

902a vi TIMOTHY HALL, b. at Rumford, 5 Jun 1757; d. at Irasburg, VT, 16 Jul 1832; m. at Concord, 15 Oct 1780, ANNA FOSTER of Bow, born about 1760; d. at Harwick, VT, 28 Feb 1853.[587][588]

903) vii STEPHEN HALL, b. at Concord, 13 May 1759; d. at Concord, 23 Nov 1808; m. PATIENCE FLANDERS, b. at Boscawen, 9 Oct 1758 daughter of Ezekiel and Sarah (Bishop) Flanders; Patience d. 17 Feb 1834.

904) viii ABIEL HALL, b. at Rumford, 31 May 1761; d. 13 Oct 1829 at Alfred, ME; m. 1st, MARY FARNUM, b. at Concord, 26 Aug 1764 daughter of Benjamin and Anna (Merrill) Farnum; Mary d. 23 Nov 1816. Abiel m. 2nd, 1819, ANNA FRANCIS (widow of Edward Grant); Anna d. 11 Dec 1857.

ix HANNAH HALL, b. 1 Nov 1764; d. 16 Nov 1765.

x HANNAH HALL, b. 2 Oct 1766; died young.

905) xi LYDIA HALL, b. at Concord, 10 Oct 1767; d. at Bow, NH, 30 Mar 1855; m. 5 Jan 1788, NATHANIEL CAVIS, b. 25 Dec 1761; Nathaniel d. 10 Sep 1842.

906) xii DEBORAH HALL, b. at Concord, 18 Sep 1769; d. 25 Oct 1791; m. at Hillsborough, 26 Oct 1787, DANIEL BARKER. Daniel perhaps married Anna Lathrop 19 Mar 1792.

222) EDWARD ABBOTT *(Edward³, Thomas², George¹)*, b. 27 Dec 1730 son of Edward and Dorcas (Chandler) Abbott; d. 15 Sep 1801; m. about 1760 DEBORAH STEVENS, origins not certain but likely the Deborah born 1738 in Rumford, NH daughter of Aaron and Deborah (Stevens) Stevens. Aaron Stevens was an early settler at Concord. Deborah d. Nov 1817.

Edward Abbott and Deborah Stevens had nine children.

907) i MARY ABBOTT, b. 1761; d. 1843; m. by 1780, THOMAS CAPEN, b. at Charlestown, 19 Apr 1762 son of Thomas and Mary (Wyman) Capen;[589] Thomas died at sea in 1808. This family settled in New Pennacook, Maine.

908) ii MEHITABLE ABBOTT, b. 23 Apr 1763; d. 16 Sep 1838;[590] m. by 1786, BENJAMIN LUFKIN, b. at Ipswich, 8 Apr 1763;[591] Benjamin d. at Roxbury, ME, Nov 1844.

909) iii SUSANNA ABBOTT, b. 1765; d. 25 Feb 1841; m. by 1786, JOHN WEEKS, b. at Portsmouth, NH, 23 Jun 1757; John d. at Concord, 6 Apr 1836.

iv EDWARD ABBOTT, b. about 1767; d. about 1784?

---

587 Revolutionary War Pension and Bounty-Land Warrant Application Files

588 Anna Hall was living with her daughter Judith Kellogg at the 1850 census.

589 Hayden and Tuttle, *The Capen Family*, p 137

590 Mehitable Lufkin's death is reported in the records of the First Congregational Church of Concord. (Reed and Thorne, History and Manual of the First Congregational Church)

591 Lapham, *History of Rumford*, p 369

910) v TIMOTHY ABBOTT, b. 12 Mar 1769; d. 23 Jan 1819; m. 1st, SARAH BRADLEY daughter of Abraham and Sarah (-) Bradley; Sarah d. 1810.[592] Timothy m. 2nd, his first cousin, LYDIA ABBOTT, b. 4 Apr 1771 daughter of Aaron and Lydia (Abbott) Abbott. Aaron and Lydia Abbott are Family # 219.

911) vi SAMUEL ABBOTT, b. 8 Apr 1771; m. at Pembroke, 4 Mar 1792, MARY "POLLY" CURRIER, b. at Concord, 13 Oct 1776 daughter of William and Mary (Carter) Currier.[593] Samuel was a carpenter and relocated to Buffalo, New York. Later, the family moved to Switzerland County, Indiana where both Samuel and Polly died in 1820.

vii DEBORAH ABBOTT, b. and d. 1773.

912) viii DEBORAH ABBOTT, b. at Concord, 29 May 1774; d. at Rumford, ME, 20 Apr 1861; m. PHINEAS HOWE, b. at Bolton, MA, 25 Mar 1769 son of Phineas and Experience (Pollard)[594] Howe; Phineas d. 27 Dec 1847.

ix ESTHER ABBOTT, b. 1777; d. 1824; m. at Concord, 13 Mar 1800, TRUEWORTHY KILGORE. Esther and Trueworthy did not have children.

223) BETSEY ABBOTT *(Edward3, Thomas2, George1)*, b. 25 Aug 1743 daughter of Edward and Dorcas (Chandler) Abbott; d. 2 Oct 1827 at Goffstown, NH; m. 1759, THOMAS SALTMARSH, b. at Watertown, 2 Mar 1736 son of Thomas and Mary (Hazen) Saltmarsh; Thomas d. at Goffstown, NH 8 May 1826.[595]

Betsey Abbott and Thomas Saltmarsh had ten children born in New Hampshire with some births recorded at Concord. Birth records for every child were not located and the Abbot genealogy was used to supplement information.[596]

913) i MEHITABLE SALTMARSH, b. at Concord, 12 Apr 1762; d. at Gilford, NH, 25 Oct 1814; m. at Goffstown, 9 Feb 1784, JAMES HOYT, b. at Kingston, 28 Mar 1762 son of Eliphalet and Mary (Peaslee) Hoyt; James d. 1834. After Mehitable's death, James married Abigail Whittier in 1815 and Huldah Fifield in 1822.

914) ii JOHN SALTMARSH, b. at Concord, 21 May 1764; d. after 1850 (living in Bedford at the 1850 U.S. Census); m. at Goffstown, 22 Nov 1785, SUSAN BURNHAM, b. at Ipswich, 1756 daughter of Samuel and Martha (Story) Burnham.

915) iii MARY "POLLY" SALTMARSH, b. at Concord, 28 Aug 1766; d. at Peterborough, 21 Apr 1848; m. at Goffstown, 31 Mar 1791, SAMUEL VOSE, b. at Bedford, 23 May 1759 son of Samuel and Phebe (Vickery) Vose; Samuel d. at Antrim, NH, 8 Aug 1830.

916) iv EDWARD ABBOTT SALTMARSH, b. 1768 likely at Goffstown; d. at Hookset, NH, 11 Mar 1851; m. at Goffstown, 19 Oct 1791, SARAH "SALLY" STORY, b. 1773 (based on age at time of death) daughter of Nehemiah and Sarah (Gold) Story; Sally d. 19 May 1860.

917) v THOMAS SALTMARSH, b. 1771; d. at Saco, ME, 1804; m. at Wolfeboro, 7 Jun 1799, BETSY EVANS, b. 21 May 1780 daughter of Benjamin and Lydia (Browne) Evans.

vi SALLY SALTMARSH, b. 1773.

918) vii SAMUEL SALTMARSH, b. 1775; d. at Goffstown, 1844; m. 28 May 1800, BETSY BURNHAM, b. about 1780; Betsy d. at Goffstown, 1840.

919) viii CATHERINE SALTMARSH, b. 1777; d. after 1850 (still living at the 1850 U.S. Census); m. her first cousin, THOMAS SALTMARSH, b. at Bedford, MA, 22 Aug 1772 son of Seth and Ruth (Bowman) Saltmarsh; Thomas d. at Gilford, NH, 18 Sep 1823.

920) ix ISAAC SALTMARSH, b. 1779; d. at Antrim, NH, 13 Mar 1823; m. at Bradford, NH, 13 Nov 1805, PHEBE STRATTON, b. at Marlboro, MA, 27 Feb 1790 daughter of Jonathan and Abigail (Barnes) Stratton; Phebe d. 13 Sep 1872.

x HAZEN SALTMARSH, b. 1781; d. 1805.

---

[592] Ancestry.com, New Hampshire, Death and Disinterment Records, 1754-1947

[593] Currier and Currier, *The Genealogy of Richard Currier*, p 26. The Abbot and Abbot genealogy gives her name as Ruth Currier, but the Currier genealogy says Mary Currier and the marriage record says Polly Currier.

[594] The division of William Pollard's estate in 1763 includes a disbursement to his daughter Elizabeth wife of Phineas Howe.

[595] The graves of Elizabeth Abbott and Thomas Saltmarsh are in the Westlawn Cemetery at Goffstown with a gravestone that lists their names as Thomas Saltmarsh and Elisabeth Abbott, his wife. (accessed through findagrave.com)

[596] Abbot and Abbot, *Genealogical Register of Descendants*, p 101

224) MARY HALL *(Deborah Abbott Hall[3], Thomas[2], George[1])*, b. 17 Mar 1743 daughter of Joseph and Deborah (Abbott) Hall; d. 12 Dec 1773; m. THOMAS WILSON who d. at Concord 23 May 1818. Thomas m. 2nd, Mary Hopkins Bancroft.

Thomas Wilson wrote his will 20 May 1818. In his will, he directs that his estate be divided equally among his five children (four children living and the children of his son Thomas who is deceased). First named is Mary Thorndike wife of John Thorndike. However, if John Thorndike brings any demand against the estate, that amount is to be deducted from Mary's share. Second named is daughter Eliza Flagg. Next named is daughter Rebecca Wilson. Then named are the children of his son Thomas. Lastly, is daughter Ruth Wilson who is to pay Eliza what she owes her.[597] Just the oldest child named, Mary Thorndike, is from Thomas's marriage to Mary Hall.

Mary Hall and Thomas Wilson had two children born at Concord.

i JEREMIAH HALL WILSON, b. at Concord 1770; d. 10 Apr 1775

921) ii MARY "MOLLY" WILSON, b. 23 Jul 1772; m. 1st, 25 Mar 1792, JOHN THORNDIKE, b. at Beverly, 30 Nov 1768 son of Larkin and Ruth (Woodbury) Thorndike. Dr. John Thorndike died at Concord, 1821. Mary m. 2nd, 27 Nov 1823, her third cousin, ABIEL WALKER, b. 5 Jul 1766 son of James and Ruth (Abbott) Walker. Abiel was first married to Judith Davis.

225) DANIEL ABBOT *(George[3], Thomas[2], George[1]* **and** *Sarah[4], Stephen[3], John[2], George[1])*, b. 7 Aug 1738 son of George and Sarah (Abbott) Abbott; d. 11 Jun 1804; m. 1st by 1761, his second cousin RACHEL ABBOTT *(Nathaniel[3], Nathaniel[2], George[1])*, b. 7 Apr 1743 daughter of Nathaniel and Penelope (Ballard) Abbott; Rachel d. 13 Jun 1788. Daniel m. 2nd 1 Jan 1789 at Boscawen, MERCY "MARY" KILBURN whose origins are not fully verified, although she is likely the daughter of Jedediah and Hannah (Platts) Kilburn. She was born about 1758 based on the birth of her last child in 1799. Mercy was living in 1830 when she was listed as a head of household in the 1830 US Census of Concord (between age 60-70).

The will of Daniel Abbot has bequests for the following persons: beloved wife Mary, beloved sons Beriah, Jeremiah, Daniel, George, Thomas, Abiel, Peter Hazeltine, Benjamin, daughters Judith, Sarah, Hannah, Lois, Susanna, son Nathan Kilburn, and son Samuel who is appointed executor along with Thomas.[598]

Children of Daniel Abbot and Rachel Abbott were born at Concord. There are birth records for all the children except the oldest child Beriah.

922) i BERIAH ABBOTT, b. about 1758; d. at Pomfret, VT, 13 Mar 1832;[599] m. about 1785 the widow MARY ANDREWS FAIRFIELD. Mary d. 29 Jul 1813; Beriah m. 2nd, MARTHA GRISWOLD, b. about 1759 and d. at Randolph, VT, 28 Jan 1841.

ii SARAH ABBOTT, b. 19 Jul 1761; d. 21 Jan 1774.

923) iii SAMUEL ABBOTT, b. 26 Mar 1764; d. at Concord, 1 Dec 1849; m. 17 Nov 1787, MARY T. "POLLY" STORY, b. 16 Oct 1764 daughter of Jeremiah and Mary "Polly" (Burnham) Story; Polly d. 21 Dec 1849.

924) iv JEREMIAH ABBOTT, b. 21 Feb 1766; d. at Pomfret, VT, 10 Feb 1811; m. 15 Jan 1795, CLARISSA PERRY, b. at Ashford, CT, 31 Mar 1770 daughter of Robert and Sarah (Hodges) Perry;[600] Clarissa d. 10 Oct 1826.

v DANIEL ABBOTT, b. 21 Feb 1768; d. 19 Sep 1769.

925) vi DANIEL ABBOTT, b. 7 Mar 1770; d. unknown; m. 29 Jan 1794, LUCY HARVEY, b. at Gilsum, NH, 15 Dec 1768 daughter of Thomas and Grace (Willey) Harvey; Lucy d. 8 Feb 1849.

926) vii GEORGE ABBOTT, b. 12 May 1772; m. BETSY EASTMAN.

927) viii THOMAS ABBOTT, b. 5 Jul 1776; d. at Concord, NH, 1845; m. 14 Apr 1801, ANNA EATON, b. in NH about 1781; d. at Concord after 1850 (living with her daughter Dorcas and her family at the 1850 census). Her parentage is not verified but she is *possibly* the daughter of Ephraim and Eunice (-) Eaton.

---

597 *New Hampshire Wills and Probate Records 1643-1982,* Probate of Thomas Wilson, Rockingham, 20 May 1818, Case number 9739.

598 *New Hampshire Wills and Probate Records 1643-1982,* Probate of Daniel Abbott, Rockingham, 27 Aug 1804, Case number 7284.

599 Ancestry.com, *Vermont, Vital Records, 1720-1908* (Provo, UT, USA: Ancestry.com Operations, Inc., 2013).

600 Robert Perry was an early settler of Windsor County, Vermont. Aldrich and Holmes, *History of Windsor County, Vermont*, p 969

928) ix ABIEL ABBOTT, b. 19 Mar 1778; d. at Waldo, ME, 1 Aug 1836;[601] m. at Lincolnville, ME, 2 Feb 1809, SARAH COMBS,[602] "of Georgetown (ME)". She is SARAH HINKLEY, b. at Georgetown, 14 Aug 1774 daughter of John and Hannah (Oliver) Hinkley[603] and the widow of Leonard Coombs. Sarah d. at Waldo, 4 Nov 1865 (age 91 years, 3 months at time of death).[604] The death record of daughter Harriet gives the maiden name of mother as Sarah Hinkley.

929) x PETER HAZELTINE ABBOTT, b. 28 Feb 1780; d. after 1860 (listed in the 1860 Census living with his son Asaph); m. 9 Mar 1815, his first cousin once removed, SARAH ABBOTT, b. 10 Sep 1781 daughter of Moses and Mary (Batchelder) Abbott; Sarah d. 10 Aug 1846.

930) xi BENJAMIN ABBOTT, b. 29 Mar 1782; m. ESTHER CURRIER, b. 5 Nov 1787 daughter of Nathaniel Currier.

931) xii JUDITH ABBOTT, b. 4 Apr 1784; d. 18 Apr 1831; m. JOHN CARPENTER.

xiii CHILD ABBOTT, b. and d. 12 Jun 1788.

Children of Daniel Abbott and Mercy Kilburn: In the 1850, 1860, and 1870 U.S. Census, Sarah, Lois, and Nathan were living together in Concord and it seems none of them married. Nathan is listed as single on his death record. Susannah also does not seem to have married.

i SARAH ABBOTT, b. 4 Apr 1790; d. after 1870.[605]

932) ii HANNAH ABBOTT, b. 28 Oct 1791; d. 13 Sep 1876; m. 16 Mar 1815, her third cousin once removed, REUBEN ABBOTT, b. at Concord, 23 Oct 1790 son of Reuben and Zerviah (Farnum) Abbott; Reuben d. 27 Jun 1869.

iii LOIS ABBOTT, b. 31 Oct 1793; d. at Concord, 18 Dec 1881.

iv SUSANNAH ABBOTT, b. 23 May 1797; d. 22 Jun 1847.[606]

v NATHAN KILBURN ABBOTT, b. 30 Aug 1799; d. at Concord 14 Jun 1878.

226) JOSEPH ABBOTT *(George³, Thomas², George¹* **and** *Sarah⁴, Stephen³, John², George¹)*, b. 23 Oct 1741 son of George and Sarah (Abbott) Abbott; d. at Concord, NH, 19 Jan 1832; m. 25 Apr 1765, his third cousin once removed, PHEBE LOVEJOY *(Phebe Chandler Lovejoy⁴, John Chandler³, Hannah Abbott Chandler², George¹)*, b. 20 Sep 1735 daughter of Henry and Phebe (Chandler) Lovejoy; Phebe d. 4 Jan 1789. Joseph m. 2nd, ABIGAIL TYLER.

Joseph Abbott and Phebe Lovejoy had ten children born at Concord.

933) i PHEBE ABBOTT, b. 22 Feb 1766; d. at Woodbury, VT, 31 May 1837;[607] m. her third cousin (and George Abbott descendant), JOSEPH BLANCHARD, b. at Dunstable, NH, 24 Nov 1761 son of John and Eleanor (Stevens) Blanchard; Joseph d. 19 Feb 1839.

934) ii MOLLY ABBOTT, b. 20 Jul 1767; d. at Concord, 15 Aug 1791; m. 22 May 1785, ISAAC HOUSTON, b. at Bedford, NH, 1760 son of James and Mary (Mitchell) Houston. Isaac m. 2nd, Ruth Gale. Isaac d. at Hanover, NH, 25 Mar 1833.

935) iii HANNAH ABBOTT, b. 3 Jan 1769; d. 31 Oct 1810; m. 10 Dec 1795, DAVID KIMBALL, b. at Rumford, 10 Oct 1757 son of Reuben and Miriam (Collins) Kimball.

936) iv SARAH ABBOTT, b. 3 Jan 1769; d. at Concord, 27 Jan 1857; m. Nov 1787, her second cousin (and George Abbott descendant), TIMOTHY CHANDLER, b. at Rumford, 25 Apr 1762 son of Timothy and Elizabeth (Copp) Chandler; Timothy d. 9 Aug 1848. This is the same as Family #259, child ii.

v LOIS ABBOTT, b. 29 Mar 1771; d. 14 Mar 1790.

---

[601] Ancestry.com, Maine, Death Records, 1761-1922

[602] "Maine Marriages, 1771-1907," database, *FamilySearch* (https://familysearch.org/ark:/61903/1:1:F4DX-WLN: 10 February 2018), Abial Abbot and Sarah Combs, 02 Feb 1809; citing Lincolnville, Waldo, Maine, reference vol 1; FHL microfilm 11,351.

[603] "Maine Births and Christenings, 1739-1900," database, *FamilySearch* (https://familysearch.org/ark:/61903/1:1:F4HY-ZPV: 10 February 2018), Sarah Hinkley, 14 Aug 1774; citing GEORGETOWN, SAGADAHOC, MAINE; FHL microfilm 873,976.

[604] Maine State Archives; Cultural Building, 84 State House Station, Augusta, ME 04333-0084; Pre-1892 Delayed Returns; Roll Number: 1; Maine State death records 1761-1922

[605] She is listed in the 1870 US Census living with Lois Abbot and Nathan K. Abbot. There is no record of her after that.

[606] Abbot and Abbot, *Genealogical Register of Descendants*, p 105

[607] *Vermont, Vital Records, 1720-1908.*

937) vi RACHEL ABBOTT, b. 2 Mar 1773; d. at Fryeburg, ME, 2 Mar 1837; m. 29 Nov 1797, JONATHAN WARD, b. at Concord, 17 Aug 1774 son of Stephen and Elizabeth (Copp) Ward; Jonathan d. 5 Feb 1822. Jonathan's mother, Elizabeth Copp, was first married to Timothy Chandler who was Rachel Abbott's first cousin, once removed.

vii DORCAS ABBOTT, b. 20 Dec 1774; d. 6 Oct 1788.

viii ISAAC ABBOTT, b. 10 Apr 1777; d. Jan 1800.

938) ix NATHAN ABBOTT, b. 27 Aug 1779; d. 26 Aug 1839; m. ELIZABETH "BETSEY" COLBY, b. 1786 daughter of John and Ann (Carter) Colby; Betsey d. 14 Dec 1819.

x RUTH ABBOTT, b. 8 May 1782; d. after 1850. Ruth did not marry. She was living alone in Concord at the 1850 U. S. Census.[608]

227) STEPHEN ABBOTT *(George³, Thomas², George¹* **and** *Sarah⁴, Stephen³, John², George¹)*, 28 Oct 1746 son of George and Sarah (Abbott) Abbott; d. 12 May 1811;[609] m. 11 Apr 1778, MARY GILE, b. about 1755 (parentage not verified at this point); Mary d. Jan 1822.

Stephen Abbott and Mary Gile had seven children born at Concord.

i EPHRAIM ABBOTT, b. 5 Feb 1779; d. Jan 1822. Ephraim did not marry.

892) ii SARAH ABBOTT, b. 20 Jun 1780; d. at Bethel, ME, 1853; m. 1 Jan 1800, her second cousin, AARON ABBOTT, b. at Concord, 11 Apr 1778 son of Aaron and Lydia (Abbott) Abbott; Aaron d. 8 Sep 1856. This is the same as Family #219, child ii.

939) iii POLLY ABBOTT, b. at Concord, 26 Apr 1782; d. after 1850 at Bethel, ME (still living at the 1850 U.S. Census); m. about 1804, JOSEPH TWITCHELL, b. at Bethel, 28 Mar 1782 son of Eleazer and Martha (Mason) Twitchell; Joseph d. after 1870.

940) iv THEODORE ABBOTT, b. 23 Feb 1784; d at George's Mill, NH, 8 May 1855; m. at New London, NH, 25 Jun 1809, MARY "POLLY" BURPEE, b. 29 Sep 1791 daughter of Thomas and Sarah (Smith) Burpee.

v STEPHEN ABBOTT, b. 19 May 1786; d. likely at Portland, ME; m. at Portland, 11 Jul 1819, the widow ABIGAIL WEBB, b. about 1787; Abigail d. 26 Aug 1846. Stephen and Abigail did not have children.

941) vi LUCY ABBOTT, b. 24 Jan 1789; m. at Springfield, NH, 2 Oct 1816, BENJAMIN HASELITNE, b. about 1785 "of Wendell."

942) vii SAMUEL ABBOTT, b. 14 May 1791; d. at Montpelier, VT, 4 May 1861; m. 5 Mar 1813, JANE DAY, b. at Boscawen, 20 Jul 1794 daughter of Daniel and Jane (Cass) Day.

228) EZRA ABBOTT *(George³, Thomas², George¹* **and** *Sarah⁴, Stephen³, John², George¹)*, b. 22 Aug 1756 son of George and Sarah (Abbott) Abbott; d. 21 Feb 1837; m. 1st 21 Nov 1782, BETTY ANDREWS, b. 12 May 1762 daughter of Thomas and Mary (Burnham) Andrews; Betty d. 25 Aug 1794. Ezra m. 2nd, 10 May 1795, ANNER CHOATE, b. at Ipswich 12 Jan 1758 daughter of Thomas and Dorothy (Proctor) Choate; Anner d. 21 Mar 1798. Ezra m. 3rd, 15 Nov 1798, JANE JACKMAN, b. at Boscawen, 20 Dec 1767 daughter of Benjamin and Jane (Woodman) Jackman; Jane d. 2 May 1847.

Ezra resided in Concord where he farmed and owned a small property. As part of his Revolutionary War pension application, Ezra provided a statement of his circumstances on 18 July 1820. The total value of his estate was appraised at $162 with $80 in real estate and $82 in personal estate. He had debts of $50. His household in 1820 was his wife aged 52 and children Betsy aged 20, Ann aged 19, George aged 17, Jane aged 14, Benjamin J. aged 12, and Sarah aged 5. The real estate was sold in 1821. Ezra reported that he suffered a rupture due to his hard labor in farming and was no longer able to work.

On 6 October 1819, Ezra Abbot aged 63 years and resident of Concord made application for a pension based on his service in the Revolution. He made a second statement of 18 July 1820 and a third statement on 9 April 1823. On 1 March 1776, he enlisted as a private in the company of Capt. James Osgood in Col. Timothy Bedel's regiment for a term of ten months. During this enlistment, he was taken prisoner at the Cedars in Canada and was released at the end of his ten-month term. He

[608] Year: 1850; Census Place: Concord, Merrimack, New Hampshire; Roll: M432_435; Page: 61A; Image: 124. Ruth Abbott, age 68, as the only member of the household.

[609] *New Hampshire, Death and Disinterment Records, 1754-1947.*

was discharged on 1 January 1777. He next enlisted in July 1777 under Col. Thomas Stickney in a New Hampshire militia company.[610] He was discharged after two months. Ezra was awarded a pension based on his service.[611]

Ezra and his first wife Betty Andrews had four children whose births are recorded at Concord.

i LUCY ABBOTT, b. 5 Apr 1784; d. at Warner, Nov 1869; m. 17 Feb 1835, OBADIAH/DIAH HUTCHINSON, b. 2 Nov 1776 son of Jonathan and Mehitable (Lovejoy) Hutchinson; Diah d. at Warner, NH, 22 Aug 1843. Lucy did not have any children.

943) ii HARRIET B. ABBOTT, b. 12 Apr 1786; d. at Hartford, VT, 1 Apr 1862; m. 20 Jun 1816, JOHN CHAMPION, b. at South Lyme, CT, 12 Dec 1792 son of Ezra and Lucretia (Tubbs) Champion;[612] John d. at Hartford, VT, 27 Oct 1879.

iii ROBERT BURNHAM ABBOTT, b. 27 Apr 1791; d. at Concord, 22 Aug 1830; m. 1st, at Hopkinton, 25 Dec 1817, RACHEL BURNHAM, b. 2 Sep 1796; Rachel d. 19 Jun 1823. Robert m. 2nd, 11 May 1823, ELIZABETH FOX, b. 2 Jun 1794; Elizabeth d. 7 Apr 1840. Robert did not have children. His will leaves his estate to his wife Elizabeth and to his sister Champion, sister Lucy, and sister Rose Dimond.[613]

944) iv ROSE B. ABBOTT, b. 26 Oct 1796; d. after 1860 (still living at the 1860 U.S. Census, but deceased before 1870); m. 11 Dec 1816, JACOB DIMOND, b. at Concord about 1790 son of Reuben and Mary (Currier) Dimond; Jacob d. at Concord, 28 Apr 1879.[614]

Ezra and Anner Choate had one child.

i ANNER ABBOTT, b. 2 Mar 1798; d. 12 Jun 1798.

Ezra and his third wife Jane Jackman had six children whose births are recorded at Concord.

945) i BETSY ABBOTT, b. 9 Aug 1799; d. 8 Aug 1856; m. Apr 1822, AMOS HOIT, b. 20 Feb 1800 son of Joseph and Polly (Elliot) Hoit. Amos m. 2nd, 6 Apr 1858, Asaneth Swain widow of Henry Swain.

946) ii ANNER ABBOTT, b. 8 Feb 1801; d. 23 Jan 1872; m. 13 Jun 1827, SAMUEL RUNNELS, b. at Boxford, 6 Dec 1796 son of Samuel and Anna (Hardy) Runnels; Samuel d. at Concord, 22 Nov 1864.

947) iii GEORGE B. ABBOTT, b. 27 Jan 1803; d. 8 May 1887; m. 1st, 22 Aug 1836, ELIZA DIDO SPAULDING, b. 6 Dec 1807 daughter of John and Elizabeth (Wheeler) Spaulding; Eliza d. 11 Oct 1856. George m. 2nd, 31 Dec 1861, CLARISSA CARTER, b. about 1815; Clarissa d. 14 Mar 1882.

iv JANE WOODMAN ABBOTT, b. 15 Sep 1805; d. at Warner, 30 Nov 1891; m. 9 Oct 1850, as his second wife, STEPHEN SANBORN, b. 21 Jun 1807 son of Daniel and Betsey (Whitcomb) Sanborn; Stephen d. 24 Jul 1869. Jane did not have children.

948) v BENJAMIN JACKMAN ABBOTT, b. 4 Feb 1808; d. 4 Mar 1869; m. about 1833, DOROTHY TEWKSBURY, b. about 1813 possibly the sister of Daniel who married Sarah, but no records have been located.

949) vi SARAH ABBOTT, b. 22 Jan 1815; d. at Stewartstown, 26 Feb 1889; m. DANIEL TEWKSBURY, b. at Warner, 1 Oct 1810 son of Stephen and Sally (Flanders) Tewksbury; Daniel d. 6 Mar 1874.

229) HANNAH ABBOTT *(Benjamin³, Thomas², George¹* **and** *Hannah (Abbott) Abbott⁴, Samuel³, John², George¹)*, b. 22 Jan 1743 daughter of Benjamin and Hannah (Abbott) Abbott; d. 22 Oct 1820; m. Sep 1783, JEREMIAH STORY (origins not fully verified, but perhaps the Jeremiah Story of Ipswich); d. at Concord, about 1806 based on the date of probate of his estate May 1806 with widow Hannah Story as administrator.

Jeremiah Story did not leave a will. His widow Hannah was administrator of the estate. The inventory of the estate gave a value of $1,000 for real estate which included a lot in Concord, a 36-acre wood lot in Hopkinton, and a 100-acre lot in Groton in Grafton County.[615]

Just two children have been identified in this family.

---

[610] This company served at the Battle of Bennington 17 August 1777, although Ezra does not relate that in his pension application statements; Bouton, History of Concord, p 623

[611] U. S. Revolutionary War Pension and Bounty Land Warrant Application Files, Case S45489

[612] Trowbridge, *The Champion Genealogy*, p 121

[613] Probate Records, 1832-1972; Probate Indexes, 1823-1973; Author: New Hampshire Probate Court (Merrimack County): Probate Place: Merrimakc, New Hampshire. Will of Robert B. Abbott, 5 Jun 1830.

[614] Ancestry.com, New Hampshire, Death and Burial Records Index, 1654-1949

[615] *New Hampshire Wills and Probate Records 1643-1982,* Probate of Jeremiah Story, Rockingham, 19 Mar 1806, Case number 7548.

950) i HANNAH STORY, b. 6 Sep 1784; d. after 1850 likely at Concord; m. 1st, 27 Feb 1806, BENNING NOYES, b. at Bow, 9 Dec 1780 son of Benjamin and Hannah (Thompson) Noyes; Benjamin d. 2 Nov 1814. Hannah m. 2nd, at Montague, 13 Apr 1816, as his second wife, EPHRAIM UPHAM, b. at Weston, 3 Nov 1778 son of Thomas and Martha (Williams) Upham; Ephraim d. 29 Mar 1844. Ephraim was first married to Hannah Cushman.

ii SARAH STORY, b. May 1787; died young.

230) BENJAMIN ABBOT *(Benjamin3, Thomas2, George1* and *Hannah (Abbott) Abbott4, Samuel3, John2, George1)*, b. 10 Feb 1750 son of Benjamin and Hannah (Abbott) Abbott; d. at Concord, 11 Dec 1815; m. 29 Jan 1778, SARAH BROWN, b. at Kingston, NH, 13 Feb 1758 daughter of Daniel and Ruth (Morrill) Brown; Sarah d. 27 Sep 1801. Benjamin m. 2nd, 17 Jun 1805, HANNAH GREENLEAF who was still living at the time of Benjamin's death.

Benjamin Abbot served in the Revolutionary War with the rank of Sargent under the commands of Captain Gordon Hutchins and Colonel John Stark.[616] He is reported to have been at the Battle of Bunker Hill.

Benjamin Abbot wrote his will 19 October 1815. His beloved wife Hannah receives the improvements of one-third part of the real and personal estate. Son Ephraim Abbot and daughter Hannah Hall each receive one dollar. Daughter Ruth Morrill Hall receives two dollars as does daughter Sarah Noyes. Son Isaac receives ten dollars and daughter Abigail Baker receives five dollars. Daughter Permelia receives fifty dollars and son Theodore Thomas Abbot receives four dollars. Son Benjamin Abbot receives all the remainder of the estate and is also named executor.[617]

Benjamin Abbot and Sarah Brown had nine children whose births are recorded at Concord, although some of the births occurred elsewhere.

951) i EPHRAIM ABBOTT, b. 28 Sep 1779; d. at Westford, MA, 21 Jul 1870; m. 1st, at Andover, 5 Jan 1814, MARY HOLYOKE PEARSON, b. 10 Mar 1782 daughter of Eliphalet and Priscilla (Holyoke) Pearson; Mary d. 15 Jul 1829. Ephraim m. 2nd, 21 Jan 1830, ABIGAIL WHITING BANCROFT, b. at Groton, 1797 daughter of Amos and Abigail (Whiting) Bancroft; Abigail d. at Groton, 17 May 1886.

952) ii HANNAH ABBOTT, b. 9 Mar 1782; d. at Westford, MA, 5 Apr 1869; m. 15 Nov 1803, her second cousin once removed (and George Abbott descendant), EBENEZER HALL, b. 9 May 1778 son of Daniel and Deborah (Davis) Hall; Ebenezer d. 14 Oct 1853.

953) iii RUTH MORRILL ABBOTT, b. 27 Jun 1784; d. after 1860 (living in Concord at the 1860 U.S. Census); m. 26 Nov 1805, her second cousin once removed (and George Abbott descendant), JAMES HALL, b. 1784 son of Daniel and Deborah (Davis) Hall.

954) iv BENJAMIN ABBOTT, b. 23 Sep 1786; d. at Whiteside, IL, 28 Feb 1854; m. 17 Sep 1807, DORCAS NOYES, b. at Bow, NH, 22 Aug 1785 daughter of Enoch and Eunice (Kinsman) Noyes; Dorcas d. 17 Feb 1877.

955) v SARAH ABBOTT, b. 3 Oct 1788; d. at Hartland, VT, 27 Jul 1878; m. 12 Sep 1805, STEPHEN NOYES, b. at Bow, NH, 5 Jul 1783 son of Enoch and Eunice (Kinsman) Noyes; Stephen d. 27 Feb 1868.

956) vi ABIGAIL LAWRENCE ABBOTT, b. 20 May 1791; d. at Chicopee, MA, 5 Dec 1856; m. 9 Feb 1809, SETH BAKER, b. at Pembroke, 21 May 1783 son of Thomas and Ruth (Peabody) Baker; Seth d. 30 Apr 1865.

957) vii ISAAC ABBOTT, b. 3 Aug 1793; d. 12 Nov 1840; m. 7 May 1817, SUSAN ELA, b. at Hooksett, 7 Jan 1797 daughter of Israel and Zebiah (Martin) Ela.[618] Susan was still living in 1880 when she was living with her daughter Fanny and her husband Leonard Beard.[619]

958) viii PARMELIA ABBOTT, b. 1 Feb 1796; d. at Pewaukee, WI, 1872; m. 7 Nov 1816, NATHANIEL GOSS, b. at Greenland, NH, 3 Nov 1788 son of Nathaniel and Mary (Nye) Goss; Nathaniel d. at Pewaukee, 7 Jul 1855.

959) ix THEODORE THOMAS ABBOTT, b. 22 Mar 1799; d. at Lunenburg, MA, 23 Mar 1887; m. at Lowell, 7 Aug 1826, MEHITABLE FROST GREENOUGH, b. at Newburyport, 1 Jan 1800 daughter of John and Elizabeth "Betsy" (March) Greenough; Mehitable d. 28 Mar 1887.

---

616 Rolls of Soldiers in the Revolutionary War, Volume 14, p 63, 181, 186

617 *New Hampshire Wills and Probate Records 1643-1982,* Probate of Benjamin Abbott, Rockingham, 17 Jan 1816, Case number 9209.

618 Ela, *Genealogy of the Ela Family*, p 17

619 Year: 1880; Census Place: Lancaster, Coos, New Hampshire; Roll: 762; Page: 153C; Enumeration District: 040

Grandchildren of Nathaniel Abbott and Dorcas Hibbert

231) MARY BLANCHARD *(Mary Abbott Blanchard³, Nathaniel², George¹)*, b. 6 Dec 1719 daughter of Benjamin and Mary (Abbott) Blanchard; m. at Andover, 11 Jan 1742/3, EDWARD TAYLOR.

Edward and Mary settled in Hollis where Edward was a farmer and had a property on the west side of Flint Hill. Three of his sons (Daniel, Joel, and Jacob) served in the Revolution.[620]

There are seven children of Mary Blanchard and Edward Taylor, the first two born at Dracut and the remainder at Hollis.

960) i EDWARD TAYLOR, b. at Dracut, 14 Jul 1744; d. at Plymouth, NH, 1777;[621] m. at Hollis, 14 Nov 1771, MARY WORCESTER daughter of Jesse and Patience (Pope) Worcester who were early settlers of Hollis. After Edward's death, Mary married Enoch Page.

ii MARY TAYLOR, b. at Dracut, 13 Aug 1746; died young.

iii DANIEL TAYLOR, b. at Hollis, 24 Mar 1749

961) iv JOEL TAYLOR, b. at Hollis, 23 Aug 1752; d. at Thornton, NH, 29 Apr 1814; m. 9 Apr 1778, as her second husband, SARAH HOBART, b. at Hollis, 15 Jan 1745 daughter of David and Sarah (Parker) Hobart; Sarah d. 1 Jan 1827. Sarah was first married to Phineas Lovejoy who died about 1777.

962) v MARY TAYLOR, b. 19 Jun 1754; m., Dec 1778, JAMES HOPKINS.[622]

963) vi JACOB TAYLOR, b. 21 Aug 1756; d. at Groton, NH, 5 Aug 1838; m. 19 Nov 1781, BETTY BOYNTON, b. at Hollis, 26 Sep 1756 daughter of John and Lydia (Jewett) Boynton; Betty d. at Grafton, 7 Feb 1843.[623]

vii ANNA TAYLOR, b. 28 Aug 1757; no further record.

232) BENJAMIN BLANCHARD *(Mary Abbott Blanchard³, Nathaniel², George¹)*, b. 19 Mar 1720/1 son of Benjamin and Mary (Abbott) Blanchard; d. 7 Mar 1791 at Canterbury, NH; m. 1st, ELIZABETH HOLT, b. 12 Mar 1719/20 daughter of Moses and Elizabeth (Russell) Holt. Benjamin m. 2nd, 27 Dec 1744, KEZIAH HASTINGS, b. at Lexington, 7 Jul 1723 daughter of Thomas and Sarah (White) Hastings; Keziah d. before 1778. Benjamin m. 3rd, SARAH BURBANK, b. Sep 1758.

Benjamin first married Elizabeth Holt who died in 1744 following the birth of their only child. This son, Benjamin, died a few weeks later. His second marriage was to Keziah Hastings by whom he had fourteen children. Following Keziah's death, Benjamin married Sarah Burbank in 1778.

This family includes sons Abiel (born 1751) and Abel (born 1761), and these two sons married sisters, Mary Eastman and Elizabeth Eastman, and both marriages were in 1784.

Children of Benjamin Blanchard and Keziah Hastings all born at Hollis:

964) i BENJAMIN BLANCHARD; b. 15 Nov 1745; d. 21 Dec 1789; m. 1st, PATTY GOODWIN who died about 1771. Benjamin m. 2nd, SARAH CURRY, b. 15 Nov 1752 daughter of William and Ann (MacFarland) Curry.[624]

816) ii KEZIAH BLANCHARD, b. 26 Mar 1747; d. 12 Aug 1789; m. 1770, JEREMIAH WHEELER son of Jeremiah and Eunice (Russell) Wheeler.

iii ABIEL BLANCHARD, b. 9 Jan 1748/9; died young

965) iv JONATHAN BLANCHARD, b. 28 Jun 1750; d. in Vermont, 31 Dec 1837; m. 13 Oct 1772, HANNAH CHADWICK, b. at Bradford, 22 Jun 1752 daughter of James and Mary (Thurston) Chadwick.

966) v ABIEL BLANCHARD, b. 1 Dec 1751; d. at Peacham, VT, 4 Jan 1803; m. 19 Feb 1784, MARY EASTMAN, b. at Rumford, 6 Apr 1758 daughter of Nathaniel and Phebe (Chandler) Eastman; Mary d. 12 Sep 1831.

---

[620] Spaulding, *An Account of Some Early Settlers of West Dunstable*, p 135

[621] Stearns and Runnels, *History of Plymouth, NH*, volume II, p 669

[622] Spaulding, *An Account of Early Settlers of West Dunstable*, p 135 reports Mary's spouse as James Hopkins. The History of Milford, p 623, has Jonathan Buxton marrying Mary Taylor born in 1754, and so it is not entirely clear who Mary married. But Spaulding's account has this listing as part of the Edward Taylor genealogy. Secomb's *History of Amherst* also has James Hopkins as her spouse. And Buxton Family Association of America states that Jonathan Buxton married Mary Taylor who was the daughter of Timothy. (Volume II, The Buxton Family, p 62)

[623] Ancestry.com, U.S., Revolutionary War Pension and Bounty-Land Warrant Application Files, 1800-1900. Death date of Jacob given in pension papers; the widow's pension was received until 1843.

[624] Lyford, *History of the Town of Canterbury*, p 28

967) vi ISAAC BLANCHARD, b. 14 Apr 1753; m. MOLLY WHEELER who may be the sister of Jeremiah Wheeler who married Isaac's sister Keziah.

vii DORCAS BLANCHARD, b. 25 Feb 1755; died young.

968) viii PETER BLANCHARD, b. 17 Aug 1756; d. at Danville, VT, 25 May 1810; m. by 1786, his second cousin (and George Abbott descendant), SARAH CHANDLER, b. at Concord, 15 Jan 1768 daughter of Abiel and Judith (Walker) Chandler; Sarah d. 21 Nov 1836. This is the same as Family #270, child i.

ix DORCAS BLANCHARD, b. 25 Feb 1757

969) x JOEL BLANCHARD, b. 27 Aug 1759; d. at Peacham, VT, 23 Jul 1816; m. by 1790, REBECCA GEORGE. Joel died from a "wrestle with a neighbor at Peacham, VT."[625]

970) xi ABEL BLANCHARD, b. 17 Feb 1761; d. at Peacham, VT, 12 Aug 1827; m. 1784, ELIZABETH EASTMAN, b. 5 Jun 1761 daughter of Nathaniel and Phebe (Chandler) Eastman.

971) xii REUBEN BLANCHARD, b. 1 Feb 1763; d. at Peacham, VT, 27 Jun 1832;[626] m. by 1790, MARY GRAY of Guy.

972) xiii BETTY BLANCHARD, b. 21 Jan 1765; d. about 1811 (husband remarried 1812); m. at Boscawen, 4 May 1783, ABNER HOYT, b. at Rumford, 15 Apr 1759 son of John and Abigail (Carter) Hoyt. Abner m. 2nd, the widow Mary Livingston Phillips. Abner d. at Wentworth, NH, 28 Dec 1852.

973) xiv SIMON BLANCHARD, b. 10 Apr 1766; d. at Peacham, VT, 22 Apr 1837; m. MARGARET GRAY or Guy, b. about 1768; Margaret d. at Peacham, 9 Aug 1824.

233) ANNE BLANCHARD *(Mary Abbott Blanchard³, Nathaniel², George¹)*, b. 22 Nov 1722 daughter of Benjamin and Mary (Abbott) Blanchard; d. at Hollis, before 1758 (when her second husband remarried); m. 26 Feb 1743, JONATHAN DANFORTH, b. at Billerica, 1 Nov 1714 son of Jonathan and Elizabeth (Manning) Danforth; Jonathan d. 1747 at Hollis, NH. Anne m. 2nd, STEPHEN MARTIN. After Anne's death, Stephen m. 21 Mar 1759, Patience Pope.

Anne Blanchard and Jonathan Danforth had three children whose births are recorded at Hollis.

974) i ANNA DANFORTH, b. 7 Feb 1744; d. at Westminster, MA, 5 Nov 1813; m. 7 Feb 1765, JAMES LAWS, b. at Billerica, 12 Mar 1741/2 son of James and Eunice (-) Laws; James d. Jul 1821.

975) ii JONATHAN DANFORTH, b. 20 Jul 1745; d. at Danville, 6 Feb 1839; m. 1770, HANNAH LEMAN, b. at Hollis, 1 Oct 1751 daughter of Abraham and Elizabeth (Hastings) Leman; Hannah d. 13 Sep 1815.

976) iii DAVID DANFORTH, b. 20 Jan 1746; d. at Washington, NH, 1 Mar 1815; m. by 1773, HANNAH PROCTOR, b. at Chelmsford, 2 Feb 1748 daughter of Israel and Sarah (Raymond) Proctor; Hannah d. 12 Jan 1842.

Anne Blanchard and Stephen Martin had two children whose births are recorded at Hollis. It is possible that Jesse married but it is not clear that the marriage was this Jesse. In any case, no children were located for either Stephen or Jesse in New Hampshire or Vermont.

i STEPHEN MARTIN, b. 1 Sep 1749[627]

ii JESSE MARTIN, b. 1 Aug 1754

234) JACOB BLANCHARD *(Mary Abbott Blanchard³, Nathaniel², George¹)*, b. 11 May 1724 son of Benjamin and Mary (Abbott) Blanchard; d. at Groton, 26 Apr 1770; m. by 1753, REBECCA LAWRENCE, b. at Groton, 17 Apr 1724 daughter of Nathaniel and Anna (Scripture) Lawrence. Rebecca m. 2nd, John Sheple 8 Dec 1772; Rebecca's date of death is not known.

The estate of Jacob Blanchard entered probate 5 March 1771. Rebecca is the administrator of the estate. There is not a will or a distribution document. The inventory gives the total value of the estate as £96.[628]

---

625 Ancestry.com, Rhode Island, Vital Extracts, 1636-1899
626 Ancestry.com, Vermont, Vital Records, 1720-1908
627 Hollis Town Records, 1739-1841, volume 1, image 175, Family Search
628 *Middlesex County, MA: Probate File Papers, 1648-1871. Probate of* Jacob Blanchard, *1771, Case number* 1878.

Records for the births of five children were found at Groton. The birth of the oldest child, Jacob, was recorded at Groton but described as occurring at Hollis. There were no births of other children found at Hollis.

i JACOB BLANCHARD, b. 16 Feb 1753; d. 21 Dec 1769.

977) ii REBECCA BLANCHARD, b. 22 Feb 1756; d. at Groton, 19 Sep 1826; m. 22 Mar 1774, DAVID LAKIN, b. at Groton, 10 Oct 1753 son of John and Lydia (Parker) Lakin; David d. 3 Mar 1846. David's death was attributed to the "decay of nature" at age 92.

iii LUCY BLANCHARD, b. 15 Dec 1757; died in early childhood.

978) iv NATHANIEL BLANCHARD, b. 29 May 1760; d.?; m. 28 Nov 1782, ANNA GREEN, b. 10 Oct 1762 daughter of Eleazer and Sarah (Parker) Green. There is an out-of-wedlock child born in Groton 14 Feb (the year missing) I believe may be a son of this Nathaniel. The child is named Nathaniel, the mother is Esther Nutting and "she saith" this is the child of Nathaniel Blanchard. Nathaniel and Anna had two children born at Groton.

v LUCY BLANCHARD, b. 29 Apr 1762; d. 30 Sep 1843; m. 6 Apr 1778, ELEAZER GREEN, b. 15 Oct 1753 son of Eleazer and Sarah (Parker) Green; Eleazer d. 13 Oct 1824. Lucy and Eleazer did have had children.

235) JOSHUA BLANCHARD *(Mary Abbott Blanchard³, Nathaniel², George¹)*, b. 29 Mar 1726 son of Benjamin and Mary (Abbott) Blanchard; d. *perhaps* 1818 at Wilton, NH; m. 23 Dec 1747, SARAH BURGE, b. 30 May 1728 daughter of John and Sarah (Taylor) Burge.

Joshua Blanchard and Sarah Burge had six children all born at Hollis.

i SARAH BLANCHARD, b. 8 Nov 1748

979) ii JOSHUA BLANCHARD, b. 21 Oct 1750; d. 11 Jan 1776; m. 16 Feb 1775, LUCY FRENCH, b. at Hollis, 21 Apr 1755 daughter of Nicholas and Priscilla (Mooar) French. Lucy m. 2nd, 6 Mar 1781, BRAY WILKINS.

iii DAVID BLANCHARD, b. 10 Nov 1752; m. May 1776, SUSANNA CHENEY, b. at Ashburnham, 2 Nov 1759 daughter of Tristram and Margaret (Joyner) Cheney. No clear records were located for this couple after their marriage.

980) iv MOLLY BLANCHARD, b. 30 Aug 1754; d. at Deering, NH, 5 Oct 1826; m. about 1774, MAJOR MILES RALEIGH, b. at Sudbury, MA, 1749 son of Philip and Susannah (Joyner) Raleigh; Major Raleigh d. at Deering, NH 6 Jun 1838.

v JOHN BLANCHARD, b. 10 Sep 1757

981) vi LUCY BLANCHARD, b. 4 Jun 1760; d. about 1798; m. about 1785, ELIAS CHENEY, b. at Sudbury, 14 Oct 1760 son of Tristram and Margaret (Joyner) Cheney. Elias m. 2nd, 6 Jun 1799, Deborah Winchester. Elias d. at Concord, VT, 1816.

236) NATHANIEL ABBOTT *(Nathaniel³, Nathaniel², George¹)*, b. 10 Mar 1726/7 daughter of Nathaniel and Penelope (Ballard) Abbott; d. at Concord 4 Feb 1806; m. by 1749, MIRIAM CHANDLER, b. at Amesbury 24 Nov 1728 daughter of Nathaniel and Susannah (Rowel) Chandler; Miriam d. at Concord Jan 1811.

Nathaniel Abbott's father was a first settler of Concord receiving land at the Plantation of Penacook in 1726.[629] Nathaniel carried on in his father's footsteps maintaining a farm in Concord. Nathaniel and his wife Miriam raised a family of ten children. Four of the sons, Nathan Chandler, Moses, Philip, and Joshua, served in the Revolutionary War.[630]

Nathaniel and Miriam had ten children, the birth of the oldest child recorded at Rumford and the others recorded at Concord.

982) i NATHANIEL CHANDLER ABBOTT, b. at Rumford, 28 Jul 1750; d. at Rumney, NH, 10 May 1814; m. 20 Jul 1778, HANNAH FARRINGTON who origins are unknown at this time.

983) ii MOSES ABBOTT, b. 19 Jun 1752; d. 11 Jul 1837; m. by 1779, MARY BATCHELDER, b. about 1756; Mary d. at Concord 2 Jul 1833.

iii JOSEPH ABBOTT, b. 24 May 1754; d. 24 Jan 1774.

---

[629] Bouton, *The History of Concord, NH*

[630] Abbot and Abbot, *Genealogical Register of Descendants*, p 118

984) iv PHILIP ABBOTT, b. 4 Feb 1757; d. at Rumford, ME, 20 Mar 1841; m. 10 Feb 1791, EXPERIENCE HOWE, b. at Bolton, MA, 1 Apr 1771 daughter of Phineas and Experience (Pollard) Howe; Experience d. 1857.

985) v JOSHUA ABBOTT, b. 15 Jun 1759; d. at Bow Junction, NH, 4 Mar 1837; m. 1st, 1780, POLLY BROWN. Joshua m. 2nd, ANN MANNING, b. 1767; Ann d. at Bow Junction, 11 Sep 1850.

986) vi SUSANNA ABBOTT, b. 21 Jan 1762; d. at Concord, 24 Jun 1832; m. 29 Nov 1791, JOHN GARVIN, b. at Bow, NH, 14 Aug 1764 son of James and Deborah (-) Garvin; John d. 16 Dec 1826.

575) vii PHEBE ABBOTT, b. 8 Aug 1764; d. at Concord, 11 Aug 1854; m. by 1791, her third cousin, NATHAN ABBOTT, b. 8 Aug 1765 son of Reuben and Rhoda (Whittemore) Abbott; Nathan d. 13 May 1849.

987) viii LEVI ABBOTT, b. 23 Sep 1767; d. 15 Dec 1825; m. 1st, 10 Jul 1791, his first cousin, ELSIE MOOR daughter of Ephraim and Hannah (Abbott) Moor; Elsie d. Apr 1795. Levi m. 2nd, POLLY CARTER, b. 1770 daughter of Joseph and Hannah (Carr) Carter; Polly d. 24 Sep 1840. Elsie Moor is a child in Family 241.

988) ix DAVID ABBOTT, b. 8 Aug 1770; d. in Oxford County, ME, 30 Jun 1836; m. BETSEY COLSON, b. at Weymouth, 24 Aug 1780 daughter of Gideon and Elizabeth (White) Colson; Betsey d. at Roxbury, ME, 16 Sep 1821.

x JOSEPH ABBOTT, b. Jan 1774. Joseph did not marry.[631]

237) DORCAS ABBOTT *(Nathaniel³, Nathaniel², George¹)*, b. 11 Nov 1728 daughter of Nathaniel and Penelope (Ballard) Abbott; d. probably at Concord date unknown; m. by 1749, MOSES MERRILL, b. at Haverhill 27 Sep 1727 son of John and Lydia (Haynes) Merrill; Moses d. at Pembroke, 1767.

Six children of Dorcas and Moses are reported in the Abbot genealogy[632] and a seventh child, Moses, is identified through probate records. Little in the way of records has yet been located for this family.

Moses Merrill of Pembroke did not leave a will and his estate entered probate 3 December 1767 with Timothy Walker, Jr. of Concord as administrator. The inventory filed 7 January 1768 gave estate value as £223.16.10. Simon Dearborn innholder of Epping gave bond on 28 September 1768 for the guardianship of Moses Merrill of Epping a minor over the age of 14 son of Moses. Claims against the estate were £23,424.10.9 old tenor or £1171.4.6 lawful money. The dower thirds were set to the widow Dorcas on 3 April 1769. The estate was sold to settle the debts.[633]

i PENELOPE MERRILL, b. at Rumford, 13 Dec 1749; m. Hoit. There is a 1777 deed record in Exeter, New Hampshire for Penelope Hoyt of Concord, NH granddaughter of John Merrill.[634] Beyond that, there are no records for this couple.

ii MOSES MERRILL, b. at Concord, 19 Nov 1751; d. 10 Apr 1752.

iii MOSES MERRILL, b. about 1753

989) iv DORCAS MERRILL, b. about 1754; d. at Reading, 30 Mar 1841; m. 3 Mar 1778, WILLIAM BEARD, b. at Reading, 5 Sep 1745 son of Andrew and Elizabeth (Burnap) Beard; William d. 15 Nov 1809.

v NEHEMIAH MERRILL, b. about 1757

vi BETSEY MERRILL, b. about 1758; m. 30 Apr 1810, as his second wife, GIDEON PIPER; Gideon d. about 1814 (will 4 Apr 1814). Betsey did not have children.

990) vii LYDIA MERRILL, b. 10 Nov 1759; d. at Concord, 10 Jan 1839; m. SAMUEL DAVIS, b. at Concord, 17 Apr 1759 son of Robert and Sarah (Walker) Davis; Samuel d. about 1848.

238) REBECCA ABBOTT *(Nathaniel³, Nathaniel², George¹)*, b. 27 May 1731 daughter of Nathaniel and Penelope (Ballard) Abbott; d. after 1799 possibly at Thetford, VT; m. 1st by 1750 JOHN MERRILL, b. at Haverhill 25 Nov 1725 son of John and Lydia (Haynes) Merrill; John d. at Bow, NH about 1758. Rebecca m. 2nd JACOB DOYEN, b. 1729 son of Francis and Abigail (Whitaker) Doyen; d. 1799 at Pembroke where his estate was probated.

---

[631] Abbot and Abbot, *Genealogical Register of Descendants*, p 118

[632] Abbot and Abbot, *Genealogical Register of Descendants*, p 121

[633] New Hampshire State Papers, 39:79-80

[634] Hoyt, *Hoyt Family*, p 122

Rebecca Abbott and John Merrill had four children, the birth of the oldest child recorded at Rumford and the youngest three at Concord.

991) i REBECCA MERRILL, b. 16 Aug 1751; m. ABNER FARNUM, b. about 1748 possibly the son of Joseph Farnum; Abner d. at Concord, 2 Aug 1820.

ii LYDIA MERRILL, b. 19 Feb 1753

iii PENELOPE MERRILL, b. 5 Oct 1754

992) iv JOHN MERRILL, b. 14 Jun 1756; d. at Tunbridge, VT, 7 Apr 1814; m. at Pembroke, 14 Mar 1782, his third cousin once removed, SARAH "SALLY" ROBERTSON, b. at Bow, 18 Apr 1757 daughter of John and Lydia (Cales) Robertson.[635]

Jacob Doyen's estate was valued at $529 and the real property was sold to pay the creditors. His five surviving children received a total of $148.[636]

Rebecca Abbott and Jacob Doyen had six children whose births are recorded at Pembroke. Two of their children married two children of James and Deborah (-) Garvin. A third child of James and Deborah Garvin, John Garvin, married Rebecca Abbott's niece, Susanna Abbott.

993) i JACOB DOYEN, b. 22 Apr 1759; d. at Somerset County, ME, 30 Apr 1830; m. Apr 1783, MERCY CRIBBS, b. about 1765; Mercy d. at Smithfield, ME, 3 Aug 1852. Mercy married 2nd, Jonathan Hibbert in October 1830. Jacob's son John married Sarah Tuck they were the parents of Dorcas Doyen, aka Helen Jewett who was murdered in New York in 1836.[637]

ii MARTHA DOYEN, b. 18 Dec 1760; d. 26 Feb 1776.[638]

994) iii SAMUEL DOYEN, b. 26 Feb 1764. Samuel completed a bounty-land warrant application for land in Maine[639] and died at Levant, ME about 1832. Samuel does marry but do not know who yet, perhaps a woman named Polly who died in Maine in 1832.

995) iv FRANCIS DOYEN, b. 17 Feb 1767; d. likely in Maine after 1830;[640] m. 7 Sep 1789, BETTY GARVIN, b. at Bow, 20 Dec 1770 daughter of James and Deborah (-) Garvin.

996) v NATHANIEL DOYEN, b. 17 Feb 1767; d. at Pembroke, 8 May 1841; m. DEBORAH SMITH.

997) vi HANNAH DOYEN, b. 1772; m. EBENEZER GARVIN, b. at Bow, 15 Sep 1768 son of James and Deborah (-) Garvin.

239) ELIZABETH ABBOTT *(Nathaniel[3], Nathaniel[2], George[1])*, b. 1 Jul 1733 daughter of Nathaniel and Penelope (Ballard) Abbott; d. at Concord 25 Jan 1834; m. by 1755, JOSEPH HAZELTINE, b. at Rumford 27 Dec 1731 son of Richard and Sarah (Barnes) Hazeltine; Joseph d. 30 May 1798.

Joseph Hazeltine wrote his will 26 May 1798. Beloved wife Elizabeth receives improvements on one-half of the real estate. His daughters each receive $25 and they are Sarah Houghton, Anne Green, Susanna Moore, Hannah Stickney, and Betty Noyes. The daughters will divide one-half of the estate after the decease of their mother. Beloved son Ballard Hazeltine receives one-half of the real estate. Ballard is also named sole executor of the estate.[641]

There are records for nine children of Elizabeth Abbott and Joseph Hazeltine, the first four birth at Rumford and the younger children at Concord.

998) i SARAH HAZELTINE, b. 24 Dec 1755; m. at Concord, 20 Jan 1777, NAHUM HOUGHTON, origin uncertain but perhaps the Nahum born in 1732 in Worcester County, MA; Nahum d. about 1800 as there is a guardianship case for his son Nahum in 1800 (son Nahum at 14 or above requests uncle Jacob Green as guardian). Sarah seems to have married 19 Jan 1812, EDMUND CARLETON.

---

[635] Some published histories/genealogies give Sarah's mother as John Robertson's first wife, Lydia Cales. However, *Bow, NH: The Town Book of Bow* identifies Elizabeth as the mother of all the children of John Robertson. *Bow, NH: The Town Book of Bow, New Hampshire, 1760-1877.* Manuscript. R. Stanton Avery Special Collections, New England Historic Genealogical Society, Boston, MA. (Online database. *AmericanAncestors.org*, New England Historic Genealogical Society, 2012.) Lydia Cales is listed here; more information is needed to resolve the issue.

[636] Rockingham County Probate Records 1799-1800, (microfilm) 77, 185, 272, 330, NEHGS

[637] Cohen, P. C. (1993). The Mystery of Helen Jewett: Romantic Fiction and the Eroticization of Violence. *Legal Stud. F.*, *17*, 133.

[638] History of Pembroke, NH 1730-1893, p 70

[639] Ancestry.com, U.S., Revolutionary War Pension and Bounty-Land Warrant Application Files, 1800-1900

[640] He is perhaps the Francis Doyen listed in the 1830 Census at Avon, Somerset, Maine as the male age 60-69. 1830; Census Place: Avon, Somerset, Maine; Series: M19; Roll: 51; Page: 174; Family History Library Film: 0497947

[641] *New Hampshire Wills and Probate Records 1643-1982,* Probate of Joseph Hazeltine, Rockingham, 18 Jul 1798, Case number 6477.

ii ABIGAIL HAZELTINE, b. 3 Sep 1758; d. at Haverhill, NH, 17 Apr 1785; m. 29 Nov 1783, as his second wife, JOHN PAGE, b. at Rindge, 16 Jul 1741 son of Nathaniel and Mercy (Gould) Page. Abigail and John had one son who died at 2 days old. John had married first, Abigail Sanders with whom he had no children. John married third, Hannah Royce who was the widow of William Green.[642]

999) iii ANNA HAZELTINE, b. 19 May 1760; d. at Bow, 13 Nov 1838; m. at Concord, 26 Sep 1776, JACOB GREEN, b. at Worcester, MA, 18 Jan 1749/50 son of Nathaniel and Lucy (Gerfield) Green; Jacob d. 17 Apr 1815.

iv PETER HAZELTINE, b. 23 Sep 1762; d. 20 Nov 1779 by drowning.

v SUSANNA HAZELTINE, b. 12 Sep 1765; m. at Bow, 21 Nov 1784, EPHRAIM MOORE. Nothing certain has been found for this family. Ephraim Moor and Hannah Abbott (Family #241) were living in Bow at this time and perhaps Ephraim is a child in that family. He may be the Ephraim Moore with an estate probated in 1830 in Beekmantown, NY with widow Susanna. Birth records for children have not been located.

1000) vi HANNAH HAZELTINE, b. 31 Aug 1767; m. 19 Apr 1787, JAMES STICKNEY, b. at Concord, 5 Dec 1766 son of Jonathan and Sarah (Webster) Stickney.

1001) vii BALLARD HAZELTINE, b. 4 Sep 1769; d. at Plattsburgh, NY, 1836; m. 19 Apr 1792, SALLY NOYES, b. at Bow, 17 Dec 1768 daughter of John and Mary (Fowler) Noyes.

1002) viii BETTY HAZELTINE, b. 3 Oct 1771; d. at Bow, 1801; m. at Pembroke, 18 Nov 1788, JOHN P. NOYES, b. at Bow, 27 Jun 1766 son of John and Mary (Fowler) Noyes; John d. in upstate New York, 1 Mar 1814 while in military service. John married second, MARTHA "PATTY" GREEN (Betty Hazeltine's niece and George Abbott descendant in the sixth generation), b. at Bow 14 Oct 1777 daughter of Jacob and Anna (Hazeltine) Green; Martha d. at Concord, 28 Jun 1843. Martha's parents and Family #995.

ix NATHANIEL HAZELTINE, b. 24 Aug 1774; d. 23 Feb 1796.

240) MARY ABBOTT *(Nathaniel³, Nathaniel², George¹)*, b. 7 Mar 1735 daughter of Nathaniel and Penelope (Ballard) Abbott; d. Mar 1795; m. by 1754, JOSEPH WALKER,[643] b. at Concord, 24 Apr 1732 son of Isaac and Sarah (Breed) Walker; Joseph d. at 1800 at Fryeburg, ME.

Joseph and Mary Walker were early settlers in Fryeburg. Joseph signed a petition in 1764 related to the opening of a road and another petition in 1776 requesting incorporation of the town.[644]

Mary Walker and Joseph Walker had eleven children at Fryeburg.[645] Three of the daughters in this family married three Stevens brothers (John, Samuel, and Ebenezer).

1003) i JOSEPH WALKER, b. 1754; m. 11 Dec 1776, JANE STERLING, b. at Conway, NH, 1755 daughter of Hugh and Isabel (Stark) Sterling.[646]

1004) ii NATHANIEL WALKER, b. 1757; d. at Fryeburg, 13 Jun 1839;[647] m. 18 Aug 1777, ABIGAIL CHARLES, b. 1758 (based on age at time of death); d. 5 Sep 1843.

1005) iii SARAH WALKER, b. 1759; m. JOHN AMES of unknown origins. Evidence of one child of this family, Jeremiah Walker Ames born at Chatham, NH has so far been located.

iv MARY WALKER, b. 1761; died in infancy.

574) v MARY WALKER, b. 1763; d. at Concord, 22 Sep 1852; m. her third cousin, EZRA ABBOTT, b. at Concord, 8 Aug 1765 son of Reuben and Rhoda (Whittemore) Abbott; Ezra d. 24 Apr 1839.

---

642 Witcher, *History of the Town of Haverhill, New Hampshire*, p 611

643 Foster and Walker, "The Walkers of Woburn, Massachusetts", *Historical Bulletin*, volumes 6-9, pp 64-65

644 Barrows, *Fryeburg, Maine: An Historical Sketch*

645 Foster and Walker, "The Walkers of Woburn", pp 64-65

646 Albert Sterling, 1909, The Sterling Genealogy, volume II, pp 1102-1103

647 The members of this family who died at Fryeburg are buried in the West Fryeburg Cemetery, Oxford County, Maine. The various gravestones with death dates and ages can be found on Find A Grave.

1006) vi ANNA WALKER, b. 1765; d. at Fryeburg, 11 Mar 1854; m. JOHN STEVENS, b. Mar 1764 (based on age at death) son of John Stevens who was perhaps born in England; John d. 30 Sep 1825.

1007) vii RUTH WALKER, b. Oct 1768; d. at Fryeburg, 19 Aug 1848; m. EBENEZER STEVENS, b. Oct 1767 son of John Stevens; John d. 1 Apr 1851.

viii JEREMIAH WALKER; b. 1771 and died in infancy.

ix NAMAH WALKER, b. 1772; died in infancy.

1008) x JEREMIAH BALLARD WALKER, b. 8 Dec 1777; d. at Whitefield, NH, 19 Oct 1841; m. his first cousin, HANNAH WALKER, b. 1781 daughter of Samuel and Hannah (Hazeltine) Walker; Hannah d. at Whitefield, 15 Jan 1855.

1009) xi NAMAH WALKER, b. Nov 1778; d. at Fryeburg, 3 Dec 1844; m. SAMUEL STEVENS, b. 11 Jun 1773 son of John Stevens; Samuel d. at Fryeburg, 7 Oct 1849.

241) HANNAH ABBOTT *(Nathaniel3, Nathaniel2, George1)*, b. 7 Mar 1736 daughter of Nathaniel and Penelope (Ballard) Abbott; d. after 1792 when dower rights were set off to her; m. EPHRAIM MOOR whose origin is not yet established but perhaps the son of James and Agnes (Colbreath) Moor;[648] Ephraim d. at Bow, NH about 1791 (when his estate was probated).

Ephraim Moor's estate entered probate 2 November 1791. Moses Moor was the administrator of his father's estate. The widow Hannah gave up her right to administer the estate and requested that her son Moses assume those responsibilities. The dower rights were set off to widow Hannah Moor. The estate had little value and there were multiple creditors.[649]

Published sources have conflicting information on this family. The Chandler and Abbot genealogies have Hannah Abbott as the wife of Ephraim Moor. The History of Pembroke (pp 230-231) states she is Hannah Rogers and that Ephraim had a second wife named Jennie Moore. However, as stated in his probate record, Ephraim's widow was Hannah. Ephraim Moor's brother William married someone named Hannah so perhaps Hannah Rogers was William's wife. One of the grandchildren of Ephraim Moor and Hannah Abbott was named Albert Abbott Moor which would support there being an Abbott connection. In addition, the published genealogies that give Ephraim's wife as Hannah Rogers have a birthdate for her of 7 March 1736 which is the birthdate of Hannah Abbott, and there is a birth record for Hannah Abbott daughter of Nathaniel and Penelope with the date 7 March 1736.

There is also discrepancy for the children in the family. The History of Pembroke and the Abbot genealogy have somewhat different lists of children. Some, but not all, the names are the same. What there does seem to be is a lack of much clear documentation for this family. There are no birth records for the children. The children given here are from the Abbot genealogy.

1010) i JAMES MOOR, b. about 1760; d. at Waterville, ME, 27 Aug 1835; m. Nov 1779, ABIGAIL NOYES, b. at Bow, 28 Jan 1764 daughter of John and Mary (Fowler) Noyes.

ii ANNA MOOR m. (-) LONG whose identity is not known. There is no information on this family.

1011) iii MOSES MOOR (twin of Aaron), b. about 1762; m. 22 Nov 1788, ESTHER MOOR, b. at Pembroke, 6 Oct 1769 daughter of Robert and Ruhamah (Mitchell) Moor.

iv AARON MOOR (twin of Moses); b. about 1762; died young.

987) v ELSIE MOOR, b. estimate 1771; d. at Concord, Apr 1795; m. 1791, LEVI ABBOTT, b. at Concord, 23 Sep 1767 son of Nathaniel and Miriam (Chandler) Abbott. Levi m. 2nd, 1 Oct 1795, Mary "Polly" Carter. Levi d. 15 Dec 1825.

vi DAVID MOOR; according to the Abbot genealogy he married, but name of his wife was not given. One possibility to explore is Janet Ross who married a David Moor at Barnet, VT in 1792.

1012) vii HANNAH MOOR, b. at Pembroke, about 1772; d. 3 Jan 1828; m. about 1791, WILLIAM NEILSON, b. 1767 at Erskine, Renfrewshire, Scotland son of William and Jean (Stewart) Neilson; William d. at Lyman, NH, 19 Sep 1830. The father of William rewrote his will 29 Sep 1830 naming the children of William, who was then deceased, among his heirs.

viii POLLY MOOR; she is reported to have married, but name of her husband is not known.

[648] According to Cutter, Volume 2, p 726 the parents of Ephraim were from Ireland and Ephraim was born in New Hampshire.

[649] *New Hampshire Wills and Probate Records 1643-1982*, Probate of Ephraim Moor, Rockingham, 2 Nov 1791, Case number 5704.

1013) ix MARTHA "PATTY" MOOR, b. 1779 (based on age at time of death); d. at Barnet, VT, 7 May 1827; m. at Barnet, VT, 6 Nov 1801, ALEXANDER BUCHANAN, b. in Scotland 4 Sep 1771 son of Peter and Anabel (Miller) Buchanan; Alexander d. at Barnet, 2 Oct 1853.[650] Alexander m. 2nd, Deborah.

1014) x DOLLY MOOR, b. about 1780; m. at Bow, 29 Jan 1801,[651] ELISHA UPTON, b. about 1779 son of Elisha and Sarah (Gilford) Upton; Elisha d. at Parishville, NY, 1854.[652][653]

xi Son who died as infant.

242) RUTH ABBOTT *(Nathaniel3, Nathaniel2, George1)*, b. 28 Jan 1738 daughter of Nathaniel and Penelope (Ballard) Abbott; d. 27 Feb 1817; m. by 1759, JAMES A. WALKER, b. at Concord 2 Sep 1739 son of Isaac and Sarah (Breed) Walker; James d. 9 Feb 1821.

James Walker wrote his will 7 December 1805 and his estate entered probate 3 May 1821. Son Bruce Walker receives $20 and a feather bed. Son John receives $80 and a feather bed. Daughter Hannah receives $150 and a feather bed as do sons James Walker and Peter Walker. Beloved wife Ruth ("in case she survives me") receives the use, occupation, and improvement of all the household goods for her natural life. These household goods will go to Hannah after her mother's decease. His wife also receives the privilege of a seat in his pew in the meeting house. Daughter Hannah also "the privilege of a seat in my pew in said meeting house so long as she remains single and unmarried." Son Abiel Walker receives a feather bed and pew number 29 in the Concord meeting house. All the rest of the estate goes to Ruth. Son Abiel is named executor.[654]

Ruth Abbott and James Walker had seven children whose births are recorded at Rumford/Concord.

1015) i BRUCE WALKER, b. at Rumford, 17 May 1760; d. at Hebron, NH, 27 Jul 1840; m. MEHITABLE CURRIER, b. at Concord, 26 Apr 1762 daughter of William and Mary (Carter) Currier; Mehitable d. 8 May 1849.

1016) ii JOHN WALKER, b. at Rumford, 8 May 1763; d. at Bethel, ME, 25 Feb 1825; m. ELIZABETH CALEF, b. at Kingston, NH, 1 Oct 1767 daughter of Joseph and Hannah (Pettingill) Calef;[655] Elizabeth d. at Bethel, 14 Nov 1829.

921) iii ABIEL WALKER, b. at Concord, 5 Jul 1766; d. 4 Apr 1855; m. 1st, 3 Feb 1807, JUDITH DAVIS; Judith d. 1 Apr 1808. Abiel m. 2nd, as her second husband, his third cousin (and George Abbott descendant), MARY "MOLLY" WILSON, b. 23 Jul 1772 daughter of Thomas and Mary (Hall) Wilson. Molly was first married to John Thorndike. This is the same as Family #224, child ii.

iv HANNAH WALKER, b. at Concord, 26 Feb 1770; d, at Concord, 10 Dec 1847; m. at Concord, 28 Nov 1819, as his second wife, WILLIAM FISK, b. at Wenham, MA, 20 Apr 1755 son of William and Susannah (Batchelder) Fisk. William d. at Amherst, 4 Jun 1831. William was married first to Eunice Nourse.[656] Hannah did not have children.

v RUTH WALKER, b. 12 Mar 1776; d. 17 May 1797.

1017) vi JAMES WALKER, b. 26 Jul 1778; d. at Milton, NH, 4 Sep 1826; m. ABIGAIL CHAPMAN, b. at Methuen, 29 Dec 1778 daughter of Eliphaz and Hannah (Jackman) Chapman; Abigail d. 3 Oct 1807. James m. 2nd, PATTY HEATH INGALLS,[657] b. 8 Aug 1786 daughter of Moses and Susan (Heath) Ingalls; Patty d. Dec 1865.[658]

1018) vii PETER WALKER, b. 6 Jul 1780; d. 2 Jun 1857; m. 3 Jan 1808, ABIGAIL SWAN, b. 15 Dec 1787 daughter of Joseph Greely and Elizabeth (Evans) Swan; Abigail d. 26 Jan 1861.[659]

---

650 The graves of Martha and Alexander Buchanan are in Barnet Center Cemetery and the gravestones include dates of death and age at time of death. Alexander's gravestone includes that he was a native of Scotland (findagrave.com)

651 *Bow, NH: The Town Book of Bow, New Hampshire, 1760-1877,* p 233 (americanancestors.org)

652 Vinton, *The Upton Memorial*, p 224

653 Year: 1850; Census Place: Parishville, Saint Lawrence, New York; Roll: M432_590; Page: 124A; Image: 517. Elisha Upton, age 71, living in a household headed by his son Guilford Upton. Dolly is apparently deceased.

654 *New Hampshire Wills and Probate Records 1643-1982,* Probate of James Walker, Rockingham, 3 May 1821, Case number 10289.

655 The 1810 will of Joseph Calef includes a bequest to his daughter Elizabeth Walker.

656 Secomb, *History of Amherst*, p 585

657 Foster and Walker, "The Walkers of Woburn," p 108

658 Burleigh, *Genealogy of the Ingalls Family*, p 96

659 Evans, *Descendants of David Evans*, p 18

243) JOSHUA ABBOT *(Nathaniel[3], Nathaniel[2], George[1])*, b. 24 Feb 1740 son of Nathaniel and Penelope (Ballard) Abbott; d. at Concord, NH, Mar 1815; m. at Bradford 23 Oct 1766, his third cousin once removed, ELIZA CHANDLER, b. at Bradford 20 Jul 1739 daughter of Josiah and Sara (-- Parker widow) Chandler; Eliza d. 27 May 1812.

Joshua served as a Captain in the Revolutionary War marching on Bunker Hill, and additional periods of service in New York in 1776, and his company was present with Gerrish's regiment in September 1777 at Saratoga.[660]

Joshua Abbot wrote his will 3 March 1815 at Concord. The will includes bequests to the following persons: daughter Betsey Abbot of Hallowell, daughter Sally Dummer who is in Hallowell, son Joshua Abbot of Concord, granddaughter Elizabeth Chandler Abbot, granddaughter Mary Faulkner Abbot, grandson Thomas Faulkner Abbot, grandson John Sullivan Abbot, and son Nathaniel Abbot of Concord. Son Nathaniel Abbot is named executor of the estate.[661]

Joshua and Eliza had six children whose births are recorded at Concord.

i NATHANIEL ABBOT, b. 25 Aug 1767; d. 31 May 1769.

1019) ii NATHANIEL ABBOT, b. 28 Oct 1769; d. 25 Nov 1848; m. 10 Feb 1793, ELIZABETH DEARBORN, b. at Chester, 1 Feb 1772 daughter of John and Mary (Emerson) Dearborn; Elizabeth d. 7 Jun 1855.

1020) iii BETSY ABBOT, b. 6 Aug 1773; d. at Farmington, ME, 30 Jul 1846; m. at Hallowell, 8 Apr 1798, her second cousin, JACOB ABBOT, b. at Wilton, 20 Oct 1776 son of Jacob and Lydia (Stevens) Abbott; Jacob d. 21 Jan 1847. This is the same as Family #255, child v.

1021) iv SARAH "SALLY" ABBOT, b. 16 Dec 1775; d. at Hallowell, 1 Dec 1841; m. 29 Apr 1802, GORHAM DUMMER, b. at Hallowell, 27 Sep 1782 son of Nathaniel and Mary (Owen) Dummer; Gorham d. 2 Jan 1805.

1022) v JOHN SULLIVAN ABBOT, b. 20 Aug 1778; d. 10 Aug 1810; m. his second cousin once removed (and George Abbott descendant) MARY FAULKNER, b. 1781 daughter of Abiel and Hannah (Abbott) Faulkner; Mary d. 17 Jun 1840.

1023) vi JOSHUA ABBOT, b. 8 Dec 1782; d. at Norfolk, VA of consumption while serving as a minister, 29 Sep 1821; m. 6 Nov 1808, ELIZA "BETSY" KIMBALL, b. 12 Jul 1787 daughter of Phineas and Lucy (Pearl) Kimball; Betsy d. at Concord 23 Jan 1870.[662]

244) JEREMIAH ABBOTT *(Nathaniel[3], Nathaniel[2], George[1])*, b. 17 Mar 1744 son of Nathaniel and Penelope (Ballard) Abbott; d. at Conway, NH 8 Nov 1823; m. ELIZABETH STICKNEY, b. at Rumford 7 Dec 1753 daughter of Thomas and Anna (Osgood) Stickney; Elizabeth d. about 1836.

Jeremiah Abbott was a prominent early settler of Conway. He was involved in making additions to a store built by Harry Merrill, and this structure was ultimately known as the Pequawket Hotel. This building was also the site of the first post office in Conway, and for a time housed the jail under a trap door in the floor – a true multi-purpose building. This hotel had several notable guests in later years including President Grant and John Greenleaf Whittier.[663]

Jeremiah was in the Battle of Bunker Hill serving in the company commanded by his brother Joshua. He also served at the Battle of Ticonderoga with the rank of Lieutenant. He also participated in the expedition against Canada.[664]

The Abbot genealogy lists ten children for this family.

1024) i ANNA ABBOTT, b. at Concord, 6 Jun 1770; m. 27 Dec 1789, RICHARD BUSWELL, b. at Kingston, 28 Mar 1761 son of Caleb and Mary (Badger) Buswell; Richard d. at Lebanon, NH, 22 Oct 1835.

ii RUTH ABBOTT; Ruth did not marry.

iii JAMES OSGOOD ABBOTT; died young.

iv JOHN ABBOTT; he was a seaman who died at Havana.

v JAMES OSGOOD ABBOTT; sea captain who died at Baltimore; he married but had no children.

vi MARY ABBOTT; died at Portland, ME; Mary did not marry.

---

660 Lyford, *History of Concord, New Hampshire*

661 *New Hampshire Wills and Probate Records 1643-1982*, will of Joshua Abbot, 3 Mar 1815, Rockingham.

662 Morrison and Sharples, *History of the Kimball Family in America, volume 1*, p 340

663 Brian P. Wiggin, 2015, Conway's Early Inns, The Conway Daily Sun, https://www.conwaydailysun.com/news/conway-s-early-inns-part-i-grant-and-maybe-lincoln/article_395a7ed7-ce14-572d-ae0e-f84b9ba68905.html

664 Abbot and Abbot, *Genealogical Register of Descendants*, p 125

1025) vii ELIZABETH "BETSY" ABBOTT, b. 1784; d. at Conway, NH, 26 Nov 1846; m. 22 Apr 1805, THOMAS ODELL, b. at Conway, 25 Apr 1775 son of Joseph and Sarah (Ingalls) Odell; Thomas d. 31 Jan 1865.

1026) viii JEREMIAH ABBOTT; m. MARY SMITH of Biddeford, ME.

1027) ix THOMAS STICKNEY ABBOTT, b. 24 Aug 1792; d. at Portland, ME, 12 Nov 1864; m. 1st, 28 Dec 1818, his third cousin once removed (and George Abbott descendant), BETSEY LOVEJOY, b. at Conway, 19 Apr 1795 daughter of Jeremiah and Elizabeth (Spring) Lovejoy; Betsey d. 1828. Thomas m. 2nd, about 1832, MARY S. TROTT.

1028) x NATHANIEL ABBOTT, b. about 1797 (based on age at census records); d. after 1850; m. his third cousin once removed (and George Abbott descendant), NANCY LOVEJOY, b. about 1805 daughter of Jeremiah and Elizabeth (Spring) Lovejoy.

245) DOROTHY ABBOTT *(Nathaniel³, Nathaniel², George¹)*, b. 28 Dec 1746 daughter of Nathaniel and Penelope (Ballard) Abbott; d. 27 Sep 1776; m. 29 May 1766, DAVID GEORGE of uncertain origins but perhaps the son of David George and Ann Cottle born in 1745 in Haverhill. There were several Haverhill families who migrated to Concord near the time of its first settlement. After Dorothy's death, David George married Hannah Colby about 1777 and they had eight children. David died at Littleton, NH about 1816.

David George was a tailor in Concord. He placed an advertisement in the newspaper giving the price for making a "genteel suit of superfine broadcloth" as three dollars and the price for an "ordinary suite of coarse cloth" as two dollars.[665] He also held several civil positions in the town.

In his will written 8 July 1811 (probate 5 November 1816), David George made bequests to the following persons: oldest son David George, George Thatcher the only son of daughter Hannah Thatcher, daughter Jane Virgin has already received her portion, daughter Dolly Morse, and daughter Betsey Martin. These first five bequests are to the children from his marriage to Dorothy Abbott. His children from his second marriage named in the will are Nanne George, daughter Ruth Gridley, daughter Polly Gennes, son Jacob Rise George, son Christopher Columbus George, son Hector Temple George, daughter Laura C. George, and son George Washington Adams George.[666]

Dorothy Abbott and David George had five children all born at Concord.

1029) i DAVID GEORGE, b. 4 Jan 1767; d. at Concord, 1838; m. 30 Aug 1789, ELIZABETH EMERY, b. at Concord, 30 Apr 1771 daughter of Benjamin and Sarah (Bailey) Emery;[667] Elizabeth d. 6 Aug 1827.

1030) ii HANNAH GEORGE, b. 23 Jun 1768; likely died by the early 1790's assuming she had just the one child mentioned in her father's will; married a Mr. Thatcher whose identity has not been found.

1031) iii JANE GEORGE, b. 22 Apr 1772; d. after 1830 at Rumford, ME;[668] m. 6 Jun 1793, JEREMIAH VIRGIN, b. at Concord, 7 Sep 1765 son of William and Mehitable (Stickney) Virgin; Jeremiah died after 1830. Jeremiah Virgin and Jane Virgin were first members of the congregational church in Rumford which was organized in 1803.[669]

1032) iv DOLLY GEORGE, b. 8 Feb 1774; d. 20 Mar 1861 at Rumford, ME;[670] m. 5 Aug 1792, BENJAMIN MORSE, b. at Amherst, NH, 24 Jun 1771 son of Benjamin and Rachel (Webster) Morse; Benjamin d. at Rumford, 4 May 1849.

1033) v BETSEY GEORGE, b. 22 Jan 1776; d. at Rumford, ME, 2 May 1832; m. 1 Jul 1798, DANIEL MARTIN, b. at Concord, 16 Jul 1772 son of Henry and Esther (Kimball) Martin; Daniel d. 15 Jun 1861.

246) SARAH ABBOTT *(Nathaniel³, Nathaniel², George¹)*, b. 3 Dec 1748 daughter of Nathaniel and Penelope (Ballard) Abbott; d. at Elizabethtown, NY. 2 Apr 1841; m. 1 Dec 1764, SAMUEL FARNUM, b. at Concord, 10 Feb 1743 son of Zebadiah and Mary (Walker) Farnum; Samuel d. at Essex County, NY, 25 Jan 1813.

---

665 Bouton, *History of Concord*, p 311

666 *New Hampshire Wills and Probate Records 1643-1982,* Probate of David George, Grafton, 5 Nov 1816.

667 The 1819 will of Benjamin Emery of Concord includes a bequest to his daughter Elizabeth George.

668 There is an 1830 Census record for Rumford for Jeremiah Virgin that includes a male and female of the ages of Jeremiah and Jane Virgin. A census record from 1840 that would fit with them was not located.

669 Lapham, *History of Rumford, Oxford County, Maine*, p 141

670 Dorothy Morse, age 86, is listed in the 1860 U.S. Census for Rumford; she is the head of household with Clarissa Morse age 43 living with her.

There is little information on this family. Samuel was born in New Hampshire, may have spent some time in Corinth Vermont where some of their children were born, and later relocated to New York. Samuel's pension application file lists eight children.

i MEHITABLE FARNUM, b. 15 Sep 1765; d. 24 Feb 1781

ii SAMUEL FARNUM, b. 1767; d. 12 Feb 1813 at Reber, NY. His gravestone has age at death as 46.

1034) iii ZEBADIAH FARNUM, b. in Vermont, 31 Mar 1769; d. at Watkins, OH, 13 Oct 1854; m. JANE MCNINCH, b. 13 Oct 1763; Jane d. 18 Mar 1853.

iv SARAH FARNUM, b. 19 Apr 1771

v POLLY FARNUM, b. 31 Aug 1774

vi Child (possibly Chloe) FARNUM, b. 17 Mar 1781

vii JOHN FARNUM, b. 5 Jul 1784

viii JOSEPH FARNUM, b. 1 Feb 1786

247) HANNAH BLANCHARD *(Sarah Abbott Blanchard³, Nathaniel², George¹)*, b. 8 Oct 1728 daughter of Joseph and Sarah (Abbott) Blanchard; d. likely at Hillsborough, NH; m. 19 May 1748, her third cousin, STEPHEN BLANCHARD, b. 9 Aug 1726 son of Stephen and Deborah (Phelps) Blanchard. Stephen had a second marriage to ELIZABETH POTTER. Stephen d. at Hillsborough between 1796 and 1802 (will written 4 Mar 1796 and proved 19 Oct 1802).

Stephen Blanchard of Milford, New Hampshire wrote his will 4 March 1796 and it was proved 19 October 1802. The will includes token bequests of one dollar to his children who have already received their full portions of the estate. The children named are son Jacob, son John, daughter Sarah, daughter Mary, and daughter Phebe. Other children receive more substantial bequests (some money or land bequests) including son Cyrus, son Joel, son James, and son Phineas. These last four sons are sons from his second marriage. He also mentions grandchildren, the sons of Stephen who is deceased, and to grandchildren the children of Hannah who is deceased. None of the last names of the daughters are given in the will nor are the names of the grandchildren. Beloved wife Elizabeth received the use of the East room and other material support for her maintenance.[671]

Hannah Blanchard and Stephen Blanchard had eight children whose births are recorded at Andover. There is one record discrepancy regarding the marriages of the children. The Batchelder genealogy[672] states that Sarah Blanchard married Uziel Batchelder while there is a marriage transcription for a marriage of Mary Blanchard and Uziel. There are baptism records in Andover for two of Uziel's children that give the mother's name as Sarah. Finally, there is a Vermont death record for Sarah Batchelder wife of Uziel.

1035) i STEPHEN BLANCHARD, b. 4 Jan 1748/9; d. at Milford, 1789; m. by 1774, LUCY ADAMS, b. at Dunstable, NH, b. 8 May 1747 daughter of Ephraim and Thankful (Blodgett) Adams.

ii PHINEAS BLANCHARD, b. 21 Jun 1750; d. at Milford, 18 Oct 1775. Phineas did not marry.

iii HANNAH BLANCHARD, b. 20 Jul 1752. It is known from the will that she married and had children and died prior to 1796. However, no good information has been located that would shed light on the name of her husband.

1036) iv SARAH BLANCHARD, b. 27 Feb 1755; d. at Chester, VT, 20 Nov 1836; m. 18 Sep 1777, UZIEL BATCHELDER, b. at Beverly, 30 Oct 1755 son of Joseph and Judith (Ray) Batchelder.

1037) v JACOB BLANCHARD, b. 22 Jun 1758; d. at Guildhall, VT, 1806; m. at Holland, MA, 6 Apr 1784, ELIZABETH CRAWFORD, b. at Union, CT, 1860 daughter of John and Mary (Rosebrooks) Crawford.[673]

vi MARY BLANCHARD, b. 9 Aug 1760; she was living at the time of her father's will in 1796.

1038) vii PHEBE BLANCHARD, b. 15 Dec 1762; d. at Wilton Center, NH, 20 Aug 1838; m. JEREMIAH BURNHAM, b. at Ipswich, 14 Sep 1763 son of Jeremiah and Mary (Burnham) Burnham; Jeremiah d. at Wilton Center, NH, 1 Nov 1844.

1039) viii JOHN BLANCHARD, b. 16 Feb 1767; d. at Chester, VT, 19 Apr 1855; m. SYBIL CRAWFORD, b. at Union, CT, about 1762 daughter of John and Mary (Rosebrooks) Crawofrd. This is confirmed by the will of John

---

[671] *New Hampshire Wills and Probate Records 1643-1982,* Probate of Stephen Blanchard, Hillsborough, will 4 Mar 1796.

[672] Pierce, *Batcheller Genealogy*, p 412

[673] Gould, *Early Families of Bradford*, p 43

Blanchard as the children named in his will have birth and death records that name parents as John and Sybil. (This John is first cousin to John born in 1768 who married Dorcas Osgood.) Both John and Sybil appear to be living in 1840 in Andover, Vermont. At the 1850 Census, John Blanchard heads a household that includes his unmarried daughter Sybil who died in 1851.

248) JOSEPH BLANCHARD *(Sarah Abbott Blanchard³, Nathaniel², George¹)*, b. 9 Feb 1730/1 son of Joseph and Sarah (Abbott) Blanchard; d. 22 Mar 1776; m. 27 Feb 1753, his third cousin, DINAH BLANCHARD, b. 28 Dec 1731 daughter of Stephen and Deborah (Phelps) Blanchard. Dinah m. 2nd, as his second wife, REUBEN ABBOTT son of James and Abigail (Farnum) Abbott; Dinah d. at Concord, NH, 11 Mar 1826.

There are births of three children of Joseph and Dinah recorded at Andover. After Joseph's death, guardians were appointed for children Joseph and John. Mother Dinah was named guardian.

i JOSEPH BLANCHARD, b. 20 May 1754; d. 3 Mar 1758.

1040) ii JOSEPH BLANCHARD, b. 10 Apr 1765; m. 27 Feb 1786, his second cousin once removed (and George Abbott descendant), HANNAH MOOAR, b. 6 Nov 1768 daughter of Benjamin and Hannah (Phelps) Mooar. Joseph served in the Revolutionary War. After Joseph's death (not yet found), Hannah married Nathan Cutler.[674] Hannah d. at Lewiston, ME, 12 Sep 1860.[675][676]

1041) iii JOHN BLANCHARD, b. 20 Feb 1768; d. at Boston, 6 Feb 1802 at age 32 or 34;[677] m. 27 Apr 1789, DORCAS OSGOOD, b. at Tewksbury, 27 Feb 1770 daughter of Stephen and Mary (Foster) Osgood. Dorcas m. 2nd, Daniel Hastings; Dorcas d. at Boston, 28 Oct 1813.

249) JEREMIAH BLANCHARD *(Sarah Abbott Blanchard³, Nathaniel², George¹)*, b. Jun 1733 son of Joseph and Sarah (Abbott) Blanchard; d. at Weston, VT, 29 Jan 1826; m. 1st, 17 May 1759, DOROTHY SMITH, b. at Andover, 26 Jan 1734/5 daughter of Benjamin and Dorothy (Ballard) Smith; Dorothy d. about 1770. Jeremiah m. 2nd, Aug 1772, SUSANNA MARTIN, b. 6 Apr 1743 daughter of John and Hannah (-) Martin.

There are three children recorded for Jeremiah Blanchard and Dorothy Smith, all born at Andover.

1042) i JEREMIAH BLANCHARD, b. 10 Oct 1759; d. at Newburyport, 4 Apr 1844; m. 20 Nov 1784, SUSANNA PEARSON; Susanna d. at Newbury, 4 Mar 1808.

ii PETER BLANCHARD, b. 12 Aug 1767; d. in Vermont, 22 Nov 1858; m. at Royalston, MA, 6 Mar 1804, HANNAH HOLDEN, b. 1776 (based on age at time of death); Hannah d. at Weston, 14 Apr 1855. Peter and Hannah do not seem to have had children. In his 1856 will, Peter leaves his entire estate to Ivers Holden and his wife Rebecca. [Ivers Holden was married to Rebecca Craggin, so there is likely a connection to the bequest in Peter's brother Eber's will mentioned just below.]

iii EBER BLANCHARD, b. 14 Jan 1769; d. at Weston, VT, 4 Feb 1842; m. MARY (last name unknown); Mary d. 4 Mar 1852. Eber and Mary do not seem to have had children. In his 1842 will, Eber leaves his entire estate to Mary, and after her death, the estate goes to her son-in-law Adna Craggin.[678]

Jeremiah Blanchard and Susannah Martin had nine children, the first four baptized at Andover, and the youngest five recorded in New Hampshire (Wilton).[679]

i HENRY BLANCHARD, baptized 25 Jul 1773; died young.

ii SARAH BLANCHARD, baptized 13 Nov 1774

---

674 Hannah Cutler received a widow's pension for Joseph Blanchard. Ancestry.com. *U.S., Revolutionary War Pension and Bounty-Land Warrant Application Files, 1800-1900*

675 Mooar, *Mooar Genealogy*, p 32

676 Hannah is buried in Hillside Cemetery in Lisbon Falls, ME with an inscription that reads wife of Nathan Cutler, died Sept 12, 1860 age 92 years. Findagrave.com

677 One record gives age at death as 32 and another as age 34.

678 Vermont Wills and Probate, Windsor County, Estate of Eber Blanchard

679 *New Hampshire: Births, Deaths and Marriages, 1654-1969.* (From microfilmed records. Online database: *AmericanAncestors.org*, New England Historic Genealogical Society, 2014.)

iii DOROTHY BLANCHARD, baptized 3 Nov 1776

1043) iv JUDITH BLANCHARD, baptized 13 Jun 1779; d. at Wilton, NH after 1860 (living at the 1860 U.S. Census); m. 12 Feb 1801, her third cousin (and George Abbott descendant) BENJAMIN STEEL, b. at Wilton, 11 Jun 1776 son of Benjamin and Hannah (Lovejoy) Steel; Benjamin d. 18 Nov 1845. This is the same as Family #288, child iv.

1044) v HENRY BLANCHARD, b. 30 Mar 1781; d. at Raymondville, NY, 22 Oct 1824; m. at Billerica, 21 Jan 1807, MARY "POLLY" CROSBY, b. at Billerica, 30 Oct 1785 daughter of Timothy and Susanna (Sanders) Crosby; Polly d. 2 Apr 1848.

1045) vi JOHN BLANCHARD, b. 26 Nov 1782; d. at Norfolk, NY, 28 Jan 1851; m. MARY; Mary d. 18 Aug 1848.

vii HANNAH BLANCHARD, b. 27 Mar 1785

1046) viii WILLIAM BLANCHARD, b. 10 Feb 1788; d. at Royalton, NY, 1861; m. ELIZABETH GILBERT, b. 1790; Elizabeth d. 10 Oct 1857.

1047) ix AARON BLANCHARD, b. 20 Jul 1791; perhaps married Sally and relocated to Norfolk, NY with his brother John. There is an Aaron of the right age with wife Sally and children in census records.

250) DANIEL BLANCHARD *(Sarah Abbott Blanchard³, Nathaniel², George¹)*, b. 15 Jul 1735 son of Joseph and Sarah (Abbott) Blanchard; d. 19 Mar 1776; m. 29 Sep 1757, JERUSHA EATON, b. 19 Sep 1737 daughter of Silas and Jerusha (Gould) Eaton.

The births of eight children are recorded at Andover for Daniel Blanchard and Jerusha Eaton.

1048) i DANIEL BLANCHARD, b. 20 Sep 1759; d. at Thetford, VT; m. at Salem, 26 Feb 1783, MARY BLANCHARD, b. 4 Feb 1762 daughter of Samuel and Ruth (Tenney) Blanchard.

ii JERUSHA BLANCHARD, b. 24 Jun 1761; d. 8 Aug 1779.

1049) iii ISAAC BLANCHARD, b. 14 Sep 1763; d. at Milford, NH, 26 Apr 1826; m. about 1786, OLIVE HOPKINS, b. at Milford, 1 Apr 1769 daughter of Ebenezer and Martha (Burns) Hopkins; Olive d. 13 Aug 1864.

1050) iv AMOS BLANCHARD, b. 22 Jan 1766; d. at Lynn 25 May 1842; m. 27 Jan 1789, LAVINA HOPKINS, b. at Milford, 1769 daughter of Benjamin and Anna (Powers) Hopkins; Lavina d. 1 Aug 1843.

v REBECCA BLANCHARD, b. May 1768; nothing else known.

1051) vi LUCY BLANCHARD, b. Jan 1771; d. at Milford, NH, 12 Feb 1855;[680] m. at Danvers, 27 Oct 1793, NATHAN PUTNAM, b. at Danvers, 18 Mar 1773 son of Nathan and Hannah (Putnam) Putnam; Nathan d. at Milford12 Mar 1842.[681]

1052) vii ABIEL BLANCHARD, b. Mar 1773; m. 1st, 9 Apr 1795, HANNAH GRAY, b. at Wilton, 17 Jun 1773 daughter of Timothy and Hannah (Blanchard) Gray. Abiel m. 2nd, at Monkton, VT, 31 May 1808, PATIENCE VARNEY.

viii HANNAH BLANCHARD, b. 4 Feb 1776; m. 13 Jan 1803, ENOCH BROWN. There is no other information found for this couple.

251) JOHN BLANCHARD *(Sarah Abbott Blanchard³, Nathaniel², George¹)*, b. 19 Jul 1737 son of Joseph and Sarah (Abbott) Blanchard; d. at Concord, NH, 10 Feb 1823; m. 5 Feb 1761, ELEANOR STEVENS, b. 1739 daughter of Samuel and Ann (Huse) Stevens; Eleanor d. 4 Dec 1799. After Eleanor's death, John married 9 Oct 1800 the widow Hannah Page.

John and Eleanor had six children, the birth of the oldest child at Dunstable, New Hampshire and the youngest five at Concord, New Hampshire.

933) i JOSEPH BLANCHARD, b. 24 Nov 1761; d. at Woodbury, VT, 19 Feb 1839; m. his third cousin once removed, PHEBE ABBOTT, b. at Concord, 22 Feb 1766 daughter of Joseph and Phebe (Lovejoy) Abbott; Phebe d. 31 May 1837.

1053) ii JOHN BLANCHARD, b. 11 Sep 1763; d. at Farmington, MI, 1844; m. HANNAH PERRIN.

---

680 Ramsdell and Colburn, *History of Milford*, vol 1, p 891

681 Burial site is Union Street Cemetery, Milford, NH, Plot 47. Findagrave.com

1054) iii STEVENS BLANCHARD, b. 15 Sep 1765; d. at Canterbury, 12 May 1792; m. 16 Oct 1788, his third cousin once removed (and George Abbott descendant), SARAH HALL, b. at Canterbury, 3 Sep 1771 daughter of Obadiah and Mary (Perham) Hall; Sarah d. at Beekmantown, NY, 1824. Sarah m. 2nd, OBADIAH MOONEY.

1055) iv SARAH BLANCHARD, b. 28 Sep 1769; d. at Concord, 11 Nov 1848; m. about 1797, EBENEZER FISK, b. at Tewksbury, 26 Jan 1766 son of Ephraim and Mehitable (Frost) Fisk; Ebenezer d. at Concord about 1857.

1056) v DAVID BLANCHARD, b. 4 Dec 1771; d. at Concord, 10 Jan 1805; m. 4 Oct 1796, HANNAH EATON, b. 31 Jun 1772 daughter of William and Sarah (Farnum) Eaton.

1057) vi MOSES BLANCHARD, b. 15 Oct 1783; d. at Stark, NH, 15 Oct 1858;[682] m. 24 Apr 1806, ELIZABETH WADLEIGH, b. about 1785; d, after 1850. Both Moses and Elizabeth were listed in the 1850 U.S. at Mexico, ME. Moses went to stay with his son Calvary in New Hampshire after the death of Elizabeth.

252) BATHSHEBA ABBOTT *(Joseph3, Nathaniel2, George1)*, b. 16 Sep 1735 daughter of Joseph and Deborah (Blanchard) Abbott; d. at Andover (at least buried at Andover), 8 Dec 1784; m. 2 Jul 1752, NATHAN BLANCHARD, b. 30 Mar 1730 son of Stephen and Deborah (Phelps) Blanchard; Nathan d. before 1784[683] probably at Wilton, NH.[684]

There is just one daughter recorded for this family at Andover. In 1763 they were dismissed from the church at Andover to a new church at Wilton. But it is not clear what happened to them after that. There are no records in Wilton for any other children. However, Charlotte Helen Abbott, identifies three other children in this family, although no other records could be located for these children.[685] There are records in Wilton and Milford for the children of the daughter Bathsheba Blanchard and her husband Daniel Barker. A probate record was not located for Nathan Blanchard.

1058) i BATHSHEBA BLANCHARD, b. at Andover, 20 Apr 1754; d. likely at Lyndeborough, NH; m. 1 Jul 1768 (intention listed, although seems very young), DANIEL BARKER, b. at Methuen, 30 May 1746 son of Zebadiah and Phebe (Merrill) Barker; Daniel is reported to have died during the Revolutionary War probably about 1784 (date of birth of youngest child).[686] Bathsheba may have remarried David Hardy in 1792.

ii MOSES BLANCHARD

iii STEPHEN BLANCHARD

iv LUCY BLANCHARD, b. 1776

253) HANNAH ABBOTT *(Joseph3, Nathaniel2, George1)*, b. 15 Jun 1742 daughter of Joseph and Deborah (Blanchard) Abbott; d. about 1770 at Wilton, NH (about this time her husband remarried); m. 15 Jan 1761, TIMOTHY DALE, b. at Danvers, 9 May 1733 son of John and Abigail (Putnam) Dale. Timothy m. 2nd Rebekah (-); date of death of Timothy is not known. He was last taxed in Wilton in 1801.

Hannah Abbott and Timothy Dale had four children born at Wilton. It is known that the oldest son, Timothy, did marry and resided in Wilton off and on. This son received a fractured skull from a tree limb falling and was partially paralyzed as a result.[687]

i TIMOTHY DALE, b. 24 Mar 1762; d. at Wilton, 18 Sep 1830. Timothy is known to have married and had children, but there are no records of who these might be.

1059) ii HANNAH DALE, b. 22 Oct 1763; she is likely the Hannah Dale who married at Wilton, 26 Feb 1793, BARNABAS GIBSON, b. at Pelham, 12 Jul 1767 son of Barnabas and Elizabeth (-) Gibson; Barnabas d. at Pelham, 4 Feb 1852.

---

682 New Hampshire, Death and Burial Records Index, 1654-1949
683 Bathsheba is listed as a widow on her death record.
684 Livermore, *History of Wilton*, NH, p 318
685 Charlotte Helen Abbott, Blanchard Family, retrieved from https://mhl.org/sites/default/files/files/Abbott/Blanchard%20Family.pdf
686 Cochrane, *Families of Antrim*, NH, p 352
687 Livermore, *History of Wilton, NH*, p 358

1060) iii JOSHUA DALE, b. 22 Jan 1765; d. at Weston, VT, 23 Mar 1845; m. at Andover, VT, 13 Apr 1789, RHODA PEASE, b. 11 May 1764 daughter of Ezekiel and Jemima (Markham) Pease; Rhoda d. at Andover, VT, 6 Jan 1821.

iv SAMUEL DALE, b. 23 Mar 1767. He might be living in Milford in the 1810 U. S. Census, in which case he married and had children, but no records have been located there. There is a Samuel Dale in Landgrove, VT who has several children at about the right time for this Samuel so perhaps Samuel went to Landgrove with his brother.

254) JOSEPH ABBOTT *(Joseph[3], Nathaniel[2], George[1])*, b. 2 Apr 1744 son of Joseph and Deborah (Blanchard) Abbott; d. at Wilton, NH about 1792; m. about 1763 MARY BARKER whose parentage is uncertain.

There are records for the births of seven children, four recorded at Andover and three at Wilton.

1061) i JOSEPH ABBOTT, b. at Andover, 6 Nov 1763; d. at Keene, NH, 23 Nov 1790; m. 30 Jun 1785, BETSY KING, b. 26 Jun 1764 daughter of Richard and Lucy (Butterfield) King. Lucy m. 2nd, Thomas Baker.

320) ii JOSHUA ABBOTT, b. at Wilton, 5 Nov 1765; d. 30 Nov 1798; m. his third cousin, HULDAH ABBOTT, b. 21 Oct 1760 daughter of Joseph and Anna (Peabody) Abbott. Huldah m. 2nd, Gideon Phillips. This is the same as Family #66, child vi.

1062) iii JAMES ABBOTT, b. at Andover, 2 Feb 1768; d. at Billerica, Jul 1810; m. 20 Feb 1791, MEHITABLE HOLT, b. at Wilton, 11 Sep 1768 daughter of Daniel and Mehitable (Putnam) Holt; Mehitable d. at Pomfret, CT, 7 Mar 1857.

1063) iv ISRAEL ABBOTT, b. at Andover, 29 Jul 1771; d. at Charlestown, NH, 26 Feb 1840; m. at Nelson, NH, 1 May 1789, ALICE BAKER, b. at Littleton, 1 Oct 1770 daughter of Timothy and Mary (Dakin) Baker; Alice d. at Whitefield, NH, 13 Aug 1858.

1064) v MOLLY ABBOTT, b. at Andover, 18 Jun 1773; d. likely at Alstead, NH; m. at Nelson, NH, 30 Aug 1789, LEVI WARREN.

1065) vi LUCY ABBOTT, b. at Wilton, 18 Jul 1775; d. at Washington County, NY, 31 Jan 1839; m. 1st, 13 Sep 1792, PEPPERELL SKINNER, b. at Mansfield, MA, 8 Jul 1773 son of Samuel and Martha (Grover) Skinner;[688] Pepperell d. at Whipple, NY, 16 Apr 1810. Lucy m. 2nd, Jonathan Pulman.

vii JEDEDIAH ABBOTT, b. at Wilton 20 Aug 1780. According to the Abiel Abbot genealogy, he was in Upper Canada and Smithville, NY. He married but it is not known to whom.

255) JACOB ABBOTT *(Joseph[3], Nathaniel[2], George[1])*, b. 9 Feb 1745/6 son of Joseph and Deborah (Blanchard) Abbott; d. 5 Mar 1820 at Brunswick, ME; m. 1 Dec 1767, LYDIA STEVENS, b. 3 May 1745 daughter of John and Lydia (Gray) Stevens; Lydia d. Jun 1821.

Jacob began his adult life as a farmer, but sold his farm in Wilton, New Hampshire to his brother in 1776. He lived in the town of Wilton involved in trade goods. He also built the first mills on the Souhegan River. He returned to Andover for a time and served on the board of Phillips Academy. He returned to New Hampshire and was later in Maine where he served on the board of Bowdoin College.[689]

Jacob and Lydia's grandson, Jacob Abbott (1803-1879), was a writer of children's books, the most well-known being the Rollo books.

Jacob and Lydia had ten children, five of whom died in childhood. A sixth child, John, graduated Harvard in 1801 but died in 1809.

i LYDIA ABBOTT, b. and d. 1 Jun 1769

1066) ii LYDIA ABBOTT, b. 1 May 1771; d. at Temple, ME, 20 Jun 1855; m. 10 Feb 1789, a fourth cousin, THOMAS RUSSELL, b. at Andover, 5 Jun 1765 son of Thomas and Bethia (Holt) Russell; Thomas d. 9 Jul 1863.

iii HANNAH ABBOTT, b. 31 Jul 1772; d. 10 May 1786.

---

688 The Genealogical Exchange, volumes 1-7, 1906, p 11

689 Abbot and Abbot, *Genealogical Register of Descendants*, p 131

799) iv PHEBE ABBOTT, b. 25 Jun 1774; d. 18 Apr 1857 (buried at Andover); m. at Andover, 17 Jan 1793, her third cousin once removed, BENJAMIN ABBOTT, b. at Wilton, 17 Mar 1770 son of Abiel and Dorcas (Abbott) Abbott; Benjamin d. at Temple, ME, 10 Sep 1823.

1020) v JACOB ABBOTT, b. 20 Oct 1776; d. at Farmington, ME, 21 Jan 1847; m. at Hallowell, ME, 8 Apr 1798, his second cousin, BETSY ABBOTT, b. at Concord, NH, 6 Aug 1773 daughter of Joshua and Eliza (Chandler) Abbott; Betsy d. 30 Jul 1846. This is the same as Family #243, child iii.

vi DORCAS ABBOTT, b. 6 Sep 1778; d. 29 Dec 1778.

vii SALVA ABBOTT, b, 6 Sep 1778; d. 16 Sep 1778.

viii JOHN S. ABBOTT, b. 25 Sep 1779; d. 9 Jun 1809. John graduated from Harvard in 1801.

ix LUCY ABBOTT, b. 19 Apr 1781; d. at Grafton, NH, 1 Apr 1866; m. DANIEL CAMPBELL, born about 1777 whose origins are not yet known; Daniel d. Oct 1849. Lucy and Daniel did not have children. In his will, Daniel left his estate to his wife Lucy as long as she was his widow and also had bequests to his brothers.

x DORCAS HIBBERT ABBOTT, b. 21 Feb 1784; d. 14 Aug 1784.

256) NATHANIEL ABBOTT *(Joseph³, Nathaniel², George¹)*, b. 27 Oct 1751 son of Joseph and Deborah (Blanchard) Abbott; d. Mar 1791 at Wilton, NH;[690] m. 31 Aug 1773, SARAH STEVENS. The identity of Sarah is not clear. Charlotte Helen Abbot suggests she was Sarah born in Andover in 1742, but that seems unlikely particularly as the last child of Nathaniel and Sarah was born in 1791. There is a Sarah daughter of James born in 1752 who is a more appropriate age. But there are no probate records for any family members yet located that would shed any light on this.

Nathaniel was a shoemaker as well as a farmer. Nathaniel and Sarah relocated from Andover to New Hampshire. The Abbot genealogy book says they located in Wilton, but their children born in New Hampshire were born at Pelham. Nathaniel did serve in the Revolutionary War which perhaps accounts for the several years gap in the births of their children.

There are records for seven children of Nathaniel and Sarah, the oldest two recorded at Andover and the youngest five at Pelham, New Hampshire.

i NATHANIEL ABBOTT, b. 20 Jun 1774; d. 11 Jul 1774.

1067) ii SARAH ABBOTT, b. 12 Oct 1775; d. 17 Feb 1854 at Acworth, ME; m. 5 Oct 1799, ABIJAH KEYES, b. at Wilton, 30 Jun 1773 son of Simon and Lucy Wheeler Keyes; Abijah d. about 1845.

1068) iii PETER ABBOTT, b. 1 Jan 1782; d. at Plainfield, NH, Feb 1850; m. 6 Mar 1806, OLIVE READ born about 1780 and *possibly* the daughter of Elisha and Welthia (Kinney) Read; Olive d. 3 Mar 1855.

iv HANNAH ABBOTT, b. 9 Mar 1784; no further record located.

v DORCAS ABBOTT, b. 24 Dec 1786; d. 6 Jul 1811.

vi PHEBE ABBOTT, b. 3 Feb 1789; no further record located.

1069) vii NATHANIEL ABBOTT, b. Nov 1791; d. at Somerville, MA, 18 Aug 1860;[691] m. at Jaffrey, 26 Mar 1823, ABIGAIL "ABI" BUTTERS, b. about 1800 (age based on census data) likely the daughter of Amos and Abi (Wilson) Butters; Abi d. after 1860 (living at the time of the 1860 census).

257) REBECCA ABBOTT *(Joseph³, Nathaniel², George¹)*, b. 19 Jun 1754 daughter of Joseph and Deborah (Blanchard) Abbott; d. 19 Apr 1795 at Wilton, NH; m. 6 Apr 1775, DANIEL BATCHELDER, b. 2 Oct 1751 son of Joseph and Judith (Rea) Batchelder. Daniel m. 2nd Sarah Kidder who was born at New Ipswich, NH; Daniel d. 23 Mar 1832.

Daniel was a farmer in Wilton. His first land holding in Wilton was 70 acres in lot seven of the first range. Over the years, he acquired other tracts of land. He served in the Revolutionary War.[692]

Rebecca and Daniel had eleven children born at Wilton.

---

[690] This is the information given in the Abbot genealogy book and is also the information used by the DAR, but there do not seem to be any records that support this.

[691] There is a death record at Somerville that includes his birthplace as Wilton, NH with parents Nathaniel and Sally and his age at death of 69 fits with this Nathaniel. This record also lists him as married.

[692] Livermore, *History of the Town of Wilton*, p 313

1070) i REBECCA BATCHELDER, b. 20 Dec 1775; d. 1805; m. 29 Jan 1799, her third cousin once removed, WILLIAM ABBOTT, b. at Wilton, 7 Jan 1779 son of William and Sara (Holt) Abbott. William m. 2nd, at Wilton, 29 Sep 1807, ABIGAIL SAWTELL; William d. at Malden, 15 Jan 1843.

1071) ii BETSY BATCHELDER, b. 4 Aug 1777; d. at Bethel, ME, 18 Nov 1864; m. 27 Jan 1799, her third cousin once removed, JONATHAN ABBOTT, b. at Andover, 11 Jun 1776 son of Jonathan and Mehitable (Abbott) Abbott; Jonathan d. 7 Jan 1843.

1072) iii JUDITH RAY BATCHELDER, b. 21 Jun 1779; d. at Wilton after 1850 (still living at 1850 U.S. Census); m. 24 Mar 1803, her third cousin once removed, JOEL ABBOTT, b. at Andover, 10 Oct 1776 son of Barachias and Sarah (Holt) Abbott; Joel d. at Wilton, 26 Mar 1863.

1073) iv DANIEL BATCHELDER, b. 15 May 1781; d. at Wilton, 28 May 1853; m. 1805, PERSIS MAYNARD, b. at Temple, 10 Apr 1782 daughter of Caleb and Elizabeth (Moore) Maynard.[693]

v JOHN BATCHELDER, b. 6 May 1783; died young.

1074) vi MARY "MOLLY" BATCHELDER, b. 11 Mar 1784; d. at Jaffrey, NH, 3 Jun 1859; m. 1806, JOHN CUTTER, b. 24 Oct 1780 son of Joseph and Rachel (Hobart) Cutter; John d. 15 Jan 1857.

vii JOSEPH BATCHELDER; b. 20 Mar 1786; d. 30 Aug 1788.

viii JOHN BATCHELDER, b. 17 Mar 1788; d. 5 Mar 1795.

1075) ix HERMAN BATCHELDER, b. 8 Aug 1790; d. at Clay, NY, 15 Aug 1876; m. 1812, POLLY BLOOD, b. at Temple, NH, about 1795 daughter of Francis and Rebecca (Parlin) Blood; Polly d. 1865 at Clay, NY.

1076) x HANNAH BATCHELDER, b. 2 May 1793; d. at Philadelphia, 2 May 1862; m. 1818, NATHANIEL RICHARDSON, b. at Weston, VT, 22 Aug 1798 son of Nathan and Hannah (Shattuck) Richardson; Nathaniel d. at Philadelphia, 17 Mar 1861.

1077) xi LYDIA BATCHELDER, b. 18 Mar 1795; d. 4 Mar 1886 at Oppenheim, NY; m. 1819, ABNER SHATTUCK, b. at Wilton, 18 Jan 1796 son of Abraham and Polly (Wright) Shattuck; Abner d. at Oppenheim, 20 Oct 1878.

258) JOHN CHANDLER *(Tabitha Abbott Chandler³, Nathaniel², George¹)*, b. 15 Aug 1730 son of John and Tabitha (Abbott) Chandler; d. at Concord, 1 Mar 1807; m. Oct 1751, MARY CARTER, b. 1729 (based on age at time of death) whose parents are unknown; Mary d. 9 Jun 1793.

John Chandler was a farmer in Concord and owned a tavern. Her served as a lieutenant in the militia. He also held the office of selectman in Concord. According to the Chandler genealogy, Mary died of an overdose of opium.[694]

John Chandler and Mary Carter had six children whose births are recorded at Concord.

1078) i JOHN CHANDLER, b. 11 Dec 1752; d. at Boscawen, NH, 24 Jan 1825; m. Mar 1780, NAOMI FARNUM, b. 20 Apr 1760 daughter of Ephraim and Judith (Hall) Farnum; Naomi d. 20 Mar 1832.

1079) ii NATHAN CHANDLER, b. 28 Apr 1754; d. 13 Apr 1781; m. 4 Mar 1775, SUSAN AMBROSE, b, at Chester about 1755 daughter of Robert Ambrose. Susan m. 2nd, Enoch Brown.

iii ISAAC CHANDLER, b. 18 Apr 1758; d. at Boscawen, NH, 25 Mar 1826; m. MARY KIMBALL. Isaac and Mary did not have children.

1080) iv JOSEPH CHANDLER, b. 18 Nov 1760; d. at Fryeburg, ME, 23 Apr 1826; m. about 1785, HANNAH FARRINGTON, b. at Andover, 9 Jul 1765 daughter of Daniel and Hannah (Farnum) Farrington; Hannah d. 29 Nov 1825.

1081) v JEREMIAH CHANDLER, b. 31 Mar 1763; d. at Lovell, ME, 12 Feb 1828; m. 3 Jun 1791, JUDITH FARNUM, b. 13 Jun 1764 daughter of Ephraim and Judith (Hall) Farnum.

1082) vi MOSES CHANDLER, b. 23 Nov 1765; d. at Fryeburg, 10 Sep 1822; m. 1st, 4 Feb 1794, SALLY GOODWIN, b. about 1770; Sally d. 24 Sep 1801. Moses m. 2nd, MARY LANGDON, b. 21 Mar 1782 daughter of Paul Langdon; Mary d. 10 May 1863.

---

[693] The 1823 will of Caleb Maynard includes a bequest to his daughter Persis "now the wife of Daniel Batchelder." New Hampshire Will and Probate Records 1643-1982.

[694] Chandler, *The Descendants of William and Annis Chandler*, p 323

259) TIMOTHY CHANDLER *(Tabitha Abbott Chandler^3, Nathaniel^2, George^1)*, b. 15 Aug 1733 son of John and Tabitha (Abbott) Chandler; d. at Concord, 24 Mar 1770; m. by 1760, ELIZABETH COPP, b. at Amesbury, 5 Apr 1740 daughter of Solomon and Elizabeth (Davis) Copp. Elizabeth m. 2nd, Stephen Ward; Elizabeth d. 20 Mar 1830.

Timothy and Elizabeth had four children born at Rumford/Concord.

1083) i TABITHA CHANDLER, b. 17 Jun 1761; d. at Randolph, VT, 22 Sep 1839; m. at Plymouth, NH, 17 Dec 1789, HUGH MCINTYRE, b. 11 May 1754 perhaps born in Scotland; Hugh d. 16 May 1837.

936) ii TIMOTHY CHANDLER, b. 25 Apr 1762; d. at Concord, 9 Aug 1848; m. Nov 1787, his second cousin, SARAH ABBOTT, b. 3 Jan 1769 daughter of Joseph and Phebe (Lovejoy) Abbott; Sarah d. 27 Jan 1857. This is the same as Family #226, child iv.

1084) iii ABIEL CHANDLER, b. 20 Oct 1765; d. at Bristol, NH, 5 Mar 1854; m. 25 Dec 1788, ABIGAIL THOMAS (whose origins are not yet verified; she seems to be living at the 1820 Census, but not in 1850).

iv ELIZABETH CHANDLER, b. 28 Jan 1768; d. 24 Jan 1791. Elizabeth did not marry.

260) DANIEL CHANDLER *(Tabitha Abbott Chandler^3, Nathaniel^2, George^1)*, b. 15 Feb 1735 son of John and Tabitha (Abbott) Chandler; d. at Concord, 25 Oct 1795; m. 1st, about 1755, SARAH EASTMAN, b. 14 Jul 1737 daughter of Ebenezer and Eleanor (-) Eastman; Sarah died by 1757 (after the birth of her only child). Daniel m. 2nd, by 1759, SARAH MERRILL, b. 24 Apr 1741 daughter of John and Lydia (Haynes) Merrill; Sarah d. at Chatham, NH, 1810.

Three of the daughters of Daniel Chandler married three Flanders brothers who were sons of Richard and Mary (Fowler) Flanders.

Daniel Chandler and Sarah Eastman had one child.

1085) i SARAH CHANDLER, b. at Concord, 15 Dec 1756; d. 26 Sep 1840 at Northfield, NH; m. 14 Aug 1773, ABNER FLANDERS, b. at South Hampton, 18 Nov 1754 son of Richard and Mary (Fowler) Flanders; Abner d. after 1840 (he was listed on the 1840 pensioners list in Northfield, NH age 85).[695] There is a gravestone in Williams Cemetery in Northfield with a death date given as 26 Nov 1843.[696]

Daniel Chandler and Sarah Merrill had nine children born at Concord.

i JOANNA CHANDLER, b. about 1759; this is a child listed in the Chandler genealogy book for whom there are no known records.

1086) ii MARY CHANDLER, b. 27 Jan 1760; d. at Concord, 1831;[697] m. 1st, about 1775, EBENEZER WEST, b. 25 Dec 1754 son of Nathaniel and Sarah (Burbank) West; Ebenezer d. about 1776. Mary m. 2nd, 20 Mar 1777, RICHARD FLANDERS, b. Mar 1752 son of Richard and Mary (Fowler) Flanders; Richard d, at Concord, 1841.

1087) iii HANNAH CHANDLER, b. 19 Jun 1763; d. 31 Mar 1828 at Rumford, ME; m. 7 Jun 1787, JOSHUA GRAHAM, b. at Rumford, 7 Jun 1763 son of George and Azubah (-) Graham; Joshua d. at Rumford, ME, 15 Mar 1830.

1088) iv LYDIA CHANDLER, b. 22 Jun 1765; d. 21 Jun 1842 at North Chatham, NH; m. 22 Feb 1784, JONAS WYMAN, b. 1759 perhaps the Jonas Wyman born at Wilmington son of Reuben and Catherine (Wyman) Wyman; Jonas d. at Chatham, 10 Oct 1818.

1089) v ABIGAIL CHANDLER, b. 4 Jul 1767; d. 2 Jan 1841; m. 18 Jan 1784, OLIVER FLANDERS, b. 21 Apr 1765 son of Richard and Mary (Fowler) Flanders; Oliver d. at West Plymouth, NH, 31 Jan 1838.

1090) vi PAUL CHANDLER, b. 5 May 1769; d. 1815 at North Chatham, NH (guardians appointed for minor children 7 Jun 1815); m. about 1795, SUSAN HARDY, b. at Fryeburg, 21 Feb 1773 daughter of David and Molly (-) Hardy; Susan d. 27 Mar 1841.

1091) vii ANN CHANDLER, b. 1771; d. at Chatham, 7 Feb 1799; m. about 1794, RICHARD WALKER.

---

695 Ancestry.com. *New Hampshire, Compiled Census and Census Substitutes Index, 1790-1890* [database on-line]. Provo, UT, USA: Ancestry.com Operations Inc, 1999.

696 Findagrave.com memorial 151316433, Abner Flanders

697 New Hampshire, Death and Disinterment Records, 1754-1947

viii ABIEL CHANDLER, b. 26 Feb 1777; d. at Walpole, NH, 22 Mar 1851; m. 15 May 1827, DORCAS SARGENT, b. at Gloucester, 15 Oct 1787 daughter of Epes and Dorcas (Babson) Sargent; Dorcas d. 2 Feb 1837. Abiel and Dorcas did not have children. Abiel was educated at Fryeburg Academy, Exeter Academy, and Harvard College. He was a school teacher, including for a year in Baltimore. He became a merchant in Boston. His will left the bulk of his estate to Dartmouth College, the legacy being used to found a scientific school at Dartmouth. Abiel and Dorcas did not have children.

1092) ix JOHN CHANDLER, b. 19 Mar 1781; d. at Chatham, 23 Apr 1815; m. 28 Nov 1805, MARY HARRIMAN, b. about 1783 daughter of Amos and Nancy (Church) Harriman. Mary m. 2nd, Nathaniel Hutchins. Mary d. 13 Jun 1844.

261) JOSHUA CHANDLER *(Tabitha Abbott Chandler³, Nathaniel², George¹)*, b. 9 Jun 1740 son of John and Tabitha (Abbott) Chandler; d. 3 Dec 1816; m. 1768, IRENE COPP, b. at Amesbury, 17 May 1745 daughter of Solomon and Elizabeth (Davis) Copp; Irene d. 7 Dec 1810.

Joshua and Irene Chandler had seven children born at Concord. Four of the children married children of Samuel and Anna (Hanson) Arlin.

1093) i DANIEL CHANDLER, b. 1 Sep 1768; d. Jun 1817; m. 3 Feb 1794, MEHITABLE ARLIN, b. 1770 daughter of Samuel and Anna (Hanson) Arlin. After the death of Daniel, Mehitable remarried Josiah Chandler.

ii RUTH CHANDLER, b. 20 Feb 1770; d. May 1792; m. 20 Mar 1791, GEORGE ARLIN, b. 1768 son of Samuel and Anna (Hanson) Arlin; George married Ruth's younger sister Sarah after Ruth's death. Ruth and George had one child who died as an infant.

iii RUHAMAH CHANDLER, b. 4 May 1772; d. after 1850 (living in Concord qt the 1850 U.S. Census);[698] m. JOHN SIMPSON 16 Feb 1824. Ruhamah did not have children.

1094) iv SARAH CHANDLER, b. 12 Feb 1774; d. after 1860 (living in Concord at the 1860 U.S. Census); m. 25 Aug 1792, GEORGE ARLIN, b. 1768 son of Samuel and Anna (Hanson) Arlin; George d. between 1850 and 1860.

v JOSHUA CHANDLER, b. 1776; d. at 16 months of age.

vi HANNAH CHANDLER, b. 2 Apr 1779; d. 18 Sep 1806. Hannah did not marry.

1095) vii JOSHUA CHANDLER, b. 4 Sep 1782; m. Aug 1802, NANCY ARLIN, b. 11 Mar 1783 daughter of Samuel and Anna (Hanson) Arlin; Nancy d. after 1870 (living in Concord at the 1870 U. S. Census).

262) HANNAH ABBOTT *(Jeremiah³, Nathaniel², George¹)*, b. 10 Oct 1735 daughter of Jeremiah and Hannah (Ballard) Abbott; d. 13 Sep 1819; m. 3 Jul 1766, OLIVER FARMER, b. 31 Jul 1728 son of Oliver and Abigail (Johnson) Farmer; Oliver d. 24 Sep 1814.

Oliver Farmer had first married Rachel Shed by whom he had six children. Hannah married Oliver when she was 31 years old. Oliver and Hannah had three children. Neither of them left a will that was located. The births of their three children are recorded at Billerica.

1096) i HANNAH FARMER, b. 17 Sep 1767; d. 21 Apr 1856; m. 10 Dec 1789, as his 2nd wife, WILLIAM ROGERS, b. 10 Dec 1789 son of Samuel and Rebekah (Farmer) Rogers. William first married Susannah Pollard in 1787. William d. 17 Aug 1838.

ii REBECCA FARMER, b. 29 Nov 1768; d. 8 Jan 1792; Rebecca did not marry.

1097) iii JEREMIAH FARMER, b. 10 Apr 1771; d. 2 Mar 1836; m. 13 Oct 1816, CLARISSA FOSTER, b. 16 Apr 1785 daughter of Timothy and Sally (Crosby) Foster; Clarissa d. at Boston, 20 Feb 1873.

263) REBECCA ABBOTT *(Jeremiah³, Nathaniel², George¹)*, b. 13 Jul 1741 daughter of Jeremiah and Hannah (Ballard) Abbott; m. 29 Oct 1761, RICHARD BOYNTON, b. at Tewksbury, 22 Mar 1741 son of Richard and Jerusha (Hutchins) Boynton.

[698] Year: 1850; Census Place: Concord, Merrimack, New Hampshire; Roll: M432_435; Page: 67A; Image: 136. Ruhamah Simpson, age 78, living in the household of George and Sarah Arlin aged 82 and 76

Richard Boynton's father died in 1754. In 1756, Richard selected William Stickney of Billerica as his guardian.[699] William Stickney was Rebecca Abbott's step-father. Hannah Ballard Abbott married William Stickney in 1749 following the death of Rebecca's father Jeremiah Abbott.

According to the *History of the Boynton Family*, this family relocated to Milford, New Hampshire, then moved on to Rindge, and ultimately settled in Weathersfield, Vermont. A death year of 1814 is also given by that source.[700]

Rebecca and Richard Boynton had ten children. Births of the first three children are recorded at Billerica. The other children were likely born in New Hampshire. Birth records were not located for all the children and record information was supplemented by information in T*he Boynton Family: A Genealogy*.

1098) i JOHN BOYNTON, b. 14 Mar 1762; d. at Chester, VT, 4 Aug 1852; m. 7 Sep 1787, PHEBE MARTIN, b. at Andover, 14 Jul 1764 daughter of Jonathan and Phebe (Farnum) Martin; Phebe d. 27 Sep 1840.

1099) ii REBECCA BOYNTON, baptized 13 Nov 1763; d. 27 Apr 1833; m. 1785, NEHEMIAH ROUNDY, b. at Beverly, 10 May 1756 son of Robert and Abigail (Presson) Roundy; Nehemiah d. at sea, Sep 1804.

1100) iii RICHARD BOYNTON, b. 3 Oct 1765; d. at Redman, NY, Jul 1841; m. BETSEY WYMAN, b. at Pelham, 20 Jun 1764 daughter of Joseph and Mary (-) Wyman. Richard married second the widow Mrs. Allen and third Jerusha Bishop.

1101) iv HANNAH BOYNTON, b. 7 Jun 1767; d. 1841 at Spencer, NY; m. at Wilton, 23 Nov 1786, NATHAN MARTIN, b. at Rockingham, VT, 3 Apr 1763 son of Samuel and Elizabeth (Osgood) Martin; Nathan d. 27 Sep 1834.

v JERUSHA BOYNTON, b. Jul 1769; d. 1788.

1102) vi SARAH BOYNTON, b. 28 Aug 1770; d. at Springfield, VT, 11 Nov 1850; m. 16 Jan 1793, DAVID KENNEY, b. about 1766 son of David Kenney; David d. at Springfield 23 Jan 1830.

1103) vii ORPHA BOYNTON, b. 10 May 1772; d. at Milford, 1851; m. about 1794, JOHN HOPKINS born at Milford about 1772 son of Ebenezer and Martha (Burns) Hopkins.

1104) viii BETSEY BOYNTON, b. 1774; d. at Athens, VT, Nov 1818; m. at Amherst, NH, 31 Oct 1802, AARON FULLER, b. 1773; Aaron d. at Crown Point, NY, 4 Apr 1847.

1105) ix DAVID BOYNTON, b. 7 Mar 1776; d. at Rockingham, VT, 14 Dec 1813;[701] m. 1 Jun 1804, LYDIA NOURSE, b. at Jaffrey, NH, 6 Jun 1783 daughter of Peter and Lydia (Low) Nourse;[702] Lydia d. 16 Oct 1874 in New York.[703]

1106) x SUSANNAH BOYNTON, b. 25 Oct 1778; m. at Rockingham, VT, 12 Jun 1804, JOSHUA EATON, b. at Reading, 3 Jul 1778 son of Thomas and Abigail (Bancroft) Eaton; Joshua d. 16 May 1840. Their oldest child was born at Wilton, but the family seems to have moved on to Vermont.

264) WILLIAM ABBOTT *(Jeremiah³, Nathaniel², George¹)*, b. 21 Jul 1746 son of Jeremiah and Hannah (Ballard) Abbott; d. after 1800 at Wheelock, VT; m. 28 Dec 1769, BRIDGET SPAULDING, b. 11 Mar 1748/9 daughter of David and Phebe (-) Spaulding; Bridget's death is not known but likely in Vermont; William married second, MEHITABLE SCOTT (according to the Abbot genealogy book).

William was a tanner and currier. William and Bridget wandered a bit in their life. They did have five children in Chelmsford, were then in Fitchburg, and then were a year in Townsend. They were warned out of Townsend, which was sometimes done by towns to encourage new arrivals who had no means of supporting themselves to leave the town. The concern was that these new arrivals might be a burden on the town for support.[704] There was this notice in Townsend: *To notify and warn out - William Abbit & Bridget his wife together with there Children named Bridget, Jedethan, Sarah, William, Joshua & David who came last from Fitchburg in the county of Worcester to Townshend the Twenty fifth of February 1783. Dated*

---

[699] *Middlesex County, MA: Probate File Papers, 1648-1871.*Online database. *AmericanAncestors.org.* New England Historic Genealogical Society, 2014. (From records supplied by the Massachusetts Supreme Judicial Court Archives. Digitized images provided by FamilySearch.org)

[700] Boynton, *The Boynton Family: A Genealogy*, p 122

[701] Hayes, *History of the Town of Rockingham Vermont*, p 810

[702] Wells, *History of Newbury, Vermont: From the Discovery of the Coös Country*, p 645

[703] At the 1860 U.S. Census, she was living in Charlotte, New York with her daughter Elvira and her husband Daniel Lake.

[704] Benton, *Warning Out in New England*

Twentyeth day of February 1784.[705] From Townsend, the family seems to have made its way to Vermont with a stay in Swanzey, New Hampshire on the way.

William Abbott served in the Revolutionary War in various companies: Captain Pollard of Billerica and in the company of Captain Edward Farmer of Billerica. He had periods of service in 1775, 1778, and 1779. It is reported that marched to the alarm of 19 April 1775 and was at Bunker Hill.[706]

The Abbot genealogy reports that William had a second marriage to Mehitable Scott with two more children from that marriage, but no records have been located for that second family.[707]

Births of five children for William and Bridget are recorded at Chelmsford. Son David is known as he is included in the "warning out" of Townsend. There is a son Calvin attributed to this family in most published genealogies and in the listings for the SAR and DAR.

1107) i BRIDGET ABBOTT, b. 13 Dec 1770; d. at Westford, 16 Jun 1849; m. 17 Dec 1807, BENJAMIN READ, b. at Westford, 19 Jan 1779 son of Abel and Rebekah (Farrar) Reed; Benjamin d. 21 Jan 1850.

ii JEDATHAN ABBOTT, b. 9 Feb 1773; he does not seem to have married; death unknown.

1108) iii SARAH ABBOTT, b. 1 Oct 1775; d. at Hancock, NH, 17 Feb 1841; m. at Swanzey, NH, 5 Nov 1794, LOTAN GASSET, b. at Northborough, MA, 31 Oct 1771 son of Levi and Vashti (Brigham) Gasset; Lotan d. 28 Jul 1861.

1109) iv WILLIAM ABBOTT, b. Apr 1778; d. at Dansville, MI, 9 Jan 1849; m. SARAH "SALLY" WOODCOCK, b. at Swanzey, NH, 1 Mar 1782 daughter of Nathan and Lovina (Goodenow) Woodcock; Sally d. 26 Mar 1854.

v JOSHUA ABBOTT, b. Apr 1780; no further record after the "warning out" of Townsend.

vi DAVID ABBOTT, b. about 1782; no record after 1784.

1110) vii CALVIN ABBOTT, b. in New Hampshire, 3 Dec 1788; d. at Ogden, NY,[708] 19 Nov 1858; m. at Danville, VT, 4 Dec 1815, CHARLOTTE CLEMENT, b. at Danville, 12 Sep 1794 daughter of William and Abigail (Hill) Clement; Charlotte d. 12 Dec 1854.

The following are the children from the proposed second marriage to Mehitable Scott. The Abbot genealogy suggests that Mehitable was from Richmond, New Hampshire. No records have been located for these children or for a marriage of William and Mehitable.

i MEHITABLE ABBOTT, b. about 1797

ii JESSE ABBOTT, b. about 1799

265) JEREMIAH ABBOTT *(Jeremiah³, Nathaniel², George¹)*, b. 11 Aug 1748 son of Jeremiah and Hannah (Ballard) Abbott; d.?; m. 19 Jan 1769, SUSANNAH BALDWIN, b. 1746 (probably the daughter of Josiah Baldwin of Tewksbury); Susanna d. 9 Apr 1825.

Jeremiah and Susannah had nine children whose births or baptisms are recorded at Chelmsford.

i SUSANNAH ABBOTT, b. 12 Jun 1769; d. likely at Milford, NH, 1 Nov 1803; m. at Lyndeborough, 18 Oct 1795, ZADOK JONES, b. at Milford, 5 Jul 1773 son of Caleb and Deborah (Hopkins) Jones; Zadok married second Susannah's sister Rebekah; Zadok d. at Milford, 31 Jul 1823. There are no children recorded for Susannah and Zadok.

1111) ii JEREMIAH ABBOTT, b. 26 Feb 1772; d. at Springfield, VT, 2 Oct 1850;[709] m. 30 May 1801, SALLY FARROR, b. at Chelmsford, 14 Apr 1776 daughter of Nathaniel and Rachel (Fletcher) Farror; Sally d. at Springfield, VT about 1815.[710]

---

[705] Massachusetts: Vital Records, 1621-1850 (Online Database: AmericanAncestors.org, New England Historic Genealogical Society, 2001-2016).

[706] Massachusetts Soldiers and Sailors of the Revolution, volume 1, p 16 and p 21; volume 5, p 507

[707] Abbot and Abbot, *Genealogical Register of Descendants*, p 143

[708] *1850 United States Federal Census*, Year: 1850; Census Place: Ogden, Monroe, New York; Roll: M432_529; Page: 83B; Image: 173. Calvin Abbott was living in Ogden in 1850.

[709] *Vermont, Vital Records, 1720-1908.*

[710] The 1810 U.S. Census for Springfield has a household for Jeremiah Abbott that includes a woman in the right age range; in the 1820 Census that older woman is no longer listed.

1112) iii HANNAH ABBOTT, b. 30 Jan 1774; d. perhaps at Vincennes, IN;[711] m. her third cousin once removed (and George Abbott descendant), DAVID CHANDLER, b. at Milford, 28 Jun 1775 son of David and Hannah (Peabody) Chandler.

iv JESSE ABBOTT, b. 22 Sep 1776; d. 26 Dec 1799.

1113) v REBEKAH ABBOTT, b. 26 Aug 1778; d. at Milford, 25 Mar 1864; m. about 1804, ZADOK JONES, b. 5 Jul 1773 son of Caleb and Deborah (Hopkins) Jones. Zadok had first married Rebekah's older sister Susannah. Zadok d. at Milford, 31 Jul 1823.

1114) vi JONAS ABBOTT, b. 29 Apr 1781; d. 11 Sep 1839 at Lyndeborough; m. 18 Jan 1807, BETSEY PARKER, b. at New Ipswich, NH, 17 Mar 1783 daughter of Joseph and Susannah (Fletcher) Parker; Betsey d. 13 Dec 1857.

vii SILAS ABBOTT, baptized 25 Jul 1784. It is not certain what became of Silas, but he is possibly the Silas Abbott who died at Chelmsford 6 Aug 1856 at age 72. This Silas was single and lived frequently in the almshouse at Chelmsford. The only issue is that the death record lists his father as Nehemiah rather than Jeremiah. However, there is no other Silas Abbott in birth records of the right age other than the son of Jeremiah. Of course, it may well be there was another Silas whose birth record has not survived.

1115) viii WILLIAM ABBOTT, b. 3 Nov 1787; d. at Lyndeborough, 14 Jan 1824; m. EUNICE CRAM, b. at Lyndeborough, 31 Aug 1785 daughter of Uriah and Eunice (Ellingwood) Cram. Eunice m. 2nd, 25 Jul 1836, William Strafford; Eunice d. 29 Feb 1868.

1116) ix SALLY ABBOTT, b. Mar 1792; d. at Lyndeborough, 31 May 1857; m. 27 Dec 1817, JOSEPH CHAMBERLAIN, b. at Lyndeborough, 12 Dec 1789 son of Samuel and Naomi (Richardson) Chamberlain; Joseph d. 30 Aug 1862.

266) JOHN MOOAR *(Elizabeth Abbott Mooar³, Nathaniel², George¹)*, b. Jun 1745 son of Timothy and Elizabeth (Abbott) Mooar; d. 1777 at Saratoga, NY during the Revolution; m. 28 Jul 1774, MARY BALLARD, b. 1754 daughter of William and Hannah (Howe) Ballard. Mary m. 2nd 13 Dec 1781, JONATHAN BOYNTON; Mary d. by 1795 when probate petition filed related to John Mooar's estate requesting administration of her widow's portion which reverted to creditors as she is deceased.

John Mooar did not leave a will; his estate entered probate 1 December 1777. Debts exceeded the value of the estate and it was deemed insolvent. Mary Mooar was administrator of the estate. One-third portion of the estate was set off to the widow for her support. She made an accounting of her expenses 1 October 1781 which was shortly before her remarriage to Jonathan Boynton. She made another accounting in 1783 in which she is listed as Mary Mooar now Mary Boynton. On 5 May 1795, Samuel Phillips made a request of the Court to be named administrator of that portion of the estate that had been set out to the widow and now reverted to the estate as the widow is deceased. Timothy Mooar had expressed his unwillingness to assume the administration and there were no other close relatives known to be living in the state.[712]

There is in published genealogies a statement that the probate includes a provision for the support of children Jacob, Sarah, and Andrew. However, I did not find that in the probate record. There are birth records in Andover in this period for children Jacob, Sarah, and Andrew but each of those births are listed with parents Abraham and Martha Mooar. The only record for a possible child in this family was Hannah baptized 26 October 1783 described as daughter of John lately deceased. Of note is that this is the same baptismal date of Mary Boynton who is the daughter of Mary Ballard Mooar and her second husband Jonathan Boynton; this at least suggests these are girls from the same family group. It is possible there are four children in this family, but none for which there are firm records. In any case, there is no information about what became of these children. In 1795, there were no living relatives of John Mooar in the State, so if there were children, they were by 1795 deceased or out of the area.

267) ELIZABETH MOOAR *(Elizabeth Abbott Mooar³, Nathaniel², George¹)*, b. 8 Mar 1747/8 daughter of Timothy and Elizabeth (Abbott) Mooar; d. 16 Mar 1818; m. 29 Jul 1766, MOSES BAILEY, b. at Bradford, 16 Jan 1743/4 son of Nathan and Mary (Palmer) Bailey; Moses d. 14 Mar 1842.

---

[711] Both the Abbot and the Chandler genealogy books list this family as going to Vincennes.

[712] *Essex County, MA: Probate File Papers, 1638-1881.* Probate of John Mooar, 1 Dec 1777, Case number 18664.

In his will, Moses makes bequests to son Moses, son John M. Bailey, son Timothy, daughters Elizabeth Downing, Sarah Ames, Hannah Abbott, Rebecca Abbott, and Rhoda Abbott, to the children of his son Joshua (deceased) namely Joshua, Hephzibah, and Elizabeth, and son Nathan who receives the remainder of the estate and is the sole executor.[713]

Elizabeth Mooar and Moses Bailey had eleven children whose births are recorded at Andover. Of the ten children who married, seven of them married fellow George Abbott descendants, and son Nathan had two wives and they were both GA descendants. Three of the spouses were children of Bixby and Hephzibah (Ames) Abbott.

1117) i MOSES BAILEY, b. 20 Oct 1766; d. 3 Jun 1846; m. 13 Sep 1787, MEHITABLE CHASE, b. at Andover, 12 Dec 1768 daughter of Emery and Mehitable (Mooar) Chase; Mehitable d. 9 Oct 1849.

1118) ii ELIZABETH BAILEY, b. 6 Jul 1768; d. at Minot, ME, 1830; m. 25 Aug 1789, SAMUEL DOWNING, b. 30 Jan 1765 son of Samuel and Abigail (Barnard) Downing; Samuel d. at Minot, 24 Jan 1836.

1119) iii JOSHUA BAILEY, b. 14 Aug 1770; d. 30 Oct 1820; m. 19 Feb 1795, his third cousin once removed, HEPHZIBAH ABBOTT, b. 17 Aug 1772 daughter of Bixby and Hephzibah (Ames) Abbott; Hephzibah d. 7 Aug 1813.

1120) iv SARAH BAILEY, b. 1 Nov 1772; d. 22 Mar 1857; m. 30 Mar 1790, her third cousin once removed (and George Abbott descendant), SIMEON AMES, b. 29 Mar 1772 son of Benjamin and Dorcas (Lovejoy) Ames; Simeon d. 29 Sep 1849.

v NATHAN BAILEY, b. 2 Feb 1775; died in infancy.

1121) vi NATHAN BAILEY, b. 4 Feb 1777; d. 16 Jan 1862;[714] m. 1st, 23 Dec 1802, his third cousin once removed, BETSY ABBOTT, b. 18 Sep 1780 daughter of Bixby and Hephzibah (Ames) Abbott; Betsy d. 24 Oct 1817. Nathan m. 2nd, 4 May 1819, his third cousin once removed (and George Abbott descendant), CHLOE POOR, b. 14 May 1779 daughter of John and Chloe (Lovejoy) Poor; Chloe d. 8 Jun 1867.

1122) vii HANNAH BAILEY, b. 3 May 1779; d. at Concord, NH, 27 Dec 1867; m. 14 Nov 1799, her third cousin once removed, WILLIAM ABBOTT, b. 14 Jul 1774 son of Bixby and Hephzibah (Ames) Abbott; William d. at Greenfield, 13 Aug 1852.

1123) viii REBECCA BAILEY, b. 10 Apr 1781; d. likely at Concord; m. 14 May 1801, her third cousin, WILLIAM ABBOTT, b. 30 Oct 1772 son of Isaac and Phebe (Chandler) Abbott; William d. at Concord, 1856 (probate 24 Jun 1856). This is the same as Family #132, child iv.

1124) ix JOHN MOOAR BAILEY, b. 20 Jul 1784; d. 3 Apr 1836; m. 5 Dec 1811, his third cousin once removed (and George Abbott descendant), ELIZABETH BOYNTON, b. 18 Jan 1789 daughter of Thomas and Hannah (Ames) Boynton.

1125) x TIMOTHY BAILEY, b. 18 Oct 1786; d. 8 Jan 1875; m. 7 Jun 1827, SALLY POOR, b. 9 Apr 1794 daughter of Theodore and Sally (Dowling) Poor; Sally d. 21 Apr 1882.

1126) xi RHODA BAILEY, b. 7 May 1789; d. at Amherst, NH, 1 Sep 1854; m. 17 Jan 1811, her third cousin once removed, HENRY ABBOTT, b. 5 Mar 1785 son of Bixby and Hephzibah (Ames) Abbott; Henry d. 28 Mar 1868.

268) JOSHUA MOOAR *(Elizabeth Abbott Mooar³, Nathaniel², George¹)*, b. 3 Jun 1751 son of Timothy and Elizabeth (Abbott) Mooar; d. at Milford, NH, 10 Sep 1824; m. 17 Sep 1776, DEBORAH CHANDLER, b. 26 Apr 1757 daughter of Zebadiah and Deborah (Blanchard) Chandler; Deborah was still living in 1822 when Joshua wrote his will.

Note of the spelling of Mooar: At some point in this transition between generations, the spelling of Mooar became Moar. The name is also at times spelled Moor or Moore.

Joshua served as a drummer in Captain Benjamin Ames's company during 1775. The Mooar genealogy includes the transcript of a letter from Joshua to his brother Timothy written 28 August 1775 which recounts some of his experiences in the war zone: ". . . the Cannon bals flew Like Smoke the regulers killed two of our men belonging to Hamshere" and goes on the request that his brother John might come to where he is in about a fortnight and bring Joshua's cloak.[715]

In his will dated 14 November 1822, Joshua Mooar has the following bequests: wife Deborah receives improvements on one-third part of the estate; his two daughters will receive the household furnishings and the library of books following the decease of their mother. Sons Joshua, Stephen C., and Timothy each receive a token bequest of $2 to make up their full portions of the estate. His daughters are Betsy Jenkins wife of Micah Jenkins and Sarah Hutchinson wife of Luther

---

713 *Essex County, MA: Probate File Papers, 1638-1881. Probate of* Moses Bailey, 5 Apr 1842, *Case number* 31843.

714 Massachusetts: Vital Records, 1841-1910. (From original records held by the Massachusetts Archives. Online database: AmericanAncestors.org, New England Historic Genealogical Society, 2004.) The death record gives his age as 84 and parents as Moses Bailey and Elizabeth. He is listed as married at the time of his death.

715 Mooar, *Mooar (Moors) Genealogy*, p 31

Hutchinson. Luther Hutchinson is named executor.[716] His daughter Deborah died in 1805 and no heirs of hers are mentioned; she had one child who died young.

Joshua and Deborah had seven children whose births are recorded at Milford.

1127) i DEBORAH MOOAR, b. 20 Jul 1777; d. at Milford, 28 Aug 1805; m. 18 Nov 1800, SIMEON GUTTERSON, b. at Andover, 8 Dec 1769 son of Samuel and Lydia (Stevens) Gutterson. Samuel m. 2nd, Phebe Burnham. Deborah and Simeon had one son, Simeon, born two months before his mother's death; Simeon died young.

1128) ii JOSHUA MOOAR, b. 2 Nov 1778; d. at Milford, 20 Jul 1831; m. at Milford, 19 Nov 1805, BEULAH BLANCHARD, b. 13 Jun 1783 daughter of Benjamin and Sarah (Griffin) Blanchard; Beulah d. 20 Nov 1824.

1129) iii STEPHEN CHANDLER MOOAR, b. 17 Aug 1780; d. at Andover, 16 Mar 1861; m. 6 Nov 1804, ELIZABETH SAWYER CHASE, b. at Leominster, 5 Jul 1782 daughter of Enoch and Sarah (Sawyer) Chase; Elizabeth d. 25 Apr 1854.

iv TIMOTHY MOOAR, b. 9 Jan and d. 19 Jan 1783.

1130) v TIMOTHY MOOAR, b. 22 Mar 1784; d. at Nashua, 1855; m. BETSY HOPKINS, b. at Milford, 8 Sep 1792 daughter of Daniel and Hannah (-) Hopkins; Betsy d. at Nashua, 1852.

1131) vi SARAH MOOAR, b. 26 Oct 1786; d. at Milford, 6 Jan 1857; m. 1808, LUTHER HUTCHINSON, b. 2 May 1783 son of Benjamin and Susannah (Peabody) Hutchinson; Luther d. 5 Sep 1861.

1132) vii BETSY MOOAR, b. 25 Jan 1790; d. 1825; m. 20 Apr 1813, MICAH JENKINS, b. 26 Jul 1786 son of Joel and Patty (Carter) Jenkins.

269) MARY MOOAR *(Elizabeth Abbott Mooar³, Nathaniel², George¹)*, b. 26 May 1760 daughter of Timothy and Elizabeth (Abbott) Mooar; d. 2 Aug 1820; m. 30 Jul 1778, WILLIAM HARRIS whose origins are not pinned down; his death is unknown but was before Mary died in 1820. Mary Harris left a will in 1820 and she was a widow at that time.

Mary Harris wrote her will 15 May 1820 and entered probate 5 September 1820. At the time of his mother's death, John M. Harris was living in Watertown as he wrote a letter from that location agreeing to the probate court for the estate to be held in Ipswich. Mary's daughter Mary Holt was living in Andover as she communicated to the probate court related to the location of the court. The will includes a bequest of one dollar to daughter Mary Holt and son John M. Harris receives the remainder of the estate both real and personal.[717]

No birth records were located for the children of William and Mary; they are known through their mother's will. There is a marriage record for the daughter Mary (Polly) and birth records for three of Polly's children including a son named William Harris Holt. Son John Moore Harris also has little in the way of records. There is a newspaper notice of his death in Watertown in 1832 at age 48. No marriage record was located, but in the 1820 and 1830 U. S. Census, there is in Watertown a John M. Harris.

1133) i MARY "POLLY" HARRIS, b. about 1779; date of death unknown but after 1820; m. at Andover, 12 Jan 1797, LOAMMI HOLT, b. 23 Jul 1775 son of Simeon and Sarah (Read) Holt; Loammi d. at Andover, 11 Jan 1827 at the almshouse.

ii JOHN MOORE HARRIS, b. about 1784; d. at Watertown, 1832. He perhaps married and had children, but no records have been located (other than census records that show a John M. Harris in Watertown with what appears to be wife and children). It is also possible that the others in the census record are his sister and her children as she was widowed in 1827.

270) ABIEL CHANDLER *(Rebecca Abbott Chandler³, Nathaniel², George¹)*, b. 11 May 1744 son of Abiel and Rebecca (Abbott) Chandler; d. 27 Aug 1776 at Long Island, NY; m. about 1766, JUDITH WALKER, b. at Rumford, 21 Dec 1744 daughter of Timothy and Sarah (Burbeen) Walker; Judith m. 2nd Nathaniel Rolfe; Judith d. at Concord 1806

Abiel and Judith lived in Concord. Abiel Chandler served as a captain in the Revolutionary War and died of smallpox while serving in New York. He earlier had been at Bunker Hill serving in John Abbott's company. The inventory of his estate

---

[716] *New Hampshire Wills and Probate Records 1643-1982,* will of Joshua Mooar, Hillsborough, 14 Nov 1822, Probate Records, Vol 34-35 1824-1827.

[717] *Essex County, MA: Probate File Papers, 1638-1881. Probate of* Mary Harris, *5* Sep 1820, *Case number* 12519.

was completed July 1777. Timothy Walker, Jr. was administrator of the estate. The final settlement of the estate (payment to creditors) occurred in 1806 following the death of Judith. There were total claims on the estate of $1,484.74 and there was $118.61 available to pay the claims.[718]

Abiel Chandler and Judith Walker had three children born at Concord.

968) i SARAH CHANDLER, b. 15 Jan 1768; d. at Danville, VT, 21 Nov 1836; m. by 1786, her second cousin (and George Abbott descendant), PETER BLANCHARD, b. at Hollis, 17 Aug 1756 son of Benjamin and Keziah (Hastings) Blanchard; Peter d. 25 May 1810.

1134) ii JUDITH CHANDLER, b. 9 Oct 1770; d. at Concord, 28 Dec 1852; m. 12 Jun 1794, TIMOTHY CARTER, b. at Concord, 6 Mar 1767 son of Ezra and Phebe (Whittemore) Carter; Timothy d. 7 Feb 1843.

iii REBECCA CHANDLER, b. 17 Dec 1773; Rebecca did not marry.

271) AMOS ABBOT *(Rebecca Abbott Abbott^3, Nathaniel^2, George^1* **and** *Amos^4, James^3, William^2, George^1)*, b. 15 Jul 1754 son of Amos and Rebecca (Abbott) Abbott; d. at Concord 11 Oct 1834; m. at Boscawen, 9 Dec 1804, JUDITH MORSE, b. at Newbury, 1 Mar 1766 daughter of Moses and Sarah (Hale) Morse; Judith d. 12 Jul 1843.

Amos Abbot wrote his will 23 February 1830. He bequeathed to his wife Judith his clock and all the household furnishings except two beds. Judith also receives the income from one-third part of the farm and use of half the dwelling house. Daughter Sarah Hale Abbot receives $300 to be paid within one year of his death. Sons John Abbot and Simeon Abbot receive all the real estate. Sons John and Simeon are named executors.[719]

Three children of Amos Abbott and Judith Morse were born at Concord.

i JOHN ABBOT, b. at Concord, 15 Nov 1805; d. at Concord, 18 Mar 1886;[720] m. at Warner, 12 Nov 1856, HANNAH MATILDA BROOKS, b. at Charlestown, MA, 14 Mar 1828 daughter of Samuel Brooks; Hannah Matilda d. at Concord, 22 Apr 1898. John and Matilda were parents of three children: Frances Matilda Abbott, John Boynton Abbott, and Walter Brooks Abbott.

1135) ii SIMEON ABBOT, b. at Concord, 3 Aug 1807; d. at Concord, 22 Feb 1895; m. 8 Feb 1837, MARY FARNUM, b. 25 Jun 1814 daughter of Simeon and Mary (Smith) Farnum; Mary d. 26 Apr 1898.

1136) iii SARAH HALE ABBOT, b. at Concord, 27 Jun 1809; d. 8 Sep 1884; m. 18 Dec 1839, her fourth cousin, DAVID ABBOTT *(Nathan^5, Jabez^4, Thomas^3, Thomas^2, George^1)*, b. 12 Jul 1809 son of Nathan and Rhoda (Brickett) Abbott; David d. at Concord, 12 Apr 1882.

272) REBECCA ABBOTT *(Rebecca Abbott Abbott^3, Nathaniel^2, George^1* **and** *Amos^4, James^3, William^2, George^1)*, b. 26 Sep 1760 daughter of Amos and Rebecca (Abbott) Abbott; d. at Loudon, NH, 24 Dec 1846; m. 9 Oct 1781, MOSES CHAMBERLAIN, b. at Hopkinton, 5 Oct 1757 son of Samuel and Martha (Mellen) Chamberlain; Moses d. 21 Oct 1811.

Rebecca Abbott Chamberlain wrote her will 7 August 1843. She left to her sons William, Moses, and John A. Chamberlain who are now living, and to the heirs of her two sons Amos and Samuel Chamberlain who are deceased, all her property that is in her possession at the time of her decease as well as one share in the Federal Bridge. The remainder of her estate to be divided among her heirs-at-law but these heirs are not named. Her son John A. Chamberlain is named executor. She does not specifically mention any of her daughters or their heirs in the will.[721]

1137) i REBECCA CHAMBERLAIN, b. 15 Mar 1783; d. 31 Jan 1868; m. 8 Feb 1805, SHADRACH CATE, b. at Loudon, 10 Aug 1779 son of Stephen and Annie (Griffin) Cate; Shadrach d. 9 Oct 1842. Rebecca m. 2nd Nathaniel True in 1852.

1138) ii JUDITH CHAMBERLAIN, b. at Loudon, 20 Apr 1785; d. at Pataskala, OH, 1843[722]; m. 16 Jun 1807, SAMUEL ELLIOT, b. at Boscawen, 13 Mar 1778 son of Jonathan and Molly (Conner) Elliot; Samuel d. 1851.

iii PATTY CHAMBERLAIN, b. at Loudon, 31 May 1786; d. at Loudon, 11 Sep 1816.

1139) iv AMOS CHAMBERLAIN, b. 24 Apr 1788; d. at Loudon, 24 Oct 1818; m. 20 Jan 1812, BETSY WOOD. Betsy m. 2nd, Joseph Baker.

---

[718] *New Hampshire Wills and Probate Records 1643-1982,* Probate of Abiel Chandler, Rockingham, 27 Nov 1777, Case number 4401.
[719] *New Hampshire Wills and Probate Records 1643-1982,* will of Amos Abbot, 23 Feb 1830, Merrimack.
[720] New Hampshire, Death and Burial Records Index, 1654-1949, John Abbot, age 80, parents Amos Abbot and Judith Morse.
[721] *New Hampshire Wills and Probate Records 1643-1982,* will of Rebecca Chamberlain, 7 Aug 1843, Merrimack.
[722] Gravestone reads Judith C. Elliot wife of Samuel Elliot 1785-1843, grave at Pataskala Cemetery. Findagrave.com

1140) v WILLIAM CHAMBERLAIN, b. 3 Apr 1790; d. at Keene, 13 Apr 1860; m. 9 Nov 1820, MARY ANN BAKER, b. at Loudon, 1805 daughter of Joseph and Anna (Hook) Baker; Mary Ann d. at Fitchburg, 10 Jan 1873.

1141) vi MOSES CHAMBERLAIN, b. 7 Feb 1792; d. at Three Oaks, MI, 12 Feb 1866; m. 18 Jun 1817, MARY "POLLY" FOSTER, b. at Canterbury, 1 Jan 1797 daughter of Abiel and Susanna (Moore) Foster; Polly d. 18 Jun 1870.

1142) vii JOHN ABBOT CHAMBERLAIN, b. at Loudon, 12 Feb 1794; d. at Concord, 28 Feb 1853; m. 10 Dec 1817, POLLY CLOUGH, b. at Canterbury, 16 Jun 1798 daughter of Jeremiah and Martha (Foster) Clough; Polly d. 11 Sep 1856.

1143) viii BETSY CHAMBERLAIN, b. 31 Aug 1796; m. 3 Oct 1815, JOSHUA EMERY, b. 16 May 1788 son of Thomas and Dolly (Sargent) Emery; Joshua d. at Loudon, 21 Jan 1870. Joshua m. 2nd, at Concord, 25 Dec 1826, ELIZA EASTMAN,[723] b. at Concord, 24 Apr 1801 daughter of Charles and Sarah (Bradley) Eastman; Eliza d. at Loudon, 18 Mar 1854.

1144) ix SAMUEL CHAMBERLAIN, b. 16 Jun 1799; d. at Loudon, 3 Nov 1838; m. 20 Nov 1823, MARTHA GERRISH, b. at Boscawen, 26 Nov 1809 daughter of Jacob and Sarah (Ames) Gerrish. Martha m. 2nd, 10 Nov 1839, Reuel Walker. Martha d. 1867.

Grandchildren of Elizabeth Abbott and Nathan Stevens

273) MARY STEVENS *(Nathan Stevens³, Elizabeth Abbott Stevens², George¹)*, b. Apr 1716 daughter of Nathan and Hannah (Robinson) Stevens; d.?; m. 3 May 1742, SAMUEL PARKER, b. at Bradford, 6 Oct 1716 son of Daniel and Anne (Morse) Parker; Samuel d. 4 Oct 1796.

The births of five children of Mary Stevens and Samuel Parker are recorded at Bradford.

i ABIGAIL PARKER, b. 13 Nov 1742; d. 23 Aug 1762.

1145) ii MOLLY PARKER, b. 18 Oct 1743; d. at Bradford, 21 Feb 1842; m. by 1768, JOHN CURTIS, b. 19 Apr 1743 whose parentage in unclear;[724] John d. at Bradford 3 Apr 1826.

1146) iii ANNA PARKER, b. 28 May 1747; d. at Haverhill, 30 Sep 1824; m. 20 Sep 1770, NATHAN PARKER, b. 14 Jul 1740 son of Nathan and Hannah (Stevens) Parker; Nathan d. 1779 (date of probate 1 Feb 1779).

1147) iv SAMUEL PARKER, b. 28 Jul 1753; d. at Bradford, 12 Jun 1822; m. 27 Mar 1777, ANNA GREENOUGH, b. at Bradford, 30 Apr 1754 daughter of William and Hannah (Atwood) Greenough; Anna d. 1 Oct 1830.

v EDMUND PARKER, b. 1 Nov 1757; d. 7 Sep 1762.

274) HANNAH STEVENS *(Nathan Stevens³, Elizabeth Abbott Stevens², George¹)*, b. about 1721 daughter of Nathan and Hannah (Robinson) Stevens; d. at Brookfield, 17 Nov 1789; m. 11 Feb 1741/2, ABNER TYLER of Boxford, b. 15 Feb 1708/9 son of John and Anna (Messenger) Tyler; Abner d. 8 Dec 1777 at Brookfield

There is another Hannah Stevens of similar age in Andover (Hannah daughter of Benjamin), but that Hannah married Aaron Gage as confirmed by Benjamin's 1748 probate record which includes a disbursement to Hannah Stevens "alias Gage."

Abner Tyler wrote his will 29 September 1773. He made a bequest to his wife Hannah including provisions for her continued maintenance. His eldest son John received all the estate, personal, real, and moveable aside from what is given in other bequests. Sons Gideon, Moses, and Joshua are to receive £100 each when they are of legal age. Daughter Hannah received a token bequest of five shillings over and above what she has received and his three other daughters, Molly, Martha, and Abigail, received bequests of £33. Son John was named sole executor.[725] Hannah Tyler did not leave a will, but her estate entered probate 19 November 1789.[726] The value of the estate after the deduction of administrative fees from the inventory value was about £48.

---

[723] Emery, *Descendants of John and Anthony Emery*, p 79, suggests Joshua married Betsy Abbott in between Betsy Chamberlain and Eliza Eastman. Stearns *Genealogical and Family History of the State of New Hampshire*, volume 3, p 1501, gives Joshua's wives were Betsy Chamberlain, Eliza Eastman, and Lydia Towle.

[724] 1743 is the year of birth based on age at time of death. The 19 Apr 1743 date is used by the DAR.

[725] *Worcester County, MA: Probate File Papers, 1731-1881, Probate of* Abner Tyler, 1778, *Case number* 60333.

[726] *Worcester County, MA: Probate File Papers, 1731-1881, Probate of* Hannah Tyler, 1789, *Case number* 60374.

Hannah Stevens and Abner Tyler had nine children, the two oldest born at Boxford and the seven younger children at Brookfield.

i NATHAN TYLER, b. Nov 1742; died in 1759 of smallpox while returning from the French and Indian War.

1148) ii JOHN TYLER, b. Mar 1744/5; d. at Bakersfield, VT, 17 Feb 1813; m. at Brookfield, Apr 1771, RACHEL CROSBY, b. at Billerica, 15 Sep 1751 daughter of David Crosby;[727] Rachel d. at Brookfield, MA, 6 Apr 1817.

1149) iii GIDEON TYLER, b. 8 Jul 1747; d. at Brookfield, 1832; m. 1 Dec 1766, ESTHER HILL daughter of Peter and Sarah (Woodbury) Hill.[728]

1150) iv HANNAH TYLER, b. 15 Feb 1749; d. at Gorham, NY, 21 May 1815; m. 27 Feb 1769, THOMAS TUFTS, b. 1749; Thomas d. 21 Jul 1811.

1151) v MARY "MOLLY" TYLER, b. 1 Sep 1753; d. at Chesterfield, NH, 16 Dec 1842; m. 9 May 1775, SAMUEL HAMILTON who was born in Ireland about 1752;[729] Samuel d. at Chesterfield, 12 Feb 1810.

1152) vi MOSES TYLER, b. 16 Mar 1756; d. at Brookfield, 8 Mar 1825; m. REBECCA TRUANT, b. about 1760; d. 17 Feb 1817. Rebecca's parents are not known. She is likely from the Trouant family of Plymouth County, the Trouants being early settlers in Marshfield.

1153) vii JOSHUA TYLER, b. 12 Aug 1758; d. at Chesterfield, NH, 11 Jun 1807; m. 1780, JUDITH AYERS, b. 12 Jan 1763 daughter of Onesiphorus and Anna (Goodale) Ayers; Judith d. 11 Aug 1854.

1154) viii MARTHA "PATTY" TYLER, b. 13 Jan 1761; m. at Brookfield, 3 Jun 1781, JOHN HUBBARD, b. at Leicester, 14 Mar 1761 son of Daniel and Elizabeth (Lynde) Hubbard; John d. at Batavia, NY 4 Jan 1850.

1155) ix ABIGAIL TYLER, b. 5 Dec 1763; m. at Brookfield, 14 Sep 1783, JESSE AYERS, b. at Brookfield, 8 Oct 1763 son of Moses and Sarah (Converse) Ayers.

275) ELIZABETH STEVENS *(Nathan Stevens³, Elizabeth Abbott Stevens², George¹)*, b. 2 Jul 1722 daughter of Nathan and Hannah (Robinson) Stevens; m. 11 Jul 1744, SAMUEL AMES, b. 1719 son of Samuel and Abigail (Spofford) Ames.

The births of nine children of Elizabeth Stevens and Samuel Ames are recorded at Andover.

i ELIZABETH AMES, b. 14 Jan 1744/5

1156) ii SAMUEL AMES, b. 19 Sep 1746; d. at Epsom, NH, 1792; m. at Andover, 10 Jul 1770, his second cousin once removed, ABIGAIL STEVENS, b. at Andover, 28 Oct 1752 daughter of David and Abigail (Martin) Stevens.

iii STEPHENS AMES, b. 24 Aug 1749

1157) iv SPOFFORD AMES, b. 23 Mar 1752; d. at Pembroke, 1835; m. 18 Apr 1780, MARY WHITE, b. 1759 daughter of John and Abigail (Bowen) Wight;[730] Mary d. at Pembroke, 6 Jul 1832.

v SOLOMON AMES, b. 21 Apr 1754

1158) vi ABIGAIL AMES, b. 1756; m. 1775, DANIEL NOYES, b. at Pembroke, 24 Nov 1748 son of John and Abigail (Poor) Noyes; Daniel d. at Pembroke, 13 Jan 1822.[731]

vii SIMON AMES, b. 28 Oct 1761

810) viii PHINEAS AMES, b. 7 Sep 1764; m. 24 Dec 1787, his third cousin, BRIDGET ABBOTT, b. about 1761 daughter of Daniel and Hannah (Chandler) Abbott. This is the same as Family #199, child iv.

ix LYDIA AMES, b. 22 Aug 1767

---

[727] Brigham, *Tyler Genealogy, the Descendants of Job Tyler*, p 118
[728] Temple, *History of North Brookfield*, p 625
[729] Bolton, *Immigrants to New England 1700-1775*, p 81
[730] Wight, "John Wight of Bristol, M.A."
[731] Noyes and Noyes, *Descendants of Nicholas Noyes*, p 82

275a) NATHAN STEVENS *(Nathan Stevens[3], Elizabeth Abbott Stevens[2], George[1])*, b. at Andover, 16 Mar 1723/4 son of Nathan and Hannah (Robinson) Stevens; d. at Wendell, MA, 14 Nov 1794;[732] m. at Andover, 22 Apr 1746, MARY POOR, b. at Andover, about 1726 *perhaps* daughter of John and Mary (Faulkner) Poor.[733]

Nathan and Mary married in Andover and the birth of the eldest child Molly is recorded at Andover and also noted in the Brookfield records. On 18 April 1748, Nathan Stevens, cordwainer of Andover, purchased seventy acres in Brookfield from David Kendall for payment of £800.[734] This was lot 22 from the original proprietor grants made to John Aiken from 1717 to 1721. Nathan was one of the original members of the Second Church of Christ in Brookfield when it was organized in 1752.[735]

The births of eleven more children are recorded at Brookfield and the family was there until 1778. The three oldest daughters married in Brookfield. On 21 May 1778, Nathan Stevens, yeoman of Brookfield, with his wife Mary sold this same 70-acre property, noted as the place he is currently living, to Samuel Hoar for payment of £1,000.[736]

The family appears next in Wendell in Franklin County and marriages of four of the children are recorded in New Salem in Franklin County. On 18 April 1788, Nathan Stevens, yeoman of Wendell, with his wife Mary sold to Joseph Emerson of Wendell a tract of 67 acres for payment of £100.[737] In the 1790 census of Wendell, Nathan headed a household of seven persons, four males and three females.[738]

Nathan Stevens and Mary Poor were parents of twelve children.[739][740]

i MOLLY STEVENS, b. at Andover, 28 Aug 1746; m. at Brookfield, 2 May 1770, JAMES HOLMES

ii REBECCA STEVENS, b. at Brookfield, 24 Aug 1748; m. at Brookfield, 8 Oct 1774, MARK NOBLES.

iii DORCAS STEVENS, b at Brookfield, 27 Sep 1750; m. at Brookfield, 9 May 1775, COMFORT GOSS, b. at Brookfield, 3 Dec 1749 son of John and Mary (Gilbert) Goss; Comfort d. at Fort Ann, NY, 21 Mar 1836. Dorcas was living in 1836 (pension record).[741]

iv JOSEPH STEVENS, b. at Brookfield, 29 Oct 1752; m. at New Salem, 10 Aug 1780, ABIGAIL HUTCHINSON.

v PHINEHAS STEVENS, b. at Brookfield, 18 Sep 1755; m. 20 Jun 1781, HANNAH KNIGHT likely daughter of Samuel and Hannah (Stacy) Knight. On 15 November 1800, Phinehas was of Amherst, MA when he sold his property in Shutesbury to Jonas Locke.[742]

vi JERUSHA STEVENS, b. at Brookfield, 7 Sep 1757

vii SARAH STEVENS, b. at Brookfield, 1 Dec 1759; d. at Oxford, NY, 20 Oct 1839; m. at Brookfield, 26 Aug 1781, JESSE HAMILTON, b. at Brookfield, 19 Jul 1754 son of Ezra and Lydia (Barnes) Hamilton; Jesse d. at Oxford, 30 Dec 1814.

viii RACHEL STEVENS, b. at Brookfield, 15 Mar 1762; d. at New Salem, 17 Apr 1834; m. at New Salem, 14 Oct 1784, WILLIAM KNIGHT, b. 1760 son of Samuel and Hannah (Stacy) Knight; William d. at New Salem, 9 Aug 1834.

ix LYDIA STEVENS, b. 1 Jul 1764

x ELIZA STEVENS, baptized 24 May 1767

xi ELIZABETH STEVENS, b. at Brookfield, 17 Feb 1768; m. at New Salem, 22 Nov 1789, DARIUS BARTLETT, b. at Brookfield, 8 May 1763 son of Obadiah and Rebecca (Adams) Bartlett; Darius d. during an epidemic, at Montague, MA, 15 May 1814.[743]

xii ABIGAIL STEVENS, b. baptized at Brookfield, 8 Jun 1777

---

732 Described as "aged"; Wendell Town Clerk Records; https://www.familysearch.org/ark:/61903/3:1:3QS7-9979-H56D?i=134&cc=2061550&cat=371001

733 Abbott, "Early Records of the Poor Family of Andover", p 7; https://mhl.org/sites/default/files/files/Abbott/Poor%20Family.pdf

734 Massachusetts Land Records, Worcester County, 27:112

735 Temple and Adams, *History of North Brookfield*, p 253, p 451

736 Massachusetts Land Records, Worcester County, 83:102

737 Massachusetts Land Records, Franklin County, 3:180

738 Year: 1790; Census Place: Wendell, Hampshire, Massachusetts; Series: M637; Roll: 4; Page: 645; Image: 700; Family History Library Film: 0568144

739 Vital Records of Brookfield, Massachusetts to the End of the Year 1849, pp 205-206

740 Temple and Adams, *History of North Brookfield*, p 743

741 U. S. Revolutionary War Pension and Bounty-Land Warrant Application Files, Case W16589

742 Massachusetts Land Records, Franklin County, 14:645

743 Bartlett, Darius, epidemic, May 15, 1814. C. R. Montague Vital Records, volume 1, p 128

276) TIMOTHY PEARL *(Elizabeth Stevens Pearl³, Elizabeth Abbott Stevens², George¹)*, b. 24 Oct 1723 son of Timothy and Elizabeth (Stevens) Pearl; d. at Willington, 19 Oct 1789; m. 6 Nov 1746, DINAH HOLT, b. at Windham, 17 Mar 1725/6 daughter of Joshua and Keturah (Holt) Holt; Dinah d. at Willington, 25 Sep 1806.

There are some double-birth records at Windham which have children (Hannah, Phineas) of the same names and birthdates with one attributed to Timothy and Dinah and one attributed to Timothy's father Timothy and his second wife Mary. [Phineas, s. of Timothy and Mary, b. 2 Aug 1753; Phineas, s. of Timothy and Dinah, b. 2 Aug 1753.] These children are all named in the will of the elder Timothy. Also, they are recorded at Windham and Timothy and Dinah were at Willington soon after their marriage. Therefore, they are not included here as it seems more likely they are the children of Timothy and Mary. There are births of nine children recorded for Timothy and Dinah, the oldest at Windham and the rest of the children at Willington.

i ALICE PEARL, b. 6 Sep 1747; d. 10 Sep 1747.

1159) ii ALICE PEARL, b. 6 Jul 1748. The birth transcription says 6 Jul 1743, but this seems an error and Durrie's Holt genealogy says 1748; her age at death in 1826 was 76. Alice d. Dec 1826; m. at Willington, 10 Oct 1767, ELEAZER SCRIPTURE, b. at Willington, 10 May 1742 son of John and Hannah (Wells) Scripture; Eleazer d. at Willington, 1813 (estate inventory 13 Oct 1813).

675) iii OLIVER PEARL, b. 9 Oct 1749; d. 4 Nov 1831; m. 1st, 1 Jan 1772, MERCY HINCKLEY; Mercy d. 15 Nov 1781. Oliver m. 2nd, 24 Apr 1782, his second cousin (and George Abbott descendant), HANNAH HOLT, b. 14 Mar 1756 daughter of Abiel and Mary (Downer) Holt; Hannah d. 20 Nov 1832. This is the same as Family #159, child i.

1160) iv JOSHUA PEARL, b. 15 Sep 1752; d. at Vernon, 11 Oct 1837; m. 14 Jan 1773, DEBORAH MARSHALL, b. at Bolton, 1755 daughter of John and Eunice (Kingsbury) Marshall; Deborah d. at Vernon, 11 May 1818.

1161) v LOIS PEARL, b. 21 Apr 1753; d. at Willington, 15 Jul 1788; m. 6 Aug 1771, SAMUEL DUNTON, b. at Wrentham, MA, 10 Nov 1748 son of Samuel and Sarah (Bennet) Dunton; Samuel d. at Willington, 1 May 1813. After Lois's death, Samuel married Lovina Marcy.

1162) vi ELIZABETH PEARL, b. 15 Jan 1756; d. 8 Jan 1779; m. 6 Aug 1771, ZOETH ELDRIDGE, b. at Willington, about 1751 son of Jesse and Abigail (Smith) Eldridge; Zoeth d. at Willington, 18 Mar 1828. Zoeth m. 2nd, Bethiah Hinkley.[744]

1163) vii SARAH PEARL, b. 16 Nov 1758; d. 11 Oct 1826; m. 17 Nov 1776, SAMUEL JOHNSON, b. 1751 (based on age 92 at time of death); Samuel d. at Willington, 22 Mar 1843. Samuel is likely the son of Daniel and Keziah (Dodge) Johnson born at Lebanon 10 Jun 1751.

1164) viii TIMOTHY PEARL, b. 6 Jun 1760; d. at Willington, 2 Jul 1834; m. 9 Jan 1783, LOIS CROCKER, b. 9 Dec 1763 daughter of Joseph and Anne (Fenton) Crocker; Lois d. 24 Sep 1850.

1165) ix PHEBE PEARL, b. 27 Nov 1765; d. at Willington, 10 Apr 1816; m. 24 Mar 1785, ZEBADIAH MARCY, b. at Woodstock, 2 Jul 1761 son of Zebadiah and Priscilla (Morris) Marcy; Zebadiah d. 24 Sep 1851.

277) NATHAN PEARL *(Elizabeth Stevens Pearl³, Elizabeth Abbott Stevens², George¹)*, b. 22 Nov 1727 son of Timothy and Elizabeth (Stevens) Pearl; d.?; m. 7 Mar 1748, ELIZABETH UTLEY, b. 22 Apr 1729 daughter of James and Annah (-) Utley.

The births of seven children are recorded for Nathan and Elizabeth, the oldest two at Windham and the youngest five at Ashford.

i STEPHEN PEARL, b. 29 Apr 1749; d. at Burlington, VT, 21 Nov 1816; m. 1st at Stockbridge, ELECTA WOODBRIDGE, b. 1 Apr 1754 daughter of Timothy and Abigail (Day) Woodbridge; Electa d. at Bennington, VT, 13 Jan 1781. Stephen m. 2nd ABIGAIL EDWARDS, b. about 1758, d. at Burlington, 21 Nov 1816. Stephen may not have had any children as there are no children named in his will.

ii JAMES PEARL, b. 27 Oct 1750; died young.

1166) iii TIMOTHY PEARL, b. 20 Apr 1752; d. at Grand Isle, VT, 15 Sep 1839; m. SARAH SWIFT, b. 18 Feb 1755 daughter of Reuben and Hannah (Dexter) Swift; Sarah d. 24 Jul 1843.

1167) iv ELIZABETH PEARL, b. 6 Jul 1757; d. unknown; m. 9 Mar 1781; SAMUEL KIMBALL, b. at Windham, 1 Feb 1761 son of Samuel and Ann (Mudge) Kimball. It is not known where this family located. There are births of four children at Ashford. Nearly all Elizabeth's siblings went to Vermont.

---

744 Eldredge, *Eldredge Genealogy*, p 8

1168) v ANNA PEARL, b. 1 Aug 1758; d. at Plattsburgh, NY, about 1830;[745] m. ABEL BRISTOL, b. at Newtown, CT, 5 May 1755 son of Ebenezer and Sarah (Lake) Bristol; Abel d. at Plattsburgh about 1830.

1169) vi AZUBAH PEARL, b. 10 Oct 1762; d. at South Hero, VT, 19 Jun 1840; m. DANIEL WADSWORTH, b. at Hartford, 4 Jan 1761 son of Hezekiah and Millicent (Seymour) Wadsworth; Daniel d. at South Hero, 7 Jan 1806.

vii NATHAN PEARL, b. 8 Mar 1764; d. Nov 1764.

278) ELIZABETH PEARL *(Elizabeth Stevens Pearl³, Elizabeth Abbott Stevens², George¹)*, b. Jan 1729/30 daughter of Timothy and Elizabeth (Stevens) Pearl; d. not known but living at the probate of her husband's estate 1805; m. 24 May 1749, JOHN HIBBARD, b. 9 Dec 1727 son of John and Martha (Durkee) Hibbard; John d. at Royalton, VT, 31 Dec 1804.

John Hibbard was one of the original grantees of Royalton, Vermont.[746] John Hibbard wrote his will 10 October 1789 with the following bequests: well-beloved daughter Abigail Hutchins, five shillings; well-beloved sons James, John, and Timothy Hibbard each receive five shillings; and well-beloved wife Elisabeth Hibbard receives the whole of the estate, "moveables and immoveables, real and personal." Elizabeth was also named executor of the estate. The will was presented to the probate court 17 January 1805.[747]

The births of seven children are recorded at Canterbury, Connecticut.

1170) i ABIGAIL HIBBARD, b. 8 May 1749; d. likely at Cherry Valley, NY; m. 22 Aug 1769, JOSHUA HUTCHINS, b. at Plainfield, 24 Feb 1747 son of Benjamin and Prudence (-) Hutchins.

ii TIMOTHY HIBBARD, b. 5 Sep 1750; d. 9 Dec 1750.

iii ELIZABETH HIBBARD, b. 25 Oct 1751; d. 25 Sep 1754.

1171) iv JAMES HIBBARD, b. 30 Jul 1753; d. at Royalton, VT likely after 1820 (he seems to be in Royalton in the 1820 census); m. 15 Aug 1773, SUSAN SHEPARD.

1172) v JOHN HIBBARD, b. 15 Sep 1755; d. at Royalton, VT, 18 Jul 1800; m. 17 Mar 1777, ABIGAIL CLEVELAND, b. at Canterbury, 6 Aug 1758 daughter of Samuel and Ruth (Darbe) Cleveland.

vi TIMOTHY HIBBARD, b. 31 Dec 1757; d. 4 Mar 1758.

1173) vii TIMOTHY HIBBARD, b. 4 Jan 1759; d. in Quebec about 1841; m. by 1780, JERUSHA LAWRENCE whose origins are unknown. There are children born in Vermont, but some vital records for the children in Quebec. Timothy received a land grant in Quebec in 1832.[748]

279) PHEBE PEARL *(Elizabeth Stevens Pearl³, Elizabeth Abbott Stevens², George¹)*, b. 12 May 1732 daughter of Timothy and Elizabeth (Stevens) Pearl; d. at Yarmouth, Nova Scotia, date unknown; m. 29 Nov 1750, PHINEAS DURKEE, b. 16 Sep 1730 son of Stephen and Lois (Moulton) Durkee; Phineas d. at Yarmouth, Nova Scotia, 5 Nov 1801.[749]

There are births for twelve children recorded in Hampden County, Massachusetts, some recorded at Wales and some at Brimfield. Additional information related to marriages for this family obtained from Brown's Yarmouth, Nova Scotia Genealogies. There is a second set of transcriptions for the Wales birth records and those transcriptions have slightly different information for the children, although that set of records has some obvious errors [e.g., attributing Moses Paine Durkee to Phineas although he was the son of Robert and Mehitable (Paine) Durkee]. The information presented here are the children from Brown's Yarmouth, Nova Scotia Genealogies.

Phineas Durkee wrote his will 19 November 1800. Loving wife Phebe receives all the household items and furniture including the looms. Phebe also receives the farming tools and the livestock. She also receives one and one-half acres marsh land in Yarmouth. She also receives other land bequests of about 200 acres. Phebe also receives all the hay and the produce. Son Pearl Durkee receives one lot of land in the third division at Yarmouth which contains 202 acres. His daughters Phebe Bancroft, Elizabeth Hayse, and Hannah Kinney each receive lots of 60 acres out of the lot numbered 114. Grandsons Phineas Allen and Nathan Bancroft receive 35 acres each.[750] The bequests to his children are to the four youngest children in the family and it

---

[745] This is the date used by DAR
[746] Lovejoy, *History of Royalton, Vermont: With Family Genealogies*, 1769-1911, Part 2, p 820
[747] Vermont Wills and Probate Records, 1749-1999, will of John Hebbard, 13 Oct 1789, Windsor, Probate Records, Vol 1-3 1783-1809.
[748] Ancestry.com, Quebec, Canada, Land Grants, 1763-1890, Letters Patent Book: L Grants; Page: 424; County Index Volume: 1; Page: 166
[749] Brown, *Yarmouth, Nova Scotia, Genealogies* [database on-line]. (ancestry.com)
[750] Nova Scotia Probate Records 1760-1993, Yarmouth, will books 1794-1859, volume 1, image 18-19, familysearch.org.

may well be that all the older children have received their portions of the estate previously. The will describes one of the land bequests being land that adjoins Amasa Durkee's land who is one of the older sons.

1174) i LOIS DURKEE, b. at Wales, 26 Sep 1752; d. at Yarmouth, Nova Scotia; m. 25 Mar 1770, SOLOMON LUFKIN, b. at Ipswich, 25 Sep 1747 son of Solomon and Mary (Knowlton) Lufkin; Solomon d. by 1780. Lois m. 2nd, 5 Mar 1780, DANIEL ALLEN, b. at Manchester, 15 Mar 1758 son of Jeremiah and Eunice (Gardner) Allen.

1175) ii AMASA DURKEE, b. at Brimfield, 6 Jul 1754; d. at Yarmouth, Nova Scotia, 1827; m. 21 Nov 1776, RUTH ROBBINS, b. about 1757; Ruth d. at Yarmouth, 1824. Amasa married the widow Mary Shurtliffe after Ruth's death.

1176) iii OLIVE DURKEE, b. 18 Jul 1756; d. at Yarmouth, Nova Scotia, 4 Jan 1846; m. 9 Nov 1775, SAMUEL TRASK, b. 27 Dec 1753 son of Elias and Abigail (Woods) Trask;[751] Samuel d. 25 Dec 1829.

1177) iv ELEANOR DURKEE, b. at Brimfield, 11 May 1758; d. at Yarmouth, 8 Mar 1817; m. about 1780; THOMAS DALTON, Thomas d. about 1809 (year of probate).[752] Eleanor m. 2nd, THOMAS RICKER.

v JOHN DURKEE, b. 1 Nov 1760; d. 30 Mar 1761.

vi PHINEAS DURKEE, b. 19 Jun 1762; died young.

1178) vii ROBERT DURKEE, b. at Wales, 22 Feb 1765; m. 1st, ABIGAIL ROGERS daughter of Cornelius and Abigail (Holmes) Rogers; Abigail d. 1817 in Nova Scotia. Robert m. 2nd, LYDIA ALLEN.

1179) viii STEPHEN DURKEE, b. 22 Sep 1766; d. at Yarmouth, Nova Scotia, 1845; m. at Yarmouth, 26 Apr 1787, LYDIA LOVITT, b. at Yarmouth, 9 Jul 1769 daughter of Andrew and Lydia (Thorndike) Lovitt; Lydia d. 6 Nov 1857.

1180) ix PEARL DURKEE (m), b. 25 May 1769; d. at Baltimore, MD, 25 Jan 1826; m. 1st, MARY HANKEY who was "of Baltimore"; Mary d. about 1812. Pearl m. 2nd, 7 Nov 1817, CHARLOTTE ROSE.

1181) x PHEBE DURKEE, b. 28 Apr 1771; d. at Carleton, Yarmouth, 16 Apr 1856; m. 31 Aug 1786, SAMUEL BANCROFT.

1182) xi ELIZABETH DURKEE, b. 22 Oct 1774; d. at Cornwallis, Nova Scotia; m. 17 Dec 1790, JOHN HAYSE "of Long Island"; John d. at Cornwallis, 17 Dec 1848.

1183) xii HANNAH DURKEE, b. 27 Jun 1781; d. at Yarmouth, Nova Scotia, 1857; m. NATHAN KINNEY, b. 1778; Nathan d. 1856.

280) LYDIA PEARL *(Elizabeth Stevens Pearl[3], Elizabeth Abbott Stevens[2], George[1])*, b. 31 Jul 1734 daughter of Timothy and Elizabeth (Stevens) Pearl; d. Sep 1819; m. 27 Nov 1753, DANIEL DENISON, b. 5 Sep 1730 son of Daniel and Hannah (Crocker) Denison; Daniel d. at Hampton, 4 Aug 1823.[753]

There are just three births recorded for Lydia and Daniel at Windham. The 1822 will of their son Daniel makes mention of his bond to care for his parents and so in his will includes a provision that a gravestone be placed on the grave of his mother and an equally suitable stone placed on the grave of his father after his father's decease.[754]

1184) i DANIEL DENISON, b. 25 Jan 1755; d. at Hampton, 10 Nov 1822; m. at Norwich, 24 Apr 1788, LUCY CLARK, b. 1763 (based on age of 80 at time of death);[755] d. at Hampton, 8 Dec 1843.

640) ii HANNAH DENISON, b. 18 Mar 1757; d. 17 Jan 1784[756]; m. 1 Jan 1778 as his first wife, her third cousin, JAMES ABBOTT, b. at Windham, 9 Mar 1753 son of Abiel and Abigail (Fenton) Abbott; James m. 2nd at Kingston, PA, 17 Jan 1798, PHEBE HOWE; James d. at Cornell, NY, 2 May 1830.[757] This is the same as Family #151, child ii.

iii DYER DENISON, b. 25 Oct 1767; d. 13 Jan 1772.

---

[751] The New England Historical and Genealogical Register, Volume 56, p 397

[752] Nova Scotia Probate Records 1760-1993, Will Books 1794-1859, volumes 1-2, p 59 (familysearch.org)

[753] Ancestry.com, *Connecticut, Hale Collection of Cemetery Inscriptions and Newspaper Notices, 1629-1934* (Provo, UT, USA: Ancestry.com Operations, Inc., 2012), Connecticut State Library; Hartford, Connecticut; The Charles R. Hale Collection of Connecticut Cemetery Inscriptions.

[754] *Connecticut Wills and Probate, 1609-1999*, Probate of Daniel Denison, Jr, Hartford, 1822, Case number 1095.

[755] Ancestry.com, Connecticut, Deaths and Burials Index, 1650-1934

[756] Ancestry.com, Connecticut Town Death Records, pre-1870 (Barbour Collection)

[757] Gravesite located at Stahl Brothers Cemetery in Steuben County, NY, findagrave.com

281) BENJAMIN AMES *(Hannah Stevens Ames³, Elizabeth Abbott Stevens², George¹)*, b. 6 Jun 1724 son of Samuel and Hannah (Stevens) Ames; d. at Andover, 10 Jan 1809; m. 1st 4 Dec 1746, his second cousin, HEPHZIBAH CHANDLER, b. 7 Apr 1726 daughter of Timothy and Hephzibah (Harnden) Chandler; Hephzibah d. 19 Jan 1768. Benjamin m. 2nd, about 1770, his second cousin once removed, DORCAS LOVEJOY *(Lydia Abbott Lovejoy⁴, Henry³, George², George¹)*, b. 18 Aug 1749 daughter of Joshua and Lydea (Abbott) Lovejoy; Dorcas d. 25 Jun 1843.

Captain Benjamin Ames was the captain of Ames's Company which served in the Revolutionary War including service at Bunker Hill. His company was part of the regiment of Colonel James Frye. Benjamin Ames first saw military service in 1757 as a private in one of Andover's militia companies.[758]

Benjamin Ames was active in the civic affairs of Andover serving as Warden and Surveyor of Highways in 1777 and served on the building committee for the new meeting house in South Parish in 1787.

The will of Benjamin Ames includes bequests to the following persons: Dorcas dearly beloved wife and Simeon is the son charged with her care; Simeon receives the lands, buildings, and husbandry utensils. The other heirs named are Benjamin Ames, Timothy Ames, Hannah Boynton wife of Thomas Boynton, heirs of daughter Hephzibah formerly the wife of Bixby Abbot, Dorcas wife of Isaac Phelps, and Abigail wife of David Johnson.[759]

There are records for nine children of Benjamin Ames and Hephzibah Chandler born at Andover.

i CHANDLER AMES, b. 14 Nov 1747; d. 24 Sep 1766

1185) ii BENJAMIN AMES, b. 9 Nov 1749; d. 23 Nov 1813; m. 30 Apr 1772, his second cousin once removed (and George Abbott descendant), PHEBE CHANDLER, b. 18 Oct 1754 daughter of Nathan and Phebe (Abbott) Chandler; Phebe d. 19 Jun 1798. The grave of Phebe Chandler Ames has the following inscription: *While o'er the grave you walk or weep, Remember here all flesh must sleep; Slender's the thread whence life depends, Begins this hour, the next it ends.*[760]

1186) iii HANNAH AMES, b. 26 Nov 1751; d. 20 Dec 1831; m. 16 Jun 1772, THOMAS BOYNTON, b. 29 Nov 1747 son of David and Mary (Stickney) Boynton; Thomas d. 10 Mar 1833.

iv RICHARD AMES, b. 16 Sep 1754; d. 6 Oct 1754

1187) v HEPHZIBAH AMES, b. 3 Nov 1755; d. 20 May 1796; m. 9 Jan 1772, her third cousin, BIXBY ABBOTT, b. 24 Nov 1750 son of William and Experience (Bixby) Abbott. Bixby m. 2nd Mary Johnson; Bixby d. at Greenfield, NH, 1813.

vi RICHARD AMES, b. 16 Aug 1758; d. 8 Sep 1758.

vii ELIZABETH AMES, b. 8 Aug 1760; d. 1 Nov 1760.

viii BETHIAH AMES, b. 22 Jul 1762; d. 11 Aug 1762.

1188) ix TIMOTHY AMES, b. 26 Sep 1765; d. at Peterborough, NH, 14 May 1835; m. 21 Mar 1787, SALLY KNEELAND, b. 1769 (based on age at time of death) who parentage is uncertain; Sally d. 13 Nov 1861.

Four children are recorded for Benjamin Ames and Dorcas Lovejoy.

1120) i SIMEON AMES, b. 29 Mar 1772; d. 29 Sep 1849; m. 30 Mar 1790, his third cousin, once removed, SARAH BAILEY, b. 1 Nov 1772 daughter of Moses and Elizabeth (Mooar) Bailey; Sarah d. 22 Mar 1857.

ii DORCAS AMES, b. 25 Jul 1773; d. 28 Sep 1775.

1189) iii DORCAS AMES, b. 31 Jul 1776; d. after 1855; m. 31 Oct 1799, ISAAC PHELPS, b. 21 Jun 1772 son of Thomas and Mary (Shattuck) Phelps; Isaac d. after 1850 (listed in the 1850 U. S. Census). Dorcas is listed in the 1855 Massachusetts census in the Andover almshouse, age 77, described as insane.[761]

---

758 Memorial Hall Library, Andover Answers, "Benjamin Ames," retrieved from https://answers.mhl.org/Benjamin_Ames

759 *Essex County, MA: Probate File Papers, 1638-1881.* Probate of Benjamin Ames, 4 May 1809, Case number 573.

760 The Essex Antiquarian, 1898, Andover Inscriptions, Old South Burying Ground

761 Ancestry.com, Massachusetts, State Census, 1855

1190) iv ABIGAIL AMES, b. 4 Oct 1779; d. after 1850 at Bradford, VT;[762] m. 15 Dec 1796, DAVID JOHNSON whose parents are not clear are there are several David Johnsons of the right age in Andover; d. after 1830 at Bradford, VT.

282) NATHAN AMES *(Hannah Stevens Ames³, Elizabeth Abbott Stevens², George¹)*, b. Apr 1729 son of Samuel and Hannah (Stevens) Ames; d. at Groton 7 Mar 1791; m. 19 Apr 1763, DEBORAH BOWERS, b. at Groton, 2 Sep 1746 daughter of Samuel and Deborah (Farnsworth) Bowers; Deborah d. 8 Apr 1782. Nathan m. 2nd by 1783, LYDIA GREEN, b. 19 Aug 1765 daughter of Jonas and Jemima (Holden) Green; d. 24 Feb 1834 at age 67. After Nathan's death, Lydia married Jeremiah Chaplin.

Nathan Ames and Deborah Bowers were married and had nine children whose births are recorded at Groton. Deborah died in 1782. After the death of Deborah, Nathan married Lydia Green in 1783. Nathan Ames died in March 1791 at age 61. The estate of Nathan Ames entered probate April 1791 with his widow Lydia as the administrator of the estate. There was no will. The current available probate papers include the inventory, but not the distribution. There are also guardianship cases for the minor children.[763] After she turned 14 years old, Anna Ames (mother Deborah) selected her brother-in-law Nathan Gray Baker as guardian. Simeon Ames (mother Deborah) selected Nathan Ames of Carlisle; it is not clear who this Nathan Ames is, but possibly his oldest brother. After he was 14 years old, Moses Ames selected Jeremiah Chaplin as his guardian.

Moses Ames, the son of Nathan and Lydia, did not marry, but he left a will in 1820. At that time, his mother was Lydia Chaplin having married Jeremiah Chaplin in 1796. Moses names several sisters in his will who were daughters of Nathan Ames and Lydia Green and then his Chaplin sisters, the daughters of Lydia and Jeremiah Chaplin. He names none of the children of Nathan and Deborah in the will. This raises the question of why he would include his half-siblings by his mother's last marriage, but not his half-siblings from his father's first marriage. Perhaps they were all adults and so not of concern. As they were adults (for the most part) at the time of Lydia's marriage to Nathan, he was not reared with them.

The age difference between Nathan Ames and Lydia Green is a concern in terms of feeling completely confident that all these relationships are correct. In 1783, Lydia had just turned 18 and Nathan was 54. Although not an impossible age difference, it was not the usual pattern. Perhaps for this family that was not so unusual, as Lydia's father, Jonas Green, married a woman 25 years younger than him when he remarried after the death of Lydia's mother.

Two of the sons of Nathan and Deborah went to Providence and two of the daughters of Nathan and Lydia went to Providence.

Nathan Ames and Deborah Bowers had nine children whose births were recorded at Groton.

i NATHAN AMES, b. 6 Feb 1764; d. at Groton 23 Mar 1851; he is listed as a bachelor on the death record. He *perhaps* married Lydia Goodhue in 1788, but there are no children recorded from that marriage.

1191) ii SAMUEL AMES, b. 7 Feb 1766; d. at Providence, RI, 16 Feb 1830; m. at Boston, 8 Sep 1801, ANNE CHECKLEY, b. at Philadelphia, 13 Aug 1785 daughter of John Webb and Anne (Wicker) Checkley; Anne d. 15 Jun 1868.

1192) iii DEBORAH AMES, b. 6 Apr 1768; d. at Andover 7 Dec 1819; m. 1st 21 Sep 1786, HENRY GRAY BAKER, b. 1 Apr 1767 son of Symonds and Lydia (Gray) Baker; Henry d. 10 Mar 1802. Deborah m. 2nd 18 Nov 1802, as his second wife, CALEB ABBOTT son of Asa and Elizabeth (Abbott) Abbott; Caleb d. 12 Apr 1837. The is the same as Family #80, child iv.

1193) iv LYDIA AMES, b. 29 Mar 1770; d. at Andover 24 Jun 1843; m. 21 Jul 1796, her third cousin once removed (and George Abbott descendant), ABBOTT WALKER, b. at Chelmsford, 24 Jul 1770 son of Benjamin and Abiel (Abbott) Walker; Abbott Walker d. 2 Aug 1831.

1194) v ASA AMES, b. 6 May 1772; d. at Providence, RI, 21 Jan 1838; m. REBECCA BRATTELL, b. 1 Jan 1776 daughter of Robert and Rebecca (Pierce) Brattell; Rebecca d. 17 Apr 1824.

vi BENJAMIN AMES, b. 22 Aug 1774; d. 24 Dec 1787.

vii ANNA AMES, b. 29 Jul 1776; she was still living in 1793 when she selected Henry Gray Baker of Andover as her guardian. She is perhaps the Anna Ames who married Peter Hutchinson in Andover in 1807, but that cannot be verified. Her sisters Deborah and Lydia had gone to Andover, so this might make sense but cannot be established. There is one child recorded for Peter and Anna Hutchinson (Lyman born in 1808) but was not tracked after that.

---

[762] In the 1850 U.S. Census, Abigail Johnson age 79 is living in Bradford, Vermont in a household that includes Abigail Dearborn who is her daughter. *United States 1850 Census.* Online database. AmericanAncestors.org. New England Historic Genealogical Society, 2014. (Original index: *United States Census, 1850.* FamilySearch, 2014.)

[763] *Middlesex County, MA: Probate File Papers, 1648-1871.* Probate of Nathan Ames, 1791, Case number 389. The guardianship cases for the children are cases 390, 391, and 392.

viii JEPHTHAH AMES, b. 29 Jun 1779; d. 30 Jun 1786.

1195) ix SIMEON AMES, b. 13 Sep 1781; d. at Sterling, CT 11 Feb 1863; m. 17 Apr 1826, BETSEY GILMORE, b. about 1809; Betsey was still living in 1870 at the time of the US Census.

Nathan Ames and Lydia Green had three children whose births are recorded at Groton.

i MOSES AMES, b. 1 Nov 1783; d. 11 Dec 1820. Moses did not marry.

1196) ii AMELIA AMES, b. 9 Apr 1788; d. at Providence, RI, 6 Apr 1874; m. 11 Oct 1812, JOSEPH WHEELOCK, b. at Westborough, 25 Jun 1788 son of Moses and Lydia (Bond) Wheelock; Joseph d. 16 May 1857.

1197) iii JEMIMA GREEN AMES, b. 14 Mar 1791; d. at Providence, RI, 11 Aug 1839; m. 10 Feb 1824, WILLIAM ALMY, b. at Westport, 23 Sep 1788 son of William and Mary "Polly" (Millett) Almy; William d. at Newport, RI aboard ship in the harbor, 16 Sep 1830.

283) AMOS AMES *(Hannah Stevens Ames³, Elizabeth Abbott Stevens², George¹)*, baptized 20 Jan 1733/4 son of Samuel and Hannah (Stevens) Ames; d. at Groton, 4 Aug 1817; m. 27 Oct 1757, ABIGAIL BULKLEY, b. at Concord, MA, 28 Oct 1733 daughter of John and Abigail (-) Bulkley; Abigail d. 20 Aug 1809.

The oldest sons in the family, Amos, Moses, and Simeon, all served in the Revolutionary War. All three were captured and were prisoners for a time on a prison ship at Halifax. Two of the brothers escaped and the third brother was later exchanged.[764]

The births of ten children are recorded at Groton.

1198) i AMOS AMES, b. 15 Apr 1758; d. at Sullivan, ME after 1810; m. 1st by 1784, POLLY ODIORNE daughter of William and Avis (Adams) Odiorne; Polly d. 29 Jul 1787. Amos next had an out-of-wedlock relationship with DEBORAH LAWRENCE with daughter recorded.[765] Amos m. 2nd MARY "POLLY" BRAGDON daughter of Ebenezer and Jane (Wilson) Bragdon; Polly d. after 1820.

ii MOSES AMES, b. 14 Nov 1759; d. 23 May 1783.

iii SIMEON AMES, b. 25 Sep 1761; d. 25 Sep 1784.

1199) iv ABIGAIL AMES, b. 28 Nov 1763; d. at Ashby, 11 Aug 1848; m. 10 Mar 1785, WILLIAM GREEN, b. at Pepperrell, 19 Jan 1755 son of William and Ruth (Colburn) Green; William d. 1 May 1843.

1200) v ELI AMES, b. 4 May 1765; reported to have gone to Virginia and perhaps Georgia;[766] m. at NH, 27 Nov 1788, EUNICE PARKER, b. Apr 1761 and d. 1843. This family was in Groton for a time and in New Ipswich, NH as the births of several children are recorded there.

1201) vi PETER AMES, b. 7 Nov 1767; d. Jun 1823; m. 7 Oct 1799, SALLY CHILD, b. at Groton, but of uncertain parentage but possibly the daughter of Abraham Child; Sarah d. 28 Feb 1838.

1202) vii HANNAH AMES, b. 30 Jan 1770; d. 22 Aug 1840; m. 7 Jun 1789, IMLAH PARKER, b. at Groton, 12 Jan 1765 son of Nathaniel and Eunice (Lakin) Parker; Imlah d. 4 Apr 1828.

1203) viii BULKLEY AMES, b. 20 Jul 1772; d. 22 Jan 1836; m. 22 Sep 1799, LYDIA PRESCOTT, b. at Westford, 8 Jan 1780 daughter of Ebenezer and Lydia (Wood) Prescott; Lydia d. 15 Feb 1848.

ix ABEL AMES, b. 3 Sep 1774; d. 14 Aug 1775.

1204) x BETSEY BULKLEY AMES, b. 10 Dec 1776; d. 28 Jul 1861; m. 21 Apr 1799, WILLIAM LIVERMORE, b. at Shirley 23 Jun 1770 son of Oliver and Catherine (Bond) Livermore; William d. 2 Mar 1846.

284) ROBERT AMES *(Hannah Stevens Ames³, Elizabeth Abbott Stevens², George¹)*, baptized 1737 son of Samuel and Hannah (Stevens) Ames; d.?; m. 1st 2 Dec 1762, SARAH WOODS, b. 19 Aug 1742 daughter of Isaac and Abigail (Stevens) Woods; Sarah d. 23 Nov 1774. Robert m. 2nd 29 Apr 1777, SUSANNA GREEN (widow of Abijah Warren), b. 20 Mar 1746 daughter of Isaac and Martha (Boyden) Green.

---

[764] Green, *Groton Historical Series*, volume 3, p 159

[765] A., d. Deborah Laurence and Amos Ames "as She Saith," Oct. 6, 1788. Massachusetts Vital Records for Groton

[766] The DAR gives his place of death as Georgia.

There are three probate records for men named Robert Ames in Massachusetts between 1786 and 1825 but none of those is this Robert. No death or probate record for Robert or Susanna was found in Massachusetts, New Hampshire, or Vermont. Robert's children scattered to further west in Massachusetts and up to New Hampshire and Vermont.

There are five births recorded at Groton for Robert Ames and Sarah Woods.

1205) i ROBERT AMES, b. 12 Oct 1763; d. 15 Nov 1789; m. 27 Mar 1783, RUTH LAWRENCE, b. 3 Jan 1758 daughter of Benjamin and Rebecca (-) Lawrence; Ruth d. at Groton 3 Jul 1825.

1206) ii SARAH AMES, b. 27 May 1765; d. at Bridport, VT, 13 Jul 1836; m. 18 Jun 1787, EPHRAIM STONE, b. at Groton, 11 Jan 1763 son of Benjamin and Prudence (Farnsworth) Stone; Ephraim d. 6 Jun 1841.[767]

1207) iii PRUDENCE AMES, b. 29 Dec 1767; d. at Ashby, MA, 6 Nov 1821;[768] m. 27 Dec 1786, ISAAC GREEN "of Ashby," b. about 1757 who parentage is uncertain; Isaac d. at Ashby 7 Nov 1821. One of Prudence's cousins married a Green from Pepperrell; there is an Isaac Green from Groton who was the much younger brother of Susanna Green who was Robert Ames's second wife.

1208) iv BETHIAH AMES, b. 30 Nov 1770; d. at Peterborough, NH, 15 Feb 1852;[769] m. 18 Feb 1788, JOHN SCOTT, b. at Dublin, NH about 1765 son of William Scott; John d. 27 Dec 1847.

v MOLLY AMES, b. 5 Dec 1772; d. 6 Aug 1775.

Two children are recorded at Groton of Robert Ames and Susanna Green. No further record was found for either of these children.

i SAMUEL AMES, b. 9 Dec 1781

ii MOLLY AMES, b. 23 Feb 1786

285) PHEBE STEEL *(Phebe Stevens Steel[3], Elizabeth Abbott Stevens[2], George[1])*, b. 27 Sep 1735 daughter of Nicholas and Phebe (Stevens) Steel; d. unknown but still living in 1783; m. 22 Nov 1776, as his second wife, JOHN ABBOTT (of the George Abbott of Rowley line), b. 10 Mar 1724/5 son of Uriah and Sarah (Mitchell) Abbott; John d. of smallpox 3 Jan 1779.

John Abbott had seven children with his first wife, Sarah Carleton. John and Phebe had one daughter born at Andover.

1209) i HANNAH ABBOTT, b. 15 Oct 1777; d. at Haverhill, 25 Nov 1853;[770] m. 27 Feb 1810 as his second wife, JOHN JOHNSON whose parentage is not yet certain, but likely the son of John and Hannah (Abbott) Johnson born in Andover 8 Dec 1777. John Johnson died 1814 (probate of estate 4 Aug 1814 with widow Hannah declining administration). John Johnson was first married to Lydia Kimball who died 1808. The 1826 will of John Kimball (Lydia's father) has a bequest for grandson Edward Johnson, who was the son of John and Lydia. John Johnson who married Hannah Abbott (of the Rowley Abbott line) was married second to Abigail Abbott of the Andover line.

286) ELIZABETH STEEL *(Phebe Stevens Steel[3], Elizabeth Abbott Stevens[2], George[1])*, b. 21 Feb 1737 daughter of Nicholas and Phebe (Stevens) Steel; date of death not known but she appears to be the Elizabeth Ingalls in Andover in the 1810 US Census; m. 9 Sep 1760, JOSHUA INGALLS, b. 13 Aug 1732 son of Joseph and Phebe (Farnum) Ingalls; Joshua d. 1785, his will probated 5 Jul 1785.

The will of Joshua Ingalls has bequests for the following persons: beloved wife Elizabeth, son Simeon, daughter Phebe Ingalls, and son Stephen.[771] The births of five children are recorded at Andover.

1210) i STEPHEN INGALLS, b. 17 Jun 1761; d. about May 1794 (will written 4 Apr 1794 and probate 3 June 1794); m. 21 Sep 1786, LYDIA KIMBALL, b. 9 Mar 1761 daughter of Andrew and Esther (Barker) Kimball; Lydia d. at Andover, 16 Dec 1831.

ii ELIZABETH INGALLS, b. 2 Sep 1762; d. before 1785.

---

[767] Ancestry.com, *Vermont, Vital Records, 1720-1908* (Provo, UT, USA: Ancestry.com Operations, Inc., 2013).

[768] This is the date engraved on her gravestone. Findagrave.com

[769] Ancestry.com, *New Hampshire, Death and Burial Records Index, 1654-1949* (Provo, UT, USA: Ancestry.com Operations, Inc., 2011).

[770] At the 1850 US Census she is listed as living with Leonard Johnson who is her son. There is a probate record for her from 1854 in which Leonard Johnson, the sole heir, is also the administrator of the estate.

[771] *Essex County, MA: Probate File Papers, 1638-1881. Probate of* Joshua Ingalls, 5 Jul 1785, *Case number* 14535.

1211) iii SIMEON INGALLS, b. 3 Sep 1764; m. 16 Jan 1787 the widow ELIZABETH FISH. The identity of Elizabeth is unknown, but she is possibly Bette Fisk who married David Fish in Andover in 1777 but just a wild guess at this point.

iv PETER INGALLS, b. 14 Jan 1766; d, before 1785.

1212) v PHEBE INGALLS, b. 30 Dec 1768; d. at Pelham, NH, 20 Jul 1847; m. 3 Jun 1790, ELIJAH BRADSTREET, b. 4 Jul 1767 son of Samuel and Ruth (Lampson) Bradstreet; Elijah d. at Pelham, 2 Dec 1850.

287) RACHEL STEEL *(Phebe Stevens Steel³, Elizabeth Abbott Stevens², George¹)*, b. 1 Jul 1739 daughter of Nicholas and Phebe (Stevens) Steel; death before 1796 when her second husband married his third wife; m. 11 Dec 1767, DUDLEY FOSTER, b. at Boxford, 21 Feb 1737/8 son of Zebadiah and Margaret (Tyler) Foster; Dudley d. by 1787 when widow Rachel Foster married James Frye (1731-1804). Rachel married James Frye in 1787 as his second wife.

There are records for four daughters in this family. For three of the daughters, the only record is the baptism and all four of the girls were baptized on the same day. There is a birth record for only one of the girls. There is marriage for one of the daughters that can be confirmed. For two of the girls, there seem to be no marriage records. Daughter Rachel was unmarried in 1801 (will written in 1801 but probate in 1804) when she receives a bequest from her step-father James Frye with whom she has lived.[772] There is uncertainty about the daughter Mary. As there is a birth record for only one daughter, the order of birth is not known.

1213) i MEHITABLE FOSTER, b. 17 Sep 1772; d. at North Andover, 16 Aug 1859; m. 3 Mar 1791, her third cousin, NATHANIEL HOLT, b. 6 Apr 1769 son of Nathaniel and Elizabeth (Stevens) Holt; Nathaniel d. 24 May 1829.

ii MARY FOSTER, baptized 14 Dec 1777

iii PHEBE FOSTER, baptized 14 Dec 1777; no further record.

iv RACHEL FOSTER, baptized 14 Dec 1777; still living but unmarried in 1801.

288) BENJAMIN STEEL *(Phebe Stevens Steel³, Elizabeth Abbott Stevens², George¹)*, b. 25 Jan 1741 son of Nicholas and Phebe (Stevens) Steel; d. at Wilton, NH 14 Nov 1817; m. 16 Jun 1768, HANNAH LOVEJOY, b. 1748 (parentage uncertain); Hannah d. at Wilton, 31 Aug 1812.

There are records for the births of seven children in this family, the two oldest born at Andover and the other five children at Wilton, New Hampshire.[773] There are no further records for the daughters in this family.

i HANNAH STEEL, b. 13 Dec 1768; died young.

ii HANNAH STEEL, b. 24 Dec 1770; no further record.

iii PHEBE STEEL, b. 28 Mar 1774; no further record.

1043) iv BENJAMIN STEEL, b. 11 Dec 1776; d. 18 Nov 1845; m. 12 Feb 1801, his third cousin, JUDITH BLANCHARD, baptized at Andover 13 Jun 1779 daughter of Jeremiah and Susanna (Martin) Blanchard; Judith d. after 1860 (still living at the 1860 US Census).[774] This is the same as Family #249, child iv.

v SARAH STEEL, b. 2 Jun 1779; no further record.

vi LYDIA STEEL, b. 19 Apr 1781; no further record.

1214) vii WILLIAM LOVEJOY STEEL, b. 28 Jun 1784; d. at Wilton, 4 Mar 1860; m. by 1820, DOLLY TARBELL, b. at Mason, NH, 3 May 1798 daughter of Samuel and Anna (Heldrick) Tarbell;[775] Dolly d. 30 Aug 1861.

---

[772] *Essex County, MA: Probate File Papers, 1638-1881.*Online database. *AmericanAncestors.org.* New England Historic Genealogical Society, 2014. (From records supplied by the Massachusetts Supreme Judicial Court Archives.)

[773] *New Hampshire, Births and Christenings Index, 1714-1904* (Provo, UT, USA: Ancestry.com Operations, Inc., 2011).

[774] Year: 1860; Census Place: Wilton, Hillsborough, New Hampshire; Roll: M653_673; Page: 388; Family History Library Film: 803673

[775] Parentage confirmed by the 1824 will of Samuel Tarbell which includes a bequest to daughter Dolly Steel. Probate Records, 1771-1921; Indexes to Probate Records, 1771-1859, 1885-1961; Author: New Hampshire. Probate Court (Hillsborough County); Probate Place: Hillsborough, New Hampshire

Generation Five

As we move through the generations, you will note that the time period for each generation expands. Children in the sixth generation who reached adulthood span 150 years in terms of dates of death, from the late-18th century to the early-20th century. The generations also expand in terms of location with descendants throughout the United States and Canada. By the end of the sixth generation, there are descendants in most of what would become the states of the continental United States. There is growing diversity in terms of occupation, education, and wealth ranging from the highly educated and prosperous to individuals living in poverty for much of their lives.

The fifth and sixth generation descendants also lived during the time of great historic events. You will read about descendants in the Revolutionary War, War of 1812, and the Civil War. It seems that most men from late adolescence through middle adulthood participated in the Revolutionary War in some way. While most descendants who served in the Civil War were with Union forces, those descendants who had migrated to the southern states served with the Confederate forces. These generations include slave owners and participants in the Underground Railroad. Gold rush fever also struck several descendants who made their way to California starting in the 1840's and 1850's. One family of descendants served as missionaries at the Cherokee mission at Brainerd and accompanied members of the Cherokee nation on the Trail of Tears.

Although there were families who stayed settled in one place, it is remarkable how much moving some families did. There are families in this generation who started in New Hampshire, went to Vermont, then traveled into New York, and headed west to Ohio by their later years. Consider that these families were moving in carts with oxen and on horseback often with several young children. Some common patterns of migration were from Connecticut into Pennsylvania, from Connecticut to western areas of Massachusetts such as Brimfield, from New Hampshire into Vermont and Maine, and from Vermont and Maine into Canada. From locations in Connecticut, Pennsylvania, or western Massachusetts, families might travel to Otsego, Allegany, or Chautauqua in New York. Some of these travelers then settled in New York, but it seemed that just as many kept moving on to Ohio or Indiana. In general, these relocations involved large family groups, for example most of the young adult children and their spouses and in-laws moving at about the same time and then perhaps followed by their parents, if parents did not initially make the trip. The one exception to this seems to be those descendants who traveled into Virginia, Tennessee, or other southern states. Often, this migration was of single young men, perhaps traveling for business or professional reasons, or perhaps getting away from poor circumstances or other challenges at home. One exception to this are a small number of couples doing missionary work in the southern states. And there were those that took off for the Gold Rush, and this was most often young men or brothers traveling together, although there are one or two instances of couples making the trip. The generations presented here also include missionary families to India and other locations in Asia.

One other change in these generations, perhaps due to the greater availability of records for these generations, is more evidence of human struggles such as suicide and divorce that seemed less common in earlier generations.

A note about the descendancy path listed in parentheses after the names: For many of the individuals in this generation, there are two or more paths that might be taken back to George Abbott and Hannah Chandler. For some individuals there are as many as five paths. For simplicity, just one path is listed.

Great-Grandchildren of John Abbott and Sarah Barker

289) PHEBE ABBOTT *(John^4, John^3, John^2, George^1)*, b. 14 Apr 1733 daughter of John and Phebe (Fiske) Abbot; d. at Andover, 26 Jul 1812; m. 18 Apr 1754, her third cousin, NATHAN CHANDLER *(Nathan Chandler^4, John Chandler^3, Hannah Abbott Chandler^2, George^1)*, b. 19 Feb 1729/30 son of Nathan and Phebe (Holt) Chandler; Nathan d. at Andover, 30 Apr 1786.

Phebe and Nathan lived in West Parish of Andover on part of the farm that had been owned by Nathan's grandfather John Chandler.[776]

In his will, Nathan left beloved wife Phebe his clock. She also has use of the northwest room of the home as long as she remains his widow. The will also notes that Nathan's mother is still living, and she is apparently living with the family, as wife Phebe will have full use of the kitchen after the decease of his mother. Phebe will have the full use of the kitchen as long as she does not interfere with Nathan's son using the kitchen. Phebe also is to have use of the well and a spot for a garden. Nathan also provides a lengthy list of provisions for her continued support to be provided by the executor. Only and well-beloved son Nathan receives all the lands and buildings. Daughter Phebe wife of Benjamin Ames receives five shillings and one-sixth of the household goods. Daughters Lucy the wife of Zebadiah Chandler and Mary wife of William Ballard receive similar bequests. In addition to the same bequest as her sisters, daughter Elizabeth has continued use of the house as long as she is unmarried. Daughters Priscilla and Rhoda receive twenty-five pounds, thirteen shillings, and four pence when they reach age 21. To beloved daughter Chloe he leaves ten shillings and "considering the difficulties she labours under not likely to be capable of

[776] Chandler, *Descendants of William and Annis Chandler*, p 329

taking care of herself I commit the care of her to my son Nathan." He also orders that his daughters Priscilla and Rhoda be raised in his house until they are of age. Nathan also specifies that son Nathan is to carry out all the bequests of the will "as I think I have given him the wherewith out of my estate to do it." Son Nathan Chandler declined to be executor writing to Judge Benjamin Greenleaf 3 July 1786 that "I utterly refuse" this responsibility. However, Judge Greenleaf responded to Nathan in a letter 6 November 1786 ordering him to assume the administration of the estate which Nathan then did carry out.[777] I can only imagine the younger Nathan's situation. He was just 30 years old, newly married, and just had his first child. As the only son in the family, he had responsibility for his widowed mother and grandmother, a disabled sister, and two sisters still underage who were living in Andover.

Phebe and Nathan Chandler had nine children whose births are recorded at Andover.[778] Of the six children who married, five married other George Abbott descendants.

i PHEBE CHANDLER, b. 18 Oct 1754; d. at Andover, 19 Jun 1798; m. 30 Apr 1772, her second cousin once removed, BENJAMIN AMES *(Benjamin Ames^{4}, Hannah Stevens Ames^{3}, Elizabeth Abbott Stevens^{2}, George^{1})*, b. at Andover, 9 Nov 1749 son of Benjamin and Hephzibah (Chandler) Ames; Benjamin d. 23 Nov 1813. Phebe Chandler and Benjamin Ames are Family 1185.

ii NATHAN CHANDLER, b. 16 Jun 1756; d. at Andover, 27 Jun 1837; m. 27 Nov 1782, his first cousin once removed, LUCY BALLARD *(Lydia Chandler Ballard^{4}, John Chandler^{3}, Hannah Abbott Chandler^{2}, George^{1})*, b. at Andover 4 Apr 1760 daughter of Hezekiah and Lydia (Chandler) Ballard; Lucy d. 29 Jun 1827. Nathan Chandler and Lucy Ballard are Family 444.

iii LUCE CHANDLER, b. 26 Jun 1758; d. at Andover, 6 Oct 1841; m. 16 Aug 1774, ZEBADIAH CHANDLER *(Zebadiah Chandler^{5}, Joshua Chandler^{4}, John Chandler^{3}, Hannah Abbott Chandler^{2}, George^{1})*, b. at Andover, 11 Nov 1752 son of Zebadiah and Deborah (Blanchard) Chandler; Zebadiah d. 5 Feb 1835.

iv EZRA CHANDLER, b. 20 Jun 1761; d. 10 Sep 1778. Ezra "died coming out of ye army."

v ELIZABETH CHANDLER, b. 15 May 1763; d. at Andover, 22 Sep 1848. Elizabeth did not marry.

vi MARY CHANDLER, b. 18 May 1766; d. at Peterborough, 12 Sep 1819; m. 11 Nov 1783, WILLIAM BALLARD, b. at Andover, Jun 1764 son of William and Hannah (How) Ballard; William d. about 1807. Mary m. 2nd, DANIEL ABBOTT "of Andover" (according to the Chandler genealogy) but I do not know what Abbott family he belongs to.

vii PRISCILLA CHANDLER, b. 30 Jun 1768; d. at Andover, 19 Feb 1831; m. 26 May 1789, her first cousin, DAVID ABBOTT *(Jonathan^{4}, David^{3}, Benjamin^{2}, George^{1})*, b. at Andover, 11 Mar 1764 son of Jonathan and Mary (Chandler) Abbott; David d. 1 Jun 1823. Priscilla Chandler and David Abbott are Family 842.

viii CHLOE CHANDLER, b. 30 Jun 1771; d. at Andover 24 Aug 1821. Chloe did not marry. She died at the almshouse.

ix RHODA CHANDLER, b. 2 Mar 1774; d. at Andover, 19 Mar 1853; m. at Andover, 26 Nov 1793, her first cousin, BENJAMIN ABBOTT *(Jonathan^{4}, David^{3}, Benjamin^{2}, George^{1})*, b. at Andover, 7 Jun 1770 son of Jonathan and Mary (Chandler) Abbott; Benjamin d. at Andover, 20 Oct 1835. "Benjamin, Oct. 20, 1835, a. 65 y." Rhoda Chandler and Benjamin Abbott are Family 845.

290) JEREMIAH ABBOT *(John^{4}, John^{3}, John^{2}, George^{1})*, b. 14 May 1743 son of John and Phebe (Fiske) Abbot; d. 2 Nov 1825 at Wilton, NH; m. 16 Sep 1766, CLOE ABBOTT (from the George Abbott of Rowley line), b. 5 Nov 1737 daughter of Zebadiah and Anne (Lovejoy) Abbott; Cloe d. at Wilton 21 Aug 1809.

Jeremiah and Cloe were married in Andover but were very soon after in Wilton, New Hampshire where they raised their family.

In his will, Jeremiah Abbot leaves six-sevenths of the household furniture and six-ninths of his books to be divided among six of his daughters: Chloe Gray, Lydia Pevey, Anna Wood, Dorcas Holt, and Sally Buss. Daughter Phebe Holt receives the other sixth portion of the household goods as well as thirty dollars. Beloved son Jeremiah Abbot, Jr. receives the pew in the meeting house in Wilton, the desk and one-ninth of the books; Jeremiah has already received his portion from the estate. Son Zebadiah receives the homestead farm in Wilton. Son Zebadiah is named executor.[779]

---

[777] *Essex County, MA: Probate File Papers, 1638-1881.* Online database. *AmericanAncestors.org. Probate of Nathan Chandler, 6 Jul 1786, case number 4963.*
[778] Massachusetts Vital Records Project. http://ma-vitalrecords.org
[779] Ancestry.com. *New Hampshire, Wills and Probate Records, 1643-1982* [database on-line]. Will of Jeremiah Abbott, 17 May 1823.

Jeremiah and Cloe had nine children whose births are recorded at Wilton.[780]

i CHLOE ABBOTT, b. 4 Jun 1767; d. at Wilton, 19 Jul 1849; m. 11 Apr 1786, JOSEPH GRAY son of Timothy and Elinor (Best) Gray; Joseph d. at Wilton, 26 Aug 1846.

ii LYDIA ABBOTT, b. 22 Oct 1768; d. at Peterborough, NH, 1 Sep 1832; m. THOMAS PEVEY, b. about 1765 *possibly* the son of Thomas and Dorcas (Holt) Pevey.

iii ANNA ABBOTT, b. 15 Jul 1770; d. at Hancock, NH, 19 Mar 1844; m. 15 Apr 1790, DAVID WOOD, b. at Andover, 1 Feb 1765 son of Israel and Sarah (Stevens) Wood; David d. at Hancock, 19 Dec 1834.

iv DORCAS ABBOTT, b. 24 Aug 1772; d. at Wilton, Jul 1847; m. 3 Feb 1795, DANIEL HOLT, b. at Wilton, 29 Oct 1769 son of Daniel and Mehitable (Putnam) Holt.

v PHEBE ABBOTT, b. 24 Aug 1772; d. at Weld, ME about 1850; m. 1st, 1 Sep 1795, WALTER FISKE, b. at Pepperrell, 17 Jun 1773 son of Daniel and Elizabeth (Vernum) Fiske. Phebe m. 2nd, 17 June 1810, CALEB HOLT, b. 16 Oct 1777 son of Daniel and Mehitable (Putnam) Holt. Caleb Holt was first married to Betsey Gray.

vi JEREMIAH ABBOTT, b. 23 Aug 1774; d. at Wilton, 30 Jun 1857; m. 30 Jun 1800, EUNICE BLANCHARD, b. at Wilton, 6 Jun 1778 daughter of Joshua and Elizabeth (Keyes) Blanchard; Eunice d. 4 Jan 1850.

vii ZEBADIAH ABBOTT, b. 20 Sep 1776; d. at Wilton, 21 Aug 1830; m. 1801, ELIZABETH HALE, b. about 1779 in Connecticut daughter of Joseph and Rebecca (Harris) Hale;[781] Elizabeth d. Apr 1845.

viii BETSEY ABBOTT, b. 21 Oct 1778; d. at Andover, 20 Jul 1835; m. 16 Oct 1807, MOSES WOOD, b. at Andover, 16 May 1779 son of Israel and Sarah (Stevens) Wood; Moses d. in New Jersey, 5 Apr 1867. Moses m. 2nd, Mrs. Pamelia Powers, 3 Apr 1836.[782]

ix SARAH ABBOTT, b. 8 Dec 1781; d. at Wilton, 26 Oct 1851; m. 8 Dec 1803, STEPHEN BUSS, b. 19 Jan 1777 son of Stephen and Phebe (Keyes) Buss; Stephen d. at Wilton, 29 Sep 1848.

291) WILLIAM ABBOT *(John⁴, John³, John², George¹)*, b. 3 Jan 1747/8 son of John and Phebe (Fiske) Abbot; d. at Wilton, NH 30 Nov 1793;[783] m. 12 Nov 1772, his third cousin, PHEBE BALLARD *(Hannah Chandler Ballard⁴, John Chandler³, Hannah Abbott Chandler², George¹)*, b. 5 Nov 1752 daughter of Timothy and Hannah (Chandler) Ballard; Phebe d. at Wilton, Jan 1846.

William and Phebe were early residents of Wilton. William was a farmer and active in community affairs. He was a representative to the State convention for the adoption of the U.S. Constitution.[784] His oldest son, William, graduated Harvard in 1797 and was an attorney. Son Herman also attended Harvard and was a physician in Waldo, Maine.[785]

William and Phebe had eleven children whose births are recorded at Wilton.

i WILLIAM ABBOTT, b. 15 Nov 1773; d. at Bangor, ME, Aug 1850; m. at Lancaster, 24 May 1802, REBECCA ATHERTON, b. about 1776 daughter of Israel and Rebecca (Stevens widow Prentice) Atherton.[786] Rebecca's death not known, but perhaps around 1852 when the remainder of William's estate was sold at auction, including the widow's dower which had been returned to the estate.[787] William Abbott graduated Harvard in 1797 and was an attorney in Castine, and later in Bangor, Maine. He was elected Mayor of Bangor in 1848 and 1850.[788] A daguerreotype of Rebecca Atherton Abbott can be found on page 15 of Castine history.[789]

ii JOHN ABBOTT, b. 6 Oct 1775; d. at Hampden, ME, 24 Nov 1861;[790] m. before 1816, MARY HAMMOND, b. at Newton, 11 Oct 1782 daughter of William and Relief (Baldwin) Hammond; Mary d. 1841.

iii TIMOTHY ABBOTT, b. 2 Sep 1777; d. at Wilton, 27 Oct 1863; m. about 1812, ELIZABETH ROCKWOOD, b. 9 Dec 1782 daughter of Ebenezer and Mary (Emerson) Rockwood; Elizabeth d. 6 Oct 1846.

iv EZRA ABBOTT, b. 10 Aug 1779; d. 29 Aug 1784.

v PHEBE ABBOTT, b. 11 Aug 1781; d. 21 Oct 1844. Phebe did not marry.

---

780 Ancestry.com. *New Hampshire, Births and Christenings Index, 1714-1904* [database on-line]. Provo, UT, USA: Ancestry.com Operations, Inc., 2011.
781 Dwight, *The History of Descendants of Elder John Strong*, p 332
782 Hayward, *History of Hancock*, NH, p 1035
783 *New Hampshire, Death and Burial Records Index, 1654-1949.*
784 Abbot and Abbot, *Genealogical Register of Descendants*, p 13
785 Harvard University, *Quinquennial Catalogue*
786 Atherton Family Papers, 1825 letter from David Atherton to Jonathan Atherton; New Hampshire Historical Society
787 Ancestry.com, Maine, Wills and Probate Records, 1584-1999, Notes: *Bonds For Sale, Vol 20,1842-1854; Petition For Sale, Vol 21, 1848-1852*
788 Wheeler, *History of Castine*, pp 212-213
789 Castine Historical Society, *Castine*, p 15
790 Ancestry.com, Penobscot County, Maine, Mount Hope Burial Index, 1861-2012

vi HERMAN ABBOTT, b. 13 Aug 1783; d. at Waldo, ME, 24 Jul 1825. Herman did not marry. He was educated at Harvard and a physician. His estate was declared insolvent when it was finally settled in 1830.

vii EZRA ABBOTT, b. 3 Jul 1785; d. at Jackson, ME, 7 Jun 1871; m. 25 Jun 1818, his first cousin, PHEBE ABBOTT *(Dorcas⁴, Benjamin³, Benjamin², George¹),* b. at Wilton, 25 Jun 1788 daughter of Abiel and Dorcas (Abbott) Abbott; Phebe d. 25 Nov 1825. Ezra Abbott and Phebe Abbott are Family 805.

viii ISAAC ABBOTT, b. 29 Jul 1787; d. 7 Nov 1788.

ix HANNAH ABBOTT, b. 17 Jul 1789; d. at Amherst, NH, 27 Aug 1871; m. 29 Jan 1818, JOHN MACK, b. at Londonderry, 7 Aug 1780 son of Andrew and Elizabeth (Clark) Mack; John d. at Amherst, 16 Jul 1854.

x BETSY ABBOTT, b. Sep 1791; d. at Wilton, 12 Mar 1828; m. 27 May 1819, TIMOTHY PARKHURST, b. 1793 son of Jonathan and Rachel (Coburn) Parkhurst; Timothy d. 18 Jul 1867.

xi ISAAC ABBOTT, b. 11 Sep 1793; d. at Jackson, ME, 9 Mar 1851; m. 16 Jul 1815, CHLOE BAYLE, b. at Wilton, 11 Jul 1794 daughter of William and Rhoda (Keyes) Bayle; Chloe d. after 1870.[791]

292) MOSES ABBOT *(Barachias⁴, John³, John², George¹)*, b. 9 Aug 1735 son of Barachias and Hannah (Holt) Abbot; d. 23 Feb 1826; m. 31 Dec 1761, his third cousin, ELIZABETH HOLT, b. 8 Jun 1743 daughter of Henry and Rebecca (Gray) Holt; Elizabeth d. 23 Sep 1838.

Moses Abbot served as a Lieutenant in the French and Indian War and later held the rank of Captain in the militia. He was a yeoman, surveyor, and schoolmaster in Andover. His homestead, which was divided between his sons Noah and Enoch, became the sites of two historic homes in Andover, 6 Stinson Road and 22 Stinson Road. The home at 6 Stinson Road was nominated to the National Register of Historical Places.[792]

The estate of Moses Abbot entered probate 18 Apr 1826. His will, written 19 March 1814, has a bequest to well-beloved wife Elizabeth who receives all the household items "proper for woman's use" to be at her own disposal. His wife and unmarried daughters also have use of and improvements of the east lower room, bedroom, and well room. The lands not bequeathed to his sons Enoch and Noah are also to be used for her support. The will includes bequests to five sons (Enoch, Noah, Moses, Henry, and Jacob) and seven daughters (Rebecca, Elizabeth, Hannah, Rhoda, Anna, Abigail, and Phebe). The bulk of the real estate goes to Enoch and Noah, although all the sons receive land bequests. Sons Moses, Henry, and Jacob also receive $300. Each of the daughters receive $150 and a cow. Moses, Noah, and Enoch are named joint executors.[793]

Moses and Elizabeth had thirteen children whose births are recorded at Andover.

i REBECCA ABBOTT, b. 2 Jan 1763; d. at Andover, 21 Jan 1844; m. 28 Jun 1798, her fourth cousin, JOSEPH PHELPS, b. at Pomfret, 17 Oct 1756 son of Joseph and Lydia (Osgood) Phelps; Joseph d. at Andover, 12 Sep 1835. Which Joseph Phelps married Rebecca Abbott is uncertain. Charlotte Helen Abbott speculates that it was Joseph son of Joseph and Ruth (French) Phelps born in 1774 and died in 1858 (although she also proposed a Joseph Phelps born in 1750 son of Thomas, but that family went to New Hampshire). Rebecca Phelps is described as a widow at her death in 1844. Joseph Phelps born in Pomfret did die in Andover in 1835 at the age of 79 and he fits better in terms of age. The family of Joseph who was born in Pomfret had returned to Andover where Joseph's father died in 1802. In addition, Joseph Phelps (son of Joseph and Ruth) born in Tewksbury in 1774 resided in Danvers (according to his Mason membership card), and there is a Joseph Phelps in Danvers married to Eunice Gardner and having children during this same period.

ii MOSES ABBOTT, b. 30 Nov 1765; d. at Andover, 9 Mar 1859; m. 1st, 5 Feb 1799, MARTHA "PATTY" FRYE, b. at Andover, 22 Mar 1772 daughter of Benjamin and Elizabeth (Clark) Frye; Martha d. at Salem, 15 Sep 1804. Moses m. 2nd, as her second husband, PRISCILLA FLINT, b. at Reading, 1784 daughter of Daniel and Priscilla (Sawyer) Flint; Priscilla d. at Andover 5 Apr 1811. Priscilla was first married to James Nelson.

iii ELIZABETH ABBOT, b. 8 May 1768; d. at Andover, 12 Feb 1829. Elizabeth did not marry.

iv NOAH ABBOTT, b. 11 May 1770; d. at Andover, 13 Jul 1849; m. 18 Feb 1806, his second cousin, HANNAH HOLT *(Lydia Ballard Holt⁵, Lydia Chandler Ballard⁴, John Chandler³, Hannah Abbott Chandler², George¹)*, b. 16 Apr 1771 daughter of Dane and Lydia (Ballard) Holt; Hannah d. 14 Jun 1862.

---

791 Year: 1870; Census Place: Brooks, Waldo, Maine; Roll: M593_560; Page: 83A; Family History Library Film: 552059. Chloe Abbott, age 75, listed in the 1870 census.

792 Andover Historic Preservation, 6 Stinson Road, retrieved from https://preservation.mhl.org/6-stinson-road

793 *Essex County, MA: Probate File Papers, 1638-1881. Probate of Moses Abbott, 18 Apr 1826, Case number 99*

v HANNAH ABBOTT, b. about 1771; d. 15 Mar 1772

vi HANNAH ABBOTT, b. Apr 1772; d. at Andover, 13 Apr 1840. Hannah did not marry.

vii ENOCH ABBOTT, b. 8 Apr 1774; d. at Andover, 26 Sep 1842; m. 4 Jul 1799, NANCY FLINT, b. at Danvers, 19 Sep 1777 daughter of Samuel and Ede (Upton) Flint;[794] Nancy d. at Andover 1 Feb 1851.

viii RHODA ABBOTT, 8 Sep 1776; d. at Andover, 6 Feb 1850. Rhoda did not marry.

ix ANNA ABBOTT, b. 8 Sep 1776; d. at Andover, 27 Jul 1834. Anna did not marry.

x HENRY ABBOTT, b. 22 Sep 1778; d. at Andover, 22 Sep 1845; m. 23 Sep 1803, his third cousin, DORCAS HOLT, b. 20 Nov 1781 daughter of David and Rebecca (Osgood) Holt; Dorcas d. 24 Mar 1842.

xi JACOB ABBOTT, b. 30 Jun 1781; d. at Andover, 12 May 1836; m. 1 Jan 1808, BETSEY BULLARD, b. at Needham, 12 Sep 1782 daughter of Nathaniel and Sarah (Saunders) Bullard; Betsey d. 28 Jul 1858.

xii ABIGAIL ABBOTT, b. 22 Dec 1783; d. 9 Aug 1827; m. 21 Dec 1811, JONATHAN PHELPS, b. at Tewksbury, 1 Sep 1780 son of Joseph and Ruth (French) Phelps;[795] Jonathan d. at Andover, 1 Mar 1866.

xiii PHEBE ABBOTT, b. Mar 1786; d. at Andover, 6 Aug 1864. Phebe did not marry. Her estate entered probate 11 Oct 1864. The estate was valued at $500 real property and $10 personal property. Her will includes bequests to the following persons: brother Moses Abbot, Eliza Moore wife of Richard Moore, Jonathan Edwin Phelps, Eliza H. Phelps, Belinda Jane Phelps, Hannah H. Phelps, and George Herbert Gutterson. George Gutterson is named executor.[796]

293) HANNAH ABBOTT *(Barachias[4], John[3], John[2], George[1])*, b. 18 May 1737 daughter of Barachias and Hannah (Holt) Abbot; d. Nov 1812 at Wilton, NH; m. 21 Apr 1756, her third cousin, JEREMIAH HOLT, b. 31 Mar 1734 son of John and Mary (Lewis) Holt; Jeremiah's death record not located, but after the 1790 US Census and perhaps in 1816.[797]

Hannah Abbott and Jeremiah Holt were parents to thirteen children.

i JEREMIAH HOLT, b. at Andover, 8 Jun 1756; d. at Wilton, 3 Oct 1776.

ii BARACHIAS HOLT, b. at Wilton, 8 Feb 1758; d. at Antrim, NH, 1846; m. 14 Oct 1783, his first cousin, ELIZABETH SHATTUCK *(Zebadiah Shattuck[5], Joanna Chandler Shattuck[4], Zebadiah Chandler[3], Hannah Abbott Chandler[2], George[1])*, b. at Andover, 16 Dec 1759 daughter of Zebadiah and Elizabeth (Abbott) Shattuck. A death record was not found for Elizabeth. Elizabeth is a daughter in Family 294.

iii AMOS HOLT, b. at Wilton, 16 Feb 1760; d. at Wilton, Dec 1782.

iv ENOCH HOLT, b. at Wilton, 20 Mar 1762

v ELIAS HOLT, b. at Wilton 5 May 1764; perhaps died at Sherburne, NY.

vi JOHN HOLT, b. at Wilton, 16 Sep 1766; d. at Sherburne, NY, 30 Jan 1835; m. at Lyndeborough, 3 May 1790, MARY MCKEAN, b. Deb 1762 (based on age at death); Mary d. at Sherburne, 30 May 1818.[798]

vii ELIJAH HOLT, b. at Wilton, 30 Jul 1768; d. at Columbus, NY, 2 Sep 1850; m. Mar 1794, ANNA DICKEY, b. at Antrim, 19 Apr 1777 daughter of James and Mary (Brown) Dickey;[799] Anna d. at Columbus, 20 Mar 1854.

viii HANNAH HOLT, b. at Wilton, 7 Jun 1770

ix PHEBE HOLT, b. at Wilton, 24 Apr 1772; d. at Columbus, NY, 28 Nov 1859.[800]

x RHODA HOLT, b. at Wilton, 3 Feb 1774; d. likely at Weston, VT; m. at Wilton, 30 Jan 1798, DAVID RIDEOUT, b. at Wilton, 27 Oct 1771 son of Benjamin and Sarah (Taylor) Rideout; David b. at Weston, Sep 1849.

xi TIMOTHY ABBOT HOLT, b. 3 Oct 1775; d. 22 Aug 1777.

xii JEREMIAH HOLT, b. at Wilton, 28 Mar 1778

xiii TIMOTHY ABBOT HOLT, b. at Wilton, 24 Aug 1781; Timothy d. at Washington Co, ME, 4 Mar 1858; m. his fourth cousin, SARAH SAWYER *(Prudence Abbott Sawyer[5], David[4], David[3], Benjamin[2], George[1])*, b. at Wilton, 25

---

[794] The 1812 will of Ede Upton Flint Dane includes a bequest to her daughter Nancy Abbott.

[795] The death record of Jonathan Phelps lists parents Joseph and Ruth. Ancestry.com. *Massachusetts, Town and Vital Records, 1620-1988*

[796] *Essex County, MA: Probate File Papers, 1638-1881. Probate of Phebe Abbott, 11 Oct 1864, Case number 30887.*

[797] Death year given as 1816 in Livermore's *History of Wilton.*

[798] Findagrave ID: 92835124; Mary wife of John Holt died May 30th1818 55 years 5 months and 26 days; Sherburne Quarter Cemetery, Sherburne, New York

[799] Cochrane, *History of the Town of Antrim*, p 453

[800] Durrie, *Holt Genealogy*, p 59

Nov 1782 daughter of Nathaniel and Prudence (Abbott) Sawyer; Sarah d. at Marion, ME, 10 Jun 1863. Sarah is a daughter in Family 825.

294) BARACHIAS ABBOT *(Barachias⁴, John³, John², George¹)*, b. 22 May 1739 son of Barachias and Hannah (Holt) Abbot; d. 29 Jan 1812; m. 6 Dec 1770, his third cousin and George Abbott descendant, SARAH HOLT *(James Holt⁴, Dorcas Abbott Holt³, Timothy², George¹)*, b. 7 Mar 1746/7 daughter of James and Sarah (Abbott) Holt; Sarah d. 11 Feb 1808.

Barachias and Sarah had their seven children in Andover, but then relocated to Wilton about 1786. Barachias owned property there which he previously cleared and established a farm. Barachias Abbot served as a selectman in Wilton 1791-1792.[801] One of the children died in infancy. The two daughters did not marry and remained in Wilton. Sons Timothy and Joel remained in Wilton, Timothy living with his father. Barachias, the oldest son, moved on to Landgrove, Vermont. Barachias and Sarah perhaps returned to Andover in their later years as both their deaths are recorded there, as well as the death of their son Timothy.

i BARACHIAS ABBOTT, b. 20 Dec 1771; d. at Landgrove, VT, 23 Mar 1855; m. at Temple, NH, 18 Jan 1798, ANNA COLBURN, b. at Temple, 20 Feb 1777 daughter of Elias and Mehitable (Wheeler) Colburn. Anna d. at Landgrove, 1 May 1856.[802] There are twelve children recorded for this family.

ii TIMOTHY ABBOTT, b. 30 Mar 1773; death recorded at Andover, 1 Jan 1837; m. at Montague, MA, 22 Sep 1801, MARY "POLLY" BANCROFT, b, about 1778 likely the daughter of Kendall and Susanna (Ewers) Bancroft;[803] Polly's death is recorded at Wilton, 13 Feb 1852. Polly was living with her son Henry in Chelmsford at the 1850 U.S. Census. Timothy and Polly had seven children. Son Henry married Caroline Abbott, Nancy Abbott from whom he was divorced,[804] and Harriet Robinson.

iii JOEL ABBOTT, b. 29 Apr 1775; d. 7 May 1775

iv JOEL ABBOTT, b. 10 Oct 1776; d. at Wilton, 26 Mar 1863; m. 24 Mar 1803, his third cousin once removed, JUDITH RAY BATCHELDER, b. 21 Jun 1779 daughter of Daniel and Rebecca (Abbott) Batchelder. Joel and Judith are the parents in Family 1072.

v SARAH ABBOTT, b. 10 Oct 1779; d. at Wilton, 19 Oct 1858. Sarah did not marry. In the 1850 U.S. Census, Sarah was living in the household next to her brother Joel in Wilton but living on her own.

vi JAMES ABBOTT, b. 30 Mar 1780; d. at Andover, 4 Oct 1858. m. 31 May 1806, MARY FOSTER, b. at Greenfield, NH, about 1784 perhaps the daughter of Isaac and Mary (Holt) Foster;[805] Mary d. at Andover 20 Feb 1862. Isaac Foster and Mary Holt are Family 868.

vii ELIZABETH ABBOTT, b. 14 Sep 1784; d. at Wilton, 9 Apr 1854. Elizabeth did not marry.

295) ELIZABETH ABBOTT *(Barachias⁴, John³, John², George¹)*, b. 2 Nov 1740 daughter of Barachias and Hannah (Holt) Abbot; d. 9 Sep 1780; m. 30 Aug 1759, her second cousin, ZEBADIAH SHATTUCK *(Joanna Chandler Shattuck⁴, Zebadiah Chandler³, Hannah Abbott Chandler², George¹)*, b. 26 Oct 1736 son of Joseph and Joanna (Chandler) Shattuck. Zebadiah m. 2nd 25 Dec 1781, SARAH CHANDLER *(Zebadiah Chandler⁵, Joshua Chandler⁴, John Chandler³, Hannah Abbott Chandler², George¹)* (widow of Ralph Holbrook), b. 8 May 1751 daughter of Zebadiah and Deborah (Blanchard) Chandler; Zebadiah d. 10 Mar 1826. Sarah d. at Andover, 4 Nov 1824.

Zebadiah Shattuck was a farmer in Andover. He served during the war with the French.[806]

Elizabeth Abbott and Zebadiah Shattuck had six children born at Andover.

---

801 Livermore, *History of Wilton*

802 The graves of Barachias and Anna are in the Old Landgrove Cemetery in Landgrove, VT; FIndagrave memorial ID 184633891

803 Kendall Bancroft lived in Montague where he died in 1806. His will includes a daughter Mary, although the will does not give the last names of any of the children. One of the children of Timothy and Polly was named Kendall Bancroft Abbott.

804 *New Hampshire, Marriage and Divorce Records, 1659-1947*, New England Historical Genealogical Society; New Hampshire Bureau of Vital Records, Concord, New Hampshire; New Hampshire, Marriage and Divorce Records, 1659–1947. Married in 1854 and divorced 1864

805 There is a possibility that Mary Foster was the daughter of Isaac's first wife Mary Hartwell. All published genealogies say mother is Mary Holt who was the second wife. Isaac Foster married Mary Hartwell in 1779 and she died in 1781, and this may be too early of a birth date for Mary Foster, but there is no birth record for Mary Foster. This is offered as an option as Mary Foster and James Abbott named one of their sons Hartwell Barachias Abbott which would be a name that honored father's father and mother's mother.

806 Shattuck, *Memorials of the Descendants of William Shattuck*, p 150

i ELIZABETH SHATTUCK, b. 16 Dec 1759; d. at Antrim, NH; m. 14 Oct 1783, her first cousin, BARACHIAS HOLT *(Hannah Abbott Holt⁵, Barachias⁴, John³, John², George¹)*, b. at Wilton, NH, 8 Feb 1758 son of Jeremiah and Hannah (Abbott) Holt; Barachias d. at Antrim, 1846. Barachias Holt is a child in Family 293.

ii HANNAH SHATTUCK, b. Dec 1761; d. at Bethel, ME, m. at Andover, 17 May 1787, JAMES SWAN, b. at Methuen, 2 Dec 1760 son of James and Mary (Smith) Swan; James d. at Bethel, about 1844 (probate 1844).

iii DOROTHY SHATTUCK, b. 14 Apr 1764; d. at Bethel, ME, 24 Jan 1852; m. 1st, at Andover, 26 Feb 1784, JACOB RUSSELL, b. at Andover, Jan 1761 son of John and Hannah (Foster) Russell; Jacob d. 1799. Dorothy m. 2nd, at Bethel, 2 Nov 1803, INGALLS BRAGG, b. at Andover, 24 Jun 1753 son of Thomas and Dorothy (Ingalls) Bragg; Ingalls d. at East Andover, ME, 1 Jan 1808. After Ingalls's death, Dorothy married at Waterford, 21 Oct 1811, DANIEL GAGE.

iv PHEBE SHATTUCK, b. Feb 1766; d. at Plainfield, VT, 16 Jun 1856; m. at Andover, 25 Jul 1786, her first cousin, ABIEL SHATTUCK *(Joseph Shattuck⁵, Joanna Chandler Shattuck⁴, Zebadiah Chandler³, Hannah Abbott Chandler², George¹)*, b. at Andover, 8 Aug 1762 son of Joseph and Anna (Johnson) Shattuck; Abiel d. at Plainfield, 29 Apr 1834. Abiel is a child in Family 337.

v JOHN SHATTUCK, b. 23 Oct 1768; no further record

vi RHODA SHATTUCK, b. 1 Sep 1776; m. about 1798, SAMUEL CLARK

Zebadiah Shattuck and Sarah Chandler had two children born at Andover.

i SARAH SHATTUCK, b. 3 Nov 1782; d. at Haverhill, MA, 29 Jan 1872; m. at Andover, 26 Nov 1801, RICHARD TROW, b. at Beverly, about 1779 son of John and Hannah (Dodge) Trow;[807] Richard d. perhaps at Nashua, NH.

ii ZEBADIAH SHATTUCK, b. at Andover, 30 Mar 1785; d. at Andover, 22 Oct 1828; m. at Andover, 29 Nov 1804, SARAH DURANT, b. at Andover, about 1786[808] daughter of Amos and Sarah (Ballard) Durant.

296) PRISCILLA ABBOTT *(Barachias⁴, John³, John², George¹)*, b. 13 Feb 1742/3 daughter of Barachias and Hannah (Holt) Abbot; d. likely at Bethel, ME; m. 16 Nov 1762, ZELA HOLT, b. 29 Dec 1738 son of James and Mary (Chandler) Holt.

Priscilla Abbott and Zela Holt married in Andover, were for a time in Wilton, New Hampshire where some of their children were born, and finally settled in Bethel, Maine around 1790.[809][810] Their six children were likely born in Wilton, although the birth of one child is recorded in Bethel and the baptism of the youngest child was recorded at Andover.

i CALVIN HOLT, b. 26 Aug 1763; d. 27 Mar 1795.

ii JAMES HOLT, b. about 1765; d. perhaps at Bethel; m. at Reading, MA, 28 Feb 1793, MEHITABLE EATON, b. at Reading, Jul 1773 daughter of Timothy and Mehitable (Burnup) Eaton.

iii PRISCILLA HOLT, b. at Wilton, 2 Jan 1768; d. at Bethel, 4 Jan 1848; m. 23 May 1791, JOHN STEARNS, b. Aug 1762 son of John and Martha (Harrington) Stearns; John d. at Bethel, 14 Dec 1826.

iv TIMOTHY ABBOT HOLT, b. 15 Aug 1773; d. at Bethel, 1856; m. at Andover, 17 Jan 1799, ANNA STEVENS, b. at Andover, 5 Jul 1774 daughter of Peter and Abigail (Johnson) Stevens; Anna d. at Bethel, 1861.

v MARY HOLT, b. about 1775; d. 18 Feb 1790.

vi BRIDGET HOLT, baptized Mar 1777; d. at Bethel, after 1850. Bridget did not marry. In 1850, she was living with her brother Timothy in Bethel.

297) LYDIA ABBOTT *(Barachias⁴, John³, John², George¹)*, b. 7 Mar 1744/5 daughter of Barachias and Hannah (Holt) Abbot; d. at Andover, 11 Jul 1829; m. 15 Aug 1771, URIAH RUSSELL, b. 1743 son of Thomas and Abigail (Ballard) Russell; Uriah d. 9 Nov 1822.

Uriah Russell wrote his will 31 March 1818 and his estate entered probate 7 January 1823.[811] His beloved wife Lydia is to have the improvements on all the household furniture during her lifetime, and after her decease, the household items will pass to his two daughters. The executor is to see that she is comfortably provided for. Sons James, Thomas, and Abiel each

---

807 Charlotte Helen Abbott, The Trow Family of Andover

808 Sarah was baptized at Andover 24 Nov 1793; the four oldest children in the family were all baptized on the same day.

809 Lapham, *History of Bethel*, p 563

810 Livermore, *History of Wilton*, p 407

811 *Essex County, MA: Probate File Papers, 1638-1881. Probate of Uriah Russell, 7 Jan 1823, Case number 24434.*

receives $125. The two daughters, Hannah Abbot the wife of Nathan Abbot and Lydia Faulkner wife of Joseph Faulkner, each receives $15. Son Joel Russell receives all the residue of the estate, both real and personal, and is named executor.

There are records for eleven children born at Andover. There is a daughter Phebe for which there is only a baptismal record. The oldest son died of yellow fever at Curacao. Of the six children who married, three married other George Abbott descendants.

i URIAH RUSSELL, b. Sep 1773; d. of yellow fever at Curacao, 1799.[812]

ii THOMAS RUSSELL, b. Dec 1774; d, Sep 1775.

iii HANNAH RUSSELL, b. Sep 1775; d. 9 Oct 1776.

iv JAMES RUSSELL, b. Nov 1777; d. about 1861 in Oxford County, ME;[813] m. at East Andover, ME, 13 Aug 1804, his first cousin once removed, DOLLY RUSSELL *(Dorothy Shattuck Russell⁶, Zebadiah Shattuck⁵, James Chandler⁴, Zebadiah Chandler³, Hannah Abbott Chandler², George¹)*, b. about 1784 daughter of Jacob and Dorothy (Shattuck) Russell; Dolly d. at Beverly, MA, 20 Sep 1863.

v THOMAS RUSSELL, b. Nov 1777 (twin of James); d. at Andover, 18 Jan 1849; m. at Albany, ME, 22 Apr 1806, ABIGAIL BELL, b. perhaps at Albany 1786 of not yet verified parents; Abigail d. at Andover 10 Oct 1833. Thomas and Abigail were parents of nine children.

vi HANNAH RUSSELL, b. Apr 1780 (based on age at death); d. at Andover, 16 Nov 1832; m. 10 Nov 1801, her third cousin, NATHAN ABBOTT *(Nathan⁵, Job⁴, Jonathan³, Benjamin², George¹)*, b. at Andover, 25 Aug 1778 son of Nathan and Sarah (Ballard) Abbott; Nathan d. 13 Feb 1837.

vii LYDIA RUSSELL, b. Sep 1782; d. Oct 1782.

viii JOEL RUSSELL, b. Aug 1783; d. at Andover, 22 Jul 1871; m. 2 Apr 1805, SARAH CURTIS, b. at Middleton, 16 Oct 1782 daughter of Israel and Elizabeth (Wilkins) Curtis; Sarah d. at Andover, 6 Feb 1857.

ix LYDIA RUSSELL, b. 5 Dec 1785; d. at Andover, 2 Dec 1865; m. 13 Jun 1809, her third cousin once removed, JOSEPH FAULKNER *(Hannah Abbott Faulkner⁵, Thomas⁴, Thomas³, Thomas², George¹)*, b. at Andover, 30 Jul 1783 son of Abiel and Hannah (Abbott) Faulkner; Joseph d. 5 Aug 1831.

x PHEBE RUSSELL, baptized 29 Jan 1786; no further record and likely died young.

xi ABIEL RUSSELL, b. Mar 1789; d. at Andover, 14 Jan 1881; m. 17 Jun 1813, his third cousin, SARAH ABBOTT *(Nathan⁵, Job⁴, Jonathan³, Benjamin², George¹)*, b. at Andover, 20 Dec 1792 daughter of Nathan and Sarah (Ballard) Abbott; Sarah d. 20 Sep 1846.

298) PHEBE ABBOTT *(Barachias⁴, John³, John², George¹)*, b. 29 Aug 1749 daughter of Barachias and Hannah (Holt) Abbot; d. at Andover, 17 Apr 1809; m. 1 Feb 1774, JOHN RUSSELL, b. 1 Jul 1746 son of John and Hannah (Foster) Russell. John m. 2nd Mary Wilkins; John d. at Andover, 12 Aug 1830. Mary Wilkins was first married to Nathaniel Sherman.

The estate of John Russell entered probate 17 August 1830.[814] The will of John Russell has bequests to the following persons: beloved wife Mary; grandson John Russell (oldest male heir with the name Russell), daughters Phebe Lovejoy, Hannah Abbot, Betsy Smith, Sally Loring, the heirs of daughter Dolly Lovejoy who is deceased, and heirs of daughter Nancy Woodbridge who is deceased; daughter-in-law Phebe Russell (this to be in the hands of a trustee);[815] and grandchildren John Russell, William Russell, Edward Russell, Phebe Russell, and Joseph Russell. Benjamin Jenkins is named executor and trustee.

Phebe Abbott and John Russell had eight children born at Andover.

i JOHN RUSSELL, b. 10 Oct 1774; d. at Andover, May 1818; m. at Andover, 21 Jul 1799, DIANA BRAY, b. at Gloucester, Oct 1775 daughter of Edward and Edith (Doane) Bray; Diana d. at Andover, 4 Mar 1858.[816]

ii PHEBE RUSSELL, b. 1776; d. at Andover, 2 Dec 1858; m. 2 Nov 1794, her third cousin, EBENEZER LOVEJOY (a descendant of William Chandler), b. at Andover, 16 Feb 1773 son of Jeremiah and Dorothy (Ballard) Lovejoy; Ebenezer d. at Andover, 1 Jun 1851.

---

[812] Uriah, jr., yellow fever, at Curacoa, ——, 1799. CR2

[813] James Russell was living at the time of the 1860 U.S. Census; his wife was a widow when she died in 1863.

[814] *Essex County, MA: Probate File Papers, 1638-1881.* Online database. *AmericanAncestors.org.* New England Historic Genealogical Society, 2014. Case number 24400

[815] It has not been determined who daughter-in-law Phebe Russell is.

[816] Diana's death record confirms Gloucester as her place of birth making Edward and Edith her likely parents.

iii HANNAH RUSSELL, b. Sep 1778; d. at Andover, 3 Jan 1840; m. 13 Aug 1801, her third cousin, STEPHEN ABBOTT *(Jonathan5, Jonathan4, Jonathan3, Benjamin2, George1)*, b. at Andover, 30 Dec 1779 son of Jonathan and Dorcas (Abbott) Abbott; Stephen d. at Andover, 1 Oct 1835. Stephen is a child in Family 321.

iv BETTY RUSSELL, b. 1780; d. at Andover, 7 Nov 1866; m. 27 Sep 1804, THOMAS SMITH, b. at Andover, 13 Mar 1781 son of Thomas and Mary (Harris) Smith; Thomas d. at Andover, 18 Sep 1832.

v SALLY RUSSELL, b. 1783; d. at Andover, 10 Jun 1848; m. at Andover, 23 Oct 1806, THOMAS LORING, born in NH, about 1780 son of John and Sarah (Foster) Loring; Thomas d. at New Orleans, 1826. Thomas was a machinist and he placed the machinery in the first steamboat to go down the Ohio River. He died of spotted fever in New Orleans.[817][818]

vi WILLIAM RUSSELL, b. 1785; d. 21 Nov 1788.

vii DOLLY RUSSELL, b. baptized 21 Sep 1788; d. at Andover, 26 Jun 1809; m. 19 May 1808, her third cousin, JOHN LOVEJOY, b. at Andover, 25 Jul 1780 son of Jeremiah and Dorothy (Ballard) Lovejoy; John d. at Andover, 26 Feb 1817. After Dolly's death, John married PERSIS BAILEY, b. at Andover, 25 May 1783 daughter of William and Rebecca (Hildreth) Bailey; Persis d. at Andover, 18 Feb 1816.

viii NANCY RUSSELL, b. Aug 1790; d. at Arlington, MA, 29 Dec 1818; m. 1812, SAMUEL WOODBRIDGE, b. at Marblehead, 13 Jan 1788 son of Dudley and Sara (Brock) Woodbridge; Dudley d. at Cambridge, 28 Jan 1867. After Nancy's death, Samuel married, 30 Sep 1821, DORCAS RUSSELL *(Mehitable Abbott Russell6, Jonathan5, Jonathan4, Jonathan3, Benjamin2, George1)*, b. at Bethel, ME, 8 Apr 1796 daughter of Benjamin and Mehitable (Abbott) Russell; Dorcas d. at Boston, 29 Nov 1877.

299) ABIGAIL ABBOTT *(Barachias4, John3, John2, George1)*, b. 25 Jul 1751 daughter of Barachias and Hannah (Holt) Abbot; d. at Greenfield, NH 1841; m. 10 Oct 1786, as his second wife, JOHN JOHNSON, b. at Andover, 1748 *perhaps* the son of John and Lydia (Osgood) Johnson (gravestone gives his age as 85); d. at Greenfield, NH 3 Oct 1833. He was *perhaps* first married to Hannah Abbott daughter of John and Hannah (Farnum) Abbott who died in 1785 and then married Abigail. Hannah Abbott and John Johnson are Family 1209. It is speculation that the same John Johnson married both Hannah Abbott and Abigail Abbot.

There are two children known for Abigail Abbott and John Johnson born at Greenfield.

i JOSEPH JOHNSON, b. 1787; d. at Greenfield, 20 Apr 1860; m. at Peterborough, 13 May 1812, MARY DIAMOND, b. at Lexington, MA, 1789 daughter of William and Rebecca (Symonds) Diamond;[819] Mary d. at Greenfield, 7 May 1858. Mary's father William was the drummer at the Battles of Lexington and Bunker Hill.

ii PHEBE JOHNSON, b. 1792; d. at West Windsor, VT, 12 May 1879; m. 1822, ROYAL SAWIN, b. at Windsor, 1798 son of Munning and Melissa (Powers) Sawin; Royal d. at West Windsor, 13 Sep 1875.

300) ASA FOSTER *(Elizabeth Abbot Foster4, John3, John2, George1)*, b. at Andover, 29 Aug 1733 son of Asa and Elizabeth (Abbot) Foster; d. at Canterbury, NH 23 Sep 1814; m. 1st HANNAH SYMONDS, b. at Boxford, 5 Nov 1733 daughter of Joseph and Mary (-) Symonds; Hannah d. 29 Jun 1775. Asa m. 2nd 1776, HANNAH PETERS, b. at Andover 11 Dec 1730 daughter of Samuel and Mary (Robinson) Peters; Hannah Peters d. 11 Jan 1815.

Asa Foster came to Canterbury with his father in 1761 where they purchased 240 acres. Asa became deacon of the church in Canterbury in 1773 and served in that position until his death.[820]

In his will written 26 July 1814, Asa Foster bequeaths to beloved wife Mrs. Hannah Foster the improvements on all the dwelling house and all the household furniture and six sheep. Son Asa Foster receives all the lands, the livestock, and the husbandry tools. Beloved daughter Susanna Parker widow of the late Frederick Parker of Canterbury receives $80. His two grandchildren Harriet Kimball and Asa Foster Kimball, children of his daughter Mrs. Mehitable Kimball who is decease, receive $30. Son Asa is named sole executor.[821]

Asa Foster and Hannah Symonds had three children born at Canterbury.

i ASA FOSTER, b. 3 Jun 1765; d. at Canterbury, 21 Aug 1861; m. at Canterbury, 10 Nov 1794, SARAH MORRILL, b. 11 May 1772 daughter of David and Abigail (Emerson) Morrill; Sarah d. 28 Mar 1868. Asa enlisted in the army at age 15 years and served for three months in West Point, NY. The *History of Canterbury* reports he was one of

[817] *New Hampshire, Death and Burial Records Index, 1654-1949.*
[818] Charlotte Helen Abbott, The Loring Family
[819] Smith and Morison, *History of Peterborough*, p 55
[820] Lyford, *History of Canterbury*, p 134
[821] *New Hampshire Wills and Probate Records 1643-1982,* Will of Asa Foster, Rockingham, 26 Jul 1814.

Benedict Arnold's bodyguards. After the Revolutionary War, Asa continued in the militia ultimately achieving a rank of Colonel.[822]

ii MEHITABLE FOSTER, b. 19 Nov 1771; d. at Concord, 23 Sep 1803; m. 14 Mar 1798, BENJAMIN KIMBALL, b. at Concord, 4 Jun 1771 son of John and Anna (Ayer) Kimball; Benjamin d. 4 Dec 1818. After Mehitable died, Benjamin married Rhoda Beaman.

iii SUSANNA FOSTER, b. 7 Feb 1775; d. at Canterbury, 24 Feb 1848; m. 24 Nov 1793, FREDERICK PARKER, b. at Shrewsbury, 4 May 1762 son of Amos and Anna (Curwen Stone) Parker; Frederick d. 20 Apr 1802. Susanna did not remarry after Frederick's death. Frederick Parker graduated from Harvard and was an ordained minister.

301) ABIEL FOSTER[823] *(Elizabeth Abbot Foster⁴, John³, John², George¹)*, b. at Andover, 8 Aug 1735 son of Asa and Elizabeth (Abbot) Foster; d. at Canterbury, NH 6 Feb 1806; m. 1st 15 May 1761, HANNAH BADGER, b. at Haverhill, 16 Nov 1742 daughter of Joseph and Hannah (Pearson) Badger; Hannah d. 10 Jan 1768. Abiel m. 2nd 11 Oct 1769, MARY ROGERS, b. 11 Nov 1745 daughter of Samuel and Hannah (Wise) Rogers; Mary d. 12 Mar 1813.

Abiel Foster graduated from Harvard in 1756 and was the pastor at Canterbury, New Hampshire from 1761-1779. He was a member of the Continental Congress from 1783 to 1785. He was a member of the First Congress of the United States from 1789 to 1791. He later served four additional terms in the United States Congress from 1795-1803.[824]

In his will dated 27 January 1806 (proved 21 May 1806), Abiel Foster bequeathed to his beloved wife all his household furniture for her natural life. After his wife's death, the furniture is to be divided among his five daughters, but with one full share going to his granddaughter Elizabeth Gerrish. His two sons William and James, and four daughters Hannah Cogswell, Sarah Tilton, Mary Gerrish, and Nancy Greenough each receive eighty dollars. Grandchildren Stephen and Elizabeth Gerrish children of his daughter Elizabeth who is deceased receive eighty dollars to divide between them. Son Abiel receives the stock, cattle, sheep, horses, farming utensils, and any surplus of notes for money and stock in trade. Abiel also receives all the books, papers, and wearing apparel. Abiel also receives eighty dollars to be held in trust for the use of daughter Martha Clough and her children. Abiel is also named sole executor.[825]

Children of Abiel Foster and Hannah Badger all born at Canterbury:

i HANNAH FOSTER, b. 25 Apr 1762; d. at Canterbury, 16 Sep 1814; m. at Canterbury, 13 Jun 1781, MOSES COGSWELL, b. 22 Sep 1757 son of Nathaniel and Judith (Badger) Cogswell; Moses d. at Canterbury, 16 Sep 1811.

ii WILLIAM FOSTER, b. 24 Dec 1763; d. at Canterbury, 10 Jul 1825; m. 10 Jun 1792, BETSEY MORRILL, b. at Concord, 30 May 1770 daughter of David and Abigail (Emerson) Morrill; Betsey d. 1848. Betsey's mother was the widow Abigail Stevens when she married David Morrill.

iii JAMES FOSTER, b. 28 Dec 1765; d. unknown; m. at Canterbury, 19 Jan 1790, BETSEY SANBORN, b. at Canterbury, 18 Aug 1764;[826] Betsey's death is not known.

iv SARAH FOSTER, b. 30 Dec 1767; m. at Belmont, NH, 10 Sep 1787, DAVID TILTON, b. at Kingston, NH, 10 Sep 1765 son of Timothy and Martha (Boynton) Tilton; David d. 1798.

Children of Abiel Foster and Mary Rogers, all born at Canterbury:

i MARTHA FOSTER, b. 19 Aug 1770; d. at Dorchester, MA, 26 Mar 1861; m. 25 Mar 1792, JEREMIAH CLOUGH, b. at Canterbury, 21 Aug 1768 son of Jeremiah and Abigail (Kezar) Clough; Jeremiah d. 15 Nov 1813 during the War of 1812.

ii ABIEL FOSTER, b. 19 Feb 1773; d. at Solon, OH, 24 Feb 1846; m. 1796, SUSANNAH MOORE, b. at Canterbury, 1775 daughter of Samuel and Susannah (-) Moore (Susannah's mother was the widow Susannah Webster). Susannah d. at Solon, 22 Jun 1853.

---

822 Lyford, *History of Canterbury*, p 136

823 An etching of Abiel Foster by Max Rosenthal is held at the Library of Congress; https://www.loc.gov/item/2004677252/

824 Abiel Foster, Biographical Directory of the United States Congress, http://bioguide.congress.gov/scripts/biodisplay.pl?index=F000297

825 *New Hampshire. Probate Court (Rockingham County)*; Probate Place: *Rockingham, New Hampshire*, Probate Records, volume 37, pp 53-55, will of Abiel Foster

826 Betsey has a birth date recorded at Canterbury, apparently listed after her marriage as name is given as Betsey Sanborn Foster, but without the names of parents.

iii MARY FOSTER, birth recorded at Concord, 1 Oct 1774; d. at Boscawen, 23 Sep 1869; m. 7 Jun 1795, HENRY GERRISH, b. at Boscawen, 29 May 1772 son of Henry and Martha (Clough) Gerrish; Henry d. at Boscawen, 11 Sep 1862.

iv ELIZABETH FOSTER, b. 9 Mar 1777; d. at Boscawen, 18 Jul 1803; m. about 1800, ENOCH GERRISH, b. at Boscawen, 30 Apr 1775 son of Enoch and Mary (Pearson) Gerrish; Enoch d. at Boscawen, 24 Apr 1834. After Elizabeth's death, Enoch married Ruth Lawrence.

v NANCY FOSTER, b. 25 May 1782; d. at Canterbury, 28 Mar 1819; m. 30 Sep 1803, JOHN GREENOUGH, b. at Haverhill, MA, 5 Apr 1780 son of Ebenezer and Mary (Flagg) Greenough; John d. 3 Sep 1862. After Nancy's death, John married Mary Bridge.

302) DANIEL FOSTER *(Elizabeth Abbot Foster^4, John^3, John^2, George^1)*, b. at Andover, 25 Sep 1737 son of Asa and Elizabeth (Abbot) Foster; d. at Canterbury 25 Jan 1833; m. 16 Dec 1760, HANNAH KITTREDGE, b. Aug 1742 daughter of Jacob and Hannah (French) Kittredge.

Daniel Foster settled in Canterbury about 1763. Daniel Foster and Hannah Kittredge had ten children, the oldest two born at Andover (although they are also recorded as Andover, New Hampshire) and the remainder at Canterbury.

Daughter Ruth Foster, who was a schoolteacher, did not marry. In her will written 2 April 1852 (proved 27 July 1858), she bequeathed to her sister widow Dorcas Norris, fifty dollars. Bequests of fifty dollars were also made to Elisabeth Fletcher wife of Jonathan Fletcher, Jonathan Sargent, Simeon B. Foster, John H. Foster (but only if he has "lineal issue" and is void if he has no children), Joseph M. Foster, Benjamin O. Foster (only if he has children), and Mary Pickard wife of James Pickard. Charles H. Foster receives one hundred dollars. To Susannah Foster, she leaves four hundred dollars, "but in case she should die without issue, and she continues to live with Jonathan B. Foster and he continues to provide for her and furnish her with a home and take good care of her in sickness and health while she lives and pays her debts and funeral charges after her decease then and in that case this legacy to go to him Jonathan B. Foster. But in case she Susannah Foster chooses at any time to leave her present home and provide one for herself then this legacy to be paid to her on demand. In any event, she Susannah is to have the interest annually at her own disposal independent of a home and living." Jonathan B. Foster receives all the rest and residue of the estate and is named executor.[827]

i DANIEL FOSTER, b. at Andover, 29 Jun 1761; m. about 1792, HARRIET BRACKETT. Daniel and Harriet had six children at Canterbury, but it is not clear what became of them after that.

ii HANNAH FOSTER, b. at Andover, 3 Feb 1763; m. 18 Jun 1785, ZEBADIAH SARGENT, b. at Kingston, 6 Sep 1760 son of Aaron and Submit (Esterbrook) Sargent; Zebadiah d. at Canterbury, 16 Nov 1828.

iii SIMEON FOSTER, b. at Canterbury, 22 Jan 1765; d. 25 Apr 1825; m. 28 Oct 1801, SUSANNAH WORTHEN, b. at Chester, 22 Feb 1777;[828] Susannah d. 16 Jan 1830.

iv BETSEY FOSTER, b. at Canterbury, 6 Apr 1767; d. at Canterbury, after 1850. Betsey did not marry.

v JONATHAN FOSTER, b. at Canterbury, 15 Aug 1769; d. 12 Sep 1778.

vi DORCAS FOSTER, b. at Canterbury, 24 Nov 1770; d. 25 Feb 1858; m. about 1798, ZEBULON NORRIS,[829] b. at Epping, 26 Mar 1763 son of Samuel and Huldah (Bartlett) Norris; Zebulon d. at Sutton, VT, 24 Oct 1820.

vii ABIAH FOSTER, b. at Canterbury, 15 Jan 1772; d. at Danville, VT, 28 Feb 1838; m. 21 Mar 1795, ELIJAH SARGENT; Elijah d. after 1830 when he was living in Danville.

viii ABIGAIL FOSTER, b. at Canterbury, 3 Apr 1776; d. at Canterbury, 5 Nov 1817; m. at Canterbury, 6 Jan 1814, JEREMIAH PICKARD, b. at Rowley, 9 Oct 1776 son of Jeremiah and Mehitable (Dresser) Pickard; Jeremiah d. at Stewartstown, 16 Feb 1860. After Abigail's death, Jeremiah married Hannah Harvey 23 Apr 1818. Jeremiah Pickard was first married to Abigail's cousin, Elizabeth Foster (a child in Family 305).

ix RUTH FOSTER, b. at Canterbury, 14 Sep 1779; d. at Canterbury, 23 Jul 1858. Ruth did not marry. She was a schoolteacher.

x JEREMIAH FOSTER, b. at Canterbury, 6 Apr 1784; d. 14 May 1839; m. at Canterbury, 14 Mar 1813, SUSANNAH BRADLEY, b. at Canterbury, 28 Jun 1784 daughter of Jonathan and Susannah (Emery) Bradley; Susannah d. at Canterbury, 5 Sep 1824.

---

[827] *New Hampshire. Probate Court (Merrimack County);* Probate Place: *Merrimack, New Hampshire, Probate Records, Vol 34, 1856-1861,* pp 158-159

[828] There is a birth transcription for Susannah that does not give the names of parents.

[829] The will of Ruth Foster includes a bequest to her sister widow Dorcas Norris.

303) DAVID FOSTER *(Elizabeth Abbot Foster^4, John^3, John^2, George^1)*, b. at Andover, 24 Sep 1741 son of Asa and Elizabeth (Abbot) Foster; d. at Canterbury, 9 Dec 1810; m. 24 Nov 1768, SARAH FOSTER, b. about 1750 who parents are not yet determined; Sarah d. about 1830.[830]

David Foster wrote his will 5 October 1810, and it was proved 16 January 1811. To daughter Sarah Hall, he leaves one-half of his land in Canterbury that is detailed in the will and includes several parcels. Beloved wife Sarah receives the other half of the parcels. Wife Sarah also receives an additional tract of land. After Sarah's death, this additional tract is to be equally divided among daughter Sarah and sons Nathaniel Foster, David Foster, and Timothy Foster. He also provides that the part of his son Joseph's estate will be divided one-third to wife Sarah and two-thirds divided among his four children. Son Nathaniel receives five dollars. Sons Timothy and David receive additional land bequests. Wife Sarah receives all the residue of the estate and is named executor.[831]

David and Sarah Foster were parents of seven children born at Canterbury.

i NATHANIEL FOSTER, b. 19 Nov 1769; d. 11 Apr 1773.

ii SARAH FOSTER, b. 21 Aug 1771; d. at Canterbury, after 1850; m. 27 Apr 1794, STEPHEN HALL, b. in Massachusetts, about 1770; Stephen d. at Canterbury, after 1850.

iii NATHANIEL FOSTER, b. 4 Sep 1773; d. likely at Canterbury, after 1840. Nathaniel does not seem to have married. He seems to be the Nathaniel listed as head of household in the 1840 census with no other member in the household.

iv DAVID FOSTER, b. 1 Apr 1776; d. at Buda, IL, 10 Sep 1843; m. at Loudon, 22 Nov 1803, SARAH DEARBORN, b. at Loudon, 1780; Sarah d. at LaSalle, IL, 1 Oct 1855.

v JOSEPH FOSTER, b. 22 Sep 1779; d. at Billerica, 21 Jul 1810. Dr. Joseph Foster did not marry.

vi TIMOTHY FOSTER, b. 21 Aug 1782; d. at Salisbury, NH, 10 Aug 1851; m. 5 Nov 1805, HANNAH CARTER, b. about 1784 daughter of John and Abigail (Bartlett) Carter. Hannah's death not known, but before 1833 when Timothy remarried. Timothy m. 2nd, at Wilmot, NH, 27 Feb 1833 the widow Dorothy Farnum (likely Dorothy Tucker widow of Ebenezer Farnum).

vii ASA FOSTER, b. 6 Aug 1784; d. 10 Jan 1785.

304) ELIZABETH FOSTER *(Elizabeth Abbot Foster^4, John^3, John^2, George^1)*, b. 14 Apr 1744 daughter of Asa and Elizabeth (Abbot) Foster; d. at Andover 24 Apr 1775; m. 3 Nov 1768, her third cousin, (General) NATHANIEL LOVEJOY *(Elizabeth Swan Lovejoy^4, Hannah Stevens Swan^3, Sarah Abbott Stevens^2, George^1)*, b. 29 Apr 1744 son of Nathaniel and Elizabeth (Swan) Lovejoy; Nathaniel d. 5 Jul 1812. Nathaniel m. 2nd, by 1776, ELIZABETH BRANDON, b. at Cambridge, 18 Nov 1750 daughter of Benjamin and Elizabeth (Foxcroft) Brandon; Elizabeth Brandon d. 19 Nov 1788. Nathaniel m. 3rd, 1 Dec 1803, his third cousin once removed, BENJAMINA WOODBRIDGE *(Dorcas March Woodbridge^5, Dorcas Osgood March^4, Hannah Abbott Osgood^3, George^2, George^1)*, b. at Salem, Mar 1772 daughter of Dudley and Dorcas (March) Woodbridge. Benjamina d. at Worcester, 6 May 1851.

Nathaniel Lovejoy served in the Essex County Militia achieving the rank of General. Earlier, he served as Captain in Colonel Johnson's 9th Company of the 4th Regiment.[832] He graduated from Harvard in 1766 and was a trader in North Andover.[833]

Nathaniel Lovejoy did not leave a will, and his probate record contains a long list of creditors who each received seventy-eight cents on the dollar for what they were owed. The widow's thirds were set off the Benjamina Lovejoy.

Elizabeth Foster and Nathaniel Lovejoy had three children born at Andover all of whom died as infants.

i Son, b. and d., 21 Jun 1771

ii ELIZABETH LOVEJOY, b. 29 May 1773; d. 8 May 1774.

iii NATHANIEL LOVEJOY, b. 13 Jan 1775; d. 18 May 1775.

---

[830] Lyford, *History of Canterbury*, p. 135

[831] *New Hampshire. Probate Court (Rockingham County)*; Probate Place: *Rockingham, New Hampshire, Probate Records, Vol 39-40, 1809-1812*, will of David Foster, pp 532-533

[832] Massachusetts Soldiers and Sailors, volume V, pp 994-995

[833] Bailey, *Historical Sketches of Andover*, p 99

Nathaniel Lovejoy and Elizabeth Brandon were parents of five children born at Andover.

i NATHANIEL LOVEJOY, b. 20 Jul 1776; d. Aug 1776.

ii MARTHA BRANDON LOVEJOY, b. 24 Jul 1779; d. at Bradford, MA, 27 Jul 1804; m. 10 May 1804, NATHANIEL THURSTON, b. at Bradford, 17 Jan 1755; Nathaniel d. at Lansingburgh, NY, 21 Oct 1811. Martha was the fifth of Nathaniel Thurston's seven wives.

iii ELIZABETH FOSTER LOVEJOY, b. 6 Aug 1780; d. at West Newbury, 3 Apr 1866; m. at Andover, 20 Dec 1798, JACOB FARNUM, b. at Andover, 10 Oct 1774 son of Benjamin and Dolly (Holt) Farnum, Jacob d, 19 Aug 1801.

iv JOHN PHILLIPS LOVEJOY, b. 3 Apr 1782; d. at West Newbury, 24 May 1864. John is listed as single on his death record. However, it is possible that he married Eliza Leman in 1807 and did not have children and was widowed early.

v NATHANIEL LOVEJOY, b. 13 Jan 1784; d. 26 Sep 1784.

305) JONATHAN FOSTER *(Elizabeth Abbot Foster⁴, John³, John², George¹)*, b. at Andover, 28 Jul 1747 son of Asa and Elizabeth (Abbot) Foster; d. about 1818 at Canterbury, NH (will dated 5 Sep 1818); m. Nov 1770, LUCY ROGERS, b. 19 Oct 1748 daughter of Samuel and Hannah (Wise) Rogers; Lucy d. about 1830.

Jonathan Foster purchased land in Canterbury from his father Asa Foster.[834] Jonathan and Lucy settled in Canterbury and raised their five children there.

In his will dated 5 September 1818, Jonathan Foster of Canterbury has bequests to son Samuel H. Foster, son John Foster, heirs of daughter Elizabeth Pickard, daughter Lucy Ames, and daughter Hannah Moody. Each of the bequests to his children is for one dollar. Beloved wife Lucy receives all the meat, cattle, hogs, sheep, and horses as well as all the personal property of every description. Lucy is also named executrix.[835]

In her will dated 14 June 1820, Lucy Rogers Foster also makes bequests to each of her children or their heirs: son Samuel H. Foster, children of daughter Elizabeth Pickard, son John, daughter Lucy Ames wife of Thomas Ames, and Hannah Moody wife of Joseph Moody. Thomas Ames is named executor.[836]

Jonathan and Lucy Foster had five children born at Canterbury.

i SAMUEL H. FOSTER, b. 6 Nov 1771; d. at New York City, 23 Mar 1847; m. 1st, at Marblehead, 11 Jul 1797, ELIZABETH SYMONDS, b. about 1767; Elizabeth d. at Newburyport, 27 Jun 1801. Samuel m. 2nd, 16 May 1802, MERCY PORTER, b. at Danvers, 7 Jul 1768 daughter of Thomas and Mercy (Clark) Porter; Mercy d. at New York City, 10 May 1846.

ii JOHN FOSTER, b. 22 Jul 1773; d. at New York City, 1834; m. about 1804, SARAH KIMBALL, b. about 1777; Sarah d. at Newark, NJ, about 1846.

iii ELIZABETH FOSTER, b. 15 May 1775; d. at Canterbury, 30 Nov 1812; m. at Canterbury, 6 Aug 1801, JEREMIAH PICKARD, b. at Rowley, 9 Oct 1776 son of Jeremiah and Mehitable (Dresser) Pickard; Jeremiah d. at Stewartstown, 16 Feb 1860. Jeremiah married second, Elizabeth's cousin Abigail Foster (a child in Family 302) and he third married Hannah Harvey.

iv LUCY FOSTER, b. 1 Sep 1777; d. at Canterbury, 22 Jul 1843; m. at Canterbury, 25 Dec 1804, THOMAS AMES, b. at Canterbury, 6 Oct 1777 son of David and Phebe (Hoyt) Ames; Thomas d. at Canterbury, 19 Nov 1840.

v HANNAH FOSTER, b. 20 Apr 1784; d. at Concord, 2 Dec 1873; m. 22 Nov 1815, JOSEPH MOODY, b. 20 May 1788 son of William and Sarah (Kimball) Moody; Joseph d. at Concord, 2 Mar 1879.

306) SARAH FOSTER *(Elizabeth Abbot Foster⁴, John³, John², George¹)*, b. at Andover, 15 Feb 1749/50 daughter of Asa and Elizabeth (Abbot) Foster; d. at Concord, NH, 8 Feb 1825;[837] m. at Andover, 23 Dec 1773, TIMOTHY BRADLEY b. at Rumford, 30 Oct 1743 son of Timothy and Abiah (Stevens) Bradley; Timothy d. 31 Jul 1811 at Concord (will 27 May 1811).

In his will dated 27 May 1811 (probate 27 August 1811), Timothy Bradley bequeaths to beloved wife Sarah all the household items and a horse and chaise. The exception is the clock which she has use of during her lifetime but goes to son Timothy after her death. There are other specific provisions made for her care and support. Her continued use of the house during her widowhood is subject to the continued maintenance of their three unmarried daughters Elizabeth, Abiah, and Anna. Beloved daughter Elizabeth is to have a good, decent maintenance provided by the income of half the farm which is not otherwise deeded and to receive $100 at the time of her marriage. The heirs of his daughter Sarah Eastman recently deceased

834 Lyford, *History of Canterbury*, p 133

835 *New Hampshire Wills and Probate Records 1643-1982,* Will of Jonathan Foster, Merrimack, 5 Sep 1818.

836 *New Hampshire Wills and Probate Records 1643-1982,* Will of Lucy Foster, Merrimack, 14 Jun 1820.

837 Published sources give Sarah's date of death as 7 Feb 1825 but the date on her will is 8 Feb 1825.

receive $6 to be divided equally among them. Daughter Abiah has provisions for her maintenance and will receive $80 at her marriage. Beloved daughter Hannah Peters Robinson receives $10. Beloved son Foster Bradley receives $100 and all the wearing apparel. Beloved son Abiel Bradley receives $500 to be paid out over several years. Beloved daughter Anna is to be provided a decent maintenance in the same way as her sisters and $80 at the time of her marriage. Beloved son Timothy Bradley, in addition to what has already been deeded to him, will receive one-half of the home farm after the decease of his mother as well as all the stock animals. This is contingent on the continued maintenance of his unmarried sisters. Timothy is the sole executor.[838]

In her will written 8 February 1825, Sarah Bradley leaves $1 to each of her three sons Timothy, Foster, and Abiel. Daughter Elizabeth Bradley receives the largest silver teaspoons and other listed household items. Daughter Abiah receives feather beds and a silver tablespoon. Daughter Nancy Hedge receives her gold necklace. Granddaughter Sarah Eastman receives one silver tablespoon as does granddaughter Sarah Robertson. Daughter Hannah Peters Robertson receives her black silk gown. Each of her four daughters, or their heirs, with the children of her daughter Sarah receiving a one-fourth part, each receive one-fourth of all the remainder of her estate. Daughters Elizabeth and Abiah also receive one cow and four sheep. Daughter Elizabeth is named sole executrix of the estate.[839]

Timothy and Sarah Bradley had nine children. Eight of the births are recorded at Concord. There is not a birth record for the youngest daughter Anna/Nancy, but the wills of Timothy and Sarah allow for her identification and the identification of her husband.

i ELIZABETH BRADLEY, b. 9 Jan 1775. Elizabeth does not seem to have married as she was unmarried at the time of her mother's will in 1825. A death record was not located.

ii ASA BRADLEY, b. 13 Dec 1776; d. 25 Jul 1778.

iii SARAH BRADLEY, b. 25 Apr 1779; d. at Concord, 7 Dec 1809; m. 27 Nov 1798, CHARLES EASTMAN, b. at Concord, 11 Dec 1774 son of Moses and Lucretia (Tyler) Eastman; Charles d. at Concord, 26 Sep 1847. After Sarah's death, Charles married Persis Chamberlain in 1813.

iv ABIAH BRADLEY, b. 7 Aug 1781; d. at Concord, 1827. Abiah did not marry.

v HANNAH PETERS BRADLEY, b. 1 Jan 1784; d. at St. Albans, ME, 16 Jul 1872; m. at Concord, 10 Jan 1809, ISAAC OSGOOD ROBERTSON, b. at Sanbornton, 5 May 1782 son of John and Abigail (Whidden) Robinson;[840] Isaac d. at St. Albans, 31 Aug 1854.

vi TIMOTHY BRADLEY, b. 24 Jan 1786; d. at Canterbury, 20 Dec 1837; m. 5 Dec 1810, ANNA "NANCY" MORRILL, b. at Canterbury, 23 Feb 1792 daughter of Laban and Sarah (Ames) Morrill; Anna d. at Canterbury, 6 Feb 1854.

vii FOSTER BRADLEY, b. 3 May 1788; d. at Topsham, ME, 10 Jul 1873; m. 1st, at Chelmsford, 10 Feb 1810, PHEBE STEVENS, b. at Chelmsford, 28 Feb 1792 daughter of Sampson and Phebe (Barker) Stevens; Phebe d. at Brunswick, ME, 14 Sep 1821. Foster m. 2nd, 6 Feb 1822, MARY MALLETT, b. about 1794 and d. at Topsham in 1879.

viii ABIEL FOSTER BRADLEY, b. 6 May 1790; d. at Columbus, OH, 16 Sep 1870; m. 1st, 6 Feb 1816, NANCY CURRY, b. at Canterbury, 2 Oct 1791 daughter of Thomas and Sarah (Blanchard) Curry; Nancy d. at Canterbury, 23 May 1851. After Nancy's death, Abiel married the widow Ruth Leavitt. After Ruth's death, Abiel went to Ohio and lived with his son Charles.

ix ANNA "NANCY" BRADLEY, b. about 1792; d. between 1825 and 1835;[841] m. at Concord, Dec 1818, GEORGE T. HEDGE, b. in Massachusetts about 1795 possibly the son of Elisha Hedge; George d. at Portland, ME, 10 Jan 1865. After Nancy's death, George m. Dorcas Judge.

---

838 *New Hampshire Wills and Probate Records 1643-1982,* Will and Probate of Timothy Bradley, Rockingham, 27 Aug 1811, Case number 8442.

839 *New Hampshire Wills and Probate Records 1643-1982,* Will of Sarah Bradley, Rockingham, 8 Feb 1825.

840 Runnels, *History of Sanbornton*, volume 2, p 604. Isaac's father was John Robinson, but Isaac transformed his named to Robertson. For example, his War of 1812 service record lists both names on his record form, Isaac O. Robinson and Isaac O. Robertson.

841 Nancy was living in 1825 when her mother wrote her will. George married his second wife in 1835.

307) JOSEPH ABBOTT *(Joseph⁴, John³, John², George¹* and *Hannah⁴, Ebenezer³, John², George¹)*, b. at Andover, 29 Mar 1742 son of Joseph and Hannah (Abbott) Abbott; d.?; m. at Lancaster, 22 Aug 1774,[842] HANNAH PITSON, b. at Boston, 28 Feb 1740 daughter of James and Rachel (Danforth) Pitson.

There are five children known for Joseph and Hannah Abbott.

i SALLY DOWN ABBOTT, b. at Lancaster, 22 Jul 1777; d. at Cobleskill, NY, 1843; m. JAMES CROSS, b. at Dutchess County, NY, 1783; James d. at Cobleskill, 1859.[843]

ii Daughter, b. 23 Aug and d. 24 Aug 1778.

iii JAMES PITSON ABBOTT, b. at Chester, 16 Jul 1779; d. at Windsor, NY, 10 Apr 1864; m. 1st, at Chester, 18 Jun 1807, THEODOSIA "DOSHA" MOORE, b. at Chester, 7 May 1784 daughter of Samuel and Elizabeth (Elder) Moore; Dosha d. about 1816. James m. 2nd, at Becket, 27 Dec 1817, SOPHRONIA KINGSLEY, b. at Becket, 16 Jul 1793 daughter of Martin and Bethena (-) Kingsley; Sophronia d. at Nineveh, NY, 1880.

iv HANNAH ABBOTT, b. at Chester, 19 Jul 1781; d. at Saratoga Springs, 8 May 1866; m. at Chester, 2 Apr 1810, SAMUEL CHAPMAN, b. about 1782 son of Joshua and Mary (Lee) Chapman; Samuel d. at Becket, MA, 28 Aug 1852.

v BETSEY ABBOTT, b. at Chester, 26 Oct 1784; d. at North Adams, 19 Jul 1881; m. 22 Aug 1806, WILLIAM HENRY, b. 15 Jan 1784 son of Andrew and Jael (Elder) Henry; William d. at North Adams, 15 Jul 1875.

308) HANNAH ABBOTT *(Joseph⁴, John³, John², George¹* and *Hannah⁴, Ebenezer³, John², George¹)*, b. at Lancaster, 23 Sep 1743 daughter of Joseph and Hannah (Abbott) Abbott; d. at Chester, 2 Mar 1802; m. at Winchendon, 27 Sep 1774, as his second wife, JOHN NEWTON PARMENTER, b. at Boston, Sep 1742 son of Benjamin and Elizabeth (Bigelow) Parmenter; John d. 6 Dec 1828. John married Mrs. Dolly Blair 19 Feb 1806. John was first married to Lydia Baldwin.

John Newton Parmenter wrote is will 27 March 1812. His wife Dolly receives a cow, household furniture, and the executor is to help her move to her house in Blandford. Eldest son John Parmenter receives one-fourth part of the farm. Son Azel receives one dollar which completes his portion with what he has already been given. Daughter Elizabeth wife of Joseph Wright receives a bed and looking glass. Son-in-law Christopher Pennimen receives a feather bed and daughter Aratusa Pennimen receives a cow and the blue bed quilt. Daughter Melinda Parmenter receives one dollar which completes her portion. Son Jonas Parmenter receives three-fourths of the farm. Jonas receives the residue of the estate and is named executor.[844] Elizabeth Wright is a daughter from John N. Parmenter's first marriage to Lydia Baldwin and Christopher Pennimen is the widower of his daughter Mary also from his first marriage. Christopher Pennimen later married Melinda Parmenter (but probably a different Melinda than John's daughter Melinda, but that has not been determined).

Hannah Abbott and John Parmenter had five children born at Chester.

i ARATHUSA PARMENTER, b. 13 Feb 1778; d. at Utica, NY, 17 Aug 1837; m. at Chester, 6 Dec 1801, WILLIAM PENNEYMAN, b. at Braintree, 12 Apr 1771 son of William and Catherine (Hivill) Penneyman; William d. at Honesdale, PA, 10 Jan 1856.

ii MELINDA PARMENTER, b. 23 Aug 1779. She was still living and unmarried in 1812 when her father wrote his will.

iii JOHN PARMENTER, b. 18 Mar 1781; d. at Pelham, NH, 27 Jan 1855; m. about 1809, HANNAH DICKINSON, b. at Hatfield, MA, about 1790 daughter of Aaron and Experience (Phelps) Dickinson;[845] Hannah d. at Pelham, 18 Apr 1862.

iv AZEL PARMENTER, b. 15 Nov 1784; d. about 1820; m. at Chester, 25 Jan 1810, REBECCA SLAYTON, b. at Brookfield, 1786 daughter of Ebenezer and Rebecca (Hamilton) Slayton; Rebecca d. at Walworth, NY, Apr 1868. After Azel's death, Rebecca married Gardner Tiffany.

v JONAS PARMENTER, b. 29 Jul 1787; d. at Worthington, MA, 4 Mar 1874; m. at Chester, 11 Oct 1810, SOPHIA STONE, b. at Chester, 1 Sep 1788 daughter of William and Mehitable (Phelps) Stone; Sophia d. at Chester, 29 Oct 1864.

---

[842] Nourse, *Register of Lancaster, Massachusetts*, p 135

[843] Roscoe, *History of Schoharie County*, Personal Statistics, p v

[844] *Probate Records of Hampden County and City of Springfield, 1806-1919 [Massachusetts], Probate Records, Vol 9, 1828-1830*, pp 201-202. Probate is in 1829 case number 8674.

[845] The 1825 will of Aaron Dickinson includes a bequest to his daughter Hannah Parmenter.

309) ELIZABETH ABBOTT *(Joseph^4, John^3, John^2, George^1* and *Hannah^4, Ebenezer^3, John^2, George^1)*, b. at Lancaster, 6 Jul 1746 daughter of Joseph and Hannah (Abbott) Abbott; d. at Pittsfield, after 1810;[846] m. 31 Jan 1779, JACOB FOWLE, b. at Lancaster, 14 Sep 1749 son of Jacob and Phebe (Osgood) Fowle; Jacob d. at Pittsfield, after 1810. Elizabeth Abbott's first cousin once removed, Priscilla Abbott, was the second wife of Jacob Fowle the elder, father of Jacob.

Jacob and Elizabeth started their family in Hampden County but relocated to Pittsfield about 1810. There are records for births of four daughters recorded at Chester in Hampden County and a fifth daughter who seems likely to be in the family based on census records (daughter Betsey living with Lucretia in 1850). In the 1810 census, there were just two daughters in the home and there are only records for two of the daughters beyond birth records.

i Daughter (unnamed), b. 25 Jul 1779

ii BETSEY FOWLE, b. 13 Dec 1780; d. at Pittsfield, 26 Apr 1864. Betsey did not marry.

iii NANCY FOWLE, b. 15 Sep 1782; no further record.

iv POLLY FOWLE, b. 27 Feb 1784; no further record.

v LUCRETIA FOWLE, b. 1786 (based on age 72 at time of death); d. at Pittsfield, 24 Nov 1858; m. at Pittsfield, 3 Oct 1812, HENRY WRIGHT TAYLOR, b. at Pittsfield, 22 Nov 1787 son of James and Sarah (Wright) Taylor; Henry d. at Pittsfield, 25 Jan 1826.

310) ABIEL ABBOTT *(Joseph^4, John^3, John^2, George^1* and *Hannah^4, Ebenezer^3, John^2, George^1)*, b. at Lancaster, about 1749 son of Joseph and Hannah (Abbott) Abbott; d. at Chester, MA, 7 Dec 1831; m. 23 Jan 1783, SARAH MANN, b. 12 Nov 1764 daughter of Nathan and Jane (Fleming) Mann; Sarah d. 22 Mar 1841.

Abiel Abbott and Sarah Mann were parents of nine children all born at Chester.

i JOSEPH ABBOTT, b. 11 Jun 1783; d. at Chester, 30 Jun 1867; m. at Chester, 9 Oct 1808, POLLY BUCKMAN, b. at Sandisfield, 3 Apr 1790 daughter of Reuben and Dolly (Kasson) Buckman;[847] Polly d. at Chester, 9 Apr 1867.

ii NATHAN ABBOTT, b. 1 Nov 1784; d. in Ashtabula County, OH, 17 Sep 1876; m. at Chester, 21 Nov 1811, DOLLY BUCKMAN, b. at Sandisfield, 3 Apr 1790 (twin of Polly) daughter of Reuben and Dolly (Kasson) Buckman; Dolly d. in Ashtabula County, 1876.

iii SALLY ABBOTT, b. 14 Apr 1787; d. 3 Sep 1802.

iv ACHSAH ABBOTT, b. 28 Jul 1789; d. at Newark, NJ, 12 Mar 1869;[848] m. at Chester, 28 Aug 1808, WILLIAM NOONEY, b. at Middlefield, MA, 19 Jan 1785 son of James and Sarah (King) Nooney; William d. at Chester, 31 Mar 1841.

v GEORGE ABBOTT, b. about 1794; d. at Chester, 15 Apr 1863. George did not marry.

vi POLLY ABBOTT, b. 11 Apr 1795; d 10 Sep 1802.

vii ASAHEL ABBOTT, b. 23 Mar 1797; d. 9 Sep 1802.

viii ELECTA ABBOTT, b. 11 Apr 1799; d. at Chester, 18 Jan 1864. Electa did not marry.

ix SALLY ABBOTT, b. 9 May 1803; d. at Chester, 5 Mar 1853; m. at Chester, 19 Aug 1821, SERENO SNOW, b. at Hinsdale, 1801; Sereno d. at Chester, 17 Sep 1881. After Sally's death, Sereno married Sarah V. Lamb on 14 Jan 1844.

311) JOHN ABBOTT *(Joseph^4, John^3, John^2, George^1* and *Hannah^4, Ebenezer^3, John^2, George^1)*, b. at Lancaster, 8 Oct 1751 son of Joseph and Hannah (Abbott) Abbott; d. 1798; m. 4 Feb 1775, LOIS BENNET, b. at Lancaster, 2 Sep 1757 daughter of Elisha and Lois (Wilder) Bennet; Lois d. at Sheffield, MA, 1829 (probate Jan 1829). After John's death, Lois married Aaron Bell 31 Jan 1811.

---

[846] In 1810, Elizabeth Fowle was dismissed from the church in Lancaster and recommended to the church in Pittsfield.

[847] Polly's father's name is given as Reuben Buckman on her death record. One of the children of Joseph and Polly Abbott is Abiel Kasson Abbott.

[848] *New Jersey, Deaths and Burials Index, 1798-1971* [database on-line]. Provo, UT, USA: Ancestry.com Operations, Inc., 2011.

Lois Bennet Abbot Bell did not leave a will. Her estate, after deductions, was valued at $185.08 which was distributed on 10 February 1829 in equal portions to her heirs: Phebe Abbot, John Abbot, Dolly Abbot, William Abbot, Jere Abbot, Lois the wife of Seymour Joyner, Eunice the wife of Josiah Loomis, and the children of Polly the late wife of Appleton Andrews.[849]

John Abbott and Lois Bennet were parents to nine children all born at Chester.

i PHEBE ABBOTT, b. 23 Nov 1777; d. 23 Jun 1779

ii PHEBE ABBOTT, b. 4 Jul 1780; d. after 1829. Phebe was living and unmarried at the time of probate of her mother's estate.

iii JOHN ABBOTT, b. 10 Mar 1783; d. at Greenwich, OH, 1847; m. at Chester, 2 Jun 1803, CLARISSA SIZER, b. in Hampshire County, MA, 4 Oct 1784 daughter of William and Abigail (Wilcox) Sizer; Clarissa d. at Greenwich, 1868.

iv DOLLY ABBOTT, b. 17 Mar 1785; d. at Egremont, 19 Apr 1855. Dolly did not marry.

v WILLIAM "BILLY" ABBOTT, b. 10 Feb 1788; d. at New Marlborough, MA, 1 Dec 1854; m. at Blandford, MA, 25 Nov 1810, BETSEY LINDSEY, b. in Hampden County, 1786 daughter of Moses and Amy (Partridge) Lindsey; Betsey d. at New Marlborough, 16 Mar 1865.

vi JERRY ABBOTT, b. 16 Jun 1790; d. at Sheffield, 26 Apr 1881; m. SARAH SIZER, b. at Middletown, CT, 9 May 1780 daughter of William and Abigail (Wilcox) Sizer; Sarah d. at Sheffield, 16 Aug 1866.

vii POLLY ABBOTT, b. 23 Oct 1792; d. before 1829; m. at Chester, 12 Nov 1812, APPLETON ANDREWS of Barrington.

viii LOIS ABBOTT, b. 25 Jan 1795; d. at Egremont, 8 Sep 1871; m. about 1816, SEYMOUR JOYNER, b. at Egremont, 6 Oct 1794 son of Octavius and Esther (Hollenbeck) Joyner; Seymour d. at Egremont, 8 Aug 1868.

ix EUNICE ABBOTT, b. 10 Aug 1797; m. about 1822, JOSIAH LOOMIS of Richmond, MA. Josiah was first married to Ruby who died 26 Dec 1821.

312) EBENEZER ABBOTT (*Joseph⁴, John³, John², George¹* and *Hannah⁴, Ebenezer³, John², George¹*), b. at Lancaster, MA, 14 Oct 1753 son of Joseph and Hannah (Abbott) Abbott; d. at Cuyahoga County, OH, about 1833;[850] m. 13 Dec 1781, ANNA WRIGHT, b. at Spencer, 23 Feb 1758 daughter of Edward and Tryphena (Hinds) Wright.

Ebenezer Abbott served as a private in Colonel Whitcomb's Regiment enlisting in April 1775 and serving for eight months. In his 1832 pension application, he reported living in Lancaster but moved to Chester about 1780 where he remained for thirty years. He was then in Worthington, Massachusetts until 1826 when the family relocated to Cuyahoga County, Ohio.[851]

Ebenezer Abbott and Anna Wright were parents of eight children born at Chester, Massachusetts. They also adopted one of their granddaughters, Amelia.[852]

i OLIVE ABBOTT, b. 23 Jan 1783; d. at Martinsburg, IL, 1 Jun 1858; m. 1st, at Middlefield, MA, 18 Jan 1808, PETER PINNEY, b. at Middlefield, MA, about 1788 son of John and Deborah (Lovett) Pinney;[853] Peter d. at Onondaga, NY, Apr 1813 (will 8 Apr 1813, probate 10 Apr 1813). Olive m. 2nd, about 1815, WILLIAM HOWLAND; William d. at Pike County, IL between 1840 and 1850.

ii RUFUS ABBOTT, b. 31 Jan 1784; d. at Payson, UT, 30 Aug 1879; m. 1st, at Chester, 17 Jan 1809, ANNA OWEN, b. at Westfield, MA, 24 Apr 1787 daughter of Asahel and Anna (Perkins) Owen; Anna d. at Salt Lake, 11 Apr 1851. Rufus m. 2nd, 11 Jun 1854, ELEANOR ELIZA BOWEN, b. about 1800 and d. at Payson before 1870. Rufus m. 3rd, by 1870, SARAH HANCOCK (widow of Thomas Crandall), b. at Bristol, NY, 13 Jun 1805 daughter of Thomas and Amy (Ward) Hancock;[854] Sarah d. at Payson, 7 Nov 1886.

iii ANNA ABBOTT, b. 4 Dec 1786

iv TRYPHENA ABBOTT, b. 24 May 1787; m. about 1810, SILAS JOY.

v LUCY ABBOTT, b. 25 May 1789

---

849 Berkshire County, MA: Probate File Papers, 1761-1917.Online database. AmericanAncestors.org. New England Historic Genealogical Society, 2017. Case 4826, probate of Lois Bell.

850 Revolutionary War Pension and Bounty-Land Warrant Application Files

851 Revolutionary War Pension and Bounty-Land Warrant Application Files, 1800-1900

852 Amelia, "adopted" granddaughter of Ebenezer and Anne baptized 2 Aug 1807.

853 Smith, *History of Middlefield, Massachusetts*, p 578

854 Information on Sarah's parents is in her obituary.

vi EBENEZER ABBOTT, b. 6 Jul 1791; d. at McHenry County, IL, 1 Nov 1852; m. at Chester, 20 Feb 1811, BERNICE "NICY" POMEROY, b. at Chester, 23 Mar 1788 daughter of Joseph and Isabel (Clark) Pomeroy; Nicy d. at McHenry County, 7 May 1854.

vii ROXANNA ABBOTT, b. 25 Oct 1793; d. at Grand Blanc, MI, 7 Jan 1853; m. by 1818, ELI DAYTON, b. in VT, about 1791; Eli d. at Binghamton, NY, 15 Apr 1858.

viii ELISHA ABBOTT, b. 9 Sep 1799; d. at St. Johns, MI, 11 Oct 1869; m. by 1822, HARRIET SMITH.

313) RELIEF ABBOTT *(Joseph^4, John^3, John^2, George^1* and *Hannah^4, Ebenezer^3, John^2, George^1)*, b. at Lancaster, 11 May 1759 daughter of Joseph and Hannah (Abbott) Abbot; d. at Chester, 9 Feb 181; m. 29 May 1784, JOHN WILLIAMS, b. at Middleborough, 23 Jan 1761 son of Larkin and Anna (Warren) Williams; John d. 28 Mar 1813.

John Williams wrote his will 27 March 1813, the day before he died. Wife Relief Williams receives one-third part of the real and personal estate. Eldest son John receives the remainder of the estate although he is to pay his brother Sumner $100 and his sisters Polisany, Nancy Warren, and Pleides, $50 each. Wife Relief Williams and Samuel Lyman were named executors.[855]

John Williams and Relief Abbott were parents to eight children born at Chester.

i Twin1, b. 7 Jul 1787

ii Twin2, b. 7 Jul 1787

iii GARDNER WILLIAMS, b. 12 Jul 1789; d. 28 Jul 1789.

iv JOHN WILLIAMS, b. 6 Aug 1792; d. after 1865; m. at Chester, 9 May 1816, SOPHIA MALLERY, b. at Montgomery, MA, 13 Jan 1789 daughter of Trueman and Olive (Hubbell) Mallery; Sophia d. at Belchertown, 16 Jun 1860.

v POLIXINA WILLIAMS, b. 19 Mar 1795; d. at Chester, 10 Oct 1880. Polixina married a Mr. Smith as she was Polixina Smith at the time of her death. She was listed as a widow in the 1865 census at Chester.

vi NANCY WARREN WILLIAMS, b. 17 Feb 1797; d. at Harwinton, CT, 20 Feb 1853. Nancy did not marry. At the 1850 census, she was living with her sister Pleades in Harwinton.

vii SUMNER WILLIAMS, b. 7 May 1799; d. at Chester, 13 Jun 1840; m. at Chester, 15 Apr 1827, MARY ANN BROWN, b. about 1802; Mary Ann d. at Austinburg, OH, after 1870. After Sumner's death, Mary Ann married Zenas Searle. A daughter of Sumner and Mary Ann, also Mary Ann, married Silas P. Searle the son of Zenas Searle and his first wife Julia Sheldon.

viii PLEADES WILLIAMS, b. 30 Jun 1801; d. at Harwinton, CT, 13 Oct 1851; m. at Chester, 15 Dec 1821, WILLIAM BENTLEY, b. about 1797 "of Tyringham."

314) DOROTHY ABBOTT *(Joseph^4, John^3, John^2, George^1* and *Hannah^4, Ebenezer^3, John^2, George^1)*, b. at Lancaster, Dec 1762 daughter of Joseph and Hannah (Abbott) Abbott; d. in IN, 8 Mar 1848; m. at Chester, 28 Dec 1784, ROBERT MOOR, *possibly* the Robert b. at Palmer, 1 May 1760 son of James and Elizabeth (Little) Moor;[856] Robert d. likely at Campbell, KY, 26 Oct 1810.[857]

Robert Moor and Dolly Abbott started their family in Chester, Massachusetts but were in Otsego County, New York by 1799 when Robert was on the tax roles in Otsego County. The family stayed in the Otsego County area for several years but were then on the move heading first to northern Kentucky. Daughter Sarah was married in Campbell County, Kentucky and that is likely where Robert Moor died. After Robert's death, most of the family settled in Indiana, first in Franklin County.

Robert Moor and Dorothy Abbott were parents of ten children, the first eight children born in Chester, Massachusetts and the two youngest children born in Worcester, New York.

---

855 Probate Records 1809-1881, Hampden County, Massachusetts

856 Moore, *John Moore Family in America* gives his parents John Moor and Rose Crawford but also give a birthdate of 6 May 1760. Robert Moor born 1 May 1760 is the son of James and Elizabeth, so it seems more likely Robert is the son of James. Also, John and Rose Moor married in 1735 and it is unlikely they were still having children in 1760.

857 Some of the vital records information is that used by the DAR.

i ARTEMAS MOOR, b. 13 Mar 1786; d. at Boone County, IN, 29 Jul 1861; m. at Franklin, IN, 18 Sep 1817, JANE MOORE; Jane d. at New Salem, IN, 1848.

ii EZRA MOOR, b. 3 May 1787; d. at Franklin County, IN, 1821; m. at Franklin County, 4 Feb 1816, VALENTINE SPEER, b. in NC, 2 May 1791; Valentine d. at Princeton, MO, 30 Oct 1858. Valentine married second Samuel Pruett 3 Oct 1829.

iii SARAH MOOR, b. 25 Feb 1789; d. at Boone County, IN, 25 May 1857; m. at Campbell, KY, 20 Jun 1810, JOHN FANCHER, b. in NY, about 1778.

iv QUARTUS MOOR, b. 1790; d. at Preble County, OH, 11 Nov 1870; m. 1st, at Preble County, 1 Apr 1813, MARIA WIMMER, b. in VA, 1 Jan 1795; Maria d. at Preble County, 10 Jul 1834. Quartus m. 2nd, at Union, OH, 5 Aug 1835, ELIZABETH PULLEN. Quartus m. 3rd, at Decatur County, IN, 17 Mar 1846, ELEANOR LONGACER who was first married to Quartus's brother Calvin (see below).

v LEVI MOOR, baptized 2 Mar 1794; d. at Culver, IN, 16 Jan 1858; m. at Franklin County, 28 Aug 1814, ELIZABETH LYONS, b. about 1795.

vi GARDNER MOOR, baptized 18 May 1794; d. at Rush County, IN, 18 Sep 1835; m. at Franklin County, 25 May 1815, PEGGY LYONS, b. 25 Dec 1795; Peggy d. at Wabash County, IN, 2 May 1850.

vii DOROTHY "DOLLY" MOOR, baptized 6 Mar 1796; d. at Connersville, IN, 1 Dec 1881; m. at Franklin County, 2 Apr 1835, WILLIAM DICKSON, b. in VA, about 1785; William d. at Connersville, 1 Mar 1867.

viii ACHSAH "AXA" MOOR, baptized 12 Jan 1800; m. at Franklin County, IN, 29 May 1823, HUGH REED, b. in PA; Hugh d. in Fayette County, IN, 1840.[858]

ix EDMUND MOOR, b. 4 May 1800; d. at Decatur County, IN, 13 Sep 1889; m. at Franklin County, 23 Dec 1824, ELIZABETH HIGGS, b. in SC, 13 Oct 1802 daughter of William and Mary (-) Higgs;[859] Elizabeth d. at Decatur County, 13 Jul 1881.

x CALVIN MOOR, b. about 1802; d. 1842; m. at Franklin County, 21 Sep 1826, ELEANOR LONGACER, b. 22 Mar 1806; Elizabeth d. at Decatur County, IN, 18 Oct 1880. Elizabeth second married Calvin's brother Quartus (see above).

315) ANNA ABBOTT *(Joseph4, Joseph3, John2, George1)*, b. at Andover, 15 Nov 1749 daughter of Joseph and Anna (Peabody) Abbott; d. at NH perhaps in 1788 (when the estate of widow Anna Stevens was probated); m. 18 Aug 1774, her third cousin, THEODORE STEVENS, b. 20 May 1750 son of John and Mary (Phelps) Stevens.

Almost no information has been found for this family. Theodore Stevens lived in Wilton and births of two children are given in Livermore's *History of Wilton*, but the family is otherwise a mystery.

i MARY STEVENS, b. at Wilton, 18 Apr 1775; d. 26 Apr 1775.

ii JOHN STEVENS, b. 17 Jan 1778; no further record found.

316) SARAH ABBOTT *(Joseph4, Joseph3, John2, George1)*, b. at Andover, 14 Sep 1751 daughter of Joseph and Anna (Peabody) Abbott; d. at Salem 19 Apr 1820; m. 1st 23 Mar 1775, BENJAMIN HERRICK, b. 6 Dec 1752 son of Edward and Mary (Kimball) Herrick; Edward d. by 1782 when his estate was probated. Sarah m. 2nd 16 Jul 1789, WILLIAM WHITTIER, b. at Newton, NH, 16 Jul 1742 son of Andrew and Elizabeth (Huntington) Whittier; William d. at Methuen, 3 Mar 1811.

Sarah Abbott's first husband Benjamin Herrick was a hatter. He did not leave a will and the only available probate document lists widow Sarah as administratrix and David Whittier, gentleman of Methuen, as surety.[860] Just one child is known for Sarah and Benjamin. There are no children known for Sarah Abbott and William Whittier.

i BENJAMIN HERRICK, b. at Methuen, 18 Jul 1775; no further record found

317) LYDIA ABBOTT *(Joseph4, Joseph3, John2, George1)*, b. at Andover, 23 Oct 1753 daughter of Joseph and Anna (Peabody) Abbott; d. at Wilton, NH 20 Sep 1826; m. by 1775, SAMUEL LOVEJOY, b. 1750 (baptized at Andover 23 Sep 1850) son of William and Hannah (Evans) Lovejoy; Samuel d. at Wilton, 6 Oct 1801.

---

858 Reifel, *History of Franklin County, Indiana*, p 944

859 Elizabeth's date of birth and death date are on her gravestone; findagrave 54576174. The 1850 will of William Higgs includes a bequest to his daughter Elizabeth Moore.

860 Essex County, MA: Probate File Papers, 1638-1881.Online database. AmericanAncestors.org. New England Historic Genealogical Society, 2014. Case number 13116

Samuel Lovejoy did not leave a will and his estate entered probate 30 October 1801 with widow Lydia as administrator.[861] The personal estate was valued as $1,318.19 and real estate at $2,590.00.

The estate of Lydia Lovejoy entered probate 8 January 1827 with Timothy Abbott as administrator, the letters of administration stating that Lydia had seven children living all of whom declined administration of the estate.[862] The personal estate was valued at $169.38.

Samuel Lovejoy and Lydia Abbott were parents to ten children all born at Wilton.

i SAMUEL LOVEJOY, b. 30 Jul 1775; d. at Townsend, MA, 21 May 1851; m. 1st, at Mason, NH, 1 Mar 1803, BETSY LAWRENCE, b. at Groton, 24 Jun 1782 daughter of Amos and Betty (Hubbard) Lawrence; Betsy d. at Townsend, 15 Oct 1826. Samuel m. 2nd, 30 Jul 1831, SARAH BARR.

ii WILLIAM LOVEJOY, b. 7 Jul 1777; d. at Milford, NH, 15 Feb 1823; m. 1st, at Brookline, NH, 27 Sep 1803, ESTHER BURNS, b. at Milford, 1780 daughter of George and Jane (McQuaid) Burns;[863] Esther d. at Milford, 11 Apr 1816. William m. 2nd, Lydia, about 1818.[864]

iii DAVID LOVEJOY, b. 16 Jul 1779; d. at Wilton, 22 May 1833; m. RACHEL HUTCHINSON, b. at Wilton, 3 Jun 1779 daughter of Samuel and Mary (Wilkins) Hutchinson; Rachel d. 21 Dec 1865.

iv HENRY LOVEJOY, b. 16 Aug 1781; d. at Milford, 23 Sep 1863; m. at Wilton, 12 Jan 1804, his third cousin, PERSIS ABBOTT *(Abiel5, John4, John3, John2, George1)*, b. at Wilton, 25 Dec 1781 daughter of Abiel and Dorcas (Abbott) Abbott; Persis d. at Milford, 13 Nov 1859. Henry and Persis are Family #803.

v LYDIA LOVEJOY, b. 11 Sep 1783; d. at Wilton, 26 Jul 1801.

vi HANNAH LOVEJOY, b. 9 Aug 1785; d. at Mason, NH, 4 Oct 1861; m. at Wilton, 7 Jun 1807, JOHN STEVENS, b. at Wilton, 21 Jul 1783 son of John and Sarah (Pierce) Stevens; John d. 25 Mar 1848.

vii ABIEL LOVEJOY, b. 22 Oct 1787; d. at Milford, 1852 (probate, 1852); m. 1st, at Milford, 11 May 1813, SUSAN COWELL WADE, b. 1792 daughter of Benjamin and Hannah (-) Wade; Susan d. 25 Aug 1840. Abiel had three further marriages to EMILY WHEELER, 11 Jul 1843; to MARIA SEARLE, 12 Mar 1850; and to ALICE E. SUMNER, 11 Dec 1851.

viii JOHN LOVEJOY, b. 11 Dec 1789; d. at Lynn, 12 Sep 1876; m. 1st, at Lynn, 30 May 1813, his fourth cousin, LAVINA BLANCHARD *(Amos Blanchard5, Daniel Blanchard4, Sarah Abbott Blanchard3, Nathaniel2, George1)*, b. at Milford, 11 Jan 1791 daughter of Amos and Lavina (Hopkins) Blanchard; Lavina d. 27 Aug 1819. John m. 2nd, 17 May 1835, RUTH V. ANDREWS (widow of Legree Johnson). Lavina Blanchard is a child in Family 1050.

ix SALLY LOVEJOY, b. 9 Jun 1792; d. at Marblehead, 25 Aug 1825; m. at Wilton, 7 Jul 1811, SILAS STOCKWELL, b. at Westborough, 21 Dec 1788 son of Daniel and Rebecca (Warren) Stockwell; Silas d. at Natchez, MS, after 1860. After Sally's death, Silas married Eunice J. Wade.

x FREDERICK LOVEJOY, b. 3 Apr 1795; d. at Milford, 27 Sep 1849; m. at Milford, 21 Jun 1818, PAMELA TUTTLE, b. at Milford, 11 Dec 1800 daughter of Charles and Hannah (Burns) Tuttle; Pamela d. at Nashua, 17 Dec 1863.

318) DORCAS ABBOTT *(Joseph4, Joseph3, John2, George1)*, b. at Andover, 26 Oct 1755 daughter of Joseph and Anna (Peabody) Abbott; d. at Salem 19 Aug 1821; m. 12 Nov 1780, her fourth cousin, JOSEPH CHANDLER, b. 30 Jan 1753 son of John and Hannah (Phelps) Chandler; Joseph d. 27 Nov 1827.

Joseph worked for Elias Hasket Derby in Salem, one of the wealthiest merchants of the era and a pioneer in trade with China. Joseph later worked for Elias's son John Derby.[865]

In his will dated 28 March 1826, Joseph Chandler named son-in-law Jonathan Kenney as executor. Son Joseph Abbot Chandler had debts to the father totaling $219.34, and the bequest to Joseph Abbot is to include this owed amount. Joseph Abbot Chandler will receive a one-third part of the estate, but this is to be held by Jonathan Kenney and all the profit from this third is to be paid to Joseph's wife Deborah as long as she remains his wife or his widow. After Deborah's decease, that third of the estate is to go to grandson Joseph T. Chandler. The remaining two-thirds of the estate goes to daughter Dorcas Chandler

---

[861] New Hampshire, County Probate Records, 1660-1973, Hillsborough, Case 05878, 9:662, 9:629, 9:650, 10:273

[862] New Hampshire. Probate Court (Hillsborough County); Probate Place: Hillsborough, New Hampshire, Probate Records, Vol 29-30, 1818-1829, volume 30, p 492

[863] Ramsdell, *History of Milford*, p 609

[864] Ramsdell, *History of Milford*, p 826

[865] McKey, Richard Haskayne. "Elias Hasket Derby, Merchant of Salem, Massachusetts, 1739-1799." PhD diss., Clark University, 1961.

and daughter Hannah Kenney. The real estate was valued at $1,325.00 and the personal estate was $1,939,15 which included about $1,700 in cash, notes, and bank deposits. The heirs-at-law providing their consent to the presentation of the will were Joseph A. Chandler and his wife Deborah Chandler, Dorcas Chandler, and Hannah Kenney.[866]

Daughter Dorcas did not marry. In her will dated 28 January 1843, Dorcas Chandler made bequests to Mrs. Hannah Kenney of one hundred dollars, her niece Dorcas Kenney to receive silver spoons, and her brother Joseph A. Chandler receives fifty dollars. There are several small bequests to what seem other relations and friends. One-half of the remainder of the estate goes to her nephew Joseph T. Chandler who is to hold this in trust and pay to his father Joseph A. Chandler the interest on the estate annually. At the decease of Joseph A. Chandler, that part of the estate is to go to Susan E. Chandler. The other half of the estate is to be equally divided among her nieces and nephews.[867] The value of the real estate was $1,200 for a house and lot and personal estate valued at $828.

Dorcas Abbott and Joseph Chandler had four children born at Danvers.

i HANNAH CHANDLER, b. 15 Dec 1781; d. at Salem, 21 Dec 1856; m. at Salem, 20 Oct 1805, JONATHAN KENNEY, b. at Middleton, 23 Aug 1771 son of Simeon and Jerusha (Johnson) Kenney; Jonathan d. at Salem, 29 Dec 1847.

ii DORCAS CHANDLER, b. 11 Jun 1785; d. at Salem, 1 Feb 1843. Dorcas did not marry.

iii JOSEPH ABBOT CHANDLER, b. 28 Dec 1789; d. at Salem, 25 Nov 1861; m. at Salem, 24 May 1812, DEBORAH SYMONDS, b. at Salem, 1796 daughter of Thorndike and Betsey (Gurley) Symonds; Deborah d. at Salm, 3 Nov 1832. Joseph was a saddler for a time and also worked as a butcher.

iv JOHN CHANDLER, b. 21 Jun 1795; d. 27 Sep 1803.

319) JOSEPH ABBOTT *(Joseph⁴, Joseph³, John², George¹)*, b. at Andover, MA, 16 Feb 1758 son of Joseph and Anna (Peabody) Abbott; d. at Andover, VT 3 May 1835;[868] m. 30 Dec 1784, LUCY KING, b. 18 May 1760 daughter of Richard and Lucy (Butterfield) King; Lucy d. at Andover, VT 2 Nov 1842.

Joseph Abbott served in the Revolution enlisting from Andover, Massachusetts in December 1775 as a private in the militia. He enlisted again at Wilton, New Hampshire in June 1780 under Captain Barnes. He applied for a pension in 1832 while living in Andover, Vermont.[869]

Joseph and Lucy started their family in Wilton and relocated to Andover, Vermont about 1790. Joseph Abbott and Lucy King were parents of six children.

i BENNING KING ABBOTT, b. at Wilton, 29 Dec 1785; d. at Rutland, VT, 28 Aug 1865; m. 1st, 3 Dec 1807, POLLY M. JOHNSON, b. at Woodstock, CT, 14 Jun 1786 daughter of Abel and Lydia (Mumford) Johnson; Polly d. 1 Sep 1848. Benning m. 2nd, at Keene, 31 Dec 1851, SARAH PEIRCE.

ii ASA ABBOTT, b. at Wilton, 30 Mar 1788; d. perhaps at Chester, VT, 16 Jun 1847. Asa may have married, but a wife has not been identified.

iii LUTHER ABBOTT, b. at Mason, NH, 1 Nov 1790; d. at Chester, 20 Sep 1869; m. 7 Jul 1816, SARAH SPAULDING, b. at Nashua, 29 Mar 1785 daughter of Samuel and Sarah (Heald) Spaulding;[870] Sarah d. 13 Dec 1863.

iv LUCY ABBOTT, b. at Andover, VT, 1793; d. at Andover, 7 May 1880; m. 1st, about 1811, JOHN GREELEY, b. at Wilton, 8 Jan 1785 son of Nathaniel and Lydia (Cram) Greeley; John d. 18 Mar 1816. Lucy m. 2nd, at Andover, 5 Dec 1819, ASA PARKER, b. at Mason, NH, 9 Feb 1781 son of Phineas and Betsey (Swan) Parker; Asa d. at Andover, VT, 24 Dec 1865.

v SALLY ABBOTT, b. at Andover, VT, 1796; d. at Conneaut, PA, after 1850; m. at Andover, 23 Mar 1826, ENOCH D. THOMAS, b. about 1798; Enoch d. at Conneaut, after 1850.

vi BETSEY ABBOTT, b. at Andover, 1799.[871]

320) HULDAH ABBOTT *(Joseph⁴, Joseph³, John², George¹)*, b. at Andover, 21 Oct 1760 daughter of Joseph and Anna (Peabody) Abbott; d. 6 Apr 1830 at Roxbury, NH; m. by 1785, her third cousin, JOSHUA ABBOTT *(Joseph⁴, Joseph³,*

---

866 Essex County, MA: Probate File Papers, 1638-1881.Online database. AmericanAncestors.org. New England Historic Genealogical Society, 2014. Case number 4951, Probate of Joseph Chandler

867 *Essex County, Massachusetts, Probate Records and Indexes 1638-1916;* Author: *Massachusetts. Probate Court (Essex County);* Probate Place: *Essex, Massachusetts, Probate Records, Vol 412-414, Book 112-114, 1843-1847*

868 Vermont, Vital Records, 1720-1908 (ancestry.com)

869 Revolutionary War Pension and Bounty-Land Warrant Application Files

870 Spalding, *Spalding Memorial*, p 206

871 Abbot, *Genealogical Register*, p 16

Nathaniel², George¹), b. at Wilton, NH, 5 Nov 1765 son of Joseph and Mary (Barker) Abbott; Joshua d. at Nelson, NH, 30 Nov 1798. Huldah m. 2nd, at Nelson, 23 Nov 1809, GIDEON PHILLIPS, b. 7 Nov 1763 son of Joshua and Freelove (Paine) Phillips;[872] Gideon d. at Roxbury, NH, 10 Jun 1840. Gideon was first married to Chloe Shattuck.

Huldah and Joshua began their family in Wilton but relocated to Nelson, New Hampshire. Joshua died when his youngest child was just one year old. There are six children known for Huldah and Joshua Abbott.

i JOSHUA ABBOTT, b. at Wilton, 19 Dec 1785; d. at Cedar Falls, IA, 21 Feb 1880;[873][874] m. 1st, 23 Jul 1809, DEBORAH WOOD, b. at Alstead, NH, 14 Jun 1790 daughter of John and Lois (Olds) Wood;[875] Deborah d. at Marcellus, NY, Apr 1817. Joshua m. 2nd, about 1817, BETSEY CARROLL, b. 5 Aug 1798; Betsey d. at Portageville, NY, 24 Dec 1830. Joshua m. 3rd, at Portage, NY. 15 May 1831, CAROLINE PERSONS, b. in New York, 31 Dec 1808; Caroline d. at Cedar Falls, 9 Mar 1879.

ii MARY "POLLY" ABBOTT, b. at Nelson, NH, 5 Apr 1788; d. at Moravia, NY after 1880 (at age 92, living with her daughter Lucetta and her husband); m. about 1817, DANIEL HOBART, b. in Massachusetts, 1792 *likely* the son of Daniel and Lois (Merrick) Hoar;[876] Daniel d. after 1865 at Genoa, NY.

iii JOSEPH ABBOTT, b. at Nelson, 12 Oct 1791; d. 29 Sep 1793.

iv HULDAH ABBOTT, b. at Nelson, 29 Mar 1794; d. at Nashua, NH, 8 Dec 1880. Huldah did not marry.

v JOSEPH ABBOTT, b. at Nelson, 30 Sep 1796; d. 6 Dec 1796.

vi SARAH ABBOTT, b. at Nelson, 19 Oct 1797; d. at Nashua, NH, 11 Jan 1876; m. at Roxbury, NH, 16 Mar 1819, GIDEON NEWCOMB, b. at Norton, MA, 4 May 1795 son of John and Lydia (Bassett) Newcomb; Gideon d. at Roxbury, 10 Sep 1838.

321) MEHITABLE ABBOTT *(Ephraim⁴, Stephen³, John², George¹)*, b. at Andover, 11 Aug 1736 daughter of Ephraim and Hannah (Phelps) Abbott; d. at Andover, 1 Jan 1777; m. about 1762, her third cousin, JONATHAN ABBOTT *(Jonathan⁴, Jonathan³, Benjamin², George¹)*, b. at Lunenburg, 29 Aug 1740 son of Jonathan and Martha (Lovejoy) Abbott. Jonathan m. 2nd, 17 Dec 1778, his third cousin, DORCAS ABBOTT *(Stephen⁴, Stephen³, John², George¹)*, b. 23 Sep 1758 daughter of Stephen and Mary (Abbott) Abbott; Jonathan d. at Andover, 26 Dec 1821. Dorcas Abbott d. at Andover, 3 Mar 1844.

Jonathan Abbott served in the Revolutionary War with the rank of Sargent in the company commanded by Captain Henry Abbott. He was a farmer and lived on the homestead inherited from his father.

In his will (probate 1 January 1822), Jonathan Abbott made bequests to the following persons: beloved wife Dorcas, beloved son Stephen, beloved son Jonathan, daughters Mehitable, Sarah, Zurviah, Nabby, and Hannah, daughter Dorcas, daughter Phebe, grandson Stephen son of Stephen, and each of his grandsons named Jonathan. Son Stephen was the sole executor.[877] The grandsons named Jonathan each receives a firelock for their bequest. Wife Dorcas is to be cared for in terms of all her needs with provisions procured by his executor and delivered to her and she is to be cared for in health and in sickness as long as she is a widow. In consideration of this care and support, Dorcas forgoes her right of dower. But if the executor fails in his responsibilities to her, then her right of dower is reinstated.

Mehitable Abbott and Jonathan Abbott were parents of six children born at Andover.

i MEHITABLE ABBOTT, b. 29 Sep 1764; d. at Newry, ME, 6 Sep 1858; m. at Andover, 20 Sep 1787, BENJAMIN RUSSELL, b. at Andover, 28 Jul 1763 son of Benjamin and Mary (Feaver) Russell; Benjamin d. at Newry, 21 Aug 1842.

ii SARAH ABBOTT, b. 22 Jun 1766; d. at Frelighsburg, Québec, 25 Jul 1845; m. at Andover, 11 Jun 1793, JONATHAN STICKNEY, b. at Rowley, 29 Jul 1763 son of Jonathan and Mary (March) Stickney; Jonathan d. at Frelighsburg, 12 Sep 1839.[878]

---

[872] Stowe, *History of the Town of Hubbardston*, p 332
[873] U.S. Federal Census Mortality Schedules, 1850-1885
[874] *War of 1812 Pension Applications*. Washington D.C.: National Archives. NARA Microfilm Publication M313, 102 rolls. Records of the Department of Veterans Affairs, Record Group Number 15.
[875] Wood, *Descendants of the Twin Brothers John and Benjamin Wood*, p 146
[876] The Hoar family relocated from Mendon, MA to New York. The family members changed their name to Hobart and this was done legally through legislation in New York from 1831-1835. New York State Legislature, Legislative Documents, volume 46, p. 634. Daniel Hobart seems to be from this family, born in Mendon in 1792.
[877] Essex County, MA: Probate File Papers, 1638-1881.Online database. AmericanAncestors.org. New England Historic Genealogical Society, 2014. Case 83
[878] *Quebec, Canada, Vital and Church Records (Drouin Collection), 1621-1968*

iii ZERVIAH ABBOTT, b. 19 Mar 1768; d. at Bethel, ME, 18 Oct 1847; m. at Andover, 29 Dec 1789, JOHN ELLENWOOD, b. at Amherst, NH, 19 Sep 1765 son of Joseph and Sarah (-) Ellenwood; John d. at Bethel, 19 Jun 1847.

iv ABIGAIL ABBOTT, b. 30 Jul 1770; d. at Bethel, ME, 2 Jun 1810; m. at Andover, 17 Sep 1789, THEODORE RUSSELL, b. at Andover, 6 Dec 1765 son of Benjamin and Mary (Feaver) Russell; Theodore, d. at Bethel, 4 Jun 1821.

v HANNAH ABBOTT, b. 18 Nov 1774; d. at Bethel, ME, 5 Aug 1854; m. 16 Aug 1795, SIMEON TWITCHELL, b. at Bethel, 18 Feb 1770 son of Eleazer and Martha (Mason) Twitchell; Simeon d. at Bethel, 4 May 1844.

vi JONATHAN ABBOTT, b. 11 Jun 1776; d. at Bethel, ME, 7 Jan 1843; m. 27 Jan 1799, his third cousin once removed, BETSY BATCHELDER *(Rebecca Abbott Batchelder[4], Joseph[3], Nathaniel[2], George[1])*, b. at Wilton, 4 Aug 1777 daughter of Daniel and Rebecca (Abbott) Batchelder; Betsy d. at Bethel, 18 Nov 1864. Jonathan Abbott and Betsy Batchelder are Family 1071.

Jonathan Abbott and Dorcas Abbott were parents of five children born at Andover.

i STEPHEN ABBOTT, b. 30 Dec 1779; d. at Andover, 1 Oct 1835; m. at Andover, 13 Aug 1801, his third cousin, HANNAH RUSSELL *(Phebe Abbott Russell[5], Barachias[4], John[3], John[2], George[1])*, b. at Andover, Sep 1778 daughter of John and Phebe (Abbott) Russell; Hannah d. at Andover, 3 Jan 1840.

ii DORCAS ABBOTT, b. 26 Mar 1782; d. at Salem, 18 Apr 1841; m. 14 Oct 1810, JOSEPH SIBLEY, b. at Salem, 13 Dec 1783; Joseph d. at Salem, 1826.

iii PATTY ABBOTT, b. 9 Jun 1785; d. 4 Jun 1797.

iv PHEBE ABBOTT, b. 17 Jan 1788; d. at Andover, 14 Apr 1870; m. 13 Nov 1810, her third cousin once removed, JOSHUA BALLARD *(Hezekiah Ballard[5], Lydia Chandler Ballard[4], John Chandler[3], Hannah Abbott Chandler[2], George[1])*, b. at Andover, 3 Jan 1785 son of Hezekiah and Mary (Chandler) Ballard; Joshua d. at Andover, 4 Feb 1871.

v POLLY ABBOTT, b. 9 Jun 1790; d. 1 Feb 1796.

322) RHODA ABBOTT *(Ephraim[4], Stephen[3], John[2], George[1])*, b. at Andover, 22 Jun 1741 daughter of Ephraim and Hannah (Phelps) Abbott; d. 12 Jan 1821 at Albany, ME; m. 22 Mar 1764, JACOB HOLT, b. 29 Mar 1739 son of Jacob and Mary (Osgood) Holt; Jacob d. 12 May 1816.

Rhoda Abbott and Jacob Holt had their twelve children in Andover, and then in 1795 went north to the new settlement of Oxford Township in Maine.

i JACOB HOLT, b. 15 Feb 1765; d. at Charlestown, MA, 22 Sep 1800; m. at Andover, 11 May 1787, his third cousin once removed, ABIGAIL HOLT, b. at Reading, Sep 1765 daughter of Joseph and Abigail (Bean) Holt; Abigail d. at Charlestown, 16 Jun 1851.

ii NEHEMIAH HOLT, b. 25 Dec 1767; d. at Bethel, ME, 26 Mar 1846; m. 24 Jan 1793, ABIGAIL TWIST, b. at Reading, about 1768; Abigail d. at Bethel, 31 Jan 1853.

iii EPHRAIM HOLT, b. 19 Mar 1769; d. at Greenfield, NH, 24 Oct 1836; m. at Andover, 27 Nov 1794, his third cousin, HANNAH HOLT *(Joshua Holt[4], Dorcas Abbott Holt[3], Timothy[2], George[1])*, b. at Andover, Jun 1771 daughter of Joshua and Phebe (Farnum) Holt; Hannah d. at Greenfield, 21 Apr 1842. Ephraim Holt and Hannah Holt are Family 872.

iv STEPHEN HOLT, b. 7 Jun 1771; d. at Norway, ME, 25 Sep 1817; m. at Albany, VT, 1 Jul 1806, his fourth cousin, MOLLY BRAGG *(Molly Frye Bragg[5], Elizabeth Osgood Frye[4], Hannah Abbott Osgood[3], George[2], George[1])*, b. at Andover, 29 Apr 1779 daughter of Ingalls and Molly (Frye) Bragg; Molly d. at Norway, 17 Aug 1823. Molly Bragg is a child in Family 508.

v RHODA HOLT, b. 5 Jul 1772; d. before 1773.

vi RHODA HOLT, b. 13 Jul 1773; d. 1 Apr 1850 (burial at Albany, ME); m. 1803, JOHN LOVEJOY, b. at Andover, 24 Mar 1773 son of Joseph and Mary (Gorden) Lovejoy; John d. at Albany, ME, 8 Nov 1832.

vii URIAH HOLT, b. 25 May 1775; d. at Norway, ME, 21 Jun 1849; m. 4 Feb 1808, HANNAH FARNUM, b. at Andover, 27 Oct 1789 daughter of Benjamin and Dolly (Holt) Farnum; Hannah d. 4 Feb 1835.

viii MARY OSGOOD HOLT, b. 21 Apr 1777; d. at Andover, 11 Feb 1856; m. 22 Dec 1802, her second cousin once removed, ZACHARIAH CHICKERING *(Samuel Chickering⁵, Hannah Osgood Chickering⁴, Hannah Abbott Osgood³, George², George¹)*, b. at Andover, 19 May 1764 son of Samuel and Mary (Dane) Chickering; Zachariah d. at Andover, 30 Jun 1841. Zachariah Chickering is a child in Family 488.

ix TABITHA HOLT, b. 11 Aug 1779; d. likely at Waterford, ME; m. at Waterford, 19 Jun 1798, THOMAS GREENE, b. at Rowley, 17 Mar 1775 son of Thomas and Lydia (Kilburn) Greene; Thomas d. at Waterford, Oct 1809 (probate 12 Dec 1809).

x HANNAH HOLT, b. 17 Jul 1781; d. at Albany, ME, 23 Dec 1856; m. 1 Oct 1801, PARSONS HASKELL, b. at Falmouth, ME, 27 Oct 1777 son of Benjamin and Lydia (Freeman) Haskell; Parsons d. at Albany, 6 Jul 1829.

xi DAVID HOLT, b. 21 Aug 1783; d. at Andover, 3 Oct 1836; m. 2 Jul 1820, his second cousin, SARAH ABBOTT *(Abner⁵, Stephen⁴, Stephen³, John², George¹)*, b. at Andover, 11 Jul 1787 daughter of Abner and Ruth (Holt) Abbott; Sarah d. at Andover, 26 Jul 1874. Sarah Abbott is a child in Family 330.

xii SARAH ABBOTT HOLT, b. 19 May 1786; d. at Phillipston, MA, 23 Jun 1845; m. Jun 1817, JOSEPH CHICKERING, b. at Dedham, 30 Apr 1780 son of Jabez and Hannah (Balch) Chickering; Joseph d. at Phillipston, 27 Jan 1844.

323) ABIEL ABBOTT (f) *(Ephraim⁴, Stephen³, John², George¹)*, b. at Andover, 14 Apr 1745 daughter of Ephraim and Hannah (Phelps) Abbott; d. May 1795; m. 1st, 4 Apr 1763, BENJAMIN WALKER, b. at Billerica 6 Aug 1741 son of Benjamin and Hannah (Frost) Walker. Benjamin was wounded at the Battle of Bunker Hill, taken prisoner, and died in prison at Boston Aug 1775.[879] Abiel m. 2nd 23 Apr 1778, as his second wife, SAMUEL FITCH, b. 9 Nov 1736 son of Jeremiah and Elizabeth (-) Fitch; Samuel Fitch d. 21 Jul 1809. Samuel Fitch was first married to Mary Blood.

Benjamin Walker held the rank of Captain. He marched on 19 April 1775 in the regiment of Moses Parker. Captain Walker was wounded at the Battle of Bunker Hill and had a leg amputated as a result of his wounds. He was taken prisoner and died at prison in Boston as a result of his injuries.[880][881][882]

Abiel Abbott and Benjamin Walker had six children births recorded at either Andover or Chelmsford.

i BENJAMIN WALKER, b. at Andover, 15 Nov 1763; d. likely in NH, about 1793; m. at Chelmsford, 25 Jan 1786, ESTHER PIERCE, b. at Chelmsford, 12 Jun 1761 daughter of Benjamin and Elizabeth (Merrill) Pierce; Esther d. at Antrim, NH, 1 Nov 1826. After Benjamin's death, Esther married Timothy Kendall on 26 Oct 1794.

ii HANNAH WALKER, b. at Andover, 20 Jul 1766; d. at Nelson, NH, 26 Apr 1844; m. at Tyngsborough, 2 Feb 1796, JOSEPH BLOOD, b. 27 Oct 1769;[883] Joseph d. at Nelson, 1 May 1839.

iii ABIEL WALKER, b. at Andover, 26 Mar 1768; d. at Westmoreland, NH, 25 Jul 1838; m. at Westmoreland, 27 Jun 1795, BETSEY VEASEY, b. at Westmoreland, 24 Feb 1775 daughter of John and Huldah (Hackett) Veasey; Betsey d. at Westmoreland, 15 Feb 1825.

iv ABBOTT WALKER, b. at Chelmsford, 24 Jul 1770; d. at Andover, 2 Aug 1831; m. at Andover, 21 Jul 1796, LYDIA AMES, b. at Groton, 29 Mar 1770 daughter of Nathan and Deborah (Bowers) Ames; Lydia d. at Salem, 24 Jun 1843.

v EPHRAIM WALKER, b. at Andover, 22 Jul 1772; d. at Springfield, VT, 21 Jul 1864; m. at Chelmsford, 4 Jan 1801, MARTHA MANNING, b. at Chelmsford, 21 Oct 1776 daughter of Jonathan and Martha (Howard) Manning; Martha d. at Springfield, 13 May, 1835.

vi RHODA WALKER, b. at Chelmsford, 12 Apr 1774; d. at Tyngsborough, 2 Apr 1822; m. at Tyngsborough, 14 Feb 1800, ELIJAH FLETCHER, b. about 1774 son of Elijah and Mercy (Butterfield) Fletcher; Elijah d. at Tyngsborough, 23 Apr 1822.

---

[879] Benjamin, Capt, wounded at Charlestown, carried captive to Boston, died in prison of sickness, in ye latter end of August, 1775. C.R.1.

[880] Colonial Soldiers and Officers in New England, 1620-1775. (Online database: AmericanAncestors.org, New England Historic Genealogical Society, 2013).

[881] Boston Public Library. American Revolutionary War Manuscripts Collection, Document certifying Capt. Benjamin Walker's capture at Bunker Hill, 1775 [manuscript], accessed through archive.org

[882] Levin, Andy, 2013, Chelmsford Bravery at the Battle of Bunker Hill, http://www.wickedlocal.com/x369947957/Chelmsford-bravery-at-the-Battle-of-Bunker-Hill

[883] Joseph's birth date calculated from age at death of 69 years, 6 months, 4 days

Abiel Abbott and Samuel Fitch had two children born at Acton. Their son Irad did not marry. In his will written 28 July 1838, Irad bequeathed one dollar each to his sister Betsey Read, half-brother Ephraim Walker, and half-brother Noah Fitch. All the remainder of the estate to be divided into seven shares and go to the following heirs: heirs of half-sister Rhoda Fletcher deceased the wife of the late Elijah Fletcher; one share to half-sister Mary Read; one share to half-brother D. Samuel Fitch; one-share to half-brother Luke Fitch; one share to half-brother Abial Walker; one share to half-sister Hannah Blood wife of Jeremiah Blood; and one share to half-brother Lot Fitch. However, he notes that he does not know where Luke Fitch and Abial Walker are living, and if they do not call for their shares within two years of Irad's decease, then the shares are to be divided among of the other five heirs who receive shares.[884]

i BETSEY FITCH, b. 1779; d. at Littleton, 26 Mar 1865; m. at Littleton, about 1854, SAMUEL REED, b. at Westford, 15 May 1774 son of Samuel and Hannah (Wright) Reed; Samuel d. at Littleton, 23 Jul 1860. Samuel Reed was first married to Betsey's half-sister Mary Fitch. Mary Fitch was the daughter of Samuel Fitch and his first wife Mary Blood. Betsey Fitch is reported to have had a first marriage to another Mr. Reed, but specific information for that marriage has not been located.[885] There is evidence that she had this earlier marriage as her brother Irad refers to her as his sister Betsey Read in his 1838 will. In her 1856 will, Betsey leaves her estate to her husband Samuel Read and then fifth parts of her estate to her sons-in-law and daughter-in-law who are the children of Samuel Read and his first wife Mary Fitch.

ii IRAD FITCH, b. 12 Jul 1781; d. at Tyngsborough, 30 Jul 1838. Irad did not marry.

324) MARY HOLT *(Mary Abbott Holt⁴, Stephen³, John², George¹)*, b. at Lunenburg, 17 Aug 1745 daughter of Joseph and Mary (Abbott) Holt; m. 26 Jun 1766, BENJAMIN DARLING, b. at Lynnfield, 28 Apr 1728 son of John and Lois (Gowing) Darling; Benjamin d. at Lunenburg, about 1783 based on date of probate.

In his young adult life, Benjamin was a mariner, but returned home and married Mary Holt. He inherited property in Lunenburg form his father and settled there.[886]

Benjamin Darling did not leave a will. The personal estate was insufficient to pay the debts and widow Mary Darling petitioned the Court to be allowed to sell as much of the real estate as was needed to pay his debts.[887]

Mary Abbott and Benjamin Darling were parents of seven children born at Lunenburg.

i PATIENCE DARLING, b. 28 Mar 1767; m. at Lunenburg, 1785, JOHN DARLING, b. at Lunenburg, 13 Aug 1759 son of Timothy and Joanna (Blood) Darling.

ii MOLLY DARLING, b. 11 Jun 1769; d. at Temple, ME; m. at Lunenburg, 22 May 1792, MITCHELL RICHARDS, b. at Lunenburg, 1759 likely the son of Mitchel and Esther (Mitchell) Richards; Mitchell d. at Temple, 2 May 1845.

iii LOIS DARLING, b. 29 Aug 1771; nothing further known.

iv EUNICE DARLING, b. 13 Apr 1774; d. at Jaffrey, NH, 27 Jul 1834; m. at Jaffrey, 25 Nov 1811, RUFUS SAWYER, b. at Lancaster, MA (baptized 20 Jul 1760) son of Bezeleel and Lois (Lawrence) Sawyer; Rufus d. at Jaffrey, 29 Sep 1845.

v BENJAMIN DARLING, b. 11 Dec 1775; d. at Northfield, MA, 4 Nov 1840; m. FANNY AMES, *perhaps* b. at Hollis, 5 Sep 1773 daughter of Jonathan Robbins and Fanny (Powers) Ames; Fanny d. at Northfield, 18 Dec 1859.

vi JAMES DARLING, b. 5 Dec 1779; d. at Northfield, 5 May 1811; m. at Lunenburg, 3 Oct 1801, OLIVE READ, b. at Westford, MA, 30 Jun 1781 daughter of Abel and Rebekah (Farrar) Read.

vii LEVI DARLING, b. 8 May 1782; d. at Northfield, after 1821. Levi may not have married. In 1821, he was being supported by the town of Northfield.[888]

325) ABIEL HOLT *(Mary Abbott Holt⁴, Stephen³, John², George¹)*, b. at Lunenburg, 14 Jul 1748 son of Joseph and Mary (Abbott) Holt; d. at Temple, NH, 7 Jan 1811; m. 25 Nov 1773, his third cousin once removed, SARAH ABBOTT *(Job⁴, Jonathan³, Benjamin², George¹)*, b. at Suncook, 1751 daughter of Job and Sarah (Abbott) Abbott; Sarah d. at Temple, 9 Oct 1854 (age at death inscribed as 103 years, 2 months, 25 days on her gravestone).[889]

---

[884] Middlesex County, MA: Probate File Papers, 1648-1871.Online database. AmericanAncestors.org. New England Historic Genealogical Society, 2014. Case number 7693

[885] There is a marriage record in Amherst, NH for 1821 for a Betsey Fitch and a Samuel Reed, but there is no good reason to think that is for this Betsey.

[886] Weeks, *The Darling Family in America*, p 14

[887] Worcester County, MA: Probate File Papers, 1731-1881. Online database. AmericanAncestors.org. New England Historic Genealogical Society, 2015. Case Number 15392

[888] Cunningham, *Cunningham's History of the Town of Lunenburg*, p 178

[889] Findagrave.com

Abiel Holt was a farmer in Temple. He and Sarah Abbott were parents of five children born at Temple, New Hampshire.

i ABIEL HOLT, b. 25 Nov 1774; d. at Temple, 11 Mar 1839; m. 31 Jan 1799, ELIZABETH "BETSEY" HOWARD, b. at Temple, NH, 15 May 1776 daughter of Samuel and Elizabeth (Barrett) Howard; Betsey d. at Temple, 30 Dec 1847.

ii ABIGAIL HOLT, b. 22 May 1779; d. at Waterford, ME, about 1806; m. 1799, JONATHAN KIMBALL, b. at Waterford, 1773 son of Isaac and Abigail (Raymond) Kimball. Jonathan Kimball married Elizabeth Bowers 26 Feb 1807.

iii JOSEPH HOLT, b. 23 Feb 1782; d. at Temple, 19 Jul 1835; m. ANNA P.,[890] b. about 1780; Anna d. at Tempe 12 Feb 1872. Joseph and Anna did not have children.

iv EMELIA HOLT, b. 11 Jun 1784; d. at Temple, 26 Sep 1834. Emelia did not marry.

v NATHAN ABBOT HOLT, b. about 1790; d. at Temple, 25 Mar 1839; m. at Temple, 7 Dec 1815, BETSY PARKHURST, b. at Temple, 10 Oct 1788 daughter of William Parkhurst; Betsy d. at Temple, 29 Dec 1875.

326) DEBORAH ABBOTT *(Stephen⁴, Stephen³, John², George¹)*, b. at Andover, 13 Oct 1745 daughter of Stephen and Mary (Abbott) Abbot; d. after 1804 (husband's probate); m. 19 Sep 1766, JONATHAN FISKE; Jonathan d. at Groton about 1804 (date of probate).

Jonathan Fiske did not leave a will and Deborah Fiske requested that son Jonathan be named administrator which was done on 14 September 1804. Real estate of 80 acres with buildings was valued at $1200 and personal estate at $348.53. The probate records mention payments made to the guardian of Reuben Fiske.[891] In 1803, Reuben of Groton had a guardian appointed for him as being a person unable to care for himself. He was described as *non compos mentis*. Samuel Lawrence was named guardian.

Deborah Abbott and Jonathan Fiske were parents of four children. There are birth records for three children and a fourth child can be identified from the probate record.

i DEBORAH FISKE, b. at Andover, 10 Jan 1769; m. at Groton, 29 Nov 1792, EBENEZER LAUGHTON, b. at Pepperell, 15 Mar 1770 son of Ebenezer and Abigail (Blood) Laughton.

ii REUBEN FISKE, b. about 1770; d. at Groton, 10 Aug 1825.

iii MARY FISKE, baptized at Andover, 24 Sep 1775; nothing further known.

iv JONATHAN FISKE, b. at Andover, 17 Jan 1779; d. at Groton, 12 Sep 1832.

327) SARAH ABBOTT *(Stephen⁴, Stephen³, John², George¹)*, b. at Andover, 1 Aug 1747 daughter of Stephen and Mary (Abbott) Abbot; d. 8 Jul 1824; m. 7 Jul 1772, JOSEPH STEVENS, baptized at Boston, Oct 1750 son of Joseph and Hephzibah (Baker) Stevens; Joseph d. 20 Feb 1803.

In his will written 18 December 1802 (probate 8 March 1803), Joseph Stevens leaves to his beloved wife Sarah the clock, the silver tankard, the great Bible, and the great looking glass to be for her benefit and use absolutely, and the easy chair. Son Joseph Stevens receives all his lands in the United States north of the River Ohio and one-half of one full share as an associate in the Ohio Company. Joseph receives all the lands lying in Wilton, New Hampshire which are held in common and undivided with John L. Abbott. All the rest of the estate is to be equally divided between wife Sarah and son Joseph who are also named executors. At the probate, Sarah declines her role as executrix and requests that son Joseph fulfill this duty.[892]

Joseph and Sarah Stevens had one child.

i JOSEPH STEVENS, b. at Danvers, Apr 1774; d. at Andover, 1 Dec 1845. Joseph did not marry.

328) STEPHEN ABBOT *(Stephen⁴, Stephen³, John², George¹)*, b. at Andover, 1 Aug 1749 son of Stephen and Mary (Abbott) Abbot; d. at Salem, 9 Aug 1813; m. 1st at Salem, 24 Sep 1769, SARAH CROWELL, b. at Salem, Dec 1750 daughter of William

[890] The will of Joseph Holt includes a bequest to his wife Anna P. Holt.

[891] Middlesex County, MA: Probate File Papers, 1648-1871.Online database. AmericanAncestors.org. New England Historic Genealogical Society, 2014. Case Number 7611

[892] Essex County, MA: Probate File Papers, 1638-1881.Online database. AmericanAncestors.org. New England Historic Genealogical Society, 2014. Case 26384

and Sarah (Stone) Crowell; Sarah d. 14 Apr 1805. Stephen m. 2nd 5 Nov 1805, MARY BADGER of Dunstable, NH, b, about 1761 daughter of Nathaniel and Mary (White) Badger;[893] Mary was still living at the time of Stephen's probate in 1813.

Stephen Abbot was a merchant in Salem, and apparently quite successful, as the value of his estate in 1813 was $25,184.67 the bulk of this in cash, bank notes, and investments.

Major General Stephen Abbot served as a Captain in the Revolutionary War. Following the war, he was Colonel of a Company of Cadets in Salem, a volunteer force. Later, he achieved the rank of Major General in 1797 leading the Second Division of Massachusetts Militia that included Essex County.[894]

Stephen Abbot was also a member of the Masons beginning in 1791 and served as treasurer of the Essex Lodge in 1802.[895]

Stephen Abbot did not leave a will and in the probate record there are three heirs signing agreeing to the administration fee of $50 for administrator Mary Abbot. The three signers as heirs are Abijah Chase, John Sneathin, and Henry Chase who are husbands of three of the daughters. There seem to be no other heirs.[896]

Daughter Mary Abbott Chase was raised in the Episcopal faith of her parents, but about age 20 joined Society of Friends. She periodically participated in ministry. She was an invalid for several years before her death.[897]

Stephen Abbot and Sarah Crowell had ten children born at Salem. Seven of their children died in childhood.

i SARAH ABBOTT, b. Aug 1770; d. 24 Jan 1776.

ii MARY ABBOTT, b. 3 Jun 1772; d. at Salem, 26 Apr 1861; m. 10 Sep 1795, ABIJAH CHASE, b. at Salem, 22 Mar 1770 son of Abner and Rebecca (Newhall) Chase; Abijah d. at Salem, 7 Aug 1851.

iii BETSY ABBOTT, b. Jan 1774; d. 5 Aug 1778.

iv HANNAH ABBOTT, b. Apr 1775; d. 5 Sep 1775.

v SARAH ABBOTT, b. Jun 1776; d. 18 Jun 1778.

vi ELIZABETH "BETSY" ABBOTT, b. 4 Nov 1778; d. at Salem, 17 Jan 1843; m. 15 Oct 1801, HENRY CHASE, b. at Salem, 8 Dec 1773 son of Abner and Rebecca (Newhall) Chase; Henry d. at Salem, 8 Jun 1846.

vii HANNAH ABBOTT, b. 8 Nov 1780; d. unknown; m. at Salem, 18 Dec 1798, JOHN SNETHEN,[898] b. at New York about 1775; John d. at Salem, 18 Jan 1845. John Snethen was a mariner and little in terms of records have been so far located; there is evidence for eight children most of whom seem to have died young. One daughter, Mary Abbott Snethen, legally changed her name to Mary Snethen Abbott in 1855.

viii STEPHEN ABBOTT, b. 22 Dec 1781; d. 17 Nov 1787.

ix PHEBE ABBOTT, b. Dec 1783; d. 25 Nov 1787.

x JOSIAH FISK ABBOTT, b. Sep 1787; d. 3 Apr 1800.

329) GEORGE ABBOTT *(Stephen⁴, Stephen³, John², George¹)*, b. at Andover, 13 Jun 1756 son of Stephen and Mary (Abbott) Abbot; d. at Salem, MA, Dec 1829; m. 1 Apr 1779, REBECCA BLANCHARD, b. at Billerica, 1754 daughter of Simon and Rebekah (Sheldon) Blanchard.

George divided his time between Wilton and Salem. George and Rebecca were parents to eight children born at Wilton.

i SAMUEL ABBOTT, b. 2 Nov 1779; d. at St. Stephen, New Brunswick; m. 1st, at Salem, 17 Nov 1803, ELIZABETH PROCTOR; Elizabeth d. by 1805. Samuel m. 2nd, at Boston, 5 Nov 1805, ANNA MARIA BURTON, b. about 1780 daughter of Thomas Burton.[899] Two of the children of Samuel and Anna Maria were adopted by Samuel's sister Sarah and her husband David Putnam.

ii REBECCA ABBOTT, b. 17 Jun 1781; d. at Wilton, 10 Feb 1801.

---

893 White, *The Descendants of William White*, p 17

894 Bentley, *The Diary of William Bentley*, volume 4, p 64

895 *Massachusetts: Grand Lodge of Masons Membership Cards, 1733-1990.* Online database. *AmericanAncestors.org.* New England Historic Genealogical Society, 2010. (From records held by the Grand Lodge of Ancient Free and Accepted Masons of Massachusetts.)

896 *Essex County, MA: Probate File Papers, 1638-1881. Probate of Stephen Abbott, 6 Sep 1813, case number 134.*

897 Society of Friends, *The American Annual Monitor for 1862*, pp 20-22

898 There are various spellings of this name: Snethen, Seathen, Sneathing

899 Abbot and Abbot, *Genealogical Register*

iii SARAH STEVENS ABBOTT, b. 12 Jun 1783; d. at Salem, 13 Dec 1856; m. at Danvers, 25 Jul 1805, DAVID PUTNAM, b. at Danvers, 23 Dec 1789 son of Nathan and Hannah (Putnam) Putnam; David d. at Salem, 15 May 1866.

iv GEORGE ABBOTT, b. 17 Jul 1785; d. at St. Stephen, New Brunswick; m. at Zanesville, OH, 18 Nov 1817, SARAH MILLS. After marrying in Ohio, George and Sarah were at St. Stephen where their children were born.

v EPHRAIM ABBOTT, b. 27 Sep 1787; d. at Zanesville, OH, Oct 1821; m. at Salem, 17 Jan 1813, SARAH CHEEVER, b. at Salem, about 1789 daughter of Samuel and Anna (Ropes) Cheever.[900]

vi ELIZABETH KNEELAND ABBOTT, b. 29 Dec 1789; d. at Salem, 14 Jan 1873. Elizabeth did not marry.

vii STEPHEN ABBOTT, b. 1 Apr 1792; d. 1800.

viii MARY ABBOTT, b. 11 Aug 1794; d. at Salem, 27 May 1847; m. at Salem, 17 Mar 1822, her fourth cousin, NATHAN PUTNAM *(Lucy Blanchard Putnam[5], Daniel Blanchard[4], Sarah Abbott Blanchard[3], Nathaniel[2], George[1])*, b. at Danvers, 7 Mar 1796 son of Nathan and Lucy (Blanchard) Putnam; Nathan d. at Salem, 25 Apr 1879. Nathan Putnam is a child in Family 1051.

330) ABNER ABBOTT *(Stephen[4], Stephen[3], John[2], George[1])*, b. at Andover, 29 Jan 1761 son of Stephen and Mary (Abbott) Abbot; d. at Albany, ME, Sep 1833; m. 29 Jan 1784, RUTH HOLT, b. 25 Feb 1765 daughter of Joseph and Ruth (Johnson) Holt; Ruth d. 17 Nov 1806. Abner m. 2nd, at Waterboro, ME, 10 Mar 1808, DORCAS J. NASON, b. 1773 and d. at Albany, 19 Jul 1862.

In his pension application file, Abner Abbott testified that he enlisted in the military in December 1775 as a private in the Regiment of Enoch Paris in General Sullivan's Brigade in New Hampshire. He served until November 1776.[901]

There are seven children known for Abner Abbott and Ruth Holt, the first six recorded at Andover, Massachusetts (either birth or baptism record) and the youngest at Albany, Maine.

i RUTH ABBOTT, b. Jul 1785; d. likely at Boston, after 1850; m. at Salem, 22 Jun 1806, THOMAS RUSSELL WILLIAMS, b. at Salem, 1783 son of Henry and Abigail (Russell) Williams; Thomas d. 1827.[902]

ii SARAH ABBOTT, b. 11 Jul 1787; d. at Andover, 26 Jul 1874; m. at Andover, 2 Jul 1820, her second cousin, DAVID HOLT *(Rhoda Abbott Holt[5], Ephraim[4], Stephen[3], John[2], George[1])*, b. at Andover, 21 Aug 1783 son of Jacob and Rhoda (Abbott) Holt; David d. at Andover, 3 Oct 1836. David Holt is a child in Family 322.

iii OBED ABBOTT, b. 14 Sep 1789; d. at Albany, ME, 3 Jan 1855; m. at Albany, 27 Jun 1813, RUTH JORDAN, b. at Gray, ME, 1793 daughter of David and Temperance (Russell) Jordan; Ruth d. at Albany, 28 Nov 1865.

iv SAMUEL ABBOTT, b. Jan 1792; d. 1 Oct 1793.

v STEPHEN ABBOTT, b. Dec 1794; d. at Andover, 29 Sep 1869; m. 1st, at Albany, 13 Jan 1820, TEMPERANCE RUSSELL JORDAN, b. at Gray, ME, 1794 daughter of David and Temperance (Russell) Jordan; Temperance d. at Andover, 9 Oct 1842. Stephen m. 2nd, at Andover, 21 Jan 1844, PHEBE DURANT, b. at Andover, about 1795 daughter of Amos and Sarah (Ballard) Durant; Phebe d. at Lawrence, 20 Jan 1875.

vi MARY ABBOTT, b. May 1797; d. likely at Taunton, after 1860; m. at Boston, 20 Jun 1819, EDWARD PHILLIPS, b. at Taunton, 25 Jul 1790 son of Edward and Bethia (Danforth) Phillips; Edward d. at Taunton, 19 Sep 1856.

vii JOSEPH STEPHENS ABBOTT, b. 22 Feb 1804; d. at Concord, 16 Mar 1871; m. at Sullivan, NH, 15 Dec 1829, GRACE STEVENS WIGGIN, b. at Concord, 6 Oct 1806 daughter of Sherburn and Margaret (Sargent) Wiggin; Grace d. at Concord, 21 Sep 1886.

Abner Abbott and Dorcas Nason were parent of two children born at Albany, Maine.

i SAMUEL STEVENS ABBOTT, b. about 1809 and d. at Albany, 24 Sep 1811.

ii MARGARET NASON ABBOTT, b. 12 Jul 1812; d. at Peabody, MA, 21 Dec 1890; m. at Albany, ME, 2 Sep 1851, WILLIAM C. LAYCOCK, b. in England, about 1803 with father's name not known but first name of mother Eva

[900] Hassam, *Genealogies: The Hassam Family, the Chilton Family, the Cheever Family*, p 14
[901] Revolutionary War Pension and Bounty-Land Warrant Application Files
[902] *U.S., Craftperson Files, 1600-1995.*

Ella; William d. at Reading 26 Jan 1887. William was first married to Ann. William arrived in Boston from England 8 Feb 1844.[903]

331) ELIZABETH ABBOTT *(Stephen^4, Stephen^3, John^2, George^1)*, b. at Andover, 22 Oct 1766 daughter of Stephen and Mary (Abbott) Abbot; d. at Salem 19 Sep 1833; m. 27 Sep 1788, ABRAHAM VALPEY, b. 1766 (based on age at time of death) son of Richard and Hannah (Ives) Valpey; Abraham d. at Ipswich 26 Feb 1848.[904]

Elizabeth Abbott and Abraham Valpey were parents of nine children born at Salem. This was a family of mariners and three of the sons died at sea.

i ABRAHAM VALPEY, b. May 1789; d. at sea.

ii STEPHEN ABBOT VALPEY, b. 1791; d. at sea, 21 Jul 1810. Stephen died in the wreck of the ship *Margaret*.

iii SAMUEL STEVENS VALPEY, b. 26 May 1795; d. at South Lawrence, MA, 22 Jun 1876; m. at Andover, 27 Nov 1817, his third cousin, ELIZABETH ABBOTT *(Caleb^5, Asa^4, Timothy^3, Timothy^2, George^1)*, b. at Andover, 27 Jul 1791 daughter of Caleb and Lucy (Lovejoy) Abbott; Elizabeth d. at Lawrence, 3 Feb 1884. Elizabeth Abbott is a child in Family 375.

iv GEORGE VALPEY, b. 13 Aug 1787; d. at sea, 1826. He was a mate on the brig *Jane*.

v SIMON VALPEY, b. 16 Mar 1800; d. 28 Aug 1801.

vi ELIZABETH VALPEY, b. about 1805; d. at Ipswich, 28 Nov 1884; m. at Boston, 11 Jul 1828, NATHANIEL ARCHER MILLETT, b. at Salem, about 1805; Nathaniel d. at Ipswich, 3 Aug 1869.

vii DORCAS VALPEY, b. 1806; d. at Salem, 19 Apr 1819. Dorcas died of consumption.

viii MARY VALPEY, b. about 1808; d. at Ipswich, 31 Jan 1886; m. 13 Jun 1832, JOHN A. KIMBALL, b. at Ipswich, 24 Jun 1807 son of Benjamin and Huldah (Wade) Kimball; John d. at Charlestown, 1 Oct 1854.

ix JOSEPH VALPEY, b. about 1809. Joseph was a mariner and he did not marry.

332) ELIZABETH ABBOTT *(Samuel^4, Stephen^3, John^2, George^1)*, b. at Andover, 2 Nov 1755 daughter of Samuel and Elizabeth (Wyman) Abbot; d. 28 Oct 1815; m. 15 Feb 1780, EBENEZER JONES, b. 1757 son of Jacob and Mary (Winn) Jones; Ebenezer m. 2nd 2 Dec 1819, Dorcas Dane, b. 1769 daughter of Joseph and Elizabeth (Wyman) Dane; Ebenezer d. 24 Aug 1832. Ebenezer's two wives, Dorcas Dane and Elizabeth Abbott, were half-sisters.

Ebenezer Jones served as private in the Revolution in Captain John Abbot's Company in Major Gage's Regiment from 30 September to 6 November 1777 in the Saratoga Campaign.[905]

In his will written 16 August 1832, Ebenezer Jones has bequests to the following persons: beloved wife Dorcas, son Jewett Jones, son Hezekiah Jones, daughter Mary wife of Abel Abbott, daughter Elizabeth Jones, and son Ebenezer Jones, and son Ebenezer is the executor. Other children Reuben Jones, Abbot Jones, and Jacob Jones have already received their portions and have no further bequest in the will.[906] The children named, other than Ebenezer, receive cash bequests and the remainder of the estate goes to Ebenezer. The real estate was valued at $4,590 and the personal estate at $402.

Ebenezer Jones and Elizabeth Abbott had nine children, the birth of the oldest child recorded at Wilmington, Massachusetts, and the other children at Andover.

i ELIZABETH "BETSEY" JONES, b. 4 Oct 1780; d. at Andover, 12 Mar 1861. Elizabeth did not marry. Her estate entered probate 7 May 1861. Hezekiah Jones was administrator and other heirs signing agreement to this are Jewett Jones, Ebenezer Jones, Mary J. Abbott, and Reuben Jones. The personal estate, in the form of bank deposits and notes, was appraised at $765.17. There was no real estate.[907]

ii JACOB JONES, b. 13 Oct 1782; d. at Weld, ME, Jan 1860; m. at Andover, 4 Oct 1807, HANNAH JENKINS, b. at Andover, 1787 daughter of Joel and Patty (Carter) Jenkins; Hannah d. at Weld, 4 Feb 1851.

---

[903] *Massachusetts, Passenger and Crew Lists, 1820-1963*, The National Archives at Washington, D.C.; Washington, D.C.; Series Title: Passenger Lists of Vessels Arriving at Boston, Massachusetts, 1820-1891

[904] Abraham, lung fever, Feb. 26, 1848, a. 82 y.

[905] Bailey, *Historical Sketches of Andover*, p 373

[906] Essex County, MA: Probate File Papers, 1638-1881.Online database. AmericanAncestors.org. New England Historic Genealogical Society, 2014. Case 15182

[907] *Massachusetts, Essex County, Probate Records;* Author: *Massachusetts. Supreme Judicial Court (Essex County);* Probate Place: *Essex, Massachusetts, Probate Records, Johnson, W-Jones, O, 1828-1991*, case 43825

iii JEWETT JONES, b. 15 Jun 1784; d. at Andover, about Dec 1867 (will 6 Dec 1867); m. at Andover, 15 Mar 1810, SUSAN "SUKEY" LOVEJOY, b. about 1788 daughter of Isaac and Ruth (Davis) Lovejoy; Sukey d. at Andover, 23 Jun 1872.

iv MARY JONES, b. 29 Jul 1786; d. at Andover, 6 Dec 1869; m. 28 Dec 1822, as his second wife, her fourth cousin, ABEL ABBOTT *(Nathan5, Job4, Jonathan3, Benjamin2, George1)*, b. at Andover 7 Sep 1786 son of Nathan and Sarah (Ballard) Abbott; Abel d. at Andover, 3 Jul 1862. Abel first married, 29 Sep 1811, his first cousin, SARAH ABBOTT *(Job5, Job4, Jonathan3, Benjamin2, George1)*, b. at Wilton, NH, 7 Apr 1789 daughter of Job and Anna (Ballard) Abbott; Sarah d. at Andover, 1 Dec 1821. Abel Abbott is a child in Family 443. Sarah Abbott is a child in Family 589.

v ABBOT JONES, b. 4 Jul 1789; d. at Methuen, 23 Jan 1848; m. at Andover, 14 Feb 1814, BETSEY FRYE, b. at Andover, 21 Mar 1784 daughter of John and Betsy (Noyes) Frye; Betsey d. after 1848 (living at the time of her husband's probate).

vi EBENEZER JONES, b. 31 Jan 1792; d. at Andover, 12 Jul 1867; m. 11 Jan 1823, MARY KIMBALL HOLT, b. at Andover, 9 Apr 1802 daughter of Henry and Mehitable (Blunt) Holt; Mary d. at Andover, 14 Oct 1845.

vii HEZEKIAH WYNN JONES, b. 14 Feb 1794; d. at Weld, ME, about 1871 (will Dec 1870); m. Jan 1821, his fourth cousin, SUSANNAH FARNUM *(Timothy Farnum5, Lydia Abbott Farnum4, Timothy3, Timothy2, George1)*, b. at Andover, 14 Jan 1799 daughter of Timothy and Susanna (Berry) Farnum; Susannah d. at Weld, after 1870 (living at time of husband's will). Susannah Farnum is child in Family 851.

viii Daughter, b. 17 Feb 1796 and d. 23 Feb 1796.

ix REUBEN JONES, b. about 1797; d. at Andover, 25 Nov 1881; m. at Andover, 21 Feb 1828, RACHEL S. WOODBRIDGE, b. at Milford, NH, about 1808 daughter of Joshua and Rachel (Jones) Woodbridge; Rachel d. at Andover, 25 Nov 1889.

333) HANNAH ABBOTT *(Samuel4, Stephen3, John2, George1)*, b. at Andover, 24 Apr 1757 daughter of Samuel and Elizabeth (Wyman) Abbot; d. 31 Dec 1837; m. 24 Apr 1777, BENJAMIN GOLDSMITH, b. at Ipswich, 1755 son of William and Hannah (Burnham) Goldsmith; Benjamin d. 5 Apr 1817.

Benjamin Goldsmith was born in Ipswich, but his father relocated to Andover when Benjamin was about eleven years old.[908] Benjamin and Hannah were parents to five children born at Andover.

i BENJAMIN GOLDSMITH, b. 3 Jan 1778; d. at Andover, 14 Jan 1797.

ii SAMUEL ABBOT GOLDSMITH, b. 24 May 1780; d. at Andover, 23 Feb 1868. Samuel did not marry. He was living with his brother-in-law James Jaquith at the 1860 Census. In 1819, a guardian was appointed for Samuel due to drunkenness and being a spendthrift.[909] Ebenezer Jones (an uncle by marriage and the father in Family 332) was his guardian. At the time of the guardianship, Samuel's estate was valued at $3,627 with debt against him of $3,685.

iii HANNAH BURNHAM GOLDSMITH, b. 10 Aug 1783; d. at Wilton, NH, after 1860 (living at the 1860 census); m. at Andover, 20 Feb 1806, SETH STORY GOLDSMITH, b. at Wilton, 11 Apr 1778 son of William and Hannah (Burnam) Goldsmith; Seth d. at Wilton, 15 Feb 1861.

iv POLLY GOLDSMITH, b. 15 Apr 1787; d. at Phillips, ME, about 1836; m. at Andover, 19 Feb 1810, WILLIAM GOLDSMITH, b. at Wilton, 8 Jun 1785 son of William and Hannah (Burnam) Goldsmith; William d. at Phillips, after 1860. After Polly's death, William married Thankful Swift.

v PHEBE GOLDSMITH, b. 4 Oct 1793; d. at Andover, 5 Jan 1846; m. at Andover, 9 Sep 1813, JAMES JAQUITH, b. at Wilmington, MA, 1 Nov 1788 son of Nathan and Anna (Crosby) Jaquith; James d. at Andover, 1 Sep 1861.

---

[908] Essex Institute Historical Collections, volume 50, p 46

[909] *Essex County, MA: Probate File Papers, 1638-1881.* Online database. *AmericanAncestors.org.* New England Historic Genealogical Society, 2014. Case 11078, Samuel A. Goldsmith, spendthrift

334) ZEBADIAH CHANDLER *(Sarah Chandler Chandler⁴, Sarah Abbott Chandler³, John², George¹)*, b. at Andover, 23 May 1729 son of Joshua and Sarah (Chandler) Chandler; d. 30 Jun 1775; m. 19 Jun 1750, DEBORAH BLANCHARD, baptized Nov 1727 daughter of Stephen and Deborah (Phelps) Blanchard; Deborah d. May 1799.

Zebadiah served in the militia in Andover, as a Corporal in 1757 in Capt. John Foster's Company and as a Lieutenant in 1762 in Capt. Benjamin Ames's Company. He worked as a cooper.[910]

In the will written 28 July 1775, beloved wife Deborah receives the use and improvement of one-third of all the lands and all of the household goods. After the decease of Deborah, the household goods will go to his four daughters Sarah, Deborah, Lydiah, and Marge. Beloved son Zebadiah receives all the lands purchased from Isaac Stevens that have not already been given to him by deed excepting one-third part of the orchard. Son Zebadiah is to make a payment to his brother Joseph. Beloved son Stephen receives all the lands in Andover not otherwise disposed of and also land that was purchased from Nathan Blanchard. Son Joseph receives the land purchased of Stephen Blanchard. The three sons Zebadiah, Joseph, and Stephen divide the wearing apparel. Beloved daughter Sarah Holbrook receives four pounds which makes her full portion when added to what she received at the time of and since her marriage. Daughters Deborah, Lydia, and Mary each receive forty pounds. Son Zebadiah is named executor. The total value of the estate was £1,273.[911]

Zebadiah and Deborah Chandler had seven children born at Andover.

i SARAH CHANDLER, b. 8 May 1751; d. at Andover, 4 Nov 1824; m. 1st, 15 Dec 1772, RALPH HOLBROOK, b. at Roxbury, 20 Aug 1748 son of Ralph and Dorothy (Williams) Holbrook; Ralph d. at Andover, 19 Mar 1775. Sarah m. 2nd, 25 Dec 1781, her first cousin once removed, ZEBADIAH SHATTUCK *(Joanna Chandler Shattuck⁴, Zebadiah Chandler³, Hannah Abbott Chandler², George¹)*, b. at Andover, 26 Oct 1736 son of Joseph and Joanna (Chandler) Shattuck; Zebadiah d. at Andover, 10 Mar 1826. Zebadiah Shattuck and Sarah Chandler are Family 295.

ii ZEBADIAH CHANDLER, b. 11 Nov 1752; d. at Andover, 5 Feb 1835; m. at Andover, 16 Aug 1774, his second cousin, LUCE CHANDLER *(Nathan Chandler⁵, Nathan Chandler⁴, John Chandler³, Hannah Abbott Chandler², George¹)*, b. at Andover, 26 Jun 1758 daughter of Nathan and Phebe (Abbott) Chandler; Luce d. at Andover, 6 Oct 1841. Luce Chandler is a child in Family 289.

iii STEPHEN CHANDLER, b. 26 Oct 1754; d. at Andover, 7 Aug 1776.

iv DEBORAH CHANDLER, b. 26 Apr 1757; d. at Milford, after 1822 (living when husband wrote his will 12 Nov 1822); m. 17 Sep 1776, her second cousin, JOSHUA MOOAR *(Elizabeth Abbott Moar³, Nathaniel², George¹)*, b. at Andover, 3 Jun 1751 son of Timothy and Elizabeth (Abbott) Mooar; Joshua d. at Milford, 10 Sep 1824. Joshua Mooar and Deborah Chandler are Family 268.

v JOSEPH CHANDLER, b. 2 May 1759; d. at Andover, 3 Nov 1815; m. at Andover, 20 Sep 1782, MARY KING, b. at Chelmsford, 24 May 1762 daughter of Richard and Lucy (Butterfield) King; Mary d. at Amesbury, 25 Sep 1854.

vi LYDIA CHANDLER, b. 18 May 1761; d. unknown but likely at Wilton; m. by 1786, ANDREW PARKHURST, b. at Chelmsford, 6 Sep 1759 son of Jonathan and Bridget (Butterfield) Parkhurst; Andrew d. likely at Wilton, after 1820. Lydia and Andrew had three children born in Temple and each of these children married in Wilton. Andrew appears to be in Wilton in the 1820 census.

vii MARY "MOLLY" CHANDLER, b. 4 Apr 1764; d. at Andover, 30 Mar 1834; m. at Andover, 10 Dec 1783, her first cousin once removed, HEZEKIAH BALLARD *(Lydia Chandler Ballard⁴, John Chandler³, Hannah Abbott Chandler², George¹)*, b. at Andover, 18 Jul 1762 son of Hezekiah and Lydia (Chandler) Ballard; Hezekiah d. 4 Oct 1848. Hezekiah Ballard and Molly Chandler are Family 445.

335) JOSHUA CHANDLER *(Sarah Chandler Chandler⁴, Sarah Abbott Chandler³, John², George¹)*, b. at Andover, 23 Jul 1732 son of Joshua and Sarah (Chandler) Chandler; d. 15 Mar 1807; m. 31 Mar 1757, his first cousin, HANNAH CHANDLER *(Nathan Chandler⁴, John Chandler³, Hannah Abbott Chandler², George¹)*, b. 20 May 1735 daughter of Nathan and Priscilla (Holt) Chandler; Hannah d. 14 Feb 1791. Joshua m. 2nd 7 Jun 1792, his first cousin, HANNAH BALLARD *(Lydia Chandler Ballard⁴, John Chandler³, Hannah Abbott Chandler², George¹)* (the widow of Obadiah Foster); Hannah Ballard b. 6 Dec 1748 daughter of Hezekiah and Lydia (Chandler) Ballard; Hannah Ballard d. 22 Dec 1838. Hannah Ballard was first married on 30 May 1769 to OBADIAH FOSTER, b. at Andover, 25 May 1741 son of John and Mary (Osgood) Foster; Obadiah d. at Andover, 25 Jul 1780.

In his will written 24 February 1806, Joshua Chandler has bequests to the following persons: beloved wife Hannah Chandler, beloved son Abiel Chandler, beloved daughter Hannah Chandler (who is under 18 at the time of the will), and beloved

[910] Chandler, *Descendants of William and Annis Chandler*, p 327

[911] Essex County, MA: Probate File Papers, 1638-1881.Online database. AmericanAncestors.org. New England Historic Genealogical Society, 2014. Case number 4987

son Joshua Chandler. Son Joshua is named executor. Hannah Chandler is his daughter from his marriage to Hannah Ballard.[912]

Joshua Chandler and Hannah Chandler were parents of three children born at Andover.

i JOSHUA CHANDLER, b. 18 Aug 1758; d. at Andover, 26 Nov 1817; m. at Andover, 18 Oct 1798, his second cousin, DORCAS FOSTER, b. at Andover, Jun 1777 daughter of Obadiah and Hannah (Ballard) Foster; Dorcas d. at Andover, 21 Dec 1830. Joshua and Dorcas were stepsiblings (see children of Hannah Ballard and Obadiah Foster just below).

ii ABIEL CHANDLER, b. 28 Aug 1760; d. at Boston, 2 Nov 1833; m. at Andover, 17 Oct 1782, his first cousin, MARY ABBOTT *(Jonathan⁴, David³, Benjamin², George¹)*, b. at Andover, 10 Jan 1762 daughter of Jonathan and Mary (Chandler) Abbott; Mary d. 1 May 1845. Mary Abbott and Abiel Chandler are Family 841.

iii HANNAH CHANDLER, b. 13 Oct 1764; d. at Andover, 30 Aug 1785; m. at Andover, 1 Jun 1784, JOSEPH SHATTUCK *(Joseph Shattuck⁵, Joanna Chandler Shattuck⁴, Zebadiah Chandler³, Hannah Abbott Chandler², George¹)*, b. at Andover, 8 Nov 1757 son of Joseph and Anna (Johnson) Shattuck; Joseph d. at Andover, 8 Jul 1847. Joseph m. 2nd, 30 Mar 1790, PHEBE ABBOTT *(Jonathan⁴, David³, Benjamin², George¹)*, b. at Andover, 22 Feb 1766 daughter of Jonathan and Mary (Chandler) Abbott; Phebe d. at Andover, 31 Dec 1848. Joseph Shattuck and Phebe Abbott are Family 843.

Joshua Chandler and Hannah Ballard had one daughter.

i HANNAH CHANDLER, b. at Andover, 1793; d. at Boston, 3 Oct 1834; m. at Andover, 9 Jan 1816, her first cousin once removed, JONATHAN CHANDLER *(Joseph Chandler⁶, Zebadiah Chandler⁵, Joshua Chandler⁴, John Chandler³, Hannah Abbott Chandler², George¹)*, b. at Andover, 6 Feb 1793 son of Joseph and Mary (King) Chandler; Jonathan d. at Boston, Nov 1837.

Obadiah Foster served in the Revolution in the 4th Andover Company of infantry commanded by Captain Joshua Holt. Obadiah Foster did not leave a will. Debts exceeded the value of the estate which was declared insolvent.[913]

Hannah Ballard and her first husband Obadiah Foster had six children all born at Andover.

i JOHN FOSTER, b. 3 Mar 1770; d. at Warner, 13 Apr 1846; m. 1st, 1799, MARY DANFORTH, b. at Billerica, 1 Mar 1780 daughter of Samuel and Mary (Toothaker) Danforth; Mary d. 27 Nov 1802. John m. 2nd, 14 Jun 1803, LUCY HASTINGS, b. at Bolton, 26 Feb 1783 daughter of Benjamin and Experience (Ball) Hastings; Lucy d. 10 Sep 1842. John m. 3rd, 25 Jan 1843, Sally Morse Couch.

ii OBADIAH FOSTER, b. 28 Nov 1771; d. at New Salem, NH, 25 Jul 1818; m. at New Salem, 25 Dec 1800, PHEBE DUTY, b. at Salem, NH, 4 Apr 1778 daughter of William and Mary (Rowell) Duty.

iii HANNAH FOSTER, b. 15 Sep 1773; d. at Methuen, 15 Jun 1832; m. at Andover, 16 Jun 1818, as his second wife, ABIJAH CROSS, b. at Methuen, 6 Jul 1758 son of William and Mary (Corliss) Cross; Abijah d. at Methuen, 21 Feb 1848. Abijah was first married to Elizabeth Parker and third married to Deborah Spofford.

iv FREDERICK FOSTER, b. 20 Jul 1775; d. at Eutaw, AL, 5 Aug 1838;[914] m. about 1804, NANCY FINCH, b. in South Carolina, 8 May 1782 daughter of Edward and Mary (Ballard) Finch;[915] Nancy d. at Eutaw, 18 Sep 1857.

v DORCAS FOSTER, b. Jun 1777; d. at Andover, 21 Dec 1830; m. 18 Oct 1798, JOSHUA CHANDLER, b. 18 Oct 1758 son of Joshua and Hannah (Chandler) Chandler; Joshua d. 26 Nov 1817. Please see Joshua just above with parents Joshua Chandler and Hannah Chandler in this same family group.

vi GIDEON FOSTER, b. Jun 1779; d. at Charlestown, MA, 24 Apr 1865; m. 1st, 14 Oct 1804, TABITHA ROBBINS, b. 1782 daughter of Thomas and Tabitha (Ireland) Robbins; Tabitha d. at Charlestown, 29 Mar 1812. Gideon m. 2nd, 28 Mar 1814, PAMELA WINN, b. at Woburn, Jan 1778 daughter of Joseph and Betsey (Poole) Winn; Pamela

---

912 *Essex County, MA: Probate File Papers, 1638-1881.* Online database. *AmericanAncestors.org.* New England Historic Genealogical Society, 2014. Case 4954

913 *Essex County, MA: Probate File Papers, 1638-1881.* Online database. *AmericanAncestors.org.* New England Historic Genealogical Society, 2014. Case 9967

914 His gravestone includes that he was born in Massachusetts and gives his birthdate of 20 July 1775. Findagrave memorial ID 28810008

915 Jacobson, Kimberly. (2007) *Greene County and Mesopotamia Cemetery*, Arcadia Publishing, p 18

d. 28 Feb 1842. Gideon m. 3rd, 13 Apr 1843, RUTH BRADSHAW, b. at Medford 1788 daughter of Thomas and Martha (Tufts) Bradshaw; Ruth d. at Charlestown, 24 Oct 1868. Ruth Bradshaw was first married to Stephen Rose.

336) HANNAH SHATTUCK *(Joanna Chandler Shattuck⁴, Sarah Abbott Chandler³, John², George¹)*, b. at Andover, 14 Jul 1729 daughter of Joseph and Joanna (Chandler) Shattuck; death record not found; m. 18 Oct 1753, SAMUEL STEVENS, b. at Methuen, 27 Aug 1730 son of Samuel and Phebe (Bodwell) Stevens; Samuel d. 10 Aug 1810.

Hannah and Samuel Stevens had four children born at Andover.

i HANNAH STEVENS, b. 22 May 1754; d. at Andover, 15 Jun 1814; m. at Andover, 8 Jan 1778, ISAAC HOLT, b. at Andover, 15 May 1752 son of Joshua and Ruth (Burnap) Holt; Isaac d. 11 Oct 1821.

ii SAMUEL STEVENS, b. 24 Apr 1757; d. at Andover, 22 Nov 1831; m. 1st at Andover, 23 Apr 1778, MARY MOOAR, b. at Andover, 16 Dec 1760 daughter of Benjamin and Abiah (Hill) Mooar; Mary d. at Andover, 5 May 1804. Samuel m. 2nd, Oct 1806, SUSANNA MANNING, baptized at Charlestown, 28 Feb 1772 daughter of James and Ann (Brown) Manning; Susanna d. at Andover, 31 Mar 1809. Samuel m. 3rd at Andover, 22 Oct 1811, his third cousin once removed, PHEBE AMES *(Benjamin Ames⁵, Benjamin Ames⁴, Hannah Stevens Ames³, Elizabeth Abbott Stevens², George¹)*, b. at Andover, 8 Apr 1775 daughter of Benjamin and Phebe (Chandler) Ames; Phebe d. at Andover, 12 Jan 1854. Phebe Ames is a child in Family 1185.

iii JOSHUA STEVENS, b. 22 Jan 1761; d. 9 Mar 1764.

iv JOSHUA STEVENS, b. 8 Jan 1765; m. at Andover, 3 Sep 1784, his third cousin once removed, MARY CHANDLER *(Timothy Chandler⁵, Abial Chandler Chandler⁴, Abiel Chandler³, Hannah Abbott Chandler², George¹)*, b. at Andover, May 1767 daughter of Timothy and Mary (Walker) Chandler. Mary Chandler is a child in Family 446.

337) JOSEPH SHATTUCK *(Joanna Chandler Shattuck⁴, Sarah Abbott Chandler³, John², George¹)*, b. at Andover, 27 Nov 1731 son of Joseph and Joanna (Chandler) Shattuck; d. at Andover, 9 Apr 1778; m. 13 Apr 1765, ANNA JOHNSON, b. at Haverhill, 6 Apr 1737 daughter of Cornelius and Lydia (Clement) Johnson; Anna reported to have died at Hillsborough.[916]

Joseph had inherited the family homestead and was a farmer in Andover. His wife Anna was described as educated.[917] Joseph Shattuck did not leave a will and his estate entered probate 15 June 1778.[918] Anna Shattuck was administratrix of the estate. In the distribution of the estate, there was a set-off of one-third part to Joseph's mother, the "elder widow", as that had not been done previously. The value of the estate was £761.

Joseph Shattuck and Anna Johnson were parents of eleven children born at Andover.

i ANNE SHATTUCK, b. 8 Oct 1756; d. 20 Mar 1776.

ii JOSEPH SHATTUCK, b. 8 Nov 1757; d. at Andover, 8 Jul 1847; m. 1st, 1 Jun 1784, his second cousin, HANNAH CHANDLER *(Joshua Chandler⁵, Joshua Chandler⁴, John Chandler³, Hannah Abbott Chandler², George¹)*, b. at Andover, 13 Oct 1764 daughter of Joshua and Hannah (Chandler) Chandler; Hannah d. at Andover, 30 Aug 1785. Joseph m. 2nd, 30 Mar 1790, his third cousin once removed, PHEBE ABBOTT *(Jonathan⁴, David³, Benjamin², George¹)*, b. at Andover, 26 Feb 1766 daughter of Jonathan and Mary (Chandler) Abbott; Phebe d. at Andover, 21 Dec 1848. Hannah Chandler is a child in Family 335. Joseph Shattuck and Phebe Abbott are Family 843.

iii ELIZABETH SHATTUCK, b. 2 Sep 1760; d. at Andover, 12 Nov 1837; m. 27 Sep 1780, PAUL HUNT, b. at Tewksbury, 19 Jul 1753 son of John and Lydia (Thorndike) Hunt; Paul d. at Andover, 28 Nov 1831.

iv ABIEL SHATTUCK, b. 8 Aug 1762; d. at Plainfield, VT, 29 Apr 1834; m. at Andover, 25 Jul 1786, his first cousin, PHEBE SHATTUCK *(Zebadiah Shattuck⁵, Joanna Chandler Shattuck⁴, Zebadiah Chandler³, Hannah Abbott Chandler², George¹)*, b. at Andover, Feb 1766 daughter of Zebadiah and Elizabeth (Abbott) Shattuck; Phebe d. at Plainfield, 16 Jun 1856. Phebe Shattuck is a child in Family 295.

v LYDIA SHATTUCK, b. 27 Apr 1765; d. at Hillsborough, NH, 1 Apr 1843; m. at Andover, 29 Jan 1795, DANIEL FLINT, b. at Reading, 27 Mar 1767 son of Ebenezer and Asenath (Holt) Flint; Daniel d. at Hillsborough, 27 Jun 1853.

---

[916] Chandler, *The Descendants of William and Annis Chandler*

[917] Shattuck, *Memorials of the Descendants of William Shattuck*, p 149

[918] *Essex County, MA: Probate File Papers, 1638-1881. Probate of Joseph Shattuck, 15 Jun 1778, Case number 25125.*

vi WILLIAM SHATTUCK, b. 26 Apr 1769; d. at Otisfield, ME, 30 Aug 1806;[919] m. at Andover, 17 Nov 1791, ABIGAIL FOSTER, b. at Andover, 13 Jan 1771 daughter of Gideon and Elizabeth (Russell) Foster; Abigail d. at Andover, 30 Dec 1846.

vii ZEBADIAH SHATTUCK, baptized 27 Jan 1771; d. at Hillsborough, 2 May 1821; m. at Andover, 15 Mar 1792, ELIZABETH MARTIN, b. at Andover, 30 Apr 1771 daughter of Joseph and Phebe (Chandler) Martin.

viii PETER SHATTUCK, b. 18 Oct 1772; d. at Andover, 9 Dec 1855; m. 5 May 1795, SUSANNA CLARK, b. at Chelsea, 1776 daughter of Samuel and Sarah (Benjamin) Clark; Susanna d. at Andover, 12 Jun 1875.

ix HANNAH SHATTUCK, b. 8 Sep 1774; d. at Andover, 4 Sep 1828; m. 1st, 16 Nov 1797, LEMUEL CLARK who was "of Dorchester"; Lemuel d. about 1819. Hannah m. 2nd, at Andover, 16 Nov 1820, her second cousin once removed, CALEB ABBOTT *(Elizabeth Abbott Abbott⁴, Ephraim³, John², George¹)*, b. at Andover, 28 Oct 1751 son of Asa and Elizabeth (Abbott) Abbott; Caleb d. at Andover, 12 Apr 1837. Caleb was first married to Lucy Lovejoy and second married to Deborah Ames. Caleb Abbot and his families with Lucy Lovejoy and Deborah Ames are Family 375.

x OBED SHATTUCK, b. Nov 1776; d. at Pembroke, NH, 6 Apr 1817; m. 29 Nov 1798, ABIGAIL LOVEJOY, b. at Pembroke, 8 Jul 1775 daughter of Caleb and Mehitable (Kimball) Lovejoy; Abigail d. at Pembroke, 9 Jan 1868.

xi ANNA SHATTUCK, b. 4 Aug 1778; d. at Andover, VT, 31 Mar 1864; m. 1798, JOHN TYRRELL, b. at Bedford, NH, 3 Mar 1773 son of Samuel and Mary (McInnes) Tyrrell; John d. at Andover, VT, 11 Jun 1854.

338) ISAAC SHATTUCK *(Joanna Chandler Shattuck⁴, Sarah Abbott Chandler³, John², George¹)*, b. at Andover, 24 Mar 1733/4 son of Joseph and Joanna (Chandler) Shattuck; d. at Andover, 27 Apr 1822; m. 24 Mar 1757, MARY BARNARD, b. 4 Dec 1739 daughter of Nathaniel and Ruth (Preston) Barnard; Mary d. at Andover, 2 Jun 1804.

Isaac Shattuck was a farmer who lived in the area of Frye Village in Andover. There are records for seven children of Isaac Shattuck and Mary Barnard born at Andover.

i ISAAC SHATTUCK, b. 12 Sep 1758; died young.

ii NATHANIEL SHATTUCK, b. 3 Aug 1760; d. at Londonderry, VT, 1835; m. 28 Nov 1782, MOLLY BURNS, b. about 1760 and of Dracut; Molly d. after 1840, at Landgrove, VT.

iii MARY SHATTUCK, b. 3 Aug 1760; died young.

iv PHEBE SHATTUCK, baptized 10 Jul 1763; no further record.

v ISAAC SHATTUCK, b. 13 Jul 1766; d. at Andover, 15 Jul 1835; m. 11 Jan 1785; his third cousin, REBECCA INGALLS *(Mary Chandler Ingalls⁵, Abial Chandler Chandler⁴, Abiel Chandler³, Hannah Abbott Chandler², George¹)*, b. at Andover, 16 Jun 1766 daughter of Isaac and Mary (Chandler) Ingalls; Rebecca d. at Andover, 15 Jun 1859. Rebecca Ingalls is a child in Family 446a.

vi SAMUEL SHATTUCK, b. 31 Mar 1772; d. at Andover, 20 Dec 1832; m. 18 Feb 1794, his second cousin once removed, LUCY CHANDLER *(Zebadiah Chandler⁶, Zebadiah Chandler⁵, Joshua Chandler⁴, John Chandler³, Hannah Abbott Chandler², George¹)*, b. at Andover, 8 Feb 1775 daughter of Zebadiah and Luce (Chandler) Chandler; Lucy d. at Andover, 22 Jul 1861.

vii MARY SHATTUCK, b. 16 Feb 1776; d. at Andover, 30 Jan 1844; m. 2 Aug 1798, her fourth cousin, ENOCH FRYE *(Lucy Lovejoy Frye⁵, Lydea Abbott Lovejoy⁴, Henry³, George², George¹)*, b. at Andover, 29 Aug 1776 son of Theophilus and Lucy (Lovejoy) Frye; Enoch d. at Andover, 8 Sep 1864. Enoch Frye is a child in Family 544.

339) SARAH SHATTUCK *(Joanna Chandler Shattuck⁴, Sarah Abbott Chandler³, John², George¹)*, b. at Andover, 9 Apr 1739 daughter of Joseph and Joanna (Chandler) Shattuck; d. 9 Jan 1832; m. 6 Jan 1757, JOHN BARNARD, b. 8 May 1728 son of John and Sarah (Osgood) Barnard; John d. 27 Feb 1802.

John Barnard wrote his will 14 April 1800 and his estate entered probate 3 May 1802.[920] In his will, wife Sarah receives the improvements for one-half of the dwelling as long as she remains a widow and one-third of the improvements for the barn and lands for the rest of her natural life. She also receives one-fourth part of the household provisions of every type.

---

[919] William, at Otisfield, ME, Aug. 30, 1806, a. 37 y. GR3

[920] *Essex County, MA: Probate File Papers, 1638-1881. Probate of John Barnard, 3 May 1802, Case number 1751.*

Son John receives $50 and one-third part of the wearing apparel which is in addition to what he has already received to complete his portion. Son Theodore receives $500 which is to be paid out on a specific schedule by son David who is the executor. Theodore also receives one-fourth part of the books. "Respecting my beloved daughter Sarah as her circumstances at present, it appears to me most likely that she will incline to remain single, and my will is she shall have liberty to live unmolested in my house, that is with her mother as she consents to it, or with her brother as may be most agreeable, and I will and order my son David to provide for her support such things as she is not able to provide for herself in her natural life in case she doth not marry." If Sarah does marry, $200 is given to son David for the use of Sarah at the time of her marriage. Son David receives all the lands except for a small portion that is specified.

Sarah Shattuck Barnard wrote her will 4 September 1815. Daughter Sarah Stickney receives a feather bed, furniture, and the use of her gold necklace (which goes to the executor after the daughter's death). Sons John and Theodore can select furniture they see as proper. Son David receives the rest of the items that belong to her as well as the loom. Any residue of the estate is to be divided among her four children. Son John is named executor.[921]

John and Sarah Barnard were parents of six children born at Andover.

i SARAH BARNARD, b. 20 Mar 1758; d. at Andover, about 1835 (husband remarried 1836); m. at Andover, 30 May 1805, BENJAMIN STICKNEY, b. at Andover, 10 Oct 1779 son of Abraham and Abigail (Bell) Stickney; Benjamin d. at Andover, 19 May 1856. After Sarah's death, Benjamin married Lydia Bodwell.

ii JOHN BARNARD, b. Apr 1761; d. at Andover, 14 Jan 1842; m. at Andover, 31 May 1788, LYDIA MOOAR, b. at Andover, 30 Aug 1766 daughter of Abraham and Sarah (Stevens) Mooar; Lydia d. at Andover, 5 Dec 1826.

iii PHEBE BARNARD, b. 20 Feb 1767; d. 10 Sep 1778.

iv THEODORE BARNARD, b. 25 Dec 1772; d. at Lawrence, 2 Dec 1850; m. 3 Feb 1800, ANNA "NANCY" MANSUR, b. at Dracut, 29 Jun 1778 daughter of Samuel and Sarah (-) Mansur. Anna's death is uncertain. Theodore Barnard married Mehitable Bailey (widow of John Goldsmith), 1 Jun 1846.

v DAVID BARNARD, b. Jan 1777; d. at Andover, 17 Sep 1838; m. 1 Dec 1803, his fourth cousin, LYDIA FRYE *(Lucy Lovejoy Frye[5], Lydia Abbott Lovejoy[4], Henry[3], George[2], George[1])*, b. at Andover, 3 May 1782 daughter of Theophilus and Lucy (Lovejoy) Frye; Lydia d. at Andover, 23 Dec 1846. Lucy Frye is a child in Family 544.

vi PHEBE BARNARD, b. Jan 1781; d. 31 Jul 1781.

340) MARY SHATTUCK *(Joanna Chandler Shattuck[4], Sarah Abbott Chandler[3], John[2], George[1])*, b. at Andover, 13 Jul 1743; d. at Andover about 1815 (probate 6 Feb 1816) daughter of Joseph and Joanna (Chandler) Shattuck; m. 17 Oct 1765, THOMAS PHELPS, b. 1 Jun 1739 son of Thomas and Prudence (Wyman) Phelps; Thomas d. at Andover, 28 May 1795.

Mary Shattuck Phelps did not leave a will and her estate entered probate 6 February 1816. The probate documents include a statement from daughter Phebe Phelps requesting that her brother Isaac be named administrator. Phebe notes that the other sons have moved out of the state for more than five years. There are five sons named: Thomas, Solomon, Henry, Joseph, and Isaac.[922]

Thomas Phelps and Mary Shattuck were parents of eight children born at Andover, Massachusetts. Marriages were identified for only two of the children.

i THOMAS PHELPS, b. 25 May 1767; living in 1816.

ii SOLOMON PHELPS, b. 17 Mar 1770; living in 1816.

iii ISAAC PHELPS, b. 21 Jun 1772; d. at Andover, after 1850; m. at Andover, 31 Oct 1799, DORCAS AMES, b. at Andover, 31 Jul 1776 daughter of Benjamin and Dorcas (Lovejoy) Ames; Dorcas d. at Andover, after 1855.

iv HENRY PHELPS, b. 16 Mar 1775; living in 1816.

v MARY PHELPS, b. 18 Sep 1777; d. at Andover, 8 Jul 1800.

vi HANNAH PHELPS, b. 17 May 1781; nothing further known.

vii JOSEPH PHELPS, b. 30 Oct 1783; living in 1816.

viii PHEBE PHELPS, b. 28 Feb 1786; d. at Andover, 24 Oct 1879; m. at Andover, 2 Nov 1827, SAMUEL THURLOW, b. at Newbury, 11 Jul 1783 son of Samuel and Sarah (Little) Thurlow; Samuel d. at West Newbury, 2 Sep 1860. Samuel was first married to Mary Tyler.

---

[921] *Essex County, MA: Probate File Papers, 1638-1881. Probate of Sarah Barnard, 7 Feb 1832, Case number 1781.*

[922] *Essex County, MA: Probate File Papers, 1638-1881. Probate of Mary Phelps, 6 Feb 1816, Case number 21656.*

341) JOSHUA PHELPS *(Priscilla Chandler Phelps[4], Sarah Abbott Chandler[3], John[2], George[1])*, b. at Andover, 25 Jun 1738 son of Samuel and Priscilla (Chandler) Phelps; d. 22 Dec 1798; m. 17 Feb 1767, his second cousin, LOIS BALLARD *(Lydia Chandler Ballard[4], John Chandler[3], Hannah Abbott Chandler[2], George[1])*, b. 19 Jul 1746 daughter of Hezekiah and Lydia (Chandler) Ballard; Lois d. 21 Dec 1836.

Joshua Phelps wrote his will 1 August 1795. Beloved wife "Louis" receives use of all the household goods (excepting one bed and some furniture) and use of the red room and half the kitchen. There is also a specific list of grains and meats to be provided to her. Other specific provisions for her support and maintenance, including having a doctor when she is sick, are also listed. Beloved daughter Louis Blunt wife of Isaac Blunt receives nine pounds ten shillings. Beloved daughter Hannah Abbot wife of Nathan Abbot receives nine pounds ten shillings. Beloved son Joshua Phelps receives all the lands and buildings. Son Joshua is the sole executor of the estate.[923]

On 11 December 1832, there was a petition filed by Isaac Blunt and Nathan Abbot requesting that a guardian be appointed for Lois Phelps as she was unable to care for herself.[924]

Joshua Phelps and Lois Ballard had four children whose births are recorded at Andover.

i LOIS PHELPS, b. 24 May 1767; d. at Andover, 10 Feb 1849; m. 13 Dec 1791, ISAAC BLUNT, b. at Andover, 26 Sep 1766 son of Isaac and Mary (Kimball) Blunt; Isaac d. 17 Oct 1833. Isaac's father Isaac Blunt had first married Mary Abbot.

ii HANNAH PHELPS, b. 10 Sep 1769; d. at Andover, 17 Dec 1853; m. 11 Dec 1792, her second cousin, NATHAN ABBOT *(Jonathan[4], David[3], Benjamin[2], George[1])*, b. at Andover, 17 May 1768 son of Jonathan and Mary (Chandler) Abbott; Nathan d. at Andover 7 Apr 1850. This couple is more fully covered in Family #844.

iii JOSHUA PHELPS, b. 8 Apr 1774; d. at Andover, 24 Aug 1807; m. at Pepperell, 13 Jan 1796, MARY GILSON, b. at Pepperell, 7 May 1771 daughter of Samuel and Elizabeth (Shed) Gilson; Mary d. at Andover, 24 Oct 1856. Mary Gilson's father Samuel Gilson was killed in the Battle of White Plains during the Revolutionary War.

iv SAMUEL PHELPS, b. 15 Aug 1777; d. 26 Sep 1778.

342) HENRY PHELPS *(Priscilla Chandler Phelps[4], Sarah Abbott Chandler[3], John[2], George[1])*, b. at Andover, 5 Sep 1740 son of Samuel and Priscilla (Chandler) Phelps; d. 31 Oct 1807; m. 31 Oct 1780, MARY BALLARD *(Lydia Chandler Ballard[4], John Chandler[3], Hannah Abbott Chandler[2], George[1])*, b. 27 Feb 1750/1 daughter of Hezekiah and Lydia (Chandler) Ballard; Mary d. 11 Aug 1835.

Henry Phelps wrote his will 15 October 1807. Beloved wife Mary receives improvements on one-third part of the lands and buildings and all the household goods as long as she is a widow. If she remarries, the household items are to be divided among his three children. Daughter Mary receives two feather beds, one-third of the household items, and $200. Beloved sons Henry and Chandler receive all the lands and all the personal estate which is to be equally divided between them. Henry and Chandler are named executors.[925] The total value of the estate was $4,844.86.

Henry Phelps and Mary Ballard had five children whose births are recorded at Andover.

i SAMUEL PHELPS, b. 9 Aug 1781; d. 4 Mar 1796.

ii MARY "MOLLY" PHELPS, b. 15 Jul 1783; d. at Andover, 29 Feb 1832; m. 18 Dec 1806, her second cousin once removed, JOSEPH CHANDLER *(Joseph Chandler[6], Zebadiah Chandler[5], Joshua Chandler[4], John Chandler[3], Hannah Abbott Chandler[2], George[1])*, b. at Andover, 18 Dec 1783 son of Joseph and Mary (King) Chandler; Joseph d. at Andover, 4 Feb 1845.

iii HENRY PHELPS, b. 15 Jul 1783; d. at Andover, 31 Jan 1865. Henry was a farmer in Andover. He did not marry.

iv CHANDLER PHELPS, b. 5 Mar 1786; d. at Andover, 27 Dec 1868; m. 1st, at Wilton, NH, his second cousin once removed, LYDIA PARKHURST *(Lydia Chandler Parkhurst[6], Zebadiah Chandler[5], Joshua Chandler[4], John Chandler[3], Hannah Abbott Chandler[2], George[1])*, b. at Mason, NH, 4 Oct 1789 daughter of Andrew and Lydia (Chandler) Parkhurst; Lydia d. at Andover, 6 Sep 1830. Chandler m. 2nd, 8 May 1834, his first cousin, HANNAH FRYE BALLARD *(Hezekiah Ballard[5], Lydia Chandler Ballard[4], John Chandler[3], Hannah Abbott Chandler[2],*

[923] *Essex County, MA: Probate File Papers, 1638-1881. Probate of Joshua Phelps, 5 Feb 1799, Case number 21651.*

[924] *Essex County, MA: Probate File Papers, 1638-1881. Probate (non compos mentis) of Joshua Phelps, 11 Dec 1832, Case number 21654.*

[925] *Essex County, MA: Probate File Papers, 1638-1881. Probate of Henry Phelps, 6 Nov 1807, Case number 21645.*

George[1]), b. at Andover, 2 Aug 1791 daughter of Hezekiah and Mary (Chandler) Ballard. Hannah died 7 Jul 1836. Hannah Frye Ballard is a child in Family 445.

v HERMAN PHELPS, b. 31 Dec 1788; d. 21 Apr 1796.

343) HANNAH PHELPS *(Priscilla Chandler Phelps[4], Sarah Abbott Chandler[3], John[2], George[1])*, b. at Andover, 5 May 1745 daughter of Samuel and Priscilla (Chandler) Phelps; d. 1826 at Lewiston, ME; m. 29 Sep 1767, BENJAMIN MOOAR, b. 28 Oct 1743 son of Benjamin and Abijah (Hill) Mooar; Benjamin d. 15 Aug 1828 at Lewiston.

Benjamin Mooar served in the Revolution in the company of Captain Benjamin Ames under Colonel James Frye.

Hannah and Benjamin had their children in Andover and relocated to Lewiston, Maine in 1794.[926] Hannah Phelps and Benjamin Mooar were parents of ten children born at Andover.

i HANNAH MOOAR, b. 6 Nov 1768; d. at Lewiston, ME, 12 Sep 1860; m. 1st, at Andover, 27 Feb 1786, her second cousin once removed, JOSEPH BLANCHARD *(Joseph Blanchard[4], Sarah Abbott Blanchard[3], Nathaniel[2], George[1])*, b. at Andover, 10 Apr 1765 son of Joseph and Dinah (Blanchard) Blanchard; Joseph d. at Baltimore, 1798.[927] Hannah m. 2nd, at Lewiston, 1 Jan 1818, NATHAN CUTLER, b. at Mendon, MA, 23 Feb 1755 son of David and Mehitable (Whitney) Cutler;[928] Nathan d. at Lewiston, 8 Dec 1827. Nathan Cutler was first married to Ruth Nelson who died in 1817. Olive Cutler, daughter of Nathan Cutler and Ruth Nelson, married Timothy Mooar who is child #9 in this family; and a son of Nathan and Ruth married Mary Mooar who is child #8 in this family. Joseph Blanchard and Hannah Mooar are Family #1040.

ii BENJAMIN MOOAR, b. 3 Sep 1770; d. at Andover, 17 Jan 1855; m. 1st, 19 Nov 1795, PHEBE CHANDLER *(Zebadiah Chandler[6], Zebadiah Chandler[5], Joshua Chandler[4], John Chandler[3], Hannah Abbott Chandler[2], George[1])*, b. at Andover, 29 Aug 1776 daughter of Zebadiah and Luce (Chandler) Chandler; Phebe d. 29 Feb 1824. Benjamin m. 2nd, 1 May 1826, SUSAN CUMMINGS, b. at Andover, 29 Apr 1789 daughter of Asa and Hannah (Peabody) Cummings; Susan d. 16 Jul 1868.

iii LOIS MOOAR, b. 15 May 1773; d. at Farmington, ME, 1 Apr 1854; m. at Andover, 18 Apr 1793, SIMEON HARDY, b. at Tewksbury, 14 Apr 1770 son of James and Jemima (Palmer) Hardy; Simeon d. at Farmington, 10 Mar 1863.

iv SAMUEL MOOAR, b. 7 Mar 1775; d. at Newport, ME, Jan 1840; m. about 1804, ELIZABETH AMES, b. at Oakham, MA, 5 Jun 1779 daughter of James and Elizabeth (Craft) Ames;[929] Elizabeth d. at Newport, 31 Dec 1864.

v JOSEPH MOOAR, b. 7 Mar 1777; d. at Wilton, ME, 23 May 1860; m. 1st, about 1803, ASENATH AMES, b. at Oakham, 13 Oct 1782 daughter of James and Elizabeth (Craft) Ames; Asenath d. at Wilton, 12 Feb 1837. Joseph m. 2nd, Sarah who has not been otherwise identified.

vi PRISCILLA MOOAR, b. 16 Nov 1778; d. at Farmington, ME, 4 Apr 1828; m. JAMES HARDY, b. at Tewksbury, 1 Apr 1773 son of James and Jemima (Palmer) Hardy; James d. at Norridgewock, ME, 4 Dec 1855.

vii JOHN MOOAR, b. 14 Aug 1780; d. at Lewiston, ME, Dec 1848; m. 3 Sep 1809, MARTHA MERRILL, b. 24 Jul 1789; Martha d. 12 Apr 1869.

viii MARY MOOAR, b. 24 Nov 1782; d. in Maine about 1822; m. 15 Mar 1800, NATHAN CUTLER, b. at Auburn, MA, 14 Sep 1779 son of Nathan and Ruth (Nelson) Cutler; Nathan d. at Farmington, ME, 1 Nov 1859. After Mary's death, Nathan married Lydia Baker.

ix TIMOTHY MOOAR, b. 5 Feb 1785, d. at Earlville, IL, 18 May 1869; m. 1st, 12 Mar 1812, OLIVE CUTLER, b. at Auburn, ME, 10 Mar 1789 daughter of Nathan and Ruth (Nelson) Cutler; Olive d. at Wilton, ME, 17 Feb 1836. Timothy m. 2nd, 13 Nov 1837, CHARLOTTE FLETCHER, b. 3 Mar 1793 daughter of Jeremiah and Elizabeth (Perham) Fletcher; Charlotte d. at Earlville, 30 Dec 1860.

x NATHAN MOOAR, b. 14 Jun 1787; d. at Stetson, ME, 24 May 1854; m. 16 Oct 1810, SARAH MERRILL, b. about 1792; Sarah d. at Stetson, 17 Jan 1854. Sarah Merrill was the sister of Martha Merrill who married John Mooar.

---

926 Abbott, Abbott Genealogies, Mooar Family of Andover

927 In her pension application file, Hannah Cutler reports that her first husband Joseph Blanchard went to Baltimore in Maryland to look for employment in 1798 and suffered a fall in a mill that killed him. Revolutionary War Pension and Bounty-Land Warrant Application Files

928 Cutler, *A Cutler Memorial*, p 341

929 Mooar, *Mooar Genealogy*, p 58

344) PRISCILLA PHELPS *(Priscilla Chandler Phelps⁴, Sarah Abbott Chandler³, John², George¹)*, b. at Andover, 10 May 1748 daughter of Samuel and Priscilla (Chandler) Phelps; d. 9 Sep 1799; m. 11 Jul 1769, her second cousin, PHILEMON DANE, b. 2 Feb 1741/2 son of John and Elizabeth (Chandler) Dane. Philemon m. 2nd 29 Jan 1801, widow Sarah French Foster of Tewksbury; Philemon d. 13 May 1816.

Philemon Dane and later his son Benjamin were owners of the historic property at 97 Argilla Road in Andover. This property had been owned by the Dane family since the time of Reverend Francis Dane who obtained the land in the 1660 land division.[930]

Philemon Dane did not leave a will. His estate entered probate 4 June 1816 with his "only sons" Henry Dane and Benjamin Dane requesting administration of the estate as his widow declined that role.[931] The value of the real property of the estate was $2,350 and personal property was valued at $205.42.

There are birth records for three children of Priscilla and Philemon.

i HENRY DANE, b. 6 Aug 1772; d. at Andover, 26 Jan 1840; m. at Andover, 7 Jun 1796, ELIZABETH F. DANE, b. at Newburyport, about 1770 *possibly* the daughter of John and Mary (Moody) Dane; Elizabeth d. at Andover, 29 Jun 1846.

ii PRISCILLA DANE, b. 27 Jul 1774; no further record found.

iii BENJAMIN DANE, b. 10 Jul 1776; d. at Andover, 7 Feb 1828; m. 13 Feb 1803, SALLY COCHRANE, b. at Andover, 1786 daughter of James and Salome (Knowlton) Cochrane;[932] Sally d. at Andover, 18 Dec 1826.

345) ELIZABETH LOVEJOY *(Mehitable Chandler Lovejoy⁴, Sarah Abbott Chandler³, John², George¹)*, b. in NH, 1738 daughter of Caleb and Mehitable (Chandler) Lovejoy; d. after 1810 at Bow, NH;[933] m. about 1766, JOHN ROBERTSON, b. at Londonderry, 9 Jun 1732 son of Samuel and Margaret (Woodend) Robertson; John d. at Bow, NH 11 Oct 1816. John was first married to Lydia Cales.

John Robertson lived in various locations including Haverhill, Ipswich, Andover, Londonderry, and Bow.[934] He served in the Revolution and received a £40 bounty 4 August 1779.

John Robertson and Elizabeth Lovejoy were likely parents of four children born at Bow.[935]

i JAMES ROBERTSON, b. 13 May 1767; d. at Bow, 1 Apr 1847; m. about 1792, MARTHA PARKER, b. at Pembroke, 4 Sep 1773 daughter of Samuel and Martha (Mitchell) Parker.

ii EBENEZER ROBERTSON, b. 5 Oct 1769; d. at Bow, 1824 (probate 9 Apr 1824); m. at Bow, 3 Sep 1795 RUHAMMAH "AMY" PARKER,[936] b. at Pembroke, 6 Apr 1777 daughter of Samuel and Martha (Mitchell) Parker.

iii MEHITABLE ROBERTSON, b. 9 Dec 1777; d. 29 Oct 1778.

iv MEHITABLE ROBERTSON, b. 20 May 1780; d. at Bow, 29 Nov 1814; m. at Bow, 19 Mar 1801, MOSES THOMPSON WILLARD, b. at Concord, 21 Jan 1783 son of Samuel and Sarah (Thompson) Willard; Moses d. 25 Jul 1814 of wounds received in battle in the War of 1812. The military record does not give the location of the battle, just that he was wounded 14 Jul 1814 and died of his wound.[937]

346) MEHITABLE LOVEJOY *(Mehitable Chandler Lovejoy⁴, Sarah Abbott Chandler³, John², George¹)*, b. in NH, 1745 daughter of Caleb and Mehitable (Chandler) Lovejoy; d. 2 Mar 1835 at Allenstown, NH; m. about 1769, JONATHAN HUTCHINSON, b. 20 Mar 1747 son of Jonathan and Theodate (Morrill) Hutchinson; Jonathan d. at Pembroke, 3 May 1830.

---

930 Andover Historic Preservation, 97 Argilla Road, https://preservation.mhl.org/97-argilla-rd

931 *Essex County, MA: Probate File Papers, 1638-1881. Probate of Philemon Dane, 4 Jun 1816, Case number 7127.*

932 Knowlton, *Errata and Addenda to Dr. Stocking's History and Genealogy of the Knowltons of England and America*, p 137

933 Elizabeth appears to still be living at the 1810 Census as a woman in her age category is in the household headed by John Robertson.

934 Stearns, Genealogical and Family History of the State of New Hampshire, p 486

935 Stearns' Genealogical and Family History of the State of New Hampshire reports that John Robertson's older children were from his first marriage to Lydia and these younger children from his marriage to Elizabeth. The Book of Bow lists all eight children with Elizabeth, but that may be a function of recording the entire family when John Robertson arrived in Bow. Just the younger children are given here.

936 The marriage record for Ebenezer gives wife's name as Amey; the wife in his will is Ruhammah. These may be two different wives, but this may also be the use of a nickname. In any event, it is Ruhammah Parker who is the daughter of Samuel and Martha Parker.

937 Letters Received By The Office Of The Adjutant General, 1805-1821 1817

Jonathan Hutchinson came to Pembroke from Kensington. After the births of their children, the family relocated to Allenstown.[938] Mehitable Lovejoy and Jonathan Hutchinson were parents of five children born at Pembroke.

i BETSY HUTCHINSON, b. 30 Jan 1770; d. at Allenstown, NH, 5 Dec 1859; m. at Pembroke, 3 Oct 1790, ROBERT BUNTIN, b. at Allenstown, 1 Dec 1767 son of Andrew and Jane (Otterson) Buntin; Robert d. at Allenstown, 26 Jan 1847.

ii JONATHAN HUTCHINSON, b. 24 Apr 1771; d. at Pembroke, 17 Jan 1843; m. his second cousin, MARY "POLLY" WARDWELL *(Molly Lovejoy Wardwell[5], Elizabeth Chandler Lovejoy[4], Zebadiah Chandler[3], Hannah Abbott Chandler[2], George[1])*, b. at Pembroke, 28 Aug 1772 daughter of Jeremiah and Molly (Lovejoy) Wardwell; Polly d. at Merrimack, NH, 31 Aug 1850. Mary Wardwell is a child in Family 352.

iii OBADIAH HUTCHINSON, b. 2 Nov 1776; d. at Warner, 22 Aug 1843; m. 1st, 30 Nov 1796, MARTHA BROWN who has not been identified; Martha d. at Warner, 25 May 1834. Obadiah m. 2nd, 17 Feb 1835, his third cousin once removed, LUCY ABBOTT *(Ezra[4], George[3], Thomas[2], George[1])*, b. 5 Apr 1784 daughter of Ezra and Betty (Andrews) Abbott; Lucy d. at Warner, Nov 1869.

iv SOLOMON HUTCHINSON, b. 2 Nov 1776; d. at Lawrence, MA, 26 Aug 1863; m. 8 Aug 1799, LYDIA POOR FARNUM, b. at Pembroke, 14 Jul 1779 daughter of David and Mary (Poor) Farnum; Lydia d. at Lawrence, 12 Feb 1867.

v LEVI HUTCHINSON, b. 12 Aug 1781; d. at Canaan, NH, 4 May 1873; m. 10 Apr 1808, SARAH PAGE, b. 15 Oct 1783;[939] Sarah d. at Canaan, 26 Jan 1840.

347) CALEB LOVEJOY *(Mehitable Chandler Lovejoy[4], Sarah Abbott Chandler[3], John[2], George[1])*, b. at Pembroke, 1749 son of Caleb and Mehitable (Chandler) Lovejoy; d. 1821 (estate probate 7 Sep 1821);[940] m. by 1773, MEHITABLE KIMBALL.[941] Caleb m. 2nd JEMIMA JUDKINS, b. about 1775; Jemima d. at Pembroke, 15 Sep 1853.

Caleb Lovejoy was a farmer in Pembroke. He did not leave a will and his estate entered probate 7 September 1821. His widow Jemima requested administration and asked that John Ladd and Jonathan Hutchinson complete the appraisal. The personal estate was appraised at $45.22.[942]

Caleb Lovejoy and Mehitable Kimball were parents of six children born at Pembroke.

i BENJAMIN LOVEJOY, b. 20 May 1773; d. at Meredith, NH, Jan 1827; m. 23 Nov 1797, BETSY MCDANIEL, b. at Pembroke, 7 Jun 1777 daughter of John and Molly (Martin) McDaniel; Betsy d. at Center Harbor, NH, Sep 1853.

ii ABIGAIL LOVEJOY, b. 8 Jul 1775; d. at Pembroke, 9 Jan 1868; m. 29 Nov 1798, OBED SHATTUCK, b. at Andover, MA, Nov 1776 son of Joseph and Anna (Johnson) Shattuck; Obed d. at Pembroke, 6 Apr 1817.

iii ZEBADIAH LOVEJOY, b. 7 Sep 1778; d. at Epsom, 7 Sep 1847; m. 1st, about 1800, SALLY FOWLER, b. at Newmarket, NH, 24 Jul 1781 daughter of Symonds and Hannah (Weeks) Fowler; Sally d. at Epsom, 3 Dec 1831. Zebadiah m. 2nd, SARAH MARDEN (widow of Benoni Critchett); Sarah d. at Epsom, 5 Aug 1864.

iv CALEB LOVEJOY, b. 11 Feb 1781; d. at Meredith, NH, Oct 1841; m. 1804, SUSAN RICHARDSON, b. at Chester, NH, 25 Apr 1780 daughter of David and Sally (Shackford) Richardson; Susan d. at Meredith, 25 Jun 1853.

v MEHITABLE LOVEJOY, b. 11 Feb 1781; d. at Pembroke, 1804; m. 26 Nov 1799, SAMUEL GARVIN, b. at Bow, 15 Sep 1777 son of James and Deborah (-) Garvin; James d. at Pembroke, 22 Apr 1837. After Mehitable's death, Samuel married, 29 Dec 1806, Susannah Ballard Holt daughter of Nathan and Sarah (Chamberlain) Holt.

vi PHEBE LOVEJOY, b. 18 Sep 1783; d. at Epsom, after 1850; m. at Epsom, 4 Feb 1802, SAMUEL TRICKEY, b. about 1777 son of Samuel Trickey; Samuel d. at Allenstown, NH, 3 Mar 1861. Most of the children of Samuel Trickey legally changed their name to Appleton.[943]

Caleb Lovejoy and Jemima Judkins were parents of three children, an unnamed son who died in infancy and two daughters.

---

[938] Carter, *History of Pembroke*, p 159

[939] Date of birth is from Wallace's *History of Canaan*, p 614

[940] Caleb's brothers-in-law Jonathan Hutchinson and John Ladd participate in the administration of the estate in addition to widow Jemima.

[941] Lovejoy, *The Lovejoy Genealogy*, p 105

[942] *New Hampshire. Probate Court (Rockingham County)*; Probate Place: *Rockingham, New Hampshire, Estate Papers, No 10302-10390, 1821-1822*, No. 10336

[943] Laws of New Hampshire: Second Constitutional Period 1829-1835, p 265

i POLLY LOVEJOY, b. perhaps 1812; nothing further known.

ii MEHITABLE LOVEJOY, b. about 1814; d. at Pittsfield, NH, 31 Jan 1887; m. 1st, about 1831, JONATHAN SARGENT, b. at Pembroke about 1795 son of Jonathan and Molly (Lucas) Sargent; Jonathan d. at Pembroke, 1849. Mehitable m. 2nd, 16 Dec 1849, her first cousin once removed, LEVI BUNTIN *(Betsy Hutchinson Buntin6, Mehitable Lovejoy Hutchinson5, Mehitable Chandler Lovejoy4, Zebadiah Chandler3, Hannah Abbott Chandler2, George1)*, b. at Allenstown, about 1797 son of Robert and Betsy (Hutchinson) Buntin; Levi d. 25 Oct 1877. Levi first married Susan Jeness and second married Elizabeth Robertson.

348) JERUSHA LOVEJOY *(Mehitable Chandler Lovejoy4, Sarah Abbott Chandler3, John2, George1)*, b. at Pembroke, 5 Oct 1753 daughter of Caleb and Mehitable (Chandler) Lovejoy; d. at Pembroke, 11 Oct 1841; m. 6 Jun 1775, JOHN LADD, b. at Kingston, 6 Jan 1755 son of Trueworthy and Lydia (Harriman) Ladd; John d. 8 Jun 1835.

Jerusha Ladd wrote her will 23 June 1836. She bequeathed to her nephew Caleb Parker the sum of five dollars and five dollars to Jerusha Ladd Parker the daughter of Caleb. Daughter Mehitable Fowler receives one-third of her personal property and granddaughter Jerusha Hutchinson also receives one-third part of the property. The final third is bequeathed to Mehitable Jenness the wife of Peter Jenness. Bailey Parker of Pembroke was appointed administrator.[944] The Mehitable Jenness mentioned is her grandniece Mehitable Garvin (the granddaughter of Jerusha's brother Caleb).

Jerusha and John Ladd had one daughter born at Pembroke.

i MEHITABLE LADD, b. 9 Mar 1776; d. 9 Sep 1853; m. 15 Jan 1795, BENJAMIN FOWLER, b. at Newmarket, 10 Jun 1769 son of Symonds and Hannah (Weeks) Fowler; Benjamin d. 24 Jul 1832.

349) MARTHA LOVEJOY *(Mehitable Chandler Lovejoy4, Sarah Abbott Chandler3, John2, George1)*, b. about 1755 at Pembroke, NH daughter of Caleb and Mehitable (Chandler) Lovejoy; death record not found; m. at Pembroke, 21 May 1781, her third cousin JOHN PARKER *(Hannah Abbott Parker4, Timothy3, Timothy2, George1)*, b. 15 Aug 1760 son of Joseph and Hannah (Abbott) Parker;[945] John d. at Pembroke 27 May 1825.

Martha Lovejoy and John Parker were parents of eleven children born at Pembroke.

i JOSEPH PARKER, b. 3 Nov 1781; d. at Lancaster, MA, after 1855; m. about 1806, ESTHER CHAPMAN, b. at Concord, 1785 *perhaps* the daughter of Benjamin and Eunice (Tuttle) Chapman; Esther d. at Charlestown, MA, 8 Jan 1849.

ii CALEB PARKER, b. 28 Feb 1785; d. at St. Johnsbury, VT, Mar 1867; m. at Pembroke, 15 Nov 1804, MARY RICHARDSON, b. at Chester, NH, 14 Apr 1779 daughter of David and Sally (Shackford) Richardson; Mary d. 4 May 1857.

iii ABIGAIL PARKER, b. 29 Jun 1787; d. at Haverhill, NH, 8 Mar 1862; m. 6 Jun 1811, JACOB CASS, b. at Hill, NH, 22 Aug 1790 son of John and Abigail (-) Cass; Jacob d. at Piermont, NH, 4 May 1830.

iv JOHN LADD PARKER, b. 1790; d. at Allenstown, NH, 21 Jan 1830; m. 1st, 12 Nov 1812, NANCY RICHARDSON, b. at Chester, 1788 daughter of David and Sally (Shackford) Richardson. John m. 2nd, 29 Aug 1815, his fourth cousin once removed, ANNA OSGOOD *(Christopher Osgood5, Elizabeth Abbott Osgood4, Thomas3, Thomas2, George1)*, b. at Concord, 2 Oct 1795 daughter of Christopher and Anna (Abbott) Osgood; Anna d. at Pembroke, 2 Aug 1868. Anna Osgood is a child in Family 880.

v EZRA PARKER, b. 12 Sep 1791; d. at Littleton, NH, 24 Sep 1863; m. 3 Feb 1820, HANNAH BURLEIGH, b. at Sanbornton, 24 Jun 1800 daughter of Josiah and Mary (Pearson) Burleigh; Hannah d. at Newbury, VT, 4 Aug 1882.

vi OBADIAH PARKER, b. about 1793; d. at New Hampton, Sep 1867; m. at Sanbornton, 4 Feb 1823, POLLY PRESCOTT, b. at Sanbornton, 1 Jan 1799 daughter of Stephen and Hannah (Prescott) Prescott.[946]

---

[944] *New Hampshire Wills and Probate Records 1643-1982,* Will of Jerusha Ladd, Merrimack, 23 Jun 1836.

[945] The Lovejoy Genealogy (and some other sources) gives his parents as Joseph Lovejoy and Elizabeth Martin, but those same sources give his birth as 15 Aug 1760 and the John with that birth date is the son of Joseph Parker and Hannah Abbott. In the Andover records, the Joseph Parker who married Hannah Abbott is "Joseph, Jr." and the Joseph who married Elizabeth Martin is "Joseph, 3d."

[946] Runnels, *History of Sanbornton*, p 589

vii JAMES PARKER, b. about 1794; m. about 1825, SALLY DEARBORN, b. at Hill, NH, 2 Feb 1800 daughter of Richard and Dolly (Underhill) Dearborn;[947] Sally d. before 1847.

viii MARY PARKER, b. 28 Mar 1796; d. at Hooksett, NH, 22 Jan 1851; m. at Pembroke, 1 Jul 1816, her fourth cousin, DANIEL AMES *(Spofford Ames[5], Elizabeth Stevens Ames[4], Nathan Stevens[3], Elizabeth Abbott Stevens[2], George[1])*, b. at Andover, MA, 29 Apr 1789 son of Spofford and Mary (White) Ames; Daniel d. at Pembroke, 1 Apr 1835. Daniel Ames is a child in Family 1157.

ix MEHITABLE LOVEJOY PARKER, b. 17 Apr 1800; d. 17 Mar 1889; m. at Sanbornton, 9 Jul 1818, BENJAMIN WALLACE PEARSON, b. 20 Feb 1797; Benjamin d. at Haverhill, NH, 3 May 1868.

x CHARLOTTE PARKER, b. 30 Apr 1803; d. at New Hampton, 4 Sep 1867; m. 6 Mar 1823, ERSKINE QUIMBY, b. at Sanbornton, 27 Jul 1799 son of Harper and Hannah (Thompson) Quimby; Erskine d. 6 Jun 1876.

xi MARTHA PARKER, b. about 1805; d. about 1823.

350) OBADIAH LOVEJOY *(Mehitable Chandler Lovejoy[4], Sarah Abbott Chandler[3], John[2], George[1])*, b. at Pembroke, 1756 son of Caleb and Mehitable (Chandler) Lovejoy; d. at Williamstown, NY, 24 Aug 1834;[948] m. about 1782, TRYPHENA WAUGH, [949] b. at South Farms, CT, 1761 daughter of Thomas and Rosanna (Watson) Waugh;[950] Tryphena d. at Williamstown after 1820 and before 1834.[951]

Obadiah Lovejoy served during the Revolution receiving his warrant as Lieutenant in the 11th Regiment from Massachusetts on 13 July 1780. He served from that time until the end of the war. He had earlier service as private and a non-commissioned officer and during that time was at the Battle of Monmouth. Obadiah made application for a pension in 1818 when he was 62 years of age. The pension documents also include a statement that on 24 August 1834 (the date of Obadiah's death) that he had three sons living and these were the only known children: Ansel and Asa who were residents of Williamstown, New York and William who lived elsewhere in New York.[952]

Obadiah Lovejoy and Tryphena Waugh were parents of three known children who were perhaps born at Litchfield, Connecticut.

i ANSEL LOVEJOY, b. 1783; d. at Williamstown, NY, 1863; m. ANGELINA GOODWIN, b. at Litchfield, 22 Aug 1782 daughter of Solomon and Anna (Waugh) Goodwin; Angelina d. at Williamstown, 18 Jul 1846.

ii WILLIAM LOVEJOY, b. about 1784; d. at Vienna, NY, after 1855; m. perhaps to Polly Colwell but that is not verified.

iii ASA LOVEJOY, b. about 1790; d. at Williamstown, NY, 2 May 1864; m. JANE, b. in NY, about 1793 who has not been identified; Jane d. at Williamstown, after 1875.

351) ELIZABETH LOVEJOY *(Elizabeth Chandler Lovejoy[4], Sarah Abbott Chandler[3], John[2], George[1])*, b. at Pembroke, 10 Jan 1742 daughter of David and Elizabeth (Chandler) Lovejoy; d. at Pembroke, 11 Apr 1815; m. 12 Jan 1764, JEREMIAH MORGAN, b. at Pembroke, 18 Aug 1741 son of Luther and Abigail (-) Morgan; Jeremiah d. 21 Jul 1819.

In his will written 27 July 1813 (proved 9 September 1819), Jeremiah Morgan left to wife Elizabeth Morgan one-third part of the proceeds of all his real estate in Pembroke, the proceeds to be delivered to her annually by the executor for the remainder of her natural life. Son Jeremiah Morgan receives the remainder of the real and personal estate and one-third of the wearing apparel and is also named executor. The remainder of the bequests are to be paid by the executor. Son David Morgan receives thirty dollars and one-third part of the wearing apparel. Son William also receives thirty dollars and one-third of the apparel. Daughter Elizabeth Mann, daughter Priscilla Johnson, and daughter Sally Holt each receives thirty dollars.[953] Although wife Elizabeth is mentioned in the will, she died between the time of the will and the probate of the estate.

Jeremiah Morgan and Elizabeth Lovejoy were parents of six children born at Pembroke.

i ELIZABETH MORGAN, b. 31 May 1765; d. not located; m. at Pembroke, 13 Dec 1787, JOSEPH MANN, b. 1762 son of William and Mary (-) Morgan; Joseph d. 25 Jan 1835.

[947] The 1847 will of Richard Dearborn of Hill, NH includes bequests to his four grandchildren Dolly Parker, Martha Parker, James Parker, and Selwin? Parker.

[948] The History of Pembroke suggests that Obadiah might have died in the Revolution but the Lovejoy genealogy reports that he married Tryphena Waugh and had children Ansel, Asa, and William. There is a pension record that supports the marriage and those three children.

[949] Lovejoy, *The Lovejoy Genealogy*, p 105

[950] The 1801 probate of the estate of Thomas Waugh includes a distribution to daughter Tryphena wife of Obadiah Lovejoy.

[951] Tryphena seems to still be living at the 1820 census but the pension file reports that Obadiah left no widow when he died in 1834.

[952] Revolutionary War Pension and Bounty-Land Warrant Application Files; Case S18952

[953] *New Hampshire. Probate Court (Rockingham County)*; Probate Place: *Rockingham, New Hampshire, Estate Papers, No 9974-10056, 1819-1920*, Case 9992

ii DAVID MORGAN, b. 18 Dec 1766; d. at Bow, 13 Dec 1854; m. 29 Jul 1788, LOIS LADD, b. 4 Jan 1767 daughter of Trueworthy and Lydia (Harriman) Ladd; Lois d. at Pembroke, 5 Dec 1835.

iii WILLIAM MORGAN, b. 21 Apr 1769; d. at Bow, 24 Nov 1825; m. 1 May 1787, BETSY RUSS, b. 4 Oct 1767;[954] Betsy d. at 20 Aug 1842.

iv PRISCILLA MORGAN, b. 13 Jul 1773; d. at Bow, 12 Apr 1862; m. 26 Dec 1797; m. 26 Dec 1797, JOHN JOHNSON of Bow; John d. Feb 1847.

v JEREMIAH MORGAN, b. 12 Aug 1776; d. at Pembroke, 12 Apr 1839 (probate 30 Apr 1839); m. 8 Oct 1799, ABIGAIL JOHNSON, b. 11 Jan 1770; Abigail d. 3 Mar 1859.

vi SALLY MORGAN, b. 31 May 1781; d. at Bow, 15 Mar 1848; m. at Pembroke, 25 Apr 1805, ENOCH HOLT, b. at Pembroke, about 1780 son of William and Betsy (Ames) Holt; Enoch d. at Salem, MA, 5 Dec 1873.

352) MOLLY LOVEJOY *(Elizabeth Chandler Lovejoy⁴, Sarah Abbott Chandler³, John², George¹)*, b. at Pembroke, 29 Apr 1748 daughter of David and Elizabeth (Chandler) Lovejoy; d. at Salisbury, NH, 23 Feb 1813; m. 21 Nov 1769, JEREMIAH WARDWELL, b. at Andover 6 Dec 1748 son of Thomas and Abigail (Gray) Wardwell; Jeremiah d. 9 Jan 1817. Jeremiah remarried to Betsy after the death of Molly.

Jeremiah Wardwell served as a private in Captain Benjamin Ames's Company of Minutemen who "marched at the alarm" 19 April 1775 and in Waldron's New Hampshire Regiment.[955]

Jeremiah and Molly had their children at Pembroke and then relocated to Salisbury about 1804 where they had a farm.[956]

In his will dated 10 May 1814 (proved 5 March 1817), wife Betsy receives a portion of the house for her use which is detailed including her right to access the cellar. She also receives twenty acres, one cow, and four sheep, and she is to have the increase of these so long as she is a widow and no longer. If she marries, she has all the furniture she brought to the marriage and all the bedding and clothing she now has. She is also to have use of a horse. Son Isaac receives all the wearing apparel and one dollar. Sons Amos, Abial, John, and Jesse each receives two dollars. Daughters Polly Hutchinson, Phebe Wester, and Sally Adams each receives two dollars. Son Abial also receives half of the household furniture. Son Reuben receives all the lands, buildings, and tenements and the right to carry on the dowry of his mother-in-law as she and he shall agree until she have done with it and then it is the be exclusively his property. Reuben also receives a specific list of household items including the eight-day clock and the farming utensils, and all the cattle, the horse, and sheep. Reuben was also named executor.[957]

Jeremiah Wardwell and Molly Lovejoy were parents of ten children born at Pembroke.

i AMOS WARDWELL, b. 17 Oct 1770; d. at Grafton, NH, 19 Apr 1817; m. Anna who has not been identified. Amos and Anna did not have children. In his will, Amos has bequests to each of his brothers and sisters and leaves the remainder of the estate to his wife Anna.

ii MARY "POLLY" WARDWELL, b. 28 Aug 1772; d. at Merrimack, NH, 31 Aug 1850; m. JONATHAN HUTCHINSON, b. at Pembroke, 24 Apr 1771 son of Jonathan and Mehitable (Lovejoy) Hutchinson; Jonathan d. at Pembroke, 17 Jan 1843.

iii ISAAC WARDWELL, b. 22 Nov 1774; d. at Lebanon, NH, 9 Jun 1848; m. at Lebanon, 16 May 1813, MARY CUSHING, b. about 1791 but not otherwise identified; Mary d. after 1860 at Brookfield, VT (living with her son in Brookfield in 1860).

iv ABIEL WARDWELL, b. 25 Nov 1777; d. at Pembroke, 9 Feb 1860; m. at Salisbury, 8 Nov 1813, SALLY WEBSTER, b. at Salisbury, 27 Aug 1779 daughter of Israel and Elizabeth (Rolfe) Webster.

v PHEBE WARDWELL, b. 29 Apr 1780; d. at Salisbury, 20 Jan 1847; m. at Pembroke, 22 Jan 1801, JEREMY WEBSTER, b. at Hampton, 19 Jun 1775 son of Jeremiah and Anna (Sleeper) Webster; Jeremy d. at Salisbury, 20 Aug 1841.

---

954 Betsy Russ's birthdate is given with the family record for William and Betsy Morgan at Bow but without names for her parents.

955 U.S. Compiled Revolutionary War Military Service Records, 1775-1783

956 Dearborn, *History of Salisbury*, p 820

957 *New Hampshire. Probate Court (Hillsborough County)*; Probate Place: *Hillsborough, New Hampshire, Probate Records, Vol 25-26, 1815-1818*, p 640, will of Jeremiah Wardwell

vi SALLY WARDWELL, b. 11 Feb 1783; d. 31 Mar 1855; m. 2 Mar 1813; JEREMIAH ADAMS, b. at New London, NH, 15 Apr 1793 son of Benjamin and Judith (Adams) Adams; Jeremiah d. at New London, 22 Aug 1832.

vii JOHN WARDWELL, b. 14 Sep 1785; d. after 1850 at Meredith, NH; m. about 1812, CLARISSA DAVIS, b. about 1794 but not identified; Clarissa d. at Laconia, after 1860.

viii JOSEPH WARDWELL, b. 3 Jul 1788; d. at Boston, 3 Feb 1814. Joseph graduated from Dartmouth College in 1813 and was a teacher.[958] He did not marry.

ix JESSE WARDWELL, b. 3 Dec 1790; d. at sea, 1821 (probate 4 Jan 1822). Jesse was a mariner lost at sea. He served as a private in the First New Hampshire Regiment in the War of 1812.[959]

x REUBEN WARDWELL, b. 23 Apr 1795; d. at Salisbury, 15 Apr 1838; m. at Newburyport, MA, 21 May 1815, MARY "POLLY" WEBSTER, b. at Salisbury, 23 Apr 1790 daughter of Israel and Elizabeth (Rolfe) Webster); Mary d. at Salisbury, 22 Sep 1836.

353) ABIGAIL LOVEJOY *(Elizabeth Chandler Lovejoy[4], Sarah Abbott Chandler[3], John[2], George[1])*, b. at Pembroke, 12 Sep 1750 daughter of David and Elizabeth (Chandler) Lovejoy; d. 18 Mar 1833; m. about 1770, her third cousin once removed, DANIEL HOLT, b. at Pembroke 14 Sep 1744 son of Benjamin and Sarah (Frye) Holt; Daniel d. 5 Dec 1813.

In his will written 18 October 1813, Daniel Holt bequeaths to beloved wife Abigail one-third of the real and personal estate while she is a widow. Children Abigail Little, Jedediah Holt, Benjamin Holt, Stephen Holt, Esther Johnson, and John Holt each receive one dollar exclusive of what they have already received. Sons Richard Holt and Daniel Holt receive all the real and personal estate in Pembroke and elsewhere not otherwise disposed of. Son Richard Holt was named executor.[960]

Abigail Lovejoy and Daniel Holt were parents of eight children all born at Pembroke.[961]

i ABIGAIL HOLT, b. 14 Apr 1771; m. at unknown date Mr. Little. Nothing else is known.[962]

ii JEDEDIAH HOLT, b. 12 Aug 1774; d. at Dorchester, NH, 25 Oct 1850; m. at Concord, 1805, MARTHA "PATTY" NOYES, b. at Bow, 28 Mar 1787 daughter of John and Mary (Fowler) Noyes.

iii BENJAMIN HOLT, b. 4 Dec 1776; d. at Loudon, 15 Jun 1867; m. at Pembroke, 28 Nov 1805, ANNA KNOX, b. at Pembroke, 12 Aug 1782 daughter of William and Elinor (McDaniel) Knox; Anna d. at Loudon, 10 Oct 1867.

iv STEPHEN HOLT, b. 16 Sep 1779; d. at Pembroke, 28 Jun 1839; m. 6 Mar 1814, POLLY KNOX, b. 15 Aug 1792 daughter of John and Mary Ann (Knox) Knox; Polly d. at Pembroke, 10 Oct 1849.

v RICHARD HOLT, b. 12 Feb 1782; d. at Pembroke, 18 Aug 1836; m. 2 Mar 1834, MARY ANN KNOX, b. 11 Aug 1796 daughter of Daniel and Rachel (McClintock) Knox; Mary Ann d. at Pembroke, 13 Aug 1865.

vi JOHN HOLT, b. 14 Feb 1784; d. at Pembroke, 22 Aug 1856; m. 19 Dec 1817, HANNAH AYER, b. at Pembroke, 15 Jul 1791 daughter of John and Abia (-) Ayer; Hannah d. at Pembroke, 22 Apr 1848.

vii ESTHER HOLT, b. 7 Jun 1787; d. at Allenstown, NH, about 1843; m. 4 Feb 1809, JOHN JOHNSON, b. at Allenstown, about 1786. By 1850, John was apparently married to Mary with whom he had a six-year child.

viii DANIEL LOVEJOY HOLT, b. 14 Jun 1791; d. at Pembroke, after 1870; m. 23 Apr 1815, SALLY HOLT, b. at Pembroke, 16 Apr 1789 daughter of Nathan and Sarah (Black) Holt; Sally d. at Pembroke, 16 Apr 1841.

354) PHEBE LOVEJOY *(Elizabeth Chandler Lovejoy[4], Sarah Abbott Chandler[3], John[2], George[1])*, b. at Pembroke, 28 Sep 1754 daughter of David and Elizabeth (Chandler) Lovejoy; d. at Pembroke, Jun 1804; m. Feb 1779, NATHANIEL AMBROSE,[963] b. about 1752 (based on age at time of death). Nathaniel m. 2nd Elizabeth Goodhue; Nathaniel d. 24 Mar 1835 at Deerfield, NH.[964]

Nathaniel Ambrose wrote his will at Deerfield 17 March 1835. Beloved wife Elizabeth is to have all the personal property she brought into the marriage. She is also to receive a good and comfortable maintenance as long as she remains a widow. The interest on $100 is to be paid to her yearly. Son Daniel receives one dollar. Daughter Martha Smith wife of William T. Smith and daughter Abigail Baker wife of Mark Baker each receives ten dollars. Daughter Jane Ambrose is to receive $150

---

958 Chapman, *Sketches of the Alumni of Dartmouth College*, p 169

959 *U.S., War of 1812 Service Records, 1812-1815* [database on-line]. Provo, UT, USA: Ancestry.com Operations Inc, 1999.

960 *New Hampshire. Probate Court (Rockingham County)*; Probate Place: *Rockingham, New Hampshire*, *Probate Records, Vol 41-42, 1812-1815*, vol 42, p 52, will of Daniel Holt

961 Durrie's Holt genealogy also reports a set of twins, unnamed, who died in early infancy.

962 The Holt genealogy and History of Pembroke report that Abigail married twice and did not have children. No records related to her marriages have been located.

963 Goodhue, *History and Genealogy of the Goodhue Family*. The Goodhue Family genealogy suggests parents of Nathaniel Ambrose as Jonathan and Abigail (Goodhue) Ambrose. The Pembroke, NH history suggests parent is Robert Ambrose.

964 Nathaniel Ambrose's will was written 17 Mar 1835 and entered probate April 1835.

within a year after Nathaniel's decease. Daughter Phebe Edmunds the wife of John Edmunds receives fifty dollars, but this is to be held in trust by the executor and paid to her from time to time as the executor thinks is required. The daughters are to divide the household belongings that were his first wife's (their mother) equally among themselves. Son Jonathan receives all the remainder of the estate and is also named executor.[965]

Nathaniel Ambrose and Phebe Lovejoy had seven children born at Pembroke.

i JONATHAN AMBROSE, b. 13 Feb 1777; d. Dec 1777.

ii PHEBE AMBROSE, b. 22 Sep 1779; d. at Chichester, NH, 6 Feb 1852; m. 12 Feb 1824, JOHN EDMUNDS, b. at Candia, NH, 7 Jul 1796 son of Edward and Molly (Bagley) Edmunds; John d. at Chichester, 29 Dec 1878.

iii MARTHA AMBROSE, b. 7 Nov 1781; d. at Wilmot, NH, 18 Feb 1862; m. 3 Mar 1801, WILLIAM TRUE SMITH, b. at Salisbury, MA, 12 Oct 1772 son of William and Anne (True) Smith; William d. at Deerfield, 9 Sep 1859.

iv ABIGAIL AMBROSE, b. 18 Apr 1784; d. at Andover, MA, 21 Nov 1849; m. about 1807, MARK BAKER, b. at Pembroke, 2 May 1785 son of Joseph and Marion (Moore) Baker; Mark d. at Tilton, NH, 6 Oct 1865. Mark married second Elizabeth Patterson.

v DAVID AMBROSE, b. 30 Sep 1786; d. at Boscawen, 8 Mar 1866; m. 21 Sep 1809, SUKEY ADAMS, b. at Pembroke, 12 Aug 1785 daughter of Thomas and Sarah (Tufts) Adams; Sukey d. at Boscawen, 10 Oct 1861.

vi JONATHAN AMBROSE, b. 18 Sep 1789; d. at Deerfield, 9 Nov 1865; m. ANNA TRUE, b. at Deerfield, 26 Dec 1790 daughter of Jacob and Abigail (Page) True; Anna d. at Deerfield, 21 Sep 1857.

vii JANE AMBROSE, b. 4 Feb 1793. Jane was single at the time of her father's will in 1835.

355) OLIVE LOVEJOY *(Elizabeth Chandler Lovejoy⁴, Sarah Abbott Chandler³, John², George¹)*, b. at Pembroke, 13 Nov 1756 daughter of David and Elizabeth (Chandler) Lovejoy; d. at Pembroke, Feb 1843; m. 6 Mar 1781, THOMAS KIMBALL, b. at Andover, 17 Jul 1753 son of Thomas and Penelope (Johnson) Kimball; Thomas d. 20 Oct 1825.

Thomas Kimball was a farmer in Pembroke, He served in Captain Samuel Johnson's Company in 1776.[966]

In his will written 3 January 1825, Thomas Kimball bequeaths to his beloved wife one-third part of all the real and personal estate during her natural life. Son John, daughter Olive Cross, daughter Sally Gooden, daughter Beckey Cochran, daughter Betsey Newel, and daughter Phebe Jonson each receives five dollars. Daughter Sukey receives a fitting out of furniture similar to his other daughters and a maintenance in his house during her single life. Son Thomas receives all the real estate not otherwise disposed of, the farming tools, the livestock, and the eight-day clock, as well as other specific furniture items. Son Thomas is named the sole executor.[967]

Thomas Kimball and Olive Lovejoy were parents of eight children all born at Pembroke.

i OLIVE KIMBALL, b. 19 Jun 1781; d. at Charlestown, MA, 3 Apr 1871;[968] m. by 1801, DAVID CROSS, b. at Salem, NH, 19 Jun 1772 son of Abiel and Sarah (-) cross; David d. at Weare, 7 Mar 1856.

ii JOHN KIMBALL, b. 5 Nov 1783; d. at Bethel, ME, 2 Mar 1863; m. 20 Feb 1813, LUCINDA "LUCIA" TWITCHELL, b. in Maine, about 1791 daughter of Eli and Rhoda (Leland) Twitchell; Lucinda d. at Bethel, 7 Jan 1875.

iii SALLY KIMBALL, b. 4 May 1786; d. at Sebec, ME, 18 Apr 1854; m. 20 Oct 1812, GEORGE W. GOODWIN who was "of Weare" but not otherwise identified; George d. at Sebec, 27 Jan 1848.

iv REBECCA "BECA" KIMBALL, b. 19 Mar 1789; m. Cochran, but nothing else is known.

v THOMAS KIMBALL, b. 20 Apr 1791; d. at Pembroke, 18 Jul 1845; m. about 1820, ELSIE GAULT, b. about 1798 daughter of Matthew and Elizabeth (Buntin) Gault; Elsie d. at Pembroke, 28 Mar 1866.

---

965 *Estate Papers, Old Series, 1771-1869;* Author: *New Hampshire. Probate Court (Rockingham County);* Probate Place: *Rockingham, New Hampshire;* Notes: *Estate Papers, No 12912-12981, 1835*

966 Carter, *History of Pembroke*, p 174

967 *New Hampshire. Probate Court (Merrimack County);* Probate Place: *Merrimack, New Hampshire, Probate Records, Vol 1, 1823-1828*, pp 163-164

968 Age at death given as 89 years, 9 months, 15 days

vi BETSEY KIMBALL, b. 15 Mar 1794; d. at Bethel, ME, 8 Jan 1873; m. at Weare, 14 Jul 1811, SETH BANNISTER NEWELL, b. at Brookfield, MA, 26 Jun 1783 son of Ebenezer and Sarah (Bannister) Newell; Seth d. at Bethel, 23 Mar 1864.

vii PHEBE KIMBALL, b. 11 Nov 1797; d. at Chicopee, MA, 19 Apr 1858; m. 28 Oct 1817, JOHN JOHNSON, b. at Weare, 11 Oct 1789 son of Robert and Abigail (Peaslee) Johnson; John d. at Weare, 8 May 1850.

viii SUSAN "SUKEY" KIMBALL, b. 25 Apr 1800. Sukey did not marry. She was living in 1825 when her father wrote his will.

356) DORCAS LOVEJOY *(Elizabeth Chandler Lovejoy⁴, Sarah Abbott Chandler³, John², George¹)*, b. at Pembroke, 1 Oct 1758 daughter of David and Elizabeth (Chandler) Lovejoy; d. at Wheelersburg, OH, 1828; m. 28 Jan 1783, BENJAMIN MILLS, b. at Plaistow, NH, 30 Dec 1755 son of Reuben and Mary (Howard) Mills; Benjamin d. at Wheelersburg, 15 Jul 1829.

Benjamin Mills and Dorcas Lovejoy were parents of eight children all born at Kingston, New Hampshire.

i AMOS HOWARD MILLS, b. 9 Nov 1783; d. at Salem, MA, 31 Mar 1852; m. at Salem, 15 Aug 1813, SARAH LEACH, b. at Manchester, MA, 24 Aug 1789 daughter of Benjamin and Sarah (Knowlton) Leach; Sarah d. at Salem, 4 Mar 1872.

ii DORCAS MILLS, b. 29 Mar 1786; d. recorded at Chester, 15 Feb 1788.

iii BENJAMIN MILLS, b. 29 Mar 1786

iv SARAH "SALLY" MILLS, b. 15 May 1788; d. at Wheelersburg, OH, 28 Nov 1876; m at Piermont, NH, 9 Feb 1818, JOSIAH MERRILL, b. at Orford, NH, 12 Jul 1792 son of Timothy and Mercy (Gage) Merrill; Josiah d. at Wheelersburg, 26 May 1876.

v BETSEY MILLS, b. 31 May 1791

vi JAMES MILLS, b. 2 Jul 1793

vii POLLY MILLS, b. 10 Apr 1796; d. at Wheelersburg, OH, 9 Oct 1831. Polly did not marry.

viii PRISCILLA MILLS, b. 19 Aug 1798

357) ESTHER LOVEJOY *(Elizabeth Chandler Lovejoy⁴, Sarah Abbott Chandler³, John², George¹)*, b. at Pembroke, 8 Mar 1764 daughter of David and Elizabeth (Chandler) Lovejoy; d. likely in Vermont;[969] m. 25 Aug 1792, AMOS LAKEMAN, b. at Bradford, NH, 7 Jan 1762 son of Samuel ad Margaret (Kimball) Lakeman; Amos d. at Woodbury, VT 20 Dec 1850.[970]

Amos Lakeman served as a private in Colonel Moses Nichols' Regiment of Militia of New Hampshire from 4 July 1780 to 24 October 1780. This regiment joined the Continental Army at West Point.[971]

There are records for five children of Esther and Amos all born at Peacham, Vermont.

i SALLY LAKEMAN, b. 7 Sep 1792. No further record was found for Sally.

ii NANCY M. LAKEMAN, b. 3 Dec 1796; d. at Woodbury, VT, 10 Feb 1866; m. at Peacham, 23 Sep 1823, CALVIN BALL, b. 19 May 1795 son of Ezekiel and Joanna (Hastings) Ball; Calvin d. 28 Oct 1865.[972]

iii ERASTUS KELLOGG LAKEMAN, b. 13 Jul 1798; d. at Fulton County, NY, about 1883 (probate 5 Feb 1883); m. at Peacham, 21 Dec 1820, RHODA WAY, likely b. at Lempster, NH 5 Sep 1801 daughter of Stephen and Clarissa (Wheeler) Way; Rhoda was still living at the time of probate of her husband's estate. Heirs-at-law mentioned in the probate records of Erastus Lakeman are widow Rhoda Lakeman, sister Laura Ball, William Weeks son of sister Eliza Weeks who is deceased, and Augusta Ball Goodell and Eliza Ball Mason only children of sister Nancy Ball who is deceased. These are the only known heirs. The heirs-at-law all consent to the approval of the will.[973] Erastus left his entire estate to his wife Rhoda in his will.

iv LAURA P. LAKEMAN, b. 19 Dec 1802; d. at Woodbury, VT, 28 Jan 1886; m. 3 Oct 1822, LUTHER BALL, b. at Royalton, VT, 4 May 1800 son of Ezekiel and Joanna (Hastings) Ball; Luther d. at Woodbury, 16 Mar 1875.

---

969 Esther was deceased before 1850 when her husband was living with one of their daughters and her family in Woodbury.

970 Vermont Vital Records, 1720-1908

971 NARA M881. Compiled service records of soldiers who served in the American Army during the Revolutionary War, 1775-1783.

972 Information from the New England Ball Project was used to supplement some of the information for this family. http://www.newenglandballproject.com/

973 Probate Records 1789-1955, General Index, 1830-1967, New York Surrogate's Court (Fulton County)

v ELIZA LAKEMAN, b. 31 Jan 1805; d. at Peacham, 23 Mar 1872; m. about 1830, HILL B. WEEKS, b. in Vermont, about 1811 son of David and Amelia (Brainerd) Weeks;[974] Hill d. at Peacham, 16 Jun 1882. After Eliza's death, Hill married widow Julia Switzer Spicer.

358) MARY GRAY *(Sarah Abbott Gray⁴, Ephraim³, John², George¹)*, b. at Rumford, 29 Dec 1743 daughter of Samuel and Sarah (Abbott) Gray; d. at Amherst, NH 19 Oct 1775; m. at Amherst, 3 Dec 1762, MOSES TOWNE, b. at Topsfield, May 1739 son of Israel and Grace (Gardner) Towne; Moses d. at Milford, NH 9 Feb 1824.

Mary Gray and Moses Towne were parents of six children all born at Amherst.

i SARAH TOWNE, b. 10 Dec 1762; d. at Hopkinton, NH, 18 Feb 1805; m. about 1785, her first cousin, JOSEPH TOWNE, b. at Amherst, 30 Sep 1758 son of Thomas and Hannah (Boutelle) Towne. Joseph married second Margaret Barker in 1806.

ii SAMUEL GRAY TOWNE, b. 25 May 1764; d. at Nashua, NH, 24 Sep 1848. Samuel did not marry.

iii MOSES TOWNE, b. 21 Oct 1766; d. at Nashua, 14 Aug 1854; m. SARAH TAYLOR, b. about 1767; Sarah d. at Nashua, 17 Apr 1851.

iv MARY TOWNE, b. 14 Sep 1768; d. at Amherst, 1 Mar 1777.

v ELIZABETH TOWNE, b. 27 Oct 1770; d. at Hopkinton, 27 Aug 1822; m. at Amherst, 20 Oct 1794, TRUEWORTHY GILMAN, b. 1769 son of Trueworthy and Elizabeth (Bartlett) Gilman; Trueworthy d. at Hopkinton, 6 Jan 1799.

vi LEMUEL TOWNE, b. 17 Jun 1773; d. 8 Oct 1775.

359) MARY ABBOTT *(Ephraim⁴, Ephraim³, John², George¹)*, b. at Andover, 11 Mar 1741 daughter of Ephraim and Mary (Abbott) Abbott; d.?; m. 9 Dec 1762, PETER GOSS, b. at Bradford, 17 Jun 1737 son of John and Mehitable (Bailey) Goss; Peter d. at Amherst after 1790.[975]

Peter Goss served as a corporal in Captain Crosby's Company and was among those men from Amherst who were at the Battle of Bunker Hill. In 1782, he was also called upon to fill the town's quota for men to serve. Two sons John Abbot Goss and Ephraim Abbott Goss also served in the Revolution.[976]

There are five children known for Peter Goss and Mary Abbott, all born at Amherst, New Hampshire.

i JOHN ABBOT GOSS, b. 5 Jun 1764; d. at Amherst, Dec 1819. John did not marry. He served in the Revolution and received a pension in 1818 due to his destitute condition. He was a laborer. The probate of his estate was 6 Jan 1820 with his brother Ephraim named as next of kin.

ii EPHRAIM ABBOTT GOSS, b. 6 Apr 1767; d. at Amherst, about 1840; m. 13 Jul 1786, ANAH BATHRICK, b. Leominster, MA, 1 Feb 1770 daughter of Stephen and Jemima (Dodge) Bathrick; Anah d. at Amherst, 20 Mar 1875.[977]

iii MARY GOSS, b. 21 May 1769; m. 2 Dec 1788, SIMEON BUCK, b. 25 Sep 1768 son of Zebadiah and Mary (Butter) Buck.

iv DANIEL GOSS, b. 20 Feb 1771; d. 18 Sep 1771.

v SARAH GOSS, b. 25 Dec 1772; m. at Amherst, 3 Dec 1797, WILLIAM RAY who has not been identified.

360) EPHRAIM ABBOTT *(Ephraim⁴, Ephraim³, John², George¹)*, b. at Andover, 5 Dec 1742 son of Ephraim and Mary (Abbott) Abbott; d. 1827 at Bedford, NH; m. by 1765, DOROTHY STILES, b. 2 Sep 1740 daughter of Caleb and Sarah (Walton) Stiles.

Deacon Ephraim Abbott lived in Deering, Greenfield, Mont Vernon, and Bedford, New Hampshire.[978]

---

[974] The names of Hill Weeks's parents are given on his death record and on his marriage record for his second marriage to Julia Switzer Spicer.

[975] Peter Goss is listed as a head of household in Amherst in 1790.

[976] Secomb, *History of the Town of Amherst*, p 397

[977] At the time Secomb's *History of Amherst* was written, Anah was the oldest person ever to have lived in Amherst, p 603

[978] Bedford, NH, *History of Bedford*, p 821

Ephraim Abbott and Dorothy Stiles had four children that survived infancy. It is possible that there were two other children, Ephraim and Samuel, who died as infants.

i SARAH ABBOTT, b. about 1767; d. at Antrim, 1848; m. at Amherst, 27 Sep 1793, JONATHAN RAND, b. at Lyndeborough, 24 Jun 1762 son of John and Sarah (Goffe) Rand; Jonathan d. at Antrim, about 1848.[979]

ii DOROTHY ABBOTT, b. at Amherst, about 1775; d. at Windham, NH, about 1822; m. at Manchester, 21 Feb 1816, as his second wife, her third cousin once removed, DAVID ABBOTT *(Solomon⁴, David³, Benjamin², George¹)*, b. at Dracut, 18 May 1775 son of Solomon and Hannah (Colbe) Abbott; David d. at Windham, 1855 (probate 8 Aug 1855). David was first married to Hannah Crosby on 13 May 1797 and third to Sarah McKinley about 1825. David Abbott and his three wives are Family 840.

iii SAMUEL ABBOTT, b. at Mont Vernon, NH, 24 Feb 1777; d. at Antrim, 1853; m. about 1798, SARAH RAND, b. at Bedford, NH, 20 Jan 1774 daughter of John and Sarah (Goffe) Rand; Sarah d. at Antrim, 24 Jun 1852. Samuel was Reverend Samuel Abbott and the inventor of what were known as "Abbott's window shades."[980]

iv EPHRAIM ABBOTT, b. at Goffstown, 1780; d. at Goffstown, 1818; m. at Hopkinton, NH, 25 Jan 1808, OLIVE PEARSON, b. at Hopkinton, 16 Jun 1779 daughter of Noah and Joanna (Bailey) Pearson. After Ephraim's death, Olive married Thomas Stevens Little on 9 Oct 1822.

361) HANNAH ABBOTT *(Ephraim⁴, Ephraim³, John², George¹)*, b. at Andover, 1 Mar 1744 daughter of Ephraim and Mary (Abbott) Abbott; d. unknown; m. *perhaps* NATHANIEL SHATTUCK; the information I have so far is a guess. Nathaniel Shattuck and a wife Hannah had two children in Hollis. The Abbot genealogy gives the name of Hannah's husband as ______ Shattuck of Hollis and I cannot locate a record.

The two children of Nathaniel Shattuck and Hannah (possibly Hannah Abbott) were born at Hollis.

i NATHANIEL SHATTUCK, b. 4 Jun 1768; d. at Monkton, VT, 6 Apr 1843; m. 1st, at Hollis, 28 Apr 1791, HANNAH KEYES, b. at Hollis, 14 Jul 1768 daughter of Abner and Mary (Shedd) Keyes; Hannah d. at Hollis, about 1793. Nathaniel m. 2nd, at Hollis, 13 Nov 1794, SUSANNAH JEWETT, b. at Hollis, 11 Feb 1767 daughter of Jacob and Mehitable (Mitchel) Jewett; Susannah d. at Monkton, 21 Mar 1839.

ii EPHRAIM SHATTUCK, b. 8 Mar 1770

362) KNEELAND ABBOTT *(Ephraim⁴, Ephraim³, John², George¹)*, b. at Andover, 17 May 1748 son of Ephraim and Mary (Kneeland) Abbott; m. BETSEY STANLEY. Kneeland m. 2nd, at Andover, VT, 3 Dec 1813, PHEBE PIERCE.

This family started in New Hampshire, were listed in Hillsborough in 1800, but then in Andover, Vermont in 1810. The Abbot genealogy gives children as Moses, Abiel, Betsy, Sarah, Mary, and Jacob. There is also evidence for Abigail and Kneeland, making a potential of eight children in this family. Records are scant.

i BETSEY ABBOTT, b. 19 Aug 1773; d. at Putney, 5 Apr 1860; m. 1st, 25 Oct 1795, JOEL MILES, b. 3 Jul 1774 son of Abner and Deborah (Underwood) Miles;[981] Joel d. at Putney, 8 Sep 1814. Betsey m. 2nd, at Winchester, NH, 5 Feb 1818, TURNER WHITE,[982] b. at Uxbridge, 4 Dec 1750 son of Ebenezer and Elizabeth (Ellis) White; Turner d. at Winchester, 6 Aug 1836. Turner White was first married to Hannah Holbrook.

ii ABIEL ABBOTT, b. about 1775; d. at Westminster, VT, 2 Nov 1858; m. at Hillsborough, 28 Jan 1798, MARY "POLLY" CLARK. In 1850, he was living in Grafton, Vermont with his nephew Kneeland Abbott (son of Jacob) and his family; Kneeland Abbott had married the daughter of Abiel and Polly, Polly Abbott.

iii KNEELAND ABBOTT, b. about 1780; d. at DeKalb County, IN, about 1846; m. 1st, 1812, LYDIA HILLS, b. at Merrimack, NH, 9 Feb 1790 daughter of Stephen and Beulah (Coburn) Hills. Kneeland m. 2nd, at DeKalb, 26 Dec 1843, MARY WILLIS, b. in CT, about 1822 daughter of Nathaniel and Huldah (-) Willis; Mary d. at Gilead Branch, MI, 4 Nov 1889. Mary was second married to Thomas Crandall Rude on 12 Feb 1849.

iv MOSES ABBOTT

v JACOB ABBOTT, b. about 1782; m. by 1803 possibly to Polly Abbott but that is not yet clear.

vi SARAH ABBOTT

---

979 Cochrane, *History of the Town of Antrim*, p 655

980 Cochrane, *History of Antrim*, p 331

981 Miles, Miles Genealogy: John Miles of Concord

982 Miles, Miles Genealogy: John Miles of Concord

vii MARY ABBOTT

viii ABIGAIL ABBOTT,[983] b. 1791; d. at Andover, VT, 12 Apr 1841; m. at Andover, 22 Feb 1814, EBENEZER FARNSWORTH, b. at Westmoreland, NH, 20 Jun 1791 son of Ebenezer and Martha (Hale) Farnsworth; Ebenezer d. at Andover, 1870. Ebenezer second married Rebecca Howard on 5 Oct 1841.

363) SARAH ABBOTT *(Ephraim[4], Ephraim[3], John[2], George[1])*, b. at Amherst, 14 Jun 1751 daughter of Ephraim and Mary (Kneeland) Abbott; d. at Hillsborough, 22 Jan 1811; m. by 1775, WILLIAM CODMAN, b. 1748 son of William and Sarah (Wilkins) Codman; William d. at Hillsborough, 9 Nov 1813. After Sarah's death, William married Mary (his widow at the time of his death).

William Codman's parents emigrated from Ireland around 1740. William Codman and Sarah Abbott lived first in Amherst, then Deering and finally to Hillsborough where they lived on what was known as Codman Farm.[984]

William Codman did not leave a will and administration of the estate was assigned to eldest son Peter Codman on 4 January 1814 as the widow had declined the administration.[985] Widow Mary Codman was allowed the value of one hundred dollars from the personal inventory for her support 20 August 1814. The personal estate was valued at $194.32 and no inventory of real estate was given. The estate was declared insolvent.

Sarah Abbott and William Codman were parents of seven children.

i WILLIAM CODMAN, b. at Amherst, 1771; d. at Deering, 1811 (probate 18 Jun 1811); m. Mary who is not yet identified.

ii SARAH CODMAN, b. at Amherst, 1773; d. at Deering, about 1799; m. about 1790, ROBERT ALCOCK-AUSTIN, b. at Salem, Nov 1768 son of Robert and Elizabeth (Marong) Alcock;[986] Robert d. at Deering, 7 Sep 1852. After Sarah's death, Robert married Ruth Blaney.

iii PETER CODMAN, b. at Amherst, 20 Apr 1775; d. at Hillsborough, 15 Jan 1857; m. 28 Nov 1805, HANNAH HADLOCK, b. at Deering 26 Nov 1786 daughter of Levi and Elizabeth (Gould) Hadlock; Hannah d. at Hillsborough, 27 Sep 1857.

iv MARY CODMAN, b. about 1779; d. at Hillsborough, Jul 1851; m. at Deering, 3 Feb 1803, DANIEL HOYT, b. at Henniker, about 1783 son of George and Rhoda (Blaisdell) Hoyt;[987] Daniel d. at Hillsborough, Jan 1848.

v ABIGAIL CODMAN, b. about 1781; d. at Bradford, NH, 10 Jun 1825; m. at Hillsborough, 15 Mar 1821, SOLOMON INGALLS, b. at Wilton, 9 Dec 1789 son of David and Anna (Winn) Ingalls; Solomon d. at Nashua, 14 Nov 1876. After Abigail's death, Solomon m. Charlotte McIntire about 1828.

vi MOSES CODMAN, b. at Deering, 24 Jun 1788; d. at Deering 4 Jan 1874; m. 1st, at Henniker, 14 Mar 1816, JANE WALLACE, b. at Henniker, 16 Jan 1791 daughter of William and Hannah (Moore) Wallace; Jane d. at Henniker, 12 Feb 1826. Moses m. 2nd, at Hillsborough, 4 Oct 1829, BETSEY BENNETT, b. 1793; Betsey d. at Hillsborough, 31 Jul 1847. Moses m. 3rd, 19 Feb 1850, JANE ROSS; Jane d. at Francestown, 2 Dec 1879.

vii EPHRAIM CODMAN, b. at Deering, 20 Nov 1789; d. at Hillsborough, 3 Jan 1856; m. 25 Dec 1813, POLLY HADLOCK, b. at Deering, 4 Feb 1793 daughter of Levi and Elizabeth (Gould) Hadlock; Polly d. at Hillsborough, 1 Jul 1873.

364) DORCAS ABBOTT *(Ephraim[4], Ephraim[3], John[2], George[1])*, b. at Amherst, 7 Aug 1752 daughter of Ephraim and Mary (Kneeland) Abbott; d. at Landgrove, VT, 23 Aug 1823; m. by 1775, JOHN WILEY,[988] b. about 1741;[989] John d. at Landgrove, Oct 1824.

John and Dorcas were married in Amherst and their one child seems to have been born there. John Wiley is on the census in Landgrove in 1810.

---

983 Littlefield, *Genealogies of the Early Settlers of Weston*, p 123

984 Browne, *The History of Hillsborough*, p 133

985 New Hampshire, County Probate Records, 1660-1973, Hillsborough, Case 01724; 19:230, 22:217, 18:465, 22:430, 18:500, 14:182

986 Stearns, *Genealogical History of New Hampshire*, p 601 reports that Robert and most of his siblings changed their name from Alcock, most of the siblings becoming Appleton but Robert seems to have used Robert Austin.

987 Browne, *History of Hillsborough*, p 321

988 The History of Amherst reports in one place that Dorcas married John Wiley, and in another place that she married George Wiley. The Abbot Genealogical Register reports her husband as John Wiley.

989 Based on age 83 at time of death.

John Wiley did not leave a will and his estate entered probate 26 April 1825 with David Wiley as administrator. Claims against the estate exceeded its value and the estate was declared insolvent.[990]

There is just one child known for John Wiley and Dorcas Abbott.[991]

i DAVID P. WILEY, b. at Amherst, 10 Aug 1776; d. at Landgrove, 8 Mar 1864; m. 1st, about 1798, BETSEY BATCHELDER, b. 18 Jul 1779 daughter of Ebenezer and Elizabeth (Thompson) Batchelder;[992] Betsey d. at Landgrove, 14 Apr 1818. David m. 2nd, at Rockingham, VT, 21 Jun 1819, SUBMIT WILDER, b. about 1787 possibly the daughter of Jacob and Lydia (Sawyer) Wilder; Submit d. at Landgrove, 22 Jan 1860. Submit was first married to Mr. Fish (she was Mrs. Submit Fish at the time of her marriage to David Wiley).

365) ESTHER ABBOTT *(Ephraim4, Ephraim3, John2, George1)*, b. at Andover, 6 Mar 1755 daughter of Ephraim and Mary (Kneeland) Abbott; d. likely at Montpelier, VT; m. at Amherst, NH, 13 Dec 1781, BENJAMIN PIKE, b. at Dunstable, NH, 1759 son of Benjamin and Elizabeth (Hardy) Pike.[993]

This family was in Amherst and Mont Vernon, New Hampshire and Montpelier, Vermont and the birth dates of most of the children are estimates. There are eight children given in *The Family of John Pike.*

i EPHRAIM PIKE, b. about 1783; d. at Burlington, VT, 20 Mar 1847; m. 10 Sep 1809, NANCY RAY, b. at Mont Vernon, 24 Mar 1791 daughter of James and Mehitable (Woodbury) Ray; Nancy d. at Lamartine, WI, 19 Aug 1866. Two do Ephraim and Nancy's children settled in Wisconsin.

ii MARY "POLLY" PIKE, b. about 1784; m. at Amherst, NH, 10 Jul 1803, JONATHAN MERRILL, b. at Amherst, 25 Jun 1779 son of Benjamin and Elizabeth (Dutton) Merrill.[994]

iii BENJAMIN PIKE, b. about 1785; reported to have lived in Boston and did not have children.

iv JAMES PIKE, b. at Mont Vernon, 1789; d. at Northfield, VT, 1877;[995] m. RHODA JONES, b. at Mont Vernon, 21 May 1790 daughter of Nathan and Esther (Butterfield) Jones.[996]

v ESTHER PIKE, b. about 1790; d. about 1841; m. at New Boston, 8 Oct 1814, ABIEZER WHEELER, b. 17 Oct 1788 son of Aaron and Mary (Knapp) Wheeler; Abiezer d. at Morristown, VT, 15 Apr 1863. After Esther's death, Abiezer Wheeler married Lydia Broad who was the widow of Esther's brother David Pike (see below). Abiezer and Lydia married 2 Mar 1842.

vi ELIZABETH PIKE, b. about 1790. Elizabeth is reported to have married first Mr. Hazelton and second Paul Upham, but records were not located for either of these marriages.[997]

vii ABIGAIL PIKE, b. at East Montpelier, 17 Sep 1791; d. at Marshfield, VT, 24 Dec 1873; m. 13 Dec 1810, EZEKIEL HOLT, b. at Amherst, NH, 19 Aug 1782 son of Ezekiel and Mary (Stewart) Holt; Ezekiel d. at Marshfield, 4 Aug 1845.

viii DAVID PIKE, b. about 1796; d. at East Montpelier, 3 Dec 1830; m. 28 Aug 1816, LYDIA BROAD, b. at Needham, MA, 3 May 1797 daughter of Seth and Azubah (Saunders) Broad;[998] Lydia d. at Montpelier, 5 Jul 1846. Lydia married second Abiezer Wheeler.

366) ABIGAIL ABBOTT *(Ephraim4, Ephraim3, John2, George1)*, b. at Amherst, 30 Jul 1756 daughter of Ephraim and Mary (Kneeland) Abbott; m. 25 Apr 1781, SAMUEL TWISS, b. at Tewksbury, 31 Jan 1755 son of John and Sarah (Patten) Twiss; Samuel d. at New Boston, NH, Oct 1799.

There is little to report for Abigail and her marriage to Samuel Twiss of New Boston, New Hampshire. Samuel died October 1799 when he was struck by a felled tree.[999] In his probate record from January 1800, his widow is Lydia (not Abigail) and the oldest male heir is Peter who is the minor child of Lydia.[1000] Lydia was still living in 1840 as the head of household in

---

990 *Vermont. Probate Court (Manchester District)*; Probate Place: *Bennington, Vermont, Probate Records, Box 77473, Wilcox, James F-Williams, James F, 1791-1935*, Estate of John Wiley, Landgrove, 1825

991 The graves of John and Dorcas Wiley, son David Wiley and his two wives Betsey and Submit are all marked by a single monument at the old Landgrove Cemetery; findagrave: 118312237

992 Pierce, *Batchelder Genealogy*, p 392

993 Pike, *The Family of John Pike of Newbury*, p 130

994 Secomb, *History of the Town of Amherst*, p 698

995 Gregory, *Centennial Proceedings and Historical Incidents of the Early Settlers of Northfield, VT*, p 186

996 Smith, *History of the Town of Mont Vernon*, p 86

997 Pike, *The Family of John Pike of Newbury*, p 130

998 Mason, *The History of Dublin, NH*, p 723

999 Cogswell, *History of New Boston*, p 232

1000 New Hampshire, County Probate Records, 1660-1973, Hillsborough; 24:4, 8:485, 9:3, 9:123, 9:157

New Boston and was age 70-79 at that time. Either Abigail Abbott married a different Samuel Twiss altogether, or she died soon after the marriage and perhaps without having children.

367) DANIEL ABBOTT *(Ephraim⁴, Ephraim³, John², George¹)*, b. at Amherst, 1 Apr 1762 son of Ephraim and Mary (Kneeland) Abbott; d. likely at Cavendish, VT; m. 28 Jul 1786, SARAH STEVENS possibly the daughter of Samuel and Rebecca (Stiles) Stevens.

On 2 October 1810, Daniel and Sally Abbott and their six children were "warned out" of Cavendish, Vermont. "To either constable of Windsor County for Cavendish in said county. . . You are hereby commanded to summon. . . Daniel Abbot and Sally, his wife, Rebecca, Dorothy, Daniel, Charity, Ruth, and Polly their children new and residing in Cavendish to depart said town."

There are six children known for Daniel Abbott and Sarah Stevens. There is a birth record for just the first child; other birthdates are estimated. The younger children may have been born at Chester, Vermont.

i MARY KNEELAND ABBOTT, b. at Goffstown, 31 Oct 1789; d. at Cavendish, VT, 25 Jul 1867; m. at Chester, VT, 12 May 1808, NATHANIEL RUSSELL FARR, b. at New Ipswich, about 1781 son of Nathaniel and Abigail (Foster) Farr; Nathaniel Russell d. at Cavendish, 12 Nov 1840.

ii REBECCA ABBOTT, b. 1791; d. at Lexington, MA, 30 Oct 1849; m. about 1815, DANIEL SNOW, b. in CT, about 1785.

iii RUTH ABBOTT, b. 1793; nothing known after the "warning out" in 1810.

iv DOROTHY DALTON ABBOTT, b. 1795; d. at Weathersfield, VT, 12 Aug 1853; m. 1st, about 1815, SILAS PUTNAM, b. at Ashburnham, 10 Mar 1790 son of Daniel and Keziah (Pollard) Putnam; Silas d. at Chester, VT, 3 May 1848 (probate 11 Jul 1848). Rhoda m. 2nd, at Cavendish, 19 Mar 1850, STEPHEN BAILEY, b. at Andover, VT, 1796 son of Nathaniel and Polly (Baldwin) Bailey; Stephen d. at Cavendish, 11 Aug 1878.

v DANIEL ABBOTT, b. at Chester, 3 Oct 1796; d. at Bethel, 7 Dec 1874; m. about 1818, SARAH LAMPSON, b. 28 Feb 1799;[1001] Sarah d. at Bethel, 18 Sep 1868.

vi CHARITY ABBOTT, b. 1798; nothing further known after the 1810 "warning out".

368) MARY READ *(Mary Abbott Read⁴, Ephraim³, John², George¹)*,[1002] b. at Litchfield 31 May 1748 daughter of Robert and Mary (Abbott) Read; d. by 1792 (date of husband's second marriage); m. by about 1775, BENJAMIN BRADFORD of Hillsborough. Benjamin m. 2nd 21 Dec 1792, Mary "Molly" Mc Adams.

Mary and Benjamin Bradford started their family in Henniker and were in Hillsborough County by 1771 when Benjamin purchased a lot in Society Land.[1003]

In the Revolution during 1777, Benjamin Bradford served as second lieutenant in Captain Peter Clark's Company of Colonel Stickney's Regiment. That company marched from Lyndeborough in July 1777 and joined the Northern Continental Army.[1004] Benjamin received a pension for his service and received his final pension payment in 1830 with a death date given of July 1830.[1005]

There are just two children known for Mary Read and Benjamin Bradford.

i ROBERT READ BRADFORD, b. at Henniker, 1776; m. at Marlow, NH, LYDIA MUNSIL, b. at Marlow, 10 May 1777 daughter of James and Esther (Miller) Munsil.

ii BENJAMIN BRADFORD, b. at Henniker, 19 Mar 1783; m. 6 Apr 1805, MARY HARTWELL, b. at Carlisle, MA, 14 Sep 1787 daughter of Simon and Mary (Hutchins) Hartwell; Mary d. at Nashua, 29 Apr 1872.

369) WILLIAM READ *(Mary Abbott Read⁴, Ephraim³, John², George¹)*, b. 14 Aug 1754 son of Robert and Mary (Abbott) Read; d. at Amherst, NH, 10 Sep 1834;[1006] m. 1st, about 1785, BRIDGET GREELEY, b. at Hudson, NH, 3 Feb 1764 daughter of

---

[1001] Sarah's birth date is given on her death record.
[1002] Browne, *The History of Hillsborough, 1735-1921*, Volume 2, p 82
[1003] Browne, *The History of Hillsborough, 1735-1921*, Volume 2, p 82
[1004] NARA M881. Compiled service records of soldiers who served in the American Army during the Revolutionary War, 1775-1783.
[1005] Index to Selected Final Payment Vouchers, 1818-1864 2 Jul 1830
[1006] Date of death is found in his Revolutionary War pension index

Ezekiel and Eunice (Lovewell) Greeley;[1007] Bridget d. at Amherst, 2 Feb 1789. William m. 2nd 26 Jun 1791, ABIGAIL HOWARD, b. 1771 and d. 15 Jun 1852.

William Read enlisted for service in the Revolutionary War at Amherst in the company of Captain Archelaus Towne. He was promoted to the rank of first corporal. He was in the service until 1 January 1776.[1008] It does not seem that he was involved in any battles. William applied for a pension in 1832 which was granted. His last pension payment was paid in the first quarter of 1835. His widow Abigail received a pension until the fourth quarter of 1852.

William resided in Amherst and served as deputy-sheriff of that town.[1009]

William Read and his first wife Bridget Greeley had one son. There are no children from his second marriage. No probate record was located.

i ROBERT READ, b. at Amherst, 19 Oct 1786; d. at Nashua, NH, 10 Mar 1857;[1010] m. 1st, 15 Dec 1818, REBECCA FRENCH, b. at Dunstable, NH, 5 Jul 1798 daughter of Frederick and Grace (Blanchard) French; Rebecca d. at Nashua, 8 Oct 1836. Robert m. 2nd, at Lowell, 22 Sep 1840, JANE M. LELAND, b. 19 Jan 1809 daughter of Joseph and Dorcas (King) Leland; Jane d. at York County, ME, 10 Aug 1872 although she is buried at Nashua with her husband. An extensive biography of Robert Read can be found in *The History of the Reed Family in Europe and America* starting on page 168.

370) OLIVE READ *(Mary Abbott Read⁴, Ephraim³, John², George¹)*, b. at Hudson, NH, 23 Jul 1757 daughter of Robert and Mary (Abbott) Read; d. at Wilton, NH, 23 Feb 1811; m. at Nottingham, 8 Nov 1779,[1011] SAMUEL GREELEY, b. at Nottingham, 29 Sep 1752 son of Samuel of Abigail (Blodgett) Greeley; Samuel d. at Wilton, 29 Sep 1798.

Olive Read and Samuel Greeley were parents of six children.

i SAMUEL GREELEY, b. at Nottingham, 2 Jul 1783; d. at Swampscott, MA, 16 Oct 1861; m. 1st, 3 May 1812, LYDIA MARIA SEWELL, b. at Marblehead, 14 Apr 1791 daughter of Samuel and Abigail (Devereux) Sewell; Lydia d. at Boston, 11 Aug 1822. Samuel m. 2nd, 19 Oct 1823, LOUISA MAY, b. at Boston, 31 Dec 1792 daughter of Joseph and Dorothy (Sewell) May; Louisa d. at Boston, 14 Nov 1828. Samuel m. 3rd, 18 Oct 1831, MARIA ANTOINETTE PAINE, b. at Boston, 2 Dec 1782 daughter of Robert Treat and Sarah (Cobb) Paine; Maria d. at Boston, 26 Mar 1842. Samuel m. 4th, at Newburyport, 8 Oct 1844, SARAH FOLLANSBEE EMERSON, b. about 1806.

ii NANCY HOLLAND GREELEY, b. at Nottingham, 13 Nov 1784; d. at Hollis, 9 Sep 1833; m. at Chelmsford, 3 Nov 1809, OLIVER SCRIPTURE, b. at Mason, NH, 16 Jun 1783 son of Oliver and Jane (Patterson) Scripture; Oliver d. at Hollis, 7 Nov 1860.

iii AUGUSTUS GREELEY, b. at Wilton, 27 Dec 1787; d. at New York, NY, 19 Aug 1843; m. 20 Dec 1820, CAROLINE CORNELIA LOVETT

iv WILLIAM GREELEY, b. at Wilton, 14 May 1790; d. at Bethany, PA, 20 Sep 1869; m. 1st, at Milton, MA, 30 Nov 1815, JANE FELT, b. at Milton, 28 Aug 1792; Jane d. 8 Nov 1832. William m. 2nd, 6 Jul 1834, OLIVE MESSENGER, b. at Plainfield, NH, 29 Jan 1809; Olive d. at Honesdale, PA, 6 Oct 1886.

v ABIGAIL GREELEY, b. at Wilton, 12 May 1793; d. at Stonington, CT, 3 Mar 1878; m. at New York, NY, 6 Oct 1818, DANIEL ELLIOT, b. at Dublin, NH, 1 Oct 1792 son of David and Lucy (Emery) Elliot; Daniel d. at New York, 30 Mar 1868.

vi ROBERT READ GREELEY, b. at Wilton, 2 Apr 1797; d. at Brooklyn, NY, 31 Mar 1871; m. Dec 1821, HARRIET RAY, b. about 1797.

371) PHEBE ABBOTT *(Joshua⁴, Ephraim³, John², George¹)*, b. at Andover, 31 Aug 1750 daughter of Joshua and Phebe (Ingalls) Abbott; m. about 1770, JOHN EVERDEN; the birth of one child for this couple is recorded at Amherst. John Everden seems to have seen service during the Revolution in Colonel Moses Nichols Regiment that marched from New Hampshire to Rhode Island in August 1778.[1012] There is a John Everden that died 21 Aug 1837 at Winchester, NH but that may not be him.

1007 Bridget's parents are confirmed by the 1793 will of Ezekiel Greeley that includes a bequest to Robert Read, Jr. son of William and his late wife Bridget. Robert Read, Jr. received one-third part of Ezekiel's estate.

1008 Pension application statements, July and August 1832, Amherst, Pension W22049

1009 Reed, *History of the Reed Family in Europe and America*, p 169

1010 Reed, *History of the Reed Family in Europe and America*, p 168

1011 New Hampshire, Marriage Records Index, 1637-1947 (ancestry.com)

1012 "New Hampshire Revolutionary War Records, 1675-1835," database with images, *FamilySearch* (https://familysearch.org/ark:/61903/1:1:Q242-NWWR: accessed 6 February 2018), John Everden, 05 Aug 1778; citing New Hampshire, United States, Archives and Records Management, Concord.

i PHEBE EVERDEN, b. at Amherst, 13 Oct 1770; nothing further known.

372) SARAH ABBOTT *(Joshua⁴, Ephraim³, John², George¹)*, b. at Andover, 19 Feb 1761 daughter of Joshua and Phebe (Ingalls) Abbott; d. at Hopkinton, NY, 5 Jan 1848; m. 29 Jan 1782, AARON NICHOLS, born at Reading, MA, 1757 son of Timothy and Mehitable (Weston) Nichols; Aaron d. at Crown Point, NY, 13 Oct 1821.[1013]

Aaron Nichols served in the Revolution with various periods of enlistment. He reported being int the battles at Lexington and Bunker Hill and enlisted from Amherst, New Hampshire in November 1775 as a private in the company of Captain Taylor in Colonel Reed's regiment. He had another enlistment in January 1776 in Colonel Bedel's New Hampshire regiment. He was taken prisoner at The Cedars on the St. Lawrence River 19 May 1776 and held until 1 June 1776. He returned to his unit for the remainder of the year. He had a subsequent enlistment in the regiment of Colonel Moses Nichols and was at the Battle of Bennington. In his pension application, he reported also serving in the New York militia during the War of 1812 and was at the Battle of Plattsburgh. Aaron, and later his widow Sarah, received a pension related to his service.

Aaron was a wanderer, and after the war lived in "Lyndeborough" Massachusetts, New Andover Vermont, Sudbury Vermont, and finally in Crown Point. From the pension file, we know also the dates of death of Aaron and his wife Sarah. In 1820, the only child at home was son Moses then age 21. Son Aaron lived in Crown Point in 1837 and was a resident of either Hopkinton or Potsdam in St. Lawrence County in 1857.[1014]

Births of eight children of Sarah Abbott and Aaron Nichols were recorded at Sudbury, Vermont.

i SARAH NICHOLS, b. 21 Mar 1783; nothing further known.

ii MEHITABLE NICHOLS, b. 5 Dec 1784; d. at Orwell, VT, 13 Jul 1841; m. 1805, WILLIS ABEL, *likely* b. at Norwich, CT, 11 Jun 1777 son of Isaiah and Rhoda (Pettis) Abel; Willis d. at Orwell, 23 Oct 1866.

iii FRANCES "FANNY" NICHOLS, b. 1 Feb 1787; d. at Sudbury, 8 Dec 1859; m. at Sudbury, 6 Apr 1806, SAMUEL SANDERS, b. at Sudbury, 3 May 1786 son of Asahel and Affia (Rich) Sanders; Samuel d. at Sudbury, 21 Nov 1869.

iv AARON NICHOLS, b. 16 Feb 1789; d. likely at Potsdam, after 1857; m. DILBIE, b. about 1789 who has not been identified; Dilbie d. at Crown Point, 10 Oct 1826.[1015]

v CHARLOTTE NICHOLS, b. 6 May 1791; nothing further known.

vi BETSEY NICHOLS, b. 8 May 1793; nothing further known.

vii TAMSON NICHOLS, b. 8 Jun 1795; d. at Addison, VT, 29 Jan 1817; m. 25 Oct 1815, ASA WATERMAN BARNET, b. 27 Mar 1787 son of Moses and Jerusha (Hyde) Barnet; Asa d. at Crown Point, 4 Apr 1860. Asa married second Jane Baldwin.

viii MOSES NICHOLS, b. 14 Jan 1798; d. at Crown Point, 15 Oct 1820.

373) PETER ABBOTT *(Joshua⁴, Ephraim³, John², George¹)*, b. at Amherst, NH, 28 Jul 1762 son of Joshua and Phebe (Ingalls) Abbott; d. unknown but likely in Oneida County, NY; m. at Amherst, NH, 23 Oct 1788, ABIGAIL FARNUM, b. at Amherst, 27 Dec 1767 daughter of Joseph and Mary (Lyon) Farnum.

Peter and Abigail married at Amherst, but were soon after in Windham, Vermont where the births of seven children are recorded. The family then traveled to what became Annsville, New York in 1806 and at least one more child was born there. Among his sons, Peter and Joshua served in the War of 1812. Sons John F. and Harvey remained in the area of Annsville and Taberg while the other family members moved West.[1016]

i PETER ABBOTT, b. 15 Apr 1789; d. at Annsville, NY, 17 Sep 1868; m. by 1815, SAPPHIRA "SOPHIA" SPINNING, b. at Ashfield, MA, 28 May 1780 daughter of John and Jerusha (Frary) Spinning; Sophia d. at Annsville, 14 May 1865.

1013 Ancestry.com. *New York Pensioners, 1835* [database on-line]. Provo, UT, USA: Ancestry.com Operations Inc, 1998. Aaron Nichols who served in the Revolution in New Hampshire received a pension beginning 30 Apr 1818 in New York. Aaron Nichols is also head of household in the 1820 Census at Crown Point, Essex, NY.

1014 Revolutionary War Pension and Bounty-Land Warrant Application Files

1015 Dilbie "Consort of Aaron Nichols" is buried in the same cemetery location as the elder Aaron Nichols and the son Moses in this family.

1016 Durant, *History of Oneida County, New York*, p 406

ii JOSHUA ABBOTT, b. 14 Apr 1791; d. at Barrington, IL, 10 Jun 1882; m. at Taberg, NY, 29 Dec 1817, EUNICE BABCOCK, b. in NY, about 1796; Eunice d. at Barrington, 8 Apr 1884.[1017]

iii POLLY ABBOTT, b. 12 Aug 1793

iv ABIGAIL ABBOTT, b. 8 Mar 1797

v JOHN F. ABBOTT, b. 25 Jun 1799; d. at Taberg, NY, 31 Jan 1890; m. 1st, about 1820, RHODA who has not been identified; Rhoda b. about 1800 and d. at Taberg, 8 Dec 1857. John m. 2nd, the widow ELLEN CLINTON who was b. about 1825 and d. 1861. John m. 3rd, about 1862, DEBORAH WICKWIRE, b. in NY, about 1814.

vi ERVIN ABBOTT, b. 28 Jan 1802

vii JEFFERSON ABBOTT, b. 15 Jan 1805; d. at Hancock, WI, 21 Mar 1856; m. ELIZA AUGUSTA HITCHCOCK, b. 5 May 1806 daughter of William and Bathsheba (Bartlett) Hitchcock;[1018] Eliza d. 28 Sep 1873 (living in WI in 1870 but interred in Iowa). Jefferson and Eliza lived in Annsville, NY until 1850 and then made the trip to Wisconsin.

viii HARVEY ABBOTT, b. at Annsville, 1810; d. at Watertown, NY, 28 Jan 1886; m. 1833, CHARLOTTE CRANDALL, b. in Stephentown, NY, 20 Mar 1813 daughter of John Dodge and Thankful (Curtis) Crandall;[1019] Charlotte d. at Toberg, 16 Jun 1881.

374) ELIZABETH ABBOTT *(Elizabeth Abbott Abbott^4, Ephraim^3, John^2, George^1)*, b. at Andover, 21 May 1747 daughter of Asa and Elizabeth (Abbott) Abbott; d. by 1802 (when husband married his third wife); m. 30 May 1779 as his 2nd wife, JESSE MANNING, b. at Billerica, 18 Aug 1745 son of Jacob and Martha (Beard) Manning. Jesse m. 3rd Abigail Baldwin; Jesse's first wife was Anne Carleton. Jesse d. at Billerica about 1825 (will probated 1825).

There are no children recorded for Elizabeth and Jesse, and the only two children mentioned in his will are from Jesse's first marriage to Anne Carleton.

375) CALEB ABBOTT *(Elizabeth Abbott Abbott^4, Ephraim^3, John^2, George^1)*, b. at Andover, 28 Oct 1751 son of Asa and Elizabeth (Abbott) Abbott; d. at Andover, 12 Apr 1837; m. 21 Jan 1779, LUCY LOVEJOY, b. 3 Aug 1757 daughter of Isaac and Mary (Peavey) Lovejoy; Lucy d. 21 Feb 1802. Caleb m. 2nd 18 Nov 1802, his third cousin, DEBORAH AMES *(Nathan Ames^4, Hannah Stevens Ames^3, Elizabeth Abbott Stevens^2, George^1)*, b. 6 Apr 1768 daughter of Nathan and Deborah (Bowers) Ames. Deborah died 7 Dec 1819. Deborah Ames was first married to Henry Gray Baker (Family #1192). Caleb married for a third time to Hannah Shattuck Clark daughter of Joseph and Anna (Johnson) Shattuck and widow of Lemuel Clark.

A note about Caleb's parentage: The Abbot genealogy and the Granite State Monthly (volume 9, p 281) both give the parents of Caleb Abbott who married Lucy Lovejoy as Nathan Abbott and Jane Paul. However, Caleb was born, had all his marriages, and died in Andover. Nathan Abbott and Jane Paul lived in New Hampshire. In addition, Caleb died in 1837 with age given at death as 86 making his birth date 1751. Nathan Abbott and Jane Paul did not marry until 1759, their two oldest children were born in Methuen, and the remainder of their children were born in Wilton.

Caleb Abbott did not leave a will, but the probate record specifies that he died 12 April 1837 and that these were his only children living at the time of the probate: Caleb Abbot, Timothy Abbot, Lucy Cummings, Charles Abbot, Gardner Abbot, Elizabeth Valpey (wife of Samuel Valpey), Mary Parker (wife of Carlton Parker), Phebe Saunders (wife of Daniel), Daniel Abbot, and Clarissa Poor (wife of Ebenezer). He left no widow.[1020]

There are records for twelve children of Caleb Abbott and Lucy Lovejoy all born at Andover. The Lovejoy genealogy[1021] reports a thirteenth child for Caleb and Lucy, Samuel Phillips born in 1801. No birth or death record was located for this child, and he was not living at the time of the probate of his father's estate.

i CALEB ABBOTT, b. 10 Nov 1779; d. at Chelmsford, 4 Dec 1846; m. at Chelmsford, 4 Nov 1806, MERCY FLETCHER, b. at Chelmsford, 29 Oct 1782 daughter of Josiah and Mercy (Richardson) Fletcher; Mercy d. at Chelmsford, 8 Feb 1834.

ii TIMOTHY ABBOTT, b. 13 Jan 1781; d. at Andover, 18 Feb 1857; m. at Andover, 7 Sep 1805, JERUSHA YORK, b. about 1773 (based on age 72 at time of death); Jerusha d. at Andover 31 Jan 1845. Her parents are unknown, but the death record transcription notes her name as Jerusha Thurston York.[1022]

[1017] War of 1812 Pension and Bounty Land Warrant Application Files

[1018] Chapin, *The Chapin Book*, p 600

[1019] Crandall, *Elder John Crandall of Rhode Island*, p 123

[1020] *Essex County, MA: Probate File Papers, 1638-1881. Probate of Caleb Abbot, 13 Jan 1838, case number 26.*

[1021] Lovejoy, *The Lovejoy Genealogy*, p 79

[1022] Jerusha [Thurston (York). CR5], w. Timothy, consumption and decay, Jan. 31, 1845, a. 72 y.

iii ORLANDO ABBOTT, b. 20 Nov 1782; d. at Andover, 4 Oct 1834; m. at Bradford, 6 Nov 1829, LYDIA C. WILLIAMS (widow of Peter Kimball)[1023], b. at Yarmouth, about 1800; Lydia d. at Jaffrey, NH, 7 Aug 1888.

iv LUCY ABBOTT, b. 20 Feb 1784; d. at Andover, 25 May 1860; m. at Andover, 27 Nov 1800, SAMUEL CUMMINGS, b. at Topsfield, 10 Sep 1774 son of Samuel and Eunice (Bradstreet) Cummings; Samuel d. at Andover, 8 Jul 1816.

v CHARLES ABBOTT, b. 8 Jan 1786; d. at Andover, 6 Mar 1856; m. at Reading, 9 Apr 1807, DORCAS HART, b. at Reading, 1788 daughter of Asa and Rachel (Flint) Hart; Dorcas d. at Andover, 31 Mar 1847.

vi GARDNER ABBOTT, b. 29 Sep 1787; d. at Andover, 17 Jan 1853; m. 30 Apr 1811, RACHEL HART, b. at Reading, about 1792 daughter of Asa and Rachel (Flint) Hart; Rachel d. at Andover, 2 Apr 1869.

vii DANIEL ABBOTT, b. 15 Jun 1789; d. at Andover, 13 Apr 1796.

viii ELIZABETH ABBOTT, b. 27 Jul 1791; d. at Lawrence, MA, 3 Feb 1880; m. at Andover, 27 Nov 1817, her third cousin, SAMUEL STEVENS VALPEY *(Elizabeth Abbott Valpey⁵, Stephen⁴, Stephen³, John², George¹)*, b. 26 May 1795 son of Abraham and Elizabeth (Abbott) Valpey; Samuel d. at South Lawrence, 22 Jun 1876. Samuel Valpey is a child in Family 331.

ix MARY ABBOTT, b. 25 Mar 1793; d. at Andover, 4 Jun 1858; m. at Andover, 4 Apr 1822, CARLTON PARKER, b. at Mont Vernon, NH, about 1795 son of Robert and Rebecca (Carleton) Parker; Carlton d. at Andover, 18 Jun 1876.

x SAMUEL ABBOTT, b. 28 Jan 1795; d. 14 Apr 1796.

xi PHEBE FOXCROFT ABBOTT, b. 8 Feb 1797; d. at Lawrence, 23 Feb 1888; m. at Andover, 21 Jun 1821, DANIEL SAUNDERS, b. at Salem, NH, 20 Jun 1796 son of James and Betty (Little) Saunders; Daniel d. at Lawrence, 8 Oct 1872.

xii DANIEL ABBOTT, b. 19 Feb 1799; d. at Andover, 9 Feb 1869; m. at Andover, 11 Jan 1827, SARAH FOSTER, b. at Andover, 14 Oct 1800 daughter of Nathan and Susannah (Barker) Foster; Sarah d. at Andover, 12 Feb 1886.

Caleb Abbott and Deborah Ames had two children whose births are recorded at Andover.

i CLARISSA ABBOTT, b. 25 Aug 1803; d. at Lawrence, 31 Jul 1898; m. at Andover, 1 Feb 1825, EBENEZER POOR, b. at Danvers, 24 Mar 1796 son of Joseph and Tamison (Sprague) Poor; Ebenezer d. at Lawrence, 18 Oct 1868.

ii AMELIA "EMILY" ABBOTT, b. 6 Apr 1805; d. at Andover, 1 Sep 1833; m. 28 Apr 1825, DAVID GRAY, b. at Andover, 15 Mar 1798 son of David and Rebecca (Jenkins) Gray; David d. at Andover, 20 Aug 1870. After Amelia's death, David married Sarah Peters.

376) NATHAN ABBOTT *(Elizabeth Abbott Abbott⁴, Ephraim³, John², George¹)*, b. at Andover, 18 Nov 1756 son of Asa and Elizabeth (Abbott) Abbott; d. at Billerica 10 Jan 1840; m. at Danvers, 22 May 1785, MARGARET "Peggy" WILSON, b. at Danvers, 25 Sep 1760 daughter of Benjamin and Lydia (Bancroft) Wilson; Margaret d. 21 Dec 1841.

Nathan and Peggy started their married life in Danvers but relocated to Billerica about 1795. When a new meeting house was constructed there in 1797, the pews were sold to raise money to pay for the building. Nathan Abbott paid $120.25 for his pew.[1024]

Nathan and Peggy had eight children, the births of the first four recorded at Danvers and the youngest four children at Billerica.

i ELIZABETH ABBOTT, b. 24 Feb 1786; d. at Chelmsford, 3 Apr 1883; m. 1st, 6 Sep 1807, EDWARD H. RUSSELL, described as "of Townsend"; Edward died at Townsend, 1826 (date of probate). Elizabeth m. 2nd, 3 May 1829 at Tyngsborough, GEORGE FREDERICK, b. about 1765 and d. at Tyngsborough, 9 Feb 1844.

1023 Morrison, History of the Kimball Family, p 519, reports her maiden name as Lydia Williams; however, the death record of one of her sons lists her maiden name as Lydia Allen.
1024 Hazen, History of Billerica, 9 263

ii MARTHA ABBOTT, b. 17 Jan 1788; d. at Waltham, 23 May 1875; m. at Billerica, 7 Apr 1825, LEONARD CUSHING, b. at Waltham, 30 Jan 1796 son of Wareham and Lucy (Harrington) Cushing; Leonard d. at Waltham, 24 Feb 1867.

iii NATHAN ABBOTT, b. 7 Feb 1790; d. at Billerica, 25 Dec 1864; m. at Billerica, 10 Nov 1825, HANNAH FARMER, b. at Billerica, 17 May 1785 daughter of Oliver and Hannah (-) Farmer; Hannah d. at Lowell, 26 Dec 1878.

iv LYDIA ABBOTT, b. 9 Aug 1792; d. at Peabody, 22 Jan 1873; m. at Roxbury, 7 Mar 1819, NATHANIEL STEVENSON, b. about 1788, Nathaniel d. at Lynn, 2 Mar 1839.

v SOPHRONIA ABBOTT, b. 20 Jun 1795; d. at Peabody, 25 Aug 1879; m. at Billerica, 26 Dec 1819, ASA BUSHBY, b. at South Danvers, 23 Jun 1792 son of Asa and Lydia (Wilson) Bushby; Asa d. at Danvers, 18 Jun 1862.

vi JUDITH ABBOTT, b. 14 Mar 1797; d. at Chelmsford, 10 Sep 1870; m. at Billerica, 3 Oct 1824, LEVI FELTON, b. at Marlboro, 17 Jan 1799 son of Levi and Susanna (Hunt) Felton; Levi d. at Westford, 21 Oct 1829.

vii ASENATH ABBOTT, b. 17 Jul 1801; d. at Danvers, 29 Mar 1859. Asenath did not marry and did not leave a will. However, at the probate of her estate, each of her heirs (seven siblings) received a distribution of $292. These heirs were Elisabeth Fredrick, Martha and Leonard Cushing, Nathan Abbott, Sophronia Bushby, Judith Felton, Lydia Stevenson, and Henry and Mary Bushby.[1025]

viii MARY ABBOTT, b. 15 Aug 1804; d. at Peabody, 8 May 1876; m. at Danvers, 24 Feb 1830, HENRY BUSHBY, b. at Danvers, 9 Mar 1805 son of Asa and Lydia (Wilson) Bushby; Henry d. at Peabody 2 Oct 1883.

377) HANNAH ABBOTT *(Josiah⁴, Ephraim³, John², George¹)*, b. at Amherst, 18 Sep 1755 daughter of Josiah and Hannah (Hobbs) Abbott; d. at Lyndeborough, NH 25 Sep 1784;[1026] m. by 1775, SAMUEL CHAMBERLAIN, b. at Chelmsford, 4 Apr 1745 son of Jonathan and Elizabeth (Cram) Chamberlain. Samuel m. 2nd 8 Nov 1785, Naomi Richardson; Samuel d. about 1812 at Lyndeborough.[1027]

Samuel Chamberlain enlisted 7 December 1776 in Captain William Walker's company and served three months in Fishkill. He had additional service in the regiment of Colonel Samuel McConnell.[1028]

Samuel and Hannah Chamberlain had five children born at Lyndeborough.

i HANNAH CHAMBERLAIN, b. 28 Apr 1775; d. at Greenfield, NH after 1850 (seems to be listed in the 1850 Census); m. at Hancock, Nov 1801, JONATHAN BURNHAM, origins unknown; Jonathan died at Greenfield, 1827 (probate 5 Jun 1827).[1029]

ii ELIZABETH CHAMBERLAIN, b. 20 May 1777; d. 13 Jun 1780.

iii SAMUEL CHAMBERLAIN, b. 4 May 1779; death not known but thought to be in Ohio or Michigan; m. 1st about 1809, OLIVE whose identity is not known. Olive died about 1818. Samuel m. 2nd, 6 May 1819, HEPHZIBAH RUSSELL, b. at 28 Oct 1783 daughter of Jedediah and Rhoda (Pratt) Russell. Hannah Russell was first married to Herman Ladd Sargent.

iv AMY CHAMBERLAIN, b. 14 Feb 1781; d. at Lyndeborough, 15 Jan 1850. Amy did not marry.

v BETSEY CHAMBERLAIN, b. 18 Apr 1783; d. at Lyndeborough, 26 Dec 1853. Betsey did not marry.

378) LEMUEL ABBOTT *(Josiah⁴, Ephraim³, John², George¹)*, b. at Amherst, 13 May 1764 son of Josiah and Hannah (Hobbs) Abbott; d. at Windham, VT 19 Jan 1840;[1030] m. by 1799, DEBORAH BALCH, b. at Dublin, NH, 13 Nov 1780 daughter of Hart and Dorcas (Somers) Balch; Deborah d. at Windham, 15 Sep 1862.

Lemuel Abbott and Deborah Balch were parents of seven children born at Windham, Vermont.

i LEMUEL ABBOTT, b. 3 Apr 1799; d. at Windham, 2 Aug 1868; m. 1st, 24 Feb 1825, FANNY SHERWIN, b. at Windham, 4 Apr 1800 daughter of Timothy and Jemima (Herrick) Sherwin; Fanny d. at Windham, 5 Dec 1841. Lemuel m. 2nd, at Weston, VT, 26 Oct 1843, MARY TEMPLE, b. in NH, about 1813; Mary d. at Windham, 2 Dec 1849. Lemuel m. 3rd, about 1850, SARAH who is perhaps Sarah Shattuck.

[1025] *Essex County, MA: Probate File Papers, 1638-1881. Probate of Aseneth Abbott, 29 Mar 1859, case number 30819.*

[1026] *New Hampshire: Births, Deaths and Marriages, 1654-1969.* (From microfilmed records. Online database: *AmericanAncestors.org*, New England Historic Genealogical Society, 2014.)

[1027] Donovan, *The History of the Town of Lyndeborough, NH*, volume II, p. 180

[1028] Donovan, *History of Lyndeborough*, volume I, p 180

[1029] Probate includes the set-off of the dower to widow Hannah. Hillsborough County, NH probate records, volume 30 p 523 and volume 35 p 480.

[1030] Ancestry.com. Vermont, Vital Records, 1720-1908

ii HART BALCH ABBOTT, b. 29 Dec 1800; d. at Windham, 1865 (probate 29 Jun 1865); m. about 1827, ELIZABETH MORSE, b. in MA, about 1806; Elizabeth d. after 1870.

iii SALLY ABBOTT, b. 17 Nov 1802; d. at Marlboro, VT, 16 Mar 1878; m. at Newfane, VT, 7 Feb 1852, EBENEZER PERSONS, b. at Windham, 1797 son of George and Abigail (Amidon) Persons; Ebenezer d. at South Newfane, 16 Jul 1889. Ebenezer was first married to Laura Gile who died in 1850.

iv LUCIUS ABBOTT, b. 3 Feb 1805; d. at South Londonderry, VT, 25 Jan 1891; m. at Windham, 30 Mar 1834, ESTHER WAITE GODDARD, b. at Windham, 21 Aug 1814 daughter of Enoch and Esther (Bliss) Goddard; Esther d. at New York, NY, 30 Aug 1900.

v LUCIA ABBOTT, b. 5 Aug 1807; d. at Windham, 1 Mar 1889; m. about 1830, JOHN FARNSWORTH, b. 1805 son of Isaac and Lydia (Wood) Farnsworth; John d. at Windham, 10 Jan 1895.

vi MARCIUS ABBOTT, b. 1 Dec 1809; d. at Montrose, NY, 25 Jun 1858; m. about 1840, ELIZABETH GRIGGS, b. at New York, 10 Jun 1817; Elizabeth d. at Montrose, 15 Feb 1890.

vii MARCIA ABBOTT, b. 26 Nov 1811. Marcia is believed to have married, about 1835, HENRY GARLICK SHERWOOD[1031], b. at Kingsbury, NY, 20 Apr 1785 son of Newcomb Sherwood; Henry d. at San Bernardino, CA, 24 Nov 1867. If Marcia did in fact marry Henry Sherwood, it is not known when she died. She was not living with him in 1850.

379) DANIEL ABBOTT *(Josiah⁴, Ephraim³, John², George¹)*, b. at Amherst, 31 Jul 1769 son of Josiah and Hannah (Hobbs) Abbott; d. at Westford, MA,[1032] 27 Jan 1854; m. 5 Jul 1798, SARAH ALLISON, b. at Londonderry, 12 Dec 1770 daughter of Samuel and Janet (McFarland) Allison; Sarah d. in New York, 22 Nov 1837.[1033]

Daniel Abbott was a grocer in New York. Daniel Abbott and Sarah Allison were parents of five children.

i Son, b. and d. May 1799

ii JANE ABBOTT, b. at Peterborough, 30 Sep 1800; d. at Brooklyn, NY, Sep 1880; m. 24 Aug 1842, as his second wife, JOHN SCOTT, b. at Peterborough, 18 Feb 1797 son of William and Catherine (Ames) Scott; John d. at Detroit, MI, 1 Sep 1846. John was first married to Sally Knowland.

iii SARAH ALLISON ABBOTT, b. recorded at Newburyport, 3 Nov 1806; d. at Rutherford, NJ, 13 Oct 1887; m. 6 May 1830, JEFFERSON FLETCHER, b. at Westford, MA, 14 Apr 1802 son of Thomas and Patty (Jewett) Fletcher; Jefferson d. at Westford, 17 Jul 1852.

iv DANIEL ABBOTT, baptized at Newburyport, Apr 1808; d. at New York, NY, 2 Sep 1854; m. 1st, 15 Feb 1838, DOROTHY EVANS CUTTER, b. at Jaffrey, NH, 20 Sep 1809 daughter of William Pope and Prudence (Evans) Cutter;[1034] Dorothy d. at New York, 19 Nov 1842. Daniel m. 2nd the widow Charlotte Foster.

v JOHN ABBOTT, b. 24 Jun 1810; d. at Monroe, MI, 30 Nov 1834; m. at Monroe, 2 Jan 1834, PAMELIA BEACH, b. at Middlebury, VT, about 1816 daughter of Hiland and Lydia (Beach) Beach; Pamelia d. at Adrian, MI, 28 Nov 1883. After John's death, Pamelia married James Murray.

380) SARAH ABBOTT *(Josiah⁴, Ephraim³, John², George¹)*, b. likely at Lyndeborough, 24 Apr 1773 daughter of Josiah and Hannah (Hobbs) Abbott; d. at Cameron, NY 12 Jun 1870;[1035] m. 19 Feb 1794, ENOCH ORDWAY, b. at Lyndeborough, 4 Aug 1762 son of John and Frances (Chase) Ordway; Enoch d. at Greenwood, NY 8 Jan 1843.

Sarah and Enoch started their family life in Lyndeborough, and all their children were born there. Around 1828, they made the move to Greenwood in Steuben County, New York. Enoch acquired a property along the creek at Greenwood. His two sons-in-law, Ezra Lovejoy and Huse Karr, settled in the same area.[1036]

1031 Josephsmithpapers.org, "Henry Garlick Sherwood" https://www.josephsmithpapers.org/person/henry-garlick-sherwood

1032 In 1850, Daniel was living with his daughter Sarah and her husband Jefferson Fletcher in Wetford.

1033 Morrison, *A History of the Alison Family*, p 63

1034 Cutter, *History of the Town of Jaffrey*, p 282

1035 In the 1870 U.S. Census, 97-year-old Sarah Ordway was living with her son Daniel and his wife Hannah. Year: 1870; Census Place: Cameron, Steuben, New York; Roll: M593_1094; Page: 506A; Family History Library Film: 552593

1036 Clayton, *History of Steuben County*, p 302

i SARAH ORDWAY, b. 27 May 1795; d. at Lyndeborough, 18 May 1826; Sarah m. 27 Dec 1821, HUSE KARR, b. at Lyndeborough, 28 Mar 1798 son of James and Sarah (Huse) Karr. In 1832, Huse remarried to Susannah Pickle and went back in Lyndeborough where he died 5 Apr 1879.[1037]

ii MARY ORDWAY, b. 13 Aug 1800; d. at Hornellsville, NY, Mar 1880; m. at Lyndeborough, 27 Dec 1821, her fourth cousin and George Abbott descendant, EZRA LOVEJOY, b. at Wilton, 2 Mar 1794 son of Henry and Elizabeth (Cummings) Lovejoy; Ezra d. at Hornellsville after 1880 (living at the 1880 Census). Ezra's parents are covered in Family #787.

iii ENOCH ORDWAY, b. 29 Jan 1803; d. at Canisteo, NY, 3 Jul 1882; m. about 1830, REBECCA MOORE, b. at Canisteo, 1801 daughter of James Moore; Rebecca d. at Canisteo, Jun 1870.

iv DANIEL ORDWAY, b. 15 Mar 1807; d. at Cameron, NY, 3 Jan 1881; m. 20 Nov 1832, HANNAH LOOMIS, b. at Tolland, 28 Jun 1810 daughter of Elisha and Eunice (Hatch) Loomis; Hannah d. at Cameron, 3 Jan 1881.

v ANNE J. ORDWAY, b. 8 Aug 1812; d. 4 Feb 1813.

381) HANNAH ABBOTT *(Ebenezer⁴, Ephraim³, John², George¹)*, b. at Andover, 27 Jun 1752 daughter of Ebenezer and Lydia (Farrington) Abbott; d. at Andover, 24 Jul 1816; m. 18 Sep 1777, ABIJAH CLARK, b. at Tewksbury, 11 May 1742 son of Nathaniel and Mary (Wyman) Clark;[1038] Abijah d. at Andover, 25 May 1818.

Abijah Clark was a farmer who came from Tewksbury to Andover and settled on property that he purchased from Nehemiah Abbott

In his will written 27 October 1814 (probate 7 October 1818), Abijah Clark bequeathed to beloved wife Hannah all the household stuff and furniture proper for woman's use. Son Nathan is to meet all his mother's needs in health and sickness as long as she remains a widow. If Nathan refuses any of his duties in her care, then Hannah shall have the improvement of as much of the real estate as is sufficient for her comfortable maintenance. Eldest and beloved son Abijah receives one hundred dollars to be paid to him from the estate by Nathan. Son John receives six hundred dollars in part wages for his services and for his part of the estate. Beloved son Nathan receives all the real and personal estate. Beloved daughters Hannah and Lydia receive fifty dollars. Beloved daughter Mary receives two hundred dollars and a privilege in the dwelling house as long as she is unmarried. Son Nathan was named executor.[1039] Real estate was valued at $3,474 and personal estate at $872.25.

Hannah Abbott and Abijah Clark were parents of six children all born at Andover.

i HANNAH CLARK, b. 12 Aug 1778; d. at North Reading, 22 Feb 1857; m. at Andover, 18 Mar 1806, NATHANIEL HAYWARD, b. at Reading, 1781 son of Jabez and Abigail (Graves) Hayward; Nathaniel d. at Medford, 3 Nov 1860.

ii ABIJAH CLARK, b. 30 Aug 1780; d. after 1818 (living at probate of father's estate) reportedly in New York.[1040]

iii JOHN CLARK, b. 20 Jul 1782; d. at Carlisle, MA, 15 Aug 1847; m. at Andover, 13 Nov 1834, as her second husband, LYDIA FROST, b. at Tewksbury, 22 Feb 1801 daughter of Aaron and Susannah (Sterns) Frost; Lydia d. at Lowell, 30 Jan 1879. Lydia was first married to Samuel Upton.

iv NATHAN CLARK, b. 16 May 1784; d. at Andover, 2 Apr 1869; m. at Andover, 30 Jan 1823, PERSIS FARNUM, b. at North Andover, 6 Mar 1799 daughter of Isaac and Persis (Stevens) Farnum; Persis d. at Andover, 17 Oct 1880.

v LYDIA CLARK, b. 17 Jul 1788; d. at Brooklyn, Apr 1852; m. at Andover, 24 Nov 1811, her fourth cousin, NATHAN AMES *(Benjamin Ames⁵, Benjamin Ames⁴, Hannah Stevens Ames³, Elizabeth Abbott Stevens², George¹)*, b. at Andover, 7 May 1787 son of Benjamin and Phebe (Chandler) Ames. Nathan Ames is a child in Family 1185.

vi MARY CLARK, b. 25 Nov 1790; d. at Andover, 13 Jun 1872. Mary did not marry. Mary left an estate valued at $3,000. Her will includes several legacies to nieces and nephews and grandnieces and grandnephews.

382) EBENEZER ABBOTT *(Ebenezer⁴, Ephraim³, John², George¹)*, b. at Andover, 15 Jan 1757 son of Ebenezer and Lydia (Farrington) Abbott; d. at Reading 1803; m. 21 Oct 1783, SARAH GRAVES, b. at Reading, Mar 1765 daughter of Daniel and Sarah (-) Graves. Sarah remarried to Lieutenant William Flint in 1804 and died at Reading, 2 Mar 1809.

Ebenezer Abbott was a cordwainer in Reading. During the Revolution, he served as a private in the Massachusetts militia.

[1037] New Hampshire, Death and Burial Records Index, 1654-1949

[1038] Andover Mass. In the Year 1863, Essex Historical Collections, 1913, p 59

[1039] Essex County, MA: Probate File Papers, 1638-1881.Online database. AmericanAncestors.org. New England Historic Genealogical Society, 2014. Case 5405

[1040] Essex Institute Historical Collections

In his will written 10 December 1802 (probate 26 April 1803), Ebenezer bequeathed to beloved wife Sarah all the personal estate and real estate in Reading and Lynnfield, all the household furniture, all the tools, and the notes and bank accounts with Sarah to pay all the other legacies in the will. Children Ebenezer, Ephraim, Eliab, Sally, Daniel, Lydia, Abigail, and Joshua are each to receive one dollar when they reach age twenty-one. Wife Sarah was named executrix.[1041]

Ebenezer Abbott and Sarah Graves were parents of nine children born at Reading.

i EBENEZER ABBOTT, b. 11 Mar 1784; d. at North Reading, 1867; m. 9 Apr 1807, BETSY SWAIN, b. at Reading, 22 Jan 1787 daughter of John and Lois (Walton) Swain; Betsy d. at Reading, 10 Aug 1852.

ii EPHRAIM ABBOTT, b. 11 Feb 1786. No clear information for Ephraim has been found. He may be the Ephraim Abbott who died at Brentwood, NH, 17 Oct 1870.

iii SALLY ABBOTT, b. 7 Feb 1798; d. 1799.

iv ELIAB ABBOTT, b. 30 Jan 1790. On 8 Jun 1812, 22-year-old Eliab enlisted from Reading as a private in the Company of Captain Chester. He was at Burlington, Vermont 13 Mar 1813 and discharged 11 Dec 1813 as his term had expired.[1042] Nothing further known.

v SALLY ABBOTT, b. 14 May 1792; d. at Salem, MA, 5 Mar 1873; m. at Danvers, 8 Oct 1815, NATHAN PEARSON, b. at Dunstable, NH, 12 Aug 1788 son of Thomas and Amy (Spaulding) Pearson; Nathan d. at Salem, 22 Feb 1863.

vi DANIEL ABBOTT, b. 2 Aug 1794; d. at Reading, 31 Jul 1851; m. at Lynn, 1 Jan 1821, ANNIS JANES (widow of Abraham Walsh), b. at Salem, 8 Jul 1792 daughter of Joseph and Annis (Orne) Janes; Annis d. at Lynn, 25 Jul 1868.

vii LYDIA ABBOTT, b. 30 Jun 1796; d. at Danvers, Apr 1852; m. at Danvers, 22 Apr 1819, ROBERT SHILLABER DANIELS, b. at Danvers, 13 Sep 1791 son of David and Elizabeth (Shillaber) Daniels; Robert d. at Danvers, 10 Nov 1865. After Lydia's death, Robert married Judith D. P. Russell on 29 Jul 1862.

viii ABIGAIL ABBOTT, b. 2 Apr 1799; d. at Danvers, 9 Sep 1888; m. at Danvers, 29 Dec 1825, as his second wife, LEVI PRESTON, b. at Danvers, 5 Dec 1783 son of Levi and Mehitable (Nichols) Preston; Levi d. at Peabody, MA, 25 Mar 1867. Levi was first married to Rebecca Felton.

ix JOSHUA ABBOTT, b. 15 Jul 1801; living in 1803 but nothing further known.

383) EPHRAIM ABBOTT *(Ebenezer⁴, Ephraim³, John², George¹)*, b. at Andover, 18 Mar 1759 son of Ebenezer and Lydia (Farrington) Abbott; d. 1 Jan 1834 at Sherbrooke, Québec; m. at Conway, NH, 18 Dec 1781, ESTHER EASTMAN of Conway, b. 6 May 1761 daughter of Richard and Mary (Lovejoy) Eastman; Esther d. at Sherbrooke, Québec, 30 Dec 1846.[1043]

Ephraim Abbott enlisted from Andover October 1775 as a private in Colonel Enoch Poor's Regiment of the Massachusetts line. His regiment was in New London, New York, Albany, Crown Point, and St. Johns. Ephraim became ill and was sent home October 1776. He enlisted again in 1777 for three months and served in New Jersey. He had an enlistment in April 1778 in the Continental line and in 1780 a further enlistment in the militia. He was present at the capture of Burgoyne. He was credited with eighteen months of service and received a pension for his service which was continued by his widow Esther.[1044]

In his pension application of 1832, Ephraim stated he was born in Andover, moved to Conway, New Hampshire when he was about 21 years old, remained there for about twenty years and then relocated to Eaton, Lower Canada.

Ephraim and Esther were parents of perhaps eleven children, although there are birth records for three children. The oldest nine children were likely born at Conway and the two youngest children at Eaton. The children who married all married in Eaton or Ascot.

i ESTHER ABBOTT, b. 29 Aug 1782; d. at Cookshire,[1045] Québec, 18 Aug 1869; m. about 1802, JOHN COOK, b. at Wallingford, CT, 20 Nov 1770 son of David and Lois (Moss) Cook; John d. at Eaton, 28 May 1819.

1041 Middlesex County, MA: Probate File Papers, 1648-1871.Online database. AmericanAncestors.org. New England Historic Genealogical Society, 2014. Case 16

1042 U.S. Army, Register of Enlistments, 1798-1914

1043 Québec, Canada, Vital and Church Records (Drouin Collection), 1621-1968 (ancestry.com)

1044 Revolutionary War Pension and Bounty-Land Warrant Application Files

1045 Cookshire-Eaton is the present name

ii POLLY ABBOTT, b. 23 May 1784; d. at Massena, NY, 1859; m. 1804, SAMUEL BRIGHAM HUDSON, b. 1777 son of Elisha and Susanna (Brigham) Hudson; Samuel d. 1853.

iii ANNA ABBOTT, b. 1785; d. at Phelps, NY, 6 May 1822; m. at Eaton, Nov 1807, CHARLES HUDSON, b. in MA, 7 Apr 1785 son of Elisha and Susanna (Brigham) Hudson; Charles d. at Arcadia, NY, after 1850.

iv LYDIA ABBOTT, b. about 1790; nothing further known.

v SUSAN ABBOTT, b. 1792; d. at Stanstead, 13 Jan 1840; m. at Ascot, 1824, JOSEPH GRIFFIN, b. about 1790.

vi SARAH ABBOTT, b. about 1793; d. at Québec, after 1861; m. about 1811, CHARLES WARD, b. 26 Aug 1790 son of Henry and Priscilla (Bixby) Ward; Charles d. at Stanstead, before 1851.

vii PATTI ABBOTT, b. about 1794; nothing further known.

viii SOPHIA ABBOTT, b. 1795; d. at Stanstead, 17 May 1887; m. 1st, at Eaton, 21 Mar 1820, HIRAM WILCOX, b. 1795; Hiram d. at Ascot, 25 Aug 1820. Sophia m. 2nd, about 1822, JOHN CHAMBERLAIN, b. about 1788; John d. at Stanstead, 24 Nov 1847. Sophia m. 3rd, 1850, ALVIN FLINT, b. at Westmoreland, NH, 4 Aug 1786 son of Jonas and Eunice (Gardner) Flint; Alvin d. at Stanstead, 6 Feb 1862. Alvin Flint was married to Joanna Barney.

ix EBENEZER ABBOTT, b. 23 Aug 1800; d. at Saratoga, MN, 23 Oct 1890; m. about 1827, CAROLINE CASWELL, b. at Eaton, 11 Oct 1807 daughter of Apthorp and Amarilla (Holden) Caswell; Caroline d. at Oshawa, Ontario, 1853.

x PHEBE ABBOTT, b. about 1802; d. in VT, 16 Jan 1851; perhaps m. at Ascot, 1825, HORACE BLODGETT.

xi SAMUEL EASTMAN ABBOTT, b. 1804; d. at Sand Hill, Québec, 11 Feb 1872; m. 1827, SALLY CHASE, b. Dec 1806; Sally d. at Sand Hill, 25 Jan 1867.

384) SARAH ABBOTT, b. at Andover, 7 Dec 1765 daughter of Ebenezer and Lydia (Farrington) Abbott; d. at Springfield, OH, 1856;[1046][1047] m. 28 Dec 1784, her third cousin, DAVID STEVENS, b. 3 Feb 1761 son of Thomas and Sarah (Gray) Stevens; David d. at Andover, 29 Jan 1834.

David Stevens served in the Revolutionary War and received a pension of $96 per year. He was a wheelwright. He struggled with alcoholism and a guardian was appointed for him in 1819 due to drunkenness and being a spendthrift. Joseph Holt, Jr. was named his guardian. This guardianship continued until David's death in 1834.[1048]

David Stevens enlisted from Andover as a private 5 July 1779 and was discharged 10 April 1780. He served in Colonel Tupper's Massachusetts Continental Regiment of Foot Soldiers and marched to West Point.[1049]

David Stevens and Sarah Abbott were parents of seven children born at Andover.

i DAVID STEVENS, b. 27 Jul 1784; d. 26 Jun 1794.

ii EBENEZER STEVENS, b. 25 Aug 1787; d. at Mt. Wealthy, OH, 11 Jun 1857; m. at Topsfield, MA, 10 Feb 1811, LUCY HERRICK, b. at Boxford, 11 Mar 1790 daughter of Edmund and Mehitable (Curtice) Herrick; Lucy d. at Mt. Healthy, 2 Feb 1883.

iii EPHRAIM STEVENS, b. 2 Feb 1790; nothing further known.

iv JACOB STEVENS, b. 26 Jul 1792; d. at Cincinnati, 10 Oct 1874; m. at Medway, MA, 10 Sep 1823, OLIVE BEALS, b. at Medfield, 25 Feb 1800 daughter of Asa and Olive (Cheney) Beals; Olive d. at Cincinnati, 10 May 1879.

v DAVID STEVENS, b. 9 Oct 1794; nothing further known.

vi SARAH STEVENS, b. 26 Apr 1797; nothing further known.

vii HERMAN ABBOT STEVENS, b. 18 Oct 1802; d. at Cincinnati, 14 Apr 1881; m. about 1829, SARAH W. BEAZY,[1050] b. at Freedom, ME, Jun 1800; Sarah d. at Cincinnati, 8 Apr 1871.

1046 Sarah was still living at the time of the probate of her husband's estate. Sarah traveled to Ohio to live with her son Ebenezer and his wife Lucy Herrick and was living with them in 1850.

1047 The Revolutionary War pension file of David Stevens includes an 1855 statement of widow Sarah Stevens who was then living in Hamilton County, Ohio.

1048 Essex County, MA: Probate File Papers, 1638-1881.Online database. AmericanAncestors.org. New England Historic Genealogical Society, 2014. Case 26319, Case 26320, Case 26321

1049 Revolutionary War Pension and Bounty-Land Warrant Application Files, 1800-1900 Case W 4823

1050 The name of Sarah's parent is given as "Beazy" on the cemetery record as well as the place of birth as Freedom, Maine.

385) PETER ABBOTT *(Peter⁴, Ephraim³, John², George¹)*, b. at Andover, 22 Jun 1758 son of Peter and Elizabeth (widow Damon)[1051] Abbott; d. at Chester, NH Nov 1828;[1052] m. 7 Mar 1782, PHEBE SPRATT[1053] who was "of Deerfield" but parents not located; Phebe d. at Chester 16 Feb 1846.

Peter Abbott served as a private in Colonel Poor's Regiment of the New Hampshire line.[1054] He received a pension of eight dollars per month. He enlisted in January 1776 for three years and was discharged January 1779. He was at the Battles of Saratoga, Stillwater, and Monmouth. In a statement made 17 August 1820 as part of his pension application, Peter reported that he worked as a laborer in agriculture but was unable to work due to his feeble health. At that time, his wife was age seventy-two and sickly. He reported a personal estate with a value of $22.

Peter Abbott did not leave a will and his estate entered probate 7 May 1829 when Jesse Mills, as the main creditor of the estate, petitioned the Court as the widow and heirs had not assumed administration of the estate.[1055] Phebe Abbott did not leave a will. The probate court noted that the next of kin did not assume administration of her estate and Stephen Palmer was named administrator. The record includes a statement that she was a pension recipient and a small number of claims against the estate for labor and groceries.[1056]

Peter and Phebe were parents of seven children, the older two children born at Kingston, New Hampshire and the younger children born perhaps at Chester. Little is known of the children in the family.

i EDMUND ABBOTT, b. 11 Nov 1782

ii PETER GRAGG ABBOTT, b. 5 Dec 1785; d. at Kingston, 1867. Peter does not seem to have married, although he may be the Peter Abbott that married Susanna Stinson (widow of Thomas Mills) in Chester in 1805.

iii HENRY ABBOTT, b. about 1788

iv CALVIN ABBOTT, b. about 1790

v GEORGE ABBOTT, b. about 1792

vi HANNAH ABBOTT, b. about 1794

vii JOHN ABBOTT, b. 3 May 1797; d. at Kingston, NH, 3 Apr 1860; m. at Brentwood, NH, 13 Dec 1825, DEBORAH WIGGIN, b. in MA, about 1805 perhaps the daughter of Barker and Deborah (Brackett) Wiggin; Deborah d. after 1850.

386) ARCHELAUS TOWNE *(Martha Abbott Towne⁴, Ephraim³, John², George¹)*, b. perhaps at Monson or Amherst, 13 Jul 1760 son of Archelaus and Martha (Abbott) Towne; d. at Hillsborough, 8 Jul 1818; m. 22 Sep 1787, ESTHER WESTON, b. at Amherst 7 Jul 1763 daughter of Ebenezer and Esther (Kendall) Weston; Esther d. 6 Apr 1850 at Amherst.

Archelaus and Esther resided in Hillsborough where Archelaus was a farmer.

Archelaus Towne served as a private during the Revolution in Colonel Bridge's Regiment for an eight-month term. He served in the area of Cambridge and was at the Battle of Bunker Hill. After the initial enlistment, he served another two years and was at the Battle of Ticonderoga.[1057] Widow Esther received a pension of $33.33 per half-year.[1058]

In Archelaus Towne's will written 24 May 1816 (proved 18 August 1818), well beloved wife Esther receives the use of one cow and one horse as long as she remains a widow and the use of one full third of all the real estate during her life and the household furniture and the wearing apparel to be entirely at her use and disposal. Son Ebenezer is named executor and he receives all the lands, stock, and farming tools. Of his six daughters, he gives Lucy nothing further as she received one hundred seventy dollars at her marriage. The other five daughters namely Esther, Patty, Polly, Harriet, and Mehitable will each receive one hundred seventy dollars at their respective marriages or at age twenty-three if they do not marry. The family also has the use of his pew as long as they continue together. The children underage are to have their maintenance and education paid from the estate.[1059]

[1051] The death records of one of the children gives her name as Elizabeth Kent. The Kingston, NH vital records book gives her name as Elizabeth Gilmon.
[1052] Peter's widow reports his death as November 1828 in the pension file. The May 1829 probate states he was deceased more than a year before probate was initiated. Nancy Mills made a statement that Peter died at her home November 1828.
[1053] Some sources give her name as Pratt, but the marriage record and the birth records for the children give her name as Phebe Spratt.
[1054] Revolutionary War Pension and Bounty-Land Warrant Application Files, 1800-1900 Case W16091
[1055] *New Hampshire. Probate Court (Rockingham County)*; Probate Place: *Rockingham, New Hampshire, Estate Papers, No 11738-11805, 1829*, Case 11802
[1056] *New Hampshire. Probate Court (Rockingham County)*; Probate Place: *Rockingham, New Hampshire, Estate Papers, No 15064-15120, 1846*, Case 15113. Probate 13 May 1846
[1057] Revolutionary War Pension and Bounty-Land Warrant Application Files
[1058] U.S., Revolutionary War Pensioners, 1801-1815, 1818-1872
[1059] *New Hampshire. Probate Court (Hillsborough County)*; Probate Place: *Hillsborough, New Hampshire*, volume 26, pp 514-515

Archelaus Towne and Esther Weston were parents of seven children all born at Hillsborough.

i LUCY TOWNE, b. 22 Apr 1789; d. at Hillsborough, 5 Dec 1863; m. 12 Nov 1812, BENJAMIN DANFORTH, b. at Hillsborough, 30 Aug 1789 son of Jonathan and Sarah (Chandler) Danforth; Benjamin d. at Unity, NH, 16 Sep 1867.

ii ESTHER TOWNE, b. 30 May 1791; d. at Weare, NH, 6 Dec 1831; m. 1822, JOHN BAKER, b. at Salisbury, NH, 22 May 1792 son of Benjamin and Mary (George) Baker; John d. at Salisbury, after 1850. After Esther's death, John next married Esther's sister Polly, and married third Lydia Hale. John Baker was a physician in Weare.

iii EBENEZER TOWNE, b. 11 Dec 1793; d. at Hillsborough, 16 Jan 1880; m. 1st, at Boston, 2 Jul 1823, RUTH FAULKNER, b. at Littleton, MA, 29 Apr 1795 daughter of John and Lydia (Whitcomb) Faulkner; Ruth d. at Hillsborough, 27 Apr 1843. Ebenezer m. 2nd, about 1844, MARY DUNCAN, b. at Antrim, 23 Apr 1801 daughter of William and Esther (Warren) Duncan; Mary d. at Hillsborough, 5 Jan 1886.

iv MARTHA "PATTY" TOWNE, b. 19 Jul 1797; d. at Boston, 25 Jan 1856; m. at Weare, 14 May 1818, JOHN KITTREDGE of Washington, NH; John d. at Boston before 1840 (Martha Kittredge was head of household in the 1840 census).

v MARY "POLLY" TOWNE, b. 26 Dec 1800; d. between 1843 and 1845 (living at time of husband's 1843 will, but he remarried about 1845); m. 1 Sep 1833, JOHN BAKER (see sister Esther above); John d. after 1850. John third married Lydia Hale.[1060]

vi HARRIET TOWNE, b 19 Dec 1804; d. at Hillsborough, 30 Sep 1885; m. 30 Dec 1832, JOHN COOLIDGE, b. at Hillsborough, 23 Sep 1800 son of Uriah and Sarah (Curtis) Coolidge; John d. at Hillsborough, 26 Jun 1885.

vii MEHITABLE TOWNE, b. 6 Nov 1809; d. at Hillsborough, 22 Apr 1837; m. 14 Jul 1835, AMOS KIDDER, b. at Dalton, NH, 15 Oct 1808 son of Amos and Susanna (Webster) Kidder; Amos d. at Newport, NH, 25 Jan 1885. After Mehitable's death, Amos married ESTHER DANFORTH, b. about 1813 daughter of Benjamin and Lucy (Towne) Danforth. Esther Danforth was Mehitable's niece (see sister Lucy above).

387) SUSANNAH TOWNE *(Martha Abbott Towne⁴, Ephraim³, John², George¹)*, b. at Amherst, NH, 29 Dec 1762 daughter of Archelaus and Martha (Abbott) Towne; d. at Norwich, VT 2 Dec 1840; m. 21 Oct 1779, TIMOTHY NICHOLS, b. at Reading, 16 Feb 1756 son of Timothy and Mehitable (Weston) Nichols; Timothy d. at Norwich, VT 22 Aug 1846.

Susannah Towne married Timothy Nichols born at Reading. Timothy's father died at the siege of Quebec in 1759. Timothy served in the Revolutionary War serving as a private in 1777 and 1778.[1061][1062]

Susannah and Timothy raised their family in Amherst, New Hampshire but relocated to Norwich, Vermont in their later years where their son Morris Lattin Nichols was living.

Two of the sons of Susannah and Timothy trained in the furniture and cabinet making trades. Two sons-in-law were Benjamin Damon and William Low partners in the Concord, New Hampshire furniture making company Low and Damon.[1063]

Timothy Nichols wrote his will 26 Jan 1829 nearly 20 years before his death. In his will, he left $1 each to son Leonard F. Nichols and daughters Susan Smith, Grace G. Low, and Sophia Damon as each of the children have already received to benefit of the estate to which they are entitled. "To my beloved friend and wife Susanna Nichols," he left all the estate, real and personal, for her use during her lifetime. Following her death, the real estate was to be divided equally among his five sons Luther W., Morris L., John P., Robert, and Charles. Wife Susanna was named executrix. Susannah Nichols died before her husband, and the administration of the estate was granted to Morris L. Nichols 6 January 1847.[1064]

Son Charles Nichols, who did not marry, wrote his will 7 September 1885 and it includes numerous bequests to his relatives, friends, and organizations. "Such is the conscious uncertainty of life with me, that I feel it necessary to have my secular matters arranged preparatory to my decease which may be near at hand."[1065] Bequests are to brother John P. Nichols and his wife Mary Ann Nichols; Dr. Arthur H. Nichols (John's son) and the three daughters of Arthur; nephews Francis H. Nichols and Horace H. Nichols; nephew Henry A. Nichols and his son Frank L. Nichols and Henry's daughter; nephew Albert Nichols and his son and daughter; niece Grace Low Knowlton and her two daughters; niece Caroline Davenport; nephew Edward F. Nichols and his four children; niece Mary Ann Eastbrook and her six children; nephew Luther W. Nichols and his sons. . . and many more too numerous to mention. The will is of interest as it includes the locations and addresses of most of the

---

1060 In his 1843 will, John Baker has bequests to wife Mary T. Baker and to his two children with Esther and his one child with Mary. In 1850, he was living in Salisbury with Lydia, Lydia's mother (Lydia Hale age 73) and his 11-year old son George O. Baker who was from his marriage with Mary Towne.

1061 Aldrich and Holmes, *History of Windsor County, Vermont*, p 498, https://archive.org/details/historyofwindsor00aldr

1062 Revolutionary War Pension and Bounty-Land Warrant Application File, www.fold3.com/image/27242315?terms=Timothy%20Nichols& ;xid=1945

1063 Ancestry.com, U.S. Craftperson Files, 1600-1995

1064 Vermont Wills and Probate, 1749-1999, Volumes 1819, 1845-1850, will and probate of Timothy Nichols

1065 *Suffolk County, MA: Probate File Papers, Will of Charles Nichols, 7 Sep 1885*

beneficiaries. One interesting side note is that one of the daughters of Dr. Arthur H. Nichols mentioned in the will is the landscape architect, suffragist, and pacifist Ruth Standish Nichols.

Susannah Towne and Timothy Nichols had nine children, eight of the births recorded at Amherst, New Hampshire and the birth of Leonard at Andover, New Hampshire.[1066]

i SUSANNAH NICHOLS, b. 22 Oct 1780; d. at Concord, 30 Apr 1855; m. 24 Oct 1820, JOHN SMITH, b. at Beverly, 6 Jun 1762 son of Job and Sarah (Allen) Smith; John d. at Bradford, 3 Feb 1845.[1067] Susannah and John did not have children. John was first married to Mary Herrick.

ii GRACE GARDNER NICHOLS, b. 23 May 1783; d. at Concord, 14 May 1868; m. at Amherst, 9 Jun 1803, WILLIAM LOW, b. at Amherst, 20 Apr 1779 son of William and Elizabeth (Crosby) Low; William d. 1847 (probate 1847). Grace and William did not have children.

iii SOPHIA NICHOLS, b. 29 Dec 1785; d. at Concord, 21 Oct 1866; m. 10 Jan 1811, BENJAMIN DAMON, b. at Amherst, 22 Dec 1783 son of Benjamin and Polly (Hosea) Damon; Benjamin d. at Concord, Sep 1872.

iv LUTHER WESTON NICHOLS, b. 23 Sep 1789; d. at Amherst, 9 Apr 1866; m. 1st, Jul 1812, HANNAH TOMPKINS, b. at Little Compton, RI, 18 Apr 1790 daughter of Gamaliel and Mary (Church) Tompkins; Hannah d. at Amherst, 25 Dec 1850. Luther m. 2nd, at Boston, 24 Nov 1852, LUCY RHOADS, b. at Amherst, 19 Apr 1801 daughter of Eleazer and Elizabeth (Bullard) Rhoads; Lucy d. at New Ipswich, NH, 9 Jun 1878. Lucy Rhoads was fist married to Joshua Horn and after Luther's death, she married James Chandler.

v LEONARD TOWNE NICHOLS, b. 16 Feb 1792; d. at Amherst, 13 Jul 1836; m. at Lyndeborough, 24 Feb 1820, FANNY BLANCHARD, b. at Lyndeborough, 29 Apr 1790 daughter of Jotham and Abigail (Crosby) Blanchard; Fanny d. 4 Dec 1862. After Leonard's death, Fanny married Oliver Willoby 3 Jun 1852.

vi MORRIS LATTIN NICHOLS, b. 31 Oct 1794; d. at Norwich, VT, 18 Mar 1870; m. 29 Jun 1824, CLARISSA SAFFORD, b. about 1795 daughter of Johnson and Clarissa (Ensworth) Safford; Clarissa d. 17 Nov 1863.

vii JOHN PERKINS NICHOLS, b. 19 Oct 1798; d. at Boston, 27 Oct 1891; m. 1 Jun 1831, MARY ANN CLARK, b. at Wilton, 19 May 1810 daughter of David and Anna Spaulding (Fiske) Clark; Mary Ann d. at Boston, 27 Dec 1885.

viii ROBERT NICHOLS, b. 13 Dec 1802; d. at Norwich, 11 Nov 1845; m. 7 Dec 1826, BETSEY ENSWORTH, b. at Norwich, 1 Jan 1801 daughter of Hezekiah and Erepta (Pike) Ensworth; Betsey d. at Boston, 16 Feb 1884.

ix CHARLES NICHOLS, b. 9 Dec 1808; d. at Boston, 24 May 1885. Charles did not marry.

388) ABIGAIL TOWNE *(Martha Abbott Towne[4], Ephraim[3], John[2], George[1])*, b. at Amherst, NH, 18 Feb 1765 daughter of Archelaus and Martha (Abbott) Towne; d. at Merrimack, NH 11 Apr 1832; m. 12 Jan 1790, Dr. PETER ALLEN, b. at Surry, NH, 13 Feb 1764 son of Abel and Elizabeth (Chapin) Allen;[1069] d. at Washington, VT, 18 Mar 1809.[1070]

Abigail Towne and Peter Allen were parents of six children, the two oldest children born at Andover, Vermont and the other children likely at Amherst, New Hampshire.[1071]

i CHAPIN ALLEN, b. 21 Dec 1790; d. at Jacksonville, IL, 18 Jul 1849; m. at Framingham, MA, 4 Dec 1817, MARY FROST, b. at Framingham, 25 Apr 1793 daughter of Samuel and Mary (Hurd) Frost; Mary d. at Quincy, IL, 19 Sep 1876.

ii ABBOTT ALLEN, b. 24 Dec 1792; d. at Arlington, MA, 23 Oct 1877; m. at Arlington, 1 May 1825, HANNAH FOSTER, b. at Hopkinton, MA, 10 Mar 1794 daughter of James and Susanna (Robberson) Foster; Hannah d. at Arlington, 8 May 1886.

iii SAMUEL ALLEN, b. 19 Dec 1795; d. at LaGrange, TX, likely after 1839; m. 1st, at Salem, MA, 10 Oct 1820, MARY SAUL, b. at Salem, about 1801 daughter of Joseph and Mary (Standley) Saul; Mary d. at Salem, 7 Sep 1821. Samuel m. 2nd, at Charlestown, 16 Dec 1821, HARRIET MAYNARD of Charlestown; Harriet d. 1826.

[1066] New Hampshire, Births and Christenings Index, 1714-1904
[1067] Gould and Beals, *Early Families of Bradford*, p 390
[1068] Morris Lattin's name is variously given as Lattin Morris and Morris Lattin.
[1069] Kingsbury, *History of the Town of Surry*, p 418
[1070] Littlefield and Pfister, *Genealogies of the Early Settlers of Weston, Vermont*
[1071] The death records of two of the children give the place of birth as Amherst.

Samuel m. 3rd, at Boston, 19 May 1828, ELIZABETH CONNELLY, b. at Boston, Apr 1802 daughter of Michael and Anna (Milton) Connelly; Elizabeth d. at LaGrange, TX, 1 Jan 1839.

iv MARY ALLEN, b. 5 Apr 1798; d. at Amherst, NH, 3 Sep 1859; m. 19 Apr 1820, ASA MCCLURE, b. at Merrimack, NH, 28 Aug 1793 son of John and Hannah (Danforth) McClure; Asa d. at Amherst, 4 Jun 1870.

v MARTHA TOWNE ALLEN, b. 25 Apr 1800; d. at Fitchburg, MA, 22 Aug 1873. Martha did not marry.

vi HEZEKIAH RICE ALLEN, b. 28 Apr 1803; d. at Jacksonville, IL, 18 Jul 1840; m. at Boston, 6 Oct 1829, CATHARINE A. CONNELLY, b. at Boston, 10 Dec 1803 daughter of Michael and Anna (Milton) Connelly; Catharine d. at Boston, 10 Jan 1887.

389) MARTHA TOWNE *(Martha Abbott Towne⁴, Ephraim³, John², George¹)*, b. at Amherst, NH, 12 Nov 1771 daughter of Archelaus and Martha (Abbott) Towne; d. about 1845 at Wells River, VT; m. 1792, DANIEL HOLT, b. 5 Feb 1767 son of Isaac and Mary (Marble) Holt; Daniel d. at Wells River, VT 18 Jun 1854.

Martha and Daniel started their family in Massachusetts with births of their first four children recorded at Concord, Chelsea, and Haverhill. They relocated to Ryegate, Vermont about 1801 and their youngest five children were born in Vermont. Daniel was a blacksmith.[1072]

Martha Towne and Daniel Holt were parents of nine children.

i NANCY HOLT, b. at Concord, MA, 18 Nov 1793; d. at Niagara County, NY, before 1850; m. 1st, 22 Sep 1821, ISAAC HOGAN, b. about 1798; Isaac d. at Glenville, NY, 16 Nov 1829. Nancy m. 2nd, at Glenville, NY, 22 Sep 1830, JOHN B. ROSS, b. in NY, Dec 1798; John d. at West Shelby, NY, 27 Jul 1883.

ii SOPHIA CAMPBELL HOLT, b. at Chelsea, MA, 8 Aug 1795; d. at Boston, MA, 3 Jul 1887. Sophia did not marry.

iii NOAH HOLT, b. at Haverhill, MA, 1 Aug 1797; d. at Renfrew, Ontario, about 1882 (living in 1881 and wife a widow in 1883); m. about 1819, ACHSAH WALKER, b. in VT, 1800; Achsah d. at Renfrew, 17 Nov 1883.

iv LOAMMI HOLT, b. at Haverhill, MA, 11 Aug 1799; d. at Ryegate, VT, 17 Sep 1836; m. 18 Nov 1830, MEREA HOOKER, b. about 1810; Merea d. at Ryegate, 9 Sep 1873. Merea married second Alexander S. Miller.

v DANIEL HOLT, b. at Newbury, VT, 2 Sep 1801; d. at Bath, NH, 5 May 1867; m. 1st, 23 Sep 1830, EUNICE F. HEYWARD, b. in NH, about 1802 daughter of Abner Heyward; Eunice d. at North Haverhill, NH, 3 Apr 1837. Daniel m. 2nd, at Bath, 12 Dec 1837, MARY SMITH, b. in NH, about 1810; Mary d. at Bath, 15 Dec 1850. Daniel m. 3rd, at Groton, VT, 10 Feb 1851, RUTH HEATH, b. in NH, about 1803 daughter of Horatio Heath; Ruth d. at Bath, after 1900.

vi MARTHA HOLT, b. at Ryegate, 19 Apr 1803; d. at Ryegate, 17 May 1852; m. about 1832, as his second wife, BENJAMIN FOLGER, b. at Charlton, NY, 1785; Benjamin d. at Ryegate, 3 May 1848. Benjamin was first married to Agnes Henderson.

vii MARY D. HOLT, b. at Ryegate, 8 Jul 1808; d. at Beebe Plain, Québec, 13 Dec 1877. Mary did not marry.

viii WILLIAM S. HOLT, b. at Ryegate, 8 Jul 1808; d. at Marshall County, IA, 1862 (will 24 May 1862; probate, 1862); m. 9 May 1833, MARGARET NELSON, b. in VT, 1811 daughter of James and Agnes (Gibson) Nelson; Margaret d. at Marshall County, after 1880.

ix JOHN HOLT, b. at Ryegate, 19 Jul 1811; d. at Boxford, 5 Sep 1898; m. LAURINDA HOOKER, b. in VT, 1812 daughter of Thomas Hooker; Laurinda d. at Danville, VT, 22 Jun 1895.

390) REBECCA ABBOTT *(John⁴, Joshua³, John², George¹)*, b. at Westford, 17 Feb 1738/9 daughter of John and Hannah (Richardson) Abbott; d. 19 Feb 1785; m. 3 Nov 1763, JOSEPH JEWETT, b. at Littleton, 15 Jun 1740 son of Ezra and Mary (Herrick) Jewett. Joseph m. 2nd 1786, Hannah Richardson; Joseph d. at Peterborough, 25 Aug 1814.

Joseph Jewett and Rebecca Abbott settled in Littleton. Joseph served in the Revolutionary War in Lieutenant Aquilla Jewett's militia company. This company "marched on the alarm" 19 April 1775.[1073] He served three days at that time. In 1777, he served in Colonel Samuel Bullard's Regiment which included a march to Saratoga.

Rebecca and Joseph had six children whose births are recorded at Littleton.

i JONATHAN JEWETT, b. 15 Aug 1764; d. at Littleton, 21 Jun 1789; m. at Littleton, 22 Jan 1789, SARAH MELVIN, b. at Littleton, 14 Mar 1767 daughter of Eleazer and Sarah (Hartwell) Melvin. After Jonathan's death,

---

1072 Miller, *History of Ryegate*, p 390.

1073 Massachusetts Soldiers and Sailors in the War of Revolution, Volume VIII

Sarah married Ezekiel Wright and relocated to Vermont. Jonathan's will written 12 Jun 1789 includes bequests to his wife Sarah, his grandfather Ezra Jewett, and other relatives.

ii JOHN JEWETT, b. 30 May 1766; d. at Peterborough, 6 Feb 1851; m. 1st, 1787, ELIZABETH CUMMINGS, b. at Westford, 7 Jul 1769 daughter of Joseph and Elizabeth (Fletcher) Cummings; Elizabeth d. 10 May 1798. John married second about 1800, MARGARET MOORE, b. Feb 1767 daughter of Samuel and Margaret (Morrison) Moore. Margaret d. 6 Jan 1850.

iii PATTY JEWETT, b. 2 May 1768; d. at Westford, 14 Aug 1824; m. at Westford, 7 Feb 1786, THOMAS FLETCHER, b. at Westford, 3 Jun 1764 son of Thomas and Sarah (Hildreth) Fletcher; Thomas d. at Westford, 22 Sep 1838.

iv LEONARD JEWETT, b. 6 Sep 1770; d. at Athens, OH, 13 May 1816 (estate probate 1816); m. at Rutland, 16 Jul 1795, MARY PORTER, b. at Rutland, 7 Nov 1774 daughter of Samuel and Sarah (Church) Porter; Mary d. at Athens, 14 Sep 1827.

v JOSHUA ABBOTT JEWETT, b. 29 Feb 1772; d. at Concord, MA, 23 Mar 1838; m. 1st, 22 Jul 1797, SARAH SPAULDING, b. 6 Jun 1773 daughter of Timothy and Hannah (Richmond) Spaulding; Sarah d. at Westford, 20 May 1798. Joshua married second, 15 May 1800, REBECCA ROBINSON, b. at Westford, 6 Jul 1774 daughter of John and Huldah (Perley) Robinson. Rebecca died 19 Oct 1854.

vi AHIMAAZ JEWETT, b. 14 Nov 1778; d. 2 Dec 1778.

391) JOHN ABBOTT *(John⁴, Joshua³, John², George¹)*, b. at Westford, 2 Dec 1743 son of John and Hannah (Richardson) Abbott; d. 8 May 1804; m. 1st Jul 1769, LUCY PROCTOR, b. at Chelmsford, 28 Nov 1746 daughter of Daniel and Susanna (Hill) Proctor; Lucy d. 27 Apr 1779. John m. 2nd 22 Jun 1780, MARY FARRAR, b. at Concord, 4 Jul 1747 daughter of Jacob and Mary (Merriam) Farrar; Mary d. 26 Feb 1815.

John Abbott served as a captain in the militia in Westford. He was active in town affairs.[1074]

John Abbott wrote his will 7 March 1804. Beloved wife Mary receives use of and improvements on one-half of the dwelling house, three hundred dollars, and three cows; Mary receives other provisions for her maintenance which are to be seen to by son Abel. Son John receives the house, land, and buildings recently purchased from Capt. Rogers King. All the rest of the lands and buildings go to son Abel Abbott who is also named executor.[1075]

John Abbott and Lucy Proctor had one son born at Westford.

i JOHN ABBOTT, b. 27 Jan 1777; d. at Westford, 30 Apr 1854; m. at Westford, 5 May 1805, SOPHIA MOSELY, b. at Hampton, CT, 16 Oct 1776 daughter of Ebenezer and Martha (Strong) Mosley; Sophia d. at Westford, 27 Mar 1821. John and Sophia had a child that died as an infant and son John William Pitt Abbott who married his fourth cousin Catherine Abbott [daughter of Jacob and Catherine (Thayer) Abbott]. John Abbott graduated Harvard in 1798, was an attorney is Westford, and served in the Massachusetts senate. John Abbott's will includes bequests to his nephew Julian Abbott, his housekeeper Rachel Blood, his "only child" John William Pitt Abbott and his four grandchildren, as well as bequests to Westford Academy and the Congregational church. John William Pitt Abbott followed in his father's footsteps attending Harvard and becoming an attorney in Westford.

John Abbott and Mary Farrar had one son born at Westford.

i ABEL ABBOTT, b. 7 Dec 1781; d. at Westford, 9 May 1810; m. 24 Nov 1805, CATHERINE CUMMINGS, b. at Westford, 28 Feb 1780 daughter of Timothy and Catharine (Fasset) Cummings; Catherine d. at Westford, 21 Jul 1809. Abel and Catherine had one son, Julian Abbott, who attended Harvard Divinity School and received an A.B. in 1826 and A.M. in 1829. He was not ordained. He later worked as an attorney in Lowell.[1076]

[1074] Hodgman, History of the Town of Westford, p 436.

[1075] *Middlesex County, MA: Probate File Papers, 1648-1871. Probate of John Abbott, 1804, Case number 31.*

[1076] Harvard Divinity School, General Catalogue of the Divinity School of Harvard University.

392) MARTHA ABBOTT *(John⁴, Joshua³, John², George¹)*, b. at Westford, 17 Sep 1755 daughter of John and Hannah (Richardson) Abbott; d. at Reading, 20 Oct 1842; m. 16 Nov 1776, JOHN PRESCOTT, b. 25 Apr 1752 son of Jonas and Rebecca (Jones) Prescott; John d. 30 Oct 1842.

Martha and John Prescott raised their family of seven children in Westford. They were married just one month short of 66 years and died 10 days apart in 1842. John was a successful farmer, and the family was able to send three of their sons to Harvard. Each of those sons became attorneys.

Deacon John Prescott wrote his will 5 June 1830. The will includes bequests to his wife Martha, son Joshua Prescott, son Aaron Prescott, grandson John Samuel Prescott son of his deceased son Samuel, John Samuel's sister Sarah (daughter of Samuel), son John Prescott (his legacy to be held in a trust for his support), after son John's death his portion to his daughter Martha Ann Prescott, daughter Hannah Prescott (also held in trust), and son Thomas Prescott (also in trust) and after Thomas's death his portion to his son Aaron Prescott and Thomas's two daughters. The legacies are monetary and are to be obtained from the sale of the estate. The legacies to John, Hannah, and Thomas each specify that they are to receive an annual interest payment from the principle of the legacy which is to be paid by the executor. John Abbot of Westford was named executor. However, at the time of John Prescott's death in 1842, John Abbot declined this responsibility and son Aaron became administrator of the estate. The personal estate was valued at $2,561.64 and the real estate at $10 (for the pew in the first parish meeting house in Westford).[1077]

Martha and John Prescott had seven children whose births are recorded at Westford.

i JOHN PRESCOTT, b. 25 Sep 1779; d. at Westford, 25 Jul 1847; m. 20 Aug 1801, ANNA KEYES, b. at Westford, 27 Oct 1780 daughter of Joseph and Ruth (Forbush) Keyes; Anna d. 21 Jan 1802. John did not remarry after Anna's death. They had one daughter, Martha Ann Prescott.

ii JOSHUA PRESCOTT, b. 15 Nov 1780; d. at North Reading, 1 Jan 1859; m. 5 Jan 1813, ABIGAIL EATON, b. at Reading, 3 Jan 1785 daughter of Thomas and Abigail (Bryant) Eaton; Abigail d. 4 Feb 1867. Joshua graduated from Harvard in 1807 and taught school for three years in Saco, ME. He studied law with Judge James Prescott and later established a practice in Reading. He was a representative to the State legislature in 1827 and 1828. He also had an interest in agriculture and supervised his successful farm.[1078] Joshua and Abigail have five children one of whom died in infancy. Joshua's son Thomas married his first cousin Abigail the daughter of Thomas Prescott.[1079]

iii SAMUEL PRESCOTT, b. 8 Jan 1782; d. at Keene, NH, 13 Nov 1813; m. about 1806, FRANCES JOHNSON, b. at Hampstead, NH, 6 Nov 1786 daughter of Moses and Sally (Holland) Johnson. It is not known if Frances remarried after Samuel's death. After graduating Harvard in 1799, Samuel was for one year a schoolteacher in Keene.[1080] He then studied law and was a counselor of the Superior Court in New Hampshire in 1806. He obtained a master's degree from Harvard in 1807.[1081] For a time, he worked with his father-in-law, Moses Johnson, in New York but later returned to Keene.[1082] Samuel left two children, Sara Elizabeth Prescott and John Samuel Prescott. Two other children died in infancy.

iv STEPHEN PRESCOTT, b. 29 Aug 1784; d. at Westford, 7 Oct 1808.

v HANNAH PRESCOTT, b. 8 Aug 1786; d. at Reading, 27 Dec 1841. Hannah did not marry.

vi AARON PRESCOTT, b. 19 Nov 1787; d. at Randolph, 24 Nov 1851. Aaron did not marry. After graduating from Harvard in 1814, Aaron was the preceptor of Framingham Academy for one year. He then studied law and established a practice in Randolph. He served as a representative to the State legislature.[1083]

vii THOMAS PRESCOTT, b. 30 May 1791; d. at Westford, 27 Aug 1854; m. 8 Dec 1814, SARAH "SALLY" HALE, b. at Stow, MA, 12 May 1793 daughter of Charles and Dorcas (Randall) Hale;[1084] Sally d. at Reading, 15 Jun 1857. Thomas's three children were Aaron Abbot Prescott, Sarah Ann Hale Prescott, and Abigail Eaton Prescott.

393) SARAH OSGOOD *(Sarah Abbott Osgood⁴, Joshua³, John², George¹)*, b. at Billerica, 28 May 1738 daughter of Christopher and Sarah (Abbott) Osgood; d. at Lancaster 24 May 1805; m. at Worcester, 10 May 1756, TIMOTHY WHITING, b. 13 Feb 1731/2 son of Samuel and Deborah (Hill) Whiting; Timothy d. at Lancaster, 12 Jul 1799.

[1077] *Middlesex County, MA: Probate File Papers, 1648-1871. Probate of John Prescott, 1842, Case number 39758.*
[1078] Palmer, Necrology of Alumni of Harvard College, pp 234-5
[1079] Prescott, The Prescott Memorial, https://archive.org/stream/prescottmemorial00pres#page/n177/mode/2up
[1080] Griffin, A history of the Town of Keene from 1732, p 338
[1081] Harvard University, Quinquennial Catalogue
[1082] Bell, The Bench and Bar of New Hampshire, p 597
[1083] Palmer, Necrology of Alumni of Harvard College, 1851-1852 to 1862-63, p 7
[1084] The 1815 probate record of Charles Hale includes Thomas Prescott signing as an heir.

Timothy Whiting served in the French and Indian War.[1085] In 1775, he and his sons Timothy and John served in the same company and were at the Battles of Lexington and Concord. A third son, Christopher, was killed at Ticonderoga.

Sarah Osgood and Timothy Whiting were parents of five children born at Lancaster.

i DEBORAH WHITING, b. 17 Jan 1757; m. at Lancaster, 21 Oct 1783, BENJAMIN BANCROFT, b. at Groton, 7 Aug 1750 son of Benjamin and Alice (Tarbell) Bancroft; Benjamin d. at Grafton, VT, 17 Mar 1828.

ii SARAH WHITING, b. 17 Jan 1757; twin of Deborah; nothing further known

iii TIMOTHY WHITING, b. 17 Jun 1758; d. at Lancaster, 12 Jan 1826; m. 1st, 21 Aug 1781, ABIGAIL KIDDER, b. at Billerica, 5 Jun 1759 daughter of Samuel and Abigail (Hill) Kidder; Abigail d. at Lancaster, 1 Oct 1798. Timothy m. 2nd, 14 Oct 1799, LYDIA PHELPS, b. at Lancaster, about 1776 daughter of John and Achsah (Whiting) Phelps; Lydia d. at Charlestown, MA, 15 Jan 1851.

iv JOHN WHITING, b. 24 Feb 1760; d. at Washington, DC, 3 Sep 1810; m. at Billerica, 24 May 1785, ORPAH DANFORTH, b. at Billerica, 7 Jun 1758 daughter of Timothy and Sarah (Patten) Danforth; Orpah d. 10 Mar 1837. John and Orpah's daughter Caroline Lee Whiting Hentz (1800-1856) was a novelist whose books featured anti-abolitionist themes. Much of Caroline's adult life was spent in Alabama.

v CHRISTOPHER WHITING, b. 27 Nov 1761; d. 10 Nov 1776 at Ticonderoga. Christopher, s. Timo[thy] and Sarah, Nov. 10, 1776, in Ticonderoga, " In the Service of his Country." (From Billerica, MA vital records)

394) MARY OSGOOD *(Sarah Abbott Osgood⁴, Joshua³, John², George¹)*, b. at Billerica, 31 Aug 1740 daughter of Christopher and Sarah (Abbott) Osgood; d. at Worcester, 5 Sep 1761; m. 14 May 1757, JOHN GREEN, b. at Leicester, 14 Aug 1736 son of Thomas and Martha (Lynde) Green. John m. 2nd MARY RUGGLES; John d. at Worcester, 29 Oct 1799.

John Green's father was a physician and John followed in his father's footsteps and had a medical practice in Worcester.[1086]

John Green wrote his will 3 October 1799.[1087] In his will, he makes bequests to his children from his second marriage and to his wife Mary. He makes provisions for the care of his younger children until they come of age. To his eldest son Thomas, he leaves one-sixth of his real and personal estate, although Thomas will not receive this until the youngest of the children come of age. Thomas was the only surviving child of John Green's marriage to Mary Osgood.

Mary Osgood and John Green had three children born at Worcester.

i JOHN GREEN, b. 1 Apr 1758; d. 20 Sep 1761.

ii MARY GREEN, b. 27 Nov 1759; d. 15 Feb 1760.

iii THOMAS GREEN, b. 3 Jan 1761; d. at Yarmouth, ME, 29 May 1814; m. at Sutton, 8 Oct 1782, SALOME BARSTOW,[1088] b. at Coventry, CT, 23 Jul 1760 daughter of Jeremiah and Rebecca (Hammond) Barstow; Salome d. at Yarmouth, 29 Nov 1799. Thomas m. 2nd, 5 Oct 1800, HULDAH STINSON, b. 1773 daughter of Samuel and Jane (Robinson) Stinson. Huldah was first married to Richard Delano.

395) CHRISTOPHER OSGOOD *(Sarah Abbott Osgood⁴, Joshua³, John², George¹)*, b. at Billerica, 12 Apr 1743 son of Christopher and Sarah (Abbott) Osgood; death uncertain;[1089] m. by 1765, HANNAH BROWN, b. at Worcester, 21 Sep 1742 daughter of Luke and Elizabeth (-) Brown; Hannah d. at Newfane, VT, 1779.

Christopher Osgood was just five years old when his father died, and Thomas Kidder was named his guardian. Christopher and Hannah started their family in Lancaster, Massachusetts and then relocated to Newfane, Vermont where Christopher was a farmer.

Christopher Osgood and Hannah Brown were parents of seven children the three oldest children born at Lancaster, Massachusetts and the youngest four children born at Newfane, Vermont.[1090]

1085 Marvin, *History of the Town of Lancaster*

1086 Vinton, *The Vinton Memorial*, p 421

1087 *Worcester County, MA: Probate File Papers, 1731-1881.* Online database. AmericanAncestors.org. Case number 25534, Probate of John Green

1088 Vinton, *The Vinton Memorial*, p 421

1089 Reported in the Osgood genealogy as being about 1780 in Massachusetts

1090 There may be an eighth, unnamed child who died as an infant.

i HANNAH OSGOOD, b. 11 Dec 1766; d. at Hinsdale, NH, 21 Apr 1816; m. about 1788, VALENTINE BUTLER, b. at Hinsdale, about 1765 son of Valentine and Lois (Willard) Butler; Valentine d. at Hinsdale, 14 Jan 1827.

ii CHRISTOPHER OSGOOD, b. 12 Jun 1769; d. at Brookline, VT, 23 Sep 1846; m. 1794, PERSIS JOY, b. at Rehoboth, MA, 11 Sep 1774 daughter of John and Persis (Wilder) Joy; Persis d. at Brookline, 28 Feb 1840.

iii JOHN OSGOOD, b. 5 Nov 1770; d. at Brookline, VT, 12 Jun 1829; m. 1802, BETSEY OSGOOD, b. at Boylston, MA, 1767 daughter of Abel and Eunice (Holland) Osgood; Betsey d. at Petersham, MA, 23 Oct 1838.

iv LUKE BROWN OSGOOD, b. 1772; d. at Brookline, VT, 9 Jan 1845; m. at Hubbardston, MA, 27 Feb 1803, SALLY THOMSON, b. at Hubbardston, 9 Jun 1782 daughter of John and Elizabeth (Beath) Thomson; Sally d. at Brookline, 14 Apr 1837.

v EMORY OSGOOD, b. 24 Jul 1774; d. at Utica, NY, 12 Sep 1824; m. about 1799, CYNTHIA STOCKWELL, b. at Marlboro, VT, 14 Dec 1780 daughter of Abel and Patience (Thomas) Stockwell; Cynthia d. at Streetsboro, OH, 5 Jan 1843. Emory was a Baptist minister.[1091]

vi SEWELL OSGOOD, b. 1776; d. at Richmond, VA, 23 Dec 1819; m. at Richmond, 14 Jan 1805, FRANCES COURTNEY, b. in VA, 1784 daughter of Thomas and Susan (Evans) Courtney; Frances d. at Richmond, 30 Apr 1859. Frances married second Richard Armstrong. Sewell was a firefighter known as the "Fire King" due to his heroic firefighting efforts. He died by suicide.[1092][1093]

vii LUTHER OSGOOD, b. 3 May 1779; d. at Joliet, IL, Mar 1859; m. at Newfane, 12 Apr 1801, LUCY SIMONDS, b. Dummerston, about 1779; Lucy d. at Preston, NY, 9 Feb 1856. Luther went to Joliet after the death of his wife.

396) REBECCA GOODWIN *(Sarah Abbott Osgood Goodwin⁴, Joshua³, John², George¹)*, b. at Worcester, 21 Oct 1751 daughter of James and Sarah (Abbott) Goodwin; m. at Worcester, 1 May 1781, AMOS JOHNSON, b. at Worcester, 13 Jan 1756 son of John and Susannah (-) Johnson; Amos d. at Worcester before 10 Mar 1825 (date of probate).[1094]

Each of the fathers of Rebecca Goodwin (James Goodwin) and Amos Johnson (John Johnson) were Captains of the two militia companies in Worcester in 1760.[1095]

There are some confusions in the records for the children in the family. There are transcriptions for marriage records for the same date, one for the marriage of Polly Johnson to Alpheus Eaton and one for the marriage of Betsy Johnson to Alpheus Eaton. A review of birth records of children for the couples, death records for the daughters, and the probate record for Betsy Eaton confirms that it was Betsy that married Alpheus Eaton. Polly's husband was Adolphus Taft.

The estate of Amos Johnson entered probate 10 March 1825.[1096] The only document available is the administrator's bond. Alpheus Eaton, Jr. is administrator and co-signers on the bond are Adolphus Taft and Thomas B. Eaton. The bond document does not mention a widow. It is not known when Rebecca died.

There are records for just three children of Rebecca and Amos born at Worcester.

i SARAH JOHNSON, b. 15 Jul 1781; d. at Worcester, 11 Feb 1844. Sarah did not marry.

ii POLLY JOHNSON, b. 26 Nov 1783; d. at Worcester, 24 Nov 1864; m. at Worcester, 19 Oct 1807, ADOLPHUS TAFT, b. at Uxbridge, 10 Jul 1784 son of Timothy and Abigail (Wright) Taft; Adolphus d. at Worcester, 8 Feb 1857.

iii BETSY JOHNSON, b. 16 Aug 1789; d. at Worcester, 3 Mar 1851; m. at Worcester, 30 Apr 1808, ALPHEUS EATON, b. at Worcester, 14 Aug 1786 son of Alpheus and Sarah (Johnson) Eaton; Alpheus d. 14 Jul 1833.

397) JOHN GOODWIN *(Sarah Abbott Osgood Goodwin⁴, Joshua³, John², George¹)*, b. at Worcester, 6 Aug 1753 son of James and Sarah (Abbott) Goodwin; d. at Putney, VT, 2 Sep 1801; m. at Leicester, 11 Feb 1773, MARTHA MOORE, b. at Worcester, 14 Jul 1752 daughter of Asa and Sarah (Hayward) Moore;[1097] Martha d. at Putney, 25 Nov 1823.[1098] After John's death, Martha married Reuben Robinson.

[1091] Osgood, *The Genealogy of the Descendants of John, Christopher, and William Osgood*, p 278

[1092] Mordecai, Samuel. 1860. *Virginia, Especially Richmond, in By-gone Days; With a Glance at the Present: Being Reminiscences and Last Words of an Old Citizen.*

[1093] Mr. Sewell Osgood, The Colombian, New York, NY, volume X, issue 2905, Dec 29, 1819, p 2

[1094] There is another Amos Johnson in Worcester County at the same time; the other Amos Johnson was a resident of Berlin, Worcester, MA and he died in November 1825.

[1095] Lincoln, *History of Worcester*, p 276

[1096] *Worcester County, MA: Probate File Papers, 1731-1881, Probate of Amos Johnson, 1825, Case number 33621.*

[1097] The will of Asa Moore written in 1798 includes a bequest to his daughter Patty Goodwin.

[1098] "Vermont Vital Records, 1760-1954," database with images, *FamilySearch* (https://familysearch.org/ark:/61903/1:1:V8MR-LV8 : 5 November 2017), Martha Robinson, 25 Nov 1823, Death; State Capitol Building, Montpelier; FHL microfilm 27,672.

John Goodwin was the first postmaster of Putney, Vermont named to that position 20 March 1797. He also owned a blacksmith shop in the town.[1099]

John Goodwin wrote his will at Putney, Vermont on 15 August 1801. Wife Martha receives all the household furnishings, the blacksmith tools, all the hay, the colt, two cows, one yearling heifer, and the silver watch. All the remainder of the estate also goes to Martha who is named executor along with John Shepard.[1100]

John Goodwin and Martha Moore were parents of six children. The births of the first five children are record both at Worcester, Massachusetts and Putney, Vermont and the youngest child at Putney.

i ELIZABETH GOODWIN, b. 30 Jun 1773; d. at Northfield, VT, about 1853;[1101] m. at Putney, 6 Feb 1791, ELEAZER NICHOLS, b. at Dighton, MA, 10 Oct 1762 son of William and Mary (Gooding) Nichols; Eleazer d. at Northfield, 2 Jun 1831.

ii SARAH GOODWIN, b. 5 May 1775; d. at Williamstown, VT, 30 Oct 1849; m. about 1794, JOHN KATHAN, b. at Dummerston, VT, 1769 son of John and Lois (Moore) Kathan; John d. at Williamstown, 17 Jan 1842.

iii MARY "POLLY" GOODWIN, b. 10 Jul 1777; d. at Jamaica, VT, 26 Nov 1859; m. at Dummerston, 23 Aug 1803, JOHN GATES, b. at Dummerston, 11 Apr 1776 son of John and Hannah (Moore) Gates; John d. at Jamaica. VT, 29 Dec 1858.

iv HANNAH GOODWIN, b. 14 Aug 1779; d. at Walpole, NH, 14 Jul 1844; m. 1st, at Putney, 15 Feb 1797, JOHN BLACK, Jr.; John d. before 1810. Hannah m. 2nd, at Westmoreland, NH, JOTHAM LORD, b. at Westmoreland, 4 Nov 1785 son of Jotham and Eunice (White) Lord; Jotham d. at Westmoreland, 17 Feb 1843.

v LUCY GOODWIN, b. 12 May 1785; d. at Putney, 8 Dec 1806.

vi JOHN GOODWIN, b. 6 Apr 1796; d. at Bridport, VT, 3 Oct 1881; m. 1st, about 1825, SALLY SMITH, b. 24 Jun 1801;[1102] Sally d. at Bridport, 4 Mar 1829. John m. 2nd, at Bridport, 17 Aug 1831, WEALTHY LEE, b. about 1803 daughter of Jeremiah and Isabel (Hamilton) Lee; Wealthy d. at Bridport, 17 Mar 1884.

398) TABITHA GOODWIN *(Sarah Abbott Osgood Goodwin⁴, Joshua³, John², George¹)*, b. at Worcester, 4 May 1756 daughter of James and Sarah (Abbott) Goodwin; d. at Shoreham, VT, 31 Jul 1825; m. 12 Jul 1776, JOEL DOOLITTLE, b. at Worcester, 8 Dec 1752 son of Ephraim and Sarah (Morton) Doolittle; Joel d. at Shoreham, 19 Dec 1829. After Tabitha's death, Joel married Mary Hall.

Colonel Joel Doolittle accompanied his father to Shoreham, Vermont about 1783. He was a mill owner along with his father.[1103]

Although the Doolittle genealogy reports two sons, John and Joel, for Tabitha and Joel Doolittle, it seems more likely that John and Joel were the sons of Joel's brother John. John Doolittle was married to Lucy Dean. John Doolittle died in 1790 leaving four children: John, Joel, Lucy, and Sally. Joel Doolittle became guardian of the minor children of his brother John. In 1803, the oldest son of John Doolittle, John Doolittle, petitioned the probate court to have his father's estate settled on him. Joel Doolittle signed his consent for this acting as guardian for Joel, Lucy, and Sally.[1104] The Doolittle genealogy reports Lucy as the only child of John and that John and Joel were the children of Joel,[1105] but it seems that all the children are the children of John Doolittle and Lucy Dean and were perhaps raised by Joel after John's death. In any event, John Doolittle born 13 January 1781 married Nancy Jones and Joel Doolittle born 26 January 1787 married Polly Janes. It appears that Tabitha Goodwin and Joel Doolittle did not have children.

399) HENRY JEFTS *(Mary Abbott Jefts⁴, Joshua³, John², George¹)*, b. at Billerica, 7 Oct 1748 son of Henry and Mary (Abbott) Jefts; d. unknown but he appears on the 1810 Census in Billerica; m. 24 Feb 1774, ELIZABETH STEARNS, b. 20 Jun 1751 daughter of Samuel and Hannah (Trask) Stearns; Elizabeth was still living when her father wrote his will 1 May 1801.

Henry Jefts and Elizabeth Stearns were parents of six children born at Billerica.

[1099] De Wulfe, *History of Putney, Vermont*, p 57 and p 85

[1100] Vermont Wills and Probate Records, 1749-1999, Probate Records, volumes 1-2, 1781-1808; will of John Goodwin, 15 Aug 1801.

[1101] Gregory, *Early Settlers of Northfield Vermont*, p 83

[1102] Sally's birthdate is given on her death record; her parents are not identified.

[1103] Goodhue, *History of the Town of Shoreham*, p 8

[1104] *New Hampshire. Probate Court (Cheshire County);* Probate Place: *Cheshire, New Hampshire, Estate Files, estate of John Doolittle, 1791, No. 23*

[1105] Doolittle, The Doolittle Family in America, p 297-298

i ELIZABETH JEFTS, b. 11 Jun 1775; d. 28 Nov 1777.

ii JOHN JEFTS, b. 1 Feb 1778; m. 25 Apr 1799, MARY SAFFORD, b. at Ipswich, 28 Feb 1773 daughter of Simeon and Deborah (Harris) Safford.

iii HENRY JEFTS, b. 11 Dec 1781

iv AARON JEFTS, b. 31 Aug 1782; m. 12 Jul 1810, HANNAH STEARNS.

v ELIZABETH JEFTS, b. 23 Jun 1784; m. at Bedford, NH, 28 Nov 1805, SMITH CAMPBELL.[1106]

vi SIMEON JEFTS, b. about 1786; d. at Lowell, 22 Oct 1848; m. 1st, at Billerica, 1 Nov 1825, his fourth cousin, LUCRETIA SNOW *(Dorcas Abbott Snow5, David4, David3, Benjamin2, George1)*, b. at Billerica, 4 Nov 1802 daughter of John and Dorcas (Abbott) Snow; Lucretia d. at Lowell, 27 Dec 1845. Simeon m. 2nd, at Lowell, 13 Apr 1847, BETSEY MCLAUGHLIN. Lucretia Snow is a child in Family 832.

400) ABIGAIL WALKER *(Elizabeth Abbott Walker4, Joshua3, John2, George1)*, b. at Billerica, 6 Oct 1746 daughter of Robert and Elizabeth (Abbott) Walker; d. at Grafton, VT, 7 Apr 1818; m. 10 Mar 1768, WILLIAM STICKNEY, b. 3 Apr 1743 son of William and Anna (Whiting) Stickney.

Abigail Walker and William Stickney began their family in Billerica. According to the Stickney Genealogy, William's father was deacon in Billerica for 32 years. After his father's death, William was elected deacon 21 November 1781, but William declined the position 31 January 1782. On 31 October 1784, William and Abigail were recommended to the church in Tomlinson, Vermont, and the family relocated there soon after. William became the deacon of the church in the area that was later incorporated as Grafton.[1107]

William and Abigail Walker were the parents of eleven children, the first eight born at Billerica and the youngest children at Grafton.

i WILLIAM STICKNEY, b. 16 Jun 1768; d. at Grafton, VT, 21 Feb 1860; m. by 1795, SARAH GIBSON, b. at Fitchburg, 23 Feb 1776 daughter of Isaac and Lois (Sampson) Gibson; Sarah d. at Grafton, 3 Aug 1856.

ii ABIGAIL STICKNEY, b. 6 Mar 1770; d. at Bridgewater, VT, 28 Apr 1847; m. 23 Jun 1793, ABIJAH BAIRD, b. at Billerica, 25 Jun 1767 son of Abijah and Hannah (Frost) Baird; Abijah d. at Grafton, 22 Oct 1844.

iii ELIZABETH STICKNEY, b. 31 May 1772; d. at Grafton, 15 May 1857; m. 18 Dec 1794, JOHN EASTMAN, b. about 1770; John d. at Grafton, 24 Jul 1827.

iv ANNA STICKNEY, b. 3 May 1774; d. May 1826; m. at Burlington, MA, 7 Feb 1818, DAVID WALKER.

v SARAH STICKNEY, b. 30 Jul 1776; d. at Billerica, 10 Mar 1846; m 16 Jul 1800, FRANCIS BLANCHARD, b. at Billerica about 1775; Francis d. at Billerica, 17 Aug 1861.

vi JOHN STICKNEY, b. 30 Aug 1778; d. at Plymouth, VT, 16 Oct 1846; m. about 1806, CELIA THATCHER, b. at Walpole, NH, 12 Sep 1784 daughter of Joseph Thatcher; Celia d. at Plymouth, 22 Jun 1847.

vii BENJAMIN STICKNEY, b. 27 Dec 1780; d. at Burton, OH, 13 Aug 1824; m. at Grafton, 2 Feb 1808, MARY "POLLY" EDSON.

viii ISAAC STICKNEY, b. 12 Oct 1782; d. at Boston, Nov 1809. Isaac did not marry. He worked at the store of Windsor Fay in Boston.

ix MARY "POLLY" STICKNEY, b. 23 Sep 1784; d. at Grafton, 17 Jan 1812; m. 26 Dec 1805, G. WASHINGTON WALKER, b. in Vermont about 1778; Washington d. at Grafton, 19 Aug 1855. After Mary's death, Washington married Polly Smith.

x SILENCE STICKNEY, b. 1 Dec 1786; d. at Grafton, 24 Dec 1863; m. at Grafton, 24 Oct 1821, JARED FARMER, b. at Grafton, 11 Mar 1791 son of Joseph and Dorcas (-) Farmer; Jared d. at Grafton, 2 Oct 1865.

xi JOSIAH STICKNEY, b. 6 Jan 1789; d. at Watertown, MA, 27 Mar 1876; m. 1st, at Boston, 30 Jan 1814, SARAH LEE, b. at Pomfret, 10 May 1791 daughter of Cyrel and Louisa (Smith) Lee; Susan d. at Boston, 23 Aug 1823. Josiah m. 2nd, at Temple, NH, 9 Oct 1824, ELIZABETH SEARLE, b. at Temple, 13 Aug 1794 daughter of Daniel and Hannah (Blood) Searle. Elizabeth Searle was first married to George Whiting.

1106 Jefts, Elizabeth (of Billerica) & Smith Campbell, Nov. 28, 1805 by Rev. David McGregore

1107 Stickney, *The Stickney Family*, p 124

401) LYDIA WALKER *(Elizabeth Abbott Walker⁴, Joshua³, John², George¹)*, b. at Billerica, 22 Mar 1752 daughter of Robert and Elizabeth (Abbott) Walker; d. after 1815; m. 20 Oct 1770, JOSIAH RICHARDSON, b. 19 Jun 1751 son of Josiah and Judith (Kendall) Richardson; Josiah d. at Billerica, 1815 (probate 3 Oct 1815).

Josiah Richardson did not leave a will and his estate entered probate 3 October 1815 with widow Lydia requesting that Josiah Crosby be named administrator. Real property consisted of 8 ½ acres of pasture valued at $212 and one-half of a pew in the meeting house valued at $50. The total value of the estate was $678.14. The debts of the estate were $999.76, and the estate was declared insolvent. The estate was sold at public auction.[1108]

There are five children known for Josiah Richardson and Lydia Walker born at Billerica.

i JOSIAH RICHARDSON, b. 11 Feb 1771; d. 1 May 1771.

ii JOSIAH RICHARDSON, b. 16 Sep 1773; d. 22 Aug 1775.

iii JUDITH RICHARDSON, b. 12 Apr 1774; d. 13 Jan 1783.

iv ABIGAIL RICHARDSON, b. 17 Nay 1776; m. at Billerica, 12 Feb 1801, ISAAC POLLARD, b. at Billerica, 27 Jun 1770 son of Solomon and Hannah (Danforth) Pollard; Isaac d. at Billerica, 27 May 1842.

v JUDITH RICHARDSON, b. 3 Feb 1783; d. at Billerica, 8 Nov 1867; m. 28 Nov 1805, FRANCIS POLLARD, b. at Billerica, 12 Dec 1772 son of Solomon and Hannah (Danforth) Pollard; Francis d. at Billerica, 1 Feb 1813.

402) REBEKAH WALKER *(Elizabeth Abbott Walker⁴, Joshua³, John², George¹)*, b. at Billerica, 12 Jun 1754 daughter of Robert and Elizabeth (Abbott) Walker; d. at Billerica, 17 May 1782; m. 25 Apr 1776, EBENEZER RICHARDSON, b. 25 Feb 1754 son of Ebenezer and Elizabeth (Shed) Richardson; Ebenezer d. at Billerica, 1818. After Rebekah's death, Ebenezer married Susanna Tufts 24 Apr 1783.

Rebekah Walker and Ebenezer Richardson were parents of three children born at Billerica.

i JOEL RICHARDSON, b. 17 Jan 1777; d. at Billerica, 3 May 1849;[1109] m. 1st, at Boston, 25 Jan 1807, ELIZA DEAN, b. about 1785; Eliza d. before 1823. Joel m. 2nd, at Boston, 3 Dec 1823, SUSAN L. BAKER, b. at Boston, Jun 1796; Susan d. at Philadelphia, PA, 7 Dec 1871 (although buried in Billerica).

ii REBECCA RICHARDSON, b. 13 Sep 1778; d. at Burlington, MA, after 1850; m. at Billerica, 8 Jun 1806, EDWARD BENNETT, b. 1782 son of James and Mary (Walker) Bennett; Edward d. at Burlington, 11 May 1865.

iii NATHANIEL RICHARDSON, b. 27 Apr 1781; there is no further clear record. He may be the Nathaniel Richardson who died in Boston in 1815.

403) HANNAH WALKER *(Elizabeth Abbott Walker⁴, Joshua³, John², George¹)*, b. at Billerica, 6 Jun 1756 daughter of Robert and Elizabeth (Abbott) Walker; m. 4 Sep 1775, JOHN WRIGHT,[1110] b. at Wilmington, 29 Jun 1756 son of Josiah and Abigail (Graves) Wright.

Hannah Walker and John Wright were parents of ten children born at Billerica. No records could be located for Hannah and John after the births of their children.

i SARAH WRIGHT, b. 21 Nov 1775; m. at Billerica, 27 Feb 1800, PHINEAS COBURN, b. at Dracut, about 1777 son of Daniel Coburn; Phineas d. of yellow fever in New Orleans, 1822.[1111]

ii JOHN WRIGHT, b. 12 Dec 1777

iii HANNAH WRIGHT, b. 11 Apr 1780

iv LUCY WRIGHT, b. 12 Apr 1782; m. at Boston, 6 May 1804, SARGENT SMITH, b. at Henniker, NH, 13 Feb 1781 son of Samuel and Hannah (Marble) Smith; Sargent d. of intemperance, at Boston, 22 Jan 1834.

[1108] Middlesex County, MA: Probate File Papers, 1648-1871.Online database. AmericanAncestors.org. New England Historic Genealogical Society, 2014. Case 19030

[1109] Joel, m., gunsmith, s. Ebenezer and Rebecca, old age, May 3, 1849, a. 72 y. 3 m. 16 d. [a. 72. GR1]

[1110] Hazen's *The History of Billerica* gives the wife of John Wright as Hannah the daughter of Joseph Walker. But Hannah the daughter of Joseph was born in 1744 making her seemingly too old for this John. In addition, the 1807 will of Joshua Abbott (the brother of Elizabeth Abbott Walker) includes a bequest for his niece Hannah Wright. Also, John and Hannah Wright's last child was born in 1796 which would rule out Hannah born in 1744 as the mother in this family.

[1111] This is according to the Coburn genealogy, but some of the information provided does not really fit for this Phineas (for example, that his mother was born in 1763). He may be the Phineas would died in Billerica in 1828 at age 51.

v JOSIAH WRIGHT, b. 20 May 1784

vi REBECCA WRIGHT, b. 23 Oct 1786; d. at Billerica, 14 Sep 1860; m., at Billerica, 1809, STEPHEN GREENLAND who has not been identified. Stephen died before 1820 when Rebecca Greenland was head of household in Billerica. In 1850, Rebecca, as Rebecca Edmunds, was living with her younger brother Jonathan. Her death record is as Rebecca Edmunds.

vii ISAAC WRIGHT, b. 9 Feb 1789

viii ELIZABETH WRIGHT, b. 1 May 1791

ix JONATHAN WRIGHT, b. 18 Aug 1793; d. at Billerica, 21 Oct 1874; m. at Billerica, 8 May 1825, HANNAH PATTEN ALLEN, b. at Littleton, 23 Nov 1801 daughter of Zadok and Sarah (Patten) Allen;[1112] Hannah d. at Billerica, 28 Jan 1883.

x LYDIA WRIGHT, b. 16 Jan 1796; d. at Boston, 13 Aug 1870; m. 1st, at Boston, 8 Jul 1815 (or 1816), BENJAMIN JORDAN, b. at Danville, ME, about 1786 son of Ebenezer and Sarah (McKenney) Jordan;[1113] Benjamin d. at Boston, 7 Jul 1831. Lydia m. 2nd, at Boston, 6 Nov 1833, GEORGE BAKER. The two children so far located for Benjamin and Lydia were born in Danville, Maine.

404) JOANNA ABBOTT *(Oliver⁴, Joshua³, John², George¹)*, b. at Billerica, 24 Jul 1755 daughter of Oliver and Joanna (French) Abbott; d. at Lexington, 2 Feb 1826; m. 21 May 1776, SIMON WINSHIP, b. at Lexington, Nov 1749 son of Samuel and Abigail (Crosby) Winship; Simon d. at Lexington 24 Jan 1813.

Joanna and Simon lived in Lexington and had two children there. Simon Winship served in the Revolutionary War with the rank of Sergeant.

Simon's estate was probated in 1813. He did not leave a will, and the estate value of $247.11 was not enough to pay the debts. His widow was allowed to keep her personal possessions and the remainder of the estate was sold to settle the debts.[1114] In July 1813, a petition was filed by Elias Maynard, a "friend and relation" of Boston, asking that a guardian be appointed for the widow Joanna Winship as she was unable to care for herself. Joanna was found *non compos mentis* 19 August 1813, and Elias Maynard was named her guardian.[1115] Elias Maynard was the second husband of Joanna the daughter of Joanna and Simon. Joanna Abbott Winship died at the home of her brother-in-law, Stephen Robbins husband of Abigail Winship, 2 February 1826.[1116]

i JOANNA WINSHIP, b. 4 May 1777; d. at Boston, 10 Mar 1848; m. 1st, at Lexington, 27 Jul 1797, DARIUS SHAW; Darius d. about 1804. Joanna m. 2nd, 10 Feb 1806, ELIAS MAYNARD, b. at Townsend, 15 Oct 1777 son of Lemuel and Sarah (Craig) Maynard; Elias d. 21 Sep 1828. Joanna and Darius had a son Oliver Abbott Shaw who attended Harvard and Yale. There is a birth record for a son Darius and there is no birth record for a son Oliver Abbott, but the Yale biographical entry for Oliver Abbott Shaw has the same birth date as the entry for Darius Shaw in the birth transcriptions; these seem to be the same person rather than twins as there is no Darius in Joanna Maynard's will. In her will, written 5 May 1845, Joanna Maynard makes bequests to daughter Joanna Maynard and to each of her sons: Oliver Abbott Shaw, Xenephon Hector Shaw, Waldo Maynard, and John Parker Maynard.

ii OLIVER ABBOTT WINSHIP, b. 5 Mar 1779; d. 1 Oct 1792.

405) DORCAS ABBOTT *(Oliver⁴, Joshua³, John², George¹)*, b. at Billerica, 19 Dec 1764 daughter of Oliver and Joanna (French) Abbott; d. after 1850 likely in Williamsburg, NY;[1117] m. 21 Apr 1783, JONATHAN BOWERS, b. at Chelmsford, 18 Feb 1761 son of William and Hannah (Kidder) Bowers; Jonathan d. 21 Feb 1804.

Dorcas and Jonathan lived in Billerica where Jonathan held the position of representative a total of four years.[1118]

Jonathan Bowers wrote his will 8 July 1799 and it includes bequests for his wife Dorcas and son Alexander. Isaac Stearns is named executor.[1119] Dorcas and Jonathan had one son born at Billerica.

[1112] The names of Hannah's parents are given as Zadok and Sarah Allen on her death record.

[1113] The names of Benjamin's parents are given as Ebenezer and Sarah on the marriage record.

[1114] *Middlesex County, MA: Probate File Papers, 1648-1871. Probate of Simon Winship, 1813, Case number 25334.*

[1115] *Middlesex County, MA: Probate File Papers, 1648-1871. Guardianship of Joanna Winship, 1813, Case number 25292.*

[1116] Hudson, *History of the Town of Lexington*, volume II, p 772

[1117] In the 1850 U.S. Census, Dorcas Bowers age 85 was in the household of Mary and Alfred Curtis in Williamsburg, NY. Mary Bowers Curtis was Dorcas's granddaughter. Also in the home was Dorcas's son (and Mary Curtis's father) Alexander Bowers. Year: 1850; Census Place: Williamsburg, Kings, New York; Roll: M432_522; Page: 400A; Image: 530

[1118] Hazen, *History of Billerica*, p 364

[1119] *Middlesex County, MA: Probate File Papers, 1648-1871. Probate of Jonathan Bowers, 1804, Case number 2293.*

Dorcas did not remarry after Jonathan's death. In the 1830 U.S. Census, she seems to be the Dorcas Bowers who is the head of a household in Boston. In the household are three women, one 60-69, one 50-59, and one 30-39. The oldest woman would be the right age for Dorcas and her son was in Boston at that time. In 1850, she was in Williamsburg, New York at the home of her granddaughter Mary Bowers Curtis.

i ALEXANDER BOWERS, b. at Billerica, 15 May 1783; d. unknown but after 1850 when he is listed in the census at his daughter's home in Williamsburg, NY. Alexander married MARY JOHNSON at Boston on 6 Jul 1805. Nothing certain is known about Mary. Alexander and Mary did have at least nine children. Alexander worked at a bank in Boston.[1120]

406) ABIGAIL ABBOTT *(Oliver⁴, Joshua³, John², George¹)*, b. at Billerica, 14 Dec 1774 daughter of Oliver and Abigail (Hall) Abbott; d. at Boston 12 Sep 1816; m. 25 Dec 1796, EPHRAIM KIDDER, b. 10 Apr 1766 son of Ephraim and Lucy (Pollard) Kidder; Ephraim d. 22 Dec 1807.

There is a record for just one child for Abigail and Ephraim. The 1800 U.S. Census for Ephraim Kidder, Jr. in Billerica seems to be a household with three children, but only one child could be located. Their daughter, Abigail E. A. Kidder, did not marry. Abigail E. A. Kidder did leave a substantial estate with a value at the time of her death of about $20,000 with $11,000 in cash and notes and a dwelling valued at $8,500. There do not seem to be any close family heirs and the only relatives mentioned in the probate papers are cousins.

i ABIGAIL ELIZABETH A. KIDDER, b. at Billerica, 1798; d. at Cambridge, 12 Oct 1875.

407) JOSEPH CHANDLER *(Mary Abbott Chandler Blunt⁴, Ebenezer³, John², George¹)*, b. at Andover, 8 Jun 1743 son of Joseph and Mary (Abbott) Chandler; d. 8 Jun 1834 at Atkinson, NH; m. at Newbury, 7 Jan 1768, ELIZABETH COOK, b. at Newbury, 22 May 1747 daughter of Samuel and Elizabeth (-) Cook; Elizabeth d. likely between 1810 and 1820.

Joseph's father died when Joseph was just two years old. He was brought up in the household of his uncle James Chandler in Rowley. As a very young man, at age 14, he went to sea and traveled to the West Indies. He did settle in Atkinson, New Hampshire and raised his family there. He was a tanner by trade and established a tannery in Atkinson.[1121] He served in the Revolutionary War and saw service at Saratoga and Stillwater.[1122]

Joseph Chandler wrote his will 6 May 1826 and the will was proved 12 February 1834.[1123] The will has the following bequests: oldest daughter Polly the wife of Stephen Heath, thirty dollars; oldest son Samuel Chandler fifteen dollars; second daughter Betsey, the wife of John Boynton, forty dollars; daughter Judith Chandler, forty dollars plus all the produce that is due to him at his decease plus all the clothing she makes and all the wool and flax; daughter Sarah wife of Silas Whiting, ten dollars; son Joseph Chandler, Jr., five dollars; and Lydia the wife of Amos Baker, five dollars. John Boynton of Londonderry is named executor. Son Samuel was living at the time of the will but died in 1831.

Joseph and Lydia had seven children all born at Atkinson. All the children married, although Judith married late in life.

i MOLLY CHANDLER, b. 12 Jan 1771; m. 27 Sep 1796, STEPHEN HEATH, b. at Sundown, NH, 24 Feb 1769 son of Moses and Sarah (Flanders) Heath; Stephen's death is not determined, but he was living at the time of the 1850 U.S. Census. Molly was deceased before 1850.

ii SAMUEL CHANDLER, b. 18 Feb 1774; d. at Campton, NH, 9 Aug 1831; m. at Plymouth, NH, 7 Nov 1798, MARY GRAVES, b. 5 Jan 1779 daughter of Benjamin Graves;[1124] Mary d. at Campton, 29 Jul 1847.

iii BETTIE CHANDLER, b. 6 Jan 1779; d. at Derry, NH, 14 Mar 1853; m. at Newburyport, 11 Oct 1805, JOHN BOYNTON, of not certain origin, but likely the son of David Boynton (and perhaps Sarah Goodhue), born in Newburyport about 1782. John d. at Derry, 28 Nov 1848.

iv JUDITH CHANDLER, b. 2 Oct 1780; d. at Hampstead, 15 Feb 1865; m. at Atkinson, 25 Nov 1847, THOMAS TEWKSBURY. The story related in the Chandler genealogy is that Thomas was from West Newbury and came to Atkinson over Thanksgiving and married Judith after very short acquaintance. The day after the wedding, he

---

1120 Ancestry,com, U.K. and U.S. Directories, 1680-1830, Alexander Bowers listed as a messenger at Boston Bank 1826-1850.

1121 Abbott, Abbott Genealogies, notes on the Chandler Family

1122 Chandler, *The Descendants of William and Annis Chandler*, p 213

1123 *New Hampshire Wills and Probate Records 1643-1982,* Probate of Joseph Chandler, Rockingham, 12 Feb 1834, Case number 12662.

1124 Stearns and Runnels, *History of Plymouth, New Hampshire*, 107

returned to West Newbury and never returned.[1125] There is a Thomas Tewksbury who died at the almshouse in West Newbury in 1859 at age 68 and perhaps that is him. At the 1860 U.S. Census, Judith was living on her own in Atkinson; she is listed as being deaf due to measles.[1126]

v SALLY CHANDLER, b. 14 Feb 1783; d. 10 Nov 1855; m. 1st, about 1802, ABIEL LOVEJOY, b. likely at Plymouth NH, 24 Apr 1780 son of Abiel and Mary (Hobart) Lovejoy; Abiel d. 18 Apr 1814. Sally m. 2nd, at Plymouth, 10 Jun 1817, as his second wife, SILAS WHITNEY, b. at Lincoln, 13 Jul 1766 son of Solomon and Mary (Fay) Whitney; Silas d. 1 Sep 1850. At the 1850 U.S. Census, Sally and Silas were living in the home of their daughter Sarah Chandler Whitney and her husband William Tyler.[1127] Silas was first married to Hopestill Sargent.

vi JOSEPH CHANDLER, b. 1 Oct 1785; d. at Atkinson, 12 Jun 1865; m. 10 Jan 1808, POLLY WOODMAN, b. at Salem, NH, 1 Jun 1784 daughter of Abner and Sarah (Emery) Woodman; Polly d. 20 Dec 1866.

vii LYDIA BARTLETT CHANDLER, b. 1 Mar 1789; d. at Westminster, MA, 7 May 1870; m. AMOS BAKER, b. in NH about 1794 (parents unknown); Amos d. at Westminster, 7 May 1870. The Chandler genealogy reported that Lydia and Amos had two children who died young. Lydia and Amos were admitted to the Plymouth, NH congregational church in 1822 and dismissed to the church in Lowell, MA August 1833.[1128] After his death, the real estate of Amos Baker was sold at auction to pay his debts. His property consisted of 93 acres of farmland in Westminster with a two-story house and barn.[1129] There did not seem to be any heirs.

408) MARY BLUNT (*Mary Abbott Chandler Blunt⁴, Ebenezer³, John², George¹*), b. at Andover, 14 Feb 1746/7 daughter of Isaac and Mary (Abbott) Blunt; d. before 1818[1130] likely at Exeter, NH; m. 2 May 1771; JEREMIAH LEAVITT, b. about 1749 and likely the son of Jeremiah and Mary (-) Leavitt; Jeremiah d. at Exeter, NH, 3 Aug 1818.

Jeremiah Leavitt did not leave a will and his estate entered probate 14 September 1818 with his son Samuel as administrator.[1131] The real estate needed to be sold to settle the estate due to indebtedness and Samuel Leavitt petitioned the Court related to the need to do this. The other heirs signing agreement with this decision were Isaac Leavitt, Mary Robinson, and Abner Merrill (who is the husband of Sarah). The sale brought $8,200 with $4,700 of that amount going to creditors.

Birth records were not located for the children and it may be there were other children who died young. Those children listed as heirs are given here with birthdates estimated based on date of marriage or age at death.

i MARY LEAVITT, b. about 1772; m. at Exeter, 12 Jul 1792, WILLIAM ROBINSON, b. at Exeter about 1770 likely the son of Caleb and Mary (Waterhouse) Robinson. William d. at Exeter about 1802 (probate of estate 8 Feb 1802). Widow Mary Robinson requested that her father Jeremiah Leavitt be granted administration of the estate.[1132]

ii ISAAC LEAVITT, b. about 1780; d. at Exeter, 13 Mar 1854. Isaac does not seem to have married. In the 1850 U.S. Census, he was living in the household of his nephew Samuel and his family; Isaac's brother Samuel was also living there.[1133]

iii SAMUEL LEAVITT, b. at Exeter about 1782; d. at Exeter 10 May 1856; m. ABIGAIL KIMBALL, b. about 1778 daughter of Nathaniel and Hannah (Wormall) Kimball;[1134] Abigail d. at Exeter, 19 Dec 1868.

iv SARAH LEAVITT, b. about 1789; d. at Exeter, 25 Mar 1870; m. 2 Jul 1816, ABNER MERRILL, b. at Newburyport, 21 Apr 1791 son of Enoch and Temperance (Little) Merrill; Abner d. 23 Jul 1877.

409) HANNAH BLUNT (*Mary Abbott Chandler Blunt⁴, Ebenezer³, John², George¹*), b. at Andover, 25 Sep 1755 daughter of Isaac and Mary (Abbott) Blunt; d. likely at Wilmington, MA before 1827; m. 10 Aug 1773, EZRA CARTER, b. at Wilmington, 26 Feb 1745/6 son of Ezra and Lydia (Jenkins) Carter; Ezra d. at Wilmington, 11 Feb 1827.

1125 Chandler, *The Descendants of William and Annis Chandler*, p 213

1126 Year: 1860; Census Place: Atkinson, Rockingham, New Hampshire; Roll: M653_679; Page: 869; Family History Library Film: 803679

1127 Year: 1850; Census Place: Thornton, Grafton, New Hampshire; Roll: M432_431; Page: 274B; Image: 546

1128 Manual of the Congregational Church of Plymouth, NH, p 38

1129 *Worcester County, MA: Probate File Papers, 1731-1881, Probate of Amos Baker, 1870, Case number 2596.*

1130 She was not living at the time of the probate of her husband's estate 14 September 1818.

1131 *New Hampshire Wills and Probate Records 1643-1982,* Probate of Jeremiah Leavitt, Rockingham, 14 Sep 1818, Case number 9777.

1132 *New Hampshire Wills and Probate Records 1643-1982,* Probate of William Robinson, Rockingham, 8 Feb 1802, Case number 6887.

1133 Year: 1850; Census Place: Exeter, Rockingham, New Hampshire; Roll: M432_438; Page: 210B; Image: 410

1134 *Reports of Cases Argued and Determined in the Superior Court of Judicature for the State of New Hampshire*, Volume 12, p 166. The 1817 will of Samuel Wormall includes a bequest to his niece Abigail Leavitt. There was a suit related to this estate when Abigail Leavitt and her husband Samuel Leavitt in 1839 made application to the judge of probate related to the handling of the estate by Thomas Kimball.

Ezra Carter did not leave a will. On 12 February 1828, eldest son Ezra Carter petitioned for administration of the estate stating his father died the year previously and left no widow. The total value of the estate was $935.74, with $850 of that value for half of the homestead buildings.[1135]

Daughter Eusebia did not marry and at the probate of her estate the following heirs-at-law were identified: sister Betsey Manning of Reading wife of Jacob Manning; sister Phebe Lewis of Fitchburg wife of Jesse Lewis; the children of sister Sarah Webster who are Isaac, Daniel, Charles, Leveret, Harriet, and Sarah Webster, and Mary Heath; children of brother Ezra Carter who are J.J. Carter, Ann C. Manning wife of Otis Manning, and Sumner Carter. Sumner Cater was administrator of the estate. The personal estate was valued at $552.39, which included $527.64 in cash and promissory notes.[1136]

Ezra Carter and Hannah Blunt were parents of nine children born at Wilmington.

i EZRA CARTER, b. 16 May 1774; d. at Westford, 22 Jun 1855; m. at Wilmington, 1 Dec 1803, ANN JAQUITH, b. at Wilmington, 21 Feb 1779 daughter of Nathan and Ann (Crosby) Jaquith; Ann d. at Westford, 29 Aug 1854.

ii HANNAH CARTER, b. 8 Aug 1776; likely died young

iii MOLLY CATER, b. 8 Aug 1776; likely died young

iv SARAH CARTER, b. 2 Oct 1778; d. at Haverhill, 28 Mar 1846; m. at Haverhill, 23 Aug 1801, ISAIAH WEBSTER, b. at Haverhill, 23 Feb 1778 son of Stephen and Elizabeth (Day) Webster; Isaiah d. at Haverhill, 30 Aug 1850.

v ELIZABETH CARTER, b. 17 Sep 1780; d. at Reading, 16 Mar 1865; m. at Wilmington, 23 Sep 1810, JACOB MANNING, b. at Tewksbury, 8 Jun 1780 son of Thomas and Abigail (Stanley) Manning; Jacob d. at Wilmington, 31 Aug 1842.

vi ABIGAIL CARTER, b. 4 May 1782; no further record but not living and without heirs at the time of her sister's probate.

vii PHEBE CARTER, b. 13 Apr 1784; d. at Fitchburg, 12 Feb 1866; m. 1st, at Burlington, MA, 16 Sep 1809, JESSE BUTTERS, b. at Wilmington, 9 Sep 1783 son of Jesse and Rebecca (Jenkins) Butters; Jesse d. at Jaffrey, NH, 25 Feb 1829. Phebe m. 2nd, about 1830, JESSE LEWIS.

viii EUSEBIA CARTER, b. 13 Jun 1786; d. at Westford, 2 Jan 1863. Eusebia did not marry.

ix ISAAC CARTER, b. 5 Nov 1789; d. at Wilmington, 9 Mar 1844. Isaac did not marry.

410) JOHN BLUNT *(Mary Abbott Chandler Blunt^4, Ebenezer^3, John^2, George^1)*, b. 31 Jan 1756 son of Isaac and Mary (Abbott) Blunt; d. at Amherst, NH, 27 Nov 1836;[1137] m. at Wilmington, 25 Oct 1780, SARAH EAMES daughter of Caleb and Mary (Harvey) Eames; Sarah d. at Milford, 25 Jan 1858.

On 5 May 1855, Sarah Blunt filed a land warrant application in Milford, New Hampshire as the widow of a Revolutionary War service member. The petition asserts that John Blunt served for more than fourteen days and was honorably discharged. The application also states that Sarah and John were married on 25 October 1780 and that John died on 27 Nov 1836. The pension file documents state that John Blunt enlisted at Andover in 1775 and was present at the Battle of Bunker Hill. He enlisted 30 September 1777 and served as a private in Captain John Abbott's company, was at the surrender of Burgoyne, and was discharged 6 November 1777.[1138]

John and Sarah Blunt started their family in Andover and then relocated to Amherst, New Hampshire. They had fifteen children.

Their son Ainsworth Emery Blunt graduated Yale and was a missionary at the Brainerd Mission in Tennessee. He accompanied the Cherokee people of the Trail of Tears.[1139]

i SALLY BLUNT, b. at Andover, 1 Jan 1782; d. at Foxborough, MA, 21 Dec 1870; m. 16 Jun 1804, DANIEL HOWE, b. at Milford, 5 Dec 1776 son of Stephen and Hannah (Duncklee) Howe; Daniel d. at Foxborough, 21 Sep 1871.

[1135] Middlesex County, MA: Probate File Papers, 1648-1871.Online database. AmericanAncestors.org. New England Historic Genealogical Society, 2014. Case number 3988

[1136] *Probate Records 1648--1924 (Middlesex County, Massachusetts)*; Author: *Massachusetts. Probate Court (Middlesex County)*; Probate Place: *Middlesex, Massachusetts*, Case 28893

[1137] The gravestone for this family has the following inscription: JOHN BLUNT DIED Nov. 27, 1836, AEt. 80; SARAH EAMES his wife Died Jan. 25, 1858, AEt. 93; Isaac 14 m's, Alva L. 3d's; Twin sons 1 d., Alva L. 17 d's & Rebecca K. 4 1/2 y's. Children of John & Sarah Blunt rest here. Blessed are the dead that die in the Lord. (findagrave.com, ID 61561179)

[1138] Revolutionary War Pension and Bounty-Land Warrant Application Files

[1139] Whitfield-Murray Historical Society, "Blunt House," http://www.whitfield-murrayhistoricalsociety.org/historicproperties/blunthouse.html

ii MARY HARVEY BLUNT, b. at Andover, 22 Mar 1784; m. at Amherst, 9 Jul 1803, CHARLES STEVENS, b. at Amherst, 9 Jan 1780 son of Daniel and Susanna (Abbott) Stevens; Charles d. at Amherst, Jul 1810.

iii JOHN BLUNT, b. at Andover, 3 Jun 1786; d. at Nashua, 25 Oct 1860; m. at Boston, 2 Aug 1814, MARY ESTEY, b. at Roxbury, 25 May 1784 daughter of Jacob and Lucy (Williams) Estey; Mary d. at Nashua, 28 Mar 1864.

iv ANNA BLUNT, b. at Andover, 5 Aug 1788; no further record.

v ISAAC BLUNT, b. at Amherst, 20 Sep 1790; d. 3 Nov 1791.

vi ELIZABETH BLUNT, b. at Amherst, 11 Jun 1793; d. at Milford, 5 Feb 1873; m. at Amherst, 11 Sep 1815, JAMES BLANCHARD, b. at Milford, 8 Oct 1786 son of Stephen and Elizabeth (Potter) Blanchard; James d. at Milford, 7 Sep 1854.

vii DAVID WEBSTER BLUNT, b. at Amherst, 25 Jul 1795; d. at Amherst, 30 Apr 1868; m. 14 Dec 1837, HANNAH BURNHAM, b. at Milford, 25 Mar 1804 daughter of Andrew and Elizabeth (Burns) Burnham; Hannah d. at Milford, 15 Jan 1882.

viii ASENATH BLUNT, b. at Amherst, 13 Jan 1798; d. at Milford, 20 Mar 1877; m. at Amherst, 1822, JACOB SARGENT, b. at Milford, 15 Feb 1796 son of Ebenezer and Mary (Marsh) Sargent; Jacob d. at Milford, 13 Jul 1873.

ix AINSWORTH EMERY BLUNT, b. at Amherst, 22 Feb 1800; d. at Dalton, GA, 21 Dec 1865; m. 1st, 17 Nov 1822, HARRIET ELLSWORTH, b. at Greensborough, VT, 22 Sep 1790 daughter of John and Sarah (Strong) Ellsworth; Harriet d. at Dalton, 10 Jun 1847. Ainsworth m. 2nd, 13 Jan 1849, ELIZABETH CHRISTIAN RAMSEY, b. at Knox, TN, 3 Aug 1816 daughter of Samuel Reynolds and Elizabeth Christian (Fleming) Ramsey; Elizabeth d. at Dalton, 16 Mar 1899.

x ALVAH L. BLUNT, b. at Amherst, 3 Mar 1802; d. 6 Mar 1802.

xi Twin1 b. and d. 15 Oct 1803

xii Twin2 b. and d. 15 Oct 1803

xiii SOPHIA BLUNT, b. at Amherst, 2 May 1805; d. at Indianapolis, IN, 28 Aug 1868; m. at Lowell, 4 Sep 1831, THURLOW HASKELL, b. at Lunenburg, 24 Oct 1807 son of Henry and Phebe (Marshall) Haskell; Thurlow d. at Indianapolis, 1866.

xiv ALVAH L. BLUNT, b. 19 Feb 1808; d. 7 Mar 1808.

xv REBECCA KENDALL BLUNT, b. 28 Jul 1809; d. 28 Jan 1814.

411) SUSANNA ABBOTT *(Isaac⁴, Ebenezer³, John², George¹)*, b. at Andover, 29 Aug 1754 daughter of Isaac and Susanna (Farnum) Abbott; d. at Fryeburg, ME, 21 Sep 1827; m. Oct 1774, SAMUEL CHARLES, b. 28 Aug 1754 son of John and Abigail (Bliss) Charles; Samuel d. 14 Dec 1843.

Samuel and Susanna Charles were parents of eleven children born at Fryeburg.

i OLIVE CHARLES, b. 1 Feb 1775; d. at Stow, ME, 6 Feb 1816; m. by 1793, JAMES WALKER, b. 25 Apr 1774 son of Samuel and Hannah (Hazeltine) Walker; James d. at Stow, 9 Nov 1810.

ii HANNAH CHARLES, b. 13 Aug 1776; d. at Freedom, IL, 1857; m. ROBERT WILEY, b. at Fryeburg, 20 Sep 1770 son of William and Elizabeth (Walker) Wiley; Robert d. at Freedom, 1857.

iii SUSANNA CHARLES, b. 6 Apr 1778; d. at Chatham, NH, 15 Aug 1851; m. about 1799, her first cousin, SOLOMON CHARLES, b. 13 May 1776 son of John and Phebe (Russell) Charles; Solomon d. at Chatham, 17 Jun 1854.

iv SAMUEL CHARLES, b. 2 Jul 1781; d. at Wethersfield, NY, 20 May 1845; m. at Fryeburg, 3 May 1803, ELIZABETH LANGDON, b. at Fryeburg, 2 Mar 1784 daughter of Peter and Mary (Kimball) Langdon; Elizabeth d. at Monroe, WI, 20 Oct 1874. After Samuel's death, Elizabeth lived with her daughter Harriet in Wisconsin.

v ESTHER C. CHARLES, b. 28 Jun 1783; d. at Fryeburg, 25 Dec 1861; m. at Fryeburg, 10 Sep 1803, JAMES WILEY, b. at Fryeburg, 24 Mar 1782 son of Benjamin and Alice (Kilgore) Wiley; James's d. not located but before 1850.

vi BLISS CHARLES, b. 3 Jun 1787; d. at Columbia, MI, 1 Aug 1857; m. SIDNEY B. TILTON, b. at Kennebec, 15 Jan 1789 daughter of Cornelius and Jedidah (Pease) Tilton; Sidney d. at Columbia, 30 Aug 1878.

vii LUCY CHARLES, b. 19 Jul 1791; d. at Fryeburg, 19 Jan 1873; m. her first cousin, ISAAC CHARLES *(Olive Abbott Charles[5], Isaac[4], Ebenezer[3], John[2], George[1])*, b. at Fryeburg, 17 Oct 1784 son of John and Olive (Abbott) Charles; Isaac d. at Fryeburg, 17 May 1865. Isaac is a child in Family 412.

viii PETER CHARLES, b. 14 Apr 1793; d. at Fryeburg, 1 Jul 1881; m. ESTHER WILEY, b. at Fryeburg, 4 Jan 1796 daughter of Benjamin and Alice (Kilgore) Wiley; Esther d. at Fryeburg, 12 Nov 1884.

ix ACHSAH CHARLES, b. 23 Jan 1795; d. at Lovell, ME, 4 Nov 1862; m. 17 Jun 1814, JOHN MERRILL, b. about 1789; John d. at Lovell, 15 Dec 1865.

x ASA GRANVILLE CHARLES, b. 3 Sep 1797; d. at Fryeburg, 30 Jan 1873; m. 15 Oct 1834, his third cousin, once removed, RUTH A. WARD *(Rachel Abbott Ward[5], Joseph[4], George[3], Thomas[2], George[1])*, b. at Fryeburg, 1 Apr 1802 daughter of Jonathan and Rachel (Abbott) Ward; Ruth d. at Fryeburg, 17 Mar 1848. Rachel is a child in Family 937.

xi NATHANIEL W. CHARLES, b. 8 Feb 1800; d. at Fryeburg, 10 Mar 1868; m. OLIVE A. CHARLES *(Olive Abbott Charles[5], Isaac[4], Ebenezer[3], John[2], George[1])*, b. at Fryeburg, 17 Sep 1795 daughter of John and Olive (Abbott) Charles; Olive d. at Fryeburg, 27 Sep 1876. Olive is a child in Family 412.

412) OLIVE ABBOTT *(Isaac[4], Ebenezer[3], John[2], George[1])*, b. at Andover, 17 Feb 1756 daughter of Isaac and Susanna (Farnum) Abbott; d. at Fryeburg, ME, 27 Aug 1828; m. about 1782, as his third wife, JOHN CHARLES, b. at Brimfield, MA, 28 Feb 1744 son of John and Abigail (Bliss) Charles; John d. at Lovell, ME, 6 Jun 1831. John was first married to Phebe Russell and second to Elizabeth Farrington.

John Charles and Olive Abbott were parents of eight children born at Fryeburg, Maine.

i DANIEL CHARLES, b. 1783; d. at Lovell, 23 Jul 1834; m. at Fryeburg, 22 Oct 1807, EXPERIENCE HOWARD, b. at Surry, NH, 29 Jul 1782 daughter of Nathan and Sarah (Smith) Howard/Hayward; Experience d. at Lovell, 10 May 1852.

ii ISAAC CHARLES, b. 17 Oct 1784; d. at Fryeburg, 17 May 1865; m. his first cousin, LUCY CHARLES *(Susanna Abbott Charles[5], Isaac[4], Ebenezer[3], John[2], George[1])*, b. at Fryeburg, 19 Jul 1791 daughter of Samuel and Susanna (Abbott) Charles; Lucy d. at Fryeburg, 19 Jan 1873. Lucy is a child in Family 411.

iii ELIZABETH FARRINGTON CHARLES, b. 2 May 1786; d. at Penobscot, ME, 22 May 1875; m. about 1807, THOMAS PAGE, b. at Conway, NH, 18 Apr 1779 son of Jeremiah and Mary (Duston) Page; Thomas d. at Penobscot, 8 Feb 1864.

iv SIMEON CHARLES, b. 28 Oct 1787; d. at Fryeburg, 4 Jun 1869; m. about 1811, SARAH WILEY, b. 28 Sep 1793 daughter of Benjamin and Alice (Kilgore) Wiley; Sarah d. at Fryeburg, 15 Jun 1886.

v DOROTHY F. CHARLES, b. 23 Dec 1789; d. at Lovell, 6 Jul 1873; m. at Lovell, 23 Nov 1813, PHINEAS EASTMAN, b. at Dracut, MA, 5 Apr 1787 son of Daniel and Sarah (Whiting) Eastman; Phineas d. at Lovell, 20 Feb 1847.

vi ELEANOR CHARLES, b. 1791; d. at Fryeburg, 28 May 1862; m. about 1816, GEORGE WILEY, b. 28 Jan 1790 son of Benjamin and Alice (Kilgore) Wiley; George d. at Fryeburg, 7 Mar 1872.

vii OLIVE A. CHARLES, b. 17 Sep 1795; d. at Fryeburg, 27 Sep 1876; m. her first cousin, NATHANIEL W. CHARLES *(Susanna Abbott Charles[5], Isaac[4], Ebenezer[3], John[2], George[1])*, b. at Fryeburg, 8 Feb 1800 son of Samuel and Susanna (Abbott) Charles; Nathaniel d. at Fryeburg, 10 Mar 1868. Nathaniel is a child in Family 411.

viii DEAN CHARLES, b. 30 Jan 1798; d. at Black Brook, NY, about 1870 (probate 19 Mar 1870); m. at Conway, 8 Jul 1823, SUSAN HOW, b. about 1800; Susan d. at Black Brook, 19 Dec 1862.

413) LUCY ABBOTT *(Isaac[4], Ebenezer[3], John[2], George[1])*, b. at Andover, 20 Mar 1759 daughter of Isaac and Susanna (Farnum) Abbott; d. at Maine about 1790; m. WILLIAM KIMBALL. William m. 2nd, BETHIAH GORDON; William d. about 1813 (date of probate).

William Kimball built the first saw and grist mills in Lovell, Maine.[1140] William did not leave a will and son William Kimball was named administrator of the estate. Real estate totaling 300 acres was valued at $1200 and personal estate at $507.70.[1141]

Lucy Abbott and William Kimball were parents to three children.

i WILLIAM KIMBALL, b. about 1782; d. at York County, ME, 11 Oct 1861; m. at Lovell, 19 Oct 1806, BETSY KILGORE, b. at Lovell, 19 Apr 1789 daughter of James and Abigail (-) Kilgore; Betsy d. at York County, 11 Apr 1864.

ii NANCY KIMBALL, b. at Fryeburg, about 1783; d. at Lovell, 25 Jun 1842; m. at Lovell, 26 Jul 1807, AMOS KENISTON.

iii JOSEPH KIMBALL, b. at Fryeburg, 20 Aug 1788; d. at Lovell, 2 Mar 1859; m. 19 Feb 1810, his fourth cousin SARAH DRESSER *(Abigail Abbott Dresser⁵, Sarah Abbott Abbott⁴, James³, William², George¹)*, b. at Lovell, 6 Aug 1792 daughter of Stephen and Abigail (Abbott) Dresser; Sarah d. at Lovell, May 1874. Sarah is a child in Family 590.

414) ISAAC ABBOTT *(Isaac⁴, Ebenezer³, John², George¹)*, b. at Andover, 16 Jun 1762 son of Isaac and Susanna (Farnum) Abbott; d. at Fryeburg, ME, 23 Jun 1861; m. by 1788, SUSANNA NOYES KNIGHT, b. about 1770 daughter of Stephen and Susanna (Noyes) Knight; Susanna d. 3 Sep 1851. Isaac is likely also the father of Enoch Eaton Abbott, an out-of-wedlock child born to Sarah Eaton in 1785.

Isaac Abbott served in the Revolution. In a statement in his pension application dated 7 August 1832, Isaac Abbott resident of Fryeburg, age 70 years, stated that in June 1780 while he was living in Fryeburg (then in Massachusetts) that "the selectman of said town engaged me into the United States service" for six months.[1142] He was at West Point in the company of Captain Benton and the Regiment of Colonel Putnam. After about a month, he was drafted into the light infantry of General Poor's Brigade. He served in various other units including being sent on scouting missions along rivers and lakes before his discharge and return to Fryeburg. He reported his total periods of service as six months in 1780, fall and winter of 1781, and four months in 1782. He was promoted to Corporal in his last period of service. Isaac had difficulty securing a pension as there was a question whether his service was "Revolutionary." He was ultimately awarded a pension of seventy dollars per annum. In 1855, at age 92, he sought bounty land for which he previously applied but never received.

Isaac Abbott did not leave a will and Charles Abbott was appointed administrator of the estate 23 January 1862. The probate concerns just the disposition of his pension.[1143]

Child of Isaac Abbott and Sarah Eaton.

i ENOCH EATON ABBOTT, b. at Fryeburg, 30 Jan 1785; d. at Conway, 22 Apr 1862; m. at Conway, 4 Jun 1818, FANNY DINSMORE, b. about 1794 daughter of John and Sally (Frye) Dinsmore; Fanny d. at Chatham, NH, Apr 1860.

Isaac Abbott and Susanna Noyes Knight were parents of nine children born at Fryeburg.

i STEPHEN ABBOTT, b. 22 Dec 1788; no further record.

ii CALEB ABBOTT, b. 1790; d. at Fryeburg, 10 Aug 1875; m. Apr 1812, MEHITABLE CHASE, b. at Fryeburg, 1791 daughter of Joseph F. and Mehitable (Day) Chase; Mehitable d. 24 Sep 1877. [Interesting connection: Sarah Eaton (mother of Isaac Abbott's out-of-wedlock child) was the third husband of Joseph F. Chase.]

iii LUCY ABBOTT, b. 8 Apr 1792; d. at Bangor, ME, 13 Jul 1881; m. at Fryeburg, 28 Nov 1811, PETER WALKER, b. at Fryeburg, 8 Jan 1787 son of Samuel and Hannah (Hazeltine) Walker; Peter d. at Fryeburg after 1840 and before 1850.

iv ASA ABBOTT, b. 2 Nov 1794; d. at Fryeburg, 23 Nov 1860; m. at Fryeburg, 6 Apr 1817, his first cousin once removed, HANNAH CHARLES *(Susanna Charles Charles⁶, Susanna Abbott Charles⁵, Isaac⁴, Ebenezer³, John², George¹)*, b. at Fryeburg, 20 Jul 1796 daughter of Solomon and Susanna (Charles) Charles; Hannah d. at Fryeburg, 21 Sep 1888.

[1140] Kimball, Sumner. "Reminiscences of Elbridge Gerry Kimball", *Yesterday's News*, volume 21, number 1, 2014. http://www.lovellhistoricalsociety.org/wp-content/uploads/2015/12/Winter-2014.pdf

[1141] *Maine. Probate Court (Oxford County);* Probate Place: *Oxford, Maine*, Probate records, volume 1, p 284

[1142] Revolutionary War Pension and Bounty-Land Warrant Application Files, 1800-1900, Case S29568

[1143] *Maine. Probate Court (Oxford County);* Probate Place: *Oxford, Maine*

v SUSANNA ABBOTT, b. 1 Feb 1797; d. at Hiram, ME, 23 Aug 1880; m. at Fryeburg, 23 Apr 1825, DANIEL GRAY SMALL, b. 12 Oct 1800 son of Reuben and Patience (Gray) Small; Daniel d. at Hiram, 27 Dec 1877.

vi DEAN ABBOTT, b. 9 Mar 1800; d. 16 May 1821.

vii CHARLES ABBOTT, b. 31 May 1803; d. at Fryeburg, 17 May 1866; m. 1st, at Fryeburg, 21 Nov 1825, MARGRETTE "PEGGY" GORDON, b. about 1800; Peggy d. at Fryeburg, 6 Feb 1842. Charles m. 2nd, 22 Jul 1843, ELIZA COLBY; Eliza d. at Fryeburg, 30 Jun 1855. Charles m. 3rd, about 1855, MARY BARKER, b. 1806; Mary d. at Fryeburg, 14 Oct 1870.

viii SALLY NOYES ABBOTT, b. 12 Jun 1805; d. 14 Mar 1832.

ix JOHN S. ABBOTT, b. 1807; d. at Fryeburg, 20 Dec 1861; m. at Fryeburg, 27 Nov 1837, CAROLINE M. WILEY, b. 8 Jun 1819; Caroline d. at Fryeburg, 8 Mar 1891.

415) SIMEON ABBOTT *(Isaac4, Ebenezer3, John2, George1)*, b. at Andover, 20 May 1764 son of Isaac and Susanna (Farnum) Abbott; d. at Stow, ME, 7 May 1851; m. 3 Jul 1791, MARY DAY, b. Feb 1768 daughter of Moses and Hannah (-) Day; Mary d. 14 Sep 1840.

Simeon and his brothers Isaac, James, and Micah settled in Fryeburg and started the first saw and grist mills in Fryeburg around 1800. The brothers later moved on to Stow where they were first settlers. Stow was incorporated in 1833. The Abbotts held a large tract of land in the area.[1144] Simeon was appointed postmaster of Stow in 1837.[1145]

There were some complications in the relationships of the children. Daughter Dolly married Abner Davis in 1831 and they had two children. By 1850, Dolly Davis was living in Stow with her brother Noyes, but Abner and the two children were living in Milan, New Hampshire along with Dolly's niece Sarah Fitch Irish (named as Sarah F. Davis on the census record). By 1860, Dolly had resumed using the name Dolly Abbott and Abner and Sarah had two children of their own. It must be assumed that Dolly and Abner divorced some time in the 1840's although a record was not located for either the divorce or the marriage of Abner Davis and Sarah Irish.

Simeon and Mary had six children.

i MOSES ABBOTT, b. at Andover, ME, 30 Aug 1792; d. at Stow, ME, 19 Feb 1862; m. 1st, at Fryeburg, Nov 1817, NANCY IRISH, b. about 1795 daughter of Ebenezer and Martha "Patty" (Morton) Irish; Nancy d. about 1829. Moses m. 2nd, about 1830, HANNAH PRIDE, b. at Falmouth, ME, about 1801; Hannah d. at Stow, 15 Mar 1863.

ii HANNAH ABBOTT, b. at Andover, ME, 7 Feb 1793; d. at Stow, 19 Jan 1881; m. at Fryeburg, 22 Mar 1817, STEPHEN IRISH, b. about 1792 son of Ebenezer and Martha (Morton) Irish; Stephen d. at Stow, 8 Jan 1863.

iii SIMEON ABBOTT, b. at Fryeburg, 12 Nov 1801; d. at Stow, Jan 1890; m. at Fryeburg, 11 Nov 1839, ABIGAIL HARDY, b. at Chatham, NH, 1 Nov 1804 daughter of Jonathan and Abigail (Walker) Hardy; Abigail d. at Paris, ME, 28 Dec 1893.

iv MARY ABBOTT, b. at Fryeburg, 6 Mar 1803; d. at Stow, 19 Jun 1866; m. 1st, about 1824, JOHN FARRINGTON, b. at Stow, 31 Oct 1801 son of Samuel and Betsy (Dresser) Farrington; John d. at Stow, 14 Nov 1825. Mary m. 2nd, about 1826, PETER HARDY, b. 1798 son of Jonathan and Abigail (Walker) Hardy; Peter d. at Stow, 25 Mar 1872. After Mary's death, Peter married Maretta Curtis 3 Jun 1869.

v NOYES ABBOTT, b. at Fryeburg, 15 Sep 1806; d. at Stow, 14 Oct 1893; m. at Fryeburg, 23 Jul 1834, his first cousin, MARY ANN DAY, b. 15 Oct 1813 daughter of Moses and Susan (McKeen) Day; Mary Ann d. at Stow, 27 Feb 1885.

vi DOLLY ABBOTT, b. at Fryeburg, 12 Dec 1808; d. at Stow, about 1870; m. at Fryeburg, 4 Jul 1831, ABNER DAVIS, b. at Standish, ME, 21 Mar 1811 son of Sylvanus and Phebe (McDonald) Davis; Abner d. at Boston, 18 Jan 1886. About 1848, Abner married Dolly's niece, SARAH FITCH IRISH, b. at Fryeburg, 29 Jun 1818 daughter of Stephen and Hannah (Abbott) Irish; Sarah d. at Bethel, ME, after 1900.

416) JAMES ABBOTT *(Isaac4, Ebenezer3, John2, George1)*, b. likely at Fryeburg, 1770 (based on age 89 at death) son of Isaac and Susanna (Farnum) Abbott; d. at Stow, ME, Dec 1859; m. at Fryeburg, 16 Aug 1795, ELIZABETH DAY, b. 18 Jun 1773 daughter of Moses and Hannah (McKeen) Day; Elizabeth d. 6 Nov 1857.

[1144] Varney, *A Gazetteer of the State of Maine*, p 530

[1145] U.S., Appointments of U. S. Postmasters, 1832-1971

James Abbott and Elizabeth Day were parents of eight children, likely all born at Stow, Maine.

i ISAAC ABBOTT, b. 27 Jan 1796; d. at Fryeburg, 6 Apr 1883; m. at Fryeburg, 1 Feb 1821, ELIZABETH IRISH, b. 1796 daughter of Elizabeth and Martha (Morton) Irish; Elizabeth d. at Fryeburg, 16 Mar 1869.

ii BENJAMIN ABBOTT, b. 4 Mar 1798; d. at Stow, 19 Mar 1842; m. MARY about whom nothing is known at this time.

iii ESTHER ABBOTT, b. at Stow, 1 Aug 1801; d. at Stow, 25 May 1894; m. 3 Apr 1832, WILLIAM COX WALKER, b. 14 Apr 1805 son of John and Nancy (Cox) Walker; William d. at Stow, 16 May 1862.

iv JAMES F. ABBOTT, b. at Stow, 5 Nov 1803; d. at Berlin, NH, 27 Sep 1884; m. about 1838, MARY F. JOHNSON, b. 10 Jan 1816 daughter of Ira B. and Nancy (Heath) Johnson;[1146] Mary d. at Paris, ME, 2 Feb 1899. A son of James and Mary Nelson Abbott was killed in action 2 Apr 1865 at Fort Gregg during the Battle of Petersburg.[1147]

v MICAH ABBOTT, b. at Stow, 13 Aug 1805; d. at Stow 17 Jun 1878; m. at Fryeburg, 7 Jun 1834, SARAH IRISH FESSENDEN, b. 1812 daughter of William and Mary (Irish) Fessenden; Sarah d. at Stow, 6 Aug 1890.

vi SEBASTIAN STREETER ABBOTT, b. 12 Jan 1810; d. at Stow, 6 Feb 1891. Sebastian did not marry.

vii ALBERT P. ABBOTT, b. about 1815; d. at Lowell, 12 Jul 1898; m. at Chatham, 29 Nov 1849, REBECCA LINELL HASKELL, b. at Standish, ME, about 1828 daughter of Ephraim C. and Eliza (Boulton) Haskell; Rebecca d. at Lowell, 14 Dec 1904.

viii FREEMAN F. ABBOTT, b. 16 Aug 1817; d. at Red Oak, IA, 7 Jan 1876; m. his first cousin once removed, MELINDA C. EASTMAN *(Jeremiah Eastman[6], Jeremy Eastman[5], Sarah Abbott Eastman[4], James[3], William[2], George[1])*, b. 14 Nov 1831 daughter of Jeremiah and Cynthia (Abbott) Eastman; Melinda d. at Red Oak, 15 May 1903.

417) MICAH ABBOTT *(Isaac[4], Ebenezer[3], John[2], George[1])*, b. at Fryeburg, 1 Nov 1774 son of Isaac and Susanna (Farnum) Abbott; d. at Stow, ME, 2 Jul 1825; m. about 1795, ALICE WILEY, b. at Stow, 20 May 1778 daughter of Benjamin and Alice (Kilgore) Wiley; Alice d. at Stow, 14 Sep 1858. After Micah's death, Alice married Samuel Huntress.

Micah Abbott and Alice Wiley were parents of eight children, the oldest six children born at Fryeburg and the two youngest children at Stow.

i SILAS ABBOTT, b. a Fryeburg, 1795; d. at Stow, 1 Sep 1883. Silas did not marry.

ii MEHITABLE ABBOTT, b. at Fryeburg, 1797; d. at Stow, 9 Apr 1884; m. at Fryeburg, 19 Apr 1817, her fourth cousin, STEPHEN DRESSER *(Abigail Abbott Dresser[5], Job[4], Jonathan[3], Benjamin[2], George[1])*, b. at Lovell, 8 Apr 1781 son of Stephen and Abigail (Abbott) Dresser; Stephen d. at Stow, 19 Aug 1858. Stephen Dresser is a child in Family 590.

iii CYNTHIA ABBOTT, b. at Fryeburg, 1800; d. at Green County, WI, 29 Dec 1867; m. 31 Mar 1823, her fourth cousin, JEREMIAH "JEREMY" EASTMAN *(Jeremy Eastman[5], Sarah Abbott Eastman[4], James[3], William[2], George[1])*, b. at Lovell, 6 Apr 1803 son of Jeremy and Betsey (Kilgore) Eastman; Jeremiah d. at Eureka County, SD, 1885.[1148] Jeremy Eastman is a child in Family 593.

iv MALINDA ABBOTT, b. 16 Mar 1802; d. at Stow, 11 Feb 1891; m. her first cousin once removed, SAMUEL CHARLES *(Susanna Charles[6], Susanna Abbott Charles[5], Isaac[4], Ebenezer[3], John[2], George[1])*, b. 23 Mar 1804 son of Solomon and Susanna (Charles) Charles; Samuel d. at Stow, 28 Sep 1889.

v ELEANOR W. ABBOTT, b. at Fryeburg, 1804; d. at Stow, 15 May 1856; m. about 1828, THOMAS COOK; Thomas d. at Milan, NH, before 1850. After the death of her husband, Eleanor returned to Maine with her two sons, Alonzo and Dustin.

vi SYLVESTER ABBOTT, b. at Fryeburg, 1806; d. at Bangor, 11 Sep 1902; m. at Fryeburg, 25 May 1833, SARAH HOBBS LEWIS, b. 21 Oct 1809 daughter of Joseph and Elizabeth (Layman) Lewis;[1149] Sarah d. at Bangor, 23 Jul 1888.

[1146] The names of Mary's parents are given on her death record as Ira B. Johnson and Nancy Heath.

[1147] *U.S., Civil War Roll of Honor, 1861-1865*, Roll of Honor, Vol. XIX.

[1148] Jeremy Eastman made a homestead application in Eureka Township in 1883. Bureau of Land Management, General Land Office Records; Washington D.C., USA; Federal Land Patents, State Volumes

[1149] Cutter and Adams, *Genealogical and Personal Memoirs Relating to the Families of the State of Massachusetts*, volume 4, p 2452

vii WILLIAM WILEY ABBOTT, b. at Stow, 11 Apr 1811; d. at Springdale, WI, 1889; m. about 1852, ELIZABETH S. GUPTIL, b. at Fryeburg, 1828 daughter of Beniah Guptil;[1150] Elizabeth d. at Springdale, before 1880.

viii PENELOPE K. "NELLIE" ABBOTT, b. at Stow, 9 Aug 1813; d. at Stow, 8 Nov 1897; m. at Fryeburg, 7 Dec 1835, her first cousin once removed, BENJAMIN W. CHARLES *(Simeon Charles⁶, Olive Abbott Charles⁵, Isaac⁴, Ebenezer³, John², George¹)*, b. at Fryeburg, 22 Mar 1812 son of Simeon and Sarah (Wiley) Charles; Benjamin d. at Stow, 4 Nov 1897. One month before their 62nd wedding anniversary, Nellie and Ben died four days apart.

418) DOROTHY "DOLLY" ABBOTT *(Isaac⁴, Ebenezer³, John², George¹)*, b. likely at Fryeburg, 16 Aug 1778 daughter of Isaac and Susanna (Farnum) Abbott; d. at Richland, MI, 11 Nov 1858; m. at Fryeburg, 26 Oct 1795, JOSEPH CHARLES, b. 7 Apr 1773 son of Abner and Sarah (Walker) Charles; Joseph d. at Wyoming County, NY, 26 Jan 1846.

Joseph Charles and Dolly Abbott had their children in Chatham, New Hampshire and were for a time in Fryeburg where the birth of the youngest child in recorded. In 1815, the family relocated to Wethersfield, New York.[1151]

i TIMOTHY WALKER CHARLES, b. 16 Sep 1796; d. at Eldred, PA, Apr 1880; m. at Wethersfield, NY, 15 Jun 1819, MIRANDA LANGDON, b. at Fryeburg, 4 Feb 1800 daughter of Paul and Mary (Kimball) Langdon; Miranda d. at Wethersfield, 16 Nov 1833.

ii ELIZABETH WALKER CHARLES, b. 21 Feb 1799; d. at Wethersfield, 1879; m. 27 Dec 1818, DANIEL CURTIS, b. at Guilford, VT, 1792; Daniel d. at Wethersfield, 13 Dec 1865.

iii JOSEPH CHARLES, b. 13 Mar 1801; d. at Wethersfield, 27 Jan 1828.

iv NEHEMIAH CHARLES, b. 18 Apr 1803; d. at North Plains, MI, 23 Sep 1888; m. ANNA MARIA LANGDON, b. 1803 likely the daughter of Paul and Mary (Kimball) Langdon; Anna d. at North Plains, 11 Oct 1887.

v SARAH WALKER CHARLES, b. 13 Apr 1805; d. at Ronald, MI, 22 Jan 1890; m. CHAUNCEY CONKEY, b. 1 Jul 1808 son of Amos and Clarissa (Conkey) Conkey; Chauncey d. at Ronald, 16 Feb 1893.

vi DOROTHY CHARLES, b. 17 Jul 1807; d. at Wethersfield, 31 Aug 1888; m. about 1830, BENJAMIN FRANKLIN LANGDON, b. at Fryeburg, 18 Jun 1806 son of Paul and Mary (Kimball) Langdon; Benjamin d. at Wethersfield, 13 May 1848.

vii MARANDA CHARLES, b. 5 Feb 1810, d. at Ronald, MI, 12 Nov 1904. Maranda did not marry.

418a) LYDIA GRIFFIN *(Phebe Abbott Griffin⁴, Ebenezer³, John², George¹)*, b. at Andover, 26 Mar 1761 daughter of James and Phebe (Abbott) Griffin; d. at Bridgton, ME, 28 Dec 1843; m. at Andover, 15 Apr 1778, her third cousin, NATHAN INGALLS (*Eunice Jennings Ingalls⁴, Phebe Stevens³, Elizabeth Abbott Stevens², George¹*), b. at Andover, 12 Jun 1755 son of Francis and Eunice (Jennings) Ingalls; Nathan d. at Bridgton, 8 Jan 1835.

Nathan and Lydia settled in Bridgton, Maine where Nathan's brother Phineas, Asa, and Francis also settled. Their property was in South Bridgton south of Choate's Hill.[1152]

On 28 August 1832, Nathan Ingalls of Bridgton aged seventy-seven provided a statement related to his application for pension. His first enlistment was in January 1776 from Andover, Massachusetts in the company of Capt. Benjamin Farnham for two months of service near Boston. He next enlisted in the company of Capt. Samuel Johnson and marched to Ticonderoga and served five months. He enlisted in the same company in April 1777 and served two months at Providence, Rhode Island. He further stated that prior to the Battle of Bunker Hill, he went to Cambridge to relieve his brother Isaiah and that he was in the battle on 17 June 1775 as a substitute for his brother. After the war, he went to Wilmington, Maine, was then in Andover, Maine, and then to Bridgton. Francis Ingalls and Phineas Ingalls of Bridgton was made statements in support of Nathan's application. On 31 August 1838, Lydia Ingalls of Bridgton aged seventy-seven made application for the widow's pension. Son Alfred Ingalls of Bridgton provided a statement supporting her application.[1153]

There are records of twelve children of Lydia Griffin and Nathan Ingalls.

1150 Pioneer Publishing, *In the Foot-Prints of the Pioneers of Stephenson County*, p 70-71
1151 *History of Wyoming County, New York*, p 298
1152 Bridgton Historical Society, *History of Bridgton, Maine*, p 26, p 264
1153 U. S. Revolutionary War Pension and Bounty Land Warrant Application Files, Case W26811

i NATHAN INGALLS, b. (recorded) at Bridgton, ME, 9 Feb 1779; d. at Stockton, ME, 1831; m. about 1808, CHARLOTTE LEIGHTON.

ii NEHEMIAH INGALLS, b. at Wilmington, ME, 19 Sep 1780; d. at Bridgton, ME, 17 Feb 1819.

iii CHARLES INGALLS, b. at Wilmington, ME, 30 Jun 1782; d. at Waterville, ME, 1 Aug 1850; m. LOUISA MOORE, b. 15 Aug 1788 daughter of Robert and Elizabeth (Hutchins) Moore; Louisa d. at Waterville, 13 Oct 1870.

iv WILLIAM INGALLS, b. at Andover, ME, 30 Jul 1784

v PHEBE ABBOTT INGALLS, b. at Bridgton, 2 Dec 1787; m. LOVELL FAIRBROTHER, b. about 1790. Phebe and Lovell were living in Bridgton in 1870.

vi JOSEPH INGALLS, b. at Andover, ME, 20 Feb 1789

vii ALFRED INGALLS, b. at Bridgton, 25 Feb 1791; d. at Bridgton, 30 May 1862; m. at Bridgton, 7 Jan 1818, HULDAH KILBOURN, b. 1794 daughter of John and Mary (Howe) Kilbourn; Huldah d. at Bridgton, 6 Jan 1875.

viii LYDIA INGALLS, b. at Bridgton, 29 Jul 1793; d. at Bridgton, 10 Oct 1879; m. EBENEZER KILBOURN, b. at Bridgton, 19 Dec 1791 son of John and Mary (Howe) Kilbourn; Ebenezer d. at Bridgton, 10 Dec 1857.

ix EBENEZER INGALLS, b. at Bridgton, 16 Oct 1795; d. 26 Oct 1795.

x SALLY INGALLS, b. at Bridgton, 4 Nov 1796

xi CHARLOTTE INGALLS, b. 31 Jan 1799; d. at Lowell, MA, 20 Jul 1874; m. at Bridgton, 28 Nov 1821, AMOS INGALLS, b. 3 Apr 1789 son of Isaiah and Phebe (Curtis) Ingalls; Amos d. at Mercer, ME, 26 Nov 1867.

xii ELIZA INGALLS, b. at Bridgton, 7 May 1801; d. at Bridgton, 12 Sep 1879; m. about 1847, as his second wife, ICHABOD WARREN, b. 23 Dec 1796 son of Ichabod and Jane (McIntire) Warren; Ichabod d. (burial at Denmark, ME), 13 Jun 1870. Ichabod was first married to Cynthia Ingalls.

419) ABIGAIL GRIFFIN *(Phebe Abbott Griffin⁴, Ebenezer³, John², George¹)*, b. at Andover, 7 Oct 1764 daughter of James and Phebe (Abbott) Griffin; d. at Middleton, 26 Jan 1860;[1154] m. 1st at Wilmington, 9 Jan 1790, SAMUEL FROST; Samuel d. by 1796. Abigail m. 2nd, 9 Oct 1796, ASA HOLT, b. 26 Mar 1768 son of Asa and Dinah (Holt) Holt.

No birth records were located for Abigail and Samuel Frost. Asa and Abigail Holt had four children whose births are recorded at Wilmington.

i SYLVESTER HOLT, b. 13 Sep 1797; d. at Brooklyn, NY, 8 Jan 1853 (while on a trip from Boston); m. 27 Jun 1820, SALLY ANN GLAZIER, b. at Ipswich, about 1799 daughter of John and Anna (Pulsipher) Glazier; Sally d. at Boston, 17 Aug 1852.

ii ABIEL HOLT, b. 18 Feb 1800; d. at Boston, 22 Jun 1833. Abiel did not marry.

iii SALLY HOLT, b. 20 Aug 1802; d. at Middleton, 2 Apr 1861; m. at Middleton, 29 Feb 1824, JOHN FLINT, b. at Middleton, 2 Jul 1782 son of Jeremiah and Sarah (Elliot) Flint; John d. at Middleton, 17 Apr 1852.

iv ASA HOLT, b. 16 Jul 1807; d. at Woburn, 14 Dec 1861; m. at Woburn, 2 Oct 1834, MARY HOLMAN, b. at Roxbury, 1807 daughter of Robert and Rachel (Skedmore) Holman; Mary d. at Somerville, 30 Jan 1892.

420) MARY "POLLY" GRIFFIN *(Phebe Abbott Griffin⁴, Ebenezer³, John², George¹)*, b. at Andover, 7 Aug 1768 daughter of James and Phebe (Abbott) Griffin; d. before 1847 (not living when husband wrote his will); m. 9 May 1796, BENJAMIN CLEMENT, b. at Haverhill, about 1760 son of Benjamin and Mary (Bartlett) Clement; Benjamin d. at Haverhill about 1853 (probate 6 Apr 1853).

Benjamin Clement wrote his will 8 July 1847. Daughter Mary B. Jones receives two undivided third parts of 30 acres of land and buildings in North parish of Haverhill where Benjamin currently lives. Daughter Abigail Clement receives one undivided third part of the same property. All the remainder of the estate is divided by thirds, one-third to Mary B. Jones, one-third to Abigail Clement, and one-third (one-sixth each) to grandsons Benjamin C. Marsh and Daniel M. Marsh.[1155]

Polly and Benjamin Clement have four children whose births are recorded at Haverhill.

[1154] New England Historic Genealogical Society; Boston, Massachusetts; Massachusetts Vital Records, 1840–1911 (accessed through ancestry.com)

[1155] *Essex County, Massachusetts, Probate Records and Indexes 1638-1916;* Author: *Massachusetts. Probate Court (Essex County);* Probate Place: *Essex, Massachusetts, Probate Records, Vol 417-418, Book 117-118, 1853-1857,* will of Benjamin Clements, 8 July 1847.

i ELIZABETH GRIFFIN CLEMENT, b. 30 Jun 1799; d. at Haverhill, 20 Mar 1833; m. 1819, SAMUEL MARSH, b. at Hudson, NH, 22 Sep 1790 son of Ebenezer and Susannah (Chase) Marsh; Samuel d. at Boylston, MA, 25 Sep 1873. After Elizabeth's death, Samuel married Persis Abbott who is from the Rowley Abbott line.

ii MARY BARTLETT CLEMENT, b. 27 Oct 1802; d. at Haverhill, 27 Aug 1895; m. at Dracut, 24 Apr 1833, as his second wife, OLIVER JONES, b. at Dracut, 12 Nov 1789 son of Oliver and Dolly (Clement) Jones; Oliver d. at Dracut, 6 Feb 1836. Oliver Jones was first married to Olive Coburn who died in 1829.

iii SARAH G. CLEMENT, b. 1809; d. at Haverhill, Sep 1838. Sarah did not marry.

iv ABIGAIL CLEMENT, b. about 1815; d. at Haverhill, about 1880 (probate 26 Jul 1880). Abigail did not marry. In her will, Abigail left her entire estate to her beloved sister Mary B. Jones.

421) EBENEZER GRIFFIN *(Phebe Abbott Griffin⁴, Ebenezer³, John², George¹)*, b. at Andover, 5 Jun 1771 son of James and Phebe (Abbott) Griffin; d. 1848 at Litchfield, NH; m. at Leominster, 20 Sep 1792, BETSY CARTER, b. 23 Nov 1774 daughter of Josiah and Elizabeth (Graves) Carter;[1156] Betsy d. at Litchfield, 1 Oct 1854.

Ebenezer Griffin and Betsey Carter were parents to twelve children recorded at various locations.

i ELIZABETH GRIFFIN, b. Leominster, MA, 13 Jan 1793; d. at Litchfield, NH, 7 Mar 1874. Elizabeth did not marry. At the 1860 census, she was living with her sister-in-law Clarissa Griffin in Litchfield.

ii MARY GRIFFIN, b. at Leominster, 8 Sep 1794; d. 1831; m. at Windham, NH, 29 Jul 1817, JAMES M. HOWE, b. at Haverhill, MA, 17 Jun 1796 son of David and Betsey (Redington) Howe.

iii PHEBE GRIFFIN, b. at Wilmington, 15 Jul 1796; d. at Lowell, after 1870; m. at Dracut, 6 Dec 1818, ABEL LINCOLN, b. at Fitchburg, 30 Jan 1793 son of Abel and Polly (Marshall) Lincoln; Abel d. at Lowell, 30 Apr 1836.

iv SOPHIA GRIFFIN, b. at Wilmington, 3 Mar 1799; d. at Manchester, MA, 11 Apr 1883; m. at Chelmsford, 2 Oct 1828, HIRAM AYERS, b. at Manchester, 28 May 1800 son of John and Patty (Allen) Ayers; Hiram d. at Manchester, 27 Mar 1882.

v EBENEZER GRIFFIN, b. at Dracut, 3 Aug 1801. The Abbot genealogy (p 22) reports that Ebenezer went to Louisiana. If so, he married, at Baton Rouge, 1829, PADLITE DAIGRE about whom nothing is known.

vi SAMUEL P. GRIFFIN, b. at Dracut, 26 Aug 1803; d. at Framingham, 17 Mar 1866; m. 1st, at Billerica, ESTHER STEVENS, b. about 1806; Esther d. at Framingham, 23 Dec 1843. Samuel m. 2nd, at Boylston, 10 Oct 1844, EMELINE FULLER, b. about 1820 daughter of Nathan and Rebecca (Brown) Fuller; Emeline d. at Framingham, 7 Nov 1889.

vii ABBOTT GRIFFIN, b. at Dracut, 22 Jun 1805; d. at Litchfield, NH, 25 Dec 1862; m. his fourth cousin, EMILY ABBOTT *(Jonathan⁵, Daniel⁴, Benjamin³, Benjamin², George¹)*, b. 18 Sep 1807 daughter of Jonathan and Dolly (Parker) Abbott; Emily d. at Litchfield, 4 Apr 1885. Emily Abbott is a child in Family 776.

viii JOSIAH GRIFFIN, b. at Dracut, 3 May 1807; d. at Litchfield, 1834.

ix NANCY GRIFFIN, b. at Dracut, 21 Aug 1809; d. at Mason, NH, 16 Oct 1891; m. at Dracut, 5 Sep 1829, DANIEL BIXBY, b. about 1806; Daniel d. at Litchfield, 1 Jun 1866.

x GEORGE GRIFFIN, b. at Chelmsford, 28 Jul 1811; d. at Litchfield, 1853; m. 27 Dec 1837, CLARISSA WHITE, b. 1818 daughter of John and Susannah (Dickey) White; Clarissa d. at Litchfield, 28 Mar 1912.

xi CAROLINE GRIFFIN, b. at Chelmsford, 16 Jul 1813; d. at Litchfield, 21 Jun 1840.

xii SARAH H. GRIFFIN, b. at Dracut, 13 Dec 1815; d. at Litchfield, 23 Jan 1910.

422) NEHEMIAH ABBOTT *(James⁴, Ebenezer³, John², George¹)*, b. at Dracut, 22 Nov 1759 son of James and Lydia (Coburn) Abbott; d. likely at Glover, VT, after 1820; m. 16 Oct 1788, ANNA VARNUM, b. at Dracut, 23 Apr 1767 daughter of Jonathan and Anna (East) Varnum.

Nehemiah and Anna married in Dracut but settled in Londonderry in their early marriage. They later relocated to Glover, Vermont. Nehemiah Abbott and Anna Varnum were parents of six children born at Londonderry.

[1156] Carter, *Carter, a Genealogy of the Descendant of Samuel and Thomas*, p 162

i JOSEPH ABBOTT, b. 24 Apr 1789. It is not clear what happened to Joseph. He may be the Joseph Abbott from New Hampshire enlisted in the War of 1812. If so, he was "left sick at Seneca" in December 1813. There is also a Joseph Abbott of the right age in Lamoille, Vermont in 1850. Joseph's sister Lydia was also in Lamoille in 1850. There is no information for a marriage.

ii LYDIA ABBOTT, b. 7 Sep 1790; d. at Glover, VT, 2 Feb 1858; m. at Londonderry, 7 Jan 1811, THOMAS BARTLETT, b. at Londonderry, 1781 son of Thomas and Sarah (Ryder) Bartlett; Thomas d. at Hyde Park, VT, 27 Jun 1869.

iii DOLLY VARNUM ABBOTT, b. 9 Feb 1793; m. about 1815, JOSEPH GARFIELD whose origins are unknown.

iv JONATHAN ABBOTT, b. 22 Oct 1795; d. at Glover, 21 Apr 1861; m. 1st, about 1825, LUCY CROSBY, b. at Dummerston, 18 Jan 1797 daughter of Timothy and Ann (-) Crosby; Lucy d. at Glover, 9 Jul 1845. Jonathan m. 2nd, about 1848, CHARLOTTE HAWKINS, b. 4 Nov 1789; Charlotte d. at Glover, 30 Oct 1889. Charlotte was first married to John Bickford who died in 1839.

v BETSEY ABBOTT, b. 3 Feb 1801; m. at Glover, VT, 11 Jan 1826, JONATHAN ROBINSON, b. at Barton, 2 Sep 1797 son of Jonathan and Hannah (-) Robinson.

vi JONAS VARNUM ABBOTT, b. 4 Mar 1804; d. at Glover, before 1850; m. at Glover, 6 Dec 1830, MARGARET KING, m. at Gilmanton, 1804 daughter of George and Sarah (-) King; Margaret d. at Glover, 7 Mar 1859. After Jonas's death, Margaret married Cephas Clark.

423) RACHEL ABBOTT *(James⁴, Ebenezer³, John², George¹)*, b. at Dracut, 22 Mar 1761 daughter of James and Lydia (Coburn) Abbott; d. at Lowell, 15 Mar 1844; m. 13 Dec 1783, JONATHAN COLBURN,[1157] b. 19 Aug 1757 son of Jonathan and Marcy (Hildreth) Colburn; Jonathan d. at Dracut, 17 Jun 1813.[1158]

Rachel Abbott and Jonathan Colburn/Coburn were parents of nine children all born at Dracut.

i RACHEL COBURN, b. 9 Jun 1784; d. at Lowell, 8 Oct 1852; m. about 1807, PETER BOWERS, b. at Dracut, 14 Jun 1778 son of John and Abiah (Goodhue) Bowers; Peter d. at Concord, MA, 30 Oct 1864.

ii JONATHAN COBURN, b. 5 Jul 1786; d. at Bethel, VT, 23 Aug 1865; m. at Bethel, 6 Jun 1820, ELIZABETH "BETSEY" PARKER of Bethel.

iii ABIAH COBURN, b. 5 Jul 1787

iv HANNAH COBURN, b. 14 Oct 1790; d. at Dracut, 23 Dec 1868; m., 22 Apr 1813, NATHANIEL BRADSTREET COBURN, b. at Dracut, 23 Mar 1786 son of Samuel and Sarah (Bradstreet) Coburn; Nathaniel d. at Dracut, 12 Apr 1854.

v SYBIL COBURN, b. 27 May 1793; d. at Lowell, 26 Sep 1877. Sybil did not marry.

vi MERCY COBURN, b. 5 Sep 1795; d. at Bethel, VT, 22 Jan 1846; m. 3 Dec 1818, IRA CRAIN, b. about 1796; Ira d. at Bethel, 1876. After Mercy's death, Ira married Servilla.

vii NEHEMIAH J. COBURN, b. 4 Jan 1799; d. at Sherman, MI, 3 Dec 1881; m. PHILURA WALES, b. at Plainfield, VT, 8 Apr 1808 daughter of Shubel and Polly (Peck) Wales; Philura d. at Sherman, 31 May 1872.

viii LEAH COBURN, b. 12 Jul 1802; d. at Lowell, 19 Mar 1879; m. by 1827, her first cousin, WILLIAM BROWN, b. at Londonderry, NH, 1799 son of Ebenezer and Relief (Abbott) Brown; William d. at Dracut, 28 Nov 1863. William Brown is a child in Family 427.

ix PRUDENCE COBURN, b. 25 Sep 1805; d. at Bethel, VT, 13 Oct 1883; m. at Randolph, VT, 3 Apr 1827, RUFUS WILSON, b. at Bethel, 1797 son of Samuel and Rachel (Holden) Wilson; Rufus d. at Bethel, 17 Sep 1857.

424) NATHANIEL ABBOTT *(James⁴, Ebenezer³, John², George¹)*, b. at Dracut, 19 Jan 1766 son of James and Lydia (Coburn) Abbott; d. at Nelson, NH, 28 Feb 1815; m. 3 Jan 1788, PHEBE CUMMINGS, b. at Westford, 2 Jun 1770 daughter of Thomas and Lucy (Laurence) Cummings; Phebe d. at Nelson, 14 Mar 1843.

Nathaniel Abbott and Phebe Cummings were first in Tyngsborough, in Stoddard, New Hampshire by 1790 and later in Nelson, New Hampshire. There are likely five children of Nathaniel Abbott and Phebe Cummings.

1157 The majority of records for Jonathan spell his last name Colburn, but many of the records for the children read Coburn.

1158 Revolutionary War Pension and Bounty-Land Warrant Application Files

i SARAH ABBOTT, b. about 1788; d. at Nelson, NH, 19 Jan 1846. Sarah did not marry.

ii MARY ABBOTT, b. 1791; d. at Nelson, 21 Jan 1846; m. at Packersfield, NH, 7 Apr 1814, TIMOTHY ADAMS TWITCHELL, b. at Dublin, NH, 29 May 1792 son of Abel and Sarah (Adams) Twitchell.

iii NATHANIEL ABBOTT, b. 1792; d. at Webster, NH, 15 Sep 1875; m. 1st, at Nelson, 7 Aug 1817, HEPHZIBAH GRIFFIN, b. at Nelson, 23 Jun 1793 daughter of Samuel and Sophia (Foster) Griffin; Hephzibah d. at Webster, NY, 22 Jan 1839. Nathaniel m. 2nd, about 1840, CHLOE HOLLY, b. in CT, about 1840; Chloe d. at Webster, 11 Mar 1880.

iv LUCY ANN ABBOTT, b. 15 May 1797; d. at Nelson, 5 Nov 1864; m. at Nelson, 3 Jun 1830, CYRUS TOLMAN, b. at Packersfield, 16 Mar 1800 son of Ebenezer and Mary (Clark) Tolman; Cyrus d. at Nelson, 15 Aug 1857.

v JAMES CUMMINGS ABBOTT, b. about 1805; d. at Sullivan, NH, 26 Apr 1880; m. at Washington, NH, 16 Mar 1831, LUCY N. BARRETT, b. at Nelson, 8 Dec 1808 daughter of John and Lucy (Nichols) Barrett; Lucy d. at South Vineland, NJ, 8 Aug 1891. James and Lucy's son Sylvester Cummings Abbott served in the 6th Regiment of New Hampshire Volunteers during the Civil War and died of disease at Hatteras Inlet, NC 3 Feb 1862.

425) HANNAH ABBOTT *(James⁴, Ebenezer³, John², George¹)*, b. at Dracut, 14 Jul 1769 daughter of James and Lydia (Coburn) Abbott; d. at Glover, VT, 15 Jan 1857; m. 17 Dec 1795, JAMES VANCE, b. at Londonderry, 15 Apr 1769 son of John and Ann (Hogg) Vance; James d. at Glover, 26 Nov 1864.

After starting their family in Londonderry, New Hampshire, James Vance and Hannah Abbott became the first settlers in Glover, Vermont. James purchased 160 acres there in 1798 for a price of one dollar per acre. James was known for his strong constitution and his amusing anecdotes about the early settlers.[1159]

Hannah Abbott and James Vance were parents of six children.

i CLARISSA VANCE, b. at Londonderry, about 1796; d. at Greensboro, VT, 12 Jun 1823; m. about 1819, ELEAZER SCOTT, b. at Hartford, VT, 21 Sep 1794 son of Luther and Esther (Whitney) Scott; Eleazer d. at Greensboro, VT, 19 Sep 1860.

ii JOHN M. G. VANCE, b. at Londonderry, Sep 1797; d. at Albany, VT, 30 Jul 1854; m. about 1818, LAURA PATTERSON, b. at Barre, VT, 12 Apr 1798 daughter of Ansel and Lucina (Colton) Patterson; Laura d. at Albany, 23 May 1856.

iii WILLIAM VANCE, b. at Glover, about 1800 (based on age 32 at military enlistment in 1832);[1160] d. after 1850; m. ROXANNA who has not been identified.

iv HANNAH VANCE, b. at Glover, about 1807; d. at Glover, 7 Jul 1887; m. AUGUSTUS KIMBALL, b. 1804 son of George Washington and Eliza (Keech) Kimball; Augustus d. at Glover, 22 Sep 1863.

v SAMUEL VANCE, b. at Glover, about 1811; d. at Glover, 1893; m. 1st, at Greensboro, VT, 3 Nov 1836, ESTHER CUTLER, b. at Greensboro, 13 Sep 1812 daughter of Obed and Azubah (Shepard) Cutler; Esther d. at Glover, 29 Jun 1863. Samuel m. 2nd, 10 Sep 1874, MARY M. BUMPS, b. at Albany, VT, about 1847 daughter of Seth and Maria (Hunter) Bumps.

vi Son, b. about 1817; d. 8 Apr 1817.

426) SYBIL ABBOTT *(James⁴, Ebenezer³, John², George¹)*, b. at Dracut, 21 Dec 1774 daughter of James and Lydia (Coburn) Abbott; d. after 1850 in NH; m. 21 Dec 1797, DAVID WILSON, b. 30 Mar 1771 son of Joseph and Abigail (Butler) Wilson;[1161] David d. at Pelham, after 1850.[1162]

Sybil and David had four children in Dracut. In 1814, they sold their property in Dracut including land, house, sawmill, and gristmill to Daniel Eams of Pelham.[1163]

1159 White, *History of Orleans County*, p 196

1160 William Vance of Glover, Vermont, age 32, a shoemaker, enlisted at Hartford, VT, 29 Nov 1832 and reported as deserted 10 Apr 1833. U.S. Army, Register of Enlistments, 1798-1914

1161 Rook, *The Butler Family*, p 32

1162 Both Sibyl and David were living at the 1850 US Census living in the home of John and Sophia Ellenwood. They are listed as Sibyl A. Wilson age 75 and David Wilson age 79. John Ellenwood married Sophia Wilson at Pelham in 1844. Unsure how they are related. It is possible that these are a different David and Sybill Wilson, but they are the right ages.

1163 NEHGR, volume 62, p 154, The Descendants of Robert Eams

There are just four children identified for Sybil Abbott and David Wilson all born at Dracut.

i DAVID WILSON, b. 11 Oct 1798

ii SYBIL WILSON, b. 23 Jun 1800; d. at Hudson, NH, 31 Mar 1878; m. about 1825, JAMES SMITH, b. at Hudson, 7 Oct 1802 son of James and Mary (Lawrence) Smith; James d. at Hudson, after 1850.

iii JOSEPH WILSON, b. 30 Sep 1803; d. at Nashua, 6 Jan 1879; m. at Nottingham, 22 Oct 1826, MINERVA STAPLES, b. at Williamstown, VT, 24 Jan 1807 daughter of Isaac and Salina (Burnham) Staples; Minerva d. at Nashua, 2 Feb 1892.

iv HERMAN WILSON, b. Jul 1805; d. 30 Jan 1806.

427) RELIEF ABBOTT *(James⁴, Ebenezer³, John², George¹)*, b. at Dracut, 8 Sep 1778 daughter of James and Lydia (Coburn) Abbott; d. likely in NH;[1164] m. 13 Aug 1796, EBENEZER BROWN, b. at Dunstable, 12 Sep 1773 son of Samuel and Bridget (Bryant) Brown; Ebenezer d. at Dracut 3 Aug 1860.

Two children were located for Relief Abbott and Ebenezer Brown.

i EBENEZER BROWN, b. at Londonderry, 1798; d. at Dracut, 14 Feb 1853; m. at Londonderry, 3 Sep 1822, MARY MELVIN, b. at Derry, 1802; Mary d. at Lowell, 5 Mar 1886.

ii WILLIAM BROWN, b. at Londonderry, 1799; d. at Dracut, 28 Nov 1863; m. about 1827, his first cousin, LEAH COBURN *(Rachel Abbott Coburn⁵, James⁴, Ebenezer³, John², George¹)*, b. at Dracut, 12 Jul 1802 daughter of Jonathan and Rachel (Abbott) Coburn; Leah d. at Lowell, 19 Mar 1879. Leah Coburn is a child in Family 423.

428) MERCY ABBOTT *(James⁴, Ebenezer³, John², George¹)*, b. at Dracut, 24 Aug 1780 daughter of James and Lydia (Coburn) Abbott; d. 1 Nov 1863 at Hancock; m. Feb 1808, EBENEZER BARTLETT, b. 10 Aug 1779 son of Thomas and Sarah (Rider) Bartlett; Ebenezer d. at Hancock, NH, 8 Nov 1854.

Ebenezer Bartlett was born in Plymouth, Massachusetts. After their marriage, Mercy and Ebenezer were in Londonderry for a time as their first children were born there. The family settled in Hancock in 1814.[1165]

Mercy Abbott and Ebenezer Bartlett were parents of eight children.[1166]

i ALMIRA BARTLETT, b. at Londonderry, 11 Nov 1808; d. at Leominster, MA, 25 Dec 1887; m. at Leominster, 27 Nov 1844, DANIEL CHESMORE, b. at Henniker, 10 Sep 1803 son of Daniel and Mary (Gibson) Chesmore; Daniel d. at Leominster, 15 Jun 1886. Daniel was first married to Mehitable Gerry who died 4 Jul 1844.

ii LYDIA BARTLETT, b. 4 Jul 1810; d. at Hancock, 28 Jan 1866; m. at Hancock, 10 Mar 1853, as the third of his four wives, WILLIAM LAKIN, b. at Hancock, 26 May 1812 son of Jacob G. and Betsey (Stanley) Lakin; William d. at Harrisville, NH, 25 Feb 1890. William married first Melvina Davis, second Mary, and fourth Melinda Norcross.

iii THOMAS BARTLETT, b. 22 Apr 1812; d. at Fitchburg, 5 Sep 1863; m. 14 Mar 1834, MARY BAILEY, b. at Nelson, NH, about 1815 daughter of John and Polly (Cobb) Bailey; Mary d. at Sterling, MA, 15 Sep 1880.

iv EBENEZER A. BARTLETT, b. at Hancock, 7 Nov 1816; d. at Sterling, MA, 4 Sep 1894; m. at Fitchburg, 18 Sep 1844, HANNAH HADLEY, b. at Sterling, Oct 1819 daughter of Samuel and Mary (Boynton) Hadley; Hannah d. at Worcester, 16 Jun 1909.

v SARAH BARTLETT, b. 25 Jan 1818; d. at Shrewsbury, MA, 31 Jan 1902; m. at Hancock, 4 Jun 1835, HENRY HARRISON FLINT, b. at Stoddard, NH, 10 Oct 1812 son of Joel and Silence (Brooks) Flint; Henry d. at Shrewsbury, 10 Sep 1886.

vi JANE M. BARTLETT, b. at Hancock, 14 Jun 1819; d. at Antrim, 11 Jan 1899; m. at Fitchburg, 15 Sep 1844, JOHN C. BROOKS, b. about 1822 son of Dickerson and Hannah (Kemp) Brooks; John d. at Antrim, 1881.

vii JOHN MILLER BARTLETT, b. at Hancock, 5 Oct 1821; d. at Medford, MA, 18 Jul 1904; m. at Lancaster, MA, 13 Oct 1853, HANNAH MARIA RIDER, b. at Hubbardston, Jul 1837 daughter of Asa and Hephzibah (Daniels) Rider; Hannah d. at Shrewsbury, 16 Jun 1909.

[1164] The births of their children are recorded at Londonderry. The family did return to Dracut but unsure whether this was before or after the death of Relief.

[1165] Hayward, *The History of Hancock*, p 336

[1166] The History of Hancock lists a ninth child, Betsey born in 1800, in this family. However, Mercy and Ebenezer were not married until 1808 so it seems unlikely that she is a child in this family. All other records for Betsey (census and death records) confirm birth in 1800.

viii MARCY MARIA BARTLETT, b. at Hancock, 20 Apr 1824; d. at Fitchburg, 5 Feb 1901; m. about 1846, IRA E. CUTLER, b. at Ashby, MA, about 1819 son of Charles and Prudence (Holden) Cutler; Ira d. at Fitchburg, 29 Jan 1872.

Great-Grandchildren of Hannah Abbott and John Chandler

429) ISAAC CHANDLER *(Nathan Chandler⁴, John Chandler³, Hannah Abbott Chandler², George¹)*, b. at Andover, 8 Apr 1732 son of Nathan and Priscilla (Holt) Chandler; d. at Andover, 6 Mar 1817; m. 14 Apr 1757, his second cousin once removed, HANNAH BALLARD, b. 3 Jan 1732/3 daughter of Josiah and Mary (Chandler) Ballard;[1167] Hannah d. 2 Oct 1824.[1168]

Isaac Chandler served one and half days at the Lexington alarm in the Company of Captain Joseph Holt.[1169]

Isaac Chandler and Hannah Ballard were the parents of eight children born at Andover.

i ISAAC CHANDLER, b. 28 Jan 1758; d. at Hamilton, MA, 30 Jan 1839; m. at Wilmington, 10 Dec 1783, ABIGAIL "NABBY" BOUTWELL, b. at Wilmington, 19 Jan 1762 daughter of Jonathan and Abigail (Eams) Boutwell; Abigail d. at Hamilton, 19 Sep 1836.

ii JOHN CHANDLER, b. 21 Nov 1759; d. at Bow, NH, Sep 1819; m. 17 Apr 1783, his first cousin once removed, DOROTHY BALLARD *(Hannah Chandler Ballard⁴, John Chandler³, Hannah Abbott Chandler², George¹)*, b. at Andover, 12 Dec 1757 daughter of Timothy and Hannah (Chandler) Ballard; Dorothy d. likely at Bow, after 1820. John Chandler and Dorothy Ballard are Family 435.

iii JAMES CHANDLER, b. 28 Nov 1761; d. at Andover, 1 Dec 1835; m. 29 Apr 1783, his third cousin, PHEBE DANE, b. at Andover, 14 May 1762 daughter of Joseph and Elizabeth (Wyman) Dane; Phebe d. at Andover, 10 Dec 1843.

iv SAMUEL CHANDLER, b. 25 Jan 1764; d. at Antrim, NH, 12 Jan 1842; m. 21 Apr 1790, SARAH JAQUES, b. at Pelham, NH, 25 Jul 1767 daughter of Nehemiah and Lucy (Colburn) Jaques;[1170] Sarah d. at Hillsborough, 20 May 1858.

v HENRY CHANDLER, b. 16 Jul 1766; d. at Concord, 3 Apr 1856; m. 11 Mar 1798, his fourth cousin, RUTH ABBOTT *(Reuben⁵, Reuben⁴, James³, William², George¹)*, b. at Concord, 25 Apr 1777 daughter of Reuben and Zerviah (Farnum) Abbott; Ruth d. at Concord, 20 Feb 1849. Ruth Abbott is a child in Family 571.

vi BENJAMIN CHANDLER, b. 17 Jan 1768; d. at Lancaster, MA, 24 Feb 1847; m. Nov 1802, ELIZABETH PRATT, b. 31 Dec 1780 daughter of James and Zerviah (Rugg) Pratt; Elizabeth d. at Lancaster, 3 Jun 1857.

vii HANNAH CHANDLER, b. 12 Jan 1771; d. 12 Apr 1818; m. at Hillsborough, 18 Oct 1791, SAMUEL BRADFORD, b. at Hillsborough, 29 Sep 1768 son of Samuel and Anna (Washer) Bradford.[1171] According to the Chandler genealogy (p 619) in 1802, Samuel went on a cattle drive from Hillsborough and was never heard from again.

viii MARY CHANDLER, b. Nov 1773; d. at Hillsborough, 16 Jun 1850; m. at Hillsborough, 14 Oct 1794, ABRAHAM ANDREWS, b. at Hillsborough, 25 Jan 1772 son of Isaac and Lucy (Perkins) Andrews; Abraham d. 23 Mar 1845.

430) TIMOTHY BALLARD *(Hannah Chandler Ballard⁴, John Chandler³, Hannah Abbott Chandler², George¹)*, b. at Andover, 1 Mar 1729/30 son of Timothy and Hannah (Chandler) Ballard; d. 12 Jul 1768; m. 21 Jan 1755, his third cousin, SARAH ABBOTT, b. 3 Aug 1733 daughter of Zebadiah and Anne (Lovejoy) Abbott. Sarah did not remarry after Timothy's death and she died 2 Aug 1809.

Sarah Abbott was descended from the Rowley Abbotts. Following the early death of her husband, Sarah ran an inn in Andover.[1172]

[1167] The 1780 will of Josiah Chandler includes a bequest to his daughter Hannah the wife of Mr. Isaac Chandler.

[1168] This is the date of death used in *The Descendants of William and Annis Chandler*, p. 330. The deaths of both Isaac and Hannah are reported by the Chandler book as occurring in Concord, NH, but the record of Isaac's death is in the Andover records with the same specific date as the Chandler book.

[1169] Chandler, *The Descendants of William and Annis Chandler*, p 330

[1170] New Hampshire, Births and Christenings Index, 1714-1904

[1171] Browne, *History of Hillsborough*, volume I, p 81

[1172] Abbott, *Descendants of George Abbott of Rowley*, p 153

Timothy Ballard did not leave a will and his estate entered probate 5 September 1768.[1173] Sarah Ballard was named administrator. The total value of the estate was £682 which included one-fourth part of a sawmill and the homestead. At the time of Timothy's death, there were guardianship cases for the following minor children: Joshua Ballard age 8 years, William Ballard age 9 years, Anna Ballard age 5 years, Sarah Ballard age 12 years, and Timothy Ballard age 11 years. In each case, the widow Sarah Ballard was named guardian.[1174]

Three of the children in this family relocated to Durham, New Hampshire. Son William Ballard did not marry, and he was a successful trader in Durham, his holdings included a wharf and a store. The inventory of his estate in 1811 included real estate that totaled over 500 acres valued at $7,737. The division of his estate included extensive land distributions to his heirs: brother Timothy Ballard, brother Joshua Ballard, sister Sarah Pinkham, and the heirs of sister Anna Abbott.[1175]

There are records for six children of Timothy Ballard and Sarah Abbott all born at Andover.

i SARAH BALLARD, b. Feb 1756; d. at Durham, NH, 16 Mar 1814; m. at Andover, 31 Mar 1774, THOMAS PINKHAM, b. 8 Jun 1755 son of Abijah and Rachel (Huckins) Pinkham; Thomas d. at Woodstock, NH, 26 May 1811.

ii TIMOTHY BALLARD, b. 28 Jul 1757; d. at Andover, 28 Feb 1828; m. at Andover, 30 Oct 1783, his third cousin once removed, MARY FOSTER *(Hannah Abbott Foster[4], George[3], George[2], George[1])*, b. at Andover, 21 Jul 1763 daughter of William and Hannah (Abbott) Foster; Mary d. at Andover, 30 Mar 1834. Timothy and Mary did not have children of their own but adopted three of their nieces and nephews. Timothy Ballard died by suicide.[1176] Mary Foster is a child in Family 127.

iii WILLIAM BALLARD, b. May 1759; d. at Durham, NH, 15 Oct 1811. William did not marry.

iv JOSHUA BALLARD, b. 24 Aug 1760; d. at Durham, NH, 27 Apr 1844; m. 16 Jun 1785, as her second husband, LYDIA BURNHAM, b. about 1751; Lydia d. at Durham, 18 Apr 1826. Lydia was first married to Moses Eastman.

v SAMUEL BALLARD, b. Nov 1761; assumed to have died young as he is not included in the guardianship cases from 1768.

vi ANNA BALLARD, b. 15 Nov 1762; d. at Wilton, 7 Apr 1805; m. at Andover, 12 Dec 1780, her third cousin once removed, JOB ABBOTT *(Job[4], Jonathan[3], Benjamin[2], George[1])*, b. at Pembroke, NH, about 1755 son of Job and Sarah (Abbott) Abbott; Job d. at Wilton, 12 Jul 1805. Anna Ballard and Job Abbott are Family 589.

431) MARY BALLARD *(Hannah Chandler Ballard[4], John Chandler[3], Hannah Abbott Chandler[2], George[1])*, b. at Andover, 1 May 1732 daughter of Timothy and Hannah (Chandler) Ballard; d. at Reading 15 Dec 1803; m. 30 Aug 1750, her third cousin once removed, DAVID CHANDLER, b. 15 Dec 1724 son of Josiah and Sarah (Ingalls) Chandler; David d. at Cambridge 1 Feb 1776. Mary m. 2nd 10 Nov 1779, Daniel Parker.

David Chandler served in the militia at Andover as a corporal in 1757. He was at the Battle of Bunker Hill as a lieutenant in Captain Benjamin Ames's company.[1177]

There are eight children known for Mary Ballard and David Chandler.[1178]

i DAVID CHANDLER, b. 10 Jun 1751; died young

ii DAVID CHANDLER, b. 9 Jul 1754; m. about 1775, HANNAH PEABODY, b. at Amherst, NH, 2 Apr 1754 daughter of William and Rebecca (Smith) Peabody.[1179]

iii DANIEL CHANDLER, b. 9 Jul 1754; d. at Amherst, NH, about 1803; m. about 1774, JOANNA STEVENS, b. at Andover, 23 Sep 1752 daughter of Asa and Mehitable (Farnum) Stevens; d. at Coventry, VT, Aug 1827. Daniel d. in debtor's prison.

iv SAMUEL CHANDLER, b. 4 Nov 1757; d. unknown but after 1801. In is not known what became of Samuel. He did graduate from Harvard in 1779 and there are various family tales and traditions related to him.[1180] In the

[1173] *Essex County, MA: Probate File Papers, 1638-1881.*Online database. *AmericanAncestors.org.* New England Historic Genealogical Society, 2014. Case 1601

[1174] *Essex County, MA: Probate File Papers, 1638-1881.*Online database. *AmericanAncestors.org.* New England Historic Genealogical Society, 2014. Case 1600

[1175] New Hampshire, County Probate Records, 1660-1973, Strafford, estate of William Ballard, 1811, 20:94, 12:481; 18:510; 15:79; 13:25; 15:250; accessed through familysearch.org

[1176] Timothy, "who cut his own throat," Feb. 29, 1828, a. 70 y. 7 m. Andover vital records

[1177] Chandler, *Descendants of William and Annis Chandler*, p 202

[1178] The Chandler genealogy lists ten children, but two of those children do not seem to go in this family. Hannah Chandler born 22 June 1755 is listed as the daughter of David, Sr. and Abiel Chandler in the Andover records. Sarah Chandler born 12 May 1761 is listed as the daughter of David and Sarah Chandler. In addition, there is a child born in January 1762 in this family which makes a child born in May 1761 not feasible.

[1179] Chandler, *Descendants of William and Annis Chandler*

[1180] The Chandler genealogy recounts these family traditions on pp 418-419

Chandler genealogy, there is a transcript of a letter written 31 January 1801 by Samuel to his mother that recounts some of his travels around the world and states that he was then on his way to the Mediterranean.

v JOSIAH CHANDLER, b. 20 Jan 1762; d. at Pomfret, VT, 22 Oct 1837; m. 15 Jan 1788, MARGARET AIKEN, b. at Bedford, 10 Jun 1767 daughter of John and Annis (Orr) Aiken;[1181] Margaret d. 17 Apr 1840.

vi BALLARD CHANDLER, b. 23 Jan 1765; d. in Oneida County, NY, 1 Mar 1838. Ballard Chandler served during the Revolution from 1781-1783 in Colonel Benjamin Tappen's Regiment of the Massachusetts line. He received a pension for his service. In his pension application file (affidavit made in 1818 when he gave his age as 53), he reports having no family. He was a farmer in Oneida County, NY but in destitute circumstances declaring that he had possessions worth about ten dollars and forty dollars in debt.[1182]

vii JOHN CHANDLER, b. 4 Jul 1771; d. at Wakefield, 12 Jun 1820; m. at Reading, 19 Sep 1793, ABIGAIL HAY, b. at Reading 1771 daughter of John and Sarah (Ring) Hay; Abigail d. at Wakefield, 20 Jun 1827.

viii MOLLY CHANDLER, b. 27 Oct 1773; d. 11 Oct 1826; m. 17 Feb 1791, DANIEL FOSTER, b. at Reading, 8 Apr 1767 son of Jonathan and Sarah (Townsend) Foster; Daniel d. at Andover, 15 Oct 1811.

432) HANNAH BALLARD *(Hannah Chandler Ballard[4], John Chandler[3], Hannah Abbott Chandler[2], George[1])*, b. at Andover, 8 Jun 1736 daughter of Timothy and Hannah (Chandler) Ballard; d. 27 Sep 1778; m. 11 Mar 1756, as his first wife, her third cousin, NEHEMIAH ABBOT, b. 24 Aug 1731 son of Zebadiah and Anne (Lovejoy) Abbot. Nehemiah m. 2nd, LYDIA CLARK; Nehemiah d. 13 Oct 1808.[1183]

Nehemiah Abbot was descended from the Rowley Abbott line. He was a trustee of Phillips Academy in Andover.

In his will written in 1807, Nehemiah leaves to beloved wife Lydia Abbot all the furniture she brought with her to the marriage, his best chaise, and a seat in his pew at the meeting house. Lydia also receives use of a specified portion of the house and a list of provisions for her support as long as she is a widow. She also receives title to a tract of salt meadow. Son Nehemiah Abbot, daughter Phebe Abbot, daughter Hannah Hawley, and son William L. Abbot receive ten dollars each which completes their portions. Son Abiel Abbot receives the remainder of the estate and is named executor.[1184] The real estate was valued at $12,923 and personal estate at $1,670.81.

All the children named in the will are from Nehemiah's marriage to Hannah Ballard. Nehemiah and his second wife Lydia Clark had two children who died in infancy.

Nehemiah Abbot and Hannah Ballard were parents of six children born at Andover.

i NEHEMIAH ABBOT, b. 10 Mar 1757; d. at Andover, 13 Dec 1822; m. 3 Mar 1785, his third cousin once removed, SARAH ABBOTT *(George[4], George[3], George[2], George[1])*, b. at Andover, 3 Oct 1762 daughter of George and Hannah (Lovejoy) Abbott; Sarah d. at Andover, 2 Mar 1848. Nehemiah and Sarah had no children. Sarah used her estate to provide funding for Abbot Female Academy in Andover which was named for her.[1185]

ii HANNAH ABBOT, b. 19 Sep 1758; d. 29 Sep 1764.

iii ABIEL ABBOT, b. 4 Sep 1760; d. at Andover, Aug 1828; m. at Dracut, 29 Sep 1793, his second cousin once removed, HANNAH FRYE, b. at Dracut, 19 May 1767 daughter of Timothy and Hannah (Carleton) Frye; Hannah d. at Andover, 13 Oct 1821.

iv PHEBE ABBOT, b. Apr 1763; d. at Andover, about 1826; m. 29 Oct 1782, her third cousin once removed, JOHN LOVEJOY ABBOTT *(George[4], George[3], George[2], George[1])*, b. at Andover, 12 Apr 1757 son of George and Hannah (Lovejoy) Abbott; John d. at Andover, 1 Nov 1837. Phebe Abbot and John Lovejoy are Family 523.

v HANNAH ABBOT, b. 18 Jan 1765; d. at Danville, VT, 29 Apr 1811; m. at Andover, 1 Jan 1788, SAMUEL HAWLEY, b. at Marblehead, Nov 1757 son of Joseph and Hannah (Pearce) Hawley; Samuel d. at Danville, 16 Dec 1829. After Hannah's death, Samuel married Sarah Frye.

1181 Treman, *History of the Treman Family*, volume 2, p 1442

1182 Revolutionary War Pension and Bounty-Land Warrant Application Files, accessed through fold3

1183 Nehemiah ["one of the Trustees of Phillips Academy," stranguary. C. R. 2.], Oct. 13, 1808, a. 77 y. 1 m. 19 d.

1184 Essex County, MA: Probate File Papers, 1638-1881.Online database. AmericanAncestors.org. New England Historic Genealogical Society, 2014.

1185 Lloyd, A Singular School: Abbot Academy 1828-1973

vi WILLIAM LOVEJOY ABBOT, b. 18 Jan 1765; d. at Haverhill, 18 Apr 1798; m. at Amesbury, 11 Mar 1792, ABIGAIL CARR, b. at Haverhill, 21 May 1770 daughter of James and Sarah (Follinsbee) Carr. After William's death, Abigail married Dr. Elias Weld.

433) NATHAN BALLARD *(Hannah Chandler Ballard^4, John Chandler^3, Hannah Abbott Chandler^2, George^1)*, b. at Andover, 1 Nov 1744 son of Timothy and Hannah (Chandler) Ballard; d. at Concord, NH 14 Jan 1835; m. 1763, his third cousin, HANNAH HOLT, b. 19 Dec 1745 daughter of Jonathan and Lydia (Blanchard) Holt; Hannah d. 1 Dec 1818.

Nathan and Hannah moved from Andover to Wilton soon after their marriage. Nathan was a farmer there from 1765-1782. He served in the Revolution in Captain Benjamin Taylor's Company in 1775 and in 1777 in the company that marched from Wilton and Amherst to Ticonderoga. He was a selectman of Wilton for several years. After 1782, the family relocated to Concord where they were first settlers at Little Pond at Concord.[1186]

Nathan and Hannah Ballard were parents of nine children, the oldest daughter born at Andover and the other children at Wilton.

i HANNAH BALLARD, b. at Andover, 12 May 1864; d. about 1809; m. at Wilton, 28 Mar 1793, DAVID MCINTIRE, b. about 1762 of undetermined origins; David's death is unknown.

ii SARAH BALLARD, b. 13 Apr 1766; d. at Wilton, 4 Jan 1856; m. at Wilton, 1 Jun 1797, WILLIAM PETTENGILL, b. at Andover, 23 Aug 1759 son of Samuel and Mary (Holt) Pettengill; William d. at Wilton, 13 Oct 1844.

iii MARY BALLARD, b. 8 May 1768; d. at Milford, after 1850; m. about 1790, her fourth cousin, AMOS HOLT, b. 20 Oct 1768 son of Amos and Jemima (Ingalls) Holt; Amos d. at Wilton, 13 Dec 1826.

iv BETSEY BALLARD, b. 19 Aug 1771; d. at Peterborough, 5 Nov 1856; m. at Wilton, 13 May 1794, RICHARD TAYLOR BUSS, b. at Wilton, 7 Sep 1772 son of Stephen and Phebe (Keyes) Buss; Richard d. at Peterborough, 20 Oct 1862.

v PHEBE BALLARD, b. 30 Apr 1773; d. at Wilton, 15 Nov 1840; m. at Concord, 23 Feb 1794, JOHN GUTTERSON, b. at Andover, 27 Aug 1766 son of Samuel and Lydia (Stevens) Gutterson; John d. at Milford, 13 Dec 1841.

vi NATHAN BALLARD, b. 21 Feb 1775; d. at Concord, 5 Jul 1856; m. HANNAH BUSS, b. at Wilton, 3 Dec 1774 daughter of Stephen and Phebe (Keyes) Buss; Hannah d. 1857.

vii JOHN BALLARD, b. 22 Feb 1778; d. at Wilton, 28 Sep 1855; m. at Wilton, 20 Jan 1808, RHODA BALES, b. at Wilton, 16 May 1779 daughter of William and Rhoda (Keyes) Bales; Rhoda d. at Wilton, 15 Jan 1839.

viii EZRA BALLARD, b. 2 Feb 1780; d. 16 Sep 1781.

ix TIMOTHY BALLARD, b. 1 Jan 1782; d. 14 Jan 1782.

434) JOSEPH BALLARD *(Hannah Chandler Ballard^4, John Chandler^3, Hannah Abbott Chandler^2, George^1)*, b. at Andover, Oct 1749 son of Timothy and Hannah (Chandler) Ballard; d. 15 Feb 1819; m. 1st 10 Sep 1771, MOLLY SMITH of Shrewsbury; Molly d. by 1773 when Joseph m. 2nd, 16 Dec 1773, his third cousin, HANNAH ABBOTT *(George^4, George^3, George^2, George^1)*, b. 10 Oct 1749 daughter of George and Hannah (Lovejoy) Abbott; Hannah d. 29 May 1784.

Joseph Ballard and Molly Smith did not have children. Joseph Ballard and Hannah Abbott had four children born at Andover, none of whom married.

i HANNAH BALLARD, b. 7 Sep 1774; d. at Andover, 9 Jan 1833.

ii JOSEPH BALLARD, b. 12 Sep 1776

iii JOHN BALLARD, b. 11 Oct 1778

iv MOLLY SMITH BALLARD, b. Apr 1781; d. at Andover, 22 Oct 1812.

435) DOROTHY BALLARD *(Hannah Chandler Ballard^4, John Chandler^3, Hannah Abbott Chandler^2, George^1)*, b. at Andover, 12 Dec 1757 daughter of Timothy and Hannah (Chandler) Ballard; d. at likely Bow, NH after 1820 (alive at the time of her husband's probate January 1820); m. 17 Apr 1783, her first cousin once removed, JOHN CHANDLER *(Isaac Chandler^5, Nathan Chandler^4, John Chandler^3, Hannah Abbott Chandler^2, George^1)*, b. 21 Nov 1759 son of Isaac and Hannah (Ballard) Chandler; John d. at Bow, NH Sep 1819.

[1186] Livermore, *History of Wilton*, p 304

Dorothy and John Chandler started their family in Andover, relocated to Concord, and finally to Bow in 1811 where they both died. John Chandler was a teamster and a farmer, and the family was of poor circumstances. Toward the end of his life, John worked at what was later known as the poor farm in Bow.[1187]

John Chandler's estate entered probate 6 January 1820. Widow Dolly requested that son John be administrator of the estate. The administration was later assumed by David White. The estate was insolvent. The whole of the real estate and the personal estate except the household furniture was sold to pay the debts. Each of the creditors received just 5% of what they were owed.[1188]

John and Dorothy Chandler were parents of seven children.

i DOLLY CHANDLER, b. at Andover, 28 Jul 1783; d. at Andover, 11 Oct 1875; m. 1st, at Concord, 26 Nov 1807, her second cousin, EZRA CHANDLER *(Zebadiah Chandler6, Zebadiah Chandler5, Joshua Chandler4, John Chandler3, Hannah Abbott Chandler2, George1)*, b. at Andover, 27 Jun 1785 son of Zebadiah and Luce (Chandler) Chandler; Ezra d. at Concord, 1 Oct 1829. Dolly m. 2nd, at Concord, 2 Sep 1832, ALEXANDER ALBEE, b. at Westmoreland, NH, 1778 son of Zuriel and Anna (Penniman) Albee;[1189] Alexander d. at Littleton, NH, 24 Jun 1843.

ii JOHN CHANDLER, b. at Andover, 11 Sep 1785; d. at Concord, 16 Nov 1887;[1190] m. 23 Aug 1821, EUPHEMIA ROWELL, b. at Bow, 25 Sep 1800 daughter of Eliphalet and Eunice (Parks) Rowell; Euphemia d. at Bow, Oct 1868.

iii HANNAH CHANDLER, b. at Andover, 20 Sep 1787; d. at Concord, 20 Jan 1883; m. at Concord, 23 Nov 1810, CALEB SMART, b. at Hopkinton, 14 Dec 1786 son of Benning and Betsey (Duda) Smart; Caleb d. at Hopkinton, 30 Oct 1836.

iv HENRY CHANDLER, b. 27 Mar 1789; d. at Concord, 29 Aug 1843. Henry did not marry.

v BETSEY CHANDLER, b. likely at Concord, 21 Sep 1796; d. at Bow after 1870 (living with her son Henry in Bow in 1870); m. 27 Jun 1813, MANLEY CLOUGH, b. at Bow, 10 Oct 1790 son of Jonathan and Ann (-) Clough; Manly d. at Bow, after 1850.

vi TIMOTHY CHANDLER, b. not known; d. at Concord, 21 Sep 1823. Timothy did not marry.

vii BALLARD CHANDLER, b. about 1800; d. at Bow, 7 Mar 1832; m. at Bow, 17 Jul 1825, ABIGAIL CLOUGH, b. at Bow, 24 Sep 1805 daughter of Jonathan and Mary (Emery) Clough; Abigail d. at Hooksett, Dec 1881.

436) ABIEL LOVEJOY *(Phebe Chandler Lovejoy4, John Chandler3, Hannah Abbott Chandler2, George1)*, b. at Andover, 25 Jul 1737 son of Henry and Phebe (Chandler) Lovejoy; d. at Conway, NH 27 May 1817; m. 1764, ANNA STICKNEY, b. at Rumford, 3 Sep 1741 daughter of Jeremiah and Elizabeth (Carleton) Stickney, Anna d. 15 Jan 1815.

Abiel Lovejoy and Anna Stickney started their family in Concord but relocated to Conway about 1771. Abiel Lovejoy served as deacon. Abiel and Anna were among the first six organizers of the church in Conway. Abiel was a member of the Committee on Safety and Correspondence and signer of the Association Test.[1191][1192]

Abiel and Anna Lovejoy were parents of six children.

i JEREMIAH LOVEJOY, b. at Concord, 23 May 1761; d. at Conway 1811 (probate 1811); m. 7 Dec 1786, ELIZABETH "BETSEY" SPRING, b. at Conway, 1764 daughter of Jedediah and Elizabeth (Saltmarsh) Spring;[1193] Betsey was living in Conway in 1811 when the dower from her husband's estate was distributed to her.

ii ABIEL LOVEJOY, b. at Concord, 10 Aug 1763; d. at Lancaster, NH, 2 Nov 1837; m. 1st, 24 Apr 1788, SALLY EASTMAN, b. about 1767 daughter of Richard and Abiah (Holt) Eastman; Sally d. at Conway, 19 Feb 1801. Abiel m. 2nd, about 1802, BETSEY WHITE, b. at Bradford, VT, 23 Jul 1777 daughter of Nathaniel and Betsey (Martin) White; Betsey d. at Lancaster, 9 Feb 1836.[1194]

[1187] Chandler, *Descendants of William Chandler*, p 614

[1188] *New Hampshire. Probate Court (Rockingham County)*; Probate Place: *Rockingham, New Hampshire, Estate Papers, No 10057-10141, 1820, case 10064*

[1189] Jackson, *History of Littleton, NH*, volume 3, p 7

[1190] John Chandler's death record gives his age as 102.

[1191] Lovejoy, *The Lovejoy Genealogy*, p 104

[1192] Merrill, *History of Carroll County, NH*, p 849

[1193] Elizabeth Spring daughter of Jedediah was baptized in Conway in 1764; Merrill, *History of Carroll County*, p 859

[1194] There is much contradictory information in published genealogies about this branch of the Lovejoy family, and the Lovejoy Genealogy suggests it was not straightened out at the time of publication of the Lovejoy genealogy. But what I have with the two wives for Abiel accounts for the eleven children attributed to him.

iii WILLIAM LOVEJOY, b. at Concord, 10 Mar 1771; d. at Lancaster, NH, 1830; m. 29 Dec 1796, MARY MOORE, b. at Northumberland, NH, 4 Jun 1777; Mary d. 1842.[1195]

iv PHEBE LOVEJOY, b. at Conway, 26 Jul 1774; d. at North Conway, 6 May 1852; m. 18 Apr 1793, JONATHAN EASTMAN, b. in Strafford County, 18 Jul 1770 son of Richard and Abiah (Holt) Eastman; Jonathan d. at North Conway, 11 May 1868.

v BETSEY LOVEJOY, b. at Conway, 22 Jan 1776; d. at North Conway, 28 Aug 1859; m. about 1800, WILLIAM RANDALL, b. at Conway, 7 Oct 1772 son of Moses and Agnes (Forrest) Randall; William d. at North Conway, 11 May 1822.

vi ANNA "NANCY" LOVEJOY, b. at Conway, 16 Apr 1785; d. at Conway, 19 Mar 1827; m. WILLIAM EASTMAN, b. 18 Apr 1784 son of Richard and Abiah (Holt) Eastman; William d. 25 Mar 1872.

437) DORCAS LOVEJOY *(Phebe Chandler Lovejoy⁴, John Chandler³, Hannah Abbott Chandler², George¹)*, b. at Andover, 10 Sep 1739 daughter of Henry and Phebe (Chandler) Lovejoy; d. likely at Rumford, ME; m. EBENEZER VIRGIN, b. at Rumford, NH, 28 May 1735 son of Ebenezer and Hannah (Foster) Virgin; Ebenezer d. at Rumford, ME.

Ebenezer was commissioned as a lieutenant of the 2nd Company of the 6th Regiment of the New Hampshire militia on 26 February 1774. He signed the Association Test in Concord.[1196]

After the births of their children, Dorcas and Ebenezer relocated to Rumford, Maine where they were first settlers.[1197] In 1792, Ebenezer Virgin received three 100-acre lots on the south side of the Great River.

Ebenezer Virgin and Dorcas Lovejoy were parents of nine children born at Rumford/Concord, New Hampshire.

i JONATHAN VIRGIN, b. 23 Nov 1758; d. at Concord, NH, 9 May 1813; m. about 1782, SARAH AUSTIN, b. about 1760; Sarah d. at Rumford, ME, 17 Sep 1825.

ii MOLLY VIRGIN, b. 3 Jan 1761; d. at Lunenburg, VT, after 1850; m. 4 May 1778, ISRAEL GLINES, b. about 1753; Israel d. at Rumford, ME, 4 Oct 1838.[1198]

iii ELIJAH VIRGIN, b. 7 Mar 1763

iv HANNAH VIRGIN, b. 5 Jun 1765; m. at Concord, 31 Dec 1789, JONATHAN MOULTON, b. at Sandown, NH, 31 May 1765 son of Henry and Elizabeth (Mace) Moulton.[1199]

v DANIEL VIRGIN, b. 5 May 1767; d. at Rumford, ME, 1815 (probate 1815); m. his fourth cousin, MARY "POLLY" WHEELER *(Keziah Blanchard Wheeler⁵, Benjamin Blanchard⁴, Mary Abbott Blanchard³, Nathaniel², George¹)*, b. at Concord, 10 Sep 1772 daughter of Jeremiah and Keziah (Blanchard) Wheeler. Mary Wheeler is a child in Family 816.

vi PHEBE VIRGIN, b. 5 Aug 1769

vii HENRY VIRGIN, b. 19 Nov 1771

viii SIMON VIRGIN, b. 21 Sep 1779; m. 27 Jul 1800, NANCY DURGIN, b. at Canterbury, 2 Jul 1782 daughter of Joseph and Abigail (Hoyt) Durgin.

ix PETER CHANDLER VIRGIN, b. 23 Jul 1783; d. at Rumford, ME, 17 Apr 1871; m. 1st, SALLY KEYES, b. at Rumford, ME, 9 Jun 1792 daughter of Francis and Dolly (Bean) Keyes; Sally d. at Rumford, 14 Nov 1853. Peter m. 2nd, at Rumford, 26 Sep 1856, NANCY KIMBALL, b. at Bethel, 25 Oct 1799 daughter of Asa and Phebe (Foster) Kimball; Nancy d. at Rumford, 17 Aug 1890. Nancy was first married to Porter Kimball.

438) CHANDLER LOVEJOY *(Phebe Chandler Lovejoy⁴, John Chandler³, Hannah Abbott Chandler², George¹)*, b. at Andover son of Henry and Phebe (Chandler) Lovejoy, 23 Jan 1741/2; d. at Concord 20 Nov 1827; m. MIRIAM VIRGIN, b. at Rumford 23 May 1744 daughter of Ebenezer and Hannah (Foster) Virgin. Chandler m. 2nd 28 Sep 1814, the widow AZUBAH

The birth records give five children born to Abiel and Sally and there is a record for Sally's death in 1801. There are then six children recorded for Abiel and Betsey, the first of these in Conway and the rest in Lancaster.

[1195] Lovejoy, *Lovejoy Genealogy*, p 137

[1196] Bouton, *History of Concord*

[1197] Lapham, *History of Rumford, Oxford County, Maine*

[1198] Revolutionary War Pension and Bounty-Land Warrant Application Files

[1199] Bouton, *History of Concord*, p 681

GRAHAM. Azubah was the widow of George Graham who died in 1813. Azubah was born about 1738 and d. at Concord, 29 Jul 1829.[1200]

Chandler Lovejoy and Miriam Virgin were parents of seven children all born at Concord.

i JOHN LOVEJOY, b. 23 Jan 1766; d. at Concord, 6 Sep 1837; m. at Concord, 26 Nov 1789, ABIGAIL AMBROSE, b. about 1768 daughter of Robert and Mary (Etheridge) Ambrose; Abigail d. at Concord, 26 Mar 1832.

ii MIRIAM LOVEJOY, b. 25 Jul 1767; d. at Stanbridge, Québec, 6 Dec 1843; m. 1785, PHINEAS THORNE, b. at Wakefield, NH, 27 Feb 1764 son of John and Mary (Selby) Thorne; Phineas d. at Sanbornton, NH, 12 Apr 1853.

iii PHINEAS LOVEJOY, b. 16 Jul 1770; d. 9 Jan 1786.

iv EBENEZER LOVEJOY, b. 17 Oct 1772; d. 1 Apr 1847; m. 1st, at Pembroke, 17 Feb 1796, SUSANNAH VIRGIN, b. at Concord, 4 Sep 1777 daughter of John and Betty (-) Virgin; Susannah d. 19 Aug 1812. Ebenezer m. 2nd, at Concord, 27 Nov 1812, MARY GLIDDEN SANBORN, b. at Northfield, NH, 6 May 1789 daughter of Jonathan and Love (Thomas) Sanborn.[1201]

v PETER CHANDLER LOVEJOY, b. 17 Oct 1776; d. 17 Aug 1778.

vi SARAH LOVEJOY, b. 27 Jun 1783; d. at Yorkshire, NY, 12 Apr 1856;[1202] m. 1st, at Concord, 29 Nov 1804, JOHN THORNE, b. 1774 son of John and Mary (Selby) Thorne; John d. at Concord, 1812. Sarah m. about 1828, WALTER HINCKLEY, b. at Chatham, CT, 13 Jun 1775 son of John and Azuba (Smith) Hinckley; Walter d. at Yorkshire, 24 Feb 1838.[1203] Walter was first married to Mercy Gibson.

vii PHINEAS LOVEJOY, b. 29 Feb 1788; nothing further known.

439) HANNAH LOVEJOY *(Phebe Chandler Lovejoy⁴, John Chandler³, Hannah Abbott Chandler², George¹)*, b. at Rumford, NH, 26 Jan 1749 daughter of Henry and Phebe (Chandler) Lovejoy; d. at Thetford, VT 29 May 1809; m. JONATHAN WEST, b. at Rumford, 20 Oct 1749 son of Nathaniel and Sarah (Burbank) West; Jonathan d. at Thetford, 30 Aug 1826.

Hannah Lovejoy and Jonathan West were parents of twelve children.

i SAMUEL WEST, b. at Concord, 17 Sep 1768; d. at North Troy, VT, 20 Nov 1855; m. at Stafford, VT, 27 Nov 1794, ABIGAIL CHILD, b. 6 Jul 1771 daughter of Richard and Abigail (Green) Child; Abigail d. at North Troy, 9 Nov 1856.

ii HANNAH WEST, b. at Boscawen, 4 Sep 1770; d. at Hartford, VT, 29 Jan 1830; m. about 1792, ELISHA BINGHAM, b. about 1768.

iii PHEBE WEST, b. at Concord, 25 Oct 1772; d. at Norwich, VT, 30 Apr 1834; m. at Norwich, 13 Aug 1820, JAMES JOHNSON, b. 1761; James d. at Norwich, 3 Jan 1835. After Phebe's death, James married Phebe Kidder 1 Jul 1834.

iv LEAVITT WEST, b. at Salisbury, 23 Sep 1774; d. at Strafford, VT, 27 Jun 1862; m. POLLY NEWTON, b. at Sutton, MA, 11 Jan 1780; Polly d. at Strafford, 21 Mar 1864.

v EBENEZER WEST, b. at Concord, 16 Sep 1777; d. at Thetford, VT, 11 Sep 1834; m. EMILIA PIERCE, b. 1783; Emilia d. at Thetford, 11 Sep 1834.

vi SARAH WEST, b. at Concord, 20 Jan 1779; d. at Thetford, 29 Oct 1815. Sarah did not marry.

vii LYDIA WEST, b. at Concord, 7 Apr 1781; d. at Strafford, VT, 11 Aug 1864. Lydia did not marry.

viii MARY WEST, b. at Strafford, VT, 22 Nov 1784; d. at Troy, VT, 2 Apr 1840; m. PELETIAH HAMILTON, b. at Waterloo, ME, 6 Apr 1785;[1204] Peletiah d. at Troy, 28 Jun 1851. Peletiah married second Lydia Mason on 4 Dec 1840.

[1200] Some published genealogies, including the Lovejoy genealogy and the Chandler genealogy, report that Azubah Graham who married Chandler Lovejoy was the daughter of Asa and Sarah (West) Graham. But Azubah the daughter of Asa and Sarah Graham was born 1795 and she married Hazen Virgin 11 October 1812. Azubah the wife of Chandler Lovejoy died at age 91 29 Jul 1829.

[1201] The 1820 will of Jonathan Sanborn includes bequests to his wife Love Sanborn and his daughter Mary Lovejoy.

[1202] In 1855, Sarah, then Sarah Hinckley, was living with her daughter Lucia and her family in Yorkshire.

[1203] New York Wills and Probate Records, Cattaraugus County, volume 001, p 225

[1204] Peletiah's date of birth is given on his death record.

ix REBECCA WEST, b. at Strafford, VT, 9 Oct 1787; d. at Strafford, 16 Mar 1866; m. JOSEPH CUMMINGS, b. in RI, 1791; Joseph d. at Norwich, VT, 15 Aug 1866.

x HENRY LOVEJOY WEST, b. 22 Nov 1789; d. at Vershire, VT, 28 May 1871; m. at Vershire, 9 Apr 1812, SERAPHINA PENNOCK, b. 1789 daughter of Aaron and Experience (Lord) Pennock; Seraphina d. at Fairlee, 3 Apr 1879.

xi SABRINA WEST, b. at Fairlee, 7 Apr 1792; d. at Stowe, VT, 30 Sep 1872; m. at Hartford, 7 Dec 1815, JAROD CAMP, b. 25 Feb 1786 son of Abel and Anna (Manning) Camp; Jarod d. at Stowe, 6 Jan 1861.

440) SARAH LOVEJOY *(Phebe Chandler Lovejoy⁴, John Chandler³, Hannah Abbott Chandler², George¹)*, b. at Rumford, 8 Jun 1752 daughter of Henry and Phebe (Chandler) Lovejoy; d. at Concord, 1815; m. about 1772, her second cousin, THEODORE FARNUM, b. at Andover, 24 Jan 1749 son of Josiah and Mary (Frye) Farnum; Theodore d. at Concord, about 1789 (probate of estate). After Theodore's death, Sarah married Jedediah Hoit 28 Feb 1796.

Theodore Farnum did not leave a will and his estate entered probate 18 February 1789. Sarah Farnum was administratrix of the estate with her brother Chandler Lovejoy and brother-in-law Ebenezer Virgin as co-signers on the surety. Real estate was valued at £150 and personal estate £48.18.3.[1205]

Sarah Lovejoy and Theodore Farnum were parents of four children born at Concord.

i ENOCH FARNUM, b. 27 Feb 1773; d. at Concord, 3 Jun 1820; m. at Concord, 13 Nov 1802, DORCAS DAVIS, b. at Concord, about 1781 daughter of Samuel and Lydia (Merrill) Davis; Dorcas d. at Concord, 14 Oct 1830.

ii DORCAS FARNUM, b. 11 May 1775; d. at Concord, 1822; m. at Concord, 17 Aug 1799, JOSEPH ELLIOT, b. about 1775 son of Joseph and Lydia (Goodwin) Elliot.[1206]

iii REBECCA FARNUM, b. 9 Jun 1782; d. at Concord, after 1850; m. at Concord, 28 Feb 1811, SAMUEL ELLIOT SCALES, b. at Concord, 24 Oct 1785 son of (-) Scales and Mehitable Elliot;[1207] Samuel d. at Concord, after 1850.

iv PHEBE FARNUM, b. 21 Apr 1785; m. at Concord, 19 Jun 1804, CHARLES ELLIOT, b. at Concord, 22 Sep 1780 son of Jonathan and Mary (Collins) Elliot.

441) LYDIA BALLARD *(Lydia Chandler Ballard⁴, John Chandler³, Hannah Abbott Chandler², George¹)*, b. at Andover, 30 Jul 1742 daughter of Hezekiah and Lydia (Chandler) Ballard; d. at Andover, 28 Nov 1813; m. 13 Dec 1763, her third cousin once removed, DANE HOLT, b. 1 Apr 1740 son of Timothy and Hannah (Dane) Holt; Dane d. 15 Dec 1818.

Dane Holt served in the Revolutionary War in Captain Henry Abbott's Andover Company. This company "marched at the alarm" 19 April 1775.[1208]

Dane Holt wrote his will 8 January 1806 and the estate entered probate 5 January 1819.[1209] "I give to Lydia my beloved wife all my household stuff and furniture proper for woman's use to be entirely at her own disposal excepting my clock which I give to my son Dane." Lydia also receives the use and improvement of the easterly end of the dwelling house and other specific provisions for her support. Beloved son Dane receives all the real estate and the personal estate that is not otherwise disposed of. Beloved daughter Lydia receives $105 and daughter Hannah receives $75. Beloved son Jacob receives $250. The wearing apparel to be equally divided between his two sons Dane and Jacob. Son Dane is named executor. Heirs signing in 1819 that they have received notification of the probate from executor Dane Holt are Lydia Cummings and Asa Cummings, Hannah Abbot and Noah Abbot, and Jacob Holt. Dane Holt's wife Lydia died in 1813 and son Dane Holt assumed administration of the estate.

Dane Holt and Lydia Ballard had four children born at Andover.

i LYDIA HOLT, b. 12 Aug 1765; d. at Albany, ME, 18 Mar 1853; m. at Andover, 25 May 1797, as his second wife, ASA CUMMINGS, b. at Ipswich, 18 Sep 1759 son of Thomas and Anne (Kittell) Cummings; Asa d. at Albany, ME, 22 May 1845. Asa was first married to Hannah Peabody. A daughter of Asa Cummings and Hannah Peabody, Susan Cummings, married Benjamin Mooar who was a descendant of George Abbott.

ii DANE HOLT, b. 11 Mar 1768; d. at Andover, 27 Nov 1839; m. 6 Dec 1798, MARY WARDWELL, b. at Andover, 28 Nov 1774 daughter of Daniel and Damaris (Faulkner) Wardwell; Mary d. at Andover, 6 Dec 1866.

[1205] *New Hampshire. Probate Court (Rockingham County);* Probate Place: *Rockingham, New Hampshire, Estate Papers, No 5396-5511, 1788-1790*

[1206] Bouton, *History of Concord*, p 653

[1207] It is possible that Samuel was an out-of-wedlock child as the birth record gives only the name of mother Mehitable Elliot.

[1208] Bailey, *Historical Sketches of Andover*, p 302

[1209] *Essex County, MA: Probate File Papers, 1638-1881. Probate of Dane Holt, 5 Jan 1819, case number 13629.*

iii HANNAH HOLT, b. 16 Apr 1771; d. at Andover, 14 Jun 1862; m. 18 Feb 1806, her second cousin, NOAH ABBOTT *(Moses⁵, Barachias⁴, John³, John², George¹)*, b. at Andover, 11 May 1770 son of Moses and Elizabeth (Holt) Abbott; Noah d. at Andover, 13 Jul 1849.

iv JACOB HOLT, b. 7 Jun 1780; d. at Merrimack, NH, 30 Mar 1847; m. 2 Apr 1807, MARY FRYE, b. at Andover, 12 Mar 1788 daughter of John and Betsy (Noyes) Frye; Mary d. at Merrimack, 19 Sep 1825. After Mary's death, Jacob married LUCY KIMBALL, b. about 1791 (based on age 84 at death) daughter of Samuel Kimball; Lucy d. at Lowell, 11 Apr 1875 but is buried at Merrimack. Jacob graduated from Dartmouth College in 1803. He was a schoolteacher and later ordained as a minister. He was ordained in 1827 and was minister of the Congregational Church of Brookline from 1827 to 1832.[1210]

442) REBECCA BALLARD *(Lydia Chandler Ballard⁴, John Chandler³, Hannah Abbott Chandler², George¹)*, b. at Andover, 15 May 1744 daughter of Hezekiah and Lydia (Chandler) Ballard; d. 15 Sep 1821; m. 1 Oct 1765, her third cousin, ZEBADIAH ABBOTT, b. 27 Sep 1739 son of Zebadiah and Anne (Lovejoy) Abbott; Zebadiah d. 24 Nov 1793. Zebadiah is a descendant of George Abbott of Rowley.

Zebadiah Abbott graduated from Harvard, was a teacher and a trader, and served as a church deacon. He also served on the committee that drafted the Massachusetts State constitution.[1211]

Zebadiah Abbott did not leave a will and his estate entered probate 6 January 1794.[1212] As part of the probate, widow Rebekah Abbot petitioned the Court for an allowance beyond the widow's thirds. "In the death of a kind and indulgent husband, I am left a sorrowing widow, deprived of that protection and assistance that the delicacy of the female constitution and the increasing infirmitys of age may require, that although I have full confidence in the dutiful and affectionate care of my children who are kind and dear to me, yet by sad experience I have been taught the uncertainty of present enjoyments, and futer prospects, as it respects this life, and that a suitable and legal provision for future support may have a tendency to cultivate and improve the harmony that present subsists in our family, therefore I pray your Honour to grant me such dower or allowance in your Wisdom shall judge my station situation in life, constitution and infirmity of age shall reasonably require and the estate of my late husband will admit."

Son Zebadiah Abbot was administrator of the estate. The inventory included merchandise apparently from a store as it includes items such as half-gross of pencils, Dutch quills, slates, English goods, 8 yards of poplin, and calico remnants among many other items. The value of the estate was £1,727.

Zebadiah Abbott and Rebecca Ballard had five children all born at Andover.

i ANNA ABBOTT, b. Sep 1767; d. at Suncook, NH, 26 Dec 1827; m. 7 Jun 1793, her third cousin, CHRISTOPHER OSGOOD *(Elizabeth Abbott Osgood⁴, Thomas³, Thomas², George¹)*, b. at Andover, 25 Apr 1769 son of Samuel and Elizabeth (Abbott) Osgood; Christopher d. at Suncook, 3 Oct 1841. After Anna's death, Christopher married 17 Feb 1829 another ANNA ABBOTT, b. at Andover, 28 Feb 1769 daughter of Thomas and Lydia (Blunt) Abbott; Anna d. 31 May 1847. Anna Abbott and Christopher Osgood are Family 880.

ii ZEBADIAH ABBOTT, b. 6 Jun 1769; d. at Andover, 31 May 1836; m. 18 Oct 1796, SARAH FARRINGTON, b. at Andover, 6 Apr 1773 daughter of Benjamin and Sarah (Batchelder) Farrington; Sarah d. at Andover, 4 Mar 1847.

iii HERMAN ABBOTT, B. 5 Mar 1771; d. at Andover, 2 Feb 1858; m. 3 Oct 1799, LYDIA FARRINGTON, b. at Andover, 26 Sep 1776 daughter of Benjamin and Sarah (Batchelder) Farrington; Lydia d. at Andover, 17 Apr 1838.

iv JOSHUA ABBOTT, b. 1 May 1773; d. 20 May 1773.

v JOSHUA ABBOTT, b. Feb 1782; d. 26 Jul 1782.

443) SARAH BALLARD *(Lydia Chandler Ballard⁴, John Chandler³, Hannah Abbott Chandler², George¹)*, b. at Andover, 28 Dec 1755 daughter of Hezekiah and Lydia (Chandler) Ballard; d. 20 Aug 1825; m. 8 May 1777, her third cousin, NATHAN ABBOTT *(Job⁴, Jonathan³, Benjamin², George¹)*, b. at Pembroke, 4 Sep 1753 son of Job and Sarah (Abbott) Abbott; Nathan d. 1801.

[1210] Chapman, *Sketches of the Alumni of Dartmouth College*, p 111

[1211] Abbot, *Genealogical Register*, p 156

[1212] Essex County, MA: Probate File Papers, 1638-1881.Online database. AmericanAncestors.org. New England Historic Genealogical Society, 2014. Case 158

Deacon Nathan Abbot wrote his will 29 December 1800 and his estate entered probate 31 March 1801.[1213] Beloved wife Sarah receives "all my household stuff and furniture proper for a woman." She also receives use and improvement of one-third part of the dwelling and son Job to provide a list of specific provisions for her support as long as she remains a widow. She also receives use of the clock while she is a widow. If she decides to remarry, she is to receive one hundred-fifty dollars so long as she quits to son Job her right in the real estate. Beloved son Nathan receives one hundred-fifty dollars. Son Job receives all the real estate, but as each of his younger brothers reaches age twenty-one, they are to receive the offer of a lot of land that Nathan owns in Oxford, York County. The selection of the value of the lots is in decreasing order starting with two hundred dollars for the first lot down to twenty dollars each for the fifth and last two lots. Each of the younger sons also receives two hundred-fifty dollars and a cow. Those beloved sons are Able, Pascal, Jeremiah, Joshua, and Amos. If any of the younger sons chooses a trade, they receive only two hundred dollars and a cow. Beloved daughters Sally and Lydia each receive one hundred thirty-three dollars and eighty-four cents when they reach age twenty-one or on the day of their marriage. Job is also responsible for the expense of the upbringing of the children who are still underage and to pay for their common schooling. Job is also to provide for Nathan's Aunt Abigail Abbot. Wife Sarah Abbot is named sole executrix. The value of the real estate was $6,058.52. This included the homestead with a cider house and lots of various types and sizes in Boston, Wilmington, Temple, and Oxford.

Nathan Abbott and Sarah Ballard were parents to twelve children born at Andover.[1214] Three of the sons in the family relocated to Dexter, Maine. Eight of the twelve marriages for the children in this family were to other descendants of George Abbott and Hannah Chandler. This includes three marriages to children of Job and Anna (Ballard) Abbott (Family 589).

i NATHAN ABBOTT, b. 25 Aug 1778; d. at Andover, 13 Feb 1837; m. 10 Nov 1801, his third cousin, HANNAH RUSSELL *(Lydia Abbott Russell[5], Barachias[4], John[3], John[2], George[1])*, b. at Andover, Apr 1780 daughter of Uriah and Lydia (Abbott) Russell; Hannah d. at Andover, 16 Nov 1832. Hannah Russell is child in Family 297.

ii Son, b. 11 Jun 1780 and d. 16 Jun 1780

iii Son, b. 2 Mar 1781 and d. 1781

iv JOB ABBOTT, b. 7 Aug 1782; d. at Andover, 15 Dec 1859; m. 9 Oct 1807, his first cousin, LUCY CHANDLER *(Lucy Ballard Chandler[5], Lucy Chandler Ballard[4], John Chandler[3], Hannah Abbott Chandler[2], George[1])*, b. at Andover, 30 Nov 1785 daughter of Nathan and Lucy (Ballard) Chandler; Lucy d. at Andover, 19 Jul 1872. Lucy Chandler is a child in Family 444.

v JOSHUA ABBOTT, b. 29 Jun 1784; d. 29 Jan 1796.

vi ABEL ABBOTT, b. 7 Sep 1786; d. at Andover, 3 Jul 1862; m. 1st, 29 Sep 1811, his first cousin, SARAH ABBOTT *(Job[5], Job[4], Jonathan[3], Benjamin[2], George[1])*, b. at Wilton, NH, 7 Apr 1789 daughter of Job and Anna (Ballard) Abbott; Sarah d. at Andover, 1 Dec 1821. Abel m. 2nd, 28 Dec 1822, his fourth cousin, MARY JONES *(Elizabeth Abbott Jones[5], Samuel[4], Stephen[3], John[2], George[1])*, b. at Andover, 29 Jul 1786 daughter of Ebenezer and Elizabeth (Abbott) Jones; Mary d. at Andover, 9 Dec 1869. Sarah Abbott is a child in Family 589. Mary Jones is a child in Family 332.

vii PASCHAL ABBOTT, b. 23 Jul 1788; d. at Dexter, ME, 30 May 1859; m. 1st, at Andover, 10 Oct 1810, his first cousin, MARY FOSTER ABBOTT *(Job[5], Job[4], Jonathan[3], Benjamin[2], George[1])*, b. at Wilton, 18 Apr 1791 daughter of Job and Anna (Ballard) Abbott; Mary d. at Andover, 28 Oct 1828. Paschal m. 2nd, at Greenfield, NH, 22 Jun 1829, HANNAH FOSTER *(Mary Holt Foster[5], Joshua Holt[4], Dorcas Abbott Holt[3], Timothy[2], George[1])*, b. at Greenfield, 18 Jun 1796 daughter of Isaac and Mary (Holt) Foster; Hannah d. at Tilton, NH, 17 Oct 1885. Mary Foster Abbott is a child in Family 589. Hannah Foster is a child in Family 868.

viii JEREMIAH ABBOTT, b. 14 Aug 1790; d. at Dexter, ME, 21 Jul 1879; m. at Dexter, 19 Mar 1826, LUCY SAFFORD, b. at Washington, NH, 30 Dec 1802 daughter of John and Olive (Puffer) Stafford; Lucy d. at Dexter, 26 Sep 1866.

ix SARAH ABBOTT, b. 20 Dec 1792; d. at Andover, 20 Sep 1846; m. 17 Jun 1813, her third cousin, ABIEL RUSSELL *(Lydia Abbott Russell[5], Barachias[4], John[3], John[2], George[1])*, b. at Andover, Mar 1789 son of Uriah and Lydia (Abbott) Russell; Abiel d. at Andover, 14 Jan 1881. Abiel Russell is a child in Family 297.

x AMOS ABBOTT, b. 13 Mar 1795; d. at Dexter, ME, 24 Dec 1865; m. at Dexter, 7 Sep 1823, MEHITABLE SAFFORD, b. at Washington, NH, 13 Jul 1798 daughter of John and Olive (Puffer) Safford; Mehitable d. at Dexter, 1870.

[1213] *Essex County, MA: Probate File Papers, 1638-1881.*Online database. *AmericanAncestors.org.* New England Historic Genealogical Society, 2014. Case 104

[1214] Perley, "Abbot Notes," *Essex Antiquarian*, volume 2, p 100 was use for some of the information on the marriages of the children.

xi JOSHUA ABBOTT, b. 22 Apr 1797; d. at Topeka, KS, 5 Jun 1855;[1215] m. 1st, at Andover, 13 Oct 1820, his first cousin, LYDIA ABBOTT *(Job5, Job4, Jonathan3, Benjamin2, George1)*, b. at Wilton, 18 Oct 1800 daughter of Job and Anna (Ballard) Abbott; Lydia d. at Dexter, ME, 11 May 1826. Joshua m. 2nd, at Dexter, 12 Oct 1826, MARY WOOD BAKER, b. at Dexter, 25 Jul 1810 daughter of Samuel and Hannah P. (-) Baker; Mary d. at Boston, 3 Apr 1870. Lydia Abbott is a child in Family 589.

xii LYDIA ABBOTT, b. 4 Nov 1800; d. at Tewksbury, 19 Oct 1883; m. at Andover, 1 May 1823, THOMAS P. KENDALL, b. at Andover, 16 Nov 1799 son of Ephraim and Molly (Harnden) Kendall; Thomas d. at Tewksbury, 27 Jun 1857.

444) LUCY BALLARD *(Lydia Chandler Ballard4, John Chandler3, Hannah Abbott Chandler2, George1)*, b. at Andover, 4 Apr 1760 daughter of Hezekiah and Lydia (Chandler) Ballard; d. 29 Jun 1827; m. 27 Nov 1782, her first cousin once removed NATHAN CHANDLER *(Nathan Chandler5, Nathan Chandler4, John Chandler3, Hannah Abbott Chandler2, George1)*, b. 16 Jun 1756 son of Nathan and Phebe (Abbott) Chandler; Nathan d. 27 Jun 1837.

Nathan Chandler was a farmer in Concord, New Hampshire and he was living there when he wrote his will in 1821, and Concord is also the location of the probate. But most of the vital records for this family are in Andover, although the events may have occurred in Concord.

In his will dated 15 July 1821 (proved 28 March 1837), Nathan Chandler bequeaths to wife Lucy Chandler her support and maintenance suitable to her circumstances and condition to be furnished by his executor. This maintenance is in lieu of her right of dower. Daughters Lucy Abbot wife of Job Abbot and Rebecca Abbot wife of Jere Abbot and sons Ezra Chandler and Herman Phelps Chandler each receive one dollar. In addition, starting on the first of April, Herman Phelps is free to act for himself as if at the full age of twenty. Daughter Dorcas Ballard Chandler receives twenty dollars to be in the form of household furniture and bedding. Son Nathan Chandler receives all the estate real and personal, not otherwise disposed of, and is also named executor.[1216]

Nathan and Lucy Chandler had seven children whose births are recorded in Andover although perhaps occurred in Concord.

i LUCY CHANDLER, b. 30 Nov 1785; d. at Andover, 19 Jul 1872; m. at Andover, 9 Oct 1807, her first cousin, JOB ABBOTT, b. at Andover, 7 Aug 1782 son of Nathan and Sarah (Ballard) Abbott; Job d. at Andover, 15 Dec 1859. Job Abbott is a child in Family 443.

ii NATHAN CHANDLER, b. 29 Mar 1788; d. at Andover, 17 Sep 1860. Nathan did not marry. The Chandler genealogy describes him as a "feeble man." He and his sister Dorcas lived together in the village of Ballardvale in Andover.

iii REBECCA CHANDLER, b. 17 Jul 1790; d. not located but between 1860 and 1870; m. 14 Jun 1821, her third cousin once removed, JEREMIAH ABBOTT *(Samuel5, Daniel4, George3, Thomas2, George1)*, b. at Concord, 29 Oct 1790 son of Samuel and Mary T. (Story) Abbott; Jeremiah d. likely at Concord, after 1870 (living with one of his children in 1870). Jeremiah Abbott is a child in Family 923.

iv EZRA CHANDLER, b. 26 Sep 1792; d. 5 Dec 1793.

v EZRA CHANDLER, b. 8 Oct 1794; d. at Lowell, 11 Apr 1872; m. 22 Mar 1824, CHARLOTTE WOOD, b. at Epsom, NH, about 1803 daughter of James and Olive (Sherburne) Wood; Charlotte d. at Lowell, 27 Dec 1890.[1217]

vi DORCAS BALLARD CHANDLER, b. 2 Oct 1797; d. at Andover, 24 Dec 1878. Dorcas did not marry.

vii HERMON PHELPS CHANDLER, b. 19 Dec 1801; d. at Andover, 9 Jan 1862; m. 17 Feb 1831, his first cousin once removed, PHEBE ABBOT BALLARD *(Joshua Ballard6, Hezekiah Ballard5, Lydia Chandler Ballard4, John Chandler3, Hannah Abbott Chandler2, George1)*, b. at Andover, 22 Aug 1811 daughter of Joshua and Phebe (Abbott) Ballard; Phebe d. at Andover, 7 Mar 1894.

1215 ABBOTT, JOSHUA, late of Dexter, Me., aged 58 yrs., d. Topeka, June 5, 1855, of dysentery. (Lawrence, Herald of Freedom, June 9), Death Notices from Kansas Territorial Newspapers, 1854-1861 by Alberta Pantle August 1950 (Vol. 18, No. 3), pages 302 to 323, Transcribed by Trudy Thurgood; digitized with permission of Kansas State Historical Society.

1216 *New Hampshire. Probate Court (Merrimack County)*; Probate Place: *Merrimack, New Hampshire*, Probate records, volume 8, 500-501

1217 *Massachusetts, Death Records, 1841-1915*, New England Historic Genealogical Society; Boston, Massachusetts; Massachusetts Vital Records, 1840–1911.

445) HEZEKIAH BALLARD *(Lydia Chandler Ballard[4], John Chandler[3], Hannah Abbott Chandler[2], George[1])*, b. at Andover, 18 Jul 1762 son of Hezekiah and Lydia (Chandler) Ballard; d. 4 Oct 1848; m. 10 Dec 1783, his first cousin once removed, MARY "Molly" CHANDLER *(Zebadiah Chandler[5], Joshua Chandler[4], John Chandler[3], Hannah Abbott Chandler[2], George[1])*, b. 4 Apr 1764 daughter of Zebadiah and Deborah (Blanchard) Chandler; Molly d. 30 Mar 1834.

Hezekiah Ballard and Molly Chandler had eight children all born at Andover.

i JOSHUA BALLARD, b. 3 Jan 1785; d. at Andover, 4 Feb 1871; m. 13 Nov 1810, his third cousin once removed, PHEBE ABBOTT *(Jonathan[5], Jonathan[4], Jonathan[3], Benjamin[2], George[1])*, b. at Andover, 17 Jan 1788 daughter of Jonathan and Dorcas (Abbott) Abbott; Phebe d. at Andover, 14 Apr 1870. Phebe Abbott is a child in Family 321.

ii HEZEKIAH BALLARD, b. 19 Feb 1787; d. 21 Jan 1796.

iii MARY BALLARD, b. 13 Feb 1789; d. about 1803.

iv HANNAH FRYE BALLARD, b. 2 Aug 1791; d. at Andover, 7 Jul 1836; m. 8 May 1834, as his second wife, her first cousin, CHANDLER PHELPS *(Henry Phelps[5], Priscilla Chandler Phelps[4], Zebadiah Chandler[3], Hannah Abbott Chandler[2], George[1])*, b. at Andover, 5 Mar 1786 son of Henry and Mary (Ballard) Phelps; Chandler d. at Andover, 27 Dec 1868. Chandler Phelps was first married to LYDIA PARKHURST *(Lydia Chandler Parkhurst[6], Zebadiah Chandler[5], Joshua Chandler[4], John Chandler[3], Hannah Abbott Chandler[2], George[1])*, b. at Temple, NH, 4 Oct 1789 daughter of Andrew of Lydia (Chandler) Parkhurst; Lydia d. at Andover, 6 Sep 1830. Chandler Phelps is a child in Family 342.

v DORCAS BALLARD, b. 17 Dec 1793; d. 19 Jan 1796.

vi SARAH BALLARD, b. 17 Jan 1793; d. 15 Apr 1801.

vii HEZEKIAH BALLARD, b. 31 Aug 1796; d. at Wakefield, 21 Dec 1837; m. SUSAN BROWN, b. at Boxford, 22 Jun 1788 daughter of John and Susan (-) Brown; Susan d. at Reading, 6 Dec 1852.[1218] Hezekiah and Susan did not have children as indicated in his probate record stating "leaving a widow and without issue."

viii NATHAN BALLARD, b. 6 Oct 1801; d. 22 Oct 1803.

446a) MARY CHANDLER *(Abial Chandler Chandler[4], Abiel Chandler[3], Hannah Abbott Chandler[2], George[1])*, b. at Andover, 8 Aug 1734 daughter of David and Abial (Chandler) Chandler; likely d. at Blue Hill, ME, 21 Mar 1830. *Likely* the wife of ISAAC INGALLS b. at Andover, 13 Sep 1733 son of Henry and Hannah (Martin) Ingalls;[1219] Isaac d. at Blue Hill, ME, 8 May 1808. Isaac Ingalls was first married to Rebecca Mooar daughter of Daniel and Martha (Osgood) Mooar.

Mary Chandler and Isaac Ingalls started their family in Andover where four children were born. They relocated to Blue Hill, Maine and their two sons settled there.[1220]

i REBECCA INGALLS, b. at Andover, 16 Jun 1766; d. at Andover, 15 Jun 1859; m. at Andover, 11 Jan 1785, her third cousin once removed, ISAAC SHATTUCK *(Isaac Shattuck[5], Joanna Chandler Shattuck[4], Zebadiah Chandler[3], Hannah Abbott Chandler[2], George[1])*, b. at Andover, 13 Jul 1766 son of Isaac and Mary (Barnard) Shattuck; Isaac d. at Andover, 15 Jul 1835. Isaac Shattuck is a child in Family 338.

ii ISAAC INGALLS, b. at Andover, 12 May 1770; d. at Blue Hill, ME, 30 Oct 1838; m. by 1795, EUNICE HORTON, b. at Blue Hill, 10 Jan 1776 daughter of Joshua and Anner (Dyer) Horton; Eunice's death not located.

iii JACOB INGALLS, b. at Andover, 27 Aug 1772; d. at Blue Hill, 6 Mar 1848; m. 1st, 1799, ABIGAIL HORTON, b. at Blue Hill, 10 Mar 1774 daughter of Joshua and Anner (Dyer) Horton; Abigail d. 16 Oct 1806. Jacob m. 2nd, 30 Nov 1809, POLLY CLOUGH, b. in Maine about 1774 but not otherwise identified. Polly was still living at the 1850 census in Blue Hill.

iv HEPHZIBAH INGALLS, b. at Andover, 10 Dec 1774; d. at Charleston, ME, 23 Dec 1848; m. at Blue Hill, 18 Apr 1797, HENRY DOUGHARTY, b. about 1772 but not otherwise identified; Henry was living at the 1830 census at Charleston. Hephzibah and Henry had eight children born at Blue Hill and were there in 1820 but then moved to Charleston.

446) TIMOTHY CHANDLER *(Abial Chandler Chandler[4], Abiel Chandler[3], Hannah Abbott Chandler[2], George[1])*, b. 5 Apr 1738 at Suncook son of David and Abial (Chandler) Chandler; m. at Townsend, 26 Aug 1762, MARY WALKER whose identity is not certain, but born about 1742 (based on age at time of death); Mary d. at Shelburne, NH, 5 Sep 1777.

[1218] Susan's parents are given as John and Susan Brown on her death record.

[1219] Porter, Bangor Historical Magazine, volume 4, p 156 gives Isaac's wife as Mary Chandler. The Ingalls genealogy, p 56, suggests she may be Mary Osgood or Mary Chandler, but the birth date they give is the birth date of Mary Chandler.

[1220] Porter, "Ingalls Family of Blue Hill," Maine Historical Magazine, volume 4, p 156

In 1757, Timothy Chandler served as a private in the company of Lieutenant Nathan Chandler that marched in defense of Fort William Henry. In 1777, he served in Captain Holt's company.[1221]

Timothy and Mary Chandler were parents of seven children born at Andover.

i MARY CHANDLER, b. May 1767[1222]; m. at Andover, 3 Sep 1784, her third cousin once removed, JOSHUA STEVENS *(Hannah Shattuck Stevens⁵, Joanna Chandler Shattuck⁴, Zebadiah Chandler³, Hannah Abbott Chandler², George¹)*, b. at Andover, 8 Jan 1765 son of Samuel and Hannah (Shattuck) Stevens. Joshua Stevens is a child in Family 336.

ii ELIZABETH CHANDLER, b. 30 Aug 1767; d. likely at Blue Hill; m. 8 May 1793, her fourth cousin once removed, JOSHUA PARKER *(Nathan Parker⁵, Hannah Swan Parker⁴, Hannah Stevens Swan³, Sarah Abbott Stevens², George¹)*, b. at Blue Hill, 25 Nov 1767 son of Nathan and Mary (Wood) Parker; Joshua d. at Blue Hill, 9 Apr 1809. Joshua Parker is a child in Family 729.

iii DAVID WALKER CHANDLER, b. Aug 1769; nothing else known. The Chandler genealogy states he went "off to work."

iv CHLOE CHANDLER, b. 30 Aug 1771; d. at Rumford, ME, 17 Mar 1859; m. 10 Nov 1795, her fourth cousin once removed, DAVID HOLT *(Hannah Abbott Holt⁵, David⁴, Jonathan³, Benjamin², George¹)*, b. at Pembroke, 12 May 1774 son of Benjamin and Hannah (Abbott) Holt; David d. at Rumford, 1 Feb 1859. David Holt is a child in Family 809.

v ABIEL CHANDLER, b. Jun 1773; d. before 1850 at East Livermore, ME; m. 1 Jun 1798, BETSEY YOUNG, b. at Deerfield, NH, 23 Sep 1773 daughter of Joshua and Mary (-) Young;[1223] Betsey d. at Melrose, MA, 17 Aug 1866.

vi TIMOTHY CHANDLER, b. Sep 1775; d. at Lovell, 29 Nov 1854; m. 13 Nov 1798, his fourth cousin once removed, PHEBE HOLT *(Hannah Abbott Holt⁵, David⁴, Jonathan³, Benjamin², George¹)*, b. 14 Jul 1772 daughter of Benjamin and Hannah (Abbott) Holt; Phebe d. at Lovell, 1 Jun 1850. Phebe Holt is a child in Family 809.

vii AMOS CHANDLER, b. Sep 1777; d. at Shelburne, NH, 24 Apr 1836; m. 7 Mar 1799, RUTH HEAD, b. at Pembroke, 16 Dec 1779 daughter of John and Lydia (Merrill) Head; Ruth d. at Shelburne, 3 Apr 1840.

447) HULDAH CHANDLER *(Abial Chandler Chandler⁴, Abiel Chandler³, Hannah Abbott Chandler², George¹)*, b. at Suncook, 16 Aug 1740 daughter of David and Abial (Chandler) Chandler; d. likely at Hillsborough;[1224] m. 1st, 27 Dec 1763, NATHAN WARDWELL, b. at Andover, 20 Jan 1740/1 son of William and Margery (Gray) Wardwell; Nathan d. 14 Aug 1769. Huldah m. 2nd at Andover, 9 Jan 1772, STEPHEN STILES, b. at Andover, 27 Mar 1741 son of Hezekiah and Hannah (Barnard) Stiles.

Huldah and Nathan Wardwell had two children before Nathan's death at age 28. Huldah then married Stephen Stiles, and after the births of their three children, the family relocated to New Hampshire finally settling in Hillsborough.

Probate records were not located for Nathan Wardwell or Stephen Stiles.

Children of Nathan and Huldah Wardwell:

i NATHAN WARDWELL, b. 10 Nov 1765; d. at Andover, 4 Nov 1838; m. at Andover, 22 May 1791, his first cousin once removed, PHEBE STEVENS, b. at Andover, 6 May 1759 daughter of Thomas and Sarah (Gray) Stevens; Phebe d. 13 Aug 1843 (age at death given as 85).

ii OLIVE WARDWELL, b. 3 Jul 1768; d. at Salem, 7 Jan 1849; m. at Andover, 9 Nov 1794, SIMEON TOWNE. Simeon's identity is uncertain. He is described as Simeon, Jr. on the marriage transcription, but he is likely Simeon Towne born in 1751 who was first married to Hannah Symonds.

Children of Stephen and Huldah Stiles:

i HULDAH STILES, b. 21 Mar 1773; d. at Bradford, NH, 24 Feb 1859; m. about 1793, ANDREW CRESSY, b. at Bradford, 10 Feb 1766 son of Daniel and Abigail (Allen) Cressy; Andrew d. 3 Apr 1860.

[1221] Chandler, *Descendants of William and Annis Chandler*, p 171

[1222] Mary was baptized in May 1767 and may have been born several months or a year earlier as there is a second child born 30 Aug 1767.

[1223] Parents are given as Joshua and Mary Young on her death record, but mother's name is not certain.

[1224] Guild, *The Stiles Family in America*, p 87

ii STEPHEN STILES, b. 18 Jul 1777; d. at Bradford, about 1852. Stephen did not marry. He worked as a shoemaker in Bradford and resided with his brother Moses.

iii MOSES STILES, b. 19 Nov 1781; d. at Bradford, NH, 5 Jan 1868; m. Oct 1803, his first cousin, MARY CHANDLER KENNEY *(Lydia Chandler Kenney[5], Abial Chandler Chandler[4], Abiel Chandler[3], Hannah Abbott Chandler[2], George[1])*, b. at Pembroke, 25 Oct 1784 daughter of Thomas and Lydia (Chandler) Kenney; Mary d. 24 Oct 1882. Mary Chandler is a child in Family 449.

448) HEPHZIBAH CHANDLER *(Abial Chandler Chandler[4], Abiel Chandler[3], Hannah Abbott Chandler[2], George[1])*, b. 16 Oct 1743 daughter of David and Abial (Chandler) Chandler; d. 25 Oct 1810; m. 12 Apr 1762, WILLIAM FARNSWORTH, b. at Pepperell, 27 Dec 1737 son of William and Ruth (Hobart) Farnsworth. William m. 2nd, 20 May 1813, Sarah Green; William d. about 1837 in New York.

William Farnsworth was a traveler. He was born in Pepperell, spent time in Conway as a young man, then on to Hawley where all the children of Hephzibah and William were born, and finally settled in Western, New York.[1225]

William served in the Revolution and applied for a pension for his service while he was living in Hawley. In May 1777, he enlisted for a term of three years in the Captain Robert Oliver's company in the Third Regiment of the Massachusetts line. He reenlisted an additional three years and was promoted to Sergeant. At the time of his pension application, he was of poor circumstances, claiming no real estate and a personal estate valued at $18.84.[1226]

Hephzibah Chandler and William Farnsworth were parents of eight children all births recorded at Hawley, Massachusetts.

i HEPHZIBAH FARNSWORTH, b. 19 Oct 1764; d. at Sangerfield, NY, 1811; m. at Conway, 17 Aug 1785, HENRY LOOK, b. at Hawley, 19 May 1763 son of Noah and Hannah (-) Look.

ii WILLIAM FARNSWORTH, b. 15 Nov 1766; d. at Madison County, NY, 3 Mar 1845; m. about 1790, DEBORAH ROGERS, b. at Monson, 1767 daughter of Nathaniel and Abiah (Ingalls) Rogers; Deborah d. 1820.

iii JOHN FARNSWORTH, b. 4 Jan 1772; d. at Molalla, OR, 1862; m. RELIEF, b. at Hawley, 21 Feb 1773.[1227]

iv LYDIA FARNSWORTH, b. about 1774; d. at Hawley, 28 Mar 1821; m. about 1793, ETHAN HITCHCOCK, b. at Hawley, 18 Oct 1773 son of Samuel and Thankful (Hawks) Hitchcock; Ethan d. at Hawley, 26 May 1866. After Lydia's death, Ethan married Catherine Parker.

v MARY FARNSWORTH, b. 21 Jun 1776; d. at Scipio, IN, 13 Feb 1860; m. at Hawley, 5 Nov 1801, PHINEAS MAYNARD

vi CHANDLER FARNSWORTH, b. 25 Feb 1782; d. at Hawley, 1860; m. at Hawley, 7 Sep 1809, BETSEY DAMON, b. about 1788.

vii REUEL FARNSWORTH, b. 10 Oct 1785; d. at Stockbridge, NY, 1870; m. at Hawley, 30 Sep 1813, RACHEL TAYLOR, b. at Hawley, 29 Sep 1785 daughter of John and Elizabeth (-) Taylor; Rachel d. at Stockbridge, 1871.

viii DAVID FARNSWORTH, b. 5 Jun 1788; d. at Perrysburg, NY, 2 Apr 1841; m. at Hawley, 29 Nov 1810, SOPHIA HOWES, b. at Ashfield, MA, 1 Aug 1790 daughter of Isaiah and Lydia (Chapman) Howes; Sophia d. at Madelia, MN, 5 Jun 1868.

449) LYDIA CHANDLER *(Abial Chandler Chandler[4], Abiel Chandler[3], Hannah Abbott Chandler[2], George[1])*, b. 28 May 1746 daughter of David and Abial (Chandler) Chandler; d. at Langdon, 27 Dec 1822; m. 1st, as his second wife, JOSEPH PARKER, b. 15 Jul 1726 son of Joseph and Mary (Emery) Parker; Joseph d. 1777. Joseph's first wife was Hannah Abbott and the children of Joseph Parker and Hannah Abbott are followed up in Family 349 and Family 819. Lydia m. 2nd, THOMAS KENNEY, b. unknown; Thomas d. about 1814 at Langdon, NH (probate of will).

Lydia Chandler and Joseph Parker were parents of three children born at Andover. There is no firm information on these children past their birth records.

i JOSEPH PARKER, b. 5 Jun 1770

ii JACOB PARKER, b. 11 Jun 1772

iii SAMUEL PARKER, b. 9 Feb 1775

[1225] Cutter, *New England Families: Genealogical and Memorial*, volume 4, p 1881

[1226] Revolutionary War Pension and Bounty-Land Warrant Application Files

[1227] Relief's birth date is listed in the Hawley town records as part of the family entry with her as mother; her maiden name is not given.

In his will written 30 Apr 1806 (probate 23 February 1814), Thomas Kenney bequeaths to beloved wife Lydia the use of one-half of the personal estate and real estate during her natural life. Daughters Hannah Kenney and Sarah Kenney receive the other half of the real and personal estate to be equally divided between them. After Lydia's decease, the half of the estate that is for her use is to be equally divided among his four children Amos Kenney, Mary Stiles, Hannah Kenney, and Sarah Kenney. Amos Kenney is named executor. The real estate was valued at $160.[1228]

Thomas Kenney and Lydia Chandler were parents of four children.

i AMOS KENNEY, baptized at Andover, Oct 1782; d. at Langdon, NH, 21 Oct 1849; m. 1st, about 1810, DEBORAH REED, b. 1785; Deborah d. at Langdon, 19 Aug 1835. Amos m. 2nd, at Bradford, NH, 4 Mar 1839, RACHEL KENDALL.

ii MARY CHANDLER KENNEY, b. at Pembroke, NH, 25 Oct 1784; d. at Bradford, NH, 24 Oct 1882; m. Oct 1803, her first cousin, MOSES STILES *(Huldah Chandler Stiles⁵, Abial Chandler Chandler⁴, Abiel Chandler³, Hannah Abbott Chandler², George¹)*, b. at Andover, 19 Nov 1781 son of Stephen and Huldah (Chandler) Stiles;[1229] Moses d. at Bradford, 5 Jan 1868. Moses Stiles is a child in Family 447.

iii HANNAH KENNEY, b. at Pembroke, 30 Jun 1787; m. about 1823, JOSEPH SMITH, b. at Beverly, MA, 17 Oct 1794 son of Joseph and Elizabeth (Jones) Smith.

iv SARAH KENNEY, b. about 1789; d. after 1846; m. at Langdon, 6 Dec 1825, JOHN FOSTER, b. 1781; John at Langdon, 13 Dec 1843.

450) JEMIMA CHAFFEE *(Dorcas Abbott Chaffee⁴, Hannah Chandler Abbott³, Hannah Abbott Chandler², George¹)*, b. at Woodstock, 12 May 1741 daughter of Thomas and Dorcas (Abbott) Chaffee; d. at Woodstock, 28 Aug 1818; out-of-wedlock relationship with Mr. Hodges 1759-1760; m. 5 Jun 1766, as his second wife, AMOS PERRIN son of Peter and Abigail (Carpenter) Perrin; Amos d. at Woodstock, 11 Jan 1811. Amos was first married to Anne Morse.

The Woodstock Vital Records have the following entry: "Asenath Hodges Daughter of Jemime Chaffe Born July 22nd 1760." The Connecticut Church Record Abstracts contain the following entries that may be related to this. On 2 August 1761, Jemima Chaffee "confessed and was pardoned." She had her daughter "Asenah" baptized on 21 February 1762.[1230] There is no information on the identity of Mr. Hodges.

i ASENATH HODGES, b. at Woodstock, 22 Jul 1760; d. at East Poultney, VT, 3 Mar 1832; m. ABIJAH WILLIAMS,[1231] b. at Pomfret, 20 May 1758 son of Abijah and Eunice (Dana) Williams; Abijah d. at East Poultney, 11 Jul 1829. Asenath used the name Perrin at the time of her marriage apparently having adopted the name of her stepfather.

In his will written 19 August 1807 (proved 5 February 1811), Amos Perrin made the following bequests. Beloved wife Jemima receives the use and improvement of all indoor moveables and real estate during her natural life. Son Abel receives $334.34 to be paid to him one year after the decease of his mother. Sons Oliver, Thomas, and Amos receive all the rest of the estate to be divided equally, this bequest to be fulfilled following the death of their mother. Wife Jemima was named sole executor. The value of the real estate was $7,268 and the personal estate $160.[1232]

Amos Perrin and Jemima Chaffe were parents of seven children born at Woodstock.

i ANNA PERRIN, b. 27 Oct 1767; died young

ii THOMAS PERRIN, b. 3 Oct 1769; d. at Woodstock, 14 Feb 1833. Thomas does not seem to have married.

iii ANNA PERRIN, b. 21 Mar 1772; d. at Woodstock, 30 May 1801; m. ASHER HYDE, b. at Norwich, 7 Oct 1770 son of Asa and Lucy (French) Hyde. After Anna's death, Asher married Mariann Bugbee. Anna and Asher do not seem to have had children.

[1228] *New Hampshire. Probate Court (Cheshire County);* Probate Place: *Cheshire, New Hampshire, Estate Files, K26-K78, 1805-1821*

[1229] Guild, *The Stiles Family in America*, p 108

[1230] Ancestry.com, *Connecticut, Church Record Abstracts, 1630-1920.* Original data: Connecticut Church Records Index. Connecticut State Library, Hartford, Connecticut.

[1231] Joslin et al., *History of Poultney*, p 363

[1232] *Connecticut State Library (Hartford, Connecticut);* Probate Place: *Hartford, Connecticut, Probate Packets, Peake, Elizabeth-Pierce, Enoch, 1752-1880*, Case 3191

iv JEMIMA PERRIN, b. 6 Oct 1776; d. at Woodstock, 26 Aug 1806.[1233] Jemima did not marry.

v OLIVER PERRIN, b. 13 Sep 1778; d. at Woodstock, 6 Nov 1822; m. at Woodstock, 27 Oct 1806, DOROTHY TRUESDELL.

vi ABEL PERRIN, b. 24 May 1781; m. at Pomfret, 5 Aug 1805, ANNE GOODELL, b. at Pomfret, 19 Oct 1779 daughter of Asaph and Huldah (Weld) Goodell.

vii AMOS PERRIN, b. 24 May 1781; d. at Woodstock, 4 May 1845; m. 1st, at Woodstock, 14 Nov 1805, POLLY LEWIS, b. at Stonington, 30 Apr 1784 daughter of Asa and Polly (Dyer) Lewis; Polly d. at Woodstock, 19 Oct 1813. Amos m. 2nd, at Woodstock, 1 Dec 1814, MARCENA BLANCHARD, b. 1794; Marcena d. at Woodstock, 2 Jun 1884.

451) DORCAS CHAFFEE *(Dorcas Abbott Chaffee[4], Hannah Chandler Abbott[3], Hannah Abbott Chandler[2], George[1])*, b. at Woodstock, 12 Jun 1747 daughter of Thomas and Dorcas (Abbott) Chaffee; d. unknown (living at time of husband's death); m. at Ashford 6 Oct 1767, FRANCIS GREEN CHAFFEE,[1234] b. 6 Apr 1745 son of Benjamin and Priscilla (Green) Chaffee; Francis d. 3 Jul 1786.

Francis Chaffee served as a private in the Revolution in the company of Captain Thomas Knowlton. This company marched from Ashford to Boston in April 1775.[1235]

In his will, Francis G. Chaffee bequeaths to beloved wife Dorcas the use and improvement on one-third part of the estate. Beloved son Benjamin receives a double portion of the real estate. Beloved daughter Dorcas receives one share in the real estate as does beloved daughter Frances and beloved son Perrin. His daughters also each receive two good sheep or the value in money for the sheep. His trusty friend Phineas Brichard of Ashford and his wife Dorcas are named executors.[1236] Real estate was valued at £190 consisting of 76 acres and buildings and personal estate was valued at £89.2.7.

Dorcas Chaffee and Francis Chaffee were parents of seven children born at Ashford, four of whom were living at the time of the father's will in 1786.

i PRISCILLA CHAFFEE, b. 17 Nov 1769; d. before 1786.

ii BENJAMIN CHAFFEE, b. 28 Jun 1771; d. at Marcellus, NY, about 1805; m. at Ashford, 29 Nov 1792, REBECCA WHITING, b. at Ashford, 9 Nov 1771 daughter of James and Mehitable (Blancher) Whiting. After Benjamin's death, Rebecca married Mr. Burgess.

iii ORRIN CHAFFEE, b. 15 Jun 1773; d. before 1786.

iv FRANCIS CHAFFEE, b. 18 Aug 1776; d. before 1786.

v DORCAS CHAFFEE, b. 29 Sep 1779. Dorcas was living in 1786. James Chaffee was named her guardian. No further record found.

vi FRANCES CHAFFEE, b. 18 Mar 1782; d. at Sabula, IA, Aug 1856; m. at Marcellus, NY, 17 Jul 1800, SAMUEL SMITH, b. at Ashford, 11 Oct 1775; Samuel d. about 1860.

vii PERRIN CHAFFEE, b. 20 Apr 1786; d. at Marcellus, NY, 1813.[1237]

452) RHODA CHAFFEE *(Dorcas Abbott Chaffee[4], Hannah Chandler Abbott[3], Hannah Abbott Chandler[2], George[1])*, b. at Woodstock, 10 May 1751 daughter of Thomas and Dorcas (Abbott) Chaffee; d. 19 Nov 1834; out-of-wedlock relationship with Mr. Corbin 1770-1771; m. by 1772, DARIUS TRUESDELL, b. at Pomfret 16 Jan 1752 son of Joseph and Mary (Holt) Truesdell; Darius d. at Woodstock 6 May 1808.

Rhoda had an out0of-wedlock child, daughter Annice Corbin born at Woodstock, 18 May 1771. Nothing further is known regarding Anice.

Rhoda Chaffee and Darius Truesdell were parents of nine children born at Woodstock.

i ASA TRUESDELL, b. 17 Jul 1773; nothing further known.

ii DARIUS TRUESDELL, b. 1 Aug 1775; d. at Hartford, 16 Mar 1814; m. at Chester, MA, 14 Sep 1794, RACHEL SIZER, b. at Middletown, CT, 12 Mar 1772 daughter of William and Abigail (Wilcox) Sizer; Rachel d. at Fishkill, NY, 16 Dec 1853.

[1233] Mis Jemima, Daughter of Mr. Amos Perrin & Jemima his Wife aged 29 years Died August-26 1806

[1234] Connecticut, Town Marriage Records, pre-1870 (Barbour Collection)

[1235] Chafee, *Chaffee Genealogy*, p 122

[1236] *Connecticut State Library (Hartford, Connecticut)*; Probate Place: *Hartford, Connecticut, Probate Packets, Carrill, Nathaniel-Chandler, Susanna, 1752-1880*, case 855

[1237] Chaffee, *Chaffee Genealogy*, p 123

iii RHODA TRUESDELL, b. 31 Jan 1778; d. at Colrain, MA, 26 Mar 1795. From the Colrain, MA records: "Truesdale, Rhode, drowned while crossing North River on a log. She was on a visit from Connecticut at the house of Ephraim Manning, Mar. 26, 1795."

iv SILAS CHAFFEE TRUESDELL, b. 14 Jan 1784; nothing further known.

v CYRUS TRUESDELL, b. about 1785; d. at Woodstock, 6 Jan 1815.

vi JOHN TRUESDELL, b. 25 Jul 1786; d. at Killingly, CT, 17 May 1860; m. at Sturbridge, MA, 4 Sep 1808, SOPHIA BAYLIS, b. at Taunton, 2 Jul 1784 daughter of Frederick and Hannah (Brown) Baylis; Sophia d. at Putnam, CT, 24 Oct 1833.

vii THOMAS TRUESDELL, b. 10 Jul 1789; d. at Montclair, NJ, 20 Mar 1874; m. 1st, at Providence, RI, 14 Oct 1811, HARRIET LEE, b. at Providence, 10 Jul 1786 daughter of William and Abigail (Kinnicutt) Lee; Harriet d. at Brooklyn, NY, 30 Jun 1862. Thomas m. 2nd, 1865, JESSIE MARGERY GUNN, b. at Thurso, Caithness, Scotland, 4 Feb 1827; Jessie d. at Caldwell, NJ, 1888.

viii SARAH TRUESDELL, b. 29 Jul 1791; d. at Woodstock, 19 Jan 1815.

ix POLLY TRUESDELL, b. 5 Feb 1794; d. at Jefferson, OH, after 1850; m. at Woodstock, about 1815, JEREMIAH C. OLNEY, b. 1 Jun 1792 son of Ithamar and Anne (Cady) Olney; Jeremiah d. at Jefferson, OH, 1860.

453) DANIEL ABBOTT *(Joseph Abbott⁴, Hannah Chandler Abbott³, Hannah Abbott Chandler², George¹)*, b. at Woodstock, 18 Oct 1740 son of Joseph and Abigail (Cutler) Abbott; d. likely at Lebanon, NH; m. at Belchertown, MA, 29 Nov 1764, MARY KENTFIELD, b. likely at Belchertown and *perhaps* the daughter of Ebenezer and Mary (-) Kentfield.[1238]

According to the Abbot Genealogical Register, Daniel married and had several children,[1239] named as Asahel, Joseph, Elisha, Chandler, Lovica, Hannah, and Susan and that Daniel resided in Lebanon, New Hampshire. There are birth records in Connecticut for the first three of those listed children (although for Elisha the record is as Elisha in one place and Elijah in another with the same date) with parents Daniel and Mary. Daniel Abbott was listed as a taxpayer in Lebanon, New Hampshire in 1800. Birth dates of the youngest four children are not known.

i ASAHEL ABBOTT, b. at Woodstock, 15 Sep 1765; m. at Lebanon, NH, 5 oct 1797, PHEBE ROSS. Asahel was living in Lebanon in 1810.

ii JOSEPH ABBOTT, b. at New Haven, 20 May 1773

iii ELIJAH ABBOTT, b. at New Haven, 14 Mar 1777; d. at Serena, IL, after 1836; m. to likely SARAH although this is not yet clear. One of Elijah's children was named Mary Kentfield Abbott.

iv CHANDLER ABBOTT

v LOVICA ABBOTT

vi FANNY ABBOTT

vii SUSAN ABBOTT

454) JOSEPH ABBOTT *(Joseph Abbott⁴, Hannah Chandler Abbott³, Hannah Abbott Chandler², George¹)*, b. at Woodstock, 17 Feb 1742/3 son of Joseph and Abigail (Cutler) Abbott; d. at Pittstown, NY, 26 Jan 1813; m. 11 Dec 1764, PERSIS PERRIN, b. 4 Jun 1742 daughter of Nathaniel and Abigail (Jackson) Perrin; Persis d. at Pittstown, 23 Jan 1817.

Joseph Abbott and Persis Perrin started their family at Woodstock and relocated to Pittstown after the births of their children.

In his will dated 3 April 1812 (probate 9 February 1813), Joseph Abbott leaves all the household furniture to wife Persis and son Royal Abbott is to care for her. Daughter Orinda Hinman receives $50 is addition to the amount she has already received. Daughter Hannah Clapp receives $200. Daughter Lucy Bennette receives the note in the sum of $134.40 that he holds

---

[1238] Mary's parents are not verified

[1239] Abbot, *Genealogical Register*, p 24

for her husband Jedediah Bennette. The other household furnishings are divided among his three daughters. The remainder of the estate goes to son Royal Abbott who is also named executor.[1240]

Joseph and Persis Abbott had five children.

i ORINDA ABBOTT, b. at Woodstock, 26 May 1766; d. likely at Hartwick, NY; m. at Brooklyn, CT, 20 Oct 1785, ASAPH ADAMS, b. at Pomfret, 30 Jun 1759 son of Noah and Merriam (Adams) Adams; Asaph d. at Hartwick, 25 Mar 1808 (probate 15 Jun 1808). Orinda later married Joshua Hinman (as evidenced by her father's will).

ii HANNAH ABBOTT, b. at Woodstock, 3 Aug 1768; d. at Waterville, OH, 20 Jun 1850; m. 1st, LEMUEL CLAPP. Hannah m. 2nd, Dr. PARIS PRAY, b. in RI, about 1786 son of John and Deborah (Wade) Pray; Paris d. at Waterville, 7 Jan 1850.

iii LUCY ABBOTT, b. at Woodstock, 20 Sep 1772; d. at Otsego County, NY, 8 Aug 1846; m. Jan 1793, JEDEDIAH BENNET, b. 16 Jun 1773; Jedediah d. at Otsego, 10 Dec 1844.

iv POLLY ABBOTT, b. at Woodstock, 23 Jul 1775; d. at Pittstown, NY, Jun 1800.

v ROYAL ABBOTT, b. at Woodstock, 9 Oct 1777; d. at Pittstown, 22 Mar 1859; m. about 1802, WILMIRA VAN WOERT, b. 24 May 1783 daughter of Johannes and Catalina Lansing (Faterh) van Woert; Wilmira d. at Pittstown, 4 Oct 1865.

455) SARAH ABBOTT *(Joseph Abbott⁴, Hannah Chandler Abbott³, Hannah Abbott Chandler², George¹)*, b. at Woodstock, 8 Jul 1748 daughter of Joseph and Abigail (Cutler) Abbott; m. at Union, CT, 24 Nov 1768, JONAS HOUGHTON, b. 17 Jan 1748 son of Edward and Abigail (Coy) Houghton;[1241] Jonas d. at Woodstock 13 Nov 1791.

Jonas Houghton did not leave a will and his estate entered probate 13 Dec 1791. The widow's dower was set off to Sarah Houghton. The estate was sold to be of most benefit to the children who are not named in the probate record.[1242]

There is conflicting information in published genealogies related to the children. There is record evidence for five children and two other children seem to be agreed on in other published sources.[1243]

i AMASA HOUGHTON, b. at Union, CT, 17 Feb 1769; d. at Springfield, VT, 30 May 1813; m. at Winchester, NH, 10 Nov 1795, POLLY HOSKINS, b. 21 Nov 1773 likely the daughter of Nehemiah and Abigail (Tisdale) Hoskins; Polly d. at Springfield, 4 May 1838.

ii SARAH HOUGHTON, b. at Union, 17 Feb 1770. Sarah likely married, but the name of her husband is not yet determined.

iii HANNAH HOUGHTON, b. at Union, 29 Jun 1773

iv POLLY HOUGHTON, b. at Woodstock, about 1783

v DANIEL HOUGHTON, b. at Woodstock, about 1785

vi WEALTHY HOUGHTON, b. at Woodstock, Nov 1787; d. at Woodstock, 14 May 1804.

vii LUCY HOUGHTON, b. at Woodstock, 20 Jul 1790; d. perhaps at Cazenovia, NY. Lucy is *perhaps* the Lucy Houghton that married at Pomfret, 17 Jan 1813, MARVIN (Charles in some records) STOWELL, b. at Union, CT, 15 Mar 1789 son of Seth and Dinah (Holt) Stowell;[1244] Marvin d. at Fabius, NY, after 1850.

456) PHEBE MURRAY *(Elizabeth Abbott Murray⁴, Hannah Chandler Abbott ³, Hannah Abbott Chandler², George¹)*, b. at Woodstock, 2 Aug 1739 daughter of Matthew and Elizabeth (Abbott) Murray; m. 16 Mar 1758, JEREMIAH JACKSON, b. 22 Aug 1739[1245] son of Joseph and Zipporah (-) Jackson; Jeremiah d. at Lafayette, NY, 10 Mar 1802.[1246]

Jeremiah Jackson served in the French and Indian War and was with General Wolfe at the Battle of Québec. He was commissioned as a Captain during the Revolution. It is reported that he enlisted in the Revolution with his three oldest sons:

[1240] *Probate Records, 1791-1921; Index to Probate Records, 1794-1916;* Author: *New York. Surrogate's Court (Rensselaer County);* Probate Place: *Rensselaer, New York, Probate Records, Vol 0002-0004, 1802-1813*, p 295.

[1241] Houghton, *The Houghton Genealogy*, p 100

[1242] *Connecticut State Library (Hartford, Connecticut);* Probate Place: *Hartford, Connecticut, Probate Packets, Holmes, T-Humphrey, E, 1752-1880*, Probate of Jonas Houghton, 1791, case number 2163

[1243] Abbot and Houghton genealogies

[1244] Stowell, *The Stowell Genealogy*, p 109

[1245] Ancestry.com, *Mayflower Births and Deaths, Vol. 1 and 2* (Provo, UT, USA: Ancestry.com Operations, Inc., 2013).

[1246] The grave of Jeremiah Jackson is in Lafayette Cemetery and includes an inscription with date of birth as 13 Aug 1739 and death as 10 Mar 1802. Findagrave.com memorial I.D. 44074277

John age 18, Jeremiah age 16, and Nathan,[1247] age 14.[1248] Later, he was involved with the militia in Onondaga County, New York with a final rank of Colonel.[1249]

Phebe and Jeremiah married in Connecticut and were in Great Barrington, Massachusetts[1250] for a time and moved to Onondaga County about 1791 where Jeremiah purchased Danforth Mills. They lived in Pompey and later in Lafayette.[1251]

Seven children have been identified for Phebe Murray and Jeremiah Jackson, although no birth records were located. Information has been gleaned from town and county histories and biographies of the children.

i JOHN JACKSON, b. about 1759. Reported to have enlisted in the Revolution with his father, but no records have been located for him.

ii JEREMIAH JACKSON, b. about 1761; d. at Onondaga, NY, 22 Aug 1837; m. 1788, SALLY LAMPHIER, b. in CT, 1766; Sally d. at Syracuse, NY, 29 Jul 1851.

iii MATTHEW MURRAY JACKSON, b. 16 Jan 1763; d. at Hamilton, OH, 14 Jul 1823; m. JANE CAMPBELL, b. at Chester, MA, 24 Jun 1770 daughter of William and Mary (Young) Campbell; Jane d. 20 Aug 1843.

iv ELIZABETH JACKSON, b. 1765; d. in NY, 1835; m. about 1785, JOHN CROSSETT.

v CALVIN M. JACKSON, b. 1767; d. in OH, 1823; m. MARY SHEW, b. 1767 daughter of Godfrey and Catherina (Frey) Shew.

vi ANSON WILLIAM JACKSON, b. in NH, 3 Oct 1773; d. at Blackman Township, MI, 20 Jun 1857; m. HANNAH BROOKS, b. at Westmoreland, NY, 1 Feb 1780; Hannah d. 4 Jan 1842.

vii PHEBE MURRAY JACKSON, b. in MA, 1780; d. at Lafayette, NY, 1858; m. 6 Jul 1797, WARHAM CAMPBELL, b. 1777; Warham d. at Lafayette, 24 Aug 1825.

457) ELIZABETH MURRAY *(Elizabeth Abbott Murray[4], Hannah Chandler Abbott [3], Hannah Abbott Chandler[2], George[1])*, b. at Woodstock, 10 Sep 1741 daughter of Matthew and Elizabeth (Abbott) Murray; d. 28 Apr 1790; m. 17 Nov 1763, ASA CHILDS, b. at Woodstock, 6 Apr 1743 son of Ephraim and Mary (Lyon) Childs; Asa d. 20 Oct 1826.[1252] After Elizabeth's death, Asa married on 20 Apr 1791, ABIGAIL ADAMS.

There are just three children known for Asa and Elizabeth Childs, all born at Woodstock.

i THEDE CHILDS, b. 24 Aug 1765; d. at Woodstock, 25 Jan 1833. Thede did not marry.

ii DEXTER CHILDS, b. 19 Feb 1767; d. at Woodstock, 19 Apr 1832. Dexter did not marry.

iii RENSELLEAR CHILDS, b. 15 Sep 1769; d. at East Woodstock, 8 Jan 1832; m. 28 Nov 1797, PRISCILLA CORBIN, b. at Woodstock, about 1775 (baptized 7 Jan 1776) daughter of Pelep and Levina (Lyon) Corbin; Priscilla d. at East Woodcock, 11 Dec 1831.

458) JAMES MURRAY *(Elizabeth Abbott Murray[4], Hannah Chandler Abbott [3], Hannah Abbott Chandler[2], George[1])*, b. at Woodstock, 8 Dec 1743 son of Matthew and Elizabeth (Abbott) Murray; m. 26 Jan 1769, SARAH REYNOLDS who is not yet identified.

James and Sarah were in Dudley, Massachusetts just after marriage, but were soon after in Woodstock where their youngest eight children were born. They were dismissed from the church in Woodstock in 4 December 1793[1253] and were next found in Bennington County, Vermont and this is perhaps where James and Sarah died, although that is not known. Three of the children are later found in Milford, New York. It is not known by me what became of the other children.

James Murray and Sarah Reynolds were parents of nine children, the birth of the oldest child recorded at Dudley, Massachusetts and the remainder of the children at Woodstock, Connecticut.

i SARAH MURRAY, b. 5 Dec 1769

[1247] This particular history says Nathan, but other sources report this son as Matthew and he seems to be Matthew.
[1248] DeLand, *DeLand's History of Jackson County, Michigan*, p 1096
[1249] Onondaga Historical Association, "Onondaga's Revolutionary Soldiers", p 185
[1250] DeLand, *DeLand's History of Jackson County, Michigan*, p 1096
[1251] Onondaga Historical Association, "Onondaga's Revolutionary Soldiers", p 185
[1252] Child, *Genealogy of the Child Families*, p 139
[1253] Connecticut Church Record Abstracts, volume 133, Woodstock

ii SANFORD MURRAY, b. 28 Dec 1771; d. at Otsego, NY, 1830 (probate 8 Nov 1830); m. MARY WHITNEY.

iii OLIVE MURRAY, b. about 1774

iv JAMES MURRAY, b. Mar 1776

v ELIZABETH MURRAY, b. 8 May 1777

vi ROCKSA MURRAY, b. 28 Aug 1781

vii ROBERT REYNOLDS MURRAY, b. 17 Apr 1784; d. at Milford, NY, 30 May 1857; m. at Pownal, VT, 26 Jan 1806, HANNAH PHILLIPS, b. about 1789; Hannah d. at Milford, 13 Jun 1842. Robert m. 2nd, ALICE who has not been identified (Alice is the wife mentioned in his will).

viii ROBAH MURRAY, b. 9 Feb 1788

ix ORRA MURRAY, b. Aug 1791; d. at Milford, NY, after 1850. Orra was unmarried and living in Milford in 1850.

459) PHEBE HOLMES *(Phebe Abbott Holmes, Hannah Chandler Abbott^3, Hannah Abbott Chandler^2, George^1)*, b. at Woodstock, 22 Jun 1743 daughter of Ebenezer and Phebe (Abbott) Holmes; d. at Dudley, MA 6 Feb 1828; m. at Dudley, 15 Jun 1766, RALPH VINTON, b. 17 Oct 1740 son of Joseph and Hannah (Baldwin) Vinton; Ralph d. 14 Apr 1832.

Ralph Vinton was a successful farmer in Dudley.

Ralph Vinton wrote his will at Dudley 9 November 1829.[1254] He bequeathed to daughter Jemima Robbins wife of Ezekiel Robbins nine hundred dollars which was to be held by a trustee and used for Jemima's support as needed. If the full nine hundred dollars is not used for her support, after her decease the residue goes to her two sons, Jefferson Putney to receive one-third and Andrew Putney to receive two-thirds. The following grandchildren receive three hundred dollars each: Nancy Bacon wife of Charles Bacon, Rebecca Haskell wife of John Haskell, and Elmira Corbin wife of Joshua Corbin. Beloved daughter Polly Dyer wife of Winthrop Dyer receives nine hundred dollars, but that amount is to put toward the note that Winthrop Dyer owes him. Grandson Jeremiah Sabin receives one dollar only as he has already received "as much as I think he ought to have from my estate." No additional bequest is made to beloved daughters Bathsheba Havens and Rebecca Lyon as they have already received their portion by deed of real estate. Son Calvin Vinton receives the outside moveables and the farming tools, but not the livestock. Calvin has already received his portion through deed of real estate. All the remainder of the estate goes to his three grandchildren who are the children of his daughter Chloe who is deceased: Nancy Bacon, Rebecca Haskell, and Elmira Corbin. John Haskell is named executor.

Phebe and Ralph Vinton had seven children all born at Dudley.

i PHEBE VINTON, b. 30 Oct 1766; d. at Hardwick, 11 Feb 1796; m. at Charlton, 4 Feb 1794, ELIJAH SABIN, b. at Dudley, 23 Aug 1768 son of Gideon and Freelove (Searles) Sabin. Phebe and Elijah had one son, Jeremiah.

ii CHLOE VINTON, b. 22 May 1769; d. 1815; m. 1st at Sturbridge, MA, 3 Mar 1799, JOSEPH BARRETT, b. at Sturbridge, 12 Jan 1772 son of Joseph and Abigail (Ross) Sturbridge; Joseph d. 12 Nov 1808. On 3 Dec 1814, Chloe married EZEKIEL ROBBINS, b. at Sturbridge, 27 Mar 1768 son of Benjamin and Elizabeth (Hemingway) Robbins. After Chloe's death, Ezekiel married Chloe's sister Jemima.

iii BATHSHEBA VINTON, b. 15 Jun 1771; d. at Dudley, 27 Jun 1831; m. 12 May 1796, ABRAM HAVENS, b. about 1770 whose parents are not determined; Abram d. 5 Jun 1839. After Bathsheba's death, Abram married Polly Shumway on 2 Sep 1832.

iv JEMIMA VINTON, b. 10 May 1774; death not found; m. 1st 1 Jan 1799, ELEAZER PUTNEY, b. at Dudley, 16 Apr 1763 son of Eleazer and Abigail (Mixer) Putney; Eleazer d. 1814 (probate 1 Nov 1814). After Eleazer's death, Jemima married Ezekiel Robbins the widower of her sister Chloe.

v POLLY VINTON, b. 13 Jul 1778; d. at Jefferson, NY, 8 Aug 1872; m. at Dudley, 22 Apr 1798, WINTHROP DYER, b. at Dudley, 22 Apr 1779 son of James and Mary (Marcy) Dyer; Winthrop d. 18 May1857.

vi CALVIN VINTON, b. 22 Sep 1782; d. at Dudley, 15 Dec 1842; m. 30 May 1809, SARAH CORBIN, b. at Dudley, 19 Feb 1782 daughter of Joshua and Rhoda (Wood) Corbin; Sarah d. 29 Aug 1828. After Sarah's death, Calvin married Mrs. Lydia Joslin (maiden name Jacobs) (intention 28 Mar 1829).

vii REBECCA VINTON, b. 22 Feb 1785; d. at Southbridge, 30 Jun 1850; m. at Dudley, 29 Mar 1809, CALEB LYON, b. at Woodstock, 19 Nov 1777 son of Jonathan and Rebecca (Corbin) Lyon; Caleb d. 22 Jun 1855. After Rebecca's death, Caleb married Elizabeth Thayer in 1852.

[1254] Massachusetts, Wills and Probate Records, 1635-1991, Probate Records volume 71-72, 1831-1833, will of Ralph Vinton.

460) DOROTHY HOLMES *(Phebe Abbott Holmes, Hannah Chandler Abbott[3], Hannah Abbott Chandler[2], George[1])*, b. at Woodstock, 13 Apr 1745 daughter Ebenezer and Phebe (Abbott) Holmes; d. after 1830 (Vinton Memorial reports Dec 1834) when she seems to be the Dorothy Vinton as head of household in the 1830 Census; m. at Dudley, 11 Jan 1770, JOHN VINTON, b. 14 Feb 1742 son of Joseph and Hannah (Baldwin) Vinton; John d. at Charlton, MA Jul 1814.[1255] John had a fist marriage to Mary Sabin with whom he had one son, John.

John was born in Dudley, but the family relocated to Charlton where he was a successful farmer. He was a private in a company of Minute Men that marched at the alarm in 1775.[1256]

John Vinton wrote his will 20 January 1814.[1257] Beloved wife Dolly receives improvements on one-third part of the real estate for her natural life and three cows that are at her disposal. Son Lyman receives the use and improvement of several tracts of land for his natural life. These tracts abut land that Lyman already owns. After his decease, this land is to be equally divided among Lyman's five daughters who are Cynthia, Caroline, Sibbel, Louisa, and Clementine. Daughter Polly Prince the wife of Jonathan Prince receives the interest on six hundred dollars to be paid to her annually. Daughter Huldah Wheeler wife of Spaulding Wheeler receives six hundred dollars which will be paid to her within one year of his decease. Daughter Susanna Vinton receives a tract of land and she also receives two hundred dollars. Son Joshua receives all the rest of the estate and will receive that property that is left for the use of Dolly after her decease.

John and Dolly Vinton had six children born at Dudley.

i PATTY VINTON, b. 14 Oct 1770; d. at Orwell, PA, 24 Nov 1831; m. at Dudley, 28 Feb 1792 (given as 31 Feb in the record), JONATHAN PRINCE, b. at Sutton, MA, 1 Feb 1769 son of Stephen and Abigail (Perkins) Prince; Jonathan d. 23 Feb 1830.

ii LYMAN VINTON, b. 5 Mar 1772; d. at Southbridge, Aug 1841; m. 28 Sep 1794, LOIS LEACH, b. about 1775 with parents not yet undetermined; Lois d. 20 Oct 1857.

iii JOSHUA VINTON, b. 6 Jul 1774; d. at Southbridge, 10 Sep 1842, m. 1794, SALLY DYER, b. at Sturbridge, 29 Dec 1776 daughter of James and Mary (Marcy) Dyer; Sally d. 28 Sep 1861.

iv HULDAH VINTON, b. 21 Dec 1777; d. 17 Oct 1778

v HULDAH VINTON, b. 16 Oct 1779; d. at Orangeville, NY, 30 Apr 1835; m. at Charlton, 4 Jun 1802, SPAULDING WHEELER, b. at Plainfield, CT, 15 Oct 1777 son of Ephraim and Mehitable (Spaulding) Wheeler; Spaulding d. at Orangeville, 2 Jun 1851.

vi SUSANNA VINTON, b. 25 Mar 1787; d. at Southbridge, 30 Sep 1851. Susanna did not marry. The total value of her estate was $900.41

461) EBENEZER HOLMES *(Phebe Abbott Holmes, Hannah Chandler Abbott[3], Hannah Abbott Chandler[2], George[1])*, b. at Woodstock, 1 Nov 1748 son Ebenezer and Phebe (Abbott) Holmes; d. at Boston 29 Jan 1810; m. 7 Apr 1778, MARCELLA COLBURN, b. at Stafford, 11 May 1760 daughter of Jonathan and Hannah (Royce) Colburn; Marcella d. at Boston 28 Apr 1815, age at death given as 55 years.

During the Revolution, Ebenezer Holmes served as a Sergeant in the Company of Captain James Green in Colonel Mead's Regiment.[1258]

Ebenezer worked as a laborer. There were ten children born in this family, all at Woodstock,[1259] and then the family relocated to Boston.

Ebenezer Holmes did not leave a will and his estate entered probate 19 March 1810 with widow Marcella Holmes as administratrix. The personal estate was valued at $116.73 and no real estate was listed in the inventory.[1260]

i EBENEZER HOLMES, b. 18 Feb 1779; nothing further known.

ii OLIVER HOLMES, b. 3 Jun 1782; possibly m. at Boston, 13 Nov 1805, LUCY JOHNSON who has not been identified. In the probate record of Ebenezer Holmes, an Oliver Holmes, dentist, co-signs the surety for the bond and that is perhaps this Oliver.

1255 The date of death is that used by the DAR Ancestor listing.

1256 Vinton, *The Vinton Memorial*, p 67

1257 Probate Records, Worcester County, volumes 43-44, 1813-1815, will of John Vinton.

1258 DAR Ancestor #: A056961

1259 Barbour, *Vital Records of Woodstock*

1260 Suffolk County, Massachusetts Probate, Case number: 23495; 202:31, 187:231, 108:553, 110:701, probate of Ebenezer Holmes, accessed through familysearch.org

iii JEREMIAH HOLMES, b. 10 Feb 1784; d. at Charlton, MA, 19 Jan 1846; m. 16 Aug 1803, TRYPHENA SHATTUCK, b. at Pepperell, 9 Mar 1785 daughter of Moses and Abigail (Wood) Shattuck; Tryphena d. at Charlton, 23 Jan 1841.

iv MARY HOLMES, b. 8 May 1786; d. at Boston, 10 Jan 1819; m. at Boston, 13 Aug 1806, MARTIN KNEELAND who has not been identified. Mary is listed as the widow Mary Kneeland, age 33, on the transcription of her death.

v PERLEY HOLMES, b. 7 Oct 1788; d. at Boston, 28 May 1864; m. at Boston, 1823, RUTH COVILLE, b. about 1806; Ruth d. at Boston, 14 Nov 1876.

vi SARAN ANN HOLMES, b. 18 Aug 1792; d. at Boston, 20 Nov 1858; m. 1st, CUMMINGS who has not been identified. Sarah m. 2nd, at Boston, 18 Jul 1826, WILLIAM G. FULLICK, b. at Salem, about 1800 son of James and Mary (Whall) Fullick; William d. at Boston, 18 Nov 1877.

vii LUCY HOLMES, b. 20 Dec 1795; nothing further known.

viii SUSAN HOLMES, b. 20 Dec 1795; nothing further known.

ix ELIZA ANN HOLMES, b. 11 Nov 1798; nothing further known.

x CHARLES HOLMES, b. 8 Apr 1801; d. at Boston, 2 Nov 1806.

462) HULDAH HOLMES *(Phebe Abbott Holmes, Hannah Chandler Abbott³, Hannah Abbott Chandler², George¹)*, b. at Woodstock, 10 Jul 1756 daughter Ebenezer and Phebe (Abbott) Holmes; d. at Woodstock, 2 Feb 1853; m. 4 Feb 1779, ZEPHANIAH TUCKER, b. at Leicester, 15 Nov 1756 son of Stephen and Mary (Pike) Tucker; Zephaniah d. 25 Apr 1817.

Huldah and Zephaniah had nine children. Two of the births are recorded at Dudley, Massachusetts and the others at Woodstock, Connecticut. Some genealogies add a tenth child, Laura, but this seems to be a confusion with daughter Lucen Lorry. There is a birth transcription in Woodstock for Laury but gives her place of birth as Dudley and does not have a year but has the same month/day as Lucen Lorry who was born in Dudley.

i LYMAN TUCKER, b. at Woodstock, 19 Sep 1779; d. at Boston, May 1846; m. at Boston, 21 Aug 1803, NANCY NEWELL, b. at Newton 29 Jan 1779 who was the out-of-wedlock daughter of Elizabeth Grimes and an unknown Newell;[1261] Nancy d. at Boston, 24 Jan 1870.

ii LUCRETIA TUCKER, b. at Woodstock, 12 Apr 1782; d. at Woodstock, 22 May 1859; m. at Woodstock, 12 Apr 1810, DANIEL HIBBARD, b. at Thompson, CT, 21 Oct 1777 son of Ebenezer and Hannah (Hagan) Hibbard; Daniel d. at East Woodstock, 1 Mar 1856.

iii CLARISSA TUCKER, b. at Dudley, 20 Mar 1784; d. at Strafford, VT, 11 Apr 1871; m. at Chelsea, VT, 23 Apr 1805, a fifth cousin, RUFUS CHANDLER, b. at Woodstock, 6 Jan 1785 son of Andrew and Relief (Haven) Chandler; Rufus d. at Strafford, 27 Jan 1866.

iv LUCEN LORRY TUCKER, b. at Dudley, 26 Feb 1786; d. at Exeter, NY, 4 Jun 1867; m. about 1806, JOHN BREWER WALKER, b. at Woodstock, 6 Apr 1785 son of Phineas and Susannah (Hide) Walker; John B. d. at Exeter, 11 Sep 1868.

v BETSY TUCKER, b. at Woodstock, 7 May 1788; d. at East Woodstock, 22 May 1858; m. 9 Sep 1817, her third cousin, WILLIAM CHAMBERLAIN *(Abiel Chamberlain⁵, Sarah Wright Chamberlain⁴, Sarah Chandler Wright³, Hannah Abbott Chandler², George¹)*, b. at Woodstock, 8 Jul 1782 son of Abiel and Grace (Ainsworth) Chamberlain; William d. 5 Mar 1853. William Chamberlain is a child in Family 480.

vi NATHAN TUCKER, b. at Woodstock, 6 Nov 1790; d. at Binghamton, NY, 1883 (probate 27 Feb 1883); m. about 1818, POLLY PHILLIPS, b. at Woodstock, 18 May 1795 daughter of John and Mehitable (May) Phillips; Polly d. at Binghamton, 1875.

vii RHODA TUCKER, b. at Woodstock, 1 Dec 1792; no further record

viii CHANDLER H. TUCKER, b. at Woodstock, 16 Feb 1795; d. at Woodstock, 1 Apr 1875; m. 3 Aug 1817, LUCY CORBIN of not determined parents; Lucy d. at East Woodstock, 24 Dec 1888. Lucy is possibly the Lucy born at Dudley March 1798 daughter of Hannah (father's name missing).

[1261] This is confirmed by the 1804 will of her maternal grandfather James Grimes that includes a bequest to "so-called" Nancy Newell.

ix HULDAH TUCKER, b. at Woodstock, 1 Apr 1797; d. at Cedar Falls, IA, 1877;[1262] m. at Woodstock, 18 Jan 1821, a fifth cousin, THEOPHILUS MAY, b. about 1796 son of Caleb and Isabel (Chandler) May; Theophilus d. at Fitzwilliam, NH, 14 Mar 1865. After her husband's death, Huldah went to live with her son in Iowa.

463) ELLINOR ABBOTT *(Nathan⁴, Hannah Chandler Abbott³, Hannah Abbott Chandler², George¹)*, b. at Woodstock, 5 May 1747 daughter of Nathan and Anna (Leach) Abbott; m. at Brimfield, 28 May 1772, EPHRAIM BOND, b. at Leicester, 3 Dec 1746 son of John and Lydia (Gray) Bond; Ephraim d. at Wilbraham, 29 Mar 1819.

Ephraim Bond did not leave a will and his estate entered probate 20 May 1819. Joseph Dow was administrator and Nathan Bond and Elias Turner were sureties for the bond. The inventory of the estate was $322.69. The estate was not sufficient to pay the debts and was declared insolvent.[1263]

Ellinor Abbott and Ephraim Bond were parents of ten children born at Brimfield.

i JACOB BOND, b. 29 Dec 1772; d. 14 Dec 1775.

ii NATHAN BOND, b. 12 Mar 1774; d. at Wilbraham, 18 Oct 1856; m. LAVINA NEEDHAM, b. 24 May 1778 daughter of Anthony and Catherine (Warner) Needham; Lavina d. 29 Jun 1852.

iii ELEANOR BOND, b. 5 Jun 1775; nothing further known.

iv JACOB BOND, b. 29 Mar 1777; d. 23 May 1781.

v EPHRAIM BOND, b. 26 Jun 1778; nothing further known.

vi SAMUEL BOND, b. 1 Dec 1779; d. at Springfield, MA, 1 Dec 1857; m. at Wilbraham, 4 Jul 1808, ABIGAIL "NABBY" TOMLIN, b. at Spencer, 25 Feb 1788 daughter of John and Hannah (Gilbert) Tomlin; Abigail d. at Springfield, 24 Aug 1845.

vii POLLY BOND, b. 18 Sep 1781; d. 15 Aug 1783.

viii PERSIS BOND, b. 12 Mar 1783; d. after 1842 (living at husband's probate); m. at Sturbridge, 20 Sep 1818, ELIAS FISKE, b. at Sturbridge, 29 Oct 1782 son of Simeon and Mary (-) Fiske; Elias d. at Sturbridge, 8 Dec 1841.

ix ASENATH BOND, b. 14 Jul 1784; d. at Wales, 25 Apr 1872; m. 1st, 28 Nov 1805, WILLARD GOULD. Asenath m. 2nd, at Chester, 28 Oct 1829, JAMES MELVIN. Asenath m. 3rd, 15 Jun 1851, JAMES BURCHAM, b. at St. Marys, GA, about 1785 son of Joseph and Jane (-) Burcham. Asenath and her last husband James Burcham do not seem to have stayed together. He was living in Minnesota in 1860.

x RUFUS BOND, b. 18 Sep 1786; d. at Ware, 13 Oct 1830; m. at Palmer, 17 May 1809, ELIZABETH RYDER, m. at Tolland, MA, about 1789 daughter of Enos and Elisabeth (-) Ryder; Elizabeth d. at Greenwich, MA, 20 Apr 1878.

464) OLIVE ABBOTT *(Nathan⁴, Hannah Chandler Abbott³, Hannah Abbott Chandler², George¹)*, b. at Woodstock, 27 May 1749 daughter of Nathan and Anna (Leach) Abbott; d. at Lebanon, CT, 7 Oct 1784; m. at Brimfield, 25 Oct 1770, ELEAZER HUTCHINSON, b. at Windham, 12 Feb 1744/5 son of Joseph and Ruth (Read) Hutchinson; Eleazer d. Apr 1824.[1264]

Olive Abbott and Eleazer Hutchinson lived in Lebanon, Connecticut where they were admitted to the church there 7 June 1772. Their deaths are recorded there, but there are no baptisms for any children in the church records.[1265] There are a total of five household members in the Eleazer Hutchinson household in Lebanon in 1790, so perhaps there are other children, but no other records were located.

i OLIVE HUTCHINSON, b. 1771; d. at Lebanon, 24 Nov 1774.

465) ZEBADIAH ABBOTT *(Nathan⁴, Hannah Chandler Abbott³, Hannah Abbott Chandler², George¹)*, b. at Woodstock, 1750 son of Nathan and Anna (Leach) Abbott; m. at Sturbridge, 25 Mar 1780, MOLLY CHUBB, b. at Needham, 14 Nov 1754 daughter of Samuel and Prudence (Fisher) Chubb.

1262 In 1870, Huldah Tucker was living in Cedar Falls with her son Theophilus Wright May.

1263 *Probate Records, 1809-1881, Hampden County, Massachusetts;* Author: *Massachusetts. Probate Court (Hampden County);* Probate Place: *Hampden, Massachusetts, Probate Records, 1339-1404, George W. Bly - Helen Bosworth*, probate of Ephraim Bond, case number 1375

1264 *Connecticut, Church Record Abstracts, 1630-1920.*

1265 Connecticut, Church Record Abstracts, 1630-1920

Zebadiah and Molly had their children in Brimfield, and in 1803 relocated to Homer, New York. Molly outlived her husband by twenty years and was blind in the last part of her life. Their three sons also settled in Homer.[1266]

Zebadiah Abbott did not leave a will. Administration of the estate was granted to widow Mary Abbott.[1267]

Zebadiah Abbott and Molly Chubb were parents of six children, the first five recorded at Brimfield. Marriages are known for two of the children and the outcomes of the other children are unknown.

i OLIVE ABBOTT, b. 16 Aug 1781; nothing further known.

ii LUCY ABBOTT, b. 6 Oct 1784; nothing further known.

iii MOLLY ABBOTT, b. 14 Sep 1786; nothing further known.

iv ASA ABBOTT, b. 12 Mar 1789; d. at Cortland, NY, 1853; m. LOUISA who is not identified but might be Louisa Bowen sister of Nancy who married Nathan Abbott (see below).

v JOSEPH ABBOTT, b. 23 Aug 1791; nothing further known.

vi NATHAN ABBOTT, b. 1 Nov 1793; d. at Homer, NY, 10 Oct 1854; m. NANCY BOWEN, b. at Hardwick, MA, 28 Sep 1798 daughter of Samuel Bowen;[1268] Nancy d. at Homer, 19 Jul 1884.

465a) MARY ABBOTT *(Nathan⁴, Hannah Chandler Abbott³, Hannah Abbott Chandler², George¹)*, b. at Brimfield, about 1752 daughter of Nathan and Anna (Leach) Abbott;[1269] d. at Brimfield, 22 Aug 1791; m. at Brimfield, 17 Jun 1773, SOLOMON CHARLES, b. at Brimfield, 8 Dec 1750 son of Jonathan and Judith (Smith) Charles; Solomon d. at Wilbraham, 7 Apr 1843. After Mary's death, Solomon married Hannah Tomblin.

Mary Abbott and Solomon Charles were parents of seven children born at Brimfield.

i MARY CHARLES, b. 6 Feb 1774

ii LEVI CHARLES, b. 22 May 1775; d. at Brimfield, 28 Apr 1841; m. about 1797, SARAH BASHFIELD, b. about 1768; Sarah d. at Brimfield, 4 Jun 1854.

iii DANFORTH CHARLES, b. 14 Mar 1777; d. 29 Sep 1778.

iv DANFORTH CHARLES, b. 20 May 1779; d. at Ballston, NY, about 1807 (probate 6 Jan 1807); m. 28 Aug 1802, INDEPENDENCE BOOTH, b. at Enfield, CT, 4 Jul 1776 daughter of Joseph and Mary (Hale) Booth; Independence d. at Ludlow, MA, 4 Nov 1828. After Danforth's death, Independence married Lewis Barber 30 Apr 1817.

v ANNA CHARLES, b. 18 Jan 1781; d. at Brimfield, 19 Jul 1817; m. at Wales, 25 May 1800, JAMES DIMMOCK, b. about 1782 son of Gideon and Sarah (Davis) Dimmock; James d. at Wales, 26 Sep 1858. James remarried to Hannah Converse 21 Jun 1840.

vi MARTHA "PATTY" CHARLES, b. 4 Feb 1785

vii PEASE CHARLES, b. 9 Apr 1791; d. 17 Apr 1791.

466) HENRY ABBOTT *(Nathan⁴, Hannah Chandler Abbott³, Hannah Abbott Chandler², George¹)*, b. at Brimfield, 30 May 1754 son of Nathan and Anna (Leach) Abbott;[1270] d. at Brimfield, 31 Jul 1797; m. TABITHA RUSSELL, b. at Brimfield, 22 Aug 1749 the daughter of Ruth Blodget and unknown father Russell (apparently a child born out of wedlock);[1271] Tabitha d. at Brimfield, 9 Mar 1832.

Henry Abbott was a blacksmith in Brimfield. It is reported that he died after being bitten by a rabid dog. The dog was raiding the piggery, and in his attempts to subdue the dog, Henry was bitten.[1272]

Henry Abbott and Tabitha Russell were parents of six children born at Brimfield.

i DANIEL ABBOTT, b. 10 Jun 1775; d. at Oshtemo, MI, after 1850; m. NANCY who has not been identified.

ii TABITHA ABBOTT, b. 23 Jul 1782

1266 Smith, *History of Cortland County*, p 195

1267 Probate Records, 1809-1935; Indexes, 1808-1970; Author: New York. Surrogate's Court (Cortland County); Probate Place: Cortland, New York

1268 Death notice, Mrs. Nancy Bowen Abbott, *The Republican*, Homer, NY, 21 Aug 1884.

1269 Mary is a presumed child of Nathan and Anna Abbott. She married in Brimfield at the time Nathan was there and no other Abbott families seem to have been there at that time. In any event, she is an Abbott even if she is later found to have other parents.

1270 Henery, s. Nathan and Annah, May 30, 1754, Brimfield births

1271 Russell, Tabitha, d. Ruth Blodget, Aug. 22, 1749. [Tabitha Blogget, C.R.]

1272 Hyde, *Historical Celebration of the Town of Brimfield*, p 165

iii CALVIN D. ABBOTT, b. 26 Jan 1785; d. at Copley, OH, 1 Mar 1871; m. LOIS EYLES, b. at Kent, CT, 17 Feb 1788 daughter of Joshua and Lois (-) Eyles; Lois d. 15 Feb 1863.

iv SAMUEL ABBOTT, b. 7 May 1787

v EPHRAIM ABBOTT, b. 21 Jul 1789; d. at Saranac, MI, 21 Dec 1866; m. MARY, b. in NY, about 1808; Mary d. at Keene, MI, after 1860. Ephraim likely also had a first marriage that has not been located.

vi LORA ABBOTT, b. 3 Feb 1792

466a) HANNAH ABBOTT *(Nathan⁴, Hannah Chandler Abbott³, Hannah Abbott Chandler², George¹)*, b. at Brimfield, about 1759 daughter of Nathan and Anna (Leach) Abbott;[1273] m. at Brimfield, 6 Nov 1788, JAMES SMITH.

No information has been found for this couple other than a marriage record. In 1777 in Brimfield, a 22-year old James Smith was admitted to the almshouse and that might be this James. In 1787, James Smith, Jr. of Brimfield served 24 days in Captain Hoar's Company during Shay's Rebellion.[1274]

467) MARY ABBOTT *(John⁴, Hannah Chandler Abbott³, Hannah Abbott Chandler², George¹)*, b. at Woodstock, 31 Aug 1753 daughter of John and Mary (Wright) Abbott; d. at Ashford, 16 Nov 1790; m. at Ashford, 21 Oct 1784, EBENEZER WRIGHT.

Births of two children of Mary and Ebenezer and Mary, but no further information was found for these children.

i ABIGAIL WRIGHT, b. at Ashford, 28 Mar 1786.

ii MARY WRIGHT, b. at Ashford, 24 Mar 1789.

468) ABIEL ABBOTT *(John⁴, Hannah Chandler Abbott³, Hannah Abbott Chandler², George¹)*, b. at Ashford son of John and Mary (Wright) Abbott, 22 Mar 1756; d. 5 Apr 1812; m. 8 Jun 1786, JANE (or Jean) BARTLETT, b. about 1766; Jane d. after 1850 at Northampton, NY (living with son Daniel at the 1850 U. S. Census).

This family started in Ashford but relocated to New York. There is not much known about the children in this family. There are perhaps five children.

i JOHN ABBOTT, b. at Ashford, 3 Jul 1787; d. 18 Oct 1790.

ii DANIEL ABBOTT, b. at Ashford, 4 Nov 1781; d. at Northampton, NY, about 1861 (probate 20 May 1861); m. BARBARY SOWLE, b. at Westport, MA, 28 Sep 1803 daughter of David and Peace (Sherman) Sowle.

iii DAVID ABBOTT

iv SALLY ABBOTT

v JOHN C. ABBOTT, b. about 1795; d. after 1850 when he was living at Ledyard, NY; m. about 1825, LYDIA HUDSON, b. in NY, about 1798.

469) DAVID ABBOTT *(John⁴, Hannah Chandler Abbott³, Hannah Abbott Chandler², George¹)*, b. at Ashford, 19 Apr 1758 son of John and Mary (Wright) Abbott; d. 27 Feb 1827; m. POLLY PAINE.

Just one child is known for David Abbott and Polly Paine.

i MARY "POLLY" ABBOTT, b. about 1783; d. likely at Westminster, VT, m. about 1804, THOMAS PAINE, b. at Westminster, 10 Apr 1782 son of Miller and Zillah (-) Paine.

470) NATHAN ABBOTT *(John⁴, Hannah Chandler Abbott³, Hannah Abbott Chandler², George¹)*, b. at Ashford, 31 Jul 1763 son of John and Mary (Wright) Abbott; d. at Cardiff, NY, 21 Mar 1836; m. 1st, 31 Aug 1785, ELIZABETH BOWEN, b. at Ashford, 13 Feb 1765 daughter of Joseph and Thankful (Chandler) Bowen; Elizabeth d. before 1808. Nathan m. 2nd, 16 Oct 1808 HULDAH SKINNER, *perhaps* b. at Stafford, 2 Feb 1777 daughter of Joseph and Mehitable (-) Skinner; Huldah d. at Cardiff, 15 Apr 1848.[1275]

[1273] Hannah is another presumed daughter of Nathan and Anna Abbott.

[1274] Hyde, *Historical Celebration of the Town of Brimfield*, p 349

[1275] The graves of Nathan and Huldah Abbott are in Cardiff Cemetery with Nathan's age on gravestone as 72 and Huldah his wife, age 70. It is not a certainty that these are the graves of this same couple.

Nathan Abbott and Elizabeth Bowen were parents of ten children, the births of the first eight children recorded at Ashford.

i ABEL ABBOTT, b. 20 Sep 1786; d. 1 Oct 1786.

ii CHARLES ABBOTT, b. 1 Oct 1787; d. at Otisco, NY, 8 Oct 1862; m. PATTY COREY, b. in NY, 1785 daughter of Peleg and Mercy (Warner) Corey; Patty d. at Otisco, 1871. Patty was first married to Mr. DeGroot.

iii PHEBE ABBOTT, b. 11 Jun 1789; d. at Otisco, 5 Sep 1836; m. about 1808, THOMAS BURLINGAME, b. at Pomfret, 30 Aug 1787 son of Nathan and Sarah (Bartlett) Burlingame; Thomas d. at Otisco, after 1870. Thomas was second married to Betsey.

iv MOLLY ABBOTT, b. 31 May 1791; d. 1819.

v LUCY ABBOTT, b. 1 Oct 1793

vi AMOS ABBOTT, b. 9 Mar 1796; d. at Woodstock, 5 May 1883; m. about 1813, ANNA SANGER, b. at Woodstock, about 1795 daughter of Perley and Anna (Chaffee) Sanger;[1276] Anna d. at Sturbridge, MA, 21 Feb 1864. Amos and Anna had their children in Woodstock, and they were then in Sturbridge, MA until Anna's death.

vii ESTHER ABBOTT, b. 14 Mar 1798; d. at Putnam, CT, 18 Feb 1873; m. JAMES RILEY HARRINGTON, b. 1798 son of William and Ann (Burgess) Harrington; James d. at Putnam, 24 Oct 1856.

viii LOIS ABBOTT, b. 18 Jun 1800

ix BENJAMIN ABBOTT, about 1802

x AMANDA ABBOTT, b. 4 Mar 1806

Nathan Abbott and Huldah Skinner were parents of three children. Very little is known of them.

i MIRANDA ABBOTT, b. at Sturbridge, MA, 12 Mar 1809; d. 1812.

ii ANNA ABBOTT, about 1810

iii JOHN ABBOTT, b. about 1812

471) JOSEPH ABBOTT *(John⁴, Hannah Chandler Abbott³, Hannah Abbott Chandler², George¹)*, b. at Ashford, 13 Feb 1771 son of John and Mary (Wright) Abbott; d. 24 Jun 1829; m. 6 Mar 1794, ANNA SKINNER, perhaps b. at Stafford, daughter of Joseph and Mehitable (-) Skinner. There are two sisters, Anna and Huldah Skinner, born at Woodstock in 1770 and 1771, but this is about six years too old for Huldah Skinner who married Nathan Abbott (based on her age at time of death). I did not locate probate records that would confirm one way of the other, so I am leaving Anna and Huldah as the sisters from Stafford for the time being.

There are records for three children of Joseph Abbott and Anna Skinner born at Ashford.

i ROXEY ABBOTT, b. 3 Sep 1794; d. 30 Mar 1795.

ii BETSEY ABBOTT, b. 9 Sep 1796; d. at Eastford, CT, 23 Sep 1848; m. at Tolland, 6 Mar 1821, AMOS BUGBEE, b. at Union, 20 Jul 1802 son of Eleazer and Surviah (Chapman) Bugbee; Amos d. at Woodstock, after 1870. After Betsey's death, Amos married Nancy S. Howard 11 Dec 1850.

iii GIRDAN ABBOTT, b. 25 Apr 1801; d. at Chicopee, MA, 11 Nov 1851; m. 1826, SALLY FAY, b. at Tolland, about 1807 daughter of Simeon and Phebe (-) Fay; Sally d. at Springfield, MA, 20 Jan 1875.

472) AMOS ABBOTT *(John⁴, Hannah Chandler Abbott³, Hannah Abbott Chandler², George¹)*, b. at Ashford, 15 Nov 1772 son of John and Mary (Wright) Abbott; d. at Otisco, NY, 21 Sep 1852; m. 9 Apr 1800, SARAH GRIGGS, b. at Ashford, 17 Sep 1776 daughter of Joseph and Rebecca (Chaffee) Griggs.

Amos and Sarah started their family in Connecticut and relocated to Otisco, New York. In 1850, Amos Abbott donated the land on which the Methodist church was built.[1277] Son Warren Abbott was one of the first trustees of the church.

Only two children have been identified for this family, although census records suggest there may have been four other children.

[1276] Chaffee, *The Chaffee Genealogy*, p 131

[1277] Clayton, History of Onondaga County, New York, p 349.

i WARNER ABBOTT, b. at Ashford, 18 May 1801; d. at Otisco, NY, 20 Sep 1867; m. at Ashford, 10 Oct 1827, SOPHIA EASTMAN, b. about 1807 daughter of Nathan and Aphia (Buck) Eastman; Sophia d. at Otisco, 3 Sep 1881.

ii BETSEY C. ABBOTT, b. about 1808; d. at Tully, NY, 5 May 1850; m. about 1826, IRA GRIGGS, b. at Ashford, 7 May 1805 son of John and Betsey (Chapman) Griggs; Ira d. at Dundas, Ontario, 1 Apr 1869. After Betsey's death, Ira married Alida who has not been identified.

473) JONATHAN CORBIN *(Sarah Abbott Corbin[4], Hannah Chandler Abbott[3], Hannah Abbott Chandler[2], George[1])*, b. at Woodstock, 22 Aug 1760 son of Jabez and Sarah (Abbott) Corbin; d. at Dudley, MA; m. at Oxford, 24 Dec 1781, ABIGAIL WIGHT, b. at Thompson, CT, 30 Jan 1757 daughter of Levi and Susannah (Barstow) Wight; Abigail d. at Dudley 31 Jul 1825.

According to the Corbin genealogy, after the death of Jonathan's father and his mother's remarriage to William Chapman, Jonathan and his sister Sarah were brought up as orphans at Muddy Brook which is now East Woodstock.[1278]

Jonathan Corbin served as a private in the Revolution in Captain William Manning's Company of Colonel Charles Webb's Regiment in Connecticut. On 26 May 1777, he enlisted for a term of eight months.[1279]

Jonathan Corbin and Abigail Wright were parents of seven children all born at Oxford, Massachusetts.

i POLLY CORBIN, b. 27 Nov 1783; m. at Dudley, 22 Oct 1802, CALEB BROWN who has not been identified, but perhaps of Thompson, CT.

ii LUCY CORBIN, b. 18 Apr 1785; d. at Monson, MA, 14 Dec 1849; m. about 1802, STEPHEN MOON of Windham, CT; Stephen d. at Monson, 26 Jun 1871.

iii SARAH CORBIN, b. 7 Dec 1787; d. at Putnam, CT, 10 Mar 1857; m. 17 Oct 1813, DANIEL WHITTEMORE, b. at Thompson, CT, 24 Mar 1791 son of Caleb and Eunice (-) Whittemore; Daniel d. at Woodstock, 3 Sep 1870.

iv ANNA CORBIN, b. 9 Feb 1790; d. at Oxford, 6 Apr 1826; m. 29 Dec 1814, JOHN EMERSON, b. at Thompson, 6 Aug 1786; John d. 9 Oct 1868.

v JOHN CORBIN, b. 26 Apr 1792; d. at Charlemont, 28 Apr 1849; m. 3 Apr 1815, MARY STONE, b. in Rhode Island, 12 Aug 1794 daughter of John and Hannah (Eddy) Stone; Mary d. 12 Oct 1841.

vi JABEZ CORBIN, b. 28 Aug 1794; d. at Dudley, 3 Oct 1846; m. at Charlton, 7 Jul 1818, MIRIAM MCINTYRE, b. at Charlton, 1792 daughter of Gardner and Miriam (McIntyre) McIntyre; Miriam d. at Webster, 9 May 1847.

vii ESTHER CORBIN, b. 27 Oct 1796; d. at Thompson, CT, 9 Oct 1842; m. at Oxford, 12 Jul 1818, ASA HANDY, b. at Smithfield, 26 Nov 1795 son of William and Thankful (-) Handy; Asa d. at Thompson, 5 Apr 1853.

474) SARAH CORBIN *(Sarah Abbott, Corbin[4], Hannah Chandler Abbott[3], Hannah Abbott Chandler[2], George[1])*, b. at Woodstock, 11 Jan 1764 daughter of Jabez and Sarah (Abbott) Corbin; d. at Centerville, NY 15 Apr 1852; m. at Oxford, 24 Oct 1782, LEVI WIGHT, b. at Thompson, CT, 3 Jul 1761 son of Levi and Susannah (Barstow) Wight;[1280] Levi d. at Centerville 2 Jan 1831.[1281]

After the births of their first six children, Levi and Sarah went with Levi's brothers to Fairfield, New York and in 1802 on to Oppenheim. In the last part of their lives, they were in Centerville where several of their children settled.

Sarah Corbin and Levi Wight were parents of eleven children.[1282]

i WILLIAM WIGHT, b. at Oxford, MA, 2 Mar 1783; d. at Centerville, NY, 31 Mar 1824; m. 1st, 6 Sep 1804, BETSEY HEWITT, b. 7 Nov 1789 daughter of Randall Hewitt; Betsey d. about 1805. William m. 2nd, 19 Oct 1806, ABIGAIL CUDWORTH, b. 1787; Abigail d. Jan 1857.

ii DANIEL WIGHT, b. at Oxford, 23 Jan 1785; d. at Centerville, 27 Nov 1841; m. 18 Nov 1810, MARY HEWITT, b. 10 Aug 1786 daughter of Randall Hewitt; Mary d. at Centerville, 7 Mar 1828.

1278 Lawson, *Corbin Genealogy*, p 52

1279 NARA M881. Compiled service records of soldiers who served in the American Army during the Revolutionary War, 1775-1783.

1280 Wight, *The Wights*, p 71

1281 The graves of Levi Wight and his wife Sarah are located at Bates Cemetery in Centerville, NY. Findagrave.com

1282 Wight, *The Wights*, p 71

iii ABBOTT WIGHT, b. at Oxford, 23 Feb 1787; d. at Alabama, NY, 15 Jun 1863; m. 5 Apr 1812, ALICE CABOT, b. at Dudley, 13 May 1788; Alice d. at Alabama, NY, 19 Oct 1872.

iv DOLLY WIGHT, b. at Oxford, 1 Sep 1789; d. at Waukon, IA; m. at Oppenheim, NY, 26 Apr 1812, NATHAN FELT, b. 18 Apr 1775; Nathan d. at Pike, NY, 1 May 1850.

v GEORGE WIGHT, b. at Oxford, 22 Sept 1791; d. at Fort George, 10 Aug 1813 during the War of 1812.

vi STEPHEN WIGHT, b. at Dudley, 6 Oct 1793; d. at Jefferson, IA, 16 Mar 1874; m. at Centerville, 23 Nov 1823, HANNAH FELT b. 26 Feb 1808; Hannah d. at Jefferson, 16 Oct 1875.

vii LYMAN WIGHT, b. at Fairfield, NY, 9 May 1796; d. at Dexter, TX, 30 Mar 1858; m. at Henrietta, NY, 5 Jan 1823, HARRIET BENTON, b. in Vermont, 1800 daughter of John and Sarah (Bradley) Benton; Harriet d. at Oakdale, NE, after 1878.

viii UZZIEL WIGHT, b. at Fairfield, NY, 16 Jun 1798; d. at Westfield, NY, 19 Aug 1850; m. at Oppenheim, 29 Dec 1821, CAROLINE VAN BUREN, b. about 1803 daughter of William and – (Miller) Van Buren; Caroline d. at Union City, PA, after 1887.

ix SUSANNAH WIGHT, b. at Fairfield, 7 Sep 1800; d. at Centerville, NY, 15 May 1847; m. at Henrietta, NY, 19 Dec 1819, MORRIS STICKEL, b. 14 Sep 1794; Morris d. at Centerville, 18 May 1851.

x SARAH WIGHT, b. at Oppenheim, NY, 4 May 1803; m. 2 Mar 1826, PETER WEAVER; Peter d. 29 Nov 1852.

xi CLARISSA WIGHT, b. at Oppenheim, NY, 4 May 1803; d. at Centerville, NY, 10 Mar 1848. Clarissa did not marry.

475) SARAH WRIGHT *(Joseph Wright[4], Sarah Chandler Wright[3], Hannah Abbott Chandler[2], George[1])*, b. at Woodstock, 24 Sep 1737 daughter of Joseph and Abigail (Chaffee) Wright; d. likely at Winchester, NH; m. 23 Apr 1761, JOSEPH NARRAMORE, b. at Thompson, CT, 11 May 1735 son of Samuel and Lydia (Davis) Narramore; Joseph d. at Winchester, 20 Feb 1802.

Joseph and Sarah had their children in Connecticut, but relocated to Winchester, New Hampshire in 1772 when Joseph purchased 57 acres of land there from Josiah Willard 23 June 1772.

Joseph Narramore and Sarah Wright were parents of six children, the births of the first five children born at Woodstock and the birth of the youngest child recorded at Pomfret.

i ABIEL WRIGHT NARRAMORE, b. 20 May 1762; d. after 1810 when he was head of household in Winchester; m. at Winchester, 26 May 1788, POLLY SMITH, b. at Dudley, MA, 18 Oct 1767 daughter of Daniel and Rebecca (Scott) Smith.

ii OLIVE NARRAMORE, b. 28 Dec 1763

iii JEMIMA "MIMA" NARRAMORE, b. 1 May 1766; d. at Winchester, 29 Nov 1850; m. at Winchester, 28 Oct 1783, ABEL SCOTT, b. at Dudley, MA, 1 Aug 1762 son of Ebenezer and Mary (Shapley) Scott; Abel d. at Winchester, 12 Sep 1845.[1283]

iv HANNAH NARRAMORE, b. 12 May 1768

v SARAH NARRAMORE, b. 13 Jul 1771

vi LUCY NARRAMORE, b. 12 Oct 1773

476) SAMUEL WRIGHT *(Joseph Wright[4], Sarah Chandler Wright[3], Hannah Abbott Chandler[2], George[1])*, b. at Woodstock, 28 Jan 1744/5 son of Joseph and Abigail (Chaffee) Wright; d. Jul 1786 at Winchester, NH; m. 27 Oct 1768, MARY COBURN, b. at Woodstock, 25 Oct 1745 daughter of John and Deborah (Goddard) Coburn.

Samuel Wright and Mary Coburn were early settlers in Winchester, New Hampshire.

Samuel Wright did not leave a will. The inventory included the homestead farm with 263 acres valued at £393 with a total value of the estate of £862. Widow's thirds were set off to Mary Wright and the remaining two-thirds of the real estate was divided among the children. After paying the claims against the personal estate, there were £64.5.5 left to be distributed to the heirs. The final distribution of the personal estate included a payment of £21.8.5 to Mary Wright, £8.11.4 to eldest son Erastus Wright and payments of £4.5.8 to the other children named in this order: Mary Gale oldest daughter, Azubah Wright, Susannah Wright, Eunice Wright, Olive Wright, Jason Wright, Clarissa Wright, and Samuel Wright.[1284]

Samuel Wright and Mary Coburn had nine children born at Winchester.

[1283] New Hampshire, Death and Disinterment Records, 1754-1947

[1284] *New Hampshire. Probate Court (Cheshire County)*; Probate Place: *Cheshire, New Hampshire, Estate Files, W1-W47, 1773-1786*, File 47

i MARY WRIGHT, b. 1769; d. at Westfield, NY, 1855; m. 1st, at Winchester, 15 Aug 1786, RICHARD GALE, b. 1769; Richard d. at Winchester, about 1801. Mary m. 2nd, about 1802, JOHN EVERDEN, b. 1770; John d. at Winchester, 11 Apr 1853.

ii AZUBAH WRIGHT, b. 10 Sep 1772; m. at Winchester, 26 Feb 1789, SAMUEL GLEASON, b. at East Sudbury, MA, 29 Jan 1766 son of Jason and Abigail (Bent) Gleason; Samuel d. at Norwich, 27 Dec 1827.

iii SUSANNAH WRIGHT, b. 27 Feb 1774; d. at Chelsea, VT, 11 May 1818; m. at Winchester, 30 Jan 1792, ROBERT PRENTISS, b. at Winchester 13 Aug 1770;[1285] Robert d. after 1830. After Susannah's death, Robert married Mary Anne Brigham 18 Nov 1818.

iv EUNICE WRIGHT, b. 1775; d. at Winchester, 27 Jun 1826; m. 1st, 26 Feb 1795, DANIEL TWITCHELL, b. about 1769; Daniel d. at Winchester, 22 Dec 1811. Eunice m. 2nd, 22 Dec 1812, JONAS HOLDEN.

v OLIVE WRIGHT, b. 1777; d. at Chelsea, VT, 21 Dec 1862; m. at Chelsea, 7 Sep 1800, DAVID HATCH, b. at Spencer, MA, 14 May 1775 son of Michael and Martha (Rice) Hatch; David d. at Chelsea, 12 May 1851.

vi ERASTUS WRIGHT, b. 27 Jan 1779; d. at Winchester, 26 Oct 1865; m. at Winchester, Apr 1805, SUSANNAH PRATT, b. at Wrentham, MA, 7 Sep 1781 daughter of Noah and Hannah (Stearns) Pratt; Susannah d. at Winchester, 10 Jun 1849.

vii JASON WRIGHT, b. Apr 1781; d. at Winchester, 13 Feb 1842; m. at Vernon, VT, 28 May 1820, ANNA NORTON, b. at Northfield, MA, 6 Oct 1792 daughter of Selah and Asenath (Stratton) Norton;[1286] Anna d. at Fitchburg, MA, 29 Apr 1871.

viii CLARISSA WRIGHT, b. about 1783; d. at Fairlee, VT, 17 Sep 1835; m. at Norwich, 26 Apr 1813, HORACE HEDGES, b. at Norwich, 1781 son of Jeremiah and Dorothy (Johnson) Hedges; Horace d. at Fairlee, 27 Feb 1830.

ix SAMUEL A. WRIGHT, b. about 1785; d. at Townsend, VT, 25 Oct 1823; m. at Norwich, 27 Dec 1810, LUCINDA HEDGES, b. 13 Dec 1787 daughter of Jeremiah and Dorothy (Johnson) Hedges.

477) HANNAH WRIGHT *(Joseph Wright⁴, Sarah Chandler Wright³, Hannah Abbott Chandler², George¹)*, b. at Woodstock, CT, 11 Dec 1747 daughter of Joseph and Mary (-) Wright; d. at Winchester, NH, 31 Mar 1812; m. 5 Nov 1767, ASAHEL JEWELL, b. 2 Aug 1744 son of Archibald and Rebecca (Leonard) Jewell; Asahel d. at Winchester, 30 Apr 1790.[1287]

Asahel Jewell's will, written 10 April 1790, includes a bequest to beloved wife Hannah of the improvements of one-third of the real and personal estate, excepting the outland, as long as she is a widow. She receives improvement on the whole of the estate until their children are of age and/or married. As the children come of age, the estate is to be equally divided into parts with each son receiving one and one-half part and each daughter one part. The exception is son Leonard whom Hannah shall provide for out of the estate as she sees proper "through his learning till he is of age." The children are not named except for Leonard. Hannah is named executor. Heirs signing agreement to a 1792 division of the estate are Hannah Jewell, William Humphrey and Elizabeth Humphrey, and James Scott and Hannah Scott.[1288]

Hannah Wright and Asahel Jewell were parents of ten children all born at Winchester, New Hampshire.

i ELIZABETH JEWELL, b. 27 Aug 1768; d. at Winchester, 16 Feb 1849; m. 27 Feb 1787, WILLIAM HUMPHREY, b. in MA, 18 Oct 1762 son of William and Olive (Pratt) Humphrey; William d. 6 Sep 1821.

ii LEONARD JEWELL, b. 18 Jun 1770; d. 20 Oct 1791. Leonard died while he was a sophomore at Dartmouth College.

iii HANNAH JEWELL, b. 21 Sep 1773; d. at Winchester, 29 Aug 1851; m. 22 Sep 1790, JAMES SCOTT, b. at Winchester, 14 Nov 1762 son of James and Rhoda (Rockwood) Scott; James d. at Winchester, 26 Mar 1847.

iv ASAHEL JEWELL, b. 16 May 1776; d. at Winchester, 29 Aug 1834; m. 21 Feb 1797, HEPHZIBAH CHAMBERLAIN, b. 1777 daughter of Moses Chamberlain; Hephzibah d. at Winchester, 25 Sep 1841.

1285 Binney, *The History and Genealogy of the Prentice Family*, p 339 reports that Robert's grandson T.W. Prentiss was able to report his grandfather's date of birth but did not know the name of Robert's father or mother.

1286 The names of Anna's parents are given on her death record.

1287 New Hampshire, Death and Disinterment Records, 1754-1947

1288 *New Hampshire Wills and Probate Records 1643-1982*, Probate of Asahel Jewell, Cheshire, 1790, Case number 14.

v REBECCA JEWELL, b. 24 Apr 1778; d. at Winchester, 4 Dec 1868; m. 10 Feb 1795, HENRY PRATT, b. at Wrentham, 14 May 1771 son of Noah and Hannah (Stearns) Pratt;[1289] Henry d. at Winchester, 28 Aug 1841.

vi SARAH JEWELL, b. 17 Apr 1780; d. 23 Mar 1788.

vii RUFUS JEWELL, b. 28 Jun 1782; d. at Winchester, 19 May 1842; m. 25 Dec 1805, OLIVIA PRATT, b. at Wrentham, 17 May 1787 daughter of Noah and Hannah (Stearns) Pratt; Olivia d. at Winchester, 28 Mar 1830. Rufus m. 2nd, about 1835, BETSEY FRENCH, b. Jul 1794; Betsey d. at Winchester, 28 Jan 1873.

viii ALVAN JEWELL, b. 6 Oct 1784; d. at Winchester, 9 May 1856; m. 1st, 6 Feb 1806, KEZIA PIERCE, b. at Jaffrey, 29 Sep 1783 daughter of Jacob and Rebecca (-) Pierce; Kezia d. at Winchester, 12 Nov 1824. Alvan m. 2nd, 19 Oct 1826, Kezia's sister, DEBORAH PIERCE, b. at Jaffrey, 4 Oct 1785; Deborah d. at Winchester, 29 Nov 1838.

ix ACHSAH JEWELL, b. 3 Feb 1787; d. at Richland, NY, 1870; m. 18 Sep 1806, JOHN ERSKINE, b. at Winchester, 22 Nov 1785 son of John and Phebe (Robinson) Erskine; John d. at Richland, 25 Mar 1872.

x EZBON JEWELL, b. 23 Nov 1789; d. at Stanstead, Canada, 3 Jul 1823;[1290] m. 20 Jul 1812, TEMPERANCE FREEMAN, b. at Norwich, VT, about 1783 daughter of Lester and Lucy (-) Freeman; Temperance d. at Bradford, VT, 1 Aug 1858.

478) BENJAMIN WRIGHT *(Joseph Wright⁴, Sarah Chandler Wright³, Hannah Abbott Chandler², George¹)*, b. at Woodstock, 25 Feb 1753 son of Joseph and Mary (-) Wright; d. at St. Johnsbury, VT, Jan 1839; m. 24 Jul 1776, SYBIL BRETT, b. at Bridgewater, MA, 16 May 1756 daughter of Seth and Patience (Curtis) Brett.

Benjamin Wright and Sybil Brett were parents of twelve children, the first four children born at Winchester, New Hampshire and the remainder at St. Johnsbury, Vermont.

i ABIGAIL WRIGHT, b. 23 Apr 1777

ii SYLVIA WRIGHT, b. 4 Nov 1778; d. at Ayer's Cliff, Memphrémagog, Quebec, Canada, 18 Mar 1860; m. at St. Johnsbury, 23 Oct 1796, THOMAS AYER, b. at Weare, NH, 7 Apr 1776 son of Samuel and Mary (Carleton) Ayer; Thomas d. at Ayer's Cliff, 8 May 1842.

iii WALTER WRIGHT, b. 23 Aug 1781; d. at St. Johnsbury, after 1870; m. about 1805, REBECCA BROCKWAY, b. at Washington, NH, about 1785 *possibly* the daughter of Jonathan and Phebe (Smith) Brockway; Rebecca d. at St. Johnsbury, 10 Oct 1840.

iv BENJAMIN WRIGHT, b. 22 Sep 1782; d. at St, Johnsbury, 14 Dec 1871; m. about 1810, RHODA CHICKERING, b. at Guilford, VT, 16 Jun 1785 daughter of Timothy and Rhoda (Wheelock) Chickering; Rhoda d. at St. Johnsbury, 8 Oct 1877.

v JOSIAH WRIGHT, b. 15 Jul 1784; d. at Newport, VT, 31 Aug 1867; m. at Lyndon, VT, 10 Oct 1807, ANN COLE, b. in RI, about 1784; Ann d. at Barton, VT, 30 Dec 1875.

vi SAMUEL WRIGHT, b. 6 Feb 1789

vii LEMUEL WRIGHT, b. 30 Sep 1791

viii EMERSON WRIGHT, b. 11 Aug 1792; d. at Lyndon, VT, after 1860; m. at St. Johnsbury, 4 Feb 1822, FANNY WARE, b. about 1805; Fanny d. at St. Johnsbury, 31 Jul 1845.

ix SALLY WRIGHT, b. 30 Sep 1794

x SYBEL WRIGHT, b. 9 Mar 1797; d. at Greenbush, WI, after 1870. Sybel did not marry.

xi CYNTHIA WRIGHT, b. 16 Aug 1799; d. at St. Johnsbury, 2 Jul 1832; m. at St. Johnsbury, 16 Mar 1818, ISAAC HARRINGTON, b. at Walpole, NH, about 1790 son of Antipas and Lavina (Brigham) Harrington; Isaac d. at St. Johnsbury, 19 Nov 1862.

xii HANNAH WRIGHT, b. 1 May 1803; d. at Greenbush, WI, 20 Oct 1878; m. at St. Johnsbury, 20 Mar 1821, THOMAS MANSFIELD, b. in CT, 13 Feb 1800; Thomas d. at Greenbush, 22 May 1859.

479) LEMUEL WRIGHT *(Joseph Wright⁴, Sarah Chandler Wright³, Hannah Abbott Chandler², George¹)*, b. at Woodstock, 15 May 1757 son of Joseph and Mary (-) Wright; d. at Quebec, Canada, 13 Feb 1846; m. 21 Dec 1779, DEBORAH ERSKINE, b. about 1755 daughter of John and Deborah (Studley) Erskine; Deborah buried at Shefford, Québec in 1843.[1291]

[1289] Van Wagenen, *Stearns Genealogy and Memoirs*, volume 1, p 89

[1290] Jewell and Jewell, *The Jewell Register*, p 39

[1291] Ancestry.com, database, The New England Historical & Genealogical Register, 1847-2011

Lemuel and Deborah Abbott were in Jericho, Vermont but relocated to Griffin Corner in Stanstead, Québec about 1800. They were parents of ten children likely all born in Vermont.[1292]

i MALINDA WRIGHT, b. about 1780; m. 1st, about 1804, WILLIAM LAMPHIRE, b. 15 Dec 1781; d. at Stanstead, 3 Jul 1813. Malinda m. 2nd, about 1815, WILLIAM BURR, b. 1789; William d. at Stanstead, after 1861.

ii GRETA WRIGHT

iii LEMUEL WRIGHT

iv BETSEY WRIGHT

v SERAPH WRIGHT, b. about 1794; d. at South Roxton, Québec, 1 Mar 1860; m. about 1814, ALANSON BALL, b. at Norwich, VT, 19 Apr 1793 son of Joseph and Olive (Phelps) Ball;[1293] Alanson d. at South Roxton, 11 May 1853.

vi IRA WRIGHT, m. at Hatley, 24 Oct 1833, his first cousin once removed, LOUISA AYER *(Sylvia Wright Ayer⁶, Benjamin Wright⁵, Joseph Wright⁴, Sarah Chandler Wright³, Hannah Abbott Chandler², George¹)*, b. about 1814 daughter of Thomas and Sylvia (Wright) Ayer; Louisa d. at Stanstead, 19 Jul 1840.

vii PHILENA WRIGHT, b. about 1797; d. at Stanstead, about 1825; m. about 1820, BARACH BURPEE, b. at Sterling, MA, 4 Jul 1797 son of Nathan and Abigail (Underwood) Burpee; Barach d. at Marlington, Québec, 2 Feb 1874. Barach married second Lucinda Royce.

viii NANCY WRIGHT, b. 1798; d. at Malahide, Ontario, 28 Oct 1880; m. at Hatley, 1822, SEBRE MACK, b. at Marlow, NH, 13 Nov 1792 son of Abijah and Lurany (Gustin) Mack; Sebre d. at Bonus. IL, before 1860. Nancy and Sebre settled in Illinois, but Nancy returned to Canada after her husband's death.

ix THEDA WRIGHT, b. about 1800; d. at Watertown, NY, 1835; m. at Derby, VT, 1820, ZADOK STEELE, b. at Randolph, VT, 11 Jan 1793 son of Zadok and Hannah (Shurtliff) Steele; Zadok d. at Watertown, Mar 1880.

x SARAH "SALLY" WRIGHT, b. 3 Jun 1800; d. after 1850; m. at Hatley, 22 Mar 1821, NATHANIEL TOWNSEND STILES, b. at Danville, VT, 5 Aug 1798 son of George and Mary (Pierce) Stiles;[1294] Nathaniel d. at Greenbush, MI, 14 Feb 1871.

480) ABIEL CHAMBERLAIN *(Sarah Wright Chamberlain⁴, Sarah Chandler Wright³, Hannah Abbott Chandler², George¹)*, b. at Woodstock, 20 Dec 1737 son of Edmund and Sarah (Wright) Chamberlain; d. at Woodstock, 12 Jan 1818; m. 1760, GRACE AINSWORTH, b. at Woodstock, 1 Jun 1743 daughter of Nathan and Huldah (Peake) Ainsworth; Grace d. at Woodstock, 10 Jan 1788.

Abiel Chamberlain and Grace Ainsworth had thirteen children all born at Woodstock.

i SARAH CHAMBERLAIN, b. 20 Sep 1762; d. at Bath, NH, 30 Apr 1827; m. about 1784, TIMOTHY HIBBARD, b. at Woodstock, 20 Feb 1757 son of Seth and Eunice (Child) Hibbard; Timothy d. at Bath, 4 Jan 1829.

ii MARSILVA CHAMBERLAIN, b. 9 Jun 1764; d. at Woodstock, 16 Mar 1822. Marsilva did not marry.

iii MARY "POLLY" CHAMBERLAIN, b. 11 Jun 1766; m. at Wilbraham, MA, 15 Nov 1787, JESSE WARNER, b. at Wilbraham, 13 Sep 1765 son of Jesse and Hannah (Colton) Warner.

iv ZERVIAH CHAMBERLAIN, b. 7 Mar 1768; d. at Greenfield, NY, 28 Apr 1843; m. at Woodstock, 11 Feb 1793, WINSLOW ALLARD, b. at Woodstock, 4 Jul 1770 son of Peter and Patience (-) Allard; Winslow d. at Greenfield, 23 Aug 1858.

v WILLOBA CHAMBERLAIN, b. 29 Aug 1772; d. at Reading, VT, 21 Jul 1852; m. at Woodstock, 3 Apr 1796, GEORGE FOSTER, b. at Dudley, MA, 7 Nov 1771 son of Timothy and Rachel (Robinson) Foster; George d. at Reading, 31 Dec 1838.

vi JOANNA CHAMBERLAIN, b. 19 Feb 1770; d. at Woodstock, 30 May 1846; m. 28 Mar 1793, ITHAMAR COOMBS, b. at Douglas, MA, 28 Oct 1769 son of Reuben and Thankful (Borden) Coombs; Ithamar d. at Woodstock, 6 Oct 1848.

[1292] Hubbard, *Forests and Clearings*, p 228

[1293] New England Ball Project

[1294] Guild, *The Stiles Family in America: Genealogies*, p 147

vii ABIEL CHAMBERLAIN, b. 19 Nov 1774; d. at Woodstock, 23 Sep 1846; m. at Woodstock, 30 Sep 1802, SALOME CHILD, b. at Woodstock, 8 Jul 1781 daughter of Abel and Rebecca (Allard) Child;[1295] Salome d. at Woodstock, 29 Jan 1850.

viii EUNICE CHAMBERLAIN, b. 2 Nov 1775; d. at Woodstock, 29 Oct 1849; m. at Woodstock, 2 Aug 1795, URIAH WALKER, b. 1767; Uriah d. at Woodstock, 18 Oct 1845.

ix OLIVE CHAMBERLAIN, b. Mar 1777; d. at East Woodstock, 6 Mar 1868. Olive did not marry.

x HULDAH PEAKE CHAMBERLAIN, b. 22 Jan 1779; d. at Holden, MA, 20 Sep 1840; m. at Thompson, CT, 30 Apr 1807, WILLARD WATERS, b. *possibly* at Pomfret, 19 Sep 1783 son of Jonathan and Mary (Parkhurst) Waters; Willard d. at Thompson, about 1818.[1296] Willard was first married to Zilpha Knapp who died in 1806.

xi WILLIAM CHAMBERLAIN, b. 8 Jul 1782; d. at Woodstock, 5 Mar 1853; m. 9 Sep 1817, BETSY TUCKER, b. at Woodstock, 7 May 1788 daughter of Zephaniah and Huldah (Holmes) Tucker; Betsy d. at East Woodstock, 22 May 1858.

xii NATHAN AINSWORTH CHAMBERLAIN, b. 21 Jul 1784; d. about 1840; m. at Thompson, 9 May 1810, POLLY GOODELL, b. at Thompson, 26 Apr 1790 daughter of Amos and Susanna (Holbrook) Goodell; Polly d. at Webster, MA, 18 Mar 1866.

xiii RENSSELAER CHAMBERLAIN, b. about 1788; nothing further known.

481) EDMUND CHAMBERLAIN *(Sarah Wright Chamberlain⁴, Sarah Chandler Wright³, Hannah Abbott Chandler², George¹)*, b. at Woodstock, 7 Mar 1742/3 son of Edmund and Sarah (Wright) Chamberlain; d. at Woodstock, 24 Oct 1824; m. 20 Nov 1766, ELIZABETH KINGSLEY possibly the daughter of Jonathan and Experience (Sabin) Kingsley b. at Pomfret 23 Jun 1747. Elizabeth d. perhaps at Sturbridge, MA, 12 Jul 1835.

Edmund Chamberlain and Elizabeth Kingsley were parents of thirteen children all born at Woodstock.

i RUFUS CHAMBERLAIN, b. 9 Sep 1767; d. 26 Sep 1790.

ii LUCINDA CHAMBERLAIN, b. 20 Jan 1769; d. 28 Sep 1790.

iii RALPH CHAMBERLAIN, b. 19 Nov 1770; d. at Plainfield, VT, 20 Jun 1826; m. about 1800, DEBORAH GOODWIN, b. at Dunbarton, NH, 12 Sep 1776 daughter of Theophilus and Abigail (-) Goodwin; Deborah d. at Plainfield, 8 Sep 1826.

iv ELIZABETH CHAMBERLAIN, b. 22 Feb 1772

v EDMUND CHAMBERLAIN, b. 6 Dec 1774; d. 27 Mar 1800.

vi JONATHAN CHAMBERLAIN, b. 13 Jan 1777; d. 1 Apr 1826; m. at Eastford, CT, 14 Oct 1802, POLLY GOULD.

vii NANCY CHAMBERLAIN, b. 2 Feb 1779; d. 25 Jan 1788.

viii SUSANNAH CHAMBERLAIN, b. 2 Feb 1781; d. at Thompson, 7 Jan 1851; m. 11 Jun 1821, TIMOTHY SHEFFIELD, b. at Thompson, 1772 son of Nathaniel and Lydia (Gibbs) Sheffield; Timothy d. at Thompson, 1 Aug 1854.

ix ADONOUGH CHAMBERLAIN, b. 16 Apr 1783; d. 24 Jun 1783.

x WYLLIS CHAMBERLAIN, b. 3 Sep 1784; d. 10 Jan 1807.

xi MYRA CHAMBERLAIN, b. 20 Jan 1786; d. at Woodstock, 5 Sep 1835; m. at Sturbridge, MA, 16 Jan 1813, COMFORT FREEMAN, b. at Sturbridge, 20 Mar 1787 son of Comfort and Lucy (Walker) Freeman; Comfort d. at Woodstock, 17 Apr 1825.

xii EXPERIENCE CHAMBERLAIN, b. 18 Jun 1789; d. at Hartford, CT, 31 Jul 1861; m. at Sturbridge, MA, 29 Nov 1807, JONATHAN TIFFANY, b. 20 Jun 1782 son of Daniel and Mary (Woodcock) Tiffany; Jonathan d. at Hartford, 12 Dec 1865.

xiii PALMER CHAMBERLAIN, b. 20 Aug 1791; d. at Woodstock, 2 Nov 1876; m. 1st, at Woodstock, 9 Mar 1820, ANN TUCKER, b. about 1793 daughter of Stephen and Ann (Cummings) Tucker; Ann d. at Woodstock, 22 Jun 1839. Palmer m. 2nd, 8 Dec 1839, his first cousin once removed, SYLVIA WALKER *(Eunice Chamberlain Walker⁶, Abiel*

[1295] Child, *Genealogy of the Child Family*, p 163

[1296] Huldah Waters was listed as the head of household in Thompson in the 1820 census. Huldah Waters presented all her children (plus Willard's child with his first wife) for membership in the church.

Chamberlain[5], Sarah Wright Chamberlain[4], Sarah Chandler Wright[3], Hannah Abbott Chandler[2], George[1]), b. about 1798 daughter of Uriah and Eunice (Chamberlain) Walker; Sylvia d. at Woodstock, 14 Mar 1885.

482) JOHN CARPENTER *(Elizabeth Wright Carpenter[4], Sarah Chandler Wright[3], Hannah Abbott Chandler[2], George[1])*, b. at Woodstock, 22 Feb 1739/40 son of John and Elizabeth (Wright) Carpenter; d. at Whitestown, NY, 12 Jan 1809; m. at Woodstock, 9 Feb 1757, MERCY MORGAN.

Captain John Carpenter served in the Revolutionary War along with his sons William and Abiel.

Just two children have been identified for John Carpenter and Mercy Morgan.

i WILLIAM CARPENTER, b. at Woodstock, 25 Jul 1757; d. at Kirkland, 5 Apr 1816; m. at Brimfield, 23 Jan 1783, SARAH SHERMAN, b. at Brimfield, 28 Mar 1765 daughter of Thomas and Anna (Blodgett) Sherman;[1297] Sarah d. at Kirkland, 5 Oct 1835.

ii ABIEL CARPENTER, b. at Brimfield, 1759; d. at Adams, NY, 1840; m. at Brimfield, 17 Apr 1788, MARY SHERMAN, b. 1764 *perhaps* the daughter of James and Mary (Stebbins) Sherman (and first cousin of Sarah Sherman who married William Carpenter); Mary d. at Adams. NY, 5 Apr 1837.

483) BEAMSLEY CARPENTER *(Elizabeth Wright Carpenter[4], Sarah Chandler Wright[3], Hannah Abbott Chandler[2], George[1])*, b. at Woodstock, 3 Jul 1743 son of John and Elizabeth (Wright) Carpenter; m. MARTHA.

There was one child found for Beamsley and Martha.

i BEAMSLEY CARPENTER, b. at Woodstock, 3 Apr 1776; d. at Madison, OH, 22 Feb 1853; m. at Lee, MA, 15 Sep 1808, OLIVE FOOTE, b. at Lee, 2 Feb 1786 daughter of Fenner and Sarah (Wilcox) Foote; Olive d. at Madison, 20 Mar 1850.[1298]

484) HANNAH BARTHOLOMEW *(Hephzibah Wright Bartholomew[4], Sarah Chandler Wright[3], Hannah Abbott Chandler[2], George[1])*, b. at Woodstock, 7 Jun 1739 daughter of Enos and Hephzibah (Wright) Bartholomew; m. 13 Jul 1758, ELKANAH STEPHENS, b. at Dighton, 18 Mar 1736 son of Nicholas and Rachel (Andrews) Stephens.

There is limited information on this family, although three children are confirmed. The family moved often. They began in Woodstock where their oldest child was born, were in Brimfield for a time where perhaps two children were born, in Amenia, New York, and finally in Alstead, New Hampshire. One child died in Amenia in 1775 (Andrew son of Elkanah and Hannah)[1299] and Elkanah signed the Association Test in Amenia in 1775.[1300] In 1790, Elkanah and his son Elkanah. Jr. were both in Alstead, New Hampshire. After 1790, just one Elkanah Stephens shows in census records, and the elder perhaps died between 1790 and 1800. Two sons, Elkanah and Henry, served in the Revolutionary War enlisting from Amenia.

i ANDREW STEPHENS, b. at Woodstock, 13 Feb 1759; d. at Amenia, NY, 19 Jul 1775.

ii ELKANAH STEPHENS, b. at Brimfield, 7 Sep 1760; d. at Chelsea, VT, after 1840 and perhaps in 1848. Elkanah does not seem to have married. His Revolutionary War application file documents the travels of the family including the time in Amenia and Alstead.[1301] Elkanah was a church deacon in Chelsea.

iii HENRY STEPHENS, b. perhaps at Brimfield, 1762; d. at Windsor, VT, 30 Jul 1848; m. by 1808, POLLY, b. in MA about 1783; Polly d. at Windsor, 6 Mar 1857. Henry and Polly had four children living at the time Henry wrote his will in 1848. Two of the children have a middle name Bartholomew adding some circumstantial support to Hannah Bartholomew as Henry's mother.

485) JOHN BARTHOLOMEW *(Hephzibah Wright Bartholomew[4], Sarah Chandler Wright[3], Hannah Abbott Chandler[2], George[1])*, b. at Woodstock, 20 Feb 1741/2; d. at Woodstock 8 Jul 1798 son of Enos and Hephzibah (Wright) Bartholomew; m. CANDACE AINSWORTH, b. at Woodstock, 31 Aug 1748 daughter of Daniel and Sarah (Bugbee) Ainsworth.

[1297] Sherman, *Sherman Genealogy*, p 27

[1298] Died/ Feb. 22, 1853/ Bemsley/ Carpenter/ Aged 77 yrs/ March 20, 1850/ Olive/ wife of B.Carpenter/ Aged 64 yrs./ Formerly from Sandisfield/ Mass./ sleep dear parents take thy rest. Findagrave: 148637737

[1299] Sharon, Connecticut and Northeast New York, Cemetery Index, 1750-1903

[1300] Hasbrouck, *History of Dutchess County, New York*, p 98

[1301] *U.S., Revolutionary War Pension and Bounty-Land Warrant Application Files, 1800-1900*

John Bartholomew was a farmer in Woodstock. He served three years from March 1777 to March 1780 in the Revolutionary War as a Sergeant in Captain William Manning's Company in the Connecticut Regiment of Foot of Colonel Charles Webb.[1302]

John Bartholomew did not leave a will and administration of the estate was assumed by Jedediah Kimball of Woodstock on 4 September 1798. Ephraim Carroll and John Bartholomew signed a one thousand-dollar surety. The estate was determined to be insolvent.[1303]

John and Candace Bartholomew had nine children born at Woodstock.[1304][1305]

i CHRISTIAN BARTHOLOMEW, b. 23 Sep 1770; d. likely at Woodstock, VT, after 1830; m. at Pomfret, VT, 17 Jun 1817, as his second wife, MARSHALL MASON, b. at Woodstock, 1765 son of Elias and Lydia (Brown) Mason; Marshall d. at Woodstock, VT, after 1830. Marshall was first married to Polly Sessions.

ii ELISHA BARTHOLOMEW, b. 17 Oct 1772; d. at Hiram, OH, 1843; m. at Woodstock, 23 Nov 1795, LOVICA HALL, described as "of Woodstock" who has not been identified. This family was in Stanstead, Québec until 1814.[1306] They were later in Irasburg, Vermont, and Elisha is reported to have died in Hiram, OH.[1307]

iii MARY "POLLY" BARTHOLOMEW, b. 1 Oct 1774; d. at Woodstock, 6 Aug 1862; m. at Woodstock, 2 Dec 1801, CYRIL CHILDS, b. at Woodstock, 15 Sep 1771 son of Nathan and Dorcas (Green) Childs; Cyril d. at Woodstock, 1842 (probate 1842).

iv JOHN BARTHOLOMEW, b. 23 Jan 1777; d. at Branford, VT, 27 Jan 1860; m. 1st, about 1801, MERCY ANGEL, b. about 1784 but not identified; Mercy d. at Greensboro, VT, Oct 1814. John m 2nd, 1816, RUTH RING.

v JOANNA BARTHOLOMEW, b. Jan 1781; m. LEVI DICKINSON.

vi SARAH BARTHOLOMEW, b. 27 Sep 1783; d. 3 Mar 1797.

vii BETSY BARTHOLOMEW, b. 25 Jun 1786; d. at Thetford, VT, 5 May 1856; m. JOHN WHEATON, *perhaps* b. at Leicester, MA, 24 Sep 1786 son of John and Phebe (Hubbard) Wheaton; John d. at West Fairlee, VT, 2 Jan 1861.

viii CLARISSA BARTHOLOMEW, b. 15 Dec 1788; m. about 1812, JOHN SIMMONS.

ix LUCY BARTHOLOMEW, b. 25 Oct 1792; d. at Peoria, IL, 5 Dec 1878; m. about 1815, JOHN JACOBS; John d. at Peoria, 10 Jul 1870.

486) MARY BARTHOLOMEW *(Hephzibah Wright Bartholomew⁴, Sarah Chandler Wright³, Hannah Abbott Chandler², George¹)*, b. at Woodstock, 28 Jun 1746 daughter of Enos and Hephzibah (Wright) Bartholomew; perhaps the widow Mary Leach who d. at Woodstock, 7 Mar 1811; likely m. 25 Jul 1765, ROBERT LEACH, *perhaps* from Bridgewater b. 4 May 1740 the son of Nehemiah and Mercy (Staples) Leach, but his parentage is unknown. Robert d. at Tolland about 1800 (probate of estate).

Robert Leach wrote his will 4 April 1800. He bequeaths to his daughter Matilda Martin the sum of two dollars. He leaves fifty pounds to his grandchildren to be equally divided among them when they reach age 21, but the grandchildren are not named. The remainder of his estate is left to beloved wife Mary who is also named executor.[1308]

There are records for three children of Robert and Mary Leach born at Woodstock. Sons Enos and Alpheus are likely twins although there are a few days difference in their birthdates in the Woodstock records.

i ALPHEUS LEACH, b. 29 Mar 1766; no further record.

ii ENOS LEACH, b. 3 Apr 1766; d. 27 May 1766.

iii MATILDA LEACH, b. about 1768; m. 14 Mar 1787, SAMUEL MARTIN, b. at Woodstock, 8 Jul 1766 son of William and Elizabeth (Crawford) Martin; Samuel's death is unknown. In 1809, Matilda had a son Hiram Howlet who seems to be an out-of-wedlock child with DIDYMUS HOWLET,[1309] b. at Woodstock, 4 Apr 1760 son of John and Rebecca (Chaffee) Howlet; Didymus d. at Hartford, 4 Dec 1836.

[1302] Compiled Service Records of Soldiers Who Served in the American Army During the Revolutionary War 1775-1785, accessed through fold3

[1303] *Connecticut State Library (Hartford, Connecticut)*; Probate Place: *Hartford, Connecticut, Probate Packets, Bacon, Joseph-Bates, M, 1752-1880*, Probate of John Bartholomew, 1798, case number 329

[1304] Bartholomew, *Record of the Bartholomew Family*, p 138

[1305] Barbour and Newton, *Vital Records of Woodstock*

[1306] Hubbard, *Forests and Clearings*, p 322

[1307] Bartholomew, *Record of the Bartholomew Family*, p 234

[1308] *Connecticut State Library (Hartford, Connecticut)*; Probate Place: *Hartford, Connecticut, Probate Packets, Kellogg, Elizabeth-Leland, 1759-1880*, Case 1335, estate of Robert Leach.

[1309] Hiram Son of Didymus Howlet by Matilda Wife of Samuel Martin born Nov. 30 1809, Woodstock Vital Records, p 241

Great-Grandchildren of George Abbott and Dorcas Graves

487) HANNAH CHICKERING *(Hannah Osgood Chickering⁴, Hannah Abbott Osgood³, George², George¹)*, b. at Andover, 13 Jul 1730 daughter of Samuel and Hannah (Osgood) Chickering; d.at Wakefield, 10 Aug 1791; m. 22 Mar 1753, BENJAMIN PETERS, b. 25 Aug 1728 son of Samuel and Mary (Robinson) Peters; Benjamin d. at Wakefield, 17 Apr 1812.

Benjamin and Hannah Peters had eight children born at Andover.

i HANNAH PETERS, b. 1753; died young

ii BENJAMIN PETERS, b. 1755; d. at Wakefield, 25 Aug 1815; m. at Wakefield, 9 Oct 1783, MARTHA BROWN, b. at Reading, 10 Dec 1763 daughter of Jeremiah and Ruth (Welman) Brown; Martha d. 5 Jun 1845.

iii MARY PETERS, b. Feb 1758; d. at Middleton, 21 Nov 1846; m. 14 Oct 1779, JONATHAN RICHARDSON, b. at Middleton, 12 Mar 1759 son of Solomon and Abigail (Buxton) Richardson; Jonathan d. at Middleton, 15 Mar 1798.

iv SAMUEL PETERS, b. May 1760; died young

v SAMUEL PETERS, b. Jun 1763; d. at Wakefield, 12 Feb 1827; m. 21 Apr 1791, ELIZABETH STEARNS, b. at New Ipswich, NH, 2 Apr 1771; d. at Wakefield, 14 Sep 1849.

vi HANNAH PETERS, b. May 1766; no further record found

vii ELIZABETH PETERS, b. Jun 1769; d. at Danvers, 20 Jun 1852; m. 29 Apr 1788, JOSIAH HUTCHINSON, b. at Reading, Feb 1764 son of Josiah and Sarah (Dean) Hutchinson; Josiah d. at Danvers, Dec 1814 (probate 3 Jan 1815).

viii NAAMAH PETERS, b. Aug 1774; no further record found

488) SAMUEL CHICKERING *(Hannah Osgood Chickering⁴, Hannah Abbott Osgood³, George², George¹)*, b. at Andover, 28 Sep 1732 son of Samuel and Hannah (Osgood) Chickering; d. 16 Mar 1814; m. 17 Apr 1755, his third cousin once removed, MARY DANE, b. 27 Sep 1733 daughter of John and Sarah (Chandler) Dane; Mary d. 24 Jun 1824.

In his will written 15 February 1808, Samuel Chickering's first request, after the payment of his just debts, is that his grave be made in such a way that his "loving wife may be laid in the same grave after death." Beloved wife Mary receives use of the southeast room on the ground floor of the house. He has a number of requests for her care and support to be provided by the executor. Daughter Molly Marston receives $50 and some household items. Daughter Hannah Chickering receives the southwest chamber for her use and a list of household items. She has privilege of use of the house as long as she remains single. Sons named are Samuel, Zachariah, Dean, Isaac, and Daniel.[1310] Daniel Chickering was named executor. The value of the real property was $7,365, the greatest value, $2,200, for the dwelling cider mill house on five acres. The personal estate was valued at $1,645. Heirs signing as agreeing to the administration of the estate are Isaac Chickering, Zachariah Chickering, Molly Marston, Dean Chickering, and Hannah Chickering.

Samuel Chickering and Mary Dane had ten children born at Andover.

i SAMUEL CHICKERING, b. 4 Feb 1756; d. at Andover, 7 Mar 1812; m. 13 Dec 1785, ESTHER KITTRIDGE, b. at Tewksbury, Aug 1762 daughter of James Kittridge.

ii MOLLY CHICKERING, b. 19 May 1758; d. at Methuen, 6 Apr 1839; m. at Methuen, 28 May 1778, PETER MARSTON, b. at Andover, 1755 son of John and Mary (Poor) Marston;[1311] Peter d. at Methuen, 13 Jun 1811.

iii DANE CHICKERING, b. 8 May 1760; d. 15 Feb 1768.

iv HANNAH CHICKERING, b. 1 Jul 1762; d. 28 Feb 1768.

v ZACHARIAH CHICKERING, b. 19 May 1764; d. at Andover, 30 Jun 1841; m. 22 Dec 1802, his second cousin once removed, MARY OSGOOD HOLT *(Rhoda Abbott Holt⁵, Ephraim⁴, Stephen³, John², George¹)*, b. at Andover, 21 Apr 1777 daughter of Jacob and Rhoda (Abbott) Holt; Mary d. at Andover, 11 Feb 1856. Mary O. Holt is a child in Family 322.

[1310] *Essex County, MA: Probate File Papers, 1638-1881.* Online database. *AmericanAncestors.org.* New England Historic Genealogical Society, 2014, case number 5300.

[1311] Marston, *The Marston Genealogy*, p 441

vi DEAN CHICKERING, b. Jun 1768; d. at North Andover, 31 Dec 1851; m. 23 Jan 1786, SARAH FARNUM, b. at Andover, 10 Nov 1767 daughter of David and Damaris (Faulkner) Farnum; Sarah d. at Andover, 10 Dec 1837.

vii ISAAC CHICKERING, b. 5 Aug 1770; d. at Amherst, NH, 13 Dec 1838; m. at Chichester, NH, 20 Feb 1799, RUTH MORRILL, b. 25 Dec 1776 daughter of Daniel and Abigail (Stevens) Morrill; Ruth d. at Amherst, 3 Sep 1834.

viii JOSEPH CHICKERING, b. 30 Aug 1772; d. at Andover, 3 Aug 1797. He was Dr. Chickering. He did not marry.

ix DANIEL CHICKERING, b. 25 Nov 1776; d. at Andover, 20 May 1834; m. 5 Sep 1797, SUSANNA STEVENS, b. at Andover, 1 Mar 1772 daughter of Daniel and Susanna (Abbott) Stevens; Susanna d. at Andover, 7 Oct 1822.

x HANNAH CHICKERING, b. 9 Jul 1779; d. at Andover, 29 Jan 1857. Hannah did not marry. In her will written 25 August 1855, Hannah Chickering, single woman of Andover, divides her estate equally between two nieces: Sarah Ellingwood wife of Ebenezer Ellingwood and Mary D. Carleton wife of James C. Carleton. James C. Carleton was named executor. Sarah Chickering Ellingwood and Mary D. Chickering Carleton were the children of Hannah's brother Daniel and his wife Susannah.[1312]

489) SARAH CHICKERING *(Hannah Osgood Chickering[4], Hannah Abbott Osgood[3], George[2], George[1])*, b. at Andover, 5 Mar 1734/5 daughter of Samuel and Hannah (Osgood) Chickering; d.?; m. 13 Dec 1753, JAMES FRYE, b. 13 Sep 1731 son of Samuel and Sarah (Osgood) Frye; James d. 17 Dec 1804. After Sarah's death, James had two additional marriages, Rachel Steel in 1787 and Eunice Carleton in 1796.

In his will date 31 August 1801, James Frye bequeaths to beloved wife Eunice all the household furniture she brought with her to the marriage. She also receives the improvement on one-third part of the real estate as long as she remains a widow. Daughter Sarah the wife of Asa Lovejoy receives two dollars as she has received her part of the estate at the time of her marriage. Daughter Betty the wife of Peter Wardwell receives ten dollars and one good cow. Son Zachariah receives twenty-five dollars and a featherbed and bedding. Sons James and Zachariah receive the wearing apparel. Rachel Foster, the daughter of his second wife who has resided with him, receives twenty dollars. Grandson James Frye Wardwell receives his firearms. The residue of the estate goes to son James who is also named executor.[1313]

James and Sarah Frye had five children born at Andover.

i SARAH FRYE, b. 19 Nov 1754; d. at Norway, ME, 1817; m. at Andover, 20 Aug 1772, ASA LOVEJOY, b. at Andover 11 Feb 1749/50 son of Joseph and Mehitable (Foster) Lovejoy; Asa d. at Norway, 2 May 1834. Asa remarried after Sarah's death.

ii JAMES FRYE, b. 20 May 1761; m. 1st, 26 Dec 1805, MARY LOVEJOY, b. at Andover, 19 Feb 1771 daughter of Joseph and Mary (Gorden) Lovejoy; Mary d. about 1807. James m. 2nd, 24 Sep 1808, DOLLY FRYE, b. at Andover, 15 Oct 1786 daughter of John and Lydia (Batchelder) Frye; Dolly d. at Andover, 19 Oct 1822. James m. 3rd, at St. Albans, ME, 30 Nov 1826, CYNTHIA CUMMINGS.

iii HANNAH FRYE, b. 22 Feb 1764; likely died young.

iv BETTY FRYE, b. 22 Oct 1768; d. at Otisfield, ME, 30 Mar 1861; m. 12 Jun 1788, PETER WARDWELL, b. at Andover, 25 Feb 1752 son of Jonathan and Rachel (Peavey) Wardwell; Peter d. at Otisfield, 9 Dec 1828.

v ZACHARIAH FRYE, b. 7 Jun 1766; d. Nov 1792; m. about 1790, ESTHER WARDWELL, b. at Andover, 25 Jun 1758 daughter of Jonathan and Rachel (Peavey) Wardwell; Esther d. at Andover, 12 Mar 1825. After Zachariah's death, Esther married Aaron Osgood.

490) ELIZABETH CHICKERING *(Hannah Osgood Chickering[4], Hannah Abbott Osgood[3], George[2], George[1])*, b. at Andover, 25 Jan 1736/7 daughter of Samuel and Hannah (Osgood) Chickering; d. at Methuen, 20 Sep 1767; m. 24 May 1757, MOSES SARGENT, b. 23 May 1738 son of Christopher and Sara (Peaslee) Sargent. Moses m. 2nd 29 Nov 1767, Esther Runnells.

Elizabeth Chickering and Moses Sargent had five children born at Methuen.

i ELIZABETH SARGENT, b. 22 May 1758; d. at Jefferson County, NY, 22 Jun 1842; m. 1st, 23 Jul 1777, PETER POOR, b. at Methuen, 20 Apr 1756 son of Peter and Sarah (Wood) Poor; Peter d. at Shelburne, NH, 2 Oct 1781. Elizabeth m. 2nd, about 1782, WILLIAM PARKINSON, b. 3 Jul 1747; William d. at Jefferson County, 20 May 1826.

ii SUSANNA SARGENT, b. 31 Jan 1761; d. at Concord, NH, 29 May 1837; m. at Methuen, 27 Aug 1777, RICHARD AYER, b. at Haverhill, 12 May 1757 son of Samuel and Ann (Hazen) Ayer; Richard d. at Concord, 17 Dec 1831.

[1312] Essex County, MA: Probate File Papers, 1638-1881.Online database. AmericanAncestors.org. New England Historic Genealogical Society, 2014. Case number: 35188

[1313] Essex County, MA: Probate File Papers, 1638-1881.Online database. AmericanAncestors.org. New England Historic Genealogical Society, 2014. Case number 10298

iii CHRISTOPHER SARGENT, b. 13 Aug 1763; d. at Danville, VT, 18 Jul 1815; m. at Plymouth, NH, 9 Jan 1789, MARY WEBSTER, b. at Plymouth, 7 Apr 1768 daughter of Stephen and Hannah (Dolbeer) Webster;[1314] Mary d. at Danville, 22 May 1853.

iv HANNAH SARGENT, b. 21 May 1765; nothing further found

v MOSES SARGENT, b. 17 Apr 1767; nothing further found

491) JOHN CHICKERING *(Hannah Osgood Chickering⁴, Hannah Abbott Osgood³, George², George¹)*, b. at Andover, 15 Aug 1744 son of Samuel and Hannah (Osgood) Chickering; d.; m. 13 Nov 1770, SARAH WEBSTER, b. 3 Oct 1748 daughter of Ebenezer and Sarah (Gage) Webster.[1315]

John Chickering did not leave a will and his estate entered probate 13 November 1807. The following heirs signed a statement requesting that widow Sarah Chickering be administrator: Ebenezer Chickering, Elizabeth Carleton, Charlotte Chickering, and Mary Chickering.[1316]

John Chickering and Sarah Webster had nine children who were born/baptized in Andover, Methuen, and Haverhill.

i SARAH CHICKERING, b. at Andover 11 Jul 1771; d. at Boston, after 1823;[1317] m. at Boston, 17 Nov 1799, ISAAC SCHOFIELD, b. in England about 1770; Isaac d. at Boston, 1849 (probate 1849).

ii ELIZABETH CHICKERING, b. at Andover, Sep 1773; d. at Charlestown, 1824 (probate 1824); m. at Haverhill, 14 Oct 1798, RICHARD CARLETON, origins not determined; Richard d. at Charlestown, 4 Nov 1803.

iii ANNA CHICKERING, b. at Methuen, 22 Jul 1776; likely died young.

iv ASA WEBSTER CHICKERING, b. at Methuen, 6 May 1778; d. at Charlestown, about 1807;[1318] m. at Newburyport, 13 Jun 1802, ANNA HART TITCOMB, b. at Newburyport, 9 Nov 1777 daughter of Michael and Lydia (Hart) Titcomb; Lydia d. at Boston, 9 May 1861.

v MARTHA CHICKERING, b. at Methuen, 8 Apr 1780; d. at Charlestown, 15 Mar 1855; m. at Charlestown, 2 May 1802, OTIS VINAL, b. at Waldoboro, ME, 21 Mar 1780 son of David and Deborah (Otis) Vinal; Otis d. at Charlestown, 6 Jan 1853.

vi CHARLOTTE CHICKERING, b. at Methuen, May 1782; d. at Charlestown, 1 Jul 1847; m. at Charlestown, 30 Apr 1809, PETER SAWYER, b. at Haverhill, 17 Nov 1780 son of William and Hannah (Snow) Sawyer; Peter d. at Haverhill, 11 Apr 1835.

vii EBENEZER CHICKERING, b. about 1785;[1319] d. at Pembroke, ME, 20 Sep 1865; m. at Dennysville, ME, 23 May 1824, ELIZABETH ALLAN, b. at Dennysville, 17 Sep 1798 daughter of Mark and Susanna (Wilder) Allan; Elizabeth d. at Pembroke, 8 Dec 1887.

viii JOHN CHICKERING, b. about 1787; likely died young

ix MARY CHICKERING, b. about 1790; d. at Charlestown, 24 Jun 1863; m. at Charlestown, 26 Dec 1810, GILBERT TUFTS, b. at Medford, 27 Apr 1778 son of Daniel and Abigail (Tufts) Tufts; Gilbert d. at Charlestown, 9 Jul 1850.

492) ZACHARIAH CHICKERING *(Hannah Osgood Chickering⁴, Hannah Abbott Osgood³, George², George¹)*, b. at Andover, 29 Mar 1747 son of Samuel and Hannah (Osgood) Chickering; d. at Hartford, ME; m. 20 Nov 1771, SARAH POOR, b. 22 May 1750 daughter of John and Rebecca (Stevens) Poor.

Zachariah and Sarah had their first eight children in Andover and then relocated to Poland, Maine about 1788 where the youngest two children were born. Later, they settled in Hartford, Maine.[1320]

1314 Stearns, *Genealogical and Family History of the State of New Hampshire*, volume 1, p 26

1315 Sarah's parentage is confirmed by the probate settlement of the estate of Ebenezer Webster which includes a disbursement to Sarah Chickering.

1316 Middlesex County, MA: Probate File Papers, 1648-1871.Online database. AmericanAncestors.org. New England Historic Genealogical Society, 2014. Case 4374

1317 Sarah was living when her sister Elizabeth wrote her will in 1823 but deceased before the probate of her husband's estate in 1849.

1318 *U.S., Newspaper Extractions from the Northeast, 1704-1930.*

1319 Ebenezer Chickering, John Chickering, and Mary Chickering were all baptized at Haverhill on 21 August 1791. Birth dates are estimates.

1320 Hayford, *History of the Hayford Family*, p 171

i HANNAH CHICKERING, b. 8 Aug 1773; d. at Hartford, ME, 17 Nov 1847; m. at Turner, ME, 26 Jan 1804, BENJAMIN ELLIS, b. at Plympton, MA, 12 Jul 1771 son of Freeman and Sarah (Bradford) Ellis; Benjamin d. at Hartford, 14 Jan 1836.

ii REBECCA CHICKERING, b. 1 Mar 1775; d. at Shirley Mills, ME, 7 Jul 1860; m. at Turner, ME, 22 Sep 1793, SIMEON DENNEN, b. at Gloucester, 1772 son of Samuel and Keziah (Bray) Dennen; Simeon d. at Shirley Mills, 28 Jan 1849.

iii FREDERICK CHICKERING, b. 20 Dec 1776; d. about 1794.

iv ZACHARIAH CHICKERING, b. 16 Aug 1778; d. at Hartford, ME, 7 Feb 1854. Zachariah did not marry.

v SARAH CHICKERING, b. 10 Aug 1780; d. at Canton, ME, 5 Oct 1845; m. 5 Apr 1799, ZERI HAYFORD, b. at Pembroke, MA, 17 Mar 1777 son of William and Elizabeth (Bonney) Hayford;[1321] Zeri d. at Canton, 14 May 1849.

vi LYDIA CHICKERING, b. 10 Aug 1780; d. at Columbia, ME, after 1850; m. at Hartford, ME, about 1804, EZEKIEL AMES whose origin is not determined; Ezekiel d. at Hartford, about 1806.

vii GEORGE OSGOOD CHICKERING, b. 18 Sep 1782; d. at Livermore, ME, 22 Sep 1877; m. Nov 1828, OLIVE H. LAZELL, b. at Pomfret, VT, 21 Sep 1796 daughter of Joshua and Susanna (-) Lazell; Olive d. at Livermore, 15 Oct 1879.

viii CLOE CHICKERING, b. 15 Oct 1785; d. at Livermore, ME, 19 Jan 1865. Cloe did not marry.

ix MARY "POLLY" CHICKERING, b. 19 Sep 1787; d. at Livermore, ME, 11 Sep 1865; m. WEBBER DORE, b. in NH about 1788 whose origins are undetermined; Webber d. at Livermore, 28 Dec 1863.

x ARTEMESIA CHICKERING, b. 6 Apr 1792; d. at Canton, ME, 10 Aug 1870; m. 17 Feb 1825, ABEL AMES, b. at Hartford, ME, 21 Apr 1796 son of Abel and Fanny (Livingston) Ames; Abel d. at Canton, after 1870.

493) MARY CHICKERING *(Hannah Osgood Chickering⁴, Hannah Abbott Osgood³, George², George¹)*, b. at Andover, 17 Jan 1749/50 daughter of Samuel and Hannah (Osgood) Chickering; d. at Danville, VT, 20 Aug 1820;[1322] m. 24 Oct 1770, JOHN SHORT, b. at Newbury, 16 Aug 1741 son of Joseph and Hannah (Prowse) Short; John d. about 1820 at Danville, VT.

John Short was the town clerk of Danville, Vermont starting in 1792, a position that he held for 26 years.[1323]

Records have been located for two children of Mary Chickering and John Short.

i JOHN SHORT, b. at Newburyport, 26 Aug 1771; m. at Danville, VT, 15 Aug 1793, ELEANOR EMERSON, b. at Chester, NH, 29 Mar 1775 daughter of Moses and Susannah (Morse) Emerson.

ii WILLIAM SHORT, b. at Newbury, 8 Oct 1780; d. At Lowell, MA, 3 Sep 1849; m. at Danville, VT, 21 Aug 1808, LYDIA EMERSON, b. at Chester, 29 Jan 1778 daughter of Moses and Susannah (Morse) Emerson; Lydia d. at Lowell, 21 Jan 1821.

494) PHEBE CHICKERING *(Hannah Osgood Chickering⁴, Hannah Abbott Osgood³, George², George¹)*, b. at Andover, 9 Nov 1751 daughter of Samuel and Hannah (Osgood) Chickering; d. likely in NH; m. 28 Jul 1778, THOMAS HUTCHINSON whose identity is uncertain, although he could be Thomas Hutchinson born in Lynn in 1750. Cutter reports he is the son of Jonathan and Elizabeth (Ganson) Hutchinson.[1324]

Thomas Hutchinson served in the Revolution in Captain David Parker's first Lexington company. He saw additional service including in the regiment of Colonel John Mansfield. Four of the children in this family (Phebe, Osgood, Charles Frye, and Nathaniel) relocated to Francestown, New Hampshire.

Phebe Chickering and Thomas Hutchinson had six children, the oldest four born at Andover and the youngest two children born at Lyndeborough, New Hampshire.

i PHEBE HUTCHINSON, b. 23 Feb 1779; d. at Francestown, NH, 18 Feb 1842. Phebe did not marry. She lived with her brother in Francestown.

1321 Hayford, *History of the Hayford Family*, pp 169-171

1322 Vermont, Vital Records, 1720-1908. Ancestry.com

1323 Deming, *Catalogue of the Principal Officers of Vermont*, p 140

1324 Cutter, *Genealogical and Personal Memoirs Relating to the Families of Boston and Eastern Massachusetts*, volume 3, p 1441

ii OSGOOD HUTCHINSON, b. 4 Jun 1780; d. at Buffalo, KS, 14 Feb 1869;[1325] m. HANNAH FULLER, b. at Lyndeborough, 21 Mar 1785 daughter of Andrew and Hannah (Smith) Fuller;[1326] Hannah d. at Jasper, NY, 5 Jan 1867.

iii EBENEZER HUTCHINSON, b. 22 Sep 1782; no further record

iv CHARLES FRYE HUTCHINSON, b. 8 Nov 1784; d. at Francestown, NH, 22 Mar 1859; m. 8 Feb 1810, BETSEY DICKERMAN, b. at Francestown, 21 Apr 1788 daughter of Samuel and Persis (Richardson) Dickerman; Betsey d. at Francestown, 29 Jun 1859.

v WARREN HUTCHINSON, b. 30 Oct 1787; no further record

vi NATHANIEL HUTCHINSON, b. 24 Jun 1790; d. at Manchester, 5 Jul 1866; m. at Francestown, 24 Jun 1814, SALLY DICKERMAN, b. at Francestown, 21 Apr 1788 daughter of Samuel and Persis (Richardson) Dickerman; Sally d. at Nashua, after 1860.

495) MARTHA OSGOOD *(John Osgood[4], Hannah Abbott Osgood[3], George[2], George[1])*, b. at Andover, 3 May 1747 daughter of John and Mary (Carleton) Osgood; d. at Exeter, NH 15 Jun 1830;[1327] m. ENOCH POOR, b. 21 Jun 1736 son of Thomas and Mary (Adams) Poor. Brigadier General Enoch Poor d. at Hackensack, NJ while serving in the military, 8 Sep 1780. The cause of death of Enoch Poor is a mystery.[1328] The National Archives have on file a letter written by George Washington to Brigadier General Enoch Poor 22 Feb 1779.[1329]

Enoch Poor served as a Brigadier General during the Revolution. He died in New Jersey during the war likely of typhoid fever, although there is legend that he died of wounds suffered during a duel.

Enoch Poor did not leave a will and his estate entered probate 31 January 1781. The estate of Enoch Poor was appraised at £196 of personal estate and about £1700 of real estate including a mansion house and acreages in excess of 100 acres in Sandwich, Effingham, Loudon, and Gilmanton. The claims against the estate totaled £600. The dower was set off to widow Martha Poor. Martha Poor was administratrix of the estate.[1330]

There are just three children known for Martha Osgood and Enoch Poor.

i MARY POOR, b. about 1769; d. at Exeter, NH, 19 Jul 1848; m. at Exeter, 13 Sep 1804, Rev. JACOB CRAM, b. at Hampton Falls, 12 Nov 1762 son of Jonathan and Mary (Cram) Cram; Jacob d. at Exeter, 1833.

ii MARTHA POOR, b. at Exeter, NH, about 1770; d. at Nottingham, NH, 20 Apr 1834; m. at Exeter, 19 Nov 1792, BRADBURY CILLEY, b. at Nottingham, 1 Feb 1760 son of Joseph and Sarah (Longfellow) Cilley; Bradbury d. at Nottingham, 17 Dec 1831.

iii HARRIET POOR, b. 31 Jan 1780; d. at Nottingham, 7 Jun 1838; m. at Nottingham, 8 Jun 1801, JACOB CILLEY, b. at Nottingham, 19 Jul 1773 son of Joseph and Sarah (Longfellow) Cilley; Jacob d. at Nottingham, 29 Jan 1831.

496) DORCAS OSGOOD *(John Osgood[4], Hannah Abbott Osgood[3], George[2], George[1])*, b. at Andover, 24 Mar 1752 daughter of John and Mary (Carleton) Osgood; d. at Roxbury 17 Oct 1810;[1331] m. 1st ISAAC MARBLE, b. 9 Jun 1740 son of Noah and Mary (Ingalls) Marble; Isaac d. by 1780. Dorcas m. 2nd as his second wife, HENRY DEARBORN, b. at Hampton, 23 Feb 1751 son of Simon and Sarah (Marston) Dearborn; Henry d. at Roxbury, 6 Jun 1829. Henry was first married to Sarah Bartlett. After Dorcas's death, Henry Dearborn married for the third time to Sarah Bowdoin.

Dorcas Osgood and Isaac Marble had three children born at Newburyport.

i MARY MARBLE, b. 26 Feb 1771; d. at Gardiner, ME, 30 Sep 1839; m. RUFUS GAY, b. at Dedham, MA, 19 Jan 1770 son of William and Margaret (Lewis) Gay; Rufus d. at Gardiner, 5 Nov 1852.

ii ISAAC MARBLE, b. Dec 1772; d. 19 Aug 1773.

[1325] Cutter, *Genealogical and Personal Memoirs Relating to the Families of Boston and Eastern Massachusetts*, volume 3, p 1441

[1326] Fuller, *Genealogy of Some Descendants of Thomas Fuller*, b. 162.

[1327] Ancestry.com. *New Hampshire, Death and Burial Records Index, 1654-1949* [database on-line]. Provo, UT, USA: Ancestry.com Operations, Inc., 2011.

[1328] A biography of Enoch Poor can be found at the site of the New Hampshire Division of Historical Resources at this link: http://rkc.org/poor/poorofnh.html

[1329] National Archives, letter from George Washington to Brigadier General Enoch Poor, retrieved from https://founders.archives.gov/documents/Washington/03-19-02-0260

[1330] *New Hampshire. Probate Court (Rockingham County);* Probate Place: *Rockingham, New Hampshire, Estate Papers, No 4566-4701, 1779-1781*, case number 4684

[1331] Ancestry.com, *U.S., Newspaper Extractions from the Northeast, 1704-1930* (Provo, UT, USA: Ancestry.com Operations, Inc., 2014).

iii DORCAS OSGOOD MARBLE, b. 1 Jun 1774; d. at Gardiner, ME, 26 Feb 1863; m. 1798, JAMES PARKER, b. at Boston, 1768 son of Cardee and Mary (Weld) Parker; James d. at Gardiner, 9 Nov 1837.

General Henry Dearborn was the Secretary of War under President Jefferson. But he began his adult life studying medicine and practiced for a time in Nottingham. At the outbreak of the Revolution, he pursued the military for the remainder of his adult life. He had numerous accomplishments including serving on George Washington's staff in Virginia during the war. He had the rank of Lieutenant Colonel during the war and achieved the rank of Brigadier General of the Massachusetts Militia in 1787. He served as a representative to the United States Congress from 1793-1797.[1332]

In his will written 30 November 1827 and proved August 1829, Henry Dearborn bequeathed to beloved son Henry Alexander Scammell Dearborn the house and land in Roxbury where he now lives and the farm in Pittstown Maine where Rufus Gay lives. Beloved daughter Julia Octavia C. Wingate received two thousand dollars. Grandson Henry G. R. Dearborn receives the farm in Monmouth, Maine. Grandson William R. Lee Dearborn also receives a farm in Monmouth. Granddaughter Pamela Augusta Sophia Dearborn receives one thousand dollars. Granddaughter Mary Ann A. S. Melwell and Sophia Blake each receive three hundred dollars. Beloved stepdaughter Mary Gay receives four hundred dollars and Dorcas Parker receives two hundred dollars. There are also bequests of two hundred and fifty dollars to each of his step-grandchildren. The remainder of the estate is divided equally between his children Julia and Henry. Son Henry Alexander Scammell Dearborn, son Joshua Wingate, Jr., and John B. Davis, Esq. are named executors.[1333]

Dorcas Osgood had three children with Henry Dearborn.

i JULIA OCTAVIA CASCALINE DEARBORN, b. 1782; d. at Portland, 11 Feb 1867; m. at Pittston, ME, 19 Nov 1799, JOSHUA WINGATE, b. at Amesbury, 28 Jun 1773 son of Joshua and Hannah (Carr) Wingate; Joshua d. at Portland, Nov 1843.

ii HENRY ALEXANDER SCAMMELL DEARBORN, b. at Exeter, NH, 3 Mar 1783; d. at Portland, ME, 29 Jul 1851; m. at Marblehead, MA, 3 May 1807, HANNAH SWETT LEE, b. at Marblehead, 1783 daughter of William R. and Mary (Lemmon) Lee; Hannah d. at Boston, 10 Oct 1868.

iii GEORGE RALEIGH DEARBORN, b. 22 Oct 1784; d. at sea, 3 Dec 1806.

497) MARY OSGOOD *(John Osgood⁴, Hannah Abbott Osgood³, George², George¹)*, b. at Andover, 30 Jun 1753 daughter of John and Mary (Carleton) Osgood; d. 22 May 1820;[1334] m. by 1771, ISAAC FARNUM, b. 19 Dec 1742 son of John and Sarah (Frye) Farnum; Isaac d. 8 Sep 1823.[1335]

In his will written 5 September 1823, Isaac Farnum has token bequests of one dollar each to his daughters that complete their portions: daughter Sally the wife of Timothy Osgood; daughter Susannah wife of Dr. Daniel Berry; and Charlotte wife of Henry P. Oxnard. Daughters Mary and Martha (who are unmarried) receive real estate, the west end of the house, use of garden, barn, and pasture, and a third of the pew in the meeting house. Son Isaac receives the remainder of the estate and is named executor.[1336]

Isaac Farnum and Mary Osgood had eight children born at Andover.

i SARAH "SALLY" FARNUM, b. 10 Mar 1771; m. 13 Nov 1788, TIMOTHY OSGOOD, b. at Andover, 17 Mar 1763 son of Peter and Sarah (Johnson) Osgood; Timothy d. at Andover, 16 Dec 1849.

ii ISAAC FARNUM, b. 3 Mar 1773; d. at Andover, 16 Apr 1839; m. 11 Jan 1798, PERSIS STEVENS, b. at Andover, 1 Dec 1773 daughter of Daniel and Susanna (Abbott) Stevens; Persis d. at Andover, 20 Jul 1853.

iii MARY FARNUM, b. 24 Feb 1775; d. at Andover, 25 Jun 1836.

iv MARTHA FARNUM, b. 12 Mar 1779; d. at North Andover, 11 Apr 1869. Martha did not marry.

v JOHN OSGOOD FARNUM, b. 24 Mar 1781; no further record. He was not living at the time of his father's will.

vi SUSANNA FARNUM, b. 2 Jan 1784; d. at St. Louis, MO, 3 Jul 1851; m. 8 Aug 1809, DANIEL BERRY, b. Feb 1777 son of Benjamin and Ruth (-) Berry (mother was the widow Ruth Estis); Daniel d. at St. Louis, 2 Sep 1851.

vii CHARLES FARNUM, b. 21 Sep 1787; d. at Andover, 7 Sep 1822.

[1332] Appletons' Cyclopedia of American Biography; Volume: Vol. II, p 117

[1333] Probate Docket Books, and Record Books (1793-1916) (Norfolk County, Massachusetts); Author: Massachusetts. Probate Court (Norfolk County); Probate Place: Norfolk, Massachusetts, volume 53, pp 252-253

[1334] Massachusetts Vital Records Project: Mary, w. Isaac, May 22, 1820, a. 66 y.

[1335] Massachusetts Vital Records Project: Isaac [h. Mary (Osgood). PR61], Sept. 8, 1823, a. 80 y. 8 m.

[1336] Essex County, MA: Probate File Papers, 1638-1881.Online database. AmericanAncestors.org. New England Historic Genealogical Society, 2014. Case Number 9236

viii CHARLOTTE FARNUM, b. 22 Feb 1793; d. at Boston, 10 Aug 1873; m. at Roxbury, 5 May 1819, HENRY OXNARD, b. at Portland, ME, 6 Jan 1789 son of Thomas and Martha (Preble) Oxnard; Henry d. at Boston, 15 Dec 1843.

498) JOHN OSGOOD *(John Osgood⁴, Hannah Abbott Osgood³, George², George¹)*, b. at Andover, 2 Jun 1770 son of John and Huldah (Frye) Osgood; d. at Haverhill, NH, 29 Jul 1840; m. SARAH PORTER, b. at Boxford, 22 Apr 1777 daughter of William and Mary (Adams) Porter; Sarah d. at Haverhill, NH 5 Feb 1858.[1337]

John Osgood was a clockmaker and silversmith particularly noted for his tall clocks which are still highly prized. He had his shop on Main Street in Haverhill, New Hampshire. He often bartered goods such as wheat and corn for his clocks. He is reported to have died of consumption.[1338]

In the will of John Osgood dated 25 June 1840, dear wife Sarah receives all the household goods, chaise and harness, and all the provisions needed for her continued support. She also receives the use of pew numbered thirteen in the brick meeting house. Son John Osgood receives $100. He directs that his farm in Haverhill and partly in Piermont plus all the stock and equipment be sold and 50% of the proceeds be put at interest for the support of Sarah as long as she remains a widow. All the rest is to be divided equally among his five children: John Osgood, Alfred Osgood, Pamela Heiler wife of Thomas G. Heiler, Charlotte Blaisdell wife of Daniel Blaisdell, and George Osgood. After the death or remarriage of Sarah, all the property that is of her use is to be divided among the children. Daniel Blaisdell of Hanover is named executor.[1339]

John Osgood and Sarah Porter had seven children born at Haverhill, New Hampshire.

i JOHN OSGOOD, b. 29 May 1798; d. at Boston, 25 Dec 1860; m. 18 Nov 1830, DELIA W. MOORE, b. at Malden, 4 Nov 1806 daughter of Joseph and Betsey (Collins) Moore; Delia d. at Danbury, CT, 27 May 1893.

ii PAMELIA OSGOOD, b. 29 Jul 1800; d. 19 Apr 1804.

iii ALFRED OSGOOD, b. 22 Jul 1802; d. at St. Louis, MO, 9 Jan 1852. Alfred does not seem to have married. He was a merchant and one of the directors of the Mercantile Library at St. Louis.

iv PAMELIA OSGOOD, b. 25 Aug 1804; d. at Boston, 16 Aug 1858; m. 17 Jan 1826, THOMAS GREENLEAF HILER, b. at Boston, 1796 son of Jacob and Grace (Greenleaf) Hiler; Thomas d. at sea, 1862.

v MARTHA OSGOOD, b. 27 Jul 1806; d. 21 Mar 1816.

vi CHARLOTTE OSGOOD, b. 25 Aug 1810; d. at Hanover, NH, 27 Nov 1898; m. 29 May 1832, DANIEL BLAISDELL, b. at Pittsfield, NH, 26 Aug 1806 son of Elijah and Mary (Fogg) Blaisdell; Daniel d. at Hanover, 24 Aug 1875.

vii GEORGE OSGOOD, b. 22 Nov 1814; d. at Conway County, AR, 4 Dec 1840.[1340]

499) ALFRED OSGOOD *(John Osgood⁴, Hannah Abbott Osgood³, George², George¹)*, b. at Andover, 7 Mar 1773 son of John and Huldah (Frye) Osgood; d. at Newburyport 25 May 1847; m. 18 Jun 1800, MARY SMITH, b. 4 Apr 1778 daughter of John and Mary (-) Smith; Mary d. at Newburyport 23 Sep 1855 at age 77. Mary's parents' names are given as John and Mary Smith on her death record.

Alfred Osgood was a shoe dealer and manufacturer in Newburyport.[1341] Alfred Osgood and Mary Smith were parents to six children all born at Newburyport.

i NATHANIEL SMITH OSGOOD, b. 23 Apr 1801; d. at Newburyport, 2 May 1881; m. at Newbury, 3 mar 1828, ELIZABETH SUTHERLAND NEWMAN, b. at Portland, ME, Jan 1801 daughter of Cornelius and Catherine (Sawyer) Newman;[1342] Elizabeth d. at Newburyport, 16 Dec 1886.

ii JOHN OSGOOD, b. 1 Sep 1803; d. at Newburyport, 28 Jun 1880; m. 23 Jan 1843, MARY DAVENPORT, b. at Newburyport, 31 Jul 1814 daughter of John and Tabitha (Russell) Davenport; Mary d. at Newburyport, 26 Dec 1868.

1337 Ancestry.com. New Hampshire, Death and Burial Records Index, 1654-1949

1338 Delaney Antique Clocks, Library of Clockmakers, John Osgood of Andover, MA and Haverhill, NH, http://delaneyantiqueclocks.com/products/maker/105/

1339 New Hampshire, Wills and Probate Records, 1643-1982, *New Hampshire. Probate Court (Grafton County)*; Probate Place: *Grafton, New Hampshire, Probate Records, Vol 17-18, 1835-1840*

1340 George's gravestone includes this inscription: of Haverhill, N.H.; aged 26 yrs; findagrave ID: 35125193

1341 Osgood, *Genealogy of the Descendants of John, Christopher, and William Osgood*, p 69

1342 Elizabeth's death record gives the names of her parents as John and Catherine, but that seems to be an error as it was Cornelius Newman that married Catherine.

iii CHARLOTTE OSGOOD, b. 30 Jan 1806; d. at Newburyport, 15 Nov 1842; m. 15 May 1837, HENRY TILDEN, b. at Boston, 14 May 1808 son of Benjamin and Mary (Wentworth) Tilden; Henry d. at Providence, RI, 31 Dec 1883. After Charlotte's death, Henry married Catherine A. Carpenter of Providence.

iv ALFRED OSGOOD, b. 1 Jun 1809; d. at Newburyport, 31 Mar 1899; m. 1st, 5 Nov 1833, LYDIA PARKER OAKES, b. at Malden, 10 Sep 1810 daughter of Jonathan and Sally (Parker) Oakes; Lydia d. at Malden, 10 Dec 1842. Alfred m. 2nd, 20 Sep 1847, SARAH ELIZABETH CALDWELL, b. at Newburyport, 3 Aug 1819 daughter of Abner and Lydia (Story) Caldwell; Sarah d. at Newburyport, 8 May 1894.

v WILLIAM H. OSGOOD, b. 5 Sep 1811; d. at Boston, 24 Oct 1862. William did not marry.

vi MARY ANN OSGOOD, b. 14 Dec 1816; d. at Newburyport, 5 Aug 1900. Mary Ann did not marry.

500) ENOCH OSGOOD *(John Osgood⁴, Hannah Abbott Osgood³, George², George¹)*, b. at Andover, 7 Nov 1775 son of John and Huldah (Frye) Osgood; d. at Newburyport 20 May 1848; m. 15 Feb 1807 MARY BROWN of not yet known origins; Mary d. Dec 1863.[1343] She was known to be living in 1859 when her daughter's estate was probated.

Enoch Osgood was involved in the start-up of The Newburyport Mutual Fire Insurance Company which was incorporated in 1829.[1344] Enoch Osgood did not leave a will. The only available documents deal with the administration of the estate which is assumed by Enoch Osgood and agreed to by widow Mary Osgood and Mary Anna Osgood. The surety for the estate was $30,000 suggesting that the value of the estate was considerable.

Enoch and Mary Osgood had four children all born at Newburyport. One child died in infancy and their son Henry died at age 21 years. Neither daughter Mary Ann nor son Enoch married, so the line of descendants ends here for this limb of the tree.

i MARY ANNA OSGOOD, b. 29 Dec 1807; d. at Somerville, 7 Jun 1858. Mary Anna did not marry.

ii ENOCH OSGOOD, b. 30 Jul 1811; d. at Chelsea, 22 Mar 1866. Enoch did not marry. In his will written 29 September 1858, Enoch left his estate to Mrs. Laura P. Holland who had cared for members of the family. The will also gives the dates of death of his siblings Henry and Mary Anna and his father Enoch. Mrs. Laura P. Holland seems to be Laura Pierce, widow of Samuel Holland daughter of Joseph (or Isaac) and Frances Pierce. She was born in 1804 and died 1892 in Chelsea.[1345]

iii JOHN FARNUM OSGOOD, b. 14 Jun 1815; d. 1 Aug 1815.

iv HENRY OSGOOD, b. 31 May 1819; d. at Newburyport, 12 May 1841.

501) ELIZABETH FRYE *(Elizabeth Osgood Frye⁴, Hannah Abbott Osgood³, George², George¹)*, b. at Andover, 7 Dec 1735 daughter of James and Elizabeth (Osgood) Frye; d. 14 May 1807; m. 24 May 1753, her second cousin once removed, SAMUEL FRYE, b. 22 Dec 1729 son of Samuel and Sarah (Osgood) Frye; Samuel d. 1819.

Samuel Frye owned saw, grist, and fulling mills in Andover. His land holdings totaled 2,000 acres and he was the second wealthiest man in town. The Frye genealogy describes his as being stern and strict in his household, but with a dignified appearance.[1346]

In his will written 3 August 1814, Samuel Frye leaves to sons Samuel Frye, Jr. and Amos Frye equal parts of a 15-acre woodland in Andover. Daughter Elizabeth the wife of John Stevens receives $100. Daughter Sarah the wife of Moses Dennis receives $100. Daughter Phebe the widow of Edward Stevens receives $200. Daughter Mary the wife of Timothy Crosby receives $200. His four daughters named also received the household items. The remainder of the estate goes to son Theophilus who is also named executor.[1347]

Samuel and Elizabeth Frye were parents to nine children born at Andover.

i THEOPHILUS FRYE, b. 12 Oct 1753; d. at Andover, 2 Apr 1830; m. 11 Apr 1776, his second cousin one removed, LUCY LOVEJOY, b. at Andover, 4 Aug 1755 daughter of Joshua and Lydea (Abbott) Lovejoy; Lucy d. at Andover, 2 Apr 1844. Theophilus and Lucy Frye are Family 544.

ii ELIZABETH FRYE, b. 2 Jun 1755; d. at Greenwich, MA, 16 Feb 1815; m. at Andover, 30 Apr 1783, JOHN STEVENS, "of Sterling," b. about 1753 (based on age at death); John d. at Greenwich, 11 Aug 1827.

[1343] Osgood, *Genealogy of Descendants. . . Osgood*, p 69
[1344] Currier, *History of Newburyport*, p 160
[1345] *Massachusetts, Wills and Probate Records, 1635-1991*, Suffolk County (Massachusetts) Probate Records, 1636-1899
[1346] Barker, *Frye Genealogy*, p 59
[1347] Essex County, MA: Probate File Papers, 1638-1881.Online database. AmericanAncestors.org. New England Historic Genealogical Society, 2014. Case number 10337

iii SARAH "SALLY" FRYE, b. 27 May 1759; d. at Hancock, NH, 12 Oct 1851; m. 11 Jun 1782, MOSES DENNIS, b. at Ipswich, 1750 son of John and Martha (Wilcomb) Dennis; Moses d. at Hancock, 18 Dec 1845.

iv PHEBE FRYE, b. 4 Apr 1762; d. after 1819 (still living at probate of father's estate); m. 23 Feb 1791, EDWARD STEVENS, b. at Andover, 30 Sep 1768 son of Thomas and Sarah (Gray) Stevens; Edward d. at Andover, of consumption, 27 Oct 1805.

v MARY FRYE, b. 5 May 1765; m. 15 Dec 1796, TIMOTHY CROSBY "of Billerica" *likely* the son of Timothy and Susanna (Sanders) Crosby; Timothy d. at Peterborough, NH, 1832 (date of probate).

vi LYDIA FRYE, b. 10 May 1767; no further record.

vii SAMUEL FRYE, b. 3 Sep 1769; d. at Andover, 16 Mar 1847; m. 21 Sep 1790, HANNAH POOR, b. at Andover, 3 Aug 1770 daughter of Jonathan and Susan (Poor) Poor; Hannah d. at Andover, 8 Aug 1847.

viii AMOS FRYE, b. Sep 1775; d. 8 Apr 1776.

ix AMOS FRYE, b. Oct 1777; d. at Andover, 28 Sep 1824; m. 30 Jun 1801, HANNAH DURANT, b. at Andover, about 1779 daughter of Amos and Sarah (Ballard) Durant; Hannah d. at Andover, 7 Sep 1865.

502) JOHANNA FRYE *(Elizabeth Osgood Frye⁴, Hannah Abbott Osgood³, George², George¹)*, b. at Andover, 19 Feb 1736/7 daughter of James and Elizabeth (Osgood) Frye; d. at Groton 24 Jun 1767; m. by 1758, THOMAS FARRINGTON, b. 8 Mar 1735/6 son of Daniel and Elizabeth (Putnam) Farrington. Thomas m. 2nd Betty Woods and he relocated to Kennebec, ME for a time. Thomas m. 3rd Jerusha Hammond. Thomas d. 9 Apr 1808 at Delhi, NY.

Thomas Farrington was a Lieutenant Colonel in the Continental army but was court-martialed for receiving counterfeit money. He was charged with receiving three hundred dollars in counterfeit money from Samuel Tarbell for which he was to pay Tarbell two hundred dollars.[1348] The following letter dated 19 May 1777 from Major General William Heath to George Washington summarizes the findings of the case: *Saturday last the General Court Martial appointed for the Tryal of Lieut. Colonel Farrington of Colo. Putnams Regiment (charged with behaving in a scandalous and infamous manner) gave in their Judgment that He was Guilty of the Charge alledged against him & have adjudged him to be discharged from the Army—Incapable to serve in the Continental Service and ordered him to be published in the News Papers. I have approved the Judgment which has this Day been put in Execution.*[1349]

Thomas Farrington and Johanna Frye were parents of five children all born at Groton, Massachusetts.

i ELIZABETH FARRINGTON, b. 2 Sep 1758. Elizabeth was living in 1776 when her grandfather James Frye wrote his will including bequests to the three children of his daughter Johanna. Nothing further found.

ii THOMAS FARRINGTON, b. 1 Oct 1760; d. at Baldwinsville, NY, 18 Feb 1815; m. at Groton, 18 Jan 1785, ELIZABETH HOLDEN, b. at Groton, 23 Sep 1763 daughter of Isaiah and Elizabeth (Shed) Holden; Elizabeth d. at Baldwinsville, 14 May 1841.

iii MARCH FARRINGTON, b. 13 Nov 1762; d. at Delhi, NY, 14 Apr 1849; m. 1788, ELIZABETH "BETSEY" COLTON, b. 17 Apr 1764;[1350] Betsey d. at Delhi, 10 Nov 1841. March was a drummer during the Revolutionary War serving in the same unit as his father.

iv FREDERICK FARRINGTON, b. 13 Nov 1764; d. Jan 1770.

v DANIEL FARRINGTON, b. Apr 1767; d. Jan 1770.

503) SARAH FRYE *(Elizabeth Osgood Frye⁴, Hannah Abbott Osgood³, George², George¹)*, b. at Andover, 8 Mar 1738/9 daughter of James and Elizabeth (Osgood) Frye; d. at Conway, MA 29 Jul 1785; m. about 1764, JOHN BOYDEN, b. at Groton, 12 Jan 1736 son of Josiah and Eunice (Parker) Boyden. John m. 2nd Esther Gilmore 16 Aug 1786; John d. at Conway, MA, 10 Oct 1819.

[1348] Continental currency was first introduced in 1775.

[1349] "To George Washington from Major General William Heath, 19 May 1777," *Founders Online,* National Archives, last modified June 13, 2018, http://founders.archives.gov/documents/Washington/03-09-02-0466. [Original source: *The Papers of George Washington*, Revolutionary War Series, vol. 9, *28 March 1777–10 June 1777*, ed. Philander D. Chase. Charlottesville: University Press of Virginia, 1999, pp. 472–475.]

[1350] Biographical Review Publishing Company, *Biographical Sketches of Delaware County*, New York, p 366

Soon after their marriage, Sarah Frye and John Boyden settled in Deerfield in an area that later became Conway. John was a farmer working land that his wife Sarah had been deeded by her father James Frye.[1351]

Sarah Frye and John Boyden were parents of nine children all born at Conway, Massachusetts.

i JOHN BOYDEN, b. 29 Jan 1764; d. at Conway, 2 Oct 1857; m. 1st, 7 Sep 1785, EUNICE HAYDEN, b. at Ashfield, May 1768 daughter of Moses and Eunice (Haroon) Hayden; Eunice d. at Conway, 29 Nov 1833. John m. 2nd, 16 May 1835, MARY "POLLY" JONES, b. at Phillipston, 29 Apr 1788 daughter of Jonathan and Lydia (Jones) Jones; Polly d. at Conway, 7 Aug 1876.

ii JAMES BOYDEN, b. 1766; d. at Conway, 4 Feb 1838; m. 1st, at Northfield, MA, 28 Feb 1789, SUSANNA NORTON, b. about 1768 and d. at Conway, about 1792. James m. 2nd, at Conway, 2 Feb 1793, LYDIA BURNHAM, b. at Montague, 9 Feb 1770 daughter of James and Dorothy (-) Burnham; Lydia d. at Conway, 11 Mar 1851.

iii FREDERICK BOYDEN, b. 1768; d. at Deerfield, MA, 12 Apr 1842; m. 1st, at Conway, 26 Aug 1793, RACHEL SPRAGUE (widow Rachel Wright), b. at Sharon, CT, 7 Oct 1769 daughter of Thomas and Prudence (Eggleston) Sprague; Rachel d. at Deerfield, 17 Jul 1834. Frederick m. 2nd, about 1835, SUSAN CHASE (widow of Levi Hawkes), b. at Royalston, Dec 1800 daughter of William and Betsey (Work) Chase;[1352] Susan d. 2 Feb 1879. After Frederick's death, Susan married his brother Daniel (see below).

iv SIMEON BOYDEN, b. Sep 1770; d. at Boston, 15 Sep 1838; m. 1st, at Northfield, 10 Sep 1795, RHODA WATRISS, b. at Northfield, MA, Jul 1777 daughter of Oliver and Lucy (Field) Watriss;[1353] Rhoda d. at Boston, 12 Nov 1813. Simeon m. 2nd, at Boston, 9 Oct 1815, LUCY EATON, b. at Gardner, 31 May 1783 daughter of John and Mary (Larkin) Eaton;[1354] Lucy d. at Gardner, 12 Aug 1855.

v HANNAH BOYDEN, b. 13 Dec 1772; d. at Deerfield, 1 Mar 1861; m. 25 Oct 1795, as his second wife, THOMAS ARMS, b. at Deerfield, 3 Aug 1759 son of Thomas and Lydia (Alvord) Arms; Thomas d. at Deerfield, 2 Jun 1832. Thomas was first married to Polly Coolidge.

vi LUCY BOYDEN, b. Oct 1774; d. at Deerfield, 14 Jan 1848; m. 15 Oct 1801, JAMES NIMS, b. at Deerfield, about 1777 son of Ariel and Anna (Brewer) Nims; James d. at Conway, 5 Apr 1848.

vii DANIEL BOYDEN, b. 1776; d. at Deerfield, 27 May 1858; m. 1st, 6 May 1800, CHARLOTTE GOODNOUGH, b. 1775; Charlotte d. at Deerfield, 2 Feb 1837. Daniel m. 2nd, about 1838, the widow ANNA ANDERSON; Anna d. at Deerfield, 3 Oct 1840. Daniel m. 3rd, at Hinsdale, NH, SUSAN CHASE who was previously married to Daniel's brother Frederick (see above).

viii SAMUEL BOYDEN, b. Mar 1779; d. 27 Sep 1782.

ix SALLY BOYDEN, b. 6 Oct 1782; d. 1865 (memorial in Brownville, NY where her daughter is buried); m. at Hinsdale, NH, Jan 1806, JOEL NIMS, b. at Deerfield, Jan 1781 son of Ariel and Anna (Brewer) Nims; Joel perhaps died in Canada, 1847.[1355]

504) JAMES FRYE *(Elizabeth Osgood Frye[4], Hannah Abbott Osgood[3], George[2], George[1])*, b. at Andover, 9 Jan 1740/1 son of James and Elizabeth (Osgood) Frye; d. 28 Jan 1826; m. 1st 21 Feb 1765, his third cousin (and George Abbott descendant), MEHITABLE ROBINSON, b. at Boxford, Oct 1742 daughter of Joseph and Mehitable (Eams) Robinson;[1356] Mehitable d. 6 Jun 1787. James m. 2nd PHEBE CAMPBELL, b. 9 Aug 1744 daughter of Alexander and Joanna (Frye) Campbell, Phebe d. 23 Jul 1838.

As a young man of just sixteen, James Frye served alongside his father for eight months in 1756 during the French and Indian War. He was also for a short period a private in Captain Nathan Lovejoy's Company in 1775.[1357]

James Frye was a farmer in Methuen. The house he built on his farm in 1775 is still standing in Methuen at 176-178 Merrimack Street, now converted into a two-family home.[1358]

In his will written 16 January 1817 (probate 7 February 1826), James Frye bequeaths to beloved wife Phebe all the furniture she brought to the marriage and the use of the household as long as she remains a widow. There are also several other specific provisions to be provided for her support. He notes that he has made advancements of money to some of his children and

1351 Boyden, *Thomas Boyden and His Descendants*, p 30

1352 Susan's parents, William and Betsey Chase, are given on her death record.

1353 Pierce, *Field Genealogy*, p 227

1354 Glazier, *History of Gardner, Massachusetts*, p 24

1355 Death notice, "Democratic Union" published at Watertown July 8, 1847: "Died, June 11, 1847, in Durham, Canada West, Joel Nims, formerly of this county, aged 66 years."

1356 The 1777 will of Joseph Robinson includes a bequest to his daughter Mehitable wife of James Frye.

1357 Barker, Frye Genealogy, p 78

1358 Methuen History, Historical Sites, http://www.methuenhistory.org/Sites/M_thru_O_Streets.html

that any amounts owed to him by his children will be canceled at his decease. Sons Francis Frye and Joseph Frye receive the livestock and farming tools. The whole of the estate, other than $1,000 that is set aside to earn interest for the support of his wife and other specific bequests in the will, is to be divided into eight equal parts. Each of the following heirs receives one-eighth: sons James Frye, Daniel Frye, and Jeremiah Frye; the children of his son Robinson Frye who is deceased; the children of daughter Joanna Kimball who is deceased; daughter Hitty Webster; and sons Francis Frye and Joseph Frye. There are also specific cash bequests to his daughters and their heirs and land bequests to his sons and their heirs.[1359]

James Frye and Mehitable Robinson were parents to nine children all born at Methuen.

i JAMES FRYE, b. 12 Jan 1766; d. at Methuen, 28 Nov 1854; m. 1st, 7 Feb 1793, ABIAH MESSER, b. at Methuen, 26 Sep 1771 daughter of Asa and Abiah (Whittier) Messer; Abiah d. at Methuen, 24 Jul 1827. James m. 2nd, at Salem, NH, 12 March 1838, ELIZABETH AYER.

ii JOANNA FRYE, b. 16 Aug 1767; d. at Lisbon, NH, 6 Dec 1810; m. at Methuen, 27 Feb 1783, BENJAMIN KIMBALL, b. at Pelham, NH, 30 Jun 1761 son of Jonathan and Phebe (-) Kimball; Benjamin d. after 1832, likely at Methuen. After Joanna's death, Benjamin married, 22 Nov 1812, Mehitable Messer.[1360]

iii ROBINSON FRYE, b. 28 May 1771; d. at Methuen, 5 Dec 1816; m. at Methuen, 25 Oct 1797, NANCY POOR, b. about 1771 daughter of Thomas and Phebe (Osgood) Poor; Nancy d. at Methuen, 9 Jan 1855.

iv DANIEL FRYE, b. 7 Jun 1773; d. at Methuen, 14 Oct 1837; m. 17 Dec 1795, SUSANNAH POOR, b. at Methuen, 14 Jan 1778 daughter of Thomas and Phebe (Osgood) Poor; Susannah d. at Methuen, 5 Feb 1834. After Susannah's death, Daniel married, 25 Oct 1835, Phebe Carleton who was perhaps a widow.

v FRANCIS FRYE, b. 24 Nov 1776; d. at Methuen, 6 Dec 1849; m. 21 Oct 1802, LYDIA WHITTIER, b. at Methuen, 5 Feb 1783 daughter of William and Elizabeth (Haseltine) Whittier.

vi JEREMIAH FRYE, b. May 1779; d. at Methuen, 11 Jan 1855; m. at Methuen, 5 Oct 1809, BETSEY HALL, b. about 1788 daughter of Jacob and Elizabeth (White) Hall; Betsey d. at Methuen, 11 Jun 1870.

vii MEHITABLE "HITTY" FRYE, b. 31 Aug 1781; d. at Methuen, 15 May 1845; m. at Methuen, 27 Jun 1813, JOSEPH WEBSTER, b. at Salem, NH, 4 Feb 1774 son of Jesse and Abigail (Eaton) Webster. Joseph was first married to Rachel Jones.

viii JOHN FRYE, b. about 1784; d. 6 Nov 1787.

ix JOSEPH FRYE, b. 4 Sep 1786; d. at Methuen, 3 Mar 1832; m. at Methuen, 11 Mar 1810, MARY EMERSON, b. at Haverhill, 10 Sep 1786 daughter of Seth and Mary (Crowell) Emerson. After Joseph's death, Mary married Stephen Gage.

505) JONATHAN FRYE *(Elizabeth Osgood Frye^4, Hannah Abbott Osgood^3, George^2, George^1)*, b. at Andover, 4 Dec 1742 son of James and Elizabeth (Osgood) Frye; d. at Bucksport, ME 12 Jul 1793; m. by 1766 to unidentified wife;[1361] no marriage record has been located.

The wife of Jonathan Frye has yet to be found, but there are seven children who are likely his children born at Methuen. These are children identified in Barker's Frye genealogy.

i JONATHAN FRYE, b. 14 Dec 1766; d. 5 Nov 1783.

ii BETTY FRYE, b. 24 Aug 1768; d. 9 Sep 1768.

iii HANNAH FRYE, b. 25 Sep 1769; d. at Newburyport, 9 Feb 1795; m. at Newburyport, 29 Jun 1794, BENJAMIN NEWMAN, baptized at Newburyport, Aug 1766 son of Benjamin and Abigail (Lewis) Newman; Benjamin d. at Newburyport, 26 Aug 1827. After Hannah's death, Benjamin married Hannah Orn 6 Jan 1799.

1359 *Essex County, MA: Probate File Papers, 1638-1881. Probate of James Frye, 7 Feb 1826, Case number 10299.*

1360 Morrison, *History of the Kimball Family*, volume I, p 305

1361 The "internet", the DAR, and even Barker's Frye genealogy identify his wife as Sarah Peabody (who was born 1729) daughter of Moses, but that is not correct. The marriage of Sarah Peabody and a different Jonathan Frye (born 1717) occurred in 1753 when this Jonathan was 11 years old. There are baptismal records for three children of Jonathan at Methuen but those records list only the father's name. Those three children can be supported as being this Jonathan's as one of the grandsons (Phineas Barnes) later placed a monument in the Wardwell Cemetery for this Jonathan. There are several other possible children born at Methuen for whom there are no available records.

iv OSGOOD FRYE, b. at Methuen, 20 Oct 1771; d. at Bucksport, ME, 5 Jan 1827; m. 7 Jul 1796, JANE RICH, b. at Wellfleet, 22 Jun 1777 daughter of Joshua and Jane (Higgins) Rich; Jane d. at Bucksport, 29 Jul 1826.

v CHARLOTTE FRYE, b. at Methuen, 12 Mar 1774; d. at Newburyport, 30 Nov 1816; m. 20 Oct 1792, JAMES POTTER, b. at Ipswich, Jun 1769 son of Richard and Lydia (Averell) Potter; James d. at Newburyport, 27 Jan 1818.

vi JONATHAN FRYE, b. at Methuen, 18 Mar 1784. Jonathan was living in Apr 1799 when he made choice of Daniel Buck of Buckstown as his guardian. It is possible that he is the Jonathan Frye that went to Nova Scotia and married Mehitable English.

vii SALLY FRYE, b. at Methuen, 1 Nov 1786; d. at Portland, ME, 6 Sep 1857; m. at Newburyport, 28 Apr 1808, PHINEAS BARNES, b. 1781; Phineas d. at Orland, ME, 1810 (probate 16 May 1811).[1362]

506) HANNAH FRYE *(Elizabeth Osgood Frye⁴, Hannah Abbott Osgood³, George², George¹)*, b. at Andover, 12 Sep 1744 daughter of James and Elizabeth (Osgood) Frye; d. 16 Jan 1824; m. 31 Mar 1763, DANIEL POOR, b. 21 Sep 1740 son of Thomas and Mary (Adams) Poor; Daniel d. 20 Jun 1814.

Daniel Poor was a wealthy farmer in Andover and served as deacon of the South Parish church. He was the builder of the Daniel Poor-Perry House, an historic home in Andover. Daniel Poor served for seven years in Captain Benjamin Ames's Company during the Revolutionary War.[1363]

The estate of Daniel Poor entered probate 8 August 1814.[1364] The total value of the estate was $14,803.63. In his will written 28 April 1808, beloved wife Hannah receives all the household goods, the tools for carrying on his tanning business, and all the stock of brute creatures. All the household goods are to be hers forever without provision. She also receives use and improvement of the real estate and the eight-day clock. Hannah also receives all the books of religious nature. Sons Daniel and Nathaniel each receive a featherbed. Nathaniel will receive the clock after his mother's death. Nathaniel and Daniel also receive all the real estate. Other bequests are as follows: daughter Elizabeth wife of Peter Coburn, one hundred dollars; daughter Hannah wife of Ezra Abbot, fifty dollars; daughter Mary wife of Joshua Bradley, two hundred dollars; daughter Sarah wife of Rev. James Kendal, fifty dollars; daughter Ann wife of Reverend Joshua Bates, fifty dollars; and daughter Pamely wife of Amos Clark, fifty dollars. The bequests to the daughters are in addition to what has already been given to them. The executors are wife Hannah, son Daniel of Portland who is a trader, and son Nathaniel. Nathaniel Poor declined being an executor of his father's estate, and those duties were assumed by Daniel.

Hannah Frye Poor's estate entered probate 4 February 1824.[1365] In her will written 6 September 1815, Hannah Poor left all her personal possessions to her daughters Elizabeth, Hannah, Mary, Ann, and Pamela, and the heirs of daughter Sarah. She also left all her notes in accounts and real property to be divided among her daughters. Mark Newman was named executor; however, by the time of the probate he was not able to fulfill these duties. Neither son was mentioned in the will.

Daniel and Hannah had twelve children born at Andover. Three of the children are known to have died in early childhood, and likely a fourth child also died young.

i HANNAH POOR, b. 19 May 1763; d. 9 Nov 1768

ii ELIZABETH POOR, b. 4 Jan 1766; d. at Dracut, 26 Nov 1841; m. 20 May 1783, PETER COBURN, b. at Dracut, 18 Dec 1764 son of Peter and Dolly (Varnum) Coburn; Peter d. at Dracut, 12 Feb 1832.

iii FRYE POOR, b. 28 Jan 1768; likely died young.

iv HANNAH POOR, b. 15 Jan 1770; d. at Andover, 11 Sep 1861; m. 24 Apr 1798, her third cousin once removed, EZRA ABBOTT *(Abigail⁴, Benjamin³, Benjamin², George¹)*, b. at Andover, 3 Dec 1760 son of John and Abigail (Abbott) Abbott; Ezra d. 22 Jan 1844. This is Family #776 covered in detail below.

v MARY POOR, b. 28 Mar 1772; d. at Dracut, 23 Jan 1843; m. 4 Nov 1790, JOSHUA BRADLEY, b. at Dracut, 2 Oct 1762 son of Amos and Elizabeth (Page) Bradley; Joshua d. at Dracut, 9 Jan 1834.

vi SARAH POOR, b. 27 Apr 1774; d. 30 Oct 1775.

vii SARAH POOR, b. 20 Aug 1776; d. at Plymouth, 13 Feb 1809; m. 22 Jul 1800, JAMES KENDALL, b. at Lancaster, 3 Nov 1769 son of James and Elizabeth (Mason) Kendall; James d. at Plymouth, 17 Mar 1859. After Sarah's death, James married Sarah Kendall.

viii DANIEL ADAMS POOR, b. 11 Sep 1778; d. 13 Jan 1780.

[1362] U.S., Newspaper Extractions from the Northeast, 1704-1930; drowned in the Penobscot River

[1363] Andover Historic Preservation, 68 Phillips Street, https://preservation.mhl.org/68-phillips-st

[1364] *Essex County, MA: Probate File Papers, 1638-1881. Probate of Daniel Poor, 8 Aug 1814, Case number 22329.*

[1365] *Essex County, MA: Probate File Papers, 1638-1881. Probate of Hannah Poor, 4 Feb 1824, Case number 22347.*

ix DANIEL ADAMS POOR, b. 11 Feb 1781; d. 6 Jul 1844;[1366] m. at Portland, 21 Dec 1806, EMILY GOODWIN, b. at Plymouth, 9 May 1789 daughter of John and Fear (Thatcher) Goodwin; Emily d. at Portland, 19 Dec 1836.

x ANNA POOR, b. 28 Feb 1783; d. in Vermont, 7 Feb 1826; m. 4 Sep 1804, JOSHUA BATES, b. 20 Mar 1776 son of Zealous and Abigail (Nichols) Bates; Joshua d. at Dudley, MA, 14 Jan 1854. Joshua Bates, D. D. was president of Middlebury College 1818-1839.

xi NATHANIEL POOR, b. 20 Apr 1785. It is not known what became of Nathaniel. He was living in Andover in 1818 at the time of the settlement of his father's estate. He is listed on the tax roles in Andover through 1823. There is not a record of a marriage, death, or probate in Massachusetts. He also does not show up on census records other than the tax list.

xii PAMELA POOR, b. 23 Dec 1787; d. 5 Apr 1871; m. 11 Oct 1807, AMOS CLARK, b. at Sherborn, 1779 son of Samuel and Elizabeth (Learned) Clark; Amos d. at Reading, 3 Sep 1863.

507) DORCAS FRYE *(Elizabeth Osgood Frye⁴, Hannah Abbott Osgood³, George², George¹)*, b. at Andover, 3 Jun 1750 daughter of James and Elizabeth (Osgood) Frye; d. 1 Dec 1821; m. 10 Nov 1768, EZEKIEL CARLETON, b. 22 Nov 1742 son of Ezekiel and Marcy (Kimball) Carleton; Ezekiel d. at Andover, 1 Jan 1831.

Dorcas Frye and Ezekiel Carleton were parents of nine children born at Andover.

i DORCAS CARLETON, b. 3 Oct 1769; d. at Salem, 26 Feb 1839; m. at Andover, 15 Jul 1790, JOHN AUSTIN, b. at Andover, 1 Jul 1764 son of Daniel and Eunice (Kimball) Austin; John d. at Andover, 3 Jun 1847.

ii MOLLY CARLETON, b. 30 Aug 1771; nothing further found.

iii FANNY CARLETON, b. 12 Dec 1773; died young.

iv FANNY CARLETON, b. 5 Dec 1774; d. at Boston, 23 Apr 1855; m. at Andover, 19 Mar 1812, PUTNAM INGALLS, b. at Andover, 18 Dec 1763 son of Henry and Sarah (Putnam) Ingalls; Putnam d. at Andover, Putnam d. at Andover, 25 May 1814.

v EZEKIEL CARLETON, b. 10 Apr 1776; d. at Andover, 20 May 1849; m. at Andover, 2 Jul 1801, PHEBE KIMBALL, b. at Andover, 14 Mar 1779 daughter of John and Hannah (Farrington) Kimball; Phebe d. at Andover, 14 Jun 1828.

vi HANNAH CARLETON, b. 11 Aug 1778; d. at Boston, 25 Mar 1861. Hannah did not marry.

vii BETSEY CARLETON, b. 26 Mar 1781; d. at Boston, 15 Aug 1855. Betsey did not marry.

viii ENOCH CARLETON, b. 20 Apr 1783; d. at Lynn, 21 May 1865; m. at Providence, RI, 5 Sep 1818, ELIZABETH GEORGE, b. 1795 *perhaps* the daughter of Henry and Betsey (Dow) George; Elizabeth d. at Chelsea, 20 Oct 1879.

ix WILLIAM CARLETON, b. Feb 1787; d. at North Andover, 21 Apr 1856. William did not marry.

508) MOLLY FRYE *(Elizabeth Osgood Frye⁴, Hannah Abbott Osgood³, George², George¹)*, b. at Andover, 9 Mar 1752 daughter of James and Elizabeth (Osgood) Frye; d. at East Andover, ME, 13 Jun 1796; m. 9 May 1776, INGALLS BRAGG, b. 24 Jun 1753 son of Thomas and Dorothy (Ingalls) Bragg; Thomas d. at East Andover, ME about 1808 the year of the probate of his estate. Ingalls m. 2nd, at Bethel, 2 Nov 1803, DOROTHY SHATTUCK *(Zebadiah Shattuck⁵, Joanna Chandler Shattuck⁴, Zebadiah Chandler³, Hannah Abbott Chandler², George¹)*, b. at Andover, 14 Apr 1764 daughter of Zebadiah and Elizabeth (Abbott) Shattuck; Dorothy d. at Bethel, 24 Jan 1852. Deborah Shattuck was first married, at Andover, 26 Feb 1784, to JACOB RUSSELL, b. at Andover, Jan 1761 son of John and Hannah (Foster) Russell; Jacob d. at Bethel, ME, 1799. Dorothy had a third married to Benjamin Gage about 1810.

Ingalls Bragg did not leave a will and his estate entered probate 16 March 1808 with Thomas Bragg as administrator. On 21 September 1809, widow Dorothy Bragg petitioned the court for an additional allowance as the income from her widow's thirds was just $25 which was not sufficient for her necessities. An undated petition by the heirs of the estate noted that the real estate could not be divided without great harm to the value and requested that the home farm be settled on son James F. Bragg who would then pay out or give satisfactory security to the other heirs. The heirs signing this petition were James F. Bragg, guardian for Pamelia Bragg, Stephen Holt, and James Russell. (James Russell seems to be the husband of Dorothy's

[1366] Daniel's death is recorded at Andover, although he was a resident of Portland.

daughter Dolly Russell from her marriage to Jacob Russell so it not sure why he is an heir.) In 1811 James F. Ingalls writes the judge that he has a letter from his sister (not named) who lives at the west and she is willing to do what the others want in terms of the division.

On 20 September 1830, William Bragg of Bridgton and Washington I. Bragg of Bethel, heirs-at-law of Ingalls Bragg, petitioned the probate court for a division of the real estate of Ingalls Bragg as that had never been done. William and Washington are the sons with Dorothy Shattuck.[1367]

Molly Frye and Ingalls Bragg were parents of eleven children, the older children born at Andover, Massachusetts and the younger children at Andover, Maine.

i INGALLS BRAGG, b. at Andover, MA, 15 Jul 1777; d. at Andover, ME, 11 Dec 1840; m. at Gloucester, MA, 13 Feb 1809, ELIZABETH "BETSEY" GARDNER, b. at Gloucester, MA, 3 Jul 1785 daughter of Coas and Lucy (Proctor) Gardner; Elizabeth d. at Andover, ME, 23 Feb 1839.

ii MOLLY BRAGG, b. at Andover, MA, 29 Apr 1779; d. at Norway, ME, 17 Aug 1823; m. at Albany, VT, 1 Jul 1806, her fourth cousin, STEPHEN HOLT *(Rhoda Abbott Holt*[5]*, Ephraim*[4]*, Stephen*[3]*, John*[2]*, George*[1]*)*, b. at Andover, MA, 7 Jun 1771 son of Jacob and Rhoda (Abbott) Holt; Stephen d. at Norway, 25 Sep 1817. Stephen Holt is a child in Family 322.

iii ELIZABETH BRAGG, b. at Andover, MA, 16 Mar 1781; d. at Andover, ME, 8 Apr 1856. Elizabeth did not marry.

iv DOROTHY "DOLLY" BRAGG, b. at Andover, MA, 4 Feb 1783; d. at Andover, ME, 16 Jun 1848; m. 6 May 1810, MOSES MERRILL, b. at Newbury, 1 Oct 1775 son of Ezekiel and Sarah (Emery) Merrill; Moses d. at Andover, ME, 5 Jan 1867.

v THOMAS BRAGG, b. at Andover, MA, 7 Apr 1785; d. at Upton, ME, 2 Feb 1840; m. SOPHIA FARRINGTON, b. at Wilton, NH, 9 Sep 1790 daughter of John and Phebe (Poor) Farrington; Sophia d. at Peru, ME, Apr 1859.

vi JAMES FRYE BRAGG, b. at Andover, MA, 4 Dec 1787; d. at Errol, NH, 30 May 1876; m. 21 Mar 1811, SARAH GRAHAM, b. at Concord, 31 May 1790 daughter of Joshua and Hannah (Chandler) Graham; Sarah d. at Errol, 30 May 1876.

vii Twin 1, b. and d. 27 Jan 1790

viii Twin 2, b. and d. 27 Jan 1790

ix PAMELA BRAGG, b. at Andover, ME, 31 Aug 1791; d. at Andover, ME, 28 Jan 1878; m. 8 Nov 1812, STEPHEN LOVEJOY, b. at Andover, MA, 10 Jul 1787 son of Abiel and Mary (Poor) Lovejoy; Stephen d. at Andover, ME between 1860 and 1870.

x SUKEY BRAGG, b. 21 Jul 1794; d. 19 Jan 1795.

xi SUKEY BRAGG, b. 19 Jan 1796; d. 23 Jun 1797.

Children of Ingalls Bragg and Dorothy Shattuck:

i WILLIAM BRAGG, b. at Andover, ME, 4 Oct 1804; d. at Boston, Jun 1853; m. 1st, about 1826, SARAH MANNING, b. at New Gloucester, ME, 22 Jul 1796 daughter of Joseph and Elizabeth (Smith) Manning; Sarah d. Bridgton, ME, 9 Aug 1831. William m. 2nd, at New Gloucester, 9 Jan 1834, Sarah's sister, ELIZA MANNING, b. at New Gloucester, 20 Sep 1794.

ii WASHINGTON INGALLS BRAGG, b. at Andover, ME, 22 Feb 1808; d. at Hartford, ME, 23 Dec 1843; m. 17 Mar 1842, CATHERINE PARCH WOODSUM, b. at Hartford, ME, 1818 daughter of Rufus and Nancy (Parch) Woodsum;[1368] Catherine d. at Mechanic Falls, ME, 16 Sep 1893. After Washington's death, Catherine married second Albert Woodsum 14 Apr 1847 and third Aranda D. Tinkham about 1851.

Dorothy Shattuck and Jacob Russell were married in Andover and perhaps some of the children were born in Andover before the family moved to Bethel, Maine. Birth dates are estimates based on census records and age at death. Four children are known for Dorothy and Jacob.[1369]

[1367] *Maine. Probate Court (Oxford County); Probate Place: Oxford, Maine, Probate Records, Box A-C, Pre 1820, probate of Ingalls Bragg*

[1368] The names of Catherin's parents are given as Rufus Woodsum and Nancy Parch on her death record and place of birth as Hartford, Maine.

[1369] Lapham, *History of Bethel, Maine*, p 611

i DOLLY RUSSELL, b. perhaps at Andover, 1784; d. at Beverly, MA, 20 Sep 1863; m. at East Andover, ME, 13 Aug 1804, her first cousin once removed, JAMES RUSSELL *(Lydia Abbott Russell[5], Barachias[4], John[3], John[2], George[1])*, b. at Andover, Nov 1777 son of Uriah and Lydia (Abbott) Russell; James d. at Paris, ME, after 1860. James Russell is a child in Family 297.

ii ABIGAIL RUSSELL, b. perhaps at Andover, 1786; d. at Rushville, NY, Jan 1859; m. at Bethel, 21 Nov 1822, as his second wife, ELI TWITCHELL, b. at Dublin, NH, 26 Jul 1786 son of Ezra and Susanna (Rice) Twitchell; Eli d. at Gorham, NY, 1874. Eli was first married to Betsy Gould 20 Jan 1807 and third married to Betsey's sister Clarissa Gould about 1862.

iii JACOB RUSSELL, b. likely at Bethel, about 1788; d. at Richland, NY, 20 May 1873 (probate 15 Oct 1873); m. 1st, by 1828, SOPHIA STARK whose parents are not identified; Sophia d. at Richland, 11 Nov 1847. Jacob m. 2nd, about 1848, Susan who has not been identified. Jacob and Sophia's daughter Lydia married her first cousin William L. Twitchell the son of Abigail Russell and Eli Twitchell.

iv CHARLES RUSSELL, b. at Bethel, about 1793; d. at Bethel, after 1850. Charles lived with his sister Dolly and her husband. He did not marry.

509) JOSEPH OSGOOD *(Joseph Osgood[4], Hannah Abbott Osgood[3], George[2], George[1])*, b. at Boston, 25 Nov 1746 son of Joseph and Margaret (Binney) Osgood; d. at Salem, Jun 1812; m. 14 Jun 1770, LUCRETIA WARD, b. at Salem, Sep 1748 daughter of Miles and Hannah (Derby) Ward; Lucretia d. Sep 1809. Lucretia's name is given as Mehitable in the Osgood genealogy, but the birth, marriage, and death record say Lucretia.

Joseph Osgood was a physician first in Danvers and later in Salem.

The sons of Joseph and Lucretia went to sea. Oldest son Joseph died in England while serving on the cargo ship *George Washington.* Son Thomas was also a seaman as evidenced by his 1813 Seamen's Protection Certificate.[1370] A third son, Benjamin, died aboard the *U.S.S. Washington* at Ann Arbor.

Dr. Joseph Osgood wrote his will 4 May 1812.[1371] Son Thomas Binney Osgood was bequeathed $1,000 and the copy of the American encyclopedia, and one share of the Lynn Mineral Spring. A trust of $500 is set aside for son Benjamin Binney Osgood and this is to be managed by the executor. Daughter Peggy Sprague wife of Joseph Sprague is to receive $1,000 although she should consider that she already received $832.50 of that at the time of her marriage. Daughter Lucy Derby wife of Samuel G. Derby also receives $1,000 again considering has already received $870. Daughter Hitty Osgood receives $1,000 and the complete dining set of India China ware. Hitty also receives privileges to use of the house as long as she lives or until she marries. Daughters Peggy and Lucy each also receive one share of the Lynn Mineral Spring. There are also bequests to grandchildren Joseph Osgood, Joseph Osgood Derby, Nathaniel Ward Osgood, and Mary Osgood. The books are to be divided among his children, except the medical books will go to son Thomas. There is also a bequest of $100 to Rebecca Sutton who for years has faithfully served the family. Son Thomas Binney Osgood was named executor. By the time of the settlement of the estate, it was noted that son Benjamin Binney Osgood was on military duty in the Mediterranean. At that time of the final settlement, daughter Lucy was deceased.

Son Thomas Binney Osgood died of consumption in 1818. His estate was valued at $25,379. In his will written 9 March 1816, Thomas left $500 to his brother-in-law Joseph Sprague with the intent that Joseph would use interest from this money to help provide care and support for Thomas's brother Benjamin (Benjamin died in January 1818 about six weeks before Thomas). Five hundred dollars was left to Mary Derby to provide care for the children of Thomas's deceased sister. The rest of the estate is to be held in trust by his brothers-in-law Joseph Sprague and Samuel G. Derby for the care of his nieces and nephews. One-quarter of the estate to go to children of his sister with Joseph Sprague, one-quarter to the children of his late sister Lucy wife of Samuel Derby, one-quarter to the children of his late brother Joseph Osgood, and one-quarter to the any children of sister Hitty and her husband Reuben Mussy.

i JOSEPH OSGOOD, b. 1772; d. in England, Jul 1806; m. 23 Oct 1796, MARY BECKFORD, b. at Salem, 23 Sep 1774 daughter of Ebenezer and Hannah (Hunt) Beckford;[1372] Mary d. at Salem 13 Mar 1822. The death notice of Joseph states the following: "Joseph, jr., supercargo of the ship George Washington, in England, Issue of July 11, 1806." NR9 [a. 34 y. PR82]

[1370] Web: US, New England Seamen's Protection Certificate Index, 1796-1871

[1371] *Essex County, MA: Probate File Papers, 1638-1881. Probate of Joseph Osgood, 20 Jul 1812, Case number 20234.*

[1372] Mary's parents are confirmed by the 1816 probate record of Ebenezer Beckford that includes heirs Mary Osgood and her son Nathaniel W. Osgood.

ii NATHANIEL WARD OSGOOD, b. Sep 1774; d. at Salem, 12 Aug 1794.

iii PEGGY OSGOOD, b. 3 Aug 1778; d. at Salem, Jun 1837; m. 6 Feb 1801, JOSEPH SPRAGUE, b. at Salem, 23 Nov 1771 son of Joseph and Elizabeth (-) Sprague; Joseph d. at Salem, 8 Jun 1833.

iv THOMAS BINNEY OSGOOD, b. Nov 1780; d. 1 Mar 1818. Thomas did not marry. He was a successful merchant. He died of consumption.

v LUCY OSGOOD, b. Oct 1782; d. at Salem, May 1812; m. at Salem, 11 Dec 1803, as his second wife, General SAMUEL GARDNER DERBY, b. at Salem, about 1767 son of Richard and Lydia (Gardner) Derby; Samuel d. at Weston, 17 Jan 1843. Samuel was first married to Margaret Barton.

vi BENJAMIN BINNEY OSGOOD, b. Jul 1787; d. at Ann Arbor on board the U.S.S. Washington, 13 Jan 1818. Benjamin graduated Harvard in 1806. The Binney genealogy reports that Benjamin was placed in the marine corps by his friends in hope to provide him a more regular life.[1373]

vii MEHITABLE "HITTY" OSGOOD, b. about 1790 (based on age 75 at death); d. at Boston, 14 May 1866; m. at Salem, 9 Jun 1813, Dr. REUBEN DIMOND MUSSEY, b. at Pelham, NH, 23 Jun 1780 son of John and Beulah (Butler) Mussey; Reuben d. at Boston, 21 Jun 1866. Reuben was a renowned physician, medical researcher, and medical academic. Details of his accomplishments can be seen in Appletons' Cyclopedia of American Biography; Volume: Vol. IV, p 471.

viii MARIA OSGOOD, b. Aug 1794; died young from injuries sustained in a fall from a window.[1374]

510) MEHITABLE OSGOOD *(Joseph Osgood⁴, Hannah Abbott Osgood³, George², George¹)*,[1375] b. at Boston, 11 Dec 1749 daughter of Joseph and Margaret (Binney) Osgood; d. 6 Oct 1788 (according to the Cushing Genealogy, but no record found); m. by 1770, JOHN CUSHING, b. at Haverhill, 11 Dec 1749 son of James and Anna (Wainwright) Cushing. John m. 2nd Mary Marsh; John d. at Goffstown, NH 1834 (will written 16 Jun 1834).

The Osgood and Cushing genealogies have different information on the children of Mehitable and John. The Osgood genealogy reports one child and the Cushing genealogy reports a son and a daughter, one of whom died in childhood. There is a baptism record for one son baptized at Andover. The 1834 will of John Cushing names wife Mary, eldest son James, youngest son Albert, eldest daughter Mary Cushing, and youngest daughter Sally Worthy specifying her bequest is to go to Sally and not to her husband. The eldest son named, James Cushing, was a son of the marriage of John Cushing and his second wife Mary suggesting that the child John had with Mehitable died before 1834 and likely did not have children.

i JOHN CUSHING, baptized in Andover 27 Jan 1771; death not known. John is mentioned in his grandfather Joseph Osgood's 1797 will stating grandson John Cushing is to be boarded for two years by his uncle George Osgood. It is not known what became of him after that.

511) JOHN OSGOOD *(Joseph Osgood⁴, Hannah Abbott Osgood³, George², George¹)*, b. at Andover 14 Nov 1754 son of Joseph and Margaret (Binney) Osgood; d. at Newbury, 5 Apr 1820; m. at Newbury, 3 Dec 1778, LYDIA NEWELL, b. at Brookline, 20 Apr 1754 daughter of Moses and Sarah (Gerrish) Newell; Lydia d. at West Newbury, 1 Feb 1836.

In his written 12 March 1812 (proved 1820), John Osgood bequeaths to son Moses the sum of one dollar and the two promissory notes owed by Moses to his father totaling $2,000. Son John receives a one-acre property in Newbury that contains the town house. This is in addition to what John has already received. In addition to what he has already received, son Samuel receives one dollar, the mahogany desk and bookcase, and a silver watch. Daughters Sally Osgood and Lydia Osgood receive $500 each. John relies on their dear and affectionate mother to make them more than equal to what their brothers have received. The remainder of the estate goes to well and dearly beloved wife Lydia who is to pay the legacies from the estate who will be free to dispose of the estate and Lydia is also named executrix.[1376]

In her will written 10 March 1832 (probate 8 March 1836), Lydia Osgood bequeathed to son Moses Osgood, one dollar. Sons John Osgood and Samuel Osgood each receive ten dollars. The remainder of the estate goes to daughter Sarah Osgood who is also named executrix.[1377]

John Osgood and Lydia Newell were parents of six children, the birth of the oldest child recorded at Andover and the other children at Newbury.

[1373] Binney, *Genealogy of the Binney Family*, p 39
[1374] Osgood, *Genealogy of the Descendants. . .*, p 70
[1375] Cushing, *The Genealogy of the Cushing Family*, p. 61
[1376] Massachusetts Wills and Probates, Essex, Probate Records vol 394-396, book 94-196, 1818-1820, pp 25-27
[1377] Essex County, MA: Probate File Papers, 1638-1881.Online database. AmericanAncestors.org. New England Historic Genealogical Society, 2014. Case 20241

i SARAH OSGOOD, b. 30 Jan 1780; d. at West Newbury, 18 Oct 1862. Sarah did not marry. In her will, Sarah made bequests to the widows of her brothers John (Dorcas) and Samuel (Rebecca N.), nieces and nephews, friends, and a bible society.

ii JOSEPH OSGOOD, b. 25 Dec 1781; d. at Newbury, 20 Jun 1804.

iii MOSES OSGOOD, b. 26 Aug 1785. Genealogies report that Moses Osgood left town when a young man and was never heard from again.

iv JOHN OSGOOD, b. 25 Apr 1788; d. at Lowell, 22 Sep 1853; m. 1st, 5 Jun 1820, MARY ANN BABSON GRIFFIN, b. at Gloucester, 5 Nov 1798 daughter of Gustavus and Anna (Babson) Griffin; Mary Ann d. at West Newbury, 31 Jul 1823. John m. 2nd, 27 Jun 1824, Nary Ann's sister, DORCAS GRIFFIN, b. 17 Jul 1802; Dorcas d. at Lowell, 16 Sep 1880.

v SAMUEL OSGOOD, b. 28 Dec 1789; d. at Newburyport, 1841 (probate 20 Jul 1841); m. 28 Oct 1813, REBECCA NOYSE FOLLANSBEE, b. at Newburyport, 12 Feb 1790 daughter of William and Rebecca (Noyse) Follansbee; Rebecca d. Newburyport, 10 Nov 1866. Samuel and Rebecca Osgood's daughter, Lydia Newell Osgood, became the adopted daughter of Matthias Plant Sawyer of Portland, Maine. Matthias Sawyer did not marry and in his 1853 will he left what is known as the Amory-Tickner House on Park Street in Boston to his adopted daughter Lydia N. the wife of Curtis Raymond.[1378]

vi LYDIA OSGOOD, b. 4 Aug 1791; d. at West Newbury, 31 Oct 1831. Lydia did not marry.

512) GEORGE OSGOOD *(Joseph Osgood⁴, Hannah Abbott Osgood³, George², George¹)*, b. at Andover, 1 Dec 1758 son of Joseph and Margaret (Binney) Osgood; d. at Andover, 24 Oct 1823; m. 7 Jan 1782, ELIZABETH OTIS, b. at Barnstable, 12 Jan 1760 daughter of Joseph and Rebecca (Sturgis) Otis; Elizabeth d. 22 May 1802. George m. 2nd 8 Mar 1803, SARAH VOSE, b. at Milton, 29 Jul 1762 daughter of Joseph and Sarah (How) Vose; Sarah d. 17 Mar 1812. After Sarah's death, George married Mary Messer, 2 Oct 1815.

The Osgoods were a family of physicians. Dr. George Osgood was a physician in Andover as his father Joseph had been. Three of George's sons (Joseph Otis, John, and George) were also physicians. Son Dr. Joseph Otis Osgood delivered "An Oration Commemorative of American Independence" on 4 July 1810. The text of this oration is readily available and provides insight into political and social mores of the times.[1379]

In his will written 16 August 1822, George Osgood bequeaths to beloved wife Mary use of east part of the house in common with his unmarried daughters, half of the household provisions, and one-third of the floor pew in the north meeting house as long as she remains a widow. Mary also receives $200. Son Joseph Otis Osgood receives the great bible, the Greek lexicon and half the wearing apparel. Son George Osgood is named executor and also receives the obstetrical instruments and his note of $160 that is owed his father. Son Benjamin Binney Osgood receives one-sixth of the real estate so long as he pays the $700 note to Edward Rand and another $500 note to Benjamin Collins. Son John Osgood receives one-sixth of the land as long as he pays the value of a note owed his father. Daughter Elizabeth Putnam receives one-sixth of the real estate deducting $278.25 and she also receives the silver pepper box. Daughter Rebecca Bridges receives one-sixth part of the real estate deducting $398. Daughter Maria Osgood receives one-sixth part of the real estate and the mahogany post bed. Daughter Sarah Osgood receives one-six of the real estate and a bedstead with bolster and pillows. His single daughters, Sarah and Maria, also have improvements on one-half of the house and property not sold to pay debts, as long as they are unmarried.[1380]

George Osgood and Elizabeth Otis had seven children, the two oldest born at Dartmouth and the younger children born at Andover.

i JOSEPH OTIS OSGOOD, b. Dec 1782; d. at Kensington, NH, 10 Aug 1845; m. 22 Mar 1811, ELIZABETH FOGG, b. at Kensington, 1782 daughter of Joseph and Mary (Sherburne) Fogg; Elizabeth d. 8 Aug 1869.

ii GEORGE OSGOOD, b. 25 Mar 1784; d. at Danvers, 26 May 1863; m. 1st, 25 Mar 1807, SARAH "SALLY" WEBSTER, b. at Danvers, 5 Dec 1784 daughter of Luke and Sarah (Holten) Webster; Sarah d. 27 Sep 1821. George and Sarah did not have children. George married 12 Mar 1822, NANCY ENDICOTT, b. 31 Aug 1788 daughter of Moses and Anna (Towne) Endicott.

iii ELIZABETH OSGOOD, b. 24 Oct 1788; d. at Syracuse, NY, 28 Jul 1848; m. 6 Aug 1816, HIRAM PUTNAM, b. at Danvers, 30 Jan 1786 son of Jethro and Mary (Holton) Putnam; Hiram d. at Syracuse, 8 Nov 1874.

1378 Lawrence, *Old Part Street and Its Vicinity*, pp 83-85

1379 Osgood, Joseph Otis, *An Oration Commemorative of American Independence*, https://archive.org/details/orationcommemora00osgo

1380 *Essex County, MA: Probate File Papers, 1638-1881. Probate of George Osgood, 4 Nov 1823, Case number 20196.*

iv BENJAMIN BINNEY OSGOOD, b. 29 Nov 1790; d. at Bangor, ME, 27 Jul 1826; m. 12 Nov 1816, CLARISSA CALL, b. at Newburyport, 9 Jan 1792 daughter of Jonathan and Hannah (Stacey) Call; Clarissa d. at Cambridge, 26 Apr 1874.

v JOHN OSGOOD, b. 12 Jul 1793; d. at Lovell, ME, 16 Mar 1826;[1381] m. at Woburn, 13 Mar 1818, ELIZA W. WOOD, b. at Woburn, 10 Aug 1798 daughter of John and Hannah (Blanchard) Wood; Eliza d. at Brooklyn, NY, 19 Sep 1854.[1382] John and Eliza had three children before his early death. After John's death, Eliza married Benjamin Wyman and they resettled in Kings County, NY.

vi REBECCA OSGOOD, b. 31 Jan 1796; d. at North Andover, 19 Nov 1856; m. 12 Jul 1819, MOODY BRIDGES, b. at Andover, 4 Sep 1784 son of James and Mary (Montgomery) Bridges; Moody d. 16 Apr 1858.

vii MARIA OSGOOD, b. 17 Jan 1802; d. at Salem, 4 Jul 1868; m. 18 Oct 1826, EDWARD AUGUSTUS HOLYOKE, b. at Boston, 12 Jul 1786 son of William and Judith (Holyoke) Turner;[1383] Edward d. at Syracuse, 17 Dec 1855.

George Osgood and Sarah Vose had one daughter born at Andover.

i SARAH VOSE OSGOOD, b. 30 Apr 1804; d. at Syracuse, 24 Jul 1901; m. 30 Nov 1836, JAMES GRANT TRACY, b. at Norwich, 16 Mar 1781 son of Jared and Margaret (Grant) Tracy; James d. 8 Nov 1850.

513) DORCAS MARCH *(Dorcas Osgood March[4], Hannah Abbott Osgood[3], George[2], George[1])*, b. at Boston, 11 Jun 1746 daughter of Thomas and Dorcas (Osgood) March; d. at Salem, Mar 1820; m. at Andover, 19 Jan 1763, DUDLEY WOODBRIDGE, b. at Salem, 3 Mar 1732/3 son of Benjamin and Mary (Osgood) Woodbridge; Dudley d. 21 Oct 1799.

Dudley Woodbridge was a merchant involved in the maritime trade that flourished in Salem following the Revolutionary War. Following his death, part of his property was acquired by the Derby family which extended their wharf to a length of one-half mile. This wharf is extant in Salem and is part of the Salem Maritime National Historic Site.[1384]

Dudley Woodbridge did not leave a will and Dorcas Woodbridge was administrator of the estate. The real property of Dudley Woodbridge was appraised at $14,325 including a dwelling house valued at $5,000 and a wharf with barn and shop located at Water Street in Salem valued at $4,500.[1385]

The estate of Dorcas Woodbridge was valued at $6,866.70 which included shares in Salem Turnpike and Salem Marine Insurance Company. Dorcas's will dated 11 September 1813 consists of canceling the debt her son Joseph Jackson Woodbridge owes to her as this amount would cancel out anything he might obtain from the estate. Otherwise, she directs that her estate be disbursed to her heirs according to law. Heirs signing agreement to the terms of the estate settlement are as follows: Thomas M. Woodbridge, Stephen Phillips an attorney who signs both as the guardian for his son and as the representative of Joseph J. Woodbridge, John W. Fenno, Louisa Fenno, and Robert J. Cloutman (he is the husband of a Fenno granddaughter).[1386]

Daughter Benjamina Woodbridge married later in life and did not have children. Benjamina Woodbridge Lovejoy wrote her will 19 February 1840 although she died in 1851. She left wearing apparel to William Woodbridge and Dudley Woodbridge who are the sons of her uncle Benjamin Woodbridge. Elizabeth Robenson wife of Dean Robinson receives $50. Eliza Storer who is the daughter of Elizabeth Robenson receives $20. Louisa Fenoe "the daughter of my sister Mary Gilman Fenoe" receives $100. Mary Cloutman, granddaughter of sister Mary, receives $100. Maria Parker daughter of Isaac Parker receives $50. Maria Rea wife of Archelaus Rea of Salem receives $100. To the surviving sons of her brother William Woodbridge, $200 each. Dr. William LeBaron of Andover receives $50. Bailey Loring receives $100. To Archelaus Rea she gives $1,000 to be held in trust with the interest from this money being used to help support her brother Joseph Jackson Woodbridge. After Joseph's death, this money is to go to her brother Thomas March Woodbridge or his heirs. The residue of the estate is given to her brother Thomas.[1387] Elizabeth Robenson wife of Dean Robenson is Benjamina's stepdaughter Elizabeth Lovejoy daughter of Nathaniel Lovejoy and his second wife Elizabeth Brandon. Maria Rea is a niece of Benjamina. The value of her personal estate at inventory in 1851 was $3,620.00.

In 1847, Benjamina who was widowed in 1812, had a guardian appointed for her due to "insanity." She was 75 years old at that time and perhaps this reflects a decline in her functioning with aging.[1388]

[1381] "Maine, Faylene Hutton Cemetery Collection, ca. 1780-1990," database with images, *FamilySearch* (https://familysearch.org/ark:/61903/1:1:QKM1-3XGY : 16 March 2018), John Osgood, 1826; citing Burial, Lovell, Oxford, Maine, United States, Maine State Library, Augusta; FHL microfilm 1,787,260.

[1382] *New York, Genealogical Records, 1675-1920,* The New York Genealogical and Biographical Record (quarterly-1932) - Extracts; Publication Place: New York; Publisher: New York Genealogical and Biographical Society.

[1383] Edward Augustus Holyoke was born Edward Turner but changed his name to Holyoke to please his grandfather Dr. Edward Augustus Holyoke. Palmer, *Necrology of Alumni of Harvard College*, p 91

[1384] https://www.nps.gov/sama/learn/historyculture/wharves.htm

[1385] *Essex County, MA: Probate File Papers, 1638-1881. Probate of Dudley Woodbridge, 8 Nov 1799, case number 30543.*

[1386] *Essex County, MA: Probate File Papers, 1638-1881. Probate of Dorcas Woodbridge, 28 Mar 1820, case number 30542.*

[1387] Massachusetts Wills and Probate Records, 1635-1991, Will of Benjamina Lovejoy, 19 Feb 1840

[1388] *Essex County, MA: Probate File Papers, 1638-1881. Guardianship case of Benjamina Lovejoy, 28 Mar 1820, case number 45618.*

Joseph Jackson Woodbridge received special mention in his mother's will forgiving his debt, and in his sister's will his inheritance was placed in trust. Joseph had a drinking problem, and in 1860 a guardian was appointed for him. A complaint was brought by the mayor and aldermen of Salem stating that due to drunkenness, idleness, and excessive spending, Joseph Woodbridge exposed himself to want and suffering and exposed the town to the expense of his maintenance and support. David P. Fitz was appointed his guardian.[1389]

Dorcas March and Dudley Woodbridge had ten children born at Salem.

i DUDLEY WOODBRIDGE, b. Jan 1764; d. 11 Aug 1771.

ii THOMAS MARCH WOODBRIDGE, b. 23 Aug 1765; d. at Salem, 18 May 1841; m. Mary born in 1763 and died 19 Jan 1838.

iii JOHN WOODBRIDGE, b. 11 Sep 1767; d. by drowning while serving on Captain Grafton's brig on 11 Mar 1784.

iv MARY GILMAN WOODBRIDGE, b. Sep 1769; d. at Salem, 3 May 1809; m. 19 Nov 1788, JOSEPH FENNO.

v BENJAMINA WOODBRIDGE, b. Mar 1772; d. at Worcester, 6 May 1851; m. 1 Dec 1803, as his third wife, NATHANIEL LOVEJOY *(Elizabeth Swan Lovejoy[4], Hannah Stevens Swan[3], Sarah Abbott Stevens[2], George[1])*, b. at Andover, 29 Apr 1744 son of Nathaniel and Elizabeth Swan Lovejoy; Nathaniel d. at Andover, 5 Jul 1812.

vi DORCAS WOODBRIDGE, b. Apr 1774; d. at Salem, Jun 1803; m. at Salem, 9 Oct 1796, STEPHEN PHILLIPS, b. at Marblehead, 1761 son of Stephen and Elizabeth (Elkins) Phillips; Stephen d. at Salem, 19 Oct 1838. After Dorcas's death, Stephen married Elizabeth Pierce. Samuel Phillips was a prominent maritime merchant.

vii DUDLEY WOODBRIDGE, b. Mar 1776; d. at Philadelphia, Dec 1795.

viii ELIZABETH GRAFTON WOODBRIDGE, b. 3 May 1778; there is no further record and she likely died young.

ix WILLIAM WOODBRIDGE, b. 10 Feb 1780; d. at Savannah, GA, 21 Aug 1820;[1390] m. about 1812, HELEN WYLLY, b. about 1785 in Georgia daughter of Hugh Wylly. William was a merchant in Savannah.

x JOSEPH JACKSON WOODBRIDGE, b. 11 Jun 1746; d. at Salem, 4 Jul 1863.

514) JOSEPH ALLEN *(Mary Osgood Allen[4], Hannah Abbott Osgood[3], George[2], George[1])*, b. at Gloucester, 24 Feb 1746/7 son of William and Mary (Osgood) Allen; d. at Gray, ME, 12 Jan 1849; m. 1st, 30 Dec 1782, MARY BAKER; Mary d. about 1810. Joseph m. 2nd, at Gray, 18 Sep 1810,[1391] DORCAS EMERY, b. about 1770; Dorcas d. at Gray, 25 Apr 1855.

Joseph served in the Revolution and in 1818 at age 59, Joseph Allen made application for his pension.[1392] In March 1777, Joseph enlisted for a term of three years as a private in the company of Captain William Ballard in the Massachusetts line. He served until March 1780 and was discharged at West Point. In 1820, the household consisted of wife Dorcas age 50, daughter Statira age 35 who is "most always sick", and a healthy boy Emery age 8. He reported no real or personal estate. The family lived in a house that had been owned by his wife's first husband. That also contained 30 acres of poor land able to support only one cow and four sheep. He reported $90 in debts. He was awarded a pension of $96 per annum. In her widow's application, Dorcas reported that her name before marriage was Dorcas Emery. The statement of the town clerk of Gray was that the marriage was between Mr. Joseph Allen of Windham and Miss (underlining in the record) Dorcas Emery of Gray.[1393] Dorcas Allen made application for bounty land in 1855.

Joseph Allen and Mary Baker were parents of thirteen children likely born at Windham, Maine where Joseph was living when he married Dorcas Emery.

i DORCAS ALLEN, b. 18 Mar 1783; m. THOMAS LEIGHTON.

ii STATIRA ALLEN, b. 20 Apr 1785 (age 35 in 1820). She perhaps m. at Gray, ME, 25 Sep 1832, ABEL GOSSOM, b. about 1780. Abel Gossom was a War of 1812 veteran who was disabled by the amputation of his arm due to a

[1389] *Essex County, MA: Probate File Papers, 1638-1881. Spendthrift case of Joseph Woodbridge, 28 Mar 1820, case number 57182.*

[1390] His grave monument includes this inscription: WILLIAM son of Dorcas and Dudley Woodbridge was born in Salem, Massachusetts Feb. 10th, 1780 and died in Savannah, Georgia Aug. 21st, 1820.

[1391] The information on the marriage given in the pension file is different from the town records of Gray available on familysearch.org. Marriages by D. Weston, Mr. Joseph Allen of Windham and Miss Dorcas Emery of Gray, Sept. 18, 1810. https://www.familysearch.org/ark:/61903/3:1:3QS7-89NW-3D9P?i=244

[1392] Revolutionary War Pension and Bounty-Land Warrant Application Files, Case W2578

[1393] No information was found related to a possible first marriage for Dorcas or information that would confirm her maiden name as Emery. But Joseph and Dorcas named their only child together Emery. It is possible that the pension application claimed she was a widow, and this was property from her first husband, as in order to be granted a pension, the pensioner needed to claim financial hardship requiring the pension.

war injury. He was widowed by 1832 and it is possible that the marriage record is for this Statira. "Mr. Abel Gossom of Poland and Miss Statira Allen of Gray" Abel Gossom d. at Poland, ME, 1837.

iii ANDREW ALLEN, b. 19 Jan 1787; d. at Windham, ME, 17 Jun 1864; m. ANNE, b. about 1792 who has not been identified; Anne d. at Windham, 12 Nov 1875.

iv LUCY ALLEN, b. 14 May 1789

v HANNAH ALLEN, b. 20 Apr 1791

vi DANIEL ALLEN, b. 10 Apr 1793; d. at Gray, 9 Apr 1855; m. 1st, about 1816, BETSEY LEIGHTON daughter of John and Leonice (Sawyer) Leighton; Betsey d. 8 Oct 1822. Daniel m. 2nd, about 1823, MARY FENLEY; Mary d. at Gray, 19 Jan 1855.

vii OTIS ALLEN, b. 20 Jul 1795; d. at Gray, 13 Mar 1873; m. at North Yarmouth, 9 Oct 1817, CLARISSA LEIGHTON, b. 20 Apr 1800 daughter of John and Leonice (Sawyer) Leighton; Clarissa d. at Gray, 16 Jun 1883.

viii JOSEPH ALLEN, b. 24 Feb 1798; d. at Gray, 25 Sep 1855; m. 2 Dec 1819, KATHERINE JANE ADAMS, b. at Gray 9 Jul 1799 daughter of Samuel and Mary (Allen) Adams;[1394] Katherine d. 3 Aug 1876.

ix LYDIA ALLEN, b. 16 Apr 1800; d. 9 Oct 1801

x SUSANNAH ALLEN, b. 9 Apr 1802

xi JOSIAH ALLEN, b. 9 Apr 1802; d. at Gray, 28 Jun 1861; m. ELEANOR "NELLY" FRANK, b. 23 Jan 1804 daughter of Josiah and Mary (Small) Frank; Nelly d. at Gray, 23 Nov 1863.[1395]

xii ELVIRA ALLEN, b. 24 Aug 1804; d. at Gray, 8 Jun 1885; m. at Portland, 10 Jan 1847, ISAAC ADAMS, b. at Limington, ME, Nov 1794 son of Samuel and Mary (Allen) Adams; Isaac d. at Gray, 24 Aug 1872. Isaac was first married to Sarah Smith who died in 1846.

xiii WILLIAM B. ALLEN, b. 8 May 1808; d. at Gray, 10 Jan 1828.[1396]

There is one child known for Joseph Allen and Dorcas Emery.

i EMERY ALLEN, b. at Windham, ME, 1 May 1812; d. at Gray, 5 May 1895; m. 1st, ANN Y. BLAKE, b. 1815; Ann d. at Gray, 1853. Emery m. 2nd, SUSAN W., b. 1815; Susan d. at Gray, 1868.

514a) MARY ALLEN *(Mary Osgood Allen⁴, Hannah Abbott Osgood³, George², George¹)*, b. at Gloucester, 3 Nov 1748 daughter and William and Mary (Osgood) Allen; d. likely at New Gloucester, about 1815; m. at New Gloucester, 8 Jul 1775, PETER GRAFFAM, b. about 1742 son of Caleb and Lois (Bennett) Graffam; Peter d. at New Gloucester, 3 May 1783. Peter was firs married to Mary Wilson.

Mary Allen and Peter Graffam were parents of four children born at New Gloucester.

i DORCAS GRAFFAM, b. 21 Oct 1776; d. at Buckfield, ME; m. at New Gloucester, 25 Oct 1798, JOSIAH BAILEY, b. about 1770; Josiah d. at Buckfield, 1834.

ii LOIS GRAFFAM, b. 29 Sep 1779; d. at Windham, ME, 2 May 1798.

iii LUCY GRAFFAM, b. 11 Mar 1782; d. at Brunswick, ME, after 1860. Lucy did not marry. She lived in the poor house in Brunswick in her later years.

iv SARAH GRAFFAM, b. 14 Jun 1783; no further record found.

515) ELIZABETH ALLEN *(Mary Osgood Allen⁴, Hannah Abbott Osgood³, George², George¹)*, b. at Gloucester, MA, 27 Oct 1752 daughter of William and Mary (Osgood) Allen; d. at Portland, ME, Apr 1850; m. 12 Oct 1773, SAMUEL STEVENS, b. at Gloucester, 12 Mar 1748 son of William and Elizabeth (Allen) Stevens; Samuel d. at Gloucester, 9 Dec 1795.

Samuel Stevens was a merchant in Gloucester, Massachusetts. In his will written 5 December 1795 (probate 4 January 1796), Samuel Stevens leaves the use and improvement of the entire estate to dear wife Elizabeth to be at her disposal for the support of Elizabeth, their children, and Samuel's only sister. He wishes that his sister remain living with the family. If his wife and only son William enter into joint business, then they will divide the profits as they think will be of the most benefit

---

1394 Adams, *A Genealogical History of Robert Adams*, p 120

1395 Josiah and his wife Eleanor (Nelly) are included in the same cemetery record as Otis Allen and his wife Clarissa Leighton and their children. Maine, Nathan Hale Cemetery Collection.

1396 The names of William's parents are given as Joseph and Mary of his gravestone.

to the family. The management of the estate is left to Elizabeth at her prudence and discretion. At Elizabeth's death, the estate is to be equally divided among his surviving children although they are not named. Elizabeth is named sole executor. The total value of the estate was $6,206.19.[1397]

Samuel and Elizabeth Stevens had seven children whose births (or baptisms) are recorded at Gloucester.

i ELIZABETH STEVENS, b. 31 Jan 1775; d. at Portland, ME, 22 Nov 1818. Elizabeth did not marry.

ii WILLIAM SAMUEL STEVENS, b. 28 Oct 1776; d. at Portland, 27 Aug 1804.

iii JUDITH STEVENS, b. 12 Mar 1780 (baptized 19 Mar 1780); d. at Portland, 18 Apr 1842; she is likely the Judith Stevens of Portland[1398] that m. 1820 as his second wife, JOSEPH BARBOUR, b. 1776 son of Joseph and Elizabeth (Goodridge) Barbour; Joseph d. at Portland, 30 May 1854. Joseph married first, Lucy Potter, and third married Agnes Archer.

iv ANNA STEVENS, b. 5 Jul 1782; d. at Cambridge, MA, 26 Dec 1861. Anna did not marry.

v MARY STEVENS, b. 20 Mar 1784; d. at Portland, 19 Nov 1803.

vi LUCY STEVENS, b. 13 Mar 1787; d. at Cambridge, MA, 30 Dec 1870; m. at Portland, 9 Jul 1812, EDWARD RUSSELL, b. 31 Aug 1782 son of Edward and Hannah (Clark) Russell; Edward d. at North Yarmouth, ME, 29 Nov 1835.

vii ESTHER STEVENS, b. 1790 (baptized 4 Apr 1790); d. at Portland, 23 Jan 1840. Esther did not marry.

516) DORCAS ALLEN *(Mary Osgood Allen[4], Hannah Abbott Osgood[3], George[2], George[1])*, b. at Gloucester, 11 Aug 1754 daughter of William and Mary (Osgood) Allen; d. at Cumberland County, ME, 27 Dec 1785; m. 24 Jun 1779, DAVID HAYES, b. 12 Oct 1755 son of John and Judith (Moulton) Hays; David d. in Cumberland County, ME, 30 Aug 1793.

Dorcas Allen and David Hayes were parents of four children born at North Yarmouth, Maine.

i JOSEPH HAYES, b. 25 Jul 1780; d. at Yarmouth, 3 Mar 1838; m. at Cumberland, 27 Mar 1803, MARY KNIGHT, b. at Boothbay, ME, about 1782 daughter of Daniel and Mary (Winslow) Knight;[1399] Mary d. at North Yarmouth, 26 Apr 1843.

ii JOHN HAYES, b. 22 Nov 1781; d. at North Yarmouth, 31 Jul 1860; m. by 1808, RACHEL HAWKS, b. about 1781; Rachel d. at North Yarmouth, 11 Mar 1866.

iii WILLIAM ALLEN HAYES, b. 20 Oct 1783; d. at South Berwick, 15 Apr 1851; m. at Berwick, 2 Jun 1811, SUSANNAH LORD, b. about 1790 daughter of John and Mehitable (Perkins) Lord; Susannah d. at South Berwick, 20 Sep 1870.

iv DORCAS HAYES, b. 17 Dec 1785; nothing further found.

517) JOHN ALLEN *(Mary Osgood Allen[4], Hannah Abbott Osgood[3], George[2], George[1])*, b. at Gloucester, 25 Mar 1756 son of William and Mary (Osgood) Allen; d. at Minot, ME, 6 Mar 1834; m. 9 Apr 1791, RACHEL WORTHLEY, b. at Yarmouth, ME, 24 Mar 1764 daughter of John and Martha (Bailey) Worthley; Rachel d. at Minot, 9 Jan 1832.

John Allen and Rachel Worthley were parents of nine children, the births recorded at either Poland or Minot, Maine.

i WILLIAM ALLEN, b. at Poland, 2 Dec 1790; d. at Minot, ME, 5 Mar 1838. William did not marry.

ii RACHEL ALLEN, b. at Poland, 20 Oct 1792; d. at Minot, 27 Dec 1807.

iii BENJAMIN ALLEN, b. 10 May 1795; d. at Minot, 21 Mar 1887; m. at Minot, 27 Sep 1817, BETSEY BRAY, b. 22 Feb 1799;[1400] Betsey d. at Minot, 18 Apr 1887.

[1397] *Essex County, Massachusetts, Probate Records and Indexes 1638-1916;* Author: *Massachusetts. Court of Insolvency (Essex County);* Probate Place: *Essex, Massachusetts, Probate Records, Vol 362-364, Book 62-64, 1792-1797*, pp 243-244. Probate case number 26428

[1398] There is a Judith Stevens born in 1780 in NH daughter of Daniel who some suggest as the wife of Joseph Barbour, but it seems more likely that it is Judith daughter of Samuel that married Joseph.

[1399] Greene, *History of Boothbay*, p 556

[1400] Date of birth is given on her cemetery index card; Maine, Faylene Hutton Cemetery Collection

iv MARTHA "PATTY" ALLEN, b. at Minot, 21 Oct 1797; d. at Minot, 7 Jul 1881; m. at Minot, 5 Sep 1822, MATTHIAS PLANT SAWYER, b. at Salisbury, MA, 6 Jun 1799 son of George and Judith (Boardman) Sawyer; Matthias d. at Minot, 24 Nov 1879.

v SARAH ALLEN, b. at Minot, 27 Nov 1800; d. at Minot, 17 Jun 1878. Sarah does not seem to have married. In 1850, she was Sarah Allen living with her sister Martha Allen Sawyer.

vi MARY ALLEN, b. at Minot, 9 Nov 1803; d. at Lincoln, ME, 23 Nov 1835; m. 1827, SAMUEL TOBIE, b. at New Gloucester, 28 Dec 1802 son of Jonathan L. and Lydia (Parsons) Tobie; Samuel d. at Lincoln, 5 Jan 1890. After Mary's death, Samuel married Polly Webber.

vii JOHN ALLEN, b. at Minot, 23 Feb 1806; d. at Lincoln, 2 May 1888; m. at Lincoln, 27 Mar 1836, HANNAH SLEEPER PEASLEE, b. at Vassalboro, 21 May 1813 daughter of William and Patience (-) Peaslee; Hannah d. at Lincoln, 21 May 1878.

viii ROSANNA ALLEN, b. at Minot, 28 Apr 1810; d. at Minot, 6 Jul 1836.

518) CHRISTOPHER ALLEN *(Mary Osgood Allen⁴, Hannah Abbott Osgood³, George², George¹)*, b. at Gloucester, 16 Apr 1765 son of William and Mary (Osgood) Allen; d. at Hebron, ME, 20 Jul 1819; m. 25 Jun 1808, DOLLY POOR, b. at Andover, 12 Oct 1772 daughter of Ebenezer and Susanna (Varnum) Poor; Dolly d. 1826.

Christopher and his brother Samuel came together to Hebron, Maine from New Gloucester. They purchased property adjoining the Craigie farm. The farms of the brothers were prosperous.[1401] Samuel did not marry. In his will dated April 1841, Samuel left his estate to the children of his brother Christopher: William Stevens Allen, Susan Varnum Allen, Mary Osgood Allen, and Martha Bridge Allen. The estate included 200 acres that was purchased by Christopher and Samuel from Andrew Craigie on 2 April 1811. Samuel added a codicil to his will in which he specifically cuts off other heirs-at-law, the children of several other siblings as it is his intent to leave all his property to the children of Christopher for whom he has "special regard."[1402]

The estate of Christopher Allen entered probate on 5 October 1819. Dolly Allen was named administrator of the estate. The value of real property was $3,200 including the homestead with 200 acres of land valued at $3,000. The personal estate was valued at $1,529.05 which included livestock, grain, and farm tools. The distribution of the estate is not included in the available probate documents.[1403]

Christopher Allen and Dolly Poor were parents of four children born at Hebron, Maine.

i WILLIAM STEVENS ALLEN, b. 24 Aug 1809; d. at Auburn, ME, 5 Jan 1882; m. at Hebron, 3 Feb 1842, ELVIRA PIKE, b. at Hebron, 6 Aug 1819 daughter of Robert and Susanna (Bickford) Pike; Elvira d. at Auburn, 17 Dec 1903.

ii SUSANNA VARNUM ALLEN, b. 1 Oct 1811; d. at Otisfield, 12 Jul 1892; m. 24 Mar 1853, SAMUEL CHAMBERS, b. at Otisfield, 10 Jan 1809 son of Thomas B. and Dorothy (Merriam) Chambers; Samuel d. at Otisfield, 14 Aug 1862.

iii MARY OSGOOD ALLEN, b. 10 Oct 1814; d. at Lewiston, 22 Nov 1888; m. at Piscataquis County, ME, 30 Jun 1847, CHARLES L. OLIVER, b. at Bethel, 27 Dec 1819 son of William and Hannah (-) Oliver; Charles d. at Lewiston, 19 Jun 1872.

iv MARTHA BRIDGE ALLEN, b. 18 Oct 1816; d. at Haverhill, MA, 17 May 1894; m. 16 Jan 1844, AARON SUMNER HILL, b. at Bucksport, 15 Feb 1814 son of Aaron and Anne (Paine) Hill; Aaron d. at Skowhegan, 20 Dec 1864.

519) AARON ALLEN *(Mary Osgood Allen⁴, Hannah Abbott Osgood³, George², George¹)*, b. at Gloucester, 17 Dec 1766 son of William and Mary (Osgood) Allen; d. before 1840; m. at New Gloucester, ME, 27 Aug 1797, MARTHA PRINCE, b. at New Gloucester, 7 Jul 1773 daughter of John and Mary (-) Prince; Martha d. after 1840 when she was head of household at Pownal, ME.

Aaron Allen and Martha Prince were parents of six children, births record at various locations.

i ABIGAIL ALLEN, b. at New Portland, 25 Nov 1797 (this may be a duplicate record for Abigail just below but the years on the birth transcriptions are different).

1401 King, *Annals of Oxford, Maine*, p 127

1402 *Maine. Probate Court (Oxford County)*; Probate Place: *Oxford, Maine, Probate Records, Vol 11-12, 1842-1846*, will of Samuel Allen.

1403 *Maine. Probate Court (Oxford County)*; Probate Place: *Oxford, Maine, Probate Records, Box A-C, Pre 1820*, probate of Christopher Allen

ii ABIGAIL ALLEN, b. at New Gloucester, 27 Nov 1798; d. after 1860 when she was living at Farmingdale, ME; m. at Richmond, ME, 15 Feb 1824, CALEB WATERHOUSE, b. about 1801 son of Elias and Mary (Waterhouse) Waterhouse; Caleb d. at Charlestown, MA, 15 Jul 1865.

iii MARTHA ALLEN, b. at Durham, ME, 21 Oct 1799

iv MARY HASKELL ALLEN, b. at Durham, ME, 25 Jan 1802

v AARON ALLEN, b. at New Gloucester, 6 Mar 1804; d. at New Portland, 6 Oct 1806.

vi JEREMIAH ALLEN, b. at New Portland, 8 Nov 1808

520) ABIGAIL HOLT *(Sarah Abbott Holt[4], Elizabeth Abbott Abbott[3], George[2], George[1])*, b. 18 Jun 1758 daughter of James and Sarah (Abbott) Holt; d. 2 Oct 1824; m. 7 Dec 1780, her fourth cousin, ISAAC CHANDLER, b. 4 Oct 1754 son of William and Rebecca (Lovejoy) Chandler; Isaac d. 12 Jan 1832. After Abigail's death, Isaac married Elizabeth Upton.

Isaac Chandler was a farmer and the family lived on the farm that had belonged to Abigail Holt's maternal grandfather Benjamin Abbott.[1404] The property owned by Isaac Chandler is the site of 17 Hidden Road in Andover. The house on the property was built by David Hidden, a son-in-law of Isaac and Abigail Chandler.[1405] The house was built in 1812 on Isaac's property and half the house was deeded to David Hidden in 1828. The house passed into the hands of the two children of David and Mary (Chandler) Hidden, Mary Elizabeth Hidden and David Isaac Chandler Hidden.

Isaac Chandler wrote his will 9 November 1831. Wife Elizabeth receives a bequest of $300 and is allowed all the household property that she brought to the marriage providing that Elizabeth quit claim and release the estate from her right of dower. Beloved granddaughter Sarah Ann Chandler receives $100 in addition to what she has already received. Beloved daughter Mary Hidden wife of David Hidden receives one-fourth part of the estate. Beloved daughter Abigail Chandler receives the remaining three-fourths of the estate. Captain Timothy Flagg was named sole executor. The real property of the estate was valued at $3,230.00 including the homestead valued at $2,200.00. The personal estate was valued at $96.33.[1406]

Isaac and Abigail Chandler had five children born at Andover.

i ABIGAIL CHANDLER, b. 13 Dec 1781; d. 20 Sep 1788.

ii ISAAC CHANDLER, b. 11 Jun 1784; d. 28 Sep 1813; m. 7 Nov 1812, SALLY THOMPSON, b. at Wilmington, 18 Jul 1789 daughter of Benjamin and Susanna (Jaquith) Thompson; Sally d. at Wilmington, 19 Sep 1853.

iii MARY CHANDLER, b. 5 Jun 1786; d. at Andover, 9 Sep 1855; m. 1 Jul 1816, DAVID HIDDEN, b. at Newbury, 21 Sep 1784 son of David and Susanna (Jaquith) Hidden; David d. at Andover, 5 Jun 1861.

iv ABIGAIL CHANDLER, b. 3 Sep 1794; d. at Andover, 22 Oct 1866. Abigail did not marry. She lived with her sister Mary and her family. Abigail's estate was valued at $2,635.00 which included real estate valued at $485.00 and $2,150.00 in amounts that were due to the estate. In her will, Abigail made bequests of $150 to her niece Sarah Ann Crocker, $300 to niece Mary E. Hidden, and the remainder of the estate to her nephew David I. C. Hidden who was also named executor.

v HANNAH CHANDLER, b. 10 Jan 1798; d. from fever 1 May 1807.

521) MARY ABBOTT *(George[4], George[3], George[2], George[1])*, b. at Andover, 29 Jun 1753 daughter of George and Hannah (Lovejoy) Abbott; d. 17 Aug 1820; m. 26 Dec 1768, JOSEPH POOR, b. 7 Nov 1748 son of Thomas and Mary (Adams) Poor; Joseph d. at Danvers 2 Mar 1815.

Joseph Poor was a tanner by trade, a business that was carried on by his son Joseph with great success. Joseph served as deacon of the church from 1796 until his death in 1815.[1407]

Rather than the traditional "In the name of God amen," Joseph Poor begins his will "This is the last will and testament of me Joseph Poor of Danvers in the county of Essex & Commonwealth of Massachusetts." His beloved wife (not named) receives all the personal estate and improvement on all the remainder of the estate not otherwise bequeathed as long as she remains a widow. Son Nathan receives half the tanyard and all the buildings that go with it. Daughter Martha receives $100 which is equivalent to what his other daughters have received. He bequeaths to his wife and each of his children (except Daniel who has received his share) $100 which is their respective share of $1000 which he had received following the death of

---

[1404] Chandler, *Descendants of William and Annis Chandler*, p 422

[1405] "17 Hidden Road," https://preservation.mhl.org/17-hidden-road

[1406] Essex County, MA: Probate File Papers, 1638-1881. Probate of Isaac Chandler, 21 Feb 1832, case number 4934.

[1407] Cutter, *Genealogical and Personal Memoirs Relating to Families of Boston, volume I*, p 144

his son George. Following the decease of his wife, all the real estate is to be divided in nine equal shares among his nine children although amounts that any of the children owe him will be figured into the amount of the bequest. Sons Nathan and Joseph are named executors. The children receiving legacies are Joseph Poor, Sylvester and Mary Proctor, Richard and Hannah Osborn, Enoch Poor, Benjamin and Sally Jacobs, Nathan Poor, Rufus and Betsey Wyman, and Martha Poor. Widow is Mary Poor. The estate was valued at $5,083.24.[1408]

Mary Abbott and Joseph Poor were parents of eleven children all born at Danvers.

i JOSEPH POOR, b. 28 Mar 1771; d. at Danvers, 19 Apr 1850; m. 1st, 9 Dec 1795, TAMISON SPRAGUE, b. at Danvers, 13 Apr 1773 daughter of Ebenezer and Hannah (Upton) Sprague; Tamison d. at Danvers, 2 Oct 1803. Joseph m. 2nd, 3 Feb 1805, SARAH REED, b. at Danvers, 20 Feb 1783 daughter of William and Elizabeth (Manning) Reed; Sarah d. at Peabody, 10 Jan 1861.

ii MARY POOR, b. 26 Apr 1773; d. at Danvers, 20 Oct 1846; m. 10 Oct 1793, SYLVESTER PROCTOR, b. at Danvers, 1 Jul 1769 son of Sylvester and Abigail (Gale) Proctor; Sylvester d. at Danvers, 20 Sep 1852.

iii HANNAH POOR, b. 30 Apr 1775; d. at Danvers, 9 Feb 1836; m. at Danvers, 13 Dec 1799, RICHARD OSBORN, b. at Danvers, 26 Aug 1769 son of James and Persis (Littlefield) Osborn; Richard d. at Danvers, 16 Aug 1826.

iv ENOCH POOR, b. 20 Jan 1777; d. at Danvers, 11 Dec 1836; m. 22 Sep 1803, SALLY SHILLABER, b. at Danvers, 23 Jun 1775 daughter of William and Mary (Waters) Shillaber; Sally d. at Salem, 2 Feb 1857.

v SARAH POOR, b. 21 Jul 1779; d. at Danvers, after 1855;[1409] m. 17 Jan 1802, BENJAMIN JACOBS, b. at South Danvers, 17 Jul 1775 son of Benjamin and Sarah (Moulton) Jacobs; Benjamin d. 11 Sep 1869.

vi GEORGE ABBOTT POOR, b. 26 Oct 1781; d. at sea, 1810. George A., s. Joseph and Mary (Abbot), "Saild from Salem, Feb. 10, 1810, not heard from."

vii NANCY POOR, b. 4 May 1784; d. 9 Mar 1804.

viii NATHAN POOR, b. 15 Sep 1786; d. at Danvers, 25 May 1842; m. 1st, 4 Feb 1810, MARGARET SILVER, b. at Salem, 14 Oct 1787 daughter of William and Jemima (Tewksbury) Silver; Margaret d. at Danvers, 18 Nov 1824. Nathan m. 2nd, 27 Feb 1826, HANNAH COOK MERRILL, b. at Salem, 2 Oct 1795 daughter of Joseph and Hannah (-) Merrill; Hannah d. at Peabody, 28 Feb 1882.

ix DANIEL POOR, b. 27 Jun 1789; d. at Manepy, Sri Lanka, 3 Feb 1855; m. 1st, at Danvers, 9 Oct 1815, SUSAN BULLFINCH, b. at Lynn, 1 Dev 1789 daughter of Jeremiah and Rebecca (Johnson) Bullfinch; Susan d. Tellippalai, Sri Lanka, 7 May 1821. Daniel m. 2nd, in Ceylon, 29 Jan 1823, ANN KNIGHT, b. at Rodborough, Gloucestershire, 10 Sep 1790 daughter of John and Elizabeth (-) Knight. Daniel Poor graduated from Dartmouth College and Andover Seminary. He was a missionary.[1410]

x BETSEY POOR, b. 21 Dec 1791; d. at Salem, 10 Nov 1844; m. at Danvers, 6 Aug 1809, RUFUS WYMAN, b. at Woburn, 14 Sep 1786 son of David and Lucy (Smith) Wyman.

xi MARTHA POOR, b. 20 Jun 1795; d. at Danvers, 28 Nov 1825; m. 5 Jun 1817, DAVID DANIELS, b. at South Danvers, 4 Mar 1796 son of David and Elizabeth (Shillaber) Daniels; David d. at Danvers, 10 Jan 1866. After Martha's death, David married Eunice Safford.

522) ELIZABETH ABBOTT *(George⁴, George³, George², George¹)*, b. at Andover, 10 Jul 1755 daughter of George and Hannah (Lovejoy) Abbott; d. 18 Aug 1821; m. 26 Jan 1775, SAMUEL LUMMUS, b. 31 Jul 1751 son of John and Hannah (Porter) Lummus; Samuel d. 10 Apr 1810.

In his will dated 29 March 1810 (proved 7 May 1810), Samuel Lummus bequeathed to beloved wife Elizabeth the improvement of one-half the real estate in Hamilton and Ipswich during her natural life. She also receives other specific provisions for her continued support. Son Samuel receives all the real estate in Hamilton, Ipswich, or any other town. There are monetary bequests to other children to be paid after the death of his wife, and with the provision that the children first satisfy any debts they have to their father. John receives one thousand two hundred dollars. Ezra receives five hundred dollars and is to learns a trade, the expenses of learning the trade to be paid by Samuel out of the estate. Daughter Betsey receives three hundred dollars but has received already two hundred-four dollars. Daughter Tamma also receives three hundred dollars with the allowance of one hundred forty-nine dollars received. Daughters Martha and Clara will each receive three hundred dollars at age eighteen or at the time of marriage. Granddaughter Hannah Ward receives four hundred dollars when eighteen or married. Son Samuel and Captain Robert Dodge were named executors. The value of the real estate at inventory was $6,024.00 and personal property of $7,441.55 with an offset of debts of $1,690.63.[1411]

[1408] Essex County, MA: Probate File Papers, 1638-1881. Probate of Joseph Poor, 19 Apr 1815, case number 22367. Will 17 March 1814

[1409] Sarah was living at the 1855 state census, but was not living in 1860.

[1410] Appletons' Cyclopedia of American Biography; Vol. VI, p 65

[1411] Essex County, MA: Probate File Papers, 1638-1881.Online database. AmericanAncestors.org. New England Historic Genealogical Society, 2014. Case 17357

Elizabeth Abbott and Samuel Lummus had ten children born at Hamilton. Several of the children (including Hannah, Samuel, Harriet, and Martha) died of consumption.

i ELIZABETH "BETTY" LUMMUS, b. 4 Feb 1776; d. at Brunswick, ME, after 1855; m. at Hamilton, 31 Dec 1795, DANIEL COGSWELL, b. at Ipswich, Sep 1769 son of Joseph and Abigail (Patch) Cogswell; Daniel d. at Ipswich, 1 Feb 1810.

ii HANNAH LUMMUS, b. 5 Oct 1777; d. at Hamilton, 15 Jun 1803; m. at Hamilton, 22 Jul 1800, JOSEPH WARD, who was "of Gorham", son of Joseph Ward.[1412] Joseph d. at Gorham, ME before 1803. Hannah was a widow at the time of her death.

iii SAMUEL LUMMUS, b. 6 Aug 1779; d. at Hamilton, 18 May 1817; m. at Gorham, ME, 31 May 1801, MARGARET ELDER, b. at Gorham, 22 Sep 1774 daughter of Isaac and (Hunnewell) Elder; Margaret d. at Beverly, 15 Aug 1833.

iv SALLY LUMMUS, b. 7 Aug 1781; d. 9 Jan 1791.

v JOHN LUMMUS, b. 9 Dec 1783; d. 1813;[1413] m. at Topsfield, 17 Sep 1804, ELIZABETH CUMMINGS, b. at Topsfield, 26 May 1783 daughter of Jonathan and Elizabeth (White) Cummings; Elizabeth d. at Wenham, 18 Aug 1851.

vi TAMISON "TAMMY" LUMMUS, b. 1 Sep 1786; d. at Wenham, 11 Jan 1878; m. at Hamilton, 11 Nov 1806, SIMON GAMMON, b. at Gorham, ME, 13 Jun 1782 son of Daniel and Mary (Blanchard) Gammon; Simon d. at sea, 1818.

vii MARTHA "PATTY" LUMMUS, b. 27 Jul 1789; d. at Hamilton, 19 Sep 1814; m. 7 Feb 1813, ELISHA BENNETT

viii HARRIET LUMMUS, b. 23 Jan 1793; d. at Hamilton, 30 Dec 1809.

ix EZRA LUMMUS, b. 17 Mar 1795; d. at Brooklyn, NY, 14 Nov 1869; m. at Newburyport, 25 Jan 1817, ANN STICKNEY, b. at Newburyport, 8 Feb 1796 daughter of Ebenezer and Mary (Pierce) Stickney; Ann d. after 1869 (living at the time of probate of her husband's estate). As directed in his father's will, Ezra learned the trade of blacksmith. He was also a hotel keeper in New York.[1414]

x CLARISSA "CLARA" LUMMUS, b. 11 Mar 1796; d. at Bradford, MA, 23 Sep 1854; m. at Wenham, 22 Dec 1829, WILLIAM FAIRFIELD PORTER, b. 18 Apr 1806 son of Jonathan and Martha (Fairfield) Porter;[1415] William d. at Jacksonville, FL, 20 Nov 1878.

523) JOHN LOVEJOY ABBOT *(George⁴, George³, George², George¹)*, b. at Andover, 12 Apr 1757 son of George and Hannah (Lovejoy) Abbott; d. 1 Nov 1837; m. 29 Oct 1782, his third cousin once removed, PHEBE ABBOT, b. Apr 1763 daughter of Nehemiah and Hannah (Ballard) Abbot; Phebe d. about 1826.

John L. Abbot was a farmer in Andover but was referred to as esquire in his community indicating his status.

In his will written 11 July 1835 (proved 7 November 1837), John L. Abbot bequeaths his wearing apparel to his sons Samuel Abbot and William Abbot. Daughter Martha J. Abbot and son William Abbot each receives five hundred dollars. Widow Elizabeth Manning formerly the wife of son Rev. John L. Abbot receives fifty dollars. The executor is authorized to sell real estate, if necessary, to pay any debts, funeral charges, and the monetary legacies. Daughter-in-law Mrs. Ruth Abbot receives two cows, six sheep, and one-half of the swine. That with what was previously given to her late husband George Abbot completes her portion of the estate. Of the residue of the estate, one-fifth part is bequeathed to son Samuel Abbot who is to hold this portion in trust for the benefit of daughter Hannah Herrick wife of Elijah L. Herrick. After Hannah's decease, this fifth portion is to go to her heirs-at-law. One-fifth part of the residue of the estate is bequeathed to Sarah Elizabeth Hull and Martha Abbot Hull, the children of his daughter Sarah and Sidney Hull. The remaining three-fifths of the residue is bequeathed to children Samuel Abbot, William Abbot, and Martha J. Abbot. Son Samuel Abbot was named executor. Real estate was valued at inventory at $9,919.00 and personal estate at $1,032.37.[1416]

John Lovejoy Abbot and Phebe Abbot were parents of ten children born at Andover.

[1412] McLellan, *History of Gorham, Maine*, p 798

[1413] The birth record of John's son John states that John was "lately deceased." John, s. John, lately deceased, bp. Oct. 10, 1813. C. R. (Hamilton, MA vital records)

[1414] Massachusetts, Mason Membership Cards, 1733-1990

[1415] Porter, A Genealogy of the Descendants of Richard Porter

[1416] Essex County, MA: Probate File Papers, 1638-1881.Online database. AmericanAncestors.org. New England Historic Genealogical Society, 2014. Case 78

i JOHN LOVEJOY ABBOT, b. 29 Nov 1783; d. at Boston, 17 Oct 1814; m. at Cambridge, 24 Oct 1813, ELIZA BELL WARLAND, b. at Cambridge, 15 Jun 1785 daughter of Thomas and Elizabeth (Bell) Warland; Eliza d. at Cambridge, 4 Mar 1880. After John's death, Eliza married Samuel Manning. Rev. John Lovejoy Abbot graduated Harvard and was a clergyman. He also served as librarian at Harvard for two years. He died of consumption.

ii GEORGE ABBOT, b. 25 Apr 1785; d. at Andover, 21 Oct 1822; m. at Andover, 3 Nov 1808, RUTH DIXON, b. at Charlestown, about 1786; Ruth d. at Andover, 8 Apr 1869.

iii SAMUEL ABBOT, b. 29 Jun 1787; d. at Charlestown, 10 Aug 1852; m. at Charlestown, 23 Nov 1817, LUCRETIA FOWLE, b. at Boston, 21 Mar 1798 daughter of Jonathan and Sarah (Makepeace) Fowle; Lucretia d. at Charlestown, 7 Oct 1859.

iv PHEBE ABBOT, b. 15 Jun 1789; d. 11 Nov 1811.

v LYDIA CLARK ABBOT, b. Jul 1791; d. 16 Mar 1796.

vi HANNAH ABBOT, b. 17 Feb 1793; d. at Rockford, IL, 28 Mar 1876; m. at Andover, 9 May 1815, ELIJAH LAWRENCE HERRICK, b. at Reading, 10 Nov 1786 son of John and Mary (Lawrence) Herrick; Elijah d. at Rockford, 15 May 1852.

vii WILLIAM LOVEJOY ABBOT, b. 25 Jan 1795; d. 27 Mar 1796.

viii SARAH KNEELAND ABBOT, b. 7 Jul 1797; d. at New Haven, CT, 2 Jan 1834; m. 1st, at Andover, 13 Oct 1822, HEZEKIAH HULL, b. at New Haven, 20 Aug 1796 son of Samuel and Mehitable "Mabel" (Bradley) Hull; Hezekiah d. at Alexandria, LA, 3 Aug 1823. Sarah m 2nd, 19 Jul 1825, Hezekiah's brother, SIDNEY HULL, b. at New Haven, 28 Aug 1784; Sidney d. at New Haven, 21 Aug 1861. Sarah was the third of Sidney Hull's five wives; Sarah's sister Martha was his fourth wife. Sidney's other marriages were to Rebecca Alling, Esther Bradley, and Ann Colburn. Hezekiah Hull was a minister having graduated from Andover Seminary. Hezekiah and Sarah were in Alexandria, Louisiana doing missionary work when Hezekiah died there of yellow fever.[1417]

ix MARTHA JENKS ABBOT, b. 26 Nov 1799; d. at New Haven, 3 Dec 1836; m. at Andover, 17 Apr 1836, as his fourth wife, SIDNEY HULL (see Sarah just above).

x WILLIAM ABBOT, b. 16 Dec 1809; d. at Andover, 28 Aug 1902; m. 1st, at New Haven, 4 Apr 1836, AMELIA HULL, b. at New Haven, 20 Apr 1809 daughter of Sidney and Rebecca (Alling) Hull (Sidney Hull was the husband of William's sisters Sarah and Martha); Amelia d. at New Haven, 16 Jul 1837. William m. 2nd, at New Haven, 11 May 1840, ELIZABETH M. BRADLEY, b. at New Haven, about 1811; Elizabeth d. at Charlestown, 16 Mar 1844. William m. 3rd, at Charlestown, 24 Dec 1845, SUSAN E. HUNT, b. Nov 1816 daughter of Enoch and Esther (Kettell) Hunt; Susan d. at Andover, 17 Jun 1902.

524) SAMUEL ABBOTT *(George⁴, George³, George², George¹)*, b. at Andover, 19 Sep 1760 son of George and Hannah (Lovejoy) Abbott; d. at Saco, ME, 8 May 1792; m. 24 Jun 1788, MARY CUTTS, b. at Saco, 19 Jul 1763 daughter of Thomas and Elizabeth (Scammon) Cutts; Mary d. 27 Mar 1796.[1418]

Little is known about this family. Samuel was born in Andover but relocated to Saco, Maine where he married. Samuel and Mary had two children before both Samuel and Mary died at young ages. Their two sons also died in young adulthood prior to marrying. Captain Samuel Phillips Abbott died by drowning at New London, Connecticut.[1419] Thomas Cutts Abbott was a midshipman aboard the USS Constellation when he died aboard ship (cause not given).[1420] At the time of his death, the Constellation was returning from service in the Second Barbary War.[1421]

i SAMUEL PHILLIPS ABBOTT, b. at Saco about 1788; d. at New London, CT, 27 Jan 1813.

ii THOMAS CUTTS ABBOTT, b. at Saco about 1789; d. aboard the USS Constellation, 13 Dec 1817.

525) MARTHA ABBOTT *(George⁴, George³, George², George¹)*, b. at Andover, 17 Oct 1764 daughter of George and Hannah (Lovejoy) Abbott; d. at Salem, 15 Sep 1798; m. 31 Aug 1788 as his second wife, JOHN JENKS, b. at Medford, 6 Dec 1751 son of John and Rebecca (Newhall) Jenks. John married first Hannah Andrew and third Annis Pauling. John d. 14 Oct 1817.

John Jenks was a successful merchant in Salem who specialized in goods imported from England.[1422]

1417 Morse-Corbin Papers, New Haven Colony Historical Society

1418 Howard, *Genealogy of the Cutts Family in America*, p. 85

1419 Connecticut, Hale Collection of Cemetery Inscriptions and Newspaper Notices, 1629-1934

1420 Ancestry.com, U.S., Navy Casualties Books, 1776-1941, volume I 1776-1885.

1421 Navy Department, Dictionary of American Naval Fighting Ships, p 171

1422 Guide to the Winterthur Library, p 290

The distribution of the estate of John Jenks included the payment of one-third part of the estate to widow Annis Jenks in the amount of $3,831.29, and each of the children received the sum of $776.25 and eight mills. The children listed are John Jenks, Sarah Furness, Hannah A. Thomas, Priscilla A. Osborne, Martha Jenks, Mary Orne Jenks, Annis Pulling Jenks, George Washington Jenks, Richard Pulling Jenks, and Horace Howard Jenks. The total value of the estate available for distribution was $11,643.87. John Jenks and Sarah Furness are children from the first marriage, Hannah Thomas, Priscilla Osborne, and Martha Jenks are from the second marriage, and the other five children are from the third marriage.[1423]

Martha Abbott and John Jenks had four children born at Salem.

i PRISCILLA ABBOT JENKS, b. 28 Jun 1789; d. at Fairfield, CT, 6 Sep 1853;[1424] m. at Salem, 14 May 1809, WILLIAM OSBORN, b. at Danvers, 29 Jul 1786 son of Joseph and Mary (Shillaber) Osborn; William d. at Fairfield, 17 Feb 1839.[1425]

ii MARTHA JENKS, b. 12 Jun 1791; d. at Norwich, CT, 9 Sep 1828. Martha did not marry.

iii HANNAH ANDREW JENKS, b. 24 May 1793; d. at Norwich, 25 May 1869; m. at Salem, 25 Oct 1815, HENRY THOMAS, b. at Norwich, 25 Aug 1780 son of Ebenezer and Chloe (Allen) Thomas;[1426] Henry d. 12 Jun 1854.

iv ANDREW JENKS, b. Jun 1796; likely died young; he is not included in the distribution of his father's estate.

526) DORCAS ABBOTT *(George⁴, George³, George², George¹)*, b. at Andover, Dec 1766 daughter of George and Hannah (Lovejoy) Abbott; d. 15 Mar 1841; m. at Andover, 6 Jan 1792, her third cousin, JOHN HOLT *(Joshua Holt⁴, Dorcas Abbott Holt³, Timothy², George¹)*, b. 12 Jan 1765 son of Joshua and Phebe (Farnum) Holt; John d. 11 Feb 1835.

Dorcas Abbott and John Holt married in Andover, but were soon after in Greenfield, New Hampshire where they reared their family.

In his will written 17 April 1827, John Holt bequeaths to beloved wife Dorcas use of one-half of the dwelling house while she remains a widow and all the household furniture not otherwise disposed of the be at her own disposal. There are also several specific provisions for the continued care and support of Dorcas. This includes provisions for medical care if needed, annual supplies of staple goods, and $200 in cash. Daughter Dorcas wife of Peter Pevey receives $50; daughter Sarah wife of Francis Dunkley, $50; daughter Tamesin, $250; daughter Phebe, $250; daughter Martha, $250; and daughter Elizabeth, $250. He also provides that the four unmarried daughters can remain in the mother's household if they choose to do so. He also wills that the four daughters, if employed, should pay some moderate amount to continue to live in the home and this is to be paid to their brother John. His only son John receives all the estate real and personal not otherwise disposed of. The wearing apparel is to be divided equally between John and his brothers-in-law. John is named sole executor.[1427]

Dorcas Abbott and John Holt were parents of eight children born at Greenfield.

i DORCAS HOLT, b. 12 Jan 1793; d. at Greenfield, 4 Jan 1856; m. about 1815, PETER PEAVEY, b. at Wilton, 27 Jul 1788 son of Peter and Lucy (Cummings) Peavey; Peter d. at Greenfield, 26 Oct 1879. After Dorcas's death, Peter married her sister Tamesin (see below).

ii SARAH HOLT, b. 10 Mar 1795; d. at Francestown, 4 Jun 1885; m. at Greenfield, 28 Feb 1817, FRANCIS DUNCKLEE, b. at Greenfield, 1791 son of Hezekiah and Mehitable (White) Duncklee; Francis d. at Francestown, 14 Feb 1859.

iii HANNAH HOLT, b. 15 Sep 1797; d. at Greenfield, 10 Nov 1821.

iv JOHN HOLT, b. 9 Aug 1799; d. at Greenfield, 16 Apr 1869; m. 1st, 1836, his first cousin, PHEBE HOLT *(Hannah Holt Holt⁵, Joshua Holt⁴, Dorcas Abbott Holt³, Timothy², George¹)*, b. 9 Jun 1797 daughter of Ephraim and Hannah (Holt) Holt; Phebe d. at Greenfield, 8 May 1862. John m. 2nd, about 1863, MARY R. HOLT, b. 1823 (based on census records) whose parents are not identified; Mary d. at Greenfield, 24 Aug 1868. Phebe Holt is a child in Family 872.

v TAMESIN HOLT, b. 23 Nov 1803; d. at Greenfield, 4 Jan 1896; m. about 1857, PETER PEAVEY who was first married to her sister Dorcas (see above).

[1423] Essex County, MA: Probate File Papers, 1638-1881.Online database. AmericanAncestors.org. New England Historic Genealogical Society, 2014.Case 14849

[1424] U.S., Newspaper Extractions from the Northeast, 1704-1930

[1425] Connecticut, Deaths and Burials Index, 1650-1934

[1426] Mayflower Births and Deaths, Vol. 1 and 2

[1427] *New Hampshire. Probate Court (Hillsborough County)*; Probate Place: *Hillsborough, New Hampshire, Probate Records, Vol 40-41, 1833-1835*, pp 32-34

vi PHEBE FARNUM HOLT, b. 1806; d. at Bennington, NH, 31 Oct 1880; m. 30 Apr 1844, as his second wife, FRANCIS BURNHAM. b. at Greenfield, 13 Jan 1784 son of Nathaniel and Mary (-) Burnham; Francis d. at Greenfield, 27 Mar 1870. Francis was first married to Mary Fletcher.

vii MARTHA HOLT, b. 24 Apr 1808; d. at Portsmouth, NH, 10 Mar 1895; m. about 1837, as his second wife, ARNOLD B. HUTCHINSON, b. at Lyndeborough, 17 Apr 1808 son of Ebenezer and Thomasin (Griffin) Hutchinson; Arnold d. at Portsmouth, 30 Jul 1888. Arnold was first married to Clarissa Fuller.

viii ELIZABETH HOLT, b. 2 Apr 1811; d. 20 Jun 1830.

527) BENJAMIN ABBOTT *(Elizabeth Abbott Abbott⁴, George³, George², George¹)*, b. at Andover, 11 Apr 1749 son of Benjamin and Elizabeth (Abbott) Abbott; d. at Hollis about 1838; m. by 1778, SARAH "SALLY" WRIGHT, b. 16 May 1763[1428] daughter of Joshua and Abigail (Richardson) Wright.

Benjamin Abbott had a reputation as a ladies' man and was prone to drinking. He neglected the care of his family and several of the sons went to sea. Benjamin Abbott died at the town poor farm.[1429]

Benjamin Abbott and Sarah Wright were parents of thirteen children born at Hollis.

i BENJAMIN ABBOTT, b. 1 Oct 1778; d. May 1793.

ii DANIEL ABBOTT, b. 28 Aug 1780

iii JACOB ABBOTT, b. 2 Oct 1782; d. at Savannah, Jun 1813.

iv SARAH ABBOTT, b. 3 Jul 1785; d. at Hollis, 8 Mar 1879; m. 1st, at Hollis, Sep 1805, NATHANIEL RIDEOUT; Nathaniel d. at Wilton, 18 Apr 1807. Sarah m. 2nd, at Hollis, 9 Feb 1810, BENJAMIN AUSTIN.

v TIMOTHY WRIGHT ABBOTT, b. 28 May 1788; d. at Bristol, England, 1816. Timothy died while a prisoner.

vi STEPHEN ABBOTT, b. 15 Dec 1790; d. 30 Jun 1831; m. NANCY DODGE.

vii BETSY ABBOTT, b. 23 Jun 1793; d. at Salem, MA, 12 Jul 1877; m. at Salem, 1 Feb 1831, EPHRAIM FELT.

viii ABIGAIL ABBOTT, b. 9 Jan 1796; d. at Salem, MA, 30 Mar 1877; m. 1820, ANDREW WARD, b. at Salem, 29 Oct 1793 son of Andrew and Matthew (Babbidge) Ward; Andrew d. at Salem, 1 Aug 1860.

ix MARY ABBOTT, b. 15 Aug 1798

x BENJAMIN ABBOTT, b. 22 Oct 1800

xi JOHN ABBOTT, b. 2 Jul 1803; d. Feb 1835.

xii ABIEL ABBOTT, b. 29 Dec 1807; d. at sea, 1841.

xiii NATHANIEL ABBOTT (child listed in the Abbot genealogy for whom no records were found).

528) ELIZABETH ABBOTT *(Elizabeth Abbott Abbott⁴, George³, George², George¹)*, b. at Hollis, 22 Feb 1751 daughter of Benjamin and Elizabeth (Abbott) Abbott; d. at Hollis, 19 Feb 1836; m. 1st about 1770, EBENEZER NUTTING of Pepperell; he died at Hollis, 1773 (probate 24 Nov 1773). Elizabeth m. 2nd 4 Aug 1774, SAMPSON POWERS, b. at Hollis, 2 Apr 1748 son of Peter and Anna (Keyes) Powers; Sampson d. 2 Jan 1822 at Hollis (will written 10 Oct 1821).

The estate of Ebenezer Nutting entered probate 24 November 1773. Widow Elizabeth Nutting requested that Stephen Powers be named administrator. The value of the estate was £48.14.9. Claims against the estate exceeded its value. In January 1774, Elizabeth petitioned the Court for relief as she had been left almost nothing from the personal estate. She found she "must submit to inconveniences and hardships altogether unknown to her while her husband lived unless your honour in his wisdom and justice should allow her something of the deceased's personal estate for the upholding of life." Elizabeth was granted £9 by the Court.[1430]

In his will written 10 October 1821, Sampson Powers made the following bequests: beloved wife Elizabeth receives improvements on one-third part of the real estate; daughter Mary A. Willoby receives $2; wearing apparel to be equally divided among his sons; the remainder of the estate goes to daughter Ursula. Jesse Worcester of Hollis is named executor. The sons are not specifically named.[1431]

Elizabeth Abbott and Ebenezer Nutting had two children born at Hollis.

[1428] This identification involves a young marriage for Sarah at age 15. However, her last child was born in 1807 so she would have to be very young at the time of the birth of the first child in 1778.

[1429] Hollis Historical Society, The Old City, http://www.windowsonhollispast.com/historicSites/sitesAcrossHollis/sites/016-001oldcity_tinklepaugh.htm

[1430] New Hampshire Probate Records, Hillsborough County, Volume 1 p 26, Volume 2 pages 92, 94, 96, 98; estate of Ebenezer Nutting, accessed through familysearch.org.

[1431] New Hampshire. Probate Court (Hillsborough County); Probate Place: Hillsborough, New Hampshire, Probate Records, Vol 31-33, 1820-1830, p 568, will of Sampson Powers

i ELIZABETH "BETSY" NUTTING, b. 18 Apr 1771; m. at Westford, 6 Feb 1794, ELEAZER WRIGHT, b. at Westford, 5 Dec 1765 son of John and Sarah (-) Wright; Eleazer d. at Westford, 31 Jul 1821.

ii EBENEZER NUTTING, b. 1772; d. at sea, 1805;[1432] m. at Salem, 3 Jul 1803, SARAH "SALLY" STEVENSON.

Elizabeth Abbott and Sampson Powers were parents of eight children born at Hollis.

i MARY ABBOTT POWERS, b. 18 Oct 1774; d. at Hollis, before 1850; m. at Hollis, 22 Feb 1816, as his second wife, WILLIAM WILLOUGHBY, b. at Hollis, 17 Jun 1774 son of Jonas and Hannah (Bates) Willoughby. William was first married to Rebecca Adams 10 Mar 1796.

ii SAMPSON POWERS, b. 17 Jan 1777; d. at Portsmouth, NH, 27 Dec 1812. Sampson did not marry.

iii PETER POWERS, b. 24 Feb 1779; d. at Bakersfield, VT, 5 Aug 1821; m. 11 Nov 1802, SARAH START, b. at New Ipswich, NH, 20 Feb 1777 daughter of George and Mary (Tucker) Start;[1433] Sarah d. at Bakersfield, 21 Dec 1873.

iv JOEL POWERS, b. 8 Aug 1781; d. at Salem, 27 Feb 1847; m. 1st, at Salem, 8 Sep 1808, RHODA BLOOD, of Salem, b. 14 Apr 1788 daughter of Jacob and Rachel (Jones) Blood; Rhoda d. at Salem, 30 Aug 1814. Joel m. 2nd, at Salem, 1 Oct 1815, Rhoda's sister, RACHEL BLOOD, b. at Salem, 14 Apr 1788; Rachel d. at Salem, Mar 1817. Joel m. 3rd, at Salem, about 1827, ELIZA FRANCIS, b. at Salem, 12 Mar 1803 daughter of William and Eliza (Pickering) Francis; Eliza d. at Salem, 31 Jul 1877.

v GRANT POWERS, b. 31 Mar 1784; d. at Goshen, CT, 10 Apr 1841; m. at Thetford, VT, 22 Sep 1817, ELIZA HOWARD HOPKINS, b. at Thetford, 22 Sep 1802 daughter of Thomas and Elizabeth (-) Hopkins; Eliza d. at Washington, DC, 25 Aug 1887. Grant Powers was a clergyman; he graduated from Dartmouth in 1810.[1434] At the time of her death, Eliza was living with her daughter Henrietta in Washington, DC.

vi LEVI POWERS, b. 20 Mar 1786; m. at Westminster, VT, 11 Mar 1817, CYNTHIA EATON, b. at Walpole, NH, 9 Nov 1794 daughter of Isaiah and Priscilla (West) Eaton; Cynthia d. at Chelsea, MA, 7 Mar 1875.

vii ANNA POWERS, b. 11 Sep 1789; d. 4 Sep 1790.

viii URSULA POWERS, b. 30 Oct 1790; d. at Hollis, 30 Aug 1857; m. at Milford, 26 Jun 1823, SIMON SAUNDERSON, b. at Hollis, 20 Mar 1790 son of Benjamin and Esther (Lawrence) Saunderson; Simon d. at Hollis, 10 Sep 1872.

529) SAMUEL ABBOTT *(Elizabeth Abbott Abbott[4], George[3], George[2], George[1])*, b. at Hollis, 13 Apr 1753 son of Benjamin and Elizabeth (Abbott) Abbott; d. Feb 1794; m. SUSAN HUBBARD.

Little is known of this family. Samuel's mother Elizabeth wrote her will 19 October 1802 and includes a bequest to Susan the daughter of her son Samuel. Just one child could be identified and no record of her following her grandmother's will.

i SUSAN ABBOTT, b. at Hollis, 15 Jul 1781; living in 1802 but no record after.

530) GEORGE ABBOTT *(Elizabeth Abbott Abbott[4], George[3], George[2], George[1])*, b. at Hollis, 29 Dec 1755 son of Benjamin and Elizabeth (Abbott) Abbott; d. at Hollis, 15 Sep 1818; m. 29 Dec 1784, NAOMI TUTTLE, b. at Littleton, MA, 28 Sep 1764 daughter of Samuel and Mary (Russell) Tuttle; Naomi d. about 1833.

George Abbott and Naomi Tuttle had six children born at Hollis.

i GEORGE ABBOTT, b. 17 Oct 1788; d. at Hollis, Nov 1841; m. at Danvers, 11 Dec 1817, BETSEY GOLDTHWAIT, b. at Danvers, 11 Apr 1798 daughter of John and Eunice (Thomas) Goldthwait; Betsey d. at Peabody, 15 Mar 1868.

ii NAOMI ABBOTT, b. 1 Feb 1790; d. at Fairwater, WI, 8 Jan 1871; m. at Hollis, 18 Jan 1810, SAMUEL FRENCH, b. at Hollis, 19 Jun 1784; Samuel d. at Glendale, WI, 22 Mar 1859.

[1432] Ebenezer, 2d, on board the ship Franklin.
[1433] Chandler, *History of New Ipswich*, p 630
[1434] Appleton's Cyclopedia of American Biography, volume V, p 97

iii BETSY ABBOTT, b. 11 Jan 1792; d. at Hollis, 16 Oct 1860; m. 25 Dec 1817, as his second wife, EBENEZER BLOOD, b. at Hollis, 15 Mar 1775 son of Josiah and Abigail (Pierce) Blood; Ebenezer d. at Hollis, 12 Nov 1853. Ebenezer was first married to Eunice Pierce.

iv MARY "POLLY" ABBOTT, b. 11 Mar 1796; d. at Sherman, NY, 1865; m. at Andover, 28 Mar 1823, LEWIS COCHRAN, b. at Andover, 1800 son of James and Salome (Knowlton) Cochran; Lewis d. at Sherman, 1863.

v WILLIAM ABBOTT, b. 14 Jun 1798; d. Dec 1827; m. 11 Apr 1819, as her second husband, RACHEL COCHRAN, b. Apr 1788 daughter of James and Salome (Knowlton) Cochran; Rachel d. at Lowell; 18 Apr 1868. Rachel was first married to JOSEPH B. ABBOTT *(Hephzibah Ames Abbott[5], Benjamin Ames[4], Hannah Stevens Ames[3], Elizabeth Abbott Stevens[2], George[1])*, b. at Andover, 1 Feb 1783 son of Bixby and Hephzibah (Ames) Abbott; Joseph d. at sea, about 1809.[1435] Joseph B. Abbott is a child in Family 1187. William Abbott is reported to have been murdered at Millbury on his way home after finishing a job at the Blackstone Canal.[1436]

vi HARRIET ABBOTT, b. 24 Jun 1802; d. Jul 1820.

531) JOEL ABBOT *(Elizabeth Abbott Abbott[4], George[3], George[2], George[1])*, b. at Hollis, 4 Dec 1757 son of Benjamin and Elizabeth (Abbott) Abbott; d. at Westford, 12 Apr 1806; m. 4 Sep 1786, LYDIA CUMMINGS, b. at Westford, 26 Nov 1769 daughter of Isaac and Elizabeth (Trowbridge) Cummings; Lydia d. at Littleton, 5 Mar 1813.[1437] After Joel's death, Lydia married Francis Kidder.

In his will dated 5 December 1805, Joel Abbot leaves beloved wife Lydia all the household items to be at her own disposal. She receives the use of and improvements on the rest of the estate as long as she is a widow. If the daughters marry and/or when sons reach age 21, two-thirds of the estate is to be divided among the children who are Elizabeth, Joel, Walter, Isaac Hotten, Lydia, and Mary Phillips. Lydia was named executor.[1438]

Joel Abbot and Lydia Cummings had eight children born at Westford.

i ELIZABETH "BETSEY" ABBOT, b. 22 Jan 1787; d. at East Windsor, CT, 30 Apr 1837; m. at Westford, 1 May 1811, Rev. Dr. JONATHAN COGSWELL, b. at Rowley, 3 Sep 1781 son of Nathaniel and Lois (Searl) Cogswell; Jonathan d. at New Brunswick, NJ, 1 Aug 1864. After Elizabeth's death, Jonathan married Jane E. Kirkpatrick.

ii JOEL ABBOT, b. 29 Jun 1789; d. 29 Jun 1789.

iii LYDIA ABBOT, b. Dec 1790; d. 20 Aug 1791.

iv JOEL ABBOTT, b. 18 Jan 1793; d. at Hong Kong, China, 14 Dec 1855; m. 1st, 1 Jan 1820, MARY WOOD, b. at Newburyport, 20 Jan 1796 daughter of Abner and Dolly (Pearson) Wood; Mary d. at Newburyport, 15 Apr 1821. Joel m. 2nd, 29 Nov 1825, LAURA WHEATON, b. at Warren, RI, 15 Mar 1801 daughter of Charles and Abigail (Miller) Wheaton; Laura d. at Warren, 10 Oct 1864. Commodore Joel Abbot was a career naval officer who died of malaria at Hong Kong while in command of the *Macedonian*.[1439]

v WALTER ABBOT, b. 17 Sep 1795; d. at Chesapeake, 12 Jul 1825. He was a lieutenant in the USN and died of a wound received on the *Chesapeake*.

vi LYDIA ABBOT, b. 5 Feb 1798, d. at Kennebunkport, ME, 13 Jun 1851; m. DANIEL WALKER LORD, b. at Arundel, ME, 29 Mar 1800 son of Nathaniel and Phebe (Walker) Lord; Daniel d. at Malden, MA, 4 Sep 1880.

vii MARY PHILLIPS ABBOT, b. 23 Nov 1801; d. 1831.

viii ISAAC HOUGHTON ABBOTT, b. 18 Jan 1804; d. in West Virginia, after 1870; m. in Washington County, VA, 13 Oct 1828, LOUISA TARKLESON, b. in Virginia, about 1806; d. in West Virginia, after 1870. Isaac also was in the Navy for a time.

532) JACOB ABBOTT *(Elizabeth Abbott Abbott[4], George[3], George[2], George[1])*, b. at Hollis, 12 Apr 1760 son of Benjamin and Elizabeth (Abbott) Abbott; d. at Westford, 11 Apr 1815; m. 14 Sep 1787, POLLY CUMMINGS, b. 12 Jul 1767 daughter of Thomas and Lucy (Laurence) Cummings; Polly d. at Westford, 4 Mar 1858.

Jacob Abbott did not leave a will and his estate entered probate 24 April 1815. Widow Polly Abbott declined administration and requested that Imla Goodhue be appointed. Real estate consisted of the homestead valued at $500 and

[1435] Errata and Addenda to Dr. Stocking's History and Genealogy of the Knowltons of England and America, part 4, p 187
[1436] Abbot, *Genealogical Register*, p 66
[1437] Lydia, w, Capt. Francis, of Littleton, formerly w. Joel Abbot, at Littleton, Mar. 5, 1813, a. 43 y. 4 m.
[1438] *Probate Records 1648--1924 (Middlesex County, Massachusetts)*; Author: *Massachusetts. Probate Court (Middlesex County)*; Probate Place: *Middlesex, Massachusetts*, *Probate Papers, No 1-39*, probate of Joel Abbott
[1439] U.S., Navy Casualties Books, 1776-1941

personal estate was valued at $129.95. The personal estate was sold at auction to settle the estate and the sale includes daughter Betsy Abbott buying a featherbed, sheets, and quilt[1440] and widow Polly Abbott buying the butter tub, an old chest, and a two-gallon keg. Polly also bought the clock valued at $12 for $7.50. The widow's dower was set off to Polly with real estate valued at $166.66. Polly Abbott, Betsy Abbott, and Silas Merriam signed a statement that they were satisfied with the setting off the dower. Also signing was Isaiah Prescott who held a $200 mortgage on the property.[1441]

Jacob Abbott and Polly Cummings were parents of six children born at Westford.

i MARY "POLLY" ABBOTT, b. 9 Apr 1788; d. at Lowell, 27 Jan 1871; m. at Westford, 2 Apr 1809, SILAS MERRIAM, b. at Mason, NH, 14 Feb 1785 son of Silas and Mary (Elliot) Merriam;[1442] Silas d. at Northborough, MA, 15 Apr 1872.

ii CUMMINGS ABBOTT, b. 2 Jan 1790; d. 11 Oct 1795.

iii BETSY ABBOTT, b. 13 Apr 1792; d. at Westford, 3 Sep 1867; m. 12 Sep 1815, TIMOTHY SMITH, b. at Westford, 25 Jun 1789 son of Thomas and Molly (Herrick) Smith; Timothy d. at Westford, 1 Nov 1859.

iv JACOB CUMMINGS ABBOTT, b. 14 Dec 1798; d. at Boston, 16 Mar 1866; m. at Boston, 22 Jan 1829, MARY W. TODD, b. at Boston, about 1809; Mary d. at Chelsea, 8 Apr 1886.

v NANCY ABBOTT, b. 29 May 1804; d. at Westford, 26 Feb 1881; m. 29 Aug 1833, JONATHAN S. HILL, b. at Danville, VT, 12 Jan 1808 son of Jonathan and Fanny (Sheldon) Hill; Jonathan d. of consumption, at Wayland, MA, 19 May 1860.[1443]

vi SAMUEL B. ABBOTT, b. 18 Oct 1812; d. at Lowell, 17 May 1864; m. at Lowell, 6 Oct 1839, HEPHZIBAH EASTMAN, b. in NH, about 1816 daughter of Samuel Batchelder and Sarah (Eastman) Eastman;[1444] Hephzibah d. at Lowell, 1882. Samuel Abbott was a dentist.

533) MARY ABBOTT *(Elizabeth Abbott Abbott⁴, George³, George², George¹)*, b. at Hollis, about 1762 daughter of Benjamin and Elizabeth (Abbott) Abbott; d. at Westford, 7 Jul 1797; m. 28 Jul 1782, ABEL BOYNTON, b. at Westford, 9 Aug 1755 son of Nathaniel and Rebekah (Barrett) Boynton. Abel m. 2nd Polly Pierce.

Abel Boynton served in the Revolution in company of Captain Oliver Bates. He received a commission as Captain in 1787. He later held the rank of Colonel in the militia. He was representative to the General Court from Westford from 1796 through 1801 (except 1800). He served as selectman in Westford most of the years from 1790 to 1801.[1445]

Son Benjamin Abbott Boynton was a career Army officer with the rank of Major.[1446] He served in the War of 1812. In his will written 18 April 1835, Major Benjamin A. Boynton of Plattsburgh left his entire estate to his wife Eleanor during her life which to be managed by the executors. After Eleanor's decease, the estate is to be divided between his sisters Sarah Ames and Elizabeth Boynton. The executors named are brothers-in-law John Palmer and Frederick Sailly.[1447]

Mary Abbott and Abel Boynton were parents of seven children born at Westford, Massachusetts.

i ABEL BOYNTON, b. 4 May 1783; d. at Bath, ME, 1817;[1448] m. about 1812, SARAH LELAND, b. at Saco, 1789 daughter of James and Dorcas (King) Leland; Sarah d. at Nashua, NH, 9 Jun 1867. Sarah married second Edmund Parker 31 Aug 1827. Abel graduated from Harvard in 1804 and was a lawyer in Bath. Abel and Sarah did not have children.

ii MARY BOYNTON, b. 3 Apr 1785; d. Nov 1810; m. 5 Apr 1809, her fourth cousin once removed, BENJAMIN AMES *(Benjamin Ames⁵, Benjamin Ames⁴, Hannah Stevens Ames³, Elizabeth Abbott Stevens², George¹)*, b. at

---

1440 Imagine having to buy your bed back at auction so you have a place to sleep.

1441 Middlesex County, MA: Probate File Papers, 1648-1871.Online database. AmericanAncestors.org. New England Historic Genealogical Society, 2014. Case 18

1442 Names of parents are given as Silas Merriam and Mary Elliot on his death record. Further information in Pope et al., *Merriam Genealogy in England and America*, p 140

1443 Although he died at Wayland, Jonathan was a resident of Westford at the time of his death.

1444 Hephzibah's father was Samuel Batchelder, but he was known as Samuel Eastman as he was adopted by an Eastman. The Eastman Family in America, p 480

1445 Hodgman, *History of Westford*

1446 Gardner, *A Dictionary of All Officers, Who Have Been Commissioned, or Have Been Appointed and Served, in the Army of the United States: Since the Inauguration of Their First President, in 1789, to the First January, 1853, p 79*

1447 New York Probate Records, Clinton County, Wills 1807-1847, Volumes A-B, pp 287-290, will of Benjamin A. Boynton.

1448 Harvard University, Quinquennial Catalogue, p 150

Andover, 30 Oct 1778 son of Benjamin and Phebe (Chandler) Ames; Benjamin d. at Houlton, ME, 28 Sep 1835. Benjamin married second Mary's sister Sally (see below).[1449] Benjamin Ames is a child in Family 1185.

iii ELIZABETH "BETSEY" BOYNTON, b. 1 Oct 1787; Betsey was living and unmarried in 1835 when her brother Benjamin wrote his will.

iv BENJAMIN ABBOTT BOYNTON, b. 28 Feb 1790; d. 23 Mar 1790.

v BENJAMIN ABBOTT BOYNTON, b. 10 Jun 1791; d. at Plattsburgh, NY, 13 Feb 1837; m. about 1818, ELEANOR M. SAILLY, b. at Plattsburgh, 1789 daughter of Peter and Maria Adelaide (Grellier) Sailly; Eleanor d. at Plattsburgh, 13 Oct 1855.

vi ISAAC NEWTON BOYNTON, b. 24 May 1793; d. 10 Jun 1793.

vii SARAH "SALLY" BOYNTON, b. 21 Jun 1794; m. at Saco, 4 May 1812, BENJAMIN AMES who was first married to Sally's sister Mary (see above).

534) SARAH HOLT *(Sarah Abbott Holt⁴, George³, George², George¹)*, b. at Danvers, 29 Oct 1758 daughter of Nathan and Sarah (Abbott) Holt; d. 17 Sep 1841; m. at Danvers, 2 Dec 1777, WILLIAM FROST, b. at New Castle, NH, 15 Nov 1754 son of William and Elizabeth (Prescott) Frost; William d. at Andover 28 Sep 1836. Sarah and William are second great grandparents of Robert Frost.

William Frost served as a lieutenant in the Continental Army during the Revolution.[1450] He was also deacon of the Congregational Church.[1451]

Sarah Holt and William Frost had twelve children all born at Andover.

i NATHAN HOLT FROST, b. 4 Sep 1778; d. 9 Jun 1784.

ii SALLY FROST, b. 28 Dec 1779; d. at Newburyport, 3 May 1863; m. at Andover, 16 Nov 1802, SAMUEL DRAKE, b. at Epping, about 1775 son of Simon and Judith (Perkins) Drake; Samuel d. at Newburyport, 27 Jun 1845.

iii BETSEY FROST, b. 21 Aug 1781; d. at Andover, 9 Aug 1819. Betsey did not marry.

iv WILLIAM FROST, b. 28 Mar 1783; d. 12 Apr 1784.

v DOROTHY CLIFFORD FROST, b. 1 Mar 1785; d. at Northwood, NH, 20 Apr 1822; m. at Andover, 7 Oct 1806, DUDLEY LEAVITT, b. about 1772 (based on age at death); Dudley d. at Northwood, 5 Feb 1838. After Dorothy's death, Dudley married her sister Mary.

vi MARY "POLLY" FROST, b. 18 Jan 1787; d. at Northwood, 17 Apr 1846; m. 5 Aug 1823, DUDLEY LEAVITT (see sister Dorothy).

vii NATHAN HOLT FROST, b. Jan 1789; d. at Rutherford County, TN, 19 Mar 1866;[1452] m. at Charlotte County, VA, 20 Nov 1817, MARTHA HEWETT JOHNSON,[1453] b. in Virginia about 1791; Martha d. at Rutherford County, 24 Oct 1873. Nathan attended Phillips Academy in Andover graduating in 1808.[1454] He was a merchant who was in Virginia from about 1810 to 1826 and then relocated to Tennessee.

viii HARRIET HOLT FROST, b. 29 Mar 1791; d. at Andover, 11 Dec 1818; m. at Salem, 29 Aug 1814, ROBERT CROWELL, b. at Salem, 9 Dec 1787 son of Samuel and Lydia (Woodbury) Crowell; Robert d. at Essex, 10 Nov 1855. After Harriet's death, Robert married Hannah Choate.

ix WILLIAM FROST, b. 12 Jun 1793; d. at Andover, 28 Mar 1866; m. 1st, 11 Dec 1823, LUCY FOSTER, b. 17 Nov 1800 daughter of Charles and Lucy (Austin) Foster; Lucy d. 4 Nov 1838. William m. 2nd, 18 Mar 1840, MARY WOMSTEAD MEAD, b. 23 Apr 1804 daughter of Levi and Susannah (Hilton) Mead; Mary d. 11 Dec 1866.

x SAMUEL ABBOTT FROST, b. 11 Jun 1795; d. at Brentwood, NH, 11 Jan 1848; m. at Eden, ME, 10 Oct 1821, MARY "POLLY" BLUNT, b. at New Castle, NH, 28 Jun 1787 daughter of William and Mary (Fernald) Blunt; Mary d. 14 Jan 1875.

xi LUCY FROST, b. 28 Nov 1798; d. at Andover, 26 Feb 1842; m. at Leicester, MA, 23 Feb 1820, JOHN RICHARDSON, b. about 1789; John d. at Andover, 3 Oct 1841.

[1449] Biographical Encyclopedia of Maine in the Nineteenth Century, p 384ff
[1450] Compiled Service Records of Soldiers Who Served in the American Army During the Revolutionary War 1775-1785, accessed through fold3
[1451] Frost, *The Nicholas Frost Family*, p 23
[1452] Year: 1860; Census Place: Murfreesboro, Rutherford, Tennessee; Roll: M653_1271; Page: 83; Family History Library Film: 805271
[1453] Virginia, Compiled Marriages, 1740-1850
[1454] Biographical catalogue of the trustees, teachers, and students of Phillips Academy, Andover, 1778-1830.

xii BENJAMIN PRESCOT FROST, b. 17 Nov 1800; d. at Andover, 25 Jun 1827.

535) MARY HOLT *(Sarah Abbott Holt⁴, George³, George², George¹)*, b. at Danvers, 3 Oct 1761 daughter of Nathan and Sarah (Abbott) Holt; d. at Beverly, 7 Jan 1850; m. 1 Nov 1781, ROBERT ENDICOTT, b. 29 Oct 1756 son of John and Elizabeth (Jacobs) Endicott; Robert d. at Beverly, 6 Mar 1819.

Mary Holt married Robert Endicott a descendant of Governor John Endicott. They settled in Beverly where they had a family of seven children. The Endicott family was instrumental in the shipping industry in Salem and three of the sons of Robert and Mary were mariners.

Son Robert Endicott went to sea at age 20,[1455] and although he did not die at sea, he died at age 28 of "decline." Son Nathan Holt Endicott went to sea at age 16 and was chief mate when he died of fever aboard the ship *Glide* in Calcutta. A son-in-law, John Ellingwood, also died at sea. He was first officer of the ship *Bramin* when he died in the Bay of Bengal.[1456]

Third oldest son, Captain Samuel Endicott, was a shipmaster in command of the ship *George* for several years. The ship *George* was built in Salem in 1814 and was part of a large fleet of merchant vessels owned by Joseph Peabody. This ship made annual trips to Calcutta and the round trip took nearly a year. The average outbound trip was 115 days and the average return took 103 days.[1457] After his seafaring days, Samuel was president of the bank in Beverly.

Youngest son, William, lived to be 99 years 10 months old. He was a successful business owner having a mercantile and drug store at the corner of Cabot and Washington Streets in Beverly.[1458]

Robert and Mary Endicott had seven children born at Beverly.

i MARY ENDICOTT, b. 29 Jul 1782; d. at Beverly, 8 Jan 1813; m. at Beverly, 18 Oct 1808, JOHN ELLINGWOOD, b. at Beverly, 20 Dec 1783 son of John and Hannah (Glover) Ellingwood; John d. aboard ship in Calcutta, 7 Nov 1816.

ii ROBERT ENDICOTT, b. 5 May 1785; d. at Beverly, 29 Aug 1813 of "decline." Robert did not marry. He was a mariner.

iii NATHAN HOLT ENDICOTT, b. 31 Jan 1788; d. aboard ship at the Bay of Bengal, 2 Jul 1816. Nathan did not marry. He died from a fever.

iv Daughter, b. 7 Jun 1790 and d. 10 Jun 1790

v SAMUEL ENDICOTT, b. 18 Jul 1793; d. at Beverly, 28 Jan 1872; m. 1st, 11 Jun 1820, his first cousin, HANNAH HOLT (descended from George Abbott by multiple lines; see Family 536), b. at Epping, NH, 4 May 1794 daughter of Peter and Hannah (Holt) Holt; Hannah d. 14 Mar 1825. Samuel m. 2nd, 21 May 1826, SARAH FARNUM HOLT, b. at Epping, 12 Feb 1809 daughter of Peter and Hannah (Holt) Holt; Sarah d. 23 Aug 1847. Samuel m. 3rd, 7 Jun 1852, MARY THORNDIKE LEECH, b. at Beverly, 3 Aug 1803 daughter of William and Ruth (Lee) Leech. Mary T. Leech had first married ship captain John Giddings. Mary d. 20 Dec 1881.

vi Daughter, b. 7 Sep 1796 and d. 11 Sep 1796

vii WILLIAM ENDICOTT, b. 11 Mar 1799; d. just two months before his 100th birthday on 8 Jan 1899; m. 26 Sep 1824, JOANNA LOVETT RANTOUL, b. at Beverly, 13 Jan 1803 daughter of Robert and Joanna (Lovett) Rantoul; Joanna d. 26 Jun 1863.[1459]

536) HANNAH HOLT *(Sarah Abbott Holt⁴, George³, George², George¹)*, b. at Danvers, 11 May 1769 daughter of Nathan and Sarah (Abbott) Holt; d. at Beverly 26 Jul 1857; m. 23 Jan 1793, her first cousin, PETER HOLT *(Joshua Holt⁴, Dorcas Abbott Holt³, Timothy², George¹)*, b. at Andover 12 Jun 1763 son of Joshua and Phebe (Farnum) Holt; Peter d. at Greenfield, NH, 25 Apr 1851.

Reverend Peter Holt graduated from Harvard in 1790.[1460] He was installed at the Presbyterian Church in Peterborough and Greenfield.[1461]

[1455] Web: US, New England Seamen's Protection Certificate Index, 1796-1871
[1456] Ancestry.com, U.S., Newspaper Extractions from the Northeast, 1704-1930
[1457] Essex Institute, *Old-Time Ships of Salem*
[1458] Hurd, *History of Essex County, Massachusetts*
[1459] Joanna Endicott's death is recorded in the Beverly records but noted as occurring in St. Louis.
[1460] Quinquennial Catalogue of the Officers and Graduates of Harvard University
[1461] The Quarterly Christian Spectator, volume 1, 1827, p 336

In his will written 26 November 1847 and proved 6 May 1851, Peter Holt bequeaths to beloved wife Hannah all his household furniture and all the farming tools to be at her own use and disposal. He notes that he has prospects of an inheritance from England, and if that occurs and it is a large amount, then he wishes for a reasonable amount of that sum to be divided among the families of his deceased brothers and the families of his deceased brothers-in-law. He also wishes that something be given to his daughter-in-law Henrietta Adams. The reside of the estate he bequeaths to his wife during her lifetime. Following that, the estate is to be divided equally between his beloved daughter Mary E. W. Holt and his beloved son-in-law Samuel Endicott.[1462]

Peter Holt and Hannah Holt were parents of seven children all born at Epping, New Hampshire. Two of the daughters of Hannah and Peter married Samuel Endicott son of Mary Holt and Robert Endicott (Family #535).

i HANNAH HOLT, b. 4 May 1794; d. at Beverly, MA, 14 Mar 1825; m. at Beverly, 11 Jun 1820, her first cousin, SAMUEL ENDICOTT *(Mary Holt Endicott5, Nathan Holt4, Dorcas Abbott Holt3, Timothy2, George1)*, b. at Beverly, 18 Jul 1793 son of Robert and Mary (Holt) Endicott; Samuel d. at Beverly, 28 Jan 1872.

ii NATHAN HOLT, b. 16 Aug 1795; d. 23 Jul 1807.

iii PETER HOLT, b. 20 Feb 1802; d. 16 Jul 1817.

iv JEREMIAH HOLT, b. 5 Sep 1803; d. 20 Nov 1817.

v JOSHUA HOLT, b. 9 Mar 1805; married at unknown date, Henrietta about whom nothing else in known at this time. Henrietta is the daughter-in-law Henrietta Adams referred to in Peter Holt's will.

vi SARAH FARNUM HOLT, b. 12 Feb 1809; d. at Beverly, 23 Aug 1847; m. 21 May 1826, SAMUEL ENDICOTT (refer to sister Hannah above).

vii MARY E. W. HOLT, b. 27 May 1812; d. at Beverly, 19 Aug 1887. Mary did not marry.

537) JAMES HOLT *(Sarah Abbott Holt4, George3, George2, George1)*, b. at Danvers, 1772 son of Nathan and Sarah (Abbott) Holt; d. in India, Aug 1807;[1463] m. 30 Aug 1796, LUCY WHIPPLE, b. 8 Mar 1778; Lucy d. at Danvers, 6 Mar 1839. Although James's death is reported as August 1807, the probate of his estate was April 1807.

James Holt was a seaman who died on a voyage to India leaving a widow with three small children. Lucy Holt was administratrix of his estate which entered probate 20 April 1807. The value of the personal estate was $61.65. After expenses of the estate, the allowance to Lucy was $45.65.[1464]

James Holt and Lucy Whipple were parents of four children born at Danvers.

i JAMES HOLT, b. 25 Feb 1797; d. at Danvers, 12 Nov 1856; m. 6 Apr 1819, MERCY SMITH, b. at Danvers, 9 Oct 1796 daughter of Israel and Margaret (-) Smith (mother was the widow Margaret Standly); Mercy d. at Danvers, 6 Nov 1856.

ii STEPHEN HOLT, b. 24 Jan 1799; d. 2 Oct 1800.

iii LUCY ANN HOLT, b. 29 Aug 1801; d. at Danvers, 28 Sep 1829; m. at Danvers, 15 May 1823, GILMAN PARKER, b. at Topsfield, 19 Sep 1802 son of Edmund and Jane (Pingrey) Parker; Gilman d. 3 Jun 1866. After Lucy's death, Gilman married Abigail Welch.

iv LYDIA HOLT, b. 27 Jan 1804; d. at Danvers, 3 Apr 1889; m. at Danvers, 28 Dec 1824, SAMUEL HARRIS, b. at Ipswich, 3 Apr 1799 son of Daniel and Sarah (Emmons) Harris; Daniel d. at Danvers, 7 Dec 1877.

538) HANNAH FOSTER *(Hannah Abbott Foster4, George3, George2, George1)*, b. at Andover, 20 Jun 1756 daughter of William and Hannah (Abbott) Foster; d. at Tewksbury 7 Nov 1830; m. 27 Feb 1777, TIMOTHY C. ROGERS, b. at Tewksbury 16 Jun 1745 son of Timothy and Rebecca (French) Rogers; Timothy d. 27 Feb 1814.

In his will, Timothy Rogers made the following bequests. Beloved wife Hannah Rogers receives the use of all the household furniture which is at her disposal forever. She also receives the use and improvement of the old house except what might be given for the use of daughter Sarah French Rogers. There is also a lengthy list of other provisions for her support and she also receives the use of the pew in the meeting house during her lifetime. Son Timothy Foster receives one good cow, a bed, and $100; this with what he has already received is his full portion. Daughter Hannah R. Kidder wife of Samuel Kidder of Charlestown receives a heifer and $150. Daughter Sarah French Rogers receives $25 from Mr. Richard Derby of Boston for her schooling and she receives an additional $25 for this purpose. Sarah also receives $475 when she comes of age or at the time of marriage. Son Samuel Abbot Rogers receives the black steer and the yellow steer which he calls his steers; these two steers are to be sold and the proceeds to be used for his schooling. Samuel also receives a bed and a cow and when he comes of age, $100

[1462] New Hampshire, County Probate Records, 1660-1973, Hillsborough, 57:213, will of Peter Holt

[1463] James, h. Lucy (Whipple), at India, Aug. —, 1807.

[1464] Essex County, MA: Probate File Papers, 1638-1881.Online database. AmericanAncestors.org. New England Historic Genealogical Society, 2014. Case 13651

for his schooling. Son William receives the clock after his mother is done with it and one good bed. His three sons equally divide the wearing apparel. All the rest of the estate goes to son William who is also named executor.[1465]

Son Samuel may have made the most of his schooling although I was not able to locate where that occurred. At his death in 1865, the bequests in his will included $5,000 to his wife. His personal estate included $6,400 in cash and stock holdings and real property valued at $2,209.[1466] His occupation was listed as farmer on census records.

Hannah Foster and Timothy Rogers had six children born at Tewksbury.

i WILLIAM ROGERS, b. 8 Jun 1778; d. at Tewksbury, 10 Apr 1865; m. 25 Apr 1850, MARTHA COGGIN, b. at Tewksbury, 27 Sep 1817 daughter of Jacob and Mary (Symmes) Coggin; Martha d. at Lowell, 30 Jan 1888. This late marriage seems to be William's only marriage. He did not have children. His will has bequests for his brother, nieces and nephews, some members of his wife's family, and the bulk of the estate to wife Martha.

ii TIMOTHY FOSTER ROGERS, b. 16 Mar 1781; d. at Bernardston, 26 Jan 1847; m. at Bernardston, 29 May 1810, MARY PIERCE, b. at Woburn, 7 Nov 1786 daughter of Jacob and Martha (Johnson) Pierce; Mary d. at Bernardston, 5 Jul 1846.

iii HANNAH PHILLIPS ROGERS, b. 25 Dec 1783; d. at Medford, 25 Oct 1852; m. at Charlestown, 19 Feb 1806, SAMUEL KIDDER, b. at Medford, 1 Sep 1781 son of Samuel and Mary (Greenleaf) Kidder; Samuel d. at Lowell, 19 Jan 1870.

iv MARY BALLARD ROGERS, b. 29 Nov 1789; d. 1 Sep 1800.

v SARAH FRENCH ROGERS, b. 9 Nov 1795; d. at Tewksbury, 1841 (probate 1841). Sarah did not marry.

vi SAMUEL ABBOT ROGERS, b. 8 Jul 1801; d. at Tewksbury, 5 Mar 1865; m. 25 Apr 1837, FRANCES E. CHAPMAN, b. about 1810 daughter of Daniel Chapman; Frances d. at Tewksbury, 9 Oct 1888.

539) WILLIAM FOSTER *(Hannah Abbott Foster[4], George[3], George[2], George[1])*, b. at Andover, 1 Jun 1758 son of William and Hannah (Abbott) Foster; d. 20 Aug 1843; m. late in life, 18 Nov 1826, SALLY WELCH KIMBALL, b. at Plaistow, NH, 20 Dec 1786 daughter of Joseph and Anna (Welch) Kimball. Sally d. 29 Jan 1850.

William Foster was a successful businessman and owner of the Eagle Hotel in Andover.[1467] At the time of the probate of his estate, real property was valued at $30, 875.61 and personal estate value was $36,378.83. He did not leave a will. His widow Sarah W. Foster was administrator of the estate. After Sarah's death in 1850, son and only heir William Phillips Foster assumed administration of the estate.[1468]

Despite their late marriage, William and Sally did have one son.

i WILLIAM PHILLIPS FOSTER, b. at Andover, 21 Jan 1830; d. at Andover, 24 Feb 1871; m. 1st, 1 Dec 1853, JANE CYNTHIA KIMBALL, b. at Newburyport, 14 Oct 1830 daughter of Charles Harrison and Mary (Foster) Kimball; Jane d. 20 May 1859. William m. 2nd, 17 Jun 1863, ANNIE MATILDA BARROWS, b. at Middleborough, MA, 22 Jan 1842 daughter of Homer and Sarah Merrill (Welch) Barrows; Annie d. at Southern Pines, NC, 29 Jan 1917.

540) SARAH "SALLY" FOSTER *(Hannah Abbott Foster[4], George[3], George[2], George[1])*, b. at Andover, 9 Sep 1765 daughter of William and Hannah (Abbott) Foster; d. at Tewksbury 30 Nov 1807; m. 8 Jun 1794, JOSEPH BROWN, b. at Tewksbury, 19 Jun 1762 son of William and Mary (Osgood) Brown; Joseph d. 21 Nov 1829.

Joseph Brown did not leave a will and his estate entered probate 8 December 1829 with eldest son George Brown and Bravity Gray as administrators. The real estate was appraised at $9,933.00 which consisted of the homestead farm in Tewksbury with 230 acres valued at $6,000, a house and lot of land in Belvidere Village, a dwelling house near the meeting house in Tewksbury, and one-half of a house and 30 acres in Andover. The personal estate was valued at $1,33330. Claims on the estate totaled $3,867.26. The subscribers signing agreement to the plan of the administrators to sell the estate to settle the claims were Sarah Gray, Mary B. Gould, Thaddeus Brown, and Hannah Brown. The final settlement of the estate was 29 May 1835 and the heirs-at-law signing that they had no further claims against the administrators George Brown and Bravity Gray were A.J. Gould and Mary B. Gould, Hannah Brown, Sarah B. Gray, and Thaddeus Brown and Susan Brown.[1469]

[1465] Middlesex County, MA: Probate File Papers, 1648-1871. Probate of Timothy Rogers, 1814, Case number 19494.

[1466] *Middlesex County, MA: Probate File Papers, 1648-1871.Online database. AmericanAncestors.org. New England Historic Genealogical Society, 2014. Case 40791*

[1467] Andover Historic Preservation, "4 Elm Square," https://preservation.mhl.org/4-elm-square

[1468] Essex County, MA: Probate File Papers, 1638-1881. Probate of William Foster, 17 Oct 1843, case number 39518.

[1469] Middlesex County, MA: Probate File Papers, 1648-1871.Online database. AmericanAncestors.org. New England Historic Genealogical Society, 2014. Case 3113

Sarah Foster and Joseph Brown were parents of five children born at Tewksbury.

i GEORGE BROWN, b. 21 Nov 1794; d. at Brooklyn, NY, 17 Apr 1882; m. 1st, Feb 1818, MARY MARSHALL, b. at Tewksbury, 14 Nov 1793 daughter of Jacob and Martha (Chapman) Marshall; Mary d. at Tewksbury, 3 Dec 1830. George m. 2nd, at Tewksbury, 24 Dec 1831, SARAH WEBSTER (widow of Charles Lee Adams), b. about 1800 about whom nothing else is known by me.

ii SARAH BROWN, b. 22 Apr 1797; d. at Methuen, 12 Apr 1887; m. 1st, 7 Mar 1817, WALTER BAILEY; Walter d. at Tewksbury, 21 Oct 1817. Sarah m 2nd, 27 Apr 1824, as his second wife, BRAVITY GRAY, b. at Tewksbury, 11 Jun 1789 son of Jonathan and Mary (Needham) Gray; Bravity d. at Tewksbury, 29 Nov 1858. Bravity was first married to Sarah Carter who died in 1818.

iii MARY BALLARD BROWN, b. 22 Feb 1799; d. at Andover, 2 Dec 1893; m. at Andover, 8 Jul 1824, as his second wife, ABRAHAM JONES GOULD, b. at Weston, 1792 son of Isaac and Esther (Jones) Gould; Abraham d. at Andover, 1868. Abraham was first married to Zerviah Griffin who died in 1823.

iv HANNAH BROWN, b. 17 Sep 1801; d. at Andover, 3 Aug 1861. Hannah did not marry. In 1850, she was living with her sister Mary Gould in Andover. She died of consumption.

v THADDEUS BROWN, b. 27 Oct 1803; d. at Billerica, 28 Sep 1839; m. 1 Nov 1832, SUSAN CROSBY, b. at Billerica, 14 Apr 1809 daughter of Josiah and Betsy (Hartwell) Crosby; Sarah d. at Billerica, 28 Jun 1845.

541) JOSHUA LOVEJOY *(Lydea Abbott Lovejoy4, Henry3, George2, George1)*, b. at Andover, 8 Jan 1743/4 son of Joshua and Lydea (Abbott) Lovejoy; d. at Sanbornton, NH 28 Jan 1832; m. 30 Apr 1769, SARAH PERKINS, b. at Middleton, 10 Mar 1744 daughter of Timothy and Phebe (Peters) Perkins; Sarah d. 3 May 1828.

Joshua Lovejoy served during the French and Indian War and was at the Battle of Bunker Hill where he was wounded. He held the rank of Sergeant while serving in the militia in Colonel James Frye's Regiment during the Revolutionary War. He was wounded in the right foot and ankle by two musket balls on 17 June 1775. As a result of this injury, he received an invalid pension under the Act of 30 April 1796 and was eligible for pension payments from 4 September 1794 through his death 28 January 1832.[1470]

Joshua and Sarah started their family in Andover, were in Amherst, New Hampshire from about 1781 to 1795, and then relocated to Sanbornton where they spent their later years. While in Amherst, Joshua was town clerk and deacon.[1471]

Joshua and Sarah were the parents of ten children, the first six born at Andover and the births of the younger children at Amherst.

i JOSHUA LOVEJOY, b. at Andover, 26 Apr 1771, d. at New York, NY, Aug 1824; m. 1st, about 1798, SARAH JOHNSON, b. at Hampstead, NH, 12 Oct 1771 daughter of Caleb and Ruth (Eastman) Johnson; Sarah d. at Buffalo, 13 Dec 1813. After Sarah's death, Joshua married Mrs. Sarah Ferris.

ii ANDREW JAMES LOVEJOY, b. at Andover, 18 Jun 1772; d. at Harlem, IL, 16 Apr 1856; m. 8 Feb 1801, MARY TAYLOR, b. 18 Apr 1783 daughter of Nathan and Hannah (Batchelder) Taylor; Mary d. at Harlem, I Oct 1840.

iii SARAH LOVEJOY, b. at Andover, 16 Dec 1773; d. in Macoupin County, IL, Oct 1849;[1472] m. at Hillsborough, 4 Mar 1805, as his second wife, VINE BINGHAM, b. at Windham, CT, 27 Mar 1765 son of Elijah and Sarah (Jackson) Bingham; Vine d. at Lempster, NH, 13 Oct 1813 (probate 1813). Vine was first married to Huldah Markham. Sarah and Vine's daughter, Sarah Perkins Bingham, married Robert Smith who served in the General Assembly of Illinois.[1473]

iv HENRY LOVEJOY, b. at Andover, 7 Dec 1775; no further record and may have died young.

v PHEBE LOVEJOY, b. at Andover, 12 Jun 1778; m. 1st, about 1805, JOSEPH CONNER, b. 1764 son of Jeremiah Conner; Joseph d. at Sanbornton, 8 Feb 1806. Phebe m. 2nd, 22 Jul 1810, GEORGE BLANCHARD, b. at Milford, 16 Aug 1783 son of Augustus and Bridget (Lovewell) Blanchard; George d. about 1831, but uncertain.[1474]

vi JONATHAN LOVEJOY, b. at Andover, Mar 1780; d. at New York, NY, 2 Mar 1845; m. 16 Mar 1812, SALLY TAYLOR, b. at Sanbornton, 25 Jan 1790 daughter of Nathan and Hannah (Batchelder) Taylor; Sally d. at Concord, NH, 23 Sep 1857.

1470 Revolutionary War Pension and Bounty-Land Warrant Application Files, file of Joshua Lovejoy, NH, R6474, accessed through fold3.
1471 Secomb, *History of Amherst*, p 675
1472 *U.S., Federal Census Mortality Schedules Index, 1850-1880.*
1473 Norton, W. T. (1916). "Forgotten Statesmen of Illinois: Hon. Robert Smith." Journal of the Illinois State Historical Society, 8:1, pp 428-429
1474 Runnels, *History of Sanbornton*, volume II, p 39

vii MARY LOVEJOY, b. at Amherst, 2 Mar 1782; d. at Sanbornton, 21 Jun 1849; m. 3 Nov 1804, THOMAS TAYLOR, b. at Sanbornton, 7 Feb 1781 son of Nathan and Hannah (Batchelder) Taylor; Thomas d. at Sanbornton, 9 Jul 1850.

viii WARREN LOVEJOY, b. at Amherst, 9 Sep 1785; d. at Boston, 30 Oct 1829; m. at Concord, 14 Oct 1810, SARAH GRIDLEY HUTCHINS, b. at Concord, 3 Jul 1788 daughter of Abel and Betsey (Partridge) Hutchins.

ix LYDIA LOVEJOY, b. at Amherst, 16 Oct 1786; d. at Manchester, NH, 26 Mar 1859; m. 1st, 17 Nov 1804, DANIEL LANE son of John and Elizabeth (Batchelder) Lane; Daniel d. at Sanbornton, 14 Apr 1814. Lydia m. 2nd, Jun 1820, as his second wife, JONATHAN MOORE, b. at Stratham, NH, 26 May 1774 son of William and Elizabeth (Piper) Moore; Jonathan d. at Sanbornton, 20 Jun 1847. Jonathan was first married to Anna Taylor another of the children of Nathan and Hannah (Batchelder) Taylor.

x PERKINS LOVEJOY, b. at Amherst, 9 May 1792; m. at Boston, 25 Sep 1815, BETSY BURBECK, b. about 1790. Runnel's History of Sanbornton reports that Perkins went to Texas, but no records were located related to his life after his marriage. He is perhaps the Perkins Lovejoy who served at Boston in 1814 in Captain Dunton's Company during the War of 1812.[1475]

542) LYDIA LOVEJOY *(Lydea Abbott Lovejoy⁴, Henry³, George², George¹)*, b. at Andover, 21 Jul 1747 daughter of Joshua and Lydea (Abbott) Lovejoy; d. at Haverhill, MA, 3 Jan 1838; m. 23 Jun 1767, third cousin once removed, ABIEL HOLT, b. 3 Apr 1746 son of Thomas and Hannah (Kimball) Holt; Abiel d. 17 Nov 1824.

Abiel Holt served in the Revolution as a private in Colonel Tupper's Regiment of the Massachusetts line. He received a pension related to his service. An inventory of his estate related to his pension conducted in 1820 found that he had no real estate and had personal property valued at $26.59. Abiel was then seventy-six years old and a laborer, although he reported recent palsy rendered him unable to go out. Living in the home was his wife age 73, daughter Hannah age 28, and a grandchild age 6 years, "a sickly feeble race totally unable to support themselves, they have been assisted by the town for the last six years."[1476]

Lydia Lovejoy and Abiel Holt were the parents of nine children all born at Andover.

i CHLOE HOLT, baptized 10 Apr 1768; d. at Norway, ME, 11 Oct 1849; m. 24 May 1785, DARIUS HOLT, b. at Andover, 6 Mar 1765 son of David and Hannah (Martin) Holt; d. at Norway, 3 Jul 1854.

ii ABIEL HOLT, baptized 10 Jan 1770; d. at Milford, NH, 11 Feb 1834; m. 1792, his fourth cousin, ELIZABETH HOLT, b. at Wilton, 5 Apr 1772 daughter of Daniel and Mehitable (Putnam) Holt; Elizabeth d. at Milford, 20 Oct 1854.

iii HANNAH HOLT, baptized 19 Jan 1772; d. 18 Sep 1775.

iv SIMEON KIMBALL HOLT, b. about 1774; d. 23 Sep 1775.

v NATHAN KIMBALL HOLT, baptized 30 Aug 1778; d. at Boscawen, NH, 10 Nov 1836; m. at Andover, 1 Apr 1800, his third cousin once removed, REBECCA HOLT, b. at Andover, 25 Aug 1776 daughter of David and Rebecca (Osgood) Holt.

vi DANIEL HOLT, baptized 30 Sep 1781; d. at Norway, ME, 15 Sep 1851; m. 1802, MARY "POLLY" HALE, b. in MA, about 1783 daughter of Israel and Esther (Taylor) Hale;[1477] Polly d. at Norway, 4 Nov 1851.

vii JONATHAN LOVEJOY HOLT, b. Jul 1784; d. at Haverhill, MA, 12 Apr 1848; m. at Andover, 9 May 1808, JANE KIMBALL, b. at Andover, 25 Jul 1789 daughter of Moses and Jane (Gordon) Kimball; Jane d. at Lowell, 20 Aug 1861.

viii THOMAS HOLT, b. 15 Jan 1790; d. at Andover, after 1858; m. 1812, RUTH BEARD, b. at Wilmington, MA, about 1789 daughter of Jacob and Anna (Evans) Beard; Ruth d. at Andover, 1 Sep 1858.

ix HANNAH KIMBALL HOLT, b. 4 Jun 1792; d at Lowell, 2 Apr 1842. Hannah did not marry.

[1475] U.S., Adjutant General Military Records, 1631-1976

[1476] Revolutionary War Pension and Bounty-Land Warrant Application Files, 1800-1900

[1477] The 1841 will of Israel Hale includes a bequest to his daughter Polly Holt.

543) CHLOE LOVEJOY *(Lydea Abbott Lovejoy⁴, Henry³, George², George¹)*, b. at Andover, 26 Mar 1753 daughter of Joshua and Lydea (Abbott) Lovejoy; d. 21 Nov 1843; m. 26 Dec 1776, her fourth cousin, JOHN POOR, b. 16 Apr 1754 son of John and Rebecca (Stevens) Poor; John d. at Andover, 7 Jul 1823.

Chloe Lovejoy and John Poor were parents of seven children born at Andover.

i JOHN POOR, b. 3 Aug 1777; d. at Medford, 24 Oct 1844; m. 28 Dec 1804, MARY OSGOOD BRADLEY, b. at Haverhill, 13 Nov 1786 daughter of Joseph and Mary (Osgood) Bradley; Mary d. at Andover, 20 Feb 1829.[1478]

ii CHLOE POOR, b. 14 May 1779; d. at Andover, 8 Jun 1867; m. at Andover, 4 May 1819, as his second wife, her third cousin once removed, NATHAN BAILEY *(Elizabeth Moar Bailey⁴, Elizabeth Abbott Moar³, Nathaniel², George¹)*, b. at Andover, 4 Feb 1777 son of Moses and Elizabeth (Moar) Bailey; Nathan d. at Andover, 16 Jan 1862. Nathan Bailey was first married to BETSY ABBOTT (1780-1817). Chloe Poor, Nathan Bailey, and Betsy Abbott are Family 1121.

iii SARAH POOR, b. 12 May 1781; nothing further known.

iv HENRY POOR, b. 12 May 1781; m. at Andover, 14 May 1807, LYDIA PARKER, b. at Andover, 20 Jan 1784 daughter of Michael and Phebe (Farrington) Parker.

v ELIZABETH "BETTY" SIBSON (or Simpson) POOR, baptized 7 Dec 1783; d. at Lawrence, 4 Apr 1869; m. at Andover, 3 Apr 1806, HEZEKIAH SMITH PLUMMER whose parents are not identified; Hezekiah d. likely before 1820 when Elizabeth Plummer was head of household in Andover with two young children in the home.

vi JOSHUA POOR, baptized 26 Aug 1787; d. at Andover, 30 May 1807.

vii TIMOTHY POOR, b. 7 Sep 1790; d. at Methuen, 16 Aug 1845; m. at Methuen, 30 Dec 1823, HANNAH BODWELL, b. at Methuen, 12 Apr 1796 daughter of Alpheus and Hannah (Bodwell) Bodwell;[1479] Hannah d. at Andover, 7 Oct 1847.

544) LUCY LOVEJOY *(Lydea Abbott Lovejoy⁴, Henry³, George², George¹)*, b. at Andover, 4 Aug 1755 daughter of Joshua and Lydea (Abbott) Lovejoy; d. at Andover, 2 Apr 1844; m. 11 Apr 1776, her second cousin once removed, THEOPHILUS FRYE *(Elizabeth Frye Frye⁵, Elizabeth Osgood Frye⁴, Hannah Abbott Osgood³, George², George¹)*, b. at Andover, 12 Oct 1753 son of Samuel and Elizabeth (Frye) Frye; Theophilus d. 2 Apr 1830.

Theophilus Frye was a clothier, miller, and farmer in Frye Village of Andover. Lucy and Theophilus Frye had eleven children born at Andover.

i ENOCH FRYE, b. 29 Aug 1776; d. at Andover, 8 Sep 1864; m. 2 Aug 1798, his fourth cousin, MARY SHATTUCK *(Isaac Shattuck⁵. Joanna Chandler Shattuck⁴, Zebadiah Chandler³, Hannah Abbott Chandler², George¹)*, b. at Andover 16 Feb 1776 daughter of Isaac and Mary (Barnard) Shattuck; Mary d. at Andover, 30 Jan 1844. Mary Shattuck is a child in Family 338.

ii LUCY FRYE, b. 4 Jul 1778; d. at Boston, 16 Jun 1854; m. at Andover, 8 Jul 1794, her third cousin, SOLOMON ABBOTT *(Jonathan⁴, David³, Benjamin², George¹)*, b. at Andover, 1 Nov 1772 son of Jonathan and Mary (Chandler) Abbott; Solomon d. at Andover, 1 Sep 1840. Solomon Abbott and Lucy Frye are Family 846.

iii THEOPHILUS FRYE, b. 23 May 1780; d. at Sackets Harbor, NY during the War of 1812, 6 Mar 1814; m. 1802, his third cousin once removed, FANNY CHANDLER *(Zebadiah Chandler⁶, Zebadiah Chandler⁵, Joshua Chandler⁴, John Chandler³, Hannah Abbott Chandler², George¹)*, b. at Andover, 18 Jun 1781 daughter of Zebadiah and Luce (Chandler) Chandler; Fanny d. likely at Hopkinton, NH. After the death of Theophilus, Fanny married 9 Jun 1818, her third cousin, ISAAC SHATTUCK *(Isaac Shattuck⁶, Isaac Shattuck⁵, Joanna Chandler Shattuck⁴, Zebadiah Chandler³, Hannah Abbott Chandler², George¹)*, b. 14 Nov 1787 son of Isaac and Rebecca (Ingalls) Shattuck.

iv LYDIA FRYE, b. 3 May 1782; d. at Andover, 23 Dec 1846; m. 1 Dec 1803, her fourth cousin, DAVID BARNARD *(Sarah Shattuck Barnard⁵, Joanna Chandler Shattuck⁴, Zebadiah Chandler³, Hannah Abbott Chandler², George¹)*, baptized at Andover, 19 Jan 1777 son of John and Sarah (Shattuck) Barnard; David d. at Andover, 17 Sep 1838. David Barnard is a child in Family 339.

[1478] Abbott, Abbott Genealogies, Poor Family of Andover, p 19: "Mary Bradley Poor broken down by grief for the loss of so many children and the cares of the house, which was too much for her, committed suicide by hanging in a fit of despondency and illness."

[1479] The 1848 probate of Alpheus Bodwell of Methuen was administered by Charles A. Poor the only heir-at-law of age and the grandchild of Alpheus Bodwell. Charles A. Poor was the child of Timothy Poor and Hannah Bodwell.

v SAMUEL FRYE, b. 22 May 1784; d. at Onondaga, MI, 18 Mar 1857; m. at Andover, 5 Mar 1805, MARY BRIDGES, b. at Andover, 21 Sep 1786 daughter of James and Mary (Montgomery) Bridges; Mary d. at Onondaga, 6 Jun 1858.

vi HENRY FRYE, b. 23 Jun 1787; d. at Lexington, VA, 13 Dec 1818.[1480] Henry did not marry.

vii REUBEN FRYE, b. 7 Aug 1789; d. at Lowell, 12 Mar 1845; m. 9 Sep 1813, his first cousin, HANNAH FRYE *(Samuel Frye⁶, Elizabeth Frye Frye⁵, Elizabeth Osgood Frye⁴, Hannah Abbott Osgood³, George², George¹)*, b. in NH, about 1792 daughter of Samuel and Hannah (Poor) Frye; Hannah d. at Boston, 21 Jan 1874.[1481]

viii JAMES FRYE, b. 23 Feb 1792; d. at Andover, 1852; m. at New York, NY, 19 Apr 1817, ELSIE HOUSTON,[1482] b. in NY, about 1793 daughter of Zebulon and Sarah (Du Bois) Houston;[1483] Elsie d. at Lawrence, 31 Jul 1880.

ix JONATHAN FRYE, b. 18 Jun 1794; d. at Pittsfield, IL, 17 Apr 1863; m. at Madison, IL, 15 Jun 1823, EMELINE DISBERRY, b. in PA, 27 Dec 1806;[1484] Emeline d. at Pittsfield, 10 Sep 1860.

x ELIZABETH FRYE, b. 25 Mar 1797; d. at Hancock, NY, 22 Jul 1822; m. at Andover, 13 Oct 1818, her first cousin, SAMUEL DENNIS *(Sally Frye Dennis⁶, Elizabeth Frye Frye⁵, Elizabeth Osgood Frye⁴, Hannah Abbott Osgood³, George², George¹)*, b. at Hancock, 26 Jan 1788 son of Moses and Sally (Frye) Dennis; Samuel d. at Jasper, NY, 18 Aug 1872. Samuel Dennis married second Lucy Whitcomb, married third Alice Whiting, and married fourth Olive M. Pettee.

xi SARAH LOVEJOY FRYE, baptized 1 Dec 1799; d. at North Andover, 14 Apr 1879; m. at Andover, 21 Nov 1835, BRADFORD BARDEN, b. at Dover, MA, 5 Oct 1808 son of Frederick and Polly (Cronnen) Barden; Bradford d. at North Andover, 2 Jul 1886.

545) PHEBE ABBOT *(Henry⁴, Henry³, George², George¹)*, b. at Andover, 25 Jan 1766 daughter of Henry and Phebe (Abbot) Abbot; d. at Medford 10 Oct 1852; m. 7 Nov 1790, as his second wife, JONATHAN PORTER, b. at Braintree, 12 Mar 1745 son of Jonathan and Hannah (Hayden) Porter; Jonathan d. at Medford, 4 Nov 1817.

Jonathan Porter as a successful merchant in Medford. He did not leave a will and his estate entered probate 14 November 1817 with sons Jonathan Porter and Henry Porter as administrators as widow Phebe declined administration. Real estate was valued at $11,824 including the homestead valued at $6,385. The personal estate includes a lengthy list of merchandise and the entire value of the estate was $83,581.55.[1485]

Jonathan Porter and Phebe Abbot were parents of seven children born at Medford.

i JONATHAN PORTER, b. 13 Nov 1791; d. at Marlborough, MA, 1 Jun 1859; m. 22 Jul 1823, CATHERINE GRAY, b. at Salem, about 1797 daughter of Samuel and Anna (Orne) Gray; Catherine d. at Medford, 18 Dec 1874.

ii HENRY PORTER, b. 5 Nov 1793; d. at Medford, 17 Apr 1869; m. 13 May 1824, SUSAN S. TIDD, b. at Boston, about 1803 daughter of Jacob and Ruth (Dawes) Tidd; Susan d. at Medford, 19 Mar 1853.

iii SALLY PORTER, b. 7 Jun 1795; d. at Andover, 3 Aug 1815.[1486] Sally did not marry.

iv CHARLOTTE PORTER, b. 2 Aug 1797; d. at Boston, 17 Feb 1878; m. at Medford, 26 Mar 1820, HEZEKIAH BLANCHARD, b. at Milton, MA, 13 Oct 1785 son of Hezekiah and Esther (Tufts) Blanchard; Hezekiah d. at Roxbury, 18 Jan 1864.

v GEORGE PORTER, b. 28 Aug 1799; d. 14 Oct 1799.

vi GEORGE WASHINGTON PORTER, b. 26 Jan 1801; d. at Medford, 21 Dec 1860; m. 17 Feb 1824, ELIZABETH HALL, b. at Brattleboro, VT, about 1801 daughter of Dr. George Holmes and Sarah (Chandler) Hall;[1487] Elizabeth d. at Medford, 6 May 1862.

1480 Barker, *Frye Genealogy*, p 76

1481 Hannah's parents are named as Samuel and Hannah on her death record.

1482 U.S., Dutch Reformed Church Records in Selected States, 1639-1989, Holland Society of New York; New York, New York; NY Marriages, Book 32

1483 Elsie's parents are named as Zebulon and Sarah on her death record.

1484 Birth calculated from age at death of 53 years, 8 months, 13 days.

1485 Middlesex County, MA: Probate File Papers, 1648-1871.Online database. AmericanAncestors.org. New England Historic Genealogical Society, 2014. Case 17782

1486 Sally's death is recorded in Medford but states that she died in Andover.

1487 The names of Elizabeth's parents are given on her death record as George Hall and (-) Chandler.

vii AUGUSTA PORTER, b. 2 Mar 1803; d. at Milford, MA, 11 Mar 1883; m. at Medford, 31 May 1827, JAMES TRASK WOODBURY, b. at Bath, 9 May 1803 son of Peter and Mary (Woodbury) Woodbury; James d. at Acton, MA, 16 Jan 1861.

546) HENRY ABBOT *(Henry⁴, Henry³, George², George¹)*, b. at Andover, 8 Apr 1777 son of Henry and Phebe (Abbot) Abbot; d. at Andover, 13 Jan 1862; m. 20 May 1807, JUDITH FOLANSBEE, b. 15 Dec 1782likely the daughter of Moody and Judith (-) Folansbee of Newbury; Judith d. at Andover, 10 Feb 1864.

Henry Abbot attended Phillips Academy in Andover and graduated from Harvard in 1796. He was in the mercantile business in Bedford for a short time, but then went to sea as the Captain's clerk on the ship *Catherine* for a voyage around the world. He was a merchant in Andover and, with his brother as a partner, had a wholesale grocery business in Boston. The grocery business failed partly related to embargoes associated with the War of 1812. Henry had other adventures including a walking trip through the Alleghany Mountains and visited Kentucky.[1488]

Henry and Judith were parents of six children.

i ELIZA JUDITH ABBOTT, b. at Boston, 16 Jun 1808; d. at Andover, 13 Jan 1862. Eliza did not marry.

ii HENRY WOODWARD ABBOTT, b. at Andover, 12 Oct 1810; d. at Andover, 3 Aug 1877; m. 10 Feb 1852, his fourth cousin once removed, ELIZA FRYE *(Priscilla Baker Frye⁶, Deborah Ames Baker⁵, Nathan Ames⁴, Hannah Stevens Ames³, Elizabeth Abbott Stevens², George¹)*, b. 30 Dec 1810 daughter of Nathaniel and Priscilla (Baker) Frye; Eliza d. at Andover, 9 Jul 1876.

iii PHEBE ABBOTT, b. at Andover, 19 Dec 1814; d. at Andover, 7 Feb 1885. Phebe did not marry. She was a dressmaker.

iv MARY JANE ABBOTT, b. at Andover, 23 Aug 1820; d. at Groveland, MA, 28 Apr 1894; m. 29 Jan 1846, as his second wife, EBEN GREENOUGH, b. at Bradford, 2 Oct 1812 son of Bailey and Betsey (Parker) Greenough;[1489] Eben d. at Groveland, 5 Oct 1890.

v ISAAC MOODY ABBOTT, b. at Andover, 24 Jan 1823; d. at Andover, 12 Sep 1842.

vi SUSAN CHARLOTTE ABBOTT, b. at Andover, 13 Dec 1827; d. at Lawrence, 19 Sep 1911. Charlotte did not marry. She was a dressmaker.

547) HENRY BUTLER *(Dorcas Abbott Butler⁴, Henry³, George², George¹)*, b. at Andover, 27 Nov 1754 son of Benjamin and Dorcas (Abbott) Butler; d. 20 Jul 1813; m. 11 Apr 1776, ISABELLA FISKE, b. at Epping, 2 Aug 1757 (or 2 Aug 1759)[1490] daughter of Ebenezer and Elizabeth (Cotton) Fiske; Isabella d. 17 Jan 1808. After Isabella's death, Henry married Ruth Parsons.

Henry Butler served in the Revolution as captain of a volunteer company. He later served as Major General of the first division of New Hampshire militia. He was the first postmaster of Nottingham. He was Master of the Sullivan Lodge of Masons.[1491]

In Henry Butler's will written 10 July 1813, beloved wife Ruth receives all the household furnishings she brought to the marriage as well as use of one-third on the land on which he is living as long as she remains a widow. She also receives use of the easterly bedroom and the privilege of the kitchen. Son Benjamin Butler receives five dollars, son Ebenezer forty dollars, son Samuel Abbot Butler receives the sword, pistols, and all the military apparatus, son Ward Cotton Butler receives the silver tankard and twenty dollars. Sons Samuel Abbot and Ward Cotton receive 50 acres of land in Nottingham. Daughter Sally Haley wife of John Haley receives one-half of the household furniture left after the death of her mother Isabella, except the largest looking glass and the feather bed which belonged to the widow Baker are to go to daughter Dorcas. Daughter Dorcas Furber wife of William Furber receives one-half of the household furniture left by her mother. His three grandchildren Joanna Norris, Betsy Norris, and William Norris each receive one dollar. The remainder of the estate goes to son Henry Butler who is also named executor.[1492]

Henry Butler and Isabella Fiske were parents of ten children born at Nottingham.

i ELIZABETH BUTLER, b. 29 Jul 1777; d. at Nottingham, 12 Jul 1808; m. about 1799, as his second wife, WILLIAM NORRIS, b. at Epping, 4 Jun 1762 son of Josiah and Eunice (Coffin) Norris; William d. at Nottingham, 1839. William Norris was first married to Eleanor Blake, and after Elizabeth's death, married for a third time to Nancy Hilton.

[1488] Palmer, *Necrology of Alumni of Harvard College*, pp 386-388

[1489] Eben's parents are confirmed on his death record.

[1490] Ancestry.com. New Hampshire, Births and Christenings Index, 1714-1904

[1491] Cogswell, *History of Nottingham*, pp 172-173

[1492] *New Hampshire. Probate Court (Rockingham County);* Probate Place: *Rockingham, New Hampshire*, Estate Paper No. 8728, accessed through ancestry.com.

ii BENJAMIN BUTLER, b. 11 Apr 1779; d. at Cornville, ME, 1 Oct 1851; m. 6 Jul 1806, HANNAH HILTON, b. at Deerfield, 11 Mar 1787 daughter of Joseph and Sarah (Thurston) Hilton; Hannah d. a Cornville, 3 Apr 1861.

iii EBENEZER BUTLER, b. 31 Mar 1781; d. at Nottingham, 25 Dec 1850; m. at Sanbornton, 19 Oct 1809, SARAH HERSEY, b. at Sanbornton, 24 Oct 1785 daughter of James and Elizabeth (Hayes) Hersey; Sarah d. at Nottingham, 27 Oct 1854.

iv HENRY BUTLER, b. 30 Jun 1783; d. after 1870, Hampden, ME; m. 1st, 1 Oct 1806, ABIGAIL FORD, b. at Nottingham, 29 Nov 1787 daughter of John and Mehitable (Ford) Ford; Abigail d. at Nottingham, 7 Jun 1817. Henry m. 2nd, 12 Mar 1818, NANCY HERSEY, b. at Sanbornton, 22 Oct 1792 daughter of James and Elizabeth (Hayes) Hersey; Nancy d. at Hampden, ME, after 1870.

v SARAH COTTA BUTLER, b. 12 Aug 1785; d. at Lee, NH, 17 Jan 1872; m. 18 Sep 1808, JOHN HALEY, b. 17 Feb 1783 son of Samuel and Martha (Nealley) Haley; John d. at Lee, 28 Nov 1874.

vi DORCAS BUTLER, b. 15 Apr 1787; d. at Nottingham, 8 Nov 1855; m. 11 Feb 1812, WILLIAM FURBER, b. 9 Feb 1783 son of Joshua and Betsy (Page) Furber; William d. at Nottingham, 18 Mar 1853.

vii SAMUEL ABBOTT BUTLER, b. 19 Jul 1789; d. near Highgate, 16 Jan 1814. Samuel was a Sergeant during the War of 1812. He died of wounds suffered in an encounter with the British infantry near Highgate.[1493]

viii Daughter, b. 16 Jun 1789 and d. Jun 1789

ix Son, b. 16 Jun 1789 and d. Jun 1789

x WARD COTTON BUTLER, b. 29 Jan 1795; d. at Philadelphia, 2 Dec 1861; m. 20 Sep 1820, MARGARET ANDERSON, b. about 1805 in New Jersey; Margaret d. after 1863 (she was listed in the Philadelphia city directory in 1863.

548) MARY BUTLER *(Dorcas Abbott Butler⁴, Henry³, George², George¹)*, b. at Nottingham, 30 Mar 1760 daughter of Benjamin and Dorcas (Abbott) Butler; d. at Northfield, 1846; m. 1776, ABRAHAM BROWN, b. at Epping, 8 May 1753 son of Abraham and Hannah (Osgood) Brown; Abraham d. at Northfield 8 Mar 1824.

Mary and Abraham Brown settled in Northfield, New Hampshire. Abraham served in the Revolutionary War as a drummer in the army for three years and as a military adjutant for four years.[1494]

Northfield was newly incorporated at the time Mary and Abraham were starting their family. Northfield began as the "north fields" of Canterbury where a garrison had been formed. The settlers in this area petitioned for separated incorporation which occurred in 1780. Mary Butler Brown was one of those known in town for the "gift of healing by the laying on of the hands."[1495]

Abraham Brown wrote his will 3 March 1824. Beloved wife Polly Brown receives the income from one-sixth part of the farm, two rooms on the north side of the house with privileges to the chamber above and the cellar, one cow, four sheep, and the use of the barn. Son Abraham is to provide his mother with the use of a horse and saddle and to provide firewood as long as she remains a widow. Daughter Hannah Brown receives forty dollars to be paid to her at age twenty-one. Daughter Sally Carr receives five dollars and daughters Phebe Brown and Clarissa Brown forty dollars each. The three unmarried daughters have the privilege to stay in the family home as long as they are unmarried. Son Benjamin Brown receives one hundred dollars to be paid with two years after he reaches age twenty-one. Daughter Polly Hills receives one dollar and son Henry Brown one hundred dollars when he reaches age twenty-one. Also, when he reaches age twenty-one, Henry is free to learn whichever mechanical art he chooses. Sons Henry and Benjamin each receive six sheep and a cow. Daughter Dorcas Osgood receives one dollar. Son Abraham Brown and Josiah Ambrose are named executors.[1496]

Mary and Abraham Brown had nine children whose births are recorded in various towns in Merrimack County, New Hampshire.

i POLLY BROWN, b. 13 Mar 1777; d. at Merrimack County, NH, Aug 1849;[1497] m. 13 Jan 1804, JOHN HILLS, b. at Haverhill, 15 Jun 1770 son of Daniel and Hannah (Emery) Hills; John d. 20 Jan 1852. John Hills was a cooper and a farmer in Northfield.

1493 Cogswell, *History of Nottingham*, p 178

1494 Cross, *History of Northfield, New Hampshire, Part I*, p 72

1495 Cross, *History of Northfield, Part I*, p 149

1496 *New Hampshire Wills and Probate Records 1643-1982,* Will of Abraham Brown, Merrimack, 3 Mar 1824.

1497 U.S., Federal Census Mortality Schedules Index, 1850-1880

ii SALLY BROWN, b. at Epping, 17 Feb 1779; d. at London, NH, 9 Dec 1849; m. at London, 12 Feb 1800, JOHN CARR, b. at Salisbury, MA, 11 Mar 1778 son of Elliot and Joanna (Dow) Carr; John d. 14 Aug 1844.

iii DORCAS BROWN, b. at Northfield, 5 Apr 1785; d. at East Andover, NH, 9 Nov 1861; m. 1807, ENOCH OSGOOD, b. at Salisbury, MA, 23 Feb 1773 son of Benjamin and Hannah (Rowell) Osgood;[1498] Enock d. at Salisbury, NH, 1832.

iv ABRAHAM BROWN, b. at Northfield, 1 Sep 1787; d. 8 Jun 1861; m. 31 Dec 1808, BETSEY FORREST, b. at Canterbury, 9 Apr 1783 daughter of William and Dorothy (Worthen) Forrest; Betsy d. at Northfield, 27 Dec 1860.

v HANNAH BROWN, b. at Northfield, 9 Dec 1791; d. at Cottage Hill, IL (where she had gone to stay with her children), 15 Mar 1859; m. 29 Sep 1817, JEREMIAH FORREST, b. at Canterbury, 25 Jun 1787 son of William and Dorothy (Worthen) Forrest; Jeremiah d. 9 Aug 1845.

vi PHEBE BROWN, b. at Pittsfield (place of record), 7 Jun 1794; d. at East Andover, NH, 28 Jan 1852. Phebe did not marry. At the 1850 U.S. census, Phebe was living with her sister Dorcas Osgood in Andover, NH.[1499]

vii BENJAMIN BUTLER BROWN, b. at Northfield, 19 Apr 1800; d. at East Andover, NH, 4 Feb 1867; m. 30 Dec 1824, PHEBE GALE, b. at Sanbornton, 24 Jan 1802 daughter of Stephen and Molly (Jewett) Gale; Phebe d. Feb 1845. After Phebe's death, Benjamin married MARY SANBORN on 4 Feb 1855.

viii HENRY BUTLER BROWN, b. at Northfield, 4 Jul 1802; d. at Big Rapids, MI, 13 Dec 1872; m. at Plainfield, NH, 24 Jan 1829, LAURA TICKNOR, b. at Lebanon, NH, 11 Jun 1804 daughter of John and Mabel (Green) Ticknor;[1500][1501] Laura d. at Rockford, IL, 20 Dec 1867. Henry Brown was a physician. The family lived in Vermont until about 1850, then relocated to Illinois. After his wife's death, Henry remarried to Sarah Hosmer, 28 Sep 1871 in Big Rapids, MI.

ix CLARISSA BROWN, b. 30 Mar 1804; d. at Meredith, NH, 1 Jun 1825; m. 24 Jan 1824, EDWARD CHASE perhaps the son of Thomas Chase. After Clarissa's death, Edward married Hannah Blake.

549) DORCAS BUTLER *(Dorcas Abbott Butler[4], Henry[3], George[2], George[1])*, b. at Nottingham, 9 Oct 1766 daughter of Benjamin and Dorcas (Abbott) Butler; d. at Colerain Township, OH, 9 Oct 1857;[1502] m. 5 Jun 1786, JONATHAN CILLEY, b. 8 Mar 1762 son of Joseph and Sarah (Longfellow) Cilley; Jonathan d. at Colerain Township, 21 Mar 1807.

Jonathan Cilley served in the Revolution as a Lieutenant in the New Hampshire line. He first attempted to enlist at the outbreak of the was when he was just fourteen. The story related in the pension application file of his widow Dorcas was that Captain Ford, who knew Jonathan's family, would not enlist him as it was against the wishes of his parents. However, Jonathan refused to go home and followed the company. The company finally met up with Jonathan's father, Colonel Joseph Cilley, and Colonel Cilley permitted his son to remain and Jonathan had a role as a waiter. Jonathan was taken prisoner for a time but was exchanged and rejoined his company. He was at the Battle of Saratoga. He rose to the rank of Lieutenant.[1503] He later held a rank of Major.[1504]

Jonathan and Dorcas started their family in Nottingham, New Hampshire where the births of the oldest five children. They were perhaps in Epsom for a time as the birth of at least one child is recorded there. In 1802, the family picked up and started the journey to Ohio, spent the winter in Wheeling and arrived in Colerain, Ohio in 1803. Jonathan purchased a section of land on the Big Miami. Jonathan died on asthma in 1807.[1505]

Jonathan Cilley and Dorcas Butler were parents of eleven children.

i JOSEPH CILLEY, b. at Nottingham, NH, 28 Dec 1786; d. at Colerain, OH, 28 Nov 1828. Joseph did not marry.

ii SARAH CILLEY, b. at Nottingham, 7 Jan 1789; d. at Miamitown, OH, 5 Oct 1862; m. 1st, 12 Mar 1812, Rev. HUGH ANDREWS, b. 22 Oct 1774;[1506] Hugh d. at Miamitown, 1 Sep 1822.

iii BENJAMIN CILLEY, b. at Nottingham, 7 Jan 1789; d. at Whitewater, OH, 11 Feb 1851; m. at Hamilton County, OH, 28 Feb 1822, MARTHA MCCORMICK, b. in OH, about 1798; Martha d. at Whitewater, 14 Oct 1873.

1498 Eastman, *History of the Town of Andover, New Hampshire*, p 262

1499 Year: 1850; Census Place: Andover, Merrimack, New Hampshire; Roll: M432_436; Page: 186B; Image: 380

1500 Laura Ticknor's parents are confirmed by the 1836 New Hampshire will of John Ticknor which includes a bequest to daughter Laura wife of Henry B. Butler.

1501 Hunnewell, *The Ticknor Family*, p 19

1502 Year: 1850; Census Place: Colerain, Hamilton, Ohio; Roll: M432_686; Page: 367B; Image: 256. In the 1850 U.S. Census, 83-year-old Dorcas Cilley, born in NH, was living in the household of Samuel and Mary Hardin who is Dorcas's daughter.

1503 Revolutionary War Pension and Bounty-Land Warrant Application Files, 1800-1900, Case W5246

1504 The Official Roster of the Soldiers of the American Revolution Buried in the State of Ohio, Vol. III. Roster Listings, p 72

1505 Ford, *History of Hamilton County, Ohio*, p 281

1506 Date of birth is on his gravestone. Findagrave: 39465712

iv JONATHAN CILLEY, b. at Nottingham, 5 Jan 1791; d. at Glendale, OH, 29 Dec 1874; m. 24 Oct 1830, SARAH LEE, b. at Saratoga County, NY, 28 Sep 1815 daughter of Rensalear and Sarah (Heisted) Lee;[1507] Sarah d. at Hartwell, OH, 25 Jun 1889.

v DORCAS CILLEY, b. at Nottingham, 22 Dec 1793; d. at Dunlap, OH, 7 Jun 1837; m. about 1825, UZAL GOULD, b. about 1799; Uzal d. at Springdale, OH, 12 Sep 1834.

vi HENRY CILLEY, b. 16 Apr 1796; d. at Colerian, Oh, 23 Mar 1845. Henry did not marry.

vii BRADBURY CILLEY, b. recorded at Epsom, NH, 16 May 1798; d. at Colerian, OH, 19 Jul 1874; m. 15 Feb 1834, HARRIET HEDGES, b. at Hamilton County, OH, 12 Apr 1810 daughter of Elias and Elizabeth (Gatsen) Hedges; Harriet d. at Colerain, 1 Sep 1885.

viii MARY CILLEY, b. 25 May 1800; d. at Colerain, 8 Mar 1873; m. 12 Nov 1829, SAMUEL DAVIS HARDIN, b. in PA, 1798 son of James and Eleanor (Davis) Hardin; Samuel d. at Colerain, 30 Aug 1851.

ix MARTHA POOR CILLEY, b. 4 Jul 1803; d. at Hamilton County, OH, 23 Oct 1848; m. at Hamilton County, OH, 22 Feb 1835, PHILIP BROWN.

x JACOB CILLEY, b. at Colerain, Jan 1807; d. Feb 1807.

xi GATES CILLEY, b. at Colerain, Jan 1807; d. Feb 1807.

550) HENRY ABBOTT HOVEY *(Mary Abbott Hovey⁴, Henry³, George², George¹)*, b. at Dracut, 15 Jan 1764 son of Thomas and Mary (Abbott) Hovey; d. at Milford, NH about 1830;[1508] m. 29 May 1791, HANNAH BRADLEY, b. at Dracut, 1 May 1768 daughter of Amos and Elizabeth (Page) Bradley; Hannah d. at Boston 14 May 1851.[1509]

Henry Abbott Hovey was a farmer in Dracut where he and his wife Hannah Bradley reared ten children.

Probate records were not located for either Henry or Hannah. Their daughter Mary did not marry and wrote her will 20 February 1875. In her will she makes monetary bequests to her siblings, nieces, nephews, and grandnieces and grandnephews. Among those receiving bequests are Angelina H. Sylvester (this is her sister with whom Mary lived for much of her adult life), and bequests to each of Angelina's children in amounts of $1,000 or $1,100 each. There are then smaller bequests ($50) to Rhoda B. Spalding, Eliza P. Hyde, Eldridge A. Hovey, Susan D. Hovey, George E. Hovey, Charles H. Hovey, Louisa J. Hovey, and a lengthy list of other heirs who seem to be grandnieces and grandnephews. Rhoda Spalding and Eliza Hyde are Mary's sisters. Eldridge Hovey is her brother and Susan D. Hovey is his wife. George E. Hovey is likely the son of Eldridge, and Charles Hovey and Louisa Hovey are the children of her brother Henry Abbot Hovey who is deceased.[1510]

Henry Abbott Hovey and Hannah Bradley had ten children whose births are recorded at Dracut.

i HANNAH HOVEY, b. 15 Oct 1791; d. at Boston, 10 Nov 1872; m. 2 May 1813, REUBEN REED, b. at Cambridge, 9 Nov 1785 son of Joseph and Eunice (Cook) Reed; Reuben d. at Boston, 17 May 1873.

ii PERMELIA HOVEY, b. 10 Oct 1793; d. at Providence, RI, 17 Aug 1835; m. at Boston, 28 Nov 1816, SAMUEL STONE, b. at Watertown, 28 Jun 1791 son of Jonathan and Sarah (-) Stone; Samuel d. at Lowell, 22 Jan 1864. After Permelia's death, Samuel m. Lydia Turner.

iii RHODA BRADLEY HOVEY, b. 17 Oct 1795; d. at Lowell, Oct 1877; m. at Chelmsford, 21 Jul 1816, SIMEON SPALDING, b. at Chelmsford, 9 Dec 1785 son of Micah and Mary (Chamberlain) Spalding; Simeon d. at Lowell, 13 Aug 1855.

iv MARY HOVEY, b. 26 Dec 1797; d. at Boston, 18 Jan 1876. Mary did not marry.[1511]

[1507] Cilley, *Cilley Family*, p 36

[1508] U.S., Newspaper Extractions from the Northeast, 1704-1930; Columbian Centinel; Henry A. Hovey died at Milford in edition 31 Jul 1830.

[1509] *Massachusetts: Vital Records, 1841-1910.* (From original records held by the Massachusetts Archives. Online database: *AmericanAncestors.org*, New England Historic Genealogical Society, 2004.)

[1510] *Suffolk County, MA: Probate File Papers, Will of Mary Hovey, Probate Records, volumes 483-484, 1875-1876.*

[1511] The Hovey Book (Daniel Hovey Association) list a husband for Mary Hovey (Joseph Swan). However, it was Mary's first cousin (Mary daughter of Benjamin) that married Joseph Swan. This is supported by the 1866 will of Benjamin Swan that includes a bequest to his granddaughter Mary Hovey Swan Emerson.

v ELIZABETH PAGE "ELIZA" HOVEY, b. 11 Jun 1800; d. at Brattleboro, VT, 1 Apr 1888;[1512] m. at Chelmsford, 30 Mar 1829, WILLIAM HYDE, b. at Lancaster, 14 Jun 1802 son of John and Mary (Marean) Hyde;[1513] William d. at Brattleboro, 23 Jul 1890.

vi HENRY ABBOT HOVEY, b. 22 Jun 1802; d. at St. Louis, MO, 1 Nov 1854; m. 6 Apr 1826, REBECCA FRANCIS, b. 27 Jun 1800 whose parents have not been identified; Rebecca d. 28 Nov 1833. Henry next married, 20 Mar 1834, JANE LOUISA GRAY, about whom nothing else is known. *The Hovey Book* reports that Henry had a third wife, but she has not been located.

vii ANGELINA HOVEY, b. 28 Jun 1804; d. at Boston, 26 Jan 1887; m. 5 Oct 1837, as his second wife, NATHANIEL SYLVESTER, b. at Hanover, MA, 12 Aug 1797 son of Nathaniel and Lucy (Clapp) Sylvester; Nathaniel d. at Boston, 6 Jul 1856. Nathaniel was first married to Nancy Farnsworth.

viii ALFRED HOVEY, b. 24 Feb 1807; d. 22 Sep 1825.

ix ELDRIDGE AUGUSTUS HOVEY, b. 28 Jan 1811; d. at Roxbury, 11 Dec 1894; m. at Boston, 2 Apr 1835, SUSAN D. BARNES, b. at Plymouth, about 1814 daughter of Lemuel and Susan (Marshall) Barnes;[1514] Susan d. at Boston, 4 Jan 1899.

x CHARLES HOVEY, b. 23 Oct 1813; d. 4 Aug 1817.

551) JAMES PLATTS HOVEY *(Mary Abbott Hovey⁴, Henry³, George², George¹)*, b. at Dracut, 21 Jul 1767 son of Thomas and Mary (Abbott) Hovey; d. at Dracut, 30 Nov 1831; m. 20 Feb 1801, REBEKAH HOVEY, b. at Boxford, about 1777 daughter of Ivory and Lucy (Peabody) Hovey; Rebekah d. at Lowell, 1 Feb 1853.

James Platts Hovey inherited the family homestead from his father. James converted the family home to a tavern which served as a stagecoach stop on the road from Boston to Concord.[1515]

James Hovey did not leave a will. On 11 April 1832, the following heirs signed a statement declining administration of the estate and requesting Nathaniel Stickney to be administrator: Rebekah Hovey, James Hovey, H. N. Hovey, Joshua Hovey, Cyrus Hovey, and George Hovey. Real estate was valued at $2,096 and personal estate at $332.75.[1516]

James Platts Hovey and Rebekah Hovey were parents of six children all born at Dracut.

i WILLIAM HOVEY, b. 10 Sep 1802; d. at Lowell, 21 Mar 1893; m. about 1832, HANNAH CARHART, b. at New York, NY, 2 Feb 1813 daughter of Zachariah and Mary (Beck) Carhart;[1517] Hannah d. at Lowell, 17 Jun 1892.

ii JAMES HOVEY, b. 8 Mar 1804; d. at Waldoboro, ME, 1 Sep 1855; m. ELIZA ANN MORSE, b. at Waldoboro, 4 Mar 1809 daughter of Samuel and Olive (Pond) Morse; Eliza d. at Boston, 10 Jun 1872.

iii HORATIO NELSON HOVEY, b. 10 Dec 1805; d. at Cambridge, MA, 18 Jan 1899; m. MARY ANN KINSLEY, b. at Cambridge, 18 Sep 1815 daughter of Henry and Mary (Pratt) Kinsley; Mary Ann d. at Cambridge, 26 Dec 1891.

iv JOSHUA HOVEY, b. 8 Jun 1808; d. at Lowell, 15 Mar 1899; m. 1st, his second cousin once removed, ELIZABETH JANE HOLT *(Joshua Holt⁶, Lydia Lovejoy Holt⁵, Lydea Abbott Lovejoy⁴, Henry³, George², George¹)*, b. at Haverhill, 4 Jun 1815 daughter of Joshua Lovejoy and Jane (Kimball) Holt; Elizabeth d. at Dracut, 17 Jul 1846. Joshua m. 2nd, 29 Nov 1849, Elizabeth's sister HARRIET HOLT, b. at Haverhill, 1819; Harriet d. at Lowell, 21 Apr 1860.

v GEORGE HOVEY, b. 26 Nov 1810; d. at Dracut, 27 Jun 1905; m. NANCY WOOD, b. at Sutton, VT, 9 Feb 1820 daughter of Uriah and Sarah (Church) Wood; Nancy d. at Dracut, 6 Jul 1891.

vi CYRUS HOVEY, b. 14 Jul 1813; d. at Lowell, 26 Mar 1890; m. at Lowell, 25 May 1853, DORCAS MAROE ELLIOTT, b. at Rumney, NH, 29 Sep 1830 daughter of Daniel and Dorcas (Baker) Elliott; Dorcas d. at Lowell, 18 May 1855.

[1512] Vermont death records give the date as 1 May 1888. It is reported on findagrave that her gravestone is engraved 1 May 1883, but there is not a photo of the gravestone so that could not be verified.
[1513] The names of his parents are given on his death record as John Hyde and Mary Narine.
[1514] The names of Susan's parents are given on her death record.
[1515] Duda, Rebecca. 2018. "At the Crossroads in Dracut Stood the Hovey Tavern." Discovering the Historic Merrimack Valley. http://blogs.lowellsun.com/history/2018/04/28/at-the-crossroads-in-dracut-stood-the-hovey-tavern/
[1516] Middlesex County, MA: Probate File Papers, 1648-1871.Online database. AmericanAncestors.org. New England Historic Genealogical Society, 2014. Case number: 11956
[1517] Hannah's parents are given as Zachariah and Mary on her death record.

552) SAMUEL HOVEY *(Mary Abbott Hovey⁴, Henry³, George², George¹)*, b. at Dracut, 26 Oct 1773 son of Thomas and Mary (Abbott) Hovey; d. after 1850;[1518] m. 12 Sep 1795, MARTHA "PATTY" BRADLEY, b. at Dracut, 31 Jan 1774 daughter of Amos and Elizabeth (Page) Bradley; Martha d. 5 Jul 1825 at Dracut.

Samuel Hovey was a carpenter. He and Martha were parents of four children born at Dracut.[1519]

i GILBERT HOVEY, b. 12 Oct 1797; d. 22 Jan 1798.

ii GEORGE HOVEY, b. 26 Oct 1801; nothing further known.

iii MARTHA HOVEY, b. 26 Nov 1801; nothing further known.

iv JULIA HOVEY, b. 10 Apr 1805; d. at Bolton, MA, 1 Apr 1879; m. at Cambridge, 26 Oct 1837, LYMAN MOORE, b. at Bolton, 8 Jun 1813 son of Levi and Betsey (Greenleaf) Moore; Lyman d. at Bolton, 20 Mar 1892.

553) BENJAMIN HOVEY *(Mary Abbott Hovey⁴, Henry³, George², George¹)*, b. at Dracut, 9 May 1775 of Thomas and Mary (Abbott) Hovey; d. at Dracut, 30 Mar 1866; m. at Medford, 2 Aug 1797, LOIS (Louisa) JENKINS, b. at Malden, 2 Aug 1767 daughter of Ezekiel and Margaret (Floyd) Jenkins;[1520] Lois d. at Dracut, 8 Aug 1846.

Benjamin Hovey had a hat factory in Dracut which was located on Pleasant Street until 1814 when the shop was moved to Sladen Street.[1521] Benjamin grew up in the historic Hovey homestead in Dracut that remained in the family 130 years; the house was demolished in 1933.[1522]

Benjamin Hovey wrote his will February 1860. He bequeaths all his personal and real estate to daughter Nancy H. Hovey. He describes at length the boundaries of the property that will go to Nancy. He makes bequests of five dollars each to his three grandchildren Mary Emerson, Joseph Swan and Edward P. Swan. The three grandchildren named are the children of his daughter Mary Hovey and her husband Joseph Swan. Mary Swan Emerson died in 1863 between the date of the will and the probate of the estate.[1523]

Daughter Nancy Heath Hovey did not marry. She lived with her father until his death and after lived on her own in the family home. In 1878, a guardian was appointed for her as she was incapable of caring for herself and was described as "insane." The petition was made by the selectmen of Dracut. Her nephew Joseph Swan was named her guardian. At the time of the guardianship, the value of her real property was $2,075 and the amount of her personal estate $1,146. The personal estate included $1,100 in cash in savings accounts. Perhaps Nancy developed dementia in her later years as she was well functioning enough to serve as executrix of her father's estate in 1866.[1524]

Benjamin and Lois Hovey had five children born at Dracut.

i MARY HOVEY, b. 9 Nov 1797; d. at Lowell, 20 May 1853; m. 27 Mar 1824, JOSEPH SWAN, b. about 1796 in NH; Joseph d. at Dracut, 1845. Mary Hovey and Joseph Swan had four children at Dracut one of whom died in infancy. These are the only grandchildren of Benjamin Hovey and Lois Jenkins.

ii BENJAMIN HOVEY, b. 26 Nov 1800; d. 12 Dec 1801.

iii BENJAMIN HOVEY, b. 7 Jun 1804; d. 2 May 1805.

iv LOUISA HOVEY, b. 30 Aug 1806; d. 1 Oct 1829. Louisa did not marry.

v NANCY HEATH HOVEY, b. 13 Nov 1808; d. at Dracut, May 1882.

554) JOSEPH HOVEY *(Mary Abbott Hovey⁴, Henry³, George², George¹)*, b. at Dracut, 25 May 1784 son of Thomas and Mary (Abbott) Hovey; d. 29 Aug 1860; m. 4 Jul 1812, MARY HOVEY, b. at Boxford, Nov 1781 daughter of Ivory and Lucy (Peabody) Hovey; Mary d. at Dracut, 13 Mar 1857.

1518 Year: 1850; Census Place: Cambridge, Middlesex, Massachusetts; Roll: M432_325; Page: 46B; Image: 98. Samuel Hovey living in Cambridge at the 1850 U.S. Census, age 76.

1519 There is an apparent error in the birth transcriptions of children George and Martha who are listed as being born one month apart. They were perhaps twins.

1520 Floyd, "Descendants of Joel Jenkins," NEHGR, p 319

1521 Coburn, History of Dracut, p 224

1522 Duda, Rebecca A. (28 April 2018), "At the Crossroads in Dracut Stood the Hovey Tavern," Lowell Sun Blogs, http://blogs.lowellsun.com/history/2018/04/28/at-the-crossroads-in-dracut-stood-the-hovey-tavern/?doing_wp_cron=1532033685.4760420322418212890625

1523 *Middlesex County, MA: Probate File Papers, 1648-1871. Probate of Benjamin Hovey, 1866, Case number 34657.*

1524 *Middlesex County (Mass.) Probate Packets (1 - 4702) (Second Series) 1872-1967 (And 4703 - 19,935)*; Author: *Massachusetts. Probate Court (Middlesex County)*; Probate Place: *Middlesex, Massachusetts*, case number 5498, guardianship of Nancy H. Hovey.

Joseph Hovey did not leave a will and his estate entered probate 27 August 1860. Joseph Hovey was named administrator and the only two heirs listed were Joseph Hovey and Augustus Hovey both of Lowell. Real estate was valued at $1,016.75 and personal estate at $1,182.99. The personal estate included a note owed by John Pierce for $936.[1525]

i JOSEPH HOVEY, b. at Dracut, 26 Sep 1812; d. at Lowell, Jul 1902; m. at Dracut, 13 Sep 1840, SARAH C. TIBBETTS, b. at Lyndon, VT, about 1812 daughter of Peter and Sarah (Richards) Tibbetts; Sarah d. at Lowell, 1 Mar 1881.

ii AUGUSTUS HOVEY, b. at Dracut, 26 Sep 1812; d. at Lowell, 20 Mar 1879; m. at Dracut, 7 Jun 1838, CLARISSA SOPHIA VARNUM, b. at Dracut, 18 Jul 1818 daughter of Prescott and Lydia (Richardson) Varnum; Clarissa d. at Lowell, 12 Oct 1905.

555) ISAAC ABBOT *(Isaac⁴, Isaac³, George², George¹)*, b. at Andover, 9 Dec 1768 son of Isaac and Phebe (Chandler) Abbot; d. at Andover, 27 Dec 1806;[1526] m. 1st, 5 Jul 1798, HEPHZIBAH FISKE, b. 21 Apr 1773 daughter of John and Hephzibah (-) Fiske; Hephzibah d. 22 Mar 1800. Isaac m. 2nd, 7 Oct 1801, MARY MOULTON, b. at Danvers, 16 Mar 1775 daughter of Ebenezer and Elizabeth (Curtis) Moulton; Mary d. 19 Aug 1851.

Isaac Abbot was a farmer in Andover. He did not leave a will and his estate entered probate 19 January 1807.[1527] Dower was set off to widow Mary Abbot. The remainder of the real estate not set aside for the dower was valued at $5,255. The distribution of the real estate in 1820 included lots to the following heirs: son Josiah Fisk Abbot, daughter Mary Fisk Abbot, daughter Phebe Fisk Abbot, son Samuel Abbot, and son Isaac Abbot.

Child of Isaac Abbott and Hephzibah Fiske:

i MARY FISK ABBOTT, b. at Andover, 14 Mar 1800; d. at Andover, 12 Feb 1881; m. 12 Dec 1823, her second cousin, NATHAN SHATTUCK *(Phebe Abbott Shattuck⁵, Jonathan⁴, David³, Benjamin², George¹)*, b. at Andover, 4 Mar 1797 son of Joseph and Phebe (Abbott) Shattuck; Nathan d. at Andover, 27 Mar 1868. Nathan Shattuck is a child in Family 843.

Isaac Abbott and Mary Moulton had five children born at Andover.

i JOSIAH FISK ABBOTT, b. 5 Dec 1801; d. at Andover, 24 Dec 1873; m. 4 Jan 1827, his third cousin, HANNAH HOLT *(Dane Holt⁶, Lydia Ballard Holt⁵, Lydia Chandler Ballard⁴, John Chandler³, Hannah Abbott Chandler², George¹)*, b. at Andover, 15 Jun 1805 daughter of Dane and Mary (Wardwell) Holt; Hannah d. at Andover, 10 Jan 1882.

ii PHEBE FISK ABBOTT, b. 9 Jul 1803; d. 20 Feb 1821.

iii SARAH FISK ABBOTT, b. about 1804, baptized at Andover, 21 Jun 1807.[1528] There is no record for Sarah other than the baptism. She is not included in the 1820 distribution of her father's estate so likely died young.

iv ISAAC ABBOTT, b. 26 Mar 1805; d. at Andover, 29 Aug 1858; m. 1st, 4 Nov 1828, DOLLY FARNUM, b. at Andover, 8 Jun 1808 daughter of Benjamin and Ruth (Saltmarsh) Farnum; Dolly d. at Andover, 21 Dec 1840. Isaac m. 2nd, at Andover, 18 Oct 1843, ELIZA ANN CURTIS, b. at Sanford, ME, 1818 daughter of Ephraim and Rhoda (Murray) Curtis; Eliza d. at Andover, 21 Jan 1889. After Isaac's death, Eliza married Moses B. Kenney 31 Jan 1860.

v SAMUEL ABBOTT, b. 22 Feb 1807; d. at Andover, 3 Sep 1869; m. 1st, 20 Jun 1839, SUSANNA BOWMAN FARNUM, b. at Andover, Dec 1812 daughter of Benjamin and Ruth (Saltmarsh) Farnum; Susanna d. at Andover, 22 Feb 1847. Samuel m. 2nd, 15 May 1849, CAROLINE TRULL, b. at Andover, 6 Apr 1818 daughter of Levi and Anna (Harnden) Trull; Caroline d. at Lowell, 23 Oct 1882.

556) WILLIAM ABBOT *(Isaac⁴, Isaac³, George², George¹)*, b. at Andover, 30 Oct 1772 son of Isaac and Phebe (Chandler) Abbot; d. at Concord, NH about 1856 (probate date 24 Jun 1856); m. 14 May 1801, his third cousin once removed, REBECCA BAILEY *(Elizabeth Mooar Bailey⁴, Elizabeth Abbott Mooar³, Nathaniel², George¹)*, b. 10 Apr 1781 daughter of Moses and

[1525] Middlesex County, MA: Probate File Papers, 1648-1871.Online database. AmericanAncestors.org. New England Historic Genealogical Society, 2014. Case number 34666

[1526] Isaac, jr., ["Oct. 16, after a muster fell from his house & was never well afterwards." C.R.2.], Dec. 27, 1806, a. 38 y. 18 d.

[1527] Essex County, MA: Probate File Papers, 1638-1881.Online database. AmericanAncestors.org. New England Historic Genealogical Society, 2014. Case 59

[1528] Sarah Fisk, d. Isaac, jr., deceased, and Mary, bp. June 21, 1807.

Elizabeth (Mooar) Bailey;[1529] Rebecca d. at Concord, 23 Dec 1863.[1530] In 1860, Rebecca was living in Concord with her son Moses.[1531]

William Abbot was a farmer in Concord.

In his will written 3 June 1848 (probate 24 June 1856), William Abbot bequeathed to beloved wife Rebecca all the household furniture and the use of all of the dwelling house that she chooses during her lifetime. She also receives $200 per year and other provisions for her support. Son William Abbot receives $100. Daughter Rebecca Abbot receives $1,000 and the right to remain in the dwelling house as long as she is unmarried. Daughter Phebe C. Lund wife of Joseph Lund receives a sum which will total $1,000 when added to what she has already received. Son Moses B. Abbot receives $2,000. Sons Isaac and Moses receive all the rest of the estate and are named executors.[1532]

William Abbot and Rebecca Bailey were parents of five children.

i WILLIAM ABBOTT, b. at Andover, 7 Sep 1801; d. at Concord, NH, 8 Jan 1888; m. 1st, 19 Nov 1846, DESDEMONA FISKE (widow of Abner Watkins), b. at Amherst, NH, 15 Mar 1792 daughter of Ebenezer and Abigail (Woodbury) Fiske; Desdemona d. at Concord, 4 Oct 1867. William m. 2nd, at Warner, NH, 12 May 1868, BETSEY WALDRON, b. at Topsham, VT, about 1803 daughter of Theodore and Lucina (McGuire) Waldron; Betsey d. at Concord, 11 Dec 1876. William m. 3rd, at Pembroke, NH, 12 Nov 1878, VASTA M. CARPENTER, b. at Deerfield, NH, about 1827 daughter of Christopher and Mary (McCrillis) Carpenter; Vasta d. at Concord, 7 Dec 1895.

ii ISAAC ABBOTT, b. at Andover, 12 Nov 1803; d. at Concord, 29 Aug 1858. Isaac did not marry.

iii REBECCA ABBOTT, b. at Andover, 6 Oct 1806; d. at Concord, 18 Feb 1873. Rebecca did not marry.

iv MOSES BAILEY ABBOTT, b. at Concord, 19 Apr 1815; d. at Concord, 12 Sep 1876. Moses did not marry.

v PHEBE CHANDLER ABBOTT, b. at Concord, 2 Oct 1817; d. at Concord, 19 Dec 1875; m. at Manchester, NH, 23 Nov 1846, as his second wife, JOSEPH S. LUND, b. at Dunstable, MA, about 1800 son of Joseph and Betsey (Whitney) Lund; Joseph d. at Concord, 27 Dec 1882. Joseph was first married to Mary Swett in 1831 and third married to Amanda J. Allen in 1877.

557) ASA ABBOTT *(Sarah Abbott Abbott[4], Isaac[3], George[2], George[1])*, b. at Andover, 15 Nov 1770 son of Timothy and Sarah (Abbott) Abbott; d. at Andover, 6 Jul 1850; m. at Billerica, 29 May 1798, JUDITH JAQUITH, b. 2 Feb 1777 daughter of Joseph and Elizabeth (Needham) Jaquith; Judith d. at Andover, 15 Jul 1843.

In the will of Asa Abbott dated 1 July 1847 (probate 18 February 1851), son Asa receives the East part of the dwelling and East part of the home lot and barn and a part of the woodlot known as the Neck. Two acres are set aside to son Sereno Timothy. Son Sylvester receives the remaining part of the home lot. Daughter Sarah A. Abbott receives the use of the chamber she now occupies. Daughter Adaline A. Manning receives one share in the Boston and Maine railroad. Daughter Hannah Jaquith Ingalls receives $100. To his daughters and daughters-in-law, he leaves a 23-acre piece of land in Billerica to be divided equally among them: Adaline A. Manning, Mehitable H. Abbot, Elizabeth J. Berry, Sarah A. Abbot, Rhoda B. Abbot, Hannah J. Ingalls, and Sarah F. Abbott. Sons Asa and Sylvester are named executors.[1533]

Asa Abbott and Judith Jaquith were parents of seven children all born at Andover.

i ASA ALBERT ABBOTT, b. 29 Mar 1799; d. at Andover, 10 Jan 1886; m. at Andover, 29 Aug 1829, MEHITABLE H. INGALLS, b. at Andover, 3 Nov 1800 daughter of Jonathan and Sarah (Berry) Ingalls; Mehitable d. at Andover, 15 May 1866.

ii ADALINE ALTON ABBOTT, b. 31 Dec 1800; d. at Andover, 28 Jul 1869; m. 2 Jan 1845, THOMAS MANNING, b. at Andover, 25 Apr 1781 son of Thomas and Mehitable (Kidder) Manning; Thomas d. at Andover, 26 Feb 1849.

iii SYLVESTER ABBOTT, b. 3 Feb 1803; d. at Andover, 20 Oct 1875; m. 18 Oct 1845, RHODA BATCHELDER, b. at Hampton Falls, NH, 25 Aug 1814 daughter of Reuben and Betsey (Tilton) Batchelder; Rhoda d. at Andover, 8 Apr 1895.

1529 The will of Moses Bailey includes a bequest to his daughter Rebecca Abbot.

1530 Reed and Thorne, *History and Manual of the First Congregationalist Church, Concord*, Catalogue of Members

1531 Year: *1860;* Census Place: *Concord Ward 7, Merrimack, New Hampshire;* Roll: *M653_675;* Page: *945;* Family History Library Film: *803675*

1532 *New Hampshire. Probate Court (Merrimack County);* Probate Place: *Merrimack, New Hampshire, Probate Records, Vol 25, 1847-1856*, will of William Abbot 3 Jun 1848

1533 *Massachusetts, Essex County, Probate Records;* Author: *Massachusetts. Supreme Judicial Court (Essex County);* Probate Place: *Essex, Massachusetts, Probate Records, Aaron, E-Abbot, H, 1828-1991*, probate of Asa Abbott, 18 Feb 1851, case number 30817

iv SERENO TIMOTHY ABBOTT, b. 17 Aug 1805; d. at Hampton Falls, NH, 10 Mar 1855; m. at North Hampton, NH, 15 Aug 1839, SARAH FRENCH, b. at North Hampton, 20 May 1820 daughter of Jonathan and Rebecca (Farrar) French; Sarah d. at Andover, 28 Apr 1905.

v ELIZABETH JAQUITH ABBOTT, b. 8 Nov 1807; d. at Danvers, 7 May 1868; m. at Danvers, 12 Dec 1831, EBENEZER GARDNER BERRY, b. at Danvers, 19 Feb 1809 son of Ebenezer and Hetta (Preston) Berry; Ebenezer d. at Danvers, 3 Aug 1895.

vi SARAH ANN ABBOTT, b. 23 Dec 1811; d. at Andover, 2 Jun 1879. Sarah did not marry.

vii HANNAH JAQUITH ABBOTT, b. 31 Aug 1815; d. at Danvers, 29 Dec 1868; m. at Andover, 16 Dec 1845, CHARLES NATHAN INGALLS, b. at Andover, 9 Jul 1820 son of Francis and Elizabeth B. (Foster) Ingalls; Charles d. at Hawley, MN, 9 Aug 1886. After Hannah's death, Charles married Mary Jane Morse Oct 1871.

558) DANIEL ABBOT *(Sarah Abbott Abbott⁴, Isaac³, George², George¹)*, b. at Andover, 25 Feb 1777 son of Timothy and Sarah (Abbott) Abbott; d. at Nashua, NH, 3 Dec 1853; m. at Salem, 11 Aug 1805, ELIZABETH PICKMAN, b. at Salem, 11 Feb 1782 daughter of William and Elizabeth (Leavitt) Pickman; Elizabeth d. at Nashua, 29 Mar 1850.

Daniel Abbot graduated from Harvard 1797 and was an attorney in Nashua. His son-in-law Charles James Fox was his law partner. Daniel Abbot served as a representative and senator in the New Hampshire state legislature. He was known as an eloquent orator. A detailed biography can be found in Parker's *History of the City of Nashua*.[1534]

In his will dated 24 November 1853, Daniel Abbot leaves to his beloved granddaughter Mary Elisabeth Abbot the only heir of his deceased son Charles D. Abbot, $10,000 in stock shares. All the residue of the estate, he leaves in equal portions to son William Pickman Abbot and daughter Catherine Pickman Dinsmoor wife of Samuel Dinsmoor. Son William is named executor.[1535]

Daniel Abbot and Elizabeth Pickman were parents of five children.

i WILLIAM PICKMAN ABBOTT, b. Aug 1806; d. 14 Sep 1809.

ii WILLIAM DUDLEY ABBOTT, b. and d. 2 May 1810.

iii WILLIAM PICKMAN ABBOTT, b. at Nashua, NH, 15 May 1811; d. at Keene, NH, 25 Aug 1880; m. 1st, at Boston, 7 Mar 1845, ABBY ANN CHANDLER, b. at Pittsburgh, 1817; Abby d. at Roxbury, MA, 22 May 1850. William m. 2nd, at Keene, 20 Feb 1855, HARRIET MEAD HANDERSON, b. at Chesterfield, 20 Dec 1820 daughter of Phineas and Hannah W. (Mead) Handerson; Harriet d. at Keene, 16 Dec 1889.

iv CHARLES DUDLEY ABBOTT, b. at Nashua, 9 Sep 1813; d. at Nashua, 3 Jan 1848; m. at Dunstable, NH, 23 May 1838, LAURINDA HOLBROOK, b. at Keene, 2 Feb 1811 daughter of Adin and Polly (Warren) Holbrook.

v CATHARINE PICKMAN ABBOTT, b. at Nashua, 19 Aug 1819; d. at Philadelphia, 11 Nov 1891; m. 1st, at Nashua, 4 Jun 1840, CHARLES JAMES FOX, b. at Hancock, NH, 25 Oct 1811 son of Jedediah and Sarah (Wheeler) Fox; Charles d. at Nashville, NH, 17 Feb 1846. Catharine m. 2nd, about 1851, SAMUEL DINSMOOR, b. at Keene, 8 May 1799 son of Samuel and Mary (Boyd) Dinsmoor; Samuel d. at Keene, 28 Feb 1869. Samuel Dinsmoor was first married to Anne Eliza Jarris. He was the governor of New Hampshire 1849 to 1852.

559) SARAH ABBOTT *(Sarah Abbott Abbott⁴, Isaac³, George², George¹)*, b. at Andover, 22 May 1783 daughter of Timothy and Sarah (Abbott) Abbott; d. at Andover, 11 Sep 1858; m. 27 Nov 1803, NATHANIEL SWIFT, b. at Dorchester, 15 Jul 1778 son of Nathaniel and Mary (Baker) Swift; Nathaniel d. at Andover, 7 Dec 1840.[1536]

Dr. Nathaniel Swift and Sarah Abbott headed a prominent family in Andover whose residence was at 35 Central Street.

Nathaniel Swift did not leave a will and his estate entered probate 19 January 1841 with Nathaniel Swift as administrator as widow Sarah Swift declined administration. Real estate was valued at $5,965 and personal estate of $2,143.08.[1537]

In her will written July 1852 (probate 4 Oct 1859), Sarah A. Swift leaves her estate to her children specifying that it be equally divided among them. Children named are Nathaniel, George, Sarah Frances, Catherine, Jonathan, and Charles. Sons Nathaniel and George were named executors.[1538]

1534 Parker, *History of the City of Nashua*, p 395

1535 *New Hampshire. Probate Court (Hillsborough County)*; Probate Place: *Hillsborough, New Hampshire*, volume 57, p 421

1536 Nathaniel, Dr., "he held many offices in the Town, was Justice of the Peace and Post Master for many years" [heart disease. CR2], Dec. 7, 1840, a. 62 y. [a. 63 y. CR2]

1537 *Massachusetts, Essex County, Probate Records*; Author: *Massachusetts. Supreme Judicial Court (Essex County)*; Probate Place: *Essex, Massachusetts, Probate Records, Sweetser, T-Simonds, B, 1828-1991*, Case 54777

1538 *Essex County, Massachusetts, Probate Records and Indexes 1638-1916*; Author: *Massachusetts. Probate Court (Essex County)*; Probate Place: *Essex, Massachusetts, Probate Records, Vol 419-420, Book 119-120, 1857-1860*

Sarah Abbott and Nathaniel Swift were parents of eight children all born at Andover.

i NATHANIEL SWIFT, b. 12 May 1805; d. at Andover, 6 Sep 1878; m. 1st, at Andover, 10 Aug 1832, MARTHA J. KIDDER, b. at Billerica, 1 Feb 1813 daughter of Francis and Nancy (Hartwell) Kidder; Martha d. at Andover, 28 Nov 1843. Nathaniel m. 2nd, 13 Oct 1847, ALMENA JACOBS, b. at Columbia, ME, about 1809 daughter of Polycarp and Rebecca (Coffin) Jacobs; Almena d. at Andover, 11 Jan 1885.

ii GEORGE BAKER SWIFT, b. 30 Jul 1806; d. at Andover, 15 Feb 1872; m. at Wrentham, MA, 3 Oct 1831, MARY BENNETT WARREN, b. at Framingham, 21 Apr 1813 daughter of Isaac and Sally (Bennett) Warren; Mary d. at Methuen, 24 May 1894.

iii SARAH FRANCES SWIFT, b. 15 Nov 1807; d. at Andover, 18 Nov 1877; m. at Andover, 19 Jun 1833, JEFFRIES HALL, b. at Cornish, NH, 3 Feb 1802 son of Timothy and Lovina (Young) Hall;[1539] Jeffries d. at Chesterfield, NH, 5 Jan 1888.

iv WILLIAM SWIFT, b. 17 Dec 1809; d. 20 Nov 1833.

v CATHERINE E. SWIFT, b. 6 Jul 1813; d. at Manhattan, NY, 21 May 1895; m. at Andover, 12 Aug 1834, JOHN FOWLER TROW, b. at Andover, 30 Jan 1810 son of John and Martha (Swan) Trow; John d. at Orange, NJ, 8 Aug 1886.

vi SAMUEL SWIFT, b. 21 Feb 1815; d. at Brooklyn, NY, 5 Dec 1851; m. at New York, NY, 22 Nov 1842, MARY PHELPS, b. at Westhampton, MA, 8 May 1818 daughter of Luke and Mary (Montague) Phelps;[1540] Mary d. at Riverdale, NY, 13 Nov 1866.

vii JONATHAN SWIFT, b. 25 Jul 1816; d. at Andover, 20 Apr 1883; m. 30 Oct 1850, ALMENA J. JACOBS, b. at Effingham, NH, 8 Jan 1831 daughter of Edward F. and Lavinia (Fickett) Jacobs; Almena d. at Andover, 20 Jan 1895.

viii CHARLES H. SWIFT, b. 25 Jul 1816; d. at Boston, 19 Jan 1892. Charles did not marry. He was a photographer.

Great-Grandchildren of William Abbott and Elizabeth Geary

560) JOSEPH BARRETT *(Elizabeth Phelps Barrett⁴, Elizabeth Abbott Phelps³, William², George¹)*, b. at Pomfret, 12 Jul 1742 son of Benoni and Elizabeth (Phelps) Barrett; date of death uncertain; m. at Pomfret, 20 Feb 1765, JEMIMA CARPENTER, b. 9 Jan 1742/3 daughter of Samuel and Keziah (Carpenter) Carpenter.

Joseph Barrett and Jemima Carpenter were parents of six children born at Pomfret.

i HANNAH BARRETT, b. 14 Nov 1765; nothing further known.

ii BENONI BARRETT, b. 20 Oct 1767; d. at Cazenovia, NY, 1807 (probate 27 Apr 1807). Benoni does not seem to have married. His estate was administered by John Linkleer and Samuel Foreman.[1541]

iii EBENEZER BARRETT, b. 7 May 1769; nothing further known.

iv NATHAN BARRETT, b. 23 Jul 1771; d. at Woodstock, 15 Mar 1849; m. 1st, SUSANNA OLNEY, b. at Providence, RI, 1775 daughter of Hezekiah and Orpha (Hawkins) Olney; Susanna d. at Putnam, 12 Jun 1802. Nathan m. 2nd, MARY who d, 27 Feb 1816 and m. 3rd, AZUBAH who d. 9 Nov 1847.[1542] Mary and Azubah have not been identified.

v KEZIA BARRETT, b. 4 Jan 1776; d. at Concord, MI, 26 Apr 1862; m. JAMES WELCH, b. in NY, 1774; James d. at Grass Lake, MI, 1857.

vi ELIZABETH BARRETT, b. 12 Dec 1777; nothing further known.

[1539] Carter, *Native Ministry of New Hampshire*, p 166

[1540] Phelps and Servin, *The Phelps Family of America*, volume 1, p 505

[1541] *New York, Wills and Probate Records, 1659-1999*, Madison County, *Vol Ax-Fx, 1806-1830*, p 22

[1542] Nathan and his three wives are interred at Grove Street Cemetery in Putnam.

561) WILLIAM BARRETT *(Elizabeth Phelps Barrett[4], Elizabeth Abbott Phelps[3], William[2], George[1])*, b. at Pomfret, 12 Apr 1751 son of Benoni and Elizabeth (Phelps) Barrett; d. at Brooklyn, CT, 7 Mar 1838; m. 26 Feb 1778, LUCY ADAMS, b. at Pomfret, 25 May 1753 daughter of Paul and Mary (Hubbard) Adams; Lucy d. 4 Apr 1834.

William Barrett and Lucy Adams began their family in Pomfret but relocated to Brooklyn, Connecticut where their youngest children were born. William was a moderately successful farmer.

William Barrett enlisted in 1776 as a private in Captain Joseph Abbott's company. He had two other enlistments, for a month in 1777 under Captain Grosvenor and for two months in 1779 under Captain Lyons.[1543]

Most often, wills are written in a matter-of-fact manner, but occasionally a will is used as a vehicle to express deeply held feelings and the will of William Barrett is one such will. He wrote his will 25 Mar 1834 and it was proved 18 April 1838. Beloved wife Lucy is to have comfortable support during her natural life to be provided by son Joseph. Son William Barrett receives twenty-five dollars. Daughter Molly Allerton receives twenty-five dollars. Daughter Lucy Barrett receives the east bedroom with the cupboard near the stairs "and as to other property she has charged me so hardily with falsehood and hypocrisy and with acts of her insolence. . . that she has forfeited her claim as child. I am under no obligation to give her more than three dollars unless she becomes a pauper and if so that her brother Joseph P. take her and keep to the expense of fifty dollars which is my will (and my prayer to God is that he will change her heart and make her a child (of) grace). Son Ebenezer receives three dollars, and his best coat and pantaloons. The remainder of the property goes to son Joseph P. Barrett. The total value of the estate was $3,110.35 which included a 70-acre house lot valued at $1,820.00.[1544]

At the time William Barrett wrote his will, daughter Lucy was 54 years old. It is difficult to imagine what behavior a middle-aged single woman who lived at home was engaging in that warranted that level of animus from her father. In any case, Lucy died in 1836 and so was deceased at the time of the probate of her father's will. She left an estate of $435, so was not a pauper.[1545]

Most of William Barrett's heirs died between the time he wrote his will and the final settlement of his estate in 1840. His wife Lucy died just two weeks after the will was written. His son Joseph Phelps Barrett died in 1836 and Joseph's widow Nancy L. W. Converse Barrett assumed administration of the estate. William's daughter Molly died about four months after her father but before the settlement of the estate. Only sons William and Ebenezer were living at the time of the settlement.

William and Lucy Barrett had eight children.

i MOLLY BARRETT, b. at Pomfret, 24 Dec 1778; d. at Brooklyn, CT, 4 Jul 1838; m. at Brooklyn, 10 Apr 1810, JOHN ALLERTON, b. at Coventry, RI, 13 Feb 1764 son of John and Rosanna (Burlingame) Allerton; John d. 3 Jan 1839.

ii LUCY BARRETT, b. at Pomfret, 2 Jul 1780; d. at Brooklyn, CT, 25 Jun 1836. Lucy did not marry.

iii WILLIAM BARRETT (twin), b. at Pomfret, 18 Jul 1782; d. at Hartland, VT, 7 May 1872; m. at Hartland, VT, 13 Feb 1809, ANNA BOREDELL DENISON, b. at Stonington, CT, 2 Dec 1785 daughter of George and Theoda (Brown) Denison. Anna likely died in the early 1850's (living at the 1850 census but William living with a different wife in 1860). After Anna's death, William married Mehitable.

iv JAMES BARRETT (twin), b. at Pomfret, 18 Jul 1782; d. at Brooklyn, CT, 20 Sep 1799.

v PHILENA BARRETT, b. at Pomfret, 16 May 1784; d. at Brooklyn, CT, 28 Feb 1799.

vi JOSEPH PHELPS BARRETT, b. perhaps at Brooklyn, CT, 9 Nov 1789; d. at Brooklyn, 23 Oct 1836; m. 11 Jun 1820, NANCY LAURA WHIPPLE CONVERSE, b. 11 Feb 1797 daughter of Jonathan and Esther (Whipple) Converse; Nancy d. 20 May 1878.

vii EBENEZER BARRETT, b. at Brooklyn, CT, about 1793; d. at Beardstown, IL, 1861; m. at Brooklyn, CT, 3 Mar 1825, ABIGAIL "ABBY" BAKER, b. in Connecticut, 22 Feb 1799 daughter of Jared and Abigail (Withie) Baker; Abby d. at Worcester, MA, 1882. Ebenezer and Abby had their four children in Connecticut and then relocated to Grafton, MA where Abby's parents also relocated.[1546] One of their children (Maria Barrett Meriam) relocated to Beardstown[1547] and Ebenezer was there with her family when he died. Abby afterwards lived in Worcester and her son J. Prescott Barrett lived there with her until his marriage about 1870.

viii HARVEY BARRETT, b. at Brooklyn, CT, 13 Apr 1796; d. 2 Jan 1817.

[1543] National Archives, Revolutionary War Pension and Bounty-Land Warrant Application Files, application of William Barrett, 1832.
[1544] Connecticut, Wills and Probate Records, 1609-1999, will and probate of William Barrett
[1545] Connecticut, Wills and Probate Records, 1609-1999, probate of Lucy Barrett
[1546] Year: 1850; Census Place: Grafton, Worcester, Massachusetts; Roll: M432_344; Page: 443B; Image: 220
[1547] Year: 1870; Census Place: Beardstown Ward 2, Cass, Illinois; Roll: M593_192; Page: 351B; Family History Library Film: 545691

562) JOSEPH LAWRENCE *(Hannah Phelps Lawrence⁴, Elizabeth Abbott Phelps³, William², George¹)*, b. at Pomfret, 9 Aug 1745 son of Samuel and Hannah (Phelps) Lawrence; d. at Pomfret 14 Oct 1775. There are births of three children at Pomfret for Joseph and wife Betty. There is no information on the identity of Betty.

i GARDNER LAWRENCE, b. 17 Oct 1769; m. at Pomfret, 1 May 1796, SILENCE TISDALE, b. at Berkley, MA, about 1775 daughter of Ephraim and Coralina (Leonard) Tisdale.

ii WARD LAWRENCE, b. 20 Feb 1772; d. 15 Feb 1782.

iii HANNAH LAWRENCE, b. 25 Dec 1774. She is perhaps the Miss Hannah Lawrence who died in Pomfret 12 Feb 1822.

562a) SARAH WALTER (*Rebecca Abbott Walter⁴, William³, William², George¹*), b. at Roxbury, 29 Mar 1736 daughter of Nathaniel and Rebecca (Abbott) Walter; d. at Leicestershire, England, 10 May 1775;[1548] m. at Quincy, MA, 31 Dec 1754, Sir ROBERT HESILRIGE, baptized at Northamptonshire, 27 Aug 1727 son of Arthur and Hannah (Sturges) Hesilrige; reported as dying at Fleet prison in London.

Sir Robert Hesilrige was 8th baronet of Noseley Hall, an only son, who spent much of his adult life in America. He was perhaps a reprobate. He and Sarah had three children in Massachusetts. Sarah and Robert went to England by 1775 and Sarah is reported dying there. Robert perhaps died at Fleet prison, but the circumstances of this are unknown.[1549]

Sarah Walter and Robert Hesilrige were parents of three children.

i ARTHUR HESILRIGE, b. 24 Feb 1756; d. at Bombay, India, 1805 while in the employ of the East India Tea Company; m. 1st ELIZABETH CHANARD, b. 1776; Elizabeth d. 1797. Arthur m. 2nd at Bengal, 27 Feb 1798, CHARLOTTE ELIZABETH GRAY, b. 1781 daughter of James Giacomo and Frances E. S. (Prince) Gray; Charlotte d. at Calcutta, 8 Jan 1817. Charlotte married second William Henry Wilkinson.

ii HANNAH HESILRIGE, b. at Quincy, 20 Aug 1757; d. at Brookline, 3 May 1789; m. at Boston, 18 Jul 1776, Rev. THOMMAS ABBOT, b. at Charlestown, 2 May 1745 son of Hull and Mary (Bradstreet) Abbot; Thomas d. at Brookline, 1 Nov 1789. Rev. Thomas Abbot graduated from Harvard in 1764 and was for a time the minister of second church at Roxbury.[1550]

iii SARAH HESILRIGE, b. at Quincy, 26 Mar 1759; d. 10 Jun 1786; m. at Boston, 21 Mar 1782, DAVID HENLEY, b. at Charlestown, MA, 12 Feb 1748 son of Samuel and Elizabeth (Cheever) Henley; David d. at Washington, D. C., 1 Jan 1823. David served throughout the Revolution as a brigade-major to Gen. Heath and was commissioned as colonel of a Massachusetts regiment on 1 Jan 1777. Gen. Burgoyne brought charges against him for cruel treatment of British prisoners, but he was exonerated at a court martial. David was a clerk in the war department in Washington.[1551]

562b) WILLIAM WALTER (*Rebecca Abbott Walter⁴, William³, William², George¹*), b. at Roxbury, 7 Oct 1737 son of Nathaniel and Rebecca (Abbott) Walter; d. at Boston, 5 Dec 1800; m. at Boston, 30 Sep 1766, LYDIA LYNDE, b. at Salem, 14 Nov 1741 daughter of Benjamin and Mary (Bowles) Lynde; Lydia d. 25 Sep 1798.

Rev. William Walter was a Doctor of Divinity and rector of Christ Church, Boston from 1791 to 1800.[1552]

In his will written 4 December 1800, William Walter notes that five of his children Lynde Walter, William Walter, Jr., Mary Lynde Smith, Thomas Walter, and Arthur Maynard Walter have received advancement as noted in his books. But his sixth child, Harriet Tyng Walter, has not, and he directs that a sum be paid to Harriet that makes her share equal to that of her brothers and sister. He directs that his estate be sold, and the proceeds divided among his children. There is a bequest to sister Maria Otis of one hundred dollars. Sister (sister-in-law) Mary Oliver is to have the portraits of her parents Hon. Benjamin Lynde and his wife returned to her. Daughter Harriet Tyng Walter is to be in the care of William Walter Smallpeace until she is of fit years to be placed in a respectable trade. To his servant Luke Smith, a black man living with him, he bequeaths a full suit

---

1548 Colonial Society of Massachusetts, Records of the Trinity Church in Boston; *Boston, MA: Deaths, 1700-1799.* (Online database: New England Historic Genealogical Society, 2007), (Dunkle, Robert J. and Lainhart, Ann S. Boston Deaths, 1700-1799, New England Historic Genealogical Society, Boston, 1999.) https://www.americanancestors.org/DB34/rd/6839850

1549 Thomas (Ed.), *The Correspondence of Richard Price, Volume II: March 1778-February 1786*, p 329

1550 "Descendants of Gov. Bradstreet", NEHGR, volume 8, 1854, p 316

1551 Appletons' Cyclopedia of American Biography, volume III, p 167

1552 Bolton, *Christ Church, Salem Street, Boston*

of black clothes to be made up from William's wardrobe. Executors named were sons Lynde and William and son-in-law Nathaniel Smith. Total estate value was $14,380.[1553]

William Walter and Lydia Lynde were parents of six children born at Boston.

i LYNDE WALTER, b. 13 Nov 1767; d. at Boston, 21 Aug 1844; m. 1st about 1794, MARIA VAN BUSKIRK, b. about 1771 (perhaps in Bergen, NJ) daughter of loyalist Abraham and Jane (Dey) Van Buskirk; Maria d. at Shelburne, Nova Scotia, 8 Dec 1796. Lynde m. 2nd at Trenton, NJ, 12 Jun 1798, ANN MINSHULL, b. at New York, 23 Aug 1773 daughter of John and Mary (Stanton) Minshull; Ann d. at Boston, 12 Dec 1853.

ii MARY LYNDE WALTER, b. about 1768; d. at Boston, 19 Aug 1844; m. at Boston, by Rev. William Walter, 11 Nov 1797, Dr. NATHANIEL SMITH, baptized at Ipswich, 7 Oct 1770 son of Nathaniel and Mary (Coffin) Smith;[1554] Nathaniel d. at Newburyport, 25 Nov 1823 at age 53.

iii WILLIAM WALTER, b. 1771; d. at Boston, 23 Apr 1814; m. at Boston, 23 Apr 1794, SARAH BICKER, b. 1774; Sarah d. at Boston, 11 Jun 1711.

iv THOMAS WALTER, b. about 1772; d. at Boston, about 1803. Thomas did not marry.

v HARRIET TYNG WALTER, b. 10 May 1776; d. at Boston, 14 Oct 1847; m. at Boston, by Rev. Samuel Parker, 4 Jun 1804, JOHN ODIN, b. 1772 son of John and Esther (Kettell) Odin; John d. at Boston, 28 Dec 1854.

vi ARTHUR MAYNARD WALTER, b. about 1781; d. at Boston, 2 Jan 1807. Arthur did not marry. His estate was administered by his brother Lynde with four heirs receiving distribution: Lynde Walter, William Walter, John Odin (husband of Harriet), and Nathaniel Smith (husband of Mary).[1555]

562c) REBECCA WALTER (*Rebecca Abbott Walter[4], William[3], William[2], George[1]*), baptized at Roxbury, 22 Apr 1739 daughter of Nathaniel and Rebecca (Abbott) Walter; d. at Boston, 23 Jul 1775; m. at Roxbury, 12 May 1761, MATHER BYLES, b. at Boston, 12 Jan 1734 son of Mather and Ann (Noyes) Byles; Mather d. at St. John, New Brunswick, 12 Mar 1814. Mather was second married to Sarah Lyde and third married Susanna *Lawlor* Reid.

Mather Byles was the great-grandson of Increase Mather. His father was a Congregational minister and Mather followed in his footsteps. He graduated from Harvard in 1751 and completed advanced degrees at Harvard and Yale.[1556] Rev. Mather Byles was ordained pastor of the First Congregational Church at New London, Connecticut on 18 November 1757.[1557] He converted to Church of England in 1768, traveled to London where he received his license from the Bishop of London. He was then minister of Christ Church, Boston. Mather was a loyalist, and at the outbreak of the war fled with British troops to Halifax.[1558] After the move to New Brunswick, Mather was the rector of Trinity church at Saint John.[1559]

Rebecca Walter and Mather Byles were parents of eight children.

i REBECCA BYLES, baptized at New London, 31 Oct 1762; d. at Halifax, Nova Scotia, 5 Jun 1853; m. at Halifax, 4 Aug 1785, Dr. WILLIAM JAMES ALMON, b. at Providence, RI, 14 Aug 1755 son of James and Ruth (Hollywood) Almon; William d. at Bath, Somerset, England, 5 Feb 1817. Dr. Almon was a loyalist and a surgeon with the Royal Artillery during the Revolution.[1560]

ii MATHER BYLES, baptized at New London, 8 Apr 1764; d. at Grenada, West Indies, 17 Dec 1802; m. at Grenada, 1 Jan 1797,[1561] MARY BRIDGEWATER, b. 1780 daughter of Chief Justice Thomas Bridgewater of Grenada.[1562] Mather was commissary general to Grenada at the time of his death.[1563]

iii WALTER BYLES, baptized at New London, 4 Aug 1765; likely died young

---

[1553] *Suffolk County, MA: Probate File Papers.* Online database. *AmericanAncestors.org.* New England Historic Genealogical Society, 2017-2019. Case 21370

[1554] The 1825 probate of the elder Nathaniel Smith includes a statement from Mary L. Smith, widow of Nathaniel of Newburyport, agreeing to the disposition of a mortgaged property in Newburyport. *Essex County, MA: Probate File Papers, 1638-1881.* Online database. *AmericanAncestors.org.* New England Historic Genealogical Society, 2014. Case 25707

[1555] *Suffolk County, MA: Probate File Papers.* Online database. *AmericanAncestors.org.* New England Historic Genealogical Society, 2017-2019. Case 22823

[1556] Byles, Mather, Dictionary of Canadian Biography; http://www.biographi.ca/en/bio/byles_mather_5E.html

[1557] Connecticut Church Record Abstracts, New London, First Congregational, 1670-1886, p 57. The baptisms of children Anna, Elizabeth, Rebecca, Mather, and Walter are recorded at New London.

[1558] Byles, Mather, Dictionary of Canadian Biography

[1559] "An Old Time Punster," The New Brunswick Magazine, volume 2, 1899. p 276

[1560] Todd, *Armory and Lineages of Canada*, p 110

[1561] Old Boston Families, "The Byles Family", NEHGR, 1915, volume 69, p 116

[1562] A portrait of Mary Bridgewater Byles is at the National Portrait Gallery of the Smithsonian; https://npg.si.edu/object/npg_VA160008

[1563] Byles Family Papers 1757-1915, Guide to the Collection, Massachusetts Historical Society, https://www.masshist.org/collection-guides/view/fa0314

iv ELIZABETH BYLES, baptized at New London, 10 May 1767; d. 13 Nov 1808; m. 1807[1564] WILLIAM SCOVIL, b. at Waterbury, CT, 21 May 1766 son of James and Amy (Nichols) Scovil; Willian d. at Saint John, New Brunswick, 26 Apr 1851. William married second Anne Davies.

v ANNA BYLES, baptized at New London, 10 May 1767; d. at Teignmouth, Devon, Apr 1830; m. at Saint John, New Brunswick, 1799, as his second wife, THOMAS DESBRISAY, b. at Thurles, Tipperary, Ireland, 1756 son of Thomas and Ellen (Landers0 DesBrisay; Thomas d. at Teignmouth, 14 Mar 1823. Thomas was first married to Sarah Proctor.

vi SARAH BYLES,[1565] b. at Boston, 1770; d. at Halifax, 8 Nov. 1855; m. at Saint John, 1801, THOMAS DESBRISAY, b. at Halifax, 14 Aug 1780 son of Thomas and Sarah (Proctor) DesBrisay; Thomas d. at Saint Vincent, West Indies, 4 Dec 1807. Thomas was the son of the Thomas that married Sarah's sister Anna.

vii MARTHA BYLES, b. 1772 and d. 1 Nov 1772.

viii MARY BYLES, baptized at Boston, 20 Nov 1774; d. at Boston, 3 Apr 1775.

562d) MARIA WALTER (*Rebecca Abbott Walter[4], William[3], William[2], George[1]*), b. at Roxbury, 19 Mar 1742/3 daughter of Nathaniel and Rebecca (Abbott) Walter; d. 19 Sep 1826; m. at Roxbury, 22 Feb 1770, as his second wife, Gen. JOSEPH OTIS, b. at Barnstable, 22 Feb 1725 son of James and Mary (Allyn) Otis; Joseph d. at West Barnstable, 21 Sep 1810. Joseph was first married to Rebeckah Sturgis.

Joseph and Maria Otis resided in Barnstable. Joseph served as a militia colonel during the Revolution and was afterwards Brigadier-General of the militia. He served on the Court of Common Pleas. He was appointed by Washington as the collector of customs at Barnstable.[1566]

In his will written 19 May 1808, Joseph Otis bequeathed to his beloved wife Mariah Otis and daughter Miss Mariah Otis all the personal estate, indoor movables, and one horse and chaise to be theirs, forever. Son William Otis and daughter Mary Gay wife of Ebenezer Gay each one moiety of the real estate. Son William receives the farming utensils, stock, and other creatures. Sons Joseph, Nathaniel Walter, and John each receives five dollars. The children of son Lemuel Williams and children of son George Osgood each receives five shillings.[1567] Wife Mariah and son William were named executors.[1568]

Maria and Joseph Otis were parents of ten children. Joseph Otis had five children with his first wife Rebeckah Sturgis.[1569]

i JOSEPH OTIS, b. 23 Sep 1771; d. at Louisville, KY, 22 Sep 1854; m. 1st at Charleston, SC, 23 Jul 1795, ANN STOLL MOORE, b. 1779; Ann d. at Sullivan's Island, SC, 4 Jul 1807. Joseph m. 2nd 10 Apr 1810, JANE MUNROE, b. at Charleston, 22 Feb 1791; Jane d. 22 Feb 1814. Joseph m. 3rd, MAHALA FOREST who d. at Louisville, 21 Aug 1846.

ii NATHANIEL WALTER OTIS, b. 9 Jan 1773; d. at New Orleans, 12 May 1841; m. 1st at Boston, 27 Oct 1794, NANCY BOURNE, b. at Barnstable, 1776 daughter of Samuel and Anne (-) Bourne; Nancy d. at Matanzas, Cuba, 31 Jul 1814. Nathaniel m. 2nd ELLEN RUDSON, b. at Nassau, Bahamas, 1798; Ellen d. at New Orleans, 29 Dec 1871.

iii JOHN OTIS, b. Apr 1774; d. at West Barnstable, 16 Jul 1854. John did not marry.

iv THOMAS OTIS, b. Nov 1775; d. at Albany, NY, 14 Aug 1803.

v CHARLES OTIS, b. Jul 1777; d. at Charleston, SC, 14 Aug 1794.

vi Son b. and d. Feb 1779

[1564] Brainard, *A Survey of the Scovils*, p 115

[1565] A needlework sampler completed by Sarah in 1781 can be seen at this link: https://www.novamuse.ca/Detail/objects/187737

[1566] Otis, *A Genealogical and Historical Memoir of the Otis Family*, p 103

[1567] Lemuel Williams and George Osgood were two sons-in-law, husbands of his daughters Rebecca and Elizabeth who were from Joseph's marriage to Rebeckah Sturgis.

[1568] Massachusetts Wills and Probate, Barnstable County, volume 35, p 194

[1569] The births of the children in this family are recorded in a family record for Barnstable, volume III, p 91; accessed through American Ancestors; https://www.americanancestors.org/DB190/i/13885/91/248781564

vii MARY ALLEYNE OTIS, b. at Barnstable, 7 Mar 1780; d. at Hingham, 18 Nov 1866; m. at Boston, 31 Jul 1800, EBENEZER GAY, b. at Boston 24 Feb 1771 son of Martin and Ruth (Atkins) Gay; Ebenezer d. at Hingham, 11 Feb 1842.

viii WILLIAM OTIS, b. Feb 1781; d. at Washington, D. C., 7 Apr 1837.

ix ARTHUR OTIS, b. Dec 1784; d. at Havana, Cuba, 24 Jul 1801.

x MARIA OTIS, baptized at Barnstable, 1 Jul 1787; d. at Bridgewater, MA, 20 May 1821; m. at Barnstable, 1 Jan 1818, as his second wife, PHILIP COLBY, b. at Sanbornton, NH, 30 Jul 1780 son of Isaac and Phebe (Hunt) Colby; Philip d. at Middleborough, MA, 27 Feb 1851. Philip was first married to Harriet Sewell and third married to Eliza Savery Standish.

563) SARAH ABBOTT *(James⁴, James³, William², George¹)*, b. at Andover, 1 Mar 1743 daughter of James and Sarah (Bancroft) Abbott; d. likely at Warner, NH, about 1772; m. by 1765, JACOB WALDRON, b. at Rumford, 2 Mar 1743 son of Isaac and Susannah (Chandler) Waldron; the date or place of death is not known. After Sarah's death, Jacob married, at Warner, 8 Sep 1774 Abigail Stevens (who was perhaps a widow).

Jacob Waldron went with his father Isaac and brother Isaac, Jr. to Warner, New Hampshire, reported to have been there by 1763.[1570] The births of two children of Sarah and Jacob were recorded at Concord, and a third child at Warner. Jacob served in the Revolution and was known as Lieutenant Jacob Waldron. He served as selectman in Warner.

There are three children known for Jacob Waldron and Sarah Abbott. Jacob likely had at least three other sons with his second wife Abigail (Abraham, Isaac, and Jacob).

i EZRA WALDRON, b. at Concord, 2 May 1765; no further record found.

ii ELIZABETH WALDRON, b. at Concord, 29 Sep 1767; m. at Warner, 30 May 1787, THOMAS ANNIS, b. about 1750 son of Daniel and Catherine (Thomas) Annis;[1571] Thomas d. at Warner, 1809.

iii SARAH WALDRON, b. at Warner, 30 Oct 1769; d. at Warner, 5 Jul 1853; m. at Warner, 19 Jun 1788, JASON WATKINS, b. 1765 son of Abner and Ruth (Annis) Watkins;[1572] Jason d. at Warner, 7 Mar 1840.

564) ABIGAIL ABBOT *(James⁴, James³, William², George¹)*, b. at Concord, 22 Jan 1745/6 daughter of James and Sarah (Bancroft) Abbot; d. at Bath, NH, 11 Feb 1815; m. 15 Apr 1767, ASA BAILEY, b. at Salem, NH, 13 May 1745 son of Edward and Elizabeth (Burbank) Bailey.

Abigail divorced Asa in 1793 following years of abuse, the last straw being the sexual abuse of one of their daughters. What happened to Asa is not clear. *The Memoirs of Mrs. Abigail Bailey* recounting the events of her marriage was published in 1815 just after her death.[1573]

Abigail Abbot and Asa Bailey were parents of seventeen children, all births recorded in towns in Grafton County, New Hampshire.

i ABIGAIL BAILEY, b. at Haverhill, NH, 11 Feb 1768; m. 13 Aug 1792, STEPHEN BARTLETT, b. at Newton, NH, 11 Mar 1762 son of Stephen and Elizabeth (Kelley) Bartlett.

ii RUTH BAILEY, b. at Haverhill, 31 Aug 1769; d. at Bath, NH, 1 Aug 1818; m. at Bath, 7 Apr 1785, EBENEZER BACON, b. 6 Aug 1754 son of John and Rhoda (Gould) Bacon; Ebenezer d. at Bath, 11 Feb 1818.

iii SAMUEL BAILEY, b. at Haverhill, 13 Jun 1771. According to the Abbot Genealogical Register, Samuel enlisted in the service in 1798. He received his discharge and discharge money and started home but was never heard from again.

iv PHEBE BAILEY, b. at Haverhill, 20 Apr 1772; d. after 1850 at the Shaker community in Canterbury, NH. In the 1850 census, Phebe was listed living in the Canterbury Shaker community.

v SARAH BAILEY, b. 28 Nov 1773; d. 1776.

vi ASA BAILEY, b. at Haverhill, 16 Oct 1775; m. at Lisbon, NH, 3 May 1803, REBECCA WEBER.

[1570] Harriman, *The History of Warner*, p 83.
[1571] Currier, *Genealogy of David Annis of Hopkinton*
[1572] Harriman, *The History of Warner*, p 443
[1573] Bailey, *Memoirs of Mrs. Abigail Bailey*

vii CALEB BAILEY, b. at Bath, 12 Aug 1777; d. at Lyme, NH, 29 Apr 1846; m. 3 Jun 1807, DEBORAH FITCH, b. 1786 daughter of Asa and Deborah (Robinson) Fitch; Deborah d. at Lyme, 17 Nov 1846.

viii ANNA BAILEY, b. at Bath, 12 Aug 1777; m. at Bradford, VT, 21 Sep 1799, LEVI PHILLIPS of Hanover, NH

ix SARAH BAILEY, b. at Bath, 21 Aug 1779; d. at Bangor, ME, 22 Feb 1852; m. 19 Nov 1807, Rev. OLIVER BEALE, b. at Bridgewater, MA, 13 Oct 1776 son of Japheth and Patience (Keith) Beale; Oliver d. at Baltimore, 30 Dec 1836. Rev. Beale had gone to Baltimore in an attempt to recover his health and died there.[1574]

x JABEZ BAILEY, b. at Landaff, 31 Jan 1781; d. at Lisbon, NH, 23 Oct 1855; m. at Bath, 29 Aug 1811, MARTHA HUNT, b. at Bath, 27 Jan 1790 daughter of Zebulon and Lucy (Whittlesey) Hunt; Martha d. at Franconia, NH, 6 Mar 1867.

xi CHLOE BAILEY, b. at Landaff, 8 Aug 1782; m. 1810, ORRIN FORD, b. in NY, about 1787; Orrin d. after 1870 at Palatine, IL. Orrin had a second marriage to Rebecca. Chloe's brother Amos also located in Palatine, IL.

xii AMOS BAILEY, b. at Landaff, 11 May 1784; d. at Palatine, IL, 19 Apr 1863; m. 1816, his first cousin, MARY ABBOTT *(Bancroft^5, James^4, James^3, William^2, George^1)*, b. at Newbury, VT, 6 Jun 1795 daughter of Bancroft and Lydia (White) Abbott; Mary d. at Chicago, 1834. Mary Abbott is a child in Family 569.

xiii OLIVE BAILEY, b. at Landaff, 25 Feb 1786; d. after 1850 (living in Washington, PA); m. 1826, STEPHEN ETHERIDGE, b. in NH, about 1787; Stephen d. after 1850.

xiv PHINEAS BAILEY, b. at Landaff, 6 Nov 1787; d. at Albany, VT, 14 Dec 1861; m. 1st, at Chelsea, VT, 22 Aug 1810, JANETTE MCARTHUR, b. at Thornton, NH, 4 Sep 1791 daughter of John and Margaret (Aiken) McArthur; Janette d. at Berkshire, VT, 4 Aug 1829. Phineas m. 2nd, 20 Oct 1839, BETSEY FISKE, b. 8 May 1804 daughter of Moses and Hannah (Batchelder) Fiske;[1575] Betsey d. at Berkshire, VT, 23 Feb 1847. Phineas m. 3rd, 1847, HANNAH EDWARDS, b. at Amherst, MA, 1 Oct 1804 daughter of Philip and Jerusha (Pomeroy) Edwards; Hannah d. at Walcott, VT, 15 May 1884.

xv JUDITH BAILEY, b. 15 Sep 1789; d. at Lyme, NH, 1865; m. at Bath, 14 Oct 1824, DAVID PELTON, b. 1792; David d. at Lyme, 1870.

xvi SIMON BAILEY, b. 15 Sep 1789; d. Oct 1789.

xvii PATIENCE BAILEY, b. at Landaff, NH, 23 May 1791; d. at Bangor, ME, 1 Apr 1874. Patience did not marry. In 1850, she was living at the town poor farm in Landaff and in 1870 living in Bangor with the family of her niece Lucinda Beal Withers.

565) MARY ABBOTT *(James^4, James^3, William^2, George^1)*, b. at Concord, 6 Feb 1748 daughter of James and Sarah (Bancroft) Abbott; m. 1st, 22 Oct 1773, RICHARD MINCHEN; Richard d. 1776. Mary m. 2nd, at Haverhill, NH, 22 Mar 1777, URIAH CROSS,[1576] b. at Mansfield, CT, 9 Jun 1752 son of Daniel and Elizabeth (Abbe) Cross;[1577] Uriah d. at Berlin Heights, OH, 1839.

Richard Minchen served as a Sergeant in Colonel Bedel's Regiment enlisting from Coos, New Hampshire.[1578] He died at Crown Point. Richard Michen and Mary Abbott were parents of one child.

i MARY MINCHEN, b. Aug 1774 (three records give three different dates in August), likely at Haverhill, NH although also recorded at Lunenburg, VT. Nothing further is known.

Mary Abbott and Uriah Cross were parents of six children born at Lunenburg, Vermont. The family was then in Champlain, New York and that is perhaps where Mary died. Uriah died in Berlin Heights, Ohio where his daughter Sally and her husband settled.

[1574] Allen, *History of Methodism in Maine*, p 402
[1575] Pierce, Batchelder Genealogy, p 394
[1576] New Hampshire Marriage Record Index 1637-1947 (ancestry.com)
[1577] Dimock, Births, marriages, baptisms, and deaths of Mansfield, CT, p 54. There are two men named Uriah Cross of similar age born in Connecticut. One married Ann Payne and one married Mary Abbott Minchen. It can be established that the Uriah who married Ann Payne was born 3 April 1750 in East Windsor (as he states this in his pension record) and Uriah born 3 April 1750 is the child of Noah and Mary (Chamberlain) Cross. By process of elimination, Uriah the son of Daniel and Elizabeth is identified as the husband of Mary Abbott.
[1578] U.S., Revolutionary War Rolls, 1775-1783

i URIAH CROSS, b. 21 Aug 1778; d. at Colden, NY, about 1863 (probate 28 Oct 1863). Uriah was married twice, and both wives are buried with Uriah in the Colden Cemetery. No other records were located for his wives who were SUSANNAH (1782-1842) and ABIGAIL (1787-1865).[1579]

ii SARAH ABBOTT CROSS, b. 2 Apr 1780; d. at Berlin Heights, OH, 29 Mar 1861; m. SYRUS CALL, b. in Windsor County, VT, 30 Oct 1772 son of Joseph and Mary (Sanderson) Call; Syrus d. at Berlin Heights, 8 Feb 1860.

iii ELIZABETH CROSS, b. 5 Nov 1781; d. at Colden, NY, 18 Oct 1866; m. ELISHA CALKINS, b. at New London, CT, 14 Mar 1775; Elisha d. at Colden, 11 May 1865.

iv MOSES CROSS, b. 7 Aug 1784; d. at Champlain, NY, 18 Nov 1857; m. EUNICE CUMMINS, b. at Mooers, NY, 2 Dec 1794 likely the daughter of Henry and Naomi (-) Cummins; Eunice d. at Champlain, 4 Aug 1852.

v HAZEN CROSS, b. 2 Aug 1787; nothing further known.

vi JAMES CROSS, b. 14 Apr 1789; d. at Hemmingford, Lower Canada, 5 Aug 1817 "by swallowing through mistake a small quantity of dilute potash prepared by his wife to rise a cake";[1580] m. NANCY DELONG, b. at Plattsburgh, 1793 daughter of Peter and Rachel (Lewis) DeLong; d. at Mooers, NY, 1886. After James's death, Nancy married Levi Dudley.

566) JAMES ABBOTT *(James⁴, James³, William², George¹)*, b. at Concord, 10 Oct 1750 son of James and Sarah (Bancroft) Abbott; d. at Portsmouth, OH, 1814; m. at Groton, VT, 29 Mar 1781, ZILPHA SMITH. James m. 2nd, at Groton, VT, 25 Jul 1785, MEHITABLE HIDDEN,[1581][1582] b. at Rowley, 7 Feb 1750, daughter of Ebenezer and Sarah (Ellsworth) Hidden;[1583] Mehitable was living in 1796 when her father wrote his will.

James Abbott was in Groton, Vermont and his third child with his first wife Zilpha, daughter Sally, was the first birth recorded in Groton, Vermont. He served on the board of selectmen when Groton was organized in 1797.[1584] In 1811, James and the family packed up and went to Scioto County, Ohio, and there purchased from Asa Boynton 176 acres of land for $522.[1585]

James Abbott and Zilpha Smith were parents of three children.

i SUSAN ABBOTT, b. at Haverhill, NH, 2 Feb 1782; d. 20 Mar 1783.

ii JOHN ABBOTT, b. at Haverhill, NH, 21 Feb 1783; nothing further known.

iii SALLY ABBOTT, b. at Groton, VT, 25 Aug 1784; d. at Woodbury, VT, 15 Aug 1839; m. at Groton, 4 Apr 1806, AARON BAILEY, b. at Grafton, NH, about 1784 son of Aaron and Elizabeth (-) Bailey; Aaron d. at Woodbury, 1 Jun 1850.

James Abbott and Mehitable Hidden were parents of six children born at Groton, Vermont.

i JAMES ABBOTT, b. 26 Mar 1786; m. at Scioto County, OH, 18 Aug 1812, DOLLY CHAMBERLAIN, b. in VT, about 1794 daughter of Wyatt and Dolly (-) Chamberlain.

ii Twin 1, b. and d. 22 Apr 1787

iii Twin 2, b. and d. 22 Apr 1787

iv JEREMIAH ABBOTT, b. 27 Apr 1788; m. at Scioto County, OH, 1 Apr 1818, BETSEY CHAMBERLAIN, b. in VT, about 1796 daughter of Wyatt and Dolly (-) Chamberlain.

v SAMUEL ABBOTT, b. 11 Jul 1790; d. at White County, IL, 8 Oct 1867; m. at Scioto County, IL, 1 Oct 1812, AURELIA CHAMBERLAIN, b. in VT, 1795 daughter of Wyatt and Dolly (-) Chamberlain.

vi EBENEZER ABBOTT, b. 16 Sep 1792; d. at Pittsfield, IL, 29 Nov 1855; m. at Scioto County, OH, 13 Feb 1817, NANCY BUCK, b. in DE, 1796 likely the daughter of John and Rachel (Beauchamp) Buck; Nancy d. at Pittsfield, 7 Feb 1866. In 1850, Nancy and Ebenezer were both is Pittsfield, but in different households, and Nancy is noted as insane. In 1860, Nancy was living with her son George.

1579 Findagrave ID: 30763828

1580 Columbian Centinel, Boston

1581 Abbott Family, Groton Families in 1790, Groton Vermont Historical Society.

1582 Vermont Vital Records 1720-1908 (ancestry.com)

1583 The 1796 will of Ebenezer Hidden, of Boscawen (but probate in Caledonia County, Vermont), includes a bequest to daughter Mehitable Abbott. The other children named are Jeremiah Hidden (who was born in Rowley in 1745) and Sarah Wells (born in Rowley in 1741 who is the half-sister of Jeremiah and Mehitable).

1584 Abbott Family, Groton Families in 1790, Groton Vermont Historical Society.

1585 Evans, *A History of Scioto County, Ohio*, p 658

567) JUDITH ABBOTT *(James⁴, James³, William², George¹)*, b. at Concord, 19 Feb 1753 daughter of James and Sarah (Bancroft) Abbott; d. at Newbury, VT, 30 Dec 1806; m. 27 Oct 1772, THOMAS BROCK, b. about 1745; Thomas d. at Newbury, 10 Jun 1811.

The origins of Thomas Brock are not clear. *The History of Newbury Vermont* suggests that he might have come from Scotland as an indentured servant under a different name. It is not known if he is connected to the Brock family that settled in Ryegate. In any event, he first shows up in records when he married Judith Abbott at Haverhill in 1772.[1586] He served in Olcott's Regiment of the Vermont Militia during the Revolution.[1587]

Judith and Thomas had fifteen children born at Newbury, twelve of whom lived to adulthood and married.

i MARY BROCK, b. 28 Dec 1773; d. at Newbury, 10 Jan 1840; m. 30 Aug 1796, SAMUEL TUCKER, b. at Oxford, MA, 26 Oct 1770 son of Samuel and Elizabeth (Livermore) Tucker; Samuel d. at Newbury, 14 Apr 1825.

ii SARAH BROCK, b. and d. 24 Jan 1775

iii THOMAS ROBINSON BROCK, b. 5 Dec 1775; d. at Newbury, 19 Jan 1839; m. at Concord, 6 Feb 1803, his second cousin, REBECCA ABBOTT *(Reuben⁵, Reuben⁴, James³, William², George¹)*, b. at Concord, 13 May 1781 daughter of Reuben and Zerviah (Farnum) Abbott; Rebecca d. at Newbury, 30 Oct 1872. Rebecca is a child in Family 571.

iv SARAH BROCK, b. 26 Sep 1777; d. at Newbury, 2 Aug 1841; m. 18 Sep 1806, SAMUEL WHITE, b. at Newbury, 12 Dec 1774 son of Ebenezer and Ruth (Emerson) White; Samuel d. at Newbury, 15 Sep 1846.

v BENJAMIN BROCK, b. 15 Jun 1779; d. 8 Jun 1841; m. 1st, 29 Dec 1806, MARGARET "PEGGY" GIBSON, b. at Newbury, 14 Jan 1784 daughter of Matthew and Betsey (McClary) Gibson; Peggy d. 27 Aug 1815. Benjamin m. 2nd, at Bradford, 22 Jan 1817, RUTH CHADWICK (widow of Tarrant Putnam), b. at Bradford, 11 Sep 1785 daughter of John and Mary (-) Chadwick; Ruth d. 12 May 1838. Benjamin m. 3rd, at Canaan, 3 Nov 1839, MARTHA C. JOHNSON who was of Enfield; Martha was still living in 1841 at the time of Benjamin's death.

vi SAMUEL BROCK, b. 18 Dec 1780; d. unknown; married NANCY FIELD, 1806. There is nothing else known. The History of Newbury reports he was dissatisfied with the settlement of his father's estate, moved away, and nothing else is known of him. There were no census records located that would fit with a Samuel Brock of his age in 1820.

vii JAMES BROCK, b. 23 Feb 1782; d. at Newbury, 23 Jul 1857; m. at Bath, 11 Jun 1813, CHLOE BUCK, b. at Bath, 17 May 1793 daughter of Amasa and Sybil (Hubbard) Buck; Chloe d. at Newbury, 15 Feb 1879.

viii JUDITH BROCK, b. 5 Aug 1783; d. 26 Jan 1797.

ix JACOB BROCK, b. 1 Nov 1784; d. at Newbury, 17 Feb 1868; b. 1st, at Haverhill, NH, 22 Jan 1807, ABIGAIL SANDERS who d. 27 Apr 1830. Jacob m. 2nd, 13 Oct 1830, BETSEY SINCLAIR, b. about 1801 and d. 16 Jul 1849. Jacob m 3rd, at Dracut, 16 Mar 1850, ABIGAIL EASTMAN. Jacob m. 4th, 16 Jan 1856, MEHITABLE KIMBALL TICE who d. 3 Jan 1870.

x SUSANNAH BROCK, b. 23 Dec 1785; d. at Dalton, NH, 15 Oct 1871; m. 11 Aug 1808, JOHN BROWN, b. in Massachusetts about 1782; John d. at Dalton, 14 Mar 1872.

xi OLIVE BROCK, b. 3 Apr 1787; d. 4 Sep 1789.

xii MOSES BROCK, b. 17 Jan 1789; d. 2 Oct 1874; m. 19 Mar 1815, LYDIA NOURSE; Lydia d. 26 Sep 1872.

xiii WILLIAM BROCK, b. 14 Sep 1790; d. 2 Oct 1857; m. 1 Nov 1818, ANN WALLACE, b. 29 Apr 1794; Ann d. at Freeport, IL, 26 Apr 1876.

xiv OLIVE BROCK, b. 13 Oct 1792; d. at Castleton, VT, 4 Jan 1875; m. at Newbury, 6 Jun 1816, JOHN WYATT, b. in New Hampshire about 1793; John d. at Castleton, VT, 5 Aug 1867.

xv ETHAN S. BROCK, b. 11 Mar 1794; d. at Newbury, 15 Nov 1870; m. at Newbury, 3 Dec 1823, MARY DOYLE, b. in New Hampshire about 1801; Mary d. after 1870.

[1586] Wells, *History of Newbury, Vermont*, p 473

[1587] Compiled Service Records of Soldiers Who Served in the American Army During the Revolutionary War 1775-1785

568) WILLIAM ABBOTT *(James⁴, James³, William², George¹)*, b. at Concord, 24 Apr 1755 son of James and Sarah (Bancroft) Abbott; d. at Bath, NH, 14 Jun 1807; m. 9 Dec 1777, MABEL WHITTLESEY, b. at Guilford, CT, 25 Jun 1757 daughter of Josiah and Elizabeth (Jackson) Whittlesey; Mabel d. at Haverhill, NH, 2 Nov 1836.

William Abbott served in the Revolutionary War as a private in the company of Captain Frederick Mordant enlisting on 27 December 1776.[1588] He was a farmer in Bath.

William Abbott did not leave a will. Mabel Abbott and Moses Abbott were administrators of the estate. Roger Sargent was named as guardian for William, Amos, and Anna each over fourteen years of age. Roger Sargent was also guardian for Nabby and Mary under age fourteen. The value of the real estate was $3,000 including the home farm of 57 acres on the Ammonoosuc River, 100 acres of farmland in Bath, an additional 100 acres in Bath called the Governor's lot, 4 acres on the Connecticut River, and two pews in the meeting house. In October 1808, Roger Sargent signed that he had received from Moses Abbott and Jacob Abbott $993.15 for the portion of the real estate for William, Amos, Anna, Nabby, and Mary. Receipts of $198.63 from Jacob Abbott and Moses Abbott were signed by Silas Buck and Lois Buck, Stephen Sly and Eliza Sly, Hitty Abbott, and Sarah Abbott. Those eleven heirs had signed agreement to the division of the estate 1 December 1807.[1589]

William Abbott and Mabel Whittlesey were parents of twelve children whose births are variously recorded at Haverhill and Bath, New Hampshire.

i MOSES ABBOTT, b. at Haverhill, NH, 16 Jun 1778; d. at Bath, 7 May 1856; m. 1st, about 1802, LUCY WILLIS, b. at Lebanon, NH, 25 Jul 1784 daughter of Abiel Willis; Lucy d. at Bath, 13 Jul 1842. Moses m. 2nd, 17 Aug 1844, the widow Lucy Wells.

ii LOIS ABBOTT, b. at Haverhill, 11 Dec 1779; d. at Napoli, NY, 15 Jul 1844; m. at Bath, 28 Nov 1805, SILAS BUCK, b. at Woodstock, CT, 22 Apr 1782 son of Amasa and Sybil (Hubbard) Buck; Silas d. at Napoli, 23 Dec 1863.

iii JACOB ABBOTT, b. at Haverhill, 15 Dec 1781; d. at Dixville, Estrie, Québec, 5 Mar 1869; m. 10 Nov 1808, NANCY WESSON, b. at Groton, VT, 1790 daughter of Ephraim and Judith (Morse) Wesson; Nancy d. at Estrie, 29 Jul 1827.

iv ELIZABETH ABBOTT, b. at Bath, 18 Jun 1783; d, at Danville, VT, 30 Sep 1840; m. Jan 1802, STEPHEN SLY, b. at Cumberland, RI, 22 May 1780 son of John and Ruth (Brown) Sly; Stephen d. at Danville, 7 Dec 1860. After Elizabeth's death, Stephen married Jane Moore.

v MEHITABLE ABBOTT, b. at Haverhill, 9 Jan 1785; d. at Bath, 7 Sep 1840; m. 1808, HORATIO BUCK, b. at Bath, 8 Feb 1787 son of Amasa and Sybil (Hubbard) Buck; Horatio d. at Bath, 29 Oct 1862.

vi SARAH ABBOTT, b. at Haverhill, 25 Oct 1786; d. at Waterford, VT, 5 Mar 1856; m. 28 Oct 1817, BENJAMIN FULLER, *possibly* b. at Montague, MA 27 Mar 1794 son of Benjamin and Hannah (Kendall) Fuller;[1590] Benjamin d. at Barnet, VT, Nov 1836 reportedly by drowning.

vii WILLIAM ABBOTT, b. at Haverhill, 19 Aug 1788; d. at Romeo, MI, 1 Jan 1862; m. at Peacham, 8 Nov 1812, PATIENCE BURBANK, b. likely at Peacham, Sep 1787; Patience d. at Romeo, 11 Jun 1829. William m. 2nd, about 1832, NANCY SABIN, b. in New York, about 1808 (census records). One of the sons of William Abbott and Nancy Sabin, Elon Abbott, died during the Civil War, 15 Mar 1862 at Lebanon, KY.

viii AMOS WHITTLESEY ABBOTT, b. at Haverhill, 3 Sep 1790; d. at Ryegate, VT, 19 Dec 1875; m. 17 Feb 1814, BETSY KNIGHT, b. at Wentworth, NH, 18 May 1794 daughter of Nathaniel and Hannah Laughlin (Smith) Knight; Betsy d. at Ryegate, 26 Apr 1874.

ix ANN ABBOTT, b. at Haverhill, 30 Jul 1792; d. at Ryegate, 3 Nov 1868; m. 2 Jul 1823, SAMUEL KNIGHT, b. at Groton, VT, 21 Jan 1799 son of Nathaniel and Hannah (Smith) Knight;[1591] Samuel d. at Ryegate, 9 Nov 1874.

x ABIGAIL ABBOTT, b. at Haverhill, 20 Aug 1794; d. at Bridgewater, MA, 29 Nov 1877; m. 1st, at Bath, 18 Mar 1819, NATHAN CULVER, b. likely at Westminster, VT, 4 Feb 1789;[1592] Nathan d. at Groton, 24 Apr 1832. Abigail m. 2nd, 14 Feb 1833, NATHAN ROBBINS, b. at Westminster, MA, 5 May 1785 son of Ephraim and Hannah (-) Robbins; Nathan Robbins d. at Bridgewater, 3 Jan 1878.

xi Son, b. and d. Aug 1797

[1588] U.S. Revolutionary Ware Rolls 1775-1783, New Hampshire, 2nd Regiment

[1589] *New Hampshire. Court of Probate (Grafton County);* Probate Place: *Grafton, New Hampshire*, Probate Estate File, William Abbott, 1807

[1590] There is circumstantial evidence for this identification based on the biography of Sarah and Benjamin's son, Benjamin Harvey Fuller, contained in Morton's *Illustrated History of Nebraska, Volume I*, p 656 which describes the circumstances of his father's and grandfather's death by drowning.

[1591] Samuel's parents are given as Nathaniel Knight and Hannah Smith on his death record.

[1592] His birthdate is given in the Groton, MA records but not as a birth that occurred there.

xii MARY ABBOTT, b. at Haverhill, 23 Nov 1802; d. at Dalton, NH, 18 Sep 1835; m. at St. Johnsbury, 13 Aug 1823, WILLIAM HUTCHINSON, b. at Lyndeborough, 4 Apr 1794 son of Ebenezer and Thomasin (Griffin) Hutchinson;[1593] William d. at Plainfield, NH, 24 Apr 1842. After Mary's death, William married Sarah Miner on 14 Dec 1836.

569) BANCROFT ABBOTT *(James⁴, James³, William², George¹)*, b. at Concord, 4 Jun 1757 son of James and Sarah (Bancroft) Abbott; d. at Newbury, VT, 29 Oct 1829;[1594] m. 1787, LYDIA WHITE, b. at Plaistow, NH, 1 Jan 1763 daughter of Ebenezer and Hannah (Merrill) White; Lydia d. 25 Jun 1853.

Bancroft Abbott was a farmer in Newbury. He was reported to be self-taught in mathematics, geometry, and surveying. He was active in town affairs.[1595] He served in the Revolutionary War in Bedel's New Hampshire Regiment[1596] and his widow Lydia received a pension until her death in 1853.[1597]

Bancroft and Lydia had eight children born at Newbury.

i THOMAS ABBOTT, b. 8 Jun 1788; d. at Georgetown, NY, 1855 (will dated 28 Mar 1855); m. 1st, 17 Sep 1812, ANNA POWERS, b. at Newbury, 12 May 1792 daughter of Stephen and Mary (Grow) Powers; Anna d. 1 Sep 1841. After Anna's death, Thomas married her sister ABIGAIL POWERS, b. 7 Sep 1797 and d. at Newbury, 24 Nov 1862. Thomas had relocated to New York and Abigail returned home to Newbury after his death.

ii MERRILL ABBOTT, b. 9 Feb 1790; d. 12 Apr 1794.

iii JAMES ABBOTT, b. 14 Feb 1792; d. at Newbury, 7 Mar 1870; m. 6 Jul 1820, ELIZABETH WYMAN MARTIN, b. at Andover, MA, 9 Jul 1791 daughter of Peter and Hannah (Dean) Martin; Elizabeth d. at Newbury, 2 Dec 1863.

iv ELIZABETH ABBOTT, b. 22 Mar 1794; died young

v MARY ABBOTT, b. 6 Jun 1795; d. at Chicago, 1834; m. 1816, her first cousin, AMOS BAILEY *(Abigail Abbott Bailey⁵, James⁴, James³, William², George¹)*, b. at Landaff, NH, 11 May 1784 son of Asa and Abigail (Abbott0 Bailey; Amos d. at Palatine, IL, 19 Apr 1863. Amos is a child in Family 564.

vi EBENEZER ABBOTT, b. 6 Nov 1797; d. at West Newbury, 10 Apr 1873; m. 11 Jun 1829, his first cousin once removed, REBECCA BROCK *(Thomas R. Brock⁶, Judith Abbott Brock⁵, James⁴, James³, William², George¹)*, b. at Newbury, 10 May 1805 daughter of Thomas Robinson and Rebecca (Abbott) Brock; Rebecca d. at West Newbury, 18 May 1897.

vii NICHOLAS ABBOTT, b. 18 Dec 1799; d. at Lafayette, IN, 29 Sep 1871; m. at St. Johnsbury, VT, 12 Aug 1829, MIRA JEWETT, b. at St. Johnsbury, 1 Nov 1809 daughter of Luther and Betsey (Adams) Jewett; Mira d. Fremont. NE, 23 Apr 1890.

viii SARAH ABBOTT, b. 11 Mar 1802; d. at Lyme, NH, Nov 1849; m. Feb 1829, MARSHALL SOUTHARD, b. at Auburn, MA, 14 Mar 1796 son of Nathaniel and Patience (Shaw) Southard; Marshal d. at Lyme, 10 Mar 1857.

570) EZRA ABBOTT *(James⁴, James³, William², George¹)*, b. at Haverhill, NH, 2 Jun 1765 son of James and Sarah (Bancroft) Abbott; d. at Irasburg, VT, 5 Jul 1842; m. at Newbury, VT, 8 Aug 1788, his first cousin, HANNAH ABBOTT *(Reuben⁴, James³, William², George¹)*, b. 29 Mar 1762 daughter of Reuben and Rhoda (Whittemore) Abbott; Hannah d. 2 Sep 1832.

Ezra was a farmer and lived in Bradford and Newbury, Vermont and was in Irasburg in his later years. Ezra and Hannah Abbott were parents to six children.

i REUBEN ABBOTT, b. perhaps at Concord, 26 Dec 1786; d. at Canton, ME, 21 Jan 1872; m. 1st, at Bath, NH, 23 Nov 1809, LYDIA HUNT, b. at Bath, 30 Dec 1786 daughter of Zebulon and Lucy (Whittlesey) Hunt; Lydia d. at Sutton, VT, 28 Jan 1842. Reuben m. 2nd, 21 Dec 1843, RUTH MARIA P. SWASEY, b. in New Hampshire, about 1807 (based on age on census records); Ruth d. at Canton, ME, 22 Jun 1866.

[1593] Carter, *Native Ministry of New Hampshire*, p 479

[1594] *Vermont, Vital Records, 1720-1908* (Provo, UT, USA: Ancestry.com Operations, Inc., 2013).

[1595] Wells, *History of Newbury Vermont*, p 421

[1596] Compiled Service Records of Soldiers Who Served in the American Army During the Revolutionary War 1775-1785

[1597] U.S., Revolutionary War Pensioners, 1801-1815, 1818-1872

ii EZRA ABBOTT, b. 11 Mar 1788; died young

iii HANNAH ABBOTT, b. at Newbury, NH, 24 Jan 1790. Hannah did not marry.

iv EZRA ABBOTT, b. at Newbury, NH, 13 Sep 1791; d. at Littleton, NH, 26 Mar 1872; m. 1st, 11 Nov 1813, MARY ANN LANG, b. at Bath, 22 Apr 1792 daughter of Moses Lang; Mary Ann d. at Littleton, 28 Sec 1849. Ezra m. 2nd, about 1850, MIRA PARKER, b. at Lyman, 30 Jun 1799; Mira d. at Bethlehem, NH, 20 Jul 1885.

v SUSAN ABBOTT, b. at Bradford, NH, 21 Feb 1792; d. at Bradford, VT, 26 Sep 1830; m. at Bath, 8 Mar 1813, THOMAS MARTIN who d. at Bradford, VT, 16 May 1868.

vi JACOB WOOD ABBOTT, b. 7 Aug 1795; died young

571) REUBEN ABBOTT *(Reuben4, James3, William2, George1)*, b. at Concord, 5 Feb 1754 son of Reuben and Rhoda (Whittemore) Abbott; d. 12 Dec 1834; m. 24 Sep 1776, his second cousin once removed (through a Farnum line), ZERVIAH FARNUM, b. at Concord, about 1752 daughter of Joseph and Zerviah (Hoit) Farnum; Zerviah d. at Concord, Dec 1818.[1598]

Reuben Abbott was a farmer in Concord. He and wife Zerviah Farnum had seven children born at Concord.

i RUTH ABBOTT, b. 25 Apr 1777; d. at Concord, 20 Feb 1849; m. 11 Mar 1798, her fourth cousin, HENRY CHANDLER *(Isaac Chandler5, Nathan Chandler4, John Chandler3, Hannah Abbott Chandler2, George1)*, b. at Andover, 16 Jul 1766 son of Isaac and Hannah (Ballard) Chandler; Henry d. at Concord, 3 Apr 1856. Henry is a child in Family 429.

ii PHEBE ABBOTT, b. 17 May 1779; d. at Concord, NH, after 1850; m. 27 Mar 1804, PETER CHANDLER FARNUM, b. at Concord, 18 Mar 1778 son of Ephraim and Abigail (Stevens) Farnum; Peter d. at Concord, 4 Apr 1816.

iii REBECCA ABBOTT, b. 13 May 1781; d. at Newbury, VT, 30 Oct 1872; m. at Concord, 6 Feb 1803, her second cousin, THOMAS ROBINSON BROCK *(Judith Abbott Brock5, James4, James3, William2, George1)*, b. at Newbury, 5 Dec 1775 son of Thomas and Judith (Abbott) Brock; Thomas d. at Newbury, 19 Jan 1839. Thomas is a child in Family 567.

iv SUSANNAH ABBOTT, b. 20 Jun 1785; death unknown. Bouton's History of Concord reports that she did not marry.

v ZERVIAH ABBOTT, b. 20 Dec 1785; d. at Concord, 1 Jul 1841; m. 13 Sep 1808, JESSE CARR TUTTLE, b. at Concord, 1779 son of Stephen and Jane (Carr) Tuttle; Jesse d. at Concord, Dec 1835.

vi POLLY ABBOTT, b. 2 Mar 1789; d. at Concord, Sep 1859; m. 8 Dec 1825, HENRY MARTIN, b. at Concord, 7 Aug 1779 son of Henry and Esther (Kimball) Martin, Henry d. at Concord, 1860.

vii REUBEN ABBOTT, b. 23 Oct 1790; d. at Concord, 27 Jun 1869; m. 16 Mar 1815, his third cousin once removed, HANNAH ABBOTT *(Daniel4, George3, Thomas2, George1)*, b. at Concord, 28 Oct 1791 daughter of Daniel and Mercy (Kilburn) Abbott; Hannah d. at Concord, 13 Sep 1876. Reuben and Hannah are the parents in Family 932.

572) RHODA ABBOTT *(Reuben4, James3, William2, George1)*, b. at Concord, 31 Dec 1755 daughter of Reuben and Rhoda (Whittemore) Abbott; d. at Boscawen, 31 Aug 1839; m. at Concord, 8 Jan 1778, JONATHAN JOHNSON, b. at Boscawen, 29 Dec 1753 son of John and Eleanor (Eastman) Johnson; Jonathan d. at Concord, 16 Sep 1820.

Rhoda Abbott and Jonathan Johnson lived in the area of Boscawen known as Horse Hill which was near the line with Concord.[1599]

In her will dated 15 March 1839, Rhoda Abbott Johnson bequeaths to John Johnson the homestead farm. Son John also receives all the household furniture. Her five daughters receive all her clothing to divide equally: Eleanor Johnson; Rhoda Abbot wife of Timothy Abbot; Hannah Eastman wife of Ezekiel Eastman; Sarah C. Johnson; and Ruth Johnson. Any residue of the estate goes to son John Johnson. Son Reuben Johnson is named executor.[1600]

In her will written 6 November 1863, daughter Sarah C. Johnson bequeathed to her sister Ruth Johnson the use of her house in Fisherville in Boscawen and support from her property. After Ruth's decease, the property will be dispersed among various heirs. Brother John to have the use of one hundred dollars and then the principle amount to his heirs; sister Rhoda Abbott, one hundred dollars; nephew Luke Eastman, twenty-five dollars; nephew Charles Johnson, one hundred dollars; heirs of brother Reuben Johnson, five dollars to be divided among them; heirs of Philip C. Johnson, twenty dollars; and nephews Phillip

---

1598 New Hampshire, Death and Disinterment Records, 1754-1947

1599 Coffin, *The History of Boscawen*, p 560

1600 *New Hampshire. Probate Court (Merrimack County)*; Probate Place: *Merrimack, New Hampshire*, volume 8, p 625, accessed through ancestry.com

Eastman and John C. Eastman each five dollars. Any residue of the estate after Ruth's death is to go to the American Home Missionary Society. Almon Harris of Fisherville in the town of Boscawen is named executor.[1601]

Jonathan and Rhoda Johnson had twelve children born at Concord.

i PHEBE JOHNSON, b. 10 Sep 1778; d. 23 Sep 1819; m. ELEAZER DAVIS likely the son of Eleazer and Sarah (Cook) Davis. Phebe was likely Eleazer's second wife and did not have children.

ii TIMOTHY JOHNSON, b. 10 Jan 1780; m. MELINDA SWEET. Nothing has been found for this family. Timothy is not mentioned in his mother's will or his sister Sarah's will and no heirs for him are mentioned in either will.

iii ELEANOR JOHNSON, b. 16 Oct 1781; d. at Boscawen, 29 Jan 1849. Eleanor did not marry.

iv RHODA JOHNSON, b. 1 Nov 1783; d. at Boscawen, 28 Nov 1864; m. at Concord, 8 Jul 1813, her first cousin, TIMOTHY ABBOTT *(Ezra^5, Reuben^4, James^3, William^2, George^1)*, b. at Concord, 21 Dec 1788 son of Ezra and Mary (Walker) Abbott; Ezra d. at Boscawen, Jan 1847. Timothy Abbott is a child in Family 574.

v HANNAH JOHNSON, b. 13 May 1785; d. at Greensboro, VT, 25 Mar 1859; m. 25 Aug 1808, EZEKIEL EASTMAN, b. about 1782; Ezekiel d. at Greensboro, 26 Nov 1847.

vi JOHN JOHNSON, b. 17 Feb 1787; d. 2 Dec 1790.

vii SARAH CARTER JOHNSON, b. 15 Mar 1791; d. at Boscawen, 1866 (probate 22 May 1866). Sarah did not marry.

viii REUBEN JOHNSON, b. 12 Jan 1792; d. at Boscawen, 16 Mar 1852; m. 16 Apr 1812, his fourth cousin once removed, JUDITH HALL CHANDLER *(John Chandler^6, John Chandler^5, John Chandler^4, John Chandler^3, Hannah Abbott Chandler^2, George^1)*, b. at Boscawen, 19 Mar 1793 daughter of John and Naomi (Farnum) Chandler; Judith d. at Boscawen, 2 Nov 1843.

ix JOHN JOHNSON, b. 15 Jan 1793; d. at Boscawen, after 1870; m. 1st, 28 Aug 1817, his first cousin, SOPHIA ABBOTT *(Nathan^5, Reuben^4, James^3, William^2, George^1)*, b. at Concord, 17 Jul 1795 daughter of Nathan and Phebe (Abbott) Abbott; Sophia d. at Boscawen, 16 Jan 1843. John m. 2nd, 27 Nov 1843, JUDITH DIMOND, b. at Concord, 29 Jan 1793 daughter of Reuben and Mary (Currier) Dimond; Judith d. at Boscawen, 18 May 1870. Sophia Abbott is a child in Family 575.

x PHILIP CARRIGAN JOHNSON, b. 9 Mar 1795; d. at Washington, DC, 10 Aug 1859; m. about 1818, his fourth cousin, MARY KIMBALL CHANDLER *(Jeremiah Chandler^5, John Chandler^4, Tabitha Abbott Chandler^3, Nathaniel^2, George^1)*, b. at Concord, 10 Oct 1796 daughter of Jeremiah and Judith (Farnum) Chandler; Mary d. at Washington, 6 Sep 1855. Mary Kimball Chandler is a child in Family 1081. Philip Carrigan Johnson was Secretary of State for Maine in 1840 and appointed by President Polk as Chief Clerk in the Bureau of Construction, Equipment, and Repair of the Navy Department

xi RUTH JOHNSON, b. 24 Aug 1797; d. at Boscawen, 6 Feb 1875. Ruth did not marry.

xii OBADIAH C. JOHNSON, b. 11 Jul 1801; d. at Lowell, MA, 10 Feb 1836; m. ELIZABETH "BETSEY" CHARLES, b. about 1805 in New Hampshire

573) ELIAS ABBOTT *(Reuben^4, James^3, William^2, George^1)*, b. at Concord, 24 Oct 1757 son of Reuben and Rhoda (Whittemore) Abbott; d. at Northfield, NH, 19 Mar 1847; m. Sep 1782, ELIZABETH BUSWELL, b. at Kingston, 4 Sep 1761 daughter of James and Elizabeth (Clough) Buswell; Elizabeth d. 25 Jan 1832.[1602]

Elias and Elizabeth had their five children in Concord, but in 1801 the family relocated to Northfield.[1603] Elias served in the Revolutionary War and received a pension for his service. He served in Captain James Osgood's Company in the Regiment of Colonel Timothy Beedle. His service included action on the St. Lawrence River in Lower Canada.[1604]

Elias and Elizabeth Abbott had five children born at Concord.

i ABIGAIL ABBOTT, b. 5 Aug 1783; d. at Sanbornton, 25 Aug 1864; m. at Northfield, 8 Feb 1827, her fourth cousin, JEREMIAH HALL *(Obadiah Hall^5, Dorcas Abbott Hall^4, Edward^3, Thomas^2, George^1)*, b. at Canterbury,

---

[1601] New Hampshire, County Probate Records, 1660-1973, Probate of Sarah C. Johnson, Case 6871, Merrimack, 26:503, 42:115, 37:391, 43:432, 22:519

[1602] Lyford, *History of the Town of Canterbury*, p 1

[1603] Cross, *History of Northfield*, part 2, genealogies, p 5

[1604] Revolutionary War Pension and Bounty-Land Warrant Application Files, application file of Elias Abbott

18 Oct 1777 son of Obadiah and Mary (Perham) Hall; Jeremiah d. at Sanbornton, 8 Jul 1867. Jeremiah was first married to Hannah Haines who died in 1826. Jeremiah is a child in Family 899.

ii ELIAS ABBOTT, b. 22 Mar 1786; d. at Northfield, 10 Sep 1862; m. 1st, 21 May 1812, LYDIA SAWYER, b. at Northfield, 23 Jul 1784 daughter of Gideon and Hannah (Sherborn) Sawyer; Lydia d. 14 May 1826. Elias m. 2nd, Aug 1826, SARAH WINSLOW, b. at Loudon, 30 Jan 1788 daughter of Zebulon and Hannah (Bagley) Winslow; Sarah d. 2 Aug 1848. Elias m. 3rd, the widow ELLINOR ROGERS, born about 1811.

iii ELIZABETH ABBOTT, b. 3 Jun 1788; d. at Northfield, 29 Mar 1847. Elizabeth did not marry.

iv CHARLOTTE ABBOTT, b. 9 Dec 1790; d. at Hopkinton, 16 Aug 1865; m. 29 Sep 1808, WILLIAM STRAW, b. at Hopkinton, 12 Jun 1787 son of James and Mary (Buswell) Straw; William d. at Hopkinton, 12 Mar 1870.

v JAMES BUSWELL ABBOTT, b. 24 Jun 1799; d. at Sanbornton, 6 Jul 1870; m. 1st, 15 Nov 1827, NANCY BUSWELL ROGERS, b. at Northfield, 6 Sep 1800 daughter of Enoch and Nancy (Buswell) Rogers; Nancy d. Nov 1837. James m. 2nd, 2 Oct 1838, ELIZABETH A. ROGERS sister of Nancy, b. 13 Mar 1803 and d. at Sanbornton, 27 Nov 1842. James m. 3rd, 1843, SARAH GERRISH, b. at Canterbury, 2 Mar 1816 daughter of Joseph and Sarah (Clark) Gerrish; Sarah d. at Sanbornton, 28 Nov 1893.

574) EZRA ABBOTT *(Reuben⁴, James³, William², George¹)*, b. at Concord, 8 Aug 1765 son of Reuben and Rhoda (Whittemore) Abbott; d. at Concord, 24 Apr 1839; m. his third cousin, MARY WALKER *(Mary Abbott Walker⁴, Nathaniel³, Nathaniel², George¹)*, b, about 1763 daughter of Joseph and Mary (Abbott) Walker; Mary d. at Concord, 22 Sep 1852.

Ezra Abbott was a farmer in Concord and both he and his wife Mary were members of the Congregational Church.[1605] Ezra and Mary had nine children born at Concord.

i JOHN ABBOTT, b. 20 Mar 1787, d. at Hopkinton, NH, 3 Dec 1839; m. at Hopkinton, 6 Dec 1811, SARAH STRAW, b. at Hopkinton, 4 Aug 1789 daughter of James and Mary (Buswell) Straw; Sarah d. at Hopkinton, 15 Feb 1838.

ii TIMOTHY ABBOTT, b. 21 Dec 1788; d. at Boscawen, Jan 1847; m. at Concord, 8 Jul 1813, his first cousin, RHODA JOHNSON, b. at Concord, 1 Nov 1783 daughter of Jonathan and Rhoda (Abbott) Johnson; Rhoda d. at Boscawen, 28 Nov 1864. Rhoda is a child in Family 572.

iii JOB ABBOTT, b. 15 Nov 1790; d. at Gilford, NH, 1876; m. at Boscawen, 6 Apr 1816, LYDIA P. MORRISON, b. in New Hampshire about 1795 (based on census records); Lydia d. a Laconia, NH, 1881.

iv NANCY ABBOTT, b. 21 Nov 1792; d. at Concord, 27 Jun 1879; m. at Concord, 31 Mar 1819, JAMES HOIT, b. at Concord, 17 Sep 1788 son of Joseph and Mary (Elliot) Hoit;[1606] James d. at Concord, 1861 (probate 26 Feb 1861).

v HERMAN ABBOTT, b. 4 Oct 1795; d. at Concord, 28 Dec 28 Dec 1828; m. at Hopkinton, 24 Jun 1819, as her third husband, SARAH CURRIER, b. at Hopkinton, 26 Dec 1788 daughter of Henry and Abigail (Burbank) Currier; Sarah d. 21 Aug 1864. Sarah was first married to Samuel Putney. Sarah Currier was second married to George Abbott descendant MOSES EASTMAN, b. 5 Mar 1790 son of Ezra and Molly (Eaton) Eastman; Moses d. 3 Mar 1817. Moses Eastman is a child in Family 585.

vi DAVID ABBOTT, b. 13 Jan 1798; d. after 1850 (living in Concord in 1850); m. at Boston, 18 May 1828, MARY HOLBROOK, b. at Boston, 4 Jan 1798 daughter of John Holbrook; Mary d. after 1850.

vii ESTHER ABBOTT, b. 30 Mar 1800; d. at Portland, ME, 1 Oct 1886; m. at Portland, 1 Nov 1832, WILLIAM E. KIMBALL, b. at Portland, about 1805 (based on census records and death records of his children); William d. at Portland, 2 Nov 1869.

viii RUTH ABBOTT, b. 9 May 1802; d. at Boscawen about 1874 (husband remarried 1875); m. at Concord, 16 Mar 1829, SAMUEL ELLSWORTH, b. at Sanbornton, about 1804 *possibly* the son of Samuel and Sally (Bean) Ellsworth; Samuel d. at Boscawen, 1883. After Ruth's death, Samuel married Sarah Elliot on 15 May 1875.

ix MARY W. ABBOTT, b. 8 Nov 1806; d. at Concord, 12 May 1836; m. at Concord, 3 Feb 1829, ALEXANDER HAMILTON PUTNEY, b. at Boscawen, 26 Feb 1804 son of Calen and Naomi (Carter) Putney; Alexander d. at Murphys, CA, 11 Sep 1861. After Mary's death, Alexander married Sarah W. Edwards on 19 May 1837.

[1605] Abbot and Abbot, *Genealogical Register*, p 37

[1606] Stearns, *Genealogical and Family History of New Hampshire*, p 82

575) NATHAN ABBOTT *(Reuben⁴, James³, William², George¹)*, b. at Concord, 8 Aug 1765 son of Reuben and Rhoda (Whittemore) Abbott; d. at Concord, 13 May 1849; m. his third cousin, PHEBE ABBOTT *(Nathaniel⁴, Nathaniel³, Nathaniel², George¹)*, b. 8 Aug 1764 daughter of Nathaniel and Miriam (Chandler) Abbott; Phebe d. at Concord, 11 Aug 1854.

Nathan Abbott and Phebe Abbott were parents of nine children born at Concord.

i RHODA ABBOTT, b. 17 May 1790; d. after 1846 (living at time of husband's probate); m. 13 Nov 1810. RICHARD WEBSTER, b. about 1783; Richard d. at Hookset, 1846 (probate Mar 1846).

ii AMOS ABBOTT, b. 16 Nov 1791; d. at Nashville, NH, Nov 1845; m. 18 Oct 1820, SALLY GOULD FOSTER, b. at Warren, 1795 daughter of Benjamin Foster; Sally d. at Nashua, Aug 1860.

iii WILLIAM ABBOTT, b. 23 Aug 1793; d. at Webster, NH, 3 Feb 1837; m. 6 Mar 1820, DORCAS CARTER, b. at Concord, 3 Dec 1797 daughter of Ephraim and Dorcas (Presby) Carter; Dorcas d. at Webster, 6 Aug 1884.

iv SOPHIA ABBOTT, b. 17 Jul 1795; d. at Boscawen, 16 Jan 1843; m. 28 Aug 1817, her first cousin, JOHN JOHNSON *(Rhoda Abbott Johnson⁵, Reuben⁴, James³, William², George¹)*, b. at Concord, 15 Jan 1793 son of Jonathan and Rhoda (Abbott) Johnson; John d. at Boscawen, after 1870. John n. 2nd, 27 Nov 1843, JUDITH DIMOND, b. at Concord, 29 Jan 1793 daughter of Reuben and Mary (Currier) Dimond; Judith d. at Boscawen, 18 May 1870. John Johnson is a child in Family 572.

v HAZEN ABBOTT, b. 6 Nov 1797; d. at Salem, NH, 12 Aug 1873; m. 1828, RUTH M. ELA, b. at Hooksett, about 1807 daughter of Enos and Betsey (Martin) Ela; Ruth d. at Salem, 2 Nov 1886.

vi SUSANNA ABBOTT, b. 13 Mar 1800; d. at Lynchburg, VA, 27 Oct 1881. Susanna did not marry. She lived with her sister Phebe and went with Phebe and her family to Lynchburg.

vii JACOB ABBOTT, b. 13 Mar 1802; d. 15 Sep 1803.

viii JACOB ABBOTT, b. 11 May 1804; d. at Nashua, after 1860; m. 11 Apr 1833, HARRIET GARVIN, b. in VT, about 1808; Harriet d. at Nashua, 1861.

ix PHEBE ABBOTT, b. 17 Oct 1806; d. at Lynchburg, VA, after 1870; m. 17 Jan 1831, SETH JUDKINS, b. about 1807 "of Bow"; Seth d. at Lynchburg, after 1860.

576) THOMAS MERRILL *(Phebe Abbott Merrill⁴, James³, William², George¹)*, b. at Conway, 31 Aug 1748 son of Thomas and Phebe (Abbott) Merrill; d. at Conway, May 1821;[1607] m. 7 Dec 1775, HANNAH AMBROSE, b, about 1750 daughter of Jonathan and Abigail (Goodhue) Ambrose.

Thomas Merrill was a farmer in Conway. Thomas and Hannah had eight children born at Conway.

i SAMUEL MERRILL, b. 20 Jan 1777; d. at Frankfort (Winterport), ME, 1 Jan 1852; m. 1st, about 1803, SARAH MASON, b. about 1780 and d. 1804. Samuel m. 2nd, about 1805, ANNA "NANCY" REED, b. about 1785; Nancy d. at Frankfort, 1849.

ii ABIGAIL MERRILL, b. 26 Oct 1778; d. at Eaton, NH, 1853; m. about 1796, DANIEL JACKSON, b. about 1775 son of James Jackson.

iii HANNAH MERRILL, b. about 1780; d. at Jefferson, NH, 1842; m. WILLIAM CHAMBERLAIN, b. at Brookfield, NH, 10 Nov 1775 son of John and Mary (Jackson) Chamberlain; William d. at Jefferson, 1857.

iv THOMAS MERRILL, b. 1783; d. at Conway, 7 Feb 1847; m. 31 Jul 1808, his first cousin, LYDIA MERRILL *(Amos Merrill⁵, Phebe Abbott Merrill⁴, James³, William², George¹)*, b. about 1789 daughter of Amos and Lois (Willey) Merrill; Lydia d. at Conway, 5 Jan 1860. Lydia is a child in Family 578.

v NATHANIEL MERRILL, b. 10 Jul 1788; d. at Gray, ME, 1 Aug 1870; m. 4 Jul 1818, OLIVE HART PLAISTED, b. at Jefferson, NH, 1794 daughter of Samuel and Elizabeth (Hart) Plaisted; Olive d. at Gray, 1843.

vi JONATHAN MERRILL, b. 29 Nov 1790; d. at Bridgton, ME, 14 Mar 1821; m. about 1813, RUTH JEWETT JORDAN, b. about 1790 daughter of Mial and Ruth (Jewett) Jordan.

vii CATHERINE MERRILL, b. about 1793; died young.

[1607] Merrill, *A Merrill Memorial*, p 294

viii NANCY MERRILL, b. 24 Aug 1796; d. at Jefferson, 18 Sep 1856; m. 6 Mar 1814, WILLIAM PLAISTED, b. about 1794 son of Samuel and Elizabeth (Hart) Plaisted; William d. at Jefferson, 6 Sep 1854.

577) ENOCH MERRILL *(Phebe Abbott Merrill⁴, James³, William², George¹)*, b. at Conway, 10 Nov 1750 son of Thomas and Phebe (Abbott) Merrill; d. 1838; m. about 1772, MARY AMBROSE, b. at Exeter, 11 Nov 1755 daughter of Jonathan and Abigail (Goodhue) Ambrose; Mary d. at Conway, 27 Mar 1815.

Three of the sons of Enoch and Mary (Josiah Goodhue, Stephen, and Henry Ambrose) were Congregationalist ministers.[1608]

Enoch Merrill and Mary Ambrose were parents of ten children born at Conway, New Hampshire. Three of the children in this family married three of the children of Nathaniel and Ann (Walker) Merrill who are first cousins once removed. Nathaniel Merrill was Enoch Merrill's uncle.

i ENOCH MERRILL, b. 27 Nov 1773; d. at Brownfield, ME, 27 Mar 1855; m. 1799, SARAH MERRILL, b. 2 May 1771 daughter of Nathaniel and Ann (Walker) Merrill; Sarah d. 14 Apr 1842.

ii PHEBE MERRILL, b. 28 Sep 1775; d. at Brownfield, ME, 16 Oct 1851; m. 13 Jun 1793, NATHANIEL MERRILL, b. at Fryeburg, 16 Jun 1767 son of Nathaniel and Ann (Walker) Merrill; Nathaniel d. at Brownfield, 19 May 1828.

iii MARY "POLLY" MERRILL, b. 11 May 1778; d. at Conway, 28 Sep 1853; m. at Conway, 10 Mar 1802, WILLIAM BROUGHTON, b. 1770; William d. at Conway, 8 Sep 1848.

iv JAMES MERRILL, b. 18 Jan 1781; d. at Conway, 16 Apr 1862; m. at Conway, 10 Dec 1809, POLLY SHERBURNE, b. at Portsmouth, NH, Aug 1780 daughter of Henry and Phebe (Dennett) Sherburne; Polly d. at Conway, 20 Apr 1862.

v SALLY MERRILL, b. 19 Mar 1783; d. at Brownfield, ME, 30 Mar 1863; m. at Conway, 23 Jan 1816, MOSES MERRILL, b. at Fryeburg, 17 Mar 1777 son of Nathaniel and Ann (Walker) Merrill; Moses d. at Brownfield, 31 Aug 1870.

vi JOSIAH MERRILL, b. 1 Jul 1785; d. Sep 1786.

vii JOSIAH GOODHUE MERRILL, b. 4 Sep 1787; d. at Lynn, MA, 18 Aug 1872; m. 1815, HARRIET JONES, b. at Standish, ME, 9 Mar 1790 daughter of Ephraim and Judith (Philbrick) Jones;[1609] Harriet d. at Lynn, 12 Feb 1865.

viii MEHITABLE MERRILL, b. 3 Apr 1790; d. at Cornish, NH, 13 Nov 1870; m. at Conway, 30 Jun 1818, HENRY SHERBURNE, b. at Portsmouth, about 1786 son of Henry and Phebe (Dennett) Sherburne. Henry's death not located. After Henry's death, Mehitable married a Mr. Kinney as she was Mehitable Kinney at the time of her death. In 1870, she was living with her son Samuel Sherburne in Cornish, NH.

ix STEPHEN MERRILL, b. 14 Oct 1793; d. at North Wolfeboro, NH, 23 Jun 1860; m. 1st, 17 Sep 1821, MARY HOIT GILMAN, b. at Epping, NH, 1790 daughter of Chase and Hannah (French) Gilman; Mary d. at Lisbon, ME, 19 Sep 1841. Stephen m. 2nd, about 1842, CLARISSA EASTMAN, b. at Conway, 28 Oct 1799 daughter of Richard and Susannah (Runnells) Eastman; Clarissa d. at Conway, 12 Jul 1869.

x HENRY AMBROSE MERRILL, b. 13 Jun 1795; d. at Granville, OH, 25 Sep 1872; m. 1st, 12 Jun 1823, ABIGAIL R. HILL, b. at Conway, 14 Feb 1795 daughter of Leavitt and Sarah (Russell) Hill; Abigail d. at Conway, 10 Apr 1837. Henry m. 2nd, at Parsonsfield, ME, 6 Nov 1838, ABIGAIL GARLAND, b. in Maine, about 1797; Abigail Garland d. at Granville, 23 Feb 1883.

578) AMOS MERRILL *(Phebe Abbott Merrill⁴, James³, William², George¹)*, b. at Conway, Jul 1752 son of Thomas and Phebe (Abbott) Merrill; d, at Conway, 13 Mar 1840; m. 30 Dec 1779, LOIS WILLEY, b. Jan 1760; Lois d. 28 Mar 1855.

Amos Merrill was a farmer whose property was along the Saco River in Conway.[1610] Amos Merrill and Lois Willey were parents of eleven children born at Conway. Some of the birth dates are estimated based on other information such as age at death or year of marriage.

i LOIS MERRILL, b. about 1781; likely died young

ii AMOS MERRILL, b. about 1785; d. at Conway, 8 Oct 1867; m. about 1820, NANCY MILLICAN, b. at Portland, ME, 1802 daughter of Harry and Mary (Brown) Millican; Nancy d. at Conway, 4 Jan 1887.

[1608] Carter, *Native Ministry of New Hampshire*, pp 161-162

[1609] The names of Harriet's parents are given as Ephraim Jones and Judith Philbrick on her death record.

[1610] Merrill, *The Merrill Memorial*, p 421.

iii HENRY MERRILL, b. estimate 1786; d. at Conway, 1829 (will 23 Dec 1828; probate Sep 1829). Henry was a trader. He did not marry. His will includes bequests to his honored father Amos and to the children of his sister Betsy Chubbuck wife of William Chubbuck.[1611]

iv LYDIA MERRILL, b. about 1789; d. at Conway, 5 Jan 1860; m. at Conway, 31 Jul 1808, her first cousin, THOMAS MERRILL, b. 1783 son of Thomas and Hannah (Ambrose) Merrill; Thomas d. at Conway, 7 Feb 1847. Thomas Merrill is a child in Family 576.

v ELIJAH MERRILL, b. about 1790; d. at Québec, 26 Sep 1813. Elijah served in U.S. land forces during the War of 1812 and died of dysentery while a prisoner of war.[1612][1613]

vi BETSY MERRILL, b. about 1792; d. after 1850 (living in Bartlett, NH in 1850); m. at Conway, 20 Jun 1818, WILLIAM BARNARD CHUBBUCK, b. estimated 1788; d. before 1850.

vii MARK MERRILL, b. 1794; d. at Conway, after 1870; m. 1st, at Conway, 1 Dec 1822, BETSY H. GIBSON, b. at Brownfield, ME, about 1804 daughter of Jonathan and Polly (Mansfield) Gibson;[1614] Betsy d. about 1830. Mark m. 2nd, about 1830, HARRIET BROUGHTON, b. about 1808 daughter of Mark and Polly (Knox) Broughton; Harriet d. after 1880 (living in Conway in 1880). Harriet was first married to Henry Gibson who was the brother of Mark Merrill's first wife.

viii PHEBE MERRILL, b. Sep 1797; d. at Conway 14 Feb 1872; m. about 1825, JACOB E. BERRY, b. at Bridgton, ME, 10 Sep 1802 son of Isaac and Phebe (Emerson) Berry; Jacob d. at Conway, 19 May 1870.

ix SAMUEL MERRILL, b. 1800; d. at Brooklyn, MN, 1862; m. 15 May 1825, MARTHA W. GREEN, b. in NH, about 1806; Martha d. at Brooklyn, MN, 1872.

x SALLY G. MERRILL, b. 1801; d. at Conway, after 1880; m. about 1825, JOHN BROUGHTON, b. about 1804 son of Mark and Polly (Knox) Broughton; John d. at Conway, after 1880.

xi ALBERT MERRILL, about 1805; d. at Conway, 1872; m. 1st, about 1832, EMILY EASTMAN, b. about 1808; Emily d. at Conway, about 1841. Albert m. 2nd, at Gilford, 10 Apr 1842, MARY K. OSGOOD, b. about 1816 daughter of Edward and Nancy (Kezar) Osgood;[1615] Mary d. after 1880 (living in Conway in 1880).

579) PHEBE MERRILL *(Phebe Abbott Merrill[4], James[3], William[2], George[1])*, b. at Conway, Dec 1753 daughter of Thomas and Phebe (Abbott) Merrill; d. at North Conway, 9 Oct 1839; m. 3 Dec 1775, her second cousin, ABIATHAR EASTMAN, b. 29 Apr 1745 son of Richard and Mary (Lovejoy) Eastman;[1616] Abiathar d. 10 Jan 1815.

Abiathar Eastman was a farmer in Conway where he served as a church deacon. He was in the Revolutionary War and had a rank of Sergeant. The Eastman genealogy reports that he was absent from duty at Chelsea in September 1785 and found unfit for duty by order of Major Watson.[1617]

Abiathar and Phebe Eastman had seven children born at Conway.

i SAMUEL EASTMAN, b. 19 Jan 1777; d. 25 Jun 1802.

ii LYDIA EASTMAN, b. 4 Sep 1779; d. at Bartlett, NH, 21 Apr 1872; m. 26 May 1801, FRYE HOLT, b. 15 Sep 1779 son of Nathan and Sarah (Chamberlain) Holt; Frye d. at North Conway, 8 Apr 1850.

iii ABIATHAR EASTMAN, b. 17 Apr 1784; d. at Plattsburgh, Dec 1813 during the War of 1812; m. at Conway, 1802, SUSAN DURGIN, b. at Conway, 17 Apr 1784 daughter of Benjamin and Sarah (Runnels) Durgin; Susan d. at Sweden, ME, 19 Apr 1853.

iv HENRY EASTMAN, b. 29 Jul 1786; d. at North Conway, 3 Jul 1838; m. 1815, ESTHER EASTMAN, b. 14 Aug 1788 daughter of Noah and Hannah (Holt) Eastman.

[1611] New Hampshire, County Probate Records, 1660-1973, Strafford, Henry Merrill, 30:252, 39:412, accessed through familysearch.org
[1612] Canada, Registers of Prisoners of War, 1803-1815, accessed through ancestry.com
[1613] National Archives, Registers of Enlistments in the United States Army, 1798-1914, accessed through fold3
[1614] Wilson, *John Gibson of Cambridge and His Descendants*, p 58
[1615] Cross, *History of Northfield*, p 244
[1616] Rix, *History and Genealogy of the Eastman Family*, p 174
[1617] Rix, *History and Genealogy of the Eastman Family*, p 174

v THOMAS EASTMAN, b. 18 Jul 1788; d. at North Conway, 7 Aug 1846; m. 18 Apr 1816, EUNICE HILL, b. at Conway, 19 Apr 1797 daughter of Leavitt and Sarah (Russell) Hill; Eunice d. at North Conway, 24 Jan 1862.

vi CALEB EASTMAN, b. 12 Aug 1790; d. 1 Jul 1791.

vii CALEB EASTMAN, b. 12 Mar 1793; d. at York, ME, 12 May 1872; m. at York, 8 May 1833, ADALINE TAPLY, b. 28 Feb 1810;[1618] Adaline d. at Portland, ME, 15 Mar 1888.

580) SIMEON EASTMAN *(Rebecca Abbott Eastman⁴, James³, William², George¹)*, b. at Hopkinton, NH, 23 Oct 1755 son of Enoch and Rebecca (Abbott) Eastman; m. about 1780, MEHITABLE PIPER.

Simeon Eastman and Mehitable Piper were parents of eight children born at Hopkinton.

i SIMEON EASTMAN, b. 3 May 1781; d. at Sunapee, NH, after 1850; m. at Newport, NH, 4 Nov 1822, MARTHA "PATTY" S. HALL, b. at Newport, 7 Apr 1782 daughter of Levi and Patty (Silver) Hall; Patty d. at Sunapee, 27 Mar 1884.

ii ENOCH EASTMAN, b. 17 Dec 1782; d. at Holley, NY, 4 Oct 1853; m. 1st, about 1805, SUSAN EASTMAN, b. in Hopkinton, 1787; Susan d. at Clarendon, NY, 30 Mar 1838. Enoch m. 2nd, about 1839, SUSAN CURTIS, b. 20 Jan 1810; Susan d. at Holley, 28 Mar 1886.

iii JOSIAH EASTMAN, b. 8 Mar 1787; d. at Lowell, MA, 5 Mar 1871; m. at Lowell, 8 May 1828, SUSAN KIMBALL, b. at Hopkinton, about 1787 daughter of John and Susan (Eastman) Kimball;[1619] Susan d. at Lowell, 26 Aug 1869.

iv STEPHEN EASTMAN, b. 30 Jan 1788; d. at Ripley, NY, after 1860; m. NANCY, b. in NY, about 1802; Nancy d. at Ripley, 1890 (probate 1890). It is possible Stephen had a first marriage as he had an older child that seems not to be the child of Nancy but that is not clear.

v TIMOTHY EASTMAN, b. 29 Jan 1790; d. at Roby, NH, 20 Dec 1879; m. 26 Mar 1820, POLLY SIBLEY, b. at Hopkinton, 30 Jul 1794 daughter of Jacob and Anna (George) Sibley;[1620] Polly d. at Warner, 30 May 1887.

vi ANNA EASTMAN, b. 3 Jun 1793; nothing further known.

vii AMOS EASTMAN, b. 3 Jun 1793; d. at Hopkinton, 18 Sep 1836; m. 31 Mar 1829, MARY P. HILLIARD, b. about 1803 likely the daughter of Daniel and Polly (Eaton) Hilliard; Mary d. at Concord, NH, 30 Nov 1878.

viii DARIUS EASTMAN, b. about 1795; this is child in the Eastman genealogy for whom no records were located.

581) ABIGAIL EASTMAN *(Rebecca Abbott Eastman⁴, James³, William², George¹)*, b. at Hopkinton, 25 Feb 1759 daughter of Enoch and Rebecca (Abbott) Eastman; d. at Hopkinton, 19 Dec 1836; m. 14 Sep 1780, MOSES COLBY, b. at Newton, NH, 7 Jun 1751 son of Moses and Mary (Sargent) Colby; Moses d. at Hopkinton, 16 Mar 1790.

Moses Colby served several enlistments during the Revolution with periods of service between 1776 and 1783. An application for the widow's pension seems to have been completed after Abigail's death with an award for arrears of $463.33 made in 1842 for the period from 4 March 1831 through her death 19 December 1836.[1621]

On 3 February 1840, Nancy Eastman, who was 59 years old and a resident of Warner, provided an affidavit for ongoing issues related to the pension even after her mother's death. Samuel Eastman (Abigail's brother), age 80 of Hopkinton, also made a statement 10 February 1841. Samuel's statement lists the names of the five children of Moses and Abigail: Anna Colby the widow of David Eastman, Enoch Colby, Hezekiah Colby, Rebekah Putney Colby the widow of David Jones, and Abby Colby. At the time of Samuel's statement, only three children were living: Anna, Hezekiah who was in Tunbridge, Vermont, and Rebecca. He also notes that Abigail was born about one month after the decease of her father. Another statement by Simeon Tyler notes that daughter Abigail died "many years hence when young."

Moses Colby and Anna Eastman were parents of five children born at Hopkinton.

i ANNA "NANCY" COLBY, b. 13 Jul 1781; d. at Hopkinton, 6 Jul 1856; m. DAVID EASTMAN, b. about 1775 (age 52 at time of death); David d. at Hopkinton, 4 Apr 1827.

ii ENOCH EASTMAN COLBY, b. 30 Mar 1784; d. at Sandusky, OH, 1828; m. about 1813, MARY HURLBURT, b. at Suffield, CT, 4 Oct 1792 daughter of John and Phebe (Harmon) Hurlburt; Mary d. 1851.

[1618] Adaline's date of birth is engraved on her gravestone; findagrave ID: 98508457

[1619] Morrison and Sharples, *History of the Kimball Family in America*, volume I, p 318

[1620] The names of Polly's parents are given on her death record.

[1621] Revolutionary War Pension and Bounty-Land Warrant Application Files

iii HEZEKIAH COLBY, b. 23 May 1786; d. at Tunbridge, VT, 1 Nov 1865; m. at Tunbridge, 19 Jan 1812, LUCY TRACY, b. at Tunbridge, 2 Sep 1787 daughter of Elijah and Jerusha (Starkweather) Tracy; Lucy d. 13 Aug 1859.

iv REBECCA PUTNEY COLBY, b. 21 Apr 1788; d. at Warner, 1844; m. 23 Nov 1809, DAVID JONES, b. at Warner, 20 Aug 1784 son of Jonathan and Judith (Jones) Jones; David d. at Warner, 30 Nov 1828.

v ABIGAIL "NABBY" COLBY, b. 16 Apr 1790. Abigail died "when young" and does not seem to have married.

582) SAMUEL EASTMAN *(Rebecca Abbott Eastman⁴, James³, William², George¹)*, b. at Hopkinton, 13 Nov 1760 son of Enoch and Rebecca (Abbott) Eastman; d. at Hopkinton, NH, 14 Feb 1841;[1622][1623] m. SARAH HARRIS, b. about 1765; Sarah d. before 1841.

Samuel Eastman enlisted in July 1780 from Hopkinton as a private in the regiment of Colonel Bartlett.[1624]

Samuel Eastman did not leave a will and his estate entered probate April 1841 with Jonathan G. Eastman as administrator. The inventory gave his estate as $9.97 in cash with nothing else noted.[1625]

Samuel Eastman and Susan Harris were parents of ten children born at Hopkinton.[1626]

i ANNA EASTMAN, b. 30 May 1785; nothing further known.

ii REBECCA EASTMAN, b. 4 Apr 1787; nothing further known.

iii JOSEPH EASTMAN, b. 28 Apr 1789; d. at Columbia, NH, 10 Aug 1875; m. at Hopkinton, Oct 1815, SARAH "SALLY" DUSTIN, b. at Tunbridge, VT, about 1793 daughter of Asa and Sarah (Martin) Dustin.

iv JAMES EASTMAN, b. 30 Jul 1791; nothing further known.

v ANNA EASTMAN, b. 13 Aug 1793; d. at Columbia, NH, before 1860; m. about 1825, as his third wife, ASA DUSTIN, b. about 1792 son of Asa and Sarah (Martin) Dustin; Asa d. at Columbia, 1 Nov 1866. Asa was first married to Anna Putney and second married to Mary Kelso.

vi ABIGAIL "NABBY" EASTMAN, b. 15 May 1796; d. at Columbia, NH, before 1850; m. at Hopkinton, 25 Dec 1817, JOEL RAY, b. at Henniker, 9 Mar 1794 son of Jonathan and Betty (Barnes) Ray;[1627] Joel d. at Columbia, 26 Mar 1870. Joel married second Betsey.

vii SAMUEL EASTMAN, b. 3 Jul 1798; d. at Columbia, NH, Feb 1840; m. 1st, 1 Feb 1824, JEMIMA "JENNIE" FLANDERS, b. 1802; Jennie d. at Columbia, 1831. Samuel m. 2nd, HANNAH.[1628]

viii JONATHAN G. EASTMAN, b. 20 Sep 1800; d. at Hopkinton, 28 Jul 1874; m. 1st, 1831, MARY SLEEPER, b. 1806 daughter of Moses and Mehitable (Peterson) Sleeper; Mary d. at Hopkinton, 7 Sep 1835. Jonathan m. 2nd, 8 May 1836, CHARLOTTE KIMBALL, b. at Hopkinton, 15 Nov 1799 daughter of John and Lydia (Clough) Kimball; Charlotte d. at Hopkinton, 28 Feb 1885.

ix SARAH EASTMAN, b. 14 Mar 1803; d. at Columbia, NH. Sarah did not marry.

x MARY EASTMAN, b. 16 Jul 1805; d. at Warner, NH, 21 Apr 1880; m. at Hopkinton, 14 Mar 1844, JAMES STEVENS COUCH, b. at Boscawen, 7 May 1811 son of Benjamin and Sally (Morse) Couch;[1629] James d. 21 Jun 1877.

583) REBEKAH EASTMAN *(Rebecca Abbott Eastman⁴, James³, William², George¹)*, b. at Hopkinton, 10 Apr 1762 daughter of Enoch and Rebecca (Abbott) Eastman; m. JAMES PUTNEY, b. at Hopkinton, 8 Feb 1761 son of John and Mary (-) Putney.

Rebekah Eastman and James Putney were parents of three children born at Tunbridge.

1622 Ancestry.com, New Hampshire, Compiled Census and Census Substitutes Index, 1790-1890. Samuel Eastman, age 79, is recorded living at Hopkinton in 1840.
1623 Date of death is given on his Revolutionary War pension records.
1624 Revolutionary War Pension and Bounty-Land Warrant Application Files
1625 New Hampshire Probate Records, Merrimack County, NH, 14:131, 12:458, case number 1873
1626 *New Hampshire, Births and Christenings Index, 1714-1904.*
1627 Cogswell, *History of Henniker*, p 704
1628 Rix, *History and Genealogy of the Eastman Family*, p 289
1629 Coffin, *History of Boscawen*, p 512

i ANNA PUTNEY, b. 18 May 1790; d. about 1813; m. at Tunbridge, 14 Nov 1813, ASA DUSTIN, b. about 1792 son of Asa and Sarah (Martin) Dustin; Asa d. at Columbia, NH, 1 Nov 1866. Asa m. 2nd, Mary Kelso 31 Dec 1820. Asa m. 3rd, about 1825, ANNA EASTMAN, b. at Hopkinton, 13 Aug 1793 daughter of Samuel and Sarah (Harris) Eastman. Anna Eastman is a child in Family 582.

ii JONATHAN PUTNEY, b. 22 Feb 1792; d. after 1820. Jonathan Putney of Tunbridge enlisted for five years in the Army in June 1818. He was at Sackett's Harbor from October 1818 to April 1820. From August to October 1820 he was listed as absent "on command at Plattsburgh." He was listed as deserted 25 November 1820.[1630]

iii BAILEY PUTNEY, b. about 1794; d. at Randolph, VT, 3 Feb 1875; m. 30 Jan 1825, HANNAH COLLINS, b. in VT, about 1805; Hannah d. at Randolph, 8 Jun 1888.

584) LUCY EASTMAN *(Rebecca Abbott Eastman⁴, James³, William², George¹)*, b. at Hopkinton, 1 Dec 1763 daughter of Enoch and Rebecca (Abbott) Eastman; d. 5 Jan 1816 at Tunbridge, VT; m. at Dunbarton, 16 Jan 1794, BENJAMIN ORDWAY, b. 1763 (based on age at time of death) perhaps the son of Moses and Susannah (Bly) Ordway; Benjamin d. 1 Dec 1849. After Lucy's death, Benjamin married Betsey Gilman.

Benjamin Ordway was a farmer in Tunbridge. He did not leave a will and Elijah Dickerman served as administrator. The estate was insolvent. Heirs signing that they think it was in the best interest of the estate for it to be sold were the following: B. F. Ordway, Shadrach Ordway, Lewis Dickerman and Diantha O. Dickerman, and Mary Ordway guardian for Elijah Ordway.[1631] Diantha Ordway wife of Lewis Dickerman was a granddaughter, the daughter of son Benjamin and his wife Mary Dickerman.

Lucy Eastman and Benjamin Ordway were parents of eight children born at Tunbridge.

i TEMPY ORDWAY, b. 1795;[1632] d. at Tunbridge, 31 Jan 1816.

ii LUCY ORDWAY, b. 1 Sep 1796; d. at Tunbridge, 5 Jan 1816.

iii MOSES ORDWAY, b. 1 Feb 1798; d. at Tunbridge, 22 Jan 1863; m. HARRIET WHITNEY, b. at Tunbridge, 6 Aug 1797 daughter of Abel and Phebe (Scott) Whitney; Harriet d. at Chelsea, VT, 15 Jun 1872.

iv FINITY ORDWAY, b. 5 Jul 1799; d. at Tunbridge, 8 Apr 1872; m. WILLIAM P. COLBY, b. at Tunbridge, 1798 son of John and Hannah (Perham) Colby; William d. at Tunbridge, 17 Mar 1868.

v BENJAMIN ORDWAY, b. 23 Dec 1801; d. at Tunbridge, 9 Jul 1840; m. MARY DICKERMAN, b. 29 Mar 1807 daughter of Elijah and Emma (Whitney) Dickerman; Mary d. at Tunbridge, 2 Feb 1881.

vi SHADRACH ORDWAY, b. 26 Apr 1803; d. at Coventry, VT, 2 Feb 1873; m. at Tunbridge, 6 Dec 1832, ANNA F. GOODWIN, b. about 1814; Anna d. at Barton, VT, after 1880.

vii DORCAS ORDWAY, b. 1804; d. at Tunbridge, 20 Apr 1824.

viii ABIGAIL ORDWAY, b. 6 Apr 1805; d. at Tunbridge, 2 Apr 1872; m. 12 Sep 1827, BEZELIEL BALLOU, b. at Lincoln, RI, 1792 son of William and Mary (Bucklin) Ballou; Bezeliel d. at Tunbridge, 15 Feb 1840.

585) EZRA EASTMAN *(Rebecca Abbott Eastman⁴, James³, William², George¹)*, b. at Hopkinton, 15 Aug 1764 son of Enoch and Rebecca (Abbott) Eastman; d. 14 Jun 1816; m. 28 Jun 1787, MOLLY EATON, b. 10 Aug 1769 daughter of Thomas and Molly (-) Eaton; Molly d. 11 Jan 1825.

Ezra Eastman and Molly Eaton were parents of eleven children all born at Hopkinton.

i SALLY EASTMAN, b. 23 Jan 1788; d. at Webster, MA, 6 Apr 1867; m. at Boscawen 21 Dec 1820, as his third wife, STEPHEN PUTNEY, b. at Hopkinton, 12 Feb 1764 son of Joseph and Mary (Eastman) Putney; Stephen d. at Boscawen, 18 Feb 1847. Stephen was first married to another Sally Eastman and second married to Susan Eastman.

ii MOSES EASTMAN, b. 5 Mar 1790; d. 3 Mar 1817; m. 1814, SARAH CURRIER, b. at Hopkinton, 26 Dec 1788; Sarah d. 21 Aug 1864. Sarah married first Samuel Putney and third married HERMAN ABBOTT (1795-1828) *(Ezra⁵, Reuben⁴, James³, William², George¹)* son of Ezra and Mary (Walker) Abbott.

[1630] *U.S. Army, Register of Enlistments, 1798-1914* [database on-line]. Provo, UT, USA: Ancestry.com Operations Inc, 2007.

[1631] *Vermont. Probate Court (Randolph District)*; Probate Place: *Orange, Vermont, Folder 59, Mann, Seth-Perkins, Daniel, 1835-1849*

[1632] Age at death given on gravestone is 21 years.

iii MOLLY EASTMAN, b. 4 Apr 1792; d. at Andover, NH, 18 Nov 1841; m. at Hopkinton, 26 Nov 1821, JOSEPH CALEF THOMPSON, b. at Andover, NH, 21 Dec 1794 son of Benjamin and Miriam (Brown) Thompson; Joseph d. at Andover, 12 Mar 1861. After Molly's death, Joseph married Lucinda Gould.

iv LUCY EASTMAN, b. 9 Mar 1794; d. 8 Jun 1815.

v IRA EASTMAN, b. 30 Mar 1796; d. 3 May 1825; m. about 1822, RHODA MORRILL

vi EZRA EASTMAN, b. 11 Apr 1798; d. at Hopkinton, 19 Apr 1884; m. 30 Sep 1828, CYNTHIA W. CONNER, b. at Henniker, 30 Sep 1805 daughter of John and Mary (Whitney) Conner; Cynthia d. at Henniker, 23 Oct 1901. Ezra was a schoolteacher and farmer.

vii CLARISSA EASTMAN, b. 17 Sep 1800; d. 22 Nov 1815.

viii Child b. and d. 30 May 1802

ix THOMAS EATON EASTMAN, b. 8 May 1803; d. at Boscawen, 9 Oct 1829; m. at St. Lawrence County, NY, 1826, OLIVE WHITNEY, b. about 1805

x ADELINE SOPHRONIA EASTMAN, b. 21 Oct 1808; d. at Hopkinton, 24 Nov 1881; m. 1st, 16 Jan 1837, JAMES DAVIS, b. at Warner, 1809 son of Aquila and Abigail (Stevens) Davis; James d. at Warner, 1 Dec 1842. Adeline m. 2nd, at Manchester, NH, 7 Mar 1854, JOHN BURNHAM, b. at Hopkinton, 30 Oct 1796 son of Thomas and Ruth (Cavis) Burnham; John d. at Hopkinton, 10 Apr 1867. John was first married to Betsey Whittier.

xi FLORA GODFREY EASTMAN, b. 18 Jul 1811; d. at Hopkinton, 26 Mar 1893; m. at Hopkinton, 25 Jan 1844, SETH LOW, b. at Dunbarton, 20 Dec 1809 son of Joseph and Apphia (Perley) Low; Seth d. at Salisbury, 18 Nov 1897.

586) TAMISON EASTMAN *(Rebecca Abbott Eastman⁴, James³, William², George¹)*, b. at Hopkinton, 19 Oct 1766 daughter of Enoch and Rebecca (Abbott) Eastman; d. after 1850; m. SAMUEL FRENCH, b. at South Hampton, 3 Apr 1762 son of Offen and Abigail (French) French;[1633] d. at Bradford, 7 Feb 1799.[1634]

Tamison Eastman and Samuel French married at Hopkinton but settled in Bradford, New Hampshire. Samuel and his brother Offen owned property there, and both served in the Revolutionary War. Samuel and Offen shared a tragic end in that both committed suicide by hanging, Samuel in 1799 and Offen in 1827.

Samuel French was a young man of 19 when he enlisted at Hopkinton 5 April 1781 to serve as a private in the Revolutionary War. He served for 17 months as a private in a company commanded by Captain Quinby in the regiment of Colonel Wingate. In the summer of 1782, Samuel was taken captive by the Indians along the Mohawk River and held captive for four years. He made his way home in 1786 and wondered how he might get his four years of back pay which was approved.[1635] Samuel and his brother Offen purchased property together in Hopkinton in 1787.

Samuel French and Tamison Eastman married in November 1790 and had three children. Their son Samuel died at three years old 6 February 1797. Almost exactly two years to the day, Samuel committed suicide by hanging on 7 February 1799. An inquest into his death concluded he had been delirious at the time of his suicide.[1636] His older brother Offen also committed suicide by hanging himself from an apple tree on his property on 5 May 1827.

Widow Tamison French filed her application for widow's pension in 1838. The application process took a considerable length of time as there are documents and affidavits of various types dated from 1838 through 1840. One of the affidavits is from Samuel Eastman attesting to the marriage of his sister Tamison to Samuel French in 1790. In one statement, Tamison states she had been delayed in making application for her pension as she did not know if she could obtain the necessary evidence. Her pension when it was finally granted was $56.66 per year. She was awarded a back payment of $283.33. On 28 November 1845, daughter Elizabeth French Eastman filed a bounty land warrant application as the heir of her father. In that statement she described herself as the only heir of the deceased soldier Samuel French.

i ENOCH FRENCH, b. 25 Feb 1792; d. 7 Dec 1815.

ii SAMUEL FRENCH, b. 30 Aug 1793; d. 6 Feb 1797.

1633 South Hampton Congregational Church, 1743-1801, marriages and baptisms, p 22

1634 Gould & Beals, *Early Families of Bradford*, p 168

1635 Revolutionary War Pension and Bounty-Land Warrant Application Files, file of Samuel French

1636 Gould & Beals, *Early Families of Bradford*, p 168

iii ELIZABETH FRENCH, b. 5 Apr 1795; d. at Spring Creek, Pennsylvania, 6 Jan 1875; m. 24 Apr 1814, JOHN EASTMAN, b. at Concord, 22 Nov 1790 son of William and Phebe (Elliot) Eastman; John d. at Spring Creek, 17 May 1865.

587) JOSEPH EASTMAN *(Rebecca Abbott Eastman⁴, James³, William², George¹)*, b. at Hopkinton, 18 Sep 1768 son of Enoch and Rebecca (Abbott) Eastman; d. at Contoocook, NH, 16 Feb 1823; m. 26 Oct 1790, BETSEY CLOUGH, b. 30 Jun 1770 daughter of James and Ruth (Webster) Clough; Betsey d. at Contoocook, NH, 1 Sep 1861.

In his will written 9 December 1821, Joseph Eastman bequeaths to beloved wife Betsy the use and improvement of all the real estate in Hopkinton except what he had on that day deeded to his son Joseph. The property set aside for Betsy's use was about 30 acres. To daughter Ruth Barnet, he bequeaths one dollar and the same amount to daughter Phebe Eastman. Son Joseph Eastman also receives one dollar. Sons Darius Eastman, Stephen C. Eastman, and Moses C. Eastman each receive fifty-three dollars. Daughters Hannah Eastman and Sally Eastman each receive twenty-five dollars. Son Darius is named executor.[1637]

Joseph Eastman and Betsey Clough were parents of eleven children born at Hopkinton.

i RUTH EASTMAN, b. 3 Sep 1791; d. at Warner, NH, 14 Apr 1822; m. about 1815, THOMAS BARNARD, b. 1781 son of Charles and Sarah (Foster) Barnard; Thomas d. at Orange, NH, 29 Jan 1859. Thomas second married, Ruth's sister PHEBE EASTMAN (see below).

ii BETTY EASTMAN, b. 28 Jul 1793; d. 25 Jun 1820.

iii PHEBE EASTMAN, b. 22 Sep 1795; d. at Orange, NH, 30 Jun 1845; m. 22 Sep 1822, THOMAS BARNARD who was first married to Phebe's sister Ruth (see above).

iv JOSEPH EASTMAN, b. 25 Oct 1797; d. at Spring Creek, PA, 1871; m. 1st, 1824, HANNAH CHASE, b. 15 Aug 1806 daughter of Enoch and Polly (Moss) Chase; Hannah d. at Orange, NH, Mar 1860. Joseph m. 2nd, at Orange, 17 Jan 1864, LOUISA ANNA BOWEN (widow Louisa Stevens), b. at Moriah, NY, about 1825; Louisa d. at Spring Creek, 2 Jun 1902. Louisa was married twice before her marriage to Joseph, and after his death she married George Noosbickle.

v DARIUS EASTMAN, b. 2 Sep 1799; d. 12 Sep 1822.

vi STEPHEN EASTMAN, b. 23 Aug 1801; d. 11 Feb 1803.

vii STEPHEN CLOUGH EASTMAN, b. 21 Apr 1803; d. at Hooksett, 13 Dec 1883; m. 6 Sep 1824, RUHAMAH ROGERS, b. about 1804 daughter of Obadiah Rogers; Ruhamah d. at Hooksett, 16 Aug 1892.

viii MOSES COLBY EASTMAN, b. 14 Jul 1805; d. 31 May 1825.

ix ENOCH EASTMAN, b. 5 Jun 1808; d. 13 Jan 1816.

x HANNAH PARSONS EASTMAN, b. 18 Jul 1812; d. 23 Dec 1822.

xi SALLY EASTMAN, b. 21 Apr 1815; d. at Hopkinton, 27 Jan 1847; m. 1832, WILLIAM DOLE EASTMAN, b. at Henniker, 24 Aug 1810 son of Jonathan and Mehitable (Dole) Eastman; William d. at Warner, 4 Jun 1894. After Sally's death, William married Mary Flanders 6 Apr 1848 and Almira Drowne 7 Jan 1886.

588) SARAH EASTMAN *(Rebecca Abbott Eastman⁴, James³, William², George¹)*, b. at Hopkinton, NH, 27 Aug 1771 daughter of Enoch and Rebecca (Abbott) Eastman; m. 5 Oct 1790, THOMAS EATON, b. 21 Jul 1771 son of Thomas and Molly (-) Eaton.

Sarah and Thomas were parents of nine children. Marriages were located for just two of the children.

i MOLLY EATON, b. at Concord, 14 Apr 1791

ii MOSES COLBY EATON, b. at Warner, 29 Dec 1792

iii STEPHEN GOULD EATON, b. at Warner, 1 Jul 1795; d. at Hanover, NY, 15 Mar 1868; m. about 1828, ABIGAIL DUTCHER, b. in NY, about 1808 daughter of John Wheaton and Eleanor (Wheeler) Dutcher; Abigail d. after 1868.

iv ENOCH EATON, b. at Warner, 4 Mar 1797

v REBECCA EATON, b. at Warner, 21 Mar 1799

[1637] *New Hampshire. Probate Court (Hillsborough County)*; Probate Place: *Hillsborough, New Hampshire, Probate Records, Vol 31-33, 1820-1830*, will of Joseph Eastman

vi SARAH EATON, b. at Warner, 27 Feb 1801

vii THOMAS EATON, b. at Warner, 17 Feb 1803

viii TRUE EATON, b. at Hopkinton, 16 Feb 1805; d. at Bradford, NH, 6 Oct 1871; m. at Bradford, 7 Jan 1838, BETSEY MARSHALL, b. at Bradford, about 1803 daughter of Joseph and Lucy (Webster) Marshall; Betsey d. at Bradford, 15 Dec 1873.

ix WALTER EATON, b. at Concord, 16 Mar 1807

589) JOB ABBOTT *(Sarah Abbott Abbott Eastman⁴, James³, William², George¹)*, b. about 1755 at Pembroke son of Job and Sarah (Abbott) Abbott; d. at Wilton 12 Jul 1805; m. at Andover, 12 Dec 1780, his third cousin once removed, ANNA BALLARD *(Timothy Ballard⁵, Hannah Chandler Ballard⁴, John Chandler³, Hannah Abbott Chandler², George¹)*, b. 15 Nov 1762 daughter of Timothy and Sarah (Abbott) Ballard; Anna d. at Wilton, 7 Apr 1805.[1638] Anna Ballard is a child in Family 430.

Job Abbott and Anna Ballard were parents of thirteen children born at Wilton. Both parents died in 1805 and the children seem to have gone to Andover after that. Three of the children married their first cousins, children of Nathan and Sarah (Ballard) Abbott (Family 443).

i SAMUEL ABBOTT, b. 14 May 1781; d. Apr 1782.

ii SAMUEL ABBOTT, b. 15 Jul 1783; d. at Dexter, ME, 22 Apr 1862; m. about 1808, SARAH PALMER, b. 14 Jul 1783; Sarah d. at Dexter, 29 Jul 1868.[1639]

iii ANNA ABBOTT, b. 28 Jul 1785; d. at Andover, MA, 9 May 1828. Anna did not marry.

iv JAMES ABBOTT, b. 14 Mar 1787; d. at Andover, 6 May 1807.

v SARAH ABBOTT, b. 7 Apr 1789; d. at Andover, 1 Dec 1821; m. at Andover, 29 Sep 1811, her first cousin, ABEL ABBOTT *(Nathan⁵, Job⁴, Jonathan³, Benjamin², George¹)*, b. at Andover, 7 Sep 1786 son of Nathan and Sarah (Ballard) Abbott; Abel d. at Andover, 3 Jul 1862. Abel m. 2nd, 28 Dec 1822, MARY JONES, b. at Andover, 29 Jul 1786 daughter of Ebenezer and Elizabeth (Abbott) Jones; Mary d. at Andover, 9 Dec 1869.

vi MARY FOSTER ABBOTT, b. 18 Apr 1791; d. at Andover, 28 Oct 1828; m. 10 Oct 1810, her first cousin, PASCHAL ABBOTT *(Nathan⁵, Job⁴, Jonathan³, Benjamin², George¹)*, b. at Andover, 23 Jul 1788 son of Nathan and Sarah (Ballard) Abbott; Paschal d. at Dexter, ME, 30 May 1859. Paschal m. 2nd, at Greenfield, 22 Jun 1829, HANNAH FOSTER, b. at Greenfield, 18 Jun 1796 daughter of Isaac and Mary (Holt) Foster; Hannah d. at Tilton, NH, 17 Oct 1885.

vii WILLIAM BALLARD ABBOTT, b. 9 Jul 1793; d. at Andover, 19 May 1840; m. 9 Dec 1816, LUCINDA FLINT, b. at Andover, 30 Oct 1796 daughter of John and Ruth (Upton) Flint; Lucinda d. at Andover, 25 Aug 1861.

viii JOB ABBOTT, b. 15 Aug 1795; d. at Andover, 15 Oct 1819.

ix TIMOTHY BALLARD ABBOTT, b. 14 Aug 1797; d. at Andover, 22 Nov 1820; m. at Wilton, 6 Apr 1819, ABIGAIL WILSON, b. at Wilton, 8 Jan 1799 daughter of Abiel and Abigail (Phillips) Wilson; Abigail d. at Wilton, 4 Jan 1831.

x ABIGAIL ABBOTT, b. 5 Jan 1799; d. at Andover, 15 Jul 1822.

xi LYDIA ABBOTT, b. 18 Aug 1800; d. at Dexter, ME, 11 May 1826; m. at Andover, 13 Oct 1820, her first cousin, JOSHUA ABBOTT *(Nathan⁵, Job⁴, Jonathan³, Benjamin², George¹)*, b. at Andover, 22 Apr 1797 son of Nathan and Sarah (Ballard) Abbott; Joshua d. at Topeka, KS, 5 Jun 1855. Joshua m. 2nd, at Dexter, Joshua m. 2nd, 12 Oct 1826, Mary Wood Baker.

xii FANNY ABBOTT, b. 7 Jan 1802; d. at Bradford, MA, 26 Nov 1887; m. at Andover, 13 Apr 1822, BENJAMIN ROBERT DOWNES, b. at Newburyport, 15 Sep 1798 son of Robert and Sarah Coffin (Knapp) Downes; Benjamin d. at Bradford, 6 Jul 1871.

xiii Son b. and d. 1804.

[1638] Date of death obtained from her gravestone which has the following inscription: Erected to the memory of Mrs. Anne Abbott, consort of Mr. Job Abbott, who died April 7, 1805, in the 43 year of her age. Findagrave Memorial ID: 34218725

[1639] Age at time of death given as 85 years, 15 days. Maine, Nathan Hale Cemetery Collection.

590) ABIGAIL ABBOTT *(Sarah Abbott Abbott Eastman^4, James^3, William^2, George^1)*, b. at Pembroke, about 1757 daughter of Job and Sarah (Abbott) Abbott; d. 1 May 1845 at Lovell, ME;[1640] m. by 1778, STEPHEN DRESSER, b. at Andover, 25 Oct 1754 son of Jonathan and Sarah (Foster) Dresser; Stephen d. at Frye, ME, 28 Sep 1829.

Stephen served in the Revolution enlisting from Fryeburg in Bedel's Regiment.[1641] Abigail Abbott and Stephen Dresser were parents of eleven children born at Lovell, Maine.[1642]

i BETSY DRESSER, b. 14 Oct 1778; d. at Stow, ME, 2 Nov 1825; m. about 1797, SAMUEL FARRINGTON, b. 22 Jun 1776 son of John and Mary (Stevens) Farrington; Samuel d. at Stow, 14 Mar 1838.

ii STEPHEN DRESSER, b. 8 Apr 1781; d. at Stow, 19 Aug 1858; m. 1st, about 1801, ABIGAIL KILGORE, b. at Lovell, about 1785 daughter of James and Abigail (-) Kilgore; Abigail d. at Lovell, 1817. Stephen m. 2nd, at Fryeburg, 19 Apr 1817, his fourth cousin, MEHITABLE ABBOTT *(Micah^5, Isaac^4, Ebenezer^3, John^2, George^1)*, b. at Fryeburg, 1797 daughter of Micah and Alice (Wiley) Abbott; Mehitable d. at Stow, 9 Apr 1884. Mehitable is a child in Family 417.

iii SARAH DRESSER, b. 1 Feb 1783; d. 9 Mar 1783.

iv ABIGAIL DRESSER, b. 1785; d. at Lovell, 1819; m. about 1805, JONATHAN FARRINGTON, b. 1780 son of John and Mary (Stevens) Farrington; Jonathan d. at Lovell, 19 Jun 1818.

v JOB ABBOTT DRESSER, b. 5 Mar 1787; d. at Lovell, 24 Apr 1882; m. at Lovell, 1 Oct 1810, HANNAH HALL, b. 18 Mar 1785; Hannah d. at Lovell, 29 May 1864.

vi MARY "POLLY" DRESSER, b. 8 May 1790; d. at Chatham, NH, 26 Aug 1879; m. at Lovell, 10 Sep 1807, JOSEPH GORDON, b. 1781; Joseph d. at Chatham, 7 Nov 1871.

vii SARAH DRESSER, b. 6 Aug 1792; d. at Lovell, May 1874; m. 19 Feb 1810, JOSEPH KIMBALL, b. at Fryeburg, 20 Aug 1788 son of William and Lucy (Abbott) Kimball; Joseph d. at Lovell, 2 Mar 1859.

viii JONATHAN FOSTER DRESSER, b. 19 Jul 1794; d. at Chatham, before 1850; m. 20 Oct 1817, BETSY WILEY, b. about 1798.

ix SUSANNA DRESSER, b. 10 Jul 1796; m. at Lovell, 22 Nov 1814, her first cousin, JAMES EASTMAN *(Daniel Eastman^5, Sarah Abbott Eastman^4, James^3, William^2, George^1)*, b. at Lovell, 25 Dec 1788 son of Daniel and Sarah (Whiting) Eastman; James d. at Lovell, 21 Feb 1870. James Eastman is a child in Family 591.

x EMILIAH HOLT DRESSER, b. 30 Jul 1799; d. at Lovell, 7 Apr 1835; m. 1817, MOSES HUTCHINS, b. at Fryeburg, 10 Dec 1791 son of Moses and Rose (Whittier) Hutchins; Moses d. at Lovell, 24 May 1872.

xi CHLOE DRESSER, b. 18 Apr 1801; d. at Lovell, 2 Oct 1835. Chloe did not marry.

591) DANIEL EASTMAN *(Sarah Abbott Abbott Eastman^4, James^3, William^2, George^1)*, b. at Pembroke, 21 Apr 1766 son of Richard and Sarah (Abbott) Eastman; d. at Lovell, ME, 16 Jan 1844; m. at Dracut, 1 Mar 1787, SARAH WHITING, b. about 1762 (based on age of 44 at time of death) of parents not yet determined; Sarah d. at Lovell, 19 Jan 1806.

Daniel Eastman and Sarah Whiting were parents of nine children, the birth of the oldest child recorded at Dracut and the remainder at Lovell, Maine.

i PHINEAS EASTMAN, b. 5 Apr 1787; d. at Lovell, 20 Feb 1847; m. at Lovell, 23 Nov 1813, DOROTHY F. CHARLES *(Olive Abbott Charles^5, Isaac^4, Ebenezer^3, John^2, George^1)*, b. at Fryeburg, 23 Dec 1789 daughter of John and Olive (Abbott) Charles; Dorothy d. at Lovell, 6 Jul 1873. Dorothy is a child in Family 412.

ii JAMES EASTMAN, b. 25 Dec 1788; d. at Lovell, 21 Feb 1870; m. 22 Nov 1814, his first cousin, SUSANNA DRESSER *(Abigail Abbott Dresser^5, Sarah Abbott Abbott Eastman^4, James^3, William^2, George^1)*, b. at Lovell, 10 Jul 1796 daughter of Stephen and Abigail (Abbott) Dresser. Susanna is a child in Family 590.

iii SALLY EASTMAN, b. 6 Mar 1791; d. at Fryeburg, 14 Jul 1871; m. 10 May 1810, THOMAS FARRINGTON, b. at Fryeburg, 16 Nov 1789 son of Putnam and Sarah (Perham) Farrington; Thomas d. at Stow, ME, 6 Nov 1864.

iv SOLOMON EASTMAN, b. 6 Dec 1792; d. at Stow, ME, 19 May 1866; m. 1st, at Lovell, 4 Dec 1817, PAMELA DRESSER, b. at Lovell, 23 Apr 1800 daughter of Levi and Pamela (-) Dresser; Pamela d. at Stow, 7 Mar 1842.

[1640] Ancestry.com, *U.S., Find A Grave Index, 1600s-Current* (Provo, UT, USA: Ancestry.com Operations, Inc., 2012).

[1641] Compiled Service Records of Soldiers Who Served in the American Army During the Revolutionary War 1775-1785

[1642] Many of the vital records for this family were obtained from Lovell Historical Society Online Collections Database, http://lovell.pastperfectonline.com/byperson?keyword=Dresser%2C+Stephen+Lt.+%281754-1829%29

Solomon m. 2nd, BETSEY who has not been identified; Betsey d. at Stow, 3 Jul 1847. Solomon m. 3rd, at Conway, NH, 29 Oct 1847, ANN S. CHASE, b. 23 Mar 1804 daughter of Joseph F. and Sarah (Eaton) Chase; Ann d. at Stow, 27 Nov 1865.

v CYRUS EASTMAN, b. 3 Dec 1795; d. 1853; m. at Lovell, 7 Jul 1823, ELIZABETH PRAY, b. at Lovell, 19 May 1806 daughter of Charles and Hannah (Hayes) Pray.

vi ASA EASTMAN, b. 7 Feb 1797; d. at Fryeburg, 16 Jul 1819.

vii DANIEL EASTMAN, b. 10 Jan 1799; d. at Lovell, 25 Oct 1877; m. 1st, at Lovell, 6 Sep 1824, LUCY WALKER, b. 1806 *possibly* the daughter of James and Olive (Charles) Walker; Lucy d. about 1835. Daniel m. 2nd, 1 Apr 1838, REBECCA L. SMART, b. about 1815 daughter of Daniel and Rhoda (Davis) Smart; Rebecca d. at Fryeburg, 1885.

viii JONAS EASTMAN, b. 28 Jan 1801; d. before 1850;[1643] m. about 1837, MARY A. YOUNG, b. at Greenwood, ME, 1814 daughter of Joshua Young;[1644] Mary d. at Boston, 21 May 1890. Mary second married George Pierson 15 Jun 1850.

ix ISAAC EASTMAN, b. 2 Mar 1803; d. at Sweden, ME, 16 Jun 1887; m. ESTHER WOODBURY, b. at Sweden, 25 Jun 1810 daughter of Andrew and Sally (Stevens) Woodbury; Esther d. at Sweden, 25 Aug 1880.

592) CYRUS EASTMAN *(Sarah Abbott Abbott Eastman⁴, James³, William², George¹)*, b. at Pembroke, 10 Jul 1767 son of Richard and Sarah (Abbott) Eastman; d. at Lovell, ME, 17 Sep 1839; m. at Fryeburg, 1799, BETSEY WEBSTER. Betsey's origins are unknown, but the births for the two sons of this marriage, according to Rix's Eastman genealogy, are 1821 and 1827, so she would be born not much earlier than 1785-1790. There is a marriage record for Cyrus "Easton" and Betsey Webster in 1799.[1645] There are questions yet to be resolved about this family. It may be that the two sons attributed to this couple are from a Cyrus from the following generation. There are other Cyrus Eastmans in the New Suncook area about 20 years younger than this Cyrus. The 1830 census for Sweden, Maine (where Cyrus was reported to have lived) has Cyrus Eastman as head of household that includes a male age 60-69, a female 40-49, 1 boy under 5, 1 boy under 9, 1 male 20-29, and 1 female 20-29. So perhaps this is Cyrus and his wife Betsey and one of his sons and his little children.[1646]

These are the two sons attributed to this family by Rix's Eastman genealogy.[1647] The birth record for the older son gives his name as Cyrus, Jr. and parents as Cyrus and Betsey and Richard's birth record also lists Cyrus and Betsey.

i CYRUS EASTMAN, b. at Sweden, ME, 6 Dec 1821; d. 14 Jun 1838.

ii RICHARD EASTMAN, b. at Sweden, ME, 4 Feb 1827; d. at Haverhill, MA, 7 Sep 1891; m. HANNAH MOULTON, b. at South Parsonsfield, ME, about 1833 daughter of Charles and Lavina (Knowles) Moulton; Hannah d. at Haverhill, 24 Dec 1904.

593) JEREMY EASTMAN *(Sarah Abbott Abbott Eastman⁴, James³, William², George¹)*, b. at Fryeburg, ME, 25 Apr 1771 son of Richard and Sarah (Abbott) Eastman; d. at Stow, ME, 8 Oct 1846; m. by 1794, BETSEY KILGORE, b. 2 Apr 1776 daughter of Joseph and Abigail (Page) Kilgore; Betsey d. at Stow, 16 Feb 1873.

Jeremy and Betsey were parents of thirteen children, the oldest three born at Fryeburg and the remainder born at Lovell.

i JOSEPH EASTMAN, b. 29 Oct 1794; d. at Andover, ME, 7 Apr 1870; m. MARY KILGORE, b. at Waterford, ME, 1796 daughter of Benjamin and Ruth (Hazeltine) Kilgore; Mary d. at Boston, 1 May 1876.

ii STEPHEN EASTMAN, b. 28 Sep 1796; d. at Conway, NH, 29 Mar 1876; m. at Conway, 25 Dec 1817, HANNAH WALKER, b. about 1795 daughter of Barnett and Hannah (Heath) Walker; Hannah d. at Conway, 7 May 1872.

1643 At the 1850 Census, the children of Jonas and Mary are living with various relatives and there is no record of Jonas in the census.

1644 Information about Mary's father and age is given on the record of her second marriage to George Pierson. The marriage record says father's names is Joshua; her death record says her father's name is Moses.

1645 "Maine Marriages, 1771-1907," database, *FamilySearch* (https://familysearch.org/ark:/61903/1:1:F4FZ-NXX: 4 December 2014), Cyrus Easton and Betsy Webster, 1799; citing Fryeburg, Oxford, Maine, reference; FHL microfilm 10,915.

1646 The Lovell Historical Society reports that Cyrus Eastman (born 1794 son of Daniel) and his wife Elizabeth Pray were parents of these children, but Cyrus born 1794 was in Stow at this time and these children were born at Sweden. Cyrus born 1794 and Cyrus born 1767 are nephew/uncle.
https://lovell.pastperfectonline.com/byperson?keyword=Eastman%2C+Cyrus+Ens.+%281794-1839%29

1647 Rix, History and Genealogy of the Eastman Family, pp 178-179

iii ABIGAIL EASTMAN, b. 26 Sep 1798; d. at Eustis, ME, 18 Feb 1884; m. at Lovell, 29 Mar 1819, THADDEUS BEMIS, b. at Fryeburg, 7 Dec 1791 son of Thaddeus and Judith (Day) Bemis; Thaddeus d. at Eustis, 8 Jun 1868.

iv CALEB EASTMAN, b. 16 Sep 1801; d. at Stow, 17 Oct 1886; m. 1st, 8 Dec 1822, LUCY BRICKETT, b. 24 Dec 1800 daughter of Jonathan and Martha (Brackett) Brickett; Lucy d. at Stow, 14 Feb 1846. Caleb m. 2nd, 9 Sep 1855, CATHERINE STILES, b. at Cape Elizabeth, ME, 14 Jul 1827 daughter of Jacob and Olive (Bryant) Stiles; Catherine d. at Cape Elizabeth, 4 Nov 1919.

v JEREMIAH EASTMAN, b. 6 Apr 1803; d. at Eureka Township, SD, 1885; m. 31 Mar 1823, his fourth cousin, CYNTHIA ABBOTT *(Micah5, Isaac4, Ebenezer3, John2, George1)*, b. at Fryeburg, 1800 daughter of Micah and Alice (Wiley) Abbott; Cynthia d. at Green County, WI, 29 Dec 1867. Cynthia Abbott is a child in Family 417.

vi SYLVANUS EASTMAN, b. 24 Feb 1805; d. at Lovell, after 1860; m. 1st, 27 Nov 1827, ABIGAIL BEAN, b. at Conway, 12 Oct 1802 daughter of Ebenezer and Catherine (Kilgore) Bean; Abigail d. 30 Oct 1832. Sylvanus m. 2nd, about 1834, MARY WALKER, b. 1804 daughter of Barnett and Hannah (Heath) Walker; Mary d. at Gorham, ME, 17 Oct 1878.

vii ELIZA EASTMAN, b. about 1807; died young.[1648]

viii RICHARD EASTMAN, b. 11 Mar 1810; d. 1811.

ix ELIZABETH EASTMAN, b. about 1814; died young.

x MOSES KILGORE EASTMAN, b. 9 May 1815; d. at Stow, ME, 9 Apr 1905; m. 1st about 1835, his first cousin once removed, ABIGAIL DRESSER *(Stephen Dresser6, Abigail Abbott Dresser5, Job4, Jonathan3, Benjamin2, George1)*, b. 30 Sep 1817 daughter of Stephen and Mehitable (Abbott) Dresser; Abigail d. at Stow, 17 Sep 1862. Moses m. 2nd, 23 Dec 1864, HANNAH CHARLES, b. 29 Jun 1839 daughter of Russell and Melinda (Ames) Charles; Hannah d. at Stow, 18 Mar 1907.

xi HANNAH W. EASTMAN, b. 24 Feb 1818; d. at Fryeburg, 12 Apr 1861; m. 4 Jul 1841, JAMES WHEELOCK RIPLEY FARRINGTON, b. 1809; James d. at Fryeburg, 14 Aug 1872.

xii BETSEY EASTMAN, b. 14 Aug 1820; d. at Fryeburg, 25 May 1888; m. 5 Nov 1842, DAVID SAWYER, b. at Otisfield, ME, 9 Mar 1816 son of Samuel and Relief (Moors) Sawyer; David d. at Fryeburg, 9 Apr 1886.

xiii MARY KILGORE EASTMAN, b. 1 Nov 1822; d. at Boston, 13 Mar 1887; m. SELDEN WENTWORTH, b. at Readfield, ME, 20 Apr 1816 son of Daniel and Elizabeth (Holt) Wentworth; Selden d. at Plymouth, ME, 14 Oct 1882.

594) JAMES TYLER *(Mary Abbott Tyler4, James3, William2, George1)*, b. at Henniker, 2 Apr 1760 son of Adonijah and Mary (Abbott) Tyler; d. at Thetford, VT, 20 Aug 1855;[1649] m. by 1779, SARAH GOULD, b. at Hampton, 24 Jul 1760 daughter of Christopher and Abigail (Shepherd) Gould; Sarah's death record was not located.

James Tyler and Sarah Gould were parents of eleven children, the birth of the oldest child recorded at Hopkinton, eight children born at Henniker, New Hampshire and the youngest children at Thetford, Vermont.

i CHRISTOPHER GOULD TYLER, b. 10 Jul 1779; d. at Black Rock, 30 Dec 1813 (probate 11 Jan 1814); m. ABIGAIL who has not been identified. Captain Gould Tyler was killed in battle during the War of 1812.

ii MARY TYLER, b. 13 Dec 1781; d. at Northfield, VT, 19 Nov 1859; m. ASA SPROUT, b. in NH, about 1778; Asa d. at Northfield, 6 Sep 1856.

iii ANNA TYLER, b. 4 Jun 1783; d. 6 Jul 1801.

iv ASA TYLER, b. about 1785; likely d. at Rockford, IL.

v JOHN TYLER, b. 4 Jun 1786

vi JOEL TYLER, b. about 1787. Reported to have lived in Philadelphia.

vii JAMES TYLER, b. 3 Jun 1789; d. at Thetford, 2 Feb 1876; m. 1 Dec 1814, BETSEY FLETCHER, b. 17 Nov 1793 daughter of Jonathan and Betsey (-) Fletcher; Betsey d. 31 Aug 1878.

viii LUCINDA TYLER, b. 18 Jul 1791; d. 24 Mar 1866; m. 21 Oct 1821, LEONARD FLETCHER, b. at Thetford, 10 Jun 1798 son of Leonard and Grace (Benton) Fletcher; Leonard, d. at West Fairlee, VT, 6 Jul 1855.

[1648] Eliza and Elizabeth are given in Rix's Eastman genealogy, but no records related to them were located.

[1649] Ancestry.com, *Vermont, Vital Records, 1720-1908* (Provo, UT, USA: Ancestry.com Operations, Inc., 2013).

ix ASHER TYLER, b. about 1793

x JEREMIAH TYLER, b. 8 Sep 1796; d. at Rockford, IL, 1877; m. about 1820, LOIS STOWELL, b. about 1800; Lois d. after 1860. Jeremiah and Lois were living in Bushnell, MI in 1860.

xi CANDICE TYLER, b. 1 Mar 1800

595) RACHEL TYLER *(Mary Abbott Tyler^4, James^3, William^2, George^1)*, b. at Henniker, 2 Mar 1762 daughter Adonijah and Mary (Abbott) Tyler; d. in New York, Feb 1843;[1650] m. about 1782, JACOB STANLEY, b. at Hopkinton, 9 Sep 1761 son of Matthew and Mary (Putney) Stanley; Jacob died after 1830 when he was head of household in Tunbridge.

Rachel Tyler and Jacob Stanley were parents of eight children, the oldest six children born at Hopkinton and the two youngest children at Tunbridge.

i ACHSAH STANLEY, b. 21 Oct 1782

ii BENJAMIN C. STANLEY, b. 16 Mar 1785; d. at Pontiac, MI, Apr 1860; m. RUTH MACK, b. 1791 daughter of Stephen and Temperance (Bond) Mack;[1651] Ruth d. at Pontiac, 15 Jan 1857.

iii MATTHEW STANLEY, b. 16 Sep 1787

iv ADONIJAH STANLEY, b. 5 Dec 1790; d. at Salmon Falls, CA, 3 Jun 1879; m. 16 Jan 1817, LYDIA OSBORN, b. at Canaan, NY, 25 Nov 1797 daughter of Asher and Lydia (Olmstead) Osborn;[1652] Lydia d. 3 Jan 1845.

v LUCY STANLEY, b. 2 Apr 1793; d. at Battle Creek, MI, 26 Dec 1881; m. JOHN STUART; John d. at Battle Creek, 1864.

vi RASWELL OLCOTT STANLEY, b. 8 Nov 1795

vii BETSEY STANLEY, b. 11 Mar 1799

viii SARAH STANLEY, b. 24 Sep 1806

596) MIRIAM TYLER *(Mary Abbott Tyler^4, James^3, William^2, George^1)*, b. at Henniker, 22 Mar 1764 daughter Adonijah and Mary (Abbott) Tyler; d. at East Canterbury, NH, 9 Aug 1841;[1653] m. 11 May 1790, MOSES HASTINGS son of James and Mary (Foster) Hastings; Moses d. at Hopkinton, 25 Jan 1815.

Miriam Tyler and Moses Hastings were parents of ten children born at Hopkinton. Daughter Edna married Rev. Abiel Silver. Edna was a published poet.[1654]

i MARY ABBOTT HASTINGS, b. 17 Apr 1791; d. at Sabula, IA, 14 Oct 1865; m. 28 Feb 1816, ENOCH LONG, b. at Hopkinton, 16 Oct 1790 son of Moses and Lucy (Harriman) Long;[1655] Enoch d. at Sabula, 19 Jul 1881.

ii JEREMIAH HASTINGS, b. 26 Jul 1793; d. 12 Mar 1795.

iii LAURA HASTINGS, b. 5 May 1796; d. at Watertown, NY, 1 Aug 1836; m. 13 Feb 1826, JOEL BLOOD, b. about 1797 *likely* the son of Jacob and Rachel (Jones) Blood; Joel d. at Watertown, Jul 1888. After Laura's death, Joel married 27 Jan 1840, IRENA HEATON TYLER, b. at Hopkinton, 15 Jan 1809 daughter of Simeon and Hannah (Rowell) Tyler; Irena d. at Watertown, 1 Feb 1852. Joel married a third time to Susan, not yet identified.

iv EDNA HASTINGS, b. 30 May 1798; d. at Boston, 12 Jan 1892; m. 16 Dec 1825, ABIEL SILVER, b. at Hopkinton, 3 Apr 1797 son of John and Mary (-) Silver;[1656][1657] Abiel d. at Boston, 27 Mar 1881.

1650 The Tyler Genealogy reports that Rachel moved to New York

1651 Mack, *The Progenitors and Descendants of Col. Stephen Mack*, p 11

1652 Olmstead and Ward, *Genealogy of the Olmstead Family*, p 90

1653 Brigham, *Tyler Genealogy*, p 236

1654 Adams, 1883, *The Poets of New Hampshire*, p 78ff

1655 Reid, *Biographical Sketch of Enoch Long: An Illinois Pioneer*, volume 2

1656 Abiel's parents are given as John and Mary on his death record.

1657 Lord, *Life and Times in Hopkinton*, p 467-468

v MARIA HASTINGS, b. 21 Jun 1800; d. at Ontwa, MI, 2 Feb 1875; m. at Hopkinton, 6 Oct 1829, JOSEPH W. LEE, b. about 1807 son of Samuel and Elizabeth (Webster) Lee; Joseph d. at Ontwa, 2 Feb 1875.[1658]

vi MOSES TYLER HASTINGS, b. 7 Oct 1802; d. at Quincy, IL, 4 Sep 1826 (probate 25 Sep 1826). The probate states there are no relatives in the state to assume administration which is assumed by John Wood.

vii BETSEY MCCONNELL HASTINGS, b. 3 Nov 1804; d. at Alfred, ME, after 1870. Betsey did not marry. She was a member of the Shaker community at Alfred.

viii HARRIET HASTINGS, b. 5 May 1807; d. at Canterbury, NH, 22 Feb 1898. Harriet was a member of the Shaker community at Canterbury.

ix CHARLOTTE HASTINGS, b. 5 Jun 1809; d. at Philadelphia, 8 Feb 1839.[1659] Charlotte does not seem to have married. It is unclear what Charlotte was doing in Philadelphia, but she may have gone there with her sister Ednah and her husband who were for a time in Philadelphia.

x MARCIA ELIZA HASTINGS, b. 1 Dec 1811; d. at Canterbury, 29 Oct 1891. Marcia was a member of the Shaker community at Canterbury.

597) JEREMIAH TYLER *(Mary Abbott Tyler⁴, James³, William², George¹)*, b. at Henniker, 6 Apr 1766 son Adonijah and Mary (Abbott) Tyler; d. perhaps at Orford, NH (but buried at Thetford, VT), 19 Jan 1844; m. 31 Oct 1802, IRENE HEATON, b. 17 Apr 1774 daughter of William and Irene (King) Heaton; Irene died at Thetford, VT, 4 May 1840.[1660]

Jeremiah and Irene Tyler were parents to three children born at Thetford.

i CYRIL S. TYLER, b. 31 Dec 1803; d. at Hopkinton, 27 May 1865; m. 29 May 1831, SARAH PUTNAM, b. about 1798 daughter of Aaron Putnam; Sarah d. at Hopkinton, 15 Apr 1880. Cyril was a physician; he graduated from Dartmouth Medical College in 1849.

ii LATIMER TYLER, b. 2 Oct 1806; d. at Elgin, IL, 3 Jun 1878; m. 8 Jan 1834, ELIZA HALL, b. at Thetford, 18 Nov 1814 daughter of John and Hannah (Lathrop) Hall; Eliza d. at Elgin, 14 Mar 1880.

iii WILLIAM MONROE TYLER, b. 5 Jul 1808; d. at Medford, MA, 3 Dec 1870; m. before 1840, MARY C. HAZELTON, b. at Orford, NH, about 1810 daughter of Nathaniel and Lucy (-) Hazelton; Mary d. at Medford, 29 Jun 1867.

598) SIMEON TYLER *(Mary Abbott Tyler⁴, James³, William², George¹)*, b. at Henniker, 22 Mar 1768 son Adonijah and Mary (Abbott) Tyler; d. at Hopkinton, 24 Dec 1855; m. 14 Mar 1799, HANNAH ROWELL, b. 1776, parents unknown; Hannah d. 28 Jun 1831. Simeon m. 2nd, SUSAN PAIGE who was born about 1786 and d. 21 Mar 1865.

Simeon and Hannah had six children born at Hopkinton.

i LYDIA TYLER, b. 24 Aug 1800; d. 20 Mar 1817.

ii PLUMY TYLER, b. 1 May 1804; d. 2 Apr 1817.

iii IRENE TYLER, b. 4 Apr 1806; d. 27 Aug 1808.

iv IRENA HEATON TYLER,[1661] b. 15 Jan 1809; d. at Watertown, NY, 1 Feb 1852; m. 27 Jan 1840, as his second husband, JOEL BLOOD, b. 1797 likely the son of Jacob and Rachel (Jones) Blood; Joel d. at Watertown, Jul 1888. Joel was first married to LAURA HASTINGS, b. 5 May 1796 and d. 1 Aug 1836 of Family 596.

v MARY JANE BALLARD TYLER, b. 29 Mar 1816; d. 20 Aug 1835.

vi LUCIUS HARVEY TYLER, b. 19 Nov 1817; d. at Hopkinton, 24 Aug 1914; m. 1st, 10 May 1852, SARAH ANNA HALL (widow Sarah Amsden), b. at Sherbrooke Québec, about 1822; Sarah d. at Hopkinton, 1 Apr 1875. Lucius m. 2nd, 16 Jan 1883, FRANCES EATON, b. at Warner, 29 Jun 1836 daughter of Elijah and Frances (Sawyer) Eaton; Frances d. at Warner, 12 Oct 1894.

599) MOSES TYLER *(Mary Abbott Tyler⁴, James³, William², George¹)*, b. at Henniker, 9 Apr 1770 son Adonijah and Mary (Abbott) Tyler; d. at Tyler's Bridge, NH, 21 Dec 1857; m. 21 Jun 1798, BETSY MCCONNELL, b. at Pembroke, 30 Jan 1774 daughter of Samuel and Ann (Cunningham) McConnell; Betsy d. 9 Sep 1866.

[1658] *Michigan, Deaths and Burials Index, 1867-1995.*

[1659] Brigham, *Tyler Genealogy*, p 236

[1660] Her grave is in Post Mills Cemetery, Vermont. Findagrave **Memorial ID** 121161310

[1661] Irena's name is reported as both Irena Heaton Tyler and Irena Eaton Tyler.

In his will written 29 May 1857, Moses Tyler has as his first request that his daughter Sarah Buswell and her husband Aaron W. Buswell have a comfortable support and maintenance during their natural lives. Daughter Nancy Childs receives fifty dollars. Granddaughters Caroline W. Perkins and Jane E. Warner each receive five dollars. His granddaughters Clara Ann Buswell, Helen L. Buswell, and Sarah J.P. Buswell each receive fifty dollars. Grandson George R. Buswell receives fifty dollars. And the residue of the estate after meeting the provision of the will for Sarah and Aaron Buswell and George Buswell, is bequeathed to grandson Edward L. Buswell. The exception to this is the land he holds in Bethlehem in Grafton County which he plans to dispose of as he seems advisable. Edward Buswell is also named executor.[1662]

Moses and Betsey were parents of three children. The third child, Calvin, was adopted and he is not mentioned in the will

i NANCY TYLER, b. at Henniker, 4 May 1799; d. at Rock City, WI, 28 Apr 1882; m. 6 Jan 1828, EBER CHILD, b. at Thetford, VT, 31 Jul 1798 son of William and Mary (Heaton) Child; Eber d. at Fulton, WI, 15 Dec 1847.

ii SARAH TYLER, b. at Hopkinton, 12 Jan 1802; d. at Hopkinton, Oct 1858; m. 18 Aug 1819, AARON WOOD BUSWELL, b. at Boxford, MA, 26 Sep 1792 son of James and Jane (Wood) Buswell; Aaron d. at Hopkinton, 20 Oct 1863.

iii CALVIN TYLER (an adopted son), b. at Hopkinton, 11 Mar 1806; d. at Hopkinton, 1 Apr 1884; m. 7 Mar 1833, ZILPHA HASTINGS, b. at Hopkinton, 22 Feb 1807 daughter of Herman and Sally (Connor) Hastings; Zilpha d. at Hopkinton, 19 Feb 1897.

600) MARY TYLER *(Mary Abbott Tyler⁴, James³, William², George¹)*, b. at Chester, 4 Jun 1773 daughter Adonijah and Mary (Abbott) Tyler; d. 1839 at Gap Grove, IL; m. 16 Nov 1797, JACOB MARTIN, b. about 1770; Jacob d. likely at Gap Grove, after 1835.

Mary and Jacob had their children in Sandwich, but relocated to Lee County, Illinois about 1835 accompanied by all their children. Mary Tyler and Jacob Martin were parents of six children born at Sandwich, New Hampshire.[1663]

i MOSES TYLER MARTIN, b. perhaps 1798; nothing further known.[1664]

ii WILLIAM MARTIN, b. about 1800; d. at Palmyra, IL, 1844; m. about 1825, ELIZABETH HILL, b. in NH, about 1804 daughter of David and Mary (Hooper) Hill. Elizabeth was living in Palmyra as head of household in 1850 and 83-year old David Hill was living with her.

iii JAMES T. MARTIN, b. 14 Jun 1802; d. at Palmyra, 3 Jul 1890; m. likely ANN EASTWOOD, b. in NY 1816 daughter of Jonas and Ann (Evarts) Eastwood; Ann d. at Palmyra, 20 Jan 1887.

iv JACOB MARTIN, b. 29 Dec 1806; d. at Palmyra, 29 Aug 1881; m. 1st, 28 Apr 1844, MARGARET CURTIS, b. in NY, about 1815; Margaret d. at Palmyra, about 1855. Jacob m. 2nd, BELLE DRYNAN, b. in Hamilton, Ontario, about 1838 daughter of William and Elizabeth (McMurty) Drynan;[1665] Belle d. at Palmyra, about 1895 (probate 6 Feb 1895).

v ELIZA MARTIN, b. 30 Jan 1809; d. at Palmyra, 11 Jan 1892; m. 1st, at Sandwich, 26 Nov 1833, OLIVER A. HUBBARD, b. at Sandwich, 1804 son of Nathaniel and Betsey (Ambrose) Hubbard;[1666] Oliver d. at Gap Grove, 16 Sep 1840. Eliza m. 2nd, 3 Nov 1843, WILLIAM W. TILTON, b. 14 Jul 1817 son of Jesse and Mary (Fifield) Tilton; William d. 11 Mar 1894.

vi SIMEON TYLER MARTIN, b. 6 May 1813; d. at Sterling, IL, 1890 (probate 18 Mar 1890); m. 1st, at Lee County, 26 Mar 1844, CATHERINE MONTGOMERY, b. in NY, about 1815; Catherine d. 7 Jun 1884. Simeon m. 2nd, ELIZABETH (his widow at probate) about whom nothing else in known. Simeon and Elizabeth had a daughter Nina May (1888-1892).

[1662] *New Hampshire. Probate Court (Merrimack County);* Probate Place: *Merrimack, New Hampshire*, volume 34, pp 112-113, will of Moses Tyler

[1663] Brigham, *The Tyler Genealogy*, p 237

[1664] This is a child in The Tyler Genealogy for whom no records were found.

[1665] *1851 Census of Canada East, Canada West, New Brunswick, and Nova Scotia*, Year: 1851; Census Place: St Mary, Hamilton City, Canada West (Ontario); Schedule: A; Roll: C_11762; Page: 130; Line: 3.

[1666] Carroll County, NH probate related to Nathaniel Hubbard includes an 8 Feb 1844 petition by Elisa A. Hubbard guardian of Moses Dudley Hubbard, a minor and son of Oliver A. Hubbard of Lee County, Illinois, heir of Nathaniel Hubbard. New Hampshire, County Probate Estate Files, 1769-1936, Carroll County, Case no 2672-2770 1840-1920, Image 892-893

601) SARAH TYLER *(Mary Abbott Tyler⁴, James³, William², George¹)*, b. at Chester, Mar 1775 daughter Adonijah and Mary (Abbott) Tyler; d. at Ogle County, IL, 7 Feb 1839; m. at Hopkinton, 14 Jun 1796, ROBERT CROWELL *possibly* the son of Aaron and Elizabeth (-) Crowell; Robert d. at Marion, IL, 22 Sep 1862.[1667]

After the births of ten children, Sarah and Robert headed to Ogle County, Illinois with nearly all the children remaining in the area of Marion, Illinois. The family was active in the community. Son Moses was the contractor and builder of the Ogle County Courthouse in 1847. [1668]

Sarah Tyler and Robert Crowell were parents of ten children all likely born at Hopkinton.

i JEREMIAH CROWELL, b. Sep 1796; d. at Marion, IL, 1 Mar 1865; m. at Hopkinton, 1815, BETSEY BICKFORD, b. 28 Dec 1799 daughter of Samuel and Ruth (Howe) Bickford; Betsey d. at Marion, 8 Jun 1880.

ii THOMAS PRITCHARD CROWELL, b. about 1798; died young.

iii WATTS TURNER CROWELL, b. 11 Nov 1803; d. at Oregon, IL, 5 Jul 1874; m. at Boston, 22 Jan 1829, HARRIET LOCKER, b. 10 Oct 1810; Harriet d. at Oregon, IL, 4 Sep 1879.

iv MOSES TYLER CROWELL, b. 9 May 1806; d. at Sacramento, CA, 10 Sep 1893; m. at Hopkinton, 3 Jul 1828, MARY HOWE BICKFORD, b. 7 Aug 1810 daughter of Samuel and Ruth (Howe) Bickford; Mary d. at Sacramento, 25 Apr 1897.

v SAMUEL PUTNEY CROWELL, b. 12 Sep 1810; d. at Oregon, IL, 20 Jul 1885; m. perhaps about 1850, BEATRICE LEAL, b. at Matanzas, Cuba, about 1815; Beatrice d. at Oregon, IL, 18 May 1872. Samuel lived for a time in Cuba where he married and where at least one child was born.

vi SIMEON SOLON CROWELL, b. 12 Sep 1812; d. at Ogle County, IL, 27 Feb 1896; m. 1st, 4 Nov 1841, MARY K. MARSHALL, b. at Plattsburgh, NY, 24 Sep 1824 daughter of Caleb and Louisa (Sanborn) Marshall; Mary d. at Ogle County, 23 Feb 1843. Simeon m. 2nd, 20 Apr 1851, SARAH KERN, b. at Madison County, NY, 18 Jan 1826 daughter of William and Elizabeth (Tackabury) Kern; Sarah d. at Ogle County, 17 May 1905.

vii LORENZO HASTINGS CROWELL, b. about 1814; likely d. in IL but does not seem to have married.

viii SARAH ANN CROWELL, b. about 1815; d. 6 Nov 1837. Sarah did not marry.

ix HANNAH CROWELL, b. about 1816; m. CHARRICE[1669]

x MARY CROWELL, b. about 1817; m. at Ogle, IL, 18 Mar 1838, JOHN WILSON

602) NATHAN ABBOTT *(Nathan⁴, Paul³, William², George¹)*, b. at Ashford, 18 May 1744 son of Nathan and Eunice (Marsh) Abbott; d. at Woodstock, 19 Jan 1794;[1670] m. JUDITH STODDARD, b. 24 Sep 1749 daughter of Ebenezer and Anna (Stowell) Stoddard. There is a probate record for Nathan Abbott from 1794 that names wife Judith as administrator of the estate with Ebenezer Stoddard as co-signer on the surety bond.[1671]

Nathan and Judith moved several times in their marriage and had children born in Union, Pomfret, and Woodstock, Connecticut. There is some evidence for seven children, five of these listed in Hammond's *History of Union Conn*,[1672] the birth of one child at Pomfret, and one birth recorded at Woodstock. Several of the children settled in Rhode Island and it is thought that Nathan and Judith may have been in Rhode Island for a time and had some children there, but no record evidence was found for other children.

Nathan and Judith were admitted as members of the church at Union 25 March 1770. Nathan was a member of the 5th Company of the 22nd Regiment that marched from Union "at the alarm" in April 1775. He served seven days at that time and his total length of service was four months.[1673]

The estate of Nathan Abbott entered probate 4 February 1794 with wife Judith as administrator. The inventory of the estate included tools and a shop related to tanning and shoe making. The inventory of the estate was valued at £522, but the debts exceeded the value of the estate. The estate, except the portion for the widow's dower, was sold in 1795 to settle the debts.[1674]

[1667] Brigham, *The Tyler Genealogy* p 237
[1668] H. F. Kett, *The History of Ogle County, Illinois*
[1669] Brigham, *The Tyler Genealogy*
[1670] *Connecticut, Hale Collection of Cemetery Inscriptions and Newspaper Notices, 1629-1934*. Newspaper notice gives age at death as 49, and states he was in the Revolutionary War.
[1671] *Connecticut Wills and Probate, 1609-1999*, Probate of Nathan Abbott, Hartford, 1794, Case number 4.
[1672] Hammond, *History of Union, Conn.*, p 255
[1673] Hammond, *History of Union, Conn.*, p 99, 117, 132
[1674] *Connecticut State Library (Hartford, Connecticut)*; Probate Place: *Hartford, Connecticut, Pomfret District, Probate Packets, Abbot-Allen, James, 1752-1880*

i ALBA ABBOTT, b. at Union, Mar 1770; d. at Homer, NY, 1836; m. 26 Nov 1795, ROENA CHILD, b. at Woodstock, 3 Dec 1775 daughter of Lemuel and Dorcas (Perry) Child.[1675]

ii HANNAH ABBOTT, b. Jul 1772 at Union. No further record was located.

iii WILLARD ABBOTT, b. at Union, 20 Apr 1774; d. at New Woodstock, NY, Aug 1831; m. 7 Jan 1799, NANCY CHILD, b. at Woodstock, 20 May 1778 daughter of Lemuel and Dorcas (Perry) Child; Nancy d. at New Woodstock, 21 Jun 1845.

iv HARVEY ABBOTT, b. at Union, 8 Sep 1778; d. at Providence, 2 Nov 1820; m. SALLY CLARK, b. at Canterbury, about 1783; Sally d. at Providence, 10 Mar 1871. Sally's parents are given as Joseph and Abigail Clark on her death record but that has not been otherwise verified.

v SALLY ABBOTT, b. at Union, 12 Jan 1782; no further record was located.

vi AMASA ABBOTT, b. at Pomfret, 11 Sep 1784; d. at Scituate, RI, 26 Feb 1842; m. RUBY CLARK, b. about 1786 and likely the sister of Sally who married Amasa's brother Harvey; Ruby d. at Providence, 27 Aug 1873.

vii ERASTUS ABBOTT, b. at Woodstock, 29 Jun 1790; d. at Providence, 1809.[1676]

603) STEPHEN ABBOTT *(Nathan⁴, Paul³, William², George¹)*, b. at Pomfret, 20 Oct 1757 son of Nathan and Eunice (Marsh) Abbott; d. at North Providence, RI, 24 Jul 1813;[1677][1678] m. 28 Jun 1781, his third cousin, ESTHER INGALLS *(Zebadiah Ingalls⁴, Mary Stevens Ingalls³, Sarah Abbott Stevens², George¹)*, b. 26 Nov 1762 daughter of Zebadiah and Esther (Goodell) Ingalls; Esther d. 4 Feb 1851.

Colonel Stephen Abbott was a tanner and currier in Providence.

Stephen Abbott did not leave a will and his estate entered probate August 1813. Widow Esther Abbott was administratrix of the estate. Personal estate was valued at $700.20.[1679]

Stephen and Esther were parents of four children.

i OLIVE ABBOTT, b. at Pomfret, 29 Mar 1782; d. at Providence, 24 Feb 1860; m. at Preston, CT, 26 Apr 1802, JEREMIAH PHILLIPS, b. at Preston, 22 Feb 1779 son of Jeremiah and Margaret (Stanton) Phillips; Jeremiah d. at Norwich, CT, 13 Jul 1816.

ii ESTHER INGALLS, b. 3 Apr 1784; d. at North Providence, 7 Nov 1803.

iii BETSEY ABBOTT, b. at Providence, 4 May 1786; d. at Providence, 17 Feb 1839; m. Dec 1803, her uncle, OLIVER INGALLS *(Zebadiah Ingalls⁴, Mary Stevens Ingalls³, Sarah Abbott Stevens², George¹)*, b. at Pomfret, 7 Apr 1770 son of Zebadiah and Esther (Goodell) Ingalls; Oliver d. at Pomfret, 10 Apr 1815. Betsey Abbott and Oliver Ingalls are Family 751.

iv LUCY ABBOTT, b. 24 Mar 1788; d. 29 Sep 1789.

604) WILLIAM ABBOTT *(William⁴, Paul³, William², George¹)*, b. at Pomfret, 27 May 1752 son of William and Jerusha (Stowell) Abbott; d. at Lisle, NY, 1806 (probate 15 Jul 1806); m. 8 Jul 1776, HANNAH SNOW, b. at Ashford, 2 Jul 1754 daughter of Samuel and Hannah (Mason) Snow.

Almost no information has been located for this family. They resided in Lisle, New York. There are birth records for two children, and it is known that son Asa lived to adulthood as he was administrator of his father's estate. William did not leave a will and estate entered probate 15 July 1806. Debts exceeded the value of the estate and it was declared insolvent.[1680]

i ASA ABBOTT, b. at Ashford, 8 Jun 1778; living in 1806.

ii BETSEY ABBOTT, b. at Ashford, 8 Jan 1780; no further record.

[1675] The 1808 will of Lemuel Child includes bequests for daughter Roene wife of Albe Abbot and daughter Nancy wife of Willard Abbot.

[16761676] Connecticut, Hale Collection of Cemetery Inscriptions and Newspaper Notices, 1629-1934

[1677] Ancestry.com, Rhode Island, Vital Extracts, 1636-1899

[1678] There is a Rhode Island probate record for Col. Stephen Abbott from August 1813 that contains an inventory and provides for widow Esther to administer the estate. Probate Files, Early to 1885 (Pawtucket, R.I.); Author: Pawtucket (Rhode Island). Court of Probate; Probate Place: Providence, Rhode Island

[1679] *Pawtucket (Rhode Island). Court of Probate;* Probate Place: *Providence, Rhode Island, Probate Files, 85-144 (1)*, Case 105

[1680] *Wills of Broome County, New York, 1806-1906;* Author: *New York. Surrogate's Court (Broome County);* Probate Place: *Broome, New York, Wills, Letters, Vol A-C, 1806-1852*

605) HENRY ABBOTT *(Benjamin⁴, Paul³, William², George¹)*, b. at Ashford, 3 Jun 1749 son of Benjamin and Mary Ann (Andrews) Abbott; d. at Brookfield, VT, 31 Mar 1807; m. at Hampton, CT, 7 Apr 1772, a fourth cousin, SARAH BURNHAM, b. 21 Aug 1750 daughter of Isaac and Eunice (Holt) Burnham; Sarah d. at Brookfield, 18 Nov 1815. Sarah had married first John Greenslit with whom she had two children.

Henry was born in Connecticut but went with his father to Brookfield, Vermont where the family settled. Henry Abbott and Sarah Burnham were parents of eight children born at Hampton, Connecticut.

i STEPHEN ANDREWS ABBOTT, b. 21 Aug 1775; d. at Brookfield, after 1840; m. about 1802, BETSY SMITH, b. about 1780; Betsy d. at Brookfield, after 1840.

ii LAVINA ABBOTT, b. 30 Oct 1777; d. at Brookfield, 11 Jan 1807; m. 2 Feb 1806, as his second wife, LUKE CLARK, b. at South Hadley, MA, 10 Feb 1762 son of Israel and Mehitable (Montague) Clark; Luke d. at Brookfield, 6 Oct 1841. Luke was first married to Sarah Smith and third married to Zerviah Cushman.

iii URIAL ABBOTT, b. 17 Jan 1780; d. at Williamston, VT, 23 Jul 1857; m. 1st, POLLY who is not yet identified; Polly d. at Brookfield, 14 Apr 1806.[1681] Urial m. 2nd, 14 May 1809, PERMELIA SMITH, b. about 1790; Permelia d. at Williamston, 19 Jan 1854.

iv SALLY ABBOTT, b. 20 May 1782; d. at Hampton, 25 Sep 1815; m. AARON FARNUM, b. 15 Nov 1776 son of Jeremiah and Lucy (Durkee) Farnum; Aaron d. at Hampton, 29 Apr 1853.

v BETSEY ABBOTT, b. 8 Oct 1784; d. about 1812; m. at Brookfield, 3 Oct 1805, JOSEPH SMITH, b. about 1784; Joseph d. at Bolton, VT, 6 Sep 1850. Joseph was second married to Betsey's sister ASENATH ABBOTT (see below).

vi HARDIN ABBOTT, b. 3 May 1787; d. at Pittsford, VT, 30 Jan 1832; m. 17 May 1814, PERSIS SMITH, b. at Brookfield, 15 Sep 1794 daughter of Josiah and Persis (Smith) Smith; Persis d. at Brookfield, 29 Jan 1873.

vii EUNICE ABBOTT, b. 2 Jul 1791; nothing further known.

viii ASENATH ABBOTT, b. 9 Oct 1793; m. 13 Apr 1813, JOSEPH SMITH who was first married to Asenath's sister Betsey (see above).

606) MARY ABBOTT *(Benjamin⁴, Paul³, William², George¹)*, b. at Windham, 4 Aug 1754 daughter of Benjamin and Mary Ann (Andrews) Abbott; d. at Brookfield, VT, 28 Feb 1811; m. 17 May 1781, THOMAS ADAMS, b. at Canterbury, CT, 24 Apr 1757 son of Eliphalet and Mary (Frost) Adams; Thomas d. at Brookfield, VT, 1803.

Mary Abbott and Thomas Adams were married in Canterbury and the births of their four children are recorded at Canterbury and Hampton. The family then settled in Brookfield, Vermont where Thomas had a small farm property.

The distribution of Thomas Adams's estate was 5 August 1803. It was determined that the real estate could not be divided without "prejudice" to the value. After the set off for the widow's third, there was a settlement of the real property to the eldest son Eliphalet and he was to pay $9.08 to each of his brothers Charles, Rufus, and John Andrews Adams.[1682]

i ELIPHALET ADAMS, b. at Canterbury, 4 Mar 1782; d. at Cabot, VT, 27 Jan 1826; m. LUCINDA WALBRIDGE, b. at Stafford, 1784 daughter of Eleazer and Abigail (Washburn) Walbridge;[1683] Lucinda d. at East Cabot, 22 Sep 1863.

ii CHARLES ADAMS, b. 15 Oct 1785; d. at Randolph, VT, 20 Jan 1839; m. at Randolph, 28 Jan 1810, PAMELIA EDGERTON, b. at Randolph, 29 Jul 1791 daughter of Oliver and Lucy (Brainerd) Edgerton;[1684] Pamelia d. at Randolph, 21 Nov 1851.

iii RUFUS ADAMS, b. at Hampton, 17 Feb 1788; d. at Brookfield, 24 Jun 1859; m. 23 Mar 1815, NANCY MORGAN, b. at Randolph, 3 Sep 1788 daughter of Justin and Martha (Day) Morgan; Nancy d. at Randolph, 1 May 1839.

iv JOHN ANDREW ADAMS, b. at Hampton, 15 Nov 1790; d. at Cabot, VT, 18 Oct 1863; m. LOIS LAIRD, b. at Strafford, 1786 daughter of John and Dorcas (Orcott) Laird; Lois d. at Cabot, 2 Nov 1862.

607) ASA ABBOTT *(Benjamin⁴, Paul³, William², George¹)*, b. at Pomfret, 25 May 1756 son of Benjamin and Mary Ann (Andrews) Abbott; d. at Hampton, 1834 (will dated 10 Apr 1834); m. by 1783, SARAH BIDLACK, b. at Hampton, 30 Sep 1756 daughter of James and Mehitable (Durkee) Bidlack. Sarah was first married to STEPHEN FULLER *(Mary Abbott Fuller⁴,*

[1681] Vermont, Vital Records, 1720-1908. Polly wife of Mr. Urial Abbott died at age 24.

[1682] *Vermont. Probate Court (Randolph District)*; Probate Place: *Orange, Vermont*, *Folder 1, Files No A-B, 1790-1890*, recorded in volume I, p 203

[1683] The 1813 Vermont will of Eleazer Walbridge includes a bequest to daughter Lucinda although the will does not give the last names of any of the daughters.

[1684] Edgerton, *The Genealogy of the Brainerd-Brainard Family in America*, volume II, p 66

Philip[3], William[2], George[1]), b. at Windham, 22 Jan 1755 son of Stephen and Mary (Abbott) Fuller. Stephen died at the Battle of Wyoming on 3 Jul 1778. These families are considered together.

Stephen Fuller was killed in the massacre at the Battle of Wyoming, a gruesome event about which much has been written. Sarah's home was ransacked in the aftermath of the massacre. She returned to Connecticut of horseback with her infant daughter.[1685]

Child of Sarah Bidlack and Stephen Fuller

i MARY FULLER, b. at Westmoreland, PA, 16 Apr 1778; d. at Hampton, CT, 18 Jun 1800; m. 21 Oct 1798, EBENEZER GRIFFIN, b. at Windham, 6 Apr 1775 son of Ebenezer and Elizabeth (Martin) Griffin; Ebenezer d. at Hampton, 14 May 1860. After Mary's death, Ebenezer married Lois Durkee and then Lydia Parsons.

In his will written 10 April 1834, Asa Abbott bequeathed to beloved wife Sarah the use and improvement of the entire estate during her natural life, and if the income from the estate is not sufficient for her comfortable support, she has the liberty to use any portion of the principal that she needs. Wife Sarah and son Warren Abbott are named executors. None of the other children are named in the will. The total value of the estate was $577.96 which included real estate valued at $425.[1686]

Asa Abbott and Sarah Bidlack were parents of eight children all born at Hampton.

i PATTY ABBOTT, b. 13 Nov 1783; d. 16 Jan 1786.

ii JAMES ABBOTT, b. 28 Oct 1785; d. at Hampton, 1839;[1687] m. at Hampton, 20 Jan 1814, ASENATH BURNET, b. at Hampton, 13 Apr 1791 daughter of James and Chloe (Martin) Burnet; Asenath d. at East Hartford, after 1860 (living with her daughter Harriet and her husband in 1860).

iii MARTHA "PATTY" ABBOTT, b. 13 Jun 1787; d. at Plainfield, CT, 2 Aug 1845; m. at Hampton, 2 Dec 1827, DORRANCE KNOX, b. in Rhode Island, about 1772 son of Andrew and Elizabeth (Dorrance) Knox; Dorrance d. at Plainfield, 11 Mar 1855. Dorrance was first married to Nancy Bennet.

iv Son b. and d. 1 Feb 1789

v OLIVE ABBOTT, b. 20 Mar 1790; d. about 1843; m. at Hampton, 16 Sep 1833, as his second wife, her second cousin, MARVIN INGALLS *(Peter Ingalls[5], Sarah Abbott Ingalls[4], Paul[3], William[2], George[1])*, b. at Pomfret, 6 Nov 1787 son of Peter and Sarah (Ashley) Ingalls; Marvin d. at Hampton, 28 Jan 1847. Marvin was first married to Amelia Spaulding 12 Dec 1811 and third married to Marietta Burnham 19 May 1844. Marvin Ingalls in a child in Family 620.

vi SALLY ABBOTT, b. 31 Jul 1792; d. at Hampton, about 1817; m. 15 Jan 1815, EBENEZER GREENSLIT, b. 17 Jul 1789;[1688] Ebenezer d. at Hampton, 22 Oct 1842. After Sally's death, Ebenezer married Lucy.

vii CHAUNCEY G. ABBOTT, b. 8 May 1794; d. at Hampton, 10 Jan 1872; m. at Hampton, 11 Mar 1821, MARY ANN FULLER, b. at Norwich, 11 Mar 1797 daughter of Rufus and Rhoda (Baldwin) Fuller; Mary Ann d. at Hampton, 12 Feb 1870.

viii WARREN W. ABBOTT, b. 3 Oct 1796; d. at Hampton, 1876; m. 12 Feb 1823, MARIA E. FRANKLIN, b. at Brooklyn, CT, 26 Mar 1803 daughter of Henry Tolman and Dorcas (Murdock) Franklin; Maria d. at Hampton, 1878.

608) HANNAH ABBOTT *(Benjamin[4], Paul[3], William[2], George[1])*, b. at Windham, 10 Feb 1759 daughter of Benjamin and Mary Ann (Andrews) Abbott; m. at Hampton, 24 May 1775, JOSIAH COLLINS, b. about 1749 (based on age 63 at time of death); Josiah d. at Hampton, 24 Feb 1812.

There are records for six children of Hannah Abbott and Josiah Collins born at Hampton.

i JOHN COLLINS, b. 10 Mar 1777

[1685] Abbot, Genealogical Register, p 55

[1686] *Connecticut. Probate Court (Windham District);* Probate Place: *Windham, Connecticut*, volume 20, pp 376-377

[1687] Abbot and Abbot, *Genealogical Register*, p 47, reported as dying when returning home from the mill during a severe snowstorm

[1688] This birthdate is given in the Hampton records but reported as the husband of Sally Abbott. It is not known where he was born, and identity of parents is not determined.

ii HANNAH COLLINS, b. 28 Feb 1780

iii JOSIAH COLLINS, b. 27 Jul 1782; d. 29 Jan 1783.

iv AURILLA COLLINS, b. 17 Mar 1784

v ERASTUS COLLINS, b. 5 Jun 1787; d. in RI, 25 Oct 1819; m. at Killingly, CT, 12 Apr 1817, MARY DAY, b. about 1795 daughter of David Day.

vi NANCY COLLINS, b. 30 Apr 1790; d. at Fabius, NY, about 1860; m. at Hampton, 4 Mar 1813, AMOS MARTIN, b. at Hampton about 1787 son of Amasa and Ursula (Utley) Martin; Amos d. at Fabius, about 1857.

609) TRYPHENA ABBOTT *(Benjamin⁴, Paul³, William², George¹)*, b. at Windham, 22 Sep 1760 daughter of Benjamin and Mary Ann (Andrews) Abbott; d. at Stafford, 21 Nov 1835; m. May 1781, ABNER ASHLEY, b. at Hampton, 19 Jan 1754 son of Abner and Mary (Crossley) Ashley; Abner d. at Tolland County 1837 (will proved 2 January 1838).

Abner and Tryphena had their children in Hampton, but later settled in Tolland, Connecticut. Abner was primarily engaged in farming, but his will suggests he also worked as a carpenter. His son Benjamin was a baker.

Abner served in the Revolutionary War including enlistments in 1775, 1778, and 1780. He took part in Sullivan's Expedition in 1778.

Abner Ashley wrote his will 13 July 1836 and it was proved 2 January 1838.[1689] The will has the following bequests: granddaughter Cordelia Ashley, fifty dollars; daughter Laura Benton, three hundred-fifty dollars in addition to what has already been paid to her; children of his daughter Maria Benton, house and land containing 10 acres located in Tolland so long as the children provide maintenance for Maria; Maria has the right to enter and improve the premises for her support; son Benjamin, all the joiner and carpentry tools; and the residue of the estate to be divided equally between Lara and Maria. Elisha Stearns was named executor although he declined that responsibility. Benjamin Ashley assumed those duties. The value of the estate was $681 which included a $366 value for the house and 9-10 acres that were bequests to the children of Maria.

There are six children of Abner and Tryphena for whom there are birth records or mention in the will. The Ashley genealogy adds a seventh child that died young.[1690]

i ABNER ASHLEY, b. 2 May 1782; d. at Stafford, 5 Oct 1829. Abner did not marry. He worked as a shoemaker and a farmer.

ii ELIJAH ASHLEY, b. 29 Jul 1784; d. at New York City, 8 Mar 1836. The Ashley genealogy reports that Elijah married twice but the names of his wives are unknown. His daughter Cordelia is the granddaughter mentioned in Abner, Sr.'s will.

iii BENJAMIN ASHLEY, b. 2 Jul 1786; d. 12 Jan 1862; m. 1st, 23 Apr 1812, LOVISA CONVERSE, b. at Tolland, 29 Jul 1788 daughter of Darius and Hannah (Hungerford) Converse; Lovisa d. 25 Sep 1848. Benjamin m. 2nd, 9 Dec 1849, SARAH STRICKLAND, b. about 1798. Sarah was the widow of Asa Bowe. Sarah died 3 Jan 1863.

iv ALVIN ASHLEY, b. 24 Jul 1788; d. 12 Dec 1792.

v TRYPHENA ASHLEY, b. 20 Jul 1792; death not known. The Ashley genealogy reports she married Mr. Phillips of Fishkill, New York. Tryphena is not mentioned in her father's will.

vi LORENDA ASHLEY, b. 1794; d. at Glastonbury, 23 Nov 1863; m. at Tolland, 18 Jul 1816, ALFRED BENTON, b. at Tolland, 6 Jan 1789 son of Ozias and Sarah (Day) Benton' Alfred d. 17 May 1865.

vii MARIA ASHLEY, b. about 1802; m. 1st, 31 Jan 1826, LEVI BENTON, b. at Tolland, 6 Feb 1799 son of Ozias and Sarah (Day) Benton; Levi d. at Tolland, 16 Jul 1841. Maria m. 2nd, at Stafford, 3 Dec 1844, SANFORD WALBRIDGE, b. about 1820 at Monson, MA. Sanford d. at Brooklyn, NY, May 1893. Maria had died by 1860 at which time Sanford was married to a woman named Ellen. Sanford was in prison in Brooklyn off and on starting about 1855 for assault and disorderly behavior.[1691]

610) LOUISA ABBOTT *(Benjamin⁴, Paul³, William², George¹)*, b. at Windham, 24 Dec 1762 daughter of Benjamin and Mary Ann (Andrews) Abbott; d. perhaps at Columbus, NY, 16 Mar 1806; m. at Canterbury, 1 Sep 1785, SAMUEL PRESTON, b. 19 Feb 1763 son of Jacob and Mary (Butts) Preston; Samuel d. at Ira, NY, 24 Mar 1836.

Louisa Abbott and Samuel Preston were parents of seven children. The first four children were born in Pomfret and the family then moved on to Columbus, New York where the youngest children were born.

[1689] *Connecticut Wills and Probate, 1609-1999*, Probate of Abner Ashley, Tolland District, 1838, Case number 43.
[1690] Trowbridge, *Ashley Genealogy*, p 301
[1691] Ancestry.com, New York, Governor's Registers of Commitments to Prisons, 1842-1908.

i HARVEY PRESTON, b. at Pomfret, 27 Jan 1786; d. at Willet, NY, 19 Aug 1835; m. MARTHA GAZLEY, b. in NY, about 1785 daughter of Jonathan and Maria (-) Gazley;[1692] Martha d. at Aetna, MI, 6 Jul 1874. After Harvey's death, Martha married Mr. Nash.

ii WALTER PRESTON, b. at Preston, 30 Jun 1787

iii ANDREWS PRESTON, b. 29 Nov 1788; d. at Cato, NY, 1858 (probate 12 Apr 1858); m. ELIZA ANN FERRIS, b. 1806 daughter of Augustus Frederick and Elizabeth (Hammond) Ferris; Eliza d. at Cato, 1854.

iv LOUISA PRESTON, b. at Pomfret, 26 Apr 1792; d. at Guilford, NY, 7 Nov 1853; m. BENJAMIN PEET, b. at Mount Upton, NY, 7 Nov 1789 son of Silas and Johanna (Leech) Peet; Benjamin d. at Guilford, 27 Sep 1860.

v MARY PRESTON, b. likely at Columbus, NY, 27 Jan 1795; nothing further known.

vi CLARINDA PRESTON, b. at Columbus, NY, 20 Jul 1797; nothing further known.

vii SAMUEL PRESTON, b. at Columbus, 16 Jul 1800; d. at Oneida, MI, 19 Jun 1883; m. about 1827, REBECCA SPRAGUE, b. at Ira, NY, 14 Oct 1807 daughter of Parmenas and Rebecca (Nobles) Sprague;[1693] Rebecca d. at Grand Lodge, MI, 1897.

611) BENJAMIN ABBOTT *(Benjamin⁴, Paul³, William², George¹)*, b. at Windham, 2 Oct 1764 son of Benjamin and Mary Ann (Andrews) Abbott; d. at Brookfield, VT, 12 Sep 1829;[1694] m. about 1786, LUCY FLINT, b. 10 Jun 1767 daughter of Nathaniel and Lucy (Martin) Flint; Lucy d. 24 Sep 1839.

Benjamin Abbott was a farmer in Brookfield. He did not leave a will and the estate entered probate 29 November 1829 with widow Lucy as administratrix. Claims against the estate exceeded the value of the estate and it was declared insolvent. The homestead consisted of 61 acres with buildings in Brookfield valued at $854.[1695]

Benjamin Abbott and Lucy Flint were parents of ten children born at Brookfield, Vermont.

i LUCY ABBOTT, b. 13 May 1788; d. at Brookfield, VT, after 1850; m. 19 Jun 1814, ALBA DAVIDSON; Alba d. at Brookfield, 1849 (probate 27 Nov 1849).

ii ANNA ABBOTT, b. 7 Mar 1790; d. at Brookfield, 10 Nov 1871; m. 9 May 1815, PHINEAS KELLOGG, b. at South Hadley, MA, 1787 son of Phineas and Jemima (Brown) Kellogg; Phineas d. at Brookfield, 4 Feb 1871.

iii EBENEZER ABBOTT, b. 31 May 1792; d. at Braintree, VT, 15 Jul 1867; m. 9 May 1815, SALLY FLINT, b. in CT, 1796 daughter of Jonathan and Mary (Amidon) Flint; Sally d. at Randolph, VT, after 1870.

iv LESTER ABBOTT, b. 31 Mar 1794; d. at Potsdam, NY, 24 Dec 1833; m. 11 Feb 1818, MEHITABLE CLARK, b. at Brookfield, VT, 10 Apr 1803 daughter of Luke and Sarah (Smith) Clark.

v WALTER ABBOTT, b. 10 Jul 1796; d. at Brookfield, 2 Jan 1879; m. 2 Dec 1820, his second cousin, SARAH AMIDON *(Keturah Holt Amidon⁵, Mary Abbott Holt⁴, Paul³, William², George¹)*, b. at Randolph, VT, about 1800 daughter of Jonathan and Keturah (Holt) Amidon; Sarah d. at Brookfield, 31 Mar 1873. Sarah Amidon is a child in Family 616.

vi BENJAMIN ABBOTT, b. 25 Feb 1799; d. at Hanover, NH, 19 Nov 1859; m. 25 Dec 1834, ADELINE REMINGTON, b. at Candia, NH, about 1814 daughter of Jesse and Polly (-) Remington; Adeline d. at Hanover, 20 Mar 1868.

vii LAURA ABBOTT, b. 16 Mar 1801; d. at Brookfield, 22 Jul 1879; m. 1st, 24 Jun 1858, JERAH EDSON, b. at Whately, MA, about 1787 son of Amasa and Hannah (Morton) Edson; Jerah d. at Brookfield, 20 Mar 1870. Laura m. 2nd, 17 Nov 1870, CALEB ALLEN STRATTON, b. at Brookfield, 22 Dec 1797 son of Ebenezer and Sarah (Smith) Stratton; Caleb d. at Brookfield, 12 Jan 1882.

viii ROYAL ABBOTT, b. 7 Jun 1803; d. at Brookfield, 29 Mar 1885; m. 29 Jan 1828, RUTH PORTER, b. at Danvers, MA, about 1802 daughter of Daniel and Ruth (Mecom) Porter; Ruth d. at Brookfield, 16 Apr 1877.

[1692] Martha's parents are given as Jonathan and Maria Gazley on her death record.
[1693] Sprague, *Sprague Families in America*, p 65
[1694] Benjamin's estate entered probate in Orange County, VT in 1830.
[1695] *Vermont. Probate Court (Randolph District)*; Probate Place: *Orange, Vermont, Folder 1, Files No A-B, 1790-1890*

ix ALBA ABBOTT, b. 18 Oct 1805; d. at Brookfield, 9 Jan 1851; m. 6 May 1835, ALZINA GRISWOLD, b. at Brookfield, 31 Jul 1805 daughter of Sylvester and Polly (Perigo) Griswold; Alzina d. at Brookfield, 19 Jan 1853.

x LOUISA ABBOTT, b. 7 Mar 1808; d. at Brookfield, 24 Sep 1839. Louisa did not marry.

612) DINAH HOLT *(Mary Abbott Holt[4], Paul[3], William[2], George[1])*, b. at Windham, 22 Mar 1750 daughter of Joshua and Mary (Abbott) Holt; d. 21 Feb 1826; m. 30 Jun 1778, SETH STOWELL, b. 29 May 1742 son of Nathaniel and Margaret (Trowbridge) Stowell; Seth d. about 1798 (when estate went to probate). Dinah m. 2nd, 27 Nov 1800, PAUL HOLT, b. 1743 and d. 1827 son of Paul and Mehitable (Chandler) Holt. Dinah was Paul Holt's third wife.

The estate of Seth Stowell entered probate 5 May 1798 with widow Dinah as administratrix with a surety bond of three thousand dollars.[1696] Four heirs, in addition to the widow Dinah, are mentioned in the probate record for Seth Stowell: Olive Stowel, Kezia Stowell, Artemisa Stowell, and Mardin Stowel.[1697]

Dinah Holt and Seth Stowell were parents of four children.[1698]

i OLIVE STOWELL, b. at Pomfret, 2 Apr 1779; d. at New Woodstock, NY, 13 Jun 1829; m. at Woodstock, 6 Feb 1803, LUTHER CORBIN, b. at Woodstock, 18 Feb 1775 son of Silas and Anna (Fisk) Corbin; Luther d. at New Woodstock, 5 Aug 1848.

ii KEZIA STOWELL, b. at Pomfret, 4 Feb 1781. Kezia was living in 1798 at the probate of father's estate but no information on her after that.

iii ARTEMESIA STOWELL, b. at Ashford, 7 Nov 1784; d. at New Woodstock, NY, 25 Jan 1853; m. at New Woodstock, 1 Jan 1806, ABIEL AINSWORTH, b. at Woodstock, 10 May 1777 son of Nathan and Phebe (Kinsley) Ainsworth; Abiel d. at New Woodstock, 4 Nov 1866.

iv MARVIN STOWELL, b. at Union, CT, 15 Mar 1789; d. likely at Cazenovia, NY, after 1830; m. at Pomfret, 17 Jan 1813, LUCY HOUGHTON, b. about 1790.[1699]

613) MARY HOLT *(Mary Abbott Holt[4], Paul[3], William[2], George[1])*, b. at Windham, 11 Jul 1752 daughter of Joshua and Mary (Abbott) Holt; d. at Hampton, CT, 23 Oct 1824; m. 7 Nov 1771, JOSEPH FULLER, b. at Ipswich, 28 Nov 1738[1700] son of John and Hannah (Lord) Fuller; Joseph d. 29 Jan 1805.

Joseph Fuller and Mary Holt were parents of seven children born at Hampton.

i MARY "POLLY" FULLER, b. 13 Oct 1772; d. at Middlefield, NY, 29 Oct 1851; m. THOMAS FULLER, b. at Windham, 21 Jul 1765 son of Thomas and Sarah (Griffin) Fuller; Thomas d. at Middlefield, 11 Jul 1837.

ii CHLOE FULLER, b. 11 Dec 1774; d. at Cooperstown, NY, 24 Aug 1854;[1701] m. 21 Nov 1803, TRUMBULL DORRANCE, b. about 1774 son of George and Alice (Trumbull) Dorrance; Trumbull d. at Dalton, MA, 9 Aug 1824.

iii ELIJAH FULLER, b. 21 Apr 1777; d. at Chenango County, NY, 30 Apr 1864; m. 5 Dec 1803, RUTH ROBINSON, b. at Tolland, CT, 10 Jan 1781 daughter of Joshua and Sybil (Webb) Robinson; Ruth d. at Chenango County, 12 Feb 1849.

iv JOSEPH FULLER, b. 6 Jan 1779; m. at Canterbury, Dec 1809, ELIZABETH FISH, b. at Canterbury, 14 Mar 1782 daughter of Darius and Sarah (Howard) Fish.

v ELISHA FULLER, b. 30 Jan 1782; d. at Hampton, 25 May 1837; m. at Hampton, 29 Oct 1805, PHEBE BURNHAM, b. 24 Apr 1788 daughter of Jedediah and Phebe (Martin) Burnham; Phebe, d. 30 Oct 1820.

vi HARVEY FULLER, b. 13 Sep 1784; d. at Hampton, 21 Apr 1860; m. 16 Dec 1810, LYDIA DENISON, b. at Hampton, 20 Jul 1789 daughter of Daniel and Lydia (Clark) Denison; Lydia d. 4 Feb 1838.

vii DANIEL FULLER, b. 14 Feb 1789; d. at Philadelphia, 12 Mar 1856; m. 1821, MARY ANN BIRD, b. at Philadelphia, 1792 daughter of William and Mary (Ross) Bird;[1702] Mary Ann d. at Philadelphia, 23 Dec 1859.

[1696] *Connecticut State Library (Hartford, Connecticut);* Probate Place: *Hartford, Connecticut, Probate Packets, Spencer, Hulda-Thompson, Calvin, 1759-1880*, case 4169, Seth Stowell

[1697] Stowell, *The Stowell Genealogy*, p 107 (This part of the probate record is not available online.)

[1698] Some of the information on the children obtained from Stowell, *The Stowell Genealogy*, pp 107-109

[1699] There is little clear information about Marvin Stowell.

[1700] Fuller, *Genealogy of Descendants of Captain Matthew Fuller*, p 216

[1701] U.S., Newspaper Extractions from the Northeast, 1704-1930; Mrs. C. Dorrance wid of the late Dr. Trumbull Dorrance of Pittsfield, Mass.

[1702] The 1903 SAR application of William A.M. Fuller, grandson of Daniel Fuller gives the names of his grandparents and names the parents of his grandmother Mary Ann Bird and William Bird and Mary Ross.

614) URIAH HOLT *(Mary Abbott Holt4, Paul3, William2, George1)*, b. at Windham, 23 Mar 1754 son of Joshua and Mary (Abbott) Holt; d. at West Springfield, MA, 22 Sep 1828; m. 1st, at Ashford, 11 Nov 1779, MARGARET MASON, b. at Ashford, 13 Aug 1754 daughter of Ebenezer and Mehitable (Holmes) Mason; Margaret d. 1817. Uriah m. 2nd, at West Springfield, 15 Oct 1818, EUNICE CHAPIN (widow of Charles Ferry), b. at Springfield, 22 Feb 1769 daughter of Elisha and Eunice (Jones) Chapin; Eunice d. at West Springfield, 1843.

Uriah and Margaret started their family in Ashford and relocated to West Springfield after the births of their first two children.

The estate of Uriah Holt was probated in 1829.[1703] Rodney Holt was administrator of the estate. The value of the estate was $230.85 and debts against the estate totaled $477.83. Widow Eunice requested relief as the value of the estate was not enough to support her in her infirm condition.

Uriah Holt and Margaret Mason were parents of seven children.

i SALLY HOLT, b. at Ashford, 18 Sep 1780; d. 9 Oct 1848; m. at Northampton, MA, 9 Apr 1803, WILLIAM SHELDON, b. at Northampton, 2 Jun 1768 son of Benjamin and Elizabeth (Hunt) Sheldon.

ii MARY "POLLY" HOLT, b. at Ashford, 2 Mar 1782; d. 1 Jun 1842; m. at West Springfield, 14 Nov 1805, ALPHEUS STEBBINS, b. at Wilbraham, 28 Jul 1780 son of Eldad and Ann (Badger) Stebbins;[1704] Alpheus d. at Wilbraham, 25 Sep 1857.

iii CLARISSA HOLT, b. at West Springfield, 11 Mar 1784; d. 4 Feb 1813. Clarissa did not marry.

iv BETSEY HOLT, b. at West Springfield, 7 May 1786; d. at Kirkland, NY, after 1865; m. 1812, as his second wife, STEPHEN BUSHNELL, b. in Connecticut, 4 Aug 1781;[1705] Stephen d. at Kirkland, 20 Jul 1862. Stephen was first married to Thankful Wilcox.

v RODNEY HOLT, b. at West Springfield, 18 Jun 1788; d. at Springfield, 25 Sep 1862; m. at West Springfield, 18 Apr 1822, CHLOE FOSTER, b. at Barkhamsted, CT, 15 Jan 1799 daughter of Eli and Catherine (Barker) Foster;[1706][1707] Chloe d. at Springfield, 9 Dec 1886.

vi JOHN HOLT, b. at West Springfield, 5 Dec 1792; d. at West Springfield, 21 Aug 1825; m. 16 May 1821, TAMAR LEONARD, b. at West Springfield, 2 Jan 1795 daughter of Rufus and Betsey (Flower) Leonard; Tamar d. at West Springfield, 1825.

vii PERLEY HOLT, b. at West Springfield, 21 Apr 1795; d. at New York, NY, after 1868 (listed in the city directory); m. at Simsbury, CT, 1824,[1708] LYDIA E. OWEN, b. in CT, about 1798 daughter of Isaac and Zerviah (Cornish) Owen;[1709] Lydia d. after 1860. Perley was a tobacco merchant in New York.

615) LEMUEL HOLT *(Mary Abbott Holt4, Paul3, William2, George1)*, b. at Windham, 28 Feb 1756 son of Joshua and Mary (Abbott) Holt; d. at Lyme, NH, 1 Aug 1836; m. 1778, his first cousin, MARY ABBOTT *(Isaac4, Paul3, William2, George1)*, b. at Pomfret, 20 Jan 1757 daughter of Isaac and Mary (Barker) Abbott; Mary d. 8 Sep 1849.

Lemuel Holt and Mary Abbott were parents of seven children.

i LESTER HOLT, b. at Windham, CT, 27 Aug 1779; d. at Lyme, 3 May 1869; m. at Hollis, 14 Feb 1809, LYDIA FRENCH, b. at Bedford, NH, 24 May 1784 daughter of David and Lydia (Parker) French; Lydia d. at Lyme, 5 Jan 1852.

ii DOROTHY "DOLLY" HOLT, b. at Windham, 3 Oct 1781; d. at Lyme, 18 Jun 1861; m. 17 Nov 1808, NATHAN PUSHEE; Nathan, b. at Lunenburg, 5 Aug 1784 son of David and Susanna (Pierce) Pushee; Nathan d. at Lyme, 16 Dec 1810. Dolly m. 2nd, May 1824, FREEMAN JOSSELYN, b. at Pembroke, MA, 25 Aug 1778 son of Joseph and Mercy (Waterman) Josselyn; Freeman d. at Lyme, 15 Dec 1868. Freeman Josselyn was first married to

---

1703 *Probate Records, 1809-1881, Hampden County, Massachusetts;* Author: *Massachusetts. Probate Court (Hampden County);* Probate Place: *Hampden, Massachusetts*. Probate of Uriah Holt, 1829, Case number 5783.

1704 Badger, *Giles Badger and His Descendants*, p 28

1705 Stephen's date of birth is on his gravestone. Findagrave: 69227383

1706 Chloe's parents are given as Eli and Catherine Foster on her death record.

1707 Chapin, *Sketches of the Old Inhabitants of Old Springfield*, p 218

1708 U.S., Newspaper Extractions from the Northeast, 1704-1930

1709 The 1825 will of Isaac Owen in Connecticut includes a bequest to daughter Lydia wife of Perly Holt.

Deborah Turner who died in 1822. When Nathan Pushee died, David Pushee was appointed guardian of Nathan's two daughters, Debby and Dolly.

iii DEBORAH HOLT, b. at Lyme, 3 Oct 1781; d. at Lyme, 4 May 1866. Deborah did not marry.

iv HARVEY HOLT, b. at Hanover, 27 Sep 1785; d. at Lyme, 23 Oct 1842; m. 21 Jun 1819, HANNAH CUMMINGS, b. at Cornish, NH, 4 Jun 1789 daughter of Isaac and Abigail (Kimball) Cummings; Hannah d. at Bradford, VT, 5 Mar 1885.

v ISAAC HOLT, b. at Hanover, 18 Nov 1792; d. at Piermont, NH, 4 Jun 1851; m. 1st, at Thetford, VT, 7 Mar 1822, RACHEL FLETCHER. Isaac m. 2nd, at Corinth, VT, PHEBE PAGE. Isaac m. 3rd, at Orange, VT, 10 Mar 1847, SALLY DINSMOOR.

vi MARY HOLT, b. at Lyme, 22 Oct 1795; d. at Lyme, 9 Aug 1884. Mary did not marry.

vii CHLOE HOLT, b. at Lyme, 30 Nov 1797; d. before 1860; m. 27 Nov 1825, ALBERT BALCH, b. at Lyme, 5 Sep 1802 son of Isaac and Elizabeth (Bell) Balch;[1710] Albert d. at Whitewater, WI, 8 Mar 1879. After Chloe's death, Albert went to Wisconsin and married Alice who has not been identified.

616) KETURAH HOLT *(Mary Abbott Holt⁴, Paul³, William², George¹)*, b. at Windham, 21 Aug 1758 daughter of Joshua and Mary (Abbott) Holt; d. at Randolph, VT, 25 Jul 1839;[1711] m. 29 Jan 1784, JONATHAN AMIDON, b. 7 Feb 1759 son of Henry and Sarah (Doubleday) Amidon; Jonathan d. at Randolph, 15 Apr 1838.

Jonathan Amidon served in the Revolutionary War with enlistments in 1777 and 1779 as a private. His war service included the battle of White Marsh and spending the winter at Valley Forge.[1712]

Jonathan Amidon did not leave a will and his estate entered probate 1 May 1838. J. K. Parish was named administrator at the request of widow Keturah Amidon. The real estate was sold for $566.00 and after the settlement of all the debts, there was $119 to be distributed to the heirs.[1713]

Jonathan Amidon and Keturah Holt were parents of eight children, the first two children born at Willington and the other children at Randolph, Vermont.

i HANNAH AMIDON, b. 28 Oct 1784; d. at Randolph, VT, after 1850; m. SAMUEL BRUCE, b. in Massachusetts, 1770 (census records); Samuel d. at Randolph, after 1850.

ii ELIJAH AMIDON, b. 1 Jul 1786; d. at Bernardston, MA, 7 Nov 1863; m. at Randolph, VT, 19 Oct 1809, REBECCA AVERILL, b. about 1793 daughter of Samuel and Molly (Barnes) Averill;[1714] Rebecca D. at Monson, MA, 30 Nov 1870.

iii ALFRED AUGUSTUS AMIDON, b. 16 May 1789; d. at Onondaga County, NY, 8 Dec 1817; m. at Barnard, VT, 1 Dec 1815, BERTHA STEVENS, b. at Barnard, about 1792 daughter of Andrew and Sarah (Clark) Stevens;[1715] Bertha d. at Barnard, 19 Apr 1837.

iv JACOB AMIDON, b. 26 Sep 1791; d. at Northfield, VT, 5 May 1866; m. 1st, 22 Apr 1816, MERCY COLE WHITTEN, b. at Cornish, NH, 31 Mar 1794 daughter of Samuel and Rebecca (-) Whitten; Mercy d. at Northfield, 9 Oct 1833. Jacob m. 2nd, 4 Dec 1834, ARMENIA RICHMOND, b. at Barnard, 4 Apr 1807 daughter of Paul and Fanny (Udall) Richmond;[1716] Armenia d. at Northfield, 22 Oct 1887.

v DYER AMIDON, b. 7 Mar 1794; d. at Richfield, MI, 26 Aug 1853; m. at Brookfield, VT, 23 Aug 1814, SABRA M. SMITH, b. 1795 daughter of Shubal and Mary (Parish) Smith; Sabra d. at Richfield, 9 Jul 1872.

vi MARY AMIDON, b. 18 Aug 1796; d. at Randolph, 18 Sep 1819.

vii SARAH AMIDON, b. about 1800; d. at Brookfield, VT, 31 Mar 1873; m. 2 Dec 1820, her second cousin, WALTER ABBOTT *(Benjamin⁵, Benjamin⁴, Paul³, William², George¹)*, b. at Brookfield, 10 Jul 1796 son of Benjamin and Lucy (Flint) Abbott; Walter d. at Brookfield, 2 Jan 1879. Walter is a child in Family 611.

viii LUCINDA AMIDON, b. 1804; d. at Moretown, VT, 3 Nov 1883; m. SOLOMON TUBBS, b. about 1800 son of Ananias Tubbs; Solomon d. at Northfield, 14 Mar 1865.

1710 Balch, *Genealogy of the Balch Families*, p 138

1711 Ancestry.com, *Vermont, Vital Records, 1720-1908* (Provo, UT, USA: Ancestry.com Operations, Inc., 2013).

1712 Best, *Amidon Family*, p 27

1713 *Vermont. Probate Court (Randolph District)*; Probate Place: *Orange, Vermont, Folder 45, Abbott, Benjamin-Brown, Enoch, 1832-1841*, probate of Jonathan Amidon, 1 May 1838

1714 Avery, *The Averell Family*, p 301

1715 The 1839 will of Andrew Stevens of Barnard includes bequests to grandson Alfred Amidon and granddaughter Harriet Rand.

1716 Richmond, *The Richmond Family*, p 150

617) SARAH HOLT *(Mary Abbott Holt^4, Paul^3, William^2, George^1)*, b. at Windham, 26 Oct 1761 daughter of Joshua and Mary (Abbott) Holt; d. at Stockbridge, VT, 19 Feb 1813; m. 1783, JOHN DURKEE, b. at Windham, 2 Jul 1762 son of Joseph and Elizabeth (Fiske) Durkee; John d. at Stockbridge, 2 May 1838. After Sarah's death, John married second Polly Webber and third Jemima Strong.

John Durkee served in the Revolution from Connecticut in Captain Robbins's company. John and his brother Ebe Durkee served in the same company. His widow Jemima was granted 160 acres of bounty land related to this service.[1717]

In his will written 14 March 1838 (probate 4 July 1838), John Durkee bequeathed to beloved wife Jemima one hundred eighty-five dollars payable in one cow and in household furniture she brought to the marriage. Jemima also receives the use of one-half of the farm and buildings in Stockbridge while she is a widow. Eunice Durkee widow of son John Durkee receives five dollars in addition to what John received during his life. Son Oren Durkee receives five dollars in addition to what he has received. Daughters Sally Morgain, Polly Bloss, and Elisa Whitcomb each receive five dollars. Harriet Durkee daughter of Harvy Durkee receives five dollars in addition to what her father received from the estate. Youngest son Fisk Durkee receives one-half of the farm and will receive the whole farm after the decease of Jemima. Justin Morgain was named sole executor.[1718]

Sarah Holt and John Durkee were parents of seven children born at Stockbridge, Vermont.

i JOHN DURKEE, b. 20 Nov 1784; d. at Stockbridge, 17 Aug 1836; m. about 1807, EUNICE RANNEY, b. at Chester, VT, 12 Dec 1784 daughter of Daniel and Eunice (Gile) Ranney; Eunice d. at Elk Grove, IL, after 1850.

ii OREN DURKEE, b. 5 Nov 1786; d. at Stockbridge, 14 Oct 1862; m. at Bethel, VT, 7 Oct 1813, PHILENA RICH, b. at Bethel, 1 Apr 1791 daughter of Justus and Mary (Tufts) Rich; Philena d. 8 Mar 1849.

iii SALLY DURKEE, b. Jun 1789; d. at Stockbridge, 18 Apr 1879; m. at Rochester, VT, 25 Mar 1814, JUSTIN MORGAN, b. at West Springfield, MA, 15 Mar 1786 son of Justin and Mary (Day) Morgan; Justin d. at Stockbridge, 4 May 1853.

iv MARY DURKEE, b. 29 Mar 1791; d. at Middlesex, VT, 28 Mar 1873; m. 1811, BENJAMIN BLOSS, b. likely at Killingly, 19 Nov 1784 son of Richard and Sarah (Barrett) Bloss;[1719] Benjamin d. 23 Sep 1862.

v ELIZABETH DURKEE, b. 26 Jun 1794; d. at Claridon, OH, 21 Oct 1872; m. 1st, at Stockbridge, VT, 17 Mar 1836, JAMES WHITCOMB, b. at Hardwick, MA, 1781 son of Lot and Lydia (Nye) Whitcomb; James d. at Burton, OH, 10 Nov 1844. Elizabeth m. 2nd, about 1848, NERI WRIGHT, b. at Westminster, VT, 1 Nov 1785 son of Medad and Mary (Willard) Wright; Meri d. at Claridon, 28 Nov 1864.

vi HARVEY DURKEE, b. 21 Dec 1797; d. at Pittsfield, 28 Nov 1826; m. 22 May 1825, HARRIET GAY, b. 1804; Harriet d. at Pittsfield, 3 Dec 1835. After Harvey's death, Harriet m. Horace Rice.

vii FISK DURKEE, b. 7 May 1803; d. at Stockbridge, 13 Feb 1885; m. 20 May 1841, ABBY S. EVERETT, b. at Stockbridge, about 1820 daughter of Ebenezer and Lucy (Kinch) Everett; Abby d. at Stockbridge, 20 Feb 1896.

618) HANNAH HOLT *(Mary Abbott Holt^4, Paul^3, William^2, George^1)*, b. at Windham, 24 May 1764 daughter of Joshua and Mary (Abbott) Holt; d. in Vermont, 7 Aug 1855; m. at Clarendon, VT, 21 Jan 1788, AARON CARPENTER, b. at Rehoboth, 9 May 1763 son of Jabez and Abigail (Dyer) Carpenter; Aaron d. at Milton, 26 Sep 1836.[1720]

In his will written 4 June 1836, Aaron Carpenter bequeathed to beloved wife Hannah the rents and profits on one-third part of the real estate during her life. She also has use of specified rooms in the house and cooking privileges. Daughters Patty Dorance, Hannah Brigham, and Dorcas Meers and son Harvey Carpenter receive one hundred dollars each. Daughter Sally Collins receives sixty dollars (as she already received forty) and daughters Polly Carpenter and Abigail Carpenter each receive one hundred dollars. Fifty dollars of each legacy is to be paid in cattle and a schedule is set out for the payments. Polly and Abigail will continue to have a room in the house. Son Alfred Carpenter receives the remainder of the estate and is responsible to pay the legacies. Alfred is named executor. Real estate, a 234-acre home farm, was valued at $3,252.50 and personal estate and personal estate at $798.59. Claims against the estate were $121.33.[1721]

Aaron Carpenter and Hannah Holt were parents of eight children born at Milton, Vermont.

[1717] Revolutionary War Pension and Bounty-Land Warrant Application Files

[1718] *Vermont. Probate Court (Hartford District)*; Probate Place: *Windsor, Vermont, Probate Records, Vol 12-13 1835-1840*, vol 13, pp 85-86

[1719] Lovejoy, *History of Royalton*, p 690

[1720] Ancestry.com, Vermont, Vital Records, 1720-1908

[1721] *Vermont. Probate Court (Chittenden District)*; Probate Place: *Chittenden, Vermont, Estate Files, Box 9, Files #914-941, 1813-1841*

i PATTIE CARPENTER, b. 5 Nov 1788; d. at Irasburg, VT, 4 Mar 1864; m. ELISHA DORRANCE, b. about 1775; Elisha d. at Colchester, 10 Dec 1846.

ii SALLY CARPENTER, b. 21 Apr 1793; d. at Craftsbury, VT, 1885; m. about 1814, NATHAN COLLINS, b. at Ira, VT, 17 May 1792 son of Nathan and Keziah (Carpenter) Collins; Nathan d. at Craftsbury, 23 Jan 1887.

iii POLLY CARPENTER, b. 5 Mar 1797; d. at Milton, 12 May 1863. Polly did not marry. In 1850, she was living with her sister Abigail.

iv HANNAH CARPENTER, b. 1 May 1799; d. at Monroe, OH, 3 Aug 1859; m. 1st, about 1829, HIRAM BRIGHAM, b. at Milton, Nov 1800 son of Leonard and Abigail (Forbush) Brigham; Hiram d. at Croton, OH, 1838. Hannah m. 2nd, at Licking, OH, 6 May 1841, ALLEN WILLIAMS, b. in NJ, about 1803; Allen d. at Robinson, IL, after 1880. Allen was first married to Elizabeth Stadden in 1825 and third married to Emeline.

v ALFRED CARPENTER, b. 6 Jun 1801; d. at Milton, 29 Mar 1863; m. 1st, 19 Oct 1835, MARY EASTMAN, b. at Westford, VT, 12 Oct 1806 daughter of Caleb and Dorcas (Faxon) Eastman; Mary d. at Milton, 14 Sep 1841. Alfred m. 2nd, 20 Apr 1842, HANNAH FULLINGTON, b. 19 Aug 1802 daughter of Ephraim and Hannah (Patten) Fullington; Hannah d. at Milton, 24 Sep 1866.

vi HARVEY CARPENTER, b. 6 Feb 1804; d. at Hartford, OH, 31 Aug 1856; m. about 1828, ALTHEA THOMAS, b. at Colchester, VT, 9 Jan 1810; Althea d. at Hartford, OH, 1891. Althea married second David Weaver.

vii ABIGAIL CARPENTER, b. 29 Jul 1807; d. at Milton, 4 Oct 1866; m. about 1838, WARREN HOLMES, b. at Westford, VT, 1810 son of Manley and Sarah (Howe) Holmes; Warren d. at Westford, 31 Mar 1884. Warren second married Anna Eliza Tucker about 1867.

viii DORCAS CARPENTER, b. about 1810; d. at Willis, KS, 1 Jan 1892; m. about 1835, TIMOTHY VILLERY MEARS, b. at Milton, 10 Feb 1812 son of Stephen and Hannah (Crittenden) Mears; Timothy d. at Willis, 5 Jan 1892.

619) DORCAS HOLT *(Mary Abbott Holt⁴, Paul³, William², George¹)*, b. at Windham, 30 Mar 1767 daughter of Joshua and Mary (Abbott) Holt; d. at Middlebury, VT, 1 Jul 1800; m. as his second wife, JOSIAH FULLER, b. 30 Oct 1764 son of David and Hannah (Fuller) Fuller; Josiah d. Potsdam, NY, 4 Dec 1835. Josiah was first married to Deliverance and third married to Olivia Moore.

Dorcas and Josiah had two children one of whom died in childhood and no further information on the second child.

i LUDOPHICUS FULLER, b. about 1797; d. at Middlebury, 11 Aug 1802.

ii MERTIA FULLER, b. at Middlebury, 4 Jul 1799; nothing further known.

620) PETER INGALLS *(Sarah Abbott Ingalls⁴, Paul³, William², George¹)*, b. at Pomfret, 12 Feb 1752 son of Joseph and Sarah (Abbott) Ingalls; d. at Pomfret, 11 Jun 1808; m. 20 Apr 1775, SARAH ASHLEY, b. at Windham, 2 Nov 1752 daughter of Joseph and Sarah (Cressy) Ashley, Sarah d. at Pomfret, 18 Nov 1811.

Peter Ingalls was a farmer in Hampton.

Peter Ingalls did not leave a will and his estate entered probate 29 Jun 1808 with Sarah Ingalls as administratrix. Personal estate was valued as $1,681.31. Real estate included the Hampton homestead of 100 acres valued at $3,333 and other smaller lots with a value of $1,553. There were ten children listed as heirs in the probate documents: sons Asa, Joseph R., Elisha, Marvin, and Chester and daughters Sally, Clarissa, heirs of Olive, Chloe, and Pamelia. In the final distribution of 17 April 1812, daughters are named Sally Childs, Clarissa Sharpe, heirs of Olive (who are not named), Chloe Ingals, and Pamelia Ingals.[1722]

Peter Ingalls and Sarah Ashley were parents of ten children, the oldest two recorded at Windham and the youngest seven children at Pomfret.

i ASA INGALLS, b. 30 Apr 1776; d. at Pomfret, 5 May 1846; m. 1st, about 1797, EDE ELLIOT, b. 11 Nov 1779 daughter of William Sibbel (Hibbard) Elliot; Ede d. at Williston, VT, 26 Jan 1834. Asa m. 2nd, at Pomfret, 17 May 1838, the widow MERCY CRAIN (widow of John Crain), b. about 1785; Mercy d. at Pomfret, 8 Jan 1850.

ii SARAH INGALLS, b. 15 Dec 1777; d. at Woodstock, 7 Nov 1836; m. at Pomfret, 18 Sep 1796, EPAPHRAS CHILD, b. at West Woodstock, 1 Sep 1767 son of Shubael and Abigail (Bowen) Child; Epaphras d. 29 Jan 1845.

[1722] *Connecticut State Library (Hartford, Connecticut)*; Probate Place: *Hartford, Connecticut, Probate Packets, Humphrey, M-Johnson, H, 1752-1880*, Case 2288, probate of Peter Ingals

iii CLARISSA INGALLS, b. about 1779; d. at Abington, 25 Jul 1844; m. at Pomfret, 6 Jun 1802, OLIVER SHARPE, b. at Pomfret, 15 Sep 1765 son of John and Lucy (Warren) Sharpe; Oliver d. at Pomfret, 14 Oct 1834.

iv OLIVE INGALLS, b. 12 Nov 1781; d. at West Winfield, NY, 6 Mar 1806; m. at Pomfret, 7 Oct 1798, ELIJAH HOLMES, b. at Pomfret, 19 Oct 1777 son of Jonathan and Eunice (Rickard) Holmes; Elijah d. at Herkimer, 1855 (probate 2 Nov 1855).

v JOSEPH ROYAL INGALLS, b. 28 Sep 1783; d. at Pomfret, 30 Mar 1819; m. at Pomfret, 26 Nov 1807, LYDIA SPAULDING, b. at Windham, 8 Oct 1783 daughter of James and Hannah (Neff) Spaulding.

vi ELISHA INGALLS, b. 31 Dec 1785; d. at Hampton, 10 Oct 1823; m. at Pomfret, 9 Feb 1814, ESTHER PALMER, b. at Windham, 8 Aug 1783 daughter of Joseph and Abigail (Lasel) Palmer; Esther d. 20 Aug 1852. After Elisha's death, Esther married Thomas Barrows.

vii MARVIN INGALLS, b. 6 Nov 1787; d. at Hampton, 28 Jan 1847; m. 1st, 12 Dec 1811, AMELIA SPAULDING, b. 8 Sep 1789 daughter of James and Hannah (Neff) Spaulding; Amelia d. at Hampton, 15 Sep 1831. Marvin m. 2nd, 16 Sep 1833, his second cousin, OLIVE ABBOTT *(Asa5, Benjamin4, Paul3, William2, George1)*, b. at Hampton, 28 Mar 1790 daughter of Asa and Sarah (Bidlack) Abbott; Olive d. about 1843. Marvin m. 3rd, at Chaplin, CT, 19 May 1844, MARIETTA BURNHAM. Olive Abbott is a child in Family 607.

viii CHLOE INGALLS, b. 29 Oct 1789. She was living in 1812 when her father's estate was settled. Otherwise, there is no clear information.

ix CHESTER INGALLS, b. 27 Dec 1791; d. at Woodstock, 29 Oct 1870; m. at Woodstock, 13 May 1818, PERSIS JOHNSON, b. at Woodstock, 30 Jul 1796 daughter of Stephen and Persis (Bugbee) Johnson; Persis d. at Woodstock, 24 Apr 1876.

x PAMELIA INGALLS, b. 14 Aug 1793; d. at Pomfret, 16 Jan 1824; m. at Hampton, 20 Mar 1816, BENJAMIN SPAULDING, b. at Windham, 8 Aug 1786 son of James and Hannah (Neff) Spaulding; Benjamin d. at Pomfret, Jul 1847. After Pamelia's death, Benjamin married Pamelia Carter.

621) DARIUS INGALLS *(Sarah Abbott Ingalls4, Paul3, William2, George1)*, b. at Pomfret, 27 Jun 1754 son of Joseph and Sarah (Abbott) Ingalls; d. at Swanton, VT, 1824; m. Mar 1796, LODEMA LEE, b. at Killingly, 3 Nov 1757 daughter of Seth and Molly (Conant) Lee.

Darius and Lodema were married in Connecticut where their first child was born and then relocated to Vermont first in Wilmington and then in Swanton. Few details have been pinned down for the children but there seem to be nine children in this family.[1723]

i PARKER INGALLS, b. about 1777; m. at Fairfax, VT, 30 Mar 1808, MARY HOLMES. Parker Ingalls was at the Battle of Plattsburgh during the War of 1812.[1724] He does seem to be living in Hayfield, PA in 1850 (where one of his sons also settled) and in 1850 he is with a wife Phebe.

ii DELIVERANCE INGALLS, b. at Wilmington, VT, 22 Apr 1779; d. at Greensburg, IN, after 1850; m. at Fairfax, VT, 24 Feb 1800, ERASTUS LATHROP, b. Aug 1776; Erastus d. at Greensburg, 22 Oct 1821.

iii MARY "POLLY" INGALLS, b. at Wilmington, 28 Jun 1782; d. at South Wayne, WI, 11 Oct 1860; m. about 1800, AMOS EASTMAN, b. 1778 son of William and Joanna (Miller) Eastman; Amos d. 1835.

iv SARAH "SALLY" INGALLS, b. at Wilmington, 23 May 1784

v HARVEY INGALLS, b. about 1786; d. at Swanton, VT, 25 Nov 1832; m. JUNIA WARNER, b. about 1791 daughter of John and Joanna (Ames) Warner.

vi ALVIN INGALLS, b. about 1788

vii ANNA INGALLS, b. 1790; d. 1862; m. about 1807, TRUMAN WARNER, b. about 1778 son of John and Joanna (Ames) Warner; Truman d. 1822. Truman was first married to Polly Caulkins who died in 1806.

1723 The names of nine children are given in the Abbot genealogy and there are records for some of these children, but not all of them. The Ingalls genealogy also lists nine children providing just their names.

1724 Aldrich, *History of Franklin and Grand Isle Counties*, p 478

viii LODERMA INGALLS, b. about 1795

ix DARIUS INGALLS, b. about 1797

622) LUTHER INGALLS *(Sarah Abbott Ingalls⁴, Paul³, William², George¹)*, b. at Pomfret, 24 Aug 1758 son of Joseph and Sarah (Abbott) Ingalls; d. at Hanover, NH, 4 Jul 1855; m. 23 Jun 1781, LUCY UTLEY, born about 1760; Lucy d. at Hanover, 7 Jan 1831.

Luther and Lucy were parents of eight children born at Hanover, New Hampshire.

i ROYAL INGALLS, b. 26 Mar 1783; d. 11 Oct 1793.

ii SYLVESTER INGALLS, b. 25 Apr 1785; d. at Hanover, 7 Nov 1846; m. at Hanover, 8 Jun 1814, MARY TURNER, b. at Hartland, VT, about 1787 daughter of Adam and Betsy (Lull) Turner; Mary d. at Hanover, 14 Mar 1866.

iii LUCY INGALLS, b. 30 May 1787; d. 3 Jan 1805.

iv SARAH INGALLS, b. 27 Aug 1789; d. at Manchester, NH, 11 Jun 1882; m. at Hanover, 9 Jun 1814, TIMOTHY OWEN, b. at Hanover, 13 Aug 1789 son of Timothy and Lydia (Perry) Owen; Timothy d. at Hanover, 17 Jun 1845.

v ELIZABETH WILLIAMS INGALLS, b. 26 Oct 1794; d. at Hanover, 21 Mar 1883; m. 18 Apr 826, REUL DURKEE, b. at Newport, NH, 11 May 1791 son of Moses Durkee; Ruel d. at Hanover, 1870.

vi MARY "POLLY" INGALLS, b. 8 Apr 1797; d. at Hanover, 9 Mar 1880; m. 19 Feb 1817, SILAS TINNEY VAUGHN, b. at Randolph, VT, 28 Aug 1797 son of Jabez and Violette (Woodward) Vaughn; Silas d. at DeKalb, IL, 20 Apr 1862.

vii LUTHER INGALLS, b. 5 May 1799; d. at Hanover, 21 Feb 1844; m. at Lebanon, NH, 10 Aug 1832, MARY ANN FERRIN, b. about 1808; Mary Ann d. at Hanover, 22 Jul 1840.

viii GEORGE INGALLS, b. 20 May 1805; d. at Hanover, 2 Jan 1843. George does not seem to have married.

623) CALVIN INGALLS *(Sarah Abbott Ingalls⁴, Paul³, William², George¹)*, b. at Pomfret, 22 Nov 1760 son of Joseph and Sarah (Abbott) Ingalls; d. at Stafford, Oct 1830; m. 1st, 28 Nov 1782, CATHERINE TERRINGTON; Catherine d. 31 Dec 1783. Calvin m. 2nd, 28 May 1795, MARY HORTON, b. at Union, 1 Oct 1759 daughter of Ezra and Mary (Hempstead) Horton; Mary d. at Stafford, 12 May 1833.

Reverend Calvin Ingalls graduated Dartmouth College in 1792.[1725] He was minister at West Stafford from 1796 to March 1803.[1726] For a time, he was a home missionary in New York.[1727]

The estate of Calvin Ingalls entered probate 5 November 1830. He did not leave a will and Nathan Bartlett was named administrator. The personal estate was valued at $173.47 which included a library valued at $40. There was a distribution of household furniture to widow Mary Ingalls.[1728]

Calvin Ingalls and Catherine Terrington had one child.

i SYLVESTER INGALLS, b. at Pomfret, 13 Nov 1783; d. 18 Nov 1783.

Calvin Ingalls and Mary Horton had two children.

i CATHERINE INGALLS, b. at Union, 12 Jun 1796; d. at Stafford, 25 Sep 1830;[1729] m. 1 Dec 1815, WILLIAM THOMPSON, b. 1785 (based on age at time of death); d. at Stafford, 27 Sep 1823. William's estate entered probate 17 Nov 1823.

ii POLLY INGALLS, b. at West Stafford, 11 Jun 1800; d. at South Hadley, MA, 7 Jul 1879; m. 17 May 1824, MILO KNIGHT, b. at Monson, 1801 son of Asher and Mary (Clark) Knight; Milo d. at South Hadley, 17 Mar 1881.

624) CHESTER INGALLS *(Sarah Abbott Ingalls⁴, Paul³, William², George¹)*, b. at Pomfret, 7 Aug 1762 son of Joseph and Sarah (Abbott) Ingalls; d. at Hanover, NH, 27 May 1842; m. 4 Apr 1784, SYLVIA STEVENS, b. 25 Mar 1763 daughter of Robert and Mary (Hathaway) Stevens.

[1725] *General Catalog of Dartmouth College*, 1769-1900, p 125

[1726] Hammond, *History of Union, Conn.*, p 376

[1727] Burleigh, *Genealogy and History of the Ingalls Family*, p 58

[1728] *Connecticut State Library (Hartford, Connecticut)*; Probate Place: *Hartford, Connecticut, Probate Packets, Hunt, P-Jennings, Benjamin, 1759-1880*, probate of Calvin Ingals

[1729] *Connecticut, Hale Collection of Cemetery Inscriptions and Newspaper Notices, 1629-1934*, Connecticut State Library; Hartford, Connecticut.

Chester and Sylvia started their family in Pomfret, were in Waitsfield, Vermont for a time, and were finally in Hanover, New Hampshire. Chester had a tavern and dancing hall in Hanover.[1730]

Chester and Sylvia were parents of four children.

i MARY INGALLS, b. at Pomfret, 27 Aug 1785

ii PERMELIA INGALLS, b. 12 Oct 1789; d. at Riceville, IA, 2 Jul 1863; m. at Hanover, 15 Dec 1810, ABIJAH CUTTING, b. at Paxton, MA, 11 Oct 1787 son of Zebulon and Abigail (Bemis) Cutting; Abijah d. at Riceville, Dec 1864.

iii ELIZABETH INGALLS, b. 1791; d. at Hanover, NH, after 1860; m. at Hanover, 25 Dec 1808, JABEZ AVERY DOUGLASS, b. 9 May 1779 son of Hezekiah and Esther (Witter) Douglass; Jabez d. at Hanover, 2 Oct 1860.

iv CHESTER INGALLS, b. about 1795

625) SARAH INGALLS *(Sarah Abbott Ingalls⁴, Paul³, William², George¹)*, b. at Pomfret, 18 Dec 1766 daughter of Joseph and Sarah (Abbott) Ingalls; d. at Jericho, VT, 24 Apr 1833;[1731] m. 22 Jan 1788, ABRAHAM FORD, b. 15 May 1764 son of Abraham and Abigail (Woodward) Ford; Abraham d. 9 Apr 1813 while on a trip to Lebanon, CT.

Abraham (whose name is sometimes given as Abram but Abraham in the probate and on his gravestone) and Sarah Ingalls started their family in Pomfret, but relocated to Jericho, Vermont about 1803. Abraham and his sons were practitioners of skilled trades such as carpentry and blacksmithing. Their son Milton was a successful carpenter and builder in Jericho, and he built many of the homes in that community.[1732]

Abraham died in 1813 while on a trip to Lebanon, Connecticut. He did not leave a will and his estate entered probate in 1813.[1733] One-half of the dwelling house and a tract of land was set off to the widow Sarah Ford. The appraised value of this set-off was $173 or one-third of the value of the real property of the estate. After all the debts were paid, the personal estate was valued at $195. One-third part, or $65 of value, went to widow Sarah Ford. The remainder was distributed among the nine living children. Son Milton agreed to not take his share. Sons Warren and Harvey received double shares of $26. The other children each received $13: Sally, Althea, Chloe, Sophia, Lovina, and Amanda.

Abraham and Sarah Ford had eleven children. There are birth records for the oldest six children in Connecticut (although the records for five children were apparently damaged, and the Barbour collection indicates the father's name could not be read and was guessed as Alvin). The other children are known through their mention in the distribution of Abraham's estate and through each of their death records that list the names of parents.

i SOPHIA FORD, b. at Hampton, 17 Dec 1788; d. at Jericho, VT, 1806.

ii ALVIN FORD, b. at Pomfret, 8 Dec 1790; d. at Jericho, 1808.

iii WARREN FORD, b. at Pomfret, 2 Aug 1792; d. at Colchester, VT, 30 Nov 1866; m. SALLY FRENCH, b. about 1797 daughter of Samuel and Sarah (Gates) French;[1734] Sally d. 31 May 1858.

iv MILTON FORD, b. at Pomfret, 10 Apr 1794; d. at Jericho, 18 Feb 1875; m. 1st, at Essex, VT, 13 Dec 1820, AMANDA BLISS, b. at Essex, 13 Nov 1797 daughter of Amos and Hannah (Clark) Bliss;[1735] Amanda d. at Jericho, 4 Nov 1833. Milton m. 2nd, about 1835, his first cousin once removed, MARIA S. INGALLS *(Asa Ingalls⁶, Peter Ingalls⁵, Sarah Abbott Ingalls⁴, Paul³, William², George¹)*, b. in Vermont about 1810 daughter of Asa and Ede (Elliott) Ingalls;[1736] Maria d. at Jericho, 25 Oct 1880.

v SALLY FORD, b. at Pomfret, 11 Jan 1796; d. at Jericho, 31 Mar 1885; m. 1st, about 1820, WILLIAM CHURCH, b, in Vermont about 1790 likely the son of Asa and Juliette (Humphrey) Church; William d. 22 Oct 1833. Sally m. 2nd, 5 Jan 1836, ELISHA SEABURY, b. in Connecticut, 26 Jul 1785 son of Benjamin and Lucretia (Kingsbury) Seabury;[1737] Elisha d. 29 Oct 1866.

[1730] Lord, *A History of the Town of Hanover, N.H.*, p 44

[1731] *Vermont, Vital Records, 1720-1908.*

[1732] Hayden, Stevens, Wilbur, and Barnum, *History of Jericho Vermont*, p 469

[1733] Vermont, Wills and Probate Records, 1749-1999, Probate Place: Chittenden, Vermont, Case Number 326, Estate of Abraham Ford.

[1734] Father's name is given on her death record. Vermont, Vital Records, 1720-1908

[1735] Bliss, *Genealogy of the Bliss Family*

[1736] The names of her parents on her death record are given as Asa and Ida.

[1737] Parents' names on death record are given as Benjamin Seabury and Lucretia Seabury.

vi ALTHEA FORD, b. at Pomfret, 4 Jan 1798; d. at Jericho, 29 Mar 1821. Althea did not marry.

vii HARVEY FORD, b. perhaps at Pomfret about 1802; d. at Jericho, 3 Feb 1876; m. CLARISSA EATON, b. about 1803 (records give birth as either Vermont or Canada) daughter of Samuel and Sarah(-) Eaton; Clarissa d. at Jericho, 8 Feb 1871.

viii CHLOE FORD, b. 1804; d. at Jericho, 26 Oct 1875; m. JOHN T. CLAPP, b. at Hinesburg, VT, 1797 and d. 10 May 1885 at the home of his son Simeon in New York.[1738]

ix SOPHIA FORD, b. about 1806 at Jericho; d. at Jericho, 5 Jun 1818.

x LOVINA FORD, b. at Jericho, 1808; d. at Jericho, 7 Jun 1852; m. at Jericho, 20 Aug 1837, EZRA CHAMBERLAIN, b. at Jericho about 1812 son of Ezra and Lydia (-) Chamberlain; Ezra d. 5 Dec 1857.

xi AMANDA FORD, b. at Jericho, 1811; d. at Jericho, 21 Sep 1851; m. 1832, HARRISON WEBSTER, b. at Chester, NH, 27 Dec 1810 son of Henry and Rebecca (Farrell) Webster; Harrison d, at Essex, VT, 18 Oct 1870. After Amanda's death, Harrison married Eleanor A. Smith.

626) HANNAH INGALLS *(Sarah Abbott Ingalls⁴, Paul³, William², George¹)*, b. at Pomfret, 22 Aug 1769 daughter of Joseph and Sarah (Abbott) Ingalls; d. at Westford, VT, about 1813; m. at Thompson, CT, 25 Jan 1791, JOSIAH INGERSOLL, baptized at Willington, CT, 1 Oct 1764 son of Richard and Zipporah (Smith) Ingersoll;[1739] Josiah d. at Plainfield, IL, 7 Feb 1853. Josiah second married Betsey Warden.

Hannah and Josiah started in Thompson, Connecticut, were in Hardwick, Massachusetts for a time, and then in Westford, Vermont. After Hannah's death, Josiah remarried and settled in Illinois.

A Genealogy of the Ingersoll Family reports seven children in this family. The Abbot genealogical register states there were ten children (names not given) and that five of the children died in a six-week period thought to around the same time that mother Hannah died. In addition to the seven children named in the Ingersoll genealogy, there are records for two other children born at Thompson, Connecticut prior to the move of the family to Vermont. The seven children named in the Ingersoll genealogy and the two children born at Thompson are given here.

i PERMELIA INGERSOLL, b. at Thompson, CT, 22 Feb 1792; d. at Wheatland, IL, after 1850; m. by 1817, CLARK TRACY COLEGROVE, b. at Fairfax, VT, 1793 son of Nathan and Olive (Tracy) Colegrove;[1740] Clark d. at Wheatland, about 1852.

ii CLARACY INGERSOLL, b. 14 Aug 1793; nothing further known.

iii CHESTER INGERSOLL, b. about 1794; d. at Maryville, CA, 2 Sep 1849; m. 1st, about 1820, MARY BURDICK, b. about 1794 daughter of Samuel and Elizabeth (Northrup) Burdick;[1741] Mary d. at Will County, IL, 1831. Chester m. 2nd, at Cook County, IL, 17 Dec 1833, PHEBE WEAVER, b. in NY, about 1810 daughter of Benjamin and Phebe (Paddock) Weaver; Phebe d. at Joliet, IL, 4 Aug 1879. Phebe married second Benjamin Russell 11 Jul 1850.

iv TIMOTHY INGERSOLL, b. perhaps 1795; nothing further known.

v AMELIA INGERSOLL, b. perhaps 1797; nothing further known.

vi SOPHIA INGERSOLL, b. about 1798; d. at Denver, MO, 1888; m. at Jericho, VT, Oct 1816, JAMES HARVEY MAXFIELD, b. at Fairfax, VT, 1798 son of William and Abigail (Belcher) Maxfield; James d. at Taylor County, IA, Jun 1875.

vii HARLEY INGERSOLL, b. at Jericho, VT, about 1802; d. at Galesburg, IL, 4 Feb 1882; m. at Essex, VT, 30 Jan 1825, SUSAN WEED, b. at Essex, VT, 15 Jan 1806 likely the daughter of Joseph and Lydia (Aldrich) Weed; Susan d. at Galesburg, 1885.

viii MELINDA INGERSOLL, b. 1804; m. 8 Oct 1827, SILAS PARKER, b. about 1795; Silas d. at Westford, VT, 1838.

ix SUSAN INGERSOLL, b. about 1808; nothing further known. She may have been born later and be a child with the second wife.

1738 Hayden, Stevens, Wilbur, and Barnum, *History of Jericho Vermont*, p 441

1739 Avery, *A Genealogy of the Ingersoll Family in America*, p 47

1740 Colegrove, *History and Genealogy of the Colegrove Family*, p 126

1741 Burdick Family Association, www.burdickfamily.org

627) HARVEY INGALLS *(Sarah Abbott Ingalls⁴, Paul³, William², George¹)*, b. at Pomfret, 7 Jul 1775 son of Joseph and Sarah (Abbott) Ingalls; d. 20 Dec 1833[1742] at Brookfield, VT; m. ELLA FORD, b. at Windham, 6 Apr 1775 daughter of Abraham and Abigail (Woodward) Ford; Ella d. at Brookfield, 1857.

Harvey Ingalls was admitted as freeman in Brookfield, Vermont in 1803.[1743]

Harvey Ingalls did not leave a will and his estate entered probate 30 January 1834. Widow Ella Ingalls declined administration and Waldo W. Ingalls assumed this duty. The real estate was valued at $1500 including 77 acres and buildings. The personal estate including stock animals was valued at $844.35.[1744]

Harvey Ingalls and Ella Ford were parents of four children all born at Brookfield.

i WALDO WOODWARD INGALLS, b. 30 Jan 1799; d. at Rockford, IL, after 1860; m. at Barre, VT, 30 Dec 1823, MINERVA WEBB, b. at Barre, 1802; Minerva d. in Cook County, IL, 22 May 1878.[1745]

ii CLARISSA INGALLS, b. 9 Oct 1802; d. at Brookfield, 29 Oct 1848; m. at Brookfield, 28 Jul 1822, ZEBINA WALCOTT, b. about 1796 son of Eliphalet and Anna (Coburn) Walcott; Zebina d. at Shields, WI, 20 Apr 1876.

iii SALLY INGALLS, b. 25 Aug 1804; nothing further known.

iv AMANDA INGALLS, b. 9 Nov 1808; d. at Brookfield, 14 Apr 1841; m. at Brookfield, 18 Oct 1828, WALTER M. WILSON, b. 1802 son of James and Amy (-) Wilson; Walter d. at Roxbury, VT, 27 May 1873. After Amanda's death, Walter married second Anna Gold and third Amanda Thompson.

628) HANNAH ABBOTT *(Isaac⁴, Paul³, William², George¹)*, b. at Pomfret, 2 Aug 1758 daughter of Isaac and Mary (Barker) Abbott; d. at Stoddard, NH, 9 Mar 1847; m. at Amherst, NH, 25 May 1781, ISRAEL TOWNE, b. at Stoddard, NH, 17 Jun 1761 son of Israel and Lydia (Hopkins) Towne; Israel d. 2 May 1848.

Hannah and Israel Towne resided in Stoddard. Israel served as the town clerk in 1785 and 1789 and served as selectman five of the years from 1783 through 1790.

Hannah Abbott and Israel Towne were parents of nine children all born at Stoddard.

i LYDIA TOWNE, b. 17 Sep 1781; d. at Stoddard, 28 Jun 1878; m. at Stoddard, 6 Jun 1805, OLIVER HODGMAN, b. about 1782 likely the son of Oliver and Submit (Locke) Hodgman; Oliver d. at Stoddard, after 1860.

ii ARCHELAUS TOWNE, b. 29 Nov 1782; d. at Langdon, 5 May 1875; m. 1st, 14 Dec 1813, CLARISSA GEROULD, b. at Stoddard, 15 Aug 1788 daughter of Samuel and Azubah (Thompson) Gerould; Clarissa d. at Stoddard, 25 May 1816. Archelaus m. 2nd, 22 Jan 1818, RUTH KENNEY, b. at Stoddard, 2 Dec 1783 daughter of Isaac and Anna (Adams) Kenney; Ruth d. at Langdon, 9 Sep 1877.

iii ISRAEL TOWNE, b. 22 Nov 1784; d. at Amherst, NH, 25 Oct 1858; m. 1st, at Boston, 14 Jun 1812, CLARISSA WELD, b. 3 Dec 1795 of undetermined parents; Clarissa d. at Boston, 13 Jan 1815. Israel m. 2nd, 23 Jul 1815, SARAH L. BRAZIER, b. 11 Jun 1796[1746] of undetermined parents; Sarah d. at Nashua, 22 May 1874.

iv HANNAH TOWNE, b. 9 Oct 1786; d. at Stoddard, 28 Jul 1864; m. at Stoddard, 2 Apr 1809, ASA COPELAND, b. at Stoddard, 9 Jun 1787 son of Jacob and Experience (Niles) Copeland; Asa d. at Stoddard, 13 Jul 1869.

v ESTHER TOWNE, b. 23 Jun 1788; d. at Sullivan, 23 Aug 1871; m. 5 Oct 1809, ISAAC HOWE, b. at Milford, 2 Jul 1781 son of Stephen and Hannah (Duncklee) Howe; Isaac d. at Stoddard, 26 Feb 1858.

vi GRACE TOWNE, b. 24 Mar 1790; d. at Stoddard 1806 or 1807 when she was killed by a falling tree limb while trying to get to a bird's nest.[1747]

vii GARDNER TOWNE, b. 16 Feb 1792; d. at Marlow, NH, 17 Feb 1872; m. 1st, at Stoddard, 23 Dec 1819, MIRIAM FLINT, b. at Stoddard, 19 Jul 1798 daughter of Joel and Silence (-) Flint; Miriam d. at Marlow, 16 Aug 1856. Gardner m. 2nd, SARAH CRAM (widow of Gilman Tenney), b. at Stoddard, 3 Jul 1806 daughter of Andrew and Sally (Towne) Cram; Sarah d. at Marlow, 7 Apr 1875.

[1742] The inscription on the gravestone gives exact age of 58 yrs. 5 mo. & 12 dys; Find a Grave Memorial # 92380131

[1743] Brookfield Historical Society, *History of Brookfield*, p 32

[1744] *Vermont. Probate Court (Randolph District)*; Probate Place: *Orange, Vermont, Folder 49, Hebard, Zebulon-Lynde, Judith, 1832-1841*

[1745] Cook County, Illinois, Deaths Index, 1878-1922

[1746] Towne, *Descendants of William Towne*, p 157

[1747] Gould, *History of Stoddard*, p 44

viii EBENEZER TOWNE, b. 31 Aug 1795; d. at Stoddard, 10 Jan 1892; m. 1823, TRYPHENA COREY, b. at Stoddard, 29 May 1800 daughter of Willard and Poll (-) Cory; Tryphena d. at Stoddard, 16 Jan 1863.

ix LUCY TOWNE, b. 16 Aug 1797; d. at Stoddard, 11 Feb 1888; m. at Stoddard, 13 Feb 1816, SAMUEL UPTON, b. 1793 parents undetermined; Samuel d. at Stoddard, 23 Dec 1862.

629) SARAH "SALLY" ABBOTT *(Isaac⁴, Paul³, William², George¹)*, b. at Pomfret, 14 Oct 1762 daughter of Isaac and Mary (Barker) Abbott; d. at Mason, NH, 16 Mar 1846; m. at Amherst, 25 Oct 1795, JAMES BROWN, b. about 1770 (based on age 84 at death); James d. at Mason, 11 Mar 1854.

Sarah Abbott and James Brown were parents of four children born at Mason.

i CHLOE BROWN, b. 14 Aug 1798; d. at Wilton, 27 Jun 1876; m. at Mason, 20 Nov 1826, JOHN BOYNTON, b. at Mason, 1 Aug 1797 son of Nathaniel and Anna (Barrett) Boynton; John d. at Mason, 27 Jun 1858.

ii SALLY BROWN, b. 13 Jul 1796; d. at Mason, 28 Oct 1831. Sally did not marry.

iii MARTHA "PATTY" BROWN, b. 4 Mar 1800; d. at Mason, 7 Feb 1883. Patty did not marry.

iv ISAAC ABBOTT BROWN, b. 6 Apr 1802; d. at Mason, 15 Aug 1878; m. 1834, LYDIA BOYNTON, b. at Mason, 14 Dec 1802 daughter of Nathaniel and Anna (Barrett) Boynton; Lydia d. at Mason, 20 Dec 1891.

630) ISAAC ABBOTT *(Isaac⁴, Paul³, William², George¹)* b. at Pomfret, 17 Jul 1766 son of Isaac and Mary (Barker) Abbott; d. at Milford, NH, 1 Sep 1831; m. 15 Oct 1793, RUTH AMES, b. at Wilmington, MA, 31 Jul 1776 daughter of Caleb and Mary (Harvey) Ames/Eams; Ruth d. at Milford, 29 Jul 1844.

Isaac was a farmer on the homestead inherited from his father in Milford.

Isaac and Ruth (Ames) Abbott had eleven children all born at Milford.[1748]

i MARY ABBOTT, b. 26 Sep 1794; d. at Portland, ME, 7 Jan 1884; m. at Boston, 20 Feb 1823, HENRY NOWELL, b. at Dracut, 19 Feb 1797 son of Moses and Patty (French) Nowell; Henry d. at Portland, 13 May 1869.

ii STEPHEN ABBOTT, b. 22 Nov 1797; d. at Hillsboro, IL, 30 Dec 1876;[1749] m. MARTHA GUTTERSON, b. at Andover, NH, 6 Nov 1805 daughter of Abiel and Sarah (Frye) Gutterson; Martha d. at Hillsboro, IL, 7 Jul 1861.

iii REBECCA ABBOTT, b. 22 Jan 1799; d. at Hollis, 11 Nov 1860; m. about 1816, JOHN MOOAR, b. at Hollis, 11 Aug 1796 son of Jacob and Dorcas (Hood) Mooar; John d. at Hollis, 13 Mar 1869. After Rebecca's death, John married her sister Deborah.

iv HARVEY ABBOTT, b. 1 Apr 1801; d. at Milford, 31 Mar 1864; m. 8 Nov 1831, ALMIRA J. LANCASTER, b. at Newburyport, about 1810 daughter of Joseph and Mary (Gutterson) Lancaster;[1750] Almira d. at Milford, 22 Mar 1861.

v WALTER ABBOTT, b. 16 Jul 1803; d. at Boston, 20 Dec 1877; m. 1st, about 1830 SARAH AVERY about whom nothing is known at this time; Sarah d. about 1840. Walter m. 2nd, at Lowell, 1 Sep 1842, ELCY PARKS EAMS, b. at Wilmington, MA, 3 Aug 1820 daughter of Caleb and Betsey (Locke) Eams; Elcy d. Wellesley, 1902.

vi DEBORAH ABBOTT, b. 15 Aug 1805; d. at Nashua, NH, 1 Jul 1872; m. 1862, JOHN MOOAR the husband of her sister Rebecca. In 1860, Deborah Abbott was living with her sister Harriet and Harriet's second husband John Morrill. In her will, Deborah Mooar left her entire estate to John Morrill.[1751]

vii FRANKLIN ABBOTT, b. 20 Aug 1807, d. at Amherst, NH, 3 May 1889; m. 1st, about 1831, INDIANNA PROCTOR, b. at Hollis, 26 Dec 1803 daughter of Nathaniel and Olive (Goddard) Proctor; Indianna d. at Milford in 1879. Franklin m. 2nd, 2 Dec 1879 at Milford, MARY PATCH, b. about 1834 daughter of Timothy and Mary (Proctor) Patch; Mary d. at Amherst, 15 Sep 1908. It is likely that Indianna Proctor and Mary Patch were related through the Proctor connection, but I have not investigated that.

viii WILLIAM B. ABBOTT, b. 7 Sep 1811; d. at St; Louis, MO, 1851.[1752] William did not marry. He was a physician. The probate of his estate included that there was no property belonging to the estate. The only thing of value was a possible patent for a sulfur bath, but it was discovered that this had already been patented by someone else.

[1748] Ramsdell & Colburn, *History of Milford*, p 560-561

[1749] Stephen's gravestone includes his date and place of birth (Milford, NH, 22 Nov 1797); findagrave memorial 66635215

[1750] The names of Almira's parents are given on her death record as Joseph and Mary G. *New Hampshire, Death and Disinterment Records, 1754-1947.*

[1751] *New Hampshire, Wills and Probate Records, 1643-1982*

[1752] The probate record of William B. Abbott includes a statement that Stephen Abbott of Hillsboro, Illinois is his brother and three brothers were living in Massachusetts. Probate Case Files, 1802-1876; Author: Missouri. Probate Court (St. Louis County); Probate Place: St Louis, Missouri

ix ROBERT B. ABBOTT, b. 20 Jan 1814; d. at Boston, 16 Apr 1881; m. at Boston, 24 Aug 1845, ARZELIA AVERILL, b. at Alna, ME, about 1812 daughter of Ebenezer and Mary (Lord) Averill;[1753] Arzelia d. at Alna, 3 Nov 1882.

x DOROTHY ABBOTT, b. 1 Aug 1816; d. at Milford, 22 Mar 1843; m. about 1840, JAMES KNIGHT about whom nothing is known at this time. There is one child known from this marriage a daughter Harriet who died 30 Nov 1842.

xi HARRIET ABBOTT, b. 20 Dec 1819; d. at Nashua, 1873; m. 1st, about 1837, WILLIAM GUTTERSON, b. at Milford, 30 May 1809 son of Abiel and Sarah (Frye) Gutterson; William d. at Milford, 30 Jun 1838. Harriet m. 2nd, about 1845, JOHN MORRILL, b. at Chichester, NH, 25 Jun 1823 son of Micajah and Sally (Shaw) Morrill;[1754] John d. at Nashua, 6 Dec 1895. After Harriet's death, John Morrill married Helen Kendall 7 Nov 1874. There is one child known for Harriet and William Gutterson, a daughter Harriet who was born and died in 1838. There are four known children for Harriet and John Morrill, three who died in early infancy and John Perley Morrill born 4 May 1856 and died 3 May 1951.

631) OLIVE ABBOTT *(Isaac4, Paul3, William2, George1)*, b. at Princeton, 28 Oct 1772 daughter of Isaac and Mary (Barker) Abbott. It is possible she is the Olive Abbott that married ISAAC PARKER 6 Feb 1794 at Amherst.[1755] The Olive Abbott that married Isaac was of Milford and she died 2 Jan 1862 at age 89 which fits for this Olive. Isaac Parker was b. at Monson, NH, 2 Mar 1769 son of Josiah and Hannah (Parkis) Parker; Isaac d. at Hollis, 22 Dec 1857.

Isaac Parker was a large landowner and successful farmer in Hollis. He was Captain of an infantry company in Hollis in 1804.[1756]

Olive Abbott and Isaac Parker were parents of five children all born at Hollis.

i OLIVE PARKER, b. 27 Jun 1795; d. at Hollis, 4 Jan 1825; m. 18 Apr 1816, JEREMIAH KIDDER NEEDHAM, b. at Milford, 20 Sep 1792 son of Stearns and Hannah (Bailey) Needham; Jeremiah d. at Hollis, 9 Apr 1862. After Olive's death, Jeremiah married second Ruhamah Whitney, third Betsey Swallow, and fourth Elizabeth Stevens.

ii HANNAH PARKER, b. 29 May 1797; d. at Hollis, 2 Nov 1816.

iii ACHSAH PARKER, b. 24 Jun 1799; d. at Exeter, ME, 6 May 1831; m. at Hollis, 10 Aug 1829, JOHN BOYNTON HILL, b. at Mason, 25 Nov 1796 son of Ebenezer and Rebecca (Bancroft) Hill; John d. at Temple, 2 May 1886.

iv ISAAC PARKER, b. 12 Apr 1801; d. 20 Aug 1813.

v JOHN PARKER, b. 30 Jul 1803; d. at Hollis, after 1870; m. 17 Apr 1828, MARY ANN GOULD, b. at Hollis, 1802 daughter of Ambrose and Susan (Farley) Gould; Mary Ann d. at Stoneham, MA, 19 Apr 1877.

632) PAUL ABBOTT *(Darius4, Paul3, William2, George1)*, b. at Andover, 18 Mar 1767 son of Darius and Mary (Holt) Abbott; death date not known but in NH; m. at Hillsborough, 30 Mar 1797, NAOMI CARR whose origins are unknown, although *perhaps* the daughter of Thomas and Hannah (-) Carr born at Londonderry, NH, 4 May 1864. Thomas Carr, who did have a daughter Naomi, was in Hillsborough at the time that Naomi married at Hillsborough.

Very little could be found for this family. The Abbot genealogy reports two children, and record evidence could be found for one of the children.

i THOMAS ABBOTT, b. about 1800; no information found

ii DARIUS ABBOTT, b. at Hillsborough, 14 May 1803; d. at Sandwich, NH, 19 May 1875; m. 1st, about 1826, BETSEY PRESCOTT whose origins are unknown; Betsey d. 22 Dec 1845. Darius m. 2nd, at Sandwich, 6 Jan 1847, MEHITABLE S. PRESCOTT (widow of Orlando Bean), b. about 1805 and d. 5 Sep 1855. Darius m. 3rd, 12 Feb 1856, NANCY HUCKINS, b. at New Hampton, 19 Jul 1809 daughter of Robert and Deborah (Gordon) Huckins; Nancy d. 7 Oct 1881.[1757]

1753 Avery, *The Averell Family*, volume 1, p 452

1754 The names of John's parents are given on his death record as Micajah Morrill and Sally Shaw.

1755 In any case, she is an Abbott and so belongs in the book even if it is later determined that she is of different parents.

1756 Spaulding, *An Account of Some Early Settlers of West Dunstable, Monson and Hollis*, N.H., p 113

1757 The 1875 will of Darius Abbott of Sandwich includes bequests to his wife Nancy and to his children from his marriage to Betsey Prescott.

633) TRYPHENA ABBOTT *(Darius⁴, Paul³, William², George¹)*, b. at Andover, 23 Feb 1769 daughter of Darius and Mary (Holt) Abbott; d. at Putney, VT, Jun 1836; m. 2 Jun 1790, JOHN WALLACE, b. at Bedford, NH, 12 May 1764 son of John and Sarah (Woodburn) Wallace; John d. 1834 (probate 25 Nov 1834).

John Wallace was in Antrim, New Hampshire with his brother James, and seems to have married Tryphena Abbott while he was there. The family then moved on to Westmoreland and finally to Putney, Vermont. Eight children have been named for this family, but five of them died in childhood.[1758] Three of the children lived to adulthood, but only two daughters were living at the time John Wallace wrote his will in 1834.

In his will dated 24 November 1834, John Wallace bequeaths to beloved wife Triphena the sole use of south front room during her natural life and all the personal property of every description. Daughter Hannah Wilbur and her husband Elisha Wilbur receive his only cow, but they need to furnish Triphena with butter. Daughter Polly Carpenter wife of David Carpenter receives one dollar and fifty cents with what has been done for her is her full share. All the real estate goes to Hannah Wilbur and Elisha Wilbur including the reversion of the dower after the decease of Triphena. Son-in-law Elisha Wilbur is the sole executor. Real estate was valued at $1,250 and personal estate at $323.10 with claims against the estate of $102.54.[1759]

Tryphena Abbott and John Wallace perhaps had eight children, five of whom died in childhood. There are no records related to the five children who died young. They are John, Sarah, Cyrus, Moseley, and Freeman. The other three children are listed below.

i MARY "POLLY" WALLACE, b. about 1792; m. at Putney, 4 Mar 1816, DAVID CARPENTER. Polly and David had four children born in Putney.

ii HANNAH WALLACE, b. about 1794; d. 16 Nov 1836; m. at Putney, 20 Apr 1820, ELISHA WILBUR, b. at Foxborough, MA, 30 Jun 1798 son of Elisha and Abi (Belcher) Wilbur; Elisha d. at Springfield, MA, 24 Jan 1893. After Hannah's death, Elisha married Esther who died in Putney 10 Mar 1887.

iii MARGARET WALLACE, b. estimated 1805; d. before 1834 when her father wrote his will.

634) CALVIN HOLT ABBOTT *(Darius⁴, Paul³, William², George¹)*, b. at Andover, 15 Apr 1771 son of Darius and Mary (Holt) Abbott; d. at Barre, VT, 14 Aug 1841; m. 10 Apr 1800, LUCY DUTTON, b. 16 May 1781 daughter of John and Elizabeth (Spaulding) Dutton; Lucy d. 15 Apr 1851.

Calvin and Lucy started their family in Hillsborough, New Hampshire, were then in Westmoreland where their youngest son was born, and finally in Barre, Vermont. He farmed throughout his life. Seven children are known for this family.

i JOHN DUTTON ABBOTT, b. at Hillsborough, 2 Jun 1800; d. at Barre, VT, 5 Mar 1870; m. at Weathersfield, VT, 24 Apr 1823, DORCAS BECKLEY, b. at Weathersfield, 26 Oct 1803 daughter of Josiah and Molly (Norton) Beckley;[1760] Dorcas d. at Barre, 16 Apr 1879.

ii LUCY ABBOTT, b. at Hillsborough, 24 Nov 1801; d. at Westmoreland, 2 Jul 1827. Lucy did not marry.

iii BETSEY ABBOTT, b. at Hillsborough, 24 Feb 1803; d. at Barre, 22 Feb 1887; m. at Barre, 23 Dec 1850, as his second wife, SAMUEL FRENCH, b. at Washington, VT, 29 Jan 1789;[1761] Samuel d. at Barre, 25 Aug 1856. Samuel was first married to Lydia Sampson.

iv CALVIN ABBOTT, b. at Hillsborough, 3 Mar 1806; d. at Coxsackie, NY, 3 Aug 1837.

v HENRY ABBOTT, b. at Hillsborough, 26 Mar 1808; d. 7 Feb 1840.[1762]

vi ALMON ABBOTT, b. 27 Feb 1810; d. at Westfield, NY, 9 Jul 1885; m. 1st, at Coxsackie, NY, 4 Sep 1837, CAROLINE SIMPSON, b. about 1815; Caroline d. at Cambridge, MA, 22 Aug 1847. Almon m. 2nd, at Cambridge, 18 Jan 1849, LUCY B. FARNSWORTH, b. in NY, about 1820 daughter of Joseph Farnsworth.

vii JOEL ABBOTT, b. 4 Oct 1820; d. at Maynard, MA, 31 Aug 1891; m. 1st, 15 May 1855, MARTHA NICHOLS, b. in VT, about 1820 daughter of Nahum and Anna (Paine) Nichols; Martha d. at Barre, VT, 17 Nov 1855. Joel m. 2nd, at Somerville, MA, 15 Apr 1858, MARIA BRAGDON BROWN, b. at Stowe, MA, 12 Mar 1838 daughter of Ezekiel S. and Lucy (Litchfield) Brown; Maria d. at Keene, NH, 22 May 1939.

635) NANCY ABBOTT *(Darius⁴, Paul³, William², George¹)*, b. at Amherst, NH about 1780 daughter of Darius and Mary (Holt) Abbott; possibly d. at North Brookfield, MA, 6 Aug 1842 (Nancy widow of Joel Jones, age 65); m. 23 Apr 1804, JOEL

[1758] Cochrane, *History of Antrim*, p 732

[1759] *Vermont. Supreme Court. Administrative Services;* Probate Place: *Windham, Vermont, Probate Records, Bundle 3, 1834-1835*

[1760] Sheppard, *The Descendants of Richard Beckley*, p 146

[1761] The birth transcription for Samuel does not give the names of his parents; it states only that his mother's residence is Salisbury.

[1762] The date of death for Henry is from the Abbot genealogical register; a record was not found.

JONES possibly the son of Joel and Mary (Bishop) Jones,[1763] b. at Hillsborough, 7 Aug 1783. Joel was first married to Nancy's sister HANNAH ABBOTT, b. 1783 (baptized 4 May 1783).[1764]

No children have been identified for Joel Jones and Hannah Abbott. Six children have been identified for Nancy Abbott and Joel Jones. A marriage has been located for only one of the children. The oldest five children were born at Hillsborough and the youngest child at Francestown.

i ADELINE JONES, b. 8 Oct 1806

ii NANCY JONES, b. 9 Aug 1808

iii CATHERINE JONES, b. 10 Apr 1810;[1765] d. at Shelby, NY, 16 Apr 1885; m. about 1830, as his second wife, CHRISTOPHER SERVOSS, b. in NY, 1787 son of Christian and Christina (Pettingill) Servoss; Christopher d. at Shelby, 19 Sep 1866. Christopher was first married to Fanny Bent.

iv ELIZA JONES, b. 14 Aug 1811

v EMELINE JONES, b. 17 Feb 1813

vi HANNAH JONES, b. 17 Apr 1816

636) ELIZABETH PHELPS *(Elizabeth Abbott Phelps[4], Paul[3], William[2], George[1])*, b. at Pomfret, 1 Mar 1765 daughter of Joseph and Elizabeth (Abbott) Phelps; d. at Lexington, 26 Jun 1835; m. about 1787, NATHAN HARRINGTON, b. at Lexington, 29 Apr 1762 son of Daniel and Anna (Munroe) Harrington; Nathan d. at Lexington, 30 Jun 1837.

Nathan Harrington was born in Lexington, but Elizabeth and Nathan lived much of their married life in Woburn returning to Lexington later in life.

Nathan Harrington did not leave a will and his estate entered probate August 1787 with his son-in-law William Chandler as administrator at the request of heirs Nathan Harrington, Abijah Harrington, Addison Gage, and Dorcas Frothingham.[1766] Real estate was valued at $2,116 for a dwelling house with about thirty-three acres and two pews in the Lexington meeting house. The personal estate was valued at under $100 and charges against the estate totaled $1,833.70.

Elizabeth Phelps and Nathan Harrington were parents of eight children likely all born at Woburn.[1767]

i BETSEY HARRINGTON, b. 27 Apr 1788; d. at Lexington, 30 Sep 1847; m. at Lexington, 17 Oct 1813, WILLIAM CHANDLER, b. 4 Oct 1788 son of Nathan and Ruth (Tidd) Chandler; William d. at Lexington, 19 Mar 1870. After Betsey's death, William married the widow Mary LaBarte.

ii DORCAS HARRINGTON, b. 25 Jun 1790; d. at Charlestown, 12 Jan 1871; m. at Woburn, 10 Jun 1813, JOSHUA PAINE FROTHINGHAM, b. at Charlestown, 13 Jan 1787 son of Thomas and Rebecca (Wait) Frothingham; Joshua d. at Cambridge, 8 May 1836.

iii NATHAN HARRINGTON, b. 29 Feb 1792; d. at Lexington, 13 Nov 1843; m. 1 Feb 1824, MARTHA MEAD, b. 1797 daughter of Josiah and Sally (Locke) Mead; Martha d. at Lexington, 13 Nov 1852.

iv TRYPHENA HARRINGTON, b. 25 Aug 1794; d. 24 Feb 1802.

v DANIEL HARRINGTON, b. 26 Aug 1796; d. at Lexington, Oct 1826; m. 16 Dec 1824, HANNAH JACOBS, b. at Littleton, 26 Jun 1799 daughter of Braddock and Sarah (Hersey) Jacobs; Hannah d. at Medford, 5 Mar 1879. After Daniel's death, Hannah married Luther Brooks.

vi ANNA HARRINGTON, b. 24 Nov 1799; d. at Arlington, MA, 22 Mar 1886; m. at Charlestown, 27 Dec 1832, ADDISON GAGE, b. at Pelham, NH, 12 Feb 1808 son of Asa and Abigail (Gage) Gage; Addison d. at Arlington, 13 Oct 1868.

vii INCREASE SUMNER HARRINGTON, b. 6 Sep 1802; d. likely in New York, NY, 18 Feb 1848; m. at Cambridge, 12 Dec 1826, ELIZA MAYNARD, b. at Waltham, about 1806 daughter of Antipas and Betsey (Child) Maynard;[1768]

[1763] Charlotte Helen Abbott suggests he is the child of William Jones and Rebecca Jenkins.

[1764] Historical Society of Amherst, Transcriptions of Baptisms of Children from Volume I of the Congregational Church of Amherst, New Hampshire, http://www.hsanh.org/Baptisms%202.htm

[1765] Birthdate is given as 12 Apr 1809 on her gravestone.

[1766] Middlesex County, MA: Probate File Papers, 1648-1871.Online database. AmericanAncestors.org. New England Historic Genealogical Society, 2014. Case 10443

[1767] Some of the information on this family was obtained from *Hudson, History of the Town of Lexington*, p 283

[1768] The names of Eliza's parents are given as Antipas Maynard and Betsey Child on her death record.

Eliza d. at Cambridge, 17 Jul 1893. I. Sumner Harrington was a successful fruit merchant in New York City[1769] and his youngest child was born in New York City in 1846, so that is likely where Sumner died.

viii ABIJAH HARRINGTON, b. 3 Sep 1804; d. at Lexington, 28 Jun 1893.

637) LYDIA PHELPS *(Elizabeth Abbott Phelps⁴, Paul³, William², George¹)*, b. at Pomfret, 5 Feb 1767 daughter of Joseph and Elizabeth (Abbott) Phelps; d. at Cambridge, 10 Nov 1834; m. PHILIP CARTERET WHITTEMORE, b. at Arlington, 1 Sep 1766 son of William and Abigail (De Carteret) Whittemore; Philip d. 30 Jun 1855.

Lydia Phelps and Philip Whittemore were parents of ten children all born at Charlestown.

i JOSEPH WHITTEMORE, b. 11 Mar 1788; d. at Arlington, 24 Sep 1819; m. at Cambridge, 20 Jun 1819, REBECCA BARKER who is not yet identified.

ii LYDIA WHITTEMORE, b. 3 Nov 1789; d. at Wakefield, 21 Aug 1879; m. at Reading, 2 Jul 1808, SUEL WINN, b. at Burlington, about 1787 son of Jeremiah Winn; Suel d. at Reading, 16 Sep 1851.

iii MARY WHITTEMORE, b. 12 Mar 1791; d. at Cambridge, 18 Mar 1874; m. at Cambridge, 14 Aug 1812, JONATHAN COOPER PRENTISS, b. at Cambridge, 23 Dec 1783 son of Nathaniel and Abigail (Logan) Prentiss; Jonathan d. at Cambridge, 15 Aug 1856.

iv ELIZABETH WHITTEMORE, b. 13 May 1793; d. at Cambridge, 9 Dec 1869; m. at Cambridge, 21 Mar 1815, ABEL LOCKE, b. at West Cambridge, 1791 son of Joseph and Mary (Butterfield) Locke; Abel d. at Arlington, 27 Feb 1848.

v PHILIP CARTERET WHITTEMORE, b. 25 Jul 1795; d. at West Cambridge, 30 Mar 1848; m. 21 Oct 1819, SARAH CUTTER, b. at Andover, 18 Aug 1800 daughter of Adam and Sarah (Putnam) Cutter; Sarah d. at Arlington, 14 May 1889.

vi ABIGAIL WHITTEMORE, b. 5 Sep 1797; d. at Ashby, MA, 4 Jun 1882; m. at West Cambridge, 5 Jun 1817, ABEL BUTTERFIELD, b. at Cambridge, 23 Feb 1797 son of Samuel and Elizabeth (Bemis) Butterfield; Abel d. at Cambridge, 25 May 1860.

vii CHARLES WHITTEMORE, b. 25 Dec 1799; d. at Arlington, 7 May 1873; m. at Arlington, 6 Aug 1826, HARRIET CARTER, b. about 1798 daughter of Mical Carter;[1770] Harriet d. at Arlington, 28 Sep 1889.

viii LEWIS WHITTEMORE, b. 9 Oct 1801; d. at Arlington, 3 May 1803.

ix LEWIS WHITTEMORE, b. 7 Jun 1804; d. 6 Jan 1828.

x EMELINE WHITTEMORE, b. 1808; d. at Reading, 31 Dec 1858; m. at Malden, 13 Aug 1835, JOSEPH O. DIX, b. at Salem, about 1810 son of William and Abigail (-) Dix;[1771] Joseph d. at Boston, 31 Jan 1884.

638) TRYPHENA PHELPS *(Elizabeth Abbott Phelps⁴, Paul³, William², George¹)*, b. at Princeton, MA, 28 Sep 1769 daughter of Joseph and Elizabeth (Abbott) Phelps; d. at Woburn, 8 Oct 1818; m. at Woburn, 19 Jun 1791, WILLIAM "BILL" RUSSELL, b. 4 May 1763 son of Jesse and Elizabeth (Whipple) Russell.[1772] After Tryphena's death, Bill Russell married Mrs. Phebe Dorman. Bill Russell d. at Billerica, 4 Jul 1842.

Bill Russel enlisted April 1779 and served eight months as a private during the Revolutionary War in the Massachusetts line. In his pension application, he reported that he did not serve in any battles. Part of his enlistment was serving as a substitute for his brother Jesse. He received an annual pension of $26.66.[1773]

The estate of Bill Russell entered probate 11 Aug 1842. Widow Phebe Russell declined administration and requested that Albert Nelson, Esq. of Woburn be named. The real estate, a fifty-acre homestead farm, was valued at $1,800 and personal estate was valued at $150.13. Debts of the estate were $1,808.94. On 11 October 1842, Phebe Russell petitioned to receive $50 from the estate for her support. The administrator petitioned to sell the real estate and those signing their agreement as all the interested parties in the estate were Cyrus P. Simonds and Mary Ann Simonds, William S. Bennett and Susan E. Bennett, and Loring Emerson and Tryphena P. Emerson.[1774]

Tryphena Phelps and Bill Russell were parents of three children born at Woburn.

1769 Cutter, *Genealogical and Personal Memoirs Relating to the Families of Boston*, volume I, p 202

1770 Parents' names are given as Michael and Sally on her death record.

1771 Names of parents are given as William and Abigail on the death record.

1772 William, s. of Jesse and Elizabeth, May 4, 1763.

1773 Revolutionary War Pension and Bounty-Land Warrant Application Files

1774 Middlesex County, MA: Probate File Papers, 1648-1871.Online database. AmericanAncestors.org. New England Historic Genealogical Society, 2014. Case 40891

i TRYPHENA RUSSELL, b. 18 Dec 1802; d. at Winchester, MA, 2 Mar 1875; m. at Woburn, 17 May 1821, LORING EMERSON, b. at Reading, 17 Feb 1796 son of Daniel and Lucy (Pratt) Emerson; Loring d. at Winchester, 24 Apr 1874.

ii SUSAN E. RUSSELL, b. 1809; d. at Woburn, 27 Apr 1878; m. at Charlestown, 31 Dec 1829, WILLIAM S. BENNETT, b. at Medford, 12 Oct 1807 son of Stephen and Lucy (Winn) Bennett; William d. at Somerville, 23 Aug 1860 when he was killed in a railroad accident.[1775]

iii MARY ANN RUSSELL, b. 23 Jul 1812; d. at Medford, 24 Jul 1864; m. at Billerica, 6 Jun 1841, CYRUS PIERCE SIMONDS, b. 10 Apr 1815 son of William and Susan (Pierce) Simonds; Cyrus d. at Waltham, 28 Apr 1889.

639) PHILIP ABBOTT *(Abiel⁴, Philip³, William², George¹)*, b. at Windham, 23 Mar 1751 son of Abiel and Abigail (Fenton) Abbott; d. at Kingston, PA, Mar 1834;[1776] m. 6 Jul 1775, ANNA HEWETT, b. at Canterbury, 1 Jul 1754 daughter of Henry and Joanna (Denison) Hewett; Anna d. at Windham 29 Dec 1796. Philip m. 2nd, 17 Mar 1815 at Wilkes-Barre, MABEL MERRITT.

Philip Abbott and Anna Hewett were parents of eight children, the oldest six children born in Windham and the two youngest children likely in Pennsylvania.

i ANNA ABBOTT, b. 27 Apr 1776. Anna did not marry.

ii AMELIA ABBOTT, b. 1 Jul 1777; d. 11 Oct 1777.

iii AURELIA ABBOTT, b. 28 Apr 1779; d. 3 Sep 1783.

iv PHILIP ABBOTT, b. 14 Apr 1781; d. at Tobyhanna, PA, 1 Aug 1854; m. 1st, 25 Dec 1805, LUCY WALLER, b. about 1784 daughter of Nathan and Elizabeth (Weeks) Waller; Lucy d. at Wilkes-Barre, 27 May 1822. Philip m. 2nd, 5 Sep 1836, SYBIL GRIDLEY, b. 17 Feb 1802 daughter of John and Sybil (-) Gridley; Sybil d. at Wilkes-Barre, Aug 1879. Sybil was first married to Edward Rohn.

v JAMES HEWETT ABBOTT, b. 1786; d. at Kingston, PA, 13 Apr 1809; m. 1806, ANNA STEPHENS, b. at Lackawaxen, PA, about 1789 daughter of Uriah and Elizabeth (Jones) Stephens; Anna d. at Hornell, NY, 30 Jul 1830. After James's death, Anna married Bazy Baker.

vi HANNAH ABBOTT, b. 28 Feb 1788; d. at Wilkes-Barre, 1858; m. 13 Jun 1807, LUTHER YARINGTON, b. at Wilkes-Barre, 1783 son of Abel and Rebecca (Keazer) Yarington; Luther d. 25 Dec 1836.

vii ABIEL ABBOTT, b. 7 Oct 1790; d. at Forty Fort, PA, 2 Oct 1838; m. at Kingston, PA, 17 Oct 1813, CELINDA ATHERTON, b. 1794 daughter of Elisha and Eunice (Carver) Atherton; Celinda d. 2 Jul 1817.

viii MARY ABBOTT, b. 10 Nov 1793; d. at Dushore, PA, 22 Jun 1851; m. 26 Feb 1822, JOSIAH JACKSON, b. at Catawissa, PA, 8 May 1791 son of Samuel and Hannah (Davis) Jackson; Josiah d. at Dushore, 9 Apr 1867. Josiah was first married to Fanny Stevenson.

640) JAMES ABBOTT *(Abiel⁴, Philip³, William², George¹)*, b. at Windham, 9 Mar 1753 son of Abiel and Abigail (Fenton) Abbott; d. at Cornell, NY, 2 May 1830; m. 1st, 1 Jan 1778, his third cousin, HANNAH DENISON *(Lydia Pearl Denison⁴, Elizabeth Stevens Pearl³, Elizabeth Abbott Stevens², George¹)*, b. 18 Mar 1757 daughter of Daniel and Lydia (Pearl) Denison; Hannah d. at Windham, 17 Jan 1784. James m. 2nd, at Kingston, PA, 17 Jan 1798, as her second husband, PHEBE HOWE (widow of John Coray), b. at Luzerne, 21 Feb 1763 daughter of John and Mary (Stephens) Howe; Phebe died at Naples, IL, 9 Sep 1842. James and Phebe may have divorced after 1813, but that is not certain.

James and Hannah were married and had their two children in Connecticut and Hannah died at Windham. James was then in in Luzerne and Lackawanna Counties in Pennsylvania before finally settling in Cornell, New York.

James Abbott and Hannah Denison were parents of two children born at Pomfret, Connecticut.

i DANIEL ABBOTT, b. 25 Oct 1778; d. 1824; m. CATHERINE HILLMAN.

1775 William S., s. of James and Lucy (b. in Medford), accidental, in Somerville, Aug. 23, 1860; 52 y. 10 m. (Although the death transcription gives parents as James and Lucy, his birth record states Stephen and Lucy.)

1776 Philip Abbott, age 70-79, is head of household in the 1830 U.S. Census; 1830; Census Place: *Plymouth, Luzerne, Pennsylvania*; Series: *M19*; Roll: *145*; Page: *431*; Family History Library Film: *0020619*

ii ELIJAH ABBOTT, b. 20 Nov 1781; d. at Ossian, NY, 22 Oct 1821 (probate 18 Feb 1822 with widow Polly); m. MARY "POLLY" LOVE.

James Abbott and Phebe Howe were parents of five children.

i JAMES ABBOTT, b. at Luzerne County, 29 Jan 1799; d. at Pike County, IL, 11 Sep 1846; m. 13 Nov 1825, MARY JONES, b. at Burns Station, NY, 6 May 1806; Mary d. 28 Dec 1878.

ii EDMOND AUSTIN ABBOTT, b. at Providence, PA, 15 Aug 1801; d. at Pokagon, MI, 1 Jan 1861; m. NANCY GREGORY, b. 22 Dec 1799; Nancy d. at Pokagon, 25 Jun 1857.

iii STEPHEN JOSEPH ABBOTT, b. at Providence, PA, 16 Aug 1804; d. at Nauvoo, IL, 19 Oct 1843; m. at Hornell, NY, 11 Dec 1825, ABIGAIL SMITH, b. at Ontario County, NY, 11 Sep 1806 daughter of James and Lydia (Harding) Smith; Abigail d. at Willard, UT, 23 Jul 1889. After Stephen's death, Abigail married James Brown.

iv ELEAZER ABBOTT, b. 5 Dec 1808; d. at New Hampton, IA, 30 Mar 1887; m. 1st, ELIZABETH GREGORY, b. at Burns, NY, 9 Dec 1810; Elizabeth d. at Mottville, MI, 16 Sep 1842. Eleazer m. 2nd, SARAH A. COOK, b. 1823; Sarah d. at New Hampton, 24 Dec 1880.

v ABIEL ABBOTT, b. at Steuben County, NY, about 1810.

641) ABIEL ABBOTT *(Abiel4, Philip3, William2, George1)*, b. at Windham, 28 Nov 1754 son of Abiel and Abigail (Fenton) Abbott; d. at Hatley, Québec, 1838; m. 13 Nov 1777, RUTH HOVEY, b. 28 Aug 1754 daughter of Nathaniel and Ruth (Parker) Hovey; Ruth d. at Hatley, 1832.

Abiel and Ruth started their family in Windham County where their children were born. In 1794,[1777] the family relocated to Hatley, Québec with a group led by his brother-in-law Ebenezer Hovey.[1778] They were one of the first four families in Hatley. Abiel was deacon of the newly formed Baptist church in Hatley, a position he held until he became blind due to cataracts two years before his death.[1779]

There are four children known for Abiel and Ruth.[1780] The Abbot genealogical register reports there were two other children who died as infants and those children are omitted here.

i ABIEL ABBOTT, b. at East Windsor, CT, 15 Aug 1778; d. at Hatley, Québec, 6 Mar 1841;[1781] m. at Hatley, 11 Dec 1800, GRACE HITCHCOCK, b. at Wilbraham, MA, 22 Jan 1778 daughter of Paul and Abigail (Pierce) Hitchcock; Grace d. at Hatley, 21 May 1867.

ii JOHN ABBOTT, b. at Willington, 27 May 1781; d. at Hatley, date unknown; m. 10 Mar 1806, LYDIA BOYNTON, b. 1788 daughter of John and Lydia (Gilson) Boynton;[1782] Lydia d. at Hatley, Feb 1836.

iii COLBE ABBOTT, b. at Willington, 21 May 1783; d. at Hatley, 1866; m. at Newport, VT, 11 Mar 1807, ESTHER OLIVER, b. 4 Mar 1792 daughter of William and Elizabeth (Kinston) Oliver;[1783] Esther d. at Hatley, 11 Feb 1866.

iv AUGUSTUS ABBOTT, b. 6 Aug 1788; d. not located but likely in Québec; m. at Newport, VT, 25 Sep 1810, LAURA JUDD, b. at Newport, 3 Mar 1791 daughter of Hawkins and Annis (Butler) Judd; Laura d. 18 Mar 1843.

642) ABIGAIL ABBOTT *(Abiel4, Philip3, William2, George1)*, b. at Windham, 21 Feb 1763 daughter of Abiel and Abigail (Fenton) Abbott; d. about 1843 perhaps in Ohio where she went to stay with her children; m. about 1784, JOSEPH UTLEY who was "of Hartford" but whose parents have not been fully verified, although *perhaps* the son of Joseph and Jerusha (Martin) Utley. Joseph d. at Hartford, 25 Feb 1822.

Abigail Abbott and Joseph Utley were parents of six children likely all born at Hartford.

i HORACE UTLEY, b. 17 Aug 1785; d. at Akron, OH, 1860. Horace did not marry.

ii RALPH UTLEY, b. 1 Jan 1790; d. at Hudson, NY, 20 Mar 1865; m. SARAH B. HUNTINGTON, b. 29 Jun 1788 daughter of Frederick and Lydia (Andrews) Huntington; Sarah d. at Hudson, 28 Feb 1870.

[1777] The Abbot genealogical register reports 1781 as the date the family went to Hatley

[1778] Skeats, *Hatley 1792-1900*

[1779] Abbot, *Genealogical Register*, p 52

[1780] Daniel Hovey Association, *The Hovey Book*, p 144

[1781] Hubbard, *Forests and Clearings*, p 261

[1782] Boynton, *The Boynton Family*, p 141

[1783] Hubbard, *Forests and Clearings*, p 266

iii ABBY UTLEY, b. 17 Jun 1792; d. at Perrysburg, OH, 31 Aug 1837; m. 17 Oct 1815, DAVID LADD, b. 9 Feb 1793 son of Daniel and Persis (-) Ladd; David d. at Perrysburg, 4 May 1856. After Abby's death, David married Eloise Cordelia Bacon.

iv ANNE L. UTLEY, b. 13 Dec 1797; d. at Akron, OH, 14 Dec 1882; m. at Franklin, OH, 30 Dec 1824, ANDREWS MAY, b. at Royalston, MA, 6 Aug 1792 son of Dexter and Sandra (Andrews) May; Andrews d. at Akron, 20 Apr 1888.

v LAURA UTLEY, b. 29 Jan 1800; d. likely at Cleveland, after 1860; m. at Portage, OH, 27 Sep 1819, AUGUSTUS PHELPS, b. at Hebron, CT, 25 Apr 1795 son of Cornelius Phelps; Augustus d. after 1860.

vi BETSEY UTLEY, b. 1804; d. at Detroit, MI, 28 Aug 1881; m. at Portage, OH, 31 Dec 1823, EDWARD FARNUM, b. about 1800; Edward d. before 1850.

643) ANNA ABBOTT *(Abiel⁴, Philip³, William², George¹)*, b. at Windham, 18 Sep 1765 daughter of Abiel and Abigail (Fenton) Abbott; d. at Armada, MI, 13 Sep 1846; m. 29 Aug 1787, SETH LATHROP, b. at Springfield, 11 Apr 1762 son of Joseph and Elizabeth (Dwight) Lathrop; Seth d. 26 Feb 1831.

Seth Lathrop was a physician in Springfield. He was involved in community affairs including being instrumental in the building of a new meeting house in Springfield in 1802.[1784]

In his will written 26 June 1830, Seth Lathrop bequeaths to beloved wife Anna the use and improvement of one-third of all the real estate and the east half of the dwelling house including the middle kitchen. There are other specific provisions for her support during her natural life. Son Solomon Lathrop receives the canes that have descended in the family from Seth's great-great grandfather Samuel Lathrop. All the remainder of the estate is disposed in the following manner: one-fifth part to daughter Betsey Andrews except that son Solomon will have the right to purchase her part of the real estate at the appraised rate; son Solomon receives two-fifths part of the estate; the remaining two-fifths of the estate goes to Samuel Lathrop and Aaron Day to hold in trust for the benefit of son Edward's family. Son Edward will have the right to occupy and improve any part of the estate set off to him as long as the trustees are assured that the proceeds are being used for the comfort and support of Edward's family. However, if at some time in the future Edward has removed "those vicious habits in view of which I have most painfully felt myself compelled by duty to him and his family to withhold from him the control and management of any portion of my property, and shall have returned to the path of temperance, industry and virtue affording a well founded expectation of his abiding in those paths, I hereby authorize and empower my said trustees to relinquish to him all the right, power and control of said property." After Edward's decease, any property still held by the trustees goes to Edward's children. If any of Edward's sons wish to obtain a public education in the gospel ministry, that will be paid for from the estate by the trustees. Wife Anna and son Solomon were named executors.[1785] The value of real estate was $4,498 and personal estate $797.28.

Apparently, son Edward got himself together. In 1860, he was living in Armada, Michigan as the head of household with his wife Emma and three of his eleven children still at home. His real property valued at $6,270 for real estate and $1,216 for personal estate.[1786]

Anna Abbott and Seth Lathrop were parents of three children born at West Springfield.

i BETSEY LATHROP, b. 28 Jul 1788; d. at Armada, MI, 5 Jun 1858; m. at West Springfield, ELISHA DEMING ANDREWS, b. at Southington, CT, 18 Feb 1783 son of Jonathan and Ruth (Deming) Andrews; Elisha d. at Armada, 12 Jan 1852.

ii SOLOMON LOTHROP, b. 11 May 1790; d. at Oakwood, MI, 11 Dec 1872; m. at West Springfield, 12 Feb 1820, SOPHIA POMEROY, b. at New Fane, VT, 5 Jun 1794 daughter of Chester and Catherine (Smith) Pomeroy; Sophia d. at Oakwood, 15 Nov 1853.

iii EDWARD LATHROP, b. 18 Apr 1792; d. at Armada, MI, 11 Sep 1863; m. 15 Oct 1815, EMMA ANDREWS, b. at Southington, CT, 7 Aug 1795 daughter of Jonathan and Ruth (Deming) Andrews; Emma d. at Richmond, MI, 21 Mar 1871.

[1784] Everts, *History of the Connecticut Family in Massachusetts*, p 908

[1785] *Probate Records of Hampden County and City of Springfield, 1806-1919 (Massachusetts)*; Author: *Massachusetts. Probate Court (Hampden County)*; Probate Place: *Hampden, Massachusetts*, volume 10, pp 288-290

[1786] 1860 U.S. Federal Census, Year: 1860; Census Place: Armada, Macomb, Michigan; Roll: M653_553; Page: 606; Family History Library Film: 803553

644) SUSANNAH ABBOTT *(Stephen⁴, Philip³, William², George¹)*, b. at Windham, 23 Cot 1752 daughter of Stephen and Freelove (Burgess) Abbott; d. at Fort Ann, NY, Oct 1815;[1787] m. 15 Sep 1773, STEPHEN BURGESS, b. at Ashford, 12 Jan 1751 son of Benjamin Burgess.

Susannah Abbott and Stephen Burgess were parents of seven children, the births of the first four children recorded at Ashford and the youngest three children likely born at Fort Ann. Very little in the way of records could be found for these children.

- i BENJAMIN BURGESS, b. 30 Aug 1775; d. at Ira, NY, after 1850; m. about 1800, JERUSHA CHASE, b. 27 Nov 1778 daughter of Caleb and Hannah (Ellison) Chase;[1788] Jerusha d. at Ira, 1844.
- ii ABIGAIL BURGESS, b. 7 Apr 1776
- iii PHILIP BURGESS, b. 30 Mar 1778; d. at Fort Ann, after 1840; m. ABIGAIL.
- iv STEPHEN BURGESS, b. 30 May 1780
- v WILLIAM BURGESS, b. about 1782
- vi FREELOVE BURGESS, b. about 1784
- vii JOSEPH BURGESS, b. about 1786. Joseph Burgess (age 26-44) was head of household in Fort Ann in 1820. If that is this Joseph, he was married with children.

645) REUBEN ABBOTT *(Stephen⁴, Philip³, William², George¹)* b. at Ashford, 15 Apr 1774 son of Stephen and Freelove (Burgess) Abbott; d. at Mansfield, CT, 1 Jan 1863; m. 8 Nov 1798, MARY "POLLY" SNOW, b. about 1773 (based on age at time of death; Abbot genealogy gives birth as 12 May 1773) whose parents are not verified; Polly d. at Mansfield, 15 Apr 1857.

Reuben Abbott and Polly Snow were parents of six children likely all born at Mansfield, Connecticut.

- i PHILIP ABBOTT, b. 6 Apr 1799; d. at Washington, NH, 7 Jul 1883; m. 1st, about 1830, REBEKAH ELKINS, b. about 1809; Rebekah d. at Shrewsbury, MA, 20 Apr 1839. Philip m. 2nd, at Shrewsbury, 19 Oct 1839, HARRIET NEWELL WILLIS, b. in VT, 1808 daughter of Joseph and Lucretia (-) Willis; Harriet d. at Boston, 5 Oct 1883. Harriet Willis was first married to Benjamin Knowlton.
- ii STEPHEN ABBOTT, b. 4 May 1803; d. at Stockton, NY, 22 Apr 1882; m. 1st, about 1830, HARRIET BUMP, b. 22 May 1809; Harriet d. at Stockton, 25 Feb 1872. Stephen m. 2nd, about 1873, ANNA K. SHEDD, b. at Stockton, 3 Apr 1813 daughter of Simeon and Lovina (Heltz) Shedd; Anna d. at Stockton, 30 May 1894. Anna Shedd was first married to Allen Richmond.
- iii BETSEY ABBOTT, b. 16 Jul 1805; d. likely at Mansfield, after 1850. Betsey did not marry. In 1850, she was living in Mansfield with her younger brother Ezra.
- iv JOSEPH ABBOTT, b. 11 Sep 1808; d. before 1857 (wife's remarriage); m. at Ashford, 7 May 1846, LUCINDA HARRIS BAKER, b. at Tolland, 23 Sep 1823 daughter of Silvanus and Clarissa (-) Baker; Lucinda d. at Coventry, 9 Mar 1907. Lucinda married second Charles Whitman 19 Oct 1857.
- v NASH ABBOTT, b. 29 Jun 1812; d. at Sheffield, PA, after 1870; m. by 1849, MARY who has not been identified.
- vi EZRA ABBOTT, b. 28 Jun 1817; d. at Mansfield, 23 Feb 1897; m. at Mansfield, 17 Feb 1847, MARY LODICIA BARROWS, b. at Mansfield, 11 Nov 1828 daughter of Enoch and Polly (Storrs) Barrows;[1789] Mary d. at Mansfield, 19 Aug 1914.

646) ABIGAIL UTLEY *(Hannah Abbott Utley⁴, Philip³, William², George¹)*, b. at Windham, 19 Nov 1749 daughter of Samuel and Hannah (Abbott) Utley; d. at Canterbury, 4 Jul 1774; m. 15 Feb 1770, JAMES BUTTS, b. 14 Jun 1748 son of Samuel and Mary (Cleveland) Butts. James m. 2nd, Elizabeth Hibbard.

Very little is known of this family. Abigail and James had two children before Abigail's early death. One child died in infancy. There is no further record for the other child.

- i ELIJAH BUTTS, b. at Canterbury, 9 Apr 1771; d. 7 Nov 1774.
- ii SALLY BUTTS, b. at Canterbury, 7 Nov 1772; no further record.

[1787] Abbot and Abbot, *Genealogical Register of Descendants*, p 54
[1788] Chase, *Seven Generations of the Descendants of Aquila and Thomas Chase*, p 163
[1789] The names of Mary's parents are given on her death record.

647) ANNA UTLEY *(Hannah Abbott Utley⁴, Philip³, William², George¹)*, b. at Windham, 6 Jan 1755 daughter of Samuel and Hannah (Abbott) Utley; m. about 1780, STEPHEN HARE, b. at Ellington, 12 Sep 1755;[1790] Stephen was living in 1810 as head of household in Ellington.

Anna Utley and Stephen Hare were parents of six children all born at Ellington.

i ANNE HARE, b. 21 Jul 1783; d. at Lincoln, OH, 28 Aug 1862; m. by 1800, JAMES KIDDER, b. at Mansfield, CT, Jun 1768 son of James Kidder; James d. at Mt. Pleasant, PA, 27 Mar 1854.[1791]

ii HANNAH HARE, b. 31 Jul 1785

iii STEPHEN ARNOLD HARE, b. 17 Aug 1788; d. at Ellington, 10 Oct 1876; m. 1st, about 1815, LOUISA SPERRY, b. 1785; Louisa d. at Ellington, 4 Aug 1839. Stephen m. 2nd, at Ellington, 28 May 1840, SARAH BUCKLAND, b. 1802; Sarah d. at Ellington, 3 Sep 1883.

iv SULLIVAN HARE, b. 7 Sep 1792; d. likely at Ashford, before 1860; m. at Willington, 4 Feb 1827, PATTY BROOKS CROCKER, b. at Willington, 19 Aug 1808 daughter of Joseph and Susannah (Sibley) Crocker; Patty d. after 1870.

v SAMUEL UTLEY HARE, b. 13 Nov 1794; d. at Cardington, OH, 24 Nov 1878; m. MARY CHARTER, b. 17 Mar 1798;[1792] Mary d. at Cardington, 8 Jun 1874.

vi SOPHIA HARE, b. 17 Nov 1799; d. at Clinton, PA, 28 Nov 1884; m. at Mt. Pleasant, PA, 21 Feb 1819, ASHBEL STEARNS, b. in PA, 24 Sep 1796 son of Joseph and Rhoda (Tingley) Stearns; Ashbel d. at Clinton, PA, 13 May 1882.

648) SAMUEL UTLEY *(Hannah Abbott Utley⁴, Philip³, William², George¹)*, b. at Windham, 2 Feb 1759 son of Samuel and Hannah (Abbott) Utley; d. at Ashford, CT, 13 Sep 1801; m. at Hampton, 7 Jan 1790, SARAH EASTMAN, b. at Ashford, 7 Aug 1761 daughter of Ebenezer and Mary (Fletcher) Eastman; Sarah d. 4 Jan 1828.

Samuel Utley did not leave a will and widow Sarah was administratrix of the estate. Real estate of 48 acres with buildings was valued at $433.33.[1793]

Samuel Utley and Sarah Eastman were parents of five children.

i MARY UTLEY, b. at Hampton, CT, 28 Aug 1791; nothing further known.

ii LYMAN UTLEY, b. at Hampton, 3 Jan 1792; d. at Eastford, CT, 14 May 1814.

iii SETH UTLEY, b. at Ashford, 27 Aug 1795; d. at Pontiac, MI, 12 Sep 1867; m. at Hampton, 21 Mar 1822, LUCY CLARK, b. 1802; Lucy d. at Pontiac, 12 Sep 1868.

iv TIMOTHY UTLEY, b. at Ashford, 10 Jul 1797; d. at Dryden, MI, 16 Jun 1857; m. at Oakland, MI, 25 Dec 1836, MARY ANN LOREE, b. in NY, 22 May 1811 daughter of William Loree;[1794] Mary Ann d. at Goodland, MI, 10 Jul 1889.

v ELIZA UTLEY, b. at Ashford, 21 Oct 1801; d. at Dryden, MI, 25 Nov 1874; m. JAMES BLISS WHITAKER, b. at North Providence, RI, 12 Jul 1797 son of Amos and Bethiah (Allen) Whitaker; James d. at Dryden, 17 May 1871.

649) STEPHEN UTLEY *(Hannah Abbott Utley⁴, Philip³, William², George¹)*, b. at Windham, 21 Nov 1762 son of Samuel and Hannah (Abbott) Utley; d. at Chaplin, CT, 1 Mar 1841; m. at Hampton, 15 Jan 1797, SARAH HOLT, b. 3 Mar 1775 daughter of Paul and Sarah (Welch) Holt; Sarah d. 10 Feb 1833.

Stephen may have had a first marriage, but no information was located for that. There are just two children known for Stephen Utley and Sarah Holt.

[1790] The birth record in the Barbour Collection lists his date of birth but not the names of parents.

[1791] Stafford, *Genealogy of the Kidder Family*, p 140

[1792] Calculated from age at death of 76 years, 2 months, 23 days

[1793] *Connecticut State Library (Hartford, Connecticut)*; Probate Place: *Hartford, Connecticut, Probate Packets, Tyler, Steven-Walker, Samuel, 1752-1880*

[1794] Mary Ann's date of birth is on her gravestone (findagrave: 81637943); father's name on death record is given as William Lowry; the marriage record and the death record of one of her children give her name as Mary Ann Loree.

i ERASTUS UTLEY, b. at Hampton, 31 May 1797; m. at Goshen, CT, 28 Dec 1820, DEBORAH MORGAN who has not been identified.

ii BETSEY UTLEY, b. at Hampton, 18 Dec 1799; d. at Chaplin, CT, 27 Jan 1881; m. at Ashford, 22 Dec 1833, EBENEZER ROBBINS, b. at Hampton, 28 Mar 1798 son of Solomon and Lois (Clark) Robbins; Ebenezer d. at Chaplin, 9 Oct 1869. Ebenezer was first married to Mary Ann Delia Pond.

650) CYRUS UTLEY *(Hannah Abbott Utley⁴, Philip³, William², George¹)*, b. at Windham, 11 Mar 1767 son of Samuel and Hannah (Abbott) Utley; d. at Homer, NY between 1820 and 1832;[1795] m. at Hampton, 4 Apr 1797, POLLY BENNET, b. at New Milford, 6 Jun 1771 daughter of Edward and Rhoda (Canfield) Bennett.

Census records from 1820 suggest there were perhaps five children in this family living at that time. Just four children have been identified one of whom died as an infant, so there may yet be two other children. The family was in Hampton, Connecticut but relocated to Homer, New York likely before 1807.[1796]

i ORREN UTLEY, b. at Hampton, CT, 4 Dec 1798; d. at Homer, NY, about 1877; m. ROXANNA, b. in CT, about 1800 who has not been identified; Roxanna d. at Homer, about 1878.

ii MARIA UTLEY, b. about 1801; d. at Hampton, 1 Jan 1802.

iii LESTER UTLEY, b. at Hampton, about 1802; d. at Homer, NY, m. EMELINE, b. about 1806; Emeline d. at Homer, 15 Apr 1867.[1797]

iv ELIJAH UTLEY, b. likely at Homer, 1807; d. at Tioga County, by 1839 (wife remarried by 1839); m. 13 Apr 1831, LOUISA B. TIDD, b. 3 Oct 1812 daughter of William and Sarah (Learned) Tidd; Louisa d. 23 Nov 1884. Louisa married second Peter Backer and married third John D. Knapp.

651) ANTIPAS UTLEY *(Hannah Abbott Utley⁴, Philip³, William², George¹)*, b. at Windham, 16 Feb 1770 son of Samuel and Hannah (Abbott) Utley; d. after 1830; m. at Hampton, 29 May 1795, POLLY LUCE daughter of Nathan and Elizabeth (Lasel) Luce.[1798] Polly seems to have died between 1816 and 1820.[1799]

Antipas Utley and Polly Luce were parents of nine children with just the birth of the oldest child recorded at Hampton.

i POLLY UTLEY, b. at Hampton, 22 Jun 1796; d. at Windham, 4 Mar 1835; m. about 1818, GEORGE BACKUS, b. about 1797 of not yet determined parents; George d. at Windham, 13 Mar 1845. After Polly's death, George married Laura Dyer 23 Mar 1836.

ii SOPHIA UTLEY, b. about 1799; d. about 1820. Sophia did not marry.

iii EBENEZER UTLEY, b. about 1801; d. at Hebron, after 1870; m. at Hampton, 14 Aug 1825, MARIA MINOR, b. at Hampton, 30 Sep 1804 daughter of Benjamin and Abigail (Holt) Minor; Maria d. at Hebron, after 1870.

iv LEWIS UTLEY, b. about 1804; d. at East Hampton, 12 Apr 1854; m. 1st, at Hartford, 20 May 1828, JERUSHA CLARK, b. 1 Dec 1807 daughter of David and Eunice (Griffith) Clark; Jerusha d. at East Hampton, 20 Dec 1842. Lewis m. 2nd, 13 Dec 1844, LAURA ALMIRA RUSS, b. at Chaplin, CT, about 1818 daughter of John and Almira (Utley) Russ; Laura d. 16 Jul 1899. After Lewis's death, Laura married Charles B. Lawton in 1860.

v CAROLINE UTLEY, b. estimate 1806; m. at Chatham, 11 Dec 1835, DANIEL PRATT.

vi WILLIAM UTLEY, b. 10 Jun 1808; d. at East Hampton, CT, 11 Dec 1893; m. at Chatham, 27 Nov 1835, JERUSHA BRAINERD, b. at Chatham, about 1814 daughter of Oliver and Anna (Strong) Brainerd; Jerusha d. 26 May 1887.

[1795] He is listed in the 1820 U.S. Census at Homer, New York, but he is listed as deceased in his brother Philip's 1832 will. *1820 United States Federal Census*, 1820 U S Census; Census Place: Homer, Cortland, New York; Page: 555; NARA Roll: M33_66; Image: 308.

[1796] Some information on children obtained from Sullivan-Rutland Genealogy Project, transcription of Jerome Utley's Family Notes. http://www.joycetice.com/bibles/backer.htm

[1797] Some suggest that it was Lester Utley son of Amos and Alice that married Emeline, but Lester the son of Amos and Alice died 25 Jul 1805 at age 4 years. The two Lester Utley are second cousins and both George Abbott descendants.

[1798] Her parents are verified by the 1816 will of Nathan Luce which includes a bequest to his daughter Polly wife of Antipas Utley. Ancestry.com. *New York, Wills and Probate Records, 1659-1999* [database on-line]. Provo, UT, USA: Ancestry.com Operations, Inc., 2015. Original data: New York County, District and Probate Courts.

[1799] Antipas is a head of household in 1800, 1810, 1820, and 1830 Census in Windham County, CT and there is a female of the right age for Polly through 1810, but not in 1820 or 1830. Polly is in her father's 1816 will.

vii MARICA UTLEY, b. about 1810; d. at Chatham, 1833.[1800]

viii LUCINDA UTLEY, b. about 1813; d. at North Windham, 1890; m. at Windham, 19 Mar 1845, FREEMAN D. SPENCER, b. at Chaplin, about 1820; Freeman d. 1905.

ix ORIGEN UTLEY, b. about 1815; d. at Middletown, 1875 (probate 1875); m. at Middletown, 12 May 1840, SUSAN M. CURTIS, b. at Meridien, 1821 daughter of Asahel Benham and Emily M. (Hubbard) Curtis; Susan d. at Middletown, 1904.

652) RUFUS UTLEY *(Hannah Abbott Utley[4], Philip[3], William[2], George[1])*, b. at Windham, 25 May 1773 son of Samuel and Hannah (Abbott) Utley; m. MARY "POLLY" SILL daughter of Ezra and Charity (Pratt) Sill; Mary d. 1847.[1801]

According to the Abbot genealogical register (p 55), Rufus married, "moved west", and committed suicide. Records for the family are scant. One child has been clearly identified, but there may be others.

i PHILIP UTLEY, b. in NY, 13 Aug 1805; d. at Masonville, NY, 22 Jul 1859; m. about 1827, HARRIET PRATT, b. in NY, 19 Oct 1806 daughter of Harriet; Harriet d. at Masonville, 3 Jun 1892.

653) ABIGAIL FULLER *(Mary Abbott Fuller[4], Philip[3], William[2], George[1])*, b. at Windham, 1 Jan 1753 daughter of Stephen and Mary (Abbott) Fuller; d. at Athens, PA, 31 Jan 1834; m. at Windham, 30 Apr 1772, JAMES BIDLACK, b. 26 Nov 1750 son of James and Mehitable (Durkee) Bidlack; James d. at Wyoming, PA, 3 Jul 1778. Abigail married 2nd, as his second wife, JOHN FRANKLIN, b. at Canaan, CT, 12 Sep 1749 son of John and Keziah (Pierce) Franklin. John Franklin d. at Athens, PA, 1 Mar 1831. John Franklin was first married to Lydia Doolittle.

James and Abigail married in Connecticut, but soon after were in Wilkes-Barre. In January 1778, James was commissioned as Captain in the 1st Company of the 24th Regiment. He was killed at the Battle of Wyoming. His estate entered probate 24 November 1778 with his widow Abigail as administratrix.[1802]

Abigail Fuller and James Bidlack were parents of four children.[1803]

i STEPHEN BIDLACK, b. at Wilkes-Barre, 5 Jan 1773; d. at Spencer, NY, 4 Mar 1849; m. 28 Mar 1793, LOIS RANSOM, b. 3 Mar 1775 daughter of Samuel and Esther (Laurence) Ransom; Lois d. at Spencer, 21 Mar 1856.

ii SARAH "SALLY" BIDLACK, b. at Wilkes-Barre, about 1773; d. at Penn Yan, NY, 14 Jun 1851; m. about 1817, as his second wife, AUGUSTUS CHIDSEY, b. at Guilford, 22 Jun 1764 son of Joseph and Zeruiah (Collins) Chidsey; Augustus d. at Penn Yan, 19 Aug 1833. Augustus was firs married to Ann Rathbone.

iii MEHITABEL "HETTY" BIDLACK, b. at Wilkes-Barre, 1 Jul 1776; d. 25 Jan 1838; m. about 1796, WILLIAM PATRICK, b. at Plainfield, CT, 6 Jan 1773 son of Jacob and Zeruah (Maxwell) Patrick; William d. at Birmingham, MI, 25 Aug 1852.

iv JAMES BIDLACK, b. at Delaware Water Gap, PA, 22 Sep 1778; d. at Sheshequin, PA, 30 Apr 1828; m. about 1803, ESTHER MOORE, b. 16 May 1787 daughter of Daniel Moore; Esther d. at Sheshequin, 23 Aug 1863.

654) MARY FULLER *(Mary Abbott Fuller[4], Philip[3], William[2], George[1])*, b. at Windham, 28 May 1759 daughter of Stephen and Mary (Abbott) Fuller; d. likely at Tioga, NY, after 1811 (living at the time of husband's probate); m. at Wilkes-Barre, 2 Jan 1782, THOMAS BALDWIN, b. 23 Feb 1755 son of Isaac and Patience (Rathburn) Baldwin; Thomas d. in Tioga, NY about 1810.

Thomas Baldwin wrote his will 11 January 1810 in Athens, Pennsylvania but the probate of his estate is in Tioga, New York and the will includes extensive description of his property in Tioga. Beloved wife Mary receives all the household furniture for her lifetime and it is at her disposal. He then notes that in addition to debts owed, there are outstanding payments due to the estate. After the settlement of the debts, the estate is to be divided among his five sons: Thomas Baldwin, Jr., Vine Baldwin, George Baldwin, Isaac Baldwin, and Morgan Baldwin. His has these bequests to his three daughters: Ency Duprey, five dollars; Mira Covel, one hundred dollars; and Hannah Baldwin, one hundred fifty dollars. There are other specifications for

---

1800 *Connecticut, Hale Collection of Cemetery Inscriptions and Newspaper Notices, 1629-1934*

1801 Sill, *Genealogy of the Descendants of John Sill*, p 86

1802 Harvey, *History of Wilkes-Barre*, volume 2, p 1000

1803 Although some sources attribute three children to Abigail Fuller from her second marriage to John Franklin, evidence currently available suggests that is not the case. Specifically, Ruth Franklin Curtis who has sometimes been reported as a daughter of Abigail and John was almost certainly the daughter of David Franklin and Hannah Simmons. Heverly, *Pioneer and Patriot Families of Bradford County, Pennsylvania, volume I*, p 182 states that Abigail Fuller and John Franklin had no children from their marriage.

the support of wife Mary and for the bringing up and education of son Morgan and daughter Hannah. These directions include how the income and interest from the farm is to be used which is given in detail. Sons Thomas and Vine Baldwin and brother Isaac Baldwin are named executors. The will was proved 18 March 1811.[1804]

Mary Fuller and Thomas Baldwin were parents of eight children. In most cases, birth dates are estimated based on other records (census, age at time of death).

i EUNICE BALDWIN, b. about 1783; d. at Lawrenceville, PA, 8 Aug 1838; m. ELIJAH DEPUY, b. at Forty Fort, PA, 17 Sep 1775; Elijah d. at Lawrenceville, PA, 17 Mar 1853.

ii THOMAS BALDWIN, b. at Tioga County, about 1783; d. in OH; m. about 1810, SALLY BALDWIN, b. 3 Mar 1791 daughter of Isaac and Alice (Haskell) Baldwin.

iii VINE BALDWIN, b. about 1785; d. at Elmira, NY, 21 Jun 1872; m. about 1810, SARAH M. "SALLY" BURT, b. at Warwick, NY, 6 Jan 1787 daughter of Thomas and Elizabeth (Hawthorn) Burt; Sarah d. at Chemung, 8 May 1864.

iv GEORGE BALDWIN, b. about 1787; d. at Wellsburg, NY, 14 May 1869; m. about 1820, POLLY BEIDELMAN, b. 7 Nov 1793 daughter of Samuel and Elizabeth (Hess) Beidelman; Polly d. at South Creek, PA, 23 May 1850.

v ISAAC BALDWIN, b. about 1788; d. at Tioga County, before 1850; m. at Elmira, 25 Jan 1816, ALICE "ELSIE" DUNN, b. 10 Nov 1798 daughter of William and Mercy Ann (Sayre) Dunn; Elsie d. at Elmira, 25 Dec 1879.

vi ALMIRA "MIRA" BALDWIN, b. about 1789; d. at Elmira, 6 Aug 1866; m. ROBERT COVELL, b. about 1787 son of Matthew and Aurelia (Tuttle) Covell; Robert d. at Elmira, 2 Apr 1864.

vii MORGAN BALDWIN, b. at Elmira, 15 Jul 1796; d. at Genesee County, 19 Jan 1880; m. 1st, about 1819, HANNAH SLY daughter of John and Mary (Hammond) Sly;[1805] Hannah d. at Southport, NY, 18 Aug 1826. Morgan m. 2nd, 14 Feb 1834,[1806] MARY JANE YANGER, b. 21 Dec 1815; Mary Jane in Genesee County, 31 Mar 1838.[1807] Morgan m. 3rd, at Genesee, 13 Dec 1838, EUNICE DART, b. in CT, 16 Jan 1815 daughter of Joshua and Susannah (Stebbins) Dart; Eunice d. 21 Mar 1905.

viii HANNAH BALDWIN, b. about 1798; living in 1810 when her father's will was written; nothing further known.

655) JOHN FULLER *(Mary Abbott Fuller4, Philip3, William2, George1)*, b. at Windham, 26 Jan 1762 son of Stephen and Mary (Abbott) Fuller; d. at Carlton, NY, 11 Mar 1817; m. about 1788, AMY SHAW, b. 1766 (based on age at time of death) whose parents are unknown to me; Amy d. 13 Nov 1834.

John Fuller had gone as a child with his parents to Wyoming, Pennsylvania, was then in Sheshequin and lastly in Carlton, New York. He donated the land for the cemetery in Carlton and was the first person buried there. He also participated in building the first school in Carlton.[1808]

In his will written 8 March 1817 (proved 1 July 1817), John Fuller bequeathed to his eldest son Stephen Fuller, one dollar. He bequeaths to his other four sons and his beloved wife three lots or one-quarter section of land on which he now lives. Son Thomas receives a described lot of 100 acres, sons John and Reuben also receive 100 acres, and son George receives 50 acres. His three daughters, Sally, Polly, and Laurenda, each receive 30 acres. The remainder of the estate goes to his beloved wife who is also named executrix.[1809]

John Fuller and Amy Shaw were parents of eight children likely all born at Sheshequin.

i SALLY FULLER, b. perhaps 1787; living in 1817 when father wrote his will, but nothing else is known.

ii STEPHEN FULLER, b. Sep 1788; d. at Carlton, NY, 23 Feb 1842; m. by 1810, JERUSHA BISHOP, b. at Suffolk County, NY, 20 Jun 1789 daughter of Stephen and Jerusha (Jagger) Bishop; Jerusha d. at Carlton, 2 Jan 1862.

iii THOMAS FULLER, b. 30 Jul 1789; d. at Carlton, NY, 8 Nov 1849; m. 1st, 15 Nov 1815, SARAH FERSTER, b. 3 Feb 1796; Sarah d. at Carlton, NY, 10 Feb 1830. Thomas m. 2nd, 3 Mar 1831, SARAH LOVEWELL, b. 19 Oct 1797; Sarah d. at Carlton, 18 Jul 1839. Thomas m. 3rd, 3 Dec 1839, ELIZABETH SHERWOOD, b. 30 Jul 1807 daughter of Timothy and Lois (Grumman) Sherwood; Elizabeth d. at Carlton, 6 Jan 1877.

1804 *Will Books (Record of Probate, Letters of Administration, Wills) 1798-1905;* Author: *New York. Surrogate's Court (Tioga County);* Probate Place: *Tioga, New York, Will Book, A-B, Vol 0002-0003, 1798-1818*, pp 30-33.

1805 History and Genealogies of the Hammond Families, volume II, part IV, p 342

1806 Ellis, *History of Genesee County, Michigan*, p 296

1807 Taken from Odell Cemetery records: Baldwin, Mary Jane (Yanger), b. 21 Dec 1815, d. 31 Mar 1838, second wife of Morgan Baldwin

1808 Fuller, *Descendants of Thomas Fuller*, p 91

1809 *Record of Wills, 1809-1911;* Author: *New York. Surrogate's Court (Genesee County);* Probate Place: *Genesee, New York, Record of Wills, Vol 0001-0003, 1809-1840*, vol 1, p 127-128

iv POLLY FULLER, b. 26 Aug 1792; d. at Dorr, MI, 2 Jul 1873; m. 7 Jan 1811, EDWARD DURFEE, b. 1 Aug 1790 son of Job and Susannah (Borden) Durfee; Edward d. at Tiskilwa, IL, 5 Aug 1846.

v JOHN FULLER, b. 2 Nov 1795; d. at Carlton, NY, 2 Mar 1863; m. about 1819, HANNAH JAGGER, b. 9 Mar 1796; Hannah d. at Carlton, 10 Oct 1840.

vi REUBEN ELMER FULLER, b. 7 May 1800; d. at Carlton, NY, 13 May 1891; m. 1st, 12 Oct 1823, JOANNA STRICKLAND, b. 1805; Joanna d. 4 Jul 1824. Reuben m. 2nd, 3 Nov 1825, FANNY MOREHOUSE, b. 1804 daughter of Adonijah and Phebe (Bennett) Morehouse; Fanny d. at Carlton, 24 Sep 1856. Reuben m. 3rd, 3 Nov 1857, HARRIET ROSS, b. 1808; Harriet d. 22 Oct 1889.

vii LAURINDA FULLER, b. 1803; d. at Vista, NY, 25 Oct 1865; m. HORACE OCTAVIUS GOOLD, b. at Lyme, CT, 12 Aug 1800 son of Walter and Sarah (Latimer) Goold; Horace d. at Lyndonville, NY, 5 Oct 1865.

viii GEORGE WASHINGTON FULLER, b. 6 Aug 1806; d. at Hastings, MI, 30 Jan 1848; m. LOUISA WICKHAM, b. 1810; Louisa d. at Hastings, MI, 1872.

656) REUBEN FULLER *(Mary Abbott Fuller4, Philip3, William2, George1)*, b. at Windham, 19 Feb 1769 son of Stephen and Mary (Abbott) Fuller; d. at Carlton, NY, 7 Jul 1837; m. 23 May 1793, MARY P. CASH, b. 10 Dec 1775 daughter of Daniel and Mary "Polly" (Tracy) Cash; Mary d. Sep 1849.

Reuben Fuller was a farmer. The family was in Sheshequin, Pennsylvania but relocated to Carlton, New York about 1811.[1810]

i ELECTA FULLER, b. at Sheshequin, 19 Nov 1794; d. at Kucksville, NY, 11 Dec 1858; m. 23 Mar 1819, Rev. GEORGE KUCK, b. in England, 23 Dec 1791 son of Garrard and Mary (Trimmer) Kuck;[1811] d. at Kucksville, NY, 16 Mar 1868.

ii HIRAM PAYNE FULLER, b. at Sheshequin, 21 Feb 1798; d. at Seneca, MI, 9 May 1856; m. 6 Dec 1820, SARAH MARVIN GOOLD, b. in NY, 21 Feb 1806 daughter of Elihu and Sarah (Marvin) Goold; Sarah d. at Broadland, SD, 21 Nov 1884.

iii HARMON FULLER, b. at Sheshequin, 16 Sep 1800; d. at Hastings, MI, 10 May 1875; m. 1 Feb 1823, POLLY BARNUM, b. in NY, 22 May 1803 daughter of Zebulon and Betsey (Ferster) Barnum; Polly d. at Hastings, 24 Feb 1872.

iv JOHN CASH FULLER, b. at Sheshequin, 20 Feb 1803; d. at Pendleton, NY, 21 Feb 1880; m. 2 Feb 1825, ELIZA GOOLD, b. 3 May 1808 daughter of Elihu and Sarah (Marvin) Goold; Eliza d. 28 Oct 1890.

v MINERVA FULLER, b. at Sheshequin, 20 Oct 1805; d. at New Windsor, IL, 1891; m. about 1822, ELIHU GOOLD, b. about 1799 son of Elihu and Sarah (Marvin) Goold; Elihu d. at New Windsor, 1883.

vi LYMAN FULLER, b. at Sheshequin, 16 Aug 1808; d. at Carlton, NY, 23 Mar 1866; m. ROXANNA BARNUM, b. at Orleans County, NY, 3 Mar 1810 daughter of Zebulon and Betsey (Ferster) Barnum; Roxanna d. at Carlton, 24 May 1875.

vii PHEBE ANN FULLER, b. at Sheshequin, 10 Nov 1810; d. 4 Aug 1813.

viii REUBEN WARREN FULLER, b. at Carlton, 23 Nov 1814; d. at Carlton, 30 Jun 1864; m. JEANETTE E. PITCHER, b. in Connecticut, 1815; Jeanette d. at Carlton, 23 Feb 1869.

ix HANNAH A. FULLER, b. at Carlton, 8 May 1817; d. at Carlton, 8 Aug 1885; m. 18 Sep 1836, WILLIAM BROWN, b. 8 Aug 1815 son of Nathaniel and Jane (-) Brown; William d. at Carlton, 4 Jun 1893.

x MARY E. FULLER, b. at Carlton, 8 Aug 1821; d. at Carlton, 5 Sep 1885; m. FRANCIS ORLANDO BENTLEY, b. 1818; Francis d. at Carlton, 1882.

657) HANNAH FULLER *(Mary Abbott Fuller4, Philip3, William2, George1)*, b. at Windham, 17 Aug 1772 daughter of Stephen and Mary (Abbott) Fuller; d. at Scipio, NY, 1 Sep 1817; m. 18 Oct 1792, WILKES DURKEE, b. at Windham, 25 Jul

[1810] Thomas, *Pioneer History of Orleans County, New York*, p 197
[1811] England, Select Births and Christenings, 1538-1975

1768 son of Andrew and Mary (Benjamin) Durkee; Wilkes d. at Franklin, MI, 23 Dec 1844.[1812] Wilkes remarried Mariah Lee Yawger after the death of Hannah.

Hannah and Wilkes had all their children in Scipio. After Hannah's death, Wilkes remarried and relocated to Franklin, Michigan about 1823.[1813]

i MARY DURKEE, b. 8 Aug 1793; d. at Nunda, NY, 25 Feb 1862; m. Mar 1815, AUSTIN DOWNS, b. at Southbury, CT, 10 Jan 1793 son of Truman and Sarah (Porter) Downs; Austin d. at Mount Norris, NY, 17 Feb 1855.

ii AURELIA DURKEE, b. 7 Mar 1795; d. at Farmington Hills, MI, 3 Aug 1856; m. JOSHUA MERWIN COONLEY, b. Oct 1790 son of Benjamin Coonley; Joshua d. at Farmington Hills, 13 Dec 1851.

iii ANNA DURKEE, b. 5 Nov 1796; d. 10 Aug 1799.

iv AMERON DURKEE, b. 16 Aug 1799; d. at Union Springs, 6 Aug 1867; m. EVELINA WRIGHT, b. 6 Nov 1800; Evelina d. at Union Springs, 30 Oct 1865.

v BALDWIN DURKEE, b. 9 Sep 1802; d. 5 Apr 1810.

vi STEPHEN FULLER DURKEE, b. 5 Jan 1805; d. at Franklin, MI, 16 Jan 1877; m. NANCY YAWGER, b. at Springport, NY, 6 May 1814 daughter of Philip Yawger; Nancy d. at Bloomfield, MI, 28 Jun 1863.

vii WILLIAM PATRICK DURKEE, b. 16 Jun 1807; d. at Bloomfield, MI, 24 Mar 1879; m. 1st, CAROLINE WARNER, b. 27 Dec 1809; Caroline d. at Franklin, MI, 27 Dec 1850. William m. 2nd, MARY ANN "POLLY" PRATT, b. 30 Jun 1830 daughter of William and Nancy (-) Pratt; Polly d. at Franklin, MI, 6 Aug 1909.

viii ROYAL DURKEE, b. 16 Jun 1811; d. at Fenton, MI, 10 Jul 1882; m. about 1850, LYDIA MARIA BRADDOCK, b. 17 Jun 1834 son of Sidney Braddock;[1814] Lydia d. at Fenton, MI, 28 Feb 1904.

ix HANNAH ANN DURKEE, b. 7 Jun 1815; d. 18 Dec 1816.

658) MARY ABBOT *(Joseph4, Philip3, William2, George1)*, b. at Pomfret, 6 Apr 1759 daughter of Joseph and Elizabeth (Stedman) Abbot; d. at Windsor, CT, 25 Dec 1835; m. 1st, about 1785, DANIEL ELLSWORTH, b. 3 Dec 1758 son of Daniel and Mary (-) Ellsworth; Daniel d. at Presque Isle, PA, 3 Mar 1798.[1815] Mary m. 2nd, EBENEZER SCARBOROUGH, b. at Pomfret, 1 Mar 1743 and d. at Brooklyn, CT, 2 Oct 1813.

In her will written 17 Aug 1827 (proved 30 Dec 1835), Mary Scarborough made the following bequests: daughter Mary Thompson wife of Samuel Thompson, $1000; daughter Nancy Scarborough, $1000; daughter Sophia Prince wife of David Prince, $1000; grandson Daniel Ellsworth Scarborough son of Nancy, $50; granddaughter Mary Thompson, silver tea spoons; Mary Abbott Prince daughter of Sophia, the large bible; her three daughters receive the wearing apparel; son John Ellsworth receives all the remainder of the estate and is named executor. The value of the estate was $4,417.[1816]

Mary Abbot and Daniel Ellsworth were parents of six children born at Ellington.

i BETSY A. ELLSWORTH, b. 24 Dec 1785; d. 24 Jul 1797.

ii MARY ELLSWORTH, b. 20 Jan 1789; d. at Ellington, 26 Feb 1868; m. 9 Nov 1809, SAMUEL THOMPSON, b. at Ellington, 1778 son of Samuel and Eleanor (-) Thompson; Samuel d. at Ellington, 22 Jun 1875.

iii NANCY ELLSWORTH, b. 12 Nov 1790; d. at Payson, IL, 4 Dec 1843; m. at Brooklyn, CT, 15 Nov 1808, LUTHER SCARBOROUGH, b. at Brooklyn, 12 May 1787 son of Joseph and Deliverance (Kingsbury) Scarborough; Luther d. at West Hartford, 16 Apr 1820.

iv JOHN ELLSWORTH, b. 22 Aug 1792; d. at West Hartford, 19 Jan 1859; m. at Hartford, 6 Apr 1836, HANNAH MAY, b. 15 Jul 1807;[1817] Hannah d. at West Hartford, 13 Jul 1872.

v SOPHIA ELLSWORTH, b. 13 Aug 1794; d. at Payson, IL, 3 May 1865; m. at Brooklyn, CT, 18 Apr 1815, DAVID PRINCE, b. 22 May 1791 son of Timothy and Prudence (Denison) Prince; David d. at Payson, 21 Nov 1873.

vi CHLOE ELLSWORTH, b. 18 Mar 1796; d. 22 Jul 1797.

[1812] Wilkes Durkee was in New York for a time but received a homestead patent 22 Apr 1824 in the Michigan-Toledo strip. United States, Bureau of Land Management. *Michigan Pre-1908 Homestead & Cash Entry Patent and Cadastral Survey Plat Index*. General Land Office Automated Records Project, 1994. (accessed through ancestry.com)

[1813] Durant, *History of Oakland County, Michigan*, p 320

[1814] Lydia's father's name is given as Sidney Braddock on her death record.

[1815] Connecticut, Hale Collection of Cemetery Inscriptions and Newspaper Notices, 1629-1934

[1816] *Connecticut. Probate Court (Hartford District)*; Probate Place: *Hartford, Connecticut, Probate Records, Vol 40-41, 1834-1838*, probate of Mary Scarborough, p 181

[1817] Hannah's date of birth is given on her death record.

659) ABIGAIL ABBOT *(Joseph[4], Philip[3], William[2], George[1])*, b. at Ellington, 17 Dec 1762 daughter of Joseph and Elizabeth (Stedman) Abbot; d. at West Hartford, 11 Sep 1844; m. about 1784, SAMUEL WHITMAN, b. 26 Jul 1753 son of John and Abigail (Pantry) Whitman; Samuel d. 7 Feb 1810 when he was kicked by a horse.

During the Revolution, Samuel Whitman served as a private in Captain Hooker's company in the Connecticut militia. His widow Abigail received an annual pension of $24.88 related to his service.[1818]

Abigail Abbot and Samuel and Whitman were parents of twelve children all born at West Hartford.

i SAMUEL WHITMAN, b. 14 Apr 1785; d. 27 Apr 1785.

ii SAMUEL WHITMAN, b. 4 May 1786; d. at West Hartford, 31 May 1852; m. 20 Apr 1813, ELIZABETH HOWARD, b. at Tolland, 27 Nov 1790 daughter of Stephen and Esther (Simon) Howard; Elizabeth d. 21 Mar 1888.

iii ELIZA WHITMAN, b. 6 Jun 1788; d. at Williamstown, MA, 28 Feb 1814. "Eliza, d. of Samuel and Abigail of Hartford, Conn., Feb. 28, 1814, in 26th year."

iv ABIGAIL WHITMAN, b. 20 Oct 1789; d. at West Hartford, 18 Dec 1812; m. at Hartford, 16 Sep 1812, TIMOTHY SEYMOUR GOODMAN, b. at West Hartford, 1787 son of Moses and Amy (Seymour) Goodman; Timothy d. at Cincinnati, 8 May 1870. After Abigail's death, Timothy married Amelia Faxon.

v HENRY WHITMAN, b. 25 Jul 1791; d. at West Hartford, 28 Feb 1814.

vi EMMA WHITMAN, b. 13 Sep 1793; d. 23 Jul 1795.

vii EMMA WHITMAN, b. 14 Aug 1795; d. 7 Sep 1797.

viii LUCY WHITMAN, b. 19 Aug 1797; d. at Ogden, NY, Feb 1831; m. at West Hartford, 22 May 1825, Rev. EVELYN SEDGWICK, b. at Ogden, about 1794 likely the son of William and Lucy (Merrill) Sedgwick; Evelyn d. at Ogden, after 1865. After Lucy's death, Evelyn married Harriet Thompson.

ix HARRIET WHITMAN, b. 20 Aug 1799; d. at Cincinnati, 1 Oct 1850; m. at West Hartford, 1 Dec 1829, EPIPHRAS GOODMAN, b. about 1790 son of Moses and Ann (Seymour) Goodman; Epiphras d. at Chicago, 5 Jun 1862.

x EMELINE WHITMAN, 4 Jul 1801; d. at Hartford, 4 Apr 1825.

xi JULIA WHITMAN, b. 28 Jul 1803; d. at Danville, IA, 10 Mar 1864. Julia did not marry. In 1850, she was living with her sister Harriet and her family in Millcreek, Ohio and in 1860 living in Chicago with her brother-in-law Epiphras Goodman and nieces and nephews.

xii LAURA WHITMAN, b. 29 Sep 1807; d. at West Hartford, 5 Sep 1833. Laura did not marry.

660) LEMUEL ABBOTT *(Joseph[4], Philip[3], William[2], George[1])*, b. at Pomfret, 9 Mar 1768 son of Joseph and Olive (Pearce) Abbot; d. at Vernon, 9 Jun 1846; m. 8 May 1792, LUCRETIA BINGHAM, b. 22 Jul 1766 daughter of Ithamar and Sarah (Kellogg) Bingham; Lucretia d. 17 Mar 1835.

In his will written 4 February 1846 (probate 14 June 1846). Lemuel Abbott states "After fulfilling the agreement entered into by myself and my son Bela Abbot respecting my support, if any of my estate remains unexpended, I dispose of it as follows." Daughter-in-law Fidelia Abbot wife of Bela receives $200. All the residue of the estate goes to son Bela, and he is also named executor. The value of the estate was $1,516.57.[1819]

Lemuel Abbott and Lucretia Bingham were parents of eight children all born at Vernon, Connecticut. The two oldest sons went to Richmond, Virginia where they both died before marrying.

i HARVEY ABBOTT, b. 3 May 1793; d. at Richmond, VA, 14 Sep 1820.

ii PERLEY ABBOTT, b. 27 Jun 1796; d. at Richmond, 24 Aug 1821.

iii CHARLES ABBOTT, b. 25 Jul 1798. He is perhaps the Charles Abbott who d. at Sugar Grove, IL, 26 Sep 1872.

[1818] Revolutionary War Pension and Bounty-Land Warrant Application Files

[1819] *Connecticut State Library (Hartford, Connecticut)*; Probate Place: *Hartford, Connecticut, Ellington District, Probate Packets, A-Bingham, Eli, 1826-1892*, Estate of Lemuel Abbott.

iv OLIVE ABBOTT, b. 3 Oct 1800; d. at Becket, MA, 1 Feb 1871; m. at Vernon, 1 Mar 1837, NEWMAN KEYES CHAFFEE, b. at Becket, 15 Dec 1796 son of Thomas and Abigail (Knowlton) Chaffee; Newman d. at Becket, 13 Dec 1858. Newman was first married to Elizabeth Phelps.

v BELA ABBOTT, b. 9 Jan 1803; d. at El Paso, IL, 2 Mar 1872; m. 30 Mar 1836, FIDELIA C. HUNT, b. 15 Jun 1815 daughter of Oliver and Roxanna (Smith) Hunt; Fidelia d. at Elmwood, IL, 13 Mar 1864.

vi LEMUEL ABBOTT, b. 14 Jun 1805; d. at Blackstone, MA, 27 Nov 1866; m. at Medway, MA, 28 Dec 1830, SARAH JOHNSON BURR, b. at Dover, VT, 26 Dec 1806 daughter of Ezekiel and Esther (Johnson) Burr;[1820] Sarah d. at Blackstone, 3 Oct 1866.

vii JOSEPH ABBOTT, b. 22 Jul 1807. He is likely the Joseph Abbott of Vernon who died at Washington, DC, 13 Jun 1852. He does not seem to have married.

viii BICKFORD ABBOTT, b. 15 Mar 1809; d. at Galesburg, IL, 21 Sep 1870; m. at East Windsor, 21 May 1835, AMELIA N. RISLEY, b. 18 Aug 1815 daughter of Whiting and Nancy (Goodale) Risley; Amelia d. at Vernon, about 1888 (probate Apr 1888).

661) DELANO ABBOT *(Joseph[4], Philip[3], William[2], George[1])*, b. at Pomfret, 16 Apr 1774 son of Joseph and Olive (Pearce) Abbot; d. at Ira, NY, 11 Mar 1852; m. 1 Jan 1801, MARY "POLLY" BINGHAM, b. 1778 daughter of Ithamar and Sarah (Kellogg) Bingham;[1821] Polly d. at Ira, 11 Mar 1852.

Delano lived in Ira, New York where he was a manufacturer of wool and satin, in addition to farming.[1822] Delano Abbott and Polly Bingham were parents of eight children born at Vernon, Connecticut.

i BETSEY ABBOTT, b. 17 Jan 1802; d. at Reading, MI, 10 May 1848; m. about 1824, JABEZ HASKELL MOSES, b. 1797 son of Martin and Roxy (Haskell) Moses; Jabez d. at Des Plaines, IL, 23 Dec 1838.[1823]

ii HORACE ABBOTT, b. 5 May 1804; d. at Auburn, NY, 1886; m. ROZELLA HEATH, b. at Ira, NY, about 1811 daughter of James and Huldah (-) Heath;[1824] Rozella d. at Auburn, 14 Jul 1899.

iii LORENZO ABBOTT, b. 4 Dec 1806; d. at Reading, MI, 14 Jan 1892; m. 1st, about 1835, CLARISSA M. HANNAH, b. 1815 daughter of David and Susannah (Sanford) Hannah; Clarissa d. at Reading, 10 Sep 1849. Lorenzo m. 2nd, at Bethlehem, CT, 2 Jun 1851, Clarissa's sister, CAROLINE HANNAH, b. 14 Feb 1811; Caroline d. at Reading, 31 Dec 1895.

iv JULIA ABBOTT, b. 22 Apr 1809; m. about 1834, DANIEL HARRISON, b. in NY, about 1800. This family was living in Manhattan in 1830 and little information has been yet found.

v DELANO BINGHAM ABBOTT, b. 22 Jul 1812; d. at Reading, MI, 30 Apr 1884; m. at Wood, OH, 23 Jun 1835, MARY FULK, b. in PA, 1815 daughter of Benjamin and Eliza (-) Fulk; Mary d. at Reading, 4 Apr 1903.

vi MARY ABBOTT, b. 3 Oct 1814; d. at Reading 1866 (probate 12 Mar 1866). Mary did not marry. In 1860, she was living with her brother Henry Kellogg and his family.

vii HENRY KELLOGG ABBOTT, b. 15 Dec 1816; d. at Reading, MI, 20 Jun 1899; m. OLIVE GRINNELL, b. in NY, about 1818 daughter of Ezra and Catherine (Degolyer) Grinnell; Olive d. at Elkhart, IN, 13 Oct 1899.

viii DELIA ANN ABBOTT, b. 19 Apr 1819; d. at Ira, NY, 22 Mar 1855; m. about 1835, BIRDSEYE CURTIS, b. at Stratford, CT, 25 Dec 1810 son of Eli and Sarah (Blakeman) Curtis; Birdseye d. at Ira, 13 Jun 1882. Birdseye married second Mary E.

662) JOHN ABBOT *(Joseph[4], Philip[3], William[2], George[1])*, b. at Pomfret, 6 Jul 1784 son of Joseph and Olive (Pearce) Abbot; d. at Vernon, 13 Mar 1859; m. 31 Mar 1813, ACHSAH CONE, b. at East Haddam, 17 Jul 1789 daughter of Daniel and Keziah (Chapman) Cone; Achsah d. 4 Aug 1882.

John Abbot was a farmer. John and Achsah were parents of four children born at Vernon, only one of whom married.

[1820] Sarah's parents' names are given as Ezekiel and Esther Burr on her death record.

[1821] Bingham, *The Bingham Family in the United States*, p 193

[1822] Abbot, *Genealogical Register*, p 57

[1823] Moses, *Historical Sketches of John Moses of Plymouth*, p 155

[1824] The 1855 probate record of James Heath of Ira, NY includes Rosilla Abbott wife of Horace Abbott as an heir.

i JOHN EDWIN ABBOTT, b. 11 Jan 1814; d. at Springfield, MA, 14 Nov 1899; m. about 1855, CAROLINE BOLLES, b. at Columbia, CT, Feb 1819 daughter of David and Mary (Carrie) Bolles;[1825] Caroline d. at Springfield, 26 Feb 1908.

ii CAROLINE NEWELL ABBOTT, b. 20 Aug 1816; d. 16 Apr 1839.

iii WILLIAM C. ABBOTT, b. 11 Feb 1820; d. 3 May 1820.

iv ABELINE ABBOTT, b. 16 Apr 1824; d. 26 Feb 1845.

663) ALICE ABBOTT *(John⁴, Philip³, William², George¹)*, b. at Windham 17 Apr 1763 daughter of John and Alice (Fuller) Abbott; d. at Hampton, 16 Jan 1809; m. 27 Apr 1790, AMOS UTLEY, b. at Windham, 22 Aug 1764 son of Amos and Grace (Martin) Utley; Amos d. at Hampton, 24 Apr 1810.

Alice Abbott and Amos Utley were parents of nine children all born at Hampton, Connecticut.

i ALICE UTLEY, b. 7 Feb 1791; d. at Chaplin, CT, 4 May 1831; m. 1st at Mansfield, CT, 27 Oct 1810, JOHN HARTSHORN, b. at Mansfield, 3 Sep 1790 son of Andrew and Elizabeth (Baldwin) Hartshorn;[1826] John d. at Mansfield, 1816 (probate 3 Apr 1816). Alice m. 2nd, about 1824, as the third of his four wives, JEREMIAH WHITE, b. at Hebron, CT, 8 Jun 1780 son of Asa and Mary (Bingham) White. Jeremiah White's other marriages were to Elizabeth Bottom, Sally Bottom, and Anna Parkhurst.

ii TRUMAN UTLEY, b. 4 May 1792; d. at Greenfield, PA, 16 Jun 1876; m. HARRIET WARREN, b. Jan 1800 daughter of Joseph and Abigail (Allen) Warren; Harriet d. at Greenfield, 19 Sep 1887.

iii AMOS UTLEY, b. 16 Jun 1793; d. at Berkshire, OH, 24 Jun 1882; m. SARAH STARK, b. 23 Feb 1802 daughter of Paul and Katherine (Rosengrant) Stark;[1827] Amos d. 9 Feb 1872.

iv ALMIRA UTLEY, b. 12 Aug 1796; d. at Chaplin, CT, 3 Jun 1867; m. at Mansfield, CT, 15 Sep 1816, JOHN RUSS, b. 1793 son of Samuel and Hannah (Owen) Russ; John d. at Chaplin, 14 Jul 1849.

v SABINA UTLEY, b. 10 Oct 1797; d. at Randolph, WI, after 1860; m. at Mansfield, CT, 20 Oct 1816, ELIJAH HARTSHORN, b. at Mansfield, 26 May 1796 son of Daniel and Hannah (Dexter) Hartshorn;[1828] Elijah's death not known, but before 1860.

vi LUCIUS UTLEY, b. 10 Jun 1799; d. at Lenox, PA, 8 Jun 1887; m. 1825, his first cousin, CATHERINE KENNEDY *(Sarah Abbott Kennedy⁵, John⁴, Philip³, William², George¹)*, b. at Wilkes-Barre, 8 Aug 1804 daughter of James and Sarah (Abbott) Kennedy; Catherine d. at Lenox, 4 Oct 1879. Catherine Kennedy is a child in Family 669.

vii LESTER UTLEY, b. 27 Jun 1801; d. 25 Jul 1805.

viii FESTUS UTLEY, b. 8 Mar 1803; d. at Berkshire, OH, 18 Aug 1872; m. ANNA TIN, b. in PA, about 1810; Anna d. at Berkshire, 11 Nov 1874.

ix JARED UTLEY, b. 21 Jul 1804; d. at Berkshire, OH, 21 May 1884; m. POLLY FISHER, b. in OH, about 1811 daughter of George and Phebe (Hopkins) Fisher; Polly d. at Berkshire, 15 Sep 1879.

664) CELINDA "LINDA" ABBOTT *(John⁴, Philip³, William², George¹)*, b. at Windham, CT, 20 May 1766 daughter of John and Alice (Fuller) Abbott; d. at Scott, PA, 8 Apr 1854; m. about 1786, REUBEN TAYLOR, b. Norwalk, CT, 28 Nov 1759 son of Reuben and Rebecca (Weeks) Taylor; Reuben d. at Greenfield, PA, 1849.

In the Revolution, Reuben Taylor served as a private in the company of Captain Seely in the Regiment of Colonel Drake in the North Fork militia. He enlisted in the winter of 1775 from Cortland Manor, New York where he was living at the time. Reuben served short periods during that first enlistment. He then moved with his father to Newbury, Connecticut and enlisted there in May 1778 in Captain Olmstead's company. He was credited with 19 months of service in determining his pension. The pension file includes an affidavit dated 13 January 1851 by Sarah Kennedy, age seventy-two, who reported she

[1825] Bolles, *Genealogy of the Bolles Family*, p 39
[1826] Dimock, *Births, Baptisms, Marriages, and Deaths, Mansfield, Connecticut*
[1827] Stark, *The Aaron Stark Family*, pp 41-42
[1828] Dimock, *Births, Baptisms, Marriages, and Deaths, Mansfield, Connecticut*

had known Celinda Abbott since a child. Celinda grew up in the area of Wilkes-Barre and married Reuben Taylor and resided in Scott Township.[1829]

In his will dated 20 July 1846, Reuben Taylor bequeaths one dollar to his son Henry Taylor and one dollar to his grandson Henry Brown. Wife Selenda receives all the personal property if she is still living at the time of his decease. Selenda also receives the use of all the property that he now owns. If she dies before Reuben, this property goes to son John A. Taylor. As a consequence of John A. Taylor receiving the entire farm, he is to pay to grandson Erastus Taylor one hundred and fifty dollars. John A. Taylor is also named executor of the estate.[1830] Grandson Erastus Taylor is the son of Henry Taylor who was deceased at the time of the will.

Reuben Taylor and Linda Abbott were parents of six children born at Providence Township, Pennsylvania.[1831]

i JOHN ABBOTT TAYLOR, b. 29 Aug 1791; d. at Scott Township, PA, 21 Sep 1867; m. 3 Jan 1812, GARTRY ACKLEY, b. at Plains Township, PA, 26 Apr 1790 daughter of Silas and Esther (Guinn) Ackley; Gartry d. at Scott Township, 3 Jun 1867.

ii HENRY TAYLOR, b. 21 May 1793; d. at Wabash, IL, 24 Apr 1849; m. 1st, about 1819, HULDAH BROWN, b. in PA, about 1800 daughter of James and Silence (Bates) Brown; Huldah d. at Montdale, PA, 1821. Henry m. 2nd, ANN who has not been identified.

iii POLLY ABBOTT TAYLOR, b. 21 Feb 1795; d. at Montdale, PA, Apr 1821; m. JAMES BROWN, b. about 1797 son of James and Silence (Bates) Brown; James d. at Montdale, Mar 1821.

iv CYNTHIA TAYLOR, b. 21 Apr 1799; nothing further known.

v REUBEN TAYLOR, b. 21 Nov 1802; nothing further known.

vi BENIRA TAYLOR, b. 21 May 1806; nothing further known.

665) CHARLES ABBOTT *(John4, Philip3, William2, George1)*, b. 3 Jun 1769 son of John and Alice (Fuller) Abbott; d. at Delaware County, OH, after 1853; m. about 1800, URANIA (also named Lorena in some sources) MANVILLE, b. 24 Mar 1775 daughter of Nicholas Manville; Urania d. at Sunbury, OH, 21 Dec 1848.[1832]

Five children have been reported for Charles Abbott and Urania Manville.[1833]

i CHARLES ABBOTT, b. 26 Apr 1803; d. at Sunbury, OH, 8 Dec 1845. Charles did not marry.

ii URANIA ABBOTT, b. about 1806; d. likely at Berkshire, OH, after 1860; m. GEORGE STILL, b. in OH, about 1806; George d. after 1860. Urania and George did not have children.

iii CAROLINE ABBOTT, b. about 1808; nothing further known.

iv LYMAN ABBOTT, b. 8 Oct 1811; d. at Berkshire, OH, 7 May 1869; m. at Delaware County, OH, 5 Jan 1845, PERMELIA NISWANER, b. in OH, 1822; Permilia d. at Galena, OH, after 1880.

v ELIZA ABBOTT, b. Nov 1815; d. at Marshalltown, IA, after 1910; m. about 1837, WILLIAM STANTON, b. in NY, 1815; William d. at Columbus, IN, 13 Sep 1869.

666) STEPHEN ABBOTT *(John4, Philip3, William2, George1)*, b. 19 Apr 1771 son of John and Alice (Fuller) Abbott; d. at Plains, PA, 22 Jul 1853;[1834] m. 14 Jul 1799, ABIGAIL SEARLE, b. at Stonington, 25 Jun 1779 daughter of William and Philena (Frink) Searle; Abigail d. 2 Jun 1842. Stephen m. 2nd, 1 Jun 1843, SARAH DENISON the widow of Thomas Ferrier and daughter of Nathan and Elizabeth (Sill) Denison.

Stephen Abbott's father was killed in the aftermath of The Battle of Wyoming (1778). Following her husband's death, Stephen's mother took her children and returned to Connecticut, but remarried and returned to Pennsylvania. Stephen Abbott settled on the property in Wyoming that had been owned by his father and lived there until his death.[1835]

Stephen and Abigail Abbott had six children born in Luzerne County, Pennsylvania.

1829 Revolutionary War Pension and Bounty-Land Warrant Application Files, 1800-1900. The pension file contains a lengthy description of Reuben's service during the war.

1830 Pennsylvania, Wills and Probate Records, 1683-1993, *Wills, 1787-1916; Index, 1787-1918;* Author: *Luzerne County (Pennsylvania). Register of Wills;* Probate Place: *Luzerne, Pennsylvania, Will Books, Vol B-C, 1839-1863*, Book B, pp 336-337

1831 The births of the children are recorded on a bible page which was copied and included with the pension application file. The places and dates of birth of Reuben and Celinda are also given in the bible record.

1832 Ancestry.com, *Web: Delaware County, Ohio, Burial Index, 1784-2011* (Provo, UT, USA: Ancestry.com Operations, Inc., 2013).

1833 Abbott, *The Courtright Family*, p 114

1834 Ancestry.com, *Pennsylvania, Deaths, 1852-1854* (Provo, UT, USA: Ancestry.com Operations, Inc., 2011), Pennsylvania State Archives; Reel Number: 671.

1835 Harvey, *History of Wilkes-Barre*, volume 5, p 723

i JOHN ABBOTT, b. at Wilkes-Barre, 18 Apr 1800; d. at Jacobs Plains, 23 Nov 1861; m. 11 Mar 1830, HANNAH COURTRIGHT, b. at Wilkes-Barre, 7 Feb 1798 daughter of Cornelius and Catherine (Kennedy) Courtright; Hannah d. 4 May 1892.

ii WILLIAM ABBOTT, b. in Luzerne County, 19 Jun 1802; d. in Knox County, OH, 9 Feb 1870; m. 2 Nov 1824, ELEANOR "ELLEN" COURTRIGHT, b. at Plains, 13 Sep 1804 daughter of Cornelius and Catherine (Kennedy) Courtright; Ellen d. 10 Mar 1886.

iii LUCY ABBOTT, b. 1 Apr 1805; d. 2 Jul 1806.

iv ELIZA ABBOTT, b. at Luzerne County, 22 Oct 1806; d. at Wilkes-Barre, 18 Aug 1846; m. 3 Jan 1826, ROBERT MINER, b. at Doylestown, PA, 17 Aug 1805 son of Abner and Mary (Wright) Miner; Robert d. 9 Dec 1843.

v STEPHEN FULLER ABBOTT, b. at Jacobs Plains, 18 Jul 1809; d. at Wilkes-Barre, 11 Feb 1856; m. 22 Feb 1838, CHARLOTTE MINER, b. 30 Jun 1816 daughter of Charles and Letitia (Wright) Miner; Charlotte d. 28 Jul 1859.

vi CHARLES M. ABBOTT, b. 24 May 1814; d. 26 Dec 1814.

667) LYDIA ABBOTT *(John⁴, Philip³, William², George¹)*, b. about 1775 daughter of John and Alice (Fuller) Abbott; d. at Know County, OH after 1853; m. ARTEMAS SWETLAND, b. in Connecticut about 1769 son of Luke and Hannah (Tiffany) Swetland; Artemas d. 1855.

Artemas and Lydia began their family in Pennsylvania and had their first five children there. They relocated to Sunbury in Delaware County, Ohio in June 1810 where their youngest child was born. In 1817, they relocated to Sparta in Morrow County where they remained.[1836][1837]

When he was 43 years old, Artemas enlisted in the Army during the War of 1812 and served as a private.[1838] He enlisted 27 October 1812 and served until 19 November 1812 in Captain Henry Slack's Company.

Artemas and Lydia had six children, one of who was unnamed and died in early infancy. The other five children are given.

i AUGUSTUS W. SWETLAND, b. 9 Oct 1797; d. at Sparta, OH, 22 Sep 1882; m. in Knox County, OH, 29 Jun 1826, HANNAH E. RICH, born about 1808 of not yet identified parents; Hannah d. at Sparta, 10 Jun 1868. Augustus Swetland was a physician, a farmer, and a postmaster at Sparta.[1839]

ii GILES TIFFANY SWETLAND, b. 19 Aug 1799; d. at Bloomfield, OH, 6 Nov 1881; m. at Knox County, OH, 28 Jun 1822, SARAH LEWIS, b. 1798 daughter of William and Rhoda (Conger) Lewis; Sarah d. at Bloomfield, 1864.

iii FULLER M. SWETLAND, b. 9 Sep 1801; d. in Morrow County, OH, 1869; m. in Knox County, 8 Feb 1832, ELIZABETH RUSSELL, born 1808 of parents not identified; Elizabeth d. 1882.

iv SETH SWETLAND, b. 14 Mar 1807; d. at Sparta, OH, 24 Oct 1891; m. at Knox County, 22 Jan 1832, PHEBE LYON, b. about 1808 in New Jersey of undetermined parents but perhaps the daughter of Benjamin Lyon; Phebe d. 1898.

v MARILLA SWETLAND, b. at Sunbury, OH, 14 Sep 1810; d. at El Paso, IL, 4 Jan 1897; m. 1832, WILLIAM SHUR, b. at Washington County, PA, 17 Sep 1806 son of Jacob and Margaret (Porter) Shur; William d. at El Paso, IL, 29 Mar 1878.

668) MARY "POLLY" ABBOTT *(John⁴, Philip³, William², George¹)*, b. about 1776 daughter of John and Alice (Fuller) Abbott; m. JOHN COURTRIGHT, b. 7 Apr 1774 son of Benjamin and Catherine (Hoover) Courtright; John d. 4 Dec 1822. [Courtright is spelled Cortwright in some records.]

In his will dated 9 August 1822 (probate 21 December 1822), John Courtright bequeathed to wife Polly fifty dollars annually to be paid by sons Cornelius and Draper Courtright, the use of one-third of the household items, and a room in the family home as long as she is unmarried. Daughter Hannah receives one hundred dollars. Son Cornelius receives one-half the landed estate to be taken from the south side of the farm. Daughter Roxanna receives one hundred-fifty dollars and son Charles receives four hundred dollars. Son Draper receives the other half of the land. Son Volany receives four hundred dollars and

[1836] Wyoming Democrat - 20 Nov 1891 - Page 3, obituary of Seth Swetland, newspapers.com
[1837] Perrin, *History of Morrow County*, p. 676
[1838] Ohio, Soldier Grave Registrations, 1804-1958; Artemas S. Swetland, born 1769, died 1855.
[1839] Ancestry.com, U.S., Appointments of U. S. Postmasters, 1832-1971

daughter Eliza Ann receives one hundred-fifty dollars. John elaborates that the real estate is to be kept undivided and jointly owned by Cornelius and Draper until Draper reaches age twenty-one. He also states that his coal bed in Wilkes-Barre can be sold if the executor thinks this in the best interest of Cornelius and Draper. Executors are wife Polly Courtright and trusty nephew John Courtright, 2nd.[1840]

Polly Abbott and John Courtright were parents of seven children all born at Plains, Pennsylvania.[1841]

i HANNAH COURTRIGHT, b. 9 Jun 1801; d. at Corning, NY, 22 Oct 1878; m. 14 Jul 1819, HORACE GRISWOLD PHELPS, b. at Simsbury, CT, 2 Feb 1797 son of Alexander and Elizabeth (Eno) Phelps; Horace d. at Corning, 1871.

ii CORNELIUS COURTRIGHT, b. 28 May 1803; d. at Newark, IL, 7 Sep 1894; m. 1st, 10 Jul 1827, HARRIET BAILEY, b. 2 Dec 1805 daughter of Benjamin and Lydia (Gore) Bailey; Harriet d. at Millington, IL, 22 Mar 1851. Cornelius m. 2nd, 4 Jul 1852 the widow SUSANNA LUTHER.

iii ROXANNA COURTRIGHT, b. 12 Oct 1805; d. at Seneca County, OH, 19 Jan 1850; m. 27 May 1833, JAMES M. CHAMBERLIN, b. in PA, 25 Aug 1806; James d. at McCutchenville, OH, 12 Aug 1888. James married second 3 Apr 1851 the widow Catherine A. Hall.

iv CHARLES A. COURTRIGHT, b. 4 Mar 1807; d. at Canaan, PA, 12 Sep 1856; m. 19 Feb 1829, REBECCA R. HART, b. in PA, 1810; Rebecca d. at Canaan, after 1870.

v JOHN DRAPER COURTRIGHT, b. 29 Dec 1808; d. at Freedom, IL, 29 Jan 1887; m. 27 Sep 1843, HANNAH RHODES, b. in England, about 1825; Hannah d. at Tacoma, WA, 14 Apr 1903.

vi VOLNEY F. COURTRIGHT, b. 17 Jun 1811; d. at Canaan, PA, 19 Aug 1855; m. at Salem, PA, 5 May 1836, PHILENA J. HAMLIN, b. at Wayne County, PA, 7 Jan 1811 daughter of Harris and Ruey (Easton) Hamlin; Philena d. at Scranton, PA, 12 Apr 1891.

vii ELIZA ANN COURTRIGHT, b. 14 May 1814; d. at Dundaff, PA, 20 Sep 1845; m. 6 Dec 1831, GEORGE CONE, b. at Kingston, NY, 31 Dec 1805 son of Doratus and Mary (Curran) Cone; George d. at Scranton, 22 Sep 1864. George married second Frances L. Courtright.

669) SARAH ABBOTT *(John⁴, Philip³, William², George¹)* b. 28 Feb 1778 daughter of John and Alice (Fuller) Abbott; d. Tunkhannock, PA; m. 16 Apr 1800, JAMES KENNEDY, b. at Deer Park, NY, 13 Jul 1775 son of John and Mary (Van Fleet) Kennedy;[1842] James d. at Tunkhannock, 19 Oct 1864.

James and Sarah started their family in the Wyoming Valley of Pennsylvania. In June 1833, James bought property in Tunkhannock in Wyoming County. He was a blacksmith by trade.[1843]

James Kennedy and Sarah Abbott were parents of five children.

i CATHERINE KENNEDY, b. at Wilkes-Barre, 8 Aug 1804; d. at Lenox, PA, 4 Oct 1879; m. 1825, her first cousin, LUCIUS UTLEY *(Alice Abbott Utley⁵, John⁴, Philip³, William², George¹)*, b. at Hampton, CT, 10 Jun 1799 son of Amos and Alice (Abbott) Utley; Lucius d. at Lenox, 8 Jun 1887. Lucius Utley is a child in Family 663.

ii LYMAN KENNEDY, b. at Canaan, PA, 14 Nov 1806; d. at South Canaan, before 1870; m. NANCY SWINGLE, b. about 1807 daughter of Jacob and Effie (Shaffer) Swingle;[1844] Nancy d. at South Canaan, after 1870.

iii JOHN A. KENNEDY, b. at Tunkhannock, 6 Aug 1808; d. at Farmingdale, IL, 6 Apr 1892; m. 11 Jan 1837, ELIZABETH CAMPBELL, b. 20 Mar 1812; Elizabeth d. at Farmingdale, 2 Nov 1892.

iv THOMAS KENNEDY, b. at Tunkhannock, 3 Jan 1811; d. at LaGrange, PA, after 1880; m. SARAH KELLEY, b. about 1827; Sarah d. after 1880.

v STEPHEN ABBOTT KENNEDY, b. at Tunkhannock, 15 Aug 1814; d. at Janesville, WI, 18 Jun 1876; m. 1st, 8 Sep 1838, MINERVA BILLINGS, b. ag Luzerne County, 1818 daughter of Jasper and Jane (Day) Billings; Minerva d. in Luzerne County, 20 May 1846. Stephen m. 2nd, Minerva's sister, HULDAH BILLINGS, b. 10 Aug 1822.

[1840] *Wills 1787-1916; Indexes 1787-1918;* Author: *Luzerne County (Pennsylvania). Register of Wills;* Probate Place: *Luzerne, Pennsylvania, Will Index, 1787-1918*, p 271

[1841] Abbott, *The Courtright Family*, p 59

[1842] Blair, *The Michael Shoemaker Book*, p 73

[1843] Blair, *The Michael Shoemaker Book*, p 74

[1844] The will of Jacob Swingle includes a bequest to his daughter Nancy Kennedy.

670) WILLIAM HOLT *(Hannah Holt Holt⁴, Hannah Abbott Holt³, William², George¹)*, b. at Windham, 15 Jul 1743 son of William and Hannah (Holt) Holt; d. at Hampton, 6 Aug 1815;[1845] m. 8 Sep 1763, his third cousin, MERCY HOLT, b. 14 Feb 1740/1 daughter of Zebadiah and Sarah (Flint) Holt; Mercy d. 15 Sep 1799.

William Holt and Mercy Holt were parents of three children born at Hampton.

i WILLIAM HOLT, b. 22 Nov 1764; d. at Hampton, 8 May 1793; m. 6 Nov 1788, his first cousin, SARAH FULLER, b. at Canterbury, 21 Oct 1768 daughter of Aaron and Sarah (Holt) Fuller; Sarah d. 1838.

ii MERCY HOLT, b. 7 Dec 1766; d. at Cooperstown, NY, 14 Sep 1834; m. 1788, JAMES AVERILL, b. at Ashford, 14 Dec 1763 son of James and Mary (Walker) Averill; James d. at St. Johnsville, NY, 17 Dec 1835.

iii ABIGAIL HOLT, b. 27 Sep 1774; nothing further known.

671) ALICE HOLT *(Hannah Holt Holt⁴, Hannah Abbott Holt³, William², George¹)*, b. at Windham, 26 Apr 1747 daughter of William and Hannah (Holt) Holt; d. at Stockbridge, VT, 28 Nov 1814;[1846] m. 13 Nov 1764, ROBERT LYON, b. at Pomfret, 30 Sep 1743 son of Peletiah and Sarah (Holt) Lyon; Robert d. at Stockbridge, 12 Feb 1809.

Robert Lyon and Alice Holt were parents of five children born at Hampton, Connecticut. They relocated to Stockbridge, Vermont after the births of their children.

i ROBERT LYON, b. 23 Dec 1765; d. at Stockbridge, VT, 17 Mar 1844; m. at Stockbridge, 26 Nov 1789, KATHERINE BURNET, b. about 1762; Katherine d. at Stockbridge, 4 Apr 1833.

ii RUFUS LYON, b. 24 Apr 1767; d. at Stockbridge, 30 Jan 1841; m. at Stockbridge, 5 Oct 1792, LOVINA WILLARD, b. in VT, about 1775; Lovina d. at Stockbridge, Aug 1852.

iii ALICE LYON, b. 14 Jun 1769; nothing further known.

iv ROSWELL LYON, b. 2 Oct 1770; d. at Stockbridge, 8 Nov 1814; m. at Stockbridge, 27 Aug 1795, LYDIA ROBERTS, b. 1778; Lydia d. at Stockbridge, 19 Jul 1859.

v CHESTER LYON, b. 25 May 1772; d. at Braintree, VT, 17 Mar 1812; m. about 1795, THIRZA POOLER, b. at Pomfret, 10 Nov 1772 daughter of Amasa and Hannah (Cady) Pooler; Thirza d. at Braintree, 18 Oct 1843.

672) SARAH HOLT *(Hannah Holt Holt⁴, Hannah Abbott Holt³, William², George¹)*, b. at Windham, 21 Jun 1748 daughter of William and Hannah (Holt) Holt; d. at Hampton, 7 Apr 1777; m. 16 Nov 1769, HENRY DURKEE, b. 29 Sep 1749 son of Henry and Relief (Adams) Durkee. Henry m. 2nd, Sarah Loomis; Henry d. at Hampton, 22 Apr 1820.

Sarah Holt and Henry Durkee were parents of three children born at Hampton.

i HENRY DURKEE, b. 25 Aug 1770; m. at Hampton, 25 Sep 1794, SALLY RUSSELL, b. at Ashford, 28 Feb 1774 daughter of Benjamin and Phebe (Smith) Russell; Sally d. at Pittsfield, MA, 23 Dec 1833.

ii ABIEL DURKEE, b. 14 Mar 1774; d. 8 Feb 1778.

iii SARAH DURKEE, b. 18 Jan 1777; d. at Hampton, 2 Jan 1806; m. 22 Dec 1796, AZEL GOODWIN, b. at Lebanon, CT, 31 Aug 1769 son of Jonathan and Anna (Clark) Goodwin; Azel d. at Coventry, 14 Apr 1829. Azel married second Clarissa Hunt.

673) MARY FENTON *(Elizabeth Holt Fenton⁴, Hannah Abbott Holt³, William², George¹)*, b. at Willington, 13 Apr 1749 daughter of Francis and Elizabeth (Holt) Fenton; d. at Willington, 14 Apr 1822; m. 1st, 21 May 1770, ISAAC SAWIN, b. 23 Sep 1748 son of George and Anna (Farrar) Sawin; Isaac d. 29 Oct 1776. Mary m. 2nd, 2 Jul 1778, as his second wife, JAMES NILES, b. at Braintree, 2 Apr 1747 son of John and Dorothy (Reynolds) Niles; James d. 18 Jan 1822. James Niles was first married to Elizabeth Vinton.

Isaac Sawin did not leave a will. The inventory of his estate was completed 5 February 1777 with a total value of £126 including house and land valued at £80. George Sawin was named guardian for three-year-old Elijah. The distribution of the estate includes a set-off of one-third part for widow Mary and the remaining two-thirds to only child Elijah.[1847]

[1845] *Connecticut, Deaths and Burials Index, 1650-1934.*

[1846] *Vermont, Vital Records, 1720-1908.*

[1847] *Connecticut Wills and Probate, 1609-1999*, Probate of Isaac Sawin, Tolland, 1777, Case number 1879.

After Isaac's death, Mary married James Niles and had four children. James had three children with his first wife, Elizabeth Vinton. James Niles wrote his will 8 June 1819 and the estate entered probate 1822. In his will, beloved wife Mary receives one cow, four sheep, the use of a west room of the house and a number of provisions to be provided by the executors. Five of the children will divide the household items after their mother's decease (Elizabeth, Phebe, Isaac, Joshua Holt, and Molly). Oldest son James receives $50. There are in-kind money bequests to Elizabeth, Phebe, and Molly. Son Isaac receives the house Isaac is living in and the land it stands upon. Son Joshua Holt receives his father's house. Sons Isaac and Joshua Holt are named executors.[1848] Children James, Elizabeth, and Phebe are children from James Nile's marriage to Elizabeth Vinton.

Mary Fenton and Isaac Sawin had two children born at Willington.

i ELIZABETH SAWIN, b. 16 Dec 1770; d. 8 Feb 1771.

ii ELIJAH SAWIN, b. 31 Oct 1774; d. at Willington, 1814 (date of probate); m. at Willington, 24 Dec 1795, AMEY POOL, b. at Willington, 7 Aug 1775 daughter of Timothy and Deborah (Presson) Pool. Amey's date and place of death are not known. Some of the children seem to have relocated to Massachusetts and perhaps Amey traveled there also.

Mary Fenton and James Niles had four children born at Willington.

i JOHN NILES, b. 2 Oct 1779; d. 26 Jun 1803.

ii MOLLY NILES, b. 3 Oct 1782. No birth or death record was located for Molly, but she was living in 1819 at the time of her father's will.

iii ISAAC NILES, b. 9 Mar 1786; d. at Tolland, 7 Oct 1858; m. at Willington, 27 Oct 1808, his third cousin, ALLICE SCRIPTURE *(Alice Pearl Scripture*[5]*, Timothy Pearl*[4]*, Elizabeth Stevens Pearl*[3]*, Elizabeth Abbott Stevens*[2]*, George*[1]*)*, b. at Willington, 14 Jul 1790 daughter of Eleazer and Alice (Pearl) Scripture; Allice d. 3 Mar 1863.

iv JOSHUA HOLT NILES, b. 6 Sep 1790; d. at Willington, 10 Apr 1850; m. at Willington, 3 Dec 1812, SIBYL HUGHES, b. at Ashford, 4 May 1795 daughter of Jonathan and Eunice (Fuller) Hughes; Sibyl d. at Willington, 29 May 1873.

674) FRANCIS FENTON *(Elizabeth Holt Fenton*[4]*, Hannah Abbott Holt*[3]*, William*[2]*, George*[1]*)*, b. at Willington, 13 Feb 1750/1 son of Francis and Elizabeth (Holt) Fenton; m. 25 May 1775, CHLOE GOODALE, b. at Pomfret, 28 Dec 1755 daughter of Ebenezer and Phebe (Holt) Goodale; Chloe d. at New Haven, Oct 1833.[1849]

Francis Fenton and Chloe Goodale were parents of six children born at Willington.

i ELIZABETH FENTON, b. 27 Mar 1777

ii OLIVER FENTON, b. 1 Nov 1778; d. 22 Nov 1781.

iii CHLOE FENTON, b. 20 May 1780; d. at South Windsor, CT, 19 Feb 1823; m. ELLIOT GRANT, b. at Windsor, CT, 23 Apr 1762 son of Edward and Hannah (Foster) Grant; Elliot d. at East Windsor, 7 Jun 1846.

iv CHESTER FENTON, b. 11 Mar 1782; d. 5 Mar 1783.

v PHEBE FENTON, b. 1 Sep 1783

vi LEISTER FENTON, b. 26 Jun 1786

675) HANNAH HOLT *(Abiel Holt*[4]*, Hannah Abbott Holt*[3]*, William*[2]*, George*[1]*)*, b. at Willington, 14 Mar 1756 daughter of Abiel and Mary (Downer) Holt; d. 20 Nov 1832; m. 24 Apr 1782, as his second wife, her second cousin, OLIVER PEARL *(Timothy Pearl*[4]*, Elizabeth Stevens Pearl*[3]*, Elizabeth Abbott Stevens*[2]*, George*[1]*)*, b. 9 Oct 1749 son of Timothy and Dinah (Holt) Pearl. Oliver was married 1st, 1 Jan 1772 MERCY HINCKLEY, b. 1749 daughter of John and Susanna (Harris) Hinckley;[1850] Mercy d. at Willington, 15 Nov 1781.

Hannah Holt and Oliver Pearl were parents of six children born at Willington.

i HANNAH PEARL, b. 29 Apr 1783; d. 23 Nov 1786.

[1848] *Connecticut Wills and Probate, 1609-1999*, Probate of James Niles, Stafford District, 1822, Case number 1554.

[1849] Connecticut, Deaths and Burials Index, 1650-1934

[1850] The 1788 Connecticut probate record of John Hinckley (widow Susanna) includes as heirs grandsons Daniel Pearl and Oliver Pearl the children of Mercy who is deceased.

ii MARCY PEARL, b. 18 Aug 1785; m. 1st, at Ashford, 1 Jan 1810, WILLIAM BUFFINGTON, b. at Ashford, 21 Jun 1789 son of William and Candace (Salisbury) Buffington; William d. at Ashford, 20 Jan 1814. Marcy m. 2nd, about 1815, LOREN FULLER.[1851]

iii OLIVER PEARL, b. 10 Nov 1788; d. at Berlin Heights, OH, 26 May 1835; m. about 1811, MARY SEXTON, b. at Ellington, 5 Dec 1795 daughter of William and Docia (Emerson) Sexton; Mary d. at Berlin Heights, 15 May 1884.

iv WALTER PEARL, b. 15 Sep 1791; m. at Mansfield, CT, 24 Nov 1814, MARIA DAVIS, b. at Mansfield, 9 Jul 1794 daughter of Thomas and Patience (Dennison) Davis.[1852]

v HANNAH PEARL, b. 17 May 1794; d. at Berlin Heights, OH, 26 Oct 1849; m. 1822, PHILIP SEELY BAKER, b. in CT, 22 Jul 1790; Philip d. at Berlin Heights, 12 May 1889. Philip married second the widow Lavinia Decker.

vi CYREL PEARL, b. 16 Sep 1797; d. at Lounsberry, NY, 20 Jul 1837; m. 29 May 1820, ROSANNAH FARMER, b. 24 Jun 1804 daughter of Thomas and Rosannah (Thompson) Farmer; Rosannah d. at Lounsberry, 17 Jun 1875.

Oliver Pearl and Mercy Hinckley were parents of five children born at Willington.

i ALICE PEARL, b. 15 Dec 1772; d. 30 Mar 1773.

ii OLIVER PEARL, b. 14 Sep 1774; d. 6 Apr 1775.

iii OLIVER PEARL, b. 15 May 1776; d. 16 Oct 1786.

iv DANIEL PEARL, b. 1779; d. 14 Jul 1779.

v DANIEL PEARL, b. 29 May 1780; d. before 1850; m. at Willington, 5 Mar 1806, POLLY HORTON, b. about 1783; Polly d. at Owego, NY, after 1860.

676) SARAH HOLT *(Abiel Holt⁴, Hannah Abbott Holt³, William², George¹)*, b. at Willington, 8 Dec 1757 daughter of Abiel and Mary (Downer) Holt; d. at Willington, 1856;[1853] m. 24 Oct 1782, ZEBULON CROCKER, b. at Willington, 5 Mar 1757 son of Ebenezer and Hannah (Hatch) Crocker; Zebulon d. at Willington, 17 Jan 1826.

The estate of Zebulon Crocker was probated in 1826 with son Zebulon Crocker as administrator. The inventory was completed 27 January 1826 with a total value of $2,081.88. The distribution of the dower was made to widow Sarah Crocker on 4 October 1826. The distribution agreement included the following children as heirs: Candace Crocker, Alpheus Crocker, Bethiah Crocker, Ira Heath and Hannah his wife, and Zebulon Crocker.[1854]

Zebulon and Sarah Crocker had six children born at Willington.

i ALPHEUS CROCKER, b. 3 Sep 1783; d. 23 May 1784.

ii CANDACE CROCKER, b. 6 Jun 1785; d. at Willington, 11 Jan 1849. Candace did not marry.

iii ALPHEUS CROCKER, b. 3 Jul 1787; d. 24 Nov 1873; m. at Willington, 28 Apr 1808, his third cousin, PHEBE MARCY *(Phebe Pearl Marcy⁵, Timothy Pearl⁴, Elizabeth Stevens Pearl³, Elizabeth Abbott Stevens², George¹)*, b. at Willington, 12 Oct 1789 daughter of Zebadiah and Phebe (Pearl) Marcy; Phebe d. at Webster, NY, 11 Jun 1871. This family lived in Webster, NY.[1855] Phebe Marcy is a child in Family 1165.

iv BETHIAH CROCKER, b. 1 Jun 1791; d. at Willington, 10 Dec 1860; m. at Willington, 3 Oct 1832, JOSEPH HULL, b. at Willington, 16 Feb 1788 son of Hazard and Abigail (-) Hull; Joseph d. at Willington, 26 Mar 1871.

v HANNAH CROCKER, b. 9 Apr 1796; m. about 1815, IRA HEATH, b. at Willington, 13 Oct 1793 son of David and Abigail (Scripture) Heath. There have been found just two records for children in this family and it is uncertain what became of Hannah and Ira. One of the sons settled in New York, so perhaps they will be found there, although there is no evidence of them in census records after 1820.

1851 Gay, *Historical Gazetteer of Tioga County, part I*, p 370

1852 Dimock, *Births, Baptisms, Marriages, and Deaths: From the Records of the Town and Churches in Mansfield, Connecticut*, p 59

1853 In the 1850 U.S. Census, 92-year old widow Sarah Crocker was living at the home of her daughter Bethiah Hull. Probate of estate was 1856 with Joseph Hull as administrator.

1854 Ancestry.com. *Connecticut, Wills and Probate Records, 1609-1999* [database on-line]. Case number 545, Probate of Zebulon Crocker

1855 Year: 1870; Census Place: Webster, Monroe, New York; Roll: M593_971; Page: 447B; Family History Library Film: 552470

vi Reverend ZEBULON CROCKER, b. 8 Mar 1802; d. at Middletown, CT, 14 Nov 1847; m. at East Windsor, 11 Oct 1830, ELIZABETH "BETSY" PORTER, b. about 1799 daughter of Daniel and Ann (Allyn) Porter;[1856] Betsy d. at Cromwell, 25 Feb 1877. Zebulon and Betsy do not seem to have had any children. Zebulon's will leaves the entire estate to Betsy.

677) MARY HOLT *(Abiel Holt⁴, Hannah Abbott Holt³, William², George¹)*, b. at Willington, 8 Dec 1760 daughter of Abiel and Mary (Downer) Holt; d. at Dracut, 6 Nov 1833;[1857] m. at Charlton, MA, 17 Feb 1783,[1858] DANIEL NEEDHAM *possibly* the son of Daniel and Hannah (Allen) Needham; Daniel d. at Paxton, MA 1801 (date of probate 6 Oct 1801; will written 4 Mar 1801).

The will of Daniel Needham written 4 March 1801 includes a bequest of the widow's third to his wife Mary, and the equal division of the remainder of the estate among his four children namely Polly, Parsons, Rachel, and Sally.[1859]

Daniel Needham and Mary Holt were parents of five children the births reported either at Paxton or Charlton.

i MARY "POLLY" NEEDHAM, b. at Paxton, 31 Mar 1784; m. at Danvers, 30 Sep 1807[1860], JOHN NEEDHAM who has not been identified.

ii JOHN NEEDHAM, baptized at Charlton, 16 Apr 1786; d. before his father's will in 1801.

iii JOSEPH PARSONS NEEDHAM, baptized at Charlton, Jun 1788; d. at Buffalo, NY, after 1865; m. at Medway, MA, 1 Feb 1815, JOANNA WIGHT, b. at Medway, 22 Jan 1794 daughter of Aaron and Jemima (Rutter) Wright; Joanna d. after 1865.

iv RACHEL NEEDHAM, b. at Paxton, 14 Dec 1791; d. at Perinton, NY, 12 Apr 1887; m. at Salem, JOSEPH BLOOD, b. 24 Jun 1787 perhaps the son of Joseph and Priscilla (French) Blood; Joseph d. 14 Sep 1840.

v SARAH NEEDHAM, baptized at Charlton, 14 Oct 1798; d. at Dracut, 22 Oct 1880; m. 26 Aug 1821, JOEL FOX, b. at Dracut, 12 Aug 1784 son of Joel and Hannah (Cheever) Fox; Joel d. at Lowell, 21 Dec 1861.

678) ABIEL HOLT *(Abiel Holt⁴, Hannah Abbott Holt³, William², George¹)*, b. at Willington, 12 Jul 1762 son of Abiel and Mary (Downer) Holt; d. at Fairfax, VT, 6 Jun 1829; m. by 1787, MARY MOSHER, b. 21 Jul 1762 daughter of Nathaniel and Elizabeth (Crandall) Mosher; Mary d. at Fairfax, 6 Sep 1827.

Abiel Holt served in the Revolution as a private in Captain Abner Robinson's company. Abiel Holt and Mary Mosher were parents of eight children.

i PHEBE HOLT, b. at Fairfax, 14 Oct 1787; d. at Sharon, VT, 11 May 1851; m. at Sharon, 19 Feb 1818, JOSEPH ROICE, b. about 1792; Joseph d. at Sharon, 7 Apr 1827.

ii LUCINDA HOLT, b. at Fairfax, 14 Oct 1789; d. at Fairfax, 24 Mar 1849; m. at Sharon, 1 Feb 1820, IRA FARNSWORTH, b. at Fairfax, 27 Nov 1799 son of Thomas and Chloe (Balch) Farnsworth; Ira d. at Fairfax, 5 Dec 1860.

iii ABIEL HOLT, b. at Sharon, 9 Sep 1791; d. at Boston, NY, 9 Dec 1869; m. at Albany, 20 Jan 1817, his third cousin, MARY ABBOTT *(Caleb⁵, William⁴, Caleb³, William², George¹)*, b. at Colden, NY, 8 Mar 1798 daughter of Caleb and Hannah (Wheat) Abbott;[1861] Mary d. at Colden, NY, 16 Oct 1879. Mary Abbott is a child in Family 713.

iv ARNOLD HOLT, b. at Sharon, 5 Jul 1794; d. at Moline, IL, about 1869 (probate Jan 1870); m. 1st, 22 Nov 1815, RUEY AUSTIN, b. at Milton, VT, 2 Jul 1797 daughter of David and Judith (Hall) Austin; Ruey d. at Colden, NY, 21 Oct 1841. Arnold m. 2nd, 19 Oct 1842, HANNAH MILLINGTON, b. in VT, 18 Sep 1819 daughter of John and Mary (Gardiner) Millington; Hannah d. at Washington, IA, 27 Sep 1906.

v ZEBINA HOLT, b. at Sharon, 7 Sep 1797; d. at Salem, MN, 19 Feb 1871; m. about 1820, his third cousin, ORINDA ABBOTT *(Caleb⁵, William⁴, Caleb³, William², George¹)*, b. at Colden, 21 Aug 1803 daughter of Caleb and Hannah (Wheat) Abbott; Orinda d. at Salem, MN, 10 Mar 1880. Orinda Abbott is a child in Family 713.

vi WORSTER HOLT, b. at Sharon, 19 Nov 1799; d. at Salem, MN, 17 Sep 1881; m. NANCY LEWIS, b. in VT, 1814; Nancy d. at Concord, NY, before 1870.

[1856] Betsy's parents are confirmed by the 1833 probate of Dr. Daniel Porter that includes a distribution to daughter Betsy Crocker.

[1857] Mary, w. Daniel, Nov. 6, 1833, a. 73.

[1858] *Massachusetts, Compiled Marriages, 1633-1850*. Daniel and Mary Holt of Willington, int. Feb. 17, 1783.

[1859] Worcester County, MA: Probate File Papers, 1731-1881. Online database. AmericanAncestors.org. New England Historic Genealogical Society, 2015.

[1860] From Danvers vital records: Needham, Mary, of Charlton, and John Needham, Sept. 30, 1807.

[1861] Durrie, Holt Genealogy, p 100; Abbot, Genealogical Register, p 62

vii NICHOLAS MOSHER HOLT, b. at Sharon, 16 Mar 1801; d. at Brecksville, OH, 1866; m. at Burlington, VT, 1 Jan 1827, ANN REYNOLDS, b. in MA, 1804; Ann d. at Brecksville, after 1880.

viii ELIZABETH HOLT, b. at Sharon, 16 Mar 1801; d. at Springville, NY, 2 Aug 1848; m. about 1823, ALVA DUTTON, b. at Fairfax, 29 Jan 1798 son of Reuben and Polly (Farnsworth) Dutton; Alva d. at Springville, 25 Jun 1878. Alva married second Martha Ann Jewett.

679) ABEL HOLT *(Abiel Holt⁴, Hannah Abbott Holt³, William², George¹)*, b. at Willington, 1770 son of Abiel and Eunice (Kingsbury) Holt; m. 1st, at Norwich, 17 Nov 1793, ANNA ABEL, b. at Norwich, 8 Jul 1771 daughter of Thomas and Zerviah (Hyde) Abel;[1862] Anna d. at Sharon, 13 Apr 1798. Abel m. 2nd, by 1798, RUTH KING, b. at Wilbraham, MA, 13 Feb 1779 daughter of Oliver and Ruth (Cooley) King.

Abel Holt and Anna Abel had one child.

i THOMAS ABEL HOLT, b. at Sharon, VT, 23 Jul 1796; d. at Sharon, 26 Aug 1815.

Abel Holt and Ruth King were parents of nine children, the first eight children born at Sharon, Vermont and the youngest child at Burlington, Vermont. After the births of their children, the family relocated to Oneida, New York.

i ANNA HOLT, b. 1 Oct 1798; m. at Sharon, 25 Oct 1824, THOMAS MOREHOUSE, b. about 1801; Thomas d. at Sharon, 6 Jun 1825.

ii RUTH HOLT, b. 22 Sep 1801; d. 11 Jul 1820.

iii EUNICE HOLT, b. 18 Jan 1804; d. at Sharon, 13 Sep 1819.

iv SAMUEL KING HOLT, b. 2 May 1806

v HORACE HOLT, b. 5 May 1808

vi CHARLES HOLT, b. 9 Aug 1810

vii ORAMEL HOLT, b. 17 Jan 1813; d. at Whittaker, MI, 5 Nov 1893; m. ELECTA GEER, b. about 1815 daughter of Thomas and Laura (-) Geer; Electa d. at Augusta, MI, 2 Nov 1875.

viii THOMAS ABEL HOLT, b. 10 Aug 1815

ix EMILY HOLT, b. 16 Feb 1818; d. at Willowvale, NY, 9 Jun 1883; m. 2 Feb 1837, AMOS ROGERS, b. at Laurens, NY, 24 Oct 1815 son of Oliver Glason and Deborah (Lewis) Rogers;[1863] Amos d. at New Hartford, NY, 2 Dec 1879.

680) ELIJAH HOLT *(Caleb Holt⁴, Hannah Abbott Holt³, William², George¹)*, b. at Willington, 24 Oct 1757 son of Caleb and Mary (Merrick) Holt; d. 4 Jul 1817; m. 5 Nov 1783,[1864] MOLLY SIMMONS, b. 1754 possibly the daughter of Paul and Mary (Isham) Simmons, but this is not confirmed; Molly d. 6 May 1814. Elijah m. 2nd, Lovina *Marcy* Dunton 17 Aug 1815. Lovina Marcy was first married to Samuel Dunton.

Elijah Holt's estate was probated in 1817. He did not leave a will. The total value of the estate was $4898.49. The distribution of the estate was made equally between Chloe wife of Chester Carpenter and Mary wife of Chester Burnham. Widow Lovina Holt received a distribution of $300 in accordance with the pre-marriage contract.[1865] The pre-marriage contract provided that Lovina would retain all the property she brought to the marriage. She had inherited real estate from her father Zebadiah Marcy and her first husband Samuel Dunton.

Elijah Holt and Molly Simmons had four children born at Willington.

i CHLOE HOLT, b. 2 Jul 1788; d. at Willington, 24 Oct 1819; m. at Willington, 16 Mar 1815, CHESTER CARPENTER, b. at Ashford, 3 Jul 1780 Jonah and Zerviah (Whittemore) Carpenter; Chester d. 3 Apr 1868. After Chloe's death, Chester married Betsey Kilbourn.

[1862] Hyde Genealogy, p 136

[1863] Rogers, *James Rogers of New London, CT*, p 404

[1864] "Connecticut Marriages, 1640-1939," database with images, *FamilySearch* (https://familysearch.org/ark:/61903/1:1:F7PB-68K: 11 February 2018), Elijah Holt and Molley Simons, Marriage 05 Nov 1783, Willington Tolland, Connecticut, United States; Connecticut State Library, Hartford; FHL microfilm 1,376,042.

[1865] Ancestry.com. *Connecticut, Wills and Probate Records, 1609-1999* [database on-line]. Provo, UT, USA: Ancestry.com Operations, Inc., 2015. Original data: Connecticut County, District and Probate Courts, Stafford Probate District. Probate of Elijah Holt, Case number 1062, 1817

ii MARY HOLT, b. 14 Sep 1790; d. at Willington, 25 Feb 1851; m. 30 Mar 1813, CHESTER BURNHAM, b. at Ashford, 28 Jun 1788 son of Roswell and Esther (Child) Burnham; Chester d. 25 Oct 1857.

iii ELIJAH HOLT, b. 23 Apr 1792; d. 8 Mar 1809.

iv CALEB HOLT, b. 30 Jun 1798; d. 16 Sep 1811.

681) CALEB HOLT *(Caleb Holt⁴, Hannah Abbott Holt³, William², George¹)*, b. at Willington, 23 Apr 1759 son of Caleb and Mary (Merrick) Holt; d. at Willington, 8 Sep 1826; m. 8 Jan 1783, SALLY GOODALE likely the daughter of Ebenezer and Phebe (Holt) Goodale; Sally d. at Willington, 4 Oct 1831.

Caleb Holt was a tanner and currier, and had a large, successful farm in Willington. He owned enough land to be able to give each of his four sons a farm.[1866]

Caleb Holt and Sally Goodale had five children born at Willington.

i HORACE HOLT, 29 Aug 1784; d. at Norwich, 30 Jan 1863; m. his second cousin, POLLY HOLT *(James Holt⁵, James Holt⁴, Hannah Abbott Holt³, William², George¹)*, b. at Willington, 7 Sep 1798 daughter of James and Mary (Pool) Holt; Polly d. at Willington, 24 Jan 1853.

ii ROYAL HOLT, b. 2 Dec 1786; d. at Willington, 20 Feb 1864; m. at Willington, 13 Aug 1809, LOVINA LAMB, b. at Randolph, VT, 17 Jan 1791 daughter of Joseph and Darias (Marcy) Lamb; Lovina d. at Willington, 5 May 1856.

iii JOSHUA HOLT, b. 17 Apr 1782; d. at Willington, 8 Nov 1834; m. 27 Oct 1831, DALUKA LEONARD, of Ashford, b. about 1806; Daluka d. at Willington, 17 Mar 1885.

iv RALPH HOLT, b. 10 Oct 1794; d. at Willington, 22 Feb 1873; m. 1819, SALLY RIDER, b. at Willington, 18 Nov 1796 daughter of Joseph and Ruanna (-) Rider; Sally d. at Willington, 26 Jun 1868.

v JULIANNA HOLT, b. 25 Apr 1796; d. at Willington, 4 Nov 1862; m. 2 Nov 1823, as his second wife, ROBERT SHARP, b. about 1791 likely the son of Solomon and Rebecca (Perkins) Sharp; Robert d. at Willington, 1 Nov 1874. Robert was first married to CELINDA HOLT *(James Holt⁵, James Holt⁴, Hannah Abbott Holt³, William², George¹)*, b. at Willington, 16 Jan 1796 daughter of James and Mary (Pool) Holt; Celinda d. at Willington, 20 May 1823. Celinda Holt is a child in Family 699.

682) NATHAN HOLT *(Nathan Holt⁴, Hannah Abbott Holt³, William², George¹)*, b. at Windham, 29 Aug 1761 son of Nathan and Abigail (Merrick) Holt; d. at Willington, 5 Sep 1820; m. his second cousin, LOIS GOODALE, b. at Pomfret, 31 Jul 1764 daughter of Ebenezer and Phebe (Holt) Goodale; Lois d. 20 May 1842.

Nathan Holt and Lois Goodale were parents of seven children all born at Willington.

i LOIS HOLT, b. 9 May 1784; d. 20 Feb 1821; m. about 1806, ASA CURTIS, b. 1785 *likely* the son of Ransom and Alice (Whitten) Curtis; Asa was living in Black Hawk, IL in 1860.

ii ASENATH HOLT, b. 26 Jan 1786; d. at Willington, 13 Feb 1813; m. 29 Dec 1809, LEONARD HOLT, b. at Willington, 15 Feb 1782 son of Isaac and Sarah (Orcutt) Holt; Leonard d. at Willington, 12 Mar 1857. Leonard m. 2nd, about 1813, JOANNA ALDEN, b. at Stafford, 14 Jul 1782 daughter of Elisha and Irene (Markham) Alden; Joanna d. at Willington, 30 Sep 1849.

iii CONSTANT HOLT, b. 11 Dec 1787; d. at Webster, NY, 15 Nov 1835; m. 1st, 9 Apr 1812, SALLY DART, b. at Manchester, CT, 1789 daughter of Joseph and Sybil (Loomis) Dart; Sally d. 8 Oct 1813. Constant m. 2nd, 13 Feb 1815, Sally's sister SYBIL DART, b. 1787; Sybil d. 12 Aug 1822. Constant m. 3rd, at Willington, 2 Feb 1823, POLLY SIBLEY, b. at Willington, 26 Mar 1781 daughter of Jonathan and Patty (Brooks) Sibley; Polly d. at Penfield, NY, 17 Dec 1858. Polly Sibley married second David Baker 24 Oct 1841.

iv BATHSHEBA HOLT, b. 13 Feb 1792; d. at Willington, 25 Sep 1880. Bathsheba did not marry.

v PHEBE HOLT, b. 12 Aug 1795; d. at Jewett City, 5 Dec 1844; m. 28 Dec 1814, STEPHEN BARROWS, b. 24 Nov 1789 son of Isaac and Rebecca (Turner) Barrows; Stephen d. at Jewett City, 28 Feb 1878. Stephen married second Hannah Hazard.

vi EBENEZER GOODALE HOLT, b. 24 Jul 1798; d. at Auburn, NY, 17 Oct 1835; m. about 1822, ANN F. WHITE, b. in NY, about 1805 daughter of Jonas White; Anna d. after 1850.

[1866] 1903, *Commemorative Biographical Record of Tolland and Windham*, volume I, p 221

vii MARILDA HOLT, b. 19 Nov 1802; d. at Willington, 31 Mar 1868; m. at Hartford, 27 Oct 1844, RICHARD SALE, b. about 1800; Richard d. at Willington, 1856 (probate 21 Jun 1856). Richard and Marilda lived in Brooklyn, NY although they seem to have been in Willington at the time of Richard's death as his will and probate are in Connecticut. They did not have children.

683) ANNE MERRICK *(Anna Holt Merrick*^{4}*, Hannah Abbott Holt*^{3}*, William*^{2}*, George*^{1}*)*, b. at Willington, 19 Sep 1756 daughter of Joseph and Anna (Holt) Merrick; d. 2 May 1809; m. 10 Jan 1782, DAVID HINCKLEY, b. 24 Feb 1754 son of John and Susannah (Harris) Hinckley; David d. 24 Jan 1835.

In his will written 18 February 1830, David Hinckley left his entire estate, real and personal, to his daughter Joanna Hinckley. But if son Benjamin was living when David died, Benjamin was to have the wearing apparel. After the payment of debts, Joanna at her discretion, might divide what was left between herself and David's other two daughters Hannah Hinckley and Betsey Torrey. Joanna was named executrix of the estate.[1867]

Anne and David Hinckley had six children whose births are recorded at Willington.

i BENJAMIN HINCKLEY, b. 23 Nov 1782; d. at Hiram, OH, 1835 (probate 1835); m. at Willington, 10 Feb 1806, SUSANNA DAVIS, b. about 1782 daughter of Avery and Amy (Lillibridge) Avery;[1868] Susanna d. at Hiram, 8 Jan 1873.

ii HANNAH HINCKLEY, b. 14 Aug 1786. Her death is uncertain, but she was living and unmarried in 1830 when her father wrote his will. It is believed she traveled with her sister Joanna and brother Benjamin to Ohio.

iii CALEB HINCKLEY, b. 3 Jun 1790; d. 26 Jul 1790.

iv EBER HINCKLEY, b. 17 Oct 1791; d. 9 May 1796.

v BETSEY HINCKLEY, b. 28 Jul 1796; d. at Union, IA, 21 Feb 1879; m. at Tolland, 21 Jun 1826, DAVID B. TORREY, b. about 1784 in Connecticut; David d. at Burlington, IA, 3 Dec 1863.

vi JOANNA HINCKLEY, b. 12 Mar 1799; d. at Windsor, OH, 19 Apr 1857; m. at Portage County, OH, 20 Jun 1840, as his second wife, Rev. RUSSELL DOWNING, b. in New York 20 Nov 1796; Russell d. at Windsor, 8 Apr 1881.[1869]

684) TIMOTHY MERRICK *(Anna Holt Merrick*^{4}*, Hannah Abbott Holt*^{3}*, William*^{2}*, George*^{1}*)*, b. at Willington, 31 Aug 1760 son of Joseph and Anna (Holt) Merrick; d. 4 Jan 1810; m. 29 Nov 1787, MEHITABLE PEARL ATWOOD, b. 1765 daughter of Thomas and Sarah (Fenton) Atwood; Mehitable d. at Wilton, 14 May 1855.

Timothy was a farmer in Willington. The Merrick genealogy reports he built one of the more pretentious houses in Willington at the time. He was respected in the town, often serving as the moderator of the town meeting.[1870]

Timothy Merrick did not leave a will and the estate entered probate 5 February 1810. The total value of the estate was $2,438 with the 101-acre homestead farm with buildings valued at $1,628.[1871]

There are two children known for Timothy and Mehitable both born at Willington.

i JOSEPH MERRICK, b. 2 Jul 1789; d. at Willington, 5 Jan 1854; m. 10 Apr 1814, LODICIA DUNTON, b. at Willington, 22 Sep 1794 daughter of Samuel and Lovina (Marcy) Dunton; Lodicia d. at Willington, 1 Sep 1857.

ii ANNE MERRICK, b. 26 Feb 1791; d. at Willington, 28 Oct 1817; m. CYREL JAMES, b. at Willington, 21 Sep 1791 son of Amos and Christian (Noble) James.

685) THOMAS MERRICK *(Anna Holt Merrick*^{4}*, Hannah Abbott Holt*^{3}*, William*^{2}*, George*^{1}*)*, b. at Willington, 6 Jan 1763 son of Joseph and Anna (Holt) Merrick; d. at Willington, 8 Sep 1840; m. 10 Jan 1790, JOANNA NOBLE, b. 8 Oct 1769 daughter of Gideon and Christian (Cadwell) Noble; Joanna d. 28 Apr 1860.

[1867] *Connecticut, Wills and Probate Records, 1609-1999*, Author: Connecticut State Library (Hartford, Connecticut); Probate Place: Hartford, Connecticut.

[1868] Susanna's parents are confirmed by the 1836 Connecticut probate record of father Avery Davis and the 1859 will of brother Avery Davis which includes a bequest to sister Susan Hinckley.

[1869] Web: Ashtabula County, Ohio, Obituary Index, 1858-2012

[1870] Merrick, *Genealogy of the Merrick Family*, p 284

[1871] *Connecticut State Library (Hartford, Connecticut)*; Probate Place: *Hartford, Connecticut, Probate Packets, McKinney, H-Nash, S, 1759-1880*, Probate of Timothy Merick, Case 1480

Thomas Merrick was a farmer in Willington. He and his wife Joanna Noble were parents of five children born at Willington.

i LOVISA MERRICK, b. 22 Mar 1791; d. at Willington, 14 May 1863; m. 14 Nov 1827, ELEAZER ROOT, b. about 1790 *likely* the son of Eleazer Root; Eleazer d. at Willington, Mar 1837 (probate 13 Mar 1837).

ii GIDEON NOBLE MERRICK, b. Jan 1793; d. at Willington, 24 Jan 1862; m. 16 Apr 1820, POLLY NILES, b. at Willington, 5 Oct 1798 daughter of James and Polly (Woodward) Niles; Polly d. at Willington, 2 Mar 1869.

iii HARRIET MERRICK, b. 24 Jan 1795; d. at Willington, 9 May 1860; m. at Willington, 22 Sep 1831, JONATHAN CASE WALKER, b. at Ashford, 5 Jan 1799 son of Samuel and Alice (Case) Walker; Jonathan d. at Willington, 2 Nov 1863.

iv MARILDA MERRICK, b. Mar 1801; d. at Wintonbury, CT, 26 Jul 1872; m. at Willington, 15 Jun 1821, RALPH R. GRIGGS, b. at Tolland, 31 Jan 1798 son of Stephen and Betsey (Lathrop) Griggs; Ralph d. at Wintonbury, 22 Aug 1874.

v HARVEY MERRICK, b. 2 May 1808; d. at Bristol, CT, 17 Aug 1887; m. at Willington, 23 Apr 1838, his second cousin once removed, ESTHER CHILDS BURNHAM *(Mary Holt Burnham⁶, Elijah Holt⁵, Caleb Holt⁴, Hannah Abbott Holt³, William², George¹)*, b. at Willington, 13 Feb 1816 daughter of Chester and Mary (Holt) Burnham; Esther d. at Bristol, 7 Feb 1905.

686) JOSEPH MERRICK *(Anna Holt Merrick⁴, Hannah Abbott Holt³, William², George¹)*, b. at Willington, 22 Feb 1765 son of Joseph and Anna (Holt) Merrick; death uncertain but about 1820 possibly by drowning; m. 21 Oct 1796, IRENA ALDEN, b. at Bellingham, MA, 24 Feb 1772 daughter of Elisha and Irene (Markham) Alden. Irena m. 2nd, Samuel Churchill; Irena d. at Pleasantville, PA, 13 Nov 1858.

Joseph Merrick and Irene Alden were parents of five children all born at Willington.

i IRENE MERRICK, b. 21 Aug 1797; d. at Willington, 29 Apr 1814.

ii LODICA MERRICK, b. 14 Dec 1798; d. at Oil Creek, PA, 1 Aug 1863; m. at Longmeadow, MA, 15 Sep 1821, AMOS HALL, b. 5 Mar 1790;[1872] Amos d. at Oil Creek, 9 Mar 1863.

iii ELISHA ALDEN MERRICK, b. 3 Apr 1800; d. at Belvidere, IL, 13 Aug 1839; m. about 1827, JERUSHA TENANT, b. at Colchester, 21 Aug 1807 daughter of John and Hannah (Atwell) Tenant; Jerusha d. at Huntington, WV, 15 Oct 1904. Jerusha married second James McClintock.

iv AUSTIN MERRICK, b. 13 Sep 1801; d. at Pleasantville, PA, 6 Aug 1876; m. 1st, 5 Feb 1839, SYLVIA WITCHER, b. at Rochester, VT, 6 May 1808 daughter of Stephen and Esther (Emerson) Witcher; Sylvia d. 1849. Austin m. 2nd, about 1851, ELIZA, b. about 1812 who has not been identified; Eliza d. 1869.

v LAURA MERRICK, b. 14 Nov 1803; d. at Adams, NE, 2 Sep 1885; m. about 1830, her second cousin, WILLIAM CURTIS *(Mary Holt Curtis⁵, Isaac Holt⁴, Hannah Abbott Holt³, William², George¹)*, b. at Willington, 20 May 1802 son of William and Mary (Holt) Curtis; William d. a Adams, 17 Mar 1879..

687) CALEB MERRICK *(Anna Holt Merrick⁴, Hannah Abbott Holt³, William², George¹)*, b. at Willington, 17 May 1767 son of Joseph and Anna (Holt) Merrick; d. at Vernon, CT, Jun 1822; m. 15 Sep 1791, CHARLOTTE NOBLE, b. at Willington, 19 Aug 1771 daughter of Gideon and Christian (Cadwell) Noble; Charlotte d. at Franklin, CT, 21 Nov 1805.

Dr. Caleb Merrick had a practice in Willington and Franklin, Connecticut.[1873]

Caleb and Charlotte had five children.

i WEALTHY MERRICK, b. at Willington, 20 Sep 1792; d. at Ellington, 12 Oct 1861; m. Mar 1818, BUELL NYE, b. at Tolland, 7 Mar 1790 son of Hezekiah and Asenath (Buell) Nye; Buell d. at Springfield, MA, 10 Apr 1833.[1874]

ii MARK MERRICK, b. at Amherst, MA, 14 Nov 1794; d. at Vernon, 18 Apr 1853; m. HANNAH SPARKS, b. at Vernon, 8 May 1794 daughter of Jonas and Olive (Smith) Sparks;[1875] Hannah d. after 1870 at Chatham, NJ (living at Chatham at the 1870 Census).

[1872] Birth date is calculated from age at death of 73 years, 4 days. Bell, *History of Venango County*, 9 734

[1873] Merrick, *Genealogy of the Merrick Family*, p 285

[1874] Nye, *Genealogy of the Nye Family*, p 354

[1875] Hannah's parents are confirmed by the 1823 Connecticut probate of Jonas Sparks which includes a distribution to daughter Hannah Merrick.

iii SOPHRONIA MERRICK, b. at Amherst, 1 Apr 1797; d. at Willington, 14 May 1843; m. at Willington, 20 Nov 1814, SPAFFORD BRIGHAM, b. 1782 son od Stephen and Hannah (Field) Brigham;[1876] Spafford d. at Ellington, 26 Sep 1866.

iv LEANDER MERRICK, b. at Tolland, 31 May 1799; d. at Amherst, 24 May 1856; m. 1st, 2 Dec 1824, HARRIET HODGE, b. 1798 daughter of John and Sarah (Dickinson) Hodge; Harriet d. at Amherst, 3 May 1825. Leander m. 2nd, 27 Nov 1827, HARRIET ELVIRA MORTON, b. 3 Feb 1808 daughter of Ebenezer and Hannah (Ingram) Morton; Harriet d. at Amherst, 18 Jun 1882.

v CHARLOTTE MERRICK, b. at Willington, 29 Jan 1802; d. at Willington, 1818.

688) CONSTANT MERRICK *(Anna Holt Merrick⁴, Hannah Abbott Holt³, William², George¹)*, b. at Willington, 14 Jan 1772 son of Joseph and Anna (Holt) Merrick; d. at Lebanon, NY, 29 Jul 1828; m. at Longmeadow, MA, 22 Sep 1796, EXPERIENCE BURT, b. 8 Aug 1776 daughter of Nathaniel and Experience (Chapin) Burt; Experience d. 1833 at Lebanon, NY, 24 Jul 1833.

Dr. Constant Merrick was a physician, but like many individuals in this era also maintained a farm. After Constant and Experience married, they relocated to Madison County, New York about 1800.[1877] The family lived near Billings Hill in Madison County and then settled in the village of Lebanon about 1806 where Dr. Merrick was the second physician in the village.[1878]

Constant Merrick and Elizabeth Burt had nine children the oldest in Longmeadow and the other children at Lebanon, New York.

i ELIZA MERRICK, b. at Longmeadow, 27 Apr 1797; d. at Lebanon, NY, 9 Jan 1815; m. 17 Apr 1814, JAMES KNAPP BENEDICT, b. 3 Feb 1790 son of Czar and Elizabeth (Knapp) Benedict;[1879] James d. at Lebanon, 9 May 1864. After Eliza's death, James married Pamelia Sweet. Eliza did not have children.

ii LAURA MERRICK, b. 17 Mar 1799; d. at Longmeadow, MA, 7 Sep 1875; m. at Lebanon, 12 Sep 1821, SAMUEL COLTON STEBBINS, b. at Longmeadow, 27 Jun 1796 son of Benjamin and Lucy (Colton) Stebbins; Samuel d. at Longmeadow, 12 Dec 1873.

iii EXPERIENCE MERRICK, b. 27 Feb 1801; d. 11 Mar 1801.

iv NATHANIEL BURT MERRICK, b. 5 Mar 1802; d. at Hudson, NY, 18 Jan 1877; m. 12 Jun 1832, LAURA H. HAMILTON, b. about 1810 daughter of Samuel and Mehitable (Bemis) Hamilton; Laura d. 27 Jan 1840. Nathaniel m. 2nd, Mar 1841, MARTHA M. BURCHARD who was "of Rochester;" Martha d. at Rochester, 7 Mar 1897.

v CONSTANT MERRICK, b. 14 Apr 1804; d. 16 Aug 1805.

vi EXPERIENCE MERRICK, b. at Lebanon, 28 Jul 1806; d. at Earlville, NY, 1870; m. 10 Jun 1830, DAVID CLARK, b. 1800 in Connecticut of as yet undetermined origins; David d. at Earlville, 1873.

vii CONSTANT MERRICK, b. at Lebanon, 22 Nov 1808; d. at Lebanon, 3 Apr 1834.

viii ANNA MERRICK, b. at Lebanon, 1 Sep 1810; d. at Chicago, 21 Jan 1886; m. 10 Jun 1830, GORDON HYDE, b. at Columbus, NY, 10 Feb 1801 son of Ambrose and Phebe (Hyde) Hyde; Gordon d. at Hamilton, NY, 1885.

ix JERUSHA MERRICK, b. at Lebanon, 8 Jun 1819; d. at Norwich, NY, 1874; m. 2 Sep 1840, ISAAC FOOTE, b. 28 May 1817 son of Isaac and Harriet (Hyde) Foote; Isaac d. at Norwich, 1893.

689) ELIZABETH MERRICK *(Anna Holt Merrick⁴, Hannah Abbott Holt³, William², George¹)*, b. at Willington, 13 Jul 1774 daughter of Joseph and Anna (Holt) Merrick; d. at Tolland, 29 Jun 1824; m. 24 Apr 1800, as his second wife, SAMUEL NYE, b. 25 Dec 1773 son of Samuel and Abigail (Benton) Nye. Samuel m. 3rd, Anna Hatch; Samuel's first wife was Elizabeth Brewster; Samuel d. at Tolland 25 Nov 1837.

[1876] Brigham, *History of the Brigham Family*, p 169

[1877] Merrick, *Genealogy of the Merrick Family*, p 286

[1878] Smith, *Our County and Its People. . .Madison County*, p 371

[1879] Benedict, *Genealogy of the Benedicts*, p 270

Samuel Nye wrote his will 24 December 1836[1880] and entered probate 29 Nov 1837. Beloved wife Ann receives the use and improvement of one-third of the real estate during her natural life. Ann also receives two shares in the Tolland County Bank. He makes other provisions for her support and she also receives the cloak. Daughter Harriet Brigham receives one hundred dollars. Son Horace and daughters Harriet and Anne receiving the wearing apparel except the cloak. The remainder of the personal estate goes to two grandchildren Buey (?) Nye and Samuel Nye. The remainder of the estate goes to son-in-law William Holman who is also named executor. Conspicuously absent from the will is Chester Nye, Samuel's son from his first marriage. Chester was living at the time the will was written. The two grandchildren mentioned are William B. Nye and Samuel Nye who were sons of Horace.

Elizabeth Merrick and Samuel Nye had four children all born at Tolland.

i HARRIET NYE, b. 15 Aug 1801; d. at Coventry, CT, 21 Mar 1879; m. 29 Nov 1827, URIAH BRIGHAM, b. at Coventry, 26 Aug 1793 son of Cephas and Amelia (Robertson) Brigham; Uriah d. at Coventry, 2 May 1860. Uriah was first married to Emily Wright who died in 1827.

ii HORACE NYE, b. 22 Aug 1803; death unknown; m. Apr 1827, BETSEY BRIGHAM, b. at Mansfield, CT, about 1805 daughter of Stephen and Huldah (Freeman) Brigham; Betsey d. at Mansfield, 17 Sep 1872.

iii SUSANNA NYE, b. 16 Feb 1805; d. 7 Feb 1828.

iv ANNA NYE, b. 12 Aug 1810; d. at Tolland, 15 Mar 1870; m. 26 Mar 1833, WILLIAM HOLMAN, b. at Ashford, 24 Oct 1811 son of Abraham and Polly (Converse) Holman; William d. at East Hoosuck, MA, 8 Oct 1887.

690) ISAAC HOLT *(Isaac Holt⁴, Hannah Abbott Holt³, William², George¹)*, b. at Willington, 3 Nov 1763 son of Isaac and Sarah (Orcutt) Holt; d. at Sharon, VT, 7 Aug 1813; m. at Sharon, 1 Jan 1789,[1881] MEHITABLE ORCUTT, b. at Stafford, CT, 17 Jan 1769 daughter of Caleb and Chloe (Parker) Orcutt; Mehitable d. 12 Nov 1851.

Isaac and Mehitable were married in Connecticut and moved soon after to Sharon, Vermont where their three children were born. Little information has been located for this couple. Probate records were not found.

i FREEMAN HOLT, b. 19 Apr 1790; d. at Sharon, 14 Jun 1865; m. 1st, LUCY PAGE, b. at Sharon, 13 Aug 1797 daughter of Samuel and Elizabeth (Mosher) Page; Lucy d. at Sharon, 10 Oct 1859. Freeman m. 2nd, 9 Jul 1860 at Gloucester, MA, MARY BRADLEY (widow Cressy), b. at Rumney, NH, 11 Feb 1801 daughter of Ebenezer and Sarah (Hall) Bradley; Mary d. at Haverhill, MA, 30 Mar 1885.

ii CALEB HOLT, b. 28 Oct 1791; d. at Sharon, 29 Jan 1880; m. 1st, at Sharon 16 Jan 1822, CLARISSA PARKER, b. at Sharon, 28 Jul 1797 daughter of James and Kezia (Weatherbee) Parker; Clarissa d. 6 Oct 1852. Caleb m. 2nd, at Rumney 20 May 1853, MARY P. HERRICK, b. at Londonderry, 17 May 1808 daughter of Nehemiah and Sarah (Day) Herrick; Mary d. at Sharon, 6 Apr 1874.

iii HANNAH HOLT, b. 11 Sep 1793; d. likely at Bethel, VT after 1850; m. at Sharon, 3 Nov 1833, as his third wife, ELISHA TERRY, b. at Bethel, 22 Nov 1786 son of Ephraim and Lucinda (Bugbee) Terry; Elisha d. at Bethel after 1850. Hannah and Elisha were both living at the 1850 Census but not located after that.

691) HANNAH HOLT *(Isaac Holt⁴, Hannah Abbott Holt³, William², George¹)*, b. at Willington, 19 May 1771 daughter of Isaac and Sarah (Orcutt) Holt; d. before 1850;[1882] m. 9 Apr 1795, ELEAZER FELLOWS, b. at Tolland, 2 Apr 1772 son of Verney and Hannah (Lathrop) Fellows; Eleazer d. after 1850 in Ohio.

Hannah and Eleazer had their children in Willington. In 1849, perhaps after the death of Hannah, Eleazer followed his son Eleazer to Clarksfield, Ohio. He bought ten acres of land there and lived with his daughter Betsey and her family.[1883]

Eleazer Fellows and Hannah Holt were parents of three children born at Willington.

i LEONARD FELLOWS, b. 23 Oct 1800; d. at Clarksfield, OH, Aug 1849; m. 24 Nov 1824, ARMINDA JOHNSON, b. at Sweden, NY, 10 Jun 1807;[1884] Arminda d. at Marion, MN, 18 Nov 1893.

[1880] Connecticut State Library (Hartford, Connecticut); Probate Place: Hartford, Connecticut, Probate Packets, Kimball, N-Warren, H, 1827-1895, Probate of Samuel Nye, case number 700.

[1881] *Vermont, Vital Records, 1720-1908.*

[1882] In the 1850 U.S. Census, Eleazer Fellows, age 78, was living in Clarksfield OH; also in the home are Betsey Haskins age 43 and five children named Haskins. Betsey is the daughter of Eleazer and Hannah. Eleazer and Hannah's son Leonard also relocated to Huron County, Ohio.

[1883] Weeks, *Pioneer History of Clarksfield*, p130

[1884] Date of birth is on her cemetery record. Dalby, John. *Minnesota Cemetery Inscription Index, Select Counties* [database on-line]. Provo, UT, USA: Ancestry.com Operations Inc, 2003.

ii LOTHROP FELLOWS, b. 4 Nov 1803; d. at Lockport, NY, 2 Jan 1845; m. 5 Dec 1827, MELINDA FISKE PARSONS, b. at Lockport, 16 Jun 1809 daughter of Seth and Achsah (Tenney) Parsons;[1885] Melinda d. at Milwaukee, 10 Mar 1891.

iii BETSEY PRIOR FELLOWS, b. 13 May 1806; m. about 1831, Mr. HASKINS, not identified but perhaps Jarius Haskins. Their youngest child was born about 1845. *Pioneer History of Clarksfield* reports that Mr. Haskins died, and Betsey married Mr. Lang but continued to use the name Haskins and she is the head of household in census records in Clarksfield. She was living in 1860.

692) MARY HOLT *(Isaac Holt⁴, Hannah Abbott Holt³, William², George¹)*, b. at Willington, 1 May 1773 daughter of Isaac and Sarah (Orcutt) Holt; d. at Willington, 6 Jun 1861; m. 27 Nov 1799, WILLIAM CURTIS, b. about 1774 *likely* the son of Ransom and Alice (Whitten) Curtis; William d. 3 Nov 1860.

In his will written 7 February 1852, William leaves his entire estate to children Sarah H. Curtis and Wilson W. Curtis stating that he has already provided for his other children (who are not named). "The said Wilson W. Curtis and Sara H. Curtis shall well and truly provide for support and maintain myself and my wife Mary Curtis during the whole period of each of our natural lives and at the death of each myself and my said wife Mary Curtis to give to each of us a decent christian burial."[1886]

Daughter Sarah Holt Curtis did not marry. In her will dated 1 August 1874, Sarah bequeaths twenty-five dollars to her brother Selden; to Chiara Ann wife of George Plimpton and daughter of her brother Oliver H. Curtis she leaves a string of gold beads to be solely her property; to brother Alfred Curtis, twenty dollars; and the remainder of the estate goes to brother Wilson W. Curtis who is also named executor.[1887]

Mary and William Curtis had nine children born at Willington. This family illustrates a pattern for this generation: a new wave of migration with children heading to the western territories, western New York, and western Massachusetts.

i SANFORD CURTIS, b. 7 Nov 1800; d. 9 May 1807.

ii WILLIAM CURTIS, b. 20 May 1802; d. at Adams, NE, 17 Mar 1879; m. about 1803, his second cousin, LAURA MERRICK *(Joseph Merrick⁵, Anna Holt Merrick⁴, Hannah Abbott Holt³, William², George¹)*, b. at Willington, 14 Nov 1803 daughter of Joseph and Irene (Alden) Merrick; Laura d. at Adams, 2 Sep 1885.

iii HORACE CURTIS, b. 9 Feb 1804; d. at Buchanan, MI, 31 Dec 1887;[1888] m. SALLY M. CLARK, b. in Pennsylvania, 3 Dec 1814 daughter of Benjamin and Esther (-) Clark; Sally d. at Buchanan, 24 Mar 1899.

iv SARAH HOLT CURTIS, b. 24 Oct 1805; d. at Willington, 30 Sep 1874. Sarah did not marry.

v ALFRED CURTIS, b. 7 Jun 1809; d. at Westfield, NY, 2 Dec 1878; m. at Willington, 5 Dec 1831, EUNICE RIDER, b. 9 Dec 1812 of undetermined parents;[1889] Eunice d. at Westfield, 3 Sep 1892.

vi OLIVER HOLT CURTIS, b. 30 Mar 1811; d. at Amherst, MA, 27 Feb 1899; m. at Tolland, 14 Nov 1837, EMILY HILLS, b. at Ellington, 12 Mar 1811 daughter of Leonard and Mary (Ladd) Hills; Emily d. at Amherst, 27 Mar 1888.

vii WILSON WHITING CURTIS, b. 25 Feb 1813; d. at Willington, 10 Aug 1890; m. at Willington, 12 Feb 1852, SARAH ELDREDGE, b. at Willington, 14 Feb 1813 daughter of Elijah and Sally (Hunt) Eldridge; Sarah d. at Willington, 13 Feb 1887.

viii SELDEN CURTIS, b. 1 Dec 1815; d. at Willington, 18 Feb 1902; m. 1st, 28 Mar 1841, MARY ELIZABETH PARSONS, b. at Somers, CT, 24 Feb 1821 daughter of Rufus and Chloe (Weston) Parsons;[1890] Mary d. at Willington, 21 Oct 1852. Selden m. 2nd, at Ashford, 5 Jun 1853, MARTHA AURELIA SKINNER, b. 14 Mar 1822 daughter of Ezekiel and Sarah (Mott) Skinner; Martha d. at Willington, 21 Sep 1892. Martha was first married to Richard Boon.

ix HENRY CURTIS, b. 1 Jun 1818; d. 3 Aug 1846.

1885 Parsons, *Parsons Family: Descendant of Cornet Joseph Parsons*, p 164

1886 *Connecticut State Library (Hartford, Connecticut)*; Probate Place: *Hartford, Connecticut, Probate Packets, Carpenter, Comfort-Kimball, J, 1833-1880*, Case number 222, accessed through ancestry.com

1887 *Connecticut State Library (Hartford, Connecticut)*; Probate Place: *Hartford, Connecticut, Probate Packets, Carpenter, Comfort-Kimball, J, 1833-1880*, Case 221

1888 *Michigan, Death Records, 1867-1950*, Michigan Department of Community Health, Division for Vital Records and Health Statistics; Lansing, Michigan. The death record includes parents as William and Mary and birth place as Connecticut. The death record for Sally Clark includes names of parents as Benjamin and Esther.

1889 Eunice's birth date is on her gravestone; findagrave ID: 87772382

1890 Parsons, *Parsons Family*, volume 2, p 319

693) OLIVER HOLT *(Isaac Holt⁴, Hannah Abbott Holt³, William², George¹)*, b. at Willington, 16 Jul 1775 son of Isaac and Sarah (Orcutt) Holt; d. 6 Mar 1869; m. 16 May 1799, MARTHA "PATTY" SIBLEY,[1891] b. 9 Feb 1776 daughter of Jonathan and Patty (Brooks) Sibley; Martha "Patty" d. 16 Dec 1846.

There are records for five children of Oliver and Patty Holt all born at Willington.

i MARCIA HOLT, b. 22 Feb 1800; d. 1 Mar 1831. Marcia did not marry.

ii SUSANNAH HOLT, b. 4 Feb 1802; d. at Mansfield, CT, 2 May 1874; m. at Willington, 18 Jun 1827, EBER DUNHAM, b. at Mansfield, 23 Jan 1798 son of Jonathan and Betty (Babcock) Dunham; Eber d. at Mansfield, 21 Oct 1878.

iii MARIAH HOLT, b. 16 Aug 1806; d. at Mansfield, 4 Jun 1867; m. 1 Jan 1846, CHAUNCEY DUNHAM, b. at Mansfield, about 1798 of undetermined parents; Chauncey d. at Mansfield, 11 Jul 1850.

iv MARTHA SIBLEY HOLT, b. 15 May 1810; d. at Tamaroa, IL, 18 Jul 1864; m. at Willington, 20 Oct 1834, BENAJAH GUERNSEY "B.G." ROOTS, b. at Fabius, NY, 20 Apr 1811 son of Peter and Elizabeth (Keep) Roots; B.G. d. at Tamaroa, 9 May 1888. After Martha's death, B.G. married Elizabeth Reynolds. Benajah Guernsey Roots was an abolitionist and is believed to have been active in the Underground Railroad.[1892]

v ELIZA HOLT, b. 7 Feb 1821; d. at Tamaroa, IL, 7 Dec 1870; m. 13 Sep 1840, her second cousin once removed, NELSON HOLT *(Constant Holt⁶, Nathan Holt⁵, Nathan Holt⁴, Hannah Abbott Holt³, William², George¹)*, b. at Penfield, NY, 6 Jan 1816 son of Constant and Sibyl (Dart) Holt;[1893] Nelson d. at Tamaroa, 29 Oct 1900.

694) ELIZABETH HOLT *(Isaac Holt⁴, Hannah Abbott Holt³, William², George¹)*, b. at Willington, 6 Aug 1777 daughter of Isaac and Sarah (Orcutt) Holt; m. 11 Apr 1799, DANIEL GLAZIER, b. 2 Jun 1776 son of Silas and Suze (Johnson) Glazier; Daniel d. 28 Dec 1852. After Elizabeth's death, Daniel married Mary G. whose last name is unknown.

Daniel Glazier was the builder and owner of the Daniel Glazier Tavern which is now the home of the Willington Historical Society.[1894]

In his will written 10 September 1852, Daniel Glazier bequeaths to beloved wife Mary all the furniture she brought to the marriage, all the furniture obtained since their marriage (except the secretary), $850, and the use of one-third part of the house as long as she remains a widow; grandson Daniel Johnson Glazier, $150 over what he has received; grandson Isaac Glazier receives 10 shares of bank stock; Elizabeth Spalden and Sarah R. Glazier receive all of his furniture (except the secretary) and $4000 to be divided equally between them; grandson Hiram Rider receives a piece of land; and son Orlen Glazier receives the remainder of the estate and is named executor.[1895] Elizabeth Spalden and Sarah R. Glazier are daughters of son Isaac. Daniel Johnson Glazier is the son of Isaac. Hiram Rider is the son of daughter Sarah.

There are records for four children of Daniel and Elizabeth Glazier. The Willington Historical Society states there were five children, but records for that child were not found and perhaps there was a fifth child that died before adulthood.

i SARAH GLAZIER, b. 17 Apr 1800; d. at Willington, 1850; m. at Willington, 3 May 1818, HIRAM RIDER, b. at Willington, 28 Apr 1790 son of Joseph and Jane (Poole) Rider; Hiram d. at Willington, 26 Sep 1851.

ii ISAAC GLAZIER, b. 19 Jan 1803; d. at Willington, 4 Feb 1835; m. 7 Mar 1824, LUCIA SNOW, b. at Ashford, 23 Nov 1804 daughter of Amos and Eunice (Burnham) Snow; Lucia d. at Willington, 30 Sep 1849.

iii ORLAN GLAZIER, b. 12 May 1805; d. at Willington, 13 Apr 1857; m. 2 Aug 1836, SOPHRONIA JOHNSON, b. at Willington, 4 Apr 1814 daughter of Abel and Deborah (Preston) Johnson; Sophronia d. at Hartford, 25 Mar 1898.

iv ELIZA GLAZIER, b. 1814; d. 2 Mar 1815.

695) LEONARD HOLT *(Isaac Holt⁴, Hannah Abbott Holt³, William², George¹)*, b. at Willington, 15 Feb 1782 son of Isaac and Sarah (Orcutt) Holt; d. 12 Mar 1857; m. 1st, 29 Dec 1809, his first cousin once removed (and George Abbott descendant), ASENATH HOLT, b. 26 Jan 1786 daughter of Nathan and Lois (Goodell) Holt; Asenath d. 13 Feb 1813. Leonard m. 2nd, about 1813, JOANNA ALDEN, b. 14 Jul 1782 daughter of Elisha and Irene (Markham) Alden; Joanna d. 30 Sep 1849. Joanna was first married to Josiah Converse.

1891 Connecticut, Marriage Index, 1620-1926; the handwritten marriage record confirms that the marriage is to Patty and not to her younger sister Polly.

1892 National Park Service. "Network to Freedom." https://www.nps.gov/subjects/ugrr/ntf_member/ntf_member_details.htm?SPFID=4068809&SPFTerritory=NULL&SPFType=NULL&SPFKeywords=NULL

1893 Durrie, *Holt Genealogy*, p 164

1894 Willington Historical Society. "About the Daniel Glazier Tavern." http://www.willingtonhistoricalsocietyct.org/html/DanielGlazierTavern2.html

1895 *Connecticut State Library (Hartford, Connecticut)*; Probate Place: *Hartford, Connecticut, Probate Packets, Carpenter, Comfort-Kimball, J, 1833-1880*, probate of Daniel Glazier, case number 354

Leonard Holt and his three children are somewhat of a mystery. His son William married twice, and one child has been identified for William. Leonard's two children by his second wife, Asenath Frances and Oliver A., led lives out of the ordinary. Oliver and Asenath lived with their father until after 1850. Asenath and her father Leonard were excommunicated from the church in Willington 31 December 1852[1896] but the reasons for this are not known. After that, Asenath attended Thetford Academy in Vermont[1897] and worked as a teacher for the remainder of her life. Oliver A. Holt married Nancy Abbe in 1853 and they had one son Leonard O. Holt who died of croup at age two years. After the birth of Leonard O., Oliver relocated to Tamaroa, IL and that is where his son Leonard O. died. Oliver lived in Tamaroa the remainder of his life, but his wife Nancy lived in Connecticut with her family. They do not seem to have divorced, and after Oliver's death, Nancy listed herself as the widow of Oliver in town registers. Asenath went to Tamaroa and was living with her brother in 1860 and she was there as a single head of household in 1880.[1898] Asenath spent her later years in Washington, D.C. where she died in 1904, although she was buried in Tamaroa.

Leonard Holt did not leave a will and the only probate document available was the administration bond given by Oliver A. Holt and Eber Dunham.

Leonard Holt and Asenath Holt had one child.

i WILLIAM HOLT, b. at Willington, 6 May 1811; d. at Willington, 5 Feb 1878; m. 1st, 21 Mar 1836, CAROLINE DELAURA CARPENTER, b. at Waterford, VT, 23 Mar 1811 daughter of Isaiah and Caroline (Bugbee) Carpenter; Caroline d. at Willington, 29 Feb 1864. William m. 2nd, at Waterford, VT, 13 Oct 1864, MARY B. PARKER, b. at New Hampton, NH, 22 Feb 1822 daughter of Ezra and Hannah (Burleigh) Parker; Mary d. at Newbury, VT, 23 Mar 1900.

Leonard and Joanna Holt had two children.

i OLIVER A. HOLT, b. at Willington about 1817; d. at Tamaroa, IL, 27 Aug 1876; m. 10 Oct 1853, NANCY AMELIA ABBE, b. at Enfield, 16 Oct 1830 daughter of Harvey C. and Mary A. (Gowdy) Abbe; Nancy d. at Bristol, CT, 5 Apr 1917.

ii ASENATH FRANCES HOLT, b. at Willington, Sep 1820; d. at Washington, D. C., 28 Jun 1904.

696) ANNE HOLT *(Isaac Holt⁴, Hannah Abbott Holt³, William², George¹)*, b. at Willington, 21 Oct 1784 daughter of Isaac and Sarah (Orcutt) Holt; d. 27 Jun 1855; m. SIMON CARPENTER, b. 13 Dec 1783 son of Elijah and Sarah (Younglove) Carpenter; Simon d. 24 Aug 1862.

Simon Carpenter did not leave a will. Lucien H. Carpenter and Elisa A. Carpenter signed the administrator's bond. Anne and Simon had two children neither of whom married. The two children lived together in Willington throughout their lives.

i LUCIEN HOLT CARPENTER, b. 21 May 1817; d. at Willington, 6 Aug 1889.

ii ELIZA A. CARPENTER, b. about 1823; d. at Willington, 31 Dec 1880.

697) ANNA HOLT *(Timothy Holt⁴, Hannah Abbott Holt³, William², George¹)*, b. at Willington, 12 Feb 1762 daughter of Timothy and Rebecca (Chamberlain) Holt; m. 17 Nov 1785, STEPHEN CROCKER, b. 14 Dec 1760 son of Ebenezer and Hannah (Hatch) Crocker. This family was in Schoharie County, New York by about 1788.[1899]

Anna and Stephen Crocker went to Rhode Island following their marriage where at least one child was born. The family was in Schoharie County by 1788 and settled in Carlisle. Stephen seems to still be living at the time of the 1820 census as the head of household, male over age 45. If so, Anna had died before that as the female in the household was age 26-44 and there are two children under age 10 in the household.

There are just three children identified for Anna and Stephen, although there may well be other children.

1896 Connecticut, Church Record Abstracts, 1630-1927, volume 127 Willington

1897 *U.S., High School Student Lists, 1821-1923.* Asenath F. Holt of Willington, CT sponsored by Leonard Holt, Thetford Academy

1898 Saints, *1880 United States Federal Census*, Year: 1880; Census Place: Tamaroa, Perry, Illinois; Roll: 241; Page: 8C; Enumeration District: 071.

1899 Roscoe, *History of Schoharie County*, p 316

i BERIAH CROCKER, b. 1785; d. at Sloansville, NY, 19 Jan 1874; m. at Reformed Protestant Church, Nassau, NY, 31 Oct 1813,[1900] SARAH GARRISON, b. about 1795; Sarah d. at Sloansville, 1 Oct 1868.

ii HANNAH CROCKER, b. about 1786; m. New London, CT, 8 Jan 1801, JOSEPH WEEKS, b. at New London, 26 May 1771 son of Joseph and Elizabeth (Grant) Weeks; Joseph d. at New London, 31 Jul 1809.

iii EDEY CROCKER, b. in RI, 1794; d. at Sloansville, NY, 23 Jan 1876; m. JACOB TEEPLE, b. 1791 son of John and Lanah (Vosseller) Teeple; Jacob d. at Sloansville, 1866.

698) TIMOTHY HOLT *(Timothy Holt[4], Hannah Abbott Holt[3], William[2], George[1])*, b. at Willington, 19 May 1765 son of Timothy and Rebecca (Chamberlain) Holt; d. 17 Apr 1850; m. 10 Dec 1789, ESTHER SCRIPTURE, b. 26 Aug 1765 son of John and Esther (Lee) Scripture; Esther d. 1 Aug 1841.

Timothy and Esther Holt lived in Willington throughout their lives and were parents to three children.

i NORMAN HOLT, b. 6 Aug 1791; d. 12 Apr 1792.

ii ORRIN HOLT, b. 13 Mar 1793; d. at Willington, 20 Jun 1855; m. 24 Sep 1819, ELIZA DUNTON, b. at Willington, 12 Apr 1801 daughter of Samuel and Lovina (Marcy) Dunton; Eliza d. at Willington, 8 Apr 1850. Orrin was a member of the Connecticut state legislature and elected to the twenty-fourth U.S. Congress as a Jacksonian. He was re-elected as a Democrat to the twenty-fifth Congress with total period of service in the U.S. Congress 1836-1839. He held positions within the Connecticut state militia up to the rank of Inspector General.[1901]

iii REBECCA HOLT, b. 1 May 1797; d. at Willington, 14 Feb 1857. Rebecca did not marry.

699) JAMES HOLT *(James Holt[4], Hannah Abbott Holt[3], William[2], George[1])*, b. at Willington, 12 Apr 1770 son of James and Esther (Owens) Holt; d. at Willington, 16 Jan 1856; m. 4 Dec 1794, MARY POOL, b. at Willington, 14 Aug 1770 daughter of Timothy and Deborah (Presson) Pool; Mary d. 18 Jan 1853.

James Holt and Mary Pool were parents to five children born at Willington.

i CELINDA HOLT, b. 16 Jan 1796; d. at Willington, 20 May 1823; m. 18 Nov 1816, ROBERT SHARP, b. about 1791 likely the son of Solomon and Rebecca (Perkins) Sharp; Robert d. at Willington, 1 Nov 1874. After Celinda's death, Robert married Julianna Holt (see Family 681).

ii POLLY HOLT, b. 7 Sep 1798; d. at Willington, 24 Jan 1853; m. her second cousin, HORACE HOLT *(Caleb Holt[5], Caleb Holt[4], Hannah Abbott Holt[3], William[2], George[1])*, b. at Willington, 29 Aug 1784 son of Caleb and Sarah (Goodale) Holt; Horace d. at Willington, 30 Jan 1863. Horace is a child in Family 681.

iii TIMOTHY HOLT, b. 12 Jul 1801; d. at Willington, 29 Dec 1864; m. 1st, at Mansfield, CT, 2 Mar 1827, THANKFUL WILSON, b. at Mendon, MA, 8 May 1801 daughter of Reuben and Joanna (Taft) Wilson; Thankful d. at Willington, 6 Dec 1835. Timothy m. 2nd, at Mansfield, 4 Mar 1836, ALMIRA A. PERKINS, b. about 1809 daughter of Ransom and Huldah (Montgomery) Perkins; Almira d. at Willington, 29 Apr 1874.

iv JAMES HOLT, b. 15 Aug 1804; d. at Webster, MA, 22 Sep 1851; m. at Willington, 5 May 1830, PHILEA WILSON, b. at Mendon, 24 Nov 1803 daughter of John and Leah (Darling) Wilson; Philea d. at Webster, 26 Apr 1858.

v ALMIRA HOLT, b. 30 Aug 1810; d. 3 Nov 1813.

700) JOSEPH HOLT *(James Holt[4], Hannah Abbott Holt[3], William[2], George[1])*, b. at Willington, 12 Apr 1770 son of James and Esther (Owens) Holt; d. at Willington, 29 Jan 1816; m. 6 Mar 1794, BETSY PARKER, b. at Willington, 23 Feb 1775 daughter of Jonathan and Betsy (Johnson) Parker; Betsy d. 7 May 1814.

The probate record for Joseph Holt includes few documents as the documents are damaged and not able to be digitally rendered. There was not a will. The surety bond for the administration was $10,000 suggesting a substantial estate. There are six guardian bonds, although the documents are not available; only folder sheets are available for minors Lucy, Mary, and Alvah.[1902] There are birth records for six children which do not include Mary, but there are six minor children at the time of probate, and son Thomas was deceased in 1814.

There is evidence for seven children of Joseph Holt and Betsy Parker, all born at Willington.

[1900] New York Marriages 1686-1980, familysearch.org

[1901] Biographical Directory of the United States Congress, Orrin Holt, http://bioguide.congress.gov/scripts/biodisplay.pl?index=H000748

[1902] Connecticut State Library (Hartford, Connecticut); Probate Place: Hartford, Connecticut, Probate Packets, Holt, Clarisa-Hunt, O, 1759-1880, case number 1064

i HANNAH HOLT, b. 16 Jan 1795, no further record

ii ESTHER HOLT, b. 27 Jan 1797; no further record

iii THOMAS HOLT, b. 27 May 1799; d. at Willington, 5 May 1814.

iv ALVAH HOLT, b. 14 Aug 1801; d. at Hartford, 30 Mar 1876; m. 13 Feb 1823, BETSEY KELSEY, b. at Hartford, 18 Mar 1794 daughter of Levi and Sarah (Burkett) Kelsey;[1903] Betsey d. at Hartford, 2 Jun 1869.

v LUCY HOLT, b. 22 Jan 1804; d. at Willington, 3 Feb 1868; m. 24 Nov 1825, ELI ELDREDGE, b. at Ashford, 18 Apr 1803 son of Elijah and Bethiah (Chapman) Eldredge; Eli d. at Willington, 31 May 1864.

vi JOSEPH PARSONS HOLT, b. 19 Jul 1806; d. at Northfield, MN, 8 May 1886; m. 23 Nov 1834, JULIA CUSHMAN, of Stafford, b. about 1817; Julia d. at Northfield, 3 Apr 1892.[1904]

vii MARY HOLT, b. about 1808; only known through guardian record and no further record.

701) SOLOMON HOLT *(James Holt⁴, Hannah Abbott Holt³, William², George¹)*, b. at Willington, 14 Apr 1772 son of James and Esther (Owens) Holt; d. at Iowa City, IA, 4 Jun 1838; m. at Franklin, CT, 7 Apr 1799, ZERVIAH ABELL, b. at Norwich, 26 Aug 1780 daughter of Thomas and Zerviah (Hyde) Abell;[1905] Zerviah d. at Johnson County, IA, 1845.

Solomon and Zerviah were married in Connecticut, but were in Exeter, New York by 1810. After 1830, they relocated to Iowa City, Iowa. Solomon Holt and Zerviah Abell were parents of eight children born at Exeter, New York.[1906]

i ESTHER HOLT, b. 16 Jun 1804; d. at Lebanon, NY, 31 May 1882; m. DANIEL ABBOTT, b. 3 Nov 1805 son of Daniel and Sally (Bellows) Abbott; Daniel d. at Lebanon, 1891. Daniel Abbott is a descendant of George Abbott of Rowley.

ii AUSTIN HOLT, b. about 1807; d. at Jefferson County, KY, about 1839; m. at Jefferson County, 17 Dec 1833, SUSANNAH WARWIC, b. about 1810. Susannah married second James Hamilton on 13 Sep 1840.

iii DIODATE HOLT, b. about 1809; d. after 1870 when he was living in Elizabethtown, KY; m. at Jefferson County, KY, 7 Mar 1834, ELIZABETH OWINGS TOY, b. in Maryland, Dec 1811 daughter of Joseph and Sarah (Owings) Toy; Elizabeth d. after 1900 when she was living in Elizabethtown, KY.

iv HARVEY HOLT, b. about 1813; d. before 1828. He was baptized in 1825 but there seems to be a second son Harvey born by 1828.

v EUNICE HITCHCOCK HOLT, b. about 1816; d. at Johnson County, IA, 22 Mar 1869; m. 20 Jul 1851, DAVID WRAY, b. at Hamilton County, OH, 15 Oct 1815 son of Richard and Catherine (Buford) Wray; David d. at Johnson County, 27 Sep 1872. David Wray was first married to Maria Alt.[1907]

vi MARY CALISTA HOLT, b. about 1820; m. at Johnson County, IA, 12 Jan 1845, JAMES M. PRICE; James d. before 1850.

vii JAMES THOMPSON HOLT, b. 22 Nov 1822; d. at Berwick, IA, 2 Mar 1901; m. 1850, PHEBE E. DUNKLE, b. in OH, 5 Nov 1832; Phebe d. at Berwick, 19 Feb 1917.

viii HARVEY HOLT, b. about 1828; d. after 1850 when he was living in Iowa City, IA with his sisters Eunice Holt and Mary C. Price.

702) ESTHER HOLT *(James Holt⁴, Hannah Abbott Holt³, William², George¹)*, b. at Willington, 20 Nov 1774 daughter of James and Esther (Owens) Holt; d. at Ashtabula County, OH; m. 9 Jan 1800, DANIEL PARKER, b. at Willington, 5 Mar 1777 son of Jonathan and Betsy (Johnson) Parker; Daniel d. at Orwell, OH, 18 Mar 1855.

Esther Holt and Daniel Parker were parents of seven children born at Willington. They then made the trip west and were in Ashtabula County, Ohio by 1820.

[1903] Barbour, *Families of Early Hartford, Conn.*, p 354

[1904] Neill, *History of Rice County*

[1905] Abell, *The Abell Family in America*, p 80

[1906] There are baptism records for children of Solomon and Zerviah Holt at the Congregational Church at Exeter: Austin, Diodate, Harvey, Eunice Hitchcock, Mary Calista, and James Thompson all on 27 March 1825. Presbyterian Historical Society; Philadelphia, Pennsylvania; *U.S., Presbyterian Church Records, 1701-1907;* Book Title: *1825 – 1861*. The names of Esther's parents, Solomon and Zeviah, are engraved on her gravestone. The younger Harvey is listed on the 1850 census as born about 1830. There may be another child born before Esther, but that information is not determined.

[1907] History of Johnson County, Iowa, p 955

i JONATHAN PARKER, b. 1 Feb 1801; d. at Madison, OH, after 1850; m. at Ashtabula County, 14 Mar 1827, ABIGAIL DEVAN, b. 1802 daughter of Talcott and Temperance (-) Devan; Abigail d. at Montville, OH, 18 Mar 1838.

ii KEZIAH PARKER, b. 16 Oct 1802; d. at Geneva, OH, 5 Jul 1833; m. at Ashtabula County, 24 Feb 1820, EZEKIEL ARNOLD, b. at Ontario, NY, 1797; Ezekiel d. at Geneva, 5 Jun 1880.

iii DANIEL PARKER, b. 2 Mar 1805; d. 7 Apr 1805.

iv HANNAH PARKER, b. 1 Mar 1806; d. at Sycamore, IL, 15 Jul 1883; m. MARSHALL CALL, b. at Randolph, VT, 24 Feb 1800 son of Rufus and Lydia (Ellis) Call; Marshall d. at Sycamore, 26 May 1873.

v NEHEMIAH PARKER, b. 2 Jun 1808; d. at Orwell, OH, 13 Mar 1871; m. 1st, at Ashtabula County, 6 Apr 1836, CHLOE SAMANTHA COOK, b. 1817 daughter of Zera and Chloe (Loomis) Cook; Chloe d. 12 Jun 1847. Nehemiah m. 2nd, 16 Nov 1848, ZILPHA FENTON, b. 1813; Zelpha d. at Orwell, 4 Jan 1898. After Nehemiah's death, Zelpha married Ichabod Clapp 27 May 1880.

vi ESTHER PARKER, b. 2 Jun 1810. Esther's marriage is uncertain, but most likely m. at Madison, OH, 14 Mar 1826, DAVID MORSE, b. in NY, about 1800 and d. at Thompson, OH, 1851. If this is Esther's marriage, she died at Thompson, OH, 20 May 1883.

vii BETSY PARKER, b. 18 Aug 1812; nothing further known.

703) JOHN HOLT *(James Holt⁴, Hannah Abbott Holt³, William², George¹)*, b. at Willington, 11 Apr 1776 son of James and Luce (Sawins) Holt; d. at Willington, 22 Apr 1841; m. 6 Sep 1804, CLARISSA HOLT, b. 1775 (based on age at time of death); Clarissa d. 25 Feb 1840. I have no idea who Clarissa Holt is and suspect she may be the widow of a Holt but have not been able to track her down.

There is little information on this family. Three children are known, all born at Willington.

i MATILDA HOLT, b. 13 Jun 1805; d. at Willington, 26 Jun 1834. Matilda did not marry.

ii JOHN HOLT, b. 15 Mar 1809; d. at Colchester, CT, 1851 (probate 15 Oct 1851 with widow Waity Holt declining administration); m. at Willington, 29 Aug 1832, WAITY MOORE, b. in Rhode Island about 1812; Waity d. at Willington, 22 Jan 1868. After John's death, Waity married Lester Carew, 29 Mar 1859.

iii LAUNDA HOLT, b. 5 Sep 1813; no further record.

704) LUCE HOLT *(James Holt⁴, Hannah Abbott Holt³, William², George¹)*, b. at Willington, 11 Jun 1778 daughter of James and Luce (Sawins) Holt; d. at Ashford, 22 Feb 1847;[1908][1909] m. at Ashford, 26 Jan 1809, AARON WALKER, b. 21 Jan 1776 son of Samuel and Alice (Case) Walker; Aaron d. at Ashford, 1 Nov 1815.

Luce did not remarry after Aaron's death and in the 1830 U.S. Census at Ashford, she is listed as Mrs. Lucy Walker with the household consisting of one female age 50-59 and one female 15-19.[1910]

The estate of Aaron Walker entered probate 1815 and the inventory was completed 29 November 1815 with a total value of $2,016.81 which included the value of the home farm and buildings of $1,164. Claims against the estate totaled $755.07. The administration of the estate included a consideration of the part of the estate which was still part of the widow's portion of Aaron's mother Alice Walker Wilson.[1911]

Luce and Aaron had two daughters whose births are recorded at Ashford.

i MARIA TRUMBULL WALKER, b. 11 Jul 1810; d. 18 May 1812.[1912]

ii LUCY MAIN WALKER, b. 11 Nov 1813; d. at Ashford, 5 May 1881; m. at Willington, 8 Apr 1840, GEORGE WHITON, b. at Ashford, 8 Jun 1816 son of Abner and Amy (Chaffee) Whiton; George d. at Ashford, 22 Sep 1887.

705) ABIEL HOLT *(James Holt⁴, Hannah Abbott Holt³, William², George¹)*, b. 14 Jan 1780 son of James and Luce (Sawins) Holt; d. at Mansfield, about 1826 (probate of estate in 1826); m. 30 Apr 1805, SALLY CONVERSE, b. at Stafford, 9 Mar 1781 daughter of Stephen and Zerviah (Sanger) Converse;[1913] Sally's date of death is uncertain. She was alive in 1823 when her

[1908] Durrie, *A Genealogy of the Holt Family*, p 50
[1909] Ancestry.com, Connecticut, Deaths and Burials Index, 1650-1934
[1910] 1830; Census Place: Ashford, Windham, Connecticut; Series: M19; Roll: 11; Page: 176; Family History Library Film: 0002804
[1911] *Connecticut Wills and Probate, 1609-1999*, Probate of Aaron Walker, Hartford, 1815, Case number 4184.
[1912] Durrie, *A Genealogy of the Holt Family*, p 103
[1913] The 1823 will of Stephen Converse includes a bequest to his daughter Sally Holt.

father wrote his will but there is no mention of her in the probate of Abiel's estate. The probate includes some provisions of the support of the two younger sons (Sanford and Arnold) who were underage at the time.

Abiel and Sally had three children whose birth are recorded at Ashford.

i ALFRED CONVERSE HOLT, b. 25 Feb 1806; d. at Hillsdale County, MI, 17 Mar 1852; m. 29 Mar 1830, ADELINE L. HURLBUT, b. at Bozrah, CT, about 1810 daughter of Asa and Salome (Arnold) Hurlbut;[1914] Adeline d. at Reading, MI, 24 Aug 1887. After Alfred's death, Adeline married Herman C. Hawse who was first married to Elvira Bacon. At the 1860 U.S. Census for Butler, MI, Adeline and H. C. Hawse are living in a household that includes two Hawse children and 10-year old Amos C. Holt.[1915]

ii SANFORD HOLT, b. 5 Feb 1815; d. at Haverhill, MA, 22 Oct 1886; m. at Willington, 30 Aug 1835, FIDELIA STUDLEY, b. 1t Mansfield, 12 Jan 1816 daughter of Ebenezer and Fidelia (Hodges) Studley. Fidelia d. at West Boylston, MA, 15 Nov 1882. After Fidelia's death, Sanford married Lydia P. Sawyer on 28 Nov 1883. Lydia Sawyer was the daughter of Timothy Sawyer and Nancy Porter Pendleton.

iii ARNOLD HOLT, b. 24 Sep 1816; d. at Hartford, 21 Dec 1862; m. at Hartford, 7 May 1838, JULIA CURTISS, b. about 1816 daughter of Lyman Curtiss. Arnold and Julia did not have children.

706) MARY HENDRICK *(Hannah Abbott Hendrick[4], Caleb[3], William[2], George[1])*, b. 5 Dec 1765 daughter of John and Hannah (Abbott) Hendrick; d. after 1845 at Putney, VT; m. 14 Sep 1786, JOHN STODDARD, b. 19 Nov 1761 son of Joshua and Sarah (Humphrey) Stoddard; John d. at Westminster, VT, 13 Aug 1831.[1916]

Mary and John Stoddard had seven children born at Westminster, Vermont.

i REUBEN STODDARD, b. 10 Apr 1788; d. at Gouverneur, NY, 1 Apr 1872; m. Oct 1817, ABIGAIL FOSTER, b. at Putney, 25 Feb 1789 daughter of David and Anne (Sessions) Foster;[1917] Abigail d. at Gouverneur, 7 Feb 1876.

ii LYDIA STODDARD, b. 9 Aug 1790; d. at Westminster, 3 Sep 1832. Lydia did not marry.

iii MELINDA STODDARD, b. 5 Mar 1794; d. at Westminster, 11 Feb 1877. Melinda did not marry.

iv JOHN HUMPHREY STODDARD, b. 21 Feb 1796; d. at Avon IL, 25 Sep 1881; m. 31 Dec 1823, SARAH PIERCE, b, at Westmoreland, NH, 8 Sep 1800 daughter of John and Hannah (Warner) Pierce; Sarah d. after 1880 (still living at the 1880 U.S. Census).

v SAREPTA STODDARD, b. 12 Jun 1800; d. at Grafton, 26 Jul 1855; m. 2 Nov 1835, as his second wife, HENRY HOLMES, b. at Grafton, about 1806 son of Given and Lucy (Palmer) Holmes;[1918] Henry d. at Grafton, 22 Sep 1871. Henry was first married to Rhoda who died in 1835.

vi SALINA STODDARD, b. 19 Nov 1802; d. at Westminster, 20 Mar 1849; m. at Westminster, 22 Oct 1828, RODNEY RANDAL BUXTON, b. at Walpole, NH, 26 Aug 1805 son of Jonathan and Margaret (-) Buxton; Rodney d. at Westminster 29 Dec 1880. After Salina's death, Rodney married Meranda Wheelock.

vii PROSPER FRANKLIN STODDARD, b. 30 Aug 1806; d. at Westminster, 2 Aug 1852; m. 15 Mar 1828, NANCY MADISON BURR, b. at Putney, 9 Jul 1809 daughter of Ephraim and Freelove (Wheeler) Burr;[1919][1920] Nancy d. at Westminster, 14 Dec 1890. After Prosper's death, Nancy married Edward Glover.

707) CALEB HENDRICK *(Hannah Abbott Hendrick[4], Caleb[3], William[2], George[1])*, b. at Union, CT, 17 Sep 1767 son of John and Hannah (Abbott) Hendrick; d. at Hartland, VT, 26 Aug 1837; m. by 1796, his first cousin, SARAH ABBOTT *(Samuel[4], Caleb[3], William[2], George[1])*, b. 15 Apr 1773 daughter of Samuel and Rachel (Ward) Abbott; Sarah d. 11 Feb 1849.

[1914] Hurlbut, *The Hurlbut Genealogy*, p 151

[1915] Year: 1860; Census Place: Butler, Branch, Michigan; Roll: M653_538; Page: 1041; Family History Library Film: 803538

[1916] *Vermont, Vital Records, 1720-1908.*

[1917] The 1848 will of Anna Foster (probate 1861) includes a bequest to her daughter Abigail wife of Reuben Stoddard.

[1918] Ancestry.com, Vermont, Vital Records, 1720-1908. Names of parents on death record of Henry Holmes are Given Holmes and Lucy Palmer.

[1919] *Vermont Births, Marriages and Deaths to 2008.* (From microfilmed records. Online database: *AmericanAncestors.org*, New England Historic Genealogical Society, 2013.) Birth of Nancy Madison Burr, parents Ephraim Burr and Freelove Wheeler.

[1920] Ancestry.com, Vermont, Vital Records, 1720-1908. Names of Nancy's parents are listed on her marriage to Edward Glover as Ephraim Burr and Freelove Wheeler. Nancy's death record gives the parents' names as John and "Frila."

Caleb and Sarah reared their family in Harland, Vermont. Caleb participated there in military preparations related to the War of 1812. Caleb served as Captain of the Artillery. "If all men were like Caleb Hendrick, there would be no use for poor-houses, jails, court houses, or prisons."[1921]

Caleb and Sarah had nine children born in Hartland, Vermont.

i MOSES S. HENDRICK, b. 16 Oct 1796; d. at Clinton, IL, 14 Jan 1861; m. 4 Apr 1822, LUCY HALL, b. 19 Jul 1794 daughter of David and Olive (Smead) Hall, Lucy d. at Clinton, 26 Feb 1884. Moses and Lucy relocated first to Ohio after 1830, but moved again after 1850 to Clinton, Illinois. Their children were born in Hartland, Vermont.

ii RACHEL HENDRICK, b. 25 Jun 1798; d. at Hartland, 13 Sep 1844. Rachel did not marry.

iii LYDIA HENDRICK, b. 7 Jul 1800; d. 28 Feb 1811.

iv MARILLA HENDRICK, b. 30 Mar 1802; d. at Morristown, VT, 16 Mar 1874; m. 17 Jun 1824, DAVID GILBERT, b. at Hartford, VT, about 1799 son of Nathaniel and Rachel (Strong) Gilbert;[1922] David d. at Morristown, 1 Jul 1894.

v DIANTHA HENDRICK, b. 13 Sep 1804; d. at Darlington, WI, 4 Mar 1860; m. 10 Dec 1833, GEORGE HOLBROOK, b. at Hartland 8 Sep 1790 son of Ebenezer and Diedamia (Durkee) Holbrook; George d. 14 Jun 1852. After George's death, Diantha received a land grant at Dane, WI on 2 Oct 1854.[1923]

vi SARAH HENDRICK, b. 13 Apr 1807; d. at Darlington, WI, 14 Apr 1882; m. 5 Dec 1838, as his second wife, ALFRED HOVEY, b. at Thetford, 20 Apr 1791 son of Amos and Clara (Calkins) Hovey; Alfred d. 5 Apr 1872. Alfred was first married to Abigail Cushman Howard who died in 1837.

vii MALINDA HENDRICK, b. 9 May 1810; d. at Hartland, 17 Dec 1880; m. 17 Dec 1857, as his second wife, Dr. LEWIS EMMONS, b. 22 May 1804 son of Solomon and Prudence (Taft) Emmons; Lewis d. 13 Aug 1878. Lewis was first married to Jane Sylvester. Malinda did not have children.

viii HANNAH HENDRICK, b. 30 Jul 1812; d. at Hartland, 17 Mar 1874; m. 24 Sep 1840, GEORGE P. HAYES, b. 1816 son of Henry and Lydia (Pierce) Hayes; George d. 20 Dec 1868.

ix MARY HENDRICK, b. 22 Jul 1815; d. at Hartland, 30 Oct 1887; m. 1 Jun 1840, EZRA L. STODDARD, b. at Westminster, 18 Jul 1814 son of Amasa and Anna (Willard) Stoddard; Ezra d. at Westminster, 19 May 1890.

708) HANNAH HENDRICK *(Hannah Abbott Hendrick^4, Caleb^3, William^2, George^1)*, b. 22 Mar 1770 daughter of John and Hannah (Abbott) Hendrick; d. at Waterford, VT, 12 Apr 1843; m. about 1800, ZEDEKIAH GOODELL, b. at Pomfret, 31 Aug 1769 son of Jacob and Mehitable (Goodell) Goodell; Zedekiah d. 11 Sep 1863.

Zedekiah Goodell and Hannah Hendrick were parents of five children all born at Waterford, Vermont.

i ZOA GOODELL, b. 8 Jun 1804; d. at Waterford, 7 May 1857. Zoa did not marry.

ii EZRA HENDRICK GOODELL, b. 2 Sep 1806; no further record

iii REUBEN GOODELL, b. 28 Apr 1807; d. at Waterford, 27 Oct 1885; m. 1st, 28 Feb 1832, TAMARA JOHNSON FAREWELL, b. at Waterford, 9 Aug 1809 daughter of Henry and Mary (Bonet) Farewell;[1924] Tamara d. about 1840. Reuben m. 2nd, the widow Betsey Dunbar, born about 1804 and died after 1860.

iv JOHN STODDARD GOODELL, b. 22 Jan 1809; d. at Barnet, VT, 19 May 1876; m. NANCY C. PEARSON,[1925] b. about 1807 and d. 1888 (last pension payment related to death of son was made Jun 1888). John and Nancy had one child, John Valentine Goodell, born 4 Feb 1843. John Valentine died 28 Nov 1864 at U.S. Hospital in Baltimore from wounds he received at the Battle of Cedar Creek.[1926]

v LYDIA A. GOODELL, b. Jul 1811; d. at Waterford, 8 Nov 1863. Lydia did not marry. She worked as a servant.

[1921] Nancy Darling, "History and Anniversary of Hartland," *The Vermonter*, volume 18, number 12, December 1913.

[1922] Lovejoy, *History of Royalton*, p 804

[1923] Ancestry.com, Bureau of Land Management, General Land Office Records; Washington D.C., USA; Federal Land Patents, State Volumes

[1924] The names of Tamara's parents are given on her marriage record as Henry Farwell and Mary Bonet.

[1925] Nancy's identity is not certain, but perhaps she is Nancy Pearson daughter of Nathaniel and Sarah (-) Pearson, born in Sanbornton and died at Lowell, MA, 24 Aug 1888.

[1926] Case Files of Approved Pension Applications of Widows and Other Dependents of Civil War Veterans, ca. 1861 - ca. 1910; John's mother Nancy C. Goodell was the recipient of the pension.

709) EZRA HENDRICK *(Hannah Abbott Hendrick^4, Caleb^3, William^2, George^1)*, b. 13 Mar 1772 son of John and Hannah (Abbott) Hendrick; d. 28 Dec 1799; m. about 1797, ESTHER GOODELL, b. at Pomfret, 1 Jul 1776 son of Jacob and Mehitable (Goodell) Goodell.

Ezra and Esther had just one child before Ezra's death at age 27 years. Daughter Esther was born just one month before her father's death. It is not known what happened to Ezra's widow after his death.

i ESTHER HENDRICK, b. at Waterford, 28 Nov 1799; d. at Waterford, 18 Jan 1879; m. 6 Jul 1817, SOWLE CUSHMAN, b. at Littleton, NH, 19 Aug 1792 son of Sowle and Thankful (Delano) Cushman. It is not known what became of Esther's husband Sowle Cushman. He left the family shortly after the birth of daughter Mary in 1833. There is no certain information about where he went. (See Cushman, "First Seven Generations of Cushman Family in New England" published in 1964, pp 83-84)

710) SARAH BURK *(Sarah Abbott Burk^4, Caleb^3, William^2, George^1)*, b. at Brimfield, MA, 18 Jan 1755 daughter of Jonathan and Sarah (Abbott) Burk; d. at Windsor, VT about 1783; m. at Windsor, 17 May 1774, LAZARUS BANNISTER, b. at Brookfield, 7 Feb 1748 son of Thomas and Mary (Wheeler) Bannister. Lazarus m. 2nd, about 1784, Anne Worcester. Lazarus d. at Windsor about 1813 (probate of estate).

The estate of Lazarus Banister entered probate 18 September 1813. Widow Anna Banister declined administration and Ebenezer Shedd assumed this duty. The demands against the estate exceeded the assets requiring the sale of the real estate and this was agreed to by the following heirs: Anna Banister, Elisha Banister, Anna Swinerton, Franklin Banister, and Sally Banister. In another document, Joseph Farwell signs as representative to the "absent heirs" but their names are not given. Abigail Banister also signs as an heir and Samuel Shedd signs as guardian to minor children who are not named. In the distribution, there are distributions of property to Norman Banister, Elisha Banister, Franklin Banister, Sukey Banister, Marcy Ruggles, and Thomas Banister.[1927]

Lazarus Banister and Sarah Burk were parents of four children all born at Windsor. Lazarus had nine children with his second wife Anne Worcester.

i MARCY BANISTER, b. 17 Sep 1776; d. at Roxbury, VT, 14 Dec 1849; m. about 1805, JONATHAN FISHER RUGGLES, b. at Windsor, 13 Jun 1779 son of Samuel and Elizabeth (Fisher) Ruggles; Jonathan d. at Roxbury, 6 Jan 1842.

ii THOMAS BURKE BANISTER, b. 19 Aug 1778; d. at Oswego, NY, 1857; m. LUCY CHASE, b. at Shirley, NH, 8 Apr 1786 daughter of Joshua and Susannah (Fitch) Chase.[1928]

iii SARAH BANISTER, b. 1 Aug 1780; d. after 1813. It is not known what became of Sarah. She was living and unmarried at the probate of her father's estate.

iv NORMAN BANISTER, b. 28 Sep 1782; living in 1813 but no further record located.

711) JOSEPH BURK *(Sarah Abbott Burk^4, Caleb^3, William^2, George^1)*, b. at Brimfield, MA, 27 Apr 1758 son of Jonathan and Sarah (Abbott) Burk; d. at Warner, NH, 7 May 1829;[1929] m. at Hartland, VT, 25 Apr 1784, JUDITH BARRELL, b. at Bridgewater, MA, 1 May 1763 daughter of John and Judith (Snow) Barrell.

There are just two children known for Joseph Burk and Judith Barrell, both born at Hartland, Vermont.

i JONATHAN BURK, b. 25 Oct 1784 d. at Hartland, 23 Oct 1861; m. 27 Jan 1808, POLLY GROW, b. at Hartland, 17 Nov 1790 daughter of Joseph and Tirzah (Sanger) Grow' Polly d. at Hartland, 27 Sep 1875.

ii SALLY BURK, b. 6 Jan 1789; m. 20 May 1806, NATHANIEL GROW, b. at Hartland, 5 May 1780 son of Joseph and Tirzah (Sanger) Grow; Nathaniel d. at Hartland, 6 Jun 1838.

[1927] *Vermont. Probate Court (Windsor District)*; Probate Place: *Windsor, Vermont, Probate Files: B, Back -- Barnard, H*, Probate of Lazarus Banister, 18 Sep 1813

[1928] Chase, *Seven Generations of the Descendants of Aquila and Thomas Chase*, p 104

[1929] Joseph's date of birth is engraved on the gravestone confirming this as his date of death. Findagrave: 7944300

712) ABIGAIL BURK *(Sarah Abbott Burk⁴, Caleb³, William², George¹)*, b. at Brimfield, MA, 12 Nov 1761 daughter of Jonathan and Sarah (Abbott) Burk; d. at Westminster, VT, 18 Oct 1801;[1930] m. 26 Aug 1779, REUBEN ROBINSON, b. at Cumberland, RI, 4 Aug 1753 son of Nathaniel and Kezia (Robbins) Robinson; Reuben d. at Bridgewater, VT, 16 Dec 1839.[1931]

Reuben Robinson and Abigail Burk were parents of eight children born at Westminster, Vermont.

i SARAH ROBINSON, b. 3 Sep 1780; d. at Morristown, VT, 8 Sep 1875; m. 11 Oct 1807, BENJAMIN RAND, b. 1775 son of Robert and Amy (Averill) Rand; Benjamin d. at Morristown, 26 Apr 1843.

ii LUCY ROBINSON, b. about 1781; d. 9 Dec 1782.

iii ELI HITCHCOCK ROBINSON, b. 25 Jan 1782; d. at Kane County, IL, 1861; m. POLLY MILLER, b. at Westminster, VT, 22 Mar 1784 daughter of Robert and Mary (Perry) Miller; Polly d. at Kane County, 1865.

iv LUCY ROBINSON, b. 9 Oct 1783; d. at Westminster, 9 Dec 1802.

v RELEFA ROBINSON, b. 21 Jun 1785; d. at Woodstock, VT, 8 Feb 1873; m. at Westminster, 8 Dec 1808, AMOS AVERILL, b. at Westminster, 2 Nov 1779 son of Thomas and Elizabeth (Robinson) Averill; Amos d. at Woodstock, 18 Sep 1862.

vi ASA ROBINSON, b. 20 Aug 1787; nothing further known.

vii ELIJAH ROBINSON, b. 31 Dec 1789. He is likely the Elijah Robinson, age 23, who enlisted from Westminster November 1812 for five years. He was listed as deserted at Sackets Harbor, July 1815.[1932]

viii BETSEY ROBINSON, b. 31 Mar 1792; d. at Westminster, 9 Mar 1874; m. JOHN MILLER, b. 26 Mar 1786 son of Robert and Mary (Perry) Miller; John d. at Westminster, 23 Jun 1867.

713) CALEB ABBOTT *(William⁴, Caleb³, William², George¹)*, b. at Union County, CT, 2 Feb 1774 son of William and Mary (Coy) Abbott; d. at Colden, NY, 25 Jan 1851; m. by 1794, HANNAH WHEAT, b. at Bernardston, MA, 6 Jan 1772 daughter of Samuel and Jerusha (Allen) Wheat;[1933] Hannah d. 4 Sep 1842.

Caleb Abbott was a farmer in Colden, New York. Caleb and Hannah Abbott were parents of ten children.

i TRYPHENA ABBOTT, b. 9 Jun 1795; d. at Sheboygan, WI, 25 Jun 1874; m. at Albany, Sep 1818, REUBEN ABBOTT, b. at Cambridge, NY, 9 Jul 1797 son of Adna and Anna (Gurley) Abbott; Reuben d. at Sheboygan, 31 Jul 1869. Reuben Abbott is descended from George Abbott of Rowley.

ii JOHN ALLEN ABBOTT, b. 28 Sep 1796; d. at Colden, 2 Aug 1855; m. about 1817, ESTHER CROCKER, b. 1800; Esther d. at Colden, 5 May 1853.

iii MARY ABBOTT, b. 8 Mar 1798; d. at Colden, 16 Oct 1879; m. at Albany, 20 Jan 1817, her third cousin, ABIEL HOLT *(Abiel Holt⁵, Abiel Holt⁴, Hannah Abbott Holt³, William², George¹)*, b. at Sharon, VT, 9 Sep 1791 son of Abiel and Mary (Mosher) Holt; Abiel d. at Boston, NY, 9 Dec 1869. Abiel is a child in Family 678.

iv SAMUEL WHEAT ABBOTT, b. 28 Sep 1799; d. at Colden, 15 Oct 1860; m. ANN AMANDA GRIGGS, b. 11 Feb 1801 daughter of Ichabod and Jerusha (Gurley) Griggs; Ann d. at Colden, 5 May 1864.

v SARAH "SALLY" ABBOTT, b. 11 Aug 1801; d. at Colden, 22 Mar 1883; m. at Albany, 1823, ICHABOD GRIGGS, b. at East Aurora, NY, 17 Nov 1793 son of Ichabod and Jerusha (Gurley) Griggs; Ichabod d. at Colden, 28 Jun 1843.

vi ORINDA ABBOTT, b. 21 Aug 1803; d. at Salem, MN, 10 Mar 1880; m. her third cousin, ZEBINA HOLT *(Abiel Holt⁵, Abiel Holt⁴, Hannah Abbott Holt³, William², George¹)*, b. at Sharon, VT, 7 Feb 1797 son of Abiel and Mary (Mosher) Holt; Zebina d. at Salem, MN, 19 Feb 1871. Zebina is a child in Family 678.

vii JERUSHA ABBOTT, b. 27 Mar 1805; d. at East Aurora, NY, 30 Jan 1888; m. at Albany, 1822, RUSSELL GREEN, b. 1800; Russell d. at Colden, after 1880.

viii MELANCTHON ABBOTT, b. 6 Sep 1807; d. at Strykersville, NY, 1889 (probate 9 Jul 1889); m. 1st, OLIVE MARANDA GRIGGS, b. about 1810 daughter of Ichabod and Jerusha (Gurley) Griggs; Olive d. 26 Aug 1867. Melancthon m. 2nd, HARRIET GRIGGS, b. at Springfield, 29 Jan 1806 daughter of Ichabod and Jerusha (Gurley) Griggs. Harriet was first married to Joe Mack.

[1930] Vermont Births, Marriages and Deaths to 2008. (From microfilmed records. Online database: AmericanAncestors.org, New England Historic Genealogical Society, 2013.)

[1931] This is given as the possible date of death. Early Vermont Settlers, 1700-1784. Nathaniel Robinson of Westminster (Original Online Database: AmericanAncestors.org, New England Historic Genealogical Society, 2015. (By Scott Andrew Bartley, Lead Genealogist.)

[1932] U.S. Army, Register of Enlistments, 1798-1914

[1933] Wheat, *Wheat Genealogy*, p 72

ix CALEB ABBOTT, b. 25 Apr 1810; d. at Cleveland, OH, 1 Jun 1875; m. 1st, 1834, JANE ANDERSON, b. 12 Oct 1810 of Schenectady, daughter of John Anderson; Jane d. at Schenectady, 22 May 1837. Caleb m. 2nd, LUCY HALE KEYES, b. at Wolcott, CT, 6 Apr 1816 daughter of John and Mary (Carmichael) Keyes;[1934] Lucy d. at Cleveland, 6 Feb 1899.

x SYLVESTER ABBOTT, b. 27 Sep 1811; d. at Concord, NY, 1879; m. at Hanover, NY, 1 Oct 1831, LOUISA WEBSTER, b. at Hanover, 6 Jul 1813 daughter of Guy and Lucretia (Mason) Webster;[1935] Louisa d. at East Aurora, 17 Dec 1905.

714) NEHEMIAH ABBOTT *(William⁴, Caleb³, William², George¹)*, b. at Union, CT, 4 Jun 1781 son of William and Esther (Green) Abbott; d. 11 Jan 1867 (probate 25 Feb 1867), Kirkland, NY; m. 4 Oct 1803, ESTHER BARKER, b. at Watertown, CT, 29 Oct 1776 daughter of Eliasaph and Mabel (Sanford) Barker; Esther d. 2 Jan 1857, Oneida County, NY.

Nehemiah Abbott was a farmer in Clinton, New York. Nehemiah and Esther were parents of five children born at Clinton.

i WILLIAM BARKER ABBOTT, b. 10 Aug 1804; d. at Syracuse, 29 Aug 1873; m. 20 Oct 1830, LUCRETIA AMANDA GREEN, b. in Massachusetts, 25 Jan 1810 daughter of Robert and Mercy (Winslow) Green; Lucretia d. at Syracuse, 31 Aug 1879.[1936]

ii EMERY ABBOTT, b. 8 Feb 1806; d. at Malta, IL, 6 Sep 1878; m. 1st, 21 May 1834, his first cousin, LAVINA HUBBARD *(Orinda Abbott Hubbard⁵, William⁴, Caleb³, William², George¹)*, b. 12 Oct 1807 daughter of Joel and Orinda (Abbott) Hubbard; Lavina d. at Harmony, NY, Oct 1849. Emery m. 2nd, about 1852, LYDIA M. DELAND, b. 22 Aug 1813 daughter of William and Mary (Bullard) Deland; Lydia d. at Malta, IL, 7 Jan 1900. Lavina is a child in Family 717.

iii SAMUEL WRIGHT ABBOTT, b. 27 Oct 1808; d. at Clinton, 1892 (probate 20 Mar 1893); m. 21 May 1829, URSULA BRYAN, b. at Camden, NY, 23 Jan 1809 daughter of John and Sophronia (Atwater) Bryan; Ursula d. at Clinton, 1900.

iv JUNIUS ABBOTT, b. 25 May 1812; d. at Syracuse, 26 Mar 1854; m. about 1850, JULIET M. GREEN, b. in New York, 14 Dec 1829 daughter of Benjamin F. and Mary (Easton) Green; Juliet d. at Fulton, NY, 20 Dec 1895. After Junius's death, Juliet married Mr. Wood.

v SHELDON SWEEZY ABBOTT, b. 1 Mar 1818; d. at Kirkland, NY, 1877; m. 21 Feb 1844, ANNA MARIA DERRAN, b. 17 Jun 1819; d. at Wampsville, NY, 31 Dec 1891.

715) PAUL ABBOTT *(William⁴, Caleb³, William², George¹)*, b. at Union, CT, 7 May 1783 son of William and Esther (Green) Abbott; d. at Lowville, NY, 18 Mar 1831; m. 1st, 6 Mar 1807, MARY GAYLORD, b. about 1783 daughter of Cheney and Mary (White) Gaylord; Mary d. 2 Sep 1809. Paul m. 2nd, 7 Mar 1811, PATTY EELS, b. 26 Oct 1787 daughter of Daniel and Martha (Hamlin) Eels;[1937] Patty d. at New Hartford, NY, 17 Apr 1873.

Paul Abbott was a merchant in Lowville, New York.

In his will written 7 February 1831 (probate 23 April 1831), Paul Abbott bequeathed to son Sylvester Abbot one thousand dollars. Daughter Elizabeth Abbot receives two hundred-fifty dollars. Wife Patty Abbot receives a certain piece of land with all the building situated in the village of Lowville for her use during her natural life. After her decease, this property goes to his children: Mary E. Abbot, Elizabeth Abbot, Henry G. Abbot, William E. Abbot, James H. Abbot, and Thomas S. Abbot. Wife Patty also has the use of all the furnishings, carriages, etc. during her life and this also is divided among the children named at her death. The custody and tuition of daughters of Mary and Elizabeth is given to Patty during the minority of the children. Custody and tuition of his sons Henry G., William E., James H., and Thomas S. is given to William Eels of the town of Whitestown.[1938]

Paul Abbott and Mary Gaylord had one child.

1934 Keyes, *Genealogy of Robert Keyes of Watertown*, p 14

1935 Mason, *Descendants of Elisha Mason*, p 31

1936 Lucretia's birth date and the names of her parents are given on the cemetery index card of Oakwood Cemetery, Syracuse, NY.

1937 Andrews, *The Hamlin Family*, p 176

1938 *Wills and Testaments, 1806-1870; Index to Wills, 1805-1940;* Author: *New York. Surrogate's Court (Lewis County);* Probate Place: *Lewis, New York, Wills, Vol A-B, 1806-1840*, Volume B, p 9

i SYLVESTER G. ABBOTT, b. at Lowville, 23 Dec 1807; d. at Oswego, NY, 9 Sep 1877; m. 4 Mar 1833, MARY FALLEY BUSH, b. at Lowville, 11 Dec 1808 daughter of Charles and Pamela (Noble) Bush;[1939] Mary d. at Oswego, after 1875.

Paul Abbott and Patty Eels had eight children born at Lowville.

i MARY E. ABBOTT, b. 27 Dec 1811; d. at Sheffield, OH, 24 Jun 1837; m. 8 Jul 1836, Rev. LORENZO DOW BUTTS, b. at Sand Hill, NY, 13 Mar 1804 son of Gideon and Elizabeth (Peck) Butts; Lorenzo d. at Alexandria, VA, 6 Dec 1882. After Mary's death, Lorenzo married Mary Ann Whittlesey 22 Jul 1839.

ii ELIZABETH ABBOTT, b. 10 Nov 1812; d. at Syracuse, 9 Sep 1894. Elizabeth did not marry.

iii HENRY ABBOTT, b. about 1814; died young

iv LUCRETIA ABBOTT, b. about 1816; died young

v HENRY GREEN ABBOTT, b. 19 Jul 1818; d. at Utica, NY, 17 Jan 1896; m. at New Hartford, NY, 9 Oct 1844, MARY CURTIS BABCOCK, b. at New Hartford, 11 Mar 1820 daughter of Charles and Nancy (Pratt) Babcock; Mary d. at Utica, 1 Jan 1894.

vi WILLIAM EELS ABBOTT, b. 19 Jan 1822; d. at Geneva, NY, 29 Apr 1899; m. 1st, 12 Aug 1845, JANE FOSTER, b. at Litchfield, NY, 26 Aug 1818 daughter of Arnold and Susan (Deming) Foster; Jane d. at Syracuse, 19 Mar 1889. William m. 2nd, 23 Dec 1890, ELIZABETH E. EELS, b. at Clinton, 15 Mar 1841 daughter of Charles W. and Mary A. (Prior) Eels; Elizabeth d. at Clinton, after 1920.

vii JAMES HAMLIN ABBOTT, b. 6 Jan 1824; d. at Chicago, 13 Apr 1911; m. at Cazenovia, NY, 24 Jan 1866, ELIZABETH ANDREWS, b. at New York Mills, 13 Sep 1836 daughter of George and Polly (Walker) Andrews; Elizabeth d. at Chicago, 2 Jan 1885.

viii THOMAS SCOTT ABBOTT, b. 31 Jan 1827; d. at Syracuse, 14 Aug 1846.

716) ESTHER ABBOTT *(William⁴, Caleb³, William², George¹)*, b. at Union, CT, 4 Oct 1784 daughter of William and Esther (Green) Abbott; d. after 1860 at Kirkland, NY (living with her daughter at 1860 Census); m. 30 Jan 1810, ELIHU WAKELEE, b. 27 Dec 1789 son of Platt and Mary (Minor) Wakelee; Elihu d. at New Hartford, NY, 1 Aug 1833.

Esther Abbott and Elihu Wakelee were parents of ten children born at Oneida County, New York.[1940]

i WILLIAM PLATT WAKELEE, b. 26 Nov 1810; d. at New Hartford, NY, 17 Nov 1891; m. 12 Sep 1844, MARY A. PARKER, b. in CT, about 1822; Mary d. at New Hartford, after 1892.

ii ELIHU WAKELEE, b. and d. 13 Jan 1812.

iii POLINA WAKELEE, b. 27 Mar 1813; d. 13 Apr 1813.

iv ANGELINA WAKELEE, b. 19 Mar 1814; d. at Tallmadge, MI, 20 Oct 1891; m. 9 Dec 1835, ALLEN GRINNELL, b. in NY, 22 Aug 1812 son of Harvey and Esther (-) Grinnell; Allen d. at Talmadge, 24 Jun 1893.

v MARY E. WAKELEE, b. 27 Jan 1816; d. after 1850 when she was living in Paris, NY and unmarried.

vi JANETTE L. WAKELEE, b. 5 May 1817; d. at Waubeka, WI, 19 Apr 1900; m. at Washington, WI, 26 Sep 1855, RUFUS C. GODFREY, b. in NY, 1 May 1820 son of Thomas and Mary (Kendall) Godfrey; Rufus d. at Waubeka, 26 Apr 1882.

vii POLINA A. WAKELEE, b. 27 Dec 1818; d. at Big Stone, MN, 2 Jun 1909; m. 8 Mar 1842, JOSEPH WILKINSON NEWELL, b. at Belchertown, MA, 2 Sep 1810 son of Theodore and Joanna (Wilkinson) Newell; Joseph d. at Big Stone, 31 Jul 1886.

viii LUMINDA WAKELEE, b. 27 Jun 1820; d. at Clinton, NY, 26 May 1898; m. 5 Sep 1839, SELAH STRONG, b. in NY, 27 Aug 1811 son of Nathan and Nancy (Beardsley) Strong; Selah d. at Clinton, 8 Aug 1881.

ix LEZEREU "LEROY" WAKELEE, b. 29 Dec 1821; d. at Bridgewater, NY, about 1855; m. 10 Aug 1843, ORILLA M. WHITING, b. in VT, 28 Oct 1823 daughter of Edmund and Mary (Whittemore) Whiting; Orilla d. at Philmont, NY, 9 Dec 1891.

[1939] Boltwood, *History and Genealogy of the Family of Thomas Noble*, p 408

[1940] Abbot, Genealogical Register, p 63.

x ZIPPHORAH WAKELEE, b. 12 Dec 1823; d. at Winfield, NY, 31 May 1855; m. at West Winfield, NY, 16 Nov 1846, CHARLES FOSKET, b. at New Hartford, NY, 22 Jul 1813 son of James and Lura (Kellogg) Fosket;[1941] Charles d. 15 Mar 1883.

717) ORINDA ABBOTT *(William⁴, Caleb³, William², George¹)*, b. at Union, CT, 1 May 1786 daughter of William and Esther (Green) Abbott; d. at Panama, NY, 11 May 1850; m. 17 Oct 1805, JOEL HUBBARD, b. 15 Mar 1784; Joel d. at Panama, 1 Apr 1862.

Orinda Abbott and Joel Hubbard were parents of twelve children, perhaps all born in Oneida County, NY.[1942] Daughter Hannah married Hiram Wilson, a prominent abolitionist and conductor in the Underground Railroad.[1943]

i HANNAH HUBBARD, b. 27 Jul 1806; d. at Dawn Mills, Ontario, about 1847; m. 17 Sep 1838, HIRAM WILSON, b. at Acworth, NH, 23 Sep 1803 son of John and Polly (McCoy) Wilson; Hiram d. at St. Catherine's, Ontario, 16 Apr 1864. Hiram had a second marriage to Mary.

ii LAVINA HUBBARD, b. 12 Oct 1807; d. at Harmony, NY, Oct 1849; m. 21 May 1834, her first cousin, EMERY ABBOTT *(Nehemiah⁵, William⁴, Caleb³, William², George¹)*, b. at Clinton, NY, 8 Feb 1806 son of Nehemiah and Esther (Barker) Abbott; Emery d. at Malta, IL, 6 Sep 1878. Emery Abbott is a child in Family 714.

iii SAMUEL B. HUBBARD, b. 13 Nov 1808; d. at Swan City, NE, after 1870; m. 1832, EUNICE RICE, b. in NY, 1806; Eunice d. at Swan City, after 1870.

iv ESTHER HUBBARD, b. 12 Dec 1809; d. Dec 1809.

v LUMAN HUBBARD, b. 31 Dec 1810; d. after 1870 when he was living in Malta, IL; m. 20 Sep 1838, PAMELIA MORTON, b. in NY, about 1816; Pamelia d. after 1870.

vi MARY A. HUBBARD, b. 14 Mar 1812; d. 1812.

vii MARY L. HUBBARD, b. 24 May 1813; d. 1813.

viii WILLIAM GREEN HUBBARD, b. at Marshall, NY[1944], 6 Sep 1814; d. at Albion, NY, after 1900; m. before 1848, LUCY AMELIA who has not been identified.

ix PAUL E. HUBBARD, b. 17 Aug 1817; no record after 1850 when he was living with his father at Harmony, NY.

x MARY HUBBARD, b. 3 Nov 1819; nothing further known.

xi JAMES HUBBARD, b. 12 Dec 1822; d. at Panama, NY, 16 May 1905; m. at Panama, NY, 10 Sep 1845[1945], ANGELINE FELCH, b. in VT, 1825 daughter of Carlton and Rhoda (Hawkins) Felch;[1946] Angeline d. at Harmony, NY, 27 Jun 1892.

xii HENRY G. HUBBARD, b. 10 Apr 1825; nothing further known.

Great-Grandchildren of Sarah Abbott and Ephraim Stevens

718) MARY ROBINSON *(Joseph Robinson⁴, Elizabeth Stevens Robinson³, Sarah Abbott Stevens², George¹)*, b. at Andover, 3 Aug 1737 daughter of Joseph and Mehitable (Eams) Robinson; d. at Methuen, 16 Nov 1811; m. 20 Sep 1759, HENRY BODWELL, b. at Methuen, 26 Jul 1729 son of Henry and Anne (Pottelle) Bodwell; Henry d. 9 Apr 1816.

Henry Bodwell was a Captain in the militia in Andover. He lived on the Bodwell homestead at the mouth of the Spigot River.[1947] Mary Robinson and Henry Bodwell were parents of eight children born at Methuen.

[1941] Hopkins, *The Kelloggs in the Old World and the New*, p 492

[1942] Abbot, Genealogical Register, pp 63-64

[1943] Oberlin College, "Hiram Wilson" http://www2.oberlin.edu/external/EOG/LaneDebates/RebelBios/HiramWilson.html

[1944] Presbyterian Ministerial Directory 1898

[1945] 10,000 Vital Records of Western New York, 1809-1850

[1946] Felch, *Memorial History of the Felch Family*, p 77

[1947] Biographical Encyclopedia of Maine in the Nineteenth Century, p 379

i HENRY BODWELL, b. 8 Jan 1762; d. at Methuen, 11 Dec 1814;[1948] m. 12 Dec 1793. SARAH "SALLY" LOWELL, b. in Massachusetts, 1771 (census records) whose parents are not identified; Sarah d. at Andover, 30 Jun 1851.

ii ISAAC BODWELL, b. 16 Oct 1765; d. at Methuen, 7 Aug 1845; m. 26 Mar 1788, ELIZABETH "BETSEY" MESSER, b. at Methuen, 2 Jun 1769 daughter of Nathaniel and Ruth (Whittier) Messer.

iii OLIVE BODWELL, b. 31 Aug 1767; d. at Milo, ME, 18 Feb 1829; m. at Methuen, 28 Dec 1786, BENJAMIN SARGENT, b. at Methuen, 2 Sep 1763 son of John and Mary (Tucker) Sargent; Benjamin d. at Milo, 12 May 1844.

iv PERSIS BODWELL, b. 30 Jul 1769; d. at Methuen, 7 Jun 1791; m. 27 Nov 1788, JOHN PINGREE, b. at Methuen, 22 Jan 1759 son of Moses and Anne (Carleton) Pingree; John d. at Scots Bay, Nova Scotia, 9 Dec 1813.[1949] After Persis's death, John married Elizabeth Pickering.

v JOSEPH BODWELL, b. 2 Nov 1771; d. at Methuen, 21 Oct 1848; m. 17 Dec 1795, MARY "MOLLY" HOWE, b. at Methuen, 15 May 1775 daughter of Joseph and Hannah (Carleton) Howe; Mary d. at Methuen, 30 Sep 1848.

vi NATHAN BODWELL, b. 12 Oct 1773; there is no clear record for Nathan after his birth. There is a Nathan Bodwell who died in Methuen in 1840, but that is the nephew of this Nathan.

vii ARNOLD BODWELL, b. 22 Mar 1776; there is no further record.

viii ELIZABETH BODWELL, b. 22 Jun 1778; m. at Methuen, 2 Jul 1799, JOSHUA DAVIS, b. at Methuen, 19 Apr 1773 son of John and Hannah (Cross) Davis.

719) JOHN ROBINSON *(Joseph Robinson⁴, Elizabeth Stevens Robinson³, Sarah Abbott Stevens², George¹)*, b. at Andover, 2 Sep 1739 son of Joseph and Mehitable (Eams) Robinson; d. at Boxford, 22 Jan 1810; m. 30 Jun 1763, REBECCA "BECCA" WOOD, b. Feb 1743/4 (baptized 12 Feb) daughter of Daniel and Sarah (Peabody) Wood; Becky d. 30 Mar 1810.

John and Becca Robinson made their home in Boxford where John was active in the community serving on the first school committee and involved in affairs of the church.[1950]

In the will of John Robinson written 28 October 1809 (probate 5 February 1810), beloved wife Becca receives all the estate, real and personal, for her use during her life. After her decease, the estate to be divided among sons Israel, Benjamin, Nathan, Aaron, and Joseph. Daughters Rebecca Barker, wife of Isaac Barker, Deborah Spofford the wife of Samuel Spofford, and Elizabeth Swan wife of Josiah Swan, and Sarah Robinson single woman receive all the household goods to divide equally. The daughters each also receive a cash payment of varying amounts. Son Benjamin receives an extra bequest of land and cash. Son Jeremy receives silver buckles and $50; Jeremy is receiving less than his brothers as he has received so much for his education and other money from his father already. A special note is made that John has been informed that son Aaron intends claims against the estate for work he did for his father after Aaron was 21 years old. The will explains that Aaron was paid $100 a year for his work and received other considerations in money and that Aaron does not have a legitimate claim against the estate. By the time of the administration of the estate, widow Becca Robinson had also died, and the following heirs signed a statement that Deacon Charles Foster of Andover be named administrator: Benjamin Robinson, Nathan Robinson, Aaron Robinson, Isaac Barker, Samuel Spofford, and Sarah Robinson.[1951]

John Robinson and Rebecca Wood were parents of eleven children born at Boxford.

i ISRAEL ROBINSON, b. 21 Mar 1764. It is not clear what happened to Israel. He was living in 1810 at the time of his father's will.

ii JOHN ROBINSON, b. 20 May 1765; d. at Boxford, 13 Aug 1790. John was a physician. He did not marry.

iii REBECCA ROBINSON, b. 16 May 1767; d. at Boxford, 18 Aug 1830; m. 13 Oct 1790, ISAAC BARKER, b. at Boxford, 17 Jul 1756 son of John and Mehitable (Goodridge) Barker; Isaac d. at Boxford, 20 Aug 1833.

iv BENJAMIN ROBINSON, b. 3 Feb 1769; d. at Boxford, 27 Mar 1841; m. 7 Apr 1794, PRISCILLA TYLER, b. at Boxford, 18 Feb 1765 daughter of Abraham and Abigail (Stickney) Tyler; Priscilla d. at Boxford, 26 Nov 1859.

v NATHAN ROBINSON, b. 30 Oct 1770; d. at Boxford, 28 Feb 1835; m. at Salem, 19 Dec 1802, EUNICE BECKFORD, b. at Salem, 19 Dec 1778 daughter of Ebenezer and Hannah (Hunt) Beckford; Eunice d. at Salem, 20 Apr 1827.

vi AARON ROBINSON, b. 29 Sep 1772; d. at North Andover, 21 Jul 1844; m. 24 Mar 1796, SARAH POOR, b. at Andover, 28 Aug 1774 daughter of Abraham and Elizabeth (Barker) Poor; Sarah d. at North Andover, 2 Dec 1830.

vii DEBORAH ROBINSON, b. 14 Oct 1774; d. at Methuen, 29 May 1842; m. 6 Oct 1793, SAMUEL SPOFFORD, b. at Boxford, 14 Jul 1764 son of Amos and Abigail (Pearl) Spofford; Samuel d. at Boxford, 8 Jan 1833.

[1948] Revolutionary War Pension and Bounty-Land Warrant Application Files

[1949] Pingry, *Genealogical Record of the Descendants of Moses Pengry, of Ipswich*

[1950] Perley, *The History of Boxford*

[1951] Essex County, MA: Probate File Papers, 1638-1881.Online database. AmericanAncestors.org. New England Historic Genealogical Society, 2014. Case number 23901

viii ELIZABETH ROBINSON, b. 30 Dec 1777; d. at Lawrence, 23 Sep 1856; m. 1st, 29 Nov 1801, JOSIAH SWAN, b. at Methuen, 1773 son of John and Abiah (Swan) Swan; Josiah d. at New Hampton, NH about 1820. Elizabeth m. 2nd, 23 Jun 1823, LEVI DOW; Levi d. at New Hampton, 1841. Levi was first married to Abigail Godfrey.

ix JOSEPH ROBINSON, b. 27 Aug 1779; d. at Boxford, 21 Aug 1817. Joseph does not seem to have married.

x SARAH ROBINSON, b. 30 Oct 1782; d. at Methuen, 3 May 1849; m. at Boxford, 29 Aug 1810, ISAAC SWAN, b. at Methuen, 8 Jul 1765 son of Francis and Lydia (Frye) Swan; Isaac d. at Methuen, 17 May 1856.

xi JEREMY ROBINSON, b. 30 May 1787; d. at Havana, Cuba, 11 Nov 1834. Jeremy does not seem to have married. He was a U.S. Agent for Commerce and Seaman in Lima, Peru in 1817 and U.S. Special Diplomatic Agent to Cuba from 1832 to 1834.[1952]

720) HANNAH ROBINSON *(Isaac Robinson⁴, Elizabeth Stevens Robinson³, Sarah Abbott Stevens², George¹)*, b. at Andover, 27 Sep 1744 daughter of Isaac and Dorothy (Poor) Robinson; m. 17 Feb 1767, JONATHAN PARKER[1953], b. at Andover, 26 Mar 1738 son of Jonathan and Hannah (Frye) Parker.

There are records for three children of Hannah and Jonathan born at Andover. Very little is known.

i JONATHAN PARKER, b. 20 Sep 1767

ii DOLLY PARKER, b. 31 Jan 1771; d. at Amherst, NH, Nov 1825;[1954] m. at Andover, 30 Aug 1798, SAMUEL FOSTER.

iii HANNAH PARKER, b. 19 Jan 1774

721) JONATHAN ROBINSON *(Isaac Robinson⁴, Elizabeth Stevens Robinson³, Sarah Abbott Stevens², George¹)*, b. at Andover, 25 Jun 1753 son of Isaac and Dorothy (Poor) Robinson; d. at Surry, NH, 17 Mar 1838;[1955] m. at Boxford, 24 Apr 1783, BETTY CHADWICK, b. at Boxford, 22 Aug 1756 daughter of John and Susannah (Peabody) Chadwick; Betty d. 23 Oct 1818. Jonathan m. 2nd, 16 Mar 1826, MARY "POLLY" PAGE, b. at Hardwick, MA, 26 Jul 1766 daughter of James and Mary (Stone) Page; Mary d. 26 Nov 1853. Mary was first married to Lemuel Page.

Jonathan Robinson served in the Revolution in the Massachusetts militia as a private and a Sergeant.[1956] He came to Surry, New Hampshire in 1789 and was active in the community there, serving as selectman. In addition to his farming enterprise, he was a merchant and kept a tavern for about 25 years.[1957]

In his will written 14 October 1835, Jonathan Robinson bequeathed to beloved wife Mary the use of one undivided third part of his real estate during her natural life and all the furniture that she brought to the marriage. The executor is to provide other provisions for her continued support. Oldest daughter Dolly Field, widow, receives one hundred dollars. Son Samuel Robinson receives one dollar. Second daughter Sukey Field wife of Eliphaz Field receives one undivided half of a tract of land in Alstead on condition that Sukey and Eliphaz pay fifty dollars to Dolly Field. Sukey also receives half the household furniture. Third daughter Sally Johnson, widow, receives one undivided half of a tract of land in Surry. Fourth daughter Clarissa Britton wife of Henry Britton receives half of Jonathan's half of Field Farm and half of the household furniture. Fifth daughter Louisa Page wife of Gilman Page receives the other undivided half of Jonathan's half of Field Farm and she is to pay fifty dollars to Dolly Field. Grandson Henry Smith receives one undivided half of a lot of land, granddaughter Mary Elizabeth Smith receives an undivided fourth of that same lot, and granddaughter Louis Ferbanks receives the remaining fourth of the lot. Second son Jonathan receives all the personal estate not otherwise disposed of including stock animals, utensils, and money. Jonathan is also named executor.[1958]

Jonathan Robinson and Betty Chadwick were parents of nine children all born at Surry.

i DOROTHY ROBINSON, b. 7 Jul 1783; d. at Delmar, PA, after 1860; m. at Surry, 22 Dec 1807, ISAAC FIELD, b. at Surry, 28 Mar 1781 son of Moses Dickinson and Patience (Smith) Field; Isaac died in Pennsylvania before 1838 (Dorothy was a widow when her father wrote his will).

1952 Political Graveyard, http://politicalgraveyard.com/bio/robinson5.html#820.45.36

1953 The 1788 (proved 18 Apr 1804) will of Isaac Robinson includes a bequest to daughter Hannah wife of Jonathan Parker.

1954 Secomb, *History of Amherst*, p 594, Dolly wife of Samuel Foster, d. in Nov, 1825, aged 54.

1955 Kingsbury, *The History of Surry, NH*

1956 U.S., The Pension Roll of 1835, Jonathan Robinson of Cheshire County, NH placed on the pension roles in 1833.

1957 Kingsbury, *The History of Surry, NH*, p 841

1958 *New Hampshire. Probate Court (Cheshire County)*; Probate Place: *Cheshire, New Hampshire, Estate Files, R181-R238, 1827-1840*, Case 228

ii SAMUEL ROBINSON, b. 29 Apr 1786; d. at Keene, NH, 7 Oct 1869; m. at Surry, 21 May 1812, NANCY HARVEY, b. about 1792 of Alstead; Nancy d. at Keene, 29 Jan 1859.

iii SUSANNAH "SUKY" ROBINSON, b. 7 Jun 1788; d. at Surry, 17 Aug 1853; m. 20 Oct 1812, ELIPHAZ FIELD, b. at Surry, 20 Feb 1784 son of Moses Dickinson and Patience (Smith) Field; Eliphaz d. at Surry, 18 Jan 1872.

iv SALLY ROBINSON, b. 20 Oct 1790; d. at Northborough, MA, 9 Feb 1879; m. at Surry, 8 Feb 1809, LEWIS JOHNSON, b. at Berlin, MA, 16 Mar 1783 son of Amos and Elizabeth (Pollard) Johnson;[1959] Lewis d. at Westmoreland, NH, 1817 (probate 1817).

v BETSEY ROBINSON, b. 14 Feb 1793; d. at Surry, 26 Dec 1821; m. at Surry, 14 May 1815, WILLARD SMITH. B. at Surry, 22 Apr 1787 son of Thomas and Arethusa (Willard) Smith; Willard d. at Surry, 22 Jul 1825.

vi CLARISSA ROBINSON, b. 13 Jan 1796; d. at Surry, 24 May 1863; m. HENRY BRITTEN, b. at Chesterfield, NH, 1803 son of John and Rhoda (Benton) Britten; Henry d. at Surry, 17 Oct 1860.

vii JONATHAN ROBINSON, b. 9 Feb 1798; d. at Keene, 30 Sep 1876; m. 1st, 2 Nov 1823, ELVIRA SHAW, b. at Alstead, NH, 15 Jul 1802 daughter of David and Prudence (-) Shaw; Elvira d. 1865. Jonathan m. 2nd, at Keene, 15 Nov 1866, his first cousin once removed, SARAH T. ROBINSON *(Daniel Robinson[6], John Robinson[5], Isaac Robinson[4], Elizabeth Stevens Robinson[3], Sarah Abbott Stevens[2], George[1])*, b. at Acworth, about 1812 daughter of Daniel and Lucy Thompson (Hills) Robinson. Sarah was first married to Winslow Allen.

viii LOUISA ROBINSON, b. 28 Sep 1800; d. at Boston, 2 Nov 1869; m. 24 Jan 1828. GILMAN PAGE, b. at Surry, 20 Jun 1799 son of Lemuel and Mary (Page) Page; Gilman d. at Boston, 1 Jun 1881. Gilman's mother Mary Page was the second wife of Louisa's father Jonathan Robinson.

ix LUCIA ROBINSON, b. 21 Dec 1802; d. at Surry, 1 Oct 1818.

722) JOHN ROBINSON *(Isaac Robinson[4], Elizabeth Stevens Robinson[3], Sarah Abbott Stevens[2], George[1])*, b. at Andover, 11 Apr 1758 son of Isaac and Dorothy (Poor) Robinson; d. at Boxford, 17 May 1807; m. at Boxford, 3 Apr 1781, SARAH TYLER, b. at Boxford, 8 Feb 1758 daughter of Gideon and Mehitable (Kimball) Tyler;[1960] Sarah d. 3 May 1840 (*Sarah, wid. John, d. Gideon Tyler, May 3, 1840, a. 82 y.* GR1).

Lieutenant John Robinson did not leave a will and his estate entered probate 3 June 1807. Widow Sarah Robinson requested that Isaac Parker be administrator. In January 1810, Jonathan Tyler, guardian of Dolly Robinson, signed that he has received $454.62 from Isaac Parker. On 14 February 1810, Sarah Robinson signed that she received $1393.87 as her dower portion. Daniel Robinson signed in February 1810 that he received his portion of $454. Daughter Sally Robinson received $454 for her portion. Dean Robinson received $162.62 for his portion and mother Sarah received $302 as part of son Dean's portion. Sarah also signed she received $464.72 for her son John's portion. Dolly Wilson and spouse Joshua sign in 1813 that they have received from Jonathan Tyler, who was her guardian during her minority, the sum of $542. Dean, age 19, made the choice of his mother as his guardian and mother was appointed guardian of John. Dolly made choice of Jonathan Tyler as her guardian.[1961]

In her will written 10 April 1840, Sarah Tyler Robinson left one dollar each to son Daniel and daughter Sarah (who signed as Sarah Emery her agreement to Dean Robinson as executor). The remainder of her estate was left to son Dean who was also named executor.[1962]

John Robinson and Sarah Tyler were parents of six children born at Andover.

i SARAH ROBINSON, b. 16 Oct 1781; d. 18 Mar 1856; m. at West Newbury, 19 Jan 1822, NICHOLAS EMERY, b. at Newbury, 16 Dec 1783 son of Nathaniel and Sarah (Short) Emery; Nicholas d. at Pembroke, 18 Mar 1856.

ii DANIEL ROBINSON, b. 14 Dec 1783; d. at Acworth, NH, 27 Oct 1856; m. 1808, LUCY THOMPSON HILLS, b. 1778 daughter of Samuel and Lucy (Thompson) Hills.

iii ISAAC ROBINSON, b. 21 Jun 1786; d. 14 Nov 1810 when he drowned in the Mohawk River.[1963]

iv DEAN ROBINSON, b. 15 Apr 1788; d. at West Newbury, 22 Aug 1863; m. at Andover, 21 Apr 1811, as her second husband, his third cousin, ELIZABETH FOSTER LOVEJOY *(Nathaniel Lovejoy[5], Elizabeth Swan Lovejoy[4], Hannah Stevens Swan[3], Sarah Abbott Stevens[2], George[1])*, b. at Andover, 6 Aug 1780 daughter of Nathaniel and Elizabeth (Brandon) Lovejoy; Elizabeth d. at West Newbury, 3 Apr 1866, Elizabeth was first married to Jacob Farnum. Elizabeth Lovejoy is a child in Family 304.

1959 Parents are confirmed by the 1825 will of his father Amos Johnson who leaves his entire estate to grandson Joshua Jewett Johnson. Joshua Jewett Johnson was born at Surry in 1809 to Lewis and Sally Johnson.

1960 The 1800 will of Gideon Tyler includes a bequest to daughter Sarah the wife of John Robinson. *Essex County, MA: Probate File Papers, 1638-1881.*

1961 Essex County, MA: Probate File Papers, 1638-1881.Online database. AmericanAncestors.org. New England Historic Genealogical Society, 2014. Case number 23900

1962 Essex County, MA: Probate File Papers, 1638-1881.Online database. AmericanAncestors.org. New England Historic Genealogical Society, 2014. Case 23922

1963 Isaac, s. John and Sarah, brother to John, drowned in Mohawk River, Nov. 14, 1810, a. 24 y. G.R.1.

v DOLLY ROBINSON, b. 3 Sep 1791; d. unknown but before mother's will in 1840; m. at Andover, 11 Feb 1813, JOSHUA WILSON, b. at Andover, 28 Apr 1787 son of Joshua and Dorothy (Stevens) Wilson; Joshua d. at Andover, 11 May 1816. Dolly and Joshua had two children both of whom died in 1816.

vi JOHN ROBINSON, b. 16 Mar 1796; d. at Andover, 24 Mar 1811.

723) PHEBE BARKER *(Sarah Robinson Barker[4], Elizabeth Stevens Robinson[3], Sarah Abbott Stevens[2], George[1])*, b. at Andover, 2 Jan 1749/50 daughter of Samuel and Sarah (Robinson) Barker; m. 19 Jun 1766, her second cousin once removed, JEDEDIAH HOLT, b. at Suncook, 23 Feb 1743/4 son of Stephen and Mary (Farnum) Holt; Jedediah d. at Andover, 12 Feb 1790.

Jedediah Holt did not leave a will and the estate entered probate 7 June 1790. Widow Phebe Holt was named administratrix. The heirs signing their agreement with the plan for inventory of the estate were Phebe Holt also signing as the guardian for Samuel Holt and Stephen Holt, Nathan Barker signing on behalf of his wife, and Phebe Holt. Real estate was valued at £455.12.4 and personal estate at £398.7.10. The children receiving distributions from the estate were Samuel Holt, Stephen Holt, Phebe Holt, and Sarah Barker.[1964]

Phebe Barker and Jedediah Holt were parents of five children born at Andover.

i SARAH HOLT, b. 16 Jan 1768; d. at Boxford, 9 Jul 1843; m. at Andover, 12 Aug 1788, NATHAN BARKER, b. at Andover, 12 Aug 1768 son of Samuel and Susannah (Foster) Barker; Nathan d. at Boxford, 17 Dec 1821.

ii PHEBE HOLT, b. 18 Feb 1771; d. at Andover, 23 Jan 1844; m. at Andover, 1805, WILLIAM FOSTER, b. about 1772 son of William and Mehitable (Fuller) Foster; William d. at Andover, 14 Nov 1833.

iii MOLLY HOLT, b. 2 Jul 1773; d. 18 Apr 1784.

iv SAMUEL HOLT, b. 24 Jan 1778; d. at Winthrop, ME, 1819 (probate 21 Dec 1819); m. at Andover, 10 May 1803, LYDIA FARNUM, b. at Andover, 14 Jul 1780 daughter of Jedediah and Rebecca (Poor) Farnum.

v STEPHEN HOLT, b. 4 Feb 1786; d. before 1850; m. *likely*, 2 Mar 1809, ABIGAIL DOLE, b. about 1790 daughter of Greenleaf and Mary (Moore) Dole; Abigail d. after 1850.[1965]

724) JONATHAN SWAN *(Robert Swan[4], Hannah Stevens Swan[3], Sarah Abbott Stevens[2], George[1])*, b. at Andover, 1 Sep 1732 son of Robert and Elizabeth (Farnum) Swan; d. at Methuen, 15 Aug 1783; m. 13 Dec 1759, as the second of her three husbands, ABIGAIL GREEN, b. at Haverhill, 7 Nov 1728 daughter of Peter and Martha (Singletary) Green.[1966] Abigail Green was first married to Moses Hall in 1750. Abigail married third, Stephen Barker on 9 Mar 1784.

In his will written 21 June 1781 (probate 29 September 1783), Jonathan Swan had the following bequests. Beloved wife Abigail receives the use of and improvements on one-third part of the real estate as long as she remains a widow. Son Jonathan receives all the real estate, lands, and buildings and one-half of a grist mill. Daughter Charlotte Swan receives a piece of land in Methuen containing about 26 acres. Daughter Abigail Swan receives a lot of about 18 acres in Methuen. Daughters Charlotte and Abigail also have the liberty of living in one room of the house so long as they are unmarried. His two daughters also receive the household goods excepting those that are needed for wife Abigail. Son Jonathan receives any other residue of the estate.[1967]

Jonathan Swan and Abigail Green had six children born at Methuen.

i BETTY SWAN, b. 9 Sep 1760; d. 10 Sep 1762.

ii JONATHAN SWAN, b. 2 May 1762; d. 13 May 1762.

iii JONATHAN SWAN, b. 9 Jun 1763; d. at Sanbornton, NH, 18 Mar 1844; m. at Methuen, 16 Mar 1786, ALICE SARGENT, b. at Methuen, 14 Aug 1761 daughter of John and Mary (Tucker) Sargent; Alice d. at Sanbornton, 12 Sep 1846.

iv ABIGAIL SWAN, b. 19 Apr 1765; d. 1 Apr 1766.

v CHARLOTTE SWAN, b. 2 May 1768; d. at Methuen, 21 Aug 1843; m. at Salem, NH, 28 Jul 1796, JOHN GAGE, of Salem, NH, b. 26 May 1757 son of Stephen and Anne (Mitchell) Gage; John d. at Methuen, 27 Aug 1846.

1964 Essex County, MA: Probate File Papers, 1638-1881.Online database. AmericanAncestors.org. New England Historic Genealogical Society, 2014. Case 13654

1965 Abigail Dole daughter of Greenleaf did marry a Stephen Holt. This is confirmed by the 1829 will of Greenleaf Dole which includes a bequest to daughter Abigail wife of Stephen Holt. The question is whether it is this Stephen Holt. The two other Stephen Holts (born 1782 and 1786) in Andover of an appropriate age can be accounted for as having other spouses. But this marriage should be considered tentative.

1966 The 1774 probate of Peter Green includes a distribution to daughter Abigail Swan.

1967 Essex County, MA: Probate File Papers, 1638-1881. Probate of Jonathan Swan, 29 Sep 1783, case number 26889.

vi ABIGAIL SWAN, b. 5 Aug 1772; d. at Methuen, 22 Jul 1824; m. at Methuen, 6 Dec 1804, STEPHEN GAGE, b. at Salem, NH, 1783 son of Stephen Gage; Stephen d. at Methuen, 30 May 1857. Stephen Gage who married Abigail Swan was the nephew of John Gage who married Charlotte Swan. After Abigail's death, Stephen married Mary Emerson.

725) ROBERT SWAN *(Robert Swan⁴, Hannah Stevens Swan³, Sarah Abbott Stevens², George¹)*, b. at Andover, 19 Jan 1748/9 son of Robert and Elizabeth (Farnum) Swan; d. at Andover, 25 Dec 1832; m. 1st, 29 Apr 1773, APHIA FARRINGTON, b. 8 Mar 1756 daughter of John and Sarah (Holton) Farrington; Aphia d. 11 Feb 1788. Robert m. 2nd, 21 May 1789, SUSANNAH EMERY, b. about 1759; Susannah d. 6 Apr 1842.[1968] Susannah's first husband was Nehemiah Abbott a descendant of George Abbott of Rowley.

Robert Swan was a silversmith and yeoman in Andover. He appears to have given up silversmithing as he had no trade tools in the estate inventory.[1969]

Robert Swan did not leave a will and the probate was 2 July 1833 with Joseph Swan as administrator. Widow Susanna Swan petitioned the Court for allowance for her necessities from the personal estate, and she was allowed to select items from the personal estate in the amount of one hundred and fifty dollars for her personal needs. The total value of the personal estate was $171.75. One-third part of the real estate was set off for the dower.[1970]

Daughter Susanna Swan did not marry. In her will written 13 May 1851, she has bequests to her brother Joseph Swan and her sister Affia Swan and numerous other bequests which seem to be to nieces, nephews, and perhaps other relatives, but just Joseph and Affia are named as siblings.

Robert Swan and Aphia Farrington were parents of seven children born at Andover.

i APHIA SWAN, b. 5 Sep 1774; d. after 1851 as she is in her sister's will. Aphia did not marry.

ii SALLY SWAN, b. 20 Mar 1776; d. at Andover 7 Jun 1812; Sally did not marry.

iii HANNAH SWAN, b. 11 Nov 1777; d. at Andover, 30 Apr 1824; m. at Andover, 30 Oct 1797, DANIEL FOSTER, b. at Andover, 26 Apr 1765 son of Stephen and Abigail (Smith) Foster; Daniel d. at Andover, 2 Jan 1821.

iv ELIZABETH SWAN, b. 20 Dec 1779; m. at Andover, 13 Jan 1801, WILLIAM FARNUM, b. at Andover, 19 Sep 1778 son of Jedediah and Rebecca (Poor) Farnum; William d. at Andover, 1 May 1822.

v BENJAMIN SWAN (twin of Joseph), b. 7 Oct 1781; nothing further known.

vi JOSEPH SWAN, b. 7 Oct 1781; d. at North Andover, 25 Mar 1868; m. at Andover, 20 Dec 1807, MARY KIMBALL ALLEN, b. in RI, about 1785 daughter of Asa and Abigail (Blunt) Allen;[1971] Mary d. at Andover, 15 Aug 1857.

vii SUSANNA SWAN, baptized 6 Apr 1783; d. at Andover, 19 Sep 1853. Susanna did not marry.

Robert Swan and Susannah Emery were parents of five children born at Andover.

i JERUSHA BARRON SWAN, b. 22 May 1791; d. at Lowell, MA, 15 Jan 1843; m. at Andover, 1 Jun 1809, JOHN FRYE, b. at Andover, 3 Sep 1782 son of John and Betsy (Noyes) Frye; John d. at Andover, 13 Jul 1825.

ii RUBY SWAN, b. 24 Mar 1793; d. at Rochester, NY, 30 Nov 1840; m. at Andover, 15 Aug 1816, JACOB GOULD, "of Schenectady", b. 10 Feb 1794 son of Jacob and Ruth (Peabody) Gould; Jacob d. at Rochester, 18 Nov 1867. Jacob married second Sarah Seward. Jacob Gould was mayor of Rochester.

iii RHODA SWAN, b. 10 Dec 1795; d. 20 Jul 1796.

iv RHODA SWAN, b. 29 Oct 1797; nothing further known.

v FIDELIA SWAN, b. 25 Jul 1800; d. at Salem, MA, 25 Nov 1830; m. at Andover, 24 Jul 1824, REUBEN REED, b. 1795 son of Amos and Lydia (Simmonds) Reed;[1972] Reuben d. at Salem, 4 Apr 1833. Reuben was first married to Abigail Foster.

726) PHINEAS SWAN *(Robert Swan⁴, Hannah Stevens Swan³, Sarah Abbott Stevens², George¹)*, b. at Andover, 14 Jun 1752 son of Robert and Elizabeth (Farnum) Swan; d. at Haverhill, NH, 16 Jan 1829; m. 21 Oct 1773, TRYPHENA WEBSTER, b. at Haverhill, 11 Sep 1754 daughter of Stephen and Susannah (Ladd) Webster; Tryphena d. 23 Mar 1843.

1968 Swan, Susanna, wid. Robert [formerly, w. Nehemiah Abbot. CR5], old age, Apr. 6, 1842, a. 83 y. [a. 86 y. CR1]

1969 American Silversmiths, "Robert Swan", https://www.americansilversmiths.org/makers/silversmiths/29661.htm

1970 *Massachusetts, Essex County, Probate Records;* Author: *Massachusetts. Supreme Judicial Court (Essex County);* Probate Place: *Essex, Massachusetts, Probate Records, Swan, R-Swasey, A, 1828-1991*, probate of Robert Swan, 3 Jul 1833, case number 26901

1971 Father's name is given as Asa Allen on Mary's death record.

1972 Reed, *History of the Reed Family in Europe and America*, p 90

Phineas and Tryphena Swan were in Haverhill, New Hampshire by 1790. Phineas was a cordwainer.[1973] There are just three children known for Phineas and Tryphena.

i PHINEAS SWAN, b. at Salem, NH, 23 Apr 1775; d. at Montgomery, VT, 14 Oct 1844; m. CYNTHIA HARDING, b. at Putney, VT, about 1782; Cynthia d. at Montgomery, 18 Feb 1868.

ii BENJAMIN SWAN, b. 1 Dec 1783; d. at Haverhill, NH, 29 Nov 1872; m. at Piermont, NH, 25 Dec 1811, GRACE CARR, b. 10 Oct 1787; Grace d. at Haverhill, 25 Apr 1851.

iii ISAAC SWAN, b. 1799; d. at Haverhill, NH, 9 Jan 1835.[1974]

727) EPHRAIM SWAN *(Ephraim Swan⁴, Hannah Stevens Swan³, Sarah Abbott Stevens², George¹)*, b. at Andover, 12 Oct 1739 son of Ephraim and Sarah (Poole) Swan; d. likely early 1777 (probate 3 Apr 1777); m. 24 Oct 1765, MARTHA FARRINGTON, b. 5 Oct 1741 daughter of John and Sarah (Holton) Farrington. Martha m. 2nd, 30 Dec 1777, Thomas Clark. Martha died after 1813 (still living in 1813 when the dower from Thomas Clark's estate was set off to widow Martha).

Ephraim Swan died a few months before his father Ephraim. Ephraim Swan, Jr. did not leave a will and his estate entered probate 3 April 1777. Martha Swan was administratrix of the estate. One-third of the estate was set-off to the widow and two-thirds of the estate for the two minor children. In 1778, Thomas Clark was named guardian of the two children.[1975]

Martha Farrington and her second husband Thomas Clark had one child, Ezra Clark, born in 1782. Ezra Clark married Hannah Chandler *(Zebadiah Chandler⁶, Zebadiah Chandler⁵, Joshua Chandler⁴, John Chandler³, Hannah Abbott Chandler², George¹)* daughter of Zebadiah and Luce (Chandler) Chandler.

Ephraim Swan and Martha Farrington had two children born at Andover.

i EPHRAIM SWAN, b. 31 Mar 1769; d. after 1778. Ephraim was living in 1778 when Thomas Clark was named his guardian. There is no record of him after that.

ii MARTHA SWAN, b. 29 Sep 1771; d. at Boston, 10 May 1857;[1976] m. at Andover, 13 Sep 1792, JOHN TROW, b. at Beverly, 22 Jan 1771 son of John and Hannah (Dodge) Trow; John d. at Manchester, NH, 6 Oct 1854.

728) MARY PARKER *(Hannah Swan Parker⁴, Hannah Stevens Swan³, Sarah Abbott Stevens², George¹)*, b. at Andover, 28 Nov 1734 daughter of Peter and Hannah (Swan) Parker; died about 1783 (and was deceased before 1795 when her father wrote his will); m. ENOCH ILSLEY, b. at Newbury, 16 Dec 1730 son of Isaac and Abigail (Moody) Ilsley; Enoch d. at Portland, ME, 10 Nov 1811. Enoch second married Elizabeth Harper about 1783 and third married Abigail Barstow 23 Jul 1803.[1977]

Enoch Ilsley was actively engaged in commerce in Portland, Maine, and at one point was the largest ship owner in town. He suffered great losses when the British burned what was then known as Falmouth 18 October 1775. His losses were estimated at £2107. He served as selectman of Portland from 1786 to 1801.[1978]

Enoch Ilsley and Mary Parker were parents of nine children born at Falmouth, Maine.[1979]

i ELIZABETH ILSLEY, b. 3 Oct 1754; d. at Portland, 26 Mar 1831; m. 1st, about 1774, PEARSON JONES, b. at Portland, 16 Jul 1746 son of Ephraim and Mary (Pearson) Jones; Pearson d. at Falmouth, ME, 10 Jan 1781. Elizabeth m. 2nd, at Portland, 7 Feb 1786, SAMUEL FREEMAN, b. at Falmouth, 15 Jun 1743 son of Enoch and Mary (Wright) Freeman; Samuel d. at Portland, 18 Jun 1831. Samuel was first married to Mary Fowle.

ii DORCAS ILSLEY, b. 30 May 1759; d. at Portland, 20 Feb 1784; m. 7 Oct 1781, EBENEZER PREBLE, b. at Portland, 15 Aug 1757 son of Jedediah and Mehitable (Bangs) Preble; Ebenezer d. at Richmond, VA, Apr 1817. Ebenezer had three other marriages after the death of Dorcas to Mary Derby, Betsey Derby, and Abigail Torrey.[1980]

iii ENOCH ILSLEY, b. 1761; lost at sea.

1973 Witcher, *History of Haverhill, NH*, p 657

1974 Witcher, *History of Haverhill, NH*, p 657

1975 Essex County, MA: Probate File Papers, 1638-1881.Online database. AmericanAncestors.org. New England Historic Genealogical Society, 2014. Case number 26884

1976 Death record of Martha S. Trow listing parents as Ephraim and Martha Swan.

1977 Smith, Deane, Freeman, and Willis, *Journals of the Rev. Thomas Smith*, p 399

1978 Willis, *History of Portland*, p 287

1979 Some sources suggest a son Joseph in this family, but he is not given in the Journals of the Rev. Thomas Smith which lists the nine children given here. There are not any clear records for a son Joseph.

1980 Preble, "Brigadier General Jedidiah Preble", New England Historical and Genealogical Register, 1868, volume 22, p 418

iv CHARLOTTE ILSLEY, b. 25 Jan 1763; d. at Portland, 22 Sep 1802; m. 1787, STEPHEN MCLELLAN, b. at Falmouth, 26 Feb 1766 son of Joseph and Mary Ann (McLellan) McLellan; Stephen d. at Portland, 25 Oct 1823. After Charlotte's death, Stephen married Charlotte's sister Hannah (see below).

v FERDINAND ILSLEY, b. about 1765; died of consumption.

vi ALMIRA ILSLEY, b. 1767; d. at Portland, Jan 1855; m. at Portland, 9 Mar 1789, JAMES DEERING, b. 1766 son of Nathaniel and Anna Margaret (Holwell) Deering; James d. at Portland, 1 Jan 1850.

vii PARKER ILSLEY, b. 1769; d. at Portland, 7 May 1839; m. at Portland, 15 Jan 1795, ELIZABETH SMITH, b. 17 Dec 1774 daughter of David and Elizabeth (Godfrey) Smith; Elizabeth d. at Portland, 13 Nov 1812.

viii HANNAH ILSLEY, b. 19 Jan 1771; d. at Portland, 26 Apr 1836; m. about 1804, STEPHEN MCLELLAN who was first married to Hannah's sister Charlotte (see above).

ix AUGUSTA ILSLEY, b. 1775; d. at Portland, 30 Sep 1851; m. at Portland, 1 Apr 1798, DANIEL ILSLEY, b. 1764 son of Daniel and Mary (Jones) Ilsley; Daniel d. at Portland, 17 Oct 1853.

729) NATHAN PARKER *(Hannah Swan Parker4, Hannah Stevens Swan3, Sarah Abbott Stevens2, George1)*, b. at Andover, 3 Jun 1739 son of Peter and Hannah (Swan) Parker; d. at Blue Hill, ME, about 1819; m. at Blue Hill, 20 Dec 1764, MARY WOOD, b. at Beverly, 15 Nov 1748 daughter of Joseph and Mary (Haskell) Wood; Mary d. a Blue Hill, 23 Sep 1806.

Nathan Parker was an early settler of Blue Hill, Maine. His marriage to Mary Wood was the first celebrated in the town and Mary's father Joseph Wood was the first settler there.[1981]

Nathan Parker did not leave a will. Andrew Whitham (who was a son-in-law) was named administrator of the estate 27 July 1819. The inventory valued real estate at $50 consisting of one-half of lot number 40 in the third division and personal estate of $27.87. The debts of the estate exceeded the value.[1982]

Nathan and Mary were parents of ten children all born at Blue Hill.[1983][1984]

i JOSEPH PARKER, b. 4 Jan 1766; d. at Blue Hill, 13 Aug 1801; m. 9 May 1789, ELIZABETH HINKLEY, b. at Blue Hill, 19 Aug 1768 daughter of Ebenezer and Susannah (Brown) Hinkley; Elizabeth d. at Bar Harbor, 11 Aug 1824. After Joseph's death, Elizabeth married John Thomas.

ii JOSHUA PARKER, b. 25 Nov 1767; d. at Blue Hill, 9 Apr 1809; m. at Blue Hill, 8 May 1793, his fourth cousin, ELIZABETH CHANDLER *(Timothy Chandler5, Abial Chandler Chandler4, Abiel Chandler3, Hannah Abbott Chandler2, George1)*, b. at Andover, 30 Aug 1767 daughter of Timothy and Mary (Walker) Chandler. Elizabeth is a child in Family 446.

iii MARY PARKER, b. 30 May 1770; d. at Blue Hill, 13 Jul 1830; m. 25 Oct 1801, as his second wife, ANDREW WHITHAM, b. at Bradford, MA, 11 Nov 1768 son of Andrew and Sarah (-) Whitham; Andrew d. at Blue Hill, 1851. Andrew was first married to Mehitable Kimball and was third married to the widow Ann Chadwick.

iv LYDIA PARKER, b. 19 Oct 1772; d. 29 Dec 1781.

v PHEBE PARKER, b. 4 Mar 1775; d. at Blue Hill, 28 Apr 1862; m. at Blue Hill, 12 Feb 1800, SAMUEL STETSON, b. at Scituate, 22 Mar 1775 son of Seth and Lucy (Studley) Stetson; Samuel d. 2 Apr 1853.

vi NATHAN PARKER, b. 4 Jun 1777; d. at Blue Hill, 23 Nov 1806; m. 26 Oct 1803, MARY "MOLLY" OSGOOD, b. 11 Oct 1783 of unidentified parents; Mary d. at Blue Hill, 28 Oct 1831. After Nathan's death, Mary married Samuel Johnson (1780-1864) son of Obed and Joanna (Wood) Johnson.

vii SIMEON PARKER, b. 13 Jun 1780; d. 2 Jan 1782.

viii RUTH PARKER, b. 23 Jul 1781; d. 8 Jun 1794.

ix LYDIA PARKER, b. 23 Sep 1784; d. at Blue Hill, 29 May 1824; m. 2 May 1808, her first cousin, SAMUEL PARKER *(Robert Parker5, Hannah Swan Parker4, Hannah Stevens Swan3, Hannah Abbott Stevens2, George1)*, b. at Blue Hill, 9 Mar 1774 son of Robert and Ruth (Wood) Parker; Samuel d. at Blue Hill, 2 Dec 1831. After Lydia's death, Samuel married Mary Matthews. Lydia and Samuel were double first cousins as their fathers were brothers and their mothers were sisters. Samuel is a child in Family 731.

x HANNAH PARKER, b. 8 Apr 1788; nothing is known

[1981] Dodge and Candage, *Families of Early Settlers in Blue Hill*, Maine, p 204

[1982] Maine, County Probate Records, 1760-1979, Hancock, Case 773; 2:339; 6:509; 6:510; 4:230; 7:141, accessed through family search.org.

[1983] Blue Hill, ME: Vital Records, 1766-1809. (Online database: AmericanAncestors.org, New England Historic Genealogical Society, 2012), (Unpublished typescripts compiled by Grace Limeburner. "Bluehill, Maine : Vital Statistics Copied from the Original Records" and "Bluehill, Maine: All Vital Statistics Recorded on the Town Books from A.D. 1799 to 1809," 1941.)

[1984] Dodge and Candage, *Families of Early Settlers in Blue Hill*, Maine

730) PETER PARKER *(Hannah Swan Parker[4], Hannah Stevens Swan[3], Sarah Abbott Stevens[2], George[1])*, b. at Andover, 28 May 1741 son of Peter and Hannah (Swan) Parker; d. at Blue Hill, 24 Oct 1822; m. 5 Jun 1766, PHEBE MARBLE, b. at Andover, 29 Jul 1744 daughter of Job and Phebe (Barker) Marble; Phebe d. 1 Oct 1805.

Peter Parker and Phebe Marble started their family in Andover, but were in Blue Hill, Maine by 1775. They were the parents of nine children,[1985] the births of the six oldest children recorded at Andover.

i PHEBE PARKER, b. 24 Apr 1767; d. at Blue Hill, 3 May 1795; m. at Andover, 11 Sep 1794, SETH KIMBALL, b. at Bradford, 31 Oct 1768 son of Isaac and Bette (-) Kimball.

ii SERENA PARKER, b. 30 Aug 1768; d. 12 Oct 1784.

iii PETER PARKER, b. 17 Oct 1769; d. at Blue Hill, 30 Apr 1855; m. 30 Sep 1794, SALLY DARLING, b. 24 Apr 1769 daughter of Jonathan and Hannah (Holt) Darling; Sally d. at Blue Hill, 16 Oct 1836.

iv HANNAH PARKER, b. 19 Feb 1771; d. at Blue Hill, 27 Oct 1855. Hannah did not marry.

v SUSANNAH PARKER, b. 27 Jul 1772; d. at Blue Hill, 17 Aug 1803; m. 11 Sep 1795, JONATHAN ELLIS, b. at Bellingham, MA, 28 Jun 1774 son of Amos and Hannah (Hill) Ellis; Jonathan d. at Blue Hill, 23 Dec 1806.

vi MARBLE PARKER, b. 1 Jul 1775; d. at Blue Hill, 17 Dec 1866; m. at Sedgwick, 17 Sep 1798, HANNAH LOVEJOY, b. at Andover, 16 Oct 1778 daughter of Joseph and Mary (Gorden) Lovejoy; Hannah d. 13 Jul 1847.

vii MARY PARKER, b. 4 Apr 1777; d. 8 Jul 1793.

viii ISAAC PARKER, b. 23 May 1782; d. at Blue Hill, 16 May 1877; m. at Blue Hill, 27 Mar 1823, HANNAH CARTER, b. 23 Jul 1796; Hannah d. at Blue Hill, 3 Jun 1855.

ix JOANNA PARKER, b. 6 May 1784; d. at Blue Hill, 4 Mar 1820; m. 15 Dec 1808, ISRAEL WOOD, b. 20 Jul 1782 son of Israel and Phebe (Holt) Wood; Israel d. 25 May 1831. After Joanna's death, Israel married Betsey Briggs Hatch.

731) ROBERT PARKER *(Hannah Swan Parker[4], Hannah Stevens Swan[3], Sarah Abbott Stevens[2], George[1])*, b. at Andover, 2 Mar 1744/5 son of Peter and Hannah (Swan) Parker; d. at Blue Hill, 12 Feb 1818; m. 29 Nov 1773, RUTH WOOD, b. at Beverly, 18 Dec 1753 daughter of Joseph and Mary (Haskell) Wood; Ruth d. 20 Jan 1825.

In his will dated 22 July 1813 (probate May 1818), Robert Parker bequeaths to beloved wife Ruth all the household goods to be at her disposal. She is also to receive her thirds or proper dower according to law. Son Samuel receives six sheep and one-half of lot 47 of the fourth division. Second son Robert receives 12 sheep. Son Simeon receives four oxen, five cows, and thirty sheep. Simeon also receives one-half of block 50 of the second division. Eldest daughter Nabby receives two hundred dollars, one cow, and twelve sheep. Daughter Ede receives two hundred dollars, one cow, and twelve sheep. Spofford Parker who is now living with him receives fifty dollars, a yoke of oxen, and two suits of clothing of a decent kind. Spofford is also to be allowed to stay with the family until he is twenty-one. The remainder of the estate goes to son Frederick who is named executor.[1986] Spofford Parker is likely Robert's grandnephew. Robert's nephew Joseph Parker (married to Elizabeth Hinkley) and father of Spofford died in 1801. Elizabeth Hinkley had remarried and moved to Bar Harbor (see Family 729).

Robert and Ruth Parker were parents of eight children all born at Blue Hill.

i SAMUEL PARKER, b. 9 Mar 1774; d. at Blue Hill, 2 Dec 1831; m. 2 May 1808, his first cousin, LYDIA PARKER, b. at Blue Hill, 23 Sep 1784 daughter of Nathan and Mary (Wood) Parker; Lydia d. at Blue Hill, 29 May 1824. Samuel m. 2nd, the widow Mary Matthews on 11 Sep 1826. Lydia is a child in Family 729.

ii MOSES PARKER, b. 1 Feb 1778; d. 13 Aug 1801.

iii ROBERT PARKER, b. 3 Feb 1780; d. 19 Dec 1781.

iv ROBERT PARKER, b. 7 Dec 1782; died at sea.

v SIMEON PARKER, b. 24 Jul 1785; d. at Blue Hill, 14 Feb 1826; m. at Blue Hill, 4 Nov 1818, his fourth cousin twice removed, LYDIA FAULKNER STEVENS *(Dorcas Osgood Stevens[5], Elizabeth Abbott Osgood[4], Thomas[3], Thomas[2], George[1])*, b. at Blue Hill, 23 May 1798 daughter of Theodore and Dorcas (Osgood) Stevens; Lydia d. 28 Mar 1860. Lydia is a child in Family 878.

[1985] Blue Hill, ME: Vital Records, 1766-1809. (Online database: AmericanAncestors.org, New England Historic Genealogical Society, 2012)

[1986] Maine, County Probate Records, 1760-1979, Hancock, Probate records 1806-1823 vol 4-6, volume 6, p 392, accessed through familysearch.org

vi FREDERICK DUNBAR PARKER, b. 30 Oct 1788; d. at Blue Hill, 6 Apr 1867; m. at Beverly, MA, 30 Apr 1818, HARRIET HASKELL, b. at Beverly, 1 Mar 1792 daughter of Robert and Sarah (Woodberry) Haskell; Harriet d. at Blue Hill, 30 Apr 1877.

vii ABIGAIL "NABBY" PARKER, b. 20 Mar 1792; d. at Blue Hill, 6 Feb 1864; m. 22 Feb 1816, her first cousin, ROBERT HASKELL WOOD, b. at Blue Hill, 27 Dec 1783 son of Robert Haskell and Mary (Coggins) Wood; Robert d. at Blue Hill, 4 Aug 1840.

viii EDITH PARKER, b. 2 Mar 1795; d. at Rockland, ME, after 1860; m. about 1818, STEPHEN HOLT, b. at Blue Hill, 10 May 1788 son of Jedediah and Sarah (Thorndike) Holt; Jedediah d. at Blue Hill, 16 May 1830. In 1860, Edith was living with her daughter Charlotte Augusta and her husband Ephraim Barrett.

732) HANNAH PARKER *(Hannah Swan Parker^4, Hannah Stevens Swan^3, Sarah Abbott Stevens^2, George^1)*, b. at Andover, 4 Apr 1747 daughter of Peter and Hannah (Swan) Parker; d. about 1782; m. at Pelham, NH, 23 May 1775,[1987] HENRY BUTLER ELWELL, b. at Gloucester, 27 Mar 1746 son of William and Elizabeth (Butler) Elwell. Henry married second Theodosia Mitchell 18 Jul 1782 and married third Lucy Pichard 17 Jan 1790.

Very little information has been found for this family. There are just two children identified for Hannah and Henry.

i PARKER ELWELL, b. about 1775; nothing further known.

ii HENRY ELWELL, b. at North Yarmouth, ME, 16 Apr 1776; nothing further known.

733) ISAAC PARKER *(Hannah Swan Parker^4, Hannah Stevens Swan^3, Sarah Abbott Stevens^2, George^1)*, b. at Andover, 29 Aug 1749 son of Peter and Hannah (Swan) Parker; d. 9 Oct 1814; m. by 1786, MARY "POLLY" PARKER, b. about 1761 (based on age at time of death) whose parents have not been verified; Mary d. at Andover 19 Nov 1834. It is also possible that Polly's maiden name is not Parker.

Isaac was an innholder in Andover. The Essex probate court for Andover was held at his house.[1988]

Isaac Parker did not leave a will and his estate entered probate 10 Nov 1814 with Timothy Osgood, Jr. of Andover as administrator. Real estate was valued at $8,120.33 and the personal estate was $2,014.91. Widow Mary Parker was allowed to take $500 in value from the personal estate for her support. Debts against the estate were $1,181. The personal estate was sold to settle the estate. The real estate was divided into nine shares for distribution among the children. In the division of the shares, the following choices were made: Mary Parker chooses share 2; Joseph Parker (who is the husband of daughter Lydia), share 3; John Baldwin (husband of Clarissa), share 7; Hannah Parker, share 1; Almira Parker, share 8; Isaac Parker, share 9; and through their guardian Timothy Osgood, Augusta Parker, share 4; Charlotte Parker, share 5; and Moses Parker, share 6.[1989]

The probate records include a guardianship case for the following minor children: Isaac, age 19, Augusta nearly 18, Charlotte age 15, who all select Timothy Osgood as their guardian; Timothy Osgood was also appointed guardian of Moses, age 13.

Isaac and Mary Parker were parents of nine children born at Andover.

i MARY "POLLY" PARKER, b. 27 Oct 1786; d. at North Andover, 12 Sep 1865. Polly did not marry.[1990]

ii LYDIA PARKER, b. 26 Mar 1788; m. 30 Dec 1806, JOSEPH PARKER, b. at Andover, 18 Jan 1782 son of Michael and Phebe (Farrington) Parker.

iii HANNAH PARKER, b. 6 Oct 1789; d. at North Andover, 29 Jul 1819. Hannah did not marry.

iv CLARISSA ELLEN PARKER, b. 2 Dec 1791; d. at Billerica, 28 May 1867; m. at Andover, 15 Nov 1810, JOHN BALDWIN, b. at Billerica, 1 Sep 1786 son of William and Susannah (Wilson) Baldwin; John d. at Billerica, 25 Jun 1875.

v ALMIRA PARKER, b. 26 Nov 1793; d. after 1870; m. at Andover, 2 Feb 1818, RICHARD KIMBALL, b. at Bradford, 20 Jan 1793 son of Benjamin and Sarah (-) Kimball;[1991] Richard d. at Lancaster, MA, 30 Dec 1867. Richard and Almira lived in Philadelphia, but in 1865 were in Lancaster, MA.

vi ISAAC PARKER, b. 18 Sep 1795; d. at Andover, 13 Jun 1851. Isaac does not seem to have married.

1987 Ancestry.com, New Hampshire, Marriage Records Index, 1637-1947

1988 As noted in the 1811 edition of *The (Old) Farmers' Almanac*

1989 Essex County, MA: Probate File Papers, 1638-1881.Online database. AmericanAncestors.org. New England Historic Genealogical Society, 2014. Case 20504

1990 The four children who did not marry (Mary, Hannah, Isaac, and Moses) share a common gravestone in the Second Burying Ground in North Andover. Findagrave: 54177918

1991 The names of Richard's parents are given as Benjamin and Sarah on his death record.

vii AUGUSTA PARKER, b. 27 Jul 1797; d. at North Andover, 21 Mar 1870; m. 26 Feb 1835, ENOCH STEVENS, b. at Andover, 16 Jan 1795 son of Peter and Susannah (Wardwell) Stevens; Enoch d. at Andover, 23 Mar 1850.

viii CHARLOTTE PARKER, b. 12 Dec 1799; d. 1 Oct 1872; m. at Andover, 14 Jun 1826, STEPHEN HUSE, b. at Methuen, 20 Apr 1797 son of Stephen and Dorothy (Rideout) Huse; Stephen d. at Edgartown, 3 Aug 1864.

ix MOSES PARKER, b. 29 Nov 1801; d. at Andover, 27 Aug 1829. Moses does not seem to have married.

734) LYDEA PARKER *(Hannah Swan Parker4, Hannah Stevens Swan3, Sarah Abbott Stevens2, George1)*, b. at Andover, 24 Apr 1752 daughter of Peter and Hannah (Swan) Parker; d. at Lowell, MA, 29 Mar 1849; m. at Dracut, 29 Oct 1774, HEZEKIAH COBURN, b. 29 Mar 1748 son of Samuel and Mary (Bradstreet) Coburn; Hezekiah d. at Dracut, 13 Mar 1816.

Hezekiah served in the Revolution as a member of the Minutemen company of Captain Peter Coburn.[1992]

Lydea Parker and Hezekiah Coburn were parents of six children born at Dracut.

i PARKER COBURN, b. 10 Dec 1775; d. at Warren, ME, 6 Aug 1842; m. 18 Mar 1804, ABIGAIL KIRKPATRICK, b. at Warren, about 1780 daughter of John and Anne (Bradbury) Kirkpatrick; Abigail d. at Warren, Mar 1860.

ii HEZEKIAH COBURN, b. 1779; d. at Dracut, 26 Mar 1805; m. at Chelmsford, 29 Jul 1804, SARAH BUTTERFIELD, b. at Chelmsford, 1 Aug 1779 daughter of Benjamin and Sarah (Chamberlain) Butterfield; Sarah d. at Lowell, 23 Aug 1868.

iii PETER COBURN, b. about 1781; d. at Dracut, 23 May 1825; m. 29 Jun 1813, MARY VARNUM, b. at Dracut, 11 Nov 1784 daughter of Thomas and Mary (Atkinson) Varnum; Mary d. at Dracut, 8 Sep 1859.

iv FANNY COBURN, b. 26 Oct 1782; d. at Blue Hill, ME, 2 Apr 1851; m. at Dracut, 7 Nov 1805, SAMUEL WOOD, b. at Blue Hill, about 1776 son of Joseph and Eleanor (Carter) Wood; Samuel d. at Blue Hill, 4 Dec 1836.

v ENOCH COBURN, b. 4 Feb 1787; d. at Fredonia, NY, 6 Aug 1873; m. MARY BARNABY, b. about 1801; Mary d. at Fredonia, 29 Nov 1866.

vi THEODORE COBURN, b. 21 Feb 1789; d. at Buffalo, NY, 3 Dec 1849; m. about 1827, SARAH TRASK, b. in MA, 3 Aug 1792 daughter of Rufus and Hannah (Stacy) Trask;[1993] Sarah d. at Buffalo, 22 Sep 1862.

735) MARY INGALLS *(James Ingalls4, Mary Stevens Ingalls3, Sarah Abbott Stevens2, George1)*, b. at Andover, 1 Dec 1745 daughter of James and Mary (Frye) Ingalls; d. at Lisbon, NH, 3 Jul 1811; m. 10 Oct 1765, her third cousin once removed, JOSHUA SWAN, b. at Methuen, 6 Aug 1745 son of Timothy and Mary (Abbott) Swan. Joshua Swan's mother Mary Abbott is from the Rowley Abbott line.

Joshua Swan captained a militia company in Salem, New Hampshire during the Revolutionary War.[1994]

Joshua Swan and Mary Ingalls were parents of nine children, the first six children born at Salem, New Hampshire, one child born at Haverhill, New Hampshire, and the youngest two children recorded at Methuen. The two youngest children have parents given as Joshua and Mary, but they are listed at Methuen and the other children were born in New Hampshire, so they are possibly children of another Joshua and Mary.

i JOSHUA SWAN, b. 23 Feb 1767; d. at Medina, OH, 17 Jul 1845; m. MARTHA COLLINS, b. about 1769; Martha d. at Medina, OH, 17 Jul 1860.

ii ISRAEL SWAN, b. 17 Dec 1768; d. at Haverhill, NH, 9 Mar 1822; m. at Haverhill, 22 Aug 1790, ABIGAIL JOHNSTON, b. at Haverhill, 20 Sep 1772 daughter of Charles and Ruth (Marsh) Johnston; Abigail d. at Haverhill, 11 May 1805.

iii MARY SWAN, b. 1 Jan 1771; d. at Woodbury, VT, 10 Apr 1845; m. at Haverhill, NH, 19 Apr 1793, DANIEL CONNOR, b. at Salisbury, MA, 10 May 1769 son of Samuel and Elizabeth (-) Connor; Daniel d. at Corinth, VT, 27 Oct 1848.

iv SILAS SWAN, b. 13 Jan 1773; d. 29 Nov 1775.

1992 Coburn, *Genealogy of the Descendants of Edward Colburn*, p 90

1993 Jordan, *Genealogical and Personal History of the Allegheny Valley*, volume 3, p 1042

1994 Gilbert, *History of Salem, N.H.*, p 236

v CHLOE SWAN, b. 18 Jan 1775; m. at Haverhill, 13 Jul 1794; BENJAMIN YOUNG, b. at Lisbon, NH, 1771 son of John and Susanna (Gatchell) Young.

vi ALICE SWAN, b. 23 Nov 1776

vii JAMES INGALLS SWAN, b. about 1779; d. at Bath, NH, 8 Apr 1820; m. at Haverhill, 13 Aug 1810, BETSY SPRAGUE, b. about 1785 daughter of Alden Sprague.

viii ALICE SWAN, b. 4 Feb 1782; nothing further known

ix RHODA SWAN, b. 5 Mar 1784; nothing further known

736) HANNAH INGALLS *(James Ingalls⁴, Mary Stevens Ingalls³, Sarah Abbott Stevens², George¹)*, b. at Andover, 27 Dec 1748 daughter of James and Mary (Frye) Ingalls; d. 10 Jul 1811; m. 18 Nov 1765, BENJAMIN HALL, *perhaps* b. at Andover, 29 Jun 1742[1995] son of Benjamin and Rebecca (Farnum) Hall; Benjamin d. at Gloversville, NY, 24 Dec 1830. Benjamin had a second marriage, but his wife's name is unknown.

Benjamin Hall was commissioned as ensign 1 January 1776 and served in Colonel John Stark's New Hampshire Regiment. He left the service 20 February 1777 but had a subsequent enlistment the details of which were not provided in his pension file. In a statement made 18 October 1820, Benjamin reported that his second wife died 3 October 1820 but did not give her name. An inquiry on behalf of son James in 1849 stated that there were three children of Benjamin living in 1849, but only James's name was given.[1996]

Benjamin and Hannah lived in Salem, New Hampshire after their marriage and their six children were born there. They relocated to Gloversville, New York. Benjamin Hall was selected as deacon of the Presbyterian church in Kingsboro (a neighborhood in Gloversville) in 1804 and served until his death in 1830.[1997]

It is possible that the two oldest children, John and Hannah, married Mudgett siblings and stayed in New Hampshire. That is not certain, but those marriages are given here.

i JOHN HALL, b. 6 Jan 1767; m. at Weare, 23 Dec 1788, MIRIAM MUDGETT, b. at Weare, 9 Aug 1766 daughter of Ebenezer and Miriam (Johnson) Mudgett.

ii HANNAH HALL, b. 12 Jun 1769; d. at Cambridge, VT, 1 Jul 1831; m. at Weare, 5 Feb 1788, WILLIAM MUDGETT, b. at Hampstead, 1 Oct 1764 son of Ebenezer and Miriam (Johnson) Mudgett; William d. at Cambridge, 8 May 1851.

iii ABIAH HALL, b. 15 Oct 1771; nothing further known.

iv BENJAMIN HALL, b. 21 Jul 1776; nothing further known.

v MARY HALL, b. 3 May 1774; d. at Cuba, NY, 6 Nov 1852; m. about 1797, ELIJAH BURR, b. at Farmington, CT, 7 Apr 1768 son of Nathaniel and Abigail (Strong) Burr; Elijah d. at Gloversville, NY, 7 Dec 1828.

vi JAMES HALL, b. 19 Oct 1778; d. at Fulton County, NY, 1849 (when he is mentioned in his father's pension file); m. HANNAH who has not been identified.

737) DORCAS INGALLS *(James Ingalls⁴, Mary Stevens Ingalls³, Sarah Abbott Stevens², George¹)*, b. at Andover, 18 Feb 1750/1 daughter of James and Mary (Frye) Ingalls; d. at Methuen, 16 Jul 1821; m. 30 Sep 1777, her third cousin once removed, CALEB SWAN, b. 4 Oct 1749 son of Timothy and Mary (Abbott) Swan.

Dorcas was born in Andover, but after her marriage, joined her husband in Methuen where they raised a family of eight children. One son, Dr. James Swan, was a physician in Springfield. Their daughter Achsah was the mother of the industrialist David Nevins, Sr. whose family wealth was used to fund the Nevins Memorial Library in Methuen.

Caleb Swan served several enlistments during the Revolutionary War beginning as a Corporal in Captain Archelaus Towne's Company which saw action in the early phases of the war including the siege of Boston. In 1777, he held the rank of Sergeant in the Continental troops. By 1781, he held the rank of Captain of a company in the 4th Regiment of Essex militia.[1998]

Captain Caleb Swan did not leave a will and his estate entered probate 3 September 1798. Dorcas Swan and James Ingalls (likely his father-in-law) administered the estate. Heirs that are mentioned in the distribution documents and receipts are Deborah Swan, Bailey Davis on behalf of his wife Hannah, Kendal Mallon and his wife Dorcas, and Dorcas Swan signing as the guardian for Achsah Swan, Caleb Swan, Fanny Swan, and James Swan. The inventory of the estate totaled $3,626.52.[1999]

1995 Benjamin Hall gave his age as 78 when he made his pension application in 1820.

1996 Revolutionary War Pension and Bounty-Land Warrant Application Files

1997 Frothingham, *History of Fulton County*, p 378

1998 Fold3.com, Compiled Service Records of Soldiers Who Served in the American Army During the Revolutionary War 1775-1785.

1999 *Essex County, MA: Probate File Papers, 1638-1881.*Online database. *AmericanAncestors.org.* New England Historic Genealogical Society, 2014. Probate of Caleb Swan, 3 Sep 1798, Case number 26880

Dorcas and Caleb Swan had eight children born at Methuen.

i DORCAS SWAN, b. 16 Jun 1778; d. at Lowell, 14 Dec 1863; m. at Methuen, 9 Jul 1799, KENDALL MALLON, b. at Methuen, 1 Jul 1771 son of James and Hannah (Parker) Mallon; Kendall d. between 1830 and 1840 likely at Charlestown.[2000] Five children have been identified for this family, the youngest of whom (Kendall Mallon) was born in Mason, NH in 1815.

ii DEBORAH SWAN, b. 10 Mar 1789; d. at Newburyport, 17 Apr 1835; m. at Methuen, 23 Nov 1802, POTTLE RICHARDSON, b. at Methuen, 3 Sep 1773 son of Francis and Mary (Ford) Richardson; Pottle d. 26 Jan 1847.

iii HANNAH SWAN, b. 19 Apr 1782; d. at Methuen, 1 Jan 1820; m. at Methuen, 11 Mar 1800, BAILEY DAVIS, b. at Methuen, 15 Nov 1776 son of John and Hannah (Cross) Davis; Bailey d. 25 Oct 1824 (probate 16 Nov 1824).

iv CALEB SWAN, b. 10 May 1784; d. 4 Jan 1788.

v ACHSAH SWAN, b. 23 Aug 1787; d. at Methuen, 15 Jan 1866; m. 4 Aug 1808, JOHN NEVENS, b. at Salem, NH, 4 Sep 1784 son of David and "Nanna" Nevens;[2001] John d. at Methuen, 15 Nov 1860. The Nevins Memorial Library in Methuen is named for their son David Nevins, Sr.

vi CALEB SWAN, b. 20 Mar 1790; d. at Methuen, 4 Dec 1863; m. 1st, 19 Jun 1814, ASENATH "SENA" TOWNE, b. at Andover, 16 Feb 1789 daughter of Peter and Rebecca (Sheldon) Towne; Sena d. 18 Feb 1831. Caleb m. 2nd, 19 Feb 1832, JUDITH PETTENGILL, b. at Methuen, 2 Apr 1797 daughter of John and Hannah (Burbank) Pettengill; Judith d. at Marblehead, 30 Dec 1870.

vii FANNY SWAN, b. 8 Jul 1792; d. at Philadelphia, 8 Nov 1862;[2002] m. 31 Dec 1811, JOHN BRADLEY, b. at Haverhill, 10 Feb 1789 son of Joseph and Mary "Polly" (Osgood) Bradley; John is likely the John Bradley who died at Haverhill 30 Nov 1830.

viii JAMES SWAN, b. 31 Oct 1794; d. at Springfield, MA, 16 Aug 1846; m. at Methuen, 24 Oct 1822, MARTHA "PATTY" SWAN, b. at Methuen, 17 Dec 1792 daughter of William and Janette (Dinsmore) Swan;[2003] Martha d. at Lee, MA, 7 Apr 1896. (Martha Swan His Wife Died at Lee, Mass. Apr. 7, 1896 Aged 103 Yrs. [Springfield Cemetery]). Dr. James Swan was a physician in Springfield.

738) DEBORAH INGALLS *(James Ingalls⁴, Mary Stevens Ingalls³, Sarah Abbott Stevens², George¹)*, b. at Andover, 28 May 1753 daughter of James and Mary (Frye) Ingalls; d. at Methuen, 20 Sep 1779; m. 24 Mar 1773, DANIEL HIBBARD, b. at Methuen, 15 Sep 1748 son of Ebenezer and Abigail (Whittier) Hibbard. Daniel m. 2nd, Sarah Lovejoy.

Deborah Ingalls and Daniel Hibbard were parents of four children born at Methuen.

i JOSHUA HIBBARD, b. 18 Jun 1773; d. 9 Sep 1775.

ii DANIEL HIBBARD, b. 4 Mar 1775; d. at Belmont, ME, May 1850; m. about 1802, KEZIAH BASS, b. about 1777; Keziah d. at Belfast, about 1810. Daniel m. 2nd, SARAH (widow Sarah Poor)[2004] who has not been identified.

iii JOSHUA INGALLS HIBBARD, b. 27 May 1777; d. at Gilford, NH, 12 Jun 1861; m. at Londonderry, 12 Oct 1802, HANNAH TENNEY, b. at Bradford, MA, 29 Jul 1781 daughter of Asa and Molly (Hale) Tenney; Hannah d. at Gilford, 14 Apr 1865.

iv DEBORAH HIBBARD, b. 20 Sep 1779; nothing further known.

739) SARAH INGALLS *(James Ingalls⁴, Mary Stevens Ingalls³, Sarah Abbott Stevens², George¹)*, b. at Methuen, 5 Oct 1761 daughter of James and Mary (Frye) Ingalls; d. at Boxford, 25 Jul 1849; m. 25 Nov 1788, JOHN FOSTER, b. at Andover, 10 Dec 1759 son of Stephen and Abigail (Smith) Foster; John d. at Andover, 30 Nov 1837.

[2000] Kendall Mallon is the head of household in Charlestown in the 1830 census and Dorcas is the head of household in the 1840 census. *1840 United States Federal Census*, Year: 1840; Census Place: Charlestown, Middlesex, Massachusetts; Page: 107

[2001] John Nevens's father's name is given as David with place of birth as Salem on John's death record. John's birth record gives the mother's name as "Nanna." *New Hampshire, Births and Christenings Index, 1714-1904.*

[2002] Fanny Bradley was living in the home of her son, John Osgood Bradley, in Philadelphia at the 1860 census. *Philadelphia, Pennsylvania, Death Certificates Index, 1803-1915*

[2003] The names of Martha's parents are given on her death record.

[2004] Hibbard, *Genealogy of the Hibbard Family*, p 81

Sarah and John Foster raised their family of six children in Andover. John Foster had trained in metal foundry and made silver buckles and sleigh bills. Later, he supported his family through farming. He also served as a deacon.[2005]

This was a family that valued both education and religious piety. Two of the sons, Stephen and Isaac, attended Dartmouth College and were ordained ministers. Stephen Foster was an educator in Tennessee and was president of East Tennessee College (now University of Tennessee) in 1834. Daughter Ruby worked as a schoolteacher before dying of fever at age 21. Their granddaughter, Sarah Jane Foster Rhea, was a missionary in Persia (present day Iran). There is a wealth of information on this family. The diary and letters of daughter Ruby were published after her death in 1812.[2006] Sarah Rhea's husband also published a memoir/diary.[2007]

John Foster's estate entered probate 12 Dec 1837.[2008] John Foster wrote his will 13 June 1836. Beloved wife Sally receives the improvements on all the real estate during her natural life. This includes the real estate he has disposed of to his children by deeds of gifts as that was a provision of the deeds. She also receives the improvements on all the livestock and household items. In addition, she receives a bequest of $1,500 to be at her own disposal. His four grandchildren who are the children of Amos Kimball each receive $375: Mary Malvina, Walter Henry, John Foster, and Lucy Foster. This money is to be held earning interest and a specific schedule for its disbursement is given. To his daughter-in-law Ann widow of son Stephen, he gives $500 in addition to the right of the real estate he deeded to Stephen. The money bequest is to assist in "bringing up her little daughter Sarah Jane." To Sarah Jane, he bequeaths $750 which is also to be held earning interest and paid on a schedule. Son Isaac Foster receives all the stock animals except two cows and receives all the farming tools. Daughters Sarah Foster and Hannah Foster are to receive all the household items after the decease of their mother. The daughters also will receive the horse, chaise, and sleigh and the floor pew in the meeting house. The American Board of the Commission of Foreign Missions and the American Educators Society receive $100 each. His three children Isaac, Hannah, and Sarah receive the remainder of any money and securities and any funds that may be remaining after the decease of their honored mother. Daughter Hannah Foster is named sole executor.

Sarah and John Foster had six children born at Andover.

i SALLY FOSTER, b. 14 Aug 1789; d. at Andover, 4 Dec 1870. Sarah did not marry. Sally and her sister Hannah lived with their brother Isaac in Andover.

ii RUBY FOSTER, b. 19 Oct 1791; d. 5 Aug 1812. Ruby did not marry. She was a teacher and a diarist. Her diary was published by her pastor, Reverend Eaton of Boxford.[2009]

iii LUCY FOSTER, b. 21 Nov 1793; d. at Boxford, 10 Feb 1825; m. 30 Oct 1817, AMOS KIMBALL, b. at Boxford, 27 Sep 1784 son of Amos and Mary (Stiles) Kimball; Amos d. at Boxford, 13 Nov 1845. After Lucy's death, Amos married Susan Foster daughter of Nathan and Susannah (Barker) Foster.

iv HANNAH FOSTER, b. 22 Sep 1795; d. at North Andover, 4 Mar 1863. Hannah did not marry. She and her sister Sarah lived with their brother Isaac in North Andover. Hannah wrote her will 25 Jan 1855. She bequeaths to her sister Sally the full use of her real estate during her lifetime. Sally has the right to dispose of any wood standing on the land and well as make any additions to the buildings. Hannah bequeaths to her brother Isaac $200. He will also receive all the real property owned by Hannah after the decease of her sister Sally. Other bequests are to her nieces and nephews and several religious and missionary organizations.

v STEPHEN FOSTER, b. 15 Feb 1798; d. at Knoxville, TN, 11 Jan 1835; m. in Knox County, TN, 30 Jun 1831, ANN A. DAVIS, b. in Tennessee, 6 Nov 1810[2010] *likely* the daughter of Samuel and Grizzy (Ross) Davis; Ann d. at Jonesboro, TN, 21 Oct 1894. In 1846, Ann married Samuel B. Cunningham (1798-1867). Stephen's only child, Sarah Jane Foster, was born five months after his death. Sarah was the second wife of Samuel Rhea and served with him as a missionary in Persia (present day Iran). Her husband died in Iran and is buried there.[2011]

vi ISAAC FOSTER, b. 7 Jul 1806; d. at North Andover, 23 Aug 1877; m. 2 Jul 1834, FRANCES B. LEE, b. at Hanover, NH, 4 Feb 1812 daughter of Ebenezer and Lydia (Burbank) Lee;[2012] Frances d. at Boxford, 8 Mar 1895. Isaac's son Charles Lee Foster died in New Orleans 8 August 1863 while serving in the Union Army.

2005 Pierce, *Foster Genealogy, Part I*, p 231, https://archive.org/stream/fostergenealogy01piergoog#page/n233/mode/2up

2006 Foster, *Miscellaneous Writings of Ruby Foster*

2007 Marsh, *The Tennesseean in Persia and Koordistan*, p 267 https://archive.org/details/tennesseeaninper00mars

2008 *Essex County, MA: Probate File Papers, 1638-1881.*Online database. *AmericanAncestors.org.* New England Historic Genealogical Society, 2014. Estate of John Foster, case number 9917, 12 Dec 1837.

2009 Pierce, *Foster Genealogy, Part I*, p 231

2010 Her date of birth is engraved on her gravestone; findagrave.com

2011 "Missionary to the Nestorians" http://biblicalcyclopedia.com/R/rhea-samuel-audley.html

2012 The will of Lydia Burbank Lee includes a bequest of to her daughter Frances B. Foster. New Hampshire Wills and Probate Records, Grafton, NH, Will of Lydia Lee, 18 Jul 1872.

740) CHARLES INGALLS *(James Ingalls⁴, Mary Stevens Ingalls³, Sarah Abbott Stevens², George¹)*, b. at Methuen, 12 Oct 1763 son of James and Mary (Frye) Ingalls; d. at Greenwich, NY, 2 Sep 1812; m. CYNTHIA RUSSELL, b. 14 Mar 1769 daughter of Thomas and Mary (Patterson) Russell; d. 17 Mar 1801.

Charles Ingalls attended Dartmouth and was an attorney in Salem, New York.[2013] He opened the first law office in Greenwich, New York. Son Charles Frye Ingalls was also an attorney, worked as a district attorney, and was a judge of the Court of Appeals, among other accomplishments.[2014]

Despite being an attorney, Charles Ingalls did not leave a will and only the assignment of administration is currently available online.

Charles and Cynthia were parents of two children born at Greenwich, New York.

i CHARLES FRYE INGALLS, b. 29 Jan 1795; d. at Greenwich, NY, 5 Mar 1870; m. MARY "MOLLY" ROGERS, b. at Canterbury, 3 Jul 1801 daughter of Nathan and Dorothea (Cleveland) Rogers; Mary d. at Greenwich, 9 Jul 1879.

ii THOMAS RUSSELL INGALLS, b. 22 Nov 1798; d. at Greenwich, 26 Jul 1868. Thomas graduate from the U.S. Military Academy and served as the president of Jefferson College in Louisiana. He did not marry.

741) ALFRED INGALLS *(James Ingalls⁴, Mary Stevens Ingalls³, Sarah Abbott Stevens², George¹)*, b. at Methuen, 16 Oct 1765 son of James and Mary (Frye) Ingalls; d. at Methuen, 15 Sep 1843; m. 1st, 9 Nov 1790, ABIGAIL "NABBY" PAGE, b. 1768 *possibly* daughter of Daniel Page; Nabby d. 29 Nov 1795. Alfred m. 2nd, 24 Jul 1797, MARY STICKNEY, b. at Bradford, 9 Aug 1766 daughter of Thomas and Sarah (Tenney) Stickney; Mary d. at Methuen, 22 Jul 1852. Mary Stickney was first married to William Carleton.

Alfred Ingalls was a farmer in Methuen. He drew the first known map of Methuen in 1794.[2015] He also drew a plan for the town of Marblehead in 1795.

In his will dated 6 December 1834, beloved wife Mary receives use and improvement on the west side of what is called the fore lot. She also receives the use of the east room, the chamber above, and the kitchen as long as Mary takes care of daughter Abigail. Mary also receives three cows, one swine, and other provisions for her support. Mary also receives one hundred dollars for her own use. Beloved son Charles receives the lot of land called Marston pasture as well as other land bequests. Part of the land adjoins land that his son James bought from Isaac Bodwell. Daughter Abigail receives four hundred dollars to be paid yearly and the use of a chamber as long as she is unmarried. After her mother's decease, Abigail is to have wood brought to her door if she is capable of living by herself. Daughter Anna Hunt receives four hundred dollars in addition to what she has received, and grandson Alfred Ingalls Hunt receives fifty dollars at age twenty-one. Son Joseph Fry Ingalls receives all the remainder of the estate. If either of his sons or daughter Abigail die without issue, their parts will be divided among the surviving children. If the money left to Abigail is not enough to support her, then Joseph F. is to pay three-fourths and son Charles is to pay one-fourth of the amount needed for her support. Son Joseph Fry Ingalls is sole executor.[2016]

Alfred Ingalls and Abigail Page had three children born at Methuen.

i JAMES INGALLS, b. 29 Oct 1791; d. 5 Jul 1793.

ii JAMES INGALLS, b. 2 Aug 1793; d. at Methuen, 4 Sep 1828. James does not seem to have married.

iii BETTY PAGE INGALLS, b. 6 Jul 1795; d. 9 Mar 1796.

Alfred Ingalls and Mary Stickney had four children born at Methuen.

i ABIGAIL INGALLS, b. 11 Jun 1798; d. at Methuen, 8 Nov 1857. Abigail was described as "deranged" on her death record. An interesting tidbit: A sampler crafted by Abigail in 1811 has been offered for sale for $4,600.[2017]

ii ANNA INGALLS, b. 11 Mar 1800; d. at Tewksbury, 4 Dec 1863; m. 10 Nov 1825, THOMAS HUNT, b. at Tewksbury, 8 Dec 1796 son of Timothy and Dolly (Worster) Hunt; Thomas d. at Tewksbury, 17 Dec 1886.

2013 Burleigh, *History and Genealogy of the Ingalls Family*, p 119

2014 G.E. Matthews Company, *Men of New York*, volume II, p 51

2015 Methuen Historical Society, http://www.methuenhistory.org/Bridges_from_the_Past_2.html

2016 Massachusetts, Essex County, Probate Records; Author: Massachusetts. Supreme Judicial Court (Essex County); Probate Place: Essex, Massachusetts, Probate Records, Hutchingson, M-Ingalls, D, 1828-1991, accessed through ancestry.com

2017 https://www.incollect.com/listings/folk-art/textiles/abigail-ingalls-sampler-by-abigail-ingalls-methuen-massachusetts-1811-166398

iii JOSEPH FRYE INGALLS, b. 27 Mar 1803; d. at Methuen, 2 Feb 1876; m. 26 Nov 1829, his third cousin once removed, PHEBE CAMPBELL FRYE *(Francis Frye6, James Frye5, Elizabeth Osgood Frye4, Hannah Abbott Osgood3, George2, George1)*, b. at Methuen, 12 Oct 1806 daughter of Francis and Lydia (Whittier) Frye; Phebe d. at Methuen, 4 Feb 1876.

iv CHARLES INGALLS, b. 25 Apr 1808; d. at Methuen, 11 Jan 1882; m. 9 Oct 1832, MARY KIMBALL, b. at Salem, NH, 1813 daughter of John and Azubah (Austin) Kimball;[2018] Mary d. at Methuen, 18 Mar 1888.

742) LYDIA INGALLS *(James Ingalls4, Mary Stevens Ingalls3, Sarah Abbott Stevens2, George1)*, b. at Methuen, 7 Dec 1767 daughter of James and Mary (Frye) Ingalls; d. at Corinth, VT, 7 Nov 1810; m. at Corinth, 28 Jan 1806, as his second wife, DAVID MCKEEN, b. at Londonderry, NH, 12 Jun 1750 son of James and Elizabeth (Dinsmore) McKeen; David d. 2 Dec 1824. David's first marriage was to Margaret McPherson. In 1818, he married Judith Johnson as his third wife.

David McKeen was a prominent early citizen of Corinth. He was constable of the town at its organization, served as justice of the peace, and built the first sawmill there.[2019] He had a large family with his first wife Margaret McPherson. After her death, he married Lydia Ingalls. The marriage date for Lydia and David is two months after the date of the record for the birth of their first child. This could be an error in the transcriptions, or they may have married after the birth.

David and Lydia had two children born at Corinth, both of whom died in childhood.

i LYDIA MCKEEN, b. 25 Nov 1805; d. 7 Nov 1808

ii DAVID INGALLS MCKEEN, b. 31 Oct 1808; d. 1 Jul 1822

743) SIMEON INGALLS *(Ephraim Ingalls4, Mary Stevens Ingalls3, Sarah Abbott Stevens2, George1)*, b. at Pomfret, 28 May 1754 son of Ephraim and Mary (Sharp) Ingalls; d. at Hartwick, NY, 23 May 1827; m. 1st, OLIVE GROSVENOR, b. 17 May 1760 daughter of Joshua and Esther (Payson) Grosvenor; Olive d. 17 Apr 1782. Simeon m. 2nd, EUNICE WHEELER, b. 1 Nov 1756 daughter of Benjamin and Prudence (Huet) Wheeler; Eunice d. 5 Oct 1807. Simeon m. 3rd, 8 Mar 1808, RACHEL HARRIS.

Simeon Ingalls was a farmer in Hartwick, New York. Simeon and his second wife Eunice were parents of four children born at Hartwick.

i OLIVE GROSVENOR INGALLS, b. 6 Nov 1788; d. 5 May 1792.

ii JARED INGALLS, b. 4 Aug 1791; d. at Cherry Creek, NY, 11 Dec 1871; m. 29 Jan 1817, ABIGAIL JONES, b. in RI, 6 Oct 1793 daughter of Seth and Nancy (Carr) Jones; Abigail d. at Cherry Creek, 13 Jan 1871.

iii OLIVE GROSVENOR INGALLS, b. 22 May 1793; d. at Hartwick, about 1865 (probate 13 Dec 1865); m. as his second wife, BENJAMIN BURLINGHAM, b. in NY about 1793; Benjamin d. at Hartwick, about 1864 (probate). Olive and Benjamin did not have children, but Benjamin had one son, also Benjamin, from his first marriage.

iv EVANDER INGALLS, b. 11 Oct 1795; d. at Hartwick, 29 Sep 1879; m. 1st, 8 Oct 1820, AMY FIELD daughter of Charles Field; Amy d. at Hartwick, 30 Sep 1821. Evander m. 2nd, 8 Sep 1824, LUCY CLARK, b. 23 Jan 1800 daughter of Caleb and Polly (-) Clark; Lucy d. 7 May 1886.

744) SARAH INGALLS *(Ephraim Ingalls4, Mary Stevens Ingalls3, Sarah Abbott Stevens2, George1)*, b. at Pomfret, 17 Feb 1762 daughter of Ephraim and Mary (Sharp) Ingalls; d. 10 Mar 1807; m. 10 Feb 1784, JOSHUA GROSVENOR, b. 24 Apr 1758 son of Joshua and Esther (Payson) Grosvenor; Joshua d. 2 Apr 1838.

In his will written 10 January 1835, Joshua Grosvenor made the following bequests. Dutiful son Jasper Grosvenor receives $200. His other dutiful children receiving bequests are Olive Osgood, $10; and Sally Reynolds, $80. Nancy C. Grosvenor the widow of son Payson P. Grosvenor receives $250. Granddaughters Francis H. Grosvenor, Elisa Ann S. Grosvenor, and Charlotte E. Grosvenor each receive $200. Grandson Alexander P. Grosvenor receives $300 and the clock. Dutiful son Charles I. Grosvenor receives all the rest of the estate and is named executor.[2020]

Sarah Ingalls and Joshua Grosvenor had seven children all born at Pomfret.

i OLIVE GROSVENOR, b. 14 Nov 1784; d. at Cincinnatus, NY, 28 Nov 1872; m. about 1808, JOHN OSGOOD, b. at Pomfret, 13 Mar 1782 son of William and Mary (Scarborough) Osgood; John d. at Cincinnatus, 19 Dec 1872.

ii PAYSON GROSVENOR, b. 1 Jul 1786; d. 13 May 1787.

iii SALLY GROSVENOR, b. 28 May 1788; d. at Cincinnatus, NY, 29 Apr 1837; m. JOHN REYNOLDS; John d. at Cincinnatus, 24 Oct 1840.

[2018] The names of Mary's parents are given on her death record as John Kimball and Arubah Austin.

[2019] Town of Corinth History Committee, *History of Corinth*, p 410

[2020] Connecticut, Wills and Probate Records, 1609-1999, *Probate Records, Vol 19-20, 1838-1857,* will of Joshua Grosvenor

iv PAYSON PEPPER GROSVENOR, b. 19 Jun 1790; d. at Pomfret, 25 Mar 1832; m. at Pomfret, 28 Sep 1815, NANCY C. GORDON, b. 1792; Nancy d. at Canterbury, CT, 24 Dec 1845.

v WALTER GROSVENOR, b. 13 Sep 1792; d. 11 Oct 1796.

vi JASPER GROSVENOR, b. 11 Oct 1794; d. at Brooklyn, NY, 7 May 1857; m. at New York, NY, 27 Sep 1834, MATILDA SIDELL, b. at New York, 9 Jan 1800 daughter of John and Elizabeth (Low) Sidell;[2021] Matilda d. at New York, 20 Jan 1885. Jasper Grosvenor was a partner in the firm Rogers, Ketchum & Grosvenor, a steam locomotive manufacturing company.[2022]

vii CHARLES INGALLS GROSVENOR, b. 18 Feb 1802; d. at Pomfret, 29 Jan 1864; m. 1st, 31 Oct 1827, ANGELINA MOSLEY, b. 1805 *likely* the daughter of Flavel and Jane (Dorrance) Moseley;[2023] Angelina d. at Hampton, 13 Feb 1832. Charles m. 2nd, about 1833, EURETTA GORDON, b. at Canterbury, 10 Jan 1803 daughter of John and Lucy (Moore) Gordon; Euretta d. at Pomfret, 2 Apr 1882.

745) EPHRAIM INGALLS *(Ephraim Ingalls4, Mary Stevens Ingalls3, Sarah Abbott Stevens2, George1)*, b. at Pomfret, 6 Sep 1764 son of Ephraim and Mary (Sharp) Ingalls; d. at Pomfret, 12 Feb 1831; m. 26 Apr 1801, LUCY GOODELL, b. at Pomfret, 22 Apr 1779 daughter of Amasa and Lucy (-) Goodell;[2024] Lucy d. 2 Apr 1829. Several sources give the name of Lucy's mother as Lydia Chandler, and that may be correct, but the birth transcription for Lucy gives her mother's name as Lucy.

In his will 16 December 1830, Ephraim Ingalls gives to son Henry L. Ingalls five hundred dollars in full compensation for his labor since he arrived at age twenty-one years. He leaves one hundred dollars each to his sons Henry L., Edmund, Charles Francis, Addison, and Ephraim. Daughters Lucy, Lydia, and Deborah receive all his stock in the Connecticut and Rhode Island turnpike and the Boston and Hartford turnpike. The rest and residue of the estate is to be divided equally among all his children when his youngest son reaches age fourteen: Mary S. Fletcher, Henry L. Ingalls, Lucy Ingalls, Lydia Ingalls, Deborah Ingalls, Edmund Ingalls, Charles F. Ingalls, Addison Ingalls, and Ephraim Ingalls, Jr. The expense of raising and educating sons Addison and Ephraim until age fourteen is to be paid by the estate. Son Henry L. Ingalls and George Sharpe, Esq. are named executors.[2025] The total value of the estate was $5,841.43 including a home lot with 154 acres valued at $4,090.96.

Ephraim Ingalls and Lucy Goodell were parents of nine children who births are records at either Pomfret or Abington and the place the birth is recorded is given with each child.[2026]

i MARY STEVENS INGALLS, b. at Abington, 4 May 1802; d. at Cavendish, VT, 30 Jul 1860; m. at Pomfret, 13 Sep 1825, as his second wife, ADDISON FLETCHER, b. at Cavendish, 25 Aug 1790 son of Asaph and Sarah (green) Fletcher; Addison d. at Cavendish, 8 Jan 1832. Addison Fletcher was first married to Mary's first cousin, Maria Ingalls (see Family 747).

ii HENRY LAURENS INGALLS, b. at Abington, 9 Jun 1805; d. at North Branch, MN, 2 Sep 1876; m. 1832, LAVINIA CHILDS, b. at Woodstock, 1 Nov 1806 daughter of Rensellear and Priscilla (Corbin) Childs; Lavinia d. at North Branch, 29 Dec 1879.

iii LUCY INGALLS, b. at Abington, 11 Apr 1807; d. at Dedham, MA, 22 Jan 1887; m. at Pomfret, 8 Jan 1833, GROSVENOR STORRS, b. at Pomfret, 1 Dec 1797 son of Amasa and Gratis (Grosvenor) Storrs; Grosvenor d. at Pomfret, 13 Dec 1867.

iv LYDIA INGALLS, b. at Pomfret, 20 Jun 1809; d. at Petersburg, IL, 3 Sep 1858; m. at Sangamon, IL, 10 Apr 1837, JONATHAN COLBY, b. at Hopkinton, NH, 10 Mar 1808 son of Timothy and Lydia (Herrick) Colby; Jonathan d. at Petersburg, 25 Oct 1885.

v DEBORAH INGALLS, b. at Abington, 3 Dec 1812; d. at Palestine, IL, about 1850; m. at LaSalle, IL, 23 Feb 1839, RICHARD FLETCHER ADAMS, b. at Tyngsborough, 20 Dec 1812 son of Richard and Sally (Fletcher) Adams; Richard d. at Lee Center, IL, 29 Sep 1895. After Deborah's death, Richard married, at Westford, MA, 28 Apr 1852, Elizabeth M. Osgood daughter of Benjamin and Nancy (Cummings) Osgood.

2021 The 1837 will of John Sidell includes a bequest to Matilda wife of Jasper Grosvenor.

2022 Morrell, Brian (1975) "The Evolution of the Rogers Locomotive Company, Paterson, NJ," *Northeast Historical Archaeology*: Vol. 44, Article 3. https://doi.org/10.22191/neha/vol4/iss1/3

2023 The 1826 distribution of the estate of Flavel Moseley includes a distribution to daughter Angelina.

2024 The 1814 will of Amasa Goodell includes a bequest to his daughters Lucy Ingalls.

2025 *Connecticut State Library (Hartford, Connecticut);* Probate Place: *Hartford, Connecticut, Probate Packets, Humphrey, M-Johnson, H, 1752-1880. case 2273*

2026 See Burleigh, *The Genealogy and History of the Ingalls Family* for additional information.

vi EDMUND INGALLS, b. at Abington, 14 Apr 1814; d. 19 Mar 1835.

vii CHARLES FRANCIS INGALLS, b. at Abington, 18 Jan 1817; d. at Chicago, IL, 2 Jan 1902; m. 1838, SARAH HAWKINS, b. at Reading, VT, 15 Mar 1819 daughter of John Sullivan and Mary (Morrison) Hawkins; Sarah d. at Chicago, 12 Feb 1908.

viii GEORGE "ADDISON" INGALLS, b. at Pomfret, 1 Feb 1820; d. at Cicero, IL, 14 Feb 1884; m. at Cook County, IL, 7 Sep 1847, MARY ELOISE CHURCH, b. at Buffalo, NY, 4 Jan 1831 daughter of Thomas and Rachel (Warriner) Church; Mary d. at Oak Park, IL, 5 Jan 1904.

ix EPHRAIM INGALLS, b. 26 May 1823; d. at Chicago, Dec 1900; m. 30 Apr 1851, MELISSA CHURCH, b. at Buffalo, 24 Mar 1834 daughter of Thomas and Rachel (Warriner) Church; Melissa d. 20 Nov 1888.

746) MOLLY INGALLS *(Ephraim Ingalls[4], Mary Stevens Ingalls[3], Sarah Abbott Stevens[2], George[1])*, b. at Pomfret, 27 Jan 1766 daughter of Ephraim and Mary (Sharp) Ingalls; d. at Dedham, MA, 14 Oct 1859;[2027] m. 1st, MOSES OSGOOD, b. 28 Nov 1766 son of Zachariah and Rachel (Kenne) Osgood; Moses d. about 1801. Molly m. 2nd, at Pomfret, 29 Jun 1803, JOHN WILSON, b. at Dedham, MA, Mar 1750 son of John and Esther (Sabin) Wilson; John d. at Dedham, 28 Sep 1812. John Wilson was first married to Abigail.

In his will written 30 May 1814, Zachariah Osgood (father of Moses) has a bequest to "my late daughter wife and widow of my son Moses deceased now Mrs. Wilson" of sixty dollars. He has bequests to his two granddaughters Polly Osgood and Maria Osgood, daughters of Moses, of five hundred thirty dollars each and one-sixth part of his household furniture.[2028]

Mary Ingalls and Moses Osgood had two daughters born at Woodstock.

i POLLY OSGOOD, b. 25 Jul 1795; d. at Dedham, MA, 18 Jan 1874; m. at Dedham, 18 Sep 1816, her step-brother, JOHN F. WILSON, b. at Dedham, about 1791 son of John and Abigail (-) Wilson; John d. at Dedham, 9 Jul 1853.

ii MARIA OSGOOD, b. 1800; d. at Dedham, 1 Dec 1826. Maria did not marry. In 1817, Maria Osgood of Dedham, daughter of Moses Osgood of Woodstock deceased, selected John Foster Wilson of Dedham as her guardian.[2029] John F. Osgood was administrator of the estate of Maria Osgood single woman of Dedham.

747) EDMUND INGALLS *(Ephraim Ingalls[4], Mary Stevens Ingalls[3], Sarah Abbott Stevens[2], George[1])*, b. at Pomfret, 7 Sep 1770 son of Ephraim and Mary (Sharp) Ingalls; d. at Cavendish, VT, 23 Dec 1850; m. 16 Apr 1801,[2030] DOROTHY WHITE, b. at Westford, MA, 26 Oct 1776 daughter of Samuel and Hephzibah (Barrett) White;[2031] Dorothy d. at Cavendish, 21 Aug 1853 (will 10 Sep 1852).

The will of Edmund Ingalls written 10 October 1850 (probate 7 January 1851) has bequests to his wife Dorothy and his granddaughter Maria D. Fletcher who has resided with him since infancy and who receives $8,000. There is a bequest to beloved niece Mary S. Fletcher widow of Addison Fletcher, and then there are several specific legacies to nieces and nephews and grandnieces.[2032] Addison Fletcher was the husband of Edmund's daughter Maria who died; Addison then married Mary Stevens Ingalls who was also Edmund's niece. In the 1850 Census, the widow Mary Fletcher was living next door to Edmund and Dorothy in Cavendish. In her will written 10 September 1852, Dorothy Ingalls has bequests to the widow Mrs. Mary Fletcher and to nieces and nephews.

Edmund and Dorothy had one child.

i MARIA INGALLS, b. at Pomfret, 20 Dec 1801; d. at Cavendish, VT, 13 May 1823; m. about 1819, ADDISON FLETCHER, b. at Cavendish, 25 Aug 1790 son of Asaph and Sarah (Green) Fletcher; Addison d. at Cavendish, 8 Jan 1832. Addison Fletcher m. 2nd, at Pomfret, CT, 13 Sep 1825, MARY STEVENS INGALLS, b. at Abington, CT, 4 May 1802 daughter of Ephraim and Lucy (Goodell) Ingalls; Mary d. at Cavendish, 30 Jul 1860. Mary Stevens Ingalls is a child in Family 745.

748) LEMUEL INGALLS *(Zebadiah Ingalls[4], Mary Stevens Ingalls[3], Sarah Abbott Stevens[2], George[1])*, b. at Pomfret, 6 Dec 1755 son of Zebadiah and Esther (Goodell) Ingalls; d. at Pomfret, 17 Nov 1839; m. 24 Aug 1780, DOROTHY SUMNER, b. 20 Aug 1759 daughter of Samuel and Dorothy (Williams) Sumner; Dorothy d. 10 Mar 1851.

[2027] The death record of Molly Wilson gives parents names as Ephraim and Mary Ingalls. New England Historic Genealogical Society; Boston, Massachusetts; Massachusetts Vital Records, 1840–1911

[2028] Connecticut. Probate Court (Pomfret District); Probate Place: Windham, Connecticut, Probate Records, Vol 12-14, 1814-1824, volume 13, p 45

[2029] Norfolk County, MA: Probate File Papers, 1793-1877. Online database. AmericanAncestors.org. New England Historic Genealogical Society, 2018. 477-13820

[2030] *Vermont, Vital Records, 1720-1908.*

[2031] Hodgman, *History of the Town of Westford*, p 480

[2032] *Vermont. Probate Court (Windsor District);* Probate Place: *Windsor, Vermont, Probate Files: Hudson, Sarah -- Hawkes, Alexander; Ide, Freeman -- Ives, Phebe*, Probate of Edmund Ingals, 7 Jan 1851

Lemuel Ingalls attended Yale College and was an attorney and Judge of probate court. He also kept a shop where he repaired arms such as swords. Dorothy Ingalls kept silkworms and spun silk which she used to make scarves.[2033]

In his will written 4 August 1828 (probate 2 December 1839), Lemuel Ingalls leaves to his beloved wife all the household furniture, a horse and a cow to be kept for her, chaise and wagon, a place to live in either of his houses as she elects, and a list of specific provisions for her care and support to be provided by his two sons. She also receives an annuity of one hundred sixty dollars to be paid annually during her natural life. All these provisions to his wife are in lieu of her dower. Son Warren Ingals receives the part of the home farm on the north side of the highway, a piece of meadow land, and one-third of the Ashford wood lot that he owns with Ephraim Ingals. Son George S. Ingals receives all the rights to the house and lot where he now lives and land south of the road by the old dwelling house. George also receives from the personal estate an inventory price of two hundred and thirty dollars and is also released from an old claim on book which is $441.67. Daughter Dolly Dresser receives one-half of the lands that he owns jointly with her husband Samuel Dresser and also the land he bought from Benjamin Ingals and Thomas Ingals and all the buildings, as well as one-third of the Ashford wood lot. Dolly is to pay forty-two dollars of her mother's annuity. Daughter Sally Cunningham receives all his rights as mortgagee from Peter Cunningham her husband for lands he occupies. Sally is to pay the same amount of the annuity as Dolly. Sally also receives a portion of the personal estate as long as the claims he has against Peter Cunningham do not exceed one thousand dollars. Daughter Nancy Holt receives all the meadow lot, four acres in Hampton, and inventory from the personal estate of fourteen hundred and twenty-four dollars. Nancy also participates in the annuity to mother. Daughter Elisa Fox receives sixteen hundred twelve dollars in inventory from the personal estate and participates in the annuity. Granddaughter Sarah J. Cunningham receives three hundred dollars to be kept by the executors until she is twenty-one or at marriage. Beloved wife Dolly Ingals and son George S. Ingals are named executors.[2034] Dorothy Ingalls declined being executrix of the estate due to infirmity.

Lemuel and Dorothy Ingalls were parents of seven children born at Pomfret.

i DOROTHY INGALLS, b. 16 Dec 1781; d. 27 Aug 1858; m. at Pomfret, 30 Nov 1806, SAMUEL DRESSER, b. at Pomfret, 31 Jan 1781 son of John and Sarah (Dresser) Dresser; Samuel d. at Abington, 18 Apr 1843.

ii WARREN INGALLS, b. 18 Aug 1783; d. at Pomfret, 18 Jan 1852; m. 1st, at Northborough, 4 May 1813, ELIZABETH FAY, b. at Northborough, MA, 15 Oct 1786 daughter of Abraham and Abigail (Martin) Fay; Elizabeth d. 5 May 1847. Warren m. 2nd, about 1848, HANNAH K. MARCY, b. 17 Dec 1811 daughter of Edward and Abigail (Hayward) Marcy; Hannah d. at Putnam, CT, 8 May 1874.

iii SARAH "SALLY" INGALLS, b. 30 Oct 1786; d. 23 Jun 1856; m. 29 Apr 1807, PETER CUNNINGHAM, b. at Pomfret, 15 Dec 1783 son of Peter and Betsey (Pierpoint) Cunningham; Peter d. at Pomfret, 4 Jun 1871.

iv GEORGE SUMNER INGALLS, b. 13 Nov 1789; d. at Pomfret, 23 Sep 1875; m. 30 Nov 1813, DELIA GOODELL, b. at Pomfret, 11 Mar 1792 daughter of Richard and Mercy (Parkhust) Goodell; Delia d. 12 Jun 1841.

v LEMUEL INGALLS, b. 22 Sep 1793; d. at Mobile, AL, 21 Sep 1819. Lemuel graduated from Yale in 1813 and was an attorney in Mobile. He died of yellow fever.[2035]

vi NANCY INGALLS, b. 23 Nov 1796; d. at Pomfret, 17 Dec 1840; m. at Pomfret, 28 May 1828, CHARLES HOLT, b. at Pomfret, about 1805 son of Oliver and Sidney (Clapp) Holt; Charles d. at Vineland, NJ, 20 Mar 1874.[2036]

vii ELIZA INGALLS, b. 16 Jul 1799; d. at Worcester, MA, 6 Apr 1855; m. at Pomfret, 10 May 1820, WILLIAM BRADLEY FOX, b. at Tolland, 27 Apr 1795 son of Thomas and Chloe (Bradley) Fox; William d. at Worcester, 18 May 1860.

749) JAMES INGALLS *(Zebadiah Ingalls[4], Mary Stevens Ingalls[3], Sarah Abbott Stevens[2], George[1])*, b. at Pomfret, 31 Dec 1760 son of Zebadiah and Esther (Goodell) Ingalls; d. at Middlefield, NY, 19 Mar 1813; m. at Brooklyn, CT, 2 Feb 1786, SARAH WILLIAMS, b. at Pomfret, 12 May 1760 daughter of Thomas and Meriam (Wolcott) Williams; Sarah d. at Middlefield, 27 Jan 1831.

There are three children known for James Ingalls and Sarah Williams all born at Middlefield, New York.

2033 Griggs, *Early Homesteads of Pomfret and Hampton*, p 118

2034 *Connecticut. Probate Court (Pomfret District)*; Probate Place: *Windham, Connecticut, Probate Records, Vol 19-20, 1838-1857*, Volume 19, pp 94-97, will of Lemuel Ingals

2035 Biographical Sketches of the Graduates of Yale College, Volume VI 1812-13, p 577

2036 New Jersey, Deaths and Burials Index, 1798-1971

i MARY ANN INGALLS, b. about 1787; d. likely at Middlefield, after 1855 (she was living with her sister Sarah in 1855). Mary Ann did not marry.

ii ERASTUS WOLCOTT INGALLS, b. about 1790; d. at Middlefield, 20 Jul 1816; m. at Burlington, NY, 16 Apr 1816, FANNY GOODSELL, b. in CT, about 1794 daughter of Peter[2037] and Elizabeth Ruth (Morehouse) Goodsell; Fanny d. at Lincoln, IL, about 1872 (probate 14 Jul 1872). After Erastus's death, Fanny married William Eager Dec 1817.

iii SARAH WILLIAMS INGALLS, b. about 1803; d. at Middlefield, 26 May 1869; m. at Middlefield, 21 Dec 1824, WILLIAM AMES WALKER, b. at Middlefield, 1797 son of Hinckley and Sarah (Fling) Walker; William d. at Middlefield (Cooperstown), 10 Sep 1852 (probate 27 Oct 1852).

750) MARY "MOLLY" INGALLS *(Zebadiah Ingalls[4], Mary Stevens Ingalls[3], Sarah Abbott Stevens[2], George[1])*, b. at Pomfret, 31 Jul 1768 daughter of Zebadiah and Esther (Goodell) Ingalls; d. at Danielson, CT, 21 Apr 1839; m. 2 Dec 1790, ELEAZER WILLIAMS, b. at Pomfret, 29 Nov 1764 son of Samuel and Susannah (Danielson) Williams; Eleazer d. at Danielson, 16 Sep 1841.

Molly Ingalls and Eleazer Williams were parents of ten children all born at Killingly, Connecticut.

i SUSANNA WILLIAMS, b. 18 Sep 1791; d. at Killingly, 11 Jul 1859. Susanna did not marry. In her will, she left her entire estate to her sister Alice H. Williams.

ii MARY WILLIAMS, b. 6 May 1793; d. at Killingly, 1 Nov 1861; m. 28 Apr 1818, JOSHUA PHIPPS WILLIAMS, b. at Brooklyn, CT, 6 Dec 1794 son of John and Susan (Farrington) Williams; Joshua d. at Brooklyn, CT, 3 Nov 1828.

iii GEORGE WILLIAMS, b. 29 Apr 1795; d. at Killingly, 14 Nov 1868; m. at Pomfret, 23 Apr 1822, MARY SHARPE, b. at Pomfret, 15 Mar 1804 daughter of Walter and Mary (Farrington) Sharpe; Mary d. after 1860.

iv ALICE H. WILLIAMS, b. 12 Apr 1797; d. at Killingly, 6 Aug 1878. Alice did not marry.

v SARAH WILLIAMS, b. 7 Mat 1799; d. at Woodstock, 7 May 1868; m. 19 May 1840, as his fourth wife, MOSES LYON, b. at Woodstock, 11 Sep 1793 son of William and Mary (Stone) Lyon; Moses d. at Woodstock, 5 Aug 1865. Moses's other marriages were to Tryphena Kendall, Sally Ann May, and Dolly May.

vi ALETHEA WILLIAMS, b. 21 Apr 1801; d. at Killingly, 16 Aug 1863. Alethea did not marry.

vii JARED WILLIAMS, b. 28 Sep 1803; d. at Pomfret, 15 Nov 1877; m. at Grafton, MA, 25 Dec 1838, SUSAN GODDARD BROWN, b. at Grafton, 11 Jul 1809 daughter of Clark and Sarah (Sherman) Brown; Susan d. 2 Oct 1888.

viii LEWIS WILLIAMS, b. 19 Nov 1805; d. at Killingly, 25 Dec 1851; m. ROXA P. BENNETT, b. at Foster, RI, about 1814 daughter of George and Azuba (-) Bennett; Roxa d. at Providence, 7 Sep 1872.[2038]

ix ESTHER WILLIAMS, b. 12 Oct 1807; d. at Killingly, 4 Feb 1888; m. 22 Oct 1833, SAMUEL SANFORD DANIELSON, b. at Killingly, 1809 son of Samuel and Sarah (Begg) Danielson; Samuel d. at Killingly, 11 May 1864.

x DAVID WILLIAMS, b. 23 Apr 1810; d. at Coventry, 7 Jun 1884; m. 1st, 12 Mar 1832, LUCINDA HYDE, b. at Killingly, 17 Feb 1806 daughter of Samuel and Ann (-) Hyde; Lucinda d. 31 Jul 1838. David m. 2nd, 17 Mar 1839, CAROLINE CHAMBERLAIN, b. in CT, about 1819; Caroline d. at Willington, 1850. David m. 3rd, 9 Mar 1851, FANNY BIRCH, b. at Middle, Shropshire, 2 Apr 1824 daughter of Thomas and Fanny (-) Birch; Fanny d. likely at Coventry, 7 Jun 1892.

751) OLIVER INGALLS *(Zebadiah Ingalls[4], Mary Stevens Ingalls[3], Sarah Abbott Stevens[2], George[1])*, b. at Pomfret, 7 Apr 1770 son of Zebadiah and Esther (Goodell) Ingalls; d. at Pomfret, 10 Apr 1815; m. Dec 1803, his niece,[2039] BETSEY ABBOTT *(Stephen[5], Nathan[4], Paul[3], William[2], George[1])*, b. likely at Providence, 4 May 1786 daughter of Stephen and Esther (Ingalls) Abbott; Betsey d. 17 Feb 1839 (will written at Providence, RI, 7 Feb 1839).

Oliver Ingalls was a farmer in Pomfret and is reported to have died by drowning.[2040]

2037 *10,000 Vital Records of Eastern New York, 1777-1834*, Genealogical Publishing Co.; Baltimore, Maryland

2038 In her 1872 will, Roxa Williams had bequests for her brothers Emery S. David H. and George W. Bennet and it can be established through guardianship records that Emery, David, and George were the sons of George and Azuba Bennet.

2039 Although the relationship between Betsey and her husband is unusual, it seems to be true. Betsey Abbott Ingalls's gravestone (buried in Swan Point Cemetery in Providence) includes an inscription that she is the wife of Oliver and the daughter of Colonel Stephen Abbott and this makes Betsey the niece of her husband Oliver Ingalls. Oliver Ingalls was the brother of Esther Ingalls who married Colonel Stephen Abbott.

2040 Burleigh, *Genealogy and History of the Ingalls Family*, p 128

Captain Oliver Ingalls did not leave a will. The bond for estate was agreed to on 2 May 1815.[2041] Widow Betsey Ingalls declined the administration of the estate. The probate records include many receipts related to notes owed by the estate for goods received (in the range of one dollar to one hundred dollars) by Oliver Ingalls in the years 1812 through January 1815 and one of these is signed also by Betsey Ingalls. The estate includes a grist mill valued at $1,800 and the total value of the estate was $3,764.33.

Betsey Abbot Ingalls wrote her will 7 February 1839.[2042] She bequeaths to her only daughter, Esther A. Ingalls, the estate on which Betsey now lives including the lot and dwelling house which lies on the westerly side of Stewart Street in Providence. Betsey goes on to specify the date of the deed and where the deed is recorded. This bequest is conditioned on Esther paying the debts and funeral charges and she is also to pay one-third of the annual revenue of the estate to Betsey's mother Mrs. Esther Abbot as long as the mother is living. After the death of daughter Esther, the estate is to be divided between sons William and Zebadiah, but Esther will have the right to sell any of the property during her lifetime. Son Zebadiah Ingalls is named sole executor.

Oliver and Betsey Ingalls had five children whose births are variously reported as Providence or Pomfret, so it is not certain where each of the children was born.

i GERARD INGALLS, b. 1804 location not certain; d. at Pomfret, 2 Jul 1812.

ii ESTHER A. INGALLS, b. 9 Jun 1807 in Rhode Island; d. at Providence, 28 Apr 1880.[2043] Esther did not marry.

iii JAMES INGALLS, b. 13 Mar 1809; d. likely in Rhode Island, 20 Apr 1828.[2044]

iv WILLIAM INGALLS, b. likely at Pomfret, 25 Feb 1811; d. at Brooklyn, NY, 26 Oct 1890. William did not marry. He lived with the family of his brother Zebadiah in Brooklyn and was employed as a shipping merchant. His estate was probated in 1890 with F. Abbott Ingalls as administrator. The value of the estate was under $1,000. The heirs identified were the children of his brother Zebadiah: Mary E. Ingalls, Charles H, Ingalls, Annie A. Ingalls, William B. B. Ingalls, F. Abbott Ingalls, and Sally A, Ingalls who are all living in Brooklyn. All the nieces and nephews, except Charles, are living at 107 State Street in Brooklyn.[2045]

v ZEBADIAH INGALLS, b. 16 Sep 1813; d. at Brooklyn, 1 Sep 1884; m. 16 Dec 1839, LUCY LIPPITT ARNOLD, b. at Warwick, RI, 2 Oct 1811 daughter of Benedict and Mary (Greene) Arnold; Lucy d. at Brooklyn, 19 Mar 1848. Zebadiah m. 2nd, 17 Feb 1852, HANNAH BOWERS BOURN (also known as Annie B.),[2046] b. Jul 1821 daughter of Francis and Mary (Bowers) Bourn; Hannah d. at Brooklyn about 1901 (living at the 1900 census and probate at Brooklyn in 1901). Zebadiah was a dry goods merchant in Brooklyn.

752) NATHANIEL ROGERS *(Abiah Ingalls Rogers[4], Mary Stevens Ingalls[3], Sarah Abbott Stevens[2], George[1])*, b. at Pomfret, 18 Nov 1755 son of Nathaniel and Abiah (Ingalls) Rogers; d. at Salem, CT, 12 Feb 1799; m. at Lyme, 23 Sep 1782, SARAH TUBBS, b. at Colchester, 1755 daughter of Alpheus Tubbs; Sarah d. likely at Harrisville, OH, about 1842.[2047]

Nathaniel Rogers was commissioned as an ensign in Captain Howell's company of the 2nd Battalion of Suffolk County, New York. He is reported to have suffered much in the war due to harsh conditions that injured his health and he died at age thirty-eight.[2048] After the death of Nathaniel, Sarah supported the family and took the family to Chenango County, New York in 1808. She and her children then relocated to Ohio, first in the area of Cleveland before finally settling in Medina County, Ohio.[2049]

Guardianship cases for the children 20 April 1807 have Matthew G. Rogers, age 18, selecting Abel Bobiah; Clarissa age 15 selecting Samuel Rathbone; and Grace, Isaac about 13, Nathaniel about 11, and Perez, about 9 had widow Sarah Rogers as guardian.[2050]

Nathaniel and Sarah were parents of eight children born at New London, Connecticut.

[2041] *Connecticut Wills and Probate, 1609-1999*, Probate of Oliver Ingalls, Pomfret, 1815, Case number 2285.

[2042] Providence, Rhode Island wills (1678-1916) and indexes (1872-1914), Author: Providence Court of Probate; wills and index volume 14-15, 1836-1848, will of Betsey Ingalls, 7 Feb 1839.

[2043] Web: Rhode Island, Historical Cemetery Commission Index, 1647-2008

[2044] Rhode Island, Vital Extracts, 1636-1899

[2045] New York, Kings County, Probate Administration Records. Probate Place: Kings, New York; Administration Records Without Wills, Ernest Bohde to Richard H. Brown (1890).

[2046] In her will written 20 May 1894, Hannah B. Ingalls gives her name as Hannah but adds she is also known as Annie B. Ingalls.

[2047] Rogers, *James Rogers of New London, Ct.*, p 120

[2048] Rogers, *James Rogers of New London, Ct.*, p 121

[2049] Wickham, *Memorial to the Pioneer Women of the Western Reserve*, volume I, p 299

[2050] Rogers, *James Rogers of New London, Ct.*, p 121

i WILLIAM T. ROGERS, b. about 1783; d. at Crawford, OH, 1861; m. in NY, about 1818, LYDIA M. BECKWITH, b. in CT, about 1793; Lydia d. at Crawford, 1859.

ii SALLY ROGERS, b. about 1787; d. likely at Bridgeport, IL, after 1860; m. about 1808, ELISHA D. BISHOP, b. at Lyme, CT, 2 Oct 1783 son of Abraham and Patience (Downing) Bishop; Elisha d. at Bridgeport, 16 Aug 1863. Sally and Elisha were in Medina County, Ohio but moved on to Illinois after 1850.

iii MATTHEW GRISWOLD ROGERS, b. 5 Feb 1789; d. at Woodstock, IL, 8 Nov 1873; m. about 184, HULDAH GILBERT, b. at Greene, NY, 28 May 1800 daughter of David Y. and Anna (Holford) Gilbert;[2051] Huldah d. at Woodstock, 3 Mar 1873.

iv CLARISSA ROGERS, b. about 1792; d. at Spencer, OH, after 1840; m. 1st, about 1810, Captain WILLIAM JOHNSON who d. about 1812 when his ship was lost. Clarissa m. 2nd, in NY, about 1813, JOHN P. MARSH, b. in VT, about 1785 son of John and Sarah (Perkins) Marsh;[2052] John d. at Spencer, after 1840 (John P. Marsh age 50-59 is head of household in 1840).[2053]

v GRACE ROGERS, about 1794; living in 1807; nothing further known.

vi ISAAC ROGERS, b. 3 Feb 1794; d. at Harrisville, OH, Feb 1861; m. about 1820, ANNA BRAINERD, b. at Rodman, NY, 8 Apr 1801 daughter of Ansel and Mary (Warren) Brainerd; Anna d. at Harrisville, 30 Oct 1847.

vii NATHANIEL ROGERS, b. about 1796; d. at Lodi, OH, 17 Oct 1851; m. at Medina County, 29 Jan 1821, HARRIET YOUNG, b. about 1800; Harriet d. before 1850 (when Nathaniel was living with his sister Sally and Harriet was not in the household).

viii PEREZ ROGERS, b. 1798; d. at Harrisville, 1 Sep 1835; m. at Medina County, 14 Jun 1827, POLLY PHELPS, b. at Jefferson County, NY, 22 Jan 1811 daughter of Roger and Cynthia (Lee) Phelps;[2054] Polly d. after 1870.

753) ABISHAI ROGERS *(Abiah Ingalls Rogers⁴, Mary Stevens Ingalls³, Sarah Abbott Stevens², George¹)*, b. at Monson, 1 Feb 1762 son of Nathaniel and Abiah (Ingalls) Rogers; d. at Sheldon, NY, 18 Jul 1831; m. 1st, Feb 1786, SARAH HAWKS, b. at Deerfield, MA, 1764 daughter of Gershom and Thankful (Corse) Hawks; Sarah d. at Hawley, 1790. Abishai m. 2nd, 15 Mar 1792, ELIZABETH RUDD, b. 28 Jun 1765 daughter of Nathaniel and Alice (Kingsley) Rudd; Elizabeth d. at Sheldon, NY, 18 Jun 1848.

Abishai served in the Revolution as a private for three enlistments: for about six weeks in June 1778, in Captain Shaw's Company from 22 July 1779 to 27 August 1779, in Captain Browning's Company from 26 August 1780 to 10 October 1780, and again in Captain Browning's Company from 20 August 1781 to 20 November 1781. His widow Elizabeth received a pension based on his service.[2055]

Abishai Rogers and Sarah Hawks were parents of three children born at Hawley.

i CYNTHIA ROGERS, b. 2 Sep 1786; d. 14 Aug 1802.

ii ABIAH ROGERS, b. 22 Aug 1788

iii SALLY ROGERS, b. 22 Nov 1790; d. 27 Jul 1808.

Abishai Rogers and Elizabeth Rudd were parents of nine children born at Hawley. Only two marriages were located for these children.

i DOLLY ROGERS, b. 15 Mar 1793; d. 13 Aug 1802.

ii ELLIS ROGERS, b. 8 Feb 1795

iii NATHANIEL ROGERS, b. 29 Jan 1797; d. at Franklinville, NY, 16 Jun 1869; m. at Hawley, 29 Oct 1825, LUCRETIA CRITTENDEN, b. at Hawley, 8 Oct 1797 daughter of Simeon and Lucretia (Chilson) Crittenden; Lucretia d. 4 Feb 1878.

2051 Rogers, *James Rogers of New London, Ct.*, p 187

2052 Wickham, *Memorial to the Pioneer Women of the Western Reserve*, volume I, p 299. This parentage is not verified.

2053 The information on Clarissa's marriages is a morass of conflicting information. The Rogers genealogy (based on information from Clarissa's nephew) is that she married Captain William Johnson in Connecticut (having stayed behind when the rest of the family went to Chenango County) and that Captain Johnson was lost at sea in 1812. She does seem to be the Clarissa that married John P. Marsh and then lived in Medina County (Wickham's *Pioneer Women* and Perrin's *History of Medina County*).

2054 Perrin, *History of Medina County*, p 873

2055 Revolutionary War Pension and Bounty-Land Warrant Application Files, Case W20031

iv BETSY ROGERS, b. 22 Apr 1799; d. at Hawley, 15 Mar 1882; m. 30 Mar 1826, ATHERTON HUNT, b. at Hawley, 29 May 1804 son of Elisha and Charity (Row) Hunt; Atherton d. at Hawley, 5 Jul 1888.

v ELIAS ROGERS, b. 10 Feb 1801; d. 29 Aug 1802.

vi SIMEON ROGERS, b. 23 Apr 1803

vii ELECTA ROGERS, b. 26 Sep 1806

viii MOSES ROGERS, b. 12 Apr 1809

ix SARAH H. ROGERS, b. 7 Feb 1811

754) SIMEON ROGERS *(Abiah Ingalls Rogers[4], Mary Stevens Ingalls[3], Sarah Abbott Stevens[2], George[1])*, b. at Monson, 1 Feb 1762 son of Nathaniel and Abiah (Ingalls) Rogers; d. at Whitestown, NY, 18 Jun 1848; m. by 1783, ANNA (-), b. 1765 and d. 1849.[2056]

Simeon Rogers served in the Revolution first entering from Munson in August 1777 as a substitute for Josiah Keep who had been drafted. He was a private in Captain Winchester's company of militia. He was at Bennington and later at White Plains under General Warner He has a second enlistment as a volunteer in 1779 as a volunteer and a third enlistment in 1781.[2057] Following the war, he was in Brimfield for six years, then in Putney. Vermont for about two years and was in Whitestown, New York in 1787 where he settled. Simeon applied for a pension in 1832 and age 70 and a pension was granted.

There are just two children known for Simeon and Anna.

i SIMEON ROGERS, b. likely at Brimfield, 1783; d. at New Hartford, NY, 1877; m. BETSEY LEWIS, b. about 1793; Betsey d. at New Hartford, 1869.

ii ARAUNAH ROGERS, b. at Whitestown, 1794; d. at Vernon, NY, 1875, m. at Belchertown, MA, 7 Nov 1822, SUSANNAH BUGBEE, b. 1804; Susannah d. at Vernon, NY, 2 Oct 1892.

755) JAMES AUGUSTUS ROGERS *(Abiah Ingalls Rogers[4], Mary Stevens Ingalls[3], Sarah Abbott Stevens[2], George[1])*, b. at Monson, 2 May 1765 son of Nathaniel and Abiah (Ingalls) Rogers; d. at Rockport, OH, 5 Aug 1837; m. 17 Nov 1790, DOROTHY LEONARD, b. at Rutland, MA, 6 Apr 1759 daughter of Andrew and Hannah (Pierce) Leonard; Dorothy d. at Pownal, VT, 5 Jun 1796. James m. 2nd, JEMIMA ROOT, b. 1769; Jemima d. at Rockport, OH, 6 Nov 1837.

James and his first wife Dorothy had their children at Charlemont, Massachusetts, moved to Pownal, Vermont where Dorothy died soon after. James and his second wife Jemima were in Fabius, New York where four children were born, and then moved again to Rockport, Ohio. James Augusts Rogers and Dorothy Leonard were parents of three children born at Charlemont.

i JAMES INGALS ROGERS, b. 24 Nov 1791; d. at Eaton Rapids, MI, 26 Sep 1886; m. SEVINA LOWELL, b. in VT, 2 Feb 1799 daughter of Timothy and Olive (Carleton) Lowell; Sevina d. at Eaton Rapids, 24 Jan 1876.

ii ELIAS ROGERS, b. 13 Jul 1793; d. at Arcade, NY, 24 Jun 1863; m. ABIGAIL, b. in NY, about 1803 who has not been identified.

iii CALVIN ROGERS, b. 5 Jun 1795; d. at Strykersville, NY, 5 Mar 1890; m. 1818, EMILY HOTCHKISS, b. 1800 daughter of Salma and Rebecca (Hall) Hotchkiss; Emily d. at Strykersville, 12 May 1878.

James Rogers and Jemima Root were parents of four children likely all born at Fabius, New York.[2058]

i ALBERT ROGERS, b. 1798; d. at Vergennes, MI, Dec 1859; m. POLLY BOYNTON, b. at Cornwall, VT, 10 Aug 1806 daughter of John and Mary (Lamb) Boynton; Polly d. after 1850.

ii ORRIN ROGERS, b. 30 Aug 1800; d. at Eaton Rapids, MI, 27 Oct 1869; m. ELSIE BEEDLE, *possibly* b. in NY, 23 Aug 1806 daughter of Robert and Susanna (Chapin) Beedle; Elsie d. at Eaton Rapids, 8 Feb 1890.

iii ANSEL ROGERS, b. 16 Sep 1806; d. at Solon, MI, Apr 1865; m. ELSIE ANN WHITE, b. at Orangeville, NY, 26 Dec 1813 daughter of Philip and Mary (Gorton) White; Elsie d. at Solon, 7 Feb 1853.

2056 Information from SAR

2057 Revolutionary War Pension and Bounty-Land Warrant Application Files, Case S14336

2058 There may be other children for James and Jemima, but no definitive information was located.

iv MARY ELIZA ROGERS, b. 1809; d. at Rockport, OH, 1888; m. SOLOMON PEASE, b. 1803 *possibly* son of Gideon and Hannah (Rood) Pease; Solomon d. at Rockport, 14 Nov 1845.

756) DEBORAH ROGERS *(Abiah Ingalls Rogers⁴, Mary Stevens Ingalls³, Sarah Abbott Stevens², George¹)*, b. about 1767 daughter of Nathaniel and Abiah (Ingalls) Rogers; m. about 1790, her third cousin once removed, WILLIAM FARNSWORTH *(Hephzibah Chandler Farnsworth⁵, Abial Chandler Chandler⁴, Abiel Chandler³, Hannah Abbott Chandler², George¹)*, b. 15 Nov 1766 son of William and Hephzibah (Chandler) Farnsworth. William Farnsworth is a child in Family 448.

Deborah and William had their children in Hawley and then relocated to Madison County, New York.

Deborah Rogers and William Farnsworth were parents of twelve children born at Hawley, Massachusetts.

i OREN ROGERS FARNSWORTH, b. 21 Aug 1791; d. at Waterloo, NY, about 1848; m. 1st, 1813, MARY "POLLY" PORTER, b. at Hatfield, MA, 1793 daughter of Silas and Mary (Graves) Porter;[2059][2060] Polly d. at Waterloo, NY, 1816. Oren m. 2nd, about 1817, LUCINDA DOPKINS, b. in NY, 1800; Lucinda d. at Waterloo, 1870.

ii TIRZAH FARNSWORTH, b. 20 Mar 1793; d. at Greenville, IN, 24 Jun 1853; m. at Hawley, 28 Oct 1813, RUFUS BLOSSOM, b. at Middlefield, MA, 6 Jun 1789 son of Thomas and Mercy (Sears) Blossom; Rufus d. at St. Louis, MO, 7 Sep 1872.

iii CALVIN FARNSWORTH, b. 16 Oct 1794; d. at Orleans, IA, after 1860. Calvin did marry and had at least eight children, but the name of his wife has not been found.

iv SOPHIA C. FARNSWORTH, b. 22 Jul 1796; d. at Rockford, IL, Aug 1869; m. 11 Mar 1819, WILLIAM M. ADAMS, b. 28 Dec 1788; William d. at Mineral Point, WI, 12 Mar 1842.[2061]

v MARSHALL LOOK FARNSWORTH, b. 12 Mar 1798; d. 27 Nov 1838; m. at Danby, NY, 20 Jun 1830, JOANNA BLAKE GOSMAN, b. at Kingston, NY, 3 May 1813 daughter of Jonathan B. and Jane (van Gassbeck) Gosman; Joanna d. at Menands, NY, 9 Jan 1907. Joanna was second married to James O. Towner.

vi JAMES INGALLS FARNSWORTH, b. 15 Mar 1800; d. at Madison, NY, Sep 1832 (probate 1 Oct 1832). James did not marry.

vii CHARLES FARNSWORTH, b. 18 Feb 1802; d. at Somerset, MI, 1851; m. ANN ELIZABETH BUSH, b. in NY, 1804.

viii WILLIAM W. FARNSWORTH, b. 28 Jan 1804

ix DEBORAH FARNSWORTH, b. 28 Oct 1806; d. likely at St. Louis, after 1860; m. at Geauga, OH, 11 Nov 1832, ANDREW ARBUCKLE, b. about 1796; Andrew d. at Painesville, OH, 21 May 1835.

x ELIZA HAWKS FARNSWORTH, b. 14 Oct 1808. Eliza perhaps married Mr. Hall but that has not been verified.

xi THOMAS SWIFT FARNSWORTH, b. 30 Oct 1810; d. at Albany, NY, 1845; m. at Glenn Falls, 1842, MARY WING, b. at Glenn Falls, 2 Dec 1824 daughter of Abraham and Abigail (Bernard) Wing;[2062] Mary d. at Jackson, MI, 10 Jun 1892. Mary married second Dwight Merriman.

xii SARAH MARIA FARNSWORTH, b. 2 Aug 1813

757) OREN ROGERS *(Abiah Ingalls Rogers⁴, Mary Stevens Ingalls³, Sarah Abbott Stevens², George¹)*, b. at Monson about 1770 son of Nathaniel and Abiah (Ingalls) Rogers; d. at Charlemont, MA, 15 Oct 1853; m. 23 Mar 1797, ABY BIRGE, b. at Deerfield, 22 Aug 1774 daughter of John and Esther (Pierce) Birge; Aby d. after 1850.

There are records for nine children of Oren and Aby born at Charlemont.

i CEPHAS ROGERS, b. 19 Jul 1797; d. at Charlemont, 10 Nov 1878; m. at Dedham, 24 Oct 1819, ELECTA BERREL GLEASON, of Dedham, b. about 1798; Electa d. at Charlemont, 6 Mar 1871.

ii ESTHER ROGERS, b. 3 Jun 1799; d. at Charlemont, 12 Sep 1859. Esther did not marry.

iii ABI ROGERS, b. 5 Jul 1801; d. at Charlemont, 9 Feb 1855. Abi did not marry.

iv SYLVIA ROGERS, b. 11 Aug 1804; d. at Charlemont, 14 Aug 1833. Sylvia did not marry.

2059 The 1837 will if Silas Porter includes a bequest to his granddaughter child of his daughter Polly Farnsworth who is deceased.

2060 Porter, *The Descendants of John Porter of Windsor, CT*, volume I, p 241

2061 Carr, *History of Rockton, Winnebago County*, p 165

2062 Fairbanks, *Emma Willard and Her Pupils*, p 256

v OREN H. ROGERS, b. 1 Dec 1806; d. at Troy, NY, about 1856; m. MARIETTA before 1844; Marietta d. likely at Troy after 1870 (she was living there with some of her children in the 1870 census).

vi JOHN BIRGE ROGERS, b. 14 Dec 1808; d. at Charlemont, 4 Jan 1877. John did not marry.

vii BOHAN B. ROGERS, b. 7 Aug 1811; d. 14 Aug 1835.

viii HANNAH ROGERS, b. 27 Aug 1813; d. at Charlemont, 18 Nov 1877; m. 26 Feb 1846, ABRAHAM VAN NESS, b. at Stuyvesant, NY, about 1813 son of Jesse and Maria (-) Van Ness;[2063] Abraham d. at Stuyvesant, 1851 (probate 29 Apr 1851).

ix JAMES MOSES ROGERS, b. 11 Nov 1815; d. at Pittsfield, MA, 10 Nov 1863; m. by 1837, SARAH DANIELS, b. at Troy, NY, about 1818 daughter of Ebenezer and Martha (Mann) Daniels; Sarah d. at Pittsfield, 22 Oct 1895.

758) MOSES ROGERS *(Abiah Ingalls Rogers[4], Mary Stevens Ingalls[3], Sarah Abbott Stevens[2], George[1])* b. about 1772 a likely son of Nathaniel and Abiah (Ingalls) Rogers; d. at Hawley, 1 Feb 1808; m. at Ashfield, 15 Feb 1800, MEHITABLE SEARS, b. at Ashfield, 21 Dec 1778 daughter of Rowland and Jedidah (Conant) Sears.[2064][2065]

Moses Rogers was a mill keeper in Hawley, MA and died when he was crushed by the wheel when trying to remove ice from the wheel.[2066] Moses Rogers did not leave a will and the estate entered probate 5 May 1808 with widow Mehitable as administratrix.[2067] Mehitable was allowed guardian for minor children under age 14: Almira, Ahira, Elias, and Polly. Real estate was valued at $975 and personal estate, $380.05.

Moses and Mehitable were parents of four children born at Hawley.

i ALMIRA ROGERS b. 11 Mar 1801; d. at Charlemont, 10 Jan 1892; m. 27 Oct 1823, ALLEN BARNARD, b. at Shelburne, MA, 4 Jan 1790 son of David and Rhoda (Allen) Barnard; Allen d. at Charlemont, 16 Sep 1876. Allen was first married to Lucy Severance.

ii AHIRA ROGERS, b. 14 Jun 1803; d. at Ithaca, NY, 11 Apr 1859; m. by 1830, MANDANA CHAPIN, b. 12 Nov 1806 likely the daughter of John and Lydia (Wedge) Chapin; Mandana d. 13 Jul 1866 (in 1865 living in Auburn, NY with her daughter).

iii ELIAS ROGERS, b. Aug 1805; d. at Ashfield, MA, 7 May 1879; m. 1832, SARAH CRANSTON, b. at Ashfield, 26 Jul 1807 daughter of Ebenezer and Abigail (Bryant) Cranston; Sarah d. at Ashfield, 24 Apr 1887.

iv POLLY ROGERS, b. 24 Sep 1807; nothing further known.

764) EUNICE CARLETON *(Samuel Carleton[4], Deborah Stevens Carleton[3], Sarah Abbott Stevens[2], George[1])*, b. at Salem, 22 Dec 1754 daughter of Samuel and Eunice (Hunt) Carleton; d. at Salem, Mar 1838; m. 23 Dec 1779, JAMES BARR, b. at Salem, 1755 son of James and Mary (Ropes) Barr; James d. 19 Jan 1848.

James Barr was a merchant in Salem where the family lived on Lynde Street. He was wealthy for the day leaving a personal estate valued at $46,937.07, much of that in investments, and real property valued at $3,800.

In his will written 4 June 1832 (probate 15 February 1848), James Barr bequeaths to beloved and affectionate wife Eunice the use and improvement of all the estate, real, personal, and mixed, during her natural life. If that is not sufficient to support her as she is accustomed, she is to receive from the capital of the estate what is necessary. After the death of Eunice, grandson Samuel George Rea will receive one thousand dollars and two shares in East India Marine. After the death of Eunice, unmarried daughters Eunice Barr and Nancy Barr will receive the use and improvement of the mansion house on Lynde Street, the land and outbuildings, and the household furniture. If either of his two other daughters come into destitute circumstances, then they will share equally with Eunice and Nancy in the household as long as they remain in destitute condition. After the deaths of daughters Eunice and Nancy, then the household items are to be divided in thirds among Sarah Rea, Priscilla Curwen, and to the children (Betsey Holman and Mary Holman) of daughter Betsey Holman who is deceased. Daughters Eunice and Nancy also receive use of pew no. 38 in St. Peter's Church in Salem. All the remainder of the estate is to be divided in equal

[2063] Parents' names and place of birth are given on transcription of marriage record.

[2064] The 1815 will of Rowland Sears includes a bequest to his daughter Mehitable Rodgers.

[2065] It is possible that Mehitable was the widow Mehitable Rogers of Hawley who married Elijah Luce in 1826. If so, she died in 1850 at age 71 (although the age is off by a month from what is should be); however, the death record for that Mehitable Luce gives the names of parents as Charles and Lydia Sears.

[2066] Atkins, *History of the Town of Hawley*, p 34

[2067] Hampshire County, MA: Probate File Papers, 1660-1889. Online database. AmericanAncestors.org. New England Historic Genealogical Society, 2016, 2017. Case 124-16

fifths among his four living daughters and one-fifth to the children of Betsey.[2068] Eunice Carleton Barr died in 1838 between the time of the will and the probate. In a codicil date 23 March 1838, James Barr named sons-in-law Samuel Rea and Jonathan Holman co-executors. Another codicil was made in 1842 after the death of his daughter Nancy Barr distributing her portion to grandchildren.

Eunice Carleton and James Barr were parents of eight children born at Salem.

i EUNICE BARR, b. 18 Feb 1781; d. at Salem, 9 Mar 1868. Eunice did not marry.

ii SARAH BARR, b. 3 Jul 1782; d. at Salem, 17 Nov 1862; m. 30 Aug 1807, SAMUEL REA, b. 3 Feb 1782 son of Archelaus and Mary (Cook) Rea; Samuel d. at Salem, 1 Oct 1842.

iii MARY BARR, b. 11 May 1784; d. at Salem, 22 Dec 1815; m. 5 Dec 1811, GEORGE C. SMITH. Mary and George do not seem to have had children.

iv BETSEY BARR, b. 18 Feb 1786; d. at Salem, 30 Dec 1827; m. 9 Nov 1815, JONATHAN HOLMAN, b. at Salem, 9 Feb 1785 son of Gabriel and Lydia (Mansfield) Holman; Jonathan d. at Salem, about 1855 (probate 1855). After Betsey's death, Jonathan married Sarah Barr daughter of John and Sarah (Pierce) Barr.

v PRISCILLA BARR, b. 31 Mar 1788; d. at Salem, 30 Nov 1863; m. 22 Mar 1818, SAMUEL CURWEN, b. at Salem, 26 Nov 1795 son of Samuel and Jane (Ward) Curwen; Samuel d. at Salem, 1833.

vi HANNAH BARR, b. 2 Jan 1791; d. 26 Nov 1809.

vii NANCY BARR, b. 31 Aug 1793; d. at Salem, 27 Jul 1842. Nancy did not marry.

viii JAMES BARR, b. 14 Jun 1799; d. 24 Aug 1800.

765) DEBORAH CARLETON *(Samuel Carleton[4], Deborah Stevens Carleton[3], Sarah Abbott Stevens[2], George[1])*, b. at Salem, 17 Dec 1759 daughter of Samuel and Eunice (Hunt) Carleton; d. at Salem, Apr 1831; m. 5 Oct 1783, HUGH HELME whose origins are unknown; Hugh d. 1792 (probate of estate 14 July 1792).

Hugh Helme was a mariner. He served for a time on the "Oliver Cromwell" with the rank of lieutenant as first mate.[2069] Later, he co-owned with Nathaniel Richardson the ship "Success." Captain Hugh Helme was the ship's master.[2070]

Deborah and Hugh Helme had two children, one of whom died in infancy and their daughter died at age 38 without marrying.

Hugh Helme's estate entered probate 14 July 1792. He did not leave a will. In her will, Deborah Helme made a bequest of $200 to her sister Hannah Carleton, $200 to sister Elizabeth Carleton, and all the remainder of her estate to John H. Andrews, a merchant of Salem. John H. Andrews was also named executor of the estate.

i THOMAS HELME, b. 1785; d. 4 Oct 1786.

ii DEBORAH HELME, b. 1792 (baptized 19 Aug 1792); d. at Salem of consumption, 29 Sep 1829.

766) BENJAMIN CARLETON *(Samuel Carleton[4], Deborah Stevens Carleton[3], Sarah Abbott Stevens[2], George[1])*, b. at Salem, 5 Jun 1765 son of Samuel and Eunice (Hunt) Carleton; d. 8 Sep 1820; m. 25 Mar 1787, his first cousin, ELIZABETH HOLMAN, b. 1762 daughter of Samuel and Ruth (Hunt) Holman; Elizabeth d. 25 Dec 1801.

In contrast to his sisters Eunice and Deborah, Benjamin Carleton lived in poor circumstances and died of consumption at the workhouse in Salem.[2071] Benjamin Carleton and Elizabeth Holman were parents of two children born at Salem.

i SAMUEL CARLETON, b. 6 Feb 1796; d. at Salem, 7 Oct 1839; m. 20 Sep 1818, FANNY ASHBY, b. at Salem, 24 Apr 1799 daughter of John Ashby; Fanny d. at Peabody, MA, 13 Sep 1884.

ii ELIZABETH CARLETON, b. 4 Nov 1798; d. at Salem, 22 Feb 1883. Elizabeth did not marry.

767) BENJAMIN CROWNINSHIELD *(Hannah Carleton Crowninshield[4], Deborah Stevens Carleton[3], Sarah Abbott Stevens[2], George[1])*, b. at Salem, 15 Feb 1758 son of Jacob and Hannah (Carleton) Crowninshield; d. at Charlestown, 22 Nov 1836; m. 9 Nov 1780, MARY LAMBERT, b. at Salem, Nov 1760 daughter of Joseph and Mary (Foote) Lambert;[2072] Mary d. at Charlestown, 21 Jun 1851.

[2068] *Essex County, Massachusetts, Probate Records and Indexes 1638-1916;* Author: *Massachusetts. Probate Court (Essex County);* Probate Place: *Essex, Massachusetts, Probate Records, Vol 412-414, Book 112-114, 1843-1847,* will of James Barr, File 34, 15 Feb 1848, pp 317-318

[2069] American War of Independence at Sea, http://www.awiatsea.com/Privateers/O/Oliver%20Cromwell%20Massachusetts%20Brig-Ship%20%5BColes%20Simmons%20Barr%20Bray%5D.html

[2070] "Ship Registers of the District of Salem and Beverly 1789-1900", Essex Institute Historical Collections, volume 41, p 373

[2071] Benjamin, consumption, at the workhouse, Sept. 8, 1820, a. 55 y. [a. 50 y. dup.]

[2072] Belknap, *The Lambert Family of Salem, Massachusetts*, p 30

Benjamin Crowninshield was a master mariner and merchant and commander of several of the Crowninshield family vessels. He was Collector of Customs for the Marblehead/Lynn district from 1821-1830.[2073]

Benjamin did not leave a will and his estate entered probate December 8136. Widow Mary and heirs James Armstrong, Benjamin Crowninshield, and J. Crowninshield all declined administration of the estate and Benjamin Merrill, Esquire, of Salem was named administrator. Real estate was valued at $7,000, $4,000 for a mansion house and 40 acres in Danvers, and $3,000 for property in Salem. There personal estate was valued at $105.20. Charges against the estate nearly equaled the value of the estate with $3,081.60 owed to Nathaniel West and $3,500 owed to the heirs of Jacob Crowninshield.[2074]

Benjamin Crowninshield and Mary Lambert were parents of five children born at Salem.

i BENJAMIN CROWNINSHIELD, b. 1782; d. at Charlestown, MA, 30 Nov 1864.

ii MARIA CROWNINSHIELD, b. about 1783; d. at Andover, 15 Sep 1870; m. at Salem, 4 Apr 1814, JOHN CROWNINSHIELD, b. 1772 son of George and Mary (Derby) Crowninshield; John d. at Boston, 10 Apr 1842.

iii HANNAH CROWNINSHIELD, baptized 28 Jun 1789; d. at Salem, 4 May 1834; m. 1819, JAMES ARMSTRONG, b. at Shelbyville, KY, 7 Aug 1794 son of James and Elizabeth (Morris) Armstrong; James d. at Salem, 25 Aug 1868. After Hannah's death, James married Hannah's sister Elizabeth (see below). Hannah Crowninshield was a portrait painter.

iv ELIZABETH CROWNINSHIELD, b. Nov 1794; d. at Salem, 17 Mar 1870; m. 1836, JAMES ARMSTRONG (see sister Hannah above).

v JACOB CROWNINSHIELD, b. Feb 1799; d. at sea, 1849; m. 1825, HARRIET WALLACH, b. at Boston, 1802 daughter of Moses and Mary (Robbins) Wallach; Harriet d. at Boston, 25 Mar 1885.

768) MARY BOWDITCH *(Mary Carleton Bowditch[4], Deborah Stevens Carleton[3], Sarah Abbott Stevens[2], George[1])*, b. at Salem, Jun 1760 daughter of John and Mary (Carleton) Bowditch; d. at Salem, 18 Mar 1829; m. 7 Apr 1782, as his second wife, LEWIS HUNT, b. 23 Mar 1746 son of William and Eunice Bowditch Hunt; Lewis d. 22 Oct 1797. Lewis Hunt was first married to Sarah Orne who died in 1781.

Lewis Hunt was a deacon in Salem. He made his living as a baker and ran his shop from a front room in the family home. The family home, known as the Lewis Hunt house, was held in the family for five generations. It was demolished in 1863.[2075] The house was originally built by Lewis's grandfather Lewis Hunt who was a mariner in Salem.

Lewis Hunt wrote his will 10 October 1797 just two weeks before his death. He makes a separate bequest of $100 each for the three children from his first marriage: William Hunt, Sarah Hunt, and Eunice Hunt to be paid five years after his decease. To allow his beloved wife Mary to keep the family together, he provides for her to have the entire income from his estate for five years. After that time, she is to receive her dower and the remainder of the estate is to be divided equally among his children and any child his wife is currently pregnant with. Children named are William, Lewis, Sarah, Eunice, Mary, Elizabeth, John, Joseph, and Benjamin. (The youngest daughter Deborah was born four days after her father's death.) Friend Deacon Thomas Hartshorne was named sole executor of the estate.[2076]

In her will written 19 July 1822, Mary Hunt specifies that her daughters Mary Hunt and Deborah Hunt are to have an undivided ninth part of their father's estate which had been left to their brother Joseph who is now deceased. Deborah and Mary also receive wearing apparel and household items. Son John Hunt, Jr. receives $10. Daughter Elizabeth Hinman receives $10. The residue of the estate is to be equally divided between Mary and Deborah and Mary is named sole executor. Both Mary and Deborah married between the time of the will and the probate of the estate (7 April 1829). Daughter Mary was Mary Ingersoll when she acted as executor of the estate. [2077]

Lewis and Mary Hunt had nine children whose births are recorded at Salem. Two of the children, John and Elizabeth, relocated to Ohio.

i LEWIS HUNT, b. 30 Jan 1783; d. 25 Jul 1800.

ii MARY HUNT, b. 22 Apr 1784; d. 10 Oct 1785

[2073] Philips Library Digital Collections, "Benjamin Crowninshield Family Papers", http://phillipslibrarycollections.pem.org/cdm/compoundobject/collection/p15928coll1/id/3965/rec/2

[2074] Middlesex County, MA: Probate File Papers, 1648-1871.Online database. AmericanAncestors.org. New England Historic Genealogical Society, 2014. Case 5404

[2075] "The Lewis Hunt House," http://www.historicsalem.org/blog/the-lewis-hunt-house

[2076] *Essex County, MA: Probate File Papers, 1638-1881. Will of Lewis Hunt, 10 Oct 1797.*

[2077] *Essex County, MA: Probate File Papers, 1638-1881. Probate of Mary Hunt, 7 Apr 1829, case number 14259.*

iii JOHN HUNT, b. 14 Dec 1785; d. in Ohio, Oct 1859; m. about 1820, LYDIA FOLGER, b. at Nantucket, 23 May 1793 daughter of Timothy and Hephzibah (Chadwick) Folger.[2078] The circumstances of John Hunt are uncertain. In her will, John Hunt's sister Mary Hunt Ingersoll Burley left John's bequest in the form of a trust managed by a trustee rather than as a direct bequest to John. Mary specified that after John's decease any remainder would be dispersed to his heirs. John Hunt's heirs in the probate document are Marcus A. Hunt, John W. Hunt, and William P. Hunt.[2079]

iv SAMUEL HUNT, b. 21 Aug 1787; d. 25 May 1790.

v JOSEPH HUNT, b. 28 Jun 1789; d. at Salem, 7 Aug 1808.

vi MARY HUNT, b. 10 May 1791; d. at Salem, 3 May 1858; m. 1 Sep 1822, her first cousin, JOHN INGERSOLL *(Hannah Bowditch Ingersoll[5], Mary Carleton Bowditch[4], Deborah Stevens Carleton[3], Sarah Abbott Stevens[2], George[1])* b. 1794 son of John and Hannah (Bowditch) Ingersoll; John d. at Salem, 5 Oct 1829. Mary remarried to John Burley on 2 Jun 1848. John Ingersoll is a child in Family 769.

vii ELIZABETH HUNT, b. 5 Jan 1793; d. at Cincinnati, OH, 30 Mar 1853; m. at Salem, 1 Feb 1815, EBENEZER HINMAN, b. at St. Martin, Birmingham, Warwickshire 31 Mar 1790 son of Whuriel and Sarah (-) Hinman;[2080][2081] Ebenezer d. at Yellow Springs, OH, 9 Feb 1868. Ebenezer Hinman served as recorder of the city council of Cincinnati from 1834-1838.[2082]

viii BENJAMIN BOWDITCH HUNT, b. 9 Sep 1795; d. at Salem, Oct 1820.

ix DEBORAH HUNT, b. 26 Oct 1797; d. at Hopkinton, NH, Oct 1831; m. at Salem, 27 Apr 1825, MICHAEL CARLETON, b. at Blue Hill, ME, about 1796 son of Moses and Mary (Webster) Carleton; Michael d. at Salem, 6 Mar 1865. Michael's uncle Edward Carleton married Phebe Abbott.

769) HANNAH BOWDITCH *(Mary Carleton Bowditch[4], Deborah Stevens Carleton[3], Sarah Abbott Stevens[2], George[1])*, b. at Salem, Dec 1761 daughter of John and Mary (Carleton) Bowditch; d. at Salem, 14 Dec 1825; m. 21 Jul 1792, as his second wife, JOHN INGERSOLL, b. Jun 1756 son of Nathaniel and Bethiah (Gardner) Ingersoll; John d. 12 Feb 1840. John was first married to Hannah Townsend and third married to the widow Elizabeth Crosby.

John Ingersoll saw several periods of service in the Revolution first enlisting as a private in Captain Ward's company 19 August 1776 and was transferred to the "Massachusetts" company at Salem for defense of the seacoast. He served as a seaman and Master's Mate and was discharged 8 May 1778. He was commissioned Commander of the brigantine "Speedwell" 24 May 1780.[2083]

In his will written 6 January 1832, John Ingersoll bequeathed to beloved wife Elizabeth the whole of personal estate, all the real estate during her natural life and she is free to sell or convey the real estate whenever she thinks this is fit. After her death, the estate goes to his children daughter Nancy Ingersoll, sons Nathaniel and David, and grandson John Ingersoll son of John who is deceased, and daughter Mary Hutchinson. Wife Elizabeth is named executrix.[2084] Nancy Ingersoll is a daughter from John's marriage to Hannah Townsend.

Hannah Bowditch and John Ingersoll were parents of five children born at Salem.

i JUDITH INGERSOLL, b. 1793; no further record and not living when her father wrote his will.

ii JOHN INGERSOLL, b. 1794; d. at Salem, 5 Oct 1829; m. at Salem, 1 Sep 1822, his first cousin, MARY HUNT *(Mary Bowditch Hunt[5], Mary Carleton Bowditch[4], Deborah Stevens Carleton[3], Sarah Abbott Stevens[2], George[1])*, b. at Salem, 10 May 1791 daughter of Lewis and Mary (Bowditch) Hunt; Mary d. at Salem, 3 May 1858. Mary Hunt is a child in Family 768.

iii NATHANIEL INGERSOLL, b. 1798; d. at Salem, 3 Dec 1854; m. at Salem, 4 May 1823, MARGARET CROWNINSHIELD FOOTE, b. at Salem, about 1793 daughter of Samuel and Anna (Crowninshield) Foote; Margaret d. at Salem, 20 Feb 1878.

[2078] Nantucket births has the following entry: Folger, Lydia w. John Hunt (widr. of Ohio formerly of Salem), d. of Timothy and Hepsabeth (Chadwick), 23rd, 5 mo. 1793. New England Historic Genealogical Society; Boston, Massachusetts; Vital Records of Nantucket, Massachusetts to the Year 1850.

[2079] In the 1850 U.S. Census, John and Lydia Hunt are living in Spencer, Ohio with sons 22-year old John W. Hunt and 16-year old Marcus A. Hunt.

[2080] *England & Wales, Non-Conformist and Non-Parochial Registers, 1567-1970*, The National Archives of the UK; Kew, Surrey, England; General Register Office: Registers of Births, Marriages and Deaths surrendered to the Non-parochial Registers Commissions of 1837 and 1857; Class Number: RG 4; Piece Number: 2972.

[2081] The name of Ebenezer's father and date of birth are given on his cemetery index card (Cincinnati Ohio, Spring Grove Cemetery).

[2082] Henry and Ford, *History of Cincinnati, Ohio*, p. 381.

[2083] Avery, *Genealogy of the Ingersoll Family*, p 44

[2084] Essex County, MA: Probate File Papers, 1638-1881.Online database. AmericanAncestors.org. New England Historic Genealogical Society, 2014. Case 14581, probate of John Ingersoll

iv MARY INGERSOLL, baptized 19 Jan 1800; d. at Salem, 12 Jun 1875; m. at Salem, 25 Apr 1826, SAMUEL HUTCHINSON, b. at Salem, about 1797 son of Benjamin and Elizabeth (Hitchins) Hutchinson; Samuel d. at Salem, 13 Dec 1885. Samuel was a master mariner.

v DAVID INGERSOLL, b. 1803; d. at sea, 17 Oct 1837;[2085] m. 15 Oct 1826, HANNAH HODGES STICKNEY, b. 14 Aug 1803 daughter of William and Elizabeth (Byrne) Stickney; Hannah d. after 1860 when she was living in Salem.

770) JOHN BOWDITCH *(Mary Carleton Bowditch⁴, Deborah Stevens Carleton³, Sarah Abbott Stevens², George¹)*, b. at Salem, Mar 1764 son of John and Mary (Carleton) Bowditch; d. at sea, Apr 1793; m. 11 Mar 1791, MARY "POLLY" WELMAN, b. about 1760 whose parents are uncertain; Polly d. at Salem 28 Apr 1844. Polly was first married to Samuel Cook 21 Mar 1778.

John Bowditch was a mariner lost at sea. He did not leave a will and widow Mary was administratrix of the estate. Personal estate was valued at £10.8.0.[2086]

John and Mary had one daughter.

i MARY BOWDITCH, b. at Salem, 19 Feb 1792; d. at Salem, 23 Jun 1872; m. 18 Sep 1814, MICHAEL PITMAN, b. at Salem, about 1790 son of Michael and Sarah (Carwick) Pitman; Michael d. at Salem, 17 Aug 1831.

771) DEBORAH BOWDITCH *(Mary Carleton Bowditch⁴, Deborah Stevens Carleton³, Sarah Abbott Stevens², George¹)*, b. at Salem, Oct 1767 daughter of John and Mary (Carleton) Bowditch; d. at Salem, 4 Jul 1823; m. 31 Oct 1782, THOMAS MORIARTY, b. in Ireland about 1760 son of John and Margaret (Moriarty) Moriarty;[2087] Thomas d. 1790 (date of probate 5 Aug 1790).

Thomas Moriarty was a mariner, born in Ireland, who came to Salem with his father John Moriarty in 1775. According to O'Laughlin's *Families of Co. Kerry, Ireland*, father John left eight other children in Ireland when he and Thomas came to Salem. During the Revolutionary War, Thomas was a privateer on a ship that was captured by the British in 1781, and he was imprisoned at St. John's Newfoundland. As part of a prisoner exchange, Thomas and the other crew members were retrieved by the sloop *Freemason* that was financed by John Moriarty.[2088] There is discrepancy about Thomas's death. Some sources suggest that Thomas died off the coast of Guinea in 1787, but the death record for that event gives the name of John Moriarty; this has been interpreted as an error for Thomas. Thomas Moriarty's estate entered probate 5 August 1790 with his widow Deborah as administrator. The estate was insolvent.[2089] Deborah was also the administrator for the estate of John Moriarty in 1797. John's estate was also insolvent.

Thomas and Deborah had two children born at Salem.

i JOHN MORIARTY, b. about 1783; d. at Salem, 16 Mar 1835; m. 26 Dec 1806, ABIGAIL MOSELEY, b. at Salem, 6 Jun 1786 daughter of Joseph and Elizabeth (Crowninshield) Moseley; Abigail d. at Boston, 16 Aug 1858.

ii THOMAS MORIARTY, b. 8 Sep 1787; d. at New York, NY, 9 Sep 1846; m. 9 Jul 1810, JEMIMA CROCKER PAUL, b. at Taunton, 7 Mar 1783 daughter of Edward and Alethia (Tobey) Paul; Jemima d. 13 Jan 1870.

772) SAMUEL BOWDITCH *(Mary Carleton Bowditch⁴, Deborah Stevens Carleton³, Sarah Abbott Stevens², George¹)*, b. at Salem, May 1769 son of John and Mary (Carleton) Bowditch; d. at sea, 21 Mar 1791; m. 15 Aug 1790; ANNA "NANCY" WELMAN, baptized 2 Sep 1770 daughter of Samuel and Mary (Kempton) Welman. Nancy m. 2nd, William Richardson (or Richardson Russell, both names are given on the transcription of the marriage record).

Samuel Bowditch was a mariner lost at sea[2090] nine months after his marriage. There was one daughter.

i NANCY BOWDITCH, b. 1791; likely died young.

773) WILLIAM CARLETON *(William Carleton⁴, Deborah Stevens Carleton³, Sarah Abbott Stevens², George¹)*, b. at Salem, 1771 (based on age at time of death) son of William and (Palfrey) Carleton; d. at Salem, 24 Jul 1805; m. at Salem, 22 May 1796,

[2085] David, Capt., of the ship Morrison, of New York, on the passage from Canton to Batavia, Oct. —, 1837, a. 37 y. Issue of Mar. 2, 1838. NR9

[2086] Essex County, MA: Probate File Papers, 1638-1881.Online database. AmericanAncestors.org. New England Historic Genealogical Society, 2014. Case 2883

[2087] O'Laughlin, *Families of Co. Kerry Ireland*, volume 2, p. 106

[2088] Massachusetts Society of the Sons of the American Revolution, Register of Members April 19, 1907, p 163

[2089] Essex County, MA: Probate File Papers, 1638-1881.Online database. AmericanAncestors.org. New England Historic Genealogical Society, 2014. Case number 18771

[2090] Samuel, m., on the brig Harriette, perished off the Texell, Mar. 21, 1791, a. 22 y. C. R. 4.

ELIZABETH COOKE, b. about 1771 daughter of Charles and (Stone) Cooke; Elizabeth d. at Salem, 22 Aug 1805. Salem vital records: *Elizabeth, d. Charles and____ (Stone) Cooke [proprietress of the Salem Register, G. R. 9.], wid. William, consumption. Aug. 25, 1805, a. 34 y.*

William Carleton was the publisher of the *Salem Register* and his wife continued as publisher after his death until her death a few months later. William was also partner in a bookstore with Thomas Cushing. Related to his news stories on a political controversy involving Thomas Pickering (an unsuccessful candidate for Congress), William was convicted of libel in 1803 and paid a $100 fine and was sentenced to two months in jail.[2091]

William and Elizabeth had four children born in Salem, three of whom died as infants.

i ELIZABETH WHITE CARLETON, b. Jun 1799; d. 21 Nov 1818. After the deaths of her parents, Elizabeth was adopted by Joseph White.

ii HANNAH CARLETON, baptized May 1801; d. 22 Jun 1802.

iii MARY CARLETON, baptized May 1801; d. 3 Nov 1801.

iv CHARLES CARLETON, b. Aug 1803; d. 14 Oct 1804.

Great-Grandchildren of Benjamin Abbott and Sarah Farnum

774) WILLIAM ABBOTT *(Daniel[4], Benjamin[3], Benjamin[2], George[1])*, b. at Dracut, 22 Feb 1760 son of Daniel and Lucy (Parker) Abbott; d. likely at Bedford, NH; m. at Dracut, 13 Nov 1784, MARTHA "PATTY" COBURN, b. at Dracut about 1765.[2092]

William Abbot is reported to have gone to Bedford, New Hampshire[2093] but no records there have been located. There are birth records for three children born at Dracut, but nothing further is known.

i POLLY ABBOTT, b. 28 Apr 1786

ii WILLIAM ABBOTT, b. 18 May 1788

iii JOHN ABBOTT, b. 22 Apr 1790

775) SAMUEL ABBOTT *(Daniel[4], Benjamin[3], Benjamin[2], George[1])*, b. at Dracut, 16 Feb 1765 son of Daniel and Lucy (Parker) Abbott; d. at Claremont, NH, 13 Apr 1840; m. by 1794, his first cousin, ELIZABETH COTTON, b. about 1768 daughter of Rev. Samuel and Elizabeth (Parker) Cotton of Claremont; Elizabeth d. at Claremont, NH, 7 Jun 1837.[2094] The mothers of Samuel Abbott and Elizabeth Cotton were sisters.

There is record evidence (death/cemetery) of three children for Samuel Abbott and Elizabeth Cotton all born at Claremont and the fourth child reported in the Abbot genealogical register.

i ELIZABETH ABBOTT, b. 1794; d. at Claremont, 3 Oct 1833.[2095] Elizabeth did not marry.

ii LUCY ABBOTT, b. 1796; d. at Claremont, 16 Mar 1855. Lucy did not marry.[2096]

iii DANIEL ABBOTT, b. about 1798; nothing further known.

iv SAMUEL C. ABBOTT, b. 1800; d. at Claremont, 14 Jul 1882; m. 1st, about 1828, his first cousin, DOROTHY "DOLLY" ABBOTT, b. 13 Apr 1803 daughter of Jonathan and Dolly (Parker) Abbott; Dolly d. at Claremont, 27 Apr 1855.[2097] Samuel m. 2nd, about 1856, his first cousin, DOLLY P. COTTON, b. 1798 daughter of Samuel and Mary (Moor) Cotton; Dolly d. at Claremont, 13 Oct 1881. Dorothy Abbott is a child in Family 776 (see just below).

2091 Hurd, *History of Essex County*, pp 120-122

2092 *The History of Dracut*, p 130, gives Patty's parents as Jacob and Lydia, but their daughter Patty died unmarried in 1802 (at least the death record gives her name as Patty Caburn).

2093 Abbot, Genealogical Register, p 67

2094 Spofford, *Gravestone Records: From the Ancient Cemeteries in the Town of Claremont*, p 6, Elizabeth (Cotton) Abbott wife of Samuel, June 7, 1837, 69y; Samuel Abbott, April 13, 1840, 76y

2095 Spofford, *Gravestone Records*, p 6; Elizabeth daughter of Samuel and Elizabeth 5 Oct 1833, age 40.

2096 "New Hampshire Death Records, 1654-1947," database with images, *FamilySearch* (https://familysearch.org/ark:/61903/1:1:FSLX-HV4 : 10 March 2018), Lucy Abbott, 16 Mar 1855; citing Claremont, Bureau Vital Records and Health Statistics, Concord; FHL microfilm 1,001,058. Lucy Abbott, single, age 59

2097 In a codicil to his will written 10 June 1855, Jonathan Abbott made bequests to his grandchildren the children of his daughter Dorothy Abbott and Samuel Abbott.

776) JONATHAN ABBOTT *(Daniel⁴, Benjamin³, Benjamin², George¹)*, b. at Dracut, 20 Jan 1772 son of Daniel and Lucy (Parker) Abbott; d. at Litchfield, NH, 4 Jul 1855; m. 1st, 21 Feb 1795, REBECCA MASSEY, b. 24 Mar 1772 daughter of Bartholomew and Mary (Fox) Massey; Rebecca d. 19 Dec 1795. Jonathan m. 2nd, 31 Dec 1800, DOLLY PARKER, b. 12 Sep 1779.[2098] Dolly died at Litchfield, 19 Sep 1824.[2099] After Dolly's death, Jonathan married a widow named Miranda (*perhaps* Miranda Knight widow of Jeduthan Kingsbury) who d. at Claremont 23 Feb 1854.

Jonathan Abbott wrote his will 23 December 1854 while he was residing in Claremont but wrote a codicil on 18 June 1855 when he was residing in Litchfield. In his original will, he made bequests of $50 each to his grandchildren Mark Campbell of Litchfield and Dorothy Knowles the wife of Henry Knowles of Nashua, but he revoked these legacies in the codicil providing each of these grandchildren one dollar and no more. Instead, he gave the $100 to his daughter Emily Griffin wife of Abbott Griffin because of her great kindness to him. He divided his estate between his grandchildren the children of Dorothy Abbott and Samuel Abbott and his daughter Emily Griffin and her husband Abbott Griffin. His daughter Dorothy Abbott died between the time of his will and the time of the codicil. The two grandchildren cut out of the will were the children of his daughter Clarissa, who was deceased, and her husband Smith Campbell. The will also includes a small bequest to Andrew Leadstone who was the husband of his daughter Rebecca Abbott who was deceased.[2100]

Jonathan Abbott and his first wife Rebecca Massey resided in Dracut where they had one child.

i REBECCA MASSEY ABBOTT, b. at Dracut, 21 Nov 1795; d. at Litchfield, NH, 18 Jul 1819; m. ANDREW LYDSTON, b. in Maine, about 1791; Andrew d. at Litchfield, 31 Dec 1858. After Rebecca's death, Andrew married Louisa Tufts.

Jonathan Abbott and Dolly Parker were parents of seven children.

i CLARISSA ABBOTT, b. at Londonderry, 20 Aug 1801; d. at Litchfield, 28 Nov 1841; m. SMITH CAMPBELL, b. at Litchfield, 3 Nov 1792 son of Daniel and Jane (Anderson) Campbell; Smith d. at Litchfield, 25 Mar 1864. After Clarissa's death, Smith married Sophia Hills.

ii DOROTHY "DOLLY" ABBOTT, b. 18 Apr 1803; d. at Claremont, 27 Apr 1855; m. about 1828, her first cousin, SAMUEL C. ABBOTT, b. at Claremont, 1800 son of Samuel and Elizabeth (Cotton) Abbott; Samuel d. at Claremont, 14 Jul 1882. Samuel is a child in Family 775 (see just above).

iii ELIZA ABBOTT, b. 5 Apr 1805; d. at Claremont, 3 Aug 1838. Eliza did not marry.

iv EMILY ABBOTT, b. 18 Sep 1807; d. at Litchfield, 4 Apr 1885; m. her fourth cousin, ABBOT GRIFFIN *(Ebenezer Griffin⁵, Phebe Abbott Griffin⁴, Ebenezer³, John², George¹)*, b. at Dracut, 22 Jun 1805 son of Ebenezer and Elizabeth (Carter) Griffin; Abbot d. at Litchfield, 25 Dec 1862. Abbot Griffin is a child in Family 421.

v THOMAS P. ABBOTT, b. 14 May 1810; d. 24 May 1810.

vi SALLY P. ABBOTT, b. 13 Sep 1811; d. 22 Se 1811.

vii MARY T. ABBOTT, b. 17 Jun 1815; d. 7 Nov 1815.

777) JOEL BARKER *(Mary Abbott Barker⁴, Benjamin³, Benjamin², George¹)*, b. at Methuen, 11 Aug 1764 son of Nehemiah and Mary (Abbott) Barker; d. at Milford, NH, 5 Dec 1832; m. at Milford, 24 Dec 1793, SARAH "SALLY" FOSTER, b. at Milford, 1774 daughter of Edward and Phebe (Pierce) Foster; Sarah d. 5 Sep 1820. Joel m. 2nd, 27 Nov 1821, CATHERINE LOVEJOY of Hollis.[2101]

Joel was a young man when he accompanied his parents to Milford. As the oldest son, he remained on the family homestead in Milford. Joel and his wife Sarah had eight children whose births are recorded at Milford.[2102]

i JOEL BARKER, b. 14 Nov 1794; d. at Milford, 10 Feb 1879; m. 15 May 1829, SARAH W. WHITNEY, b. at Marlborough, NH, 28 Apr 1799 daughter of Benjamin and Nancy (Fuller) Whitney; Sarah d. at Milford 23 Jun 1887.

[2098] Family Tree Samplers, 1759-1894. Online database. AmericanAncestors.org. New England Historic Genealogical Society, 2013. (From the collection of Dan and Marty Campanelli.) Vital records for this family are contained in a sampler stitched by Dolly Parker.

[2099] Findagrave.com memorial ID 167676976

[2100] *New Hampshire. Probate Court (Hillsborough County)*; Probate Place: *Hillsborough, New Hampshire, Probate Records, Vol 57-58, 1848-1856*, will of Jonathan Abbott, p 527.

[2101] Ramsdell, *History of Milford, Volume 1*, p 576

[2102] *New Hampshire, Births and Christenings Index, 1714-1904* [database on-line]

ii SARAH "SALLY" BARKER, b. 9 Jul 1797; d. at Merrimack, 11 Apr 1865; m. 13 Nov 1827, AARON HOOD, b. at Nashua about 1797 son of Aaron and Hannah (Richardson) Hood; Aaron d. at Merrimack, 6 Dec 1874. After Sarah's death, Aaron married Sally Davis 7 Dec 1865.[2103]

iii MARY "POLLY" BARKER, b. 6 Mar 1800; d. at Nashua, 6 Mar 1860; m. 25 Dec 1832, HIRAM WHEELER, b. at Merrimack, about 1800 son of Reuben and Mary (Conant) Wheeler; Reuben d. at Nashville, NH, about 1849 (will dated 30 May 1849). Mary and Hiram do not seem to have children that lived past infancy (there may be two children who died as young infants). Hiram's will mentions his father Reuben, brother Gilman, and leaves the estate to wife Mary B. Wheeler.[2104] Mary seems to have remarried to Mr. Tinker after Hiram's death as evidenced by the bequest in the will of her brother James to Mary B. Tinker.

iv BENJAMIN BARKER, b. 8 Aug 1802; d. at Milford, 6 Oct 1843 (will dated 23 Aug 1843); m. about 1835, as her second husband, ALMA AVERILL, b. about 1796 daughter of Ebenezer and Anna (Johnson) Averill; Alma d. 3 Aug 1855. Alma was first married to Daniel Johnson. Benjamin and Alma did not have children. Alma had one son from her first marriage.

v JOHN BARKER, b. 23 Sep 1805; d. at Milford, 14 Aug 1845; m. 22 Dec 1840, MARTHA WOOLSON, b. at Milford, 28 Aug 1800 daughter of David and Sarah (Crosby) Woolson; Martha d. at Quincy, 10 Jan 1879.

vi JAMES BARKER, b. 28 Jun 1808; d. at Milford, 7 Oct 1859. James was a cooper. He did not marry. James wrote his will 27 Sep 1859. The will includes bequests to brother Joel Barker, sister Sarah B. Hood, sister Mary B. Tinker, and sister Hannah B. Spaulding.[2105]

vii HANNAH BARKER, b. 15 Jul 1810; d. at Salisbury, MA, 19 Jul 1887; m. 18 Dec 1838, her first cousin, BENJAMIN SPAULDING *(Mary Barker Spaulding[5], Mary Abbott Barker[4], Benjamin[3], Benjamin[2], George[1])*, b. at Hollis, 27 Aug 1800 son of Jacob and Mary (Barker) Spaulding; Benjamin d. at Salisbury, 29 Mar 1892. Benjamin Spaulding is a child in Family 778.

viii NANCY BARKER, b. 18 Jul 1812; d. Feb 1835.

778) MARY BARKER *(Mary Abbott Barker[4], Benjamin[3], Benjamin[2], George[1])*, b. at Methuen, 18 Dec 1767 daughter of Nehemiah and Mary (Abbott) Barker; d. at Hollis, 3 Sep 1824; m. at Hollis, 6 Jan 1791, JACOB SPAULDING, b. at Chelmsford, 13 Dec 1767 son of Benjamin and Mary (Spaulding) Spaulding. Jacob m. 2nd, Susanna Robertson. Jacob d. at Hollis, 14 May 1838.

Deacon Jacob Spaulding and Mary Barker settled in Hillsborough soon after their marriage in 1791.

Mary Barker and Jacob Spaulding were parents of nine children born at Hillsborough.

i POLLY SPAULDING, b. 21 Apr 1792; d. at Antrim, 2 Jul 1886; m. 20 Sep 1808, DANIEL COOLIDGE, b. at Hillsborough, 10 Mar 1789 son of Paul and Martha (Jones) Coolidge; Daniel d. at Antrim, 25 Feb 1869.

ii ABIGAIL SPAULDING, b. 14 Mar 1794; m. 16 Mar 1837, as his second wife, JOHN DUNLAP, b. at Bedford, NH, 20 Dec 1784 son of John and Martha (Gilmore) Dunlap; John d. at Nashua, NH, 15 Dec 1869. John was first married to Jenny Nesmith (1787-1835).

iii JACOB SPAULDING, b. 26 Apr 1796; d. at New York, NY, 14 Oct 1818.[2106] Jacob did not marry.

iv SALLY SPAULDING, b. 8 May 1798; Sally d. at Hillsborough, 9 Jun 1820. Sally did not marry.

v BENJAMIN SPAULDING, b. 27 Aug 1800; d. at Salisbury, MA, 29 Mar 1892; m. 18 Dec 1838, his first cousin, HANNAH BARKER *(Joel Barker[5], Mary Abbott Barker[4], Benjamin[3], Benjamin[2], George[1])*, b. at Milford, 15 Jul 1810 daughter of Joel and Sarah (Foster) Barker; Hannah d. at Salisbury, 19 Jul 1887. Hannah is a daughter in Family 777.

vi CYRUS SPAULDING, b. 28 Sep 1802; d. at Chicopee, MA, 22 May 1880; m. at Watertown, 4 Sep 1831, SUSAN GRANT, b. at Lyman, ME, about 1808 daughter of Silas and Betsy (Straw) Grant; Susan d. at Springfield, MA, 23 Feb 1895.

vii FRANKLIN SPAULDING, b. 13 Jan 1806; d. at Chicopee, 23 Jan 1873; m. 1st, 1831, THIRZA EUNICE KIDDER, b. at Roxbury, NH, 29 Mar 1811 daughter of Aaron Bush and Persis (Hemenway) Kidder; Thirza d. 1851. Franklin m. 2nd, at Chicopee, 21 Oct 1852, EUNICE HOLTON, of Dummerston, VT, b. about 1808.

[2103] The names of Aaron's parents are given on the 1865 marriage record to Sally Davis. New Hampshire, Marriage Records Index, 1637-1947

[2104] New Hampshire Probate Court, Hillsborough, will of Hiram Wheeler, 30 May 1849, Probate Records, volumes 57-58, 1848-1856.

[2105] New Hampshire Probate Court, Hillsborough, will of James Barker, Probate Records, volume 68, 1856-1869.

[2106] The names of Jacob's parents are on his gravestone. Findagrave memorial: 170785505

viii NANCY BARKER SPAULDING, b. 2 Feb 1809; d. at Tewksbury, 25 Jun 1887; m. EPHRAIM PARKHURST SPAULDING, b. at Chelmsford, 23 Nov 1813 son of Henry and Jemima (Spaulding) Spaulding; Ephraim d. at Tewksbury, 18 Nov 1885.

ix EMELINE SPAULDING, b. 1 Dec 1812; d. at Augusta, ME, after 1880; m. JOEL SPAULDING, b. at Chelmsford, 2 Feb 1816 son of Henry and Jemima (Spaulding) Spaulding; Joel d. at Augusta, 21 Jun 1900.

779) DORCAS BARKER *(Mary Abbott Barker⁴, Benjamin³, Benjamin², George¹)*, b. at Methuen, 4 Sep 1770 daughter of Nehemiah and Mary (Abbott) Barker; d. at Peterborough, NH, 25 Jul 1840; m. About 1792, MERRILL PIERCE, b. at Chelmsford, 29 Jan 1764 son of Benjamin and Elizabeth (Merrill) Pierce. Merrill Pierce was the brother of Phebe Pierce (born 1748) who was the mother of Sarah Foster who married Dorcas's older brother Joel.

Merrill Pierce was the uncle of President Franklin Pierce.[2107]

Dorcas Barker and Merrill Pierce were parents of nine children likely all born at Hillsborough.

i BENJAMIN PIERCE b. and d. Feb 1793.

ii POLLY PIERCE, b. 4 Sep 1794; d. at Peterborough, 11 Jul 1867; m. at Hillsborough, 25 Dec 1823, MOSES CHAPMAN, b. at Peterborough, 16 Mar 1796 son of Dudley and Eliza (-) Chapman; Moses d. at Peterborough, 3 Mar 1859.

iii MERRILL PIERCE, b. about 1798; d. likely at Utica, NY; m. about 1828, MARY DICKINSON. Merrill was living in Utica at the 1830 census and one child of this couple died in 1832. Nothing further is known.

iv JESSE PIERCE. Jesse is a son reported in the Pierce genealogy and reported to have not married.

v MARY ANN PIERCE, b. 4 Sep 1803; d. at Peterborough, 5 Feb 1849; m. 22 Nov 1826, WILLIAM B. KIMBALL, b. at New Andover, VT, 24 May 1801 son of Isaac and Sarah (Cutler) Kimball; William d. at Peterborough, 20 Feb 1889.

vi ADALINE PIERCE, b. 26 Mar 1807; d. at Marlboro, NH, 10 Nov 1870; m. at Peterborough, 23 Nov 1831, BENJAMIN B. CUSHING, b. 29 Sep 1808 son of Nehemiah and Deborah (Briggs) Cushing; Benjamin d. at Hingham, MA, 29 Nov 1888.

vii LOUISA PIERCE, b. 31 Aug 1809; d. at Sharon, NH, 22 Nov 1873; m. 25 Dec 1851, THOMAS MCCOY, b. about 1786 son of Gilbert and Elizabeth (Stewart) McCoy; Thomas d. at Sharon, 10 Mar 1870.

viii NANCY PIERCE, b. 16 Oct 1812; d. at Nashua, NH, 16 Aug 1895; m. 4 Sep 1834, EDWARD P. EMERSON, b. at Francestown, about 1809 son of Timothy and Miriam (Pelty) Emerson; Edward d. at Nashua, 23 Feb 1882.

ix ELIZABETH M. PIERCE, b. 10 Dec 1816; d. at Nashua, 18 Apr 1882; m. at Henniker, 16 Nov 1835, CORNELIUS G. FENNER, b. at Providence, RI, 16 Aug 1799 son of Arthur and Lydia (Sabin) Fenner; Cornelius d. at Dauphin, PA, 19 Oct 1887.

780) EZRA ABBOT *(Abigail Abbott Abbot⁴, Benjamin³, Benjamin², George¹)*, b. at Andover, 3 Dec 1760 son of John and Abigail (Abbott) Abbot; d. at Andover, 22 Jan 1844; m. 24 Apr 1798, his third cousin once removed, HANNAH POOR *(Hannah Frye Poor⁵, Elizabeth Osgood Frye⁴, Hannah Abbott Osgood³, George², George¹)* b. 15 Jan 1770 daughter of Daniel and Hannah (Frye) Poor; Hannah d. 11 Sep 1861. Hannah Poor is a child in Family 506.

In his will written 5 July 1839 and proved 20 February 1844, Ezra Abbot bequeathed to his son Daniel P. Abbot land in Andover known as "Pole's Hill." Daughter Hannah Mansfield the wife of Rev. Daniel Mansfield of Wenham receives four hundred dollars. Son Ezra Abbot, of Canton in the County of Norfolk, physician, receives any notes that the father holds against him. His wife Mrs. Hannah Abbot receives use of and improvement of any of the household items she chooses, and the use and improvement of all the buildings and lands wherever they are situated. All the remainder of the estate goes to son John Abbot who is also responsible to pay any just debts. John Abbot is also named executor.[2108]

Ezra and Hannah Abbot had six children born at Andover.

i EZRA ABBOTT, b. 30 Mar 1799; d. 12 Jan 1804.

[2107] Pierce, *Pierce Genealogy*, p 100

[2108] *Essex County, MA: Probate File Papers, 1638-1881. Probate of Ezra Abbot, 20 Feb 1844, case number 30841.*

ii JOHN ABBOTT, b. 17 Mar 1801; d. 6 Aug 1803.

iii DANIEL POOR ABBOTT, b. 9 Mar 1803; d. at Andover, 11 Nov 1881; m. at Andover, 21 Jan 1837, MEHITABLE FOSTER, b. at Andover, 7 Apr 1813 daughter of Charles and Mehitable (Chandler) Foster; Mehitable d. 20 Jan 1863.

iv HANNAH FRYE ABBOTT, b. 16 Jun 1806; d. at Boston, 29 Jun 1862; m. at Andover, 23 Jul 1838, DANIEL MANSFIELD, b. at Lynnfield, 24 Aug 1807 son of Andrew and Eunice (Perkins) Mansfield; Daniel d. at Wenham, MA, 8 Apr 1847.

v EZRA ABBOTT, b. 27 Nov 1808; d. at Canton, MA, 21 Apr 1872; m. at Canton, 23 Dec 1839, HARRIET MOODY LINCOLN, b. at Abington, 1819 daughter of Louis and Mary (Knight) Lincoln; Harriet d. at Canton, 22 Jul 1844.

vi JOHN ABBOTT, b. 9 Feb 1812; d. at Andover, 4 Feb 1881. John was a farmer in Andover. He did not marry. In his will dated 17 Dec 1880, he made disposition of his various properties to siblings, nieces, and nephews. He described his homestead property of 5 ¾ acres lying between Abbot Street and Central Street in Andover and his desire for this property to stay in the family as long as possible.[2109]

781) BENJAMIN ABBOT *(Abigail Abbott Abbot[4], Benjamin[3], Benjamin[2], George[1])*, b. at Andover, 17 Sep 1762 son of John and Abigail (Abbott) Abbot; d. at Exeter, NH, 25 Oct 1849; m. 1st, HANNAH TRACY EMERY, b. at Exeter, 7 Mar 1771 daughter of John and Margaret (Gookin) Emery; Hannah d. 6 Dec 1793. Benjamin m. 2nd, at Boston, 1 May 1798, MARY PERKINS, b. at Boston, 24 May 1769 daughter of James and Elizabeth (Peck) Perkins; Mary d. at Exeter, 13 Mar 1863.

Benjamin Abbot attended Phillips Andover Academy and graduated from Harvard in 1788 where he was salutatorian. In October 1788 he was named temporary preceptor of Phillips Exeter Academy. He was subsequently named to the position permanently and held that post for fifty years.[2110]

Hannah Tracy Emery was mentioned in the diary of John Quincy Adams his having met her on a visit to a Mr. Carter. "Miss H. Emery was there, a young lady with a beautiful countenance, an elegant person, and (I am told) an amiable mind."[2111]

In his will written 24 August 1846 (proved 14 November 1849), Benjamin Abbot bequeaths to beloved wife Mary the house and land in Exeter now occupied by David W. Gorham for use during her life, and after Mary's death, this property goes to daughter Elizabeth P. Gorham. Elizabeth also receives five shares in the Boston and Maine Railroad. His son Charles B. Abbot and wife Henrietta receive all the real estate in Glenburn, Maine. After the deaths of Charles and Henrietta, the property goes to their son Francis Peabody Abbot. Charles also receives two hundred dollars. All the amounts Charles and Elizabeth owe him are forgiven. Each grandchild receives one share in the Boston and Maine Railroad. All the residue of the estate goes to wife Mary during her life, and after her decease to be equally divided between his two children. David W. Gorham and Charles B. Abbot were named executors. In a codicil written 16 October 1849, Benjamin adds to his bequest to Charles B. and Henrietta by giving them the island in Pushaw Lake in Orono, Maine called "Dollar Island" but Charles is responsible for the mortgage.[2112]

Benjamin Abbot and Hannah Emery had one child.

i JOHN EMERY ABBOTT, b. at Exeter, NH, 6 Aug 1793; d. at Exeter, 7 Oct 1819. John graduated Boston College 1810, was ordained in 1815, and was minister of the North Church in Salem.

Benjamin Abbot and Mary Perkins had three children all born at Exeter.

i MARY P. ABBOTT, b. 14 Feb 1799; d. 22 Jun 1802.

ii ELIZABETH P. ABBOTT, b. 14 Nov 1801; d. at Exeter, 16 Aug 1873; m. 3 May 1826, DAVID WOOD GORHAM, b. at Charlestown, 1 Feb 1800 son of Nathaniel and Ruth (Wood) Gorham; David d. at Exeter, 11 Oct 1873.

iii CHARLES BENJAMIN ABBOTT, b. 19 Jan 1805; d. at Bangor, ME, 8 Mar 1874; m. HENRIETTA PEABODY THURSTON, b. about 1804 daughter of James and Elizabeth (Peabody) Thurston; Henrietta d. after 1870.

782) ABIGAIL ABBOTT *(Abigail Abbott Abbot[4], Benjamin[3], Benjamin[2], George[1])*, b. at Andover, 15 Sep 1764 daughter of John and Abigail (Abbott) Abbot; d. at Portland, ME, 22 Apr 1841; m. at Andover, 21 Apr 1791, WILLIAM DOUGLAS, baptized at Rutland, MA, 29 Mar 1761 son of Robert and Elinor (Fales) Douglas; William d. at Portland, 4 Dec 1827.

[2109] *Essex County, Massachusetts, Probate Records and Indexes 1638-1916;* Author: *Massachusetts. Probate Court (Essex County);* Probate Place: *Essex, Massachusetts*, volume 436, pp 142-143

[2110] Crosbie, *The Phillips Exeter Academy*, p 53

[2111] John Quincy Adams, Charles Francis Adams, 1903, Life in a New England Town 1787, 1788: Diary of John Quincy Adams While a Student in the Office of Theophilus Parsons at Newburyport, p 45

[2112] *New Hampshire. Probate Court (Rockingham County);* Probate Place: *Rockingham, New Hampshire, Probate Records, Vol 84, 1849-1851*, pp 202-204, will of Honorable Benjamin Abbot and codicil

William Douglas was a merchant in Portland. Abigail and William were parents of four children born at Portland.

i JOHN ABBOT DOUGLAS, b. 4 Feb 1792; d. at Waterford, ME, 8 Aug 1878; m. 1st, at Andover, 22 Oct 1822, his first cousin, ELIZABETH ABBOTT *(Elizabeth Abbott Abbot5, Abigail Abbott Abbot4, Benjamin3, Benjamin2, George1)*, b. at Peterborough, 22 May 1798 daughter of Abiel and Elizabeth (Abbott) Abbot; Elizabeth d. at Waterford, 12 Oct 1823. John m. 2nd, about 1825, his second cousin, LUCY ABBOTT *(Benjamin5, Dorcas Abbott Abbott4, Benjamin3, Benjamin2, George1)*, b. at Wilton, 6 May 1802 daughter of Benjamin and Phebe (Abbott) Abbott; Lucy d. at Waterford, after 1870. Lucy Abbott is a child in Family 799. Elizabeth Abbott is a child in Family 783.

ii ABIGAIL DOUGLAS, b. 22 Oct 1793; d. at Portland, 15 Oct 1826; m. at Portland, 19 Aug 1817, CHARLES FARLEY, b. at Ipswich, MA, 4 Jun 1791 son of Jonathan and Susannah (Dodge) Farley; Charles d. at Boston, 20 Dec 1877. Charles Farley married second Rebecca Faulkner Hamlin.

iii HARRIET DOUGLAS, b. 9 Oct 1795; d. at Portland, 12 Jul 1818.

iv ALMIRA DOUGLAS, b. 4 Feb 1804; d. at Portland, 15 Mar 1848; m. at Portland, 29 Mar 1831, EBENEZER STEELE, b. at Gloucester, MA, 1801 son of Joseph and Judith (Haskell) Steele; Ebenezer d. at Portland, 8 Aug 1871.

783) ELIZABETH ABBOTT *(Abigail Abbott Abbot4, Benjamin3, Benjamin2, George1)*, b. at Andover, 2 Aug 1766 daughter of John and Abigail (Abbott) Abbot; d. at Peterborough, NH, 6 Apr 1853; m. 19 May 1796, her first cousin, ABIEL ABBOT, b. at Wilton, 14 Dec 1765 son of Abiel and Dorcas (Abbott) Abbot; Abiel d. at Cambridge, MA, 31 Jan 1859. This is a quadruple Abbott marriage; all four of the parents of this couple are Abbotts.

Dr. Abiel Abbot was a distinguished minister and scholar. He graduated from Harvard in 1787 and was awarded a Doctor of Divinity from Harvard in 1838. After graduating from Harvard, Abiel taught at Phillips Academy for two years. He then pursued the ministry and was ordained October 1795.[2113] Dr. Abbot was co-compiler of the 1847 *Genealogical Register of the Descendants of George Abbot of Andover.*

Abiel Abbot did not leave a will and his estate entered probate 22 February 1859. Abby Abbot requested that Samuel A. Smith be named administrator of the estate and noted that she, a daughter, and Samuel A. Smith, a grandson, were the only heirs-at-law.[2114]

Elizabeth and Abiel Abbot were parents of three children all born at at Coventry, Connecticut.

i ELIZABETH ABBOT, b. 22 May 1798; d. at Waterford, ME, 12 Oct 1823; m. at Andover, 22 Oct 1822, JOHN ABBOT DOUGLAS *(Abigail Abbott Douglas5, Abigail Abbott Abbot4, Benjamin3, Benjamin2, George1)*, b. at Portland, 4 Feb 1792 son of William and Abigail (Abbot) Douglas; John d. at Waterford, 8 Aug 1878. After Elizabeth's death, John married LUCY ABBOTT *(Benjamin5, Dorcas Abbott Abbott4, Benjamin3, Benjamin2, George1)* daughter of Benjamin and Phebe (Abbott) Abbott. John Abbot Douglas is a child in Family 782.

ii ABIGAIL ABBOT, b. 17 Oct 1799; d. at Peterborough, 30 Mar 1881. Abigail did not marry.

iii SARAH DORCAS ABBOT, b. 20 Jun 1801; d. at Peterborough, 11 Jun 1831; m. 21 Jul 1828, SAMUEL GARFIELD SMITH, b. at Peterborough, about 1799 son of Samuel and Sally (Garfield) Smith; Samuel d. at Peterborough, 9 Sep 1842.

784) PHEBE ABBOTT *(Abigail Abbott Abbot4, Benjamin3, Benjamin2, George1)*, b. at Andover, 18 Nov 1768 daughter of John and Abigail (Abbott) Abbot; d. at Portland, ME, 30 Apr 1852; m. 9 Apr 1789, EDWARD CARLETON, b. at Bradford, 2 Jul 1762 son of Dudley and Abigail (Wilson) Carleton; Edward d. at Portland, 12 Jun 1825.

Edward Carleton and Phebe Abbott were in Blue Hill, Maine during their early marriage. Edward was the surveyor of lumber in Blue Hill in 1789 and served on a committee to keep the fish course near Carleton Mills clear.[2115] They were then in Portland where Edward associated with founders of a Baptist church, and he was chosen one of the first two deacons in 1802.[2116]

2113 Smith and Morison, *History of the Town of Peterborough, Genealogical Register*, pp 4-5 for a detailed biography

2114 Middlesex County, MA: Probate File Papers, 1648-1871.Online database. AmericanAncestors.org. New England Historic Genealogical Society, 2014. Case 26033

2115 Candage, *Historical Sketches of Blue Hill*, Maine, p 10

2116 Willis, *History of Portland*, p 688

Phebe Abbott and Edward Carleton were parents of ten children, and it is likely their older children were born at Blue Hill and the younger children at Portland.[2117]

i ABIGAIL CARLETON, b. 17 Mar 1790; d. at Andover, MA, 22 May 1834; m. 1816, ABIEL UPTON, b. at Andover, Apr 1792 son of Abiel and Mary (Jenkins) Upton; Abiel d. after 1865. Abiel married second Mary Blaisdell.

ii PHEBE CARLETON, b. 13 Feb 1792; d. at Portland, 24 Jun 1853. Phebe did not marry.

iii HANNAH EMERY CARLETON, b. 6 Sep 1794; d. at Portland, Mar 1844.

iv ELIZABETH A. CARLETON, b. 14 Dec 1796; d. at Portland, after 1860. Elizabeth did not marry.

v EDWARD CARLETON, b. 20 Sep 1799; d. at Waterford, ME, 22 Aug 1856; m. 22 Jul 1824, ACHSAH MUNROE, b. in MA, about 1802 daughter of William and Achsah (Sawyer) Munroe;[2118] Achsah d. at Waterford, 5 Feb 1875.

vi WILLIAM CARLETON, b. 4 Feb 1802; d. at Port Townsend, WA, 1873; m. at Rockton, IL, 23 Sep 1840, MELISSA JANE AUSTIN, b. at Buckfield, ME, 1814 daughter of Silas and Lydia (Briggs) Austin; Melissa d. at Port Townsend, 1881.

vii JOHN CARLETON, b. 12 Jul 1804; d. 15 Aug 1805.

viii MARY CARLETON, b. 9 Mar 1807; d. at Calais, ME, 3 Apr 1857; m. 1833, PHINEAS HOLDEN "P.H." GLOVER, b. at Dorchester, MA, Nov 1807 son of Samuel and Martha (Holden) Glover; Phineas d. at Quincy, MA, 28 Feb 1884. Phineas married second Irene C. Nash 19 Aug 1860.

ix HARRIET CARLETON, b. 6 Dec 1809; d. at Port Townsend, WA, 1882; m. about 1830, EDWARD SIDNEY DYER, b. in ME, 1804 son of Jones and Lydia (Knight) Dyer; Edward d. at Port Townsend, 5 Oct 1875.

x ABIEL CARLETON, b. 23 Mar 1813; d in IL, April 1846.

785) ABIEL ABBOT *(Abigail Abbott Abbot⁴, Benjamin³, Benjamin², George¹)*, b. at Andover, 17 Aug 1770 son of John and Abigail (Abbott) Abbot; d. at New York in transit from Cuba, 7 Jun 1828;[2119] m. at Haverhill, 19 Jul 1796, EUNICE WALES, b. at Roxbury, 21 Sep 1772 daughter of Ebenezer and Eunice (Davis) Wales; Eunice d. at Dorchester, 29 Dec 1831.

Abiel Abbot was a prominent clergyman. He graduated from Harvard in 1787 and received the Doctor of Divinity in 1792. He was pastor of the Beverly Congregational Church. He died of yellow fever on the ship *Othello* in New York. In 1827, having spent the winter in Charleston, South Carolina and in Cuba.[2120]

In his will dated 21 October 1818 (probate 19 August 1828), Abiel Abbot left the income of his estate in trust to his brother-in-law Ebenezer Wales for the support of Abiel's wife and children until the youngest child arrives at age fourteen. After the youngest child reaches fourteen, the estate is to be divided as follows. One-third of the estate to his wife forever exclusive of her dower provided she relinquish her right of dower. The remaining two thirds to be divided equally among his children (who are not named). Ebenezer Wales was named executor. Real estate was valued at $1,525 and personal estate at $1,962.15 the bulk of which was cash received from the parish at Beverly.[2121]

Abiel and Eunice Abbot had nine children, the oldest four births recorded at Haverhill and the remainder at Beverly.

i EUNICE ADELINE ABBOT, b. at Haverhill, 17 Aug 1797; d. at Beverly 8 Dec 1828; m. 25 Nov 1824, JOSIAH GOULD, b. at Beverly, 1793 (baptized 8 Sep 1793) son of Josiah and Abigail (Williams) Gould; Josiah died 21 Nov 1836 of typhoid fever while at sea.

ii EMILY ABBOT, b. at Haverhill, 4 Sep 1799; d. at Cambridge, MA, 23 Sep 1904; m. 4 Feb 1824, STEVENS EVERETT, b. at Dorchester, 14 Dec 1797 son of Moses and Hannah (Gardner) Everett; Stevens d. 23 Feb 1833 (buried at Dorchester).

iii ABIEL ABBOT, b. at Haverhill, 25 Oct 1800; d. at Cambridge, 18 Sep 1847. Abiel did not marry. In his will, he left his estate to his siblings with his brother-in-law Charles Vaughan as executor.

iv MARY SUSANNA ABBOT, b. at Haverhill, 10 Jan 1803; d. at Cambridge, 3 Sep 1866; m. at Dorchester, 1 Jul 1832, CHARLES VAUGHAN, b. 1804 at Hallowell, ME son of Charles and Frances Western[2122] (Apthorp) Vaughan; Charles d. at Cambridge, 6 Sep 1878.

2117 Dates of birth for the children in this family are from the Abbot *Genealogical Register, p 5*

2118 Warren, *History of Waterford, Maine*, p 273

2119 Abbot, Abiel, Rev. Dr., yellow fever, on his passage from Charleston, S. C, to New York, June 7, 1828, a. 58 y. C. R. 1.

2120 Abbot, *Genealogical Register*, p 6

2121 Essex County, MA: Probate File Papers, 1638-1881.Online database. AmericanAncestors.org. New England Historic Genealogical Society, 2014. Case number 7.

2122 Frances's middle name is variously spelled Western or Weston.

v WILLIAM WALES ABBOT, b. at Beverly, 12 Aug 1805; d. 16 Feb 1806.

vi ANNE WALES ABBOT, b. at Beverly, 10 Apr 1808; d. at Cambridge, 1 Jun 1908.

vii WILLIAM EBENEZER ABBOT, b. at Beverly, 2 May 1810; d. at Boston, 4 May 1888; m. 20 Apr 1837, his first cousin, ANNA SUSAN WALES, b. at Augusta, ME, 1810 daughter of Joseph and Betsy (Wales) Wales; Anna d. at Boston, 20 Dec 1891.

viii JOHN JOSEPH ABBOT, b. at Beverly, 4 Feb 1812; d. 17 Jul 1816.

ix ELIZABETH ABBOT, b. at Beverly, 24 Mar 1815; d. at Cambridge, 27 Feb 1849. Elizabeth did not marry. She died of typhoid fever.

786) BENJAMIN ABBOTT *(Abiel⁴, Benjamin³, Benjamin², George¹)*, b. at Andover, 28 May 1763 son of Abiel and Phebe (Ballard) Abbott; d. at Newburyport, 18 Aug 1821; m. 21 Nov 1786, JOANNA HOLMES, b. at Newburyport, 1765 daughter of Francis and Mary (Smith) Holmes; Joanna d. at Newburyport, 11 Aug 1828.

Benjamin Abbott was a deacon in Newburyport. He and Joanna Holmes were parents of ten children born at Newburyport.

i PHEBE BALLARD ABBOTT, b. 10 Oct 1787; d. at Rockingham, NH, about 1875. Phebe did not marry. For a time, she lived with her sister Sarah and her husband Jonathan Palmer in Rockingham.

ii JOANNA ABBOTT, b. 4 Jan 1790; d. at Chester, NH, 30 Apr 1842; m. at Newburyport, 25 Jul 1825, JOHN PICKET, b. at Marblehead, about 1788 son of William and Dorothy (Skinner) Picket; John d. at Chester, 14 Apr 1851. After Joanna's death, John married Elizabeth Morrill 14 Dec 1842.

iii MARY SMITH ABBOTT, b. 21 Oct 1791; d. at Newburyport, 9 Dec 1848. Mary did not marry.

iv ELIZABETH ABBOTT, b. 1 Feb 1793; d. at Kensington, 5 Mar 1866; m. at Newbury, 2 Apr 1826, WILLIAM FITTS, b. at Kensington, 1802 son of Richard and Elizabeth (Currier) Fitts;[2123] William d. at Kensington, 26 Aug 1844.

v BENJAMIN ABBOTT, b. 10 Dec 1794; d. at sea, Aug 1818.

vi FRANCIS HOLMES ABBOTT, b. 4 Jan 1797; d. at Orange, NJ, 12 May 1874; m. 1st, at Newbury, 18 Dec 1820, EMILY DODGE, b. at Newbury, 5 Jun 1801 daughter of Robert and Elizabeth (Wade) Dodge; Emily d. at Newburyport, 10 Oct 1824. Francis m. 2nd, at Newbury, 20 Apr 1826, MARY WADE, b. at Ipswich, 24 Oct 1804 daughter of Thomas and Elizabeth (Mansfield) Wade.

vii ABIEL ABBOTT, b. 26 Jul 1798; d. at Jersey City, NJ, 20 Dec 1871; m. 1st, at Lowell, 26 Nov 1826, CHARLOTTE MORRILL, b. at Amesbury, 12 Dec 1805 daughter of John and Catherine (Gerrish) Morrill; Charlotte d. at Lowell, 26 Mar 1827. Abiel m. 2nd, 24 Feb 1828, RUTH MORRILL, b. at Amesbury, 23 Jan 1807 daughter of John and Catherine (Gerrish) Morrill; Ruth d. at Jersey City, 9 Dec 1877.

viii SARAH ABBOTT, b. 19 Jun 1800; d. at Kensington, NH, 29 Apr 1867; m. at Newburyport, 6 Jan 1848, as his second wife, JONATHAN PALMER, b. at Kensington, 1800 son of Daniel and Sarah (Dole) Palmer; Jonathan d. at Kensington, 8 Aug 1881. Jonathan was first married to Dorothy Locke and third married to Mary Packard.

ix REBECCA ABBOTT, b. Jul 1802; d. 9 Aug 1802.

x JOHN OWEN ABBOTT, b. 5 Aug 1803; d. at sea, Dec 1830. John Owen, Capt., "perished in the wreck of the Brig Samaritan on the coast of Maryland Dec. —, 1830, a. 27 y."

787) ELIZABETH CUMMINGS *(Elizabeth Abbott Cummings⁴, Benjamin³, Benjamin², George¹)*, b. at Hollis, 23 Nov 1759 daughter of Ebenezer and Elizabeth (Abbott) Cummings; d. 3 Oct 1812; m. 13 Jun 1780, her third cousin, HENRY LOVEJOY, b. at Andover, 23 Nov 1753 son of William and Hannah (Evans) Lovejoy; Henry d. at Wilton, 14 Feb 1835.

Henry Lovejoy served in the Revolution first enlisting from Wilton as a private in May 1775 in the New Hampshire regiment of Colonel Read for a period of eight months. In May 1777 he served one month as a Sergeant in the company of Captain Boardman for one month and was a private for two in July to August 1777. He had additional service in 1778 as a private in the company of Captain Ballard.

[2123] Fitts, *Genealogy of the Fitts Family*, p 30

In his pension application, Henry stated he lived in Wilton after the war and removed to Hillsborough in 1799. From there, he went to Lyndeborough and Temple and was back in Wilton in 1830.[2124]

Elizabeth Cummings and Henry Lovejoy were parents of eight children, the births of the oldest six children recorded at Wilton and the two youngest children at Hillsborough.[2125]

i ELIZABETH LOVEJOY, b. 31 Jan 1782; d. at Wilton, 26 Apr 1846. Elizabeth did not marry.

ii HENRY LOVEJOY, b. 26 Feb 1784; died in infancy.

iii HENRY LOVEJOY, b. 2 May 1786; d. at Hillsborough, 26 May 1864; m. HANNAH LITTLE, b. 18 Nov 1786 daughter of George and Esther (Cole) Little; Hannah d. at Hillsborough, 7 Nov 1865.

iv JACOB LOVEJOY, b. 28 Oct 1788; m. 27 Oct 1812, POLLY FLETCHER, b. at Wilton, 17 Jun 1791 daughter of Oliver and Molly (Wilson) Fletcher.[2126]

v EZRA LOVEJOY, b. 2 Mar 1794; d. at Hornellsville, NY, after 1880; m. at Lyndeborough, 27 Dec 1821, his fourth cousin, MARY ORDWAY *(Sarah Abbott Ordway[5], Josiah[4], Ephraim[3], John[2], George[1])*, b. at Lyndeborough, 13 Aug 1800 daughter of Enoch and Sarah (Abbott) Ordway; Martha d. at Hornellsville, Mar 1880. Mary Ordway is a child in Family 380.

vi AMOS LOVEJOY, b. 27 Nov 1796; nothing further known.

vii POLLY LOVEJOY, b. 27 Mar 1800; d. at Temple, 28 Dec 1878; m. at Temple, 21 Jun 1856, DAVID MOORE, b. about 1790; David d. at Temple, after 1870. Polly and her sister Sally were living together in Wilton in 1850. Polly married after Sally's death.

viii SALLY LOVEJOY, b. 10 Mar 1801; d. at Wilton, 20 Oct 1854. Sally did not marry.

788) EBENEZER CUMMINGS *(Elizabeth Abbott Cummings[4], Benjamin[3], Benjamin[2], George[1])*, b. at Hollis, 15 Sep 1761 son of Ebenezer and Elizabeth (Abbott) Cummings; d, about 1842;[2127] m. at Surry, NH, 29 May 1787, HANNAH WASHER, b. at Amherst, about 1767 daughter of Stephen and Sarah (Wilkins) Washer; Hannah d. at Andover, VT, 6 Aug 1837.

Ebenezer Cummings lived in Andover, Vermont where he had a business in dressing cloth. His daughter Betsey was also in the cloth trade working as a tailoress.[2128] Ebenezer was living in Ludlow, Vermont in 1839 when he pursued a pension for his war service, the pension being previously denied.

Ebenezer served as a private in Regiment of Colonel Peabody from October to December 1780. He also reported enlisting in March 1781 for a period of three years.[2129]

Ebenezer Cummings and Hannah Washer were parents of eight children born at Andover, Vermont.

i HANNAH CUMMINGS, b. 5 Sep 1787; d. at Andover, VT, 2 Sep 1803.

ii BRIDGET CUMMINGS, b. 26 May 1789; d. at Ludlow, VT. Bridget did not marry.

iii EBENEZER CUMMINGS, b. 10 Jul 1793; d. 30 Aug 1803.

iv BETSEY CUMMINGS, b. 26 Aug 1795; d. at Waukesha, WI, 31 Dec 1862; m. JONATHAN CRAM, b. at Salisbury, NH, 2 Jun 1773 son of Jonathan and Martha (French) Cram; Jonathan d. at Waukesha, 7 Jun 1861.

v STEPHEN CUMMINGS, b. 28 Mar 1797; d. perhaps at Peoria, IL, 1861;[2130] m. 1823, MARY ANN WOODWORTH, b. in CT, 1798 daughter of Ezra and Susan (Gager) Woodworth;[2131] Mary Ann d. at Cook County, IL, 23 Jun 1884.

vi LEONARD CUMMINGS, b. 24 Aug 1798; d. at Beaver Dam, WI, before 1860; m. at Sandwich, MA, 17 May 1827, DEBORAH HAMBLEN, b. at Sandwich, 20 Nov 1807 daughter of Nathaniel and Fear (Fish) Hamblen; Deborah d. at Beaver Dam, after 1860.

[2124] Revolutionary War Pension and Bounty-Land Warrant Application Files, 1800-1900

[2125] *The History of Wilton* reports a ninth child in this family, William (no birth date given) who was reported to die of consumption as a young man, but no records were located for him.

[2126] Livermore, History of Wilton, p 367

[2127] His death is reported by several sources as occurring in Wisconsin. However, he seems to have still been in Vermont in 1839 when his son Stephen made an appeal related to his father not having received his military service pension which he first applied for in 1832. It is possible that he relocated to Wisconsin in his very last years, perhaps to be with one of his children, but that needs further investigation. There is a death record for Ebenezer's wife 6 Aug 1837 in Vermont, so Ebenezer was still in Vermont in 1837. Some of his children did relocate to Wisconsin.

[2128] Gutterson, *The Local History of Andover, Vermont*, p 21

[2129] Revolutionary War Pension and Bounty-Land Warrant Application Files, 1800-1900

[2130] Stephen was living in Peoria in 1860.

[2131] The 1836 will of Ezra Woodworth of Ludlow, VT includes a bequest to his daughter Mary Ann Cummings.

vii JACOB CUMMINGS, b. 17 Jul 1800; d. at Deerfield, IA, after 1880; m. at Andover, VT, 13 Mar 1820, LYDIA R. DODGE, b. in VT, 1799 daughter of Moses Ritter and Peggy (Knight) Dodge; Lydia d. at Deerfield, after 1880.

viii BENJAMIN FRANKLIN CUMMINGS, b. 24 Jan 1803; d. at Ludlow, VT, 6 May 1833; m. about 1830, ALMIRA BATES, b. at Ludlow, VT, 3 May 1805 daughter of Oren and Lois (McKinstry) Bates; Almira d. at Ludlow, 4 Jul 1887.

789) ABIGAIL CUMMINGS *(Elizabeth Abbott Cummings⁴, Benjamin³, Benjamin², George¹)*, b. at Hollis, 1 Jul 1763 daughter of Ebenezer and Elizabeth (Abbott) Cummings; d. likely at Bartlett, 14 Nov 1801; m. at Conway, 8 Apr 1788, JOSEPH SEAVEY, b. 1762 son of Jonathan and Comfort (Cates) Seavey; Joseph d. at Bartlett, NH, about 1812.

Little information has been located for this family. There is evidence of four children likely born at Bartlett, New Hampshire.

i JOSEPH SEAVEY, b. 16 Oct 1788; *possibly* m. at Boston, 25 Mar 1814, MARY PARK.

ii HANNAH SEAVEY, b. 22 Apr 1790; d. at Hart's Location, NH, 26 Aug 1839; m. about 1814, as his third wife, ELIAS HALL, b. at Falmouth, ME, 16 Aug 1777 son of Joseph and Mary (Cox) Hall; Elias d. at Jefferson, NH, 16 Oct 1851. Elias was first married to Hannah Tyman, second to Polly Hubbard, and fourth to Sarah Mead.

iii EBENEZER CUMMINGS SEAVEY, b. 13 Jan 1792

iv BENJAMIN SEAVEY, b. 11 Jan 1794

790) LUCY CUMMINGS *(Elizabeth Abbott Cummings⁴, Benjamin³, Benjamin², George¹)*, b. at Hollis, 9 Jul 1767 daughter of Ebenezer and Elizabeth (Abbott) Cummings; d. 15 Oct 1854; m. 8 Apr 1788, PETER PEAVEY, b. at Andover, 14 Apr 1762 son of Thomas and Dorcas (Holt) Peavey; Peter d. at Greenfield, NH, 28 Jul 1836.

Peter Peavey served in the Revolution and was present at the surrender of Burgoyne. He continued service in the militia following the war achieving the rank of Major. He was a mill owner in Greenfield.[2132]

Lucy Cummings and Peter Peavey were parents of twelve children all born at Greenfield.

i PETER PEAVEY, b. 27 Jul 1788; d. at Greenfield, 26 Oct 1879; m. 1st, about 1815, his fourth cousin once removed, DORCAS HOLT *(John Holt⁵, Joshua Holt⁴, Dorcas Abbott Holt³, Timothy², George¹)*, b. at Greenfield, 12 Jan 1793 daughter of John and Dorcas (Abbott) Holt; Dorcas d. at Greenfield, 4 Jan 1856. Peter m. 2nd, about 1857, Dorcas's sister, TAMESIN HOLT, b. 23 Nov 1803; Tamesin d. at Greenfield, 4 Jan 1896. Dorcas and Tamesin Holt are children in Family 526.

ii SALLY PEAVEY, b. 11 Jul 1790; d. at Greenfield, 18 Sep 1874; m. 2 Jun 1855, as his second wife, WILLIAM WRIGHT, b. about 1790 *perhaps* the son of Jonas and Rebecca (Boynton) Wright; William d. after 1874. William was first married to Nancy Flynn.

iii LUCY CUMMINGS PEAVEY, b. 3 Jul 1792; d. at Milford, NH, 13 Feb 1874; m. 14 Jun 1816, her fourth cousin, FARNUM HOLT *(Joshua Holt⁵, Joshua Holt⁴, Dorcas Abbott Holt³, Timothy², George¹)*, b. at Greenfield, 15 Apr 1791 son of Joshua and Hannah (Ingalls) Holt; Farnum d. at Greenfield, 27 Feb 1865. Farnum Holt is a child in Family 867.

iv BENJAMIN ABBOTT PEAVEY, b. 25 Sep 1794; d. at Boylston, MA, 16 Nov 1864; m. about 1822, CLARISSA WHITTEMORE, b. at Greenfield, 11 Dec 1799 daughter of Amos and Polly (Savage) Whittemore; Clarissa d. at Barre, MA, 19 May 1871.

v JACOB S. PEAVEY, b. 24 Dec 1797; d. at Londonderry, 5 Mar 1872; m. 1st, at Henniker, 2 Nov 1824, SUSAN CAMPBELL, b. at Henniker, 5 Aug 1805 daughter of Phineas and Susanna (Bowman) Campbell; Susan d. at Henniker, 16 Feb 1838. Jacob m. 2nd, 26 Mar 1840, SARAH MARSH, b. at Henniker, 7 Aug 1802 daughter of Joseph and Mehitable (Harriman) Marsh; Sarah d. at Londonderry, 15 Aug 1884.

vi ABIEL PEAVEY, b. 27 Mar 1799; d. 29 Nov 1799.

vii DORCAS PEAVEY, b. 8 Oct 1801; d. at Wilton, 19 Mar 1884; m. 1st, at Lyndeborough, 2 Mar 1824, EDWARD PRATT, b. at Reading, 2 Sep 1797 son of Edward and Asenath (Flint) Pratt; Edward d. at Wilton, 1 Feb 1838.

[2132] Livermore, *History of Wilton*, p 467

Dorcas m. 2nd, about 1847, WILLIAM SHELDON, b. at Wilton, 9 May 1810 son of Samuel and Phebe (Keyes) Sheldon; William d. at Wilton, 14 Nov 1891.

viii ELIZABETH PEAVEY, b. 6 Apr 1803; d. 5 Nov 1803.

ix ELIZABETH PEAVEY, b. 30 Aug 1804; d. at Lowell, MA, 28 Oct 1882; m. 4 Jun 1833, NEHEMIAH LOWE, b. at Greenfield, about 1805 son of Simon and Mary (Burnham) Lowe; Nehemiah d. at Lowell, 1 Nov 1891.

x ABIEL PEAVEY, b. 17 Jan 1807; d. at Lowell, 14 Sep 1886; m. at Swanzey, NH, 4 Dec 1832, LOUISA STONE, b. at Swanzey, 9 Mar 1813 daughter of Martin and Betsey (Valentine) Stone; Louisa d. at Lowell, 23 Nov 1904.

xi JOHN MERRILL PEAVEY, b. 30 Nov 1809; d. 2 Dec 1809

xii MERRILL C. PEAVEY, b. 7 Aug 1812; d. at Lowell, 8 Aug 1873; m. at Swanzey, 3 Jun 1841, ELIZABETH STONE, b. at Swanzey, 24 Feb 1817 daughter of Martin and Betsey (Valentine) Stone; Elizabeth d. at Lowell, 1 Mar 1890.

791) MARY CUMMINGS *(Elizabeth Abbott Cummings[4], Benjamin[3], Benjamin[2], George[1])*, b. at Hollis, 22 Oct 1770 daughter of Ebenezer and Elizabeth (Abbott) Cummings; d. at Francestown, NH, 6 Apr 1856; m. 8 Dec 1810, WILLIAM BIXBY, b. 4 Nov 1779 son of Edward and Lucy (Barnes) Bixby; William d. at Francestown, 30 Oct 1862.

William Bixby was a bank president in Francestown. Mary and William had one adopted child[2133] who was the biological child of Merrill Pierce and Dorcas Barker (Family 779).

i NANCY PIERCE, b. at Hillsborough, 16 Oct 1812 biological child of Merrill and Dorcas (Baker) Pierce); d. at Nashua, 16 Aug 1895; m. 4 Sep 1834, EDWARD P. EMERSON, b. at Francestown, about 1809 son of Timothy and Miriam (Pelty) Emerson; Edward d. at Nashua, 23 Feb 1882.

792) JACOB ABBOT CUMMINGS *(Elizabeth Abbott Cummings[4], Benjamin[3], Benjamin[2], George[1])*, b. at Hollis, 2 Nov 1772 son of Ebenezer and Elizabeth (Abbott) Cummings; d. at Boston, 24 Feb 1820; m. 9 Aug 1807, ELIZABETH MERRILL, b. at Haverhill, 10 Mar 1781 daughter of Gyles and Lucy (Cushing) Merrill; Elizabeth d. at Portland, ME, 24 Dec 1867.

Jacob Cummings was a teacher and bookseller in Boston. He was the author of spelling book.[2134]

In his will, Jacob leaves to wife Elizabeth all the household furniture and his private library for her use. He bequeathed to his sister Sally Cummings one thousand dollars. All the remainder of the estate is to be held in trust and used for the care and support of his wife Elizabeth and son James Merrill Cummings. Henry Foster of Boston Merchant is named executor. The estate includes his portion of a book selling business.[2135]

Jacob Abbot Cummings and Elizabeth Merrill had two children born at Boston.

i JAMES MERRILL CUMMINGS, b. 27 Jul 1810; d. at Portland, ME, 20 Jul 1883; m. at Portland, 4 Nov 1835, SARAH THURSTON PHILLIPS HALL, b. at Portland, 10 Sep 1804 daughter of Joel and Sarah (Thurston) Hall; Sarah d. at Portland, after 1880.

ii JOHN S. CUMMINGS, b. 5 Nov 1812; d. 16 Jul 1813.

793) JOHN MERRILL *(Elizabeth Abbott Merrill[4], Benjamin[3], Benjamin[2], George[1])*, b. 2 Mar 1782 son of Thomas and Elizabeth (Abbott) Merrill; d. at Portland, ME, 7 Jun 1855; m. at Portland, 26 Sep 1820, MARY SOUTHGATE BOYD, b. at Portland, 20 Jan 1797 daughter of Joseph Coffin and Isabella (Southgate) Boyd; Mary d. Apr 1861.[2136]

John Merrill attended Exeter Academy, graduated from Harvard in 1804, and completed medical school training at Harvard in 1807.[2137] He was a physician in Portland.

John and Mary Merrill had five children. One son, John Cummings, was a physician and son Charles Benjamin was an attorney. Sons John Cummings and Charles Benjamin served on opposite sides in the Civil War. Dr. John Cummings Merrill was working in Natchez, Mississippi when the war broke out and joined the Confederate army enlisting as a private (serving as a physician) in Captain Henry Lathrop's Company.[2138] Dates of service were 3 December 1861 through 20 January 1862. John Cummings Merrill returned to Portland after the war where he practiced medicine. Lieutenant Colonel Charles Benjamin Merrill served in the 17th Maine Regiment.[2139]

2133 Cochrane and Wood, *History of Francestown*, p 518

2134 Merrill, *A Merrill Memorial*, p 363

2135 *Suffolk County (Massachusetts) Probate Records, 1636-1899;* Author: *Massachusetts. Probate Court (Suffolk County);* Probate Place: *Suffolk, Massachusetts, Probate Records, Vol 118, 1819*, pp 204-205

2136 Chapman, *Monograph of the Southgate Family*, p 27

2137 Harvard University, Quinquennial Catalogue

2138 National Archives, Compiled Service Records of Confederate Soldiers Who Served in Organizations from the State of Mississippi.

2139 National Archives, Letters Received by the Commission Branch of the Adjutant General's Office, 1863-1870.

Five children of John and Mary Merrill were born at Portland, Maine.

i ISABELLA SOUTHGATE MERRILL, b. 2 Jul 1823; d. at Portland, 6 Feb 1871. Isabella did not marry.

ii An infant daughter, born and died about 1825.

iii CHARLES BENJAMIN MERRILL, b. 14 Apr 1827; d. at Portland, 5 Apr 1891; m. 24 Sep 1856, ABBA ISABELLA LITTLE, born about 1835 daughter of Josiah S. and Abba I. (Chamberlain) Little; Abba d. at Portland, 8 Oct 1891.

iv JOHN CUMMINGS MERRILL, b. 8 Nov 1831; d. at Portland, 6 Aug 1900; m. 18 Oct 1886, CLARA BROOKS, b. at Portland, 31 Dec 1852 daughter of John Cotton and Caroline Whitman (Parris) Brooks; Clara d. 11 Nov 1931. Despite their late marriage, John and Clara had two children. Their daughter, Janet Boyd Merrill, died 2 Feb 1951.

v MARY BOYD MERRILL, b. 7 May 1837; d. at Portland, 23 Apr 1919. Mary did not marry. The Southgate Monograph reports she lived in New York; however, in each census record located for her she was living in Maine (Portland or Gorham) with family members. No occupation was listed.

794) ANNA BURGE *(Anna Abbott Burge⁴, Benjamin³, Benjamin², George¹)*, b. at Hollis, 20 Nov 1762 daughter of Ephraim and Anna (Abbott) Burge; d. at Dunstable, 31 Oct 1794; m. 17 Nov 1783, PHINEAS FLETCHER, b. 28 Nov 1757 son of Joseph and Elizabeth (Underwood) Fletcher. Phineas m. 2nd, Alice Ames; Phineas d. 31 Jul 1833.

Anna married Phineas Fletcher of Dunstable, Massachusetts and resided there with him.

In his will written 26 January 1816, Phineas Fletcher bequeaths to beloved wife Allis Fletcher her full one-third part right of dower. She also receives $175, two cows, and half the household furniture. Daughter Anna receives $100, half the furniture that was her mother's, and the great bible. Daughter Betsey receives $100 and the remaining half of the furniture that was her mother's. Daughters Indiana, Sally, Lucy, and Jane each receive $100. Jane's legacy is to be held in trust until she is capable of taking care of herself. The remaining half of his furniture is to be equally divided among his six daughters. All the remainder of the estate goes to son Mark Fletcher who is also named executor. There is a codicil to the will dated 26 January 1823 in which he bequeaths an additional $25 to Allice and all the provisions that he dies possessed of. She also has use of all his library while she remains a widow. After his death, the library is to be divided among his six youngest children. Phineas also provides that any of his daughters that remain unmarried can have use of the house.[2140] Indiana, Sally, Lucy, and Jane are Phineas's daughters from his second marriage to Alice Ames.

Anna Burge and Phineas Fletcher had six children born at Dunstable.

i ANNA FLETCHER, b. 29 Oct 1784; d. at Mason, NH, 1 Feb 1837; m. 4 Jun 1816, as his second wife, NATHANIEL CUMMINGS, b. at Westford, 15 Sep 1778 son of Nathaniel and Rebecca (Wilson) Cummings;[2141] Nathaniel d. at Townsend, MA, 1 Sep 1854. Nathaniel was first married to Martha Fletcher.

ii SEWALL FLETCHER, b. 19 Oct 1786; d. 29 May 1795.

iii MARK FLETCHER, b. 19 Aug 1788; d. 16 Nov 1789.

iv MARK FLETCHER, b. 14 Sep 1790; d. at Dunstable, 4 Aug 1851; m. 27 Dec 1817, RHODA FLETCHER, b. at Dunstable, 24 Dec 1796 daughter of Samuel and Rhoda (Kendall) Fletcher; Rhoda d. at Dunstable, 25 Oct 1858.

v ELIZABETH "BETSEY" FLETCHER, b. 2 Aug 1792; d. at Derry, NH, 10 Nov 1858; m. 1st, 12 Apr 1825, SAMUEL W. SLOAN, b. about 1791; Samuel d. at Roxbury, 17 May 1826. Elizabeth m. 2nd, 27 Oct 1833,[2142] as his third wife, GILBERT BROOKS, b. 1785 and d. at Derry, 28 Feb 1854. Elizabeth and Gilbert had one son who died at age six months. In her will written 10 October 1856, Elizabeth made a bequest of a looking glass to Lucretia Fletcher of Dunstable and the remainder of her estate to stepdaughter Martha Ann Brooks. Martha Ann was the child of Gilbert and his second wife, Martha Burge. Martha Burge and Elizabeth Fletcher were first cousins.

vi CHARLOTTE FLETCHER, b. 19 May 1794; d. 30 Sep 1794.

[2140] Middlesex County, MA: Probate File Papers, 1648-1871.Online database. AmericanAncestors.org. Case number 7906

[2141] Cummins, *Cummings Genealogy*, p 351

[2142] New England Historic Genealogical Society, *Massachusetts, Town Marriage Records, 1620-1850, marriage of Mrs. Elizabeth Sloan and Gilbert Brooks*

795) EPHRAIM BURGE *(Anna Abbott Burge⁴, Benjamin³, Benjamin², George¹)*, b. at Hollis, 7 Jun 1764 son of Ephraim and Anna (Abbott) Burge; d. at Hollis, 2 Mar 1853; m. 28 Jan 1793, PATTY BALDWIN, b. at Amherst, NH, 2 Mar 1764 daughter of Nahum and Mary (Lowe) Baldwin; Patty d. 2 Aug 1822.

In his will written 5 March 1830 and proved 6 June 1843, Ephraim Burge bequeaths all his real estate to his only son Cyrus Burge. Cyrus also receives all the personal estate excepting some notes and personal securities. The will also refers to agreements relating to Cyrus's sisters and it seems, although not entirely clear, that there have already been financial arrangements made related to Ephraim's daughters. Cyrus's receipt of the estate is provisioned on Cyrus caring for his father by providing him comfortable clothing, wholesome food in sickness and health, and the use of horse and carriage to visit his friends. Ephraim also states that Cyrus will have benefit of Ephraim's labor, given at Ephraim's discretion, in order to pay other of Ephraim's necessary expenses and charitable donations, not to exceed 10 dollar per year. Cyrus is named sole executor. At inventory, real estate was valued at $3,980 including $3,000 for the home farm. Personal estate was valued at $551.64.[2143]

Ephraim and Patty had seven children born at Hollis.

i EPHRAIM BURGE, b. 8 Nov 1794; d. at Hollis, Oct 1825. Ephraim does not seem to have married.

ii MARTHA BURGE, b. 9 May 1796; d. 3 Apr 1830; m. at Medford, MA, 13 May 1826, as the second of his three wives, GILBERT BROOKS, b. 1785[2144] of not known parentage; Gilbert d. at Derry, NH, 28 Feb 1854. Gilbert was first married to Betsey Barstow. His third marriage was to another George Abbott descendant, ELIZABETH "BETSEY" FLETCHER. Elizabeth Fletcher is a child in Family 794.

iii ANNA BURGE, b. 13 Jul 1798; d. at Manchester, MA, 19 Sep 1882; m. at Middleton, 13 Jul 1839, as his second wife, ANDREW MERRIAM, b. at Middleton, 24 May 1780 son of Silas and Lydia (Peabody) Merriam;[2145] Andrew d. at Middleton, 15 Apr 1863. Andrew was first married to Ann Jane Nixon.

iv NAHUM BURGE, b. 5 Sep 1800; d. 3 Nov 1801.[2146]

v CLARISSA BURGE, b. 12 May 1802; d. 2 Dec 1820.

vi CYRUS BURGE, b. 7 Sep 1804; d. at Hollis, 24 Jun 1884; m. 1835, JOANNA CUMMINGS, b. at Hudson, NH, 26 Nov 1806 daughter of Samuel and Joanna (Wyman) Cummings;[2147] Joanna d. at Hollis, 9 Aug 1886.

vii EMMA BURGE, b. 7 Nov 1807; d. not located but living in Lawrence, MA in 1850; m. at Hollis, 11 May 1834, GEORGE W. HUBBARD, b. at Hanover, NH, 2 Dec 1808 son of John and Rebecca (Preston) Hubbard;[2148] George d. in California in 1849. George and Emma were missionaries and embarked for a mission assignment in India just ten days after their marriage.[2149]

796) SUSANNAH "SUKEY" BURGE *(Anna Abbott Burge⁴, Benjamin³, Benjamin², George¹)*, b. at Hollis, 21 Jul 1773 daughter of Ephraim and Anna (Abbott) Burge; d. at Hollis, 6 Sep 1816; m. 16 Apr 1799, THOMAS FARLEY, b. 28 Dec 1769 son of Caleb and Elizabeth (Farley) Farley; Thomas d. 17 Mar 1832. Thomas was first married to Polly Jewett who died in 1795. After Sukey's death, he married Polly (-).

Sukey and Thomas Farley reared their family in Hollis, New Hampshire. Thomas was chosen a deacon of Hollis Congregational Church in 1803 a position he held until his death.[2150] One of their sons, Thomas Abbot Farley, attended Andover Theological Seminary.

In his will written 16 September 1831, Thomas Farley leaves to beloved wife Polly Farley all the household goods and furniture that she brought to the marriage. Polly also has use of a room in the house and of the kitchen and scullery as long as she remains a widow. He bequeaths to daughters Polly Farley and Anna Farley each two hundred and the use of chambers in the house. Wife Polly and daughters Polly and Anna will share a section of the house. Youngest son Thomas Abbot Farley receives $120. Eldest son Asa Farley receives all the remainder of the estate and is named executor. Asa is charged with providing for the needs of his mother (his stepmother) and a specific list of provisions is provided.[2151]

Thomas and Sukey Farley had nine children born at Hollis.

i Stillborn son, 19 Nov 1799

ii SUSANNA FARLEY, b. 13 Jun 1801; d. 7 Dec 1822.

[2143] New Hampshire County Probate Records, 1660-1973, Hillsborough County, probate of Ephraim Burge, 48:268, 44:291, 49:485. Accessed through familysearch.org.
[2144] Gilbert's birth year only is report in Medford records.
[2145] Pope, *Merriam Genealogy*, p 86
[2146] Nahum is a child included in the Abbot genealogy but he is not in other sources.
[2147] Cummins, *Cummings Genealogy*, p 132
[2148] Day, *One Thousand Years of Hubbard History*, p 323
[2149] Tracy, *History of American Missions*, p 227
[2150] Worcester, *History of the Town of Hollis*, p 242.
[2151] *New Hampshire. Probate Court (Hillsborough County)*; Probate Place: *Hillsborough, New Hampshire, Probate Records, Vol 38-39, 1829-1833*, will of Thomas Farley 16 Sep 1831

iii POLLY FARLEY, b. 2 Jun 1803; d. at Hollis, 30 Aug 1876; m. 21 Mar 1833, DANIEL FARLEY, b. at Hollis, 4 Dec 1806 son of Ebenezer and Abigail Minot (Farmer) Farley; Daniel d. at Hollis, 8 Feb 1887.

iv ASA FARLEY, b. 7 Apr 1804; d. at Medina, MI, 10 Oct 1885; m. 22 Sep 1831, SYBIL CYRENE HOLT, b. at Hollis, 13 Sep 1806 daughter of Nathan Taylor and Sybil (Phelps) Holt; Sybil d. at Medina, 30 Aug 1888.

v ANNA FARLEY, b. 3 Jun 1806; d. 27 Jul 1809.

vi JOSIAH BURGE FARLEY, b. 11 Jun 1808; d. 17 Jan 1816.

vii ANNA FARLEY, b. 8 Jan 1811; d. 14 Jun 1837. Anna did not marry.

viii THOMAS ABBOT FARLEY, b. 1 Jul 1813; d. 26 Aug 1841.

ix EPHRAIM B. FARLEY, b. 12 Jul 1816; d. 28 Jul 1816.

797) SAMUEL BURGE *(Anna Abbott Burge⁴, Benjamin³, Benjamin², George¹)*, b. at Hollis, 28 Mar 1779 son of Ephraim and Anna (Abbott) Burge; d. at Francestown, NH, 5 Sep 1824; m. by 1805, ANNA MAY,[2152] b. 1787 (age 30 at time of death); d. 30 Oct 1817. Samuel m. 2nd, 5 Feb 1822, DEBORAH STARETT, b. 26 Dec 1782 daughter of William and Abigail (Fisher) Starett.

Samuel Burge lived in Francestown and there is some discrepancy about the names of and the number of his wives (refer to the footnote). There is evidence for six children, one son from a first wife Charlotte Morrill and five children with his second wife Anna May. In any event, only three children were living at the time Samuel wrote his will in 1824 and these are all children with his wife Anna May.

Samuel was a blacksmith in Francestown and built his shop there in 1820 replacing a shop he had run out of a smaller location.[2153]

In his will written 27 May 1824, Samuel Burge leaves to beloved wife Deborah all the wearing apparel and household goods that she brought to the marriage. In addition, during the period of minority of son Benjamin Burge, Deborah has use of the homestead farm and outland and she is to keep the fences and tools in good repair. If Deborah remarries, this use will cease. Beloved son Benjamin receives all the real estate including the homestead farm and all the lands in Francestown when he reaches age twenty-one. The exception is the dower payment to Deborah. The personal estate is to be divided among his three children daughters Anna Abbot Burge and Mary Burge and Benjamin Burge, except that each of the daughters will receive $50 more in value of the personal estate than Benjamin. While they remain single, daughters Anna and Mary have use of the west room and west bedroom and access to the cellar. The daughters will also receive a set of summer and winter bedding when they reach age twenty-one or marry. The blacksmith shop and tools can be sold at the executor's discretion. Daughter Mary is to have benefit of the town school and three months of public school if any is kept in the town until she is eighteen. Son Benjamin is to be provided a suitable place until he is sixteen and then if he chooses a trade, he can be set out to learn one by his guardian. Daniel Lewis is named sole executor.[2154]

Samuel Burge had six children born at Francestown. The oldest child, Samuel, may be from a first marriage to Charlotte Morrill. The other five children are from Samuel's marriage to Anna May.

i SAMUEL BURGE, b. 24 Aug 1805. There is no further record and he is not mentioned in his father's will.

ii ANNA ABBOT BURGE, b. 23 Apr 1807; d. at Francestown, 8 Nov 1830. Anna did not marry.

iii SALLY BURGE, b. Aug 1808; d. 25 Nov 1810.

iv MARY BURGE, b. 1810; d. at Watertown, WI, 22 Apr 1879; m. 21 Jan 1834, JACOB TAYLOR FULLER, b. at Milford, 7 Apr 1811 son of Robert and Rhoda (French) Fuller; Jacob d. at Watertown, WI, 30 Jan 1883.[2155]

v BENJAMIN BURGE, b. 25 Apr 1812; d. at Enfield, NH, 3 Sep 1858; m. 25 Nov 1841, LUCRETIA DEWEY, b. at Hanover, 27 Jun 1817 daughter of Andrew and Harriet (Pinneo) Dewey;[2156] Lucretia d. at Toulon, IL, 28 Sep 1905.

[2152] Cochrane's *History of Francestown, NH* suggests her name might be Charlotte Morrill. However, her grave stone gives her name as Anna wife of Samuel. In addition, the son of Samuel and Anna, Benjamin, was a graduate of Dartmouth College. Benjamin's biographical sketch for the alumni of Dartmouth College gives his mother's name as Anna May. (Chapman, *Sketches of the Alumni of Dartmouth College*, p 275.) On the other hand, the birth record for the first child Samuel (the only record so far located) lists mother as Charlotte Morrill. It is possible that Samuel was married three times.

[2153] Cochrane, *History of Francestown*, p 414

[2154] *New Hampshire. Probate Court (Hillsborough County)*; Probate Place: *Hillsborough, New Hampshire*, Notes: *Probate Records, Vol 34-35 1824-1827*, will of Samuel Burge, 27 May 1824

[2155] *U.S., Newspaper Extractions from the Northeast, 1704-1930.*

[2156] Dewey, *Life of George Dewey*, p 596

vi Infant b. 10 Jul 1813 and d. 13 Jul 1813

798) JACOB ABBOT *(Dorcas Abbot Abbot[4] Benjamin[3], Benjamin[2], George[1])*, b. at Wilton, 7 Jan 1768 son of Abiel and Dorcas (Abbot) Abbot; d. at Windham, 2 Nov 1834; m. 11 Feb 1802, CATHERINE THAYER, b. at Hampton, 28 Sep 1779 daughter of Ebenezer and Martha (Cotton) Thayer;[2157] Catherine d. at Windham, NH, 27 Jan 1843.

Jacob Abbot graduated from Harvard in 1792 and served as the pastor of the church at Hampton Falls. He served in this role for nineteen years but was dismissed 23 October 1827. There were theological disagreements and Jacob adopted Unitarianism. Following his dismissal, he relocated to Windham, New Hampshire. Jacob died by drowning when his boat overturned while he was crossing a pond near his home.[2158]

Neither Jacob or Catherine left a will and each of their estates were administered by son Ebenezer T. Abbot.

Jacob and Catherine had eleven children born at Hampton.

i SARAH WHITE ABBOTT, b. 11 Nov 1802, d. at Washington, DC, 18 Jul 1879; m. at Windham, NH, 25 Oct 1830, ROBERT MOORE, b. at Nashua, 16 Nov 1798 son of Hugh and Susannah (McAllister) Moore; Robert d. at Nashua, 8 Feb 1871.

ii EBENEZER T. ABBOTT, b. 27 May 1804; d. at Windham, NH, 2 Mar 1853; m. 1st, 1 Feb 1838, ELIZABETH NESMITH, b. at Windham, 19 Aug 1815 daughter of Jacob and Margaret (Dinsmoor) Nesmith; Elizabeth d., at Windham, 31 Dec 1846. Ebenezer m. 2nd, 7 Jul 1849, BETSEY DOW, b. at Windham, 26 Jun 1818 daughter of Abel and Elizabeth (Morrison) Dow; Betsey d. at Windham, 30 Dec 1854.

iii MARTHA THAYER ABBOTT, b. 29 Mar 1806; d. at Hampton, 10 Aug 1891; m. at Windham, 2 Jun 1828, NEHEMIAH PORTER CRAM, b. at Hampton Falls, 3 Aug 1799 son of Jonathan and Rhoda (Tilton) Cram; Nehemiah d. at Hampton, 12 Nov 1879.

iv CATHERINE ABBOTT, b. 18 Mar 1808; d. at Westford, MA, 14 Apr 1891; m. at Windham, 18 Jul 1833, her fourth cousin, JOHN WILLIAM PITT ABBOTT *(John[6], John[5], John[4], Joshua[3], John[2], George[1])*, b. at Hampton, CT, 27 Apr 1806 son of John and Sophia (Mosley) Abbott; John d. at Westford, 16 Aug 1872.

v ELIZABETH DORCAS ABBOTT, b. 24 Mar 1810; d. at Boston, 13 Sep 1879; m. 17 May 1838, her first cousin, ABIEL ABBOT LIVERMORE *(Abigail Abbott Livermore[5], Dorcas Abbott Abbott[4], Benjamin[3], Benjamin[2], George[1])*, b. at Wilton, 30 Oct 1811 son of Jonathan and Abigail (Abbott) Livermore; Abiel d. at Wilton, 28 Nov 1892. After Elizabeth's death, Abiel married Mary A. Keating daughter of William Keating. Abiel was a graduate of Harvard and Cambridge Divinity School. Abiel is a child in Family 802.

vi GEORGE JACOB ABBOT, b. 14 Jul 1812; d. at Goderich, Ontario, 21 Jan 1879;[2159] m. 30 Aug 1841, ANN TAYLOR GILMAN EMERY, b. at Portland, ME, 15 May 1815 daughter of Nicholas and Ann Taylor (Gilman) Emery; Ann d. at Washington, DC, 31 Jan 1861. George graduated from Harvard in 1835 and was a teacher in Washington, DC.

vii ABIGAIL ABBOTT, b. 29 Sep 1814; d. at Lowell, MA, 18 Sep 1905; m. at Windham, 11 Mar 1835, HORATIO WOOD, b. at Newburyport, 1 Dec 1807 son of John and Elizabeth (Smith) Wood; Horatio d. at Lowell, 12 May 1891.

viii PHEBE ABBOTT, b. 1816 and d. 5 Nov 1816.

ix MARY ANN TOPPAN ABBOTT, b. 2 Dec 1817; d. at Peterborough, 9 Aug 1856; m. at Windham, 22 Feb 1844, as his second wife, JAMES WALKER, b. at Rindge, NH, 10 Mar 1784 son of Joshua and Mary (Whitmore) Walker;[2160] James d. at Peterborough, 31 Dec 1854. James was first married to Sally Smith.

x LUCY ELIOT ABBOTT, b. 22 May 1820; d. at Winchester, MA, 24 Jun 1909; m. at Lowell, 19 Aug 1846, JOHANNES/JOHN KEBLER (Kübler), b. at Kingdom of Wür Limberg, Germany, 1 Feb 1819 son of Johann Friederich and Anna Barbara (Mutschler) Kübler; John d. at Cincinnati, 4 Apr 1885.[2161][2162] John Kebler was an attorney educated at Harvard.

[2157] Dow, *History of the Town of Hampton*, volume 2, p 993

[2158] Dow, *History of the Town of Hampton*, volume 2, p 583

[2159] Ontario, Canada, Deaths and Deaths Overseas, 1869-1946, the death records lists George Jacob Abbott, age 66, United States Commercial Agent, died of heart disease.

[2160] Smith, *History of Peterborough*, p 329

[2161] Ancestry.com, *Württemberg, Germany, Family Tables, 1550-1985.*

[2162] U.S. Passport Applications, 1795-1925, Passport application of John Kebler gives place and date of birth

xi CHARLES ELIOT ABBOT, b. 5 Nov 1822; d. at Tuscarora, NV, 11 May 1900; m. in San Francisco, by 1868, SUSAN FOLGER OSBORNE, b. in NY about 1840 daughter of Homer B. and Sarah (Folger) Osborne;[2163] Susan d. at Tuscarora between 1875 and 1880. Although, not a certainty, I believe that this is information for this Charles Eliot Abbot as all the information on census records beginning in 1852 fit with his information including birth year, place of birth, and places of birth of parents. If so, he went to California by 1852[2164] and lived in Eldorado and San Francisco. Charles and Susan had a son Charles Elliot Abbott in San Francisco in 1868[2165] and then relocated to Tuscarora, Nevada by 1870 and a second son, Homer Osborne Abbott, was born there. Charles E. Abbot was elected Justice of the Peace for Annaville Justice Court in Elko County, Nevada on 7 November 1876 and his term of office ran from 1 January 1877 through 6 January 1879.[2166] His death notice refers to him as Judge Charles E. Abbot.

799) BENJAMIN ABBOTT *(Dorcas Abbot Abbot[4] Benjamin[3], Benjamin[2], George[1])*, b. at Wilton, 17 Mar 1770 son of Abiel and Dorcas (Abbot) Abbot; d. at Temple, ME, 10 Sep 1823; m. at Andover, 17 Jan 1793, his third cousin, PHEBE ABBOTT, b. at Wilton, 25 Jun 1774 daughter of Jacob and Lydia (Stevens) Abbott; Phebe d. 18 Apr 1857.

Benjamin and Phebe lived at Greenfield, New Hampshire and Wilton, New Hampshire during their early marriage and relocated to Temple, Maine in February 1803 where they were early settlers. Benjamin was greatly respected in Temple earning the title of "the patriarch."[2167]

The estate of Benjamin Abbot entered probate on 18 March 1824 with Benjamin Abbott, Jr. noted as executor of the will. Bond surety was given by Phebe Abbot, widow, John Barker, physician of Wilton, Maine, and Lafayette Perkins, physician of Weld, Maine.[2168]

In her will written 9 August 1851 (probate 1857), Phebe Abbot of Farmington bequeathed the household furniture to her six daughters: Hannah A. Merrill, Dorcas A. Perkins, Salva A. Freeman, Lucy A. Douglas, Lydia A. Titcomb, and Abigail A. Hamlin. Her granddaughters Phebe Barker and Emily Barker, daughters of her daughter Phebe A. Barker deceased, also receive a portion of the household goods. Bequests were also made to sons Benjamin, John S., Abiel, and Ezra, and the children of son George Abbot, deceased. Son Abiel Abbot was named executor. In a codicil in January 1857, Phebe changed the executor of the will to Hon. Thomas Parker.[2169]

Benjamin and Phebe had fourteen children, the older children born at Greenfield and Wilton and the younger children at Temple.

i PHEBE ABBOTT, b. at Greenfield, 25 Mar 1794; d. at Norwich, CT, 8 Mar 1843; m. 1813, JOHN BARKER, b. at Londonderry, 17 Aug 1785 son of John and Mary (Barker) Jackman; John d. at Norwich, 4 Feb 1858.

ii HANNAH ABBOTT, b. at Greenfield, 6 Jul 1795; d. at Farmington, ME, 19 Dec 1876; m. at Temple, 19 Nov 1820, ENOS MERRILL, b. at Falmouth, ME, 18 Mar 1786 son of Humphrey and Hannah (Lunt) Merrill; Enos d. at Oxford, NH, 22 Mar 1861.

iii DORCAS ABBOTT, b. at Greenfield, 25 Feb 1797; d. at Farmington, ME, 31 Mar 1887; m. 30 Dec 1817, LAFAYETTE PERKINS, b. at Boston, 26 Mar 1786 son of William and Abigail (Cox) Perkins; Lafayette d. at Farmington, 9 May 1874.

iv SALVA ABBOTT, b. at Wilton, 12 Nov 1798; d. at Chelsea, MA, 4 Nov 1867; m. 1827, CHARLES FREEMAN, b. at Portland, ME, 3 Jun 1794 son of Samuel and Elizabeth (Ilsley) Freeman; Charles d. at Limerick, ME, 19 Sep 1853. Charles was first married to Nancy Pierce.

v BENJAMIN ABBOTT, b. at Wilton, 10 Aug 1800; d. at Douglas, MA, 7 Jan 1861; m. about 1824, MARY CHASE BLANCHARD, b. in ME, 1804 whose parents are not identified; Mary d. at Douglas, 15 Aug 1883.

vi LUCY ABBOTT, b. at Wilton, 6 May 1802; d. at Waterford, ME, after 1870; m. about 1825, her second cousin, JOHN ABBOT DOUGLAS *(Abigail Abbott Douglas[5], Abigail Abbott Abbott[4], Benjamin[3], Benjamin[2], George[1])*, b. at Portland, ME, 4 Feb 1792 son of William and Abigail (Abbott) Douglas; John d. at Waterford, 8 Aug 1878. John

[2163] Homer B. Osborne was a hardware merchant from New York City who relocated to San Francisco in the 1850's.
[2164] California State Census, 1852
[2165] California, County Birth, Marriage, and Death Records, 1849-1980
[2166] Nevada Judicial History Database, https://nvcourts.gov/AOC/JudicialHistory/detail.aspx?id=1627
[2167] Dennison, *Benjamin Abbott of Temple Maine and His Descendants*, Sprague's Journal of Maine History, volume 11, pp 22-31
[2168] Maine Probate, Kennebec County, Volume 20, Orders of Notice, p 145; volume 14, Executors Bonds, p 247
[2169] Maine Probate, Franklin County, Estate of Phebe Abbott, May 1857, No. 720

first married, at Andover, 22 Oct 1822, his first cousin, ELIZABETH ABBOTT *(Abiel⁵, Dorcas Abbott Abbott⁴, Benjamin³, Benjamin², George¹)*, b. at Peterborough, 22 May 1798 daughter of Abiel and Elizabeth (Abbott) Abbott; Elizabeth d. at Waterford, 12 Oct 1823. John Abbot Douglas is a child in Family 782. Elizabeth Abbott is a child in Family 783.

vii Son b. and d. 19 Apr 1804.

viii LYDIA ABBOTT, b. at Temple, 19 Feb 1805; d. at Farmington, 26 Dec 1883; m. 18 Feb 1828, JOHN TITCOMB, b. at Farmington, 24 Feb 1794 son of Stephen and Elizabeth (Henry) Titcomb; John d. at Farmington, 1 Oct 1861.

ix JOHN STEVENS ABBOTT, b. at Temple, 6 Jan 1807; d. at Watertown, MA, 12 Jun 1881; m. 1835, ELIZABETH ALLEN, b. at Norridgewock, ME, 25 Sep 1813 daughter of William and Hannah (Titcomb) Allen; Elizabeth d. Norridgewock, 27 Jul 1858.

x RHODA ABBOTT, b. 26 Sep 1808; d. 29 Mar 1809.

xi ABIEL ABBOTT, b. at Temple, 28 Dec 1809; d. at Watertown, MA, 21 Apr 1884; m. about 1848, SARAH SMITH DAVIS, b. at Farmington, 1823 daughter of Nathan Smith and Elizabeth (Cooper) Davis; Sarah d. at Watertown, 27 May 1896.

xii M. GEORGE ABBOTT, b. at Temple, 22 Feb 1813; d. at Thomaston, ME, 18 Aug 1850; m. 1837, MELINA ALDEN, b. at Union, ME, 16 Jun 1811 daughter of Ebenezer and Patience (Gilmore) Alden; Melina d. at Watertown, MA, 2 Jul 1875.

xiii ABIGAIL ABBOTT, b. at Temple, 20 Jun 1815; d. at Waverly, MA, 1 Jun 1867; m. 5 Feb 1835, HANNIBAL HAMLIN, b. at Waterford, ME, 30 Jan 1809 son of Hannibal and Susannah (Faulkner) Hamlin; Hannibal d. at Washington, DC, 16 Nov 1862. Hannibal was working in the U.S. Treasury Department at the time of his death.

xiv EZRA ABBOTT, b. 18 Sep 1817; d. at Richmond, ME, 28 Dec 1859. Ezra did not marry. He attended Bowdoin College and was an attorney admitted to the bar in 1842.

800) EZRA ABBOT *(Dorcas Abbot Abbot⁴, Benjamin³, Benjamin², George¹)*, b. at Wilton, NH, 8 Feb 1772 son of Abiel and Dorcas (Abbot) Abbot; d. at Wilton, 3 Apr 1847; m. at Coventry, CT, 6 Oct 1799, REBEKAH HALE, b. at Coventry, 9 Jan 1781 daughter of Joseph and Rebecca (Harris) Hale; Rebekah d. 5 May 1860.[2170]

Ezra Abbot married Rebekah Hale of Coventry, Connecticut. Rebekah was the niece of Nathan Hale. The marriage was performed by Ezra's brother, Reverend Abiel Abbot. The family settled in Wilton. Ezra was primarily a farmer and took over the large homestead that was acquired by his father.

Ezra had a wide range of interests one of which was working with his brother Samuel in the manufacture of potato starch which was used as sizing in the textile industry. Samuel Abbot had invented machinery for processing the starch.[2171]

Ezra and Rebekah Abbot were parents who valued education including education of their daughters. Three of the daughters were schoolteachers. In his young adult life, Ezra did some teaching in the community.

In his will written 15 December 1846, Ezra Abbot bequeaths to beloved wife Rebekah H. Abbot the use of that part of the dwelling house she finds convenient. She also receives $2,000 to be paid over a period of three years with interest. Rebekah also receives the household furniture and the use of the library. There are several other provisions for her maintenance. Granddaughter Emily Marie Knight is the receive $500 held by a guardian and to earn interest which is reinvested. The money is to be used for her education. If Emily dies before age twenty-one, the bequest will go to Emily's mother, beloved daughter Rebecca A. Knight. Son Joseph Hale Abbot receives $420. Beloved son Ezra Abbot receives $400 which will make his full portion when added to what he has already received. Son Abiel receives $500, daughter Harriet $500, son Nelson $2,400, daughter Abby Ann Rockwood $500, daughter Sarah Jane Abbot $1,500, and son John Hale Abbot $2,250. Son Harris Abbot receives all the real estate and personal property not otherwise distributed. Harris will be responsible for paying any debts owed and to pay out all the legacies given in the will. Harris is named executor.[2172]

Ezra and Rebekah had thirteen children born at Wilton.

i REBECCA ABBOT, b. 16 Jul 1800; d. at Wilton, 5 Apr 1882; m. 20 Jan 1841, as his second wife, Reverend ISAAC KNIGHT, b. at Waterford, ME, 29 Dec 1797 son of Abel and Mercy (Watson) Knight;[2173] Isaac d. at Boscawen, NH, 24 Jul 1850. Isaac was first married to Phebe Beaman who died in 1840. Sadly, Emily Marie Knight died in 1864 at age 19 and so was not able to use her legacy from her grandfather for her education. Rebecca was a teacher.

[2170] Abbott, *Family Tree of Ezra Abbot*. See this source of additional information.

[2171] Abbot, "Biographical Memoir of Henry Larcom Abbot"

[2172] *New Hampshire Wills and Probate Records 1643-1982,* Will of Ezra Abbot, Hillsborough, 15 Dec 1846.

[2173] Warren, *The History of Waterford, Oxford County, Maine*, p 270

ii SON ABBOT, b. and d. 13 Sep 1801

iii JOSEPH HALE ABBOT, b. 25 Sep 1802; d. at Cambridge, MA, 7 Apr 1873; m. at Beverly, 13 May 1830, FANNY ELLINGWOOD LARCOM, b. at Beverly, 14 Jun 1807 daughter of Henry and Fanny (Ellingwood) Larcom; Fanny d. at Cambridge, 26 Jun 1883.

iv DORCAS ABBOT, b. 24 Jan 1804; d. at Wilton, 2 Nov 1833; m. 21 Sep 1825, EBENEZER BISHOP, b. at Lisbon, CT, 1798 son of Cyrus and Susannah (Bishop) Bishop; Ebenezer d. at Lisbon, 6 Jan 1827. Dorcas and Ebenezer had no children.

v EZRA ABBOTT, b. 27 Nov 1805; d. at Owatonna, MN, 16 Aug 1876; m. 29 Apr 1846, SARAH HOOKER, b. at New York, NY, 7 Aug 1824 daughter of William and Eliza Carlton (Blunt) Hooker; Sarah d. 13 Feb 1905.

vi ABIEL ABBOT, b. 11 May 1808; d. at Wilton, 23 Aug 1896. Abiel did not marry. He was a teacher. He spent some time with his brother in Minnesota helping him establish his property.

vii EMILY ABBOT, b. 16 Aug 1810; d. at Wilton, 10 Jun 1835. Emily was a teacher. She did not marry.

viii HARRIS ABBOT, b. 19 Sep 1812; d. at Wilton, 20 Mar 1884; m. at Dracut, 8 Dec 1860, CAROLINE ANN GREELEY, b. at Pelham, NH, 20 Oct 1836 daughter of Jonathan Butler and Lucy Ann (Coburn) Greeley; Caroline d. at Wilton, 8 Nov 1911.

ix HARRIET ABBOT, b. 19 Jun 1814; d. at Wilton, 16 Jul 1886; m. 5 Jan 1837, her second cousin, HERMAN ABBOT *(Jeremiah[6], Jeremiah[5], John[4], John[3], John[2], George[1])*, b. at Wilton, 20 Feb 1814 son of Jeremiah and Eunice (Blanchard) Abbot; Herman d. 17 Nov 1878.

x NELSON ABBOT, b. 17 Nov 1816; d. at Wilton, 9 Jan 1890; m. 17 Aug 1848, his second cousin once removed, HANNAH HOLT PEAVEY *(Peter Peavey[6], Lucy Cummings Peavey[5], Elizabeth Abbott Cummings[4], Benjamin[3], Benjamin[2], George[1])*, b. at Greenfield, 13 Aug 1821 daughter of Peter and Dorcas (Holt) Peavey; Hannah d. at Wilton, 21 Mar 1891.

xi ABBY ANN ABBOT, b. 13 Dec 1818; d. at Boston, 12 May 1912; m. 1 May 1845, LUBIN BURTON ROCKWOOD, b. at Wilton, 8 Aug 1816 son of Lubin and Lydia (Burton) Rockwood; Lubin d. at Boston, 7 May 1872.

xii SARAH JANE ABBOT, b. 15 May 1821; d. at Wilton, 18 Jun 1857. Sarah did not marry.

xiii JOHN HALE ABBOT, b. 5 Sep 1825; d. at Wilton, 19 Jan 1905. John did not marry. He was a civil engineer and a surveyor. He went to Owatoona with his brother Ezra and lived there about 30 years but returned to Wilton in his later years.

801) DORCAS ABBOT *(Dorcas Abbot Abbot[4], Benjamin[3], Benjamin[2], George[1])*, b. at Wilton, 30 Jan 1774 daughter of Abiel and Dorcas (Abbot) Abbot; died after 2 Oct 1846, the date of her will;[2174] m. 3 Jan 1795, ELIPHALET PUTNAM, b. at Wilton, 23 Jan 1766 son of Nathaniel and Mary (Eastman) Putnam; Eliphalet d. 25 Feb 1826.

As a youth, Eliphalet Putnam did a seven-year apprenticeship with Samuel Rockwood of Groton to learn the cloth-dresser's trade. He built a clothing mill in Wilton and in 1817 built a two-story building to house carding machines. He was a selectman in Wilton for ten years.[2175]

Dorcas Abbot Putnam wrote her will 2 October 1846. "I give to my daughter Rachel Dascombe my least valuable bed." Son Eliphalet also receives a bed. She leaves in trust with the executor for daughter Dorcas Putnam the amount of $302.27. Daughter Abigail wife of George Buss receives $377.45. Daughters Rachel, Abigail, and Dorcas receive the kitchen and household items. Son Samuel receives the great bible and the remainder of her books. She orders her executor to sell her farm in Milford now occupied by Calvin Dascombe and authorizes the executor to provide a promissory note to the trustees of Philips Academy for $500. Sons Abiel Putnam, Eliphalet Putnam, and Sewell Putnam receive all the residue of the estate. Son Eliphalet is named executor.[2176] [I know I am not supposed to editorialize, but I must wonder what daughter Rachel and husband Calvin Dascombe did to warrant "the least valuable bed" and having the farm sold out from under them.]

A clue to the issue with Rachel and Calvin might come from the settlement of Eliphalet Putnam's estate. In the settlement, it was determined that the homestead property could not be reasonably divided and so was given as a unit to the

---

2174 *Probate Records, 1771-1921; Indexes to Probate Records, 1771-1859, 1885-1961*; Author: New Hampshire. Probate Court (Hillsborough County); *Probate Place: Hillsborough, New Hampshire*

2175 Livermore, *History of the Town of Wilton*, pp 478-479

2176 *New Hampshire Wills and Probate Records 1643-1982,* Will of Dorcas Putnam, Hillsborough, 2 Oct 1846.

three oldest sons. The other children received a payment of $129.43. However, it was determined that Rachel Dascomb was previously advanced the sum of $224.28 by her father, and this was more than her share, so she received nothing from the estate.[2177] The total value of Eliphalet's estate was $4,996 which include a $4000 value of the homestead farm and an additional 22 acres of woodland.

Dorcas and Eliphalet Putnam had twelve children born at Wilton.

i RACHEL PUTNAM, b. 14 Feb 1796; d. at Milford, 10 Oct 1856; m. 23 Jul 1820, CALVIN DASCOMB, b. at Lyndeborough, 29 Oct 1790 son of Jacob and Rachel (Dale) Dascomb; Calvin d. at Milford, 13 Oct 1859.

ii ELIPHALET PUTNAM, b. 25 Oct 1797; d. 7 Oct 1799.

iii ELIPHALET PUTNAM, b. 26 Oct 1799; d. at Wilton, 16 Oct 1862; m. 1st, 27 Jul 1823, HANNAH RUSSELL, b. at Wilton, 11 Aug 1800 daughter of Daniel and Elizabeth (Dascomb) Russell; Hannah d. 14 Mar 1857. Eliphalet m. 2nd, 15 Oct 1857, PERSIS LOVEJOY, b. at Milford, 13 May 1817 daughter of Henry and Persis (Abbott) Lovejoy; Persis d. at Milford, 8 Dec 1908. Eliphalet taught school in the winters. He also worked in cloth-dressing and carding and later manufactured bobbins.[2178] Persis Lovejoy is a child in Family 803.

iv ABIEL ABBOT PUTNAM, b. 29 Jul 1801; d. at Wilton, 30 Dec 1881; m. 12 Feb 1835, MARY ANN RADDIN, b. at Saugus, 18 Jul 1803[2179] of undetermined parentage; Mary Ann d. at Wilton 9 Dec 1859.

v SEWALL PUTNAM, b. 10 Oct 1803; d. 31 Oct 1803.

vi SEWALL PUTNAM, b. 27 Apr 1805; d. at Goffstown, 16 Mar 1895; m. 27 Aug 1835, HANNAH MORRILL GLIDDEN, b. at Gilmanton, 6 Aug 1813 daughter of Caleb and Diantha (Gilman) Glidden;[2180] Hannah d. at Wilton, 21 Feb 1867.

vii SAMUEL PUTNAM, b. 9 May 1807; d. 5 Dec 1814.

viii DORCAS PUTNAM, b. 5 Sep 1809; d. 5 May 1810.

ix DORCAS PUTNAM, b. 8 Apr 1811; d. at Wilton, 15 Mar 1887; m. at Wilton, 2 Sep 1834, AMOS PUTNAM, b. at Andover, VT, 14 Apr 1804 son of Jacob and Mary (Burton) Putnam; Amos d. at Nashua, 4 Nov 1888.

x MARY EASTMAN PUTNAM, b. 31 Jul 1813; d. 14 Jul 1830.

xi ABIGAIL PUTNAM, b. 11 Mar 1817; d. at Wilton, 19 Jun 1871; m. 27 Aug 1835, her second cousin, GEORGE BUSS *(Sarah Abbott Buss⁶, Jeremiah⁵, John⁴, John³, John², George¹)*, b. at Wilton, 27 Sep 1812 son of Stephen and Sarah (Abbott) Buss; George d. at Wilton, 12 Mar 1897. After Abigail's death, George married Hannah L. Colby who was the widow of Joseph Upton.

xii SAMUEL PUTNAM, b. 14 Sep 1819; d. at Wilton, 11 Nov 1853; m. 14 May 1845, PHEBE S. JONES, b. at Wilton, 4 Sep 1822 daughter of Asa and Lucy (Flint) Jones; Phebe d. at Wilton, 18 Feb 1905.

802) ABIGAIL ABBOTT *(Dorcas Abbot Abbot⁴, Benjamin³, Benjamin², George¹)*, b. at Wilton, 13 Jul 1779 daughter of Abiel and Dorcas (Abbot) Abbot; d. at Wilton, 5 Jun 1812; m. 19 May 1808, JONATHAN LIVERMORE, b. at Wilton, 10 Jul 1770 son of Jonathan and Elizabeth (Kidder) Livermore; Jonathan d. 24 Dec 1845.

Jonathan Livermore's father graduated from Harvard in 1760 and was the first pastor of the Congregational church in Wilton. As the oldest son, Jonathan inherited and lived on the family homestead and was a farmer.[2181] Abigail and Jonathan had two children before her early death. Jonathan did not remarry.

i JONATHAN LIVERMORE, b. 24 Apr 1809; d. at Wilton, 18 Jun 1887; m. 15 Aug 1833, his second cousin, DORCAS HOLT *(Dorcas Abbott Holt⁶, Jeremiah⁵, John⁴, John³, John², George¹)*, b. at Wilton, 23 May 1809 daughter of Daniel and Dorcas (Abbott) Holt; Dorcas d. 13 Feb 1887. Dorcas was first married to NEHEMIAH BLODGETT, born at Dunstable, NH about 1800 son of Oliver Blodgett. Nehemiah died 16 Nov 1829 very soon after the marriage. His will includes a bequest to wife Dorcas for the household goods she brought to the marriage and the remainder of the estate to his father Oliver Blodgett.

2177 New Hampshire, County Probate Records, 1660-1973, Hillsborough, probate of Eliphalet Putnam, 1826, 24:44, 39:338, 30:424, 35:51, 38:289, 39:557, 20:417, accessed through familysearch.org

2178 Livermore, *History of Wilton*, p 479

2179 This is the date and place of birth given in the History of Wilton. There is a birth transcription at Groton for Mary Ann with this birth date. Mary Ann is described as "of Dunstable" at the time of her marriage. Two possible sets of parents are John Raddin and Hannah Copp or Robert Raddin and Betsey Danforth. As John Raddin and Hannah Copp were in Dunstable, perhaps they are more likely.

2180 The 1840 will of Caleb Glidden of Gilmanton includes a bequest to his daughter Hannah M. Putnam.

2181 Livermore, *History of the Town of Wilton*, p 436

ii ABIEL ABBOT LIVERMORE, b. 30 Oct 1811; d. at Wilton, 28 Nov 1892; m. 1st, 17 May 1838, his first cousin, ELIZABETH DORCAS ABBOT *(Jacob5, Dorcas Abbott Abbott4, Benjamin3, Benjamin2, George1)*, b. at Hampton, 24 Mar 1810 daughter of Jacob and Catherine (Thayer) Abbot; Elizabeth d. 13 Sep 1879. After Elizabeth's death, Abiel married the widow Mary A. (Keating) Moore who was born at Searsmont, ME, 11 Aug 1831 daughter of William Keating. Mary d. 16 Jun 1919. Abiel attended Harvard and Cambridge Divinity School. In the 1850's, he was pastor of a Unitarian church in Cincinnati and later in New York at Hope Church. He was also president of Meadville Theological School at its original location in Meadville, Pennsylvania.[2182]

803) PERSIS ABBOTT *(Dorcas Abbot Abbot4, Benjamin3, Benjamin2, George1)*, b. at Wilton, 25 Dec 1781 daughter of Abiel and Dorcas (Abbot) Abbot; d. at Milford, NH, 13 Nov 1859; m. 12 Jan 1804, her third cousin, HENRY LOVEJOY *(Lydia Abbott Lovejoy5, Joseph4, Joseph3, John2, George1)*, b. 16 Aug 1781 son of Samuel and Lydia (Abbott) Lovejoy; Henry d. 23 Sep 1863.

Persis and Henry Lovejoy started their married life in Greenfield, New Hampshire and their first six children were born there. They relocated to Milford in 1816[2183] where their youngest four children were born.

i HENRY LOVEJOY, b. 8 Nov 1804; d. at Brooklyn, NY, 7 May 1887; m. 1st, at Boston, 19 Oct 1832, ELIZABETH FRANCIS, b. about 1815 of undetermined parents; Elizabeth d. at Bangor, ME, 8 Feb 1837. Henry m. 2nd, 5 Oct 1837, MALINDA C. WHEELER, b. at Bangor, 19 Mar 1817 daughter of John and Welthia (Gorton) Wheeler; Malinda d. at Brooklyn, 1883.

ii SAMUEL LOVEJOY, b. 3 Nov 1806; d. at Milford, 26 Sep 1881; m. 29 Sep 1859, NANCY WRIGHT, b. at Milford, 12 Mar 1826 daughter of Oliver and Susan (Smith) Wright; Nancy d. at Milford, 5 Nov 1905.

iii ABIEL A. LOVEJOY, b. 14 Dec 1808; d. 26 Dec 1822.

iv LYDIA LOVEJOY, b. 18 Jun 1811; d. 4 Aug 1811.

v WILLIAM LOVEJOY, b. 22 Jul 1812; d. at Milford, 21 May 1880; m. at Milford, 9 Sep 1852, SYRENA HOLT, b. at Temple, NH, 5 Jul 1827 daughter of Nehemiah and Mary (Wright) Holt; Syrena d. at Milford, 29 Jan 1918.

vi JACOB ABBOT LOVEJOY, b. 23 Jul 1815; d. 25 Sep 1815.

vii PERSIS LOVEJOY, b. 13 May 1817; d. at Milford, 8 Dec 1908; m. 15 Oct 1857, her first cousin, ELIPHALET PUTNAM, b. 26 Oct 1799 son of Eliphalet and Dorcas (Abbott) Putnam; Eliphalet d. at Wilton, 16 Oct 1862. Eliphalet is a child in Family 801.

viii SARAH LOVEJOY, b. 13 Oct 1819; d. at Milford, 27 Apr 1852. Sarah did not marry.

ix ABIGAIL LOVEJOY, b. 13 Jan 1823; d. at Milford, 8 Jun 1852. Abigail did not marry.

x PHEBE LOVEJOY, b. 14 Feb 1826; d. at Milford, 9 Jun 1918. Phebe did not marry.

804) RHODA ABBOTT *(Dorcas Abbot Abbot4, Benjamin3, Benjamin2, George1)*, b. at Wilton, 17 Mar 1784 daughter of Abiel and Dorcas (Abbot) Abbot; d. at Peterborough, 19 Mar 1853; m. 14 Nov 1805, EPHRAIM PEABODY, b. at Wilton, 17 Jun 1776 son of Ephraim and Sarah (Hutchinson) Peabody; Ephraim d. 5 Jul 1816.

Ephraim Peabody was a blacksmith in Wilton and a prominent man in town serving as a selectman and representative to the legislature in 1815 and 1816.[2184] His probate record refers to him as Esquire reflecting his status in the community. Ephraim did not leave a will. The inventory of his estate valued real estate at $2,353 and personal estate at $1,445.85. The inventory includes blacksmith tools and a supply of iron and steel.[2185] There were also books valued at $7. The dower was set off to widow Rhoda Peabody on 30 October 1817.

Ephraim and Rhoda had two children born at Wilton.

i EPHRAIM PEABODY, b. 22 Mar 1807; d. at Boston, 28 Nov 1856; m. at Salem, MA, 5 Aug 1833, MARY JANE DERBY, b. at Salem, 30 Jan 1807 daughter of John and Eleanor (Coffin) Derby; Mary Jane d. at Marion, MA, 15 Jul 1892. Ephraim Peabody was a renowned Unitarian clergyman and planner of the Boston school system about

[2182] Livermore, *History of the Town of Wilton*, p 436

[2183] Brooks, *History of Milford*, p 827

[2184] Livermore, *History of the Town of Wilton*, p 462

[2185] New Hampshire County Probate Records, 1660-1973, Hillsborough, probate of Ephraim Peabody, 19:408, 25:522, 26:286, 29:44, 18:558; accessed through familysearch.org

whom much has been written. There are several sources for his biography including one in Eliot's *Heralds of a Liberal Faith*, volume 3, pp 297-302.

ii DORCAS PEABODY, b. 25 Apr 1809; d. at Milford, 12 Apr 1896. Dorcas did not marry. Dorcas wrote her will 15 August 1895 and made bequests to her cousin Mary Ann Peabody (who had lived with Dorcas and who receives the bulk of the estate) and cousin Lydia Parker, her nieces and nephews, and grandnieces and grandnephews. Any residue of the estate following the payment of the legacies is to go to A. M. Pendleton who is also named executor.

805) PHEBE ABBOTT *(Dorcas Abbot Abbot[4], Benjamin[3], Benjamin[2], George[1])*, b. at Wilton, 25 Jun 1788 daughter of Abiel and Dorcas (Abbot) Abbot; d. at Jackson, ME, 25 Nov 1825, m. 25 Jun 1818, her first cousin, EZRA ABBOTT *(William[5], John[4], John[3], John[2], George[1])*, b. at Wilton, 3 Jul 1785 son of William and Phebe (Ballard) Abbott; Ezra d. 7 Jun 1871.

Ezra was a farmer in Jackson, Maine. At the 1870 census, his real estate had an estimated value of $3,000 and personal property of $1.165. Ezra and Phebe Abbott had two children born at Jackson, Maine.

i EZRA ABBOTT, b. 28 Apr 1819; d. at Cambridge, MA, 21 Mar 1884; m. 1st, at Jackson, 17 Dec 1843, CATHERINE MEDER, b. 1821 and d. at Jackson, 25 Jul 1847. Ezra m. 2nd, at Cambridge, 21 Dec 1855, EMILY EVERETT, b. Hallowell, ME, 1829 daughter of Stevens and Emily (Abbott) Everett; Emily d. at Cambridge, 5 Nov 1888.

ii PHEBE DORCAS "ABIGAIL" ABBOTT, b. 28 Oct 1822; d. at Jackson, 17 Dec 1892; m. 1st, at Jackson, 6 Aug 1840, WILLIAM GROUT, b. 1817 of not yet determined parents; William d. at Jackson, 23 Jan 1846. Abigail m. 2nd, 21 Aug 1855, NATHANIEL EMMONS CARPENTER, b. at Brooklyn, CT, 28 Feb 1816[2186] son of Job and Susannah (Daniels) Carpenter; Nathaniel d. at Jackson, 16 May 1884. Nathaniel was first married to Ruth T. White.

806) WILLIAM ABBOT *(Jonathan[4], Jonathan[3], Benjamin[2], George[1])*, b. at Lunenburg, 24 Nov 1745 son of Jonathan and Martha (Lovejoy) Abbot; d. Wilton, NH, Oct 1807;[2187] m. at Andover, 26 Aug 1766, his third cousin, SARA HOLT, b. 11 Aug 1746 daughter of Timothy and Hannah (Dane) Holt.

William Abbot and Sarah Holt were parents of six children.

i HANNAH ABBOTT, b. at Andover, 11 Jun 1767; d. at Temple, NH, 13 Mar 1858; m. at Temple, 10 Feb 1791, DANIEL HEALD, b. at Temple, 5 Sep 1761 son of Oliver and Lydia (Spaulding) Heald; Daniel d. at Temple, 26 Aug 1836.

ii SARAH ABBOTT, b. at Andover, 3 Jun 1769; m. EZRA UPTON. Sarah and Ezra did not have children.[2188]

iii MARTHA ABBOTT, b. at Wilton, 11 Dec 1772; d. at Temple, 15 Dec 1861; m. 17 Feb 1795, ELISHA CHILD, b. at Groton, MA, 31 Oct 1767 son of Moses and Sarah (Stiles) Child; Elisha d. at Temple, 1 Apr 1853.

iv MARY ABBOTT, b. at Wilton, 5 Apr 1775; d. 20 Aug 1777.

v WILLIAM ABBOTT, b. at Wilton, 7 Jan 1779; d. at Malden, MA, 15 Jan 1843; m. 1st, at Wilton, 29 Jan 1799, his third cousin once removed, REBECCA BATCHELDER *(Rebecca Abbott Batchelder[4], Joseph[3], Nathaniel[2], George[1])*, b. at Wilton, 20 Dec 1775 daughter of Daniel and Rebecca (Abbott) Batchelder; Rebecca d. 1805. William m. 2nd, 4 Jun 1806, APPHIA TYLER, b. 22 Nov 1784; Apphia d. 29 Sep 1806. William m. 3rd, 29 Sep 1807, ABIGAIL SAWTELL, b. at Groton, 31 Jul 1779 daughter of Richard and Elizabeth (Bennett) Sawtell; Abigail d. at Lynn, 14 Nov 1864. William Abbott, Rebecca Batchelder, and Abigail Sawtell are Family 1070.

vi MOLLY ABBOTT, b. at Wilton, 23 Apr 1782; d. at Boston, Jun 1806; m. at Malden, 15 Sep 1805, SAMUEL TUFTS, b. at Malden, 1 Apr 1783 son of Samuel and Martha (Upham) Tufts; Samuel d. at Cleveland, OH, Dec 1863. Samuel married second Sarah F. Loring and third Clarissa Pool.

807) MARTHA ABBOT *(Jonathan[4], Jonathan[3], Benjamin[2], George[1])*, b. at Andover, 23 Jan 1749/50 daughter of Jonathan and Martha (Lovejoy) Abbot; d. at Temple, NH, 10 Jan 1842; m. 3 May 1774; OLIVER WHITING, b. at Pelham, NH, 6 Apr 1750 son of Eleazer and Dorothy (Crosby) Whiting; Oliver d. 28 Sep 1829.

2186 Birth is reported in the Northbridge, MA records as occurring in Brooklyn, CT.

2187 Livermore, *History of the Town of Wilton*, p 550; no death record was located to support this information.

2188 This is a marriage reported by the Abbot genealogical register for which records have not yet been located.

Oliver Whiting saw service in the New Hampshire militia during the Revolution serving for six weeks in 1779.[2189] Oliver and Martha married in Andover but were soon after in Temple where they remained.

Oliver Whiting and Martha Abbot were parents of nine children, the oldest child born at Andover and the remainder at Temple, New Hampshire.

i PATTY WHITING, b. 22 Jul 1775; d. at Temple, 9 Aug 1778.

ii OLIVER WHITING, b. 5 Jan 1778; d. at Wilton, 9 Aug 1849; m. at Temple, 2 Jan 1800, FANNY STILES, b. at Temple, 30 Mar 1778 daughter of Asa and Hannah (Bixby) Stiles;[2190] Fanny d. at Wilton, 25 May 1866.

iii PATTY WHITING, b. 13 Feb 1780; d. at Temple, 17 Jan 1800; m. 1799, EPHRAIM BLOOD, b. at Concord, MA, 6 Mar 1779 son of Francis and Elizabeth (Spaulding) Blood. Ephraim married second Rebecca Maynard and third Mrs. Goldsmith.

iv SALLY WHITING, b. 1 Jul 1782; d. 3 Jun 1785.

v HANNAH WHITING, b. 8 Oct 1784; d. at Temple, 9 Dec 1817; m. 28 Mar 1804, ELIAS BOYNTON, b. at Temple, 15 May 1782 son of Elias and Elizabeth (Blood) Boynton. After Hannah's death, Elias married Mary Ferguson 16 Jul 1817.

vi NATHAN ABBOT WHITING, b. 20 Apr 1787; d. at Cicero, NY, after 1860; m. at Temple, 2 Apr 1811, BETSEY BLOOD, b. 1793 daughter of Francis and Rebecca (Parlin) Blood; Betsey d. at Cicero, after 1855.

vii BENJAMIN WHITING, b. 13 Apr 1789; d. at Temple, 23 Jan 1856; m. 18 Jun 1811, REBECCA BLOOD, b. at Temple, about 1792 daughter of Francis and Rebecca (Parlin) Blood.

viii GEORGE WHITING, b. 16 Feb 1791; d. at Temple, 13 Sep 1822; m. 1813, ELIZABETH SEARLE, b. at Temple, 13 Aug 1794 daughter of Daniel and Hannah (Blood) Searle. After George's death, Elizabeth married Josiah Stickney *(Abigail Walker Stickney[5], Elizabeth Abbott Walker[4], Joshua[3], John[2], George[1])* 9 Aug 1824.

ix DAVID WHITING, b. 22 Apr 1793; d. at Temple, 7 Feb 1827; m. 1 Jun 1815, POLLY FARRAR, b. at Temple, 1795 daughter of Simon and Mehitable (Thompson) Farrar.

808) JOB ABBOT *(David[4], Jonathan[3], Benjamin[2], George[1])*, b. likely in NH about 1742 son of David and Hannah (Chandler) Abbot; d. at West Barnet, VT, 15 Dec 1815; m. PHEBE FARNUM whose parentage is unknown at this time.

Job Abbott and Phebe Farnum were parents likely of ten children, the oldest six children born at Pembroke, New Hampshire and the youngest four born perhaps at Barnet, Vermont.[2191] Of the six children who married, four of them married children from newly arrived families from Scotland, three of them children of Walter and Janet (Stuart) Brock.

i SARAH ABBOTT, b. at Pembroke, 21 Mar 1772; d. at Barnet, VT, 14 Sep 1851; m. ALEXANDER STUART, b. in Scotland, 1768 son of Claudius and Janet (McFarlane) Stuart; Alexander d. at Barnet, 2 Mar 1840.

ii HANNAH ABBOTT, b. at Pembroke, 30 Dec 1773; m. JONATHAN DARLING, b. at Hampstead, NH, 20 Dec 1767 son of John and Phebe (Robards) Darling; Jonathan d. at Groton, VT, 9 Oct 1820.

iii PHEBE ABBOTT, b. at Pembroke, 28 Feb 1775; d. at Barnet, VT, 5 Oct 1873; m. JOHN BROCK, b. Glasgow, Lanarkshire, Scotland, 31 Oct 1768 son of Walter and Janet (Stuart) Brock;[2192] John d. at Barnet, 5 Nov 1852.

iv SUSANNA ABBOTT, b. at Pembroke, Dec 1778; d. at Cabot, VT, 24 Sep 1862; m. about 1798, JOSIAH DARLING, b. at Hampstead, NH, 14 Jun 1772 son of John and Phebe (Robards) Darling' Josiah d. at Ryegate about 1830. Susanna m. 2nd, Mr. Lane (or Laird) who has not been identified. Susannah m. 3rd, at Cabot, 16 Apr 1849, ANTHONY PERRY, b. at Cabot, 7 Apr 1774 son of Benjamin and Susannah (Potter) Perry; Anthony d. at Cabot, 1 Dec 1854.

v JOHN ABBOTT, b. at Pembroke, 27 Aug 1780; d. at Barnet, VT, 5 Sep 1854; m. ANNA BROCK, b. at Barnet, 1 Sep 1780 daughter of Walter and Janet (Stuart) Brock; Anna d. at Barnet, 15 Dec 1870.

2189 Compiled Service Records of Soldiers Who Served in the American Army During the Revolutionary War 1775-1785

2190 Gould, *The Stiles Family in America*, p 84

2191 The four youngest children are given in the *History of Ryegate*, but not in other sources and there are no other records associated with them. Of these four youngest children, three are reported to have died in childhood and the fourth, son Job, is reported to have "gone West."

2192 *Scotland, Select Births and Baptisms, 1564-1950.*

vi MARY ABBOTT, b. at Pembroke, 1782; d. at Peacham, VT, 20 Jul 1864; m. at Barnet, 18 Feb 1805, JAMES BROCK, b. at Barnet, 27 Sep 1783 son of Walter and Janet (Stuart) Brock; James d. at Barnet, 27 Jul 1847.

vii JEROME JEREMIAH ABBOTT, b. about 1785; d. 1802.

viii PRISCILLA ABBOTT, b. about 1786; likely died young.

ix JOB ABBOTT, b. likely at Barnet, about 1788; reported to have "gone West" with no records located.

x JANET ABBOTT, b. about 1789; likely died young.

809) HANNAH ABBOT *(David⁴, Jonathan³, Benjamin², George¹)*, b. in NH, 7 Sep 1743 daughter of David and Hannah (Chandler) Abbot; d. at Pembroke, 17 Mar 1813; m. her third cousin, BENJAMIN HOLT, b. 28 Feb 1741 son of Benjamin and Sarah (Frye) Holt; Benjamin d. at Pembroke, 28 Feb 1826.

In his will written 7 January 1811 and proved 1 March 1826, Benjamin Holt directs that his executor David Holt pay the legacies in the will. Beloved wife Hannah receives a full one-third part of the real estate and full use of all the household furniture during her natural life. Son Nicolas receives twenty-two dollars which completes his portion. Son David receives all the real and personal estate except Benjamin reserves one yolk of oxen. To complete their full portions daughter Sarah Chandler receives twenty-two dollars, daughters Hannah Mason, Molly Russell, Mehitable Shannon, and Phebe Chandler each receive twenty-five dollars, and daughter Dolly Shannon twenty-two dollars. Daughter Betty Holt receives one hundred dollars. Granddaughter Hannah Norris with what she has received is her full share. Daughter Betty Holt and granddaughter Hannah Norris receive use of part of the house as long as they remain unmarried. Hannah and Betty will also share equally in the household furniture after his wife's demise.[2193]

Hannah Abbot and Benjamin Holt were parents of eleven children likely all born at Pembroke.

i SARAH HOLT, b. 23 Jan 1764; d. at Danbury, NH, after 1830; m. at Pembroke, 17 Apr 1787, JOSIAH CHANDLER, b. 1763 of undetermined parents;[2194] Josiah d. at Danbury, after 1830. Josiah served as a private in the Revolution and received a pension as an invalid.

ii NICHOLAS HOLT, b. 4 Aug 1766; d. at Danbury, NH, 24 Jun 1816; m. at Concord, 9 Jun 1790, ACHSAH RUSSELL, b. at Haverhill, MA, 14 Sep 1758 daughter of Edward and Mary (Page) Russell; Achsah d. at Warrensburg, NY, 26 May 1851.

iii HANNAH HOLT, b. 15 Sep 1768; d. at Pembroke, 22 Aug 1831; m. 18 Oct 1789, ISAAC MORRISON, b. at Nottingham, NH, 3 Feb 1760 son of James and Martha (White) Morrison; Isaac d. at Pembroke, 9 Jan 1846.

iv MOLLY HOLT, b. 7 Apr 1770; m. 3 Mar 1791, JOHN RUSSELL, *perhaps* b. at Haverhill, MA, 16 Jun 1767 son of James and Susannah (Richardson) Russell. Molly and John had seven children born at New London, NH, but have not located clear information on their deaths.

v PHEBE HOLT, b. 14 Jul 1772; d. at Lovell, ME, 1 Jun 1850; m. 13 Nov 1798, her fourth cousin, TIMOTHY CHANDLER *(Timothy Chandler⁵, Abial Chandler Chandler⁴, Abiel Chandler³, Hannah Abbott Chandler², George¹)*, b. at Andover, Sep 1775 son of Timothy and Mary (Walker) Chandler; Timothy d. at Lovell, 29 Nov 1854. Timothy is a child in Family 446.

vi DAVID HOLT, b. 12 May 1774; d. at Rumford, ME, 1 Feb 1859; m. 10 Nov 1795, his fourth cousin, CHLOE CHANDLER *(Timothy Chandler⁵, Abial Chandler Chandler⁴, Abiel Chandler³, Hannah Abbott Chandler², George¹)*, b. at Andover, 30 Aug 1771 daughter of Timothy and Mary (Walker) Chandler; Chloe d. at Rumford, 17 Mar 1859. Chloe is a child in Family 446.

vii MEHITABLE HOLT, b. 28 Jul 1776; d. 16 Jan 1778.

viii MEHITABLE HOLT, b. 17 Jul 1778; d. at Cottage, NY, 28 Jan 1855; m. 1st, at Pembroke, NH, Sep 1798, as his second wife, JOHN SHANNON, b. 1 Feb 1769;[2195] John d. at Perrysburg, NY, about 1840. Mehitable m. 2nd, about 1842, AZARIAH DARBEE, b. in CT, 1762 son of Jedediah and Lucretia (Cleveland) Darbee; Azariah d. at Dayton, NY, 18 Aug 1851. John Shannon was first married to Ruth Whittemore daughter of Benjamin and Abigail (Abbott) Whittemore. Azariah Darbee was first married to Susannah Phelps.

ix ELIZABETH HOLT, b. 7 May 1780; d. at Chichester, NH, after 1844; m. at Pembroke, 12 Feb 1835, as his third wife, JONATHAN LEAVITT, b. at Chichester, 17 Nov 1772 son of Jonathan and Anna (Tilton) Leavitt; Jonathan

---

[2193] New Hampshire County Probate Records, 1660-1973, Merrimack, case 282, probate of Benjamin Holt, 1:211, 6:523. Accessed through familysearch.org

[2194] There is another Josiah Chandler born 1762 son of David and Mary (Ballard) Chandler who married Margaret Aiken.

[2195] John's birth date is from a family bible record.

d. at Chichester, 24 Dec 1844. Jonathan was first married to Rebecca Lake and second married to Hannah Perkins.

x DORCAS HOLT, b. 7 May 1783; d. 27 Feb 1810.

xi DOLLY HOLT, b. 1 May 1785; d. at Leon, NY, 1851; m. Mar 1802, SAMUEL SHANNON, b. 1774;[2196] Samuel d. at Leon, NY, 1 Oct 1849.

810) BRIDGET ABBOT *(David⁴, Jonathan³, Benjamin², George¹)*, b. in NH, about 1761 daughter of David and Hannah (Chandler) Abbot; d. at Harmony, OH, after 1850; m. 1st, 24 Dec 1787, her third cousin, PHINEAS AMES *(Elizabeth Stevens Ames⁴, Nathan Stevens³, Elizabeth Abbott Stevens², George¹)*, b. 7 Sep 1764 son of Samuel and Elizabeth (Stevens) Ames; Phineas d. about 1792. Bridget m. 2nd, 17 Dec 1793, STEPHEN HARRIMAN, b. at Haverhill, MA, 10 Mar 1757 son of Stephen and Sarah (Mascraft) Harriman; Stephen d. at Lisbon, OH, 25 Feb 1828. Stephen Harriman was first married to Lucy Story.

No children were identified for Bridget Abbot and Phineas Ames. Following the death of Phineas, Bridget married Stephen Harriman who was also widowed and had four children from his first marriage. After spending time in Tunbridge, Vermont the family relocated to Clark County, Ohio.

Stephen Harriman did not leave a will and a report on the inventory of the estate was made 22 April 1828 with the final settlement in March 1834. George W. Harriman was administrator. The heirs-at-law, in addition to George W. Harriman, were Bridget Harriman, Noah and Sarah Norton, Isaac and Mary Chamberlain, Stephen Harriman, Ira Harriman, James and Betty Hackett, Thomas Harriman, John and Sophronia Lasky, and Flanders children (Lucy, Charlotte, Walter, James, Stephen, Sarah, William, and Arthur). The real estate was sold to settle the debts of the estate. The sale of the property brought $3,465 and $1,033.97 was paid to creditors.[2197] Sarah Norton, Mary Chamberlain, Stephen Harriman, and the Flanders grandchildren are heirs from Stephen Harriman's first marriage to Lucy Story.

Bridget Abbot and Stephen Harriman had four children who were living at the time of the probate of Stephen's estate in 1828. There are birth records in Tunbridge, Vermont for three of the children. It is possible there were other children who died before adulthood.

i IRA HARRIMAN, b. 24 Nov 1795; d. at Madison, OH, 7 Jul 1857; m. at Ashtabula, OH, 16 Jan 1823, LOEY BROWN, b. 18 Sep 1803 daughter of Solomon and Lydia (Walton) Brown; Loey d. at Madison, OH, 24 May 1884.

ii SOPHRONIA HARRIMAN, b. at Tunbridge, 18 Sep 1800; m. 1st, at Clark County, OH, 14 Jun 1829, JOHN LASKY; John d. before 1850. Sophronia m. 2nd, at Kane, IL, 27 May 1850, EDWARD GRAY, b. in Germany, about 1790; Edward d. before 1857. Sophronia m. 3rd, at Houston, MN, 14 Jun 1857, GEORGE HOLLIDAY, b. in England, about 1815.

iii THOMAS JEFFERSON HARRIMAN, b. at Tunbridge, 25 May 1801; *perhaps* m. at Champaign, OH, 20 May 1830, MARGERY ALEXANDER.

iv GEORGE WASHINGTON HARRIMAN, b. at Tunbridge, 2 Sep 1803; d. at Garnett, KS, 16 Feb 1875; m. 1st, at Clark County, OH, 22 Nov 1835, ELIZABETH MORRIS, b. likely at Clark County, about 1815 daughter of Joseph and Lavina (Drake) Morris;[2198] Elizabeth d. before 1850. George m. 2nd, 23 Aug 1851, SARAH ANN CAMPBELL, b. in OH, Apr 1835 of undetermined parents; Sarah was still living in 1900 in Indianapolis with her daughter Ida and her husband.

811) EPHRAIM BLUNT *(Zerviah Abbott Blunt⁴, Jonathan³, Benjamin², George¹)*, b. at Danville, VT, 20 Jun 1754 son of Ephraim and Zerviah (Abbott) Blunt; d. at Danville, 15 Feb 1829; m. 21 Nov 1776, MARTHA ORDWAY, b. at Amesbury, 28 Mar 1753 daughter of Moses and Anna (-) Ordway.

Ephraim Blunt and Martha Ordway were parents of eight children born at Danville, Vermont.

[2196] John Shannon and Samuel Shannon are likely brothers, but they do not seem to be the children of Samuel and Lydia (Leavitt) Shannon. The 1817 probate of Samuel Shannon of Rockingham County (a Revolutionary War pensioner with widow Lydia), NY includes a statement that Lydia Taber Shannon, Thomas Shannon, and Sarah Shannon are the only children of the deceased.

[2197] Ohio Probate Records, Clark County, Administration Records 1828-1836, pp 62-63; Settlements 1827-1844, volume 1, pp 327-329

[2198] At the 1850 Census, the three young children of George and Elizabeth Harriman were living with Lavina Morris Murray and her husband George Murray. Lavina Morris is the daughter of Joseph and Lavina (Drake) Morris. It might be assumed that the children went to live with their aunt after mother's death. In 1850, G. W. Harriman was living with his elderly mother Bridget.

i DAVID BLUNT, b. 7 Jun 1777; d. at Shefford, Québec, 13 Aug 1839; m. at Danville, 13 Sep 1801, POLLY DAVIS *perhaps* the daughter of Dudley and Mary (Straw) Davis; Polly d. at Shefford, 1831.[2199]

ii EPHRAIM BLUNT, b. 10 Nov 1778; d. at Danville, 27 Oct 1845; m. 1st, about 1807, LYDIA MORRILL, b. at Londonderry, 9 Sep 1787 daughter of Samuel and Sally (Blunt) Morrill; Lydia d. at Danville, 25 Aug 1814. Ephraim m. 2nd, BETSEY PEABODY, b. in NH, 1790; Betsey d. at Danville, 25 Mar 1875.

iii ANNA BLUNT, b. 27 Aug 1780; m. at Danville, 3 Oct 1808, JOSIAH BATCHELDER.

iv MARTHA BLUNT, b. 31 May 1782; died young.

v MOSES BLUNT, b. 6 Dec 1783; d. at Stanstead, Québec, 12 Sep 1834; m. LYDIA BOYNTON, b. 15 Aug 1791 daughter of John and Lydia (Dow) Boynton;[2200] Lydia d. likely at Stanstead, after 1871.[2201]

vi MARTHA BLUNT, b. 24 Oct 1785; m. ISAAC WHEELER STANTON, b. 10 Apr 1781 son of Isaac and Ruth (Ayer) Stanton; Isaac d. at Danville, 26 Oct 1870.

vii ASA BLUNT, b. 13 Nov 1787; d. at Stanstead, Québec, 1819; m. about 1814, NANCY BOYNTON, b. 11 Oct 1794 daughter of John and Lydia (Dow) Boynton; Nancy d. at Derby, VT, 23 Mar 1878. After Asa's death, Nancy married Heman Lindsey.

viii SARAH BLUNT, b. 26 Mar 1790

812) ZERVIAH BLUNT *(Zerviah Abbott Blunt⁴, Jonathan³, Benjamin², George¹)*, b. at Suncook, NH, 1759 daughter of Ephraim and Zerviah (Abbott) Blunt;[2202] d. at Calais, VT, 18 Jan 1860; m. at Canterbury, NH, 26 Feb 1778, AARON HARTSHORN, b. at Reading, 1754 son of Thomas and Abia (-) Hartshorn; Aaron d. at Danville, VT, 19 Jun 1799.

During the Revolution, Aaron Hartshorn served as a private in the company of Captain Batchelder and addition service in the company of Captain Abbot. Periods of service were claimed from December 1775 and in 1776 and 1777 and a total of eight months service were allowed. Widow Zerviah Hartshorn received a pension of $26.66 per annum related to Aaron's service. In 1855 at age 96 years, Zerviah made a claim for bounty land and was determined to be entitled to 160 acres.[2203]

The obituary for Zerviah Hartshorn included the following information. Mrs. Hartshorn was born in Suncook, Massachusetts. The family came to Danville, Vermont in 1787. Aaron died at the young age of 40 leaving his widow with ten children. Zerviah remained a widow for 61 years. She was an active member of the Free Will Baptist church.[2204]

The pension file includes a summary of the 19 July 1800 probate of Aaron Hartshorn in which the real estate was divided among the following heirs: widow Zerviah Hartshorn and children Thomas, Aaron, Susan, Ephraim, Zerviah, Mary S., Sarah, Abigail, Abraham S., and Charles C. P. Hartshorn.

Zerviah Blunt and Aaron Hartshorn were parents of twelve children born in Vermont and the youngest seven children at Danville.

i SUSANNAH HARTSHORN, b. 30 Sep 1779; d. at Danville, 20 Jan 1881; m. 1st, at Danville, 18 Mar 1804, DANIEL SMITH; Daniel d. at Danville, 6 Jul 1823. Susannah m. 2nd, at Danville, 17 Jun 1827, EBENEZER EATON, b. at Mansfield, CT, 1777 son of Nathaniel and Sarah (Johnson) Eaton; Ebenezer d. at Danville, 31 Jan 1859.

ii THOMAS HARTSHORN, b. 1780; d. at Danville, 1802.

iii AARON HARTSHORN, b. 1781; d. at Middlesex County, Ontario, Canada, 6 Feb 1847; m. at Danville, 12 Jan 1806, HANNAH PEASLEY, b. at Danville, 1787 daughter of Jedediah and Judith (Hunt) Peasley; Hannah d. in Middlesex County, 1843.

iv Son (name not known), b. about 1783; d. before 1800.[2205]

v EPHRAIM HARTSHORN, b. 1785; d. at McHenry, IL, Feb 1849; m. at Danvers, MA, 25 May 1807, MARTHA "PATTY" CROWELL, b. at Danvers, 12 Dec 1780 daughter of John and Mary (Masury) Crowell; Martha d. at Danville, 1 Jul 1877.

2199 *Quebec, Canada, Vital and Church Records (Drouin Collection), 1621-1968*, Institut Généalogique Drouin

2200 Boynton, *The Boynton Family*, p 40

2201 Lydia was living in Stanstead at the 1871 Canada census.

2202 Zerviah Hartshorn's death record lists her parents as Zerviah Blunt and Ephraim "Hartshorn" although this seems just to be a confusion of the name of her spouse and the name of her father. Her age on the death record is 100 years, 11 months, 21 days. *Vermont Vital Records 1720-1908*

2203 Revolutionary War Pension and Bounty-Land Warrant Application Files, 1800-1900, Case W19694

2204 *The Caledonian*, St. Johnsbury, Vermont, February 3, 1860. "Death of a Centenarian"

2205 The gravestone for Hartshorn in Danville has three unmarried sons on the stone: Benjamin, Thomas, and a third son whose name is broken off; this son is not in the estate distribution of his father and so is deceased before 1800.

vi BENJAMIN HARTSHORN, b. 1787; d. at Danville, Dec 1798.

vii ZERVIAH HARTSHORN, b. 1789; d. at St. Johnsbury, VT, 19 Feb 1851; m. 15 Apr 1812, PETER KNAPP, b. at Duanesburg, NY, 15 Apr 1793 son of Peter and Priscilla (Owen) Knapp; Peter d. at Barnet, VT, 12 Jul 1861. After Zerviah's death, Peter married Electa Sayre.

viii MARY SHORT HARTSHORN, b. 1790; d. at Danville, 6 Mar 1826; m. NATHAN FULLER, b. 1778; Nathan d. at Danville, 24 Oct 1839. After Mary's death, Nathan married Freelove Fuller.

ix SARAH HARTSHORN, b. about 1792; d. at Claremont, NH, 15 Jun 1869; m. at Danville, 9 Oct 1814, BENNAGER RODGERS, b. in CT, 3 Oct 1782 son of Joseph and Lois (Hall) Rodgers; Bennager d. at Claremont, 31 Mar 1864.

x ABIGAIL HARTSHORN, b. 3 Sep 1793; d. at Danville, 8 Sep 1862; m. 1816, JOHN FARNSWORTH, b. at Washington, NH, 3 Jun 1787 son of Manassah and Charity (Rounsevel) Farnsworth; John d. at Danville, 1 Apr 1837.

xi ABRAHAM SILVER HARTSHORN, b. 1795; d. at Moira, NY, 25 Apr 1869; m. at Danville, 9 Feb 1818, SARAH GREEN, b. at Danville, 1800; Sarah d. at Moira, 22 Oct 1885.

xii CHARLES COTESWORTH PINKEY HARTSHORN, b. 1799; d. at Danville, 4 Apr 1887; m. at Danville, 11 Feb 1823, HANNAH WEST, b. 1791; Hannah d. at Danville, 22 1876. Charles m. 2nd, 4 Jun 1878, ABIGAIL SANBORN (widow Parker).

813) SAMUEL ABBOTT *(Samuel4, Jonathan3, Benjamin2, George1)*, b. at Pembroke, 16 Apr 1750 son of Samuel and Miriam (Stevens) Abbott; d. at North Pembroke, 11 Mar 1836; m. 22 Mar 1781, LYDIA PERRIN, b. about 1752 (based on age at time of death) parents not yet certain; Lydia d. at North Pembroke, 1 Apr 1829.

Samuel Abbott was a farmer in Pembroke.[2206] He and Lydia Perrin were parents of seven children born at Pembroke.

i EBENEZER ABBOTT, b. 22 Dec 1780; d. at Northfield, NH, after 1850; m. COMFORT SIMONDS, b. at Northfield, 25 Apr 1786 daughter of John and Dorothy (Batchelder) Simonds; Comfort d. after 1860.

ii AMOS ABBOTT, b. 6 Feb 1783; m. at Belmont, NH, 21 Nov 1811, DEBORAH BUSWELL, b. at East Kingston, NH, 12 Dec 1792 daughter of James and Ruth (Lord) Buswell; Deborah d. at Monroe, MO, about 1870.

iii JOB ABBOTT, b. about 1785; died young.

iv JOHN ABBOTT, b. 2 Nov 1788; d. at Peabody, MA, 15 Dec 1872; m. 1st, at Pembroke, 2 Jun 1814, SALLY DAVIS, b. about 1792 and d. about 1815. John m. 2nd, at Danvers, MA, Dec 1815, LYDIA CARRIAGE, b. at Danvers, 21 Dec 1800 daughter of William and Elizabeth (Fairn) Carriage; Lydia d. at Lynn, Sep 1821. John m. 3rd, at Danvers, 20 Oct 1822, ANNA LARRABEE, b. at Lynn, about 1791 daughter of Joseph and Lydia (Collis) Larrabee; Anna d. at Danvers, 5 May 1864.

v BETSY ABBOTT, b. 3 Jan 1790; m. at Epping, NH, 17 Jun 1813, BENJAMIN BROWN son of Benjamin Brown.

vi HANNAH ABBOTT, b. 23 Nov 1792; m. A STEVENS who has not been identified.[2207]

vii JOB ABBOTT, b. about 1794; m. at Manchester, NH, 16 Oct 1817, CHARLOTTE "LOTTIE" MERRILL, b. about 1795 "of Manchester."

814) ABIGAIL ABBOTT *(Samuel4, Jonathan3, Benjamin2, George1)*, b. at Pembroke, 6 Sep 1753 daughter of Samuel and Miriam (Stevens) Abbott; m. 23 Nov 1773, BENJAMIN WHITTEMORE, b. 4 Dec 1750 son of Aaron and Abigail (Coffin) Whittemore; Benjamin d. at Concord, 8 Oct 1822.

The History of Salisbury reports that Benjamin Whittemore, known as Button Whittemore, was often in legal disputes including once with his son who had his father jailed. The family was in Salisbury after 1791 when Benjamin purchased

---

2206 Carter, *History of Pembroke, Genealogies*, p 2

2207 Carter, *History of Pembroke, Genealogies*, p 2

property there, and later relocated to Danbury. Benjamin is reported to have had a second wife, but that information is not clear.[2208]

Abigail Abbott and Benjamin Whittemore were parents of ten children born at Pembroke.[2209]

i RUTH WHITTEMORE, b. 15 Sep 1775; d. Oct 1797; m. at Salisbury, 18 Aug 1795, JOHN SHANNON, b. at Canterbury, 1 Feb 1769;[2210] John d. at Perrysburg, NY, about 1840. John m. 2nd, Sep 1798, MEHITABLE HOLT *(Hannah Abbott Holt5, David4, Jonathan3, Benjamin2, George1)*, b. 17 Jul 1778 daughter of Benjamin and Hannah (Abbott) Holt. Mehitable Holt is a child in Family 809.

ii JOHN WHITTEMORE, b. 7 Feb 1776; d. at Dixville, NH, 19 Jan 1846; m. 1st, 1 Jan 1799, BETSEY PILLSBURY, b. at Salisbury, 24 Apr 1779 daughter of Samuel and Elizabeth (Pingrey) Pillsbury; Betsey d. at Dixville, 15 Dec 1815. John m. 2nd, at Stewartstown, 3 Feb 1834, OLIVE BRAINERD, b. at Rumney, NH, 5 Dec 1790 daughter of Brazillai and Hannah (Blodgett) Brainerd;[2211] Olive d. at Colebrook, 17 Sep 1860.

iii EBENEZER WHITTEMORE, b. 2 Feb 1778; d. at Springfield, NH, 30 Oct 1863; m. at Boscawen, 20 Feb 1800, LYDIA S. RICHARDS, b. 1778 daughter of Daniel and Eunice (Somerby) Richards; Lydia d. at North Wilmot, NH, 13 Jul 1845.

iv JUDITH WHITTEMORE, b. 6 Feb 1780; d. about 1813; m. 8 Aug 1799, JOSEPH ADAMS, b. at Newbury, 1 May 1779 *likely* the son of Abraham and Mary (Bricket) Adams; Joseph d. at Bright, IN, 12 Mar 1843. After Judith's death, Joseph married Sarah Judd on 29 Jan 1814.

v BENJAMIN WHITTEMORE, b. 29 Sep 1782; d. at Concord, NH, 19 May 1871; m. 1st, 27 Sep 1821, RUTH D. HILDRETH, b. about 1799; Ruth d. at Salisbury, 15 Jul 1828. Benjamin m. 2nd, at Andover, NH, 4 Oct 1829, SARAH SAWYER, b. at Hopkinton, about 1790 daughter of Samuel and Lucy (Perley) Sawyer;[2212] Sarah d. at Concord, 8 Sep 1880.

vi AMOS WHITTEMORE, b. 22 Aug 1785; d. at Princeton, IL, before 1855; m. 1st, at Salisbury, 28 Nov 1822, JUDITH CAMP (or Kemp), b. about 1796; Judith d. at Salisbury, 14 Mar 1835. Amos m. 2nd, 22 Aug 1841, MEHITABLE MARCH (widow of John Quimby), b. at Springfield, NH, 1 Jul 1799 daughter of David and Eunice (Persons) March; Mehitable was still living in 1860 in Concord, IL.

vii ESTHER WHITTEMORE, b. Jul 1788; d. at Salisbury, 22 Jun 1825. Esther did not marry.

viii AMELIA WHITTEMORE, b. 1790; nothing further known.

ix SAMUEL WHITTEMORE, b. 10 Nov 1792; d. at Charleston, IL, before 1860; m. 10 Jan 1821, MARTHA PERRIN, b. at Salisbury, about 1796 daughter of Stephen and Achsah (Heath) Perrin.[2213]

x SARAH WHITTEMORE, b. 8 Jul 1795; d. 1799.

815) JEREMIAH ABBOTT *(Samuel4, Jonathan3, Benjamin2, George1)*, b. at Pembroke, 9 May 1757 son of Samuel and Miriam (Stevens) Abbott; d. at Montville, ME, 27 Jan 1816; m. at Pembroke, NH, 29 Nov 1787, ELIZABETH "BETSEY" FRYE, b. 18 Feb 1767 daughter of Ebenezer and Hannah (Baker) Frye; Betsey d. at Montville, 27 Aug 1841.

Jeremiah Abbott served as a private during the Revolution initially in Colonel Wingate's regiment of New Hampshire militia. He saw other service in Colonel Thomas Stickney's regiment under General Stark and was at the Battle of Bennington. He served a total of 21 months and 6 days for which his widow Betsey received a pension of $70.66 per annum. As part of the pension application, son Joel Abbott made an affidavit giving the date of his father's death and that his mother Betsey Abbott was now living in Montville with Joel.[2214]

The family started in New Hampshire, were in Vermont for a time where at least one child was born, and were lastly in Montville, Maine. Five children have been identified for Jeremiah Abbott and Betsey Frye. There are no birth records, but the children are identified through death records giving Jeremiah Abbott and Betsey Frye as parents and from information in the pension application file. The information is consistent with census records as the siblings lived with each other off and on during their adult years. Given that the first child known was born ten years after the marriage, there may well be other children who have not been identified.

2208 Dearborn, *History of Salisbury*, p 857. The two names of second wives suggested by Dearborn, Ruth D. and Sarah Sawyer, were the wives of Benjamin's son Benjamin.

2209 *The History of Salisbury* suggests there were 16 children, but record evidence was found just for these ten

2210 The is a transcription of a birth at Canterbury, but no names of parents on the card.

2211 Brainard, *Descendants of Daniel, James and Joshua Brainerd*, p 79

2212 The names of Sarah's parents are given on her death record. Other census and probate records establish her siblings which further confirms parents.

2213 Dearborn, *History of Salisbury*, p 687

2214 Revolutionary War Pension and Bounty-Land Warrant Application Files

i JOEL ABBOTT, b. in VT, about 1797; d. after 1870 perhaps at China, ME; m. at Montville, 11 Mar 1824, JANE CARTER, b. at Montville, 11 Oct 1804 daughter of Thomas and Joanna (Perkins) Carter; Jane d. at Montville, after 1880.

ii HANNAH A. ABBOTT, b. in NH (according to census records), 1804; d. at Montville, ME, 23 Jul 1890; m. before 1833, REUBEN G. BLAKE, b. in ME, Apr 1803;[2215] Reuben d. at Montville, 4 May 1887.

iii EBENEZER GUY ABBOTT, b. in ME, 1808; d. at Morrill, ME, 12 Jan 1892; m. at Knox, ME, 29 Nov 1849, DESIRE BLAKE, b. about 1810; Desire d. after 1880.

iv LEONARD W. ABBOTT, b. about 1810; d. at Montville, 16 Mar 1814.

v LYDIA FRYE ABBOTT, b. at Montville, Jan 1811; d. at Montville, 14 May 1901; m. about 1847, as his second wife, HATHERLY VARNEY, b. about 1810; Hatherly d. at Levant, ME, 5 Aug 1851. Hatherly was first married to Adeline Smith.

816) SARAH ABBOTT *(Samuel[4], Jonathan[3], Benjamin[2], George[1])*, b. at Pembroke, 21 Jul 1759 daughter of Samuel and Miriam (Stevens) Abbott; m. 4 Nov 1790, as his second wife, JEREMIAH WHEELER, b. at Concord, MA, Feb 1745 son of Jeremiah and Esther (Russell) Wheeler; Jeremiah d. at Concord, NH, 17 Oct 1827. Jeremiah Wheeler was first married, 15 Feb 1770 to KEZIAH BLANCHARD *(Benjamin Blanchard[4], Mary Abbott Blanchard[3], Nathaniel[2], George[1])*, b. at Hollis, 26 Mar 1747 daughter of Benjamin and Keziah (Hastings) Blanchard; Keziah d. at Concord, 12 Aug 1789.

Jeremiah Wheeler and Keziah Blanchard were parents of seven children born at Concord.

i DORCAS WHEELER, b. 4 Feb 1771; d. at Rumford, ME, 1 Dec 1864; m. DAVID FARNUM, b. at Concord, 24 Dec 1767 son of Stephen and Martha (Hall) Farnum; David d. at Rumford, 1839.

ii MARY "POLLY" WHEELER, b. 10 Sep 1772; m. her fourth cousin, DANIEL VIRGIN, b. at Concord, 5 May 1767 son of Ebenezer and Dorcas (Lovejoy) Virgin; Daniel d. at Rumford, 1815.

iii ABEL WHEELER, b. 2 Sep 1774; d. at Rumford, 30 Sep 1852; m. about 1800, BETSEY AUSTIN, b. in ME, 1775; Betsey d. at Rumford, 21 May 1851.

iv BETSEY WHEELER, b. 25 May 1776; m. at Concord, 15 Feb 1797, DANIEL KNIGHT, b. at Rumford, 9 Sep 1769 son of Joseph and Phebe (Libby) Knight; Daniel d. at Rumford, 1819 (probate 5 Oct 1819).

v HANNAH WHEELER, b. 21 Feb 1778; d. at Mexico, ME, 27 Mar 1857; m. at Rumford, 24 Nov 1808, JOHN KIMBALL, b. in NH, 6 Jul 1785 son of Moses and Phebe (Cole) Kimball; John d. at Mexico, ME, 6 Dec 1864.

vi SALLY WHEELER, b. 27 May 1780; d. at Rumford, 14 Apr 1864; m. at Concord, 27 Jan 1801, NATHAN BROWN, b. in NH, about 1775; Nathan d. at Rumford, 1 May 1852.

vii WILLIAM WHEELER, b. 5 Jul 1782; d. at Peacham, VT, 1851; m. 1st, at Concord, 8 Mar 1804, PATTY VIRGIN, b. at Concord, 21 May 1783 daughter of Jonathan and Sarah (Austin) Virgin; Patty d. at Rumford, 4 Jan 1826. William m. 2nd, at Peacham, 12 Oct 1826, RHODA SKEELE, b. at Peacham, 28 Jun 1794 daughter of John and Phebe (Webster) Skeele; Rhoda d. at Peacham, 18 May 1864.

Sarah Abbott and Jeremiah Wheeler were parents of seven children born at Concord.

i LYDIA WHEELER, b. 8 Jan 1791; nothing further known.

ii KEZIAH BLANCHARD WHEELER, b. 25 Feb 1793; d. at Rumford, ME, 26 Nov 1873; m. at Concord, 13 Mar 1814, COLMAN GODWIN, b. 6 May 1782 son of William and Rachel (Harper) Godwin; Colman d. at Rumford, 24 Aug 1852.

iii JOHN WHEELER, b. 25 Feb 1793; d. at Concord, after 1870; m. 1st, 19 Feb 1817, MAHALA COCHRAN, b. at Pembroke, 1 Feb 1797 daughter of James and Lettice (Duncan) Cochran; Mahala d. at Concord, 24 Oct 1832. John m. 2nd, about 1834, MARY who has not been identified, but described as "of Warner" in the death record of one of the children; Mary d. by 1841. John m. 3rd, at Sanbornton, 3 Apr 1842, EUNICE HILLIARD, b. at

[2215] It is possible that Reuben Blake who married Hannah Abbott and Desire Blake who married Ebenezer Guy Abbott are siblings and the children of Moses and Hannah (Mayo) Blake.

Sanbornton, about 1814 daughter of Daniel and Polly (Eaton) Hilliard; Eunice d. at Concord, 26 Oct 1885. Eunice Hillard was first married to Edwin D. Fogg.

iv JEREMIAH WHEELER, b. 15 Feb 1795; d. at Manchester, NH, 27 Jan 1873; m. at Concord, 28 Mar 1820, SARAH WHIDDEN, b. in NH, about 1798 daughter of Josiah and Polly (Currier) Whidden.

v RUTH W. WHEELER, b. 4 Jan 1799; d. at Concord, 19 Mar 1880; m. at Concord, 16 Feb 1829, ANDREW MOODY, b. at Penobscot, ME, 2 Nov 1796 son of William and Mary (Dresser) Moody; Andrew d. at Concord, 10 Jan 1881.

vi JUDITH WHEELER, b. 10 Aug 1802; d. at Manchester, NH, after 1850; m. at Concord, 13 Feb 1823, SAINT LUKE MORSE, b. in NH, 11 Dec 1797 son of Benjamin and Dolly (George) Morse; Saint Luke d. after 1850.

vii MIRIAM WHEELER, b. 21 Jun 1805; may have died young.

817) LYDIA ABBOTT *(Samuel⁴, Jonathan³, Benjamin², George¹)*, b. at Pembroke, 14 Jul 1761 daughter of Samuel and Miriam (Stevens) Abbott; d. at Bethel, VT, 9 Dec 1840; m. 29 Mar 1787, NATHANIEL MORRILL, b. at South Hampton, NH, 10 Jun 1761 son of Paul and Martha (Worthen) Morrill; Nathaniel d. at Bethel, 17 Nov 1832.

This family was in Chichester, New Hampshire and Tunbridge, Vermont, and finally in Bethel, Vermont. Lydia and Nathaniel were parents of ten children.[2216]

i WILLIAM MORRILL, b. 1788; d. at Macon, MO, 1865; m. at Pembroke, 11 Feb 1813, MARY MARTIN, b. at Pembroke, 27 Jul 1790 daughter of Robert and Abigail (McCriss) Martin.

ii JUDITH MORRILL, b. at Chichester, 16 Aug 1789; d. at Royalton, VT, 3 Sep 1869; m. at Tunbridge, 11 Jan 1811, THOMAS RUSS, b. at Royalton, 31 Mar 1789 son of Jeremiah and Eunice (Moxley) Russ; Thomas d. at Royalton, 29 Apr 1868.

iii ABIGAIL MORRILL, b. 1791; d. at Royalton, 20 Apr 1836; m. 3 Dec 1812, JOHN GOULD DUTTON, b. at Clarendon, VT, 18 Nov 1789 son of Amasa and Sarah (Parmalee) Dutton;[2217] John d. at Northfield, VT, 7 Nov 1877.

iv SARAH "SALLY" MORRILL, b. 1792; d. at Tunbridge, after 1860; m. about 1817, LYMAN WIGHT, b. about Tunbridge, about 1792; Lyman d. at Randolph, VT, 1 May 1869.

v NATHANIEL MORRILL, b. 28 Jan 1795; d. at Concord, MI, 14 Oct 1865; m. at Canaan, NH, 8 Mar 1820, HANNAH MARTIN, b. at Pembroke, 15 Dec 1792 daughter of Robert and Abigail (McCriss) Martin; Hannah d. at Concord, MI, 14 Jun 1873.

vi JEREMIAH MORRILL, b. 1796; d. at Danville, VT, 17 Aug 1859; m. SARAH MORRILL, b. in VT, 25 Jul 1805 daughter of Jacob and Abigail (-) Morrill; Sarah d. at Lowell, MA, 8 Dec 1870.

vii SAMUEL MORRILL, b. 1799; d. at Orleans, VT, 14 Aug 1872; m. at Bethel, 1820, ACHSAH PEARSON, b. at Randolph, VT, 9 Jan 1804 daughter of John T. and Polly (-) Pearson; Achsah d. at Troy, VT, 18 Sep 1873.

viii LYDIA MORRILL, b. 1801; d. at Walcott, VT, 10 Feb 1885; m. ZIBA GIFFORD, b. at Tunbridge, 23 Aug 1792 son of Ziba and Sarah (McKnight) Gifford; Ziba d. at Walcott, 1 May 1870.

ix EZEKIEL MORRILL, b. 1803; d. at Tunbridge, 2 Jan 1836.

x SUSAN MORRILL, b. 1809; d. at Troy, VT, 1 Mar 1876; m. at Tunbridge, 8 Jan 1843, DANIEL KELSEY, b. at Tunbridge, 8 Apr 1797 son of James and Parmelia (Pratt) Kelsey; Daniel d. at Troy, VT, 22 May 1875.

818) EZRA ABBOTT *(Samuel⁴, Jonathan³, Benjamin², George¹)*, b. at Pembroke, 4 Aug 1763 son of Samuel and Miriam (Stevens) Abbott; d. at Sanbornton, NH, 16 Nov 1824; m. 30 Nov 1794, MOLLY BROWN, b. about 1770 daughter of William and Ruth (McDuffee) Brown;[2218] Molly d. at Cabot, VT, 1836.

Ezra Abbott and Molly Brown made the move from Pembroke to Sanbornton soon after their marriage and their five children were born in Sanbornton.

2216 Morrill Kindred in America, volume 2, p 39.
2217 Lovejoy, *History of Royalton*, part 2, p 776
2218 Chase, *History of Old Chester*, p 478

i SARAH ABBOTT, b. 23 Aug 1795; d. at Sanbornton, 16 May 1817; m. at Sanbornton, 14 Dec 1815, JOHN ABRAMS, b. at Sanbornton, 18 Jan 1793 son of John and Mehitable (Harriman) Abrams; d. at sea, 4 Jul 1853.[2219] John was second married to Nancy Rollins and third married to Ruth Sanborn.

ii JOHN ABBOTT, b. 30 Apr 1797; d. at Allenstown, NH, 21 Dec 1855; m. 31 Dec 1818, his fourth cousin once removed, MARY BUNTIN *(Betsy Hutchinson Buntin⁶, Mehitable Lovejoy Hutchinson⁵, Mehitable Chandler Lovejoy⁴, Zebadiah Chandler³, Hannah Abbott Chandler², George¹)*, b. at Pembroke, 25 Feb 1795 daughter of Robert and Betsy (Hutchinson) Buntin; Mary d. at Allenstown, 9 Feb 1858.

iii MARY ABBOTT, b. 5 Sep 1798; d. at Sanbornton, 27 Jun 1827; m. 28 Dec 1819, ASAHEL QUIMBY, b. at Sanbornton, 20 Jun 1797 son of Harper and Hannah (Thompson) Quimby; Asahel d. at Hill, NH, 25 Jul 1849. Asahel married second Sarah Bennett.

iv WILLIAM ABBOTT, b. 21 Feb 1800; d. at Medford, MN, 1862; m. at Hebron, 30 Dec 1824, LOIS SAWYER, b. at Newport, NH, 19 Dec 1801 daughter of Richard K. and Mary B. (Bean) Sawyer;[2220] Lois d. at Medford, 20 Jun 1863.

v CHAUNCEY ABBOTT, b. about 1802. He is reported to have left Sanbornton for New York in 1832 with nothing further heard of him.[2221]

Great-Grandchildren of Timothy Abbott and Hannah Graves

819) WILLIAM ABBOTT *(Samuel⁴, Jonathan³, Benjamin², George¹)*, b. at Pembroke, 10 Sep 1765 son of Samuel and Miriam (Stevens) Abbott; d. at Pembroke, 22 Jul 1838; m. his third cousin, DORCAS PARKER *(Hannah Abbott Parker⁴, Timothy³, Timothy², George¹)*, b. at Andover, 17 Feb 1769 daughter of Joseph and Hannah (Abbott) Parker; Dorcas d. at Pembroke, 9 Nov 1853.

William Abbott and Dorcas Parker were parents of nine children born at Pembroke.

i NATHANIEL ABBOTT, b. 10 Feb 1793; d. 27 Aug 1814.

ii WILLIAM ABBOTT, b. 15 Aug 1794; d. at Chichester, 23 May 1874; m. 1st, 22 Oct 1816, ESTHER FOWLER, b. at Pembroke, 16 Mar 1797 daughter of Benjamin and Mehitable (Ladd) Fowler; Esther d. at Pembroke, 31 Dec 1831. William m. 2nd, at Epsom, 5 Feb 1833, NANCY D. CAMPBELL, b. at Pembroke, about 1815 daughter of David and Deborah (Goss) Campbell; Nancy d. at Dover, NH, 22 Sep 1890.

iii HANNAH ABBOTT, b. 10 Jul 1796; d. at Pembroke, 3 Apr 1863; m. at Pembroke, 12 Sep 1828, her fourth cousin once removed, HERMAN ABBOT OSGOOD *(Christopher Osgood⁵, Elizabeth Abbott Osgood⁴, Thomas³, Thomas², George¹)*, b. at Pembroke, 20 Jul 1797 son of Christopher and Anna (Abbott) Osgood; Herman d. at Pembroke, 12 Feb 1858. Herman Osgood is a child in Family 880.

iv MIRIAM ABBOTT, b. 3 Mar 1798; d. at Worcester, VT, 17 Apr 1873; m. 24 Dec 1816, her first cousin, SAMUEL KELLY *(Rachel Abbott Kelly⁵, Samuel⁴, Jonathan³, Benjamin², George¹)*, b. at Pembroke, 23 Sep 1792 son of John and Rachel (Abbott) Kelly; Samuel d. at Worcester, VT, 2 Apr 1871. Samuel Kelly is a child in Family 820.

v MARY ABBOTT, b. 29 Jan 1800; d. at Pembroke, 20 Aug 1845; m. 15 Dec 1841, JONATHAN ROBINSON, b. at Epsom, 27 Jun 1785 son of David and Hannah (Fowler) Robinson; Jonathan d. at Pembroke, 19 Sep 1853.

vi ADRIAN ABBOTT, b. 21 Dec 1802; d. at Beddington, ME, 18 Apr 1881; m. about 1836, FANNY SCHOPPE, b. at Beddington, 23 Sep 1814 daughter of John and Eliza (Weston) Schoppe; Fanny d. at Pittsburg, NH, 28 Oct 1902.

2219 According to the History of Sanbornton, John died on a return trip from Oregon where he had been for two years; died when crossing the Gulf of Mexico.
2220 Dearborn, *History of Salisbury*, p 470
2221 Runnels, *History of Sanbornton, Genealogies*, p 1

vii LAVINIA ABBOTT, b. 12 Apr 1807; d. at North Pembroke, 25 Oct 1880; m. at Pembroke, 12 Mar 1824, JOHN LADD FOWLER, b. at Pembroke, 1 Aug 1801 son of Benjamin and Mehitable (Ladd) Fowler; John d. at North Pembroke, 27 Mar 1871.

viii SAVALLA ABBOTT, b. 24 Aug 1809; d. at Goffstown, after 1860; m. 1st, 16 Mar 1830, NATHAN LIBBEY, b. at Epsom, 25 Jun 1808 son of Nathan and Abigail (Fowler) Libbey; Nathan d. at Philadelphia, PA, 15 Oct 1874. It is possible that Savalla and Nathan Libbey divorced. In 1860, Savalla was in Goffstown listed as Savalla Thrasher with some of the children from her marriage to Nathan Libbey living with her. In 1860, Nathan Libbey was living in Philadelphia with what seems to be a new wife. If Savalla married a Mr. Thrasher, he was not in the home with her in 1860.

ix Stillborn child, 26 Aug 1811.

820) RACHEL ABBOTT *(Samuel4, Jonathan3, Benjamin2, George1)*, b. at Pembroke, 15 Jun 1768 daughter of Samuel and Miriam (Stevens) Abbott; d. at Pembroke, 28 Dec 1854; m. 30 Dec 1789, JOHN KELLEY, b. 22 Jul 1764 son of Samuel and Sarah (Barker) Kelley; John d. at Pembroke, 1 Jan 1817.

John Kelley was a farmer and he and Rachel raised their family in Pembroke, John did not leave a will and his estate entered probate 15 January 1817. His widow declined administration and this duty was assumed by son John Kelley. Real estate was valued at $800 and personal estate at $282.68.[2222]

Rachel Abbott and John Kelley were parents of ten children born at Pembroke.

i MIRIAM KELLEY, b. 23 Aug 1790; d. at Epsom, NH, 26 Sep 1879; m. at Pembroke, 30 Nov 1830, LEVI BAKER, b. at Pembroke, 22 Feb 1798 son of Joseph and Hannah (Haggett) Baker; Levi d. at Pembroke, 7 Oct 1844.

ii SAMUEL KELLEY, b. 23 Sep 1792; d. at Worcester, VT, 2 Apr 1871; m. 24 Dec 1816, his first cousin, MIRIAM ABBOTT, b. at Pembroke, 3 Mar 1798 daughter of William and Dorcas (Parker) Abbott; Miriam d. at Worcester, 17 Apr 1873. Miriam Abbott is a child in Family 819.

iii JOHN KELLEY, b. 10 Dec 1794; d. at Pembroke, 23 Apr 1864; m. 1st at Chichester, 10 Dec 1818, PHEBE STEVENS, b. 1802 daughter of Phebe and Olive (Locke) Stevens; Phebe d. at Pembroke, about 1851. John m. 2nd, 13 Aug 1856, ABIGAIL TIBBETTS (widow of William Caldwell), b. at Madbury, NH, about 1802; Abigail d. at Pembroke, 18 Apr 1877.

iv ALVA KELLEY, b. 14 Feb 1797; d. at Boston, MA, 4 May 1872; m. at Charlestown, 20 Jun 1824, LUCY BEAVERSTOCK, b. at Charlestown, 1 Jun 1800 daughter of Samuel and Olive (Read) Beaverstock; Lucy d. at Boston, 19 Dec 1878.

v HEPHZIBAH KELLEY, b. 6 Mar 1799; d. at Epsom, 24 Jan 1881; m. 20 Nov 1823, STEPHEN BAKER, b. at Pembroke, 4 May 1796 son of Joseph and Hannah (Haggett) Baker; Stephen d. at Epsom, 30 May 1869.

vi DAVID KELLEY, b. 10 Mar 1801; d. at Boston, 20 Jul 1846; m. at Charlestown, 25 Jan 1827, OLIVE BEAVERSTOCK, b. at Charlestown, 17 May 1809 daughter of Samuel and Olive (Reed) Beaverstock.

vii JASON ABBOTT KELLEY, b. 16 Feb 1803; d. at West Bridgewater, MA, 22 Feb 1882; m. at Chichester, 13 May 1830, MARINDA GILES DEARBORN, b. at Pembroke, 30 Apr 1805 daughter of Joseph and Sally (Bellamy) Dearborn; Marinda d. at Concord, 29 Dec 1867.

viii SALLY KELLEY, b. 17 Nov 1804; d. at Pembroke, 17 Jan 1878; m. 19 Aug 1828, MALACHI HAINES, b. at Chichester, 29 Oct 1802 son of Malachi and Sally (Fife) Haines; Malachi d. at Chichester, 1 Apr 1863.

ix BENAIAH KELLEY, b. 10 Dec 1807; d. at Hillsboro, IL, 17 Oct 1888; m. 1st at Montgomery County, IL, 10 Oct 1841, SARAH ANN MCADAMS, b. in IL, about 1820; Sarah d. at Hillsboro, about 1875. Benaiah m. 2nd, at Montgomery County, 23 Oct 1879, CYNTHIA E. KING, b. about 1839.

x MEHITABLE KELLEY, b. 12 Aug 1809; d. at North Pembroke, 23 Jan 1895; m. 21 Jan 1834, DARIUS SNELL, b. at Barnstead, NH, 15 Apr 1808 son of Thomas and Hannah (Merrill) Snell; Darius d. at North Pembroke, 16 Jan 1892.

821) MARIAM ABBOTT *(Samuel4, Jonathan3, Benjamin2, George1)*, b. at Pembroke, 5 Sep 1771 daughter of Samuel and Miriam (Stevens) Abbott; d. at Randolph, VT, 21 Jun 1820; m. JOHN MORRILL, b. 17 Jan 1759 son of Paul and Martha (Worthen) Morrill; John d. at Randolph, 21 Sep 1849.

[2222] *New Hampshire. Probate Court (Rockingham County);* Probate Place: *Rockingham, New Hampshire, Estate Papers, No 9415-9493, 1816-1817,* Case 9460

John Morrill and Mariam Abbott settled in Randolph, Vermont soon after their marriage. They had a farm there and were the parents of eleven children all born at Randolph.[2223]

i NANCY MORRILL, b. 5 Aug 1794; d. at Hampton, MN, 5 Mar 1860; m. at Randolph, 22 Feb 1815, WILLIAM PERRIN, b. at Royalton, VT, 11 Feb 1793 son of Greenfield and Sally (Ashcroft) Perrin;[2224] William d. at Hampton, 13 Feb 1865.

ii BETSEY MORRILL, b. 6 Feb 1796; d. at Chelsea, VT, 20 Jul 1852; m. 31 Mar 1818, PETER M. LOUGEE, b. Jan 1791;[2225] Peter d. at Randolph, 10 Dec 1857. Peter married second Betsey Worthley.

iii IRA MORRILL, b. 5 Sep 1797; d. at Randolph, VT, after 1870; m. 1st, at Randolph, 3 Jan 1822, MARY PICKENS, b. about 1799; Mary d. at Randolph, 25 Feb 1839. Ira m. 2nd, 22 Jun 1839, MARY B. SMITH, b. about 1810; Mary d. after 1870.

iv MARIAM MORRILL, b. 19 Sep 1799; d. at Randolph, 17 Mar 1833; m. 4 Feb 1854, ASAHEL BRAINERD, b. at Randolph, 15 Nov 1798 son of Asahel and Lydia (Loveland) Brainerd; Asahel d. at Randolph, 5 Aug 1851.

v JOHN MORRILL, b. 1 Jun 1801; d. at Randolph, 1852 (probate 19 Nov 1852); m. 1827, ABIAH OSGOOD, b. at Randolph, 11 Dec 1804 daughter of Abijah and Betsey (Sprague) Osgood; Abiah d. 29 Oct 1853.

vi MARY "POLLY" MORRILL, b. 15 Apr 1802; d. at Wolcott, VT, Nov 1885; m. 1 Dec 1825, PHILANDER SMITH, b. at Randolph, about 1805 son of Jonathan and Abigail (Edgerton) Smith; Philander d. at Wolcott, 24 May 1875.

vii MARTHA MORRILL, b. 15 May 1805; d. at Wolcott, VT, 25 May 1900; m. Feb 1827, IRA WALBRIDGE, b. at Cabot, VT, 25 Aug 1799 son of Oliver and Elizabeth (Smith) Walbridge; Ira d. at Wolcott, 29 Jun 1877.

viii Son, b. 10 Jun 1807

ix Son, b. 20 Aug 1809

x WILLIAM MORRILL, b. 11 Jan 1811; d. at Lewiston, WI, 2 Oct 1893; m. ANNA FOLSOM, b. at Tunbridge, 4 Aug 1808 daughter of John and Anna (Fifield) Folsom; Anna d. at Briggsville, WI, 28 Jan 1892.

xi GILBERT MORRILL, b. 11 Feb 1812; d. at Randolph, 3 Dec 1893; m. 1837, SALLY SPRAGUE, b. at Randolph, 2 Feb 1817 daughter of John and Sally (Story) Sprague; Sally d. at Randolph, 29 Mar 1886.

822) JONATHAN LANE *(Sarah Abbot Lane[4], David[3], Benjamin[2], George[1])*, b. at Bedford, 15 Oct 1763 son of John and Sarah (Abbot) Lane; d. at Bedford, 4 Mar 1808; m. 1 Feb 1787, his second cousin, HANNAH LANE *(Samuel Lane[4], Hannah Abbott Lane[3], Timothy[2], George[1])*, b. 26 Feb 1765 daughter of Samuel and Elizabeth (Fitch) Lane; Hannah d. at Lowell, 1848 (date of probate).

Jonathan Lane was a farmer in Bedford. He died of consumption at age 40 leaving eight children.

In his will written 3 February 1808 (probate 13 April 1808), Jonathan Lane bequeathed to wife Hannah half of the household property and the other half divided among his daughters Hannah, Arinda, and Sarah. Clothing is equally divided among his five sons Jonathan Lane, Josiah Abbot Lane, George Lane, Charles Lane, and Samuel John Lane. Only if needed for the care of his younger children, some of his property may be sold if the family circumstances require that. Each of the sons is to have double the amount from the estate of each of the daughters. He wills that his son Jonathan will continue to work on the family farm after he reaches the age of twenty. If he continues to work on the family place, he will receive wages the same as other men generally receive. His land is not to be sold until at least seven years after his death unless this is necessary for the support of the family. Deacon Moses Fitch and wife Hannah Lane are named executors. Real estate was valued at $2408 including a 40-acre homestead valued at $1900. Personal estate was valued at $288.15 which included an 8-day clock valued at $38.[2226]

Hannah Lane wrote her will 10 December 1839 (probate 1848). She bequeaths $50 to her son John Samuel Lane and this amount is to be paid before any of the other legacies so that he receives this full amount. Daughter Hannah Putnam wife of Elijah Putnam receives $50. Son Josiah Abbott Lane receives her mahogany framed likeness. Daughter Arinda Fiske wife of George Fiske receives the best carpet and other furniture items. Daughter Sarah Hayward wife of Ebenezer Hayward receives $50. Granddaughter Hannah E. Moore wife of Daniel P. Moore receives her gold necklace. Grandson Jonathan Lane Fiske

---

2223 Nickerson and Cox, *Illustrated Historical Souvenir of Randolph, Vermont*, p 79

2224 Aldrich and Holmes, *History of Windsor County, Vermont*, p 783

2225 Birth date is given on his death record.

2226 Middlesex County, MA: Probate File Papers, 1648-1871.Online database. AmericanAncestors.org. New England Historic Genealogical Society, 2014. Case number 13580

(when he reaches age 21) receives her woodlot of about 40 rods that she received by deed in 1823. Her three daughters will equally divide her household items. All the remainder of the estate to be equally divided among her children Jonathan Lane, Hannah Putnam, Josiah Abbott Lane, Arinda Fiske, Sarah Hayward, George Lane, Charles Lane, and John Samuel Lane. Son Jonathan Lane is named sole executor.[2227]

Jonathan Lane and Hannah Lane were parents of eleven children born at Bedford, Massachusetts.

i JONATHAN LANE, b. 27 Jan 1788; d. at Bedford, 12 Nov 1860; m. 27 Jul 1815, RUHAMAH PAGE, b. at Bedford, 1 May 1788 daughter of Nathaniel and Sarah (Brown) Page; Ruhamah d. at Bedford, 19 Jun 1882.

ii HANNAH LANE, b. 11 Oct 1789; d. at Bedford, 22 Apr 1874; m. at Bedford, 27 Sep 1838, as his second wife, ELIJAH PUTNAM, b. at Rindge, NH, 5 Jan 1780 son of Jonathan and Lucy (Lane) Putnam; Elijah d. at Amherst, NH, 18 Oct 1855. Elijah was first married to Lucy Weber.

iii JOSIAH ABBOTT LANE, b. 17 Aug 1791; d. at Brooklyn, NY, 15 Jan 1870; m. in NY, 17 May 1818, PHEBE SPINNING, b. in NY, 14 Sep 1801;[2228] Phebe d. at Brooklyn, 29 Oct 1880.

iv ARINDA LANE, b. 26 May 1793; d. at Lowell, 24 Jan 1885; m. at Bedford, 6 May 1824, GEORGE FISKE, b. at Merrimack, NH, 22 Aug 1794 son of David and Edith (-) Fiske; George d. at Lowell, 20 Feb 1869.

v ROLLIN LANE, b. 9 Apr 1795; d. 9 Jan 1800.

vi SARAH LANE, b. 1 May 1797; d. at Boston, 28 Jun 1871; m. at Bedford, 15 May 1817, EBENEZER HAYWARD, b. about 1792 perhaps the son of John and Abigail (Haynes) Hayward; Ebenezer d. at Boston, 1861.

vii ELIZABETH LANE, b. 13 Jun 1799; d. 15 Jan 1800.

viii MYRA LANE, b. 24 Nov 1800; d. 20 May 1801.

ix GEORGE LANE, b. 8 May 1802; d. at Boston, 11 Feb 1882; m. 1st, at Charlestown, 28 Oct 1826, LUCY MARIA DUNN, b. about 1804 daughter of John and Polly (Puffer) Dunn;[2229] Lucy d. at Charlestown, 13 Feb 1831. George m. 2nd, 22 Nov 1831, SARAH E. BARRY, b. at Barnstable, about 1810 daughter of Watson and Elizabeth (Nickerson) Barry; Sarah d. at Boston, 17 Nov 1897.

x CHARLES S. LANE, b. 4 Aug 1804; d. at Boston, 14 Oct 1872; m. at Boston, 22 Nov 1827, SARAH BARCROFT WHEELER, b. 1804; Sarah d. at Dorchester, 5 Apr 1844. Charles m. 2nd, at Dorchester, 10 Apr 1845, ELIZABETH S. CARLETON, b. about 1816 daughter of William L. and Mary J. (-) Carleton; Elizabeth d. at Boston, 22 Aug 1887.

xi JOHN SAMUEL LANE, b. 15 Jan 1808; d. at New York, NY, 21 Jul 1857; m. at Harlem, NY, 12 May 1834, SARAH ANN VERMILYEA,[2230] b. at New York, 11 Feb 1816 daughter of Abraham and Mary (Seaman) Vermilyea; Sarah d. at New York, 24 Aug 1878.

823) SARAH LANE *(Sarah Abbot Lane⁴, David³, Benjamin², George¹)*, b. at Bedford, 1 Oct 1765 daughter of John and Sarah (Abbot) Lane; d. at Billerica, 11 Jun 1849; m. 1 Nov 1787, TIMOTHY STEARNS, b. at Billerica, 25 Sep 1763 son of Isaac and Sarah (Abbott) Stearns; Timothy d. 8 Aug 1816. Sarah's mother and Timothy's mother were both named Sarah Abbott. Timothy's mother Sarah Abbott was from the Rowley Abbott lane.

Timothy Stearns was a farmer and Sarah and Timothy raised their family in Billerica. Two of the younger children, Sarah and Timothy, were educators.

In Timothy Stearns's will written 29 Jan 1816 (proved 28 Aug 1816), his beloved wife receives all the household goods, the horse and chaise, and $100 to dispose of as she pleases. She also receives use of one-third part of the real estate and a seat in the pew during her life. She has use of the clock while she is a widow. Son Eckly receives one-half of the pasture in Ashburnham and $100 to be paid to him when he reaches age 19. Son Timothy receives the other half of the pasture and $100 when he is 19. Daughter Sarah Abbot Stearns receives $250 to be paid at age 18 or on the day of her marriage if she marries earlier. Son Sewal Stearns receives his watch and a yoke of oxen. All the remainder of the estate is to be divided between sons Sewal and Obed. Elijah Stearns of Bedford and son Sewal Stearns were named executors. Real estate was valued at $3,715 and personal estate at $1,637.72.[2231]

Sarah Lane and Timothy Stearns were parents of ten children born at Billerica.

[2227] Middlesex County, MA: Probate File Papers, 1648-1871.Online database. AmericanAncestors.org. New England Historic Genealogical Society, 2014. Case number 36074

[2228] Chapman and Fitts, *Lane Genealogies*, p 116

[2229] Cary, *John Ainsworth Dunn*, p 58

[2230] New York City, Marriages, 1600s-1800s

[2231] Middlesex County, MA: Probate File Papers, 1648-1871.Online database. AmericanAncestors.org. New England Historic Genealogical Society, 2014. Case 21346

i TIMOTHY STEARNS, b. 8 Sep 1788; d. 22 Nov 1791.

ii SALLY STEARNS, b. 21 Sep 1790; d. 23 Feb 1793.

iii TIMOTHY STEARNS, b. 12 Nov 1792; d. 6 Apr 1795.

iv JOHN STEARNS, b. 5 Sep 1794; d. 3 Mar 1809.

v SEWALL STEARNS, b. 21 Sep 1796; d. at Billerica, 31 Oct 1849; m. 23 Jun 1836, LUCRETIA HILL, b. at Billerica, 3 Mar 1807 daughter of Job and Susannah (Blanchard) Hill; Lucretia d. at Billerica, 17 Feb 1874.

vi SARAH STEARNS, b. 8 Jul 1798; d. 18 Jun 1800.

vii OBED STEARNS, b. 21 Mar 1801; d. at Winchester, MA, 7 Jul 1863; m. at Billerica, 27 May 1827, MEHITABLE CARLETON, b. at Billerica, 17 Jan 1803 daughter of Amos and Esther (Manning) Carleton; Mehitable d. at Elmira, NY, 18 Dec 1876.

viii SARAH ABBOT STEARNS, b. 27 Feb 1803; d. at Amherst, NH, 15 Sep 1865; m. at Billerica, 16 Dec 1842, as his second wife, AARON LAURENCE, b. at Hollis, 23 Dec 1804 son of Aaron and Lucy (Putnam) Laurence; Aaron d. at Amherst, 1 Sep 1867. Aaron was first married to Lucy Clagett. Before her marriage, Sarah was the principal of a female seminary in Chillicothe, Ohio.[2232]

ix ECKLEY STEARNS, b. 12 Jun 1805; d. at Woburn, 9 Aug 1872; m. 11 Sep 1831, HANNAH LORING PRATT, b. at Weymouth, MA, 23 May 1811 daughter of Jacob and Hannah (Loring) Pratt; Hannah d. at Woburn, 30 Oct 1888.

x TIMOTHY STEARNS, b. 23 Jan 1810; d. at Fort Madison, IA, 19 Jul 1861; m. 13 Dec 1837, CATHERINE TAYLOR, b. at Athens, OH, 10 Dec 1816 daughter of Isaac and Lydia (Perkins) Taylor; Catherine d. at Lafayette, IN, 16 Oct 1879. Timothy attended Andover Seminary and for a time was a principal of a high school in Columbus, Ohio. For a time, he was an assistant at the female seminary where his sister Sarah was principal.[2233]

824) ELIZABETH ABBOTT *(David[4], David[3], Benjamin[2], George[1])*, b. at Andover, 26 Feb 1754 daughter of David and Prudence (Sheldon) Abbot; d. at Mount Holly, VT, about 1807; m. at Cavendish, VT, 19 Aug 1792, WILLIAM D. DOUGLASS, b. about 1750; William d. at Mount Holly, VT, after 1810. After Elizabeth's death, William married Sarah Pratt 1 Mar 1808.

Very little information is known for Elizabeth Abbott and William Douglass. There were two children born at Mount Holly, Vermont.

i DAVID DOUGLASS, b. 23 Oct 1793; nothing further known.

ii WILLIAM D. DOUGLASS, b. 7 Jul 1796. There is a record for a birth of a daughter Annis Douglass at Mount Holly on 15 Jan 1816 daughter of William and Prudence Douglass. It is not known if this is a child of this William or a child of his father William with a third wife.

825) PRUDENCE ABBOTT *(David[4], David[3], Benjamin[2], George[1])*, b. at Andover, 3 Oct 1757 daughter of David and Prudence (Sheldon) Abbot; d. at Salina, NY, 15 Dec 1839;[2234] m. 13 Oct 1778, NATHANIEL SAWYER, b. at Methuen, 16 Jun 1750 son of Josiah and Hannah (Gowing) Sawyer; Nathaniel d. at Wilton, 15 Oct 1807.

Hurd's *History of Hillsborough County* includes a personal reminiscence of her father written by Achsah Sawyer Allen. Achsah notes her father's service in the Revolution, his move to Wilton in 1781, eighteen years of toil on his farm, and later taking over the general store previously operated by Jacob Abbot.[2235]

Prudence Abbott and Nathaniel Sawyer were parents of eleven children, the oldest two born at Amherst and the other children at Wilton.

i FANNY SAWYER, b. 5 Jul 1779; d. at Temple, NH, 31 Oct 1853; m. 10 Mar 1800, SILAS BUSS, b. about 1776 son of Silas and Hannah (Pierce) Buss; Silas d. at Temple, 11 Dec 1854.

[2232] Renick, *Che-le-co-the, Glimpses of Yesterday*, p 186ff for detailed information on Sarah Stearns and her leadership of the seminary.

[2233] Bond, *Genealogies and Descendants of the Early Settlers of Watertown*, p 941

[2234] Livermore, *History of Wilton*, p 495

[2235] Hurd, *History of Hillsborough County*, pp 705-707. This source includes many additional details of the life and times in Wilton during the time of Nathaniel Sawyer written by Mrs. Achsah Allen and is available on archive.org.

ii HANNAH SAWYER, b. 5 Dec 1780; d. at Salem, NY, 15 Jul 1864; m. 31 May 1804, LEONARD BARKER, b. 1778 likely the son of Phineas and Sarah (Howe) Barker; Leonard, d. at Salem, NY, 26 Mar 1864.

iii SARAH "SALLY" SAWYER, b. 25 Nov 1782; d. at Marion, ME, 10 Jun 1863; m. her fourth cousin once removed, TIMOTHY ABBOT HOLT *(Hannah Abbott Holt[5], Barachias[4], John[3], John[2], George[1])*, b. at Wilton, 24 Aug 1781 son of Jeremiah and Hannah (Abbott) Holt; Timothy d. at Edmonds, ME, 4 Mar 1858. Timothy A. Holt is a child in Family 293.

iv NATHANIEL SAWYER, b. 25 Nov 1784; d. at Cooper, ME, 20 Jun 1875; m. at Machias, ME, 2 Apr 1818, JANE CHRISTY WATERHOUSE, b. in New Brunswick, Canada, 13 Mar 1800 daughter of Elias and Martha (Greenlaw) Waterhouse; Jane d. at Cooper, ME, after 1880.

v OLIVE SAWYER, b. 11 Feb 1787; d. at Parkesburg, PA, 31 Jan 1871; m. 12 May 1808, JOSEPH PARKER, b. about 1783 son of Hananiah and Hephzibah (Warren) Parker; Joseph d. at Chester, VT, 12 Mar 1831.

vi ASAPH SAWYER, b. 11 May 1789; d. 6 Feb 1790.

vii ANNA SAWYER, b. 17 Jan 1791; d. 30 May 1809.

viii ASAPH SAWYER, b. 15 Jul 1793; d. at Cooper, ME, 1 Aug 1875; m. 1st, 23 Feb 1819, BETSEY RUSSELL, b. at Wilton, 4 Mar 1797 daughter of Daniel and Elizabeth (Dascombe) Russell; Betsey d. about 1844. Asaph m. 2nd, about 1845, ALICE CRANE ALLAN, b. at Whiting, ME, 7 Oct 1818 daughter of Horatio Gates and Charlotte (Crane) Allan; Alice d. at Brockton, MA, 1 Aug 1896.

ix AMOS SAWYER, b. 26 Oct 1795; d. 20 Oct 1799.

x Infant (unnamed), b. and d. Dec 1797.

xi ACHSAH SAWYER, b. 15 Sep 1800; d. at Marion, ME, 28 May 1886; m. 12 Oct 1825, JOHN CRANE ALLAN, b. 31 Jan 1800 son of William and Alice (Crane) Allan; John d. at Dennysville, ME, 27 Dec 1867.

826) JOSIAH ABBOTT *(David[4], David[3], Benjamin[2], George[1])*, b. at Andover, 29 Dec 1759 son of David and Prudence (Sheldon) Abbot; d. at Lemington, VT, Feb 1837; m. 1st, 15 May 1784, RUTH BODWELL; Ruth d. by 1790. Josiah m. 2nd, 30 Mar 1790, ANNA FURBUSH, b. Oct 1768 daughter of Charles and Sarah (Corey) Furbush; Anna d. at Colebrook, NH, 11 Feb 1842.

Josiah and his first wife Ruth lived in Andover. During his second marriage, Josiah relocated to Bath, New Hampshire, and finally settled in Lemington, Vermont.

During the Revolution, Josiah served as Ensign for a period of two years in Colonel Tupper's Regiment of the Massachusetts Line which he joined in July 1781. Prior to that time, he reported six shorter enlistments as a private. In 1818, at age 59, he made application for a pension. Josiah reported he had worked as a laborer and was now debilitated. His wife was age 53 and two minor children were still at home, Moses S. Abbot aged 12 and Maria F. Abbot aged 9.[2236]

Josiah Abbott and Ruth Bodwell were parents of three children born at Andover.

i CHARLES ABBOTT, b. 25 Nov 1784; d. at Lemington, VT, 29 Dec 1833; m. at Bath, NH, 31 Dec 1813, ANN "NANCY" SALTER LANG, b. at Bath, 26 Jun 1788 daughter of Samuel and Susan (Salter) Lang; Nancy d. at Bath, 14 Aug 1873.

ii RUTH BODWELL ABBOTT, b. 1 Jan 1786; d. at East Hardwick, VT, 17 Jun 1858; m. at Lyman, NH, 11 Nov 1813, ASA HOLMES "of Dalton, NH."[2237] The children of this couple were born in Newbury, VT.

iii FANNY ABBOTT, b. 20 Dec 1787; d. at Landaff, NH, after 1850; m. at Bath, 27 Nov 1806, JEREMIAH CLOUGH, b. at Salem, NH, 20 Jan 1782 son of William and Abigail (Bailey) Clough; Jeremiah d. after 1850.

Josiah Abbott and Anna Furbush were parents of eight children, the oldest five at Andover and the three youngest children at Bath, New Hampshire.

i NANCY ABBOTT, b. 30 Nov 1790; d. 10 Jul 1818. Nancy did not marry.

ii SARAH F. ABBOTT, b. 10 Nov 1791; d. at Troy, NY, 18 Sep 1876; m. at Lynn, 24 Oct 1819, AARON HALL, b. 28 Apr 1792;[2238] Aaron d. at Troy, 13 Jun 1868.

[2236] Revolutionary War Pension and Bounty-Land Warrant Application Files

[2237] Asa Holmes is perhaps the son of Lemuel and Abigail (Bicknell) Holmes who was born in 1765 in Walpole, NH. If so, he had two earlier marriages.

[2238] Aaron's date of birth is on his gravestone.

iii SOPHIA C. ABBOTT, b. 20 Aug 1793; d. at Chazy, NY, after 1850; m. about 1813, HENRY GOSS, b. at Vernon, VT, 3 Jan 1788 son of Daniel and Anna (Inder) Goss; Henry d. after 1850.

iv DORCAS ABBOTT, b. 4 Mar 1796; d. at Troy, NY, 11 Jun 1842; m. about 1820, ARTEMUS W. BUFFINGTON, b. 11 Dec 1798 son of Comens and Laura (Lamkin) Buffington;[2239] Artemus d. at Lemington, 27 Jun 1835.

v WALTER STUART ABBOTT, b. 23 Feb 1798; d. at Milford, OH, after 1860; m. BETSEY G. LADD, b. about 1796 daughter of James and Elizabeth (Gould) Ladd;[2240] Betsey d. at Milford, 1858.

vi GEORGE WASHINGTON ABBOTT, b. 24 Dec 1799; d. at Lyman, NH, 13 Mar 1853; m. 1817, LUCINDA ROWELL, b. at Bennington, NY, 3 Mar 1800 daughter of William and Anna (-) Rowell;[2241] Lucinda d. at Barnet, VT, 22 Feb 1890.[2242]

vii MOSES SEWELL ABBOTT, b. 22 Oct 1806; d. at Mellette, SD, 27 Feb 1885; m. SOPHRONIA LADD, b. Sep 1809 daughter of James and Elizabeth (Gould) Ladd; Sophronia d. at Prairie de Sac, WI, 12 Apr 1872.

viii MARIA F. ABBOTT, b. 18 Jul 1809; d. at Stewartstown, NH, 3 Aug 1869; m. about 1830, STEPHEN HARRIS, b. at Vernon, VT, 27 Mar 1809 son of Stephen and Elizabeth (Johnson) Harris; Stephen d. at Westfield, MA, 14 Aug 1882.

827) HANNAH ABBOTT *(David⁴, David³, Benjamin², George¹)*, b. at Andover, 5 Jan 1762 daughter of David and Prudence (Sheldon) Abbot; d. at Compton, Québec, 1856; m. at Billerica, 21 Jan 1787, AARON PARKER, b. at Methuen, 22 Feb 1759 son of Timothy and Priscilla (Carleton) Parker; Aaron d. 1857; living in Compton in 1851 listed as 93 years old.[2243]

Aaron Parker and Hannah Abbott were parents of six children the oldest five born at Hancock, New Hampshire and the youngest child at Compton, Québec.

i DAVID ABBOT PARKER, b. 28 Feb 1791; d. at Monroe, OH, after 1860; m. 1st, at Eaton, Québec, 1820, FANNY HASKELL, b. at Chesterfield, NH, 16 Dec 1793 daughter of Benjamin and Susannah (Stone) Haskell;[2244] Fanny d. about 1832. David m. 2nd, EMILY STARKS, b. in NY, 1813 daughter of Henry and Priscilla (Harris) Starks; Emily d. 1891 (memorial marker at Calhoun, IA).[2245]

ii HANNAH PARKER, b. 22 Jul 1792; d. at Hancock, 7 Oct 1799.

iii PRISCILLA PARKER, b. 22 May 1794; d. at Hancock, 1 Oct 1799.

iv JAMES PARKER, b. 22 Jan 1796; d. at Ascot, Sherbrooke, Québec, 1857; m. about 1831, HARRIET LOWELL, b. in VT, about 1815.

v LEMUEL PARKER, b. 11 Jun 1797; nothing further known.

vi ALFRED CARLTON PARKER, b. at Compton, 13 Nov 1804; d. at Coaticook, Stanstead, 20 Mar 1882; m. at Ascot, 1825, ZERVIAH WHITCOMB, b. about 1807 daughter of Joshua and Clarissa (Bailey) Whitcomb;[2246] Zerviah d. at Compton, 15 Apr 1866.

828) SAMUEL ABBOTT *(David⁴, David³, Benjamin², George¹)*, b. at Andover, 27 Mar 1764 son of David and Prudence (Sheldon) Abbot; d. at Bennington, NH, 29 Mar 1833; m. 1st, at Billerica, 26 Jan 1786, his second cousin once removed, RHODA BLANCHARD, b. 17 Nov 1762 daughter of Samuel and Mary (Brown) Blanchard;[2247] Rhoda d. about 1800. Samuel m. 2nd at Hancock, NH, 22 Dec 1801, ANNA (MOORE) WALLACE,[2248] b. at Londonderry, about 1768; Anna d. at Bennington, NH, 24 Sep 1836.

Samuel Abbott and Rhoda Blanchard were parents of seven children.

2239 Wilkins, *The Descendants of Thomas Lamkin*, p 163

2240 Ladd, *The Ladd Family*, p 119

2241 Lucinda's parents are given as William and Anna on her death record.

2242 Obituary of Lucinda Abbott, Caledonian, St. Johnsbury, VT, 27 Feb 1890

2243 1851 Census of Canada East, Canada West, New Brunswick, and Nova Scotia; Year: 1851; Census Place: Compton, Sherbrooke County, Canada East (Quebec); Schedule: A; Roll: C_1142; Page: 89; Line: 41

2244 Haskell Family Association, hfa.haskells.net

2245 David and Emily's son Rollin D. Parker lived in Iowa and Emily perhaps was living there before her death.

2246 Whitcomb, *The Whitcomb Family in America*, p 440

2247 Burrage, *Genealogical and Family History of the State of Maine*, volume I, p 382

2248 She is named as Anna Wallace on the marriage transcription, but there are sources who give her name as Anna Moore. Perhaps she was a widow.

i HENRY BLANCHARD ABBOTT, b. at Andover, 11 Feb 1787; nothing further known.

ii RHODA ABBOTT, b. 18 Oct 1788; nothing further known.

iii SAMUEL SHELDON ABBOTT, b. at Andover, 23 Sep 1790; d. at Matinicus, ME, 15 Jun 1872; m. 29 Sep 1821, ABIGAIL BURGESS, b. at Matinicus, 13 Aug 1805 daughter of Ezekiel and Lydia (Eldredge) Burgess;[2249] Abigail d. 11 Feb 1858.

iv WILLIAM ABBOTT, b. at Andover, 18 Oct 1792

v DAVID ABBOTT, b. at Milford, NH, 10 Jul 1794

vi PAMELA ABBOTT, b. recorded at Wilton, 7 Dec 1796. She is *perhaps* the Pamela Abbott who married JAMES FLETCHER at Morgan, IL, 22 Feb 1836. If so, she died at Eagle, AR, 1869. James Fletcher was the son of John Gould and Mary (Lewis) Fletcher. Pamela Fletcher, born in NH in 1797, is listed on the Census at Eagle in both 1850 and 1860.

vii HANNAH ABBOTT, b. 14 Jan 1799

Samuel Abbott and Anna Wallace were parents of three children born at Bennington, New Hampshire.

i BETSY ABBOTT, b. 1803

ii SARAH ABBOTT, b. 23 Sep 1804; d. at Deering, NH, 22 Dec 1892; m. at Deering, 9 Oct 1839, HIRAM DODGE, b. at Amherst, NH, 2 Jan 1803 son of Levi and Eunice (Fiske) Dodge; Hiram d. at Amherst, 4 Aug 1876.

iii ROBERT M. ABBOTT, b. 24 Sep 1806; d. 16 Aug 1810.

829) DAVID ABBOTT *(David[4], David[3], Benjamin[2], George[1])*, b. at Andover, 4 Mar 1766 son of David and Prudence (Sheldon) Abbot; d. at Barton, VT, 11 Mar 1847; m. at Fryeburg, ME, Sep 1786, SARAH "SALLY" KEZAR;[2250] Sally d. at Barton, May 1816.

David served in the last part of the Revolution enlisting on 11 August 1781 from Andover as a private in the company of Captain John Robinson in Colonel William Turner's Massachusetts Regiment. He was discharged at Rhode Island 11 November 1781.

David was in Parsonsfield, Maine, went to Sheffield, Vermont in 1796 and then settled in Barton. David and Sally Abbott were parents of six children.[2251]

i POLLY ABBOTT, b. 10 Oct 1787

ii PRUDENCE ABBOTT, b. 20 Jan 1791; d. at Barton, 6 Jan 1865; m. about 1815, JOHN BUSWELL, b. at East Kingston, NH, 14 Feb 1789 son of John and Ruth (Lord) Buswell; John d. at Barton, 1 Jan 1839.

iii GEORGE ABBOTT, b. about 1793; d. 20 Jul 1797.

iv DAVID ABBOTT, b. about 1794; d. 7 Aug 1797.

v DAVID S. ABBOTT, b. 6 Oct 1797; d. at Barton, 14 May 1885; m. 1st, at Sheffield, Mar 1830, SARAH COLLEY, b. about 1804; Sarah d. at Sheffield, VT, 6 Jun 1853. David m. 3rd. at Glover, VT, 15 Jan 1867, OLIVE R. SCOTT, b. about 1805 and likely a widow. David m. 4th, at Barton, 19 Nov 1877, JANE KENNISON (widow of Isaiah Evans), b. at Sandwich, NH, about 1800 daughter of Simeon and Mary (Mudgett) Kennison;[2252] Jane d. at Sutton, VT, 24 Sep 1881. David may have married four times, but the second marriage is not yet located, or perhaps he has just three marriages.

vi HANNAH PARKER ABBOTT, b. 19 Mar 1803

830) BENJAMIN ABBOTT *(David[4], David[3], Benjamin[2], George[1])*, b. at Andover, 26 Jun 1768 son of David and Prudence (Sheldon) Abbot; d. at Ashtabula, OH, 22 May 1856; m. at Hancock, 6 Oct 1793, BETSEY NOONING whose origins are unknown; Betsey d. 4 Sep 1854.

[2249] Long, *Matinicus Isle: Its Story and Its People*, p 145

[2250] Published genealogies give her name as Sarah Keyser, but every birth record for this couple lists her name as Sarah Parker and Parker is included as the middle name of one of their children. Son David has mother's name as Keizer on a marriage record. Daughter Prudence has mother as Parker on her death record.

[2251] Child, *Gazetteer and Business Directory of Lamoille and Orleans Counties, Vt., for 1883-84*, p 205

[2252] The names of Jane's parents are given on her marriage record as Simeon Kennison and Mary Hagget and on her death record as Simeon Kennison and Mary Mudgett, but it seems to be Mudgett. Simeon Kennison married Mary Mudgett 20 Sep 1792.

Benjamin and Betsey Abbott were wanderers. They started their family in Billerica (although they were married likely in Hancock, NH) and were next in Hancock, New Hampshire for three or four years. They were then in Lower Canada where their two youngest children were born. *The History of Hancock* reports that the family then, with the family of David Parker, traveled in a boat built by Benjamin up the St. Lawrence River to Lake Ontario and were for a time in Genesee. Before 1819, they were in Ashtabula County, Ohio.[2253] The family settled in the north part of Monroe Township.[2254] Benjamin was a township trustee in 1819 and was Justice of the Peace in 1821.

Benjamin and Betsey were parents of eight children.

i BETSEY ABBOTT, b. at Billerica, 1 Jan 1795; nothing further known.

ii ANNA ABBOTT, b. at Billerica, 22 Apr 1796; nothing further known.

iii HANNAH P. ABBOTT, b. at Billerica, 16 Nov 1797; d. at Conneaut, OH, after 1880; m. at Ashtabula County, OH, 9 Mar 1820, 9 Mar 1820, BENJAMIN FIFIELD, b. in VT, about 1794 son of Josiah and Miriam (-) Fifield; Benjamin d. at Conneaut, 26 Dec 1871.

iv FRANKLIN ABBOTT, b. at Hancock, NH, Apr 1799; d. 6 Aug 1800.

v DORCAS ABBOTT, b. Jan 1801; d. 8 Sep 1802.

vi AUGUSTUS ABBOTT, b. in VT, about 1803; d. at Ashtabula County, OH, 1871; m. 8 Feb 1838, OBEDIENCE EVARTS, b. at Burlington, VT, 11 Nov 1811 daughter of Jesse and Dorcas (-) Evarts; Obedience d. at Burlington, NJ at the home of her daughter, 7 Mar 1894. Obedience was first married to Robert Quigley.

vii PRISCILLA ABBOTT, b. at England, Ottawa, Ontario, 1806; d. at Miami, OH, after 1880; m. at Ashtabula County, OH, 27 Sep 1826, WOODBURY HATCH, b. at Chelsea, VT, 3 Oct 1802 son of Rufus and Selah (Hall) Hatch; Woodbury d. at Miami, OH, after 1860.

viii SOPHIA ABBOTT, b. in Lower Canada, 30 Jun 1808; d. at Conneaut, OH, 6 May 1853; m. 1st, at Ashtabula County, 1 Apr 1833, SOLOMON SPALDING, b. at Chelsea, VT, 20 Aug 1801 son of Elisha and Urania (Woodard) Spalding;[2255] Solomon d. at Conneaut, 11 Jun 1846. Sophia m. 2nd, about 1848, ALONZO GEORGE FERGUSON, b. in VT, about 1823; Alonzo d. after 1880 (last record in Monroe, OH). Two of the sons of Sophia Abbott and Solomon Spalding were killed in the Civil War. Asa Blodget Spalding died at the Battle of Perryville 8 Oct 1862. Elisha Abbott Spalding died 26 Sep 1863 of wounds received six days earlier at the Battle of Chickamauga.

831) OLIVE ABBOTT *(David4, David3, Benjamin2, George1)*, b. at Andover 24 Jul 1770 daughter of David and Prudence (Sheldon) Abbot; d. at Thurso, Quebec, 27 Jun 1834; m. 1st, ALEXANDER MCDOLE, b. 15 Jun 1760 son of William McDowell and Rosannah (McLaughlin) McDole; Alexander d. 1814.[2256] Olive m. 2nd 31 Mar 1816, as his second wife, DAVID TOWN, b. 25 Jun 1762 son of Edmund and Abigail (Brewer) Town;[2257] David d. at Waterbury, VT, 4 Sep 1828. David Town was first married to Lydia Slate.

Alexander McDole served in the Revolution and served in the War of 1812. He enlisted as a private 21 June 1813 for one year and joined Captain Aikens company of 31st Infantry on 31 August 1813 and was discharged 28 January 1814 for "inability."[2258]

David Town served as a private in the company of Captain Henry Wiley in the regiment of Colonel Michael Jackson of the Massachusetts line from April 1777 to January 1778. He served an additional term from Mary 1778 to 10 March 1779. David received a pension for his service. At the time of his pension application in 1827, he reported having two boys living at home, one age 12 and one age 10.[2259]

Olive Abbott and Alexander McDole were parents of eleven children. Several of the children dropped the "Mc" from their name and were known as Dole.

2253 Hayward, *History of Hancock*, p 297

2254 Williams, *History of Ashtabula County*, p 201

2255 Spalding, *Spalding Memorial*, p 293

2256 The circumstances of Alexander's death are not clear. The War of 1812 pension application of his son David McDole reports that Alexander was wounded at the Battle of Plattsburgh 11 Sep 1814 and died of his wounds. However, the pension records also give a death date of 17 January 1814 at Grand Isle, Vermont reportedly dying of wounds, but this is eight months before the Battle of Plattsburgh. The official records in the pension file report he was discharged for "inability" 28 Jan 1814. Perhaps he was wounded and died while traveling home, just not wounded at the Battle of Plattsburgh.

2257 Briggs, *Verses and Pioneer Memories*, p 28

2258 War of 1812 Pension and Bounty Land Warrant Application Files; information on Alexander McDole's 1812 war service is in the pension application of his son David McDole.

2259 Revolutionary War Pension and Bounty-Land Warrant Application Files, 1800-1900

i ROSANNA MCDOLE, b. 2 Jan 1791; d. at Waterbury, VT, 2 Oct 1849; m. at Waterbury, 9 Jan 1814, EBENEZER HILL, b. at Wakefield, NH, 7 Jan 1787 son of Ebenezer and Sarah (Bryant) Hill; Ebenezer d. at Waterbury, 22 Jan 1877.

ii DAVID MCDOLE, b. 18 Apr 1793; d. at Mendota, IL, 10 Dec 1865; m. at England, Ontario, 7 Feb 1819, CHLOE CALVIN, b. in Québec, about 1804; Chloe was still living in 1891 in Ste Angelique, Québec. Chloe seems to have remarried to Leo Montreuil as her widow's pension for David's War of 1812 service was suspended in 1888 due to the belief that she had been remarried while she was receiving the widow's pension (with a criminal action initiated). Chloe, listed as Chloe Montreuil, was living with Leo Montreuil in Canada in 1861 while David was in Indiana and Illinois.

iii WILLIAM MCDOLE, b. 11 Mar 1795; d. at Thurso, Québec, 23 Jul 1885; m. 1st, 30 Aug 1826, MARIA MILLER, b. about 1793; Maria d. about 1856. William m. 2nd, at Cumberland, Ontario, 9 Jun 1857, MARIA MCPHEE; Maria d. at Las Vegas, NV, 11 Jan 1911.

iv OLIVE A. MCDOLE, b. 9 Apr 1797; d. at Irasburg, VT, 22 Oct 1886; m. 12 Jan 1817, BENJAMIN EDMONDS, b. in RI, 1780 son of Joseph and Rosamond (Barton) Edmonds; Benjamin d. at Irasburg, 6 Nov 1863.

v THOMAS MCDOLE, b. 17 Mar 1799; d. 20 Aug 1800.

vi CLARISSA MCDOLE, b. 10 Mar 1801; d. 24 Feb 1824.

vii CYNTHIA MCDOLE, b. 10 Feb 1803; d. at Thurso, 26 Sep 1841; m. at Wardsboro, VT, 21 Jan 1822, AUSTIN SMITH, b. about 1799; Austin d. at Waterbury, VT, 6 Jan 1877. Austin Smith second married Susannah.

viii PRUDENCE DOLE, b. 16 Aug 1805; d. at Franklin Grove, IL, 4 Feb 1878; m. 1st, 30 Jan 1823, HOLLIS GOSS, b. at Vernon, VT, 3 May 1795 son of Daniel and Anna (Inder) Goss; Hollis d. about 1829. Prudence m. 2nd, Mr. Griswold who has not been identified; Mr. Griswold d. likely at Oswego County, NY, before 1850 when Prudence was head of household in Oswego County. Prudence m. 3rd, by 1860, ELISHA PRATT, b. in CT, 1798; Elijah d. at Franklin Grove, after 1870. Elisha Pratt was first married to Lucy Robbins.

ix JOHN M. DOLE, b. at Antrim, NH, 8 Sep 1807; d. at Thurso, 11 Jul 1877; m. 2 Dec 1834, MARY HILLMAN; Mary d. in SD, 2 Aug 1892.

x DORCAS MCDOLE, b. 5 Mar 1811; d. at Jeffersonville, VT, 31 May 1892; m. about 1830, ROBERT MCKAY WHITCOMB, b. about 1807 son of Robert and Mary (McKay) Whitcomb; Robert d. at Jeffersonville, 1894.

xi ALEXANDER M. DOLE, b. 1 Mar 1814; d. at Minneapolis, MN, 21 Oct 1888; m. 11 Jul 1857, SANTA MARIA STILES, b. in VT, 20 Oct 1814 daughter of Abial and Azubah (Hawley) Stiles; Santa Maria d. at Minneapolis, 8 Mar 1903. Santa Maria was first married to Horatio Nelson Blaisdell.

Olive Abbott and David Town were parents of one child.

i HOSEA TOWN, b. at Waterbury, VT, 13 Apr 1817; d. at Pueblo, CO, 11 Jul 1908; m. at Paw Paw, IL, 17 Oct 1850, OLIVE HAWLEY, b. in KY, 5 May 1819 daughter of Abijah and Mercy (Woodberry) Hawley;[2260] Olive d. at Pueblo, 21 Feb 1907.[2261]

832) DORCAS ABBOTT *(David⁴, David³, Benjamin², George¹)*, b. at Andover, 5 Dec 1773 daughter of David and Prudence (Sheldon) Abbot; d. at Burlington, MA, 22 Sep 1856; m. 4 Feb 1798, JOHN SNOW, b. 5 Jul 1774 son of Richard and Lydia (Wright) Snow; John was living in 1830 as head of household in Billerica.

Dorcas Abbott and John Snow were parents of eight children all born at Billerica.

i JOHN SNOW, b. 20 Jul 1798; d. at Billerica, 31 Aug 1824.

ii DAVID ABBOT SNOW, b. 13 Nov 1799; nothing further found.

iii SEWAL SNOW, b. 24 Feb 1801; d. at Chester, IN, 18 Mar 1864; m. at Grafton, VT, 5 Apr 1830, MARIEL GATES, b. in VT, 17 Mar 1806; Mariel d. at Chester, 27 Mar 1870.

2260 Memorial Record of Northeastern Indiana, p 704, Lewis Publishing Company, 1896

2261 In the 1860 Census at Brooklyn, IL, Hosea Town headed a household that included his wife Clara Hawley, his mother-in-law Mercy Hawley then age 73, and his nephew Sherman A. Griswold, then age 21, who was the son of Prudence Dole and her second husband Mr. Griswold.

iv LUCRETIA SNOW, b. 4 Dec 1802; d. at Lowell, 27 Dec 1845; m. at Billerica, 1 Nov 1825, SIMEON JEFTS, b. about 1786 son of Henry and Elizabeth (Stearns) Jefts; Simeon d. at Lowell, 22 Oct 1848. After Lucretia's death, Simeon married Mrs. Betsey McLaughlin.

v LAVINA SNOW, b. 1 May 1804; d. at Billerica, 25 Jun 1900; m. 2 Apr 1833, THOMAS K. RICHARDSON, b. at Woburn, 8 Oct 1801 son of Joseph and Anna (Knight) Richardson; Thomas d. at Billerica, 4 Aug 1890.

vi JULIA SNOW, b. 20 Dec 1805; d. 28 Jul 1807.

vii JULIA L. SNOW, b. 15 Jan 1808; d. at Lowell, 27 Nov 1872; m. at Chelmsford, 13 Sep 1835, JOHN TURNER, b. at Hanover, MA, about 1813 son of Ezekiel and Lydia (Stetson) Turner; John d. at Lowell, 24 Aug 1879.

viii CLARISSA JANE SNOW, b. 5 Dec 1811; d. at Boston, 3 Sep 1881; m. at Boston, Mar 1834, JAMES G. HUNT, b. 1811 son of Cyrus and Polly (Merrick) Hunt; James d. at Boston, 15 Sep 1874.

833) JEREMIAH ABBOTT *(David[4], David[3], Benjamin[2], George[1])*, b. at Billerica, 18 May 1776 son of David and Prudence (Sheldon) Abbot; d. in New York, 28 Mar 1835;[2262] Jeremiah lived in Portland, Maine much of his adulthood. He did marry and had some children. One child has been identified, but the identity of his wife has not been found. The most likely candidate for a wife is Susanna Centre who married Jeremiah Abbott at Boston in 1797. There is a Maine death record for Susanna Abbott wife of Jeremiah S. for 22 Feb 1844 with age of 74 at time of death. There are gravestones in Portland for Jeremiah and his wife Susanna with the appropriate death years so perhaps that is this Jeremiah and Susannah. There is one son who may be the child of this Jeremiah.

i ALEXIS ABBOTT, b. in MA (according to census records), Jan 1804; d. at Portland, ME, 6 Feb 1889; m. at Portland, 4 May 1832, ABIGAIL MITCHELL CHANDLER, b. at Portland, 9 Aug 1814 daughter of Joel and Pamela (Lincoln) Chandler; Abigail d. at Chicago, IL, 7 Jan 1912.

834) HANNAH ABBOTT *(Solomon[4], David[3], Benjamin[2], George[1])*, b. at Andover, 1 May 1757 daughter of Solomon and Hannah (Colbe) Abbot; d. after 1827 (living at the probate of her second husband's estate); m. 1st, 27 Feb 1776, PARKER BODWELL, b. at Methuen, 29 Oct 1750 son of Daniel and Abigail (Ladd) Bodwell; Parker d. 7 Aug 1795. Hannah m. 2nd, as his third wife, DAVID JONES, b. 12 Feb 1740/1 son of David and Hannah (Fox) Jones; David d. at Dracut, 1826 (probate).

Parker Bodwell did not leave a will and his estate entered probate 3 November 1795. Real estate was valued at $690 and personal estate at $365.33. Two-thirds of the real estate was settled on son Herman and the other children received payments of $60 each from Herman for their share. Those acknowledging the payments in 1801 were Parker L. Bodwell; William Whittier guardian for Susannah Morse a minor; mother Hannah Bodwell acting as guardian for Fanny Bodwell, Hannah Bodwell, Charles Bodwell, Samuel Bodwell, and Nabby Bodwell;[2263] and Sally Boles with Reuben Boles also signing.[2264]

Hannah Abbott and Parker Bodwell were parents of nine children born at Methuen.

i PARKER LADD BODWELL, b. 23 Mar 1776; d. at Methuen, 16 Jan 1858; m. 1st, 24 Jun 1798, ELIZABETH MERRILL, b. at Methuen, 8 Mar 1779 daughter of John and Elizabeth (Teppets) Merrill; Elizabeth d. at Methuen, Jan 1808. Parker m. 2nd, 8 Apr 1810, NANCY MERRILL, b. at Haverhill, 1783 daughter of Dean and (Swett) Merrill; Nancy d. at Methuen, 4 Nov 1867. Nancy was first married to David Hemphill who died about 1805.

ii HERMAN BODWELL, b. 3 Oct 1777; d. at Methuen, 1837 (probate 2 Mar 1837); m. 7 Sep 1813, ELIZABETH HALL, b. at Methuen, 15 Jul 1790 daughter of Farnum and Sarah (Bailey) Hall.

iii SARAH BODWELL, b. 20 Jan 1780; d. at Methuen, 1868; m. at Methuen, 12 Feb 1800, REUBEN BOLES, b. about 1770 son of Reuben Boles; Reuben d. at Methuen, 4 Jul 1866.

iv SUSANNAH BODWELL, b. 13 Mar 1782; d. at Lawrence, 1856; m. 14 Dec 1800, NATHANIEL MORSE, b. 3 Apr 1779 son of Paine and Martha (Sprague) Morse; Nathaniel d. at Lawrence, 5 Jan 1867.

[2262] Ancestry.com, *U.S., Newspaper Extractions from the Northeast, 1704-1930* (Provo, UT, USA: Ancestry.com Operations, Inc., 2014). This notice gives place of death as New York but notes that he was until recently in Portland, Maine. Age at death given as 60.

[2263] Abigail "Nabby" Bodwell died between the time of her father's death and the settlement of the estate. The payment for Nabby included the amount for her support before her death.

[2264] Essex County, MA: Probate File Papers, 1638-1881.Online database. AmericanAncestors.org. New England Historic Genealogical Society, 2014. Case 2760

v FANNY BODWELL, b. 20 Feb 1784; d. at Methuen, 26 Aug 1857; m. 7 Oct 1802, TRUEWORTHY WHITE, b. at Methuen, 3 Sep 1781 son of John and Elizabeth (Haynes) White; Trueworthy d. at Methuen, 31 Oct 1838.

vi HANNAH BODWELL, b. 28 Aug 1786; d. at Peabody, MA, 20 Sep 1873; m. at Danvers, 14 Jan 1813, ENOCH POOR, b. 17 May 1783 son of Abraham and Elizabeth (Barker) Poor.

vii CHARLES BODWELL, b. 25 Aug 1788; d. at Dracut, 7 Jul 1862; m. at Dracut, 10 Mar 1810, SARAH VARNUM, b. at Dracut, 21 Oct 1791 daughter of Thomas and Mary (Atkinson) Varnum; Sarah d. at Dracut, 30 Aug 1853.

viii ABIGAIL BODWELL, b. 25 Apr 1791; d. 4 Dec 1796.

ix SAMUEL A. BODWELL, b. 25 Apr 1791; d. at Methuen, 2 Apr 1861; m. 24 Apr 1815, ELIZABETH MITCHELL, b. about 1790; Elizabeth d. at Methuen, before 1850. Elizabeth was first married to James Ordway.

835) SOLOMON ABBOTT *(Solomon⁴, David³, Benjamin², George¹)*, b. at Dracut, 7 May 1759 son of Solomon and Hannah (Colbe) Abbot; d. at Dracut, 5 Jan 1842; m. about 1785, RACHEL BOWERS, b. 16 Jul 1763 daughter of John and Rachel (Varnum) Bowers; Rachel d. at Dracut, 7 Jan 1845.

Solomon Abbott and Rachel Bowers were parents of ten children born at Dracut.

i DORCAS ABBOTT, b. 19 Sep 1786; d. 20 Sep 1801.

ii DOLLY ABBOTT, b. 17 Jul 1789; d. at Lowell, 25 Feb 1852; m. at Dracut, 22 Dec 1814, PRESCOTT COBURN, b. at Pelham, NH, 19 Nov 1788 son of Benjamin and Alice (Hardy) Coburn; Prescott d. at Lowell, 28 Aug 1874.

iii SALLY ABBOTT, b. 13 Jun 1791; d. at Somerville, 31 Jan 1864; m. at Dracut, 20 May 1810, REUBEN UPTON, b. at Wilmington, 31 May 1783 son of Paul and Jerusha (Richardson) Upton; Reuben d. at Dracut, 3 Aug 1825.

iv POLLY ABBOTT, b. 4 Apr 1793; d. 20 Jul 1799.

v RACHEL ABBOTT, b. 3 Apr 1795; d. at Lowell, 18 Nov 1859; m. at Dracut, 12 Apr 1814, ALLEN PIERCE, b. at Lowell, 1782; Allen d. at Tyngsborough, 23 May 1849.

vi ABIGAIL ABBOTT, b. 13 Mar 1797; d. at Dracut, 1 Oct 1868; m. at Dracut, 22 Apr 1824, THOMAS BOWERS, b. about 1795; Thomas d. at Dracut, 2 Aug 1882.

vii SAMUEL BOWERS ABBOTT, b. 22 Sep 1799; d. at Chicago, before 1870; m. 1st, 1 Jun 1822, SALLY J. VARNUM; Sally d. at Lowell, 5 Oct 1826. Solomon m. 2nd, at Methuen, 5 Feb 1828, RACHEL U. WHITING, b. about 1801

viii SOLOMON ABBOTT, b. 1 Sep 1801; d. 15 Aug 1805.

ix LYDIA ABBOTT, b. 2 Nov 1804; d. at Lowell, 23 Sep 1855; m. 1st, at Dracut, 2 Dec 1824, SOLOMON COMBS; Solomon d. before 1839. Lydia m. 2nd, at Woburn, 4 Jul 1839, JOSHUA HALE, b. at Worcester, 8 Feb 1806 son of Joshua and Sarah (Clement) Hale; Joshua d. after 1855.

x EMILY ABBOTT, b. 10 Jan 1807; m. at Dracut, 2 Sep 1827, JOEL PIERCE, b. about 1800; Joel d. at Dracut, 1843 (probate Apr 1843).[2265]

836) SARAH ABBOTT *(Solomon⁴, David³, Benjamin², George¹)*, b. at Dracut, 22 Mar 1761 daughter of Solomon and Hannah (Colbe) Abbot; m. at Methuen, 16 Mar 1786, SAMUEL MORSE, b. at Methuen, 28 Mar 1759 son of Joseph and Lydia (Huse) Morse.

There are three children known for Sarah and Samuel.

i SAMUEL MORSE, b. 9 Sep 1786; nothing further known.

ii SARAH "SALLY" MORSE, b. 13 Dec 1789; d. at Loudon, NH, after 1850; m. at Methuen, 7 Mar 1811, ABEL AUSTIN, b. at Methuen, 7 Mar 1787 son of Isaac and Elizabeth (Huse) Austin; Abel d. at Loudon, after 1850.

iii CHARLES ABBOTT MORSE, b. 28 Dec 1792; d. at Canterbury, NH, 19 Apr 1864; m. EUNICE LAKE, b. at Chichester, NH, 19 Feb 1798 daughter of James and Mehitable (Berry) Lake; Eunice d. at Canterbury, 22 Nov 1880.

[2265] Abbot, *Genealogical Register* reports that Emily died 14 Dec 1842, so perhaps she is not the Emily Abbott who married Joel Pierce. Emily Pierce was living in April 1843 at the probate of her husband's estate. There is no further record of her.

837) DANIEL COLBY ABBOT *(Solomon[4], David[3], Benjamin[2], George[1])*, b. at Dracut, 26 Oct 1766 son of Solomon and Hannah (Colbe) Abbot; d. at Dracut, 18 Sep 1842; m. about 1792, PATIENCE COBURN, b. at Methuen, 1768 daughter of Aaron and Phebe (Harris) Coburn; Patience d. 15 Apr 1830.

Daniel Colby Abbot was a carpenter and owned a farm on what is now Hildreth Street in Dracut. Daniel Colby Abbott was the town treasurer of Dracut for 21 years and was Representative to the General Court.[2266]

Daniel Colby Abbot wrote his will 11 April 1842. Sons Luther Abbot and Ziba Abbot receive $400 each in addition to what they have received. Son Daniel Abbot receives all the remaining real estate except a specified one-acre lot. Daughters Patience Ames and Dolly Peabody each receive $300 in addition to what they previously received. Son Daniel Abbot is named executor. The following heirs, indicating they are all the heirs, signed a statement agreeing to make a division of the estate among themselves respecting the wishes of their father in his will: William Ames and Patience Ames, Luther C. Abbot, Ziba Abbott, Leonard Peabody and Dolly A. Peabody, and Daniel Abbot.[2267]

Daniel Colby Abbot and Patience Coburn were parents of six children born at Dracut.

i PATIENCE ABBOTT, b. 7 Dec 1792; d. at Hollis, NH, 19 Apr 1860; m. at Dracut, 9 Apr 1829, as his third wife, WILLIAM AMES, b. at Hollis, 3 Mar 1786 son of Burpee and Hannah (Pool) Ames; William d. at Hollis, 10 Apr 1847. William was first married to Sarah Brooks and second married to Lydia Merrill.

ii LUTHER ABBOT, b. 20 May 1795; d. at Stoddard, NH, 2 Mar 1872; m. at Sullivan, NH, 27 Dec 1825, NANCY LOCKE, b. at Sullivan, 10 Apr 1802 daughter of Calvin and Sarah (Jewett) Locke; Nancy d. at Goffstown, 15 Jul 1885. After Luther's death, Nancy married David Wilkinson.

iii DANIEL ABBOT, b. 19 Jan 1799; d. 4 Dec 1799.

iv ZIBA ABBOTT, b. 11 Nov 1800; d. at Lowell, 16 Feb 1878; m. at Lowell, 16 May 1833, ELIZABETH THAYER, b. at Hollis, NH, 24 Mar 1811 daughter of Nathan and Hannah (Jewett) Thayer; Elizabeth d. at Lowell, 4 Feb 1880.

v DOLLY ABBOTT, b. 30 Mar 1803; d. at Bradford, MA, 16 May 1879; m. at Dracut, 11 May 1836, LEONARD PEABODY, b. at Bradford, 7 Feb 1800 son of John and Alice (Carleton) Peabody; Leonard d. at Bradford, 11 Jan 1888.

vi DANIEL ABBOT, b. 20 Oct 1805; d. at Concord, MA, 9 May 1864; m. at Hollis, 17 May 1832, ELSIE MARSHALL, b. at Hollis, about 1810 daughter of Thaddeus and Harriet (Colburn) Marshall; Elsie d. at Dracut, 21 Nov 1899.

838) ELIZABETH DANFORTH ABBOTT *(Solomon[4], David[3], Benjamin[2], George[1])*, b. at Dracut, 11 Oct 1768 daughter of Solomon and Hannah (Colbe) Abbot; d. at Walpole, NH, 5 Jul 1856; m. 18 Sep 1793, EPHRAIM LANE, b. at Bedford, 11 Mar 1767 son of Samuel and Ruth (Davis) Lane; Ephraim d. 15 Aug 1837.

Elizabeth Danforth Abbott is reported to have come from poor economic circumstances and as a child worked out as a servant for 25 cents per week.[2268] The reason for the dire financial circumstances is not clear. Her father Solomon Abbot had owned 110 acres of land in Dracut as well as a ferry and fishing rights. Solomon, however, sold 57 acres of his property as well as the ferry in 1761.[2269]

Elizabeth's husband, Ephraim Lane, is described in Aldrich's Walpole history as a frugal man who loaned money at high rates of interest. He was not a believer in education beyond the very basics. He is reported to have left a considerable estate, although I could not locate the inventory of the estate.

In his will written 19 November 1830, Ephraim Lane left to beloved wife Elizabeth D. Lane the use and improvement of the homestead farm in Walpole consisting of about 50 acres, the use of all the household furniture, and the use of all the sleighs and horses. She is also to be paid sixty dollars per year by the executor. These bequests are to continue as long as she remains a widow. Eldest son George Lane and his other son Lewis Lane each receive seven hundred-fifty dollars. George Lane also receives 100 acres of land in the town of Peacham, Vermont. Lewis Lane will receive the homestead farm in Walpole contingent on the allowance of his mother's use of the property during her widowhood. Daughters Rebecca Pulsipher, Susan Pulsipher, Betsey Lane, Mary Hooper, Phebe Wise, Sophia Lane, and Almira Lane will divide the household furniture after the decease of their mother. All the residue of the estate is to be divided equally among his nine children, although several

2266 Coburn, *History of Dracut*, p 365

2267 Middlesex County, MA: Probate File Papers, 1648-1871. Online database. AmericanAncestors.org. New England Historic Genealogical Society, 2014. (From records supplied by the Massachusetts Supreme Judicial Court Archives. Digitized images provided by FamilySearch.org); Probate of Daniel Colby Abbot, 1842, Case number 26041

2268 Aldrich, *Walpole as It Was and Is*, p. 309

2269 Coburn, *History of Dracut*, p 365

daughters have already received amounts that are to be accounted for in the division of the property. Captain James Hooper of Walpole and son Lewis Lane were named executors.[2270] James Hooper was the husband of daughter Mary.

Elizabeth and Ephraim reared their nine children, seven daughters and two sons, in Walpole, New Hampshire. The children were all born at Walpole.[2271] As was common, two of the daughters married two Pulsipher brothers and two of the other daughters married two Hooper brothers. Several of the children relocated to Vermont.

i REBECCA LANE, b. 7 Apr 1794; d. at Rockingham, VT, 5 Feb 1847; m. at Walpole, 15 Mar 1815, DAVID PULSIPHER, b. at Rockingham, VT, 6 Dec 1791 son of David and Priscilla (Russell) Pulsipher; David d. 14 Dec 1865.

ii SUSAN LANE, b. 1 Oct 1796; d. at Rockingham, VT, 7 Jun 1880; m. at Walpole, 30 Jan 1820, ELIAS PULSIPHER, b. at Rockingham, 20 Jun 1794 son of David and Priscilla (Russell) Pulsipher; Elias d. at Rockingham, 1858.

iii BETSEY LANE, b. 25 Jan 1799; d. at Westmoreland, NH, 1886; m. at unknown date, HORACE REYNOLDS, b. at Putney, VT, about 1803 son of Benjamin and Mary (Sheffield) Reynolds; Horace d. at Putney, 27 Apr 1882. Betsey was living with her son Horace in Westmoreland in 1880.

iv MARY LANE, b. 3 Sep 1801; d. at Cambridge, MA, 31 Mar 1895; m. at Walpole, 19 Jan 1826, JAMES HOOPER, b. at Walpole, 31 Aug 1803 son of James and Eleanor (Wellington) Hooper; James d. at Cambridge, 31 Dec 1877.

v GEORGE LANE, b. 25 Nov 1803; d. at Putney, VT, 21 Jun 1878; m. 1st, at Walpole, 4 Apr 1831, SARAH DUNSHEE, b. at Walpole, 6 Oct 1805 daughter of Hugh and Cynthia (Allen) Dunshee; Sarah d. at Putney, 21 Sep 1841. George married second ELIZABETH BAILEY, b. at Coventry, VT, 14 Dec 1823 daughter of Hosea and Susan (Hodgson) Bailey;[2272] Elizabeth d. at Brattleboro, 14 Apr 1895.

vi PHEBE LANE, b. 25 Jan 1806; d. at Walpole, 24 Sep 1880; m. 3 Mar 1829, CHESTER WIRE, JR., b. at Kirby, VT, 9 Dec 1804 son of Chester and Affie (Lumbad) Wire; Chester d. at Walpole, 22 Jan 1837. Phebe did not remarry after the death of her husband.

vii SOPHIA LANE, b. 10 Jul 1808; d. at Rockingham, VT, 3 Jul 1890; m. at Walpole, 31 Mar 1835, OLIVER HUNTINGTON, b. at Walpole, 24 Oct 1795 son of Gamaliel and Keturah (Armstrong) Huntington; Oliver d. at Walpole, 27 Jan 1857.

viii ALMIRA LANE, b. 8 Jan 1811; d. at Walpole, 18 Jan 1891; m. 23 May 1839, CHARLES HOOPER, b. at Walpole, 16 Dec 1809 son of James and Eleanor (Wellington) Hooper; Charles d. at Walpole, 25 Dec 1890. Almira and Charles were married 50 years and died three weeks apart.

ix LEWIS LANE, b. 22 Apr 1813; d. at Keene, NH, 17 Mar 1886; m. at Walpole, 20 Oct 1841, MARY PHILENA ANGIER, b. at Walpole, 20 Nov 1820 daughter of Elisha and Sally (Russell) Angier; Mary d. at Keene, 12 Nov 1891.

839) LYDIA ABBOTT *(Solomon⁴, David³, Benjamin², George¹)*, b. at Dracut, 22 May 1771 daughter of Solomon and Hannah (Colbe) Abbot; d. at Hooksett, after 1840; m. JOSHUA MARTIN, "of Hooksett" b. about 1765; Joshua d. at Hooksett, after 1840.[2273]

Very little information was located for this family. The Abbot Genealogical Register reports children Lydia and Daniel and there is record evidence for Joshua Martin, Jr. in Hooksett and he *perhaps* also goes in this family.

i LYDIA MARTIN; report in the Abbot Genealogical Register; no records found.

ii JOSHUA MARTIN, b. at Hooksett, 29 Apr 1794; d. at Hooksett, 20 Nov 1844; m. 1st, at Dunbarton, 12 Mar 1818, HANNAH HOYT, b. about 1793; Hannah d. at Hooksett, 10 May 1822. Joshua m. 2nd, 18 Nov 1824, SARAH C. PALMER, b. at Candia, NH, 27 Nov 1804 daughter of Josiah and Betsey (Carr) Palmer; Sarah d. at Hooksett, 14 Mar 1879.

iii DANIEL MARTIN

840) DAVID ABBOTT *(Solomon⁴, David³, Benjamin², George¹)*, b. at Dracut, 18 May 1775 son of Solomon and Hannah (Colbe) Abbot; d. at Windham, NH, 1855 (probate 8 Aug 1855); m. 1st, 13 May 1797, HANNAH CROSBY, b. 20 Sep 1773

[2270] New Hampshire, County Probate Records, 1660-1973, Cheshire, Wills 1799-1848 vol 76-78, 78:104, will of Ephraim Lane, accessed through familysearch.org.

[2271] "New Hampshire, Birth Records, through 1900." Online index and digital images. *New England Historical Genealogical Society*. Citing New Hampshire Bureau of Vital Records, Concord, New Hampshire.

[2272] The names of Elizabeth Bailey's parents are given on her death record. Her maiden name is confirmed by the death records of several of her children.

[2273] This is a marriage reported in Abbot and Abbot, *Genealogical Register of Descendants* but have yet to find records associated with the family.

daughter of Jonathan and Hannah (Goodhue) Crosby; Hannah d. before 1816. David m. 2nd, 21 Feb 1816, DOLLY ABBOTT, b. at Amherst, 1775 daughter of Ephraim and Dorothy (Stiles) Abbott; Dolly d. 1822. David m. 3rd, about 1827, SARAH MCKINLEY, b. 1789 daughter of Robert and Sarah (Harriman) McKinley; Sarah d. at Windham, NH, 30 Jan 1869.

Rev. David Abbott was a preacher in Windham, New Hampshire. He did not leave a will and his estate was probated in 1855 with Sarah Abbott as administratrix. There was no real estate and the personal estate was valued at $104.16.[2274]

David Abbott and Hannah Crosby were parents of four children.

i HANNAH ABBOTT, b. at Dracut, 23 Oct 1798

ii LUCRETIA ABBOTT, b. at Windham, NH, about 1802

iii DAVID ABBOTT, b. at Manchester, 16 Jul 1804; d. at Windham, NH, 15 Dec 1870. David did not marry. In 1870, he was listed in the census as a town pauper.

iv DORCAS ABBOTT, b. at Manchester, 23 Jul 1807; d. at Manchester, 22 Nov 1864; m. 1st, at Dracut, 15 Jun 1829, CALVIN KIMBALL, b. 21 Mar 1806 son of Ezra and Sarah (Elliot) Kimball; Calvin d. 1837. Dorcas m. 2nd, about 1840, ELVIRESS PARMENTER, b. 13 Dec 1799 son of Asahel and Mary (Stoughton) Parmenter. Elviress was first married to Electa Howard.

David Abbott and Sarah McKinley were parents of two children both born at Windham, New Hampshire.

i SARAH JANE ABBOTT, b. about 1828; d. at Windham, 1 Aug 1885; m. 16 Nov 1855, EDWARD TITCOMB, b. at Newburyport, MA, 22 Mar 1802 son of Jonathan and Mary (Bradish) Titcomb;[2275] Edward d. at Windham, 24 Nov 1870 (probate 7 Dec 1870). Sarah was a teacher.

ii DANIEL COLBY ABBOTT, b. 1830; d. at Manchester, NH, 16 Feb 1896; m. ELIZA A. TOTMAN, b. at Hudson, NH, about 1844 daughter of Daniel and Ann (Hamblett) Totman; Eliza d. at Manchester, 19 Aug 1905.

841) MARY ABBOTT *(Jonathan[4], David[3], Benjamin[2], George[1])*, b. at Andover, 10 Jan 1762 daughter of Jonathan and Mary (Chandler) Abbot; d. 1 May 1845; m. 17 Oct 1782, her first cousin, ABIEL CHANDLER *(Joshua Chandler[5], Joshua Chandler[4], John Chandler[3], Hannah Abbott Chandler[2], George[1])*, b. 28 Aug 1760 son of Joshua and Hannah (Chandler) Chandler; Abiel d. at Boston, 2 Nov 1833.

Mary and Abiel lived in Andover for much of their lives, but later moved to Boston where they had a boarding house.

Their son Joshua graduated from Harvard in 1807. He was a Congregationalist minister who held and was dismissed from several posts in Swansey, New Hampshire and Orange, Massachusetts.[2276]

i JOSHUA CHANDLER, b. at Andover, 15 May 1785; d. at Boston, 31 May 1854.

842) DAVID ABBOT *(Jonathan[4], David[3], Benjamin[2], George[1])*, b. at Andover, 11 Mar 1764 son of Jonathan and Mary (Chandler) Abbot; d. 1 Jun 1823; m. 26 May 1789, his first cousin, PRISCILLA CHANDLER *(Nathan Chandler[5], Nathan Chandler[4], John Chandler[3], Hannah Abbott Chandler[2], George[1])*, b. 30 Jun 1768 daughter of Nathan and Phebe (Abbott) Chandler; Priscilla d. 19 Feb 1831.

David Abbot did not leave a will and his estate entered probate 1 July 1823 with Jonathan Abbot, Jr. as administrator. The request that Jonathan be named administrator was signed by the following heirs: widow Priscilla Abbot, Priscilla Abbot, Samuel Bailey and Mary Bailey, David Abbot, Nathan Abbot, and Ezra Abbot. Real estate was valued at $4,057 and personal estate at $1,136.83. Debts were $5,160.52. Some of the real estate was under mortgage, and widow Priscilla petitioned to have the dower set off to her in real estate that was not mortgaged. Real estate was sold to settle debts.[2277]

Son Nathan Abbott did not marry. At the probate of his estate in 1870, the following were listed as heirs: sister Mary Bailey of Andover; brother David Abbott of Andover; brother Ezra Abbott of Andover; sister Phebe Wilson of Peabody; sister

[2274] *New Hampshire. Probate Court (Rockingham County)*; Probate Place: *Rockingham, New Hampshire, Estate Papers, No 17104-17164, 1855, Case number 17106*
[2275] Morrison, *The History of Windham in New Hampshire*, p 801
[2276] Chandler, *The Descendants of William and Annis Chandler*, p 608
[2277] Essex County, MA: Probate File Papers, 1638-1881. Online database. AmericanAncestors.org. Essex Cases 1-1999, Case number 29

Serena Abbott of Andover; brother Hermon Abbott of Groton; niece Sarah J. Tuck of Haverhill, and nephew Charles H. Abbott of Brookline, NH.[2278] David A. Abbott was administrator of the estate.

David Abbot and Priscilla Chandler were parents of eleven children born at Andover.

i PRISCILLA ABBOTT, b. 10 Jun 1790; d. at Andover, 11 Nov 1857. Priscilla did not marry, but she had an out-of-wedlock child with WILLIAM BAILEY who has not been otherwise identified. The death record of Sarah Jane Bailey Tuck lists parents as Priscilla Abbott and William Bailey.[2279]

ii MARY ABBOTT, b. Jun 1791; d. at Andover, 11 Jul 1880; m. at Andover, 18 Mar 1815, SAMUEL BAILEY, b. at Tewksbury, 7 Jun 1789 son of Daniel and Molly (Standley) Bailey; Samuel d. at Andover, 21 Jun 1859.

iii DAVID ABBOTT, b. 23 Dec 1792; d. at Middleton, 23 Jul 1882; m. at Peterborough, NH, 5 Sep 1833, MARY GRANT, b. at Hancock, NH, 25 Sep 1810 daughter of Charles and Mary (Ballard) Grant; Mary d. at Middleton, 15 Mar 1889.

iv JONATHAN ABBOTT, b. 12 Jun 1796; d. at Boston, 8 Apr 1869; m. at Andover, 16 Feb 1826, LYDIA PHELPS, b. at Andover, 10 Nov 1804 daughter of Joshua and Mary (Gilson) Phelps; Lydia d. at Andover, 16 Jul 1839.

v NATHAN ABBOTT, b. 5 Jul 1799; d. at Westford, 29 Oct 1870. Nathan did not marry.

vi EZRA ABBOTT, b. 19 Apr 1801; d. at Andover, 24 Feb 1890; m. 1st, at Andover, 19 Apr 1849, HANNAH BAILEY, b. at Andover, 13 Mar 1813 daughter of William and Rebecca (Gilson) Bailey; Hannah d. at Taunton, 8 Nov 1860. Ezra m. 2nd, 14 Mar 1863, MARY INGALLS, b. at Andover, 9 Sep 1819 daughter of Ezra and Dolly (Wilson) Ingalls; Mary d. at Methuen, 30 Jan 1911.

vii PHEBE ABBOTT, b. 5 Aug 1803; d. at Peabody, MA, 24 Apr 1880; m. 30 Apr 1833, ELIJAH WILSON, b. at Danvers, 23 Jan 1796 son of Isaac and Dolly (Dickinson) Wilson; Elijah d. at Danvers, 18 Aug 1865.

viii SERENA ABBOTT, b. 8 Jul 1805; d. 20 Sep 1805.

ix JOSHUA ABBOTT, b. 1 Sep 1806; nothing further known. Neither he nor any children of his are listed as heirs in the probate of brother Nathan's estate.

x SERENA ABBOTT, b. 8 Sep 1808; d. at Andover, 20 Sep 1880. Serena did not marry.

xi HERMON ABBOTT, b. 15 Jan 1814; d. at Nashua, NH, 11 Jul 1878; m. 1st, at Andover, 19 Aug 1837, MARY NEEDHAM GRAY, b. at Tewksbury, 15 Aug 1815 daughter of Jonathan and Mary (Batchelder) Gray; Mary d. at Reading, 19 Nov 1845. Hermon m. 2nd, ELVINA BANCROFT, b. at Reading, 15 Mar 1818 daughter of Timothy and Rhoda (Emerson) Bancroft; Elvina d. at Tyngsborough, 19 Sep 1865. Hermon m. 3rd, at Groton, 25 Apr 1866, DIANTHA MAHALA FISHER, b. at Townsend, VT, about 1812 daughter of Noah and Clarissa (Knapp) Fisher;[2280] Diantha d. at Nashua, 28 Jan 1884.

843) PHEBE ABBOTT *(Jonathan⁴, David³, Benjamin², George¹)*, b. at Andover, 26 Feb 1766 daughter of Jonathan and Mary (Chandler) Abbot; d 1 Dec 1848; m. 30 Mar 1790, her third cousin once removed, JOSEPH SHATTUCK *(Joseph Shattuck⁵, Joanna Chandler Shattuck⁴, Zebadiah Chandler³, Hannah Abbott Chandler², George¹)*, b. 8 Nov 1757 son of Joseph and Anna (Johnson) Shattuck; Joseph d. 8 Jul 1847. Joseph had first married Hannah Chandler (a 6th generation descendant) who died in the first year of the marriage.

Joseph Shattuck served as a Corporal in the Revolutionary War and received a promotion to the rank of Third Sergeant 28 January 1780 while serving in the fourth company of the 11th Massachusetts Bay Regiment. "To Mr. Joseph Shattuck of the Eleventh Massachusetts Bay Regiment in the service of the United States of America, Greeting. Possessing especial trust and confidence in your prudence and good conduct, I by these presents appoint you third Sergeant in the fourth company in said regiment in the service of the United States. You are therefore carefully and diligently to discharge the duty of a Sergeant by doing and performing all manner of things." This document was signed by Lieutenant Jonathan Libby and Major Moses Knap.[2281] His military service included the Battles of Bennington and Saratoga.

Joseph did not leave a will and his estate entered probate 2 November 1847. Eldest son Joseph Shattuck was administrator of the estate. The real property was valued at $4,874.33 and personal property at $329.25. The real estate included the homestead with 44 acres valued at $2,500. On 1 November 1847, widow Phebe Shattuck petitioned the Court

2278 *Massachusetts, Essex County, Probate Records;* Author: *Massachusetts. Supreme Judicial Court (Essex County);* Probate Place: *Essex, Massachusetts, Probate Records, Abbot, I-Abbot, S,, 1828-1991*

2279 The 1870 probate record of Priscilla's brother Nathan lists his niece Sarah J. Tuck as an heir.

2280 Diantha's parents are given on her death record as Noah Fisher and Clarissa Knapp.

2281 National Archives. Revolutionary War Pension and Bounty-Land Warrant Application Files. www.fold3.com/image/1/16444125?xid=1945

requesting the required certificate in order to receive the arrears from her husband's Revolutionary War pension, and this request was granted.[2282]

Joseph and Phebe had four children born at Andover.

i HANNAH CHANDLER SHATTUCK, b. 2 Aug 1791; d. at Andover, 25 Oct 1847. Hannah did not marry.

ii JOSEPH SHATTUCK, b. 18 Oct 1793; d. at Andover, 24 Aug 1873; m. 25 May 1826, HANNAH BAILEY, b. at Andover, 14 Aug 1796 daughter of James and Lucy (Brown) Bailey; Hannah d. at Andover, 9 Aug 1866.

iii NATHAN SHATTUCK, b. 4 Mar 1797; d. at Andover, 27 Mar 1868; m. 12 Dec 1823, his second cousin, MARY FISK ABBOTT *(Isaac⁴, Isaac⁴, Isaac³, George², George¹)*, b. at Andover, 14 Mar 1800 daughter of Isaac and Hephzibah (Fisk) Abbott;[2283] Mary d. at Andover 12 Feb 1881.

iv PHEBE AUGUSTA SHATTUCK, b. 21 Feb 1807; d. at Lawrence, 24 Oct 1897; m. 4 Feb 1836, WILLIAM MERRILL, b. at Andover, 5 Aug 1814 son of John and Jane (Cochran) Merrill;[2284] William d. at Lawrence, 19 Apr 1870.

844) NATHAN ABBOT *(Jonathan⁴, David³, Benjamin², George¹)*, b. at Andover, 17 May 1768 son of Jonathan and Mary (Chandler) Abbot; d. at Andover, 7 Apr 1850; m. 11 Dec 1792, his second cousin, HANNAH PHELPS *(Joseph Phelps⁵, Priscilla Chandler Phelps⁴, Zebadiah Chandler³, Hannah Abbott Chandler², George¹)*, b. 10 Sep 1769 daughter of Joshua and Lois (Ballard) Phelps; Hannah d. 17 Dec 1853.

Nathan Abbot was a farmer, but apparently struggled financially in his later years as he died at the almshouse in Andover at age 82. There is one child known for Nathan Abbot and Hannah Phelps.

i NATHAN ABBOTT, b. at Andover, 25 Feb 1799; d. at Andover, 26 Apr 1872; m. at Andover, 27 Apr 1854, his fourth cousin once removed, DOLLY LOVEJOY *(Dolly Russell Lovejoy⁶, Phebe Abbott Russell⁵, Barachias⁴, John³, John², George¹)*, b. about 1799 daughter of John and Dolly (Russell) Lovejoy; Dolly d. at Andover, 17 Nov 1889. Nathan was a laborer.

845) BENJAMIN ABBOTT *(Jonathan⁴, David³, Benjamin², George¹)*, b. at Andover, 7 Jun 1770 son of Jonathan and Mary (Chandler) Abbot; d. at Andover, 20 Oct 1835;[2285] m. 26 Nov 1793, his first cousin, RHODA CHANDLER *(Nathan Chandler⁵, Nathan Chandler⁴, John Chandler³, Hannah Abbott Chandler², George¹)*, b. 2 Mar 1774 daughter of Nathan and Phebe (Abbott) Chandler; Rhoda d. 19 Mar 1853.

Benjamin Abbott and Rhoda Chandler were parents of seven children all born at Andover.

Son Jonathan Abbott did not marry, and his estate entered probate 1 May 1838 with Solomon Abbott (perhaps his uncle) as administrator.[2286] Jonathan was a cordwainer and his personal estate was valued at $3,623.18. Heirs receiving equal payments of $404.58 were Ebenezer Ricker, Benjamin Abbot, Nathan C. Abbott, Daniel Knowlton (his payment $408.36), and Solomon Holt.

i BENJAMIN ABBOTT, b. 29 Mar 1795; d. at Holden, 21 Sep 1853; m. at Andover, 24 Dec 1818, his fourth cousin once removed, REBECCA BOYNTON *(Thomas Boynton⁶, Hannah Ames Boynton⁵, Benjamin Ames⁴, Hannah Stevens Ames³, Elizabeth Abbott Stevens², George¹)*, b. at Andover, 18 Oct 1800 daughter of Thomas and Rebecca (Bailey) Boynton; Rebecca d. at Manchester, NH (at the home of her son William Otis Abbott), 13 Jan 1895.

ii RHODA ABBOTT, b. 24 Oct 1796; d. at Concord, NH, 5 Nov 1871; m. at Andover, 18 Nov 1817, DANIEL KNOWLTON, b. at Concord, 14 Jan 1795 son of Robert and Ede (Allen) Knowlton; Daniel d. at Concord, 6 Jan 1874. After Rhoda's death, Daniel married the widow Mrs. Ruth Knowlton.

iii PHEBE ABBOTT, b. 27 Nov 1798; d. at Andover, 18 Oct 1872; m. at Andover, 25 Nov 1824, her fourth cousin, SOLOMON HOLT *(Solomon Holt⁵, Joshua Holt⁴, Dorcas Abbott Holt³, Timothy², George¹)*, b. at Andover, 1799

2282 Essex County, MA: Probate File Papers, 1638-1881.Online database. AmericanAncestors.org. Case number 52994

2283 Both of Mary's parents died when she was a young child. She was raised by her grandfather Isaac Abbott. She was baptized in 1807: Mary Fisk, d. the late Isaac and Hepzibah, grandd. Dea. Isaac Abbot, bp. May 10, 1807

2284 The names of William's parents are given as Joseph and Jane Merrill on his death record. However, parents are John and Jane.

2285 Benjamin, Oct. 20, 1835, a. 65 y.

2286 Essex County, MA: Probate File Papers, 1638-1881.Online database. AmericanAncestors.org. New England Historic Genealogical Society, 2014. Case 85

son of Solomon and Mary (Cummings) Holt; Solomon d. at Andover, 3 Apr 1883. Solomon Holt is a child in Family 871.

iv JONATHAN ABBOTT, b. 15 Nov 1801; d. at Andover, 8 Mar 1838. Jonathan did not marry.

v NATHAN CHANDLER ABBOTT, b. 16 Jan 1807; d. at Andover, 20 May 1879; m. at Andover, 6 Dec 1836, his first cousin once removed, HANNAH BALLARD GRANT *(Mary Ballard Grant[7], Mary Chandler Ballard[6], Nathan Chandler[5], Nathan Chandler[4], John Chandler[3], Hannah Abbott Chandler[2], George[1])*, b. at Andover, 19 Sep 1815 daughter of Charles and Mary (Ballard) Grant; Hannah d. at Andover, 24 Jul 1873.

vi MARY ABBOTT, b. 17 Nov 1809; d. at Lyman, ME, 16 Feb 1903; m. at Andover, 11 Feb 1836, EBENEZER RICKER, b. 1810; Ebenezer d. at Lyman, 9 Jul 1882.

vii GILBERT ABBOTT, b. 5 Apr 1812; d. 1 Jan 1835. Gilbert did not marry.

846) SOLOMON ABBOTT *(Jonathan[4], David[3], Benjamin[2], George[1])*, b. at Andover, 1 Nov 1772 son of Jonathan and Mary (Chandler) Abbot; d. 1 Sep 1840; m. 8 Jul 1794, his third cousin once removed, LUCY POOR FRYE *(Lucy Lovejoy Frye[5], Lydea Abbott Lovejoy[4], Henry[3], George[2], George[1])*, b. 4 Jul 1778 daughter of Theophilus and Lucy (Lovejoy) Frye; Lucy d. at Boston, 16 Jun 1854.

Solomon Abbott and Lucy Frye were parents of five children born at Andover.

i LUCY ABBOTT, b. 30 Oct 1794; d. at Temple, NH, 30 Dec 1820; m. at Andover, 7 Mar 1813, JOSEPH BURTT, b. at Andover, 18 Oct 1788 son of Joseph and Mary (Carleton) Burtt; Joseph d. at Temple, 28 Mar 1872. After Lucy's death, Joseph married Roxalany Lawrence.

ii Son b. 7 Nov 1796

iii SOLOMON ABBOTT, b. 22 Sep 1802; no further record and may have died young.

iv JOSHUA ABBOTT, b. 6 Feb 1805; d. at Lowell, 12 Jan 1840; m. at Lowell, 27 Dec 1827, FANNY DAVIS, b. at Chelmsford, 15 Apr 1801 daughter of Joshua and Betty (Bowers) Davis; Fanny d. at Medford, 21 Dec 1884.

v ANDREW ABBOTT, b. 8 Aug 1808; d. at Boston, 15 Oct 1884; m. at Boston, 3 Nov 1831, ROSALIE YOUNET, b. in France, about 1807 daughter of Alexis and Madeline (-) Younet;[2287] Rosalie d. at Boston, 22 Nov 1878.

847) TIMOTHY ABBOTT *(Nathan[4], Timothy[3], Timothy[2], George[1])*, b. at Wilton, 15 Oct 1762 son of Nathan and Jane (Paul) Abbott; d. at Thetford, 8 Sep 1831; m. by 1788, SARAH SMITH, b. 1765 daughter of Ezekiel and Ruth (Childs) Smith; Sarah d. at Waterbury, VT, 9 Nov 1848.

Timothy and Sarah lived in Henniker, New Hampshire during their early marriage and eight children were born there. They relocated to Thetford, Vermont about 1803 where two more children were born.

i JAMES ABBOTT, b. at Henniker, 17 Feb 1788; d. at Thetford, after 1870; m. at Thetford, 14 Jan 1813, HANNAH LADD, b. at Hopkinton, NH, 21 May 1789 daughter of Thaddeus and Hannah (Dow) Ladd; Hannah d. at Springfield, VT, 11 Dec 1874.

ii DANIEL ABBOTT, b. at Henniker, 12 Mar 1790; d. at Worcester, VT, 27 Mar 1872; m. at Thetford, 16 Dec 1819, HANNAH CLOSSON, b. at Thetford, 15 Jan 1796 daughter of Simon and Sarah (Wood) Closson; Hannah d. at Worcester, VT, 29 Jul 1860.

iii NATHAN ABBOTT, b. at Henniker, 22 Dec 1791; nothing further known.

iv SEBA ABBOTT, b. at Henniker, 28 Jun 1794; nothing further known.

v SALLY ABBOTT, b. at Henniker, 25 Jul 1796; d. at Middlesex, VT, 29 Oct 1867; m. at Thetford, 21 Jan 1821, NATHAN JACKMAN, b. at Bradford, NH, 22 Feb 1797 son of Nathan and Catherine (-) Jackman; Nathan d. at Middlesex, 1871 (probate 1871).

vi JANE "JENNIE" ABBOTT, b. at Henniker, 1 Apr 1798; d. at Waterbury, VT, Sep 1867. Jennie did not marry.

vii APPLETON ABBOTT, b. at Henniker, 4 May 1800; d. at Boston, 20 Jul 1864; m. at Boston, 30 Jun 1822, LOUISA SMITH,[2288] b. in England, about 1799; Louisa d. after 1860.

[2287] Names of Rosalie's parents are given on her death record.

[2288] Louisa's name is not certain. The marriage record says Louisa Smith, but the death record of one of the children gives her name as Louisa Walker.

viii JONAS ABBOTT, b. at Henniker, 1 Feb 1802; d. at Worcester, VT, 5 Apr 1875; m. at Worcester, 6 Jan 1826, MINERVA E. VAIL, b. at Pomfret, VT, about 1802 daughter of Allan and Elizabeth (Tuthill) Vail; Minerva d. at Boston, 30 Jun 1888.

ix TIMOTHY ABBOTT, b. at Thetford, 1806; d. at Boston, 16 Jun 1871; m. about 1830, MARY M. (last name unknown), b. in NH, about 1802; Mary d. after 1871.

x MARY ANN ABBOTT, b. at Thetford, 1809; d. at Waterbury, VT, 5 May 1884; m. at Westbury, VT, 24 Dec 1839, SYLVANUS SAYRE BROWN, b. about 1807; Sylvanus d. at Waterbury, 22 Sep 1867.

848) ASA ABBOTT *(Nathan⁴, Timothy³, Timothy², George¹)*, b. at Wilton, 24 Jan 1765 son of Nathan and Jane (Paul) Abbott; d. at Bradford, NH, 5 Nov 1852; m. 1st, MIRIAM SMITH, b. 1770 daughter of Ezekiel and Ruth (Childs) Smith; Miriam d. at Bradford, 12 Feb 1819. Asa m. 2nd, 23 Dec 1819, AZUBA FARNSWORTH (widow of Francis Bowman), b. at Harvard, MA, 31 Aug 1771 daughter of Phineas and Lydia (Whitcomb) Farnsworth; Azuba d. at Bradford, after 1860.

Asa Abbott was born in Wilton and he and Miriam were in Bradford, New Hampshire by 1794. Asa was a shoemaker in Bradford.[2289]

Asa Abbott and Miriam Smith were parents of ten children, the youngest eight born at Bradford and birthplace of the oldest two children uncertain.

i LYDIA ABBOTT, b. 1789; d. at Plainfield, NH, Jul 1869; m. at Bradford, 7 Jan 1813, DANIEL MORRILL, b. at Warner, NH, 12 May 1786 son of Enoch and Eunice (Pearson) Morrill; Daniel d. at Plainfield, 24 May 1867.

ii ASA ABBOTT, b. about 1792; d. at Mason City, IA, 11 Oct 1875; m. 7 Jun 1815, MARY SARGENT, b. 1789 daughter of James and Polly (Roach) Sargent; Mary d. at Mason City, 10 Dec 1870.

iii MARY ABBOTT, b. 1794; d. at Cornish, NH, 25 Apr 1877; m. at Sutton, 8 Mar 1816, TRUEWORTHY SARGENT, b. at Bradford, about 1795 son of James and Polly (Roach) Taylor; Trueworthy d. at Bradford, about 1840.[2290]

iv EZEKIEL ABBOTT, b. 1796; d. at Manchester, NH, 20 Sep 1880; m. at Cornish, 20 Nov 1823, PHEBE MORSE, b. at Reading, VT, 24 May 1802 daughter of Jonathan and Sally (Cummings) Morse; Phebe d. at Bedford, NH, 13 Apr 1875.

v PATTY ABBOTT, b. 1798; d. at Bradford, 9 Apr 1872; m. before 1827, STEPHEN CHENEY, b. 20 Oct 1795 son of Jonathan and Lavina C. (Ward) Cheney;[2291] Stephen d. at Bradford, 9 Dec 1872.

vi RUTH ABBOTT, b. about 1801; d. at Sutton, NH, 25 Apr 1861; m. 1st, at Henniker, 21 Dec 1820, her step-brother, LEVI BOWMAN, b. about 1795 son of Francis and Azubah (Farnsworth) Bowman; Levi d. 25 Oct 1841. Ruth m. 2nd, at Henniker, 3 May 1860, WILLIAM CHENEY, b. at Bradford, about 1798 son of Jonathan and Lavina C. (Ward) Cheney; William d. at Sutton, 20 Nov 1874. William was first married to Sally Emery.

vii HANNAH ABBOTT, b. 10 Oct 1803; d. at Plainfield, 2 Apr 1891; m. at Bradford, 26 Mar 1832, CYRUS SMITH, b. at Grantham, NH, 2 Aug 1804 son of James and Mary (Colby) Smith; Cyrus d. at Plainfield, 25 Jun 1891.

viii SILAS ABBOTT, b. 1806; d. at Ridott, IL, 24 Jan 1872; m. 18 Apr 1833, JUDITH HALE, b. at Bradford, 17 Apr 1806 daughter of Daniel and Betsey (Fellows) Hale;[2292] Judith d. at Ridott, 14 Jun 1872.

ix DORCAS ABBOTT, b. 13 Dec 1810; d. at Enfield, NH, 17 Jul 1894; m. ABIJAH EMERSON, b. at Sunapee, about 1815 son of Samuel Emerson;[2293] Abijah d. at Enfield, 14 May 1877.

x CLARISSA ABBOTT, b. 19 Feb 1814; d. at Hanover, NH, 8 Sep 1896; m. 1st, 22 Dec 1841, STEPHEN LEAVITT, b. at Grantham, 31 Mar 1807 son of Dudley and Hannah (Prescott) Leavitt; Stephen d. 3 Oct 1850. Clarissa m. 2nd, at Plainfield, 1 Feb 1860, NATHANIEL PURMORT, b. at Enfield, about 1809 son of Mark and Abigail (Dole) Purmort; Nathaniel d. at Enfield, 4 Nov 1884.

[2289] Gould and Beals, *Early Families of Bradford*, p 1

[2290] According to Gould and Beals, *Bradford Early Families*, the widow Mary Sargent was on the tax rolls in Bradford in 1843. Trueworthy is listed as a head of household in Bradford in 1830.

[2291] Pope, *The Cheney Genealogy*, p 362

[2292] Hale, *Genealogy of the Descendants of Thomas Hale*, p 278

[2293] Abijah's death record gives father's name as Samuel Emerson and mother's name as Baker.

849) PHEBE FARMER *(Sarah Abbott Farmer⁴, Timothy³, Timothy², George¹)*, b. in Hillsborough County, NH, 21 Sep 1761 daughter of Edward and Sarah (Abbott) Farmer; d. at Pelham, 23 Apr 1839; m. ENOS HADLEY, b. at Amesbury, 24 Oct 1755 son of Eliphalet and Elizabeth (Davis) Hadley; Enos d. at Pelham, about 1838.

Enos Hadley did not leave a will and son Caleb was appointed administrator 6 February 1839. However, Caleb died in 1839 as did the widow Phebe and administration was granted to Samuel Simpson at the request of six surviving children. In his will written 7 October 1839, son Caleb Hadley make token bequests of one dollar each to siblings Hannah Hadley, Mary Hadley, Betsey Hadley, James V. Hadley, and Almira Fulton. The remainder of the estate was divided roughly in thirds (with some complicated provisions) to siblings Sarah Hadley, John Hadley, and Athaliah Hadley. Friend Colburn Blood was named executor.[2294] In her will in 1867, daughter Hannah made bequests to her brother John Hadley, heirs of brother James V. Hadley, and sisters Sally Hadley, Polly Hadley, and Almira Fulton.

Phebe Farmer and Enos Hadley were parents of nine children born at Pelham. Only two of the children married.

i BETSEY HADLEY, b. about 1787; d. before 1850. Betsey did not marry.

ii MARY "POLLY" HADLEY, b. 1788; Polly d. at Pelham, 3 May 1881. Polly did not marry.

iii CALEB HADLEY, b. about 1790; d. at Pelham, about 1839. Caleb did not marry.

iv JOHN HADLEY, b. about 1792; d. uncertain but after 1867. John does not seem to have married and he may be the John Hadley who was living at the poor farm in Hudson, NH in 1850 and 1860.

v HANNAH HADLEY, b. about 1794; d. at Hudson, 1867. Hannah did not marry.

vi SARAH HADLEY, b. about 1800; d. after 1867. Sarah did not marry.

vii JAMES VARNUM HADLEY, b. 1802; d. at Augusta, ME, 2 Sep 1850; m. at Tyngsborough, MA, 30 Dec 1827, CLARISSA COBURN, b. 1803 daughter of James and Mary (Bailey) Coburn; Clarissa d. at Augusta, 21 Aug 1855.

viii ATHALIAH HADLEY, b. about 1806; d. after 1839. Athaliah does not seem to have married.

ix ALMIRA HADLEY, b. about 1807; d. after 1867; m. at Pelham, 23 Apr 1839, SAMUEL FULTON, b. at Hancock, 10 Feb 1812 son of Jonathan and Mary (Wallace) Fulton. Almira and Samuel divorced 5 Jun 1861.[2295] Samuel remarried to Elizabeth Farmer 12 Oct 1861, and after Elizabeth died in 1871, he married Sarah J. Towns who was 18 years old at the time of the marriage. Sarah had a marriage in 1886 so Samuel is assumed to have died prior to 1886. Almira Hadley and Samuel Fulton were parents of six children.

849a) LYDIA FARNUM *(Lydia Abbott Farnum⁴, Timothy³, Timothy², George¹)*, b. 10 Nov 1756 daughter of Thomas and Lydia (Abbott) Farnum; m. 27 Oct 1774, her second cousin (and George Abbott descendant), THOMAS HOLT, b. 15 Jun 1750 son of Thomas and Dorcas (Holt) Holt; Thomas and Lydia d. after 1794 when they were living at Lyndeborough.

Thomas and Lydia married in Andover and baptisms of three children are recorded there. The family was then in Amherst, New Hampshire. In 1779, Thomas Holt of Andover purchased property in Amherst from Isaac and Hannah Holt of Andover. Thomas and Lydia sold their property in Amherst in 1793 and 1794 and were of Lyndeborough in 1794 when they sold the last of their property in Amherst. They perhaps were next in Greenfield, but that is not known.[2296]

Thomas Holt's household was six persons in Amherst in 1790: two males 16 and over, one male under 16, and three females.[2297] Three children were identified for Thomas Holt and Lydia Farnum.

i STEPHEN HOLT, baptized at Andover, 27 Apr 1777

ii LYDIA HOLT, baptized at Andover, 12 Jul 1778; d. at Greenfield, NH, 25 Nov 1869; m. at Lyndeborough, 30 Apr 1793, JOHN SAVAGE, b. at Marblehead, MA, 13 Sep 1771 son of John and Mary (Jackson) Savage; John d. at Greenfield, 5 Oct 1850.

iii PHEBE HOLT, baptized 11 Jun 1780; *perhaps* m. at Andover, 15 Mar 1805, SAMUEL EATON, b. at Reading, 17 Oct 1782 son of Samuel Phillips and Sarah (Evans) Eaton; Samuel d. at Lynn, 14 Nov 1871.

[2294] *New Hampshire, Wills and Probate Records, 1643-1982, Hillsborough, Probate Records, Vol 48-49, 1839-1846*, volume 48, pp 1-3

[2295] *New Hampshire, Marriage and Divorce Records, 1659-1947*, New England Historical Genealogical Society; New Hampshire Bureau of Vital Records, Concord, New Hampshire.

[2296] New Hampshire Land Records, Hillsborough County, 8:179, 30:450, 30:452, 35:272

[2297] Year: 1790; Census Place: Amherst, Hillsborough, New Hampshire; Series: M637; Roll: 5; Page: 227; Image: 144; Family History Library Film: 0568145

850) ISRAEL FARNUM *(Lydia Abbott Farnum⁴, Timothy³, Timothy², George¹)*, b. at Andover, 14 Jun 1758 son of Thomas and Lydia (Abbott) Farnum; d. at Mont Vernon, NH, 1842; m. 3 Aug 1786, PHEBE SHELDON; Phebe d. 2 Feb 1824. Israel m. 2nd, 17 May 1825, SUSANNAH FARNUM, b. 22 Mar 1772 daughter of Asa and Susannah (Town) Farnum.[2298]

Israel Farnum and Phebe Sheldon were parents of three children.

i PHEBE FARNUM, b. at Andover, 31 Mar 1788; d. at Landgrove, VT, 8 Sep 1863; m. at Mont Vernon, NH, 19 Jul 1810, her fourth cousin, EBENEZER HOLT LAMPSON *(Rebecca Holt Lampson⁵, Ebenezer Holt⁴, Mehitable Stevens Holt³, Sarah Abbott Stevens², George¹)*, b. at Amherst, NH, 23 Dec 1784 son of Jonathan and Elizabeth (Holt) Lampson; Ebenezer d. at Landgrove, 10 Apr 1855. Ebenezer is a child in Family 759.

ii ISRAEL FARNUM, b. at Mont Vernon, 8 Jun 1790; d. at Mont Vernon, 30 Dec 1861; m. 4 Nov 1816, CATHERINE TALBERT, b. 5 Apr 1788; Catherine d. at Mont Vernon, 16 May 1875.

iii AMOS FARNUM, b. at Mont Vernon, 17 May 1792; d. 17 Oct 1812.

851) TIMOTHY FARNUM *(Lydia Abbott Farnum⁴, Timothy³, Timothy², George¹)*, b. at Andover, 13 May 1759 son of Thomas and Lydia (Abbott) Farnum; m. 23 Sep 1786, SUSANNA BERRY, b. 27 Apr 1767 daughter of Nathaniel and Susanna (Easty) Berry; Susanna d. 16 Jul 1854.

Timothy Farnum did not leave a will and his estate entered probate 26 March 1811.[2299] Susanna Farnum was named administratrix. Real estate was valued at $3,512.35 and personal estate at $1,028.76. For reasons that are not stated, Susanna did not petition to have her right of dower set off to her until 18 August 1835 and the one-third was set off in 1835. Her son Jesse died 31 July 1835 and that may be related to her delay of requesting the dower.

Timothy Farnum and Susanna Berry were parents of twelve children born at Andover.

i LEVI FARNUM, b. 26 Oct 1787; d. at North Andover, 27 Apr 1870; m. 14 May 1816, BETSY LACY, b. at Andover, 21 Oct 1787 daughter of Ephraim and Mehitable (Kimball) Lacy; Betsy d. at North Andover, 11 Sep 1875.

ii LUCY FARNUM, b. 23 Mar 1789; d. at Andover, 11 May 1857; m. at Andover, 20 Jul 1812, JOSEPH VIALL ALLEN, b. at Barrington, RI, 12 May 1783 son of Asa and Abigail (Blunt) Allen; Joseph d. at Andover, 16 Mar 1868.

iii NANCY FARNUM, b. 13 Mar 1791; d. at Middleton, MA, 30 Sep 1874; m. at Andover, 12 Mar 1812, DAVID STILES, b. at Middleton, 1 Nov 1784 son of Ezekiel and Miriam (Richardson) Stiles; David d. at Middleton, 7 Aug 1863.

iv JESSE FARNUM, b. 4 Feb 1793; d. at Andover, 31 Jul 1835; m. 19 Jun 1834, ELIZABETH ANGIER, b. at North Reading, 14 Apr 1800 daughter of Asa and Abigail (Carter) Angier; Elizabeth d. at Andover, 10 Sep 1892. After Jesse's death, Elizabeth married Mr. Clark. Jesse and Elizabeth did have one daughter Amlet Augusta Farnum.

v LYDIA FARNUM, b. 28 Feb 1795; no further clear information, but she may be the Lydia Farnum who died in Andover in 1816.

vi JERE FARNUM, b. 17 Mar 1797; d. at Andover, 11 May 1848; m. 1 Apr 1824, SARAH WARDWELL, b. at Andover, 7 Sep 1803 daughter of John and Sarah (Trussel) Wardwell; Sarah d. at Andover, 18 Aug 1884. Sarah Wardwell m. 2nd, 18 Mar 1857, EBENEZER LOVEJOY *(Phebe Russell Lovejoy⁶, Phebe Abbott Russell⁵, Barachias⁴, John³, John², George¹)*, b. at Andover, 7 Feb 1795 son of Ebenezer and Phebe (Russell) Lovejoy.

vii SUSANNAH FARNUM, b. 14 Jan 1799; d. at Weld, ME, after 1870 (living when husband wrote his will); m. at Andover, Jan 1821, her fourth cousin, HEZEKIAH WYNN JONES *(Elizabeth Abbott Jones⁵, Samuel⁴, Sarah Stevens Abbott³, Sarah Abbott Stevens², George¹)*, b. at Andover, 14 Feb 1794 son of Ebenezer and Elizabeth (Abbott) Jones; Hezekiah d. at Weld, ME, about 1871 (will Dec 1870). Hezekiah Jones is a child in Family 332.

viii PHEBE FARNUM, b. 21 Nov 1800; d. at Saugus, MA, 8 May 1872; m. 1st, at Andover, 8 Oct 1823, OLIVER PARKER, b. about 1795 son of Simeon and Mary (Tarbox) Parker; Oliver d. at North Reading, 31 Aug 1854. Phebe m. 2nd, 29 Apr 1860, JACOB BROWN, b. at Cape Ann, about 1799 son of Vincent and Anna (Stanwood) Brown; Jacob d. at North Reading, 23 Apr 1885. Jacob was first married to Phebe's sister Ruby (see below).

2298 Smith, *History of Mont Vernon*, p 63

2299 Essex County, MA: Probate File Papers, 1638-1881.Online database. AmericanAncestors.org. New England Historic Genealogical Society, 2014. Case 9257

ix HANNAH FARNUM, b. 30 Sep 1804; d. at Malden, 25 May 1886; m. at Andover, 16 Nov 1825, RICHARD LEWIS, b. at Lynn, 6 Nov 1802 son of Nathaniel and Rebecca (Richards) Lewis; Richard d. at Malden, 18 Jan 1878.

x RUBY FARNUM, b. Mar 1806; d. at Andover, 21 Dec 1857; m. 4 Mar 1824, JACOB BROWN, b. at Cape Ann, about 1799 (see entry with Ruby's sister Phebe above).

xi MARY FARNUM, b. 3 Aug 1808; d. at Malden, 24 May 1895; m. 1 Nov 1830, GEORGE NICHOLS, b. at Malden, 14 Jan 1809 son of Ebenezer and Esther (Sargent) Nichols; George d. at Malden, 29 Nov 1852.

xii FANNY FARNUM, b. 31 May 1810; d. at Methuen, 28 Jun 1903; m. at Andover, 3 Dec 1835, BENJAMIN PARKER GRANT, b. in Maine, about 1802 son of Benjamin and Mahala (-) Grant;[2300] Benjamin d. at Methuen, 16 Oct 1884.

852) PHEBE FARNUM *(Lydia Abbott Farnum⁴, Timothy³, Timothy², George¹)*, b. at Andover, 25 Jul 1762 daughter of Thomas and Lydia (Abbott) Farnum; m. SAVAGE (according to Charlotte Helen Abbott). No records for this marriage were located, but it may be that this is the Phebe that married David Hovey, but that has not been verified. There is nothing definitive known at this time.

853) SARAH FARNUM *(Lydia Abbott Farnum⁴, Timothy³, Timothy², George¹)*, b. at Andover, 21 Sep 1764 daughter of Thomas and Lydia (Abbott) Farnum; m. at Andover, MA, 10 Sep 1793, ENOS ABBOTT of Andover, ME, b. 7 Feb 1769 son of Jonathan and Ruth (Bragg) Abbott of The Rowley Abbott line; Enos d. at Upton, ME, 28 Feb 1839.

Sarah Farnum and Enos Abbott were parents of eight children born at Andover, Maine.

i ENOS ABBOTT, b. 1 Jan 1795; d. at Rumford, ME, 27 Apr 1867; m. 9 Dec 1821, POLLY HUTCHINS, b. at Rumford, 25 Jan 1804 son of Hezekiah and Sally (Elliot) Hutchins; Polly d. at Andover, ME, 4 Nov 1883.

ii ASA ABBOTT, b. 26 Jan 1796; d. at Rumford, ME, 1832 (probate 1833); m. at Rumford, 1 Jun 1820, ESTHER WOOD, b. at Rumford, 3 Jun 1802 daughter of Phineas and Martha (Spalding) Wood; Esther d. at Rumford, 1871.

iii SARAH ABBOTT, b. 24 Feb 1798; m. Jul 1817, DAVID HUTCHINS, b. at Concord, 4 Jul 1795 son of Hezekiah and Sally (Elliot) Hutchins.

iv THOMAS ABBOTT, b. 9 May 1800; d. at Welchville, ME, 26 Mar 1879; m. 30 Nov 1820, ELIZABETH SAMPSON, b. at Concord, 23 Apr 1801 daughter of William and Abigail (Gilman) Sampson; Elizabeth d. 3 Feb 1889.

v STEPHEN ABBOTT, b. 7 Sep 1801; d. at Rumford, after 1860; m. at Rumford, 25 Dec 1823, LUCY MANSUR, b. at Methuen, MA, 13 Oct 1794 daughter of Elijah and Lucy (Messer) Mansur; Lucy d. at Rumford, 29 Mar 1861.

vi FARNUM ABBOTT, b. 21 Nov 1802; d. at Andover, ME, 1870; m. at Andover, ME, 23 Dec 1828, MARY CHAPMAN, b. at Worcester, MA, 17 Jun 1802 daughter of Abel and Pamela (Rice) Chapman; Mary d. at Andover, 8 Jul 1855.

vii MARY FARNUM ABBOTT, b. 12 Dec 1804; d. likely at Monroe, ME, after 1880 (where she was living with her son); m. 1st, 1826, ABEL CHAPMAN, b. at Worcester, 1 Apr 1804 son of Abel and Pamela (Rice) Chapman; Abel d. at Rumford, 1841. Mary m. 2nd, 17 Nov 1845, SPARROW KING, b. about 1798 son of Sparrow and Elizabeth (Brown) King). Mary m. 3rd, at Corinth, ME, 18 Jun 1863, PETER ELLIOT, b. about 1799; Peter d. at Frankfort, ME, 1869.

viii JACOB FARNUM ABBOTT, b. 13 Sep 1808; d. at Paradise, UT, May 1877; m. 1st, at Andover, ME, 15 Sep 1830, MARY GOUD, b. at Dresden, ME, 1 Sep 1811 daughter of James and Nancy (Cane) Goud; Jacob and Mary divorced about 1845. Jacob m. 2nd, about 1847, MARY SOPHRONIA CHAPMAN, b. at Eugene, IN, 1826; Mary d. Oct 1849. Jacob m. 3rd, at Indian Creek, IA, 9 Jan 1850, MARTHA JANE BICKMORE, b. at Madison, IL, 24 Jan 1832 daughter of Isaac and Martha (Harvell) Bickmore. Jacob was a stagecoach driver in New Mexico. He was an early Mormon.

854) DORCAS FARNUM *(Lydia Abbott Farnum⁴, Timothy³, Timothy², George¹)*, b. at Andover, 27 Dec 1766 daughter of Thomas and Lydia (Abbott) Farnum; d. at Andover, 6 May 1856; m. 25 Dec 1788, NATHAN JONES, b. at Andover, 1767 son of Jacob and Mary (Winn) Jones; Nathan d. at Andover, 14 Aug 1804.

Nathan Jones did not leave a will and his estate entered probate 1 October 1804 with widow Dorcas as administratrix.[2301] The personal estate was valued at $154.98.

Nathan and Dorcas were parents of nine children all born at Andover.

[2300] The names of Benjamin's parents are given as Benjamin and Mahala on his death record.

[2301] Essex County, MA: Probate File Papers, 1638-1881. Online database. AmericanAncestors.org. Case 15216

i JACOB JONES, b. 8 May 1789; d. at Salem, 7 May 1821; m. at Salem, 15 Jun 1817, ELIZA DUTCH, b. at Salem, 7 Sep 1789 daughter of John and Fanny (Jones) Dutch;[2302] Eliza d. at Boston, 22 Apr 1836.

ii LYDIA JONES, b. 25 Oct 1790; d. at Lyndon, VT, 29 Dec 1875; m. at Andover, 15 Apr 1813, her fourth cousin, NATHAN WHITE AMES *(Spofford Ames⁵, Elizabeth Stevens Ames⁴, Nathan Stevens³, Elizabeth Abbott Stevens², George¹)*, b. at Andover, 11 Feb 1785 son of Spofford and Mary (White) Ames; Nathan d. at Lyndon, 24 Jul 1865. Nathan is a child in Family 1157.

iii NATHAN JONES, b. 8 Mar 1792; d. 8 Aug 1799.

iv HERMAN JONES, b. 27 Oct 1793; d. at Andover, 9 Feb 1869; m. at Andover, Jul 1820, his fourth cousin once removed, SALLY WARDWELL *(Nathan Wardwell⁶, Huldah Chandler Wardwell⁵, Abial Chandler Chandler⁴, Abiel Chandler³, Hannah Abbott Chandler², George¹)*, b. at Andover, 29 Jun 1798 daughter of Nathan and Phebe (Stevens) Wardwell; Sally d. at Andover, 10 Sep 1845.

v PHEBE JONES, b. 22 Sep 1795; d. 20 Feb 1798.

vi GARDNER JONES, b. 3 Oct 1798; d. before 1850 at Jefferson County, NY; m. at Lyndeborough, NH, 12 Sep 1820, EUNICE THOMPSON, b. 1795; Eunice d. at Depauville, NY, 4 Mar 1894.

vii PHEBE JONES, b. 16 Apr 1799; d. at Stoneham, MA, 21 Apr 1881; m. 29 May 1822, JONATHAN ATKINSON. The story is that Phebe married sailor Jonathan Atkinson and he ran away the next day.[2303] Phebe worked as a nurse. In her 1869 will, she left her estate to siblings, nieces, and nephews. In 1878, a guardian was appointed for her as she was "insane." The guardianship was obtained after the death of her sister Anna with whom she lived.

viii ANNA JONES, b. 17 Jul 1801; d. at Andover, 18 May 1878. Anna did not marry.

ix DORCAS JONES, b. 24 Oct 1803; d. 14 Jul 1826.

855) PHEBE DANE *(Phebe Abbott Dane⁴, Timothy³, Timothy², George¹)*, b. at Andover, 18 Dec 1767 daughter of William and Phebe (Abbott) Dane; d. at Greenfield, NH, 12 Sep 1854; m. 10 Nov 1794, BENJAMIN HARDY, b. at Tewksbury, 10 Aug 1768 son of James and Jemima (Palmer) Hardy; Benjamin d. at Greenfield, 16 Apr 1834.

Phebe and Benjamin started their family in Andover, but soon settled in Greenfield, New Hampshire where they had a farm.

In his will written 13 April 1833, Benjamin Hardy bequeaths to his wife Phebe one hundred dollars, the use and occupancy of one-third of his real estate, and all the household furniture, one cow to be at her disposal, the use of a horse and carriage, and firewood to be brought to her door. Oldest son Benjamin receives two hundred dollars as does second son John Dean. Third son Herman receives two hundred and twenty dollars. Oldest daughter Phebe Richardson receives thirty-three dollars as does as does second daughter Betsey Bailey. Third daughter Hannah Hardy receives one hundred and fourteen dollars and a home in the family home as long as she lives single. Fourth son Hiram receives one-half of the real estate, one-half the stock, and one-half the farming tools as long as he carries on said farm in a husband-like manner. Hiram is responsible to pay and doctor's and nurse's bills for his parents and is responsible for debts of the estate. At the decease of both his parents, Hiram receives all the real estate. Hiram is also named executor.[2304]

Benjamin Hardy and Phebe Dane were parents of seven children, the first two births at Andover and the other children were likely born at Greenfield.

i BENJAMIN HARDY, b. about 1795; d. at Greenfield, 20 Jun 1879; m. about 1820, MEHITABLE HOLT, b. at Greenfield, 24 May 1799 daughter of William and Mehitable (Stiles) Holt; Mehitable d. at Greenfield, 1866.

ii JOHN DEAN HARDY, b. 24 Nov 1796; d. at Greenfield, 12 May 1875; m. 1st, about 1825, SALLY JAQUITH, b. 1803 daughter of Benjamin and Phebe (Ames) Jaquith; Sally d. at Greenfield, 9 Aug 1833. John m. 2nd, about 1834, his third cousin once removed, HANNAH ABBOTT *(Hannah Bailey Abbott⁵, Elizabeth Mooar Bailey⁴, Elizabeth Abbott Mooar³, Nathaniel², George¹)*, b. at Greenfield, 7 Sep 1807 daughter of William and Hannah (Bailey) Abbott; Hannah d. at Greenfield, 1 Jul 1880.

[2302] Stickney, *The Fowler Family*, p. 88

[2303] Abbott, Early Records of the Jones Family of Andover

[2304] *New Hampshire. Probate Court (Hillsborough County);* Probate Place: *Hillsborough, New Hampshire*, volume 40, p 407

iii HERMAN HARDY, b. about 1800; d. at Francestown, NH, 31 Aug 1865; m. at Francestown, 20 Jan 1828, RELIEF HOPKINS, b. at Francestown, 6 Apr 1804 daughter of William and Rachel (Brewster) Hopkins; Relief d. at Cambridge, MA, 19 Oct 1875.

iv PHEBE HARDY, b. about 1802; d. at Greenfield, 21 Jun 1833; m. at Malden, MA, 22 Nov 1828, LEWIS RICHARDSON, b. 3 Aug 1801 son of Jacob and Sarah (Lewis) Richardson; Lewis d. at Greenfield, 21 Aug 1878. Lewis married second Elizabeth Wade and third Charlotte Sprague.

v BETSEY HARDY, b. 30 May 1804; d. at Greenfield, 14 Jun 1873; m. about 1825, LEONARD BAILEY, b. at Greenfield, 20 Jun 1800 son of James and Dorothy (Worcester) Bailey; Leonard d. at Greenfield, 7 Jul 1885. After Betsey's death, Leonard married Dorothy C. Mansfield 12 Jan 1874.

vi HANNAH HARDY, b. Sep 1808; d. at Greenfield, 13 Jan 1888; m. at Hancock, NH, 26 Jun 1834, her third cousin once removed, HERMAN ABBOTT *(Hannah Bailey Abbott[5], Elizabeth Mooar Bailey[4], Elizabeth Abbott Mooar[3], Nathaniel[2], George[1])*, b. at Greenfield, 23 Nov 1804 son of William and Hannah (Bailey) Abbott; Herman d. at Greenfield, 7 Dec 1891.

vii HIRAM HARDY, b. about 1810; d. at Greenfield, 7 Feb 1866; m. 1st, 1830, ABIGAIL DODGE, b. 1812 daughter of Levi and Keziah (Stanley) Dodge; Abigail d. at Greenfield, 21 Sep 1838. Hiram m. 2nd, about 1839, Abigail's sister, MARIA DODGE, b. 1819; Maria d. at Greenfield, 17 Oct 1894.

856) DORCAS DANE *(Phebe Abbott Dane[4], Timothy[3], Timothy[2], George[1])*, b. at Andover, 22 Apr 1771 daughter of William and Phebe (Abbott) Dane; m. 9 Oct 1794, her first cousin, EZRA HOLT, b. 20 Mar 1762 son of Timothy and Hannah (Dane) Holt.

Dorcas and Ezra started their family in Andover and then settled in Wilton. Ezra Holt was a farmer in Wilton where he lived on lot 6 of the ninth range.[2305] Ezra Holt and Dorcas Dane were parents of seven children.

i EZRA HOLT, b. at Andover, 9 Aug 1795; d. at Milford, NH, 7 Apr 1860; m. 1st, at Dracut, 13 Feb 1821, JOANNA MARSHALL, b. at Dracut, 30 Aug 1797 daughter of Joshua and Esther (Moors) Marshall; Joanna d. at Wilton, 20 Dec 1839. Ezra m. 2nd, at Mont Vernon, NH, 28 May 1840, DOLLY B. GOULD, b. at Alstead, 3 Jan 1812;[2306] Dolly d. at Lexington, MA, 11 Feb 1897.

ii DORCAS HOLT, b. at Andover, 24 Dec 1797; d. at Wilton, 11 Nov 1869. Dorcas did not marry.

iii SARAH ABBOT HOLT, b. 1 Sep 1800; d. 26 Aug 1801.

iv JOSEPH HOLT, b. at Andover, May 1803; d. at Wilton, after 1870; m. Oct 1840, his third cousin once removed, BETSEY FRYE *(Joshua Frye[6], Elizabeth Holt Frye[5], Timothy Holt[4], Dorcas Abbott Holt[3], Timothy[2], George[1])*, b. in VT, about 1808 daughter of Joshua and Lois (Farrington) Frye; Betsey d. at Wilton, 5 Jun 1885.

v HERMAN HOLT, b. at Wilton, 1807; d. at Wilton, 21 Jun 1836.

vi DANE HOLT, b. at Wilton, 1810; d. at Wilton, 23 Dec 1858; m. Dec 1839, ESTHER BLANCHARD, b. at Milford, 5 May 1816 daughter of Phineas and Sarah (Stevens) Blanchard; Esther d. at Milford, 21 Feb 1893.

vii MARY HOLT, b. at Wilton, 1816; d. at Wilton, 11 Feb 1853. Mary did not marry.

857) TIMOTHY DANE *(Phebe Abbott Dane[4], Timothy[3], Timothy[2], George[1])*, b. at Andover, 9 May 1773 son William and Phebe (Abbott) Dane; d. at Hillsborough, Aug 1856; m. 1st, 2 Apr 1806, ESTHER WHEELER, b. at Hillsborough, 24 Mar 1778 daughter of Oliver and Hephzibah (Munroe) Wheeler; Esther d. about 1812. Timothy m. 2nd, about 1814, SARAH TUCKER (widow Sarah Howe), b. at Henniker, 27 Nov 1772 daughter of Ezra and Hephzibah (Pressy) Tucker; Sarah d. at Hillsborough, before 1850.

Timothy succeeded his father on the family homestead in Hillsborough.[2307] Timothy Dane and Esther Wheeler were parents of three children born at Hillsborough.

i PHEBE DANE, b. about 1808; d. at Lempster, NH, about 1858; m. Apr 1828, JOHN BUTTERFIELD, b. at Francestown, about 1808 son of Oliver and Hannah (Dane) Butterfield; John d. at Goshen, NH, after 1870. After Phebe's death, John married Emily Sleeper 5 Feb 1859.

[2305] Livermore, *History of Wilton*, p 407
[2306] Ramsdell, *History of Milford*, volume 1, p 749
[2307] Browne, *History of Hillsborough*, p 165

ii JOHN DANE, b. about 1809; d. at Amador County, CA, after 1880; m. at Boston, 5 Jul 1836, ELIZABETH COVELL, b. at Boston, about 1808 *likely* the daughter of Edmund and Elizabeth (Daniels) Covell; Elizabeth d. at Amador County, after 1870.

iii TIMOTHY DANE, b. about 1810; d. at Nashua, 13 Oct 1887; m. 2 Feb 1834, RHODA PROCTOR, b. at Andover, NH, Aug 1807 daughter of William and Rhoda (Bailey) Proctor; Rhoda d. at Franklin, NH, 4 Jun 1895.

Timothy Dane and Sarah Tucker were parents of four children born at Hillsborough.

i MOSES DANE, b. at Hillsborough, about 1815; d. at Dorchester, MA, 20 May 1868;[2308] m. at Dorchester, 11 Aug 1839, MARY COVELL, b. at Boston, about 1814 daughter of Edmund and Elizabeth (Daniels) Covell;[2309] Mary d. at Boston, 28 Oct 1893. Moses was a stone mason.

ii JOSEPH DANE, b. about 1816; likely died young

iii SARAH DANE, b. at Hillsborough, 1817; d. at Hillsborough, 28 Nov 1886. Sarah did not marry.

iv ESTHER DANE, b. at Hillsborough, 7 Aug 1820; d. at Hillsborough, 2 Mar 1906. Esther did not marry. She was a seamstress at Bridge Village.

858) DORCAS LANE *(Samuel Lane⁴, Hannah Abbott Lane³, Timothy², George¹)*, b. at Bedford, MA, 8 Feb 1771 daughter of Samuel and Elizabeth (Fitch) Lane; d. 11 Feb 1849; m. 3 Jan 1788, NATHAN WHITE.

Dorcas and Nathan remained in Bedford and five children were born there. No information has been located for Nathan. He was in the 1790 Census as a head of household at Bedford, but no record after that time. There is no probate record.

i ELIZABETH "BETSEY" WHITE, b. 19 Jul 1788; d. at Cambridge, 8 Apr 1856; m. 1st, 18 May 1817, AARON WELLS, b. about 1790 son of Aaron Wells; Aaron d. at Boston, 7 Sep 1819. Betsey m. 2nd. 5 Mar 1820, THOMAS WISE SHORT, b. at Cork, Ireland, 1784; Thomas d. at Cambridge, 29 Jul 1842. Thomas W. Short was a merchant who immigrated to Cambridge in 1815.[2310]

ii Twin Son1, b. 22 Jul 1789; d. 22 Jul 1789

iii Twin Son2; b. 22 Jul 1789; d. 26 Jul 1789

iv DORCAS WHITE, b. 15 Nov 1790; d. at Rindge, NH, 4 Apr 1856; m. at Bedford, 3 Apr 1811, BENJAMIN HUBBARD, b. at Rindge, 9 Sep 1782 son of Hezekiah and Rebecca (Hutchinson) Hubbard;[2311] Benjamin d. at Rindge, 9 Jun 1841.

v SAMUEL LANE WHITE, b. 23 Dec 1792; no further record found.

859) MARY "POLLY" LANE *(Samuel Lane⁴, Hannah Abbott Lane³, Timothy², George¹)*, b. at Bedford, MA, 15 Aug 1776 daughter of Samuel and Elizabeth (Fitch) Lane; d. at Billerica, 30 Nov 1815; m. 10 Feb 1801, JOHN STEARNS, b. 18 Sep 1765 son of Isaac and Sarah (Abbott of the Rowley Abbott line) Stearns; John d. at Woburn, 4 Nov 1836.

On 4 November 1836, John Stearns who was 71 years old and partially deaf, was walking along the railroad track in Woburn. The engineer of the locomotive Phoenix of the Boston and Lowell Railroad had no cars and was going at a slow rate of speed. The engineer saw John on the track but thought he was getting off. There was so much smoke from the locomotive that the engineer could not see, but he kept going and hit John killing him.[2312]

Despite the tragedy of their father's death, two of his sons were active in the early railroad business. John Owen Stearns was Director and Superintendent of the Central Railroad of New Jersey from 1849 to his death in 1862. The Central Railroad was built by John Owen Stearns and Coffin Colkett between 1834 and 1842 and connected Somerville and Elizabethport.[2313]

Son Onslow went with his brother John to Virginia and was employed in the engineering department of the construction of the Chesapeake and Ohio Canal. He was then involved in building railroads in Philadelphia and Baltimore. He

---

2308 His parents' names are given as Timothy and Sarah on his death record and place of birth as Hillsborough.

2309 Names of parents are given as Edmund Corel and Elizabeth Daniels on her death record. Edmund Covell and Elizabeth Daniels were married in Boston in 1801.

2310 *Massachusetts, State and Federal Naturalization Records, 1798-1950*, National Archives at Boston

2311 Stearns, *History of the Town of Rindge*, p. 561

2312 Christian Watchman (Boston, Massachusetts), Friday, November 11, 1836, p. 2.

2313 Van Buskirk, "Bayonne and South Hudson," Papers Read Before the Historical Society of Hudson County, volume 1, 1909, p 18.

returned to New England about 1837 and completed the Nashua and Lowell Railroad in 1838. He was then involved in building the Northern Railroad from Concord to West Lebanon, New Hampshire. He was also superintendent of the Vermont Central Railroad. In 1874, he became president of the Concord Railroad.[2314] He was the first superintendent of the Nashua and Lowell Railroad. The first president of the Nahua and Lowell was sixth generation descendant Daniel Abbot (1777-1853).[2315] He was also president of the New Hampshire state senate and the governor of New Hampshire.

John Stearns wrote his will 12 April 1836. Beloved wife Susannah Stearns receives all the household furniture she brought at the time of her marriage. Daughters Mary Whitford and Elisa Ann Billings each receive $100. Son John O. Stearns receives $250 as does son Onslow Stearns. Sons Lorenzo Stearns and Barnard Stearns each receive $300. The remainder of the estate goes to son Franklin Stearns who is named executor.[2316]

Mary and John Stearns had eight children born at Billerica.

i FRANKLIN STEARNS, b. 25 Jan 1802; d. at Billerica, 29 May 1886; m. 28 Dec 1828, SALLY LANE, b. at Ashburnham, 8 Oct 1801 daughter of Benjamin and Isabel (Hill) Lane; Sally d. at Billerica, 27 Nov 1894.

ii MARY STEARNS, b. 28 Dec 1803; b. at Concord, NH, 7 Apr 1882; m. at Billerica, 13 May 1832, WILLIAM WHITFORD, b. at Middleton, 5 Oct 1799 son of William and Lucy (Dale) Whitford; William d. at Billerica, 5 Dec 1863.

iii JOHN OWEN STEARNS, b. 3 Aug 1805; d. at Elizabeth, NJ, 1 Nov 1862; m. 1842, MARGARET C. WALKER, of Rehoboth, PA, b. 9 Oct 1821 daughter of William and Sarah (Pennypacker) Walker; death no known, but Margaret was still living in Elizabeth, NJ in 1895.

iv ONSLOW STEARNS, b. 2 Feb 1807; d. 23 Feb 1808.

v ELIZA ANN STEARNS, b. 4 Oct 1808; d. at Boston, 3 Mar 1875; m. at Billerica, 17 May 1832, JOHN DENNIS BILLINGS, b. at Lincoln, 10 Nov 1805 son of John and Lydia (Bowen) Billings; John d. at Bedford, 27 Mar 1871.

vi ONSLOW STEARNS, b. 30 Aug 1810; d. at Concord, 29 Dec 1878; m. 26 Jun 1845, his fourth cousin once removed, MARY ABBOTT HOLBROOK *(Polly Warren Holbrook^6, Molly Abbott Warren^5, Joseph^4, Joseph^3, Nathaniel^2, George^1)*, b. at Athol, 10 Feb 1819 daughter of Adin and Polly (Warren) Holbrook; Mary d. at Concord, 27 Jul 1895.

vii LORENZO STEARNS, b. 13 May 1813; d. at Elizabeth, NJ, 13 May 1836.

viii BERNARD STEARNS, b. 23 Nov 1815; d. at Elizabeth, NJ, 28 May 1880; m. 30 Dec 1851, LAVINIA BEATRICE HAINES, b. at New York, 29 Jan 1830 daughter of Simeon and Elsey Ann (Holmes) Haines; Lavinia d. at Poughkeepsie, 2 Sep 1877. Simeon Haines was a skilled cabinetmaker in the company Holmes and Haines whose pieces are now in museums.

860) ELIZABETH HOLT *(Timothy Holt^4, Dorcas Abbott Holt^3, Timothy^2, George^1)*, b. at Andover, 25 Nov 1748 daughter of Timothy and Elizabeth (Holt) Holt; m. 1 Jun 1769, ISAAC FRYE, b. at Andover, 6 Feb 1748 son of Abiel and Abigail (Emery) Frye; Isaac d. at Wilton, NH, 3 Nov 1791.

A few days after the Battle of Lexington, Isaac Frye enlisted in the 3rd New Hampshire Regiment of Colonel Reed. On 4 March 1776, he was charged with raising a Company of Colonel Scammel's Regiment. He was appointed Captain in the 3rd New York Regiment. He was appointed muster master 5 April 1782. He achieved the rank of Major in 1783.[2317]

Elizabeth Frye wrote to her husband while he was at war. On 7 October 1776, she wrote the following: "Loveing Husband after my love to you I would inform you that through the goodness of God we are all well at this time. Blessed be God for it I have had a letter from you dated September 18 which gave me joy." She goes on to detail items she is sending to him with the bearer of the letter which included two pounds of butter and ginger. She also expresses her hope to see him before the next season, although she does not want him to neglect his duty.

Isaac Frye came to Wilton in 1770 or 1771 and maintained a farm there. He was well-respected in the community. Isaac Frye Highway in Wilton is named for him.

Elizabeth Holt and Isaac Frye were parents of ten children, the oldest child born at Andover and the remainder at Wilton.

i ISAAC FRYE, b. Dec 1769; d. at Wilton, 14 Sep 1814; m. at Wilton, 19 Jun 1794, HANNAH PHELPS, b. at Andover, 18 Jan 1774 daughter of Joseph and Abigail (Smith) Phelps; Hannah d. at Wilton, 28 Oct 1861.

[2314] Hazen, *History of Billerica*, p. 142.

[2315] Bradlee, *The Boston and Lowell Railroad*, p 14.

[2316] Middlesex County, MA: Probate File Papers, 1648-1871.Online database. AmericanAncestors.org. New England Historic Genealogical Society, 2014, case number 21266, probate of John Stearns.

[2317] Stearns, Genealogical and Family History of the State of Maine, p 908.

ii TIMOTHY FRYE, b. 21 Sep 1773; d. 17 Mar 1776.

iii ABIEL FRYE, b. 28 Jul 1774; d. about 1820. Abiel did not marry.

iv JOHN FRYE, b. 23 Aug 1775; d. at Edinboro, PA, 11 Sep 1851; m. LUCY WELLMAN, b. 1782 daughter of Timothy and Lucy (Skinner) Wellman;[2318] Lucy d. at Edinboro, 1867.

v TIMOTHY FRYE, b. 27 Oct 1777; d. at Weld, 7 Jan 1830; m. 8 Jan 1809. RACHEL HOLT, b. at Wilton, 7 Feb 1793 daughter of Simeon and Mary (Dale) Holt; Rachel d. at Weld, after 1860.

vi JOSHUA FRYE, b. 21 Dec 1779; d. at Wilton, 20 Jun 1864; m. 1st, about 1805, LOIS FARRINGTON, b. at Hubbardston, MA, 4 Mar 1783 daughter of Elijah and Elizabeth (Sawin) Farrington; Lois d. at Athens, VT, 17 Aug 1815. Joshua m. 2nd, 19 May 1831, LUCY JONES, b. at Hillsborough, 27 Apr 1787 daughter of Joel and Mary (Bishop) Jones; Lucy d. at Wilton, 17 Dec 1875.

vii BETSY FRYE, b. 21 Dec 1781; d. at Wilton, 9 Jun 1862. Betsy did not marry.

viii HANNAH FRYE, b. 30 May 1785; d. at Wilton, 31 Oct 1863; m. 26 Oct 1813, BENJAMIN BLANCHARD, b. at Wilton, 5 Apr 1781 son of Benjamin and Sarah (Griffin) Blanchard; Benjamin d. at Wilton, 12 Jul 1855.

ix ALFRED FRYE, b. 28 Feb 1787; d. at Wilton, 25 Sep 1867; m. 1st, 19 Aug 1817, LUCY FARRINGTON, b. at Hubbardston, 29 Apr 1787 daughter of Elijah and Elizabeth (Sawin) Farrington; Lucy d. at Wilton, 12 Dec 1835. Alfred m. 2nd, about 1836, BETSEY BLANCHARD, b. at Milford, 9 Jul 1801 daughter of Phineas and Sarah (Stevens) Blanchard; Betsey d. at Wilton, 11 Feb 1863.

x SARAH "SALLY" FRYE, b. 20 Sep 1790; d. at Wilton, 18 May 1835. Sally did not marry.

861) HANNAH HOLT *(Timothy Holt[4], Dorcas Abbott Holt[3], Timothy[2], George[1])*, b. at Andover, 18 Jan 1754 daughter of Timothy and Elizabeth (Holt) Holt; d. at Brookline, VT, Apr 1833; m. about 1774, as his second wife, RICHARD WHITNEY, b. at Oxford, MA, 22 Apr 1743 son of Israel and Hannah (Blodgett) Whitney' Richard d. at Brookline, 20 Oct 1816. Richard was first married to Sarah Butterfield who died in 1773.

Hannah and Richard lived in Wilton until 1795 then relocated to Brookline, Vermont after the births of nine children. Their youngest daughter was born in Vermont.

i ISRAEL WHITNEY, b. 4 Jul 1774; d. at Brookline, VT, 14 Dec 1850; m. at Wilton, 27 Nov 1794, ELIZABETH HOLT, b. at Wilton, Sep 1775 daughter of Timothy and Hannah (Johnson) Holt; Elizabeth d. at Brookline, 24 Nov 1874.

ii TIMOTHY HOLT WHITNEY, b. 21 Nov 1776; d. at Athens, VT, 16 Mar 1859; m. 11 Feb 1800, ABIGAIL BLANCHARD, b. at Wilton, 11 Jun 1777 daughter of Benjamin and Sarah (Griffin) Blanchard; Abigail d. at Athens, 27 Apr 1843.

iii EBENEZER WHITNEY, b. 3 Jul 1778; d. at Brookline, VT, 12 Apr 1869; m. DEBORAH JOY, b. 1778; Deborah d. at Brookline, 20 Sep 1850.

iv ABRAM WHITNEY, b. 8 Jan 1780; d. at Lindley, NY, Mar 1860; m. BETSEY, b. in VT about 1783; Betsey d. at Hornby, NY, after 1865.

v ISAAC WHITNEY, b. 21 Jan 1782; d. at Weston, VT, 22 Nov 1860; m. at Chester, VT, Dec 1806, ABIGAIL EDSON.

vi JACOB WHITNEY, b. 15 Jan 1784; d. 9 Jul 1785.

vii HANNAH WHITNEY, b. 15 Aug 1785; d. at Newfane, VT, 27 Jan 1871; m. JAMES CAMPBELL (whom she divorced). Hannah m. 2nd, JOSEPHUS ORVIS, b. 28 Feb 1780 son of Waitstill and Elizabeth (Church) Orvis; Josephus d. at South Newfane, 24 Dec 1855.

viii SARAH BUTTERFIELD WHITNEY, b. 1 Nov 1787; d. at Brookline, VT, 17 Sep 1873; m. JOEL HARWOOD, b. 1786; Joel d. at Brookline, 11 Dec 1849.

[2318] Wellman, *Descendants of Thomas Wellman*, p 213

ix SOLOMON WHITNEY, b. 26 Aug 1790; d. at Austinburg, OH, 1862 (probate); m. SARAH LEE, b. 1794; Sarah d. at Austinburg, after 1862.

x CHLOE WHITNEY, b. 22 Nov 1795; d. at Putney, VT, after 1870; m. DAVID KIDDER, b. at Oxford, MA, 11 May 1797 son of David and Sophia (Fressenden) Kidder; David d. at Putney, after 1870.

862) DORCAS HOLT *(Dorcas Holt Holt4, Dorcas Abbott Holt3, Timothy2, George1)*, b. at Andover, 19 Mar 1753 daughter of Thomas and Dorcas (Holt) Holt; m. 25 Nov 1773, her third cousin, MOSES LOVEJOY, b. 9 Sep 1751 son of Daniel and Mary (Holt) Lovejoy; Moses d. at Wilton, 19 Mar 1807.

Moses Lovejoy served in the Revolution in Nichols Regiment of militia in New Hampshire. He enlisted 29 September 1777 and was discharged 25 October 1777. This unit joined the northern Continental Army at Saratoga.[2319]

Moses and Dorcas were parents of six children born at Wilton.

i MOSES LOVEJOY, b. Feb 1776; died young

ii MOSES LOVEJOY, b. at Wilton, 29 Mar 1778; d. at Wilton, 13 Nov 1846; m. at Mason, 6 Nov 1807, NANCY TARBELL, b. at Mason, NH, 4 Jun 1786 daughter of Samuel and Anne (Heldrick) Tarbell;[2320] Nancy d. at Mason, NH, 16 Oct 1851.

iii DORCAS LOVEJOY, b. 30 May 1780; d. at Wilton, 8 Jul 1858. Dorcas did not marry.

iv HENRY LOVEJOY, b. at Wilton, 14 May 1782; d. at Weston, VT, 15 May 1848; m. 1st, about 1807, BETSEY PEASE, b. at Weston, 31 Oct 1788 daughter of Augustus and Tirzah (Hall) Pease; Betsey d. 16 Jan 1819. Henry m. 2nd, 2 Dec 1819, SALLY AUSTIN, b. at Weston, 11 Jun 1798 daughter of David and Dorcas (Barker) Austin; Sally d. at Weston, 17 Jul 1868.

v EZEKIEL LOVEJOY, b. at Wilton, 14 Nov 1784; d. at Weston, VT, 30 Jan 1840; m. at Wilton, 15 Feb 1810, EUNICE GAGE, b. at Pelham, NH, 7 Apr 1786 daughter of Pierce and Eunice (Eaton) Gage;[2321] Eunice d. at Weston, 7 Aug 1872.

vi HANNAH LOVEJOY, b. at Wilton, 22 Jun 1787; d. at Weld, ME, 5 Nov 1843; m. about 1815, STEPHEN HOLT, b. at Andover, 11 Apr 1786 son of William and Elizabeth (Jones) Holt; Stephen d. at Weld, 7 Dec 1855. After Hannah's death, Stephen married Phebe Douglas.

863) LOIS HOLT *(Dorcas Holt Holt4, Dorcas Abbott Holt3, Timothy2, George1)*, b. at Andover, 29 Oct 1760 daughter of Thomas and Dorcas (Holt) Holt; d. at Andover, 17 Apr 1852; m. 4 Jan 1785, MOSES PEARSON, b. at Wilmington, 6 Nov 1750 son of Nathan and Mary (Wilson) Pearson; Moses d. recorded at Andover 11 Aug 1836 (1835).[2322] Moses Pearson was first married to Hephzibah Jones.

Moses Pearson served in the Revolution as a private first enlisting in September 1776 in the militia company of Captain Putnam of Wilton, New Hampshire. In his pension application, Moses reported he was living in Amherst, New Hampshire at the time of his enlistment. He saw service at White Plains, New York. He had another enlistment for nine months in 1778 and marched to Fishkill for two months and was later in Hampstead, Connecticut. The total period of service was credited at twelve months. Moses and later his widow Lois received a pension related to his service.[2323]

Moses and Lois lived in Wilmington (although their deaths are recorded in Andover) and they were parents of nine children all born at Wilmington.

i THOMAS PEARSON, b. 28 Oct 1785; d. at Haverhill, 1 Aug 1863; m. at Andover, 24 Nov 1811, LUCY TROW, b. at Beverly, 1786 daughter of John and Hannah (Dodge) Trow; Lucy d. at Haverhill, about 1863.

ii NATHAN PEARSON, b. 20 Aug 1787; d. at Wilmington, 20 Feb 1855; m. LYDIA ANN HOWE.

iii HEPHZIBAH PEARSON, b. 28 Mar 1790; d. at North Andover, 29 Aug 1880; m. at Wilmington, 30 Nov 1815, WILLIAM TUCKER, b. at Wilmington, 10 Aug 1789 son of William and Hannah (Holt) Tucker; William d. 26 Mar 1861.

iv JOSEPH J. PEARSON, b. 5 Sep 1792; d. at Andover, 15 Jul 1841; m. at Andover, 23 Oct 1814, SARAH FOSTER, b. at Ashby, about 1790; Sarah d. at Andover, 11 Feb 1853.

2319 Compiled Service Records of Soldiers Who Served in the American Army During the Revolutionary War

2320 The 1824 will of Samuel Tarbell includes a bequest to his daughter Nancy Lovejoy.

2321 Gage, *A Record of Pierce Gage and His Descendants*, p 17

2322 The transcription of the death record says 1835 but the pension application and the gravestone say 1836.

2323 U.S., Revolutionary War Pension and Bounty-Land Warrant Application Files, 1800-1900

v ABIEL PEARSON, b. 8 Jun 1795; d. at Wilmington, 9 Nov 1851; m. at Reading, 18 Apr 1822, JERUSHA DAMON, b. about 1804 perhaps the daughter of Edmund and Lucy (Flint) Damon; Lucy d. at Andover, 21 Feb 1884.

vi JABEZ PEARSON, b. 1 Aug 1797; d. at Boston, 28 Apr 1850; m. at Andover, 15 Sep 1823, OLIVE P. TUCKER.

vii JAMES PEARSON, b. 21 Dec 1799. Nothing further certain is known, but it is possible he was the James Pearson who married ELIZA ANN BRADLEY in Boston 6 Dec 1827. James's brother Jabez was in Boston. This is speculation at this point. If so, James died in Boston in 1836 (probate May 1836) leaving two sons, James Bradley Pearson and Joel F. Pearson.

viii AMOS PEARSON, b. 5 oct 1802; d. at Haverhill, MA, 3 Jul 1866; m. at Boston, 13 Feb 1836, ANNIS TROW, b. at Andover, 10 May 1800 daughter of Dudley and Annis (Johnson) Trow; Annis d. at Medford, 20 Apr 1873.

ix KENDALL PEARSON, b. 30 Jan 1805; d. recorded at Andover, 16 May 1824.

864) WILLIAM HOLT *(Dorcas Holt Holt⁴, Dorcas Abbott Holt³, Timothy², George¹)*, b. at Andover, 7 Sep 1763 son of Thomas and Dorcas (Holt) Holt; d. at Wilton, 23 Dec 1810; m. 29 Jul 1784, ELIZABETH JONES, b. at Andover, about 1763 daughter of Jacob and Mary (Winn) Jones;[2324][2325] Elizabeth d. at Weld, ME, 1829.

William Holt and Elizabeth Jones were parents of eight children, the oldest six at Andover and youngest two at Wilton, New Hampshire.

i JACOB HOLT, b. 13 Dec 1784; d. by suicide in Boston Harbor, Dec 1817; m. at Beverly, 19 Oct 1806, HANNAH RAYMOND, b. at Beverly, 19 Mar 1781 daughter of David and Hannah (Giles) Raymond. Jacob was a sea captain. He committed suicide by jumping into Boston Harbor.[2326]

ii STEPHEN HOLT, b. 11 Apr 1786; d. at Weld, ME, 7 Dec 1855; m. 1st, about 1815, his first cousin, HANNAH LOVEJOY *(Dorcas Holt Lovejoy⁵, Dorcas Holt Holt⁴, Dorcas Abbott Holt³, Timothy², George¹)*, b. at Wilton 22 Jun 1787 daughter of Moses and Dorcas (Holt) Lovejoy; Hannah d. at Weld, 5 Nov 1843. Stephen m. 2nd, about 1846, PHEBE DOUGLAS. Hannah Lovejoy is a child in Family 862.

iii WILLIAM HOLT, b. 6 Mar 1788; d. at sea, 22 Oct 1820; m. 28 Nov 1812, LUCY WOODBURY, b. at Beverly, 31 May 1789 daughter of Thomas and Jane (Homan) Woodbury; Lucy d. at Beverly, 19 Aug 1870. William was master of a ship out of Beverly and died while on voyage.

iv ELIZABETH HOLT, b. 12 Mar 1790; d. Mar 1797.

v JOSEPH HOLT, b. 28 Jan 1792; d. at Wilton, 20 Jun 1864; m. at Wilton, 31 Jan 1813, BETSEY SMITH, b. at Wilton, 9 Jan 1791 daughter of Uriah and Lydia (Keyes) Smith; Betsey d. at Wilton, 8 Sep 1869.

vi ASA HOLT, b. 5 May 1794; d. at Weld, ME, 12 Jul 1825; m. at Brattleboro, VT, 24 Jul 1822, SYBIL BUTTERFIELD, b. at Brattleboro, 5 Apr 1792 daughter of Benjamin and Lois (Herrick) Butterfield; Sybil d. at Weld, 22 Dec 1830. After Asa's death Sybil married Joshua Eaton.

vii ELIZABETH HOLT, b. about 1798; d. at Weld, ME, 23 Mar 1867; m. at Andover, MA, 16 Feb 1818, BENJAMIN HOUGHTON, b. about 1790; Benjamin d. at Weld, 6 Mar 1882.

viii NATHAN HOLT, b. about 1801; d. at Weld, ME, after 1880; m. Nov 1824, PHEBE SEVERY, b. in ME, 5 Dec 1803 daughter of Aaron and Phebe (Tucker) Severy; Phebe d. 16 Nov 1884.

865) JOSEPH HOLT *(Dorcas Holt Holt⁴, Dorcas Abbott Holt³, Timothy², George¹)*, b. at Andover, 29 Sep 1766 son of Thomas and Dorcas (Holt) Holt; d. at Andover, 8 Jun 1791; m. 27 Nov 1788, his third cousin once removed, ABIGAIL HOLT, b. 19 May 1767 daughter of Samuel and Abigail (Blanchard) Holt; Abigail d. 13 May 1821.

Joseph Holt died at the young age 24 of nervous fever.[2327] Joseph and Abigail had two children at Andover, the younger child born after Joseph's death.

[2324] A birth record was not located for Elizabeth, but the will of Jacob Jones includes a bequest to his daughter Betty.
[2325] Bartlett, *Hugh Jones of Salem*, p 18
[2326] Newspaper Extractions from the Northeast, 1704-1930
[2327] Joseph, jr., nervous fever, bur. June 8, 1791, a. 24 y. 9 m. CR2

i JOSEPH HOLT, b. 20 Jan 1790; d. at Andover, 4 Jul 1866; m. 18 Oct 1821, ELIZABETH BRADDOCK, b. in ME, 1792 daughter of John Braddock; Elizabeth d. at Andover, 3 Dec 1875.

ii SAMUEL HOLT, b. 24 Sep 1791; d. 1 Apr 1802.

866) PHEBE HOLT *(Joshua Holt⁴, Dorcas Abbott Holt³, Timothy², George¹)*, b. at Andover, 28 Nov 1756 daughter of Joshua and Phebe (Farnum) Holt; d. at Greenfield, 1849; m. 11 Dec 1778, JOSEPH BATCHELDER, b. 6 Mar 1748 son of Joseph and Judith (Rea) Batchelder; Joseph d. 1826.

This family started in Andover, were in Lyndeborough where at least one child was born, and were in Greenfield by about 1786. Joseph was a deacon in Greenfield. Phebe Holt and Joseph Batchelder were parents of ten children.[2328]

i ANNA CARLTON BATCHELDER, b. at Andover, 2 Apr 1781; d. after 1850 when she and Hezekiah were living in Lyndeborough; m. 25 Feb 1813, HEZEKIAH DUNKLEE, b. at Greenfield, 16 Feb 1784 son of Hezekiah and Mehitable (White) Duncklee; Hexekiah d. at Francestown, 16 Nov 1863.

ii PHEBE BATCHELDER, b. at Lyndeborough, 2 Nov 1782; d. at Mont Vernon, NH, 20 Feb 1866; m. Apr 1820, WILLIAM RICHARDSON, b. at Billerica, MA, 20 Aug 1778 son of Jacob and Sarah (Brown) Richardson; William d. at Mont Vernon, 16 Mar 1863.

iii FANNY BATCHELDER, b. 30 Aug 1784

iv JOSEPH BATCHELDER, b. 13 Mar 1786; d. at Peoria, IL, 27 Nov 1849; m. 1st, at Athol, MA, 20 May 1819, MARY TILESTON HUMPHREY, b. at Athol, 5 Jul 1795 daughter of John and Hannah (Brinton) Humphrey; Mary d. at Athol, 20 Aug 1825. Joseph m. 2nd, 5 Jan 1832, RACHEL STONE, b. at Jericho, NY, 26 Sep 1796 daughter of William and Tamson (Graves) Stone;[2329] Rachel d. at Peoria, 22 Aug 1842.

v CHLOE BATCHELDER, b. at Greenfield, 22 Feb 1788; d. at Tioga, NY, after 1870; m. 30 Mar 1817, MOSES CARLETON, b. at Lyndeborough, 7 Sep 1792 son of Jeremiah and Lois (Hoyt) Carleton; Moses d. at Tioga, after 1860.

vi BETSEY BATCHELDER, b. 29 May 1789; d. at Greenwood, NY, 4 Aug 1856; m. 30 Dec 1813, JOHN JOHNSON HOLT, b. at Wilton, 21 Jul 1787 son of Simeon and Mary (Dale) Holt; John d. at Jasper, NY, after 1870.

vii JOHN BATCHELDER, b. 7 May 1791; d. 27 May 1792.

viii PERSIS BATCHELDER, b. 6 May 1793

ix JUDITH BATCHELDER, b. 19 May 1795

x LUCY BATCHELDER, b. 3 Jul 1797

867) JOSHUA HOLT *(Joshua Holt⁴, Dorcas Abbott Holt³, Timothy², George¹)*, b. at Andover, 17 Jan 1758 son of Joshua and Phebe (Farnum) Holt; d at Greenfield, 14 Mar 1835; m. 31 Oct 1782,[2330] HANNAH INGALLS, b. 20 Feb 1759 daughter of David and Priscilla (Howe) Ingalls; Hannah d. 1 Dec 1838.

Joshua served in the Revolutionary War. After the war, he settled in New Hampshire in the area later known as Greenfield on land his father had purchased prior to 1780.[2331][2332] He received a pension of thirty-six dollars per year for his war service.[2333]

In his will dated 13 March 1835, left five dollars each to his children Joshua, Farnum, Hannah Balch, and Mary. His son Herman, who "has been absent for many years," also receives five dollars whenever he returns. All the remainder of the estate is bequeathed to his beloved wife Hannah and it is to be at her entire use and disposal. Executors of the estate are Hannah and Joshua's brother Stephen Holt.[2334]

Hannah Ingalls Holt did not leave a will. Her estate was probated in 1839 when Stephen Holt petitioned to be administrator as her "several children" had not stepped forward to administer the estate. The total value of her estate was $1722 which included real estate valued at $850 being one undivided half of the old Holt farm consisting of 170 acres and buildings.[2335]

Joshua Holt and Hannah Ingalls had six children born at Greenfield.

[2328] Pierce, Batchelder Genealogy, p 410

[2329] Stone, The Family of John Stone, p 27 (This genealogy was written by William Leete Stone who was Rachel's brother.)

[2330] This is the marriage date give by Hannah in her widow's pension application.

[2331] Durrie, Holt Genealogy, p 44

[2332] Hurd, *History of Hillsborough County, NH*, p 344

[2333] Revolutionary War Pension and Bounty-Land Warrant Application Files, fold3

[2334] New Hampshire, County Probate Records, 1660-1973, Hillsborough, 41:65, 37:255, 41:116, 41:285, Probate of Joshua Holt

[2335] New Hampshire, County Probate Records, 1660-1973, Hillsborough, 44:66, 43:499, 27:385, 46:212, probate of Hannah Holt

i JOSHUA HOLT, b. 13 Jun 1788; d. at Roseville Park, IA, 21 Jun 1848;[2336] m. at Antrim, 11 May 1815, ISABELLA READ NESMITH, b. at Antrim, 16 Oct 1784 daughter of James and Elizabeth (Brewster) Nesmith; Isabella d. at Indianapolis, after 1850. Joshua graduated from Dartmouth in 1814 and was a teacher in Harrisburg, PA and later in Indianapolis.[2337] Durrie's Holt genealogy describes him as having superior intellect "but intemperance wrought his ruin."[2338]

ii FARNUM HOLT, b. 15 Apr 1791; d. at Greenfield, 27 Feb 1865; m. 14 Jun 1816, his fourth cousin, LUCY CUMMINGS PEAVEY *(Lucy Cummings Peavey⁵, Elizabeth Abbott Cummings⁴, Benjamin³, Benjamin², George¹)*, b. at Greenfield, 3 Jul 1792 daughter of Peter and Lucy (Cummings) Peavey; Lucy d. at Milford, 13 Feb 1874. Lucy is a child in Family 1790.

iii NATHAN HOLT, b. and d. 1792 at age 11 weeks.

iv HERMAN HOLT, b. 4 Apr 1793. According to the Holt genealogy, he went to Mississippi. No records were located for him and he does not show up in any census records.

v HANNAH HOLT, b. 3 May 1796; d, at Francestown, 7 Oct 1856; m. about 1832, as his second wife, MASON BALCH, b. at Francestown, 23 Oct 1800 son of Isiah and Elizabeth (Epps) Balch; Mason d. at Greenfield, 21 Jul 1873. Mason was first married to Sabrina Holmes, and after Hannah's death, he married Elizabeth Gould (the widow Elizabeth Stiles).

vi MARY HOLT, b. 19 Aug 1798; d. at Greenfield, 23 Mar 1856. Mary was a teacher. She did not marry.

868) MARY HOLT *(Joshua Holt⁴, Dorcas Abbott Holt³, Timothy², George¹)*, b. at Andover, 5 Dec 1759 daughter of Joshua and Phebe (Farnum) Holt; d. at Greenfield, 9 Jul 1819; m. at Andover, 26 Aug 1784, ISAAC FOSTER, b. 23 Dec 1751 son of Jacob and Abigail (Frost) Foster. Isaac Foster was first married to Mary Hartwell who died in 1781.

Isaac Foster had his first marriage in Andover and his wife Mary Hartwell died there; they did not have children. Isaac Foster and Mary Holt married in Andover, although Mary's family was already in Greenfield. Isaac and Mary settled in Greenfield where their nine children were born.

i MARY FOSTER, b. about 1785; d. at Andover, 20 Feb 1862; m. 31 May 1806, her second cousin, JAMES ABBOTT *(Barachias⁵, Barachias⁴, John³, John², George¹)*, b. at Andover, 30 Mar 1780 son of Barachias and Sarah (Holt) Abbott; James d. at Andover, 4 Oct 1858. James Abbott is a child in Family 294.

ii DORCAS FOSTER, b. about 1787; d. at Greenfield, 8 May 1879; m. about 1838, JOSIAH TAYLOR, b. at Boxborough, MA, 3 Mar 1778 son of Silas and Mary (Wilkins) Taylor; Josiah d. at Temple, NH, 4 Oct 1850. Josiah Taylor was first married to Elizabeth Sargent.

iii ISAAC H. FOSTER, b. 1789; d. at Greenfield, 8 Mar 1882; m. about 1847, LUCINDA WOODWARD, b. at Lyndeborough, 1812 daughter of Ephraim and Hannah (Badger) Woodward; Lucinda d. at Bennington, NH, 29 Oct 1887.

iv TIMOTHY FOSTER, b. 1790; d. at Greenfield, 19 Nov 1863. Timothy did not marry.

v AMOS FOSTER, b. 31 Jul 1794; d. at Greenfield, 10 Oct 1882; m. 1st, about 1823, BETSEY PRATT, b. at Easthampton, MA, 13 Feb 1800 daughter of Joshua and Sylvia (Smith) Pratt;[2339] Betsey d. at Greenfield, 10 Dec 1853. Amos m. 2nd, about 1854, MARY M. DYKE, b. at Greenfield, 1810 daughter of Gideon and Mary (Fuller) Dyke; Mary d. at Peterborough, 29 Dec 1905. Mary Dyke was first married to Samuel Gould.

vi HANNAH FOSTER, b. 18 Jun 1796; d. at Tilton, NH, 17 Oct 1885; m. at Greenfield, 22 Jun 1829, her fourth cousin once removed, PASCHAL ABBOTT *(Nathan⁵, Job⁴, Jonathan³, Benjamin², George¹)*, b. at Andover, 23 Jul 1788 son of Nathan and Sarah (Ballard) Abbott; Paschal d. at Dexter, ME, 30 May 1859. Paschal Abbott was first married to MARY FOSTER ABBOTT (1791-1828) daughter of Job and Anna (Ballard) Abbott. Paschal Abbott is a child in Family 443. Mary Foster Abbott is a child in Family 589.

[2336] Joshua was living in Indianapolis at the time of his death but was on a trip to Iowa when he died.
[2337] Chapman, *Sketches of the Alumni of Dartmouth College*, p 172
[2338] Durrie, Holt Genealogy, p 94
[2339] Pratt, *The Pratt Family*, p 54

vii ABIGAIL FOSTER, b. 1799; d. at Lyndeborough, 7 Mar 1853; m. about 1848 as the third of his five wives, DAVID PUTNAM, b. at Lyndeborough, 19 Jun 1790 son of David and Abigail (Carleton) Putnam; David d. at Lyndeborough, 10 Jun 1870. David Putnam's other marriages were to Tryphena Butler, Sarah Fletcher, Nancy Pierce, and Sarah Brown.

viii PHEBE FOSTER, b. 1802; d. at Andover, 2 May 1886; m. at Brentwood, NH, as his second wife, JOSEPH CUMMINGS, b. at Andover, 6 Dec 1792 son of Stephen and Deborah (Peabody) Cummings; Joseph d. at Andover, 10 Oct 1860. Joseph was first married to Mary Poor.

ix ANN FOSTER, b. about 1805; d. at Medford, MA, 7 Mar 1869; m. at Medford, 1 Jan 1837, as his second wife, THOMAS OLIVER PRATT, b. at Chelsea, 26 Apr 1792 son of Daniel and Abigail (Wilcott) Pratt; Thomas d. at Medford, 24 Jun 1870. Thomas was first married to Phebe Hudson.

869) ABIAH HOLT *(Joshua Holt[4], Dorcas Abbott Holt[3], Timothy[2], George[1])*, b. at Andover, 16 Apr 1761 daughter of Joshua and Phebe (Farnum) Holt; d. at Hancock, NH, 4 May 1841; m. 21 Jun 1791, as his second wife, DANIEL KIMBALL, b. at Ipswich, 20 Oct 1755 son of Daniel and Hephzibah (Howe) Kimball; d. 24 May 1843. Daniel's first wife was Elizabeth Osgood.

Daniel Kimball and Abiah Holt made their home in Hancock, New Hampshire where Daniel served as a deacon and selectman. He had served in the Revolution and worked at a powder mill making gunpowder for the Continental army.[2340]

Daniel had three children with his first wife Elizabeth Osgood. Daniel and Abiah Kimball were parents of eight children all born at Hancock.

i BETSEY KIMBALL, b. 1 Apr 1793; d. at Unadilla, NY, 6 Mar 1872; m. at Hancock, NH, 30 Jan 1817, EPHRAIM SMITH, b. 18 Apr 1789 son of James and Keturah (Putnam) Smith; Ephraim d. at Unadilla, 1 Aug 1862.

ii PHEBE KIMBALL, b. 28 Mar 1795; d. at Andover, 18 Jan 1836; m. at Andover, 20 Oct 1814, RALPH HOLBROOK CHANDLER, b. at Andover, 17 Feb 1791 son of John and Mary (King) Chandler; Ralph d. at Andover, Aug 1861. After Phebe's death, Ralph married Phebe's sister Mary (see below).

iii HANNAH KIMBALL, b. 17 Nov 1796; d. at Hancock, 1881; m. 16 Sep 1818, LUKE BOWERS, b. at Hancock, 25 Oct 1792 son of John and Elizabeth (Boutelle) Bowers; Luke d. at Hancock, 11 Aug 1834.

iv ANNA KIMBALL, b. 23 Jul 1798; d. Nov 1800.

v JOSEPH KIMBALL, b. 6 Dec 1799; d. Nov 1800.

vi JOSEPH KIMBALL, b. 21 Jan 1801; d. at Somerville, MA, Sep 1864; m. 20 Oct 1831, LUCY BOYD, b. at Antrim, 6 Oct 1802 daughter of James and Fanny (Baldwin) Boyd; Lucy d. at Antrim, 10 Feb 1879.

vii BENJAMIN KIMBALL, b. 8 Feb 1803; d. at Hancock, 18 Mar 1877; m. 27 Oct 1829, SALLY MATTHEWS, b. 5 Jan 1804 daughter of Thomas and Sally (Goodhue) Matthews; Sally d. at Hancock, 31 Mar 1887.

viii MARY KIMBALL, b. 14 Oct 1805; d. at Andover, 28 Jul 1891; m. at Hancock, 20 Oct 1836, RALPH HOLBROOK CHANDLER who was first married to Mary's sister Phebe (see above).

870) TIMOTHY HOLT *(Joshua Holt[4], Dorcas Abbott Holt[3], Timothy[2], George[1])*, b. at Andover, Apr 1767 son of Joshua and Phebe (Farnum) Holt; d. at Peterborough, 1856; m. 7 Nov 1793, his second cousin once removed, LYDIA HOLT, b. 18 Apr 1767 daughter of Joseph and Ruth (Johnson) Holt; Lydia d. 22 Nov 1825. Timothy m. 2nd, 11 Mar 1830, CHARITY SAVAGE, b. 1779 and d. at Peterborough, 28 Feb 1846.

Timothy and Lydia Holt located in Peterborough immediately after their marriage. Their farm was at East Mountain on the border of Peterborough and Greenfield. Timothy was deacon at the Congregational Church in Greenfield.[2341]

In his will written 29 April 1847 (proved 5 November 1856), Timothy Holt bequeathed to son Timothy Holt ten dollars. Daughter Chloe Baldwin wife of Ziba Baldwin and Ruth Hovey wife of Timothy Hovey each receive five dollars. Daughters Lydia Holt and Tabitha Holt have the privilege of occupying the southeast chamber, but if the executor disposes of the dwelling, they are to be paid five dollars each. Son Joseph Holt receives all the real estate and all the residue of the personal estate and is named executor.[2342]

Timothy and Lydia were parents of eight children. The births of the three oldest children are recorded at Andover, although the births may have occurred in Peterborough.

i LYDIA HOLT, b. 19 Apr 1795; d. at Peterborough, 5 Nov 1867. Lydia did not marry.

[2340] Hayward, *History of Hancock*, p 694

[2341] Smith and Morison, *History of Peterborough: Genealogy and History of Peterborough Families,* p 117

[2342] *New Hampshire. Probate Court (Hillsborough County);* Probate Place: *Hillsborough, New Hampshire, Probate Records, Vol 68, 1856-1869*, p 62

ii CHLOE HOLT, b. 30 Mar 1797; d. at Peterborough, 1876; m. 1834, ZIBA BALDWIN, b. at Milford, 1787 son of Jeremiah Baldwin; Ziba d. at Peterborough, 28 Oct 1872. Ziba was first married to Eliza Morse who died in 1831.

iii TABITHA HOLT, b. 16 Sep 1799; d. at Peterborough, 22 Jan 1855. Tabitha did not marry.

iv TIMOTHY HOLT, b. 16 Mar 1802; d. at Concord, 22 Apr 1867; m. 1825, MARY JACKMAN, b. at Boscawen, 12 Nov 1802 daughter of Nehemiah and Ruth (Flanders) Jackman; Mary d. at Concord, 12 Mar 1884.

v JOSEPH HOLT, b. 4 Apr 1804; d. at Peterborough, 13 Dec 1861; m. at Peterborough, 17 Jan 1832, MARY JANE MILLER, b. 1806 daughter of Adams and Ann (Robertson) Miller; Mary Jane d. at Lowell, 16 Jul 1870.

vi JOSHUA HOLT, b. 17 Mar 1807; d. 6 Jul 1811.

vii RUTH HOLT, b. 8 Feb 1809; d. 18 Jul 1811.

viii RUTH HOLT, b. 19 May 1812; d. at Peterborough, 29 Jul 1874; m. at Peterborough, 17 Nov 1836, TIMOTHY L. HOVEY, b. at Peterborough, 9 Aug 1813 son of Richard and Asenath (Baxter) Hovey; Timothy d. at Peterborough, 31 Mar 1887. After Ruth's death, Timothy married Myra Parker (widow of Charles Hutchinson) daughter of Jonathan and Alice (Gutterson) Parker.

871) SOLOMON HOLT *(Joshua Holt⁴, Dorcas Abbott Holt³, Timothy², George¹)*, b. at Andover, Dec 1768 son of Joshua and Phebe (Farnum) Holt; d. 15 Apr 1830; m. 22 May 1798, MARY CUMMINGS, b. about 1775 daughter of Justin and Mary (-) Cummings;[2343] Mary d. 8 Oct 1852.

Solomon Holt inherited the homestead from his father Joshua Holt. The historic home is at 111 Reservation Road in Andover. Solomon served as a deacon of the newly formed West Parish church in Andover.[2344]

In his will written 24 Feb 1830, Solomon Holt bequeaths to beloved wife Mary the use and improvement of one-third part of the homestead farm in Andover and several provisions for her support. Son Solomon is to furnish his mother with a horse and chaise. Sons Solomon and Nathan each receive $450. Son Abiathar receives his support including board and tuition to prosecute his studies "till he is fitted to enter college" and his executor is to furnish this support to Abiathar out of the estate. When he enters college, Abiathar will receive $450, and if he does not enter college, he will receive that amount when he is age twenty-one. Son Stephen will also receive $450 at age twenty-one, and until that time he is to labor on the farm for son Solomon, and Solomon will provide his support. Daughters Mary and Phebe C. each receive $200 and the improvements on the northeast chamber as long as they remain single. Mary and Phebe each receive a seat in the pew at the west parish meeting house. His wearing apparel is to be divided among his five sons, the books are to be equally divided among all the children, and his military equipment goes to Solomon. The remainder of the estate goes to Solomon who is also named executor.[2345]

Solomon Holt and Mary Cummings were parents of eight children born at Andover.

i SOLOMON HOLT, b. 1799; d. at Andover, 3 Apr 1883; m. 25 May 1824, his fourth cousin, PHEBE ABBOTT *(Benjamin⁵, Jonathan⁴, David³, Benjamin², George¹)*, b. at Andover, 27 Nov 1798 daughter of Benjamin and Rhoda (Chandler) Abbott; Phebe d. at Andover, 18 Oct 1872. Phebe is a child in Family 845.

ii MARY HOLT, b. 8 Mar 1801; d. 17 Feb 1803.

iii JOSHUA HOLT, b. 6 Mar 1804; d. at Haverhill, 24 Sep 1886; m. 1st, 26 Nov 1829, REBECCA BAILEY, b. at Andover, 19 Nov 1804 daughter of William and Rebecca (Gillson) Bailey; Rebecca d. 4 Sep 1834. Joshua m. 2nd, 2 Apr 1836, CHARLOTTE GAGE, b. at Andover, 18 Jun 1806 daughter of Nathaniel and Betsey (Kimball) Gage; Charlotte d. at Bradford, 30 Nov 1846. Joshua m. 3rd, 25 Oct 1848, his first cousin once removed, SARAH ABBOTT *(James⁶, Barachias⁵, Barachias⁴, John³, John², George¹)*, b. at Andover, 23 Jul 1814 daughter of James and Mary (Foster) Abbott; Sarah d. at Bradford, 10 Jul 1857. Joshua m. 4th, 7 Apr 1859, MARY A. SARGENT, b. at Walton, NH, about 1811 daughter of William and Susan (Stackpole) Sargent; Mary d. at Lawrence, 26 Sep 1891. Mary Sargent was first married to Charles Gault.

iv MARY HOLT, b. 20 Feb 1806; d. at Lyndon, VT, 23 Feb 1900; m. at Andover, 6 Jun 1837, as his second wife, SAMUEL READ HALL, b. at Croydon, NH, 27 Oct 1795 son of Samuel Read and Elizabeth (Hall) Hall; Samuel d. at Brownington, VT, 24 Jun 1877. Samuel was first married to Mary Dascomb.

2343 These are the parents given by Durrie's Holt family genealogy. There are no records that support this.

2344 Andover Historic Preservation, 111 Reservation Road, https://preservation.mhl.org/111-reservation-road

2345 Essex County, MA: Probate File Papers, 1638-1881.Online database. AmericanAncestors.org. New England Historic Genealogical Society, 2014. Case number 13695, probate of Solomon Holt

v NATHAN HOLT, b. 18 Apr 1808; d. at Lawrence, MA, 26 Dec 1891; m. at Andover, 21 Aug 1832, ABIGAIL COCHRAN, b. at Andover, 13 Apr 1812 daughter of Samuel and Mary (Bailey) Cochran; Abigail d. at Lawrence, 5 Sep 1892.

vi PHEBE CUMMINGS HOLT, b. 30 Apr 1810; d. at Andover, Aug 1858; m. at Andover, 19 Oct 1835, TIMOTHY DWIGHT PORTER STONE, b. at Cornwall, CT, 21 Jul 1811 son of Timothy and Mary (Merwin) Stone; Timothy d. at Andover, 11 Apr 1887. After Phebe's death, Timothy married Susan Margaret Dickinson.

vii ABIATHER HOLT, b. 31 Jan 1813; d. at Lowell, 18 Aug 1846; m. at Andover, 15 Sep 1836, ELIZABETH PLUNKETT, b. at Belfast, Ireland, 8 Feb 1814 daughter of John and Elizabeth (Keenan) Plunkett; Elizabeth d. at Matagorda, TX, 7 Jan 1887.[2346] Elizabeth immigrated with her parents around 1830.[2347] Abiather was a manufacturer in Lowell.

viii STEPHEN P. HOLT, b. 12 Feb 1816; d. at Andover, 17 Nov 1860; m. at Andover, 2 Dec 1847, JEANETTE M. SMITH, b. at Andover, 14 May 1824 daughter of Peter and Rebecca (Bartlett) Smith; Jeanette d. at Andover, 23 May 1872.

872) HANNAH HOLT *(Joshua Holt[4], Dorcas Abbott Holt[3], Timothy[2], George[1])*, b. at Andover, Jun 1771 daughter of Joshua and Phebe (Farnum) Holt; d. at Greenfield, 21 Apr 1842; m. 27 Nov 1794, her third cousin once removed, EPHRAIM HOLT *(Rhoda Abbott Holt[5], Ephraim[4], Stephen[3], John[2], George[1])*, b. 19 Mar 1769 son of Jacob and Rhoda (Abbott) Holt; Ephraim d. 24 Oct 1836. Ephraim Holt is a child in Family 322.

Ephraim and Hannah lived in Greenfield where Ephraim was a selectman from 1811 to 1827 and a representative to the General Court from 1829 to 1832.[2348]

Ephraim and Hannah Holt were parents of seven children born at Greenfield.

i HANNAH HOLT, b. 19 Oct 1795; d. at Peterborough, 15 Nov 1879. Hannah did not marry.

ii PHEBE HOLT, b. 9 Jun 1797; d. at Greenfield, 8 May 1862; m. 1836, her first cousin, JOHN HOLT *(John Holt[5], Joshua Holt[4], Dorcas Abbott Holt[3], Timothy[2], George[1])*, b. 9 Aug 1799 son of John and Dorcas (Abbott) Holt; John d. at Greenfield, 19 Apr 1869. After Phebe's death, John married Mary R. Holt, b. 1823 and d. at Greenfield, 24 Aug 1868. John Holt is a child in Family 526.

iii EPHRAIM HOLT, b. 2 Jul 1799; d. 26 Apr 1801.

iv JACOB HOLT, b. 23 Apr 1801; d. 26 Apr 1811.

v EPHRAIM HOLT, b. 12 Dec 1803; d. at Greenfield, 26 Aug 1867; m. SELINDA HILL, b. 26 May 1809 daughter of Job and Betsey (Perry) Hill; Selinda d. at Peterborough, 25 Aug 1891.

vi RHODA HOLT, b. 26 Dec 1809; d. 1 Jul 1811.

vii RHODA HOLT, b. 7 Aug 1815; d. at Pepperell, MA, 15 Feb 1849; m. 7 Oct 1845, JOHN VARNUM AMES, b. at Pepperell, 16 Jul 1821 son of John and Jane (Varnum) Ames; John d. after 1865. After Rhoda's death, John married Jane M. Wolcott in 1852 and Harriet R. Perry in 1855.

873) STEPHEN HOLT *(Joshua Holt[4], Dorcas Abbott Holt[3], Timothy[2], George[1])*, b. at Andover, May 1773 son of Joshua and Phebe (Farnum) Holt; d. at Greenfield, 26 Mar 1868; m. 1799, FANNY BOWERS, b. at Chelmsford, Jun 1773 daughter of Francis and Elizabeth (Holt) Bowers; Fanny d. 18 Apr 1828. Stephen married in 1831, MARGARET BATCHELDER, b. Sep 1784 and d. at Greenfield, 17 Aug 1867.

Stephen and Fanny Holt resided in Greenfield, New Hampshire where Stephen was a selectman in 1805 and 1806. Son Stephen Holt, Jr. operated the first steam mill in Greenfield.[2349]

In his will dated 2 September 1867, Stephen Holt bequeaths to Jane Bradford wife of Robert Bradford all the household furniture her mother brought at the time of our marriage. The remaining household items, books, and wearing apparel are to be divided among the following heirs: son Stephen Holt, Jr., daughter Mary Jaquith wife of Benjamin Jaquith, daughter Ann Jaquith widow of Ambrose Jaquith, and Benjamin F. Jaquith and Fannie Hardy children of daughter Fannie Jaquith deceased. All the rest and residue of the estate real and personal is to be divided among the same heirs with the addition of the children of daughter Rhoda Dane who is deceased. The children of Rhoda are Maria, Moses, and Dexter. He also

---

[2346] *Texas, Death Certificates, 1903-1982*, Texas Department of State Health Services; Austin Texas, USA.

[2347] "John Plunkett" Veteran Biographies, San Jacinto Museum of History, https://www.sanjacinto-museum.org/Library/Veteran_Bios/Bio_page/?id=677&army=Texian

[2348] Hurd, *History of Hillsborough County, New Hampshire*

[2349] Hurd, *History of Hillsborough County, New Hampshire*

directs the erection of gravestones for deceased family members. Ephraim Holt of Greenfield, New Hampshire was named executor.[2350]

Stephen Holt and Fanny Bowers were parents of eight children all born at Greenfield.

i FANNY HOLT, b. 3 Jun 1800; d. at Greenfield, 20 Nov 1834; m. at Lyndeborough, 26 Dec 1826, BENJAMIN JAQUITH, b. at Wilmington, MA, 13 Apr 1798 son of Benjamin and Phebe (Ames) Jaquith; Benjamin d. at Greenfield, 8 Dec 1881. Benjamin married second, Fanny's sister MARY BOWERS HOLT (see below). After Mary's death, Benjamin married Hannah Marshall.

ii BETSEY HOLT, b. 11 Jun 1802; d. 1816.

iii STEPHEN HOLT, b. 4 Mar 1804; d. 12 Mar 1804.

iv MARY BOWERS HOLT, b. 5 Jul 1805; d. at Greenfield, 1870; m. 1835, BENJAMIN JAQUITH (see sister Fanny above).

v RHODA HOLT, b. 11 Sep 1807; d. at Lowell, MA, 2 Apr 1846; m. MOSES DANE, b. about 1800 son of John and Deborah (Bailey) Dane; Moses d. at Cedar, IA, 24 Mar 1888. After Rhoda's death, Moses married Lavina Lane.

vi STEPHEN HOLT, b. 24 Apr 1810; d. at Francestown, NH, 24 Nov 1879; m. 2 Jun 1839, SARAH A. SPAULDING, b. at Lyndeborough, 2 Jan 1820 daughter of Henry and Lucy (Dunklee) Spaulding; Sarah d. at Francestown, 30 Mar 1890.

vii ANNA DANDRIDGE HOLT, b. 13 Jul 1812; d. at Peterborough, 17 Jan 1895; m. AMBROSE JAQUITH, b. 1810 son of Benjamin and Phebe (Ames) Jaquith; Ambrose d. at Greenfield, 6 Jan 1864.

viii BENJAMIN HOLT, b. 25 Nov 1816; d. 19 Apr 1827.

874) CHLOE HOLT *(Joshua Holt⁴, Dorcas Abbott Holt³, Timothy², George¹)*, b. at Andover, Jun 1775 daughter of Joshua and Phebe (Farnum) Holt; d. at Peterborough, 6 Nov 1849; m. 23 Oct 1798, FRANCIS BOWERS, b. at Chelmsford, 20 May 1775 son of Francis and Elizabeth (Holt) Bowers; Francis d. 15 Oct 1835.

Francis Bowers and Chloe Holt came to Peterborough about 1800. He had a homestead farm, but from about 1820 to 1835 he operated what was known as Holmes' Mills.[2351]

Francis Bowers did not leave a will. His widow declined administration, and this was assumed by Samuel Miller December 1835. On 18 June 1836, an allowance of one hundred-fifty dollars was made to the widow for her support. Real estate was valued at $1,075 and personal estate $1,483.97.[2352]

Francis Bowers and Chloe Holt were parents of eight children born at Peterborough.

i CHLOE BOWERS, b. 15 Jan 1799; d. at Francestown, 7 Oct 1844; m. JOHN DANE, b. at Andover, 22 Nov 1786 son of John and Deborah (Bailey) Dane; John d. at Francestown, 8 Jul 1850.

ii RUTH D. BOWERS, b. 20 Jan 1803; d. at Lowell, MA, 10 Dec 1883; m. 1831, SAMUEL MILLER, b. at Peterborough, about 1796 son of Hugh and Jane (Templeton) Miller; Samuel d. at Peterborough, 9 May 1872.

iii BENJAMIN BOWERS, b. 16 Mar 1807; d. 16 Mar 1811.

iv PHEBE F. BOWERS, b. 18 Apr 1809; d. 28 Feb 1811.

v FRANCIS H. BOWERS, b. 24 Feb 1811; d. at Billerica, MA, 5 Feb 1864; m. at Lowell, 16 Jan 1845, MARTHA A. SHERBURN, b. at Epsom, NH, about 1825 daughter of John and Abigail (Page) Sherburn; Martha d. at Somerville, MA, 23 Feb 1904.

vi HANNAH BOWERS, b. 11 Jun 1812; d. at Carrollton, MN, 11 May 1886; m. 1st, about 1835, EZRA DANE, b. at Greenfield, about 1802 son of John and Deborah (Bailey) Dane; Ezra d. before 1866. Hannah m. 2nd, at Lowell, 5 Aug 1867, LUKE MILLER, b. at Wakefield, NH, 18 Aug 1815 son of Andrew and Jenny (Ames) Miller; Luke d. at Lanesboro, MN, 5 Sep 1881. Luke Miller was first married to Abby D. Lovell.

[2350] *New Hampshire. Probate Court (Hillsborough County);* Probate Place: *Hillsborough, New Hampshire, Probate Records, Vol 81-84, 1865-1890*, p 218, will of Stephen Holt

[2351] Smith and Morison, *History of Peterborough: Genealogy and History of Peterborough Families*, p 21

[2352] New Hampshire, County Probate Records, 1660-1973, Hillsborough, 37:272, 41:229, 41:1, 27:308, probate of Francis Bowers, 1835

vii BETSEY H. BOWERS, b. 28 Nov 1820; d. at Peterborough, 15 Oct 1861. Betsey did not marry. She lived with her sister Ruth and her husband.

viii PHEBE F. BOWERS, b. 12 Oct 1823; d. at Lowell, 19 Apr 1910; m. at Lowell, 29 Nov 1883, NATHANIEL GAY, b. at Raymond, ME, 22 Apr 1814 son of Luther and Mary (Cash) Gay; Nathaniel d. at Lowell, 30 Jun 1889.

875) DANIEL HOLT *(Daniel Holt^4, Dorcas Abbott Holt^3, Timothy^2, George^1)*, b. at Andover, Dec 1761 son of Daniel and Hannah (Holt) Holt; d. at Fitchburg, 27 Nov 1830; m. 5 Jan 1790, MARY JONES, b. at Andover, about 1769 daughter of Jacob and Mary (Winn) Jones.[2353]

Daniel and Mary Holt had one daughter and Mary likely died soon after that. Deacon Daniel Holt lived in Fitchburg and does not seem to have remarried.

Daniel Holt did not leave a will and John Andrews assumed administration of the estate. Debts exceeded the value of the estate, the estate was sold, and creditors received eighty cents on the dollar.[2354]

i MARY "POLLY" HOLT, b. at Fitchburg, 14 Mar 1792; d. at Fitchburg, 19 Oct 1818; m. at Fitchburg, 7 Aug 1810, JOHN ANDREWS, b. at Ipswich, about 1786 son of Daniel and Susan (Choate) Andrews; John d. at Fitchburg, 1 Apr 1874. After Mary's death, John married Zoa Lawrence.

876) ABIEL HOLT *(Daniel Holt^4, Dorcas Abbott Holt^3, Timothy^2, George^1)*, b. at Andover, 8 Jun 1765 son of Daniel and Hannah (Holt) Holt; d. at Rindge, NH, 18 Jun 1825; m. 26 Jul 1791, PHEBE PUTNAM, b. at Fitchburg, 20 Sep 1770 daughter of Daniel and Rachel (-) Putnam; Phebe d. at Fitchburg, 12 Nov 1827.

Abiel and Phebe Holt spent their early married life in Fitchburg where four children were born. They relocated to Rindge, New Hampshire in 1806 where a fifth child was born. Abiel died in Rindge and Phebe seems to have returned to Fitchburg.[2355]

Abiel Holt did not leave a will. Widow Phebe Holt declined administration of the estate and requested oldest son Abiel to be named administrator. This document is also signed by Nathan Holt and Edah Holt. On 15 October 1825, widow Phebe Holt was allowed to take $150 from the estate account. A committee was named to set off the dower to widow Phebe.[2356]

i ABIEL HOLT, b. 16 Aug 1791; d. at Winthrop, MA, 10 Jun 1864; m. at Rindge, NH, Nov 1815, EDAH DARLING, b. at Rindge, 14 Apr 1792 daughter of Amos and Ede (Stone) Darling; Edah d. at Ashburnham, 30 Oct 1864.

ii DANIEL HOLT, b. about 1795. The History of Rindge reports that Daniel went to New York, had a family there, and died 1871. A tentative marriage is being suggested for him. Only one Daniel Holt of the correct age was found in the census records in the state of New York. That Daniel was married in Worcester County, MA which would fit for him. Daniel Holt, m. at Warren, MA, 16 Sep 1820, FRANCES BRIGHAM, b. at Brookfield, 27 Nov 1798 daughter of Tilly and Rachel (Walker) Brigham. Daniel Holt who married Frances was a grocer in New York. He died in New York City, 1866 (probate Sep 1866). Frances d. after 1870. Daniel and Frances Holt had two daughters, Sarah and Maria.

iii NATHAN HOLT, b. about 1798; d. 25 Oct 1827. Nathan did not marry.

iv EDAH PUTNAM HOLT, b. at Lunenburg, 29 Sep 1804; d. at Fitchburg, 9 Jul 1861; m. at Fitchburg, 18 Sep 1859, WILLIAM BASCOM PHELPS, b. at Fitchburg, 2 Mar 1811 son of Samuel and Elizabeth (Hartwell) Phelps; William d. at Fitchburg, 2 Apr 1882.

v LIBERTY HOLT, b. at Rindge, 9 Nov 1813; d. at Ashburnham, 29 Jun 1887; m. 1st, at Westminster, MA, 7 Nov 1837, LUCY WHEELER, b. at Westminster, 5 Oct 1812 daughter of Haman and Sally (Wheeler) Wheeler; Lucy d. at Fitchburg, 18 Jul 1863. Liberty m. 2nd, at Ashburnham, 30 Oct 1864, SARAH WHEELER, b. at Sudbury, about 1813 daughter of Nathan and Dolly (-) Wheeler; Sarah d. at Ayer, MA, 12 Sep 1899. Sarah Wheeler was first married to Elnathan Haynes.

[2353] The 1810 will of Jacob Jones includes a bequest to his granddaughter Mary Holt the child of his daughter Mary who is deceased.

[2354] Worcester County, MA: Probate File Papers, 1731-1881. Online database. AmericanAncestors.org. New England Historic Genealogical Society, 2015. Case 30625

[2355] Stearns, *History of the Town of Rindge*, p 556

[2356] *New Hampshire. Probate Court (Cheshire County)*; Probate Place: *Cheshire, New Hampshire, Estate Files, H324-H374, 1822-1826*, probate of Abiel Holt

Great-Grandchildren of Thomas Abbott and Hannah Gray

877) JOSEPH OSGOOD *(Elizabeth Abbott Osgood[4], Thomas[3], Thomas[2], George[1])*, b. at Andover, 5 Oct 1760 son of Samuel and Elizabeth (Abbott) Osgood; d. at Blue Hill, ME, 15 Mar 1854; m. 31 May 1785, HANNAH BAILEY, b. at Andover, 21 Dec 1765 daughter of Nathan and Deborah (Johnson) Bailey.

Joseph and Hannah Osgood started their family in Andover but were in Blue Hill, Maine by 1790 where their younger children were born. They were parents of eight children.

i HANNAH OSGOOD, b. May 1786 (baptized at Andover); d. at Blue Hill, 6 Jun 1806; m. 29 Jul 1805, SAMUEL DARLING, b. at Blue Hill, 28 Jul 1781 son of Jonathan and Hannah (Holt) Darling; Samuel d. at Patten, ME, 1859. After Hannah's death, Samuel married Polly Jellison. Hannah and Samuel did have one child, son Anson who married Eliza Long.

ii JOSEPH OSGOOD, b. 11 Aug 1788; d. 17 Aug 1788.

iii ELIZABETH OSGOOD, baptized at Andover, Nov 1789; d. at Blue Hill, 4 Feb 1858; m. Nov 1808, a distant Holt cousin, JEREMIAH THORNDIKE HOLT, b. at Beverly, MA, 12 May 1781 son of Jedediah and Sarah (Thorndike) Holt; Jeremiah d. at Blue Hill, Apr 1832.[2357]

iv PHEBE OSGOOD, b. at Blue Hill, 29 Mar 1792; d. at Blue Hill, 12 Feb 1847; m. Nov 1812, LEMUEL SMITH OSGOOD, b. at Blue Hill, 3 Jul 1788 son of Phineas and Mary (Smith) Osgood; Lemuel d. at Blue Hill, 3 Jul 1865. After Phebe's death, PHEBE PETERS HINCKLEY who was the widow of Phebe Osgood's brother Joseph Osgood (see below).

v SALLY OSGOOD, b. at Blue Hill, 3 Jun 1794; d. at Blue Hill, 7 Dec 1814; m. Mar 1810, as his second wife, NATHAN ELLIS, b. at Bellingham, MA, 7 Mar 1777 son of Amos and Hannah (Hill) Ellis; Nathan d. at Blue Hill, Apr 1848. Nathan was first married to Mary Bass and third married to Dolly b. Newell.

vi JOSEPH OSGOOD, b. at Blue Hill, 2 Aug 1796; d. at Blue Hill, 28 May 1834; m. Mar 1817, PHEBE PETERS HINCKLEY, b. at Blue Hill, 12 Jan 1794 daughter of Isaiah and Annie (Horton) Hinckley; Phebe d. at Blue Hill, 24 Dec 1876. After Joseph's death, Phebe married LEMUEL SMITH OSGOOD who had been married to Joseph's sister Phebe.

vii NATHAN BAILEY OSGOOD, b. 17 Aug 1799; d. at Manchester, NH, 15 Oct 1854; m. 4 Jan 1829, CLARISSA DOW, "of Gilmanton", b. about 1800. Clarissa was living in Manchester in 1866.

viii SEWELL OSGOOD, b. at Blue Hill, 10 Dec 1801; d. 18 Jun 1823.

878) DORCAS OSGOOD *(Elizabeth Abbott Osgood[4], Thomas[3], Thomas[2], George[1])*, b. at Andover, Mar 1763 daughter of Samuel and Elizabeth (Abbott) Osgood; d. at Blue Hill, ME, 27 Apr 1832; m. at Andover, 4 Oct 1791, THEODORE STEVENS, b. 12 Jul 1763 son of Benjamin and Hannah (Varnum) Stevens; Theodore d. 15 May 1820.

Theodore and Dorcas married in Andover 4 October 1791 and very soon after headed to Blue Hill, Maine where they arrived 7 November 1791.[2358]

In Theodore Stevens's will written 19 April 1820 (proved 27 June 1820, beloved wife Dorcas receives all the household furniture and one-third of all the estate real and personal. The rest of the estate goes to his two eldest sons Varnum Stevens and Benjamin Stevens. Varnum and Benjamin are then to pay the other legacies from the estate. These are eldest daughter Elizabeth O. Holt, seventy-five dollars; second daughter Lydia F. Parker, seventy-five dollars; youngest daughter Elvira Stevens, one hundred seventy-five dollars to be paid at the time of her marriage and she also has use of a room while she remains unmarried; and youngest son John Stevens, six hundred dollars when he comes of age and one yoke of oxen. There was an additional bequest of one hundred dollars to Congregational Society in Bluehill to be used for the pedobaptist congregational minister of the Calvinistic denomination while it should have such a minister; if not, then the money is to be used for the support of the missions to the Indians at Brainard. His two oldest sons Varnum and Benjamin are named executors.[2359]

Theodore Stevens and Dorcas Osgood were parents of seven children all born at Blue Hill.

[2357] Dodge and Cadage, *Families of Early Settlers in Blue Hill, ME*

[2358] Dodge and Candage, *Families of Early Settlers in Blue Hill, ME*, p 211

[2359] *Hancock, Maine, Estate Files, No 645-767, 1790-1915*, will of Theodore Stevens, will 19 April 1820, proved 27 June 1820

i ELIZABETH OSGOOD STEVENS, b. 8 Dec 1793; d. at Blue Hill, 20 Nov 1847; m. 27 Feb 1811, JONAH HOLT, b. at Blue Hill, 2 Nov 1783 son of Jedediah and Sarah (Thorndike) Holt; Jonah d. at Blue Hill, 19 Feb 1860. After Elizabeth's death, Jonah married Almira Wilcox.

ii VARNUM STEVENS, b. 10 Oct 1794; d. at Blue Hill, Nov 1869; m. 2 Dec 1819, SUSANNAH BROWN HINCKLEY, b. at Blue Hill, 21 Feb 1793 daughter of Nehemiah and Edith (Wood) Hinckley; Susannah d. at Blue Hill, 18 May 1857.

iii BENJAMIN STEVENS, b. 1 Jun 1796; d. at Blue Hill, 22 May 1873; m. 11 Nov 1829, MARY "POLLY" FISHER, b. at Blue Hill, 12 Feb 1808 daughter of Jonathan and Dolly (Battle) Fisher; Mary d. at San Francisco, CA, 28 Mar 1878. Mary died at the home of her daughter Harriet Stevens Morton In San Francisco.[2360]

iv LYDIA FAULKNER STEVENS, b. 23 May 1798; d. at Blue Hill, 28 Mar 1860; m. at Blue Hill, 4 Nov 1818, SIMEON PARKER, b. at Blue Hill, 24 Jul 1785 son of Robert and Ruth (Wood) Parker; Simeon d. at Blue Hill, 14 Feb 1826.

v LUCRETIA STEVENS, b. 18 Mar 1801; d. 31 Mar 1801.

vi ELVIRA STEVENS, b. 7 May 1802; d. at Blue Hill, 1891; m. about 1837, as his second wife, JOSEPH HINCKLEY, b. at Blue Hill, 8 Jan 1798 son of Nehemiah and Edith (Wood) Hinckley; Joseph d. at Blue Hill, 7 Nov 1884. Joseph was first married to Ruby Kimball (1804-1836) daughter of Seth and Molly (Peters) Kimball.

vii JOHN STEVENS, b. 12 Jun 1804; d. at Blue Hill, after 1890; m. Nov 1838, MARY JANE PERKINS, b. a Castine, ME, about 1811 daughter of Robert and Miriam (Plummer) Perkins;[2361] Mary Jane d. at Blue Hill, 19 Dec 1878.

879) THOMAS OSGOOD *(Elizabeth Abbott Osgood[4], Thomas[3], Thomas[2], George[1])*, b. at Andover, 11 Jun 1767 son of Samuel and Elizabeth (Abbott) Osgood; d. at Charlestown, MA, 21 Mar 1818; m. 15 Mar 1792, HANNAH STEVENS, b. at Andover, 23 May 1770 daughter of Benjamin and Hannah (Wilkins) Stevens; Hannah d. 1 Sep 1830.

Thomas Osgood was a housewright in Charlestown.

On 7 April 1818, widow Hannah Osgood declined administration of the estate and requested Oliver Brown be appointed and Isaac Osgood joined in that request. The eldest daughter Eliza Osgood was said to be insane and the second daughter Hannah W. Osgood also requested Mr. Brown to administer. Isaac, Eliza, and Hannah were the only children of age. The surety bond was fifteen thousand dollars. The personal estate was valued at $805.20 and the real estate at $4,718.50 which included a house on Salem Street and a house on Brook Street. The inventory listed each of the book titles and these were all religious texts excepting a dictionary, copies of American Clerk magazine, and copies of the Constitution. There were charges against the estate, and part of the estate was sold to settle debts. The settlement of the personal estate yielded a total of $16.87 for distribution to the heirs, $5.62 to the widow Hannah Osgood and $1.25 to each of the children: Isaac, Eliza, Hannah W., Harriet, Sarah, Mary, Thomas, Samuel, and Abigail. The final settlement of the real estate was 26 May 1828 with real estate valued at $4,500 and one-third of that set off to the widow.[2362]

Thomas and Hannah Osgood were parents of twelve children. Most of the children either did not marry or married late in life. At the 1850 census, children Isaac, Hannah, Harriet, Sarah, Mary, and Abigail were living together in Charlestown.[2363] Only son Samuel had children.

i ISAAC OSGOOD, b. at Andover, 28 Jan 1793; d. at Charlestown, 22 Jun 1865. Isaac did not marry. He was a successful merchant and tailor in Charlestown. At probate, real estate was valued at $15,348.40 and personal estate at $29,733.22.

ii ELIZABETH OSGOOD, b. at Andover, 17 Jul 1794; d. at Charlestown, 15 Jun 1860.

iii HANNAH WILKINS OSGOOD, b. at Andover, 3 Jun 1796; d. after 1865. Hannah did not marry. She was living in Charlestown in 1865 when her brother Isaac's estate was probated.

iv MARY OSGOOD, b. 19 Oct 1799; d. 6 Oct 1801.

v HARRIET OSGOOD, b. at Charlestown, 2 Feb 1802; d. at Fairfield, CT, Sep 1879; m. 11 Jun 1863, as his third wife, THOMAS MANDELL, b. 1793 son of Thomas and Sarah (Dillingham) Mandell; Thomas d. at New Bedford, 13 Feb 1870. Thomas was first married to Sophia Hart; his second wife was Harriet's sister Abigail.

vi SARAH PAGE OSGOOD, b. at Charlestown, 19 Jan 1804; d. at Somerville, 27 Dec 1874. Sarah did not marry. At the settlement of her brother Isaac's estate, Sarah was represented by *guardian ad litem,* but I could not locate a guardianship case for her.

[2360] Daily Alta California, San Francisco, p 4, "In this city, March 28, Mrs. Benjamin Stevens, a native of Maine, mother of Mrs. Reuben Morton, aged 70 years."
[2361] The 1854 will of Robert Perkins of Castine includes a bequest to his daughter Mary J. Stevens.
[2362] Middlesex County, MA: Probate File Papers, 1648-1871.Online database. AmericanAncestors.org. New England Historic Genealogical Society, 2014. Case 16284
[2363] *1850 United States Federal Census*, Year: 1850; Census Place: Charlestown, Middlesex, Massachusetts; Roll: M432_322; Page: 184B; Image: 374.

vii MARY OSGOOD, b. at Charlestown, 25 Aug 1805; d. after 1879 when living at New York City. Mary did not marry.

viii THOMAS ABBOTT OSGOOD, b. at Charlestown, 8 Feb 1807; d. at Charlestown, 4 May 1833. Thomas Abbott Osgood and his brother Isaac had a firm in Charlestown, I. & T.A. Osgood.

ix SAMUEL OSGOOD, b. 9 Oct 1808; d. 6 Oct 1809.

x SAMUEL OSGOOD, b. 16 Nov 1810; d. 9 Sep 1811.

xi SAMUEL OSGOOD, b. at Charlestown, 30 Aug 1812; d. at Fairfield, CT, 14 Apr 1880; m. 24 May 1843, ELLEN HASWELL MURDOCK, b. at Boston, 9 Dec 1820 daughter of George and Mary (Haswell) Murdock; Ellen d. at Fairfield, 9 Dec 1906. Reverend Samuel Osgood attended Harvard, completed his divinity studies at Cambridge, and later completed the D.D. degree at Harvard. He was a pastor in New York City and was a prolific writer on religious topics.[2364]

xii ABIGAIL OSGOOD, b. at Charlestown, 30 Sep 1814; d. at New Bedford, 22 Jan 1862; m. 11 Dec 1857, as his second wife, THOMAS MANDELL (see above the entry for sister Harriet).

880) CHRISTOPHER OSGOOD *(Elizabeth Abbott Osgood⁴, Thomas³, Thomas², George¹)*, b. at Andover, 25 Apr 1769 son of Samuel and Elizabeth (Abbott) Osgood; d. at Pembroke, 3 Oct 1841; m. 1st, 7 Nov 1793, his third cousin once removed, ANNA ABBOTT *(Rebecca Ballard Abbott⁵, Lydia Chandler Ballard⁴, John Chandler³, Hannah Abbott Chandler², George¹)*, b. Sep 1767 daughter of Zebadiah and Rebecca (Ballard) Abbott; Anna d. 26 Dec 1827. Anna Abbott is a descendant of both George Abbott of Andover and George Abbott of Rowley. Christopher m. 2nd, at Derry, NH, 17 Feb 1829, *another* ANNA ABBOTT *(Thomas⁴, Thomas³, Thomas², George¹)*, b. at Andover, 28 Feb 1769 daughter of Thomas and Lydia (Blunt) Abbott; Anna d. 31 May 1847.

Christopher Osgood was a sawmill and gristmill owner and operator in Pembroke. He also served as deacon on the Congregational church.

In his will dated 4 March 1840 (proved 4th Tuesday of October 1841), Christopher Osgood leaves to sons Herman A. Osgood and Ira B. Osgood three-fourths of the sawmill, sawmill yard, and water privileges, also his hundred-acre lot known as the Gulf lot. Son John H. Osgood receives three-fourths of the gristmill, gristmill yard, and water privileges, also a piece of land lying near the crossroad leading from the mill to the village, and thirty acres of land in Hooksett. Daughter Anna O. Parker receives privileges and occupancy of the dwelling house during her natural life, and after her decease the house goes to Herman. All the remainder of the estate is to be divided equally among his three sons. Herman is named executor.[2365] The Osgood genealogy reports that the second Mrs. Anna Osgood died in 1847 but there is no mention of her in the will.

Christopher Osgood and Anna Abbott were parents of four children.

i ANNA OSGOOD, b. at Concord, 2 Oct 1795; d. at Pembroke, 2 Aug 1868; m. 29 Aug 1815, as his second wife, her fourth cousin once removed, JOHN LADD PARKER *(John Parker⁵, Hannah Abbott Parker⁴, Timothy³, Timothy², George¹)*, b. at Pembroke, 1790 son of John and Martha (Lovejoy) Parker; John d. at Allenstown, NH, 21 Jan 1830. John was first married to Nancy Richardson in 1812. John Ladd Parker is a child in Family 349.

ii HERMAN ABBOT OSGOOD, b. at Pembroke, 20 Jul 1797; d. at Pembroke, 12 Feb 1858; m. 12 Sep 1828, his fourth cousin once removed, HANNAH ABBOTT *(William⁵, Samuel⁴, Jonathan³, Benjamin², George¹)*, b. at Pembroke, 10 Jul 1796 daughter of William and Dorcas (Parker) Abbott; Hannah d. at Pembroke, 3 Apr 1863. Hannah Abbott is a child in Family 819.

iii JOHN HALL OSGOOD, b. at Pembroke, 23 Apr 1801; d. at Pembroke, 1 Apr 1868; m. at Lowell, 12 May 1828, CYNTHIA STEWART, b. at Dunbarton, NH, 2 Feb 1808 daughter of William and Ann (Sargent) Stewart;[2366][2367] Cynthia d. at Pembroke, 22 Feb 1891.

iv IRA BALLARD OSGOOD, b. at Pembroke, 30 Dec 1804; d. at Allenstown, NH, 29 Oct 1869; m. 27 Nov 1831, ALICE PRESCOTT, b. at Pembroke, 3 Nov 1807 daughter of Samuel and Betsey (Clement) Prescott; Alice d. after 1880 (living with her son Alvah in Allenstown in 1880).

2364 Osgood, *Genealogy of the Descendants of John, Christopher, and William Osgood*, pp 293-294

2365 *New Hampshire. Probate Court (Merrimack County)*; Probate Place: *Merrimack, New Hampshire, Probate Records, Vol 16, 1839-1875*, p 81

2366 Stewart, George W. (1923) "John Stewart of Haverhill, Mass." Stewart Clan Magazine, vol 1, number 12, p 43

2367 The 1863 probate of Ann Sargent Stewart of Billerica names Cynthia Osgood of Suncook as an heir-at-law.

881) LYDIA ABBOTT *(Thomas⁴, Thomas³, Thomas², George¹)*, b. at Andover, 10 Apr 1757 daughter of Thomas and Lydia (Blunt) Abbot; d. at Deering, NH, 12 Nov 1826; m. at Andover, 4 May 1779, THOMAS ELIPHALET MERRILL, b. at South Hampton, NH, 25 Oct 1751 son of Eliphalet and Mary (Clough) Merrill; Thomas d. at Weare, NH, 19 Oct 1830.

Thomas and Lydia started their family in Andover, but relocated to Deering, New Hampshire where they were pioneers.[2368]

In his will written 3 August 1828, Thomas Merrill makes the following bequests: to Thomas Azro Merrill son of his deceased son Nathaniel, $60 which is to be held in trust by William Dickey; the other children of his son Nathaniel each receive $60 and these are Lydia, John, William, Martha, and Mary Merrill; Jonathan Clement late husband of deceased daughter Charlotte Lucretia receives $100 to aid him in educating his children; grandchildren Charlotte Lucretia Clements and Jonathan D. Clements, Jr. each receive $350 this amount to be held in trust; if the grandchildren do not live until they come of age, their shares will be divided among his sons Thomas A., Enos, and John; the wearing apparel is equally divided among the three sons. Additional provisions are made for Enos in the form of a trust; after Enos's death, the remainder of the trust is to be divided among Enos's wife and children. There are some complicated contingencies related to the legacy to Enos based on who dies when, although it is clear that Enos's legacy is to be held in trust for him. Son Thomas A. Merrill is named sole executor.[2369]

Thomas E. Merrill and Lydia Abbott were parents of five children.

i THOMAS ABBOT MERRILL, b. at Andover, 18 Jan 1780; d. at Middlebury, VT, 29 Apr 1855; m. 1st, at Bradford, MA, 18 Jun 1812, ELIZA "BETSEY" ALLEN, b. about 1787 daughter of Jonathan and Elizabeth (Kent) Allen; Eliza d. at Middlebury, 6 Aug 1834. Thomas m. 2nd, at Concord, NH, 13 Nov 1837, LYDIA BOARDMAN, b. at South Reading, MA, about 1791 daughter of Amos and Mary (Lewis) Boardman; Lydia d. at Rupert, VT, 3 Aug 1879.

ii NATHANIEL MERRILL, b. at Andover, 21 Nov 1782; d. at Deering, 16 Jul 1816; m. at Henniker, 20 Oct 1805, ANNA WILKINS, b. at Deering, 16 Feb 1785 daughter of Bray and Lucy (French) Wilkins; Anna d. at Deering, after 1850. After Nathaniel's death, Anna married Stephen M. Carr.

iii ENOS MERRILL, b. at Deering, 24 Mar 1786; d. at Weare, NH, 3 Jan 1836; m. at Francestown, 28 May 1811, ANNA GREGG, b. at Deering, 21 Aug 1789 daughter of Alexander and Mary (Christie) Gregg; Anna d. at Deering, 4 Sep 1834.

iv JOHN MERRILL, b. at Deering, 31 Oct 1790; d. at Weare, 29 Dec 1844 (will 23 Dec 1844, proved 8 Jan 1845); m. at Weare, 14 Nov 1833, NANCY BERNARD who has not been identified. In his will, he left his estate to Nancy during her life and it goes to his brother Thomas A. Merrill after her death.

v CHARLOTTE LUCRETIA MERRILL, b. at Deering, 19 Jan 1800; d. at Deering, 22 Mar 1828; m. 6 Apr 1824, JONATHAN D. CLEMENT, b. at Deering, 12 Aug 1794 son of Carleton and Kezia (Dow) Clement; Jonathan d. at Weare, 24 Jun 1862. After Charlotte's death, Jonathan married Cynthia Hanson.

882) HANNAH ABBOTT *(Thomas⁴, Thomas³, Thomas², George¹)*, b. at Andover, 5 May 1759 daughter of Thomas and Lydia (Blunt) Abbot; d. 14 Nov 1789; m. at Andover, 16 Feb 1777, ABIEL FAULKNER, b. at Andover, 4 Sep 1755 son of Abiel and Mary (Poor) Faulkner; Abiel d. 26 Nov 1818. After Hannah's death, Abiel married LYDIA OSGOOD (1754-1818) daughter of Samuel and Elizabeth (Abbott) Osgood *(Elizabeth Abbott Osgood⁴, Thomas³, Thomas², George¹)*. Abiel had a third marriage to Clarissa Dillaway.

Abiel served in the Revolution. He was a musical instrument maker.[2370]

Hannah Abbott and Abiel Faulkner were parents of six children all born at Andover.

i ABIEL FAULKNER, b. 6 Mar 1778; d. 1 Sep 1794.

ii HANNAH FAULKNER, b. Jul 1779; d. at Deering, NH, 1833; m. JAMES FULTON, b. at Francestown, 18 Oct 1777 son of Robert and Sarah (Brown) Fulton;[2371] James d. at Deering, 1844.

iii MARY FAULKNER, b. Jul 1781; d. 17 Jun 1840; m. 1802, her second cousin once removed, JOHN SULLIVAN ABBOTT *(Joshua⁴, Nathaniel³, Nathaniel², George¹)*, b. at Concord, 20 Aug 1778 son of Joshua and Eliza (Chandler) Abbott; John d. at Concord, 10 Aug 1810. Mary Faulkner and John Sullivan Abbott are Family 1022.

iv JOSEPH FAULKNER, b. 30 Jul 1783; d. at Andover, 5 Aug 1831; m. 13 Jun 1809, his fourth cousin, LYDIA RUSSELL *(Lydia Abbott Russell⁵, Barachias⁴, John³, John², George¹)*, b. at Andover, 5 Dec 1785 daughter of Uriah and Lydia (Abbott) Russell; Lydia d. at Andover, 2 Dec 1865. Lydia Russell is a child in Family 297.

[2368] Merrill, *A Merrill Memorial*, p 395

[2369] *New Hampshire. Probate Court (Hillsborough County)*; Probate Place: *Hillsborough, New Hampshire, Probate Records, Vol 38-39, 1829-1833*, will of Thomas Merrill, 3 Aug 1828.

[2370] Abbott, Charlotte Helen, Faulkner Family of Andover, https://www.mhl.org/sites/default/files/files/Abbott/Faulkner%20Family.pdf

[2371] Hurd, *History of Hillsborough County*, p 377

v JOHN FAULKNER, b. 7 mar 1785; d. 27 Jan 1823; m. 14 Jun 1812, HANNAH HOLT, b. at Andover, 7 Apr 1787 daughter of Joseph and Ruth (Johnson) Holt.

vi THOMAS FAULKNER, b. 5 Sep 1787; d. at Redfield, NY, 21 Jun 1813. Thomas served in the War of 1812. He died at the home of Dr. David Dickinson in Redfield. Thomas did not marry.[2372]

883) THOMAS ABBOTT *(Thomas⁴, Thomas³, Thomas², George¹)*, b. at Andover, 25 May 1761 son of Thomas and Lydia (Blunt) Abbot; d. at Providence, 11 Jun 1826;[2373] m. at Providence, 5 Jan 1800, RUTH OWEN, b. 21 Feb 1766 daughter of Joseph and Mary (Tripp) Owen; Ruth d. 26 Apr 1849.

Thomas Abbott did not leave a will and his estate entered probate 10 July 1826 with widow Ruth as administratrix.[2374] The available probate documents give a personal estate inventory with a value of $66.55.

Thomas Abbott and Ruth Owen had four children born at Providence. Only one of the children married.

i MARY ANN ABBOTT, b. 10 Jun 1802; d. at Providence, 10 Jan 1840. Mary Ann did not marry.

ii ELIZABETH OWEN ABBOTT, b. 19 May 1804; d. at Providence, 25 Mar 1833.

iii THOMAS BLUNT ABBOTT, b. 10 Mar 1806; d. at Providence, 26 Jan 1835. Thomas was a mariner. He did not marry.

iv NATHANIEL D. ABBOTT, b. 15 Apr 1808; d. at sea, 26 Apr 1851;[2375] m. 24 Feb 1840, ELIZABETH SIMMONS PALMER, b. 12 Jun 1813 daughter of Gideon and Elizabeth (Simmons) Palmer; Elizabeth d. at New York, NY, 13 Jan 1850. Captain Nathaniel Abbott was a master mariner. In 1850, after Elizabeth's death, Nathaniel Abbott and his children were living with Gideon and Elizabeth Palmer in Providence.

884) BETTE ABBOTT *(Thomas⁴, Thomas³, Thomas², George¹)*, b. at Andover, 25 Jun 1763 daughter of Thomas and Lydia (Blunt) Abbot; d. at Temple, ME, 12 Feb 1842; m. 17 Dec 1789, JONATHAN BALLARD, b. May 1761; Jonathan d. at Temple, 28 Nov 1830.

Jonathan Ballard was a farmer in Temple, Maine. Jonathan Ballard served a three-year enlistment from February 1777 through February 1780 as a private in Captain Farnum's Company and Colonel Francis's Regiment in the Massachusetts line. He was at Ticonderoga, Valley Forge, and West Point. He enlisted for another three-year term in 1781. His final honorable discharge was December 1783.

At the time of his pension application on 3 April 1818, Jonathan was in poor circumstances holding no deed to any real estate and would have been unable to meet any demands against him if required. He had sold his property to his son Jonathan A. Ballard for $700. In 1820, he was described as unable to work and his wife aged 57 was crippled. The total household consisted of six persons including daughter Lydia age 27 in feeble health, son Jonathan Adams age 24, John age 16 who was sick and under the care of a doctor, and daughter Hannah age 13 who was healthy.[2376]

Jonathan Ballard and Bette Abbott were parents of nine children all born at Temple, Maine.

i ELIZA ANN BALLARD, b. 8 Jun 1790; d. at Island Falls, ME, 30 Oct 1884; m. 29 Nov 1816, TIMOTHY CURRIER, b. 6 Apr 1789 son of Joseph and Elizabeth (Tweed) Currier;[2377] Timothy d. at Farmington, ME, 10 Oct 1858.

ii ALPHEUS BALLARD, b. 3 Jan 1792; d. in 1815 while a soldier (probate 13 Dec 1815 with father Jonathan Ballard as administrator).

iii LYDIA ABBOT BALLARD, b. 4 Apr 1793; d. at Farmington, 21 Feb 1890. Lydia did not marry.

[2372] Abbott, Charlotte Helen, Faulkner Family of Andover

[2373] *Rhode Island, Vital Extracts, 1636-1899.*

[2374] *Rhode Island. Court of Probate (Providence County);* Probate Place: *Providence, Rhode Island, Letters of Administration and Guardianship, 1804-1840, Probate Files, A4969-A5047, 1826-1827*

[2375] U.S., Newspaper Extractions from the Northeast, 1704-1930; Captain of the ship *Carrington*

[2376] Revolutionary War Pension and Bounty-Land Warrant Application Files

[2377] Butler, *A History of Farmington*, p 446

iv FREDERICK BALLARD, b. 19 Feb 1795; d. at Farmington, 11 Jun 1866; m. 1st, LYDIA TUCK, b. about 1795 daughter of Lemuel and Susanna (Fellows) Tuck;[2378] Lydia d. at Farmington, 11 Feb 1843. Frederick m. 2nd, ANNA, b. about 1793 who has not been identified; Anna d. at Farmington, 1890.

v JONATHAN ADAMS BALLARD, b. 24 Jan 1797; d. at Lawrence, MA, 11 Jun 1875; m. CAROLINE TAGGERT, b. at Temple, about 1807 daughter of John and Hannah (Hawes) Taggert;[2379] Caroline d. at Lawrence, 23 Oct 1890.

vi ANNA A. BALLARD, b. 8 Sep 1799; d. at Farmington, 9 Feb 1887; m. JONATHAN SCOTT ELLIS, b. at Nova Scotia, 10 Aug 1793 son of Ebenezer and Lydia (Scott) Ellis; Jonathan d. at Farmington, 30 Mar 1895.[2380]

vii SALVA ABBOT BALLARD, b. 5 Jan 1802; d. at Temple, ME, 13 Feb 1833. Salva did not marry.

viii JOHN BALLARD, b. 12 Dec 1803; d. at Perry, IL, 13 Feb 1867; m. at Dorchester, MA, 26 Jun 1835, ELIZABETH SIMMONS, b. at Dorchester, 16 Jun 1815 daughter of Benjamin and Elizabeth (Gould) Simmons; Elizabeth d. at Perry, 15 May 1853. John graduate from Boston College 1831 and was Reverend John Ballard and was a minister at Griggsville, IL.[2381]

ix HANNAH BALLARD, b. 11 Oct 1806; d. at Farmington, 8 Apr 1891. Hannah did not marry.

885) CHLOE ABBOTT *(Thomas⁴, Thomas³, Thomas², George¹)*, b. at Andover, 4 Nov 1771 daughter of Thomas and Lydia (Blunt) Abbot; d. at Melbourne, Québec; m. 19 Jan 1799, PETER FRYE, b. about 1771; Peter d. at Melbourne, Québec, 29 Jul 1843.[2382]

Peter Frye and Chloe Abbott had two children in Danville, Vermont and relocated to Melbourne, Québec by 1803.[2383] There were perhaps other children born in Canada, but none have been identified.

i TIMOTHY FRYE, b. at Danville, about 1800; d. at Melbourne, Québec, 1868; m. at Shipton, Québec, 1834, NANCY BEAMAN, b. at Canada East, 1813 daughter of Jonas and Abigail (Leighton) Beaman; Nancy d. at Windsor, 1892.

ii HERMAN ABBOTT FRYE, b. at Danville, about 1802; d. after 1871; m. 1st, at Ascot, Québec, 4 Jan 1827, his first cousin, MARY HOLT FRYE, b. at Danville, VT, about 1806 daughter of Samuel and Mary (Fletcher) Frye; Mary d. at Melbourne, Québec, 4 Feb 1852. Herman m. 2nd, at Windsor, 24 Mar 1854,[2384] MARY ANN WEBSTER who has not been identified; Mary Webster d. before 1871.

886) JOSEPH ABBOTT *(Jabez⁴, Thomas³, Thomas², George¹)*, b. at Concord, 5 Aug 1759 son of Jabez and Phebe (Abbott) Abbott; d. at Boscawen, NH, 7 Oct 1837; m. at Salisbury, 3 Apr 1794, MOLLY MELOON, b. at Salisbury, 25 Jan 1769 daughter of Nathaniel and Bathsheba (Tucker) Meloon; Molly d. 17 Dec 1847.

Joseph was a farmer in Boscawen in the area that is now Webster, New Hampshire. Joseph Abbott and Molly Meloon were parents of eight children born at Boscawen.

i PHEBE ABBOTT, b. 17 Dec 1794; d. 27 Mar 1796

ii NATHANIEL ABBOTT, b. 11 Aug 1796; d. at Fisherville (Penacook), NH, 28 Jan 1865; m. at Sandown, NH, 3 Dec 1827, MARY FITTS, b. at Sandown, 29 May 1797 daughter of Richard and Dorothy (Kimball) Fitts;[2385] Mary d. at Penacook, 3 Aug 1880.

iii JOSEPH ABBOTT, b. 23 Apr 1798; d. at Oakland, CA, 3 Dec 1878; m. at Salisbury, NH, 30 Jan 1834, MARY ELKINS, b. at Hampton, 26 May 1805 daughter of John and Mary (Brown) Elkins;[2386] Mary d. at Oakland, 22 Dec 1877.

[2378] Butler, *A History of Farmington*, p 593
[2379] The names of Caroline's parents are given on her death record.
[2380] The newspaper obituary of Jonathan corroborates his age as 101.
[2381] Abbot, *Genealogical Register*, p 86
[2382] Ancestry.com, *Quebec, Canada, Vital and Church Records (Drouin Collection), 1621-1968* (Provo, UT, USA: Ancestry.com Operations, Inc., 2008), Institut Généalogique Drouin; Montreal, Quebec, Canada; Author: Gabriel Drouin, comp..
[2383] Day, *History of the Eastern Townships*, p 434
[2384] Institut Généalogique Drouin; Montreal, Quebec, Canada; Drouin Collection; Author: Gabriel Drouin, comp. Widower Herman Abbott Frye married Mary Ann Webster.
[2385] Greeley, *Genealogy of the Greely-Greeley Family*, p 174
[2386] The 1866 will of John Elkins of Concord includes a bequest to daughter Mary E. Abbott wife of Joseph Abbott.

iv JABEZ ABBOTT, b. 3 Jul 1800; d. at Webster, NH, 8 Oct 1886; m. at Boscawen, 10 Dec 1828, EUNICE KNIGHT MOODY, b. 1803 *likely* the daughter of Benjamin and Abigail (George) Moody; Eunice d. at Webster, 21 Jul 1877.

v CLARISSA ABBOTT, b. 3 Jan 1803; d. 24 Sep 1804.

vi PHEBE ABBOTT, b. 26 Feb 1805, d. at Polk, MO, 16 Sep 1864; m. about 1831, her fourth cousin once removed, JASON D. WATKINS *(Sarah Waldron Watkins^{6}, Sarah Abbott Waldron^{5}, James^{4}, James^{3}, William^{2}, George^{1})*, b. at Warner, NH, 24 Jul 1809 son of Jason and Sarah (Waldron) Watkins; Jason d. at Polk, 21 Jul 1879.

vii IRA ABBOTT, b. 10 Sep 1807; d. at Concord, 2 Mar 1883; m. at Lowell, 12 Nov 1837, ALMIRA ELKINS, b. Jul 1812; Almira d. 26 Mar 1877.

viii NATHAN ABBOTT, b. 7 Feb 1811; d. at Concord, 14 Jul 1880; m. at Plymouth, NH, 1838, JENNETTE C. RYAN, b. at Plymouth, 1811 daughter of Isaac and Mehitable (Bradbury) Ryan;[2387][2388] Jennette d. at Boscawen, 7 Apr 1858.

887) PHEBE ABBOTT *(Jabez^{4}, Thomas^{3}, Thomas^{2}, George^{1})*, b. at Concord, 29 Oct 1762 daughter of Jabez and Phebe (Abbott) Abbott; d. at Boscawen, 14 Sep 1819; m. 29 Dec 1791, PAUL CLARK, b. at Newbury, 23 May 1762 son of Daniel and Mehitable (Hale) Clark;[2389] Paul d. 11 Jan 1808.

Just one child is known for Phebe Abbott and Paul Clark.

i MARY CLARK, b. at Boscawen, 30 Sep 1800; d. at Webster, NH, 17 Jun 1891; m. 28 Feb 1846, CALVIN MORRILL, b. at Boscawen, 6 Dec 1805 son of John Hobson and Lydia Jacques (Pearson) Morrill; Calvin d. at Webster, 14 May 1875.

888) NATHAN ABBOTT *(Jabez^{4}, Thomas^{3}, Thomas^{2}, George^{1})*, b. at Concord, 29 Jun 1765 son of Jabez and Phebe (Abbott) Abbott; d. at Concord, 19 Mar 1844; m. 24 Feb 1801, RHODA BRICKETT, b. at Newbury, MA, 24 Jul 1769 daughter of Thomas and Mary (Noyes) Brickett.

Nathan Abbott and Rhoda Brickett were parents of four children all born at Concord.

i NANCY BRICKETT ABBOTT, b. 2 Dec 1801; d. at Webster, NH, 24 Oct 1865; m. at Concord, 5 Feb 1823, JOSEPH CALEB MORSE, b. at Boscawen, b. 16 Aug 1796 son of Ezekiel and Mary (Prescott) Morse; Joseph d. at Webster, Sep 1863.

ii ALFRED CHANDLER ABBOTT, b. 29 Mar 1804; d. at Concord, 15 Apr 1887; m. 1st, at Concord, 21 Dec 1830, SARAH B. KNOWLES, b. at Epsom, about 1806 daughter of John and Temperance (Blake) Knowles; Sarah d. at Concord, 10 Mar 1836. Alfred m. 2nd, 12 Apr 1837, his third cousin once removed, JUDITH FARNUM *(Abner Farnum^{6}, Rebecca Merrill Farnum^{5}, Rebecca Abbott Merrill^{4}, Nathaniel^{3}, Nathaniel^{2}, George^{1})*, b. at Concord, 10 Sep 1808 daughter of Abner and Mary (Martin) Farnum; Judith d. at Concord, 27 Jun 1885.

iii PHEBE ABBOTT, b. 16 Mar 1806; d. at Irasburg, VT, after 1870 and before 1876; m. 2 Oct 1833, SIMON KNOWLES LOCKE, b. at Lyman, NH, 2 Nov 1802 son of William and Esther (Knowles) Locke; Simon d. at Barton, VT, after 1880. After Phebe's death, Simon married Cardelia Campbell at Barton on 11 Sep 1876.

iv DAVID ABBOTT, b. 12 Jul 1809; d. at Concord, 12 Apr 1882; m. 18 Dec 1838, his fourth cousin, SARAH HALE ABBOTT *(Amos^{3}, Rebecca Abbott Abbott^{3}, Nathaniel^{2}, George^{1})*, b. at Concord, 27 Jun 1809 daughter of Amos and Judith (Morse) Abbott; Sarah d. at Concord, 8 Sep 1884. David Abbott and Sarah Hale Abbott are Family 1136.

889) LYDIA ABBOTT *(Jabez^{4}, Thomas^{3}, Thomas^{2}, George^{1})*, b. at Concord, 10 Jun 1773 daughter of Jabez and Hephzibah (Stevens) Abbott; d, 23 Mar 1841; m. at Concord, 27 Oct 1796, CHRISTOPHER ROWELL, b. at Hampstead, 22 Aug 1769 son of Christopher and Ruth (Moors) Rowell.

Lydia and Christopher were parents of two children born at Concord.

[2387] The names of Jennette's parents are given and Isaac Ryan and Mehitable on her death record.

[2388] Stearns, *History of Plymouth*, p 605

[2389] Hale, *Genealogy of the Descendants of Thomas Hale*, p 248

i IRA ROWELL, b. 29 May 1797; d. at Concord, 14 Jun 1876; m. 1st, at Pembroke, 30 Dec 1824, ELIZABETH THOMPSON, b. at Pembroke, 13 Oct 1796 daughter of John and Margaret (Hemphill) Thompson;[2390] Elizabeth d. at Concord, 28 Apr 1826. Ira m. 2nd, 9 Par 1828, REBECCA KIMBELL, b. at Pembroke, 15 Jan 1802 daughter of Edward and Elizabeth (McAllister) Kimball; Rebecca d. at Concord, 12 Dec 1871.

ii THOMAS E. ROWELL, b. 12 Aug 1799; d. at Concord, 20 Apr 1832; m. at Concord, 27 Mar 1828, his fourth cousin once removed, BRIDGET WALKER FARNUM *(Phebe Abbott Farnum⁶, Reuben⁵, Reuben⁴, James³, William², George¹)*, b. at Concord, 19 Jan 1809 daughter of Peter Chandler and Phebe (Abbott) Farnum; Bridget d. at Concord, 19 Jan 1891. After Thomas's death, Bridget married Timothy Hoyt.

890) DYER ABBOTT *(Jabez⁴, Thomas³, Thomas², George¹)*, b. at Concord, 18 Jun 1778 son of Jabez and Hephzibah (Stevens) Abbott; d. at Henniker, 8 Mar 1832; m. at Boscawen, 1 Oct 1807, SARAH ATKINSON, b. at Boscawen, 19 Jul 1785 daughter of Benjamin and Jane (Varney) Atkinson.

Dyer Abbott was a farmer and worked as a joiner in Henniker. The family was first in Concord and Dyer was the chorister of the North Church in Concord in 1805[2391] and later the choir master at the church in Henniker. His musical talent seems to have been passed on as his granddaughter was Emma Almira Abbott founder of the Abbott English Opera Company.[2392]

Dyer Abbott and Sarah Atkinson were parents of twelve children, the oldest two births recorded at Concord and the remainder of the children at Henniker. Three of the children died in a four-day period in 1832.

i CHARLES ABBOTT, b. 20 Aug 1808; d. at Lowell, 29 Jan 1863; m. 1st, at Lowell, 23 Nov 1833, JANE WHITTEMORE, b. at Weston 17 Dec 1811 daughter of Aaron and Lucy (Sanderson) Weston; Jane d. at Weston, 2 Feb 1837. Charles m. 2nd, 30 Aug 1838, MARY PLUMMER, b. at Boscawen, 25 Aug 1805 daughter of John and Hannah (Jackman) Plummer; Mary d. Dec 1868.

ii SARAH JANE ABBOTT, b. 20 Jan 1810; d. at Holliston, MA, 20 Jun 1841; m. at Holliston, 22 Nov 1832, CHARLES OCTAVIUS MESSENGER, b. at Holliston, 1807 son of Samuel and Olive (Chase) Messenger; Charles d. at Rochester, NY, after 1875. After Sarah's death, Charles married Sarah's sister Maria (see below).

iii HERMAN ABBOTT, b. 16 Oct 1811; d. at Lowell, 16 May 1888; m. at Lowell, 24 Nov 1842, ELIZABETH R. SANBORN, b. about 1811; Elizabeth d. at Lowell, 1 May 1846.

iv MARIA ABBOTT, b. 24 Jul 1813; d. at Rochester, NY, after 1892; m. 1 Oct 1842, CHARLES OCTAVIUS MESSENGER who was first married to Maria's sister Sarah (see above).

v JOHN ABBOTT, b. 14 Aug 1815; d. at Carlisle, MA, 28 Nov 1883; m. at Lowell, 26 Oct 1845, HANNAH E. NOTTING, b. at Carlisle, 12 May 1818 daughter of Cyrus and Hannah (Wilkins) Notting; Hannah d. at Brockton, 5 Mar 1893.

vi SETH ABBOTT, b. 12 Mar 1817; d. at Chicago, 22 Oct 1901; m. at Woodstock, VT, 3 Oct 1842, ALMIRA PALMER, b. perhaps in New York, Jun 1815; Almira d. at Chicago, 25 Mar 1898.

vii FRANCIS BROWN ABBOTT, b. 12 Jan 1819; d. at Rockford, IL, 4 Oct 1903; m. at Lowell, 17 Mar 1842, HANNAH F. DODGE, b. about 1824; Hannah d. at Rockford, 17 Feb 1914.

viii PHEBE C. ABBOTT, b. 10 Feb 1821; d. 17 Feb 1832.

ix MARY ABBOTT, b. 26 Jan 1823; d. 12 Feb 1832.

x BENJAMIN ABBOTT, b. 20 Jan 1825; d. 13 Feb 1832.

xi PAUL C. ABBOTT, b. 6 Feb 1827; likely died young

xii BENJAMIN ABBOTT, b. 10 Jun 1832; d. 5 Jan 1833.

891) ASENATH ABBOTT *(Jabez⁴, Thomas³, Thomas², George¹)*, b. at Concord, 3 Oct 1781 daughter of Jabez and Hephzibah (Stevens) Abbott; d. at Pembroke, NH, 13 Apr 1854;[2393] m. 24 Feb 1804, THOMAS BRICKETT, b. at Pembroke, 7 Aug 1778 son of Thomas and Mary (Noyes) Brickett; Thomas d. at Pembroke, 10 Sep 1855 (probate of estate 25 Sep 1855).

Thomas Brickett was a farmer in Pembroke.

2390 Carter, *History of Pembroke*, p 308

2391 Cogswell, *History of Henniker*, p 439

2392 Martin, *The Life and Professional Career of Emma Abbott*

2393 Asenath and her husband Thomas Brickett are both listed in the 1850 U.S. Census living at Pembroke.

In his will written 1 April 1853, Thomas Brickett leaves to beloved wife Aseneth, in addition to her dower, the use of all the household furniture except one of the beds and the brass clock. After her decease, the household furniture is to go to daughters Mary, Sarah, and Aseneth. Wife Aseneth also receives one cow. Beloved son Irad Brickett receives one dollar. Son Abbott Brickett receives the use and improvement of, during his natural life, the property that Thomas purchased from Asa Moore in Pembroke where Abbott now lives. After Abbott's decease, this property is to go to Abbott's children who are Lovina Brickett, Sarah H. Brickett, Mary K. Brickett, Esther Brickett, Charles Brickett, and Gilford B. Brickett. Daughter Mary wife of Jeremiah Austin receives ten dollars in addition to what she has already received. Son Barnard Brickett receives three hundred dollars. Daughter Sarah H. Brickett receives two hundred dollars. Daughter Aseneth A. wife of David L. Holt receives one hundred dollars in addition to what she has received. Son Charles Brickett also receives two hundred dollars. All the remainder of the estate goes to sons Thomas W. Brickett and Josiah K. Brickett who are also named executors.[2394] Wife Asenath was living at the time of the will but died before the probate of the estate.

Thomas Brickett and Asenath Abbott were parents of eleven children all born at Pembroke.

i IRAD BRICKETT, b. 7 Oct 1804; d. at Cincinnati, OH, 1884; m. 18 Apr 1827, ESTHER KNOWLES BLAKE, b. at Chichester, NH, 16 Dec 1805 daughter of James and Jane (Sherburne) Blake; Esther d. at Cincinnati, 1882. This family seems to have been in Buffalo for a time before settling in Cincinnati.

ii ABBOTT BRICKETT, b. 17 Sep 1806; d. at Pembroke, 17 Jul 1875; m. about 1830, THEODATE DAVIS, b. at Chichester, about 1811 daughter of Joseph and Esther (Blake) Davis; Theodate d. at Northwood, NH, 27 Feb 1896. After Abbott's death, Theodate married Hiram Carter 27 Oct 1875.

iii MARY BRICKETT, b. 18 Nov 1808; d. at Bow, 18 Apr 1873; m. 24 Jun 1831, JEREMIAH AUSTIN, b. at Landaff, 19 Apr 1802 son of Benjamin and Anna (McConnell) Austin;[2395] Jeremiah d. at Bow, 10 Dec 1885.

iv BARNARD BRICKETT, b. 24 Feb 1811; d. at Pembroke, 12 Aug 1869. Barnard did not marry.

v SARAH HALE BRICKETT, b. 7 Mar 1813; d. 5 Feb 1815.

vi THOMAS WORSTER BRICKETT, b. 21 Apr 1815; d. at Pembroke, 14 Feb 1867. Thomas did not marry.

vii SARAH HALE BRICKETT, b. 18 Apr 1817; d. at Henniker, NH, 16 Mar 1891; m. 1st, 17 Apr 1857, MATTHIAS NUTTER, b. in NH, about 1807 *perhaps* the son of Matthias and Ruth (Smith) Nutter; Matthias d. at Pembroke, 6 Nov 1862; Matthias was first married to Sarah Gault. Sarah m. 2nd, 4 Sep 1871, ASA MOORE, b. at Pembroke, 13 Jun 1807 son of Daniel and Hannah (Martin) Moore; Asa d. at Henniker, 16 Aug 1881. Asa was first married to Serepta Pennock. Asa Moore and his first wife lived for a time in Ellicott, NY where two of Sarah's brothers lived.

viii CHARLES STEVEN BRICKETT, b. 22 Nov 1820; d. 8 Mar 1821.

ix JOSIAH KITTRIDGE BRICKETT, b. 15 Dec 1821; d. after 1865. Josiah does not seem to have married. He lived in Pembroke with two of his brothers in 1860 and in 1865 was living with his brother Charles in Ellicott, NY.

x ASENATH A. BRICKETT, b. 15 Jan 1824; d. at Pembroke, 7 Jan 1911; m. 26 Jan 1853, as his second wife, her fifth cousin, DAVID LOVEJOY HOLT *(Stephen Holt^6, Abigail Lovejoy Holt^5, Elizabeth Chandler Lovejoy^4, Zebadiah Chandler^3, Hannah Abbott Chandler^2, George^1)*, b. at Pembroke, 21 Apr 1821 son of Stephen and Polly (Knox) Holt; David d. at Pembroke, 2 Feb 1891. David was first married to Abby White Ames.

xi CHARLES BRICKETT, b. 6 Jul 1826; d. at Jamestown, NY, 2 Jan 1903; m. 20 Mar 1856, WELTHIA A. MOORE, b. in NH, about 1832 (parents not identified); Welthia d. after 1910, likely at Jamestown, NY.

892) AARON ABBOTT *(Aaron^4, Thomas^3, Thomas^2, George^1)*, b. at Concord, 11 Apr 1778 son of Aaron and Lydia (Abbott) Abbott; d. at Bethel, ME, 8 Sep 1856; m. 1 Jan 1800, his second cousin, SARAH ABBOTT *(Stephen^4, George^3, Thomas^2, George^1)*, b. at Concord, 26 Jun 1780 daughter of Stephen and Mary (Gile) Abbott; Sarah d. at Bethel, 1853.

Aaron Abbott was a farmer and tailor at Bethel, Maine. Aaron and Sarah Abbott were parents of seven children born at Bethel.

i CLARISSA ABBOTT, b. 25 May 1800; d. 20 Sep 1856. Clarissa did not marry.

[2394] *New Hampshire. Probate Court (Merrimack County)*; Probate Place: *Merrimack, New Hampshire, Probate Records, Vol 25, 1847-1856*, will of Thomas Brickett, pp 611-612

[2395] Carter, *History of Pembroke*, p 12

ii AARON ABBOTT, b. 20 Dec 1802; d. at Bethel, 15 Aug 1878; m. at Wells, ME, 27 Jun 1829, MARY DAY, b. at Wells, 8 May 1802 daughter of Moses W. and Elizabeth (Littlefield) Wells; Mary d. after 1870.

iii SARAH ABBOTT, b. 12 Mar 1806; d. at Bethel, 14 Apr 1874; m. about 1831, as his second wife, her second cousin, TIMOTHY CAPEN *(Mary Abbott Capen[5], Edward[4], Edward[3], Thomas[2], George[1])*, b. 1793 son of Thomas and Mary (Abbott) Capen; Timothy d. at Bethel, 1872. Timothy was first married to Ruth York. Timothy Capen is a child in Family 907.

iv LYDIA ABBOTT, b. 18 Jul 1809; d. 1 Jan 1834. Lydia did not marry.

v STEPHEN ABBOTT, b. 18 Feb 1812; d. at Bethel, 30 Oct 1861; m. at Harrison, ME, 4 May 1841, NANCY GODDARD, b. 28 Jun 1819 daughter of Oliver and Tryphena (Bardens) Goddard; Nancy d. at Bethel, 30 Mar 1901.

vi SAMUEL ABBOTT, b. 1 Aug 1815; d. 18 Jul 1823.

vii JOHN ABBOTT, b. 27 Apr 1819; d. at Bethel, 29 Jan 1902; m. 31 Mar 1841, his second cousin once removed, SARAH ACKLEY *(Deborah Capen Ackley[6], Mary Abbott Capen[5], Edward[4], Edward[3], Thomas[2], George[1])*, b. at Rumford, 22 Jan 1820 daughter of William and Deborah (Capen) Ackley; Sarah d. at Bethel, 1865.

893) JACOB ABBOTT *(Nathan[4], Thomas[3], Thomas[2], George[1])*, b. at Concord, NH, 16 Jan 1769 son of Nathan and Betty (Farnum) Abbott; d. at Rumford, ME, 13 Jan 1838; m. 1802, BETSEY KNAPP, b. 4 Mar 1782;[2396] Betsey d. at Rumford, ME, 18 Mar 1831.

Jacob Abbott and Betsey Knapp were parents of seven children all born at Rumford, Maine.

i NATHAN ABBOTT, b. 18 Nov 1804; d. at Rumford, 23 Feb 1872; m. 18 May 1824, BETSEY WOOD, b. at Rumford, 4 Mar 1804 daughter of Phineas and Martha (Spalding) Wood; Betsey d. at Rumford, 23 Sep 1870.

ii ESTHER ABBOTT, b. 27 May 1809; d. at Rumford, 5 Aug 1882; m. at Rumford, ME, 27 Nov 1842, LEANDER HOWARD, b. 1819; Leander d. at Mexico, ME, 14 May 1865. Leander registered for the draft in the Civil War 1 July 1863 at Mexico, ME.

iii JOHN M. C. ABBOTT, b. 14 May 1813; m. at Waldo, ME, 14 Aug 1836, CHARLOTTE HAYCOCK.

iv DANIEL S. ABBOTT, b. 21 Feb 1816; m. 14 Jan 1841, CYNTHIA WHEELER FARNUM, b. at Rumford, 13 Oct 1820 daughter of Merrill and Sarah (Virgin) Farnum.

v BETSEY F. ABBOTT, b. 8 Jan 1819; d. at Newport, ME, 28 Nov 1896; m. 9 May 1837, PETER D. BRACKETT, b. 1817; Peter d. at Rumford, ME, 1865.

vi ROSILLA ABBOTT, b. 9 Jun 1822; d. at Putnam, CT, 22 Dec 1865; m. at Rumford, 8 Dec 1838, DANIEL PORTER, b. at Mexico, ME, 4 Jun 1815 son of Daniel and Abigail (-) Porter.

vii MELISSA ABBOTT, b. 3 May 1828; d. at Rumford Falls, ME, 21 Nov 1904. Melissa did not marry.

894) DAVID ABBOTT *(Nathan[4], Thomas[3], Thomas[2], George[1])*, b. at Concord, NH, 22 Sep 1772 son of Nathan and Betty (Farnum) Abbott. The Abbot genealogy reports he went to New York in 1794 and left no trace after that. He was a house-joiner. The Rutherford County Tennessee Historical Society suggests that this David Abbott made his way to Tennessee and died in Gibson County, TN 2 Dec 1856. The historical society has prepared a summary on David and reports he married Elizabeth Cummins 15 Oct 1811.[2397] ELIZABETH CUMMINS, b. in TN, 1795 daughter of John and Elizabeth (Waller) Cummins; Elizabeth d. at Gibson County, 31 May 1877.

David Abbott owned a mill and received a pension for service in the War of 1812.[2398] There is an 1850 U.S. Census Record for Fall Creek, Rutherford, TN which lists David Abbott born about 1772 in NH as head of the household.[2399]

During the War of 1812, David Abbott was a Major in the 13th Regiment of Tennessee militia in the Brigade of General Jackson, He was at the Battle of New Orleans in December 1814. He applied for and received a 40-acre land bounty for his service. His widow Elizabeth received a pension.

David Abbott wrote his will 24 August 1855 that was in probate in Gibson County, TN in February 1857.[2400] In his will, David Abbott made the following bequests: to beloved wife Elizabeth, he leaves "all my black people and servants" during

---

2396 Lapham, *History of Rumford, Maine*, p 290

2397 Rutherford County Tennessee Historical Society, "Some of the Earliest People in Rutherford County by Their Date of Birth Prior to 1800," retrieved from http://rutherfordtnhistory.org/wp-content/uploads/2017/10/Pioneers-before-1800.pdf

2398 National Archives, War of 1812 Pension and Bounty Land Warrant Application Files, www.fold3.com/image/270301070?xid=1945

2399 Year: 1850; Census Place: Fall Creek, Rutherford, Tennessee; Roll: M432_894; Page: 164B; Image: 321

2400 Tennessee Wills and Probate Records, 1779-2008, Gibson County, TN, Will Books Vol D-F, 1846-1862, Will of David Abbott.

her natural life and on her death, these same to be divided equally among his four youngest sons Fayette, James, Samuel, and George. All the remainder of his property is to be equally divided among his four sons and son Fayette is named executor.

David Abbott and Elizabeth Cummins had six children likely all born in Gibson County, Tennessee for whom there is clear evidence. However, David and Elizabeth married in 1811 so it is likely that are several more children not listed here. It has been speculated that there are as many as thirteen children in this family, but the evidence for the older children in the family is murky at this point.

i LETITIA ABBOTT, b. 23 Mar 1824; d. at Rutherford County, 17 Sep 1850; m. at Rutherford County, TN, 29 Jan 1845, DRURY DANCE, b. at Dinwiddie County, 28 Oct 1800 son of Drury and Mary (Russell) Dance; Drury d. at Gibson County, 5 Jun 1874. After Letitia's death, Drury married her sister Mary Jane (see below).

ii MARY JANE ABBOTT, b. 29 Mar 1826; d. at Gibson County, 15 Jan 1899; m. 17 Dec 1853, DRURY DANCE (see sister Letitia above).

iii LAFAYETTE M. D. ABBOTT, b. 1831; d. unknown but after 1878; m. at Gibson County, 6 Oct 1875, EMMA LEA WRIGHT, b. 13 Apr 1847 daughter of Griffin and Violet (Jetton) Wright. Lafayette served in the Confederate forces and was taken prisoner at Franklin, TN 30 Nov 1864 by forces under Major General Thomas. He was released 9 Jun 1865 after taking the oath of allegiance to the United States and was provided transportation to Gibson, TN.

iv JAMES ABBOTT, b. 1833; nothing further specific known.

v SAMUEL ABBOTT, b. 1836

vi GEORGE ABBOTT, b. 1838. He is thought to be the George Abbott who d. at Winchester, TN, 11 Mar 1904; m. at Franklin, TN, 16 Nov 1882, MARTHA CATHERINE "MATTIE" SANDERS, b. at Winchester, TN, 21 Feb 1853 daughter of James and Patsy (Hecon) Sanders; Mattie d. at Winchester, 4 Nov 1939.

895) HENRY ABBOTT *(Nathan⁴, Thomas³, Thomas², George¹)*, b. at Concord, NH, 22 Sep 1774 son of Nathan and Betty (Farnum) Abbott; d. at Rumford, ME, 1 Feb 1862; m. 1 Jun 1798, his second cousin once removed, SUSANNAH HALL *(Stephen Hall⁵, Dorcas Abbott Hall⁴, Edward³, Thomas², George¹)*, b. at Concord, 13 Nov 1781 daughter of Stephen and Patience (Flanders) Hall; Susannah d. 20 Mar 1867. Susannah Hall is a child in Family 903.

Henry Abbott was a tanner and was known for his hunting skill.[2401] Henry Abbott and Susannah Hall were parents of twelve children all born at Rumford.

i DAVID ABBOTT, b. 26 Sep 1798; d. at Rumford, after 1860; m. at Rumford, 29 Aug 1821, AZUBAH MORSE, baptized at Northborough, MA, 14 Jun 1807 daughter of William and Sally (Wood) Morse; Azubah d. at Rumford, after 1880.

ii HARRIET ABBOTT, b. 23 Sep 1800; d. at Concord, after 1867; m. about 1828, WESLEY BALCH PALMER, b. at Bradford, MA, 1 May 1801 son of William and Mehitable (Balch) Palmer; Wesley d. at Concord, after 1850.

iii JACOB ABBOTT, b. 28 Aug 1802; d. at Rumford, 1884; m. about 1826, PRUDENCE PUFFER, b. at Rumford, 30 Jul 1803 daughter of John and Elizabeth (Putnam) Puffer; Prudence d. at Rumford, Sep 1875.

iv JUDITH ABBOTT, b. 1 Sep 1804; d. at Barnstead, NH, 23 Mar 1879; m. 1st, about 1829, TRUEWORTHY CHESLEY, b. at Gilmanton, NH, about 1802 son of Trueworthy and Sally (Powers) Chesley; Trueworthy d. at Barnstead, 2 Nov 1854. Judith m. 2nd, at Barnstead, 22 Feb 1858, JONATHAN PICKERING.

v NANCY ABBOTT, b. 20 Sep 1806; d. at Rumford, 31 Aug 1884; m. at Rumford, 11 May 1828, HAINES STEVENS, b. at Rumford, 15 Apr 1806 son of Samuel and Miriam (-) Stevens; Haines d. at Rumford, 29 Dec 1883.

vi SUSAN ABBOTT, b. 21 Sep 1808; d. at Nelson, NH, 11 May 1873; m. about 1830, MARK TARBOX, b. at Stoddard, NH, 17 Jun 1801 son of Ebenezer and Mary (Blodgett) Tarbox; Mark d. at Nelson, 17 Dec 1889. After Susan's death, Mark married Mary A. Andrews in 1880.

[2401] Lapham, *History of Rumford*, p 290

vii STEPHEN HALL ABBOTT, b. 12 Oct 1810; d. at Bethel, 6 May 1881; m. 26 Nov 1835, SARAH JANE SMALL, b. at North Yarmouth, ME, 16 Jul 1816 daughter of Edward and Rebecca (Pratt) Small;[2402] Sarah d. at Springvale, ME, 29 Apr 1888.

viii BENJAMIN E. ABBOTT, b. 8 Sep 1812; d. at Rumford, 3 Jul 1884; m. 5 Sep 1840, MAHALA GODWIN, b. at Rumford, 30 Nov 1818 daughter of Colman and Keziah Blanchard (Wheeler) Godwin; Mahala d. at Rumford, 4 Dec 1882.

ix ASA ABBOTT, b. 10 Sep 1814; d. at Rumford, 7 Aug 1854; m. at Rumford, 13 Jun 1852, JULIA OCTAVIA GODWIN, b. at Rumford, 20 Nov 1820 daughter of Colman and Keziah Blanchard (Wheeler) Godwin; Julia d. at Rumford, 4 Oct 1903.

x LOREN ABBOTT, b. and d. 1816.

xi LYDIA H. ABBOTT, b. 1818; d. at Rumford, 16 Feb 1894; m. at Rumford, 26 Sep 1836, KIMBALL MARTIN, b. 27 Oct 1811 son of Kimball and Rachel (Godwin) Martin; Kimball d. at Rumford, 14 Oct 1881.

xii HENRY ABBOTT, b. 8 Feb 1824; d. at Rumford, 29 Oct 1895; m. 1st, 4 Mar 1847, ROZILLA W. HALL, b. at Rumford, 30 Dec 1826 daughter of Daniel and Sally (Johnson) Hall; Rozilla d. at Rumford, 4 May 1853. Henry m. 2nd, 15 Mar 1854, CHARLOTTE A. WAITE, b. at Dixfield, 7 Feb 1826 daughter of Aaron and Charlotte (Chesley) Waite; Charlotte d. at Rumford, 25 Feb 1908.

896) ANNA ABBOTT *(Nathan4, Thomas3, Thomas2, George1)*, b. at Concord, NH, 8 Jan 1781 daughter of Nathan and Betty (Farnum) Abbott; m. Feb 1806, her third cousin once removed, EDMUND BLANCHARD *(Jonathan Blanchard5, Benjamin Blanchard4, Mary Abbott Blanchard3, Nathaniel2, George1)*, b. at Canterbury, NH, 27 Jan 1778 son of Jonathan and Hannah (Chadwick) Blanchard; Edmund d. in Vermont, 29 Nov 1836.[2403] Edmund Blanchard is a child in Family 965.

Edmund Blanchard and Anna Abbott were parents of ten children born at Greensboro, Vermont.

i NATHAN A. BLANCHARD, b. 12 Nov 1806; d. at Glover, VT, 15 Nov 1882; m. 1st, HULDAH PHILLIPS, b. at Williamstown, VT, 1802 daughter of Zedakiah and Hannah (Brown) Phillips; Huldah d. at Glover, 10 Jun 1880. Nathan m. 2nd, 18 Nov 1880, MARY SPOONER, b. at Lisbon, NH, 27 Oct 1811 daughter of Simeon and Priscilla (Priest) Spooner; Mar d. at Glover, 12 Mar 1886.

ii HAMMOND BLANCHARD, b. Jul 1808; d. Nov 1808.

iii ASA ABBOTT BLANCHARD, b. about 1810; d. at Concord, 9 Mar 1889; m. JULIA ANN GILMAN, b. at Loudon, NH, about 1815 daughter of Joseph and Eunice (Bickford0 Gilman; Julia d. at Concord, 2 Jan 1883.

iv ERASTUS BLANCHARD, b. 8 Oct 1811; d. at Greensboro, 9 Feb 1850. Erastus does not seem to have married.

v BETSEY BLANCHARD, b. 11 Jul 1814; d. at Barnet, VT, 1860; m. 1841, PETER BUCHANAN, b. at Barnet, 4 May 1808 son of James and Elizabeth (Hurd) Buchanan; Peter d. at McIndoe Falls, VT, 13 Mar 1886.

vi EMILY BLANCHARD, b. 23 Apr 1817; d. at Glover, 15 May 1906; m. JOSIAH B. PHILLIPS, b. at Glover, 28 Sep 1814 Jonas and Dorothy (Bean) Phillips; Josiah d. at Glover, 1 Aug 1864.

vii SAMUEL SEWELL BLANCHARD, b. 20 Sep 1818; d. at Glover, 30 Sep 1888; m. EMILY BAKER, b. at Glover, 29 Mar 1821 daughter of Thomas and Huldah (Dwinell) Baker; Emily d. at Glover, 15 Oct 1881.

viii EDMUND HARVEY BLANCHARD, b. 16 Jan 1821; d. at Bloomington, IL, 22 Oct 1891; m. 16 May 1860, ANNE CLIFFORD, b. at Loudon, 3 Dec 1828 daughter of Joseph and Jane (Martin) Clifford; Anne d. at Bloomington, 29 Aug 1897.

ix ESTHER BLANCHARD, b. 1824; d. at Craftsbury, VT, 24 Feb 1912. Esther did not marry.

x MARY ANN BLANCHARD, b. 3 Sep 1828; d. at Craftsbury, VT, 27 Feb 1906; m. 1852, MOSES ROOT, b. at Sunderland, MA, 1821 son of Salmon and Eliza (Carpenter) Root; Moses d. at Craftsbury, 2 Jul 1903.

897) CHLOE ABBOTT *(Nathan4, Thomas3, Thomas2, George1)*, b. at Concord, NH, 10 Jun 1783 daughter of Nathan and Betty (Farnum) Abbott; d. at Hollis, ME, after 1850; m. 19 Dec 1809, ZEBADIAH FARNUM, b. at Concord, 4 Mar 1781 son of John and Sally (West) Farnum; Zebadiah d. at Hollis, after 1850.

Chloe Abbott and Zebadiah Farnum were parents of six children born at Rumford, Maine.

[2402] Underhill, *Descendants of Edward Small*, volume 1, p 252
[2403] *Vermont, Vital Records, 1720-1908.*

i BETSEY ABBOTT FARNUM, b. 10 Apr 1811; d. at Lyman, ME, after 1870; m. at Boston, 30 Mar 1835, JEFFERSON MOULTON, b. about 1806 son of Samuel and Jerusha (Dodge) Moulton; Jefferson d. at Lyman, 15 Jan 1893.

ii ASA ABBOT FARNUM, b. 12 Dec 1812; d. 3 Mar 1824.

iii ANNA FARNUM, b. 9 Oct 1814; d. at Hollis, ME, before 1860; m. WILLIAM ROBERTS, b. about 1801; William d. at Dayton, ME, after 1870.

iv CHLOE FARNUM, b. 17 Sep 1817; nothing further known.

v ZEBADIAH FARNUM, b. 11 Dec 1821; d. at Watertown, MA, 20 Mar 1868; m. at Waltham, 17 Sep 1851, MARY LARKIN, b. in Ireland, about 1826 daughter of Thomas and Margaret (-) Larkin;[2404] Mary d. at Watertown, 28 Dec 1879.

vi ASA FARNUM, b. 16 Dec 1824; d. 9 Sep 1840.

898) HEPHZIBAH HALL *(Dorcas Abbott Hall⁴, Edward³, Thomas², George¹)*, b. at Rumford, 29 Mar 1747 daughter of Ebenezer and Dorcas (Abbott) Hall; d. at Concord, 23 Nov 1817; m. about 1765, RICHARD HAZELTINE, b. 5 Apr 1742 son of Richard and Sarah (Barnes) Hazeltine; Richard d. 21 Apr 1817.

Hephzibah Hall and Richard Hazeltine were parents of nine children born at Concord.[2405]

i MARY HAZELTINE, b. 25 May 1766; d. at Concord, 29 Sep 1793; m. 1784, EBENEZER DUSTIN, b. about 1751 (based on age 67 at time of death); Ebenezer d. at Bow, 28 Dec 1818. After Mary's death, Ebenezer married Betsy Bryant.

ii ABIGAIL HAZELTINE, b. 24 Apr 1768; d. at Salisbury, NH, 9 May 1846; m. at Pembroke, 28 Feb 1787, BENJAMIN THOMPSON, b. at Chester, NH, 1761; Benjamin d. at Salisbury, 9 May 1846.

iii JOSEPH HAZELTINE, b. 17 Nov 1770; d. at Sandwich, NH, May 1829; m. at Concord, 3 Aug 1791, RUTH CHASE, b. at Haverhill, NH, 20 Feb 1772 daughter of Daniel and Susan (Wilson) Chase; Ruth d. at Henniker, 10 Feb 1861.

iv RICHARD HAZELTINE, b. 28 Nov 1773; d. at Lynn, 10 Jul 1836; m. at Concord, 9 Jun 1799, PHEBE CARTER, b. at Concord, 25 Dec 1775 daughter of Ezra and Phebe (Whittemore) Carter; Phebe d. at Lynn, 25 Sep 1840.

v TIMOTHY HAZELTINE, b. 28 Aug 1776; d. at Concord, 24 Jul 1811; m. 25 Feb 1799, LYDIA BRICKETT, b. at Newbury, MA, 1775 daughter of Thomas and Mary (Noyes) Brickett;[2406] Lydia d. 1823. After Timothy's death, Lydia married Abel Baker 26 Feb 1818.

vi BARNES HAZELTINE, b. 3 Nov 1778; d. 6 Nov 1799.

vii SALLY HAZELTINE, b. 23 Jan 1781; m. at Concord, 24 May 1801, PETER ROBERTSON.

viii HANNAH HAZELTINE, b. 29 Apr 1783; m. at Concord, 22 Feb 1803, NATHANIEL DICKEY, b. at Francestown, 13 Dec 1777 son of John and Jannet (McClintock) Dickey.

ix BETSEY HAZELTINE, b. 23 May 1785; d. at Concord, 2 Dec 1851; m. at Concord, 6 Jun 1809, her fourth cousin, WILLIAM HOIT *(Elizabeth Blanchard Hoit⁵, Benjamin Blanchard⁴, Mary Abbott Blanchard³, Nathaniel², George¹)*, b. at Peacham, VT, 21 Nov 1783 son of Abner and Elizabeth (Blanchard) Hoit; William d. at Pembroke, 28 Dec 1854. William Hoit is a child in Family 972.

899) OBADIAH HALL *(Dorcas Abbott Hall⁴, Edward³, Thomas², George¹)*, b. at Rumford, 13 Oct 1748 son of Ebenezer and Dorcas (Abbott) Hall; d. at Northfield, NH, 24 Mar 1831; m. 3 Nov 1770, MARY PERHAM,[2407] b. 3 May 1749 daughter of Samuel and Mary (-) Perham of New Ipswich; Mary d. at Northfield, 27 Feb 1822. After Mary's death, Obadiah married at Sanbornton,

---

[2404] Names of Mary's parents and country of birth are given on the marriage record.

[2405] Bouton, *History of Concord*, p 709

[2406] The 1820 will of Thomas Brickett includes a bequest to daughter Lydia Baker.

[2407] Published genealogies disagree about the identity of Obadiah's first wife. For example, the *History of Sanbornton* gives her name as Hannah Lyford. The death record of son Obadiah gives mother's name as Mary and the will of Obadiah written in 1816 gives wife's name as Molly. In addition, the father of Hannah Lyford, John Lyford, wrote his will in 1788 and at that time his daughter Hannah Lyford was unmarried.

17 Sep 1822, ABIGAIL LIBBEY (widow of John Morrison), b. at Rye, 13 Nov 1763 son of Abraham and Abigail (Page) Libbey;[2408] Abigail d. at Sanbornton, 4 Feb 1840.

Obadiah Hall was a farmer. Obadiah and Mary had their children while in Canterbury and later settled in Northfield where they were members of the Congregational church.

Obadiah Hall wrote his will 18 April 1816, fifteen years before his death. In his will, he makes provisions for the care and support of his beloved consort Molly Hall. (Molly died in 1822.) He made bequests of one dollar to each of the following children: eldest daughter Sarah wife of Obadiah Mooney, second daughter Hannah wife of Thomas Lyford, third daughter Polly wife of Joseph Kimball, eldest son Jeremiah, and daughter Ruth wife of Charles Glydden. Son Obadiah Hall receives all the real estate, some furniture, the clock, and the personal estate. Youngest daughter Lydia Hall is to receive one hundred dollars at the time of her marriage unless she has married between the time of the will and Obadiah's decease. There are also provisions for Lydia's support if she remains unmarried. There is an additional bequest to David Sawyer, a boy age five years at the time, a decent and comfortable support until he is age fourteen. His five daughters are to divide the household furniture except the books. The great bible goes to Obadiah. All the books are to be kept by Obadiah as a family library to be open to the perusal of son Jeremiah and Thomas Lyford. Son Obadiah is named the sole executor.[2409]

Obadiah Hall and Mary Perham were parents of eight children all born at Canterbury.

i SARAH HALL, b. 3 Sep 1771; d. at Beekmantown, NY, 1824; m. 1st, 16 Oct 1788, her third cousin once removed, STEVENS BLANCHARD *(John Blanchard[4], Sarah Abbott Blanchard[3], Nathaniel[2], George[1])*, b. at Concord, 15 Sep 1765 son of John and Eleanor (Stevens) Blanchard; Stevens d. at Canterbury, 12 May 1792 (probate 19 Sep 1792). Sarah m. 2nd, 16 Jun 1793, OBADIAH MOONEY, b. at Durham, NH, 26 Jun 1748 son of Hercules and Elizabeth (Evans) Mooney; Obadiah d. at Beekmantown, 1836. The families of Sarah Hall and Stevens Blanchard and Sarah Hall and Obadiah Mooney are Family 1054.

ii HANNAH HALL, b. 29 Jul 1773; d. at Northfield, 28 Jul 1839; m. at Canterbury, 7 Apr 1793. THOMAS LYFORD, b. 12 Nov 1768 son of John and Lydia (Folsom) Lyford; Thomas d. at Northfield, 4 Mar 1846.

iii MARY "POLLY" HALL, b. 11 Jul 1775; d. 6 Feb 1817; m. 3 Dec 1795, JOSEPH KIMBALL, b. at Exeter, NH, 23 May 1772 son of Joseph and Sarah (Smith) Kimball; Joseph d. at Gilmanton, 19 Jun 1863. Joseph married Mary Sanborn 1 May 1817.

iv JEREMIAH HALL, b. 18 Oct 1777; d. at Sanbornton, 8 Jul 1867; m. 1st, 15 Sep 1801, HANNAH HAINES, b. at Canterbury, 31 Jan 1780 daughter of Richard and Prudence (Brickett) Haines; Hannah d. at Northfield, 14 Oct 1826. Jeremiah m. 2nd, at Northfield, 8 Feb 1827, his fourth cousin, ABIGAIL ABBOTT *(Elias[5], Reuben[4], James[3], William[2], George[1])*, b. at Concord, 5 Aug 1783 daughter of Elias and Elizabeth (Buswell) Abbott; Abigail d. at Sanbornton, 25 Aug 1864. Abigail Abbott is a child in Family 573.

v BETSEY HALL, b. 2 Nov 1779; d. 12 Nov 1795.

vi RUTH HALL, b. 26 Sep 1782; d. at Ironton, 3 Aug 1874; m. at Northfield, 28 Jun 1802, CHARLES GLIDDEN, b. at Northfield, 23 Feb 1780 son of Charles and Alice (Mills) Glidden; Charles d. at Wheelersburg, OH, 11 Sep 1836.

vii OBADIAH HALL, b. 23 Mar 1785; d. at Northfield, 25 May 1870; m. 17 Sep 1812, HANNAH FORREST, b. at Canterbury, 15 May 1785 daughter of William and Dorothy (Worthen) Forrest; Hannah d. after 1850.

viii LYDIA HALL, b. 26 Nov 1787; d. at Stow, ME, 1 Aug 1861; m. about 1824, JOSIAH BEMIS DAY, b. 10 Mar 1795 son of Ebenezer and Mary (Bemis) Day; Josiah d. at Stow, 23 Sep 1872.

900) DORCAS HALL *(Dorcas Abbott Hall[4], Edward[3], Thomas[2], George[1])*, b. 13 Jan 1751 daughter of Ebenezer and Dorcas (Abbott) Hall; d. at Concord, 5 Sep 1813 (probate 18 Jan 1815 with Bela Carter as administrator); m. EPHRAIM CARTER, b. at Concord, 21 Oct 1746 son of Ezra and Ruth (Eastman) Carter' Ephraim d. at Concord, 1802 (probate 13 Aug 1802). Dorcas m. 2nd, at Weare, NH, 20 Aug 1809, BENJAMIN CILLEY.

In his will written 14 December 1801. Ephraim Carter bequeaths to beloved wife Dorcas the use of and improvement on all the homestead during her natural life or while she is a widow, and if she dies before son Gross reaches age twenty-one, then the estate is to be used for the support of the children who remain at home. Dorcas also receives three small tracts of land (one of about six acres) in Bow and Concord that are at her own disposal. Daughter Hannah and son Ezra each receive one dollar which constitutes their whole portion with what they previously received. If son Gross conducts himself prudently and conducts business with discretion and continues to work on the farm with his mother, when he reaches age twenty-one, he will receive one-third of the real estate. At the decease or remarriage of his mother, he will receive the other two-thirds of the real estate but is required to make the payments to his siblings from the estate. The personal estate including all the stock animals, but excluding the household furniture, is to be equally divided among all the children except Hannah and Ezra. The household

[2408] Runnels, *History of Sanbornton*, p 502

[2409] *New Hampshire. Probate Court (Merrimack County)*; Probate Place: *Merrimack, New Hampshire, Probate Records, Vol 8-9, 1827-1839*, volume 8, pp 153-155

furniture will go to daughters Dorcas, Ruth, Judith, Polly, and Sally. There are also money payments of varying amounts from the estate to Dorcas, Ruth, Polly, Sally, Bela, and Hubbard. Daughter Sally is to have a comfortable maintenance from the estate so long as her bodily and mental infirmities prevent her from being able to maintain herself. There are several other stipulations and son Ezra will be the sole judge of Ephraim's intentions in the will. Dorcas was named sole executrix. In her last accounting of the estate in 1809, Dorcas signed as Dorcas Cilley.[2410]

Dorcas Hall and Ephraim Carter were parents of twelve children born at Concord.

i EZRA CARTER, b. 24 Oct 1769; d. 4 Nov 1769.

ii HANNAH CARTER, b. 31 Oct 1770; m. 30 Jun 1789, JAMES RUSSELL, b. at Haverhill, MA, Aug 1760 son of Edward and Mary (Page) Russell; James d. at Bow, NH, 1798 (probate 27 May 1798).[2411]

iii EZRA CARTER, b. 15 Feb 1773;[2412] d. at Peacham, VT, 10 Oct 1811; m. at Peacham, 4 Dec 1800, MARTHA ELLSWORTH, b. at Middletown, CT, 22 Aug 1773 daughter of John and Martha (Elton) Ellsworth;[2413] Martha d. after 1830 (listed as head of household, age 50-59, in the 1830 census of Peacham).

iv EBENEZER CARTER, b. 2 Apr 1775; d. at Charleston, SC, 8 Oct 1795. The death is recorded in Concord, NH but notes that Ebenezer's death occurred at Charleston. Ebenezer was buried at Concord.[2414]

v DORCAS CARTER, b. 22 Oct 1777; d. at St. Louis, MO, 13 Aug 1871;[2415] m. at Peacham, 30 Oct 1803, EPHRAIM CHAMBERLAIN, b. at Hopkinton, MA, 20 Feb 1770 son of Abiel and Lois (Whitney) Chamberlain; Ephraim d. at Lyndon, VT, 4 Feb 1836.

vi RUTH CARTER, b. 21 Sep 1780. It is not clear what happened to Ruth. It is possible that she married George Knight and lived in New Brunswick, Canada, but that is not confirmed.

vii JUDITH CARTER, b. 21 Sep 1780; m. at Barret, VT, 20 Oct 1803, JACOB PAGE, b. at Newbury, VT, 24 Apr 1781 son of Jacob and Sarah (Johnson) Page.

viii MARY "POLLY" CARTER, b. 1 Jul 1783; d. at Hudson, MA, 8 Apr 1880; m. about 1810, DANIEL CARTER

ix THOMAS GROSS CARTER, b. 21 May 1786. Thomas was a seaman. There is no clear evidence of what happened to him.

x BELA CARTER, b. 12 Jul 1789; d. at Natick, MA, 20 Jun 1846; m. at Concord, 21 Dec 1813, JUDITH CARTER, b. at Concord, 2 May 1783 daughter of Ezra and Phebe (Whittemore) Carter.

xi FRANKLIN HUBBARD CARTER, b. 2 Apr 1791; d. at Conneaut, OH, 17 Jun 1860; m. 1825, CLARISSA PUTNEY, b. 8 Jul 1801; Clarissa d. at Conneaut, 27 Dec 1842. Franklin m. 2nd, Emily, b. about 1821.

xii SALLY CARTER, b. 6 Jun 1794. It is not known what became of Sally, but her father's will suggests that she was in some way disabled an unable to care for herself.

901) SARAH HALL *(Dorcas Abbott Hall⁴, Edward³, Thomas², George¹)*, b. at Rumford, 4 Feb 1753 daughter of Ebenezer and Dorcas (Abbott) Hall; d. May 1845; m. by 1774, WILLIAM HAZELTINE, b. at Rumford, 16 Jun 1744 son of Richard and Sarah (Barnes) Hazeltine; William d. at Canterbury, Jan 1826.

Sarah Hall and William Hazeltine were in Concord for a time where Sarah Hall Hazeltine was a member of the Congregational Church. They were in Canterbury by 1790 when William was one of the ten signers of the covenant adopted by the Congregational Church.[2416]

In his will written 16 Jun 1825, William Hazeltine left to beloved wife Sarah, in addition to her right of dower, the use and improvement of all the household as well as all the notes owed to her to be at her own disposal. Beloved daughter Judith Rolfe receives $300, one-half of the household furniture after the decease of her mother, one-half of the farm utensils, and one-third of the neat cattle, sheep, hogs, and horses. Beloved daughter Sarah Jones receives the same bequest as Judith. Well-beloved daughter-in-law Sarah Hazeltine widow of son Samuel C. receives the privilege of living with the family as long as she

---

[2410] *New Hampshire. Probate Court (Rockingham County);* Probate Place: *Rockingham, New Hampshire*, volume 34, pp 173-175

[2411] In the probate record of James Russell, widow Hannah Russell of Bow requests that her father Ephraim Carter be named administrator.

[2412] There are two Ezra Carters born in Concord in 1773, Ezra the son of Ephraim born in Feb 1773 and Ezra the son of Ezra (Ephraim's brother) in Mar 1773. Ezra the son of Ezra married Sarah Fabyan and lived in Scarborough, Maine.

[2413] Mathews, *The Descendants of Governor Thomas Welles*, p 2, p 815

[2414] New Hampshire, Death and Burial Records Index, 1654-1949

[2415] In 1870, Dorcas was living with her daughter Louisa and her family in St. Louis.

[2416] Lyford, *History of Canterbury*, p 188

remains a widow. Beloved son Abiel receives all the real estate, the other one-third of the animals, the clock, and the sleigh and harness. The remainder of his personal effects and clothing are to be divided equally among his three children. Abiel Hazeltine was name executor.[2417]

Sarah Hall and William Hazeltine were parents of four children likely born at Concord or Canterbury. There was perhaps a fifth child that died before adulthood.

i JUDITH HAZELTINE, b. 10 Jun 1774; d. at Boscawen, Jan 1847; m. about 1800, WILLIAM ROLFE, b. 14 Mar 1773 son of William and Lavina (Harriman) Rolfe; William d. at Groton, NH, 23 Jan 1837.

ii ABIEL HAZELTINE, b. 22 Jun 1777; d. at Canterbury, 1838 (probate 1838); m. at Boscawen, 28 Nov 1805, HANNAH ADAMS, b. 1 May 1779;[2418] Hannah d. at Canterbury, 24 Jan 1849.

iii SARAH HAZELTINE, b. 13 Oct 1779; d. at Wheelock, VT, 11 Nov 1853; m. HENRY JONES, b. about 1782; Henry d. at Wheelock, 27 Apr 1834.

iv SAMUEL C. HAZELTINE, b. 5 Sep 1781; d. Aug 1824; m. 19 Mar 1818, SARAH CLOUGH, b. at Canterbury, 5 Aug 1786 daughter of Nehemiah and Sarah (Clough) Clough; Sarah d. at Sanbornton, 1843. After Samuel's death, Sarah married Joseph G. March 9 Mar 1826.

902) DANIEL HALL *(Dorcas Abbott Hall⁴, Edward³, Thomas², George¹)*, b. at Rumford, 13 Jan 1755 son of Ebenezer and Dorcas (Abbott) Hall; d. at Concord, 18 Feb 1835; m. 26 Sep 1775, DEBORAH DAVIS, b. at Concord, 15 Jul 1757 daughter of Robert and Sarah (Walker) Davis; Deborah d. at Concord, 31 Oct 1822. Daniel married 2nd, 17 Nov 1825, ELIZABETH BURNUM FELLOWS, b. 9 Nov 1757; Elizabeth d. at Concord, Dec 1831.

Daniel Hall was a farmer in Concord. Daniel Hall and Deborah Davis were parents of fourteen children all born at Concord.

i DORCAS HALL, b. 14 Aug 1776; d. at Concord, 5 Mar 1856; m. at Concord, 13 Nov 1800, JOSEPH SHERBURNE, b. at Epsom, NH, 20 Oct 1770 son of Joseph and Olive (Pitman) Sherburne; Joseph d. at Epsom, 29 Jul 1807.

ii EBENEZER HALL, b. 9 May 1778; d. at Westford, MA, 14 Oct 1853; m. at Concord, 15 Nov 1803, his second cousin once removed, HANNAH ABBOTT *(Benjamin⁴, Benjamin³, Thomas², George¹)*, b. at Concord, 9 Mar 1782 daughter of Benjamin and Sarah (Brown) Abbott; Hannah d. at Westford, 5 Apr 1869. Ebenezer Hall and Hannah Abbott are Family 952.

iii ROBERT HALL, b. 16 Jun 1780; d. at St, Croix, West Indies, 18 Aug 1805.[2419]

iv JOSEPH HALL, b. 4 May 1782; d. at Rumford, ME, 3 Dec 1874; m. at Rumford, 3 Mar 1805, JUDITH BLANCHARD, b. at Boscawen, NH, 27 Jan 1784 daughter of Simeon and Dorothy (Elliot) Blanchard; Judith d. at Rumford, 22 Dec 1871.

v JEREMIAH HALL, b. 4 May 1782; d. at Rumford, ME, Nov 1857; m. at Rumford, 8 Aug 1805, JUDITH ROLFE, b. at Concord, 17 Mar 1787 daughter of Benjamin and Mary (Swett) Rolfe; Judith d. at Rumford, 1844.

vi JAMES HALL, b. 19 Jun 1784; d. at Concord, 1861 (probate Nov 1861); m. at Concord, 26 Nov 1805, his second cousin once removed, RUTH MORRILL ABBOTT *(Benjamin⁴, Benjamin³, Thomas², George¹)*, b. at Concord, 27 Jun 1784 daughter of Benjamin and Sarah (Brown) Abbott; Ruth d. about 1861. James Hall and Ruth Abbott are Family 953.

vii SIMEON HALL, b. 16 Mar 1786. According to the Abbot Genealogical Register (p 96), Simeon did not marry and lived in Cleveland.

viii SALLY HALL, b. 11 Sep 1788; d. at Rumford, ME, 26 Sep 1859; m. at Concord, 16 Jan 1811, JEREMIAH FARNUM, b. at Concord, 29 Jul 1785 son of Benjamin and Anna (Merrill) Farnum; Jeremiah d. at Rumford, 21 Nov 1869.

ix POLLY HALL, b. 9 May 1790; d. 28 Sep 1798.

x DANIEL HALL, b. 17 Jun 1792; d. at Rumford, 15 Dec 1862; m. at Hopkinton, NH, 4 Jun 1820, SALLY JOHNSON, b. in NH, 1791; Sally d. at Rumford, 20 Jul 1867.

xi HANNAH HALL, b. 12 Mar 1794; d. 16 Mar 1794.

2417 *New Hampshire. Probate Court (Merrimack County)*; Probate Place: *Merrimack, New Hampshire, Probate Records, Vol 1, 1823-1828*, will of William Hazeltine, pp 204-205

2418 Abbot, *Genealogical Register*, p 95

2419 New Hampshire, Death and Burial Records Index, 1654-1949; death record notes place of death as West Indies.

xii IVORY HALL, b. 25 Aug 1795; d. at Concord, 15 Nov 1882; m. 1st, Jul 1821, PAMELA L. CLEMENT, b. at Pembroke, 16 Jul 1801 daughter of Joshua and Abigail (Head) Clement; Pamela d. at Concord, 11 Jan 1835. Ivory m. 2nd, 8 Aug 1837, SARAH DOW, b. at Canaan, NH, 10 Apr 1813 daughter of Jacob and Phebe (Wells) Dow; Sarah d. at Everett, MA, 15 May 1891.

xiii JOHN CALVIN HALL, b. 12 Sep 1798; d. at Bedford, OH; m. 1st, the widow PHEBE PARKER KIMBALL; Phebe d. 1826. John had a second marriage, but she is yet to be identified, but perhaps Hannah Bartlett.

xiv POLLY HALL, b. 27 Jul 1801; d. 8 Jul 1803.

902a) TIMOTHY HALL *(Dorcas Abbott Hall4, Edward3, Thomas2, George1)*, b. at Rumford, 5 Jun 1757 son of Ebenezer and Dorcas (Abbott) Hall; d. at Irasburg, VT, 16 Jul 1832; m. at Concord, 15 Oct 1780, ANNA FOSTER of Bow, born about 1760 *perhaps* the daughter of Ephraim and Hannah (Moor) Foster; Anna d. at Hardwick, VT, 28 Feb 1853.[2420][2421]

Timothy Hall was a tanner by trade and had some success in his business as a result of hard work. Problems started when Timothy served as surety for a loan related to a business started by three of his sons, Abiel, Moses, and Ebenezer. The business failed and, in 1819, a warrant was issued for Timothy and son Ebenezer related to the debt and Timothy was taken to debtor's prison in Danville. Timothy was still in debtor's prison in 1827 but it is not known if he was there continuously.

On 21 June 1820, Timothy Hall, age 64, made an affidavit related to his pension application. He served in the company commanded by Captain Joshua Abbott in the Regiment of Colonel John Stark. He received a pension 2 October 1819, pension number 15,609. He declared having possession of property valued at $1,589.41 which was property transferred to him 26 February 1820 from the late firm A. E. & M. Hall & Co. of Barnet as partial indemnity for what the firm owed him. He also states he is bound for the amount of $4,814.20. The company is now bankrupt, and he expects to not get one cent of what is owed him. As a consequence of his debts, he is now confined as a prisoner within the limits of the prison at Danville. This is for a judgment against him for money owed to John Dickson. The total amount of all his property including what was transferred to him from A. E. & M. Hall is $1,903.41. He reports his occupation as tanner and being in good health for his age. His current family consists of wife Anna age 61 and in good health and daughter Hephzibah age 36 and in good health. The accounting includes property of $1,903.41 and debts of $4,814.20 which leaves nothing. In 1838, Lydia Cavis wife of Nathaniel Cavis, made a deposition related to the widow's pension application of Anna Hall. In that deposition, she states she was Lydia Hall who lived in Concord with her father Ebenezer, and that two of her brothers, Timothy and Stephen, served in the Revolutionary War. She further states that Timothy married Anna Foster of Bow and removed to Peacham, Vermont.[2422] On 1 January 1839, widow Anna Hall made an affidavit. Timothy and Anna were married at Concord in October 1781 by the Reverend Timothy Walker. Before her marriage, she was Anna Foster and lived in the town of Bow, New Hampshire. For two or three years after their marriage, they lived on a house on the farm that belonged to her husband's father. After that, they moved to Peacham where they lived for thirty years and after that is Irasburg, except for short periods in Danville and Barnett Vermont.

There is evidence for seven children of Timothy and Anna. Four births recorded at Peacham and three additional children mentioned in Timothy's Revolutionary War pension application file.

i JUDITH HALL, b. at Peacham, 12 Nov 1781; d. at Peacham, 19 Dec 1856; m. 3 Dec 1801, ERASTUS KELLOGG, b. at South Hadley, MA, 4 Apr 1776 son of Jabez and Abigail (Catlin) Kellogg; Erastus d. at Peacham, 16 Jul 1853.

ii HEPHZIBAH HALL, b. 17 Aug 1784; d. at Irasburg, after 1839. Hephzibah did not marry. She was of Irasburg when she made an affidavit related to her father's pension application in 1839.

iii ELIZABETH HALL, b. at Peacham, 9 Jan 1787; nothing further known.

iv ABEL HALL, b. at Peacham, 7 Jun 1790; likely d. before 1819 when his father and brother were sent to debtor's prison for the failed business.

v MOSES HALL, b. about 1792; reported to have gone to Kentucky and/or Alabama.

vi OREN HALL, b. about 1797; nothing definite known other than he was living in 1825 when he made an affidavit related to his father's pension application.

[2420] Revolutionary War Pension and Bounty-Land Warrant Application Files

[2421] Anna Hall was living with her daughter Judith Kellogg at the 1850 census.

[2422] Revolutionary War Pension and Bounty-Land Warrant Application Files, File of Timothy Hall, p 89

vii EBENEZER HALL, b. perhaps 1798 or earlier; he was listed on the warrant for detention for debtor's prison in 1819 and he made a statement in 1823 related to the failed business. A *very remote possibility* is that he later went to Carroll, Mississippi and worked as a toll gate keeper. If that is him, he married Barbary Gedder who was 30 years younger than him.

903) STEPHEN HALL *(Dorcas Abbott Hall⁴, Edward³, Thomas², George¹)*, b. at Concord, 13 May 1759 son of Ebenezer and Dorcas (Abbott) Hall; d. at Concord, 23 Nov 1808; m. PATIENCE FLANDERS, b. at Boscawen, 9 Oct 1758 daughter of Ezekiel and Sarah (Bishop) Flanders; Patience d. 17 Feb 1834.

Stephen Hall served alongside his brother Timothy in the Revolutionary War.

Stephen Hall did not leave a will, and his estate entered probate 21 Dec 1808. Widow Patience Hall was administrator of the estate. The children listed as heirs are Moses Hall, Nancy Hall, Susanna Hall Abbot, John Hall, Lydia Hall Emery, Abiel Hall, Deborah Hall, Sally Hall, Harriet Hall, Stephen Hall, and Ebenezer Hall. The value of the real property was $2,075 and the personal estate $1,148.02.[2423]

In her will written 28 August 1833 (proved fourth Tuesday of Feb 1834), Patience Hall bequeathed on dollar to each of the children of her daughter Lydia Emery now deceased. Bequests of one dollar are also made to each of the children of her other children who are now deceased: Moses Hall, John C. Hall, and Nancy Darling. These one-dollar payments are to be the full legacies of those grandchildren. The remainder of the estate is to be divided among daughters Susan Abbot, Sally Clark, and Harriet Elkins; sons Stephen Hall and Ebenezer Hall; and the children of Abiel Hall, this division to be in one-sixth part to each heir. Peter Elkins was named sole executor.[2424]

Stephen Hall and Patience Flanders were parents of eleven children born at Concord.

i MOSES HALL, b. 12 May 1780; d. at Concord, 4 Jun 1833; m. about 1814, LUCY BRADLEY, b. 1787 daughter of Samuel Bradley; Lucy d. at Concord, 3 Jun 1843.

ii SUSANNAH HALL, b. 13 Nov 1781; d. at Rumford, ME, 20 Mar 1867; m. at Concord, 1 Jun 1798, her second cousin once removed, HENRY ABBOTT *(Nathan⁴, Thomas³, Thomas², George¹)*, b. at Concord, 22 Sep 1774 son of Nathan and Betty (Farnum) Abbott; Henry d. at Rumford, 1 Feb 1862. Susannah Hall and Henry Abbott are Family 895.

iii NANCY HALL, b. 17 Feb 1784; d. at Hopkinton, NH, 21 May 1823; m. at Concord, 3 Dec 1809, TIMOTHY DARLING, b. at Hopkinton, 6 May 1784 son of Timothy and Ann (Chase) Darling.

iv JOHN COFFIN HALL, b. 21 Jan 1786; d. at Westminster, VT, 30 Sep 1820; m. at Westminster, 22 Aug 1811, MERCY SMITH, b. at Westminster, 4 Sep 1787 daughter of Benjamin and Sarah (Paul) Smith; Mercy d. at Westminster, 7 Jun 1829.

v LYDIA HALL, b. 2 Mar 1788; d. at Concord, 29 Jun 1818; m. at Concord, 9 Apr 1786, BENJAMIN EMERY, b. at Concord, 9 Apr 1786 son of Benjamin and Sarah (Bailey) Emery.

vi ABIEL HALL, b. 21 Jan 1790; d. Nov 1826; m. at Portland, ME, 25 Aug 1811, MARTHA CARVER.

vii DEBORAH HALL, b. 16 Mar 1792; d. 21 May 1825. Deborah did not marry.

viii SALLY HALL, b. 30 Apr 1794; d. at Concord, 1 Sep 1870; m. DANIEL CLARK, b. at Concord, 26 Mar 1793 son of Daniel and Mary (Whitemarsh) Clark; Daniel d. at Concord, about 1862 (probate 24 Jun 1862).

ix HARRIET HALL, b. 13 May 1796; m. at Concord, 5 Nov 1823, PETER ELKINS, b. about 1797; Peter d. at Concord, 16 Mar 1838.

x STEPHEN HALL, b. 15 Apr 1798; d. at Claremont, NH, 3 Aug 1858; m. at Concord, 25 Feb 1821, CHARLOTTE BRADLEY, b. about 1803.

xi EBENEZER HALL, b. 3 Jan 1800; m. 15 Jan 1824, ABIGAIL E. HODGDON, b. at Portsmouth, NH, about 1806 likely the daughter of Benjamin and Mary (Emerson) Hodgdon; Abigail d. at Concord, 1859.[2425]

904) ABIEL HALL *(Dorcas Abbott Hall⁴, Edward³, Thomas², George¹)*, b. at Rumford, 31 May 1761 son of Ebenezer and Dorcas (Abbott) Hall; d. 13 Oct 1829 at Alfred, ME; m. 1st, MARY FARNUM, b. at Concord, 26 Aug 1764 daughter of Benjamin and Anna (Merrill) Farnum; Mary d. 23 Nov 1816. Abiel m. 2nd, 1819, ANNA FRANCIS (widow of Edward Grant); Anna d. 11 Dec 1857.

[2423] *New Hampshire. Probate Court (Rockingham County);* Probate Place: *Rockingham, New Hampshire, Estate Papers, No 8000-8076, 1808-1809, Case number 8038, probate of Stephen Hall of Concord.*

[2424] *New Hampshire. Probate Court (Merrimack County);* Probate Place: *Merrimack, New Hampshire*, volume 8, pp 282-283, will of Patience Hall

[2425] Manual of the First Congregational Church, Concord, 1888, p 42

Abiel Hall was a physician and the first resident physician of Sanford, Maine.[2426] He served in the Revolutionary War at Ticonderoga. In 1780, he left Concord and settled in what is now Alfred, Maine. He son Abiel was also a physician and took over his father's practice.

Abiel and Mary (Farnum) Hall had eight children born at Alfred, Maine.[2427]

i IVORY HALL, b. about 1785; died young

ii ABIEL HALL, b. 16 Sep 1787; d. at Alfred, ME, 11 Dec 1869; m. 16 Nov 1815, ELIZABETH FROST, b. 1795 daughter of William and Betsey (Goodwin) Frost of Sanford; Elizabeth d. 24 Mar 1863.

iii JOHN HALL, b. about 1789; d. before 1850; m. about 1817, LETITIA LITTLEFIELD, b. in Maine about 1796 *possibly* the daughter of Aaron and Lydia (Taylor) Littlefield; Letitia d. after 1850 likely at Alfred, ME (living at the 1850 U.S. Census).

iv DAVID HALL, b. 8 Oct 1791; d. at Portland, 12 Mar 1863; m. 10 Dec 1818, ANN "NANCY" MERRILL CONANT, b. at Alfred, 27 Dec 1796 daughter of John and Lydia (Farnum) Conant; Nancy d. Nov 1865.

v IVORY HALL, b. 22 Oct 1796; d. at Alfred, 5 Apr 1873; m. 12 Jun 1820, CHARLOTTE APPLETON KENT, b. at Scituate, 12 Jan 1800 daughter of Samuel and Hannah (Brooks) Kent; Charlotte d. 3 Jan 1885.

vi MARY HALL, b. 21 May 1798; d. at Alfred, 16 Nov 1872; m. 2 Feb 1819, RUFUS SAYWARD, b. 19 May 1789 son of John and Elizabeth (Trafton) Sayward; Rufus d. 11 Apr 1838.

vii JULIA HALL, b. 13 Jan 1804; d. at Portland, 17 Jul 1880; m. 1826, NATHAN DANE APPLETON, b. at Ipswich, 20 May 1794 son of Samuel and Mary (White) Appleton; Nathan d. 12 Nov 1861. Nathan was a state legislator in Maine and served a term as attorney general for Maine.[2428]

viii PORTER HALL, b. 12 Mar 1807; d. at Kennebunk, 18 Jun 1853; m. 1st, MARY DANE, b. at Kennebunk, 14 Nov 1810 daughter of Joseph and Mary (Clark) Dane; Mary d. at Kennebunk, 14 Apr 1843. Porter m. 2nd, MARIA PERKINS, b. in Maine, 18 Jul 1825; Maria d. Dec 1894.[2429]

905) LYDIA HALL *(Dorcas Abbott Hall⁴, Edward³, Thomas², George¹)*, b. at Concord, 10 Oct 1767 daughter of Ebenezer and Dorcas (Abbott) Hall; d. at Bow, NH, 30 Mar 1855; m. 5 Jan 1788, NATHANIEL CAVIS, b. 25 Dec 1761[2430] son of Nathaniel and Mary (-) Cavis; Nathaniel d. 10 Sep 1842. Nathaniel was first married to Sally Heath.

Nathaniel Cavis wrote his will 7 June 1826 and it was proved on the fourth Tuesday of September 1842.[2431] Nathaniel left one dollar to each of his children as they had already received their portions: sons Jonathan, Nathaniel, John, and Solomon and daughters Sarah Cilley wife of Seth Newell Cilley and Mary Gault wife of Obed Gault. All the personal estate including money, just demands, and movables went to beloved wife Lydia who was also named executrix. Son Jonathan was Nathaniel's son from his first marriage to Sally Heath.

The births of seven children of Lydia and Nathaniel are recorded at Bow.[2432]

i NATHANIEL CAVIS, b. 30 Sep 1789; d. at Lawrence, MA, 3 Jun 1855; m. at Bow, 28 Sep 1819, ANN "NANCY" VEASY, b. at Brentwood, NH, about 1798 daughter of Jonathan and Anna (-) Veasy;[2433] Nancy d. at Boston, 31 May 1868.

ii SARAH "SALLY" CAVIS, b. 23 May 1791; d. at Weare, NH, 14 Nov 1850; m. at Bow, 24 May 1813, SETH NOBLE CILLEY, b. at Weare, 3 Dec 1783 son of John and Elizabeth (Fowler) Cilley; Seth d. at Weare, 27 May 1861.

iii MARY "POLLY" CAVIS, b. 13 Mar 1793; d. at Bow, 1 Jul 1869; m. 20 Oct 1818, OBED GAULT, b. at Bow, 7 Jan 1791 son of Samuel and Anna (Gile) Gault; Obed d. at Bow, 17 Jul 1872.

2426 Emery, *History of Sanford*, Maine, p 464

2427 Most of the birth dates are on the gravestones; NEHGR, 1937, volume 91, p 222 and p 227, "Cemetery Inscriptions at Alfred Maine"

2428 Cleaveland, *History of Bowdoin College*, p 171

2429 Maria's date of birth is engraved on her gravestone as well as her maiden name; parents not yet located; findagrave.com ID 74446095

2430 Abbot, *Genealogical Register of Descendants of George Abbot*, p 98

2431 *New Hampshire. Probate Court (Merrimack County)*; Probate Place: *Merrimack, New Hampshire, Probate Records, Vol 16, 1839-1875*, pp 116-117

2432 *Bow, NH: The Town Book of Bow, New Hampshire, 1760-1877.* Manuscript. R. Stanton Avery Special Collections, New England Historic Genealogical Society, Boston, MA., p 249

2433 The 1833 New Hampshire will of Jonathan Veazy includes a bequest to his daughter Nancy Cavis.

iv EBENEZER HALL CAVIS, b. 22 Jan 1795; died young

v JOHN CAVIS, b. 28 Nov 1796; d. at Hopkinton, NH, about 1843 (probate Apr 1843); m. 21 Oct 1823, NANCY MILLS, b. at Dunbarton, NH, 4 May 1797 daughter of Caleb Mills; Nancy d. at Holyoke, MA, 22 Mar 1867.

vi SOLOMON CAVIS, b. 22 Nov 1800; d. at Bristol, NH, 2 Feb 1884; m. at Bristol, 16 Oct 1828, ALMIRA MINOT, b. at New London, NH, 23 Nov 1804 daughter of James and Sally (Wilson) Minot; Almira d. at Bristol, 13 Sep 1884.

vii LYDIA LOISA CAVIS, b. 24 May 1809; d. at Bow, 9 Jul 1826.

906) DEBORAH HALL *(Dorcas Abbott Hall^4, Edward^3, Thomas^2, George^1)*, b. at Concord, 18 Sep 1769 daughter of Ebenezer and Dorcas (Abbott) Hall; d. 25 Oct 1791;[2434] m. at Hillsborough, 26 Oct 1787, DANIEL BARKER. Daniel perhaps married Anna Lathrop 19 Mar 1792.

Virtually no information was found for this family. Two children are reported in the Abbot genealogical register (p 98).

i ROBERT BARKER, b. about 1789

ii HANNAH BARKER, b. about 1791

907) MARY ABBOTT *(Edward^4, Edward^3, Thomas^2, George^1)*, b. 1761 daughter of Edward and Deborah (Stevens) Abbott; d. 1843; m. by 1780, THOMAS CAPEN, b. at Charlestown, 19 Apr 1762 son of Thomas and Mary (Wyman) Capen;[2435] Thomas died at sea in 1808.

Thomas Capen was born in Charlestown, married Mary Abbott in Concord, where the birth or their first child is recorded, and then settled in Rumford, Maine by 1788. Thomas and Molly Capen had several land transactions there between 1788 and 1794; they were described as "of New Penacook."[2436]

There are seven, and perhaps eight, children of Mary and Thomas. The Abbot genealogy reports a daughter Mary who is not included in the Capen genealogy or in the *History of Rumford*. She is included here, although there are no records for her. There is specific information on births for three of the children; other birthdates are estimated.

i EBENEZER CAPEN, b. at Concord, 30 Dec 1780; d. at Concord, after 1850; m. 1st, at Concord, 31 Jul 1805, ABIGAIL CARTER, b. 17 Jul 1780 daughter of Joseph and Hannah (Carr) Carter); Abigail d. 5 Jul 1840. Ebenezer m. 2nd, at Lowell, 27 Aug 1840, NANCY E. BUNTIN, b. in NH about 1822; Nancy d. at Lowell, 19 Dec 1907.

ii JAMES CAPEN, b. about 1785; m. by 1809, HANNAH. The Capen genealogy lists children for James born in Concord[2437] and those children have a mother Hannah, but last name of mother is not given. The oldest of those children was Lydia born 30 Aug 1809. Records were found for seven children of James and Hannah, but no other information.

iii MARY CAPEN, b. about 1790; no other information.

iv TIMOTHY CAPEN, b. 1793; d. at Bethel, ME, 1872; m. 1st, at Rumford, 13 Jul 1815, RUTH YORK (widow of Ezekiel Duston), b. at Standish, ME, 21 Apr 1778 daughter of John and Abigail (Bean) York; Ruth d. at Bethel, 6 Jun 1830. Timothy m. 2nd, about 1831, his second cousin, SARAH ABBOTT *(Aaron^5, Aaron^4, Thomas^3, Thomas^2, George^1)*, b. at Bethel, 12 Mar 1806 daughter of Aaron and Sarah (Abbott) Abbott; Sarah d. at Bethel, 14 Apr 1874. Sarah Abbott is a child in Family 892.

v DEBORAH CAPEN, b. 7 Jun 1796; d. at Bethel, 1881; m. at Rumford, 21 Mar 1816, WILLIAM ACKLEY, b. 12 Dec 1792 son of Samuel and Elizabeth (Moody) Ackley; William d. at Rumford, 2 Nov 1874.

vi SAMUEL A. CAPEN, b. 1798; d. at Chelsea, MA, 7 May 1847; m. at Boston, 28 Jun 1830, ABIGAIL R. GREENE (widow of Thomas Bickford), b. at New York, NY, about 1788 daughter of John and Sarah (-) Greene; Abigail d. at Boston, 15 Jan 1878.

vii OLIVER BEAL CAPEN, b. 1800; d. at Colebrook, NH, 28 Dec 1866; m. 10 Jun 1827, SUSAN B. CHASE, b. 13 May 1808 daughter of Thomas and Tabitha (Piper) Chase; Susan d. at Colebrook, 29 Jul 1870.

viii ESTHER CAPEN, b. 14 Jan 1805; d. at Portland, 10 Feb 1866; m. at Portland, 30 Aug 1829, URIAH FURLONG, b. 27 Nov 1807 son of Thomas and Elizabeth (Jordan) Furlong; Uriah d. at Portland, 15 Oct 1865.

[2434] The death is recorded at Concord but reported as occurring at "Lebanon or Grantham." New Hampshire, Death and Burial Records Index, 1654-1949

[2435] Hayden and Tuttle, *The Capen Family*, p 137

[2436] Lapham, *History of Rumford, Maine*

[2437] Hayden and Tuttle, *The Capen Family*, p 206

908) MEHITABLE ABBOTT *(Edward^4, Edward^3, Thomas^2, George^1)*, b. 23 Apr 1763 daughter of Edward and Deborah (Stevens) Abbott; d. 16 Sep 1838;[2438] m. at Concord, 18 May 1786, BENJAMIN LUFKIN, b. at Ipswich, 8 Apr 1763;[2439] Benjamin d. at Roxbury, ME, Nov 1844. Benjamin m. 2nd, Sarah Elliot Bunker.

Benjamin Lufkin served as a private in the revolution in four different enlistments with a total service of about 24 months. One enlistment was in Captain Fogg's company of Massachusetts troops. Benjamin and later his widow Sarah received a pension based on his service.[2440]

Benjamin Lufkin did not leave a will. The only documents in the probate file are a statement that he was a pensioner and that his widow was Sarah.

Mehitable Abbott and Benjamin Lufkin were parents of eleven children, all but the oldest child born at Rumford. Son Samuel was the first child born in Rumford. Three of the sons, Joseph, Moses, and Benjamin, were ministers.

i JOSEPH LUFKIN, b. 19 Aug 1786; d. at Rumford, 16 Jan 1872; m. 22 Apr 1811, LORUHAMAH S. KIMBALL, b. at Rumford, 15 Feb 1792 daughter of Moses and Phebe (Cole) Kimball; Loruhamah d. at Rumford, 27 Nov 1871.

ii SAMUEL LUFKIN, b. 15 Aug 1788; d. at Rumford, 4 Apr 1845; m. at Rumford, 28 Nov 1816, PAMELLA SEGAR, b. at Bethel, 18 Apr 1790 daughter of Nathaniel and Mary (Russell) Segar; Pamella d. at Rumford, 23 May 1855.

iii JACOB LUFKIN, b. 22 Jul 1790; d. at Chesterville, ME, 1 Feb 1879; m. 1st, about 1816. ELEANOR ELLIOT, b. at Concord, NH, 5 Mar 1794 daughter of Joseph and Lydia (Goodwin) Elliot; Eleanor d. 12 Apr 1851. Jacob m. 2nd, LUCY ADAMS.

iv JOHN LUFKIN, b. 16 Dec 1792; d. at Wilton, ME, 14 May 1855; m. at Rumford, 29 Nov 1821, PHEBE KIMBALL, b. at Rumford, 23 May 1796 daughter of Moses and Phebe (Cole) Kimball; Phebe d. at Rumford, after 1870 (living with daughter Sarah in 1870).

v AARON LUFKIN, b. 26 May 1795; d. at Mexico, ME, 14 May 1869; m. 5 Apr 1825, LUCY BROWN, b. 23 Jul 1801 daughter of Nathan and Sally (Wheeler) Brown; Lucy d. at Mexico, ME, 17 Oct 1869.

vi ESTHER LUFKIN, b. 4 Jun 1797; d. at Springfield, NH, by 1849 (when husband remarried); m. about 1825, BARNARD CARTER STEVENS, b. about 1800 but not yet identified; Barnard d. at Springfield, Oct 1874. After Esther's death, Barnard married Sarah Stevens on 16 Nov 1849.

vii MOSES LUFKIN, b. 12 Feb 1800; d. at Strong, ME, after 1870; m. about 1833, HANNAH VIRGIN, b. at Rumford, 6 Sep 1807 daughter of Ebenezer and Elizabeth (Quinby) Virgin;[2441] Hannah d. at Strong, after 1860.

viii BENJAMIN LUFKIN, b. 12 Apr 1802; m. at Boston, 23 Apr 1850, ELIZABETH THORNTON, b. at Duxbury, about 1806 daughter of William and Deborah (-) Thornton; Elizabeth d. at Boston, 25 Apr 1881.

ix MARY LUFKIN, b. 2 Jul 1804; d. 10 Oct 1812.

x DAVID LUFKIN, b. 17 Feb 1807; d. 16 Jan 1832.

xi HANNAH LUFKIN, b. 19 Nov 1809; d. at Dummerston, VT, 14 Feb 1875; m. at Dover, NH, 3 Jul 1836, JESSE JAQUITH MANSFIELD, b. at Alstead, NH, 7 Jul 1809 son of Aaron and Betsey (Jaquith) Mansfield; Jesse d. at Dummerston, 7 Nov 1886.

909) SUSANNA ABBOTT *(Edward^4, Edward^3, Thomas^2, George^1)*, b. 1765 daughter of Edward and Deborah (Stevens) Abbott; d. at Concord, 25 Feb 1841; m. by 1786, JOHN WEEKS, b. at Portsmouth, NH, 23 Jun 1757[2442] possibly the son of James Weeks; John d. at Concord, 6 Apr 1836.

John Weeks served as a private on the New Hampshire for four years during the Revolution in Colonel Alexander Scammel's Regiment. In his position, he was attached as a steward to the families of several high-ranking officers including General Enoch Poor, Colonel Henry Dearborn, and General John Stark.[2443]

2438 Mehitable Lufkin's death is reported in the records of the First Congregational Church of Concord. (Reed and Thorne, History and Manual of the First Congregational Church)

2439 Lapham, *History of Rumford*, p 369

2440 Revolutionary War Pension and Bounty-Land Warrant Application Files, Case W8068

2441 Lapham, *History of Rumford, Maine*, p 412

2442 Ancestry.com. *U.S., Sons of the American Revolution Membership Applications, 1889-1970* [database on-line].

2443 Revolutionary War Pension and Bounty-Land Warrant Application Files, Case W18324

James and Susanna had ten children born at Concord.[2444]

i ABIGAIL WEEKS, b. 29 Jul 1786; d. at Concord, 11 Aug 1872. Abigail did not marry.

ii MARY "POLLY" WEEKS, b. 13 Jul 1788; d. at Concord, 25 Aug 1820; m. at Concord, 6 Sep 1810, KEYES POWELL, b. at Concord, May 1787 son of Benjamin and Elizabeth (Bradley) Powell; Keyes d. at Strafford, 1 Nov 1841. After Polly's death, Keyes married Lydia Lougee.

iii NANCY WEEKS, b. 7 Apr 1791; d. after 1870; m. at Concord, 23 Mar 1815, EBENEZER FLANDERS, b. at Concord, 30 Apr 1790 son of Oliver and Abigail (Chandler) Flanders; Ebenezer d. at Concord, about 1836 (will 24 Jun 1836).

iv JOSEPH WEEKS, b. 21 Jul 1793; d. 19 May 1813.

v JAMES WEEKS, b. 22 Nov 1795; d. at Concord, 1865 (probate 28 Nov 1865); m. at Epsom, 19 Feb 1822, MARY LOCKE, b. at Epsom, 20 Sep 1800 daughter of Jonathan and Alice (Pearsons) Locke;[2445] Mary d. at Concord, about 1845. James m. 2nd, 31 May 1847, HANNAH MCCRILLIS, b. about 1795 daughter of William and Hannah (Brown) McCrillis.[2446] Hannah was living at the time of her husband's probate in 1865.

vi TIMOTHY ABBOT WEEKS, b. 17 Sep 1797; d. at Concord, 8 Nov 1807.

vii SAMUEL WEEKS, b. 25 May 1799; d. at Epsom, 28 Dec 1878; m. at Epsom, 28 Oct 1824, BETSY HEATH, b. at Epsom, 2 Dec 1798 daughter of Simon and Elizabeth (McClary) Heath; Betsy d. at Epsom, 1 Mar 1853.

viii GEORGE WEEKS, b. 26 Oct 1801; d. 8 Nov 1801.

ix ELIZA R. WEEKS, b. 17 Nov 1802; d. at Concord, 22 Apr 1881; m. 23 Jan 1829, JOHN BAILEY CRUMMETT, b. 3 Jan 1807 of undetermined parents; John d. at the almshouse in Concord, 7 Dec 1880. John was a tinsmith and died of "softening of the brain."

x HARRIET STICKNEY WEEKS, b. 11 Apr 1806; d. at Concord, 18 Apr 1893; m. at Concord, 28 Dec 1827, ROBERT CRUMMETT, b. about 1805 at Greenland; Robert d. at Concord, 17 Dec 1879.

910) TIMOTHY ABBOTT *(Edward⁴, Edward³, Thomas², George¹)*, b. 12 Mar 1769 son of Edward and Deborah (Stevens) Abbott; d. 23 Jan 1819; m. 1st, SARAH BRADLEY daughter of Abraham and Sarah (-) Bradley; Sarah d. 1810.[2447] Timothy m. 2nd, at Concord, 17 Apr 1811, his first cousin, LYDIA ABBOTT *(Aaron⁴, Aaron³, Thomas², George¹)*, b. 4 Apr 1771 daughter of Aaron and Lydia (Abbott) Abbott; Lydia d. at Concord, 25 May 1853.

Timothy was placed under guardianship as *non compos* in 1817. Benjamin Kimball, Jr. was named his guardian. The inventory included about 12 acres with buildings valued at $900.00 and a personal estate valued at $24.50. The guardianship of Benjamin Kimball was revoked 16 February 1818. That petition was made by the selectman of Concord as they thought the misdemeanors (which seem to be intemperance) of which Timothy Abbott was guilty were far removed and that he no longer needed a guardian. The original request for a guardian dated 19 May 1817 notes excessive drinking, neglect and wasting of his estate and causing his family want and suffering circumstances as a consequence.[2448] But after that, his property was perhaps transferred to the town which supported Timothy and his wife. After Timothy's death, his wife Lydia suffered a fractured hip as the result of a fall and was afterwards supported by the town.[2449]

Timothy Abbott and Sarah Bradley had three children born at Concord.

i ESTHER ABBOTT, b. 8 Apr 1802; m. at Fryeburg, ME, 29 Sep 1827, JAMES WALKER.

ii PHILBRICK BRADLEY ABBOTT, b. 26 Feb 1804; d. at Standish, ME, 1844; m. SUSAN D. USHER, b. at Hollis, ME, 25 Feb 1811 daughter of Abijah and Susan (Nason) Usher;[2450] Susan d. at Standish, 1855.

iii GEORGE S. ABBOTT, b. Jan 1809; d. at Lovell, ME, 14 May 1893; m. at Lovell, 10 Mar 1832, his fourth cousin once removed, BETSEY H. KIMBALL *(William Kimball⁶, Lucy Abbott Kimball⁵, Isaac⁴, Ebenezer³, John², George¹)*, b. at Lovell, 1814 daughter of William and Betsey (Kilgore) Kimball; Betsey d. at Boston, 17 Mar 1880.

2444 The Abbot genealogy adds an eleventh child, Edward Abbot Weeks, as a twin of Timothy Abbot Weeks. However, John's pension file includes a list of each child and his/her birth date and there is no Edward.

2445 Locke, *History and Genealogy of Captain John Locke*, p 93

2446 Epsom Historical Association, Sanborn Hill, part 2, http://epsomhistory.blogspot.com/2015/08/sanborn-hill-part-2-weeks-langley-house.html

2447 Ancestry.com, New Hampshire, Death and Disinterment Records, 1754-1947

2448 *New Hampshire. Probate Court (Rockingham County)*; Probate Place: *Rockingham, New Hampshire, Estate Papers, No 9494-9576, 1817*, Case 9549, accessed through ancestry.com

2449 Bouton, *History of Concord*, p 366

2450 Clayton, *History of York County, Maine*, p 364

911) SAMUEL ABBOTT *(Edward⁴, Edward³, Thomas², George¹)*, b. 8 Apr 1771 son of Edward and Deborah (Stevens) Abbott; d. at Switzerland County, IN, 1822 (probate 5 Jul 1822); m. at Pembroke, 4 Mar 1792, MARY "POLLY" CURRIER, b. at Concord, 13 Oct 1776 daughter of William and Mary (Carter) Currier;[2451] Polly d. 1822.

Samuel was a carpenter in New Hampshire where he had a business as a chairmaker. The family relocated to Buffalo, New York and then about 1818, the family moved to Switzerland County, Indiana[2452] where both Samuel and Polly died in 1822 perhaps in a flu epidemic.

Samuel Abbott did not leave a will and his estate entered probate 5 July 1822 with James Dugan as administrator. Sylvanus S. Kingsley was guardian for at least two of the children, Mary and Samuel.[2453]

Samuel Abbott and Polly Currier were parents of thirteen children, the first six children likely born in New Hampshire, the next children born at Buffalo, and the youngest child in Switzerland County.[2454]

i ELIZABETH "BETSEY" ABBOTT, b. 9 Oct 1793; d. at Indianapolis, 4 Feb 1881; m. about 1814, SYLVANUS SABIN "SILAS" KINGSLEY, b. at Rutland, VT, 29 Oct 1786 likely the son of Sylvanus and Naomi (-) Kingsley; Silas d. 25 Dec 1865.

ii MARY ABBOTT, b. 26 Aug 1795; d. 21 Oct 1811.

iii BELINDA BRIDGET ABBOTT, b. 3 Sep 1797; d. at Franklin, IN, after 1880; m. EPHRAIM DEAN, b. in MD, about 1790; Ephraim d. at Franklin, after 1880.

iv HARRIET ABBOTT, b. 28 Sep 1799

v HANNAH ABBOTT, b. 29 Jan 1802; d. 21 Nov 1811.

vi HIRAM ABBOTT, b. 23 Nov 1803; d. at Dearborn, IN, 1 Jan 1854; m. at Versailles, IN, 3 Apr 1828, NANCY ANDERSON, b. at Hancock County, PA, 18 Dec 1806; Nancy d. at Ripley County, IN, 28 Jan 1890. Nancy was second married to Thomas Coen.

vii ISAAC ABBOTT, b. 22 Feb 1805; d. at Meeker County, MN, 4 May 1872; m. at Dearborn County, IN, 14 Oct 1827, ELIZABETH FAULKNER, b. at Genesee, NY, 24 Mar 1809 daughter of Cornelius and Lucinda (Halstead) Faulkner; Elizabeth d. about 1854.

viii JOHN ABBOTT, b. 15 May 1807; d. Jan 1819.

ix RUTH ABBOTT, b. 22 Dec 1808; d. at Lawrenceburg, IN, 9 Jun 1889; m. 1st, about 1831, Mr. OLMSTEAD who has not been identified. Ruth m. 2nd, at Dearborn, 28 Oct 1841, JOSHUA NOTHERN, b. in OH, about 1814.

x EDWARD ABBOTT, b. 5 Nov 1811; d. at Center, IN, 8 Oct 1903; m. 8 Mar 1835, IRENA SCHOONOVER, b. at Genesee, NY, 17 Jul 1814 daughter of Levi and Jane (Peabody) Schoonover; Irena d. at Lebanon, IN, 28 Jan 1908.

xi MARY ABBOTT, b. 2 Mar 1814; d. at Switzerland County, IN, 22 Dec 1846; m. at Switzerland County, 20 Jul 1833, JOHN H. CASE, b. 1806; John d. at Sadorus, IL, 19 Sep 1888. John was second married to Fannie Weaver.

xii SAMUEL ABBOTT, b. 15 Sep 1817; d. 21 Mar 1818.

xiii SAMUEL ABBOTT, b. 21 Feb 1819; d. at Andrews, IN, 1 Dec 1903; m. at Wabash, IN, 30 Aug 1840, ELIZA ANN LESTER, b. at Switzerland County, 5 Mar 1821 daughter of David and Sarah (Applebee) Lester; Eliza d. at Andrews, 24 Jun 1906.

912) DEBORAH ABBOTT *(Edward⁴, Edward³, Thomas², George¹)*, b. at Concord, 29 May 1774 daughter of Edward and Deborah (Stevens) Abbott; d. at Rumford, ME, 20 Apr 1861; m. PHINEAS HOWE, b. at Bolton, MA, 25 Mar 1769 son of Phineas and Experience (Pollard) Howe;[2455] Phineas d. 27 Dec 1847.

Deborah Abbott and Phineas Howe were parents of five children born at Rumford.

[2451] Currier and Currier, *The Genealogy of Richard Currier*, p 26. The Abbot and Abbot genealogy gives her name as Ruth Currier, but the Currier genealogy says Mary Currier and the marriage record says Polly Currier.

[2452] A. W. Bowen Publishers, A Portrait and Biographical Record of Boone and Clinton Counties, p 193

[2453] Switzerland County, Probate Order Book, Volume 1, pp 172-173; volume A, p. 108; volume A, p 122

[2454] It is possible there was a youngest fourteenth child, Isaiah, who was born in 1821 and died as an infant.

[2455] The division of William Pollard's estate in 1763 includes a disbursement to his daughter Elizabeth wife of Phineas Howe.

i CHARLOTTE HOWE, b. 21 Aug 1800; d. at Carthage, ME, 24 May 1882; m. at Rumford, 27 Feb 1823, SAMUEL JACKSON BUNKER, b. about 1797 son of John and Sally (-) Bunker; Samuel d. at Carthage, 16 Jan 1884.

ii PHINEAS HOWE, b. 25 Feb 1802; d. at Canton, ME, 22 Sep 1870; m. at Rumford, 17 Jun 1828, PHILA PARK HOLLAND, b. about 1809 likely the daughter of Samuel and Phila (Park) Holland of Dixfield, ME; Phila d. at Canton, 14 May 1883.

iii LOUISA HOWE, b. 19 Dec 1805; d. at Rumford, 21 Aug 1862; m. 26 Dec 1824, MERRILL FARNUM, b. at Rumford, 29 Sep 1794 son of Benjamin and Sarah (Thompson) Farnum; Merrill d. at Rumford, 14 Sep 1871.

iv GEORGE W. HOWE, b. 3 Jul 1810; d. at Rumford, after 1860. George did not marry. At the 1850 and 1860 census, George was living with his mother in Rumford.

v MARY HOWE, b. 29 Jan 1817; d. at Buckfield, ME, 25 Jun 1885; m. about 1837, GEORGE WASHINGTON BISBEE, b. at Buckfield, 6 Jul 1812 son of Elisha and Joanna (Sturtevant) Bisbee; George d. at Peru, ME, 27 Jan 1872.

913) MEHITABLE SALTMARSH *(Betsey Abbott Saltmarsh⁴, Edward³, Thomas², George¹)*, b. at Concord, 12 Apr 1762 daughter of Thomas and Betsey (Abbott) Saltmarsh; d. at Gilford, NH, 25 Oct 1814; m. at Goffstown, 9 Feb 1784, JAMES HOYT, b. at Kingston, 28 Mar 1762 son of Eliphalet and Mary (Peaslee) Hoyt; James d. 1834. After Mehitable's death, James married Abigail Whittier in 1815 and Huldah Fifield in 1822.

In his will written 9 July 1826 (probate 11 August 1834), James Hoyt bequeaths to beloved wife Huldah the income on one-fourth part of his property. She also has use of part of the dwelling house and the barn. There are other provisions made for her support and maintenance. Beloved daughter Sally Hoyt receives $100 to be paid to her by her brother Peaslee Hoyt within three years. Beloved daughter Betsy Weeks also receives $100 to be paid by Peaslee. Beloved son Eliphalet also receives $100. Grandson Nathan Weeks receives $50. Son Peaslee receives the property in Gilford on which Peaslee is now living. All the remainder of the real property is bequeathed to son Thomas. Thomas is the sole executor of the estate.[2456]

Mehitable and James Hoyt were parents of six children born at Gilford, New Hampshire.

i SALLY HOYT, b. about 1786; d. at Readfield, ME, Mar 1850; m. 22 Jan 1806, her first cousin, ELIPHALET HOYT, b. 9 Jul 1779 son of Peaslee and Margaret (Hubbard) Hoyt; Eliphalet d. 15 Aug 1856.

ii BETSY HOYT, b. about 1788; d. at Gilford, NH, 15 May 1843; m. 28 Jun 1806, BENJAMIN WEEKS, b. at Gilford, 4 Apr 1788 son of Benjamin and Sarah (Weed) Weeks; Benjamin d. at Gilford, 29 Dec 1863. After Betsy's death, Benjamin married Lucinda.

iii ELIPHALET HOYT, b. about 1790; d. at Readfield, after 1860; m. 1812, his first cousin, JOANNA HOYT, b. 5 May 1787 daughter of Peaslee and Margaret (Hubbard) Hoyt; Joanna d. at Belgrade, ME, after 1870.

iv THOMAS HOYT, b. 4 Aug 1796; d. at Gilford, 13 Dec 1857; m. MIRIAM HOYT, b. at Gilmanton, about 1790 daughter of Simeon and Miriam (Morrill) Hoyt; Miriam d. at Gilford, 26 Oct 1880.

v NATHAN HOYT, b. about 1798; no further record but died before 1826 when his father wrote his will.

vi PEASLEE HOYT, b. about 1799; d. at Gilford, 11 May 1851; m. Hannah who is not yet identified; Hannah d. at Gilford, 23 Jul 1865.

914) JOHN SALTMARSH *(Betsey Abbott Saltmarsh⁴, Edward³, Thomas², George¹)*, b. at Concord, 21 May 1764 son of Thomas and Betsey (Abbott) Saltmarsh; d. after 1850 (living in Bedford at the 1850 U.S. Census); m. at Goffstown, 22 Nov 1785, SUSAN BURNHAM, b. at Ipswich, 1756 daughter of Samuel and Martha (Story) Burnham; Susan d. Jun 1851.

As many as six children have been reported for this family. The History of Goffstown reports just two children[2457] for this family and marriage records were located for just those two children who are listed here. Names of the other proposed children are Samuel, Jabez, Thomas, and Nehemiah.

i JOHN SALTMARSH, b. 1786; m. at Goffstown, 29 Mar 1810, SALLY GOLDSMITH.

ii BETSEY SALTMARSH, b. about 1790; d. at Goffstown, 31 Mar 1878; m. 29 Mar 1810, AMOS HARRIMAN, b. at Goffstown, 1781 son of Peter and Lydia (Jackman) Harriman; Amos d. at Goffstown, 7 Mar 1864.

[2456] New Hampshire, Wills and Probate Records, 1643-1982, *New Hampshire. Probate Court (Strafford County)*; Probate Place: *Strafford, New Hampshire, Probate Records, Vol 45-46, 1833-1834*

[2457] Hadley, *History of the Town of Goffstown*, volume II, p 446

915) MARY "POLLY" SALTMARSH *(Betsey Abbott Saltmarsh[4], Edward[3], Thomas[2], George[1])*, b. at Concord, 28 Aug 1766 daughter of Thomas and Betsey (Abbott) Saltmarsh; d. at Peterborough, 21 Apr 1848; m. at Goffstown, 31 Mar 1791, SAMUEL VOSE, b. at Bedford, 23 May 1759 son of Samuel and Phebe (Vickery) Vose; Samuel d. at Antrim, NH, 8 Aug 1830.

Deacon Samuel Vose came to Antrim about 1788. Samuel and Mary lived in a log cabin in Antrim during their early family life.[2458] Samuel and Mary Vose had nine children born at Antrim.

i SAMUEL VOSE, b. 2 Aug 1792; b. at New Portland, 4 Nov 1860; m. RUTH D. HANSON, b. at New Portland, 12 Sep 1810 daughter of Nathan and Dorcas (True) Hanson; Ruth d. at Portland, 4 May 1895.

ii THOMAS VOSE, b. 2 Aug 1792; d. at Antrim, 22 Mar 1849; m. 1st, 20 May 1823, SALLY MUZZEY, b. at Wear, Mar 1798 daughter of Dimond and Mary (Waldron) Muzzey; Sally d. 9 Dec 1845. Thomas m. 2nd, 1 Jun 1847, ISABELLA WALDRON.

iii POLLY VOSE, b. 26 Sep 1795; d. at Peterborough, NH, 28 Mar 1838; m. 25 Sep 1834, as his second wife, PHILIP AVERILL, b. at Amherst, NH, 27 Feb 1788 son of Thomas and Mary (Dresser) Averill; Philip d. at Peterborough, 27 Sep 1858. Philip was first married to Hannah Boutwell and third married to Hannah Barber.

iv ISAAC VOSE, b. 10 Jun 1797; died young.

v DERBY VOSE, b. 15 May 1799; died young.

vi JOHN VOSE, b. 28 Aug 1801; d. at Peterborough, 4 Jun 1867; m. at Peterborough, 4 May 1829, JULIANNA HUNT, b. 14 Mar 1802 daughter of Timothy and Nancy (Wade) Hunt; Julianna d. at Antrim, 23 Dec 1831. John m. 2nd, about 1832, MARIA POORE, b. at Antrim, 14 Aug 1804 daughter of Frederick and Mercy (Barber) Poore; Maria d. at Peterborough, 19 Aug 1888.

vii HAZEN S. VOSE, b. 12 Jul 1804; d. 26 Sep 1828.

viii EDWARD LUKE VOSE, b. 16 Aug 1806; d. at Antrim, 1 May 1868; m. 28 Oct 1835, AURELIA WILSON, b. at Stoddard, about 1815 son of Joel Wilson; Aurelia d. at Antrim, 3 May 1889.

ix HARRIET VOSE, b. 9 Mar 1810; d. 1840. Harriet did not marry. She died of consumption.

916) EDWARD ABBOTT SALTMARSH *(Betsey Abbott Saltmarsh[4], Edward[3], Thomas[2], George[1])*, b. 1768 likely at Goffstown son of Thomas and Betsey (Abbott) Saltmarsh; d. at Hookset, NH, 11 Mar 1851; m. at Goffstown, 19 Oct 1791, SARAH "SALLY" STORY, b. 1773 (based on age at time of death) daughter of Nehemiah and Sarah (Gold) Story; Sally d. 19 May 1860.

Edward and Sally Saltmarsh had thirteen children born at Goffstown.

i NEHEMIAH SALTMARSH, b. 5 Jan 1792; d. at Plattsburgh, NY, in 1813 during the War of 1812.

ii AARON SALTMARSH, b. 1793; d. at Concord, 1842; m. about 1820, JOANNA GEORGE, b. at Bradford, NH, about 1799 daughter of Austin and Lydia (George) George;[2459] Joanna d. at Concord, 5 May 1878.

iii ABBOTT SALTMARSH, b. 10 Nov 1795; d. at Concord, 25 Jan 1876; m. 1st, at Newport, NH, 12 Mar 1823, POLLY J. STEVENS, b. at Newport, 5 Jun 1803 daughter of John and Lois (Buswell) Stevens; Polly d. at Concord, 22 Nov 1851. Abbott m. 2nd, about 1852, Polly's sister, LOIS STEVENS, b. at Newport, 29 Jan 1806; Lois d. at Concord, 26 Jun 1889. Lois Stevens was first married to Amos Kempton.

iv LUCY SALTMARSH, b. about 1798; d. at Henniker, 20 Jan 1859; m. at Goffstown, 2 Mar 1820, JOHN POPE, b. at Washington, VT, 5 Nov 1797 sons of Thomas and Sally (Jones) Pope; John d. at Aurora, IL (at the home of his son Oramel), 22 Apr 1882.

v BETSEY SALTMARSH, b. 20 Apr 1800; d. at Hooksett, 3 Aug 1883; m. at Goffstown, 1 Jun 1819, JAMES PUTNAM, b. at Hancock, NH, 19 Jun 1797 son of Joseph and Rebecca (Barton) Putnam; James d. at Hooksett, 16 Mar 1874.

vi THOMAS SALTMARSH, b. about 1802; d. at Weare, 5 Aug 1885; m. 1826, SOPHIA MUZZY, b. at Henniker, 1809 daughter of Benjamin and Lydia (Peaslee) Muzzy; Sophia d. at Weare, 30 Jan 1888.

2458 Cochrane, *History of Antrim*, p 725

2459 Gould, *Early Families of Bradford*, p 174

vii HENRY SALTMARSH, b. 2 Feb 1804; d. at Auburn, NH, 1 Sep 1888; m. KEZIA BATCHELDER, b. 17 Dec 1804 *perhaps* the daughter of James P. and Rebecca (Wintworth) Batchelder; Kezia d. at Hooksett, 21 Nov 1868.

viii HAZEN SALTMARSH, b. 1806; d. at Hooksett, 10 Nov 1890; m. 1st, at Goffstown, 1829, SALLY BATCHELDER; Sally d. at Hooksett, 17 Jan 1855. Hazen m. 2nd, at Epsom, 29 Oct 1856, MARY MATTHEWS, b. at Milton Mills, NH, about 1822; Mary d. at Bow, 20 Nov 1898.

ix SUSAN SALTMARSH, b. 9 Jul 1808; d. at Hooksett, 2 Jul 1884; m. at Pembroke, 14 Apr 1825, ERI POOR, b. at Hooksett, 20 Jul 1800 son of Samuel and Ann (Bridges) Poor; Eri d. at Hooksett, 28 Jan 1874.

x GILMAN SALTMARSH, b. 1810; d. at Bow, 25 Apr 1899; m. LYDIA WARREN CLOUGH, b. at Bow, 28 Dec 1818 daughter of Daniel and Margaret (Shirley) Clough; Lydia d. at Bow, 26 May 1896.

xi FRANKLIN SALTMARSH, b. 1812; d. at Clintonville, NY, 6 Apr 1878; m. at Washington, VT, 20 Apr 1834, BETSEY STEVENS RING, b. at Washington, VT, 30 Aug 1814 daughter of Moses and Bethiah (Story) Ring; Betsey d. at Clintonville, 9 May 1900.

xii SALLY S. SALTMARSH, b. 1814; d. at Hooksett, 1834; m. at Goffstown, 25 Sep 1832, DAVID PAGE, b. at Bow, 8 Jul 1799; David d. at Bow, after 1860. David was second married to Lucinda.

xiii ABIGAIL SALTMARSH, b. 19 May 1817; d. at Cedar, IA, 1903; m. 5 Jul 1842, CYRUS SARGENT, b. at Bow, 3 Mar 1816 son of James and Betsey (Stewart) Sargent; Cyrus d. at Cedar, 1903.

917) THOMAS SALTMARSH *(Betsey Abbott Saltmarsh⁴, Edward³, Thomas², George¹)*, b. at Goffstown, 1771 son of Thomas and Betsey (Abbott) Saltmarsh; d. at Saco, ME, 1804; m. at Wolfeboro, 7 Jun 1799, BETSY EVANS, b. 21 May 1780 daughter of Benjamin and Lydia (Browne) Evans. Elizabeth was second married to Joseph Young.

Very little could be found for this family. Thomas was a physician in Saco, Maine. Records for two children were located for this family, and there may be two other children but that is not clear.

i BETSEY SALTMARSH, b. at New Durham, NH, 6 Feb 1799; d. at Dover, NH, after 1870; m. at Dover, 27 Feb 1827, THEODORE LITTLEFIELD, b. in ME, about 1797; Theodore d. at Dover, 1865 (probate Nov 1865).

ii LYDIA SALTMARSH, b. at New Durham, 12 Aug 1801; d. at Dover, after 1850. Lydia did not marry.

918) SAMUEL SALTMARSH *(Betsey Abbott Saltmarsh⁴, Edward³, Thomas², George¹)*, b. at Goffstown, 1775 son of Thomas and Betsey (Abbott) Saltmarsh; d. at Goffstown, 1844; m. 28 May 1800, BETSY BURNHAM, b. about 1780; Betsy d. at Goffstown, 1840.

In his will written 28 February 1840 (probate 7 May 1844), Samuel Saltmarsh bequeathed $375 to his eldest daughter Betsey B. Talent. The entirety of his real estate was left to his three daughters Sally Saltmarsh, Hannah B. Saltmarsh, and Mary Saltmarsh. Sally, Hannah, and Mary also receive all the personal property. Daughter Hannah B. Saltmarsh was named sole executor.[2460]

Samuel and Betsey Saltmarsh had four daughters born likely at Goffstown. The eldest daughter, Betsey, relocated to New York. The three other daughters remained in New Hampshire and each of them married, although married relatively later in life and each married a man several years younger than themselves. One child was located for one of the daughters, and it is possible that this child is the only grandchild of Samuel and Betsey Saltmarsh.

i ELIZABETH B. "BETSEY" SALTMARSH, b. about 1801; d. at Guilderland, NY, 4 Oct 1882; m. at Goffstown, 6 Mar 1821, ANTIPAS D. TALLENT, b. about 1795 whose origins unknown to me; Antipas d. at Menands, NY, 13 Aug 1847. I have not located any children for this couple.

ii SALLY SALTMARSH, b. about 1805; d. at Goffstown, 24 Aug 1884; m. at Goffstown, 6 Jan 1859, JEREMIAH S. PARKER, b. at St. Johnsbury, VT, about 1826 son of John Parker. Sally and Jeremiah seem to have lived together only briefly. In the 1860 U. S. Census, Sally was living with her sister Hannah. Jeremiah filed for divorce from Sally on grounds of abandonment and they were divorced 6 Dec 1865.

iii HANNAH B. SALTMARSH, b. at Goffstown, 28 Jul 1809; d. at Goffstown, 14 Jun 1888; m. 12 Mar 1855, CHARLES MORGRAGE, b. at Goffstown, 1 Mar 1832 son of Charles and Lucy (Hadley) Morgrage. After Hannah's death, Charles married Mandana Potter. Charles died at Goffstown, 26 Aug 1922. Hannah Morgrage wrote her will 5 Jul 1887. She bequeaths to her husband household items which are to go to her grandnephew Charles Blake after her husband's decease. Her husband also receives the income of the real estate during his lifetime. After his death, all the real estate goes to Hannah's niece, Mary E. Blake, or to her heirs. Hannah also includes a bequest for her grandniece Bessie Blake. Mary E. Blake is the only child of Hannah's sister Mary.

[2460] New Hampshire, Wills and Probate Records, 1643-1982, Hillsborough, Probate Records volume 48-49, 1839-1846, will of Samuel Saltmarsh.

iv MARY SALTMARSH, b. at Goffstown, 9 Feb 1814; d. at Goffstown, 16 Nov 1844; m. by 1844, THOMAS STEVENS, b. 9 Jun 1823 son of Jonathan and Samantha (Kidder) Stevens; Thomas d. at Goffstown, 1 Jul 1876. Mary and Thomas had one daughter, Mary, who married Leonard Blake.

919) CATHERINE SALTMARSH *(Betsey Abbott Saltmarsh⁴, Edward³, Thomas², George¹)*, b. at Goffstown, 1777 daughter of Thomas and Betsey (Abbott) Saltmarsh; d. after 1850 (still living at the 1850 U.S. Census); m. her first cousin, THOMAS SALTMARSH, b. at Bedford, MA, 22 Aug 1772 son of Seth and Ruth (Bowman) Saltmarsh; Thomas d. at Gilford, NH, 18 Sep 1823.

Catherine and Thomas Saltmarsh were the parents of possibly seven children, although the information is limited. There is record evidence related to five of the children. The oldest child was born at Goffstown and the other children likely born at Gilford, New Hampshire.

i WILLIAM SALTMARSH, b. 10 Feb 1798; nothing further known.

ii SETH SALTMARSH, b. about 1799; d. likely at Gilford, after 1850; m. 5 Feb 1824, MARY "POLLY" GILMAN, b. at Gilford, 25 Jun 1804 daughter of Levi and Sally (Hunt) Gilman;[2461] Polly d. at Woodstock, NH, 1 Jan 1890.

iii MARTHA SALTMARSH, b. about 1802

iv MARY SALTMARSH, b. about 1804

v ELIZA SALTMARSH, b. 1808; d. at Gilford, 21 May 1825.

vi THOMAS SALTMARSH, b. about 1809; d. at Gilford, after 1870; m. at Gilford, 16 Oct 1835, SALLY H. GILMAN, b. at Gilford, Oct 1818 daughter of Levi and Mary (Folsom) Gilman;[2462] Sally d. after 1870.

vii MATILDA SALTMARSH, b. 1819; d. at Gilford, 1 Aug 1856; m. 7 Dec 1837, MOSES BROWN DOCKHAM, b. at Tuftonboro, 1811 son of Ephraim and Dolly (Brown) Dockham; Moses d. at Gilmanton, after 1882. Moses has three further marriages to Mary C. Gilman, Hannah, and Louisa Maxfield.

920) ISAAC SALTMARSH *(Betsey Abbott Saltmarsh⁴, Edward³, Thomas², George¹)*, b. at Goffstown, 1779 son of Thomas and Betsey (Abbott) Saltmarsh; d. at Antrim, NH, 13 Mar 1823; m. at Bradford, NH, 13 Nov 1805, PHEBE STRATTON, b. at Marlboro, MA, 27 Feb 1790 daughter of Jonathan and Abigail (Barnes) Stratton; Phebe d. 13 Sep 1872.

Isaac Saltmarsh came to Antrim in 1793 where he married and raised his family.

Isaac Saltmarsh did not leave a will and the estate entered probate 2 April 1823. Phebe Saltmarsh was named administrator of the estate. The total value of the estate was $1,275.21 including the $900 value of the farm. On 7 July 1830, John Worthley guardian of minor child Betsey and Phebe Saltmarsh guardian of minor Reed, petitioned to sell the 80-acre farm in order to be able to provide support for the two minor children. The dower rights were set-off to Phebe 6 April 1831.[2463]

Son Reed P. Saltmarsh did not marry. In his will dated 2 March 1894, he made small monetary bequests to Hattie F. Burnham (who is a minor) daughter of George F. Burnham and granddaughter of Elizabeth Burnham and Clinton F. Saltmarsh (who is a son of George F. Saltmarsh[2464] and Mary Gore). He also leaves a bequest of fifty dollars to Maple Wood Cemetery Association to be used to take care of lot 119. He leaves all his real estate and personal property to Hannah B. Saltmarsh (widow of his brother Cyrus Saltmarsh) for her use during her life. After her decease, the estate goes to the town of Antrim for support of the poor.[2465]

The History of Antrim and History of Goffstown report four children in this family. The Abbot genealogy adds three other children for whom no records could be located. These additional three children perhaps all died in childhood. Those three children are named as Jackson, Abigail, and Thomas in the Abbot genealogy and are not included here.[2466][2467] After the death of her husband Isaac, Phebe Saltmarsh and her two unmarried children, Betsey and Reed, lived with Cyrus and his wife Hannah.[2468] There was just one grandchild in this family, and she died without marrying.

[2461] The names of Polly's parents are given on her death record as Levi Gilman and Sally Hunt.

[2462] Folsom, *A Genealogy of the Folsom Family*, p 84

[2463] New Hampshire County Probate Records, Hillsborough, 30:273; 32:308; 38:60; 38:296; 39:39; Guardianships for Betsey and Reed, 23:464; 23:465; 38:373; 38:374

[2464] George F. Saltmarsh was the son of Reed's first cousin Thomas Saltmarsh and his wife Sophia Muzzey.

[2465] *New Hampshire. Probate Court (Hillsborough County)*; Probate Place: *Hillsborough, New Hampshire*, Probate Records volume 161, p 112

[2466] Abbot, *Genealogical Register*, p 102

[2467] According to the History of Antrim, p 670, Reed P. Saltmarsh, one of the children in this family, provided some of the background information for that text as he was still living at the time it was written. As the History of Antrim lists only four children in the family that suggests that perhaps that is correct.

[2468] Year: 1860; Census Place: Antrim, Hillsborough, New Hampshire; Roll: M653_672; Page: 593; Family History Library Film: 803672

i CYRUS SALTMARSH, b. 21 May 1809; d. at Antrim, 5 Aug 1872; m. HANNAH B. HOWE, b. at Stockbridge, VT, 8 May 1823 daughter of Otis and Hannah B. (Carr) Howe; Hannah d. at Antrim, 7 Dec 1903. Cyrus and Hannah had one daughter Mary J. Saltmarsh born in 1861 and died in 1885 without marrying.

ii STILLMAN SALTMARSH, b. 12 Dec 1811; died young.

iii BETSEY A. SALTMARSH, b. 1815; d. at Antrim, 11 Jan 1870. Betsey did not marry; she was reported to be an invalid (History of Antrim).

iv REED P. SALTMARSH, b. 4 Dec 1820; d. at Antrim, 14 May 1898.

921) MARY "MOLLY" WILSON *(Mary Hall Wilson⁴, Deborah Abbott Hall³, Thomas², George¹)*, b. at Concord, 23 Jul 1772 daughter of Thomas and Mary (Hall) Wilson; m. 1st, 25 Mar 1792, JOHN THORNDIKE, b. at Beverly, 30 Nov 1768 son of Larkin and Ruth (Woodbury) Thorndike. Dr. John Thorndike died at Concord, 19 Mar 1821. Mary m. 2nd, 27 Nov 1823, her third cousin, ABIEL WALKER *(Ruth Abbott Walker⁴, Nathaniel³, Nathaniel², George¹)*, b. at Concord, 5 Jul 1766 son of James and Ruth (Abbott) Walker. Abiel 1st married, 3 Feb 1807, JUDITH DAVIS, b. at Concord, 24 Feb 1775 daughter of Robert and Sarah (Walker) Davis; Judith d. at Concord, 1 Apr 1808.

John Thorndike was a physician in Concord. Dr. John Thorndike did not leave a will and widow Mary Thorndike requested that she be named administrator of the estate. The value of real estate was $1725 and personal estate was $847.03.[2469]

Mary's second husband, Abiel Walker, had one child from his first marriage to Judith Davis. That daughter died at thirteen. The will of Abiel Walker includes bequests to his numerous nieces and nephews and to his brother Peter Walker.

Mary Wilson and John Thorndike had four children born at Concord.

i MARY THORNDIKE, b. 12 Oct 1793; d. at Concord, 23 Feb 1878; m. 19 May 1812, CHARLES HUTCHINS, b. at Concord, 6 Nov 1786 son of Abel and Betsey (Partridge) Hutchins; Charles d. at Concord, 1868 (probate, 1868). Charles's father Abel Hutchins was a skilled clockmaker whose clocks are still highly sought after in the antique auction market.

ii JOHN LARKIN THORNDIKE, b. 23 Apr 1796; d. at Pittsfield, NH, 23 Jan 1884; m. 28 Nov 1824, MARIA JOY, b. at Pittsfield, 25 Apr 1804 daughter of Jacob and Sarah (Pickering) Joy;[2470] Maria d. at Pittsfield, 20 Sep 1845.

iii THOMAS WILSON THORNDIKE, b. 26 Nov 1797; d. at Weare, NH, 26 Jan 1888; m. at Henniker, 19 Nov 1823, RUTH GAGE DOW, b. at Henniker, 8 Dec 1794 daughter of Winthrop and Mary (-) Dow;[2471] Ruth d. at Weare, 17 Apr 1873.

iv HENRY THORNDIKE, b. 22 May 1800; d. 11 May 1824.

Abiel Walker and Judith Davis had one child.

i JUDITH WALKER, b. 23 Mar 1808; d. 15 Oct 1825.

922) BERIAH ABBOTT *(Daniel⁴, George³, Thomas², George¹)*, b. at Concord, about 1758 son of Daniel and Rachel (Abbott) Abbot; d. at Pomfret, VT, 13 Mar 1832;[2472] m. about 1785 the widow MARY ANDREWS (widow Mary Fairfield). Mary d. 29 Jul 1813; Beriah m. 2nd, MARTHA GRISWOLD, b. about 1759 and d. at Randolph, VT, 28 Jan 1841.

In January 1776, Beriah Abbott enlisted for a term of one year in Captain Joshua Abbott's foot company. Beriah Abbott served as a private in the New Hampshire regiment enlisting 22 March 1777 for a three-year term and was discharged 20 March 1780. He again enlisted 29 May 1781 for a three-year term in Captain Daniel Livermore's company. He was discharged 7 June 1783, the last year of his enlistment being provided by a substitute that Beriah procured. He applied for a pension on 20 April 1818 giving his age as 60 years old. He related that he had infirmities and a broken constitution which he attributed to his hard and long military service. He further reported having to care for his 75-year old sister-in-law which was a great bother to him. He reported just one child, Moses then age 33 who had a large family to support and was greatly in debt. The inventory included as part of the pension application showed real estate valued at $850 for 53 acres of land with buildings, $50 as the value of a share in the New Hampshire turnpike road, and a personal estate of $52.28.[2473]

There is just one child known for Beriah Abbott and Mary Andrews.

[2469] *New Hampshire. Probate Court (Rockingham County)*; Probate Place: *Rockingham, New Hampshire*, Estate paper 10288

[2470] Joy, *Thomas Joy and His Descendants*, p 42

[2471] The 1830 will of Winthrop Dow includes a bequest to his daughter Ruth Thorndike. New Hampshire Probate, Hillsborough, volume 41, p 83

[2472] Ancestry.com, *Vermont, Vital Records, 1720-1908* (Provo, UT, USA: Ancestry.com Operations, Inc., 2013).

[2473] Revolutionary War Pension and Bounty-Land Warrant Application Files, accessed through fold3

i MOSES ABBOTT, b. at Lebanon, NH, 21 Apr 1787; d. at Windsor, VT, 12 May 1850; m. at Canaan, NH, RELIEF STRAW, of Canaan, b. about 1803 daughter of Jacob and Abigail (Young) Straw; Relief d., likely at Charleston, VT, after 1860. After Moses's death, Relief married Richard Gile.

923) SAMUEL ABBOTT *(Daniel⁴, George³, Thomas², George¹)*, b. at Concord, 26 Mar 1764 son of Daniel and Rachel (Abbott) Abbot; d. at Concord, 1 Dec 1849; m. 17 Nov 1787, MARY T. "POLLY" STORY, b. 16 Oct 1764 daughter of Jeremiah and Mary "Polly" (Burnham) Story; Polly d. 21 Dec 1849.

Samuel was a farmer in Concord. Samuel and Mary Abbott had seven children all born at Concord. Of the six children who married, five of them married other descendants of George and Hannah Abbott.

i RACHEL ABBOTT, b. 31 Aug 1788; d. at Concord, 1876; m. 31 May 1812, her third cousin, JOHN FLANDERS *(Mary Chandler Flanders⁵, Daniel Chandler⁴, Tabitha Abbott Chandler³, Nathaniel², George¹)*, b. at Concord, 19 Jan 1787 son of Richard and Mary (Chandler) Flanders; John d. at Concord, 1856. John is a child in Family 1086.

ii JEREMIAH ABBOTT, b. 29 Oct 1790; d. at Concord, after 1870; m. 14 Jun 1821, his fourth cousin once removed, REBECCA CHANDLER *(Lucy Ballard Chandler⁵, Lydia Chandler⁴, John Chandler³, Hannah Abbott Chandler², George¹)*, b. at Andover, 17 Jul 1790 daughter of Nathan and Lucy (Ballard) Chandler. Rebecca is a child in Family 444.

iii POLLY ABBOTT, b. 30 Apr 1794; d. at Bridgewater, VT, 8 May 1873; m. about 1820, her second cousin, CALVIN ABBOTT *(Moses⁵, Nathaniel⁴, Nathaniel³, Nathaniel², George¹)*, b. at Concord, 14 Jul 1791 son of Moses and Mary (Batchelder) Abbott; Calvin d. at Bridgewater, 28 Oct 1856. Calvin is a child in Family 983.

iv HULDAH ABBOTT, b. 30 Mar 1797; d. at Concord, 8 Jul 1880; m. at Concord, 15 Apr 1819, her third cousin, JACOB FLANDERS *(Mary Chandler Flanders⁵, Daniel Chandler⁴, Tabitha Abbott Chandler³, Nathaniel², George¹)*, b. at Concord, 7 Feb 1796 son of Richard and Mary (Chandler) Flanders; Jacob d. at Concord, 10 Jul 1847. Jacob is a child in Family 1086.

v JOSEPH STORY ABBOTT, b. 28 May 1800; d. at Concord, 10 Apr 1878; m. 26 Dec 1827, ESTHER FARNUM, b. at Concord, 2 Nov 1803 daughter of Isaac and Hannah (Martin) Farnum; Esther d. at Concord, 15 Oct 1890.

vi GEORGE DANIEL ABBOTT, b. 14 Aug 1804; d. at Concord, 29 Sep 1868; m. 8 Nov 1832, his third cousin, PHEBE BALLARD *(Nathan Ballard⁶, Nathan Ballard⁵, Hannah Chandler Ballard⁴, John Chandler³, Hannah Abbott Chandler², George¹)*, b. at Concord, 4 Apr 1807 daughter of Nathan and Hannah (Buss) Ballard; Phebe d. at Concord, 3 Jan 1860.

vii ABIGAIL STORY ABBOTT, b. 10 May 1807; d. at Concord, 1828.

924) JEREMIAH ABBOTT *(Daniel⁴, George³, Thomas², George¹)*, b. at Concord, 21 Feb 1766 son of Daniel and Rachel (Abbott) Abbot; d. at Pomfret, VT, 10 Feb 1811; m. 15 Jan 1795, CLARISSA PERRY, b. at Ashford, CT, 31 Mar 1770 daughter of Robert and Sarah (Hodges) Perry;[2474] Clarissa d. 10 Oct 1826.

Jeremiah was a farmer in Lebanon, New Hampshire and about 1800 relocated to Pomfret, Vermont. He owned 300 acres in Pomfret. His wife Clarissa died of spotted fever.[2475]

Jeremiah and Clarissa were parents of eight children.

i ALFREDA ABBOTT, b. at Lebanon, NH, 3 Jul 1796; d. at Pomfret, VT, 25 Mar 1813; m. Mar 1812, JOSHUA REED of undetermined parentage; Joshua d. at Pomfret, about May 1818 (will proved 18 Jun 1818). In his will, Joshua left his estate to his brother George.[2476]

ii AMANDA ABBOTT, b. at Lebanon, 5 Apr 1798; d. at Royalton, VT, 4 Nov 1875; m. at Pomfret, 3 Jun 1818, WILLIAM MAXHAM, b. in Vermont 1797; William d. at Royalton, 13 Jul 1867 of "the effects of smoking."[2477]

[2474] Robert Perry was an early settler of Windsor County, Vermont. Aldrich and Holmes, *History of Windsor County, Vermont*, p 969

[2475] Vail and White, *Pomfret Vermont*, volume II, p 426

[2476] *Vermont. Probate Court (Hartford District)*; Probate Place: *Windsor, Vermont, Probate Records, Vol 4-5 1809-1816, p 607*

[2477] "Vermont Vital Records, 1760-1954," database with images, *FamilySearch* (https://familysearch.org/ark:/61903/1:1:XFK4-BPB : 3 November 2017), William Maxham, 13 Jul 1867, Death; State Capitol Building, Montpelier; FHL microfilm 27,624.

iii ROBERT P. ABBOTT, b. at Pomfret, VT, 23 Jan 1801; d. at West Windsor, 13 Jul 1849; m. 11 May 1822, SARAH CADY, b. at Reading, VT, 30 Jul 1800 daughter of Nebadiah and Sarah (Washburn) Cady;[2478] Sarah d. at Windsor, 18 Jul 1861.

iv DANIEL ABBOTT, b. at Pomfret, 25 Feb 1802; d. at Pomfret, 18 Apr 1890; m. 27 Oct 1828, DEBORAH DEWOLFE, b. at Luzerne, NY, 5 Dec 1809 daughter of Daniel Shays and Mary (Hodges) DeWolfe;[2479] Deborah d. at Woodstock, VT, 20 Feb 1893.

v POLLY ABBOTT, b. at Pomfret, 12 Feb 1804; d. at Pomfret, 20 May 1888; m. 24 Mar 1822, EDMUND HODGES, b. at Pomfret, 24 Apr 1799 son of Seth and Martha (Hodges) Hodges;[2480] Edmund d. at Pomfret, 27 Feb 1864.

vi IRA ABBOTT, b. 5 Jan 1806; d. 25 Jan 1813.

vii CLARISSA ABBOTT, b. 7 Aug 1807; d. 8 Jul 1827.

viii SARAH H. ABBOTT, b. 19 Apr 1810; d. 21 Apr 1811.

925) DANIEL ABBOTT *(Daniel⁴, George³, Thomas², George¹)*, b. at Concord, 7 Mar 1770 son of Daniel and Rachel (Abbott) Abbot; d. unknown; m. 29 Jan 1794, LUCY HARVEY, b. at Gilsum, NH, 15 Dec 1768 daughter of Thomas and Grace (Willey) Harvey; Lucy d. at Surry, NH, 8 Feb 1849.

Daniel was a tailor and farmer in Surry, New Hampshire, arriving there as early as 1795. There is conflicting information about what became of him. One report is that he went to the conflict at Lake Champlain in 1812 and was never heard from again. Another report is that he enlisted as a private from May to July 1814 in Captain Andrew Pierce's Company. In any case, he seems to be gone from Surry by 1814, although his wife and children remained there.[2481]

Daniel and Lucy had four children born at Surry.

i BETSEY ABBOTT, b. 16 May 1795; d. at Moira, NY, 6 Apr 1864; m. 5 Sep 1816, GEORGE LEONARD, b. about 1792 perhaps in Massachusetts, of uncertain parentage; George d. at Moira, 17 Nov 1859. Published genealogies disagree on parents of George Leonard, but more likely is Benjamin and Judith (Macomber) Leonard. Another wife, Molly Ryder, has been suggested for Benjamin Leonard and the History of Surry suggests this is a second wife.[2482]

ii LUCY ABBOTT, b. 10 Jan 1797; d. at Winchester, 2 Jan 1870. Lucy did not marry.

iii DANIEL ABBOTT, b. 13 Dec 1798; d. at Surry, 18 Jun 1869; m. 23 May 1823, POLLY BROWN, b. at Westmoreland, 17 Sep 1798 daughter of Nehemiah and Susannah (Ward) Brown; Polly d. at Surry, 3 Oct 1887.

iv LYNA ABBOTT, b. 10 May 1800; d. at Surry, 16 Mar 1882; m. 5 Mar 1820, JOSEPH ALLEN, b. at Surry, 28 May 1798 son of Abel and Susannah (Wilbur) Allen; Joseph d. at Surry, 28 Jun 1877.

926) GEORGE ABBOTT *(Daniel⁴, George³, Thomas², George¹)*, b. at Concord, 12 May 1772 son of Daniel and Rachel (Abbott) Abbot; m. BETSY EASTMAN.

George Abbott and Betsy Eastman resided in St. Johnsbury, Vermont. The Abbot genealogy reports six children for this family and records related to five of the children were located.[2483]

i LUCINDA ABBOTT, b. about 1792; d. at St. Johnsbury, 9 Oct 1800.

ii MIRANDA ABBOTT, b. about 1795. The Abbot genealogy reports that Miranda married, but no information related to her marriage could be located.

iii ARTIMUS ABBOTT, b. about 1797; d. at St. Johnsbury, 8 Oct 1800.

iv ARTIMUS ABBOTT, b. at St. Johnsbury, 15 Sep 1801

v BARKER BARNABUS ABBOTT, b. at St. Johnsbury, 10 Feb 1804; d. 30 Sep 1849.[2484] Barker was a ships carpenter in the Navy. Barnabas enlisted at Boston 2 Aug 1828.[2485]

[2478] Allen, *Descendants of Nicholas Cady*, p 75
[2479] Hodges, *Genealogical Record of the Hodges Family*, p 211
[2480] Vail and White, *Pomfret, Vermont*, volume 2, p 512
[2481] Kingsbury, *History of Surry*, p 408
[2482] Kingsbury, *History of Surry*, p 751
[2483] Abbot, Genealogical Register, p 107
[2484] Death was reported in the New York Evening Post.
[2485] U.S. Army, Register of Enlistments, 1798-1914

vi GEORGE EDSON ABBOTT, b. at St. Johnsbury, 15 Feb 1806; d. after 1870 when he was living in Lawrence, NY; m. HANNAH, b. about 1817. George also seems to have had a first marriage as he has a daughter born 1832. He was in Canada for a time as at least one child was born there.

927) THOMAS ABBOTT *(Daniel⁴, George³, Thomas², George¹)*, b. at Concord, 5 Jul 1776 son of Daniel and Rachel (Abbott) Abbot; d. at Concord, NH, 22 Sep 1845; m. 14 Apr 1801, ANNA EATON, b. in NH about 1781; d. after 1860 (living with her daughter Dorcas and her family at the 1850 census in Concord and with her daughter Judith at the 1860 census in Auburn, NH). Her parentage is not verified but she is *possibly* the daughter of Ephraim and Eunice (-) Eaton.

Thomas Abbott and Anna Eaton were parents of eleven children all born at Concord.

i EUNICE BUSS ABBOTT, b. 22 Nov 1801; d. at Concord, 1865; m. 12 Dec 1826, ABRIA FISK, b. at Concord, 9 Mar 1800 son of Ebenezer and Sarah (Blanchard) Fisk; Abria d. at Manchester, NH, 1 Nov 1877. After Eunice's death, Abria married her sister SARAH ELIZABETH ABBOTT (see below).

ii JUDITH ABBOTT, b. 17 Dec 1803; d. at West Boylston, MA, 5 Dec 1899; m. at Concord, 13 Jan 1835, WILLIAM MOORE, b. at Freeport, ME, 1797 son of James and Anna (Todd) Moore;[2486] James d. at Worcester, MA, 20 Sep 1876 (will naming wife Judith and son William J. written August 1876).

iii PETER ABBOTT, b. 8 Apr 1806; d. 17 Dec 1813.

iv HARRIET ABBOTT, b. 9 May 1808; d. at Concord, 27 May 1893; m. at Concord, 19 Oct 1859, as his second wife, GILMAN SCRIBNER, b. at Salisbury, NH, about 1807 son of Benjamin and Martha (Peaslee) Scribner; Gilman d. at Henniker, NH, 26 Jun 1881. Gilman was first married to Louisa Baron.

v RUFUS ABBOTT, b. 7 Feb 1810; d. at Concord, 15 Jan 1890; m. at Andover, NH, 19 Jun 1845, the widow SUSAN LADD, b. in NH about 1817; Susan d. at Concord, 26 Mar 1874. Rufus and Susan do not seem to have children as in his will, Rufus leaves his estate to other relatives. Susan is almost certainly Susan H. Keyser who was the widow of Artemus C. Ladd. Susan and Artemus had two children; their son William M. Ladd married Susan M. Abbott (daughter of Levi Abbott and Elizabeth Dimond). William M. Ladd died during the Civil War.

vi LUCRETIA ABBOTT, b. 6 Mar 1812; d. at Concord, 29 Dec 1899; m. at Boston, 22 Aug 1837, as his second wife, DOLLIVER JOHNSON, b. at Bradford, VT, 6 Jul 1800 son of Joseph and Betsey (Beckford) Johnson;[2487] Dolliver d. at Nachusa, IL, 3 Nov 1884.[2488]

vii LUCY EASTMAN ABBOTT, b. 30 Apr 1815; d. after 1880 when she was living with her husband in Enfield; m. at Beverly, MA, 1 Aug 1846, SAMUEL NOYES, b. at Enfield, NH, 3 Apr 1805 son of David and Emily (Clough) Noyes;[2489] Samuel d. at Enfield, 10 Dec 1881.

viii DORCAS MERRILL ABBOTT, b. 16 Apr 1817; d. at Concord, 26 Jun 1881; m. JOHN STICKNEY, b. at Concord, 16 Feb 1798 son of William and Susanna (Emerson) Stickney; John d. at Concord, 18 Feb 1854. Dorcas and John do not seem to have had children. In her will, Dorcas left her estate to her brother Francis B. Abbott and other relatives. After John's death, Dorcas worked as a nurse.

ix CLARISSA ANN ABBOTT, b. 6 Nov 1819; d. at Cresbard, SD, 1 Nov 1903; m. 1st, at Concord, 28 Apr 1846, JOHN DOLE PILLSBURY, b. in NH, 4 Nov 1817 son of Joshua and Sarah (Fletcher) Pillsbury;[2490] John d. at Andover, IL, 25 Oct 1847. Clarissa m. 2nd, at Bureau, IL, 17 Nov 1851, JOHN THOMPSON, b. at Royalston, MA, 25 Apr 1817 son of Robert and Lydia (Jones) Thompson;[2491] John d. at Bureau, 13 May 1895. Clarissa had a son Daniel Pillsbury with her first husband and was living with him in South Dakota in 1900.

x FRANCIS BROWN ABBOTT, b. 11 Aug 1821; d. at Hillsborough, NH, 15 Jan 1898; m. 1 Aug 1844, NANCY GOLDTHWAITE, b. 29 Jun 1825 daughter of Alvin and Polly (Metcalf) Goldthwaite;[2492] Nancy d. at Hillsborough, 20 Aug 1913.

2486 Names of William's parents are given on his death record.

2487 New Hampshire Historical Society, "Johnson, Dolliver (1800-1884)", https://www.nhhistory.org/object/252681/johnson-dolliver-1800-1884

2488 Place and date of death are given on his Mason membership card.

2489 Names of parents on Samuel's death record are given as David Noyes and Mary Clough, but this may be a confusion with David's two wives who were Emily Clough and Mary Carter.

2490 Pilsbury and Getchell, *The Pillsbury Family*, p 80

2491 John's birthdate is engraved on his gravestone which allowed verification of parents.

2492 Browne, *The History of Hillsborough*, p 17

xi SARAH ELIZABETH ABBOTT, b. 15 Jul 1823; d. at Manchester, NH, 14 Jul 1895; m. 24 Oct 1866, ABRIA FISK who was first married to Sarah's sister EUNICE BUSS ABBOTT (see above).

928) ABIEL ABBOTT *(Daniel[4], George[3], Thomas[2], George[1])*, b. at Concord, 19 Mar 1778 son of Daniel and Rachel (Abbott) Abbot; d. at Waldo, ME, 1 Aug 1836;[2493] m. at Lincolnville, ME, 2 Feb 1809, SARAH COMBS,[2494] "of Georgetown (ME)". She is SARAH HINCKLEY,[2495] b. at Georgetown, 14 Aug 1774 daughter of John and Hannah (Oliver) Hinckley[2496] and the widow of Leonard Coombs. Sarah d. at Waldo, 4 Nov 1865 (age 91 years, 3 months at time of death).[2497]

Abiel was a farmer in Waldo, Maine. The Abbot genealogy reports five children in this family and records were located for four of those children.[2498] Birth dates are estimates.

i CLARISSA ABBOTT, b. about 1810; m. JOSEPH ROWLANDSON. No information has been located for this couple.

ii ABIEL ABBOTT, b. at Waldo, 18 Apr 1811; d. at Seaport, ME, 20 Mar 1877; m. about 1833, ELEANOR JANE WEST, b. in ME, about 1816; Eleanor d. at Stockton, CA, 30 Jan 1875. This couple lived in Waldo until 1850.

iii HANNAH ABBOTT, b. about 1812; m. at Lincolnville, ME, 20 Nov 1836, ANDREW MCKENNEY.

iv HARRIET ABBOTT, b. about 1814; d. at Portsmouth, NH, 22 Oct 1901; m. about 1835, CHARLES G. CURTIS, b. in NH, about 1804; Charles d. at Portsmouth, 8 Oct 1881.

v CHARLES ABBOTT, b. about 1815; likely died young.

929) PETER HAZELTINE ABBOTT *(Daniel[4], George[3], Thomas[2], George[1])*, b. at Concord, 28 Feb 1780 son of Daniel and Rachel (Abbott) Abbot; d. at Concord, about 1862 (will written 4 Feb 1862); m. 9 Mar 1815, his first cousin once removed, SARAH ABBOTT *(Moses[5], Nathaniel[4], Nathaniel[3], Nathaniel[2], George[1])*, b. 10 Sep 1781 daughter of Moses and Mary (Batchelder) Abbott; Sarah d. 10 Aug 1846. Sarah Abbott is a child in Family 983.

Peter and Sarah started their family in Pomfret, Vermont where their children were born, although the birth records are conflicting with some recorded both at Hanover, New Hampshire and Pomfret, Vermont. Later, the family was in Concord where Peter was a farmer.

In his will dated 4 February 1862, Peter H. Abbott has the following bequests: son Jeremiah Abbott of Hopkinton receives $250; son John Carpenter Abbott of Nevada, California receives $50; all the rest of the estate goes to son Asaph Abbott who is also named executor.[2499]

Peter and Sarah were parents of three children born at Pomfret, Vermont. After Sarah's death, Peter lived with his son Asaph in Concord.

i ASAPH ABBOTT, b. (recorded at Hanover) 11 Sep 1815; d. at Webster, NH, 9 Apr 1903; m. 1st, at Concord, 15 Jun 1842, HEPHZIBAH DOW, b. at Concord, about 1808 daughter of Joseph and Hannah (Farnum) Dow; Hannah d. after 1860. Asaph m. 2nd, perhaps about 1862, Catherine A. who has not been identified.

ii JEREMIAH ABBOTT, b. at Pomfret, 31 Jul 1817; d. at Concord, 9 Apr 1901; m. 25 Jun 1855, HANNAH K. BUSWELL, b. at Concord, 14 Jun 1821 daughter of Andrew and Zilphah (Diamond) Buswell; Hannah d. at Concord, 21 Aug 1905.

iii JOHN CARPENTER ABBOTT, b. at Pomfret, 31 Jul 1820; d. at Nevada, CA, 18 May 1891; m. about 1862, MARY CALL, b. at Boscawen, 29 Jun 1830 daughter of David and Polly (Fellows) Call; Mary d. at Nevada, CA, 18 May 1905. Mary was still living in Nevada, CA at the 1900 census. John Carpenter Abbott was a carpenter working in the gold rush area of Nevada, CA. John and Mary had two sons, Wilfred Abbott and Ira Warren Abbott. Ira Warren Abbott was a blacksmith convicted of second-degree murder for killing a business rival during an argument and spent nine years in Folsom Prison prior to being paroled 24 Dec 1903.[2500][2501]

2493 Ancestry.com, Maine, Death Records, 1761-1922

2494 "Maine Marriages, 1771-1907," database, *FamilySearch* (https://familysearch.org/ark:/61903/1:1:F4DX-WLN: 10 February 2018), Abial Abbot and Sarah Combs, 02 Feb 1809; citing Lincolnville, Waldo, Maine, reference vol 1; FHL microfilm 11,351.

2495 The death record of daughter Harriet gives the maiden name of mother as Sarah Hinkley.

2496 "Maine Births and Christenings, 1739-1900," database, *FamilySearch* (https://familysearch.org/ark:/61903/1:1:F4HY-ZPV: 10 February 2018), Sarah Hinkley, 14 Aug 1774; citing GEORGETOWN, SAGADAHOC, MAINE; FHL microfilm 873,976.

2497 Maine State Archives; Cultural Building, 84 State House Station, Augusta, ME 04333-0084; Pre-1892 Delayed Returns; Roll Number: 1; Maine State death records 1761-1922

2498 Abbot, Genealogical Register, p 107

2499 *New Hampshire. Probate Court (Merrimack County)*; Probate Place: *Merrimack, New Hampshire, Probate Records, Vol 39-43, 1861-1892*, will of Peter H. Abbott, accessed through ancestry.com

2500 The San Francisco Call, 28 July 1894, p 7

2501 California, Prison and Correctional Records, 1851-1950, California State Archives; Sacramento, California; Register and Descriptive List of Convicts - Folsom

930) BENJAMIN ABBOTT *(Daniel⁴, George³, Thomas², George¹)*, b. at Concord, 29 Mar 1782 son of Daniel and Rachel (Abbott) Abbot; d. at Concord, after 1860 (living with his son James B. at the 1860 census); m. at Concord, 21 Oct 1805, ESTHER CURRIER, b. 5 Nov 1787 daughter of Nathaniel Currier; Esther d. between 1850 and 1860.

Benjamin Abbott was a shoemaker in Concord. Benjamin and Esther had seven children born at Concord.

i JEDEDIAH ABBOTT, b. 4 Sep 1806; d. at Goffstown, 14 Nov 1889; m. 11 Mar 1833, SALLY M. BARTLETT, b. at Northwood, NH, 30 Jan 1815 daughter of Samuel and Mary (Pinkham) Bartlett;[2502] Sally d. at Northfield, 13 Apr 1886.

ii NATHANIEL C. ABBOTT, b. 14 Sep 1808; d. at Concord, 8 Jan 1870; m. 1840, JULIA H. FELLOWS, b. at Norwich, VT, 9 Nov 1812 daughter of Ebenezer and Lucy (Miles) Fellows; Julia d. at Concord, 3 May 1893.[2503]

iii BENJAMIN K. ABBOTT, b. 1 Jun 1811; d. at Concord, 17 Feb 1872; m. at Concord, 4 Jun 1836, MARY ANN HOOK, b. 1814 daughter of Jacob and Hannah (Griffin) Hook; Mary Ann d. at Concord, 24 Sep 1876.

iv HORACE S. ABBOTT, b. 12 Oct 1812; d. at Concord, 3 Feb 1891; m. 1st, 26 Nov 1835, LEVINA P. BARTLETT, b. at Northwood, 25 Jul 1810 daughter of Samuel and Hannah (Pinkham) Bartlett; Levina d. at Concord, 10 Oct 1869. Horace m. 2nd, 6 Sep 1876, AUGUSTA THOMPSON, b. at Concord, May 1845 daughter of Luther P. Thompson; Augusta d. at Concord, 28 Aug 1923. In the 1870 Census, 24-year old Augusta Thompson was living with Horace S. Abbott and listed as his housekeeper. Horace and Augusta did have two children the younger child born when Horace was 71.

v THOMAS W. ABBOTT, b. 4 Jul 1815; d. at Concord, 1 Mar 1884; m. at Pittsfield, NH, 13 Nov 1842, ADALINE NANCY VENT, b. in Vermont, 3 Nov 1818;[2504] Adaline Nancy (or Nancy A. as she is listed on her gravestone), d. at Concord, 22 Jun 1867.

vi JAMES B. ABBOTT, b. 24 Jul 1818; d. at Concord, 20 Jun 1896; m. at Concord, 3 Jul 1851, LOVILLA B. WARD, b. at Bradford, NH, 7 Apr 1826 daughter of Sylvester and Lydia (Cheney) Ward;[2505] Lovilla d. at Concord, 20 Dec 1864.

vii WILLIS S. ABBOTT, b. 9 Oct 1820; d. at Manchester, NH, 18 May 1883; m. 30 Oct 1845, BETSEY BROWN HADLEY, b. at Bow, 13 Mar 1828 daughter of Rodney and Lydia (Brown) Hadley;[2506] Betsey d. at Goffstown, 9 Sep 1892.

931) JUDITH ABBOTT *(Daniel⁴, George³, Thomas², George¹)*, b. at Concord, 4 Apr 1784 daughter of Daniel and Rachel (Abbott) Abbot; d. at Hanover, NH, 18 Apr 1831; m. about 1808, JOHN CARPENTER, b. in NH, about 1787; John d. at Hanover, NH, after 1860. John married second Nancy who has not been identified.

John Carpenter was a store owner in Hanover. Judith Abbott and John Carpenter were parents of six children born at Hanover.

i EMILY CARPENTER, b. 3 Jun 1808; d. at Nantucket, MA, 11 May 1881;[2507] m. 1st, about 1828, IRA POWELL, b. at Strafford, VT, 24 Jul 1800 son of John and Lydia (Robinson) Powell; Ira d. at Strafford, 3 Apr 1832. Emily m. 2nd, at Nantucket, 11 Sep 1842, EDWARD COLEMAN, b. at Nantucket, 4 Feb 1807 son of Joseph Gorham and Phebe (Bunker) Coleman; Edward d. at Nantucket, 20 Nov 1876.

ii ABIGAIL CARPENTER, b. 16 Nov 1810; d. at Strafford, VT, 21 Mar 1890; m. about 1840, EDWIN HYDE, b. at Strafford, 29 May 1817 son of James and Eunice (Pennock) Hyde;[2508] Edwin d. at Strafford, 2 Jul 1878.

iii JOHN CARPENTER, b. 10 Nov 1812; d. 1814.

[2502] Cogswell, *History of Nottingham, Deerfield, and Northwood*, p 624

[2503] The names of Julia's parents are given on her death record as Ebenezer Fellows and Lucy Miles.

[2504] Adaline's birthdate is engraved on her gravestone.

[2505] Gould and Beals, *Early Families of Bradford*, p 437

[2506] Betsey's parents are given on her death record.

[2507] Emily Coleman daughter of John Carpenter, born at Hanover, died 11 May 1881; Nantucket births, marriages, and deaths

[2508] Names of parents are given on Edwin's death record.

iv SUSAN A. CARPENTER, b. 28 Jan 1816; m. JOHN FORD, of Hudson, NY; John d. at Pittsburgh, PA, about 1852. Susan and John's son, Henry Parker Ford, was mayor of Pittsburgh from 1896-1899.[2509]

v LUCIA CARPENTER, b. about 1821; d. at Jersey City, NJ, after 1880; m. about 1841, JOHN GEAR,[2510] b. in NH, about 1817; John d. at Jersey City, 21 Sep 1884.

vi SARAH J. A. CARPENTER, b. about 1823; d. at Strafford, VT, 18 Jun 1883; m. 19 Oct 1846, WINTHROP S. BRADBURY, b. at Strafford, VT, 30 Jun 1823 son of Benjamin and Betsey (Poole) Bradbury; Winthrop d. at Strafford, 1904.

932) HANNAH ABBOTT *(Daniel⁴, George³, Thomas², George¹)*, b. at Concord, 28 Oct 1791 daughter of Daniel and Mercy (Kilburn) Abbot; d. 13 Sep 1876; m. 16 Mar 1815, her third cousin once removed, REUBEN ABBOTT *(Reuben⁵, Reuben⁴, James³, William², George¹)*, b. at Concord, 23 Oct 1790 son of Reuben and Zerviah (Farnum) Abbott; Reuben d. 27 Jun 1869. Reuben Abbott is a child in Family 571.

Reuben Abbott was a farmer in Concord. There are birth records for seven children of Reuben and Hannah Abbott born at Concord. Bouton's History of Concord and the Abbot genealogy include an eighth child (Henry C.) and he is included here.

i REUBEN KILBURN ABBOTT, b. 20 Nov 1815; d. at Concord, 15 Dec 1889; m. 19 Oct 1847, MARY MANUEL EMERSON, b. at Concord, 3 Nov 1817 daughter of John and Hannah (Nudd) Emerson; Mary d. at Concord, 5 Nov 1896.

ii CATHERINE WHEELER ABBOTT, b. 16 Dec 1817; d. at Concord, 16 Oct 1903; m. 1 Apr 1841, DANIEL FARNUM, b. at West Concord, 4 Feb 1815 son of Abner and Mary (Martin) Farnum; Daniel d. at Farnum, 9 Nov 1887.

iii HANNAH GERRISH ABBOTT, b. 9 Jan 1820; d. at Concord, 6 May 1897; m. 22 May 1845, JOHN BALLARD, b. at Concord, 1 Jan 1818 son of Nathan and Hannah (Buss) Ballard; John d. at Concord, 19 Sep 1902.

iv ELIZABETH BRADLEY ABBOTT, b. at Concord, 29 Mar 1822; d. at Concord, 11 Mar 1872; m. 2 Mar 1847, FRANKLIN B. CARTER, b. at Concord, about 1823 son of Abiel C. and Martha (Farnum) Carter; Franklin d. at Concord, 1 Mar 1897.

v ESTHER MARTIN ABBOTT, b. 1825; d. at Concord, 19 Aug 1893; m. at Epsom, 19 May 1846, ALBERT G. DOW, b. at Concord, 3 Jan 1820 son of Timothy and Margaret (Sawyer) Dow; Albert d. at Concord, 20 Mar 1900.

vi EZRA CARTER ABBOTT, b. 16 Mar 1827; d. at Couderay, WI, 13 Jan 1916; m. at Clayton, IA, 16 Nov 1854, DEVILAH STOOPS, b. at Portage, OH, 14 Sep 1835 daughter of Washington H. and Cynthia E. (Carter) Stoops; Devilah d. at Couderay, Apr 1927.

vii PETER GREEN ABBOTT, b. 14 Feb 1830; d. at Hawkeye, IA, 1915; m. 1st, 7 Sep 1856, EMILY PALMER, b. at Fairfax, VT, 25 Jan 1836; Emily d. at Fayette County, IA, 11 May 1873. Peter m. 2nd, at Lawler, IA, 13 Nov 1879, ACHSAH OATMAN, b. in New York, about 1829 daughter of Simeon and Martha (Miller) Oatman;[2511] Achsah d. at Bethel, IA, 18 Sep 1925. Achsah was Achsah Morse when she married Peter Abbott and was on the 1870 census, she was in Honey Creek, IA and working as a teacher. Perhaps she was married and early widowed, but that marriage has not been located.

viii HENRY C. ABBOTT, b. 1 Oct 1833; d. at LeRoy, KS, 30 Sep 1911; m. 1st, at Concord, 20 Aug 1851, ADELINE CURRIER, b. about 1827 daughter of William and Eleanor (Whittemore) Currier; Adeline d. at Concord, 8 Jan 1903. On 1 Oct 1872, Adeline divorced Henry on grounds of his "willing absence" and he was at that time "of parts unknown" to Adeline. Adeline went on to marry John Bodwell about 1875. Henry C. Abbott seems to have gone off to Kansas and started a second family there and was living with Amanda starting around 1860. On one census record, Henry and Amanda report marrying in 1861, but no record has been located. The Henry C. in Kansas seems to be this Henry C. as his birth date and place of birth as New Hampshire fit with him. Henry and Adeline had just one child, son Francis, who was born in Concord in 1854.

2509 Biographical Review, volume XXIV, Life Sketches of Leading Citizens of Pittsburgh, p 30

2510 This is a child and marriage reported in the Abbot genealogy, but there seems to be another Lucia Carpenter born about the same time and so this is somewhat uncertain.

2511 Parents are confirmed by census records on which she identifies her father as Simeon Oatman and death record gives mother's maiden name as Miller.

933) PHEBE ABBOTT *(Joseph⁴, George³, Thomas², George¹)*, b. at Concord, 22 Feb 1766 daughter of Joseph and Phebe (Lovejoy) Abbott; d. at Woodbury, VT, 31 May 1837;[2512] m. her third cousin (and George Abbott descendant), JOSEPH BLANCHARD, b. at Dunstable, NH, 24 Nov 1761 son of John and Eleanor (Stevens) Blanchard; Joseph d. 19 Feb 1839.

In the Revolution, Joseph Blanchard served in the Continental army from New Hampshire in the Regiment of Colonel Stark enlisting in January 1776 for a period of one year. In 1778, he served seven months in Colonel Peabody's Regiment, served four months in 1780 with Colonel Stark, and a further four months in 1782 in Colonel Runnel's Regiment. While living in Cabot, Vermont he made application for a pension. As part of his pension application in 1820, Joseph claimed personal property with a value of $69 and $100 in debts. He reported he was a carpenter but in poor health. In the home in 1820 were wife Phebe age 54, son John age 20, daughter Hannah age 13 described in poor health, and daughter Ruth age 11.[2513]

Phebe Abbott and Joseph Blanchard were parents of twelve children.

i ISAAC BLANCHARD, b. at Plainfield, NH, 9 Apr 1787; d. at Gros Cap, MI, 10 Jun 1866; m. in Michigan, Nov 1824, MARY BABBEAU, b. at Mackinac, MI, 20 Apr 1805 daughter of Louis and Josephine (Anse) Babbeau; Mary d. 15 Nov 1875.

ii PHEBE BLANCHARD, b. at Plainfield, NH, 9 Jun 1789; d. at Woodbury, VT, 12 Apr 1861; m. 17 May 1811, JOEL CILLEY, b. at Andover, NH, 7 Jul 1789 son of Elisha and Sally (Keniston) Cilley;[2514] Joel d. 19 Jul 1849.

iii LOIS BLANCHARD, b. at Plainfield, NH, 19 Mar 1791; d. at Cabot, VT, 27 Mar 1880; m. at Cabot, 18 Jun 1809, PETER LYFORD, b. 1774 son of Thomas and Mehitable (Robinson) Lyford; Thomas d. at Cabot, 10 Dec 1861.

iv JAMES BLANCHARD, b. at Plainfield, NH, 9 Mar 1793; d. at Cabot, VT, 24 Nov 1869; m. 1st, 4 Feb 1819, ABIGAIL HOYT, b. 2 Sep 1799 daughter of Joseph F. and Hannah (Batchelder) Hoyt; Abigail d. at Cabot, 5 Mar 1837. James m. 2nd, 31 Oct 1838, SUSAN EVERETT, b. at Barre, VT, 21 Jan 1799 daughter of Stephen of Susanna (Mirick) Everett; Susan d. at Cabot, 20 Nov 1878.

v JOSEPH BLANCHARD, b. at Plainfield, NH, 20 Jun 1795; d. at Barre, VT, 16 Feb 1859; m. at Calais, VT, 1 Apr 1821, LUCY DAVIS WHEELOCK, b. at Calais, 28 Mar 1803 daughter of Gideon and Sally (Davis) Wheelock;[2515] Lucy d. at Barre, 31 May 1869.

vi MARY "POLLY" BLANCHARD, b. at Plainfield, NH, 19 Aug 1797; d. at Woodbury, VT, 9 Mar 1862; m. 9 Jan 1818, as his second wife, THOMAS HARVEY, b. about 1785 son of Thomas and Elizabeth (Tripe) Trickey;[2516] Thomas d. at Woodbury, 16 Apr 1871. Thomas Harvey (as Trickey) was first married to Fannie Bartlett.

vii JOHN BLANCHARD, b. at Cabot, VT, 26 Sep 1799; d. at Conneaut, OH, 28 Mar 1865; m. 1824, ANNA HOYT, b. in Vermont, 1803 daughter of Enoch and Mary (Smith) Hoyt;[2517] Anna d. at Conneaut, 1884.

viii ELEANOR BLANCHARD, b. at Cabot, 15 Jul 1801; d. at Cabot, 20 Jul 1882; m. 25 Nov 1824, JAMES RICHMOND NORCROSS, b. at Rockingham, VT, 17 Dec 1802 son of Noah and Fanny (Rollins) Norcross; James d. at Montpelier, 29 Apr 1875.

ix SALLY BLANCHARD, b. at Cabot, 19 May 1804; d. Feb 1816.

x HANNAH BLANCHARD, b. at Cabot, 3 Aug 1806; d. at Montpelier, 27 Aug 1895; m. at Barre, 20 May 1847, as his third wife, HORACE BECKLEY, b. at Weathersfield, VT, 13 Feb 1792 son of Zebedee and Elizabeth (Belding) Beckley; Horace d. at Barre, 15 Sep 1877. Horace's first two marriages were to Abigail Willington and Mrs. White.

xi RUTH BLANCHARD, b. at Cabot, 24 Aug 1808; d. at Woodbury, 18 Nov 1838; m. 4 Mar 1829, ELIAS HEATH, b. at Newport, NH, 14 Jan 1801 son of Elias and Lucy (Cutler) Heath; Elias d. at Woodbury, 24 Aug 1879.

xii NATHAN A. BLANCHARD, b. 23 Oct 1811; d. 15 Mar 1813.

[2512] *Vermont, Vital Records, 1720-1908.*

[2513] Revolutionary War Pension and Bounty-Land Warrant Application Files Case 41442

[2514] Eastman, *History of the Town of Andover, New Hampshire*, p 77

[2515] Davis, *Samuel Davis of Oxford, Mass.*, p 104

[2516] Acts and Laws Passed by the Legislature of the State of Vermont, October Session 1838, p 104. In 1838, Thomas Trickey of Woodbury changed his name and the names of his wife Polly and all his children with Polly to the last name of Harvey. "It is hereby entered by the General Assembly of the State of Vermont, That Thomas Trickey of Woodbury, shall hereafter be known by the name of Thomas Harvey", etc.

[2517] Hoyt, *The Hoyt Family: A Genealogical History*, p 104

934) MOLLY ABBOTT *(Joseph4, George3, Thomas2, George1)*, b. at Concord, 20 Jul 1767 daughter of Joseph and Phebe (Lovejoy) Abbott; d. at Concord, 15 Aug 1791; m. 22 May 1785, ISAAC HOUSTON, b. at Bedford, NH, 1760 son of James and Mary (Mitchell) Houston. Isaac m. 2nd, Ruth Gale. Isaac d. at Hanover, NH, 25 Mar 1833.

Isaac Houston was a blacksmith in Concord. Molly had four children before her early death, three of whom died as infants.

i SARAH "SALLY" HOUSTON, b. at Concord, 20 Sep 1786; d at Waterford, NY, about 1857 (probate 9 Jun 1857); m. 1st, at Hanover, 13 Dec 1814, JOEL AMSDEN, b. about 1780 son of Joseph and Mary (Andrews) Amsden; Joel d. 15 Jan 1830. Sarah m. 2nd, 30 Aug 1831, MANLY AMSDEN, b. about 1786 son of Joseph and Ann (-) Amsden; Manly d. at Waterford, about 1848 (probate 25 Jul 1848). Joel Amsden and Manly Amsden were half-brothers. Sarah did not have children.

ii PHEBE HOUSTON, b. 24 Feb 1789; d. 7 Nov 1789.

iii Son, b, 16 Aug 1790; died young

iv Son, b. 1 Jun 1791; died young

935) HANNAH ABBOTT *(Joseph4, George3, Thomas2, George1)*, b. at Concord, 3 Jan 1769daughter of Joseph and Phebe (Lovejoy) Abbott; d. 31 Oct 1810; m. 10 Dec 1795, DAVID KIMBALL, b. at Rumford, 10 Oct 1757 son of Reuben and Miriam (Collins) Kimball; David d. at Northfield, 1826 (will written 10 Dec 1825 and proved 16 Jan 1826. After Hannah's death, David married Lydia.

Hannah and David Kimball started their family in Concord but relocated to Northfield where David purchased the property that his brother Benjamin had there.[2518]

In his will written 10 December 1825 (proved 16 January 1826), David bequeathed to beloved wife Lydia household items that she brought with her to the marriage. Eldest son David, Jr. receives one dollar, second son Joseph receives a cow. Third son John and fourth son Joseph receive all the farm not heretofore disposed of, all the stock and farming tools, and the household furniture not bequeathed to Lydia. Fifth son Simeon receives one good bed and bedding and one hundred-forty dollars. Josiah Ambrose was named sole executor.[2519]

Hannah Abbott and David Kimball were parents of eight children, three of whom died in childhood. The children may have been born in Concord or Northfield.[2520]

i SIMEON KIMBALL, b. 30 Sep 1796; d. 16 Mar 1799.

ii DORCAS KIMBALL, b. 7 Jan 1799; d. 10 Feb 1799.

iii DAVID KIMBALL, b. 30 Mar 1800; d. at Northfield, 1875; perhaps a relationship in 1823 with MARY CARR. According to the *History of Northfield*, p 199, David never established himself independently and was said to be somewhat unstable owing to an early romance. He is not known to have married, but there is a death record for a David Kimball born in Northfield in 1824 and died 1896 with parents David Kimball and Mary Carr. Mary Carr, born 1806, was the daughter of Jesse and Jane (Dustin) Carr; Mary married Moses Evans in 1839. The son David Kimball was raised by Stephen and Martha Carr in South Hampton, NH.

iv ISAAC KIMBALL, b. 19 Jun 1802; d. at Lowell, 1875; m. 16 Dec 1832, as her second husband, SARAH MOODY, b. at Sanbornton, 2 Feb 1795 daughter of Bradstreet and Ednah (Gale) Moody;[2521] Sarah d. at Lowell, 20 Aug 1871. Sarah was first married to Samuel Bellows.

v Daughter, b. and d. 1804

vi JOHN KIMBALL, b. 26 Feb 1806; d. at Northfield, 22 Dec 1868; m. 30 Jun 1831, SUSAN WEEKS, b. at Sanbornton, 15 Aug 1798 daughter of William and Sally (Calley) Weeks;[2522] Susan d. at Northfield, 22 Jul 1874.

vii JOSEPH KIMBALL, b. 16 Mar 1808; d. at Northfield, 9 Nov 1865; m. 6 Dec 1832, HARRIET ROGERS, b. at Northfield, 7 Nov 1812 daughter of Benjamin and Lucy (Hoag) Rogers.[2523]

viii SIMEON KIMBALL, b. 11 May 1810; d. at Tilton, NH, 1865; m. 5 Sep 1837, FANNY ROGERS, b. 20 Nov 1802 daughter of Benjamin and Lucy (Hoag) Rogers.

2518 Cross, *History of Northfield*, p 198

2519 *New Hampshire. Probate Court (Merrimack County)*; Probate Place: *Merrimack, New Hampshire*, volume 1, pp 209-210, will of David Kimball

2520 Birthdates are from the Abbot genealogical register.

2521 Rocks Village Historic District, "Moody Family", http://www.rocksvillage.org/families/moody-family

2522 Runnels, *History of Sanbornton*, p 834

2523 Cross, *History of Northfield*, p 270

936) SARAH ABBOTT *(Joseph⁴, George³, Thomas², George¹)*, b. at Concord, 3 Jan 1769 daughter of Joseph and Phebe (Lovejoy) Abbott; d. at Concord, 27 Jan 1857; m. Nov 1787, her second cousin, TIMOTHY CHANDLER *(Timothy Chandler⁴, Tabitha Abbott Chandler³, Nathaniel², George¹)*, b. at Rumford, 25 Apr 1762 son of Timothy and Elizabeth (Copp) Chandler; Timothy d. 9 Aug 1848.

Timothy Chandler was only eight years old when his father died. As the family was left destitute, Timothy was apprenticed at the young age of eight to Jonathan Hale of Concord who made hand-cards for carding wool. He went with Mr. Hale to Connecticut and finished his apprenticeship there at age 21. Timothy returned to Concord and was in the trade of making hand-cards, but that process soon was mechanized and he was out of business. He switched to gold and silver smithing and developed a business in jewelry and clock making. He lost his house and shop to fire in 1809 but was able to rebuild and had a successful business.[2524] He became noted for his tall clocks which are still sold at antique auctions.[2525] Sons Peregrine, Timothy, and Abiel were also clockmakers and jewelers, Abiel taking over the business after his father's death. Daughter Sally's husband, Abel Eastman, was also a clockmaker.[2526]

Timothy was public-minded, involved in the opening of a "signing" school for the deaf and was involved in the opening of the New Hampshire asylum in 1842.[2527] This latter interest was perhaps triggered by the circumstances of his children, four of whom suffered from psychological disorders.

Timothy and Sarah's son Peregrine Chandler committed suicide in 1828 at age 35.[2528] In 1848, son Timothy Jay Chandler was declared insane and his younger brother Abiel was appointed his guardian. Daughter Sally Eastman was also decreed to be insane and Chandler Eastman was appointed her guardian when she was in her 40's. Chandler Eastman may have been her brother-in-law, the brother of Abel Blanchard Eastman. The appointment of guardians for Timothy Jay and Sally was done as part of the settlement of their father's estate and these guardians were to represent their legal interests, so it is not clear how long mental illness was present.

A fourth child, John Bradley Chandler, died at the New Hampshire asylum in Concord in 1864. John Bradley Chandler was a church deacon who was fervent in his religious beliefs. He was dismissed from the South Church in Concord in 1842 due to his "abolition and come-outer sentiments." A come-outer was a person who advocated for political reform, so it seems that John Bradley was too far ahead of the times for the South Church at Concord. Later, he was described as "deranged by spiritualism" and was institutionalized at the New Hampshire Asylum.

Timothy Chandler did not leave a will. Richard Bradley was administrator. There was a set-off to the widow Sarah for her dower. The final property division was made in February 1849 with the following heirs receiving shares in the estate: Abiel Chandler, Timothy J. Chandler (with Abiel Chandler as guardian), Judith Chandler, John B. Chandler, and Sally Eastman (with Chandler Eastman as guardian).[2529]

Sarah and Timothy Chandler had twelve children born at Concord.

i PEREGRINE WHITE CHANDLER, b. 10 Jul 1788; d. 28 Aug 1792.

ii SALLY CHANDLER, b. 11 Feb 1791; d. at Concord, 25 Apr 1856; m. 11 Oct 1808, ABEL BLANCHARD EASTMAN, b. at Concord, 12 Jan 1788 son of Jacob and Abigail (Noyes) Eastman; Abel d. at Belfast, ME, 13 Nov 1822.

iii PEREGRINE HALE WHITE CHANDLER, b. 6 Mar 1793; d. at Concord, by suicide, 18 Jul 1828.

iv Infant, b. 8 Feb 1795 and d. 18 Feb 1795

v JUDITH CHANDLER, b. 16 Feb 1796; d. at Concord, 4 Jun 1851. Judith did not marry.

vi TIMOTHY JAY CHANDLER, b. 21 May 1798; d. unknown but after 1848. Timothy did not marry and was declared insane in 1848.

vii DORCAS CHANDLER, b. 22 Jul 1800; d. 22 Aug 1800.

viii ISAAC ABBOT CHANDLER, b. 2 Oct 1801; d. at Concord, 11 Oct 1819.

[2524] Chandler, *The Descendants of William and Annis Chandler*, pp 592-593
[2525] Delaney Antique Clocks, http://delaneyantiqueclocks.com/search/?q=timothy+chandler
[2526] *U.S., Craftperson Files, 1600-1995* [database on-line]. Provo, UT, USA: Ancestry.com Operations, Inc., 2014
[2527] Chandler, *The Descendants of William and Annis Chandler*, p 593
[2528] New Hampshire, Death and Disinterment Records, 1754-1947
[2529] New Hampshire County Probate Records, 1660-1973, Merrimack County, 14:456, 21:192, 24:19, 13:139, 29:9, 20:138, accessed through familysearch.org

ix JOHN BRADLEY CHANDLER, b. 13 Feb 1805; d. at Concord, 3 Aug 1864; m. 23 Apr 1843, MARIA FRENCH, b. about 1821 of uncertain origins but described as the adopted daughter of Mr. French of Salem. Maria's death is unknown, but she was living in Ithaca, NY in 1880 with her two daughters.

x ABIEL CHANDLER, b. 2 Apr 1807; d. at Concord, 22 Apr 1881; m. 31 Oct 1833, MARIA LAMSON FELT, b. at Charlestown, 3 Aug 1813 daughter of Jacob and Eliza (Neagle) Felt; Maria d. at Concord, 12 Jan 1886.

xi SENECA CHANDLER, b. 10 Sep 1809 and d. 1810.

xii ELIZABETH CHANDLER, b. 4 Feb 1812; d. at Concord, 4 Sep 1844. Elizabeth did not marry.

937) RACHEL ABBOTT *(Joseph⁴, George³, Thomas², George¹)*, b. at Concord, 2 Mar 1773 daughter of Joseph and Phebe (Lovejoy) Abbott; d. at Fryeburg, ME, 2 Mar 1837; m. 29 Nov 1797, JONATHAN WARD, b. at Concord, 17 Aug 1774 son of Stephen and Elizabeth (Copp) Ward; Jonathan d. 5 Feb 1822. Jonathan's mother, Elizabeth Copp, was first married to Timothy Chandler who was Rachel Abbott's first cousin, once removed.

Jonathan Ward was a clockmaker in Fryeburg. He participated as a Sergeant in an artillery company that marched from Fryeburg to Portland in 1814 as part of the War of 1812.[2530]

Jonathan Ward and Rachel Abbott had eight children all born at Fryeburg.

i FANNY WARD, b. 27 Sep 1798; d. at Limington, ME, 12 Sep 1829; m. 4 Nov 1822, as his second wife, PARMENIO LIBBY, b. at Scarborough, 22 Nov 1791 son of Abner and Anna (Harding) Libby; d. at Limington, 11 Oct 1875. Parmenio was first married to Eunice Jewell and third married to Eliza Larrabee.

ii RACHEL WARD, b. 20 Sep 1800; d. at Fryeburg, 5 Jan 1892; m. 11 Jul 1832, as his second wife, EDWARD WESTON, b. at Fryeburg, 13 Aug 1781 son of Ephraim and Ruth (Richardson) Weston; Edward d. at Fryeburg, 3 Apr 1851. Edward was first married to Jane Webster.

iii RUTH A. WARD, b. 1 Apr 1802; d. at Fryeburg, 17 Mar 1848; m. 15 Oct 1834, as his second wife, her fourth cousin, ASA GRANVILLE CHARLES *(Susanna Abbott Charles⁵, Isaac⁴, Ebenezer³, John², George¹)*, b. at Fryeburg, 3 Sep 1797 son of Samuel and Susanna (Abbott) Charles; Asa d. at Fryeburg, 30 Jan 1873. Asa was first married to Ruth's sister Harriet (see below). Asa G. Charles is a child in Family 411.

iv JONATHAN HALE CHANDLER WARD, b. 23 Feb 1804; d. at Fryeburg, 28 Oct 1841; m. 22 Feb 1834, HARRIET DURGIN, b. at Fryeburg, 19 Sep 1811 daughter of Joshua and Sarah (Pratt) Durgin; Harriet d. at Worcester, 27 Mar 1889.

v HARRIET H. WARD, b. 29 Jul 1806; d. at Fryeburg, 31 Jul 1833; m. 1826, ASA GRANVILLE CHARLES who is described above with Harriet's sister Ruth who was his second wife.

vi GEORGE AUGUSTUS FREDERICK WARD, b. 3 Sep 1809; d. 1 Jan 1820.

vii AMOS J. COOK WARD, b. 4 Jan 1811; d. at Fryeburg, 2 Jan 1886; m. BETSY H. EASTMAN, b. at Conway, NH, 9 Nov 1818 daughter of Stephen and Hannah (Walker) Eastman;[2531] Betsy d. at Fryeburg, 25 Aug 1876.

viii TIMOTHY CHANDLER WARD, b. 29 Dec 1813; d. at Fryeburg, after 1870; m. Jul 1841, ELIZABETH CLEMENT FESSENDEN, b. about 1814 daughter of Ebenezer and Rebecca (Perley) Fessenden; Elizabeth d. at West Orange, NJ, 30 Dec 1880.

938) NATHAN ABBOTT *(Joseph⁴, George³, Thomas², George¹)*, b. at Concord, 27 Aug 1779 son of Joseph and Phebe (Lovejoy) Abbott; d. 26 Aug 1839; m. ELIZABETH "BETSEY" COLBY, b. 1786 daughter of John and Ann (Carter) Colby; Betsey d. 14 Dec 1819.

Nathan Abbott and Betsey Colby were parents of three children born at Concord.

i ISAAC COLBY ABBOTT, b. 9 Jul 1804; d. at Belfast, ME, 1895; m. MARY OSGOOD EVANS, b. at Fryeburg, ME, 22 Mar 1809 daughter of William and Anna (Webster) Evans;[2532] Mary d. at Belfast, 29 Apr 1893.

ii HIRAM ABBOTT, b. 1 Oct 1806; d. at Concord, 6 Aug 1844. Hiram did not marry.

iii JOHN COLBY ABBOTT, b. 19 Feb 1810; d. at Boston, 11 Dec 1893; m. 1st, at Lynn, MA, 1836, LYDIA MARIA BREED, b. at Lynn, 22 Feb 1816 daughter of Aaron and Mary (Kemp) Breed; Lydia d. at Lynn, 20 Apr 1838. John m. 2nd, at Lynn, 12 Jun 1842, MARY ELLEN FULLER, b. at Lynn, about 1822 daughter of James and Betsey

---

2530 Barrows, *Fryeburg, Maine: An Historical Sketch*, p 160

2531 Rix, *History of the Eastman Family*, p 372

2532 Evans, *Descendants of David Evans*, p 34

(Rich) Fuller; Mary d. at Lynn, 2 Jan 1853. John m. 3rd, at Brookline, 16 Feb 1857, ELIZABETH CUSHING LINCOLN, b. at Hingham, 21 Jan 1819 daughter of Gorham and Mary (Cushing) Lincoln; Elizabeth d. at Boston, 27 Sep 1900. Elizabeth was first married to William Edward Doane.

939) POLLY ABBOTT *(Stephen4, George3, Thomas2, George1)*, b. at Concord, 26 Apr 1782 daughter of Stephen and Mary (Gile) Abbott; d. after 1850 at Bethel, ME (still living at the 1850 U.S. Census); m. about 1804, JOSEPH TWITCHELL, b. at Bethel, 28 Mar 1782 son of Eleazer and Martha (Mason) Twitchell; Joseph d. at Bethel, 24 Nov 1871.

Joseph Twitchell was a farmer in Bethel and is reported as "the first white child" born at Bethel Hill.[2533]

Polly Abbott and Joseph Twitchell were parents of eight children all born at Bethel.

i DEBORAH TWITCHELL, b. 3 Jan 1805; d. at Bethel, 9 Apr 1844; m. at Woodstock, ME, 15 May 1829, LEARNED WHITMAN, b. at Woodstock, ME, 17 Feb 1808 son of Luther and Polly (Berry) Whitman; Learned d. at Bethel, 18 Jun 1893. After Deborah's death, Learned married Angeline Stiles 15 Feb 1846.

ii MARTHA TWITCHELL, b. 12 Nov 1806; d. 23 Jan 1831. Martha did not marry. She was a teacher.

iii MARY TWITCHELL, b. 8 Jul 1809; d. 9 Aug 1810.

iv ALMON TWITCHELL, b. 14 Sep 1811; d. at Bethel, 29 Oct 1859; m. PHEBE BUXTON, b. at Cumberland, ME, 3 Dec 1813 daughter of Jeremiah and Jane (Drinkwater) Buxton; Phebe d. at Bethel, 25 Dec 1883. Almon Twitchell was a physician.

v ALBERT TWITCHELL, b. 25 Jun 1814; d. 23 Jul 1823.

vi ALFRED TWITCHELL, b. 25 Jun 1814; d. at Bethel, 19 Nov 1900; m. at Sweden, ME, 27 Dec 1837, MARTHA A. STEVENS, b. at Sweden, 18 Dec 1812 daughter of Ebenezer and Mary (Barnard) Stevens; Martha d. at Bethel, 13 Nov 1897.

vii JOSEPH ABBOT TWITCHELL, b. 19 May 1817; d. at Bethel, 2 May 1890; m. 12 Dec 1839, ORINDA LEONARD MASON, b. at Bethel, 12 Apr 1812 daughter of John and Bethiah (Houghton) Mason; Orinda d. at Bethel, 19 Sep 1894.

viii OSMON MASON TWITCHELL, b. 29 Jun 1819; d. at Madison, WI, 20 Oct 1899; m. 2 Sep 1849, his fifth cousin once removed, DONNA ROSALBA CHANDLER *(Hazen Chandler7, Amos Chandler6, Timothy Chandler5, Abial Chandler Chandler4, Abiel Chandler3, Hannah Abbott Chandler2, George1)*, b. at Gilead, ME, 21 Jun 1829 daughter of Hazen and Betsy (Lary) Chandler; Donna d. at Madison, 9 Mar 1912.

940) THEODORE ABBOTT *(Stephen4, George3, Thomas2, George1)*, b. at Concord, 23 Feb 1784 son of Stephen and Mary (Gile) Abbott; d at George's Mill, NH, 8 May 1855; m. at New London, NH, 25 Jun 1809, MARY "POLLY" BURPEE, b. 29 Sep 1791 daughter of Thomas and Sarah (Smith) Burpee; Mary d. at Sunapee, NH, 9 Aug 1878. After Thomas's death, Mary married Jacob Worthen.

In his will written 25 April 1855 (probate 28 June 1855), Theodore Abbott leaves to beloved wife Mary all the income from his real and personal estate for her natural life. Mary receives all the household furniture to dispose of at her pleasure. Sons Amasa L. Abbott, Stephen Abbott, Elias B. Abbott, and Thomas B. Abbott receive one dollar each. Each of the daughters receive fifty cents: Sally Worthen, Mary Ann Chase, Abigail Chase, Lois Eastman, and Lydia Jane Abbott. After the decease of their mother, the estate will be divided among the children with the sons receiving twice the amount of the daughters. Wife Mary is named sole executor.[2534]

In her will written 8 August 1874, Mary Burpee Abbott Worthen left her entire personal estate to her two youngest daughters, Lois S. Eastman and Lydia Jane Jones. They are to use the proceeds of the estate to provide for Mary a suitable burying place and gravestone. William Russell of Sunapee was named executor.[2535]

Theodore Abbott and Mary Burpee were parents of eleven children, the first ten births recorded at New London and the youngest child born at Wendell, New Hampshire.

i AMASA ABBOTT, b. 21 Apr 1810; d. at Springfield, NH, 13 May 1898; m. 11 Jan 1835, MAHALA CHASE, b. at Springfield, 30 Jul 1817 daughter of Asa and Huldah (Towle) Chase; Mahala d. at Sunapee, 10 Jan 1900.

2533 Lapham, *History of Bethel, Maine*, p 628

2534 *New Hampshire. Probate Court (Sullivan County)*; Probate Place: *Sullivan, New Hampshire, Wills, Vol 19, 1852-1864*, will of Theodore Abbott

2535 *New Hampshire. Probate Court (Sullivan County)*; Probate Place: *Sullivan, New Hampshire, Wills, Vol J-K, 1827-1855*, volume J, p 603

ii STEPHEN ABBOTT, b. 25 Feb 1812; d. at Sunapee, 19 Mar 1895; m. 24 Jan 1844, SARAH KIDDER, b. at Sunapee, 8 Jul 1817 daughter of Jacob and Mehitable (Johonett) Kidder; Sarah d. at Warner, NH, 3 Feb 1896.

iii SALLY ABBOTT, b. 1 Aug 1814; d. at Sutton, NH, 30 Jul 1891; m. 20 Apr 1834, ALBERT S. WORTHEN, b. at Amesbury, MA, 21 Jan 1812 son of Jacob and Betsey (Sergeant) Worthen; Albert d. at Sutton, 12 May 1885. Albert's father Jacob Worthen was the second husband of Sally's mother.

iv MARY ANN ABBOTT, b. 11 Oct 1816; d. at Springfield, 5 Feb 1886; m. 12 Jun 1836, ASA CHASE, b. 12 Mar 1812 son of Asa and Huldah (Towle) Chase; Asa d. at Sunapee, 3 Dec 1882.

v MARTHA ABBOTT, b. 20 Dec 1818; d. 27 Jun 1819.

vi ELIAS B. ABBOTT, b. 25 Jul 1820; d. at Lempster, NH, 7 May 1900; m. 4 Dec 1844, LORINDA BARTLETT, b. at Sunapee, about 1820 daughter of Joshua and Patsy (Chase) Bartlett; Lorinda d. at Lempster, 12 Oct 1893.

vii ABIGAIL ABBOTT, b. 7 Nov 1823; d. at Warner, NH, 13 Mar 1907; m. at Sunapee, 29 Dec 1842, ELBRIDGE G. CHASE, b. at Deering, 30 Oct 1815; Elbridge d. at Warner, 1 Jul 1895.[2536]

viii THOMAS B. ABBOTT, b. 25 Dec 1826; d. at Derry, 1 Dec 1910; m. about 1850, MEHITABLE MUDGETT KIDDER, b. 29 Aug 1832 daughter of Thomas and Ruth (Mudgett) Kidder; Mehitable d. Oct 1876. Thomas m. 2nd, at Derry, 23 Apr 1887, ANNIE M. TUCK, b. at London, England, 1844; Annie d. 1916. Annie was first married to William S. Smart.

ix LOIS S. ABBOTT, b. 27 Sep 1829; d. at New London, 24 Mar 1920; m. at Danvers, MA, 8 Jun 1849, JAMES R. EASTMAN, b. at Sunapee, 11 Jan 1825 son of Moses and Mary (Hersey) Eastman; James d. at Springfield, 4 May 1898.

x HARRIS ABBOTT, b. 5 Dec 1831; d. at New London, 10 Nov 1850.

xi LYDIA JANE ABBOTT, b. 9 Apr 1834; d. at Sunapee, 21 May 1887; m. DAVID B. JONES, b. at Lewiston, about 1824; David d. at Sunapee, 13 Apr 1899.

941) LUCY ABBOTT *(Stephen⁴, George³, Thomas², George¹)*, b. at Concord, 24 Jan 1789 daughter of Stephen and Mary (Gile) Abbott; d. at Hampton, MN after 1870; m. at Springfield, NH, 2 Oct 1816, BENJAMIN HASELITNE, b. about 1791 "of Wendell."

Lucy Abbott and Benjamin Haseltine lived in Springfield, New Hampshire where they had a farm. It is not known when Benjamin died, but likely between 1840 and 1850. He seems to be listed as head of household in Springfield in 1840, but no evidence of him in 1850. By 1857, Lucy was living in the Minnesota Territory with the family of her son Jonathan.

Lucy Abbott and Benjamin Abbott were parents of six children all born at Springfield, New Hampshire.

i FRANCIS P. HASELTINE, b. 4 Apr 1818; d. in Arkansas, Oct 1838.[2537]

ii JONATHAN S. HASELTINE, b. 31 Jan 1819; d. at Northfield, MN, 20 Aug 1900; m. 5 Oct 1843, his fourth cousin once removed, ESTHER B. WEBSTER *(Rhoda Abbott Webster⁶, Nathan⁵, Reuben⁴, James³, William², George¹)*, b. at Hooksett, 2 Oct 1820 daughter of Richard and Rhoda (Abbott) Webster; Esther d. at Northfield, 7 Sep 1907.

iii MARTHA HASELTINE, b. 8 May 1821; d. at Boscawen, NH, 5 Sep 1861; m. at Concord, 13 Mar 1845, her fifth cousin, CHARLES ABBOTT *(Timothy⁶, Ezra⁵, Reuben⁴, James³, William², George¹)*, b. at Boscawen, 29 Jul 1823 son of Timothy and Rhoda (Johnson) Abbott; Charles d. at Concord, 21 Apr 1901.

iv MARY JANE HASELTINE, b. 8 Jun 1826; d. in MN, after 1880; m. 1st, at Springfield, NH, 1 Jun 1842, TRUMAN SCOLLAY, b. at Concord, 1819; Truman d. at Lowell, 4 Sep 1847. Mary Jane m. 2nd, at Lowell, 16 Jul 1854, ORIN W. AVERY, b. at Alexandria, NH, about 1827; Orin d. at Hampton, MN, before 1870. Mary Jane m. 3rd, at Northfield, MN, 9 Mar 1870, JOHN KARKER, b. in NY, about 1814; John d. at Hampton, MN, before 1880.

v HARRIET HASELTINE, b. 20 Dec 1827; d. at Billerica, 30 Oct 1880; m. at Billerica, 26 Sep 1853, ISAAC NEWTON HOLDEN, b. at Lowell, about 1832 son of Isaac and Louisa (Wellington) Holden; Isaac d. at Lawrence, 13 Oct 1897.

vi CLARA HASELTINE, b. 2 Mar 1831; d. at Hastings, MN, 7 Jan 1904; m. 25 Jul 1853, NATHAN EMERSON, b. at Concord, 19 Nov 1834;[2538] Nathan d. at Hastings, 28 Jun 1898.

[2536] There are discrepancies related to the parents of Elbridge Chase. His death record reports parents as Stephen Chase and Esther Hall. Some suggest his father was Metaphor Chase. The Chase genealogy does not list this Elbridge and states that Stephen Chase and Esther Hall did not have children which perhaps is just mistaken.

[2537] Abbot, Genealogical Register

[2538] Nathan's birthdate and place of birth are given on his cemetery index.

942) SAMUEL ABBOTT *(Stephen⁴, George³, Thomas², George¹)*, b. at Concord, 14 May 1791 son of Stephen and Mary (Gile) Abbott; d. at Montpelier, VT, 4 May 1861; m. 5 Mar 1813, JANE DAY, b. at Boscawen, 20 Jul 1794 daughter of Daniel and Jane (Cass) Day; Jane d. after 1860.

Samuel was a clockmaker, watchmaker, and jeweler. The family started in Dover where Samuel developed his trade. Between 1827 and 1831, he had his business in Boston. Later, he was in Montpelier and was in a partnership known as Abbott & Freeman. His son John Sullivan Abbott followed in his father's footsteps as a clockmaker and jeweler.[2539][2540]

Samuel Abbott and Jane Day were parents of two children born at Dover, New Hampshire.

i MARY ANN ABBOTT, b. 22 Aug 1814; d. at Montpelier, 24 Nov 1874; m. at Woodbury, VT, 7 Oct 1832, GEORGE WASHINGTON HARRAN, b. at Danville, VT, 8 Jul 1798 son of James and Dolly (-) Harran; George d. after 1850. George was first married to Laura Kimball.

ii JOHN SULLIVAN ABBOTT, b. 20 Jan 1817; d. at Conneaut, OH, 1875;[2541] m. 14 Aug 1839, his second cousin once removed, MARY JANE CILLEY *(Phebe Blanchard Cilley⁶, Joseph Blanchard⁵, John Blanchard⁴, Sarah Abbott Blanchard³, Nathaniel², George¹)*, b. at Woodbury, VT, 18 Aug 1819 daughter of Joel and Phebe (Blanchard) Cilley; Mary Jane d. at Colchester, VT, 23 Mar 1905.

943) HARRIET B. ABBOTT *(Ezra⁴, George³, Thomas², George¹)*, b. at Concord, 12 Apr 1786 daughter of Ezra and Betty (Andrews) Abbott; d. at Hartford, VT, 1 Apr 1862; m. 20 Jun 1816, JOHN CHAMPION, b. at South Lyme, CT, 12 Dec 1792 son of Ezra and Lucretia (Tubbs) Champion;[2542] John d. at Hartford, VT, 27 Oct 1879.

John Champion was born in Connecticut and was apprenticed to Ira Gates when he was just five years old. Mr. Gates relocated to Lebanon, New Hampshire and John went with him. When John reached adult age, he returned to Connecticut and discovered his mother had died and father remarried. John returned to Lebanon, was married there and his four children were born there. The family then relocated to Hartford, Vermont.[2543]

Harriet Abbott and John Champion were parents of four children born at Lebanon, New Hampshire.

i LUCY CHAMPION, b. 29 Mar 1817; d. at Hartford, VT, 28 Aug 1841. Lucy did not marry.

ii SARAH ANN CHAMPION, b. 23 Feb 1819; d. at Bridgewater, VT, 13 Feb 1900; m. at Hartford, VT, 8 Mar 1840, LEMUEL SHATTUCK, b. at Canaan, NH, about 1816 son of Peter and Ruxbey (Whiting) Shattuck; Lemuel d. at Bridgewater, VT, 14 Jan 1895.

iii EZRA ABBOTT CHAMPION, b. 7 Apr 1825; d. at Hartford, VT, 14 Feb 1914; m. at Hartford, 2 Jan 1851, ELLEN JULIA PERKINS, b. at Unity, NH, 21 Jun 1826 daughter of John and Elmira (Newton) Perkins; Ellen d. at Hartford, 8 Sep 1911.

iv HARRIET CHAMPION, b. 25 May 1828; d. at Brattleboro, VT, 29 Apr 1904; m. at Hartford, VT, 20 Sep 1852, ISAAC B. TAFT, b. at Newfane, about 1823 son of Caleb and Mary (Burnett) Taft; Isaac d. at Brattleboro, 3 Aug 1901.

944) ROSE B. ABBOTT *(Ezra⁴, George³, Thomas², George¹)*, b. at Concord, 26 Oct 1796 daughter of Ezra and Betty (Andrews) Abbott; d. after 1860 (still living at the 1860 U.S. Census, but deceased before 1870); m. 11 Dec 1816, JACOB DIMOND, b. at Concord about 1790 son of Reuben and Mary (Currier) Dimond; Jacob d. at Concord, 28 Apr 1879.[2544]

Jacob Dimond did not leave a will and son Elbridge was named administrator. Rose and Jacob had one child.

i ELBRIDGE DIMOND, b. at Concord, 4 Aug 1818; d. at Concord, 24 Dec 1902; m. 11 Apr 1843, JANETTE HOIT, b. at Concord, 24 Jun 1823 daughter of Enoch and Mary (French) Hoit; Janette d. at Concord, 23 Sep 1895.

[2539] Delaney Antique Clocks, Samuel Abbott of Dover, Boston, and Montpelier, http://delaneyantiqueclocks.com/products/maker/104/

[2540] U.S., Craftperson Files, 1600-1995

[2541] The 1905 probate record of Mary Jane Abbott contains information that her husband was buried in Conneaut, Ohio.

[2542] Trowbridge, *The Champion Genealogy*, p 121

[2543] Trowbridge, *The Champion Genealogy*, p 123

[2544] Ancestry.com, New Hampshire, Death and Burial Records Index, 1654-1949

945) BETSEY ABBOTT *(Ezra⁴, George³, Thomas², George¹)*, b. at Concord, 9 Aug 1799 daughter of Ezra and Jane (Jackman) Abbott; d. at Concord, 8 Aug 1856; m. Apr 1822, AMOS HOIT, b. 20 Feb 1800 son of Joseph and Polly (Elliot) Hoit. Amos m. 2nd, 6 Apr 1858, Asaneth Swain widow of Henry Swain.

Amos Hoit and Betsey Abbott lived on the Hoit homestead farm at Horse Hill in Concord.[2545]

In her will dated 5 July 1856, Betsey Hoit wife of Amos Hoit made the following bequests. Daughter Rose Anner Hoit receives a feather bed and bedding, ten dollars, one dessert silver spoon, and half the silver tea spoons. Daughter Ruth Ann S. Hoit receives a feather bed and bedding, five dollars, one dessert spoon, and half the tea spoons. Daughter Martha Dow wife of Timothy Dow receives one dollar. Grandson Edwin Sawyer son of John and Polly Elizabeth Sawyer receives one dollar. Sons Sylvester G. Hoit and Joseph S. Hoit each receives one feather bed and bedding, five dollars, one large silver spoon, and two tea spoons from the last six that she bought. Son George A. Hoit receives a bed and bedding, all the remainder of the money, a large silver spoon, the last two silver tea spoons, and all the household furniture. The money legacies are to be paid within six months, the household items when each of them leaves the home or marries, and the silver spoons only after the death of her husband Amos. Amos Hoit was named executor.[2546]

Betsey Abbott and Amos Hoit were parents of nine children born at Concord.

i MARTHA JANE HOIT, b. 18 Jan 1823; d. at Concord, 9 Sep 1880; m. 30 Mar 1843, TIMOTHY DOW, b. at Concord, 15 Jan 1821; Timothy d. at Concord, 15 Sep 1863. Timothy served as a lieutenant during the Civil War. He mustered out on 22 Aug 1863 and died three weeks later.[2547]

ii ROSE ANNA HOIT, b. 3 Aug 1824; d. at Concord, 12 Jun 1896. Rose did not marry.

iii POLLY ELIZABETH HOIT, b. 23 Apr 1826; d. at Concord, about 1851; m. at Concord, 23 Jan 1844, JOHN SAWYER, b. at Hopkinton, 13 Jan 1821 son of Amos and Martha (Austin) Sawyer; John d. at Boscawen, 3 Dec 1908. John married second Charlotte A. Stone on 8 Oct 1863 and third married Elizabeth Stevens on 6 Jun 1889.

iv HARRIET EMELINE HOIT, b. 20 Jan 1828; d. 28 Sep 1829.

v SYLVESTER GOIN HOIT, b. 29 Jan 1830; d. at Warner, NH, 2 Feb 1913. Sylvester was a farmer. He did not marry.

vi SARAH EVELINE HOIT, b. 4 Apr 1832; d. at Concord, 30 Mar 1853.

vii GEORGE ABBOTT HOIT, b. 14 Apr 1834; d. at Concord, 20 Apr 1928; m. 29 Apr 1858, ADELINE MAHALA HOLMES, b. at Boscawen, 8 Jan 1840 daughter of Ezra and Mahala (Colby) Holmes; Adeline d. at East Concord, 1 Mar 1892.

viii RUTH ANN SEMIRA HOIT, b. 6 Sep 1836; d. at Concord, 16 Jan 1910; m. 14 May 1884, DAVID CRANE TENNEY, b. at Newbury, VT, 9 Nov 1819 son of Jonathan and Lydia (Crane) Tenney; David d. at Concord, 6 Jan 1899. David was first married to Judith D. Little.

ix JOSEPH SULLIVAN HOIT, b. 28 Oct 1838; d. at Concord, 16 Jun 1873; m. LOUISE FRANCES DIX, b. at Webster, NH, 24 Jan 1837; Louise d. at Deland, FL, 25 Apr 1922.

946) ANNER ABBOTT *(Ezra⁴, George³, Thomas², George¹)*, b. at Concord, 8 Feb 1801 daughter of Ezra and Jane (Jackman) Abbott; d. at Concord, 23 Jan 1872; m. 13 Jun 1827, SAMUEL RUNNELS, b. at Boxford, 6 Dec 1796 son of Samuel and Anna (Hardy) Runnels; Samuel d. at Concord, 22 Nov 1864.

Samuel Runnels had his property on part of his father's homestead which was near the Contoocook River in Concord. He served as selectman from his ward and was actively involved in the Congregational Church.

In his will written 23 August 1864 (proved fourth Tuesday of December 1864), Samuel Runnels bequeathed to beloved wife Anner A. Runnels two hundred dollars, all the household furniture, and all the provisions on hand. Daughter Emily R. Freeze wife of Joseph M. Freeze receives one hundred-thirty dollars. Daughter Louisa Runnels receives one hundred-eighty dollars. Daughter Almira R. Long wife of Moses E. Long receives ten dollars. Daughter Anner A. Runnels receives one hundred thirty-five dollars. Daughters Louisa and Anner have right to occupy the north chamber as long as they are unmarried. Any remaining personal property goes to son Cyrus Runnels. His wife receives the use of all the real estate in Concord, which is more than 100 acres, for her natural life and this is in lieu of her dower. After the decease of his wife, all the real estate goes to son Cyrus.[2548]

Anner Abbott and Samuel Runnels were parents of seven children born at Concord.[2549]

[2545] Stearns, *Genealogical and Family History of the State of New Hampshire*, volume 1, p 82

[2546] *New Hampshire. Probate Court (Merrimack County)*; Probate Place: *Merrimack, New Hampshire, Vol 25, 1847-1856*, pp 704-705

[2547] U.S., Civil War Soldier Records and Profiles, 1861-1865

[2548] *New Hampshire. Probate Court (Merrimack County)*; Probate Place: *Merrimack, New Hampshire, Vol 39-43, 1861-1892*, Vol 39, pp 437-438

[2549] Runnels, *A Genealogy of the Runnels and Reynolds Families*, p 78. The author of this compilation notes that Anner Abbot Runnels contributed the information on her family.

i SAMUEL RUNNELS, b. 21 Jan 1828; d. 22 Jan 1828.

ii JOANNA RUNNELS, b. 28 Aug 1829; d. 1 Oct 1830.

iii CYRUS RUNNELS, b. 6 Apr 1832; d. at Concord 7 Jul 1905. Cyrus graduated from Chandler Scientific School at Dartmouth College in 1855 and a surveyor in Iowa and Illinois for nine years. He returned to Concord after his father's death. He did not marry.

iv LOUISA JANE RUNNELS, b. 18 Jan 1835; d. at Concord, 18 Jan 1914. Louisa did not marry.

v EMILY RUNNELS, b. 24 May 1838; d. at Concord, 5 Nov 1882; m. at Ipswich, 6 Oct 1863, as his second wife, JOSEPH M. FREEZE, b. at Tuftonboro, NH, about 1827 son of Joseph and Alice (Leavitt) Freeze; Joseph d. at Lawrence, MA, 12 Dec 1875.

vi ALMIRA RUNNELS, b. 16 May 1841; d. at Concord, 6 Feb 1919; m. at Concord, 20 Oct 1859, MOSES EDWIN LONG, b. at Amesbury, MA, 6 Apr 1837 son of Nathan and Sally (Ordway) Long; Moses d. at Concord, 15 Mar 1890.

vii ANNER RUNNELS, b. 1 May 1844; d. at Northfield, NH, 20 May 1908; m. at Hopkinton, 13 Nov 1867, FRANK B. CHASE, b. at Hopkinton, NH, about 1845 son of Ambrose and Abigail (Gould) Chase; Frank d. at Tilton, NH, 3 Dec 1909.

947) GEORGE B. ABBOT *(Ezra⁴, George³, Thomas², George¹)*, b. at Concord, 27 Jan 1803 son of Ezra and Jane (Jackman) Abbott; d. 8 May 1887; m. 1st, 22 Aug 1836, ELIZA DIDO SPAULDING, b. at Orford, NH, 6 Dec 1807 daughter of John and Elizabeth (Wheeler) Spaulding; Eliza d. at Concord, 11 Oct 1856. George m. 2nd, 31 Dec 1861, CLARISSA CARTER, b. about 1815; Clarissa d. 14 Mar 1882.

In his will written 9 March 1885 (proved fourth Tuesday of May 1887), George Abbot bequeathed to daughter Betsey Jane Abbot a specific list of household items, the polyglott bible, Barnes' notes on the new testament, and other specified religious volumes. Son George Abbot, Jr. receives all the rest and residue of the estate and is also named executor.[2550]

George Abbot and Eliza Spaulding were parents of two children born at Concord.

i GEORGE ABBOT, b. 13 Nov 1838; d. at Concord, 30 Aug 1928; m. at Concord, 5 Apr 1864, JOANNA G. FISKE, b. at Concord, about 1844 daughter of John and Elizabeth (Kittredge) Fiske; Joanna d. at Concord, 26 Jan 1919.

ii BETSEY JANE "JENNIE" ABBOT, b. 9 Feb 1849; d. at Hooksett, NH, 16 May 1938. Betsey did not marry. She was a teacher.

948) BENJAMIN JACKMAN ABBOTT *(Ezra⁴, George³, Thomas², George¹)*, b. at Concord, 4 Feb 1808 son of Ezra and Jane (Jackman) Abbott; d. 4 Mar 1869; m. about 1833, DOROTHY TEWKSBURY, b. about 1813 possibly the sister of Daniel Tewksbury who married Benjamin's sister Sarah, but no records have been located.

Benjamin Jackman Abbott and Dorothy Tewksbury were parents of six children, the oldest two born at Stewartstown, New Hampshire and the younger children at Hartford, Vermont.

i ZILPHA ABBOTT, b. at Stewartstown, 29 Oct 1833; d. at Stewartstown, 15 Sep 1876; m. ABIAL GLINES, b. at Canterbury, NH, 19 Feb 1821 son of Obadiah and Keziah (Blanchard) Glines; Abial d. at Stewartstown, 27 Jul 1909.

ii MERRIAM ABBOTT, b. at Stewartstown, 25 Jan 1835; d. at Stewartstown, after 1880; m. at Concord, 12 Jul 1855, STEPHEN J. SWAIN, b. at Meredith, NH, about 1835 son of Benjamin and Polly (Davis) Swain; Stephen d. at West Stewartstown, 4 Apr 1898.

iii SARAH JANE ABBOTT, b. 28 Dec 1836; d. at Hartford, VT, 3 Oct 1837.

iv GEORGE BENJAMIN ABBOTT, b. at Hartford, VT, 26 May 1838; d. at Canaan, VT, 20 Mar 1914; m. at Eaton, Québec, 1870, IRENA BISHOP, b. at Dudswell, Québec, 14 May 1834 daughter of Major Naphthali and Caroline (Gilbert) Bishop; Irena d. at Stewartstown, 13 Jun 1911.

[2550] *New Hampshire. Probate Court (Merrimack County)*; Probate Place: *Merrimack, New Hampshire*, volume 68, p 358

v MARTIN VAN BUREN ABBOTT, b. 8 Jun 1840; d. at Hartford, 22 Mar 1841.

vi ROXANA ABBOTT, b. at Hartford, 18 Jan 1842; d. at Stewartstown, 21 Oct 1876; m. at Stewartstown, 10 Oct 1863, ALVAH BUNNELL, b. at Whitefield, NH, Dec 1842 son of Horatio and Sally (Chamberlain) Bunnell; Alvah d. at Colebrook, NH, 3 oct 1909.

949) SARAH ABBOTT *(Ezra⁴, George³, Thomas², George¹)*, b. at Concord, 22 Jan 1815 daughter of Ezra and Jane (Jackman) Abbott; d. at Stewartstown, 26 Feb 1889; m. DANIEL TEWKSBURY, b. at Warner, 1 Oct 1810 son of Stephen and Sally (Flanders) Tewksbury; Daniel d. at Stewartstown, 6 Mar 1874.

Sarah Abbott and Daniel Tewksbury were parents of six children.

i Daughter, b. and d. 19 Jul 1838

ii Son b. and d. 17 Mar 1839

iii MARTHA G. TEWKSBURY, b. at Hartford, VT, 17 May 1841; d. at Stewartstown, NH, 2 Jul 1913; m. at Stewartstown, 24 Nov 1858, ALANSON OWEN, b. at Stewartstown, about 1837 son of Ethan and Huldah (Heath) Owen; Alanson d. at Stewartstown, 11 Jan 1893.

iv AMOS H. TEWKSBURY, b. at Stewartstown, 21 Oct 1846; d. at Stewartstown, 21 Jul 1922; m. at Canaan, VT, LYDIA CHAMBERLAIN, b. at Clarksville, NH, 22 Mar 1853 daughter of Walter and Achsah (Towle) Chamberlain; Lydia d. at Colebrook, NH, 13 May 1937.

v BETSEY JANE TEWKSBURY, b. at Stewartstown, 27 Aug 1848; d. at Stewartstown, 18 Jun 1893; m. 11 Jan 1873, her first cousin, ALVA SAWYER, b. at Topsham, VT, about 1846 son of George and Mary M. (Tewksbury) Sawyer; Alva d. at Littleton, NH, 29 May 1930.

vi CHARLES E. TEWKSBURY, b. at Stewartstown, 14 Jul 1854; d. at Chickasaw, OK, 25 Apr 1913; m. at Stewartstown, 7 Aug 1881, LUCINDA SUSAN REED, b. at Bury, Québec, 17 Jul 1862 daughter of John and Susan (Ellis) Reed;[2551] Lucinda d. at Chickasaw, 25 Apr 1945.

950) HANNAH STORY *(Hannah Abbott Story⁴, Benjamin³, Thomas², George¹)* b. 6 Sep 1784 daughter of Jeremiah and Hannah (Abbott) Story; d. at Concord, after 1850; m. 1st, 27 Feb 1806, BENNING NOYES, b. at Bow, 9 Dec 1780 son of Benjamin and Hannah (Thompson) Noyes; Benjamin d. at Bow, 2 Nov 1814. Hannah m. 2nd, at Montague, MA, 13 Apr 1816, as his second wife, EPHRAIM UPHAM, b. at Weston, 3 Nov 1778 son of Thomas and Martha (Williams) Upham; Ephraim d. at Bow, 29 Mar 1844. Ephraim was first married to Hannah Cushman.

After the death of Ephraim, Hannah lived with her son Jeremiah and his family in Concord.[2552]

Hannah Abbott and Benjamin Noyes were parents of four children.

i HANNAH NOYES, b. at Concord, 12 Jul 1807; d. 10 Feb 1809.

ii BENJAMIN ABBOT NOYES, b. at Concord, 10 Jul 1807; d. at Bow, 2 Jan 1892; m. 1st, 27 May 1832, JANE ROACH, b. about 1807; Jane d. at Bow, 21 Jul 1868. Benjamin m. 2nd, at Hooksett, NH, 28 Aug 1890, MARY FOWLER, b. at Pembroke, about 1835 daughter of William and Salome (Stickney) Fowler; Mary d. at Manchester, NH, 1 Sep 1908.

iii JEREMIAH S. NOYES, b. at Bow, 7 Jun 1811; d. at Concord, 16 Jan 1894; m. 13 Sep 1831, CAROLINE BATES, b. a Nashua, about 1812 daughter of Stephen and Anne (Thurston) Bates; Caroline d. at Concord, 20 Dec 1893.

iv HANNAH NOYES, b. at Bow, 3 Aug 1813; d. at Manchester, 18 Jun 1888; m. 1st, at Concord, 18 Sep 1832, JOHN PARKER, b. about 1800; John d. at Bow, 4 Sep 1836. Hannah m. 2nd, MESCHECK CATE, b. at Starksboro, VT, 12 Mar 1812 son of Jonathan and Charlotte (Blanchard) Cate; Mescheck d. at Manchester, 17 Apr 1905. Mescheck married second Mary Wallace Holt.

Hannah Abbott and Ephraim Upham were parents of two children.

i MARY A. UPHAM, b. at Bow, 7 Jul 1817; d. at Concord, 4 Mar 1882; m. at Portland, ME, 7 Nov 1839, JOHN SCALES; John d. before 1850.

[2551] Lucinda's place of birth and names of her parents are given on the marriage record of Lucinda Reed and Charles Saltmarsh.

[2552] Year: 1850; Census Place: Concord, Merrimack, New Hampshire; Roll: M432_435; Page: 56A; Image: 114

ii CHARLOTTE UPHAM, b. at Bow, 10 Feb 1827; d. at Washington, DC, 2 Nov 1924; m. 31 Dec 1848, JOHN MERRILL, b. at Andover, about 1826; John d. at Washington, about 1874. John was a clerk in the War Department.

951) EPHRAIM ABBOT *(Benjamin[4], Benjamin[3], Thomas[2], George[1])*, b. at New Castle, ME, 28 Sep 1779 son of Benjamin and Sarah (Brown) Abbot; d. at Westford, MA, 21 Jul 1870; m. 1st, at Andover, 5 Jan 1814, MARY HOLYOKE PEARSON, b. 10 Mar 1782 daughter of Eliphalet and Priscilla (Holyoke) Pearson; Mary d. 15 Jul 1829. Ephraim m. 2nd, 21 Jan 1830, ABIGAIL WHITING BANCROFT, b. at Groton, 1797 daughter of Amos and Abigail (Whiting) Bancroft; Abigail d. at Groton, 17 May 1886.

Rev. Ephraim Abbot was co-compiler of the *Genealogical Register of the Descendants of George Abbot.* He graduated from Harvard in 1806 and Andover Seminary in 1810 as part of the first graduating class. He was a missionary in Eastern Maine from 1811 to 1812. He was pastor of the Congregational Church in Greenland until 1828 when he left that post due to ill health. He was preceptor of Brackett Academy in Greenland from 1825 to 1828. Following that, he was principal at Westford Academy for nine years.[2553][2554]

Ephraim Abbot was twice married. He and Mary Holyoke Pearson did not have children. Ephraim and his second wife, Abigail Whiting Bancroft, had six children whose births are record at Westford. Three of the children lived to adulthood, but none married. In 1880, the three surviving children were living with their mother in Groton, and in 1900, the three of them shared a household in Groton.

Ephraim Abbot did not leave a will. Son George E. H. Abbot was named administrator, and heirs noted are widow Abigail W. Abbot and two daughters Lucy M. B. Abbot and Sarah B. Abbot.[2555]

i ABBA MARIA ABBOT, b. 14 Nov 1830; d. 30 Oct 1831.

ii LUCY MIRANDA BANCROFT ABBOT, b. 10 Apr 1832; d. at Groton, 2 Dec 1908.

iii AMOS B. ABBOT, b. 11 Nov 1833; d. 25 Jan 1835.

iv EPHRAIM E. P. ABBOT, b. 9 Aug 1835; d. 20 Apr 1841.

v GEORGE EDWARD HENRY ABBOT, b 15 Feb 1838; d. at Groton, 24 Dec 1911. George was a teacher.

vi SARAH BASS ABBOT, b. 13 Jul 1841; d. at Groton, 9 Feb 1908.

952) HANNAH ABBOTT *(Benjamin[4], Benjamin[3], Thomas[2], George[1])*, b. at Concord, 9 Mar 1782 daughter of Benjamin and Sarah (Brown) Abbot; d. at Westford, MA, 5 Apr 1869; m. 15 Nov 1803, her second cousin once removed, EBENEZER HALL *(Daniel Hall[5], Dorcas Abbott Hall[4], Edward[3], Thomas[2], George[1])*, b. 9 May 1778 son of Daniel and Deborah (Davis) Hall; Ebenezer d. 14 Oct 1853. Ebenezer is a child in Family 902.

Ebenezer and Hannah started their family in Concord and relocated to Westford. They were the parents of five children.

i LUTHER HALL, b. at Concord, 2 Oct 1804; d. at Boston, 21 Dec 1869; m. 1st, 19 Oct 1834, LYDIA ELIZABETH WHITE, b. at Dorchester, Aug 1806 daughter of Samuel and Lydia (Blumer) White; Lydia d. at Dorchester, 5 Mar 1837. Luther m. 2nd, at Boston, 26 Jun 1837, OLIVIA PORTER, b. at Rye, NH, 15 Feb 1811 daughter of Huntington and Sarah Emery (Moulton) Porter; Olivia d. at Newton, 7 Apr 1896.

ii SARAH BROWN HALL, b. at Concord, 13 Feb 1806; d at Westford, 28 Sep 1859; m. 2 Dec 1836, RUFUS PATTEN, b. at Westford, 7 Sep 1802 son of Isaac and Lydia (Keyes) Patten; Rufus d. at Westford, 7 Sep 1881. After Sarah's death, Rufus married Dolly Bryant, 12 Mar 1862.

iii EPHRAIM A. HALL, b. at Concord, 27 Jun 1812; d. before 1870 likely at Malden;[2556] m. at Boston, 2 May 1839, LOUISA LYDIA GLOVER, b. at Boston, about 1818 daughter of Elisha and Lydia (Wooly) Glover; Louisa d. after 1870.

iv MARY HOLYOKE PEARSON HALL, b. 1 Dec 1816; d. at Boston, 18 Aug 1838.

2553 Abbot, *Descendants of George Abbot*, p 115

2554 NEHGS, *Memorial Biographies of the New England Historical and Genealogical Society*, pp 394-395

2555 *Middlesex County, MA: Probate File Papers, 1648-1871.*Online database. *AmericanAncestors.org.* New England Historic Genealogical Society, 2014.

2556 Ephraim was living in Malden at the 1860 census; his wife was living there in 1870 and a widow.

v ANGELINA D. HALL, b. at Westford, 29 Oct 1821; d. at Everett, 8 May 1903; m. at Marblehead, 29 Aug 1841, JOHN BROOKS PARKER, b. at Brighton, 12 Aug 1817 son of John and Harriet (Green) Parker; John d. at Everett, 29 Mar 1896.

953) RUTH MORRILL ABBOTT *(Benjamin⁴, Benjamin³, Thomas², George¹)*, b. at Concord, 27 Jun 1784 daughter of Benjamin and Sarah (Brown) Abbot; d. after 1860 (living in Concord at the 1860 U.S. Census but not mentioned in her husband's 1861 will); m. 26 Nov 1805, her second cousin once removed, JAMES HALL *(Daniel Hall⁵, Dorcas Abbott Hall⁴, Edward³, Thomas², George¹)*, b. 1784 son of Daniel and Deborah (Davis) Hall. James is a child in Family 902.

In his will written 10 September 1861, James Hall notes that he has already made provisions for four of his children so that there is no further bequest for son Benjamin A., the heirs of son Theodore A. who is deceased, daughter Sarah, or daughter Mary. Son John C. Hall receives one-fourth part of the estate real and personal, and the remainder of the estate is bequeathed to son Robert Hall who was also named executor.[2557]

James and Ruth were the parents of eight children.

i MARY HALL, b. at Concord, 28 Dec 1806; d. unknown but after 1855 when she was living in Lowell; m. 5 Jun 1838, ALBERT GALLATIN CAPEN, b. at Stewartstown, 30 Jan 1806 son of Ebenezer and Abigail (Carter) Capen. Albert's death is uncertain but in 1870 he was living in the country of Panama. A. G. Capen wrote his will 8 February 1870 while a resident of Panama, South America (sic). The will was filed in New Hampshire. In his will, Albert left his entire estate to George Smith Hall, the son of his brother-in-law Theodore Hall, whom A. G. regards as his adopted son. George Smith Hall was named executor of the estate.[2558] Mary and Albert Capen had one son, George Hall Capen.

ii SARAH HALL, b. at Concord, 29 Aug 1808; d. at Lawrence, 14 Sep 1888; m. 1st, Apr 1829, LEONARD RUSSELL, b. about 1806 son of Jeremiah and Betsy (Merrill) Russell; Leonard d. at Lowell, 7 Dec 1848. Sarah m. 2nd, at Lowell, 6 Apr 1852, BRADLEY VARNUM LYON, b. at Pelham, 13 Apr 1823 son of William Read and Molly (-) Lyon; Bradley d. at Westford, 1875.

iii ROBERT HALL, b. at Concord, 7 Nov 1810; d. at Concord, 10 Jan 1902; m. 1 Jun 1833, LUCINDA S. CAPEN, b. at Stewartstown, 13 Jul 1815 daughter of Ebenezer and Abigail (Carter) Capen; Lucinda d. at Concord, 27 Aug 1890.

iv ISAAC A. HALL, b. at Concord, 21 Jul 1812; d. at Concord, 4 Dec 1834. Isaac was a silversmith in Concord as was his uncle Ivory Hall.[2559]

v JUDITH D. HALL, b. at Concord, 22 May 1817; d. at Lowell, 9 Jan 1835.

vi BENJAMIN A. HALL, b. at Lowell, 22 Jul 1819; d. at Concord, 21 Nov 1883; m. at Lowell, 2 Oct 1842, ELEANOR STONE, b. at Dunbarton, 11 Dec 1818 daughter of James and Mary (Beard) Stone; Eleanor d. at Concord, 17 Jan 1893.[2560]

vii JOHN CALVIN HALL, b. at Concord, 8 Oct 1821; d. at Concord about1863; m. at Lowell, 18 Oct 1842, ELIZABETH CARRIGAN, b. at Epsom, about 1819 daughter of Obadiah and Sarah (-) Carrigan; Elizabeth d. 22 Sep 1878.[2561]

viii THEODORE A. HALL, b. at Concord, 17 Oct 1824; d. about 1848;[2562] m. at Lowell, 16 Mar 1846, SUSAN BATCHELDER SMITH, b. 1 May 1823 daughter of Benjamin and Hannah (Mudgett) Smith; Susan d. at Concord, 17 May 1892. After Theodore's death, Susan married William T. Clough.

954) BENJAMIN ABBOTT *(Benjamin⁴, Benjamin³, Thomas², George¹)*, b. at Concord, 23 Sep 1786 son of Benjamin and Sarah (Brown) Abbot; d. at Ustick, IL, 28 Feb 1854; m. 17 Sep 1807, DORCAS NOYES, b. at Bow, NH, 22 Aug 1785 daughter of Enoch and Eunice (Kinsman) Noyes; Dorcas d. at Ustick, IL, 17 Feb 1877.

Deacon Benjamin Abbott and Dorcas Noyes lived in New Hampshire and Hartland, Vermont and all their children were born and reared in New England. In 1848, Benjamin and Dorcas relocated to Ustick, Illinois.[2563] Their son Asa MacFarland Abbott settled there a few years earlier. Benjamin and Dorcas were original members of the Congregational church at Unionville. Dorcas died at the age of 91 at the home of her son Asa.

2557 *New Hampshire. Probate Court (Merrimack County)*; Probate Place: *Merrimack, New Hampshire, Probate Records, Vol 34, 1856-1861, p 552, will of James Hall*

2558 *New Hampshire. Probate Court (Merrimack County)*; Probate Place: *Merrimack, New Hampshire*. volume 43, p 61

2559 New Hampshire Historical Society, Ivory Hall, https://www.nhhistory.org/object/250264/hall-ivory-1795-1880

2560 *New Hampshire, Death and Disinterment Records, 1754-1947*. The names of Eleanor's parents are given on her death record as James Stone and Mary Beard.

2561 *New Hampshire, Death and Burial Records Index, 1654-1949*. Elizabeth's parents are given as Obadiah and Sarah G. Carrigan on her death record.

2562 Theodore and Susan had a son in 1848, but Theodore died before the 1850 census.

2563 Bent, *History of Whiteside County, Illinois*, p 472

Benjamin and Dorcas were the parents of eight children.

i EPHRAIM ABBOTT, b. 25 Oct 1808; d. 10 Apr 1813.

ii SUSANNAH MANNING ABBOTT, b. 3 Dec 1810; d. at Moline, IL, 12 Mar 1898; m. 12 Nov 1842, JESSE FRYE, b. at Cattaraugus County, NY, 15 Feb 1818 son of Jesse and Betsey (Noyes) Frye;[2564] Jesse d. at Boston, 24 Feb 1887. Jesse Frye was the inventor of what was known as the Gang Plow which was an innovation in plow technology.[2565]

iii EPHRAIM ABBOTT, b. 25 Feb 1813; d. at St, Louis, MO, 30 Oct 1861; m. at Boston, 28 Jul 1835, MARY HUNT, b. about 1818 whose parents have not been identified; Mary d. at St. Louis, after 1880.

iv PETER GREEN ABBOTT, b. 8 May 1815; d. at Windsor County, VT, 7 Nov 1829.

v ENOCH N. ABBOTT, b. at Hartland, VT, 16 Dec 1817; d. at Lowell, MA, 18 Feb 1855; m. at Manchester, NH, 11 Apr 1843, MARIA HANNAH WOOD, b. at Hancock, NH, 11 Dec 1820 daughter of John and Hannah (Hills) Wood;[2566] Maria Hannah d. at Manchester, NH, 1860.

vi ASA MCFARLAND ABBOTT, b. at Hartland, VT, 16 Nov 1820; d. at Ustick, IL, 9 Apr 1889; m. at Henderson County, IL, 10 Dec 1846, SARAH SPERRY, b. 18 Feb 1822 daughter of Jay and Mary (Lamoret) Sperry; Sarah d. at Ustick, 12 May 1900.

vii LAURA D. ABBOTT, b. 31 Mar 1824 (recorded at Manchester, NH); d. at Springville, NY, 14 Feb 1853; m. about 1845, ALANSON P. MORTON, b. at Boston, NY, 16 May 1812 son of Wendell Morton; Alanson d. at Springville, 4 Mar 1872.

viii RUTH M. ABBOTT, b. 28 Feb 1828; d. 30 Sep 1832.

955) SARAH ABBOTT *(Benjamin⁴, Benjamin³, Thomas², George¹)*, b. at Concord, 3 Oct 1788 daughter of Benjamin and Sarah (Brown) Abbot; d. at Hartland, VT, 27 Jul 1878; m. 12 Sep 1805, STEPHEN NOYES, b. at Bow, NH, 5 Jul 1783 son of Enoch and Eunice (Kinsman) Noyes;[2567] Stephen d. 27 Feb 1868.

Sarah and Stephen started their family in Bow, were for a time in Concord, and settled in Hartland, Vermont by 1820. They were parents of four children.

i ENOCH NOYES, b. at Bow, 16 Jul 1806; d. at Concord, 18 May 1811.

ii SUSAN PARKER NOYES, b. 12 Nov 1808; d. at Hartland, VT, 31 Jan 1846; m. at Hartland, 28 Jun 1829, JOSHUA DICKINSON ALLEN, b. at Waterford, VT, 25 Oct 1804 son of Zadok and Abigail (Dickinson) Allen; Joshua d. at Hartland, 1869. After Susan's death, Joshua married Abigail.

iii BENJAMIN NOYES, b. 16 Mar 1811; d. at Hannibal, MO, 13 Feb 1865; m. 1st, 6 Jun 1830, LUCIA ANN W. THOMPSON, b. at Hartland, 31 Aug 1808 daughter of Jonah and Patience (Cushman) Thompson; Lucia d. at Hartland, 18 Jul 1831. Benjamin m. 2nd, 17 Sep 1834, JULIA A. BARTLETT, b. about 1811 daughter of Amos and Eunice K. (Noyes) Bartlett; Julia d. at Kansas City, MO, 7 Apr 1894.

iv STEPHEN NOYES, b. 26 May 1817; d. at Hartland, 22 Mar 1822.

956) ABIGAIL LAWRENCE ABBOTT *(Benjamin⁴, Benjamin³, Thomas², George¹)*, b. at Concord, 20 May 1791 daughter of Benjamin and Sarah (Brown) Abbot; d. at Chicopee, MA, 5 Dec 1856; m. 9 Feb 1809, SETH BAKER, b. at Pembroke, 21 May 1783 son of Thomas and Ruth (Peabody) Baker; Seth d. 30 Apr 1865.

Seth Baker was a carpenter in Chicopee. He and Abigail were parents of three children.

i THOMAS BAKER, b. at Pembroke, NH, 2 Oct 1810; d. at Chicopee, 24 Sep 1832; m. at Boston, MARY EARYS, b. at Boston, about 1810.

[2564] Barker, *Frye Genealogy*, p 88, p 114

[2565] US Patent US16912A, https://patents.google.com/patent/US16912A/en

[2566] Hayward, *History of Hancock, NH*, p 1041

[2567] Noyes, *Descendants of Nicholas Noyes*, p 114

ii TIMOTHY HALL BAKER, b. at Pembroke, 2 May 1812; d. at Chicopee, 1 Aug 1835; m. at Lowell, 5 Jun 1834, EMELINE SIMMONS.

iii CHARLOTTE G.D. BAKER, b. at Chicopee, 3 Oct 1821; d. at Springfield, 12 Jul 1907; m. 8 Dec 1840, JOSEPH WARREN HITCHCOCK, b. at Brimfield, 10 Jun 1816 son of Nathan and Esther (Bigelow) Hitchcock; Joseph d. at Springfield, 11 Feb 1895.

957) ISAAC ABBOTT *(Benjamin⁴, Benjamin³, Thomas², George¹)*, b. at Concord, 3 Aug 1793 son of Benjamin and Sarah (Brown) Abbot; d. 12 Nov 1840; m. 7 May 1817, SUSAN ELA, b. at Hooksett, 7 Jan 1797 daughter of Israel and Zebiah (Martin) Ela.[2568] Susan was still living in 1880 when she was living with her daughter Fanny and her husband Leonard Beard.[2569]

Isaac and Susan started their family in Hartland, Vermont, were then in Merrimack County, New Hampshire, and finally in Lancaster, New Hampshire. Isaac Abbott and Susan Ela were parents of thirteen children.

i ERASTUS I. ABBOTT, b. at Hartland, VT, about 1818; d. at Peru, ME, 24 Jan 1903; m. at Lancaster, NH, 21 Mar 1843, LYDIA ANN ACKLEY, b. at Lancaster, 24 Apr 1823; Lydia d. at Peru, 27 Feb 1867.

ii RODERICK T. ABBOTT, b. at Hartland, VT, 11 Aug 1819; d. at Boston, after 1882; m. at Lancaster, Apr 1846, SUSAN JANE JONES, b. about 1828 daughter of Clark and Susan (Brown) Jones; Susan d. at Boston, 8 Oct 1915.

iii EDWIN L. ABBOTT, b. at Hartland, 2 Jun 1821; nothing further known.

iv ROE ANN ABBOTT, b. 25 Apr 1823; d. at Bethel, VT, 16 Jan 1898; m. 7 Jan 1850, JOSEPH M. CHAMBERLAIN, b. 15 Aug 1820 son of Joseph T. and Fanny (Bullard) Chamberlain; Joseph d. 11 Jan 1864 at Marine G. H., New Orleans, LA. Joseph was a private during the Civil War.

v SARAH ANN ABBOTT, b. 27 Mar 1825; d. at Dunbarton, NH, 17 Mar 1888; m. at Manchester, NH, 1 Oct 1856, EDWARD P. WILLIAMS, b. at Pepperell, MA, about 1825 son of Peter and Annie (Lakin) Williams; Edward d. at Goffstown, 17 Oct 1895.

vi MARY O. ABBOTT, b. recorded at Bow, 29 Apr 1827; d. at Hooksett, NH, 28 Apr 1913; m. about 1852, DAVID A. KIMBALL, b. at Gilmanton, 24 Oct 1822 son of John and Nancy (Adams) Kimball; David d. at Hooksett, 30 Jan 1894.

vii SUSAN EASTER ABBOTT, b. 17 Sep 1829; d. at Portland, ME, 23 Feb 1911; m. at Lowell, 14 Nov 1850, HARVEY SCRIBNER, b. 15 Jul 1828 son of Harvey and Martha (Winship) Scribner; Harvey d. at Gardiner, ME, 1 Jul 1896.

viii JOHN ISAAC ABBOTT, b. 17 Sep 1829; d. at Lancaster, NH, after 1880. John does not seem to have married. In 1880, he was living with his sister Fanny and her husband.

ix WILLIAM NATHANIEL ABBOTT, b. at Lancaster, 19 Sep 1832; d. at Lamoni, IA, 14 Aug 1917; m. at Bethel, 20 Jul 1858, ALMA BILLINGS, b. 3 Apr 1835; Alma d. at Lamoni, 11 Jan 1917.

x ELIZABETH P. ABBOTT, b. at Lancaster, 19 Sep 1832 d. at Brattleboro, after 1882; m. at Bethel, VT, 24 Dec 1861, HARRY H. DEAN, b. about 1831 son of Wyman and Susan (Adams) Dean; Harry d. at Brattleboro, 25 Apr 1885.

xi LUCRETIA D. ABBOTT, b. at Lancaster, 18 Mar 1835; likely died young as she is not listed with the family in the 1850 census.

xii FANNY F. ABBOTT, b. at Lancaster, 12 Nov 1837; d. at Goffstown, 9 Mar 1897; m. at Lancaster, 28 Nov 1867, LEONARD M. BEARD, b. at Needham, MA, 1 Sep 1839 son of Cleveland and Elizabeth (Crawford) Beard; Leonard d. at Goffstown, 21 Feb 1924.

xiii LUTHER ERASMUS ABBOTT, b. 15 May 1840; likely d. before 1850 as he is not listed with the family at that census.

958) PARMELIA ABBOTT *(Benjamin⁴, Benjamin³, Thomas², George¹)*, b. at Concord, 1 Feb 1796 daughter of Benjamin and Sarah (Brown) Abbot; d. at Pewaukee, WI, 1872; m. 7 Nov 1816, NATHANIEL GOSS, b. at Greenland, NH, 3 Nov 1788 son of Nathaniel and Mary (Nye) Goss; Nathaniel d. at Pewaukee, 7 Jul 1855.

[2568] Ela, *Genealogy of the Ela Family*, p 17

[2569] Year: 1880; Census Place: Lancaster, Coos, New Hampshire; Roll: 762; Page: 153C; Enumeration District: 040

Parmella and Nathaniel had their four children in New Hampshire, but Nathaniel lost his property in New Hampshire and the family with four adolescent children headed to Wisconsin.[2570]

Son Nathaniel Stickney Goss married but was early widowed and had no children. In his will written 22 August 1889 (probate 13 March 1891), he made bequests related to his extensive bird collection donating his specimens to the State of Kansas. Following detailed instructions related to this bequest, he directs that the remainder of the estate be sold, held in trust, and that semi-annual payments of the interest be made to his three siblings: sister Mrs. Sarah L. Clark and her husband T. L. Clark of Neosho Falls, Kansas, sister Mrs. Mary N. Waterman and her husband J. H. Waterman of Pewaukee, Wisconsin, and brother Captain B. F. Goss and his wife Abby B. Goss of Pewaukee, Wisconsin.[2571]

i SARAH ABBOT GOSS, b. at Greenland, NH, 7 Jan 1818; d. at Neosho Falls, KS, 8 Nov 1890; m. 7 Jul 1840, TIMOTHY LYMAN CLARK, b. in Vermont, 27 Aug 1813 son of Asa and Naomi C. (Lyman) Clark; Timothy d. at Neosho Falls, 17 Oct 1897.

ii MARY NYE GOSS, b. at Greenland, 28 Mar 1820; d. at Pewaukee, WI, 1893; m. 25 Jun 1844, JAMES HENRY WATERMAN, b. at Lee, NY, 11 Jul 1813 son of West and Sophia (Bartlett) Waterman; James d. at Pewaukee, 1894.

iii BENJAMIN FRANKLIN GOSS, b. at Lancaster, NH, 24 Apr 1823; d. at Pewaukee, WI, 6 Jul 1893; m. at Pewaukee, 21 Jan 1851, ABBY BRADLEY, b. at Cayuga County, NY, 6 Oct 1832 daughter of Lyman and Elizabeth (-) Bradley; Abby d. at Pewaukee, 2 Nov 1916.

iv NATHANIEL STICKNEY GOSS, b. at Lancaster, NH, 7 Jun 1826; d. at Neosho Falls, KS, 10 Mar 1891; m. at Waukesha, WI, 26 Oct 1854, his first cousin, EMELINE F. "EMMA" BROWN, b. in New Hampshire, about 1834 daughter of William J. and Lydia Emeline (Goss) Brown; Emma d. at Waverly, IA, 1856. Nathaniel Stickney Goss was known as the Kansas Audubon for his extensive identification and collection of bird species.[2572]

959) THEODORE THOMAS ABBOT *(Benjamin⁴, Benjamin³, Thomas², George¹)*, b. at Concord, 22 Mar 1799 son of Benjamin and Sarah (Brown) Abbot; d. at Lunenburg, MA, 23 Mar 1887; m. at Lowell, 7 Aug 1826, MEHITABLE FROST GREENOUGH, b. at Newburyport, 1 Jan 1800 daughter of John and Elizabeth "Betsy" (March) Greenough; Mehitable d. 28 Mar 1887.

Theodore and Mehitable were married 60 years and died five days apart.

Theodore Abbot served roles as a farmer and a machinist. He was mayor of Manchester, New Hampshire from 1855-1857 and 1862-1863.[2573]

i MARGARET HOLYOKE ABBOTT, b. 13 May 1827; d. at Sauk City, WI, 8 Aug 1854; m. at Manchester, NH, 20 May 1851, JOHN WARREN JOHNSON, b. about 1826 of Mason, NH. Margaret had one son who died in infancy. John Warren Johnson was an attorney[2574] but his parents are not yet located.

ii THEODORE EDSON ABBOTT, b. 5 Mar 1830; d. unknown. It is not clear what became of Theodore. He may be the Theodore E. Abbott age 20 living at Calaveras District, CA in 1850. The Calaveras District was a gold rush area.

iii EDWARD PAYSON ABBOTT,[2575] b. 1 Apr 1832; d. at Vernon, NJ, 26 Jun 1901. Edward served in the Civil War enlisting as a Quarter Master Sergeant in Company E of the Rhode Island 1st Calvary 3 Mar 1862. He was promoted to First Lieutenant 15 Apr 1864 and mustered out 15 Jul 1865 at Cloud's Mills, Virginia. He was wounded and a POW,[2576] but the details on that have not been located. In the 1900 Census, Edward P. Abbott born Apr 1832 was living in Vernon as a boarder with occupation listed as civil engineer. He reported being a widower. No marriage record has been located for him and no record of children. He did receive an invalid pension related to his service in the Civil War.

[2570] Jackson, Mary E. "Col. N. S. Goss", *Topeka pen and camera sketches*. GW Crane, 1890, pp 124-130.

[2571] Kansas, Wills and Probate Records, 1803-1987, *Will Record, Vol B, 1884-1903*, pp 245-247

[2572] Lantz, D. E. "A List of Birds Collected by Col. N. S. Goss in Mexico and Central America." *Transactions of the Annual Meetings of the Kansas Academy of Science* 16 (1897): 218-24. doi:10.2307/3623718.

[2573] New Hampshire Historical Society, "Abbot, Theodore Thomas." https://www.nhhistory.org/object/463823/abbot-theodore-thomas-1799-1887

[2574] New Hampshire Historical Society, "Johnson, Margaret Holyoke." https://www.nhhistory.org/object/550778/johnson-margaret-holyoke-1827-1854

[2575] There are several Edward P. Abbotts of about the same age and they are often confused. The Edward P. Abbott who married Martha Tarbell was the son of Hugh and Minerva (Cragin) Abbott.

[2576] U.S., Civil War Soldier Records and Profiles, 1861-1865

iv ELIZABETH MARCH ABBOTT, b. at Canton, NH, 22 Apr 1834; d. at Litchfield, NH, 8 Feb 1927; m. at Manchester, 15 Jan 1863, as his second wife, JOHN PLUMMER NEWELL, b. at Barnstead, NH, 30 Jul 1823 son of William H. and Olive (Dennett) Newell; John d. 22 Nov 1917. John was first married to Mary W. Bell who died in 1858.

v OSSIAN FRANK ABBOTT, b. 16 May 1836; d. at Ann Arbor, MI, 26 Jun 1856. Ossian died while a student at the University of Michigan.

vi EPHRAIM ELIPHALET PEARSON ABBOTT, b. at Concord, 20 Sep 1841; d. at San Diego, CA, 11 Aug 1919; m. 30 Jun 1868, CAROLINE HARVEY, b. at Ryegate, VT, 9 Mar 1837 daughter of Alexander and Elizabeth (-) Harvey; Caroline d. 9 Oct 1916. Ephraim graduated from Dartmouth College and the Andover Theological Seminary.[2577]

Great-Grandchildren of Nathaniel Abbott and Dorcas Hibbert

960) EDWARD TAYLOR *(Mary Blanchard Taylor[4], Mary Abbott Blanchard[3], Nathaniel[2], George[1])*, b. at Dracut, 14 Jul 1744 son of Edward and Mary (Blanchard) Taylor; d. at Plymouth, NH, 1777;[2578] m. at Hollis, 14 Nov 1771, MARY WORCESTER daughter of Jesse and Patience (Pope) Worcester who were early settlers of Hollis. After Edward's death, Mary married Enoch Page.

Edward Taylor and Mary Worcester were parents of four children born at Plymouth, New Hampshire.

i MOLLY TAYLOR, b. 23 Aug 1772; d. at Grafton, NH, 1842; m. at Plymouth, 8 Jun 1794, JARAHMAEL CUMMINGS, b. at Plymouth, 9 Dec 1771 son of Jotham and Anna (Brown) Cummings;[2579] Jarahmael d. at Grafton, 25 Dec 1831.

ii PATIENCE TAYLOR, b. 3 Mar 1773; nothing further known.

iii EDWARD TAYLOR, b. 11 Nov 1775; nothing further known.

iv JOHN TAYLOR, b. 21 Nov 1777; m. 1802, LYDIA CLIFFORD, b. at Dorchester, NH, about 1780 daughter of John and Mary (Worthen) Clifford.[2580]

961) JOEL TAYLOR *(Mary Blanchard Taylor[4], Mary Abbott Blanchard[3], Nathaniel[2], George[1])*, b. at Hollis, 23 Aug 1752 son of Edward and Mary (Blanchard) Taylor; d. at Thornton, NH, 29 Apr 1814; m. 9 Apr 1778, as her second husband, SARAH HOBART, b. at Hollis, 15 Jan 1745 daughter of David and Sarah (Parker) Hobart; Sarah d. 1 Jan 1827. Sarah was first married to Phineas Lovejoy who died about 1777.

Joel Taylor was in Plymouth, New Hampshire from 1776 to 1793 when he was on the tax rolls there.[2581] The family was then in Thornton, New Hampshire.

In his will written 10 September 1813, Joel Taylor bequeaths to dearly beloved wife Sarah the improvement on one-third of all of his estate. He bequeaths to "only and dearly beloved child" Katharine Taylor fifty dollars, and as she was entitled to wages after she was eighteen, she can take the wages owed to her in the form of household furnishings. He leaves to the town of Thornton two-thirds of his personal and real estate for the building of a meeting house as long as it is built within five years and is the size of the Compton meeting house. In addition, one hundred dollars is to be used for the settlement of a good gospel minister. After Sarah's decease, her thirds also go to the town. Deacon Moses Foss was named executor. On 18 March 1814, Joel Taylor added a codicil in which the dower thirds are to be in the hands of the town but retained for the use of Katharine and her heirs if she has any. On 18 April 1814, he added another codicil as he believed his bequest to Katharine was deficient and increased the bequest to two hundred-fifty dollars.[2582]

Sadly, Katharine did not have the opportunity to enjoy her increased bequest as she died three days after her father. Katharine wrote her will 2 May 1814 in which she bequeathed all her honored father had given her to Sarah Ramsey and her children.

Joel and Sarah Taylor had three children.

i KATHARINE TAYLOR, b. about 1780; d. at Thornton, 2 May 1814.

2577 A detailed biography of Rev. Ephraim E. P. Abbott can be found in Scales, *Biographical Sketches of the Class of 1863 Dartmouth College*, pp 126-134, available on Google Books.

2578 Stearns and Runnels, *History of Plymouth, NH*, volume II, p 328

2579 Stearns and Runnels, *History of Plymouth, New Hampshire*, volume II, Genealogies, p 162

2580 Stearns and Runnels, *History of Plymouth*, volume II, p 132

2581 Stearns, *History of Plymouth, NH*, volume II, p 669

2582 *New Hampshire. Probate Court (Grafton County)*; Probate Place: *Grafton, New Hampshire, Probate Records, Vol 1-2, 1773-1814*, p 654, will of Joel Taylor.

ii DAVID TAYLOR, b. 1785; d. at Thornton, 10 Sep 1811.

iii JOEL TAYLOR, b. 1786; d. at Thornton, 30 Dec 1811.

962) MARY TAYLOR *(Mary Blanchard Taylor⁴, Mary Abbott Blanchard³, Nathaniel², George¹)*, b. at Hollis, 19 Jun 1754 daughter of Edward and Mary (Blanchard) Taylor; d. at Mont Vernon, after 1812; m. Dec 1778, JAMES HOPKINS.[2583] James d. at Mont Vernon, NH, 1809. James seems to have had a first marriage, although there is conflicting information on her name, but which is more likely Martha.

James Hopkins was a farmer in Mont Vernon. He had a daughter Sarah from his first marriage,[2584] although the History of Mont Vernon attributes this daughter to Mary Taylor.

James Hopkins did not leave a will and his estate entered probate 20 December 1809. Only son James Hopkins was named administrator as the widow declined administration. The real estate inventory included home farm of $1,050, lot in Lyndeborough at $415, a small lot at $10, and a pew in the meeting house, $45. On 1 Apr 1812, widow Mary Hopkins was allowed $100 from the personal estate for support of life.[2585]

There are just two children known for Mary Taylor and James Hopkins.

i JAMES HOPKINS, b. at Amherst, 10 Jun 1781; d. at Mont Vernon, 26 Sep 1862; m. at Mont Vernon, 9 Aug 1804, AZUBA CURTIS, b. at Lyndeborough, about 1781; Azuba d. at Mont Vernon, 26 Sep 1855. After Azuba's death, James married Mrs. Nancy Gould who died in 1857.

ii MOLLY HOPKINS, b. at Amherst, 15 Mar 1783; d. at Amherst, Feb 1803.

963) JACOB TAYLOR *(Mary Blanchard Taylor⁴, Mary Abbott Blanchard³, Nathaniel², George¹)*, b. at Hollis, 21 Aug 1756 son of Edward and Mary (Blanchard) Taylor; d. at Groton, NH, 5 Aug 1838; m. 19 Nov 1781, BETTY BOYNTON, b. at Hollis, 26 Sep 1756 daughter of John and Lydia (Jewett) Boynton; Betty d. at Grafton, 7 Feb 1843.[2586]

Jacob Taylor served in the Revolution as a private in the regiment of Colonel Prescott of the Massachusetts line for one year. He received a pension of $96 per year. The pension file states that at his death, Jacob left a widow Betsy Taylor and one daughter Betsey Tenney.[2587] There is just one child known for Jacob and Betty.

i BETSEY TAYLOR, b. at Groton, NH, 1782; d. at Groton, 3 Oct 1852; m. 14 Jun 1803, BENJAMIN TENNEY, b. at Temple, 23 Aug 1781 son of Benjamin and Ruth (Blanchard) Tenney; Benjamin d. at Groton, 12 Sep 1871.

964) BENJAMIN BLANCHARD *(Benjamin Blanchard⁴, Mary Abbott Blanchard³, Nathaniel², George¹)*; b. at Hollis, 15 Nov 1745 son of Benjamin and Keziah (Hastings) Blanchard; d. 21 Dec 1789; m. 1st, PATTY GOODWIN who died about 1771. Benjamin m. 2nd, SARAH CURRY, b. 15 Nov 1752 daughter of William and Ann (MacFarland) Curry.[2588]

In his will written 17 December 1789, Benjamin Blanchard bequeaths to his beloved wife one-third part of his real and personal estate as the law directs. Sons Amos, Ralph, and John each receive £30 lawful money. The remainder of the estate, real and personal, is to be divided equally among his three sons Amos, Ralph, and John and his three daughters Keziah, Martha, and Sarah. Trusty friend Samuel Gerrish was named executor.[2589]

There are no known children of Benjamin Blanchard and Patty Goodwin. Benjamin Blanchard and Sarah Curry were parents of seven children born at Canterbury.[2590]

i AMOS BLANCHARD, b. 8 Jun 1773; d. at Greensboro, VT, 10 Mar 1829; m. ELIZABETH TOLMAN, b. about 1773 whose parents are not identified; Elizabeth d. at Greensboro, 10 Jan 1829.

[2583] Spaulding, *An Account of Early Settlers of West Dunstable*, p 135 reports Mary's spouse as James Hopkins. The History of Milford, p 623, has Jonathan Buxton marrying Mary Taylor born in 1754, and so it is not entirely clear who Mary married. But Spaulding's account has this listing as part of the Edward Taylor genealogy. Secomb's *History of Amherst* also has James Hopkins as her spouse. And Buxton Family Association of America states that Jonathan Buxton married Mary Taylor who was the daughter of Timothy. (Volume II, The Buxton Family, p 62)

[2584] Sarah Hopkins daughter of James and Martha Hopkins born at Amherst, NH, 7 Dec 1769.

[2585] New Hampshire, County Probate Records, 1660-1973, Hillsborough; 21:231, 16:506; 18:471

[2586] Ancestry.com, U.S., Revolutionary War Pension and Bounty-Land Warrant Application Files, 1800-1900. Death date of Jacob given in pension papers; the widow's pension was received until 1843.

[2587] U.S., Revolutionary War Pension and Bounty-Land Warrant Application Files, 1800-1900

[2588] Lyford, *History of the Town of Canterbury*, p 28

[2589] *New Hampshire. Probate Court (Rockingham County)*; Probate Place: *Rockingham, New Hampshire, Estate Papers, No 5396-5511, 1788-1790*, File 5511

[2590] Lyford, *History of Canterbury*, p 28

ii RALPH BLANCHARD, b. 11 Jan 1775; d. at Peacham, VT, 1796 (probate at Rockingham County, NH, 2 Dec 1796).

iii WILLIAM BLANCHARD, b. about 1778; d. young and before 1789.

iv KEZIAH BLANCHARD, b. 20 May 1781; d. at Greensboro, VT, 21 Oct 1866; m. about 1800, OBADIAH B. GLINES, b. at Canterbury, 4 May 1774 son of Nathaniel and Elizabeth (Moore) Glines; Obadiah d. at Greensboro, 7 Jul 1857.

v MARTHA BLANCHARD, b. 18 Jun 1783; d. at Glover, VT, 17 Apr 1853; m. at Boscawen, 23 Jan 1803, NATHAN CUTLER, b. 1773; Nathan d. at Glover, 16 Apr 1818.

vi SARAH BLANCHARD, b. 11 May 1786; m. at Chichester, NH, 6 Mar 1820, BENJAMIN EMERY.

vii JOHN BLANCHARD, b.. 18 Feb 1788. John did marry and is reported in the History of Canterbury to have lived in Canada, but records have not been located.

965) JONATHAN BLANCHARD *(Benjamin Blanchard⁴, Mary Abbott Blanchard³, Nathaniel², George¹)*, b. at Hollis, 28 Jun 1750 son of Benjamin and Keziah (Hastings) Blanchard; d. in Vermont, 31 Dec 1837; m. 13 Oct 1772, HANNAH CHADWICK, b. at Bradford, 22 Jun 1752 daughter of James and Mary (Thurston) Chadwick.

Jonathan Blanchard and Hannah Chadwick were parents of eight children, the oldest six births at Canterbury and the births of the youngest two children at Boscawen.

i JAMES BLANCHARD, b. 15 Jan 1774; d. at Greensboro, VT, 30 Apr 1843; m. PHEBE CARTER, b. about 1777; Phebe d. at Greensboro, 21 Feb 1840.

ii JACOB BLANCHARD, b. 13 Nov 1775; d. 1779.

iii EDMUND BLANCHARD, b. 27 Jan 1778; d. at Greensboro, VT, 29 Nov 1836; m. Feb 1806, his third cousin once removed, ANNA ABBOTT *(Nathan⁴, Thomas³, Thomas², George¹)*, b. at Concord, 8 Jan 1781 daughter of Nathan and Betty (Farnum) Abbott; Anna d. at Craftsbury, VT, 27 Oct 1868. Edmund Blanchard and Anna Abbott are the parents of Family 896.

iv JACOB BLANCHARD, b. 10 May 1780; d. at Canterbury, Jun 1848; m. 11 Nov 1807, HANNAH MCCRILLIS, b. at Canterbury, 13 Feb 1782 daughter of David and Susannah (Moore) McCrillis; Hannah d. 25 Oct 1869.

v POLLY BLANCHARD, b. 1781; d. 1785.

vi SALLY BLANCHARD, b. 21 May 1782; d. at Bethel, ME, 1865; m. at Canterbury, 19 Sep 1805, BAXTER LYON, b. at Sturbridge, MA, 15 Mar 1782 son of Nehemiah and Betty (Bugbee) Lyon; Baxter d. at Bethel, 1862.

vii HANNAH BLANCHARD, b. about 1784; d. at Gilmanton, NH, 1816; m. at Canterbury, 26 Dec 1809, JONATHAN LOUGEE, b. 29 Apr 1782 son of Jonathan and Elizabeth (Fletcher) Lougee; Jonathan d. at Gilmanton, 19 Mar 1863. Jonathan married second Elizabeth Morgan (widow of Gilbert Hewitt).

viii SAMUEL BLANCHARD, b. about 1786; d. at Canterbury, 10 Nov 1819; m. 1819, SUSAN DIMOND, b. at Concord, 1 Mar 1795 daughter of Reuben and Mary (Currier) Dimond; Susan d. at Boston, 23 Dec 1877.

966) ABIEL BLANCHARD *(Benjamin Blanchard⁴, Mary Abbott Blanchard³, Nathaniel², George¹)*, b. at Hollis, 1 Dec 1751 son of Benjamin and Keziah (Hastings) Blanchard; d. at Peacham, VT, 4 Jan 1803; m. 19 Feb 1784, MARY EASTMAN, b. at Rumford, 6 Apr 1758 daughter of Nathaniel and Phebe (Chandler) Eastman; Mary d. at Peacham, 12 Sep 1831.

In his will written 30 November 1802, Abiel Blanchard bequeathed to beloved wife Mary the whole and sole use and improvement of the estate for a period of seven years provided she continues a widow. This is so she can provide for and see to the education of their children. Eldest daughter Phebe receives one-half of a 100-acre lot in Peacham for her sole use as well as $500 which will come from an obligation owed him by John William Barns, Martha Buckminster, and William Moore. Sons John Blanchard and Jacob Blanchard receive $1,000 when they reach age twenty-one that will come from the same amount owed to Abiel. John and Jacob also receive the home farm to be equally divided. Sons Enoch and Nathaniel each receive $1,000 when they reach age twenty-one. Daughter Pamelia and Polly will receive $500 when they reach age eighteen. There are other stipulations related to the care of the children if their mother remarries while the children are young. Reuben Blanchard and William Chamberlain were named executors. Real estate was valued at $3,100 ($3,000 for the home farm and $100 for the 50-acre lot) and personal estate of $8,323.03 which largely consists of notes and mortgages that he holds.[2591]

Abiel Blanchard and Polly Eastman were parents of seven children born at Peacham, Vermont.

[2591] Vermont Wills and Probates, 1749-1999, Caledonia, volume 2, pp 75-87

i PHEBE BLANCHARD, b. 3 Jan 1785; d. at Barnet, VT, 20 Jun 1861; m. at Peacham, 1 Feb 1816, WALTER HARVEY, b. at Barnet, VT, 12 Feb 1789 son of Alexander and Jenet (Brock) Harvey; Walter d. at Barnet, 9 Apr 1863.

ii JOHN BLANCHARD, b. 30 Sep 1787; d. at Columbia, PA, 9 Mar 1849; m. by 1824, MARY MILES, b. at Milesburg, PA, 23 Mar 1799 daughter of Evan and Rebecca (George) Miles;[2592] Mary d. at Bellefonte, PA, 9 Jan 1857. John graduated from Dartmouth in 1812 and located in York, Pennsylvania where he studied law and was admitted to the bar in 1815. He served as a member of Congress from 1844 to his death in 1849.[2593]

iii JACOB BLANCHARD, b. 1790; d. at Peacham, 7 May 1870; m. 1st at Ryegate, 27 Jan 1824, THOMAS J. "JEFFY" CAMERON, b. at Ryegate, 13 May 1804 daughter of John and Elizabeth (Stark) Cameron; Jeffy d. 1843. Jacob m. 2nd, at Peacham, 6 Jan 1846, MYRA JERUSHA COWLES, b. at Marshfield, VT, about 1806 daughter of Timothy and Susan (Fairchild) Cowles; Myra d. at Peacham, 28 Nov 1898.

iv PAMELIA BLANCHARD, b. 1791; d. at Peacham, 21 Nov 1821. Pamelia did not marry.

v ENOCH BLANCHARD, b. 9 Jan 1793; d. at Paoli, IN, 27 Jul 1822. Enoch was a physician. He does not seem to have married.

vi POLLY BLANCHARD, b. about 1796; living in 1802 but nothing further known.

vii NATHANIEL BLANCHARD, b. about 1799; d. at Hardwick, VT, 15 Sep 1836. Nathaniel graduated from Yale in 1821. In 1822, he went to Georgia to teach. He studied law and had a practice in Fayetteville, GA. He died while visiting friends in Vermont.[2594]

967) ISAAC BLANCHARD *(Benjamin Blanchard⁴, Mary Abbott Blanchard³, Nathaniel², George¹)*, b. at Hollis, 14 Apr 1753 son of Benjamin and Keziah (Hastings) Blanchard; m. MOLLY WHEELER *perhaps* the daughter of Jeremiah and Esther (Russell) Wheeler.

Isaac and Molly lived in Concord and there are records for six children the oldest two children born at Groton and the younger children born at Concord. Marriages were not located for any of the children.

i HASTINGS BLANCHARD, b. 31 Jan 1777; died young

ii JOHN BLANCHARD, b. 7 Jan 1779

iii DORCAS BLANCHARD, b. 7 Nov 1781

iv KATY BLANCHARD, b. 2 Oct 1784

v MOLLY BLANCHARD, b. 20 Oct 1786

vi HASTINGS BLANCHARD, b. 24 Aug 1788; d. at Peacham, VT, 10 Dec 1853. Hastings did not marry. He enlisted in the Army from Concord 18 January 1819 and was discharged 30 September 1819 as *non compos.*[2595]

968) PETER BLANCHARD *(Benjamin Blanchard⁴, Mary Abbott Blanchard³, Nathaniel², George¹)*, b. at Hollis, 17 Aug 1756 son of Benjamin and Keziah (Hastings) Blanchard; d. at Danville, VT, 25 May 1810; m. by 1786, his second cousin, SARAH CHANDLER *(Abiel Chandler⁴, Rebecca Abbott Chandler³, Nathaniel², George¹)*, b. at Concord, 15 Jan 1768 daughter of Abiel and Judith (Walker) Chandler; Sarah d. 21 Nov 1836.

After their marriage, Peter and Sarah relocated to Peacham, Vermont and then to Danville, Vermont.

In her will dated 13 May 1833, Sarah Chandler Blanchard leaves to William A. Palmer, to hold in trust, ten shares at the bank in Caledonia and he is to use the dividends on those shares to provide support for her daughter Rebecca Porter during her life. At Rebecca's decease, those shares are to be equally divided among Rebecca's children. The other ten shares are bequeathed to daughter Sarah Palmer. Sarah also receives the farm stock, farming tools, and personal estate excluding the furniture. Rebecca and Sarah will equally divide the furniture and clothing. William Palmer is named executor.[2596]

[2592] Linn, *History of Centre and Clinton Counties, Pennsylvania*, p 215

[2593] Linn, *History of Centre and Clinton Counties, Pennsylvania, p 162*

[2594] Dexter, *Biographical Notices of Graduates of Yale College*, p 69

[2595] "United States Registers of Enlistments in the U.S. Army, 1798-1914," database with images, *FamilySearch* (https://familysearch.org/ark:/61903/1:1:QJD5-PQ4P : 13 March 2018), Hastings Blanchard, 18 Jan 1819; citing p. 154, volume 027, Concord, , New Hampshire, United States, NARA microfilm publication M233 (Washington D.C.: National Archives and Records Administration, n.d.), roll 14; FHL microfilm 350,320.

[2596] *Vermont. Probate Court (Caledonia District);* Probate Place: *Caledonia, Vermont, Probate Records, Vol 12-13, 1830-1851,* volume 13, p 157, will of Sarah Blanchard

Peter Blanchard and Sarah Chandler were parents of four children likely all born at Peacham.

i REBECCA BLANCHARD, b. 4 Jan 1787; d. at Danville, VT, 11 Oct 1847; m. 2 Nov 1807, AARON PORTER, b. at Boxford, MA, 27 Jun 1773 son of William and Mary (Adams) Porter; Aaron d. at Danville, 23 Mar 1860.

ii SOPHIA BLANCHARD, b. 7 Sep 1790; d. at Danville, VT, 16 Apr 1833; m. 1808, AUGUSTINE CLARK, b. about 1781 (baptized at Richmond, MA, 15 Mar 1786) son of Joseph and Rebecca (Jacobs) Clark; Augustine d. at Montpelier, VT, 17 Jun 1841. Augustine was second married to Julia Jewett. Augustine was an attorney and banker.

iii SARAH BLANCHARD, b. 6 Nov 1792; d. at Danville, VT, 12 Jan 1853; m. 18 Oct 1813, WILLIAM ADAMS PALMER, b. at Hebron, CT, 12 Sep 1791 son of Stephen and Susannah (Sawyer) Palmer; William d. at Danville, 3 Dec 1860. William Palmer was U.S. Senator from Vermont 1818-1825 and was governor of Vermont for three years.[2597]

iv ABIEL BLANCHARD, died young.[2598]

969) JOEL BLANCHARD *(Benjamin Blanchard[4], Mary Abbott Blanchard[3], Nathaniel[2], George[1])*, b. at Hollis, 27 Aug 1759 son of Benjamin and Keziah (Hastings) Blanchard; d. at Peacham, VT, 23 Jul 1816; m. by 1790, REBECCA GEORGE. Joel died from a "wrestle with a neighbor at Peacham, VT."[2599]

Joel Blanchard and Rebecca George were parents of twelve children born at Peacham, Vermont.[2600]

i REBECCA BLANCHARD, b. 1 May 1787; d. at Peacham, about 1812; possibly m. at Peacham, 2 Apr 1807, DAVID C. KIMBALL, b. at Hopkinton, NH, 18 Nov 1787 son of Smith and Elizabeth (Buswell) Kimball. David married second Rachel Goss 17 Oct 1813.

ii SAMUEL BLANCHARD, b. 13 Aug 1788

iii THEODORE BLANCHARD, b. 31 Jan 1790; d. at Peacham, 11 May 1850; m. at Peacham, 17 Mar 1813, ANNA JONES.

iv IRA BLANCHARD, b. 9 Feb 1791

v BETSEY BLANCHARD, b. 13 Feb 1793; d. at Barnet, VT, 24 Apr 1859; m. at Peacham, 18 Apr 1820, CURTIS NORRIS, b. at Danville, VT, 7 Feb 1798 son of Benjamin and Lucy (Kittredge) Norris; Curtis d. at Peacham, 25 Aug 1864.

vi NANCY BLANCHARD, b. 17 Sep 1794; d. at Barnet, 2 May 1862; m. 23 Mar 1827, CLAUDIUS GILFILLAN, b. Nov 1801 son of Thomas and Janet (Somers) Gilfillan;[2601] Claudius d. at Danville, VT, 27 Mar 1855.

vii JOEL RALPH BLANCHARD, b. 3 Sep 1796; d. at Peacham, 12 Oct 1867; m. 1st, at Peacham, 16 Nov 1824, his fourth cousin once removed, MARIA KELLOGG *(Judith Hall Kellogg[6], Timothy Hall[5], Dorcas Abbott Hall[4], Edward[3], Thomas[2], George[1])*, b. at Peacham, 13 Sep 1802 daughter of Erastus and Judith (Hall) Kellogg; Maria d. at Peacham, 17 Oct 1852. Joel m. 2nd, NANCY MCLAUGHLIN.

viii SUSANNA BLANCHARD, b. 17 Nov 1798

ix AMOS BLANCHARD, b. 8 Sep 1800; d. at Barnet, 6 Jan 1869; m. at Barre, VT, 2 Aug 1829, MARY BULLOCK, b. at Barre, 21 Nov 1805 daughter of Lovell and Betsey (Southwick) Bullock;[2602] Mary d. at Peacham, 21 Nov 1887.

x ELECTA BLANCHARD, b. 28 Dec 1802

xi ABIEL BLANCHARD, b. 29 Feb 1805; d. at Lenox, NY, 1850; m. about 1827, EDAH NOURSE, b. in VT 1799 likely the daughter of Francis and Anna (Pettit) Nourse; Edah d. at Concord, NY, 6 Aug 1886. Edah married second Sillick Canfield.

xii RUTH BLANCHARD, 30 Nov 1805

[2597] Biographical Directory of the United States Congress, William Adams Palmer (1781-1860). http://bioguide.congress.gov/scripts/biodisplay.pl?index=P000045

[2598] Abiel is a child listed in the Abbot Genealogical Register as dying young; no records were located.

[2599] Ancestry.com, Rhode Island, Vital Extracts, 1636-1899

[2600] *Vermont, Vital Records, 1720-1908.*

[2601] Wells, *History of Barnet*, p 438

[2602] Caller, *Genealogy of the Descendants of Lawrence and Cassandra Southwick*, p 356

970) ABEL BLANCHARD *(Benjamin Blanchard⁴, Mary Abbott Blanchard³, Nathaniel², George¹)*, b. at Hollis, 17 Feb 1761 son of Benjamin and Keziah (Hastings) Blanchard; d. at Peacham, VT, 12 Aug 1827; m. 1784, ELIZABETH EASTMAN, b. 5 Jun 1761 daughter of Nathaniel and Phebe (Chandler) Eastman; Elizabeth d. 10 Jul 1850.

Abel and Elizabeth married in New Hampshire but were in Caledonia County, Vermont by 1785. The parents remained in Peacham, but most of the children left the area when they reached there adolescent and young adult years. Several of the children spent time in Lower Canada, but most of them eventually settled in Allegany County, New York.

The children corresponded with their parents after leaving home and an archive of some of the family letters in available in a collection at the University of Notre Dame Hesburgh Libraries. For example, son Lewis, then age 22, wrote to his father Captain Abel Blanchard from Montreal on 7 May 1810. "Dear Father, I now take this opportunity to converse with you by the way of a letter. . .. I have not forgot you nor none of the rest of the family and friends and relations. I have been absent a year or more and have had as good luck as possible or at least as can be expected for a young man to start out into the world."[2603]

Abel Blanchard and Elizabeth Eastman were parents of eleven children born at Peacham.

i RUTH BLANCHARD, b. 12 Apr 1784; d. at Barnet, VT, 11 Nov 1862; m. 1st, about 1805 JOSEPH CHAMBERLAIN; Joseph d. about 1814. Ruth m. 2nd, Mar 1815, as his second wife, WILLIAM GILFILLAN, b. at Balfron, Scotland, 29 May 1767 son of William and Helen (Stevenson) Gilfillan;[2604] William d. at Barnet, 14 Aug 1840. William was first married to Janet Waddell.

ii BENJAMIN BLANCHARD, b. 16 Jan 1786; d. at Rushford, NY, 10 Jul 1869; m. RUHAMA GLEASON, b. 1787; Ruhama d. 1868.

iii LEWIS BLANCHARD, b. 15 Feb 1788; d. at Centerville, NY, 1847; m. about 1820, DEBORAH WHEELER, b. Fairfield, CT, 1793 daughter of John and Lydia (Squire) Wheeler; Deborah d. at Centerville, 1852. Deborah was first married to Peter Hotchkiss about 1811.

iv MARK BLANCHARD, b. 25 Nov 1789; d. at Centerville, NY, 10 Oct 1838; m. 1st, 1814, JERUSHA SPENCER, b. about 1795 daughter of Zacheus Spencer;[2605] Jerusha d. about 1824. Mark m. 2nd, about 1825, CYNTHIA LYON, b. about 1793 daughter of James and Jerusha (Miller) Lyon; Cynthia d. at Centerville, 23 Sep 1835. Mark m. 3rd, about 1835, LYDIA DELANO; Lydia d. at Centerville, 1842.

v HAZEN BLANCHARD, b. 10 Jan 1792; d. at Peacham, 17 Jul 1867; m. at Peacham, 15 Aug 1815; SARAH EMERY BURBANK, b. at Sanbornton, NH, 28 Dec 1793 daughter of Wells and Mercy (Hooker) Burbank; Sarah d. at Peacham, 19 Jul 1877.

vi JUDITH BLANCHARD, b. 18 Oct 1793; d. at Landis, NJ, 11 Feb 1890; m. at Peacham, 1 Jan 1828, TIMOTHY ELLIS, b. in NH, 1798 son of Timothy and Anna (Page) Ellis; Timothy d. at Landis, Feb 1880. Timothy was first married to Susannah Thompson.

vii CLARISSA BLANCHARD, b. 19 Dec 1795; d. at Peacham, 15 Sep 1851; m. at Peacham, 7 Dec 1815, SIMEON BROWN, b. in MA, 1794 son of David and Olive (Lamb) Brown; Simeon d. at Peacham, 17 Feb 1852.

viii ABEL BLANCHARD, b. 10 Nov 1797; d. at Centerville, 25 Jun 1867; m. 1820, HARRIET TRAIL, b. at Vernon, CT, 1798 daughter of Russell and Tirzah (Thatcher) Trail;[2606] Harriet d. at Centerville, 5 Nov 1855.

ix PETER BLANCHARD, b. 17 Jan 1800; nothing further known.

x CYNTHIA BLANCHARD, b. 30 Oct 1802; d. at Peacham, 21 Nov 1881; m. at Peacham, 27 Sept 1831, THOMAS MORSE, b. at Peacham, about 1796 son of Moody and Mary (Foster) Morse; Thomas d. at Peacham, 4 Sep 1872.

xi BARNES BLANCHARD, b. 21 Dec 1807; d. at Rushford, NY, 11 Aug 1872; m. at Peacham, 25 Apr 1832, ROSINA C. CLEASBY, b. at Plymouth, NH, about 1808 daughter of Zachariah and Elizabeth (Wilson) Cleasby; Rosina d. at Rushford, 20 Oct 1885.

[2603] Guide to the Abel Blanchard Family Correspondence, https://rbsc.library.nd.edu/finding_aids/und:ks65h991878

[2604] Wells, *History of Barnet, Vermont*, p 430

[2605] Blanchard, History of Centerville, NY

[2606] Blanchard, *History of Centerville, NY*

971) REUBEN BLANCHARD *(Benjamin Blanchard[4], Mary Abbott Blanchard[3], Nathaniel[2], George[1])*, b. at Hollis, 1 Feb 1763 son of Benjamin and Keziah (Hastings) Blanchard; d. at Peacham, VT, 27 Jun 1832;[2607] m. by 1790, MARY GRAY of Guy.

Reuben Blanchard and Mary Gray were parents of seven children born at Peacham, Vermont.

i KEZIAH BLANCHARD, b. 21 Dec 1790

ii MARY "POLLY" BLANCHARD, b. 19 May 1792; m. at Peacham, 7 Mar 1809, AMASA FARRINGTON, b. at Pomfret, 28 Feb 1781 son of Ephraim and Elizabeth (Sabin) Farrington.

iii MATILDA BLANCHARD, b. 17 Mar 1794

iv JOHN WINTHROP BLANCHARD, b. 27 Jul 1795; d. 30 Jul 1795.

v BETSEY BLANCHARD, b. 30 Aug 1797

vi REUBEN BLANCHARD, b. 14 Nov 1801; d. at Peacham, 12 Mar 1811.

vii GEORGE WASHINGTON BLANCHARD, b. 29 Mar 1803; d. at Randolph, PA, 1880; m. at Peacham, 19 Nov 1826, JANE ELIZA COBURN, b. about 1805; Jane d. at Randolph, May 1880.

972) BETTY BLANCHARD *(Benjamin Blanchard[4], Mary Abbott Blanchard[3], Nathaniel[2], George[1])*, b. at Hollis, 21 Jan 1765 daughter of Benjamin and Keziah (Hastings) Blanchard; d. at Peacham, VT, Mar 1811 (husband remarried 1812); m. at Boscawen, 4 May 1783, ABNER HOIT, b. at Rumford, 15 Apr 1759 son of John and Abigail (Carter) Hoit. Abner m. 2nd, the widow Mary Livingston Phillips. Abner d. at Wentworth, NH, 28 Dec 1852.

Betty Blanchard and Abner Hoit were parents of twelve children born at Peacham, Vermont.[2608]

i WILLIAM HOIT, b. 21 Nov 1783; d. at Pembroke, NH, 28 Dec 1854; m. at Concord, 6 Jun 1809, BETSEY HAZELTINE, b. at Concord, 23 May 1785 daughter of Richard and Hephzibah (Hall) Hazeltine; Betsey d. at Concord, 2 Dec 1851. William was a publisher and printer.

ii REUBEN HOIT, b. 30 Jun 1785; d. at Canterbury, 17 Mar 1837. Reuben was a member of the Shaker community at Canterbury and did not marry.

iii MIRIAM HOIT, b. 12 Feb 1787; d. Danville, Estrie, Québec, 23 Jan 1861; m. at Peacham, 20 Oct 1807, ASHLEY MARTIN, b. at Woodbury, CT, 17 Mar 1781 son of Elijah and Annie (Smith) Martin;[2609] Ashley d. at Danville, 29 Sep 1873.

iv MARY "POLLY" HOIT, b. 28 Jan 1789; d. unknown but perhaps in Ohio; m. at Peacham, 23 May 1808, HENRY SUMNER, b. at Peacham, 24 Jun 1788 son of Edward C. and Abigail (Clark) Sumner.

v MARTHA "PATTY" HOIT, b. 30 Apr 1791; d. 1863; m. at Peacham, 5 Feb 1809, ELIPHALET MARTIN, b. at Woodbury, CT, 5 Sep 1772 son of Elijah and Annie (Smith) Martin.

vi BENJAMIN HOIT, b. 18 Dec 1792; d. at Chelsea, MA, 2 Aug 1817. Benjamin served on the frigate *Constitution* during the War of 1812. He died at the marine hospital in Chelsea.

vii ABNER HOIT, b. 20 Dec 1794; d. at Albany, NY, 1835; m. at Ryegate, 7 Jan 1822, MARY WHITE, b. at Ryegate, 4 Mar 1800 daughter of Nicholas and Eunice (Johnson) White;[2610] Mary d. at Haverhill, NH, about 1860. After Abner's death, Mary married John Milton Morse.

viii JOHN HOIT, b. 9 May 1797; d. at Lawrence, MA, 14 May 1826; m. Mar 1819, DOLLY P. PAGE, b. at Wentworth, Dec 1794 daughter of Benjamin and Mary (-) Page;[2611] Dolly d. at Lawrence, 12 Dec 1863.

ix CHARLES HOIT, b. 9 Apr 1799; d. at Wentworth, NH, 21 Jan 1884; m. MARY HARRIMAN, b. about 1805 perhaps the daughter of John Harriman of Bridgewater, NH; Mary d. at Wentworth, after 1870 and before 1880.

x MATILDA B. HOIT, b. 1 Apr 1801; d. at Cincinnati, OH, 27 Sep 1827; m. Sep 1819, JOHN LANGDON WHITE son of John and Betty (French) White.

[2607] Ancestry.com, Vermont, Vital Records, 1720-1908

[2608] Hoyt, *Genealogical History of the Hoyt Families*, pp 82-82

[2609] Hay, *Martin Genealogy*, p 33

[2610] Miller, History of Ryegate gives parents as Nicholas White and Rachel Johnson but the marriage record of Nicholas says Eunice Johnson as do other records related to births and deaths.

[2611] Dolly's parents are given as Benjamin and Mary on her death record.

xi DAVID ELKINS HOIT, b. 20 Apr 1805; d. at Wentworth, NH, 6 Aug 1851; m. May 1834, LYDIA CONE, b. 1811 daughter of Thomas and Alice (Burbank) Cone.[2612]

xii PETER HOIT, b. 18 Nov 1810; d. Feb 1814.

973) SIMON BLANCHARD *(Benjamin Blanchard⁴, Mary Abbott Blanchard³, Nathaniel², George¹)*, b. at Hollis, 10 Apr 1766 son of Benjamin and Keziah (Hastings) Blanchard; d. at Peacham, VT, 22 Apr 1837; m. MARGARET GRAY or Guy, b. about 1768; Margaret d. at Peacham, 9 Aug 1824. After Margaret's death, Simon married Miriam Sumner on 13 Nov 1825.

Three children are known for Simon Blanchard and Margaret Gray.[2613]

i LOCADA BLANCHARD, b. at Peacham, 24 Oct 1792; d. at Peacham, 20 Apr 1855; m. at Peacham, 7 Apr 1811, PHINEAS VARNUM, b. about 1783 son of William and Sarah (Colburn) Varnum; Phineas d. at Peacham, 11 Mar 1863.

ii HARVEY BLANCHARD, b. at Peacham, 4 Nov 1793; d. at Peacham, 10 Mar 1849; m. at Peacham, 6 Mar 1817, BETSEY MARTIN, b. in Connecticut, about 1793 (based on census records); Betsey d. at Peacham, 11 Oct 1866.

iii SIMON BLANCHARD, b. at Peacham, 6 Sep 1795; d. at Peacham, 11 Jan 1871; m. 1st, at Peacham, 13 Sep 1818, BETSEY SPENCER, b. 3 Sep 1796 daughter of Ebenezer and Mehitable (Buzzell) Spencer;[2614] Betsey d. at Peacham, 25 Apr 1852. Simon m. 2nd, 12 Apr 1855, JEAN PADDLEFORD, b. at Monroe, NH, 11 Jan 1820 daughter of Comer and Hannah (Nelson) Paddleford;[2615] Jean d. at Monroe, 17 Feb 1873. Jean Paddleford was first married to John Moore in 1844.

974) ANNA DANFORTH *(Anne Blanchard Danforth⁴, Mary Abbott Blanchard³, Nathaniel², George¹)*, b. at Hollis, 7 Feb 1744 daughter of Jonathan and Anne (Blanchard) Danforth; d. at Westminster, MA, 5 Nov 1813; m. 7 Feb 1765, JAMES LAWS, b. at Billerica, 12 Mar 1741/2 son of James and Eunice (Hosley) Laws; James d. Jul 1821.

In his will written 17 May 1821, James Laws made the following bequests. Eldest son James Laws, Jr. receives all the farming tools. Son William receives $300. Sons James and William divide the wearing apparel. The heirs of oldest daughter Elizabeth Gibbs, who is deceased, receive $150. Daughter Anna Sawyer wife of Eli Sawyer receives $150; daughter Lucy Sawin wife of Benjamin, $150; and daughter Rhoda Locke, $150. The remainder of the estate is divided in sixth parts, one part to each of the children including the heirs of Elizabeth. Son James has a $500 note and he is to pay back this amount by giving $100 to each of his siblings. Eli Sawyer is named executor.[2616]

James Laws and Anna Danforth were parents of six children.

i ELIZABETH LAWS, b. at Billerica, 28 Jul 1766; d. at Ashburnham, 10 Nov 1809; m. at Ashburnham, 9 Jul 1787, JOSEPH GIBBS, b. at Rutland, 12 Oct 1756 son of Joseph and Hannah (Howe) Gibbs; Joseph d. at Ashburnham, 19 Mar 1829. After Elizabeth's death, Joseph married Sally Fairbank.

ii ANNA LAWS, b. at Billerica, 18 Feb 1768; d. at Fitchburg, 3 Oct 1856; m. at Westminster, 1 Jul 1790, ELI SAWYER, b. at Reading, 18 Oct 1765 son of Nathaniel and Jerusha (Flint) Sawyer; Eli d. at Westminster, 30 Jun 1841.

iii LUCY LAWS, b. at Westminster, 14 Feb 1770; m. at Westminster, 3 Feb 1793, BENJAMIN SAWIN, b. at Westminster, 13 Dec 1764 son of Samuel and Mary (Wesson) Sawin.

iv JAMES LAWS, b. at Westminster, 13 Dec 1772; d. at Ashburnham, 14 Aug 1860; m. at Ashburnham, 21 Mar 1797, THANKFUL METCALF, b. at Ashburnham, 18 May 1775 daughter of Joseph and Margaret (Shattuck) Metcalf; Thankful d. at Ashburnham after 1850.

v WILLIAM LAWS, b. at Westminster, 18 Oct 1774; *likely* m. at Chelmsford, 9 Sep 1804, ABIGAIL LAWS who has not been identified. Two children for this family were born at New Ipswich, NH. William was still living in 1821 when his father wrote his will.

[2612] Cone, *Some Account of the Cone Family in America*, p 327

[2613] Lyford, *History of Canterbury*, p 28

[2614] The 1847 will of Ebenezer Spencer of Peacham includes a bequest to his daughter Betsy Blanchard.

[2615] Wells, *History of Barnet, Vermont*, p 575

[2616] *Probate Records (Worcester County, Massachusetts); Index 1731-1881;* Author: *Massachusetts. Probate Court (Worcester County);* Probate Place: *Worcester, Massachusetts, Probate Records, Vol 56-57, 1821-1825*, will of James Laws, 17 May 1821

vi RHODA LAWS, b. at Westminster, 4 Oct 1776; d. at Jaffrey, NH, 4 Oct 1852; m. at Westminster, Apr 1801, EDWARD JEWET LOCKE, b. at Rindge, NH, 8 Aug 1778 son of Ebenezer and Phebe (Moore) Locke; Edward d. at Peterborough, NH, 2 Feb 1808.

975) JONATHAN DANFORTH *(Anne Blanchard Danforth⁴, Mary Abbott Blanchard³, Nathaniel², George¹)*, b. at Hollis, 20 Jul 1745 son of Jonathan and Anne (Blanchard) Danforth; d. at Danville, 6 Feb 1839; m. 1770, HANNAH LEMAN, b. at Hollis, 1 Oct 1751 daughter of Abraham and Elizabeth (Hastings) Leman; Hannah d. at Danville, 13 Sep 1815.

Jonathan Danforth wrote his will 28 March 1828 (proved 1839). In his will, he left his entire estate to his son Leonard and made no other bequests.

Jonathan Danforth and Hannah Leman were parents of twelve children, perhaps all born at Hollis, but with records for the first nine children in Hollis.

i HANNAH DANFORTH, b. 5 May 1770; d. at Danville, after 1830 (living at time of husband's probate); m. at Hollis, 10 Feb 1791, JERATHMAEL BOWERS, b. at Chelmsford, 11 Mar 1765 son of Oliver and Esther (-) Bowers; Jerathmael d. at Danville, 11 May 1830.

ii JONATHAN DANFORTH, b. 27 Jul 1772; d. at Danville, VT, 11 May 1854; m. 2 Feb 1797, MARY "POLLY" SINCLAIR, b. at Brentwood, NH, 15 May 1775 daughter of James and Anna (Veasey) Sinkler; Polly d. at Danville, 25 Apr 1817.

iii ELIZABETH "BETSEY" DANFORTH, b. 10 May 1774; d. at Stanstead, Québec, 14 Feb 1843;[2617] m. at Danville, VT, 1 Sep 1795, WILLIAM CLARK, b. at Andover, MA,[2618] 15 Feb 1769 son of William and Rebecca (Ballard) Clark; William d. at Stanstead, 28 Mar 1846.

iv LEONARD DANFORTH, b. 9 Apr 1777; d. at Danville, 9 Feb 1851; m. MARY HENRY, b. 11 Sep 1780 of unclear parentage;[2619] Mary d. at Danville, 16 Dec 1867.

v DAVID DANFORTH, b. 15 May 1779; d. at Fort Covington, NY, 9 Jul 1832;[2620] m. PAULINA "POLLY" RICHMOND, b. at New Milford, CT, 13 Jun 1788 daughter of Jonathan and Amarillis (Chambers) Richmond; Paulina d. at Fort Covington, 11 Apr 1866.

vi LUTHER DANFORTH, b. 23 Oct 1781; d. at Fort Covington, 4 Apr 1857; m. 14 Jun 1807, HENRIETTA ELLSWORTH, b. at Fort Covington, 1 May 1786 *likely* the daughter of Elijah Ellsworth; Henrietta d. 2 Apr 1841.

vii ANNA DANFORTH, b. 19 Jul 1783

viii ASA DANFORTH, b. 14 Oct 1785; d. at Malone, NY, after 1860; m. about 1807, MIRANDA RICHMOND.

ix REBECCA DANFORTH, b. 23 Mar 1788; m. at Danville, 3 Dec 1807, SAMUEL HENRY.

x CALVIN DANFORTH, b. about 1791; d. at Danville, 22 Nov 1813.

xi SOPHIA DANFORTH, b. about 1792; d. at Lima, NY, 13 Nov 1819; m. at Danville, 7 May 1813, MANNING HARDY, b. at Danville, 25 Mar 1781 son of David and Rebecca (Manning) Hardy; Manning d. a Lima, 3 Oct 1875. After Sophia's death, Manning m. Catherine Moses.

xii RALPH DANFORTH, b. about 1794; d. at Danville, 28 Mar 1811.

976) DAVID DANFORTH *(Anne Blanchard Danforth⁴, Mary Abbott Blanchard³, Nathaniel², George¹)*, b. at Hollis, 20 Jan 1746 son of Jonathan and Anne (Blanchard) Danforth; d. at Washington, NH, 1 Mar 1815; m. by 1773, HANNAH PROCTOR, b. at Chelmsford, 2 Feb 1748 daughter of Israel and Sarah (Raymond) Proctor; Hannah d. 12 Jan 1842.

David and Hannah Danforth came to the town of Camden, New Hampshire before 1773. David was one of thirty signers on the petition requesting changing the name of the town from Camden to Washington in honor of George Washington.[2621] David served in the Revolution in July 1777 in the company of Captain Jonathan Brockway, and for a second period in October 1777 in the regiment of Colonel Bellows.

David and Hannah were parents of six children born at Camden and then Washington, New Hampshire. Their oldest child Eli is said to be the first birth recorded in the town.[2622]

[2617] *Quebec, Canada, Vital and Church Records (Drouin Collection), 1621-1968*, Institut Généalogique Drouin; Montreal, Quebec, Canada; Drouin Collection

[2618] Hubbard, *Forests and Clearings*, p 206

[2619] Mary's death record gives parents as Samuel and Hannah; published genealogies give her father as William and suggest several different mothers.

[2620] May, *Danforth Genealogy*, p 204

[2621] Proctor, *Genealogy of Robert Proctor*, p 17

[2622] Gage, *History of Washington, NH*, p 364

i ELI DANFORTH, b. 27 Oct 1773; d. at Washington, 7 Dec 1866; m. LODEMA HOSKINS, b. at Torrington, CT, 17 May 1771 daughter of Elisha and Delight (Holmes) Hoskins;[2623] Lodema d. at Washington, 6 Jan 1861. Lodema was the widow Lodema Bryant when she married Eli. Although Eli was born and died in Washington, for much of his adult life he was in Ohio, returning to his birthplace in his later years.

ii ISRAEL DANFORTH, b. 25 Jun 1775; d. at Norridgewock, ME, 14 Aug 1855; m. 16 Jan 1806, SARAH WAITE, b. at Marlboro, MA, 4 Feb 1782 daughter of David and Abigail (Brigham) Waite; Sarah d. at Norridgewock, 2 Jan 1866.

iii HANNAH DANFORTH, b. 21 Mar 1777; d. at Washington, 15 Nov 1843; m. at Washington, 20 May 1800, REUBEN FARNSWORTH, b. at Harvard, MA, Aug 1771 (baptized 12 Aug 1771) son of Simeon and Lucy (Atherton) Farnsworth;[2624] Reuben d. at Washington, 2 Sep 1842.

iv DAVID DANFORTH, b. 5 Apr 1779; d. at Claremont, NH, after 1850; m. at Washington, 12 Dec 1804, ELEANOR HAYNES, b. in Massachusetts, about 1780 daughter of Joshua and Hephzibah (-) Haynes; Eleanor d. at Claremont, Nov 1859.

v JONATHAN DANFORTH, b. 13 Feb 1782; d. at Washington, 26 Nov 1863; m. 1st, 4 Apr 1805, MARTHA C. "PATTY" BARNEY, b. 1780 daughter of John and Comfort (Sparhawk) Barney; Martha d. at Washington, 27 Jul 1827. Jonathan m. 2nd, ANNA DRAPER, b. at Washington, 25 Jan 1784 daughter of Nathaniel and Anna (Jones) Draper; Anna d. at Washington, 10 Feb 1875.

vi ISAAC DANFORTH, b. 10 Sep 1785; d. at Concord, 11 Mar 1862;[2625] m. at Concord, 26 Oct 1815, DOLLY HUTCHINS, b. at Concord, 18 Jul 1790 daughter of Abel and Betsey (Partridge) Hutchins; Dolly d. at Concord, 9 Jun 1857.

977) REBECCA BLANCHARD *(Jacob Blanchard[4], Mary Abbott Blanchard[3], Nathaniel[2], George[1])*, b. at Groton, 22 Feb 1756 daughter of Jacob and Rebecca (Lawrence) Blanchard; d. at Groton, 19 Sep 1826; m. 22 Mar 1774, DAVID LAKIN, b. at Groton, 10 Oct 1753 son of John and Lydia (Parker) Lakin; David d. 3 Mar 1846. David's death was attributed to the "decay of nature" at age 92.

David Lakin and Rebecca Blanchard were parents of nine children all born at Groton.

i SIBBEL LAKIN, b. 22 May 1774; d. at Harrison, ME, about 1808; m. at Groton, 7 Nov 1793, LEVI GILSON, b. at Groton, 16 Feb 1770 son of Solomon and Mary (Shattuck) Gilson; Levi d. at Harrison, about 1830. After Sibbel's death, Levi married Philena Bucknell.

ii JACOB LAKIN, b. 13 Sep 1776; d. at Groton, 3 Dec 1826; m. at Lincoln, 21 Nov 1802, SARAH "SALLY" UNDERWOOD, b. at Lincoln, 8 Mar 1777 daughter of Moses and Mary (Pierce) Underwood; Sally d. at Lincoln, 4 Jul 1865. After Jacob's death, Sally married Daniel Bathrick.

iii LUCY LAKIN, b. 3 Nov 1778; m. at Groton, 26 Jun 1802, JOHN BROWN.

iv REBECCA LAKIN, b. 14 Apr 1781; m. at Groton, 12 Feb 1806, JOHN HAYMAN who was "of Salem" perhaps the John Hayman born in England about 1783.

v JOHN LAKIN, b. 6 Jul 1783; d. at Groton, 6 Oct 1817; m. at Groton, 2 Jan 1808, ANNA JEWETT, b. at Pepperell, 8 Dec 1787 daughter of Caleb and Elizabeth (Green) Jewett; Anna d. at Pepperell, 12 Apr 1865. After John's death, Anna married John's brother David (see below).

vi DANIEL LAKIN, b. 22 Feb 1786; m. HANNAH CROCKETT, b. 1790; Hannah d. at Durham, NH, 7 Mar 1852.

vii RACHEL LAKIN, b. 1 Oct 1788; d. about 1812; m. at Groton, 1 Mar 1809, WILLIAM LAWRENCE, b. at Groton, 7 Sep 1783 son of Samuel and Susannah (Parker) Lawrence; William d. 14 Oct 1843. After Rachel's death, William married Sarah Ruggles Boardman.

viii ABEL LAKIN, b. 1 Nov 1793; d. at Lowell, 16 Mar 1868; m. at Tewksbury, Aug 1826, PRISCILLA HOBSON, b. at Ipswich, about 1806 daughter of Samuel and Bethia (Chase) Hobson; Priscilla d. at Lowell, 9 Mar 1888.

[2623] Lodema's place of birth and name of father are given on her death record.

[2624] Gage, *History of Washington, NH*, p 396

[2625] Isaac was living in Concord just before his death. He and Dolly are buried at Mt. Auburn Cemetery in Cambridge.

ix DAVID LAKIN, b. 19 Feb 1796; d. at Pepperell, 19 Sep 1879; m. at Groton, 19 May 1822, ANNA JEWETT who was first married to David's brother John (see above).

978) NATHANIEL BLANCHARD *(Jacob Blanchard⁴, Mary Abbott Blanchard³, Nathaniel², George¹)*, b. at Groton, 29 May 1760 son of Jacob and Rebecca (Lawrence) Blanchard; d.?; m. 28 Nov 1782, ANNA GREEN, b. 10 Oct 1762 daughter of Eleazer and Sarah (Parker) Green.

There is an out-of-wedlock child born in Groton 14 Feb (the year missing) I believe may be a son of this Nathaniel. The child is named Nathaniel, the mother is Esther Nutting and "she saith" this is the child of Nathaniel Blanchard. Esther was born in 1759 so that would fit. I cannot find what happened to Nathaniel and Anna after the births of their two children at Groton.

Child of Nathaniel Blanchard and Esther Nutting.

i NATHANIEL BLANCHARD, b. 14 Feb 1780; nothing further known.

Children of Nathaniel Blanchard and Anna Green.

i JACOB BLANCHARD, b. 20 Feb 1793; nothing further known.

ii SQUIRE BLANCHARD, b. 3 Jul 1798; d. at Manchester, NH, about 1845; m. at Dunstable, NH, 13 Apr 1819, RACHEL SEARLES, b. at Dunstable, MA, 7 Oct 1800 daughter of Samuel and Lois (-) Searles; Rachel d. at Manchester, 14 Jan 1847.

979) JOSHUA BLANCHARD *(Joshua Blanchard⁴, Mary Abbott Blanchard³, Nathaniel², George¹)*, b. at Hollis, 21 Oct 1750 son of Joshua and Sarah (Burge) Blanchard; d. at Hollis, 11 Jan 1776; m. 16 Feb 1775, LUCY FRENCH, b. at Hollis, 21 Apr 1755 daughter of Nicholas and Priscilla (Mooar) French. Lucy m. 2nd, 6 Mar 1781, BRAY WILKINS.

Joshua Blanchard served in the Revolution and returned to Hollis after his duty[2626] but died soon after. Joshua and Lucy were parents of one child born at Hollis.

i JOSHUA MOORE BLANCHARD, b. at Hollis, 26 Jul 1775; d. at Washington, NH, 7 Dec 1860; m. about 1800, RHODA COLBY, b. at Hopkinton, 22 Jun 1772 daughter of Isaac and Hannah (Allen) Colby; Rhoda d. at Washington, 11 Dec 1848.

980) MOLLY BLANCHARD *(Joshua Blanchard⁴, Mary Abbott Blanchard³, Nathaniel², George¹)*, b. at Hollis, 30 Aug 1754 daughter of Joshua and Sarah (Burge) Blanchard; d. at Deering, NH, 5 Oct 1826; m. about 1774, MAJOR MILES RALEIGH,[2627] b. at Sudbury, MA, 1749 son of Philip and Susannah (Joyner) Raleigh; Major Raleigh d. at Deering, NH 6 Jun 1838.

In his pension application file, Miles Raleigh stated he enlisted at Concord, Massachusetts for eight months in April 1775 immediately after the battle at Lexington. He served until December 1775. After his service, he continued to live in Concord about two years, was then to Hillsborough, after that in Antrim, and finally in Deering.[2628]

Major Miles Raleigh and Molly Blanchard were parents of four children.

i DOLLY RALEIGH, b. at Concord, 20 Nov 1774; d. about 1786.

ii MAJOR RALEIGH, b. at Hillsborough, 10 Jan 1778; died young.

iii MAJOR RALEIGH, b. at Antrim, 15 Mar 1785; d. at Burlington, PA, 1848; m. at Goffstown, 14 Oct 1806, NANCY ORDWAY, b. about 1787; Nancy d. at Goffstown, 1863.

iv JAMES L. RALEIGH, b. at Antrim, 11 Mar 1790; d. at Hillsborough, 2 Jun 1864; m. at Amherst, 21 Feb 1816, SUSAN H. MCCOY, b. about 1800; Susan d. at Hillsborough, 14 Oct 1885.

981) LUCY BLANCHARD *(Joshua Blanchard⁴, Mary Abbott Blanchard³, Nathaniel², George¹)*, b. at Hollis, 4 Jun 1760 daughter of Joshua and Sarah (Burge) Blanchard; d. about 1798; m. about 1785, ELIAS CHENEY, b. at Sudbury, 14 Oct 1760 son of Tristram and Margaret (Joyner) Cheney. Elias m. 2nd, 6 Jun 1799, Deborah Winchester. Elias d. at Concord, VT, 7 Aug 1817.

2626 Worcester, *History of Hollis*, p 158

2627 Major is his first name, not his rank.

2628 Revolutionary War Pension and Bounty-Land Warrant Application Files

Elias Cheney served as a private in the New Hampshire Line during the Revolution. He enlisted from Andover, New Hampshire for a period of three years on 17 Dec 1777. He saw service in New York, New Jersey, Maryland, and Virginia. His widow Deborah (then Deborah Clifford) received a pension based on his service.[2629]

Lucy Blanchard and Elias Cheney were parents of seven children, the oldest six children born at Antrim and the youngest child perhaps born at Concord, Vermont.

i WILLIAM CHENEY, b. 31 Dec 1787; d. at Stowe, VT, 8 Sep 1875; m. 1st, MEHITABLE CARR, b. at Grantham, NH, 5 Apr 1789 daughter of Parker and Judith (Preston) Carr; Mehitable d. at Stowe, 22 Mar 1847. William m. 2nd, 26 Jun 1851, PALACE LAMPHER (widow of Ruel Loomis), b. about 1808 daughter of William and Palace (Davis) Lampher; Palace d. at Stowe, 16 Oct 1888.

ii ELIAS CHENEY, b. 31 Dec 1787; d. at Waterford, VT, 16 Dec 1810 when struck by a falling tree; m. at Cabot, VT, 10 Sep 1809, NANCY CARR, b. at Grantham, 16 Mar 1786 daughter of Parker and Judith (Preston) Carr; Nancy d. 27 Nov 1865. After Elias's death, Nancy married Benjamin Powers.

iii JESSE CHENEY, b. 3 Oct 1788; d. at Manchester, NH, 23 Jun 1863; m. 25 Nov 1813, ALICE STEELE, b. at Antrim, 12 Aug 1791 daughter of James and Alice (Boyd) Steele; Alice d. at Manchester, 28 Jul 1849.

iv JOHN CHENEY, b. about 1790; d. at Lyndon, VT, Sep 1827; m. at Waterford, VT, 1 Jan 1809, ELIZA "BETSEY" NEWTON, b. about 1790; Eliza d, at Lyndon, 27 Oct 1846.

v JOEL CHENEY, b. 19 Mar 1791; d. at Albany, VT, 26 Jul 1849; m. 1819, OLIVE HILL, b. 1796 daughter of Samuel and Olive (Sawyer) Hill; Olive d. at Albany, 6 Jul 1861.

vi SARAH CHENEY, b. 23 Feb 1793; d. at Hardwick, VT, 26 Jan 1878; m. at Concord, VT, 15 Jan 1815, BENJAMIN WELLS, b. about 1791 son of Paul and Rachel (Webster) Wells; Benjamin d. at Hardwick, 23 Jul 1849.

vii LUCY CHENEY, b. about 1795; d. likely at Bethlehem, NH, after 1850; m. at Concord, VT, 6 Mar 1814, JESSE WELLS, b. about 1789 son of Paul and Rachel (Webster) Wells; Jesse d. after 1850.

982) NATHANIEL CHANDLER ABBOTT *(Nathaniel⁴, Nathaniel³, Nathaniel², George¹)*, b. at Rumford, 28 Jul 1750 son of Nathaniel and Miriam (Chandler) Abbott; d. at Rumney, NH, 10 May 1814; m. 20 Jul 1778, HANNAH FARRINGTON who origins are unknown at this time; Hannah d. at Warren, NH 1844.

Nathaniel served in the Revolution and widow Hannah was granted a pension based on his service.[2630] Nathaniel enlisted at Concord for a period of eight months in May 1775 in the company of Captain Joshua Abbot. He was at the Battle of Bunker Hill. In February 1776, he enlisted for a one-year term in the company of Captain James Osgood and during this enlistment marched into Canada and to Ticonderoga. He had further enlistments in May 1777, and the fall of 1778. On 22 November 1837, daughter Mary Merrill of Warren, then age 40, provided a statement in support of her mother's application for a pension. Daughter Abigail Batchelder also provided a statement.

Hannah Farrington Abbott did not leave a will and her estate entered probate 17 September 1844. True Merrill requested to be made administrator noting that Hannah's daughter has neglected for more than a month to assume administration of the estate. The accounting for the estate includes just her widow's pension.[2631]

Nathaniel Chandler Abbott and Hannah Farrington were parents of seven children, the eldest six children born at Concord and youngest child Mary born at Rumney.

i JOSEPH ABBOTT, b. 14 Dec 1778; m. AFFA BRAINARD, b. about 1782 daughter of Daniel Brainard.[2632]

ii SUSY ABBOTT, b. 25 Sep 1782; nothing further known.

iii KATY ABBOTT, b. 21 Jan 1785; nothing further known.

iv ABIGAIL ABBOTT, b. 4 Jan 1787; d. at Warren, 29 Jan 1875; m. at Warren, 12 Nov 1812, NATHANIEL BATCHELDER, b. about 1785; Nathaniel d. at Warren, 4 Jul 1837.

v DAVID ABBOTT, b. 6 May 1789; nothing further known.

vi SALLY ABBOTT, b. 5 Sep 1791; nothing further known.

[2629] Revolutionary War Pension and Bounty-Land Warrant Application Files

[2630] Revolutionary War Pension and Bounty-Land Warrant Application Files, Case W15502

[2631] New Hampshire County Probate Records 1660-1973, Grafton County, 19:55; 23:205

[2632] Child, *Gazetteer of Grafton County*, p 605

vii MARY ABBOTT, b. at Rumney, 26 Nov 1797; d. at Warren, NH, about 1841; m. about 1825, TRUE W. MERRILL, b. about 1801; True d. at Warren, 23 Mar 1883. True m. 2nd, 19 Jan 1842, Sally Clough.

983) MOSES ABBOTT *(Nathaniel4, Nathaniel3, Nathaniel2, George1)*, b. at Concord, 19 Jun 1752 son of Nathaniel and Miriam (Chandler) Abbott; d. at Concord, 11 Jul 1837; m. by 1779, MARY BATCHELDER, b. about 1756; Mary d. at Concord 2 Jul 1833.

There are ten children reported in the Abbot *Genealogical Register*[2633] and there are birth records for the oldest seven children at Concord and the youngest three children can be confirmed as of this family through death and probate records.

i JOHN ABBOTT, b. 6 Sep 1779; d. at Rumford, ME, 18 Jun 1870; m. at Concord, 17 Mar 1801, his third cousin, HANNAH FLANDERS *(Mary Chandler Flanders5, Daniel Chandler4, Tabitha Abbott Chandler3, Nathaniel2, George1)*, b. at Concord, 29 Jul 1781 daughter of Richard and Mary (Chandler) Flanders; Hannah d. at Rumford, ME, 27 Apr 1849. Hannah Flanders is a child in Family 1086.

ii SARAH ABBOTT, b. 10 Sep 1781; d. 16 Aug 1846; m. at Concord, 9 Mar 1815, her first cousin once removed, PETER HAZELTINE ABBOTT *(Daniel4, George3, Thomas2, George1)*, b. at Concord, 28 Feb 1780 son of Daniel and Rachel (Abbott) Abbott; Peter d. at Concord, 1862 (probate 1862). Sarah Abbott and Peter Hazeltine Abbott are the parents in Family 929.

iii MOSES ABBOTT, b. 3 Aug 1783; d. at Quincy, MA, 18 Oct 1867;[2634] m. at Concord, 27 Sep 1814, EUNICE CALL, b. about 1793 daughter of John and Dorothy (Sanborn) Call;[2635] Eunice d. at Quincy, 23 Apr 1846.

iv LIZA ABBOTT, b. 22 Jun 1785; d. 1803.

v NATHANIEL ABBOTT, b. 23 Jun 1787; m. at Rumford, ME, 7 Mar 1813, SABRINA MORSE, b. at Concord, 14 Nov 1793 daughter of Benjamin and Dolly (George) Morse.

vi LEVI ABBOTT, b. 21 Apr 1789; d. at Concord, 16 Apr 1859; m. at Concord, 25 Jan 1816, ELIZABETH DIMOND, b. Aug 1798 daughter of John and Sarah (Emerson) Dimond;[2636] Elizabeth d. at Concord, 31 Oct 1858.

vii CALVIN ABBOTT, b. 14 Jul 1791; d. at Bridgewater, VT, 28 Oct 1856; m. about 1820, his second cousin, POLLY ABBOTT *(Samuel5, Daniel4, George3, Thomas2, George1)*, b. at Concord, 30 Apr 1794 daughter of Samuel and Mary T. (Story) Abbott; Polly d. at Bridgewater, 8 May 1873. Polly Abbott is a child in Family 923.

viii LUTHER ABBOTT, b. about 1795; d. at Hopkinton, NH, 8 Oct 1873.[2637] Luther did not marry. The administration of his estate was assumed by his nephew Jeremiah Abbott who was the son of Sarah Abbott and Peter Hazeltine Abbott.

ix ELSIE ABBOTT, b. about 1796; d. at Hopkinton, 3 Dec 1882;[2638] m. 28 Dec 1820, MOSES COLBY, b. 31 Dec 1796 son of James Bryant and Susannah (Story) Colby;[2639] Moses d. at Hopkinton, 28 Jan 1876.

x MARY ABBOTT, b. about 1798; d. Apr 1822; m. at Concord, 31 May 1821, CARTER BUSWELL, b. at Hopkinton, 24 Jan 1795 son of Benjamin and Johanna (Carter) Buswell. Carter second married Rachel Flanders.

984) PHILIP ABBOTT *(Nathaniel4, Nathaniel3, Nathaniel2, George1)*, b. at Concord, 4 Feb 1757 son of Nathaniel and Miriam (Chandler) Abbott; d. at Rumford, ME, 20 Mar 1841; m. 10 Feb 1791, EXPERIENCE HOWE, b. at Bolton, MA, 1 Apr 1771 daughter of Phineas and Experience (Pollard) Howe; Experience d. at Rumford, 1857.

Philip Abbott settled what would become Rumford, Maine in 1784. He served on the committee that in 1799 petitioned for incorporation. Rumford, Maine was incorporated in 1800 and Philip Abbott was one of the first selectmen of the town. Philip was also one of those in the town licensed to sell strong liquors.[2640]

In Philip Abbott's will written 1 April 1831 (probate 25 May 1841), wife Experience Abbott receives the use of and income from one-third part of the homestead farm during her natural life. He gives one dollar to each of the following children: Susannah Virgin wife of Rufus Virgin, Betsy Baxter widow of Joseph Baxter, Philip Abbott, Jr., Levi Abbott, Sophia Parlin wife of Simon Parlin, and Charlotte Abbott. The rest of the estate goes to son David Abbott who is also named executor.[2641]

Philip and Experience were parent of nine children all born at Rumford, Maine.

[2633] Abbot, *Genealogical Register*, pp 118-119

[2634] The death record notes that Moses the son of Moses and Mary was born at Concord and was 85 years old at time of death.

[2635] Dearborn, *History of Salisbury, NH*, p 521

[2636] Dimond, *Genealogy of the Dimond Family*, p 136

[2637] Father's name of Moses Abbott is given on his death record.

[2638] Parents names are given as Moses Abbott and Mary Batchelder on her death record.

[2639] Lord, *Life and Times in Hopkinton*, p 340

[2640] Lapham, *History of Rumford, Oxford County, Maine*

[2641] *Maine. Probate Court (Oxford County);* Probate Place: *Oxford, Maine, Estate Files, Asa Abbott-John Akley, 1822-1854*, probate of Philip Abbott

i SUSANNA ABBOTT, b. 26 Jun 1793; d. at Rumford, 1868; m. at Rumford, 20 Jun 1815, RUFUS VIRGIN, b. 2 Jan 1792 son of Jonathan and Susan (Austin) Virgin; Rufus d. at Rumford, 1858.

ii BETSY ABBOTT, b. 10 Aug 1795; d. at Rumford, 1863; m. at Rumford, 1 Oct 1822, JOSEPH BAXTER, b. at Boston, 17 Dec 1769 son of Joseph Baxter; Joseph d. at Fayette, ME, 25 Aug 1828.

iii PARNA ABBOTT, b. 10 Apr 1797; d. 8 Apr 1801.

iv DAVID ABBOTT, b. 5 Feb 1799; d. 1 Jul 1808.

v PHILIP ABBOTT, b. 11 Dec 1800; m. 16 Feb 1823, LUCINA TRASK (widow Lucina White), b. at Dixfield, ME, 2 May 1786 daughter of Amos and Lucy (Park) Trask; Lucina d. at Dixfield, 24 Jun 1841.

vi LEVI ABBOTT, b. 4 Nov 1802; d. at Dixfield, 3 Jan 1871; m. 4 Feb 1825, VASHTI WHEELER, b. at Rumford, 28 Nov 1806 daughter of William and Patty (Virgin) Wheeler; Vashti d. at Dixfield, 27 Apr 1870.

vii SOPHIA ABBOTT, b. 4 Apr 1805; d. at Weld, ME, 26 May 1876; m. 10 Jan 1824, SIMON PARLIN, b. at Sumner, ME, 13 Jun 1801 son of Simon and Elizabeth (Robinson) Parlin; Simon d. at Weld, 30 Mar 1877.

viii CHANDLER ABBOTT, b. 10 Oct 1807; d. at Rumford, 22 Mar 1897; m. 1st at Rumford, 31 May 1831, CHARITY DURGAN, b. at Bowdoin, ME, 23 Feb 1813; Charity d. at Rumford, 10 Nov 1850. Chandler m. 2nd, 4 Nov 1858 MARY CHADBORN, b. about 1826 and d. after 1880.

ix DAVID W. ABBOTT, b. 16 Nov 1809; d. at Rumford, 13 Feb 1863. David did not marry.

985) JOSHUA ABBOTT *(Nathaniel4, Nathaniel3, Nathaniel2, George1)*, b. at Concord, 15 Jun 1759 son of Nathaniel and Miriam (Chandler) Abbott; d. at Bow Junction, NH, 4 Mar 1837; m. 1st, 1780, POLLY BROWN. Joshua m. 2nd, ANN MANNING, b. at Charlestown, MA, 1767 daughter of James and Ann (Brown) Manning;[2642] Ann d. at Bow Junction, 11 Sep 1850.

Joshua Abbott was a farmer and innholder in Hooksett Falls, New Hampshire. He was the first settler in the area of the falls where there was not a school resulting his children needing to walk the path through the woods to Bow to attend school.[2643]

Joshua Abbott and Polly Brown were parents of six children born at Hooksett.

i PHILIP ABBOTT, b. about 1780; m. at Goffstown, 8 Sep 1808, POLLY COCHRAN, b. at Hooksett, about 1788 daughter of Thomas and Rachel (Patterson) Cochran; Polly d. at Hooksett, 9 Mar 1869.

ii BETSEY ABBOTT, b. about 1782

iii MIRIAM ABBOTT, b. about 1785

iv MARY "POLLY" ABBOTT, b. about 1786; d. at Carthage, ME, 23 Feb 1882; m. at Dunbarton, 12 Nov 1809, JAMES RUSSELL KITTREDGE, b. Jan 1784; James d. at Carthage, 8 Jul 1852.

v JOSHUA ABBOTT, b. about 1787; m. at Hooksett, 19 May 1825, MARY EVANS.

vi Son, b. and d. about 1789

Joshua Abbott and Ann Manning were parents of eleven children born at Hookset.

i SUSAN ABBOTT, b. 23 May 1790; d. at Hooksett, after 1860. Susan did not marry and lived in the almshouse in Hooksett in her later years.

ii SALLY ABBOTT, b. 24 May 1793; d. 1 May 1825. Sally did not marry.

iii MARGARET SWAN ABBOTT, b. 7 Sep 1795; d. at Hooksett, 25 Feb 1854; m. about 1820, JOHN PRESCOTT, b. at Chester, NH, 14 Mar 1790 son of John and Molly (Merrill) Prescott; John d. at Hooksett, 25 Oct 1861.

iv DOROTHY MERRILL ABBOTT, b. 19 Oct 1797; m. at Dunbarton, 1 Dec 1814, SAMUEL HOSMER.

2642 Manning, *Genealogical and Biographical History of the Manning Families*, p 308

2643 Hurd, *History of Merrimack and Belknap Counties*, p 375

v NANCY ABBOTT, b. 11 Nov 1799; d. at Lebanon, NH, 21 Feb 1893; m. AMASA HURLBURT, b. at Hanover, NH, 5 May 1785 son of Asher and Hannah (Wright) Hurlburt; Amasa d. at Lebanon, 6 Apr 1870.

vi WILLIAM PRESCOTT ABBOTT, b. 11 Nov 1801; d. at Hooksett, 29 Sep 1862; m. about 1832, SARAH LOCKLAN (widow of Samuel McMurphy), b. about 1794; Sarah d. at Hooksett, 2 Dec 1876.

vii ELMIRA ABBOTT, b. 6 Dec 1803; d. at Concord, 1870; m. about 1835, WILLIAM CARR, b. at Cabot, VT, 1800 son of Peter and Roxanna (Ryder) Carr; William d. at Concord, 3 Apr 1876. After Elmira's death, William married Mary A. West 9 Oct 1871.

viii BENJAMIN FRANKLIN ABBOTT, b. 20 Apr 1806; d. 15 Mar 1811.

ix JOSEPH WARREN ABBOTT, b. 23 Jun 1808; d. 1808.

x CYNTHIA JANE ABBOTT, b. 23 Jan 1811; d. at Boston, 16 Mar 1880; m. about 1835, RALPH BUTLER, b. at Farmington, ME, 5 May 1813 son of Ralph and Mary (Stevens) Butler; Ralph d. at Dorchester, 14 Feb 1915. Ralph second married Harriet A. Chapman.

xi WALTER HARRIS ABBOTT, b. 19 Jun 1815; d. at Laconia, NH, 24 Feb 1892. Walter does not seem to have married. He worked on the county poor farm in Laconia.

986) SUSANNA ABBOTT *(Nathaniel⁴, Nathaniel³, Nathaniel², George¹)*, b. at Concord, 21 Jan 1762 daughter of Nathaniel and Miriam (Chandler) Abbott; d. at Concord, 24 Jun 1832; m. 29 Nov 1791, JOHN GARVIN, b. at Bow, NH, 14 Aug 1764 son of James and Deborah (-) Garvin; John d. at Concord, 16 Dec 1826.

Susanna and John resided in Concord where John was active in the town affairs such as a committee to develop schools and surveyor of highways.[2644]

In his will written 16 June 1826, John Garvin bequeaths to beloved wife Susanna improvements on one-third part of the property during her widowhood plus the privilege in the kitchen "to wash and do other work" and "a privilege in the oven to bake." Other provisions for her support are specified. Son Nathaniel Garvin receives $100, son James Garvin $150, son Hubbard Garvin $300, and son Jeremiah Garvin $100. Daughter Mariam Rogers receives $50. Son Seth Garvin receives $150. Sons Nathaniel and Jeremiah receive the remainder of the estate and they are named joint executors.[2645]

John Garvin and Susanna Abbott were parents of six children born at Concord.

i NATHANIEL GARVIN, b. 15 Sep 1792; d. at Concord, 1858 (probate 1858); m. about 1825, MARY ROGERS, b. at Londonderry, 11 May 1793 daughter of Josiah and Sarah (-) Rogers; Mary d. at Concord, 9 Jan 1880.

ii JAMES GARVIN, b. 20 Dec 1794; d. 8 Dec 1829.

iii HUBBARD GARVIN, b. 26 Jun 1796; d. at Nashua, NH, Apr 1850; m. at Sharon, VT, 14 Mar 1819, LYDIA GARVIN whose parents have not been identified; Lydia d. at Nashua, 15 Jun 1843.

iv JEREMIAH GARVIN, b. 28 Nov 1798; d. at Exeter, ME, 20 Jun 1869; m. at Andover, MA, 15 Aug 1826, MARY F. HUTCHINSON, b. at Pembroke, 3 May 1807 daughter of Solomon and Lydia Poor (Farnum) Hutchinson;[2646] Mary d. at Bangor, 5 Mar 1899.

v MIRIAM C. GARVIN, b. 23 Jul 1802; d. at Exeter, ME, after 1870; m. at Concord, 12 Dec 1822, FRANCIS W. ROGERS, b. 15 Dec 1795 son of Josiah and Sarah (-) Rogers; Francis d. at Exeter, after 1870.

vi SETH N. GARVIN, b. 17 May 1807; d. after 1840. In 1840, Seth was head of household as the only member of the household. He was employed in the "navigation of canals, lakes, and rivers"

987) LEVI ABBOTT *(Nathaniel⁴, Nathaniel³, Nathaniel², George¹)*, b. at Concord, 23 Sep 1767 son of Nathaniel and Miriam (Chandler) Abbott; d. 15 Dec 1825; m. 1st, 10 Jul 1791, his first cousin, ELSIE MOOR *(Hannah Abbott Moor⁴, Nathaniel³, Nathaniel², George¹)* daughter of Ephraim and Hannah (Abbott) Moor; Elsie d. at Concord, Apr 1795. Levi m. 2nd, POLLY CARTER, b. 1770 daughter of Joseph and Hannah (Carr) Carter; Polly d. at Concord, 24 Sep 1840.

Levi Abbott and Elsie Moor were parents of one child.

i ANNE ABBOTT, b. at Concord, about 1792; d. 1817; m. SAMUEL MOORE.[2647]

[2644] Bouton, *History of Concord*

[2645] *New Hampshire. Probate Court (Merrimack County)*; Probate Place: *Merrimack, New Hampshire, Probate Records, Vol 1, 1823-1828*, will of John Garvin 16 June 1826

[2646] The names of Mary's parents are given on her death record as Solomon and Lydia Hutchinson.

[2647] Bouton, *History of Concord*, p 626

Levi Abbott and Polly Carter were parents of eleven children born at Concord.

i JOSEPH C. ABBOTT, b. 2 Apr 1796; d. 23 Jul 1825; m. at Hartford, VT, 6 Apr 1817, SUSAN FURBER, b. 8 Nov 1795 daughter of Nathaniel and Abigail (Kimball) Furber; Susan d. 20 Sep 1874.

ii CHARLES ABBOTT, b. 30 Nov 1797; d. at Concord, 18 Apr 1879; m. 13 Dec 1827, SARAH CARTER, b. at Concord, 13 Jun 1805 daughter of Moses and Molly (Robinson) Carter; Sarah d. at Concord, 15 Aug 1884.

iii AARON ABBOTT, b. 28 Sep 1799; d. at Concord, 29 Dec 1868; m. at Concord, 5 Oct 1824, NANCY BADGER, b. in ME, about 1801; Nancy d. at Concord, after 1880.

iv ALICE ABBOTT, b. 28 Jun 1801; d. at Bow, 1 Nov 1893; m. at Bow, 26 Sep 1821, MENDELL SAMPSON, b. in ME, 20 Oct 1799 *possibly* the son of Phineas and Rachel (White) Sampson; Mendell d. at Bow, 1872.

v MARY ABBOTT, b. 1 Jun 1803; d. at Concord, 27 Oct 1825. Mary did not marry.

vi IRA ABBOTT, b. 14 Feb 1805; d. at Concord, 27 Aug 1878; m. 20 Feb 1831, HANNAH ALICE CAPEN, b. at Stewartstown, NH, 14 Oct 1812 daughter of Ebenezer and Abigail (Carter) Capen; Hannah d. at Concord, 8 Nov 1906.

vii ELIZA ABBOTT, b. 3 Apr 1807; d. at Derry, NH, 29 Nov 1891; m. 12 Dec 1827, SIMEON CARTER, b. at Concord, 15 Feb 1797 son of Moses and Molly (Robinson) Carter; Simeon d. at Concord, before 1850.

viii HANNAH J. ABBOTT, b. 1 Jul 1809; d. at Greenfield, MA, 23 Sep 1891; m. Apr 1844, as his second wife, LEMUEL WILSON PAIGE, b. at Antrim, NH, 3 Aug 1807 son of Reuben and Sally (-) Paige; Lemuel d. at Chicopee, MA, 31 Dec 1857. Lemuel was first married to Harriet Little.

ix SUSAN G. ABBOTT, b. 17 Nov 1811; d. at Washington, DC, after 1880; m. 17 Nov 1839, JOHN C. WILSON, b. in NH 1813 with parents not determined but mother's name Sarah; John d. at Washington, Jun 1879.

x CLARA C. ABBOTT, b. 4 May 1813; d. at Hanover, NH, 31 Oct 1895; m. 13 Jan 1841, her fourth cousin once removed, ABIEL ROLFE *(Judith Hazeltine Rolfe[6], Sarah Hall Hazeltine[5], Dorcas Abbott Hall[4], Edward[3], Thomas[2], George[1])*, b. about 1814 son of William and Judith (Hazeltine) Rolfe;[2648] Abiel d. at Lowell, 8 Sep 1896.

xi RUTH W. ABBOTT, b. 23 Dec 1816; d. at Lowell, 10 Feb 1845; m. 10 Dec 1843, as his second wife, JOHN ORR MONROE LADD, b. 10 Sep 1816 son of Alexander Park and Charlotte (Hackett) Ladd; John d. at Meredith, NH, 16 Aug 1855. John was first married to Nancy J. Coombs.

988) DAVID ABBOTT *(Nathaniel[4], Nathaniel[3], Nathaniel[2], George[1])*, b. at Concord, 8 Aug 1770 son of Nathaniel and Miriam (Chandler) Abbott; d. in Oxford County, ME, 30 Jun 1836; m. BETSEY COLSON, b. at Weymouth, 24 Aug 1780 daughter of Gideon and Elizabeth (White) Colson; Betsey d. at Roxbury, ME, 16 Sep 1821. David m. 2nd, at Bethel, 28 Mar 1833, BETSEY TWITCHELL, b. 1781 daughter of Jacob and Sally (Matthews) Twitchell; Betsey d. at Palermo, ME, 4 Apr 1857. Betsey Twitchell was married five times: Mr. Carey, Isaac Knight, David Abbott, Matthew Randall, and Jonathan Worthen.

David Abbott was proprietor of Abbot's Mills on the Concord River in Rumford, Maine.[2649]

David Abbott did not leave a will and his estate entered probated 1 Aug 1836 with Timothy Walker as administrator. The homestead farm in Rumford of about 150 acres was valued at $1200 and personal estate at $527.97. Debts were $679. On 22 August 1836, widow Betsey Abbott petitioned the court for an allowance from the personal estate. The real property was sold to settle the debts of the estate.[2650]

David Abbott and Betsey Colson were parents of ten children born at Rumford, Maine.

i VESTA ABBOTT, b. 20 Dec 1802; d. at Rumford, Dec 1840; m. Nov 1822, JOHN ACKLEY, b. 24 Dec 1798 son of Samuel and Elizabeth (Moody) Ackley; John d. at Rumford, 7 May 1849.

ii LAURA ABBOTT, b. Aug 1804; d. at Rumford, 13 Jun 1892; m. at Rumford, 10 Jun 1824, WILLIAM MOODY, b. 1 Jan 1799 son of William and Mary (Dresser) Moody; William d. at Rumford, 12 May 1873.

iii LUNA ABBOTT, b. 25 Feb 1806; d. 29 Sep 1807.

2648 The names of Abiel's parents are given as William Rolfe and Judith Hazelton on his death record.

2649 Lapham, *History of Rumford Maine*, p 289

2650 *Probate Court (Oxford County)*; Probate Place: *Oxford, Maine, Letters of Administration, Vol 1-3, 1811-1860*, volume 1, p 485; *Probate Records, Vol 8-9, 1836-1841*, volume 8, p 43-44; volume 8, p 294; volume 8, p 442

iv ARVILLA ABBOTT, b. 30 Dec 1807; d. at Rumford, 11 Jun 1894; m. 7 Dec 1834, JOHN MARTIN, b. 4 Dec 1804 son of Kimball and Rachel (Godwin) Martin; John d. at Rumford, 21 Jan 1894.

v GIDEON COLSON ABBOTT, b. Nov 1809; d. at Rumford, 1 Mar 1898; m. 17 Nov 1833, CEVILIA BARKER, b. at Rumford, 17 Dec 1812 daughter of Samuel and Rachel (Sessions) Barker; Cevilia d. at Rumford, 27 Dec 1901.

vi LUNA ABBOTT, b. 1 Oct 1811; d. at Rumford, 27 Apr 1890; m. 16 Apr 1835, TIMOTHY WALKER, b. at Concord, NH, 10 Jul 1813 son of Charles and Hannah (Pickering) Walker; Timothy d. at Rumford, 29 Jan 1882.

vii ELIZABETH ABBOTT, b. May 1813; d. at Rumford, 3 Dec 1897; m. Apr 1837, CHARLES ADAMS KIMBALL, b. at Rumford, 10 Dec 1816 son of Moses F. and Mary (Bean) Kimball; Charles d. 27 Dec 1895.

viii SAMUEL VINCENT ABBOTT, b. 22 May 1816; d. at Rumford, 22 Feb 1907; m. May 1843, MARY KYLE, b. 28 Oct 1819 daughter of William and Rebecca (Walker) Kyle; Mary d. at Rumford, 14 Oct 1875.

ix JAMES WEBSTER ABBOTT, b. Aug 1818; d. at Groveton, NH, 1872; m. at Northumberland, NH, ANN RICHIE, b. about 1820 who has not been identified; Ann was living in 1870.

x DEBAN RENSALIER ABBOTT, b. 16 Feb 1821; d. at sea, 18 Aug 1850. Deban did not marry. He died during passage to California.

989) DORCAS MERRILL *(Dorcas Abbott Merrill[4], Nathaniel[3], Nathaniel[2], George[1])*, b. about 1754 daughter of Moses and Dorcas (Abbott) Merrill; d. at Reading, 30 Mar 1841; m. 3 Mar 1778, WILLIAM BEARD, b. at Reading, 5 Sep 1745 son of Andrew and Elizabeth (Burnap) Beard; William d. at Reading, 15 Nov 1809. William was first married to Sarah Nichols.

William Beard did not leave a will. Timothy Wakefield was administrator of the estate acting as the agent for the widow Dorcas Beard. The estate was sold at public auction. The heirs to the estate signing a request for appraisers of the estate were Dorcas Beard widow, Daniel Temple (who is the husband of Sarah Beard), William Beard, Fanne Beard, Merrill Beard, and Langdon Beard. Another document includes heirs Dorcas Beard widow, Fanny Beard, William Beard, Edmund Beard, Merrill Beard, and Langdon Beard. William Beard had a first marriage and heirs from the first marriage are Edmund, William, Fanny, and Sarah Beard Temple.[2651]

Dorcas Merrill and William Beard had four children born at Reading.

i MERRILL BEARD, b. about 1781; d. at Reading, 24 Dec 1831; m. at Reading, 28 Nov 1802, OLIVE YOUNG, b. at Woburn, 13 Feb 1779 daughter of William and Elizabeth (Johnson) Young.

ii LANGDON BEARD, b. 2 Apr 1788; d. at Reading, 2 Jul 1864; m. at Salem, 17 May 1828, ABIAH ANN BADGER, b. at Warner, NH, 13 Nov 1798 daughter of Stephen and Betsey (Eastman) Badger; Abiah d. at Charlestown, MA, 7 Nov 1873.

iii POLLY BEARD, b. 29 May 1790; d. at Reading, 21 Oct 1857. Polly did not marry.

iv BETSEY BEARD, b. 10 Jun 1793; d. at Reading, 6 Feb 1826. Betsey did not marry.

990) LYDIA MERRILL *(Dorcas Abbott Merrill[4], Nathaniel[3], Nathaniel[2], George[1])*, b. 10 Nov 1759 daughter of Moses and Dorcas (Abbott) Merrill; d. at Concord, 10 Jan 1839; m. SAMUEL DAVIS, b. at Concord, 17 Apr 1759 son of Robert and Sarah (Walker) Davis; Samuel d. at Concord, 19 May 1848.

Lydia Merrill and Samuel Davis were parents of nine children all born at Concord.

i DORCAS DAVIS, b. about 1781; d. at Concord, 14 Oct 1830; m. at Concord, 13 Nov 1802, her fourth cousin, ENOCH FARNUM *(Sarah Lovejoy Farnum[5], Phebe Chandler Lovejoy[4], John Chandler[3], Hannah Abbott Chandler[2], George[1])*, b. at Concord, 27 Sep 1773 son of Theodore and Sarah (Lovejoy) Farnum; Enoch d. at Concord, 3 Jun 1820. Enoch Farnum is a child in Family 440.

ii SARAH DAVIS, b. 1782; d. at Concord, about 1831; m. at Concord, 5 Aug 1810, JAMES BUSWELL, b. at Concord, 7 Aug 1782 son of Caleb and Mary (Badger) Buswell; James d. 2 Nov 1847. After Sarah's death, James married her sister Judith (see below).

iii NANCY DAVIS, b. about 1785; d. at Concord, 30 Aug 1836; m. at Concord, 28 Apr 1813, LABAN PAGE, b. at Dunbarton, 4 Aug 1783 son of William and Hannah (Heath) Page; Laban d. at Concord, 9 Jun 1854.

iv RUTH DAVIS, b. about 1789; d. at Lowell, 23 Mar 1855; m. 14 Apr 1808, EPHRAIM COLBY.

[2651] Middlesex County, MA: Probate File Papers, 1648-1871.Online database. AmericanAncestors.org. New England Historic Genealogical Society, 2014. Case number 1454

v ROBERT DAVIS, b. 14 Sep 1790; d. at Concord, 28 Jan 1825; m. at Concord, 19 Sep 1818, ALMIRA BROWN DEARBORN, b. at Concord, 12 May 1798 daughter of Trueworthy "T. G." and Sarah (Brown) Dearborn; Almira d. at Concord, 7 Mar 1861. After Robert's death, Almira married Asaph Evans.

vi SAMUEL DAVIS, b. about 1793; d. at Concord, 12 Jan 1853. Samuel did not marry.

vii JUDITH DAVIS, b. 1795; d. at Concord, 8 Jul 1876; m. 25 Feb 1832, JAMES BUSWELL who was first married to her sister Sarah (see above).

viii MOSES DAVIS, b. 1797; d. at Concord, 7 Jun 1875; m. at Concord, 27 Dec 1825, ESTHER MARTIN, b. at Rumford, ME, 27 Jan 1799 daughter of Daniel and Betsey (George0 Martin; Esther d. at Boscawen, 27 Sep 1886.

ix DAVID DAVIS, b. 1800; d. at Somerville, MA, 25 Nov 1864; m. at Lowell, 10 Jan 1850, ELIZA C. PHELPS, b. at Lowell, about 1825 daughter of Jesse and Catherine (Shattuck) Phelps; Eliza d. at Boston, 12 May 1898.

991) REBECCA MERRILL *(Rebecca Abbott Merrill Doyen[4], Nathaniel[3], Nathaniel[2], George[1])*, b. at Rumford, 16 Aug 1751 daughter of John and Rebecca (Abbott) Merrill; d. at Concord, by 1778; m. by 1769, ABNER FARNUM, b. about 1748 son of Joseph and Zerviah (Hoit) Farnum; Abner d. at Concord, 2 Aug 1820.

Bouton's *History of Concord* reports just three children for Rebecca Merrill and Abner Farnum and states that the other children of Abner were from his second marriage to Sarah Elliot.[2652]

i THOMAS FARNUM, b. 31 Dec 1769; d. at Concord, 7 Sep 1793.

ii JOHN FARNUM, b. about 1772; died young.

iii MOSES FARNUM, b. about 1774; d. at Cornish, NH, 19 Sep 1828; m. at Lebanon, NH, 30 Oct 1800, REBECCA DEAN, b. about 1773; Rebecca d. at Cornish, 27 Oct 1828.

992) JOHN MERRILL *(Rebecca Abbott Merrill Doyen[4], Nathaniel[3], Nathaniel[2], George[1])*, b. at Concord, 14 Jun 1756 son of John and Rebecca (Abbott) Merrill; d. at Tunbridge, VT, 7 Apr 1814; m. at Pembroke, 14 Mar 1782, SARAH "SALLY" ROBERTSON, b. at Bow, 18 Apr 1757 daughter of John and Elizabeth (Lovejoy) Robertson.[2653]

John Merrill and Sally Robertson were parents of four children.

i JOHN MERRILL, b. at Concord, 17 Oct 1783; d. at Merrillsville, NY, 19 Oct 1872; m. 4 Jan 1807, SARAH C. DEGROFF, b. likely in Saratoga County, NY, about 1787 daughter of Abraham and Catherine (Voorhees) DeGroff;[2654] Sarah d. at Merrillsville, 1863.

ii JAMES MERRILL, b. at Bow, 1785; d. at Chelsea, VT, 3 Dec 1879; m. at Chelsea, 17 Jun 1810, MARY BEAN, b. about 1790 daughter of Levi and Elizabeth (Moody) Bean; Mary d. at Chelsea, 21 Oct 1878.[2655]

iii MOSES MERRILL, b. about 1788; nothing further known.

iv EBENEZER MERRILL, b. at Tunbridge, VT, 10 Aug 1794; d. 19 Sep 1794.

993) JACOB DOYEN *(Rebecca Abbott Merrill Doyen[4], Nathaniel[3], Nathaniel[2], George[1])*, b. at Pembroke, 22 Apr 1759 son of Jacob and Rebecca (Abbott) Doyen; d. at Somerset County, ME, 30 Apr 1830; m. Apr 1783, MERCY CRIBBS, b. about 1765; Mercy d. at Smithfield, ME, 3 Aug 1852. Mercy was second married to Jonathan Hibbert in October 1830.

On 1 March 1818, Jacob Doyen of Temple, Maine, then age 50, made application for a pension based on his service in the Revolution. He stated that he enlisted 1 March 1777 for a period of three years in the company of Captain Ebenezer Frye in

---

2652 The birth transcriptions for all the children of Abner give the mother's name as Rebecca, although those may just be errors. Only one death record for the younger children included a mother's name and that record gave the mother as Sarah.

2653 Some published histories/genealogies give Sarah's mother as John Robertson's first wife, Lydia Cales. However, *Bow, NH: The Town Book of Bow* identifies Elizabeth as the mother of all the children of John Robertson. *Bow, NH: The Town Book of Bow, New Hampshire, 1760-1877.* Manuscript. R. Stanton Avery Special Collections, New England Historic Genealogical Society, Boston, MA. (Online database. *AmericanAncestors.org*, New England Historic Genealogical Society, 2012.)

2654 The 1818 will of Abraham DeGroff with wife Catherine of Orange, NY includes a bequest to his daughter Sally Merrill.

2655 The Merrill Memorial reports that James son of John Merrill and Sally Robertson married Susan Silver of Bow. However, that James died before 1872 in New Hampshire. There is a death record for James Merrill in Chelsea, Vermont for 3 Dec 1879 that states the names of his parents as John Merrill and Sally Robertson and birthplace of Bow, NH. The James Merrill of Chelsea was married to Mary Bean.

the Regiment of Colonel Joseph Cilley. He was discharged near Fishkill in March 1780. He was at the taking of Burgoyne, spent one winter at Valley Forge, went into Indian territory with General Sullivan in 1779, and was at the Battle of Monmouth.[2656]

Following the death of her second husband, Mercy Hibbert applied for the widow's pension of Jacob Doyen. In her statement of 1 August 1843, Mercy reported that she and Jacob were parents of nine children, five of whom were living in 1843. The clerk of Temple, Maine provided a list of the birthdates of seven children for the family that were registered in Temple. Mercy Hibbert was granted a pension of $80 per year.

In December 1853, after the death of Mercy Cribbs Doyen Hibbert, Mary Doyen of Plymouth, Maine made application for Jacob's pension stating she was Jacob's widow and that she and Jacob were married March 1820 and that her maiden name was Mary Cribbs. She stated Jacob died 15 April 1829 and she had been a widow since that time. This application was rejected as Jacob had another widow who had received his pension.

Jacob Doyen and Mercy Cribbs were parents of seven known children who were registered at Temple, Maine. Jacob and Mercy's son John married Sarah Tuck and they were the parents of Dorcas Doyen, aka Helen Jewett who was murdered in New York in 1836.[2657]

i JOHN DOYEN, b. 8 Mar 1785; d. at Avon, ME, after 1850; m. 1st, about 1806, SALLY TUCK, b. about 1785; Sally d. about 1822. John m. 2nd, about 1823, LYDIA DUTTON; Lydia d. at Augusta, ME, about 1837. JOHN m. 3rd, BETSY; Betsy d. at Dixfield, ME, 20 May 1856.

ii BENJAMIN DOYEN, b. 17 Mar 1794; d. at Dixfield, ME, 9 Aug 1831; m. DOROTHY SUMNER WHEELER, b. at Worcester, 5 Sep 1795 daughter of Joseph and Lucy (Sumner) Wheeler; Dorothy d. at Worcester, 20 Nov 1865.[2658] Dorothy married second Elisha Hayden.

iii JOEL DOYEN, b. 3 Aug 1796; d. at Smithfield, ME, 5 Mar 1874; m. MAHALA, b. in ME, about 1796; Mahala d. at Smithfield, 24 Sep 1877.

iv JEREMIAH DOYEN, b. 17 Feb 1798; d. at Farmington, ME, 6 Apr 1869; m. 1st, at Industry, ME, 30 Nov 1826, LYDIA PRATT. Jeremiah m. 2nd, Oct 1842, SARAH L. SAWYER, b. 20 Oct 1801; Sarah d. at Smithfield, 2 May 1866.

v SAMUEL DOYEN, b. 13 Sep 1800

vi RACHEL DOYEN, b. 6 Jun 1803; d. after 1860 when the family was in Cornville, ME; m. about 1829, JOHN POMEROY, b. in ME, about 1806; John d. after 1860.

vii ABBOTT DOYEN, b. 5 Oct 1805; d. at Norridgewock, ME, 8 Jan 1879; m. KATHERINE COLLINS, b. at Stark, ME, 2 Apr 1809 daughter of John and Dorcas (Greenleaf) Collins; Katherine d. at Norridgewock, Jun 1892.

994) SAMUEL DOYEN *(Rebecca Abbott Merrill Doyen⁴, Nathaniel³, Nathaniel², George¹)*, b. at Pembroke, 26 Feb 1764 son of Jacob and Rebecca (Abbott) Doyen. Samuel completed a bounty-land warrant application for land in Maine[2659] and died at Levant, ME between 1832 and 1840. Samuel married POLLY who has not been identified and who died in Maine in 1832.

Of the families in this fifth generation, the Doyens are perhaps the most difficult to pin down. They were highly mobile, seemed to live on the fringes of their communities, and in the case of Samuel and his family were repeatedly "warned out" of nearly every place they arrived.

Samuel did serve in the Revolution and in 1780 was in the rolls of the 2nd Company of Captain Jonas Kidder. After his marriage to Polly, the young family was in Hallowell, Maine in 1790 and in 1800 were in Vassalboro. They were then in Vermont where Samuel and his family were "warned out" of Thetford 20 January 1807 and were warned out of Randolph, Vermont on 27 February 1810. And, again, warned out of Brookfield, Vermont on 5 February 1812. The family ultimately made their way to Maine and were living in Levant by 1832.[2660]

The children in this family are not certain, but these are four possible children. The children were likely born in Maine, but the family was frequently on the move.

i SAMUEL DOYEN, b. about 1787

ii NATHANIEL DOYEN, b. about 1788; d. after 1850 when he was living in Levant, ME; m. at York County, New Brunswick, Canada, 26 Jun 1817, HULDAH MOREHOUSE, b. at New Brunswick, 15 May 1786 daughter of Daniel Morehouse.

[2656] Revolutionary War Pension and Bounty-Land Warrant Application Files, Case W27513

[2657] Cohen, P. C. (1993). The Mystery of Helen Jewett: Romantic Fiction and the Eroticization of Violence. *Legal Stud. F.*, *17*, 133.

[2658] Wheeler, *Genealogy of Some of the Descendants of Obadiah Wheeler*, p 27. Also, names of parents are given as Joseph and Lucy on Dorothy's death record.

[2659] Ancestry.com, U.S., Revolutionary War Pension and Bounty-Land Warrant Application Files, 1800-1900

[2660] Otten, "Discovering Doyen Descendants", *The Maine Genealogist*, May 1996, volume 18, p 63ff

iii HANNAH DOYEN, b. about 1795; d. at Story County, IA, Apr 1880; m. about 1813, DANIEL ROGERS, b. at Lincoln County, ME, 11 Aug 1791; Daniel d. at Honey Creek, IA, 11 Nov 1871. The children of Hannah and Daniel include Daniel Abbott Rogers and Samuel Doin Rogers.

iv JACOB DOYEN, b. about 1797; d. at Vassalboro, ME, 4 Nov 1815 when he drowned in the Kennebec River.

995) FRANCIS DOYEN *(Rebecca Abbott Merrill Doyen⁴, Nathaniel³, Nathaniel², George¹)*, b. at Pembroke, 17 Feb 1767 son of Jacob and Rebecca (Abbott) Doyen; d. likely in Maine after 1830;[2661] m. 7 Sep 1789, BETTY GARVIN, b. at Bow, 20 Dec 1770 daughter of James and Deborah (-) Garvin.

There may be as many as eight children in this family, but just three have so far been identified.

i HANNAH DOYEN, b. about 1791; d. at Sullivan, PA, about 1840; m. at Royalton, VT, 9 Mar 1806, SAMUEL WELCH, b. at Brookline, MA, 1784 son of Nathaniel and Lura (Dickinson) Welch; Samuel d. at Sullivan, after 1860.[2662]

ii FRANCIS DOYEN, b. in VT, about 1801; d. after 1880 when he was living in Farmington, ME; m. 1st, ELIZABETH POMEROY, b. about 1803; Elizabeth d. at Livermore Falls, ME, 12 Jul 1874. Francis m. 2nd, DOROTHY F. (widow of Gilman Hobbs), b. in ME, Sep 1826; Dorothy d. after 1900 when she was living in Phillips, ME.

iii LUCINDA DOYEN, b. Jun 1805; d. at Wilton, ME, 25 Sep 1873; m. at Wilton, 18 Nov 1820, MOSES AVERILL, b. 1799 son of Moses and Eunice (-) Averill; Moses d. at Wilton, 11 Feb 1887.

996) NATHANIEL DOYEN *(Rebecca Abbott Merrill Doyen⁴, Nathaniel³, Nathaniel², George¹)*, b. at Pembroke, 17 Feb 1767 son of Jacob and Rebecca (Abbott) Doyen; d. at Pembroke, 8 May 1841; m. at Goffstown, 2 May 1791, DEBORAH SMITH.

Nathaniel Doyen and Deborah Smith were parents of four children born at Pembroke.[2663]

i REBECCA DOYEN, b. about 1796; m. NATHANIEL KENISTON.

ii BETSEY DOYEN, b. about 1798; m. JOHN HENDERSON.

iii SOPHIA ROBINSON DOYEN, b. 10 Jul 1799; d. at Plymouth, NH, 29 Apr 1866; m. 22 Feb 1826, WILLIAM CURRIER, b. at Concord, 21 Mar 1800 son of Daniel and Mary (Smith) Currier; William d. at Holderness, NH, 13 Mar 1877.

iv SARAH DOYEN, b. about 1800; d. at Concord between 1870 and 1880; m. before 1828, JOSEPH H. EMERY, b. at Epping, 26 Jul 1801 son of Nehemiah and Mary (Henderson) Emery; Joseph d. at Concord, 27 Aug 1886.

997) HANNAH DOYEN *(Rebecca Abbott Merrill Doyen⁴, Nathaniel³, Nathaniel², George¹)*, b. at Pembroke, 1772 daughter of Jacob and Rebecca (Abbott) Doyen; m. EBENEZER GARVIN, b. at Bow, 15 Sep 1768 son of James and Deborah (-) Garvin.

Just one child has been identified for Ebenezer Garvin and Hannah Doyen.

i JEREMIAH ABBOTT GARVIN, b. at Concord, 12 Aug 1793; d. at Shelby, NY, 24 Aug 1866; m. LYDIA MARIA MOYER, b. in NY, about 1798; Lydia d. at Shelby, 24 Jul 1874.

998) SARAH HAZELTINE *(Elizabeth Abbott Hazeltine⁴, Nathaniel³, Nathaniel², George¹)*, b. at Rumford, 24 Dec 1755 daughter of Joseph and Elizabeth (Abbott) Hazeltine; m. at Concord, 20 Jan 1777, NAHUM HOUGHTON, origin uncertain but perhaps the Nahum born in 1732 in Worcester County, MA; Nahum d. at Bridport, VT, 29 Aug 1802.[2664]

On 25 February 1800, Nahum Houghton over the age of 14 selected his uncle Captain Jacob Green as his guardian. Jacob Green was the husband of Anna Hazeltine who was Sarah's sister. Nahum's statement is the he has "no parents capable of contributing to my support."[2665] The wording of the statement does not suggest/state that his parents are deceased.

2661 He is perhaps the Francis Doyen listed in the 1830 Census at Avon, Somerset, Maine as the male age 60-69. 1830; Census Place: Avon, Somerset, Maine; Series: M19; Roll: 51; Page: 174; Family History Library Film: 0497947

2662 Tice, Sullivan-Rutland Genealogy Project, http://www.joycetice.com/srgp/doynewelch.pdf

2663 Carter, *History of Pembroke*, p 70. No records/information was located for Rebecca and Betsey other than that given in the *History of Pembroke*.

2664 Vermont, Vital Records, 1720-1908

2665 *New Hampshire. Probate Court (Rockingham County)*; Probate Place: *Rockingham, New Hampshire, Estate Papers, No 6644-6749, 1800*

Nahum Houghton and Sarah Hazeltine were parents of eleven children, the births of the first ten children at Shoreham, Vermont and the youngest child at Bridport, Vermont.

i SALLY HOUGHTON, b. 17 Apr 1777

ii NAHUM HOUGHTON, b. 10 Apr 1783; d. at Brunswick, ME, 12 Jun 1860; m. about 1812, DIANA ROGERS, b. at Topsham, ME, 1 Apr 1781 daughter of John and Jane (Potter) Rogers; Diana d. at Brunswick, ME, 20 May 1860.

iii SOPHIA HOUGHTON, b. 10 Apr 1783

iv WILLIAM HOUGHTON, b. 12 Nov 1784

v ELIZABETH HOUGHTON, b. 22 Feb 1786

vi PETER HAZELTINE HOUGHTON, b. 9 Feb 1788; d. at Bridport, VT, 9 Mar 1865; m. at Bridport, 14 Mar 1818, ELECTA SMITH, b. in VT, about 1788 daughter of Asher and Eunice (Lum) Smith; Electa d. at Bridport, after 1870.

vii LUCINDA HOUGHTON, b. 28 Aug 1788

viii SUSANNAH HOUGHTON, b. 7 Jun 1793; d. at Crown Point, NY, 25 Mar 1872;[2666] m. JOHN BURWELL, b. 3 at Bridport, VT, Sep 1792 son of David and Christian (Baldwin) Burwell; John d. at Crown Point, 12 Mar 1861.

ix ROSANNA HOUGHTON, b. 7 Jun 1793

x POLLY HOUGHTON, b. 18 Jun 1795

xi AMELIA HOUGHTON, b. 9 Mar 1799; d. at Bridport, 15 Sep 1802.

999) ANNA HAZELTINE *(Elizabeth Abbott Hazeltine[4], Nathaniel[3], Nathaniel[2], George[1])*, b. at Rumford, 19 May 1760 daughter of Joseph and Elizabeth (Abbott) Hazeltine; d. at Bow, 13 Nov 1838; m. at Concord, 26 Sep 1776, JACOB GREEN, b. at Worcester, MA, 18 Jan 1749/50 son of Nathaniel and Lucy (Gerfield) Green; Jacob d. at Bow, 17 Apr 1815.

Jacob Green did not leave a will and his estate entered probate 23 May 1815 with widow Anna as administratrix. The real property consisting of a farm with buildings was valued at $1,000 and personal property was valued at $377.78. The demands against the estate exceeded $1,500 and the estate was declared insolvent. The estate was sold to pay the debts.[2667]

Anna Hazeltine and Jacob Green were parents of thirteen children born at Bow.

i MARTHA "PATTY" GREEN, b. 14 Oct 1777; d. at Concord, 28 Jun 1843; m. 28 Jan 1802, as his second wife, JOHN P. NOYES, b. at Bow, 27 Jun 1766 son of John and Mary (Fowler) Noyes; John d. in NY during the War of 1812 on 1 Mar 1814.[2668] John Noyes was first married to Martha's aunt, BETTY HAZELTINE (1771-1801). John P. Noyes, Betty Hazeltine, and Martha Green are Family 1002.

ii JACOB GREEN, b. 24 Apr 1779; d. at Gilmanton, NH, 30 Nov 1856; m. about 1800, SARAH DOW, b. at Bow, 11 May 1779 daughter of Richard and Mary (Loeffler) Dow; Sarah d. at Gilmanton, 10 Feb 1862.

iii PETER HAZELTINE GREEN, b. 30 Nov 1780; d. at Brookline, MA, 19 Oct 1862; m. 1st, about 1806, MARGARET FOSTER, b. at Topsham, ME, 1786 daughter of Steel and Martha (Potter) Foster; Margaret d. 1836. Peter m. 2nd, at Bath, 19 Apr 1837, LOUISA MEACHAM daughter of Asa Meacham.

iv NATHANIEL GREEN, b. 11 Aug 1782; d. at Topsham, ME, 3 Apr 1842; m. 1808, MARGARET ROGERS, b. 1784 daughter of Alexander and Margaret (Wilson) Rogers; Margaret d. at Topsham, 14 Dec 1875.

v BETSEY GREEN, b. 28 Nov 1784; nothing further known.

vi GARDNER GREEN, b. 26 Sep 1786; d. at Topsham, ME, 10 Jan 1840; m. at Lewiston, 28 Dec 1817, MARY W. STONE,[2669] b. in ME, 1799; Mary d. at Topsham, 25 Aug 1867.

vii BALLARD GREEN, b. 26 Sep 1786; d. at Thomaston, ME, 20 Feb 1831; m. at Brunswick, ME, 9 Jun 1819, JANE NOYES, b. at Brunswick, 22 Oct 1793 daughter of Cutting and Anne (Martin) Noyes; Jane d. at Thomaston, 6 Feb 1832.

[2666] The birthdate is engraved on her gravestone and this corresponds with her birth record. Findagrave ID: 93608148

[2667] *New Hampshire. Probate Court (Rockingham County);* Probate Place: *Rockingham, New Hampshire, Estate Papers, No 9082-9174, 1815*, case 9087

[2668] At the 13 Apr 1814 probate of John Noyes, widow Martha Noyes requested that her father Jacob Green of Bow be named administrator.

[2669] "Maine Marriages, 1771-1907," database, *FamilySearch* (https://familysearch.org/ark:/61903/1:1:F4X3-X8W : 10 February 2018), Gardner Green and Mary Stone, 28 Dec 1817; citing Civil, Lewiston, Androscoggin, Maine, reference ; FHL microfilm 223,931.

viii ABIGAIL GREEN, b. 20 Dec 1788; d. at Bow, 26 Jan 1852; m. at Concord, 6 May 1846, as his second wife, WILLIAM GAULT, b. at Bow, 4 Feb 1793 son of Samuel and Anna (Gile) Gault; William d. at Concord, 7 Apr 1853. William was first married to Harriet Stickney.

ix TIMOTHY DIX GREEN, b. 1 Mar 1791; d. at Bow, 10 Apr 1815.

x LUCY GREEN, b. 4 May 1793; d. at Topsham, 4 Mar 1879; m. at Topsham, 27 Jan 1818, HUGH PATTEN, b. at Topsham, 29 Jul 1789 son of Actor and Jane (McLellan) Patten; Hugh d. at Phippsburg, ME, 18 Feb 1860.

xi ANNA GREEN, b. 1 Jul 1795; d. at Concord, 28 Jun 1842; m. at Bow, 20 Nov 1821, OREN SHAW, b. about 1797; Oren d. at Concord, 2 Mar 1837.

xii MARY GREEN, b. 20 Jul 1798; d. 8 Feb 1852 (buried at Bow). Mary did not marry. In 1850, she was living in Concord with her sister Abigail and her husband William Gault.

xiii REBECCA GREEN, b. 20 Oct 1800; d. at Bow, 3 Dec 1841; m. about 1838, DAVID TOWLE, b. at Chichester, NH, about 1815 son of Jonathan and Betty (Fellows) Towle;[2670] David d. at Canterbury, 13 Jan 1871. David married second Nancy Kezer 4 Jul 1846.

1000) HANNAH HAZELTINE *(Elizabeth Abbott Hazeltine⁴, Nathaniel³, Nathaniel², George¹)*, b. at Concord, 31 Aug 1767 daughter of Joseph and Elizabeth (Abbott) Hazeltine; m. 19 Apr 1787, JAMES STICKNEY, b. at Concord, 5 Dec 1766 son of Jonathan and Sarah (Webster) Stickney.

Hannah Hazeltine and James Stickney were parents of nine children, the oldest child born at Concord and the other children likely all born at Lebanon, New Hampshire. Death records have not been located for either Hannah or James.

i SARAH STICKNEY, b. 10 Aug 1788; d. at Springfield, NH, 19 Jan 1868; m. 1st, at Newport, NH, 22 Apr 1881, URIAH HALL, b. about 1782; Uriah d. at Newport, 1814 (probate 1814). Sarah m. 2nd, at Newport, 25 Oct 1815, JOHN WORTHEN, b. at Enfield, 2 Mar 1778; John d. at Enfield, 2 Jul 1841. Sarah m. 3rd, about 1842, JOSEPH GOODHUE, b. about 1771; Joseph d. at Enfield, 21 Feb 1847.

ii ELIZABETH A. STICKNEY, b. 26 Aug 1790; d. at Salem, NY, 1 Sep 1856; m. 1805, ADRIAL PARTRIDGE, b. 4 Nov 1790 son of Stephen and Esther (Emerson) Partridge;[2671] Adrial d. at Shushan, NY, 27 Jun 1874.

iii SAMUEL STICKNEY, b. 2 Sep 1791; d. at Elk Grove, CA, 6 Nov 1883; m. at Lebanon, NH, 27 Jan 1816, BETSEY WELLS, b. at Lebanon, about 1796 daughter of Eliphalet and Ruth (Lyman) Wells; Betsey d. at Lebanon, 14 Aug 1864.

iv PETER STICKNEY, b. 2 Sep 1791; nothing further known.

v ROBERT STICKNEY, b. 1796; d. 1797.

vi ROBERT STICKNEY, b. Oct 1799; nothing further known.

vii NATHANIEL STICKNEY, b. about 1801; d. after 1860, likely at Orange, OH; m. at Meigs, OH, 3 Jul 1828, JANE CONANT, b. in OH, about 1810; Jane d. after 1860.

viii JONATHAN STICKNEY, b. 10 Mar 1803; d. at Newport, ME, 4 Jul 1846; m. at Brewer, ME, 7 Aug 1830, MARY SPRAGUE, b. 4 Mar 1810 daughter of Ephraim and Esther (Bigelow) Sprague; Mary d. 22 Nov 1889. Mary married second Samuel Young.

ix DAVID STICKNEY, b. about 1804; d. after 1850 when he was living in Jay, New York; nothing further known.

1001) BALLARD HAZELTINE *(Elizabeth Abbott Hazeltine⁴, Nathaniel³, Nathaniel², George¹)*, b. at Concord, 4 Sep 1769 son of Joseph and Elizabeth (Abbott) Hazeltine; d. at Plattsburgh, NY, 1836; m. 19 Apr 1792, SALLY NOYES, b. at Bow, 17 Dec 1768 daughter of John and Mary (Fowler) Noyes; Sally d. at Concord, 1854.

Ballard was a farmer in Concord who continued on the homestead he inherited from his father. He sold out his farm by 1835 and was in Plattsburgh, New York where he died.[2672] Ballard Hazeltine and Sally Noyes were parents of nine children born at Concord, New Hampshire.

[2670] Lyford, *History of Canterbury*, p 330.
[2671] Partridge, *Partridge Genealogy: Descendants of John Partridge of Medfield*, p 25
[2672] Bouton, *History of Concord*, p 709

i PETER HAZELTINE, b. 7 Jan 1793; d. at Marengo, MI, 22 Dec 1846; m. Nov 1820, SARAH PIERCE, b. in RI, 1787; Sarah d. at Homer, MI, 1852.

ii JOHN HAZELTINE, b. 12 Oct 1794; nothing further known.

iii NATHANIEL HAZELTINE, b. 2 Dec 1797; nothing further known.

iv JOSEPH HAZELTINE, b. 29 Nov 1799; d. at Concord, 31 Dec 1880; m. at Lyndeborough, 9 Jun 1824, ABIGAIL WHITEMARSH, b. at Lyndeborough, 1800 daughter of Charles and Anna (Faxon) Whitemarsh; Abigail d. at Concord, 1834.

v ELIZA HAZELTINE, b. 5 Dec 1802; d. at WI, after 1880; m. at Concord, 18 Nov 1823, AARON CARTER, b. at Bow, 28 May 1796 son of John and Lucy (-) Carter; Aaron d. at Waupaca County, WI, 15 Apr 1855.

vi MARY NOYES HAZELTINE, b. 21 May 1805; d. at Ela, IL, Apr 1868; m. at Goffstown, 18 Oct 1832, GEORGE ELA, b. 17 Jun 1805 son of Benjamin and Abigail (Emerson) Ela; George d. at Barrington, IL, 12 Dec 1882. George married second Caroline E. Hazeltine 28 Oct 1870.

vii EMILY HAZELTINE, b. 3 Aug 1807; d. at Concord, 27 Feb 1895; m. Jan 1841, HIRAM READ, b. in NH, about 1811; Hiram d. likely at Portsmouth, NH, after 1860.

viii SARAH STICKNEY HAZELTINE, b. 16 Jul 1809

ix NANCY JANE HAZELTINE, b. 24 Sep 1812; d. at Glenholme, Nova Scotia, 13 Mar 1886; m. at Boston, 22 Jul 1855, ALEXANDER CUMMINGS, b. at Truro, Nova Scotia, 18 Oct 1819 son of John and Letitia (Barnhill) Cummings; Alexander d. at Middle Londonderry, Nova Scotia, after 1891.

1002) BETTY HAZELTINE *(Elizabeth Abbott Hazeltine⁴, Nathaniel³, Nathaniel², George¹)*, b. at Concord, 3 Oct 1771 daughter of Joseph and Elizabeth (Abbott) Hazeltine; d. at Bow, 1801; m. at Pembroke, 18 Nov 1788, JOHN P. NOYES, b. at Bow, 27 Jun 1766 son of John and Mary (Fowler) Noyes; John d. in upstate New York, 1 Mar 1814 while in military service. John married second, MARTHA "PATTY" GREEN (Betty Hazeltine's niece) *(Anna Hazeltine Green⁵, Elizabeth Abbott Hazeltine⁴, Nathaniel³, Nathaniel², George¹)*, b. at Bow 14 Oct 1777 daughter of Jacob and Anna (Hazeltine) Green; Martha d. at Concord, 28 Jun 1843. Martha is a child in Family 995.

John Noyes did not leave a will and his estate entered probate 13 April 1814. Widow Martha Noyes requested that her father Jacob Green of Bow be named administrator. Jacob Green died in 1815 and administration was then assumed by Samuel Green of Concord. Real estate consisted of twenty acres with buildings valued at $300 and twenty-five acres of woodland valued at $150. Personal estate was valued at $156.12. Claims against the estate exceeded the inventory. A petition was made by Samuel Green to sell two-thirds of the real estate noting also the need to provide support for the widow and two minor children under age seven years.[2673]

John Noyes and Betty Hazeltine were parents of seven children born at Bow.[2674]

i BALLARD HAZELTON NOYES, b. 12 Apr 1789; d. after 1820; m. at Boston 5 Jan 1818, SALLY HENLEY. Ballard Noyes was a Sergeant in the War of 1812. His first marriage intention to Betsey Brown was forbidden. He was living in Boston in 1820, but there is no record after.

ii ABIGAIL NOYES, b. 10 Dec 1790; d. at Bow, 23 Jan 1861; m. at Bow, 26 Jul 1818, THOMAS COLBY, b. at Bow, 20 Jan 1790 son of Thomas and Susannah (-) Colby; Thomas d. at Bow, 15 Jun 1856.

iii ABNER NOYES, b. 28 Oct 1792; d. at Tate, OH 1869 (probate 1869); m. at Brown County, IN, 5 Apr 1821, MARGARET CRISS, b. in PA, about 1802.

iv NATHANIEL NOYES, b. 17 Jul 1795; nothing further known.

v ELIZABETH "BETSEY" NOYES, b. 28 Dec 1797; m. at Bow, 24 Mar 1822, ABRAHAM GATES, b. at Bow, 20 May 1797 son of Abraham and Judith (Tenney) Gates.

vi MARY NOYES, b. 24 Sep 1799; d. at Iowa City, IA, 16 Nov 1872; m. at Dorchester, 1816, WINTHROP FOLSOM, b. at Epping, NH, 27 Jan 1794 son of James and Abigail (Blake) Folsom; Winthrop d. at Iowa City, 18 Sep 1856.

vii RUTH NOYES, b. 6 Mar 1801; d. at Bow, after 1850; m. at Bow, 21 Sep 1820, TIMOTHY HAMMOND, b. at Dunbarton, NH, 27 Aug 1797 son of Thomas and Esther (Dole) Hammond; Timothy d. at Bow, after 1870.

[2673] *New Hampshire. Probate Court (Rockingham County)*; Probate Place: *Rockingham, New Hampshire, Estate Papers, No 8833-8916, 1814*, Case 8845

[2674] Noyes, *Genealogical Record of Some of the Noyes Descendants*, p 108 includes a son John in this family. However, there are no records related to John and there are records for the other children, so John is omitted here as no record could be found for him. John should be considered an other possible child.

John Noyes and Martha Green were parents of four children born at Bow.

i MATILDA NOYES, b. 20 Sep 1802; d. at Sharon, VT, 18 Nov 1870; m. at Foxborough, MA, 12 Jun 1824, JOB WILLIS, b. at Foxborough, about 1803 son of Job and Lela (Bromard) Willis; Job d. at Warren, NH, 28 Jun 1891.

ii HIRAM NOYES, b. 11 Sep 1804; d. at Warren, NH, after 1880; m. at Hooksett, 9 Mar 1828, RELIEF QUIMBY, b. at Hooksett, about 1810; Relief d. at Warren, 13 May 1885.

iii LUCY G. NOYES, b. 20 Sep 1807; d. at Concord, 30 May 1882; m. at Concord, 22 Jan 1827, JONATHAN SANBORN, b. at Epping, about 1804 son of James and Sally (Avery) Sanborn; Jonathan d. at Concord, 27 May 1888.

iv PETER G. NOYES, b. 7 Nov 1810; d. at Patten, ME, after 1880; m. HENRIETTA BONNEY, b. in ME, about 1815 daughter of Andrew and Millie (Balkam) Bonney; Henrietta d. at Patten, 14 Mar 1892.

1003) JOSEPH WALKER *(Mary Abbott Walker⁴, Nathaniel³, Nathaniel², George¹)*, b. at Fryeburg, 1754 son of Joseph and Mary (Abbott) Walker; m. 11 Dec 1776, JANE STERLING, b. at Conway, NH, 1755 daughter of Hugh and Isabel (Stark) Sterling.[2675]

Joseph and Jane settled in Chatham, New Hampshire and four children have been reported, but little is known of them.

i ARCHIBALD WALKER, b. Aug 1777; d. at Portland, ME, 28 Dec 1835; m. PATIENCE who has not been identified; Patience d. at Portland, 15 Dec 1825.[2676]

ii HUGH WALKER, b. about 1780

iii MOLLY WALKER, b. about 1783

iv ANN STARK WALKER; b. about 1785

1004) NATHANIEL WALKER *(Mary Abbott Walker⁴, Nathaniel³, Nathaniel², George¹)*, b. at Fryeburg, 1757son of Joseph and Mary (Abbott) Walker; d. at Fryeburg, 13 Jun 1839;[2677] m. 18 Aug 1777, ABIGAIL CHARLES, b. at Brimfield, MA, 24 Sep 1758 daughter of John and Abigail (Bliss) Charles; Abigail d. at Fryeburg, 5 Sep 1843. Abigail was the widow Abigail Wiley at the time of her marriage to Nathaniel Walker; her first husband was likely William Wiley.

During the Revolution, Nathaniel Walker served as a private for one year in the regiment of Colonel Beedle in the New Hampshire line enlisting in December 1775. He applied for and was granted a pension in 1818 based on his reduced circumstances. In records related to Abigail's widow's pension, it was noted that in 1843 there were three surviving children: Charles Walker, William Walker, and Abigail Shirley.[2678]

There are four likely children of Nathaniel and Abigail all born at Fryeburg, Maine.

i WILLIAM WILEY WALKER, b. about 1778; m. at Conway, NH, 26 Nov 1801, POLLY WALKER who has not otherwise been identified.

ii DOROTHY WALKER, b. 1779; d. at Fryeburg, 19 Mar 1811; m. at Chatham, 23 Dec 1802, WILLIAM SHIRLEY, b. 6 Jul 1775 son of Edward and Sally (Hutchins) Shirley; William d. at Fryeburg, 18 Dec 1845. After Dorothy's death, William married Betsey S. Chase.

iii CHARLES WALKER, b. 5 Sep 1780; d. at Fryeburg, 11 Mar 1862; m. at Fryeburg, 25 Oct 1801, BETSEY PALMER, b. at Cambridge, 14 Apr 1783 daughter of Stephen and Mary (Bemis) Palmer; Betsey d. at Fryeburg, 14 Feb 1860.

iv ABIGAIL BLISS WALKER, b. 28 May 1788; d. at Fryeburg, 24 Jun 1863; m. EDMUND SHIRLEY, b. at Fryeburg, 25 Oct 1790 son of Edward and Abigail (Kelley) Shirley; Edmund d. at Fryeburg, 25 Apr 1876. Edmund Shirley was the half-brother of William Shirley who married Abigail's sister Dorothy.

[2675] Albert Sterling, 1909, *The Sterling Genealogy*, volume II, pp 1102-1103

[2676] Maine, Death Records, 1761-1922

[2677] The members of this family who died at Fryeburg are buried in the West Fryeburg Cemetery, Oxford County, Maine. The various gravestones with death dates and ages can be found on Find A Grave.

[2678] U.S., Revolutionary War Pension and Bounty-Land Warrant Application Files, 1800-1900, pension of Nathaniel Walker, Case W.25867

1005) SARAH WALKER *(Mary Abbott Walker⁴, Nathaniel³, Nathaniel², George¹)*, b. at Fryeburg, 1759 daughter of Joseph and Mary (Abbott) Walker; m. JOHN AMES of unknown origins.

Little can be found for this family and, so far, there is evidence for one child.

i JEREMIAH WALKER AMES, b. at Chatham, 14 Oct 1794; d. at Hallowell, ME, 29 Dec 1828; m. at Hallowell, 22 Oct 1817, MARY ELIZABETH SAGER, b. at Hallowell, 3 Mar 1796 daughter of Robert and Hannah (Jarvis) Sager; Mary d. after 1860. After Jeremiah's death, Mary married Stuart Foster.

1006) ANNA WALKER *(Mary Abbott Walker⁴, Nathaniel³, Nathaniel², George¹)*, b. at Fryeburg, 1765 daughter of Joseph and Mary (Abbott) Walker; d. at Fryeburg, 11 Mar 1854; m. JOHN STEVENS, b. Mar 1764 (based on age at death) son of John Stevens who was perhaps born in England; John d. at Fryeburg, 30 Sep 1825.

In his will written 22 September 1825, John Stevens bequeathed three hundred dollars each to daughters Betsey Atwood and Nancy Walker. All the remainder of the estate goes in equal portions to sons John Stevens, Jr. and Joseph Stevens on condition that they provide suitable maintenance for his wife as long as she is a widow. His wife's name is not given, and he makes no specific provision for her in the will other than his sons should provide for her. Eldest son John Stevens, Jr. was named executor. On 16 January 1826, widow Anna Stevens wrote to the probate court stating "I do hereby wave the provision made for me in the will of my late husband John Stevens late of Fryeburg deceased, and claim my dower of his estate. I therefore pray that your Honour would order the same to be assigned and set off to me as the law in such cases directs."[2679] Real estate was valued at $6,480 and personal estate at $1,745.43.

Anna Walker and John Stevens were parents of four children born at Fryeburg.

i ELIZABETH "BETSEY" STEVENS, b. 1789; d. at Fryeburg, 16 Apr 1852; m. JAMES ATWOOD, b. 1785; James d. at Fryeburg, 16 May 1855.

ii JOHN STEVENS, b. 1790; d. at Fryeburg, 1863; m. at Fryeburg, 8 Sep 1823, JUDITH KELLEY, b. at Conway, NH, 12 May 1799 daughter of Edmund and Elizabeth (Walker) Kelley;[2680] Judith d. at Fryeburg, 1887.

iii JOSEPH STEVENS, b. 26 Mar 1792; d. at Fryeburg, 17 Sep 1873; m. at Fryeburg, 12 Dec 1817, MARY L. STEELE, b. 11 Mar 1793; Mary d. at Fryeburg, 30 Apr 1863.

iv ANNA "NANCY" STEVENS, b. 4 Apr 1794; d. at Fryeburg, 8 Jul 1872; m. 5 Nov 1813, SAMUEL WALKER, b. 6 Dec 1784 son of Samuel and Hannah (Hazeltine) Walker; Samuel d. at Fryeburg, 17 Jan 1860.

1007) RUTH WALKER *(Mary Abbott Walker⁴, Nathaniel³, Nathaniel², George¹)*, b. at Fryeburg, Oct 1768 daughter of Joseph and Mary (Abbott) Walker; d. at Fryeburg, 19 Aug 1848; m. EBENEZER STEVENS, b. Oct 1767 son of John Stevens; John d. 1 Apr 1851.

Ruth and Ebenezer lived in Fryeburg and little is known of their family. There is one child known, son William. It is also possible that Mary Stevens born in Fryeburg is their daughter, but this cannot be established. However, she is listed here. Mary Stevens married the brother of the wife of William Stevens.

i WILLIAM STEVENS, b. at Fryeburg, 1792; d. at Fryeburg, 4 Dec 1866; m. at Conway, 30 Nov 1817, DEBORAH PAGE KELLEY, b. at Conway, 21 May 1795 daughter of Edmund and Elizabeth (Walker) Kelley; Deborah d. at Fryeburg, 19 Mar 1884.

ii MARY STEVENS, b. at Fryeburg, Oct 1794; d. at Conway, 15 Apr 1878; m. at Fryeburg, 29 Mar 1819, ISAAC WALKER KELLEY, b. at Conway, 9 Aug 1791 son of Edmund and Elizabeth (Walker) Kelley; Isaac d. at Conway, 14 Nov 1882.

1008) JEREMIAH BALLARD WALKER *(Mary Abbott Walker⁴, Nathaniel³, Nathaniel², George¹)*, b.at Fryeburg, 8 Dec 1777 son of Joseph and Mary (Abbott) Walker; d. at Whitefield, NH, 19 Oct 1841; m. his first cousin, HANNAH WALKER, b. 1781 daughter of Samuel and Hannah (Hazeltine) Walker; Hannah d. at Whitefield, 15 Jan 1855.

Jeremiah and Hannah Walker were parents of eight children born at Chatham, New Hampshire.

i POLLY ABBOTT WALKER, b. 9 Jan 1804; d. at Whitefield, NH, 5 Mar 1862; m. RALPH FISKE, b. at Lunenburg, 7 May 1804 son of Asa and Betsey (Henry) Fiske; Ralph d. at Whitefield, 26 Dec 1893.

[2679] Maine, Oxford County, Probate Estate Files, File Number S96, 1822-1833, Estate File of John Stevens, accessed through familysearch.org

[2680] Kelly, *Genealogical Account of the Descendants of John Kelly*, p 76

ii HENRY STEVENS WALKER, b. 23 Apr 1805; d. at Whitefield, NH, 24 Aug 1874; m. at Bethlehem, NH, 23 Nov 1842, ELVIRA KELSO, b. at Bethlehem, 26 Mar 1814 daughter of William and Zerviah (Woodbury) Kelso; Elvira d. at Whitefield, 29 Jun 1884. Elvira married second Jeremiah W. Stevens at Whitefield 1 Apr 1876.

iii HAZEN CLEMENT WALKER, b. 18 Feb 1807; Hazen d. at Lancaster, NH, 30 Sep 1872; m. at Whitefield, 14 Jan 1841, FANNY E. GREENWOOD, b. at Bethel, 3 Dec 1820 daughter of Holica and Julia (Twitchell) Greenwood; Fanny d. at Lancaster, 14 Feb 1877.

iv CALEB WALKER, b. 1 Apr 1809; d. at Whitefield, 16 Jan 1885; m. 1st, at Whitefield, 16 Oct 1835, MARY CAMPBELL MONTGOMERY, b. at Whitefield, 27 Jun 1814 daughter of Thomas and Martha (Woodbury) Montgomery; Mary d. 15 Apr 1855. Caleb m. 2nd, ANN ESTHER WHEEDON, b. at Dartford, Kent, England, 1819 daughter of Charles and Elizabeth (Allard) Wheedon; Ann d. 20 Oct 1893.

v JAMES WALKER, b. 5 Jul 1811; d. at Whitefield, 8 Apr 1863; m. 13 Mar 1846, SARAH WEARE, b. at Whitefield, 25 Aug 1823 daughter of Nathaniel and Elsie (Couch) Weare; Sarah d. at Whitefield, 27 Jul 1902.

vi ANNA MARIAH WALKER, b. 7 Apr 1813; d. at Whitefield, 18 Jul 1876; m. at Whitefield, 28 Mar 1837, BELA JOHNSON, b. 1812, "of Whitefield"; Bela d. at Whitefield, 22 Jun 1851.

vii JEREMIAH WALKER, b. 5 Jun 1815. It is not clear what became of Jeremiah. He is possibly the Jeremiah Walker that married Mary Jane E. Jones in Boston on 1 Nov 1840, but that cannot be determined.

viii SETH C. WALKER, b. 14 Aug 1817; d. at Philadelphia, 13 Jan 1890; m. at Boston, 3 Aug 1848, SARAH ELIZABETH JANES, b. at Charlestown, MA, 19 Mar 1827 daughter of Elihu and Sarah (Jarvis) Janes; Sarah d. at Somerville, 3 Oct 1898.

1009) NAMAH WALKER *(Mary Abbott Walker⁴, Nathaniel³, Nathaniel², George¹)*, b. at Fryeburg, Nov 1778 daughter of Joseph and Mary (Abbott) Walker; d. at Fryeburg, 3 Dec 1844; m. SAMUEL STEVENS, b. 11 Jun 1773 son of John Stevens; Samuel d. at Fryeburg, 7 Oct 1849.

Namah Walker and Samuel Stevens resided in Fryeburg throughout their lives.

Daughter Mary Stevens did not marry. In her will dated 9 December 1862 (proved third Tuesday of March 1863), Mary Stevens bequeathed one hundred dollars to each of three sisters: Judith Clarke wife of John Clarke, Namah Bucknell formerly Namah Stevens, and Ruth Thoms wife of Zenos P. Thoms. Brothers Samuel Stevens and Joseph W. Stevens each receive one dollar. Sister Abigail Tibbetts wife of Samuel Tibbetts receives two hundred dollars, two shawls, and a cloak. Niece Mary Abby Tibbetts receives two hundred dollars and bedding. Niece Esther Thoms receives a gold necklace. Niece Ann B. Thoms receives a bosom pin and ear drops. The remainder of the wardrobe is to be divided among her sisters and nieces. The remainder of the estate goes to brother-in-law Samuel Tibbetts who is also named executor.[2681]

Namah Walker and Samuel Stevens were parents of eight children all born at Fryeburg, Maine.

i JUDITH WALKER, b. 29 Mar 1801; d. at Hiram, ME, 8 May 1883; m. at Hiram, 29 Mar 1857, JOHN CLARKE, b. about 1797; John d. at Hiram, after 1870.

ii NAMAH STEVENS, b. about 1804; d. at Hiram, 20 Sep 1864; m. about 1839, JOHN BUCKNELL, b. about 1785; John d. at Hiram, 1861. John was first married to Hannah who died in 1838.

iii DOROTHY STEVENS, b. 14 Sep 1806; d. 14 Jan 1839. Dorothy did not marry.

iv RUTH STEVENS, b. 29 Dec 1808; d. at Fryeburg, 12 Jan 1890; m. 28 Nov 1836, ZENOS P. THOMS, b. 6 Mar 1806; Zenos d. at Fryeburg, 6 Jan 1866. Zenos was first married to Esther Wiley who died in 1835.

v SAMUEL STEVENS, b. 4 Feb 1811; d. at Fryeburg, 7 Mar 1881; m. his first cousin once removed, MARY ANN STEVENS, b. at Fryeburg, 6 Dec 1817 daughter of Joseph and Mary L. (Steele) Stevens; Mary Ann d. at Chatham, NH, 19 May 1910.

vi MARY STEVENS, b. 4 Jun 1813; d. at Fryeburg, 4 Jan 1863. Mary did not marry.

vii JOSEPH WALKER STEVENS, b. about 1815; d. at Fryeburg, 3 Oct 1886; m. at Chatham, NH, 31 Dec 1849, SARAH C. GORDON, b. 6 Mar 1823 daughter of Joseph and Mary (Dresser) Gordon; Sarah d. at Fryeburg, 2 Feb 1901.

[2681] *Maine. Probate Court (Oxford County);* Probate Place: *Oxford, Maine, Drawer S100, Scribner, William P -Sylvester, Hervey, 1862-1868*

viii ABIGAIL STEVENS, b. 5 Apr 1818; d. at Fryeburg, 12 Aug 1867; m. SAMUEL TIBBETTS, b. 8 Dec 1809; Samuel d. at Fryeburg, 13 Sep 1883.

1010) JAMES MOOR *(Hannah Abbott Moor⁴, Nathaniel³, Nathaniel², George¹)*, b. at Pembroke, about 1760 son of Ephraim and Hannah (Abbott) Moor; d. at Waterville, ME, 27 Aug 1835; m. Nov 1779, ABIGAIL NOYES, b. at Bow, 28 Jan 1764 daughter of John and Mary (Fowler) Noyes; Abigail d. at Monroe, NH, 1 Feb 1842.

James and Abigail had their children in Bow, but then relocated to Stanstead, Québec in 1804 and were later in Hatley.[2682] They did return to the United States and James died at Waterville, Maine.

In her will written 16 March 1841 (probate March 11842), Abigail Moor bequeathed one dollar to each of her children or their heirs: eldest son John Moor, eldest daughter Hannah Farnum, son Rodney Moor, son Thomas Moor, heirs-at-law of son James Moor, heir-at-law of son Washington Moor, son Jacob Moor, son Isaac W. Moor, son Ephraim Moor, and daughter Nancy Moor. The rest of the estate is to be used by the executor to purchase real estate for the sole use of daughter Nancy during her natural life. After Nancy's decease, this bequest goes to Nancy's heirs. Richard P. Moor is named executor.[2683] Richard P. Moor is Nancy's son with her husband Archibald Moore.

James Moor and Abigail Noyes were parents of ten children born at Bow, New Hampshire.

i JOHN MOOR, b. 5 Oct 1781; d. at Waterville, ME, after 1850; m. BETSEY, b. in MA, about 1787.

ii HANNAH MOOR, b. 23 Nov 1784; m. at Bow, 10 Apr 1806, JOHN FARNUM, b. at Pembroke, 6 May 1782 son of David and Mary (Poor) Farnum.

iii RODNEY MOOR, b. 23 Oct 1786; d. at Farmington, ME, 1872; m. HANNAH PERRY, b. at Hopkinton, MA, 14 Nov 1796 daughter of Moses and Hannah (Adams) Perry; Hannah d. at Farmington, 1880.

iv THOMAS MOOR, b. 5 Dec 1787; d. at Hatley, Québec, after 1871; m. about 1813, MARGARET DICKEY, b. at Epsom, 1795; Margaret d. after 1871.

v JAMES MOOR, b. 29 Mar 1791; d. at Greenwich, NY, 18 Jul 1831; m. his third cousin, SILVA SKINNER *(Lucy Abbott Skinner⁵, Joseph⁴, Joseph³, Nathaniel², George¹)*, b. at Nelson, NH, 26 Mar 1795 daughter of Pepperell and Lucy (Abbott) Skinner; Silva d. at Greenwich, 10 Oct 1837. Silva Skinner is a child in Family 1065.

vi WASHINGTON MOOR, b. 27 Mar 1793; d. before 1841 (mother's will); he did marry and have children, but his family has not been identified.

vii JACOB GREEN MOOR, b. 23 Feb 1796; d. at Belleville, Ontario, 15 Dec 1850; m. 27 Oct 1821, NANCY HICKEY, b. at Williamsburg, Ontario, 6 Dec 1804 daughter of John and Margaret (Casselman) Hickey; Nancy d. at Stormont, Ontario, 3 Sep 1869.

viii ISAAC WHITE MOOR, b. 24 May 1798; d. at Swanville, ME, 3 Feb 1881; m. MALINDA, b. at Swanville, about 1802; Malinda d. at Monroe, ME, 9 May 1877.

ix EPHRAIM MOOR, b. 4 Jul 1800; d. after 1841.

x NANCY MOOR, b. 8 Mar 1802; d. at Monroe, NH, 1 Sep 1884; m. 19 Feb 1824, ARCHIBALD MOORE, b. in NH, 1798 son of William and Martha (-) Moore; Archibald d. at Monroe, 1 Oct 1881.

1011) MOSES MOOR *(Hannah Abbott Moor⁴, Nathaniel³, Nathaniel², George¹)* (twin of Aaron), b. at Pembroke, about 1762 son of Ephraim and Hannah (Abbott) Moor; m. 22 Nov 1788, ESTHER MOOR, b. at Pembroke, 6 Oct 1769 daughter of Robert and Ruhamah (Mitchell) Moor; Esther d. at Monroe, 6 Sep 1830. Moses m. 2nd, about 1831, MIRIAM BLAKE, b. about 1786; Miriam d. after 1870 when she was living in Littleton, NH.[2684]

Moses and Esther Moor were parents of eight children, the births of the oldest four children recorded at Bath, New Hampshire and the younger children likely born at Monroe.[2685]

i ELIZABETH "LIZZIE" MOOR, b. about 1790; d. at Newbury, VT, 3 Sep 1854; m. at Monroe, NH, 10 Jan 1805; ALEXANDER FERGUSON, b. in Scotland, 1778 son of Alexander and Agnes (Heatherick) Ferguson; Alexander d. at Monroe, 21 Mar 1830.

[2682] Hubbard, *Forests and Clearings*, p 291

[2683] *New Hampshire. Probate Court (Grafton County);* Probate Place: *Grafton, New Hampshire*, volume 24, p 355

[2684] The History of Ryegate suggests there was a second son named Moses who married Miriam Blake, but the census records clearly show that Moses the elder married Miriam who was about 25 years his junior.

[2685] Johnson, *History of Monroe, NH*, p 641

ii NANCY MOOR, b. 1790; m. 15 Jul 1813, RICHARD LAKEMAN, b. at Pembroke, 20 Jun 1784 son of Nathaniel and Elizabeth (Haggett) Lakeman; Richard d. at Groton, NH, 16 Sep 1824.

iii SAMUEL F. MOOR, b. 1796; m. at Bath, 7 Sep 1819, HANNAH LANG, b. in NH, about 1800.

iv MOSES MOOR, b. 1799; d. 10 Nov 1855; m. 1st, at Bath, 14 Mar 1832, ADELINE DODGE, b. about 1810; Adeline d. about 1842. Moses m. 2nd, 17 Jul 1843, MARGARET ANN BURBANK, b. at Barnet, VT, about 1825 daughter of Hazen and Hannah (Garland) Burbank.

v HANNAH MOOR, b. Jul 1806; d. at St. Johnsbury, VT, 24 Jul 1871; m. at Bath, 14 Mar 1832, CALVIN JEWETT WRIGHT, b. 19 Jun 1806 son of Walter and Rebecca (Brockway) Wright; Calvin d. at St. Johnsbury, 21 Dec 1883.

vi ROBERT MOOR, b. about 1805; reported to have gone to Chicago;[2686] nothing further known.

vii MARY ANN MOOR, b. 1807; d. at Monroe, 2 Dec 1830.

viii RUHAMAH MOOR, b. about 1811; m. at Bath, 25 Apr 1832, CHARLES NEGUS, b. in MA, about 1811. Charles and Ruhamah were living in Lyman, NH in 1850.

Moses Moor and Miriam Blake were parents of one child.

i ROBERT B. MOORE, b. at Monroe, NH, 27 Aug 1832; d. at Chicago, IL, 19 Apr 1919; m. at Chicago, 16 Jan 1858, CAROLINE S. ELKINS, b. in VT, 14 Nov 1838 daughter of John G. and Lucina (Titus) Elkins;[2687] Caroline d. at Chicago, 20 May 1911.

1012) HANNAH MOOR *(Hannah Abbott Moor⁴, Nathaniel³, Nathaniel², George¹)*, b. at Pembroke, about 1772 daughter of Ephraim and Hannah (Abbott) Moor; d. 3 Jan 1828; m. about 1791, WILLIAM NEILSON, b. 1767 at Erskine, Renfrewshire, Scotland son of William and Jean (Stewart) Neilson;[2688] William d. at Lyman, NH, 19 Sep 1830. William married second Hannah Nelson. The father of William rewrote his will 29 Sep 1830 naming the children of William, who was then deceased, among his heirs.

William was born in Scotland and came to America with his parents in 1774. William was first with his brother Robert in Ryegate, Vermont and later settled in Monroe, New Hampshire.

In his will written 29 September 1830, grandfather William Neilson of Ryegate made bequests to his grandchildren the children of his son William: William Nelson, Hannah Stevens wife of Michael Stevens, John Nelson, Richard A. Nelson, Robert S. Nelson, Benjamin Nelson, Maria Nelson, and Horatio Nelson.[2689]

Hannah Moor and William Neilson were parents of nine children, the births of the oldest eight children record at Lyman, New Hampshire and the birth of the youngest child recorded at Monroe.

i WILLIAM NEILSON, b. 2 Jul 1793; d. 9 Nov 1840; m. at Bath, 8 Jan 1818, LIMA HIBBARD, b. at Bath, 11 Jun 1796 daughter of Aaron and Sarah (Merrill) Hibbard; Lima d. at Newbury, VT, after 1854. Lima married second William Scott.

ii ELSIE NEILSON, b. 9 Apr 1795; d. at Lyman, 3 Aug 1818.

iii HANNAH NEILSON, b. 22 Oct 1799; d. at Bath, 15 Feb 1833; m. about 1825, MICHAEL M. STEVENS, b. at Lyman, 1800 son of Timothy and Mary (Sanborn) Stevens; Michael d. at Bethlehem, NH, 11 Apr 1851.

iv JOHN NEILSON, b. 16 Oct 1801; d. at Monroe, 15 Feb 1865; m. 15 Jan 1823, HARRIET KELSEA, b. at Derby, VT, about 1803 daughter of Daniel Kelsea; Harriet d. at Monroe, 23 Apr 1885.

v RICHARD A. NEILSON, b. 1806; d. at Monroe, 19 Nov 1849; m. his first cousin once removed, MARGARET FERGUSON *(Elizabeth Moor Ferguson⁶, Moses Moor⁵, Hannah Abbott Moor⁴, Nathaniel³, Nathaniel², George¹)*, b. at Monroe, 12 Sep 1809 daughter of Alexander and Elizabeth (Moor) Ferguson; Margaret d. at Monticello, IL, 1878.

2686 Johnson, *History of Monroe, NH*, p 641

2687 The names of Caroline's parents are given on her death record as John G. Elkins and Lucina Titus.

2688 Genealogical and Family History of the State of Maine, volume 4, p 1910

2689 *New Hampshire. Probate Court (Grafton County)*; Probate Place: *Grafton, New Hampshire*, Probate Records, volume 14, pp 297-298

vi ROBERT STEWART NEILSON, b. 1808; d. at Hillsborough, IL, 1858; m. at Lyman, 25 Apr 1830, ELIZA KELSEA, b. at Derby, about 1811 daughter of Daniel and Mary (Mansfield) Kelsea; Eliza d. 20 Aug 1860. Eliza is the half-sister of Harriet Kelsea who married Robert's brother John.

vii BENJAMIN NEILSON, b. 9 Aug 1812; d. in IL, 1884; m. 18 Apr 1833, EMILY MOORE, b. at Lyman, 18 Feb 1816 daughter of James Moore.

viii MARY GARDNER "MARIA" NEILSON, b. at Lyman, 10 Jan 1815; d. at Littleton, NH, 15 Mar 1885; m. 13 Jan 1836, EBEN W. BLAKE, b. Bridgton, ME, 13 Apr 1810 son of Freeman and Mary (-) Blake; Eben d. at Littleton, 25 Aug 1875.

ix HORATIO NEILSON, b. 11 Sep 1818; d. at Bunker Hill, IL, 29 Jul 1898; m. 1836, ANGELINE MOORE, b. at Lyman, 21 Apr 1818 daughter of James Moore; Angeline d. 18 Jun 1877.

1013) MARTHA "PATTY" MOOR *(Hannah Abbott Moor⁴, Nathaniel³, Nathaniel², George¹)*, b. at Pembroke, 1779 (based on age at time of death) daughter of Ephraim and Hannah (Abbott) Moor; d. at Barnet, VT, 7 May 1827; m. at Barnet, VT, 6 Nov 1801, ALEXANDER BUCHANAN, b. in Scotland 4 Sep 1771 son of Peter and Anabel (Miller) Buchanan; Alexander d. at Barnet, 2 Oct 1853.[2690] Alexander m. 2nd, Deborah.

Patty Moor and Alexander Buchanan were parents of eight children born at Barnet.

i PETER BUCHANAN, b. Apr 1801; d. at Barnet, 24 Nov 1853; m. about 1822, MARGARET KENNEDY, b. in Scotland, 1 Aug 1798 daughter of Ronald and Jane (Buchanan) Kennedy; Margaret d. at Barnet, 8 Apr 1877.

ii JAMES BUCHANAN, b. 2 Apr 1802; d. at Johnson County, IA, 18 Nov 1887; m. but name of spouse not yet found. One son of James, William Henry Buchanan born in 1851, has been identified.

iii NANCY AGNES BUCHANAN, b. 3 Apr 1809; d. at Ryegate, VT, 22 Dec 1876; m. at Ryegate, 16 Nov 1828, PETER GIBSON, b. at Renfrewshire, Scotland, 6 Mar 1801 son of William and Margaret (Aitken) Gibson;[2691] Peter d. at Ryegate, 1 May 1866.

iv HENRY BUCHANAN, b. Oct 1810; d. at Cedar County, IA, 30 Jun 1843; m. about 1840, MALINDA MASON, b. in OH, 1823 daughter of William and Margaret (Morgan) Mason; Malinda d. at Cedar County, 30 Oct 1842.

v MARGARET BUCHANAN, b. 18 Jan 1813; d. at Ryegate, 19 Aug 1897; m. about 1830, WILLIAM MCCOLE, b. at Balfron, Stirlingshire, Scotland, 15 May 1802 son of William and Margaret (Lackie) McCole; William d. at Ryegate, 29 Sep 1865.

vi ALEXANDER BUCHANAN, b. about 1816; d. at Montague, MA, 18 Feb 1896. Alexander did not marry.

vii WILLIAM BUCHANAN, b. 1818; d. at Barnet, 27 Apr 1849.

viii JOHN BUCHANAN, b. about 1821; d. at Danville, VT, 29 Jul 1887; m. at Danville, 1 Jan 1851, ELIZABETH CLIFFORD, b. about 1829; Elizabeth was living in Danville in 1880.

1014) DOLLY MOOR *(Hannah Abbott Moor⁴, Nathaniel³, Nathaniel², George¹)*, b. at Pembroke, about 1780 daughter of Ephraim and Hannah (Abbott) Moor; m. at Bow, 29 Jan 1801,[2692] ELISHA UPTON, b. about 1779 son of Elisha and Sarah (Gilford) Upton; Elisha d. at Parishville, NY, 1854.[2693][2694]

Dolly and Elisha married in Bow, but were then in Bath, New Hampshire, then Jay, New York and finally in Parishville. *The Upton Memorial* lists seven children for this family[2695] and little information was located for them.

i JOHN UPTON, b. about 1809; d. at Brattleboro, VT, 13 Jan 1889; m. ORINDA W., b. Sep 1809;[2696] Orinda d. at Troy, 16 Dec 1865.

ii SUSAN UPTON

iii OTIS UPTON

[2690] The graves of Martha and Alexander Buchanan are in Barnet Center Cemetery and the gravestones include dates of death and age at time of death. Alexander's gravestone includes that he was a native of Scotland (findagrave.com)

[2691] Miller, *History of Ryegate*, p 352

[2692] *Bow, NH: The Town Book of Bow, New Hampshire, 1760-1877, p 233 (americanancestors.org)*

[2693] Vinton, *The Upton Memorial*, p 224

[2694] Year: 1850; Census Place: Parishville, Saint Lawrence, New York; Roll: M432_590; Page: 124A; Image: 517. Elisha Upton, age 71, living in a household headed by his son Guilford Upton. Dolly is apparently deceased.

[2695] Vinton, *The Upton Memorial*, p 224

[2696] Birth calculated based on age 56 years 3 months at time of death

iv HORACE UPTON

v DOLLY UPTON

vi MARY UPTON

vii GUILFORD E. UPTON, b. 3 May 1820; d. at Green Lake, WI, 23 Mar 1905; m. about 1840, LOUISA WARNER,[2697][2698] b. in VT, 1823; Louisa d. at Stevens Point, WI, 1882.

1015) BRUCE WALKER *(Ruth Abbott Walker⁴, Nathaniel³, Nathaniel², George¹)*, b. at Rumford, 17 May 1760 son of James A. and Ruth (Abbott) Walker; d. at Hebron, NH, 27 Jul 1840; m. MEHITABLE CURRIER, b. at Concord, 26 Apr 1762 daughter of William and Mary (Carter) Currier; Mehitable d. at Haverhill, NH, 8 May 1849.

Bruce Walker served as a private in the Revolution and was credited with total service of sixteen months over four enlistments from August 1776 through September 1778.[2699] He made application for his pension 30 August 1832 when he was living in Hebron and the pension was granted. Widow Mehitable Walker received a pension of $44.10 per annum.

Bruce Walker and Mehitable Currier were parents of eleven children born at Concord.[2700]

i DANIEL CARTER WALKER, b. 8 Jan 1781; d. at Bridgewater, NH, 27 May 1859; m. 1st, 9 Nov 1805, HANNAH HAZELTON, b. at Hebron, 18 Jan 1784 daughter of Samuel and Mary (Farley) Hazelton; Hannah d. at Hebron, 2 Feb 1850. Daniel m. 2nd, 7 Jul 1850, HULDAH PIKE (widow of Peter Sanborn), b. at Hollis, 1784 daughter of James and Ruth (-) Pike; Huldah d. at Bridgewater, NH, 10 Sep 1874.

ii MARY WALKER, b. 4 Dec 1782; d. at Hebron, 25 Dec 1870; m. 1804, DANIEL HAZELTON, b. at Hebron, 6 Jun 1781 son of Samuel and Mary (Farley) Hazelton; Daniel d. at Hebron, 31 Aug 1850.

iii NATHANIEL WALKER, b. 4 Jan 1785; d. at Haverhill, NH, 27 Jun 1844; m. at Plymouth, NH, 23 Jan 1817, LUCY DOE, b. at Rumney, 1794 daughter of John and Mary (Sanborn) Doe; Lucy d. at Manchester, NH, 9 Feb 1883.

iv ISAAC WALKER, b. 1 Feb 1787

v JOHN WALKER, b. 4 May 1789

vi SARAH WALKER, b. about 1791

vii ELIZA WALKER, b. about 1793; died young

viii NANCY WALKER, b. 29 Aug 1796; d. at Havana, IL, 12 Nov 1860; m. 22 Jun 1815, JONATHAN DEARBORN, b. at Plymouth, NH, 18 Jun 1793 son of Samuel and Abigail (Ward) Dearborn; Jonathan d. at Havana, 5 Mar 1862.

ix RUTH WALKER, b. about 1799

x ELIZA WALKER, b. about 1801

xi JAMES WALKER, b. at Hebron, about 1802; d. at Windsor, MA, 28 Apr 1880; m. 1st, at Hebron, 1 Jul 1824, ELIZA STAFFORD; Eliza d. about 1835. James m. 2nd, at Lowell, 11 Oct 1835, LUCINDA DUNBAR, b. at Haverhill, NH, 1814 likely daughter of Sylvester and Hannah (Powers) Dunbar; Lucinda d. at Goshen, MA, 30 Apr 1855. James m. 3rd, at Great Barrington, 15 Feb 1863, BELINDA AXTELL (widow of Adolphus Draper),[2701] b. at Sutton, MA, 1799 daughter of William and Rebekah (Axtell) Axtell; Belinda d. at Windsor, 22 May 1882.

1016) JOHN WALKER *(Ruth Abbott Walker⁴, Nathaniel³, Nathaniel², George¹)*, b. at Rumford, 8 May 1763 son of James A. and Ruth (Abbott) Walker; d. at Bethel, ME, 25 Feb 1825; m. ELIZABETH CALEF, b. at Kingston, NH, 1 Oct 1767 daughter of Joseph and Hannah (Pettingill) Calef;[2702] Elizabeth d. at Bethel, 14 Nov 1829.

John Walker and Elizabeth Calef were parents of seven children, the two oldest children born at Salisbury, New Hampshire and the younger children at Bethel, Maine.

2697 Louisa's maiden name is given on the death record of her daughter Lucy.

2698 In 1850, father Elisha Upton was living in the household with Guilford and Louisa Upton in Parishville, NY.

2699 Revolutionary War Pension and Bounty-Land Warrant Application Files, Case W18272

2700 Abbot, *Genealogical Register*, p 124

2701 The marriage record for James and Belinda gives the names of James's parents as Bruce and Mehitable.

2702 The 1810 will of Joseph Calef includes a bequest to his daughter Elizabeth Walker.

i JAMES WALKER, b. 8 Jul 1791; d. at Bethel, 7 Dec 1866; m. 21 Feb 1822, HANNAH JACKMAN BARKER, b. at Londonderry, NH, 26 Jul 1801 daughter of John and Mary (Jackman) Barker; Hannah d. at Bethel, 27 Aug 1874.

ii JOSEPH CALEF WALKER, b. 1793; d. at Waterford, ME, 10 Apr 1881; m. LUCINDA HALE, b. at Waterford, about 1798 daughter of Oliver and Eunice (Fletcher) Hale; Lucinda d. at Waterford, after 1860.

iii HANNAH WALKER, b. 12 Mar 1796; m. at Mercer, ME, 15 Oct 1819, ISAAC PRESSEY.

iv ABIEL WALKER, b. about 1797; d. at Milan, NH, after 1870; m. 1st, about 1830, ARMINA STEVENS, b. about 1805; d. at Dummer, NH, before 1850. Abiel m. 2nd, at Dummer, 15 Apr 1860, 15 Apr 1860, CHRISTINA ROBBINS, b. at Milan, NH, 29 Jun 1824 daughter of Moses and Hannah (-) Robbins.

v RUTH WALKER, b. about 1799; d. *perhaps* at Concord, 5 May 1845. Ruth does not seem to have married.

vi ELIZA WALKER, b. Aug 1802; d. at Bethel, 11 Jan 1835.

vii CHARLES WALKER, b. 7 Aug 1809; m. at Bridgton, ME, 23 Nov 1835, LOUISA BARKER, b. 1807; Louisa d. at Lovell, 14 Aug 1839.

1017) JAMES WALKER *(Ruth Abbott Walker4, Nathaniel3, Nathaniel2, George1)*, b. at Concord, 26 Jul 1778 son of James A. and Ruth (Abbott) Walker; d. at Milton, NH, 4 Sep 1826; m. ABIGAIL CHAPMAN, b. at Methuen, 29 Dec 1778 daughter of Eliphaz and Hannah (Jackman) Chapman; Abigail d. 3 Oct 1807. James m. 2nd, PATTY HEATH INGALLS,[2703] b. 8 Aug 1786 daughter of Moses and Susan (Heath) Ingalls; Patty d. at Somersworth, NH, Dec 1865.[2704]

James Walker and Abigail Chapman were parents of three children born at Bethel.

i MILTON CHAPMAN WALKER, b. 1805; d. at Lincoln, MA, 4 Sep 1872; m. at Wakefield, NH, 28 Jan 1828, ELIZA M. RICHARDS, b. at Brookfield, NH, 5 Oct 1808 daughter of Ichabod and Anna (Hurd) Richards; Eliza d. at Lincoln, 16 Jul 1881.

ii ABIGAIL CHAPMAN WALKER, b. 1806; d. before 1810.

iii JAMES MILTON WALKER, b. and d. 1807.

James Walker and Patty Ingalls were parents of four children born at Bethel.

i ABIGAIL CHAPMAN WALKER, b. 14 Jun 1811; d. at Somersworth, NH, 6 Jun 1888. Abigail did not marry.

ii ROBERT INGALLS WALKER, b. 24 Sep 1813; d. at Somersworth, 17 May 1857; m. 5 Oct 1848, MEHITABLE MORSE CHAMBERLAIN, b. at Lebanon, ME, 10 Feb 1822 daughter of Amos and Charlotte (Tarr) Chamberlain; Mehitable d. at Somersworth, 15 Apr 1904.

iii JAMES ABBOTT WALKER, b. 14 Dec 1815; d. 1 Dec 1825.

iv BETSY INGALLS WALKER, b. 22 Mar 1818; d. at Somersworth, 1 Apr 1900. Betsy did not marry.

1018) PETER WALKER *(Ruth Abbott Walker4, Nathaniel3, Nathaniel2, George1)*, b. at Concord, 6 Jul 1780 son of James A. and Ruth (Abbott) Walker; d. at Fryeburg, ME, 2 Jun 1857; m. 3 Jan 1808, ABIGAIL SWAN, b. 15 Dec 1787 daughter of Joseph Greely and Elizabeth (Evans) Swan; Abigail d. at Boston, 26 Jan 1861.[2705][2706]

Peter Walker and Abigail Swan were parents of seven children.

i WILLIAM SWAN WALKER, b. 12 Dec 1810; d. 1 Apr 1836. William did not marry.

ii GALEN CARTER WALKER, b. at Bethel, 4 Dec 1814; d. at Charlestown, MA, 15 Dec 1856; m. at Wethersfield, CT, 10 Nov 1845, LOIS CLEVELAND PILLSBURY, b. in NH, about 1820 daughter of Moses Cross and Lois (Cleveland) Pillsbury; Lois d. at Jacksonville, IL, 2 Apr 1900.

iii LYMAN ABBOTT WALKER, b. at Bethel, 28 Oct 1817; d. at Concord, NH, 25 Apr 1893; m. 14 Nov 1843, LUCY ANN PRATT, b. at Hebron, NH, 20 Jul 1817 daughter of Joseph S. and Sarah (Walker) Pratt; Lucy d. at Concord, 13 Feb 1891.

2703 Foster and Walker, "The Walkers of Woburn," p 108

2704 Burleigh, *Genealogy of the Ingalls Family*, p 96

2705 Evans, *Descendants of David Evans*, p 18

2706 Abigail Swan Walker died at the asylum in Boston. She was living in Concord in 1860.

iv CLEMENT ADAMS WALKER, b. at Fryeburg, 3 Jul 1820; d. at Boston, 26 Apr 1883; m. 30 Jan 1856, GEORGIANNA NICHOLS, b. in CT, about 1832 daughter of William Hanford and Mary Burr (Bartram) Nichols; Georgianna d. likely at Bridgeport, CT, after 1910. Clement was a physician. He graduated Dartmouth College in 1842 and Harvard Medical School in 1850.

v CHARLES WEBSTER WALKER, b. at Fryeburg, 25 Nov 1822; d. at Plainfield, NJ, 21 Jun 1861. Charles was commissioned as an officer with rank of 1st Lieutenant at his enlistment 11 May 1861. He served in Company B of the New Hampshire 2nd Infantry beginning 1 June 1861 and died at Plainfield, NJ, 21 Jun 1861.[2707]

vi JUDITH WALKER, b. at Fryeburg, 26 Apr 1826; d. at Boston, 29 Aug 1914; m. 15 Jan 1857, as his second wife, JOSEPH ANDREWS, b. at Salem, 10 Dec 1808 son of Joseph and Mary (Bell) Andrews; Joseph d. at Boston, 8 Feb 1869. Joseph Andrews was first married to Elizabeth Maria Sprague.

vii HENRY DURGIN WALKER, b. at Fryeburg, 1 Sep 1829; d. at Boston, 9 Jan 1882; m. at Boston, 15 Aug 1853, SUSAN LAURETTA ANDREWS, b. about 1831.

1019) NATHANIEL ABBOT *(Joshua⁴, Nathaniel³, Nathaniel², George¹)*, b. at Concord, 28 Oct 1769 son of Joshua and Eliza (Chandler) Abbot; d. at Concord, 25 Nov 1848; m. at Chester, NH, 10 Feb 1793, ELIZABETH DEARBORN, b. at Chester, 1 Feb 1772 daughter of John S. and Mary (Emerson) Dearborn;[2708] Elizabeth d. 7 Jun 1855.

Nathaniel Abbot was a selectman in Concord and served as a member of the state legislature.[2709]

In his will written 5 February 1844 (proved 4 February 1849), Nathaniel Abbot bequeaths to beloved wife Betsey the use of and improvements on all the real and personal estate during her natural life. He gives a bequest of five dollars to each of his children: Fanny Low, John D. Abbott, Mary West, and Emeline Estabrook. After their mother's decease, the children will divide the estate in equal portions. Joseph Low of Concord was named sole executor. In a codicil also written in February 1844, he allows for his daughter Emeline Estabrook to reside in the family home as long as she is unmarried.[2710]

Nathaniel Abbot and Elizabeth Dearborn were parents of four children born at Concord.

i FANNY ABBOTT, b. 26 Oct 1794; d. at Concord, 24 Feb 1867; m. 16 Nov 1815, JOSEPH LOW, b. at Amherst, NH, 24 Jul 1790 son of William and Elizabeth (Crosby) Low; Joseph d. at Concord, 28 Aug 1859.

ii JOHN DEARBORN ABBOTT, b. 22 Feb 1796; d. at Brooklyn, NY, 28 Jul 1854; m. at Concord, 12 Sep 1826, MARY ELIZABETH BARTLETT, b. at Pembroke, 10 Feb 1800 daughter of Caleb and Ruth (McClintock) Bartlett; Mary d. after 1855.

iii MARY ABBOTT, b. 8 Mar 1797; d. at Concord, 1872 (probate 21 Jul 1872); m. at Concord, 29 Oct 1818, JOSEPH CARTER WEST, b. at Salisbury, 29 Apr 1794 son of Edward and Merriam (Badger) West.

iv EMELINE ABBOTT, b. 21 Feb 1811; d. at Concord, 7 Feb 1887; m. 1st, 6 Jul 1829, JOHN ESTABROOK, b. at Hopkinton, NH, 9 Sep 1805 son of Joseph and Emma (Stocker) Estabrook; John d. at Essex, CT, 9 Oct 1833 in an explosion of the boilers of the steamboat *New England*.[2711] Emeline m. 2nd, ROBERT EASTMAN PECKER, b. at Concord, 29 Apr 1807 son of Jeremiah and Ruth (Kimball) Pecker; Robert d. at Concord, 19 Sep 1867. Robert was first married to Esther J. Lang.

1020) BETSY ABBOT *(Joshua⁴, Nathaniel³, Nathaniel², George¹)*, b. at Concord, 6 Aug 1773 daughter of Joshua and Eliza (Chandler) Abbot; d. at Farmington, ME, 30 Jul 1846; m. at Hallowell, 8 Apr 1798, her second cousin, JACOB ABBOT *(Jacob⁴, Joseph³, Nathaniel², George¹)*, b. at Wilton, 20 Oct 1776 son of Jacob and Lydia (Stevens) Abbott; Jacob d. at Farmington, 21 Jan 1847.

Jacob and Betsy Abbot had their children in Hallowell, Maine, but then relocated to Weld, Maine where Jacob had large land holdings. In later life, they were in Farmington.[2712]

2707 U.S., Civil War Soldier Records and Profiles, 1861-1865

2708 The will of John S. Dearborn includes a bequest to his daughter Betsy Abbot; New Hampshire Probate, Rockingham County, 42:30

2709 Bouton, *History of Concord*, p 626

2710 *New Hampshire. Probate Court (Merrimack County)*; Probate Place: *Merrimack, New Hampshire, Probate Records, Vol 25, 1847-1856*, p 83, will 5 Feb 1844, proved 4 Feb 1849.

2711 Bouton, *History of Concord*, p 417

2712 Butler, *A History of Farmington*, p 351

Jacob Abbot did not leave a will, and his estate entered probate February 1847 with Jacob Abbot as administrator.[2713] In the first accounting, personal property was valued at $11,915.89 (inventory not given). Those heirs signing agreement to the accounting by Jacob Abbot were Sallucia Abbot, John S.C. Abbot, Gorham D. Abbot, Clara A. Cutler, Samuel P. Abbot, and Charles E. Abbot.

Jacob and Betsy Abbot were parents of seven children born at Hallowell, Maine.

i SALLUCIA ABBOT, b. 7 Aug 1801; d. at Hallowell, 8 Apr 1886.

ii JACOB ABBOT, b. 14 Nov 1803; d. at Farmington, 31 Oct 1879; m. 18 May 1828, HARRIET VAUGHAN, b. 1808 daughter of Charles and Frances Western (Apthorp) Vaughan; Harriet d. at Farmington, 11 Sep 1843. Jacob Abbott was a writer of children's books best known for the *Rollo* books.

iii JOHN STEVENS CABOT ABBOT, b. 18 Sep 1805; d. at New Haven, CT, 17 Jun 1877; m. at Boston, 1 Aug 1830, JANE WILLIAMS BOURNE, b. in NY, 1810 daughter of Abner and Abigail (Williams) Bourne; Jane d. at New Haven, 18 May 1896.

iv GORHAM DUMMER ABBOT, b. 3 Sep 1807; d. at Natick, MA, 3 Aug 1874; m. at Natick, 11 Feb 1834, REBECCA S. LEACH, b. at Lancaster, MA, 24 Feb 1807 daughter of Joseph and Rebecca (Flagg) Leach; Rebecca d. at Fair Haven, CT, 29 Mar 1876.

v CLARA ANN ABBOT, b. 28 Oct 1809; d. at King, NY, 24 Dec 1888; m. 24 Apr 1843, ELBRIDGE GERRY CUTLER, b. 14 Mar 1812 son of Nathan and Hannah (Moore) Cutler; Elbridge d. at Reading, PA, 28 Apr 1846.

vi CHARLES EDWARDS ABBOT, b. 24 Dec 1811; d. at Hartford, CT, 25 Jul 1880; m. at Nantucket, 25 Nov 1841, MARY ELIZABETH SPAULDING, b. at Ceylon (in current Sri Lanka), about 1822 daughter of the missionaries Levi and Mary (Christie) Spaulding; Mary d. at Los Angeles, 7 Nov 1913.

vii SAMUEL PHILLIPS ABBOTT, b. 8 Dec 1815; d. at Farmington, ME, 29 May 1849; m. at Roxbury, 2 May 1841, HANNAH BARKER, b. at Nottinghamshire, about 1821; Hannah d. at Farmington, 21 Jun 1849. Samuel graduated from Bowdoin College in 1836 and Andover Seminary in 1840.

1021) SARAH "SALLY" ABBOT *(Joshua⁴, Nathaniel³, Nathaniel², George¹)*, b. at Concord, 16 Dec 1775 daughter of Joshua and Eliza (Chandler) Abbot; d. at Hallowell, 1 Dec 1841; m. 29 Apr 1802, GORHAM DUMMER, b. at Hallowell, 27 Sep 1782 son of Nathaniel and Mary (Owen) Dummer; Gorham d. 2 Jan 1805.

The Dummer family was prominent in Kennebec County, Maine having a street named for the family, the donation of a family home to Bowdoin College, and the founding of Dummer Academy through a bequest from Lieutenant Governor William Dummer.[2714] Gorham's father Nathaniel Dummer was the builder of historic Dummer House on Dummer's Lane in Hallowell. This house was slated for relocation in 2018 to make way for a parking lot which will also absorb Dummer's Lane.[2715]

Sarah and Gorham Dummer had one daughter.

i LUCY GORHAM DUMMER, b. at Hallowell, 20 Aug 1802; d. at Hallowell, 13 Aug 1875; m. 24 Apr 1821, SAMUEL KINSMAN GILMAN, b. at Exeter, 2 May 1796 son of Samuel and Martha (Kinsman) Gilman; Samuel d. at Hallowell, 26 Dec 1882.

1022) JOHN SULLIVAN ABBOT *(Joshua⁴, Nathaniel³, Nathaniel², George¹)*, b. at Concord, 20 Aug 1778 son of Joshua and Eliza (Chandler) Abbot; d. 10 Aug 1810; m. his second cousin once removed MARY FAULKNER *(Hannah Abbott Faulkner⁵, Thomas⁴, Thomas³, Thomas², George¹)*, b. 1781 daughter of Abiel and Hannah (Abbott) Faulkner; Mary d. 17 Jun 1840. Mary Faulkner is a child in Family 882.

John Sullivan Abbott and Mary Faulkner were parents of four children.

i ELIZABETH CHANDLER ABBOTT, b. at Boscawen, 18 Feb 1804; d. at Concord, NH, 18 Feb 1895; m. at Littleton, MA, 17 Jun 1824, JOHN C. PILLSBURY, b. at Ipswich, MA 31 May 1802 son of Moses Cross and Lois (Cleveland) Pillsbury; John d. at Concord, 18 Mar 1885.

[2713] *Probate Court (Franklin County);* Probate Place: *Franklin, Maine*, Case 292, Probate of Jacob Abbot, Feb 1847

[2714] Kingsbury, *History of Kennebec County*, p 495.

[2715] Pafundi, Jason, 2018, "Hallowell Planning Board . . ." https://www.centralmaine.com/2018/03/21/hallowell-planning-board-approves-plan-to-relocate-dummer-house/

ii MARY FAULKNER ABBOTT, b. at Boscawen, 22 Apr 1805; d. at Littleton, MA, 19 Dec 1874; m. at Littleton, 22 Sep 1825, HENRY LAWRENCE, b. at Littleton, 28 Oct 1803 son of David and Martha (Adams) Lawrence; Henry d. at Littleton, 27 Oct 1873.

iii THOMAS FAULKNER ABBOTT, b. 20 Feb 1808; d. at Detroit, MI, 29 Apr 1881; m. at Hamilton, OH, 5 Jan 1852, ELIZABETH MILTIMON HALE, b. in NH, 1 Aug 1828 son of Leonard and Elizabeth (Miltimon) Hale; Elizabeth d. at Detroit, 30 May 1908.

iv JOHN SULLIVAN ABBOTT, b. at Concord, 1 Dec 1810; d. 16 Aug 1811.

1023) JOSHUA ABBOT *(Joshua⁴, Nathaniel³, Nathaniel², George¹)*, b. at Concord, 8 Dec 1782 son of Joshua and Eliza (Chandler) Abbot; d. at Norfolk, VA of consumption while serving as a minister, 29 Sep 1824; m. 6 Nov 1808, ELIZA "BETSY" KIMBALL, b. 12 Jul 1787 daughter of Phineas and Lucy (Pearl) Kimball; Betsy d. at Concord 23 Jan 1870.[2716]

Joshua served as a Captain in a cavalry company of Eleventh Regiment of the New Hampshire militia on 21 June 1814, re-appointed in 1817, achieved the rank of Major in 1819 and served until 1820. He was licensed to preach which he undertook in Virginia where he died.[2717]

Joshua Abbot and Eliza Kimball were parents of seven children born at Concord.

i JOSHUA KIMBALL ABBOTT, b. 23 Dec 1810; d. at Cairo, IL, 4 Feb 1863; m. at Detroit, MI, 23 Apr 1842, CYNTHIA H. STORER, b. at East Berlin, PA, 14 Jun 1824; Cynthia d. likely at Grand Blanc, MI, after 1880. After Joshua's death, Cynthia married Joseph T. Dayton.

ii JOHN SULLIVAN ABBOTT, b. 21 Feb 1812; d. at Bloomington, IA, 30 Aug 1840. John did not marry. He was one of the first settlers of Bloomington, Iowa and built the first frame house there.[2718]

iii ANN MATILDA ABBOTT, b. 21 Oct 1813; d. at Concord, 14 Dec 1908; m. 26 Jan 1841, STEPHEN HALL PARKER, b. at Methuen, 16 Dec 1809 son of Winthrop and Lydia (Hall) Parker; Stephen d. at North Andover, MA, 19 Apr 1865.

iv SARAH DUMMER ABBOTT, b. 29 May 1815; d. at Nashville, TN, 6 Nov 1896; m. 21 Sep 1841, WILLIAM KELSEA, b. at Boston, 12 May 1815; d. at Nashville, 10 Aug 1890.

v CHARLES HENRY ABBOTT, b. 7 Sep 1817; d. 28 Sep 1818.

vi CHARLES HENRY ABBOTT, b. 25 Feb 1819; d. at Vicksburg, MS, 22 May 1863; m. at Catskill, NY, 29 Aug 1853, JULIA ANN BEACH, b. in MI about 1835 daughter of John Beach; Julia d. at El Paso, CO, 9 Apr 1886. Julia married second George W. Barnhart. Charles was a Colonel in the 30th Iowa Infantry and killed in battle near Vicksburg. He had a banking house in Muscatine, IA.

vii NATHANIEL PEARL ABBOTT, b. 2 Mar 1821; d. at Concord, 30 Dec 1900. Nathaniel did not marry.

1024) ANNA ABBOTT *(Jeremiah⁴, Nathaniel³, Nathaniel², George¹)*, b. at Concord, 6 Jun 1770 daughter of Jeremiah and Elizabeth (Stickney) Abbott; m. 27 Dec 1789, RICHARD BUSWELL, b. at Kingston, 28 Mar 1761 son of Caleb and Mary (Badger) Buswell; Richard d. at Lebanon, NH, 22 Oct 1835.

Richard Buswell and Anna Abbott resided in Lebanon where they had a farm. In his will dated December 1834 (proved 8 November 1835), Richard Buswell bequeaths to wife Ann one undivided half of all the real estate land and tenements in Lebanon during her natural life. Anna also receives six shares in the Concord Bank and all the household furniture. The other half of the real estate was bequeathed to son Hammond Buswell as well as half of the stock animals. Son James O. Buswell receives five shares in the Bank of Lebanon and five hundred dollars. Daughters Almira Dustin and Anna Thom each receive three hundred dollars. Sons James and Hammond were named executors. In a codicil he adds five shares in the Merrimack County Bank to the bequest to James.[2719]

Anna Abbott and Richard Buswell were parents of six children all born at Lebanon, New Hampshire.

i HAMMOND BUSWELL, b. 7 Jan 1792; d. 18 Nov 1794.

[2716] Morrison and Sharples, *History of the Kimball Family in America, volume 1*, p 340
[2717] Morrison and Sharples, *History of the Kimball Family in America, volume 1*, p 340
[2718] Morrison and Sharples, *History of the Kimball Family in America, volume 1*, p 340
[2719] *New Hampshire. Probate Court (Grafton County)*; Probate Place: *Grafton, New Hampshire, Probate Records, Vol 15-16, 1833-1838*, will of Richard Buswell, p 483

ii HAMMOND BUSWELL, b. 25 Nov 1795; d. at Lebanon, 4 Mar 1859; m. 1st, 25 Dec 1828, MARTHA HALE CONNER, b. 1806 daughter of Daniel and Sarah (Adams) Conner;[2720] Martha d. at Lebanon, 30 Apr 1842. Hammond m. 2nd, about 1843, EMILY M. ROLLINS, m. at Gilmanton, NH, about 1813 daughter of Moses and Betsey (Osgood) Rollins; Emily d. at Lebanon, 15 Sep 1893.

iii JAMES OSGOOD BUSWELL, b. about 1797; d. at Conway, NH, about 1882; m. 17 Nov 1828, HARRIET SAXTON, b. at Lebanon, about 1803; Harriet d. at Derry, NH, 9 Mar 1870.

iv ALMIRA BUSWELL, b. 26 Aug 1801; d. at Galena, OH, 25 Jan 1850; m. 4 Aug 1828, NATHAN DUSTIN, b. 14 Nov 1791 son of Samuel and Eunice Stanley (Martin) Dustin; Nathan d. at Galena, 12 Nov 1872.

v ANNA BUSWELL, b. 12 Jul 1805; d. at Conway, NH, Jul 1869; m. 8 Nov 1830, SAMUEL THOMS, b. about 1807; Samuel d. at Conway, 1858.

vi HAZEN BUSWELL, b. 6 Aug 1807; d. 30 Aug 1821.

1025) ELIZABETH "BETSY" ABBOTT *(Jeremiah4, Nathaniel3, Nathaniel2, George1)*, b. likely at Conway, 1784 daughter of Jeremiah and Elizabeth (Stickney) Abbott; d. at Conway, NH, 26 Nov 1846; m. 22 Apr 1805, THOMAS F. ODELL, b. at Conway, 25 Apr 1775 son of Joseph and Sarah (Ingalls) Odell; Thomas d. 31 Jan 1865.

The executors bond related to the estate of Thomas F. Odell was entered 1 May 1865 and the will was proved 4 April 1865. Unfortunately, the entire first page of the will is missing from the record. The portion of the will that is available includes bequests to daughter Ann B. Atkinson wife of John M. Atkinson, daughter Almira Maxwell wife of George Maxwell, and granddaughter Elizabeth Odell. The remainder of the estate is bequeathed to daughter Sarah F. Sparhawk with son-in-law Charles Sparhawk named executor.[2721]

Betsey Abbott and Thomas Odell were parents of ten children born at Conway, New Hampshire.

i JOHN ABBOTT ODELL, b. 13 May 1805; d. at Conway, 24 Feb 1876; m. at Gorham, ME, 27 Oct 1831, REBECCA SANBORN, b. at Gorham, 1808 daughter of Josedeck and Martha (Murch) Sanborn;[2722] Rebecca d. at Conway, 1 Dec 1873.

ii ARTHUR ODELL, b. 12 Nov 1806. Arthur was a seaman still living in 1836, but further information was not found.

iii MARY STICKNEY ODELL, b. 6 Aug 1809; d. at Mendon, MA, 9 Oct 1884; m. at Paris, ME, about 1836, PRESTON ROBINSON, b. at Paris, ME, 16 Nov 1802 son of John and Susan (Blake) Robinson; Preston d. at West Paris, ME, 29 Jan 1877. Mary and Preston divorced May 1863 in Oxford County ME.[2723] Preston remarried to Phebe Ann.

iv DANIEL INGALLS ODELL, b. 6 Apr 1811; d. at Carleton, Ontario, Canada, 11 Aug 1899; m. HANNAH E. PEAVEY, b. at Portsmouth, NH, about 1815 daughter of Charles and Elizabeth (Johnson) Peavey; Hannah d. at Needham, MA, 6 Apr 1891.

v ELIZABETH ODELL, b. about 1815; d. at Conway, 3 Jan 1887; m. ARNOLD FLOYD, b. at Warner, 20 Jan 1806 son of Daniel and Sarah (Hall) Floyd; Arnold d. at Ossipee, NH, 12 Mar 1885.

vi RICHARD E. ODELL, b. about 1818; d. at Dunleith, IL, after 1900; m. at Erie, OH, 16 Feb 1856, MARY E. MARSHALL, b. in OH, about 1832; Mary d. at Dunleith, after 1880.

vii LUCY JANE ODELL, b. Dec 1818; d. at Newark, NJ, after 1905; m. at Conway, 16 Jun 1859, as his second wife, JAMES C. ODELL, b. about 1817; James d. at Newark, after 1880. James was first married to Mary.

viii ANN B. ODELL, b. about 1822; d. at Madison, NH, 2 Sep 1893; m. JOHN M. ATKINSON, b. about 1822 son of Samuel and Abigail (March) Atkinson; John d. at Madison, 1867 (probate Apr 1867).

ix SARAH F. ODELL, b. about 1824; d. at Conway, 15 Jan 1892; m. 23 Dec 1858, CHARLES SPARHAWK, b. 20 Apr 1812 son of George King and Abigail (Humphreys) Sparhawk; Charles d. at Conway, 30 Sep 1870.

x ALMIRA ODELL, b. about 1829; d. at Eastport, ME, 9 Dec 1915; m. at Conway, 9 Feb 1858, GEORGE H. MAXWELL, b. at Sweden, ME, 23 Apr 1822 son of George and Anna (Town) Maxwell; George d. at Lovell, ME, after 1870.

2720 The 1863 will of Daniel Conner includes a bequest to his daughter Martha Hale Buswell.

2721 *New Hampshire. Probate Court (Carroll County)*; Probate Place: *Carroll, New Hampshire, Probate Packets, No 3835-3931, 1840-1920*

2722 McLellan, *History of Gorham, Maine*, p 754

2723 Maine, Divorce Records, 1798-1891

1026) JEREMIAH ABBOTT *(Jeremiah⁴, Nathaniel³, Nathaniel², George¹)*, b. likely at Conway, about 1785 son of Jeremiah and Elizabeth (Stickney) Abbott; d. not known but before 1846 when his mother's estate was probated (and probably before 1830); m. by 1812, MARY SMITH[2724] of Biddeford, ME.

Jeremiah Abbott and Mary Smith were parents of eight children,[2725] the birth of the oldest child recorded at Saco, Maine and the other children likely at Conway, New Hampshire.

i HIRAM CALVIN ABBOTT, b. 15 May 1812; d. at Conway, 14 Jan 1886; m. 1st, 28 Dec 1846, LAURA A. CHASE daughter of Jonathan T. and Fanny Moody (Bean) Chase; Laura d. at Conway, 29 Nov 1875. Hiram m. 2nd, 8 Nov 1876, MARGARET T. HALL, b. at Bartlett, about 1838 daughter of Jonathan and Lydia (Carleton) Hall.

ii ELEANOR M. ABBOTT, b. about 1815; d. at Lowell, 22 Oct 1879; m. at Lowell, 29 Oct 1842, JAMES H. GREEN, b. in ME, about 1821 son of William and Sophia (-) Green; James d. at Lowell, 10 Jun 1867.

iii ELIZABETH S. ABBOTT, b. 19 Mar 1817; d. at Conway, 18 Nov 1895; m. at Conway, 24 Dec 1842, THOMAS TAYLOR, b. at Sanbornton, 8 Aug 1810 son of Thomas and Sarah (Jewett) Taylor; Thomas d. at Conway, 28 Mar 1858.

iv JOHN ABBOTT, b. about 1820

v MARY ABBOTT, b. about 1822

vi WILLIAM S. ABBOTT, b. about 1827; d. at Conway, 26 Apr 1894; m. 1st, at Boston, 27 Jun 1864, ADELINE M. HUXFORD, b. at Portland, ME, about 1839 daughter of Hiram and Nancy (-) Huxford; Adeline d. about 1875. William m. 2nd, at Boston, 5 Nov 1878, MINNIE AYER, bat Salem, about 1852 daughter of Abel and Clara (McMillan) Ayer; Minnie d. at Boston, 3 Feb 1881. William m. 3rd, about 1884, FANNIE CARSON, b. at Fryeburg, ME, Jun 1855 daughter of John and Sarah (Dinsmore) Carson; Fannie d. at Conway, 13 May 1929.

vii OSGOOD ABBOTT, b. about 1828; d. at Lowell, 6 Mar 1852.

viii HORACE C. ABBOTT, b. about 1829; d. at Madison, NH, 20 Mar 1916; m. at Lowell, 4 Mar 1855, HARRIET C. MASON, b. at Madison, NH, about 1836 daughter of Nathaniel and Abigail (Cook) Mason; Harriet d. at Conway, 6 May 1891.

1027) THOMAS STICKNEY ABBOTT *(Jeremiah⁴, Nathaniel³, Nathaniel², George¹)*, b. at Conway, 24 Aug 1792 son of Jeremiah and Elizabeth (Stickney) Abbott; d. at Portland, ME, 12 Nov 1864; m. 1st, 28 Dec 1818, his third cousin once removed (and George Abbott descendant), BETSEY LOVEJOY, b. at Conway, 19 Apr 1795 daughter of Jeremiah and Elizabeth (Spring) Lovejoy; Betsey d. 1828. Thomas m. 2nd, about 1832, MARY SAYWARD TROTT, b. at Georgetown, ME, 25 Aug 1798 daughter of Joseph Payson and Rachel (McCobb) Trott;[2726] Mary d. at Portland, 16 Mar 1859.

Thomas S. Abbott kept a boarding house in Portland, Maine. He and Betsey Lovejoy were parents of two children born at Conway.

i JAMES ALEXANDER ABBOTT, b. at Conway, 1822; d. at Boston, 11 Jan 1859; m. at Boston, 15 May 1847, HANNAH KITTREDGE, b. at Dover, NH, about 1826 daughter of Jacob Kittredge; Hannah d. at Boston, 15 Apr 1882. James graduated from Dartmouth in 1840 and Harvard Law School in 1843.[2727]

ii JEREMIAH "JERE" ABBOTT, b. at Conway, 16 Mar 1824; d. at Boston, 18 Mar 1895; m. ELLEN MARIA BANGS, b. at Boston, 14 Jul 1831 daughter of George P. and Elizabeth (Simpkins) Bangs;[2728] Ellen d. at Boston, 22 Mar 1920. Jere Abbott was a successful merchant in the iron and steel industry.

Thomas S. Abbott and Mary S. Trott were parents of two children.

[2724] There are discrepancies in the records as to whether her name is Mary or Betsey Smith, but most of the records, such as death records of children, say Mary Smith although at least one of the birth records and one of the death records say Betsey Smith. It is also possible there are two different wives, but there is not a pattern in terms of mother's name given in records (older versus younger children, for example). The *History of Carroll County* gives her name as Mary Smith and the Abbot genealogy says Betsey.

[2725] Merrill, *History of Carroll County, New Hampshire*, p 899

[2726] U.S., Newspaper Extractions from the Northeast, 1704-1930. Mary S. Trott daughter of late Capt. Joseph Trott m. Thomas S. Abbott of Cornish, NH in Bath, ME (Columbian Centinel Sept. 12, 1832)

[2727] Davis, *Professional and Industrial History of Suffolk County, Massachusetts*, volume 1, p. 456

[2728] Names of Elizabeth's parents are given on her death record.

i GEORGE ABBOTT, b. 1834; d. at Portland, 18 Apr 1842.

ii MARGARET ABBOTT, b. at Portland, about 1837; d. at Portland, 24 Aug 1856.

1028) NATHANIEL ABBOTT *(Jeremiah⁴, Nathaniel³, Nathaniel², George¹)*, b. at Conway, about 1797 (based on age at census records) son of Jeremiah and Elizabeth (Stickney) Abbott; d. after 1850; m. his third cousin once removed (and George Abbott descendant), NANCY LOVEJOY, b. about 1805 daughter of Jeremiah and Elizabeth (Spring) Lovejoy.

On 30 January 1864, Nancy Abbott petitioned the probate court for allowance of four hundred dollars from the estate of Nathaniel Abbott for support of life. Nancy also petitions that Samuel B. Shackford be named administrator. In this petition, she states the only heirs are the widow, a son living in California, and a daughter in Maine. The estate was decreed to be insolvent. Claims against the estate totaled $9,070. Samuel Shackford petitioned to sell the entire estate including the widow's dower as selling the whole was thought to be of the most benefit. Nancy assented to the sale on 3 January 1865. The estate was sold for $7,253 and the dower for Nancy was to be based on her current age of fifty-nine. Nancy received the original allowance of $400 and a payment for her dower of $1,294.55.[2729]

There are just two children known for Nathaniel and Nancy Abbott and a possible third child. In addition to the two known children as noted in the probate record, in the 1850 census, there is a 3-year old Walter in the household and Walter is also in the household in 1860, age 12, and a 4-year old Nellie is there is 1860. Nellie likely does not go in this family as Nancy would have been in her 50's when Nellie was born. Walter perhaps is a child in this family, but he had died prior to 1864 when Nathaniel's estate was probated.

i ELIZABETH ABBOTT, b. at Conway, 17 Dec 1832; d. at Bridgton, ME, 9 Nov 1900; m. at Conway, 27 Nov 1862, CHARLES E. HILTON, b. at Bridgton, 12 Mar 1830 son of Nathaniel and Betsey (-) Hilton; Charles d. at Bridgton, 17 Sep 1883. Elizabeth was a teacher prior to her marriage.

ii HENRY ABBOTT, b. at Conway, Nov 1838; d. at Anderson, CA, 1901 (will 6 Dec 1900; probate May 1901); m. 1884, ANNIE L., b. in Tennessee, Sep 1848 (from census records); Annie was living in 1901. Henry was a stage driver, and after settling in California was a fruit grower. Henry and Annie did not have children. The probate notes only Annie as a next of kin, the closest next family being some cousins in Boston whose names were unknown to Annie.

iii WALTER ABBOTT, b. about 1846; d. before 1864 (if he is a child in this family).

1029) DAVID GEORGE *(Dorothy Abbott George⁴, Nathaniel³, Nathaniel², George¹)*, b. at Concord, 4 Jan 1767 son of David and Dorothy (Abbott) George; d. at Concord, 1838; m. 30 Aug 1789, ELIZABETH EMERY, b. at Concord, 30 Apr 1771 daughter of Benjamin and Sarah (Bailey) Emery;[2730] Elizabeth d. 6 Aug 1827.

In his will written 11 April 1838, David George bequeaths to the three children of his son David B. George, one hundred dollars to be divided as follows: $49.50 to Henry Harrison George, $49.50 to Mary E. Fry, and one dollar to Emily George. Daughter Elizabeth Moulton receives $100. Daughter Ruth E. receives $200. Daughter Dolly Osgood receives all the residue of the estate and is named executrix.[2731]

David and Elizabeth George had nine children born at Concord.

i DAVID BAILEY GEORGE, b. 12 Apr 1790; d. at Concord, 18 Dec 1824; m. 21 Jan 1812, his fourth cousin once removed, RHODA CHANDLER *(Zebadiah Chandler⁶, Zebadiah Chandler⁵, Joshua Chandler⁴, John Chandler³, Hannah Abbott Chandler², George¹)*, b. at Andover, 1 Jul 1793 daughter of Zebadiah and Luce (Chandler) Chandler; Rhoda d. at Andover, 20 Jan 1847. After David's death, Rhoda married PHINEAS SHATTUCK *(Isaac Shattuck⁶, Isaac Shattuck⁵, Joanna Chandler Shattuck⁴, Zebadiah Chandler³, Hannah Abbott Chandler², George¹)* as his second wife.

ii CHARLES HENRY GEORGE, b. 11 Aug 1792; d. at New Orleans, 8 Feb 1824.

iii DOLLY GEORGE, b. 23 May 1794; d. after 1850; m. at Concord, 30 Nov 1815, REUBEN OSGOOD, b. about 1792 possibly the son of Reuben and Hannan (Morrill) Osgood; Reuben d. at Concord, 18 Jan 1836.

iv ELIZABETH GEORGE, b. 10 May 1797; d. after 1838 (living at the time of her father's will); m. 24 May 1821, BENNING MOULTON, b. about 1793; Benning's death is not known but was after 1850 when he was serving time in the county jail at Augusta for stealing.[2732]

[2729] *New Hampshire. Probate Court (Carroll County)*; Probate Place: *Carroll, New Hampshire, Probate Packets, No 1-20, 1840-1920*, accessed through ancestry.com

[2730] The 1819 will of Benjamin Emery of Concord includes a bequest to his daughter Elizabeth George.

[2731] *New Hampshire, Wills and Probate Records, 1643-1982*, Author: New Hampshire. Probate Court (Merrimack County); Probate Place: Merrimack, New Hampshire.

[2732] *1850 United States Federal Census*, Year: 1850; Census Place: Augusta, Kennebec, Maine; Roll: M432_256; Page: 6B; Image: 19.

v HANNAH GEORGE, b. 29 Jul 1800; d. at Concord, 11 Apr 1835. Hannah did not marry.

vi RUTH EMERY GEORGE, b. 14 Aug 1802; d. at Hiram, ME, Dec 1876; m. about 1840, JOHN WADSWORTH, b. about 1782 son of Peleg and Elizabeth (Bartlett) Wadsworth; John d. at Hiram, 22 Jun 1860.

vii SARAH GEORGE, b. 26 Feb 1806; d. about 1837 (husband remarried about 1838); m. 24 Dec 1828, AARON PALMER, b. at Bradford, MA, 1805 son of William and Mehitable (Balch) Palmer; d. unknown but after 1850. After Sarah's death, Aaron married Elizabeth Prouse Ladd.

viii MATTHEW OLIVER GEORGE, b. 30 Jun 1809; d. May 1817.

ix GRACE LOW GEORGE, b. 14 Aug 1812; d. at Concord, 29 Mar 1838. Grace did not marry.

1030) HANNAH GEORGE *(Dorothy Abbott George[4], Nathaniel[3], Nathaniel[2], George[1])*, b. 23 at Concord, Jun 1768 daughter of David and Dorothy (Abbott) George; likely died by the early 1790's assuming she had just the one child mentioned in her father's will; married a Mr. Thatcher whose identity has not been found.

The 1816 will of Hannah's father, David George, included a bequest to his grandson George Thatcher the only son of his daughter Hannah who was deceased. To this point nothing else has been discovered about this family.

i GEORGE THATCHER, b. about 1790 and still living in 1816

1031) JANE GEORGE *(Dorothy Abbott George[4], Nathaniel[3], Nathaniel[2], George[1])*, b. at Concord, 22 Apr 1772 daughter of David and Dorothy (Abbott) George; d. after 1830 at Rumford, ME;[2733] m. 6 Jun 1793, JEREMIAH VIRGIN, b. at Concord, 7 Sep 1765 son of William and Mehitable (Stickney) Virgin; Jeremiah died after 1830.

Jane and Jeremiah had their three children in Concord and then relocated to Rumford, Maine. Jeremiah Virgin and Jane Virgin were first members of the congregational church in Rumford which was organized in 1803.[2734] The family had their farm on the Swift River.

Three children have been identified for this family and only one marriage.

i JONATHAN STICKNEY VIRGIN, b. 29 Oct 1793; he is perhaps the Stickney Virgin living in Mexico, ME at the 1860 Census living in the household of Moses Kimball. If this is Jonathan Stickney, he seems to not have married or had children.

ii JOHN VIRGIN, b. 16 Jul 1795

iii HARRIET VIRGIN, b. 1 May 1805; d. at Rumford, 16 Oct 1874; m. at Rumford, 25 Mar 1830, JEREMIAH RICHARDSON, b. in Maine, 16 Sep 1804 son of Jeremiah and Hannah (Connor) Richardson; Jeremiah d. at Rumford, 27 May 1888.

1032) DOLLY GEORGE *(Dorothy Abbott George[4], Nathaniel[3], Nathaniel[2], George[1])*, b. at Concord, 8 Feb 1774 daughter of David and Dorothy (Abbott) George; d. 20 Mar 1861 at Rumford, ME;[2735] m. 5 Aug 1792, BENJAMIN MORSE, b. at Amherst, NH, 24 Jun 1771 son of Benjamin and Rachel (Webster) Morse; Benjamin d. at Rumford, 4 May 1849.

Benjamin was a shoemaker and wool-carder. The family started out in Concord but relocated to Rumford some time after the birth of their third child.

Benjamin and Dolly had three children born in Concord and record of a fourth child born in Rumford, but with a gap of fourteen years between the third and fourth child, so it might be that there are several children missing. The History of Rumford identifies just these four children.[2736]

i SABRINA MORSE, b. at Concord, 14 Nov 1793; m. at Rumford, 7 Mar 1813, her second cousin, NATHANIEL ABBOTT *(Moses[5], Nathaniel[4], Nathaniel[3], Nathaniel[2], George[1])*, b. at Concord, 23 Jun 1787 son of Moses and Mary (Batchelder) Abbott. Nathaniel is a child in Family 983.

[2733] There is an 1830 Census record for Rumford for Jeremiah Virgin that includes a male and female of the ages of Jeremiah and Jane Virgin. A census record from 1840 that would fit with them was not located.

[2734] Lapham, *History of Rumford, Oxford County, Maine*, p 141

[2735] Dorothy Morse, age 86, is listed in the 1860 U.S. Census for Rumford; she is the head of household with Clarissa Morse age 43 living with her.

[2736] Lapham, *History of Rumford*, p. 379.

ii DOLLY MORSE, b. at Concord, 1 Aug 1795; d. at Canton, ME, 3 Nov 1882; m. at Rumford, 1 Jan 1818, THOMAS BRADBURY, b. in Maine, 18 Feb 1791 son of Daniel and Mary (Wingate) Bradbury; Thomas d. at Rumford, 15 Oct 1857.

iii SAINT LUKE MORSE, b. at Concord, 11 Dec 1797; d. after 1850 likely at Manchester, NH; m. at Concord, 13 Feb 1823, his fourth cousin, JUDITH WHEELER *(Sarah Abbott Wheeler^5, Samuel^4, Jonathan^3, Benjamin^2, George^1)*, b. about 1802 daughter of Jeremiah and Sarah (Abbott) Wheeler; Judith d. after 1850. Judith is a child in Family 816.

iv CLARISSA MORSE, b. at Rumford, 13 Jan 1811; d. at Rumford, Dec 1889. Clarissa did not marry.

1033) BETSEY GEORGE *(Dorothy Abbott George^4, Nathaniel^3,* [2737] *Nathaniel^2, George^1)*, b. at Concord, 22 Jan 1776 daughter of David and Dorothy (Abbott) George; d. at Rumford, ME, 2 May 1832; m. 1 Jul 1798, DANIEL MARTIN, b. at Concord, 16 Jul 1772 son of Henry and Esther (Kimball) Martin; Daniel d. 15 Jun 1861.

Daniel Martin was an early settler of Rumford, Maine. He was active in town affairs serving in officer positions in the town and surveyor of highways.

Betsey George and Daniel Martin were parents of ten children born at Rumford, Maine.

i ESTHER MARTIN, b. 27 Jan 1799; d. at Boscawen, NH, 27 Sep 1886; m. at Concord, 27 Dec 1825, her second cousin, MOSES DAVIS *(Lydia Merrill Davis^5, Dorcas Abbott Merrill^4, Nathaniel^3, Nathaniel^2, George^1)*, b. at Concord, 1797 son of Samuel and Lydia (Merrill) Davis; Moses d. at Concord, 7 Jun 1875. Moses is a child in Family 990.

ii DOROTHY MARTIN, b. 13 Mar 1801; d. at Rumford, 1823.

iii HANNAH MARTIN, b. 12 Jun 1802; d. at Rumford, 1892; m. her second cousin once removed, HAZEN F. ABBOTT *(John^6, Moses^5, Nathaniel^4, Nathaniel^3, Nathaniel^2, George^1)*, b. in NH about 1801 son of John and Hannah (Flanders) Abbott; Hazen d. at Rumford, 20 Oct 1870.

iv MEHITABLE MARTIN, b. 11 Feb 1804; d. at Columbia, NH, 23 Jun 1845; m. HARVEY WILLARD.

v BETSEY MARTIN, b. 30 Oct 1805; d. 1806

vi DANIEL MARTIN, b. 6 Sep 1807; d. at Rumford, 1876; m. 28 Nov 1831, ISABEL C. BROWN, b. at Brunswick, 22 Nov 1812 daughter of Benjamin and Mary (O'Donahue) Brown;[2738] Isabel d. after 1880.

vii GEORGE MARTIN, b. 29 Aug 1809; d. 23 Mar 1810.

viii BETSEY MARTIN, b. 1812; d. at Bethel, ME after 1880; m. PHINEAS STEARNS, b. at Bethel, 17 Dec 1803 son of Charles and Thankful (Bartlett) Stearns; Phineas d. at Bethel after 1880.[2739]

ix POLLY MARTIN, b. 1814; d. at Caribou, ME, 13 Jan 1875; m. CYRUS SMALL, b. about 1816; Cyrus d. at Caribou, 9 Apr 1878.

x DAVID GEORGE MARTIN, b. 1816; d. at Rumford, 17 Oct 1864; m. 13 Oct 1845, his first cousin, SARAH G. MARTIN, b. at Rumford, 11 Jun 1816 daughter of Kimball and Rachel (Godwin) Martin; Sarah d. at Rumford, 8 Jan 1894.

1034) ZEBADIAH FARNUM *(Sarah Abbott Farnum^4, Nathaniel^3, Nathaniel^2, George^1)*, b. in Vermont, 31 Mar 1769 son of Samuel and Sarah (Abbott) Farnum; d. at Watkins, OH, 13 Oct 1854; m. JANE MCNINCH, b. 13 Oct 1763; Jane d. 18 Mar 1853.

Zebadiah and Jane started their family of thirteen children in Essex County, New York and relocated to Union County, Ohio about 1823 and settled in Watkins.[2740] They cleared land and established a homestead where they remained until their deaths. Their children nearly all stayed in the Union County area, although son Chester relocated to Illinois, but with his health failing attempted to return to Ohio but died before arriving.

Zebadiah and Jane had thirteen children likely all born in Westport in Essex County, New York.

[2737] Lapham, *History of Rumford, Oxford County Maine*

[2738] Lapham, *History of Rumford*, p 374

[2739] *1880 United States Federal Census*, Year: 1880; Census Place: Bethel, Oxford, Maine; Roll: 484; Page: 26A; Enumeration District: 117.

[2740] Durant, *History of Union County, Ohio*, p 334

i POLLY FARNUM, b. Dec 1792, d. at Watkins, OH, 14 Feb 1832; m. in New York, about 1815, ASAHEL ROSE, b. about 1792. Polly and Asahel came to Union County before her parents. Asahel was listed as a head of household in Millcreek, OH in 1830, but no record of him after that.

ii SAMUEL FARNUM, b. about 1794; d. at Shelby County, OH, about 1841; m. in New York, about 1818, HANNAH RANDALL. After Samuel's death, Hannah married James Milna, 10 Oct 1846. Samuel was the first member of the family to make the trip to Union County, OH arriving about 1820.

iii HENRY FARNUM, b. 1796; d. at Marysville, OH, about 1862 (probate 12 Dec 1862); m. at Franklin, OH, 15 Feb 1825, FANNY HAMILTON, b. in PA, about 1798; Fanny d. at Watkins, Nov 1867.

iv BETSEY FARNUM, b. about 1798; died young

v SALLIE FARNUM, b. about 1800; died young

vi PRISCILLA FARNUM, b. 8 Oct 1802; d. at Millcreek, OH, 9 Jul 1883; m. SEYMOUR WILKINS, b. in Windsor County, VT, 29 Feb 1796; Seymour d. in Union County, 1 Jan 1881.

vii CHESTER FARNUM, b. 13 Sep 1804; d. at Monticello, IL, 7 Aug 1844; m. SARAH LONGBRAKE, b. in Clark County, OH, 4 Jul 1813 daughter of George and Susanna (Catrow) Longbrake; Sarah d. at Union County, OH, 26 May 1897.

viii ISAAC FARNUM, b. about 1806; d. at Watkins, OH, 2 Oct 1829.

ix JANE FARNUM, b. about 1809; d. at Scioto, OH, after 1880; m. at Union County, OH, 3 Dec 1838, ELIJAH NEWHOUSE, b. in Ohio, about 1815 son of Anthony and Nancy (Coons) Newhouse; Elijah d. at Scioto, 31 Oct 1854.

x SUSAN FARNUM, b. 17 Sep 1811; d. at Marysville, OH, 5 Feb 1904; m. 12 Dec 1833, JACOB LONGBRAKE, b. at Fairfield County, OH, 17 Jan 1808 son of George and Susanna (Catrow) Longbrake; Jacob d. at Marysville, 10 Jan 1865.

xi SOPHRONIA FARNUM, b. 1812; d. at Union County, OH, 23 Aug 1884; m. ADAM RICHEY, b. 1807 in Pennsylvania; Adam d. at Dover, OH, 25 Sep 1871.

xii EMILY FARNUM, b. about 1812; d. at Watkins, OH, 12 Nov 1903; m. 22 Dec 1844, WARRET OWEN, b. at Champaign County, OH, 3 Jul 1823 son of James and Rebecca (Henry) Owen;[2741] Warret d. at Watkins, 10 Nov 1903.

xiii CAROLINE FARNUM, b. about 1813; d. at Larue, OH, 1 Dec 1894; m. 1st, 9 Jan 1834, WILLIAM CORY, b. 17 Dec 1807 son of Stephen and Rhoda (Wright) Cory; William d. at Frankfort, OH, 21 Jul 1834. Caroline m. 2nd, 5 Sep 1837, SAMUEL SHERWOOD, b. at Plattsburgh, NY, May 1797; Samuel d. at Marysville, OH, 29 Dec 1859.

1035) STEPHEN BLANCHARD *(Hannah Blanchard Blanchard[4], Sarah Abbott Blanchard[3], Nathaniel[2], George[1])*, b. at Andover, 4 Jan 1748/9 son of Stephen and Hannah (Blanchard) Blanchard; d. at Milford, 27 Jul 1789; m. by 1774, LUCY ADAMS, b. at Dunstable, NH, b. 8 May 1747 daughter of Ephraim and Thankful (Blodgett) Adams.

Stephen Blanchard and Lucy Adams were parents of eight children born at Milford, New Hampshire.

i LUCY BLANCHARD, b. 20 Jun 1774; d at Wheelock, VT, 27 Oct 1815; m. 2 May 1799, JOHN WHITE, b. at Gloucester, 28 Sep 1774 (baptized 2 Oct 1774) son of William and Molly (Griffin) White;[2742] John d. at Calais, VT, 26 Jul 1863.

ii MOSES BLANCHARD, b. 28 Oct 1776 (recorded at Wilton). He is likely the Moses that married at Wilton, 8 May 1800, ELIZABETH BOUTWELL, b. at Amherst, 10 Mar 1775 daughter of Amos and Eleanor (Lewis) Boutwell. If so, Moses d. at Belgrade, ME, about 1827 (probate Mar 1827).

iii MEHITABLE BLANCHARD, b. 3 Oct 1778; d. at Lisbon, NH, 20 Mar 1865; m. at Wilton, 24 Aug 1800, FARNUM MORSE, b. at Salem, NH, 1 Nov 1778 son of Asa and Hannah (Austin) Morse; Farnum d. at Lisbon, 29 Jun 1859.

iv ENOS BLANCHARD, b. 1 Jul 1800; nothing further known.

[2741] Durant, *History of Union County*, OH, p 348

[2742] White Family Quarterly, volumes 1-3, p 67

v FANNY BLANCHARD, b. 18 Aug 1782; nothing further known.

vi HANNAH BLANCHARD, b. 18 Aug 1782; d. at Wilmot, NH, 27 Dec 1831; m. at Wilton, 25 Dec 1830, JABEZ MORRILL, b. at Weare, 23 Feb 1777 son of Jabez and Hannah (Clough) Morrill; Jabez d. at Wilmot, 2 Apr 1854.

vii STEPHEN BLANCHARD, b. 24 Aug 1784; d. at Cynthian Township, OH, 6 Nov 1856; m. CHRISTIANA PENNEY, b. at Belgrade, ME, 12 May 1788 daughter of George and Abigail (Wormwood) Penney; Christiana d. at Cynthian, 10 Feb 1873.

viii PERSIS BLANCHARD, b. 21 Apr 1786; m. 16 Nov 1809, JAMES ADAMS, b. at New Boston, NH, 1 Aug 1785 son of James and Lydia (-) Adams. Persis and James were living in New Boston, NH in 1820.

1036) SARAH BLANCHARD *(Hannah Blanchard Blanchard⁴, Sarah Abbott Blanchard³, Nathaniel², George¹)*, b. at Andover, 27 Feb 1755 daughter of Stephen and Hannah (Blanchard) Blanchard; d. at Chester, VT, 20 Nov 1836; m. 18 Sep 1777, UZIEL BATCHELDER, b. at Beverly, 30 Oct 1755 son of Joseph and Judith (Ray) Batchelder.

Uziel Batchelder served in the Revolutionary War from August to December 1781 with the rank of corporal in Captain Mellon's company.[2743]

Uziel Batchelder and Sarah Blanchard were parents of seven children.[2744] The family was in Massachusetts and their first children were likely born there, and were later in Putney, Vermont.

i SARAH BATCHELDER, baptized at Andover, 6 Jun 1779; d. at Plattsburgh, NY; m. at Wilton, 11 Sep 1800, SIMON DALE, b. at Wilton, 22 Oct 1772 son of Timothy and Rebekah (-) Dale; Simon d. at Plattsburgh, after 1840.

ii UZIEL RAY BATCHELDER, baptized at Andover, 5 Nov 1780; d. at Jasper, NY, after 1850; m. 19 Feb 1804, LUCY ROSS, b. at Ipswich, MA, 15 Aug 1786 daughter of Timothy and Mary (Burnham) Ross; Lucy d. at Rupert, VT, 18 Jun 1832.

iii MARY "POLLY" BATCHELDER, b. about 1781; d. at Stevensville, MI, 6 Nov 1857; m. at Landgrove, VT, 6 Dec 1804, LEONARD ARCHER, b. at Keene, NH, 10 Apr 1774 son of Benjamin and Elizabeth (Ellis) Archer.

iv JAMES BATCHELDER, b. about 1782; reported to have gone to northern Vermont; nothing further known.

v HENRY BATCHELDER, b. 11 Oct 1786; d. at Londonderry, VT, 2 Dec 1834; m. 21 Nov 1811, BETSEY KIDDER, b. at Amherst, NH, 25 Nov 1782 daughter of Daniel and Betsey (Melendy) Kidder;[2745] Betsey d. at Landgrove, VT, 1 Mar 1870.

vi MELINDA BATCHELDER, b. about 1789; d. at Putney, VT, 14 Dec 1863; m. NORMAN SEAVER WHITNEY, b. at Westminster, MA, 22 May 1791 son of Elisha and Eunice (Seaver) Whitney; Norman d. at Putney, 19 Feb 1863.

vii JOSEPH BATCHELDER, b. about 1791; d at Steuben County, NY, after 1850. Joseph was married twice. The name of his first wife has not been found. His second wife was Hannah who has not been identified.

1037) JACOB BLANCHARD *(Hannah Blanchard Blanchard⁴, Sarah Abbott Blanchard³, Nathaniel², George¹)*, b. at Andover, 22 Jun 1758 son of Stephen and Hannah (Blanchard) Blanchard; d. at Guildhall, VT, 1806; m. at Holland, MA, 6 Apr 1784, ELIZABETH CRAWFORD, b. at Union, CT, 1860 daughter of John and Mary (Rosebrooks) Crawford.[2746]

Jacob and Elizabeth settled in Bradford, New Hampshire, but planned to relocate to Guildhall, Vermont. In 1806, Jacob traveled to Guildhall ahead of his family and died during the first winter there.[2747] The family did go to Vermont and lived in the house that Jacob built with then oldest son Rial taking charge of the household.[2748]

Jacob Blanchard and Elizabeth Crawford were parents of seven children.

i JACOB BLANCHARD, b. at Wilton, 10 Jun 1785; d. before 1806 when Rial was named as oldest son.

ii DOTHA BLANCHARD, b. at Milford, 22 Dec 1786; d. at Bradford, 12 Aug 1790.

iii RIAL BLANCHARD, b. at Bradford, 16 Dec 1788; d. at West Windsor, VT, 13 Nov 1859; m. MINDWELL WOOSTER, b. 5 Apr 1790; Mindwell d. at Windsor, 30 Mar 1860.

[2743] Pierce, *Batchelder Genealogy*, p 411

[2744] Pierce, *Batchelder Genealogy*, p 412

[2745] Secomb, *History of Amherst*, p 659

[2746] Gould, *Early Families of Bradford*, p 43

[2747] Cutter, *New England Families*, volume 2, pp 868-869

[2748] Gould, *Early Families of Bradford*, p 44

iv STEPHEN BLANCHARD, b. at Bradford, 10 Apr 1791; d. at Lenox, MI, 16 Apr 1859; m. at Vergennes, VT, 16 Apr 1813, LOIS GOODRICH, b. at West Haven, VT, about 1794; Lois d. at Macomb, MI, Apr 1870.

v ROXANNA BLANCHARD, b. at Bradford, 10 Apr 1792; d. at Guildhall, VT, 3 Jan 1880; m. at Guildhall, 17 Nov 1822, SIMEON CALL, b. about 1795; Simeon d. at Guildhall, 28 Sep 1874.

vi JOSEPH BLANCHARD, b. 1795; nothing further known.

vii CYNTHIA BLANCHARD, b. 3 Mar 1797; d. at Harmony, NY, 27 Jan 1832; m. at Hartland, VT, 29 Jan 1817, CLINTON MARCY, b. 24 Dec 1791 son of William and Lydia (Pike) Marcy; Clinton d. at Magnolia, NY, 10 Jan 1859. Clinton married second Charlotte Hurlburt.

1038) PHEBE BLANCHARD *(Hannah Blanchard Blanchard[4], Sarah Abbott Blanchard[3], Nathaniel[2], George[1])*, b. at Andover, 15 Dec 1762 daughter of Stephen and Hannah (Blanchard) Blanchard; d. at Wilton Center, NH, 20 Aug 1838; m. JEREMIAH BURNHAM, b. at Ipswich, 14 Sep 1763 son of Jeremiah and Mary (Burnham) Burnham; Jeremiah d. at Wilton Center, NH, 1 Nov 1844.

Phebe Blanchard and Jeremiah Burnham were parents of nine children born at Wilton where Jeremiah was a farmer.

i PHEBE BURNHAM, b. 18 Sep 1787; d. at Charlestown, MA, 3 Oct 1868; m. 1st, 24 Apr 1810, as his second wife, SIMEON GUTTERSON, b. at Andover, 8 Dec 1769 son of Samuel and Lydia (Stevens) Gutterson; Simeon d. at Milford, 1 Mar 1846. Phebe m. 2nd, about 1848, DANIEL FULLER, b. about 1785 son of Enoch and Sarah (Putnam) Fuller; Daniel d. at Wilton, 3 Oct 1858. Simeon Gutterson was first married to Deborah Mooar (1777-1805). Daniel Fuller was first married to Phebe's sister Betsey Burnham (see below).

ii MARY "POLLY" BURNHAM, b. 25 Apr 1789; d. at Andover, VT, 5 May 1867; m. 24 Jun 1813, SAMUEL PUFFER, b. at Ashby, 25 Sep 1788 son of Ephraim and Abigail (Smith) Puffer;[2749] Samuel d. in CA, 1852.[2750]

iii BETSEY BURNHAM, b. 16 Apr 1791; d. 4 Oct 1847; m. 1810, DANIEL FULLER who was second married to Betsey's sister Phebe (see above).

iv HANNAH BURNHAM, b. 15 May 1793; d. at Wilton, 1872; m. 1st, 21 Jul 1841, WILLIAM FOSTER of Ashby; William d. about 1845. Hannah m. 2nd, 27 May 1845, ISAAC PRESTON, b. at New Ipswich, NH, 3 Jun 1786 son of Isaac and Susanna (Fletcher) Preston; Isaac d. at Wilton, 29 Sep 1869.

v LOIS BURNHAM, b. 11 Aug 1795; d. at Milford, 19 Feb 1874; m. 1818, SAMUEL LOVEJOY, b. at Milford, Sep 1798 son of Samuel and Elizabeth (Elliot) Lovejoy; Samuel d. at Canaan, NH, 27 Mar 1881.

vi LUCY BURNHAM, b. 15 Aug 1797; d. at Wilton, 4 Jun 1863; m. at New Boston, NH, 26 Nov 1835, ISRAEL DODGE, b. at Hamilton, MA, 15 Nov 1793 son of John and Mary (Dodge) Dodge; Israel d. at New Boston, 11 Sep 1862.

vii SALLY BURNHAM, b. 24 Sep 1799; d. at Brookline, NH, 13 Mar 1894; m. about 1841, as his second wife, ABEL SHATTUCK, b. at Pepperell, MA, 24 Jul 1802 son of Nathaniel and Hannah (Ball) Shattuck; Abel d. at Brookline, 23 Aug 1870. Abel was first married to Deverd Verder.

viii STEPHEN BURNHAM, b. 31 Dec 1802; d. at New Boston, NH, 31 Mar 1878; m. at Townsend, MA, 1 Jun 1826, MARY ROCKWOOD, b. at Groton, 5 Dec 1805 daughter of Joseph and Lucy (Fletcher) Rockwood; Mary d. at Milford, NH, 22 Dec 1885.

ix REBECCA BURNHAM, b. 24 Apr 1805; d. at Wilton, 18 Dec 1850; m. WILLIAM CURRIER, b. about 1804; William d. at Wilton, 8 Nov 1854.

1039) JOHN BLANCHARD *(Hannah Blanchard Blanchard[4], Sarah Abbott Blanchard[3], Nathaniel[2], George[1])*, b. at Andover, 16 Feb 1767 son of Stephen and Hannah (Blanchard) Blanchard; d. at Chester, VT, 19 Apr 1855; m. SYBIL CRAWFORD, b. at Union, CT, about 1762 daughter of John and Mary (Rosebrooks) Crawford. This is confirmed by the will of John Blanchard as the children named in his will have birth and death records that name parents as John and Sybil. (This John is first cousin to John born in 1768 who married Dorcas Osgood.) Both John and Sybil appear to be living in 1840 in Andover, Vermont. At the 1850 Census, John Blanchard heads a household that includes his unmarried daughter Sybil who died in 1851.

[2749] Null, *Descendants of George Puffer of Braintree*, p 62

[2750] The recording of Samuel's death in Putney, Vermont states that he died in California.

Although a resident of Chester, Vermont, the probate of the estate of John Blanchard was in Cheshire County, New Hampshire. At the probate, the only children living in the state identified as heirs were Miranda Goodnow and Irene B. Carpenter and they requested that Lauris G. Whiting be named administrator. Property consisted of $1,153.47 in cash at a savings bank.[2751]

John Blanchard and Sybil Crawford were parents of seven children, the oldest daughter likely born in New Hampshire and the other children at Andover, Vermont.

i SYBIL BLANCHARD, b. 1791; d. at Andover, VT, 17 Apr 1851. Sybil did not marry.

ii WILLARD BLANCHARD, b. 3 Jun 1795; d. at Peterborough, NH, 2 Feb 1845; m. CHARLOTTE P. whose identity was not found; she was b. about 1797 and d. at Peterborough, 13 Dec 1844. Willard's brother-in-law Sumner Carpenter was administrator of his estate and states that Willard left no children and his heir-at-law was his father John Blanchard. Willard was listed as a widower on his death record and he and his wife are buried in Peterborough.

iii LEONARD BLANCHARD, b. 30 Jan 1797; d. at Putney, VT, 12 Oct 1884; m. at Andover, VT, 14 Dec 1826, ELEANOR SPAULDING, b. 30 Nov 1799 daughter of Samuel and Sarah (Heald) Spaulding;[2752] Eleanor d. at Putney, 1876.

iv MIRANDA BLANCHARD, b. 11 Aug 1798; d. at Keene, NH, 28 Jan 1865; m. GEORGE GOODNOW, b. at Sudbury, MA, 29 Apr 1799 son of William and Mary (Brown) Goodnow; George d. at Keene, about 1866 (probate 1866).

v ROXY BLANCHARD, b. 14 Dec 1800; d. at Boston, 26 Apr 1878; m. at Andover, VT, 12 Nov 1829, JOHN MARSHALL BARNARD, b. at Hollis, 9 Mar 1798 son of Stephen and Martha (Marshall) Barnard; John d. at Boston, 22 Aug 1880.

vi IRENE BLANCHARD, b. 17 Jul 1802; d. at Chester, VT, 26 Jun 1875; m. SUMNER CARPENTER, b. at Peru, VT, 23 Sep 1802 son of David and Azubah (Allen) Carpenter; Sumner d. at Chester, 3 May 1875.

vii MARY "POLLY" BLANCHARD, b. 7 Oct 1804; d. at Chester, VT, 17 Jan 1891; m. at Londonderry, VT, 16 Feb 1826, PARKER STEVENS, b. about 1801 son of Parker and Catherine (Parkhurst) Stevens; Parker d. at Chester, 1886 (probate 10 Jun 1886).

1040) JOSEPH BLANCHARD *(Joseph Blanchard⁴, Sarah Abbott Blanchard³, Nathaniel², George¹)*, b. at Andover, 10 Apr 1765 son of Joseph and Dinah (Blanchard) Blanchard; d. at Baltimore, MD, 1798;[2753] m. 27 Feb 1786, his second cousin once removed, HANNAH MOOAR *(Hannah Phelps Mooar⁵, Priscilla Chandler Phelps⁴, Zebadiah Chandler³, Hannah Abbott Chandler², George¹)*, b. 6 Nov 1768 daughter of Benjamin and Hannah (Phelps) Mooar; Hannah d. at Lewiston, 12 Sep 1860.[2754][2755] Hannah m. 2nd, 1 Jan 1818, NATHAN CUTLER,[2756] b. at Mendon, MA, 23 Feb 1755 son of David and Mehitable (Whitney) Cutler; Nathan d. at Lewiston, ME, 8 Dec 1827. Nathan Cutler was first married to Ruth Nelson. Hannah Mooar is a child in Family 343.

Joseph served in the Revolutionary War as a fifer. In her 22 August 1843 application for a widow's pension, Hannah reported that she and Joseph settled in Lewiston, Maine and were parents of five children. About 1798, Joseph traveled to Baltimore to find work and prepare to bring his family there. He found work at a mill where he died in a fall. She also related that she had remarried but was widowed in 1827.

Joseph Blanchard and Hannah Mooar were parents of five children born at Lewiston.[2757]

i HANNAH BLANCHARD, b. 8 Mar 1787; d. at Levant, ME, 9 May 1852; m. 1st, 14 Mar 1806, her step-brother, HENRY CUTLER., b. at Auburn, ME, 26 Aug 1781 son of Nathan and Ruth (Nelson) Cutler;[2758] Henry d. 26 Mar 1815. Hannah m. 2nd, at New Gloucester, 7 Dec 1817, as his third wife, JOB HASKELL, b. at New Gloucester, 11 May 1765 son of Nathaniel and Deborah (Bailey) Haskell;[2759] Job d. at Levant, 18 Apr 1847. Job was first married to Judith Dwinal and second married to Mary Cox.

[2751] *New Hampshire. Probate Court (Cheshire County);* Probate Place: *Cheshire, New Hampshire, Estate Files, B826-B877, 1854-1857,* number 851

[2752] Spalding, *Spalding Memorial*, p 206

[2753] The Revolutionary War pension application of widow Hannah states that Joseph went to Baltimore to find work and died there from a fall.

[2754] Mooar, *Mooar Genealogy*, p 32

[2755] Hannah is buried in Hillside Cemetery in Lisbon Falls, ME with an inscription that reads wife of Nathan Cutler, died Sept 12, 1860 age 92 years. Findagrave.com

[2756] Hannah Cutler received a widow's pension for Joseph Blanchard. Ancestry.com. *U.S., Revolutionary War Pension and Bounty-Land Warrant Application Files, 1800-1900,* Case W22876

[2757] Hannah's widow's pension file includes her statement that she and Joseph had five children.

[2758] Cutler, *A Cutler Memorial*, p 404

[2759] Little, *Genealogical and Family History of the State of Maine*, volume 2

ii MARY BLANCHARD, b. 16 Apr 1789; d. at Lisbon, ME, 6 Jun 1848; m. JOSEPH SAWYER, b. at Lisbon, 27 Sep 1791 *likely* the son of George and Hannah (Dain) Sawyer; Joseph d. at Lisbon, 14 May 1882.

iii JOSEPH BLANCHARD, b. 15 Jul 1791; d. at Corrina, ME, 13 May 1842; m. at Monmouth, ME, 21 Jan 1822, HANNAH ROWELL, b. 16 Nov 1792 *perhaps* the daughter of Joseph and Mary (Colby) Rowell; Hannah d. at Corrina, 3 Jun 1871.

iv ISAAC BLANCHARD, b. 9 Sep 1793. The Mooar Genealogy reports that Isaac was blind. He did not marry.

v HERMAN BLANCHARD, b. 11 Mar 1796. Herman was also blind. He did not marry.

1041) JOHN BLANCHARD *(Joseph Blanchard[4], Sarah Abbott Blanchard[3], Nathaniel[2], George[1])*, b. at Andover, 20 Feb 1768 son of Joseph and Dinah (Blanchard) Blanchard; d. at Boston, 6 Feb 1802 at age 32 or 34;[2760] m. 27 Apr 1789, DORCAS OSGOOD, b. at Tewksbury, 27 Feb 1770 daughter of Stephen and Mary (Foster) Osgood. Dorcas m. 2nd, Daniel Hastings; Dorcas d. at Boston, 28 Oct 1813.

John and Dorcas Blanchard started their family in Andover, were soon after in Topsham, Maine, and lastly in Boston where John was a merchant.

John Blanchard did not leave a will and the estate entered probate 15 February 1802 with widow Dorcas Blanchard named administratrix. The inventory included details on the contents of his shop such as 11 gross of pewter spoons, one dozen spectacle cases, 5 chalk lines, and a long list of other items for the well-stocked store. Real estate was valued at $7500 and personal estate including merchandise totaled $4125.60. The distribution of the estate on 20 January 1806, included payments of $998 to each of the following heirs all children of the deceased: John Blanchard, Harriet Blanchard, Mary Blanchard, Charles Blanchard, and Caroline Blanchard. This accounting was made by Daniel Hastings acting as administrator on behalf of his wife Dorcas. The final distribution from the estate was in 1812 at which time the five children mentioned above were living.[2761]

John Blanchard and Dorcas Osgood were parents of six children.

i JOHN BLANCHARD, b. at Andover, 2 May 1790; still living in 1812 at the final distribution of father's estate but no clear records for him otherwise.

ii HARRIET BLANCHARD, b. at Topsham, ME, 27 Nov 1792; d. at Boston, 30 Aug 1827; m. at Boston, 26 Aug 1813, her step-brother, JOSEPH S. HASTINGS, b. at Newton, MA, 25 Jun 1789 son of Daniel and Mary (Morse) Hastings; Joseph d. at Hoboken, NJ, 18 Dec 1872. Joseph remarried to Jane Nichols in 1855.

iii MARY BLANCHARD, b. at Topsham, 28 Nov 1793; d. at Cambridge, 12 Jun 1823; m. at Boston, 25 Jan 1813, NATHANIEL DANA, b. at Natick, 2 May 1787 son of Samuel and Mehitable (Goddard) Dana; Nathaniel d. at Brookline, MA, 18 Jan 1856. After Mary's death, Nathaniel married Lois Walker Lord.

iv CHARLES BLANCHARD, b. at Topsham, 15 Mar 1795; d. at Chelsea, 24 Sep 1876; m. at Portland, 6 Dec 1818, MARY WINSHIP DANA, b. at Boston, 29 Nov 1800 daughter of Dexter and Sarah Wyman (Winship) Dana; Mary d. at Chelsea, 13 Sep 1869.

v LOUISA BLANCHARD, b. at Topsham, Jul 1797 d. at Boston, 30 Mar 1801.

vi CAROLINE BLANCHARD, b. at Boston, 1800; d. after 1837 (living at time of probate of husband's estate); m. at Boston, 24 Apr 1820, JOHN HALL, b. at Burslem, Staffordshire, England,[2762] 10 May 1795 son of John and Elizabeth (Pedley) Hall;[2763] John d. at Roxbury, 16 Aug 1837.

1042) JEREMIAH BLANCHARD *(Jeremiah Blanchard[4], Sarah Abbott Blanchard[3], Nathaniel[2], George[1])*, b. at Andover, 10 Oct 1759 son of Jeremiah and Dorothy (Smith) Blanchard; d. at Newburyport, 4 Apr 1844;[2764] m. 20 Nov 1784, SUSANNA PEARSON; Susanna d. at Newbury, 4 Mar 1808. Jeremiah married second, 14 Jan 1810, Sarah Allen who seems to have been a widow; Sarah was born about 1769 (age 84 in 1853) and died about 1853 (last pension payment April 1853).

[2760] One record gives age at death as 32 and another as age 34.

[2761] Suffolk County, Massachusetts probate records, accessed through familysearch.org, probate of John Blanchard, 100:48, 100:83, 100:378, 103:48, 103:75, 103: 141, 104:9, 114:241

[2762] John Hall, Jr. of Burslem, England married Caroline Blanchard in Boston Apr. 26 1820. U.S., Newspaper Extractions from the Northeast, 1704-1930

[2763] England & Wales, Non-Conformist and Non-Parochial Registers, 1567-1970

[2764] Jeremiah, master mariner, palsy, Sept. 13, 1844, a. 83 y.

In 1775, Jeremiah Blanchard enlisted as a private in the company of Captain Charles Furbush, served an initial term of six months, and then a subsequent enlistment of ten months. In 1777, he enlisted in an artillery company, served a term of three years, and was honorably discharged 9 May 1780.[2765]

Jeremiah Blanchard and Susanna Pearson were parents of seven children, the birth of the oldest child record at Andover and the remainder at Newbury.

i POLLY BLANCHARD, b. 14 Feb 1786; d. at Newbury, 10 May 1820; m. at Newbury, 6 Oct 1805, MOSES CHASE, b. at Newbury, 2 Sep 1784 son of Moses and Joanna (Lunt) Chase; Moses d. at Newbury, 19 Dec 1858. After Polly's death, Moses married Hannah Allen 20 Jan 1821.

ii DOROTHY "DOLLY" BLANCHARD, b. 12 Jan 1789; d. at Newburyport, 11 Aug 1855. Dolly did not marry. In 1850, she was living at the poor farm in Newbury and died at the almshouse in Newburyport.

iii JEREMIAH BLANCHARD, b. 16 Dec 1790; no further record found.

iv LOIS PEARSON BLANCHARD, b. 2 Mar 1793; d. at Newburyport, 4 Sep 1876; m. 1st, 22 Oct 1812, JEREMIAH LUNT, b. at Newburyport, 4 Mar 1786 son of Daniel and Sarah (Knight) Lunt; Jeremiah d. at Newburyport, 21 Apr 1832. Lois m. 2nd, at Newburyport, 24 Dec 1833, JOHN F. NILES, b. about 1802; John d. at Trinidad, Cuba, 7 Jul 1846.[2766]

v REBECCA BLANCHARD, b. 15 Feb 1796; d. at Newburyport, 21 Feb 1885; m. 1st, at Newbury, 26 Aug 1815, SAMUEL BARTLETT, b. at Amesbury, 7 Apr 1793 son of Enoch and Mary (Barnard) Bartlett; Samuel d. at Amesbury, 17 Apr 1830. Rebecca m. 2nd, at Newburyport, 4 Mar 1831, JOHN PUTNAM, b. about 1807 (age 41 at death); John d. Feb 1849 when lost at sea.

vi FANNY BLANCHARD, b. 14 Apr 1798; d. at Newburyport, 19 Aug 1863. Fanny did not marry.

vii JOHN PEARSON BLANCHARD, b. 29 Aug 1801; d. at Salisbury, MA, 12 Dec 1872; m. at Salisbury, 3 Apr 1829, MARY ANN TOWLE, b. at Salisbury, 30 Apr 1799 daughter of Elisha and Sarah (Bragg) Towle; Mary Ann d. at Salisbury, 13 Aug 1872.

1043) JUDITH BLANCHARD *(Jeremiah Blanchard⁴, Sarah Abbott Blanchard³, Nathaniel², George¹)*, baptized at Andover, 13 Jun 1779 daughter of Jeremiah and Susannah (Martin) Blanchard; d. at Wilton, NH after 1860 (living at the 1860 U.S. Census); m. 12 Feb 1801, her third cousin (and George Abbott descendant) BENJAMIN STEEL, b. at Wilton, 11 Jun 1776 son of Benjamin and Hannah (Lovejoy) Steel; Benjamin d. 18 Nov 1845.

Benjamin Steel was a farmer in Wilton. He and Judith were parents of five children born at Wilton.

i ALVAH STEEL, b. 7 Mar 1801; d. at Milledgeville, GA, 16 Aug 1836; m. at Wilton, 1826, his fourth cousin once removed, ELIZA HALE ABBOTT *(Zebediah⁶, Jeremiah⁵, John⁴, John³, John², George¹)*, b. at Wilton, 7 Sep 1802 daughter of Zebadiah and Elizabeth (Hale) Abbott; Eliza d. at Wilton, 1853. Alvah attended Yale and for a time was an executive at Phillips Academy. He taught school in Georgia and started the school in Milledgeville. After his death, Eliza returned to Wilton.[2767]

ii ABIEL STEEL, b. 1 May 1803; d. at Harvard, MA, 28 Dec 1878; m. at Hollis, 4 Nov 1838, BETSEY HARDY, b. at Hollis, 13 Apr 1803 daughter of Phineas and Sybil (Shattuck) Hardy; Betsey d. at Harvard, 28 Mar 1877.

iii HANNAH STEEL, b. 14 Dec 1804; d. at Wilton, 17 Jul 1882; m. 22 Dec 1834, LEONARD PETTENGILL, b. at Wilton, 4 Mar 1806 son of William and Sarah (Ballard) Pettengill; Leonard d. at Wilton, 28 Sep 1868.

iv NANCY STEEL, b. 1 Nov 1806; d. at Lowell, 21 Oct 1901; m. 18 Dec 1832, FRANCIS GREEN, b. at Weathersfield, VT, 7 Sep 1809 son of Samuel and Mary (-) Green; Francis d. at Lowell, 7 Feb 1891.

v RUBY STEEL, b. 10 Jan 1819; d. at Wilton, 4 Feb 1848; m. at Nashville, NH, 7 May 1846, PETER HAMILTON PUTNAM, b. at Wilton, 11 Sep 1819 son of Joseph and Lucy (Rumrill) Putnam; Peter d. at Nashua, 9 Sep 1897. After Ruby's death, Peter second married Lavinia Lane Oct 1848 and third Hannah W. Perkins Jul 1862.

1044) HENRY BLANCHARD *(Jeremiah Blanchard⁴, Sarah Abbott Blanchard³, Nathaniel², George¹)*, b. at Wilton, 30 Mar 1781 son of Jeremiah and Susannah (Martin) Blanchard; d. at Raymondville, NY, 22 Oct 1824; m. at Billerica, 21 Jan 1807,

[2765] Revolutionary War Pension and Bounty-Land Warrant Application Files

[2766] "Died at Trinidad, Cuba aged 44 years." Findagrave: 55480381

[2767] Carpenter, *Biographical Catalogue of the Trustees, Teachers and Students of Phillips*, p 127

MARY "POLLY" CROSBY, b. at Billerica, 30 Oct 1785 daughter of Timothy and Susanna (Sanders) Crosby;[2768] Polly d. 2 Apr 1848.

Henry and Polly married in Billerica where Polly was born, and they seem to have been in Vermont for a time where their children were born. Henry along with his brothers John, William, and Aaron relocated to New York with Henry, John, and Aaron all in St. Lawrence County and William finally in Niagara County.

Four children have been identified for Henry Blanchard and Polly Crosby likely born in Vermont (census records available give place of birth as Vermont for each of the children). Only one of the children married.

i HENRY BLANCHARD, b. 1807; d. at Raymondville, NY, 17 Aug 1877. Henry did not marry. In 1850, he was unmarried and living with his brother Charles in Norfolk, NY.

ii MARY BLANCHARD, b. 1811; d. at Raymondville, 19 Jun 1853. Mary did not marry. Mary and her sister Eveline are both buried in the same lot as their parents Henry and Mary at the Raymondville Cemetery.[2769]

iii EVELINE BLANCHARD, b. 1814; d. at Raymondville, 12 Jun 1843. Eveline did not marry.

iv CHARLES EDWARD BLANCHARD, b. 1817; d. at Norfolk, NY, 21 Mar 1887; m. ELEANOR STEBBINGS, b. in Canada, 22 Aug 1815 daughter of Levi and Sarah (Price) Stebbings;[2770] Eleanor d. at Norfolk, NY, 6 Aug 1888.

1045) JOHN BLANCHARD *(Jeremiah Blanchard[4], Sarah Abbott Blanchard[3], Nathaniel[2], George[1])*, b. at Wilton, 26 Nov 1782 son of Jeremiah and Susannah (Martin) Blanchard; d. at Norfolk, NY, 28 Jan 1851; m. by 1820, MARY DUDLEY HASKELL, b. at Rochester, VT, 22 Nov 1784 daughter of David and Elizabeth (Putnam) Haskell; Mary d. 18 Aug 1848.

There are five children known for John and Mary Blanchard likely all born at Norfolk, New York. Daughter Elizabeth Blanchard did not marry. The list of heirs at the probate of Elizabeth's estate were given as Clarissa B. Smith, Gratia A. Blanchard, Ida M. Blanchard Kennen all of Norfolk, NY and Silas A. Blanchard of Pittsburgh.[2771] Clarissa and Gratia are Elizabeth's sisters, Ida is the daughter of her brother Samuel, and Silas is the son of her brother Dudley.

i CLARISSA BLANCHARD, b. 15 Jun 1820; d. at Raymondville, NY, 11 Sep 1898; m. REUBEN SMITH, b. at Weathersfield, VT, 7 Apr 1806 son of Reuben and Persis (Hutchins) Smith; Reuben d. at Raymondville, 8 Apr 1896.

ii DUDLEY BLANCHARD, b. about 1822; d. at Pittsburgh, PA, Dec 1890 (probate 8 Dec 1890); m. SARAH A. BURCHARD,[2772] b. about 1818 and d. after 1880.

iii SAMUEL BLANCHARD, b. 27 Mar 1823; d. at Norfolk, NY, 7 Apr 1894; m. about 1849, JANETTE, b. 31 Mar 1829; Janette d. at Norfolk, 26 Dec 1908.

iv ELIZABETH BLANCHARD, b. 2 Oct 1824; d. at Raymondville, NY, 13 Sep 1895. Elizabeth did not marry.

v GRATIA ANN BLANCHARD, b. 25 Jun 1827; d. at Raymondville, 17 Apr 1910. Gratia did not marry.

1046) WILLIAM BLANCHARD *(Jeremiah Blanchard[4], Sarah Abbott Blanchard[3], Nathaniel[2], George[1])*, b. at Wilton, 10 Feb 1788 son of Jeremiah and Susannah (Martin) Blanchard; d. at Royalton, NY, 1861; m. ELIZABETH GILBERT, b. at Hebron, CT, 1 Mar 1790 daughter of Gardner and Ann (Lathrop) Gilbert; Elizabeth d. 10 Oct 1857. After Elizabeth's death, William married Catherine Heywood.

In his will dated 11 June 1861 and proved 23 December 1861, William Blanchard bequeathed to his wife Catherine the village lot in the village of Gasport, all the household furniture, and all the stock, cows, and swine, fifty dollars, and a one-thousand-dollar annuity. Catherine also receives one-third of his interest in the Gasport oil well. The residue of the estate is left to his children Polly L. Randall, William H. Blanchard, Lavina Davis, Lorin G. Blanchard, Caroline Hubbard, Leonard W. Blanchard, Charles A. Blanchard, and Betsey Hoyt to be equally divided among them. John Gill, son-in-law of his daughter

---

[2768] Hazen, *History of Billerica*, p 31

[2769] Findagrave ID 67070074

[2770] Greenlee and Greenlee, *The Stebbins Genealogy*, p 1150

[2771] *Probate Records, 1830-1919; Indexes, 1830-1955 [St. Lawrence County, New York]*; Author: *New York. Surrogate's Court (St. Lawrence County)*; Probate Place: *St Lawrence, New York*, Volume 29, p 191

[2772] The death record of Silas Wright Blanchard, son of Dudley and Sarah, gives the maiden name of his mother as Burchard.

Polly Louisa, was named trustee for Polly's portion of the estate to be used for her benefit.[2773] Friend John Sybrant was named executor.

William Blanchard and Elizabeth Gilbert were parents of nine children born in Niagara County, New York.

i POLLY LOUISA BLANCHARD, b. 13 Sep 1810; d. at Ridgeway, NY, 29 Jan 1891; m. 6 Aug 1829, WILLIAM RANDALL, b. 14 Jan 1808 son of Abraham and Elishaba (Talbot) Randall;[2774] William d. at Knowlesville, NY, 29 Oct 1884.

ii NANCY MARIA BLANCHARD, b. 17 Jul 1812; d. 1814.

iii WILLIAM HAMILTON BLANCHARD, b. 23 Sep 1814; d. at Polkton, MI, 31 May 1899; m. 1st, at Lockport, NY, 18 Apr 1841, MARIA CONNIT, b. about 1825; Maria d. at Talmadge, MI, 1871. William m. 2nd, Oct 1873, MARY ELIZABETH WEATHERWAX, b. at Adrian, MI, 15 May 1848 daughter of Peter and Jane (Steele) Weatherwax; Mary d. at Coopersville, MI, 16 Oct 1938.

iv SUSANNAH LAVINA BLANCHARD, b. 23 Mar 1817; d. at Battle Creek, MI, 16 Aug 1897; m. GILBERT DAVIS, b. 25 Dec 1811;[2775] Gilbert d. at Battle Creek, 26 Sep 1870.

v LORING GILBERT BLANCHARD, b. 10 Nov 1819; d. at White Pigeon, MI, 22 Feb 1890; m. 1st, 11 Aug 1843, HULDAH HARRIMAN, b. 23 Aug 1824 daughter of Reuben and Abigail (Davis) Harriman; Huldah d. at White Pigeon, 1 Nov 1851. Loring m. 2nd, about 1852, MARIA WHITNEY, b. Dec 1826 daughter of Emery and Lydia (Locke) Whitney; Maria d. at White Pigeon, 26 Oct 1909.

vi ELIZABETH MARIA BLANCHARD, b. 6 Apr 1823; d. at Edgar, NE, 2 Feb 1910; m. CHARLES E. HOYT, b. 19 Aug 1819; Charles d. at Edgar, 9 Mar 1897.

vii CAROLINE ELIZA BLANCHARD, b. 12 Jul 1826; d. at Battle Creek, MI, 22 May 1905; m. 1847, PELEG A. HUBBARD, b. 17 Jan 1817 son of Daniel and Lavina (Andrews) Hubbard; Peleg d. at Hart, MI, 24 Jun 1901.

viii LEONARD WESLEY BLANCHARD, b. 12 Mar 1830; d. at Lockport, NY, 2 Jul 1876; m. MARY JANE (perhaps Batten), b. about 1833; Mary Jane d. after 1884.

ix CHARLES AUGUSTUS BLANCHARD, b. 12 Apr 1833; d. in IA, after 1870; m. AUGUSTA LEACH, b. in NY, about 1836; Augusta d. after 1901 when she was listed in the city directory for Council Bluffs, IA.

1047) AARON BLANCHARD *(Jeremiah Blanchard[4], Sarah Abbott Blanchard[3], Nathaniel[2], George[1])*, b. at Wilton, 20 Jul 1791 son of Jeremiah and Susannah (Martin) Blanchard; perhaps married Sally and relocated to Norfolk, NY with his brother John. There is an Aaron of the right age with wife Sally and children in census records in Norfolk.

Four children have been identified for Aaron Blanchard and Sally all born at Norfolk, New York. There may be other children for this couple.

i HANNAH BLANCHARD, b. about 1825, d. at Lowell, MA, 2 Jun 1906; m. JOSEPH HASKELL, b. 1817 son of Israel P. and Polly (Williams) Haskell; Joseph d. at Madrid, NY, 8 Nov 1874.

ii ALVA BLANCHARD, b. 1828; d. at Eaton County, MI, 1886; m. JULIA MEERS, b. about 1828 in NY; Julia d. at Benton, MI, 22 Dec 1911.

iii CALVIN BLANCHARD, b. 1831; d. at Buckhorn, IA, 22 May 1913; m. 1860, LOUISA GRANDY, b. in NY, 1834 daughter of John and Fidelia (Gilson) Grandy; Louisa d. at Buckhorn, 25 Aug 1913.

iv LYDIA BLANCHARD, b. 1837; d. in Lawrence County, NY, 1883. Lydia did not marry. In 1880, she was living with her sister Hannah Haskell.

1048) DANIEL BLANCHARD *(Daniel Blanchard[4], Sarah Abbott Blanchard[3], Nathaniel[2], George[1])*, b. at Andover, 20 Sep 1759 son of Daniel and Jerusha (Eaton) Blanchard; d. at Thetford, VT; m. at Salem, 26 Feb 1783, MARY BLANCHARD, b. at Andover, 4 Feb 1762 daughter of Samuel and Ruth (Tenney) Blanchard.

Daniel and Mary were based in the area of Thetford, Vermont, but it is possible that they relocated prior to their deaths.

[2773] *New York, Wills and Probate Records, 1659-1999* [database on-line]. Provo, UT, USA: Ancestry.com Operations, Inc., 2015. Wills 1860-1866, volume 8, pp 253-255

[2774] Randall, *Randall and Allied Families*, p 56

[2775] Gilbert's date of birth is on his gravestone.

Five children have been identified as likely children of Daniel Blanchard and Mary Blanchard.[2776]

i RUTH TENNEY BLANCHARD, b. at Thetford, 8 Jul 1784; d. at Swampscott, MA, 19 May 1862; m. 1st, at Thetford, 24 Dec 1802, SYLVESTER CUSHMAN ABBOTT, b. about 1778 (of Thetford) son of Walter and Persis (Cushman) Abbott;[2777] Sylvester d. at South Fairlee, Oct 1815. Ruth m. 2nd, at Lynn, MA, 16 Jul 1835, CYRUS B. SCALES, b. in NH about 1799; Cyrus d. at Salem, 21 Sep 1863.

ii JERUSHA EATON BLANCHARD, b. at Thetford, 29 May 1786; nothing further known.

iii SUSAN BLANCHARD, b. at Fairlee/Thetford, 1794; d. at Lynn, 21 Jun 1866; m. at Charlestown, MA, 18 Jul 1817, JOHN THOMAS, b. at Duxbury about 1793; John d. at Swampscott, 3 Jun 1876.

iv NATHANIEL BLANCHARD, b. at Thetford, 13 Nov 1795; d. at Swampscott, 3 Jun 1871; m. at Lynn, 2 Apr 1820, ALICE PHILLIPS BLANEY, b. at Lynn, 9 Sep 1805 daughter of Joseph and Ruth (Phillips) Blaney; Alice d. at Swampscott, 8 Mar 1889.

v PETER BLANCHARD,[2778] b. perhaps at Salem, 1801; d. at Rutland, VT, 15 Mar 1867; m. by 1830, ROSANNA LITTLEFIELD, b. in VT, about 1797 daughter of Levi and Jemima (Bragg) Littlefield;[2779] Rosanna d. at Rutland, 5 Apr 1878.

1049) ISAAC BLANCHARD *(Daniel Blanchard4, Sarah Abbott Blanchard3, Nathaniel2, George1)*, b. at Andover, 14 Sep 1763 son of Daniel and Jerusha (Eaton) Blanchard; d. at Milford, NH, 26 Apr 1826; m. about 1786, OLIVE HOPKINS, b. at Milford, 1 Apr 1769 daughter of Ebenezer and Martha (Burns) Hopkins; Olive d. 13 Aug 1864.

Isaac Blanchard was a farmer in Milford.

Isaac Blanchard did not leave a will. A probate record dated 4 March 1827 listed the following heirs-at-law: widow Olive Blanchard; Isaac Blanchard of Fitchburg, Massachusetts; Olive Howe wife of Jeremiah Howe of Milford; Jerusha Goss wife of Samuel Goss of Merrimack; Sophia Blanchard, single woman of Milford; Charlotte Hutchinson wife of Silvester Hutchinson of Wilton; Rachel Howard wife of Jacob Howard of Milford; Nancy Blanchard single woman of Milford; Melora Blanchard single woman of Milford; Rebecca Blanchard; and Charles Blanchard. The last three named were under twenty-one years of age.[2780]

Isaac Blanchard and Olive Hopkins were parents of ten children, the birth of the oldest child record at Amherst, New Hampshire and the remainder at Milford.

i ISAAC BLANCHARD, b. 5 Nov 1786; d. at Fitchburg, before 1850; m. at Milford, 30 Dec 1810, HANNAH HERRICK, b. at Portland, Sep 1791 daughter of Joseph and Lydia (Lowell) Herrick; Hannah d. at Fitchburg, 16 Sep 1852.

ii OLIVE BLANCHARD, b. 5 Aug 1789; d. at Milford, 11 Dec 1864; m. at Milford, 3 Jan 1809, JEREMIAH HOWE, b. at Montpelier, 1786;[2781] Jeremiah d. at Milford, 3 Sep 1854.

iii JERUSHA BLANCHARD, b. 4 Nov 1791; d. at Milford, 11 Mar 1878; m. at Milford, 28 Aug 1814, SAMUEL GOSS, b. at Amherst, 14 Jun 1788 son of John and Elizabeth (-) Goss; Samuel d. at Milford, 7 Aug 1863.

iv SOPHIA BLANCHARD, b. 17 Apr 1794; d. at Milford, 16 Oct 1884. Sophia did not marry.

v CHARLOTTE BLANCHARD, b. 4 Nov 1796; d. at Wilton, 26 Jan 1871; m. 15 Dec 1815, SYLVESTER HUTCHINSON, b. at Wilton, 21 Jun 1789 son of Ebenezer and Phebe (Sawtell) Hutchinson; Sylvester d. at Wilton, 29 Mar 1858.

vi RACHEL BLANCHARD, b. 4 Oct 1799; d. at Milford, 3 May 1889; m. at Milford, 10 Mar 1824, JACOB HOWARD, b. at Lyndeborough, 3 Mar 1795 son of Silas and Rebecca (Reed) Howard; Jacob d. at Milford, 5 May 1873.

2776 There is another Daniel Blanchard (born 1755) who married Mary Vinson and based in Weymouth having children at the same time. As a result, the death records that give parents as Daniel and Mary may not be definitive, but the movement patterns of these children (for example, siblings living near each other in Lynn at the same time) suggests that these five children likely go with these parents.

2777 Walter Abbott is a bit of a mystery. He seems not at all connected to either the Andover or Rowley Abbott lines. The idea is that there was an Abbott line that came from England and settled in Stonington, CT but there seems to be no firm information related to that.

2778 Peter's parents are given as Daniel and Mary on his death record, but his placement in this family is tentative.

2779 Parents are given as Levi and Jemima Littlefield on her death record.

2780 *New Hampshire. Probate Court (Hillsborough County)*; Probate Place: *Hillsborough, New Hampshire*, Probate records 1818-1829, volume 30, p 512

2781 Ramsdell. *History of Milford*, p 765

vii NANCY BLANCHARD, b. 23 Feb 1804; d. at Nashua, 31 Dec 1850; m. 12 Feb 1828, JOSEPHUS BALDWIN, b. at Nashua, 15 Oct 1803 son of James and Priscilla (Keyes) Baldwin; Josephus d. at Nashua, 4 Mar 1872. Josephus married widow Lydia Hunt in 1863.

viii MELORA BLANCHARD, b. 3 Oct 1806; d. at Wilton, 25 Feb 1889. Melora did not marry.

ix REBECCA BLANCHARD, b. 1 Jun 1809; d. at Nashua, 8 Apr 1870; m. at Milford, 8 Apr 1834, WILLIAM FAXON WHITMARSH, b. at Lyndeborough, 6 Dec 1805 son of Charles and Anna (Faxon) Whitmarsh; William d. at Nashua, 9 Apr 1846.

x CHARLES BLANCHARD, b. 20 Oct 1812; d. at Nashua, 29 Mary 1880; m. 15 Jul 1847, his third cousin, SALLY CHAMBERLAIN *(Sally Abbott Chamberlain[5], Jeremiah[4], Jeremiah[3], Nathaniel[2], George[1])*, b. at Milford, 11 Mar 1823 daughter of Joseph and Sally (Abbott) Chamberlain; Sally d. at Nashua, 10 Apr 1907. Sally is a child in Family 1116.

1050) AMOS BLANCHARD *(Daniel Blanchard[4], Sarah Abbott Blanchard[3], Nathaniel[2], George[1])*, b. at Andover, 22 Jan 1766 son of Daniel and Jerusha (Eaton) Blanchard; d. at Lynn 25 May 1842; m. 27 Jan 1789, LAVINA HOPKINS, b. at Milford, 1769 daughter of Benjamin and Anna (Powers) Hopkins; Lavina d. 1 Aug 1843.

Amos Blanchard was a fifer during the Revolution with his rank given as musician. He enlisted March 1781 in Captain Nehemiah Emerson's company in the 10th Regiment of the Massachusetts line. He served until December 1783. Amos made application for a pension in 1818 while a resident of Lynn. An inventory completed as part of the pension application valued his entire estate at $65. He had no real estate and no income. His wife and a 17-year-old son were described as invalids and a daughter and three other sons between ages 8 and 15 were in the home. The pension application file includes a page torn from the family bible which provides the ancestry of Amos. Amos received a pension of $8 per month and Lavina, as his widow, continued to receive a pension.[2782]

Eleven children have been identified for Amos Blanchard and Lavina Hopkins. Perhaps as a result of their poverty and uncertain circumstances, this family seems to have moved several times with birthplaces of children given in various locations in New Hampshire and Massachusetts.

i AMOS BLANCHARD, b. at Amherst, NH, 30 Jun 1789; nothing further known.

ii LAVINA BLANCHARD, b. in NH, 17 Jan 1791; d. at Lynn, MA, 27 Aug 1819; m. at Lynn, 30 May 1813, her fourth cousin, JOHN LOVEJOY *(Lydia Abbott Lovejoy[5], Joseph[4], Joseph[3], John[2], George[1])*, b. at Wilton, 11 Dec 1789 son of Samuel and Lydia (Abbott) Lovejoy; John d. at Lynn, 12 Sep 1876. John married second Ruth V. Andrews. John Lovejoy is a child in Family 317.

iii LEVI BLANCHARD, b. at Lynnfield, 4 Mar 1793. Levi was a seaman[2783] and nothing further is known.

iv DANIEL BLANCHARD, b. at Lynnfield, 23 Nov 1794; d. at Lynn, 26 Sep 1823; m. at Lynn, 9 Mar 1820, MARY HARRIS, b. in MA, about 1802; Mary d. at Baltimore, MD, 26 May 1874. Mary did not remarry. She lived with her son Daniel Harris Blanchard in Baltimore.

v ELIAS BLANCHARD, b. at Lynnfield, Oct 1796; d. at Lynn, 4 oct 1817.

vi ELIZA BLANCHARD, b. about 1798; d. at Lynn, 9 Sep 1881; m. at Lynn, 11 Nov 1819, JOHN STOCKER BANCROFT, b. at Lynn, 5 Dec 1796 son of Ebenezer and Nancy (Sargent) Bancroft; John d. at Boston, 21 Oct 1852.

vii CYRENE BLANCHARD, b. at Andover, 12 Oct 1800; d. at Lynn, 24 Sep 1819.

viii MARIA BLANCHARD, b. at Lynn, about 1803; m. 1st, at Lynn, 20 Jun 1824, ALFRED TUFTS, b. at Malden, 15 May 1802 son of Samuel and Martha (Upham) Tufts. Maria m. 2nd, at Lynn, 12 Sep 1830, JOSEPH A. PITMAN.

ix MARTIN LUTHER BLANCHARD, b. at Lynnfield, about 1807; d. at Lynn, 1 Mar 1832; m. SARAH N. SARGENT, b. at Lynn, 9 May 1808 daughter of Samuel and Keturah (Newhall) Sargent; Sarah d. at Lynn, 26 Jun 1834.

x WILLIAM H. BLANCHARD, b. perhaps at Portsmouth, 1809; d. at Marlborough, MA, 3 Sep 1885; m. 1st, at Lynn, 20 Jun 1832, LYDIA FARRINGTON, b. at Lynn, 27 Sep 1807 daughter of Amos and Polly (Newhall) Farrington; Lydia d. 10 May 1843. William m. 2nd, at Lynn, 9 Jun 1845, MARY JANE HOLLAND, b. about 1819 and d. after 1885.

2782 Revolutionary War Pension and Bounty-Land Warrant Application Files
2783 Web: US, New England Seamen's Protection Certificate Index, 1796-1871

xi CHARLES EDWARD BLANCHARD, b. at Lynn, 22 Oct 1811; d. at Lynn, 18 Sep 1841; m. at Lynn, 10 Nov 1833, EMILY SARGENT, b. at Lynn, 16 Nov 1812 daughter of Samuel and Keturah (Newhall) Sargent; Emily d. at Lynn, 12 Aug 1835.

1051) LUCY BLANCHARD *(Daniel Blanchard⁴, Sarah Abbott Blanchard³, Nathaniel², George¹)*, b. at Andover, Jan 1771 daughter of Daniel and Jerusha (Eaton) Blanchard; d. at Milford, NH, 12 Feb 1855;[2784] m. at Danvers, 27 Oct 1793, NATHAN PUTNAM, b. at Danvers, 18 Mar 1773 son of Nathan and Hannah (Putnam) Putnam; Nathan d. at Milford, 12 Mar 1842.[2785]

Lucy and Nathan started their family in Danvers but relocated to Milford, New Hampshire in 1797. They were the parents of nine children, the oldest two born at Danvers and the other children at Milford.

i LUCY PUTNAM, b. 17 Feb 1794; d. 30 Aug 1797.

ii NATHAN PUTNAM, b. 7 Mar 1796; d. at Salem, MA, 25 Apr 1879; m. 1st, at Salem, 17 Mar 1822, his fourth cousin, MARY ABBOTT *(George⁵, Stephen⁴, Stephen³, John², George¹)*, b. at Wilton, 11 Aug 1794 daughter of George and Rebecca (Blanchard) Abbott; Mary d. at Salem, 27 May 1847. Nathan m. 2nd, about 1848, CAROLINE MESSER, b. at Piermont, NH, 11 Sep 1821 daughter of Daniel and Ruth (Rodman) Messer; Caroline d. at Salem, 13 Aug 1887. Mary Abbott is a child in Family 329.

iii PERLEY PUTNAM, b. 5 Mar 1798; d. at Milford, 15 Sep 1825. Perley did not marry. His will has bequests to his father Nathan, mother Lucy, brother Daniel, and brother Nathan of Salem.

iv LUCY PUTNAM, b. 3 Aug 1800; d. at Milford, 5 Apr 1845; m. about 1818, NATHANIEL WOOLSON, b. at Amherst, NH, 24 Apr 1795 son of Ezra and Susannah (Elliott) Woolson; Nathaniel d. at Milford, 4 Dec 1844.

v CYRENE PUTNAM, b. 22 Oct 1802; d. at New Ipswich, NH, 2 Sep 1834; m. 12 Mar 1829 as his second of three wives, JAMES DAVIS, b. at New Ipswich, 6 Apr 1793 son of Silas and Mary (Preston) Davis; James d. at New Ipswich, 26 May 1865. James was first married to Patty Bacon and third married to Ann Giles.[2786]

vi DANIEL PUTNAM, b. 12 Aug 1804; d. at Milford, 31 May 1881; m. at Newburyport, MA, 8 May 1832, ELIZABETH HALE, b. at Newburyport, 6 Dec 1807 daughter of Moses and Susan (Tappan) Hale; Elizabeth d. at Milford, 3 May 1891.

vii AMOS PUTNAM, b. 15 Aug 1806; d. at Milford, 23 Aug 1859; m. 15 Dec 1841, DEBORAH HILL, b. at Mont Vernon, 23 Oct 1824 daughter of James and Huldah (Peabody) Hill; Deborah d. at Milford, 10 Apr 1904.

viii MARY JANETTE PUTNAM, b. 18 May 1809; d. at Chicago, IL, 16 Feb 1891; m. 9 May 1832, JOHN GRAFTON GREENOUGH, b. at Newburyport, 20 Dec 1806 son of John and Elizabeth (March) Greenough; John d. at Chatham, NY, 1873.

ix DAVID PUTNAM, b. 9 Jul 1816; died in infancy.

1052) ABIEL BLANCHARD *(Daniel Blanchard⁴, Sarah Abbott Blanchard³, Nathaniel², George¹)*, b. at Andover, Mar 1773 son of Daniel and Jerusha (Eaton) Blanchard; d. at Clermont County, OH, 1821; m. 1st, 9 Apr 1795, HANNAH GRAY, b. at Wilton, 17 Jun 1773 daughter of Timothy and Hannah (Blanchard) Gray;[2787] Hannah d. about 1807. Abiel m. 2nd, at Monkton, VT, 31 May 1808, PATIENCE VARNEY, *possibly* b. at Berwick, ME, 1 Oct 1780 daughter of Hezekiah and Hannah (Rogers) Varney;[2788] Patience d. at Clermont, OH, after 1840.

Abiel Blanchard and Hannah Gray were parents of seven children, the four oldest children born at Landgrove and the younger children at Ferrisburgh, Vermont.

i HANNAH BLANCHARD, b. 28 Oct 1795

ii ACHSAH BLANCHARD, b. 5 Feb 1797

2784 Ramsdell and Colburn, *History of Milford*, vol 1, p 891

2785 Burial site is Union Street Cemetery, Milford, NH, Plot 47. Findagrave.com

2786 Chandler and Lee, *The History of New Ipswich*

2787 The 1807 New Hampshire will of Timothy Gray includes a bequest to his daughter Hannah Blanchard.

2788 Hezekiah Varney was in Monkton, Vermont at the time of his death in 1795. Hezekiah and Hannah (Rogers) Varney did have a daughter Patience born in Berwick, Maine in 1780.

iii ABIEL BLANCHARD, b. 9 Mar 1799

iv HERMAN BLANCHARD, b. 1 Aug 1800; d. at Clermont County, OH, 1844; m. 26 Mar 1833, SARAH DAVIS.

v REUBEN BLANCHARD, b. 14 Mar 1802

vi CLARE BLANCHARD, b. 19 Nov 1803

vii DEAMUS BLANCHARD, b. 6 Jan 1806; d. after 1860 when he was living in Starksboro, VT; m. 1st MARY who died about 1849 and m. 2nd, JULIA

Abiel Blanchard and Patience Varney were parents of four children.

i ABEL BLANCHARD, b. 1809

ii EZRA BLANCHARD, b. 1811; m. 1st, at Clermont County, OH, 10 Jan 1833, CATHERINE WOOD, b. in OH about 1815; Catherine d. at Marion, IN, about 1854. Ezra m. 2nd, at Jennings, IN, 19 Jul 1855, JANE SUMMERFIELD.

iii LUCY BLANCHARD, b. 1813

iv AMOS BLANCHARD, b. in PA, 1815; d. at Montgomery, IN, after 1870; m. 1st, at Clermont County, 11 Aug 1833, SARAH LAVER, b. in PA, about 1806; Sarah d. at Montgomery, about 1858. Amos m. 2nd, 6 Mar 1859, SARAH ANN BRANHAM. Amos m. 3rd, 11 Nov 1860, LUCINDA GOODHUE.

1053) JOHN BLANCHARD *(John Blanchard⁴, Sarah Abbott Blanchard³, Nathaniel², George¹)*, b. at Concord, 11 Sep 1763 son of John and Eleanor (Stevens) Blanchard; d. at Farmington, MI, 1844; m. HANNAH PERRIN.

On 9 July 1834 while a resident of Farmington in the Michigan Territory, John Blanchard made application for a pension related to his service in the Revolution. In his affidavit, John reported that in 1778 at age 15 while living in Dunbarton, he enlisted in the company of Captain Burnham, marched to Rhode Island, and joined the army under General Sullivan. He returned to Dunbarton after two months. H enlisted as a private in July 1779 for one year, again from Dunbarton. He was with the first and second New Hampshire Regiments commanded by Colonels Cilley and Read. He returned home after this enlistment where he remained until May 1782 when he again enlisted at Concord and was in the light infantry company commanded by Captain Monroe. After June of that year, he was at West Point until November when his father sent a man to be his substitute and John returned home.

After his time in the army, John reported he was in Concord, New Hampshire for five years, then in Vermont for about ten years, next to the province of Lower Canada where he lived nineteen years, then to Lockport, New York where he lived until 1832. He then relocated to Farmington. He noted that he had never been in such reduced circumstances that he needed to apply for a pension, but the infirmities of old age now required that he make the application. In the application, he states he was born in Concord on 11 September 1763.[2789]

This is a family with conflicting information about marriages and children. It is not clear if John was married more than once. There is evidence for four children, although there may well have been more. The four children known were born in Lower Canada.

i SOPHIA BLANCHARD, b. 25 Dec 1799; d. at Riley, MI, 6 Mar 1889; m. at LaChute, Québec, 20 Feb 1819, ABRAHAM LACKEY, b. at Spencer, MA, 25 May 1793 son of Abraham and Mary (Stone) Lackey; Abraham d. at Riley, MI, 2 Aug 1866.

ii JOHN BLANCHARD, b. about 1800; d. at Farmington, MI about 1838;[2790] m. at Farmington, 16 Jun 1829, ELIZABETH "BETSEY" WIXOM, b. at Hector, NY, 1805 daughter of Robert and Phebe (Lewis) Wixom; Betsey d. at Farmington, 1 Sep 1848.

iii DAVID BLANCHARD, b. 5 Oct 1808; d. at Riley, MI, 9 Sep 1895; m. at Elba, NY, 25 Jan 1831, SARAH MILLER, b. 12 Jul 1812; Sarah d. at Riley, 19 Aug 1876. David and Sarah's son Charles E. Blanchard died 10 Apr 1862 of pneumonia during the Civil War; he was just 16.

iv LOVINA BLANCHARD, b. 1811; d. at Cascade, MI, about 1861; m. 1833, EZRA COLLINS MILLER, b. at Seneca County, NY, 15 May 1805; Ezra d. at Cascade, 29 Dec 1882. After Lovina's death, Ezra married Rachel Clark 30 Nov 1862.

[2789] U.S., Revolutionary War Pension and Bounty-Land Warrant Application Files, 1800-1900

[2790] John has a child born in 1836, but his widow Betsey is the head of household in the 1840 census at Farmington.

1054) STEVENS BLANCHARD *(John Blanchard[4], Sarah Abbott Blanchard[3], Nathaniel[2], George[1])*, b. at Concord, 15 Sep 1765 son of John and Eleanor (Stevens) Blanchard; d. at Canterbury, 12 May 1792; m. 16 Oct 1788, his third cousin once removed, SARAH HALL *(Obadiah Hall[5], Dorcas Abbott Hall[4], Edward[3], Thomas[2], George[1])*, b. at Canterbury, 3 Sep 1771 daughter of Obadiah and Mary (Perham) Hall;[2791] Sarah d. at Beekmantown, NY, 1824. Sarah m. 2nd, 16 Jun 1793, OBADIAH MOONEY, b. at Durham, NH, 26 Jun 1748 son of Hercules and Elizabeth (Evans) Mooney; Obadiah d. at Beartown, NY, 1836.

Stevens Blanchard did not leave a will and his estate entered probate 19 September 1792. Obadiah Hall and John Blanchard were appointed guardians for the two minor children, Sally Blanchard and Parker Blanchard. The claims against the estate were such that the estate was sold to settle the claims.[2792]

Stevens Blanchard and Sarah Hall were parents of two children both born at Canterbury.

i SARAH BLANCHARD, b. 3 Apr 1788; d. at Beekmantown, NY, 27 May 1873; m. at Northfield, NH, Oct 1809, LEVITT C. DURGIN, b. at Canterbury, 21 May 1787 son of Joseph and Abigail (Hoyt) Durgin; Levitt d. at Beekmantown, NY, 14 Apr 1842.[2793]

ii PARKER BLANCHARD, b. 13 Jan 1791; d. at Point Au Roche, NY, 6 Oct 1877; m. MARY, b. about 1790 who has not been identified; Mary d. 2 Dec 1874.

Obadiah Mooney and Sarah Hall were parents of seven children born at Canterbury.

i STEVENS MOONEY, b. 4 May 1794; d. at Champlain, NY, 9 Jun 1875; m. 1819, ELIZABETH ALLEN, b. at South Hero, VT, 1804 daughter of Eleazer Hawkes and Eunice (Gilbert) Allen;[2794] Elizabeth d. 20 Feb 1840.

ii OBADIAH MOONEY, b. 11 Jan 1796; d. at Beekmantown, 8 May 1870; m. NANCY CONNOR,[2795] b. at South Hero, VT, 1804 daughter of Stephen and Polly (Barnes) Connor; Nancy d. at Plattsburgh, 16 Sep 1887.

iii HERCULES MOONEY, b. 8 Jan 1798; d. at Moira, NY, 21 Mar 1881; m. at South Hero, 4 Jul 1819, MARY KINNEY, b. at South Hero, 25 Apr 1802 daughter of Thomas and Mary (Bishop) Kinney; Mary d. at South Hero, 8 Apr 1868.

iv JOHN MOONEY, b. 7 Apr 1800; d. at Beekmantown, 22 Jul 1887; m. EUNICE CONNOR, b. at South Hero, about 1805 daughter of Stephen and Polly (Barnes) Connor; Eunice d. at Beekmantown, 5 Apr 1897.

v JEREMIAH MOONEY, b. 15 Sep 1802; d. 30 Sep 1802.

vi BENJAMIN F. MOONEY, b. 28 Nov 1804; nothing further found

vii ASA MOONEY, b. 11 May 1808; d. at North Hero, VT, 3 Sep 1866; m. LOIS HUTCHINS, b. at North Hero, 1809 daughter of Nathan and Lois (Hatch) Hutchins;[2796] Lois d. at Alburgh, VT, 4 Jun 1878.

1055) SARAH BLANCHARD *(John Blanchard[4], Sarah Abbott Blanchard[3], Nathaniel[2], George[1])*, b. at Concord, 28 Sep 1769 daughter of John and Eleanor (Stevens) Blanchard; d. at Concord, 11 Nov 1848; m. about 1797, EBENEZER FISK, b. at Tewksbury, 26 Jan 1766 son of Ephraim and Mehitable (Frost) Fisk; Ebenezer d. at Concord about 1857.

Ebenezer Fisk was born in Tewksbury but relocated to Concord with his family when he was about six years old. He was one of the first settlers at Little Pond in Concord.[2797]

In his will written 22 April 1848 (proved 1857), Ebenezer Fisk bequeaths to beloved wife Sarah all the household furniture, provisions, and one cow. Sarah receives use of the house farm during her natural life which is in lieu of her dower. Daughter Betsey Seavey wife of Andrew receives $200. Son Abria Fisk and daughter Eleanor Fisk receive all the residue of the estate. Abria is appointed executor.[2798]

[2791] The 1816 will of Obadiah Hall includes a bequest to his eldest daughter Sarah Mooney wife of Obadiah Mooney.

[2792] *New Hampshire. Probate Court (Rockingham County);* Probate Place: *Rockingham, New Hampshire, Estate Papers, No 5706-5815, 1791-1792*, Case 5804

[2793] War of 1812 Pension and Bounty Land Warrant Application Files. The application of Sarah Blanchard Durgin for a widow's pension based on her husband's War of 1812 service confirms the marriage date and date of death of husband.

[2794] The 1828 will of Eleazer Hawkes Allen of South Hero includes a bequest to his daughter Elizabeth Mooney.

[2795] Cutter, *Genealogical and Family History of Northern New York*, volume 2, p 705

[2796] In his 1833 will, Nathan Hutchins of North Hero leaves half his estate to Asa Mooney and his wife.

[2797] Bouton, *History of Concord*, p 661

[2798] *New Hampshire. Probate Court (Merrimack County);* Probate Place: *Merrimack, New Hampshire, Probate Records, Vol 25, 1847-1856*, pp 650-651, will of Ebenezer Fisk, 22 April 1848

Ebenezer Fisk and Sarah Blanchard were parents of six children all born at Concord. Two of the children, Henry and Mehitable, were teachers but both these children died in their 20's.

i BETSY FISK, b. 3 Aug 1798; d. at Hopkinton, NH, 6 Mar 1880; m. at Concord, 29 May 1828, ANDREW SEAVEY, b. at Nottingham, NH, 21 May 1798; Andrew d. at Contoocook, NH, 23 Sep 1881.

ii ABRIA FISK, b. 9 Mar 1800; d. at Manchester, NH, 1 Nov 1877; m. 1st, at Concord, 12 Dec 1826, his third cousin, EUNICE BUSS ABBOTT *(Thomas5, Daniel4, George3, Thomas2, George1)*, b. at Concord, 22 Nov 1801 daughter of Thomas and Anna (Eaton) Abbott; Eunice d. 1865. Abria m. 2nd, 24 Oct 1866, Eunice's sister, SARAH ELIZABETH ABBOTT, b. 15 Jul 1823; Sarah d. at Manchester, 14 Jul 1895. Eunice and Sarah are children in Family 927.

iii ELEANOR S. FISK, b. 12 Jul 1801; d. at Canterbury, 26 Apr 1882. Eleanor did not marry. Eleanor left her estate to her nephew Francis Fisk with whom she lived in her later years.

iv HENRY FISK, b. 30 Oct 1803; d. at Concord, 26 May 1831. Henry was a teacher.

v SARAH FISK, b. 8 Jun 1805; d. at Concord, 30 Oct 1840; m. at Concord, 5 Apr 1832, HAZEN RUNNELS, b. at Concord, 21 Sep 1801 son of Joseph and Joanna (Farnum) Runnels; Hazen d. at Concord, about 1859. After Sarah's death, Hazen married Sarah E. Corlis 19 Apr 1842.

vi MEHITABLE F. FISK, b. 4 May 1809; d. at Concord, 19 Aug 1832. Mehitable was a teacher.

1056) DAVID BLANCHARD *(John Blanchard4, Sarah Abbott Blanchard3, Nathaniel2, George1)*, b. at Concord, 4 Dec 1771 son of John and Eleanor (Stevens) Blanchard; d. at Concord, 10 Jan 1805;[2799] m. 4 Oct 1796, HANNAH EATON, b. 31 Jun 1772 daughter of William and Sarah (Farnum) Eaton.

David was a farmer in Concord. David Blanchard did not leave a will. As part of the probate, widow Hannah Blanchard was appointed guardian for four minor children: Herman Blanchard, Matilda Blanchard, William Blanchard, and Susannah Blanchard.[2800]

David Blanchard and Hannah Eaton were parents of four children born at Concord.

i HERMAN BLANCHARD, b. 12 Feb 1797; d. at Cooper, MI, 4 May 1882; m. 1st, 23 Nov 1824, BETSEY MARIA TAYLOR,[2801] b. 20 Jan 1803 daughter of Stephen and Ruth (Lovejoy) Taylor;[2802] Betsey d. at Persis, NY, 6 Jan 1838. Herman m. 2nd, at Wales, NY, 3 Jan 1839, LAURA WEED, b. at Saratoga County, NY, 11 Mar 1810 daughter of John D. and Betsey (Wood) Weed; Laura d. at Cooper, 24 Jan 1886.

ii MATILDA BLANCHARD, b. 5 Nov 1798; d. at Dakota, WI, 8 Feb 1852; m. at Brownville, NY, 18 Jan 1822, GEORGE THORNGATE, b. at Marlborough, Wiltshire, 30 Apr 1798 son of William and Hannah (-) Thorngate;[2803][2804] George d. at North Loup, NE, 29 Nov 1881.

iii WILLIAM BLANCHARD, b. about 1801; no further record found other than he was living in 1810.

iv SUSANNAH BLANCHARD, b. about 1804; d. at Bethel, ME, 30 Nov 1892; m. about 1828, SILAS GROVER, b. at Bethel, 21 May 1801 son of Jedediah and Hannah (Wheeler) Grover; Silas d. at Bethel, 19 Jun 1855.

1057) MOSES BLANCHARD *(John Blanchard4, Sarah Abbott Blanchard3, Nathaniel2, George1)*, b. at Concord, 15 Oct 1783 son of John and Eleanor (Stevens) Blanchard; d. at Stark, NH, 15 Oct 1858;[2805] m. 24 Apr 1806, ELIZABETH WADLEIGH, b. about 1785; d, after 1850. Both Moses and Elizabeth were listed in the 1850 U.S. at Mexico, ME. Moses went to stay with his son Calvary in New Hampshire after the death of Elizabeth.

Moses Blanchard was a musician and held the position of musician during his military service. He enlisted 24 September 1808 for a five-year term. He enlisted again 14 October 1813 for a period of eighteen months and was in Captain Howland's Company of U.S. Light Dragoons.[2806][2807] Moses claimed in his bounty-land application that in June 1814 he suffered a severe injury to his hand when a splinter thrown from a tree by a cannon ball pierced his hand. Since that time, he was unable

2799 There is a New Hampshire death record for 1805, but the probate record is date 1810, and unsure of the reason for that.
2800 *New Hampshire. Probate Court (Rockingham County)*; Probate Place: *Rockingham, New Hampshire, Estate Papers, No 8161-8265, 1809-1810*
2801 War of 1812 Pension Application Files Index, 1812-1815
2802 Durant, *History of Kalamazoo, Michigan*, p 403
2803 Rood, *Historical Sketch of the Thorngate-Rood Family*, p 11
2804 England, Select Births and Christenings, 1538-1975
2805 New Hampshire, Death and Burial Records Index, 1654-1949
2806 National Archives. Bounty-Land Warrant Applications Index
2807 War of 1812 Pension and Bounty Land Warrant Application Files

to follow his profession as a musician. Dr. Farwell of Mexico, Maine made an affidavit in support of Moses's account of his injuries, his physician also noting that Moses had an injury to his left side that prevented him from performing labor.

Moses Blanchard and Elizabeth Wadleigh were parents of seven children.

i DAVID S. BLANCHARD, b. 7 Apr 1807; d. at Rumford, ME, about 1857; m. 1st, 30 Apr 1829, MEHITABLE TAYLOR, b. 14 Oct 1808 daughter of Simeon and Mary (-) Taylor; Mehitable d. at Rumford, 1 Jan 1851. David m. 2nd, Nov 1851, his fourth cousin once removed, DEBORAH DAVIS HALL *(Joseph Hall6, Daniel Hall5, Dorcas Abbott Hall4, Edward3, Thomas2, George1)*, b. at Rumford, 11 Jan 1811 daughter of Joseph and Judith (Blanchard) Hall; Deborah d. at Rumford, 17 Apr 1891. Deborah Hall was first married to Philip Wheeler in 1846.

ii BENJAMIN H. BLANCHARD, b. 29 Jan 1810; d. at Mexico, ME, 23 Jan 1852; m. about 1835, MARY P. BERRY, b. 28 Aug 1812 daughter of Joseph and Sarah (Greenleaf) Berry;[2808] Mary d. after 1860, likely at Rumford. After Benjamin's death, Mary married Oliver S. Lang 24 Sep 1853.

iii LUCY M. BLANCHARD, b. 22 Dec 1819; d. in IA, about 1848; m. at Mexico, ME, 6 Feb 1840, GEORGE S. WALTON, b. 3 Oct 1818; George d. at Medford, OR, 1 Sep 1895. After Lucy's death, George married Samantha H. C. Amy 16 Apr 1849.

iv CALVARY M. BLANCHARD, b. 18 Feb 1822; d. at Dummer, NH, 18 Sep 1872; m. 1842, MARY F. SMITH, b. in ME, 1819; Mary d. at Milan, NH, 7 Sep 1895.

v ZEBADIAH M. BLANCHARD, b. 12 May 1824; d. at Cuyahoga County, OH, 1870 (probate 1870); m. at Cuyahoga, 24 Jun 1853, JANE A. RUDGE, b. in CT, 1826; Jane d. at Cleveland, OH, 8 Oct 1901.

vi NICHOLAS G. BLANCHARD, b. 4 Jan 1828; was living in 1850 but no record after.

vii HESTER ANN BLANCHARD, b. 25 Sep 1830; no further record.

1058) BATHSHEBA BLANCHARD *(Bathsheba Abbott Blanchard4, Joseph3, Nathaniel2, George1)*, b. at Andover, 20 Apr 1754 daughter of Nathan and Bathsheba (Abbott) Blanchard; d. likely at Lyndeborough, NH; m. 1 Jul 1768 (intention listed, although seems very young), DANIEL BARKER, b. at Methuen, 30 May 1746 son of Zebadiah and Phebe (Merrill) Barker; Daniel is reported to have died during the Revolutionary War probably about 1784 (date of birth of youngest child).[2809] Bathsheba m. 2nd, at Lyndeborough, 25 Dec 1792, DAVID HARDY.

Bathsheba Blanchard and Daniel Barker were parents of seven children the oldest six children and Wilton and the youngest child at Lyndeborough.

i BATHSHEBA BARKER, b. 6 Sep 1769; m. at Lyndeborough, 19 Aug 1788, BENJAMIN HOLT, b. about 1765 possibly the son of William and Beulah (-) Holt of Lyndeborough.

ii DORCAS BARKER, b. 30 May 1771; d. at Weston, VT, 4 Jan 1857; m. at Temple, NH, 17 Sep 1790, DAVID AUSTIN, b. at Temple, 20 Mar 1769 son of Timothy and Elizabeth (Ames) Austin; David d. at Weston, 15 Feb 1844.

iii PHEBE BARKER, b. 3 May 1773; m. 1st, at Lyndeborough, 19 May 1791, JOHN FLETCHER, b. about 1766 son of Simeon and Mary (Davis) Fletcher; John d. at Greenfield, 1792. Phebe m. 2nd, at Lyndeborough, 3 Oct 1793, WILLIAM TAYLOR.

iv LOIS BARKER, b. 19 Apr 1775; m. at Lyndeborough, 26 Sep 1795, BENJAMIN FARNUM.

v SARAH MERRILL BARKER, b. 15 Apr 1777

vi RHODA BARKER, b. 12 Apr 1779

vii NATHAN BLANCHARD BARKER, b. 1784; d. at Lewiston, NY, 1864; m. about 1807, HANNAH PARKER, b. at Peterborough, NH, 1 Feb 1781 daughter of Abel and Sarah (-) Parker; Hannah d. at Lewiston, Apr 1860.

1059) HANNAH DALE *(Hannah Abbott Dale4, Joseph3, Nathaniel2, George1)*, b. at Wilton, 22 Oct 1763 daughter of Timothy and Hannah (Abbott) Dale; she is likely the Hannah Dale who married at Wilton, 26 Feb 1793, BARNABAS GIBSON, b. at

2808 Greenleaf, *Genealogy of the Greenleaf Family*, p 406

2809 Cochrane, *Families of Antrim*, NH, p 352

Pelham, 12 Jul 1767 son of Barnabas and Elizabeth (-) Gibson; Barnabas d. at Pelham, 4 Feb 1852. After Hannah's death, Barnabas married Betsey Chase about 1802.

Hannah Dale and Barnabas Gibson were parents of four children born at Pelham. Barnabas had five children with his second wife Betsey Chase.

i SAMUEL D. GIBSON, b. 26 Apr 1794; d. at Pelham, 29 Jul 1864; m. SUSAN F., b. about 1788; Susan d. at Pelham, 28 May 1865.

ii MARY "POLLY" GIBSON, b. 12 Sep 1795; d. at Pelham, 1 Aug 1826. Mary did not marry.

iii ROBERT GIBSON, b. 4 Nov 1797; d. at Londonderry, NH, 22 Aug 1881; m. 6 Apr 1828, ELIZA ANN FOX, b. about 1804; Eliza d. at Londonderry, 28 Feb 1886.

iv HANNAH GIBSON, b. 1801; d. at Pelham, 1 Dec 1801.

1060) JOSHUA DALE *(Hannah Abbott Dale⁴, Joseph³, Nathaniel², George¹)*, b. at Wilton, 22 Jan 1765 son of Timothy and Hannah (Abbott) Dale; d. at Weston, VT, 23 Mar 1845; m. at Andover, VT, 13 Apr 1789, RHODA PEASE, b. 11 May 1764 daughter of Ezekiel and Jemima (Markham) Pease; Rhoda d. at Andover, VT, 6 Jan 1821.

Joshua Dale and Rhoda Pease were parents of ten children, the oldest eight children born at Landgrove and the younger children at Weston, Vermont.

i RHODA DALE, b. 1789; d. at Landgrove, 25 Jan 1790.

ii JOSHUA DALE, b. 4 Mar 1791; d. at Marlborough, MA, 25 Aug 1875; m. at Enfield, CT, 22 Jan 1818, HANNAH PHELPS, b. at Enfield, 4 Jan 1800 daughter of Peletiah and Sarah (Simmons) Phelps; Hannah d. at Winn, ME, 10 May 1859.

iii ABBOT DALE, b. 3 Aug 1793; d. at LaGrange, OH, 8 Sep 1872; m. at Weston, VT, 3 Dec 1818, MALINDA PEASE, b. at Landgrove, 5 Jun 1800 daughter of Elijah and Polly (Allen) Pease; Malinda d. at LaGrange, 4 Jun 1873.

iv JOSEPH DALE, b. 15 Jul 1794; d. 16 Jul 1794.

v TIMOTHY DALE, b. and d. 4 Feb 1796.

vi SAMUEL DALE, b. 1 Aug 1797; d. at Boston, 9 Apr 1858; m. 15 Feb 1821, MELINDA TARBELL, b. at Chester, VT, 20 Aug 1798 daughter of Reuben and Elizabeth (Blood) Tarbell; Melinda d. at Chelsea, MA, 6 May 1868.

vii ANSON DALE, b. 31 Jan 1800; d. at Walpole, NH, 17 Jan 1855; m. at Boston, 2 Dec 1830, SARAH NELSON, b. at Salem, about 1805.

viii JOHN DALE, b. 9 Nov 1803; d. at Weston, 24 Sep 1832; m. SARAH SMITH, b. at Mont Vernon, NH, 2 Aug 1806 daughter of Rogers and Sarah (Dodge) Smith;[2810] Sarah d. Aug 1851. After John's death, Sarah married Elijah Munson.

ix CEPHAS DALE, b. 19 Oct 1806; d. at Denmark, IA, 16 Mar 1868; m. REBECCA SMITH, b. at Mont Vernon, 12 Nov 1808 daughter of Rogers and Sarah (Dodge) Smith; Rebecca d. at Denmark, IA, 11 Mar 1877.

x JONAS DALE, b. 9 Jun 1809; d. at Weston, 29 Jul 1845; m. 24 Sep 1839, ROXANNA BATCHELDER, b. at Townsend, VT, 5 Oct 1817 daughter of Edmund and Betsey (Jones) Batchelder; d. at Londonderry, NH, 28 Nov 1867. After Jonas's death, Roxanna married William S. Waterman.

1061) JOSEPH ABBOTT *(Joseph⁴, Joseph³, Nathaniel², George¹)*, b. at Andover, 6 Nov 1763 son of Joseph and Mary (Barker) Abbott; d. at Keene, NH, 23 Nov 1790; m. 30 Jun 1785, BETSY KING, b. 26 Jun 1764 daughter of Richard and Lucy (Butterfield) King. Lucy m. 2nd, Thomas Baker.

Joseph Abbott did not leave a will and his estate entered probate 7 Dec 1790 with widow Betsy declining administration and requesting Nathan Blake, Jr. as administrator. The estate was valued at £17:19:9.[2811]

There are three children known for Joseph Abbott and Betsy King born at Keene, New Hampshire.

i JOSEPH ABBOTT, b. 22 Apr 1786; nothing further known.

ii ISAAC ABBOTT, b. 26 Sep 1788; nothing further known.

[2810] Secomb, *History of the Town of Antrim*, p 772

[2811] *New Hampshire. Probate Court (Cheshire County)*; Probate Place: *Cheshire, New Hampshire, Estate Files, A1-A61, 1771-1813*, No. 18

iii BETSY ABBOTT, b. 27 Mar 1791; d. at Glover, VT, 9 Mar 1840; m. at Keene, 25 Oct 1814, ISAAC WYMAN, b. at Keene, 14 Nov 1787 son of Isaac and Lucretia (Hammond) Wyman; Isaac d. at Glover, 8 Oct 9 Mar 1840.

1062) JAMES ABBOTT *(Joseph⁴, Joseph³, Nathaniel², George¹)*, b. at Andover, 2 Feb 1768 son of Joseph and Mary (Barker) Abbott; d. at Billerica, Jul 1810; m. 20 Feb 1791, MEHITABLE HOLT, b. at Wilton, 11 Sep 1768 daughter of Daniel and Mehitable (Putnam) Holt; Mehitable d. at Pomfret, CT, 7 Mar 1857.

James Abbott was a merchant in Billerica and served as town clerk in 1797. He was also involved in the development of the Middlesex Turnpike.[2812] After James's death, the family seems to have moved to Waltham where three of the children married.

James did not leave a will and his estate entered probate 27 August 1810 with widow Mehitable requesting that Joseph Locke be named administrator. Real estate consisted of two pews in the meeting house, one on the floor and one in the gallery, valued at $110 and personal estate was $569.05. Claims against the estate were $1,450.01. The widow was allowed $300 from the estate.[2813]

James Abbott and Mehitable Holt were parents of nine children born at Billerica. Marriages were located for just three of the children.

i SOPHRONIA ABBOTT, b. 7 Dec 1791; d. at Pomfret, CT, 1 Dec 1869; m. at Waltham, MA, 21 Aug 1845, PAYSON GROSVENOR, b. at Pomfret, 13 Dec 1776 son of Oliver and Zerviah (Payson) Grosvenor; Payson d. at Pomfret, 10 Oct 1861.

ii JAMES ABBOTT, b. 2 Jun 1793

iii JOSEPH ABBOTT, b. 8 May 1795

iv DANIEL ABBOTT, b. 23 May 1797

v MEHITABLE ABBOTT, b. Feb 1799

vi ISAAC ABBOTT, b. Nov 1800; died young

vii ISAAC ABBOTT, b. 15 Jul 1804

viii JOHN ABBOTT, b. May 1806; d. at Waltham, 28 Nov 1842; m. 1st, at Lowell, 7 Sep 1826, MARY ANN GOVE, b. 1811; Mary Ann d. at Waltham, 13 Dec 1831. John m. 2nd, at Sudbury, 27 Sep 1832, OLIVE HAYNES, b. at Sudbury, 15 Apr 1811 daughter of Josiah and Lydia (Conant) Haynes; Olive d. at Waltham, 19 Jan 1899.

ix CLARISSA ABBOTT, b. Mar 1808; d. at Waltham, MA, 5 Mar 1895; m. at Waltham, 30 Oct 1845, JOHN DAVIS, b. at Weston, 1806 son of John and Lydia (Bowman) Davis; John d. at Waltham, 18 Nov 1890.

1063) ISRAEL ABBOTT *(Joseph⁴, Joseph³, Nathaniel², George¹)*, b. at Andover, 29 Jul 1771 son of Joseph and Mary (Barker) Abbott; d. at Charlestown, NH, 26 Feb 1840; m. at Nelson, NH, 1 May 1789, ALICE BAKER, b. at Littleton, 1 Oct 1770 daughter of Timothy and Mary (Dakin) Baker; Alice d. at Whitefield, NH, 13 Aug 1858.

Israel Abbott was born in Wilton. After his marriage, the family seems to have been in Stoddard and Acworth before settling finally in Charlestown, New Hampshire in 1807.[2814]

Israel Abbott and Alice Baker were parents of ten children.

i ISRAEL ABBOTT, b. 13 Nov 1791; d. at Putney, VT, 1 Jan 1867; m. 1st, at Charlestown, 2 Nov 1811, LYDIA KITTREDGE; Lydia d. about 1815. Israel m. 2nd, at Springfield, VT, 7 Jan 1816, PHEBE PIERCE, b. about 1793; Phebe d. at Putney, 25 Aug 1854.

ii LEVI ABBOTT, b. at Stoddard, NH, 24 Jan 1794; d. at Wilmington, MA, 23 Feb 1867; m. 1st, about 1816, SOPHIA TIDD, b. about 1796; Sophia d. at Woburn, Dec 1830. Levi m. 2nd, at Wilmington, 4 Oct 1838, RHODA BUCK (widow of Harvey Colcord), b. at Wilmington, 14 Apr 1800 daughter of Nathan and Elizabeth (Thompson) Buck; Rhoda d. at Woburn, 3 Feb 1874.

[2812] Hazen, *History of Billerica, Massachusetts*

[2813] Middlesex County, MA: Probate File Papers, 1648-1871.Online database. AmericanAncestors.org. New England Historic Genealogical Society, 2014. Case 19

[2814] Saunderson, *History of Charlestown, New Hampshire*, p 275

iii ISAAC ABBOTT, b. 20 Sep 1796; d. at Lancaster, NH, after 1870; m. SUSAN LABEREE; Susan d. at Lancaster, 1870.

iv JOSEPH ABBOTT, b. 11 Aug 1798; d. 19 Jul 1816.

v BENJAMIN ABBOTT, b. 11 Aug 1798; d. at Cumberland, RI, 1864; m. LYDIA HARRINGTON, b. at Cumberland, 1804; Lydia d. at Cumberland, 1869.

vi LURA ABBOTT, b. 7 Jul 1800; m. at Charlestown, 15 Oct 1822, IRA GOWEN, likely b. at Rockingham, VT, 21 Sep 1795 son of Levi and Achsah (Hill) Gowen. Lura and Ira were living in Cold Spring, WI in 1850.

vii TRYPHENA ABBOTT, b. 27 Mar 1803; d. at Waterford, VT, 11 Oct 1867; m. 2 Jan 1828, WILLARD BOWMAN, b. at Henniker, 4 Jul 1800 son of Jonathan and Anna (Conner) Bowman; Willard d. at Littleton, NH, 28 Feb 1860.

viii HARVEY ABBOTT, b. at Acworth, 28 Dec 1804; d. at Keene, NH, 15 Apr 1886; m. 4 Oct 1831, SOPHRONIA HEWS, b. at Weston, MA, 1 Jun 1804 daughter of Abraham and Martha (Griffin) Hews; Sophronia d. at Keene, 3 Nov 1881.

ix ALICE ABBOTT, b. at Acworth, 30 Jan 1806; d. likely at Abington, MA, after 1855; m. 16 Jan 1828, SILAS BOND, b. at Charlestown, 12 Feb 1799 son of William and Sarah (Parks) Bond; Silas d. before 1850.

x SOPHRONIA ABBOTT, b. at Charlestown, 20 Jun 1807; d. at Whitefield, NH, 10 Feb 1885; m. 2 May 1830, BAKER DODGE, b. at Francestown, 26 Feb 1801 son of Simeon and Mary (Balch) Dodge; Baker d. at Whitefield, 26 Jan 1867.

1064) MOLLY ABBOTT *(Joseph⁴, Joseph³, Nathaniel², George¹)*, b. at Andover, 18 Jun 1773 daughter of Joseph and Mary (Barker) Abbott; d. at Alstead, NH, 1817; m. at Nelson, NH, 30 Aug 1789, LEVI WARREN, b. at Upton, MA, 24 oct 1867 son of Samuel and Elizabeth (-) Warren;[2815] Levi d. at Alstead, 1827 (probate 1827).

Levi Warren and Molly Abbott were parents of nine children born at Alstead.

i POLLY WARREN, b. 21 Mar 1790; d. at Athol, MA, 1 Sep 1849; m. about 1810, ADIN HOLBROOK, b. at Lowell, MA, 2 May 1780 son of Adin and Hannah (Day) Holbrook; Adin d. at Lowell, 17 Apr 1864.

ii BETSEY WARREN, b. 2 Oct 1791; m. 13 Dec 1821, ELISHA SMITH who has not been identified.

iii LUCY WARREN, b. 31 Jul 1796; nothing further known.

iv AMORY WARREN, b. 10 Feb 1799; d. at Groton, 24 Oct 1874; m. at Uxbridge, 17 May 1821, PARLA PARILLA TAFT, b. at Uxbridge, MA, 5 Mar 1798 daughter of Frederic and Abigail (Wood) Taft;[2816] Parla d. 26 Sep 1852.

v SAMUEL WARREN, b. 6 Feb 1802; nothing further known.

vi GARDNER WARREN, b. 6 Nov 1804; d. at Boston, 6 Mar 1879; m. about 1836, MARION FORD, b. at Saratoga Springs, NH, about 1821 daughter of John and Hannah (Smith) Ford;[2817] Marion d. at Manchester, NH, 4 Jan 1850.[2818]

vii FRANKLIN WARREN, b. 7 Dec 1807; nothing further known.

viii HARVEY WARREN, b. 30 Sep 1811; d. at Rochester, NY, 4 Dec 1883; m. about 1842, CATALINA SCHERMERHORN[2819], b. in NY, 25 Aug 1818; Catalina d. at Rochester, 2 Nov 1900.

ix CHARLES FRANKLIN WARREN, b. 26 Feb 1814; d. at Manchester, 11 Feb 1899; m. at Dunstable, MA, 11 Apr 1839, ABBY PARKER, b. at Lexington, MA, 30 Dec 1813 daughter of John A. and Esther (Reed) Parker; Abby d. at Manchester, 18 May 1897.

1065) LUCY ABBOTT *(Joseph⁴, Joseph³, Nathaniel², George¹)*, b. at Wilton, 18 Jul 1775 daughter of Joseph and Mary (Barker) Abbott; d. at Washington County, NY, 31 Jan 1839; m. 1st, 13 Sep 1792, PEPPERELL SKINNER, b. at Mansfield, MA, 8 Jul 1773 son of Samuel and Martha (Grover) Skinner;[2820] Pepperrell d. at Whipple, NY, 16 Apr 1810. Lucy m. 2nd, about 1816,

[2815] The Compendium of American Genealogy, volume VI, p 604

[2816] Guild, Howard Redwood, "Frederic Taft, Esquire of Uxbridge, Mass.", Dedham Historical Register, volume 8, 1897

[2817] After Marion's early death at age 29, her children went to live with Marion's parents John and Hannah Ford in Saratoga Springs (U.S. Census 1850).

[2818] *U.S. Federal Census Mortality Schedules, 1850-1885*

[2819] The probate record of Catalina Warren gives her name as Catalina Schermerhorn Warren. In the 1855 census, Catalina's aunt Maria Schermerhorn was living with the family.

[2820] The Genealogical Exchange, volumes 1-7, 1906, p 11

JONATHAN PULMAN, b. 3 Mar 1754 son of Nathaniel and Sarah (Kenyon) Pullman; Jonathan d. at Easton, NY, 24 Sep 1839. Jonathan Pulman was first married to Sarah Tefft.

Lucy Abbott and Pepperell Skinner were parents of four children.

i AMOS SKINNER, b. at Nelson, NH, 8 Aug 1793; d. about 1860 likely at Onondaga, NY; m. BETSEY LESLIE, b. about 1796; Betsey d. at Onondaga County, 9 May 1853.

ii SILVA SKINNER, b. at Nelson, 26 Mar 1795; d. at Greenwich, NY, 10 Oct 1837; m. JAMES MOOR, b. at Bow, NH, 29 Mar 1791 son of James and Abigail (Noyes) Moor; James d. at Greenwich, 18 Ju; 1831.

iii SAMUEL SKINNER, b. at Nelson, 18 Jan 1797; d. at Nunda Village, NY, after 1870; m. LUANNA SATTERLY, b. at Greenwich, NY, 1 Aug 1796 daughter of Sylvester and Bethany (Coon) Satterly; Luanna d. at Nunda Village, after 1855.

iv ABBOTT SKINNER, b. about 1806; d. at Elgin, PA, after 1880; m. MARILLA BARBER, b. about 1808 daughter of West and Thankful (Pulman) Barber; Marilla d. after 1880.

Lucy Abbott and Jonathan Pulman were parents of one child.

i MARY PULMAN, b. in Washington County, NY, about 1819. Mary was unmarried and living in Greenwich, NY in 1850.

1066) LYDIA ABBOTT *(Jacob[4], Joseph[3], Nathaniel[2], George[1])*, b. at Wilton, 1 May 1771 daughter of Jacob and Lydia (Stevens) Abbott; d. at Temple, ME, 20 Jun 1855; m. 10 Feb 1789, a fourth cousin, THOMAS RUSSELL, b. at Andover, 5 Jun 1765 son of Thomas and Bethia (Holt) Russell; Thomas d. at Temple, ME, 9 Jul 1863.

Lydia Abbott and Thomas Russell were parents of twelve children, the older children born at Wilton, New Hampshire and the younger children at Temple, Maine.

i THOMAS RUSSELL, b. 7 Aug 1791; d. 26 Aug 1791.

ii THOMAS RUSSELL, b. 3 Sep 1792; d. at Temple, ME, 22 Oct 1840; m. 18 Aug 1813, MARTHA TRUE, b. at Farmington, ME, 14 Jan 1799 daughter of Zebulon and Martha (Kennedy) True; Martha d. at Millbury, MA, 25 Feb 1873.

iii HANNAH ABBOTT RUSSELL, b. at Wilton, 3 May 1794; d. at Temple, 16 Mar 1838; m. about 1813, WILLIAM TRUE, b. at Farmington, 12 Apr 1789 daughter of Zebulon and Martha (Kennedy) True; William d. at Temple, 9 May 1865.

iv JACOB ABBOTT RUSSELL, b. at Wilton, 25 Jul 1795; d. at Temple, May 1866; m. 1st, 28 Dec 1820, APHIA STAPLES, b. at Temple, 29 May 1803 daughter of George and Phebe (Kennison) Staples; Aphia d. at Temple, 25 Nov 1836. Jacob n. 2nd, 4 Dec 1839,

v LYDIA RUSSELL, b. at Wilton, 27 Feb 1797; d. at Temple, 24 Nov 1874; m. 27 Nov 1817, SAMUEL STAPLES, b. at Temple, 10 Jul 1795 son of George and Phebe (Kennison) Staples; Samuel d. at Temple, 22 Oct 1840.

vi POLLY RUSSELL, b. 10 Aug 1799; d. at Farmington, ME, 10 May 1894; m. 5 Jan 1828, AARON DRESSER, b. 23 Apr 1801; Aaron d. at Farmington, 31 Oct 1890.

vii JOHN RUSSELL, b. at Temple, 24 May 1801; d. at Weld, ME, 21 Feb 1851; m. 20 Oct 1822, ELEANOR BURNHAM, b. at Farmington, 7 Mar 1804; Eleanor d. at Weld, 5 Dec 1859. After John's death, Eleanor married Samuel Stowers 20 Aug 1852.

viii JOSEPH RUSSELL, b. 23 Feb 1803; d. 27 Aug 1804.

ix SAMUEL P. RUSSELL, b. at Temple, 17 Feb 1805; d. at Springfield, MA, 19 Jan 1880; m. at Princeton, MA, 6 Oct 1829, CAROLINE WILDER, b. at Princeton, 26 Nov 1805 daughter of Nahum and Hannah (Woods) Wilder; Caroline d. after 1870.

x BENJAMIN W. RUSSELL, b. at Temple, 22 Jan 1807; d. at Temple, 23 Sep 1883; m. 7 Apr 1840, HANNAH B. EDES, b. at Temple, 27 Jun 1813 daughter of Joseph and Hannah (Baker) Edes; Hannah d. at Temple, 1 Aug 1888.

xi JOSEPH RUSSELL, b. at Temple, 18 Feb 1809; d. at Temple, after 1850; m. 28 Feb 1832, ALICE ABBOTT, b. 23 Apr 1811 daughter of Jeremiah Abbott; Alice d. at Douglas, MA, 3 Nov 1880. (Alice's Abbott lineage has not been identified.)

xii FISK RUSSELL, b. at Temple, 12 Nov 1810; d. at Cambridge, MA, 3 Apr 1892; m. 26 Mar 1837, ELIZABETH MOORS BATCHELDER, b. at Wilton, 15 Aug 1813 daughter of Daniel and Persis (Maynard) Batchelder; Elizabeth d. at Boston, 29 May 1848.

1067) SARAH ABBOTT *(Nathaniel⁴, Joseph³, Nathaniel², George¹)*, b. at Andover, 12 Oct 1775 daughter of Nathaniel and Sarah (Stevens) Abbott; d. 17 Feb 1854 at Acworth, ME; m. 5 Oct 1799, ABIJAH KEYES, b. at Wilton, 30 Jun 1773 son of Simon and Lucy (Wheeler) Keyes; Abijah d. at Pelham, 25 Dec 1844.

Abijah Keyes lived in Wilton until 1811 and then moved his family to Pelham where he was a farmer. His son Abijah was his partner in the farm.[2821]

In his will dated 11 May 1842, Abijah Keyes bequeaths to beloved wife Sarah Keyes the income from one-fifth of the combined farm that he and his son Abijah own together. She also receives the improvement of the house east of the easterly chimney from the top to the bottom, and some other areas of the house that are specified in the will. Son Solomon receives one hundred-sixty dollars. Son Nathaniel Abbot receives one hundred-eighty dollars. Grandson Calvin Tupper receives one hundred dollars nine years after Abijah's decease. Solomon's three little sons Edward, Abbot, and Kimball receive five dollars each. The remainder of the estate goes to son Abijah who is also named executor.[2822]

Sarah Abbott and Abijah Keyes were parents of seven children, the first five children born at Wilton and the youngest two children at Pelham.

i ABIJAH WHEELER KEYES, b. 5 Oct 1799; d. at Pelham, 25 Apr 1881; m. at Windham, NH, 27 May 1841, MARGARET C. BUTLER, b. 1817 daughter of Joseph and Hannah (Butler) Butler;[2823] Margaret d. at Pelham, 23 Aug 1849.

ii SOLOMON KEYES, b. 10 Nov 1800; d. at Crystal Lake, IL, 1866; m. 1826, ELIZA CARLTON TODD, b. at Rowley, MA, 25 Jul 1805 daughter of Wallingford and Hannah (Todd) Todd;[2824] Eliza d. after 1880 (she was living in Alden, IL in 1880).

iii SALLY KEYES, b. 14 Oct 1802; d. at Barnard, VT, Jun 1827; m. at Pelham, 11 Nov 1824, SILAS TUPPER, b. at Barnard, 14 Mar 1799 son of Samuel and Mary (Green) Tupper; Silas d. at Barnard, 2 Apr 1869. After Sally's death, Silas married Nancy Stone.

iv POLLY KEYES, b. 3 Feb 1804; d. 1806.

v NATHANIEL ABBOT KEYES, b. 26 Dec 1807; d. at Griggsville, IL, 30 Mar 1857; m. 26 Sep 1839, MARY PETTIGREW, b. at Weathersfield, VT, 26 May 1813 daughter of William and Mary (Alden) Pettigrew; Mary d. at Princeton, IL, 7 Mar 1913.

vi JOHN CALVIN KEYES, b. 3 Feb 1814; d. 5 Aug 1818.

vii POLLY KEYES, b. 14 Nov 1820; d. at Pelham, 10 Jan 1841.

1068) PETER ABBOTT *(Nathaniel⁴, Joseph³, Nathaniel², George¹)*, b. at Pelham, 1 Jan 1782 son of Nathaniel and Sarah (Stevens) Abbott; d. at Plainfield, NH, Feb 1850; m. 6 Mar 1806, OLIVE READ born about 1780 and *possibly* the daughter of Elisha and Welthia (Kinney) Read; Olive d. 3 Mar 1855.

Just two children have been identified for Peter Abbott and Olive Read.

i HARRIET HOLT ABBOTT, b. 1815; d. likely at Plainfield, NH, before 1850; m. about 1835, ROBERT MOORE DAVIDSON, b. about 1810; Robert d. before 1850.

ii SARAH ABBOTT, b. 30 Mar 1818; d. at Cornish, NH, 23 Feb 1862; m. at Cornish, 11 Oct 1843, ARIEL K. SPAULDING, b. at Plainfield, about 1818 son of Zebina and Abigail (Spaulding) Spaulding; Ariel d. at Cornish, 30 Nov 1890. After Sarah's death, Ariel married Eleanor Nichols 13 May 1873.

[2821] Keyes, *Genealogy of Robert Keyes of Watertown*, Appendix to Part First

[2822] *New Hampshire. Probate Court (Hillsborough County)*; Probate Place: *Hillsborough, New Hampshire*, volume 48, p 422

[2823] Butler, *Deacon John Butler and His Descendants*, NEHGR, volumes 3-4, 1849, p 354

[2824] In 1850, Wallingford and Hannah Todd were living in Illinois in the home of their daughter and son-in-law Eliza and Solomon Keyes.

1069) NATHANIEL ABBOTT *(Nathaniel⁴, Joseph³, Nathaniel², George¹)*, b. at Wilton, Nov 1791 son of Nathaniel and Sarah (Stevens) Abbott; d. at Somerville, MA, 18 Aug 1860;[2825] m. at Jaffrey, 26 Mar 1823, ABIGAIL "ABI" BUTTERS,[2826] b. about 1800 (age on census data) daughter of Amos and Abi (Wilson) Butters;[2827] Abi d. after 1860 (living at the time of the 1860 census).

Nathaniel Abbott was a shoemaker in Somerville. He and Abi were parents of three children.

i CHARLES ABBOTT, b. at Bedford, MA, 16 Feb 1824; d. at Lexington, MA, Sep 1849.

ii LEVI ABBOTT, b. at Woburn, 22 Feb 1832; d. at Tewksbury, 28 Oct 1912; m. at Boston, 1 Jul 1855, HARRIET ELIZABETH HALL, b. at Troy, NY, about 1839[2828] daughter of Henry and Esther (Hersey) Hall;[2829] Harriet d. at Medford, 1 May 1904.

iii NATHANIEL WARREN ABBOTT, b. at Woburn, 1835; m. at Boston, 30 Dec 1857, ELIZABETH "ELIZA" HAMMOND, b. in Nova Scotia, about 1832 daughter of James Hammond; Eliza d. at Boston, 13 Jan 1873.

1070) REBECCA BATCHELDER *(Rebecca Abbott Batchelder⁴, Joseph³, Nathaniel², George¹)*, b. at Wilton, 20 Dec 1775 daughter of Daniel and Rebecca (Abbott) Batchelder; d. 1805; m. 29 Jan 1799, her third cousin once removed, WILLIAM ABBOTT *(William⁵, Jonathan⁴, Jonathan³, Benjamin², George¹)*, b. at Wilton, 7 Jan 1779 son of William and Sara (Holt) Abbott; William d. at Malden, 15 Jan 1843. William m. 2nd, 4 Jun 1806, to Apphia Tyler who died just three months after the marriage. William m. 3rd, at Wilton, 29 Sep 1807, ABIGAIL SAWTELL, b. at Groton, 31 Jul 1779 daughter of Richard and Elizabeth (Bennet) Sawtell; Abigail d. at Lynn, 14 Nov 1864. William Abbott is a child in Family 806.

Rebecca Batchelder and William Abbott were parents of one child.

i WILLIAM ABBOTT, b. at Wilton, 23 Jun 1800; nothing further known.

William Abbott and Abigail Sawtell were parents of eight children, the oldest two children born at Wilton, five children born at Malden, and the youngest child perhaps at Stoneham. Son Richard Sawtell Abbott did not marry. In his 1853 (proved 1856) will, Richard left his entire estate to his sister Maria Abbott specifying it is to be hers free of interference from any future husband. George W. Townsend was executor.

In the 1850 U.S. Census for Malden, Maria Abbott was living with Richard Abbott and their mother Abigail. A few houses away was the household of George W. Townsend and his wife Mary Abbott whom he married in 1829. Information available is consistent daughters named Maria and Mary.

i NATHAN ABBOTT, b. 11 Jul 1808; nothing further known.

ii MARIA ABBOTT, b. about 1810. She was still living and unmarried in 1853 when her brother wrote his will and no record found after.

iii MARY ABBOTT, b. 21 Jan 1811; d. at Malden, 6 Dec 1881;[2830] m. at Malden, 8 Nov 1829, GEORGE W. TOWNSEND, b. at Malden, 12 Mar 1805 son of John and Ann (Ramsdell) Townsend; George d. at Malden, 14 Apr 1890.

iv WALTER LONGLEY ABBOTT, b. 15 Jan 1814; d. at Malden, 21 Jul 1851. Walter does not seem to have married. He was a seaman.

v RICHARD SAWTELL ABBOTT, b. 5 Sep 1815; d. at Malden, 1856. Richard was a seaman.

vi SARAH TARBELL ABBOTT, b. 1 Nov 1816; nothing further known.

vii ELIZABETH WAIT ABBOTT, b. 12 Jul 1818; d. 5 Apr 1819.

2825 There is a death record at Somerville that includes his birthplace as Wilton, NH with parents Nathaniel and Sally and his age at death of 69 fits with this Nathaniel. This record also lists him as married.

2826 *New Hampshire, Marriage Records Index, 1637-1947*.

2827 Butters, *Genealogical Register of the Butters Family*, p 74

2828 Age at death given as 66 years, 9 months, 19 days

2829 The names of Harriet's parents are given on her death record.

2830 Death records names William and Abigail as parents and age at death as 70 years, 10 months, 15 days.

viii ELIZABETH WAIT ABBOTT, b. about 1820;[2831] d. at Medford, 3 Oct 1896; m. about 1841, as his second wife, JOSEPH HENRY WAITE, b. at Malden, 13 Aug 1813 son of Aaron and Nancy (Cheever) Waite; Joseph d. at Malden, 11 Jun 1875. Joseph was first married to Harriet A. Sylvester.

1071) BETSY BATCHELDER *(Rebecca Abbott Batchelder⁴, Joseph³, Nathaniel², George¹)*, b. at Wilton, 4 Aug 1777 daughter of Daniel and Rebecca (Abbott) Batchelder; d. at Bethel, ME, 18 Nov 1864; m. 27 Jan 1799, her third cousin once removed, JONATHAN ABBOTT *(Jonathan⁵, Jonathan⁴, Jonathan³, Benjamin², George¹)*, b. at Andover, 11 Jun 1776 son of Jonathan and Mehitable (Abbott) Abbott; Jonathan d. at Bethel, 7 Jan 1843. Jonathan Abbott is a child in Family 321.

Betsy Batchelder and Jonathan Abbott came to Bethel about 1803 where Jonathan had a farm and was, for a time, owner of the mills at South Bethel.[2832]

Betsy Batchelder and Jonathan Abbott were parents of twelve children born at Bethel.

i BETSEY ABBOTT, b. 15 Jan 1801; d. at Rumford, 14 Apr 1821; m. Jan 1819, JOHN HOWE, b. at Marlborough, MA, 1792 son of John and Mary (Newton) Howe;[2833] John d. at Rumford, ME, 1861. John married the widow Nancy Brown and the widow Clarissa Estes.

ii POLLY ABBOTT, b. 13 Nov 1802; died in infancy.

iii PATTY ABBOTT, b. 13 Nov 1802; died in infancy.

iv ADDISON ABBOTT, b. 25 Jul 1803; d. at Paris, ME, 1855; m. 1842, REBEKAH CHASE, b. at Paris, ME, 7 May 1807 daughter of Peter and Rebekah (Doble) Chase; Rebekah d. at Paris, 18 May 1896. Rebekah was second married to William H. Drake and third married to Mr. Lewis.

v MARY ABBOTT, b. 16 Nov 1804; d. at Bethel, ME, 1861; m. 1st, about 1827, NATHAN EAMS, b. at Dublin, NH, 30 Apr 1797 son of Ebenezer and Elizabeth (Coolidge) Eams; Nathan d. at Bethel, 8 Jun 1838. Mary m. 2nd, about 1840, ELIHU BEAN, b. at Bethel, 30 May 1796 son of Jesse and Rhoda (Coffin) Bean; Elihu d. at Bethel, 25 Sep 1865. Elihu was first married to Abigail Grover.

vi REBEKAH ABBOTT, b. 23 Dec 1806; d. at Bethel, 10 Nov 1824.

vii JONATHAN ABBOTT, b. 7 Aug 1808; d. at Bethel, 29 Jun 1887; m. 1 Feb 1848, ELIZA CHASE, b. at Paris, 14 Dec 1821 daughter of Peter and Rebekah (Doble) Chase; Eliza d. at Bethel, 6 Oct 1886.

viii DANIEL ABBOTT, b. 16 May 1810; d. 2 Apr 1812.

ix MEHITABLE ABBOTT, b. 13 Oct 1812; d. at Newton, MA, 25 Mar 1882; m. at Andover, 8 Feb 1840, her first cousin, JOSHUA BALLARD *(Joshua Ballard⁶, Hezekiah Ballard⁵, Lydia Chandler Ballard⁴, John Chandler³, Hannah Abbott Chandler², George¹)*, b. at Andover, 28 Jan 1813 son of Joshua and Phebe (Abbott) Ballard; Joshua d. at Newton, 25 Mar 1882.

x DORCAS ABBOTT, b. 9 Sep 1814; d. at Bethel, 11 May 1882; m. about 1853, as his second wife, CHRISTOPHER BRYANT, b. at Woodstock, ME, 12 Nov 1798 son of Christopher and Susanna (Swan) Bryant; Christopher d. at Woodstock, ME, 21 Dec 1868. Christopher was first married to Sally Flint.

xi STEPHEN ABBOTT, b. 9 Sep 1817; d. at Boston, 18 Jan 1872. Stephen did not marry.

xii SYBIL B. ABBOTT, b. 4 Jun 1821; d. at Southbridge, MA, 1 Aug 1866; m. at Southbridge, 21 Sep 1846, her first cousin, GAYTON BALLARD *(Joshua Ballard⁶, Hezekiah Ballard⁵, Lydia Chandler Ballard⁴, John Chandler³, Hannah Abbott Chandler², George¹)*, b. at Andover, 8 Jul 1821 son of Joshua and Phebe (Abbott) Ballard; Gayton d. at Brooklyn, NY, 27 Jan 1904. Gayton married second at Southbridge, 15 Sep 1869, SARAH L. FISKE, b. at Southbridge, 3 Sep 1834 daughter of Henry and Sarah (Belknap) Fiske; Sarah d. 24 Feb 1918.

1072) JUDITH RAY BATCHELDER *(Rebecca Abbott Batchelder⁴, Joseph³, Nathaniel², George¹)*, b. 21 Jun 1779 daughter of Daniel and Rebecca (Abbott) Batchelder; d. at Wilton after 1850 (still living at 1850 U.S. Census); m. 24 Mar 1803, her third cousin once removed, JOEL ABBOTT *(Barachias⁵, Barachias⁴, John³, John², George¹)*, b. at Andover, 10 Oct 1776 son of Barachias and Sarah (Holt) Abbott; Joel d. at Wilton, 26 Mar 1863. Joel Abbott is a child in Family 294.

Judith and Joel lived in Wilton where Joel was a carpenter and a farmer. He also served as Justice of the Peace.[2834]

Judith Batchelder and Joel Abbott were parents of seven children born at Wilton.

2831 Elizabeth's death record gives her place of birth as Stoneham and parents as William Abbott and Abigail Sawtell.

2832 Lapham, *History of Bethel*, p 458

2833 Lapham, *History of Rumford, Maine*, p 351

2834 Livermore, *History of Wilton*, p 555

i FANNY ABBOTT, b. 25 Jul 1804; d. at Wilton, 25 May 1849. Fanny did not marry.

ii JOHN ABBOTT, b. 30 Jul 1805; d. at Andover, 10 May 1848; m. SALLY BROWN of Reading whose parents have not been identified; Sally d. 11 Apr 1840.

iii REBECCA JANE ABBOTT, b. 5 Aug 1807; d. at Wilton, 28 Aug 1864. Rebecca did not marry.

iv JAMES MADISON ABBOTT, b. 30 May 1810; d. 5 Jul 1837.

v HANNAH ABBOTT, b. 9 Sep 1812; d. 15 Aug 1813.

vi GEORGE CLINTON ABBOTT, b. 30 Oct 1817; d. 3 Feb 1839.

vii HARVEY LAFAYETTE ABBOTT, b. 18 Dec 1822; d. at Wilton, 18 Jun 1894; m. at Melrose, MA, 4 Jul 1856, AMANDA LOUISE WILSON, b. at Tyngsborough, 12 Apr 1829 daughter of Stephen and Louisa (Gould) Wilson; Amanda d. at Wilton, 10 Feb 1889. Amanda was first married to William Levingston.

1073) DANIEL BATCHELDER *(Rebecca Abbott Batchelder[4], Joseph[3], Nathaniel[2], George[1])*, b. at Wilton, 15 May 1781 son of Daniel and Rebecca (Abbott) Batchelder; d. at Wilton, 28 May 1853; m. at Temple, NH, 1805, PERSIS MAYNARD, b. at Temple, 10 Apr 1782 daughter of Caleb and Elizabeth (Moore) Maynard; Persis d. at Wilton, 18 Aug 1850.[2835]

Daniel Batchelder was a farmer in Wilton. He served as a selectman in Wilton, was a representative to the General Court from 1835 to 1837 and was state senator from 1849-1850.[2836]

Daniel Batchelder and Persis Maynard were parents of six children born at Wilton.

i PERSIS BATCHELDER, b. 31 May 1808; d. at Wilton, 27 Mar 1897; m. at Wilton, 30 Sep 1830, ZIMRI BARRETT, b. at Westford, MA, 3 Nov 1795 son of Ebenezer and Jane (Reed) Barrett; Zimri d. at Wilton, 8 May 1860.

ii REBECCA ABBOTT BATCHELDER, b. 7 Apr 1810; d. 4 Mar 1895; m. at Boston, 6 May 1834, FRANKLIN BROOKS, b. at Lincoln, MA, 22 Dec 1807 son of Joshua and Sarah (Davis) Brooks; Franklin d. at Boston, 6 Apr 1869.

iii CALEB MAYNARD BATCHELDER, b. 26 Jan 1812; d. at Wilton, 29 Mar 1897; m. 13 Feb 1859, his fourth cousin once removed, EMILY A. BUSS *(Sarah Abbott Buss[6], Jeremiah[5], John[4], John[3], John[2], George[1])*, b. at Wilton, 30 Aug 1829 daughter of Stephen and Sarah (Abbott) Buss; Emily d. at Wilton, 25 Mar 1897.

iv ELIZABETH MOORS BATCHELDER, b. 15 Aug 1813; d. at Boston, 29 May 1848; m. 26 Mar 1837, her second cousin, FISK RUSSELL *(Lydia Abbott Russell[5], Jacob[4], Joseph[3], Nathaniel[2], George[1])*, b. at Temple, NH, 12 Nov 1810 son of Thomas and Lydia (Abbott) Russell; Fisk d. at Cambridge, 3 Apr 1892. Fisk Russell is a child in Family 1066.

v EMILY BATCHELDER, b. 11 Sep 1815; d. at Wilton, 5 Feb 1849. Emily did not marry.

vi ADELINE BATCHELDER, b. 26 Aug 1817; d. at Boston, 8 Oct 1885. Adeline did not marry.

1074) MARY "MOLLY" BATCHELDER *(Rebecca Abbott Batchelder[4], Joseph[3], Nathaniel[2], George[1])*, b. at Wilton, 11 Mar 1784 daughter of Daniel and Rebecca (Abbott) Batchelder; d. at Jaffrey, NH, 3 Jun 1859; m. 1806, JOHN CUTTER, b. 24 Oct 1780 son of Joseph and Rachel (Hobart) Cutter; John d. at Jaffrey, 15 Jan 1857.

John Cutter was a successful farmer and wool grower in Jaffrey. This family valued education. Son Benoni graduated from Vermont Medical College at Woodstock.[2837] Their granddaughter Carrie Cutter (daughter of Calvin and Caroline) was a nurse who served in the Civil War and died of typhoid fever on the steamship Northerner at New Bern, North Carolina 24 March 1862.[2838] Son Calvin was Brigade Surgeon during the war.

Molly Batchelder and John Cutter were parents of eleven children born at Jaffrey, New Hampshire.

[2835] The 1823 will of Caleb Maynard includes a bequest to his daughter Persis "now the wife of Daniel Batchelder." New Hampshire Will and Probate Records 1643-1982.

[2836] Pierce, Batchelder Genealogy, p 470

[2837] Cutter, *History of Jaffrey*, p 267

[2838] "Nurse Carrie Cutter" https://civilwartalk.com/threads/nurse-carrie-cutter-remembered-because-clara-did.150094/

i LUTHER CUTTER, b. 1 May 1807; d. at Jaffrey, 22 Sep 1876; m. 15 Sep 1830, CAROLINE CUTTER, b. at Jaffrey, 1809 daughter of Moses and Rachel (Turner0 Cutter; Caroline d. at Jaffrey, 26 Dec 1861.

ii CALVIN CUTTER, b. 1 May 1807; d. at Warren, MA, 19 Jun 1873; m. 1st, at Dunstable, 5 Apr 1835, CAROLINE HALL, b. 1808 daughter of Nathan and Ruth (Waterman) Hall; Caroline d. at Milford, 1842. Calvin m. 2nd, 10 Dec 1843, EUNICE N. POWERS, b. at Warren, about 1819 daughter of Chester and Eunice (Haskell) Powers; Eunice d. at Warren, 10 Mar 1893.

iii REBECCA CUTTER, b. 5 Aug 1808; d. at Marlborough, NH, 11 Apr 1896; m. 22 Apr 1834, IRA HASTINGS, b. at Marlborough, 5 Mar 1801 son of Thaddeus and Asenath (Rice) Hastings; Ira d. at Marlborough, 5 Apr 1888.

iv JOHN ABBOTT CUTTER, b. 7 Jan 1810; d. at Marlborough, 29 Aug 1886; m. 27 Jan 1832, NANCY H. WHEELOCK, b. 20 Jan 1811 daughter of Emery and Martha (Hill) Wheelock; Nancy d. at Jaffrey, 16 Oct 1885.

v Child, b. and d. 28 Feb 1811

vi CALEB CUTTER, b. 29 Oct 1812; d. at Shirley, MA, 17 Oct 1873; m. 26 Mar 1835, SUSAN A. NORRIS, b. at Windham, VT, about 1816 daughter of Nealy and Anna (Belding) Norris; Susan d. at Shirley, 28 Jan 1890.

vii MARY CUTTER, b. 3 Jul 1814; d. at Peterborough, 14 Oct 1886; m. 14 Oct 1836, SAMUEL MCCOY, b. at Sharon, NH, 24 May 1812 son of William and Lucy (Ryan) McCoy; Samuel d. at Peterborough, 8 Apr 1893.

viii BENONI CUTTER, b. 14 Feb 1816; d. at Webster, ME, 4 Sep 1851; m. 1st, 19 May 1842, OLIVE S. DRINKWATER daughter of Edward and Elizabeth (Locke) Drinkwater; Olive d. 11 Mar 1847. Benoni m. 2nd, about 1848, Olive's sister, JANE B. DRINKWATER, b. 1815; Jane d. at Augusta, ME, after 1880.

ix CHARLES CUTTER, b. 11 Sep 1817; d. at East Jaffrey, 1 Mar 1896; m. 1 Apr 1841, MARIAH EUNICE HATHORN, b. at Jaffrey, 7 Mar 1819 daughter of Ebenezer and Mary (Thompson) Hathorn; Mariah d. at Jaffrey, 8 Apr 1907.

x SIBEL CUTTER, b. 14 Oct 1819; d. at Jaffrey, 31 Aug 1865; m. 1st, 7 Mar 1839, JOEL HOBART CUTTER, b. at Jaffrey, 23 Nov 1816 son of Joel and Mary S. (Jones) Cutter; Joel d. at Jaffrey, 17 Sep 1839. Sibel m. 2nd, 12 Nov 1840, JOHN WARD POOLE, b. at Jaffrey, 13 Aug 1812 son of Ebenezer and Olive (Ward) Poole; John d. at Jaffrey, 7 Jan 1877.

xi GEORGE CUTTER, b. 23 May 1821; d. 25 Aug 1827.

1075) HERMAN BATCHELDER *(Rebecca Abbott Batchelder[4], Joseph[3], Nathaniel[2], George[1])*, b. at Wilton, 8 Aug 1790 son of Daniel and Rebecca (Abbott) Batchelder; d. at Clay, NY, 15 Aug 1876; m. 1812, MARY "POLLY" BLOOD, b. at Temple, NH, about 1795 daughter of Francis and Rebecca (Parlin) Blood; Polly d. 1865 at Clay, NY.

The Batchelder Genealogy reports Herman and Polly had four daughters born at Wilton and later relocated to the area of Cicero, New York.[2839] The youngest daughter in the family, Rebecca Jane, spent her last years in a poor house in Onondaga, New York. Her personal information card for the poor house indicates that she had one brother and two sisters.[2840] The son in the family, Francis H. Batchelder, can be identified as it is in his family grave plot that father Herman and mother Mary are buried and the members of the family share a gravestone.[2841]

i MARY BATCHELDER, b. at Wilton, 3 Mar 1815; d. at Harrisville, NH, 23 Apr 1879; m. about 1836, SYLVANDER HARDY, b. at Nelson, NH, 23 Feb 1814 son of Noah and Jerusha (Kimball) Hardy; Sylvander d. at Pepperrell, MA, 10 Apr 1850.

ii FIDUCIA BATCHELDER, b. at Wilton, 2 May 1818; no further record.

iii SARAH ANN BATCHELDER, b. at Wilton, 7 May 1820; no further record.

iv REBECCA JANE BATCHELDER, b. at Wilton, 10 Feb 1823; d. at Onondaga, NY, after 1900; m. about 1844, FRANCIS H. EDWARD, b. in NH about 1825; Francis seems to have died between 1850 and 1855 (when he is not listed on the census with Rebecca). Rebecca spent the last years of her life at the poor house in Onondaga County.

v FRANCIS H. BATCHELDER, b. likely at Cicero, NY, 1825; d. at Brewerton, NY, 31 Aug 1902; m. ADELINE ERIN POTTER, b. at Bennington, VT, 15 Mar 1839 daughter of Lyman and Harriet (Elwell) Potter; Adeline d. at Clay, 1914. After Francis's death, Adeline married Asa Shank 20 Aug 1910.

2839 Pierce, *Batchelder Genealogy*, p 470
2840 New York State Archives; Albany, New York; Census of Inmates in Almshouses and Poorhouses, 1875-1921; Series: A1978; Reel: A1978:153; Record Number: 1341, accessed through ancestry.com
2841 Findagrave ID: 60336779

1076) HANNAH ABBOT BATCHELDER *(Rebecca Abbott Batchelder[4], Joseph[3], Nathaniel[2], George[1])*, b. at Wilton, 2 May 1793 daughter of Daniel and Rebecca (Abbott) Batchelder; d. at Philadelphia, 2 May 1862; m. 1818, NATHANIEL RICHARDSON, b. at Weston, VT, 22 Aug 1798 son of Nathan and Hannah (Shattuck) Richardson; Nathaniel d. at Philadelphia, 17 Mar 1861.[2842]

Nathaniel Richardson was a hydraulic engine maker in Philadelphia. Three children were identified for this family, all living together in Philadelphia in 1850. The children were born in New Hampshire.

i HANNAH J. RICHARDSON, b. about 1826; she was living in Philadelphia with her parents in 1860 and was unmarried.

ii REBECCA A. RICHARDSON, b. Aug 1827; d. at Elmhurst, IL, 1906.[2843] Rebecca did not marry.

iii NATHANIEL S. RICHARDSON, b. about 1828; m. KATE, b. in PA, about 1836 who has not been identified. Nathaniel and his wife Kate were living with his parents and sisters in 1860. Nothing further is known.

1077) LYDIA ABBOTT BATCHELDER *(Rebecca Abbott Batchelder[4], Joseph[3], Nathaniel[2], George[1])*, b. at Wilton, 18 Mar 1795 daughter of Daniel and Rebecca (Abbott) Batchelder; d. 4 Mar 1886 at Oppenheim, NY; m. 1819, ABNER SHATTUCK, b. at Wilton, 18 Jan 1796 son of Abraham and Polly (Wright) Shattuck; Abner d. at Oppenheim, 20 Oct 1878.

Shortly after their marriage, Lydia and Abner relocated from Wilton to Temple, New Hampshire and their youngest four children were born in Temple. After the births of all the children, the family moved to Oppenheim, New York.[2844]

i ABNER SHATTUCK, b. at Wilton, 28 Nov 1819; d. at Montague, MA, 12 Aug 1843 (probate 19 Sep 1843). Abner owned one-half of a shingle mill. He does not seem to have married.

ii DANIEL B. SHATTUCK, b. at Temple, 20 Dec 1821; d. at Brown, OH, 4 Jan 1895; m. 1st, at Fulton County, NY, 3 Jun 1847, MARGARET ELIZABETH ROBINSON,[2845][2846] b. in NH about 1823; Margaret Elizabeth d. at Oppenheim, 26 Sep 1862. After Margaret's death, Daniel married Mary identified on census records as being born about 1823 in Connecticut. Mary was still living in 1903 in Marion, IN.

iii REBECCA SHATTUCK, b. at Temple, 27 Dec 1823; d. at Oppenheim, NY, 25 Feb 1916. Rebecca did not marry. She and her younger sister Mary Jane lived together.

iv ORIN SHATTUCK, b. at Temple, 15 Nov 1829; d. at Port Orchard, WA, 27 Dec 1905; m. 1862, JULIA PELCHER, b. in New York, about 1844 daughter of John and Mary (-) Pelcher;[2847] Julia d. at Seattle, WA, 13 May 1937.

v MARY JANE SHATTUCK, b. at Temple, 7 Sep 1831; d. after 1900 at Oppenheim, NY. Mary Jane did not marry.

1078) JOHN CHANDLER *(John Chandler[4], Tabitha Abbott Chandler[3], Nathaniel[2], George[1])*, b. 11 Dec 1752; d. at Boscawen, NH, 24 Jan 1825 son of John and Mary (Carter) Chandler; m. Mar 1780, NAOMI FARNUM, b. 20 Apr 1760 daughter of Ephraim and Judith (Hall) Farnum; Naomi d. 20 Mar 1832.

Captain John Chandler was the builder of the Bonney Tavern in Boscawen. The tavern built in 1787 remained at its original site on the corner of North Maine and Eel Streets in Boscawen until 1937.[2848]

John Chandler did not leave a will and son John Chandler was administrator of the estate. The real estate was valued at $1,780 including an $800 value on the homestead farm which was one undivided half of a 70-acre farm. The personal estate was valued at $632.03. Claims against the estate exceeded its value and the estate was declared insolvent 6 September 1825.[2849]

John and Naomi Chandler were parents of seven children all born at Boscawen.

2842 There were two Nathaniel Richardsons both with a wife Hannah who were in Philadelphia at the same time. The other Nathaniel married Hannah Yarnell and that Nathaniel died in Philadelphia in 1862.

2843 Although Rebecca died in Illinois, she is buried in Woodlands Cemetery in Philadelphia in the same plot as Nathaniel and Hannah Richardson. Findagrave: 142587790

2844 Shattuck, *Memorials of the Descendants of William Shattuck*, p 345

2845 New York, County Marriage Records, 1847-1849, 1907-1936, ancestry.com

2846 Margaret's name is given as Margaret Elizabeth on some records and Elizabeth Margaret on others.

2847 Julia's parents' names are given as John and Mary on her death certificate.

2848 Boscawen Historical Society. http://www.boscawenhistoricalsociety.org/online-resources/links/

2849 New Hampshire, County Probate Records, 1660-1973, Merrimack County, probate of John Chandler, 3:52, 2:173, 6:127, 7:6, 2:279, 6:228, 1:320, 7:278

i JOHN CHANDLER, b. 25 Oct 1780; d. at Manchester, NH, 6 Mar 1859; m. 28 Sep 1806, PRISCILLA KIMBALL, b. at Boscawen, 7 Aug 1781 daughter of Peter and Elizabeth (Thurston) Kimball; Priscilla d. at Manchester, 24 Mar 1868.

ii NATHAN CHANDLER, b. 14 Apr 1782; d. at Concord, Apr 1835; m. at Concord, 17 Apr 1805, JANE ROLFE, b. at Concord, 21 Jan 1783 daughter of Nathaniel and Judith (Walker) Rolfe; Jane d. at Concord, 5 Jun 1863.

iii EPHRAIM CHANDLER, b. 4 Sep 1784; d. at Boscawen, 12 Mar 1837; m. about 1815, TABITHA CURRIER, b. at Warner, NH, 9 Feb 1793 daughter of Theophilus and Sarah (Hacket) Currier; Tabitha d. at Boscawen, 16 Jul 1877.

iv MARY CHANDLER, b. 3 Sep 1786; d. at Concord, 27 Feb 1872; m. at Boscawen, 9 Aug 1804, JONATHAN EASTMAN, b. at Concord, 14 Nov 1781 son of Jonathan and Esther (Johnson) Eastman; Jonathan d. at Concord, 23 Mar 1867.

v SUSANNA FARNUM CHANDLER, b. 7 Dec 1788; d. at Boscawen, 6 Feb 1870; m. 8 Feb 1806, RICHARD GAGE, b. at Methuen, 11 Dec 1776 son of Thaddeus and Abigail (Merrill) Gage; Richard d. at Boscawen, 18 May 1855.

vi JUDITH HALL CHANDLER, b. 19 Mar 1793; d. at Boscawen, 2 Nov 1843; m. 16 Apr 1812, her fourth cousin, REUBEN JOHNSON *(Rhoda Abbott Johnson⁵, Reuben⁴, James³, William², George¹)*, b. at Concord, 12 Jan 1792 son of Jonathan and Rhoda (Abbott) Johnson; Reuben d. at Boscawen, 16 Mar 1852. Reuben Johnson is a child in Family 572.

vii RHODA CARTER CHANDLER, b. 10 Jul 1799; d. at Brodhead, WI, about 1881; m. 29 Oct 1829, her first cousin, JOSEPHUS CHANDLER *(Joseph Chandler⁵, John Chandler⁴, Tabitha Abbott Chandler³, Nathaniel², George¹)*, b. at Fryeburg, ME, 20 Aug 1796 son of Joseph and Hannah L. (Farrington) Chandler; Josephus d. at Primrose, WI, 11 Feb 1859. Josephus first married SARAH COLBY, b. 22 Mar 1802 daughter of Joseph and Elizabeth (Evans) Colby; Sarah d. at Fryeburg, 9 Jul 1828. Josephus Chandler is a child in Family 1080.

1079) NATHAN CHANDLER *(John Chandler⁴, Tabitha Abbott Chandler³, Nathaniel², George¹)*, b. at Concord, 28 Apr 1754 son of John and Mary (Carter) Chandler; d. 13 Apr 1781; m. 4 Mar 1775, SUSAN AMBROSE, b, at Chester about 1755 daughter of Robert Ambrose. Susan m. 2nd, Enoch Brown.

Nathan Chandler was a farmer at Boscawen. He died at age 26 leaving two small children.

i MARY "POLLY" CHANDLER, b. at Boscawen about 1776; d. about 1781.

ii JUDITH CHANDLER, b. at Boscawen, 16 Feb 1778; d. at Philipsburg, Québec, 18 Oct 1821; m. at Concord, Feb 1800, ENOCH GERRISH, b. at Canterbury, 20 Feb 1775 son of Samuel and Lucy (Noyes) Gerrish; Enoch d. 1856. After Judith's death, Enoch married Martha Foster.[2850]

iii SALLY CHANDLER, b. at Boscawen, 30 Mar 1780; d. at Boscawen, 14 Nov 1812; m. 1800, JOSEPH GERRISH, b. at Canterbury, 7 Mar 1777 son of Samuel and Lucy (Noyes) Gerrish. After Sally's death, Joseph married Sarah Church.

1080) JOSEPH CHANDLER *(John Chandler⁴, Tabitha Abbott Chandler³, Nathaniel², George¹)*, b. at Concord, 18 Nov 1760 son of John and Mary (Carter) Chandler; d. at Fryeburg, ME, 23 Apr 1826; m. about 1785, HANNAH L. FARRINGTON, b. at Andover, 9 Jul 1765 1764 daughter of Daniel and Hannah (Farnum) Farrington; Hannah d. 29 Nov 1825.

Joseph was a farmer in North Fryeburg and had settled there by his young adulthood.[2851] Joseph and Hannah had all thirteen of their children in Fryeburg, but only the third child, John, remained there. Several of the children ultimately settled in Wisconsin via Wethersfield, New York. Two of the children settled in Iowa.

Joseph served as a private in Bedel's New Hampshire Regiment in 1776.[2852] In Fryeburg, he was active in the community and was a selectman for thirteen years.

Joseph Chandler did not leave a will and his estate entered probate 15 May 1826. The inventory of his estate included real property valued at $4,763.00 with a homestead of 124 acres and additional lots totaling about 200 acres. The personal estate was valued at $2,261.51. The heirs receiving distributions from the estate were as follows: Luther Richardson's children, Jere Chandler, John Chandler, Hazen Chandler, Josephus Chandler, Susan Farrington wife of Stephen, Nathan Chandler,

---

2850 Lyford, *History of Canterbury*, p 158

2851 Chandler, *The Descendants of William and Annis Chandler*, p 588.

2852 NARA M881. Compiled service records of soldiers who served in the American Army during the Revolutionary War, 1775-1783.

Molly Wiley wife of America, Daniel Chandler, Isaac Chandler, Peter Chandler, and George Chandler. There was no distribution to the heirs of son Moses who died in 1825. Luther Richardson was administrator of the estate.[2853]

Joseph and Hannah Chandler had thirteen children whose births are recorded at Fryeburg.[2854]

i MOSES CHANDLER, b. 13 Mar 1786; d. at Concord, 2 Sep 1825. Moses was a physician. He did have a son, Joseph Addison Chandler born in 1811, who was raised by Moses's parents. However, this seems to be a child born out-of-wedlock. In the probate of Moses's estate, father Joseph Chandler is administrator and reports himself as the only heir.[2855] The distribution of Joseph Chandler's estate includes no distribution to Moses's heir although the heirs of Moses's deceased sister are included. Taken together, these suggest that Moses's son was not considered an heir-at-law. There is no record of a marriage. Published genealogies list the son, but none of them mention or suggest a wife.[2856]

ii DANIEL CHANDLER, b. 20 Nov 1787; d. at Union, IA, 9 Sep 1870; m. MEHITABLE COLBY, b. at Fryeburg, 8 Apr 1796 daughter of David and Sally (Farrington) Colby; Mehitable d. at Union, Sep 1878.[2857]

iii JOHN CHANDLER, b. 4 Apr 1793; d. at Fryeburg, 31 May 1868; m. 9 Mar 1820, HANNAH WILSON BARKER, b. at Fryeburg, 15 Jan 1803 daughter of Richard and Margaret (Gordon) Barker; Mehitable d. at North Fryeburg, 17 Nov 1888.

iv HANNAH CHANDLER, b. 7 Jul 1789; d. 25 Nov 1825; m. Nov 1814, LUTHER RICHARDSON, b. at Sanford, ME, 1787 son of Zebadiah and Rebecca (Snow) Richardson; Luther d. at North Fryeburg, 27 Feb 1864.

v ISAAC CHANDLER, b. 4 Jul 1790; d. at Pleasant Grove, IA, 12 Oct 1878; m. 1st at Fryeburg, May 1812, JUDITH WALKER *(Olive Charles Walker⁶, Susanna Abbott Charles⁵, Isaac⁴, Ebenezer³, John², George¹)*, b. at Fryeburg, 1793 daughter of James and Olive (Charles) Walker; Judith d. at Union, IA, Aug 1842. Isaac m. 2nd 20 Aug 1845, JEMIMA DECKER (widow of Frederick Westfall), b. in New York, 31 Jan 1803 daughter of Isaac and Mary (-) Decker;[2858] Jemima d. at Washington Township, IA, 9 Oct 1888.[2859]

vi NATHAN CHANDLER, b. 28 Dec 1794; d. at Wethersfield, NY, 10 Sep 1857; m. Dec 1818, RHODA TILTON, b. about 1800 *perhaps* the daughter of Cornelius Tilton; Rhoda d. at Primrose, WI, 10 Sep 1876.[2860]

vii JOSEPHUS CHANDLER, b. 20 Aug 1796; d. at Primrose, WI, 11 Feb 1859; m. 1st, about 1824, SALLY COLBY, b. 22 Mar 1802 daughter of Joseph and Elizabeth (Evans) Colby; Sally d. at North Fryeburg, 9 Jul 1828. Josephus m. 2nd, 29 Oct 1829, his first cousin, RHODA CARTER CHANDLER *(John Chandler⁵, John Chandler⁴, Tabitha Abbott Chandler³, Nathaniel², George¹)*, b. at Boscawen, 10 Jul 1799 daughter of John and Naomi (Farnum) Chandler; Rhoda d. at Brodhead, WI, 1881.[2861] Rhoda is a child in Family 1078.

viii MARY CARTER CHANDLER, b. 28 Apr 1798; d. at Bangor, 29 Aug 1875; m. MYRICK "AMERICA" WILEY, b. about 1798 son of Benjamin and Alice (Kilgore) Wiley; America d. at Bangor, 4 Mar 1872.

ix SUSAN CHANDLER, b. 6 May 1801; d. at Gorham, NH, 9 Jan 1892; m. 4 Jan 1819, STEPHEN FARRINGTON *(Betsy Dresser Farrington⁶, Abigail Abbott Dresser⁵, Sarah Abbott Abbott⁴, James³, William², George¹)*, b. about 1797 son of Samuel and Betsy (Dresser) Farrington; Stephen d. at Gorham, 29 Apr 1886.

x JERE CHANDLER, b. 8 Mar 1803, d. at Monroe, WI, 18 Jun 1874; m. at Wethersfield, NY, 25 Apr 1830, HARRIET CHARLES *(Samuel Charles⁶, Susanna Abbott Charles⁵, Isaac⁴, Ebenezer³, John², George¹)*, b. at Fryeburg, 25 Apr 1810 daughter of Samuel and Elizabeth (Langdon) Charles; Harriet d. at Monroe, 24 Mar 1894.

2853 *Maine. Probate Court (Oxford County)*; Probate Place: *Oxford, Maine, Estate Files, Drawer C21, Caldwell, Zenas-Chapman, Samuel, 1820-1832*, estate of Joseph Chandler

2854 *New Hampshire, Death and Disinterment Records, 1754-1947.*

2855 New Hampshire Wills and Probate, Merrimack County, images at familysearch.org, estate of Moses Chandler, volume 3:80; additional information on the probate in 2:274, 6:409, 2:465, 6:267, 9:201, and 9:284.

2856 For example, Chandler, *Descendants of William Chandler*, p 978

2857 Daniel and Mehitable were living at Union at the time of the 1870 Census.

2858 Chandler, *Descendants of William and Annis Chandler*, volume 3, p 979

2859 *Iowa, Deaths and Burials, 1850-1990.*

2860 Rhoda's grave site is Mount Pleasant Cemetery in Primrose (findagrave ID 54818377); Rhoda's daughter Maria Chandler Randall lived in Primrose.

2861 Rhoda was living in Brodhead at the time of the 1880 census with her daughter Kate Chandler Thompson.

xi PETER CHANDLER, b. 19 Feb 1805; d. at Monroe, WI, 8 May 1884; m. at Wethersfield, NY, 7 Sep 1843, ELIZA ANN WESCOTT, b. at Milton, NY, 21 Feb 1810 daughter of John and Eunice (Reed) Wescott; Eliza d. at Monroe, 21 Dec 1893.

xii HAZEN CHANDLER, b. 4 Feb 1807; d. at Boston, 25 Nov 1878; m. 1st, at Wethersfield, 25 Apr 1825, LUCINDA EMMONS, b. in New York, 12 Apr 1807 daughter of Squire and Rhoda (Fuller) Emmons; Lucinda d. at Wethersfield, 29 May 1841. Hazen m. 2nd, 20 Nov 1841, PAULINA STOWE, b. at Wethersfield, 29 Jul 1807 daughter of Daniel and Mercy (Southgate) Stowe; Paulina d. at Independence, KS, 18 Sep 1901.

xiii GEORGE CHANDLER, b. 1 Feb 1810; d. at Delavan, WI, 6 May 1895; m. at Des Moines, IA, 28 Mar 1844, MATILDA GODDARD (widow Lisloff), b. 15 Mar 1813 (at locations reported as Kentucky, Tennessee, and Mississippi) of undetermined parents; Matilda d. at Burlington, IA, 28 Mar 1878.

1081) JEREMIAH CHANDLER *(John Chandler⁴, Tabitha Abbott Chandler³, Nathaniel², George¹)*, b. at Concord, 31 Mar 1763 son of John and Mary (Carter) Chandler; d. at Lovell, ME, 12 Feb 1828; m. 3 Jun 1791, JUDITH FARNUM, b. 13 Jun 1764 daughter of Ephraim and Judith (Hall) Farnum; Judith d. at Gorham, ME, 21 Feb 1851.

Jeremiah was a farmer in Boscawen and later relocated to Lovell, Maine. Jeremiah and Judith had just three children, one who died as a young infant.

i Infant b. and d. 1793

ii JOHN CARTER CHANDLER, b. at Concord, 28 Jul 1794; d. at Lovell, ME, 1866; m. MEHITABLE HAZELTINE, b. about 1795 daughter of Abraham and Polly (-) Hazeltine; Mehitable d. at Lovell, 8 Mar 1846.

iii MARY KIMBALL CHANDLER, b. at Concord, 10 Oct 1796; d. at Washington, DC, 6 Sep 1855; m. about 1818, her fourth cousin, PHILIP CARRIGAN JOHNSON *(Rhoda Abbott Johnson⁵, Reuben⁴, James³, William², George¹)*, b. at Concord, 7 Mar 1795 son of Jonathan and Rhoda (Abbott) Johnson; Philip d. at Washington, 10 Aug 1859. Philip Carrigan Johnson was Secretary of State for Maine in 1840 and appointed by President Polk as Chief Clerk in the Bureau of Construction, Equipment, and Repair of the Navy Department. Philip Johnson is a child in Family 572.

1082) MOSES CHANDLER *(John Chandler⁴, Tabitha Abbott Chandler³, Nathaniel², George¹)*, b. at Concord, 23 Nov 1765 son of John and Mary (Carter) Chandler; d. at Fryeburg, 10 Sep 1822; m. 1st, 4 Feb 1794, SALLY GOODWIN, b. about 1770; Sally d. 24 Sep 1801. Moses m. 2nd, MARY LANGDON, b. 21 Mar 1782 daughter of Paul Langdon; Mary d. 10 May 1863.

Dr. Moses Chandler owned and managed a farm but was also a practicing physician first in Newmarket, New Hampshire and then in Lovell, Maine.[2862]

In June 1782, Moses joined the military as a private in the regiment of Colonel Dearborn and served for a period of eighteen months. Moses later received a pension with an annual payment of $96 starting in 1818. His widow Mary received a widow's pension of $56.66 per year.[2863]

Moses wrote his will while a resident of Fryeburg, Maine but the probate of his estate was in New Hampshire. In his will, he leaves his estate to beloved wife Mary except for the specific bequests to his children. Each of the children received a legacy of two dollars: Jeremiah Chandler, Enoch F. Chandler, Mary Anne Frye wife of Frederick, Nathan Chandler, David S. Chandler, Sally G. Chandler, Samuel S. Chandler, Joseph Chandler, Moses Chandler, Betsey C. Chandler, Isaac Chandler, Paul Chandler, and Anna Maria Chandler. Brother Joseph Chandler of Fryeburg was named executor.[2864]

Moses Chandler and his first wife Sally Chandler were parents of four children.

i JEREMIAH CHANDLER, b. at Newmarket, NH, 23 Mar 1794; d. at Conway, NH, 16 May 1864; m. 1st, 21 Oct 1822, POLLY CUMMINGS EASTMAN, b. at Conway, 7 Jul 1801 daughter of Noah and Hannah (Holt) Eastman; Polly d. at Conway, 12 Nov 1855. Jeremiah m. 2nd, 9 Oct 1858, CORDELIA E. SWEETSER, b. at New Gloucester, ME, 12 Jul 1825 daughter of Nicholas and Celia (Cushman) Sweetser; Cordelia d. at Portland, 6 Jan 1876.

ii ENOCH FOLSOM CHANDLER, b. at Lee, NH, 29 Apr 1796; d. at Bethel, ME, 13 Sep 1864; m. about 1827, HANNAH SHIRLEY, b. at Fryeburg, 18 Jun 1803 daughter of William and Dorothy (Walker) Walker Shirley; Hannah d. at Bethel, 30 Oct 1879.

2862 Chandler, *Descendants of William and Annis Chandler*, p 590

2863 Revolutionary War Pension and Bounty-Land Warrant Application Files

2864 *New Hampshire. Probate Court (Strafford County);* Probate Place: *Strafford, New Hampshire, Probate Records, Vol 35-36, 1827-1827*, will of Moses Chandler, pp 154-156

iii MARY ANN CHANDLER, b. at Fryeburg, 16 Nov 1798; d. at Fryeburg, 9 May 1880; m. 7 Jan 1819; FREDERICK FRYE, b. at Fryeburg, 6 Jun 1796 son of Nathaniel and Dorothy (Swan) Frye; Frederick d. at Fryeburg, 23 Nov 1823.

iv NATHAN CHANDLER, b. at Fryeburg, 15 Feb 1801; d. at Kearsarge, NH, 10 Mar 1880; m. 6 Apr 1833, SARAH BARNES, b. at Conway, 24 May 1803 daughter of Amos and Polly (Eastman) Barnes; Sarah d. at Conway, 27 Dec 1890.

Moses Chandler and Mary Langdon were parents of eleven children all born at Fryeburg.

i DAVID SEWALL CHANDLER, b. 27 Jun 1804; d. 14 Oct 1825.

ii SARAH GOODWIN CHANDLER, b. 27 Dec 1805; d. 26 Oct 1823.

iii SAMUEL LANGDON CHANDLER, b. 7 Oct 1807; d. at Fryeburg, 16 Feb 1882; m. at Bartlett, NH, 16 Nov 1832, MARY STEARNS KILGORE, b. at Lovell, ME, 13 Dec 1813 daughter of James and Mehitable (Stearns) Kilgore; Mary d. at Amherst, NH, 17 Apr 1904.

iv JOSEPH CHANDLER, b. 27 Nov 1809; d. at Pembroke, MA, 26 Aug 1900; m. 18 Apr 1842, MARY SPRING CHASE, b. at Fryeburg, 9 Nov 1823 daughter of Seth S. and Elizabeth (Shirley) Chase; Mary d. at Pembroke, MA, 28 Dec 1911.

v MOSES CHANDLER, b. 27 Jan 1809; d. at Fryeburg, 17 Jan 1899; m. 29 Jun 1852, JUDITH WALKER, b. at Fryeburg, 6 Feb 1817 daughter of Samuel and Anna (Stevens) Walker; Judith d. at Fryeburg, 17 Mar 1871.

vi BETSEY CHASE CHANDLER, b. 9 Feb 1812; d. at Fryeburg, 27 Apr 1893; m. 2 Mar 1832, JUSTUS CHARLES, b. at Fryeburg, Dec 1809 son of James and Sarah (Stevens) Charles; Justus d. at Fryeburg, 6 Jul 1872.

vii ISAAC CHANDLER, b. 27 Jul 1814; d. 6 Oct 1814.

viii JUDITH CHANDLER, b. 27 Jul 1814; d. 21 Oct 1814.

ix ISAAC CHANDLER, b. 27 Sep 1815; d. at Lovell, 1889; m. 6 Dec 849, OLIVE G. BRYANT, b. at South Portland, 7 Dec 1829 daughter of Walter L. and Mary (-) Bryant; Olive d. at Lovell, 19 Apr 1900.

x PAUL LANGDON CHANDLER, b. 27 Jul 1818; d. at Wendell, MA, 14 Jan 1904; m. 28 Aug 1846, MARY MESSENGER DOW, b. at Boston, Feb 1820 daughter of Levi and Elizabeth (Horton) Dow; Mary d. after 1900, likely at Minneapolis.[2865] Paul and Mary divorced by about 1870. Paul m. 2nd, 27 Mar 1874 Almeda Page Osgood (widow of Pearl Kimball) of Oberlin, OH.[2866] Almeda and Paul apparently also divorced. In 1880, Almeda Chandler was living with her sister Sarah Osgood in Oberlin, but by the time of her death in 1889, she was using the name Almeda Kimball. Paul m. 3rd, 1882 (marriage date given on 1900 census), Etta (likely Etta Achilles), b. about 1830, although Paul and Etta were living together in 1880 as Paul and Etta Chandler.

xi ANNA MARIA CHANDLER, b. 7 Jun 1821; d. at Fryeburg, 9 Aug 1849; m. 1845, JAMES MADISON GORDON, b. at Fryeburg, 1810 son of James and Patty (Farrington) Gordon; James d. after 1880 (still living at the 1880 census). After Anna's death, James married Betsey Frye.

1083) TABITHA CHANDLER *(Timothy Chandler⁴, Tabitha Abbott Chandler³, Nathaniel², George¹)*, b. at Rumford, 17 Jun 1761 daughter of Timothy and Elizabeth (Copp) Chandler; d. at Randolph, VT, 22 Sep 1839; m. at Plymouth, NH, 17 Dec 1789, HUGH MCINTIRE, b. 11 May 1754[2867] perhaps born in Scotland;[2868] Hugh d. at Randolph, 16 May 1837.

The origins of Hugh McIntire are not entirely clear, but it is most likely that he was born in Scotland and emigrated as an adolescent or young man. In his early adult life, he was in Plymouth, New Hampshire (there in 1790), then for a time in Bradford, Vermont before finally settling in Randolph, Vermont. Hugh and Tabitha were the parents of seven children.

Daughter Mary McIntire did not marry. Mary McIntire wrote her will 17 March 1864 and the estate entered probate 22 October 1874. In her will, Mary left to her brother James the use of all her estate during his natural life. She left bequests of one hundred dollars to children of her brother James: Hamden W. McIntire and Elizabeth C. Temple widow of George Temple.

[2865] At the 1900 Census, Mary M. Chandler, divorced, was living with her son Philip in Minneapolis. Paul Chandler was living in Wendell with wife Etta.

[2866] Cleaveland, *History of Bowdoin College*, p 567

[2867] McIntire, *Descendants of Philip McIntire*, p 189

[2868] In the 1880 Census, daughter Nancy McIntire Grsiwold gives the birthplace of her father as Scotland.

After the death of her brother James, her estate is to be divided with one-half to her niece Abbie P. McIntire, and the other half to be divided equally between Hugh Henry McIntire and Benjamin G. McIntire who are children of James. Nephew Hugh Henry McIntire was named executor.[2869]

i MARY MCINTIRE, b. at Plymouth, NH, 9 Mar 1790; d. at Randolph, VT, 15 Sep 1874. Mary did not marry.

ii ELIZA MCINTIRE, b. at Merrimack, NH, 7 Dec 1791; d. at Moretown, VT, 1 Feb 1865; m. at Northfield, VT, 5 Feb 1815, JOHN POOR, b. at Goffstown, NH, 26 Apr 1786 son of Samuel and Ann (Bridges) Poor; John d. at Moretown, 26 Jan 1865.

iii JACOB MCINTIRE, b. at Bradford, VT, about 1794; d. at Montpelier, VT, 13 Oct 1872; m. about 1817, FANNIE "MARIA" CULVER, b. at Groton, CT,[2870] about 1794; Maria d. at Montpelier, 9 Dec 1861.

iv JANE MCINTIRE, b. at Randolph, 8 Apr 1797; d. at Randolph, 13 Dec 1862. Jane did not marry.

v TIMOTHY CHANDLER MCINTIRE, b. at Randolph, about 1798 (age 23 at time of death); d. at Randolph, 11 Aug 1821.

vi NANCY MCINTIRE, b. at Randolph, about 1801; d. at Waterbury, VT, after 1880 (still living at the 1880 census); m. 4 May 1829, HOWARD GRISWOLD, b. at Randolph, 24 Oct 1804 son of Benjamin and Selinda (Howard) Griswold; Howard d. at Randolph, 11 Feb 1855.

vii JAMES MCINITIRE, b. at Randolph, about 1803; d. at Randolph, 19 Aug 1883; m. 1834, CHARLOTTE BLODGETT, b. at Randolph, 6 Mar 1807 daughter of Henry and Abigail (Parmalee) Blodgett; Charlotte d. at Randolph, 11 Jul 1854.

1084) ABIEL CHANDLER *(Timothy Chandler[4], Tabitha Abbott Chandler[3], Nathaniel[2], George[1])*, b. at Concord, 20 Oct 1765 son of Timothy and Elizabeth (Copp) Chandler; d. at Bristol, NH, 5 Mar 1854; m. 25 Dec 1788, ABIGAIL THOMAS, born about 1769 reported as the daughter of Jonathan Thomas of Sanbornton.[2871][2872] Abigail died some time between 1820 and 1850 likely at Stewartstown, but exact date is not known.

Abiel Chandler served as a private in the Revolution in the company of Captain Ellis and the First New Hampshire Regiment under Colonel Henry Dearborn. Abiel enlisted April 1781 and served for about two years until the close of the war.[2873]

Abiel and Abigail started their family in Sanbornton where their first three children were born. They were then in Bridgewater, New Hampshire until 1819 and then relocated to Stewartstown where Abigail died. Abiel then went to Bristol where his son Timothy was living. Abiel and Abigail were parents to eleven children.

i ELIZA CHANDLER, b. at Sanbornton, 28 Jul 1789; d. at Stewartstown, 10 Sep 1891; m. at Bristol, 22 Nov 1810, DANIEL H. KIDDER, b. at Bridgewater, 22 Aug 1788 son of Benjamin and Molly (Heath) Kidder; Daniel d. at Stewartstown, 16 Oct 1864.

ii ABIGAIL CHANDLER, b. at Sanbornton, 4 Apr 1791; d. 17 Aug 1791.

iii TIMOTHY CHANDLER, b. at Sanbornton, 4 Jun 1792; d. at Bristol, 18 Mar 1881; m. Apr 1821, LOIS GURDY, b. at Bridgewater, 20 Jun 1794 daughter of Jacob and Mary (Favor) Gurdy; Lois d. at Bristol, 9 May 1872.

iv TABITHA CHANDLER, b. at Bridgewater, 18 Apr 1794; d. at Brompton, Québec, 1881; m. at Shipton, Québec, 22 Jan 1822, STEPHEN CASWELL, b. at Lisbon, NH, 17 Jul 1799 son of Joseph and Ruth (Bishop) Caswell;[2874] Stephen d. at Brompton, 1 Dec 1878.[2875]

v JONATHAN CHANDLER, b. at Bridgewater, 14 May 1795; d. at Paola, KS, 26 Oct 1881; m. 1st, about 1824, SARAH SMALL, b. about 1804 and died about 1844 in Missouri. Jonathan m. 2nd, at St. Clair, MO, ELIZABETH HARRIS, b. in Tennessee, about 1813 whose parents are not yet identified; Elizabeth d. at St. Genevieve, MO, after 1880. About 1875, Jonathan Chandler deeded his property in St. Genevieve to his son Thomas. He left his wife and his children in Missouri and he went to Kansas where he died in 1881.

2869 *Vermont. Probate Court (Randolph District);* Probate Place: *Orange, Vermont, Folder 97, Lock, John-Noyes, Mary L, 1871-1879*

2870 Most sources give her name as just Maria Culver, but the death record of one of her daughters gives her name as Fannie Maria and her birthplace as Groton, CT.

2871 Musgrove, *History of Bristol, New Hampshire*, p 91

2872 One of the supporting affidavits in Abiel Chandler's pension file is by Jacob Thomas one of Jonathan Thomas's sons.

2873 U.S., Revolutionary War Pension and Bounty-Land Warrant Application Files, 1800-1900

2874 Furber, *History of Littleton, New Hampshire*, p 117

2875 *Quebec, Canada, Vital and Church Records (Drouin Collection), 1621-1968*

vi GEORGE WASHINGTON CHANDLER, b. at Bridgewater, 30 Jun 1797; d. 25 Jan 1832 perhaps in Ohio;[2876] m. 7 Apr 1825, HARRIET LADD, b. at Stewartstown, about 1796 daughter of Daniel and Elizabeth (Goodwin) Ladd; d. not known but after 1850 when she was living in Stewartstown in a household that included her son Asa Chandler and her step-son Joseph Taylor. After George W.'s death, Harriet married Joseph Taylor.

vii AZUBA CHANDLER, b. at Bridgewater, 29 Sep 1800; d. at Stewartstown, 19 Jan 1891; m. 10 Nov 1825, SETH TIRRELL, b. at Canterbury, 12 Nov 1798 son of William and Hannah (Fellows) Tirrell; Seth d. at Stewartstown, 4 Sep 1872.

viii SALOME CHANDLER, b. 6 Aug 1802; d. 7 Nov 1802.

ix LUCETTA CHANDLER, b. at Bridgewater, 30 Sep 1803; d. at Stewartstown, 13 Aug 1864; m. 27 Aug 1823, CALEB STEVENS DALTON, b. at Northfield, 12 Jun 1796 son of Samuel and Mary (Merrick) Dalton; Caleb d. at Stewartstown, 28 Mar 1847.

x MATILDA CHANDLER, b. at Bridgewater, 7 Jan 1805; d. at Stewartstown, 28 May 1871; m. 28 Sep 1828, JOSHUA TIRRELL, b. at Canterbury, 29 Jul 1800 son of William and Hannah (Fellows) Tirrell; Joshua d. at Stewartstown, 18 Mar 1860.

xi ABIEL WALKER CHANDLER, b. at Bridgewater, 26 Nov 1807; d. at Union County, OH, 17 Apr 1871; m. at Lowell, 8 Feb 1835, EMILY JANE PIERCE, born about 1810 of not yet determined parents (*perhaps* Daniel and Jane (Foss) Pierce of Campton, NH); d. not known but still living in 1880 in Union County, OH.

1085) SARAH CHANDLER *(Daniel Chandler⁴, Tabitha Abbott Chandler³, Nathaniel², George¹)*, b. at Concord, 15 Dec 1756 daughter of Daniel and Sarah (Eastman) Chandler; d. 26 Sep 1840 at Northfield, NH; m. 14 Aug 1773, ABNER FLANDERS, b. at South Hampton, 18 Nov 1754 son of Richard and Mary (Fowler) Flanders; Abner d. after 1840 (he was listed on the 1840 pensioners list in Northfield, NH age 85).[2877] There is a gravestone in Williams Cemetery in Northfield with a death date given as 26 Nov 1843.[2878]

Abner Flanders was a miller in Concord. He served in the Revolution first as a private in Colonel Stark's Regiment and applied for a pension in 1833.[2879] Abner had five separate enlistments from April 1775 through July 1781 and was credited with fifteen months of service. He achieved the rank of Sergeant by the end of his service. He was at the Battle of Bennington.

Sarah Chandler and Abner Flanders were parents of ten children born at Concord.

i MOLLY FLANDERS, b. 26 Feb 1774; m. at Hopkinton, 11 Mar 1789, JONATHAN CARTER, b. at Concord, 17 Sep 1772 son of Daniel and Mary (Chase) Carter.

ii CHARLES FLANDERS, b. 5 Aug 1776; m. at Concord, 15 Nov 1795, ANNA "NANCY" SHUTE, b. at Concord, 15 Jun 1773 daughter of John and Anna (Colby) Shute;[2880] Anna d. at Concord, after 1850 when she was living with her son Origen.

iii SARAH FLANDERS, b. 7 Nov 1779; d. at Concord, 17 Nov 1863; m. at Concord, 24 Dec 1799, ABNER DIMOND, b. 1765 son of Ezekiel and Miriam (Fowler) Dimond; Abner d. at Concord, 11 Feb 1848.

iv NATHAN FLANDERS, b. 13 Mar 1782; d. at Concord, 11 Dec 1834; m. 23 Mar 1806, ALICE CONREY, b. at Concord, about 1783 daughter of Samuel and Alice (Blood) Conrey; Alice d. at Hopkinton, NH, 4 Jan 1877.

v SAMUEL WOOD FLANDERS, b. 26 Jun 1785; m. at Hopkinton, 15 Sep 1806, MARY FARWELL, b. at Groton, NH, 19 Apr 1787 daughter of Ephraim and Anne (Bartlett) Farwell;[2881] Mary d. at Washington, NH, 11 Feb 1848.

vi CHRISTOPHER PAIGE FLANDERS, b. 11 May 1788; d. at Groton, NH, after 1860; m. 25 Apr 1811, SARAH POWERS

[2876] Musgrove, History of the Town of Bristol, p 93. Several published genealogies report that George W. Chandler was a farmer in New Hampshire and Ohio and that he died in Ohio. There is an August 1833 probate case in Ross County, Ohio for a George W. Chandler, but his widow's name was Julianne, so it is not clear that our George W. Chandler is the one who died in Ohio, or perhaps there were two George W. Chandler's who died in Ohio within a year of each other.

[2877] Ancestry.com. *New Hampshire, Compiled Census and Census Substitutes Index, 1790-1890* [database on-line]. Provo, UT, USA: Ancestry.com Operations Inc, 1999.

[2878] Findagrave.com memorial 151316433, Abner Flanders

[2879] Revolutionary War Pension and Bounty-Land Warrant Application Files, 1800-1900 Case number S9887

[2880] The 1828 will of John Shute of Concord includes a bequest to his daughter Anna Flanders.

[2881] Gage, *History of Washington, NH*, p 409

vii ABNER FLANDERS, b. 21 May 1790; d. at Equality, IL, 21 Jun 1878; m. about 1815, DEBORAH HILL, b. in NY, 1794 daughter of John and Sarah (Colyer) Hill; Deborah d. at Equality, after 1860.

viii NANCY FLANDERS, b. 27 Jul 1794; d. at Sanbornton, NH, 1866; m. at Concord, 17 Nov 1830, JOHN HANNAFORD, b. at Northfield, 20 Oct 1787 son of John and Cordelia (Russell) Hannaford.[2882] John was first married to Jane Sanborn.

ix ORIGEN FLANDERS, b. 10 Mar 1797; d. 16 Jul 1798.

x APHIA FLANDERS, b. 4 Aug 1801; d. at Equality, IL, 4 Mar 1854. Aphia did not marry.

1086) MARY CHANDLER *(Daniel Chandler[4], Tabitha Abbott Chandler[3], Nathaniel[2], George[1])*, b. at Concord, 27 Jan 1760 daughter of Daniel and Sarah (Merrill) Chandler; d. at Concord, 1831;[2883] m. 1st, about 1775, EBENEZER WEST, b. 25 Dec 1754 son of Nathaniel and Sarah (Burbank) West; Ebenezer d. about 1776. Mary m. 2nd, 20 Mar 1777, RICHARD FLANDERS, b. Mar 1752 son of Richard and Mary (Fowler) Flanders; Richard d. at Concord, 1841.

Ebenezer West and Mary Chandler were parents of one child.

i SARAH WEST, b. at Concord, about 1776; d. at Concord, about 1798; m. 7 Jun 1794, ASA GRAHAM, b. at Concord, 3 Nov 1771 son of George and Azubah (-) Graham. Asa married second Rachel Morse 27 Sep 1798.

Mary Chandler and Richard Flanders were parents of nine children born at Concord.

i DANIEL FLANDERS, b. 17 Dec 1778; d. 9 Dec 1854. Daniel did not marry.

ii HANNAH FLANDERS, b. 29 Jul 1781; d. at Rumford, ME, 27 Apr 1849; m. at Concord, 17 Mar 1801, her third cousin, JOHN ABBOTT *(Moses[5], Nathaniel[4], Nathaniel[3], Nathaniel[2], George[1])*, b. at Concord, 6 Sep 1779 son of Moses and Mary (Batchelder) Abbott; John d. at Rumford, 18 Jun 1870. John Abbott is a child in Family 983.

iii EBENEZER FLANDERS, b. 23 Aug 1784; d. 24 Dec 1788.

iv JOHN FLANDERS, b. 19 Jan 1787; d. at Concord, 1856; m. at Concord, 31 May 1812, his third cousin, RACHEL ABBOTT *(Samuel[5], Daniel[4], George[3], Thomas[2], George[1])*, b. at Concord, 31 Aug 1788 daughter of Samuel and Mary (Story) Abbott; Rachel d. at Concord, 1876. Rachel Abbott is a child in Family 923.

v JACOB FLANDERS, b. 22 Mar 1791; d. 9 Nov 1795.

vi LYDIA FLANDERS, b. 11 Aug 1793; d. at Concord, 1861. Lydia did not marry.

vii JACOB FLANDERS, b. 7 Feb 1796; d. at Concord, 10 Jul 1847; m. at Concord, 15 Apr 1819, his third cousin, HULDAH ABBOTT *(Samuel[5], Daniel[4], George[3], Thomas[2], George[1])*, b. at Concord, 30 Mar 1797 daughter of Samuel and Mary (Story) Abbott; Huldah d. at Concord, 8 Jul 1880. Huldah Abbott is a child in Family 923.

viii SARAH FLANDERS, b. 17 Apr 1800; d. at Rumford, ME, 2 Jan 1890; m. at Concord, 13 Jan 1820, her third cousin once removed, HENRY MARTIN *(Hannah Wheeler Martin[6], Keziah Blanchard Wheeler[5], Benjamin Blanchard[4], Mary Abbott Blanchard[3], Nathaniel[2], George[1])*, b. at Rumford, 1 Oct 1798 son of John and Hannah (Wheeler) Martin; Henry d. 15 Nov 1872.

ix MARY FLANDERS, b. 21 Feb 1803; d. at Concord, 12 Feb 1871; m. at Concord, 16 Jun 1825, her third cousin, EZRA BALLARD *(Nathan Ballard[6], Nathan Ballard[5], Hannah Chandler Ballard[4], John Chandler[3], Hannah Abbott Chandler[2], George[1])*, b. at Concord, 12 May 1802 son of Nathan and Hannah (Buss) Ballard; Ezra d. at Concord, 7 May 1872.

1087) HANNAH CHANDLER *(Daniel Chandler[4], Tabitha Abbott Chandler[3], Nathaniel[2], George[1])*, b. at Concord, 19 Jun 1763 daughter of Daniel and Sarah (Merrill) Chandler; d. 31 Mar 1828 at Rumford, ME; m. 7 Jun 1787, JOSHUA GRAHAM, b. at Rumford, 7 Jun 1763 son of George and Azubah (-) Graham; Joshua d. at Rumford, ME, 15 Mar 1830.

Joshua filled many roles in Rumford, Maine working as a merchant, farmer, innkeeper, and mill man.[2884] He served as a private in the Revolutionary War in the company of Captain Nathaniel Hutchins in the First New Hampshire Battalion commanded by Colonel Joseph Cilley in 1780. He served five months, twenty days from June 1780 through December 1780.[2885]

Joshua and Hannah were parents of eight children.

[2882] Cross, *History of Northfield, NH*, p 165

[2883] New Hampshire, Death and Disinterment Records, 1754-1947

[2884] Lapham, *History of Rumford*, Maine, p 338

[2885] Compiled Service Records of Soldiers Who Served in the American Army During the Revolutionary War 1775-1785, accessed through fold3

i AARON GRAHAM, b. at Concord, 6 Mar 1788; d. at Rumford, ME, 9 Sep 1875; m. 21 Apr 1811, GENEVA MOORE, b. at Rumford, 24 Jan 1790 daughter of Aaron and Salome (Goss) Moore; Geneva d. at Rumford, 7 Jan 1866.

ii SARAH GRAHAM, b. at Concord, 31 May 1790; d. at Errol, NH, 2 May 1868; m. 21 Mar 1811, her fourth cousin, JAMES FRYE BRAGG *(Molly Frye Bragg⁵, Elizabeth Osgood Frye⁴, Hannah Abbott Osgood³, George², George¹)*, b. at Andover, MA, 4 Dec 1787 son of Ingalls and Molly (Frye) Bragg; James d. at Errol, 30 May 1876. James Frye Bragg is a child in Family 508.

iii NANCY GRAHAM, b. at Concord, 30 May 1792; d. at Bethel, ME, 16 Oct 1866; m. 7 Jun 1810, ELIJAH BARTLETT, b. 30 Oct 1788 son of Jonathan and Mary (Shaw) Bartlett; Elijah d. at Bethel, 18 Mar 1860.

iv GEORGE GRAHAM, b. at Rumford, ME, 24 Feb 1795; d. at Milton, ME, 1 Jul 1851; m. 21 Mar 1818, HANNAH EASTMAN, b. at Rumford, ME, 28 Nov 1799 daughter of Caleb and Comfort (Haines) Eastman; d. after 1850 (living in Milton at the 1850 census).

v ASA GRAHAM, b. at Rumford, ME, 2 Aug 1797; d. at Portland, ME, 1 Feb 1857; m. 1st, 7 Feb 1817, LUCINDA FARNUM, b. at Rumford, 1799 daughter of Stephen and Stephen (Jackman) Farnum; Lucinda d. at Rumford, 2 Mar 1840. Asa m. 2nd, at Portland, 8 Nov 1840, NANCY M. GERRISH, b. 6 Jul 1803 daughter of Nathaniel and Alice (Abbott) Gerrish;[2886] Nancy d. at Portland, 5 Oct 1859.

vi ABIEL C. GRAHAM, b. 24 Aug 1799; d. 12 Jan 1802.

vii JOHN C GRAHAM, b. and d. 1 Jan 1802

viii JOSHUA GRAHAM, b. at Rumford, 4 Mar 1804; d. at Rumford, 24 Aug 1856; m. 1st, 27 Dec 1825, HANNAH PETERS GODDARD, b. at Rumford, 10 May 1807 daughter of Robert and Sybil (Peters0 Goddard; Hannah d. at Rumford, 10 Dec 1837. Joshua m. 2nd, at Portland, 23 Aug 1839, RUTH STUART TREADWELL, b. 18 Apr 1817 daughter of Jonathan and Ruth (Stuart) Treadwell; Ruth d. at Rumford, 13 Jan 1843. Joshua m. 3rd, SARAH H. LEAVITT, b. about 1817; Sarah d. at Hollis, ME, 1888.

1088) LYDIA CHANDLER *(Daniel Chandler⁴, Tabitha Abbott Chandler³, Nathaniel², George¹)*, b. at Concord, 22 Jun 1765 daughter of Daniel and Sarah (Merrill) Chandler; d. 21 Jun 1842 at North Chatham, NH; m. at Concord, 4 Mar 1784, JONAS WYMAN, b. 1759 perhaps the Jonas Wyman born at Wilmington son of Reuben and Catherine (Wyman) Wyman; Jonas d. at Chatham, 10 Oct 1818.

Jonas Wyman served in the Revolution as a private with a total service period of fourteen months. His widow Lydia received a pension related to his service with a pension application in 1839.[2887]

Daughter Betsey Wyman married Joseph Hobart later in life and she did not have children. In her will written 8 March 1854, she leaves bequests to each of her brothers and sisters: Mary Baker, Lydia Heath, Sally How, Abigail Stevens, Nancy Greely, Reuben Wyman, and Merrill Wyman. Merrill Wyman was named executor.[2888]

Lydia and Jonas Wyman were parents of ten children.

i MARY WYMAN, b. 30 Apr 1784; d. at Salisbury, NH, after 1860 (living with daughter Caroline in 1860); m. at Salisbury, 19 Jun 1806, BENJAMIN BAKER, b. at Salisbury, 23 Oct 1783 son of Benjamin and Mary (George) Baker; Benjamin d. at Salisbury before 1829 (deceased when his father wrote his will in 1829).

ii ELIZABETH "BETSEY" WYMAN, b. 28 May 1786; d. at Salisbury, NH, 27 Mar 1854; m. Sep 1838, JOSEPH HOBART who is not yet identified; Joseph was deceased prior to 1854 when Betsey wrote her will.

iii REUBEN WYMAN, b. at Chatham, 22 Jul 1789; d. at Bartlett, NH, 1859 (probate 12 Nov 1859); m. 1st, 15 Apr 1811, SARAH WALKER about whom nothing is known; Sarah d. by 1833. Reuben m. 2nd, at Salisbury, 20 Mar 1834, MARY BAKER, b. in NH, about 1793; Mary d. at Concord, 21 Jul 1867.

2886 Little, *Genealogical History of the State of Maine*, volume III, p 1261

2887 U.S., Revolutionary War Pension and Bounty-Land Warrant Application Files, 1800-1900

2888 *New Hampshire. Probate Court (Merrimack County)*; Probate Place: *Merrimack, New Hampshire, Probate Records, Vol 25, 1847-1856*, pp 474-475, will of Betsey Hobart

iv JONAS WYMAN, b. at Chatham, 15 Jan 1791; d. at Chatham, 22 Jun 1853; m. at Chatham, 12 Sep 1816, his fourth cousin, SARAH NOYES *(Abigail Ames Noyes⁵, Elizabeth Stevens Ames⁴, Nathan Stevens³, Elizabeth Abbott Stevens², George¹)*, b. at Pembroke, 2 Nov 1791 daughter of Daniel and Abigail (Ames) Noyes; Sarah d. at Chatham, 23 Aug 1860. Sarah Noyes is a child in Family 1158.

v SARAH WYMAN, b. at Chatham, 14 May 1793; d. at Rensselaer Falls, NY, 11 May 1874; m. at Chatham, 16 Aug 1816; GARDNER HOWE, b. in NH, about 1794; d. at Lisbon, NY, after 1860.

vi LYDIA WYMAN, b. at Chatham, 16 May 1795; d. at Waldwick, WI, 20 Mar 1871; m. 15 Aug 1820, CHANDLER GRAHAM HEATH, b. at Rumford, ME, 18 Oct 1795 son of Benjamin and Dorothy (Wiley) Heath; Chandler d. at Fryeburg, 2 Feb 1888.

vii ABIEL CHANDLER WYMAN, b. at Chatham, 20 Feb 1798; Abiel d. at Chatham, before 1850 (not living at 1850 census); m. at Chatham, 15 Aug 1820, HANNAH K. STEVENS, b. at Alfred, ME, about 1796; Hannah d. at Stow, ME, after 1880 (living with her daughter Caroline at the 1880 census).

viii NANCY WYMAN, b. at Chatham, 19 Jul 1801; d. at Thornton, NH, 2 Apr 1863; m. at Chatham, 13 Feb 1831, NATHANIEL GREELEY, b. at Salisbury, 1802 son of Nathaniel and Mary (Maloon) Greeley; Nathaniel d. at Thornton, 18 Oct 1885.

ix MERRILL WYMAN, b. at Chatham, 4 Jul 1804; d. at Chatham, 14 Nov 1873; m. at Bartlett, 12 Mar 1845, MARTHA P. MESERVE, b. 13 Mar 1821 daughter of Daniel and Betsey (Poindexter) Meserve; Martha d. at Conway, 12 Oct 1909.

x ABIGAIL WYMAN, b. at Chatham, 20 Sep 1809; d. at Waldwick, WI, 5 Feb 1867; m. Sep 1839, HUBBARD STEVENS, b. in NH about 1808; d. at Waldwick, WI, after 1870.

1089) ABIGAIL CHANDLER *(Daniel Chandler⁴, Tabitha Abbott Chandler³, Nathaniel², George¹)*, b. at Concord, 4 Jul 1767 daughter of Daniel and Sarah (Merrill) Chandler; d. 2 Jan 1841; m. 18 Jan 1784, OLIVER FLANDERS, b. 21 Apr 1765 son of Richard and Mary (Fowler) Flanders; Oliver d. at West Plymouth, NH, 31 Jan 1838.

Oliver Flanders was a miller and farmer in Plymouth, New Hampshire.

In his will written 11 August 1834 and proved 16 February 1838, Oliver Flanders refers to his real estate consisting of a farm and a grist mill which he received by deed from Moses Flanders 16 May 1828. He conveys this land and mill to his son Oliver Flanders, Jr. upon the conditions set forth in the will. Oliver, Jr. is to provide maintenance and support for Oliver and his wife and provide all things necessary for them in sickness and in health. Oliver is also to provide a comfortable home for his three unmarried sisters. If any of these sisters marry, Oliver will pay them thirty dollars at marriage. If Oliver, Jr. fails in his duties, then the real estate will be divided among the unmarried daughters, but if they all marry before the deaths of both parents, then it will be divided equally among all the daughters namely Martha, Susan, Abigail, Ann, Betsey, Mary, and Orilla. Oliver has already provided for his other sons Peter, Moses, and Ebenezer, and makes no further provision for them. Abigail Flanders is named executor.[2889]

Abigail and Oliver Flanders were parents to fourteen children.

i PETER FLANDERS, b. at Concord, 19 Jun 1784; d. at Plymouth, 23 Aug 1856; m. at Plymouth, 26 Dec 1807, HANNAH HEATH, b. at Bow, NH, about 1786 daughter of Solomon and Abiah (Carleton) Heath; Hannah d. at Plymouth, 25 Feb 1879.

ii MOSES FLANDERS, b. at Concord 21 Apr 1786; d. at Plymouth, 28 Jun 1846; m. 1st, at Rumney, 10 Sep 1811, RUTH BEAN, b. 23 Sep 1790 daughter of Samuel and Dorothy (Wells) Bean; Ruth d. at Concord, about 1813. Moses m. 2nd, SARAH BEAN, b. 13 Apr 1788, the sister of Ruth; Sarah d. at Plymouth, 2 Jan 1855.

iii RICHARD FLANDERS, b. at Haverhill, NH, 23 Apr 1788; d. at Concord, 16 Mar 1833; m. 29 Sep 1814, ABIGAIL FURBER, b. in NH, about 1791 and still living in Concord in 1870.

iv EBENEZER FLANDERS, b. at Concord, 30 Apr 1790; d. at Concord, about 1836 (will 24 June 1836); m. at Concord, 23 Mar 1815, his fourth cousin once removed, NANCY WEEKS *(Susannah Abbott Weeks⁵, Edward⁴, Edward³, Thomas², George¹)*, b. at Concord, 7 Apr 1791 daughter of John and Susannah (Abbott) Weeks; Nancy d. at Concord, after 1870. Nancy Weeks is child in Family 909.

v Child b. 1791 and d. 1792

vi ABIEL CHANDLER FLANDERS, b. 7 Jan 1793; d. at Plymouth, 13 Feb 1824; m. 11 May 1818, SARAH FELLOWS.

2889 *New Hampshire. Probate Court (Grafton County)*; Probate Place: *Grafton, New Hampshire*, volume 17, pp 58-59, will of Oliver Flanders

vii MARTHA FLANDERS, b. at Concord, 13 Feb 1796; d. at Concord, about 1859; m. at Concord, 29 Apr 1816, STEPHEN LANG, b. at Concord, about 1793 son of Stephen and Abigail (Weare) Lang.

viii SUSAN FLANDERS, b. at Concord, 5 Mar 1799; d. at Norwich, VT, 22 Feb 1886; m. 19 Feb 1828, NATHANIEL LANCASTER, b. at Rowley, MA, about 1798 son of Samuel and Mehitable (Lambert) Lancaster; Nathaniel d. at Norwich, 6 Mar 1878.

ix ABIGAIL FLANDERS, b. 24 Apr 1801; d. at Plymouth, 3 Sep 1837; m. 28 Nov 1833, SAMUEL MORSE, b. at Plymouth, 13 Apr 1787 son of Samuel and Sarah (Webster) Morse; Samuel d. at Plymouth, 6 May 1870. After Abigail's death, Samuel married Ruth Witcher.

x OLIVER FLANDERS, b. 28 Mar 1803; d. at Plymouth, 2 Feb 1878; m. 29 Apr 1830, HANNAH F. GREEN, b. about 1809 daughter of Ephraim and Sally (French) Green; Hannah d. at Plymouth, 2 Nov 1871.

xi ELIZABETH FLANDERS, b. at Plymouth, 17 Apr 1805; d. at Plymouth, 8 Jun 1877. Elizabeth did not marry. In 1870, she was living with her sister Orilla and her family.

xii ANNA FLANDERS, b. 5 Oct 1807; d. at Rumney, 20 Jan 1884; m. 3 Feb 1830, JAMES RALSTON PAYNE, b. at Lebanon, NH, 5 Jun 1801 son of Elijah and Lydia (Collins) Payne; James d. at Rumney, 25 Jul 1881.

xiii MARIA FLANDERS, b. 20 Feb 1809; d. at Plymouth, 28 Apr 1840. Maria did not marry.

xiv ORILLA FLANDERS, b. 5 Mar 1811; d. at Rumney, 5 Sep 1887; m. 1st, 13 Sep 1852, JOHN R. WEST who died before 1870. Orilla m. 2nd, at Rumney, 5 May 1870, LEVI S. GORDON, b. 15 Aug 1821 son of Levi and Hannah (Jewett) Gordon; Levi d. at Laconia, NH, 29 Jan 1906. Levi Gordon was first married to Nancy Gove who died in 1869. In her will written 15 May 1885, Orilla Gordon bequeathed to her husband Levi S. Gordon, one thousand dollars. She bequeathed two hundred dollars each to her adopted nephew Charles F. Chandler and his wife Helen S. Chandler. Her adopted niece Ellen J. Penniman and her husband Charles D. Penniman each receive one hundred dollars. Other bequests are to her stepson Albertis S. Gordon and his wife Anna, her sister Susan Lancaster wife of Nathaniel, nephew George R. Lang, and niece Ruth T. Lang. Samuel P. Fletcher of Plymouth was named executor.[2890]

1090) PAUL CHANDLER *(Daniel Chandler4, Tabitha Abbott Chandler3, Nathaniel2, George1)*, b. at Concord, 5 May 1769 son of Daniel and Sarah (Merrill) Chandler; d. 1815 at North Chatham, NH (guardians appointed for minor children 7 Jun 1815); m. about 1795, SUSAN HARDY, b. at Fryeburg, 21 Feb 1773 daughter of David and Molly (-) Hardy; Susan d. at Chatham, 27 Mar 1841.

Paul Chandler and Susan Hardy were parents of nine children born at Chatham.

i DORCAS CHANDLER, b. 23 Mar 1796; d. at Chatham, 1869; m. 14 Nov 1816, 14 Nov 1816, JOHN LEAVITT, b. in ME, 1795; John d. at Chatham, 1873.

ii DAVID HARDY CHANDLER, b. 23 Mar 1798; d. at Chatham, 15 Jul 1845; m. at Chatham, 27 May 1821, his fourth cousin once removed, MEHITABLE CHARLES *(Susanna Charles Charles6, Susanna Abbott Charles5, Isaac4, Ebenezer3, John2, George1)*, b. at Fryeburg, ME, 1 Jul 1800 daughter of Solomon and Susanna (Charles) Charles; Mehitable d. at Chatham, 28 Sep 1869.

iii DANIEL CHANDLER, b. 19 Apr 1800; d. at Concord, 10 Aug 1879; m. at Chatham, 1 Nov 1832, JANE WALKER, b. 4 May 1804; Jane d. at Stow, ME, 14 Aug 1882.

iv MOSES CHANDLER, b. 10 Oct 1802; d. at Bethel, ME, 29 Jul 1875; m. 28 Mar 1827, NANCY FARRINGTON SWAN, b. at Bethel, 11 Jul 1805 daughter of Elijah and Eunice (Barton) Swan; Nancy d. at Bethel, 23 Jul 1884.

v ABIEL CHANDLER, b. 14 Jan 1805; d. at Bethel, ME; m. 11 Mar 1827, HANNAH CHANDLER BARTLETT, b. at Bethel, 13 Oct 1810 daughter of Elijah and Nancy (Graham) Bartlett.

vi JOHN CHANDLER, b. 11 Mar 1807; d. at Fryeburg, 12 Nov 1892; m. at Chatham, 23 Nov 1834, BETSEY FIFE, b. at Chatham, 6 Feb 1812 daughter of Moses and Betsey (Noyes) Fife; Betsey d. at Stow, ME, 17 Feb 1884.

[2890] *New Hampshire. Probate Court (Grafton County)*; Probate Place: *Grafton, New Hampshire*, volume 63, pp 316-317, will of Orilla F. Gordon

vii SUSAN HARDY CHANDLER, b. 19 Apr 1809; d. at Stow, ME, 19 Feb 1887; m. at Chatham, 29 Dec 1825, her fourth cousin once removed, HENRY S. FARRINGTON *(Betty Dresser Farrington[6], Abigail Abbott Dresser[5], Job[4], Jonathan[3], Benjamin[2], George[1])*, b. at Stow, 8 Nov 1803 son of Samuel and Betsey (Dresser) Farrington; Henry d. at Stow, 30 Jun 1878.

viii STEPHEN CHANDLER, b. 27 Dec 1810; d. at Aroostook County, ME, 8 Dec 1829.

ix OLIVER PERRY CHANDLER, b. 30 Oct 1813; d. at Fryeburg, 8 Dec 1837; m. 1837, EUNICE SANBORN, b. in ME, about 1822; Eunice d. at Bridgton, ME, 22 May 1901. After Oliver's death, Eunice married Paul C. Leavitt.

1091) ANN CHANDLER *(Daniel Chandler[4], Tabitha Abbott Chandler[3], Nathaniel[2], George[1])*, b. at Concord, 1771 daughter of Daniel and Sarah (Merrill) Chandler; d. at Chatham, 7 Feb 1799; m. about 1794, RICHARD WALKER.

Ann Chandler and Richard Walker were parents of two children born at Chatham.

i HANNAH C. WALKER, b. 29 Dec 1795; d. at Paris, ME, 1 Jun 1877; m. about 1816, OTIS BENT, b. at Middleboro, MA, 23 Aug 1793 son of William and Olive Cushman (Bessey) Bent; Otis d. at Paris, 31 Mar 1871.

ii DANIEL WALKER, b. 1797; died young

1092) JOHN CHANDLER *(Daniel Chandler[4], Tabitha Abbott Chandler[3], Nathaniel[2], George[1])*, b. at Concord, 19 Mar 1781 son of Daniel and Sarah (Merrill) Chandler; d. at Chatham, 23 Apr 1815; m. 28 Nov 1805, MARY HARRIMAN, b. about 1783 daughter of Amos and Nancy (Church) Harriman. Mary m. 2nd, Nathaniel Hutchins. Mary d. in ME, 13 Jun 1844.

John Chandler and Mary Harriman were parents of five children born at Chatham, New Hampshire.

i HANNAH CHANDLER, b. 30 Jan 1806; d. at Norway, ME, 15 May 1880; m. 31 Mar 1836, her third cousin, LEWIS EASTMAN *(Phebe Lovejoy Eastman[6], Abiel Lovejoy[5], Phebe Chandler Lovejoy[4], John Chandler[3], Hannah Abbott Chandler[2], Geroge[1])*, b. at Conway, 7 Aug 1809 son of Jonathan and Phebe (Lovejoy) Eastman; Lewis d. at Paris, ME, 10 Dec 1873.

ii SARAH MERRILL CHANDLER, b. 16 Apr 1808; d. at Lowell, 28 Jun 1866; m. 1833, her fourth cousin once removed, JONATHAN S. FARRINGTON *(Abigail Dresser Farrington[6], Abigail Abbott Dresser[5], Job[4], Jonathan[3], Benjamin[2], George[1])*, b. at Lovell, ME, about 1805 son of Jonathan and Abigail (Dresser) Farrington; Jonathan d. at Lovell, about 1866 (probate 16 Jan 1867).

iii JOHN C. CHANDLER, b. 18 Aug 1809; m. 1st, about 1839, LUCY HORN, about 1815; Lucy d. about 1851. John m. 2nd, about 1854, SUSAN HALEY, b. at Chatham, 8 Aug 1829; Susan d. at Janesville, MN, 6 Jun 1911.

iv CHARLES H. CHANDLER, b. 1814; d. at Concord, 20 Aug 1848; m. LAVINA KENNISTON, b. in NH, about 1815.

v PAUL CHANDLER, b. about 1815; d. at Wiota, WI, 9 Nov 1858; m. at Green, WI, 5 Jul 1849, JERUSHA LUCRETIA BUTLER, b. in PA, about 1832; Jerusha d. at Wiota, about 1855.

1093) DANIEL CHANDLER *(Joshua Chandler[4], Tabitha Abbott Chandler[3], Nathaniel[2], George[1])*, b. at Concord, 1 Sep 1768 son of Joshua and Irene (Copp) Chandler; d. at Concord, Jun 1817; m. 3 Feb 1794, MEHITABLE ARLIN, b. 1770 daughter of Samuel and Anna (Hanson) Arlin. After the death of Daniel, Mehitable married Nathaniel Merrill in 1820 and married Josiah Chandler in 1829.

Daniel Chandler served as a private with the New Hampshire militia in the War of 1812. Daniel Chandler and Mehitable Arlin were parents of twelve children born at Concord.

i NATHANIEL L. CHANDLER, b. about 1796. Nothing definite is known. The Chandler genealogy reports he "went off and had a large family."

ii JUDITH CHANDLER, b. 1797; d. at Concord, after 1850. Judith did not marry. In 1850, she was living at the almshouse in Concord.

iii SARAH CHANDLER, b. about 1799; d. about 1811.

iv NANCY CHANDLER, b. about 1801; m. at Concord, 30 Jan 1821, JEREMIAH ARLIN, b. about 1796; Jeremiah d. at Concord, after 1871. Jeremiah married second Sarah Dearborn. According to the Chandler genealogy, Nancy abandoned the family. Nancy was excommunicated from the church in Concord 8 Jul 1824.

v ELIZABETH CHANDLER, b. about 1804; d. at Concord, 29 Jan 1883; m. 1st, MOSES POWELL. Elizabeth m. 2nd, 13 May 1853, JEREMIAH QUIMBY.

vi Infant, b. and d. 1805

vii Infant, b. and d. 1809

viii JEREMIAH CHANDLER, b. 10 Mar 1810; d. at Concord, 16 Mar 1874; m. 1st, 24 Dec 1829, PHIDELIA ESTABROOK CHASE, b. 15 Oct 1815 daughter of Moses and Lydia (Kimball) Chase; Phidelia d. 9 Jun 1834. Jeremiah m. 2nd, 22 Oct 1835, MERCY FRENCH MERRILL, b. 15 Jan 1813 daughter of Parker and Rebecca (Kimball) Merrill; Mercy d. 4 Nov 1840. Jeremiah m. 3rd, 14 Feb 1841, SARAH PAGE SHED, b. at Saco, ME, 19 Apr 1818 daughter of Zachariah and Mary (Foster) Shed; Sarah d. at Strafford, NH, 20 Jul 1891.

ix SARAH CHANDLER, b. about 1811; d. at Allenstown, NH, after 1880; m. 1st, about 1831, JOHN SLEEPER; John d. at Grafton, NH, about 1843. Sarah m. 2nd, about 1850, JONATHAN B. PRESCOTT, b. about 1800; John d. at Allenstown, after 1880.

x MOSES CHANDLER, b. 7 May 1812; d. at Los Angeles, CA, 6 Feb 1899; m. 7 Oct 1842, ABIGAIL LADD, b. in VT, 8 Dec 1814 daughter of Caleb and Tamma (Dunham) Ladd; Abigail d. at Los Angeles, 25 Mar 1900.

xi SAMUEL B. CHANDLER, b. Apr 1814; m. 1st, at Lowell, 25 Sep 1840, PHILINDA JANE BALL, b. about 1815; Philinda d. before 1860. Samuel m. 2nd, 30 Jul 1860, RUHAMMAH TANDY (widow of Charles Libby), b. at Epsom, about 1818. Samuel m. 3rd, at Hopkinton, 3 Apr 1864, CAROLINE JEWETT (widow of Moses Swett), b. at Bradford, about 1815.

xii BENJAMIN CHANDLER, b. about 1816; d. at Concord, about 1872. Benjamin had two marriages that have not been located. His third marriage was 24 Jan 1869 to MELISSA A. WISER, b. at Concord, 1846 daughter of Nathan and Sarah (Nichols) Wiser; Melissa d. at Concord, 10 Mar 1917. Melissa was second married to Daniel Davis and third married to Frank St. John.

1094) SARAH CHANDLER *(Joshua Chandler[4], Tabitha Abbott Chandler[3], Nathaniel[2], George[1])*, b. at Concord, 12 Feb 1774 daughter of Joshua and Irene (Copp) Chandler; d. after 1860 (living in Concord at the 1860 U.S. Census); m. 25 Aug 1792, GEORGE ARLIN, b. 1768 son of Samuel and Anna (Hanson) Arlin; George d. between 1850 and 1860. George was first married to Sarah's sister Ruth Chandler who died May 1792.

Sarah Chandler and George Arlin were parents of twelve children born at Concord.

i IRENE ARLIN, b. 19 Apr 1793; m. at Weare, 18 Jul 1816, DAVID GOVE, b. at Weare, 10 Jun 1793 son of Edmund and Mary (Breed) Gove; David d. at Alden, WI, 7 Mar 1882.

ii PRISCILLA ARLIN, b. 7 Jun 1795; d. at Concord, 13 May 1881; m. Jun 1817, AMOS PERRY.

iii Infant, b. and d. 20 Oct 1797

iv SARAH ARLIN, b. 5 Jan 1799; m. NATHAN BROWN who died before 1850.

v ZACHARIAH CHANDLER ARLIN, b. 23 Nov 1801; d. at Concord, 23 Jun 1880; m. 1st, about 1828, HARRIET DANIELS, b. about 1801; Harriet d. at Concord, 22 Aug 1833. Zachariah m. 2nd, 7 Feb 1839, LAVINA ARLIN, b. at Concord, 10 Nov 1815; Lavina d. at Pembroke, 16 Mar 1903.

vi HANNAH ARLIN, b. 8 Jul 1804; m. 1st, at Concord, 16 Sep 1825, HENRY L. EMERSON. Hannah m. 2nd, about 1847, JOSEPH WALLACE, b. about 1804.

vii ABIGAIL ARLIN, b. 22 May 1807; d. at Randolph, VT, before 1880; m. at Concord, 11 Jan 1830, JOHN EASTMAN DODGE, b. at Tunbridge, VT, 31 Dec 1799 son of Ammi and Polly (Howe) Dodge; John d. at Tunbridge, 7 Aug 1848.

viii MARY ARLIN, b. 15 Jun 1809; d. 18 Mar 1840; m. EPHRAIM WENTWORTH.

ix CATHERINE ARLIN, b. 11 Dec 1811; d. at Medford, MA, 6 Apr 1902; m. 24 Nov 1831, NATHANIEL ARLIN, b. about 1808; Nathaniel d. Apr 1844.

x ANNA ARLIN, b. 5 May 1814; d. at Hopkinton, NH, 31 Jan 1894; m. 1st, about 1839, JOHN TIBBITS, b. about 1809; John d. at Concord, after 1860. Anna m. 2nd, about 1871, LEVI CONNOR, b. about 1800; Levi d. at Henniker, before 1880.

xi ELIZABETH Y. ARLIN, b. 6 Jul 1816; d. at Concord, 1 Jan 1891; m. 1st, 23 Jan 1834, ENOCH J. QUIMBY, b. in VT, about 1806; Enoch d. at Concord, 1871. Elizabeth m. 2nd, about 1872, Mr. Morse who d. about 1876. Elizabeth m. 3rd, 14 May 1878, ISAIAH J. WEBBER, b. at Hopkinton, about 1819 son of Josiah and Hannah (-) Webber. Elizabeth m. 4th, 10 Aug 1885, JOSIAH LEAVITT, b. at Sanbornton, about 1814 son of Josiah and Susan (Copp) Leavitt.

xii HARRIET E. ARLIN, b. 6 Jun 1819; d. at Concord, 14 Feb 1905; m. at Concord, 7 Feb 1839, THOMAS JEFFERSON BARNES, b. at Rochester, VT, 1 Dec 1815 son of Thomas and Abigail (Eaton) Barnes; Harriet d. at Concord, 14 Feb 1905.

1095) JOSHUA CHANDLER *(Joshua Chandler4, Tabitha Abbott Chandler3, Nathaniel2, George1)*, b. at Concord, 4 Sep 1782 son of Joshua and Irene (Copp) Chandler; d. at Concord, after 1850 when he was living at the town poor farm; m. Aug 1802, NANCY ARLIN, b. 11 Mar 1783 daughter of Samuel and Anna (Hanson) Arlin; Nancy d. after 1870 (living in Concord at the 1870 U. S. Census).

Joshua was a shoemaker. He died at the poor farm in Concord. Joshua Chandler and Nancy Arlin were parents of ten children born at Concord.

i CHARLES CHANDLER, b. about 1811; d. at Concord, 1863. Charles does not seem to have married. He died at the almshouse.

ii MARY CHANDLER, b. about 1813; d. about 1821.

iii SARAH CHANDLER, b. 11 Aug 1814; m. 17 Sep 1829, WARREN PUFFER, b. about 1805 son of Thomas and Mary (Gload) Puffer.

iv DANIEL CHANDLER, b. 1816; d. at Concord, 1859; m. 3 May 1852, ADELINA DIADAMIA PECK.

v SUSAN CHANDLER, b. Jan 1818. Susan did not marry. She was developmentally disabled.

vi DORCAS C. CHANDLER, b. 14 Jul 1819; d. at Hillsborough, NH, 15 Jul 1895; m. 1st, 25 Nov 1841, THOMAS PUFFER, b. about 1819 son of Thomas and Mary (Gload) Puffer; Thomas d. 1848. Dorcas m. 2nd, 4 Jun 1848, JESSE S. BLACK, b. at Berlin, VT, 9 Feb 1823 son of Daniel and Polly (-) Black; Thomas d. at Weare, NH, 9 Jan 1882.

vii ANN CHANDLER, b. 1821; d. 1823.

viii JOSEPH CHANDLER, b. 11 Apr 1823; d. at Boscawen, 7 Aug 1893; m. 16 May 1848, JANE HUNT, b. at Webster, about 1831 daughter of Ephraim and Rhoda (Jackman) Hunt; Jane d. at Boscawen, 11 Sep 1891.

ix MARY CHANDLER, b. about 1824; m. at Concord, 8 Jul 1855, DANIEL BROWN; Daniel d. about 1863.

x SAMUEL CHANDLER, b. about 1825; d. 1 May 1891; m. 5 Nov 1855, MARIA MOODY.

1096) HANNAH FARMER *(Hannah Abbott Farmer4, Jeremiah3, Nathaniel2, George1)*, b. at Billerica, 17 Sep 1767 daughter of Oliver and Hannah (Abbott) Farmer; d. at Billerica, 21 Apr 1856; m. 10 Dec 1789, as his 2nd wife, WILLIAM ROGERS, b. 10 Dec 1789 son of Samuel and Rebekah (Farmer) Rogers. William first married Susannah Pollard in 1787. William d. at Billerica, 17 Aug 1838.

Hannah Farmer and William Rogers were parents of eleven children born at Billerica.

i WILLIAM ROGERS, b. 23 Dec 1790; d. at Billerica, 24 Feb 1862; m. at Medford, about 1822, MARY HOWE, b. at Boston, 6 Apr 1788 daughter of Joseph and Margaret (Cotton) Howe;[2891] Mary d. at Boston, 4 Jan 1841.

ii JEREMIAH ROGERS, b. 26 Oct 1792; d. at Londonderry, NH, 27 Apr 1877; m. at Billerica, 16 Apr 1822, ABIGAIL CROSBY, b. at Billerica, 15 May 1799 daughter of John and Abigail (Cook) Crosby; Abigail d. at Londonderry, 19 Dec 1886.

iii CALVIN ROGERS, b. 30 Aug 1794; d. at Billerica, 9 Mar 1879; m. at Billerica, 30 Apr 1820, ANN FAULKNER, b. at Watertown, 1799 daughter of Francis and Ann (Robbins) Faulkner; Ann d. at Billerica, 12 Dec 1894.

[2891] Howe, *Howe Genealogies, volume 2, Abraham of Roxbury*, p 33

iv HANNAH ROGERS, b. 11 May 1796; d. at Salem, 8 Feb 1876; m. at Salem, 10 May 1821, CHARLES ROUNDY *(Rebecca Boynton Roundy5, Rebecca Abbott Boynton4, Jeremiah3, Nathaniel2, George1)*, b. at Beverly, 15 Oct 1794 son of Nehemiah and Rebecca (Boynton) Roundy; Charles d. at Salem, 26 Feb 1886.

v CHARLES ROGERS, b. 25 May 1798; d. 27 May 1799.

vi REBECCA FARMER ROGERS, b. 18 May 1800; d. at Watertown, MA, 15 Feb 1889; m. at Billerica, 14 Jul 1822, JABEZ WARD BARTON, b. in VT, 1801 son of Caleb and Rachel (Thompson) Barton; Jabez d. at Watertown, 1 Nov 1888.

vii SUSAN "SUKEY" ROGERS, b. 1 Apr 1802; d. at Billerica, 22 May 1878; m. 1st, at Billerica, 24 Nov 1824, JOB KITTREDGE, b. at Tewksbury, 1 Apr 1802 son of Job and Eleanor (Wright) Kittredge; Job d. at Tewksbury, about 1836. Susan m. 2nd, 27 Apr 1837, OLIVER CLARK ROGERS, b. at Tewksbury, 16 Sep 1806 son of Philip and Lydia (Clark) Rogers; Oliver d. at Harrisville, NH, 8 Jul 1893.

viii HARRIET R. ROGERS, b. 17 Apr 1805; d. at Lowell, 17 Jul 1872; m. at Lowell, 4 Dec 1828, SAMUEL BURBANK, b. at West Nottingham, NH, 9 Jul 1792 son of Jonathan and Elizabeth (Cummings) Burbank; Samuel d. at Lowell, 17 Mar 1868.

ix LOUISA ROGERS, b. 23 Aug 1808; d. at Billerica, 12 Feb 1850. Louisa did not marry.

x ELVIRA ROGERS, b. 5 Aug 1810; d. 22 Feb 1830.

xi AUGUSTUS ROGERS, b. 25 Nov 1813; d. at Guilford, NH, 21 Apr 1889; m. 1st, at Salem, MA, 22 Dec 1844, SARAH HALEY, b. about 1820; Sarah d. before 1850. Augustus m. 2nd, about 1855, ABIGAIL HOYT, b. in NH, about 1820; Abigail d. at Gilford, 21 Apr 1889.

1097) JEREMIAH FARMER *(Hannah Abbott Farmer4, Jeremiah3, Nathaniel2, George1)*, b. at Billerica, 10 Apr 1771 son of Oliver and Hannah (Abbott) Farmer; d. 2 Mar 1836; m. 13 Oct 1816, CLARISSA FOSTER, b. 16 Apr 1785 daughter of Timothy and Sally (Crosby) Foster; Clarissa d. at Boston, 20 Feb 1873.

Jeremiah Foster did not leave a will and the estate entered probate 12 April 1836 with Clarissa Farmer as administrator. Real property was valued at $3,440 and debts were $1,535.62. In December 1836 the farm was sold at auction in two lots to Seth Crosby and Dudley Foster for a total of $1,950.[2892]

There are two children known for Jeremiah and Clarissa, both born at Billerica.

i SARAH CLARISSA FARMER, baptized 7 Jan 1818; d. at Boston, 17 Nov 1907; m. at Billerica, 8 Jun 1841, HENRY BLANCHARD, b. at Billerica, 25 Sep 1811 son of Joseph and Sarah (Brown) Blanchard; Henry d. at Boston, 10 Feb 1897.

ii TIMOTHY FOSTER FARMER, baptized 3 Oct 1824; d. at Billerica, 27 May 1871; m. 24 Jul 1862, JANE LEAVITT, b. at Clinton, ME, 2 Feb 1838 daughter of Nathan and Elizabeth (Hanson) Leavitt; Jane d. at Billerica, about 1909.

1098) JOHN BOYNTON *(Rebecca Abbott Boynton4, Jeremiah3, Nathaniel2, George1)*, b. at Billerica, 14 Mar 1762 son of Richard and Rebecca (Abbott) Boynton; d. at Chester, VT, 4 Aug 1852; m. 7 Sep 1787, PHEBE MARTIN, b. at Andover, 14 Jul 1764 daughter of Jonathan and Phebe (Farnum) Martin; Phebe d. at Chester, 27 Sep 1840.

John Boynton and Phebe Martin were parents of eleven children, all the births except the youngest recorded at Rockingham, Vermont and the youngest child at Springfield, Vermont.

i PHEBE BOYNTON, b. 3 Aug 1788; d. at Rockingham, 16 Sep 1848; m. at Springfield, 23 Dec 1807, JOSEPH DAMON, b. 1785 son of Samuel and Anne (Bowker) Damon; Joseph d. 18 Jun 1845.

ii JOHN BOYNTON, b. 4 Mar 1790; d. at Springfield, 8 Oct 1879; m. 17 Jun 1822, LAURA MASON, b. at Springfield, 1794 daughter of Allen and Molly (Weaver) Mason; Laura d. at Springfield, 24 Oct 1874.

iii JAMES BOYNTON, b. 25 Dec 1791; d. at Boston, 18 Jun 1856; m. 6 Feb 1831, ELIZA B. BACON, b. about 1805; Eliza d. at Boston, 4 May 1832.

2892 Middlesex County, MA: Probate File Papers, 1648-1871.Online database. AmericanAncestors.org. New England Historic Genealogical Society, 2014. Case 7187

iv WILLIAM BOYNTON, b. 16 Oct 1793; d. at Springfield, 18 May 1867; m. 28 Mar 1821, FRINDA CUTLER, b. at Springfield, 14 Feb 1802 daughter of Silas and Olive (Holbrook) Cutler; Frinda d. at Chester, VT, 26 Nov 1876.

v JERUSHA BOYNTON, b. 12 Aug 1795; d. 29 Mar 1796.

vi LOAMMI BOYNTON, b. 17 Jan 1797; d. 3 Feb 1797.

vii HANNAH BOYNTON, b. 16 Feb 1798; d. 23 Apr 1809.

viii ORPHA BOYNTON, b. 22 Mar 1800; d. at Chester, VT, 12 May 1876; m. at Springfield, 26 Apr 1821, NOAH PARKER, b. about 1791; Noah d. at Rockingham, 20 Par 1849.

ix MARY BOYNTON, b. 1 Feb 1802; d. at Weathersfield, VT, 19 Dec 1889; m. Nov 1835, NAPOLEON BONAPARTE ROUNDY, b. at Rockingham, 22 Jan 1801 son of Ralph and Rosalinda (Wright) Roundy; Napoleon Bonaparte d. at Weathersfield, 13 Aug 1871.

x MATILDA BOYNTON, b. 4 May 1804; d. 16 May 1818.

xi HASKELL BOYNTON, b. 15 Apr 1808; d. at Rockingham, 6 Jun 1882; m. 19 Mar 1837, MARTHA MANNING WALKER, b. at Springfield, 12 May 1813 daughter of Ephraim and Martha (Manning) Walker; Martha d. 17 Mar 1889.

1099) REBECCA BOYNTON *(Rebecca Abbott Boynton⁴, Jeremiah³, Nathaniel², George¹)*, b. at Billerica, baptized 13 Nov 1763 daughter of Richard and Rebecca (Abbott) Boynton; d. 27 Apr 1833; m. 1785, NEHEMIAH ROUNDY,[2893] b. at Beverly, 10 May 1756 son of Robert and Abigail (Presson) Roundy; Nehemiah d. at sea, Sep 1804.

Captain Nehemiah Roundy was a master mariner on the brig *Minerva* which was owned by William Gray.[2894] He was lost a sea in a great gale.[2895]

Nehemiah Roundy did not leave a will and his estate entered probate 15 October 1805. The widow's dower was set off to Rebecca and the remainder of the estate was sold.

Rebecca Boynton and Nehemiah Roundy were parents of six children born at Beverly.

i GEORGE ROUNDY, b. 9 Sep 1786; d. at New York, Mar 1826. George was a mariner. He did not marry.

ii BETSEY ROUNDY, b. 17 Sep 1788; d. at Beverly, 10 Feb 1871; m. 29 Jan 1809, WARWICK PALFREY, b. at Salem, 1787 son of Warwick and Hannah (Chapman) Palfrey; Warwick d. at Salem, 23 Aug 1838. Warwick Palfrey was editor of the *Essex Register* from 1805 until his death.[2896]

iii CHARLES ROUNDY, b. about 1790; died young.

iv CHARLES ROUNDY, b. 15 Oct 1794; d. at Salem, 26 Feb 1886; m. at Salem, 10 May 1821, HANNAH ROGERS, b. at Billerica, 11 May 1796 daughter of William and Hannah (Farmer) Rogers; Hannah d. at Salem, 8 Feb 1876.

v ABIGAIL ROUNDY, b. 26 Jun 1797; d. at Salem, 24 Jan 1856; m. at Salem, 8 Oct 1815, JOHN CHAPMAN, b. at Salem, 4 Sep 1793 son of John and Ruth (Henfield) Chapman; John d. at Salem, 19 Apr 1873.

vi OLIVER ROUNDY, b. 6 Feb 1801; d. 1813.

1100) RICHARD BOYNTON *(Rebecca Abbott Boynton⁴, Jeremiah³, Nathaniel², George¹)*, b. at Billerica, 3 Oct 1765 son of Richard and Rebecca (Abbott) Boynton; d. at Redman, NY, Jul 1841; m. BETSEY WYMAN, b. at Pelham, 20 Jun 1764 daughter of Joseph and Mary (-) Wyman. Richard married second Mary who died 1831, and third Jerusha Bishop.

Richard and Betsey were likely married in Massachusetts and perhaps their first few children were born there, although the births are all recorded in Vermont. They resided in Rockingham, Vermont before relocating to Jefferson County, New York before 1809.

Richard Boynton and Betsey Wyman were parents of eight children, births recorded at Rockingham, Vermont.

i WILLIAM BOYNTON, b. 5 Jun 1791; d. at Watertown, NY, about 1863;[2897] m. 1818,[2898] LOVICA HANCOCK, b. about 1799; Lovica d. at Watertown, 1868 (probate Mar 1869).

[2893] Nehemiah Roundy is also likely the father of Nehemiah Roundy born at Beverly 20 Oct 1777, an out-of-wedlock child with Jane Leavitt.
[2894] Gray, *William Gray of Salem, Merchant*, p 101
[2895] Massachusetts, Town and Vital Records, 1620-1988
[2896] Appletons' Cyclopedia of American Biography; Volume: Vol. IV
[2897] A March 1865 probate document is a petition summoning Lovica Boynton to explain why she has not attending to the administration of her husband's estate.
[2898] Boynton, *The Boynton Family*

ii ELIZABETH BOYNTON, b. 15 Mar 1793; d. at Rodman, NY, 10 Apr 1829;[2899] m. about 1813, WILLIAM WINSLOW, b. in CT, 1790 son of Jesse and Kezia (Spicer) Winslow; William d. at Rodman, 2 Jun 1852. After Elizabeth's death, William married Julia Kinney (who is the sister of Jonathan Boynton's wife Maria Kinney).

iii JONATHAN BOYNTON, b. 2 Mar 1795; d. at Rodman, NY, 3 Feb 1883; m. 1819, MARIA KINNEY, b. 1800 daughter of Daniel and Rachel (Stephens) Kinney; Maria d. at Rodman, 30 Jul 1841.

iv RICHARD BOYNTON, b. 2 Oct 1797; d. at Clarendon, NY, 23 Feb 1873; m. about 1825, ABIGAIL MOODY, b. about 1796; Abigail d. at Ellisburg, NY, 1838. Richard and Abigail had a daughter Harriet and Richard lived with Harriet and her husband. He did not remarry.

v SIMEON BOYNTON, b. 25 Jun 1798; d. at Elyria, OH, 1873 (probate 21 Jun 1873); m. about 1822, SEREPTA BAKER who d. before 1840. Simeon m. 2nd, about 1840, NANCY WIGHTMAN, b. at Rodman, 1806 daughter of Nathan and Betsey (Osgood) Wightman;[2900] Nancy d. at Norwalk, OH, 8 May 1891.

vi DAVID BOYNTON, b. 22 Nov 1800; d. at Rodman, NY, 20 Jan 1892. David did not marry. He lived with his sister Sarah and her son. His nephew Isaac Wood was administrator of his estate.

vii SARAH BOYNTON, b. 22 May 1803; d. at Rodman, NY, 23 Feb 1872; m. 1 May 1826, DARIUS MORRIS WOOD, b. at Wilbraham, MA, 1 May 1804 son of Isaac S. and Betsey (Morris) Wood; Darius d. at Rodman, 19 Apr 1840.

viii LYDIA BOYNTON, b. 20 Aug 1805; nothing further known.

Richard Boynton and Mary were parents of one child.

i ZOBIDA BOYNTON, b. at Rodman, NY, 1816; d. at Rodman, 20 Feb 1856; m. about 1837, SILAS KINNEY, b. at Rodman, about 1814 son of Daniel and Rachel (Stephens) Kinney; Silas d. at Rodman, 27 Mar 1859. Silas married second the widow Mary Jackson.

1101) HANNAH BOYNTON *(Rebecca Abbott Boynton[4], Jeremiah[3], Nathaniel[2], George[1])*, b. 7 Jun 1767 daughter of Richard and Rebecca (Abbott) Boynton; d. 1841 at Spencer, NY; m. at Wilton, 23 Nov 1786, NATHAN MARTIN, b. at Rockingham, VT, 3 Apr 1763 son of Samuel and Elizabeth (Osgood) Martin; Nathan d. at Spencer, 27 Sep 1834.

Hannah and Nathan had their eleven children in Rockingham, Vermont and then relocated to Spencer, New York.

i NATHAN MARTIN, b. 11 Feb 1787; d. 21 Mar 1795.

ii SAUL MARTIN, b. 23 May 1789

iii REBECCA ABBOTT MARTIN, b. 10 Jul 1791; d. at Rockingham, 20 Apr 1825; m. 4 Feb 1813, WARD CLARK, b. at Rockingham, 2 Feb 1790 son of Ward and Jane (-) Clark.

iv JERUSHA BOYNTON MARTIN, b. 3 Mar 1793

v MARY "POLLY" MARTIN, b. 4 Feb 1795; d. about 1832; m. 1818, NOAH EMERY, b. 27 Oct 1794 son of Noah and Elizabeth (Philbrick) Emery;[2901] Noah d. at Spencer, NY, Jul 1880. Noah married second Sophia Hugg in 1833.

vi SAMUEL MARTIN, b. 3 Nov 1796; d. at Catharine, NY, 1868; m. 1821, CLARISSA CAROLINE HUGG, b. at New Marlborough, MA, 2 Sep 1804 daughter of Daniel and Achsah (Brown) Hugg;[2902] Caroline d. at Havana, NY, 1880.

vii HANNAH MARTIN, b. 28 Feb 1799

viii NATHAN MARTIN, b. 17 Jan 1801

ix SUSANNAH MARTIN, b. 14 Feb 1803; d. at Spencer, NY, 28 Oct 1870; m. at Spencer, about 1828, DAVID HOWELL, b. 1798; David d. at Spencer, 2 Oct 1870.

x IRA MARTIN, b. 16 Apr 1805; d. at Spencer, NY, 16 Apr 1882; m. 1st, unknown. Ira m. 2nd, JANE, b. in NY, about 1822. Census records show that Ira has older children who are likely from a first wife who died about 1845. The name of his first wife has not been found.

[2899] Early Settlers of New York State, Volume II, p 13

[2900] Wightman, *The Wightman Ancestry*, volume I, p 149

[2901] Emery, *Genealogical Records of the Descendants of John and Anthony Emery*, p 345

[2902] The 1856 will of Daniel Hugg includes a bequest to his daughter Clarissa C. the wife of Samuel Martin.

xi EZRA MARTIN, b. 26 Jan 1807; d. at Chippewa County, WI, May 1874; m. 1st, about 1830, LUCY WOODFORD, b. 10 Oct 1805 daughter of Truman and Lucy (Hawley) Woodford; Lucy d. at Candor, NY, 8 Nov 1858. Ezra m. 2nd, about 1859 the widow MALINDA HENDRIX, b. about 1816.

1102) SARAH BOYNTON *(Rebecca Abbott Boynton⁴, Jeremiah³, Nathaniel², George¹)*, b. 28 Aug 1770 daughter of Richard and Rebecca (Abbott) Boynton; d. at Springfield, VT, 11 Nov 1850; m. 16 Jan 1793, DAVID KENNEY, b. about 1766 son of David Kenney;[2903] David d. at Springfield, VT, 23 Jan 1830.

David and Sarah Kenney started their family in Wilton where four children were born. In 1808, the family relocated to Springfield, Vermont. Births of other children after the move have not been located.

i DAVID KENNEY, b. 2 Dec 1799; d. at Montrose, WI, after 1870; m. 4 Feb 1824, LUCY C. RICHMOND, b. at Athens, VT, 8 Feb 1800 daughter of Amaziah and Sarah (Field) Richmond;[2904] Lucy d. at Montrose, after 1870.

ii HIRAM KENNEY, b. 2 Nov 1802; d. at Springfield, VT, 10 Nov 1873; m. 20 May 1838, ELIZABETH BLACKBURN, b. in England, about 1810; Elizabeth d. at Springfield, 10 Oct 1856.

iii SARAH KENNEY, b. 4 Oct 1804; d. at Springfield, VT, 20 Mar 1869; m. 22 Feb 1827, GEORGE B. CLARKE, b. at Helene, NH, about 1800 son of Paul and Hannah (Hodgman) Clark; George d. at Springfield, 17 Oct 1871.

iv CLEMENS KENNEY, b. 24 Oct 1808; nothing further known.

1103) ORPHA BOYNTON *(Rebecca Abbott Boynton⁴, Jeremiah³, Nathaniel², George¹)*, b. in New Hampshire, 10 May 1772 daughter of Richard and Rebecca (Abbott) Boynton; d. at Milford, 1851;[2905] m. about 1794, JOHN HOPKINS born at Milford about 1772 son of Ebenezer and Martha (Burns) Hopkins; John d. at Milford about 1850.

Orpha Boynton was the seventh oldest of ten children of Richard and Rebecca (Abbott) Boynton. Around the time of her birth, the family relocated from Massachusetts and settled in Milford, New Hampshire. It was there that she met and married John Hopkins. The couple had nine children, five sons and four daughters, all born in Milford. This is a family that struggled financially and ended in poverty. There were also disruptions in the families of their children including one son leaving his wife and going to seek his fortunes in the California gold rush.

By the time of their deaths around 1850, Orpha and John were living apart. At the 1850 census, Orpha was a pauper living at the poor house in Milford.[2906] John at age 76 was still working as a laborer and living next to his granddaughter Harriet and her family.[2907]

The four daughters located in Waltham, Massachusetts where daughter Jerusha ran a boarding house. Three of the daughters (Jerusha, Olive, and Eliza) did not marry and lived with each other.[2908] Daughter Fanny married and had four children with her husband Reuben Wright, but Reuben left the family taking the oldest son and going to Michigan where they were farmers. Fanny then lived with her younger children in Waltham. The oldest son, Almon, returned to Waltham by 1855 and stayed with his mother for a time, then returned to Michigan with his father before finally resettling in Massachusetts. Fanny's husband died in Michigan.

Son Frye died as a young man without marrying. Oldest son Jotham settled with his wife and children in Springfield, Vermont. Son Luther and his wife and children started in Massachusetts and spent time in New York before settling in Michigan. Son Holland married and remained in Milford where he had seven children. The History of Milford states that Holland moved to Ohio in 1848 and died there,[2909] but he was listed in Milford in the 1850 census. Four of his children died in Milford between 1852 and 1858, so if Holland went to Ohio he did so without his family. Holland's wife did remain in Milford and she died in Wilton, New Hampshire in 1878.

Son John B. Hopkins married Cassendana (Cassandra) Hutchinson in 1837. The couple did not have children and by 1850 John left his wife and went to California where he died in 1857. It is believed that John joined the gold rush perhaps working in the area near Tuolumne in the Sierra Nevada.[2910] His wife continued living in Milford before relocating to Massachusetts in her later years.

i JOTHAM HOPKINS, b. 19 Jan 1795; d. at Springfield, VT, 21 Apr 1874; m. 1st, 3 Mar 1822, RUTHENA BURR, b. at Rockingham, VT, 4 Jan 1794 daughter of Samuel and Susannah (-) Burr; Ruthena d. about 1833. Jotham

---

2903 Livermore, *History of Wilton*, p 423
2904 Richmond, *The Richmond Family*, p 152
2905 *U.S., Find A Grave Index, 1600s-Current, memorial ID* 81442211.
2906 *1850 United States Federal Census*, Year: 1850; Census Place: Milford, Hillsborough, New Hampshire; Roll: M432_434; Page: 176B; Image: 346.
2907 *1850 United States Federal Census*, Year: 1850; Census Place: Milford, Hillsborough, New Hampshire; Roll: M432_434; Page: 188A; Image: 369.
2908 *1860 United States Federal Census*, Year: 1860; Census Place: Waltham, Middlesex, Massachusetts; Roll: M653_511; Page: 642; Family History Library Film: 803511.
2909 Ramsdell and Colburn, The History of Milford, Volume 1, p 933 ff
2910 *1850 United States Federal Census*, Year: 1850; Census Place: Chinese Camp, Tuolumne, California; Roll: M432_36; Page: 99A; Image: 207.

second married 25 Nov 1834 ESTHER PERRY, b. at Springfield, about 1803 daughter of Jonathan and Anna (Lawrence) Perry; Esther d. 10 Jun 1876.

ii JERUSHA B. HOPKINS, b. about 1797; d. at Waltham, MA, 21 May 1879. Jerusha ran a boarding house in Waltham.

iii FANNY HOPKINS, b. about 1799; d. at Waltham, MA, 27 Dec 1874; m. at Waltham, 17 May 1829, REUBEN WRIGHT, b. in NH 1802 likely the son of Reuben and Olive (Atwood) Wright; Reuben d. in Michigan after 1860.[2911] Fanny and Reuben had four children. Reuben and the oldest son went to Michigan before 1850 and Fanny and the younger children stayed in Massachusetts.

iv HOLLAND HOPKINS, b. 4 Apr 1802; d. unknown but perhaps in Ohio after 1850; m. at Milford, 3 Feb 1823, ELIZA HUTCHINSON, b. at Milford, 4 Oct 1803 daughter of Bartholomew and Phebe (Hagget) Hutchinson; Eliza d. at Wilton, NH, 27 Jan 1878. Holland and Eliza had seven children. The Milford history book reports Holland went to Ohio, but his family apparently remained in Milford.

v JOHN B. HOPKINS, b. Sep 1803; d. likely in California, 11 Apr 1857; m. 25 Dec 1837, his third cousin, CASSENDANA HUTCHINSON *(Sarah Moar Hutchinson[5], Joshua Moar[4], Elizabeth Abbott Moar[3], Nathaniel[2], George[1])*, b. at Milford, May 1812 daughter of Luther and Sarah (Moar) Hutchinson; Cassendana d. at Worcester, MA, 23 Feb 1871 (although a resident of Lynn at the time of death).[2912] John and Cassendana did not have children. John left the area by 1850 and is perhaps the John Hopkins listed on the 1850 Census for Chinese Camp, Tuolumne, CA. Cassendana is a child in Family 1131.

vi FRYE HOPKINS, b. about 1807; d. 17 Aug 1838. Some sources report he died in Rhode Island, but he is buried in Milford. Frye did not marry.

vii OLIVE HOPKINS, b. about 1809; d. at Waltham, MA, 10 Aug 1848. Olive did not marry.

viii ELIZA HOPKINS, b. about 1813; d. at Waltham, MA, 1 May 1881. Eliza did not marry.

ix LUTHER B. HOPKINS, b. about 1814; d. at Comstock, MI after 1860; m. at Cambridge, MA, 25 Jul 1837, LUCY ANN C. SEAVER, born in Maine about 1818 likely the daughter of Richard Crafts Seaver; Lucy d. at Otsego, MI after 1870. Luther and Lucy were in Massachusetts and New York before finally settling in Michigan.

1104) BETSEY BOYNTON *(Rebecca Abbott Boynton[4], Jeremiah[3], Nathaniel[2], George[1])*, b. 1774 daughter of Richard and Rebecca (Abbott) Boynton; d. at Athens, VT, Nov 1818; m. at Amherst, NH, 31 Oct 1802, AARON FULLER, b. at Wilton 1773 son of Amos and Hannah (Putnam) Fuller;[2913] Aaron d. at Crown Point, NY, 4 Apr 1847. Aaron second married Betsy Locke.

This family started in Wilton where two children were born and were then in Athens, Vermont where Betsey died. Aaron remarried and relocated to Crown Point, New York. Betsey Boynton and Aaron Fuller were parents of five children.[2914]

i AMOS FULLER, b. at Wilton, 6 Jul 1803; d. at Ellisburg, NY, after 1860; m. MARY D. who had not been identified.

ii AARON FULLER, b. at Wilton, 26 Jul 1805

iii ACHSAH FULLER, b. at Athens, VT, 21 Jul 1808; d. at Raymond, WA, 26 Jan 1881; m. in NY, about 1831,[2915] TIMOTHY MERRILL ADAMS, b. at Rockingham, VT, 19 Jan 1805 son of Joseph and Sarah (-) Adams; Thomas d. at Raymond, 8 Jun 1864.

iv PUTNAM FULLER, b. at Athens, about 1809

v BETSY FULLER, b. at Athens, about 1811

[2911] *1860 United States Federal Census*, Year: 1860; Census Place: Lexington, Sanilac, Michigan; Roll: M653_558; Page: 917; Family History Library Film: 803558.

[2912] *Massachusetts, Death Records, 1841-1915*, New England Historic Genealogical Society; Boston, Massachusetts; Massachusetts Vital Records, 1840–1911.

[2913] Cutter, *New England Families, Genealogical and Memorial: A Record of the Achievements of Her People in the Making of Commonwealths and the Founding of a Nation,* Volume 3, p 1457

[2914] Boynton, *History of the Boynton Family*, p 124

[2915] Oregon, Early Oregonians Index, 1800-1860

1105) DAVID BOYNTON *(Rebecca Abbott Boynton⁴, Jeremiah³, Nathaniel², George¹)*, b. 7 Mar 1776 son of Richard and Rebecca (Abbott) Boynton; d. at Rockingham, VT, 14 Dec 1813;[2916] m. 1 Jun 1804, LYDIA NOURSE, b. at Jaffrey, NH, 6 Jun 1783 daughter of Peter and Lydia (Low) Nourse;[2917] Lydia d. 16 Oct 1874 in Charlotte, NY.[2918]

David and Lydia Boynton were the parents of four children born at Rockingham, Vermont.

i JEREMIAH BOYNTON, b. 29 Sep 1805; d. at Newbury, VT, 6 Mar 1876; m. at Newbury, 26 Sep 1831, DEBORAH CROSS BAILEY, b. at Newbury, 2 Jun 1803 daughter of Jacob and Mary (Ladd) Bailey; Deborah d. at Newbury, 28 Nov 1863.

ii ELVIRA BOYNTON, b. 4 Dec 1806; d. at Charlotte, NY,[2919] 23 Sep 1890; m. 1 Sep 1829, DANIEL BIXBY LAKE, b. at Rockingham, VT, 9 Sep 1802 son of Henry and Prudence (Lovejoy) Lake; Daniel d. at Charlotte, 4 Jul 1879.

iii CLARISSA BOYNTON, b. 12 Mar 1808; d. at Charlotte, NY, 25 Nov 1888; m. 1836, FREEMAN LAKE, b. at Rockingham, VT, 11 Jul 1808 son of Henry and Prudence (Lovejoy) Lake; Freeman d. at Charlotte, 12 Oct 1881.

iv DAVID F. BOYNTON, b. 24 Feb 1810; d. at Westfield, VT, 22 Oct 1894; m. 23 Mar 1837, LYDIA ROBERTS, b. at Groton, VT, about 1812 daughter of Stephen and Lydia (Gray) Roberts; Lydia d. at Westfield, 29 Sep 1877.

1106) SUSANNAH BOYNTON *(Rebecca Abbott Boynton⁴, Jeremiah³, Nathaniel², George¹)*, b. in Vermont, 25 Oct 1778 daughter of Richard and Rebecca (Abbott) Boynton; d. after 1850 perhaps in Greece, NY;[2920] m. at Rockingham, VT, 12 Jun 1804, JOSHUA EATON, b. at Reading, 3 Jul 1778 son of Thomas and Abigail (Bancroft) Eaton; Joshua d. 16 May 1840.

Joshua and Susannah lived in Rockingham, Vermont but relocated to Jefferson County, New York. The oldest child of Susannah and Joshua was born at Wilton, and the younger two children were likely born in Vermont. Just three children are known.

i JOSHUA EATON, b. at Wilton, 23 Mar 1805; d. at Charlotte, NY, 27 Aug 1879; m. 1st, about 1829, HARRIET KINNEY, b. about 1809; Harriet d. at Sackets Harbor, NY, 12 Apr 1844. Joshua m. 2nd, 1845, ADELINE F. BAKER, b. about 1811; Adeline d. at Charlotte, 1878 (probate 10 Jul 1878 with brother Isaac N. Baker as administrator).

ii REBECCA EATON, b. 26 Mar 1806; m. 7 Jan 1828, GEORGE H. FREEMAN, b. about 1800 son of Bradley and Eunice (Noyes) Freeman; George d. at Leslie, MI, 15 Oct 1846.

iii ABIGAIL EATON, b. 7 Nov 1809; d. at Jefferson County, NY, May 1841; m. May 1830, LUTHER MILLS, b. about 1807; Luther d. at Henderson, NY, 16 Sep 1858 (probate 22 Sep 1858). After Abigail's death, Luther married Anna Maria.

1107) BRIDGET ABBOTT *(William⁴, Jeremiah³, Nathaniel², George¹)*, b. 13 Dec 1770 daughter of William and Bridget (Spaulding) Abbott; d. at Westford, 16 Jun 1849; m. 17 Dec 1807, BENJAMIN READ, b. at Westford, 19 Jan 1779 son of Abel and Rebekah (Farrar) Read; Benjamin d. 21 Jan 1850.

As a young child, Bridget along with all her family had been "warned out" of Townsend a procedure used by towns to remove newcomers who seemed unable to support themselves. There was this notice in Townsend: *To notify and warn out - William Abbit & Bridget his wife together with there Children named Bridget, Jedethan, Sarah, William, Joshua & David who came last from Fitchburg in the county of Worcester to Townshend the Twenty fifth of February 1783. Dated Twentyeth day of February 1784.*[2921]

Bridget married later in life to Benjamin Read, a farmer in Westford. They had one son born in Westford. Benjamin's father Abel Read had served in the Revolutionary War and fought in the Battle of White Plains 28 October 1776.[2922]

i BENJAMIN ABBOTT READ, b. 30 Jan 1810; d. at Westford, 11 Jul 1871; m. 29 Jan 1835, BETSY HUNT, b. at Westford, 25 Oct 1803 daughter of Simon and Lydia (Proctor) Hunt; Betsy d. at Westford, 15 Mar 1881. Benjamin continued his father's work as a farmer. Benjamin and Betsy had four children.

[2916] Hayes, *History of the Town of Rockingham Vermont*, p 810

[2917] Wells, *History of Newbury, Vermont: From the Discovery of the Coös Country*, p 645

[2918] At the 1860 U.S. Census, she was living in Charlotte, New York with her daughter Elvira and her husband Daniel Lake.

[2919] *New York, State Census, 1855.*

[2920] *1850 United States Federal Census*, Year: 1850; Census Place: Greece, Monroe, New York; Roll: M432_529; Page: 133B; Image: 273. Susannah Eaton, age 70, living in the household of Joshua Eaton, age 45.

[2921] Massachusetts: Vital Records, 1621-1850 (Online Database: AmericanAncestors.org, New England Historic Genealogical Society, 2001-2016).

[2922] Hodgman, *History of the Town of Westford*, p 125

1108) SARAH ABBOTT *(William⁴, Jeremiah³, Nathaniel², George¹)*, b. at Chelmsford, 1 Oct 1775 daughter of William and Bridget (Spaulding) Abbott; d. at Hancock, NH, 17 Feb 1841; m. at Swanzey, NH, 5 Nov 1794, LOTAN GASSETT, b. at Northborough, MA, 31 Oct 1771 son of Levi and Vashti (Brigham) Gassett; Lotan d. 28 Jul 1861. After Sarah's death, Lotan married Elizabeth Dearborn.

Sarah and Lotan began their family in Townsend, Massachusetts. About 1820, the family relocated to Hancock, New Hampshire.

Both Lotan and his son Lotan were widowed in early 1841. *The History of Hancock* suggests that Lotan, Jr. remarried to Elizabeth Dearborn in December 1841,[2923] but it seems that Lotan, Sr. is the one who remarried. In the 1850 U.S. Census, Lotan, Sr. is living with a woman Elizabeth of the right age to be Elizabeth Dearborn.

The spouses of two of the daughters, Franklin Saunders and Jacob Saunders, are likely first cousins. Both these Saunders families received "warnings out" from Townsend in 1785. Sarah Abbott's family received a warning out in 1784 (see Bridget Abbott above). It is interesting that all these families "warned out" of Townsend wound up settling there.

Sarah and Lotan Gassett had nine children, most of the births recorded at Townsend. Additional information on births was obtained from Hayward's *History of Hancock*.

i SABRIA GASSETT, b. 15 Feb 1795; d. at Townsend, 29 Aug 1875; m. at Townsend, 26 Nov 1812, JACOB SAUNDERS, b. at Townsend, 9 Mar 1787 son of Jacob Saunders; Jacob d. at Townsend 16 Mar 1865.

ii LEVI GASSETT, b. 20 Nov 1797; d. likely in Iowa after 1855;[2924] m. at Peterborough, 4 Apr 1820, ALMIRA HILDREATH of undetermined parentage. It is not known when Almira died, but might have been by 1823 when Levi might have remarried.

iii SALLY GASSETT, b. 30 May 1801; d. at Townsend, 18 Oct 1838; m. 16 Mar 1828, FRANKLIN SAUNDERS, b. at Townsend, 8 Jun 1800 son of Solomon and Lydia (Landon) Saunders; Franklin d. at Townsend, 30 Mar 1878.

iv MARY BRIGHAM "POLLY" GASSETT, b. 27 Mar 1803; d. about 1836; m. at Hancock, 1 Jan 1829, as his second wife, STEPHEN WYMAN THAYER, b. in NH about 1802 son of William and Abigail (Wyman) Thayer; Stephen d. 10 Aug 1883 in Wayne County, NY. William perhaps had three more wives after the death of Polly.

v VASHTI GASSETT, b. 10 Jul 1806; d. at Hancock, NH, 20 Aug 1855; m. at Hancock, 10 Oct 1826, ROYAL A. WILKINS, b. at Hillsborough, 11 Apr 1801 son of Asaph and Ruth (Curtis) Wilkins; Royal d. in California in 1856.

vi LOTAN GASSETT, b. 20 Feb 1808; d. at Cambridge, MA, 22 Oct 1888; m. at Hancock, 14 Jul 1833, SYBIL AUGUSTA DAVIS, b. 1814 daughter of Joshua and Sally (Lee) Davis; Sybil d. at Hancock, 19 Apr 1841.

vii ABBOT GASSETT, b. 24 Jun 1810; d. at Hancock, 18 Mar 1837.

viii WILLIAM GASSETT, b. 13 Sep 1815; m. MARY E. MAY, b. at Hancock, 10 Dec 1825 daughter of Whitcomb and Mary (Felch) May. William and Mary had a daughter Eliza Adeline who was later adopted by Josiah Cram. This adoption was not through the Court[2925] and it is not clear why this occurred, but Eliza used the name Cram on her marriage record. William Gassett and Mary May divorced Sep 1856.[2926]

ix CHARLES R. GASSETT, b. at Hancock, 24 Mar 1822; d. at Boston, 1 Jul 1884; m. 16 Jun 1853, LOUISIANA AUGUSTA BLANCHARD, b. at Charlestown, Apr 1831 daughter of Simon and Louisiana (Farley) Blanchard; Augusta d. at Melrose, 3 Jul 1900.

1109) WILLIAM ABBOTT *(William⁴, Jeremiah³, Nathaniel², George¹)*, b. Apr 1778 son of William and Bridget (Spaulding) Abbott; d. at Dansville, MI, 9 Jan 1849; m. at Swanzey, NH, 30 Oct 1804, SARAH "SALLY" WOODCOCK, b. at Swanzey, NH, 1 Mar 1782 daughter of Nathan and Lovina (Goodenow) Woodcock; Sally d. at Mason, MI, 26 Mar 1854.

William and Sally had their children in Wheelock and Shoreham, Vermont and then relocated to Ingham County, Michigan.

There are seven children known for William Abbott and Sarah Woodcock.[2927]

[2923] Hayward, *The History of Hancock*, p 593

[2924] Year: 1850; Census Place: Monticello, Jones, Iowa; Roll: M432_185; Page: 203B; Image: 412. Levi Gassett, age 53, is living in the home of his son George W. Gassett. Levi is also listed in the 1855 Iowa census, age 64 and widowed.

[2925] Hayward, *History of Hancock*, p 470

[2926] Ancestry.com, Maine, Divorce Records, 1798-1891

[2927] Some sources suggest two additional children in this family, William and Elmira, but I did not locate good evidence for them. As there is a nine-year gap between the 1804 marriage and birth of the first known child in 1813, there are likely other children.

i NANCY ABBOTT, b. at Wheelock, VT, 3 Mar 1813; d. at Detroit, 14 Nov 1902; m. about 1841, Dr. MINOS MCROBERT, b. at Springfield, VT, 14 Feb 1804 son of William and Lydia (Safford) McRobert; Minos d. at Mason, MI, 5 Oct 1884.

ii WILLIAM ABBOTT, b. 1814; d. at Shoreham, VT, 31 May 1831.

iii RHODA ARVILLA ABBOTT, b. at Wheelock, 12 May 1815; d. at Mason, MI, 27 Oct 1886; m. AMAZIAH WINCHELL, b. at Prattsville, NY, 25 Nov 1810 son of Jason and Sarah (Phillips) Winchell; Amaziah d. at Mason, 27 Oct 1887.

iv LOVINA ABBOTT, b. at Wheelock, 24 Feb 1819;[2928] d. at Mason, MI, 10 Jun 1885; m. at White Oak, MI, 2 Nov 1842, JOHN COATSWORTH, b. in Lower Canada, about 1815; John d. at Stockbridge, MI, 15 Nov 1893.

v LEVI ABBOTT, b. at Wheelock, 14 May 1819; d. at White Oak, MI, 10 Apr 1907; m. 1st, at Ingham County, 11 Mar 1847, SUSAN LAMBRIGHT, b. 18 Nov 1828; Susan d. at White Oak, 27 Jan 1850. Levi m. 2nd, SALOME BURGESS, b. in NY, 23 Jan 1830 daughter of William Burgess; Salome d. at Dansville, MI, 20 Jun 1917.

vi JULIET ABBOTT, b. about 1827; d. at Shoreham, VT, 14 Apr 1831.

vii MYRON ABBOTT, b. at Shoreham, VT, 21 Jan 1827; d. at White Oak, MI, 24 Feb 1901; m. at Mason, MI, 31 Dec 1854, HANNAH REEVES, b. at Macedon, NY, 1831 daughter of Levi Henry and Elizabeth (Freer) Reeves; Hannah d. at Dansville, MI, 13 May 1876.

1110) CALVIN ABBOTT *(William⁴, Jeremiah³, Nathaniel², George¹)*, b. in New Hampshire, 3 Dec 1788 son of William and Bridget (Spaulding) Abbott; d. at Ogden, NY,[2929] 19 Nov 1858; m. at Danville, VT, 4 Dec 1815, CHARLOTTE CLEMENT, b. at Danville, 12 Sep 1794 daughter of William and Abigail (Hill) Clement; Charlotte d. 12 Dec 1854.

Calvin was of humble beginnings, with his parents being "warned out" of Townsend, Massachusetts when the family had several young children. But Calvin and his children went on to become prosperous and important members of their communities. Calvin was raised in Vermont, but after his marriage relocated to Ogden, New York where he was a farmer. Of Calvin and Charlotte's eight children, only Edwin remained in Ogden, the rest of their children seeking their fortunes to the west including Michigan, Illinois, Nebraska, Iowa, and California.

Calvin Abbott wrote his will 23 Sep 1854 and the estate entered probate 30 December 1858.[2930] In his will, Calvin makes bequests to each of his eight children so that the total legacy received by each is $525. The older children already received $500 in cash and so have additional bequests of $25. The other children receive $525 with the condition that the two youngest children, Silas and Cyrus, will receive their legacies when they become of age. All the rest of the estate, real and personal, is bequeathed to his beloved wife Charlotte, and after her death the estate will be equally divided among the heirs. Son Edwin is named executor.

i HANNAH ADELINE ABBOTT, b. at Ogden, 20 Apr 1817; d. at Paw Paw, MI, 3 Jan 1895; m. 1st, ALVAH GREGORY BRACE, b. at Wilkes-Barre, PA, 11 Feb 1814 son of Chester and Asenath (Strong) Brace; Alvah d. at Grand Rapids, MI, 22 Feb 1867. After Alvah's death, Hannah married Joseph Gilman as his second wife.

ii MARIA HILL ABBOTT, b. at Ogden, 3 Mar 1821; d. at Wyoming, MI, 3 Nov 1858; m. about 1839, PHILIP FRANKLIN COVELL, b. at Cabot, VT, 12 Dec 1811 son of Philip and Lois (Nye) Covell; Philip d. in Kent County, MI, 3 Jul 1895. After Maria's death, Philip married Sarah Thompson.

iii EDWARD D. ABBOTT, b. at Ogden, 2 Aug 1822; d. at Ogden, 7 Jan 1892; m. about 1839, MARY COVELL, b. at Ogden, 6 Jun 1822 daughter of Edward and Mary (Gilman) Covell; Mary d. at Ogden, 13 May 1913.

iv CLEMENT W. ABBOTT, b. at Ogden, 13 Dec 1825; d. at Sheffield, IL, 4 Oct 1910; m. 6 May 1857, MARTHA M. BATTEY, b. at Bristol, RI, 1836 daughter of Silas and Mercy (Bennett) Battey; Martha d. at Sheffield, IL, 22 Nov 1906. Clement was a farmer in Sheffield, Illinois and was prosperous. He served in several civic positions including assessor and the county board of supervisors.[2931]

v FOSTER ABBOTT, b. at Ogden, 30 Aug 1828; d. 15 Apr 1890 likely in Michigan although there is a cemetery marker for him where his brother Cyrus is buried in California; m. before 1856, ELIZABETH ROSE, b. in New York about 1836 daughter of Harvey K. and Lucy (-) Rose; Elizabeth died after 1880 (living at the time of the 1880 Census in Michigan with Foster).

[2928] There is likely an error in the birth transcription for either Levi or Lovina as their births are recorded as being three months apart.

[2929] *1850 United States Federal Census*, Year: 1850; Census Place: Ogden, Monroe, New York; Roll: M432_529; Page: 83B; Image: 173. Calvin Abbott was living in Ogden in 1850.

[2930] Ancestry.com. *New York, Wills and Probate Records, 1659-1999, Wills, Vol 003, 1856-1860, Will of Calvin Abbott*

[2931] Harrington, *Bureau County, Illinois*, p 540

vi CHARLOTTE CLEMENT ABBOTT, b. at Ogden, 6 Apr 1831; d. at Lincoln, NE, 19 Mar 1897; m. 6 Jun 1855, HARVEY WESLEY HARDY, b. at Perry, NY, 29 Oct 1825 son of Samuel and Polly (Parker) Hardy; Harvey d. Jan 1913. Harvey Wesley Hardy was twice elected mayor of Lincoln, Nebraska in 1877 and 1878.[2932] He was also prominent in the temperance movement.

vii CYRUS HARLAN ABBOTT, b. at Ogden, 30 Sep 1835; d. at Alameda, CA, 21 Jun 1923; m. about 1857, MARTHA ALICE GRUNENDYKE, b. in Monroe County, NY, 26 Oct 1835 daughter of Abraham and Margaret (Petty) Grunendyke; Martha d. at Stanislaus, CA, 11 Jun 1905. Cyrus served in the Civil War enlisting in Illinois as a private but ended with a rank of 1st Lieutenant. He filed his Civil War pension application in 1888.[2933] He moved to California in 1872.

viii SILAS D. "S.D." ABBOTT, b. at Ogden, 30 Sep 1835; d. at Shelby, IA, 13 Aug 1909; m. in Spencer County, KY, 8 Oct 1863, INDIANA "ANNA" HENRY, b. in Kentucky, about 1841 daughter of David and Hannah (Brown) Henry; Anna d. after 1900. Silas attended school in Hanover, Indiana and for eight years taught school in Kentucky where he was known as the Yankee schoolmaster. Due to his strong Union sentiments, he moved to Bureau County, Illinois where his brother Clement settled. Later, Silas relocated with his family to Shelby County, Iowa in 1882.[2934]

1111) JEREMIAH ABBOTT *(Jeremiah⁴, Jeremiah³, Nathaniel², George¹)*, b. at Chelmsford, 26 Feb 1772 son of Jeremiah and Susannah (Baldwin) Abbott; d. at Springfield, VT, 2 Oct 1850;[2935] m. 30 May 1801, SALLY FARROR, b. at Chelmsford, 14 Apr 1776 daughter of Nathaniel and Rachel (Fletcher) Farror; Sally d. at Springfield, VT about 1815.[2936]

Jeremiah and Sally settled in Springfield, Vermont and Jeremiah took the freeman's oath there in 1803.[2937]

The estate of Jeremiah Abbott entered probate 21 October 1850. Heirs signing that they received notice related to the estate are Hiram Harlow, Rachel Harlow, Sarah Abbott, Olive Dunshee, Mary Ann Abbott, Emily Abbott, and Jeremiah Abbott. These same heirs signed a statement related to the distribution of the estate acknowledging that Jeremiah, Olive, and Rachel received money from their father when starting out in life and requesting adjustment to the distribution so that all the heirs will benefit equally. The total value of the estate was $1,212.37 including a farm valued at $700.[2938]

Jeremiah and Sally had eight children born at Springfield, Vermont.

i OLIVE ABBOTT, b. at Springfield, VT, 23 Sep 1801; d. after 1850 likely in NH (still living at the 1850 census); m. at Springfield, 20 Mar 1832, as his second wife, JOHN DUNSHEE, b. at Walpole, NH, about 1790 son of Hugh and Cynthia (Allen) Dunshee;[2939] John d. at Walpole, 20 Oct 1848. John was first married to Annette Wires who died in 1830.

ii JAMES ABBOTT, b. 9 Nov 1803; d. 9 Jul 1804.

iii MARY ANN ABBOTT, b. 9 Jul 1805; d. at Springfield, 25 Dec 1864. Mary Ann did not marry.

iv SARAH ABBOTT, b. 31 May 1807; d. at Springfield, 18 Jul 1869; m. in the 1850's, JOHN FARNUM, b. at Milton, NH, 20 Jan 1803 son of John and Mary (Martin) Farnum; John d. at Springfield, 23 Nov 1882. After 1850, Sarah married John Farnum who was widowed. John Farnum had lived with the Abbott family during his adolescent years. John's father died when John was about three years old. He stayed with his mother until age seven, but was then sent to live with Timothy Goodnow, then Hugh Henry, and at age 14 to Jeremiah Abbott.[2940] John Farnum was first married to Mary Parker, and after Sarah Abbott's death, he married Cynthia Brown.

v SUSAN ABBOTT (twin of Sarah), b. 31 May 1807; d. at Springfield, 25 Mar 1826.

2932 Chapman Brothers, *Lancaster County, Nebraska*, p 637

2933 National Archives. Organization Index to Pension Files of Veterans Who Served Between 1861 and 1900. Abbott, Cyrus H. www.fold3.com/image/83019?terms=Cyrus%20Abbott&xid=1
945

2934 State Historical Society of Wisconsin, *Biographical History of Shelby*, p 447

2935 *Vermont, Vital Records, 1720-1908*.

2936 The 1810 U.S. Census for Springfield has a household for Jeremiah Abbott that includes a woman in the right age range; in the 1820 Census that older woman is no longer listed.

2937 Hubbard and Dartt, *History of Springfield*, p 528

2938 Probate Files 1709-1906; Vermont Probate Court (Windsor District), Probate of Jeremiah Abbott

2939 Aldrich, *Walpole As It Was*, p 244

2940 Hubbard and Dartt, *History of the Town of Springfield*, p 291

vi EMILY ABBOTT, b. 25 Apr 1809; d. at Springfield, 9 Nov 1872. Emily did not marry. At the 1870 U.S. Census, Emily was living with her younger sister Rachel and her husband.

vii JEREMIAH ABBOTT, b. 25 Jul 1811; d. at Springfield, 13 Jul 1886; m. 4 Apr 1839, OLIVE METCALF HAYWOOD, b. at Gilsum, NH, 1819 daughter of Amherst and Betsey (Cole) Haywood;[2941] Olive d. at Springfield, 11 Nov 1908.

viii RACHEL S. ABBOTT, b. 23 Aug 1813; d. at Windsor, VT, 2 Jan 1893; m. 23 Mar 1836, HIRAM HARLOW, b. at Springfield, about 1811 son of William and Margaret (Campbell) Harlow; Hiram d. at Windsor, 26 Jul 1886.

1112) HANNAH ABBOTT *(Jeremiah⁴, Jeremiah³, Nathaniel², George¹)*, b. at Chelmsford, 30 Jan 1774 daughter of Jeremiah and Susannah (Baldwin) Abbott; d. perhaps at Vincennes, IN;[2942] m. her third cousin once removed, DAVID CHANDLER *(David Chandler⁶, Mary Ballard Chandler⁵, Hannah Chandler Ballard⁴, John Chandler³, Hannah Abbott Chandler², George¹)*, b. at Milford, 28 Jun 1775 son of David and Hannah (Peabody) Chandler.[2943]

There is little information on this family. The Chandler genealogy reports three children and further information could be located for just one of these children.

i ABIGAIL CHANDLER, b. about 1800

ii HANNAH CHANDLER, b. about 1805

iii IRA PEABODY CHANDLER, b. about 1810; d. at Van Buren County, IA, 1853 (probate 6 Apr 1853); m. Hannah who has not been identified.

1113) REBEKAH ABBOTT *(Jeremiah⁴, Jeremiah³, Nathaniel², George¹)*, b. at Chelmsford, 26 Aug 1778 daughter of Jeremiah and Susannah (Baldwin) Abbott; d. at Milford, 25 Mar 1864; m. about 1804, ZADOK JONES, b. 5 Jul 1773 son of Caleb and Deborah (Hopkins) Jones. Zadok had first married Rebekah's older sister Susannah who died 1 Nov 1803; there were no children from Zadok's first marriage. Zadok d. at Milford, 31 Jul 1823.

Zadok Jones did not leave a will. His estate entered probate 21 August 1823 with David Stiles as administrator at the request of the widow. Real property was valued at $3,750.00 and personal estate was $807.10. The claims against the estate required some of the estate to be sold with a balance after the sale of the estate and settlement of debts of $2,931.75.[2944]

Rebekah Abbott and Zadok Jones were parents of nine children born at Milford.

i STEPHEN JONES, b. 26 Sep 1804.

ii SUSANNA JONES, b. 16 Jun 1806; d. at New Boston, NH, 17 Sep 1872; m. 24 May 1827, PETER HOPKINS, b. at Milford, 22 Sep 1791 son of Peter and Hannah (Burnham) Hopkins; Peter d. at New Boston, 27 Sep 1874.

iii ZADOK JONES, b. 24 May 1808; d. after 1870 likely at Milford; m. ELEANOR SANBORN, b. at Dorchester, NH, about 1812 daughter of Jacob and Elenora (-) Sanborn; Eleanor d. before 1860.

iv DAVIS JONES, b. 27 May 1810; d. at Cohoes, NY, after 1865; m. LYDIA A., b. about 1812 who has not been identified; Lydia d. at Cohoes, 16 Jul 1891.

v HANNAH JONES, b. 30 Dec 1812; d. at Wilton, 13 Dec 1887. Hannah did not marry.

vi FANNY JONES, b. about 1814; d. at Saratoga Springs, NY, 27 Oct 1896; m. at Lowell, 20 Nov 1836, EDWARD FLANDERS SANBORN, b. at Dorchester, NH, about 1808 son of Jacob and Elenora (-) Sanborn; Edward d. at Lowell, 5 Nov 1853.

vii CALEB JONES, b. 26 Nov 1816; d. at Milford, 6 May 1868.

viii WILLIAM JONES, b. 13 Jan 1819; d. at Milford, 26 Oct 1896; m. 1st, HARRIET HOPKINS, b. at Milford, 30 Jul 1826 daughter of Holland and Eliza (Hutchinson) Hopkins; Harriet d. at Milford, 1854. William m. 2nd, LAURA THURSTON, b. 1841; Laura d. at Milford, 1913.

ix SARAH "SALLY" JONES, b. 17 Dec 1821; d. at Lowell, 2 Jul 1877; m. at Lowell, 30 Oct 1851, WILLIAM M. JONES, b. at Durham, ME, about 1823 son of Samuel and Sarah (-) Jones.

[2941] Vermont, Vital Records, 1720-1908. The names of Olive's parents are on her death record.

[2942] Both the Abbot and the Chandler genealogy books list this family as going to Vincennes.

[2943] Chandler, *Descendants of William and Annis Chandler*, p 763

[2944] New Hampshire, County Probate Records, 1660-1973, Hillsborough, Case 05441; 30:285, 32:381, 27:110, 18:604, 32:532, 20:323, 20:390, 35:355

1114) JONAS ABBOTT *(Jeremiah⁴, Jeremiah³, Nathaniel², George¹)*, b. at Chelmsford, 29 Apr 1781 son of Jeremiah and Susannah (Baldwin) Abbott; d. 11 Sep 1839 at Lyndeborough; m. 18 Jan 1807, BETSEY PARKER, b. at New Ipswich, NH, 17 Mar 1783 daughter of Joseph and Susannah (Fletcher) Parker; Betsey d. 13 Dec 1857.

Jonas and Betsey started their family in Chelmsford, but after the birth of their first child, they relocated to Lyndeborough along with Jonas's brother William and their father Jeremiah.[2945]

Jonas and Betsey were parents of eleven children, the oldest born at Chelmsford and the remainder at Lyndeborough.

i ELIZA ABBOTT, b. 12 May 1808; d. at Francestown, NH, 22 Jun 1890; m. 14 Mar 1832, as his second wife, WILLIAM TERREN, b. at Boston, 10 Nov 1801 son of William Terren; William d. at Francestown, 6 May 1883. William was first married to Sarah Sleeper.

ii JONAS PARKER ABBOTT, b. 27 Aug 1809; d. at Hill, NH, 5 Aug 1868; m. at Lowell, 9 Apr 1837, ARALETTA "ANN" CASS, b. at Corinth, VT, 1812 daughter of Jacob and Betsey (Bean) Cass;[2946] Ann d. at Hill, 31 Mar 1866. After Ann's death, Jonas married her sister MARY G. CASS, b. 1808 likely in Lower Canada; Mary d. at Morgan County, TN, 16 Feb 1899 at the home of one of her daughters. Mary had been married three times previously.

iii MARY A. ABBOTT, b. 30 Mar 1811; d. at Littleton, MA, 1 Jan 1897; m. 19 Jun 1841, ITHAMAR WRIGHT, b. at Littleton, 1805 son of Isaac and Rhoda (Woster) Wright; Ithamar d. at Littleton, 15 May 1848.

iv RACHEL P. ABBOTT, b. 11 Dec 1812; d. at Lyndeborough, 27 Oct 1872; m. 1st, at Lowell, 1 Jun 1834, MOSES BUSWELL; Moses d. before 1848. Rachel m. 2nd, at Lyndeborough, 30 Nov 1848, MANLEY KIDDER, b. at Lyndeborough, 24 Jul 1810 son of Phineas and Ann (Manley) Kidder; Manley d. at Lyndeborough, 10 Jun 1877.

v JEREMIAH ABBOTT, b. 3 Apr 1815; d. 30 Oct 1820.

vi HANNAH W. ABBOTT, b. 2 Sep 1817; d. at Lowell, 31 May 1891; m. at Lowell, 24 Nov 1858, SEWELL N. WATSON, b. at Fayette, ME, 8 Aug 1808 son of Henry and Dolly (Batchelder) Watson; Sewell d. at Fayette, 26 Aug 1886.

vii PRUDENCE ABBOTT, b. 2 Sep 1819; d. at Lyndeborough, 20 Feb 1909; m. 23 May 1842, her fourth cousin once removed, MORRIS FRYE *(Alfred Frye⁶, Elizabeth Holt Frye⁵, Timothy Holt⁴, Dorcas Abbott Holt³, Timothy², George¹)*, b. in VT, 21 May 1818 son of Alfred and Lucy (Farrington) Frye; Morris d. at Lyndeborough, 4 Apr 1900.

viii HEZEKIAH ABBOTT, b. 26 Apr 1822; d. at Tewksbury, 11 Jan 1890; m. 1 Jun 1858, as her second husband, ANNETTE RACHEL COLBURN, b. 1 Aug 1833 daughter of Jacob Taylor and Rachel (Colburn) Colburn. Annette was first married to Leonard Robbins and third married to Edward P. Crosby.

ix WILLIAM ABBOTT, b. 30 Jun 1825; d. at Lyndeborough, 30 Jul 1858 of consumption. William did not marry. He was a carpenter.

x EMILY ABBOTT, b. 21 Nov 1827; d. at Lyndeborough, 19 Dec 1914; m. at Lyndeborough, 8 Dec 1858, CHARLES L. AVERY, b. at Lyndeborough, 12 Apr 1836 son of Solomon and Lavina (Morse) Avery; Charles d. at Lyndeborough, 22 Dec 1914.

xi SUSAN ABBOTT, b. 5 May 1829; d. 18 Aug 1830.

1115) WILLIAM ABBOTT *(Jeremiah⁴, Jeremiah³, Nathaniel², George¹)*, b. at Chelmsford, 3 Nov 1787 son of Jeremiah and Susannah (Baldwin) Abbott; d. at Lyndeborough, 14 Jan 1824; m. EUNICE CRAM, b. at Lyndeborough, 31 Aug 1785 daughter of Uriah and Eunice (Ellingwood) Cram. Eunice m. 2nd, 25 Jul 1836, William Strafford. Eunice d. at Lyndeborough, 29 Feb 1868.

William settled in Lyndeborough with his brother Jonas and their father Jeremiah. William Abbott and Eunice Cram had six children born at Lyndeborough.

i LYDIA C. ABBOTT, b. 5 Jun 1809; d. at Hancock, 15 Sep 1895; m. 27 Dec 1827, DAVID CARKIN, b. at Lyndeborough, 1 Jan 1806 son of Aaron and Betsey (Duncklee) Carkin; David d. at Hancock, 6 Jul 1892.

ii WILLIAM B. ABBOTT, b. 28 Jun 1811; d. at Lyndeborough, Dec 1862; m. at Greenfield, 4 Dec 1854, as her second husband, NANCY BROWN, b. at Amherst, about 1797 daughter of William H. and Annie (-) Brown; Nancy d. at Lyndeborough, 26 Sep 1875. Nancy was first married to Abram Boutwell.

[2945] Donovan, *History of Town of Lyndeborough*, p 651

[2946] Musgrove, *History of the Town of Bristol*, p 88

iii ABIGAIL C. ABBOTT, b. 26 Jan 1814; d. at Lyndeborough, 9 Oct 1893; m. 1st, 13 May 1833, JAMES MARSHALL; James d. 13 May 1840. Abigail m. 2nd, 6 May 1846, ISRAEL PUTNAM, b. at Lyndeborough, 30 Oct 1794 son of Daniel and Hannah (Johnson) Putnam; Israel d. at Lyndeborough, 2 Feb 1869. Israel was first married to Ruth Sargent.

iv CHARLES D. ABBOTT, b. 31 Mar 1817; d. at Lyndeborough, 28 Mar 1854. Charles did not marry.

v HENRY N. ABBOTT, b. 16 Feb 1820; d. at Lyndeborough, 14 May 1859. Henry did not marry.

vi CALVIN ABBOTT, b. 5 May 1824; d. at Lyndeborough, 23 Oct 1868; m. about 1854, MARY JANE BOUTWELL, b. at Lyndeborough, 1833 daughter of Abram and Nancy (Brown) Boutwell; Mary Jane d. at Hancock, 30 May 1901. Mary Jane is a step-niece of Calvin as her mother was the wife of Calvin's brother William (see above).

1116) SALLY ABBOTT *(Jeremiah4, Jeremiah3, Nathaniel2, George1)*, b. at Chelmsford, Mar 1792 daughter of Jeremiah and Susannah (Baldwin) Abbott; d. at Lyndeborough, 31 May 1857; m. 27 Dec 1817, JOSEPH CHAMBERLAIN, b. at Lyndeborough, 12 Dec 1789 son of Samuel and Naomi (Richardson) Chamberlain; Joseph d. 30 Aug 1862.

Joseph Chamberlain served as a private in the 3rd Regiment of New Hampshire Militia during the War of 1812. Joseph Chamberlain was a brick maker. After their marriage, Joseph and Sally were in Milford for several years but returned to Lyndeborough about 1825.[2947] They were the parents of seven children.

i RUFUS CHAMBERLAIN, b. at Milford, 5 Jun 1819; d. at Lyndeborough, 22 Nov 1907; m. 20 May 1843, MARTHA JANE UPTON, b. at Lyndeborough, 21 Jan 1821 daughter of Elijah and Alice (Putnam) Upton; Martha d. 24 May 1892.

ii JOSEPH CHAMBERLAIN, b. at Milford, 22 Feb 1821; d. at Paxton, MA, 18 Sep 1886; m. 31 Oct 1844, MARY A. DREW, b. 3 Apr 1824 daughter of Edwin and Elizabeth (-) Drew; Mary d. at Cambridgeport, MA, 6 Dec 1886.

iii SALLY CHAMBERLAIN, b. at Milford, 11 Mar 1823; d. at Nashua, NH, 10 Apr 1907; m. 15 Jul 1847, her third cousin, CHARLES BLANCHARD *(Isaac Blanchard5, Daniel Blanchard4, Sarah Abbott Blanchard3, Nathaniel2, George1)*, b. 20 Oct 1812 son of Isaac and Olive (Hopkins) Blanchard; Charles d. at Nashua, 29 May 1880. Charles is a child in Family 1049.

iv OTIS CHAMBERLAIN, b. at Lyndeborough, 8 Jan 1826; d. at Orange, NH, 24 Apr 1904; m. 1st, May 1849, CLARISSA S. HOLT, b. about 1830; Clarissa d. at Lyndeborough, 10 Jun 1852. Otis m. 2nd, 24 Nov 1852, MARTHA K. WHEELER, b. at Lyndeborough, 23 Nov 1834 daughter of Jonas and Mary (Hall) Wheeler; Martha d. at Boston, 9 Mar 1924.

v OLIVE CHAMBERLAIN, b. at Lyndeborough, 20 Jan 1828; d. at Lyndeborough, 9 Oct 1898; m. 24 Sep 1847, EDWIN N. PATCH, b. at Hollis, 15 Jul 1824 son of Thomas and Lucinda (Nutting) Patch; Edwin d. at Lyndeborough, 9 Jun 1892.

vi SUSAN CHAMBERLAIN, b. 29 Oct 1830; d. 17 Aug 1832.

vii HARVEY CHAMBERLAIN, b. at Lyndeborough, 2 Mar 1833; d. at Riviere du Loup, Québec, 9 Sep 1867; m. at Warren, NH, 21 Sep 1862, SARAH JANE LIBBEY, b. at Warren, 4 Feb 1842 daughter of Ezra Bartlett and Mary Gibbin (Haman) Libbey;[2948] Sarah d. after 1910 (living in Lynn at the 1910 census).

1117) MOSES BAILEY *(Elizabeth Moar Bailey4, Elizabeth Abbott Moar3, Nathaniel2, George1)*, b. at Andover 20 Oct 1766 son of Moses and Elizabeth (Moar) Bailey; d. 3 Jun 1846; m. 13 Sep 1787, MEHITABLE CHASE, b. at Andover, 12 Dec 1768 daughter of Emery and Mehitable (Moar) Chase; Mehitable d. 9 Oct 1849.

Moses and Mehitable had their first three children in Andover, but then relocated to Dracut where their youngest children were born.

Moses Bailey wrote his will 27 June 1840. In his will, he left all his personal estate to his wife Mehitable except bequests of one dollar to each of the following heirs: daughter Fanny Wells, Mehitable Richardson, Elizabeth Richardson, the heirs of John Bailey, Moses Bailey, Jr., and James Richardson, Jr. Benjamin Stevens was named executor. The heirs signing 4 November 1846 that they were satisfied with the disposition of the estate were the following: Elizabeth M. Richardson, Moses Bailey, James Richardson, Jr., Hephzibah Bailey, Zachariah Wells, and Fanny Wells.[2949] James Richardson, Jr. was the husband of daughter Hannah Bailey Hannah Bailey Richardson died in 1827 four months after her marriage to James Richardson. Hephzibah Bailey was the widow of son John Bailey.

Moses and Mehitable had six children.

2947 Donovan, *History of Lyndeborough*, p 693

2948 Libby, *The Libby Family in America*, p 456

2949 *Middlesex County, MA: Probate File Papers, 1648-1871. Probate of Moses Bailey, 1846, Case number 26704*

i FANNY BAILEY, b. at Andover, 19 Nov 1797; d. at Princeton, MA, 1 Oct 1856; m. at Dracut 1809, ZACHARIAH WELLS, b. at Methuen about 1782 son of Daniel and Susan (-) Wells;[2950] Zachariah d. at Dracut, 30 Sep 1857.

ii JOHN BAILEY, b. 19 Jun 1790; d. at Dracut, 8 Jul 1835; m. at Dracut, 7 Mar 1823, his first cousin, HEPHZIBAH BAILEY *(Joshua Bailey⁵, Elizabeth Moar Bailey⁴, Elizabeth Abbott Moar³, Nathaniel², George¹)*, b. at Andover, 2 Oct 1795 daughter of Joshua and Hephzibah (Abbott) Bailey; Hephzibah d. at Dracut, 23 Oct 1866.

iii MOSES BAILEY, b. at Andover, 13 Jan 1793; d. recorded at Rowley, 23 Dec 1870; m. 1st, 18 Oct 1822, FANNY CARLETON, b. about 1800 daughter of Asa and Elsy (Burns) Carleton;[2951] Fanny d. at Pelham, NH, 13 Aug 1838. Moses m. 2nd, date unknown, RHODA AUSTIN, b. at Dracut, 29 Aug 1793 daughter of William and Hannah (-) Austin.[2952] Rhoda's death record not located but death was before 1860 when Moses was living in his son's home in Salem. Moses lived in Pelham, NH with his first wife. Just one child has been located for Moses and Fanny.

iv MEHITABLE BAILEY, b. at Dracut, 25 Jul 1795; d. at Dracut, 18 Jul 1840; m. at Dracut, 26 Nov 1812, JOHN CUMMINGS RICHARDSON, b. at Methuen, 1785 son of Samuel and Lucy (Parker) Richardson; John d. at Methuen, 2 Nov 1823.

v ELIZABETH MOAR BAILEY, b. at Dracut, 17 Jul 1798; d. at Dracut, 18 Jun 1867; m. 1st, 1 Dec 1814, DANIEL MANSUR, b. at Dracut, 19 Mar 1791 son of James and Mary (Harris) Mansur; Daniel d. 26 Jul 1829. Elizabeth m. 2nd, 21 Sep 1831, SAMUEL RICHARDSON, b. 5 Oct 1808 son of Samuel and Abigail (Mansur) Richardson; Samuel d. at Dracut, 12 Feb 1833. Daniel Mansur was the uncle of Elizabeth's second husband Samuel Richardson.

vi HANNAH BAILEY, b. at Dracut, 16 Sep 1804; d. at Dracut, 27 Jul 1827; m. 28 Mar 1827, JAMES RICHARDSON, JR., b. at Dracut, 16 Apr 1803 son of James and Polly (Taylor) Richardson; James d. at Dracut, 31 Jul 1879. After Hannah's death, James married Lucy Jane Richardson.

1118) ELIZABETH BAILEY *(Elizabeth Moar Bailey⁴, Elizabeth Abbott Moar³, Nathaniel², George¹)*, b. at Andover, 6 Jul 1768 daughter of Moses and Elizabeth (Moar) Bailey; d. at Minot, ME, 1830; m. 25 Aug 1789, SAMUEL DOWNING, b. at Andover, 30 Jan 1765 son of Samuel and Abigail (Barnard) Downing; Samuel d. at Minot, 24 Jan 1836.

Samuel Downing served in the Revolutionary War serving from Massachusetts in Jackson's Regiment. His Revolutionary War pension application from 1820 includes a statement that he owns no real estate, lists a small amount of livestock, and reports $240 in debts. At the time of the application, there were five minor children at home: Amos age 20 able to support himself; Timothy age 17 who is feeble; Clarissa age 14 described as very unwell; Sumner age 12 who was weakly since infancy; and Alvina (sic) age 9 who is partially able to earn her support. Wife Elizabeth is age 52 and described as a "weakly woman."[2953]

Samuel and Elizabeth had ten children, the births of the oldest five children recorded at Poland, Maine[2954] and the youngest five at Minot, Maine.

i ELIZABETH DOWNING, b. 3 Dec 1789; d. at Minot, 23 Oct 1871; m. at Minot, 9 Oct 1814, EBENEZER HODGKINS, b. at Poland, ME, 20 Aug 1787 son of Ebenezer and Elizabeth (-) Hodgkins; Ebenezer d. at Minot, 13 Jan 1834.

ii SAMUEL DOWNING, b. 20 May 1792; d. at Auburn, ME, 7 Sep 1856; m. 3 Jun 1821, his first cousin, PHEBE LANE, b. at Gloucester, ME, 21 Jan 1802 daughter of Benjamin F. and Hannah (Downing) Lane; Phebe d. at Auburn, 17 Jun 1873.

iii MOSES DOWNING, b. 24 Apr 1794; nothing further known.

iv NATHAN DOWNING, b. 20 Oct 1796; d. at Minot, 7 Apr 1884; m. about 1830, WATY VERRILL, b. at Auburn, 2 Feb 1804; Waty d. at Minot, 11 Oct 1887.

2950 A birth record was not located for Zachariah; the names of his parents are given as Daniel and Susan Wells on his death record.

2951 A birth record was not located; Fanny's gravestone includes an inscription that she is wife of Moses Baily and daughter of Asa and Alcy. findagrave.com

2952 The 1846 probate record of William Austin has a listing of heirs that includes Rhoda Bailey wife of Moses Bailey.

2953 White, "Maine Estate Schedules from Revolutionary War Pensions"

2954 Early Vital Records of Poland, Maine, Vital Records from the NEHGS Register, https://www.americanancestors.org/DB522/r/264640924

v RICHARD DOWNING, b. 20 Feb 1798; d. at Minot, 7 Apr 1833; m. at Minot, 21 Jan 1832, his first cousin, SALLY DAVIS LANE, b. at Minot, 30 May 1811 daughter of Benjamin F. and Hannah (Downing) Lane; Sally d. in IL, after 1870. Sally married second David B. Johnson and third John H. Meserve.

vi AMOS DOWNING, b. 24 Jul 1800; d. at Norway, ME, about 1884 (probate 15 Aug 1884); m. 1st, 23 Sep 1828, LURA WING, "of Winthrop", b. 1805; Lura d. at Winthrop, ME, 16 Feb 1837. Amos m. 2nd, 14 Jun 1838, LUCY M. ORCUTT, b. about 1808; Lucy d. at Bangor, 4 Dec 1896.

vii TIMOTHY DOWNING, b. 15 Dec 1802; d. at Chesterville, ME, 10 Jul 1871; m. about 1832, HANNAH WHITEHOUSE, b. about 1811; d. at Minot, 3 May 1856.

viii CLARISSA DOWNING, b. 31 Mar 1805; d. at Auburn, after 1870; m. by 1830, EBENEZER ROWE; Ebenezer d. at Minot, before 1850.

ix SUMNER B. DOWNING, b. 11 Feb 1808; d. at Wayne, ME, 27 Apr 1875; m. 1st, ABIGAIL BROWNELL MACOMBER, b. 8 Mar 1818 daughter of John and Abigail (Miller) Macomber;[2955] Abigail d. at Wayne, ME, 7 Apr 1853. Sumner m. 2nd, 30 May 1854, ABBIE B. ROWELL, b. 1819 daughter of Abijah and Sophia (Warren) Rowell; Abbie d. at Livermore, ME, 16 Jan 1893.

x ELMIRA AMES DOWNING, b. 18 Sep 1810; d. at Minot, 10 Apr 1892. Elmira did not marry. She worked as a dressmaker. Elmira wrote her will 10 Dec 1886. She gave detailed instructions for her burial and the gravestone which should read "Elmira Ames youngest child of Major Samuel Downing formally of Minot." She leaves the house she lives in including the land to Samuel D. Hodgkins; and he can have the tools (including the snow shovel) and rocking chair. Other belongings are left to Richard and Lizzy. She wants Lizzy and Abby to have her quilts. Samuel D. Hodkins is named executor.[2956] Samuel D. Hodgkins was her nephew, son of her sister Elizabeth.

1119) JOSHUA BAILEY *(Elizabeth Moar Bailey[4], Elizabeth Abbott Moar[3], Nathaniel[2], George[1])*, b. at Andover, 14 Aug 1770 son of Moses and Elizabeth (Moar) Bailey; d. at Andover, 30 Oct 1820; m. 19 Feb 1795, his third cousin once removed, HEPHZIBAH ABBOTT *(Hephzibah Ames Abbott[5], Benjamin Ames[4], Hannah Stevens Ames[3], Elizabeth Abbott Stevens[2], George[1])*, b. 17 Aug 1772 daughter of Bixby and Hephzibah (Ames) Abbott; Hephzibah d. 7 Aug 1813.

Joshua Bailey did not leave a will and his estate entered probate 2 January 1821.[2957] Joshua Bailey was administrator. The value of real estate was $3,800 including a "mansion house" and 85 acres of land including pasture, tillage, mowing, and wood land. The personal estate was valued at $2,993.46. Claims against the estate totaled $1,799.31. Signing that they have examined the accounting for the estate and are satisfied that it was just and true are Hephzibah Bailey and Joshua Bailey. Heirs signing agreement to the final settlement in 1826 are Joshua Bailey, Hephzibah Bailey, and Samuel McCoy. Samuel McCoy was the husband of daughter Elizabeth Bailey.

Joshua and Hephzibah had three children whose births are recorded at Andover. Daughter Hephzibah married a cousin and relocated to Dracut. Joshua and Elizabeth both married spouses from Peterborough, New Hampshire and relocated there about 1822.

i HEPHZIBAH BAILEY, b. 2 Oct 1795; d. at Dracut, 23 Oct 1866; m. at Dracut, 7 Mar 1823, her first cousin, JOHN BAILEY, b. at Dracut, 19 Jun 1790 son of Moses and Mehitable (Chase) Bailey; John d. at Dracut, 6 Jul 1835. This is the same as Family #1117, child ii.

ii JOSHUA BAILEY, b. 7 May 1798; d. at Peterborough, NH, 18 Feb 1873; m. 6 Feb 1824, MARY SPRING, b. at Peterborough, 21 Dec 1799 son of Silas and Margaret (Stuart) Spring;[2958] Mary d. 4 Apr 1862.

iii ELIZABETH BAILEY, b. 4 Jul 1802; d. at Peterborough, NH, 4 Aug 1883; m. 25 Nov 1822, SAMUEL MCCOY, b. at Peterborough, 11 Sep 1797 son of Charles and Jane (Templeton) McCoy; Samuel d. 4 Sep 1871.

1120) SARAH BAILEY *(Elizabeth Moar Bailey[4], Elizabeth Abbott Moar[3], Nathaniel[2], George[1])*, b. at Andover, 1 Nov 1772 daughter of Moses and Elizabeth (Moar) Bailey; d. 22 Mar 1857; m. 30 Mar 1790, her third cousin once removed, SIMEON AMES *(Benjamin Ames[4], Hannah Stevens Ames[3], Elizabeth Abbott Stevens[2], George[1])*, b. 29 Mar 1772 son of Benjamin and Dorcas (Lovejoy) Ames; Simeon d. 29 Sep 1849.

[2955] Stackpole, *Macomber Genealogy*, p 147

[2956] Maine Wills and Probate Records, 1584-1999, online database at ancestry.com, case number 3183.

[2957] *Essex County, MA: Probate File Papers, 1638-1881. Probate of Joshua Bailey, 2 Jan 1821, Case number 1361.*

[2958] History of the Town of Peterborough, p 290

Simeon Ames was a farmer in Andover. His father was Captain Benjamin Ames who led one of the companies responding from Andover at the Lexington alarm. Simeon's mother Dorcas lived with the family until her death in 1843 at the age of 93.[2959]

Simeon Ames wrote his will 10 November 1842. He made a bequest of one dollar to each of his grandchildren who are the children of his son Simeon who is deceased: Mehitable Ames, Moses Bailey Ames, Gayton Osgood Ames, Mary Poor Ames, and Benjamin Ames. Daughter Hannah Ames received $100. The entire remainder of the estate was left to wife Sarah Ames to have and to hold to her, her heirs, and assigns forever. Solomon Holt of Andover is named executor. Those signing their consent to the accounting of the estate were Sarah Ames, Francis Smiley, Sarah Smiley, John Tuck, Elizabeth A. Tuck, Hannah Ames, Dorcas P. Ames, William Bailey, Jr., Rhoda Bailey, Eben Woodbury, Mehitable Woodbury, Moses B. Ames, Gayton O. Ames, Carlton Payson, Mary P. Payson, and Benjamin Ames.[2960] The personal estate was valued at $234.50. The real property was valued at $1215.00 including a 50-acre home farm, a small wood lot, and one undivided half of a pew at the West Parish meeting house.

In her will written 11 March 1850, Sarah Ames bequeaths to her daughter Hannah Ames fifty dollars and the use of the northeast bed chamber for the remainder of her life. The remainder of the estate is to be divided equally among her four daughters: Sarah Smiley of Peterborough, NH, Elizabeth Abbot Tuck of Andover, Hannah Ames, and Rhoda Bailey of Andover. Deacon Solomon Holt is named executor. On the same date of 11 March 1850, Sarah added a codicil to the will increasing the payment to Hannah to one hundred dollars plus an additional payment of fifty dollars. Hannah would also have the use of the whole dwelling house rather than two rooms.[2961]

Sarah Bailey and Simeon Ames had five children whose births are recorded at Andover.

i SARAH AMES, b. 14 Aug 1790; d. at Peterborough, NH, 24 Sep 1877; m. 4 Feb 1810, FRANCIS SMILEY, b. at Peterborough, 9 Sep 1787 son of David and Rachel (Johnson Smiley); Francis d. at Peterborough, 19 Feb 1867.

ii ELIZABETH ABBOT AMES, b. 3 Jan 1794; d. at Andover, 8 Aug 1870; m. 13 Oct 1811, JOHN TUCK, b. at Beverly, 13 Nov 1793 son of Samuel and Hannah (Marston) Tuck; John d. at Chelmsford, 16 Feb 1875.

iii HANNAH AMES, b. 4 Nov 1796; d. at Andover, 29 Apr 1858. Hannah did not marry and lived in the family home. She died about one year after her mother. Hannah Ames did not leave a will. On 24 May 1858, the following heirs-at-law signed a request that Solomon Holt be named administrator: Sarah Smiley, John Tuck, Elizabeth A. Tuck, William Bailey, Rhoda Bailey, Moses B. Ames, Gayton O. Ames, Mehitable A. Woodbury, Benjamin Ames, and Mary P. Payson. The total value of the estate was $509.23 and after payment of funeral expenses, each of the following heirs received $76.72: sister Sarah Smiley, sister, Betsey Tuck, sister Rhoda Bailey, and legal representatives of Simeon Ames deceased brother.[2962]

iv SIMEON AMES, b. 23 Dec 1799; d. at Andover, 22 Jun 1831; m. 20 Nov 1823, DORCAS POOR, b. at Andover, 13 Oct 1802 daughter of Theodore and Sally (Downing) Poor; Dorcas d. at Andover, 24 Jul 1883.

v RHODA AMES, b. 6 Nov 1814; d. at Andover, 29 Mar 1872; m. 13 Nov 1832, WILLIAM BAILEY, b. at Andover, 20 Sep 1808 son of William and Rebecca (Gillson) Bailey; William d. at Andover, 27 Oct 1889.

1121) NATHAN BAILEY *(Elizabeth Moar Bailey[4], Elizabeth Abbott Moar[3], Nathaniel[2], George[1])*, b. at Andover, 4 Feb 1777 son of Moses and Elizabeth (Moar) Bailey; d. 16 Jan 1862;[2963] m. 1st, 23 Dec 1802, his third cousin once removed, BETSY ABBOTT *(Hephzibah Ames Abbott[5], Benjamin Ames[4], Hannah Stevens Ames[3], Elizabeth Abbott Stevens[2], George[1])*, b. 18 Sep 1780 daughter of Bixby and Hephzibah (Ames) Abbott; Betsy d. 24 Oct 1817. Nathan m. 2nd, 4 May 1819, his third cousin once removed, CHLOE POOR *(Chloe Lovejoy Poor[5], Lydea Abbott Lovejoy[4], Henry[3], George[2], George[1])*, b. 14 May 1779 daughter of John and Chloe (Lovejoy) Poor; Chloe d. 8 Jun 1867.

[2959] In 1840, Simeon Ames of Andover was listed as the head of household where a Revolutionary War pensioner was living which would be his mother Dorcas Ames. L. M. Cromwell, A Census of Pensioners for Revolutionary or Military Service, 1841, p 41.

[2960] *Massachusetts, Essex County, Probate Records;* Author: *Massachusetts. Supreme Judicial Court (Essex County);* Probate Place: *Essex, Massachusetts, Probate Records, Ambler, S-Amory, C, 1828-1991*, case number 31284, Simeon Ames yeoman of Andover.

[2961] Essex County, MA: Probate File Papers, 1638-1881.Online database. AmericanAncestors.org. New England Historic Genealogical Society, 2014. (From records supplied by the Massachusetts Supreme Judicial Court Archives.) Case 31283, Sarah Ames of Andover.

[2962] *Massachusetts, Essex County, Probate Records;* Author: *Massachusetts. Supreme Judicial Court (Essex County);* Probate Place: *Essex, Massachusetts, Probate Records, Ambler, S-Amory, C, 1828-1991*, case 31271, Hannah Ames, single woman of Andover.

[2963] Massachusetts: Vital Records, 1841-1910. (From original records held by the Massachusetts Archives. Online database: AmericanAncestors.org, New England Historic Genealogical Society, 2004.) The death record gives his age as 84 and parents as Moses Bailey and Elizabeth. He is listed as married at the time of his death.

Nathan Bailey inherited from his father Moses Bailey a farm property which is now the historic property at 72 Brundrett Avenue in Andover.[2964] This property stayed in the family until the death of Nathan's grandson Moses Bailey Abbott in 1891. Moses's widow Susan sold the property to the Brundrett family.

This family has the distinction of having nearly every person as a descendant of George Abbott and Hannah Chandler. Nathan Bailey and his wives Betsy Abbott and Cloe Poor were all descendants as well as Pamelia Frye the wife of son Nathan Bailey. The husband of daughter Mary Palmer Bailey, William Abbott, is not a descendant as he comes from the Rowley Abbott line.

Nathan Bailey and Betsy Abbott had three children born at Andover.

i ELIZABETH BAILEY, b. 1 Mar 1805; d. 4 Oct 1817. Elizabeth died three weeks before her mother.

ii MARY PALMER BAILEY, b. 24 Jun 1810; d. at Andover, 7 Sep 1876; m. 30 Dec 1832, WILLIAM ABBOTT, b. at Andover, 27 May 1805 son of Jeduthan and Betsey (Bridges) Abbott; William d. at Andover, 10 Apr 1869.

iii NATHAN BAILEY, b. 28 Apr 1816; d. at Andover, 8 Jan 1854; m. 6 Apr 1839, his fourth cousin once removed, PAMELIA FRYE *(Joseph Frye[6], Mehitable Robinson Frye[5], Joseph Robinson[4], Elizabeth Stevens Robinson[3], Sarah Abbott Stevens[2], George[1])*, b. at Andover, 10 Jul 1820 daughter of Joseph and Mary (Emerson) Frye; Pamelia d. 22 Jun 1861.

Nathan Bailey and Chloe Poor had one daughter.

i ELIZA BAILEY, b. 23 May 1820; d. at Andover, 21 Oct 1883. Eliza did not marry.

1122) HANNAH BAILEY *(Elizabeth Moar Bailey[4], Elizabeth Abbott Moar[3], Nathaniel[2], George[1])*, b. at Andover, 3 May 1779 daughter of Moses and Elizabeth (Moar) Bailey; d. at Concord, NH, 27 Dec 1867; m. 14 Nov 1799, her third cousin once removed, WILLIAM ABBOTT *(Hephzibah Ames Abbott[5], Benjamin Ames[4], Hannah Stevens Ames[3], Elizabeth Abbott Stevens[2], George[1])*, b. 14 Jul 1774 son of Bixby and Hephzibah (Ames) Abbott; William d. at Greenfield, 13 Aug 1852.

Hannah Bailey and William Abbott started their family in Andover where their oldest son was born. The family relocated to Greenfield, New Hampshire about 1801 and settled at the base of Peterborough Mountain. There were thirteen children born in this family, but just seven children lived to adulthood.[2965] No records were located for five of the children who died young. This family group is also one that takes us into the 20th century with one daughter living until 1915.

i WILLIAM ABBOTT, b. at Andover, 5 Jan 1801; d. at Greenfield, 6 Jun 1813.

ii HUGH ADAMS ABBOTT, b. at Greenfield, 3 Nov 1802; d. at Greenfield, 1 May 1883; m. 1st, at Mount Vernon, 29 Jun 1830, MINERVA CRAGIN, b. at Greenfield, 13 May 1807 daughter of Paul and Polly (Whittemore) Cragin;[2966] Minerva d. 15 Oct 1856. Hugh m. 2nd, about 1857, SARAH STILES, b. at Temple, NH, about 1810 daughter of Ebenezer and Sarah (Putnam) Stiles; Sarah d. at Milford, 21 Jan 1886.

iii HERMAN ABBOTT, b. 23 Nov 1804; d. at Greenfield, 7 Dec 1891; m. at Hancock, NH, 26 Jun 1834, his third cousin once removed, HANNAH HARDY *(Phebe Dane Hardy[5], Phebe Abbott Dane[4], Timothy[3], Timothy[2], George[1])*, b. Sep 1808 daughter of Benjamin and Phebe (Dane) Hardy; Hannah d. at Greenfield, 13 Jan 1888. Hannah Hardy is a child in Family 855.

iv HANNAH ABBOTT, b. 7 Sep 1807; d. at Greenfield, 1 Jul 1880; m. about 1834, his third cousin once removed, JOHN DEAN HARDY *(Phebe Dane Hardy[5], Phebe Abbott Dane[4], Timothy[3], Timothy[2], George[1])*, b. at Andover 24 Nov 1796 son of Benjamin and Phebe (Dane) Hardy; John d. at Greenfield, 12 May 1875. John was first married to SALLY JAQUITH, b. 1803 daughter of Benjamin and Phebe (Ames) Jaquith; Sally d. at Greenfield, 9 Aug 1833. John Dean Hardy is a child in Family 855.

v ALBERT ABBOTT, b. 27 Feb 1810; d. at Andover, 5 Apr 1882; m. 1st, 6 May 1834, SARAH BARNARD ABBOTT, b. at Andover, 10 Apr 1814 daughter of Amos and Esther Mackey (West) Abbott; Sarah d. 10 Aug 1834. Albert m. 2nd, 12 Dec 1835, ABIGAIL HALE CUTLER, b. at Winchendon, 8 Jun 1816 daughter of William and Abigail Hale (Lowe) Cutler; Abigail d. at Andover, 11 Aug 1894. Sarah Barnard Abbott descends from the Rowley Abbott line.

vi WILLIAM ABBOTT, b. 16 Jul 1814; d. at Andover, 16 Jan 1885; m. at Andover, 30 May 1838, his fourth cousin once removed, SARAH JOB ABBOTT *(Job[6], Nathan[5], Job[4], Jonathan[3], Benjamin[2], George[1])*, b. at Andover, 19 Jul 1818 daughter of Job and Lucy (Chandler) Abbott; Sarah d. at Andover, 10 Nov 1863.

2964 Andover Historic Preservation, https://preservation.mhl.org/72-brundrett-avenue

2965 Browne, *The History of Hillsborough County*, p 344

2966 The 1852 will of Paul Cragin includes a bequest to son-in-law Hugh A, Abbott.

vii ELIZABETH ELVIRA ABBOTT, b. 28 Feb 1817; d. at Greenfield, 9 May 1915; m. DAVID RAMSEY, b. at Greenfield, 27 Dec 1811 son of David and Hannah (Marshall) Ramsey; David d. 10 Oct 1889. Elizabeth Elvira went by Elvira E. Ramsey although her probate and other records are in the name Elizabeth E.

viii CAROLINE ABBOTT, b. 14 Aug 1823; d. at Woburn, 26 Mar 1899; m. at Andover, 1 Jan 1849, GAWIN RIDLE GAGE, b. at Bedford, NH, about 1820 son of Benjamin and Annis (Moor) Gage; Gawin d. at Woburn, 25 Nov 1892. Gawin was a merchant tailor in Woburn.

1123) REBECCA BAILEY *(Elizabeth Moar Bailey⁴, Elizabeth Abbott Moar³, Nathaniel², George¹)*, b. at Andover, 10 Apr 1781 daughter of Moses and Elizabeth (Moar) Bailey; d. likely at Concord; m. 14 May 1801, her third cousin, WILLIAM ABBOTT *(Isaac⁴, Isaac³, George², George¹)*, b. 30 Oct 1772 son of Isaac and Phebe (Chandler) Abbott; William d. at Concord, 1856 (probate 24 Jun 1856).

Rebecca and William started their family in Andover but relocated to Concord after the births of their first three children.

William Abbott wrote his will 3 June 1848 and the estate entered probate 24 June 1856. In the will, beloved wife Rebecca receives all the household furniture and the use of all the dwelling house that she chooses during her lifetime. She also receives $200 per year and other provisions for her support. Son William Abbot receives $100. Daughter Rebecca Abbot receives $1,000 and the right to remain in the dwelling house as long as she is unmarried. Daughter Phebe C. Lund wife of Joseph Lund receives a sum which will total $1,000 when added to what she has already received. Son Moses B. Abbot receives $2,000. Sons Isaac and Moses receive all the rest of the estate and are named co-executors.[2967]

There are records for five children for Rebecca and William, only two of whom married. At the 1850 census, children Isaac, Rebecca, and Moses were living with their parents in Concord. At the 1870 census, children Moses and Rebecca were living together in Concord. The estate of Moses Bailey Abbott entered probate 26 September 1876. Brother William was administrator stating that he was the only heir-at-law and that Moses had neither widow, children, father, mother, sister, or brother except William.[2968] The two children who did marry, William and Phebe, did not have children.

i WILLIAM ABBOTT, b. at Andover, 7 Sep 1801; d. at Concord, 8 Jan 1888. William married later in life but had three marriages to three widows. First, 19 Nov 1846, married DESDEMONA FISKE (widow of Abner Watkins), b. at Amherst, NH, 15 Mar 1792 daughter of Ebenezer and Abigail (Woodbury) Fiske. Desdemona died at Concord, 4 Oct 1867. Second, William married 12 May 1868, BETSEY WALDRON (widow Davis), b. at Topsham, VT, about 1803 daughter of Theodore and Lucina (McGuire) Waldron. Betsey d. at Concord, 11 Dec 1876. William third married on 12 Nov 1878, VASTA M. CARPENTER (widow of Albert Dolby), b. at Deerfield, about 1827 daughter of Christopher and Mary (McCrillis) Carpenter. Vasta died at Concord, 7 Dec 1895. William did not have children.

ii ISAAC ABBOTT, b. at Andover, 12 Nov 1803; d. at Concord, 29 Aug 1858.

iii REBECCA ABBOTT, b. at Andover, 6 Oct 1806; d. at Concord, 18 Feb 1873.

iv MOSES BAILEY ABBOTT, b. at Concord, 19 Apr 1815; d. at Concord, 12 Sep 1876.

v PHEBE CHANDLER ABBOTT, b. at Concord, 2 Oct 1817; d. at Concord, 19 Dec 1875; m. at Manchester, 23 Nov 1846, JOSEPH S. LUND, b. at Dunstable, MA, about 1800 son of Joseph and Betsey (Whitney) Lund; Joseph d. at Concord, 27 Dec 1882. Joseph was first married to Mary Swett. After Phebe's death, Joseph married Amanda Allen. Phebe did not have children.

1124) JOHN MOAR BAILEY *(Elizabeth Moar Bailey⁴, Elizabeth Abbott Moar³, Nathaniel², George¹)*, b. at Andover, 20 Jul 1784 son of Moses and Elizabeth (Moar) Bailey; d. 3 Apr 1836; m. 5 Dec 1811, his third cousin once removed, ELIZABETH BOYNTON *(Hannah Ames Boynton⁵, Benjamin Ames⁴, Hannah Stevens Ames³, Elizabeth Abbott Stevens², George¹)*, b. 18 Jan 1789 daughter of Thomas and Hannah (Ames) Boynton; Elizabeth d. at Andover, 25 Jun 1856.

There is little available in terms of records for this family. John and Elizabeth lived in Andover throughout their lives. John's estate entered probate 19 April 1836 but the only records available is the assignment of the administration of the estate to Daniel Fox at the request of widow Elizabeth. John and Elizabeth Bailey had six children all born at Andover.

[2967] *New Hampshire. Probate Court (Merrimack County)*; Probate Place: *Merrimack, New Hampshire, Probate Records, Vol 25, 1847-1856*, will of William Abbot 3 Jun 1848

[2968] *New Hampshire. Probate Court (Merrimack County)*; Probate Place: *Merrimack, New Hampshire, Probate Records, Vol 53-54, 1872-1894, probate of Moses B. Abbott*

i HANNAH AMES BAILEY, b. 22 Jan 1813; d. at Andover, 29 Jan 1899; m. 21 Mar 1835, JOHN TUCK, b. at Andover, 5 Nov 1810 son of John Tuck and Mary Abbott;[2969] John d. at Andover, 7 Feb 1880. The family of Mary Abbott has not been identified and it is possible that John Tuck and Mary Abbott were not married. Hannah Bailey's husband John Tuck is the one known as John Tuck, II in town records. There was also John Tuck, III, who is a George Abbott descendant through his parents John Tuck and Elizabeth Abbot Ames. John Tuck, III married Sarah Jane Bailey the out-of-wedlock child of Pricilla Abbott (1790-1857) and William Bailey.

ii LUCY A. BAILEY, b. 11 Apr 1815; d. at Lynn, 21 Dec 1884; m. 21 Jul 1836, JOSEPH BAILEY, b. at Andover, 29 Nov 1810 son of William and Rebecca (Gillson) Bailey; Joseph d. at Tewksbury, 21 Dec 1884.

iii JOHN MOAR BAILEY, b. 16 Oct 1817; d. at Andover, 9 Sep 1885; m. 31 May 1843, LUCY JONES, b. at Andover, 18 Dec 1817 daughter of Abiel and Lucy (Carter) Jones; Lucy d. at Lawrence, 10 Sep 1894.

iv HARRIET BAILEY, b. 23 Jan 1820; d. at Andover, 17 Dec 1899; m. 12 Dec 1850, HENRY HARDY, b. at Tewksbury, 6 Aug 1811 son of Stephen and Sarah (Bailey) Hardy; Henry d. at Andover, 26 May 1887.

v CHARLES BAILEY, b. 26 Nov 1821; d. 4 Nov 1847.

vi WALTER BAILEY, b. 30 Aug 1827; d. at Andover, 28 Aug 1906. Walter did not marry.

1125) TIMOTHY BAILEY *(Elizabeth Moar Bailey[4], Elizabeth Abbott Moar[3], Nathaniel[2], George[1])*, b. at Andover, 18 Oct 1786 son of Moses and Elizabeth (Moar) Bailey; d. 8 Jan 1875; m. 7 Jun 1827, SALLY POOR, b. 9 Apr 1794 daughter of Theodore and Sally (Dowling) Poor; Sally d. 21 Apr 1882.

Timothy Bailey was a successful farmer in Andover and builder of the now historic home at 221 Chandler Road in Andover.[2970] His farm property exceeded 300 acres and his son Timothy Palmer Bailey bought the estate for $11,250 after his father's death.

Timothy and Elizabeth Bailey had two children born at Andover.

i TIMOTHY PALMER BAILEY, b. 25 May 1828; d. at Andover, 9 Dec 1902; m. at Manchester, NH, 28 Nov 1856, MARY JANE MORSE, b. at Springfield, NH, 31 Dec 1825 daughter of Gilbert and Betsey (Jones) Morse; Mary Jane d. at Andover, 21 Apr 1915.

ii MOSES ALBERT BAILEY, b. 5 Mar 1835; d. at Andover, 20 Oct 1904; m. 23 Jan 1864, his fourth cousin twice removed, HANNAH ELIZA MERRILL *(Phebe Shattuck Merrill[6], Phebe Abbott Shattuck[5], Jonathan[4], David[3], Benjamin[2], George[1])*, b. at Andover about 1842 daughter of William and Phebe Abbot (Shattuck) Merrill; Hannah d. at Lawrence, 20 Oct 1870.

1126) RHODA BAILEY *(Elizabeth Moar Bailey[4], Elizabeth Abbott Moar[3], Nathaniel[2], George[1])*, b. at Andover, 7 May 1789 daughter of Moses and Elizabeth (Moar) Bailey; d. at Amherst, NH, 1 Sep 1854; m. 17 Jan 1811, her third cousin once removed, HENRY ABBOTT *(Hephzibah Ames Abbott[5], Benjamin Ames[4], Hannah Stevens Ames[3], Elizabeth Abbott Stevens[2], George[1])*, b. 5 Mar 1785 son of Bixby and Hephzibah (Ames) Abbott; Henry d. 28 Mar 1868.

Rhoda and Henry started their lives in Andover, were for a time in Greenfield, then were in Milford, and finally settled in Amherst, New Hampshire.

Some published genealogies list ten children for this family, but there are no records found for three of these children. They are nevertheless included here but noted as having no records found. Daughters Rhoda and Sylvia did not marry. They lived with their parents and following the deaths of their parents lived with their brother Azel in Harvard, Massachusetts.

i NATHAN P. ABBOTT, b. at Greenfield, NH, 16 Nov 1811; d. at Hampstead, NH, 1 Aug 1889; m. at Nashua, 25 Apr 1849, BETSEY ANN SMITH, b. at Derry, about 1828 daughter of James and Mary D. (Warner) Smith; Betsey d. at Hampstead, 17 Sep 1889.

ii TIMOTHY BIXBY ABBOTT, b. at Greenfield, 20 Jan 1814; d. at Passaic, NJ, 2 Dec 1898;[2971] m. at Blauvelt, NY, 24 Sep 1839,[2972] ELIZA BRADY, b. in New York, about 1818 daughter of David and Mary (Coleman) Brady; Eliza d. at New York, NY, after 1880.

iii RHODA BAILEY ABBOTT, b. at Greenfield, 9 Apr 1817; d. at Amherst, NH, 19 Mar 1895. Rhoda did not marry.

iv MARY ABBOTT, b. and d. about 1818; no records located.

2969 *Massachusetts, Town and Vital Records, 1620-1988.*

2970 Andover Historic Preservation, 221 Chandler Road. https://preservation.mhl.org/221-chandler-rd

2971 *U.S., Dutch Reformed Church Records in Selected States, 1639-1989*, The Archives of the Reformed Church in America; New Brunswick, New Jersey; Old First Church, Records, Consistory Minutes, 1810-1944.

2972 *U.S., Presbyterian Church Records, 1701-1970*, Presbyterian Historical Society; Philadelphia, Pennsylvania; Book Title: 1812 - 1841.

v ELIZA ABBOTT, b. about 1819; no records located

vi AZEL BAILEY ABBOTT, b. at Milford, 28 Jul 1820; d. at Harvard, MA, 7 Mar 1900; m. 18 Oct 1843, MARY B. CORNELL, b. at Newport, RI, about 1820 daughter of Robert and Ann B. (Tew) Cornell; Mary d. at Harvard, 25 Nov 1901.

vii MARY BAILEY ABBOTT reported as a twin of Azel, b. 28 Jul 1820. There were no records located.

viii ARCHER PENN ABBOTT, b. at Milford, 6 Dec 1822; d. at Postville, IA, 6 Dec 1901; m. 22 Feb 1858, ESTHER A. CALLBREATH, b. at Bethel, NY, 27 Sep 1834 daughter of Thomas and Esther Solis (Brady) Callbreath; Esther d. at Chicago, 3 Mar 1917.

ix SYLVIA ANN ABBOTT, b. at Milford, 24 Aug 1826; d. at Andover, 11 Oct 1883. Sylvia did not marry.

x ASA WARREN ABBOTT, b. at Milford, 5 Sep 1829 and d. 1 Nov 1829.

1127) DEBORAH MOAR *(Joshua Moar[4], Elizabeth Abbott Moar[3], Nathaniel[2], George[1])*, b. at Milford, 20 Jul 1777 daughter of Joshua and Deborah (Chandler) Moar; d. at Milford, 28 Aug 1805; m. 18 Nov 1800, SIMEON GUTTERSON, b. at Andover, 8 Dec 1769 son of Samuel and Lydia (Stevens) Gutterson. Samuel m. 2nd, PHEBE BURNHAM *(Phebe Blanchard Burnham[5], Hannah Blanchard Blanchard[4], Sarah Abbott Blanchard[3], Nathaniel[2], George[1])*, b. at Wilton, 18 Sep 1787 daughter of Jeremiah and Phebe (Blanchard) Burnham; Phebe d. at Charlestown, MA, 3 Oct 1868. After Simeon's death, Phebe married Daniel Fuller.

Simeon Gutterson was a farmer in Milford, New Hampshire and her married two descendants of George Abbott and Hannah Chandler. Deborah Moar and Simeon had one son, Simeon, who died as an infant. Simeon and his second wife Phebe Burnham had one daughter who died at age two years. Simeon and Phebe also adopted a daughter Harriet.

In his will dated 7 February 1844, Simeon Gutterson left to his adopted daughter Harriet wife of Peter C. Jones, five dollars. All the remainder of the estate he left to his beloved wife Phebe Gutterson who was also named executrix of the estate.[2973]

Child of Simeon and Deborah:

i SIMEON GUTTERSON, b. 20 Aug 1801; died young

Children of Simeon Gutterson and Phebe Burnham:

i DEBORAH GUTTERSON, b. at Milford, 5 Dec 1817; d. 1819.

ii HARRIET GUTTERSON, adopted child, b. 23 May 1823; d. at Holliston, MA, 11 Aug 1909; m. 1st, 9 Apr 1840, PETER C. JONES. Harriet m. 2nd, at Charlestown, 29 Aug 1859, JOHN STEVENS, b. at Wells, ME, about 1826 son of James and Adeline (Hilton) Stevens. Harriet m. 3rd, at Boston, 30 Sep 1875, WILLIAM STUART, b. at Wells, ME, 5 Dec 1813 son of William and Mary (Rhines) Stuart.

1128) JOSHUA MOAR *(Joshua Moar[4], Elizabeth Abbott Moar[3], Nathaniel[2], George[1])*, b. at Milford, 2 Nov 1778 son of Joshua and Deborah (Chandler) Moar; d. at Milford, 20 Jul 1831; m. at Milford, 19 Nov 1805, BEULAH BLANCHARD, b. 13 Jun 1783 daughter of Benjamin and Sarah (Griffin) Blanchard; Beulah d. 20 Nov 1824.

Joshua was a farmer in Milford, New Hampshire. His wife Beulah died at age 41 leaving seven children, the youngest of whom was four years old.

On 2 August 1831, administration of the estate of Joshua Moar was granted to Solomon Swinmore of Milford noting that there was no widow and the seven children were all underage. The inventory listed homestead land with building valued at $1,100 and personal estate of $564.67. It was later determined that the property was overvalued, and that the estate needed to be sold to settle the accounts. After the sale of the estate and settlement of accounts, $803.68 was left in the estate.[2974]

Joshua and Beulah were parents of eight children born at Milford.[2975][2976]

2973 New Hampshire. Probate Court (Hillsborough County); Probate Place: Hillsborough, New Hampshire, Probate Records, volume 48, p 510, accessed through ancestry.com

2974 New Hampshire, County Probate Records, 1660-1973, Hillsborough County, probate of Joshua Moar, Case 06493, 37:74, 39:128, 27:236, 39:460

2975 Brooks, *History of Milford*, p 854

2976 Mooar, *Mooar Genealogy*, p 47

i LOUISA MOAR, b. 31 Aug 1806; d. at Wilton, 13 Oct 1869; m. 19 Feb 1823, FREEMAN HUTCHINSON, b. 24 Oct 1805 son of Samuel and Martha (Howard) Hutchinson; Freeman d. at Wilton, 25 Jul 1873.

ii SARAH MOAR, b. 1808; d. 22 Oct 1809.

iii ROXANNA MOAR, b. 30 Sep 1810; d. at Cavendish, VT, 26 Dec 1858; m. SEWELL PARKER, b. at Chelmsford, 23 Nov 1801 son of Joseph and Tabitha (Warren) Parker; Sewell d. at Cavendish, 9 Dec 1844.

iv CHARLES MOAR, b. 17 Sep 1812; d. at Claremont, NH, 11 May 1880; m. at Chelmsford, 17 Feb 1838, LAURA ANN MOORE, b. at Lempster, NH, 1819 daughter of Thomas and Laura A. (Way) Moore; Laura d. at Lempster, 9 Aug 1897.

v DORINDA MOAR, b. 18 Aug 1814; d. at Somersworth, NH, 7 Nov 1871; m. at Chelmsford, MA, 21 Dec 1834, JOTHAM M. STEVENS, b. 1811; Jotham d. at Berwick, ME, 21 Aug 1844.

vi TIMOTHY MOAR, b. 22 Jul 1816; d. at Milford, 14 Sep 1840. The Mooar genealogy reports that Timothy married but his wife has not been identified.

vii SARAH MOAR, b. 29 Jul 1818; m. at Andover, MA, 3 Feb 1836, JESSE GAY.

viii JOHN MOAR, b. 1 Sep 1820; d. at Rockingham, VT, 18 Aug 1882; m. 2 Jul 1844, MARY MARINDA SNELL, b. at Chester, VT, 3 Nov 1819 daughter of Amasa and Rebecca (Houghton) Snell; Mary d. at Rockingham, 12 Dec 1897.

1129) STEPHEN CHANDLER MOAR *(Joshua Moar⁴, Elizabeth Abbott Moar³, Nathaniel², George¹)*, b. at Milford, 17 Aug 1780 son of Joshua and Deborah (Chandler) Moar; d. at Andover, 16 Mar 1861; m. 6 Nov 1804, ELIZABETH SAWYER CHASE, b. at Leominster, 5 Jul 1782 daughter of Enoch and Sarah (Sawyer) Chase; Elizabeth d. 25 Apr 1854.

Stephen Moar was a farmer who lived in Milford, Peterborough, and lastly in Andover where he died.[2977]

Daughter Eliza Chase Moar did not marry. In her will written 31 July 1871, Eliza C. Moar bequeathed to brother Stephen Moar and her sister-in-law Sarah Jane Moar, twenty-five dollars each. There are numerous other bequests to nieces, nephews, and friends. The remainder of the estate is to be equally divided between the American Home Missionary Society and the American Board of Commissioners for Foreign Missions. Sarah J. Moar was the second wife of Stephen Moar.[2978]

Stephen and Elizabeth Moar were parents of three children.

i ELIZA CHASE MOAR, b. at Peterborough, 17 Aug 1806; d. at Andover, MA, 15 Feb 1872. Eliza did not marry.

ii STEPHEN MOAR, b. at Peterborough, 10 Apr 1810; d. at Chester, NH, 24 Nov 1876; m. 1st, at Andover, 20 Mar 1833, HANNAH STEVENS, b. at Andover, 11 Aug 1812 daughter of Phineas and Rebecca (Farnum) Stevens; Hannah d. at Lowell, 16 Dec 1852. Stephen m. 2nd, 29 Mar 1854, SARAH J. POOR, b. at Raymond, NH, 1818 daughter of Benjamin and Alice (Moore) Poor; Sarah d. at Raymond, 14 Feb 1911.

iii JOSHUA MOAR, b. at Milford, 12 Jul 1812; d. at Andover, 18 Nov 1867; m. at Andover, 23 Mar 1841, his fourth cousin once removed, MARY E. ABBOTT *(Gardner⁶, Caleb⁵, Asa⁴, Timothy³, Timothy², George¹)*, b. at Andover, 16 Mar 1822 daughter of Gardner and Rachel (Hart) Abbott; Mary d. at Andover, 22 Oct 1864.

1130) TIMOTHY MOAR *(Joshua Moar⁴, Elizabeth Abbott Moar³, Nathaniel², George¹)*, b. at Milford, 22 Mar 1784 son of Joshua and Deborah (Chandler) Moar; d. at Nashua, 1855; m. BETSY HOPKINS, b. at Milford, 8 Sep 1792 daughter of Daniel and Hannah (-) Hopkins; Betsy d. at Nashua, 1852.

Timothy Moar and Betsy Hopkins were parents of ten children.

i MARSENA MOAR, b. at Peterborough, 2 Oct 1810; d. at Wichita, KS, 7 Jul 1898; m. 1st, 21 Sep 1837, MARY BLANCHARD, b. at Milford, about 1812 daughter of Isaac and Hannah (Herrick) Blanchard; Mary d. before 1877. Marsena m. 2nd, at Boston, 10 May 1877, LOUISA WYMAN, b. at Nashua, NH, about 1842 daughter of Paul and Luvilla (Morrill) Wyman; Marsena and Louisa were divorced before 1880 when Marsena was living alone in Kansas and listed as divorced on the 1880 census.

ii DANIEL HOPKINS MOAR, b. at Peterborough, 3 Jan 1813; d. at Milford, 21 Oct 1833.

iii JOSHUA ABBOT MOAR, b. at Peterborough, 10 Nov 1814; d. at Londonderry, 26 Sep 1872; m. 6 Aug 1837, LOVINA WITHERSPOON, b. at Chester, 8 Apr 1814 daughter of John and Nancy (Linn) Witherspoon; Lovina d. at Bedford, 26 Dec 1882.

[2977] Ramsdell, *History of Milford*, p 854

[2978] *Essex County, Massachusetts, Probate Records and Indexes 1638-1916;* Author: *Massachusetts. Probate Court (Essex County);* Probate Place: *Essex, Massachusetts*, volume 427, pp 455-457, will of Eliza C. Moar.

iv MARIA JOSEPHINE MOAR, b. at Peterborough, 5 Feb 1817; d. at Nashua, 23 Jan 1892; m. 10 Feb 1844, DAVID BLANCHARD, b. at Peterborough, 10 Oct 1813 son of Cyrus and Mary (Blanchard) Blanchard; David d. at Peterborough, 9 Jun 1889.

v ELVIRA MOAR, b. at Peterborough, 17 Feb 1820; d. at Nashua, 1 Feb 1906; m. 1 Jan 1848, FREDERIC W. DOW, b. at Vermont, about 1811 son of Moses and Hannah (Phillips) Dow; Frederic d. at Nashua, 25 Jul 1885. Elvira and Frederic divorced 5 Jun 1861.

vi MANUEL MOAR, b. at Peterborough, 10 Jan 1823; d. at Nashua, 6 Jan 1896; m. 1st, at Londonderry, 23 Apr 1850, SARAH PLUMMER, b. 1829 daughter of Abel and Mary (Anderson) Plummer;[2979] Sarah d. at Nashua, 1867. Manuel m. 2nd, at Boston, 11 Dec 1867, ELLEN "NELLIE" BUTTERFIELD, b. 1841 daughter of John and Celestia (-) Butterfield; Nellie d. at Nahua, 23 Aug 1878.

vii MORRILL C. MOAR, b. at Peterborough, 10 Oct 1825; d. at Nashua, 2 Apr. 1865. Morrill may have married, but at the time of his death, he had no wife, child, mother, or father and his brother Manuel Moar and sister Jennie Moar were listed as next of kin.[2980]

viii ELIZA JENNIE MOAR, b. at Peterborough, 31 Aug 1828; d. at Nashua, 26 Nov 1910. Eliza did not marry.

ix MARY ANN MOAR, b. at Milford, 15 Feb 1831; d. 6 Jan 1837.

x DANIEL H. MOAR, b. at Milford, 7 Jan 1833; d. 3 Feb 1837.

1131) SARAH MOAR *(Joshua Moar⁴, Elizabeth Abbott Moar³, Nathaniel², George¹)*, b. at Milford, 26 Oct 1786 daughter of Joshua and Deborah (Chandler) Moar; d. at Milford, 6 Jan 1857; m. 1808, LUTHER HUTCHINSON, b. 2 May 1783 son of Benjamin and Susannah (Peabody) Hutchinson; Luther d. 5 Sep 1861. After Sarah's death, Luther married Betsey (Tay) Crosby.

Luther Hutchinson was a farmer and worked the property which had one time been owned by his father-in-law Joshua Moar.[2981]

Luther Hutchinson wrote his will 28 January 1859 and it was proved 27 September 1861. Beloved wife Betsey is to have use of all the household furnishings and the interest on the money in-hand and all of the railroad stock as long as she remains a widow. Son Elbridge Hutchinson receives one dollar which with what he has already received constitutes his full share. Daughter Cassandra H. Hopkins receives all the household furniture, one-third of the money and one-third of the railroad stock. Son Gerry Hutchinson receives one-third of the money and one-third of the railroad stock. Son Evelyn Milton Hutchinson receives the final third of the money and stock. The legacies are to be paid following the decease of Luther and Betsey or Betsey ceasing to be a widow. Any reside of the estate goes to Evelyn Milton who is also named executor.[2982]

There are records for four children of Sarah and Luther born at Milford, and Ramsdell's history of Milford list two other children who died in young childhood.

i MILTON HUTCHINSON, b. 1809 and d. 1812.

ii CASSENDANA HUTCHINSON, b. May 1812; d. at Worcester, MA, 23 Feb 1871; m. 25 Dec 1837, her third cousin, JOHN B. HOPKINS *(Orpha Boynton Hopkins⁵, Rebecca Abbott Boynton⁴, Jeremiah³, Nathaniel², George¹)*, b. at Milford, Sep 1803 son of John and Orpha (Boynton) Hopkins; John d. in California, 11 Apr 1857. According to Ramsdell's History of Milford, John went to California for the gold rush, and there is a John B. Hopkins of the right age at Chinese Camp in the 1850 census. Cassendana did not go to California and was living in Milford with siblings in 1850.

iii EVELYN MILTON HUTCHINSON, b. 17 Aug 1815; d. at Waltham, 2 Mar 1875; m. at Waltham, 1 Nov 1840, ESTHER P. HAWES, b. at Boston, about 1819 daughter of Ebenezer O. and Cynthia (Brown) Hawes; Esther d. at Waltham, 4 Dec 1890.

iv ELBRIDGE HUTCHINSON, b. 9 Dec 1817; d. at Milford, 27 Jan 1877; m. 3 Nov 1844, CYNTHIA KNIGHT, b. at Hancock, NH, 9 Feb 1820 daughter of Asa and Melinda (Adams) Knight; Cynthia d. at Milford, 15 Feb 1897.

[2979] Morrison, *The History of the Morrison Family*, p 264

[2980] *New Hampshire. Probate Court (Hillsborough County)*; Probate Place: *Hillsborough, New Hampshire*, volume 79, p 72

[2981] Ramsdell, *History of Milford*, p 775

[2982] *New Hampshire. Probate Court (Hillsborough County)*; Probate Place: *Hillsborough, New Hampshire, Probate Records, Vol 75-78, 1861-1877, will of Luther Hutchinson, pp 17-18*

v GERRY HUTCHINSON, b. 21 Mar 1820; d. at Worcester, 22 Jan 1882; m. at Waltham, 22 Jan 1848, ELIZABETH R. ROBBINS, b. at Wilton, ME, Sep 1822 daughter of John and Lydia (Harris) Robbins; Elizabeth d. at Worcester, 9 Oct 1905.

vi BETSEY HUTCHINSON, daughter who died in infancy for whom there are no records.

1132) BETSY MOAR *(Joshua Moar[4], Elizabeth Abbott Moar[3], Nathaniel[2], George[1])*, b. at Milford, 25 Jan 1790 daughter of Joshua and Deborah (Chandler) Moar; d. 1825; m. 20 Apr 1813, MICAH JENKINS, b. 26 Jul 1786 son of Joel and Patty (Carter) Jenkins; Micah d. after 1860.

Micah and Betsy had their three children in Mont Vernon, New Hampshire where Betsy died. Micah later relocated to Andover where he was living with his son Luther in 1860. Micah does not seem to have remarried.

i OSMORE JENKINS, b. at Mont Vernon, 3 Dec 1815; d. at Melrose, MA, 18 Dec 1904; m. at New Bedford, MA, 29 Nov 1838, DELILAH R. HART, b. at Dartmouth, about 1820 daughter of Benjamin and Delilah (Russell) Hart; Delilah d. at Stoughton, 18 Jan 1901.

ii DEBORAH M. JENKINS, b. at Mont Vernon, 13 Apr 1819; d. at Montague, MA, 10 Mar 1885; m. at Andover, 7 Sep 1847, JOTHAM CLARK, b. at Granby, MA, 12 Nov 1820 son of Augustus and Mary (Ayers) Clark; Jotham d. at Northampton, MA, 25 Nov 1896.

iii LUTHER L. JENKINS, b. at Mont Vernon, 27 Aug 1822; d. at Northampton, MA, 10 Apr 1898; m. 1st, at Andover, 28 Apr 1849, NANCY JANE PUTNAM, b. at Andover, 13 Oct 1827 daughter of Israel and Mary (Hawks) Putnam; Nancy d. at Andover, 22 Aug 1850. Luther m. 2nd, at Reading, 27 Feb 1851, Nancy's sister CAROLINE ELIZABETH PUTNAM, b. at Andover, 12 Aug 1829.

1133) MARY "POLLY" HARRIS *(Mary Moar Harris[4], Elizabeth Abbott Moar[3], Nathaniel[2], George[1])*, b. at Andover, about 1779 daughter of William and Mary (Moar) Harris; date of death unknown but after 1820; m. at Andover, 12 Jan 1797, LOAMMI B. HOLT, b. 23 Jul 1775 son of Simeon and Sarah (Read) Holt; Loammi d. at Andover, 11 Jan 1827 at the almshouse.

Durrie's Holt genealogy (p 87) sums up Loammi and Polly (Harris) Holt this way: "He was a hatter at Andover but failed in business: removed and never returned. His wife was of ill repute, and subsequently lived at the Alms House; had twins b. Mar. 12 1816, 1 d. 1816, 1 d. 1817." But a search of records suggests there was more to this family than that.

Polly Harris was the daughter of William and Mary (Moar) Harris. Mary Moar Harris was a widow when she died at Andover on 2 August 1820. Mary Harris wrote her will 15 May 1820 and the estate entered probate 5 September 1820. The will includes a bequest of one dollar to daughter Mary Holt, and son John M. Harris receives the remainder of the estate both real and personal. John M. Bailey was named executor. The probate records include statements from each of the two children agreeing to the location of the probate hearing. Son John M. Harris was living in Watertown and daughter Mary Holt was living in Andover.

Loammi B. Holt was the son of Simeon and Sarah (Read) Holt. Loammi and Polly married at Andover on 12 January 1797. Loammi was living in the West District of South Parish for at least some periods of time as he was on the tax role lists there from 1810 to 1818. In the 1810 U.S. Census, Loammi Holt is listed as the head of household in Andover with a household that consists of one male over age 45, one female over age 45, one male 26-44, one female 26-44, and three males under the age of 10. The couple also seem to have been in Gloucester, Massachusetts, or at least connected to a church there, as there are records for four children of Loammi baptized there from 1800 to 1809. These children were named John Harris Holt, two children William Harris Holt in 1802 and 1809, and Mary Harris Holt. The Andover records report births of three infants, twin sons born 12 March 1816 (one of whom died 14 March 1816) and a "child" born 1 August 1817 who died 26 August 1817. It is assumed that the second twin born in 1816 also died as an infant.

One son of Loammi and Polly, William Harris Holt, married and had a family. The 1896 death record for William Harris Holt lists his birthplace as Gloucester and his parents as Loammi B. Holt and Mary Harris. It is not known what became of the other children born at Gloucester, although the 1810 census records list three males under the age of 10 so it may be that there were two other sons who lived at least through part of their childhoods. Loammi Holt died at the almshouse in Andover 11 January 1827. It is not known what became of Polly. She is known to be living when her mother wrote her will in 1820.

There are birth records for seven children of Loammi Holt and Mary Harris.

i MARY HARRIS HOLT, baptized at Gloucester, Aug 1800; no further record.

ii WILLIAM HARRIS HOLT, baptized at Gloucester, Aug 1802; died young.

iii JOHN HARRIS HOLT, baptized at Gloucester, Dec 1806; no further record.

iv WILLIAM HARRIS HOLT, b. at Gloucester, 9 Jul 1809; d. at Lynn, 21 Aug 1896; m. at Lynn, 28 May 1837, CLARISSA EMMONS, b. in Maine, 23 Aug 1814 daughter of John and Huldah (Shockley) Emmons; Clarissa d. at Lynn, 3 Dec 1890.

v Twin1 Holt (m); b. at Andover 12 Mar 1816; d. 14 Mar 1816.

vi Twin2 Holt (m); b. at Andover 12 Mar 1816; no further record.

vii Child Holt, b. at Andover, 1 Aug 1817; d. 26 Aug 1817.

1134) JUDITH CHANDLER *(Abiel Chandler[4], Rebecca Abbott Chandler[3], Nathaniel[2], George[1])*, b. at Concord, 9 Oct 1770 daughter of Abiel and Judith (Walker) Chandler; d. at Concord, 28 Dec 1852; m. 12 Jun 1794, TIMOTHY CARTER, b. at Concord, 6 Mar 1767 son of Ezra and Phebe (Whittemore) Carter; Timothy d. 7 Feb 1843.

Timothy Carter's father, Ezra Carter, was the first physician in Concord. His family owned the Carter Hill Orchard in Concord and son Abiel Chandler Carter inherited and ran the orchard. The orchard is still in business.[2983]

Timothy Carter wrote his will 8 March 1833 and was proved on the fourth Tuesday of February 1843. Wife Judith receives all the household furniture, $100 in cash, and provisions for her maintenance for her natural life or as long as she is a widow. Son Ezra Carter receives $100, daughter Judith W. Carter $400, and son-in-law Augustin C. Pierce $50. All the remainder of the estate goes to son Abiel C. Carter who was also named executor.[2984]

Judith Chandler and Timothy Carter had four children born at Concord.

i ABIEL CHANDLER CARTER, b. 8 Jan 1796; d. at Concord, 26 Aug 1856; m. Dec 1819, MARTHA "PATTY" FARNUM, b. at Boscawen, 10 May 1797 daughter of Stephen and Susan (Jackman) Farnum; Patty d. at Concord, 29 Nov 1855.

ii EZRA CARTER, b. 27 Dec 1798; d. at Concord, 28 Jan 1879; m. 8 May 1830, ABBY T. CLARK, b. at Portsmouth, NH, 29 May 1807 daughter of George and Charlotte (Turner) Clark; Abby d. after 1870. Dr. Ezra Carter was a physician in Concord. He attended lectures at Yale 1821-1822 and received his M.D. degree from Bowdoin College. He was also a member of the state legislature 1836-1837.[2985]

iii SARAH RUMFORD CARTER, b. 16 Feb 1801; d. at Concord, 25 Jul 1829; m. at Concord, 15 May 1826, AUGUSTINE C. PIERCE, b. at Montpelier, 11 Apr 1801 son of Lyman and Lucinda (Clark) Pierce; Augustine d. at Concord, 5 Sep 1883. After Sarah's death, Augustine had two other marriages to Martha Hutchins and Hannah Hutchins.

iv JUDITH WALKER CARTER, b. 4 Dec 1807; d. at Worcester, MA, 18 Nov 1889; m. at Portland, 11 Oct 1834, her first cousin, EZRA CARTER, b. at Scarborough, ME, 1804 son of Ezra and Sarah (Fabyan) Carter; Ezra d. at Portland, 11 May 1887.

1135) SIMEON ABBOTT *(Amos[4], Rebecca Abbott Abbott[3], Nathaniel[2], George[1])*, b. at Concord, 3 Aug 1807 son of Amos and Judith (Morse) Abbot; d. at Concord, 22 Feb 1895; m. 8 Feb 1837, MARY FARNUM, b. 25 Jun 1814 daughter of Simeon and Mary (Smith) Farnum; Mary d. 26 Apr 1898.

Simeon Abbott was born and died on the homestead farm in Concord. He was educated at local schools and as a young man worked as a teacher. He was known for his skill as a farmer. His property also included part of Rattlesnake Hill from which Concord granite is obtained. He was interested in genealogy and much of the information on the Abbott and Farnum families in Bouton's History of Concord was contributed by Simeon.[2986]

Simeon and Mary Abbott were the parents of ten children born at Concord.

i AMOS SMITH ABBOTT, b. 24 Dec 1837; d. at Concord, 3 Dec 1909; m. at Concord, 1 Jul 1860, HARRIET A. WILLIAMS, b. at Lowell, MA, 1840 daughter of Otis and Philena (Read) Williams; Harriet d. at Concord, 27 Jul 1900.

ii REBECCA CHANDLER ABBOTT, b. 24 Aug 1839; d. at Concord, 18 Jun 1931. Rebecca did not marry.

iii MARY SMITH ABBOTT, b. 26 Aug 1841; d. at Concord, 25 May 1925; m. 21 Jun 1877, her third cousin once removed, FREDERICK GRAY CHANDLER *(Nathan Chandler[7], Nathan Chandler[6], John Chandler[5], John Chandler[4], Tabitha Abbott Chandler[3], Nathaniel[2], George[1])*, b. at Penacook, 21 Dec 1845 son of Nathan and Louisa (Ferrin) Chandler; Frederick d. at Concord, 5 Jan 1930.

[2983] "The History of Carter Hill Orchard" http://www.carterhillapples.com/history.html

[2984] *New Hampshire. Probate Court (Merrimack County)*; Probate Place: *Merrimack, New Hampshire, Probate Records, Vol 16, 1839-1875*, will of Timothy Carter, pp 131-132

[2985] Cogswell, *The New Hampshire Repository*, volume I, p 142

[2986] Stearns, *Genealogical and Family History of the State of New Hampshire*, volume I, pp 358-359

iv ABIAL CHANDLER ABBOTT, b. 17 Oct 1843; d. at Concord, 21 Dec 1928; m. 25 Dec 1872, MARY FRANCIS, b. at Lowell, Sep 1851 daughter of James and Sarah (Haggis) Francis; Mary d. at Concord, 15 Mar 1915.

v CALVIN FARNUM ABBOTT, b. 29 Jan 1846; d. 24 Mar 1847.

vi STEPHEN FARNUM ABBOTT, b. 11 Jan 1849; d. at Concord, 26 Apr 1878. Stephen did not marry. His father Simeon was administrator of his estate.

vii LOUISE GOULD ABBOTT, b. 30 Dec 1850; d. at Omaha, NE, 19 Mar 1891; m. at Concord, 9 Sep 1874, GEORGE HALL CAPEN, b. at Lowell, about 1847 son of Albert Gallatin and Mary (Hall) Capen; George d. at Los Angeles, 19 Sep 1935.

viii CLARA ANN ABBOTT, b. 20 Dec 1852; d. at Concord, 5 Apr 1905. Clara did not marry.

ix MARTHA WARDE ABBOTT, b. 3 May 1855; d. at Concord, 9 Jul 1896.

x ANDREW JAMES ABBOTT, b. 19 Dec 1856; d. at Concord, 9 May 1938. Andrew did not marry.

1136) SARAH HALE ABBOT *(Amos[4], Rebecca Abbott Abbott[3], Nathaniel[2], George[1])*, b. at Concord, 27 Jun 1809 daughter of Amos and Judith (Morse) Abbot; d. at Concord, 8 Sep 1884; m. 18 Dec 1839, her fourth cousin, DAVID ABBOTT *(Nathan[5], Jabez[4], Thomas[3], Thomas[2], George[1])*, b. 12 Jul 1809 son of Nathan and Rhoda (Brickett) Abbott; David d. at Concord, 12 Apr 1882.

David Abbott was a farmer in Concord. Records for eight children of Sarah Hale Abbott and David Abbott were located.[2987] The children were born at Concord.

i JUDITH MORSE ABBOTT, b. Oct 1839; d. at Concord, 25 Sep 1907; m. 1st, at Canterbury, 21 May 1861, ALFRED BULLOCK, b. at Boscawen, 1834 son of Jesse and Candace (Mason) Bullock; Alfred d. at Boscawen, 31 Mar 1868 (probate 28 Apr 1868). Judith m. 2nd, at Penacook, 12 Nov 1869, CHARLES COUCH, b. at West Salisbury, 1830 son of Samuel and Susan (Call) Couch; Charles d. at Concord, 25 May 1907.

ii JOHN C. ABBOTT, b. 1841; d. at Fort Steilacoom, WA, 25 Sep 1915; m. at Elba, MN, 10 Aug 1883, ANNIE PUCHEIT, b. in Germany, Oct 1865. John and Annie divorced 1898. Annie was living in Blaine, WA in 1910.[2988]

iii GEORGE M. ABBOTT, b. about 1844; d. at Concord, 1856.[2989]

iv ELIZA E. ABBOTT, b. Feb 1846; d. at Penacook, 3 Jan 1925; m. at Concord, 27 Feb 1866, JOHN E. S. FIFIELD, b. at Bridgewater, NH, 21 Mar 1842 son of Samuel and Elmira (Martin) Fifield; John d. at Webster, 11 Feb 1909.

v RHODA B. ABBOTT, b. 1848; d. at Concord, 5 May 1918. Rhoda did not marry. On 12 Nov 1907, Charles H. Sanders were appointed guardian for Rhoda due to her being an insane person.[2990]

vi SARAH E. ABBOTT, b. 1851; d. at Penacook, 17 May 1930; m. before 1880, CHARLES HENRY SANDERS, b. at Penacook, 12 Sep 1851 son of Jacob and Sarah (Dutton) Sanders; Charles d. at Concord, 2 Jan 1934.

vii ELLEN C. ABBOTT, b. 1853; d. at Concord, 21 Jan 1909; m. at Concord, 26 Nov 1873, WALTER SCOTT MUZZEY, b. at Bristol, NH, 13 Jul 1849 son of Samuel and Sally (Blake) Muzzey; Walter d. at Northampton, MA, 31 Mar 1920 (resident of Springfield at time of death).

viii MARY A. ABBOTT, b. 8 Jan 1855; d. at Concord, 18 Sep 1887. Mary did not marry.

1137) REBECCA CHAMBERLAIN *(Rebecca Abbott Chamberlain[4], Rebecca Abbott Abbott[3], Nathaniel[2], George[1])*, b. 15 Mar 1783 daughter of Moses and Rebecca (Abbott) Chamberlain; d. at Loudon, NH, 31 Jan 1868; m. 8 Feb 1805, SHADRACH CATE, b. at Loudon, 10 Aug 1779 son of Stephen and Annie (Griffin) Cate; Shadrach d. 9 Oct 1842. Rebecca m. 2nd Nathaniel True in 1852.

In his will written 27 February 1840 and proved October 1842, Shadrach Cate bequeaths to beloved wife Rebecca all the corn, grain, meat, and potatoes and the other provisions now on hand. Rebecca also receives the clock, one cow, and one shoat (young pig). Oldest son Hiram Cate and oldest daughter Hannah Chase each receive one dollar. Daughter Rebecca C. Cate receives five dollars; daughter Eliza Ann Morrill, one dollar; daughter Sally W. Cate, five dollars; and daughter Judith E. Cate, five dollars. Sons Shadrach M. Cate and Moses C. Cate receive the residue of the estate both real and personal to be divided equally between them. His brother Stephen Cate was named sole executor.[2991]

2987 Stearns, *Genealogical and Family History of the State of New Hampshire, volume I*, p 356 reports there were ten children in this family.

2988 1900; Census Place: Blaine, Whatcom, Washington; Page: 5; Enumeration District: 0232; FHL microfilm: 1241753. In the 1900 Census is listed as divorced and her two children are with her.

2989 Cemetery Index from Selected States, 1847-2010; burial at Maple Grove Cemetery in Concord with engraving son of David and Sarah H.

2990 New Hampshire County Probate Records, Merrimack County, volume 122, p 29, Case 20739 ½

2991 New Hampshire. Probate Court (Merrimack County); Probate Place: Merrimack, New Hampshire, volume 16, pp 118-119, will of Shadrach Cate

In her will written 11 April 1867 and proved 23 February 1869, Rebecca C. True left to sons Hiram and Moses C. Cate five dollars each. Son Shadrach M. Cate receives the eight-day clock. Daughter Eliza Ann the wife of Alpheus Morrill receives fifty dollars. The children of her daughters Hannah B. and Judith E. who are now deceased receive her love and goodwill. Daughters Eliza Ann and Sally W. receive the household furniture. Daughter Sally W. Dickerman receives the residue of the estate. William Emery of Loudon was named sole executor.[2992]

Shadrach and Rebecca Cate had eleven children born at Loudon.

i REBECCA CATE, b. 28 May 1805; d. 12 Jan 1808.

ii HIRAM CATE, b. 1 Apr 1807; d. at Loudon, 8 Jun 1892; m. at Concord, 4 May 1831, MARY SHUTE POTTER, b. at Concord, 18 Jul 1794 daughter of Anthony and Dolly (Goodwin) Potter. After Mary's death, Hiram married Abigail Austin on 12 Jan 1874.

iii HANNAH B. CATE, b. 1 Apr 1807; d. 16 Dec 1850; m. 10 Jan 1827, IRA ALLEN CHASE, b. at Loudon, 22 Jan 1804 son of Isaiah and Abigail (Batchelder) Chase; Ira d. at Loudon, 25 Apr 1853.[2993]

iv REBECCA CHAMBERLAIN CATE, b. 4 Jun 1809; d. at Solon, OH, 15 Sep 1858;[2994] m. at Geauga, OH, 6 Jan 1841, EBENEZER GOVE, b. at Sanbornton, NH, 17 Feb 1814 son of Ebenezer and Hannah (Haynes) Gove; Ebenezer d. at North Hampton, NH, 28 May 1897. After Rebecca's death, Ebenezer married Miranda Fuller and Abigail Philbrook. Ebenezer Gove was a scale manufacturer and lived for a time in Ohio. Rebecca and Ebenezer had two children. A daughter died as a young child. Son Page M. Gove served with the 103rd Ohio Volunteers during the Civil War and died of typhoid pneumonia at the field hospital at Frankfort, KY, 7 Mar 1863.[2995]

v ELIZA ANN CATE, b. 13 Oct 1811; d. at Concord, 1888 (probate 11 Dec 1888); m. 1838, ALPHEUS MORRILL, b. at Canterbury, 26 Jun 1808 son of Ezekiel and Betsey (Stevens) Morrill; Alpheus d. at Concord, 9 May 1871.

vi JUDITH CHAMBERLAIN CATE, b. 26 Nov 1813; d. 24 Jul 1815.

vii MARTHA CATE, b. about 1816; d. 13 Apr 1823.

viii SALLY W. CATE, b. 1819; d. at Loudon, 14 May 1897; m. 26 Jan 1844, THOMAS T. DICKERMAN, b. 11 Nov 1819 son of Moses and Lydia (Wales) Dickerman; Thomas d. 28 Aug 1856.[2996]

ix JUDITH E. CATE, b. 1821; d. at Salem, MA, 30 Nov 1866; m. at Cuyahoga, OH, 29 Sep 1840, CHARLES MORRILL, b. at Canterbury, NH, 17 Jul 1819 son of Ezekiel and Betsey (Stevens) Morrill; Charles d. Cleveland, 1892.

x SHADRACH MELLEN CATE, b. about 1824; d. at Danvers, MA, 22 Apr 1898; m. at Salem, MA, 1 Jan 1849, MARTHA JANE MESSER, b. in Canada, Sep 1826 daughter of Amos and Sarah (Colby) Messer; Martha d. at Danvers, 1917.

xi MOSES CHAMBERLAIN CATE, b. 23 Aug 1818; d. at Solon, MI, 28 Jul 1916; m. MARY LOUISE BARNARD, b. at Adams, NY, 1833 daughter of William B. and Mary (Kilborn) Barnard. Mary d. at Solon, 23 Mar 1897.

1138) JUDITH CHAMBERLAIN *(Rebecca Abbott Chamberlain[4], Rebecca Abbott Abbott[3], Nathaniel[2], George[1])*, b. at Loudon, 20 Apr 1785 daughter of Moses and Rebecca (Abbott) Chamberlain; d. at Pataskala, OH, 1843;[2997] m. 16 Jun 1807, SAMUEL ELLIOTT, b. at Boscawen, 13 Mar 1778 son of Jonathan and Molly (Conner) Elliot; Samuel d. at Pataskala, 1851.

Judith and Samuel were married in New Hampshire and had their seven children there before relocating to Pataskala, Ohio.

Son Samuel Barnard Elliott died in 1886 without leaving a will and with no wife or children. His heirs-at-law were Moses C. Elliott, Charles H. Elliott, and William C. Elliott of Pataskala, Ohio, Mary Morrill of Concord, NH, niece Mary Atkinson and nephew Joseph Atkinson of Pataskala, Samuel Peabody of Champaign, IL, and nephew George Atkinson of Columbus, OH.[2998]

[2992] New Hampshire. Probate Court (Merrimack County); Probate Place: Merrimack, New Hampshire, volume 43, p 150, will of Rebecca C. True

[2993] Dale, Raymond E. 1944. "Some Descendants of Aquila Chase of Newbury, Massachusetts", The Nebraska and Midwest Genealogical Record, volume XXII, number 1.

[2994] Rebecca is buried at Roselawn Cemetery in Solon, OH. Her gravestone includes her birth date of 4 June 1809.

[2995] *Registers of Deaths of Volunteers, compiled 1861–1865.* ARC ID: 656639. Records of the Adjutant General's Office, 1780's–1917. Record Group 94. National Archives at Washington, D.C.

[2996] Dickerman, *Dickerman Genealogy*, p 132

[2997] Gravestone reads Judith C. Elliot wife of Samuel Elliot 1785-1843, grave at Pataskala Cemetery. Findagrave.com

[2998] *Applications for Letters of Administration, 1875-1897;* Probate Place: *Licking, Ohio*, volume 3, p 75

Samuel Elliott and Judith Chamberlain were parents of seven children.

i SAMUEL BARNARD ELLIOTT, b. at Loudon, NH, 7 Sep 1808; d. at Pataskala, 1 oct 1886. Samuel did not marry.

ii MARANDA ELLIOTT, b. at Loudon, 19 Sep 1810; d. at Pataskala, 3 Dec 1866; m. at Boscawen, 31 Oct 1831, PEABODY ATKINSON, b. at Boscawen, 30 Dec 1804 son of Joseph and Anna (Atkinson) Atkinson; Peabody d. at Pataskala, 1863.

iii MOSES CHAMBERLAIN ELLIOTT, b. at Loudon, 11 Dec 1812; d. at Pataskala, 1891; m. at Licking County, OH, 16 Dec 1841, SARAH HERRON, b. in OH, about 1818; Sarah d. at Pataskala, 1898.

iv CHARLES HENRY EASTMAN ELLIOTT, b. at Boscawen, 17 Mar 1821; d. at Pataskala, 18 Apr 1902; m. at Licking County, OH, 11 Sep 1852, JANE BAIRD, b. in OH, Dec 1831 daughter of Joseph and Margery (Ferrel) Baird;[2999] Jane d. at Pataskala, 20 Jun 1912.

v JOHN NEWTON ELLIOTT, b. at Boscawen, 18 Nov 1825; d. 1845.

vi WILLIAM CHAMBERLAIN ELLIOTT, b. at Boscawen, 27 Feb 1827; d. at Pataskala, 1901; m. 1854, AMY BEACH, b. in OH, Oct 1829; Amy d. at Pataskala, 16 Nov 1911.

vii MARY REBEKAH ELLIOTT, b. at Boscawen, 14 Mar 1830; d. at Concord, NH, 9 Nov 1907; m. at Concord, 24 Nov 1857, LUTHER M. MORRILL, b. at Canterbury, 12 Jun 1814 son of Ezekiel and Betsey (Stevens) Morrill; Luther d. at Concord, 7 Jun 1880.

1139) AMOS CHAMBERLAIN *(Rebecca Abbott Chamberlain[4], Rebecca Abbott Abbott[3], Nathaniel[2], George[1])*, b. at Loudon 24 Apr 1788 son of Moses and Rebecca (Abbott) Chamberlain; d. at Loudon, 24 Oct 1818; m. 20 Jan 1812, ELIZABETH "BETSY" WOOD, b. about 1790; Betsey d. after 1850 when she was living in Boscawen. Betsy m. 2nd, 29 Nov 1820, Joseph Baker.

Amos and Betsy lived in Loudon. Amos Chamberlain did not leave a will and his estate entered probate 8 November 1818 with widow Elizabeth requesting that William Chamberlain be named administrator. On 7 September 1820, Eliphalet Wood of Loudon was named guardian for four minor children under age fourteen: Luisa Chamberlain, Julia Ann Chamberlain, Moses Chamberlain, and Eliza Wood Chamberlain. Other documents report payments made from the estate for the support of these four minor children. Real estate was valued at $2,000 and personal estate, $1,015.80. The widow's dower was set off the Betsy Baker 25 November 1833.[3000]

There are five children known for Amos Chamberlain and Betsy Wood, all born at Loudon.[3001]

i LOUISA CHAMBERLAIN, b. about 1813; d. at Fulton County, OH, 1900; m. at Loudon, 7 Oct 1833, SAMUEL HARTFORD DURGIN, b. at Loudon, 16 Jan 1809 son of Samuel and Hannah (Shaw) Durgin; Samuel d. at Fulton County, 1872.

ii JULIA ANN CHAMBERLAIN, b. about 1814; d. at Lucas County, OH, 1892; m. at Lucas County, 1 Feb 1841, AUGUSTUS DAVENPORT WILLIAMS, b. at Tolland, CT, 24 Dec 1805 son of William and Sarah (Burt) Williams; Augustus d. at Waynesfield, OH, 17 Sep 1894.

iii MOSES CHAMBERLAIN, b. about 1815

iv ELIZA WOOD CHAMBERLAIN, b. about 1816; d. 1839.

v AMOS CHAMBERLAIN, d. before 1820 as he is not included in the children who are named a guardian.

1140) WILLIAM CHAMBERLAIN *(Rebecca Abbott Chamberlain[4], Rebecca Abbott Abbott[3], Nathaniel[2], George[1])*, b. 3 Apr 1790 son of Moses and Rebecca (Abbott) Chamberlain; d. at Keene, 13 Apr 1860; m. 9 Nov 1820, MARY ANN BAKER, b. at Loudon, 1805 daughter of Joseph and Anna (Hook) Baker; Mary Ann d. at Fitchburg, 10 Jan 1873.

William Chamberlain was a mechanic in Boscawen and was also in Sanbornton and Keene where he died.

William Chamberlain wrote his will at Sanbornton 1 January 1860. Son William B. Chamberlain receives one hundred dollars, and in addition he is released and discharged from a five hundred-dollar charge against him on his book account. He bequeaths two hundred dollars to each of his daughters Mary C. Whittier and Ann Eliza Freeland. Son William B. Chamberlain receives an undivided third part of a plot of land of Boscawen. Each daughter also receives an undivided third of the same land in Boscawen which is woodland of about 38 acres. Beloved wife Mary Ann receives the use of and income from all his real and personal estate for the remainder of her natural life as long as she does not remarry. Mary Ann also has full

---

[2999] The names of Jane's parents are given on her death record as Joseph Baird and Margery Ferrel.

[3000] *New Hampshire. Probate Court (Rockingham County)*; Probate Place: *Rockingham, New Hampshire, Estate Papers, No 9749-9827, 1818*, Number 9827

[3001] Williams Family Papers Finding Aid, William L. Clements Library Manuscript Division, https://quod.lib.umich.edu/c/clementsmss/umich-wcl-M-4500.1wil?view=text

authority to dispose of the property during her lifetime for the necessities and benefit of their children. After Mary Ann's decease, the estate is to be divided equally among his three children.[3002]

There are four children known for William Chamberlain and Mary Ann Baker. Son William B. Baker was a physician in Worcester, and son-in-law Daniel B. Whittier did early training in medicine with his brother-in-law. Dr. Daniel Whittier attended Harvard Medical School and the New York Homeopathic College.[3003]

i AMOS CHAMBERLAIN, b. 1823; d. at Boscawen, 29 Dec 1846.[3004]

ii WILLIAM B. CHAMBERLAIN, b. at Loudon, about 1828; d. at Worcester, 19 Apr 1889; m. at Boston, 23 Nov 1859, LOUISE BRAINERD, b. at Randolph, VT, 7 Mar 1833 daughter of Asahel and Mariam (Morrill) Brainerd; Louise d. at Worcester, 2 Apr 1913.

iii MARY C. CHAMBERLAIN, b. at Loudon, 23 Aug 1835; d. at Fitchburg, MA, 9 Mar 1915; m. at Sanbornton, 14 Oct 1858, DANIEL BRAINARD WHITTIER, b. at Goffstown, 21 Oct 1834 son of Israel and Fanny Parker (McQuestion) Whittier; Daniel d. at Fitchburg, 16 Ap r1895.

iv ANNA ELIZA CHAMBERLAIN, b. at Canterbury, 1838; d. at Worcester, 11 Oct 1911; m. at Sanbornton, 2 May 1859, JAMES CHESTER FREELAND, b. at Becket, MA, about 1832 son of Chester and Marcia (Austin) Freeland; James d. at Fitchburg, 23 Apr 1871.

1141) MOSES CHAMBERLAIN *(Rebecca Abbott Chamberlain[4], Rebecca Abbott Abbott[3], Nathaniel[2], George[1])*, b. at Loudon, 7 Feb 1792 son of Moses and Rebecca (Abbott) Chamberlain; d. at Three Oaks, MI, 12 Feb 1866; m. 18 Jun 1817, MARY "POLLY" FOSTER, b. at Canterbury, 1 Jan 1797 daughter of Abiel and Susanna (Moore) Foster; Polly d. 18 Jun 1870.

As a young man, Moses Chamberlain worked on his father's farm and in mills. About 1815, he went to Pembroke and engaged in trade until 1835. Moses and Polly had their children in Pembroke. Moses then went to Ohio and Michigan for a year or two and purchased a large tract of land. In 1843, Moses and Polly and four of their children went to Michigan. The tract of land Moses purchased is now Three Oaks, Michigan.[3005] Three Oaks was incorporated in 1867 and Moses's son Henry Chamberlain was the founder of Three Oaks Village.[3006]

In his will written 13 May 1853 (probate 26 Mar 1866), Moses Chamberlain bequeaths to daughter Mary F. the wife of Hale E. Crosby ten dollars which is in addition to what he had previously given her. Son Mellen Chamberlain receives one hundred dollars in addition to previous amounts. Son Henry Chamberlain receives ten dollars. Son William receives the East half of Section Fifteen of Town Eight South and Range Twenty West. This bequest to his son is subject to William providing support for Moses's wife Mary for the remainder of her natural life. If at any time Mary is dissatisfied with the support from William, and if the Judge of Probate of Berrien County finds she has reasonable cause for complaint, then Mary will receive an annual payment of seventy-five dollars paid quarterly. William also receives all the stock animals and tools. Wife Mary Chamberlain receives the rest of the real estate and all of the personal estate. This bequest to Mary is in full satisfaction of her dower thirds. Mary Chamberlain was named executrix.[3007]

There are records of five children of Moses Chamberlain and Polly Foster born at Pembroke.[3008]

i MARY FOSTER CHAMBERLAIN, b. 3 Nov 1818; d. at Three Oaks, MI, 7 Jan 1890; m. Oct 1838, HALE ESTERBROOK CROSBY, b. at Ashburnham, MA, 18 Oct 1816 son of Fitch and Rebecca (Davis) Crosby; Hale d. at Three Oaks, 28 Dec 1900.

ii MELLEN CHAMBERLAIN, b. 4 Jun 1821; d. at Chelsea, MA, 25 Jun 1900; m. 6 Jun 1846, MARTHA ANN PUTNAM, b. at Danvers, 19 Aug 1819 daughter of Jesse and Elizabeth (Merriam) Putnam; Martha d. at Chelsea, 25 Apr 1887.

iii HENRY CHAMBERLAIN, b. 17 Mar 1824; d. at Three Oaks, 9 Feb 1907; m. 1st, at Berrien County, MI, 16 Jan 1851, SARAH JANE NASH, b. at Jefferson County, IN, 11 Sep 1830 daughter of Vincent and Catherine (Magness) Nash; Sarah d. at Three Oaks, 1 Jun 1852. Henry m. 2nd, at Grant, IN, 19 Nov 1856, REBECCA VAN

3002 *New Hampshire. Probate Court (Cheshire County)*; Probate Place: *Cheshire, New Hampshire, Wills, Vol 79-80, 1848-1869*, volume 80, pp 17-18
3003 Bacon, *Men of Progress*, p 616
3004 The gravestone of Amos Chamberlain has engraved he was the son of William and Mary Ann. Findagrave: 186744993
3005 Pierce, *Foster Genealogy, Part I*, p 277
3006 Tatina and Baird, "The Three Oaks of Three Oaks", *Chronicle: Membership Magazine of the Historical Society of Michigan*, Fall 2016, volume 39, no 3
3007 *Michigan Probate Court (Berrien County); Berrien County Historical Association (Berrien Springs, Michigan)*; Probate Place: *Berrien, Michigan, Estate Files, 445-490*
3008 Pierce, *Foster Genealogy*, part I, p 277; detailed information in this family can be found in the Foster Genealogy

DEVENTER, b. at Delaware County, OH, 7 Aug 1825 daughter of Jacob and Lydia (Fee) Van Deventer;[3009] Rebecca d. at Three Oaks, 27 Aug 1896. Rebecca was first married to Joseph Gerrish Ames.

iv ELIZABETH CHAMBERLAIN, b. 18 Oct 1826; d. at Three Oaks, 27 Mar 1850; m. JOHN GARDINER MASON, b. at Sempronius, NY, 13 Apr 1819; d. at Howell, MI, after 1880. After Elizabeth's death, John married Mary.

v WILLIAM CHAMBERLAIN, b. 7 Feb 1834; d. at Jackson, MI, 7 Nov 1901; m. 1857, his first cousin, CAROLINE SAWYER CHAMBERLAIN, b. at Londonderry, NH, 29 Oct 1834 daughter of John Abbot and Polly (Clough) Chamberlain; Caroline d. at Three Oaks, 6 Nov 1926. Caroline Chamberlain is a child in Family 1142.

1142) JOHN ABBOT CHAMBERLAIN *(Rebecca Abbott Chamberlain⁴, Rebecca Abbott Abbott³, Nathaniel², George¹)*, b. at Loudon, 12 Feb 1794 son of Moses and Rebecca (Abbott) Chamberlain; d. at Concord, 28 Feb 1853; m. 10 Dec 1817, POLLY CLOUGH, b. at Canterbury, 16 Jun 1798 daughter of Jeremiah and Martha (Foster) Clough; Polly d. 11 Sep 1856.

After the births of their first two children, John and Polly Chamberlain relocated from Loudon to Canterbury. John was active in the community and deacon of the Congregational church in Canterbury.

John Abbot Chamberlain was active in the anti-slavery movement and was a delegate to the first Free Soil convention in Portsmouth.[3010] He and his wife Polly Clough participated in the Underground Railroad. They received refuges at their farmhouse outside Canterbury and directed them to a safe house along Meredith Ridge in Belknap, New Hampshire.[3011]

In his will written 30 December 1852, John A. Chamberlain bequeathed to beloved wife Polly all the household furniture and two-thirds of all of the estate, both real and mixed. The remainder is to be divided among his four beloved children: Martha C. Bradley, Elizabeth E. Chamberlain, Jeremiah C. Chamberlain, and Caroline S. Chamberlain. His beloved son John has received his full share. Brother William Chamberlain was named sole executor.[3012]

John A. Chamberlain and Polly Clough were the parents of seven children with birth records at Loudon and Londonderry.

i MARTHA CLOUGH CHAMBERLAIN, b. at Loudon, 23 Apr 1820; d. at 3 Oaks, MI, 11 Nov 1902; m. at Canterbury, 28 Sep 1818, her second cousin once removed, THOMAS CURRY BRADLEY *(Abiel F. Bradley⁶, Sarah Foster Bradley⁵, Elizabeth Abbott Foster⁴, John³, John², George¹)*, b. at Canterbury, 28 Sep 1818 son of Abiel Foster and Nancy (Curry) Bradley; Thomas d. at 3 Oaks, 4 May 1886.

ii JOHN CHAMBERLAIN, b. at Loudon, 27 Nov 1821; at Northfield, NH, 1 Jan 1893; m. 1st, 9 May 1848, AMANDA M. JOHNSON, b. 29 Sep 1829; Amanda d. at Bedford, NH, 23 Jul 1867. John m. 2nd, 29 Sep 1868, IRENE BATCHELDER, b. about 1844 daughter of Moses and Mary (Davis) Batchelder; Irene d. at Concord, 16 Mar 1907. After John's death, Irene married Charles Noyes in 1902.

iii MARY GERRISH CHAMBERLAIN, b. at Loudon, 26 Apr 1824; d. at Canterbury, 23 Jul 1843.

iv ELIZABETH EMERY CHAMBERLAIN, b. at Londonderry, 11 Aug 1826; d. at Cass County, MI, 19 Oct 1905; m. at Canterbury, 18 Apr 1854, CYRUS C. RYTHER, b. at Niagara County, NY, 11 Dec 1830 son of Elkenath and Catherine (Corwin) Ryther; Cyrus d. at Cass County, 28 Mar 1915.

v REBECCA ABBOT CHAMBERLAIN, b. at Loudon, 5 Mar 1829; d. at Canterbury, 28 Sep 1843.

vi JEREMIAH C. CHAMBERLAIN, b. at Londonderry, 15 Apr 1832; d. at Chelsea, MA, 17 Aug 1901; m. at Berrien County, MI, 12 Nov 1861, MARY GRACE BURLEIGH, b. in NH, about 1835 daughter of Hilton and Sarah (Gilman) Burleigh; Mary d. at Chelsea, after 1910.

vii CAROLINE SAWYER CHAMBERLAIN, b. at Londonderry, 29 Oct 1834; d. at 3 Oaks, MI, 6 Nov 1926; m. her first cousin, WILLIAM CHAMBERLAIN *(Moses Chamberlain⁵, Rebecca Abbott Chamberlain⁴, Rebecca Abbott Abbott³, Nathaniel², George¹)*, b. at Pembroke, NH, 7 Feb 1834 son of Moses and Mary (Foster) Chamberlain; William d. at Jackson, MI, 7 Nov 1901. William Chamberlain is a child in Family 1141.

1143) BETSY CHAMBERLAIN *(Rebecca Abbott Chamberlain⁴, Rebecca Abbott Abbott³, Nathaniel², George¹)*, b. at Loudon, 31 Aug 1796 daughter of Moses and Rebecca (Abbott) Chamberlain; m. 3 Oct 1815, JOSHUA EMERY, b. 16 May 1788 son of Thomas and Dolly (Sargent) Emery; Joshua d. at Loudon, 21 Jan 1870. Joshua m. 2nd, at Concord, 25 Dec 1826, ELIZA EASTMAN *(Sarah Bradley Eastman⁶, Sarah Foster Bradley⁵, Elizabeth Abbott Foster⁴, John³, John², George¹)*,[3013] b. at

---

[3009] Van Deventer, The Van Deventer Family, p 84

[3010] Lyford, History of Canterbury, volume II, p 54

[3011] Snodgrass, Mary Ellen. 2015. *The Underground Railroad: An Encyclopedia of People, Places, and Operations*, Routledge.

[3012] *New Hampshire. Probate Court (Merrimack County)*; Probate Place: *Merrimack, New Hampshire, Probate Records, Vol 25, 1847-1856*, p 353, will of John A. Chamberlain

[3013] Emery, *Genealogical Records of Descendants of John and Anthony Emery*, p 79, suggests Joshua married Betsy Abbott in between Betsy Chamberlain and Eliza Eastman, but that may not be correct. Stearns *Genealogical and Family History of the State of New Hampshire*, volume 3, p 1501, gives Joshua's wives as Betsy Chamberlain, Eliza Eastman, and Lydia Towle.

Concord, 24 Apr 1801 daughter of Charles and Sarah (Bradley) Eastman; Eliza d. at Loudon, 18 Mar 1854. Joshua married a third time, perhaps to Ruth Hayes (widow of Nathan Towle who died in 1851).

Joshua Emery was a cabinet maker in Loudon.[3014]

Joshua Emery and Betsy Chamberlain were parents of four children born at Loudon, New Hampshire.

i JOHN CHAMBERLAIN EMERY, b. Aug 1816; d. at Montpelier, VT, 27 Dec 1888; m. at Loudon, 4 Feb 1847, MARY MORSE BROWN, b. at Loudon, 27 Apr 1817 daughter of Levi and Mary (Morse) Brown;[3015] Mary d. at Montpelier, 19 Mar 1913.

ii WILLIAM C. EMERY, b. 31 Aug 1819; d. at Montpelier, 11 Jun 1882. William did not marry. The probate of his estate was administered by John C. Emery his "brother and only heir."

iii ELIZABETH EMERY, b. 23 Jan 1822; d. 1833.

iv THOMAS EMERY, b. 24 Jan 1824; d. 1846.

Joshua Emery and Eliza Eastman were parents of three children born at Loudon.

i CHARLES E. EMERY, b. 8 Oct 1827; d. 1849.

ii ROBERT A. EMERY, b. 18 Jun 1831; d. about 1866. In 1850, he was living with his half-brother John C. Emery in Montpelier.

iii ELLEN M. EMERY, b. 18 Dec 1842; d. 25 Jun 1881. Ellen did not marry. She was a teacher.

1144) SAMUEL CHAMBERLAIN *(Rebecca Abbott Chamberlain[4], Rebecca Abbott Abbott[3], Nathaniel[2], George[1])*, b. at Loudon, 16 Jun 1799 son of Moses and Rebecca (Abbott) Chamberlain; d. at Loudon, 3 Nov 1838; m. 20 Nov 1823, MARTHA GERRISH, b. at Boscawen, 26 Nov 1809 daughter of Jacob and Sarah (Ames) Gerrish. Martha m. 2nd, 10 Nov 1839, Reuel Walker. Martha d. 1867 (probate of estate 1867).

Samuel Chamberlain did not leave a will and his estate entered probate December 1838 with widow Martha as administratrix. In January 1840, Jacob Gerrish assumed administration of the estate after Martha remarried. The real estate was valued at $2,200.00 including the homestead farm worth $1,900.00 The personal estate was valued at $951.19.[3016]

Samuel and Martha Chamberlain had three children born at Loudon.

i MARTHA ANN CHAMBERLAIN, b. 1 Mar 1824; d. at Los Angeles, 28 Sep 1910; m. about 1846, ORVILLE MESSER, b. about 1820 son of Amos and Sarah (Colby) Messer; Orville d. at Laconia, 1847. Martha did not remarry. She lived with her mother and stepfather until her mother's death. She then lived with her brother Jacob in Ohio and then in Los Angeles. In her later life, she is listed as a boarder in Los Angeles.[3017]

ii SAMUEL WOOD CHAMBERLAIN, b. 19 Mar 1827; d. at 3 Oaks, MI, 17 Oct 1865; m. at Lebanon, NH, 1 Jan 1850, SARAH W. KENDRICK, b. at Lebanon, 14 Feb 1831 daughter of Egbert Benson and Emma (Wood) Kendrick; Sarah d. 30 Aug 1870.[3018]

iii JACOB GERRISH CHAMBERLAIN, b. 11 Sep 1829; d. at Los Angeles, 30 May 1897; m. 1852, HARRIET BUGBEE, b. at Stockton, NY, 8 Mar 1830 daughter of Andrew and Harriet (Putnam) Bugbee; Harriet d. at Windber, PA, 10 Jul 1908.[3019]

[3014] Stearns, *Genealogical and Family History of New Hampshire*, volume 3, p 1501

[3015] The 1854 will of Levi Brown includes a bequest to his daughter Mary M. Emery wife of John C. Emery.

[3016] New Hampshire, County Probate Records, 1660-1973, Merrimack County, Case number 1572, Samuel Chamberlain, 14:17, 12:298, 13:37, 6:466, 15:33, accessed through familysearch.org

[3017] Martha's gravestone includes that she was born in Loudon and the date of birth; findagrave ID: 71957894

[3018] Stearns, *Genealogical and Family History of New Hampshire*, volume I, p 304

[3019] *Pennsylvania, Death Certificates, 1906-1966*, Pennsylvania Historic and Museum Commission; Pennsylvania, USA; Pennsylvania, Death Certificates, 1906-1965; Certificate Number Range: 066801-070600. Parents names of Andrew Bugbee and Harriet Putnam are given on death certificate.

Great-Grandchildren of Elizabeth Abbott and Nathan Stevens

1145) MOLLY PARKER *(Mary Stevens Parker⁴, Nathan Stevens³, Elizabeth Abbott Stevens², George¹)*, b. at Bradford, MA, 18 Oct 1743 daughter of Samuel and Mary (Stevens) Parker; d. at Bradford, 21 Feb 1842; m. by 1768, JOHN CURTIS, b. 19 Apr 1743 whose parentage in unclear;[3020] John d. at Bradford 3 Apr 1826.

John Curtis and Molly Parker were parents of four children born at Bradford, Massachusetts.

i WILLIAM CURTIS, b. 10 Mar 1768; d. at Dunbarton, NH, 28 Apr 1839; m. at Bradford, 28 Oct 1797, SARAH "SALLY" CHANDLER, b. 1774; Sally d. at Dunbarton, 12 Mar 1847.

ii JOHN BRITTAN CURTIS, b. 1773; d. at Mercer, ME, after 1860; m. at Boxford, 6 Dec 1795, MARGARET "PEGGY" ROBINSON, b. at Boxford, 22 May 1774 daughter of Asa and Margaret (Hovey) Robinson; Peggy d. at Mercer, 1860.

iii NATHANIEL CURTIS, b. about 1790; d. at Lowell, after 1855; m. at Sutton, NH, 11 Jul 1820, LYDIA HILLS FOWLER, b. about 1796 daughter of Benjamin and Sarah (Stevens) Fowler; Lydia d. at Lowell, 21 Dec 1858.

iv LYDIA CURTIS, b. 18 Mar 1791; d. at Groveland, MA, 21 Apr 1876; m. at Rowley, MA, 9 Mar 1820, JOSIAH GOODRIDGE TYLER, b. at Newburyport, 26 Jul 1797 son of Isaac and Dorcas (Goodridge) Tyler; Josiah d. at Groveland, 20 Jun 1881.

1146) ANNA PARKER *(Mary Stevens Parker⁴, Nathan Stevens³, Elizabeth Abbott Stevens², George¹)*, b. at Bradford, MA, 28 May 1747 daughter of Samuel and Mary (Stevens) Parker; d. at Haverhill, MA, 30 Sep 1824; m. 20 Sep 1770, NATHAN PARKER, b. 14 Jul 1740 son of Nathan and Hannah (Stevens) Parker; Nathan d. 1779 (date of probate 1 Feb 1779).

Nathan did not leave a will. Widow Anna was administratrix. The estate was declared insolvent. Anna Parker and Nathan Parker were parents of two children born at Andover.

i FREDERICK PARKER, b. 20 Jan 1771; d. at Haverhill, 8 Jul 1820; m. at Haverhill, 5 Mar 1796, ABIGAIL BOROUGHS who has not been identified. Frederick and Abigail did not have children. The probate of his estate gave heirs as widow Abigail, mother Anna Parker, and sister Nancy Parker. It is possible that Abigail was the Mrs. Abigail Parker who married Deacon Moses Brown in Haverhill in 1832.

ii ANNA "NANCY" PARKER, b. Sep 1772; she was living and unmarried at the probate of her brother's estate in 1820.

1147) SAMUEL PARKER *(Mary Stevens Parker⁴, Nathan Stevens³, Elizabeth Abbott Stevens², George¹)*, b. at Bradford, MA, 28 Jul 1753 son of Samuel and Mary (Stevens) Parker; d. at Bradford, 12 Jun 1822; m. 27 Mar 1777, ANNA GREENOUGH, b. at Bradford, 30 Apr 1754 daughter of William and Hannah (Atwood) Greenough; Anna d. at Bradford, 1 Oct 1830.

Samuel Parker and Anna Greenough were parents of seven children born at Bradford.

i NATHAN PARKER, b. 19 Jul 1777; d. at Bradford, 1841; m. 4 Aug 1800, ABIGAIL BURBANK, b. at Bradford, 11 Jun 1782 daughter of Stephen and Bette (Hopkinson) Burbank; Abigail d. at Bradford, 11 Dec 1847.

ii ABIGAIL PARKER, b. 16 Oct 1779; d. at Westport, NY, after 1850; m. at Bradford, 10 Aug 1801, JOSEPH HILL ORDWAY, b. at Haverhill, 1 Apr 1779 son of Edward and Elizabeth (Eaton) Ordway; Joseph d. at Westport, about 1866 (probate 16 Apr 1866).

iii SARAH PARKER, b. 17 Apr 1782; d. at Groveland, MA, 16 Jan 1857; m. at Bradford, 2 Jul 1806, ELIJAH CLARKE, b. at Topsfield, 22 Jan 1779 son of Daniel and Hannah (Perley) Clarke; Elijah d. at Groveland, 29 Mar 1857.

iv THEODORE PARKER, b. 5 Dec 1784; d. at Groveland, 5 Feb 1872; m. 1st, at Bradford, 15 Sep 1807, MARY "POLLY" MARDEN, b. at Bradford, 5 Nov 1786 daughter of David and Mary (Marden) Marden; Polly d. at Bradford, 8 Nov 1825. Theodore m. 2nd, at Bradford, 8 Dec 1828, ELIZABETH SPOFFORD (widow of Joseph Noyes), b. at Georgetown, MA, 13 Jan 1789 daughter of Jacob and Mary (Tenney) Spofford; Elizabeth d. at Bradford, 4 Nov 1832. Theodore m. 3rd, at Bradford, 29 Dec 1833, HANNAH HARDY, b. at Bradford, 20 Sep 1795 daughter of Jacob and Hannah (Hardy) Hardy; Hannah d. at Groveland, 23 Dec 1868.

[3020] 1743 is the year of birth based on age at time of death. The 19 Apr 1743 date is used by the DAR.

v DEAN PARKER, b. 18 Mar 1788; d. at Bradford, 3 Oct 1814. Dean did not marry.

vi WILLIAM PARKER, b. 17 Mar 1791; d. at Groveland, 24 Jul 1868; m. at Bradford, 7 Nov 1815, ABIGAIL HOPKINSON, b. at Bradford, 28 Jun 1796 daughter of Silas and Hannah (Balch) Hopkinson; Abigail d. at Groveland, 16 Sep 1867.

vii ANNA PARKER, b. 15 Nov 1799; d. at Groveland, 18 Aug 1890; m. at Bradford, 30 Apr 1822, DANIEL BALCH STICKNEY, b. at Bradford, 21 Jul 1798 son of Daniel and Sarah (Balch) Stickney; Daniel d. at Groveland, 17 Dec 1863.

1148) JOHN TYLER *(Hannah Stevens Tyler[4], Nathan Stevens[3], Elizabeth Abbott Stevens[2], George[1])*, b. at Boxford, Mar 1744/5 son of Abner and Hannah (Stevens) Tyler; d. at Bakersfield, VT (while visiting his son), 17 Feb 1813; m. at Brookfield, Apr 1771, RACHEL CROSBY, b. at Billerica, 15 Sep 1751 daughter of David Crosby;[3021] Rachel d. at Brookfield, MA, 6 Apr 1817.

John Tyler was a farmer in Brookfield. He did not leave a will and son John Tyler was named administrator 5 March 1813. Personal estate was valued at $817.18 and real estate totaled $3,155 including the home farm valued at $3,000. Total debts were $3.131.39. The widow's dower was set off to Rachel Tyler. The estate was sold to settle the debts.[3022]

John Tyler and Rachel Crosby were parents of six children born at Brookfield.

i ROYAL TYLER, b. 30 Aug 1772; m. at Brookfield, 19 Sep 1793, PHEBE DOANE, b. at Eastham, 1774 daughter of Benjamin and Ruth (Smith) Doane.[3023] Royal and Phebe lived in Geneva, NY.

ii ELI TYLER, b. 1 Mar 1774. Eli was a physician in Malone, NY. He did not marry.

iii POLLY TYLER, b. 10 Jul 1776; d. at Ware, MA, 19 Jul 1833; m. 1st, 21 Sep 1796, MICHAEL BRIGHAM, b. at North Brookfield, 2 Mar 1772 son of Jonas and Hannah (Draper) Brigham; Michael d. at Bakersfield, VT, 19 Sep 1802. Polly m. 2nd, 17 Apr 1805, WILLIAM BOWDOIN; William d. at Ware, 23 Sep 1831.

iv SALLY TYLER, b. 20 Sep 1778; d. at Brookfield, 14 Oct 1805; m. 17 Feb 1801, SILAS BALL, perhaps b. at Rutland, MA, 23 Oct 1777 son of Zerubabel and Mary (Bruce) Ball.

v JOHN TYLER, b. 20 Nov 1780; d. at North Brookfield, 23 Aug 1857; m. 1st, 25 Apr 1813, ELIZABETH HILL, b. at Brookfield, 15 Sep 1785 daughter of Thomas and Eleanor (Bartlett) Hill;[3024] Elizabeth d. 4 Nov 1819. John m. 2nd, 15 Apr 1821, MYRA BAILEY, b. at Berlin, MA, 15 Nov 1795 daughter of Stephen and Sarah (Crosby) Bailey; Myra d. at North Brookfield, 21 Nov 1868.

vi ABNER TYLER, b. 4 Aug 1785; d. at Malone, NY, May 1840; m. at Barnard, VT, 5 Feb 1812, DEBORAH TUPPER, b. 1790 daughter of Israel and Deborah (Tobey) Tupper.

1149) GIDEON TYLER *(Hannah Stevens Tyler[4], Nathan Stevens[3], Elizabeth Abbott Stevens[2], George[1])*, b. 8 Jul 1747; d. at Brookfield, 1832 son of Abner and Hannah (Stevens) Tyler; m. 1 Sep 1766, ESTHER HILL daughter of Peter and Sarah (Woodbury) Hill.[3025]

Gideon Tyler was a farmer in Brookfield. *The Tyler Genealogy* reports nine children in this family all born at Brookfield, Massachusetts.[3026] Three of the children were reported as dying young. Birth years of the other children are estimates based on time of marriage or age at death.

i WARREN TYLER; died young

ii ABNER TYLER; died young

iii THEODORE TYLER; died young

[3021] Brigham, *Tyler Genealogy, the Descendants of Job Tyler*, p 118
[3022] Worcester County, MA: Probate File Papers, 1731-1881. Online database. AmericanAncestors.org. New England Historic Genealogical Society, 2015. Case 60391
[3023] Doane, *The Doane Family*, p 99
[3024] Adams, *Genealogical Register of North Brookfield*, p 625
[3025] Temple, *History of North Brookfield*, p 625
[3026] Brigham, *The Tyler Genealogy*, p 119

iv PHINEAS TYLER, b. about 1770; d. before 1848 (when his wife died as a widow); m. 30 Mar 1794, JOANNA BARNES, b. at North Brookfield, 18 May 1774 daughter of Jonathan and Dorothy (How) Barnes; Joanna d. at Braintree, 27 Apr 1848.

v NATHAN TYLER, b. about 1770; possibly m. at Warren, MA, 20 Feb 1798, PHEBE BLISS.[3027]

vi JOSHUA TYLER, b. about 1780; possibly m. at Brookfield, 26 Nov 1807, PRUDENCE SANDERS.

vii AMOS TYLER, b. 1784; d. at Hinsdale, MA, 4 Jul 1838; m. at Pelham, NH, 5 Dec 1807, PERSIS NICKOLS, b. at Brookfield, 19 Mar 1764 daughter of James and Ruth (Rich) Nickols; Persis d. at Hinsdale, 26 Aug 1853. Persis was first married to Jonathan Larrabee.

viii ESTHER TYLER, b. 1784; d. at North Brookfield, Mar 1853; m. 1st, 17 Mar 1814, as his second wife, THADDEUS DODGE, b. at Brookfield, 17 Jun 1758 son of Joshua and Thankful (Morse) Dodge; Thaddeus d. at Brookfield, 18 Feb 1837. Esther m. 2nd, as his second wife, EPHRAIM DEWING, b. at North Brookfield, about 1785 son of Solomon and Lydia (Pickard) Dewing; Ephraim d. at North Brookfield, 12 Jan 1855. Thaddeus Dodge was first married to Susan Halloway. Ephraim Dewing was first married to Jemima Hinds and third married to Catherine O'Neal.

ix MARY "POLLY" TYLER, b. about 1785; d. at Brookfield, 24 Nov 1858; m. at Brookfield, 8 Oct 1809, PHINEAS GILBERT, b. at Brookfield, 1 Oct 1779 son of Lemuel and Ruth (Gilbert) Gilbert; Phineas d. at Brookfield, 25 Jan 1834.

1150) HANNAH TYLER *(Hannah Stevens Tyler[1], Nathan Stevens[3], Elizabeth Abbott Stevens[2], George[1])*, b. at Brookfield, 15 Feb 1749 daughter of Abner and Hannah (Stevens) Tyler; d. at Gorham, NY, 21 May 1815; m. 27 Feb 1769, THOMAS TUFTS, b. at West Brookfield, 1749; Thomas d. at Gorham, 21 Jul 1811.

Hannah and Thomas were in Brookfield and later in Gorham, New York. There are birth/baptism records for seven children at Brookfield, although the family baptized several children on a single date, so it is not known when they were born in most cases. Marriages were located for just two children.

i THOMAS TUFTS, baptized 18 Apr 1773; likely died young.

ii BETTY TUFTS, baptized 18 Apr 1773

iii SARAH TUFTS, b. 12 Jun 1780; d. at Gorham, NY, 4 May 1860; m. JONATHAN STEARNS,[3028] b. at Upton, MA, 28 Jun 1781 son of Ebenezer and Rebecca (Lackey) Stearns; Jonathan d. at Gorham, 7 Apr 1863.

iv THOMAS TUFTS, b. 17 Jun 1783; d. at Gorham, NY, 19 Mar 1866; m. about 1818, CLARISSA HATFIELD, b. 1799 daughter of Mason and Elizabeth (-) Hatfield; Clarissa d. at Gorham, 5 Jul 1847. The children of Thomas and Clarissa Tufts include Mason Tufts.

v SUKEY TUFTS, baptized 10 Mar 1799

vi HANNAH TUFTS, baptized 10 Mar 1799

vii PATTY TUFTS, baptized 10 Mar 1799

1151) MARY "MOLLY" TYLER *(Hannah Stevens Tyler[1], Nathan Stevens[3], Elizabeth Abbott Stevens[2], George[1])*, b. at Brookfield, 1 Sep 1753 daughter of Abner and Hannah (Stevens) Tyler; d. at Chesterfield, NH, 16 Dec 1842; m. 9 May 1775, SAMUEL HAMILTON who was born in Ireland about 1752;[3029] Samuel d. at Chesterfield, 12 Feb 1810.

Samuel Hamilton was the son of a linen weaver and merchant. He came to Chesterfield, New Hampshire between 1780 and 1785 where he had a farm. He was also a linen weaver.[3030]

Samuel Hamilton did not leave a will and son Samuel was administrator of the estate. The following heirs, the children of Samuel, each received a payment of $133.44: John Hamilton, Hannah wife of Joseph Hill, Hance Hamilton, Loami Hamilton, James Hamilton, Ara Hamilton, Fanny Hamilton, Uri Hamilton, and Amadella Hamilton. The widow's dower was set off to Molly.[3031]

Molly Tyler and Samuel Hamilton were parents of ten children all born at Chesterfield.

[3027] Nathan Tyler "of Brookfield" married Phebe Bliss
[3028] Aldrich, *History of Ontario County, New York*, p 179
[3029] Bolton, *Immigrants to New England 1700-1775*, p 81
[3030] Randall, *History of Chesterfield*, p 328
[3031] *New Hampshire. Probate Court (Cheshire County)*; Probate Place: *Cheshire, New Hampshire, Estate Files, H136-H208, 1806-1813*, case 176, probate of Samuel Hamilton.

i JOHN HAMILTON, b. 11 Jul 1775; d. at Windham, VT, 29 Sep 1827; m. AMY CHURCHILL, b. 1773; Amy d. at Windham, 30 Aug 1861.

ii HANNAH HAMILTON, b. about 1777; d. at Madison, OH, after 1850; m. about 1797, JOSEPH HILL, b. 1765; Joseph d. at Madison, 23 Oct 1823.

iii HANCE HAMILTON, b. 18 Mar 1780; d. at Weston, VT, 11 May 1859; m. 12 Sep 1809, BETSY MARK, b. at Gilsum, NH, 15 Aug 1779 daughter of John and Ann (McCurdy) Mark; Betsy d. at Weston, 15 Aug 1870.

iv LOAMMI HAMILTON, b. 11 May 1782; d. likely at Northampton, MA; m. at Northampton, 17 Nov 1805, RUTH WILDER, b. at Northampton, about 1786 daughter of Shubael and Sarah (Wright) Wilder; Ruth d. at Northampton, 7 Sep 1836.

v JAMES HAMILTON, b. 3 Feb 1784; d. at Chittenango, NY, 3 Apr 1872; m. at Richmond, NH, 3 Aug 1817, REBECCA BACON, b. in RI, 4 Jan 1790; Rebecca d. at Chittenango, 17 Mar 1880.

vi SAMUEL HAMILTON, b. 22 Jan 1787; d. at Chesterfield, 19 Oct 1878; m. at Surry, 14 Mar 1814, POLLY MCCURDY, b. at Surry, 25 Jul 1788 daughter of John and Sarah (Watts) McCurdy; Polly d. at Chesterfield, 12 Mar 1872.

vii ARA HAMILTON, b. 22 May 1789; d. at Chesterfield, 24 Jul 1865; m. 8 Feb 1815, SALLY ROBERTSON, b. at Chesterfield, 30 Jul 1794 daughter of James and Ede (Fasset) Robertson; Sally d. 11 Dec 1823. Asa m. 2nd, Feb 1824, ALMIRA FULLAM, b. 8 May 1806 daughter of Phineas and Bathsheba (Britton) Fullam; Almira d. at Chesterfield, 24 Apr 1883.

viii FANNY HAMILTON, b. 1 Jul 1791; d. about 1813. Fanny did not marry.

ix URIAH HAMILTON, b. 27 Apr 1793; d. at Pavilion, MI, 15 Oct 1844; m. about 1827, MARY JENKINS, b. in CT, about 1807; Mary d. at Comstock, MI, after 1860.

x AMADELLA HAMILTON, b. Aug 1796; m. VERANUS ALLEN. The family was in Madison, Ohio in 1830.

1152) MOSES TYLER *(Hannah Stevens Tyler⁴, Nathan Stevens³, Elizabeth Abbott Stevens², George¹)*, b. at Brookfield, 16 Mar 1756 son of Abner and Hannah (Stevens) Tyler; d. at Brookfield, 8 Mar 1825; m. REBECCA TRUANT, b. about 1760; d. 17 Feb 1817. Rebecca's parents are not known. She is likely from the Trouant family of Plymouth County, the Trouants being early settlers in Marshfield.

In his will written 1 February 1818 (proved 12 April 1825), Moses Tyler bequeaths one hundred dollars to daughter Betsey Howe, the house farm to son David Tyler, $1,100 to son Eli Tyler to be paid by David from the estate, $1,100 to son Warren to be paid by David, $600 to daughter Hannah Tyler, $500 to daughter Matilda Tyler, and $300 to daughter Polly the wife of Joseph Dean. There are other stipulations regarding the division of the household furniture and personal estate and son Eli receives all the residue of the estate. Son Eli was named executor.[3032]

Moses Tyler and Rebecca Truant were parents of ten children born at Brookfield, Massachusetts.

i ELIZABETH TYLER, b. 25 Apr 1779; d. after 1839 (living at the time of her second husband's death); m. 1st, at Brookfield, 25 Mar 1802, ABRAHAM HOWE, b. at North Brookfield, 13 Oct 1776 son of Eli and Elizabeth (Smith) Howe; Abraham d. before 1818. Elizabeth m. 2nd, 1818, ZADOK HINSDALE, b. at East Hartford, Apr 1763 son of Isaac and Leah (Merry) Hinsdale;[3033] Zadok d. at East Granby, CT, 3 Apr 1839.

ii DAVID TYLER, b. 20 Aug 1781; d. at North Brookfield, 29 Feb 1864; m. 13 Feb 1817, NANCY BARTLETT, b. at North Brookfield, 16 May 1798 daughter of Wyman and Elizabeth (Smith) Bartlett; Nancy d. at North Brookfield, 29 Apr 1866.

iii HANNAH TYLER, b. 9 Feb 1783; d. at West Brookfield, 24 May 1878. Hannah did not marry.

iv POLLY TYLER, b. 20 Feb 1785; d. at West Brookfield, 7 Dec 1862; m. 23 Nov 1814, JOSEPH DANE, b. at North Brookfield, 7 Oct 1782 don of Joseph and Lucy (Gilbert) Dane; Joseph d. at West Brookfield, 17 Apr 1863.

v MOSES TYLER, b. 28 Apr 1787; d. 12 Jun 1807.

3032 *Probate Records (Worcester County, Massachusetts); Index 1731-1881*, volume 59, pp 29-30

3033 Barbour, *Families of Early Hartford*, p 306

vi ELI TYLER, b. 25 Mar 1789; d. at West Brookfield, 1 Jul 1858; m. at Brookfield, 8 Oct 1820, CLARISSA WHITE, b. 1798; Clarissa d. at Est Brookfield, 21 Sep 1871.

vii MELINDA TYLER, b. 7 Sep 1791; d. at West Brookfield, 1 Feb 1872; m. 20 Sep 1821, GEORGE WYLLYS, b. at Hartford, CT, 28 Aug 1787 son of Hezekiah and Amelia (-) Wyllys; George d. at Hartford, 27 Jun 1822.

viii PATTY TYLER, b. 21 Sep 1795; d. 8 Oct 1796.

ix WARREN TYLER, b. 11 Sep 1797; d. at Natchez, MS, Jun 1822[3034] (probate 23 Sep 1822 Adams County, MS).

x FANNY TYLER, b. 12 Mar 1800; d. 15 Sep 1805.

1153) JOSHUA TYLER *(Hannah Stevens Tyler[1], Nathan Stevens[3], Elizabeth Abbott Stevens[2], George[1])*, b. at Brookfield, MA, 12 Aug 1758 son of Abner and Hannah (Stevens) Tyler; d. at Chesterfield, NH, 11 Jun 1807; m. 1780, JUDITH AYERS, b. at Brookfield, 12 Jan 1763 daughter of Onesiphorus and Anna (Goodale) Ayers; Judith d. at Chesterfield, 11 Aug 1854.

Dr. Joshua Tyler was a physician who came to Chesterfield between 1776 and 1781.[3035] Joshua Tyler and Judith Ayers were parents of fourteen children all born at Chesterfield, New Hampshire.

i JOSHUA TYLER, b. 16 Aug 1781; d. at Clara, PA, 19 Mar 1858; m. 1st, at Chesterfield, 2 Oct 1803, LYDIA FARR, b. at Chesterfield, 28 Jan 1783 daughter of William and Lydia (Trowbridge) Farr; Lydia d. at Chesterfield, 13 Jan 1805. Joshua m. 2nd, about 1810, LOIS BACON, b. about 1791 daughter of Philip and Lydia (Wilson) Bacon;[3036] Lois d. at Clara, PA, after 1880.

ii JUDITH TYLER, b. 4 Dec 1782; d. at Burlington, VT, 12 Mar 1843; m. at Chesterfield, 8 Dec 1806, DANIEL DAVIS, b. 1785; Daniel d. at Burlington, 16 Aug 1860.

iii JASON TYLER, b. 21 Jan 1784; d. at Keene, 10 Mar 1843; m. THIRZY KING, b. at Chesterfield, 7 May 1785 daughter of Samuel and Molly (Whitney) King; Thirzy d. at Winchester, NH, 18 Aug 1852.

iv AYERS TYLER, b. 5 Sep 1785; d. 1787.

v MARTHA "PATTY" TYLER, b. 14 Jan 1787; d. at Tunkhannock, PA, after 1860; m. at Chesterfield, 10 Apr 1808, JOSHUA KELLY; Joshua d. at Tunkhannock, after 1860.

vi ANNA AYERS TYLER, b. 8 Sep 1789; d. at Chesterfield, 14 Apr 1868. Anna did not marry.

vii BETSEY TYLER, b. 29 Aug 1791; d. at Chesterfield, 31 Mar 1872; m. 1st, KING. Betsey m. 2nd, ATWOOD.[3037] Betsey m. 3rd, 8 Mar 1850, ANDREW COMMINGS, b. about 1777; Andrew d. after 1850 when he was living in Cornish, NH.

viii BUCKLEY O. TYLER, b. 13 May 1793; d. 1794.

ix JOSEPH WARREN TYLER, b. 9 Dec 1795; d. at Hinsdale, NH, 23 Nov 1849; m. ELEANOR THOMAS, b. at Hinsdale, 8 Apr 1804; d. at Hinsdale, 18 Sep 1890.

x BUCKLEY OLCOTT TYLER, b. 13 Feb 1798; d. at Montpelier, VT, 21 May 1878; m. 8 Dec 1824, MARY TOWNE, b. at Windsor, 7 Apr 1807 daughter of Benjamin and Sarah (Burt) Towne; Mary d. at Montpelier, 26 Jun 1851.

xi FANNY S. TYLER, b. 14 Sep 1799; d. at Chesterfield, 1837.

xii ROYAL TYLER, b. 21 Jan 1801; d. 1803.

xiii ROLSTON TYLER, b. 14 Aug 1804; d. 1804.

xiv ROLSTON GOODELL TYLER, b. 7 Aug 1805; d. at Orange, MA, 19 Aug 1882; m. MARY JANE DUDLEY.

1154) MARTHA "PATTY" TYLER *(Hannah Stevens Tyler[1], Nathan Stevens[3], Elizabeth Abbott Stevens[2], George[1])*, b. at Brookfield, 13 Jan 1761 daughter of Abner and Hannah (Stevens) Tyler; d. about 1787; m. at Brookfield, 3 Jun 1781, JOHN HUBBARD, b. at Leicester, 14 Mar 1761 son of Daniel and Elizabeth (Lynde) Hubbard; John d. at Batavia, NY 5 Dec 1849.[3038] John had at least two further marriages to Eunice Moore and Patience Wheeler.

Dr. John Hubbard enlisted as a private in 1777 for a term of two years of service in the Revolution in the Massachusetts line. John received a pension based on his service and following his death, his widow Patience Wheeler Hubbard continued the pension.[3039]

3034 Tyler, *Tyler Genealogy*, p 120
3035 Randal, *History of Chesterfield*, p 473
3036 Randall, *History of Chesterfield*, p 221
3037 Marriages are as given in The Tyler Genealogy but records were not located.
3038 10,000 Vital Records of Western New York, 1809-1850
3039 Revolutionary War Pension and Bounty-Land Warrant Application Files, 1800-1900

Patty Tyler and John Hubbard were parents of three children likely all born at Salem, New York.

i JOHN HUBBARD, b. 31 Dec 1781; nothing further known

ii DANIEL HUBBARD, b. 22 Jan 1784; d. at Providence, RI, 1840; m. at Holden, MA, 23 Apr 1806, TAMISON WHEATON, b. at Leicester, MA, 12 Mar 1784 daughter of Christopher and Abigail (Brewer) Wheaton; Tamison d. at Providence, 5 Jan 1865.

iii POLLY HUBBARD, b. 1786; d. at Jackson County, MI (where she was living with her daughter), 14 Apr 1866; m. 1st, at Salem, NY, 9 Apr 1807, JOHN HUGGINS, b. about 1782; John d. at Salem, about 1815. Polly m. 2nd, DANIEL DEMOTT, b. about 1786; Daniel d. at Pembroke, NY, after 1850.

1155) ABIGAIL TYLER *(Hannah Stevens Tyler[1], Nathan Stevens[3], Elizabeth Abbott Stevens[2], George[1])*, b. at Brookfield, 5 Dec 1763 daughter of Abner and Hannah (Stevens) Tyler; m. at Brookfield, 14 Sep 1783, JESSE AYERS, b. at Brookfield, 8 Oct 1763 son of Moses and Sarah (Converse) Ayers; Jesse d. at Leverett, 26 Jul 1844.

Abigail Tyler and Jesse Ayers were parents of eleven children, the births of the oldest two children at Brookfield, Massachusetts and the remainder at Leverett.

i HANNAH AYERS, b. 7 Feb 1784; d. at Chester, about 1820; m. at Leverett, 16 Apr 1808, HENRY WARNER, b. at Chester, 15 May 1789 son of James and Achsah (Sanderson) Warner; Henry d. at Middlefield, MA, 11 Apr 1838. Henry second married Beulah White.

ii SARAH "SALLY" AYERS, b. 29 Jan 1786; d. at Hinsdale, MA, 13 Sep 1875; m. (intention 25 Feb 1812), LUTHER COLE, b. at Peru, MA, 13 Mar 1783 son of Ezra and Susan (Cole) Cole; Luther d. at Hinsdale, 8 Nov 1866.

iii JOHN AYERS, b. 21 May 1788; d. at Erie, PA, 10 Nov 1878; m. MIRANDA who has not been identified, b. in Massachusetts, about 1795; Miranda d. at Erie, 1866.

iv MARY AYERS, b. 20 Jun 1790; d. of typhoid fever, at Leverett, 9 Oct 1857; m. JOHN COMINGS, b. at Spencer, MA, 27 Apr 1799 son of Gershom and Ruth (Newton) Comings; John d. at Amherst, MA, 16 Feb 1880.

v MOSES AYERS, b. 20 Aug 1792; d. at Peru, MA, 15 Mar 1874; m. 1st, at Peru, MA, 24 Mar 1815, JANE N. GAMWELL, b. at Chester, 19 Jun 1790 daughter of John and Jane (-) Gamwell; Jane d. at Hawley, 23 Apr 1854. Moses m. 2nd, at Hawley, 13 Aug 1857, LOVINA SQUIRE, b. at Hinsdale, 21 Dec 1815 daughter of Solomon and Betsey (Whitney) Squire; Lovina d. at Hinsdale, 25 Feb 1900.

vi JESSE AYERS, b. 23 Apr 1795; d. at Springfield, NY, 19 May 1888; m. NANCY C. who has not been identified, b. in MA, 1797; Nancy d. at Springfield, 22 Feb 1863.

vii ABIGAIL AYERS, b. 5 Oct 1797

viii BETSEY AYERS, b. 26 Dec 1800; d. 26 Oct 1803.

ix TYLER AYERS, b. 26 Apr 1804; d. at Pittsfield, MA, 12 May 1882; m. MARIAM JANE POTTER, b. at Stephentown, NY, 1808; Mariam d. at Pittsfield, 1880.

x GEORGE AYERS, b. 19 Aug 1807; d. at Monson, MA, 9 Dec 1888; m. at Shutesbury, MA, 5 Oct 1828, ABIGAIL JUCKET, b. at Shutesbury, about 1813 daughter of Daniel and Judith (Kimball) Jucket;[3040] Abigail d. at Monson, 23 May 1887.

xi ELI AYERS, b. 25 Jul 1810

1156) SAMUEL AMES *(Elizabeth Stevens Ames[4], Nathan Stevens[3], Elizabeth Abbott Stevens[2], George[1])*, b. at Andover, 19 Sep 1746 son of Samuel and Elizabeth (Stevens) Ames; d. at Epsom, NH, 1792; m. at Andover, 10 Jul 1770, his second cousin once removed, ABIGAIL STEVENS, b. at Andover, 28 Oct 1752 daughter of David and Abigail (Martin) Stevens.

Samuel Ames resided in Epsom and was there by 1774, and his father deeded property to him in 1786.[3041] Samuel and Abigail were parents of six children.[3042]

[3040] Abigail's parents are named as Daniel and Juda Jucket on her death record. Morrison, History of the Kimball Family, p 221 reports that Judith Kimball (father Ebenezer of Shutesbury) married Daniel Jucket.

[3041] Epsom Historical Society

[3042] Carter, *History of Pembroke* identifies five children. The Epsom Historical Society (www.epsomhistory.com) identifies six children.

i ISAAC AMES, b. about 1772; d. at Epsom, Apr 1825; m. by 1812, HANNAH who has not been identified.

ii STEPHEN AMES, b. about 1775; d. at Stow, ME, 19 Dec 1861; m. at Pembroke, 30 Mar 1797, LYDIA HEAD, b. at Pembroke, 28 Jan 1778 daughter of John and Lydia (Merrill) Head; Lydia d. at Chatham, NH, 6 Jan 1854.

iii AMOS AMES, b. about 1786; d. at Epsom, May 1836; m. at Epsom, 18 Jul 1816, SUSANNAH MOSES, b. at Epsom, about 1796 daughter of Samuel and Abigail (Robertson) Moses.

iv LYDIA AMES, b. about 1788; m. at Pembroke, 2 Mar 1815, PETER JENNESS "of Meredith".

v ELIZABETH "BETSEY" AMES, b. about 1790; d. of consumption, at Epsom, 13 Apr 1855. Betsey did not marry. She was a pauper.

vi PARKER AMES, b. 15 Jul 1792; d. at Pembroke, 28 Jun 1830; m. at Pembroke, 4 Feb 1813, PHEBE LULL, b. 26 Feb 1787 daughter of Simon and Tabitha (Frye) Lull; Phebe d. at Pembroke, 19 Feb 1837.

1157) SPOFFORD AMES *(Elizabeth Stevens Ames[4], Nathan Stevens[3], Elizabeth Abbott Stevens[2], George[1])*, b. at Andover, 23 Mar 1752 son of Samuel and Elizabeth (Stevens) Ames; d. at Pembroke, 1835; m. 18 Apr 1780, MARY WHITE, b. 1759 daughter of John and Abigail (Bowen) Wight;[3043] Mary d. at Pembroke, 6 Jul 1832.

Spofford Ames and Mary White were parents of eight children all born at Andover.

i MARY AMES, b. 19 Jan 1782; d. at Pembroke, 23 Nov 1816.

ii NATHAN WHITE AMES, b. 11 Feb 1785; d. at Lyndon, VT, 24 Jul 1865; m. at Andover, 15 Apr 1813, LYDIA JONES, b. at Andover, 25 Oct 1790 daughter of Nathan and Dorcas (Farnum) Jones; Lydia d. at Lyndon, 29 Dec 1875.

iii STEPHEN AMES, b. 14 Apr 1787; d. at Allenstown, NH, Oct 1870; m. at Pembroke, 9 Jul 1811, DOLLY BAKER, b. at Pembroke, 30 Oct 1790 daughter of Thomas and Ruth (Peabody) Baker; Dolly d. at Hooksett, NH, 1829.

iv DANIEL AMES, b. 29 Apr 1789; d. at Pembroke, 1 Apr 1835; m. at Pembroke, 1 Jul 1816, MARY PARKER, b. at Pembroke, 28 Mar 1796 daughter of John and Martha (Lovejoy) Parker; Mary d. at Hooksett, 22 Jan 1851.

v JOHN AMES, b. 8 Apr 1792; d. at Atkinson, NH, 1866; m. at Andover, 16 Mar 1816, MARY WILSON, b. in NH, about 1790; Mary d. at Atkinson, after 1850.

vi SAMUEL AMES, b. 4 Nov 1795; d. at Pembroke, 9 Aug 1841; m. 1834, SARAH P. LANE, b. about 1800; Sarah d. at Chichester, NH, 22 Mar 1863.

vii SARAH AMES, b. Jan 1798; d. at Pembroke, 6 Dec 1888. Sarah did not marry.

viii FREDERICK AMES, b. 12 Aug 1800; d. at Concord, NH, 25 Jan 1882; m. at Charlestown, MA, NANCY TILTON, "of Meredith, NH" b. about 1794; Nancy d. at Pembroke, 22 Mar 1878.

1158) ABIGAIL AMES *(Elizabeth Stevens Ames[4], Nathan Stevens[3], Elizabeth Abbott Stevens[2], George[1])*, b. at Andover, 1756 daughter of Samuel and Elizabeth (Stevens) Ames; m. 1775, DANIEL NOYES, b. at Pembroke, 24 Nov 1748 son of John and Abigail (Poor) Noyes; Daniel d. at Pembroke, 13 Jan 1822.[3044]

Abigail Ames and Daniel Noyes were parents of twelve children all born at Pembroke.

i BETSEY NOYES, b. 9 Jan 1778; d. at Chatham, NH, 15 Jul 1843; m. at Pembroke, 22 Jan 1809, MOSES W. FIFE, b. in Pembroke about 1783 son of William and Phebe (White) Fife;[3045] Moses d. at Chatham, 1859.

ii DANIEL NOYES, b. 10 Jun 1780; d. at Newburyport, MA, 17 Jul 1850; m. at Portland, ME, 25 Feb 1808, NANCY DAVIS, b. at Newburyport, 14 Jun 1789 daughter of Moses and Rebecca (Plummer) Davis; Nancy d. at Newburyport, 20 Feb 1831.

iii ABIGAIL NOYES, b. 15 Jun 1782; d. at Warner, NH, 30 Sep 1868; m. 1st, 11 Jul 1799, ENOCH NOYES, b. at Pembroke, 18 Dec 1777 daughter of Enoch and Eunice (Kinsman) Noyes; Enoch d. 1800. Abigail m. 2nd, 1808, BENJAMIN CURRIER, b. at Warner, 13 Jul 1782 son of Joseph and Nancy (Stevens) Currier; Benjamin d. at Warner, 9 Dec 1864.

3043 Wight, "John Wight of Bristol, M.A."

3044 Noyes and Noyes, *Descendants of Nicholas Noyes*, p 82

3045 Carter, *History of Pembroke*, p 93

iv PETER NOYES, b. 29 May 1785; d. at Pembroke, 26 Dec 1828; m. at Pembroke, 30 Jul 1815, EUNICE MESERVE, b. about 1795; Eunice d. at Concord, after 1872.

v REBECCA NOYES, b. 19 Mar 1786; d. at Epsom, 1862; m. at Epson, 3 Apr 1857, SAMUEL BICKFORD, b. at Epsom, 13 May 1779 son of Benjamin and Hannah (Locke) Bickford; Samuel d. at Epsom, 1863.

vi JOSEPH NOYES, b. 24 Mar 1788; d. at Pembroke, 18 Sep 1838; m. at Newburyport, 7 Feb 1813, MEHITABLE CHASE, b. at Newburyport, 1 Jul 1793 daughter of James and Abigail (Bickford) Chase; Mehitable d. at Concord, 28 Sep 1867.

vii JACOB NOYES, b. 1 Nov 1789; d at Oxford, Ontario, 21 Nov 1881;[3046] m. at Newcastle, Ontario, 21 Mar 1842, ANNA MARIA EDE,[3047] baptized at Botus Fleming, Cornwall, England, 5 Jun 1825 daughter of David and Anna (Ternouth) Ede;[3048] Anna Maria d. at Oxford, Ontario, 20 Feb 1913.

viii SARAH NOYES, b. 2 Nov 1791; d. at Chatham, NH, 23 Aug 1860; m. at Chatham, 12 Sep 1816, JONAS WYMAN, b. 15 Jan 1791 son of Jonas and Lydia (Chandler) Wyman; Jonas d. at Chatham, 22 Jun 1853.

ix FANNY NOYES, b. 14 Feb 1794; d. 3 May 1856.

x NANCY NOYES, b. 23 Feb 1796; d. at Bradford, NH, 15 Mar 1826; m. 9 May 1819, PAINE DAVIS BADGER, b. at Warner, NH, 31 Jul 1796 son of Stephen and Betsey (Eastman) Badger; Paine d. at Peterborough, after 1860. Paine married second Dorothy Hold 30 Apr 1827 and third Rebecca Harrington 6 Oct 1845.

xi MICAJAH NOYES, b. 7 Aug 1798; d. at Nashua, 17 Sep 1836; m. about 1824, ELIZABETH CHAMBERLAIN, b. 1807; Elizabeth d. at Nashua, 27 Jan 1840.

xii ELIPHALET SWETT NOYES, b. 7 Mar 1802; d. 17 Apr 1820.

1159) ALICE PEARL *(Timothy Pearl^4, Elizabeth Stevens Pearl^3, Elizabeth Abbott Stevens^2, George^1)*, b. at Willington, 6 Jul 1748 daughter of Timothy and Dinah (Holt) Pearl. The birth transcription says 6 Jul 1743, but this seems an error and Durrie's Holt genealogy says 1748; her age at death in 1826 was 76. Alice d. Dec 1826; m. at Willington, 10 Oct 1767, ELEAZER SCRIPTURE, b. at Willington, 10 May 1742 son of John and Hannah (Wells) Scripture; Eleazer d. at Willington, 1813 (estate inventory 13 Oct 1813).

Eleazer Scripture did not leave a will and his estate entered probate October 1813 with Alpheus Scripture as administrator. The widow's dower was set off to Alice Scripture. The estate was insolvent and sold to pay debts.[3049]

Alice Pearl and Eleazer Scripture were parents of ten children born at Willington.

i ROSWELL SCRIPTURE, b. 18 Apr 1768; d. at Stafford, CT, 8 Feb 1839; m. SOPHIA DANA, b. 1777 daughter of James and Elizabeth (Whittemore) Dana; Sophia d. at Cobleskill, NY, 17 Dec 1861.

ii HIRAM SCRIPTURE, b. 2 Apr 1772; d. at Westmoreland, NY, 17 Apr 1849; m. ELIZABETH PARKER, b. about 1773; Elizabeth d. at Westmoreland, 23 Aug 1862.

iii ZEVINAH SCRIPTURE, b. 24 Dec 1774; nothing further known.

iv ALPHEUS SCRIPTURE, b. 1 Sep 1777; d. at Willington, 23 Oct 1846; m. ELIZABETH, b. 1777; Elizabeth d. at Willington, 21 Sep 1865.

v IRENE SCRIPTURE, b. 24 Mar 1779; d. at Willington, 31 Aug 1861; m. RUFUS FISK, b. at Willington, 10 Feb 1773 son of Rufus and Dorcas (Gleason) Fisk; Rufus d. at Willington, 22 Sep 1848.

vi ELIZABETH SCRIPTURE, b. 14 Oct 1781; d. at Rushville, NY, 1 Jan 1864; m. PORTER HINKLEY, b. at Willington, 19 Oct 1781 son of John and Ann (Whipple) Hinkley; Porter d. at Gorham, NY, 6 Jun 1849.

vii ELEAZER SCRIPTURE, b. 24 Mar 1783. What became of Eleazer is not clear. On 2 September 1805, Eleazer Scripture born in Connecticut was convicted in Oneida County of grand larceny and sentenced to one year in Newgate Prison. Eleazer's older brother Hiram was in Oneida County at this time, so perhaps that is this

[3046] Ontario, Canada, Deaths and Deaths Overseas, 1869-1946

[3047] Ontario, Canada, Marriages, 1826-1936

[3048] England, Select Births and Christenings, 1538-1975

[3049] *Connecticut State Library (Hartford, Connecticut)*; Probate Place: *Hartford, Connecticut, Probate Packets, Rockwell, N-Sessions, O, 1759-1880*, probate of Eleazer Scripture, 1813, case number 1893

Eleazer. There is also an Eleazer Scripture from Connecticut who died in Pewaukee, IL, after 1855. That Eleazer was married to Susan Saunders who was born in RI in 1796 daughter of Thomas and Elizabeth (Cross) Saunders.

viii CYRREL SCRIPTURE, b. 17 Mar 1785; d. at Willington, 15 Feb 1853; m. ABIGAIL HALL, b. 1788; Abigail d. at Willington, 15 Apr 1845.

ix LOIS SCRIPTURE, b. 11 Sep 1788; d. at Rushville, NY, 17 Sep 1846; m. at Willington, 17 Jul 1808, STEPHEN CARD, b. 1785 who has not been identified.

x ALLICE SCRIPTURE, b. 14 Jul 1790; d. at Tolland, 3 Mar 1863; m. at Willington, 27 Oct 1808, ISAAC NILES, b. at Willington, 9 Mar 1786 son of James and Mary (Fenton) Niles; Isaac d. at Tolland, 7 Oct 1858.

1160) JOSHUA PEARL *(Timothy Pearl⁴, Elizabeth Stevens Pearl³, Elizabeth Abbott Stevens², George¹)*, b. at Willington, 15 Sep 1752 son of Timothy and Dinah (Holt) Pearl; d. at Vernon, 11 Oct 1837; m. 14 Jan 1773, DEBORAH MARSHALL, b. at Bolton, 1755 daughter of John and Eunice (Kingsbury) Marshall; Deborah d. at Vernon, 11 May 1818.

Joshua Pearl and Deborah Marshall were parents of eleven children, nine of the births recorded at Bolton, Connecticut and two additional children whose parents are identified on death records.

i JOHN MARSHALL PEARL, b. at Bolton, 28 Apr 1774; d. at Belchertown, MA, 26 Apr 1853; m. 1797, ACHSAH FENTON, b. at Willington, 10 Aug 1773 daughter of Eleazer and Elizabeth (Davis) Fenton; Achsah d. at Belchertown, 17 Jan 1863.

ii TIMOTHY PEARL, b. at Bolton, 19 Jul 1776; d. at Belchertown, 10 Dec 1837; m. SALLY PERRY, b. about 1774 daughter of Joseph Perry; Sally d. at Belchertown, 30 Oct 1837.

iii JOSHUA PEARL, b. at Bolton, 8 Nov 1778; d. at Vernon, CT, 27 Jan 1817; m. 14 May 1801, EUNICE STEDMAN who has not been identified. Eunice was living in Vernon in 1830 as head of household.

iv ELIZABETH PEARL, b. at Bolton, 24 Oct 1780; no further information.

v LYDIA PEARL, b. at Bolton, 6 Mar 1783; d. at Vernon, 6 Nov 1841; m. at Vernon, 27 Oct 1808, ELIJAH CHAPMAN, likely the Elijah b. 1783 who d. at Vernon, 31 Aug 1872.

vi EUNICE PEARL, b. 13 Jan 1786; d. 13 Mar 1797.

vii WALTER PEARL, b. 6 Mar 1788; d. 16 Feb 1789.

viii CYRIL PEARL, b. 1790; d. 11 Mar 1797.

ix POLLY PEARL, b. likely at Bolton, 1792; d. at Belchertown, 24 Sep 1857; m. at Vernon, 12 May 1825, as his second wife, ISRAEL COWLES, b. at Belchertown, 5 Nov 1788 son of Josiah and Chloe (Mehuren) Cowles; Israel d. at Belchertown, 11 Feb 1857. Israel was first married to Lois Dunton.

x ACHSAH PEARL, b. at Bolton, 15 May 1795; d. at Vernon, 13 Dec 1857; m. about 1816, ANSON ROGERS, b. likely at Vernon, about 1790; Anson d. at Vernon, 22 Dec 1872.

xi EUNICE PEARL, b. at Vernon, 1798; d. at Belchertown, 4 Jan 1873;[3050] m. as his second wife, HORATIO RICE, b. at Belchertown, 5 Feb 1787 son of Timothy and Elizabeth (Howe) Rice; Horatio d. at Belchertown, 9 Mar 1871. Horatio was first married to Elizabeth Allen.

1161) LOIS PEARL *(Timothy Pearl⁴, Elizabeth Stevens Pearl³, Elizabeth Abbott Stevens², George¹)*, b. at Willington, 21 Apr 1753 daughter of Timothy and Dinah (Holt) Pearl; d. at Willington, 15 Jul 1788; m. 6 Aug 1771, SAMUEL DUNTON, b. at Wrentham, MA, 10 Nov 1748 son of Samuel and Sarah (Bennet) Dunton; Samuel d. at Willington, 1 May 1813. After Lois's death, Samuel married Lovina Marcy.

Samuel Dunton served as a Sergeant during the Revolution in Wadsworth Brigade.[3051]

In his will written 21 February 1810 (probate 6 November 1813), Samuel Dunton notes that his five first children namely Amasa, Josiah, Leonard, Sally, and Lois have received £40 each, except Josiah received £33 10 shillings; Josiah will receive an amount to bring his up to £40. Sons Amasa, Josiah, and Leonard also receive land in Willington. Two oldest daughters, Sally Stewart and Lois Eldridge, each receives $33 to bring their portion to £50 which is their full portion of the estate. His two youngest daughters, Lodicia and Eliza, each receives one dollar and the remainder of the estate both real and personal goes to his beloved wife Lovina. Wife Lovina Dunton was named executrix.[3052]

Lois Pearl and Samuel Dunton were parents of seven children born at Willington. Samuel had three children with his second wife Lovina Marcy.

[3050] The death record of Eunice Rice gives parents names as Joshua and Deborah.

[3051] Eldridge, *Eldridge Genealogy*, p 11

[3052] *Connecticut. Probate Court (Stafford District);* Probate Place: *Tolland, Connecticut, Probate Records, Vol 7-8, 1809-1815*, volume 8, pp 98-100

i AMASA DUNTON, b. 5 Jan 1772; d. at Earlville, NY, 11 Apr 1836; m. at Willington, 9 Apr 1793. MERCY TAYLOR, b. at Mansfield, CT, 21 Jun 1777 daughter of Thomas and Experience (Freeman) Taylor; Mercy d. at Earlville, 5 Mar 1848.

ii LEONARD DUNTON, b. 20 Mar 1774; d. 29 Oct 1775.

iii JOSIAH DUNTON, b. 20 Nov 1777; d. at Cambridge, NY, 24 Nov 1866; m. SARAH CROCKER, b. 4 Mar 1779 daughter of Seth and Mary (Hinckley) Crocker;[3053] Sarah d. at Cambridge, NY, 10 May 1863.

iv SARAH "SALLY" DUNTON, b. 8 Dec 1779; b. at Fort Edward, NY, after 1850; m. by 1810, JOSEPH STEWART, b. 14 Mar 1778 son of Joseph and Rosanna (Harmon) Stewart;[3054] Joseph d. after 1850.

v LEONARD DUNTON, b. 2 Jul 1782; d. at Rome, NY, Jan 1832; m. at Ellington, CT, 4 Nov 1806, ROSINA MCKINSTRY, b. at Ellington, 25 Jan 1783 daughter of Ezekiel and Rosina (Chapman) McKinstry; Rosina d. at Rome, 1 Sep 1847.

vi LOIS DUNTON, b. 4 Oct 1784; d. likely at Syracuse; m. at Willington, 8 Oct 1804, ZOETH ELDRIDGE, b. 1 Apr 1782 son of Zoeth and Bethiah (Hinkley) Eldridge; Zoeth d. at Syracuse, 1844.

vii SAMUEL DUNTON, b. 13 Dec 1787; d. 2 Jun 1798.

1162) ELIZABETH PEARL *(Timothy Pearl⁴, Elizabeth Stevens Pearl³, Elizabeth Abbott Stevens², George¹)*, b. at Willington, 15 Jan 1756 daughter of Timothy and Dinah (Holt) Pearl; d. 8 Jan 1779; m. 6 Aug 1771, ZOETH ELDRIDGE, b. at Willington, about 1751 son of Jesse and Abigail (Smith) Eldridge; Zoeth d. at Willington, 18 Mar 1828. Zoeth m. 2nd, Bethiah Hinkley.[3055]

Zoeth Eldridge was a farmer in Willington. He served in the Revolution first as part of the Minute Men militia and later in the Second Connecticut Regiment which participated in the siege of Boston.

Elizabeth Pearl and Zoeth Eldridge were parents of five children born at Willington. Zoeth's son with his second wife Bethiah Hinkley (Zoeth) married Elizabeth's niece Lois Pearl.

i ZOETH ELDRIDGE, b. 29 Jan 1772; d. 6 Sep 1780.

ii TIMOTHY ELDRIDGE, b. 8 Sep 1773; d. 3 Jul 1775.

iii ERASTUS ELDRIDGE, b. 30 Apr 1775; d. at Springfield, MA, 6 May 1820; m. at Enfield, CT, 1 Nov 1795, RUBY ALLEN, b. at Enfield, 14 May 1778 daughter of Moses and Mary (Adams) Allen; Ruby d. at Whitehall, NY, 15 Sep 1844.

iv TIMOTHY ELDRIDGE, b. 16 Feb 1777; d. likely in western New York; m. by 1804, CLARISSA HAZEN, b. at Hartford, VT, 9 Nov 1784 daughter of Solomon and Theodore (Pease) Hazen; Clarissa d. at Greenville, IL, about 1857.[3056] Timothy and Clarissa were in Hartford, Vermont for about twenty years where they had nine children.

v ELIJAH ELDRIDGE, b. 26 Dec 1778; d. at sea, 1799. He shipped from Boston on the *Pickering* 15 Feb 1799 and was never heard from again.[3057]

1163) SARAH PEARL *(Timothy Pearl⁴, Elizabeth Stevens Pearl³, Elizabeth Abbott Stevens², George¹)*, b. at Willington, 16 Nov 1758 daughter of Timothy and Dinah (Holt) Pearl; d. at Willington, 11 Oct 1826; m. 17 Nov 1776, SAMUEL JOHNSON, b. 1751 (based on age 92 at time of death); Samuel d. at Willington, 22 Mar 1843. Samuel is likely the son of Daniel and Keziah (Dodge) Johnson born at Lebanon, CT 10 Jun 1751.

Samuel Johnson and Sarah Pearl were parents of ten children born at Willington. Marriages were identified for just two of the children.

i DINAH JOHNSON, b. 1 May 1777

ii DAVID JOHNSON, b. 15 Jan 1779; d. 4 Jun 1785.

3053 The 1806 will of Seth Crocker of Cambridge, NY includes a bequest to his daughter Sarah Dunton.

3054 Stewart Clan Magazine, volume 1, number 3, 1922, p 28, Stewarts of Londonderry, NH

3055 Eldredge, *Eldredge Genealogy*, p 8

3056 Hazen, *The Hazen Family in America*, p 290

3057 Eldridge, *Eldridge Genealogy*, p 9. The Eldridge genealogy suggests the Pickering was a pirate ship, but it was the USS Pickering and there is no information on the history of that ship that suggests it was a pirate ship.

iii KETURAH JOHNSON, b. 8 Jan 1781

iv JOHN JOHNSON, b. 28 Nov 1782

v SAMUEL JOHNSON,[3058] b. 21 Oct 1784; d. at Medfield, MA, 28 Jan 1840; m. 1st, at Medfield, 31 Mar 1812, BETSEY FISHER; Betsey d. at Medfield, 12 Dec 1814. Samuel m. 2nd, 28 Mar 1816, CATHERINE HARTSHORN, b. at Medfield, 1 Sep 1792 daughter of Moses and Catherine (Clark) Hartshorn; Catherine d. at Medfield, 27 Dec 1860.

vi DAVID JOHNSON, b. 15 Sep 1786

vii DANIEL JOHNSON, b. 29 Sep 1788

viii SARAH JOHNSON, b. 11 Jun 1791

ix IRA JOHNSON, b. 3 Nov 1794; d. at Willington, 15 Aug 1878; m. 21 Oct 1819, CYNTHIA SWIFT CUSHMAN, b. at Willington, 29 Mar 1797 daughter of Joab and Hannah (Swift) Cushman; Cynthia d. at Willington, 23 Sep 1892.

x RALPH JOHNSON, b. 27 Jun 1798; d. at Willington, 6 Oct 1826.

1164) TIMOTHY PEARL *(Timothy Pearl⁴, Elizabeth Stevens Pearl³, Elizabeth Abbott Stevens², George¹)*, b. at Willington, 6 Jun 1760 son of Timothy and Dinah (Holt) Pearl; d. at Willington, 2 Jul 1834; m. 9 Jan 1783, LOIS CROCKER, b. 9 Dec 1763 daughter of Joseph and Anne (Fenton) Crocker; Lois d. 24 Sep 1850.

Timothy Pearl did not leave a will and his estate entered probate 15 July 1834. There was a $150 surety provided by Austin Pearl as principal and Chloe Pearl both of Willington.[3059]

Timothy Pearl and Lois Crocker were parents of five children born at Willington.

i ELIJAH CROCKER PEARL,[3060] b. 18 Jun 1783; d. at Georgetown, WV, 21 Mar 1864; m. at Willington, 6 Dec 1804, POLLY ELDRIDGE, b. at Willington, 29 Jun 1786 daughter of Zoeth and Bethiah (Hinkley) Eldridge; Polly d. at Amsterdam, NY, 23 Jun 1874.

ii LOIS PEARL, b. 23 Aug 1785; d. at Willington, 19 Sep 1807.

iii CHLOE PEARL, b. 24 Jan 1792; d. at Willington, 1 Jun 1835. Chloe did not marry.

iv ANNA PEARL, b. 24 Apr 1794; d. 1 Jan 1800.

v AUSTIN PEARL, b. 21 Aug 1798; d. at Willington, 14 Jul 1863; m. at Willington, 24 Oct 1824, SOPHRONIA ELDRIDGE, b. at Willington, 11 Dec 1799 daughter of Zoeth and Bethiah (Hinkley) Eldridge; Sophronia d. at Brookfield, MA, 6 Aug 1882.

1165) PHEBE PEARL *(Timothy Pearl⁴, Elizabeth Stevens Pearl³, Elizabeth Abbott Stevens², George¹)*, b. at Willington, 27 Nov 1765 daughter of Timothy and Dinah (Holt) Pearl; d. at Willington, 10 Apr 1816; m. 24 Mar 1785, ZEBADIAH MARCY, b. at Woodstock, 2 Jul 1761 son of Zebadiah and Priscilla (Morris) Marcy; Zebadiah d. at Willington, 24 Sep 1851. Zebadiah married second Mary "Polly" Britt.

Phebe Pearl and Zebadiah Marcy were parents of eleven children born at Willington. Zebadiah also had several children with his second wife.

i PRISCILLA MARCY, b. 29 Nov 1786; d. at Worcester, MA, 4 Aug 1874; m. 1st, about 1808, JESSE OAKLEY. Priscilla m. 2nd, JONAS GREEN, b. in MA, about 1784; Jonas d. at Tolland, 1860.

ii ELIZABETH MARCY, b. 14 Feb 1788; m. at Willington, 1 Sep 1804, JOHN GIPSON.

iii PHEBE MARCY, b. 12 Oct 1789; d. at Webster, NY, 11 Jun 1871; m. at Willington, 28 Apr 1808, her third cousin, ALPHEUS CROCKER *(Sarah Holt Crocker⁵, Abiel Holt⁴, Hannah Abbott Holt³, William², George¹)*, b. at Willington, 3 Jul 1787 son of Zebulon and Sarah (Holt) Crocker; Alpheus d. at Webster, 24 Nov 1873. Alpheus Crocker is a child in Family 676.

[3058] Tilden, *History of Medfield*, reports that Samuel Johnson was born in 1784 and came from Ashford, CT. He was a stagecoach driver. The death record of one of his children gives Samuel's place of birth as Willington.

[3059] *Connecticut State Library (Hartford, Connecticut)*; Probate Place: *Hartford, Connecticut, Probate Packets, Kimball, N-Warren, H, 1827-1895*

[3060] *Biographical Review: This Volume Contains Biographical Sketches of Leading Citizens of Clinton and Essex Counties, New York, Part 1*, p 479, Biographical Review Publishing Company, 1896; details on Elijah's biography and business ventures can be found at this source.

iv LOIS MARCY, b. 7 Aug 1791; d. at Franklin, IL, 20 Dec 1860; m. PETER STOLP, b. at Claverack, NY, 19 Aug 1791 son of Johannes Pieter and Catrina (Chrysler) Stolp;[3061] Peter d. at Franklin, 17 Oct 1853.

v LUCY MARCY, b. 21 Apr 1793; d. at Concord, NY, 19 Mar 1859; m. at Skaneateles, NY, 1 Jan 1816, ABIJAH SIBLEY, b. at Willington, 1 Nov 1788 son of Jonathan and Patty (Brooks) Sibley; Abijah d. at Concord, NY, 3 Jun 1856.

vi HANNAH MARCY, b. 21 Aug 1795

vii SARAH MARCY, b. 2 Sep 1797

viii THOMAS J. MARCY, b. 16 Sep 1780; d. at Coventry, CT, 16 Jul 1866; m. at Somers, 9 Dec 1824, AMELIA KIBBE, b. in CT, about 1805; Amelia d. at Coventry, 11 Sep 1866.

ix TIMOTHY MARCY, b. 6 Aug 1803; d. at Willimantic, CT, 6 Sep 1858; m. ANGELINE GAGER, b. 1805 daughter of Samuel and Fanny (Woodworth) Gager; Angeline d. at Willimantic, 5 Jun 1891.

x ZEBADIAH MARCY, b. 26 Jan 1806; d. at Riverhead, NY, 1878; m. at Willington, 5 Nov 1827, ABIGAIL STILES, b. at Willington, 7 Feb 1795 daughter of Isaac and Abigail (Case) Stiles.

xi LUCINDA MARCY, b. 30 Nov 1808; d. at West Haven, CT, 13 Sep 1881; m. at Hartford, 9 Jan 1825, ELIAS H. SNOW, b. in CT, about 1797; Elias d. after 1870 when he was living in New Haven.

1166) TIMOTHY PEARL *(Nathan Pearl⁴, Elizabeth Stevens Pearl³, Elizabeth Abbott Stevens², George¹)*, b.at Windham, 20 Apr 1752 son of Nathan and Elizabeth (Utley) Pearl; d. at Grand Isle, VT, 15 Sep 1839; m. by 1775, SARAH SWIFT, b. 18 Feb 1755 daughter of Reuben and Hannah (Dexter) Swift; Sarah d. 24 Jul 1843.

Timothy Pearl served as a Sergeant in Ira Allen's Regiment of Vermont Militia in 1781 and 1783.[3062]

Timothy and Sarah started their family in Connecticut and their first two children are reported to be born in Kent, Connecticut. They were then in Vermont in Bennington County and later were in South Hero.

For much of his adult life, Timothy Pearl was active in public affairs serving as Justice of the Peace for Bennington County, Vermont 1787-1788, was a selectman in South Hero, and in 1797 was representative from South Hero to the Vermont General Assembly. He was involved in land speculation which perhaps did not go well as he was jailed from 1805 through 1817 at Burlington jail as a debtor.[3063]

Timothy Pearl and Sarah Swift were parents of ten children, the oldest two or three children born in Connecticut and the others likely in Bennington County, Vermont.

i THEODOTIA PEARL, b. about 1775; d. at South Hero, VT, 17 Sep 1811; m. AARON GRAHAM.

ii SOPHIA PEARL, b. Feb 1776; d. at Milton, VT, 15 Jan 1859; m. about 1795, ALEXANDER PHELPS, b. at Goshen, CT, 1768 son of Abel and Lucy (Beardsley) Phelps; Alexander d. at Milton, 7 Sep 1842.

iii CLARISSA PEARL, b. 1781; d. at South Hero, 16 Dec 1857; m. 1st, about 1803, EDWARD BARNES; Edward d. about 1809. Clarissa m. 2nd, at South Hero, 18 Sep 1810, JOSEPH PHELPS, b. at Windsor, VT, 1771 son of Joseph and Huldah (Wilcox) Phelps; Joseph d. before 1850.

iv STEPHEN PEARL, b. Dec 1784; d. at South Hero, 31 Oct 1859; m. 1st, about 1808, RHODA GRIFFITH, b. 29 Jan 1786 daughter of Jonathan and Hannah (Deuel) Griffith; Rhoda d. at South Hero, 24 Jul 1836. Stephen m. 2nd, ALMIRA LADD, b. at Norwich, CT, 20 Jan 1795 daughter of Andrew and Hannah (Sanford) Ladd; Almira d. at South Hero, 14 Feb 1860.

v ASAPH PEARL, b. 7 Sep 1787; d. at Leelanau County, MI, Dec 1860; m. 1st, HANNAH WOOD who d. before 1820. Asaph m. 2nd, NANCY HOWARD (widow of Charles Flannagan), b. 20 Sep 1782; Nancy d. at Antrim County, MI, 10 Dec 1866.

vi CHAUNCEY PEARL, b. 27 Dec 1788; d. at Champlain, NY, 3 Mar 1868; m. 1st, about 1806, ZILPHA ALLEN daughter of Samuel and Zilpha (Hawks) Allen; Zilpha and Chauncey seem to have divorced before 1810. Chauncey m. 2nd, about 1810, SYLVIA E. PELTON, b. 1 Jul 1793 daughter of Ephraim and Statira (Holcomb) Pelton; Sylvia divorced Chauncey about 1813. Chancey m. 3rd, about 1813, EUNICE ALLEN (the niece of his first

[3061] Peter's date of birth is on his gravestone; findagrave: 7580071

[3062] Compiled Service Records of Soldiers Who Served in the American Army During the Revolutionary War 1775-1785

[3063] Stratton, *History of the South Heroe Island*, pp 730-731

wife and the mother of an out-of-wedlock child with Chauncey during his marriage to Sylvia), b. 23 Aug 1792 daughter of Eleazer Hawks and Eunice (Gilbert) Allen; Eunice d. 11 Nov 1831. Chauncey m. 4th, 3 Sep 1837, ELIZABETH MCINTIRE, b. about 1798; Elizabeth d. before 1850.[3064]

vii SALLY PEARL, b. 15 May 1789; d. at Milton, VT, 11 Feb 1873; m. 1st, JERONEMUS SEEGER, b. about 1785; Jeronemus d. at Burlington, VT, 6 Apr 1817. Sally m. 2nd, at Colchester, 27 Jun 1823, LUTHER S. DIXON, b. at Kent, CT, 20 Dec 1769 son of Archibald and Eleanor (Miller) Dixon; Luther d. at Milton, VT, 17 Dec 1846.

viii CHARLOTTE PEARL, b. 10 Mar 1791; d. at Milton, VT, 10 Oct 1864; m. ALPHEUS HALL, b. 6 Dec 1790 son of Alpheus and Mercy (Blinn) Hall; Alpheus d. at Milton, 18 Oct 1855.

ix BETSEY PEARL, b. 5 Mar 1794; d. at Grand Isle, 26 Apr 1881; m. at Chazy, NY, 19 Dec 1813, HARMON GRAVES, b. 1790 son of Benjamin Graves; Harmon d. at Grand Isle, 26 Nov 1856.

x MARCIA PEARL; no information

1167) ELIZABETH PEARL *(Nathan Pearl[4], Elizabeth Stevens Pearl[3], Elizabeth Abbott Stevens[2], George[1])*, b. at Windham, 6 Jul 1757 daughter of Nathan and Elizabeth (Utley) Pearl; d. unknown; m. 9 Mar 1781; SAMUEL KIMBALL, b. at Windham, 1 Feb 1761 son of Samuel and Ann (Mudge) Kimball. Death records were not located for Elizabeth or Samuel. There are births of four children at Ashford. Nearly all Elizabeth's siblings went to Vermont.

i LUCY KIMBALL, b. 22 Sep 1781; nothing further known.

ii ORRA KIMBALL, b. 1 Jun 1783. He may be the Orra Kimball who d. at East Windsor, 20 Feb 1812; m. about 1808, CLARISSA SIMONS, b. in CT, 1785 daughter of Silas and Abigail (Lord) Simons; Clarissa d. at Jonesville, MI, 1 Jun 1853. Clarissa married second Simon Drake.

iii BETSEY KIMBALL, b. 22 Feb 1785; d. 19 Nov 1785.

iv ELEAZER KIMBALL, b. 24 Dec 1787. He may be the Eleazer Kimball who d. at Hillsdale County, MI, 10 Dec 1866; m. about 1805, MARY "POLLY" STONE. Eleazer m. 2nd, EXPERIENCE who has not been identified. Experience was born in NY, 1802 and d. at Somerset, MI, 17 Aug 1871. Eleazer was in Westfield, NY in 1850 and Sugar Grove, IL in 1860.

1168) ANNA PEARL *(Nathan Pearl[4], Elizabeth Stevens Pearl[3], Elizabeth Abbott Stevens[2], George[1])*, b. at Windham, 1 Aug 1758 daughter of Nathan and Elizabeth (Utley) Pearl; d. at Plattsburgh, NY, about 1830;[3065] m. about 1780, ABEL BRISTOL, b. at Newtown, CT, 5 May 1755 son of Ebenezer and Sarah (Lake) Bristol; Abel d. at Plattsburgh about 1830.[3066]

Anna and Abel made several moves. Abel was born in Newtown, Connecticut and the family was in Manchester, Vermont through 1790 where at least the first five children were born, then in Grand Isle, Vermont, and finally at Plattsburgh.[3067] Abel served in Warren's Regiment during the Revolution enlisting from Manchester.[3068]

Anna and Abel were parents of nine children, the first five children born at Manchester and the youngest four children likely at Grand Isle.

i EBENEZER BRISTOL, b. 14 Jun 1781. Ebenezer is reported to have gone to Ohio and died there unmarried.[3069]

ii NATHAN PEARL BRISTOL, b. 22 Apr 1783; d. at Hamburg, NY, 4 Nov 1866; m. RACHEL CUMMINS, b. in NY, 15 Mar 1784;[3070] Rachel d. at Hamburg, 3 Feb 1861.

iii TIMOTHY BRISTOL, b. 17 Aug 1785; d. at Prescott, Ontario, Canada, 23 Jan 1873; m. REBECCA WILLISTON, b. 19 Nov 1793 daughter of Elijah and Lucy (Kellogg) Williston;[3071] Rebecca d. after 1861.

iv RUTH BRISTOL, b. 27 Aug 1787; m. about 1810, ERASTUS CURTIS.

v ELIZABETH BRISTOL, b. 1789; d. at Plattsburgh, after 1860; m. at Middle Hero, VT, 17 Jul 1808, JOHN HOBBS, b. at Sturbridge, MA, 9 May 1782 son of William and Experience (McKinstry) Hobbs; John d. at Plattsburgh, after 1860.

[3064] The details of Chauncey's various marital and legal adventures are detailed in Stratton's *History of South Heroe*, pp 734-735
[3065] This is the date used by DAR
[3066] Bristol, "Bristol Notes", NYGBR, vol 45, p 171
[3067] Bristol, "Bristol Notes", NYGBR, vol 45, p 171
[3068] Revolutionary War Rolls, 1775-1783
[3069] Bristol, "Bristol Notes", NYGBR, vol 45, p 171
[3070] Rachel's birth date is on her gravestone; findagrave: 91698796
[3071] Hopkins, *The Kelloggs in the Old World and New*, p 200

vi SARAH BRISTOL, b. 1791; d. at Collins, NY, before 1865; m. IRA CHAMBERLAIN, b. at Chelmsford, MA, about 1782 son of Aaron and Sarah (Adams) Chamberlain; Ira d. at Grand Isle, VT, 10 Feb 1874.

vii HULDAH BRISTOL, b. 1793; d. after 1870 when she was living in Plattsburgh; m. about 1825, JAMES WILTON, b. in England, about 1795; James d. after 1850.

viii ANNA BRISTOL, b. 1795; d. at Grand Isle, 25 Jan 1837; m. at South Hero, 7 Oct 1821, REUBEN SAMSON, b. at Grand Isle, 20 Apr 1794 son of Daniel and Anna (Griswold) Samson; Reuben d. at Grand Isle, 6 Jan 1865.

ix ARESTUS BRISTOL, b. 18 Dec 1802; d. at Plattsburgh, 4 Aug 1883; m. about 1840, ALTHEA WORTHINGTON, b. in CT, 1817; Althea d. at Plattsburgh, after 1880.

1169) AZUBAH PEARL *(Nathan Pearl⁴, Elizabeth Stevens Pearl³, Elizabeth Abbott Stevens², George¹)*, b. at Windham, 10 Oct 1762 daughter of Nathan and Elizabeth (Utley) Pearl; d. at South Hero, VT, 19 Jun 1840; m. by 1792, DANIEL WADSWORTH, b. at Hartford, 4 Jan 1761 son of Hezekiah and Millicent (Seymour) Wadsworth;[3072] Daniel d. at South Hero, 7 Jan 1806.

Azubah Pearl and Daniel Wadsworth were parents of six children born at South Hero.

i STEPHEN PEARL WADSWORTH, b. 22 Sep 1792; d. at South Hero, 5 Sep 1882; m. MARY TARDIFF, b. in Canada, 20 May 1795 daughter of Isaac and Jane (Nichols) Tardiff; Mary d. at South Hero, 13 Oct 1863.

ii ABIGAIL WADSWORTH, b. 10 Oct 1794; d. at Iberville, Le Haut-Richelieu, Québec, Canada, 2 Jan 1834; m. JOHN GRIGGS, b. 12 Jun 1789 son of Simon and Letitia (Brevoort) Griggs; John d. at Noyan and Foucault, Québec, Canada, 5 Mar 1856.

iii LUCRETIA WADSWORTH, b. 6 Mar 1796; d. 22 Feb 1797.

iv ELIZABETH WADSWORTH, b. 16 Feb 1798; d. at South Hero, 11 Jul 1859. Elizabeth did not marry.

v HORACE WADSWORTH, b. 19 Nov 1800; d. at South Hero, 4 Apr 1864; m. at South Hero, 11 Nov 1833, JULIETTE KEELER, b. at South Hero, 3 Oct 1812 daughter of Abner and Philena (Tehune) Keeler; Juliette d. at South Hero, 20 Mar 1863.

vi MILLICENT WADSWORTH, b. 23 Mar 1802; d. at South Hero, 3 Apr 1888. Millicent did not marry.

1170) ABIGAIL HIBBARD *(Elizabeth Pearl Hibbard⁴, Elizabeth Stevens Pearl³, Elizabeth Abbott Stevens², George¹)*, b. at Canterbury, CT, 8 May 1749 daughter of John and Elizabeth (Pearl) Hibbard; d. likely at Cherry Valley, NY; m. at Canterbury, 22 Aug 1769, JOSHUA HUTCHINS, b. at Plainfield, 24 Feb 1747 son of Benjamin and Prudence (-) Hutchins; Joshua d. at Cherry Valley, NY, 1789.

Joshua Hutchins and Abigail Hibbard were parents of five children.

i ELIZABETH HUTCHINS, b. at Canterbury, 20 Mar 1770

ii AMY HUTCHINS, b. at Canterbury, 15 Jul 1772

iii ABIGAIL HUTCHINS, b. at Canterbury, 1774

iv JOHN HUTCHINS, b. at Mansfield, CT, 9 Jun 1776; d. at Cherry Valley, NY, Sep 1803; m. about 1800, SARAH OLIN, b. 1774; Sarah d. at Ovid, NY, 16 Mar 1843. Sarah married second Abijah Barnum.

v JOSHUA HUTCHINS, b. at Cherry Valley, about 1783; d. at Junius, NY, 15 Apr 1850; m. about 1805, OLIVE, b. in NY, about 1788 who has not been identified; Olive d. after 1850 (living at probate of husband's estate).

1171) JAMES HIBBARD *(Elizabeth Pearl Hibbard⁴, Elizabeth Stevens Pearl³, Elizabeth Abbott Stevens², George¹)*, b. at Canterbury, CT, 30 Jul 1753 son of John and Elizabeth (Pearl) Hibbard; d. at Royalton, VT, 1807; m. at Canterbury, CT, 15 Aug 1773, SUSAN SHEPARD *perhaps* the daughter of Nathan and Susannah (Wheeler) Shepard of Plainfield, CT.

James and Susan were from Connecticut and births of two children are reported at Canterbury. James was in Royalton, Vermont by 1791 when he was listed on the tax rolls,[3073] and the family was perhaps there by 1785. Little other is known.

[3072] Stratton, *History of South Heroe*, volume 2, pp 767-768
[3073] Lovejoy, *History of Royalton, Vermont*, p 531

i General LOVELL HIBBARD, b. at Canterbury, CT, 28 Mar 1774; d. at Royalton, VT, 20 May 1848; m. 1st, at Tunbridge, 4 Dec 1793, LOIS WHITNEY, b. at Willington, CT, 30 Mar 1768 daughter of Peter and Mary (Case) Whitney; Lois d. at Royalton, 15 Oct 1818. Lovell m. 2nd, 24 Nov 1819, ELIZABETH WOODWORTH (widow of Ebenezer Paul), b. 1786 daughter of Benjamin and Ruth (Pinney) Woodworth; Elizabeth d. at Royalton, 1 Jul 1837. Lovell m. 3rd, at Royalton, 20 Mar 1839, EUNICE PARKHURST, b. at Royalton, 27 Nov 1798 daughter of Simon and Rachel (Spaulding) Shepard; Eunice d. at Royalton, 30 Apr 1860.

ii MARY HIBBARD, b. 7 May 1777; d. at Royalton, 20 May 1817; m. at Royalton, 7 May 1795, CHESTER CLEVELAND, b. at Canterbury, 28 Mar 1771 son of Samuel and Ruth (Darbe) Cleveland; Chester d. at Tunbridge, 6 Feb 1864.

1172) JOHN HIBBARD *(Elizabeth Pearl Hibbard[4], Elizabeth Stevens Pearl[3], Elizabeth Abbott Stevens[2], George[1])*, b. at Canterbury, CT, 15 Sep 1755 son of John and Elizabeth (Pearl) Hibbard; d. at Royalton, VT, 18 Jul 1800; m. 17 Mar 1777, ABIGAIL CLEVELAND, b. at Canterbury, 6 Aug 1758 daughter of Samuel and Ruth (Darbe) Cleveland.

John and Abigail started their family in Canterbury and then relocated to Royalton, Vermont. John was a Baptist preacher and made preaching tours in this rural area.[3074]

John Hibbard did not leave a will and his estate entered probate 22 August 1800 with the letter of administration signed by Abigail Hibbard and John Billings. Personal estate was valued at $425.83 and real estate at $1,200. Charges against the estate were $170.36. The dower was set off to widow Abigail 22 June 1802. The settlement of the estate July 1806 included distributions to the following heirs: oldest son Arunah Hibbard, son Samuel, son John, son Elmore, daughter Polly Woodard, daughter Abigail Sanborn, daughter Zerviah, daughter Sarah, and daughter Philena.[3075]

John Hibbard and Abigail Cleveland were parents of ten children, the oldest child born at Canterbury and the other children recorded at Royalton, Vermont.

i ARUNAH HIBBARD, b. 28 Dec 1777; d. at Sturgis, MI, 19 Oct 1851; m. 7 Dec 1797, ESTHER WHITNEY, b. at Ashford, CT, 1 Nov 1778 daughter of Peter and Mary (Case) Whitney; Esther d. at Sturgis, MI, 29 Sep 1847.

ii MARY "POLLY" HIBBARD, b. 6 Feb 1780; d. at Royalton, 25 Jun 1858; m. by 1802, DANIEL WOODWARD, b. at Windham, CT, 26 Feb 1776 son of Ebenezer and Patience (Orms) Woodward; Daniel d. at Royalton, 27 Jul 1836.

iii SAMUEL HIBBARD, b. 20 Jan 1782; d. at Walden, VT, after 1860; m. about 1805, CHARLOTTE FRASIER, b. at Pomfret, VT, 12 Jun 1780 daughter of John and Anna (-) Frasier; Charlotte d. after 1860.

iv JOHN HIBBARD, b. 3 Aug 1783; d. at Richfield, MI, 10 Jul 1872; m. at Norwich, VT, 13 Jun 1805, ROXA BARTLETT, b. at Norwich, 14 Jun 1787 likely the daughter of Samuel and Irene (Strong) Bartlett; Roxa d. at Richfield, 21 Feb 1872.[3076]

v ABIGAIL HIBBARD, b. about 1785; d. at Peru, NY, after 1860; m. at Tunbridge, VT, 26 Jan 1804, ISAAC SANBORN, b. at Sandown, NH, 6 Dec 1777 son of Peter and Martha (Dow) Sanborn; Isaac d. at Barry County, MI, 23 Jun 1834.

vi ZERVIAH HIBBARD, b. about 1786; d. at Bethel, VT, about 1815; m. at Royalton, 4 Feb 1808, ELISHA TERRY, b. at Bethel, 22 Nov 1786 son of Ephraim and Lucina (Bugbee) Terry; Elisha d. at Bethel, after 1850. Elisha married second Hannah Holt on 25 Sep 1815 and married third Parmelia Moseley on 3 Nov 1833.

vii SARAH ENSWORTH HIBBARD, about 1787; d. at Tunbridge, Jan 1850; m. at Royalton, 6 Jul 1812, HORACE FARNHAM, b. about 1790 son of Philip and Hannah (Bement) Farnham;[3077] Horace d. at Tunbridge, 1868

viii ELMORE DARBE HIBBARD, b. about 1789; m. at Royalton, 20 Aug 1818, LYDIA LYMAN, b. about 1800 daughter of Asa and Submit (Mitchell) Lyman. This appears to be the Elmore and Lydia Hibbard who made their way to Brazoria County, TX with Lydia moving on to Fort Bend after Elmore's death.[3078] If so, Elmore died about 1837 at Brazoria County, TX and Lydia died at Fort Bend, after 1860 when she was living in the same/next household of sons Luther and Levi.

ix PHILANDA HIBBARD, b. about 1795; d. at Mooers, NY, Apr 1870; m. 26 Sep 1816, LYMAN EATON, b. in VT, about 1794; Lyman d. at Peru, NY, about 1871 (probate 30 Jan 1871).

[3074] Hibbard, *Genealogy of the Hibbard Family*, p 90

[3075] *Vermont. Probate Court (Hartford District), Royalton, Windsor; 2:268, 3:30, 3:39, 3:57, 3:258, 3:287, 3:293, estate of John Hibbard*

[3076] The Hibbard genealogy reports that John married Roxa Bartlett and the History of Royalton says he married Achsah Kingsbury, but his marriage seems to be to Roxa Bartlett. John Hibbard's nephew, Daniel Woodward (son of Polly Hibbard and Daniel Woodward) married Achsah Kingsbury.

[3077] Child, *Gazetteer of Orange County Vermont, 1762-1888*, Part First, p 479

[3078] Sowell, *History of Fort Bend County*, p 264

x JAMES HIBBARD, b. 11 Feb 1794; d. 4 Mar 1794.

1173) TIMOTHY HIBBARD *(Elizabeth Pearl Hibbard⁴, Elizabeth Stevens Pearl³, Elizabeth Abbott Stevens², George¹)*, b. at Canterbury, CT, 4 Jan 1759 son of John and Elizabeth (Pearl) Hibbard; d. in Québec about 1841; m. by 1780, JERUSHA LAWRENCE whose origins are unknown.

Timothy Hibbard served as a musician in the Connecticut militia during the Revolution.

Timothy and Jerusha lived in Bethel, Vermont where their six children were born. After the War of 1812, Timothy went to the British Provinces. He was living in Fief Marianne in 1825[3079] and received a land grant in Québec in 1832.[3080]

i SAMUEL L. HIBBARD, b. 30 Sep 1781; d. at Louiseville, Québec, 3 Oct 1849; m. about 1820, MARIE JOSEPHTE BERCIER, b. at Québec.

ii ELIZABETH HIBBARD, b. 8 Apr 1783; d. at Louiseville, Québec, 6 Nov 1851; m. about 1805, BENJAMIN PAGE, b. about 1770; Benjamin d. after 1852.

iii TIMOTHY HIBBARD, b. 29 Jun 1784; d. 1790.

iv MARY HIBBARD, b. 1785; d. at Louiseville, 14 Aug 1862; m. at Trois-Rivières, Québec, 25 Dec 1809, CHARLES DUNN, b. at Maskinongé, about 1786 son of Charles and Rebecca (Logie) Dunn; Charles d. at Louiseville, 15 May 1860.

v JOHN HIBBARD, b. 23 Jul 1787; d. at Rivière-du-Loup, 2 May 1864; m. at Trois-Rivières, 30 May 1813, MARY ARMSTRONG, b. at Poughkeepsie, NY, 15 Jul 1793 daughter of Jesse and Hannah (Crocker) Armstrong; Mary d. 2 Aug 1870.

vi JOSIAH HIBBARD, b. 6 Mar 1789;[3081] d. at St. Didace, Canada East, 1858; m. at Louiseville, 7 Jan 1822, ANNA HUNTER, b. in NY, 1797; d. at St. Didace, after 1852.

1174) LOIS DURKEE *(Phebe Pearl Durkee⁴, Elizabeth Stevens Pearl³, Elizabeth Abbott Stevens², George¹)*, b. at Wales, 26 Sep 1752 daughter of Phineas and Phebe (Pearl) Durkee; d. at Yarmouth, Nova Scotia; m. 25 Mar 1770, SOLOMON LUFKIN, b. at Ipswich, 25 Sep 1747 son of Solomon and Mary (Knowlton) Lufkin; Solomon d. by 1780. Lois m. 2nd, 5 Mar 1780, DANIEL ALLEN, b. at Manchester, 15 Mar 1758 son of Jeremiah and Eunice (Gardner) Allen; Daniel d. at Yarmouth, Nova Scotia, 20 Jan 1838.

No children were located for Lois Durkee and Solomon Lufkin. Four children have been identified for Lois Durkee and Daniel Allen all born at Yarmouth, Nova Scotia.[3082]

i JOHN ALLEN, b. 3 Dec 1780; m. LYDIA LANDERS, b. at Yarmouth, 24 Sep 1784 daughter of John and Lydia (Sollows) Landers.

ii PHINEAS ALLEN, b. 30 Oct 1782; d. at Yarmouth, 9 Jun 1864; m. about 1805, BETHIAH STRICKLAND, b. 1782 daughter of Christopher and Olivia (Landers) Strickland; Bethiah d. at Yarmouth, 30 Apr 1861.

iii SAMUEL ALLEN, b. 8 Jan 1785; d. before 1832 (wife remarried); m. about 1807, SARAH PERRY, b. at Yarmouth, 25 Jul 1785 daughter of John and Tryphena (Smith) Perry; Sarah d. at Beverly, MA, 9 Apr 1873. After Samuel's death, Sarah married Edward Bethune 3 Jan 1832.

iv CLARISSA ALLEN, b. 2 May 1793; d. at Johnstown, OH, 8 Nov 1861; m. SIMEON DEWOLFE, b. at Yarmouth, 28 Apr 1787 son of Charles and Sabra (Harding) DeWolfe;[3083] Simeon d. at Johnstown, 11 Sep 1849.

1175) AMASA DURKEE *(Phebe Pearl Durkee⁴, Elizabeth Stevens Pearl³, Elizabeth Abbott Stevens², George¹)*, b. at Brimfield, 6 Jul 1754 son of Phineas and Phebe (Pearl) Durkee; d. at Yarmouth, Nova Scotia, 1827; m. 21 Nov 1776, RUTH

[3079] 1825 Census of Lower Canada

[3080] Ancestry.com, Quebec, Canada, Land Grants, 1763-1890, Letters Patent Book: L Grants; Page: 424; County Index Volume: 1; Page: 166

[3081] The Hibbard Genealogy reports that there were two Josiahs in this family, one born in 1789 who died in 1797 and a second born in 1798, but that is an error. When Josiah Hibbard was baptized as an adult at Louiseville, Québec on 22 Dec 1821, he gave his birthdate as 6 Mar 1789.

[3082] Brown, *Yarmouth, Nova Scotia Genealogies*

[3083] Perry, *Charles DeWolf of Guadaloupe*, p 235

ROBBINS, b. about 1757 daughter of James and Ruth (Prince) Robbins;[3084] Ruth d. at Yarmouth, 1824. Amasa married the widow Mary Shurtliffe after Ruth's death.

Amasa had moved to Nova Scotia with his parents and he remained there maintaining a farm and a wharf.

In his will written 11 May 1827, Amasa Durkee bequeaths to "true and loving wife Martha" the use of whatever she wants of every kind of the household furniture. As long as she remains a widow, she receives other specific provisions for her support, and she is to be paid £100 yearly by son Lyman Durkee. The bequests to Martha are in lieu of her dower. Son Amasa Durkee receives the lot of land he now occupies and an additional wood lot. Beloved daughter Ruth Bacon receives £40 to be paid by the executor within four years. Beloved son John receives half of a wood land, half of a saltmarsh, and half of the wharf and landing, and a place suitable to set a store if he chooses to do so. Amasa bequeaths 30 acres to his grandson son of James and Phebe Durkee. Granddaughter Mary Jane, also daughter of James and Phebe, receives a feather bed, bedding, and a cow and granddaughter Ruth receives a cow and four sheep. James's widow Phebe receives £5. Beloved son Lyman receives the homestead, all the farming utensils, all the stock animals, any remainder of the estate, and he is named executor.[3085]

Amasa Durkee and Ruth Robbins were parents of six children born at Yarmouth, Nova Scotia.[3086]

i AMASA DURKEE, b. Aug 1777; d. 25 Jul 1779.

ii RUTH LYDIA DURKEE, b. 6 Jul 1779, d. at North Yarmouth, ME, 6 Dec 1848; m. about 1802, SAMUEL BACON, b. at North Yarmouth, 16 Mar 1779 son of Samuel and Lucy (Lufkin) Bacon; Samuel d. at North Yarmouth, 19 Mar 1849.

iii AMASA DURKEE, b. 23 Jul 1782; d. at Yarmouth, 16 Feb 1859; m. HANNAH CROSBY, b. 16 Sep 1779 daughter of Ebenezer and Elizabeth (Robinson) Crosby; Hannah, d. 3 Oct 1866.

iv JOHN DURKEE, b. 18 Sep 1783; d. at Yarmouth, 3 Dec 1877; m. 1807, HANNAH DAVIS, b. at Westport, Nova Scotia, 1785 *likely* the daughter of Ethel and Margaret (Hubbard) Davis; Hannah d. at Yarmouth, 10 Jul 1877.

v JAMES DURKEE, b. 1788; d. 26 Jan 1814; m. PHEBE ROBBINS, b. 11 May 1792 daughter of Joseph and Elizabeth (Stephens) Robbins; Phebe d. Sep 1859.

vi LYMAN DURKEE, b. 1794; d. 12 Sep 1867; m. 1818, HANNAH KELLEY, b. 15 Dec 1795 daughter of Samuel and Hannah (Dennis) Kelley; Hannah d. 13 Apr 1844.

1176) OLIVE DURKEE *(Phebe Pearl Durkee[4], Elizabeth Stevens Pearl[3], Elizabeth Abbott Stevens[2], George[1])*, b. at Brimfield, 18 Jul 1756 daughter of Phineas and Phebe (Pearl) Durkee; d. at Yarmouth, Nova Scotia, 4 Jan 1846; m. 9 Nov 1775, SAMUEL TRASK, b. 27 Dec 1753 son of Elias and Abigail (Woods) Trask;[3087] Samuel d. 25 Dec 1829.

Three children are known for Olive Durkee and Samuel Trask all born at Yarmouth.

i OLIVE TRASK, b. 23 Nov 1778; d. at Yarmouth, 1847; m. 1795, EBENEZER ELDRIDGE, b. at Yarmouth, 9 Oct 1772 son of Barnabas and Temperance (Stewart) Eldridge; Ebenezer d. at Yarmouth, 27 Mar 1863. After Olive's death, Ebenezer married Anna Ellenwood.

ii ABIGAIL TRASK, b. 3 Jan 1781; nothing further known.

iii SAMUEL TRASK, b. 8 Mar 1793; d. 10 Nov 1812.[3088]

1177) ELEANOR DURKEE *(Phebe Pearl Durkee[4], Elizabeth Stevens Pearl[3], Elizabeth Abbott Stevens[2], George[1])*, b. at Brimfield, 11 May 1758 daughter of Phineas and Phebe (Pearl) Durkee; d. at Yarmouth, 8 Mar 1817; m. about 1780; THOMAS DALTON, Thomas d. about 1809 (year of probate).[3089] Eleanor m. 2nd, THOMAS RICKER.

Thomas Dalton did not leave a will and inventory was taken 1 April 1809 with real property valued at £130 and personal property at £27.[3090]

There is just one child known for Eleanor Durkee and Thomas Dalton.

i THOMAS DALTON, b. at Yarmouth, about 1784; d. at Yarmouth, about 1807; m. about 1804, ELIZABETH POOLE, b. at Yarmouth, 15 May 1785 daughter of Samuel Sheldon and Elizabeth (Barnes) Poole; Elizabeth d. at Yarmouth, after 1871. After Thomas's death, Elizabeth married Benjamin Lewis.

[3084] Brown, *Yarmouth Genealogies*, p 200

[3085] Nova Scotia Probate Records, 1760-1993, Yarmouth, Will books, 1794-1859, vol 1-2, pp 137-140, accessed through familysearch.org.

[3086] Brown, *Yarmouth Genealogies*

[3087] The New England Historical and Genealogical Register, Volume 56, p 397

[3088] Trask, The Trasks of Nova Scotia

[3089] Nova Scotia Probate Records 1760-1993, Will Books 1794-1859, volumes 1-2, p 59 (familysearch.org)

[3090] Nova Scotia Probate Records, 1760-1993, Yarmouth, Estate files, 1799-1863, vol D

1178) ROBERT DURKEE *(Phebe Pearl Durkee[4], Elizabeth Stevens Pearl[3], Elizabeth Abbott Stevens[2], George[1])*, b. at Wales, MA, 22 Feb 1765 son of Phineas and Phebe (Pearl) Durkee; m. 1st, ABIGAIL ROGERS, b. at Yarmouth, 9 Mar 1766 daughter of Cornelius and Abigail (Holmes) Rogers; Abigail d. 1807 in Nova Scotia. Robert m. 2nd, about 1808, LYDIA ALLEN, b. at Yarmouth, 25 Jul 1785 daughter of Nathaniel and Sarah (Robbins) Allen; Lydia d. at Yarmouth, 28 Sep 1851.

Robert Durkee and Abigail Rogers were parents of five children born at Yarmouth, Nova Scotia.[3091]

i JOHN DURKEE, b. 16 Feb 1787; d. at Ohio, Yarmouth, 8 Oct 1873; m. 1st, about 1812, CATHERINE MOSES, b. at Yarmouth, 15 May 1788 daughter of William and Sarah (Tinkler) Moses; Catherine d. at Ohio, Yarmouth, 15 Aug 1857. John m. 2nd, about 1858, LOIS BUTLER (widow of William Crosby), b. at Yarmouth, 28 Jun 1797 daughter of Eleazer and Joanna (Ellenwood) Butler; Lois d. after 1881 (living at Ohio, Yarmouth at 1881 census).

ii ROBERT DURKEE, b. about 1789; d. not known by me; m. 1st, about 1815, FRANCES TEDFORD, b. at Yarmouth, 16 Jun 1793 daughter of Jacob and Ann (Porter) Tedford; Frances d. at Yarmouth, 22 Jul 1848. Robert m. 2nd, about 1849, MARY SULLIVAN (widow of Nathan Crosby), b. at Yarmouth, 17 Mar 1794 daughter of Patrick and Mary (Gillfian) Sullivan; Mary d. by 1854. Robert m. 3rd, 1854, MARTHA HARRIS, b. a Yarmouth, about 1817 daughter of Jonathan and Martha (Harris) Harris. Martha Harris was first married to Nathan Rodney and second married to Moses Sollows.

iii ABIGAIL DURKEE, b. and d. about 1791.

iv ABIGAIL DURKEE, b. about 1793; m. about 1820 (first child born 1822), NATHAN BAKER, b. at Yarmouth, 17 Aug 1794 son of Jonathan and Hannah (Clements) Baker.

v PEARL DURKEE, b. about 1795; m. HANNAH TRASK, b. 11 Apr 1800 daughter of Elias and Margaret (Williams) Trask.

Robert Durkee and Lydia Allen were parents of five children born at Yarmouth.

i JOSEPH R. DURKEE, b. about 1808; d. at Ohio, Yarmouth, after 1881; m. 1st, about 1831, HANNAH PORTER, b. about 1811 daughter of John and Bethia (Bent) Porter); Hannah d. at Ohio, Yarmouth, about 1871. Joseph m. 2nd, about 1872, ANNIE PORTER (widow of Waterman Allen and Hannah's sister), b. about 1813; Annie d. after 1881.

ii HENRY A. DURKEE, b. 1809; d. at Ohio, Yarmouth, 1892; m. Feb 1835, OLIVIA MAGRAY, b. at Yarmouth, 12 Apr 1814 daughter of John and Abigail (Robbins) Magray; Olivia d. 10 Jul 1888.

iii OLIVE DURKEE, b. 1815; d. in infancy.

iv ZILPHA DURKEE, b. 1817; d. about 1826.

v SARAH ROBBINS DURKEE, b. Dec 1822; d. at Providence, RI, after 1900; m. at Yarmouth, 22 Jun 1846, JOSEPH ROBBINS MAGRAY, b. at Yarmouth, 4 Dec 1818 son of John and Abigail (Robbins) Magray; Joseph d. at Providence, 27 Aug 1874.

1179) STEPHEN DURKEE *(Phebe Pearl Durkee[4], Elizabeth Stevens Pearl[3], Elizabeth Abbott Stevens[2], George[1])*, b. at Wales, MA, 22 Sep 1766 son of Phineas and Phebe (Pearl) Durkee; d. at Brooklyn, Yarmouth, Nova Scotia, 1845; m. at Yarmouth, 26 Apr 1787, LYDIA LOVITT, b. at Yarmouth, 9 Jul 1769 daughter of Andrew and Lydia (Thorndike) Lovitt; Lydia d. at Beaver River, Yarmouth, 6 Nov 1857.

Stephen Durkee and Lydia Lovitt were parents of ten children all born at Yarmouth.[3092]

i ANDREW DURKEE, b. 22 Nov 1789; nothing further known.

ii LYDIA DURKEE, b. 2 Jun 1792; m. about 1818, JOHN STEPHENS, b. about 1792 son of William Stephens.

iii FREEBORN MOULTON DURKEE, b. 7 Nov 1794; d. at Yarmouth, 16 Jan 1869; m. SARAH G. DOANE, b. at Yarmouth, 28 May 1801 daughter of Israel and Mehitable (Kenney) Doane.

[3091] Brown, *Yarmouth, Nova Scotia Genealogies*

[3092] Brown, *Yarmouth, Nova Scotia Genealogies*

iv DEBORAH DURKEE, b. 22 Sep 1797; d. at Brooklyn, Yarmouth, 22 May 1874; m. MOSES MORRILL, b. at Yarmouth, 6 Jun 1798 son of Moses and Sarah (-) Morrill; Moses d. at Brooklyn, 7 Oct 1878.

v ELEANOR DURKEE, b. 10 Nov 1797; d. at Sudbury, MA, after 1860; m. about 1825, as his second wife, JOSEPH TUPPER ARCHER, b. at Cherryfield, ME, about 1783 son of John and Elizabeth (Tupper) Archer; Joseph d. at Sudbury, 1 Oct 1863.

vi STEPHEN DURKEE, b. 21 Aug 1800; d. at Ohio, Yarmouth, after 1871; m. 1st, about 1824, ABIGAIL BUTLER, b. at Yarmouth, 14 Jun 1804 daughter of Eleazer and Joanna (Ellenwood) Butler; Abigail d. at Yarmouth, 13 Mar 1840. Stephen m. 2nd, 27 Apr 1842, PHEBE SCOTT (widow of Daniel Allen), b. at Yarmouth, 13 Jun 1808 daughter of John Flavel and Margaret (Dennis) Scott; Phebe d. at Ohio, Yarmouth, 7 Sep 1880.

vii GEORGE W. DURKEE, b. 28 Nov 1802; d. at Yarmouth, 23 Jan 1870; m. 1st, about 1825, MEHITABLE CORNING, b. at Yarmouth, 26 Sep 1802 daughter of Samuel and Sarah (Killam) Corning; Mehitable d. 28 Dec 1848. George m. 2nd, 12 Nov 1851, SARAH K. ALLEN daughter of Phineas and Bethiah (Strickland) Allen; Sarah d. 25 Mar 1894.

viii HANNAH LOVITT DURKEE, b. 28 Nov 1804; m. 15 Nov 1825, RICHARD PATTEN CROSBY, b. at Yarmouth, 31 Oct 1800 son of James and Mary (Patten) Crosby; Richard d. at Lake George, Yarmouth, 28 Aug 1862.

ix ZILPHA DURKEE, b. 31 Aug 1807; d. at Winona, MN, 8 Aug 1887; m. about 1835, WILLOUGHBY WADE POWELL, b. about 1806 son of Evan and Philena (Sabean) Powell; Willoughby d. at Winona, 2 May 1881.

x FRANCES DURKEE, b. 1810; m. about 1832, JEFFERSON CORNING, b. at Yarmouth, 26 Nov 1807 son of Samuel and Sarah (Killam) Corning.

1180) PEARL DURKEE *(Phebe Pearl Durkee⁴, Elizabeth Stevens Pearl³, Elizabeth Abbott Stevens², George¹)*, b. at Wales, MA, 25 May 1769 son of Phineas and Phebe (Pearl) Durkee; d. at Baltimore, MD, 25 Jan 1826; m. 1st, MARY HANKEY who was "of Baltimore"; Mary d. about 1812. Pearl m. 2nd, 7 Nov 1817, CHARLOTTE ROSE, b. about 1785; Charlotte d. at Baltimore before Nov 1825 (not living at time of husband's will).

Captain Pearl Durkee was a ship master based in Baltimore.

In his will written 16 November 1825, Pearl Durkee requests that his remains be deposited beside those of his last wife Charlotte Durkee formerly Charlotte Rose. He leaves all his lands in Yarmouth, Nova Scotia to his children to be equally divided among them: sons Robert, John, Pearl, and Stephen Durkee and daughters Ellenor Green, Charlotte Eugenia Constancia Phebe and Mary Elizabeth Durkee. As he has laid out considerable money for son Robert's education, that will be considered his full portion except he also receives the gold-headed cane. Son John receives all the books and charts related to navigation. Daughter Ellenor receives the kind letters that she sent to her stepmother. Daughters Charlotte Eugenia Constancia Phebe and Mary Elizabeth are to be educated equal to the rest of the children. The remainder of the estate is to be divided among sons Pearl and Stephen and daughters Charlotte and Mary. He also specifies if any of these last four children (who were all minors at the time) become intemperate or profligates, then the executor is to retain their portions and disperse to that child as the executor feels is needed. Friends Abraham Price and Benjamin Buck were named executors.[3093]

Pearl Durkee and Mary Hankey were parents of five children born at Baltimore.

i ROBERT ALOYSIUS DURKEE, b. about 1799; death unknown; m. about 1830, ELIZABETH GREEN. Dr. Robert Durkee graduated from University of Pennsylvania in 1822. He was in Baltimore working as a physician in 1840, but it is not known where he was after that.

ii ELEANOR DURKEE, b. 11 Nov 1800; d. at New Orleans, LA, 13 Jan 1878; m. at Baltimore, 19 Sep 1820, HENRY GREEN, b. at Baltimore, 8 Jan 1800 son of Josiah and Mary (-) Green; Henry d. at New Orleans, 14 May 1882.

iii JOHN ALOYSIUS DURKEE, b. 11 Nov 1800; d. at Cecil County, MD, 24 Jan 1866; m. 1st, 7 Apr 1823, MARY ADALINE WHEELER, b. at Baltimore, 15 Sep 1802 daughter of Leonard and Theresa (Green) Wheeler; Mary d. at Baltimore, 11 Nov 1834. John m. 2nd, Mary's sister, ELIZABETH C. WHEELER, b. 20 Mar 1798; Elizabeth d. 25 Jun 1867.

iv PEARL FRANCIS BEESTON DURKEE, b. about 1805; d. at Baltimore, about 1842; m. JANE MARY DREW, b. about 1811; Jane d. at Baltimore, after 1850.

v STEPHEN DURKEE, b. about 1807. According to Brown's Yarmouth genealogies, Stephen left Baltimore about 1840 and his whereabouts after then are unknown.

Pearl Durkee and Charlotte Rose were parents of two children.

3093 Maryland Register of Will Records, Baltimore, Wills 1824-1827, volume 12, Folio 225, will of Pearl Durkee, 16 Nov 1825

i CHARLOTTE EUGENIA "CONSTANTIA" PHEBE DURKEE, b. about 1818; d. at Galena, IL, after 1870; m. at Baltimore, 1 Mar 1836, ROBERT WILLIAM CARSON, b. in VA, about 1818; Robert d. at Galena, after 1860.

ii MARY ELIZABETH DURKEE, b. about 1820; she was living in 1825 when her father wrote his will; nothing further known.

1181) PHEBE DURKEE *(Phebe Pearl Durkee4, Elizabeth Stevens Pearl3, Elizabeth Abbott Stevens2, George1)*, b. at Wales, MA, 28 Apr 1771 daughter of Phineas and Phebe (Pearl) Durkee; d. at Carleton, Yarmouth, 16 Apr 1856; m. at Yarmouth, 31 Aug 1786, SAMUEL BANCROFT, b. about 1786.

There are three children known for Phebe Durkee and Samuel Bancroft born at Yarmouth.

i MATILDA BANCROFT, b. 1791; d. at Yarmouth, Aug 1870; m. about 1812, RUFUS KINNEY, b. at Barrington, Nova Scotia, 3 Dec 1791 son of John and Hannah (Weston) Kinney; Rufus d. at Yarmouth, 24 Jun 1875.

ii SOPHIA BANCROFT, b. about 1795. Sophia did not marry. Nothing further known.

iii WILLIAM BANCROFT, b. 1797; d. at sea, 28 Oct 1861 while on the schooner *Melrose*; m. about 1820, THANKFUL AMELIA CANN, b. at Yarmouth, 25 Nov 1800 daughter of John and Thankful (Corning) Cann; Thankful d. at Yarmouth, 1863.

1182) ELIZABETH DURKEE *(Phebe Pearl Durkee4, Elizabeth Stevens Pearl3, Elizabeth Abbott Stevens2, George1)*, b. at Wales, MA, 22 Oct 1774 daughter of Phineas and Phebe (Pearl) Durkee; d. at Cornwallis, Nova Scotia; m. 17 Dec 1790, JOHN HAYSE "of Long Island"; John d. at Cornwallis, 17 Dec 1848.

John Hayse was a Loyalist originally from Long Island. John and Elizabeth were parents of eleven children likely all born at Horton, Kings, Nova Scotia.[3094]

i ALFRED HAYSE, b. 11 Nov 1791; d. at sea, 1830.

ii JOHN HAYSE, b. 25 Dec 1794; m. at Digby, Nova Scotia, 29 Dec 1819, MARY HINES, b. at Digby, about 1800 daughter of Richard and Sarah (Sypher) Hines.

iii LYDIA HAYSE, b. 13 Jun 1796; m. 1st Mr. DENTON and 2nd, Mr. FRASER. These are marriages reported in Yarmouth Genealogies but have not been identified.

iv PHEBE HAYSE, b. 10 Nov 1798; d. at Whitneyville, ME, 6 Oct 1872; m. about 1825, FREDERICK SCHOFIELD, b. at Horton, about 1800 son of William and Hannah (Bennett) Schofield; Frederick d. at Grand Manon, New Brunswick, after 1881.

v THOMAS HAYSE, b. about 1800; nothing further known.

vi FRANCES HAYSE, b. 13 Apr 1801; d. at Boston, 10 Dec 1858; m. 1818, EZEKIEL MASTERS, b. at Cornwallis, Nova Scotia, 19 Oct 1794 son of Abraham and Elizabeth Seaborn (Woodworth) Masters;[3095] Ezekiel d. at Centerville, Nova Scotia, Apr 1883.

vii PHINEAS DOWNING HAYSE, b. 1 Jul 1803; m. Miss PURDY who has not been identified.

viii SARAH HAYSE, b. 9 Jul 1805; d. at Aylesford, Nova Scotia, after 1881; m. about 1825, JOHN GATES, b. about 1800.

ix BENJAMIN HAYSE, b. about 1806; m. MARIA who has not been identified.

x ELIZABETH HAYSE, b. 23 Aug 1807; m. 1st, 22 Feb 1830, WILLIAM HARRINGTON, b. about 1802 son of Stephen Harrington. Elizabeth m. 2nd, TIMOTHY NICHOLS, b. about 1800.

xi MATILDA HAYSE; nothing further known.

1183) HANNAH DURKEE *(Phebe Pearl Durkee4, Elizabeth Stevens Pearl3, Elizabeth Abbott Stevens2, George1)*, b. at Wales, MA, 27 Jun 1781 daughter of Phineas and Phebe (Pearl) Durkee; d. at Yarmouth, Nova Scotia, 10 May 1857; m. about

---

3094 Brown, *Yarmouth, Nova Scotia Genealogies*

3095 Eaton, *History of Kings County, Nova Scotia*, p 745

1799, NATHAN KINNEY, b. at Yarmouth, 25 Dec 1778 son of Nathan and Sarah (Nickerson) Kinney; Nathan d. at Yarmouth, 13 Feb 1856.

Hannah Durkee and Nathan Kinney were parents of eleven children all born at Yarmouth.[3096]

i PEARL DURKEE KINNEY, b. 4 Jul 1800; d. at Yarmouth, 29 Oct 1848; m. about 1825, ELIZA MAGRAY, b. at Yarmouth, 16 Dec 1804 daughter of John and Abigail (Robbins) Magray; Eliza d. at Bridgewater, Nova Scotia, 30 May 1885. Eliza married second Sylvanus Morton.

ii NATHAN KINNEY, b. 1 Nov 1801; d. at Yarmouth, 9 Jul 1839; m. about 1825, ELIZABETH PERRY, b. at Yarmouth, 1803 daughter of Thomas and Mercy (Robbins) Perry; Elizabeth d. 28 Feb 1854. Elizabeth married second Nehemiah Porter.

iii LYDIA KINNEY, b. 2 Oct 1803; d. at Yarmouth, 22 Feb 1865; m. about 1822, EDWARD PERRY, b. at Yarmouth, 27 Oct 1801 son of Thomas and Mercy (Robbins) Perry; Edward d. at Yarmouth, 22 Feb 1870. After Lydia's death, Edward married MARY DURKEE widow of Joseph Perry and Ebenezer Parry. Mary Durkee, b. 5 Jun 1803 was the daughter of Amasa and Hannah (Crosby) Durkee.

iv DAVID SMITH KINNEY, b. 3 Jan 1806; d. at Weymouth, Nova Scotia, 23 Apr 1891; m. about 1830, LOUISA COOK PINKNEY, b. about 1808 daughter of John and Louisa (Cook) Pinkney; Louisa d. at Weymouth, after 1881.

v PRINCE WHITNEY KINNEY, b. 29 Oct 1807; d. at Chebogue, Nova Scotia, 19 Oct 1880; m. about 1830, HARRIET KELLEY, b. at Yarmouth, 23 Mar 1812 daughter of Jacob and Abigail (Butler) Kelley; Harriet d. at Chebogue, 20 Jan 1898.

vi WILLIAM KINNEY, b. 2 Sep 1809; d. at Chebogue, 18 Aug 1891; m. ORPHA R. ROBBINS, b. at Yarmouth, 22 Aug 1810 daughter of Joseph and Hannah (Raymond) Robbins; Orpha d. at Chebogue, 10 Oct 1891.

vii HANNAH KINNEY, b. 24 Sep 1811; d. at Chebogue, 22 Jan 1887; m. ALEXANDER ANDREWS, b. 1798 son of Samuel and Mary (-) Andrews; Alexander d. at Chebogue, 1880.

viii ROBERT KINNEY, b. 16 Aug 1813; d. at Rockville, Nova Scotia, 14 Mar 1873; m. 1836, MARGARET PINKNEY, b. at Yarmouth, 14 Sep 1815 daughter of John and Abigail (Clements) Pinkney; Margaret d. at Rockville, 14 Mar 1873.

ix WENTWORTH KINNEY, b. 13 Aug 1816; d. at Chebogue, Nova Scotia, 9 Apr 1881; m. about 1843, LOUISA SHERLOCK, b. in ME, about 1825 daughter of George Sherlock. This family lived in Cape Elizabeth, Maine and were also in Brooklyn, New York where they were living in 1870. Louisa was living in 1870.

x ELEANOR KINNEY, b. 29 Mar 1818; d. at Yarmouth, 4 Apr 1886; m. 1 Feb 1837, WALLACE FLINT, b. at Yarmouth, 2 May 1810 son of David and Catherine (Telford) Flint; Wallace d. Dec 1858.

xi LOIS ELIZABETH KINNEY, b. 25 Jul 1823; d. at Yarmouth, 1 Jul 1849; m. JACOB UTLEY, b. at Yarmouth, 15 Sep 1811 son of Nathan and Mary (Crosby) Utley; Jacob d. 15 Jun 1857.

1184) DANIEL DENISON *(Lydia Pearl Denison[4], Elizabeth Stevens Pearl[3], Elizabeth Abbott Stevens[2], George[1])*, b. at Windham, 25 Jan 1755 son of Daniel and Lydia (Pearl) Denison; d. at Hampton, 10 Nov 1822; m. at Norwich, 24 Apr 1788, LUCY CLARK, b. 1763 (based on age of 80 at time of death);[3097] d. at Hampton, 8 Dec 1843.

In his will written 7 September 1822, Daniel Denison leaves to beloved wife Lucy one-third of all the personal estate for her use forever and use of one-third of the real estate during her natural life. Son Daniel Denison is at liberty to choose his part of the real estate except that to be set off to Lucy. Daughters Lydia, Lucy, and Hannah receive the remainder of the estate, real and personal, to be divided equally among them, and to make the total amounts equal considering Lydia has already received $300. Daniel also notes he has given his bond to support his honored father and mother during their lives and he expects his wife and children to fulfill this bond. Son Samuel is named executor.[3098] Real estate was valued at $4,438 and personal estate at $1,105.

In her will written 8 June 1842 (probate 12 January 1844), Lucy Denison left her entire estate, both real and personal, to daughter Hannah Clark wife of William Clark. John Tweedy, Esq. was named executor.[3099]

Daniel Denison and Lucy Clark were parents of four children all born at Hampton.

[3096] Brown, *Yarmouth, Nova Scotia Genealogies*

[3097] Ancestry.com, Connecticut, Deaths and Burials Index, 1650-1934

[3098] *Connecticut State Library (Hartford, Connecticut)*; Probate Place: *Hartford, Connecticut, Probate Packets, Decker, Joseph-Durkee, M, 1719-1880*, probate of Daniel Denison, Jr.

[3099] *Connecticut. Probate Court (Norwich District)*; Probate Place: *New London, Connecticut, Probate Records, Vol 17-18, 1842-1849*, vol 17, p 177, will of Lucy Denison

i LYDIA DENISON, b. 20 Jul 1789; d. at Hampton, 4 Feb 1838; m. 16 Dec 1810, HARVEY FULLER, b. at Hampton, 13 Sep 1784 son of Joseph and Mary (Holt) Fuller; Harvey d. at Hampton, 21 Apr 1860.

ii DANIEL DENISON, b. 6 Jun 1791; d. at Hampton, 25 Feb 1838; m. at Hampton, 27 Mar 1821, SUSAN CUNNINGHAM, b. at Pomfret, 4 Apr 1799 daughter of Peter and Betsey (Pierpoint) Cunningham; Susan d. at Newark, NJ, 13 Mar 1883.

iii LUCY DENISON, b. 16 Jan 1798; d. at Hampton, 11 Oct 1877; m. 9 Apr 1827, JOSIAH C. JACKSON, b. "of Chaplin", about 1803; Josiah d. at Hampton, 1 Sep 1855.

iv HANNAH DENISON, b. 13 Jul 1803; d. at Hampton, 22 Mar 1875; m. 29 Nov 1832, WILLIAM CLARK, b. at Hampton, 4 May 1804 son of Amasa and Eleanor (Fuller) Clark;[3100] William d. at Hampton, 16 Apr 1866.

1185) BENJAMIN AMES *(Benjamin Ames[4], Hannah Stevens Ames[3], Elizabeth Abbott Stevens[2], George[1])*, b. at Andover, 9 Nov 1749 son of Benjamin and Hephzibah (Chandler) Ames; d. at Andover, 23 Nov 1813; m. 30 Apr 1772, his second cousin once removed, PHEBE CHANDLER *(Nathan Chandler[5], Nathan Chandler[4], John Chandler[3], Hannah Abbott Chandler[2], George[1])*, b. 18 Oct 1754 daughter of Nathan and Phebe (Abbott) Chandler; Phebe d. 19 Jun 1798. The grave of Phebe Chandler Ames has the following inscription: *While o'er the grave you walk or weep, Remember here all flesh must sleep; Slender's the thread whence life depends, Begins this hour, the next it ends.*[3101] Phebe Chandler is a child in Family 289.

Benjamin Ames built Ye Ames Tavern in Andover which was later known as Elm House.[3102] He was a large landowner and is reported to have, at one time, owned most of the township of Hebron, Maine.[3103] However, he was in debt at the time of his death.[3104]

Benjamin Ames and Phebe Chandler were parents of eleven children born at Andover.

i BENJAMIN AMES, b. 24 Feb 1773; d. 10 Oct 1775.

ii PHEBE AMES, b. 8 Apr 1775; d. at Andover, 12 Jan 1854; m. 22 Oct 1811, as his third wife, her third cousin once removed, SAMUEL STEVENS *(Hannah Shattuck Stevens[5], Joanna Chandler Shattuck[4], Zebadiah Chandler[3], Hannah Abbott Chandler[2], George[1])*,[3105] b. at Andover, 24 Apr 1757 son of Samuel and Hannah (Shattuck) Stevens; Samuel d. at Andover, 22 Nov 1831. Samuel was first married to Mary Mooar and second married Susannah Manning. Samuel Stevens is a child in Family 336.

iii HEPHZIBAH AMES, b. 20 Jan 1777; d. at Montreal, Québec, 28 Jan 1802; m. at Andover, 17 Nov 1793, NATHANIEL STIMPSON, baptized at Charlestown, 18 Jul 1773 son of John and Susannah (Fosdick) Stimpson;[3106] d. about 1840.

iv BENJAMIN AMES, b. 30 Oct 1778; d. at Houlton, ME, 28 Sep 1835; m. 1st, 5 Apr 1809, his fourth cousin, MARY BOYNTON *(Mary Abbott Boynton[5], Elizabeth Abbott Abbott[4], George[3], George[2], George[1])*, b. at Westford, 3 Apr 1785 daughter of Abel and Mary (Abbott) Boynton; Mary d. Nov 1810. Benjamin m. 2nd, Mary's sister, SARAH BOYNTON, b. at Westford, 21 Jun 1794. Benjamin Ames graduated from Harvard and was an attorney and politician in Maine.[3107] Mary and Sarah Boynton are children in Family 533.

v HANNAH AMES, b. 19 Jul 1781; d. at Haverhill, after 1860; m. 1st, 30 Jun 1801, DANIEL CUMMINGS, b. at Andover, 2 Sep 1778 son of Jonathan and Mary (-) Cummings; Daniel d. 26 Dec 1827. Hannah m. 2nd, 21 Jun 1842, LEONARD WHITE, b. at Haverhill, 3 May 1767 son of John and Sarah (LeBaron) White; Leonard d. at Haverhill, 10 Oct 1849.

vi MARY AMES, b. 3 Jul 1783; d. at Charlestown, MA, by 1814; m. at Andover, 9 Apr 1805, JOSEPH WILSON, b. at Andover, 20 Aug 1781 son of Joshua and Dorothy (Stevens) Wilson; Joseph d. at Charlestown, 1834 (probate 19 Aug 1834). Joseph m. 2nd, 6 Nov 1814, Lucy Boynton daughter of Moses and Lucy (Howe) Boynton.

3100 The names of William's parents are given as Amasa Clark and Eleanor Fuller on his death record.
3101 The Essex Antiquarian, 1898, Andover Inscriptions, Old South Burying Ground
3102 Bailey, *Historical Sketches of Andover*, p 126
3103 Chandler, *Descendants of William and Annis Chandler*, p 609
3104 Whittier, *Genealogy of the Stimpson Family*, p 49
3105 The Chandler genealogy reports Phebe had a first marriage to Searls but she was Phebe Ames when she married Samuel Stevens.
3106 Whittier, *Genealogy of the Stimpson Family*, p 48
3107 A detailed biography of Benjamin Ames can be found in *Biographical Encyclopedia of Maine in the Nineteenth Century*, p 384ff

vii EZRA CHANDLER AMES, b. 1 Jan 1785; d. at Haverhill, MA, 14 Jan 1865; m. 1st, 19 Nov 1815, JOANNA EAMES, b. at Haverhill, 17 Oct 1790 daughter of Daniel and Hannah (Winter) Eames; Joanna d. 6 Oct 1822. Ezra m. 2nd, 4 Mar 1824, NANCY PORTER, b. at Haverhill, 17 Oct 1789 daughter of Dudley and Sarah (Davis) Porter; Nancy d. 11 May 1840. Ezra m. 3rd, 26 Apr 1842, ELIZABETH MARSH, b. at Haverhill, 16 Jan 1792 daughter of Moses and Hannah (Lampson) Marsh; Elizabeth d. at Haverhill, 21 Feb 1868.

viii NATHAN AMES, b. 7 May 1787; d. unknown (might have died in New York); m. 24 Nov 1811, his fourth cousin, LYDIA CLARK *(Hannah Abbott Clark5, Ebenezer4, Ephraim3, John2, George1)*, b. at Andover, 17 Jul 1788 daughter of Abijah and Hannah (Abbott) Clark; Lydia d. about 1851 perhaps in NY. Nathan was deputy sheriff of Lincoln County, ME but was involved in political controversy related to his being engaged in "trade with the enemy" during the War of 1812.[3108] Lydia Clark is a child in Family 381.

ix ELIZABETH AMES, b. 19 Jan 1789; d. at Haverhill, 27 Apr 1867; m. at Andover, 29 Nov 1810, her first cousin, DAVID BOYNTON *(Hannah Ames Boynton5, Benjamin Ames4, Hannah Stevens Ames3, Elizabeth Abbott Stevens2, George1)*, b. at Andover, 4 Jan 1784 son of Thomas and Hannah (Ames) Boynton; David d. at Andover, 26 Mar 1826. David Boynton is a child in Family 1186.

x RHODA AMES, b. 12 Jan 1792; d. 31 Jan 1792.

xi ISAAC AMES, b. 13 Nov 1795; d. at Richmond, VA, 5 Nov 1818. Isaac did not marry. He was a commission merchant.[3109]

1186) HANNAH AMES *(Benjamin Ames4, Hannah Stevens Ames3, Elizabeth Abbott Stevens2, George1)*, b. at Andover, 26 Nov 1751 daughter of Benjamin and Hephzibah (Chandler) Ames; d. 20 Dec 1831; m. 16 Jun 1772, THOMAS BOYNTON, b. 29 Nov 1747 son of David and Mary (Stickney) Boynton; Thomas d. 10 Mar 1833.

Thomas Boynton was a carpenter in Andover. He served as a sergeant in Captain Benjamin Ames's company under Colonel James Frye's Lexington Alarm Unit (Minute Men) in the Revolutionary War for which he received a pension.

Thomas did not leave a will and his estate entered probate 15 July 1834. His probate record mentions his pension as a veteran of the Revolutionary War. The children given as the only heirs to the estate were as follows: Thomas Boynton, Amos Boynton, Benjamin Boynton, Sally Boynton, Betsey Bailey, Mary Pearl, and Hephzibah Chandler.[3110]

Hannah Ames and Thomas Boynton were parents of eleven children all born at Andover.

i HANNAH BOYNTON, b. 11 Mar 1773; d. at Greenfield, NH, 13 Jun 1817; m. 19 Apr 1793, JOHN CROSBY, b. about 1772;[3111] John d. at Cambria, NY, after 1860.

ii THOMAS BOYNTON, b. 7 Jan 1775; d. at Lowell, 26 Feb 1856; m. 19 Nov 1799, REBECCA BAILEY, b. at Andover, 25 Aug 1774 daughter of William and Rebecca (Hildreth) Bailey; Rebecca d. at Andover, May 1830.

iii AMOS BOYNTON, b. 27 Oct 1776; d. at Lowell, 19 Jan 1849; m. 3 Apr 1809, CLARISSA RICHARDSON, b. at Dracut, 24 Mar 1787 daughter of Obadiah and Hannah (Hildreth) Richardson; Clarissa d. at Lowell, 31 Jan 1880. After Amos's death, Clarissa married Samuel Law.

iv MARY BOYNTON, b. 1 Aug 1778; d. at Boxford, 1 Oct 1863; m. 1st, 26 May 1801, ISAAC CARLETON, b. at Andover, 27 Oct 1772 son of Asa and Hannah (Kimball) Carleton; Isaac d. at Andover, 13 Jun 1816. Mary m. 2nd, 15 Aug 1820, SIMEON PEARL, b. at Boxford, 21 Sep 1781 son of John and Eunice (Kimball) Pearl; Simeon d. at Boxford, 18 May 1864.

v BENJAMIN BOYNTON, b. 24 Jul 1780; d. at Amesbury, 12 Sep 1854; m. 7 Mar 1817, BELINDA RICHARDSON PEARSON, b. at Lynnfield, 31 Jan 1797 daughter of Samuel and Keziah (Richardson) Pearson; Belinda d. at Andover, 10 Jul 1872.

vi SARAH BOYNTON, b. 30 Jan 1782; d. at Andover, 14 Apr 1844. Sarah did not marry.

vii DAVID BOYNTON, b. 4 Jan 1784; d. at Andover, 26 Mar 1826; m. 29 Nov 1810, his first cousin, ELIZABETH AMES *(Benjamin Ames5, Benjamin Ames4, Hannah Stevens Ames3, Elizabeth Abbott Stevens2, George1)*, b. at Andover, 19 Jan 1789 daughter of Benjamin and Phebe (Chandler) Ames; Elizabeth d. at Haverhill, 27 Apr 1867. Elizabeth Ames is a child in Family 1185.

viii SAMUEL BOYNTON, b. 8 Nov 1785; d. 2 Aug 1787.

ix ELIZABETH BOYNTON, b. 18 Jan 1789; d. at Andover, 25 Jun 1856; m. 5 Dec 1811, her third cousin once removed, JOHN MOOAR BAILEY *(Elizabeth Mooar Bailey4, Elizabeth Abbott Mooar3, Nathaniel2, George1)*, b. at

[3108] Reed, *History of Bath and Environs*, p 86

[3109] Chandler, *Descendants of William and Annis Chandler*, p 610

[3110] Essex County, MA: Probate File Papers, 1638-1881.Online database. AmericanAncestors.org. New England Historic Genealogical Society, 2014. Case 2977

[3111] John is *possibly* the son of Simon and Dorothy (Farmer) Crosby.

Andover, 20 Jul 1784 son of Moses and Elizabeth (Mooar) Bailey; John d. at Andover, 3 Apr 1836. Elizabeth Boynton and John Mooar Bailey are Family 1124.

x SAMUEL BOYNTON, b. Sep 1791; d. 11 Jan 1792.

xi HEPHZIBAH BOYNTON, b. 1792; d. at Dudley, MA, 1 Jan 1870; m. 22 Sep 1814, her fourth cousin once removed, JAMES CHANDLER *(James Chandler[6], Isaac Chandler[5], Nathan Chandler[4], John Chandler[3], Hannah Abbott Chandler[2], George[1])*, b. at Andover, 16 May 1788 son of James and Phebe (Dane) Chandler; James d. at Andover, 12 Oct 1831.

1187) HEPHZIBAH AMES *(Benjamin Ames[4], Hannah Stevens Ames[3], Elizabeth Abbott Stevens[2], George[1])*, b. at Andover, 3 Nov 1755 daughter of Benjamin and Hephzibah (Chandler) Ames; d. at Andover, 20 May 1796; m. 9 Jan 1772, her third cousin, BIXBY ABBOTT, b. 24 Nov 1750 son of William and Experience (Bixby) Abbott (the Rowley Abbott line). Bixby m. 2nd Mary Johnson; Bixby d. at Greenfield, NH, 1813.

Bixby served in the Revolutionary War as a corporal in Captain Benjamin Ames's company. Captain Ames was Bixby's father-in-law.

Bixby Abbot did not leave a will and Asa Abbot was named administrator. The inventory included 122 acres, dwelling house, and half of a barn with a value of $950, value of crops on the stalk if brought to maturity valued at $55, and personal estate including stock animals valued at $503.29. Administrator Asa Abbot was licensed to sell all the personal estate.[3112]

Hephzibah Ames and Bixby Abbott were parents of twelve children all born at Andover. After the death of Hephzibah, Bixby relocated to Greenfield, New Hampshire.

i HEPHZIBAH ABBOTT, b. 17 Aug 1772; d. at Andover, 7 Aug 1813; m. 19 Feb 1795, her third cousin once removed, JOSHUA BAILEY *(Elizabeth Mooar Bailey[4], Elizabeth Abbott Mooar[3], Nathaniel[2], George[1])*, b. at Andover, 14 Aug 1770 son of Moses and Elizabeth (Mooar) Bailey; Joshua d. at Andover, 30 Oct 1820. Hephzibah Abbott and Joshua Bailey are the parents in Family 1119.

ii WILLIAM ABBOTT, b. 14 Jul 1774; d. at Greenfield, NH, 13 Aug 1852; m. 14 Nov 1799, his third cousin once removed, HANNAH BAILEY *(Elizabeth Mooar Bailey[4], Elizabeth Abbott Mooar[3], Nathaniel[2], George[1])*, b. at Andover, 3 May 1779 daughter of Moses and Elizabeth (Mooar) Bailey; Hannah d. at Concord, NH, 27 Dec 1867. William Abbott and Hannah Bailey are the parents in Family 1122.

iii BENJAMIN ABBOTT, b. 8 Nov 1776; d. at Andover, 13 Aug 1852; m. 1st, 19 May 1798, MARY KIDDER, b. at Medford, 1 Apr 1779 daughter of Samuel and Mary (Greenleaf) Kidder; Mary d. at Andover, 26 May 1816. Benjamin m. 2nd, ELIZABETH GOLDSMITH, b. at Andover, 29 Aug 1791 daughter of Jeremiah and Sarah (Converse) Goldsmith; Elizabeth d. 25 Mar 1867.

iv JOSEPH ABBOTT, b. Jun 1778; d. Aug 1778.

v BETSEY ABBOTT, b. 18 Sep 1780; d. at Andover, 24 Oct 1817; m. 23 Dec 1820, her third cousin once removed, NATHAN BAILEY *(Elizabeth Mooar Bailey[4], Elizabeth Abbott Mooar[3], Nathaniel[2], George[1])*, b. at Andover, 4 Feb 1777 son of Moses and Elizabeth (Mooar) Bailey; Nathan d. at Andover, 16 Jan 1862. Nathan m. 2nd, 4 May 1819, CHLOE POOR *(Chloe Lovejoy Poor[5], Lydea Abbott Lovejoy[4], Henry[3], George[2], George[1])*, b. at Andover, 14 May 1779 daughter of John and Chloe (Lovejoy) Poor; Chloe d. at Andover, 8 Jun 1867. Betsey Abbott and Nathan Bailey are the parents in Family 1121. Chloe Lovejoy is a child in Family 543.

vi JOSEPH B. ABBOTT, b. 1 Feb 1783; d. at sea, about 1809; m. 28 Jul 1808, RACHEL COCHRAN, b. Apr 1788 daughter of James and Salome (Knowlton) Cochran;[3113] Rachel d. at Lowell, 18 Apr 1868. Rachel m. 2nd, 11 Apr 1819, WILLIAM ABBOTT *(George[5], Benjamin[4], Benjamin[3], Benjamin[2], George[1])*, b. at Hollis, 14 Jun 1798 son of George and Naomi (Tuttle) Abbott; William d. Dec 1827 when he was murdered at Millbury when on his way home after finishing a job at the Blackstone Canal. William Abbott is a child in Family 530.

vii HENRY ABBOTT, b. 5 Mar 1785; d. at Amherst, NH, 28 Mar 1868; m. 17 Jan 1811, his third cousin once removed, RHODA BAILEY *(Elizabeth Mooar Bailey[4], Elizabeth Abbott Mooar[3], Nathaniel[2], George[1])*, b. at Andover, 7 May 1789 daughter of Moses and Elizabeth (Mooar) Bailey; Rhoda d. at Amherst, 1 Sep 1854. Henry Abbott and Rhoda Bailey are the parents in Family 1126.

viii ASA ABBOTT, b. 7 Mar 1787; m. 21 Nov 1811, HANNAH BAILEY who has not been identified.

[3112] New Hampshire, County Probate Records, 1660-1973, Hillsborough, probate of Bixby Abbot, Case 094, 19:152, 21:526, 13:543

[3113] Knowlton, *Errata and Addenda to Dr. Stocking's History and Genealogy of the Knowltons of England and America*, p 187

ix SAMUEL ABBOTT, b. 28 Jan 1789; d. at Woburn, 28 Apr 1855; m. at Woburn, 28 Apr 1855, RUTH WINN, b. at Woburn, 22 Feb 1796 daughter of Abel and Ruth (Richardson) Winn; Ruth d. at Woburn, 8 Apr 1871.

x NEHEMIAH ABBOTT, b. 18 Oct 1790; d. at Georgetown, 14 Jan 1860; m. 6 Aug 1832, his second cousin once removed, REBECCA SHATTUCK *(Isaac Shattuck⁶, Isaac Shattuck⁵, Joanna Chandler⁴, Zebadiah Chandler³, Hannah Abbott Chandler², George¹)*, b. at Andover, 18 Jun 1795 daughter of Isaac and Rebecca (Ingalls) Shattuck; Rebecca d. at Andover, 30 Dec 1874.

xi TIMOTHY ABBOTT, b. 22 Feb 1793; d. 1813.[3114]

xii WARREN ABBOTT, b. 14 Jul 1796; d. at Bradford, 12 Jul 1825; m. at Bradford, 6 Sep 1824, MYRA GREENOUGH, b. at Bradford, 4 Mar 1799 daughter of William and Abigail (Parker) Greenough; Myra d. at Cambridge, 30 Jan 1881. Dr. Warren Abbott received the Doctor of Medicine degree from Harvard in 1823.[3115] He died of consumption.

1188) TIMOTHY AMES *(Benjamin Ames⁴, Hannah Stevens Ames³, Elizabeth Abbott Stevens², George¹)*, b. at Andover, 26 Sep 1765 son of Benjamin and Hephzibah (Chandler) Ames; d. at Peterborough, NH, 14 May 1835; m. 21 Mar 1787, SALLY KNEELAND, b. 1769 (based on age at time of death) who parentage is uncertain;[3116] Sally d. at Peterborough, 13 Nov 1861.

Timothy and Sally started their family in Andover but relocated to Peterborough in 1793. He struggled to provide for his large family, but was described as cheerful and industrious, He played the violin and provided music for dance parties in the area.[3117]

Timothy Ames did not leave a will and his estate entered probate 5 August 1835 with Timothy K. Ames as administrator as the widow declined administration. Real estate was valued at $350 and personal estate at $141.22 which included a violin valued at $12. The personal estate was insufficient to settle the demands against the estate and the real estate was sold. Widow Sally Ames received an allowance from the estate of $141.22 (value of the personal estate) on 3 November 1835. The real estate was sold for $300. After the debts were paid, there was a balance of $179.87.[3118]

Timothy Ames and Sally Kneeland were parents of eleven children, the oldest three children born at Andover and the other children at Peterborough.

i SALLY ADAMS AMES, b. 21 Feb 1788; d. at Peterborough, 13 May 1825; m. at Peterborough, 16 Aug 1812, GEORGE HENRY, b. at Charlestown, NH, 6 Aug 1790 son of Robert B. and Sarah (Bellows) Henry.[3119] *The Bellows Genealogy* reports that George was mentally ill in his later life, that he got away from an attendant who was caring for him, then fell in a pond and drowned.

ii TIMOTHY KNEELAND AMES, b. 16 Aug 1789; d. at Peterborough, 25 Aug 1874; m. 16 Jan 1813, DOROTHY EVANS, b. at Peterborough, 24 Apr 1790 daughter of Asa and Dorothy (Buss) Evans; Dorothy d. at Peterborough, 1 Apr 1873.

iii SAMUEL AMES, b. 6 Oct 1791; d. at Peterborough, 31 Jan 1872; m. SALLY SCOTT who has not been identified. Samuel and Sally lived in Constantia, NY for a time, but Samuel returned to Peterborough prior to his death.

iv JOHN AMES, b. 3 Aug 1793; d. 16 Jul 1816.

v BENJAMIN AMES, b. 30 Jul 1795; d. 6 Jul 1797.

vi BENJAMIN AMES, b. 25 Jun 1797; d. 24 Mar 1812.

vii MARY KNEELAND AMES, b. 1 Jun 1799; d. at Peterborough, 21 Oct 1844; m. at Peterborough, 12 May 1818, STEPHEN FELT, b. at Temple, NH, 15 Sep 1793 son of Peter and Lucy (Andrews) Felt; Stephen d. at Peterborough, 3 May 1879.

viii RUTHY S. AMES, b. 12 Mar 1802; d. at Fitchburg, MA, 26 Nov 1880; m. at Peterborough, 1 May 1821, JOHN HADLEY, b. about 1796; John d. at Peterborough, 1850.

ix HEPHZIBAH C. AMES, b. 25 Dec 1803; d. at Peterborough, 13 Sep 1871; m. 10 Mar 1831, JACOB LONGLEY, b. at Shirley, MA, 1 Jul 1801 son of Ezekiel and Mary (Swan) Longley; Jacob d. at Peterborough, 30 Jan 1888.

x ALVAH AMES, b. 5 Apr 1806; d. at Peterborough, 7 May 1890; m. 1st, 21 May 1828, BETSEY LITTLE, b. at Belmont, ME, about 1804 daughter of Thomas and Relief (White) Little; Betsey d. at Peterborough, 27 Mar 1872. Alvah m. 2nd, at Peterborough, 26 Nov 1872, RACHEL A. DUVALL (widow of Thomas Watts), b. at Fort

---

3114 Perley, Abbot Genealogy, Essex Antiquarian, volume 1, p 108

3115 Quinquennial Catalogue of Harvard University

3116 Possible parents of Sally are John Kneeland and his second wife Abigail Adams of Boston.

3117 Smith and Morison, *History of the Town of Peterborough, Genealogical*, p 10

3118 New Hampshire, County Probate Records, 1660-1973, Hillsborough, case 0174, probate of Timothy Ames; 37:262, 41:177; 41:1; 37:442; 46:79

3119 Peck, *The Bellows Genealogy*, p 117

Montgomery, NY, about 1831 daughter of George and Martha (Farrington) Duvall; Rachel d. at Meriden, CT, 23 Jan 1913.

xi JOSEPH H. AMES, b. 9 Apr 1808; d. at Peterborough, 6 Sep 1888; m. 28 Aug 1832, MARY MELVIN, b. at Peterborough, 22 Oct 1806 daughter of Reuben and Sarah (Marshall) Melvin; Mary d. at Peterborough, 14 May 1880.

1189) DORCAS AMES *(Benjamin Ames⁴, Hannah Stevens Ames³, Elizabeth Abbott Stevens², George¹)*, b. at Andover, 31 Jul 1776 daughter of Benjamin and Dorcas (Lovejoy) Ames; d. after 1855; m. 31 Oct 1799, ISAAC PHELPS, b. 21 Jun 1772 son of Thomas and Mary (Shattuck) Phelps; Isaac d. after 1850 (listed in the 1850 U. S. Census). Dorcas is listed in the 1855 Massachusetts census in the Andover almshouse, age 77, described as insane.[3120]

There is little known of this family. They were perhaps beset by misfortune as Dorcas died likely at the almshouse in Andover described as insane. In the 1850 census, Isaac is listed as living in the household of Benjamin and Elizabeth Abbott, this likely being Dorcas Ames's nephew Benjamin Abbott and his second wife Elizabeth Goldsmith. There is just one child recorded in this family.

i DORCAS PHELPS, b. at Andover, 24 May 1801; d. 8 Aug 1822.

1190) ABIGAIL AMES *(Benjamin Ames⁴, Hannah Stevens Ames³, Elizabeth Abbott Stevens², George¹)*, b. at Andover, 4 Oct 1779 daughter of Benjamin and Dorcas (Lovejoy) Ames; d. after 1850 at Bradford, VT;[3121] m. 15 Dec 1796, DAVID JOHNSON, b. at Andover, 11 Jul 1772 son of Jacob and Sarah (Doliver) Johnson;[3122] David d. after 1830 at Bradford, VT.

Soon after their marriage, Abigail and David Johnson were in Bradford, Vermont. Three children have been identified for Abigail Ames and David Johnson. Census records suggest there were at least three other children who have not been identified. In the 1850 Census, Abigail Johnson was living in the household of Simeon and Hannah Fuller with daughter Abigail Dearborn also in the household.

i ABIGAIL JOHNSON, baptized at Andover, 17 Sep 1797; d. at Bradford, VT, Dec 1872;[3123] m. about 1821, HENRY DEARBORN, b. about 1790; Henry d. at Orange, VT, 1840 (probate Mar 1840 with widow Abigail as administrator).

ii DAVID JOHNSON, b. at Bradford, about 1800. In 1830, he was a head of household in Bradford and with a female age 20-29 and one female under age 5. He appears to have married but that has not been located.

iii HANNAH JOHNSON, b. at Bradford, about 1802; d. at Bradford, 8 Nov 1865;[3124] m. at Bradford, 6 Sep 1829, SIMEON FULLER, b. about 1808; Simeon d. at Bradford between 1850 and 1860.

1191) SAMUEL AMES *(Nathan Ames⁴, Hannah Stevens Ames³, Elizabeth Abbott Stevens², George¹)*, b. at Groton, 7 Feb 1766 son of Nathan and Deborah (Bowers) Ames; d. at Providence, RI, 16 Feb 1830; m. at Boston, 8 Sep 1801, ANNE CHECKLEY, b. at Philadelphia, 13 Aug 1785 daughter of John Webb and Anne (Wicker) Checkley; Anne d. 15 Jun 1868.

Samuel Ames and his brother Asa located in Providence, Rhode Island where they were shopkeepers. Samuel was apparently successful as he could afford to send his son Samuel to Phillips Academy in Andover and to Brown University.[3125]

Samuel Ames did not leave a will and widow Anne Ames was appointed administratrix of the estate 12 August 1830 with an administrator's bond of ten thousand dollars. The moveable estate was valued at $1,510.51. Samuel also held stock in the Sterling Cotton Manufacturing Company with principal and interest valued at $7,424.86.[3126]

In her will written 14 September 1857, proved in 1868, Anne Ames left her entire estate to her two daughters Anne Ckeckley Ames and Sophia Bicker Greene.[3127] She also added a separate list of "remembrances" in which certain personal items

---

3120 Ancestry.com, Massachusetts, State Census, 1855

3121 In the 1850 U.S. Census, Abigail Johnson age 79 is living in Bradford, Vermont in a household that includes Abigail Dearborn who is her daughter. *United States 1850 Census.* Online database. AmericanAncestors.org. New England Historic Genealogical Society, 2014. (Original index: *United States Census, 1850.* FamilySearch, 2014.)

3122 According to Charlotte Helen Abbott, David Johnson who married Abigail Ames was the brother of Osgood Johnson and Osgood's parents were Jacob and Sarah Johnson. Early Records of the Ames Family of Andover

3123 Death record for Abigail Dearborn daughter of David and Abigail Johnson.

3124 Death record for Hannah Fuller daughter of David Johnson.

3125 American Historical Society, *American Biography: A New Cyclopedia*, volume 12, pp 180-181

3126 Providence (Rhode Island). Court of Probate; Probate Place: Providence, Rhode Island, File A5296. Accessed through ancestry.com

3127 Providence (Rhode Island). Court of Probate; Probate Place: Providence, Rhode Island, File A9496. Accessed through ancestry.com

are left to her children and other relatives. These included bequests to son Samuel C. Ames of his choice of plates (after his sister Sophia's death), daughter Elizabeth a locket containing a lock of hair of Anne's son William, granddaughter Mary Keighler a favorite miniature, to daughter Elizabeth Keighler a mosaic pin that Anne received from her sister, and many similar small bequests to extended family members. Anne's personal estate was valued at $4,698.85 about $4,500 of this in stocks and cash.

Samuel Ames and Anne Checkley had seven children born at Providence.

i ANNE CHECKLEY AMES, b. 19 Jul 1802; d. at Providence, 18 May 1860. Anne did not marry. In her 1860 will, Anne C. Ames left her entire estate to her sister Sophia B. Greene.

ii SOPHIA BICKER AMES, b. 23 Mar 1804; d. at Providence, 27 Dec 1866; m. at Providence, 1 Aug 1836, WILLIAM PERRY GREENE, b. at Newport, RI, 19 Jun 1784 son of Perry and Betsey (Belcher) Greene; William d. at Philadelphia, 23 Apr 1855.

iii SAMUEL C. AMES, b. 6 Sep 1806, d. at Providence, 20 Dec 1865; m. about 1839, MARY THROOP DORR, b. at Providence, 16 Oct 1811 daughter of Sullivan and Lydia (Allen) Dorr; Mary d. at Providence, 14 Feb 1869.

iv JOHN CHECKLEY AMES, b. 21 Jul 1808; d. at Sterling, CT, 5 Oct 1854; m. at Sterling, 16 Apr 1835, SARAH MALVINA CAMPBELL, b. at Voluntown, CT, 19 May 1818 daughter of James and Mary (Terry) Campbell; Sarah d. at Norwich, 22 Aug 1891.

v FRANCIS "FRANK" AMES, b. 14 Mar 1811; d. at San Diego, 20 Jun 1861. Frank was a merchant in San Diego. He does not seem to have married.

vi ELIZABETH LATHROP AMES, b. about 1816; d. at Scituate, RI, 1861; m. at Providence, 5 Nov 1835, WILLIAM HENRY KEIGHLER, b. at Baltimore, about 1804; William d. at Baltimore, 9 Jan 1855.

vii WILLIAM SHAW AMES, b. 18 Feb 1818; d. at Providence, 13 Dec 1840.

1192) DEBORAH AMES *(Nathan Ames⁴, Hannah Stevens Ames³, Elizabeth Abbott Stevens², George¹)*, b. at Groton, 6 Apr 1768 daughter of Nathan and Deborah (Bowers) Ames; d. at Andover 7 Dec 1819; m. 1st 21 Sep 1786, HENRY GRAY BAKER, b. 1 Apr 1767 son of Symonds and Lydia (Gray) Baker; Henry d. of consumption, at Andover, 10 Mar 1802. Deborah m. 2nd 18 Nov 1802, as his second wife, CALEB ABBOTT son of Asa and Elizabeth (Abbott) Abbott; Caleb d. 12 Apr 1837. The family of Deborah Ames and Caleb Abbott is covered in Family 375.

Henry Gray Baker did not leave a will and his estate entered probate 30 March 1802 with Moses Abbot as administrator at the request of widow Deborah. Personal estate was valued at $246.14. Debts were $353.11.[3128]

Three children are known for Deborah Ames and Henry Gray Baker all born at Andover.

i DEBORAH BOWERS BAKER, b. 10 Dec 1786; d. at Andover, 19 Aug 1861; m. 1 Dec 1808, DANIEL POOR, b. at Andover, 27 Mar 1782 son of Daniel and Hannah (Frye) Poor; Daniel d. at Andover, 9 Jul 1846.

ii PRISCILLA BAKER, b. 17 Apr 1789; d. at Andover, 2 Nov 1838; m. 21 Jun 1810, NATHANIEL FRYE, b. at Andover, 23 May 1786 son of John and Betsey (Noyes) Frye; Nathaniel d. at Andover, 11 Feb 1822.

iii THOMAS BAKER, b. 18 Mar 1792; d. at Salem, 3 Aug 1817; m. at Salem, 30 Jan 1816, NANCY BROWN, b. at Salem, 1798 daughter of Peletiah and Hannah (Brown) Brown; Nancy d. at Salem, 27 Jun 1847. Nancy married second, Peter E. Webster on 9 Sep 1822.

1193) LYDIA AMES *(Nathan Ames⁴, Hannah Stevens Ames³, Elizabeth Abbott Stevens², George¹)*, b. at Groton, 29 Mar 1770 daughter of Nathan and Deborah (Bowers) Ames; d. at Andover 24 Jun 1843; m. 21 Jul 1796, her third cousin once removed, ABBOTT WALKER *(Abiel Abbott Walker⁵, Ephraim⁴, Stephen³, John², George¹)*, b. at Chelmsford, 24 Jul 1770 son of Benjamin and Abiel (Abbott) Walker; Abbott Walker d. 2 Aug 1831.

If his gravestone inscription is any indication, Major Abbott Walker was highly esteemed in his community: "He was, but words are wanting/to say what. Ask what a man should be and he was that."[3129]

Little could be found about the specific circumstances of this family. Two of the sons, Samuel and Benjamin, were educated at Phillips Academy. Benjamin was a hotel keeper and lived in Salem, Boston, Newburgh New York, and Plainfield, Connecticut. Samuel was a mariner and later U.S. Gauger in the Boston Custom House.[3130]

There are four children known for Abbott Walker and Lydia Ames.

3128 Essex County, MA: Probate File Papers, 1638-1881.Online database. AmericanAncestors.org. New England Historic Genealogical Society, 2014. Case 1428

3129 findagrave.com, ID: 119837513

3130 Carpenter, Biographical Catalogue of the Trustees, Teachers and Students of Phillips Academy: Andover, 1778-1830, p74

i ABBOT WALKER, b. at Greenfield, NH, 8 Jan 1797; d. at Salem, MA, 14 Jan 1873; m. at Salem, 1 Feb 1826, ELIZABETH KING SMITH, b. at Salem, 9 Jul 1803 daughter of George and Lydia (King) Smith; Elizabeth d. at Salem, 30 Mar 1879.

ii LYDIA WALKER, b. at Andover, 10 Nov 1799; d. at Danvers, 29 Apr 1884. Lydia did not marry. She died at the Danvers asylum of senile dementia. She lived for a time with the Cogswell family in Andover and then with her brother Abbot Walker in Salem.

iii BENJAMIN WALKER, b. at Andover, 6 Sep 1801; d. at Plainfield, CT, 26 Feb 1871; m. at Plainfield, 7 Aug 1825, SUSAN PERKINS WILBUR, b. at Plainfield, 22 Nov 1798 daughter of John and Mehitable (Jones) Wilbur; Susan d. at Plainfield, 13 Apr 1886.

iv SAMUEL WALKER, b. at Andover, 12 Jul 1803; d. at Chelsea, MA, 4 Jul 1864; m. at Newburyport, 12 Sep 1833, LOUISA WOOD, b. at Newburyport, about 1810 daughter of Abner and Dolly (Pearson) Wood; Louisa d. at Chelsea, 4 Sep 1869.

1194) ASA AMES *(Nathan Ames[4], Hannah Stevens Ames[3], Elizabeth Abbott Stevens[2], George[1])*, b. at Groton, 6 May 1772 son of Nathan and Deborah (Bowers) Ames; d. at Providence, RI, 21 Jan 1838; m. REBECCA BRATTELL, b. 1 Jan 1776 daughter of Robert and Rebecca (Pierce) Brattell;[3131] Rebecca d. 17 Apr 1824.

Asa Ames and his brother Samuel settled in Providence where they were shopkeepers.[3132] Asa Ames and Rebecca Brattell were parents of seven children born at Providence, Rhode Island.

i SUSAN BRATTELL AMES, b. 9 Aug 1799; d. at Providence, 14 Mar 1877; m. at Providence, 16 Aug 1821, ISAAC ARNOLD, b. in RI, about 1785; Isaac d. at New York, NY, Jan 1869.

ii ROBERT NATHAN AMES, b. 1800; d. at Sands Point, NY, 25 Mar 1837; m. 1st, at Warren, RI, 26 May 1822, MARIA MAXWELL SISSON, b. at Warren, 10 Feb 1802 daughter of Freeborn and Jane (Maxwell) Sisson; Maria d. 26 Jun 1828. Robert m. 2nd, about 1829, MARY ELIZA SANDS, b. at Sands Point, 11 Dec 1808; Mary d. at Brooklyn, NY, 28 Mar 1872.

iii REBECCA BRATTELL AMES, b. about 1801; d. at Providence, 28 Apr 1837; m. at Providence, 19 Mar 1828, JOSEPH WARREN FEARING, b. at Wareham, MA, 6 Sep 1800 son of Benjamin and Salome (Pope) Fearing; Joseph d. at Providence, 24 Nov 1862. Joseph married Matilda Perkins 13 Dec 1854.[3133]

iv JAMES B. AMES, b. 1807; d. at Providence, 13 Jun 1870; m. in NY, 13 Sep 1843, ANGELINA DOWNING, b. 2o Dec 1824 daughter of George and Sarah (Sands) Downing; Angelina d. at Providence, 14 May 1899.

v AMELIA W. AMES, b. 1810; d. at North Providence, 14 Feb 1868; m. at Providence, 4 Dec 1829, CHARLES F. MANCHESTER, b. in RI, 1805 son of Niles and Phebe (Fenner) Manchester; Charles d. at North Providence, 5 Apr 1878.

vi FISHER AMES, b. 7 Aug 1812; d. at Providence, 21 May 1867; m. at Providence, 8 May 1837, ALMA F. WESTCOTT, b. 20 May 1814; Alma d. at Providence, 1 Jul 1891.

vii JOHN BRATTELL AMES, b. 15 May 1815; d. at Providence, 30 Mar 1904; m. at Plainfield, CT, 13 May 1840, HARRIET F. BURGESS, b. at Plainfield, 14 Feb 1818 daughter of Mowry and Martha (Green) Burgess; Harriet d. at Providence, 21 Apr 1893.

1195) SIMEON AMES *(Nathan Ames[4], Hannah Stevens Ames[3], Elizabeth Abbott Stevens[2], George[1])*, b. at Groton, 13 Sep 1781 son of Nathan and Deborah (Bowers) Ames; d. at Sterling, CT 11 Feb 1863; m. 17 Apr 1826, BETSEY GILMORE, b. about 1809; Betsey was still living in 1870 at the time of the US Census.

There are four children known for Simeon Ames and Betsey Gilmore.

[3131] The 1806 Rhode Island will of Robert Brattell includes a bequest to his grandson James Ames son of Asa and Rebecca and to his beloved daughter Rebecca wife of Asa.

[3132] Cutter, American Biography: A New Cyclopedia, volume 12, p 181

[3133] The Biographical Cyclopedia of Representative Men of Rhode Island, p 289

i GEORGE BOWERS AMES, b. at Sterling, CT, 19 Jul 1831; d. at Providence, 12 Mar 1899; m. 7 Oct 1855, CAROLINE J. SPRAGUE, b. in MA, Feb 1839 daughter of John Sprague;[3134] Caroline d. at Taunton, MA, 23 Aug 1920.

ii CHARLES FISHER AMES, b at Sterling, 16 Apr 1833; d. at Montclair, NJ, after 1910; m. 1865, ELLEN LOUISE GOODELL, b. at Ellington, 8 May 1847 daughter of Francis and Sophia (Burpee) Goodell.

iii SAMUEL AMES, b. at Sterling, 13 Dec 1835; d. at Plainfield, CT, after 1910; m. about 1865, CYNTHIA S., b. in RI about 1829; Cynthia d. at Plainfield, after 1880.

iv HARRIET T. AMES, b. at Hebron, Apr 1840; d. at Plainfield, 26 Mar 1911; m. 1st, about 1858, ELHENAN WAKEFIELD, b. 1839 son of Otis and Mary (Parker) Wakefield; Harriet and Elhenan divorced about 1865. Elhenan died about 1887. Harriet m. 2nd, about 1866, JOSEPH MEDBURY, b. 1837 son of Nathaniel and Prudence (Angell) Medbury; Joseph d. at Plainfield, 13 Feb 1875.

1196) AMELIA AMES *(Nathan Ames⁴, Hannah Stevens Ames³, Elizabeth Abbott Stevens², George¹)*, b. at Groton, 9 Apr 1788 daughter of Nathan and Lydia (Green) Ames; d. at Providence, RI, 6 Apr 1874; m. 11 Oct 1812, JOSEPH WHEELOCK, b. at Westborough, 25 Jun 1788 son of Moses and Lydia (Bond) Wheelock; Joseph d. at New York, NY, 16 May 1857.

Amelia Ames and Joseph Wheelock were parents of nine children born at Providence.[3135]

i AMELIA AMES WHEELOCK, b. 29 Jul 1813; d. at Providence, 1 Jun 1855; m. at Providence, 24 May 1835, EDWARD WALCOTT, b. at Cumberland, RI, 3 Apr 1797 son of Benjamin Stewart and Marcy (Dexter) Walcott; Edward d. at Providence, 5 Feb 1870. Edward was first married to Anna Witherspoon Greene who died in 1832.

ii OTIS AMMIDON WHEELOCK, b. 1815; d. at Providence, 13 Jun 1872; m. at New York, NY, 12 Sep 1849, ELIZA JANE ROSENBURGH, b. in VT, about 1821; Eliza d. at Providence, 22 Mar 1902.

iii ELIZABETH SLATER WHEELOCK, b. 1816; d. at Providence, 16 Nov 1820.

iv MARY ELIZABETH WHEELOCK, b. 1818; d. at Providence, 15 Apr 1830.

v MOSES AMES WHEELOCK, b. 14 Apr 1821; d. at Brooklyn, NY, 23 Jun 1878; m. JENNETTE M. PHYFE, b. in NY, 1824 daughter of John and Jane (McNiesh) Phyfe; Jennette d. at New York, NY, 19 Feb 1901.

vi JOSEPH BOND WHEELOCK, b. 1823; d. at Boston, 15 Nov 1873; m. 1st, about 1860, MARTHA PECK (widow of James Bickford), b. at Rehoboth, MA, 15 Apr 1833 daughter of Edwin and Martha W. (Burr) Peck; Martha d. 13 Jul 1862. Joseph m. 2nd, ABBIE WILMARTH (widow of George Palfrey), b. at Boston, 8 Dec 1841 daughter of Seth and Mary (Sylvester) Wilmarth; Abbie d. at Boston, 26 May 1873.

vii WILLIAM ALMY WHEELOCK, b. 23 Mar 1825; d. at East Hampton, NY, 6 Jul 1905; m. 20 Feb 1850, HENRIETTE EFFNER, b. 5 Oct 1827 daughter of Elijah and Sophia (Dorchester) Effner.

viii EDWARD WHEELOCK, b. 1827; d. 1 May 1829.

ix EDWARD WHEELOCK, b. 1829 d. at the hospital at Fairfax Seminary, VA, 26 Oct 1862. Edward was a private in the Civil War; he died of wounds suffered at the Battle of Bull Run 30 Aug 1862.

1197) JEMIMA GREEN AMES *(Nathan Ames⁴, Hannah Stevens Ames³, Elizabeth Abbott Stevens², George¹)*, b. at Groton, 14 Mar 1791 daughter of Nathan and Lydia (Green) Ames; d. at Providence, RI, 11 Aug 1839; m. 10 Feb 1824, WILLIAM ALMY, b. at Westport, 23 Sep 1788 son of William and Mary "Polly" (Millett) Almy; William d. at Newport, RI aboard ship in the harbor, 16 Sep 1830.

No information has been found for this family. It is known that Jemima and William had one son as Jemima's gravestone bears this inscription: "ERECTED BY AN ONLY SON". But the name of this son is unknown.

1198) AMOS AMES *(Amos Ames⁴, Hannah Stevens Ames³, Elizabeth Abbott Stevens², George¹)*, b. at Groton, 15 Apr 1758 son of Amos and Abigail (Bulkley) Ames; d. at Sullivan, ME after 1810 and before 1820;[3136] m. 1st by 1784, MARY "POLLY" ODIORNE, b. about 1760 daughter of William and Avis (Adams) Odiorne;[3137] Polly d. at Groton, 29 Jul 1787. Amos next had an out-of-wedlock relationship with DEBORAH LAWRENCE with daughter recorded.[3138] Amos m. 2nd,9 Dec 1790, MARY "POLLY" BRAGDON daughter of Ebenezer and Jane (Wilson) Bragdon;[3139] Mary Bragdon d. at Sullivan, after 1820.

3134 Name of father is given on her death record.

3135 Colonial Families of the U.S., volume II, p 748 also lists a son Frank in this family (and only one Edward), but no type of record could be found for Frank.

3136 Amos Ames is head of household in Sullivan in 1810, but Mary Ames is the head of household in 1820.

3137 Odiorne, *Genealogy of the Odiorne Family*, p 32 and p 46

3138 A., d. Deborah Laurence and Amos Ames "as She Saith," Oct. 6, 1788. Massachusetts Vital Records for Groton

3139 The 1806 will of Ebenezer Bragdon includes a bequest to daughter Mary wife of Amos Ames.

Ames Amos enlisted from Groton for six months service in the Revolution on 7 July 1777. He served in Colonel John Robinson's Regiment.[3140]

After the death of his first wife Polly Odiorne and his out-of-wedlock child, Amos went to Sullivan, Maine where he married Mary Bragdon. There are no known children of Amos Ames and Mary Bragdon, but the 1810 census includes a boy under age ten so there is perhaps one additional child of Amos not yet identified.

Amos Ames and Polly Odiorne were parents of two children born at Groton.

i SALLY AMES, b. 29 Jan 1784; d. at Sullivan, ME, 1808; m. JOSHUA DYER, b. at Sullivan, 1783 son of Ephraim and Hannah (Thorndike) Dyer; Joshua d. at Sullivan, 1 Jan 1865. After Sally's death, Joshua married Betsey Sawyer.

ii MARY "POLLY" AMES, b. 19 Mar 1786. Mary did not marry.

Child of Amos Ames and Deborah Lawrence:

i Daughter, b. 6 Oct 1788; nothing further known.

1199) ABIGAIL AMES *(Amos Ames⁴, Hannah Stevens Ames³, Elizabeth Abbott Stevens², George¹)*, b. at Groton, 28 Nov 1763 daughter of Amos and Abigail (Bulkley) Ames; d. at Ashby, 11 Aug 1848; m. 10 Mar 1785, WILLIAM GREEN, b. at Pepperrell, 19 Jan 1755 son of William and Ruth (Colburn) Green; William d. 1 May 1843.

William Green did not leave a will and his estate entered probate 8 August 1843 with Moses Green as administrator. Real estate was valued at $584 and personal estate at $2,095.24 most of which was notes that were owed to him by others. Son Emerson had notes totaling $1,042.91. The distribution included $653 to widow Abigail Green and payments of $186.59 to each of the following children: Moses Green, Isaac Hapgood in the right of his wife, Silas Wetherbee in the right of his wife, William Green, Noah Andrews in the right of his wife, Emerson Green, and Amos Green.[3141]

Abigail Ames and William Green were parents of nine children born at Ashby.

i MOSES GREEN, b. 10 Feb 1786; d. at Ashby, 1 Jul 1857; m. at Ashby, 18 Feb 1805, POLLY KENDALL, b. at Ashby, 25 Apr 1787 daughter of Asa and Molly (Wallis) Kendall; Polly d. at Ashby, 8 Nov 1843.

ii ABIGAIL GREEN, b. 1 Mar 1789; d. 14 Jan 1790.

iii ABIGAIL GREEN, b. 3 Jul 1791; d. at Ashby, 19 Mar 1866; m. 2 Sep 1817, ISAAC HAPGOOD, b. at Marlborough, 8 Mar 1791 son of Joseph and Ruth (Jackson) Hapgood; Joseph d. at Ashby, 24 Nov 1852.

iv LUCY GREEN, b. 15 Jul 1793; d. at Ashby, 4 Feb 1858; m. about 1815, SILAS WETHERBEE, b. at Ashby, 27 Mar 1786 son of Israel and Sarah (Howe) Wetherbee; Silas d. at Ashby, 14 May 1863. After Lucy's death, Silas married Sally Whitcomb who was the widow of Lucy's brother William Green (see below).

v WILLIAM GREEN, b. 25 Jul 1795; d. at Ashby, 3 Sep 1858; m. at Littleton, 4 Jun 1821, SALLY WHITCOMB, b. at Boxborough, 20 Aug 1795 daughter of Moses and Anna (Hayward) Whitcomb; Sally d. at Chelmsford, 27 May 1878. After William's death, Sally married Silas Wetherbee (widower of Lucy Green) on 1 May 1859.

vi SOPHIA GREEN, b. 13 Sep 1797; d. at Ashby, 13 Apr 1880; m. 18 Mar 1815, NOAH ANDREWS, b. at Fitchburg, 1792 son of Daniel and Susanna (Choate) Andrews; Noah d. at Ashby, 8 Aug 1849.

vii EMERSON GREEN, b. 25 Sep 1799; d. at Ashby, 13 Nov 1851; m. about 1829, CLARISSA D. WRIGHT, b. at Ashby, 12 Sep 1809 daughter of Henry and Bette (Lawrence) Wright; Clarissa d. at Ashby, 22 Sep 1857.

viii AMOS GREEN, b. 23 Jul 1801; d. at Ashby, 29 Jul 1886; m. about 1826, ASENATH RAND, b. at Harvard, MA, 28 Oct 1804 daughter of Jonathan and Mercy (Taylor) Rand; Asenath d. at Ashby, 9 Jan 1892.

ix ADALINE GREEN, b. 15 May 1805; d. 22 Aug 1807.

1200) ELI AMES *(Amos Ames⁴, Hannah Stevens Ames³, Elizabeth Abbott Stevens², George¹)*, b. at Groton, 4 May 1765 son of Amos and Abigail (Bulkley) Ames; reported to have gone to Virginia and perhaps Georgia;[3142] m. at NH, 27 Nov 1788,

[3140] Massachusetts Soldiers and Sailors in the Revolutionary War (Images Online)

[3141] Middlesex County, MA: Probate File Papers, 1648-1871.Online database. AmericanAncestors.org. New England Historic Genealogical Society, 2014. Case 33154

[3142] The DAR gives his place of death as Georgia.

EUNICE PARKER, b. at New Ipswich, NH, Apr 1761 daughter of Samuel and Abijah (Cook) Parker;[3143] Eunice d. likely at Covesville, VA, 1843.[3144]

Eli and Eunice started their family in New Ipswich where two children were born and were then back in Groton where the younger children were born. The family did go to Virginia where the two youngest children settled. Their daughter Lucy married Elizur Butler and they were missionaries at the Brainerd Mission in Tennessee. While serving at a mission in Georgia, Elizur Butler was arrested for residing in the Cherokee Nation without a permit and imprisoned from 16 September 1831 to 18 January 1833.[3145][3146] As the death Eli Ames is reported to have occurred in Georgia, perhaps he had some connection with the mission work of his daughter and son-in-law.

Eli Ames and Eunice Parker were parents of five children.

i ABIGAIL AMES, b. at New Ipswich, 1 May 1789; nothing further known.

ii LUCY AMES, b. 13 Jul 1790; d. 4 Jul 1791.

iii LUCY AMES, b. at Groton, 25 Apr 1793; d. at Fort Smith, AK, 5 Jun 1870; m. 14 Aug 1830, ELIZUR BUTLER, b. at Norfolk, CT, 11 Jun 1794 son of Hezekiah and Hephzibah (Burr) Butler; Elizur d. at Van Buren, AK, 4 Feb 1857.

iv ELI AMES, b. at Groton, 23 Apr 1795; d. at Covesville, VA, 12 Mar 1870; m. at Franklin, VT, 25 Mar 1819, NANCY WINCH, b. about 1794 (reported as NH on census records); Nancy d. likely at Sam Miller Township (Covesville), VA, after 1870.

v PHILLIS AMES, b. about 1799; d. at Covesville, VA, after 1850. Phillis did not marry. In 1850, she was living with her brother Eli.

1201) PETER AMES *(Amos Ames[4], Hannah Stevens Ames[3], Elizabeth Abbott Stevens[2], George[1])*, b. at Groton, 7 Nov 1767 son of Amos and Abigail (Bulkley) Ames; d. Jun 1823; m. 7 Oct 1799, SALLY CHILD, b. at Groton, of uncertain parentage but possibly the daughter of Abraham and Rebecca (Stowell) Child; Sally d. at Groton, 29 Aug 1828.[3147] After Peter's death, Sally m. John Rockwood, 6 May 1827.

Peter Ames did not leave a will and widow Sally Ames was named administratrix of the estate 30 September 1823. The real property included 150 acres with house and barn valued at $1200. The personal estate was valued at $272.27. Parcels of real property with total value of $400 were set off to the widow. The real estate was sold in 1825 to settle the estate. There were guardianship cases for Charles Ames (William Livermore selected) and Adaline Ames (William Livermore). Charles was over fourteen in 1824 when he selected his guardian and Adeline was over age fourteen in 1826.[3148]

Peter Ames and Sally Child were parents of six children born at Groton.

i EDWARD AMES, b. 1 Feb 1800; m. 22 Sep 1822, MARY TILLA "of New London". Nothing further is known.

ii SALLY AMES, b. 14 Nov 1802; d. at Groton, Dec 1842; m. at Groton, 15 Oct 1823, CALVIN HUBBARD, b. 1 Oct 1797 son of Thomas and Susannah (Patterson) Hubbard; Calvin d. at Groton, 16 Mar 1837.

iii CHARLES AMES, b. 24 Jul 1805; d. 2 Nov 1808.

iv CHARLES AMES, b. about 1810; living in 1824 when he selected William Livermore as his guardian. One possibility is that he is the Charles Ames who shows up in Cass County, Texas in the 1830's. On census records, his birth is estimated as 1810 and was born in Massachusetts. If so, he married Harriet Ann Moore as her third husband. Names of the children of Charles and Harriet include Charles Peter Ames, Edward York Ames, and Adeline Ames.

v ADELINE AMES, b. about 1812 (baptized 24 Nov 1816); d. at Harvard, MA, 1 Aug 1893; m. at Groton, 31 May 1836, OLIVER HUMPHREY ATHERTON, b. at Harvard, MA, 20 Jun 1809 son of Philemon and Elizabeth (Patterson) Atherton; Oliver d. at Harvard, 24 Jul 1898.

vi ABIGAIL BULKLEY AMES, b. 28 Jun 1819; d. May 1824.

3143 Cutter, *History of the Town of Jaffrey, New Hampshire*, p 417

3144 There is a memorial marker in Cove Presbyterian Cemetery in Covesville, Virginia with the inscription: Mrs. Eunice Ames mother of Eli and Phillis Ames born Apr 16 1761 in the 82nd year of her age.

3145 Kurian and Lamport, *Encyclopedia of Christianity in the United States*, volume 5, p 362

3146 "Death of Dr. Butler" The Daily Dispatch, Richmond, Virginia, March 24, 1857

3147 Rockwood, Sally, w. John, formerly w. Peter Ames, and d. Abraham Child, Aug. 29, 1828. From Groton vital records

3148 Middlesex County, MA: Probate File Papers, 1648-1871.Online database. AmericanAncestors.org. New England Historic Genealogical Society, 2014. Case number 393

1202) HANNAH AMES *(Amos Ames[4], Hannah Stevens Ames[3], Elizabeth Abbott Stevens[2], George[1])*, b. at Groton, 30 Jan 1770 daughter of Amos and Abigail (Bulkley) Ames; d. 22 Aug 1840; m. 7 Jun 1789, IMLA PARKER, b. at Groton, 12 Jan 1765 son of Nathaniel and Eunice (Lakin) Parker; Imla d. 4 Apr 1828.

In his will written 21 February 1828, Imla Parker bequeaths to beloved wife Hannah one hundred eighty dollars in household furniture, real stock, and provisions to be selected by her from the personal inventory. She also receives use and improvement on one-third of the real estate during her natural life. Daughter Hannah wife of Billings Fisher receives two hundred dollars, son Imla two hundred eighty dollars, daughter Clarissa wife of William Buttrick two hundred dollars. Sons Eber and Moses receive two hundred dollars in trust for the use of daughter Mary wife of Winslow Ames, and Eber and Moses are to use this sum and interest on the sum for the convenience and comfort of Mary and her children. After Winslow Ames dies, the money is to be paid to Mary. Son Moses receives two hundred eighty dollars. Daughter Abigail receives two hundred eighty dollars. The remainder of the estate goes to son Eber who is also named executor.[3149]

Imla and Hannah Parker had nine children whose births are recorded at Groton.

i HANNAH PARKER, b. 27 Sep 1789; d. at Dedham, 29 Aug 1849; m. at Groton, 19 Nov 1821, BILLINGS FISHER, b. at Dedham, about 1781 son of Oliver and Sarah (Billings) Fisher; Billings d. at Dedham, 4 Feb 1854.

ii IMLA PARKER, b. 4 Sep 1791; d. at Littleton, 1836 (probate 12 Apr 1836); m. at Lexington, 1 Jan 1823, HARRIET SMITH, b. at Lexington, 6 Jan 1791 daughter of Jonathan and Abigail (Marrett) Smith; Harriet d. at Boston, 15 Apr 1876.

iii EBER PARKER, b. 16 Sep 1793; d. at Boston, 23 Jun 1869; m. at Boston, 16 Sep 1818, MARY ANN WILD, b. at Boston, about 1800 daughter of Barnabas and Betsy (-) Wild; Mary Ann d. at Boston, 11 Mar 1887.

iv CLARISSA PARKER, b. 18 Sep 1795; d. at Pepperell, 10 Aug 1865; m. at Groton, 25 Dec 1814, WILLIAM BUTTRICK, b. at Pepperell, 25 Feb 1792 son of Francis and Lydia (Howe) Buttrick; William d. at Harvard, MA, 23 Mar 1844.

v MARY PARKER, b. 15 Mar 1798; d. at New Ipswich, NH, 23 Oct 1881; m. 1st at Groton, 27 Feb 1818, WINSLOW AMES, b. at Pepperell, 7 Nov 1780 son of Elijah and Sarah (Blood) Ames; Winslow d. at Groton, 7 May 1837. Mary m. 2nd, 30 Nov 1837, JOSEPH DAVIS, b. at New Ipswich, 2 Jan 1778 son of Silas and Mary (Clark) Davis; Joseph d. at New Ipswich, 10 Mar 1876.

vi MOSES PARKER, b. 17 Jul 1800; d. at West Roxbury, 3 Apr 1873; m. at Boston, 2 Aug 1824, ANNIS N. WILSON, b. in NH, 24 Mar 1798[3150] of unknown parents; Annis d. at Boston, 28 Mar 1886.

vii ABIGAIL PARKER, b. 23 Nov 1802; d. 30 Nov 1802

viii PAMELA PARKER, b. 6 Nov 1803; d. 7 Mar 1815

ix ABIGAIL PARKER, b. 13 Sep 1806; d. at Groton, 30 Jun 1900; m. at Groton, Dec 1829, RUFUS MOORS, b. at Groton, 17 Jan 1805 son of Rufus and Lucy (Sewell) Moors; Rufus d. at Groton, 23 Aug 1880.

1203) BULKLEY AMES *(Amos Ames[4], Hannah Stevens Ames[3], Elizabeth Abbott Stevens[2], George[1])*, b. at Groton, 20 Jul 1772 son of Amos and Abigail (Bulkley) Ames; d. 22 Jan 1836; m. 22 Sep 1799, LYDIA PRESCOTT, b. at Westford, 8 Jan 1780 daughter of Ebenezer and Lydia (Wood) Prescott; Lydia d. 15 Feb 1848.

Bulkley Ames was a farmer in Groton. He was the recipient of the last tract of common land in Groton in 1829.[3151] At the time of his death in 1836, he held a total of 244 acres including the homestead farm of 137 acres. The total value of real property was $249.00. Widow Lydia Ames received the set-off of the dower. The heirs-at-law signing as being satisfied with the accounting of the estate were widow Lydia Ames, Asa Ames, Simeon Ames, Luther F. Potter (husband of daughter Lydia Ames), and William Ames.[3152]

Bulkley and Lydia Ames had four children whose births are recorded at Groton.

3149 *Probate Records 1648--1924 (Middlesex County, Massachusetts)*; Author: *Massachusetts. Probate Court (Middlesex County)*; Probate Place: *Middlesex, Massachusetts*, Case number 16580.

3150 Annis's age at death is given as 88 years, 4 days.

3151 Butler, *History of Groton*, p 32

3152 *Probate Records 1648--1924 (Middlesex County, Massachusetts); Author: Massachusetts. Probate Court (Middlesex County); Probate Place: Middlesex, Massachusetts, Case 368*

i ASA AMES, b. 3 Nov 1799; d. at Groton, 14 Apr 1846; m. at Groton, 28 Mar 1836, MARY ADAMS, b. at Ashburnham, 29 Oct 1808 daughter of Walter Russel and Mercy (Fairbanks) Adams;[3153] Mary d. at Groton, 19 Jun 1864. After Asa's death, Mary married Calvin Childs.

ii SIMEON AMES, b. 14 Aug 1803; d. at Groton, 28 Feb 1874; m. at Groton, 25 Nov 1830, SIBBEL BLOOD, b. at Groton, 22 Jul 1810 daughter of Timothy and Sibbel (Woods) Blood; Sibbel d. at Groton, 23 May 1903.

iii WILLIAM AMES, b. 6 Aug 1807; d. at Dedham, 29 Nov 1892; m. at Dedham, 23 Sep 1832, SUSAN LEWIS, b. at Dedham, 24 Apr 1814 daughter of Samuel and Ann (MacFarlane) Lewis; Susan d. at Dedham, 13 Feb 1880.

iv LYDIA PRESCOTT AMES, b. 11 May 1814; d. at Dade, FL, 1907;[3154] m. at Groton, LUTHER FITCH POTTER, b. at Sebago Lake, ME, 10 Dec 1810 son of David and Sibyl (Fitch) Potter; Luther d. at Cincinnati, 2 Dec 1884.

1204) BETSEY BULKLEY AMES *(Amos Ames[4], Hannah Stevens Ames[3], Elizabeth Abbott Stevens[2], George[1])*, b. at Groton, 10 Dec 1776 daughter of Amos and Abigail (Bulkley) Ames; d. 28 Jul 1861; m. 21 Apr 1799, WILLIAM LIVERMORE, b. at Shirley 23 Jun 1770 son of Oliver and Catherine (Bond) Livermore; William d. 2 Mar 1846.

William Livermore was a carpenter and a builder, but later focused on farming.[3155] He represented Groton in the State Legislature in 1829 and 1830.[3156]

In his will written 31 July 1843 (probate 1846), William Livermore makes the following bequests. Beloved wife Betsey receives all the household furniture, two cows, $800, and one-fourth part of the income form the produce of the homestead farm. There are several other specific provisions for her maintenance. Son Daniel receives the rest of the livestock, farming tools, and homestead farm which he is to cultivate and improve in a good husband-like manner. Son Nathaniel receives all the wearing apparel. The rest of the estate goes equally to daughter Catherine, sons William and Nathaniel, and daughter Betsey the wife of Charles Prescott. Son William is the sole executor. The total value of the estate was $9,125,38 with $5,075 value to the real estate.[3157]

William and Betsey Livermore had seven children born at Groton.

i CATHERINE LIVERMORE, b. 15 Jun 1800; d. at Groton, 9 Apr 1877. Catherine did not marry. She lived with her mother until her mother's death and afterward lived with her sister Betsey.

ii DANIEL LIVERMORE, b. 18 May 1802; d. 18 Aug 1802.

iii WILLIAM LIVERMORE, b. 9 Jul 1803; d. at Groton, 4 Nov 1894; m. 1st at Cohasset, 7 Sep 1830, SARAH CAROLINE LAWRENCE, b. about 1809 daughter of Jonathan and Mary (Steele) Lawrence; Sarah d. 30 Aug 1831. William m. 2nd at Boston, 11 Nov 1832, HARRIET LIVERMORE, b. at Alstead, NH, 16 Nov 1804 daughter of William and Tabitha (Tilton) Livermore;[3158] Harriet d. at Groton, 17 May 1891.

iv DANIEL LIVERMORE, b. 26 Mar 1805; d. at Shirley, 9 Jan 1882; m. 15 May 1831, ABIGAIL TUCK, b. at Hambleton, NY, 30 May 1805 daughter of William and Hannah (Porter) Tuck; Abigail d. at Shirley, 25 Feb 1881.[3159]

v NATHANIEL LIVERMORE, b. 8 Mar 1807; d. at Groton, 2 Oct 1893; m. 1st at Boston, ELIZABETH WOOD LAWRENCE, b. at Cohasset (baptism Oct 1819) daughter of Jonathan and Mary (Steele) Lawrence; Elizabeth d. before 1850 when Nathaniel remarried. Nathaniel m. 2nd 16 Jan 1850, NANCY BLOOD, b. at Groton, 5 Jun 1812 daughter of Thomas and Milley (Fitch) Blood; Nancy d. at Groton, 7 Dec 1875. Nathaniel m. 3rd at Bedford, NH, 1 Sep 1881, REBECCA MILLER CHAMPNEY, b. 6 Aug 1822 daughter of Francis and Rebecca (Miller) Champney.

vi LUTHER LIVERMORE, b. 17 Feb 1809; d. at Groton, 24 May 1834.

vii BETSEY LIVERMORE, b. 29 Aug 1811; d. at Groton, 1 Jan 1871; m. at Groton, 3 May 1835, CHARLES PRESCOTT, b. at Groton, 21 Nov 1809 son of Abel and Hannah (Spaulding) Prescott; Charles d. at Groton, 31 May 1875.

1205) ROBERT AMES *(Robert Ames[4], Hannah Stevens Ames[3], Elizabeth Abbott Stevens[2], George[1])*, b. at Groton, 12 Oct 1763 son of Robert and Sarah (Woods) Ames; d. at Groton, 15 Nov 1789; m. 27 Mar 1783, RUTH LAWRENCE, b. 3 Jan 1758 daughter of Benjamin and Rebecca (-) Lawrence; Ruth d. at Groton 3 Jul 1825.

3153 Mary's place of birth and names of her parents as Walter R. and Mercy Adams are given on her death record.
3154 Lydia was living with her son George at Lake Worth, FL at the 1900 U.S. Census.
3155 Thwing, *The Livermore Family*, p 119
3156 Butler, *History of Groton*, p 464
3157 *Middlesex County, MA: Probate File Papers, 1648-1871.*Online database. *AmericanAncestors.org.* New England Historic Genealogical Society, 2014. Case number 36518
3158 Harriet's parents' names are given as William and Tabitha Livermore on her death record.
3159 Abigail's place of birth and names of parents as William and Hannah Tuck are given on her death record.

Ruth Lawrence Ames did not leave a will and her estate entered probate 27 Sep 1825. Son Gideon Ames wrote the probate court noting that he was living in a remote part of the state and requested his brother Mial be named administrator. The probate document naming Mial as administrator notes that there were just the two children living at the time of their mother's death. The estate was valued at $733.[3160]

Robert Ames and Ruth Lawrence were parents of four children born at Groton.

i GIDEON AMES, b. 5 Sep 1783; d. at Belchertown, MA, 22 Jul 1855; m. at Belchertown, 2 Nov 1812, MEHITABLE WARD, b. at Royalston, MA, about 1782 daughter of Eneas and Rebecca (Newton) Ward; Mehitable d. at Belchertown, 30 Oct 1855.

ii MIAL AMES, b. 1784; d. 31 Mar 1785.

iii MIAL AMES, b. 24 Jan 1787; d. at Pepperell, 1 Feb 1846; m. at Pepperell, 21 May 1812, ELIZABETH "BETSEY" LAWRENCE, b. at Pepperell, 2 Nov 1788 daughter of Jeremiah and Anna (Woods) Lawrence; Betsey d. at Pepperell, 4 Oct 1850.

iv BOAZ AMES, b. 12 May 1789; nothing further known.

1206) SARAH AMES *(Robert Ames[4], Hannah Stevens Ames[3], Elizabeth Abbott Stevens[2], George[1])*, b. at Groton, 27 May 1765 daughter of Robert and Sarah (Woods) Ames; d. at Bridport, VT, 13 Jul 1836; m. 18 Jun 1787, EPHRAIM STONE, b. at Groton, 11 Jan 1763 son of Benjamin and Prudence (Farnsworth) Stone; Ephraim d. 6 Jun 1841.[3161]

Ephraim Stone and Sarah Ames were parents of twelve children born at Bridport, Vermont.

i EPHRAIM STONE, b. 16 Mar 1788; d. at Ironville, NY, 14 Mar 1841; m. at Bridport, 21 Dec 1810, HULDAH WILCOX, b. at Bridport, 24 Oct 1792 daughter of James and Eunice (Vickery) Wilcox; Huldah d. at Ironville, 20 Mar 1841.

ii SIMEON STONE, b. 15 Apr 1790; d. 11 Jun 1790.

iii SALLY STONE, b. 23 May 1791; d. 21 Jun 1791.

iv ISAAC STONE, b. 16 May 1792; d. at Mexico, NY, 4 Feb 1848; m. in VT, 20 Jul 1815, LYDIA HURLBURT, b. at Sudbury, VT, 1 Feb 1796 daughter of Samuel and Jerusha (Higgins) Hurlburt; Lydia d. at Mexico, NY, 26 Apr 1875.

v SALLY STONE, b. 18 Apr 1794; d. at Bridport, 21 May 1838. Sally did not marry.

vi MAIL STONE, b. 18 Jul 1795; d. at East Troy, WI, Dec 1869; m. about 1822, LUCY BEEBE, b. about 1798; Lucy d. at East Troy, 4 Mar 1872.

vii ENOS STONE, b. 25 Apr 1799; no further information.

viii ROBERT AMES STONE, b. 25 Jun 1801; d. at Potsdam, NY, 5 Feb 1851; m. about 1824, PHILA BOSWORTH, b. 15 Jul 1799; Phila d. at Potsdam, 4 Apr 1862.

ix PHILIP STONE, b. 12 Oct 1803; d. at Bridport, 26 Mar 1882; m. at Bridport, 31 Dec 1840, JULIA LINCOLN, b. 1824; Julia d. at Bridport, 16 Feb 1888.

x SIMEON STONE, b. 12 Jun 1805; d. at Canton, NY, 1870; m. at Bridport, 23 Aug 1832, JOANNA B. JOHNSON, b. in VT, 1807; Joanna d. at Canton, 1882.

xi HENRY STONE, b. 15 Dec 1808; d. 24 Dec 1808.

xii HENRIETTA STONE, b. 15 Dec 1808; d. at Bridport, 29 Jan 1868. Henrietta did not marry.

1207) PRUDENCE AMES *(Robert Ames[4], Hannah Stevens Ames[3], Elizabeth Abbott Stevens[2], George[1])*, b. at Groton, 29 Dec 1767 daughter of Robert and Sarah (Woods) Ames; d. at Ashby, MA, 6 Nov 1821;[3162] m. 27 Dec 1786, ISAAC GREEN "of Ashby," b. about 1757 who parentage is uncertain; Isaac d. at Ashby 7 Nov 1821. One of Prudence's cousins married a Green from

[3160] Middlesex County, MA: Probate File Papers, 1648-1871.Online database. AmericanAncestors.org. New England Historic Genealogical Society, 2014. Case 399

[3161] Ancestry.com, *Vermont, Vital Records, 1720-1908* (Provo, UT, USA: Ancestry.com Operations, Inc., 2013).

[3162] This is the date engraved on her gravestone. Findagrave.com

Pepperrell and there is an Isaac Green born at Pepperell of the right age. There is an Isaac Green from Groton who was the much younger brother of Susanna Green who was Robert Ames's second wife.

There are records for three children of Prudence Ames and Isaac Green born at Ashby.

i POLLY GREEN, b. 1 Jun 1787; d. at Ashby, 24 oct 1805.

ii SALLY GREEN, b. 27 Mar 1789; d. at Woburn, MA, 17 Apr 1865; m. about 1812, DANIEL RAYMOND, b. at Ashby, 18 May 1788 son of Daniel and Molly (Kingsley) Raymond; Daniel d. at Ashburnham, 5 Jan 1846.

iii ISAAC GREEN, b. 11 Jun 1793; d. at Okaw, IL, after 1870; m. at West Boylston, 28 May 1818, ABIGAIL LOVELL, b. at West Boylston, about 1799 daughter of Asa and Betty (Raymond) Lovell; Abigail d. at Okaw, after 1870.

1208) BETHIAH AMES *(Robert Ames^4, Hannah Stevens Ames^3, Elizabeth Abbott Stevens^2, George^1)*, b. at Groton, 30 Nov 1770 daughter of Robert and Sarah (Woods) Ames; d. at Peterborough, NH, 15 Feb 1852;[3163] m. 18 Feb 1788, JOHN SCOTT, b. at Dublin, NH about 1765; John d. at Peterborough, 27 Dec 1847.

John Scott accompanied his father Major William Scott in the Revolution, John being a teenager at the time. John served as selectman of Peterborough for eight of the years from 1810 to 1818. He was a farmer, but late in life, sold his farm and moved to a house in town.[3164]

In his will dated 26 November 1847, John Scott bequeaths to wife Bethia during her life "the entire use and control of the house I now live in" as well as all the buildings and land they stand on. She also receives use of and income from other parcels of real estate. To daughter Clarissa Scott, he leaves the use of one undivided half of the house and she will have full use of the house after the death of her mother. After the death of his wife, one undivided half of the house is bequeathed to granddaughter Mary Sophia Fuller as long as she pays to her brother Charles Fuller $200. Daughter Sally Scott receives $350 and daughter Harriet Gray $400. His grandchildren who are the children of his daughter Elizabeth Jewett who is deceased each receive $50: Elizabeth Hales, George Jewett, Charles Jewett, Sarah Jewett, John Jewett, Henry Jewett, and Mary Jewett. His grandchildren who are the children of his deceased son William Scott also receive $50 each: Albert S. Scott, Susan A. Scott, Will H. Scott, Sophia D. Scott, Charles Scott, Kendall Scott, Philenda Scott, Walter Scott, Mary S. Scott, and John Scott. He also bequeaths $30 to his niece Jane McCoy "as a token of my esteem." He specifies that these legacies are not to be paid until after the decease of his wife. John H. Steele and James Scott are named executors. (James Scott is the husband of daughter Sally Scott.) Daughter Nancy is not mentioned in the will although she was living at the time and there is other evidence that she is a daughter in this family.[3165][3166]

John Scott and Bethiah Ames were parents of nine children born at Peterborough.

i SALLY SCOTT, b. 22 Dec 1789; d. at Stoddard, NH, 23 Feb 1865; m. at Peterborough, 7 Jun 1812, JAMES SCOTT, Jr., b. at Stoddard, about 1782 son of James and Hannah (-) Scott; James d. at Stoddard, 19 Apr 1863.

ii HARRIET SCOTT, b. 30 Jul 1792; d. at Peterborough, 28 Jan 1885; m. 14 Apr 1811, WILLIAM GRAY, b. at Peterborough, 3 Dec 1781 son of Kelso and Phebe (Gray) Gray; William d. at Peterborough, 31 Mar 1855.

iii JOHN SCOTT, b. 20 Jun 1794; d. at Barre, MA, 19 Mar 1837 (buried in Village Cemetery, Peterborough; m. at Adams, MS, 14 May 1821, SUSAN ANN MABIN, "of Natchez".

iv CLARISSA SCOTT, b. 26 Nov 1795; d. at Peterborough. 1 Apr 1873. Clarissa did not marry.

v NANCY SCOTT, b. 20 Apr 1797; d. at Peterborough, 29 Dec 1886; m. at Peterborough, 24 Nov 1818, SAMUEL BULLARD, b. about 1794 son of Isaac and Betsey (Jackson) Bullard;[3167] Samuel d. at Hancock, 3 Jan 1839. Nancy m. 2nd, at Hancock, 14 Sep 1841, JOSEPH COBB, b. at Nelson, NH, 18 Jan 1792 son of Samuel Cobb; Joseph went to California for the gold rush where he died 9 Mar 1855. Joseph had two marriages prior to his marriage to Nancy.

vi ELIZABETH SCOTT, b. 11 Jun 1799; d. at Peterborough, 12 Oct 1842; m. 27 Feb 1821, AMIHAZ JEWETT, b. 19 Jan 1794 son of John and Elizabeth (Cummings) Jewett; Amihaz d. at Peterborough, 2 Nov 1860.

vii WILLIAM SCOTT, b. 19 Feb 1801; d. at Peterborough, 24 Sep 1846; m. 1st, 19 Jan 1823, PHILENDA CROSSFIELD, b. at Keene, NH, 9 Apr 1798 daughter of Samuel Crossfield; Philenda d. at Peterborough, 23 May 1839. William m. 2nd, about 1840, MALINDA WARD, b. 18 Jan 1807; Malinda d. at Peterborough, 13 Sep 1862.

3163 Ancestry.com, *New Hampshire, Death and Burial Records Index, 1654-1949* (Provo, UT, USA: Ancestry.com Operations, Inc., 2011).

3164 Smith and Morison, *History of Peterborough*, p 249

3165 *New Hampshire. Probate Court (Hillsborough County);* Probate Place: *Hillsborough, New Hampshire, Probate Records, Vol 55-56, 1846-1849*, pp 104-105, will of John Scott

3166 The marriage record for Nancy's marriage to Samuel Bullard gives her parents' names as John Scott and Bethiah Ames.

3167 Hayward, *History of Hancock*, p 407

viii MARY SCOTT, b. 5 Jan 1806; d. at Peterborough, 17 Nov 1842; m. CHARLES L. FULLER, b. 1808; Charles d. at Peterborough, 7 Jul 1832.

ix CHARLES SCOTT, b. 26 Jan 1808; d. 2 Oct 1826.

1209) HANNAH ABBOTT *(Phebe Steel Abbott[4], Phebe Stevens Steel[3], Elizabeth Abbott Stevens[2], George[1])*, b. at Andover, 15 Oct 1777 daughter of John and Phebe (Steel) Abbott (father John is of the Rowley Abbott line); d. at Haverhill, 25 Nov 1853;[3168] m. 27 Feb 1810 as his second wife, JOHN JOHNSON whose parentage is not yet certain, but likely the son of John and Hannah (Abbott) Johnson born in Andover 8 Dec 1777. John Johnson died 1814 (probate of estate 4 Aug 1814 with widow Hannah declining administration). John Johnson was first married to Lydia Kimball who died 1808. The 1826 will of John Kimball (Lydia's father) has a bequest for grandson Edward Johnson, who was the son of John and Lydia.

John Johnson was a mariner. His estate entered probate 4 Aug 1814 with William Johnson, the third as administrator. Personal estate was valued at $137.63.[3169] The estate of Hannah Johnson entered probate 7 November 1854.[3170] Stephen Roberts was named administrator at the request of only heir Leonard Johnson. Real estate was valued at $1,300 and personal estate at $388.

Hannah Abbott and John Johnson were parents of two children born at Andover.

i JOHN ABBOTT JOHNSON, b. 21 Jul 1810; nothing further known but deceased before 1853 when brother Leonard was listed as the only heir of mother's estate.

ii LEONARD JOHNSON, b. 16 Jan 1812; d. at Haverhill, 2 Jan 1865; m. at Haverhill, 9 Dec 1832, SARAH ANN DAVIS, b. in VT, about 1814; Sarah d. of consumption, at Haverhill, 12 Oct 1855.

1210) STEPHEN INGALLS *(Elizabeth Steel Ingalls[4], Phebe Stevens Steel[3], Elizabeth Abbott Stevens[2], George[1])*, b. at Andover, 17 Jun 1761 son of Joshua and Elizabeth (Steel) Ingalls; d. about May 1794 (will written 4 Apr 1794 and probate 3 June 1794); m. 21 Sep 1786, LYDIA KIMBALL, b. 9 Mar 1761 daughter of Andrew and Esther (Barker) Kimball; Lydia d. at Andover, 16 Dec 1831.

In his will written 5 April 1794 (probate 3 June 1794), Stephen Ingalls bequeaths to beloved wife Lydia the use of and improvement on all the real estate while she is a widow as well as other provisions for her support. Lydia also receives seven pounds 10 shillings to be used for the support and education of their daughters Lydia and Lodemia during their minority. Honored mother Elizabeth Ingalls receives one seat in his pew. Daughter Lydia receives his watch and daughter Lodemia receives his desk. Lydia and Lodemia will also divided all the remainder of the estate. Brother-in-law Ephraim Lacy is named executor.[3171]

Stephen Ingalls and Lydia Kimball were parents of three children born at Andover.

i LYDIA INGALLS, b. 11 Nov 1787; d. at Andover, 30 Jul 1824; m. 5 Jun 1823, ANDREW KIMBALL LACY, b. at Andover, 16 Oct 1792 son of Ephraim and Mehitable (Kimball) Lacy; Andrew d. at Newburyport, 28 Aug 1861.

ii LODEMIA INGALLS, b. 30 Oct 1789; d. at Andover, 18 Jul 1868. Lydia did not marry.

iii STEPHEN INGALLS, b. Jun 1793; d. before date of father's will.

1211) SIMEON INGALLS *(Elizabeth Steel Ingalls[4], Phebe Stevens Steel[3], Elizabeth Abbott Stevens[2], George[1])*, b. at Andover, 3 Sep 1764 son of Joshua and Elizabeth (Steel) Ingalls; m. 1st, 1 Jan 1784, PRISCILLA BERRY, b. at Andover, 20 May 1760 daughter of Benjamin and Mary (-) Berry; Priscilla d. about 1786. Simeon m. 2nd, 16 Jan 1787 the widow ELIZABETH FISH whose identity is unknown.

There are no children known for Simeon Ingalls and Priscilla Berry. There are two children known for Simeon and Elizabeth Ingalls, both born at Andover, but no further information.

i PETER INGALLS, b. 18 Nov 1787

ii BETTY INGALLS, b. 20 Dec 1789

[3168] At the 1850 US Census she is listed as living with Leonard Johnson who is her son. There is a probate record for her from 1854 in which Leonard Johnson, the sole heir, is also the administrator of the estate.

[3169] Essex County, MA: Probate File Papers, 1638-1881.Online database. AmericanAncestors.org. New England Historic Genealogical Society, 2014. Case 15070

[3170] Essex County, MA: Probate File Papers, 1638-1881.Online database. AmericanAncestors.org. New England Historic Genealogical Society, 2014. Case 43685

[3171] Essex County, MA: Probate File Papers, 1638-1881.Online database. AmericanAncestors.org. New England Historic Genealogical Society, 2014. Case 14560

1212) PHEBE INGALLS *(Elizabeth Steel Ingalls[4], Phebe Stevens Steel[3], Elizabeth Abbott Stevens[2], George[1])*, b. at Andover, 30 Dec 1768 daughter of Joshua and Elizabeth (Steel) Ingalls; d. at Pelham, NH, 20 Jul 1847; m. 3 Jun 1790, ELIJAH BRADSTREET, b. 4 Jul 1767 son of Samuel and Ruth (Lampson) Bradstreet; Elijah d. at Pelham, 2 Dec 1850.

Elijah Bradstreet and Phebe Ingalls married in Andover and their first child was born there. The family relocated to Greenfield where five other children were born, and after the birth of their youngest child, moved on to Pelham, New Hampshire.

i ELIZABETH INGALLS BRADSTREET, b. at Andover, 28 May 1791; d. at Andover, 12 Apr 1828; m. 12 Dec 1815, CALEB WHEELER, b. at Salem, 22 Dec 1782 son of Abner and Sarah (Stickney) Wheeler; Caleb d. at Andover, 10 Apr 1836.

ii ELIJAH BRADSTREET, b. 15 Dec 1792; d. at Bradford, 29 Jun 1882; m. 1 Apr 1824, HANNAH CARLETON, b. at Bradford, 10 Dec 1798 daughter of Bazaleel and Mary (Richardson) Carleton; Hannah d. at Lawrence, 20 Feb 1875.

iii STEPHEN INGALLS BRADSTREET, b. at Greenfield, MA, 27 Oct 1794; d. at Cleveland, OH, Jun 1837; m. 5 Aug 1824, ANNA DANA SMITH, b. at Amherst, NH, 19 Sep 1801 daughter of Jonathan and Amelia (Dana) Smith;[3172] Anna d. at Cleveland, 27 May 1838. Stephen Ingalls Bradstreet attended Dartmouth, was an ordained minister, and was one of the first trustees of Case Western Reserve University.

iv PHEBE BRADSTREET, b. at Greenfield, MA, 29 Sep 1796; d. at Amherst, MA, 10 Feb 1875; m. 27 Dec 1827, ARTEMAS HERRICK, b. at Boxford, 3 Jul 1788 son of Edmund and Mehitable (Curtice) Herrick; Artemas d. at Methuen, 4 Aug 1861.

v RUTH EMERSON BRADSTREET, b. at Greenfield, MA, 20 Jul 1798; d. at East Cambridge, 17 Aug 1886; m. 18 Oct 1827, WILLIAM WYMAN, b. at Pelham, NH, 15 Jul 1797 son of William and Elizabeth (Tenney) Wyman; William d. at Cambridge, 8 Apr 1877.

vi RUBY BRADSTREET, b. at Greenfield, MA, 4 Jul 1800; d. 21 Jun 1843; m. at Methuen, 25 Sep 1827, THOMAS THAXTER, b. at Machias, ME, 2 Mar 1791 son of Marshal and Lucy (Drew) Thaxter; Thomas d. at Methuen, 27 Jun 1842.

1213) MEHITABLE FOSTER *(Rachel Steel Foster[4], Phebe Stevens Steel[3], Elizabeth Abbott Stevens[2], George[1])*, b. at Andover, 17 Sep 1772 daughter of Dudley and Rachel (Steel) Foster; d. at North Andover, 16 Aug 1859; m. 3 Mar 1791, her third cousin, NATHANIEL HOLT, b. 6 Apr 1769 son of Nathaniel and Elizabeth (Stevens) Holt; Nathaniel d. at Andover, 24 May 1829.

Mehitable Foster and Nathaniel Holt were parents of twelve children born at Andover.

i DUDLEY FOSTER HOLT, b. 6 Dec 1791; d. at Haverhill, 10 Dec 1856; m. 1st, 14 Jun 1813, SALLY BRADLEY who has not been identified; Sally d. by 1821. Dudley m. 2nd, 25 Apr 1822, JUDITH A. CHASE, b. at Haverhill, about 1796 daughter of Josiah and Ruth (Bradley) Chase; Judith d. at Haverhill, 31 Oct 1864.

ii NATHANIEL HOLT, b. 6 Aug 1793; d. 28 Nov 1813. Nathaniel served in the War of 1812 and died in service: "Nathaniel, jr., d. in the Army, Nov. 28, 1813, a. 21 y."[3173]

iii PHEBE FOSTER HOLT, b. 27 Jul 1795; d. at Millville, MA, 1870; m. at Boston, 19 Nov 1825, her first cousin, JAMES WILEY, b. at Andover, Feb 1790 son of David and Chloe (Holt) Wiley; James d. at Andover, 9 Jan 1850.

iv ELIPHALET MARTIN HOLT, b. 15 Jul 1797; d. at Andover, 8 Feb 1868; m. at Haverhill, 31 Mar 1829, MARY ANN COLBY, b. at Haverhill, 1 Sep 1806 daughter of Ephraim and Lydia (Chase) Colby; Mary Ann d. at North Andover, 4 Apr 1872.

v POLLY HOLT, b. 2 Jun 1799; d. at Andover, 9 Mar 1826. Polly did not marry.

vi HANNAH HOLT, b. 16 Sep 1801; m. at Boston, 14 Dec 1824, JAMES FRAZER who has not been identified.

vii ELIZABETH HOLT, b. 7 Jan 1804; d. at Andover, 15 Sep 1832. Elizabeth did not marry. She was deaf and died of consumption.

viii CHARLES HOLT, b. 17 Jun 1806; d. at Exeter, NH, after 1870; m. 1st, about 1834, MELINDA TUCKER, b. at Plaistow, NH, 4 Jul 1812 daughter of Elisha and Mehitable (Davis) Tucker; Melinda d. at Amesbury, 2 Nov 1848.

3172 Carter, *Native Ministry of New Hampshire*, p 600

3173 Massachusetts: Vital Records, 1621-1850

Charles m. 2nd, at Amesbury, 11 May 1849, NANCY SANBORN, b. at Exeter, NH, 1809 daughter of Jesse and Elizabeth (Lovering) Sanborn; Nancy d. at Haverhill, 12 Jan 1892.

ix SUSANNA HOLT, b. 23 Aug 1808; d. after 1860; m. 9 Sep 1832, WILLIAM FRYE, b. at Andover, 26 Oct 1801 son of Philip and Sarah Smith (Wilkins) Frye; William d. at Andover, 26 Sep 1844.

x TIMOTHY PARKER HOLT, b. 27 Feb 1811; d. at Andover, 23 Nov 1892; m. at Andover, 27 Nov 1834, MARY H. LOVEJOY, b. at Andover, 24 Sep 1811 daughter of Orlando and Abiah (Gray) Lovejoy; Mary d. at Andover, 4 Feb 1888.

xi REBECCA HOLT, b. 29 Nov 1813; d. at Stoughton, MA, 19 Jul 1886; m. 1st, 15 Sep 1834, JOSEPH STEVENS, b. at Andover, 20 Feb 1801 son of Joseph and Phebe (Frye) Stevens; Joseph d. at Andover, 13 Jul 1849. Rebecca m. 2nd, at Tisbury, 14 Jun 1853, BENJAMIN MAGOON who was b. at Kingston, NH about 1807.

xii HARRIET BRADSTREET HOLT, b. 11 Nov 1816; d. 17 Oct 1826.

1214) WILLIAM LOVEJOY STEEL *(Benjamin Steel4, Phebe Stevens Steel3, Elizabeth Abbott Stevens2, George1)*, b. at Wilton, 28 Jun 1784 son of Benjamin and Hannah (Lovejoy) Steel; d. at Wilton, 4 Mar 1860; m. by 1820, DOLLY TARBELL, b. at Mason, NH, 3 May 1798 daughter of Samuel and Anna (Heldrick) Tarbell;[3174] Dolly d. 30 Aug 1861.

William Lovejoy Steel was a farmer in Wilton and he and Dolly raised their four children there. A probate record was not located.

i BENJAMIN FRANKLIN STEEL, b. 1 Sep 1820; d. at Wilton by early 1872 (probate date 22 Feb 1872); m. 16 Nov 1846, RACHEL COLBURN, b. at Hollis, 27 Jan 1822 daughter of Nathan and Lydia (Jewett) Colburn. After Benjamin's death, Rachel married Parker Jewett. She lived in Illinois, but likely died in Cass, Iowa where she was living with one of her stepchildren in 1900. Rachel died 26 Dec 1900. Benjamin and Rachel took in a young boy, Albert W. Whiting, who was born in Massachusetts in 1852.[3175] They later adopted Albert and his named was changed to Albert W. Steel.

ii ELIZA STEEL, b. 3 Nov 1822; d. at Hollis, 24 Jan 1885. Eliza did not marry. She wrote her will 8 December 1873 in which she left all her estate to her sister Elvira Steel.

iii ELVIRA STEEL, b. 2 Sep 1825; d. at Hollis, 12 Jun 1891. Elvira did not marry. Elvira and her sister Eliza lived with their parents until the death of their father and mother. They then lived with their brother Benjamin, but in 1880, Elvira and Eliza lived together in Hollis.

iv ELMIRA (Almira) STEEL (twin of Elvira), b. 2 Sep 1825; d. at Hollis, 3 Aug 1902; m. 13 May 1852, ENOCH JEWETT COLBURN, b. at Hollis, 27 Apr 1830 son of Nathan and Lydia (Jewett) Colburn; Enoch d. at Brookline, NH, 2 Mar 1905.

[3174] Parentage confirmed by the 1824 will of Samuel Tarbell which includes a bequest to daughter Dolly Steel. Probate Records, 1771-1921; Indexes to Probate Records, 1771-1859, 1885-1961; Author: New Hampshire. Probate Court (Hillsborough County); Probate Place: Hillsborough, New Hampshire

[3175] Year: 1860; Census Place: Wilton, Hillsborough, New Hampshire; Roll: M653_673; Page: 373; Family History Library Film: 803673. Albert W. Whiting, age 7, living in the household of Benjamin and Rachel Steel.

References

Abbot, Abiel. 1829. *History of Andover: From its Settlement to 1829.* Andover, MA: Flagg and Gould.

Abbot, Abiel, and Ephraim Abbot. 1847. *Genealogical Register of the Descendants of George Abbot of Andover, George Abbot of Rowley, Thomas Abbot of Andover, Arthur Abbot of Ipswich, Robert Abbot of Branford, CT, and George Abbot of Norwalk, CT.* Boston: James Munroe and Company.

Abbot, Charles Greeley. 1929. "Biographical Memoir of Henry Larcom Abbot 1831-1927." *National Academy of Sciences Annual Meeting.*

Abbott, Charlotte Helen. n.d. "Abbott Genealogies." http://www.mhl.org/abbott-genealogies.

Abbott, John Howard. 1922. *The Courtright (Kortright) Family: Descendants of Bastian Van Kortryk, a Native of Belgium Who Emigrated to Holland about 1615.* New York: T. A. Wright.

Abbott, Lemuel Abijah. 1906. *Descendants of George Abbott of Rowley, Mass., of His Joint Descendants of George Abbott, Sr., of Andover, Mass. . .* Boston: Published by the compiler, T. R. Marvin Printing.

Abbott, Margaret T. 1952. "Ten Generations of Abbotts in America." Unpublished manuscript. https://www.mhl.org/sites/default/files/files/Abbott/Abbott%20Family.pdf.

Abbott, Stanley Hale. 1961. *The Family Tree of Ezra Abbot.* Hastings, NE: Stanley Hale Abbott.

Abell, Horace Avery. 1940. *The Abell Family in America: Robert Abell of Rehoboth, Mass., his English Ancestry and his Descendants, other Abell Families and Immigrants, Abell Families in England.* Rutland, VT: Tuttle Publishing.

Adams, Charles. 1887. *A Genealogical Register of North Brookfield Families: Including the Records of Many Early Settlers of Brookfield.* Town of North Brookfield.

Adams, John Quincy, and Charles Francis Adams. 1903. *Life in a New England Town, 1787, 1788: Diary of John Quincy Adams While a Student in the Office of Theophilus Parsons at Newburyport.* Newburyport, MA: Little, Brown.

Aldrich, George. 1880. *Walpole As It Was and As It Is.* Claremont, NH: Claremont Manufacturing.

Aldrich, Lewis Cass, and Frank R. Holmes. 1891. *History of Windsor County, Vermont.* Syracuse, NY: D. Mason and Co.

Allen, Orrin Peer. 1910. *Descendants of Nicholas Cady of Watertown, Mass. 1645-1910.* Palmer, MA: Published by the author.

American Historical Society. 1922. *American Biography: A New Cyclopedia, Volume XII.* New York: American Historical Society.

American Series of Popular Biographies. 1901. *Biographical Skethces of Representative Citizens of the Commonwealth of Massachusetts.* Boston, MA: Graves and Steinbarger.

Andrews, H. Franklin. 1900. *The Hamlin Family: A Genealogy of Capt. Giles Hamlin of Middletown,Connecticut. 1654-1900.* Exira, IA: Published by the author.

Avery, Clara Arlette. 1914. *The Averell-Averill-Avery Family: A Record of the Descendants of William and Abigail Averell of Ipswich, Mass.* Cleveland, OH: Evangelical Publishing House.

Avery, Lillian Drake. 1926. *A Genealogy of the Ingersoll Family in America, 1629-1925: Comprising Descendants of Richard Ingersoll of Salem, Massachusetts, John Ingersoll of Westfield, Mass., and John Ingersoll of Huntington, Long Island.* Salem, MA: Higginson Book Co.

Bacon, Edwin Monroe. 1896. *Men of Progress: One Thousand Biographical Sketches and Portraits of Leaders in Business and Professional Life in the Commonwealth of Massachusetts.* Boston, MA: New England Magazine.

Badger, John Cogswell. 1909. *Giles Badger and His Descendants.* Manchester, NH: J.B. Clarke Printers.

Bailey, Abigail Abbot. 1815. *Memoirs of Mrs. Abigail Bailey, Who Had Been the Wife of Major Asa Bailey.* Boston: Samuel T. Armstrong.

Bailey, Sarah Loring. 1880. *Historical Sketches of Andover: Comprising the Present Towns of Andover and North Andover.* Boston: Houghton.

Barbour, Lucius Barnes, and Case Brainard Newton. 1914. *Vital Records of Woodstock, 1686-1854.* Hartford: The Case, Lockwood, and Brainard Co.

Barker, Elizabeth Frye. 1920. *Frye Genealogy; Adrian of Kittery, Me., John of Andover, Mass., Joshua of Virginia, Thomas of Rhode Island.* New York: T. A. Wright.

Barrows, John Stuart. 1938. *Fryeburg, Maine: An Historical Sketch.* Fryeburg, ME: Pequawket Press.

Bartholomew, George Wells. 1885. *Record of the Bartholomew Family: Historical, Genealogical and Biographical.* Austin, TX: Printed by the compiler.

Bartlett, Joseph Gardner. 1908. *Hugh Jones of Salem, Mass., and His Descendants.* Boston, MA: New England Historic Genealogical Society.

Bedford, NH. 1903. *History of Bedford, New Hampshire, from 1737, being Statistics Compiled on the Occasion of the One Hundred and Fiftieth Anniversary of the Incorporation of the Town, May 15, 1900.* Concord, NH: Rumford Printing.

Belknap, Henry Wyckoff. 1918. *The Lambert Family of Salem, Massachusetts.* Salem, MA: Essex Institute.

Bell, Charles Henry. 1894. *The Bench and Bar of New Hampshire: Including Biographical Notices of Deceased Judges of the Highest Court, and Lawyers of the Province and State, and a List of Names of Those Now Living.* Boston: Houghton-Mifflin.

Benedict, Henry Marvin. 1870. *The Genealogy of the Benedicts in America.* Albany: J Munsell.

Bent, Charles. 1877. *History of Whiteside County, Illinois, from its First Settlement to the Present Time.* Morrison, IL: L. P. Allen printer.

Bentley, William. 1914. *The Diary of William Bentley: Pastor of the East Church, Salem, Massachusetts, Volume 4.* Salem, MA: Newcomb & Gauss.

Benton, Josiah Henry. 1911. *Warning Out in New England 1656-1817.* Boston: W. B. Clarke.

Best, Frank Eugene. 1904. *Amidon Family: A Record of the Descendants of Roger Amadowne of Rehoboth, Mass.* Chicago, IL: F. E. Best.

Bingham, Theodore Alfred. 1927. *The Bingham Family in the United States, Especially of the State of Connecticut.* Easton, PA: The Bingham Association.

Binney, Charles James Fox. 1886. *Genealogy of the Binney Family in the United States.* Albany, NY: J. Munsell's Sons.

Blair, Williams T., and Jacob I. Shoemaker. 1924. *The Michael Shoemaker Book : (Schumacher).* Scranton, PA: International Textbook Press.

Blake, Francis E. 1915. *History of the Town of Princeton in the County of Worcester and the Commonwealth of Massachusetts.* Princeton, MA: Published by the town.

Blanchard, Marvin. 1908. "History of Centerville, New York." Accessed April 23, 2019. https://centerville.files.wordpress.com/2009/05/history-of-centervillenew-yorkbymarvin-blanchard1908-centerville1.pdf.

Bliss, John Homer. 1881. *Genealogy of the Bliss Family in America, from about the Year 1550-1880.* Boston, MA: Printed by the author.

Bolton, Charles Knowles. 1923. *Christ Church, Salem Street, Boston, 1723: A Guide, 200th Anniversary Edition.* Boston, MA: Published by the Church.

Bolton, Ethel Stanwood. 2009. *Immigrants to New England, 1700-1775.* Heritage Books.

Boltwood, Lucius Manlius. 1878. *History and Genealogy of the Family of Thomas Noble, of Westfied, Massachusetts.* Hartford, CT: Case, Lockwood & Brainard.

Bouton, Nathaniel. 1856. *The History of Concord from Its First Grant in 1725 to the Organization of the City Government in 1853.* Concord, NH: Benning W. Sanborn.

Boyden, Wallace Clarke. 1901. *Thomas Boyden and His Descendants.* Boston, MA: T. R. Marvin Printers.

Boynton, John Farnham, and Caroline Harriman Boynton. 1897. *The Boynton Family. A Genealogy of the Descendants of William and John Boynton, who Emigrated from Yorkshire, England, in 1638, and Setted at Rowley, Essex County, Massachusetts.* Groveland, MA.

Bradlee, Francis B. C. 1918. *The Boston and Lowell Railroad, the Nashua and Lowell Railroad, and the Salem and Lowell Railroad.* Salem, MA: Essex Institute.

Bradsby, Henry C. (Ed.). 1893. *History of Luzerne County, Pennsylvania, with Biographical Selections.* Chicago: S. B. Nelson.

Brainard, Homer Worthington. 1915. *A Survey of the Scovils or Scovills in England and America; Seven Hundred Years of History and Genealogy.* Hartford, CT: Privately printed.

Brainard, Lucy Abigail. 1908. *The Genealogy of the Brainerd-Brainard Family in America, 1649-1908.* Hartford Press.

Brigham, Willard. 1907. *The History of the Brigham Family: A Record of Several Thousand Descendants of Thomas Brigham the Emigrant, 1603-1653.* New York: The Grafton Press.

—. 1912. *The Tyler Genealogy; the Descendants of Job Tyler, of Andover, Massachusetts, 1619-1700.* Plainfield, NJ: C. B. Tyler.

Bristol, Theresa Hall. 1914. "Bristol Notes." *The New York Genealogical and Biographical Record* 45: 68ff.

Brookfield Historical Society. 1987. *The History of Brookfield, Vermont.* Brookfield, VT: Published by the society.

Brown, George Stayley. 1993. *Yarmouth, Nova Scotia, Genealogies: Transcribed from the Yarmouth Herald.* Genealogical Publishing Company.

Browne, George Waldo. 1921-22. *The History of Hillsborough, New Hampshire, 1735-1921.* Manchester, NH: John B. Clarke.

Burleigh, Charles. 1903. *The Genealogy and History of the Ingalls Family in America.* Malden, MA: G. E. Dunbar.

Butler, Francis Gould. 1885. *A History of Farmington, Franklin County, Maine, from the Earliest Explorations to the Present Time, 1776-1885.* Farmington, ME: Press of Knowlton, McLeary, and Co.

Caller, James Moore, and Maria A. Ober. 1881. *Genealogy of the Descendants of Lawrence and Cassandra Southwick of Salem, Mass.* Salem, MA: J. H. Choate.

Carter, Clarabel Augusta Lincoln. 1887. *Carter, a Genealogy of the Descendants of Samuel and Thomas, Sons of Rev. Samuel Carter: 1640-1886.* Clinton, MA: Printer for the Carter Association.

Carter, Nathan Franklin. 1906. *The Native Ministry of New Hampshire.* Rumford: Rumford Printing Company.

Carter, Nathan Franklin, and Trueworthy Ladd Fowler. 1895. *History of Pembroke, N. H. 1730-1895.* Concord, NH: Republican Press Association.

Castine Historical Society. 1996. *Castine.* Arcadia Publishing.

Caulfield, Ernest. 1950. "The Pursuit of a Pestilence." *Pocessdings of the American Antiquarian Society* 60 (1): 21-52.

Chaffee, William Henry. 1909. *The Chaffee Genealogy.* New York: Grafton Press.

Chandler, Charles Henry, and Sarah Fiske Lee. 1914. *The History of New Ipswich, New Hampshire, 1735-1914: With Genealogical Records of the Principal Families.* Fitchburg, MA: Sentinel Printing Company.

Chandler, George. 1883. *The Descendants of William and Annis Chandler who Settled in Roxbury, Mass., 1637.* Worcester: Press of C. Hamilton.

Chapin, Charles Wells. 1893. *Sketches of the Old Inhabitants and Other Citizens of Old Springfield of the Present Century.* Springfield, MA: Springfield Printing and Binding Company.

Chapin, Gilbert Warren. 1924. *The Chapin Book of Genealogical Data.* Hartford, CT: Chapin Family Association.

Chapman Brothers. Chicago. *Portrait and Biographical Album of Lancaster County, Nebraska.* 1888: Chapman Brothers.

Chapman, George T. 1867. *Sketches of the Alumni of Dartmouth College, from the First Graduation in 1771 to the Present Time, with a Brief History of the Institution.* Cambridge, MA: Riverside Press.

Chapman, Leonard Bond. 1907. *Monograph on the Southgate Family of Scarborough, Maine: Their Ancestors and Descendants.* Portland, ME: H. W. Bryant.

Chase, Benjamin. 1869. *History of Old Chester.* Auburn, NH: Published by the author.

Chase, John Carroll, and George Walter Chamberlain. 1928. *Seven Generations of the Descendants of Aquila and Thomas Chase.* Haverhill, MA: Record Publishing Co.

Child, Elias. 1881. *Genealogy of the Child, Childs and Childe Families, of the Past and Present in the United States and the Canadas, from 1630 to 1881.* Utica, NY: Published for the author.

Child, Hamilton. 1888. *Gazetteer of Orange County, VT. 1762-1888, Part First.* Syracuse, NY: Syracuse Journal Company, Printers.

Clayton, W. Woodford. 1879. *History of Steuben County, New York, with Illustrations and Biographical Sketches of Some of its Prominent Men and Pioneers.* Philadelphia: Lewis, Peck, & Co.

Cleaveland, Nehemiah. 1882. *History of Bowdoin College with Biographical Sketches of Its Graduates.* Boston: James Ripley Osgood.

Coburn, Silas Roger. 1922. *History of Dracut, Massachusetts, Called by the Indians Augumtoocooke and before Incorporation, the Wildernesse North of the Merrimac. First Permanment Settlement in 1669 and Incorporated as a Town in 1701.* Lowell, MA: Press of the Courier-Citizen.

Coburn, Silas Roger, and George Augustus Gordon. 1913. *Genealogy of the Descendants of Edward Colburn/Coburn; Came from England, 1635.* Lowell, MA: W. Coburn.

Cochrane, Warren Robert. 1880. *History of the Town of Antrim, New Hampshire, from its Earliest Settlement to June 27, 1877, with a Brief Genealogical Record of all the Antrim Families.* Manchester, NH: Mirror Steam Printing Press.

Cochrane, Warren Robert, and George K. Wood. 1895. *History of Francestown, N. H., from its Earliest Settlement April, 1758, to January 1, 1891: With a Brief Genealogical Record of all the Francestown Families.* Nashua, NH: Published by the town.

Coffin, Charles Carleton. 1878. *The History of Boscawen and Webster [N.H.] from 1733 to 1878.* Concord, NH: Republican Press Association.

Cogswell, Elliott C. 1878. *History of Nottingham, Deerfield, and Northwood, Comprised Within the Original Limits of Nottingham, Rockingham County, N.H., with Records of the Centennial Proceedings at Northwood, and Genealogical Sketches.* Manchester, NH: J. B. Clarke.

Cogswell, Leander Winslow. 1880. *History of the Town of Henniker, Merrimack County, New Hampshire, from the Date of the Canada Grant by the Province of Massachusetts, in 1735, to 1880; with a Genealogical Register of the Families of Henniker.* Concord, NH: Republican Press Association.

Cogswell, William. 1846. *The New Hampshire Repository: Devoted to Education, Literature and Religion.* Gilmanton, NH: Printed by Alfred Prescott.

Colegrove, William. 1894. *History and Genealogy of the Colegrove Family in America.* Chicago, IL: Published by the author.

1903. *Commemorative Biographical Record of Tolland and Windham Counties, Connecticut, Volume I.* Chicago: J. H. Beers.

1897. *Commemorative Historical and Biographical Record of Wood County, Ohio, Volume 2.* Chicago: J. H. Beers and Company.

Cone, William Whitney. 1903. *Some Account of the Cone Family in America Principally of the Descendants of Daniel Cone, Who Settled in Haddam, Connecticut, in 1662.* Topeka, KS: Crane and Company.

Crandall, John Cortland. 1931. *Elder John Crandall of Rhode Island and His Descendants* . New Woodstock, NY: J. C. Crandall.

Crosbie, Laurence M. 1924. *The Phillips Exeter Academy: A History.* Published by The Academy.

Cross, Lucy Rogers Hill. 1905. *History of Northfield, New Hampshire, 1780-1905. In Two Parts with Many Biographical Sketches and Portraits.* Concord, NH: Rumford Printing.

Cummins, Albert Oren. 1904. *Cummings Genealogy: Isaac Cummings, 1601-1677 of Ipswich in 1638 and Some of His Descendants.* Montpelier, VT: Argus and Patriot Printing House.

Currier, Harvey Lear, and John McNabb Currier. 1910. *Genealogy of Richard Currier of Salisbury and Amesbury, Massachusetts (1616--1686-7) and Many of His Descendants.* Newport, VT: Orleans County Historical Society.

Currier, John J. 1906. *History of Newburyport, Mass., 1764-1905.* Newburyport, MA: Published by the author.

Cushing, James Stevenson. 1905. *The Genealogy of the Cushing Family, an Account of the Ancestors and Descendants of Matthew Cushing, Who Came to America in 1638.* Montreal: Perrault Printing Co.

Cutler, Nahim Sawin. 1889. *A Cutler Memorial and Genealogical History: Containing the Names of a Large Proportion of the Cutlers in the United States and Canada, and a Record of Many Individual Members of the Family.* Greenfield, MA: E. A. Hall & Co.

Cutter, William Richard. 1914. *New England Families, Genealogical and Memorial: A Record of the Achievements of Her People in the Making of Commonwealths and the Founding of a Nation, Volume 2.* Lewis Historical Publishing.

—. 1915. *New England Families, Genealogical and Memorial; a Record of the Achievements of Her People in the Making of Commonwealths and the Founding of a Nation, Volumes 1-4.* New York: Lewis Historical Publishing Co.

Daniel Hovey Association. 1914. *The Hovey Book: Describing the English Ancestry and American Descendants of Daniel Hovey of Ipswich, Massachusetts.* Ipswich, MA: Lewis R. Hovey.

Darling, Nancy. 1913. "History and Anniversary of Hartland, Vermont." *The Vermonter, Volume 18.*

Day, Catherine Matilda. 1869. *History of the Eastern Townships, Province of Québec, Dominion of Canada.* Montreal: J. Lovell.

Day, Edward Warren. 1895. *One Thousand Years of Hubbard History, 866 to 1895. From Hubba, the Norse Sea King, to the Enlightened Present.* New York: H. P. Hubbard.

De Wolfe, Edity. 1953. *The History of Putney, Vermont, 1753-1953.* Putney, VT: Fortnightly Club.

Dearborn, John Jacob. 1890. *The History of Salisbury, New Hampshire: From Date of Settlement to the Present Time.* Manchester, NH: Printed by W.E. Moore.

Deming, Leonard. 1851. *Catalogue of the Principal Officers of Vermont, as Connected with its Political History, from 1778 to 1851, with Some Biographical Notices.* Middlebury, VT: Published by the author.

Dewey, Adelbert Milton, Louis Marinus Dewey, William Tarbox Dewey, and Orville C. Dewey. 1898. *Life of George Dewey, Rear Admiral, U.S.N.; and Dewey Family History: Being an Authentic Historical and Genealogical Record of More Than Fifteen Thousand Persons in the United States by the Name of Dewey, and Their Descendants.* Westfield, MA: Dewey Publishing Company.

Dickerman, Edward Dwight. 1922. *Dickerman Genealogy: Descendants of Thomas Dickerman, an Early Settler of Dorchester, Massachusetts.* New Haven: Tuttle, Morehouse, & Taylor Press.

Dimock, Susan Whitney. 1898. *Births, Baptisms,Mmarriages and Deaths, from the Records of the Town and Churches in Mansfield, Connecticut, 1703-1850.* New York, NY: The Baker and Taylor Company.

Dimond, Edwin R. 1891. *The Genealogy of the Dimond or Dimon Family, of Fairfield, Conn.: Together with Records of the Dimon or Dymont Family of East Hampton, Long Island, and of the Dimond Family of New Hampshire.* Albany, NY: Published for the compiler by J. Munsell.

Doane, Alfred A. 1902. *The Doane Family: 1. Deacon John Doane, of Plymouth, 2. Doctor John Done, of Maryland, and Their Descendants.* Boston, MA: A. A. Doane.

Dodge, Joseph Thompson. 1894. *Genealogy of the Dodge Family of Essex County, Mass. 1629-1894.* Madison, WI: Democrat Printing Co.

Dodge, R.G.W., and R.G.F. Candage. 1890. "Families of Early Settlers in Blue Hill Maine." *Maine Historical Magazine (Bangor Historical Magazine)*, April, May: 181-217.

Donovan, Dennis. 1906. *The History of the Town of Lyndeborough, New Hampshire.* Tufts College Press.

Doolittle, Wiliam Frederick. 1901. *The Doolittle Family in America.* Cleveland, OH: Press of National Printing Company.

Dow, Joseph, and Lucy Ellen Dow. 1893. *History of the Town of Hampton, New Hampshire, from its Settlement in 1638 to the Autumn of 1892.* Salem, MA: L. E. Dow.

Durant, Pliny A. 1883. *The History of Union County, Ohio, Containing a History of the County; Its Townships, Towns ... Military Record.* Chicago: W. H. Beers.

Durant, Samuel W. 1880. *History of Kalamazoo County, Michigan: With Illustrations and Biographical Sketches of Its Prominent Men and Pioneers.* Philadelphia, PA: Everts & Abbott.

—. 1878. *History of Oneida County, New York: With Illustrations and Biographical Sketches of Some of its Prominent Men and Pioneers.* Philadelphia, PA: Everts and Farris.

Durrie, Daniel S. 1864. *A Genealogical History of the Holt Family in the United States More Particularly the Descendants of Nicholas Holt of Newbury and Andover, Mass.* Albany: Munsell.

Eastman, John Robie. 1910. *History of the Town of Andover New Hampshire, 1751-1906.* Concord, NH: Rumford Printing.

Ela, David Hough. 1896. *Genealogy of the Ela Family: Descendant of Israel Ela, of Haverhill, Mass.* Manchester, CT: Elwood S. Ela, Printer.

Eldredge, Zoeth Skinner. 1896. *Eldredge Genealogy.* Boston: D. Clapp Printers.

Emery, Edwin. 1901. *The History of Sanford, Maine, 1661-1900.* Salem, MA: Salem Press Company.

Emery, Rufus. 1890. *Genealogical Records of Desendants of John and Anthony Emery, of Newbury, Mass. 1590-1890.* Salem, MA: Emery Cleaves.

Essex Institute. 1922. *Old-Time Ships of Salem, 2nd Edition.* Salem, MA: Nichols Press Printers.

Evans, Nelson Wiley. 1903. *A History of Scioto County, Ohio.* Portsmouth, OH: N. W. Evans.

Evans, Simeon Adams. 1893. *Descendants of David Evans of Charleston, Massachusetts: To which is Appended Partial Records of Certain Families Connected with Them by Marriage.*

Fairbanks, Mary Mason. 1898. *Emma Willard and Her Pupils; or, Fifty Years of Troy Female Seminary, 1822-1872.* New York, NY: Mrs. Russell Sage.

Farnham, Russell Clare. 1999. *The New England Descendants of the Immigrant Ralph Farnum of Rochester, Kent County, England, and Ipswich, Massachusetts.* Peter Randall Publishing.

Fernald, Natalie R. 1906. "Corrections and Additions to Thomas Skinner's Descendants." *The Genealogical Exchange*, June: 9-11.

Fitts, James Hill. 1869. *Genealogy of the Fitts Or Fitz Family in America.* Clinton: Printed by Wm. J. Coulter.

Floyd, C. Harold. 1912. "Some Descendants of Joel Jenkins of Braintree and Malden, Mass." *New England Historical and Genealogical Register* 268 ff.

Ford, Henry A., and Kate B. Ford. 1881. *History of Cincinnati, Ohio, with Illustrations and Biographical Sketches.* Cleveland, OH: L. A. Williams and Co.

—. 1881. *History of Hamilton County, Ohio, with Illustrations and Biographical Sketches.* Cleveland, OH: L. A. Williams.

Foster, E. W., and Philip Walker. 1905. "The Walkers of Woburn, Massachusetts." *Historical Bulletin, Volumes 6-9* 64-65.

Foster, Ruby. 1813. *Miscellaneous Writings of Ruby Foster Who Died in Andover, Mass., August 5th, 1812, in the 21st Year of Her Age Selected from Her Diary, Other Private Papers, and Letters to Her Friends.* Boston: Printed by Samuel T. Armstrong and sold by him.

Frost, John Eldridge. 1943. *The Nicholas Frost Family.* Milford, NH: Cabinet Press.

Frothingham, Washington. 1892. *History of Fulton County: Embracing Early Discoveries, the Advance of Civilization. . .* Syracuse, NY: D. Mason.

Fuess, Claude Moore. 1959. *Andover: Symbol of New England: The Evolution of a Town.* Andover, MA: Andover Historical Society.

Fuller, William Hylsop. 1914. *Genealogy of some descendants of Captain Matthew Fuller, John Fuller of Newton, John Fuller of Lynn, John Fuller of Ipswich, Robert Fuller of Dorchester and Dedham.* Printed for the Compiler.

Fuller, William Hyslop. 1919. *Genealogy of Some Descendants of Thomas Fuller of Woburn.* Palmer, MA: C. B. Fiske.

Gage, George N. 1894. *A Record of Pierce Gage and His Descendants.* East Washington, NH: Printed by the author.

—. 1886. *History of Washington, New Hampshire, from the First Settlement to the Present Time, 1768-1886.* Claremont, NH: The Claremont Manufacturing Company.

George E. Matthews and Company. 1898. *The Men of New York: A Collection of Biographies and Portraits of Citizens of the Empire State Prominent in Business, Professional, Social, and Political Life During the Last Decade of the Nineteenth Century.* Buffalo, NY: George E. Matthews and Company.

Gilbert, Edgar. 1907. *History of Salem, N.H.* Concord, NH: Rumford Printing.

Glazier, Lewis. 1860. *History of Gardner, Massachusetts: From its Earliest Settlement to 1860.* Worcester, MA: C. Hamilton Printer.

Goodhue, Jonathan Elbridge. 1891. *History and Genealogy of the Goodhue Family : In England and America to the Year 1890.* Rochester, NY: E. R. Andrews.

Goodhue, Josiah Fletcher. 1861. *History of the Town of Shoreham, Vermont: From the Date of its Charter, October 8th, 1761, to the Present Time.* Middlebury, VT: A. H. Copeland.

Gould, Isaiah. 1897. *History of Stoddard, Cheshire County, N.H.* Keene, NH: W. L. Metcalf, printer.

Gould, Sherry L, and Kathleen C. Beals. 2004. *Early Families of Bradford, NH.* Bradford, NH: Bradford Historical Society.

Gove, William Henry. 1922. *The Gove Book: History and Genealogy of the American Family of Gove, and Notes of European Goves.* Salem, MA: S. Perley.

Green, Samuel Abbott. 1893. *Groton Historical Series: A Collection of Papers Relating to the History of the Town of Groton, Massachusetts, Volume 3.* Cambridge, MA: John Wilson and Son.

Greenleaf, James Edward. 1896. *Genealogy of the Greenleaf Family.* Boston, MA: Frank Wood Printer.

Greenlee, Ralph Stebbins, and Robert Lemuel Greenlee. 1904. *The Stebbins Genealogy.* Chicago: Privately printed.

Gregory, John. 1878. *Centennial Proceedings and Historical Incidents of the Early Settlers of Northfield, Vt.* Montpelier, VT: Argus and Patriot Book and Job Printing.

—. 1878. *Centennial Proceedings and Historical Incidents of the Early Settlers of Northfield, Vt.* Montpelier, VT: Argus and Patriot Book.

Greven, Philip. 1970. *Four Generations: Population, Land, and Family in Colonial Andover, Massachusetts.* Ithaca: Cornell University Press.

Griffin, Simon G. 1904. *A History of the Town of Keene from 1732, When the Township Was Granted by Massachusetts, to 1874, When it Became a City.* Keene, NH: Sentinel Printing Company.

Griggs, Susan Jewett. 1950. *Early Homesteads of Pomfret and Hampton.* Abington, CT.

Guild, Mary Stiles Paul. 1892. *The Stiles Family in America: Genealogies of the Massachusetts Family, Descendants of Robert Stiles of Rowley, Mass. 1659-1891. And the Dover, N. H., Family, Descendants of William Stiles of Dover, N. H., 1702-1891.* Albany, NY: Joel Munsell's Sons.

H. F. Kett and Company. 1878. *The History of Ogle County, Illinois, Containing a History of the County, its Cities, Towns, etc.* Chicago, IL: H. F. Kett Publishers.

Hadley, George Plummer. 1924. *History of the Town of Goffstown 1733-1920.* Goffstown, NH: Published by the town.

Hale, Robert Safford. 1889. *Genealogy of Descendants of Thomas Hale of Walton, England, and of Newbury, Mass.* Albany, NY: Weed, Parsons, and Co.

Hammond, Charles. 1893. *The History of Union, Conn.* New Haven: Price, Lee & Adkins.

Harrington, George B. 1906. *Past and Present of Bureau County, Illinois: Together with Biographical Sketches of Many of Its Prominent and Leading Citizens and Illustrious Dead, Volume 1.* Chicago: Pioneer Publishing.

Harvard University. 1905. *Quinquennial Catalogue of the Officers and Graduates of Harvard University.* Cambridge, MA: Harvard University.

Harvey, Oscar Jewell. 1909. *A History of Wilkes-Barré, Luzerne County, Pennsylvania: From Its First Beginnings to the Present Time, Including Chapters of Newly-discovered Early Wyoming Valley History, Together with Many Biographical Sketches and Much Genealogical Material, Volume 5.* Wilkes-Barre, PA: Reader Press.

Haskell, T. H. 1875. *The New Gloucester Centennial.* Portland, ME: Hoyt, Fogg, and Donham.

Hatch, Louis C. 1920. *History of Bowdoin College.* Portland, ME: Loring, Short, and Harmon.

Hay, Thomas Arthur. 1911. *Martin Genealogy. Descendants of Lieutenant Samuel Martin of Wethersfield, Conn., Showing Descent from Royalty.* Printed for the comiler.

Hayden, Charles Albert, and Jessie Hale Tuttle. 1929. *The Capen Family: Descendants of Bernard Capen of Dorchester, Mass.* Minneapolis, MN: Augsburg Publishing House.

Hayden, Chauncey H., Luther C. Stevens, LaFayette Wilbur, and S. H. Barnum. 1916. *The History of Jericho Vermont.* Burlington, VT: Free Press Printing.

Hayes, Lyman Simpson. 1907. *History of the Town of Rockingham, Vermont, Including the Villages of Bellows Falls, Saxtons River, Rockingham, Cambridgeport and Bartonsville, 1753-1907, with Family Genealogies.* Bellows Falls, VT: Published by the town.

Hayford, Otis. 1901. *History of the Hayford Family, 1100-1900: With Biographical Sketches and Illustrations.* Rumford, ME: Rumford Falls Printing.

Hayward, William Willis. 1889. *The History of Hancock, New Hampshire, 1764-1889.* Lowell, MA: Vox Populi Press.

Hazen, Henry Allen. 1883. *History of Billerica, Massachusetts, with a Genealogical Register.* Boston: A. Williams and Co.

Hibbard, Augustine George. 1901. *Genealogy of the Hibbard Family Who are Descendants of Robert Hibbard of Salem, Massachusetts.* Hartford, CT: Case.

Hodges, Almon Danforth. 1896. *Genealogical Record of the Hodges Family of New England, Ending December 31, 1894.* Boston, MA: Published by the author.

Hodgman, Edwin Ruthven. 1883. *History of the Town of Westford, in the County of Middlesex, Massachusetts, 1659-1883.* Lowell, MA: Morning Mail Co.

Holt Association of America. 1930. *The First Three Generations of Holts in America.* Newburgh, NY: Moore Printing Company.

Hopkins, Timothy. 1903. *The Kelloggs in the Old World and the New.* San Francisco, CA: Sunset Press.

Howard, Cecil Hampden Cutts. 1892. *Genealogy of the Cutts Family in America.* Albany, NY: Munsell.

Howe, Gilman Bigelow. 1890. *Genealogy of the Bigelow Family of America, from the Marriage in 1642 of John Biglo and Mary Warren to the Year 1890.* Worcester, MA: Charles Hamilton.

Hoyt, David Webster. 1871. *A Genealogical History of the Hoyt, Haight, and Hight Families: With Some Account of the Earlier Hyatt Families, a List of the First Settlers of Salisbury and Amesbury, Mass.* Providence, RI: Printed for the author.

—. 1857. *Hoyt Family: A Genealogical History of John Hoyt of Salisbury, and David Hoyt of Deerfield, (Massachusetts,) and Their Descendants: With Some Account of the Earlier Connecticut Hoyts.* Boston, MA: C. Benjamin Richardson.

Hubbard, Benjamin F. 1874. *Forests and Clearings: The History of Stanstead County, Province of Quebec.* Montreal: Printed for the publisher.

Hubbard, Charles Horace, and Justus Dartt. 1895. *History of the Town of Springfield, Vermont.* Boston: G. H. Walker.

Hudson, Charles. 1868. *History of the Town of Lexington, Middlesex County, Massachusetts in Two Volumes, Bi-Centenniel Edition.* Boston: Wiggin and Lunt.

Hunnewell, James Melville. 1919. *The Ticknor Family in America: Being an Account of the Descendants of William Ticknor of Scituate, and of Other Immigrants Named Ticknor or Tickner.* Boston: Published by the author.

Hurd, Duane Hamilton (Ed.). 1885. *History of Merrimack and Belknap Counties, New Hampshire.* Philadelphia: J. W. Lewis.

Hurd, Duane Hamilton. 1888. *History of Essex County, Massachusetts: With Biographical Sketches of Many of Its Pioneers and Prominent Men, Volume 1.* Philadelphia: J. W. Lewis.

—. 1885. *History of Hillsborough County, New Hampshire.* Philadephia: J. W. Lewis.

Hurlbut, Henry Higgins. 1888. *The Hurlbut Genealogy: Or, Record of the Descendants of Thomas Hurlbut, of Saybrook and Wethersfield, Conn.* Albany, NY: Joel Munsell's Sons.

Hyde, Charles McEwan. 1879. *Historical Celebration of the Town of Brimfield, Hampden County, Mass.* Springfield, MA: C. W. Bryan.

Jackson, James Robert. 1905. *History of Littleton, New Hampshire.* Cambridge, MA: Published for the Town of Littleton.

Jewell, Pliny, and Joel Jewell. 1860. *The Jewell Register: Containing a List of the Descendants of Thomas Jewell, of Braintree, Near Boston, Mass.* Hartford, CT: Case, Lockwood.

Jordan, John Woolf. 1913. *Genealogical and Personal History of the Allegheny Valley, Pennsylvania, volume 3.* New York, NY: Lewis Historical Publishing.

Joy, James Richard. 1900. *Thomas Joy and His Descendants: In the Lines of His Sons Samuel of Boston, Joseph of Hingham, Ephraim of Berwick: A Portfolio of Family Papers.* New York: Published by the author.

Kelly, Giles Merrill. 1886. *Genealogical Account of the Descendants of John Kelly of Newbury, Massachusetts.* Albany, NY: Munsell.

Keyes, Asa. 1880. *Genealogy of Robert Keyes of Watertown, Mass., 1633, Solomon Keyes of Newbury and Chelmsford Mass., 1653.* Brattleboro, VT: G.E. Selleck.

King, Marquis Fayette. 1903. *Annals of Oxford, Maine.* Hebron, ME: New England History Press.

Kingsbury, Frank B. 1925. *History of the Town of Surry, Cheshire County, New Hampshire: From Date of Severance from Gilsum and Westmoreland, 1769-1922, with a Genealogical Register and Map of the Town.* Surry, NH: Published by the town.

Kneeland, Stillman Foster. 1897. *Seven Centuries in the Kneeland Family.* New York: Published by the author.

Lamson, William J. 1917. *Descendants of William Lamson of Ipswich, Mass. 1634-1917.* New York: T. A. Wright.

Lapham, William Berry. 1890. *History of Rumford, Oxford County, Maine, from Its First Settlement in 1779, to the Present Time.* Augusta, ME: Press of the Maine Farmer.

Lawson, Harvey Merrill. 1905. *History and Genealogy of the Descendants of Clement Corbin of Muddy River (Brookline), Mass. and Woodstock, Conn. with Notices of Other Lines of Corbins.* Hartford, CT: Hartford Press.

Leonard, Levi Washburn, and Josiah Lafayette Seward. 1920. *The History of Dublin, N.H.: Containing the Address by Charles Mason, and the Proceedings at the Centennial Celebration, June 17, 1852, with a Register of Families.* Dublin, NH: Published by the town.

Libby, Charles Thornton. 1882. *The Libby Family in America,1602-1881.* Portland, ME: B. Thurston.

Lincoln, William. 1862. *History of Worcester, Massachusetts, from its Earliest Settlement to September, 1836: With Various Notices Relating to the History of Worcester County.* Worcester: Charles Hersey.

Linn, John Blair. 1883. *History of Centre and Clinton Counties, Pennsylvania.* Philadelphia, PA: Louis H. Everts.

Littlefield, Peter F., and Karl Pfister. 2001. *Genealogies of the Early Settlers of Weston, Vermont, Second Edition.* Weston, VT: Weston Historical Society.

Livermore, Abiel Abbot, and Putnam Sewall. 1888. *History of the Town of Wilton, Hillsborough County, New Hampshire, with a Genealogical Register.* Lowell, MA: Marden and Rowell.

Lloyd, Susan McIntosh. 1979. *A Singular School: Abbot Academy, 1828-1973.* Andover, MA: Phillips Academy.

Locke, Arthur Horton. 1916. *A History and Genealogy of Captain John Locke (1627-1696) of Portsmouth and Rye, N.H., and His Descendants.* Concord, NH: Rumford Press.

Long, Charles A. E. 1926. *Matinicus Isle: Its Story and Its People.* Lewiston Journal Print Shop.

Lord, Charles Chase. 1890. *Life and Times in Hopkinton, N.H.* Concord, NH: Republican Press.

Lord, John King. 1928. *A History of the Town of Hanover, N.H.* Hanover, NH: The Dartmouth Press.

Lovejoy, Clarence Earle. 1930. *The Lovejoy Genealogy with Biographies and History.* New York: Published by the author.

Lovejoy, Mary Elevyn Wood. 1911. *History of Royalton, Vermont, with Family Genealogies, 1769-1911.* Burlington, VT: Free Press Printing Company.

Lyford, James Otis. 1912. *History of the Town of Canterbury, New Hampshire, 1727-1912.* Concord, NH: Rumford.

Manning, William Henry. 1902. *The Genealogical and Biographical History of the Manning Families of New England and Descendants.* Salem, MA: Salem Press.

Mansfield, David Lufkin. 1902. *History of Captain John Kathan: The First Settler of Dummerston, Vt. and His Associates and Family Descendants.* Brattleboro, VT: E. L. Hildreth & Co.

Marsh, Dwight W. 1869. *The Tennesseean in Persia and Koordistan. Being the Scenes and Incidents in the Life of Samuel Audley Rhea.* New York: A.D.F. Randolph for the Philadelphia Presbyterian Publication Committee.

Marston, Nathan Washington. 1888. *The Marston Genealogy: In Two Parts.* Lubec, ME.

Martin, Sadie E. 1891. *The Life and Professional Career of Emma Abbott.* Minneapolis, MN: L. Kimball Printing Company.

Mason, George W. 1911. *Ancestors and Descendants of Elisha Mason, Litchfield, Connecticut, 1759-1858, and His Wife Lucretia Webster, 1766-1853.* Waterbury, CT: Mattatuck Press.

McIntire, Robert Harry. 1941. *Descendants of Philip McIntire, a Scottish Highlander who was Deported by Oliver Cromwell Following the Battle of Dunbar, September 3, 1650, and Settled at Reading, Mass., about 1660.* Lancaster, PA: Lancaster Press.

McKeen, Phebe Fuller. 1880. *Annals of Fifty Years: A History of Abbot Academy, Andover, Mass., 1829-1879.* Andover, MA: W. F. Draper.

McLellan, Hugh Davis. 1903. *History of Gorham, Me.* Gorham, ME: Portland, Smith & Sale.

Meriam, Rufus N. 1892. "John and Thomas Totman and Their Descendants." *Proceedings of Worcester Society of Antiquity for the Year 1891, Volume XIII* 45-75.

Merrick, George Byron. 1902. *Genealogy of the Merrick--Mirick--Myrick Family of Massachusetts.* Madison, WI: Tracy, Gibbs & Company.

Merrill, Georgia Drew. 1889. *History of Carroll County, New Hampshire.* Boston, MA: W. A. Ferguson.

Merrill, Samuel. 1917-1928. *A Merrill Memorial: An Account of the Descendants of Nathaniel Merrill, an Early Settler of Newbury, Massachusetts.* Cambridge, MA.

Miller, Edward. 1913. *History of Ryegate, Vermont, from its Settlement by the Scotch-American Company of Farmers to Present Time.* St. Johnsbury, VT: Celdonian Company.

Mitchell, Donald T. 1883. *The Woodbridge Record: Being an Account of the Descendants of the Rev. John Woodbridge, of Newbury, Mass.* New Haven, CT: Private printing by Tuttle, Morehouse & Taylor.

Mooar, George. 1901. *Mooar (Moors) Genealogy: Abraham Mooar of Andover, and His Descendants.* Boston: Press of David Clapp.

—. 1903. *The Cummings Memorial: A Genealogical History of the Descendants of Isaac Cummings, an Early Settler of Topsfield, Massachusetts.* New York: B. F. Cummings.

Moriarty, G. Andrews. 1931. "Ancestry of George Abbott of Andover." *New England Historic and Genealogical Register* 85: 79-86.

Morrison, Leonard Allison. 1893. *The History of the Alison, or Allison Family in Europe and America, A.D. 1135 to 1893; Giving an Account of the Family in Scotland, England, Ireland, Australia, Canada, and the United States.* Boston, MA: Damrell & Upham.

—. 1880. *The History of the Morison or Morrison Family with Most of the "Traditions of the Morrisons" (Clan MacGillemhuire).* Boston, MA: A. Williams & Co.

—. 1883. *The History of Windham in New Hampshire (Rockingham County).* Boston, MA: Cupples, Upham, and Co.

Morrison, Leonard Allison, and Stephen Paschall Sharples. 1897. *History of the Kimball Family in America, from 1634 to 1897 : and of its Ancestors the Kemballs or Kemboldes of England; with an Account of the Kembles of Boston, Massachusetts.* Boston: Damrell & Upham.

Moses, Zebina. 1890. *Historical Sketches of John Moses, of Plymouth, a Settler of 1632 to 1640; John Moses, of Windsor and Simsbury, a Settler Prior to 1647; and John Moses, of Portsmouth, a Settler Prior to 1640.* Hartford, CT: Press of Case, Lockwood, and Brainard.

Moyer, Paul B. 2006. "A Dangerous Combination of Villains: Pennsylvania's Wild Yankees and the Social Context of Agrarian Resistance in Early America." *Pennsylvania History: A Journal of Mid-Atlantic Studies* 73 (1): 37-68.

NEHGS. 1905. *Memorial Biographies of the New England Historic Genealogical Society.* Boston: Published by the society.

Nourse, Henry S. 1993. *The Birth, Marriage, and Death Register, Church Records and Epitaphs of Lancaster, Massachusetts, 1643-1850.* Heritage Books.

Noyes, Henry E., and Harrlette E. Noyes. 1904. *Genealogical Record of Some of the Noyes Descendants: Volume I, Descendants of Nicholas Noyes.* Boston, MA.

Nye, George Hyatt. 1907. *A Genealogy of the Nye Family.* Cleveland, OH: The Nye Family of America Association.

OLaughlin, Michael. 1994. *Families of Co. Kerry, Ireland.* Kansas City, MO: Irish Genealogical Foundation.

Onondaga Historical Association. 1913. "Onondaga's Revolutionary Soldiers." *Publications of the Onondaga Historical Association* 1 (2).

Osgood, Ira. 1894. *A Genealogy of the Descendants of John, Christopher and William Osgood, Who Came from England and Settled in New England Early in the Seventeenth Century.* Salem, MA: Salem Press.

Otis, William A. 1924. *A Genealogical and Historical Memoir of the Otis Family in America.* Chicago, IL: [Schulkins, Inc.].

Otten, Marjorie Wardell. 2000. "The Two George Abbot Families of Andover, Massachusetts." *The Essex Genealogist* 20: 19-23.

Otten, Marjorie Wardwell. 1996. "Discovering Doyen Descendants." *The Maine Genealogist* 18: 63.

Oviatt, F. C. 1906. "Historical Study of Fire Insurance in the United States." *The Annals of the American Academy of Political and Social Science* 26: 155-178.

Palmer, Joseph. 1864. *Necrology of Alumni of Harvard College, 1851-1852 to 1862-1863.* Boston: John Wilson and Son.

Parker, Edward Everett. 1897. *History of the City of Nashua, N. H., from the Earliest Settlement of Old Dunstable to the Year 1895; with Biographical Sketches of Early Settlers, Their Descendants and Other Residents.* Nashua, NH: Telegraph Publishing.

Parsons, Henry. 1912. *Parsons Family: Descendants of Cornet Joseph Parsons, Springfield, 1636--Northampton,1655; Volume 2.* New York: Frank Allaben Genealogical Company.

Peck, Thomas Bellows. 1898. *The Bellows Genealogy; or John Bellows, the Boy Emigrant of 1635 and His Descendants.* Keene, NH: Sentinel Printing.

Perley, Sidney (Ed.). 1897. "Abbot Genealogy." *Essex Antiquarian* 1 (3): 35-42.

Perley, Sidney. 1880. *The History of Boxford, Essex County, Massachusetts, from the Earliest Settlement Known to the Present Time.* Boxford, MA: Published by the author.

Perrin, William Henry. 1881. *History of Medina County and Ohio.* Chicago, IL: Baskin & Battey, Historical Publishers.

—. 1880. *History of Morrow County and Ohio.* Chicago: O. L. Baskin.

Peters, Eleanor Bradley. 1903. *Peters of New England: A Genealogy, and Family History.* Knickerbocker Press.

Phelps, Oliver Seymour, and Andrew Tinkey Servin. 1899. *The Phelps Family of America and Their English Ancestors.* Pittsfield, MA: Eagle Publishing.

Pierce, Frederic Beech. 1882. *Pierce Genealogy: Being the Record of the Posterity of Thomas Pierce, an Early Inhabitant of Charlestown, and Afterwards Charlestown Village (Woburn), in New England.* Worcester, MA: Press of C. Hamilton.

Pierce, Frederick Clifton. 1898. *Batchelder, Batcheller genealogy. Descendants of Rev. Stephen Bachiler, of England ... Who Settled the Town of New Hampton, N.H., and Joseph, Henry, Joshua and John Batcheller of Essex Co., Mass.* Chicago: W. B. Conkey.

—. 1899. *Foster Genealogy, Part I.* Chicago: Published by the author, Press of W. B. Conkey.

Pierce, Frederick Clinton. 1901. *Field Genealogy.* Chicago, IL: Hammond Press.

Pike Family Association. 1907. *Records of the Pike Family Association 1906.* Saco, ME: The Streeter Press.

Pike, Allen Raymond. 1995. *The Family of John Pike of Newbury, Massachusetts (Some Descendants), 1635-1995.* Carmel, NY: Penobscot Press.

Pilsbury, David Brainard, and Emily A. Getchell. 1898. *The Pillsbury Family: Being a History of William and Dorothy Pillsbury (or Pilsbery) of Newbury in New England, and Their Descendants to the Eleventh Generation.* Everett, MA: Massachusetts Publishing Co.

Pingry, William Morrill. 1881. *A Genealogical Record of the Descendants of Moses Pengry, of Ipswich, Mass: So Far as Ascertained.* Ludlow, VT: Warner & Hyde Printers.

Pioneer Publishing. 1900. *In the Foot-Prints of the Pioneers of Stephenson County, Illinois: A Genealogical Record.* . Freeport, IL: Pioneer Publishing.

Pitkin, Ozias C,, and Fred E. Pitkin. 1941. "History of Marshfield, VT." Unpublished manuscript. https://dcms.lds.org/delivery/DeliveryManagerServlet?dps_pid=IE103298.

Poore, Alfred. 1913. "A Genealogical-Historical Visitation of Andover, Mass. in the Year 1863." *Essex Institute Historical Collections* 49: 50-64.

Pope, Charles Henry, Charles Pierce Merriam, C. E. Gildersome Dickinson, and James Sheldon Merriam. 1906. *Merriam Genealogy in England and America.* Boston: C. H. Pope.

Porter, Joseph Whitcomb. 1878. *A Genealogy of the Descendants of Richard Porter, Who Settled at Weymouth, Mass., 1635, and Allied Families.* Bangor, ME: Burr & Robinson.

Prescott, William. 1870. *The Prescott Memorial, or, A Genealogical Memoir of the Prescott Families in America, in Two Parts.* Boston: H.W. Dutton.

Proctor, William Lawrence. 1898. *A Genealogy of Descendants of Robert Proctor of Concord and Chelmsford, Mass.* Ogdensburg, NY: Republican & Journal Print.

Ramsdell, George Allen, and William P. Colburn. 1901. *The History of Milford, Volume 1.* Milford, NH: Rumford Press.

Reed, Jacob Whittemore. 1861. *History of the Reed Family in Europe and America.* Boston: Printed by J. Wilson and Son.

Reid, Harvey. 1884. *Biographical Sketch of Enoch Long: An Illinois Pioneer, Volume 2.* Alton, IL: Fergus Printing Company.

Richmond, Joshua Bailey. 1897. *The Richmond Family, 1594-1896, and Pre-American Ancestors, 1040-1594.* Boston, MA: Published by the compiler.

Rix, Guy Scoby. 1901. *History and Genealogy of the Eastman Family of America: Containing Biographical Sketches and Genealogies of both Males and Females.* Concord, NH: I. C. Evans.

Rogers, James Swift. 1902. *James Rogers of New London, Ct: And His Descendants.* Boston, MA: Published by the compiler.

Rood, Hosea Whitford. 1910. *A Historical Sketch of the Thorngate-Rood Family, Descendants of George Thorngate, Senior, and Matilda Blanchard, 1798-1906.* Ord, NE: H. M. Davis.

Rook, Albert Wilmot. 1901. *The Butler Family.* Chicago, IL: Lakeside Press.

Roscoe, William E. 1882. *History of Schoharie County, New York, with Illustrations and Biographical Sketches of Some of its Prominent Men and Pioneers.* Syracuse, NY: D. Mason & Co.

Runnels, Moses Thurston. 1873. *A Genealogy of Runnels and Reynolds Families in America.* Boston, MA: Alfred Mudge & Son.

—. 1882. *History of Sanbornton, New Hampshire, Volume II.* Boston, MA: Mudge.

Secomb, Daniel F. 1883. *History of the Town of Amherst, Hillsborough County, New Hampshire.* Concord, NH: Evans, Sleeper, and Woodbury.

Shattuck, L'emuel. 1855. *Memorials of the Descendants of William Shattuck, the Progenitor of the Families in America that Have Borne His Name.* Boston: Dutton and Wentworth, printed for the family.

Sheppard, Caroleen Beckley Clark. 1948. *The Descendants of Richard Beckley of Wethersfield, Connecticut.* Hartford, CT: Connecticut Historical Society.

Skeats, Phyllis Emery, and Terry Skeats. 2000. *Hatley, 1792-1900: History of a Village in Hatley Township.* North Hatley, Québec: P. E. Skeats.

Smith, Albert, and John Hopkins Morison. 1876. *History of the Town of Peterborough, Hillsborough County, New Hampshire.* Boston: Press of G.H. Ellis.

Smith, Charles James. 1907. *History of the Town of Mont Vernon, New Hampshire.* Boston: Blanchard Printing Company.

Smith, Edward Church, and Philip Mack Smith. 1924. *A History of the Town of Middlefield, Massachusetts.* Menasha, WI: Private printing.

Smith, Henry Perry. 1885. *History of Cortland County, with Illustrations and Biographical Sketches of some of its Prominent Men and Pioneers.* Syracuse, NY: D. Mason & Co.

Smith, John E. 1899. *Our County and Its People: A Descriptive and Biographical Record of Madison County, New York.* Boston: Boston History Company.

Smith, Thomas, Samuel Deane, Samuel Freeman, and William Willis. 1849. *Journals of the Rev. Thomas Smith, and the Rev. Samuel Deane, Pastors of the First Church in Portland: with Notes and Biographical Notices: and a Summary History of Portland.* Portland, ME: J. S. Bailey.

Society of Friends. 1862. *The American Annual Monitor for 1862.* New York: Published for the Tract Association of Friends.

Sowell, Andrew Jackson. 1904. *History of Fort Bend County, Containing Biographical Sketches of Many Noted Characters.* Houston, TX: W. H. Coyle.

Spalding, Samuel J. 1872. *Edward Spalding of Massachusetts Bay and His Descendants.* Boston, MA: Alfred Mudge and Son, Printers.

Spaulding, Charles S. 1915. *An Account of Some of the Early Settlers of West Dunstable, Monson and Hollis, N. H.* Nashua, NH: Telegraph Press.

Spofford, Charles B. 1896. *Grave Stone Records: Rrom the Ancient Cemeteries in the Town of Claremont, New Hampshire, with Historical and Biographical Notes.* Claremont, NH: G. I Putnam.

Sprague, Warren Vincent. 1913. *Sprague Families in America.* Rutland, VT: Tuttle Co.

Sprague, William Buell. 1859. *Annals of the American Pulpit, Volume 1.* R. Carter and Brothers.

Stafford, Morgan Hewitt. 1941. *A Genealogy of the Kidder Family Comprising the Descendants in the Male Line of Ensign James Kidder, 1626-1676, of Cambridge and Billerica in the Colony of Massachusetts Bay.* Rutland, VT: Tuttle Publishing.

Stark, Charles R. 1927. *The Aaron Stark Family, Seven Generations of the Descendants of Aaron Stark of Groton, Connecticut.* Boston, MA: Wright and Potter.

State Historical Society of Wisconsin. 1889. *Biographical History of Shelby and Audubon Counties, Iowa.* Chicago: W. S. Dunbar.

Stearns, Ezra S. 1875. *History of the Town of Rindge, New Hampshire, from the Date of the Rowley Canada or Massachusetts Charter, to the Present Time, 1736-1874, with a Genealogical Register of the Rindge Families.* Boston: G. H. Ellis.

Stearns, Ezra S., William F. Witcher, and Edward E. Parker. 1908. *Genealogical and Family History of the State of New Hampshire: A Record of the Achievements of Her People in the Making of a Commonwealth and the Founding of a Nation.* New York: Lewis Publishing.

Stearsns, Ezra Scollay, and Moses Thurston Runnels. 1906. *History of Plymouth, New Hampshire: Vol. I. Narrative--vol. II. Genealogies.* Plymouth, NH: Printed for the town by University Press.

Sterling, Albert Mack, and Sterling Edward Boker. 1909. *The Sterling Genealogy, Vol II.* New York: Grafton Press.

Stickney, Matthew Adams. 1883. *The Fowler Family: A Genealogical Memoir of the Descendants of Philip and Mary Fowler, of Ipswich, Mass.* Salem, MA: Printed for the author.

—. 1867. *The Stickney Family: A Genealogical Memoir.* Salem, MA: Printed for the Author, Essex Institute Press.

Stone, William Leete. 1888. *The Family of John Stone: One of the First Settlers of Guilford, Conn.* Albany, NY: J. Munsell's Sons.

Stowell, William Henry Harrison. 1922. *The Stowell Genealogy: A Record of the Descendants of Samuel Stowell of Hingham, Mass.* Rutland, VT: Tuttle Company.

Stratton, Allen L. 1980. *History of the South Heroe Island: Being the Towns of South Hero and Grand Isle, Vermont.* North Hero, VT: A. L. Stratton.

Temple, Josiah Howard. 1887. *History of North Brookfield, Massachusetts: Preceded by an Account of Old Quabaug, Indian and English Occupation, 1647-1676; Brookfield Records, 1686-1783.* Boston: Rand Avery Company.

The Essex Antiquarian. 1898. "Andover Inscriptions Old South Burying Ground." August.

Thomas, Arad. 1871. *Pioneer History of Orleans County, New York: Containing Some Account of the Civil Divisions of Western New York.* Albion, NY: H. A. Bruner.

Thomas, D. O. (Ed.). 1991. *The Correspondence of Richard Price, Volume II: March 1778 - February 1786.* Durham, NC: Duke University Press.

Thwing, Walter Eliot. 1902. *The Livermore Family in America.* Boston, MA: W. B. Clarke.

Todd, Herbert George. 1913. *Armory and Lineages of Canada: Comprising Pedigrees with Historical Notes, Brief Biographies and Family Registers of Prominent Men of Canada.* Yonkers, NY: Herbert George Todd.

Town of Corinth History Committee. 1964. *History of Corinth, Vermont, 1764-1964.* Corinth, VT: Corinth History Committee.

Towne, Edwin Eugene. 1901. *The Descendants of William Towne.* Newtonville, MA: Published by the author.

Tracy, Joseph, Solomon Peck, Enoch Mudge, William Cutter, and Enoch Mack. 1840. *History of American Missions to the Heathen, from Their Commencement to the Present Time.* Worcester: Spooner & Howland.

Trask, William Blake. 1902. "Captain William Trask and Some of HIs Descedants." *New England Historical and Genealogical Record* 56: 397-401.

Treman, Ebenezer Mack. 1901. *The History of the Treman, Tremaine, Truman Family in America.* Ithaca, NY: Press of the Ithaca Democrat.

Trowbridge, Francis Bacon. 1896. *The Ashley Genealogy: A History of the Descendants of Robert Ashley of Springfield, Massachusetts.* New Haven : Printed for the author.

—. 1891. *The Champion Genealogy: A History of the Descendants of Henry Champion, of Saybrook and Lyme, Connecticut, Together with Some Account of Other Families of the Name.* New Haven, CT: Printed for the author by Tuttle, Morehouse & Taylor.

Trussell, John B. B. 1976. "The Battle of Wyoming and Hartley's Expedition." *Historical Pennsylvania Leaflet, No. 40.* Harrisburg: Pennsylvania Historical and Museum Commission.

Vail, Henry Hobart, and Emma Chandler White. 1930. *Pomfret, Vermont.* Boston, MA: Cockayne.

Van Deventer, Christobelle. 1943. *The Van Deventer Family.* Columbia, MO: E. W. Stephens.

Vinton, John Adams. 1874. *The Upton Memorial: A Genealogical Record of the Descendants of John Upton, of North Reading, Mass. ... Together with Short Genealogies of the Putnam, Stone and Bruce Families.* E. Upton and Sons.

—. 1858. *The Vinton Memorial: Comprising a Genealogy of the Descendants of John Vinton of Lynn, 1648: Also, Genealogical Sketches of Several Allied Families.* S. K. Whipple, Published for the Author.

Wallace, William Allen. 1910. *The History of Canaan, New Hampshire.* Concord, NH: Rumford Press.

Ward, Robert Leigh. 1999. "The Footloose Joshua Whitney (1687-1771) and Some of His Descendants." *The American Genealogist* 74: 197-208.

Warren, Henry Pelt. 1879. *The History of Waterford: Oxford County, Maine, Comprising Historical Address, by Henry P. Warren; Record of Families, by Rev. William Warren, D.D.; Centennial Proceedings, by Samuel Warren, Esq.* Waterford, ME: Hoyt, Fogg & Donham.

Weaver, William L. 1867. *A Genealogy of the Fenton Family : Descendants of Robert Fenton, an Early Settler of Ancient Windham, Conn. (Now Mansfield).* Willimantic, CT.

Webster, Kimball, and George Waldo Browne. 1913. *History of Hudson, N.H.: Formerly a Part of Dunstable, Mass., 1673-1733, Nottingham, Mass., 1733-1741, District of Nottingham, 1741-1746, Nottingham West, N.H., 1746-1830, Hudson, N.H., 1830-1912.* Manchester, NH: Granite State Publishing.

Weeks, Frank Edgar. 1908. *Pioneer History of Clarksfield.* Clarksfield, OH: Published by the author.

Weeks, Lyman Horace. 1913. *The Darling Family in America: Being an Account of the Founders and First Colonial Families, an Official List of the Heads of Families of the Name Darling, Resident in the United States in 1790, and a Bibliography.* New York, NY: W. W. Clemens.

Weis, Frederick Lewis. 1936. *The Colonial Clergy and the Colonial Churches of New England.* Lancaster, MA: Society of the Descendants of the Colonial Clergy.

Wells, Frederic Palmer. 1923. *History of Barnet, Vermont: from the Outbreak of the French and Indian War to Present Time, with Genealogical Records of Many Families.* Burlington, VT: Free Press Printing Co.

—. 1902. *History of Newbury, Vermont, from the Discovery of the Coös Country to Present Time. With Genealogical Records of Many Families.* St. Johnsbury, VT: The Caledonian Company.

Wheeler, George Augustus. 1875. *History of Castine, Penobscot, and Brooksville, Maine: Including the Ancient Settlement of Pentagöet.* Bangor, ME: Burr and Robinson.

Whitcomb, Charlotte. 1904. *The Whitcomb Family in America: A Biographical Genealogy with a Chapter on Our English Forbears "by the name of Whetcombe".* Minneapolis, MN.

White, Daniel Appleton. 1889. *The Descendants of William White, of Haverhill, Mass.* Boston: American Printing & Engraving.

White, Paul R. 1991. "Maine Estate Schedules from Revolutionary War Pensions." *NEHGR* 145: 45.

White, Pliny H. 1882. *The History of Orleans County, Vermont. Civil, Ecclesiastical, Biographical and Military.* White River Junction, VT: White River Paper Company.

Wickham, Gertrude Van Rensselaer. 1896. *Memorial to the Pioneer Women of the Western Reserve, Volume 1.* Jefferson, OH: Ashtabula County Genealogical Society.

Wiggin, Brian P. 2015. "Conway's Early Inns, Part I: Grant (and Maybe Lincoln) Slept Here." *The Conway Daily Sun*, September 9. https://www.conwaydailysun.com/news/conway-s-early-inns-part-i-grant-and-maybe-lincoln/article_395a7ed7-ce14-572d-ae0e-f84b9ba68905.html.

Wight, William Ward. 1888. "John Wight, of Bristol, M.A." *New England Historical and Genealogical Record* 42: 91-93.

—. 1890. *The Wights: A Record of Thomas Wight of Dedham and Medfield and His Descendants 1635-1890.* Milwaukee: Swain and Tate Printers.

Wightman, Wade C., and Mary Ross Whitman. 1994. *The Wightman Ancestry: Including George Wightman of Quidnessett, RI (1632-1721/2) and His Descendants / by Mary Ross Whitman.* Chelsea, MI: Bookcrafters.

Wilkins, Harold E. 2001. *The Descendants of Thomas Lamkin of the Northern Neck of Virginia.* Boston, MA: Newbury Street Press.

Williams, William W. 1878. *History of Ashtabula County, Ohio.* Philadelphia, PA: Williams Brothers.

Willis, William. 1833. *The History of Portland, from its First Settlement, Part II From 1700 to 1833.* Portland, ME: Charles Day & Co. Printers.

Wilson, Mehitable Calef Copenhagen. 1900. *John Gibson of Cambridge, Massachusetts, and His Descendants, 1634-1899.* Washington, DC: McGill & Wallace.

Witcher, William. 1919. *The History of the Town of Haverhill, NH.*

Wood, James Amasa. 1902. *Descendants of the Twin Brothers John and Benjamin Wood.* Concord, NH: Rumford Press.

Worcester Society of Antiquity. 1881. *Proceedings of the Worcester Society of Antiquity for the Year 1880, Volume XIII.* Published by the Society.

Worcester, Samuel T. 1879. *History of the Town of Hollis, New Hampshire, from its First Settlement to the Year 1879: with Many Biographical Sketches of its Early Settlers, Their Descendants, and Other Residents.* Boston: A. Williams.

Master List of Families

Name Index

www.ingramcontent.com/pod-product-compliance
Lightning Source LLC
Chambersburg PA
CBHW080127270326
41926CB00021B/4380

9780578515953